WHY YOU SHOULD CONSIDER

ALGEBRA, STRUCTURE AND METHOD, BOOK 1

■ **This sound, carefully developed course** meets the needs of a wide range of students. (See Contents, pages v–xiii.)

■ **Helpful worked-out examples** supported by clear explanations help students understand concepts and skills. (See pages 107, 126, 350.)

■ An abundance of **carefully developed exercise sets** provides practice with skills, applications, and theory at A, B, and C levels of difficulty. (See pages 85, 97, 118.) The worked-out examples provide clear models for A and early B level exercises. Geometric models provide concrete examples. (See pages 163, 211, 214.) *Challenge* exercises provide extra motivation for very capable students. (See pages 9, 223, 437.)

■ **Real-life applications** throughout the text and problem sets show the usefulness of mathematics. (See pages 165, 360, 394.) Special *Application* sections connect algebra with the real world. (See pages 378, 499, 614.)

■ **Frequent reviews** boost students' retention. Short *Mixed Reviews* follow each lesson. (See pages 340, 358.) *Chapter Reviews, Cumulative Reviews, Maintaining Skills* pages, and *Mixed Problem Solving* sets provide both mixed and sequential review at the ends of chapters. (See pages 178–179, 181, 182, 245.)

■ **Calculators and computers** help students explore new concepts and solve realistic problems. Suggestions for computer graphing techniques and calculator use are included throughout. (See pages 309, 335, 384.) *Calculator Key-Ins, Computer Key-Ins,* and *Computer Exercises* support and extend the lessons. (See pages 13, 87, 145.)

■ **Explorations** provide students with activities for exploring concepts using manipulatives, scientific and graphing calculators, and software. (See pages 685–700.)

■ **Portfolio Projects** offer students nonroutine problem-solving experiences and help students develop their ability to communicate mathematical ideas. (See pages 701–708.)

Supplementary materials (See pages CA4 and T4–T5 for descriptions.)

The **California Teacher's Edition** begins with correlations to the California Content Standards. It includes six interleaved pages of teaching material for each chapter, *Strategies for Teaching, Lesson Commentary*, and annotated student book pages with side column notes. (See Contents, page CA3, and pages T1 and T8–T9.)

The **Study Guide for Reteaching and Practice** accommodates students who need reteaching or who miss a class lesson. Colorful **Overhead Visuals** help you present abstract concepts in a more concrete way. The disk **Algebra Plotter Plus** and the booklet **Using Algebra Plotter Plus** help you and your student graph with ease and explore concepts on a computer.

California support materials are described on page CA4. Other ancillaries include **Teacher's Resource Files, Resource Book, Practice Masters, Tests, Computer Activities, Test Generator** software with **Test Bank,** and **Solution Key.**

Algebra

Structure and Method
Book 1

California Teacher's Edition

Richard G. Brown
Mary P. Dolciani
Robert H. Sorgenfrey
William L. Cole

Contributing Authors
Cleo Campbell
Joan MacDonald Piper

Teacher Consultants
Alma Aguirre
Gail Gismondi
Celia Lazarski
Ron Pelfry
Edward VanderTook

California

McDougal Littell

A HOUGHTON MIFFLIN COMPANY

Evanston, Illinois • Boston • Dallas

Printed in U.S.A.

ISBN: 0-395-97724-X 　　　　　　　　　23456789-VJM-03 02 01

Contents of the California Teacher's Edition

California Teaching Resources and Correlations to the California Curriculum

---

Annotated Student Edition with Answers and Teaching Suggestions

Using the California Teacher's Edition

The California Teacher's Edition for *Algebra, Structure and Method, Book 1* provides all the information you need to effectively coordinate your teaching with California curriculum guidelines and assessment. Correlations to the California Mathematical Content Standards begin on page CA5.

California Standards Practice Workbook

This helpful workbook includes
- Practice Tests
- Practice Worksheets
- Supplemental Content Lessons
- Answer Sheets
- Correlation Charts, Student Record Forms, and Answers in the accompanying Teacher's Guide

Algebra Readiness Book

This resource book of blackline masters includes
- Diagnostic Test on pre-algebra skills
- Instruction and practice in pre-algebra topics
- Assessment by topic, plus Cumulative Assessment
- Answer Key

Algebra Skills Resources Book

This resource book of blackline masters includes
- Practice Worksheets for every lesson of the student book
- Practice Activities and Assessments for every chapter of the student book
- Answer Key

Correlation to California Standards

California Standards for Algebra 1	Student Edition Teacher's Edition	Additional Resources
1 Students identify and use the arithmetic properties of subsets of integers, rational, irrational and real numbers. This includes closure properties for the four basic arithmetic operations where applicable.	**SE/TE: pp. 45–48, 49–53, 65–69, 70–73, 79–82;** 88, 89, 90, 507–511, 685, 696; **Additional TE: pp.** T83–T84, T86–T87, T88	**PM:** pp. 5, 7, 8, 9 **SG:** pp. 19–22, 27–30, 33–34 **T:** pp. 9–18
1.1 Students use properties of numbers to demonstrate that assertions are true or false.	**SE/TE:** Occurs throughout the book. See, for example, pp. 45–48, 49–53, 130–133, 239, 254 (Challenge), 457–458 (Example 2), 459 (Exs. 1–12), 460 (Exs. 15–22), 475 (Challenge), 488 (Exs. 19–24), 507–511, 524, 696, 715–717, 718–719, 720; **Additional TE:** pp. T83–T84, T86, T94	**PM:** pp. 3 (Exs. 22–24), 4 (Exs. 16, 17), 16 (Exs. 29–32), 65 (Exs. 1–4), 66 (Exs. 1–6) **SG:** pp. 18 (Exs. 23–31), 51–52, 167–168 (Examples 2, 3; Exs. 13–24), 170 (Exs. 1–3), 183–184 (Example 2; Exs. 7–18) **T:** pp. 4 (Exs. 14, 17, 20), 6 (Exs. 17, 18, 20), 8 (Exs. 17, 18, 20), 10 (Exs. 13, 14, 21, Challenge), 12 (Exs. 17, 19, Challenge), 13 (Exs. 1, 6, 7), 14 (Ex. 13, Challenge), 24 (Exs. 5–13), 26 (Exs. 14–18), 28 (Exs. 14–18), 99 (Exs. 13–15)
2 Students understand and use such operations as taking the opposite, reciprocal, raising to a power, and taking a root. This includes the understanding and use of the rules of exponents.	**SE/TE: pp. 36, 38, 79–82, 141–144, 152–154, 155–157, 517–520, 521–524, 525–528;** 50–51, 178–179, 190–193, 251–254, 529–534, 551–553, 645, 660–661; **Additional TE:** pp. T82, T88, T94–T95, T96–T97	**PM:** pp. 8, 18, 19, 67, 68 **SG:** pp. 33–34, 53–54, 57–60, 187–192 **T:** pp. 13–14, 29–30, 33, 35, 99, 101, 104–107
3 Students solve equations and inequalities involving absolute values.	**SE/TE: pp. 482–485, 486–488;** 36–39, 502 (Exs. 7–10), 659; **Additional TE:** pp. T129–T130	**PM:** p. 63 **SG:** pp. 175–176, 177–178 **T:** pp. 92–93, 94–95, 96–97
4 Students simplify expressions prior to solving linear equations and inequalities in one variable such as $3(2x - 5) + 4(x - 2) = 12$.	**SE/TE: pp. 95–98, 102–104, 107–110, 116–118, 462–467;** 2–4, 6–9, 46, 65–69, 70–73, 79–81, 641–642, 643, 658; **Additional TE:** pp. T89–T91, T92, T95, T127	**PM:** pp. 11, 12, 13, 15, 61 **SG:** pp. 37–42, 45–46, 169–170 **T:** pp. 19–20, 21, 25, 27, 90–91
5 Students solve multi-step problems, including word problems, involving linear equations and linear inequalities in one variable, with justification of each step.	**SE/TE: pp. 107–110, 112–115, 116–119, 121–125, 126–129, 462–467;** 135, 136, 469–474, 478–481, 643, 644, 658, 667–668, 677; **Additional TE:** pp. T90–T92, T127	**PM:** pp. 12, 13, 14, 15, 61 **SG:** pp. 41–50, 169–170 **T:** pp. 20–23, 25–28, 90–91

KEY: Boldface – Key page references are indicated in boldface type.
PM – Practice Masters, **SG** – Study Guide, **T** – Tests

Correlation to California Standards

California Standards for Algebra 1	Student Edition Teacher's Edition	Additional Resources
6 Students graph a linear equation, and compute the x- and y- intercepts (e.g., graph $2x + 6y = 4$). They are also able to sketch the region defined by a linear inequality (e.g., sketch the region defined by $2x + 6y < 4$).	**SE/TE: pp. 353–359, 490–494;** 366–370, 407 (Exs. 9, 10), 502 (Exs. 11, 12), 653, 659; **Additional TE: pp. T118, T130**	**PM: pp. 46, 64** SG: pp. 135–136, 179–180 T: pp. 69–70, 93
7 Students verify that a point lies on a line given an equation of the line. Students are able to derive linear equations using the point-slope formula.	**SE/TE: pp. 349–352, 371–373, 713–714;** 405 (Exs. 1, 2), 406 (Exs. 9, 10), 407–408 (Exs. 1, 2, 27–31), 653, 654; **Additional TE: pp. T117–T118, T120**	**PM: pp. 46, 48, 51** SG: pp. 133–134, 141–142 T: pp. 69, 71
8 Students understand the concepts of parallel and perpendicular lines and how their slopes are related. Students are able to find the equation of a line perpendicular to a given line that passes through a given point.	**SE/TE: pp. 366–370, 713–714;** 373 (Exs. 35, 36), 406 (Ex. 8), 407 (Exs. 19–22); **Additional TE: pp. T119–T120**	SG: pp. 139–140 T: p. 77 (Ex. 11)
9 Students solve a system of two linear equations in two variables algebraically, and are able to interpret the answer graphically. Students are able to use this to solve a system of two linear inequalities in two variables, and to sketch the solution sets.	**SE/TE: pp. 413–415, 417–420, 426–429, 430–436, 495–500;** 421–425, 438–443, 444–449, 451 (Exs. 1–5), 452 (Exs. 1–11), 656–657, 695; **Additional TE: pp. T123, T124**	**PM: pp. 54–56, 58, 64** SG: pp. 153–156, 159–162, 181–182 T: pp. 81–83, 86, 88, 93, 95, 97
10 Students add, subtract, multiply and divide monomials and polynomials. Students solve multistep problems, including word problems, using these techniques.	**SE/TE: pp. 146–150, 152–154, 158–160, 161–164, 189–193, 274–277;** 167–171, 172–174, 175–177, 178–180, 194–199, 645–646, 647, 651, 668–669, 689–690; **Additional TE: pp. T95–T96, T97–T98, T101, T111**	**PM: pp. 18, 19, 20, 23, 24, 36** SG: pp. 55–58, 61–64, 75–76, 111–112 T: pp. 29–30, 33, 35, 39, 45, 47, 52, 54, 56
11 Students apply basic factoring techniques to second and simple third degree polynomials. These techniques include finding a common factor to all of the terms in a polynomial and recognizing the difference of two squares, and recognizing perfect squares of binomials.	**SE/TE: pp. 194–199, 204–207, 208–212, 213–216, 217–219, 220–223, 224–226, 227–229, 239;** 230–233, 234–238, 240–242, 647–648; **Additional TE: pp. T101, T102–T105**	**PM: pp. 25–29, 31** SG: pp. 77–78, 81–94 T: pp. 39–45, 47
12 Students simplify fractions with polynomials in the numerator and denominator by factoring both and reducing to lowest terms.	**SE/TE: pp. 194–197, 247–250;** 258 (Exs. 1, 2), 280 (Exs. 1, 2), 282 (Exs. 1–4), 649 (Exs. 1–16); **Additional TE: pp. T107–T108**	**PM: pp. 25, 33, 37** SG: pp. 77–78, 99–100 T: pp. 39–40, 49, 53, 55

KEY: Boldface – Key page references are indicated in boldface type.
PM – Practice Masters, **SG** – Study Guide, **T** – Tests

Correlation to California Standards

California Standards for Algebra 1	Student Edition Teacher's Edition	Additional Resources
13 Students add, subtract, multiply, and divide rational expressions and functions. Students solve both computationally and conceptually challenging problems by using these techniques.	**SE/TE: pp. 251–254, 255–258, 264–268;** 259–262, 270–273, 274–277, 278–279, 280–282, 649–651; **Additional TE: pp. T108–T110**	**PM:** pp. 33–35, 37 **SG:** pp. 101–104, 107–108 **T:** pp. 49–51, 53, 55
14 Students solve a quadratic equation by factoring or completing the square.	**SE/TE: pp. 230–233, 564–566;** 234–238, 576–578, 648–649 (Exs. 119–140), 663 (Exs. 19–37); **Additional TE: pp. T106, T137–T138**	**PM:** pp. 29, 31, 73, 76 **SG:** pp. 95–96, 205–206 **T:** pp. 44, 45, 47, 108–109, 112, 114
15 Students apply algebraic techniques to solve rate problems, work problems, and percent mixture problems.	**SE/TE: pp. 167–171, 321–325, 326–330;** 126–128, 302–303, 434–436, 438–442, 646, 652, 668–669, 672–673; **Additional TE: pp. T98, T114–T116**	**PM:** pp. 21, 23, 43, 45 **SG:** pp. 67–68, 125–128 **T:** pp. 31, 34, 36, 62–63, 66, 68
16 Students understand the concepts of a relation and a function, determine whether a given relation defines a function, and give pertinent information about given relations and functions.	**SE/TE: pp. 374–377, 379–382, 389–390;** 383–387, 654–655 (Exs. 71–88); **Additional TE: pp. T120–T121**	**PM:** pp. 48, 49, 51 **SG:** pp. 143–146 **T:** pp. 72–73, 76, 78
17 Students determine the domain of independent variables and the range of dependent variables defined by a graph, a set of ordered pairs, or a symbolic expression.	**SE/TE: pp. 374–377, 379–381, 389–390;** 383–387, 406 (Exs. 11–13), 408 (Exs. 32–34, 37, 38), 654–655 (Exs. 71–88); **Additional TE: pp. T120–T121**	**PM:** pp. 49, 51 **SG:** pp. 143–146 **T:** pp. 72–73, 76, 78
18 Students determine whether a relation defined by a graph, a set of ordered pairs, or a symbolic expression is a function and justify the conclusion.	**SE/TE: pp. 389–390**	
19 Students know the quadratic formula and are familiar with its proof by completing the square.	**SE/TE: pp. 567–570;** 564–566, 663; **Additional TE: p. T138**	**PM:** p. 74 **SG:** pp. 207–208 **T:** pp. 109, 112, 114
20 Students use the quadratic formula to find the roots of a second-degree polynomial and to solve quadratic equations.	**SE/TE: pp. 567–570;** 576–578, 579–581, 595 (Exs. 5, 6), 596 (Exs. 5, 6), 663 (Exs. 31–39, 49–62); **Additional TE: p. T138**	**PM:** p. 74 **SG:** pp. 207–208 **T:** pp. 109, 112, 114
21 Students graph quadratic functions and know that their roots are the x-intercepts.	**SE/TE: pp. 383–387, 572–575;** 408 (Ex. 39), 700; **Additional TE: pp. T138–T139**	**PM:** pp. 49, 74 **SG:** pp. 147–148, 209–210 **T:** pp. 73, 110, 112, 114

KEY: Boldface – Key page references are indicated in boldface type.
PM – Practice Masters, **SG** – Study Guide, **T** – Tests

Correlation to California Standards

California Standards for Algebra 1	Student Edition Teacher's Edition	Additional Resources
22 Students use the quadratic formula and/or factoring techniques to determine whether the graph of a quadratic function will intersect the *x*-axis in zero, one, or two points.	**SE/TE: pp. 572–575; 581–582, 595** (Exs. 7, 8), 596 (Exs. 7, 8), 663 (Exs. 40–45), 700; **Additional TE:** pp. T138–T139	**PM:** pp. 74, 76 **SG:** pp. 209–210 **T:** pp. 110, 112, 114
23 Students apply quadratic equations to physical problems such as the motion of an object under the force of gravity.	**SE/TE: pp. 234–238, 579–581;** 244 (Ex. 5), 595 (Ex. 10), 596 (Ex. 11), 669–670; **Additional TE:** pp. T106–T107	**PM:** pp. 30, 75 **SG:** pp. 97–98, 213–214 **T:** pp. 44, 111
24 Students use and know simple aspects of a logical argument.	**SE/TE: pp. 715–717, 718–719, 720**	
24.1 Students explain the difference between inductive and deductive reasoning and identify and provide examples of each.	**SE/TE: pp. 715–717;** 9 (Challenge), 35 (Challenge), 130–134, 193 (Exs. 61, 62), 233 (Ex. 55), 382 (Challenge), 524, 543	
24.2 Students identify the hypothesis and conclusion in logical deduction.	**SE/TE: pp. 718–719**	
24.3 Students use counterexamples to show that an assertion is false and recognize that a single counterexample is sufficient to refute an assertion.	**SE/TE: pp. 716–717, 720**	
25 Students use properties of the number system to judge the validity of results, to justify each step of a procedure and to prove or disprove statements.	**SE/TE: pp. 130–134, 715–717, 718–719, 720;** 48 (Exs. 35, 36), 73 (Exs. 59, 60), 193 (Exs. 61, 62), 207 (Exs. 65, 66), 233 (Ex. 55), 524; **Additional TE:** p. T94	**PM:** p. 14 **SG:** pp. 51–52 **T:** pp. 24, 26, 28
25.1 Students use properties of numbers to construct simple valid arguments (direct and indirect) for, or formulate counterexamples to, claimed assertions.	**SE/TE: pp. 130–134, 715–717, 718–719, 720;** 48 (Exs. 35, 36), 73 (Exs. 59, 60), 193 (Exs. 61, 62), 207 (Exs. 65, 66), 233 (Ex. 55), 524; **Additional TE:** p. T94	**PM:** p. 14 **SG:** pp. 51–52 **T:** pp. 129 (Challenge), 14 (Challenge), 24, 26, 28
25.2 Students judge the validity of an argument based on whether the properties of the real number system and order of operations have been applied correctly at each step.	**SE/TE: pp. 715–717, 718–719;** 249 (Exs. 39, 40), 254 (Challenge), 475 (Challenge)	

KEY: **Boldface** – Key page references are indicated in boldface type.
PM – Practice Masters, **SG** – Study Guide, **T** – Tests

Correlation to California Standards

California Standards for Algebra 1	Student Edition Teacher's Edition	Additional Resources
25.3 Given a specific algebraic statement involving linear, quadratic or absolute value expressions, equations or inequalities, students determine if the statement is true sometimes, always, or never.	**SE/TE: pp. 716–717, 718–719;** 39 (Ex. 45), 48 (Exs. 37–40), 93 (Ex. 6), 296 (Ex. 46), 393 (Exs. 17–20), 460 (Exs. 39–42), 467 (Exs. 59–66), 481 (Ex. 39), 488 (Exs. 19–24), 511 (Exs. 37, 38), 599 (Exs. 6, 7)	**T:** pp. 4 (Exs. 14, 17, 20), 10 (Exs. 21, Challenge), 11 (Exs. 1, 8), 13 (Exs. 1, 7), 19 (Ex. 1, 8), 29 (Ex. 10), 30 (Exs. 14, 21), 33 (Exs. 1, 3), 35 (Exs. 1, 3), 37 (Ex. 10), 39 (Ex. 10), 57 (Ex. 7), 91 (Challenge), 108 (Ex. 1), 112 (Ex. 4)

KEY: Boldface – Key page references are indicated in boldface type.
PM – Practice Masters, **SG** – Study Guide, **T** – Tests

Correlation to Algebra, Structure and Method, Book 1

Lesson	California Standards	California Key Concepts Book	California Standards Practice Workbook	Practice Masters	Tests	Study Guide
1-1	4					1–2
1-2	4					3–4
Challenge	24.1					
1-3				1		5–6
1-4						7–8
1-5						9–10
1-6					1–2	11–12
1-7				2		13–14
1-8			47–48			15–16
Challenge	24.1					
1-9	2, 3, 25.3		22, 23	3, 4	3–4, 5–8	17–18
2-1	1, 1.1, 4, 25, 25.1, 25.3		21, 49–51			19–20
2-2	1, 1.1, 2		21, 22	5		21–22
2-3			52–53			23–24
2-4			54–55	6	9–10	25–26
2-5	1, 4		21			27–28
2-6	1, 4, 25, 25.1		21	7		29–30
2-7					11–12	31–32
2-8	1, 2, 4		21, 22			33–34
2-9				8, 9–10	13–14, 15–18	35–36
3-1	4		56–57			37–38
3-2	4			11		39–40
3-3	4, 5	S10–S14	24, 25		19–20	41–42
3-4	5	S18–S21	25	12		43–44
3-5	4, 5	S10–S14	24, 25			45–46
3-6	5	S18–S21	25	13	21–22	47–48
3-7	5, 15	S18–S21	25, 35			49–50
3-8	1.1, 24.1, 25, 25.1	S92–S95	21	14, 15, 16–17	23–24, 25–28	51–52

Correlation to Algebra, Structure and Method, Book 1

Lesson	California Standards	California Key Concepts Book	California Standards Practice Workbook	Practice Masters	Tests	Study Guide
4-1	2		22			53–54
4-2	10	S56–S58	30	18		55–56
4-3	2, 10	S2–S3	22, 30			57–58
4-4	2	S2–S3	22	19		59–60
4-5	10		30, 58–59			61–62
4-6	10	S59–S62	30, 58–59	20	29–30	63–64
4-7						65–66
4-8	5, 10, 15	S18–S21, S78–S80	30, 35	21		67–68
4-9	5, 10	S18–S21	30			69–70
4-10	10		30	22, 23	31–32, 33–36, 37–38	71–72
5-1						73–74
5-2	2, 10, 24.1, 25, 25.1		22, 30	24		75–76
5-3	10, 11, 12	S63–S64	30, 31, 32			77–78
5-4	10	S59–S62	30, 60–61	25	39–40	79–80
5-5	10, 11, 25, 25.1	S59–S62, T13–T16	30, 31			81–82
5-6	10, 11	S59–S62, T13–T16	30, 31	26		83–84
5-7	11		31, 62–63			85–86
5-8	11		31	27		87–88
5-9	11		31		41–42	89–90
5-10	11		31	28		91–92
5-11	11		31			93–94
5-12	11, 14, 24.1, 25, 25.1		31, 34	29		95–96
5-13	11, 14, 23		31, 34, 43	30, 31, 32	43–44, 45–48	97–98
Sums and Differences of Cubes	1.1, 11		21, 31			

Correlation to Algebra, Structure and Method, Book 1

Lesson	California Standards	California Key Concepts Book	California Standards Practice Workbook	Practice Masters	Tests	Study Guide
6-1	12, 25.2	S63–S64	32			99–100
6-2	2, 13	S66–S69	22, 33	33		101–102
Challenge	1.1, 25.2					
6-3	13	S66–S69	33		49–50	103–104
6-4	13		33, 64–65	34		105–106
6-5	13	S70–S72	33, 85–86			107–108
6-6	13		33	34		109–110
6-7	10, 13		30, 33	36, 37, 38–39	51–52, 53–56, 57–59	111–112
Complex Fractions	13		33			
7-1						113–114
7-2	25.3		66–67	40		115–116
7-3						117–118
7-4				41		119–120
7-5					60–61	121–122
7-6	5	S18–S21		42		123–124
7-7	5, 15	S18–S21, S84–S86	35			125–126
7-8	5, 15	S18–S21, S81–S83	35	43		127–128
7-9	2	S4–S6, S7–S9	22			129–130
7-10				44, 45	62–64, 65–68	131–132

► Correlation to Algebra, Structure and Method, Book 1

Lesson	California Standards	California Key Concepts Book	California Standards Practice Workbook	Practice Masters	Tests	Study Guide
8-1	7	S26–S27	27			133–134
8-2	6	S28–S31	26	46		135–136
8-3		S37–S39, T4–T7	68–69			137–138
8-4	6, 8	S40–S42	26, 28, 70–71	47		139–140
Perpendicular Lines	8		28			
8-5	7, 8	S43–S46	27		69–71	141–142
8-6	16, 17		36, 37	48		143–144
8-7	16, 17	S88–S91	36, 37, 87–88			145–146
Challenge	24.1					
8-8	16, 17, 21		36, 37, 41, 72–73	49	72–73	147–148
Relations	16, 17, 18	S88–S91	36, 37, 38			
8-9	25.3					149–150
8-10				50, 51, 52–53	74, 75–78	151–152
9-1	9		29, 74–75			153–154
9-2	9	S48–S52	29	54		155–156
9-3	9		29			157–158
9-4	9	S48–S52	29	55		159–160
9-5	9, 15	S48–S52	29, 35	56	81–83	161–162
9-6	9, 15		29, 35			163–164
9-7	9		29	57, 58, 59–60	84–85, 86–89	165–166
10-1	1.1, 25.3		21			167–168
10-2	4, 5, 25.3	S15–S16	24, 25, 76–77	61		169–170
10-3	5	S22–S24	25		90–91	171–172
Challenge	1.1, 25.2					
10-4	5, 25.3		25	62		173–174
10-5	3		23			175–176
10-6	1.1, 3, 25.3		21, 23	63		177–178
10-7	6	S32–S35	26			179–180
10-8	9	S53–S54	29	64, 65	92–93, 94–97	181–182

Correlation to Algebra, Structure and Method, Book 1

Lesson	California Standards	California Key Concepts Book	California Standards Practice Workbook	Practice Masters	Tests	Study Guide
11-1	1, 1.1, 25.3		21			183–184
11-2		T17–T21	78–79	66		185–186
11-3	2		22		98–99	187–188
11-4	2	T8–T12	22	67		189–190
Irrationality of $\sqrt{2}$	1.1, 24.1, 25, 25.1		21			
11-5	2		22			191–192
11-6	2	T22–T25	22, 80–82	68	100–101	193–194
11-7						195–196
11-8				69		197–198
Proving Divisibility Tests	24.1					
11-9						199–200
11-10				70, 71, 72	102–103, 104–107	201–202
Fractional Exponents	2		22			
12-1		S74–S77				203–204
12-2	14, 19	S74–S77	34, 39	73		205–206
12-3	19, 20		39, 40		108–109	207–208
12-4	21, 22		41, 42, 83–84	74		209–210
12-5	14, 20		34, 40			211–212
12-6	20, 23		40, 43			213–214
Quadratic Inequalities	22		42			
12-7						215–216
12-8				75, 76, 77, 78–80	110–111, 112–115, 116–118, 119–121	217–218

►Correlation to Algebra, Structure and Method, Book 1

Lesson	California Standards	California Key Concepts Book	California Standards Practice Workbook	Practice Masters	Tests	Study Guide
Expl. 1-8	1		21			
Expl. 2-3						
Expl. 2-4						
Expl. 3-1						
Expl. 4-5–4-6	10		30			
Expl. 5-7						
Expl. 6-4						
Expl. 7-2						
Expl. 8-4						
Expl. 9-1	9		29			
Expl. 10-2	1, 1.1		21			
Expl. 11-2						
Expl. 11-6						
Expl. 12-4	21, 22		41, 42			
Appendix 1						
Appendix 2	7, 8	S43–S46	27, 28			
Appendix 3	1.1, 24, 24.1, 24.3, 25, 25.1, 25.2, 25.3	S92–S95	21, 44, 45, 89–92			
Appendix 4	1.1, 24, 24.2, 25, 25.1, 25.2, 25.3	S92–S95	21, 44, 45, 93–96, 97–100			
Appendix 5	1.1, 24, 24.3, 25, 25.1	S92–S95	21, 44, 45, 101–102			

Algebra

Structure and Method
Book 1
Teacher's Edition

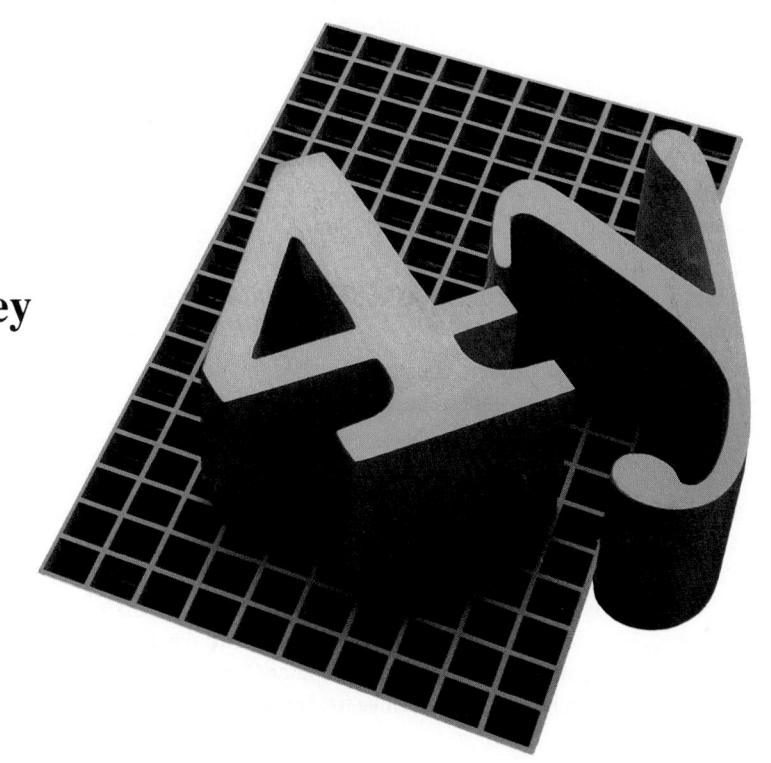

Richard G. Brown
Mary P. Dolciani
Robert H. Sorgenfrey
William L. Cole

Contributing Authors
Cleo Campbell
Joan MacDonald Piper

Teacher Consultants
Alma Aguirre
Gail Gismondi
Celia Lazarski
Ron Pelfrey
Edward VanderTook

McDougal Littell
A HOUGHTON MIFFLIN COMPANY
Evanston, Illinois • Boston • Dallas

Authors

Richard G. Brown, Mathematics Teacher, Phillips Exeter Academy, Exeter, New Hampshire

Mary P. Dolciani, formerly Professor of Mathematical Sciences, Hunter College of the City University of New York

Robert H. Sorgenfrey, Professor Emeritus of Mathematics, University of California, Los Angeles

William L. Cole, Associate Professor of Mathematics Education, Michigan State University

Contributing Authors

Cleo Campbell, Coordinator of Mathematics, Anne Arundel County Public Schools, Annapolis, Maryland

Joan MacDonald Piper, Mathematics Editor, Westborough, Massachusetts, and former Mathematics Teacher, Concord Academy, Concord, Massachusetts

Teacher Consultants

Alma Cantu Aguirre, Mathematics Department Chairperson, Thomas Jefferson High School, San Antonio, Texas

Celia Lazarski, Mathematics Teacher, Glenbard North High School, Carol Stream, Illinois

Edward M. VanderTook, former Assistant Director for Instruction, Math/Science/Computer Unit, Tucson Unified School District, Tucson, Arizona

Gail Girvan Gismondi, Mathematics Teacher, Log College Middle School, Warminster, Pennsylvania

Ron Pelfrey, Mathematics Coordinator, Fayette County School, Lexington, Kentucky

The authors wish to thank Celia Lazarski, Mathematics Teacher, Glenbard North High School, Carol Stream, Illinois; James M. Sconyers, Math/Science Resource Teacher, Garrett County, Maryland; Robert H. Cornell, Mathematics Department Head, Milton Academy, Milton, Massachusetts; and Douglas Burmbaugh, University of Central Florida, Orlando, Florida, for their valuable contributions to the Teacher's Edition. The authors also wish to thank David L. Myers, Computer Coordinator and Mathematics Teacher, Winsor School, Boston, Massachusetts, for writing the Portfolio Projects.

ISBN: 0-395-97724-X   23456789-VJM-03 02 01

Contents

Challenges of the Future

Experts predict that in the 21st century many jobs will require employees to have greater mathematical knowledge and better problem solving skills than they do today. In addition, citizens will need strong quantitative-reasoning skills to make effective decisions in their daily lives. Preparing students to meet the challenges of the future is our mutual goal. No textbook can guide or inspire students in the same way as a teacher. But we can help make your teaching job easier by providing a comprehensive textbook program that helps students build their thinking and problem solving skills as well as their understanding of algebra.

A Course for Today's Students

In planning this new edition, we have spoken with many algebra teachers throughout the country and have been guided by their suggestions. We have also been guided by the recommendations of professional organizations, such as the *Standards* of the National Council of Teachers of Mathematics. The result is a contemporary course that works in the classroom.

In this book, **problem solving** is introduced early and is integrated throughout.

Contemporary curriculum

Applications of algebra are presented in chapter-opening pages, lesson developments, special *Application* sections, and interesting and varied word problems. **Reasoning skills** such as analyzing information, making conjectures, and giving convincing arguments are developed throughout the course. **Geometric models** are used to illustrate abstract algebraic concepts. Suggestions for appropriate use of **technology** are included in the text and the exercises. **Explorations** activities help students develop understanding of concepts.

Puts Algebra Within Reach

This book has been designed to make algebra accessible to a wide range of students — without sacrificing complete content and challenge for capable students. The following features help bring algebra within reach:

Classroom-tested for effectiveness

Accessible to a wide range of students

Readable text, with clear, concise, language; **visual highlighting** of important results; **numerous worked-out examples**; **exercise sets** that start with straightforward skill development and build gradually in difficulty; **frequent mixed reviews**; special sections on **reading algebra**.

A Proven Program Improved

The *Algebra, Structure and Method*, series has been used successfully in many algebra classrooms. This new edition builds on the strengths of earlier editions that teachers have valued, such as **complete topic coverage, clear development of mathematical concepts**, and **carefully sequenced exercise sets**. At the same time, the books have been enhanced to provide a more contemporary and more accessible course — a course that will help prepare a wide range of students for the challenges of the future.

The
Classic Algebra
for the new
Millennium

Algebra

Structure and Method
Book 1

Houghton Mifflin

Teaching the Course

Teacher's Edition

- Designed to help you teach algebra.
- Special articles discuss a variety of teaching strategies.
- Pages interleaved between chapters provide alternative strategies for teaching lessons.
- Easily accessible assignment and supplementary materials guides interleaved between chapters.
- Contains reduced facsimiles of key supplementary materials.
- Includes extra tests and reviews.

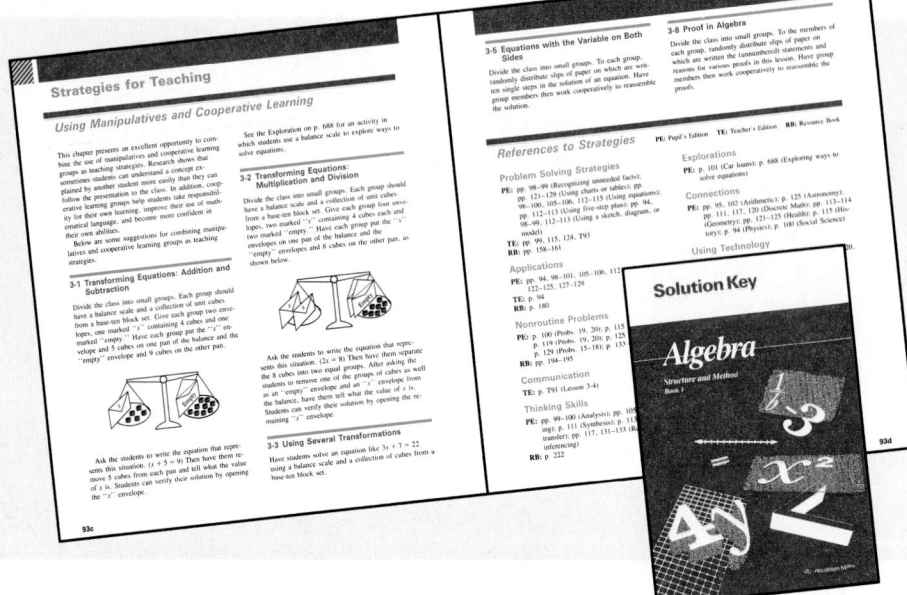

Overhead Visuals

- Full-color overhead transparencies, some with moving parts, provide concrete modeling to enhance presentations.
- Printed folders include objectives, textbook references, and questions and answers for using the visuals.

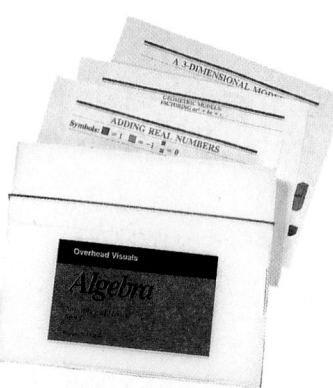

Study Guide for Reteaching and Practice

- Contains alternative two-page lessons for each textbook lesson.
- Provides vocabulary review.
- Has worked-out examples, exercises mainly at the "A" level, and mixed reviews.
- Accompanied by a separate *Answer Key*.

Algebra Plotter Plus

- *Disk* can be used independently by students or by the teacher for classroom presentations.
- Plots lines, conics, functions, inequalities, and absolute value.
  - Utilities includes matrix reducer, statistics spreadsheet, and a sampling experiment simulation.
  - Apple II, Macintosh, and IBM versions.
  - Available for 5 1/4" or 3 1/2" disk drives.
- *Using Algebra Plotter Plus* booklet includes worked examples, scripted demonstrations, enrichment topics, activity sheets, and user's manual.

Additional Support

Teacher's Resource Files

- *Teachers Resource Book* tests, practice, mixed review, problem solving, applications, enrichment, technology, thinking skills, warm-up exercises, diagram masters
- *Study Guide for Reteaching and Practice*
- *Algebra Plotter Plus* Demo disk and booklet
- *Overhead Visuals* sample
- *Tests* (blackline)
- *Practice Masters* (blackline)
- Topic and Chapter folders

Practice Masters

offer concentrated practice in worksheet format including periodic cumulative reviews on blackline masters and duplicating masters.

Tests

contain quizzes, chapter tests (in two parallel forms), and cumulative tests on black-line masters and duplicating masters.

Computer Activities

provide worksheets that extend and reinforce students' understanding of algebraic concepts through BASIC programming.

Test Generator

software for generating your own tests either manually or by random selection, with options for customizing the format and level of difficulty.

Organization of the Textbook

- **Chapters** divided into several groups of related lessons.

- **Objectives** stated at the start of lessons.

- **Lesson Text** focuses on the underlying structure of algebraic content, as well as methods and applications.

- **Worked-Out Examples** illustrate and reinforce the content and skills taught.

- **Vocabulary** words are boldfaced in the text and appear in the glossary.

- **Important Information** is boxed for easy reference and review.

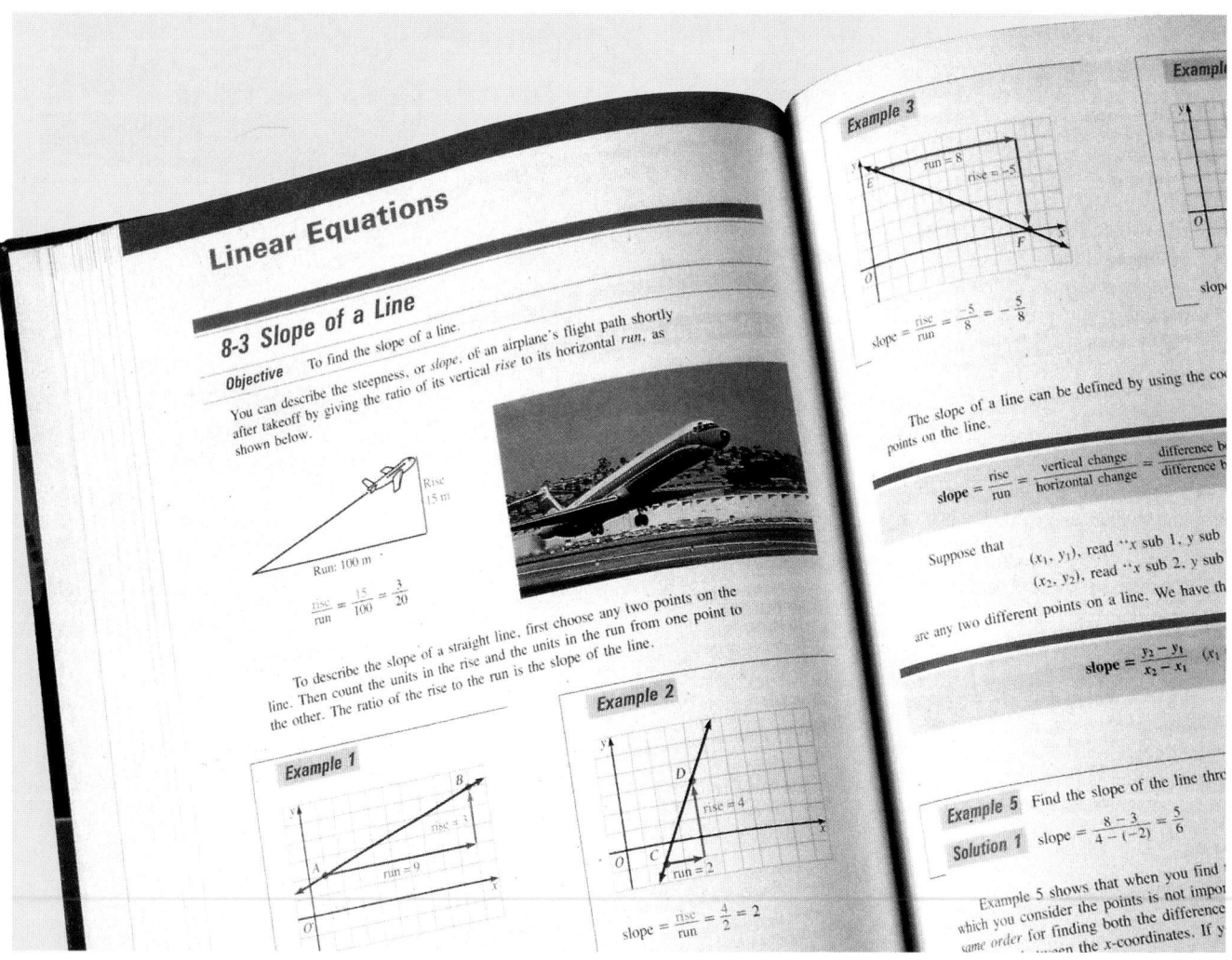

Exercises

Oral Exercises provide students and teachers with immediate feedback of lesson comprehension.

Written Exercises are graded for varying levels of student ability.

Problems put skills practice in a problem-solving context.

Exercises include suggestions for using *calculators* and *computers*.

Computer Exercises provide students opportunities to use programs for lesson enrichment.

Mixed Review exercises at the end of lessons maintain previously taught skills.

Applications

For example, p. 101

Applications relate algebra to other disciplines and everyday life, enriching the course for all students.

Study Skills

For example, p. 64

Reading Algebra features help students read and use their textbooks.

Challenges and Extras

For examples, pp. 292 and 570

Challenges are high interest problems where students utilize their problem solving and thinking skills.

Extras are for those students who are able to extend lesson content.

Enrichment

For examples, pp. 125, 269, and 477

Career Notes relate algebra to everyday life and the work place.

Historical and **Biographical Notes** provide historical background and human interest for all students.

Technology

For examples, pp. 82 and 359

Calculator Key-In features indicate ways of using calculators to enhance algebra.

Computer Key-In features show students how computers can also be used to enhance content.

Testing and Review

Self-Test lists important vocabulary and tests key concepts every 3-4 lessons.

Chapter Summary capsulizes important information highlighted within chapters.

Chapter Reviews and **Chapter Tests** provide checks of lesson objective comprehension.

Cumulative Reviews review skills and concepts from previous chapters.

Maintaining Skills review arithmetic and basic algebra skills at the end of each chapter.

Preparing for College Entrance Exams help students develop test-taking skills.

Using the Teacher's Edition

This Teacher's Edition provides pupil pages with answers and side columns. As illustrated below, the side columns include time-saving material for your lesson presentation, from Warm-Up Exercises to lesson summary. Other side-column entries include **Computer** and **Calculator Key-In Commentaries, Additional Answers,** and **Application** descriptions and activities. A number of aids for checking students' understanding are suggested in the side columns, including notes on **Check for Understanding, Guided Practice, Chalkboard Examples,** and **Common Errors**.

For each lesson, page references are given for the corresponding Lesson Commentary, which includes **Teaching Suggestions, Suggested Extensions, Group Activities, Reading Algebra,** and **Using Manipulatives.**

Warm-Up Exercises practice skills taught in previous lessons.

Motivating the Lesson connects new concepts to prior ones or to real-world applications.

Thinking Skills, Common Errors, Problem Solving Strategies, and techniques for **Reading Algebra** are identified.

Chalkboard Examples provide additional examples to use in presenting the lesson.

Check for Understanding suggests a use of the Oral Exercises to assess how well students have understood one lesson concept before you move on to the next.

Teaching Suggestions p. T102
Using Manipulatives p. T102
Suggested Extensions p. T102

Warm-Up Exercises
Find each product.
1. $(x + 1)(x - 1)$ $x^2 - 1$
2. $(y + 5)(y - 5)$ $y^2 - 25$
3. $(2t + 3)(2t - 3)$ $4t^2 - 9$

Motivating the Lesson
Ask students what pattern they see in the answers found in the Warm-Up Exercises. This pattern is important in simplifying products of the form $(a + b)(a - b)$ and factoring the difference of two squares.

Thinking Skills
Before multiplying or factoring, students are encouraged to *analyze* and *classify* given expressions to see whether the pattern $(a + b)(a - b) = a^2 - b^2$ applies.

Chalkboard Examples
Write each product as a binomial.
1. $(y + 2)(y - 2)$
   $y^2 - 2^2 = y^2 - 4$
2. $(2a + 9b)(2a - 9b)$
   $(2a)^2 - (9b)^2 = 4a^2 - 81b^2$

Check for Understanding
Oral Exs. 1–12: use at the beginning of the lesson.

Common Errors
A common error is to factor $x^2 - 49$ as $(x - 7)(x - 7)$. In reteaching the pattern, encourage students to check their factorization by multiplying the two binomials.

5-5 Differences of Two Squares   SIMULATED PAGE

Objective To simplify products of the form $(a + b)(a - b)$ and to factor differences of two squares.

The shaded area below can be thought of as the product $(a + b)(a - b)$. Notice on the right that when you multiply, the product can be simplified to $a^2 - b^2$, the difference of two squares.

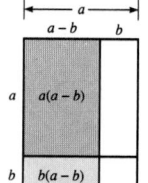

$$
\begin{array}{r}
a - b \\
a + b \\
\hline
a^2 - ab \\
ab - b^2 \\
\hline
a^2 \qquad - b^2
\end{array}
$$

$$(a + b)(a - b) = a^2 - b^2$$

$$\left(\begin{array}{c}\text{Sum of two}\\\text{numbers}\end{array}\right) \times (\text{Their difference}) = \left(\begin{array}{c}\text{First}\\\text{number}\end{array}\right)^2 - \left(\begin{array}{c}\text{Second}\\\text{number}\end{array}\right)^2$$

Example 1 Write each product as a binomial.
  a. $(x + 3)(x - 3)$ **b.** $(2n + 5)(2n - 5)$

Solution **a.** $(x + 3)(x - 3) = x^2 - 3^2$ **b.** $(2n + 5)(2n - 5) = (2n)^2 - 5^2$
                    $= x^2 - 9$ $= 4n^2 - 25$
                    Answer   *Answer*

Example 2 Write each product as a binomial.
  a. $(a^2 - 2b)(a^2 + 2b)$ **b.** $(xy + z^2)(xy - z^2)$

Solution **a.** $(a^2 - 2b)(a^2 + 2b) = (a^2)^2 - (2b)^2$
                    $= a^4 - 4b^2$ *Answer*
              b. $(xy + z^2)(xy - z^2) = (xy)^2 - (z^2)^2$
                    $= x^2y^2 - z^4$ *Answer*

Before each chapter, the Teacher's Edition provides six pages of support materials for that chapter, including **Objectives, Assignment Guide, Supplementary Materials Guide,** guides to available **Software** and **Overhead Visuals,** strategies and activities for teaching the lessons, and facsimiles of key supplementary materials pages.

The front of the Teacher's Edition provides chapter-by-chapter **Lesson Commentary, permission-to-reproduce tests** and **reviews,** and other support materials. See Contents, page T1, for a complete listing.

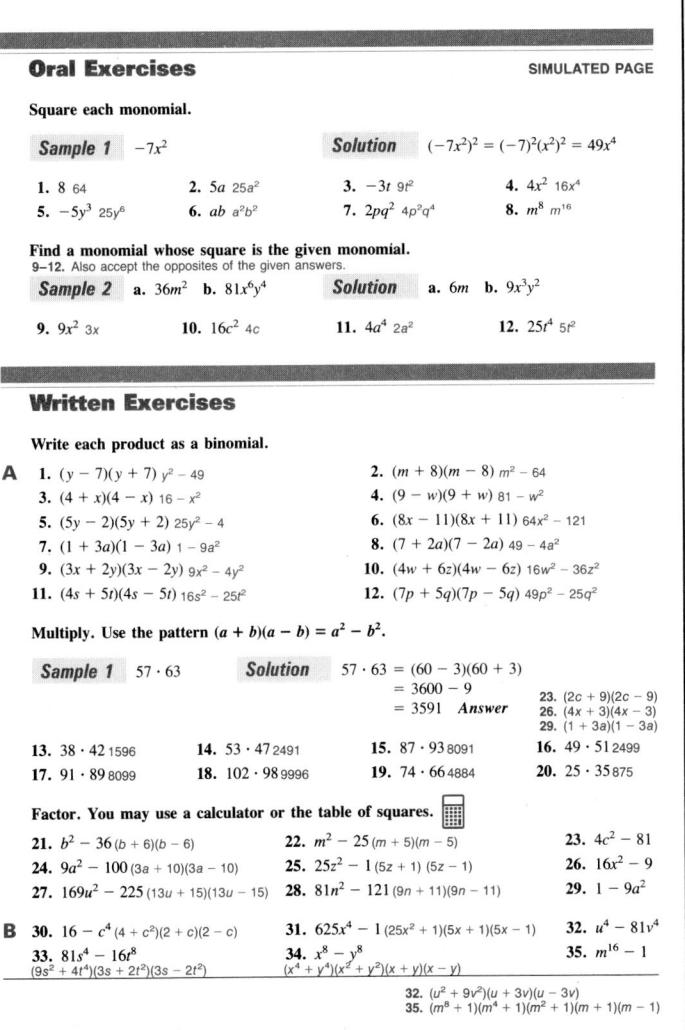

Oral Exercises

SIMULATED PAGE

Square each monomial.

Sample 1 $-7x^2$ **Solution** $(-7x^2)^2 = (-7)^2(x^2)^2 = 49x^4$

1. 8 $_{64}$ 2. $5a$ $_{25a^2}$ 3. $-3t$ $_{9t^2}$ 4. $4x^2$ $_{16x^4}$
5. $-5y^3$ $_{25y^6}$ 6. ab $_{a^2b^2}$ 7. $2pq^2$ $_{4p^2q^4}$ 8. m^8 $_{m^{16}}$

Find a monomial whose square is the given monomial.
9–12. Also accept the opposites of the given answers.

Sample 2 a. $36m^2$ b. $81x^6y^4$ **Solution** a. $6m$ b. $9x^3y^2$

9. $9x^2$ $_{3x}$ 10. $16c^2$ $_{4c}$ 11. $4a^4$ $_{2a^2}$ 12. $25t^4$ $_{5t^2}$

Written Exercises

Write each product as a binomial.

A 1. $(y - 7)(y + 7)$ $_{y^2 - 49}$ 2. $(m + 8)(m - 8)$ $_{m^2 - 64}$
3. $(4 + x)(4 - x)$ $_{16 - x^2}$ 4. $(9 - w)(9 + w)$ $_{81 - w^2}$
5. $(5y - 2)(5y + 2)$ $_{25y^2 - 4}$ 6. $(8x - 11)(8x + 11)$ $_{64x^2 - 121}$
7. $(1 + 3a)(1 - 3a)$ $_{1 - 9a^2}$ 8. $(7 + 2a)(7 - 2a)$ $_{49 - 4a^2}$
9. $(3x + 2y)(3x - 2y)$ $_{9x^2 - 4y^2}$ 10. $(4w + 6z)(4w - 6z)$ $_{16w^2 - 36z^2}$
11. $(4s + 5t)(4s - 5t)$ $_{16s^2 - 25t^2}$ 12. $(7p + 5q)(7p - 5q)$ $_{49p^2 - 25q^2}$

Multiply. Use the pattern $(a + b)(a - b) = a^2 - b^2$.

Sample 1 $57 \cdot 63$ **Solution** $57 \cdot 63 = (60 - 3)(60 + 3)$
                                  $= 3600 - 9$
                                  $= 3591$ ***Answer***

13. $38 \cdot 42$ $_{1596}$ 14. $53 \cdot 47$ $_{2491}$ 15. $87 \cdot 93$ $_{8091}$ 16. $49 \cdot 51$ $_{2499}$
17. $91 \cdot 89$ $_{8099}$ 18. $102 \cdot 98$ $_{9996}$ 19. $74 \cdot 66$ $_{4884}$ 20. $25 \cdot 35$ $_{875}$

Factor. You may use a calculator or the table of squares. 🖩

21. $b^2 - 36$ $_{(b + 6)(b - 6)}$ 22. $m^2 - 25$ $_{(m + 5)(m - 5)}$ 23. $4c^2 - 81$
24. $9a^2 - 100$ $_{(3a + 10)(3a - 10)}$ 25. $25z^2 - 1$ $_{(5z + 1)(5z - 1)}$ 26. $16x^2 - 9$
27. $169u^2 - 225$ $_{(13u + 15)(13u - 15)}$ 28. $81n^2 - 121$ $_{(9n + 11)(9n - 11)}$ 29. $1 - 9a^2$

B 30. $16 - c^4$ $_{(4 + c^2)(2 + c)(2 - c)}$ 31. $625x^4 - 1$ $_{(25x^2 + 1)(5x + 1)(5x - 1)}$ 32. $u^4 - 81v^4$
33. $81s^4 - 16t^8$ 34. $x^8 - y^8$ 35. $m^{16} - 1$
$_{(9s^2 + 4t^4)(3s + 2t^2)(3s - 2t^2)}$ $_{(x^4 + y^4)(x^2 + y^2)(x + y)(x - y)}$

32. $(u^2 + 9v^2)(u + 3v)(u - 3v)$
35. $(m^8 + 1)(m^4 + 1)(m^2 + 1)(m + 1)(m - 1)$

Guided Practice
Write each product as a binomial.
1. $(x + 3)(x - 3)$ $x^2 - 9$
2. $(2 + 3b)(2 - 3b)$ $4 - 9b^2$

Summarizing the Lesson
Tell the students that they have learned to multiply two binomials that differ only in the sign of the second term. Ask some students to write the pattern on the board and give an example of using the pattern in reverse to factor the difference of two squares.

Suggested Assignments
Minimum
  206/1–43 odd
Average
  206/3–60 mult. of 3
  S 207/Mixed Review
Maximum
  206/3–66 mult. of 3
  S 207/Mixed Review

🖩   **Using a Calculator**
Remind students to enter, for example, 225 *before* pressing the square root key to calculate $\sqrt{225}$ when using a calculator in Exercises 21–35.

Supplementary Materials
Study Guide   pp. 81–82
Computer Activity   13
Resource Book   p. 182

Quick Quiz
Write each product as a polynomial.
1. $(y + 3)(y + 5)$
    $y^2 + 8y + 15$
2. $(x - 4)(x - 6)$
    $x^2 - 10x + 24$

Guided Practice provides additional "A" exercises for students to do in class under the teacher's guidance after the presentation of the lesson.

Summarizing the Lesson suggests how to bring closure to the lesson.

Suggested Assignments for minimum, average, and maximum courses are also given in the **Assignment Guide** before each chapter and on pp. T59–T71. The letters R and S designate review and spiral assignments.

A red logo of a calculator or a computer highlights suggestions for using technology with the course.

Supplementary Materials include references to the Resource Book, Study Guide, Tests, Practice Masters, and Computer Activities that accompany the textbook.

For each Self-Test in the textbook, there is a corresponding **Quick Quiz.**

Key Topics and Approaches

Problem Solving

Problem Solving Strategies

Checking solution, 26–29, 234–235, 294, 404, 579, 584
Choosing a strategy, 404
Recognizing no solution possible, 175–177
Recognizing patterns, 9, 35, 53, 69, 208, 213–214, 217, 220–221, 239, 273, 382, 685, 694–695, 697–699
Recognizing similar types, 322, 327
Recognizing unneeded facts, 98–99
Using alternate methods, 395–396
Using charts or tables, 121–129, 167–169, 175, 307, 321–324, 326–328, 421–422, 438–439, 444–445
Using dimensional analysis, 302
Using equations, 23–24, 27–28, 75–78, 98–100, 105–106, 112–115
Using estimation, 294, 404, 693
Using factoring, 234–238
Using five–step plan, 23–24, 26–29, 112–113, 244, 404, 469–474
Using inequalities, 468–474
Using quadratic equations, 234–238, 579–581, 700
Using a sketch, diagram, or model, 23–24, 29, 94, 98–99, 112–113, 167–169, 172–173, 238–239, 533, 686–691
Using square roots, 527, 529–533
Using trigonometry, 633–634
Using two variables, 421–424, 428–429, 434–436

Applications

Age, 445–448
Architecture, 8, 140, 229, 477
Astronomy, 30, 125, 145, 336–337, 339–340, 591
Bicycle gears, 286
Boyle's gas law, 583
Business, 44, 57, 73, 313–319, 422–424, 434
Car loans, 101
Chemistry, 322–325, 434
Cost, income, and value, 127–129, 253, 302–303, 307, 350, 352, 421–424, 434

Distance/rate/time, 167–171, 424, 438–442, 472–474, 580
Energy, 5, 333, 550, 589, 591–592
Engineering, 165, 341, 443
Games, 184, 412, 560
Geometry, 29, 113, 140, 172–174, 197–199, 236–238, 253, 291, 358–359, 365, 396, 400, 416, 434, 470–471, 477, 527, 533, 580
Health, 18, 121–125, 396, 425, 461, 489
Illumination, 593
Investment, 313–314, 316, 319, 422–424, 434
Line of best fit, 378
Linear programming, 499–500
Map coordinates, 100, 348, 359
Misuse of statistics, 614–615
Mixtures, 321–325, 434–435
Photography, 172, 246, 297, 587
Physics, xviii, 94, 236–237, 339–340, 394–395, 398, 400–402, 456, 549–550, 560, 586–587, 591–592
Puzzle problems, 444–449
Surveying, 359, 506, 633
Understanding product prices, 74
Units of measurement in problem solving, 302–303
Various word problems, 17–18, 22, 28–29, 56–58, 62–63, 98–100, 105–106, 112–115, 119, 122–125, 176–177, 235–238, 253, 272, 288–297, 300–301, 306–308, 313–319, 335, 350, 352, 369, 395–396, 400–402, 421–424, 434–436, 470–474, 549–550, 580–581, 586–592
Wind and water current, 438–442
Work problems, 326–330

Nonroutine Problems

Exercises, 9 (Exs. 39–46), 12 (Exs. 39–46), 35 (Exs. 55–58), 39 (Ex. 45), 48 (Exs. 37–40), 53 (Ex. 39), 62 (Exs. 61–62), 63 (Ex. 12), 73 (Exs. 57–60), 78 (Exs. 17–18), 86 (Exs. 34–35), 133 (Exs. 9–11), 154 (Exs. 36–40), 157 (Exs. 51–53), 160 (Exs. 39–44), 163–164 (Exs. 47–50), 193 (Exs. 61–62), 202 (Exs. 45–49), 207 (Exs.

Reasoning

Thinking Skills

Explorations

Communication

Reading

Reading Algebra/Problem Solving, 26
Reading Algebra/Independent Study, 64
Reading Algebra/Problem Solving Strategies, 404
Reading Algebra/Inequalities, 468

Discussion

Discussion, 53 (Ex. 39c), 62 (Ex. 62), 249 (Ex. 39)

Translating, 14–26, 459–460
Convincing argument, 39 (Ex. 45), 48 (Ex. 39), 53 (Ex. 39), 143 (Exs. 35–36), 176–177 (Exs. 1–16), 211 (Ex. 57b), 232 (Exs. 7–12), 254 (Challenge), 272 (Ex. 39), 296 (Ex. 46), 475 (Challenge), 524 (Extra), 529 (Informal proof), 543 (Extra), 577 (Ex. 13), 615 (Exs. 1–3), 628 (Ex. 13), 631 (Ex. 13), 685 (Ex. 7)

Connections

Mathematics

Arithmetic, 45–46, 50–51, 70–71, 79–80, 95, 102, 251, 255, 259, 264
Data Analysis, 44, 287, 296, 320, 377–378, 600–607, 609–610, 614–615
Discrete Math, 10, 31–32, 111, 117, 120, 145, 185, 195, 203, 273, 320, 382, 388, 436, 476, 499–500, 507–508, 521–522, 570, 575, 600–605
Geometry, 4, 8–9, 15, 19–22, 29, 66, 113–114, 140–141, 154, 158, 161, 165, 174, 197–199, 204, 208, 211, 213–214, 221, 236–238, 253, 265, 267–268, 291, 300–301, 358, 365, 396, 400, 416, 434, 436, 470–471, 473–474, 527, 532–533, 549, 580, 586–591, 616–626
Statistics, 320, 374–378, 600–615
Trigonometry, 633–634

Other Disciplines

Astronomy, 30, 125, 145, 287, 336–337, 339–340, 591
Business, 44, 57, 73, 313–319, 422–424, 434
Chemistry, 322–325, 434
Engineering, 165, 341, 443
Health, 18, 121–125, 396, 425, 461, 489
History, 62–63, 87, 115, 239, 301, 303, 359, 450, 477, 523–524
Language Arts, 40
Physics, xviii, 94, 236–237, 336–340, 394–395, 398, 400–402, 456, 549–550, 560, 578, 583, 586–587, 591–593
Social Science, 100, 318, 333, 335, 348

Technology

Calculator

Explorations, 74, 685, 697

Exercises, 7, 74, 187, 205–206, 223, 235–236, 309–314, 318–319, 335, 515, 517, 519, 521–523, 527, 532–534, 565–566, 569, 579–581, 586–587, 590–592, 631–632, 635

Key-Ins, 13, 58, 82, 106, 111, 145, 193, 203, 258, 341, 365, 403, 498, 528, 554

Computer

Explorations, 494, 500, 693–695, 700

Exercises, 111, 120, 129, 145, 151, 187, 203, 250, 273, 319–320, 352, 354, 357, 368, 382, 384, 386–388, 399, 414–416, 436, 460, 481, 494, 532, 570, 575

Key-Ins, 87, 188, 263, 359

Algebra Plotter Plus Disk

Line Plotter, 353, 354, 360, 366, 367, 385, 413, 414, 426

Line Quiz, 371

Parabola Plotter, 385, 561, 572

Parabola Quiz, 385

Absolute Value Plotter, 490, 494

Function Plotter, 383, 397, 399, 521, 547

Inequality Plotter, 490, 495, 500

Conics Plotter, 399

Statistics Spreadsheet, 391, 607

Using Algebra Plotter Plus

Scripted Demonstrations

Slope of a Line, 360

The Graphing Method, 413

Graphing Linear Inequalities, 490

Quadratic Equations: The Discriminant, 572

Enrichment Topics

Determining Direct Variation, 391

The Addition-or-Subtraction Method, 426

Real-World Applications of Linear Inequalities, 495

Finding Irrational Square Roots by Graphing, 521

Solving Simple Radical Equations by Graphing, 547

Quadratic Equations with Perfect Squares, 561

Activity Sheets

Graphs of Linear Equations in Standard Form, 353

Slope-Intercept Form, 366

Zeros of Functions, 383

Inverse Variation, 397

Solving Systems of Linear Equations, 413

Absolute Value Graphs, 490

Linear Programming, 495

Diagnostic Test on Pre-Algebra

The following test can help you to assess the strengths and weaknesses of your incoming class. Part I is devoted to a review of pertinent arithmetic skills, and Part II addresses several early algebra topics often covered in pre-algebra courses. Your class's average performance on Part I can assist you in determining the amount of review required by your class. For this review, the **Maintaining Skills** material found at the end of each chapter will be helpful, particularly that following the first three chapters. Your class's responses to Part II will provide you with an idea of their familiarity with algebraic topics and will help you choose appropriate assignments. (See the Assignment Guide, page T59.)

Part I

Simplify.

1. $425 + 275$

2. $760 - 230$

3. 15×200

4. $7 \cdot 16$

5. $800 \div 50$

6. $2.5\overline{)37.5}$

7. 52.1×9

8. $36.9 \div 2.4$

9. 12×0.01

10. $\frac{2}{5} + \frac{1}{5}$

11. $\frac{1}{6} + \frac{2}{3}$

12. $\frac{7}{10} - \frac{3}{10}$

13. $\frac{5}{8} - \frac{1}{4}$

14. $\frac{7}{9} \cdot \frac{1}{3}$

15. $\frac{2}{5} \cdot \frac{7}{11}$

16. $\frac{3}{8} \div \frac{1}{8}$

17. $\frac{5}{9} \div \frac{1}{3}$

18. $\frac{6}{5} \div 3$

19. Estimate: $2001 \div 49$.

20. Round 3.9619 to the nearest hundredth.

21. Write 0.625 as a fraction.

Write as a ratio in lowest terms.

22. 20 g to 50 g

23. 7 cm to 1 m

24. 8 in. to 2 ft

25. $\frac{1}{4}$ of 20 is what number?

26. $\frac{4}{5}$ of 72 is what number?

27. 5 is what percent of 50?

28. 6 is what percent of 120?

29. 50% of 26 is what number?

30. 15% of 80 is what number?

31. 9 is 25% of what number?

32. 3 is 12% of what number?

33. Write the decimals in order from least to greatest:

$$3.08, \ 3.0, \ 3.006, \ 3.0008, \ 3.7$$

34. Joyce correctly answered 15 out of 20 questions on her French test. What percent did she answer correctly?

35. Find the area of a rectangle with length of 10 in. and width of 6 in.

Part II

Simplify.

36. $3 - 5$

37. $11 - (-2)$

38. $(-4)(-6)$

39. $-15 \div 3$

40. $3 + 6x + 4$

41. $5x + 1 - 3x$

Solve for x.

42. $x + 4 = 11$

43. $4x = 28$

44. $2x + 5 = 25$

45. $\frac{x}{10} = 5$

Write a variable expression for each phrase.

46. 7 plus x

47. three times y

48. 14 divided by x

49. Lisa's dog is 11 lb heavier than Marcia's dog. Let m represent the weight of Marcia's dog. What is the weight of Lisa's dog?

50. Robin earned twice as much money this week as she did last week. Let d represent the amount of money she earned last week. How much did she earn this week?

Chapter Tests

Chapter 1 Test

1. Evaluate if $x = 5$, $y = 8$, $z = 1$, $r = 6$, and $s = 2$: **a.** $(x + y)(s + z)$ **b.** $\dfrac{y + rs}{x - z}$

2. Simplify: **a.** $3 + 9 \cdot 7 - 8 \div 2$ **b.** $\dfrac{15 \times 4 + 9}{(2 + 1)(2 - 1)}$ **c.** $\dfrac{15 \times (4 + 9)}{(2 + 1)2 - 1}$

3. Solve if $x \in \{0, 1, 2, 3, 4, 5, 6, 7\}$:   **a.** $8x - 6 = 10$ **b.** $\frac{2}{3}x = 4$

4. A bag of peanuts costs c cents. A box of granola bars costs 15¢ more than a bag of peanuts. Represent (a) the cost of 3 boxes of granola bars and (b) the change you would receive after buying a bag of peanuts and a box of granola bars if you gave the salesperson $2.00.

5. Translate the following problem into an equation.
   (1) Kevin ran 4 miles more than Steve.
   (2) The sum of the distances they ran was 22 miles. How far did each run?

6. Use the five-step plan to solve the following problem: The number of international units (I.U.) of vitamin A in a cup of skim milk is one ninth the number in a stalk of cooked broccoli. A person who has both the skim milk and the broccoli has received the recommended daily allowance of 5000 I.U. of vitamin A. How many I.U.'s of vitamin A are contained in a cup of skim milk? Choices for broccoli: 500, 4500, 450

7. Graph the given numbers on a number line: -2, $\dfrac{-1}{2}$, 0, $\dfrac{3}{2}$.

8. On a number line, point P has coordinate -4. Write the coordinate of the point halfway between the origin and P.

9. Simplify: **a.** $|-8.5| + |-5.8|$ **b.** $-|-(-\frac{2}{3})|$ **c.** $|-7| + [-(-1)]$

Tell how many solutions each equation has.

10. $|m| = 9$ 11. $|n| = -9$ 12. $|-q| = \dfrac{1}{9}$

13. Translate into symbols: The absolute value of negative two is greater than the opposite of seven.

Complete using < or > to make a true statement.

14. $-\frac{2}{3} \underline{\quad ? \quad} -\frac{3}{2}$ 15. $-|-1| \underline{\quad ? \quad} |-(-1)|$ 16. $-0 \underline{\quad ? \quad} -(5 + 6)$

Chapter 2 Test

Simplify each expression.

1. $1.7 + 0.5 + 8.5 + 4.3$
2. $2 \times 9 \times 50 \times 11$
3. $a + 6 + b + 2$
4. $(-7 + 2) + 5$
5. $[-3 + (-4)] + (-9)$
6. $-\frac{5}{4} + 2 + \frac{1}{4} + (-8)$

7. Solve the equation $-20 + x = -10$ if $x \in \{-10, 10, 30\}$.
8. Simplify: $-39 + 18 + 53 + (-72) + (-6) + 75$.
9. Evaluate $-x + y + (-3)$ if $x = -2$ and $y = -4$.
10. Oxygen has a melting point of $-218.4°$ C. If the boiling point is $35.4°$ C higher than the melting point, find the boiling point of oxygen.

Simplify.

11. $51 - (7 - 104)$
12. $-3.6 - (-9.15)$
13. $-(r - 4) - (-r)$

14. Find the difference in the latitudes of Athens, Greece, latitude 38°N, and Sydney, Australia, latitude 34°S.

Simplify.

15. $(17 \times 19) + (3 \times 19)$
16. $3(a - 2) + 5(a + 6)$
17. $-9 + (-5)j + 3 + (-2)j$
18. $(-2)(-3)(-5)$
19. $-7(-2a + b) - (-3b)$
20. $(-9)(-8) - 9(-8)$

21. Write an equation to represent the following: The lengths in centimeters of the sides of a triangle are consecutive odd integers. The perimeter of the triangle is 45 cm.

22. If $x \neq 0$, what is the reciprocal of $-\frac{2}{x}$?

Simplify.

23. $\left(-\frac{1}{2}\right)(-72)\left(-\frac{t}{9}\right)$
24. $\left(-\frac{1}{11}\right)(-132x + 66y - 110)$
25. $8\left(-\frac{1}{2}a - \frac{1}{8}b\right) - 75\left(-\frac{1}{3}a\right)$
26. $-27 \div \left(-\frac{1}{3}\right)$
27. $\frac{-j}{12}(-24)\left(\frac{k}{-2}\right)$
28. $\frac{266z}{-14z}$, $z \neq 0$

29. Evaluate $\frac{b - 7c}{a - c}$ if $a = -3$, $b = -1$, and $c = 2$.

Chapter 3 Test

Solve.

1. $r + 115 = -27$

2. $-9 + j = |-8 + 2|$

3. $11 - (t - 7) = 0$

4. $-\frac{v}{4} = -8$

5. $\frac{2a}{15} = -12$

6. $-29d = 377$

7. $-15x - 5x = -40$

8. $1 - 9y = 100$

9. $-\frac{1}{3}z + 7 = -5$

10. $6b - 2(b - 1) = -14$

11. $h + 21 - 2h = 12$

12. The Chans' electric bill for September was $40.70, which included a tax of $1.98. If the Chans used 320 kW · h of electricity that month, find the cost per kilowatt-hour.

Solve. If the equation is an identity or has no solution, state that fact.

13. $7 - 5x = 3x + 31$

14. $3r - 1 + r = -2(1 - 2r)$

15. $\frac{3}{4}(8k - 4) = -3 + 6k$

16. $6(n - 8) = 7(n + 8)$

17. The sum of two numbers is -2. If twice the smaller number is added to three times the larger, the result is 1. Find the numbers.

18. Helen has 2 more than twice as many stamps as Gail. If Gail buys 10 more stamps she and Helen will have the same number of stamps. How many stamps does each person have now?

19. The manager of the Craft Shoppe bought some rug kits for $16 each, sold all but 6 of them for $22 each, and made a total profit of $168. How many kits were originally bought?

20. Write the missing reasons.

If $a + b = 0$, then $a = -b$.

1. $a + b = 0$ 1. __?__
2. $(a + b) + (-b) = 0 + (-b)$ 2. __?__
3. $a + [b + (-b)] = 0 + (-b)$ 3. __?__
4. $a + 0 = 0 + (-b)$ 4. __?__
5. $a = -b$ 5. __?__

Chapter 4 Test

1. Write in exponential form: the cube of three more than x.

2. Simplify: $(1 - 3^2) \div (1 - 3)^2 - (-20)$.

3. Evaluate $\dfrac{-x^3 - 1}{(x + 1)^3}$ when $x = -2$.

Simplify.

4. $(3r^2 - 5r - 2) + (-3r^2 + 6r - 8)$

5. $(2a - 9ab + b) - (8b - ab + 7a)$

6. $(-4a^2b)\left(\dfrac{5}{2}b^2c\right)$

7. $5^k \cdot 5 \cdot 5^{k-1}$

8. $7t^3(-t^3) + 5t(3t^5)$

9. $\left(\dfrac{1}{3}x^3y\right)^3$

10. $-8z(-2z^3)^4$

11. $(3n^x)^2 \cdot (n^4)^x$

12. Multiply: $4y^2(y^3 - 7y - 1)$

13. Simplify: $-2j[7 - j(3j - 5) + j^2]$

14. Solve: $\dfrac{3}{4}(12n - 20) + 2n^2 = 2n(n + 3)$

Multiply.

15. $(x + 2)(3x^2 + 2x - 1)$

16. $(3c - d)(2c - 5d)$

17. $(7x - 2y)(3x^2 + 4xy)$

18. Solve $P = R(1 + bt)$:   **a.** for R **b.** for t

Solve each problem that has a solution. If a problem has no solution, explain why.

19. Find three consecutive odd integers such that the sum of the two least integers is 11 more than the greatest integer.

20. The Ortiz family drove from Dawson to Linbury in 1.75 h. The return trip in the rain took 15 min more. If the average speed on the first part of the trip was 10 km/h faster than the speed on the return trip, find the distance from Dawson to Linbury.

21. A rectangular park was 15 m longer than it was wide. When a border of bushes 0.5 m wide was planted around the edges of the park, the area of the park increased by 56 m². Find the original dimensions of the park.

22. Marla has 3 dimes and half as many nickels as pennies. If her coins are worth 50¢ in all, how many nickels does she have?

Chapter 5 Test

1. List all the pairs of integral factors of -66.

2. Give the prime factorization of 504.

Simplify. Assume that no denominator equals zero.

3. $\dfrac{(-3xy^2)^3}{36x^2y^6}$

4. $\dfrac{4a^4b \cdot 25abc^4}{10ab^2c^3}$

5. $\dfrac{-3(ab + c)^3}{-9(ab + c)}$

6. $\dfrac{16g^5h^2 - 8g^6h + 4g^7}{4g^5}$

7. $\dfrac{21t + 49}{7} - \dfrac{5t^3 - 9t}{t}$

8. Find the greatest common factor of $252r^2(r + 1)^3$ and $392(r + 1)^4$.

9. Express $3x^4y^2 - 6x^2y^4 + 9y^6$ as the product of its greatest monomial factor and another polynomial.

Express each product as a polynomial.

10. $(3m - 2)(m - 1)$

11. $c(4c + 5)(2c - 3)$

12. $(5e - f)(7e + 4f)$

13. $(z^2 + 7)(z^2 - 7)$

14. $(5a - 8b)(5a + 8b)$

15. $(r - 3)^2$

16. $(s + 6t)^2$

17. $(-2j^3 + k)^2$

18. $(mn^2 - p)^2$

Factor completely. If the polynomial is not factorable, write "prime."

19. $289x^2 - 36y^2$

20. $4v^6 - 9$

21. $25u^2 - 10u + 1$

22. $49h^2 - 28hk + k^2$

23. $n^2 - 17n + 60$

24. $y^2 - 20yz + 56z^2$

25. $r^2 + 18r - 63$

26. $1 - 11ab - 12a^2b^2$

27. $4j^2 - 13j - 10$

28. $7x^2 - 11xy - 6y^2$

29. $3g^5 - 7g^4 + 6g - 14$

30. $9 - (a + 2b)^2$

31. $-6c^3 + 8c^2 + 8c$

32. $m^4 - 24m^2 - 25$

33. $x^2 + 2xy + y^2 - z^4$

Solve.

34. $27x^3 = 3x$

35. $18y^2 + 8 = 24y$

36. $z^3 + 10z^2 = 24z$

37. The sum of two integers is 8, and the sum of their squares is 19 more than their product. Find the integers.

38. The base of a triangle is 3 cm shorter than the altitude. If the area is $20\ \text{cm}^2$, find the length of the base.

Chapter 6 Test

Simplify. Give the restrictions on the variables.

1. $\dfrac{6a^2 + 4ab}{6a^2 + 13ab + 6b^2}$

2. $\dfrac{m^2 - 2m + 1}{5 - m - 4m^2}$

3. $\dfrac{2x^2 - 98}{28x^2 + 4x^3}$

4. $\dfrac{9c^4d}{7de^2} \cdot \dfrac{14ce^3}{27c^6}$

5. $\left(-\dfrac{3x}{y^2}\right)^4 \cdot \dfrac{xy^6}{18}$

6. $\dfrac{(a-5)^3}{3a^3} \cdot \dfrac{6a^6}{5-a}$

7. $\left(-\dfrac{2a}{3b}\right)^3 \div 6a^2b$

8. $\dfrac{4r^2 + 4s^2}{8rs} \div \dfrac{8r + 8s}{4r^2s^2}$

9. $\dfrac{t^4 - 1}{t^3 + t} \div \left(\dfrac{t-1}{t}\right)^2$

10. $\dfrac{x^2 + 2x - 3}{x^2 + 5x + 6} \cdot \dfrac{4 - x^2}{x^2 - x}$

11. $-12yz^2 \div 4y^2z \div 9z$

12. Find the missing numerator: $\dfrac{2}{c - 3d} = \dfrac{?}{c^2 - cd - 6d^2}$

Rewrite each group of fractions with their LCD.

13. $\dfrac{x+1}{8}, \dfrac{x-1}{28}$

14. $\dfrac{1}{3a - 9}, \dfrac{8}{21 - 7a}$

15. $\dfrac{5}{4bc^2}, \dfrac{7}{10c^3}, \dfrac{4}{b^2c}$

Simplify.

16. $\dfrac{2ab}{a - 2b} + \dfrac{a^2}{2b - a}$

17. $\dfrac{1}{6n^2} - \dfrac{5}{4n}$

18. $\dfrac{7}{9} + \dfrac{8x}{45} - \dfrac{x}{15}$

19. $\dfrac{y}{x + y} - \dfrac{x}{x + y}$

20. $\dfrac{z+3}{z^2 + 2z} - \dfrac{z+4}{z^2 - 4}$

21. $h - \dfrac{2}{h - 1}$

22. $\dfrac{2c + 1}{3c - 1} + 2$

23. $\dfrac{t}{2t - 1} + \dfrac{1}{2t + 1} - 1$

24. $\left(x - \dfrac{2}{x}\right)\left(2 - \dfrac{x}{2}\right)$

Divide. Write your answer as a polynomial or mixed expression.

25. $\dfrac{2 + 4x + 6x^2}{3x - 1}$

26. $\dfrac{6a^3 - 11a^2 + 1}{3a - 1}$

27. $\dfrac{b^2 + 5bc + 4c^2}{b + 2c}$

28. Factor $6x^3 - 23x^2 - 5x + 4$ completely given that $2x + 1$ is a factor.

Chapter 7 Test

State each ratio in simplest form.

1. 72 s:0.5 h

2. A rectangle has sides 60 cm long and 2.2 m wide, and a square has sides 80 cm long. Find the ratio of (a) the perimeters and (b) the areas.

Solve.

3. $\dfrac{3x + 2}{8} = 4$

4. $\dfrac{5n - 9}{2} = \dfrac{5n + 4}{3}$

5. $\dfrac{4}{2a + 5} = \dfrac{7}{10a - 1}$

6. $\dfrac{3x + 5}{2} - \dfrac{8x + 1}{6} = 3$

7. $3y - \dfrac{2y}{3} = \dfrac{3y}{2} + 10$

8. $\dfrac{5}{6}(z + 2) - 8 = \dfrac{3}{8}(z - 1)$

9. $\dfrac{9r - 30}{17r + 2} = \dfrac{2}{5}$

10. $\dfrac{b + 4}{6b} = \dfrac{b}{b + 8}$

11. $\dfrac{9}{x^2 - 3x} + \dfrac{x}{3 - x} = 1$

12. The sum of a number and twice its reciprocal is 3. Find the number.

13. Express (a) $8\frac{1}{4}\%$ and (b) 320% as fractions in simplest form.

14. Find (a) 5.7% of 80 and (b) 108% of 5.

15. 5.6 is 42% of what number?

16. The number of hospital volunteers recently increased from 25 to 30. What was the percent increase?

17. Sue and Lois live 13.5 km apart. At 10:00 A.M. each girl leaves her house and jogs toward the other. The ratio of Sue's speed to Lois's speed is 5:4. If the girls meet at 11:15 A.M., how fast does each jog?

18. A chemist mixed a 20% acid solution with a 60% acid solution to make 10 L of a 30% solution. How many liters of each solution were used?

19. Emily can paint her fence in 6 h. If she does the job with her son, it takes 2.5 h less. How long would it take her son working alone?

20. Express 0.0059 in (a) scientific notation and (b) expanded notation.

21. Evaluate: **a.** $\dfrac{5^{-3}}{5^0 \cdot 5^{-5}}$ **b.** $(7 \cdot 2^{-3})^{-2}$

Simplify. Give answers using positive exponents.

22. $(a^0 b^{-1})^2$

23. $\dfrac{e^{-3}}{e^3}$

24. $\left(\dfrac{g}{g^{-2}}\right)^{-1}$

25. $x^{-2} \cdot x^2$

Chapter 8 Test

1. State whether each ordered pair is a solution of $3x + 4y = 1$.

    a. $(-5, 4)$ **b.** $\left(-3, \frac{3}{2}\right)$ **c.** $\left(\frac{2}{3}, -\frac{3}{4}\right)$

Solve each equation if x and y are whole numbers.

2. $4x + 6y = 12$ **3.** $y = \dfrac{12}{x + 1}$

4. Plot the points $A(-4, 2)$, $B(0, -4)$, $C(3, 0)$, and $D(-5, -1)$ in a coordinate plane.

Graph each equation.

5. $4x - 2y = 8$ **6.** $y = 3x - 4$

7. Find the slope of the line through the points $(-8, 1)$ and $(-5, -8)$. If $(-1, b)$ lies on the line, find the value of b.

8. Write an equation in standard form of the line that has a slope of $\frac{3}{2}$ and a y-intercept of $-\frac{1}{4}$. Draw the graph of the equation.

Write an equation in slope-intercept form for each line described.

9. parallel to the graph of $y + x = 7$ and with y-intercept 0

10. passing through points $(5, 5)$ and $(0, 5)$

Find the range of each function.

11. $f\!: x \rightarrow \dfrac{1}{2x - 1}$, $D = \{-1, 0, 1\}$ **12.** $g(x) = x^2 + x$, $D = \{-2, -1, 0\}$

13. The table at the right shows a function based on consumer prices in 1967.
    a. State the domain and range of the function.
    b. Make a broken-line graph of the function.

Average Purchasing Power of Dollar

Year	1967	1972	1977	1982
Value	$1.00	$0.84	$0.55	$0.35

14. Find the coordinates of the vertex and the equation of the axis of symmetry of the graph of the equation $y = 3x^2 + 6x$. Use the vertex and at least four other points to graph the equation.

15. Given: $x_1 = 6$, $x_2 = 2.5$, and $y_1 = 2.4$. Find y_2 if (x_1, y_1) and (x_2, y_2) are ordered pairs of (a) the same direct variation and (b) the same inverse variation.

16. An employee's wages are directly proportional to the time worked. If Shelli received $114 for 30 hours of work, how much will she receive for 40 hours of work?

Chapter 9 Test

1. Solve by the graphic method: $y = \frac{2}{3}x + 3$
$$2x - 3y = -9$$

2. Solve by the substitution method: $7x + 3y = 11$
$$3x - y = 23$$

3. Show that the following system has infinitely many solutions:

$y = 2x - 8$
$6x - 3y = 24$

4. Show that the following system has no solution:

$2x - y = 2$
$y = 2x + 10$

Solve by the addition-or-subtraction method.

5. $2x + 3y = 0$
$4x + 3y = 3$

6. $5a + b = 23$
$5a - 6b = 2$

Solve by using multiplication with the addition-or-subtraction method.

7. $2a + b = 4$
$5a + 2b = -26$

8. $5a + 4b = 6$
$2a - 3b = 7$

Solve by using a system of two equations in two variables.

9. Joan has $1.45 in dimes and nickels. She has 20 coins altogether. How many coins of each kind does she have?

10. Kate is three years less than twice as old as her brother, Brett. Next year Brett's age will be three-fourths Kate's age. How old is each now?

11. A canoeist paddles 21 km downstream in 3 h. The return trip takes 1.2 h longer. What is the rate of the current?

12. A two-digit number is three times the sum of its digits. When the number is subtracted from the number obtained by reversing the digits, the result is 45. Find the original number.

13. If the numerator of a fraction is increased by 1, the value of the resulting fraction is $\frac{2}{3}$. If the numerator and the denominator are both increased by 5, the value of the resulting fraction is $\frac{7}{10}$. Find the original fraction.

Chapter 10 Test

Find the solution set of each open sentence if $x \in \{-3, -2, -1, 0, 1, 2, 3\}$.

1. $4 - 3x \geq 1$ **2.** $x^2 > 3x$ **3.** $|x| \leq 1.5$

4. Of all the pairs of consecutive even integers whose sum is greater than 44, find the pair whose sum is the least.

Solve each open sentence and graph its solution set.

5. $-7j > -35$ **6.** $4 + \dfrac{5}{3}k \leq k$

7. $3(3a + 1) < -2(1 - 5a)$ **8.** $2\left(2b + \dfrac{1}{4}\right) \geq \dfrac{5}{4}(b - 15)$

Solve each open sentence.

9. $-8 \leq c - 3 \leq -1$ **10.** $5x + 8 > 3$ or $7x - 9 \leq 5$

11. $8 > -2 - 3d > -8$ **12.** $4f > -24$ or $f + 5 \leq -1$

13. $|g + 7| \geq 2$ **14.** $|9 - h| = 0$

15. $11 - 8|n| > -13$ **16.** $-\dfrac{1}{2}(5 + 3|t|) = -7$

Draw the graph of each open sentence.

17. $|2y - 13| \leq 3$ **18.** $\left|1 - \dfrac{3z}{2}\right| > 2$

19. $|4q - (3 - 2q)| = 1$ **20.** $9|5w + 4| - 7 > 29$

Graph each inequality in a coordinate plane.

21. $2x - y < -6$ **22.** $x + 1 \geq -2$ **23.** $5x + 2y > 8 - 2x$

Graph the solution set of each system.

24. $y \geq x - 3$
    $y < 3x + 1$
25. $y < -2x$
    $y > -3 - 2x$
26. $2x - y \geq 5$
    $x + 2y \leq 7$

Chapter 11 Test

1. Arrange $-\frac{59}{24}$, $-\frac{89}{36}$, and -2.5 in order from least to greatest.

2. Find the rational number halfway between $\frac{3}{5}$ and $\frac{2}{3}$.

3. Express (a) $\frac{7}{45}$ and (b) $\frac{19}{16}$ as decimals.

4. Express (a) 0.725 and (b) $0.3\overline{45}$ as fractions in simplest form.

Simplify.

5. $\sqrt{\dfrac{100}{9}}$

6. $\sqrt{0.0121}$

7. $\sqrt{1225}$

8. $-\dfrac{\sqrt{98}}{\sqrt{8}}$

9. $\sqrt{72}$

10. $3\sqrt{112}$

11. $\sqrt{\dfrac{3r^7s}{27rs^3}}$

12. $\sqrt{z^2 + 2z + 1}$

Find both roots of each equation to the nearest tenth. You may use your calculator or the Table of Square Roots at the back of the book.

13. $m^2 - 81 = 0$

14. $12a^2 = 75$

15. $x^2 = 320$

16. A rectangle has width 10 and diagonals of length 26. Find its length.

17. The hypotenuse of a right triangle is 3 cm longer than one leg. If the other leg is 9 cm long, find the perimeter of the triangle.

Express in simplest form. Assume that $x > 0$.

18. $\dfrac{6\sqrt{2}}{\sqrt{15}}$

19. $\sqrt{\dfrac{8}{3}} \cdot \sqrt{\dfrac{45}{32}}$

20. $\sqrt{x}(\sqrt{x^5} - \sqrt{4x})$

21. $\sqrt{75} - \sqrt{48}$

22. $\sqrt{\dfrac{21}{2}} + \sqrt{\dfrac{3}{14}}$

23. $\sqrt{6}\left(\sqrt{18} - \sqrt{\dfrac{1}{2}}\right)$

24. $(\sqrt{3} + 3\sqrt{2})^2$

25. $(1 + \sqrt{5})(1 - 2\sqrt{5})$

26. $(\sqrt{2} + \sqrt{7})(\sqrt{2} - \sqrt{7})$

27. Rationalize the denominator of $\dfrac{4}{1 - \sqrt{3}}$.

Solve.

28. $\sqrt{\dfrac{a}{3}} - 2 = 2$

29. $\sqrt{4x - 1} = \dfrac{1}{2}$

30. $\sqrt{2s^2 - 3} = 1$

Chapter 12 Test

Solve. If the equation has no solution, so state.

1. $64y^2 = 81$ **2.** $4y^2 + 169 = 0$ **3.** $2(x - 1)^2 = 32$

Solve by completing the square. Give irrational roots in simplest radical form.

4. $a^2 - 8a = 2$ **5.** $3b^2 - 12b = 15$ **6.** $c^2 - 3c = -1$

Solve by the quadratic formula.

7. $r^2 + 2r = 1$ **8.** $3s^2 - 5s + 1 = 0$ **9.** $6t^2 + t - 15 = 0$

Solve.

10. $m^2 - 1 = -\dfrac{3}{2}m$ **11.** $2v^2 + 0.5 = 5v$ **12.** $\dfrac{x + 1}{3x + 2} = \dfrac{x + 2}{2x - 1}$

State the number of real roots.

13. $9d^2 - 6d + 1 = 0$ **14.** $3e^2 + 7e - 3 = 0$ **15.** $f^2 + 6f + 10 = 0$

16. How many points does the graph of the parabola with equation $y = 2 - 3x + 4x^2$ have in common with the x-axis? Does its vertex lie above, below, or on the x-axis?

17. The sum of a number and twice its square is 6. Find the number.

18. A picture that is 5 inches by 7 inches is placed in a frame of uniform width. Framing the picture increases the area by 20 square inches. Find the width of the frame.

19. The brightness of the illumination of an object varies inversely as the square of the distance from the object to the source of light. How far from a bulb does an object receive four times as much illumination as it does when it is 8 m from the bulb?

20. If z varies directly as x and inversely as the cube of y, and $z = 12$ when $x = 3$ and $y = 0.5$, find x when $z = 16$ and $y = 0.75$.

Cumulative Reviews

Review for Chapters 1–3

Simplify.

1. $\dfrac{30 \div 5 - 2}{2(5 - 3)}$

2. $|-7.2| - |-2.7|$

3. $-1 + 7 + (-13) + 4$

4. $-4 - (-1) - 6$

5. $3(2a - b) + b - 7a$

6. $-\dfrac{2}{3}(-9x + 3y)$

7. $(-360)\left(-\dfrac{1}{18}\right)\left(-\dfrac{1}{4}\right)$

8. $\dfrac{-222t}{6t}, \ t \neq 0$

9. $\dfrac{-30}{-\frac{1}{2}}$

10. $56 \div 8 - 6 \div 2$

11. $56 \div (8 - 6) \div 2$

12. $0.9 - 1.02 + 0.54$

13. $-7(-5r - 1) + 2(4 - 3r)$

14. $3j - 2k - 3k(5 - j)$

15. $|3 - 1| - |1 - 3|$

Evaluate each expression if $r = -2$, $s = |-3|$, $t = \dfrac{1}{3}$, and $v = 6$.

16. $-4r(t + v)$

17. $\dfrac{st + 4v}{r - 3}$

18. $\dfrac{(v + r)(v - r)}{t(s + r)}$

Solve each equation over the domain $\{-3, -2, -1, 0, 1, 2, 3\}$.

19. $(x + 1)(x - 2) = 0$

20. $x = -x$

21. $2 - (-x) = 1$

22. Graph the given numbers on one number line: $2, -5, -1.5, 3.5$

23. True or false: $-(3 - 7)(-2) < \dfrac{-|-27|}{3}$

24. Complete the statement with a variable expression: The Cabot Theatre opened y years ago. Ten years from now it will be __?__ years old.

25. Translate the sentence into an equation: I have 9 dimes and quarters worth $1.65.

26. Translate the sentences into an equation: A rectangle has a perimeter of 64 cm. The lengths in centimeters of its adjacent sides are consecutive odd integers.

Solve. If the equation is an identity or has no solution, say so.

27. $|a| = 8$

28. $|b| = -1$

29. $-10 = -3 + k$

30. $15 - (5 - n) = 1$

31. $100 - d = 0$

32. $24 = \dfrac{c}{-2}$

33. $-12j = -84$

34. $2m - 8m + 1 = 55$

35. $4 + \dfrac{5}{2}(t - 3) = 24$

Solve. If the equation is an identity or has no solution, say so.

36. $-5(2h - 1) - 8 = 7$ **37.** $\frac{2}{5}x + 16 = 0$ **38.** $-2(3 - b) = 2b + 6$

39. $2y - 17 = 7y + 13$ **40.** $3\left(2g - \frac{1}{3}\right) = 2\left(3g - \frac{1}{2}\right)$ **41.** $\frac{5}{6}(7r - 15) = 4r + 4$

42. By increasing the speed of her car by 5 km/h, Alice was able to drive 12 km in 0.2 h. What was her original speed?

43. Six times a number, decreased by 5, is -14. Find the number.

44. Pedro bought five more 20¢ stamps than his friend George. If the average amount of money spent was $1.70, how many stamps did each buy?

45. The numbers of fish in Rick and Lisa's aquariums are consecutive integers. When they each had three less fish, together they had 15 fish. How many fish does each have now if Lisa has more fish?

46. When Kate worked 10 h overtime she earned $8 more than one third the amount she earns for 40 h of work at her usual rate. If her overtime rate is $2.40 per hour more than her usual rate, find her overtime rate.

47. On a number line, point R has coordinate -7 and point S has coordinate -13. Find the coordinate of the point one third of the way from R to S.

Write the missing reasons. Assume that each variable represents any real number.

48. *Prove:*   If $7x + 1 = 15$, then $x = 2$.
   Proof: 1. $7x + 1 = 15$ 1. ?
              2. $(7x + 1) + (-1) = 15 + (-1)$ 2. ?
              3. $7x + [1 + (-1)] = 15 + (-1)$ 3. ?
              4. $7x + 0 = 15 + (-1)$ 4. ?
              5. $7x = 15 + (-1)$ 5. ?
              6. $7x = 14$ 6. Substitution principle
              7. $\frac{1}{7}(7x) = \frac{1}{7}(14)$ 7. ?
              8. $\left(\frac{1}{7} \cdot 7\right)x = \frac{1}{7}(14)$ 8. ?
              9. $1 \cdot x = \frac{1}{7}(14)$ 9. ?
              10. $x = 2$ 10. ?

49. *Prove:* $-(-a + b) = a - b$
   Proof: 1. $-(-a + b) = -(-a) + (-b)$ 1. ?
              2. $= a + (-b)$ 2. ?
              3. $= a - b$ 3. ?

50. Write a proof including statements and reasons. *Prove: If $a + b = 0$, then $a = -b$.*

Review for Chapters 4–6

Simplify. Assume that no denominator equals 0.

1. $(3 - 5)^2 - (5 - 3)^3$

2. $(5r^2 - 3r + 1) + (-6r^2 + 3r - 7)$

3. $(2x^2 + xy - 3y^2) - (x^2 + 5xy - 4y^2)$

4. $\left(-\dfrac{20}{3}a^5b^2c\right)\left(\dfrac{21}{8}ac^3\right)$

5. $5^x \cdot 5^{x-1} \cdot 5$

6. $(-3c^2d)^3\left(\dfrac{2}{3}cd^2\right)^2$

7. $7h(1 - 2h) - 3h(4h + 2)$

8. $-5d^2(-2 + 3d - 4d^2)$

9. $(5x + y)(2x^2 + 4xy - 5y^2)$

10. $\dfrac{(2n)^3(-n)^3}{(-4n)^2}$

11. $\dfrac{36r^3s^4 - 8r^4s^3 - 2r^5s^2}{4r^2s}$

12. $2t(3t - 1)(t + 4)$

13. $(5d^2 - 2e)(d^2 + 3e)$

14. $(11m - 4)(11m + 4)$

15. $(9k + 4)^2$

16. $(-3ab + 2c)^2$

17. Solve the formula $S = \dfrac{a}{1 - r}$ for r.

18. Give the prime factorization of 504.

19. Find the GCF of $60x^3yz^2$ and $84y^3z^2$.

Factor completely. If the polynomial is not factorable, write *prime*.

20. $-16r^3s + 8r^2s - 32rs$

21. $9a^2 - 121b^2$

22. $16c - c^9$

23. $d^2 - 10d + 100$

24. $4m^2 + 20mn + 25n^2$

25. $z^2 - 12z + 35$

26. $x^2 - 2xy - 63y^2$

27. $j^2 + 10j - 28$

28. $4t^2 + 19t + 12$

29. $15k^2 - 7k - 4$

30. $3 + 2x^3 - x^2 - 6x$

31. $(x - 1)^2 - 4y^2$

32. $g^4 - 22g^2 - 25$

33. $-30q^3 + 65q^2 - 30q$

34. $4r^3s^2 - 28r^2s^3 + 49rs^4$

Solve.

35. $(2k - 7) - (3k + 5) = 5(k - 3)$

36. $(2r + 5)(r - 6) = (2r + 3)(r - 4)$

37. $9x^2 + 3x = 2$

38. $a^3 = 81a$

39. $4y^4 - 4y^3 + y^2 = 0$

40. $8z^2 = 11z - 3$

41. Paul walked to school at 6 km/h and rode home from school at a speed 6 times as fast. If his total traveling time was 56 min, how many minutes did he spend walking?

42. A rectangular garden is 8 m long and 4 m wide. When the garden is widened on all four sides by x meters, the area is tripled. Find the value of x.

Solve each problem. If a problem has no solution, explain why.

43. Find three consecutive odd integers whose sum is 10 less than 4 times the least integer.

44. The sum of two integers is 15. Their product is 9 more than the difference of their squares. Find the integers.

45. Tickets to a basketball game were $2.50 each for students and $4.00 each for adults. If $2800 was collected in all, how many student tickets were sold?

Simplify.

46. $\dfrac{3x^2 + 7x + 2}{3x^2 + 8x + 4}$

47. $\dfrac{9r^3 - 4rs^2}{2s^2 - 5sr + 3r^2}$

48. $\dfrac{b^2 + b}{1 - b} \cdot \dfrac{1 + b}{b^3 - b}$

49. $\left(\dfrac{3x}{2}\right)^4 \cdot \left(\dfrac{4}{x}\right)^3$

50. $(4n)^2 \div \left(\dfrac{n}{2}\right)^5$

51. $\dfrac{a^4 - 81}{3 + a} \div (7a - 21)$

Find the LCD for each group of fractions.

52. $\dfrac{29}{36}, \dfrac{29}{30}, \dfrac{15}{16}$

53. $\dfrac{1}{b^2 + 2b}, \dfrac{1}{3b + 6}$

54. $\dfrac{1}{m + n}, \dfrac{1}{m - n}, \dfrac{1}{(m + n)^2}$

Write as a polynomial or a fraction in simplest form.

55. $\dfrac{p}{p - 3} - \dfrac{2}{3 - p} - \dfrac{2p - 1}{p - 3}$

56. $\dfrac{2x - 7}{12} + \dfrac{5(x - 2)}{18}$

57. $\dfrac{3}{g - 3} - \dfrac{2}{g + 2}$

58. $\dfrac{3}{9t^2 + 6t + 1} - \dfrac{1}{3t^2 + t}$

59. $\dfrac{1}{m + 1} + \dfrac{9}{5m^2 + m - 4}$

60. $\dfrac{y}{y - 4} - 1$

61. $\dfrac{1}{x} + 3 + \dfrac{2}{x - 1}$

62. $\left(\dfrac{3y^2}{z^2} - 3\right) \div \left(\dfrac{y}{z} + 1\right)$

63. Express the square of $3d^2 + 2d - 5$ as a polynomial.

64. Find (a) the perimeter and (b) the area of the rectangle shown at the right in terms of x.

Ex. 64

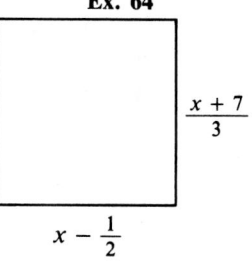

$x + 7 \over 3$

$x - \dfrac{1}{2}$

Divide. Write the answer as a polynomial or a mixed expression.

65. $\dfrac{6c^3 - c^2 + c + 9}{2c + 3}$

66. $\dfrac{n^3 - 11n + 6}{n - 3}$

67. $\dfrac{3x^3 - 10x^2y + 9xy^2 - 2y^3}{x - 2y}$

68. Factor $5z^3 + 34z^2 + 53z - 12$ given that $z + 3$ is a factor.

Review for Chapters 7–9

1. Write the ratio of 9 months to 2 years in simplest form.
2. Find the ratio of x to y if $5(x + 2y) = 7(y - x)$.

Solve.

3. $\dfrac{4x + 3}{5} = \dfrac{9x + 5}{11}$

4. $\dfrac{8}{y - 2} = 3$

5. $\dfrac{m}{m + 4} = \dfrac{m - 2}{m}$

6. $\dfrac{a + 1}{4} - \dfrac{a - 3}{5} = \dfrac{1}{2}$

7. $b + \dfrac{1}{3}b = 2 - \dfrac{7b}{6}$

8. $\dfrac{1}{4}(c - 7) = \dfrac{1}{10}(c - 4)$

9. $\dfrac{5r - 1}{8r} + \dfrac{1}{3} = 1$

10. $\dfrac{s - 7}{4} = \dfrac{5}{s + 1}$

11. $\dfrac{1}{t - 2} - \dfrac{4}{t^2 - 4} = 0$

12. Write as a fraction in simplest form: **a.** 15.6% **b.** 240%
13. $7\frac{1}{2}\%$ of 32 is what number? **14.** 49 is 35% of what number? **15.** What percent of 30 is 75?
16. Write 531,000 in (a) scientific notation and (b) expanded notation.

Simplify. Give your answers using positive exponents.

17. $\left(\dfrac{2^{-3} \cdot 2}{2^{-5}}\right)^{-1}$

18. $(3^{-1} - 2^0)^{-2}$

19. $(5x^{-1})^{-3}$

20. $(-2y^{-3})^2$

21. $\left(\dfrac{t}{t^{-2}}\right)^{-1}$

22. The ratio of Jake's compact discs to those of Andrea is $3:2$. When they each had two fewer discs it was $5:3$. How many discs does Jake have now?

23. A poll of 500 voters found that 320 favored a tax reform proposal. If there are 15,600 voters, find (a) the percent in favor of the proposal and (b) the approximate number of voters in favor of it.

24. The numerator of a fraction is 3 less than the denominator. The sum of twice the fraction and the reciprocal of the fraction is $\frac{57}{20}$. Find the fraction.

25. Leon spent $20.25 for a camera lens that had been marked down 10%. What was the original price of the lens?

26. How many grams of acid must be added to 80 g of a 25% acid solution in order to produce a 40% acid solution?

27. Carmen can retile the kitchen floor in 8 h, but if Joe helps her, the job will take only $3\frac{1}{2}$ h. How long would it take Joe to do the job alone?

28. Is $(-2, -6)$ a solution of $3x^2 - 4xy + y^2 = 0$?

29. Solve $x + 3y = 8$ if x and y are whole numbers.

30. Plot $A(4, -2)$, $B(-1, 5)$, and $C(0, -3)$ in a coordinate plane.

31. Graph $4x - y = -8$ in a coordinate plane.

32. Solve the system by the graphing method:

$3x + y = 1$

$x - y = -5$

33. Solve the system by the substitution method:

$\frac{a}{2} = b - 3$

$3b - 2a = 12$

34. Determine whether the system has no solution or infinitely many solutions:

$y = -4x + 2$

$8x + 2y = 5$

35. Solve by using a system of two equations in two variables:
Samantha invested $2000, part at $5\frac{1}{2}\%$ and part at $9\frac{1}{2}\%$. If her annual income from the investments is $170, how much is invested at each rate?

Solve by the addition-or-subtraction method.

36. $5c - 2d = 1$

$3c + 2d = -9$

37. $2s + 3t = 20$

$4s - 5t = 18$

38. $7j - 2k = -11$

$3j - 5k = 16$

39. A motorboat traveled a certain distance upstream in exactly 2 h. The return trip took 40 min less. During both trips the rate of the current was 4 km/h. How far upstream did the boat travel? How long would this trip have taken if there were no current?

40. A two-digit number is two more than three times the sum of its digits. If the digits are reversed, the number is increased by 36. Find the original number.

41. Find the slope of the line through $(-7, -1)$ and $(2, -7)$.

42. Graph the line through $(2, -4)$ with slope $\frac{3}{2}$.

Write an equation in standard form for each line described.

43. slope $\frac{1}{4}$ and y-intercept $-\frac{1}{2}$

44. y-intercept 0 and parallel to the graph of $5x + 2y = 10$

45. slope -3 and through point $(2, 0)$

46. through points $(0, 5)$ and $(8, 11)$

47. Find the range of the function: $f(t) = t^2 - t + 3, D = \{-2, -1, 0, 1, 2\}$

48. Draw the graph of $g: x \rightarrow \frac{1}{2}x^2 + 2x$. Then give the least value of the function.

49. Given: $x_1 = 18$, $y_1 = 6$, and $y_2 = 4$. Find x_2 if (x_1, y_1) and (x_2, y_2) are ordered pairs of (a) the same direct variation and (b) the same inverse variation.

50. If a 9 g mass is 20 cm from the fulcrum of a lever, find the mass of an object, 24 cm from the fulcrum, that balances it.

51. The surface area of a cube varies directly as the square of the length of a side. If a cube with sides of length 3 has a surface area of 54, find the surface area of a cube with sides of length 5.

Review for Chapters 10–12

Classify each statement as true or false.

1. $|-3.5| < |-3.4|$

2. $-2 \geq -5 > -4$

3. $2^{-3} > 3^{-2}$

4. Solve $2y \leq 10$ if $y \in$ {the positive integers}.

Solve each inequality.

5. $7x + 5 < 3x - 11$

6. $\frac{3}{4}m - 2 \geq 2(m - 6)$

7. $\frac{5}{2}(4 + k) \leq \frac{2}{3}(7k + 2)$

Graph the solution set of each open sentence.

8. $3 > -2 - x > -4$

9. $3 < 2y + 1$ or $\frac{1}{2}y + 1 < -3$

10. $-5z \leq -15$ or $2(1 - z) > -4$

11. $|2 + v| = \frac{3}{2}$

12. $|-4 - m| \geq 4$

13. $9 - 5|j| > -1$

14. $|3 - 2k| < 5$

15. $\left|\frac{1}{2}a + 1\right| \geq 2$

16. $3q - 7 < -4$ and $3q - 7 > 4$

17. $0 = |(d + 3) - (5d + 1)|$

18. A wallet contains nickels and dimes worth more than \$1.05. If the ratio of the number of dimes to the number of nickels is 2:3, find the minimum number of nickels.

19. A scientist has 50 mL of a 40% ammonia solution. At least how much water should she add to produce a solution that is no more than 32% ammonia?

Graph each inequality or system of inequalities.

20. $3x - y > 5$

21. $4(x + 2y) \leq 5y - 12$

22. $3x > -6$
$y \leq x + 5$

23. $3x + 4y \leq 0$
$x + 2y > 3$

24. Arrange this group of numbers in order from least to greatest: $\frac{4}{5}, \frac{13}{18}, \frac{53}{66}, \frac{23}{29}$

25. Find the number one third of the way from $-\frac{5}{6}$ to $\frac{1}{4}$.

26. Express each rational number as a terminating or repeating decimal:

    a. $4\frac{7}{16}$ **b.** $-\frac{2}{27}$

27. Express $0.\overline{72}$ and 1.98 as fractions in simplest form. Then find their product.

Simplify.

28. $-\sqrt{676}$

29. $\sqrt{\frac{49}{900}}$

30. $\pm\sqrt{0.0256}$

31. $\sqrt{\frac{35}{140}}$

32. $4\sqrt{150}$

33. $\frac{2}{3}\sqrt{243}$

34. $-\sqrt{45a^3b^4}$ **35.** $\sqrt{1.21x^2}$ **36.** $\sqrt{g^2 - 4g + 4}$ **37.** $\sqrt{\dfrac{m^{10}}{16n^8}}$ **38.** $\sqrt{3388}$ **39.** $\sqrt{32k^5}$

40. Use the Table of Square Roots on page 682 to approximate $\sqrt{2511}$ to the nearest tenth.

41. A circle has area 1386 cm². Find the diameter of the circle. (Use $\pi \approx \frac{22}{7}$.)

42. Is a triangle with sides of lengths 10, 15, and 18 a right triangle?

43. A triangle has three sides of length 8. Find the length of an altitude to the nearest hundredth. (*Hint:* The altitude of this triangle divides the base into two equal parts.)

Simplify.

44. $\sqrt{\dfrac{14}{27}} \cdot \sqrt{\dfrac{6}{7}}$ **45.** $\sqrt{\dfrac{20}{7}}$ **46.** $\sqrt{15} \cdot 3\sqrt{40}$ **47.** $(x\sqrt{3x})^2$ **48.** $3\sqrt{18} - \sqrt{8} + 2\sqrt{64}$

49. $4\sqrt{12} - \sqrt{\dfrac{100}{3}} - \sqrt{\dfrac{1}{75}}$ **50.** $7\sqrt{5}(\sqrt{15} + 2\sqrt{125})$ **51.** $(\sqrt{19} + 2\sqrt{3})(\sqrt{19} - 2\sqrt{3})$

52. $(5\sqrt{6} + \sqrt{3})^2$ **53.** $(2\sqrt{2} - \sqrt{11})(3\sqrt{2} + 5\sqrt{11})$ **54.** $\dfrac{6}{2\sqrt{3} - 3}$

Solve. If the equation has no solution, write *No solution*. In Exercises 61–63, complete the square. In Exercises 64–66, use the quadratic formula.

55. $\sqrt{x - 7} = 5$ **56.** $\sqrt{y} - 2 = \dfrac{3}{4}$ **57.** $\sqrt{z + 2} = z$ **58.** $7p^2 - 10 = 46$

59. $(2j - 1)^2 = -4$ **60.** $\dfrac{1}{5}k^2 - 1 = \dfrac{1}{4}$ **61.** $t^2 + 4t = 21$ **62.** $3n^2 - 24n = 1$

63. $x = \dfrac{x + 3}{x - 5}$ **64.** $2y^2 - 8y + 3 = 0$ **65.** $4m^2 + 7m = 1$ **66.** $25s^2 + 0.04 = -2s$

Write the value of the discriminant of each equation. Then use it to decide how many different real-number roots the equation has.

67. $4c^2 - c + 2 = 0$ **68.** $5x^2 + 7x = 6$ **69.** $\dfrac{1}{6}d^2 + \dfrac{27}{2} = 3d$

Solve each quadratic equation by using the most appropriate method.

70. $2h^2 = 2h + 3$ **71.** $x^2 + 4x = 1$ **72.** $\dfrac{1}{r} = \dfrac{r - 1}{r + 3}$

Solve. Find each answer to the nearest tenth.

73. The sum of a number and its reciprocal is 3. Find the number.

74. If the area of the region inside the rectangle and outside the square is 720, find the value of x.

75. The gravitational attraction, G, between two objects is directly proportional to the product of the masses, m and n, and inversely proportional to the square of the distance, d, between their centers of gravity. Translate this statement into a formula.

Ex. 74

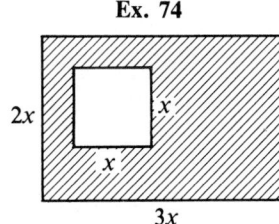

Topical Reviews

Review of Factoring Polynomials

Factor completely.

1. $x^2 + 13x - 14$
2. $3p^2 - 12q^2$
3. $m^2 + 16m - 192$
4. $-4p^2 + 25q^2$
5. $22x^2 - 7x - 2$
6. $36r^2 - 16$
7. $4cx + 6cy - 3ay - 2ax$
8. $6x^2 - 73x + 12$
9. $1 - 81w^8x^4$
10. $4acz - 4bcz + 3ay - 3by$
11. $6x^2 + 15x - 21$
12. $200c^2 + 80c + 8$
13. $9 + 18y - 16y^2$
14. $3 + 20x^2 - 16x$
15. $76x^2y - 19y^5$
16. $4x^2 + 8x - 12$
17. $0.16ax^4 - 0.09ay^2$
18. $4 - 4x - 3x^2$
19. $12x^2 + 57xy - 21y^2$
20. $6(3 - x) + y(x - 3)$
21. $32x^2 - 44x + 5$
22. $14a^3 - 29a^2 - 15a$
23. $30fg - 5fk + 12gh - 2hk$
24. $14x^4 + 21x^3 - 35x^2$
25. $-x^2 - x + 2$
26. $2p^3 - 3p^2 - 8p + 12$
27. $(a - b)^2 + 4ab$
28. $32x^4 - 32x^2 + 2$
29. $2(c - d)^2 - 8$
30. $5c^2d^2 + 30cd + 45$
31. $9 - (a + b)^2$
32. $-p^2 - q^2 - 2pq$
33. $m^4 - 23m^2 - 50$
34. $63x^2y - 28x^2y^3$
35. $-30x^2 - 61x - 30$
36. $4ax - 5mx + 12am - 15m^2$
37. $2a^3 + 2a^2 + a + 1$
38. $(3x - 5)(x + 3) - 4(x + 3)$
39. $(x + 1)(x + 2) - 12$
40. $2x^3 - 12x^2 + x - 6$
41. $(x - 2)(x^2 - 7) + 3(x - 2)$
42. $a^{14} + 4a^{13} - 5a^{12}$
43. $4c^2 - 4c + 1 - 9d^2$
44. $x^4 - 2x^2 + 1$
45. $(x + 1)^2 + 6(x + 1) + 8$
46. $m^2 - n^2 - (m - n)^2$
47. $a(b - c) - (b - c)^2$
48. $x^2 - 6xy + 9y^2 - 1$

Challenge Problems

49. $2a^2 + a - 2 - a^3$
50. $x^4 - (x - 1)^4$

Review of Simplifying Expressions

Simplify. Rationalize denominators where appropriate. Assume that no denominator equals 0.

1. $(5x^7)(-23x^{17})$
2. $(4\sqrt{18})(-2\sqrt{20})$
3. $\dfrac{3x^2 - 12}{x^2 - 2x - 8}$
4. $\dfrac{a^2 - b^2}{2a^3} \div \dfrac{4b - 4a}{a^3 + a^2b}$
5. $\dfrac{4a - 7}{12} + \dfrac{a + 1}{9} - \dfrac{a + 2}{6}$
6. $\dfrac{2^5 \div 8 + 3}{4 + 3}$

7. $\sqrt{\dfrac{14}{5}} \cdot \sqrt{\dfrac{35}{2}}$

8. $\dfrac{2x^3 + 7x^2 + 16}{x + 4}$

9. $\left(\dfrac{3x}{7}\right)^2$

10. $\left(1 + \dfrac{3}{x}\right)\left(1 + \dfrac{4}{x - 4}\right)$

11. $5\sqrt{8}(8\sqrt{3} - 6\sqrt{2})$

12. $\dfrac{-32x^7y^4z^9}{18xy^{10}z^{10}}$

13. $\dfrac{cd}{c^2 - 4cd + 4d^2} + \dfrac{c}{3c - 6d}$

14. $\left(\dfrac{a}{-6c^2}\right)^3$

15. $3^4 - 3^2 \div 3^2 - 3$

16. $(y - 5)(2y^2 + 4y - 3)$

17. $\dfrac{2}{3 - \sqrt{5}}$

18. $(4a)^2\left(\dfrac{1}{2}a\right)(-a)^3$

19. $\dfrac{4x - 1}{x^2 - 9} \cdot \dfrac{x^2 - 3x}{2 - 8x}$

20. $\dfrac{m - 3}{m^2 + 7m} - \dfrac{m + 7}{m^2 - 3m}$

21. $\dfrac{p^3 - 4p^2}{4p^4} \div \dfrac{48 - 3p^2}{6p^2 + 24p}$

22. $(-3x^2)^4$

23. $\dfrac{6x^2 + x - 2}{2x^2 + 9x - 5}$

24. $\dfrac{4ab^2}{4a - 2b} \cdot \dfrac{4a^2 - b^2}{4a^3 + 4a^2b + ab^2}$

25. $\left(\dfrac{4a^2}{3b}\right)^2$

26. $\dfrac{1}{a + 4} + 2 - \dfrac{1}{a - 4}$

27. $\dfrac{15x^4 - 4x^3 + 13x + 4}{3x + 1}$

28. $(5 - 7\sqrt{2})^2$

29. $-2(x^6)^4$

30. $(18 \div 2) \times 3 - 5 - 20$

31. $\dfrac{(-6a)^3}{-6a^3}$

32. $(4x + 7)(x + 1)(x + 2)$

33. $\dfrac{x^2 + 3x - 28}{2x - 4x^2} \div \dfrac{2x^2 - 7x - 4}{1 - 4x^2}$

34. $\dfrac{xy^2 - x^3}{2x^2 - 9xy + 7y^2}$

35. $3\sqrt{\dfrac{4}{7}} + \dfrac{2}{3}\sqrt{28}$

36. $\dfrac{5 - 2x}{2x^2 + 5x + 3} + \dfrac{7x}{4x^2 + 16x + 15}$

37. $\dfrac{3}{4x^2 + 4x + 1} - \dfrac{2}{2x^2 - x - 1}$

38. $\left(x - 5 + \dfrac{6}{x}\right) \div \left(x - \dfrac{9}{x}\right)$

39. $\dfrac{(x + 3y)^3}{3x^2 + xy - 24y^2} \cdot \dfrac{8xy - 3x^2}{x^2 + 6xy + 9y^2}$

40. $(4\sqrt{3x})^2\sqrt{9x}$

41. $\dfrac{2a^3 + a^2 - 17a + 5}{2a - 5}$

42. $\left(\dfrac{5c}{2d^5}\right)^4$

43. $(12a^2 - 2a) \div \dfrac{108a^3 - 3a}{6a^2 - 35a - 6}$

44. $\dfrac{a}{2a - 3} + \dfrac{a + 1}{a + 2}$

45. $c^{2n}(c^{3n})^2c^4$

46. $(2x^3 - 3y)^2$

47. $(-4p^2q^3)(3pq^5)(3p^7q)^2$

48. $\dfrac{2}{3p + 1} - \dfrac{1}{3p + 2} - 4$

49. $\dfrac{(4x^3)^3x^2y^2}{22x^7y^5}$

50. $7\sqrt{\dfrac{27}{8}}$

51. $\dfrac{8}{4 - 3x} + \dfrac{6x}{3x - 4}$

52. $a^{m+6} \cdot a^m \cdot a^{2m-1}$

53. $\dfrac{4x^4 - 14x^2 + 3x^3 - 9x + 6}{4x^2 + 3x - 2}$

54. $\dfrac{a^2 - ab - ac + bc}{a^2 - 2ab + b^2}$

55. $\left(\dfrac{3a^2c}{2d}\right)^3$

56. $\dfrac{5\sqrt{6}}{1 - \sqrt{2}}$

57. $\dfrac{4x^2 - 21x - 18}{2x^2 - 72} \div \dfrac{12x^2 - 7x - 12}{x^2 + 7x + 6}$

58. $(3xy^2)^3 \cdot 2(x^2y)^2$

59. $\dfrac{12x - 3}{x^3 - 5x^2} \cdot \dfrac{2x^2 - 10x}{2 - 32x^2}$

60. $4\sqrt{32} - 5\sqrt{98} + \sqrt{162}$

61. $(a - 5)^3$

62. $\dfrac{x - 5}{10 - 2x} + \dfrac{5}{3x + 15}$

63. $\dfrac{(7x^2y^5z^7)^5}{(7x^2y^5z^7)^3}$

64. $\dfrac{4a - 4c}{6c^3} \cdot \dfrac{a^2c + 4ac^2 + 4c^3}{a^2 + ac - 2c^2}$

65. $\left(\dfrac{4x}{7y}\right)^2 \div \dfrac{(3x^2)^2}{-7y^3}$

66. $3c(4c^2c)^3\left(\dfrac{1}{2}c^3\right)^2$

Simplify. Rationalize denominators where appropriate. Assume that no denominator equals 0.

67. $\left(a - \dfrac{4}{a+3}\right) \div \left(2a + \dfrac{a+3}{a-3}\right)$

68. $\dfrac{4 - x^2}{x^2 + 3x - 10} \cdot \dfrac{2x^2 - 9x + 7}{2x^2 - 3x - 14}$

69. $\dfrac{3}{p^2 - 6p + 5} + \dfrac{4}{p^2 - 25}$

70. $3(2 + 3\sqrt{2})^2$

71. $\dfrac{4x + 2y}{6y} \div \dfrac{2x^2 + xy}{4}$

72. $\dfrac{15x^3 + 38x - 14 - 41x^2}{7 - 5x}$

73. $(\sqrt{2x^3})(5\sqrt{8x^6})$

74. $\dfrac{2x - 7}{3x^2 + 4x + 1} + \dfrac{x + 4}{9x^2 - 1}$

75. $\dfrac{16x^3 - 36x}{-4x^2 - 12x - 9} \div (6 - 4x)$

76. $\left(\dfrac{x^2}{3} - x\right)\left(1 + \dfrac{7}{x}\right)$

77. $\dfrac{3\sqrt{2} - 7}{3\sqrt{2} + 7}$

78. $\dfrac{4x - y}{8xy + 2y^2} \cdot \dfrac{16x^2 + 8xy + y^2}{y^2 - 16x^2}$

79. $\dfrac{3x}{x^2 - 1} - \dfrac{1}{5 - 5x}$

80. $\dfrac{3\sqrt{2} - \sqrt{3}}{\sqrt{8}} - \sqrt{\dfrac{3}{2}}$

81. $5^{2n} \cdot 5^{4n+2} \cdot 5$

82. $(2\sqrt{6} + 3\sqrt{7})(2\sqrt{6} - 3\sqrt{7})$

83. $\sqrt{\dfrac{6}{5}} + \sqrt{\dfrac{5}{6}} - \dfrac{\sqrt{120}}{15}$

84. $(3a)^2(2a^2b^4)^3 - (-3a^4b)^2(b^2)^5$

85. $8y^{-3}$

86. $c^{-3}d^4e^0$

87. $(x^{-1}y^2)^{-1}$

88. $\dfrac{3a^{-1}b^{-2}}{2^{-1}c^{-1}}$

89. $\dfrac{3^{-1}u^{-1}v^2}{2u^3v^{-4}}$

90. $\dfrac{p^{-4}q^5r^{-6}}{pq^{-2}r^3}$

Challenge Problems

91. $\dfrac{\dfrac{1}{a^2} + \dfrac{1}{ab}}{\dfrac{1}{ab} + \dfrac{1}{b^2}}$

92. $\dfrac{\dfrac{c}{d} - 3 + \dfrac{2d}{c}}{\dfrac{4d}{c} - \dfrac{c}{d}}$

93. $\dfrac{x^3 - y^3}{x^4 + xy^3} \cdot \dfrac{6x^3 - 6xy^2}{4x^2 + 4xy + 4y^2}$

Review of Solving Equations, Inequalities, and Systems

Solve the following equations and inequalities. If a problem has no solution, write *No solution*.

1. $4y - 1 = 31$

2. $-2n + 9n - 343 = 0$

3. $3y + 82 = 58 - y$

4. $7n - 6 = 9n - 114$

5. $2(2x - 1) + 4 = 26$

6. $3(y + 4) + y = 20$

7. $5a - 1 - 3(a + 7) = 2(a - 6)$

8. $4 + 6(2x - 3) \le (1 - 3x)2 + x$

9. $\dfrac{3}{x^2 - 7x + 6} + \dfrac{1}{x^2 - 1} = \dfrac{x + 3}{x^2 - 5x - 6}$

10. $4\left(\dfrac{1}{2}x + 7\right) - 3x = \dfrac{1}{3}(9 - 6x) + 23$

11. $2x + \dfrac{2}{3}(4 - x) = \dfrac{1}{6}(4x + 5) + \dfrac{9}{2}$

12. $\dfrac{5}{2}(1 - 4a) \le \dfrac{3}{2} - \dfrac{7}{5}(6a + 5)$

Solve the following equations, inequalities, and systems. If a problem has no solution, write _No solution_. Graph the solution sets for Exercises 14, 31, 46, 64, and 75, which are marked with a ᵍ.

13. $\sqrt{3x - 2} = x - 2$

ᵍ14. $|3x - 8| \geq 4$

15. $0.5y + 0.1 = y^2$

16. $\begin{aligned} 4x - y &= 7 \\ x - 5y &= -3 \end{aligned}$

17. $\begin{aligned} 0.1y - 0.02x &= 0.02 \\ 0.1x - 0.16y &= 0.24 \end{aligned}$

18. $\begin{aligned} y &= 6 - 3x \\ 5x - 4y &= 10 \end{aligned}$

19. $\dfrac{3}{x^2 - 9} + \dfrac{2}{x + 3} = \dfrac{7}{x - 3}$

20. $\dfrac{a + b}{c} = d$ (Solve for a.)

21. $3 - \dfrac{2}{3x} = x$

22. $\dfrac{7x + 2}{4} = \dfrac{5}{x - 3}$

23. $\dfrac{5}{4a - 4} + \dfrac{3}{6a - 6} - 2 = \dfrac{1}{a - 1}$

24. $\sqrt{\dfrac{5a + 4}{2}} = 4$

25. $x - 4x^2 = 1 - 7x$

26. $3|x - 2| = 6$

27. $3 + 5(x - 7) > 3x + 7$

28. $\dfrac{3(2x - 7)}{11} - \dfrac{2 - 3x}{3} = \dfrac{17}{33}$

29. $\dfrac{x + 1}{x^2 - x} - \dfrac{13}{2x} = 2$

30. $\dfrac{3}{a + 5} - \dfrac{2}{2a + 3} = 0$

ᵍ31. $|-3 - 2a| \leq 11$

32. $3cx - a = c(5 - x)$ (Solve for x.)

33. $7 - 2x^2 = 0$

34. $x^2 + 6x - 2 = 0$

35. $\sqrt{2w^2 + 7} = 6$

36. $6\left(5 - \dfrac{1}{3}x\right) \leq 3 - x$

37. $\dfrac{4x - 5}{x + 2} = \dfrac{1 - 5x}{x + 6}$

38. $\dfrac{x}{x - 1} + \dfrac{12}{x + 1} = \dfrac{2}{x^2 - 1}$

39. $\dfrac{9}{4x + 1} - \dfrac{2}{2x - 3} = -1$

40. $m^3 + 4m^2 - 9m - 36 = 0$

41. $(a - 5)(2a + 3) = -11$

42. $2\sqrt{x - 3} = 5$

43. $\begin{aligned} \dfrac{m - n}{3} &= 5 \\ \dfrac{m + n}{3} &= -1 \end{aligned}$

44. $\begin{aligned} 4a + 4 &= 7b \\ \dfrac{a}{3} + b + 2 &= 0 \end{aligned}$

45. $\begin{aligned} y &= -\dfrac{5}{2}x + 3 \\ x &= -\dfrac{2}{5}y + 1 \end{aligned}$

ᵍ46. $|2x + 1| < 7$

47. $2x^2 - 4x = 3$

48. $81p^4 - 18p^2 + 1 = 0$

49. $\dfrac{5}{2x} - \dfrac{4}{3x} = \dfrac{7}{12}$

50. $\dfrac{3}{5x + 3} = \dfrac{1}{3x - 7}$

51. $\dfrac{1}{x + 3} + \dfrac{2}{x^2(x + 3)} = \dfrac{2}{x^2}$

52. $\dfrac{cx - a}{2c} = d$ (Solve for x.)

53. $3 - 2(c + 1) + 3c = 28 - 8c$

54. $\dfrac{x^2}{3x - 2} = -2$

55. $2\sqrt{t} = 2\sqrt{3} - 6$

56. $|5x - 2| = 0$

57. $10x^2 - 6 = 7x$

58. $-\dfrac{3x - 1}{8} \geq \dfrac{x}{3} + \dfrac{71}{24}$

59. $\dfrac{4}{x} = \dfrac{x}{3}$

60. $\dfrac{3}{x - 4} + \dfrac{1}{2x - 8} = -1$

61. $\dfrac{x}{3} - \dfrac{3}{x} = 3$

62. $\dfrac{2x}{x - 2} - \dfrac{3}{x + 2} = \dfrac{7}{x^2 - 4}$

63. $\dfrac{1}{x - 4} - \dfrac{1}{x} = 2$

ᵍ64. $|4 - y| > |-2 - 4|$

65. $0.02x^2 + 0.2x - 2 = 0$

66. $\sqrt{3x^2 + 4x} = 8$

67. $s = vt - \dfrac{1}{2}gt^2$ (Solve for v.)

68. $\dfrac{3w - 1}{7} + \dfrac{5 - 2w}{2} = -\dfrac{15}{14}$

69. $\dfrac{4}{3} - \dfrac{3c + 1}{2} > 12$

Solve the following equations, inequalities, and systems. Graph the solution set for Exercise 75, which is marked with a ^{g}.

70. $t = \dfrac{1 - 6s}{5}$

$\qquad s = \dfrac{2 - 6t}{7}$

71. $\dfrac{1}{5}(3x - 5y) = 5$

$\qquad x = -2y - 10$

72. $y = \dfrac{1}{6}(x - 5)$

$\qquad 3x - 18y = 15$

73. $3c^3 + 48c = 24c^2$

74. $\sqrt{2x + 3} = \sqrt{x^2 - 5}$

^{g}**75.** $\left| -\dfrac{4x}{7} \right| \le 3$

Challenge Problems

76. $\dfrac{4x + 1}{3x^2 - 12x} + \dfrac{x}{16 - 4x} = \dfrac{1}{12x} - \dfrac{1}{4}$

77. $\dfrac{8}{2x^2 + 9x - 5} + \dfrac{3x - 1}{1 - 4x^2} = \dfrac{x + 1}{2x^2 + 11x + 5}$

78. $\sqrt{3x - 5} = \sqrt{x - 2} + 1$

79. $\sqrt{2x - 2} = \sqrt{x} + 1$

Review of Solving Word Problems

Solve. Use a calculator or the Table of Square Roots on page 682 where applicable.

1. Four brothers decided to buy a color television set that cost $392. Their contributions were in the ratio 4:2:3:5. How much did each contribute?

2. Marie and Tony went shopping together. Marie bought 2 L of milk and 10 oranges for $3.44. Tony bought 3 L of milk and 8 oranges for $3.69. What was the cost of one liter of milk? of one orange?

3. The hypotenuse of a right triangle is 3 cm longer than twice the length of the shorter leg. The longer leg measures 12 cm. Find the lengths of the shorter leg and the hypotenuse.

4. Card reader A can read decks of punched cards in half the time it takes card reader B. Together they can read a certain deck in eight minutes. How long would it take each reader alone to read the deck?

5. How many grams of a 5% antiseptic solution must be added to 300 g of a 10% solution to produce an 8% solution?

6. Anthony has $6.10 in coins. He has six more quarters than nickels and half as many dimes as quarters. He also has three half dollars. How many coins of each type does he have?

7. John Kennedy's picture appears on 8% of Pedro's collection of presidential campaign buttons. If he has 34 Kennedy buttons, how many buttons has he in all?

8. Two years ago Seth was one third as old as his father. If he is now 22 years younger than his father, how old is Seth now?

9. A square and a rectangle have the same area. If the length of the rectangle is 4 cm greater and the width is 3 cm less than the length of a side of the square, what are the dimensions of the rectangle?

Solve. Use a calculator or the Table of Square Roots on page 682 where applicable.

10. Colin and Maureen receive $3.50/h and $4.00/h respectively for working in Brendan's garden. Colin works on Saturdays and Maureen works on Sundays. How much money did each one earn if they received $42 between them for a total of 11 h of work one weekend?

11. The ratio of the lengths of the sides of two squares is $3:7$. The sum of their areas is 522 cm². Find the area of each square.

12. Find the three smallest consecutive odd integers whose sum is at least 99.

13. The volume of a cylinder varies directly as the square of the radius of the base. If the volume is 18 cm³ when the radius is 3 cm, find the volume when the radius is 4 cm.

14. Heather paid $650 for some stock in Newcar, Inc. If she sold the stock for $728, what was the percent gain on her original investment?

15. The width of a rectangle is 5 cm less than half its length. Its area is 72 cm². Find the length and the width of the rectangle.

16. The denominator of a fraction is 1 more than twice the numerator. If 1 is subtracted from the numerator, the resulting fraction is equivalent to $\frac{1}{3}$. Find the original fraction.

17. The first cyclist in a two-leg relay race rode at a speed of 40 km/h. The second cyclist rode at 30 km/h. If they completed the 170 km course in 4 h 50 min, how far did each cyclist ride?

18. A sample quilt is made from 150 small squares. It is possible to make a quilt of the same size using 100 squares, 1 cm longer on each side than the smaller squares. What is the length of a side of each smaller square?

19. Inge invested part of her $6000 savings in common stock and the rest in rare stamps. At the end of the year, she realized a gain of 9% on the stock and 12% on the stamps. If her savings now amount to $6615, how much did she invest in stamps?

20. A 3 m by 5 m rectangular wall hanging is hung in the center of a wall. The uncovered part of the wall is a border strip of uniform width. How wide is the border strip if the area of the wall hanging is three sevenths of the area of the entire wall?

21. A tea merchant prepares a blend of 30 kg of tea to sell at $2.95/kg. The merchant blends two types of tea, one selling at $2.70/kg, the other at $3.00/kg. How much of each type should the merchant use?

22. The sum of the digits of a two-digit number is 11. If the digits are reversed, the new number is 7 more than twice the original number. Find the original number.

23. Paula leaves her house at 1:20 P.M. to get to the ball park by 2:00 P.M. Malcolm leaves his house for the ballpark at 1:30 P.M. Paula lives 2 km farther away from the ball park than Malcolm, but can walk 2 km/h faster. How fast can Paula walk?

24. A boat can travel 6 km downstream in 40 min. The return trip takes one hour. Find the rate of the boat in still water and the rate of the current.

25. Flying with the wind, a small airplane can travel 1080 mi in 6 h. Flying against the wind, the plane can travel only 720 mi in 6 h. Find the speed of the plane in still air and the speed of the wind.

Challenge Problems

26. Louise can trim the shrubs in 6 h working alone. Her father can do it in 5 h. They worked together until dinner but trimmed only $\frac{11}{15}$ of the shrubs. How long did they work?

27. On their way to a campsite, Edie and Wilma walked 5 km west and 8 km north. After lunch they walked 3 more km west and 7 km north, arriving at the campsite at 5 P.M. How far would they have walked had they taken the more dangerous, straight-line route through the forest?

Review of Lines and Graphing

Solve each system by the graphing method.

1. $x - y = 6$
   $x + y = -2$

2. $y = 3x - 6$
   $2x + y = 4$

3. $y = -\frac{2}{3}x + 3$
   $4x + 6y = 18$

Write an equation in standard form of the line passing through the given points.

4. $(-3, 6), (4, -1)$
5. $(0, 3), (-2, -2)$
6. $(7, -4), (11, -10)$
7. $(4, -3), (4, 0)$
8. $(1, 8), (4, 7)$
9. $(-5, -1), (7, -1)$
10. $(6, -2), (2, -6)$
11. $(-4, 5), (-6, 1)$

Solve each open sentence and graph each solution set that is not empty.

12. $4 < 2x \leq 8$
13. $-2x \leq 4$ and $x < 3.5$
14. $-4x > 2$ and $x + 1 > 6$
15. $2 - 3x < 5$ or $2x - 5 < -3$
16. $5a - 1 \leq 9$ or $7 - 3a \geq -2$
17. $|1 - 2x| > 3$

Write an equation in standard form for each line whose graph is shown.

18.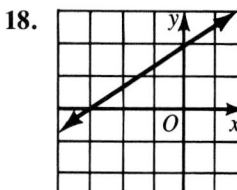

19.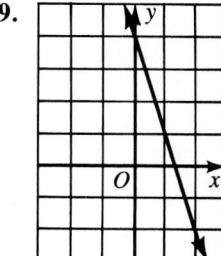

20.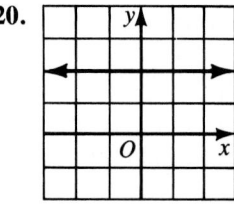

21.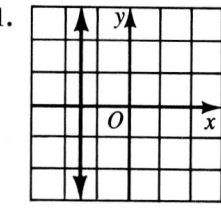

Find the coordinates of the vertex of the graph of each equation. Use the vertex and at least four other points to graph the equation.

22. $y = x^2 - 2x$

23. $y = -2x^2 + 5x - 3$

24. $y = x^2 + 4x + 1$

Graph each pair of inequalities and indicate the solution set of the system with crosshatching or shading.

25. $y \geq x + 3$
$\quad y > -2x - 1$

26. $x + 2y > 4$
$\quad x \geq 3$

27. $3x - 5y \leq 5$
$\quad x - 3y \geq 0$

Write an equation in standard form of the line that has the given slope and passes through the given point.

28. $m = \frac{4}{3}$; $(0, 4)$

29. $m = \frac{2}{3}$; $(-3, -3)$

30. $m = -\frac{1}{4}$; $(6, 0)$

31. $m = \frac{3}{8}$; $(1, -3)$

32. $m = -5$; $(5, -2)$

33. $m = 0$; $(6, 4)$

34. The points $(3, -4)$ and $(-2, a)$ lie on a line with slope $\frac{3}{5}$. Find the value of a.

Write an equation in standard form for each line described.

35. The line that passes through $(2, 3)$ and is parallel to $3x - y = 2$

36. The line that passes through $(-1, 4)$ and is parallel to $x + 2y = 5$

Graph the line whose equation or slope and y-intercept is given.

37. $m = -\frac{3}{4}$, $b = -1$

38. $\frac{x}{2} + \frac{y}{4} = 1$

39. $x = 2\frac{1}{2}$

40. $y = \frac{1}{2}x + 3$

41. $m = -\frac{2}{3}$, $b = 3$

42. $4y - 3x = 4$

Determine whether the given points are collinear.

43. $(4, 7)$, $(2, -1)$, $(-6, -33)$, $(-1, -13)$

44. $(3, -7)$, $(-1, -4)$, $(6, -10)$, $(-9, 2)$

Challenge Problems

Solve each open sentence and graph each solution set that is not empty.

45. $-1 \leq t \leq 3$ and $|t| \geq 2$

46. $\frac{1}{2}|3x - 6| + 3 < 2$

47. $x > 3\frac{1}{2}$ or x is an integer.

Answers

Diagnostic Test

1. 700 **2.** 530 **3.** 3000 **4.** 112 **5.** 16 **6.** 15

7. 468.9 **8.** 15.375 **9.** 0.12 **10.** $\frac{3}{5}$ **11.** $\frac{5}{6}$ **12.** $\frac{2}{5}$

13. $\frac{3}{8}$ **14.** $\frac{7}{27}$ **15.** $\frac{14}{55}$ **16.** 3 **17.** $\frac{5}{3}$, or $1\frac{2}{3}$ **18.** $\frac{2}{5}$

19. ~40 **20.** 3.96 **21.** $\frac{5}{8}$ **22.** $\frac{2}{5}$ **23.** $\frac{7}{100}$ **24.** $\frac{1}{3}$

25. 5 **26.** 57.6 **27.** 10% **28.** 5% **29.** 13 **30.** 12
31. 36 **32.** 25 **33.** 3.0, 3.0008, 3.006, 3.08, 3.7
34. 75% **35.** 60 in.^{2} **36.** -2 **37.** 13 **38.** 24 **39.** -5
40. $7 + 6x$ **41.** $2x + 1$ **42.** $\{7\}$ **43.** $\{7\}$ **44.** $\{10\}$

45. $\{50\}$ **46.** $7 + x$ **47.** $3y$ **48.** $\frac{14}{x}$ **49.** $11 + m$

50. $2d$

Chapter Tests

Chapter 1 Test

1. a. 39 **b.** 5 **2. a.** 62 **b.** 23 **c.** 39 **3. a.** $\{2\}$
b. $\{6\}$ **4. a.** $3(c + 15)$, or $3c + 45$ **b.** $200 - (2c + 15)$,
or $185 - 2c$ **5.** $s + 4$; $s + (s + 4) = 22$

6. 500 I.U. **7.** **8.** -2 **9. a.** 14.3

b. $-\frac{2}{3}$ **c.** 8 **10.** 2 **11.** none **12.** 2 **13.** $|-2| > -7$

14. $>$ **15.** $<$ **16.** $>$

Chapter 2 Test

1. 15 **2.** 9900 **3.** $a + b + 8$ **4.** 0 **5.** -16 **6.** -7
7. $\{10\}$ **8.** 29 **9.** -5 **10.** $-183°C$ **11.** 148 **12.** 5.55
13. 4 **14.** $72°$ **15.** 380 **16.** $8a + 24$ **17.** $-6 - 7j$
18. -30 **19.** $14a - 4b$ **20.** 144 **21.** $x + (x + 2) +$
$(x + 4) = 45$, or $3x + 6 = 45$ **22.** $-\frac{x}{2}$ **23.** $-4t$

24. $12x - 6y + 10$ **25.** $21a - b$ **26.** 81 **27.** $-jk$
28. -19 **29.** 3

Chapter 3 Test

1. $\{-142\}$ **2.** $\{15\}$ **3.** $\{18\}$ **4.** $\{32\}$ **5.** $\{-90\}$
6. $\{-13\}$ **7.** $\{2\}$ **8.** $\{-11\}$ **9.** $\{36\}$ **10.** $\{-4\}$ **11.** $\{9\}$
12. 12.1¢ **13.** $\{-3\}$ **14.** no solution **15.** identity
16. $\{-104\}$ **17.** -7 and 5 **18.** Gail, 8; Helen, 18
19. 50 **20.** (1) Given (2) Add. prop. of equality
(3) Assoc. prop. of addition (4) Prop. of opposites
(5) Identity prop. for addition

Chapter 4 Test

1. $(x + 3)^3$ **2.** 18 **3.** -7 **4.** $r - 10$
5. $-5a - 8ab - 7b$ **6.** $-10a^2b^3c$ **7.** 5^{2k}, or 25^k **8.** $8t^6$
9. $\frac{1}{27}x^9y^3$ **10.** $-128z^{13}$ **11.** $9n^{6x}$ **12.** $4y^5 - 28y^3 - 4y^2$
13. $-14j + 4j^3 - 10j^2$ **14.** $\{5\}$ **15.** $3x^3 + 8x^2 + 3x - 2$
16. $6c^2 - 17cd + 5d^2$ **17.** $21x^3 + 22x^2y - 8xy^2$
18. a. $R = \dfrac{P}{1 + bt}$ **b.** $t = \dfrac{P - R}{Rb}$ **19.** 13, 15, 17
20. 140 km **21.** 20 m by 35 m **22.** No solution; unrealistic result

Chapter 5 Test

1. $(1)(-66)$, $(2)(-33)$, $(3)(-22)$, $(6)(-11)$, $(11)(-6)$,
$(22)(-3)$, $(33)(-2)$, $(66)(-1)$ **2.** $2^3 \cdot 3^2 \cdot 7$ **3.** $-\dfrac{3x}{4}$

4. $10a^4c$ **5.** $\dfrac{(ab + c)^2}{3}$ **6.** $4h^2 - 2gh + g^2$

7. $3t - 5t^2 + 16$ **8.** $28(r + 1)^3$ **9.** $3y^2(x^4 - 2x^2y^2 + 3y^4)$
10. $3m^2 - 5m + 2$ **11.** $8c^3 - 2c^2 - 15c$
12. $35e^2 + 13ef - 4f^2$ **13.** $z^4 - 49$ **14.** $25a^2 - 64b^2$
15. $r^2 - 6r + 9$ **16.** $s^2 + 12st + 36t^2$
17. $4j^6 - 4j^3k + k^2$ **18.** $m^2n^4 - 2mn^2p + p^2$
19. $(17x - 6y)(17x + 6y)$ **20.** $(2v^3 - 3)(2v^3 + 3)$
21. $(5u - 1)^2$ **22.** prime **23.** $(n - 12)(n - 5)$ **24.** prime
25. $(r + 21)(r - 3)$ **26.** $(1 - 12ab)(1 + ab)$ **27.** prime
28. $(7x + 3y)(x - 2y)$ **29.** $(g^4 + 2)(3g - 7)$
30. $(3 - a - 2b)(3 + a + 2b)$ **31.** $-2c(3c + 2)(c - 2)$
32. $(m - 5)(m + 5)(m^2 + 1)$ **33.** $(x + y - z^2)(x + y + z^2)$
34. $\left\{0, \dfrac{1}{3}, -\dfrac{1}{3}\right\}$ **35.** $\dfrac{2}{3}$ **36.** $\{0, 2, -12\}$ **37.** 3 and 5
38. 5 cm

Chapter 6 Test

1. $\dfrac{2a}{2a + 3b}$; $a \neq -\dfrac{2}{3}b$, $a \neq -\dfrac{3}{2}b$ 2. $-\dfrac{m - 1}{4m + 5}$; $m \neq 1$,

$m \neq -\dfrac{5}{4}$ 3. $\dfrac{(x - 7)}{2x^2}$; $x \neq 0$, $x \neq -7$ 4. $\dfrac{2e}{3c}$; $c \neq 0$,

$d \neq 0$, $e \neq 0$ 5. $\dfrac{9x^5}{2y^2}$; $y \neq 0$ 6. $-2a^3(a - 5)^2$; $a \neq 0$,

$a \neq 5$ 7. $-\dfrac{4a}{81b^4}$; $a \neq 0$, $b \neq 0$ 8. $\dfrac{rs(r^2 + s^2)}{4(r + s)}$; $r \neq 0$,

$s \neq 0$, $r \neq -s$ 9. $\dfrac{t(t + 1)}{t - 1}$; $t \neq 1$, $t \neq 0$ 10. $\dfrac{2 - x}{x}$; $x \neq 0$,

$x \neq 1$, $x \neq -2$, $x \neq -3$ 11. $-\dfrac{1}{3y}$; $y \neq 0$, $z \neq 0$

12. $2(c + 2d)$ 13. $\dfrac{7(x + 1)}{56}$, $\dfrac{2(x - 1)}{56}$ 14. $\dfrac{7}{21(a - 3)}$,

$-\dfrac{24}{21(a - 3)}$ 15. $\dfrac{25bc}{20b^2c^3}$, $\dfrac{14b^2}{20b^2c^3}$, $\dfrac{80c^2}{20b^2c^3}$ 16. $-a$

17. $\dfrac{2 - 15n}{12n^2}$ 18. $\dfrac{7 + x}{9}$ 19. $\dfrac{y - x}{x + y}$ 20. $-\dfrac{3}{z(z - 2)}$

21. $\dfrac{(h - 2)(h + 1)}{h - 1}$ 22. $\dfrac{8c - 1}{3c - 1}$ 23. $\dfrac{-t(2t - 3)}{(2t - 1)(2t + 1)}$

24. $\dfrac{4x^2 - x^3 - 8 + 2x}{2x}$ 25. $2x + 2 + \dfrac{4}{3x - 1}$

26. $2a^2 - 3a - 1$ 27. $b + 3c - \dfrac{2c^2}{b + 2c}$

28. $(2x + 1)(3x - 1)(x - 4)$

Chapter 7 Test

1. $1:25$ 2. a. $7:4$ b. $33:16$ 3. $\{10\}$ 4. $\{7\}$ 5. $\left\{\dfrac{3}{2}\right\}$

6. $\{4\}$ 7. $\{12\}$ 8. $\{13\}$ 9. $\{14\}$ 10. $\left\{4, -\dfrac{8}{5}\right\}$

11. $\left\{-\dfrac{3}{2}, 3\right\}$ 12. 1 or 2 13. a. $\dfrac{33}{400}$ b. $\dfrac{16}{5}$

14. a. 4.56 b. 5.4 15. $\dfrac{40}{3}$ 16. 20% 17. Sue, 6 km/h;

Lois, 4.8 km/h 18. 7.5 L of 20%, 2.5 L of 60%
19. 8.4 h 20. a. 5.9×10^{-3} b. $0 \times 10^{-1} +$

$0 \times 10^{-2} + 5 \times 10^{-3} + 9 \times 10^{-4}$ 21. a. 25 b. $\dfrac{64}{49}$

22. $\dfrac{1}{b^2}$ 23. $\dfrac{1}{e^6}$ 24. $\dfrac{1}{g^3}$ 25. 1

Chapter 8 Test

1. a. yes b. no c. no 2. $(0, 2)$, $(3, 0)$ 3. $(0, 12)$,
$(1, 6)$, $(2, 4)$, $(3, 3)$, $(5, 2)$, $(11, 1)$

4. 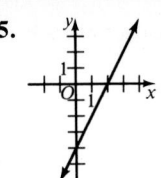 5. 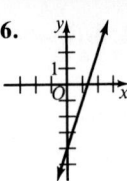 6.

7. -3; -20 8. $6x - 4y = 1$ 9. $y = -x$

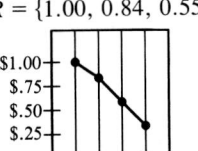

10. $y = 5$

11. $\left\{-\dfrac{1}{3}, -1, 1\right\}$

12. $\{2, 0\}$

13. a. $D = \{1967, 1972, 1977, 1982\}$. 14. $(-1, -3)$;
    $R = \{1.00, 0.84, 0.55, 0.35\}$ $x = -1$

b.

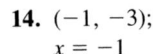
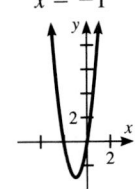

15. a. 1 b. 5.76 16. $\$152$

Chapter 9 Test

1. There are infinitely many solutions. 2. $(5, -8)$
3. $6x - 3y = 24$, $-3y = -6x + 24$, $y = 2x - 8$; the equations are equivalent; $\therefore$ there are infinitely many solutions.
4. $2x - y = 2$

$\underline{2x - y = -10}$

$0 = 12$ $\therefore$ there is no solution.

5. $\left(\dfrac{3}{2}, -1\right)$ 6. $(4, 3)$ 7. $(-34, 72)$ 8. $(2, -1)$

9. 9 dimes, 11 nickels 10. Kate, 7 years old; Brett,

5 years old 11. 1 km/h 12. 27 13. $\dfrac{9}{15}$

Chapter 10 Test

1. $\{-3, -2, -1, 0, 1\}$ 2. $\{-3, -2, -1\}$
3. $\{-1, 0, 1\}$ 4. $(22, 24)$
5. $\{$the real numbers less than $5\}$

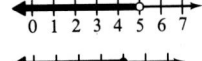

6. $\{$the real numbers less than or equal to $-6\}$

7. $\{$the real numbers greater than $5\}$

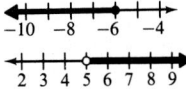

8. $\{$the real numbers greater than or equal to $-7\}$

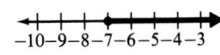

9. {−5, 2, and the real numbers between −5 and 2}

10. {all real numbers} **11.** {the real numbers between $-\frac{10}{3}$ and 2} **12.** {all real numbers} **13.** {−5, −9, and the real numbers greater than −5 or less than −9} **14.** {9}

15. {the real numbers between −3 and 3} **16.** {3, −3}

17. (number line from 3 to 9, shaded)

18. (number line from −2 to 3, with $-\frac{2}{3}$ marked)

19. (number line 0 to 2, with $\frac{1}{3}$, $\frac{2}{3}$, 1 marked)

20. (number line −2 to 1, with −1.6 marked)

21.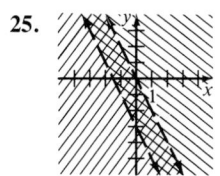

22. (graph)

23. (graph)

24. (graph)

25. (graph)

26. (graph)

Chapter 11 Test

1. -2.5, $-\frac{89}{36}$, $-\frac{59}{24}$ **2.** $\frac{19}{30}$ **3. a.** $0.1\overline{5}$ **b.** 1.1875

4. a. $\frac{29}{40}$ **b.** $\frac{19}{55}$ **5.** $\frac{10}{3}$ **6.** 0.11 **7.** 35 **8.** -3.5

9. $6\sqrt{2}$ **10.** $12\sqrt{7}$ **11.** $\frac{1}{3}\left|\frac{r^3}{s}\right|$ **12.** $|z + 1|$ **13.** {9, −9}

14. {2.5, −2.5} **15.** {17.9, −17.9} **16.** 24 **17.** 36 cm

18. $\frac{2\sqrt{30}}{5}$ **19.** $\frac{\sqrt{15}}{2}$ **20.** $x^3 - 2x$ **21.** $\sqrt{3}$ **22.** $\frac{4}{7}\sqrt{42}$

23. $5\sqrt{3}$ **24.** $21 + 6\sqrt{6}$ **25.** $-9 - \sqrt{5}$ **26.** -5

27. $-2(1 + \sqrt{3})$ **28.** {48} **29.** $\left\{\frac{5}{16}\right\}$ **30.** {$\sqrt{2}$, $-\sqrt{2}$}

Chapter 12 Test

1. $\left\{-\frac{9}{8}, \frac{9}{8}\right\}$ **2.** no solution **3.** {5, −3}

4. {$4 + 3\sqrt{2}$, $4 - 3\sqrt{2}$} **5.** {5, −1}

---

6. $\left\{\frac{3 + \sqrt{5}}{2}, \frac{3 - \sqrt{5}}{2}\right\}$ **7.** {$-1 + \sqrt{2}$, $-1 - \sqrt{2}$}

8. $\left\{\frac{5 + \sqrt{13}}{6}, \frac{5 - \sqrt{13}}{6}\right\}$ **9.** $\left\{-\frac{5}{3}, \frac{3}{2}\right\}$ **10.** $\left\{-2, \frac{1}{2}\right\}$

11. $\left\{\frac{5 + \sqrt{21}}{4}, \frac{5 - \sqrt{21}}{4}\right\}$ **12.** $\left\{\frac{-7 + \sqrt{29}}{2}, \frac{-7 - \sqrt{29}}{2}\right\}$

13. one **14.** two **15.** no real roots **16.** none; above

17. -2 or $\frac{3}{2}$ **18.** 0.74 in. **19.** 4 m **20.** 13.5

Cumulative Reviews

Review for Chapters 1–3

1. 1 **2.** 4.5 **3.** −3 **4.** −9 **5.** $-a - 2b$ **6.** $6x - 2y$

7. −5 **8.** −37 **9.** 60 **10.** 4 **11.** 14 **12.** 0.42

13. $29r + 15$ **14.** $3j - 17k + 3jk$ **15.** 0 **16.** $\frac{152}{3}$

17. −5 **18.** 96 **19.** {−1, 2} **20.** {0} **21.** {−1}

22. (number line from −4 to 4) **23.** F **24.** $y + 10$

25. $10d + 25(9 - d) = 165$ **26.** $2x + 2(x + 2) = 64$, or $4x + 4 = 64$ **27.** {8, −8} **28.** no solution **29.** {−7}

30. {−9} **31.** {100} **32.** {−48} **33.** {7} **34.** {−9}

35. {11} **36.** {−1} **37.** {−40} **38.** no solution

39. {−6} **40.** identity **41.** {9} **42.** 55 km/h **43.** $-\frac{3}{2}$

44. George, 6 stamps; Pedro, 11 stamps **45.** Rick, 10 fish; Lisa, 11 fish **46.** $7.20 per hour **47.** −9

48. (1) Given (2) Addition prop. of equality (3) Associative prop. of add. (4) Prop. of opposites (5) Identity prop. of add. (7) Mult. prop. of equality (8) Associative prop. of mult. (9) Prop. of reciprocals (10) Substitution principle **49.** (1) Prop. of the opp. of a sum (2) Def. of opp. (3) Def. of subtraction

50.

Statements	Reasons
1. $a + b = 0$	1. Given
2. $a + b + (-b) = 0 + (-b)$	2. Addition prop. of equality
3. $a + [b + (-b)] = 0 + (-b)$	3. Assoc. prop. of add.
4. $a + 0 = 0 + (-b)$	4. Prop. of opposites
5. $a = -b$	5. Identity prop. of add.

Review for Chapters 4–6

1. -4 2. $-r^2 - 6$ 3. $x^2 - 4xy + y^2$ 4. $-\dfrac{35}{2}a^6b^2c^4$

5. 5^{2x} 6. $-12c^8d^7$ 7. $-26h^2 + h$

8. $10d^2 - 15d^3 + 20d^4$ 9. $10x^3 + 22x^2y - 21xy^2 - 5y^3$

10. $-\dfrac{n^4}{2}$ 11. $9rs^3 - 2r^2s^2 - \dfrac{1}{2}r^3s$ 12. $6t^3 + 22t^2 - 8t$

13. $5d^4 + 13d^2e - 6e^2$ 14. $121m^2 - 16$

15. $81k^2 + 72k + 16$ 16. $9a^2b^2 - 12abc + 4c^2$

17. $\dfrac{S - a}{S} = r; r \neq 1$ 18. $2^3 \cdot 3^2 \cdot 7$ 19. $12yz^2$

20. $-8rs(2r^2 - r + 4)$ 21. $(3a - 11b)(3a + 11b)$

22. $c(2 - c^2)(2 + c^2)(4 + c^4)$ 23. prime 24. $(2m + 5n)^2$

25. $(z - 5)(z - 7)$ 26. $(x - 9y)(x + 7y)$ 27. prime

28. $(4t + 3)(t + 4)$ 29. $(3k + 1)(5k - 4)$

30. $(x^2 - 3)(2x - 1)$ 31. $(x - 1 + 2y)(x - 1 - 2y)$

32. prime 33. $-5q(3q - 2)(2q - 3)$ 34. $rs^2(2r - 7s)^2$

35. $\left\{\dfrac{1}{2}\right\}$ 36. $\{-9\}$ 37. $\left\{\dfrac{1}{3}, -\dfrac{2}{3}\right\}$ 38. $\{0, 9, -9\}$

39. $\left\{0, \dfrac{1}{2}\right\}$ 40. $\left\{\dfrac{3}{8}, 1\right\}$ 41. 48 min 42. 2 m 43. No
solution; the only possible integers are 16, 18, and 20,
which are even. 44. 6 and 9, or 39 and -24 45. No solution; we need to know the total number of tickets sold.

46. $\dfrac{3x + 1}{3x + 2}$ 47. $\dfrac{r(3r + 2s)}{r - s}$ 48. $-\dfrac{1 + b}{(b - 1)^2}$ 49. $324x$

50. $\dfrac{512}{n^3}$ 51. $\dfrac{a^2 + 9}{7}$ 52. 720 53. $3b(b + 2)$

54. $(m + n)^2(m - n)$ 55. -1 56. $\dfrac{16x - 41}{36}$

57. $\dfrac{g + 12}{(g - 3)(g + 2)}$ 58. $-\dfrac{1}{t(3t + 1)^2}$ 59. $\dfrac{5}{5m - 4}$

60. $\dfrac{4}{y - 4}$ 61. $\dfrac{3x^2 - 1}{x(x - 1)}$ 62. $\dfrac{3(y - z)}{z}$

63. $9d^4 + 12d^3 - 26d^2 - 20d + 25$ 64. $\dfrac{8x + 11}{3}$;

$\dfrac{2x^2 + 13x - 7}{6}$ 65. $3c^2 - 5c + 8 - \dfrac{15}{2c + 3}$

66. $n^2 + 3n - 2$ 67. $3x^2 - 4xy + y^2$

68. $(z + 3)(5z - 1)(z + 4)$

Review for Chapters 7–9

1. 3:8 2. $-1:4$ 3. $\{8\}$ 4. $\left\{\dfrac{14}{3}\right\}$ 5. $\{4\}$ 6. $\{-7\}$

7. $\left\{\dfrac{4}{5}\right\}$ 8. $\{9\}$ 9. $\{-3\}$ 10. $\{9, -3\}$ 11. no solution

12. a. $\dfrac{39}{250}$ b. $\dfrac{12}{5}$ 13. 2.4 14. 140 15. 250%

16. (a) 5.31×10^5 (b) $5 \times 10^5 + 3 \times 10^4 + 1 \times 10^3 +$

$0 \times 10^2 + 0 \times 10^1 + 0 \times 10^0$ 17. $\dfrac{1}{8}$ 18. $\dfrac{9}{4}$ 19. $\dfrac{x^3}{125}$

20. $\dfrac{4}{y^6}$ 21. $\dfrac{1}{t^3}$ 22. 12 compact discs 23. (a) 64%

(b) 9984 24. $\dfrac{12}{15}$ or $\dfrac{5}{8}$ 25. $22.50 26. 20 g 27. $6\dfrac{2}{9}$ h

28. yes 29. $\{(8, 0), (2, 2), (5, 1)\}$

30. 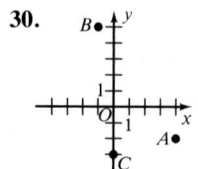 31. 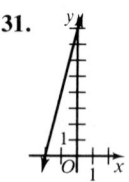 32.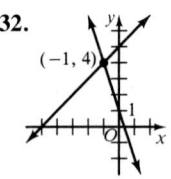

33. $(-6, 0)$ 34. no solution 35. $500 at 5.5%, $1500 at
9.5% 36. $(-1, -3)$ 37. $(7, 2)$ 38. $(-3, -5)$

39. 32 km; 1.6 h 40. 26 41. $-\dfrac{2}{3}$

42.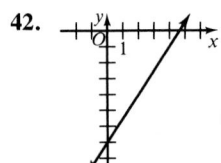

43. $-x + 4y = -2$
44. $5x + 2y = 0$
45. $3x + y = 6$
46. $-3x + 4y = 20$
47. $\{9, 5, 3\}$

48. 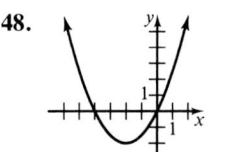 -2

49. a. 12 b. 27
50. 7.5 g
51. 150

Review for Chapters 10–12

1. F 2. F 3. T 4. $\{1, 2, 3, 4, 5\}$

5. {the real numbers less than -4}

6. {the real numbers less than or equal to 8}

7. {the real numbers greater than or equal to 4}

8. 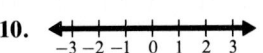 9.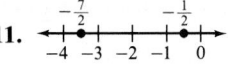

10. 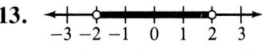 11.

12. 13.

14. 15.

16. 17.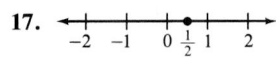

18. 9 nickels 19. 12.5 mL

20. 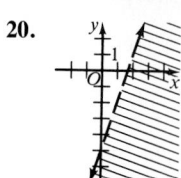   **21.**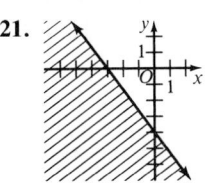

22. 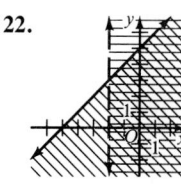   **23.**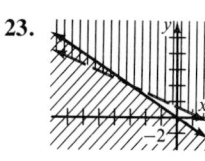

24. $\frac{13}{18}, \frac{23}{29}, \frac{4}{5}, \frac{53}{66}$ **25.** $-\frac{17}{36}$ **26. a.** 4.4375

b. $-0.\overline{074}$ **27.** $\frac{8}{11}; \frac{99}{50}; \frac{36}{25}$ **28.** -26 **29.** $\frac{7}{30}$

30. ± 0.16 **31.** $\frac{1}{2}$ **32.** $20\sqrt{6}$ **33.** $6\sqrt{3}$

34. $-3|a|b^2\sqrt{5a}$ **35.** $1.1|x|$ **36.** $|g - 2|$ **37.** $\frac{|m^5|}{4n^4}$

38. $22\sqrt{7}$ **39.** $4k^2\sqrt{2k}$ **40.** 50.1   **41.** 42 cm   **42.** no

43. 6.93   **44.** $\frac{2}{3}$ **45.** $\frac{2\sqrt{35}}{7}$ **46.** $30\sqrt{6}$ **47.** $3x^3$

48. $16 + 7\sqrt{2}$ **49.** $\frac{23\sqrt{3}}{5}$ **50.** $35\sqrt{3} + 350$ **51.** 7

52. $153 + 30\sqrt{2}$ **53.** $-43 + 7\sqrt{22}$ **54.** $4\sqrt{3} + 6$

55. 32   **56.** $\frac{121}{16}$ **57.** 2   **58.** $\{2\sqrt{2}, -2\sqrt{2}\}$

59. no solution   **60.** $\left\{\frac{5}{2}, -\frac{5}{2}\right\}$ **61.** $\{-7, 3\}$

62. $\left\{\frac{12 + 7\sqrt{3}}{3}, \frac{12 - 7\sqrt{3}}{3}\right\}$ **63.** $\{3 + 2\sqrt{3}, 3 - 2\sqrt{3}\}$

64. $\left\{\frac{4 + \sqrt{10}}{2}, \frac{4 - \sqrt{10}}{2}\right\}$ **65.** $\left\{\frac{-7 + \sqrt{65}}{8}, \frac{-7 - \sqrt{65}}{8}\right\}$

66. $-\frac{1}{25}$ **67. a.** -31 **b.** none   **68. a.** 169   **b.** two

69. a. 0   **b.** one   **70.** $\left\{\frac{1 + \sqrt{7}}{2}, \frac{1 - \sqrt{7}}{2}\right\}$

71. $\{-2 + \sqrt{5}, -2 - \sqrt{5}\}$ **72.** $\{3, -1\}$ **73.** $\{2.6, 0.4\}$

74. 12   **75.** $G = \frac{kmn}{d^2}$

Topical Reviews

Review of Factoring Polynomials

1. $(x + 14)(x - 1)$ **2.** $3(p + 2q)(p - 2q)$
3. $(m + 24)(m - 8)$ **4.** $(5q + 2p)(5q - 2p)$
5. $(11x + 2)(2x - 1)$ **6.** $4(3r + 2)(3r - 2)$

7. $(2x + 3y)(2c - a)$ **8.** $(6x - 1)(x - 12)$
9. $(1 + 9w^4x^2)(1 + 3w^2x)(1 - 3w^2x)$ **10.** $(a - b)(4cz + 3y)$
11. $3(2x + 7)(x - 1)$ **12.** $8(5c + 1)^2$
13. $(3 + 8y)(3 - 2y)$ **14.** $(10x - 3)(2x - 1)$
15. $19y(2x + y^2)(2x - y^2)$ **16.** $4(x + 3)(x - 1)$
17. $a(0.4x^2 + 0.3y)(0.4x^2 - 0.3y)$ **18.** $(2 - 3x)(2 + x)$
19. $3(4x^2 + 19xy - 7y^2)$ **20.** $(x - 3)(y - 6)$
21. $(4x - 5)(8x - 1)$ **22.** $a(7a + 3)(2a - 5)$
23. $(6g - k)(5f + 2h)$ **24.** $7x^2(2x + 5)(x - 1)$
25. $(x + 2)(1 - x)$ **26.** $(2p - 3)(p + 2)(p - 2)$
27. $(a + b)^2$ **28.** $2(16x^4 - 16x^2 + 1)$
29. $2(c - d + 2)(c - d - 2)$ **30.** $5(cd + 3)^2$
31. $(3 + a + b)(3 - a - b)$ **32.** $-(p + q)^2$
33. $(m + 5)(m - 5)(m^2 + 2)$ **34.** $7x^2y(3 + 2y)(3 - 2y)$
35. $-(6x + 5)(5x + 6)$ **36.** $(4a - 5m)(x + 3m)$
37. $(2a^2 + 1)(a + 1)$ **38.** $3(x + 3)(x - 3)$
39. $(x + 5)(x - 2)$ **40.** $(x - 6)(2x^2 + 1)$
41. $(x - 2)^2(x + 2)$ **42.** $a^{12}(a + 5)(a - 1)$
43. $(2c + 3d - 1)(2c - 3d - 1)$ **44.** $(x - 1)^2(x + 1)^2$
45. $(x + 3)(x + 5)$ **46.** $2n(m - n)$ **47.** $(b - c)(a - b + c)$
48. $(x - 3y + 1)(x - 3y - 1)$ **49.** $(a + 1)(a - 2)(1 - a)$
50. $(2x^2 - 2x + 1)(2x - 1)$

Review of Simplifying Expressions

1. $-115x^{24}$ **2.** $-48\sqrt{10}$ **3.** $\frac{3x - 6}{x - 4}$ **4.** $-\frac{(a + b)^2}{8a}$

5. $\frac{10a - 29}{36}$ **6.** 1   **7.** 7   **8.** $2x^2 - x + 4$ **9.** $\frac{9x^2}{49}$

10. $\frac{x + 3}{x - 4}$ **11.** $80\sqrt{6} - 120$ **12.** $-\frac{16x^6}{9y^6z}$ **13.** $\frac{c^2 + cd}{3(c - 2d)^2}$

14. $-\frac{a^3}{216c^6}$ **15.** 77   **16.** $2y^3 - 6y^2 - 23y + 15$

17. $\frac{3 + \sqrt{5}}{2}$ **18.** $-8a^6$ **19.** $-\frac{x}{2x + 6}$

20. $\frac{-20m - 40}{m(m + 7)(m - 3)}$ **21.** $-\frac{1}{2p}$ **22.** $81x^8$ **23.** $\frac{3x + 2}{x + 5}$

24. $\frac{2b^2}{2a + b}$ **25.** $\frac{16a^4}{9b^2}$ **26.** $\frac{2a^2 - 40}{(a + 4)(a - 4)}$

27. $5x^3 - 3x^2 + x + 4$ **28.** $123 - 70\sqrt{2}$ **29.** $-2x^{24}$

30. 2   **31.** 36   **32.** $4x^3 + 19x^2 + 29x + 14$ **33.** $\frac{x + 7}{2x}$

34. $\frac{-x(y + x)}{2x - 7y}$ **35.** $\frac{46\sqrt{7}}{21}$ **36.** $\frac{3x^2 + 7x + 25}{(2x + 3)(x + 1)(2x + 5)}$

37. $\frac{-x - 5}{(2x + 1)^2(x - 1)}$ **38.** $\frac{x - 2}{x + 3}$ **39.** $-x$ **40.** $144x\sqrt{x}$

41. $a^2 + 3a - 1$ **42.** $\frac{625c^4}{16d^{20}}$ **43.** $\frac{2(a - 6)}{3}$

44. $\frac{3a^2 + a - 3}{(2a - 3)(a + 2)}$ **45.** c^{8n+4} **46.** $4x^6 - 12x^3y + 9y^2$

47. $-108p^{17}q^{10}$ **48.** $\frac{-36p^2 - 33p - 5}{(3p + 1)(3p + 2)}$ **49.** $\frac{32x^4}{11y^3}$

50. $\frac{21\sqrt{6}}{4}$ 51. 2 52. a^{4m+5} 53. $x^2 - 3$ 54. $\frac{a-c}{a-b}$

55. $\frac{27a^6c^3}{8d^3}$ 56. $-5\sqrt{6} - 10\sqrt{3}$ 57. $\frac{x+1}{2(3x-4)}$

58. $54x^7y^8$ 59. $-\frac{3}{x(4x+1)}$ 60. $-10\sqrt{2}$

61. $a^3 - 15a^2 + 75a - 125$ 62. $\frac{-3x-5}{6(x+5)}$ 63. $49x^4y^{10}z^{14}$

64. $\frac{2(a+2c)}{3c^2}$ 65. $\frac{-16y}{63x^2}$ 66. $48c^{16}$ 67. $\frac{(a+4)(a-3)}{(2a-3)(a+3)}$

68. $\frac{1-x}{x+5}$ 69. $\frac{7p+11}{(p-1)(p+5)(p-5)}$ 70. $66 + 36\sqrt{2}$

71. $\frac{4}{3xy}$ 72. $-3x^2 + 4x - 2$ 73. $20x^4\sqrt{x}$

74. $\frac{7x^2 - 18x + 11}{(3x+1)(3x-1)(x+1)}$ 75. $\frac{2x}{2x+3}$ 76. $\frac{(x-3)(x+7)}{3}$

77. $\frac{42\sqrt{2} - 67}{31}$ 78. $-\frac{1}{2y}$ 79. $\frac{16x+1}{5(x+1)(x-1)}$

80. $\frac{6-3\sqrt{6}}{4}$ 81. 5^{6n+3} 82. -39 83. $\frac{7\sqrt{30}}{30}$

84. $63a^8b^{12}$ 85. $\frac{8}{y^3}$ 86. $\frac{d^4}{c^3}$ 87. $\frac{x}{y^2}$ 88. $\frac{6c}{ab^2}$ 89. $\frac{v^6}{6u^4}$

90. $\frac{q^7}{p^5r^9}$ 91. $\frac{b}{a}$ 92. $\frac{d-c}{2d+c}$ 93. $\frac{3(x-y)^2}{2(x^2-xy+y^2)}$

Review of Solving Equations, Inequalities, and Systems

1. 8 2. 49 3. -6 4. 54 5. 6 6. 2 7. no solution
8. {the real numbers less than or equal to $\frac{16}{17}$} 9. $\{0, 2\}$
10. -2 11. 4 12. {the real numbers greater than or equal to 5} 13. 6 14. {the real numbers greater than or equal to 4 or less than or equal to $\frac{4}{3}$}

15. $\left\{\frac{5+\sqrt{65}}{20}, \frac{5-\sqrt{65}}{20}\right\}$ 16. $(2, 1)$ 17. $(4, 1)$

18. $(2, 0)$ 19. $\frac{-24}{5}$ 20. $cd - b$

21. $\left\{\frac{9+\sqrt{57}}{6}, \frac{9-\sqrt{57}}{6}\right\}$ 22. $\left\{-1, \frac{26}{7}\right\}$ 23. $\frac{11}{8}$

24. $\frac{28}{5}$ 25. $\left\{\frac{2+\sqrt{3}}{2}, \frac{2-\sqrt{3}}{2}\right\}$ 26. $\{0, 4\}$ 27. {the real numbers greater than $\frac{39}{2}$} 28. 2 29. $\left\{-3, \frac{5}{4}\right\}$ 30. $\frac{1}{4}$

31. $\{-7, 4,$ and the real numbers between -7 and $4\}$ 32. $\frac{5c+a}{4c}$

33. $\left\{\frac{\sqrt{14}}{2}, -\frac{\sqrt{14}}{2}\right\}$ 34. $\{-3 + \sqrt{11}, -3 - \sqrt{11}\}$

35. $\left\{\frac{\sqrt{58}}{2}, -\frac{\sqrt{58}}{2}\right\}$ 36. {the real numbers greater than or equal to 27} 37. $\left\{-4, \frac{8}{9}\right\}$ 38. -14 39. $\{2, -2\}$

40. $\{-4, -3, 3\}$ 41. $\left\{4, -\frac{1}{2}\right\}$ 42. $\frac{37}{4}$ 43. $(6, -9)$

44. $\left(-\frac{54}{19}, -\frac{20}{19}\right)$ 45. no solution 46. {the real numbers between -4 and 3}

47. $\left\{\frac{2+\sqrt{10}}{2}, \frac{2-\sqrt{10}}{2}\right\}$ 48. $\left\{-\frac{1}{3}, \frac{1}{3}\right\}$ 49. 2 50. 6

51. $\{1 + \sqrt{5}, 1 - \sqrt{5}\}$ 52. $\frac{2cd+a}{c}$ 53. 3

54. $\{-3 + \sqrt{13}, -3 - \sqrt{13}\}$ 55. $12 - 6\sqrt{3}$ 56. $\frac{2}{5}$

57. $\left\{\frac{6}{5}, -\frac{1}{2}\right\}$ 58. {the real numbers less than or equal to -4} 59. $\{2\sqrt{3}, -2\sqrt{3}\}$ 60. $\frac{1}{2}$

61. $\left\{\frac{9+3\sqrt{13}}{2}, \frac{9-3\sqrt{13}}{2}\right\}$ 62. $\left\{-1, \frac{1}{2}\right\}$
63. $\{2 + \sqrt{6}, 2 - \sqrt{6}\}$ 64. {the real numbers greater than 10 or less than -2}

65. $\{-5 + 5\sqrt{5}, -5 - 5\sqrt{5}\}$ 66. $\left\{4, -\frac{16}{3}\right\}$

67. $\frac{2s + gt^2}{2t}$ 68. 6 69. {the real numbers less than $-\frac{67}{9}$}

70. $(-4, 5)$ 71. $(0, -5)$ 72. infinite set of solutions
73. $\{0, 4\}$ 74. 4 75. $\left\{-\frac{21}{4}, \frac{21}{4},\right.$ and the real numbers between $-\frac{21}{4}$ and $\left.\frac{21}{4}\right\}$

76. $-\frac{8}{3}$

77. $\left\{\frac{1+\sqrt{281}}{10}, \frac{1-\sqrt{281}}{10}\right\}$ 78. $\{2, 3\}$ 79. 9

Review of Solving Word Problems

1. $112, $56, $84, $140 2. 1 L milk, $.67; 1 orange, $.21 3. side = 5 cm, hyp. = 13 cm
4. Reader A, 12 min; Reader B, 24 min 5. 200 g
6. 8 nickels, 14 quarters, 7 dimes, 3 half dollars
7. 425 buttons 8. 13 years old 9. 9 cm by 16 cm
10. Colin, $14.00; Maureen, $28.00 11. 81 cm^2, 441 cm^2
12. 31, 33, 35 (Divide 99 by 3 to find the middle number.)
13. 32 cm^3 14. 12% 15. 4 cm by 18 cm 16. $\frac{4}{9}$

17. first cyclist, 100 km; second cyclist, 70 km 18. about 4.45 cm 19. $2500 20. 1 m 21. 5 kg at $2.70, 25 kg at $3.00 22. 38 23. 6 km/h 24. boat, 7.5 km/h; current, 1.5 km/h 25. airplane, 150 mph; wind, 30 mph
26. 2 h 27. 17 km

T46

Review of Lines and Graphing

1.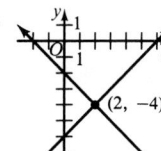

2.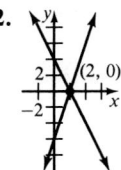

3.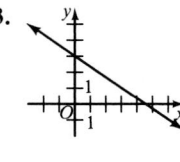

4. $x + y = 3$ **5.** $5x - 2y = -6$ **6.** $3x + 2y = 13$

7. $x = 4$ **8.** $x + 3y = 25$ **9.** $y = -1$ **10.** $x - y = 8$

11. $2x - y = -13$

12. {4, and the real numbers between 2 and 4}

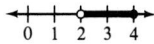

13. {−2, and the real numbers between −2 and 3.5}

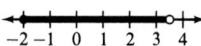

14. no solution **15.** {all real numbers}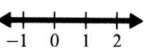

16. {the real numbers less than or equal to 3}

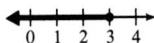

17. {the real numbers greater than 2 or less than −1}

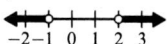

18. $2x - 3y = -6$ **22.** 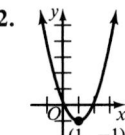 **23.**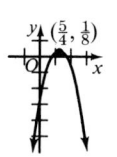

19. $3x + y = 4$

20. $y = 2$

21. $x = -\dfrac{3}{2}$

24.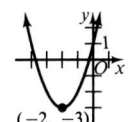

25.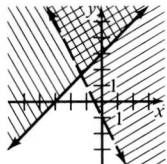

26.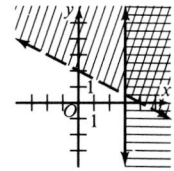

27.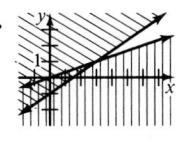

28. $4x - 3y = -12$ **29.** $2x - 3y = 3$ **30.** $x + 4y = 6$

31. $3x - 8y = 27$ **32.** $5x + y = 23$ **33.** $y = 4$ **34.** -7

35. $3x - y = 3$ **36.** $x + 2y = 7$

37. 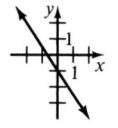 **38.** 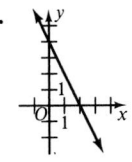 **39.**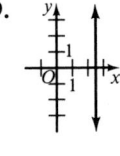

40. 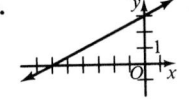 **41.** 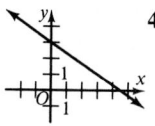 **42.**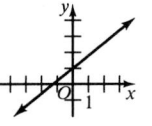

43. Yes; $m = 4$ **44.** No **45.** {2, 3, and the real numbers between 2 and 3} **46.** no solution

47. {the real numbers greater than 3.5 or all integers less than or equal to 3}

Strategies for Teaching

Varying the Mode of Instruction

Using Manipulatives

We commonly think of manipulatives as being most appropriate for elementary school; they are viewed as being needed less frequently at the middle school or junior high school level and rarely at the senior high level. However, concrete approaches also enhance the introduction of algebraic concepts and aid student understanding of mathematical principles when re-teaching is needed. Algebra 1 students may need assistance in making the transition from arithmetic to the new world of symbols. Algebra 2 students who previously focused on learning the algorithms may need help in understanding the concepts underlying the symbolic procedures. Teachers can diminish students' anxieties by using concrete approaches to introduce or to reteach many of the topics in algebra. The goal is to have the students progress to the point where they can work entirely on the abstract level.

In many of the **Explorations** on pages 685–700, students use manipulatives to explore concepts. Below are also a few suggestions for using manipulatives, which can be either commercially made or made by you and your students. See the Lesson Commentary for others.

- **Operations with integers using colored tiles or chips**

   Students gain an understanding of the operations with integers as they physically represent the problems, draw a picture of the process, record the numerical results, and arrive at the algorithms inductively by looking for patterns in their results. (See **Explorations** on pages 686–687.)

   Use: □ ▨ ▨
           1 −1 0

   Record: □□ ▨▨▨ $2 + (-3) = -1$

- **Operations with polynomials using algebra tiles**

   When a teacher says "x-squared" a student's mental image may be the abstract expression "x^2." It is equally valuable for the student to realize that this expression represents the area of a square having x as the length of side. Area models are effective for multiplying binomials and factoring trinomials. (See **Explorations** on pages 689–691.)

   $$(x+1)(x+2) = x^2 + 3x + 2$$

- **Solving equations using a balance scale**

   An equation can be represented as a balance of unknown and known quantities, say, $x + 5 = 9$. Solving for x is represented physically by the removal of equal quantities from both sides in order to maintain the balance. (See **Explorations** on page 688.)

   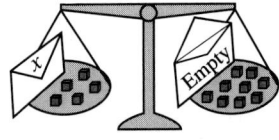

- **Studying lines and their slopes using a geoboard**

   Taking the central peg on a geoboard as (0, 0), a rubber band can "draw" the line between two points and then be stretched to show the rise and run of the slope. (See, for example, p. T119.)

   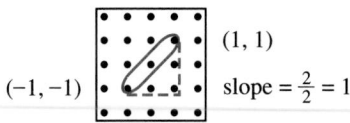

   $(-1, -1)$ (1, 1)   slope $= \frac{2}{2} = 1$

Cooperative Learning

Cooperative learning is most easily accomplished in small groups in which students see themselves as members of a team working together to achieve a specific goal. This does not mean that all the members of a group must be of equal ability or that maximum achievement is demanded of each member. It means that each member contributes according to his or her ability, that everyone's contribution is respected, and that the team does achieve its goal.

Sometimes students can understand a concept explained by another student more easily than they can follow the presentation to the class as a whole. The process of explaining and teaching is in itself a learning process. In a small group, students may find it easier to ask questions and advance ideas.

Groups involved in cooperative learning may vary in size. An even number of members is recommended (four has worked well). In setting up the group you should try to choose students who work well together. However, it is advisable to re-form the groups at intervals in order to achieve maximum interaction.

Cooperative learning can be used in several ways. You may prefer to have students work in small groups for a short time every day, or you may prefer longer but less frequent group sessions. In any case, be sure to choose material that lends itself well to group work—discovery and exploration of a concept, solution of a challenging problem, making a model, for example. You may wish to move among the groups as a counselor and resource person.

The **Explorations** activities on pages 685–700 are well-suited for cooperative learning. Also, in the Lesson Commentary for some lessons, you will find sections headed Group Activities. Many of these can be used for cooperative learning. (For example, see pages T81 and T87.) Some of them involve team activities; others call for group discussion of conclusions individually reached.

Using Technology

Competence in the use of calculators and computers is already recognized as one of the basic skills needed in many careers. Computers and related electronic devices have liberated students from a great deal of routine calculation and have vastly increased the range of information available to them.

The computer has many uses beyond that of saving students' time. Computer simulations make it possible for students to examine some concepts (function, for example) in depth and to test a variety of hypotheses. In statistics, use of computers facilitates the collection and analysis of data. The graphic presentation of data is made much easier if a graphing calculator or a computer is available.

When students become involved in writing programs, they are obliged to learn to communicate with the computer in its own language and to organize their thoughts in logical sequence. In the words of a recent report issued by the National Science Board, writing programs motivates students "to think algorithmically and develop problem solving skills."

Throughout the textbook, students will find features entitled Calculator Key-In and Computer Key-In, which can be used by students with no prior programming experience. Special sets of Computer Exercises extend some lessons for students who have had some programming experience. Suggestions for use of a calculator, a graphing calculator, or a computer appear within some of the text discussions and in directions for groups of exercises where use of these aids is particularly appropriate. In many of the **Explorations** on pages 685–700, students explore concepts using calculators and computers.

These references to the use of technology are highlighted by a special calculator or computer logo on the annotated student pages and in the side columns in this Teacher's Edition. (See, for example, pages 7 and 354.)

Communicating in Mathematics

Effective communication involves skills in four areas—listening, speaking, reading, and writing. Students need to be able to understand directions and follow them accurately, to explain processes and concepts clearly, to read with understanding, and to express their ideas clearly in writing. Much more is involved than the ability to repeat vocabulary and manipulate symbols previously learned. Students who cannot verbalize their ideas may not be able to think clearly and to evaluate their own thinking.

The symbolism of algebra is a powerful language in itself, and students need much experience in using it if they are to realize its value as a concise way of expressing ideas that would require many words. One of the goals of mathematics education is to bring students to a point where they can use the language of algebra as a natural way of expressing mathematical ideas, and not as a foreign language.

Verbalization

Working in small groups is one way in which students can improve their communication skills. In such groups students can gain experience in explaining a concept, restating a definition, justifying a conclusion, or thinking aloud through the steps in solving a problem. Certain exercises on the pages listed in the Index under *Proof, informal,* that ask students to "explain" or to "give a convincing argument" can be used in this context. Group discussion exposes students to others' thought processes and helps them clarify their own. Try to monitor these discussions unobtrusively and to act as a coach and facilitator when help is needed.

Whole-class discussions, with you as moderator, can be valuable on occasion. The questions you raise should be aimed at encouraging independent thinking, not at eliciting specific information. An occasional brainstorming session involving a particularly difficult concept may be worth trying.

Insist that your students use the correct word for a concept or procedure. "The number in front of this thing combines with those, and the whole thing cancels." Sound familiar? Using words like *coefficient, term, factor, root, evaluate,* and *function* will keep your students aware of important and subtle differences in meaning.

Writing in Algebra

Here are a few ways to help students acquire competence in writing mathematics.

1. Have students keep a journal while working through a lesson or a section of the textbook—not as a literary exercise, but as a record of a student's false starts, frustrations, questions, and triumphs.

2. Ask students to take one of the biographies or career notes in the textbook, find additional information, and write an expansion of the article.

3. Have students write a group of word problems related to a concept being studied. Or, for a problem that a student has found particularly difficult, ask the student to try rewriting it in a way that can be more easily understood.

4. Have students prepare a list of questions for an interview of a well-known mathematician or scientist.

5. Ask students to write a set of step-by-step directions for a procedure familiar to them (not necessarily mathematical) but not well known to everyone. Other students may then evaluate these directions. Similarly, students may try writing a definition or a generalization.

6. Occasionally use five to ten minutes of class time to have students write a paragraph on an assigned topic—perhaps an explanation of a recently learned concept. This might be followed by small-group discussions.

Reading Algebra

Difficulties that students encounter in algebra are often the result of difficulties in reading. Since reading is a "learning-to-learn" skill, students become independent learners as their ability to read improves.

Clearly, successful reading calls for practice and patience on the part of both teacher and students. Consistent work on reading that is integrated into the content of the course seems to be the method most likely to lead to success. To help the learner, this textbook has been organized in a way that is easy to follow, with important material highlighted. Six major reading objectives are stressed throughout. These objectives are interrelated; it is hardly possible to teach one without the others. The Lesson Commentary and side-column material suggest practical ways of accomplishing the objectives (for example, see pp. T79 and T96). We encourage you to take advantage of every opportunity throughout the year to help your students gain proficiency in the following reading skills.

1. *Reading and communicating orally*

   Since the transition from what is written to what is spoken is often difficult, students need much experience in verbalizing material that is expressed in symbolic form. You may find it helpful to have them work in small groups, reading parts of a lesson aloud and explaining the examples to one another.

2. *Reading silently*

   It is important for students to realize that the speed of silent reading depends on one's purpose—is one *skimming* for a quick preview or review of the material or is one *studying* to learn the concepts discussed in a lesson? To help students gain study skills, you may want to provide a list of questions in advance.

3. *Using symbols*

   The language of algebra is very compact because of the extensive use of symbols. Students need much help in the correct interpretation and use of symbols. By writing out a few solutions in words, they can gain an appreciation of the value of symbols as savers of time and effort.

4. *Using mathematical words*

   Algebra not only introduces students to its own specialized vocabulary, it also introduces them to new meanings for familiar words such as *power* and *variable*. Encourage your students to learn and use correct terminology and to turn to the Glossary and Index when they need help.

5. *Reading charts, graphs, and diagrams*

   These visual aids are freely used throughout the textbook. Students need to realize that these visual aids are essential parts of the text and examples and must be read along with the words. You can help students to a better understanding of charts and graphs by demonstrating how they are constructed.

6. *Reading word problems*

   Reading a problem with comprehension is the first and most essential step in its solution. You will need to work through a variety of problems with your students, applying the plan discussed on page 27 of the textbook. Help students recognize problems that are similar in structure although considerably different in wording.

Learning Strategies

One of the goals of education is to help students become independent thinkers. The purpose of this section is to provide some suggestions for you when your students need help in learning mathematics.

You can help your students by pointing out that a great deal of learning takes place by trial and error, and that the neat and orderly presentation in the textbook is the final result. When you sense that your students are having difficulty with a lesson, explain that real learning takes place through asking questions, trying guesses, starting down false paths, and trying new methods of approach.

No doubt students have often come to you with questions and statements of frustration like those that follow. The suggestions below each quotation are intended to help you respond in a way that will encourage independent thinking.

"I don't understand the book when I try to read it. What should I do?"

1. Be an active reader; as you study an example in the book, write out the solution in your notebook. In that way you'll understand why certain things are done because you'll be doing them as the authors explain them.

2. Learn the boldface words and their meanings. If a paragraph talks about factors, for example, and you don't know what a factor is, then the paragraph will not make any sense. Look up the words you don't know in the Glossary or in the Index at the back of the book. Finally, use the words when describing to someone else how you did a mathematics problem.

"When you explain a problem in class I understand it, but when I try to do my homework I just don't know how to begin."

1. If you *think* that you can do a problem, then you're ahead of the game. By saying "I can't do this problem," you're defeating yourself and giving yourself an excuse to stop trying. Your teacher believes you can do the problem; otherwise he or she wouldn't have assigned it.

2. Before your teacher or another student explains a problem in class, write the problem in your notebook. Try not to take notes while the explanation is going on, but listen carefully to get a feel for the direction of the solution and the order of the steps. When the explanation is finished, write up the solution in your notebook. If there's any confusion, or if you have forgotten any step in the solution, ask about it right then and there. Perhaps several others are stuck at the same place you are; someone had better clear up the confusion, and it might as well be you.

3. Before doing your homework it's a good idea to look at the assignment from the previous day; part of your homework is probably review.

4. Look again at the discussion preceding the exercises in the textbook and at the notes you made in class. Be sure to review the examples that are worked out in the book.

5. Here are some questions to ask yourself:
   a. What is the problem asking for? Do I understand all the words? Can I rewrite the question in another way? Have I seen a problem like this before? What does this problem have in common with others I've seen before?
   b. What is known? What are the conditions within which I must work? Can I rewrite the given items or the conditions in another way? Can I guess an answer?

6. Remember that there can be more than one way to do a mathematics problem. If the first method you try doesn't work, look for another way. Once you've solved a problem see if there are others that you can solve in the same way.

"I can't seem to organize my solutions to word problems. What do I write down first?"

1. Usually you can begin by using x or another letter to represent the quantity you are asked to find. Then see if you can express other quantities and relationships in terms of x. As the book suggests, it is often helpful to set up a chart, as in the rate-time-distance problems.

2. Read the problem carefully to find the relationships that are involved. Look for phrases such as "is twice" or "is equal to," since some form of the verb "to be" often indicates where the equals sign in an equation will be located.

3. Sometimes it is helpful to guess an answer and then test your guess to see whether or not it is correct. The process you go through in testing your guess is often the same process that is used to set up an equation to solve the problem.

"My friend and I work together on our homework a lot. It's helpful to have someone to work with, but most of the time she ends up doing the problem before I've even started."

It's fun to work with someone so you can share ideas and feel a sense of cooperation. Be sure to take turns in talking through the problems. When one person is talking through a problem, the other has to listen carefully to what is being said in order to understand each step. If you are doing the talking, just think out loud so your friend can hear the answers to all the questions you are asking yourself. Listen carefully if your friend makes a suggestion because she may say something that turns out to be the missing link you need.

"How should I study for the next test?"

Most studying for tests actually takes place through your daily homework assignments and class work. Don't think that the only preparation for a test should take place the night before.

Here are some study suggestions:

1. Review the meanings of the boldface words.

2. Review the examples worked out in the book by covering up each solution, writing out your solution, and then seeing if you are right.

3. Review the problems done in class that are in your notebook.

4. Do the Self-Test and Chapter Review exercises.

5. Pick out the problems from your homework that you could not do. Can you do them now?

6. Have a friend make up a problem for you to do. Then make up one for your friend.

These examples of student frustration imply that one of your major tasks is to raise students' levels of confidence—especially in problem solving. Here are a few specific suggestions:

1. Before showing your students how to do a problem, spend some time discussing the three steps shown on page 23.

2. Have your students make up their own problems. You will get a sense of the sophistication of their understanding of the material and you may get some good test questions!

3. Take some time in class for your students to work together. Encourage cooperation and sharing.

4. There is often more than one way to do a problem. Help your students see these various ways. For example, one student may let x represent the time in a motion problem, and a second student may let x represent the distance.

5. Finally, give your students plenty of time in class to write in their notebooks and to think about a question before attempting to answer it.

Problem Solving Strategies

A problem solving strategy is simply a plan or technique for solving a problem. There are a number of well-known problem solving strategies that relate specifically to algebra. For example, transforming an equation into an equivalent equation whose solution is obvious is a strategy for solving linear equations, and applying the quadratic formula is a strategy for solving quadratic equations. One of the goals of an algebra course is to familiarize students with these standard techniques and to give students enough practice with these techniques so that they can use them confidently and successfully to solve algebra problems.

These rather specific strategies are not the only ones that students can use in solving algebra problems, however. Other, more general, strategies, such as looking for a pattern or drawing a diagram, can be very effective problem solving tools. These general strategies can help not only with algebra problems but also with problems in other branches of mathematics and in other subject areas. Since these general strategies provide an *approach* to solving a problem rather than a specific method of solution, they are particularly useful for attacking a problem when the method of solution is not obvious.

For example, suppose several algebra students are confronted with a word problem that they do not know how to solve. One student might ask, ''Is this problem similar to any of the types of problems I have seen before?'' Another student might try to organize information in a table or a chart or a diagram. Still another might guess an answer and by checking it with the words of the problem discover a general method of solution. Each of these approaches can be a useful strategy.

Below is a list of general problem solving strategies and skills that are helpful in an Algebra 1 course. Each of these strategies is used in the textbook in several different contexts. By using strategies such as these, students can become better problem solvers and may also grow to enjoy problem solving more.

- look for a pattern in the data
- use a table or a chart
- draw a diagram
- generalize from specific examples
- write and solve an equation, an inequality, or a system of equations or inequalities
- use the 5-step problem solving plan discussed on page 27
- apply a standard formula
- recognize a problem as a standard type
- solve a simpler, related problem
- use trial and error and the process of elimination
- reason backward
- make a deductive argument
- recognize the possibility of no solution

In the side columns of the annotated student pages in this Teacher's Edition, problem-solving strategies related to topics presented on the pages are discussed (see, for example, pages 99 and 124).

Nonroutine Problems

Learning how to solve common types of problems helps students develop their problem solving abilities. To become independent problem solvers, they must then learn how to extend familiar procedures and apply them in new situations; that is, they must learn how to solve *nonroutine* problems. There is no single strategy for solving nonroutine problems.

In order to develop their ability to solve nonroutine problems, students need frequent opportunities to extend and apply what they have learned. In this program, see the Resource Book *(Applications, Enrichment, Thinking Skills);* the Tests *(Challenge* problems); this Teacher's Edition *(Suggested Extensions);* and the student book pages listed below.

Ch.	Written Exercises	Problems	Challenges
1	p. 9: 39–46; p. 12: 39–46; p. 35: 55–58; p. 39: 45	p. 29: 16–18	p. 9; p. 35
2	p. 48: 37–40; p. 53: 39; p. 62: 61–62; p. 63: 12; p. 73: 57–60; p. 78: 17–18; p. 86: 34–35	p. 58: 15–16	p. 48; p. 53; p. 69
3	p. 133: 9–11	p. 100: 19–20; p. 115: 31–33; p. 119: 19–20; p. 125: 20; p. 129: 15–18	
4	p. 154: 36–40; p. 157: 51–53; p. 160: 39–44; pp. 163–164: 47–50	p. 171: 17–20; p. 174: 9–13; pp. 176–177: 5, 8, 10–16	
5	p. 193: 61–62; p. 202: 45–49; p. 207: 65–66; pp. 211–212: 62–64, 66; p. 233: 55	pp. 198–199: 1–11; pp. 237–238: 30–32	p. 188; p. 223
6	p. 249: 39–40; p. 262: 45; pp. 267–268: 31–34; p. 272: 39, 44–46; p. 277: 31–38		p. 254; p. 263; p. 273
7	p. 290: 43–45; p. 296: 46–50; pp. 334–335: 68–71	p. 292: 17–19; p. 297: 10–13; p. 301: 16; p. 308: 13–14; p. 314: 15; p. 325: 24–25; p. 330: 22–23; pp. 339–340: 1–3	p. 292
8	p. 352: 44–45; pp. 357–358: 44–48; p. 365: 39–42; p. 369: 41–45; p. 373: 38–42; p. 377: 9–10; p. 381: 47–48; p. 387: 31–32, 41–42; p. 395: 23–24	p. 396: 15; p. 402: 15–18	p. 382
9	p. 416: 22–24; p. 420: 37–41; p. 428: 29–31; pp. 432–433: 36–46	p. 424: 21–22; p. 429: 9–10; pp. 435–436: 27–32; p. 442: 23; p. 449: 31–34	p. 425; p. 437
10	p. 460: 39–42; p. 467: 51–66; p. 481: 39–40; p. 488: 19–25; p. 493: 34–39; pp. 497–498: 19–28	p. 474: 21–23	p. 475
11	pp. 510–511: 33–38; p. 516: 41–43; p. 546: 41–44; p. 549: 47–50	p. 527: 10–12; p. 533: 9–12; p. 550: 9–11	p. 520; p. 534; p. 536
12	p. 563: 49; p. 566: 28–30; p. 569: 29–31; p. 574: 19–20; p. 578: 28–31; p. 590: 7–10	p. 581: 15; p. 587: 11–12; p. 592: 11–14	
	Probability p. 602: 6–7; p. 605: 7 Statistics p. 608: 12–16 Geometry p. 618: 19–22 Trig. p. 629: 10–16; p. 632: 32–33	p. 623: 12–13; p. 626: 9 p. 636: 12–14	p. 632

Making Connections

To appreciate the power of mathematics, students need to see the connections between the mathematics they are studying and other mathematics courses, other subject areas, and everyday and career applications. Many opportunities to explore these connections are provided in this book, as detailed below.

Connections with Earlier Math Courses

Comparing previously acquired and new concepts helps students transfer prior learning to new situations. For example, the algebraic representation of the distributive property is related to mental arithmetic techniques (page 65) and to manipulative models of area (page 66) from earlier grades. Arithmetic examples parallel new skills with algebraic fractions (e.g., pages 251 and 259).

Connections with Geometry

Strong connections between algebra and geometry occur throughout the course in the use of geometric formulas in early work with variables, in the geometric modeling of algebraic concepts, and in problem solving (e.g., pages 8–9; 143 and 208; 172–174 and 198). In the Looking Ahead section, lessons on topics in geometry (pages 616–626) prepare students for formal courses in geometry and trigonometry. For additional examples of the integration of geometry with algebra in this book, refer to the Index under *Geometry, Area formulas and problems, Perimeter formulas and problems,* and *Problems, geometry*.

Connections with Data Analysis, Statistics, and Probability

Throughout this algebra book, students meet techniques for dealing with data. In the illustrations facing page 1 and on page 44, they see three different graphic presentations of data, one of them on a computer to emphasize the current use of technology in statistical work. In Lesson 7-1 (page 287) students compare data using ratios and then use proportions (page 296) to solve problems involving statistical sampling techniques. They later learn how to use scientific notation for very large or very small items of data (pages 336–340). In Lesson 8-6 (pages 374–377) students draw and interpret graphs of data and then use a line of best fit to make predictions from data they gather (page 378). In addition to the integration of statistical work throughout, formal lessons on statistical techniques (beginning on page 606) introduce students to frequency distributions, statistical measures, stem-and-leaf and box-and-whisker plots, and the misuse of statistics.

Students are prepared for future coursework in statistics and probability with a discussion of random experiments, sample spaces, and events (beginning on page 600) and with practice in finding the probability of equally likely events.

Connections with Discrete Mathematics

Topics in discrete mathematics, such as sets, using recursion relations, writing algorithms in computer programming, and linear programming, are listed in the Index under *Discrete Mathematics*.

Connections with Real-World Applications

The connections between mathematics and other curriculum areas can be seen throughout, such as the science connection (e.g., pages 246, 335, 456, and 583), the social science connection (e.g., pages 100, 333, and 348), and the historical connection (e.g., pages 87, 115, and 477). Some of the innumerable applications are highlighted in the Applications features and in the problems throughout (see the Index under *Applications, Formulas,* and *Problems*). In Biographical Notes and Career Notes students can see the contribution of others to past and contemporary society and can see that the study of mathematics opens the door to possible contributions they themselves can make.

Thinking Skills

Thinking skills are woven into the whole fabric of algebra. While such topics as proofs and problem solving may make special demands on students' thinking skills, no real understanding of any of the concepts presented in this course can take place without good thinking skills.

Your students are likely to come to you with a variety of thinking skills, not always well developed or even recognized by the students themselves. You can help students improve these skills, use them more efficiently, and acquire additional skills.

The side-column notes in this Teacher's Edition point out specific thinking skills that come into play in particular lessons (for example, pp. 9 and 204). These skills are key in the study of algebra:

Recall and transfer
Applying concepts
Analysis
Interpreting
Reasoning and inferencing
Spatial perception
Synthesis

In the Index under "Thinking Skills" you will find a list of some of the areas in which these skills are applied by students. Among these are the *recall* of methods learned earlier and their *transfer* or extension to new material; and the *application* of important concepts to the mathematical modeling of situations familiar to students.

Throughout the course, the skills of *analysis* and *interpretation* of information will be called upon. Encourage your students to be on the lookout for likenesses, differences, and patterns; and to recognize similarities among problems that appear at first glance to be quite different. In attacking a problem, students will need to examine and interpret the given information and discard any irrelevant material. In working through the solution of an equation or an inequality, they will need to analyze possible values to see whether they fit the given conditions. In problem solving, they will need to interpret their solutions to see whether all the solutions make sense (see, for example, pages 165 and 175).

Reasoning comes into play whenever students consider information in an if-then format. They draw *inferences* about number relationships on the basis of observed patterns and from statistical data and graphs.

Spatial perception is required to picture all views of an object in space in order to calculate the total surface area.

Synthesis is employed when ideas come together to form something new; for example, when data are plotted to form a graph and commands are organized to create a computer program.

In the Resource Book there are *Thinking Skills* pages that define these critical thinking skills and provide the opportunity to practice them in the context of this algebra course.

Here are some ways to help students develop their thinking skills:

1. *Be a role model.* Talk through the steps in your own solution of an exercise or a problem. By following your reasoning, a student can often learn to organize his or her own thinking in a more logical way.

2. *Use helpful questioning techniques.* Be sure that many of your questions to students address the way in which they have arrived at answers rather than to their recall of specific information.

3. *Encourage active participation by students.* Take full advantage of Oral and Written Exercises that ask students to "explain," "show," or "give a convincing argument." These phrases indicate that an informal proof is expected of the students. (See *Proof, informal,* in the Index.) As the basis for a group activity, such exercises provide the opportunity for one student to present an explanation and the others to judge whether the argument is convincing.

You will need to emphasize the importance of attacking a problem analytically—of trying to see the problem as a whole and planning one's solution. Point out also that there may be a variety of ways of approaching a problem, and that there is nothing wrong with abandoning one strategy and trying another.

Error Analysis

Since mathematics builds on previously learned symbols, concepts, and skills, error patterns that are left uncorrected will impede students' progress. Of course, there are many different reasons for errors, but certain types of errors are more common than others. If you are aware of these common errors, you can help students avoid them and you can be better prepared to help students overcome them if they do occur. Throughout the book, in the side columns next to the textbook pages, common errors have been identified and suggestions for avoiding them have been provided. (See, for example, "Common Errors" on pages 66 and 224.) The errors discussed in the side columns are fairly specific. However, many of them can be grouped into one or more of the following categories:

Errors in Reading and Translating

(See, for example, pp. 20 and 170.)

Students often have difficulty in translating English phrases and sentences into mathematical expressions and sentences. For example, students may translate the expression "five less than a number" as $5 - n$. Not reading word problems carefully, with concentration on their meaning, is another frequent cause of difficulty. Students may make mistakes because they do not fully understand the meanings of mathematical terms—for example, "maximum value of a function." Words such as *or*, which have a different meaning in mathematics than in everyday speech, may cause confusion.

Failure to Understand Symbols

(See, for example, pp. 144, 332, and 380.)

Students often do not fully understand the meanings of mathematical symbols. As a result, they may make the following errors:

$$\frac{6}{0} = 0 \qquad -x^2 = (-x)^2 \qquad b^n = nb$$

$$2^{-2} = -4 \qquad (a + b)^2 = a^2 + b^2 \qquad -2 > x > 3$$

$$0.\overline{5} = \frac{1}{2} \qquad 2\sqrt{3} = \sqrt{6} \qquad \sqrt{x^2} = x$$

Misunderstanding of Properties

(See, for example, pp. 296, 300, and 464.)

Recurring errors often stem from students' misapplying properties in the ways shown below.

Addition property of equality: $x + 2 = 6$
$$x = 8$$

Multiplication property of equality: $\frac{x}{2} + \frac{x}{3} = 5$
$$3x + 2x = 5$$

Division property of equality: $3x(x + 2) = 0$
$$x + 2 = 0$$

Multiplication property of order: $2x > -8$
$$x < -4$$

Distributive property $-4(x + 1) = 9$
$$-4x + 1 = 9$$

Zero-product property: $(x - 3)(x + 2) = 14$
$$x - 3 = 14 \text{ or } x + 2 = 14$$

Rule for simplifying fractions: $\dfrac{x}{\cancel{3}_1} = \dfrac{\cancel{6}^2}{5}$

Errors in Using Standard Forms

(See, for example, pp. 531 and 568.)

Although students may have memorized the Pythagorean theorem or the quadratic formula, they may not understand the importance of using the standard form when they apply these formulas.

Consequently, they often try to work with an expression or an equation without first putting it into standard form. This means that they may substitute incorrect values in the formula $a^2 + b^2 = c^2$ or try to solve an equation by the quadratic formula before transforming it so that one side is 0. Other errors that students are liable to make are illustrated below.

$$2x + 3y = 6 \qquad y = 1 - 3x$$
$$\text{slope} = 2 \qquad \text{slope} = 1$$
$$y\text{-intercept} = -3$$
$$x^2 + 1 - 2x = 0$$
$$a = 1, \ b = 1, \ c = -2$$

Use of Incorrect Formulas

(See, for example, pp. 361, 368, and 531.)

Many errors are the result of students' using formulas that are incorrect. Some of the more common "impostors" are shown below.

$$p = l + w \qquad C = \pi r^2 \qquad \text{slope} = \frac{x_2 - x_1}{y_2 - y_1}$$

$$x = -b \pm \frac{\sqrt{b^2 - 4ac}}{2a} \qquad \text{discriminant} = \sqrt{b^2 - 4ac}$$

Errors in Simplifying

(See, for example, pp. 190, 197, and 522.)

In addition to some of the reasons already given, students may make errors in simplifying expressions because of incorrect assumptions such as $\sqrt{a^2 - b^2} = \sqrt{a^2} - \sqrt{b^2}$. They may also make errors because they do not take notice of grouping symbols such as the fraction bar or because they do not follow the pre-

scribed order of operations or because they add unlike terms. Students sometimes confuse the rules of exponents—multiplying exponents when they are multiplying and dividing exponents when they are dividing. Students may forget to (or not realize that they must) change the sign of every term of a polynomial that they are subtracting. Simplifying fractions seems to be particularly troublesome. Thinking that $\frac{n}{n} = 0$ can lead to errors such as $6x^2 + 8x + 2 = 2(3x^2 + 4x)$.

Errors such as $\frac{\not{x} + 3}{\not{x}} = 3$ and $\dfrac{\overset{3}{\not{6}}y(x + 3)}{\underset{1}{\not{2}}y^2(x + 1)} = \dfrac{3(x + 3)}{2(x + 1)}$ are common.

Errors in Checking

(See, for example, pp. 236 and 549.)

Checking can help students develop self-confidence and alert them to errors. However, a check that is incorrectly performed is not useful. Students often fail to realize that it is not only helpful but necessary to check the roots of fractional and radical equations. The following checking errors may occur: Students may occasionally substitute a value for a variable such as 8 for x, get a true statement such as $4 = 4$, and conclude that the solution is 4. Students may not realize that they must check their answers with the *words* of word problems or that they must check their solutions to systems of linear equations in *both original* equations. Some students may think that they should always discard negative solutions. Students may not think of checking their answers when the method involves, for example, considering whether an answer is reasonable or multiplying to check factoring.

Reteaching

Effective reteaching involves a variety of approaches and activities. Factors to be considered include the nature of the material to be retaught, the maturity and ability level of the students involved, the particular point of difficulty, and the number of students affected.

Prerequisite to reteaching is error analysis. This is discussed more fully in the article on page T56, as well as in the side-column notes headed "Common Errors." These notes not only identify frequently occurring errors; they also suggest methods of reteaching to correct them. The Cautions that appear in the student textbook are intended to anticipate students' errors and prevent their occurrence. The Mixed Review exercises at the end of each lesson will help to minimize the need for extensive reteaching of skills.

The primary focus in reteaching needs to be on concepts that have been imperfectly understood or that students have difficulty in applying. Reteaching of concepts must be more than reiteration of what has previously been presented. In most cases a fresh approach is needed, perhaps with the aid of manipulative or visual materials. In addition to the model lesson plan that is provided for each lesson in the side columns, the Lesson Commentary (pages T77–T144) offers alternate teaching suggestions. The articles on varying the mode of instruction and communicating in mathematics under "Strategies for Teaching" (pages T48–T51) suggest new approaches that may be useful for reteaching. Also, the student textbook itself sometimes highlights alternate methods of attacking a problem (see, for example, pages 54, 288, and 482).

The ancillaries provide much help in the reteaching of concepts. The Study Guide, the Resource Book, and the tutorial material in Algebra Action offer a variety of approaches aimed at enhancing students' understanding. The Overhead Visuals will be helpful to students who learn best from a graphic or visual approach. The disk Algebra Plotter Plus provides software for classroom demonstration or independent use, enabling users to explore concepts using computer graphing techniques. Students who are having difficulty with word problems may be directed to the problem solving pages in the Resource Book. Each lesson on these pages takes students step by step through the analysis and solution of a few problems.

Many of the errors that call for reteaching are the result of forgetting or of failure to stay with a concept or skill long enough for mastery. Built into this program are provisions for detecting and correcting errors of this type at an early stage. Students should be encouraged to use the Self-Tests, the Chapter Summaries, Reviews, and Tests, and the Cumulative Reviews as means of detecting their own weaknesses.

Students who need additional reinforcement of skills imperfectly learned will benefit from the additional "A" exercises in the Guided Practice section in the side columns. Further materials for reteaching and reinforcing skills are provided by the Practice Masters and the practice pages in the Resource Book.

Reading References

The National Council of Teachers of Mathematics produces a number of helpful publications that give additional information about the topics discussed in the preceding pages. Here are a few suggestions:

Classroom Ideas from Research on Secondary School Mathematics, Part 1: Algebra, 1983

Curriculum and Evaluation Standards for School Mathematics, 1988

Effective Mathematics Teaching, 1987

The Ideas of Algebra, K-12, 1988

Research Within Reach: Secondary School Mathematics, 1982

Assignment Guide

The following guide offers suggestions for planning separate minimum, average, and maximum courses that you can adapt as necessary to fit the needs of your particular classes.

Because students' interests and backgrounds differ widely from class to class, most of the optional features, including the **Explorations** on pp. 685–700, are not listed. You will want to choose those features which best suit your classes. If you have access to a computer that accepts BASIC, you may wish to allow some time for your students to do the Computer Key-Ins or the Computer Exercises. Please see the note on page xiii regarding these features.

All the assignments refer to written exercises, with the letter "P" indicating word problems. Spiraled review assignments, denoted by the letter "S," provide a mixed review, while sequential review assignments, denoted by the letter "R," review topics in the same order as presented in the textbook. "EP" refers the teacher to the Extra Practice section, which contains extra exercises and problems to be used as needed.

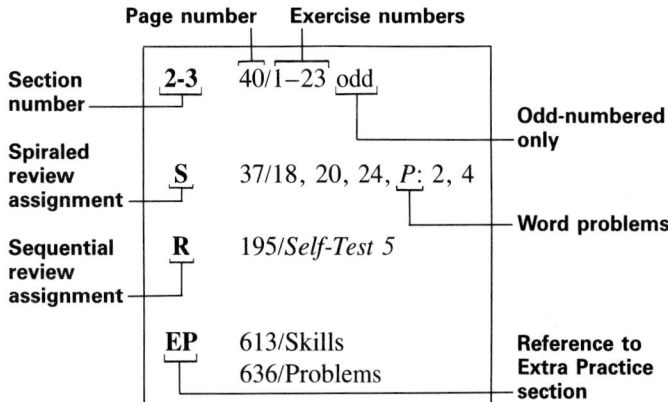

Summary Time Schedule for the Assignments

Chapter	1	2	3	4	5	6	7	8	9	10	11	12	Looking Ahead	Total
Minimum Course	13	12	14	15	19	13	15	15	14	10	14	6	0	160
Average Course	12	11	13	15	20	12	15	14	14	11	13	10	0	160
Maximum Course	10	11	12	14	16	11	14	13	13	10	14	10	12	160

Trimester **Semester** Trimester

LESSON	MINIMUM COURSE	AVERAGE COURSE	MAXIMUM COURSE
1	**1-1** 3/1–37 odd **S** 5/*Mixed Review*	**1-1** 3/1–47 odd **S** 5/*Mixed Review*	**1-1** 3/3–48 mult. of 3 **1-2** 8/3–45 mult. of 3 **S** 9/*Mixed Review*
2	**1-2** 8/1–29 odd, 35, 36 **S** 9/*Mixed Review*	**1-2** 8/1–33 odd, 37–39 **S** 9/*Mixed Review*	**1-3** 11/1–25 odd, 33–42 **S** 12/*Mixed Review*
3	**1-3** 11/1–29 odd **S** 12/*Mixed Review*	**1-3** 11/1–39 odd **S** 12/*Mixed Review*	**1-4** 16/2–42 even, 51–53 **S** 18/*Mixed Review* **R** 13/*Self-Test 1*
4	**1-4** 16/1–25 odd **R** 13/*Self-Test 1*	**1-4** 16/1–41 odd **R** 13/*Self-Test 1*	**1-5** 20/2–36 even **S** 22/*Mixed Review*

LESSON	MINIMUM COURSE		AVERAGE COURSE		MAXIMUM COURSE	
5	**1-4**	17/27–41 odd	**1-4**	18/42–52 even	**1-6**	24/*P*: 2–18 even, 19–22
	S	18/*Mixed Review*	**S**	18/*Mixed Review*	**S**	26/*Mixed Review*
	1-5	20/1–7	**1-5**	20/2–16 even		
6	**1-5**	21/9–29 odd	**1-5**	21/17–35 odd	**1-7**	28/*P*: 2–14 even, 16–18
	S	22/*Mixed Review*	**S**	22/*Mixed Review*	**S**	29/*Mixed Review*
7	**1-6**	24/*P*: 1–12	**1-6**	24/*P*: 1–18	**1-8**	33/3–57 mult. of 3
					S	35/*Mixed Review*
					R	30/*Self-Test 2*
8	**1-6**	25/*P*: 13–19 odd	**1-6**	25/*P*: 19–22	**1-9**	38/2–38 even, 43–45
	S	26/*Mixed Review*	**S**	26/*Mixed Review*	**S**	39/*Mixed Review*
9	**1-7**	28/*P*: 1–10	**1-7**	28/*P*: 1–15 odd	*Prepare for Chapter Test*	
	S	29/*Mixed Review*	**S**	29/*Mixed Review*	**R**	39/*Self-Test 3*
			R	30/*Self-Test 2*		41/*Chapter Review*
					EP	639/*Skills;* 665/*Problems*
10	**1-8**	33/3–36 mult. of 3	**1-8**	33/3–48 mult. of 3	*Administer Chapter 1 Test*	
	S	35/*Mixed Review*	**S**	35/*Mixed Review*	**R**	43/*Maintaining Skills*
	R	30/*Self-Test 2*	**1-9**	38/3–42 mult. of 3		
11	**1-9**	38/3–33 mult. of 3	*Prepare for Chapter Test*		**2-1**	47/1–35 odd, 37–40
	S	34/39–49 odd	**R**	39/*Self-Test 3*	**S**	48/*Mixed Review*
		39/*Mixed Review*		41/*Chapter Review*		
			EP	639/*Skills;* 665/*Problems*		
12	*Prepare for Chapter Test*		*Administer Chapter 1 Test*		**2-2**	52/1–39 odd
	R	39/*Self-Test 3*	**R**	43/*Maintaining Skills*	**S**	53/*Mixed Review*
		41/*Chapter Review*				
	EP	639/*Skills*				
		665/*Problems*				
13	*Administer Chapter 1 Test*		**2-1**	47/1–37 odd	**2-3**	55/3–42 mult. of 3
	R	43/*Maintaining Skills*	**S**	48/*Mixed Review*		56/*P*: 2–16 even
					S	58/*Mixed Review*
14	**2-1**	47/1–33 odd, 35	**2-2**	52/1–33 odd, 37	**2-4**	61/15–60 mult. of 3, 61
	S	48/*Mixed Review*	**S**	53/*Mixed Review*		62/*P*: 2–12 even
					S	63/*Mixed Review*
15	**2-2**	52/1–29 odd, 31–32	**2-3**	55/1–39 odd	**2-5**	67/3–75 mult. of 3
	S	53/*Mixed Review*		56/*P*: 2–12 even	**S**	69/*Mixed Review*
			S	58/*Mixed Review*	**R**	63/*Self-Test 1*
16	**2-3**	55/1–35 odd	**2-4**	61/2–48 even, 55–58	**2-6**	72/3–57 mult. of 3, 59
	S	58/*Mixed Review*		62/*P*: 2–10 even	**S**	73/*Mixed Review*
			S	63/*Mixed Review*		
17	**2-3**	56/*P*: 1–10	**2-5**	67/3–69 mult. of 3	**2-7**	77/2–18 even
	2-4	61/2–46 even	**S**	69/*Mixed Review*	**S**	78/*Mixed Review*
			R	63/*Self-Test 1*		

LESSON	MINIMUM COURSE	AVERAGE COURSE	MAXIMUM COURSE
18	**2-4** 62/*P*: 1–10 **S** 63/*Mixed Review*	**2-6** 72/2–34 even, 36–51 mult. of 3 **S** 73/*Mixed Review*	**2-8** 81/3–36 mult. of 3 **S** 82/*Mixed Review* **R** 78/*Self-Test 2*
19	**2-5** 67/3–54 mult. of 3, 67–68 **S** 69/*Mixed Review* **R** 63/*Self-Test 1*	**2-7** 77/2–16 even **S** 78/*Mixed Review*	**2-9** 85/1–33 odd, 34–35 **S** 86/*Mixed Review*
20	**2-6** 72/1–43 odd **S** 73/*Mixed Review*	**2-8** 81/1–31 odd **S** 82/*Mixed Review* **R** 78/*Self-Test 2*	*Prepare for Chapter Test* **R** 86/*Self-Test 3* 89/*Chapter Review* **EP** 641/*Skills;* 665/*Problems*
21	**2-7** 77/1–13 **S** 78/*Mixed Review*	**2-9** 85/1–33 odd **S** 86/*Mixed Review*	*Administer Chapter 2 Test* **R** 91/*Cum. Review:* 1–35 odd **S** 93/*Preparing for College Entrance Exams*
22	**2-8** 81/1–25 odd **S** 82/*Mixed Review* **R** 78/*Self-Test 2*	*Prepare for Chapter Test* **R** 86/*Self-Test 3* 89/*Chapter Review* **EP** 641/*Skills;* 665/*Problems*	**3-1** 97/3–57 mult. of 3 98/*P*: 6–18 mult. of 3 **S** 100/*Mixed Review*
23	**2-9** 85/1–27 odd **S** 86/*Mixed Review*	*Administer Chapter 2 Test* **R** 91/*Cum. Review:* 1–35 odd **S** 93/*Preparing for College Entrance Exams*	**3-2** 104/3–51 mult. of 3 105/*P*: 8, 10, 12, 15, 17 **S** 106/*Mixed Review*
24	*Prepare for Chapter Test* **R** 86/*Self-Test 3* 89/*Chapter Review* **EP** 641/*Skills;* 665/*Problems*	**3-1** 97/1–39 odd 98/*P*: 1–9 odd	**3-3** 109/3–60 mult. of 3 **S** 110/*Mixed Review*
25	*Administer Chapter 2 Test* **R** 92/*Maintaining Skills*	**3-1** 98/40–48 even 99/*P*: 10, 12, 13 **S** 100/*Mixed Review* **3-2** 104/3–21 mult. of 3	**3-4** 113/*P*: 2–26 even **R** 111/*Self-Test 1*
26	**3-1** 97/1–29 odd 98/*P*: 2, 3, 5, 8	**3-2** 104/24–39 mult. of 3 105/*P*: 7–15 odd **S** 106/*Mixed Review* **3-3** 109/1–11 odd	**3-4** 114/*P*: 27–33 **S** 115/*Mixed Review*
27	**3-1** 97/26–42 even 99/*P*: 9, 11, 13 **S** 100/*Mixed Review*	**3-3** 110/15–57 mult. of 3 **S** 110/*Mixed Review*	**3-5** 118/3–48 mult. of 3 118/*P*: 3–18 mult. of 3 **S** 120/*Mixed Review*
28	**3-2** 104/1–35 odd; 105/*P*: 1–13 odd **S** 106/*Mixed Review*	**3-4** 113/*P*: 1–21 odd **R** 111/*Self-Test 1*	**3-6** 122/*P*: 2–8 even, 10–14 **R** 120/*Self-Test 2*
29	**3-3** 109/1–39 odd	**3-4** 114/*P*: 23–26, 27, 29, 31 **S** 115/*Mixed Review*	**3-6** 124/*P*: 15, 17, 19, 20 **S** 125/*Mixed Review* **3-7** 127/*P*: 2–10 even

LESSON	MINIMUM COURSE	AVERAGE COURSE	MAXIMUM COURSE
30	**3-3** 110/32–48 even **S** 110/*Mixed Review*	**3-5** 118/6–42 mult. of 3 118/*P*: 3–18 mult. of 3 **S** 120/*Mixed Review*	**3-7** 128/*P*: 11–18 **S** 129/*Mixed Review*
31	**3-4** 113/*P*: 1–17 odd **R** 111/*Self-Test 1*	**3-6** 122/*P*: 1–3, 6, 7, 9, 11, 12 **R** 120/*Self-Test 2*	**3-8** 131/2–8 even, 9–11 **S** 133/*Mixed Review*
32	**3-4** 113/*P*: 8–22 even **S** 115/*Mixed Review*	**3-6** 124/*P*: 14, 16, 18, 19 **S** 125/*Mixed Review* **3-7** 127/*P*: 2, 4, 6	*Prepare for Chapter Test* **R** 134/*Self-Test 3* 135/*Chapter Review* **EP** 643/*Skills;* 666/*Problems*
33	**3-5** 118/1–29 odd 118/*P*: 1–6	**3-7** 128/*P*: 7–17 odd **S** 129/*Mixed Review*	*Administer Chapter 3 Test* **R** 137/*Cum. Review:* 1–39 odd **S** 139/*Mixed Problem Solving:* 1–17 odd
34	**3-5** 118/16–32 even 119/*P*: 7–9 **S** 120/*Mixed Review*	**3-8** 131/1–9 odd **S** 133/*Mixed Review*	**4-1** 143/1–31 odd, 33–48 mult. of 3 **S** 144/*Mixed Review*
35	**3-6** 122/*P*: 1–6 **R** 120/*Self-Test 2*	*Prepare for Chapter Test* **R** 134/*Self-Test 3* 135/*Chapter Review* **EP** 643/*Skills;* 666/*Problems*	**4-2** 148/3–51 mult. of 3 150/*P*: 4–10 even
36	**3-6** 124/*P*: 8–11 **S** 125/*Mixed Review* **3-7** 127/*P*: 1–5	*Administer Chapter 3 Test* **R** 137/*Cum. Review:* 1–39 odd **S** 139/*Mixed Problem Solving:* 1–17 odd	**4-2** 149/53–56 150/*P*: 11–14 **S** 150/*Mixed Review*
37	**3-7** 128/*P*: 6–11 **S** 129/*Mixed Review*	**4-1** 143/1–31 odd, 33–45 mult. of 3 **S** 144/*Mixed Review*	**4-3** 153/3–48 mult. of 3 **S** 154/*Mixed Review* **R** 151/*Self-Test 1*
38	*Prepare for Chapter Test* **R** 134/*Self-Test 3* 135/*Chapter Review:* 1–11 **EP** 643/*Skills;* 666/*Problems*	**4-2** 148/3–48 mult. of 3 150/*P*: 2–8 even	**4-4** 156/3–51 mult. of 3 **S** 157/*Mixed Review*
39	*Administer Chapter 3 Test* **R** 138/*Maintaining Skills* **S** 139/*Mixed Problem Solving:* 1–7 odd	**4-2** 149/49–54 150/*P*: 9–11 **S** 150/*Mixed Review*	**4-5** 159/3–42 mult. of 3, 43 **S** 160/*Mixed Review*
40	**4-1** 143/1–35 odd **S** 144/*Mixed Review*	**4-3** 153/3–36 mult. of 3, 38, 41, 42 **S** 154/*Mixed Review* **R** 151/*Self-Test 1*	**4-6** 162/3–48 mult. of 3, 50 **S** 164/*Mixed Review*
41	**4-2** 148/2–40 even 150/*P*: 2–8 even	**4-4** 156/2–36 even, 39 **S** 157/*Mixed Review*	**4-7** 166/4–28 even **S** 166/*Mixed Review* **R** 164/*Self-Test 2*

LESSON	MINIMUM COURSE	AVERAGE COURSE	MAXIMUM COURSE
42	**4-2** 149/42–50 even 150/*P*: 9, 10 **S** 150/*Mixed Review* **4-3** 153/2–18 even	**4-5** 159/3–36 mult. of 3, 40–42 **S** 160/*Mixed Review*	**4-8** 170/*P*: 1–11
43	**4-3** 153/19–37 odd **S** 154/*Mixed Review* **R** 151/*Self-Test 1*	**4-6** 162/3–42 mult. of 3, 43, 45 **S** 164/*Mixed Review*	**4-8** 171/*P*: 13–17 odd **S** 171/*Mixed Review* **4-9** 173/*P*: 2, 4
44	**4-4** 156/1–20 **S** 157/*Mixed Review*	**4-7** 166/2–26 even **S** 166/*Mixed Review* **R** 164/*Self-Test 2*	**4-9** 173/*P*: 6–9, 10, 12 **S** 174/*Mixed Review*
45	**4-4** 157/22–34 even **4-5** 159/2–18 even	**4-8** 170/*P*: 1–5, 7, 9, 10	**4-10** 176/*P*: 2–16 even
46	**4-5** 159/19–37 odd, 40 **S** 160/*Mixed Review*	**4-8** 170/*P*: 11, 13, 15 **S** 171/*Mixed Review*	*Prepare for Chapter Test* **R** 177/*Self-Test 3* 178/*Chapter Review* **EP** 645/*Skills;* 668/*Problems*
47	**4-6** 162/1–31 odd	**4-9** 173/*P*: 1–6	*Administer Chapter 4 Test* **R** 181/*Cum. Review:* 1–39 odd **S** 183/*Preparing for College Entrance Exams*
48	**4-6** 163/33–43 odd **S** 164/*Mixed Review*	**4-9** 174/*P*: 8–11 **S** 174/*Mixed Review*	**5-1** 186/3–48 mult. of 3 **5-2** 192/3–57 mult. of 3 **S** 193/*Mixed Review*
49	**4-7** 166/2–22 even **S** 166/*Mixed Review* **R** 164/*Self-Test 2*	**4-10** 176/*P*: 2–14 even	**5-3** 196/3–54 mult. of 3 197/*P*: 2–10 even **S** 199/*Mixed Review*
50	**4-8** 170/*P*: 1–5, 7, 9	*Prepare for Chapter Test* **R** 177/*Self-Test 3* 178/*Chapter Review* **EP** 645/*Skills* 668/*Problems*	**5-4** 201/3–48 mult. of 3 **S** 203/*Mixed Review* **R** 199/*Self-Test 1*
51	**4-8** 170/*P*: 11, 13 **S** 171/*Mixed Review* **4-9** 173/*P*: 1, 3, 5	*Administer Chapter 4 Test* **R** 181/*Cum. Review:* 1–39 odd **S** 183/*Preparing for College Entrance Exams*	**5-5** 206/3–66 mult. of 3 **S** 207/*Mixed Review*
52	**4-9** 173/*P*: 7–9 **S** 174/*Mixed Review* **4-10** 176/*P*: 1, 3, 5, 7	**5-1** 186/3–39 mult. of 3, 41–46 **S** 187/*Mixed Review*	**5-6** 210/3–66 mult. of 3 **S** 212/*Mixed Review*
53	*Prepare for Chapter Test* **R** 177/*Self-Test 3* 178/*Chapter Review* **EP** 645/*Skills;* 668/*Problems*	**5-2** 192/1–45 odd	**5-7** 215/3–51 mult. of 3, 56 **S** 216/*Mixed Review* **R** 212/*Self-Test 2*

LESSON	MINIMUM COURSE		AVERAGE COURSE		MAXIMUM COURSE	
54		*Administer Chapter 4 Test* **R** 182/*Maintaining Skills*	**5-2** **S** **5-3**	192/47–57 odd 193/*Mixed Review* 196/1–19 odd	**5-8** **S**	218/3–54 mult. of 3, 55 219/*Mixed Review*
55	**5-1** **S**	186/1–31 odd, 41–43 187/*Mixed Review*	**5-3** **S**	196/21–51 odd 197/*P*: 2, 6, 7 199/*Mixed Review*	**5-9** **S**	222/3–45 mult. of 3, 46 223/*Mixed Review*
56	**5-2**	192/2–38 even, 47, 49	**5-4** **S** **R**	201/3–45 mult. of 3 203/*Mixed Review* 199/*Self-Test 1*	**5-10** **S** **R**	225/3–63 mult. of 3 226/*Mixed Review* 223/*Self-Test 3*
57	**5-2** **S** **5-3**	192/39–54 mult. of 3 193/*Mixed Review* 196/1–17 odd	**5-5** **S**	206/3–60 mult. of 3 207/*Mixed Review*	**5-11**	228/1–39 odd
58	**5-3** **S**	196/21–49 odd; 197/*P*: 1, 3, 5 199/*Mixed Review*	**5-6**	210/2–46 even	**5-11** **S**	228/41–57 odd 229/*Mixed Review*
59	**5-4** **R**	201/2–30 even 199/*Self-Test 1*	**5-6** **S**	211/48–64 even 212/*Mixed Review*	**5-12**	232/1–41 odd
60	**5-4** **S**	202/32–44 even 203/*Mixed Review*	**5-7** **S** **R**	215/3–48 mult. of 3 216/*Mixed Review* 212/*Self-Test 2*	**5-12** **S** **5-13**	233/43–55 odd 233/*Mixed Review* 235/*P*: 2, 4, 6, 8
61	**5-5**	206/1–43 odd	**5-8** **S**	218/3–48 mult. of 3 219/*Mixed Review*	**5-13** **S**	236/*P*: 9–31 odd 238/*Mixed Review*
62	**5-5** **S** **5-6**	207/45–53 odd 207/*Mixed Review* 210/1–19 odd	**5-9** **S**	222/1–37 odd 223/*Mixed Review*		*Prepare for Chapter Test* **R** 238/*Self-Test 4* 240/*Chapter Review* **EP** 647/*Skills;* 669/*Problems*
63	**5-6** **S**	210/21–49 odd, 58 212/*Mixed Review*	**5-10** **R**	225/1–41 odd 223/*Self-Test 3*		*Administer Chapter 5 Test* **R** 243/*Cum. Review:* 1–41 odd **S** 245/*Mixed Problem Solving*
64	**5-7** **S** **R**	215/2–36 even, 37 216/*Mixed Review* 212/*Self-Test 2*	**5-10** **S**	226/43–59 odd 226/*Mixed Review*	**6-1** **S**	248/3–54 mult. of 3 250/*Mixed Review*
65	**5-8** **S**	218/1–33 odd, 36 219/*Mixed Review*	**5-11** **S**	228/1–6, 9–51 mult. of 3 229/*Mixed Review*	**6-2** **S**	253/3–57 mult. of 3, 59 254/*Mixed Review*
66	**5-9** **S**	222/1–33 odd 223/*Mixed Review*	**5-12**	232/1–41 odd	**6-3** **S**	256/3–45 mult. of 3 258/*Mixed Review*
67	**5-10** **R**	225/1–15 odd, 21, 23, 25, 39 223/*Self-Test 3*	**5-12** **S**	232/38–54 even 233/*Mixed Review*	**6-4** **S** **R**	261/3–45 mult. of 3 262/*Mixed Review* 258/*Self-Test 1*
68	**5-11** **S**	228/1–6, 11–29 odd 229/*Mixed Review*	**5-13**	235/*P*: 1–23 odd	**6-5**	267/3–30 mult. of 3, 31–34

LESSON	MINIMUM COURSE	AVERAGE COURSE	MAXIMUM COURSE
69	**5-12** 232/1–39 odd	**5-13** 236/*P*: 14–30 even **S** 238/*Mixed Review*	**6-5** 268/36–58 even **S** 268/*Mixed Review* **R** 269/*Self-Test 2*
70	**5-12** 232/28–44 even **S** 233/*Mixed Review*	*Prepare for Chapter Test* **R** 238/*Self-Test 4* 240/*Chapter Review* **EP** 647/*Skills;* 669/*Problems*	**6-6** 271/3–45 mult. of 3 **S** 273/*Mixed Review*
71	**5-13** 235/*P*: 2–18 even **S** 238/*Mixed Review*	*Administer Chapter 5 Test* **R** 243/*Cum. Review:* 1–41 odd **S** 245/*Mixed Problem Solving:* 1–13 odd	**6-7** 276/2–30 even, 31, 35
72	*Prepare for Chapter Test* **R** 238/*Self-Test 4* 240/*Chapter Review* **EP** 647/*Skills;* 669/*Problems*	**6-1** 248/2–38 even	**6-7** 277/32–34, 36–38 **S** 277/*Mixed Review*
73	*Administer Chapter 5 Test* **R** 244/*Maintaining Skills* **S** 245/*Mixed Problem Solving:* 1–5 odd	**6-1** 249/39–48 **S** 250/*Mixed Review*	*Prepare for Chapter Test* **R** 277/*Self-Test 3* 280/*Chapter Review* **EP** 649/*Skills*
74	**6-1** 248/2–30 even	**6-2** 253/3–54 mult. of 3, 55 **S** 254/*Mixed Review*	*Administer Chapter 6 Test* **R** 283/*Cum. Review:* 1–39 odd **S** 285/*Preparing for College* *Entrance Exams*
75	**6-1** 249/31–37 odd, 41–45 odd **S** 250/*Mixed Review*	**6-3** 256/2–32 even, 33, 36, 39, 42 **S** 258/*Mixed Review*	**7-1** 289/3–45 mult. of 3 291/*P*: 3–18 mult. of 3 **S** 292/*Mixed Review*
76	**6-2** 253/1–23 odd, 29, 30, 35–53 odd **S** 254/*Mixed Review*	**6-4** 261/2–44 even **S** 262/*Mixed Review* **R** 258/*Self-Test 1*	**7-2** 295/3–48 mult. of 3 296/*P*: 3, 6, 9, 12, 13 **S** 297/*Mixed Review*
77	**6-3** 256/1–19 odd, 22	**6-5** 267/2–30 even, 31–33, 35–37	**7-3** 299/3–33 mult. of 3 300/*P*: 3–15 mult. of 3 **S** 301/*Mixed Review* **R** 297/*Self-Test 1*
78	**6-3** 257/21–41 odd **S** 258/*Mixed Review*	**6-5** 268/34, 38–54 even **S** 268/*Mixed Review*	**7-4** 305/3–36 mult. of 3 306/*P*: 2, 4, 6
79	**6-4** 261/1–31 odd, 33, 36, 37, 41 **S** 262/*Mixed Review* **R** 258/*Self-Test 1*	**6-6** 271/2–32 even **R** 269/*Self-Test 2*	**7-4** 306/39, 40 307/*P*: 8, 10, 12, 14 **S** 308/*Mixed Review*
80	**6-5** 267/1–31 odd, 35, 37, 39	**6-6** 272/34, 36, 38, 40 **S** 273/*Mixed Review* **6-7** 276/2–22 even	**7-5** 312/3–60 mult. of 3 313/*P*: 3–15 mult. of 3 **S** 314/*Mixed Review* **R** 308/*Self-Test 2*

LESSON	MINIMUM COURSE	AVERAGE COURSE	MAXIMUM COURSE
81	**6-5** 267/32–46 even **S** 268/*Mixed Review*	**6-7** 276/24–34 even **S** 277/*Mixed Review*	**7-6** 317/3–21 mult. of 3 318/*P*: 3–15 mult. of 3 **S** 320/*Mixed Review*
82	**6-6** 271/1–37 odd **R** 269/*Self-Test 2*	*Prepare for Chapter Test* **R** 277/*Self-Test 3* 280/*Chapter Review* **EP** 649/*Skills*	**7-7** 324/*P*: 1–8, 9, 12, 15, 18, 21 **R** 320/*Self-Test 3*
83	**6-6** 272/30–36 even **S** 273/*Mixed Review* **6-7** 276/1–21 odd	*Administer Chapter 6 Test* **R** 283/*Cum. Review:* 1–39 odd **S** 285/*Preparing for College Entrance Exams*	**7-7** 325/*P*: 22–25 **S** 325/*Mixed Review* **7-8** 328/*P*: 1–8
84	**6-7** 276/23–33 odd **S** 277/*Mixed Review*	**7-1** 289/2–34 even 291/*P*: 2, 4, 6, 8, 10	**7-8** 329/*P*: 9, 12, 15, 18, 21–23 **S** 330/*Mixed Review*
85	*Prepare for Chapter Test* **R** 277/*Self-Test 3* 280/*Chapter Review* **EP** 649/*Skills*	**7-1** 290/36, 38, 40, 42 291/*P*: 12, 14, 16 **S** 292/*Mixed Review* **7-2** 295/3–30 mult. of 3	**7-9** 333/3–69 mult. of 3 335/*P*: 3, 5 **S** 335/*Mixed Review* **R** 330/*Self-Test 4*
86	*Administer Chapter 6 Test* **R** 284/*Maintaining Skills*	**7-2** 295/33–45 mult. of 3 296/*P*: 3, 5, 7, 9, 11 **S** 297/*Mixed Review*	**7-10** 339/3–30 mult. of 3 339/*P*: 1, 2 **S** 340/*Mixed Review*
87	**7-1** 289/1–25 odd, 31–33 291/*P*: 2, 4, 6, 8	**7-3** 299/1–4, 6–21 mult. of 3 300/*P*: 2, 4, 6, 8 **R** 297/*Self-Test 1*	*Prepare for Chapter Test* **R** 341/*Self-Test 5* 342/*Chapter Review* **EP** 651/*Skills;* 670/*Problems*
88	**7-1** 290/18, 20, 28, 32, 34 291/*P*: 10, 12 **S** 292/*Mixed Review* **7-2** 295/1–15 odd	**7-3** 300/25–27 301/*P*: 10, 12, 14 **S** 301/*Mixed Review* **7-4** 305/1–6, 8, 10, 12	*Administer Chapter 7 Test* **R** 345/*Cum. Review:* 1–39 odd **S** 347/*Mixed Problem Solving:* 1–13 odd
89	**7-2** 295/17–35 odd 296/*P*: 3, 5, 7, 9 **S** 297/*Mixed Review*	**7-4** 306/14–32 even 306/*P*: 2, 4, 6, 8, 10 **S** 308/*Mixed Review*	**8-1** 351/1–45 odd **S** 352/*Mixed Review*
90	**7-3** 299/1–15 odd 300/*P*: 1, 3, 5 **R** 297/*Self-Test 1*	**7-5** 312/3–48 mult. of 3 313/*P*: 2, 5, 8, 10, 12 **S** 314/*Mixed Review* **R** 308/*Self-Test 2*	**8-2** 357/1–35 odd, 43–48 **S** 358/*Mixed Review*
91	**7-3** 299/14, 16, 18 300/*P*: 7, 9, 10 **S** 301/*Mixed Review* **7-4** 305/1–6	**7-6** 317/3–21 mult. of 3 318/*P*: 3, 5, 7, 9, 11 **S** 320/*Mixed Review*	**8-3** 363/1–35 odd, 38, 40, 42 **S** 365/*Mixed Review* **R** 358/*Self-Test 1*
92	**7-4** 305/7–29 odd 306/*P*: 1–3, 5 **S** 308/*Mixed Review*	**7-7** 324/*P*: 1–8, 10, 12, 14, 16 **R** 320/*Self-Test 3*	**8-4** 368/3–45 mult. of 3 **S** 369/*Mixed Review*

LESSON	MINIMUM COURSE	AVERAGE COURSE	MAXIMUM COURSE
93	7-5 312/1–31 odd 313/*P*: 1–3 R 308/*Self-Test 2*	7-7 325/*P*: 18, 20, 22 S 325/*Mixed Review* 7-8 328/*P*: 1–8, 10	8-5 372/3–42 mult. of 3 S 373/*Mixed Review*
94	7-5 312/34–40 even; 314/*P*: 5–7 S 314/*Mixed Review*	7-8 329/*P*: 11–14, 16, 18, 20 S 330/*Mixed Review*	8-6 377/1–9 odd, 10 R 373/*Self-Test 2*
95	7-6 317/1–15 odd 318/*P*: 1, 3, 5, 7, 9 S 320/*Mixed Review*	7-9 333/3–30 mult. of 3, 36–66 mult. of 3; 335/*P*: 1–3 S 335/*Mixed Review* R 330/*Self-Test 4*	8-7 380/1–27 odd S 377/*Mixed Review*
96	7-7 324/*P*: 1–8, 10, 12, 16 R 320/*Self-Test 3* S 325/*Mixed Review*: 5–10	7-10 339/3–30 mult. of 3 339/*P*: 1, 2 S 340/*Mixed Review*	8-7 381/24–48 even S 382/*Mixed Review*
97	7-8 328/*P*: 1–11 odd S 330/*Mixed Review*	*Prepare for Chapter Test* R 341/*Self-Test 5* 342/*Chapter Review* EP 651/*Skills*; 670/*Problems*	8-8 386/1–41 odd S 387/*Mixed Review*
98	7-9 333/1–27 odd, 29–31 335/*P*: 1, 2 S 335/*Mixed Review* R 330/*Self-Test 4*	*Administer Chapter 7 Test* R 345/*Cum. Review*: 1–39 odd S 347/*Mixed Problem Solving*: 1–13 odd	8-9 393/3–24 mult. of 3 395/*P*: 3–15 mult. of 3 S 396/*Mixed Review* R 388/*Self-Test 3*
99	7-10 339/3–21 mult. of 3 R 341/*Self-Test 5*: 1–3, 10–12	8-1 351/1–35 odd, 39–41 S 352/*Mixed Review*	8-10 399/3–18 mult. of 3 400/*P*: 3–18 mult. of 3 S 402/*Mixed Review*
100	*Prepare for Chapter Test* R 342/*Chapter Review* EP 651/*Skills* 670/*Problems*	8-2 357/1–39 odd, 45, 46 S 358/*Mixed Review*	*Prepare for Chapter Test* R 403/*Self-Test 4* 405/*Chapter Review* EP 653/*Skills*; 674/*Problems*
101	*Administer Chapter 7 Test* R 346/*Maintaining Skills* S 347/*Mixed Problem Solving*: 1–7 odd	8-3 363/1–39 odd S 365/*Mixed Review* R 358/*Self-Test 1*	*Administer Chapter 8 Test* R 409/*Cum. Review*: 1–33 odd S 411/*Preparing for College Entrance Exams*
102	8-1 351/1–23 odd, 29, 33, 37 S 352/*Mixed Review*	8-4 368/1–35 odd S 369/*Mixed Review*	9-1 415/1–23 odd S 416/*Mixed Review*
103	8-2 357/1–37 odd, 45 S 358/*Mixed Review*	8-4 369/37–43 odd 8-5 372/1–15 odd	9-2 419/1–39 odd S 420/*Mixed Review*
104	8-3 363/1–33 odd, 37 S 365/*Mixed Review* R 358/*Self-Test 1*	8-5 372/17–39 odd S 373/*Mixed Review*	9-3 424/*P*: 1–21 odd S 425/*Mixed Review*
105	8-4 368/1–27 odd S 369/*Mixed Review*	8-6 377/1–9 odd, 10 S 377/*Mixed Review* R 373/*Self-Test 2*	9-4 427/1–27 odd S 429/*Mixed Review*

LESSON	MINIMUM COURSE		AVERAGE COURSE		MAXIMUM COURSE	
106	8-4	368/28–38 even	8-7	380/1–43 odd	9-4	428/28–31
	8-5	372/2–16 even	S	382/*Mixed Review*		428/*P*: 1–9 odd
107	8-5	372/17–35 odd	8-8	386/1–29 odd, 31, 33	9-5	432/3–45 mult. of 3
	S	373/*Mixed Review*	S	387/*Mixed Review*	R	433/3, 6, 9, 12, 15, 18
108	8-6	377/1–6	8-9	393/1–21 odd	9-5	434/*P*: 1–23 odd
	S	377/*Mixed Review*	R	388/*Self-Test 3*	S	436/*Mixed Review*
	R	373/*Self-Test 2*				
109	8-7	380/1–23 odd	8-9	395/*P*: 1–11 odd	9-5	435/*P*: 25–31 odd
			S	396/*Mixed Review*	R	437/*Self-Test 1*
			8-10	399/1–13 odd		
110	8-7	381/24–34 even	8-10	400/15–19 odd; *P*: 1–13 odd	9-6	440/*P*: 3–21 mult. of 3, 23
		382/*Mixed Review*	S	402/*Mixed Review*	S	443/*Mixed Review*
111	8-8	386/1–21 odd	*Prepare for Chapter Test*		9-7	447/*P*: 1–21 odd
	S	387/*Mixed Review*	R	403/*Self-Test 4*	S	449/*Mixed Review*
				405/*Chapter Review*		
			EP	653/*Skills;* 674/*Problems*		
112	8-9	393/1–21 odd	*Administer Chapter 8 Test*		9-7	448/*P*: 23–33 odd
	R	388/*Self-Test 3*	R	409/*Cum. Review:* 1–33 odd	R	450/*Self-Test 2*
			S	411/*Prep. for Coll. Ent. Exams*		
113	8-9	395/*P*: 1–9 odd	9-1	415/1–21 odd	*Prepare for Chapter Test*	
	S	396/*Mixed Review*	S	416/*Mixed Review*	R	451/*Chapter Review*
	8-10	399/1–11 odd			EP	656/*Skills;* 675/*Problems*
114	8-10	400/15, 17	9-2	419/1–19 odd	*Administer Chapter 9 Test*	
		400/*P*: 1–9 odd	S	420/*Mixed Review*	R	453/*Cum. Review:* 1–31 odd
	S	402/*Mixed Review*			S	455/*Mix. Prob. Solv.:* 1–13 odd
115	*Prepare for Chapter Test*		9-2	419/18–40 even	10-1	459/1–29 odd, 36–40
	R	403/*Self-Test 4*			S	461/*Mixed Review*
		405/*Chapter Review*				
	EP	653/*Skills;* 674/*Problems*				
116	*Administer Chapter 8 Test*		9-3	424/*P*: 1–9 odd	10-2	466/1–10, 12–48 mult. of 3,
	R	410/*Maintaining Skills*	S	425/*Mixed Review*		51, 56, 61, 63
					S	467/*Mixed Review*
117	9-1	415/1–17 odd, 18	9-3	424/*P*: 6–22 even	10-3	471/3–18 mult. of 3
	S	416/*Mixed Review*				473/*P*: 3–21 mult. of 3
					S	475/*Mixed Review*
118	9-2	419/1–17 odd	9-4	427/1–19 odd	10-4	480/3–39 mult. of 3
	S	420/*Mixed Review*	S	429/*Mixed Review*	S	481/*Mixed Review*
					R	475/*Self-Test 1*
119	9-2	419/18–30 even	9-4	428/22, 24, 26, 28	10-5	484/3–36 mult. of 3
				428/*P*: 1, 3, 5, 7	S	485/*Mixed Review*

LESSON	MINIMUM COURSE	AVERAGE COURSE	MAXIMUM COURSE
120	**9-3** 424/*P*: 1–9 odd **S** 425/*Mixed Review*	**9-5** 432/3–33 mult. of 3 **R** 433/3, 6, 9, 12, 15	**10-6** 488/1–25 odd **S** 488/*Mixed Review*
121	**9-3** 424/*P*: 11–19	**9-5** 434/*P*: 1–17 odd **S** 436/*Mixed Review*	**10-7** 492/3–39 mult. of 3 **S** 494/*Mixed Review* **R** 489/*Self-Test 2*
122	**9-4** 427/1–11 odd, 17, 20 **S** 429/*Mixed Review*	**9-5** 435/*P*: 19, 21, 25 **9-6** 440/*P*: 1–11 odd **R** 437/*Self-Test 1*	**10-8** 496/3–24 mult. of 3 **S** 498/*Mixed Review*
123	**9-4** 427/12, 15, 18, 19 428/*P*: 1–4	**9-6** 442/*P*: 12, 15, 18, 21 **S** 443/*Mixed Review* **9-7** 447/*P*: 1–6, 7, 9	*Prepare for Chapter Test* **R** 498/*Self-Test 3* 501/*Chapter Review* **EP** 657/*Skills;* 677/*Problems*
124	**9-5** 432/1–21 odd **R** 433/2, 5, 8, 11, 14	**9-7** 448/*P*: 14–28 even **S** 449/*Mixed Review*	*Administer Chapter 10 Test* **R** 503/*Cum. Review:* 1–39 odd **S** 505/*Prep. for Coll. Ent. Exams*
125	**9-5** 434/*P*: 1–15 odd **S** 436/*Mixed Review*	*Prepare for Chapter Test* **R** 450/*Self-Test 2* 451/*Chapter Review* **EP** 656/*Skills;* 675/*Problems*	**11-1** 510/2–38 even **S** 511/*Mixed Review*
126	**9-5** 434/*P*: 12, 14, 16 **9-6** 440/*P*: 1–4, 7 **R** 437/*Self-Test 1*	*Administer Chapter 9 Test* **R** 453/*Cum. Review:* 1–39 odd **S** 455/*Mix. Prob. Solv.:* 1–13 odd	**11-2** 515/2–42 even **S** 516/*Mixed Review*
127	**9-6** 440/*P*: 5, 6, 9, 10, 11 **S** 443/*Mixed Review* **9-7** 447/*P*: 1–7	**10-1** 459/1–37 odd **S** 461/*Mixed Review*	**11-3** 519/3–48 mult. of 3 **S** 520/*Mixed Review*
128	**9-7** 447/*P*: 9–13 **S** 449/*Mixed Review*	**10-2** 466/1–10, 12–45 mult. of 3 **S** 467/*Mixed Review*	**11-4** 522/3–48 mult. of 3 **S** 523/*Mixed Review* **R** 520/*Self-Test 1*
129	*Prepare for Chapter Test* **R** 450/*Self-Test 2* 451/*Chapter Review:* 1–8 **EP** 656/*Skills;* 675/*Problems*	**10-3** 471/1–15 odd 473/*P*: 2, 5, 10, 13, 15 **S** 475/*Mixed Review*	**11-5** 526/3–51 mult. of 3 527/*P*: 3, 6, 9, 12 **S** 528/*Mixed Review*
130	*Administer Chapter 9 Test* **R** 454/*Maintaining Skills* **S** 455/*Mixed Problem Solving:* 2–6 even	**10-4** 480/1–15 odd, 23–26 **S** 481/*Mixed Review* **R** 475/*Self-Test 1*	**11-6** 532/3–30 mult. of 3 533/*P*: 3, 6, 9, 12 **S** 534/*Mixed Review*
131	**10-1** 459/1–35 odd **S** 461/*Mixed Review*	**10-5** 484/3–36 mult. of 3 **S** 485/*Mixed Review*	**11-7** 538/3–57 mult. of 3 **S** 539/*Mixed Review* **R** 534/*Self-Test 2*
132	**10-2** 466/1–10, 12, 15, 22, 23, 41 **S** 467/*Mixed Review*	**10-6** 488/1–21 odd **S** 488/*Mixed Review*	**11-8** 541/3–36 mult. of 3 **S** 542/*Mixed Review*

LESSON	MINIMUM COURSE		AVERAGE COURSE		MAXIMUM COURSE	
133	**10-2** 467/26, 35, 43 **10-3** 471/1–11 odd **S** 475/*Mixed Review*		**10-7** 492/3–33 mult. of 3 **S** 494/*Mixed Review* **R** 489/*Self-Test 2*		**11-9** 545/3–45 mult. of 3 **S** 546/*Mixed Review*	
134	**10-3** 472/6, 8, 10; 473/*P*: 1–3 **10-4** 480/1–15 odd **R** 475/*Self-Test 1*		**10-8** 496/1–17 odd **S** 498/*Mixed Review*		**11-10** 548/3–48 mult. of 3 549/*P*: 3, 6, 9, 10 **S** 550/*Mixed Review*	
135	**10-4** 480/12–22 even **S** 481/*Mixed Review* **10-5** 484/1–6		**10-8** 496/16, 18–22 **R** 498/*Self-Test 3*		*Prepare for Chapter Test* **R** 550/*Self-Test 3* 555/*Chapter Review* **EP** 659/*Skills;* 677/*Problems*	
136	**10-5** 485/13–21 odd **S** 485/*Mixed Review* **10-6** 488/1–5		*Prepare for Chapter Test* **R** 501/*Chapter Review* **EP** 657/*Skills;* 677/*Problems*		*Administer Chapter 11 Test* **R** 557/*Cum. Review:* 1–41 odd **S** 559/*Mix. Prob. Solv.:* 1–13 odd	
137	**10-6** 488/9–12 **S** 488/*Mixed Review* **10-7** 492/1–11 odd		*Administer Chapter 10 Test* **R** 503/*Cum. Review:* 1–39 odd **S** 505/*Prep. for Coll. Ent. Exams*		**12-1** 563/3–48 mult. of 3, 49 **S** 563/*Mixed Review*	
138	**10-7** 492/10, 12–14, 25–28 **S** 494/*Mixed Review* **10-8** 496/1–11 odd		**11-1** 510/1–35 odd **S** 511/*Mixed Review*		**12-2** 566/2–30 even **S** 566/*Mixed Review*	
139	*Prepare for Chapter Test* **R** 489/*Self-Test 2* 501/*Chapter Review* **EP** 657/*Skills;* 677/*Problems*		**11-2** 515/1–39 odd **S** 516/*Mixed Review*		**12-3** 569/1–31 odd **S** 570/*Mixed Review*	
140	*Administer Chapter 10 Test* **R** 504/*Maintaining Skills*		**11-3** 519/3–45 mult. of 3 **S** 520/*Mixed Review*		**12-4** 574/1–19 odd **S** 575/*Mixed Review*	
141	**11-1** 510/1–31 odd **S** 511/*Mixed Review*		**11-4** 522/3–45 mult. of 3 **S** 523/*Mixed Review* **R** 520/*Self-Test 1*		**12-5** 577/1–31 odd **S** 578/*Mixed Review* **R** 575/*Self-Test 1*	
142	**11-2** 515/1–37 odd **S** 516/*Mixed Review*		**11-5** 526/3–48 mult. of 3 527/*P*: 2, 5, 8 **S** 528/*Mixed Review*		**12-6** 580/*P*: 1–15 odd **S** 581/*Mixed Review*	
143	**11-3** 519/1–35 odd **S** 520/*Mixed Review*		**11-6** 532/3–27 mult. of 3 533/*P*: 2, 5, 8 **S** 534/*Mixed Review*		**12-7** 586/*P*: 1–11 odd **S** 587/*Mixed Review* **R** 582/*Self-Test 2*	
144	**11-4** 522/1–35 odd **S** 523/*Mixed Review* **R** 520/*Self-Test 1*		**11-7** 538/3–51 mult. of 3 **S** 539/*Mixed Review* **R** 534/*Self-Test 2*		**12-8** 590/1–9 odd 590/*P*: 1–13 odd **S** 592/*Mixed Review*	
145	**11-5** 526/1–37 odd 527/*P*: 1, 3, 5 **S** 528/*Mixed Review*		**11-8** 541/3–33 mult. of 3 **S** 542/*Mixed Review*		*Prepare for Chapter Test* **R** 594/*Self-Test 3* 595/*Chapter Review* **EP** 662/*Skills;* 679/*Problems*	

LESSON	MINIMUM COURSE	AVERAGE COURSE	MAXIMUM COURSE
146	**11-6** 532/1–21 odd 533/P: 1, 3 S 534/*Mixed Review*	**11-9** 545/3–42 mult. of 3 S 546/*Mixed Review*	*Administer Chapter 12 Test* R 597–598/*Cumulative Review:* 3–84, mult. of 3 S 599/*Prep. for Coll. Ent. Exams*
147	**11-7** 538/1–25 odd R 534/*Self-Test 2*	**11-10** 548/2–42 even S 550/*Mixed Review*	*Looking Ahead* 602/1–7
148	**11-7** 538/14–36 even S 539/*Mixed Review*	**11-10** 549/P: 1–6, 8, 10 R 550/*Self-Test 3*	*Looking Ahead* 604/1–7
149	**11-8** 541/1–14 S 533/P: 5	*Prepare for Chapter Test* R 555/*Chapter Review* EP 659/*Skills;* 677/*Problems*	*Looking Ahead* 608/1–16
150	**11-8** 541/15–27 S 542/*Mixed Review*	*Administer Chapter 11 Test* R 557/*Cum. Review:* 1–41 odd S 559/*Mix. Prob. Solv.:* 1–13 odd	*Looking Ahead* 613/1–7 615/1–3
151	**11-9** 545/1–27 odd, 31 S 546/*Mixed Review*	**12-1** 563/1–39 odd S 563/*Mixed Review*	*Looking Ahead* 618/1–22
152	**11-10** 548/1–25 odd; 549/P: 1–3 S 550/*Mixed Review*	**12-2** 566/1–27 odd S 566/*Mixed Review*	*Looking Ahead* 620/1–10
153	*Prepare for Chapter Test* R 550/*Self-Test 3* 555/*Chapter Review* EP 659/*Skills;* 677/*Problems*	**12-3** 569/1–31 odd S 570/*Mixed Review*	*Looking Ahead* 622/1–25 odd 623/P: 3, 6, 9, 12
154	*Administer Chapter 11 Test* R 558/*Maintaining Skills* S 559/*Mix. Prob. Solv.:* 2, 4, 6	**12-4** 574/1–17 odd S 575/*Mixed Review*	*Looking Ahead* 625/1–15 odd 626/P: 3, 6, 9
155	**12-1** 563/1–31 odd S 563/*Mixed Review*	**12-5** 577/1–27 odd S 578/*Mixed Review* R 575/*Self-Test 1*	*Looking Ahead* 629/1–16
156	**12-2** 566/1–10 S 563/33	**12-6** 580/P: 1–13 odd S 581/*Mixed Review*	*Looking Ahead* 632/1–33 odd
157	**12-2** 566/11–18 S 566/*Mixed Review*	**12-7** 586/P: 1–5, 7, 9 S 587/*Mixed Review* R 582/*Self-Test 2*	*Looking Ahead* 635/1–15 odd
158	**12-3** 569/1–12 S 570/*Mixed Review*	**12-8** 590/1–6; P: 1–11 odd S 592/*Mixed Review*	*Looking Ahead* 635/P: 1–14
159	**12-3** 569/13–18 R 575/*Self-Test 1,* 1–5 595/*Chapter Review:* 1–3, 5–6	*Prepare for Chapter Test* R 594/*Self-Test 3;* 595/*Chap. Rev.* EP 662/*Skills;* 679/*Problems*	*Prepare for Chapter Test* 637/*Review*
160	*Administer Chapter 12 Test* (through Lesson 12-3)	*Administer Chapter 12 Test*	*Administer Looking Ahead Test*

Supplementary Materials Guide

For use with Lesson	Practice Masters	Tests	Study Guide (Reteaching)	Resource Book		
				Tests	Practice Exercises	Mixed Review (MR) Prob. Solving (PS) Applications (A) Enrichment (E) Technology (T) Thinking Skl. (TS)
1-1			pp. 1–2	pp. 1–5		p. 178 (A)
1-2			pp. 3–4		p. 79	
1-3	Sheet 1		pp. 5–6			
1-4			pp. 7–8			
1-5		Test 1	pp. 9–10			
1-6			pp. 11–12			
1-7	Sheet 2		pp. 13–14		p. 80	pp. 220–221 (TS)
1-8			pp. 15–16			
1-9	Sheet 3	Test 2	pp. 17–18		p. 81	
Chapter 1	Sheet 4	Tests 3, 4		pp. 6–9		p. 190 (E)
2-1			pp. 19–20			p. 179 (A)
2-2	Sheet 5		pp. 21–22			
2-3			pp. 23–24		p. 82	
2-4	Sheet 6	Test 5	pp. 25–26			
2-5			pp. 27–28		p. 83	
2-6	Sheet 7		pp. 29–30			
2-7		Test 6	pp. 31–32		p. 84	
2-8			pp. 33–34			
2-9	Sheet 8	Test 7	pp. 35–36		p. 85	pp. 213–219 (T)
Chapter 2	Sheet 9	Tests 8, 9		pp. 10–13		pp. 191–193 (E)
Cum. Rev. 1–2	Sheet 10					
3-1			pp. 37–38			p. 180 (A)
3-2	Sheet 11		pp. 39–40			
3-3		Test 10	pp. 41–42		p. 86	pp. 213–219 (T)
3-4	Sheet 12		pp. 43–44			p. 222 (TS)
3-5			pp. 45–46		p. 87	
3-6	Sheet 13	Test 11	pp. 47–48			pp. 158–159 (PS)
3-7			pp. 49–50			pp. 160–161 (PS)
3-8	Sheet 14	Test 12	pp. 51–52		p. 88	
Chapter 3	Sheet 15	Tests 13, 14		pp. 14–17		pp. 194–195 (E)
Cum. Rev. 1–3	Sheets 16, 17			pp. 18–19	pp. 89–90	pp. 146–147 (MR)
4-1			pp. 53–54			p. 181 (A)
4-2	Sheet 18		pp. 55–56		p. 91	
4-3			pp. 57–58			
4-4	Sheet 19		pp. 59–60		p. 92	
4-5			pp. 61–62			
4-6	Sheet 20	Test 15	pp. 63–64		p. 93	
4-7			pp. 65–66			
4-8	Sheet 21		pp. 67–68		p. 94	pp. 162–165 (PS)
4-9			pp. 69–70			pp. 166–167 (PS)
4-10	Sheet 22	Test 16	pp. 71–72		p. 95	
Chapter 4	Sheet 23	Tests 17, 18		pp. 20–23		p. 196 (E)
Cum. Rev. 1–4		Test 19				

For use with Lesson	Practice Masters	Tests	Study Guide (Reteaching)	Resource Book		
				Tests	Practice Exercises	Mix. Rev., Prob. Solv., Applications, Enrich., Tech., Think. Skl.
5-1			pp. 73–74			p. 182 (A)
5-2	Sheet 24		pp. 75–76			
5-3			pp. 77–78		p. 96	
5-4	Sheet 25	Test 20	pp. 79–80			
5-5			pp. 81–82			
5-6	Sheet 26		pp. 83–84	pp. 24–25	p. 97	
5-7			pp. 85–86			
5-8	Sheet 27		pp. 87–88			
5-9		Test 21	pp. 89–90		p. 98	
5-10	Sheet 28		pp. 91–92			
5-11			pp. 93–94		p. 99	
5-12	Sheet 29		pp. 95–96			
5-13	Sheet 30	Test 22	pp. 97–98		p. 100	p. 223 (TS)
Chapter 5	Sheet 31	Tests 23, 24		pp. 26–29		p. 197 (E)
Cum. Rev. 4–5	Sheet 32					
6-1			pp. 99–100			p. 183 (A)
6-2	Sheet 33		pp. 101–102		p. 101	
6-3		Test 25	pp. 103–104			
6-4	Sheet 34		pp. 105–106		p. 102	
6-5			pp. 107–108			
6-6	Sheet 35		pp. 109–110		p. 103	
6-7	Sheet 36	Test 26	pp. 111–112		p. 104	
Chapter 6	Sheet 37	Tests 27, 28		pp. 30–33		p. 198 (E)
Cum. Rev. 4–6	Sheets 38, 39			pp. 34–35	pp. 105–106	
Cum. Rev. 1–6		Test 29		pp. 36–41	pp. 107–108	pp. 148–150 (MR)
7-1			pp. 113–114			p. 184 (A)
7-2	Sheet 40		pp. 115–116		p. 109	pp. 224–225 (TS)
7-3			pp. 117–118			
7-4	Sheet 41		pp. 119–120		p. 110	
7-5		Test 30	pp. 121–122			
7-6	Sheet 42		pp. 123–124		p. 111	
7-7			pp. 125–126			pp. 168–170 (PS)
7-8	Sheet 43		pp. 127–128		p. 112	pp. 171–172 (PS)
7-9			pp. 129–130		p. 113	
7-10	Sheet 44	Test 31	pp. 131–132	pp. 42–45		
Chapter 7	Sheet 45	Tests 32, 33				p. 199 (E)
8-1			pp. 133–134			p. 185 (A)
8-2	Sheet 46		pp. 135–136		p. 114	p. 206 (T)
8-3			pp. 137–138		p. 115	
8-4	Sheet 47		pp. 139–140			pp. 206–207 (T)
8-5		Test 34	pp. 141–142		p. 116	p. 226 (TS)
8-6	Sheet 48		pp. 143–144			
8-7			pp. 145–146		p. 117	
8-8	Sheet 49	Test 35	pp. 147–148		p. 118	pp. 208–209 (T)
8-9			pp. 149–150			
8-10	Sheet 50	Test 36	pp. 151–152		p. 119	p. 210 (T)
Chapter 8	Sheet 51	Tests 37, 38		pp. 46–49		pp. 200–201 (E)
Cum. Rev. 7–8	Sheets 52, 53					
Cum. Rev. 5–8		Test 39				

For use with Lesson	Practice Masters	Tests	Study Guide (Reteaching)	Resource Book		
				Tests	Practice Exercises	Mixed Review (MR) Prob. Solving (PS) Applications (A) Enrichment (E) Technology (T) Thinking Skl. (TS)
9-1			pp. 153–154			p. 186 (A) pp. 210–211 (T)
9-2	Sheet 54		pp. 155–156		p. 120	
9-3			pp. 157–158			
9-4	Sheet 55		pp. 159–160			
9-5	Sheet 56	Test 40	pp. 161–162		p. 121	
9-6			pp. 163–164		p. 122	pp. 173–175 (PS)
9-7	Sheet 57	Test 41	pp. 165–166		p. 123	pp. 176–177 (PS)
Chapter 9	Sheet 58	Tests 42, 43		pp. 50–53		p. 202 (E)
Cum. Rev. 7–9	Sheets 59, 60			pp. 54–55	pp. 124–125	
Cum. Rev. 1–9						pp. 151–154 (MR)
10-1			pp. 167–168			p. 187 (A)
10-2	Sheet 61		pp. 169–170		p. 126	
10-3		Test 44	pp. 171–172		p. 127	
10-4	Sheet 62		pp. 173–174		p. 128	
10-5			pp. 175–176			
10-6	Sheet 63		pp. 177–178		p. 129	
10-7		Test 45	pp. 179–180			p. 212 (T)
10-8	Sheet 64		pp. 181–182		p. 130	
Chapter 10	Sheet 65	Tests 46, 47		pp. 56–59		p. 203 (E)
11-1			pp. 183–184			p. 188 (A)
11-2	Sheet 66		pp. 185–186		p. 131	
11-3		Test 48	pp. 187–188			
11-4	Sheet 67		pp. 189–190		p. 132	
11-5			pp. 191–192			
11-6	Sheet 68	Test 49	pp. 193–194		p. 133	p. 227 (TS)
11-7			pp. 195–196			
11-8	Sheet 69		pp. 197–198		p. 134	
11-9			pp. 199–200			
11-10	Sheet 70	Test 50	pp. 201–202		p. 135	
Chapter 11	Sheet 71	Tests 51, 52		pp. 60–63		p. 204 (E)
Cum. Rev. 10-11	Sheet 72					
12-1			pp. 203–204			p. 189 (A)
12-2	Sheet 73		pp. 205–206		p. 136	
12-3		Test 53	pp. 207–208		p. 137	
12-4	Sheet 74		pp. 209–210		p. 138	
12-5			pp. 211–212			
12-6			pp. 213–214		p. 139	
12-7			pp. 215–216			
12-8	Sheet 75	Test 54	pp. 217–218		p. 140	
Chapter 12	Sheet 76	Tests 55, 56		pp. 64–67		p. 205 (E)
Cum. Rev. 10–12	Sheets 77, 78			pp. 68–69	pp. 141–142	
Cum. Rev. 9–12		Test 57				
Cum. Rev. 7–12		Test 58		pp. 70–72	pp. 143–145	
Cum. Rev. 1–12	Sheets 79, 80			pp. 73–78		pp. 155–157 (MR)
Looking Ahead			pp. 219–240			

Software

The chart correlates textbook pages in *ALGEBRA, Structure and Method, Book 1,* with the supporting menu items on the disk *Algebra Plotter Plus.* Suggestions for using the disk for classroom demonstration or independent use are found in the side-column material of this Teacher's Edition under the heading "Using a Computer or a Graphing Calculator." Also, the booklet that accompanies the disk, *Using Algebra Plotter Plus,* includes worked examples, scripted demonstrations, enrichment topics, and activity sheets correlated to lessons in Chapters 8–12 of this text.

The chart also correlates the textbook with the *Computer Activities* booklet of blackline masters and the optional disk. A more detailed correlation appears in the contents of the booklet itself.

For use with Chapter	Disk for algebra; Algebra Plotter Plus		Computer Activities
	Menu Item	**Suggested Use**	
1			Activities 1–4
2			Activity 5
3			Activities 6–9
4			Activities 10, 11
5			Activities 12–14
6			Activities 15–18
7			Activities 19–22
8	Line Plotter Parabola Plotter Parabola Quiz Conics Plotter Function Plotter	pp. 354, 367, 385 p. 385 p. 385 p. 399 p. 399	Activities 23–26
9	Line Plotter	p. 414	Activities 27–29
10	Absolute Value Plotter Inequality Plotter	p. 494 p. 500	Activities 30–32
11			Activities 33–35
12			Activities 36, 37
Looking Ahead	Statistics Spreadsheet	p. 607	Activity 38

Test Generator

This software, available for Apple II and IBM computers, is for generating your own tests. There are 21 test items for every lesson of *ALGEBRA, Structure and Method, Book 1*. To generate a test, you can manually choose the items or choose by random selection, and customize the content and format of your test.

The Test Generator package includes Program Disks, Data Disks, and a Test Bank with User's Guide booklet. The Test Bank includes all the test items available in the Test Generator.

Lesson Commentary

1 Introduction to Algebra

This chapter develops some of the basic symbolism and terminology that students may have seen before but still need to master. The concepts of variables, expressions, and equations are presented in meaningful examples in an intuitive manner. This in turn leads to an introduction to algebraic problem solving that will be the basis for problem solving throughout the course. The chapter concludes with the development of certain important concepts related to the real numbers using the one-to-one correspondence between numbers and points on a number line.

1-1 (pages 1–5)

Key Mathematical Ideas

- simplifying numerical expressions
- using the substitution principle to evaluate variable expressions

Teaching Suggestions

The concept of a variable may be difficult for some students to grasp. You may find it helpful to use the photo on page xviii to stress the idea that $0.44 \times d$ is a *general* expression for water pressure, which depends upon how the depth, d, *varies*. Ask your students for other examples of variable expressions. Possibilities include the variable expression for the total cost of buying n items at a fixed price p per item or the variable expression for the perimeter of a square having sides of length s.

Students are generally more willing to adopt the convention of omitting the multiplication symbol in variable expressions once they realize how easily a handwritten multiplication symbol can be mistaken for the variable x or vice versa.

Parentheses are used to indicate which calculation comes first in expressions that involve more than one operation. (Other grouping symbols and conventions for order of operations are presented in the next lesson.)

When doing Example 1 with your students, you might want to review the meaning of *sum, difference, product,* and *quotient*. Also, be sure to point out that the word *quantity* is a key word used to indicate that parentheses are needed in writing a mathematical expression.

Suggested Extensions

Ask students to simplify each of the following, performing operations in parentheses first and then in order from left to right.

1. $(200 - 20) \div (10 - 4) + 2$ 32
2. $(200 - 20) \div 10 - (4 + 2)$ 12
3. $200 - (20 \div 10) - (4 + 2)$ 192
4. $200 - (20 \div 10) - 4 + 2$ 196

To lead into the next lesson, ask your students if $200 - 20 \div 10 - 4 + 2$ is equal to any of the expressions above. It is equal to the expression in 4.

1-2 (pages 6–9)

Key Mathematical Ideas

- simplifying expressions containing grouping symbols
- using the correct order of operations to simplify expressions in which grouping symbols have been omitted

Teaching Suggestions

Emphasize that mathematics is a language that attempts to express statements as concisely as possible. Thus, multiplication symbols are often omitted from expressions when grouping symbols are used.

Point out that brackets are generally used in expressions that already contain parentheses to make them easier to read.

Many teachers use the mnemonic device **My Dear Aunt Sally** to remind students of the agreed-upon order of operations. If you use this device, be sure to stress that multiplication and division have equal "status" and that these operations are done in the order in which they appear when reading an expression from left to right. The same applies to addition and subtraction.

The symbol π (pi) is used in Exercises 32 and 33. Many students will already know its value from previous mathematics courses. Take a moment, however, to remind them that the fraction $\frac{22}{7}$ and the decimal 3.14 are *approximations* for π, not its exact value.

Suggested Extension

Have students place grouping symbols in the following expressions so that each will have the stated value.

1. $9 + 35 \div 7 - 2$; 16
   $9 + 35 \div (7 - 2)$

2. $2 \times 8 - 3 + 6 \div 2$; 13
   $2 \times (8 - 3) + (6 \div 2)$

3. $20 - 4 \times 2 + 8 \div 16$; 10
   $(20 - 4) \times (2 + 8) \div 16$

1-3 (pages 10–13)

Key Mathematical Ideas

- using the terminology and symbolism associated with equations
- determining the solution set of an equation over a specified domain

Teaching Suggestions

Students may have learned synonyms for some of the terms introduced in this lesson, such as *element*, rather than *member, of a set*, and *member*, rather than *side, of an equation*. This text avoids referring to *members* of an equation because of possible confusion with *members* of a set.

To introduce students to the concept of an open sentence, have the students consider sentences like "He is 5'8" tall" and "She is 14 years old." The students should realize that unless the referents of the pronouns *he* and *she* are known, the sentences cannot be judged true or false. By taking the domain of *he* to be {boys in the class} and the domain of *she* to be {girls in the class}, you can use the names of your students as replacements for the pronouns. The solution set of each open sentence can then be determined by asking the students to judge the appropriate sentence true or false as it applies to them.

Emphasize that the members of the solution set of an open sentence must (1) be in the domain of the open sentence and (2) make the open sentence true. Point out that the domain of a variable is sometimes called its replacement set because the members of this set are the only *replacements* for the variable that can be considered for inclusion in the solution set of an open sentence.

If your students have trouble remembering what the symbol $\in$ means, point out that it resembles the letter E and can be thought of as meaning *is an element of*.

After considering the solution set of an equation whose solution set is its domain (see the next-to-last paragraph on page 10), you may want to challenge your students to find the solution set of an equation such as $x = x + 1$, which has no solution.

Suggested Extension

Have students write an equation whose solution set over the domain {1, 2, 3, 4} is the following.
Answers may vary. Examples are given.

1. {1} $x - 1 = 0$
2. {1, 2, 3, 4} $(x - 1) + 1 = x$
3. { } (the empty set) $x - 1 = x$
4. {1, 2} $(x - 1)(x - 2) = 0$

1-4 (pages 14–18)

Key Mathematical Idea

- translating word phrases involving numerical relationships into mathematical expressions

Teaching Suggestions

Remind students that mathematics is a language that people throughout the world use. Have your students think of themselves as translators who will be translating English into mathematical symbols. In preparation for solving word problems in Lesson 1-7, this lesson provides students with practice translating numerical relationships into mathematical expressions. The next lesson involves translating English sentences into equations.

Students may initially have trouble expressing a number in terms of another number represented by a variable when their sum or product is known (see Exercises 31 and 32 on page 17). To guide their thinking, ask your students a question like "What number and 6 have a sum of 17?" Then ask them what they did to the sum to find the unknown number.

Reading Algebra

Sometimes students wonder why they can't write $5 < x$ for "five less than a number." Emphasize that "five less than a number" is a phrase; there is no verb; it does not express a complete thought. On the other hand, $5 < x$ (read "five *is* less than x") is a sentence.

Be sure to point out that the word *of* in a word phrase expressing relationships between numbers indicates multiplication. In fact, it would be helpful at this time to develop a list of various ways the symbols for all four operations can be verbalized.

Suggested Extension

Have students represent their own age as x and write an expression for each of the following in terms of x.

1. their mother's (or father's) age Answers will vary.
2. their own age four years ago $x - 4$
3. three times their age $3x$
4. twice their age in three years $2(x + 3)$

1-5 (pages 19–22)

Key Mathematical Idea

- translating word sentences involving numerical relationships into equations

Teaching Suggestion

This lesson builds upon the foundation laid in the previous lesson. Many students will feel that they are supposed to find an "answer" because that is what they have usually been asked to do. Explain that translating sentences into equations is just part of the problem-solving process and that finding the answer, or solution, will come later.

Reading Algebra

Emphasize that an English sentence must contain a verb and that in sentences about numerical relationships, that verb will often be some form of the verb *to be*. If your students can substitute *is equal to* for *is*, they have identified the part of the sentence that should be represented by the equality symbol when the word sentence is translated into an equation. Be sure to point out that other forms of the verb *to be*, such as *are, was,* and *will be,* would also be represented by an equals sign. Sometimes students will find it helpful to restate a given problem using the word *is*. For example, Exercise 24 on page 22 can be restated as "The cost of a dozen eggs *is* $1.19."

Suggested Extension

Ask students to (a) restate each of the following sentences using the word *is* and (b) write an equation to represent each sentence in terms of the specified variable. Answers may vary. Examples are given.

1. In a class of 25 students there are three more girls than boys. Let b = the number of boys in the class. In a class with 3 more girls than boys, the number of students *is* 25; $b + (b + 3) = 25$.

2. Lance and Rita drove 400 miles, or $\frac{2}{3}$ of the way from Kansas City, Missouri, to Denver, Colorado. Let d = the number of miles from Kansas City, Missouri, to Denver, Colorado.
   Two thirds of the distance from Kansas City, Missouri, to Denver, Colorado, *is* 400 miles;
   $\frac{2}{3}d = 400$.

3. Fred has a collection of quarters worth $18.75. Let q = the number of quarters.
   The value of Fred's collection of quarters *is* $18.75; $0.25q = 18.75$.

4. Clair bought a tennis racquet for $60. The frame cost $16 more than the strings. Let s = the cost of the strings. The cost of the strings plus the cost of the frame *is* $60; $s + (s + 16) = 60$.

1-6 (pages 23–26)

Key Mathematical Idea

- translating simple word problems into equations

Teaching Suggestions

As with the previous lesson, students may think that they are to determine the solution of a given word problem. All that is required, however, is an equation for the problem.

Students sometimes have difficulty deciding which quantity in a word problem should be represented by a variable. They should ask themselves, "To which quantity are the other quantities in the problem being compared?" In Example 1, for instance, the problem states that Marta has twice as much money as Heidi, so it makes sense to represent Heidi's amount as h and Marta's amount as $2h$. Although h could be used to represent Marta's amount, Heidi's amount would then be $\frac{h}{2}$. Since this approach involves a fraction it is best avoided.

You might want to show students that the order in which the facts of a problem are used doesn't matter. Example 1 could have been solved by using the sec-

ond fact to represent the unknowns (h = Heidi's amount and $36 - h$ = Marta's amount) and the first fact to write an equation ($36 - h = 2h$). Students should come to realize that there is often more than one way to approach a problem.

Be sure to encourage students to draw sketches when appropriate, as Example 2 illustrates. For reluctant students, point out that sketches need not be detailed or even very accurate. They simply serve as visual "hooks" on which to hang mathematical symbols and see mathematical relationships.

Using Manipulatives

To emphasize the need to read carefully, ask each student to bring a newspaper or magazine to class. The students should then look for articles containing numerical information. After choosing one sentence or paragraph from the article, each student should write down questions that the sentence or paragraph raises but does not answer.

For instance, in a newspaper article about an insurance company, the company was described as "the fifth largest seller of auto insurance in the state with 6.7 percent of the total market." A few questions arising from this description might be: How is the "total market" measured—in terms of the number of customers, the volume of sales, or something else? How many customers or how much money does "6.7 percent" actually represent? Who are the four larger sellers of auto insurance in the state, and what are their shares of the total market?

As a follow-up activity, you can ask students to read the entire article to see which of their questions are actually answered. You might also ask them what they should do to get more information about any unanswered questions.

Suggested Extension

Have students write a word problem for which each of the following equations would be an appropriate mathematical translation. Answers will vary.

1. $x + (x + 5) = 13$ 2. $y + 3y = 24$
3. $m + (m - 6) = 14$ 4. $4n = n + 9$
5. $21 - p = 2p$

T80

1-7 (pages 27–30)

Key Mathematical Idea

- using the five-step plan to solve word problems

Teaching Suggestions

Students often have trouble solving word problems. Point out the relevance of this lesson; most problems that anyone has to solve outside the classroom are word problems.

Students may recognize that being given choices for one of the unknown quantities in a word problem is unrealistic. Point out that what you are most interested in at this time is that they learn a problem-solving process that they can use to help them solve more difficult problems as the course proceeds. Because the five-step plan will be used throughout the course, you may wish to post it where students can refer to it when necessary.

Encourage students to check their answers (Step 5 of the five-step plan), because doing so will give them confidence if they have gotten the correct answer or give them a chance to find their own mistake if they have made a careless error. Students should be cautioned to check their answers with the *words* of the problem. Substituting the value they got for the variable into their equation will not help them find their error if their equation does not correctly represent the given information.

Reading Algebra

Step 1 of the five-step problem solving plan tells the student to read the problem carefully. Although few would question the need for this step, students should be given specific guidance concerning how to do so. Some components of careful reading are: (1) reading the problem at least twice, once to get a "feel" for the problem and once to concentrate on the details; (2) recognizing what is unknown, that is, what needs to be "found"; (3) selecting the essential facts from the statement of the problem and organizing them in a chart, a sketch, or some other format; and (4) questioning the given information with respect to its completeness (Are relevant facts missing?) and its

consistency (Do any facts contradict each other?). Students who take the time to read carefully will find that the rest of the problem solving process becomes considerably easier.

Group Activity

To give students experience in cooperative problem solving, divide the class into groups and give each group member a slip of paper that has both a general statement of the problem and one fact needed for its solution. After each group has read and discussed the problem statement, one member at a time should read his/her given fact to the group and discuss its implications for the solution of the problem. By the time all the members have contributed their facts, the solution should be evident to everyone in the group.

An example of a problem for a four-person group is the following.

Problem: The four officers of a club are lined up for a yearbook photo. Who is the club president?

Fact 1: Tom stands at the opposite end of the line from the treasurer.

Fact 2: Mary stands next to the secretary.

Fact 3: Joe stands the farthest from the vice president.

Fact 4: Sue stands between the president and the vice president.

Mary is the club president.

Suggested Extension

Students may enjoy making up word problems from their own experience for their classmates to solve.

Example: Our basketball team won three more games this year than it did last year. During the two years it won 27 games. How many games did it win this year? 15 games

1-8 (pages 31–35)

Key Mathematical Idea

- correspondence of the real numbers and points on a number line

Teaching Suggestions

In developing the number line, point out to your students that "0" (the origin) can be placed anywhere on the line and that the unit length is also of their choosing. You may wish to mark the location of several integers on your number line with a compass to stress that once the location of the origin and the unit distance have been determined, every number that your students are familiar with is associated with some point of the line and that every point on the line is associated with some "real" number.

As you discuss number lines with your class, point out the following: Although each tick placed on a number line usually indicates the location of an integer, other numbers exist at points between the ticks; be sure to show students how to locate points corresponding to numbers like 1.5 and $-2\frac{1}{3}$. The arrowheads on a number line indicate that the line extends in both directions indefinitely; be sure to emphasize that one or both arrowheads are shaded when an infinite set, such as the set of whole numbers or the set of real numbers, is graphed. On a horizontal number line, larger numbers are always to the right of smaller numbers; be sure to point out the usefulness of this fact when ordering numbers, especially negative numbers.

If students think the term "real" number strange, point out that they will learn about other kinds of numbers, such as imaginary numbers, in future mathematics courses. For now, all they need to know is that the set of real numbers includes any numbers that they will encounter in this course.

Suggested Extension

Have the students use the number line to name the points with the given coordinates.

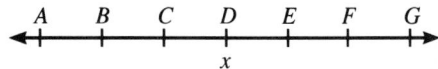

1. $x + 1$ E **2.** $x - 1$ C

3. $x - 3$ A **4.** $2 + x$ F

5. Give the coordinate of G in terms of x. $x + 3$

6. Give the coordinate of B in terms of x. $x - 2$

1-9 (pages 36–39)

Key Mathematical Idea

- opposites and absolute value

Teaching Suggestions

The number line can be very useful in presenting this lesson. Draw a number line on the chalkboard and use a compass to locate the opposite of several numbers. Be sure to include 0 and some positive and negative integers, fractions, and decimals. Point out that each number and its opposite are the same distance from the origin but are in opposite directions (hence the name "opposite").

Be sure your students understand that numbers like -3 ("the opposite of 3") and $^-3$ ("negative 3") are the same. Understanding this now will make subtracting real numbers (Lesson 2-4) much easier for them.

Emphasize that $-a$ is not necessarily a negative number. Use numerical examples to show students that when a is negative, $-a$ is positive; that when $a = 0$, $-a = 0$; and that when a is positive, $-a$ is negative.

Students will probably have less trouble understanding the notion of absolute value if you emphasize that the absolute value of a number is the distance from the origin to the graph of the number on the number line. Using a compass, show your students that the distance from the origin to -3, for example, is the same as the distance from the origin to 3, or $|-3| = |3| = 3$. Point out that since distance can never be negative, the absolute value of a number can never be negative.

Suggested Extension

Have students use a number line to answer the following questions. **1.** $-5, 5$ **2.** $-2, 8$ **3.** $-8, 2$

1. What numbers are 5 units from the origin?

2. What numbers are 5 units from the graph of 3?

3. What numbers are 5 units from the graph of -3?

4. What numbers are 5 units from the graph of x?
$x - 5, x + 5$

5. If x is a positive number, what numbers are x units from the graph of 5? $5 - x, 5 + x$

2 Working with Real Numbers

This chapter focuses on using the four operations and the properties of real numbers to simplify numerical and algebraic expressions.

The commutative, associative, distributive, and other properties are introduced to help students simplify numerical and algebraic expressions. Students learn to add real numbers, first by using a number line and then by developing rules consistent with the results suggested by the number line.

Subtraction is defined in terms of addition. The rules for multiplication are introduced, and division is defined in terms of multiplication. The properties of real numbers and problem-solving skills are developed further in Lesson 2-7.

2-1 (pages 45–48)

Key Mathematical Idea

- using the commutative and associative properties to simplify expressions

Teaching Suggestions

When discussing the closure properties, be sure to point out that they are not as simple as they may seem. Not all sets are closed under addition and multiplication. For example, since the sum of two odd integers is even, the set of odd integers is *not* closed under addition.

Students may already be familiar with the commutative and associative properties for addition and multiplication. Present a variety of examples to illustrate each property. Exercises 37–39 on page 48 can be used to show students that the commutative and associative axioms do not hold for subtraction and division. Point out that the commutative properties have to do with *order:* no matter what *order* you choose to add or multiply two numbers, you get the same sum or product. Point out that the word *associative* is similar to the word *association,* meaning a *group,* and has to do with *grouping:* no matter how you *group*

numbers to be added or multiplied, you get the same sum or product.

Suggested Extension

The operation # is defined for all real numbers a and b as follows: $a \# b = a + ab + b$. For example, $3 \# 5 = 3 + 15 + 5 = 23$.

1. Have the students complete the following table.

a	2	4	5	1
b	3	2	1	2
c	1	2	2	0
$a \# b$	11	14	11	5
$b \# a$	11	14	11	5
$(a \# b) \# c$	23	44	35	5
$a \# (b \# c)$	23	44	35	5

2. Ask the students whether # is **(a)** a commutative operation and **(b)** an associative operation.
   a. Yes
   b. Yes

2-2 (pages 49–53)

Key Mathematical Ideas

- addition of real numbers on the number line
- using the identity property of addition and the property of opposites

Teaching Suggestions

Some students may find it helpful to relate number line addition to adding gains and losses, with the sum being the net gain (positive) or net loss (negative). They are familiar with games involving gains and losses with the possibility of going "in the hole." Suggest a game in which a person has scores of 30, −80, and 20, and ask the students what the net score would be. (−30)

Reading Algebra

This lesson provides a good opportunity for you to show how diagrams must be read along with the text discussion. You might draw the first diagram on page 49 on the chalkboard and ask a student to read aloud the paragraph above the diagram. Have the reader pause after "at the origin," "3 units to the left," and "6 more units to the left" as you show the corresponding moves on the diagram. Then ask students to relate the text and the second diagram in the same way, by moving a finger along the diagram.

Using Manipulatives

You can show how to find the sum $3 + (-2)$ using unit tiles of different color. In the figure below, a white tile represents $+1$, and a gray tile represents -1. Thus, three white tiles and two gray tiles are used to represent 3 and -2, respectively.

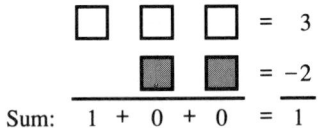

Notice in the figure that whenever a white tile and a gray tile are together (that is, vertically aligned), the pair represents 0. The sum of 3 and -2, therefore, consists of two white-gray pairs and one white tile left over. In other words, the sum is 1.

Have your students use tiles to find other sums like $-3 + 2$ and $-3 + (-2)$. Be sure to have students record their results, and encourage them to generalize the results in preparation for the next lesson, which presents the rules for adding positive and negative numbers.

Suggested Extension

The first three plays of a football team starting from its own 20-yard line are described below. Using a diagram of a football field like the one that follows, have students draw arrows to represent the sequence of plays. Then have them represent these plays as the sum of three integers and state the net gain or loss as a positive or negative number.

1. gain of 7 yd, loss of 3 yd, loss of 6 yd
   $7 + (-3) + (-6) = -2$
2. loss of 5 yd, loss of 2 yd, gain of 12 yd
   $-5 + (-2) + 12 = 5$
3. gain of 8 yd, loss of 5 yd, gain of 9 yd
   $8 + (-5) + 9 = 12$
4. loss of 1 yd, loss of 4 yd, loss of 10 yd
   $-1 + (-4) + (-10) = -15$
5. loss of 3 yd, no gain or loss, gain of 3 yd
   $-3 + 0 + 3 = 0$

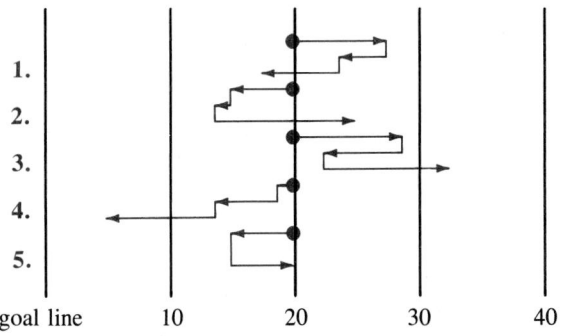

2-3 (pages 54–58)

Key Mathematical Ideas

- general rules for adding real numbers
- using addition to solve word problems

Teaching Suggestions

Your students learned to add real numbers using a number line in the previous lesson. The rules for addition stated in this lesson are intended to help them find sums more quickly. Students should be encouraged to use a number line to find a sum whenever they are unsure of their answer.

To check students' understanding of the rules of addition, you might ask them to correlate the enumerated rules in the box on page 54 with the summary of the rules in the paragraph that follows.

When several numbers, some positive and some negative, are to be added, students may find the work easier if the sums of the positive numbers and of the negative numbers are found separately and then added, as shown in the lesson examples.

Suggested Extension

The sum of each row, column, and diagonal of the magic square below is always the same number. Have the students use this fact to complete the square.

7	−7	−6	4
−4	2	1	−1
0	−2	−3	3
−5	5	6	−8

2-4 (pages 59–63)

Key Mathematical Ideas

- using the definition of subtraction to simplify expressions involving differences
- using subtraction to solve word problems

Teaching Suggestions

This is a difficult lesson for many students. Encourage students to express each difference as a sum and apply the rules they learned in the previous lesson. By using the definition of subtraction, students are less likely to become confused when one or both of the numbers involved are negative.

To convince students that their answers are correct, have them check their answers using addition. Examples: $7 - 8 = -1$ and $-1 + 8 = 7$; $-5 - (-3) = -2$ and $-2 + (-3) = -5$.

If students still need to be convinced that the correct answer is reasonable, try this approach using the number line. Remind students that when they subtract two positive numbers a and b with $a > b$, the difference, $a - b$, is positive. Point out that this holds for all real numbers a and b. Likewise, if $a < b$, $a - b$ is negative for all real numbers. Thus, the difference of a and b can be found by first finding the distance between a and b on the number line and then determining whether the difference is positive or negative based on whether $a > b$ or $a < b$. Show several examples like those at the top of the next column.

1.

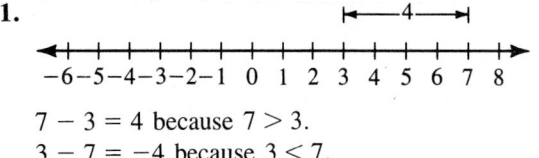

$7 - 3 = 4$ because $7 > 3$.
$3 - 7 = -4$ because $3 < 7$.

2.

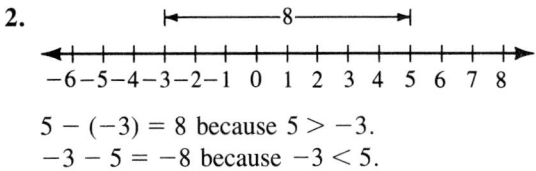

$5 - (-3) = 8$ because $5 > -3$.
$-3 - 5 = -8$ because $-3 < 5$.

3.

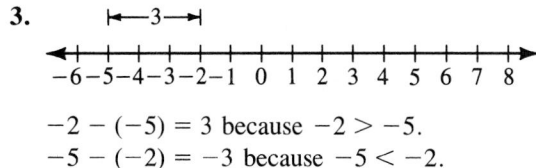

$-2 - (-5) = 3$ because $-2 > -5$.
$-5 - (-2) = -3$ because $-5 < -2$.

Using Manipulatives

Just as unit tiles were used to illustrate the addition of positive and negative numbers (see Using Manipulatives for Lesson 2-2), they can be used to illustrate subtraction. For example, the difference $3 - (-2)$ involves "taking away" two gray tiles from three white ones. To do so, you must first "build up" the three white tiles by adding two white-gray tile pairs (each representing 0). Once the two gray tiles are removed, five white tiles remain. In other words, the difference is 5.

First "build up" 3:

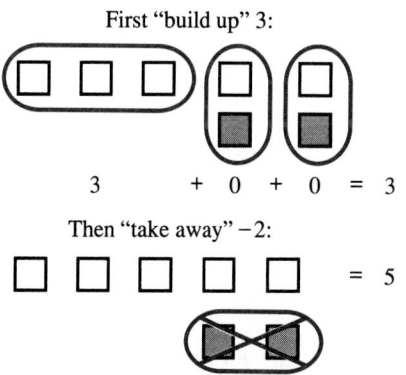

Have your students use tiles to find other differences like $-3 - 2$ and $-3 - (-2)$. Be sure to have them record their results for later discussion.

Suggested Extension

Have students find the following pairs of differences using a number line (see Teaching Suggestions). Then have them check their answers using addition.

1. **a.** $6 - 2$ 4
   b. $2 - 6$ -4

2. **a.** $-4 - (-1)$ -3
   b. $-1 - (-4)$ 3

3. **a.** $-3 - 2$ -5
   b. $2 - (-3)$ 5

4. **a.** $8 - 0$ 8
   b. $0 - 8$ -8

5. **a.** $0 - (-5)$ 5
   b. $-5 - 0$ -5

6. **a.** $7 - (-2)$ 9
   b. $-2 - 7$ -9

2-5 (pages 65–69)

Key Mathematical Idea

- using the distributive property to simplify expressions

Teaching Suggestions

You can point out to students that they have used the distributive property before, probably without realizing it. The algorithm for multiplying, say, 7 and 23 is based on the fact that $23 = 20 + 3$:

$$
\begin{array}{r}
23 \\
\times\ 7 \\
\hline
(7 \times 3) = \quad 21 \\
(7 \times 20) = \ 140 \\
\hline
161
\end{array}
$$

or
$$
\begin{aligned}
7 \times 23 &= 7 \times (20 + 3) \\
&= 7 \times 20 + 7 \times 3 \\
&= 140 + 21 \\
&= 161
\end{aligned}
$$

When discussing the distributive property, you might use arrows to reinforce the concept of distributing:

$$a(b + c) = ab + ac$$

Emphasize that terms are separated by "+" or "−" and that the distributive property is used to combine like terms.

Using Manipulatives

You can have students become familiar with the distributive property through the use of tiles or manipulatives cut from graph paper. For example, the fact that $3(x + 2) = 3x + 6$ is apparent from the areas of the rectangles shown below.

Have students consider the areas of other pairs of rectangles, both joined and separated, and record their observations.

Suggested Extension

Ask students which of the following statements would be true for all real numbers. 2, 3, and 5

1. $3(2x + 5) = 6x + 5$
2. $4p - 8q = 4(p - 2q)$
3. $35 + 5(4a - b) = 5[7 + (4a - b)]$
4. $5[2(3c + 4)] = 10(6c + 8)$
5. $12m - 9n + 15 = 3(4m - 3n + 5)$

2-6 (pages 70–73)

Key Mathematical Idea

- using rules and properties to find the products of real numbers

---

Teaching Suggestions

Students often confuse the new rules for multiplication with the rules for addition. Many students who would have added -5 and -3 correctly before might now say that $(-5) + (-3)$ is 8 because "two minuses make a plus." Require precise language as in the following statements.

1. The product of two negative numbers is positive.
2. The sum of two negative numbers is negative.
3. The product of a positive and a negative number is negative.
4. The sum of a positive and a negative number may be either positive or negative.

To illustrate the multiplicative property of -1, you might use the diagram below. It emphasizes the fact that multiplying a number by -1 is equivalent to taking the opposite of the number.

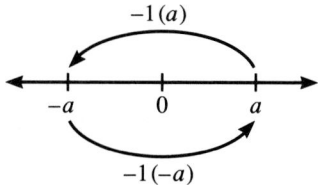

Group Activity

Divide the class into small groups to discuss the following situations. Ask the members of each group to agree upon an equation involving a product of signed numbers that models each situation.

1. Suppose you earn money at the rate of $5 per day. Will you be richer or poorer in 3 days than you are now? By how much? Richer; $15; 3(5) = 15
2. Suppose you spend money at the rate of $5 per day. Will you be richer or poorer in 3 days than now? By how much? Poorer; $15; 3(−5) = −15
3. Suppose you earn money at the rate of $5 per day. Were you richer or poorer 3 days ago than you are now? By how much? Poorer; $15; −3(5) = −15
4. Suppose you spend money at the rate of $5 per day. Were you richer or poorer 3 days ago than now? By how much? Richer; $15; −3(−5) = 15

Using Manipulatives

Students can use unit tiles (see Using Manipulatives for Lesson 2-2) to find a product like $3(-2)$. By taking three groups of two gray tiles each, they should see that $3(-2) = -6$.

Suggested Extension

Have your students simplify each of the following.

1. a. $(-8)(-3)$ 24
   b. $(-8) + (-3)$ −11
2. a. $(9)(-2)$ −18
   b. $(9) + (-2)$ 7
3. a. $(4)(-6)$ −24
   b. $(4) + (-6)$ −2
4. a. $(-7)(0)$ 0
   b. $(-7) + (0)$ −7
5. a. $(2)(-3)(-1)(4)(-2)$ −48
   b. $(2) + (-3) + (-1) + (4) + (-2)$ 0
6. a. $(-1)(-2)(-3)(-4)$ 24
   b. $(-1) + (-2) + (-3) + (-4)$ −10

2-7 (pages 75–78)

Key Mathematical Idea

- translating relationships among integers into equations

Teaching Suggestions

This lesson provides practice in using parentheses as grouping symbols in writing equations. Consecutive integers, consecutive even integers, and consecutive odd integers are the basis of the equations.

Use several examples to illustrate that n, $n + 2$, $n + 4$, and so on can represent either consecutive even or consecutive odd integers. You might want to select three consecutive odd integers (15, 17, and 19, for example) and then show how the equation expressing their sum can be written in terms of the smallest integer:

$$15 + (15 + 2) + (15 + 4) = 51$$

Stress that there is more than one correct way to write an equation about consecutive, consecutive even, or consecutive odd integers. For example, given that the sum of three consecutive integers is 27, students can write

$$n + (n + 1) + (n + 2) = 27,$$
$$(n - 1) + n + (n + 1) = 27,$$
or $\qquad (n - 2) + (n - 1) + n = 27,$

depending on whether n represents the smallest, the middle, or the largest integer. The second of these equations has the advantage of its left side, when simplified, being just $3n$.

Group Activity

Divide the class into small groups. Give each group a different list of three consecutive, consecutive even, or consecutive odd integers. Ask each group member to write a word problem about the integers and give a domain for one of them. Then have each group exchange its word problems with another group. Ask the members of each group to solve the word problems they were given and compare their solutions to make sure they all agree on the same three integers.

Suggested Extension

Have each student select three consecutive integers, complete the following statements about them, and write an equation to represent each statement. Answers will vary.

1. The sum of three consecutive integers is __?__ .

2. Three times the smallest integer is __?__ more than the sum of the two larger integers.

3. Twice the sum of the two smaller integers is __?__ less than five times the largest.

2-8 (pages 79–82)

Key Mathematical Idea

- using the property of reciprocals to simplify products

Teaching Suggestions

It would be worthwhile to review the property of opposites as you introduce the property of reciprocals. You can review the relationships between numbers and their opposites using a number line similar to the one shown on page 36 and contrast this with a number line like the one below, which shows some numbers and their reciprocals.

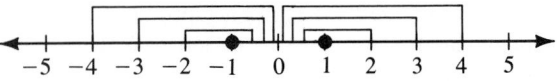

Point out that the sum of opposites, or additive inverses, is 0, the identity element for addition, and that the product of reciprocals, or multiplicative inverses, is 1, the identity element for multiplication. Using the number line above, also point out the following facts about reciprocals.

1. The numbers 1 and -1 are their own reciprocals.
2. The number 0 has no reciprocal.
3. The reciprocal of a positive number less than 1 is a number greater than 1, and vice versa. Likewise, the reciprocal of a negative number greater than -1 is a number less than -1, and vice versa.

Some students may want to write the reciprocal of, say, $\frac{2}{3}$ in the form $\frac{1}{\frac{2}{3}}$, which is correct but awkward. Point out that the simplest form for the reciprocal of $\frac{2}{3}$ is $\frac{3}{2}$. You might also want to show that

$$\frac{3}{2} = \frac{1}{\frac{2}{3}} \cdot \frac{3}{3}.$$

Suggested Extension

Have students replace each __?__ with a number to make a true statement.

1. $-1 + $ __?__ $= 0$ 1

2. $-1($ __?__ $) = 1$ -1

3. $2 + $ __?__ $= 0$ -2

4. $2($ __?__ $) = 1$ $\frac{1}{2}$

5. $-\frac{3}{4} + $ __?__ $= 0$ $\frac{3}{4}$

6. $-\frac{3}{4}($ __?__ $) = 1$ $-\frac{4}{3}$

2-9 (pages 83–86)

Key Mathematical Ideas

- using the definition of division to express quotients as products
- simplifying quotients

Teaching Suggestions

Point out to your students that they used the definition of division whenever they found the quotient of two fractions by inverting the second one and multiplying. Also point out that division is defined in terms of multiplication just as subtraction is defined in terms of addition. Make sure students understand that the rules for dividing real numbers are similar to the rules for multiplying real numbers because the definition of division permits replacing any quotient by a product.

Point out that the properties of division given in the box on page 84 are directly related to the distributive properties of multiplication.

Using Manipulatives

Students can use unit tiles (see Using Manipulatives for Lesson 2-2) to find a quotient like $\frac{-6}{3}$: By separating six gray tiles into three equal groups, they should see that $\frac{-6}{3} = -2$.

Suggested Extension

Have students replace each __?__ with a number to make a true statement.

1. If $14 \div (-2) = $ __?__ , then __?__$(-2) = 14.$ $-7, -7$

2. If $-8 \div \frac{1}{2} = $ __?__ , then __?__ $\cdot \frac{1}{2} = -8.$ $-16, -16$

3. If $\frac{4}{5} \div 3 = $ __?__ , then __?__ $\cdot 3 = \frac{4}{5}.$ $\frac{4}{15}, \frac{4}{15}$

4. If $-\frac{1}{2} \div \left(-\frac{1}{4}\right) = $ __?__ , then __?__$\left(-\frac{1}{4}\right) = -\frac{1}{2}.$ $2, 2$

3 Solving Equations and Problems

Algebraic methods of solving equations are developed using the properties of equality. Multistep solutions require the use of many properties from earlier lessons.

The algebraic method of problem solving is now considered in its entirety. The use of charts is introduced as an aid to organizing information in various types of word problems, including cost and value problems.

An introduction to proofs of algebraic theorems is presented in the last lesson.

3-1 (pages 95–101)

Key Mathematical Ideas

- using the addition and subtraction properties of equality to solve equations
- solving simple word problems using addition or subtraction

Teaching Suggestions

Begin with some simple examples, emphasizing that the solution of an equation is a number and not another equation. For example, the solution to Example 1 is 25, not $x = 25$.

Some students want to show steps of a solution horizontally as, for example, $x - 4 = 9 = x = 13$. Point out that the equivalence symbol $\leftrightarrow$ can be used

for this purpose, but that the equals sign cannot. Stress that the vertical form, with the equals signs lined up, is generally preferred.

Point out to students that the goal when solving an equation is to isolate the variable on one side.

Using Manipulatives

Divide the class into small groups. Each group should have a balance scale and a collection of unit cubes from a base-ten block set. Give each group two envelopes, one marked "x" containing 4 cubes and one marked "empty." Have each group put the "x" envelope and 5 cubes on one pan of the balance and the "empty" envelope and 9 cubes on the other pan.

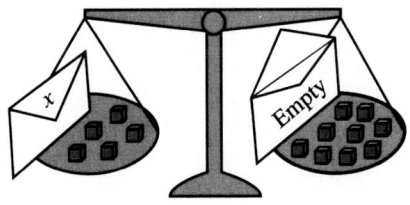

Ask the students to write the equation that represents this situation. ($x + 5 = 9$) Then have them remove 5 cubes from each pan and tell what the value of x is. Students can verify their solution by opening the "x" envelope.

Suggested Extension

Have your students match each equation on the left with an equivalent equation on the right.

1. $4 - x = 7$ d   **a.** $4 - x = -7$

2. $-x = 7$ b   **b.** $x = -7$

3. $x - 4 = 7$ a   **c.** $x + 4 = -7$

4. $4 + x = 7$ e   **d.** $x - 4 = -7$

5. $-x = -7$ f   **e.** $-4 - x = -7$

6. $4 + x = -7$ c   **f.** $7 - x = 0$

3-2 (pages 102–106)

Key Mathematical Ideas

- using the multiplication and division properties of equality to solve equations
- solving simple word problems using multiplication or division

---

Teaching Suggestions

Remind students that the goal in solving an equation is to transform it into an equation that has only the variable on one of the sides. Point out that an equation of the form $ax = b$ $(a \neq 0)$ can be solved by multiplying each side by $\frac{1}{a}$ or by dividing each side by a.

Point out that $\frac{1}{3}x$ and $\frac{x}{3}$ represent the same number and that $3\left(\frac{1}{3}x\right)$ and $3 \cdot \frac{x}{3}$ are each equal to $1x$ or x.

Be sure that students understand why zero cannot be used as a multiplier or as a divisor in transforming equations.

Using Manipulatives

Divide the class into small groups. Each group should have a balance scale and a collection of unit cubes from a base-ten block set. Give each group four envelopes, two marked "x" containing 4 cubes each and two marked "empty." Have each group put the "x" envelopes on one pan of the balance and the "empty" envelopes and 8 cubes on the other pan, as shown at the top of the next column.

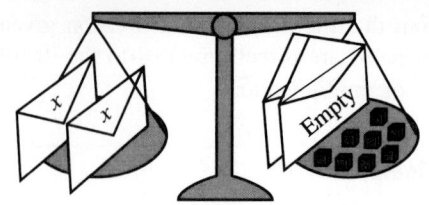

Ask the students to write the equation that represents this situation. ($2x = 8$) Then have them separate the 8 cubes into two equal groups. After asking the students to remove one of the groups of cubes as well as an "empty" envelope and an "x" envelope from the balance, have them tell what the value of x is. Students can verify their solution by opening the remaining "x" envelope.

Suggested Extension

Ask your students to solve equation (a) and then predict the solutions of equations (b)–(f).

a. $5x = 75$ {15}   **b.** $0.5x = 7.5$ {15}

c. $0.05x = 0.75$ {15}   **d.** $50x = 750$ {15}

e. $0.5x = 75$ {150}   **f.** $5x = 7.5$ {1.5}

3-3 (pages 107–111)

Key Mathematical Idea

- using several transformations to solve equations

Teaching Suggestions

Encourage students who have difficulty solving multi-step equations to show the actual application of inverse operations. You might even have these students verbalize what they do and why, like "I added 5 to both sides of $2x - 5 = 7$ to undo the subtraction of 5 from $2x$." The ultimate goal is to produce condensed solutions, as shown in the examples on page 108.

Since the solutions of multistep equations are not as "obvious" as those of one-step equations, you might now give more emphasis to checking solutions.

The "helpful tips" given at the top of page 109 need not be considered inviolable rules. For instance, the equation in Example 5 can be solved without using the distributive property to simplify the left side, as shown below.

$$4(y + 8) - 7 = 15$$
$$4(y + 8) = 22$$
$$y + 8 = \frac{11}{2}$$
$$y = -\frac{5}{2}$$

Using Manipulatives

Have students solve an equation like $3x + 7 = 22$ using a balance scale and a collection of cubes from a base-ten block set. (Refer to "Using Manipulatives" in the commentary for Lessons 3-1 and 3-2.)

Suggested Extension

Write the equation $0.024(x - 50) = -4.8$ on the chalkboard.

1. Ask students to solve the equation by using the distributive property first. $\{-150\}$

2. Ask students to solve the equation by dividing each side by 0.024 first. $\{-150\}$

3. Ask students to solve the equation by multiplying each side by 1000 first. $\{-150\}$

4. Ask individual students to discuss why they prefer one method over another.
   Answers will vary.

3-4 (pages 112–115)

Key Mathematical Idea

• using the five-step plan to solve word problems

Teaching Suggestions

You will need to discuss many examples and to stress the importance of organization and neatness. Remind students that accurate problem solving requires careful reading.

Example 2 on page 112 is full of words whose meaning might be unclear to students. Be sure to dis-cuss what is meant by *perimeter, trapezoid,* and so on. Some students might also need to be reminded that 2 must be added in going from one odd integer to the next, so that x and $x + 2$ represent consecutive odd integers if x is odd.

To emphasize the need to check a problem's solution against the original statement of the problem, you might ask the students, "How would the solution of Example 2 be affected if the lengths of the trapezoid's legs were supposed to be consecutive *even* integers?" The students should recognize that nothing would change until Step 5, where an odd length would have to be rejected; Example 2 would therefore have no solution.

Reading Algebra

As students begin more difficult work with problems, you may want to remind them of the material on reading problems on page 26. You may also discuss with them the ideas presented in the article on problem solving strategies on page T54.

Emphasize the value of looking for words in problems that suggest the operations involved in the solution. Examples are: *perimeter* of a triangle (addition); *area* of a rectangle (multiplication); and *average* (addition and division).

Suggested Extension

Have each student make up a problem with the answer "12." Use the following examples.

1. $30 + 10(12) = 150$

   Bart wants to buy a bike that costs $150. He has $30 saved and plans to put aside $10 each week. In how many weeks will Bart have enough money to buy the bike?

2. $8 + 2(10) + 3(12) = 64$

   I'm thinking of three consecutive even integers. When I add the smallest, twice the second, and three times the largest, the result is 64. Find the largest integer.

3. $2(12) + 2(23) = 70$

   The length of a rectangle is 1 cm less than twice the width. If the perimeter of the rectangle is 70 cm, find the width.

3-5 (pages 116–120)

Key Mathematical Ideas

- solving equations when the variable appears on both sides
- solving problems leading to equations with the variable on both sides

Teaching Suggestions

Review the concept of *equivalent equations,* that is, equations with the same solution set over a specified domain. Stress that the following transformations produce equivalent equations:

1. simplifying one side or both sides
2. adding the same number to both sides or subtracting the same number from both sides
3. multiplying or dividing both sides by the same *nonzero* number

Suggest that students check each solution to an equation in the *original* equation. If the solution does not check, students should examine each step of the solution to locate errors. Common errors include: miscopying an equation from one step to the next; ignoring a negative sign; and not distributing completely, for example rewriting $2(x + 3)$ as $2x + 3$.

Point out that while most of the equations in this chapter have one solution, some equations in this lesson have no solution and others are satisfied by every real number. Students should be aware of the three possibilities that exist for a linear equation in one variable: the equation has a unique root, has no root, or is an identity.

When an equation has no solution, you may wish to have students use { } instead of $\emptyset$ to denote the empty set. Be sure to warn students not to write $\{\emptyset\}$.

Group Activity

Divide the class into small groups. To the members of each group, randomly distribute slips of paper on which are written single steps in the solution of an equation like $3(x - 2) + 5 = 7x - 3$. (For instance, one slip would have $3x - 6 + 5 = 7x - 3$.) The group members should then work cooperatively to reassemble the solution.

Suggested Extension

Each of the following solutions is incorrect. Have students identify which two consecutive equations are not equivalent and state why.

1. a. $2x + 5 = 3(x - 4)$
    b. $2x + 5 = 3x - 12$
    c. $\qquad 5 = x - 12$
    d. $\qquad -7 = x$

2. a. $\frac{1}{3}(6x - 12) = 6 + 4(x - 2)$
    b. $\qquad 2x - 4 = 10(x - 2)$
    c. $\qquad 2x - 4 = 10x - 20$
    d. $\qquad -4 = 8x - 20$
    e. $\qquad 16 = 8x$
    f. $\qquad 2 = x$

3. a. $5(x + 4) - x = -6(x - 10)$
    b. $5x + 20 - x = -6x + 60$
    c. $\qquad 4x + 20 = -6x + 60$
    d. $\qquad 10x + 20 = 60$
    e. $\qquad x + 20 = 6$
    f. $\qquad x = -14$

1. c and d; $5 + 12 = x - 12 + 12$ is equivalent to $17 = x$.
2. a and b; $6 + 4(x - 2) = 6 + 4x - 8 = 4x - 2$; $10(x - 2) = 10x - 20$; $4x - 2 \neq 10x - 20$.
3. d and e; $\frac{1}{10}(10x + 20) = \frac{1}{10}(60)$ gives $x + 2 = 6$.

3-6 (pages 121–125)

Key Mathematical Idea

- using charts to solve word problems

Teaching Suggestions

Point out that a chart is particularly useful in problems involving two or more numbers that we do not know. It helps us represent the unknown numbers in terms of a single variable before writing an equation.

Many students find that once they have set up a chart and filled it in, they can complete the solution process with little difficulty. The Oral Exercises provide good practice in completing charts.

Put the calendar of any month on the board. Ask a student to pick any date that is surrounded by other dates. Then ask the students to give you the total of the four diagonally opposite numbers. You can tell the date the students picked by dividing the sum by 4. The following chart shows why this works. The x stands for the date chosen.

$x - 8$	$x - 7$	$x - 6$
$x - 1$	x	$x + 1$
$x + 6$	$x + 7$	$x + 8$

3-7 (pages 126–129)

Key Mathematical Idea

- solving problems involving cost, income, and value

Teaching Suggestions

Returning to Example 1 on page 121 in Lesson 3-6, you might want to continue the example by introducing another fact like "The areas of the carpets are the same." After pointing out that the length of each roll of carpet can now be determined, show how each chart given in the example leads to a different equation, yet the same solution.

Present the following problem and help students develop the chart used in solving the problem.

Eric has 8 nickels, twice as many dimes as nickels, and 4 more quarters than nickels. What is the total value of his coins?

	Number × Value of Coin = Total Value		
Nickels	8	5	5(8)
Dimes	$2 \cdot 8$	10	$10(2 \cdot 8)$
Quarters	$8 + 4$	25	$25(8 + 4)$

The total value is

$$5(8) + 10(2 \cdot 8) + 25(8 + 4) =$$
$$40 + 160 + 300 = 500, \text{ or } \$5.00.$$

Now have students make a chart for the following problem by replacing 8 by n.

Erica has some nickels, twice as many dimes as nickels, and 4 more quarters than nickels. The total value of all her coins is $6.50. How many coins of each type does she have?

	Number × Value of Coin = Total Value		
Nickels	n	5	$5n$
Dimes	$2n$	10	$10(2n)$
Quarters	$n + 4$	25	$25(n + 4)$

Help students write and solve an equation and answer the question. Discuss why $6.50 must be expressed in terms of cents.

$$5n + 10(2n) + 25(n + 4) = 650$$
$$5n + 20n + 25n + 100 = 650$$
$$50n = 550$$
$$n = 11 \quad \text{11 nickels}$$
$$2n = 22 \quad \text{22 dimes}$$
$$n + 4 = 15 \quad \text{15 quarters}$$

Emphasize that the various types of problems in this lesson are variations of this basic type:

(number of units) · (unit value) = total value

When solving problems like these, students should remember the need for uniformity in the choice of units (for example, cents or dollars).

Suggested Extension

Have students determine the better buy by comparing unit prices.

1. A 24 oz can of corn that costs $.96 or a 16 oz can that costs $.68. 24 oz can

2. A roll of paper towels that has 500 sheets and costs $1.20 or a roll that has 400 sheets and costs $.90. Roll that has 400 sheets

3. A package of 6 blank video cassettes that costs $19.08 or a package of 8 that costs $25.20. Package of 8

4. A roll of 50 ft² of aluminum foil that costs $.75 or a roll of 75 ft² that costs $1.15. 50 ft² roll

3-8 (pages 130–134)

Key Mathematical Idea

- proving theorems in algebra

Teaching Suggestions

This will probably be the first exposure to proof of any kind for your students. A good way to begin is to review the properties learned thus far. (See the summaries on page 88.)

For the most part, students will be asked in this lesson to provide reasons for proofs, not to write complete proofs. Encourage your students to become familiar with the two-column proof format.

Most students will have little success writing original proofs and some may become discouraged. Tell students that it is more important for them to be able to understand a proof.

Group Activity

Divide the class into small groups. To the members of each group, randomly distribute slips of paper on which are written the (unnumbered) statements and reasons for the proof of the multiplicative property of zero (shown below). The group members should then work cooperatively to reassemble the proof.

For every real number a, $a \cdot 0 = 0$ and $0 \cdot a = 0$.

1. $0 + 0 = 0$	1. Identity prop. of addition
2. $a(0 + 0) = a \cdot 0$	2. Mult. prop. of equality
3. $a \cdot 0 + a \cdot 0 = a \cdot 0$	3. Distributive prop.
4. $a \cdot 0 + a \cdot 0 = 0 + a \cdot 0$	4. Identity prop. of addition
5. $a \cdot 0 = 0$	5. Subtr. prop. of equality
6. $0 \cdot a = 0$	6. Commutative prop. of mult.

4 Polynomials

The concept of an exponent and the first rules of exponents are introduced. The addition, subtraction, and multiplication of polynomials are developed and applied in conjunction with additional rules of exponents. Previous work with equations is extended to transforming formulas. The chapter concludes with further development of problem solving skills, uniform motion, and area problems. They provide an opportunity to apply the skills developed in the chapter. Students also learn to recognize problems without solutions.

4-1 (pages 141–144)

Key Mathematical Idea

- simplifying expressions with exponents

Teaching Suggestions

Write the following examples on the chalkboard:

$$5^3 \quad (-2)^4 \quad 2x^3 \quad 1 + 3^2$$
$$-5^3 \quad -2^4 \quad (2x)^3 \quad (1 + 3)^2$$

Ask students to identify the base and exponent in each and to write the expressions as a product of factors. Be sure students understand the difference between each pair of examples. The Oral Exercises and A-level exercises provide excellent practice with exponents and help uncover some mistakes the students commonly make when working with exponents. Caution students against evaluating b^n as $b \cdot n$ and $(b - a)^n$ as $b^n - a^n$.

Review the order of operations on page 142. Emphasize that the second step, simplifying expressions with powers, is a new one on the list.

Point out that Exercises 32 and 33 on page 144 use powers of 10 to show place value.

Reading Algebra

Math teachers need to stress the use of oral language by having students verbalize in sentences, summarize, repeat, say another way, and read aloud. It is not uncommon for a set of symbols to be verbalized in several ways within one class lesson. For example, a^2 may be called the square of a, the second power of a, a squared, or a to the second power. Practice is necessary if the relationship between the spoken and the written is to be understood.

Suggested Extensions

Write each expression on the chalkboard and ask students to place grouping symbols so that the expression has the given value.

1. $2 \cdot 1 + 7 - 10^2 \cdot 3 \div (-4) + 2$ **a.** -12 **b.** 93
   a. $2 \cdot (1 + 7 - 10)^2 \cdot 3 \div [(-4) + 2] = -12$
   b. $2(1 + 7) - 10^2 \cdot 3 \div (-4) + 2 = 93$

2. $3 \cdot 4 - 3 \cdot 2^4 - 4^3 \div 2$ **a.** -8 **b.** 42,592
   a. $[3(4 - 3 \cdot 2)^4 - 4^3] \div 2 = -8$
   b. $[3 \cdot (4 - 3) \cdot 2^4 - 4]^3 \div 2 = 42{,}592$

4-2 (pages 146–151)

Key Mathematical Idea

- adding and subtracting polynomials

Teaching Suggestions

Write the following monomials on the chalkboard: $-5x^2y^3z$, $2a^7b^9$, and $9pq^2r^3s^4t^5$. For each monomial, have students state the degree in each variable and the degree of the monomial. If they have difficulty, ask them to think about the factored form of the monomial.

Demonstrate both the horizontal and the vertical formats for addition and subtraction of polynomials. Suggest the use of the operation symbols $+$ and $-$ for those using the vertical format.

Emphasize that in simplifying $6x^2 + 4x^2 = (6 + 4)x^2 = 10x^2$, the distributive property is used. This should help avoid the common error of adding exponents as well as coefficients when adding similar terms.

Errors in subtraction are very common. Caution students to work carefully, consistently, and to check their work. Some students may find it helpful to think

of a subtraction problem as multiplying the second polynomial by -1 and then finding the sum. Emphasize that $(a + b) - (c + d) = a + b - c - d$ and remind students to combine like terms.

Reading Algebra

Guide students in understanding the new vocabulary introduced in this lesson by relating the new terms to words they already know. Discuss the words *monorail*, *bicycle*, and *tripod*. Ask students for the meaning of the prefixes *mono*, *bi*, and *tri* and for examples of words using each prefix. Relate the meaning of these prefixes to the terms *monomial*, *binomial*, and *trinomial*.

Group Activities

In a magic square, each horizontal and vertical row and the two diagonals must have the same sum. Have each member of a group test a different row or diagonal of the following box. Have them compare their results and decide if it is a magic square.

$6x - y$	$4x - y$	$4x - 6y$
$3x - 4y$	$5x + y$	$6x + 6y$
$5x + 2y$	$5y - 2y$	$3x - 3y$

no

Alternate Square

$4a - 6b$	$9a - b$	$2a - 8b$
$3a - 7b$	$5a - 5b$	$7a - 3b$
$8a - 2b$	$a - 9b$	$6a - 4b$

yes

Suggested Extensions

Instruct students to find the missing polynomial P for each of the following.

1. $4x^2 + 3x - 7 + P = 0$
   $-4x^2 - 3x + 7$

2. $8ab - a^3 - 9a^2b + b^3 - P = 0$
   $-a^3 - 9a^2b + 8ab + b^3$

4-3 (pages 152–154)

Key Mathematical Idea

- using the rule of exponents for the product of powers when multiplying monomials

Teaching Suggestions

The rules of exponents often cause difficulty. Students will appear to be successful with one rule treated in isolation, but once all the rules are established, students tend to become confused. Therefore, place emphasis on the concept behind the rule. That is, students are likely to be successful if you stress the definition of an exponent, which is the basis of the rules of exponents.

You might want to begin the lesson with a numerical example like $2^3 \cdot 2^5 = 8 \cdot 32 = 256 = 2^8$. Some students may want to multiply exponents rather than add them; point out that $2^3 \cdot 2^5 \neq 2^{15}$. Also, some students may want to multiply the bases; point out that $2^3 \cdot 2^5 \neq 4^8$.

When working through algebraic examples, remind students that x can be written as x^1.

Suggested Extensions

1. Ask students to find the volume of each of the figures in Exercises 38–40 on page 154. (The volume can be found by multiplying the area of the bottom or top of the solid by the height.)

    38. $6a^3$ **39.** $15x^3$ **40.** $18a^3$

2. Ask students to tell whether each statement is true or false. If it is false, students should give a counterexample. If it is true, students should prove it.

    a. $a^{m \cdot n} = a^m \cdot a^n$

    b. $a^{m+n} = a^m + a^n$

    c. $(ab)^m = a^m \cdot b^m$

    d. $(a + b)^m = a^m + b^m$

    a. False; counterexample:
    $3^{2 \cdot 3} = 3^6 = 729; 3^2 \cdot 3^3 = 9 \cdot 27 = 243$

    b. False; counterexample:
    $3^{2+3} = 3^5 = 243; 3^2 + 3^3 = 9 + 27 = 36$

    c. True; $(ab)^m = ab \cdot ab \cdot ab \cdots ab$ (m factors)
    $= (a \cdot a \cdot a \cdots a)(b \cdot b \cdot b \cdots b)$
    (m factors of a, m factors of b)
    $= a^m \cdot b^m$

    d. False; counterexample:
    $(3 + 4)^2 = 7^2 = 49; 3^2 + 4^2 = 9 + 16 = 25$

4-4 (pages 155–157)

Key Mathematical Ideas

- using two more rules of exponents
- finding powers of monomials

Teaching Suggestions

Point out that the second rule of exponents in this lesson, $(ab)^m = a^m b^m$, can easily be generalized to any number of factors by the same reasoning, $(abcd \ldots)^m = a^m b^m c^m d^m \ldots$.

The Oral and Written exercises of this lesson provide good exercises to compare power of power problems with the product of power problems of Lesson 4-3.

The B exercises of this lesson require students to use all three rules that have been established this far. Caution students to use only one rule at a time until they are experienced enough to skip steps.

Reading Algebra

You will find it worthwhile to focus on the symbolism used in this lesson. Example 1 and the rules of exponents might be read aloud. Point out that an expression such as $(x^3)^2$ can be read in several different ways—for example, "x cubed to the second power," "x cubed [pause] squared," "the square of the cube of x." Any word form that makes the meaning clear is acceptable. Ask students to respond to the Oral Exercises with complete sentences—for example, "The square of the fourth power of x is x to the eighth power."

Suggested Extension

Ask students to simplify each expression. Assume that each variable represents a positive integer.

1. $[a^na^2]^3$
$= [a^n \cdot a^2]^3$
$= a^{3n} \cdot a^6$
$= a^{3n+6}$

2. $[(2b)^3]^n$
$= [2^3 \cdot b^3]^n$
$= [8b^3]^n$
$= 8^n b^{3n}$

3. $[(3a)^m]^n \cdot (3a^m)^n$
$= [3^m a^m]^n \cdot (3^n a^{mn})$
$= 3^{mn} a^{mn} \cdot 3^n a^{mn}$
$= 3^{mn+n} \cdot a^{2mn}$

4-5 (pages 158–160)

Key Mathematical Idea

- multiplying a polynomial by a monomial

Teaching Suggestions

The new skill introduced in this lesson, multiplying a polynomial by a monomial, is based on the distributive property and the rules of exponents. Point out that once the distributive property is applied, the resulting expression is of the type found in Lessons 4-3 and 4-4.

$$3y^2(2y^3 - 4y - 9) =$$
$$(3y^2)(2y^3) + (3y^2)(-4y) + (3y^2)(-9)$$

You can prepare the students for the next lesson by introducing both the horizontal and vertical forms of multiplication.

Caution students that it is easy to confuse signs when multiplying and simplifying expressions. They should be especially careful when working on Exercises 19–38 on pages 159 and 160.

Using Manipulatives

Using tiles or manipulatives cut from grid paper (a conveniently sized square to represent one unit, a strip of 10 ones to represent x, and a 10-by-10 square to represent x^2), you can have students confirm that $x^2 + 3x$ is the area of a rectangle with sides x and $x + 3$.

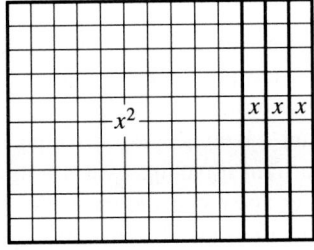

Suggested Extensions

To help develop students' spatial perception, ask them to draw the figure in Exercise 43 on page 160 if viewed straight on from each of the six sides. You may wish to include the figures in Exercises 39 and 40 on page 154 in this activity.

4-6 (pages 161–164)

Key Mathematical Idea

- multiplying polynomials

Teaching Suggestions

You can develop the multiplication of polynomials by showing the steps in the multiplication of numbers, both in vertical and horizontal format. For example, $(27)(13)$ can be written as

$$
\begin{array}{r}
20 + 7 \\
\times\ 10 + 3 \\
\hline
200 + 70 \\
60 + 21 \\
\hline
200 + 130 + 21 = 351
\end{array}
$$

and

$$(20 + 7)(10 + 3)$$
$$20(10 + 3) + 7(10 + 3)$$
$$20(10) + 20(3) + 7(10) + 7(3)$$
$$200 + 60 + 70 + 21 = 351$$

You may wish to show the horizontal form for multiplying the polynomials in Example 1 on page 161 and correlate the steps to the vertical form shown.

Stress the fact that simplest form requires that similar terms be combined. However, you need not require students to do this mentally at this point. Note that in Lesson 5-4 a shortcut method will be developed for multiplying binomials.

Using Manipulatives

Using tiles or manipulatives cut from grid paper as described in Lesson 4-5, students can work in pairs to demonstrate that $6x^2 + 19x + 10$ is the area of a rectangle with sides $2x + 5$ and $3x + 2$ as illustrated on page 161.

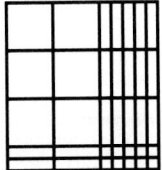

Suggested Extensions

Use the following example and ask the class to discover a short rule for multiplying polynomials.

$$(a + b)(c + d + e)$$
$$= (a + b)c + (a + b)d + (a + b)e$$
$$= ac + bc + ad + bd + ae + be$$

Multiply each term of the first polynomial by each term of the second polynomial.

Also ask the class to discover a rule for determining the number of terms, before combining, in a product of two polynomials. Multiply the number of terms in the first by the number of terms in the second.

4-7 (pages 165–166)

Key Mathematical Idea

- transforming formulas

Teaching Suggestions

Write the formula for the area of a trapezoid, $A = \frac{1}{2}h(a + b)$, on the chalkboard and ask for the value of a if $A = 84$, $h = 7$, and $b = 15$. 9 Point out that if the original formula is solved for a first, then the computation is much simpler.

Illustrate how the steps carried out for a specific number parallel the steps indicated in the general solution:

$$84 = \frac{1}{2}(7)(a + 15) \qquad A = \frac{1}{2}h(a + b)$$
$$2 \cdot 84 = 7(a + 15) \qquad 2A = h(a + b)$$
$$\frac{2 \cdot 84}{7} = a + 15 \qquad \frac{2A}{h} = a + b$$
$$\frac{2 \cdot 84}{7} - 15 = a \qquad \frac{2A}{h} - b = a$$

Suggested Extension

Have students make a paper model of the pyramid in Example 2 on page 165 and use it to demonstrate that $A = s^2 + 2rs$.

4-8 (pages 167–171)

Key Mathematical Idea

- solving uniform motion problems

Teaching Suggestions

Students are still inexperienced at problem solving. They may wonder how they are supposed to know what to let the variable represent when there is more than one unknown number in the problem. Show them that in Example 1, page 167 they may choose to let r = Brent's speed. The alternate solution would be as follows:

	Rate	× Time =	Distance
Brent	r	1.5	$1.5r$
Jane	$r - 4$	1.5	$1.5(r - 4)$

The equation would then be $1.5r + 1.5(r - 4) = 60$. The last step would be $r = 22$ and $r - 4 = 18$. The answers to the question are the same as the text answers. This approach emphasizes the importance of precisely identifying the variable so we know its significance when we have solved for it. Point out that the choice in the text is made because Brent's speed is given in terms of Jane's speed in the problem.

You may want to ask students to solve Example 2, page 168, by letting t = the helicopter's flying time.

Emphasize the usefulness of preparing a chart and drawing a sketch when solving a uniform motion problem. Also, point out that each example in the text represents a different type of distance problem: motion in opposite directions, motion in the same direction, and round-trip travel. Students should have enough practice to feel comfortable with each of these types.

Suggested Extensions

Encourage students to draw a sketch to help them solve the following problem.

Station A is d miles due west of station B. From station A a train traveling west at r mph leaves a hours before a train traveling east at v mph leaves station B. How far apart will the trains be t hours after the departure of the second train? $(d + rt + ar + vt)$ mi

4-9 (pages 172–174)

Key Mathematical Idea

• solving problems involving area

Teaching Suggestions

Some students may see different methods of dissecting the border in the example on page 172 which yield equations equivalent to the text equation.

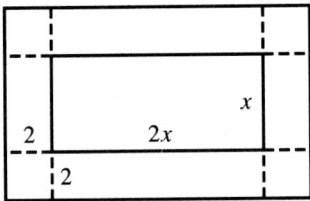

$$2(2(x + 4)) + 2(2(2x)) = 76$$
$$12x + 16 = 76$$
$$x = 5$$

Suggested Extensions

Present the following problem to the class:

A hole in the shape of a parallelogram is cut from a piece of cardboard as shown. The base of the parallelogram is 1 cm more than the height. The area of the remaining cardboard is 34 cm². Find the base and height of the hole.

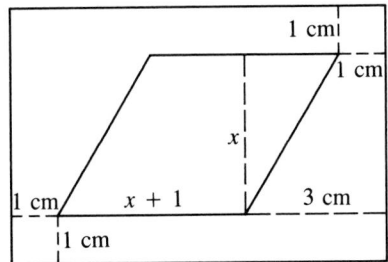

base, 5 cm;
height, 4 cm

4-10 (pages 175–177)

Key Mathematical Idea

• recognizing problems that do not have solutions

Teaching Suggestions

Point out that a problem does not necessarily have a solution. Example 1 on page 175 cannot be solved because there is not enough information to determine a unique solution. Ask, "What type of information is needed?" Information relating the expressions within the chart.

Example 2 has no solution because it leads to the unrealistic result that a width of a lawn is a negative number. The associated equation for a problem may itself have no solution, as illustrated in Example 3. Remind students that it is important to establish the domain of a variable. Then, as students solve equations, they can determine if the solution is in the domain of the variable. For example, the domain of n, if n = the number of dimes, cannot include $22\frac{6}{7}$, if that is the computed answer.

Group Activities

Have students work in groups of four. Direct each group to write a problem relating to something in the classroom and to write out a step-by-step solution. Then have each group alter its problem so that it has no solution because of one of the reasons listed on page 175.

Suggested Extensions

Ask the students to fill in the blanks in each of the following problems that have integral solutions and identify those that do not have integral solutions.

1. $x + \Box$ 2
    $x + \Box$ 3
    $\overline{x^2 + 2x}$
    $\quad\quad 3x + 6$
    $\overline{x^2 + 5x + 6}$

2. $2x - \Box$ 3
    $x + \Box$ 4
    $\overline{2x^2 + \Box}$ $-3x$
    $\quad\quad 8x - 12$
    $\overline{2x^2 + 5x - 12}$

3. $x + 1$
    $x + \Box$
    $\overline{x^2 + \Box}$
    $\quad\quad \Box + 1$
    $\overline{x^2 + x + 1}$
    no solution

4. $3x + \Box$
    $x + \Box$
    $\overline{3x^2 + \Box}$
    $\quad\quad \Box + 2$
    $\overline{3x^2 + 6x + 2}$
    no solution

5 Factoring Polynomials

This chapter develops the factorization of composite numbers, monomials, and polynomials. Division of monomials is presented as a related skill along with the rule of exponents for division. Several lessons are devoted to special techniques of factoring polynomials, and one lesson provides practice in multiplying binomials mentally. The last part of the chapter uses factoring and the zero-product property to solve polynomial equations and application problems.

5-1 (pages 185–188)

Key Mathematical Ideas

- finding the prime factorization of composite numbers
- finding the greatest common factor of several integers

Teaching Suggestions

Use the examples on page 185 to illustrate the factors of a number. Stress that if an integer is a factor of a number, then it is a divisor of that number. Likewise, if an integer is a divisor of a number, then it is a factor of that number.

Another method of prime factoring is commonly known as a "factor tree." Students can start out with any pair of integral factors of a number and then keep factoring (in tree form) until all branches end in primes. For instance, Example 2, page 185, could be done with the following tree:

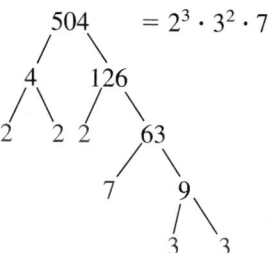

$$504 \quad = 2^3 \cdot 3^2 \cdot 7$$

In either case, remind students that the only prime factors of 504 are 2, 3, and 7, *not* 2^3 or 3^2, which are, of course, composite.

Students can check their answer to finding the GCF of 882 and 945 in Example 3, page 186, by noting that $\frac{882}{63} = 14$, $\frac{945}{63} = 15$, and 14 and 15 have no common prime factor.

Point out the two special cases involving the GCF. Note that the GCF of two numbers can be 1, or it can be the smaller number. For example, the GCF of 15 and 26 is 1, and the GCF of 14 and 70 is 14.

Reading Algebra

You might use this lesson to give students practice in skimming (reading quickly) to acquire specific information. Ask them to read the lesson rapidly first, looking for the main ideas and finding out what types of exercises are involved. Discuss and list their findings on the chalkboard. factor integers; find prime factorizations; find the GCF of two or more numbers

Suggested Extensions

1. Some students may enjoy finding all the primes less than a specified number by using the Sieve of Eratosthenes, presented on page 239.

2. Ask a student to study the following proof and present it to the class.

   Prove: There are infinitely many prime numbers.

   Plan: Assume that there are only finitely many primes and show that it leads to a contradictory conclusion.

   Proof: Suppose there are finitely many primes: 2, 3, 5, . . . , p. Let $Q = 2 \cdot 3 \cdot 5 \cdots \cdot p$, the product of all the primes. Then $Q + 1$ cannot be prime, since $Q + 1 > p$ and p is the largest prime. But if $Q + 1$ is not prime, it must be divisible by one of the primes 2, 3, 5, . . . , p. This is impossible, since each of these primes divides Q and therefore leaves a remainder of 1 when divided into $Q + 1$. Therefore there must be infinitely many primes, since the assumption that there are only finitely many leads to a contradiction.

5-2 (pages 189–193)

Key Mathematical Ideas

- simplifying the quotients of monomials
- finding the GCF of several monomials

Teaching Suggestions

Discuss the restrictions $b \neq 0$ and $d \neq 0$ as stated in the property of quotients on page 189. The fact that a denominator cannot equal 0 can be explained the following way: If $\frac{15}{3} = 5$ because $15 = 5 \times 3$, then

$\frac{15}{0} = 0$ should mean $15 = 0 \times 0$, which is, of course, impossible, as is $\frac{15}{0} = 15$. It is therefore impossible to divide by 0, and dividing by 0 is undefined.

Some students might feel more comfortable doing Example 2, page 189, the following way:

$$\frac{-4xy}{10x} = \frac{{}^1\!2\!x \cdot (-2y)}{{}_1\!2\!x \cdot 5}, \text{ with the ``1's'' showing.}$$

Also discuss the acceptability of equivalent answers $\frac{-2y}{5}, -\frac{2y}{5}, \text{ or } \frac{2y}{-5}$.

Use this opportunity to review the rules for exponents from Lessons 4-3 and 4-4 (pages 152 and 155).

Suggested Extensions

Simplify. Assume $x \neq 0$ and m and n are positive integers.

1. $\dfrac{(x^{m+1})^2}{x^2(x^m)^2} = \dfrac{x^{2m+2}}{x^2 \cdot x^{2m}} = \dfrac{x^{2m+2}}{x^{2m+2}} = 1$

2. $\dfrac{(x^{m+1})^{n+1}}{(x^m)^n} = \dfrac{x^{(m+1)(n+1)}}{x^{mn}} = \dfrac{x^{mn+n+m+1}}{x^{mn}}$
   $= x^{m+n+1}$

5-3 (pages 194–199)

Key Mathematical Ideas

- dividing polynomials by monomials
- finding monomial factors of polynomials

Teaching Suggestions

Place strong emphasis on checking division exercises and factoring exercises by multiplication. You might ask students to verify Examples 1 and 2 in this way.

Some students have difficulty factoring when the greatest common monomial factor is one of the terms of the polynomial. For example,
$12x^3y^2 + 18x^2y^3 + 6x^2y = 6x^2y(2xy + 3y^2 + 1)$.
Such students will fail to write the 1. But if they think in terms of multiplication, they will think "What must I multiply by $6x^2y$ to get $6x^2y$?" Stress the following two points in this type of factoring problem.

1. The polynomial factor in parentheses must have the same number of terms as the original polynomial.

2. The greatest common monomial factor of the terms of the polynomial in parentheses should be 1.

Suggested Extension

Use the formulas for the areas of a triangle, $A = \frac{1}{2}hb$, and of a trapezoid, $A = \frac{1}{2}h(\text{sum of bases})$, to show that the total cross-sectional area of the river is $h(a + b + c)$, where a, b, and c are the depths of the water at equal distances across a river.

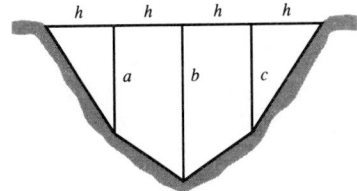

$$A = \frac{1}{2}h \cdot a + \frac{1}{2}h(a + b) + \frac{1}{2}h(b + c) + \frac{1}{2}h \cdot c$$

$$= \frac{1}{2}h(a + a + b + b + c + c)$$

$$= \frac{1}{2}h(2a + 2b + 2c)$$

$$= \frac{2}{2}h(a + b + c)$$

$$= h(a + b + c)$$

5-4 (pages 200–203)

Key Mathematical Idea

- finding the product of two binomials mentally

Teaching Suggestions

Review the definitions of monomial, binomial, and trinomial. Be sure to point out that a polynomial is the *sum* of monomials, so that $6x^2 - 7x - 20$ really is $6x^2 + (-7x) + (-20)$.

FOIL is the most common memory device used in multiplying two binomials. When you present this device, stress the fact that it is not a "method," but rather a means of remembering the shortcut that allows us to skip the writing of $ax(cx + d) + b(cx + d)$ when applying the distributive property to write $(ax + b)(cx + d)$ as a trinomial.

Point out that if the first and last terms of the binomials are similar, then the outside and inside products always are similar and can be combined. Make the point that the ability to combine these terms mentally will be important later in the chapter when factoring is introduced.

Suggested Extensions

Find each of the following products, where m and n are positive integers.

1. $(x^{mn} - y^{mn})(x^{mn} + y^{mn})$ $x^{2mn} - y^{2mn}$
2. $(x^n - y^n)^2$ $x^{2n} - 2x^n y^n + y^{2n}$
3. $(x^n - y^{n+1})(x^n - y^{n-1})$ $x^{2n} - x^n y^{n-1} - x^n y^{n+1} + y^{2n}$
4. $(x^n - y^n)^3$ $x^{3n} - 3x^{2n}y^n + 3x^n y^{2n} - y^{3n}$

5-5 (pages 204–207)

Key Mathematical Ideas

- simplifying products of the form $(a + b)(a - b)$
- factoring the difference of two squares

Teaching Suggestions

Both the multiplication and factoring exercises of this section depend upon students' recognition of the specified pattern. Be sure students get enough practice to recognize the pattern even when other patterns are present.

The two types of exercises can be illustrated and reinforced with numerical examples as follows:

$$
\begin{array}{c|c}
(8 + 5)(8 - 5) & 8^2 - 5^2 \\
13 \cdot 3 & 64 - 25 \\
\multicolumn{2}{c}{39 = 39}
\end{array}
$$

$$
\begin{array}{c|c}
15^2 - 7^2 & (15 + 7)(15 - 7) \\
225 - 49 & 22 \cdot 8 \\
\multicolumn{2}{c}{176 = 176}
\end{array}
$$

Point out the table of squares on page 681 of the text. You might also encourage students to make and memorize their own tables of squares from $1^2 = 1$ through $15^2 = 225$. Knowing these perfect squares will be helpful throughout the course. Also illustrate the pattern of perfect squares involving exponents.

$$(x^1)^2 = x^2, \ (x^2)^2 = x^4, \ \ldots, \ (x^n)^2 = x^{2n}$$

Using Manipulatives

For a change of pace, you may wish to demonstrate $(a + b)(a - b)$ on an overhead projector, as shown in the diagram on page 204, before having the students duplicate the geometric model using manipulatives.

Suggested Extension

The Extra on page 239 discusses factoring patterns for the sum and the difference of cubes. This feature provides an interesting extension of the lesson.

5-6 (pages 208–212)

Key Mathematical Ideas

- finding the squares of binomials
- factoring trinomial squares

Teaching Suggestions

Two of the most universal errors that algebra teachers encounter are the two related false statements $(a + b)^2 = a^2 + b^2$ and $a + b = \sqrt{a^2 + b^2}$.

Along with the text development, the concept of the square of a binomial can be reinforced by both arithmetic and geometry. $(3 + 4)^2 = 7^2 = 49$ and $3^2 + 2(3 \cdot 4) + 4^2 = 9 + 24 + 16 = 49$ but $3^2 + 4^2 = 9 + 16 = 25 \neq 49$.

For geometric interpretations of the trinomial square formulas, refer to Exercises 62–64, page 211.

Emphasize that in both trinomial square patterns, a plus sign precedes the last term. Thus, it should be obvious to students that a polynomial like $9x^2 + 6x - 4$ cannot be a trinomial square.

Using Manipulatives

Using algebra tiles or manipulatives cut from grid paper as described on page T97, students can work in pairs to discover what happens when they square binomials; for example, $(x + 1)^2 = x^2 + 2x + 1$ and $(x + 3)^2 = x^2 + 6x + 9$. Then the geometric model of $(a + b)^2$ on page 208 can be presented as a generalization of their results.

Suggested Extensions

Ask students to factor each polynomial, assuming that n is a positive integer.

1. $x^{2n} + 2x^n y^{2n} + y^{4n}$ $(x^n + y^{2n})^2$
2. $4x^{6n} - 20x^{3n} + 25$ $(2x^{3n} - 5)^2$
3. $x^{2n} - 2x^n + 1 - y^{2n}$ $(x^n - 1 + y^n)(x^n - 1 - y^n)$
4. $2x^{9n} - 4x^{5n} + 2x^n$ $2x^n(x^{4n} - 1)^2$

5-7 (pages 213–216)

Key Mathematical Idea

- factoring quadratic trinomials of the form $x^2 + bx + c$, c positive

Teaching Suggestions

Write the following multiplication problems on the chalkboard and call on class members to use the short method to find the products.

$$(x + 1)(x + 24) = x^2 + 25x + 24$$
$$(x - 1)(x - 24) = x^2 - 25x + 24$$
$$(x + 2)(x + 12) = x^2 + 14x + 24$$
$$(x - 2)(x - 12) = x^2 - 14x + 24$$
$$(x + 3)(x + 8) = x^2 + 11x + 24$$
$$(x - 3)(x - 8) = x^2 - 11x + 24$$
$$(x + 4)(x + 6) = x^2 + 10x + 24$$
$$(x - 4)(x - 6) = x^2 - 10x + 24$$

Stress the common form of these trinomials: $x^2 \underline{\hspace{1cm}} + 24$. Then choose one of these eight trinomials, say $x^2 - 14x + 24$. Point out that to factor this trinomial we need to discover what two numbers we used to get the middle term when we multiplied. That is, $x^2 - 14x + 24 = (x - \underline{\ ?\ })(x - \underline{\ ?\ })$. Emphasize that factoring is the "reverse process" of multiplying.

The examples on pages 213 and 214 offer alternate ways of finding the factors of a trinomial. Some students feel more comfortable listing all pairs of factors and their sums as done in Example 3, page 213. Others prefer scanning the list mentally and then selecting the correct pair.

Using Manipulatives

If students used manipulatives as suggested on page T97 to make geometric models of the products of polynomials, they can easily reverse the process now. For example, to factor the trinomial $x^2 + 3x + 2$, have them represent it as follows:

Tell them to move the tiles around to try to form a rectangle. Trial and error will yield:

Point out that the length and width of the rectangle are the factors: $x^2 + 3x + 2 = (x + 2)(x + 1)$.

Suggested Extensions

Have students find all possible values of r and c such that $x + r$ is a factor of both trinomials.

1. $x^2 - 24x + 143$ and $x^2 - 26x + c$
   $r = -11$ and $c = 165$,
   or $r = -13$ and $c = 169$

2. $x^2 + 40x + 204$ and $x^2 + 77x + c$
   $r = 34$ and $c = 1462$,
   or $r = 6$ and $c = 426$

required pair of factors of -54 must have opposite signs. Also, remind students that it is important for them to check factors by multiplying.

Suggested Extensions

Ask students to factor each trinomial, assuming that n is a positive integer.

1. $(x^2 - 1)^2 - 3(x^2 - 1) - 40$
   (*Hint:* Let $y = x^2 - 1$.)
   $(x + 3)(x - 3)(x^2 + 4)$

2. $(x^2 + 4x)^2 - 9(x^2 + 4x) - 36$
   (*Hint:* Let $z = x^2 + 4x$.)
   $(x + 1)(x + 3)(x + 6)(x - 2)$

3. $x^{6n} - 2x^{3n} - 35$
   $(x^{3n} - 7)(x^{3n} + 5)$

4. $x^{4n} + 2x^{2n}y^{2n} - 3y^{4n}$
   $(x^{2n} + 3y^{2n})(x^n + y^n)(x^n - y^n)$

5-8 (pages 217–219)

Key Mathematical Idea

- factoring quadratic trinomials of the form $x^2 + bx + c$ with c negative

Teaching Suggestions

Present the following multiplication problems to the class as in the previous section.

$$(x + 1)(x - 54) = x^2 - 53x - 54$$
$$(x - 1)(x + 54) = x^2 + 53x - 54$$
$$(x + 2)(x - 27) = x^2 - 25x - 54$$
$$(x - 2)(x + 27) = x^2 + 25x - 54$$
$$(x + 3)(x - 18) = x^2 - 15x - 54$$
$$(x - 3)(x + 18) = x^2 + 15x - 54$$
$$(x + 6)(x - 9) = x^2 - 3x - 54$$
$$(x - 6)(x + 9) = x^2 + 3x - 54$$

Once again point out the common form of each of these trinomials: $x^2 \underline{\hspace{2em}} - 54$. Now discuss the procedure for factoring a trinomial of this form. Emphasize that since the constant term is negative, the

5-9 (pages 220–223)

Key Mathematical Idea

- factoring quadratic trinomials of the form $ax^2 + bx + c$ with integral coefficients

Teaching Suggestions

Explain that the purpose of this lesson is to learn to factor general trinomials regardless of the coefficient of the quadratic term. Emphasize that the basic method of factoring is the same as in previous lessons, but now there are more possibilities.

Point out the orderly system of charts presented in Examples 1 and 2 on page 220. Remind students that the most important factoring clue is the sign of the constant term.

Encourage students who are having difficulty factoring expressions such as $3(a + 1)^2 - 5(a + 1) - 2$ to substitute for $a + 1$. For example, if $u = a + 1$, the expression becomes $3u^2 - 5u - 2$, which factors into $(3u + 1)(u - 2)$. Replace u with $a + 1$ to get $[3(a + 1) + 1][(a + 1) - 2]$ or $(3a + 4)(a - 1)$.

Group Activities

Divide the class into groups of three or four students. The goal of each group's activity is to factor $12x^2 + 76x + 24$. Suggest that the members of each group devise a plan for working cooperatively toward the goal. Then have all groups begin at the same time. When the goal has been met by each group, have the class compare the working plans of the fastest and slowest groups.

Suggested Extensions

Ask students to determine all integral values for k for which the trinomial can be factored.

1. $4t^2 + kt + 2$ 6, 9, -6, -9
2. $3x^2 + kx + 10$ 11, 13, 17, 31, -11, -13, -17, -31
3. $2m^2 + km + 9$ 9, 11, 19, -9, -11, -19
4. $12y^2 + ky + 5$ 16, 17, 19, 23, 32, 61, -16, -17, -19, -23, -32, -61

5-10 (pages 224–226)

Key Mathematical Idea

- factoring polynomials by grouping terms

Teaching Suggestions

Emphasize the role of the distributive property in factoring by grouping terms. Point out that many problems require a sign-change step that gives an equivalent expression with matching groups, as shown in the second solution of Example 3, page 225.

Some students may question whether they should group the first two, the first three, or the last three terms. Encourage them to try different combinations of groups and to expect some combinations not to lead anywhere. Some students will feel that $x(x + 10) + (5 + 2y)(5 - 2y)$ is an appropriate factorization. Point out that $x(x + 10) + (5 + 2y)(5 - 2y)$ is an indicated sum and $(x + 5 + 2y)(x + 5 - 2y)$ is an indicated product. Stress that *factoring* a polynomial means expressing it as an indicated *product*.

Suggested Extensions

Ask students to give a value of k that will make these polynomials factorable.

1. $x^2 - y^2 + ky - 4$ -4
2. $x^3 + kx^2 - 2x - 6$ 3
3. $9a^2 - 30a + k - b^2$ 25

5-11 (pages 227–229)

Key Mathematical Idea

- factoring polynomials completely

Teaching Suggestions

This lesson ties together the various methods of factoring polynomials. Since these methods are applied in the last two lessons of the chapter and throughout the course, it is important to spend enough time to master the techniques of factoring. The guidelines on page 227 are an excellent starting point for students having difficulty. Stress the importance of not skipping the first step, factoring out the greatest common monomial factor.

Group Activities

Assign groups of five students to work together as an assembly-line factoring team. Each team member is assigned to carry out one of the first five steps in the Guidelines for Factoring on page 227. Have the teams work cooperatively on Oral Exercises 7–12 on page 228.

Suggested Extensions

Ask students to show that there are infinitely many integral values of c for which $x^2 + x + c$ is factorable. What is the general form of the factorization?
- c must have factors whose sum is 1, the coefficient of the linear term x.
- Possible values are factors with a sum of 1 and will have opposite signs. For example, 4 and -3; in general n and $1 - n$.
- The general pattern will be $(x + n)(x + 1 - n)$.

5-12 (pages 230–233)

Key Mathematical Idea

- solving polynomial equations by factoring and using the zero-product property

Teaching Suggestions

You can use this opportunity to review the term "degree of a polynomial." Remind students that a linear equation has degree 1, a quadratic equation has degree 2, and a cubic equation has degree 3. Relate the degree of a polynomial equation to the number of roots it has (the degree gives the maximum number of roots).

It is very common for students to try to apply the zero-product property without expressing the equation in standard form. For example, they will write $x^2 + 2x = 3$, $x(x + 2) = 3$, and so $x = 0$ or $x = -2$. Caution students to check that one side of a polynomial equation is zero before they attempt to factor the polynomial. Discuss the warning at the top of page 232; it will help students avoid "losing roots."

Suggest that when students solve polynomial equations, they write each factor in a separate column as shown in the examples. Encourage students to check their answers by substituting them in the original equations.

Suggested Extensions

Each of the following solutions is wrong. Have students identify the two consecutive steps that are not equivalent.

1. **a.** $x^2 + 70 = 10 - 16x$
   b. $x^2 + 16x + 60 = 0$
   c. $(x + 6)(x + 10) = 0$ c and d;
   d. $x = 6$ or $x = 10$ $x = -6$ or $x = -10$

2. **a.** $x(2x + 15) = 27$
   b. $2x^2 + 15x = 27$
   c. $2x^2 + 15x - 27 = 0$ c and d;
   d. $(2x + 3)(x - 9) = 0$ $x = \frac{3}{2}$ or $x = -9$
   e. $x = -\frac{3}{2}$ or $x = 9$

3. **a.** $x^2 + 5x - 14 = 10$
   b. $(x + 7)(x - 2) = 10$ b and c;
   c. $x + 7 = 0$ or $x - 2 = 0$ $x = 3$ or $x = -8$
   d. $x = -7$ or $x = 2$

5-13 (pages 234–238)

Key Mathematical Idea

- solving word problems by writing and factoring quadratic equations

Teaching Suggestions

Review the five-step plan for solving problems (see Lesson 1-7). Remind students to define each variable carefully and to draw a sketch or chart when possible.

An alternate solution to Example 1, page 234, is to use the following chart.

	Length	× Width	= Area
Room	12	9	108
Rug	$12 - 2x$	$9 - 2x$	$(12 - 2x)(9 - 2x)$

The equation would still be

$$(12 - 2x)(9 - 2x) = \frac{1}{2}(9 \cdot 12).$$

Point out that the fifth step, checking the solution, is especially important in this lesson because many quadratic equations have solutions that do not satisfy the requirements of the associated word problem. Example 1, page 234, illustrates this idea.

Group Activities

One effective way to handle word problems is to have students work in pairs. Students can often help each other with minor problems and you can concentrate on students with major difficulties.

Another way is to have students work in groups of four using the five-step word problem plan.

1. Assign groups of four students at least four word problems to solve together.

2. One student is responsible for reading the problem carefully and drawing a sketch, chart, or diagram to accompany it. The same student is also responsible for explaining the problem to the group (Steps 1 and 2).

3. The second member is responsible for writing an equation that fits the problem (Step 3).

4. The third member solves the equation (Step 4).

5. The fourth member checks the solutions with the conditions in the problem and determines if the solutions are accurate and reasonable (Step 5).

6. The group members switch roles, go on to the next problem, and repeat the process until every student has had a chance to practice each of the steps.

Suggested Extension

Ask students to solve the following problem:
A bus that can carry 45 people is to be rented for an excursion at the rate of $40 per person if 20 or fewer people go. If more than 20 people go, each passenger's fare is reduced 50¢ for each person over 20. How many passengers can go for a rental fee of $1200? Is $1200 the maximum rental fee? 40 passengers; No, when 45 people go, the fee is $1237.50.

6 Fractions

A thorough treatment of algebraic fractions and operations with fractions and mixed expressions is presented in this chapter. Emphasis is placed on expressing fractions in simplest form and on dividing polynomials using the long division form.

6-1 (pages 247–250)

Key Mathematical Idea

- simplifying algebraic fractions

Teaching Suggestions

It will be helpful to begin this lesson with a review of the rule for simplifying fractions (page 189). Tell students that to simplify a quotient of polynomials they must divide the numerator and the denominator by their greatest common factor. Stress that restrictions on the variable are important when simplifying algebraic fractions, and students should note them after factoring a fraction and before simplifying it. For example, $\dfrac{5x^2 - 17x + 6}{x^2 - 7x + 12}$ factors into $\dfrac{(x - 3)(5x - 2)}{(x - 3)(x - 4)}$ with the restrictions $x \neq 3$ and $x \neq 4$. If students simplify the fraction first and get $\dfrac{5x - 2}{x - 4}$, they might think the only restriction is $x \neq 4$. Also point out that restrictions can be literal, like $a \neq -b$ in Example 1.

A common error is for students to cancel single terms of binomial factors. Use the following examples to caution students against this mistake:

$$\frac{\cancel{2x + 1}}{x^2 + \cancel{2x + 1}} \neq \frac{1}{x^2}$$

$$\frac{(\cancel{3x + 2}) + 1}{(\cancel{3x + 2})(x + 5)} \neq \frac{1}{x + 5}$$

$$\frac{(\cancel{x + 5})(x - 2) + (\cancel{x - 7})(x + 1)}{(\cancel{x + 5})(\cancel{x - 7})} \neq (x - 2) + (x + 1)$$

When students cancel common factors have them use a line for each prime factor. Do not permit cancellations like $\dfrac{(x + 2)(\cancel{2x + 5})}{(\cancel{2x + 5})(x + 4)} = \dfrac{x + 2}{x + 4}$.

Emphasize the importance of recognizing factors that are opposites of each other. After discussing Example 3, ask students to name the opposite of each expression: $5 + 2t$, $2t - 5$, $5 - 2t$, $-5 - 2t$.

Reading Algebra

This lesson includes several important instructions in the discussion of the solutions in Examples 1–4, pages 247–248. Have the students read the instructions as you go over the examples and emphasize the importance of reading such helpful tips.

Simplify. Give any restrictions on the variables.

1. $\dfrac{4x^{2n} + 4x^n + 1}{2x^n + 1} \cdot \dfrac{(2x^n + 1)(2x^n + 1)}{2x^n + 1} =$

$\quad 2x^n + 1;\ 2x^n \neq -1$

2. $\dfrac{x^{2n} - y^{2n}}{x^n - y^n} \cdot \dfrac{(x^n + y^n)(x^n - y^n)}{x^n - y^n} =$

$\quad x^n + y^n;\ x^n \neq y^n$

3. $\dfrac{x^{2n} + 2x^n y^n + y^{2n}}{x^n + y^n} \cdot \dfrac{(x^n + y^n)(x^n + y^n)}{x^n + y^n} =$

$\quad x^n + y^n;\ x^n \neq -y^n$

6-2 (pages 251–254)

Key Mathematical Idea

- multiplying algebraic fractions

Teaching Suggestions

Some students will want to begin working on a problem like $\dfrac{2x + 2}{x^2 + 3x + 2} \cdot \dfrac{x^2 - 3x - 10}{x^2 - 25}$ by multiplying the numerators and multiplying the denominators. Emphasize that the multiplication rule for fractions is the last property that should be used. The first step in simplifying the expression is to factor each polynomial:

$$\dfrac{2(x + 1)}{(x + 1)(x + 2)} \cdot \dfrac{(x + 2)(x - 5)}{(x + 5)(x - 5)} = \dfrac{2}{x + 5}$$

Show students how an arithmetic check may be helpful. Let $x = 3$:

$$\dfrac{2(3) + 2}{3^2 + 3(3) + 2} \cdot \dfrac{3^2 - 3(3) - 10}{3^2 - 25} \ \Big|\ \dfrac{2}{3 + 5}$$

$$\dfrac{8}{20} \cdot \dfrac{-10}{-16} \ \Big|\ \dfrac{2}{8}$$

$$\dfrac{2}{5} \cdot \dfrac{5}{8}$$

$$\dfrac{1}{4} = \dfrac{1}{4} \ \checkmark$$

Point out that if the equation is true for $x = 3$, it is probably, but not necessarily, true for all x in the domain of x. However, if the equation is false for $x = 3$, there is definitely a mistake in the work. You may wish to discuss the concept of a counterexample.

Group Activities

Through this activity students will have practice in communicating mathematical ideas orally and in writing.

Have students form groups to discuss an answer to the following question: What should have been done before reaching the solution in the following problem?

$$\dfrac{21}{12} \cdot \dfrac{33}{28} = \dfrac{693}{336} = \dfrac{3 \times 3 \times 7 \times 11}{2 \times 2 \times 2 \times 2 \times 3 \times 7} = \dfrac{33}{16}$$

When a group agrees on an answer to the question, it should be written down by the group's recording secretary. The answer must be a clearly written English paragraph including the use of these words: numerator, denominator, common factor, and simplify.

Suggested Extension

Find the total area and volume for the rectangular solid below.

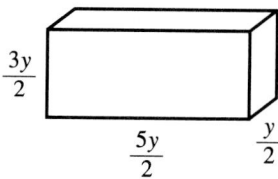

$$A = 2\left(\dfrac{3y}{2} \cdot \dfrac{5y}{2}\right) + 2\left(\dfrac{5y}{2} \cdot \dfrac{y}{2}\right) + 2\left(\dfrac{3y}{2} \cdot \dfrac{y}{2}\right)$$

$$= 2\left(\dfrac{15y^2}{4}\right) + 2\left(\dfrac{5y^2}{4}\right) + 2\left(\dfrac{3y^2}{4}\right)$$

$$= 2\left(\dfrac{23y^2}{4}\right)$$

$$= \dfrac{23y^2}{2}$$

$$V = \dfrac{3y}{2} \cdot \dfrac{5y}{2} \cdot \dfrac{y}{2}$$

$$= \dfrac{15y^3}{8}$$

6-3 (pages 255–258)

Key Mathematical Idea

- dividing algebraic fractions

Teaching Suggestions

Division of real numbers was presented in Lesson 2-9. Point out that dividing algebraic fractions involves a similar procedure: to divide, multiply by the reciprocal.

You can emphasize the relationship between division and multiplication by reminding students that $a \div b = x$ is equivalent to $bx = a$. Also, have students use this equivalence as follows:

1. Ask students to simplify

$$\frac{6x - 6}{x^2 + 3x + 2} \div \frac{2x - 2}{x^2 - x - 6}.$$

$$\frac{6(x - 1)}{(x + 2)(x + 1)} \cdot \frac{(x + 2)(x - 3)}{2(x - 1)} = \frac{3(x - 3)}{x + 1}$$

$$= \frac{3x - 9}{x + 1}$$

2. Have them check their work by multiplying the quotient and the divisor.

$$\frac{3x - 9}{x + 1} \cdot \frac{2x - 2}{x^2 - x - 6} = \frac{3(x - 3)}{x + 1} \cdot \frac{2(x - 1)}{(x - 3)(x + 2)}$$

$$= \frac{6(x - 1)}{(x + 1)(x + 2)}$$

$$= \frac{6x - 6}{x^2 + 3x + 2} \quad \checkmark$$

Suggested Extensions

Simplify.

1. $\dfrac{x^n}{y^n} \div \dfrac{x}{y} \quad \dfrac{x^n}{y^n} \cdot \dfrac{y^1}{x^1} = \dfrac{x^{n-1}}{y^{n-1}}$

2. $\dfrac{x^n}{y^n} \div \dfrac{y^n}{x^n} \quad \dfrac{x^n}{y^n} \cdot \dfrac{x^n}{y^n} = \dfrac{x^{2n}}{y^{2n}}$

3. $\dfrac{x^n}{y^n} \div \left(\dfrac{x^n}{y^n}\right)^2 \quad \dfrac{x^n}{y^n} \cdot \dfrac{y^{2n}}{x^{2n}} = \dfrac{y^n}{x^n}$

6-4 (pages 259–263)

Key Mathematical Idea

- expressing a group of fractions with their least common denominator

Teaching Suggestions

Students frequently confuse the GCF and LCM of a set of numbers. Show how the prime factorization can be used to find the GCF and the LCM and emphasize the difference between them. For example, for $60 = 2^2 \cdot 3 \cdot 5$ and $75 = 3 \cdot 5^2$:

GCF $= 3 \cdot 5 = 15$	LCM $= 2^2 \cdot 3 \cdot 5^2 = 300$
$60 = 15 \cdot 4$	$300 = 60 \cdot 5$
$75 = 15 \cdot 5$	$300 = 75 \cdot 4$

Also remind students of the two special cases that were referred to in Lesson 5-1 of this commentary.

$15 = 3 \cdot 5$	$14 = 2 \cdot 7$
$26 = 2 \cdot 13$	$70 = 2 \cdot 5 \cdot 7$
GCF $= 1$	GCF $= 2 \cdot 7$
LCM $= 2 \cdot 3 \cdot 5 \cdot 13$	LCM $= 2 \cdot 5 \cdot 7$

Generalize these results with the following statements and then point out that both generalizations hold for polynomials.

1. If the GCF of two numbers is 1, the LCM is their product.

2. If the GCF of two numbers is the smaller number, the LCM is the larger number.

If some students have difficulty doing Exercises 1–20, suggest that they leave space in which a multiplier can be written. For example, to do Exercise 15, they can write

$$\frac{4}{a - 1} = \frac{4}{a - 1} \cdot \underline{\hspace{1cm}} = \frac{}{2(a - 2)}.$$

Then they can go back and fill in the missing multipliers and numerator. This procedure may also be helpful when students are expressing a group of fractions with their LCD.

Suggested Extension

Have students find the LCD of any two fractions and the GCF of their denominators. Ask students to find the LCD by using the GCF. (*Hint:* Numerical examples are simplest to use.) Multiply the two denominators together and divide the product by the GCF to obtain the LCD.

6-5 (pages 264–269)

Key Mathematical Idea

- adding and subtracting algebraic fractions

Teaching Suggestions

Adding and subtracting algebraic fractions are among the most difficult skills for beginning algebra students. It might be helpful for students to organize their work in the following way on the more difficult problems.

1. Factor each denominator but leave space for the multiplication.

$$\frac{x^2}{x^2 - 9} + \frac{1}{x + 3} + \frac{x}{2x + 6} =$$

$$\frac{x^2 \quad \cdot}{(x + 3)(x - 3) \cdot} +$$

$$\frac{1 \quad \cdot}{(x + 3) \cdot} + \frac{x \quad \cdot}{2(x + 3) \cdot}$$

2. Write the LCD separately in factored form.
   LCD $= 2(x + 3)(x - 3)$

3. Now complete the expression above by writing the necessary factor(s) first in the denominators, checking that each denominator is the LCD.

$$\frac{x^2 \quad \cdot 2}{(x + 3)(x - 3) \cdot 2} +$$

$$\frac{1 \quad \cdot 2(x - 3)}{(x + 3) \cdot 2(x - 3)} + \frac{x \quad \cdot (x - 3)}{2(x + 3) \cdot (x - 3)}$$

4. Complete the problem with the students.

It is also necessary once again to stress the fact that a fraction bar is a grouping symbol, particularly in subtraction.

$$\frac{5x - 1}{6} - \frac{3x - 7}{10} = \frac{25x - 5}{6 \cdot 5} - \frac{9x - 21}{10 \cdot 3}$$

$$= \frac{(25x - 5) - (9x - 21)}{30}$$

$$= \frac{25x - 5 - 9x + 21}{30}$$

$$= \frac{16x + 16}{30}$$

$$= \frac{2(8x + 8)}{2 \cdot 15} = \frac{8x - 8}{15}$$

The use of the parentheses shown in red may help avoid one of the most common errors in this type of problem, forgetting to distribute the minus sign.

Suggested Extensions

Find the value of A that makes the expressions equal.

1. $\dfrac{3y - 6}{(y - 4)(y + 2)} = \dfrac{1}{y - 4} + \dfrac{A}{y + 2}$ 2

2. $\dfrac{2y - 22}{(y - 5)(y - 1)} = \dfrac{A}{y - 5} + \dfrac{5}{y - 1}$ -3

6-6 (pages 270–273)

Key Mathematical Idea

- writing mixed expressions as fractions in simplest form

Teaching Suggestions

Although this lesson is an extension of the previous one, students still have a great deal of difficulty simplifying expressions like $x + \dfrac{3}{x}$ or $4 + \dfrac{3}{x - 1}$.

Point out that a mixed number has the addition implied: $4\dfrac{2}{5}$ means $4 + \dfrac{2}{5}$. A mixed expression, on the other hand, requires a plus sign.

Suggested Extensions

Have students identify each of the following statements as true or false. If a statement is false, have them change the right side to make it true.

1. $2 + \dfrac{x}{5} = \dfrac{2 + x}{5}$ false; $2 + \dfrac{x}{5} = \dfrac{10 + x}{5}$

2. $x + 2 + \dfrac{1}{3} = \dfrac{3(x + 2) + 1}{3}$ true

3. $\dfrac{x}{3} + 4 + \dfrac{3}{x} = \dfrac{x^2 + 12x + 9}{3x}$ true

4. $5 - \dfrac{x + 2}{2} = \dfrac{12 - x}{2}$ false; $5 - \dfrac{x + 2}{2} = \dfrac{8 - x}{2}$

5. $\dfrac{x + 2}{2} - 5 = \dfrac{x - 8}{2}$ true

6-7 (pages 274–279)

Key Mathematical Idea

- dividing a polynomial by another polynomial

Teaching Suggestions

Use the examples on page 274 to point out the parallels between long division with numbers and with polynomials. Emphasize the following points:

1. The identity

    dividend = quotient × divisor + remainder

    should be used to check divisions.

2. The terms in the divisor and dividend should be written in order of decreasing degree in the variable.

3. If a degree is missing in the dividend, insert (add) it using a coefficient of 0 so that the polynomial is equivalent.

4. Divide the first term of the dividend or partial remainder by the first term of the divisor at each step in the division.

If the remainder is zero, then both the divisor and the quotient are factors of the dividend. If the remainder is not zero, the answer should be given as a mixed expression.

Suggested Extensions

1. Ask students to find each quotient.

    a. $\dfrac{x^3 - y^3}{x - y}$ $x^2 + xy + y^2$

    b. $\dfrac{x^4 + y^4}{x + y}$ $x^3 - x^2y + xy^2 - y^3 + \dfrac{2y^4}{x + y}$

    c. $\dfrac{x^5 - y^5}{x - y}$ $x^4 + x^3y + x^2y^2 + xy^3 + y^4$

    d. $\dfrac{2x^4 - x^3y + xy^3 - 2y^4}{x^2 - y^2}$ $2x^2 - xy + 2y^2$

2. Assign the Extra on pages 278–279, which introduces complex fractions. This topic requires students to use many of the skills developed in the chapter.

---

7 Applying Fractions

This chapter presents a wide variety of equations and word problems related to algebraic fractions. Ratios are introduced and proportions are solved as a special case of fractional equations. Extensive treatment is given to solving equations with fractional coefficients and fractional equations.

The first lesson on percent presents the three cases of percent; the next lesson provides further applications. The lessons on mixture and work problems both extend and reinforce problem solving skills. The concluding lessons provide further work with both exponents and fractions.

7-1 (pages 287–292)

Key Mathematical Ideas

- meaning of ratio
- forms of expressing a ratio
- solving problems involving ratios

Teaching Suggestions

Emphasize the three ways of expressing ratios stated on page 287. Point out that because ratios can be expressed as fractions, they have the properties of fractions. These properties can be used to simplify ratios, as shown in Example 2 on page 287.

Some students may want to solve Example 5, pages 288–289, as follows.

Step 2: Let a = the number of acres of alfalfa. Then $160 - a$ = the number of acres of wheat.

Step 3: $\dfrac{a}{160 - a} = \dfrac{3}{5}$

Point out that while this approach is correct, solving an equation like the one in Step 3 is the topic of the next lesson.

Be sure students understand that a compound ratio of the form $a:b:c$ incorporates three simple ratios: $a:b$, $b:c$, and $a:c$.

Using Manipulatives

Give each student 40 chips, tiles, or cubes. Ask the students to separate the objects into two groups having the ratio $2:3$ by using the "2 for you, 3 for me" technique. They can do the same for other ratios like $3:5$, $1:3$, and $3:7$. For each ratio, have students record the number of objects in each of the two groups.

Suggested Extension

Ask one of your students to prepare a report about sports statistics, many of which are based on ratios. The sports pages of a newspaper can provide the basis for a class discussion about ratios.

7-2 (pages 293–297)

Key Mathematical Ideas

- solving proportions
- solving problems involving proportions

Teaching Suggestions

When discussing the proportion $a:b = c:d$, point out that the extremes are the numbers farthest from the equals sign and that the means are the numbers closest to the equals sign.

Some students have difficulty solving problems involving proportions because they do not set up the proportion correctly. Point out that there is a choice in the order of the first ratio, but that the second ratio must correspond to the first. For example, if the first ratio is $\dfrac{\text{number of miles}}{\text{number of gallons}}$, the second ratio must also have the number of miles in the numerator and the number of gallons in the denominator.

Group Activity

Divide the class into small groups. Give each group different maps of the same regions. Have the members of each group use the maps' scales to determine the straight-line distance between two given cities or towns. Ask the group members to suggest explanations for any variations in the distance found among the maps.

Suggested Extension

Ask your school's yearbook sponsor for a cropping tool. This device is used not only to crop photos but also to indicate enlargements and reductions of photos on yearbook dummy sheets. With a cropping tool you can demonstrate to the class that the ratio of length to width for various enlargements and reductions of a given rectangle remains constant.

7-3 (pages 298–303)

Key Mathematical Ideas

- solving equations with fractional coefficients
- solving problems involving fractional coefficients

Teaching Suggestions

Let students compare two solutions to the same equation:

Solution 1 $\quad \dfrac{1}{2}x + \dfrac{1}{3}(x - 2) = 11$

$$\dfrac{1}{2}x + \dfrac{1}{3}x - \dfrac{2}{3} = 11$$

$$\dfrac{1}{2}x + \dfrac{1}{3}x = 11 + \dfrac{2}{3}$$

$$\frac{3}{6}x + \frac{2}{6}x = \frac{33}{3} + \frac{2}{3}$$

$$\frac{5}{6}x = \frac{35}{3}$$

$$x = \frac{35}{3} \cdot \frac{6}{5} = 14$$

Solution 2
$$\frac{1}{2}x + \frac{1}{3}(x - 2) = 11$$

$$6\left[\frac{1}{2}x + \frac{1}{3}(x - 2)\right] = 6 \cdot 11$$

$$3x + 2(x - 2) = 66$$

$$3x + 2x - 4 = 66$$

$$5x - 4 = 66$$

$$5x = 70$$

$$x = 14$$

Point out the need to find the LCD, 6, in both solutions. Stress the desirability of eliminating the fractions as soon as possible.

Suggested Extension

Have students solve each equation.

1. $\dfrac{5x(x - 1)}{4} - \dfrac{x + 2}{2} = 5$ $\left\{-\dfrac{8}{5}, 3\right\}$

2. $\dfrac{y^2}{3} + \dfrac{y}{12} = \dfrac{1}{8}$ $\left\{-\dfrac{3}{4}, \dfrac{1}{2}\right\}$

3. $\dfrac{5}{4}z^2 + \dfrac{1}{5} = z$ $\left\{\dfrac{2}{5}\right\}$

4. $\dfrac{(t + 1)(t - 2)}{6} - \dfrac{5(t + 3)}{8} = \dfrac{37}{4}$ $\left\{-\dfrac{25}{4}, 11\right\}$

7-4 (pages 304–308)

Key Mathematical Ideas

- solving fractional equations
- solving problems involving fractional equations

Teaching Suggestions

Point out that students will find solving a fractional equation easier if they multiply both sides by the LCD and clear all the fractions than if they rewrite each fraction with the LCD as the denominator.

Emphasize that an apparent root of a fractional equation may not satisfy the original equation. Suggest that students begin solving fractional equations by listing the values of the variable for which any fractions are meaningless, that is, values that make a denominator equal to zero. Tell students to eliminate any apparent roots that are on the list and to check the remaining ones in the original equation.

Suggested Extension

Ask students to solve each equation.

1. $1 + \dfrac{9}{x^4} = \dfrac{10}{x^2}$ $\{-3, -1, 1, 3\}$

2. $12 - \dfrac{13}{t} + \dfrac{3}{t^2} = 0$ $\left\{\dfrac{1}{3}, \dfrac{3}{4}\right\}$

3. $\dfrac{3}{y + 1} + \dfrac{y}{y - 1} + \dfrac{4}{y - 4} = 1$ $\left\{\dfrac{1}{4}, 2\right\}$

4. $\dfrac{a + 3}{a^2 - 1} + \dfrac{a - 3}{a^2 - a} = \dfrac{2a}{a^2 + a}$ no solution

---

7-5 (pages 309–314)

Key Mathematical Ideas

- working with percents
- solving equations with decimal coefficients
- solving problems involving percents

Teaching Suggestions

Students should know the fraction, decimal, and percent equivalents for all fractions with denominators 2, 3, 4, 5, 8, and 10. It may be helpful to have each student make a table of these equivalents and memorize the entries. Encourage students to use these facts for estimating answers to percent problems.

Students frequently have difficulty with percents less than 1% or greater than 100%. Stress that $1\% = 0.01$ and that $100\% = 1.0$. To drive home the point, you might want to have students express each of the following as a decimal: 300%, 30%, 3%, 0.3%, and 0.03%. Then have them express each of the following decimals as a percent: 0.0075, 0.075, 0.75, 7.5, and 75.

Some students may have learned how to solve percent problems by using proportions. Point out that the "proportion method" is an acceptable alternative to the solutions presented in Examples 3, 4, and 5 on page 310. For instance, Example 3 can be done as follows:

$$\frac{15}{100} = \frac{x}{180}$$
$$100x = 15 \cdot 180$$
$$x = \frac{2700}{100} = 27$$

Reading Algebra

Examples 3, 4, and 5 on page 310 present the three basic types of percent problems. The problems are all based on the formula

$$\text{percent} \cdot \text{base} = \text{percentage}.$$

For example, the statement "15% of 180 is 27" is equivalent to the equation $\frac{15}{100} \cdot 180 = 27$, where $\frac{15}{100}$ is the *percent,* 180 is the *base,* and 27 is the *percentage.* After discussing these words with your students, you might have them identify the formula's missing element in each of Examples 3, 4, and 5.

Suggested Extension

Present the following situation to the students and have them answer the related questions.

To reduce operating expenses, a business cut a worker's salary by 10%. Later, when the business was in better financial shape, the worker's salary was raised 10%.

1. How did the final salary compare with the initial salary? The final salary was 1% less than the initial salary.

2. How would receiving the cut and raise in reverse order have affected the final salary? Reversing the order makes no difference.

7-6 (pages 315–320)

Key Mathematical Ideas

- solving problems involving percent of increase or percent of decrease
- solving investment problems

Teaching Suggestions

When discussing percent-of-increase and percent-of-decrease problems, be sure to stress the formula given in the box on page 315. Point out that the change in price is always found by subtracting the original price from the new price, where a positive difference indicates an increase and a negative difference indicates a decrease. Also point out that the change in price is always compared with the original price, not the new price, to obtain the percent of increase or decrease.

Encourage students to estimate the answer to a percent problem before actually solving it. In this way the reasonableness of the answer can be judged. In Example 4 on page 316, for instance, students might guess that an equal amount of money ($3000) is invested at 6% and at 11%. If so, the total interest would be 0.06(3000) + 0.11(3000), or $510. Since the actual interest is $460, something more than $3000 must be invested at the lower rate (and something less than $3000 at the higher rate).

Suggested Extension

Have students calculate the amount of interest earned over 3 years on a $2000 savings account if the annual interest rate is 5% and the interest is (a) not compounded, (b) compounded annually, and (c) compounded quarterly. Note that in part (c) a *quarterly* interest rate of $\frac{5}{4}$% must be used.

a. $300 b. $315.25 c. $321.51

7-7 (pages 321–325)

Key Mathematical Idea

- solving mixture problems

Teaching Suggestions

Some students may find a sketch helpful in visualizing a problem. The sketch below might be used

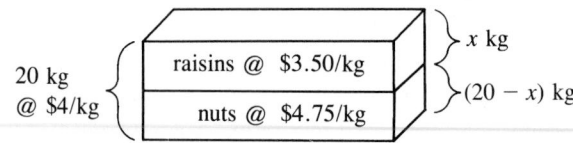

20 kg @ $4/kg | raisins @ $3.50/kg | } x kg
| nuts @ $4.75/kg | } (20 − x) kg

to explain Example 1 on page 321. Note that although the nuts and raisins are to be mixed, they can be considered separately in the sketch.

You might point out the following alternate solution for Example 2 on page 322. The chart and the equation are based on the amount of water in the solution rather than the amount of acid.

Step 2: Let x = the number of milliliters of water to be added.

	Total amount	% water	Amount of water
		$\times$	$=$
Original sol.	300	40%	0.40(300)
Water	x	100%	1.00x
New sol.	300 + x	55%	0.55(300 + x)

Step 3: Original amount of water + added water = new amount of water

$$0.40(300) + 1.00x = 0.55(300 + x)$$

Step 4:
$$40(300) + 100x = 55(300 + x)$$
$$12,000 + 100x = 16,500 + 55x$$
$$45x = 4500$$
$$x = 100$$

Reading Algebra

To use charts effectively in the solution of problems, students must understand their organization. Since many students find mixture problems difficult, you may want to spend some time in discussing the charts in Examples 1 and 2. Point out that each of the words in the equation at the top of the chart identifies the quantities in the column below. Thus, in Example 1, under "Cost" we have successively the total cost (in dollars) of the raisins, the total cost of the nuts, and the total cost of the mixture. These quantities can then be used to set up the equation in Step 3.

Suggested Extension

Have students show that each of the following problems has no solution and ask them to explain why this is so.

1. Dan has 100 coins worth $12.50. He has twice as many nickels as quarters, 5 more quarters than dimes, and the rest are pennies. How many pennies does he have?

   Let q = number of quarters.
   Since $25q + 10(q - 5) + 5(2q) + [100 - (q + q - 5 + 2q)] = 1250$ gives a nonintegral value for q, there is no solution.

2. Lori Eigenbrode invested a sum of money partly at 8% and partly at 5.5%. If her annual income from these investments was $270, how much did she invest at each rate?

   There is not enough information to write an equation, so there are infinitely many solutions and thus no unique solution.

3. How many grams of water must be evaporated from 100 g of a 30% acid solution to produce a 25% acid solution?

   There is no need to write an equation, since evaporating water *increases* the acid concentration; the facts of the problem are inconsistent.

7-8 (pages 326–330)

Key Mathematical Idea

- solving problems involving rate of work

Teaching Suggestions

When discussing Example 2 on page 326, be sure students understand that the column headed "Work rate" in the chart for Step 2 refers to the fraction of the whole job done per unit of time. Thus, when this rate is multiplied by time, the result is the fraction of the whole job done. The sum of the fractions in the third column of the chart must of course be 1.

You might show students an alternate solution of Example 2 based on the equation below.

Fractional part done by Josh in one unit of time		Fractional part done by father in one unit of time		Fractional part done by both in one unit of time
$\frac{1}{4}$	$+$	$\frac{1}{2}$	$=$	$\frac{1}{x}$

Emphasize the importance of checking a solution to see if it makes sense. When two or more people work together, the time it takes them must be less than the time the fastest worker can do the job alone.

Using Manipulatives

Students can solve Example 2 on page 326 using manipulatives as follows.

1. Cut three equal strips of paper so that each is 4 units wide. (Note that the width is the LCD of 4 and 2, the times needed for Josh and his father each to do the job alone.)

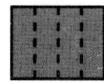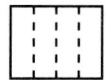

2. Cut one strip into 4 equal parts, representing the 4 days it takes Josh to do the job alone, and label each part "J." Cut another strip into 2 equal parts, representing the 2 days it takes Josh's father to do the job alone, and label each part "F." Label the third strip "Whole job."

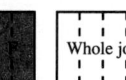

3. Place as many J-F pairs onto the "Whole job" strip as will fit. (In this case, only one pair fits.) Each pair represents the part of the whole job done by Josh and his father in *one* day.

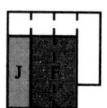

4. The width of the "Whole job" strip that remains uncovered (1 unit) divided by the width of a J-F pair (3 units) gives the additional fraction of a day needed to finish the job $\left(\frac{1}{3}\text{ day}\right)$.

5. Therefore, the total time needed to complete the job is $1 + \frac{1}{3}$ days, or $1\frac{1}{3}$ days.

You might have students solve Oral Exercises 5 and 6 on page 328 in a similar fashion.

T116

Suggested Extension

Have your students solve the following problem.

At 12:00 P.M. Professor Lopez began to grade a set of test papers. At 1:15 her assistant joined her and together they finished the job at 5:00 P.M. If the assistant would need 2 hours more than the professor to grade the papers working alone, how long would Professor Lopez need to grade all the papers by herself? 8 hours

7-9 (pages 331–335)

Key Mathematical Ideas

- using negative and zero exponents
- solving problems involving zero and negative exponents

Teaching Suggestions

You can introduce zero and negative exponents by having students consider the pattern at the right. Point out that the left sides are obtained by successively dividing by 2. Ask the class what the missing exponents would have to be for the pattern to continue.

$$8 = 2^3$$
$$4 = 2^2$$
$$2 = 2^1$$
$$1 = 2^?\quad 0$$
$$\frac{1}{2} = 2^?\quad -1$$
$$\frac{1}{4} = 2^?\quad -2$$
$$\frac{1}{8} = 2^?\quad -3$$

Explain to the class that many definitions are made in mathematics on the basis of consistency with previously established rules. The rule $\frac{a^m}{a^n} = a^{m-n}$ was established for positive integral exponents only. The symbol a^{-4} cannot have meaning in terms of the number of factors of a, so it is defined to be consistent with the rule above, as developed on page 331.

Emphasize the fact that a positive number raised to *any* power is always positive. Many students confuse the two problems $2^{-3} = \frac{1}{8}$ and $(-2)^3 = -8$.

Suggested Extension

Have students write each of the following without exponents.

$\frac{1}{125}$		-125		$-\frac{1}{125}$
1. 5^3 125	**2.** 5^{-3}	**3.** $(-5)^3$		**4.** $(-5)^{-3}$
5. $\left(\frac{1}{5}\right)^3$	**6.** $\left(\frac{1}{5}\right)^{-3}$	**7.** $\left(-\frac{1}{5}\right)^3$		**8.** $\left(-\frac{1}{5}\right)^{-3}$
$\frac{1}{125}$	125	$-\frac{1}{125}$		-125

7-10 (pages 336–341)

Key Mathematical Ideas

- writing numbers in scientific notation
- performing computations with numbers in scientific notation

Teaching Suggestions

As you define scientific notation and discuss Examples 1 and 2 on pages 336–337, emphasize that a number written in scientific notation with 10 raised to the nth power is equivalent to the number obtained by moving the decimal point n places to the right if n is positive and n places to the left if n is negative.

To reinforce the idea of powers of ten, ask students to match equal numbers below.

1. 1,230,000 d	**a.** 123×10^2
2. 123,000 e	**b.** 1.23×10^{-3}
3. 12,300 a	**c.** 1230×10^{-4}
4. 1230 g	**d.** 1.23×10^6
5. 1.23 h	**e.** 0.0123×10^7
6. 0.123 c	**f.** 12.3×10^{-5}
7. 0.00123 b	**g.** 0.123×10^4
8. 0.000123 f	**h.** 0.00123×10^3

Encourage students to interpret the solutions to the problems in this lesson. This will not only help them spot errors but will also make the results of the computations more meaningful. For instance, the solution to Example 4 on page 337 means that Pluto is about 10 times farther away from the sun than Mercury.

Using Manipulatives

When very large or very small numbers are reported in newspaper and magazine articles, words are used to indicate size, as in "1.8 billion dollars" and "one millionth of an inch." Have students bring to class examples of these quantitative phrases and then rewrite them using scientific notation.

---

8 Introduction to Functions

This chapter introduces the basic tools for working with linear equations in two variables. Solution sets of linear equations are represented graphically using the coordinate plane. The slope of a line is defined, and the standard and slope-intercept forms of a line's equation are examined. Lines are graphed from given equations, and equations are determined from given facts about a line.

Functions are defined by tables, graphs, and equations. Special attention is given to linear and quadratic functions.

The chapter concludes with direct and inverse variations. Practical examples of each type of variation are examined.

8-1 (pages 349–352)

Key Mathematical Ideas

- selecting ordered pairs that are solutions of equations in two variables
- solving equations in two variables over specified domains of the variables

Teaching Suggestions

The material in this section may be completely new to some students, so the idea of an equation in two variables should be explained carefully.

Emphasize that if an equation contains two variables, each of its solutions must be an ordered pair of numbers. If the idea of an *ordered* pair is not familiar to students, be sure to point out the importance of giving the numbers in a solution pair in the appropriate order.

Emphasize that a linear equation in two variables usually has many solutions, as illustrated on page 349. Show how substitution is used to determine whether or not a given ordered pair is a solution of a given equation.

When you discuss Examples 2 and 3 on page 350, stress the value of solving for one variable in terms of the other. (Recall that transforming formulas was discussed in Lesson 4-7.) Point out that it is sometimes easier to solve for a certain variable than to solve for the other. Ask students which variable would be easiest to solve for in Written Exercises 13, 18, and 35.

Suggested Extension

Have students solve for y in terms of x and identify the smallest whole-number value for x such that the value of y is negative.

1. $3x + y = 4$

$y = 4 - 3x; x = 2$

2. $x + 3y = 3$

$y = \frac{3 - x}{3}; x = 4$

3. $3x + 2y = 20$

$y = \frac{20 - 3x}{2}; x = 7$

4. $7x + 15y = 90$

$y = \frac{90 - 7x}{15}; x = 13$

8-2 (pages 353–359)

Key Mathematical Ideas

- graphing ordered pairs in the coordinate plane
- graphing linear equations in two variables

Teaching Suggestions

Many students are confused initially when plotting points or reading the coordinates of a given point, so considerable practice is necessary. Be sure to cover all combinations of signs of coordinates and emphasize the two special cases in which the x-coordinate is

0 (points on the y-axis) and the y-coordinate is 0 (points on the x-axis).

Point out that when students graph a line that is neither horizontal nor vertical, they may select any convenient values for x and y and use these values to find two ordered-pair solutions. Frequently the intercepts are convenient values to compute but when the intercepts are not integers, other values may be more convenient. For example, to graph $2x + 3y = 7$ it is helpful to note that $2(2) + 3(1) = 7$ and $2(5) + 3(-1) = 7$ and so the line contains $(2, 1)$ and $(5, -1)$.

You may want the students to generalize from Examples 2 and 3 on page 355 by stating what type of line the graph of $ax + by = c$ is if $a \neq 0$ and $b \neq 0$ (a slanted line), if $a \neq 0$ and $b = 0$ (a vertical line), and if $a = 0$ and $b \neq 0$ (a horizontal line).

Suggested Extensions

1. Have students graph the equation $y = x$. On the same set of axes have them plot the following points in pairs.

a. $(5, 2), (2, 5)$ **b.** $(3, -2), (-2, 3)$
c. $(-5, 1), (1, -5)$ **d.** $(4, 0), (0, 4)$
e. $(-6, -2), (-2, -6)$ **f.** $(0, -3), (-3, 0)$

2. Ask students to state an observation based on their graph. The points (x, y) and (y, x) are symmetric with respect to the line $y = x$.

3. Challenge students to complete this statement: The points (x, y) and $(\underline{}, \underline{})$ are symmetric with respect to the line $y = -x$. $(-y, -x)$

8-3 (pages 360–365)

Key Mathematical Ideas

- defining slope
- finding the slope of a line

Teaching Suggestions

A simple classroom model can be used to illustrate the concept of slope. Place a stack of books on a desk and prop a ruler up on the books as shown at the top of the next page.

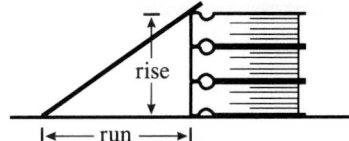

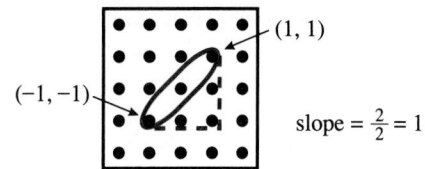

slope $= \frac{2}{2} = 1$

Point out that the steepness of the ruler depends on the number of books in the pile.

Draw several lines, emphasizing that the slope of a straight line is constant—positive if the line rises from left to right and negative if it falls from left to right.

The difference between zero slope and no slope causes a great deal of difficulty for many students. Stress the significance of a zero numerator or denominator. You may wish to try this approach: Use the line whose equation is $y = x$ with slope 1 as a starting point, pointing out that it makes a 45° angle with both axes. As the steepness decreases, the line approaches the horizontal and the numerical value of the slope approaches 0. (See the figure at the left below.) Therefore the slope of a horizontal line is 0.

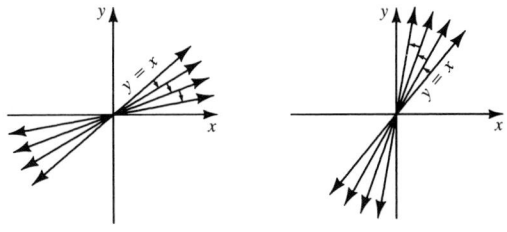

As the steepness increases from 1, the line approaches the vertical and the numerical value of the slope just gets larger and larger without approaching any specific number. (See the figure at the right above.) Therefore it seems reasonable that there is no number that can be assigned to the slope of a vertical line.

Using Manipulatives

Using the center peg of a geoboard as $(0, 0)$, students can find the slope of the line containing $(1, 1)$ and $(-1, -1)$ by placing a rubber band on the proper pegs and stretching it to show the rise and the run as shown in the diagram that follows.

Suggested Extension

Challenge students to use their answers to Written Exercises 13–24 to find an expression for the slope of the line with equation $ax + by = c$, $b \neq 0$.

$$\text{slope} = -\frac{a}{b}$$

8-4 (pages 366–370)

Key Mathematical Idea

• using the slope-intercept form of a linear equation

Teaching Suggestions

Be sure to emphasize Example 2 on page 367. Some students continue to rely on a table of values when graphing a linear equation. Emphasize the advantage of using the slope and the y-intercept to locate points on the graph. Have students begin the "stair-stepping" process by graphing the point $(0, b)$, which can be found by inspection from $y = mx + b$. For example, to graph $3x - 2y = 8$, have students use $y = \frac{3}{2}x - 4$, graph $(0, -4)$, and then use the slope to locate other points. Suggest that students verify their work by substituting the coordinates of one point in the original equation: $3(4) - 2(2) = 8$, so $(4, 2)$ does lie on the line.

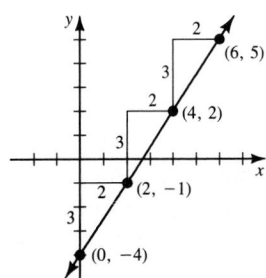

When discussing parallel lines, you can refer to the graphs of $y = 2x$ and $y = 2x + 4$ on page 366. Point out that these parallel lines have the same slope.

Group Activity

Divide the class into small groups. Have each group investigate the relationship between the slopes and between the graphs of $ax + by = c$ and $bx - ay = c$. Ask each group member to choose specific values for a, b, and c ($a \neq 0$ and $b \neq 0$), find the slopes, and draw the graphs (on the same coordinate plane). Then ask the group members to pool their work, discuss it, and arrive at a general conclusion. The lines are perpendicular and their slopes are negative reciprocals.

8-5 (pages 371–373)

Key Mathematical Idea

- finding an equation of a line given the slope and one point on the line, or given two points on the line

Teaching Suggestions

Reinforce the idea that every line has an equation. Information that determines a line can be given in various ways. This information can be used to find an equation either in standard form or in slope-intercept form. The latter is preferred in this lesson.

In discussing the examples on page 371, remind students of the significance of m and b. Students should use the given information to find and substitute numerical values for m and b in the equation $y = mx + b$.

In Example 3, the point $(4, 8)$ is used to find b. Be sure to mention that the other point, $(-2, 5)$, can be used to check the answer by substituting -2 for x and 5 for y in the equation $y = \frac{1}{2}x + 6$.

Suggested Extension

Have students draw, on a coordinate plane, an ''A,'' ''K,'' or other capitalized letter of the alphabet composed only of straight line segments. Ask the students to find equations for the lines containing the segments that form the letter.

8-6 (pages 374–378)

Key Mathematical Idea

- defining functions by using tables, bar graphs, and broken-line graphs

Teaching Suggestions

This lesson introduces the concept of a function in a concrete way. Here functions are specified by tables, bar graphs, and broken-line graphs. In the next lesson a more abstract approach involving equations is taken.

You can illustrate the idea of a function as an association by pointing out that each student in the class has a particular grade point average (GPA). Stress that this association follows the requirements of a function: no one student will have two GPA's at a given point in time, but two different students may have the same GPA.

When discussing Examples 2 and 3 on page 375, you might want to point out the circumstances for which bar graphs and broken-line graphs are appropriate. If the domain of a function is ''discrete'' (that is, the members of the domain are ''independent,'' with no natural progression from one member to the next), a bar graph is used to display the function. On the other hand, if the domain is ''continuous'' (that is, the members of the domain are ''tied together,'' with one element naturally leading to the next), a broken-line graph is used.

Using Manipulatives

Have students bring in examples of bar graphs and broken-line graphs from newspapers and magazines. Ask them to write down the ordered pairs that can be read from the graphs.

Conversely, have students bring in examples of tabular data from newspapers and magazines. Ask them to draw bar graphs and broken-line graphs for the data.

Suggested Extension

Have students use the graph in Example 3 on page 375 to estimate each of the following. Accept reasonable estimates.

1. The population in 1950 about 150 million
2. The population in 1975 about 210 million
3. The year in which the population was 200 million about 1970
4. The year in which the population was 100 million about 1915

8-7 (pages 379–382)

Key Mathematical Ideas

- using equations to define functions
- finding values of functions

Teaching Suggestions

Point out that the values of a function defined by an equation can be found without using a table or a graph, as in the previous lesson. For any member of the domain, the equation tells how to find the corresponding member of the range.

Be sure to discuss the two types of notation used to specify a function. While students may find arrow notation more appealing, functional notation is more commonly used.

You might want to stress the concept of a function as a set of ordered pairs, as introduced in the previous lesson. In Example 1 on page 379, for instance, the function g can be specified by $\{(-1, 0), (0, 4), (1, 6), (2, 6)\}$.

Reading Algebra

The verbalizations of functions given in symbolic form can be reinforced as students do the Oral Exercises on page 380. Ask individual students to read the directions aloud, read each exercise aloud, and give each answer as a complete sentence.

Suggested Extension

Point out to students that the square root key on a calculator can be thought of as a function f that pairs each number x with $\sqrt{x}$. Have each student enter a different positive value for x and repeatedly press the square root key to find $f(x)$, $f(f(x))$, $f(f(f(x)))$, and so on. Ask the students to describe what happens. The values approach 1 no matter what x is.

8-8 (pages 383–390)

Key Mathematical Idea

- graphing linear functions and quadratic functions

Teaching Suggestions

Students are already familiar with linear functions from their work with linear equations. Encourage students to think of a linear function in terms of a domain, a rule, and a range. Point out that if the domain is not specified, it is assumed to be the set of real numbers.

Understanding quadratic functions may be difficult for some students. Discuss the quadratic functions developed on pages 383, 384, and 385. Discuss why each graph represents a function. Stress the fact that the coefficient of x^2 determines whether the parabola opens upward or downward, and thus whether the function has a minimum point or a maximum point.

Once the general equation for a parabola's axis of symmetry has been discussed (see the box on page 385), have the students confirm that this general equation "works" for the parabolas in Examples 1 and 2 on pages 383–384. Encourage students to draw the axis of symmetry when they are graphing a parabola. Remind them that the axis of symmetry always contains the vertex of a parabola.

Reading Algebra

This lesson gives you a good opportunity to help students understand how equations, tables, and graphs are used together to describe a given function. As an aid in interpreting the tables and graphs, you might give students some specific questions to consider as they read the lesson. For example, the following questions relate to the table and graph at the bottom of page 383.

1. What part of the table would be filled in first?
   the top row
2. Would the numbers under x or those under $x^2 - 2x - 2 = y$ usually be filled in first?
   those under x

3. Where do the numbers in the left-hand column come from? They are chosen by the person making the table.

4. How do you know what equations to write in the right-hand column? Substitute the chosen values of x in the equation at the top of the column.

5. Where do the ordered pairs shown on the graph come from? They are the values of x and y from the table.

Suggested Extension

Let $f(x) = x - 1$ and $g(x) = x^2$. Have students graph the following functions.

1. $y = f[g(x)]$
$f[g(x)] = x^2 - 1$

2. $y = g[f(x)]$
$g[f(x)] = (x - 1)^2$
$= x^2 - 2x + 1$

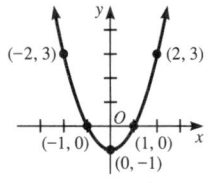

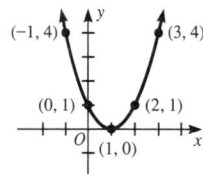

8-9 (pages 391–396)

Key Mathematical Idea

- solving problems involving direct variation

Teaching Suggestions

To introduce direct variation, ask students if they have watched the dials on a pump at a gas station: The amount to be paid for the gas varies directly as the number of gallons pumped. Point out that the constant of variation in this case is the price per gallon. Also mention that in most practical situations the constant of variation is a positive number.

When you introduce the relationship $\dfrac{y_1}{x_1} = \dfrac{y_2}{x_2}$, review the meaning of subscripts. Stress that each variable with a subscript represents a particular value of the variable. Point out that the proportion $\dfrac{y_1}{x_1} = \dfrac{y_2}{x_2}$ indicates that the quotient, or ratio, of the variables is

constant. Remind students of the procedure used to solve proportions. (See Lesson 7-2.)

The following example may appeal to students: Jan worked 7 hours last week and earned \$28. If her wages vary directly as the number of hours worked, find the constant of variation and the amount she will earn if she works 17.5 hours.

$k = $ hourly rate $= \dfrac{28}{7} = 4$ and $w = 4(17.5) = 70$;

or $\dfrac{28}{7} = \dfrac{w}{17.5}$ and $w = \dfrac{28(17.5)}{7} = 70$

Use these computations to illustrate the general formulas $y = kx$, $\dfrac{y}{x} = k$, and $\dfrac{y_1}{x_1} = \dfrac{y_2}{x_2}$.

Suggested Extension

Point out that the number of times that the tires on a car have turned and the car's odometer reading vary directly. Have students approximate what the constant of variation is if a car's tires have radius 1 ft. For each turn of the tires the car travels approximately $2 \cdot 3.14 \cdot 1$, or 6.28 ft. Convert 6.28 ft to miles: $6.28 \div 5280 \approx 0.0012$ (mi). $\therefore k \approx 0.0012$

8-10 (pages 397–404)

Key Mathematical Idea

- solving problems involving inverse variation

Teaching Suggestions

You can introduce the concept of inverse variation by using the following table showing the values of various coins and the number of each coin needed to equal one dollar. Emphasize that one value increases as the other decreases and that $vn = 100$ for each coin.

Coin	Value in Cents	No. needed for \$1
Penny	1	100
Nickel	5	20
Dime	10	10
Quarter	25	4
Half-dollar	50	2
Dollar	100	1

9 Systems of Linear Equations

This chapter shows how to find the solutions that are common to two linear equations in two variables. Three methods of solving a system of linear equations are presented: the graphing method, the substitution method, and the addition-or-subtraction method.

Problem solving skills are extended to include many types of problems associated with systems of linear equations. Applications include wind- and water-current problems as well as age, digit, and fraction puzzle problems.

9-1 (pages 413–416)

Key Mathematical Idea

- solving a system of linear equations by graphing

Teaching Suggestions

The three examples in this lesson show that two lines on a coordinate plane may intersect, be parallel, or coincide. Since each solution of a system of two linear equations is a point on both graphs, a system can have either a unique solution, no solution, or infinitely many solutions.

Ask the class if it would be possible to have exactly two ordered pairs as solutions. Also ask for a convincing argument to explain why or why not.

Students may produce inaccurate graphs when solving a system. If a system has a unique solution, be sure to have students check it using both equations.

Group Activity

Pair students so that one has a graph such as the first graph on page 413 and the other has a sheet of graph paper with only the x- and y-axes drawn. The first student describes the graph orally, and the second student tries to draw it from the description. After the graph has been completed and checked, the students exchange roles, using another graph. Hints for the first graph on page 413 might be: "The two lines pass through the point $(3, -2)$. One line passes through the point $(0, 1)$. The other line has slope 2."

Suggested Extension

Have students identify the two equations for which each ordered pair is a solution.

1. $(1, 3)$	**a.** $x - 2y = 2$	**1.** b, d
2. $(-2, 5)$	**b.** $2x + 3y = 11$	**2.** b, c
3. $(4, 1)$	**c.** $3x + 2y = 4$	**3.** a, b
4. $(-4, -3)$	**d.** $6x - 5y = -9$	**4.** a, d

9-2 (pages 417–420)

Key Mathematical Idea

- solving a system of linear equations by substitution

Teaching Suggestions

Introduce the substitution method as a technique that gives more accurate solutions than the graphing method. For example, the system $\begin{aligned} x + y &= 12 \\ 6x - 7y &= -2 \end{aligned}$ is easily solved by substitution but difficult to solve by graphing. Point out that the substitution method is usually used only when at least one of the four coefficients of the variables is 1 or -1.

A common error is shown in the following example. Caution students against solving for $-y$ or for $-x$.

$$2x - y = 3 \rightarrow -y = 3 - 2x$$
$$3x + 2y = 8$$
$$3x + 2(3 - 2x) = 8$$

Emphasize the importance of solving for just x or just y before substituting.

Suggested Extensions

Solve by the substitution method.

1. $y = x^2$	**2.** $y = x^2 + 3x$	**3.** $x + y = 4$
$x + y = 6$	$y = 5x$	$x^2 + y^2 = 10$
$(2, 4), (-3, 9)$	$(0, 0), (2, 10)$	$(1, 3), (3, 1)$

9-3 (pages 421–425)

Key Mathematical Idea

* using systems of linear equations in two variables to solve word problems

Teaching Suggestions

The two solutions of Example 1 show that some problems can be solved using either one equation and one variable or two equations and two variables. Stress that students should use systems of equations in this lesson to gain practice in writing and solving systems.

For most students, the chief difficulty in solving the problems in this lesson is in identifying two independent relationships on which to base two equations in two variables. The Oral Exercises provide excellent practice in setting up systems of equations.

Point out that both sides of an equation must be in the same units. In Example 1, the right-hand side of the equation is 255 cents because the chart uses 10 cents per dime and 25 cents per quarter.

The C-level exercises require students to set up and solve systems of three equations in three variables. You may wish to modify these exercises by having students write but not solve the equations.

Suggested Extension

Have students solve the following problem. Find three numbers in decreasing order that satisfy all of the following conditions:
a. the first two numbers have a difference of 4
b. the sum of the greatest and least numbers is 2
c. the sum of the three numbers is 3. 5, 1, −3

9-4 (pages 426–429)

Key Mathematical Idea

* solving a system of linear equations by addition or subtraction

Teaching Suggestions

The addition-or-subtraction method is based on the addition property of equality. Review with the class the two versions of that rule:

$$\text{If } a = b, \text{ then } a + c = b + c$$
$$\text{If } a = b \text{ and } c = d, \text{ then } a + c = b + d.$$

Instruct students to write equations in standard form before deciding to add or subtract. (See Written Exercises 19–27.) Remind students to write similar terms in the same column to avoid addition or subtraction errors. Point out that all the systems in Written Exercises 1–18 have been designed so that the coefficients of one variable are the same or are opposites. In the next lesson students will learn to solve systems that cannot be solved simply by adding or subtracting.

After the value of one variable is known, the value of the second variable should be found. The value of the first variable can be substituted in either equation to find the value of the second variable. Be sure to list members of the ordered pair solution of a system of equations in alphabetical order; for example, (m, n) not (n, m) in Written Exercise 5.

Suggested Extensions

Have students use addition or subtraction to solve each system. The solution will be an ordered triple (x, y, z).

1. $x + y - z = 0$
    $x - y - z = 10$
    $3x - y + z = 8$
    $(2, -5, -3)$

2. $3x - 2y + z = 5$
    $2y - z = 7$
    $3x - 2y - 5z = 47$
    $(4, 0, -7)$

9-5 (pages 430–437)

Key Mathematical Idea

* using multiplication with the addition-or-subtraction method to solve a system of linear equations

Teaching Suggestions

In this lesson, if a student uses the addition-or-subtraction method immediately, the resulting equation will still contain two variables. In order to eliminate a variable, one must find an equivalent system in which the coefficients of this variable are equal or opposites.

It may be helpful to point out that the required coefficients of the variable to be eliminated are equal to a common multiple of its original coefficients, preferably the LCM. In Example 2 the LCM of the coefficients of a is 15.

Be sure to assign some of the Mixed Practice exercises on page 433 to ensure that students are comfortable with the graphing method, the substitution method, and the addition-or-subtraction method. You may want to ask students to solve the system $\begin{array}{l}5x + 2y = -4 \\ x - 2y = -8\end{array}$ by all three methods. $(-2, 3)$

Reading Algebra

This lesson is a good one for students to study independently before it is discussed in class. You might provide the following key questions to guide students as they read:

1. Where is the addition-or-subtraction method explained in your book? Lesson 9-4

2. Why can't you use this method immediately with the given equations in Example 1 on page 430? The equations in the system don't have the same or opposite coefficients for one of their terms.

3. What must you do before you can use the addition-or-subtraction method? Use the mult. prop. of equality to make two terms the same or opposites.

4. Can you explain the solution of Example 1 without looking at the directions? See Steps 1–4 of the solution to Example 1, page 430.

Suggested Extensions

If students are interested in solving a system of linear equations by using a computer or a calculator, have them rewrite the equations in the form

$$Ax + By = C$$
$$Dx + Ey = F.$$

The ordered pair (x, y) is a solution if and only if

$$(x, y) = \left(\frac{CE - BF}{AE - BD}, \frac{AF - CD}{AE - BD}\right).$$

Refer students to the Computer Exercises on page 436.

9-6 (pages 438–443)

Key Mathematical Idea

- solving wind and water current problems using systems of equations

Teaching Suggestions

Previous motion problems were solved with one variable only. Point out that the same relationship involving distance, rate, and time still holds, but with the introduction of wind or current, the rate of the current or wind has to be added to or subtracted from the rate of the object that is traveling. Two rates can be added or subtracted as long as they are rates in the same or opposite directions.

Some students fail to notice common factors that occur in equations. Emphasize Step 3 in the example on page 439. Point out that it is considerably easier to solve $\begin{array}{l}r + w = 1000 \\ r - w = 850\end{array}$ than to solve

$$6.8r + 6.8w = 6800$$
$$8r - 8w = 6800.$$

Using Manipulatives

The problem below shows what can happen when the wind is not blowing along the line of motion of the object.

An airplane takes off to fly north at 120 km/h. The pilot ignores the fact that the wind is blowing from the west at 50 km/h.

1. Use a coordinate plane to represent the motion during the first 6 minutes as follows:
   a. Draw an arrow from the origin to the point $(0, 12)$ to represent the motion due to the engine.
   b. Draw an arrow from $(0, 12)$ to $(5, 12)$ to represent the motion due to the wind.
   c. Draw an arrow from the origin to $(5, 12)$ to represent the actual motion of the plane.

2. Use the edge of a second piece of graph paper as a ruler to measure the length of the arrow drawn in part (c), above. How far will the plane actually travel in 6 minutes? in one hour? 13 km; 130 km

3. How far will the plane be from the expected location at the end of six minutes? at the end of one hour? 5 km east; 50 km east

Have students solve the following problem.

A boat can go 20 km downstream in 2 h. The return trip takes 5 h. What is the speed of the current? If there is also a strong wind of 2 km/h blowing against the current, how long will the same trip take downstream? upstream? current, 3 km/h;

time downstream, $2\frac{1}{2}$ h;

time upstream, $3\frac{1}{3}$ h

9-7 (pages 444–450)

Key Mathematical Idea

- solving digit, age, and fraction problems using systems of equations

Teaching Suggestions

Emphasize the value of making a chart when solving digit or age problems. Remind students to check their results against the conditions of the problem. Caution them that the sum of the digits of a number is not the same as the number. The number 345 has 12 as the sum of its digits.

When you discuss fraction problems, you may need to review the procedure for solving proportions.

Suggested Extension

Have students solve the following problem to find each person's age.

Bertha was twice as old as Carla twelve years ago. Carla is now four times as old as Andrew, who is half the age of Doug. In sixteen years Doug will be the same age as Carla is now. $A = 8$, $B = 52$, $C = 32$, $D = 16$

10 Inequalities

The introduction to inequality symbols in Lesson 1-8 provides the background for a more formal study of inequalities in this chapter. The order of the real numbers leads to the study of inequalities in one variable and their graphs.

Techniques for solving inequalities, similar to those for solving equations, are developed. Methods for simple inequalities are extended to include conjunctions, disjunctions, and absolute value. Problems that are best expressed with inequalities are solved.

Linear inequalities in two variables and systems of such inequalities are investigated, with emphasis on their graphs.

10-1 (pages 457–461)

Key Mathematical Ideas

- reviewing order and the number line
- understanding the meaning of the solution of an inequality

Teaching Suggestions

Begin with a review of the inequality signs and their meanings, and of how to graph a real number on a number line. Review the meaning of solution of an open sentence in general, and show that possible solutions of an inequality can be tested by substituting values for the variable in the inequality.

Emphasize the difference between the symbols $<$ and $\le$, and between $>$ and $\ge$. Also, remind students that a statement such as $x \ge 5$ is equivalent to the statement $5 \le x$.

The significance of the words "and" and "or" is developed more thoroughly in Lesson 10-4, but begin to stress the idea of true and false statements.

$-5 < -2$ and $-2 < 0$ true $-1 < -2$ and $-2 < 0$ false	An "and" statement is true only if both parts are true.
$5 > 2$ or $5 < 9$ true $7 > 4$ or $7 = 4$ true $-2 > 0$ or $-2 < -4$ false	An "or" statement is true if either part is true.

Suggested Extension

Define the "greatest integer" symbol [ ] as follows: $[x]$ is the greatest integer that is less than or equal to x. For example, $[5] = 5$, $[-3] = -3$, $[2.3] = 2$, and $[-9.6] = -10$.

Solve each inequality over the domain {the positive real numbers}.

1. $[x] > 3$ **2.** $[x] \leq 5$ **3.** $2 < [x] < 6$

1. {the real numbers greater than or equal to 4}
2. {the positive real numbers less than 6}
3. {the real numbers less than 6 and greater than or equal to 3}

10-2 (pages 462–468)

Key Mathematical Ideas

- using transformations to solve any linear inequality in one variable
- graphing solution sets of inequalities over the real numbers

Teaching Suggestions

Build on students' earlier work with equations by discussing the transformations that produce equivalent inequalities. Point out that these are the same as those for equations, with the exception of transformation number 4 in the list on page 463.

Suggest a quick check on the reasonableness of a solution. Substitute a number that is obviously in the solution set of the transformed inequality in the original inequality, and see if it satisfies the original.

Using Manipulatives

Lead students through some simple activities to reinforce their understanding of the addition and multiplication properties of order. Sample activities are described.

1. Use a double pan balance. Place objects with different weights in the pans. Write a statement using $<$ or $>$ for the weights. Then add identical items to the two pans. Observe that the heavier pan is

still heavier, and so on. Students can even write more formal statements, such as if $L < R$ (if the left pan is higher), then $L + A < R + A$ (where A is the identical item added to each pan).

2. Use coins or play money. Make two small piles of different values. Write a statement using $<$ or $>$ for the two money amounts. Then make three more piles identical to each of the original piles. Have students identify the collection with the greater value. Guide them to see that if $L < R$ then, in this case, $4L < 4R$.

Suggested Extension

Have students determine which of these transformations will always produce equivalent inequalities.

1. Squaring each side. no
2. Taking the absolute value of each side. no
3. Taking the reciprocal of each side. no
4. Taking the opposite of each side and reversing the inequality sign. yes

10-3 (pages 469–477)

Key Mathematical Ideas

- translating problems from verbal statements to algebraic inequalities
- solving problems involving inequalities

Teaching Suggestions

Discuss that in everyday life, it is common to deal with measurements and conditions best described by inequalities rather than equations. Some students may be familiar with the use of "tolerances" in machine work. Others may have had experience writing statements such as "IF ABS(X − Y) <= 0.00001 THEN ..." in BASIC programs when what was really meant was "IF X = Y THEN ...".

This section builds on previous work. The emphasis should be on writing the inequalities. Once this has been done, solutions should not pose a major difficulty; students simply use the methods developed in Lesson 10-2. The Written Exercises allow students to concentrate on the crucial skill of translating problems into mathematical terms, without concerning themselves with the mechanics of solving the inequalities.

The list at the bottom of page 469, while not exhaustive, should help students develop a feel for which inequality sign is implied by a given expression.

Reading Algebra

The five-step plan for solving word problems encourages students to read and reread problems and to break them down into comprehensible portions. This may counter the expectation of many students that they should be able to read a problem and write a solution immediately. Students should be encouraged to read word problems with pencil in hand, to jot notes as they read, and to refine their notes when rereading. The notes should reveal relationships and patterns that are likely to elude a student who simply reads the problem. Tell students that they are "working smart" when they use pencil and paper.

Suggested Extension

For the given inequality, have students write or describe a corresponding problem.

1. $70 + 50x > 300$

2. $465 - 25x < 200$

3. $20(x - 6) > 950$

Answers will vary.

Samples are given.

1. At noon you were 70 mi from home. After driving for some time at 50 mi/h you were then more than 300 mi from home. How long did you drive?
2. A piggy bank held $4.65. You took out some quarters, and then there was less than $2.00 left in the bank. How many quarters did you remove?
3. You own stocks worth $20 a share. After you sell 6 shares, your remaining shares are still worth more than $950. How many shares did you have to begin with?

10-4 (pages 478–481)

Key Mathematical Ideas

- using "or" and "and" in inequalities
- solving combined inequalities

Teaching Suggestions

The mathematical meanings of the words "or" and "and" are matters of definition. The word "or," in particular, has more than one meaning in ordinary English and, hence, must be clearly defined in a mathematical context. The meaning used is usually expressed "either or both" in ordinary English. Encourage students to work through the Extra on pages 476–477 if they haven't already done so. It can be helpful to explain solutions of conjunctions and disjunctions in terms of intersections and unions.

Many students will benefit from a graphic breakdown of combined inequalities. To solve $2x + 3 > 9$ and $12 - x > 5$, graph the two component inequalities individually, then look for the overlapping portion (intersection).

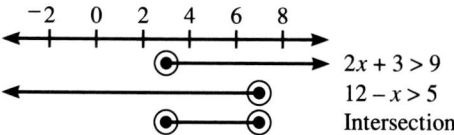

Using Manipulatives

Borrow simple equipment from the science or electronics classes to build some parallel and series circuits. Incorporate a buzzer or light to signal when the circuit is complete. Have students determine which circuit corresponds to a conjunction and which to a disjunction by experimenting with the switches in the circuits. They'll discover that the parallel circuit is complete when either switch is closed (disjunction), while both switches must be closed to complete the series circuit (conjunction).

Suggested Extension

Combined inequalities may have more than two components. Have students solve more complicated combined inequalities.

1. $(3 - 2x > 5$ and $3(4 + x) > 0)$ or $3 + x > 9 - x$

$-4 < x < -1$ or $x > 3$

2. $(2x - 1 > 0$ or $-5x > 0)$ and $-3 < 3 - 2x < 5$

$-1 < x < 0$ or $\frac{1}{2} < x < 3$

10-5 (pages 482–485)

Key Mathematical Ideas

- using absolute value to represent the distance between points on a number line
- writing open sentences with absolute values as conjunctions and disjunctions
- solving equations and inequalities involving absolute value

Teaching Suggestions

Review the definition of absolute value on page 37. Use numerical examples as in Example 1 to establish that the distance between points is the absolute value of the difference of their coordinates. Emphasize that the distance is always determined by a subtraction; some students have informal rules in mind that sometimes involve subtraction and sometimes addition. The advantage of the rule given is its uniformity—always subtract.

Students will appreciate the alternative methods of solving inequalities with absolute values shown in Examples 1, 2, and 3. Some will prefer the algebraic approach, others the graphing technique. Students are often surprised at the ease of solution using the number line approach and find this method preferable, especially for simpler inequalities. For more difficult or complicated inequalities students often prefer the more mechanical, algorithmic approach of expressing them as conjunctions or disjunctions and applying transformation rules.

Suggested Extension

Challenge students to graph the solution set of each inequality.

1. $2 \le |x| \le 3$

2. $1 \le |x - 2| \le 4$

3. $4 < |3 - x| \le 6$

1.

2.

3.

10-6 (pages 486–489)

Key Mathematical Ideas

- recognizing that $|ab| = |a| \cdot |b|$
- solving more difficult open sentences involving absolute value

Teaching Suggestions

Use many numerical examples along with those that follow Example 1 to remind students that the absolute value of a product is the product of the absolute values. Generalize the results with a concise statement:

$$|ab| = |a|\,|b|.$$

Point out that this statement says that if a number is factored from an absolute value quantity, it must be positive. For example, $|3x| = 3|x|$ and $|-3x| = 3|x|$.

Work through Example 2 carefully. Once students grasp the procedure for "factoring out" the coefficient, be sure they realize that the rest of the solution is the same as that in the previous lesson. Of course, one major reason for presenting this technique here is to enable students to use the graphing method studied in Lesson 10-5, which students usually consider easy.

Group Activity

Prepare a blank chart with the following column headings:

a	b	$|a|$	$|b|$	ab	$|ab|$	$|a|\,|b|$

Have students break up into groups of five. Distribute one copy of the chart to each group. The first person in the group should fill in at least ten values for a and b. Encourage them to use all kinds of combinations—positive and negative, integers, decimals, and so on.

The next person should fill in columns 3 and 4 based on the given values of a and b.

The remaining group members fill in columns 5, 6, and 7, respectively.

Once the chart is complete, the group should examine it and attempt to generalize the results. Students will probably conclude that, no matter what the values of a and b, $|ab| = |a|\,|b|$.

Suggested Extension

Have students determine the conditions on a and b for which each statement is true.

1. $|ab| = a|b|$ $a \geq 0$
2. $|ab| = ab$ a and b both positive or both negative, or either zero
3. $|ab| = |a||b|$ always true
4. $|ab| > ab$ a or b negative, but not both, and neither zero
5. $|ab| < ab$ never true

10-7 (pages 490–494)

Key Mathematical Ideas

- transforming inequalities in two variables to have y alone as one side
- graphing open and closed half-planes

Teaching Suggestions

Review how to graph a line using slope–intercept form. The steps in the box on page 491 and in Example 1 involve expressing a line in slope-intercept form. Graphing this line produces the boundary of the half-plane that is the graph of the inequality under consideration. Relate the symbols $\leq$, $\geq$, $<$, and $>$ to the inclusion or exclusion of the boundary line in the graph and remind students to use care in drawing either a solid or a dashed boundary line. This topic is one in which students should be encouraged very strongly to check their work. First, the check is easy. Students simply substitute the coordinates of a test point as in Example 1. Second, the check prevents students from graphing the half-plane opposite the correct one because of errors in solving the original inequality for y.

Inequalities whose graphs have horizontal or vertical boundaries as in Examples 2 and 3 are usually easier for students to graph.

Suggested Extension

Challenge students to graph more difficult open sentences.

1. $|x| + |y| < 4$

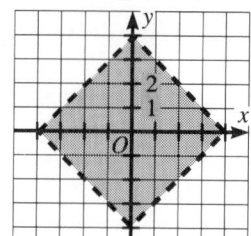

2. $|x + y| = 4$

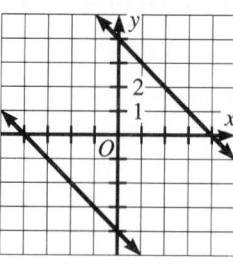

10-8 (pages 495–498)

Key Mathematical Idea

- graphing a system of two or more linear inequalities

Teaching Suggestions

Review intersections of sets and solutions of conjunctions. A system of open sentences is a conjunction; the solution of the system is the intersection of the solution sets of the component open sentences. In a sense, no new skills are required for this lesson. To graph a system of two inequalities, show students that they merely graph the inequalities separately, just as they did in Lesson 10-7, and then indicate the intersection of these separate graphs. The procedure can be extended to systems with any number of inequalities.

Point out that some systems have graphs that are closed polygonal regions (Exercises 23 and 24) while others have graphs that are open regions (Exercises 19–22). Systems with closed polygonal regions for their solutions are involved in linear programming, the Application beginning on page 499.

Suggested Extension

Students are often curious about the usefulness of the algebra they are learning. Discuss the theory of linear programming. Mention that this is a practical technique used as a decision-making tool in business, agriculture, and medicine. Emphasize that linear programming is a relatively recent mathematical development and it is still the subject of much vital research. Encourage students to work through the Application on pages 499–500.

11 Rational and Irrational Numbers

Rational numbers and their properties are defined and then examined in both the decimal and square root form. Irrational numbers are then introduced in terms of irrational square roots. Finding the square root of a variable expression leads to the Pythagorean Theorem and its applications.

The last part of the chapter is devoted to radical expressions and equations. Operations involving radicals are discussed along with various techniques for simplification. The chapter concludes with the solution of simple radical equations and of word problems involving radical equations.

11-1 (pages 507–511)

Key Mathematical Ideas

- defining rational numbers
- comparing rational numbers
- understanding the density property for rational numbers

Teaching Suggestions

Point out that all integers, mixed numbers, and terminating decimals are rational since each can be expressed as the quotient of two integers. Be sure to stress the words "can be expressed" in the definition of rational numbers.

You can emphasize the density property by using a number line. Have the class locate the rational number halfway between 0 and 1, halfway between $\frac{1}{2}$ and 1, and so on. $\frac{1}{2}, \frac{3}{4}, \frac{7}{8}, \ldots$

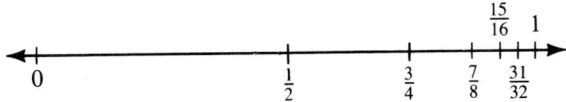

Ask the class how many rational numbers are between $\frac{1}{99}$ and $\frac{1}{100}$. infinitely many

Suggested Extension

Students can determine the greater of two rational numbers having the same sign by writing them with the same positive numerators, comparing the denominators, and reversing the order to compare the fractions. Use this method to compare the following.

1. $\frac{5}{8}$ and $\frac{5}{6}$ $8 > 6$ so $\frac{5}{8} < \frac{5}{6}$.

2. $\frac{3}{4}$ and $\frac{2}{3}$ Change to $\frac{6}{8}$ and $\frac{6}{9}$.

         Since $8 < 9$, $\frac{3}{4} > \frac{2}{3}$.

3. $\frac{-4}{8}$ and $\frac{-4}{5}$ Change to $\frac{4}{-8}$ and $\frac{4}{-5}$.

         $-8 < -5$ so $\frac{-4}{8} > \frac{-4}{5}$.

11-2 (pages 512–516)

Key Mathematical Ideas

- expressing rational numbers as terminating or repeating decimals
- expressing terminating or repeating decimals as common fractions

Teaching Suggestions

It is possible to determine whether a common rational fraction in simplest form can be expressed as a terminating or repeating decimal by the following rules:

1. If the prime factors of the denominator are only twos and/or fives (the prime factors of 10), the decimal is terminating. Illustration:

$$\frac{23}{80} = \frac{23}{2^4 \cdot 5} \cdot \frac{5^3}{5^3} = \frac{23 \cdot 5^3}{10^4} = \frac{2875}{10,000} = 0.2875$$

2. If the denominator contains a prime factor other than 2 or 5, the decimal is repeating. Illustration:

$$\frac{11}{60} = \frac{11}{2^2 \cdot 3 \cdot 5} = 0.18\overline{3}$$

Ask students to use these rules to identify whether the decimal representation of the number would terminate (T) or repeat (R).

$\frac{7}{15}$ R $\frac{9}{16}$ T $\frac{29}{375}$ R $\frac{59}{180}$ R $\frac{37}{8000}$ T

Emphasize that students should be familiar with the two definitions of a rational number:

1. Any real number that can be expressed as a ratio of two integers.

2. Any number whose decimal representation is a terminating decimal or a repeating decimal.

Most students will not be familiar with the method for converting a repeating decimal to a fraction. Be sure they understand how to determine the power of ten to use as a multiplier.

Reading Algebra

After a brief discussion of this lesson, you might want to have students read certain portions aloud, both to reinforce the sight–sound relationship and to assist with comprehension. Suggested ideas:

1. Have a student read the boxed generalization on page 513. Follow the reading with a discussion of the statement and include specific examples.

2. Have one student read Example 4 aloud while another student writes it on the board. (A good way to read $0.5\overline{42}$ is "zero point five four two, with the four two repeating.")

3. Have a student read the material on approximations at the bottom of page 514. Follow the reading with a discussion of where approximations are used in real life.

Suggested Extension

Students may be surprised by the results they obtain when they express $3.\overline{9}$ and $0.7\overline{9}$ as common fractions. (In lowest terms, the numbers are $\frac{4}{1}$ and $\frac{4}{5}$.) Ask students to show that the value of any repeating decimal of the form $x.\overline{9}$, where x is a whole number, is $x + 1$.

Let $N = x.\overline{9}$. Then $10N = x9.\overline{9}$

$$10N = x9.\overline{9}$$
$$\underline{N = x.\overline{9}}$$
$$9N = x9 - x$$
$$= (x \cdot 10 + 9) - x$$
$$= 10x + 9 - x$$
$$= 9x + 9 = 9(x + 1)$$
$$N = \frac{9(x + 1)}{9} = x + 1$$

11-3 (pages 517–520)

Key Mathematical Idea

• finding square roots that are rational

Teaching Suggestion

It may be helpful to review the methods for factoring presented in Chapter 5. Emphasize the need to look for factors with known square roots like 4, 9, 25, and 36.

Some students may be inclined to evaluate $\sqrt{87^2}$ by first writing $\sqrt{7569}$. Point out that evaluating 87^2 to evaluate $\sqrt{87^2}$ is a waste of effort.

Many students have difficulty with square roots of decimals. Help them discover that if the radicand is a perfect square, the number of digits to the right of the decimal point must be even. Then the number of digits to the right of the decimal point in the square root is half that number. Elaborate on Sample 2, page 519, by pointing out that the denominator in the fraction form must be an even power of 10, and the exponent of 10 in the square root is half the exponent in the radical. Another example:

$$\sqrt{0.000144} = \sqrt{\frac{144}{10^6}} = \frac{12}{10^3} = \frac{12}{1000} = 0.012.$$

Encourage students to read $\sqrt{x}$ as "the positive square root of x." This will help them remember that the principal square root of a number is not negative.

Using Manipulatives

Students can "see" numbers that are perfect squares and their square roots if you demonstrate the following activity with unit squares and an overhead projector. Then have students use manipulatives to "see" other perfect squares.

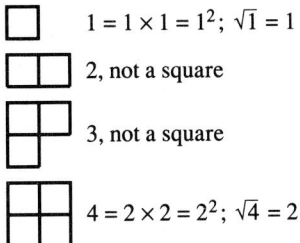

$1 = 1 \times 1 = 1^2$; $\sqrt{1} = 1$

2, not a square

3, not a square

$4 = 2 \times 2 = 2^2$; $\sqrt{4} = 2$

Suggested Extension

Ask students to find the value(s) of x for which the statement is true.

1. $\sqrt{(x - 1)^2} = x - 1$ $x \geq 1$

2. $\sqrt{x} + 3 = 0$ $x = -3$

3. $\sqrt{x^2} = -x$ $x \leq 0$

4. $\sqrt{x^2} = -1$ no solution

5. $\sqrt{(x - 4)^2} = 0$ $x = 4$

6. $\sqrt{(x + 1)^2} = 2$ $x = 1$ or $x = -3$

11-4 (pages 521–524)

Key Mathematical Ideas

- defining irrational numbers
- simplifying radicals
- approximating irrational square roots

Teaching Suggestions

Write the square roots $\sqrt{64}$, $\sqrt{74}$, and $\sqrt{81}$ on the chalkboard. Point out that $\sqrt{64} = 8$, $\sqrt{81} = 9$ and that 74 is between 49 and 81, so $\sqrt{74}$ is between 8 and 9. Ask, "Is 8.5 too large or too small?" It is too small because $8.5^2 = 72.25$. Ask the class to try 8.6 and 8.7. Discuss the fact that since 74 is not the square of an integer, $\sqrt{74}$ is not a rational number.

Point out that the symbol $\sqrt{}$ has previously been used to indicate an operation. Now students can think of $\sqrt{x}$ as naming a unique real number. Show students that we can approximate an irrational number like $\sqrt{74}$ to as many decimal places as we please. Have students use a calculator or the Table of Square Roots (page 682) to approximate $\sqrt{74}$ to three decimal places. $\sqrt{74} \approx 8.602$.

Emphasize that every real number is either rational or irrational and that no number can be both.

When discussing Oral Exercises 11–15 and Written Exercises 1–30, remind students that for a radical to be in simplest form, the radicand must contain no square integral factor other than 1.

Suggested Extension

Students can find an approximation to an irrational square root without access to a calculator or a square root table by using the divide-and-average method.

To approximate $\sqrt{28}$ to the nearest hundredth, have students use the following technique.

1. Select the integer whose square is nearest 28 as the first approximation, a. Since $5^2 = 25$, let $a = 5$.

2. Divide by a, carrying out the division to two more digits than are in the divisor: $28 \div 5 = 5.60$.

3. Find the average of a and $\dfrac{28}{a}$: $\dfrac{1}{2}(5 + 5.6) = 5.3$.

4. Use the average as the new value for a. Continue repeating steps 2 and 3 as often as necessary.

   Step 2: $28 \div 5.3 \approx 5.283$

   Step 3: $\dfrac{1}{2}(5.3 + 5.283) = 5.2915$

   Step 2: $28 \div 5.2915 \approx 5.2915$

Then $\sqrt{28}$ is approximately 5.29 to the nearest hundredth.

11-5 (pages 525–528)

Key Mathematical Ideas

- finding square roots of variable expressions
- solving equations and problems involving square roots

Teaching Suggestions

Write the chart below on the chalkboard with the first column filled in. Ask the class to help you complete the chart.

a	$\lvert a \rvert$	a^2	$\sqrt{a^2}$
-3	3	9	3
-2	2	4	2
-1	1	1	1
0	0	0	0
1	1	1	1
2	2	4	2
3	3	9	3

Point out that columns 2 and 4 are always equal: $\lvert a \rvert = \sqrt{a^2}$. Students should realize that if $x \geq 0$, they can write $\sqrt{x^2} = x$; if $x < 0$, they can write $\sqrt{x^2} = -x$.

Now add columns with the headings a^4 and $\sqrt{a^4}$. Help students realize that $\sqrt{a^4} = a^2$ for every real value of a since $a^2 \geq 0$ for every value of a. Generalize so that students understand that absolute values are needed for square roots only if the exponent of the variable in the answer is an odd number.

Suggested Extension

Ask students to find the values of x and y for which the radicand is nonnegative.

1. $\sqrt{xy}$ **2.** $\sqrt{x^2 y}$ **3.** $\sqrt{x^3 y}$ **4.** $\sqrt{x^4 y^3}$

1. $x > 0$ and $y > 0$; $x < 0$ and $y < 0$; if either x or $y = 0$, the other can be any real number.
2. x can be any real number, $y \geq 0$.
3. $x > 0$ and $y > 0$; $x < 0$ and $y < 0$; if either x or $y = 0$, the other can be any real number.
4. x can be any real number, $y \geq 0$.

11-6 (pages 529–536)

Key Mathematical Idea

- applying the Pythagorean Theorem and its converse

Teaching Suggestions

Although students have probably studied the Pythagorean Theorem in previous courses, some of them will not remember it. Thus, some review is recommended. You may want to check their understanding of the terms used throughout the lesson.

Help students to see the relationship between a theorem and its converse. Point out that while every theorem has a converse, not all converses are true. As an example, the converse of "If an animal is a collie, then it's a dog" is "If an animal is a dog, then it's a collie." The converse in this case is false. Ask a student to state the converse of "If a shape is a square, then it has four sides" and to tell whether the converse is true or false. *"If a shape has four sides, then it's a square." False*

Using Manipulatives

In addition to discussing the proof given on page 529, you can have students investigate the Pythagorean Theorem independently. Give each student a piece of graph paper and these directions: Draw a right triangle with legs 3 units and 4 units long. Then draw squares using each side of the right triangle as a side of the square.

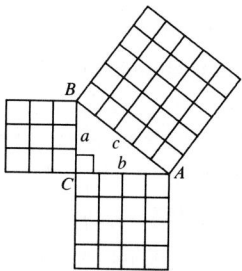

Have students count the unit squares to verify that $c^2 = a^2 + b^2$. (Have them devise their own methods for counting the unit squares in the square on the hypotenuse.)

Suggested Extensions

Define Pythagorean triples as three positive integers $\{a, b, c\}$ such that $a^2 + b^2 = c^2$.

Ask students to use the equations $a = 2xy$, $b = x^2 - y^2$, and $c = x^2 + y^2$ to verify that $\{2xy, x^2 - y^2, x^2 + y^2\}$ is a Pythagorean Triple.

$$a^2 + b^2 = (2xy)^2 + (x^2 - y^2)^2$$
$$= 4x^2y^2 + (x^4 - 2x^2y^2 + y^4)$$
$$= x^4 + 2x^2y^2 + y^4 = (x^2 + y^2)^2 = c^2$$

Use the given values of x and y and verify that the resulting values of a, b, and c form a Pythagorean triple.

1. $x = 2$, $y = 1$ $\quad 4^2 + 3^2 = 5^2$

2. $x = 3$, $y = 2$ $\quad 12^2 + 5^2 = 13^2$

3. $x = 5$, $y = 2$ $\quad 20^2 + 21^2 = 29^2$

4. $x = 4$, $y = 3$ $\quad 24^2 + 7^2 = 25^2$

5. $x = 7$, $y = 4$ $\quad 56^2 + 33^2 = 65^2$

11-7 (pages 537–539)

Key Mathematical Idea

• simplifying products and quotients of radicals

Teaching Suggestions

Review the product and quotient properties of square roots before introducing the new material.

Emphasize that when students are rationalizing a denominator, they should select the *smallest* multiplier that will produce a perfect square radicand in the denominator. For instance, to simplify $\sqrt{\frac{7}{8}}$ in Example 3, page 538, use $\sqrt{2}$ as the multiplier, not $\sqrt{8}$.

Students need to realize that the Quotient Property can be used in two ways: to write $\sqrt{\frac{a}{b}}$ as $\frac{\sqrt{a}}{\sqrt{b}}$ and to write $\frac{\sqrt{a}}{\sqrt{b}}$ as $\sqrt{\frac{a}{b}}$. Oral Exercises 2, 3, 7, 8, and 9 should be discussed, advising students to look for the

easiest way to simplify a quotient. For example, $\frac{\sqrt{18}}{\sqrt{3}} = \sqrt{\frac{18}{3}} = \sqrt{6}$. Multiplying $\frac{\sqrt{18}}{\sqrt{3}}$ by $\frac{\sqrt{3}}{\sqrt{3}}$ merely complicates the process.

Suggested Extension

Present the following problem to your students: A square with sides of length s is inscribed in a circle as shown. Find, in terms of s,

a. the radius of the circle.

b. the circumference of the circle.

c. the area of the circle.

d. the ratio of the perimeter of the square to the circumference.

e. the ratio of the area of the square to the area of the circle.

a. $\frac{1}{2} s\sqrt{2}$ **b.** $\pi s\sqrt{2}$ **c.** $\frac{1}{2}\pi s^2$ **d.** $\frac{2\sqrt{2}}{\pi}$ **e.** $\frac{2}{\pi}$

11-8 (pages 540–543)

Key Mathematical Idea

• simplifying sums and differences of radicals

Teaching Suggestions

To develop the idea of simplifying sums and differences of radicals, draw an analogy with simplifying sums and differences of polynomials:

$$2x + 3x = (2 + 3)x = 5x$$
$$2\sqrt{7} + 3\sqrt{7} = (2 + 3)\sqrt{7} = 5\sqrt{7}$$

Discuss the Examples on page 540, emphasizing that each term must be in simplest form before the terms can be combined.

It may be helpful to stress the differences between the addition and multiplication of radicals with the following examples.

$$\sqrt{9} \cdot \sqrt{16} \stackrel{?}{=} \sqrt{9 \cdot 16} \qquad \sqrt{9} + \sqrt{16} \stackrel{?}{=} \sqrt{9 + 16}$$
$$3 \cdot 4 \stackrel{?}{=} \sqrt{144} \qquad\qquad 3 + 4 \stackrel{?}{=} \sqrt{25}$$
$$12 = 12 \quad \checkmark \qquad\qquad 7 \neq 5$$

You can then generalize:

$$\sqrt{a} \cdot \sqrt{b} = \sqrt{ab}, \text{ but } \sqrt{a} + \sqrt{b} \neq \sqrt{a + b}.$$

Group Activity

Have each student write five statements involving sums and differences of radicals, some true and others false. For example, $\sqrt{18} + \sqrt{8} = \sqrt{50}$ (true) or $\sqrt{16} + \sqrt{9} = \sqrt{25}$ (false). These statements can then be exchanged with other students in the class who determine which are true and which are false.

Suggested Extensions

Have students solve the following equations and express the solution in simplest form.

1. $4x\sqrt{5} + 8 = 3\sqrt{5} + 8$ $\left\{\frac{3}{4}\right\}$

2. $2\sqrt{48} + 4x = 3\sqrt{27}$ $\left\{\frac{\sqrt{3}}{4}\right\}$

3. $x\sqrt{2} - \sqrt{6} = \sqrt{24} - x\sqrt{8}$ $\{\sqrt{3}\}$

4. $5x\sqrt{7} + 2 = 7x\sqrt{7} + 10$ $\left\{\frac{-4\sqrt{7}}{7}\right\}$

5. $\sqrt{175} - y\sqrt{63} = y\sqrt{112} - \sqrt{448}$ $\left\{\frac{13}{7}\right\}$

Develop the idea of rationalizing denominators by asking the class what value of x will produce a rational denominator:

$$\frac{4}{3 + \sqrt{7}} \cdot \frac{x}{x} = \frac{}{\text{rational}}$$

Show that if $x = \sqrt{7}$ or if $x = 3 + \sqrt{7}$, the denominator will be irrational. Complete the example using the conjugate value $3 - \sqrt{7}$ for x.

Suggested Extension

Have students mentally name the number from the list of products below that is the product of the given binomial and its conjugate.

Binomial	Product	
a. $3 + \sqrt{5}$	2	a. 4
b. $\sqrt{3} + 5$	4	b. -22
c. $\sqrt{3} + \sqrt{5}$	22	c. -2
d. $5 - \sqrt{3}$	-2	d. 22
e. $\sqrt{5} - 3$	-4	e. -4
f. $\sqrt{5} - \sqrt{3}$	-22	f. 2

11-9 (pages 544–546)

Key Mathematical Ideas

- multiplying binomials containing square-root radicals
- using conjugates to rationalize denominators

Teaching Suggestions

It will be helpful to begin the lesson with a review of the FOIL method and these product patterns.

$$(a + b)(a - b) = a^2 - b^2$$
$$(a + b)^2 = a^2 + 2ab + b^2$$
$$(a - b)^2 = a^2 - 2ab + b^2$$

Point out the similarity between simplifying $(a + b)(a - b)$ and $(6 + \sqrt{11})(6 - \sqrt{11})$ in Example 1, page 544.

Remind students to combine similar terms when multiplying binomials containing square roots.

11-10 (pages 547–553)

Key Mathematical Ideas

- solving simple radical equations
- solving word problems involving square roots

Teaching Suggestions

The idea of inverse operations should be reviewed. Point out that taking a square root and squaring are inverse operations; thus squaring a radical equation can eliminate the square root.

Stress the Property of Square Roots of Equal Numbers stated on page 526: $r^2 = s^2$ if and only if $r = s$ or $r = -s$. Thus, if we are given $x = 4$ and we square both sides, we obtain $x^2 = 16$. Since $x = 4$ has the solution set $\{4\}$ and $x^2 = 16$ has the solution set $\{4, -4\}$, the equations are not equivalent. Be sure students understand that squaring may introduce extraneous roots and that solutions of radical equations should always be checked in the original equation.

The solution to Example 2, page 547, shows the importance of isolating the radical before squaring. You may want to emphasize this idea by squaring each side of the original equation:

$$(5x + 1) + 2 \cdot 2\sqrt{5x + 1} + 4 = 36.$$

Students should see that this new equation is even more complicated than the original one.

Suggested Extension

Some of your students may be interested in exploring fractional exponents. Refer them to the Extra on pages 551–553 which includes text and exercises on this topic.

12 Quadratic Functions

In previous chapters students learned to solve quadratic equations by factoring and by using the property of square roots of equal numbers. This chapter supplements these methods by the methods of completing the square and using the quadratic formula. Graphs of quadratic functions are related to solutions of quadratic equations by means of the discriminant.

Following this, a lesson ties together all the methods of solving quadratic equations by listing guidelines for selecting the most appropriate method. These techniques of solution are then applied in a variety of word problems, some of which have irrational solutions.

The chapter concludes with an important application of quadratic functions: direct and inverse variations with practical examples of each type.

12-1 (pages 561–563)

Key Mathematical Idea

- solving quadratic equations involving perfect squares

Teaching Suggestions

Emphasize the three possible cases for an equation of the form $x^2 = k$. Stress, as noted on page 561, that such an equation can have two different real-number solutions, one real-number solution, or no real-number solution depending on the value of k. Write the following equations on the chalkboard and ask the class to tell without solving how many real-number roots each equation has.

$$(3x - 1)^2 = 9 \quad 2 \qquad (x - 4)^2 + 16 = 0 \quad 0$$

$$x^2 + 2 = 6 \quad 2 \qquad \left(x - \frac{1}{3}\right)^2 = 0 \quad 1$$

Remind students that irrational roots should be written in simplest form (see page 537).

Suggested Extension

1. Challenge students to solve each equation.
   a. $(\sqrt{2y} - 1)^2 = 9$ {8}
   b. $(\sqrt{x + 1} - 8)^2 = 25$ {8, 168}
   c. $(\sqrt{z} + 2)^2 = 3$ no solution
   d. $(4 - \sqrt{t})^2 = 18$ {34 + 24$\sqrt{2}$}

2. The Extra on pages 570 and 571 introduces imaginary numbers and solutions of equations of the form $x^2 = k$ where $k < 0$. This material offers excellent preparation for future work.

12-2 (pages 564–566)

Key Mathematical Idea

- solving quadratic equations by completing the square

Teaching Suggestions

Write the equation $(x - 6)^2 = 2$ on the chalkboard and have the class complete the solution. $x = 6 \pm \sqrt{2}$. Then write the following sequence on the chalkboard:

$$(x - 6)^2 = 2$$
$$x^2 - 12x + 36 = 2$$
$$x^2 - 12x + 34 = 0$$

Point out that since each equation is equivalent, each has the same solution set, $6 \pm \sqrt{2}$. Introduce the method of completing the square as a way of obtaining an equation like $(x - 6)^2 = 2$ from an equation like $x^2 - 12x + 34 = 0$.

The Oral Exercises offer valuable practice in completing the square, the only new skill taught in this lesson. Stress that this technique will only provide valid results if the coefficient of the quadratic term is 1.

Be sure to discuss Example 3 on page 565, emphasizing the need to divide each side of the equation by 5 and to add $\left(\dfrac{4}{5}\right)^2$ to *both* sides.

Suggested Extensions

Students may extend their knowledge of completing the square by solving the following equations. Since the greatest exponent in each equation is four, students should realize before solving the equation that there are at most four real-number solutions.

1. $x^4 - 4x^2 = 0$ $\{-2, 0, 2\}$
2. $x^2 - 10x - 9 = 0$ $\{5 + \sqrt{34}, 5 - \sqrt{34}\}$
3. $x^4 - 4x^2 + 3 = 0$ $\{-\sqrt{3}, -1, 1, \sqrt{3}\}$

12-3 (pages 567–571)

Key Mathematical Idea

- solving quadratic equations by using the quadratic formula

Teaching Suggestions

The derivation of the quadratic formula on page 567 may be difficult for some students to understand. Nevertheless, it is worthwhile to discuss the derivation step by step. Emphasize that the formula is obtained by completing the square of the general quadratic equation $ax^2 + bx + c = 0$. While students should not be expected to derive the formula, they should memorize it. Encourage students to write the formula every time they use it so that they will avoid errors.

Students often make errors substituting for a, b, and c. Stress the importance of expressing an equation

in the form $ax^2 + bx + c = 0$ before applying the quadratic formula. Students may find it helpful to write a "skeleton form" of the formula as shown below and then to substitute the appropriate values.

$$x = \frac{-(\ ) \pm \sqrt{(\ )^2 - 4(\ )(\ )}}{2(\ )}$$

If a student asks about equations for which $b^2 - 4ac < 0$, point out that such an equation has no *real* roots.

Group Activity

Divide the class into groups of three to five students and give each student a slip of paper showing a single step in the derivation of the quadratic formula. Students may be given more than one slip of paper. Have each group derive the quadratic formula by placing their individual slips of paper in the proper sequence. Students should explain why their step appears next in the solution.

Suggested Extension

1. Have students solve each equation, writing roots in simplest radical form.

    a. $2t^2 - 4t\sqrt{3} + 1 = 0$ $\left\{\dfrac{2\sqrt{3} \pm \sqrt{10}}{2}\right\}$

    b. $\sqrt{2} \cdot y^2 + 5y + 2\sqrt{2} = 0$ $\left\{-\dfrac{\sqrt{2}}{2}, -2\sqrt{2}\right\}$

    c. $x^2 - 4x\sqrt{3} - 6 = 0$ $\{2\sqrt{3} \pm 3\sqrt{2}\}$

2. Ask students to find the value(s) of k for which the equation has exactly one solution.

    a. $2m^2 - km + 3 = 0$ $k = \pm 2\sqrt{6}$
    b. $kv^2 - 6v + k = 0$ $k = \pm 3$

    c. $(k + 1)r^2 + 2kr + (k + 2) = 0$ $k = -\dfrac{2}{3}$

    d. $x^2 + (k + 1)x - k = 0$ $k = -3 \pm 2\sqrt{2}$

12-4 (pages 572–575)

Key Mathematical Idea

- using the discriminant to analyze quadratic equations and functions

Teaching Suggestions

Point out that students have spent a great deal of time studying quadratic equations and quadratic functions. This lesson shows the strong relationship between the two topics. Emphasize that the value of the discriminant tells us the number of roots that $ax^2 + bx + c = 0$ has and also the number of x-intercepts that the parabola $y = ax^2 + bx + c$ has. Be sure students realize that the discriminant equals $b^2 - 4ac$, not $\sqrt{b^2 - 4ac}$.

Be sure to discuss Example 3, on page 573, in which the discriminant is negative. You may want to graph a parabola that lies entirely below the x-axis, such as $y = -x^2 + 2x - 7$, pointing out that its discriminant is also negative.

The chart on page 573 provides a helpful summary of the important facts.

Suggested Extension

This lesson concentrates on finding the point(s) of a parabola for which $y = 0$. We can also consider quadratic inequalities to find points for which

$$y < ax^2 + bx + c \text{ or } y > ax^2 + bx + c.$$

The Extra, pages 581–582, relates the graph of a quadratic function to quadratic inequalities.

12-5 (pages 576–578)

Key Mathematical Idea

- choosing the most appropriate method for solving a quadratic equation

Teaching Suggestions

Be sure students realize that more than one method may be suitable for solving a particular quadratic equation. Encourage students to use the guidelines on page 576 to select a method that will simplify the computations.

Stress that any quadratic equation can be solved by applying the quadratic formula. Students should memorize the quadratic formula.

It may be helpful to assign and/or discuss as many of the A-level and B-level Written Exercises as possi-

ble. These exercises provide the full range of forms of quadratic equations, reinforcing the four methods of solution.

Suggested Extension

The discriminant can be used to determine if a quadratic equation in the form $ax^2 + bx + c = 0$ can be factored or not. If a, b, and c are integers and $b^2 - 4ac$ is greater than zero and a perfect square, the given quadratic equation can be solved by factoring and the solutions will be rational numbers.

Have students determine if the following can be solved by factoring. **1.** yes **2.** yes **3.** no **4.** yes

1. $x^2 + 5x - 14 = 0$ **2.** $12x^2 - 5x - 2 = 0$

3. $4x^2 - 3x - 3 = 0$ **4.** $14x^2 - 25x + 6 = 0$

12-6 (pages 579–581)

Key Mathematical Idea

- solving problems involving quadratic equations

Teaching Suggestions

If needed, have students review the five-step method of solving problems before attempting to write an equation. Be sure to have students check their answers in the original word problem so that they can reject inappropriate roots.

Reading Algebra

As you discuss the example on page 579, point out that Step 4 yields a solution in simplest radical form: $x = -2 \pm \sqrt{29}$. Stress that practical problems require solutions that make sense under the given conditions. In this particular case:

1. An answer in radical form is not useful.
2. Only the positive root makes sense.
3. The answers must be rounded to usable approximations.
4. The check using approximate values cannot be exact.

Emphasize the importance of always going back to the words of the problem as a final test.

Challenge students to solve each equation. As a hint, you may suggest that students rewrite the original equation by multiplying each term by the LCM. Students should check their solutions in the original equation.

1. $\frac{1}{x} = 2 - x$ {1}

2. $\frac{8}{x} + \frac{4}{5 + x} = 2$ {5, −4}

3. $\frac{1}{x} + \frac{4}{x + 3} = 1$ {3, −1}

4. $\frac{3x + 5}{6x + 5} = x - 1$ $\left\{\frac{5}{3}, -1\right\}$

12-7 (pages 584–587)

Key Mathematical Ideas

- solving problems involving quadratic direct variation
- solving problems involving inverse variation as the square

Teaching Suggestions

A simple example of quadratic direct variation is given by the formula for the area of a square, $A = s^2$. Show the class that its graph is half the parabola $y = x^2$.

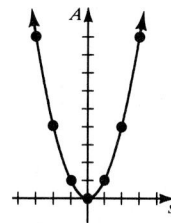

s	$A = s^2$
1	1
2	4
3	9
4	16

Generalize to any relationship of the form $y = kx^2$. Ask students to identify the value of k in the example above.

It may be helpful to graph $y = 2x^2$, $y = 4x^2$, and $y = \frac{1}{4}x^2$ on the chalkboard to review the effect that changes in the value of k have on the graph of $y = kx^2$. Point out that the value of k influences the rate at which y changes with respect to x.

Using Manipulatives

To illustrate another inverse variation, a flashlight can be used to show that illumination decreases as the distance between the flashlight and the lit surface increases.

Students having difficulty visualizing inverse variation involving squares may benefit from the following activity. Obtain two different graduated cylinders from the physics or chemistry department, each with a different radius. Partially fill the cylinder with the greater radius with water. Ask students whether the height of the water will be higher or lower when poured into the second cylinder (higher). You can repeat with different quantities of water. Finally, predict the height before pouring water into the second cylinder. (Formula: $h = \frac{V}{\pi r^2}$, or $h_1 r_1^2 = h_2 r_2^2$)

Suggested Extension

The Application on page 593 illustrates how the illumination of a light source varies inversely as the square of the distance from the light source.

12-8 (pages 588–594)

Key Mathematical Idea

- solving problems involving joint variation and combined variation

Teaching Suggestions

Joint and combined variations are examples of functions of more than one variable. Be sure students understand that joint variation is always direct variation. In combined variation the words "directly" and "inversely" are specified.

Point out a difference between inverse variation and joint variation: in inverse variation, the constant equals the product ($k = xy$) and in joint variation, the constant is a factor of the product ($z = kxy$).

The text shows the proportion method of solving variation problems. It is equally possible to solve these problems by finding the value of k first.

Looking Ahead

This unit provides an overview of probability, statistics, geometry, and numerical trigonometry. The probability lessons present the concepts of sample space and events of random experiments as well as how to evaluate the probabilities of events. The statistics lessons discuss the mean, median, mode, and range of a frequency distribution and how to represent the statistical data by means of stem-and-leaf and box-and-whisker plots. The geometry lessons, building upon the abstract ideas of point and line, explore the properties of angles, triangles, and similar triangles. The final lessons, on trigonometry, develop the skills needed to solve problems using the sine, cosine, and tangent ratios and a trigonometric table. The topics of this unit are introductory, but sufficiently varied for students to see what future mathematics courses have to offer.

Sample Spaces and Events (pages 600–602)

Key Mathematical Idea

- listing the sample space and events for a random experiment

Teaching Suggestions

Discuss the importance of organizing results of an experiment and the need for a precise notation to clarify these results. Stress the intuitive approach in the problems, but require students to use the correct language. In particular, stress the importance of identifying the set of *all possible outcomes* and that it is called the sample space.

You can conduct some random experiments in your classroom to motivate the students. For example, place known numbers of differently colored marbles in an opaque container. Ask the class to identify the sample space and the simple events when one marble is drawn at random. Discuss the sample space when two marbles are chosen at a time and ask students to specify events such as "the two marbles are of different colors."

Probability (pages 603–605)

Key Mathematical Idea

- finding the probability that an event will occur

Teaching Suggestions

Discuss the nature of probability in general and the fact that some probabilities are not of the type considered in this lesson: the probability of rain tomorrow, the probability that Jason will get a hit in his next time at bat. Stress the intuitive idea of probability of an event as a number between 0 and 1. The less likely an event is to occur, the closer the probability is to 0, and the more likely, the closer to 1.

It is not always feasible to write out the sample space (drawing cards from a 52-card deck), but Written Exercise 4, page 605, shows how helpful it is to have it clearly identified.

Using Manipulatives

Give each student a cup and a thumbtack. Ask students to put the thumbtack in the cup, shake it, "pour" the thumbtack onto the desk, and record whether the thumbtack lands point up or point down. After, say, 20 such trials, have students determine the empirical probabilities of the thumbtack's landing point up or point down. Then pool the students' point up and point down counts to obtain probabilities for the entire class. Ask students to hypothesize how these probabilities might change if the head of the thumbtack were wider or if the shaft were longer.

Group Activity

Divide the class into small groups. Have one member of each group secretly create a spinner by drawing a circle, dividing it into sectors (not necessarily of equal area), and numbering each sector. Then, using the tip of a pencil to anchor a paper clip at the center of the circle, the student should spin the paper clip a number of times and announce the number obtained from each spin to the other members of the group. These students should use the sequence of spin results to draw what they think the spinner looks like. After discussing their drawings among themselves, they should compare them with the actual spinner.

Frequency Distributions (pages 606–610)

Key Mathematical Ideas

- working with frequency distributions and histograms
- finding the mean, median, mode, and range of a frequency distribution

Teaching Suggestions

Point out that the mean, median, and mode all measure the "center" of a distribution. Discuss with students situations in which one or more of these statistics is useful. You might want to show students how their grade point average, which is a mean, is calculated. Also point out that the owner of a shoe store would be interested in the mode of shoe sizes sold, since the modal size would require additional inventory. Finally, note that very high or low values can greatly affect the mean; for this reason, a median income or median test score might tell more about the central position for a large group of people than a mean would.

Note that the range uses only two values, the largest and the smallest, to measure the variability of a distribution. Point out that there are other measures of variation that are "stronger" than the range, because they use all the values of a distribution. You might have interested students read the Extra on pages 609–610 to learn about two such measures, variance and standard deviation.

Presenting Statistical Data (pages 611–615)

Key Mathematical Idea

- constructing stem-and-leaf and box-and-whisker plots

Teaching Suggestions

Point out that in a histogram some information is lost: the frequency of the data is shown but the actual values are suppressed. A stem-and-leaf plot is similar to a histogram in shape but all the original data can still be determined.

When students draw a stem-and-leaf plot, have them do so in two steps, first writing the leaves next to the stems without regard to order and then ordering the leaves for each stem. Students should find that this two-step approach is actually faster than trying to write the leaves and order them simultaneously.

When discussing box-and-whisker plots, emphasize that the data must first be arranged in order. Point out that roughly 25% of the data should be less than the first quartile, 50% should be less than the median, and 75% should be less than the third quartile. Also note that the length of the box in a box-and-whisker plot gives the variability in the middle half of the data; this number is called the *interquartile range,* just as the distance between the endpoints of the whiskers is the range.

Have students examine the box-and-whisker plots at the bottom of page 612 to answer questions like "Which set of scores is more dispersed?" (about the same for mathematics and history) and "Which class has the better set of scores?" (history).

Group Activity

Divide the class into small groups and assign to each group a different question for which data needs to be collected. The questions might involve such topics as the height of students, the time they go to bed, the distance they live from school, and the number of minutes they study mathematics each night. Once the groups have collected the data, they can analyze and present the data using statistics and graphs.

Points, Lines, and Angles (pages 616–618)

Key Mathematical Ideas

- representing points, lines, and angles
- measuring and classifying angles

Teaching Suggestions

This lesson presents a few basic geometric ideas. Most of your students will probably be familiar with some, if not all, of the vocabulary. Students often tend to think of points, lines, angles, and planes as concrete objects. Discuss the abstract nature of geometry and geometric figures. For example, lines and planes extend indefinitely, although their representations do not.

Stress the importance of notation in precisely naming figures and their measures. Be sure that students differentiate between $\overleftrightarrow{AB}$, $\overline{AB}$, $\overrightarrow{AB}$, and AB. When introducing the notation for angles, emphasize that the middle letter names the vertex.

Point out that the numbers on a protractor are reference numbers just as they are on a number line. Note that for every ray there is exactly one number between 0 and 180, and for every number between 0 and 180 there is exactly one ray.

Most protractors have two scales, one with 0 on the right and one with 0 on the left. Be sure students know which scale to use when measuring angles.

Reading Algebra

In reading geometric notations, students may encounter some confusion. For example, $\overleftrightarrow{AB}$ is the same as $\overleftrightarrow{BA}$, $\overline{AB}$ is the same as $\overline{BA}$, and $\angle ABC$ is the same as $\angle CBA$; however, $\overrightarrow{AB}$ is *not* the same as $\overrightarrow{BA}$ and $\angle ABC$ is *not* the same as $\angle BCA$. Emphasize the importance of recognizing the symbols and identifying when the order is important.

Pairs of Angles (pages 619–620)

Key Mathematical Idea

- using vertical angles, complementary angles, and supplementary angles

Teaching Suggestions

Draw the diagrams shown at the top of the next column. Challenge students to write an equation to represent each diagram.

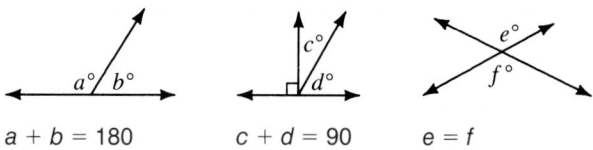

$a + b = 180 \qquad c + d = 90 \qquad e = f$

Use these diagrams and equations to introduce the concepts of supplementary angles, complementary angles, and vertical angles.

You can justify the idea that vertical angles have equal measures by pointing out that in the figure below $x + z = 180$. (Together they form a straight angle.) Also, $y + z = 180$. Since $x = 180 - z$ and $y = 180 - z$, $x = y$ by substitution.

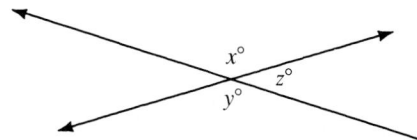

Point out that this lesson uses both geometric and algebraic concepts.

Triangles (pages 621–623)

Key Mathematical Idea

- using properties of general and special triangles

Teaching Suggestions

Be sure students understand the characteristics of a right triangle, an isosceles triangle, and an equilateral triangle. You might ask them questions like "Can a right triangle be isosceles?" (yes), "If a base angle of an isosceles triangle is $x°$, what are the measures of the other two angles?" ($x°$, $(180 - 2x)°$), and "If the perimeter of an equilateral triangle is 48 cm, what is the length of each side?" (16 cm).

Be sure to review the Pythagorean theorem and its converse. Since radicals often result from using the Pythagorean theorem, also review how to simplify radicals.

Using Manipulatives

Have students tear off the corners of a paper triangle to see that they fit together to form a straight angle. (See page 621.)

Similar Triangles (pages 624–626)

Key Mathematical Idea

- solving problems involving similar triangles

Teaching Suggestions

Discuss the idea of similarity as indicating objects with the same shape but not necessarily the same size. Photographs, maps, and scale drawings can provide good intuitive examples of similar figures.

Stress the idea that a statement like $\triangle GHK \sim \triangle STR$ establishes a correspondence and implies that $\frac{GH}{ST} = \frac{HK}{TR} = \frac{GK}{SR}$. Point out the need to write a similarity statement carefully; the statement $\triangle GHK \sim \triangle RST$ establishes a different correspondence than the one above.

Trigonometric Ratios (pages 627–629)

Key Mathematical Idea

- finding the sine, cosine, and tangent of an acute angle

Teaching Suggestions

When discussing the trigonometric ratios presented on page 627, you might mention the mnemonic device "SOHCAHTOA" (Sine: Opposite over Hypotenuse, Cosine: Adjacent over Hypotenuse, Tangent: Opposite over Adjacent).

Remind students that the hypotenuse of a right triangle is always the longest side. Show that this implies that the sine and the cosine of an acute angle must each be less than 1. However, the tangent of an acute angle can be any positive number, as illustrated in Example 1 on page 627.

Point out the use of the Pythagorean theorem in Example 2. Mention that students will need to use the theorem in the Written Exercises.

Finally, draw students' attention to the discussion on page 628 that shows that the values of the trigonometric ratios of an angle depend only on the measure of the angle and not on the size of the triangle that contains the angle.

Using Trigonometric Tables (pages 630–632)

Key Mathematical Idea

- using a trigonometric table to find decimal values for measures of angles

Teaching Suggestions

When you introduce the trigonometric table on page 683, mention the following characteristics:

1. The sine and cosine of an acute angle are always less than 1.
2. As the angle increases from 0° to 90°, the sine increases between 0 and 1 and the cosine decreases between 1 and 0.
3. $\tan 45° = 1$.
4. If $\angle A < 45°$, $\tan A < 1$ and if $\angle A > 45$, $\tan A > 1$.

Point out that there are three exact values in the table: $\sin 30°$, $\tan 45°$, and $\cos 60°$. All other values are approximations to four decimal places.

Problem Solving Using Trigonometry (pages 633–637)

Key Mathematical Idea

- using trigonometric ratios to solve problems

Teaching Suggestions

Encourage students to draw a diagram to solve a trigonometric problem if one is not given. Suggest that it is helpful to draw diagrams that are reasonably accurate. With a little practice, students should be able to draw acute angles of specified measure by using a 45° angle as a guide.

Some students may inadvertently use a vertical ray as a side of an angle of depression. Stress that both an angle of depression and an angle of elevation must have a horizontal ray as one side.

Point out that sometimes one trigonometric ratio is more helpful than another. For instance, to find the value of x in Example 2, one might write $\tan 22° = \frac{166}{x}$, but this is more difficult to solve for x than the equation given in the solution of Example 2.

Algebra

Structure and Method   *Book 1*

Algebra

Structure and Method
Book 1

Richard G. Brown
Mary P. Dolciani
Robert H. Sorgenfrey
William L. Cole

Contributing Authors
Cleo Campbell
Joan MacDonald Piper

Teacher Consultants
Alma Cantu Aguirre
Gail Girvan Gismondi
Celia Lazarski
Ron Pelfrey
Edward M. VanderTook

McDougal Littell
A HOUGHTON MIFFLIN COMPANY
Evanston, Illinois ◆ Boston ◆ Dallas

Authors

Richard G. Brown, Mathematics Teacher, Phillips Exeter Academy, Exeter, New Hampshire

Mary P. Dolciani, formerly Professor of Mathematical Sciences, Hunter College of the City University of New York

Robert H. Sorgenfrey, Professor Emeritus of Mathematics, University of California, Los Angeles

William L. Cole, Associate Professor of Mathematics Education, Michigan State University

Contributing Authors

Cleo Campbell, Coordinator of Mathematics, Anne Arundel County Public Schools, Annapolis, Maryland

Joan MacDonald Piper, Mathematics Editor, Westborough, Massachusetts, and former Mathematics Teacher, Concord Academy, Concord, Massachusetts

Teacher Consultants

Alma Cantu Aguirre, Mathematics Department Chairperson, Thomas Jefferson High School, San Antonio, Texas

Gail Girvan Gismondi, Mathematics Teacher, Log College Middle School, Warminster, Pennsylvania

Celia Lazarski, Mathematics Teacher, Glenbard North High School, Carol Stream, Illinois

Ron Pelfrey, Mathematics Coordinator, Fayette County School, Lexington, Kentucky

Edward M. VanderTook, former Assistant Director for Instruction, Math/Science/Computer Unit, Tucson Unified School District, Tucson, Arizona

The authors wish to thank **David L. Myers**, Computer Coordinator and Mathematics Teacher, Winsor School, Boston, Massachusetts, for writing the Portfolio Projects.

Printed in U.S.A.

ISBN: 0-395-97722-3

123456789-VJM-03 02 01 00 99

Contents

1 Introduction to Algebra

2 Working with Real Numbers

3 Solving Equations and Problems

4 Polynomials

5 Factoring Polynomials

6 Fractions

7 Applying Fractions

8 Introduction to Functions

9 Systems of Linear Equations

10 Inequalities

11 Rational and Irrational Numbers

12 Quadratic Functions

Looking Ahead

Using Technology with This Course

There are three types of optional technology material in this text: Computer Key-In features, Computer Exercises, and suggestions for using graphing calculators and software to explore concepts and confirm results.

The Computer Key-In features can be used by students without previous programming experience. They include a program that students can run to explore an algebra topic covered in the chapter. Some writing of programs may be required in some of these features.

The optional Computer Exercises are designed for students who have some familiarity with programming in BASIC. Students are usually asked to write one or more programs related to the lesson just presented.

The suggestions for applying computer graphing techniques are appropriate for use with a graphing calculator or with graphing software such as *Algebra Plotter Plus* or *McDougal Littell Mathpack*.

Calculator Key-In features and certain exercise sets also suggest appropriate use of scientific and graphing calculators with this course.

Reading Your Algebra Book

An algebra book requires a different type of reading than a novel or a short story. Every sentence in a math book is full of information and logically linked to the surrounding sentences. You should read the sentences carefully and think about their meaning. As you read, remember that algebra builds upon itself; for example, the method of multiplying binomials that you'll study on page 200 will be useful to you on page 544. Be sure to read with a pencil and paper: Do calculations, draw sketches, and take notes.

Vocabulary

You'll learn many new words in algebra. Some, such as *polynomial* and *parabola,* are mathematical in nature. Others, such as *power* and *proof,* are used in everyday speech but have different meanings when used in algebra. Important words whose meanings you'll learn are printed in **heavy type.** They are also listed at the beginning of each Self-Test. If you don't recall the meaning of a word, you can look it up in the Glossary or the Index at the back of the book. The Glossary will give you a definition, and the Index will give you page references for more information.

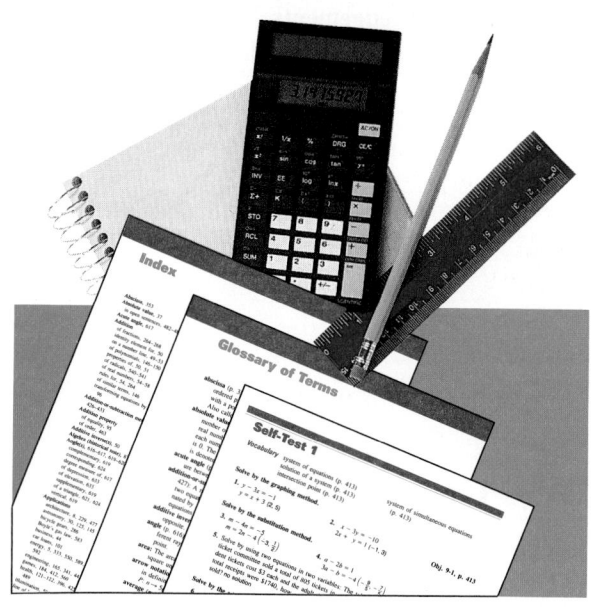

Symbols

Algebra, and mathematics in general, has its own symbolic language. You must be able to read these symbols in order to understand algebra. For example, $|x| > 2$ means "the absolute value of x is greater than 2." If you aren't sure what a symbol means, check the list of symbols on page xvi.

Diagrams

Throughout this book you'll find many diagrams. They contain information that will help you understand the concepts under discussion. Study the diagrams carefully as you read the text that accompanies them.

$$x(x+3) = x^2 + 3x$$

Displayed Material

Throughout this book important information is displayed in gray boxes. This information includes properties, definitions, methods, and summaries. Be sure to read and understand the material in these boxes. You should find these boxes useful when reviewing for tests and exams.

> If a is a real number and m and n are positive integers, then $a^m \cdot a^n = a^{m+n}$.

This book also contains worked-out examples. They will help you in doing many of the exercises and problems.

Example   Simplify $x^3 \cdot x^5$.

Solution $x^3 \cdot x^5 = x^{3+5} = x^8$ **Answer**

Reading Aids

Throughout this book you will find sections called Reading Algebra. These sections deal with such topics as independent study and problem solving strategies. They will help you become a more effective reader and problem solver.

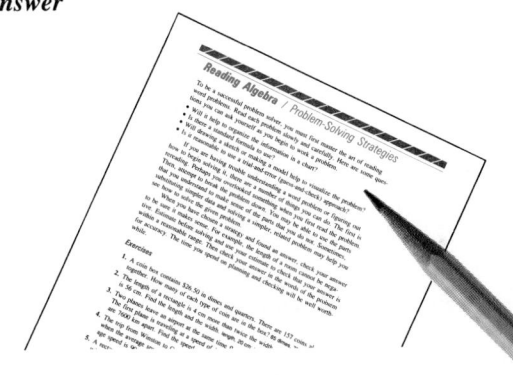

Exercises, Tests, and Reviews

Each lesson in this book is followed by Oral, Written, and Mixed Review Exercises. Lessons may also include Problems and optional Computer Exercises. Answers for all Mixed Review Exercises and for selected Written Exercises, Problems, and Computer Exercises are given at the back of this book.

Within each chapter you will find Self-Tests that you can use to check your progress. Answers for all Self-Tests are also given at the back of this book.

Each chapter concludes with a Chapter Summary that lists important ideas from the chapter, a Chapter Review in multiple-choice format, and a Chapter Test. Lesson numbers in the margins of the Review and Test indicate which lesson a group of questions covers.

Reading Algebra/Symbols

		Page			Page
·	× (times)	1	(a, b)	ordered pair whose first component is a and second component is b	349
=	equals, is equal to	2	$f(x)$	f of x, the value of f at x	379
≠	is not equal to	2	≥	is greater than or equal to	457
( )	parentheses—a grouping symbol	2	≤	is less than or equal to	457
[ ]	brackets—a grouping symbol	6	∩	the intersection of	476
π	pi, a number approximately equal to $\frac{22}{7}$	8	∪	the union of	476
∈	is a member of, belongs to	10	≈	is approximately equal to	514
∴	therefore	11	$\sqrt{}$	principal square root	517
$\stackrel{?}{=}$	is this statement true?	27	$P(A)$	probability of event A	603
−	negative	31	$\overleftrightarrow{AB}$	line AB	616
+	positive	31	$\overline{AB}$	segment AB	616
<	is less than	32	AB	the length of $\overline{AB}$	616
>	is greater than	32	$\overrightarrow{AB}$	ray AB	616
$-a$	opposite or additive inverse of a	36	∠	angle	616
$|a|$	absolute value of a	37	°	degree(s)	617
$\frac{1}{b}$	reciprocal or multiplicative inverse of b	79	△	triangle	621
∅	empty set, null set	117	~	is similar to	624
$a:b$	ratio of a to b	287	$\cos A$	cosine of A	627
			$\sin A$	sine of A	627
			$\tan A$	tangent of A	627

Reading Algebra/*Table of Measures*

Metric Units

Length		
	10 millimeters (mm)	= 1 centimeter (cm)
	100 centimeters 1000 millimeters	= 1 meter (m)
	1000 meters	= 1 kilometer (km)

Area		
	100 square millimeters (mm²)	= 1 square centimeter (cm²)
	10,000 square centimeters	= 1 square meter (m²)

Using proper notation:

Metric Units

Length
10 millimeters (mm) = 1 centimeter (cm)
100 centimeters } = 1 meter (m)
1000 millimeters }
1000 meters = 1 kilometer (km)

Area
100 square millimeters (mm^2) = 1 square centimeter (cm^2)
10,000 square centimeters = 1 square meter (m^2)

Volume
1000 cubic millimeters (mm^3) = 1 cubic centimeter (cm^3)
1,000,000 cubic centimeters = 1 cubic meter (m^3)

Liquid Capacity
1000 milliliters (mL) = 1 liter (L)
1000 cubic centimeters = 1 liter

Mass
1000 milligrams (mg) = 1 gram (g)
1000 grams = 1 kilogram (kg)

Temperature in degrees Celsius (°C)
0°C = freezing point of water
100°C = boiling point of water

United States Customary Units

Length
12 inches (in.) = 1 foot (ft)
36 inches } = 1 yard (yd)
3 feet }
5280 feet } = 1 mile (mi)
1760 yards }

Area
144 square inches (in.²) = 1 square foot (ft^2)
9 square feet = 1 square yard (yd^2)

Volume
1728 cubic inches (in.³) = 1 cubic foot (ft^3)
27 cubic feet = 1 cubic yard (yd^3)

Liquid Capacity
16 fluid ounces (fl oz) = 1 pint (pt)
2 pints = 1 quart (qt)
4 quarts = 1 gallon (gal)

Weight
16 ounces (oz) = 1 pound (lb)

Temperature in degrees Fahrenheit (°F)
32°F = freezing point of water
212°F = boiling point of water

Time

60 seconds (s) = 1 minute (min)
60 minutes = 1 hour (h)

1 Introduction to Algebra

Objectives

1-1 To simplify numerical expressions and evaluate algebraic expressions.

1-2 To simplify expressions with and without grouping symbols.

1-3 To find solution sets of equations over a given domain.

1-4 To translate phrases into variable expressions.

1-5 To translate word sentences into equations.

1-6 To translate simple word problems into equations.

1-7 To use the five-step plan to solve word problems over a given domain.

1-8 To graph real numbers on a number line and to compare real numbers.

1-9 To use opposites and absolute values.

Assignment Guide

See p. T59 for Key to the format of the Assignment Guide

Day	Minimum Course		Average Course		Maximum Course	
1	**1-1** S	3/1–37 odd 5/*Mixed Review*	**1-1** S	3/1–47 odd 5/*Mixed Review*	**1-1** **1-2** S	3/3–48 mult. of 3 8/3–45 mult. of 3 9/*Mixed Review*
2	**1-2** S	8/1–29 odd, 35, 36 9/*Mixed Review*	**1-2** S	8/1–33 odd, 37–39 9/*Mixed Review*	**1-3** S	11/1–25 odd, 33–42 12/*Mixed Review*
3	**1-3** S	11/1–29 odd 12/*Mixed Review*	**1-3** S	11/1–39 odd 12/*Mixed Review*	**1-4** S R	16/2–42 even, 51–53 18/*Mixed Review* 13/*Self-Test 1*
4	**1-4** R	16/1–25 odd 13/*Self-Test 1*	**1-4** R	16/1–41 odd 13/*Self-Test 1*	**1-5** S	20/2–36 even 22/*Mixed Review*
5	**1-4** S **1-5**	17/27–41 odd 18/*Mixed Review* 20/1–7	**1-4** S **1-5**	18/42–52 even 18/*Mixed Review* 20/2–16 even	**1-6** S	24/*P:* 2–18 even, 19–22 26/*Mixed Review*
6	**1-5** S	21/9–29 odd 22/*Mixed Review*	**1-5** S	21/17–35 odd 22/*Mixed Review*	**1-7** S	28/*P:* 2–14 even, 16–18 29/*Mixed Review*
7	**1-6**	24/*P:* 1–12	**1-6**	24/*P:* 1–18	**1-8** S R	33/3–57 mult. of 3 35/*Mixed Review* 30/*Self-Test 2*
8	**1-6** S	25/*P:* 13–19 odd 26/*Mixed Review*	**1-6** S	25/*P:* 19–22 26/*Mixed Review*	**1-9** S	38/2–38 even, 43–45 39/*Mixed Review*
9	**1-7** S	28/*P:* 1–10 29/*Mixed Review*	**1-7** S R	28/*P:* 1–15 odd 29/*Mixed Review* 30/*Self-Test 2*	*Prepare for Chapter Test* R EP	 39/*Self-Test 3* 41/*Chapter Review* 639/*Skills;* 665/*Problems*
10	**1-8** S R	33/3–36 mult. of 3 35/*Mixed Review* 30/*Self-Test 2*	**1-8** S **1-9**	33/3–48 mult. of 3 35/*Mixed Review* 38/3–42 mult. of 3	*Administer Chapter 1 Test* R	 43/*Maintaining Skills*

Assignment Guide (continued)

Day	Minimum Course	Average Course	Maximum Course
11	**1-9** 38/3–33 mult. of 3 **S** 34/39–49 odd 39/*Mixed Review*	*Prepare for Chapter Test* **R** 39/*Self-Test 3* 41/*Chapter Review* **EP** 639/*Skills;* 665/*Problems*	
12	*Prepare for Chapter Test* **R** 39/*Self-Test 3* 41/*Chapter Review* **EP** 639/*Skills* 665/*Problems*	*Administer Chapter 1 Test* **R** 43/*Maintaining Skills*	
13	*Administer Chapter 1 Test* **R** 43/*Maintaining Skills*		

Supplementary Materials Guide

For Use with Lesson	Practice Masters	Tests	Study Guide (Reteaching)	Resource Book		
				Tests	Practice Exercises	Applications (A) Enrichment (E) Thinking Skl. (TS)
1-1			pp. 1–2	pp.1–5		p. 178 (A)
1-2			pp. 3–4		p. 79	
1-3	Sheet 1		pp. 5–6			
1-4			pp. 7–8			
1-5		Test 1	pp. 9–10			
1-6			pp. 11–12			
1-7	Sheet 2		pp. 13–14		p. 80	pp. 220–221 (TS)
1-8			pp. 15–16			
1-9	Sheet 3	Test 2	pp. 17–18		p. 81	
Chapter 1	Sheet 4	Tests 3, 4		pp. 6–9		p. 190 (E)

Overhead Visuals

For Use with Lesson	Visual	Title
1-8	A	Multi-Use Packet 1
1-8	B	Multi-Use Packet 2

Software

Software	Computer Activities	Test Generator
Software	Activities 1–4	189 test items
For Use with Lessons	1-1, 1-4, 1-8	all lessons

Strategies for Teaching

Communication

Effective communication involves skills in four areas—listening, speaking, reading, and writing. Students need to be able to understand directions and follow them accurately, to explain processes and concepts, to read with understanding, and to express their ideas clearly in writing.

The symbolism of algebra is a powerful language in itself, and students need much experience in using it if they are to realize its value as a concise way of expressing ideas that would require many words. One of the current goals of mathematics education is to bring students to a point where they can use the language of algebra as a natural way of expressing mathematical ideas, and not as a foreign language.

Chapter 1 introduces students to the terminology that shapes algebraic thought: variables, grouping symbols, and the language of equations. Below are some specific strategies for strengthening students' communication skills and their understanding of the language of algebra.

1-1 Variables

The concept of a variable may be difficult for some students to grasp. You may find it helpful to use the chapter opener photo on page xviii to stress the idea that $0.44 \times d$ is a *general* expression for water pressure, which depends upon how the depth, d, *varies*. Ask your students for other examples of variable expressions. Possibilities include the variable expression for the total cost of buying n items at a fixed price p per item or the variable expression for the perimeter of a square having sides of length s.

Students are generally more willing to adopt the convention of omitting the multiplication symbol in variable expressions once they realize how easily a handwritten multiplication symbol can be mistaken for the variable x or vice versa.

1-2 Grouping Symbols

Emphasize that mathematics is a language that attempts to express statements as concisely as possible. Thus, multiplication symbols are often omitted from expressions when grouping symbols are used.

Point out that brackets are generally used in expressions that already contain parentheses to make them easier to read.

1-3 Equations

Students may have learned synonyms for some of the terms introduced in this lesson, such as *element*, rather than *member, of a set*, and *member*, rather than *side, of an equation*. This text avoids referring to *members* of an equation because of possible confusion with *members* of a set.

1-4 Translating Words into Symbols

Students may initially have trouble expressing a number in terms of another number represented by a variable when their sum or product is known (see Exercises 31 and 32 on page 17). To guide their thinking, ask your students a question like "What number and 6 have a sum of 17?" Then ask them what they did to the sum to find the unknown number.

Sometimes students wonder why they can't write $5 < x$ for "five less than a number." Emphasize that "five less than a number" is a phrase; there is no verb; it does not express a complete thought. On the other hand, $5 < x$ (read "five *is* less than x") is a sentence.

Be sure to point out that the word *of* in a word phrase expressing relationships between numbers indicates multiplication. In fact, it would be helpful at this time to develop a list of various ways the symbols for all four operations can be verbalized.

1-5 Translating Sentences into Equations

Emphasize that an English sentence must contain a verb and that in sentences about numerical relationships, that verb will often be some form of the verb *to be*. If your students can substitute *is equal to* for *is*, they have identified the part of the sentence that should be represented by the equality symbol.

1-6 Translating Problems into Equations

Remind students that mathematics is a language that people throughout the world use. Have your students think of themselves as translators who translate English into mathematical symbols, and vice versa.

1-7 A Problem Solving Plan

Step 1 of the five-step problem solving plan tells the student to read the problem carefully. Some components of careful reading are: (1) reading the problem at least twice, once to get a "feel" for the problem and once to concentrate on the details; (2) recognizing what is unknown, that is, what needs to be "found"; (3) selecting the essential facts from the statement of the problem and organizing them in a chart, a sketch, or some other format; and (4) questioning the given information with respect to its completeness (Are relevant facts missing?) and its consistency (Do any facts contradict each other?). Students who read carefully will find that problem solving becomes easier.

References to Strategies

PE: Pupil's Edition   **TE:** Teacher's Edition   **RB:** Resource Book

Problem Solving Strategies

PE: pp. 26–29 (Checking solutions); pp. 9, 35 (Recognizing patterns); pp. 23–24, 27–28 (Using equations; using five-step plan; using a sketch, diagram, or model)
TE: p. T79 (Sugg. Extension)

Applications

PE: pp. xviii, 5, 8, 17, 18, 22, 28–30
TE: pp. xviii, 15
RB: p. 178

Nonroutine Problems

PE: p. 9 (Exs. 39–46, Challenge); p. 12 (Exs. 39–46); p. 29 (Probs. 16–18); p. 35 (Exs. 55–58, Challenge); p. 39 (Ex. 45)
RB: p. 190

Communication

PE: p. 26 (Reading Algebra); p. 39 (Ex. 45, convincing argument)
TE: p. T79, T81, 20 (Reading Algebra)

Explorations

PE: pp. 5, 685

Thinking Skills

PE: pp. 9, 35 (Reasoning and inferencing)
TE: pp. 9, 25
RB: pp. 220–221

Connections

PE: p. 30 (Astronomy); pp. 10, 31-32 (Discrete Math); pp. 4, 8–9, 15, 19–22, 29 (Geometry); p. 18 (Health); p. 40 (Language Arts); p. xviii (Physics)

Using Technology

PE: p. 7 (Calculator Exs.); p. 13 (Calculator Key-In)
RB: pp. 213–219 (Summary of BASIC)
Computer Activities: pp. 1–9

Using Manipulatives/Models

TE: p. T80 (Lesson 1-6)
Overhead Visuals: A, B

Cooperative Learning

TE: p. T81 (Lesson 1-7)

Teaching Resources

For use in implementing the teaching strategies referenced on the previous page.

Application
Resource Book, p. 178

Application—Diving Competition Scoring (for use with Chapter 1)

Many contests have more than one judge—skating, diving, surfing, and skiing, for example. Each judge evaluates an individual's performance and awards a point value for the performance. Often, the high and low scores are disregarded and the sum of the remaining scores, called the *aggregate score*, is the final score awarded for the performance. In some sports contests, diving for example, individual performances vary in difficulty level and therefore a numerical difficulty factor is assigned to each performance. An individual's final score from one judge is the product of the difficulty factor and the judge's score.

A diving competition is judged by 7 judges using a scale from 0 to 10 in half-point increments. The degree of difficulty is rated from 1.2 to 3.5 in increments of one-tenth of a point. Thus, a dive with a degree of difficulty of 2 scoring 9.5 with a single judge would be worth 19 points to the diver. Use the information in the table below to answer the questions that follow.

Diver	Difficulty Factor	1	2	Judges 3	4	5	6	7	Final Aggregate Score
A	2.4	6.5	7.0	8.0	7.5	6.5	6.0	7.0	
B	2.7	8.5	9.5	9.0	8.0	8.0	7.5	8.0	
C	3.1	4.0	5.0	5.5	5.0	5.0	4.0	4.5	
D	2.6	7.5	8.5	8.5	8.5	8.5	8.5	8.5	

1. Disregarding the highest and lowest scores for each diver, find the final aggregate score for each diver and enter this information in the table above.

2. Which diver placed first? _____ What was the winning score? _____

3. Which diver placed last? _____ What was the lowest score? _____

4. What is the highest possible score for a dive with a degree of difficulty of 1.5? _____

5. If a diver needs a score of 89 to take the lead, can that be accomplished in one dive, assuming the dive is performed perfectly? _____

6. What is the highest possible score a diver can make with one dive? _____

7. What is the lowest possible score a diver can make with one dive? _____

8. Is a score of zero likely? _____

Enrichment/Nonroutine Problems
Resource Book, p. 190

Puzzles (For use with Chapter 1 of text)

1. Three boxes are in a room. You know that one contains apples, one contains oranges, and one contains a mixture of apples and oranges, but you don't know the contents of the specific boxes. The boxes are labeled "apples," "oranges," and "apples and oranges," but each box has the wrong label on it. You must identify the contents of each box by picking only one piece of fruit from only one box. You are not allowed to feel the fruit! How can you identify the contents of each box?

_____

2. Susan Teacher, John Writer, and Mary Potter work as a teacher, a writer, and a potter. No one, however, works at the occupation that corresponds to his or her last name. Each person has a child with the same last name that assists one of the other two. No child works at the occupation that corresponds to his or her last name. If John Writer is not a potter, what does Susan Teacher's child do?

3. You probably know someone who will be x years old in the year x^2. When was that person born?

4. In a set of eight coins, seven weigh the same amount and one is lighter than the others. How can you find the lighter coin in only two weighings using a pair of balance scales?

_____

5. Suppose the following statements are true.
   It takes a minimum of four United States coins to buy an apple.
   To buy two apples, you need a minimum of six coins.
   To buy three apples you need no more than two coins.
   How much does the apple cost?

_____

6. This 6×8 rectangle has just as many square tiles along its border as there are square tiles in the interior—namely, 24. Can you find any other rectangle that has as many square tiles along its border as there are in its interior? If so, name it.

Thinking Skills
Resource Book, p. 220

Thinking Skills in the Study of Algebra (For use after Chapter 1)

Here are some thinking skills you'll be using as you study algebra. Use your skills to answer the questions.

Recalling knowledge || You'll be using facts, formulas, and ideas that you've already learned in your study of mathematics.

1. Describe a rectangle. _____

2. What is the formula for the perimeter of a rectangle? _____

3. What is the formula for the area of a rectangle? _____

Interpreting information || You'll be reading information about a problem situation. You'll be trying to make sense of the information, translating it into mathematical terms, and perhaps organizing it in a chart.

4. If the length of a rectangle is twice the width w, write a variable expression in terms of w for:
   a. the length _____ b. the perimeter _____ c. the area _____

5. Complete the chart at the right to organize the following information:
   The length of a kitchen is 2 ft more than the width, which is w ft. The furnace room beneath the kitchen is 1 ft shorter and 1 ft narrower than the kitchen.

   Labels →
   ↓

Applying concepts || You'll be recalling what you've already learned and then transferring or extending the ideas to new situations.

6. What is the cost of a 9 ft by 12 ft rug that sells for $12.99/ft²? _____

7. If you budget $600 for a 6 ft by 9 ft rug, what is the most you can pay per square foot? _____

Reasoning and drawing inferences || You'll be making conjectures, gathering evidence, reaching conclusions, and defending your conclusions.

8. A carpenter intends to build a rectangular frame for a sandbox. He cuts four boards so that opposite sides of the frame will have equal length. Will this guarantee a rectangle when the boards are nailed together? Explain.

9. Suppose the carpenter of Exercise 8, after building the frame, measures the distances between diagonally opposite corners and finds them to be equal. Does this guarantee that the frame is rectangular? Explain.

(continued)

Thinking Skills
Resource Book, p. 221

Thinking Skills (Chapter 1) (continued)

Analysis || You'll be looking at mathematical objects in detail. You'll try to find similarities, differences, and patterns in data, in mathematical expressions, and in problem types. You'll also be looking for relationships between ideas.

10. Suppose a farmer has 160 ft of wire fencing and wants to create a rectangular pen. The length and width of the pen can vary, however.

Length (ft)	Width (ft)	Area (ft²)
10		
20		
30		
40		
50		
60		
70		

   a. Complete the table at the right to determine the areas enclosed by rectangular pens having variable dimensions but a constant perimeter of 160 ft.
   b. From the table, what are the dimensions of the pen enclosing the greatest area?
   c. Is there anything special about your answer to part (b)?

Synthesis || You'll be combining ideas to generate a new idea and combining steps to generate a new result.

11. Find the area of the ground floor of a house with dimensions shown at the right.

12. Describe a general procedure for finding the area of the ground floor of any house having outer walls that are straight and meet at right angles.

Spatial perception || You'll be picturing how three-dimensional objects look, perhaps from different sides. You'll also be visualizing moves in space.

13. Indicate by letter which of the patterns shown at the right can be folded along the dashed lines to form completely closed cubes.

e

Communication
Study Guide, p. 9

1–5 Translating Sentences into Equations

Objective: To translate word sentences into equations.

Example 1 Twice the sum of a number and 3 is twelve.

Translation $2 \cdot \qquad (n + 3) \qquad = 12$

Example 2 The sum of one half of the number x and 10 is 24.

Translation $\frac{1}{2}x + 10 \qquad = 24$

Match the sentence in the first column with the corresponding equation in the second column.

1. Three more than twice a number is nine.
2. Two less than three times a number is nine.
3. Three times the number which is two less than x is nine.
4. Two times the number which is three less than x is nine.
5. Two times the quantity three more than x is nine.
6. Three less than the product of two and x is nine.
7. Two decreased by three times a number is nine.
8. Three times the quantity two decreased by x is nine.

a. $2 - 3x = 9$
b. $3(x - 2) = 9$
c. $2x + 3 = 9$
d. $2(x + 3) = 9$
e. $3(2 - x) = 9$
f. $2(x - 3) = 9$
g. $2x - 3 = 9$
h. $3x - 2 = 9$

Translate each sentence into an equation.

9. One half of a number is four.
10. Three more than a number is eight.
11. Six less than a number is nine.
12. Two less than three times a number is eleven.
13. Twice a number is 12 more than five times the number.
14. The number x is seven more than one fourth of itself.
15. Five less than twice a number is 15.
16. Two times the quantity x minus 1 is 12.
17. Eleven more than twice x is five less than x.
18. Nine times x is twice the sum of x and five.

Vocabulary

Formulas Equations that state rules about relationships. Examples:

$A = lw$ **Area of rectangle** = length of rectangle × width of rectangle
$P = 2l + 2w$ **Perimeter of rectangle** = (2 × length) + (2 × width)
$D = rt$ **Distance traveled** = rate × time traveled
$C = np$ **Cost** = number of items × price per item

9

Communication
Study Guide, p. 10

1–5 Translating Sentences into Equations *(continued)*

Example 3 Use the figure and the information below it to write an equation involving x.

Solution Perimeter = the sum of the lengths of the sides.
$20 = 5 + 7 + x$
$20 = 12 + x$

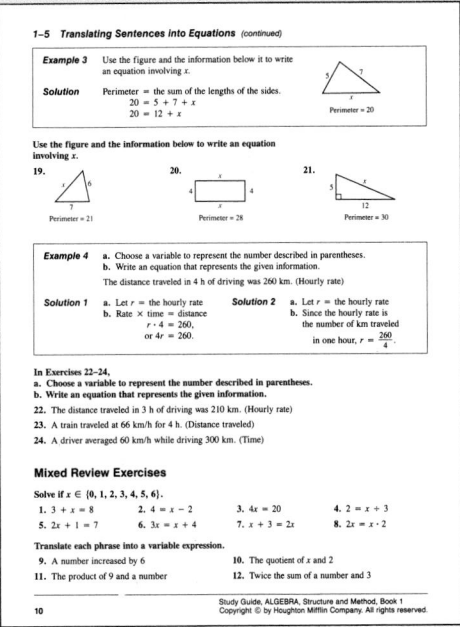

Perimeter = 20

Use the figure and the information below to write an equation involving x.

19. Perimeter = 21   20. Perimeter = 28   21. Perimeter = 30

Example 4 a. Choose a variable to represent the number described in parentheses.
b. Write an equation that represents the given information.

The distance traveled in 4 h of driving was 260 km. (Hourly rate)

Solution 1 a. Let r = the hourly rate
b. Rate × time = distance
$r \cdot 4 = 260$,
or $4r = 260$.

Solution 2 a. Let r = the hourly rate
b. Since the hourly rate is the number of km traveled in one hour, $r = \frac{260}{4}$

In Exercises 22–24,
a. Choose a variable to represent the number described in parentheses.
b. Write an equation that represents the given information.

22. The distance traveled in 3 h of driving was 210 km. (Hourly rate)
23. A train traveled at 66 km/h for 4 h. (Distance traveled)
24. A driver averaged 60 km/h while driving 300 km. (Time)

Mixed Review Exercises

Solve if $x \in \{0, 1, 2, 3, 4, 5, 6\}$.

1. $3 + x = 8$ 2. $4 = x - 2$ 3. $4x = 20$ 4. $2 = x + 3$
5. $2x + 1 = 7$ 6. $3x = x + 4$ 7. $x + 3 = 2x$ 8. $2x = x \cdot 2$

Translate each phrase into a variable expression.

9. A number increased by 6
10. The quotient of x and 2
11. The product of 9 and a number
12. Twice the sum of a number and 3

Using Technology
Resource Book, p. 213

Summary of BASIC

BASIC is one of the so-called "higher-level" languages in which programs may be written for computers. It is translated by a *compiler* or an *interpreter* inside the computer into a "machine language" that tells the computer what to do.

BASIC is essentially linear in character. A BASIC program contains *statements* that are numbered in succession. The numbering may be 1, 2, 3, . . ., but it is customary to use 10, 20, 30, . . . so that additional statements can be inserted if necessary. The computer follows the statements in numerical order and carries out the instruction in each statement as the computer comes to it.

The END statement

In some versions of BASIC, the last statement of a program must be an END statement. In other versions, no END statement is needed.

Besides having statements found within programs, BASIC has several *commands* that operate on programs. Since commands are not part of any program, they are not given line numbers.

The RUN command

The RUN command tells the computer to execute (carry out) a program.

The LIST command

The LIST command tells the computer to display the statements in numerical order. This is especially useful after changes have been made in a program and you want to see a "clean" copy of it.

The symbols for operations in BASIC are:

+ for addition   * for multiplication
− for subtraction   / for division
( ) for grouping   ↑ or ^ for raising to a power

The same order-of-operations rules are followed as in algebra.

Other symbols used in BASIC are:

= for *is equal to*   < for *is less than*
> for *is greater than*   < > for *is not equal to*
< = for *is less than or equal to*   > = for *is greater than or equal to*

Very large and very small numbers are expressed in E-notation, which is a version of scientific notation. For example, 1.002E + 09 means 1.002×10^9, and 0.000001 would be written as 1E − 06.

BASIC handles variables much as you do in algebra. A variable can be denoted by a single letter, a letter followed by a digit, or possibly other combinations of symbols as allowed for the various versions of BASIC. Values are given to variables, and operations are performed on them.

(continued)

USING TECHNOLOGY   213

Using Technology
Computer Activities, p. 8

ACTIVITY 4. *Dividing a Segment* *(for use with Section 1-8)*

Directions: Write all answers in the spaces provided.

PROBLEM

Given the coordinates of the endpoints of a segment on a number line, divide the segment into n equal parts.

PROGRAM

```
10  PRINT "WHAT ARE THE COORDINATES OF THE ENDPOINTS: A, B";
20  INPUT A, B
30  PRINT "DIVIDE THE SEGMENT INTO HOW MANY PARTS";
40  INPUT N
50  PRINT "THE COORDINATES, INCLUDING ORIGINAL ENDPOINTS, ARE:"
60  FOR I = A TO B STEP (B − A) / N
70  PRINT I,
80  NEXT I
90  END
```

PROGRAM CHECK

Type in the program. To test whether you entered it correctly, run the program. Enter 1, 3 after the first question, and 4 after the second question. The computer should print

THE COORDINATES, INCLUDING ORIGINAL ENDPOINTS, ARE:
1   1.5   2   2.5   3

ANALYSIS

The results obtained in the program check indicate that points with coordinates 1.5, 2, and 2.5 divide the segment with endpoints 1 and 3 into 4 equal parts.

USING THE PROGRAM

Run the program to solve the following problems.

1. Find points that divide the segment with endpoints −1 and 3 into 5 equal parts.

2. Find the midpoint of the segment with endpoints:

   a. 2 and 13
   b. 16 and 38
   c. 12 and −6
   d. 9 and −9
   e. −7 and −15
   f. 4 and −23

(continued)

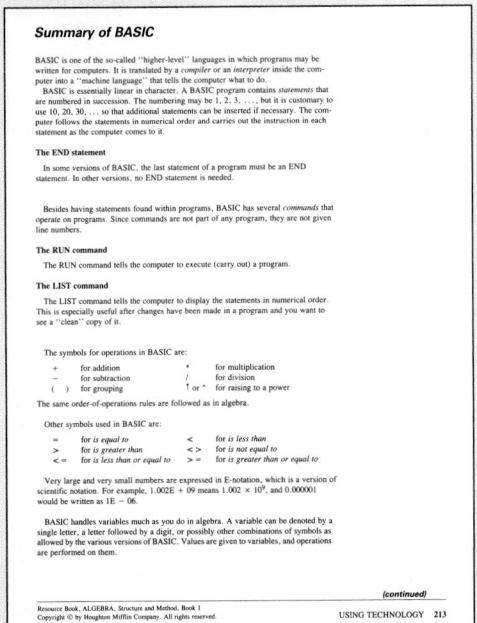

f

Application

When more than a few feet below the surface of the water, you have probably noticed pressure in your ears. On the surface, only the atmosphere is pressing on you. Below the surface, the water begins to press on you, and the atmosphere continues to push on you as it pushes on the surface of the water.

When diving, the volume of air in your lungs gets squeezed by these forces. To keep your lungs from collapsing, you need more air pressure in them. A SCUBA (Self-Contained Underwater Breathing Apparatus) helps accomplish this. When the depth is great enough to provide twice the normal atmospheric pressure, the SCUBA equipment provides twice the amount of air to maintain the same volume inside your lungs.

Research Activities

Students can interview a local scuba diving instructor about the mathematics of scuba diving and report to the class.

Students can write a paper or give an oral report about the effects of water pressure on fish and submarines, or about the effects of air pressure on airplane cabins. They might also research the mathematics behind the decompression tables used by divers. Students who would like to learn more about the history of diving can study hard hat or saturation diving.

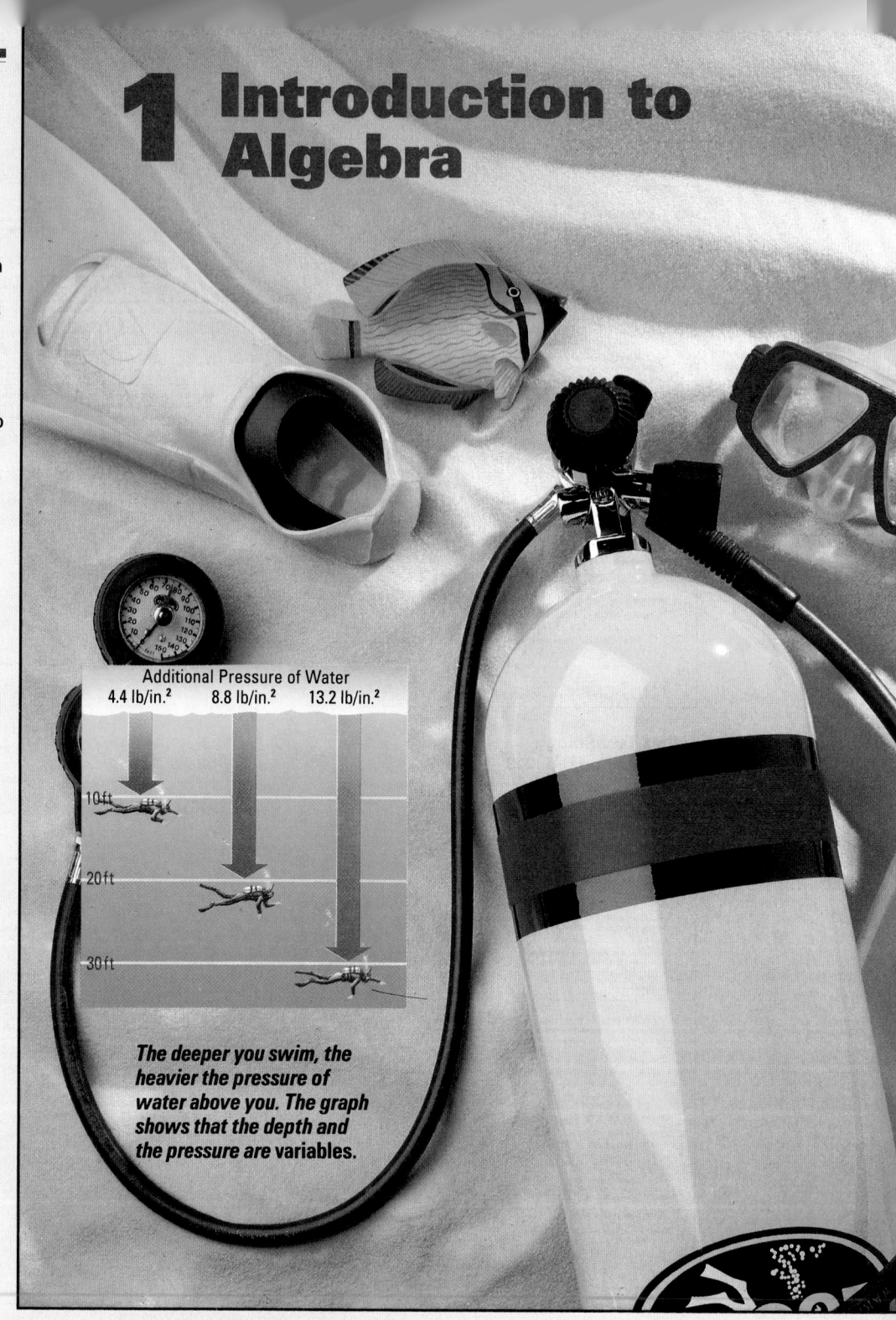

Additional Pressure of Water
4.4 lb/in.²   8.8 lb/in.²   13.2 lb/in.²

10 ft

20 ft

30 ft

The deeper you swim, the heavier the pressure of water above you. The graph shows that the depth and the pressure are variables.

Variables and Equations

1-1 Variables

Objective To simplify numerical expressions and evaluate algebraic expressions.

When you go to an ocean beach, you may find small shops that rent recreational equipment, such as scuba gear, surfboards, and snorkeling gear. Suppose the rental charge for snorkeling gear is $4.50 per hour. The amount you'll pay for using the gear depends on the amount of time you have it.

Number of hours	Rental charge
1	$4.50 × 1 = $4.50
2	$4.50 × 2 = $9.00
3	$4.50 × 3 = $13.50
4	$4.50 × 4 = $18.00

The rental charge follows this pattern:

$$\text{Rental charge} = \$4.50 \times \text{number of hours}$$
$$= \$4.50 \times h$$

The letter h stands for the hours shown in the table: 1, 2, 3, or 4. Also, h can stand for other hours not in the table. We call h a *variable*.

A **variable** is a symbol used to represent one or more numbers. The numbers are called **values of the variable.** An expression that contains a variable, such as the expression $4.50 \times h$, is called a **variable expression.** An expression, such as 4.50×4, that names a particular number is called a **numerical expression,** or **numeral.**

Another way to indicate multiplication is to use a raised dot, for example, $4.50 \cdot 4$. In algebra, products that contain a variable are usually written without the multiplication sign because it looks too much like the letter x, which is often used as a variable.

$$19 \times n \quad \text{can be written as} \quad 19n.$$
$$a \times b \quad \text{can be written as} \quad ab.$$
$$\frac{1}{2} \times x \quad \text{can be written as} \quad \frac{1}{2}x.$$

The number named by a numerical expression is called the **value of the expression.** Since the expressions $4 + 2$ and 6 name the same number, they have the same value. To show that these expressions have the same value, you use the equals sign, $=$.

Introduction to Algebra **1**

Teaching References
Lesson Commentary,
  pp. T77–T82
Assignment Guide,
  pp. T59–T60
Supplementary Materials
  Practice Masters 1–4
  Tests 1–3
  Resource Book
    Practice Exercises,
    pp. 79–81
    Tests, pp. 6–9
    Enrichment Activity,
    p. 190
    Application, p. 178
  Study Guide, pp. 1–18
  Computer Activities 1–5
  Test Generator
  California Standards
  Support Workbook
    Exploration for
    Lesson 1-8
Alternate Test, p. T12

Teaching Suggestions, p. T77

Suggested Extensions, p. T77

Warm-Up Exercises
Simplify.
1. $9 \div 9$ 1
2. $44 \div 11$ 4
3. $20 \div 22$ $\frac{10}{11}$
4. $7 \times \frac{1}{7}$ 1
5. $1234 \times \frac{5678}{1234}$ 5678

Motivating the Lesson

The skills used in the Warm-Up Exercises are the skills that today's lesson builds on. The only difference is that variables will be used to represent numbers.

1

Simplify.

1. $12 + (4 \div 2)$
$12 + 2 = 14$

2. $12 \div (4 + 2)$
$12 \div 6 = 2$

3. $(3 + 2) \div (6 - 1)$
$5 \div 5 = 1$

4. $12 \times (12 - 2)$
$12 \times 10 = 120$

Evaluate each expression when $m = 1$ and $n = 2$.

5. $3 \cdot (n + 4)$
$3 \cdot (2 + 4) =$
$3 \cdot 6 = 18$

6. $(mn) + 4$
$(1 \cdot 2) + 4 =$
$2 + 4 = 6$

7. $m + (14n)$
$1 + (14 \times 2) =$
$1 + 28 = 29$

8. $\dfrac{(m + 14)}{5} + \dfrac{(n + 14)}{4}$
$\dfrac{(1 + 14)}{5} + \dfrac{(2 + 14)}{4} =$
$\dfrac{15}{5} + \dfrac{16}{4} =$
$3 + 4 = 7$

Evaluate the expression for the given values of the variables.

9. Area of a rectangle: lw
$l = 22$ and $w = 4$
$22 \times 4 = 88$

You write $\qquad$ $4 + 2 = 6$

and say "four plus two *equals* (or *is equal to* or *is*) six." The *simplest*, or most common, name for the number six is 6.

The symbol $\neq$ means "is not equal to." You write

$$4 + 2 \neq 5$$

to show that the expressions $4 + 2$ and 5 do not have the same value.

Replacing a numerical expression by the simplest name for its value is called **simplifying the expression.** When you simplify a numerical expression, you use the following principle.

Substitution Principle

An expression may be replaced by another expression that has the same value.

Example 1 Simplify each expression. **a.** $(42 \div 6) + 8$ **b.** $54 \div (8 - 2)$

Solution The parentheses ( ) show how the numerals in the expression are to be grouped. The expression within the parentheses is simplified first.

a. $(42 \div 6) + 8 = 7 + 8 = 15$ *Answer*
Note that to read the symbols "$(42 \div 6) + 8$," you may say "the *quantity* forty-two divided by six, plus eight."

b. $54 \div (8 - 2) = 54 \div 6 = 9$ *Answer*

Replacing each variable in a variable expression by a given value and simplifying the result is called **evaluating the expression** or **finding the value of the expression**.

Example 2 Evaluate each expression if $a = 5$. **a.** $7a$ **b.** $(3a) + 2$

Solution **a.** Substitute 5 for a. **b.** Substitute 5 for a.
$7a = 7 \cdot 5$ $\qquad (3a) + 2 = (3 \cdot 5) + 2$
$\quad = 35$ *Answer* $\qquad\qquad = 15 + 2 = 17$ *Answer*

In Examples 1 and 2 the parentheses show how the variables and numbers in the expression are to be grouped. Notice that *expressions within parentheses should be simplified first.*

Example 3 Evaluate $(5x) - (3 + y)$ if $x = 12$ and $y = 9$.

Solution First replace x with 12 and y with 9, and insert the necessary multiplication symbol.

---

2 *Chapter 1*

Then simplify the result.

$$(5x) - (3 + y)$$
$$(5 \cdot 12) - (3 + 9)$$
$$60 - 12 = 48 \quad \textit{Answer}$$

Oral Exercises

Tell whether each statement is true or false. Give a reason for your answer.

Sample   **a.** $7 \cdot 5 = 20 + 15$ **b.** $3 \cdot 4 = 3 + 4$ **c.** $2 + 2 \neq 2 \cdot 2$

Solution   **a.** True, because the value of both $7 \cdot 5$ and $20 + 15$ is 35.
  b. False, because $3 \cdot 4 = 12$, but $3 + 4 = 7$.
  c. False, because the value of both $2 + 2$ and $2 \cdot 2$ is 4.

1. $6 \cdot 3 = 3 \cdot 6$ True; 18 = 18 **2.** $4 \cdot 0 = 0 \cdot 6$ True; 0 = 0

3. $8 \div 1 \neq 1 \div 8$ True; $8 \neq \frac{1}{8}$ **4.** $54 \times \frac{1}{2} \neq 54 \times 0.5$ False; 27 = 27

5. $3 \cdot (4 \cdot 2) = (3 \cdot 4) \cdot 2$ True; 24 = 24 **6.** $(14 - 3) - 1 = 14 - (3 - 1)$ False; 10 ≠ 12

7. $\frac{(8 - 2)}{2} = 8 - 1$ False; 3 ≠ 7 **8.** $0.23 \times 5 = 2.3 \times 0.5$ True; 1.15 = 1.15

Simplify each expression.

9. $9 + (5 \cdot 4)$ 29 **10.** $(9 + 5) \cdot 4$ 56 **11.** $18 - (4 \cdot 4)$ 2

12. $(17 - 3) \cdot 3$ 42 **13.** $\frac{(22 - 7)}{5}$ 3 **14.** $\frac{(13 + 11)}{(6 - 2)}$ 6

Evaluate each expression if $a = 1$, $b = 2$, and $c = 3$.

15. $7b$ 14 **16.** $6a$ 6 **17.** $c - 3$ 0 **18.** $9 - b$ 7

19. $\frac{2}{b}$ 1 **20.** $(5c) - 4$ 11 **21.** $b + (ac)$ 5 **22.** $a + (bc)$ 7

23. $3 \cdot (a - 1)$ 0 **24.** $2 \cdot (b + 2)$ 8 **25.** $(a + b) \div c$ 1 **26.** $a \div (c - b)$ 1

Written Exercises

Simplify each expression.

A **1.** $(8 - 3) + 3$ 8 **2.** $9 + (18 - 2)$ 25 **3.** $5 \cdot (11 + 1)$ 60

  4. $(13 - 6) - 7$ 0 **5.** $(6 + 12) \div 3$ 6 **6.** $6 + (12 \div 3)$ 10

Introduction to Algebra   **3**

Check for Understanding
Many teachers like to assess how well students have understood the explanation of a concept just presented by having students try a few exercises immediately, before a new concept is introduced. Here is a suggested use of the Oral Exercises to provide this check.
Oral Exs. 1–14: use after Example 1.
Oral Exs. 15–26: use after Example 3.

Guided Practice
After the presentation of the lesson, some teachers like to have students work some exercises under their guidance in preparation for a homework assignment. Here are some additional A exercises that can be used for this purpose.

Simplify each expression.
1. $9 + (17 + 4)$ 30
2. $(3 \times 16) \div (2 \times 4)$ 6
3. $(72 \div 6) \div 3$ 4
Evaluate each expression if $x = 2$, $y = 0$, $a = 11$, and $b = 22$.
4. $(5x) + 2$ 12
5. $(4xy) - (5ay)$ 0
6. $\frac{(x + y)}{b}$ $\frac{1}{11}$

Summarizing the Lesson
Review the key points of today's lesson by having students define and give examples of a variable, a variable expression, and a numerical expression. Remind them that to evaluate a variable expression, they substitute and then simplify.

Suggested Assignments

Minimum
   3/1–37 odd
   S 5/Mixed Review

Average
   3/1–47 odd
   S 5/Mixed Review

Maximum
   3/3–48 mult. of 3
   8/3–45 mult. of 3
   S 9/Mixed Review

This assignment covers
Lesson 1-1 and Lesson 1-2.

Supplementary Materials

Study Guide   pp. 1–2
Computer Activities   1, 2

Simplify each expression.

7. $29 - (0 \cdot 9)$ 29

8. $5 - (16 \div 4)$ 1

9. $(8 \cdot 17) + (12 \cdot 17)$ 340

10. $(12 \cdot 11) - (2 \cdot 11)$ 110

11. $(26 + 4) \div (30 \div 2)$ 2

12. $(40 \div 10) \div (1 \cdot 4)$ 1

Evaluate each expression if $x = 2$, $y = 3$, and $z = 4$.

13. $5x$ 10

14. $6y$ 18

15. xy 6

16. yz 12

17. $(4x) + 7$ 15

18. $(3y) - 9$ 0

19. $(5z) - 7$ 13

20. $(8x) + 7$ 23

21. $(2x) + (2y)$ 10

22. $(3z) - (4x)$ 4

23. $8 \cdot (y + z)$ 56

24. $7 \cdot (y - x)$ 7

25. $\frac{1}{2} \cdot (z - x)$ 1

26. $\frac{2}{3} \cdot (y + 6)$ 6

27. $\frac{(y + x)}{(y - x)}$ 5

28. $\frac{(z + y)}{(z - y)}$ 7

29. $(4x) - 8$ 0

30. $4z - (8x)$ 0

31. $(5yz) - x$ 58

32. $8 + (9xy)$ 62

Evaluate each expression in color for the given values of the variables.

B   **33.** Area of a rectangle: lw
   if $l = 25$ and $w = 12$ 300

34. Perimeter of a rectangle: $(2l) + (2w)$
   if $l = 25$ and $w = 12$ 74

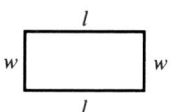

Exs. 33 and 34

35. Perimeter of a triangle: $(a + b) + c$
   if $a = 10$, $b = 24$, and $c = 26$ 60

36. Area of a right triangle: $\frac{1}{2} \cdot (ab)$
   if $a = 10$ and $b = 24$ 120

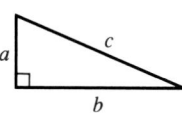

Exs. 35 and 36

37. Temperature in degrees Fahrenheit, given degrees Celsius:
   $(1.8C) + 32$ if $C = 37$ 98.6

38. Distance in meters traveled by an object falling for t seconds:
   $\left(\frac{1}{2} \cdot g\right)(t \cdot t)$ if $g = 9.8$ and $t = 16$ 1254.4

39. Simple interest on a loan of P dollars: Prt
   if $P = 5000$ (dollars), $r = 0.125$ (12.5% per year), and $t = 2$ (years) 1250

40. Cost in cents of electricity to operate an electric light for one hour:
   $\frac{(p \cdot c)}{1000}$ if $p = 75$ (watts) and $c = 9.5$ (cents) per kilowatt hour 0.7125

For each variable find a value that will make a true statement. If possible, find more than one value.

41. $4n = 12$ 3

42. $8x = 16$ 2

43. $y + 3 = 3 + y$ any number

44. $m + 5 = 5$ 0

45. $6\frac{1}{2} - y = 3 \cdot 2$ $\frac{1}{2}$

46. $\frac{3}{4} + y = 0.75 + y$ any number

C   **47.** $a \cdot a = 2a$ 0, 2

48. $z \cdot 8 = z$ 0

49. $(b \cdot b) + 3 = 4b$ 1, 3

Mixed Review Exercises

Perform the indicated operation.

1. $(0.3) \cdot (1.2)$ 0.36
2. $21.25 + 8.07$ 29.32
3. $1.6 \div 0.4$ 4
4. $7.2 - 3.8$ 3.4

5. $212.1 + 6.9$ 219
6. $6.32 - 4.7$ 1.62
7. 72.34×2.1 151.914
8. $33.6 \div 2.1$ 16

9. $\frac{2}{3} + \frac{3}{10}$ $\frac{29}{30}$
10. $\frac{5}{7} \times \frac{14}{16}$ $\frac{5}{8}$
11. $\frac{1}{2} \div \frac{3}{8}$ $\frac{4}{3}$
12. $\frac{3}{8} - \frac{1}{4}$ $\frac{1}{8}$

13. $\frac{7}{20} \times \frac{16}{21}$ $\frac{4}{15}$
14. $\frac{5}{12} - \frac{1}{15}$ $\frac{7}{20}$
15. $\frac{4}{7} + \frac{2}{3}$ $\frac{26}{21}$
16. $\frac{4}{7} \div \frac{3}{14}$ $\frac{8}{3}$

Application / *Energy Consumption*

Power is associated with the flow of electricity in a circuit. Your electric company determines your monthly electric bill based on how much electricity you have used. Electrical power is measured in watts (W).

When p watts are used for t hours, the amount of energy measured in watt-hours is represented by the expression $p \cdot t$. The electric meter for your home measures the amount of electricity you use in units called *kilowatt-hours* (kW · h). A kilowatt is 1000 watts.

To find the number of kilowatt-hours an appliance uses, use the expression $p \cdot t$ to determine the number of *watt-hours* used and then divide by 1000. You can get an idea of what 1 kW · h of electricity is by thinking of a 100-watt light bulb. To use 1 kW · h of electricity, you need to burn the 100-watt light bulb for 10 hours.

Example   An air conditioner uses 1330 watts for 6 hours.
How many kilowatt-hours does it use?

Solution   In the expression $p \cdot t$,
$p = 1330$ and $t = 6$.

$1330 \cdot 6 = 7980$ (watt-hours)
$7980 \div 1000 = 7.98$ (kW · h)
Answer

Exercises

1. An iron using 1008 watts is plugged in for 2 hours. How many kilowatt-hours are used? 2.016 kW · h

2. A clothes dryer uses 4856 watts. How many kilowatt-hours are used if it runs for 10 hours? 48.56 kW · h

Introduction to Algebra   **5**

1-2 Grouping Symbols

Objective To simplify expressions with and without grouping symbols.

Parentheses have been used to show you how to group the numerals in an expression. Different groupings may produce different numbers.

$$(150 \div 10) + 5 \text{ means } 15 + 5, \text{ or } 20.$$
$$150 \div (10 + 5) \text{ means } 150 \div 15, \text{ or } 10.$$

A **grouping symbol** is a device, such as a pair of parentheses, used to enclose an expression that should be simplified first. Multiplication symbols are often left out of expressions with grouping symbols.

Example 1 Simplify: **a.** 6(5 − 3) **b.** 6(5) − 3

Solution **a.** 6(5 − 3) stands for 6 × (5 − 3).
The parentheses tell you to simplify 5 − 3 first. Then multiply by 6.
6(5 − 3) = 6(2) = 12 *Answer*

b. 6(5) stands for 6 × 5.
6(5) − 3 = 30 − 3 = 27 *Answer*

In Example 1, note that 6(5) stands for 6 × 5. Other ways to write this product using parentheses are (6)5 and (6)(5).

In a fraction such as $\frac{12 + 4}{15 - 7}$ the bar is a grouping symbol as well as a division sign.

Example 2 Simplify $\frac{12 + 4}{15 - 7}$.

Solution $\frac{12 + 4}{15 - 7} = \frac{16}{8} = 16 \div 8 = 2$ *Answer*

Throughout your work in algebra you will use these symbols:

Grouping Symbols

Parentheses	Brackets	Fraction Bar
6(5 − 3)	6[5 − 3]	$\frac{12 + 4}{15 - 7}$

If an expression contains more than one grouping symbol, *first simplify the expression in the innermost grouping symbol*. Then work toward the outermost grouping symbol until the simplest expression is found.

6 *Chapter 1*

Example 3 Simplify $18 - [52 \div (7 + 6)]$.

Solution

$$18 - [52 \div \underbrace{(7 + 6)}]$$
$$18 - [\underbrace{52 \div \quad 13}]$$
$$\underbrace{18 - \quad 4}$$
$$14 \quad \textit{Answer}$$

When there are no grouping symbols, simplify in the following order:

1. Do all multiplications and divisions in order from left to right.
2. Do all additions and subtractions in order from left to right.

Example 4 Simplify: **a.** $29 + 15 \cdot 4$ **b.** $19 - 7 + 12 \cdot 2 \div 8$

Solution **a.** $29 + \underbrace{15 \cdot 4}$ **b.** $19 - 7 + \underbrace{12 \cdot 2} \div 8$
$$\underbrace{29 + \quad 60} \qquad \qquad 19 - 7 + \underbrace{24 \quad \div 8}$$
$$89 \qquad \qquad \quad \underbrace{19 - 7} + \quad 3$$
$$\textit{Answer} \qquad \qquad \underbrace{12 \quad + \quad 3}$$
$$\qquad \qquad \qquad \qquad 15 \quad \textit{Answer}$$

Example 5 Evaluate $\dfrac{4x + 5y}{3x - y}$ if $x = 3$ and $y = 8$.

Solution Replace x with 3 and y with 8. Then simplify the result.
$$\frac{4x + 5y}{3x - y} = \frac{4 \cdot 3 + 5 \cdot 8}{3 \cdot 3 - 8} = \frac{12 + 40}{9 - 8} = \frac{52}{1} = 52 \quad \textit{Answer}$$

You may wish to use a calculator to evaluate some expressions. If you do, be sure to read the Calculator Key-In on page 13 first.

Oral Exercises

Describe the operation(s) for each expression.

Sample $3(x + 1) + 5$

Solution 1 Multiply 3 by the sum of x and 1; then add 5 to the product.

Solution 2 Add x and 1; multiply the sum by 3; then add 5 to the product.

1. $7y$ **3.** $9x + 4$ **4.** $8z - 5$ **5.** $4(z + 6)$
2. $z - 2$

6. $4(2x - 1)$ **7.** $\dfrac{z}{x + y}$ **8.** $\dfrac{z - y}{x}$ **9.** $\dfrac{13 - x}{y}$ **10.** $\dfrac{6x + 9}{8 + z}$

11–20. In Exercises 1–10, evaluate each expression if $x = 1$, $y = 3$, and $z = 7$.

Evaluate if $a = 4$, $b = 7$, and $c = 10$.

6. $\dfrac{4a + 2b}{c - a}$
$$\frac{4(4) + 2(7)}{10 - 4} = \frac{16 + 14}{6} =$$
$$\frac{30}{6} = 5$$

Check for Understanding

Here is a suggested use of the Oral Exercises to check students' understanding as you teach the lesson.
Oral Exs. 1–20: use after Example 5.

 Using a Calculator

Students need to be warned to check out the order in which operations are performed on their calculators, as suggested on page 13.

Additional Answers
Oral Exercises

1. Multiply 7 by y.
2. Subtract 2 from z.
3. Multiply 9 by x, and then add 4.
4. Multiply 8 by z, and then subtract 5.
5. Add z and 6, and then multiply the sum by 4.
6. Multiply 2 by x, subtract 1, and then multiply the difference by 4.
7. Add x and y, then divide z by the sum.
8. Subtract y from z, and then divide the difference by x.
9. Subtract x from 13, and then divide the difference by y.
10. Multiply 6 by x and add 9; add 8 and z. Then divide the sum of $6x$ and 9 by the sum of 8 and z.

(continued)

7

Guided Practice
Simplify.

1. $3 + 8 \times 2$ 19

2. $(9 + 2)5$ 55

3. $\frac{12 - 6}{20 - 18}$ 3

4. $\frac{2(2 + 3)}{5(3 - 2)}$ 2

Evaluate if $x = 4$ and $y = 3$.

5. $x + 4 \cdot y - 1$ 15

6. $(x + 4)(y - 1)$ 16

7. $9x - xy$ 24

8. $\frac{xy - 5}{x + y}$ 1

Summarizing the Lesson
Review the major points of today's lesson by having students identify the different grouping symbols and state the rules for the order of operations with and without grouping symbols.

Suggested Assignments

Minimum
  8/1–29 odd, 35, 36
S 9/Mixed Review

Average
  8/1–33 odd, 37–39
S 9/Mixed Review

Maximum
Lesson 1-2 is covered in the assignment for Lesson 1-1.

Written Exercises

Simplify each expression.

A   **1. a.** $8 + 3 \cdot 4$ 20   **2. a.** $9 + 5 \cdot 2$ 19   **3. a.** $6 - 3 \div 3$ 5   **4. a.** $5 + 10 \div 5$ 7
      b. $(8 + 3)4$ 44   **b.** $(9 + 5)2$ 28   **b.** $(6 - 3) \div 3$ 1   **b.** $(5 + 10) \div 5$ 3

5. $\frac{6 + 5 \cdot 3}{6 + 1}$ 3   **6.** $\frac{8 + 3 \cdot 2}{4 + 3}$ 2   **7.** $\frac{3(12 - 8)}{2 \cdot 5 - 4}$ 2   **8.** $\frac{8 \cdot 5 + 2 \cdot 7}{2(7 - 4)}$ 9

Evaluate each expression if $t = 6$, $x = 3$, $y = 4$, and $z = 5$.

9. a. $2x + 7$ 13   **10. a.** $5y - 3$ 17   **11. a.** $18 - 4x$ 6   **12. a.** $7z + 8$ 43
     b. $2(x + 7)$ 20   **b.** $5(y - 3)$ 5   **b.** $(18 - 4)x$ 42   **b.** $7(z + 8)$ 91

13. a. $xy + z$ 17   **14. a.** $zt - y$ 26   **15. a.** $4xz + 3y$ 72   **16. a.** $9xyz - t$ 534
     b. $x(y + z)$ 27   **b.** $z(t - y)$ 10   **b.** $4(xz + 3y)$ 108   **b.** $9x(zy - t)$ 378

17. $5(3y - 4x)$ 0   **18.** $6y - 2xy$ 0   **19.** $xyz - 4z$ 40   **20.** $(y \cdot y + z) \cdot z$ 105

21. $\frac{9x + z}{x + z}$ 4   **22.** $\frac{4y - 2t}{y + 2t}$ $\frac{1}{4}$ **23.** $\frac{10t - z}{10(t - z)}$ $\frac{11}{2}$ **24.** $\frac{2(y + x)}{2y + x}$ $\frac{14}{11}$

B   **25.** $2[x + 4(y + z)]$ 78   **26.** $3[z + 5(2y - x)]$ 90
    27. $[(5y + 6z) - 3t] \div y$ 8   **28.** $2t - [7z \div (y + x)]$ 7

Evaluate each expression in color for the given values of the variables.

29. Perimeter of a parallelogram: $2(a + b)$
    if $a = 7.5$ and $b = 19.5$ 54

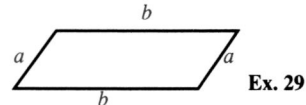

Ex. 29

30. Perimeter of an isosceles trapezoid: $2a + b + c$
    if $a = 20$, $b = 16$, and $c = 48$ 104

Exs. 30-31

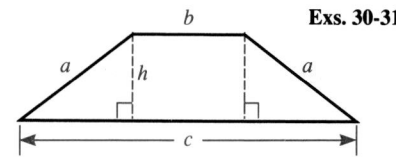

31. Area of a trapezoid: $\frac{1}{2}h(b + c)$
    if $h = 12$, $b = 16$, and $c = 48$ 384

32. Area of a circle: $(\pi r)r$ if $r = 28$
    Use $\frac{22}{7}$ as an approximate value for π. 2464

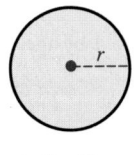

Ex. 32

33. Perimeter of a Norman window: $2(r + h) + \pi r$
    if $r = 2.00$ and $h = 3.00$
    Use 3.14 as an approximate value for π. 16.28

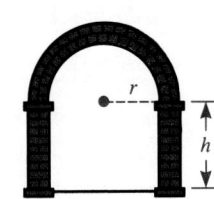

Ex. 33

---

34. Surface area of a rectangular solid: $2(lw + wh + lh)$
if $l = 14$, $w = 12$, and $h = 10$ 856

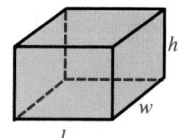

Simplify the expression on each side of the __?__. Then complete using one of the symbols = or ≠ to make a true statement.

35. $\dfrac{24 \cdot 8}{12 + 4}$ __?__ $\dfrac{12 \cdot 4}{6 + 2}$ 12 ≠ 6

36. $\dfrac{23 + 19}{7 \cdot 2}$ __?__ 54 ÷ 9 − 3 3 = 3

37. 2[3(12 − 7)] __?__ 5 · 5 + 5 30 = 30

38. 3[36 ÷ (3 + 6)] __?__ 30 − [(36 ÷ 3) + 6] 12 = 12

Insert grouping symbols in the expression 5 · 8 − 6 ÷ 2 so that its value is:

C
39. 5
5 · (8 − 6) ÷ 2

40. 17
(5 · 8 − 6) ÷ 2

41. 25
5 · (8 − 6 ÷ 2)

42. 37
(5 · 8) − (6 ÷ 2)

Insert grouping symbols in 5 · 2 + 8 − 4 ÷ 2 so that its value is:

43. 15
5 · (2 + 8 − 4) ÷ 2

44. 16
(5 · 2) + 8 − (4 ÷ 2)

45. 7
[(5 · 2) + 8 − 4] ÷ 2

46. 12
5 · 2 + [(8 − 4) ÷ 2]

Mixed Review Exercises

Simplify.

1. $(10 − 4) ÷ 2$ 3

2. $40 · 10 + 18 · 2$ 436

3. $8 × (26 − 8)$ 144

4. $7 + 15 ÷ 3$ 12

5. $(28 + 4) ÷ (16 ÷ 2)$ 4

6. $(6 + 5) · (8 − 3)$
55

Evaluate if $a = 3$, $b = 2$, $x = 8$, and $y = 5$.

7. $x + ay$ 23

8. $(5 − a)y$ 10

9. $3a − 2b$ 5

10. $\frac{1}{4}x + 3$ 5

11. $\frac{1}{2}axy$ 60

12. $x · (2a − b)$ 32

Challenge

Notice that: $2(1 + 2 + 3) = 3 \cdot 4$
$2(1 + 2 + 3 + 4) = 4 \cdot 5$
$2(1 + 2 + 3 + 4 + 5) = 5 \cdot 6$

If this pattern continues to hold, predict the value of:

a. $2(1 + 2 + 3 + 4 + 5 + 6 + 7 + 8 + 9 + 10)$. 110

b. the sum of the integers from 1 to 100. 5050

Introduction to Algebra   **9**

Supplementary Materials
Study Guide   pp. 3–4
Resource Book   p. 79

Thinking Skills
Recognizing patterns is an important thinking skill as well as a useful problem solving strategy. In this challenge problem students are asked to look for a pattern and *draw inferences* from it.

Warm-Up Exercises

If $a = 11$ and $b = 22$, which of the following variable expressions will be equal?

1. $2a + b$ **2.** $2b + a$

3. $2(a + b)$ **4.** $2a + 2b$

5. $6a + 22 - b$

6. $[3(a + b) - 3a]$

3, 4, 5, and 6 are equal to 66.

Motivating the Lesson

Remind students that in the previous lesson they learned how to find the value of a variable expression. Point out that this lesson goes one step further. Students will learn how to find the value or values of the variable that make an expression equal to a given amount. For example, ask students what value of x will make the expression $x - 3$ equal to 8.

Chalkboard Examples

1. Solve the equation $x + 4 = 11$ if the domain of x is $\{1, 3, 5, 7, 11\}$. $\{7\}$

2. Solve the equation $2x - 5 = 13$ if $x \in \{3, 6, 9, 12\}$. $\{9\}$

3. Solve the equation $m(3 - m) = 2$ if $m \in \{0, 1, 2, 3\}$. $\{1, 2\}$

4. Solve over the domain $\{1, 2, 5, 6\}$.
Two more than six times a number is 14. What is the number? $\{2\}$

1-3 Equations

Objective   To find solution sets of equations over a given domain.

An **equation** is formed by placing an equals sign between two numerical or variable expressions, called the **sides** of the equation.

$$\underbrace{11 - 7 = 4}_{\text{the two sides}} \qquad \underbrace{5x - 1 = 9}_{\text{the two sides}} \qquad \underbrace{y + 2 = 2 + y}_{\text{the two sides}}$$

Sentences containing variables (like the equations $5x - 1 = 9$ and $y + 2 = 2 + y$) are called **open sentences.** The given set of numbers that a variable may represent is called the **domain** of the variable.

A variable in an equation can be replaced by any of the numbers in its domain. The resulting equation may be either true or false.

You may use *braces* $\{\ \}$ to show a set of numbers. A short way to write "the set whose members are 1, 2, and 3" is $\{1, 2, 3\}$.

Example 1   The domain of x is $\{1, 2, 3\}$.
Is the equation $5x - 1 = 9$ true when $x = 1$? when $x = 2$? when $x = 3$?

Solution   Replace x in turn by 1, 2, and 3.

x	$5x - 1 = 9$	
1	$5 \cdot 1 - 1 = 9$	False
2	$5 \cdot 2 - 1 = 9$	True
3	$5 \cdot 3 - 1 = 9$	False

In Example 1, when x is replaced by 2, the resulting equation is true. Any value of a variable that turns an open sentence into a true statement is a **solution,** or **root,** of the sentence and is said to **satisfy** the sentence.

The set of all solutions of an open sentence is called the **solution set** of the sentence. Finding the solution set is called **solving** the sentence. In Example 1, there is only one solution. For the equation $5x - 1 = 9$ you may say either "The solution is 2," or "The solution set is $\{2\}$."

Some equations have more than one solution, and some equations have no solutions. The sentence $y + 2 = 2 + y$ is true no matter what number is substituted for y. Therefore the solution set is the set of *all* numbers. If you are asked to solve this equation *over the domain* $\{0, 1, 2, 3\}$, you state that the solution set is the domain itself, $\{0, 1, 2, 3\}$.

Here is another way to show that the domain of a variable y is $\{0, 1, 2, 3\}$:

$$y \in \{0, 1, 2, 3\}$$

(Read "y belongs to the set whose members are 0, 1, 2, and 3.")

10   *Chapter 1*

Example 2 Solve $y(4 - y) = 3$ if $y \in \{0, 1, 2, 3\}$.

Solution

y	$y(4 - y) = 3$	
0	$0 \cdot (4 - 0) = 3$	False
1	$1 \cdot (4 - 1) = 3$	True
2	$2 \cdot (4 - 2) = 3$	False
3	$3 \cdot (4 - 3) = 3$	True

The solutions are 1 and 3.

∴ (read "therefore") the
solution set is $\{1, 3\}$.
Answer

Example 3 Solve over the domain $\{6, 8, 12\}$:
Five more than twice a number is 29. What is the number?

Solution Use mental math to see which members of the given domain are solutions.

Number	Five more than twice a number is 29.	
6	Five more than twice 6 is 29.	False
8	Five more than twice 8 is 29.	False
12	Five more than twice 12 is 29.	True

∴ the number is 12. *Answer*

Oral Exercises

**Solve each equation if $x \in \{0, 1, 2, 3, 4, 5, 6\}$. If there is no solution over
the given domain, say "No solution."**

1. $x + 2 = 6$ {4} **2.** $x - 1 = 4$ {5} **3.** $2x = 6$ {3} **4.** $x + 5 = 1$ No sol.

5. $x - 3 = 3$ {6} **6.** $x + 1 = 5$ {4} **7.** $x + 4 = 4 + x$ **8.** $x + 4 = x$ No sol.
                                              {0, 1, 2, 3, 4, 5, 6}

Solve each problem over the domain $\{1, 3, 5, 7, 9\}$. Use mental math.

9. Three more than twice a number is 13. What is the number? 5

10. Eight times the sum of 4 and a number is 56. What is the number? 3

Written Exercises

Solve each equation if $x \in \{0, 1, 2, 3, 4, 5\}$.

A **1.** $x + 5 = 9$ {4} **2.** $6 + x = 11$ {5} **3.** $x - 2 = 3$ {5} **4.** $x - 3 = 1$ {4}

5. $7 - x = 2$ {5} **6.** $6 - x = 3$ {3} **7.** $2x = 8$ {4} **8.** $5x = 10$ {2}

9. $8x = 16$ {2} **10.** $2x = 10$ {5} **11.** $3x = 0$ {0} **12.** $0 = 4x$ {0}

13. $x \div 3 = 1$ {3} **14.** $x \div 2 = 2$ {4} **15.** $\frac{1}{2}x = 2$ {4} **16.** $\frac{1}{3}x = 1$ {3}

17. $x \cdot x = 1$ {1} **18.** $9x = 9$ {1} **19.** $x - x = 0$ **20.** $x \cdot x = 25$ {5}
                                                      {0, 1, 2, 3, 4, 5}

Introduction to Algebra **11**

Check for Understanding

Here is a suggested use of
the Oral Exercises to check
students' understanding as
you teach the lesson.
Oral Exs. 1–8: use after
  Example 2.
Oral Exs. 9–10: use after
  Example 3.

Guided Practice

Solve each equation if
$x \in \{0, 1, 2, 3, 4, 5, 6\}$.

1. $x + 6 = 7$ {1}
2. $12 - x = 12$ {0}
3. $4x = 24$ {6}
4. $40 \div x = 8$ {5}

Solve over the domain
$\{10, 12, 14, 16\}$.

5. Seven less than a number
is 9. What is the num-
ber? {16}

Summarizing the Lesson

Ask a student to read the
lesson objective on page 10
and explain how the objective was met, using an example to illustrate.

Suggested Assignments

Minimum
  11/1–29 odd
  S 12/Mixed Review
Average
  11/1–39 odd
  S 12/Mixed Review
Maximum
  11/1–25 odd, 33–42
  S 12/Mixed Review

Supplementary Materials

Study Guide   pp. 5–6
Practice Master   1

Solve each problem over the domain {0, 2, 4, 6, 8}.

21. Eight times a number is 32. What is the number? 4

22. Twelve more than a number is 20. What is the number? 8

23. A number divided by four is 2. What is the number? 8

24. Three less than a number is 3. What is the number? 6

B 25. Three more than twice a number is 7. What is the number? 2

26. Four times a number is 6 more than the number. What is the number? 2

Solve each equation over the domain {0, 1, 2, 3, 4, 5, 6, 7, 8, 9}.

27. $2a + 9 = 17$ {4}

28. $3b - 4 = 11$ {5}

29. $10 = 8c - 6$ {2}

30. $13 = 6d - 5$ {3}

31. $9 + 9r = 81$ {8}

32. $5 + 5n = 50$ {9}

33. $2x = x + 7$ {7}

34. $3w = w \cdot 3$ {0, 1, 2, 3, 4, 5, 6, 7, 8, 9}

35. $2f = f \cdot f$ {0, 2}

36. $y(8 - y) = 0$ {0, 8}

37. $(6 - v)(1 + v)v = 0$ {0, 6}

38. $27k = (3k)(3k)(3k)$ {0, 1}

Suppose the domain for each equation is {1, 2, 3, 4,...}. (The dots show that the set goes on without end.) Determine the number of solutions for each equation. Write "None," "One," or "More than one." For those equations with one solution, try to determine what the solution is.

C 39. a. $x + 3 = 3 + x$ More than one
b. $x + 4 = x + 3$ None
c. $x + 4 = 8$ One; {4}

40. a. $x - x = 1$ None
b. $x + x = 2x$ More than one
c. $x - x = 2x$ None

41. a. $4x = 8$ One; {2}
b. $4 \cdot x = x \cdot 4$ More than one
c. $4x = 4x + 1$ None

42. a. $3 \cdot x = x \cdot 3$ More than one
b. $x - 3 = x$ None
c. $x - 3 = 3 - x$ One; {3}

Write two different equations for which the solution set over the domain {0, 1, 2, 3, 4} is the given set. Answers vary; examples are given.

43. {3}
$1 \cdot x = 3$
$x + 1 = 4$

44. {0}
$x + x = x$
$x \cdot 1 = 0$

45. {0, 1, 2, 3, 4}
$x - x = 0$
$4x \div 2 = x + x$

46. {0, 3}
$x(3 - x) = 0$
$x \cdot x \cdot x = 9x$

Mixed Review Exercises

Simplify.

1. $11 \cdot 9 + 3 \cdot 11$ 132

2. $7 + (15 \div 5)$ 10

3. $(17 - 8) \div 3$ 3

4. $(3 + 2 \cdot 2) \div 8$ $\frac{7}{8}$

5. $7 - 4 \div 2 \div 2$ 6

6. $42 \div 7 \div (2 + 1)$ 2

Evaluate if $a = 3$, $x = 2$, $y = 5$, and $z = 4$.

7. $3x + 4z$ 22

8. $6 \cdot (z - x)$ 12

9. $4(yz + 2)$ 88

10. $5xz + 3y$ 55

11. $axz \div (2y)$ 2.4

12. $2y - [4a \div (x + 1)]$ 6

Calculator Key-In

Does your calculator follow the steps for simplifying an expression stated on page 7? Experiment with your calculator by entering the following example exactly as it appears here: $8 + 3 \times 4 =$

If your calculator displays the answer 20, it followed the order of operations you learned: multiplication before addition. Your calculator has an algebraic operating system. The answer 20 is correct.

If your calculator displays the answer 44, it performed the addition and the multiplication in the order in which you pressed the keys. One way to get the correct answer on your calculator is to multiply 3 and 4 first and then add 8, just as you would if you were using pencil and paper.

Exercises

Use a calculator to simplify each expression.

1. $21 - 2.8 \times 7.5$ 0

2. $0.8 + 1.2 \div 0.4$ 3.8

3. $0.75 \div 0.25 \times 0.5 - 1.4$ 0.1

4. $0.45 \times 369 + 0.55 \times 369$ 369

5. $364 \div 13 \times 15{,}873 - 5291 \times 7 \times 3$ 333,333

6. $432 \times 0.25 - 24 \div 0.25$ 12

7. Evaluate $C = 5(F - 32) \div 9$ for each value of F:
   a. $F = 212$ 100   **b.** $F = 32$ 0   **c.** $F = 98.6$ 37

Self-Test 1

Vocabulary variable (p. 1)
value of a variable (p. 1)
variable expression (p. 1)
numerical expression (p. 1)
value of a numerical expression (p. 1)
simplify an expression (p. 2)
substitution principle (p. 2)
evaluate an expression (p. 2)

grouping symbol (p. 6)
equation (p. 10)
side of an equation (p. 10)
open sentence (p. 10)
domain of a variable (p. 10)
solution or root (p. 10)
satisfy an open sentence (p. 10)
solution set (p. 10)
solve an open sentence (p. 10)

Evaluate if $x = 4$, $y = 2$, and $z = 5$.

1. $(5x + y)(z - 4)$ 22

2. $3x(y + z)$ 84   **Obj. 1-1, p. 1**

3. $8x - 3(z - y)$ 23

4. $\dfrac{2(x + 5)}{4y - z}$ 6   **Obj. 1-2, p. 6**

Solve if $x \in \{0, 1, 2, 3, 4, 5\}$.

5. $12 - 2x = 2$ {5}

6. $2x = x + 3$ {3}   **Obj. 1-3, p. 10**

Check your answers with those at the back of the book.

Introduction to Algebra **13**

Quick Quiz

Evaluate each expression if $x = 3$, $y = 2$, and $z = 1$.

1. $(4x - 1) - (y + z)$ 8

2. $x + \dfrac{x + y}{5}$ 4

3. $5 + x(2y - z)$ 14

4. $(5 + x)(2y - z)$ 24

Solve each equation if $x \in \{0, 1, 2, 3, 4\}$.

5. $2x - 7 = 1$ {4}

6. $x = 6 - x$ {3}

For each of the following words, write two sentences that demonstrate two different meanings of the word.

Examples: His good batting average is the *product* of years of practice. The *product* of 3 and 8 is 24.

1. times   **2.** add

3. divide   **4.** decrease

Answers will vary.

Motivating the Lesson

Ask if anyone speaks a foreign language. If so, have those students translate the names of classroom objects and familiar expressions from English into their languages. Discuss the problems that can arise when translating from one language to another. Point out that algebra has a language of its own and that, in today's lesson, students will learn how to translate phrases into algebraic expressions.

Chalkboard Examples

Translate each phrase into a variable expression. Let the letter n stand for the number.

1. Four times a number $4n$

2. One half a number $\frac{1}{2}n$

3. Eight more than twice a number $8 + 2n$

4. Six less than a number $n - 6$

Applications and Problem Solving

1-4 Translating Words into Symbols

Objective   To translate phrases into variable expressions.

To solve problems using algebra, you must often translate phrases about numbers into expressions containing variables.

	Phrase	Translation
Addition	The *sum of* 8 and x A number *increased* by 7 5 *more than* a number	$8 + x$ $n + 7$ $n + 5$
Subtraction	The *difference* between a number and 4 A number *decreased* by 8 5 *less than* a number 6 *minus* a number	$x - 4$ $x - 8$ $n - 5$ $6 - n$
Multiplication	The *product of* 4 and a number Seven *times* a number One third *of* a number	$4n$ $7n$ $\frac{1}{3}x$
Division	The *quotient of* a number and 8 A number *divided* by 10	$\frac{n}{8}$ $\frac{n}{10}$

Caution: Be careful with phrases involving subtraction.
The phrase "5 less than x" is translated $x - 5$ and *not* $5 - x$.
The phrase "5 more than x" can be translated as either $5 + x$ or $x + 5$.

Example 1 Translate each phrase into a variable expression.
a. 3 less than half of x **b.** Half the difference between x and 3

Solution   **a.** $\frac{1}{2}x - 3$ **b.** $\frac{1}{2}(x - 3)$

Notice that the answer to Example 1 (b) is $\frac{1}{2}(x - 3)$, *not* $\frac{1}{2}(3 - x)$. In this book when we say "the difference between x and y," we mean $x - y$. Also, "the quotient of x and y" means $\frac{x}{y}$, or $x \div y$.

Example 2 If the length of a board in centimeters is l,
then the length of a board 7 cm *shorter* is $l - 7$,
and the length of a board 6 cm *longer* is $l + 6$.

Formulas are often used in algebra. **Formulas** are equations that state rules about relationships. Here are four useful formulas:

$A = lw$ **Area of rectangle** = length of rectangle × width of rectangle

$P = 2l + 2w$ **Perimeter of rectangle** = (2 × length) + (2 × width)

$D = rt$ **Distance traveled** = rate × time traveled

$C = np$ **Cost** = number of items × price per item

Example 3 Find the area and perimeter of a rectangle with length 10 and width w.

Solution

$Area$	= length × width	$Perimeter$	= (2 × length) + (2 × width)
	= $10 \cdot w$		= $(2 \cdot 10) + (2 \cdot w)$
	= $10w$ **Answer**		= $20 + 2w$ **Answer**

Example 4 You and your friends buy 2 pizzas at p dollars each and 4 salads at s dollars each. How much do you and your friends spend?

Solution
Cost = number × price
Pizza cost = $2p$ Salad cost = $4s$
Total cost = $2p + 4s$
You spend $(2p + 4s)$ dollars. **Answer**

Example 5 You travel $(h + \frac{1}{2})$ hours at 80 km/h. How far do you travel?

Solution
Distance = rate × time
        = $80(h + \frac{1}{2})$
You travel $80(h + \frac{1}{2})$ km.
Answer

Introduction to Algebra   **15**

Kip has n books. Use n to write an expression for each of the following numbers.

5. The number of books Kip has after he buys 3 more books $3 + n$

6. The number of books Kip has after he gives away 3 books $n - 3$

Use the given variable to write an expression for the measure required.

7. The area of a rectangle whose length is l and whose width is $(l - 4)$
$l(l - 4)$

8. The distance you travel if you travel 4 h at $(x + 30)$ mi/h
$4(x + 30)$ mi

Check for Understanding
Here is a suggested use of the Oral Exercises to check students' understanding as you teach the lesson.
Oral Exs. 1–8: use after Example 1.
Oral Exs. 9–20: use after Example 5.

Guided Practice
Translate each phrase into a variable expression.

1. 12 more than a number
$n + 12$

2. 7 times a number $7n$

3. 8 less than a number
$n - 8$

4. 9 times the sum of a number and 3 $9(n + 3)$

5. 10 more than one fourth of a number $10 + \frac{1}{4}n$

Complete each statement with a variable expression.

6. The sum of two numbers is 25. If one number is x, then the other is _?_ .
$25 - x$

(continued)

7. Wendy weighs 8 lb less than Jean. If Jean's weight is p lb, then Wendy's weight is __?__ lb. $p - 8$

8. Eric has one third as much money as Ted. If Eric has d dollars, then Ted has __?__ dollars. $3d$

Summarizing the Lesson

Point out that being able to translate a phrase into a variable expression lays the foundation for understanding the language of algebra. Discuss which phrases the students found most difficult to translate. Elicit suggestions on how to translate these phrases more easily. Let students take turns writing phrases on the chalkboard for the class to translate into expressions. Then, provide practice with the opposite skill, translating an expression into a word phrase.

Suggested Assignments

Minimum
Day 1: 16/1–25 odd
    R 13/Self-Test 1
Day 2: 17/27–41 odd
    S 18/Mixed Review
Assign with Lesson 1-5.
Average
Day 1: 16/1–41 odd
    R 13/Self-Test 1
Day 2: 18/42–52 even
    S 18/Mixed Review
Assign with Lesson 1-5.
Maximum
    16/2–42 even, 51–53
    S 18/Mixed Review
    R 13/Self-Test 1

Oral Exercises

Translate each phrase into a variable expression. Use n for the variable.

1. Eight times a number $8n$
2. The product of three and a number $3n$
3. Five more than a number $5 + n$
4. One fourth of a number $\frac{1}{4}n$
5. A number decreased by four $n - 4$
6. A number divided by five $\frac{n}{5}$
7. Nine less than half a number $\frac{1}{2}n - 9$
8. Nine more than twice a number $9 + 2n$

Complete each statement with a variable expression.

9. A rectangle has width 6 units and length x units. Its area is __?__ square units. $6x$

10. A rectangle has width y and length 13. Its perimeter is __?__. $2(y + 13)$

11. You travel for $(t - 2)$ hours at 75 km/h. You travel __?__ km. $75(t - 2)$

12. You buy $(m + 5)$ bagels at 35 cents each. The cost is __?__ cents. $35(m + 5)$

13. Al earns $(p + 3)$ dollars per hour. In 8 hours, he earns __?__ dollars. $8(p + 3)$

14. Our house is y years old. Four years ago it was __?__ years old. $y - 4$

15. The Golden Gate Bridge was built n years ago. Three years from now it will have been standing __?__ years. $n + 3$

16. A sports arena was d years old 15 years ago. It is now __?__ years old. $d + 15$

17. Nine years from now Fenway Park will be g years old. It is now __?__ years old. $g - 9$

18. Mike jogs for half an hour at y mi/h. He jogs __?__ mi. $\frac{1}{2}y$

19. Workers on an assembly line produce $(x + 10)$ cars each day. In 5 days they produce __?__ cars. $5(x + 10)$

20. A conveyor belt moves at n yd/min. In 10 minutes it moves __?__ yd. $10n$

Written Exercises

Translate each phrase into a variable expression.

A
1. 8 more than a number $8 + n$
2. Four times a number $4n$
3. A number decreased by 11 $n - 11$
4. The sum of 3 and a number $3 + n$
5. Half of a number $\frac{1}{2}n$
6. A number increased by 10 $n + 10$
7. The quotient of 17 and d $\frac{17}{d}$
8. A number divided by 3 $\frac{n}{3}$
9. The product of 11 and x $11x$
10. The difference between a number and 2 $n - 2$
11. 7 more than twice y $7 + 2y$
12. 4 less than five times a number $5n - 4$
13. 8 less than half of n $\frac{1}{2}n - 8$ $5 + \frac{n}{8}$
14. 11 more than one third of a number $11 + \frac{1}{3}n$
15. 5 plus the quotient of a number and 8
16. 10 times the sum of a number and 9 $10(n + 9)$

Match each phrase in the first column with the corresponding variable expression in the second column.

17. Seven decreased by three times a number i
18. Twice the sum of a number and three a
19. Five times the sum of a number and two g
20. The difference between three times a number and one d
21. Six times the difference of a number and five h
22. Five less than six times a number j
23. One more than three times a number b
24. Twice a number, increased by three f
25. Seven less than three times a number c
26. Two increased by five times a number e

a. $2(x + 3)$
b. $3x + 1$
c. $3x - 7$
d. $3x - 1$
e. $5x + 2$
f. $2x + 3$
g. $5(x + 2)$
h. $6(x - 5)$
i. $7 - 3x$
j. $6x - 5$

Complete each statement with a variable expression.

27. Leann is 3 cm taller than Fred.
    If Fred's height is f cm, $f + 3$
    then Leann's height is __?__ cm.

28. Adam is 9 in. shorter than Jeff.
    If Jeff's height is j in., $j - 9$
    then Adam's height is __?__ in.

29. Maria has $10 more than Luisa.
    If Maria has m dollars,
    then Luisa has __?__ dollars. $m - 10$

30. Dale has twice as much money as Leo.
    If Dale has d dollars,
    then Leo has __?__ dollars. $\frac{1}{2}d$

31. The sum of two numbers is 17.
    If one number is x, $17 - x$
    then the other number is __?__ .

32. The product of two numbers is 18.
    If one number is y,
    then the other number is __?__ . $\frac{18}{y}$

B 33. Seiji is 3 in. taller than Dan.
    a. If Seiji's height is s in., $s - 3$
       then Dan's height is __?__ in.
    b. If Dan's height is d in., $d + 3$ •
       then Seiji's height is __?__ in.

34. Ruth weighs 5 lb less than Erin.
    a. If Ruth's weight is r lb, $r + 5$
       then Erin's weight is __?__ lb.
    b. If Erin's weight is e lb, $e - 5$
       then Ruth's weight is __?__ lb.

35. There are 12 fewer boys than girls.
    a. If the number of girls is g,
       then there are __?__ boys. $g - 12$
    b. If the number of boys is b,
       then there are __?__ girls. $b + 12$

36. Two numbers differ by 12.
    a. If the smaller number is s, $s + 12$
       then the larger number is __?__ .
    b. If the larger number is l, $l - 12$
       then the smaller number is __?__ .

Answer each question. Use the formulas on page 15.

37. I drove for 3 hours at r mi/h. How far did I go? $3r$ mi
38. Dick drove for h hours at 85 km/h. How far did he go? $85h$ km
39. Pencils cost p cents each. How much will 5 pencils cost? $5p$ cents
40. Yogurt costs 75 cents per container. How much will x containers cost? $75x$ cents
41. Sketch a rectangle having length l and width 5. What is its area? $5l$

Supplementary Materials
Study Guide   pp. 7–8
Computer Activity   3

Answer each question. Use the formulas on page 15.

42. Sketch a rectangle having length 7 and width w. What is its perimeter? $14 + 2w$

43. Pencils cost p cents each and notebooks cost n cents each. How much will 3 pencils and 2 notebooks cost? $(3p + 2n)$ cents

44. Shirts cost 20 dollars each and ties cost 12 dollars each. How much will s shirts and t ties cost? $(20s + 12t)$ dollars

45. How many minutes are in 3 hours? In h hours? 180 min; $60h$ min

46. How many days are in 4 weeks? In w weeks? 28 days; $7w$ days

47. How many years are in 36 months? In m months? 3 years; $\frac{m}{12}$ years

48. How many minutes are in 330 seconds? In s seconds? 5.5 min; $\frac{s}{60}$ min

Complete each statement with a variable expression.

49. Oranges sell for c cents per pound at Carl's Convenience Store. They cost 5 cents per pound less at the local supermarket. Ten pounds of oranges cost __?__ cents at Carl's and __?__ cents at the supermarket. $10c$; $10(c - 5)$

50. Vera drove at the rate of r km/h. Kim's average speed was 3 km/h faster. In two hours, Vera traveled __?__ km and Kim traveled __?__ km. $2r$; $2(r + 3)$

51. The difference between two numbers is five. The greater number is n. The smaller number is __?__. $n - 5$

52. The difference between two numbers is eight. The smaller number is m. The larger number is __?__. $m + 8$

C 53. An apple has 29 more calories than a peach and 13 fewer calories than a banana. If a peach has p calories, then there are __?__ calories in a fruit salad made with one apple, two peaches, and one banana. $(p + 29) + 2p + (p + 42)$

54. A cup of peanuts contains 8 more grams of carbohydrates than a cup of walnuts and 1 less gram than a cup of almonds. If a cup of walnuts contains w grams of carbohydrates, then a mix of one cup each of peanuts, walnuts, and almonds contains __?__ grams of carbohydrates. $(w + 8) + w + (w + 9)$

Mixed Review Exercises

Evaluate if $t = 2$, $x = 3$, $y = 4$, and $z = 5$.

1. $7x - 2y$ 13
2. $4 + 3yz$ 64
3. $(2x - t) \cdot 3$ 12
4. $4z + 3x - t$ 27
5. $txy + 2$ 26
6. $ty + z + x$ 16

Solve if $x \in \{0, 1, 2, 3, 4\}$.

7. $x + 4 = 8$ {4}
8. $3x = 12$ {4}
9. $4x = 4$ {1}
10. $5x = 0$ {0}
11. $2x + 1 = 7$ {3}
12. $5 = 3x - 1$ {2}
13. $x \div 2 = 2$ {4}
14. $2x = x + 3$ {3}

1–5 Translating Sentences into Equations

Objective   To translate word sentences into equations.

Applications of algebra frequently require you to translate word sentences about numbers into equations. Sometimes you can translate the words in order. You may need grouping symbols.

Example 1 Twice the sum of a number and four is ten.

Translation $2 \cdot \qquad (n + 4) \qquad = 10$

Example 2 When a number is multiplied by four and the result decreased by six, the final result is 10.

Translation $4x - 6 = 10$

Caution: Be careful when the words "less than" are used. You may not be able to translate the words in order.

Example 3 Three less than the number x is 12.

Translation $x - 3 = 12$

Sometimes you will need to use a formula in order to write an equation. Examples 4 and 5 illustrate how this may be done.

Example 4 Use the figure and the information below it to write an equation involving x.

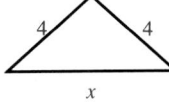

Perimeter = 14

Solution   Perimeter = the sum of the lengths of the sides.
$$14 = 4 + 4 + x$$
$$14 = 8 + x \quad \textbf{\textit{Answer}}$$

Example 5 **a.** Choose a variable to represent the number described by the words in parentheses.
b. Write an equation that represents the given information.
The distance traveled in 3 hours of driving was 240 km. (Hourly rate)

Solution 1 **a.** Let r = the hourly rate.
b. Since rate $\times$ time = distance, $r \cdot 3 = 240$, or $3r = 240$.

Introduction to Algebra   **19**

Warm-Up Exercises

Answer each question. Write a variable expression as needed.

1. How many days are there in 3 weeks? in w weeks?   21; 7w

2. How many minutes are there in 8 hours? in h hours?   480; 60h

3. How many yards are there in 36 inches? in t inches?   1; $\frac{t}{36}$

Motivating the Lesson

Remind students that in the previous lesson they learned how to translate phrases into algebraic expressions. Point out that this lesson extends that skill to translating sentences into algebraic equations.

Chalkboard Examples

Write an equation for each word sentence.

1. The sum of a number and 12 is equal to 78.
   $x + 12 = 78$

2. If a number is decreased by 5 and the result is multiplied by 2, then the result is 26.
   $2(x - 5) = 26$

3. Three less the number x equals 44. $3 - x = 44$

4. The sides of a rectangle are x and $(x - 4)$. The perimeter is 87.
   $87 = 2x + 2(x - 4)$

(continued)

19

Solution 2   **a.** Let r = the hourly rate.
       b. Since the hourly rate is the number of miles traveled in one hour, $r = \frac{240}{3}$.

Notice that the equations obtained in the Solutions to Example 5 are not the same. As soon as you become more familiar with algebra, you will see that these equations have the same solution set.

Oral Exercises

Translate each sentence into an equation.

1. Twelve more than the number p is 37. $12 + p = 37$
2. Eight is 5 less than twice the number r. $8 = 2r - 5$
3. Forty decreased by the number m is 24.5. $40 - m = 24.5$
4. The number a increased by 2.3 is 8.3. $a + 2.3 = 8.3$
5. The sum of one third of the number s and 12 is 23. $\frac{1}{3}s + 12 = 23$
6. The product of 58 and the number n is 1. $58n = 1$
7. The quotient of the number b and 4 is 8. $\frac{b}{4} = 8$
8. Three fourths of the number h is 192. $\frac{3}{4}h = 192$
9. The product of 12 and the quantity 1 less than the number d is 84. $12(d - 1) = 84$
10. The product of 7 and the sum of twice the number x and 3 is 126. $7(2x + 3) = 126$

Use the figure and the information below it to write an equation involving x.

11.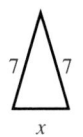

Perimeter = 18
$x + 7 + 7 = 18$

12.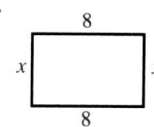

Perimeter = 26
$(2 \cdot 8) + (2 \cdot x) = 26$

13.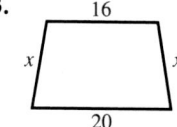

Perimeter = 60
$x + 16 + x + 20 = 60$

Written Exercises

Tell whether equation (a) or equation (b) is a translation of the given statement.

A   **1.** One third of a number is seven.   **ⓐ** $\frac{1}{3} \cdot n = 7$ **b.** $\frac{1}{3} \cdot 7 = n$

     2. Six less than a number is twelve.   **a.** $6 - n = 12$ **ⓑ** $n - 6 = 12$

     3. Half of the sum of three and a number is four   **ⓐ** $\frac{1}{2}(3 + n) = 4$ **b.** $\frac{1}{2} \cdot 3 + n = 4$

20   *Chapter 1*

4. Four less than twice a number is nine.
    (**a.**) $2x - 4 = 9$ **b.** $4 - 2x = 9$

5. Twice a number is 18 more than five times the number.
    a. $2x + 18 = 5x$ (**b.**) $2x = 18 + 5x$

6. A number is 9 more than one third of itself.
    (**a.**) $n = 9 + \frac{1}{3}n$ **b.** $n = \frac{1}{3}(n + 9)$

7. Eleven less than twice n is seven more than n.
    a. $(11 - 2)n = 7 + n$ (**b.**) $2n - 11 = 7 + n$

8. Ten times x is twice the sum of x and eight.
    a. $10x = 2x + 8$ (**b.**) $10x = 2(x + 8)$

Match the sentence in the first column with the corresponding equation in the second column.

9. Three less than twice a number is eight. e

10. Three times the quantity two less than x is eight. a

11. Two less than the product of three and x is eight. b

12. Two times the number which is three less than x is eight. f

13. Three times two decreased by x is eight. d

14. Three diminished by twice a number is eight. g

15. Two decreased by three times a number is eight. h

16. Three times the number which is x less than two is eight. c

a. $3(x - 2) = 8$

b. $3x - 2 = 8$

c. $3(2 - x) = 8$

d. $3 \cdot 2 - x = 8$

e. $2x - 3 = 8$

f. $2(x - 3) = 8$

g. $3 - 2x = 8$

h. $2 - 3x = 8$

Use the figure and the information below it to write an equation involving x.

17.

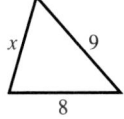

Perimeter = 24
$24 = x + 17$

18.

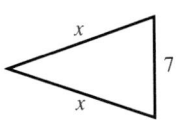

Perimeter = 29
$29 = x + x + 7$

19.

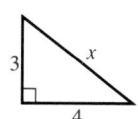

Perimeter = 12
$12 = 7 + x$

20.

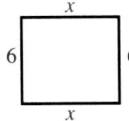

Rectangle
Perimeter = 26
$26 = 2x + 12$

21.

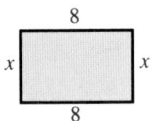

Rectangle
Area = 40
$40 = 8x$

22.

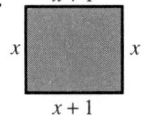

Rectangle
Area = 42
$42 = (x + 1)x$

Introduction to Algebra   **21**

In Exercises 23–36,
a. **Choose a variable to represent the number described by the words in parentheses.**
b. **Write an equation that represents the given information.**

B 23. The perimeter of a square is 116 m. (Length of a side) s; $4s = 116$

24. A dozen eggs cost \$1.19. (Cost of one egg) e; $12e = 1.19$

25. Seven years from now a coin will be 50 years old. (Coin's age now) c; $c + 7 = 50$

26. Nine days ago a new radio station had been on the air for 13 days. (Station's age now) r; $r - 9 = 13$

27. A bookstore has sold all but 12 of the dictionaries in a shipment of 120 dictionaries. (Number of dictionaries sold) d; $d + 12 = 120$

28. A student solved all but the last four exercises in a homework assignment of 30 exercises. (Number of exercises solved) x; $x + 4 = 30$

29. One eighth of a pizza sold for \$.95. (Cost of the whole pizza) p; $\frac{1}{8}p = 0.95$

30. A sixteen-year-old building is one fourth as old as a nearby bridge. (Bridge's age now) b; $16 = \frac{1}{4}b$

31. A train traveled 462 km at a rate of 132 km/h. (Number of hours traveled) t; $462 = 132t$

32. A rectangular floor is tiled with 928 square tiles. The floor is 32 tiles long. (Number of tiles in the width) w; $928 = 32w$

33. In the floor plan of a house, dimensions are shown $\frac{1}{100}$ of actual size. The length of the family room in the plan is 8.5 cm. (Actual length of the room) l; $\frac{1}{100}l = 8.5$

34. A season ticket good for 39 basketball games costs \$1092. (Cost of one admission with this ticket) c; $39c = 1092$

C 35. Each car in a fleet of 24 rental cars is either red or blue. There are 3 more blue cars than twice the number of red ones. (Number of red cars) r; $24 - r = 3 + 2r$

36. The sum of three numbers is 120. The second of the numbers is 8 less than the first, and the third is 4 more than the first. (First number)
n; $n + (n - 8) + (n + 4) = 120$

Mixed Review Exercises

Solve if $x \in \{0, 1, 2, 3, 4, 5, 6\}$.

1. $3 + x = 7$ $\{4\}$
2. $2 = x - 4$ $\{6\}$
3. $5x = 25$ $\{5\}$
4. $3 = x \div 2$ $\{6\}$

5. $3x + 1 = 10$ $\{3\}$
6. $4x = x + 6$ $\{2\}$
7. $x + 5 = 2x$ $\{5\}$
8. $4x = x \cdot 4$ $\{0, 1, 2, 3, 4, 5, 6\}$

Translate each phrase into a variable expression.

9. A number decreased by 5 $n - 5$
10. 5 more than a number $5 + n$

11. The quotient of 5 and a number $\frac{5}{n}$
12. Twice the sum of 5 and a number $2(5 + n)$

1-6 Translating Problems into Equations

Objective   To translate simple word problems into equations.

A word problem describes a situation in which certain numbers are related to each other. Some of these numbers are given in the problem and are considered to be known numbers. Other numbers are at first unknown. You must determine their values by using the facts of the problem.

   Simple word problems often give two facts involving two unknowns. The following steps can be used to translate such problems into equations. (In a later section, you will learn to find the solution of the problem by solving the equation.)

Step 1 **Read the problem carefully.**
   • Decide what the unknowns are.
   • Decide what the facts are.

Step 2 **Choose a variable and represent the unknowns.**
   • Choose a variable for one unknown.
   • Write an expression for the other unknown using the variable and one of the facts.

Step 3 **Reread the problem and write an equation.**
   • Use the other fact from the problem to write an equation.

Example 1   Translate the problem into an equation.
   (1) Marta has twice as much money as Heidi.
   (2) Together they have $36.
   How much money does each have?

Solution   Use the three steps shown above.

Step 1 The unknowns are the amounts of money Marta and Heidi have. Each of the numbered sentences gives you a fact.

Step 2 Choose a variable: Let h = Heidi's amount.
   Use h and sentence (1):   Then $2h$ = Marta's amount.

Step 3 Use sentence (2) to write an equation: $h + 2h = 36$

If a word problem involves lengths or distances, a sketch can help you to analyze the problem. Example 2 illustrates this.

Example 2   Translate the problem into an equation.
   (1) A wooden rod 60 in. long is sawed into two pieces.
   (2) One piece is 4 in. longer than the other.
   What are the lengths of the pieces?

Introduction to Algebra   **23**

Warm-Up Exercises

Translate each equation into a sentence where *n* is a number.   Answers may vary.

1. $9n + 2 = 44$
Two more than 9 times a number is 44.

2. $9(n + 2) = 44$
Nine times the sum of a number and 2 is 44.

3. $9(n - 2) = 44$
Nine times the quantity 2 less than a number is 44.

4. $9n - 2 = 44$
Two less than 9 times a number is 44.

Motivating the Lesson

Pose the following problem to the students.

Pretend that you are an architect. You have many ideas for a new house but you aren't sure which ones will work. How can you find out?

Discuss such possible solutions as drawing a blueprint or making a scale model. Point out that in algebra, as in architecture, problems can be solved by creating models. State that in today's lesson students will learn how to write an equation that will serve as a model of a situation described in a problem.

Let p = the number of people who prefer item A. Use the first sentence to write a variable expression for the number of people who prefer item B. Use the second sentence to write an equation.

1. There were twice as many people who preferred item B to item A. 300 people were questioned.
$2p; p + 2p = 300$

2. 45 fewer people preferred item B to item A. 234 people were questioned.
$p - 45; p + (p - 45) = 234$

Guided Practice

Translate each problem into an equation.

1. The area of a rectangle is 102 cm². The length of the rectangle is 6 cm. Find the width of the rectangle.
$6w = 102$

2. There are 22 students in a classroom. There are 12 more girls than boys. Find the number of boys in the classroom.
$22 = (12 + b) + b$

3. Claire sold 25 more cards than Alice. Claire and Alice sold a total of 211 cards. Find the number of cards Alice sold.
$211 = (a + 25) + a$

4. The perimeter of a rectangle is 36 cm. The length is twice as long as the width. Find the width of the rectangle.
$36 = 2w + 2(2w)$

5. Allan has $6.00 more than Bill. Together they have $30. Find how much money Bill has.
$30 = b + (b + 6)$

Solution Use the three steps shown on page 23.

Step 1 The unknowns are the lengths of the pieces. Sentences (1) and (2) each give a fact.

Step 2 Choose a variable:
Let x = the shorter length.

Use x and sentence (2):
Then $x + 4$ = the longer length.

Step 3 Use sentence (1) to write an equation: $x + (x + 4) = 60$

Problems

Translate each problem into an equation.

A 1. (1) Luke has $5 more than Sam.
(2) Together they have $73. $s + (s + 5) = 73$
How much money does each have?

2. (1) Lyn has twice as much money as Jo.
(2) Together they have $63. $j + 2j = 63$
How much money does each have?

3. (1) There were 12 people on the jury.
(2) There were 4 more men than women.
How many men were there? $w + (4 + w) = 12$

4. (1) State College has 620 students.
(2) There are 20 more women than men.
How many women are there?
$m + (20 + m) = 620$

5. (1) Lee bicycled 3 km farther than Wing.
(2) The sum of the distances they bicycled was 25 km. $w + (3 + w) = 25$
How far did each bicyclist go?

6. (1) Brenda drove three times as far as Jan.
(2) Brenda drove 24 miles more than Jan.
How far did Jan drive? $3j = j + 24$

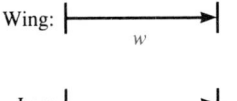

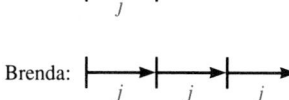

7. (1) Lisa walked 8 km more than Tim.
(2) Lisa walked twice as far as Tim.
How far did each walk? $t + 8 = 2t$

8. (1) The Ravens won twice as many games as they lost.
(2) They played 96 games. $l + 2l = 96$
How many games did they win?

9. (1) Shelley made five more sales calls than Clark.
(2) Shelley and Clark made a total of 33 sales calls.
How many sales calls did each make?
$c + (5 + c) = 33$

10. (1) Skip had eight fewer job interviews than Woody.
(2) Together they had 20 interviews.
How many interviews did each have?
$w + (w - 8) = 20$

11. (1) Amanda spent $2 more than Barry on school supplies.
(2) Together they spent $34.
How much money did each spend?
$b + (2 + b) = 34$

12. (1) The number of items on two grocery lists differs by 7.
(2) The total number of items is 33.
How many items are on each list?
$n + (n - 7) = 33$

Translate each problem into an equation. Drawing a sketch may help you.

B **13.** A ribbon 9 feet long is cut into two pieces. One piece is 1 foot longer than the other. What are the lengths of the pieces? $x + (x + 1) = 9$

14. The height of a tower is three times the height of a certain building. If the tower is 50 m taller than the building, how tall is the tower? $3b = 50 + b$

15. The length of a rectangle is twice its width. If the perimeter is 60, find the dimensions of the rectangle. $2(2w) + 2w = 60$

16. The length of a rectangle is one unit more than its width. If the area is 30 square units, find the dimensions of the rectangle. $30 = (w + 1)w$

17. The sides of a triangle have lengths 7, x, and $x + 1$. If the perimeter is 30, find the value of x. $30 = 7 + x + (x + 1)$

18. A triangle has two equal sides and a third side that is 15 cm long. If the perimeter is 50 cm, how long is each of the two equal sides? $50 = x + x + 15$

Translate each problem into an equation. Note that Problems 19–22 involve three facts about three unknowns.

Sample

Ling is three times as heavy as her packed suitcase. Her suitcase is 20 lb heavier than her knapsack. The weights of Ling, her suitcase, and her knapsack total 170 lb. How much does each weigh?

Solution

Step 1 The unknowns are the weights of Ling, her suitcase, and her knapsack. We know three facts that relate these weights to each other.

Step 2 Let k = the knapsack weight.
Then $k + 20$ = the suitcase weight, and $3(k + 20)$ = Ling's weight.

Step 3 $k + (k + 20) + 3(k + 20) = 170$.

$x + (x + 1) + [(x + 1) + 2] = 12$

C **19.** A hockey team played 12 games. They won two more than they lost. They lost one more than they tied. How many games did they win, lose, and tie?

20. Tina, Dawn, and Harry have $175 together. Tina has three times as much money as Dawn. Dawn has twice as much money as Harry. How much money does each have? $h + 2h + 3(2h) = 175$

21. A board ten feet long is cut into three pieces. One piece is one foot longer than the shortest piece and two feet shorter than the longest piece. How long is each piece?

$x + (x + 1) + [2 + (1 + x)] = 10$

Introduction to Algebra **25**

Summarizing the Lesson

Ask a volunteer to read the objective of this lesson as stated on page 23. Then ask the class why this lesson concentrates only on writing an equation for a problem and not on solving the problem. Discuss difficulties students encountered in writing equations for word problems. Encourage students to offer suggestions for overcoming these difficulties. Emphasize again the value of drawing a sketch to analyze a problem that involves lengths or distances.

Thinking Skills

In the sample problem a variable could have been assigned to any of the three unknowns. If a variable had been assigned to Ling's weight, the resulting equation would have involved the fraction $\frac{1}{3}$. Students should *analyze* the conditions of a problem and choose the most convenient assignment of a variable.

Suggested Assignments

Minimum
Day 1: 24/*P*: 1–12
Day 2: 25/*P*: 13–19 odd
      S 26/Mixed Review

Average
Day 1: 24/*P*: 1–18
Day 2: 25/*P*: 19–22
      S 26/Mixed Review

Maximum
      24/*P*: 2–18 even,
      19–22
      S 26/Mixed Review

Supplementary Materials

Study Guide   pp. 11–12

22. Terri has $\frac{1}{4}$ as many Canadian stamps as her father has in his collection. She has $\frac{1}{7}$ as many Canadian stamps as her grandfather has. How many stamps do they each have if together they have 120 Canadian stamps?

$x + 4x + 7x = 120$

Mixed Review Exercises

Solve if $x \in \{0, 1, 2, 3, 4, 5, 6\}$.

1. $2x + 3 = 5$ {1} **2.** $x \div 2 = 1$ {2} **3.** $16 = 4x$ {4} **4.** $3 = 2x - 5$ {4}

5. $6 + 6x = 36$ {5} **6.** $7 = 2x - 3$ {5} **7.** $3x = x + 4$ {2} **8.** $x \cdot x = 16$ {4}

Translate each phrase into a variable expression.

9. One third of a number $\frac{1}{3}x$

10. 2 less than 4 times a number $4x - 2$

11. 5 more than twice a number $5 + 2x$

12. 4 less than one fourth of a number

$\frac{1}{4}x - 4$

Reading Algebra / Problem Solving

Accurate reading is a vital part of problem solving. When you read a problem, do so slowly and carefully to be sure you fully understand every word, fact, and idea. Look up any words that you do not know in a dictionary or in the glossary at the back of this book. Remember that more information than you need may be given.

When you have read the problem carefully and answered the questions, check your answers with those printed at the back of the book or with your teacher. If your answer is wrong, reread the problem and try to find your error. Good problem solvers learn from their mistakes as well as their successes.

A good way to find your error is to explain to a classmate how you reached your answer. Explaining to someone else—or even explaining aloud to yourself—often helps you clarify your own thinking.

Exercises

One day a cafeteria served twice as much milk as apple juice and three times as much milk as fruit punch. A total of 660 cartons of the three drinks was served. This is 100 more than 80% of the usual number served.

1. What given information do you need in order to find the number of cartons of milk served? Twice as much milk as apple juice and three times as much milk as fruit punch was served; a total of 660 cartons was served.

2. Which is greater, the number of cartons of apple juice served, or the number of cartons of fruit punch served? The number of cartons of apple juice

3. Rob found the number of cartons of milk served by using the equation $x + 2x + 3x = 660$, where x represents the number of cartons of milk served. Was this method correct? Explain. No; the amount of apple juice served was $\frac{1}{2}x$, not $2x$, and the amount of punch served was $\frac{1}{3}x$, not $3x$.

26 *Chapter 1*

1-7 A Problem Solving Plan

Objective   To use the five-step plan to solve word problems over a given domain.

To solve a word problem using algebra you can use the five-step plan below. Notice that you already know how to do the first three steps!

Plan for Solving a Word Problem

Step 1 Read the problem carefully. Decide what unknown numbers are asked for and what facts are known. Making a sketch may help.

Step 2 Choose a variable and use it with the given facts to represent the unknowns described in the problem.

Step 3 Reread the problem and write an equation that represents relationships among the numbers in the problem.

Step 4 Solve the equation and find the unknowns asked for.

Step 5 Check your results with the words of the problem. Give the answer.

In this section you will be asked to check which number in a given domain satisfies the equation you write for Step 3. Later you will learn how to solve an equation (Step 4) using other algebraic methods.

Example 1   Solve using the five-step plan. Write out each step. A choice of possible numbers for one unknown is given.

Phillip has $23 more than Kevin. Together they have $187. How much money does each have?
Choices for Kevin's amount: 72, 78, 82

Solution

Step 1 The unknowns are the amounts of money that Phillip and Kevin have.

Step 2 Let k = Kevin's amount. Then $k + 23$ = Phillip's amount.

Step 3 $k + (k + 23) = 187$

Step 4 Replace k in turn by 72, 78, and 82.

k	$k + (k + 23) = 187$	
72	$72 + (72 + 23) \overset{?}{=} 187$	False
78	$78 + (78 + 23) \overset{?}{=} 187$	False
82	$82 + (82 + 23) \overset{?}{=} 187$	True

Kevin's amount: $k = 82$ Phillip's amount: $k + 23 = 82 + 23 = 105$

Introduction to Algebra   **27**

(continued)

Teaching Suggestions, p. T81
Reading Algebra, p. T81
Group Activities, p. T81
Suggested Extensions, p. T81

Warm-Up Exercises
Which of the following equations have {12} as their solution set?

1. $12x - 12 = 12$
2. $12x - 144 = 0$
3. $12(x - 2) = 120$
4. $\dfrac{x + 12}{x - 2} = 2.4$
5. $2x = x + 2$
   2, 3, and 4

Motivating the Lesson
Pose the following problem. It's 7:00 P.M. and you have an algebra test tomorrow, but you left your algebra book at school. What do you do?

Discuss possible solutions. Emphasize that the solution to every problem involves making a plan. Point out that, in this lesson, students will learn a *five-step plan* for solving word problems in algebra.

Chalkboard Example
Solve using the five-step plan. Write out each step. A choice of possible numbers for one unknown is given.

A board is 17 ft long and a hole is 1 ft farther from one end than it is from the other. How far is the hole from each end of the board? Choices for the shorter distance: 6, 8, 10

Step 1 The problem asks for the distance of the hole from each end.

Step 2 Let x = distance of the hole from one end. Then $17 - x$ = the distance of the hole from the other end.

Step 3 $x + 1 = 17 - x$

Step 4 $6 + 1 \stackrel{?}{=} 17 - 6$ F
$\quad\;\, 8 + 1 \stackrel{?}{=} 17 - 8$ T
$\quad 10 + 1 \stackrel{?}{=} 17 - 10$ F

Step 5 The hole is 8 ft from one end and 9 ft from the other end.

Guided Practice

Solve using the five-step plan. A choice of possible numbers for one unknown is given.

1. Two numbers have a sum of 44. The larger number is 8 more than the smaller. Find the numbers. Choices for the smaller number: 18, 19, 20
   18 and 26

2. A puppy weighs 12 lb more than a kitten. The puppy weighs seven times as much as the kitten. Find the weights of the puppy and kitten. Choices for the weight of the kitten: 1, 2, 3, 5 kitten 2 lb; puppy 14 lb

3. Jason has one and a half times as many books as Ramon. Together they have 45 books. How many books does each boy have? Choices for the number of books Ramon has: 16, 18, 20, 22
   Ramon 18; Jason 27

Step 5 Check the results of Step 4 with the words of the problem.

Phillip has $23 more than Kevin. $105 \stackrel{?}{=} 23 + 82$
$\qquad\qquad\qquad\qquad\qquad\qquad\qquad\quad 105 = 105\;\checkmark$

Together they have $187. $105 + 82 \stackrel{?}{=} 187$
$\qquad\qquad\qquad\qquad\qquad\qquad\quad\; 187 = 187\;\checkmark$

$\therefore$ Kevin has $82 and Phillip has $105.   **Answer**

Problems

Solve using the five-step plan. Write out each step. A choice of possible numbers for one unknown is given. In Problems 11–16, drawing a sketch may help you.

A 1. An oil painting is 16 years older than a watercolor by the same artist. The oil painting is also three times older than the watercolor. How old is each? Choices for the watercolor's age: 4, 8, 12 water color, 8; oil painting, 24

2. The gym is 21 years newer than the auditorium. The gym is also one fourth as old as the auditorium. How old is each building? Choices for the auditorium's age: 26, 27, 28 auditorium, 28; gym, 7

3. Two numbers differ by 57. Their sum is 185. Find the numbers. Choices for the smaller number: 54, 64, 74 smaller, 64; larger, 121

4. One number is four times another number. The larger number is also 87 more than the smaller number. Find the numbers. Choices for the smaller number: 29, 30, 33 smaller, 29; larger, 116

5. A bus went 318 km farther than a car. The car went one third as far as the bus. How far did each vehicle travel? Choices for the car's distance: 147, 151, 159 car, 159 km; bus, 477 km

6. A clown weighs 60 lb more than a trapeze artist. The trapeze artist weighs two thirds as much as the clown. How much does each weigh? Choices for the weight of the trapeze artist: 110, 120, 125 trapeze artist, 120 lb; clown, 180 lb

7. The U.S. Senate has 100 members, all Democrats or Republicans. Recently there were 12 more Democrats than Republicans. How many Senators from each political party were there at that time? Choices for the number of Republicans: 38, 42, 44 44 Republicans; 56 Democrats

8. The ninth grade class has 17 more girls than boys. There are 431 students in all. How many boys are there? How many girls are there? Choices for the number of boys: 191, 202, 207 207 boys; 224 girls

9. Elena has one and a half times as much money as Ramon. Together they have $225. How much money does each have? Choices for Ramon's amount: 80, 90, 95 Ramon, $90; Elena, $135

10. Western State College is 18 years older than Southern State. Western is also $2\frac{1}{2}$ times as old as Southern. How old is each? Choices for Southern State's age: 12, 14, 18 Southern, 12; Western, 30

---

28   *Chapter 1*

B **11.** The height of the flagpole is three fourths the height of the school. The difference in their heights is 4.5 m. What is the height of the school? Choices for school's height: 18, 20, 24 School, 18 m

12. Leah and Barb started at school and jogged in opposite directions. After 30 min they were 10.5 km apart. Barb had traveled 1.5 km farther than Leah. How far did each jog? Choices for Leah's distance: 4.5, 4.6, 4.7 Leah, 4.5 km; Barb, 6 km

13. A rectangle is 12 m longer than it is wide. Its perimeter is 68 m. Find its length and width. Choices for the width: 10, 11, 12 width, 11 m; length, 23 m

14. The length of a rectangle is $3\frac{1}{2}$ times its width. Its perimeter is 108 cm. Find its length and width. Choices for the width: 12, 18, 24 width, 12 cm; length, 42 cm

15. A rectangle is 15 ft longer than it is wide and its area is 324 ft². Find its length and width. Choices for the width: 10, 12, 16 width, 12 ft; length, 27 ft

C **16.** A rectangle and a square have the same width but the rectangle is 5 m longer than the square. Their total area is 133 m². Find the dimensions of each figure. Choices for the square's width: 6, 7, 8 rectangle: width, 7 m; length, 12 m square: width, 7 m; length, 7 m

17. Luis weighs 5 lb more than Carla. Carla weighs 2 lb more than Rita. Together their weights total 333 lb. How much does each weigh? Choices for Luis's weight: 110, 115, 120 Luis, 115 lb; Carla, 110 lb; Rita, 108 lb

18. Tony has twice as much money as Alicia. She has $16 less than Ralph. Together they have $200. How much money does each have? Choices for Ralph's amount: 59, 62, 63 Ralph, $62; Alicia, $46; Tony, $92

Mixed Review Exercises

Simplify.

1. $\dfrac{7 \cdot 2 + 6 \cdot 6}{10 - 6 + 1}$ 10

2. $(30 - 4 + 4 \div 2) \div (21 \div 3)$ 4

3. $30 - (12 \div 3 + 2)$ 24

4. $6 \cdot 17 + 17 \cdot 3$ 153

Translate each sentence into an equation.

5. Six times a number is 36. 6x = 36

6. Six is two less than a number. 6 = x − 2

7. Two more than twice a number is ten. 2x + 2 = 10

8. One third of a number is six. $\frac{1}{3}x = 6$

Introduction to Algebra **29**

Problem Solving Strategies

Understanding the problem, planning, solving, and looking back are the key parts of a problem solving plan. In this lesson the planning focuses on choosing a variable and writing an equation. Ask your students to recall other problem solving strategies studied in prior courses (e.g., using a formula, a sketch, trial and error; working backwards).

Summarizing the Lesson

Have students recall the five-step plan for solving word problems. You may wish to extend the objective of this lesson by writing a few simple equations on the chalkboard and asking the students to think of a problem that corresponds to each equation. Sample equations could include:

$$x + 2x = 15$$
$$x + (6 + x) = 50$$

Suggested Assignments

Minimum
  28/P: 1–10
S 29/Mixed Review

Average
  28/P: 1–15 odd
S 29/Mixed Review
R 30/Self-Test 2

Maximum
  28/P: 2–14 even,
    16–18
S 29/Mixed Review

Supplementary Materials

Study Guide   pp. 13–14
Practice Master   2
Computer Activity   5
Resource Book   p. 80

Self-Test 2

Vocabulary   formula (p. 15)

1. A variable expression for eight times the sum of a number n and four is __?__. $8(n + 4)$

   Obj. 1-4, p. 14

Translate into an equation.

2. Twice a number x is two more than x. $2x = 2 + x$

   Obj. 1-5, p. 19

3. A rope 11 ft long is cut so that one piece is 2 ft longer than twice the other piece. What are the lengths of the pieces? $x + (2 + 2x) = 11$

   Obj. 1-6, p. 23

4. Use the five-step plan to solve the following problem.

   A rectangle has an area of 55 ft². Its length is 6 ft more than its width. Find the length and the width. Choices for the width: 5, 7, 9 length, 11 ft; width, 5 ft

   Obj. 1-7, p. 27

Check your answers with those at the back of the book.

Biographical Note / Maria Mitchell

Maria Mitchell (1818–1889) was the first woman in the United States to be recognized for her work in astronomy. Born on the island of Nantucket, off the coast of Massachusetts, Mitchell helped her father with calculations needed to rate the chronometers of whaling ships.

Mitchell became the librarian of the Nantucket Atheneum in 1836 and continued to study mathematics and astronomy. On October 1, 1847, while conducting telescope observations, Mitchell discovered a new comet that was later named for her. She gained worldwide recognition for this discovery.

In 1865 Mitchell became the first professor of astronomy and the director of the observatory at Vassar College. In 1869 she became the first woman elected to the American Philosophical Society for her scientific achievements.

Numbers on a Line

Explorations, p. 685

Teaching Suggestions, p. T82

Suggested Extensions, p. T82

1-8 Number Lines

Objective   To graph real numbers on a number line and to compare real numbers.

The numbers used in elementary algebra can be pictured as points on a *number line* as shown below. The point labeled zero is called the **origin.** The origin separates the line into a **positive side** and **negative side.** For a horizontal line, the side to the right of the origin is the positive side.

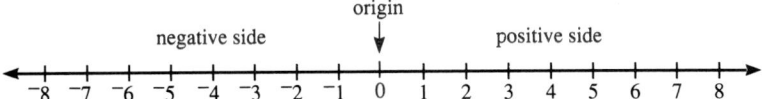

Equal units of distance are marked on both sides of the origin. The end-points of successive units are paired with *negative and positive integers.* The number $^-1$ is read "negative one." The number "positive one" can be written either as 1 or $^+1$. Zero is neither positive nor negative.

> **Positive integers:** $\{1, 2, 3, 4, \ldots\}$
>
> **Negative integers:** $\{^-1, ^-2, ^-3, ^-4, \ldots\}$

The three dots are read "and so on." They indicate that the list continues without end. The positive integers, negative integers, and zero make up the set of **integers.**

> **Integers:** $\{\ldots, ^-3, ^-2, ^-1, 0, 1, 2, 3, \ldots\}$

The set of **whole numbers** consists of zero and all positive integers.

> **Whole numbers:** $\{0, 1, 2, 3, \ldots\}$

A number line contains points corresponding to fractions and decimals as well as integers. A **positive number** is a number paired with a point on the positive side of a number line. A **negative number** is a number paired with a point on the negative side of a number line. For example:

A is 1.5 units from 0 on the positive side.
The *positive* number 1.5 is paired with *A.*

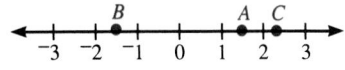

B is 1.5 units from 0 on the negative side.
The *negative* number $^-1.5$ is paired with *B.*

On a number line, the point paired with a number is called the **graph** of the number. The number paired with a point is called the **coordinate** of the point. Point *C,* above, is the graph of $2\frac{1}{3}$, and $2\frac{1}{3}$ is the coordinate of *C.*

Introduction to Algebra   **31**

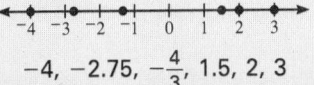

Check for Understanding

Here is a suggested use of the Oral Exercises to check students' understanding as you teach the lesson.
Oral Exs. 1–16: use after Example 1.
Oral Exs. 17–24: use after Example 2.

Guided Practice

Write a number to represent each situation. Then write the opposite of that situation and write a number to represent it.

1. Eight steps up
8; eight steps down; −8

2. Two miles west
−2; two miles east; 2

3. Translate into symbols:
Negative 3 is greater than negative 33.
−3 > −33

4. State two inequalities, one with > and one with <, for the coordinates of the points shown below.

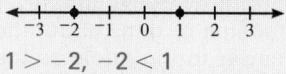

1 > −2, −2 < 1

Complete using < or > to make a true statement.

5. −5 _?_ −4   <

6. $\frac{1}{2}$ _?_ $\frac{1}{3}$ >

7. −10 _?_ 0.1   <

Any number that is either positive, negative, or zero is called a **real number.** When you graph real numbers, you take the following for granted.

1. Each real number is paired with exactly one point on a number line.
2. Each point on a number line is paired with exactly one real number.

Thus, the graphs of *all* the real numbers make up the entire number line:

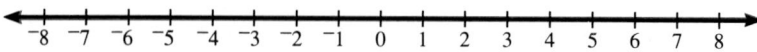

The arrowheads indicate that the number line and the graphs go on without end in both directions.

Because positive and negative numbers suggest opposite directions, they are sometimes called *directed numbers.* You use them for measurements that have *direction* as well as size.

Example 1   Write a number to represent each situation.

a. A temperature rise of 6°:   6
A temperature drop of 6°:   ⁻6

b. 7.3 km north: 7.3
7.3 km south: ⁻7.3

c. A wage increase of $15:   15
A wage decrease of $15:   ⁻15

Inequality symbols are used to show the *order* of two real numbers.

< means "is less than"   3 < 7
> means "is greater than"   7 > 3

The greater number is always placed at the greater (or open) end of the inequality symbol. The statements 3 < 7 and 7 > 3 give the same information and are interchangeable.

On a horizontal number line, such as the one above, the numbers increase from left to right and decrease from right to left. By studying the number line, you can see that the following statements are true.

⁻5 < ⁻2	⁻5 < 0	⁻5 < 3
⁻2 > ⁻5	0 > ⁻5	3 > ⁻5

Example 2   Graph the numbers ⁻1, 2.5, 0, ⁻3, $\frac{7}{3}$, and ⁻3.75 on a number line. Then list them in increasing order.

Solution

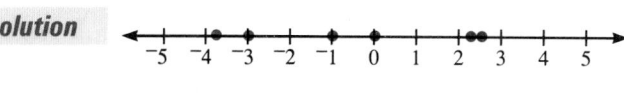

From least to greatest: ⁻3.75, ⁻3, ⁻1, 0, $\frac{7}{3}$, 2.5

32   *Chapter 1*

Oral Exercises

Exercises 1–16 refer to the number line below.

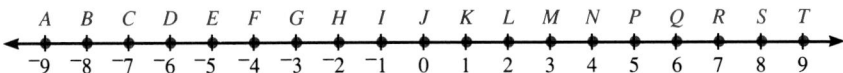

Name the point that is the graph of the given coordinate.

Sample 1 $^-7$ **Solution**   Point C

1. 8 S 2. 0 J 3. $^-1$ I 4. $^-6$ D 5. 4 N 6. $^-4$ F

State the coordinate of the given point.

7. G $^-3$ 8. R 7 9. T 9 10. H $^-2$ 11. B $^-8$ 12. J 0

Sample 2   The point halfway between P and Q **Solution**   5.5

13. The point halfway between L and M 2.5
14. The point halfway between D and E $^-5.5$
15. The point one third of the way from E to K $^-3$
16. The point one fourth of the way from I to A $^-3$

Read aloud each inequality statement. Tell whether it is true or false.

17. $2 < 5$ True   18. $^-4 < 0$ True   19. $^-3 > ^-2$ False   20. $^-5 < \frac{1}{4}$ True

21. $8 > ^-9$ True   22. $^-3 > ^-4$ True   23. $7 > 0$ True   24. $^-2 < ^-2.01$ False

Written Exercises

Write a number to represent each situation. Then write the opposite of that situation and write a number to represent it.

A
1. Five steps down $^-5;\ 5$
2. Two rooms to the right 2; $^-2$
3. 190 m above sea level 190; $^-190$
4. Nine degrees below freezing (0° C) $^-9;\ 9$
5. A profit of $18 18; $^-18$
6. Four losses $^-4;\ 4$
7. 15 km west $^-15;\ 15$
8. Latitude of 41° north 41; $^-41$
9. Receipts of $85 85; $^-85$
10. A bank withdrawal of $25 $^-25;\ 25$
11. One foot below ground $^-1;\ 1$
12. 3 bonus points 3; $^-3$
13. A loss of $50 $^-50;\ 50$
14. 10 lb lost $^-10;\ 10$

Introduction to Algebra   **33**

Translate each statement into symbols.

15. Six is greater than negative nine. $6 > {}^-9$

16. Negative eleven is less than negative one. $^-11 < {}^-1$

17. Negative eight is greater than negative ten. $^-8 > {}^-10$

18. Ten is greater than seven. $10 > 7$

19. Six is less than six and five tenths. $6 < 6.5$

20. Zero is greater than negative three tenths. $0 > {}^-0.3$

21. Negative thirteen is less than zero. $^-13 < 0$

22. One eighth is less than one seventh.
$\frac{1}{8} < \frac{1}{7}$

List the letters of the points whose coordinates are given.

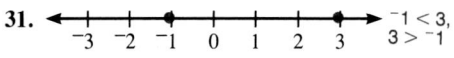

R S Z U A M T P L K B D N H C F J V E Q I Y G W

$^-9$ $^-8$ $^-7$ $^-6$ $^-5$ $^-4$ $^-3$ $^-2$ $^-1$ 0 1 2 3 4 5 6 7 8 9

23. $^-8$, 2 *S, F*

24. $^-5$, 4 *M, V*

25. 0, $^-9$ *N, R*

26. $^-6$, 8 *A, G*

27. 6, $^-6$, $^-6\frac{1}{2}$ *Q, A, U* **28.** 1, $^-1$, $^-1\frac{1}{2}$ *H, D, B* **29.** $^-5$, $^-4\frac{1}{2}$, $^-4$ *M, T, P* **30.** $^-8$, $^-7$, $7\frac{1}{2}$ *S, Z, Y*

State two inequalities, one with > and one with <, for the coordinates of the points shown in color.

Sample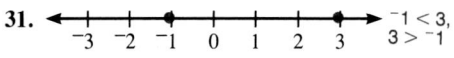
$^-3$ $^-2$ $^-1$ 0 1 2 3

Solution $^-2 < 1, \; 1 > {}^-2$

31.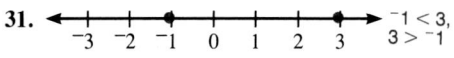
$^-3$ $^-2$ $^-1$ 0 1 2 3
$^-1 < 3,$
$3 > {}^-1$

32.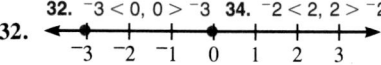
$^-3$ $^-2$ $^-1$ 0 1 2 3

32. $^-3 < 0, 0 > {}^-3$ **34.** $^-2 < 2, 2 > {}^-2$

33.
$^-1$ 0 1 2 3 4 5
$0 < 2,$
$2 > 0$

34.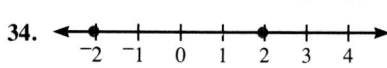
$^-2$ $^-1$ 0 1 2 3 4

35.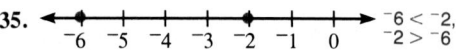
$^-6$ $^-5$ $^-4$ $^-3$ $^-2$ $^-1$ 0
$^-6 < {}^-2,$
$^-2 > {}^-6$

36.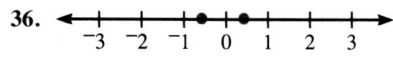
$^-3$ $^-2$ $^-1$ 0 1 2 3

37.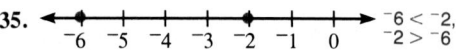
0 1 2 3 4 5 6
$0 < 5,$
$5 > 0$

38.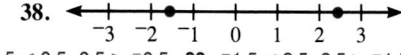
$^-3$ $^-2$ $^-1$ 0 1 2 3

36. $^-0.5 < 0.5, 0.5 > {}^-0.5$ **38.** $^-1.5 < 2.5, 2.5 > {}^-1.5$

Complete using one of the symbols < or > to make a true statement.

39. $^-4 \underline{\;?\;} 0$ $<$

40. $0 \underline{\;?\;} {}^-5$ $>$

41. $6 \underline{\;?\;} 5 + 4$ $<$

42. $8 - 7 \underline{\;?\;} {}^-1$ $>$

43. $0 \underline{\;?\;} {}^-1$ $>$

44. $0 \times 0 \underline{\;?\;} 1$ $<$

45. $^-3.1 \underline{\;?\;} {}^-3.2$ $>$

46. $-\frac{2}{5} \underline{\;?\;} -\frac{1}{5}$ $<$

Graph the given numbers on a number line. Draw a separate line for each exercise. Then list the numbers in increasing order.

$^-1$, $^-0.5$, 0, 1.5

B **47.** 1, 2, $^-2$, $^-1$ $^-2$, $^-1$, 1, 2 **48.** 3, $^-3$, 6, $^-6$ $^-6$, $^-3$, 3, 6 **49.** 0, 1.5, $^-1$, $^-0.5$

50. $^-1$, $^-2$, $^-1.5$, 0 $^-2$, $^-1.5$, $^-1$, 0 **51.** $^-1\frac{2}{3}$, $^-3$, 0, $\frac{-1}{3}$ $^-3$, $^-1\frac{2}{3}$, $\frac{-1}{3}$, 0 **52.** 0, $^-4$, 1, $\frac{1}{2}$

$^-4$, 0, $\frac{1}{2}$, 1

53. $^-1\frac{1}{4}$, $\frac{3}{4}$, $\frac{-1}{4}$, $2\frac{1}{4}$ $^-1\frac{1}{4}$, $\frac{-1}{4}$, $\frac{3}{4}$, $2\frac{1}{4}$ **54.** $\frac{5}{3}$, $\frac{10}{3}$, $\frac{2}{3}$, $\frac{-2}{3}$ $\frac{-2}{3}$, $\frac{2}{3}$, $\frac{5}{3}$, $\frac{10}{3}$

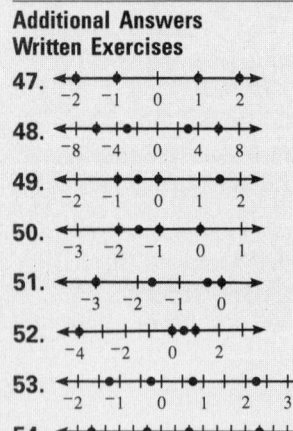

55. Freida is taller than Cora but shorter than Stu.
Stu is taller than Freida but shorter than Janelle. Cora, Freida, Stu, Janelle
List the names of these people in order from shortest to tallest.

56. Jack and Nick are both older than Mona.
Pete is older than Jack but younger than Nick. Nick, Pete, Jack, Mona
List the names of these people in order from oldest to youngest.

C **57.** On a number line, point M has coordinate 2 and point T has coordinate 5.
What is the coordinate of the point between M and T that is half as far
from M as it is from T? 3

58. On a number line, point C has coordinate ⁻2 and point D has coordinate 4.
What is the coordinate of the point between C and D that is twice as far
from C as it is from D? 2

Mixed Review Exercises

Evaluate if $a = 2$, $b = 5$, $c = 4$, $x = 3$, and $y = 7$.

1. $3ab - 2x$ 24   **2.** $4x(y - b)$ 24   **3.** $a \cdot (3y \div 7)$ 6

4. $\frac{1}{5}(4c - 1)$ 3   **5.** $3y - (2a + c \div 2)$ 15   **6.** $\left(\frac{1}{2}ac\right) + (5 - x)b$ 14

Translate each sentence into an equation.

7. Thirty decreased by a number is twelve. $30 - x = 12$ **8.** Four more than a number is two. $x + 4 = 2$

9. The product of a number and 6 is 2. $6x = 2$ **10.** One fourth of a number is one. $\frac{1}{4}x = 1$

Challenge

1, 3, 6, 10, 15, . . . are called triangular numbers because they can be
represented by dots arranged to form equilateral triangles.

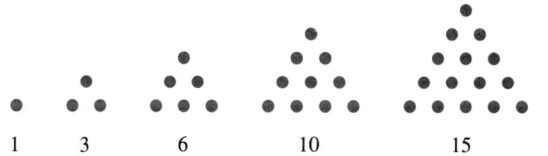

1   3   6   10   15   and so on

1. Find the next five triangular numbers. 21, 28, 36, 45, 55

2. Let n represent the position of a particular triangular number in the list
($n = 1$ for 1, $n = 2$ for 3, and so on). Show that for $n = 1, 2, . . . , 10$,
the nth triangular number $= \frac{n(n + 1)}{2}$.

Introduction to Algebra   **35**

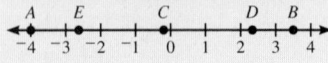
1-9 Opposites and Absolute Values

Objective   To use opposites and absolute values.

The paired points on the number line below are the same distance from the origin but on opposite sides of the origin. The origin is paired with itself.

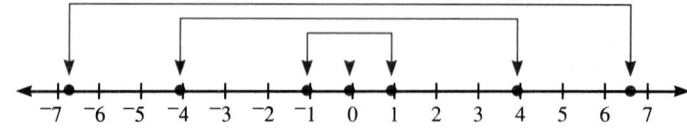

The coordinates of the paired points can also be paired:

0 with 0 $^-1$ with 1 $^-4$ with 4 $^-6.8$ with 6.8

Each number in a pair such as 4 and $^-4$ is called the **opposite** of the other number. The opposite of a is written $-a$. For example:

$$-4 \quad = \,^-4, \quad \text{read "The opposite of four equals negative four."}$$
$$-(^-4) = \quad 4, \quad \text{read "The opposite of negative four equals four."}$$
$$-0 \quad = \quad 0, \quad \text{read "The opposite of zero equals zero."}$$

The numerals -4 (lowered minus sign) and $^-4$ (raised minus sign) name the same number. Thus, -4 can mean "negative four" or "the opposite of four."

To simplify notation, lowered minus signs will be used to write negative numbers throughout the rest of this book.

Caution: $-a$, read "the opposite of a," is not necessarily a negative number. For example, if $a = -2$, then $-a = -(-2) = 2$.

1. If a is positive, then $-a$ is negative.
2. If a is negative, then $-a$ is positive.
3. If $a = 0$, then $-a = 0$.
4. The opposite of $-a$ is a; that is, $-(-a) = a$.

Example 1   Simplify: **a.** $-(7 + 9)$ **b.** $-(-1.8)$

Solution   **a.** -16 **b.** 1.8

Example 2   Evaluate $-n + 14$, if $n = -8$.

Solution $-n + 14 = -(-8) + 14$
$$= 8 + 14$$
$$= 22 \quad \textbf{Answer}$$

In any pair of nonzero opposites, such as −4 and 4, one number is negative and the other is positive. The positive number of any pair of opposite nonzero real numbers is called the **absolute value** of each number in the pair.

The absolute value of a number a is denoted by $|a|$.
1. If a is positive, $|a| = a$.   Example: $|8| = 8$
2. If a is negative, $|a| = -a$.   Example: $|-8| = -(-8) = 8$
3. If a is zero, $|a| = 0$.   Example: $|0| = 0$

The absolute value of a number may also be thought of as *the distance between the graph of the number and the origin on a number line*. The graphs of both 4 and −4 are 4 units from the origin.

Example 3 Simplify: **a.** $|-7| + |5|$ **b.** $|-15| + 8|-3|$

Solution   **a.** $|-7| + |5| = 7 + 5$ **b.** $|-15| + 8|-3| = 15 + 8(3)$
$= 12$ *Answer* $= 15 + 24$
$= 39$ *Answer*

Example 4 Solve $|x| = 3$.

Solution   Think of which numbers are 3 units from the origin. They are 3 and −3, so the replacements for x that make $|x| = 3$ true are 3 and −3. Therefore $x = 3$ or $x = -3$.
∴ the solution set is $\{3, -3\}$.   *Answer*

Oral Exercises

Name the opposite and the absolute value of each number.

1. 7 −7, 7   **2.** 5 −5, 5   **3.** −1 1, 1   **4.** −9 9, 9   **5.** 24 −24, 24

6. −56 56, 56   **7.** 0 0, 0   **8.** 0.3 −0.3, 0.3   **9.** 6.5 −6.5, 6.5   **10.** $-2\frac{1}{3}$ $2\frac{1}{3}$, $2\frac{1}{3}$

Read each expression aloud. Then simplify.

11. $-(-2)$ 2   **12.** $-\left(-\frac{1}{2}\right)$ $\frac{1}{2}$ **13.** $|12|$ 12   **14.** $-(9 + 8)$ −17

15. $-(9 - 8)$ −1   **16.** $-[-(-8)]$ −8   **17.** $-[-(-0)]$ 0   **18.** $|-14|$ 14

19. $|-3.4|$ 3.4   **20.** $-|-4|$ −4   **21.** $-|0|$ 0   **22.** $6 - |-6|$ 0

Introduction to Algebra   **37**

Solve for x.
7. $|x| = 88$ 88 or −88
8. $|x| = 12.9$ 12.9 or −12.9

Check for Understanding
Here is a suggested use of the Oral Exercises to check students' understanding as you teach the lesson.
Oral Exs. 1–10: use after Example 3.
Oral Exs. 11–22: use after Example 4.

Guided Practice
Simplify.
1. $-(12 - 12)$ 0
2. $-[-(4)]$ 4
3. $|2.6| + |-0.4|$ 3
4. $|-246| + 4$ 250
Translate each statement into symbols.
5. The absolute value of 6 is less than the absolute value of −20. $|6| < |-20|$
6. The opposite of −3 is greater than the opposite of 2. $-(-3) > -2$

Summarizing the Lesson
Write the following statements on the chalkboard. Ask whether each is true or false. Have students give an example to verify their answer.
• The absolute value of a number is always positive. false
• A number and its absolute value can never be equal. false
• If b is a negative number, then the opposite of b is also negative. false

Suggested Assignments

Minimum
   38/3–33 mult. of 3
S 34/39–49 odd
   39/Mixed Review

Average
Lesson 1-9 is covered in the
assignment for Lesson 1-8.

Maximum
   38/2–38 even, 43–45
S 39/Mixed Review

Supplementary Materials

Study Guide   pp. 17–18
Practice Masters   3, 4
Test Master   2
Resource Book   p. 81

Complete each statement.

23. If n is a negative number, then $-n$ is a ___?___ number. positive

24. If n is a positive number, then $-n$ is a ___?___ number. negative

25. The only number whose absolute value is zero is ___?___. 0

26. A real number that is its own opposite is ___?___. 0

27. How many solutions are there for the equation $|x| = -7$? Explain.
None, the absolute value of a number cannot be negative.

Written Exercises

Simplify.

A   **1.** $-(7 + 5)$ –12

2. $-(8 - 2)$ –6

3. $-(13 - 13)$ 0

4. $-(0 + 0)$ 0

5. $[-(-9)] + 10$ 19

6. $[-(-7)] + 1$ 8

7. $6 + [-(-2)]$ 8

8. $3 - [-(-1)]$ 2

9. $8 + |-3|$ 11

10. $|-11| + 4$ 15

11. $|-8| + |6|$ 14

12. $|2| + |-9|$ 11

13. $\left|-\dfrac{3}{2}\right| + |0|$ $\dfrac{3}{2}$

14. $|-1| - |0|$ 1

15. $|-0.7| + |-3.3|$ 4

16. $|-2.8| + |2.8|$ 5.6

17. $\left|\dfrac{1}{2}\right| + \left|-\dfrac{1}{2}\right|$ 1

18. $\left|-\dfrac{3}{4}\right| - \left|\dfrac{1}{4}\right|$ $\dfrac{1}{2}$

19. $|6| - |6|$ 0

20. $|6| - |-6|$ 0

Complete using one of the symbols >, <, or = to make a true statement.

21. $-(-8)$ ___?___ (-8) >

22. $-(-2)$ ___?___ $|-3|$ <

23. $|-8|$ ___?___ $|-10|$ <

24. $|-15|$ ___?___ $|-6|$ >

25. $-|-8|$ ___?___ -8 =

26. -3 ___?___ $-|-3|$ =

Translate each statement into symbols.

27. The absolute value of negative five is greater than two. $|-5| > 2$

28. Four is less than the absolute value of negative ten. $4 < |-10|$

29. The opposite of negative two is greater than the opposite of negative one. $-(-2) > -(-1)$

30. The opposite of eight is less than the opposite of four. $-8 < -4$

Solve each equation over the set of real numbers. If there is no solution, explain why there is none.

B   **31.** $|n| = 0$ {0}

32. $|p| = 2$ {2, –2}

33. $|t| = \dfrac{1}{2}$ $\left\{\dfrac{1}{2}, -\dfrac{1}{2}\right\}$

34. $|z| = 0.3$ {0.3, –0.3}

35. $|a| = -2$ No sol.

36. $|b| = -9$ No sol.

37. $|-q| = 1$ {1, –1}

38. $|-x| = 5$ {5, –5}

Evaluate each expression if $a = 1.5$, $b = -2$, and $c = -1.7$.

39. $|a| + |b|$ 3.5

40. $a + |-b|$ 3.5

41. $4a - |b| - |c|$ 2.3

42. $2|b| - |a| + |c|$ 4.2

43. $(a + 8.5) - [(-b) + |c|]$ 6.3

44. $(10.5 - a) - [|c| + (-b)]$ 5.3

C 45. Two of the following statements are true and one is false. Which one is false? Explain why you think it's false.

    a. The absolute value of every real number is a positive number.

    b. There is at least one real number whose absolute value is zero.

    c. The absolute value of a real number is never a negative number.

    (a) is false. 0 is a real number and |0| = 0 which is not a positive number.

Mixed Review Exercises

Simplify.

1. $6 - (2 + 3)$ 1

2. $6 - 2 + 3$ 7

3. $6 \div (2 + 1)$ 2

4. $(4 - 2) \cdot (5 - 1)$ 8

5. $7 - 2 \cdot 3$ 1

6. $15 - 6 \div (2 + 1)$ 13

Write a number to represent each situation. Then write the opposite of that number.

7. Three steps down −3, 3

8. A bank withdrawal of $50 −50, 50

9. A profit of $1000 1000, −1000

10. A pay raise of $.50 per hour 0.5, −0.5

Self-Test 3

Vocabulary   origin (p. 31)
                positive side (p. 31)
                negative side (p. 31)
                positive integer (p. 31)
                negative integer (p. 31)
                integers (p. 31)
                whole numbers (p. 31)
                positive number (p. 31)

negative number (p. 31)
graph (p. 31)
coordinate (p. 31)
real number (p. 32)
inequality symbols (p. 32)
opposite (p. 36)
absolute value (p. 37)

1. Graph the given numbers on the same number line: 2, ⁻3, 3, ⁻2   **Obj. 1-8, p. 31**

Simplify.

2. $-(4 + 3)$ −7

3. $|-11| + |3|$ 14   **Obj. 1-9, p. 36**

4. $-[-(-3)]$ −3

5. $\left|-\dfrac{1}{3}\right| + \left|\dfrac{1}{3}\right|$ $\dfrac{2}{3}$

Check your answers with those at the back of the book.

Introduction to Algebra   **39**

Quick Quiz

1. Graph the given numbers on the same number line:

$2\dfrac{1}{2}$, −3, −1.5, 0

Simplify.

2. $-(-3) + 12$ 15

3. $|-8| - 1$ 7

4. $2|-4| + |-3|$ 11

5. Which of the following numbers are less than −23?

23, −24, −239, 239, 0, −23.5, −22.5

−24, −239, −23.5

6. Which is smaller −44.4 or −43.4? −44.4

Math teachers with Spanish-speaking students might assign this problem:

Cuarenta obreros construyen en 28 días 1220 m de un camino. ¿Que longitud construiran 24 obreros en 28 días?

Here is a translation:

Forty workers construct 1220 m of road in 28 days. How many meters will 24 workers construct in 28 days?

Can you follow the solution below?

Solución:

40 obr. 1220 m

1 obr. $\dfrac{1220 \text{ m}}{40}$

24 obr. $\dfrac{1220 \text{ m} \times 24}{40} = 732$ m

Bilingual teachers are fluent in two languages. For certification in public schools, a bachelor's degree with courses in education and mathematics is required.

Chapter Summary

1. A numerical expression represents a particular number. To simplify a numerical expression, replace it with the simplest name for its value.

2. A variable expression is evaluated by replacing each variable with a given value and simplifying the resulting numerical expression.

3. Grouping symbols are used to enclose an expression that should be simplified first. (When there are no grouping symbols, follow the steps listed on page 7.)

4. Replacing each variable in an open sentence by each of the values in its domain is a way to find solutions of the open sentence.

5. A word problem can often be solved by writing an equation based on the given facts and then solving the equation as outlined on page 27.

6. The positive numbers, the negative numbers, and zero make up the real numbers. These numbers can be paired with the points on a number line, thereby showing their order.

7. The opposite of a number a is written as $-a$. The positive number of any pair of opposite nonzero real numbers is called the absolute value of each number in the pair. The absolute value of a is written as $|a|$.

Supplementary Materials

Practice Master   4
Resource Book   p. 190

Chapter Review

Write the letter of the correct answer.

1. Simplify $36 \div (9 \cdot 4)$.   1-1
   a. 19   **b.** 0   **c.** 81   (**d.**) 1

2. Evaluate $(x + y) - 3z$ if $x = 7$, $y = 8$, and $z = 0$.
   a. 12   **b.** 0   (**c.**) 15   **d.** 5

3. Evaluate $\dfrac{3x - y}{3(x - y)}$ if $x = 5$ and $y = 3$.   1-2
   a. 1   (**b.**) 2   **c.** 3   **d.** 6

4. Solve $9 = 3c - 6$ over the domain $\{0, 1, 2, 3, 4, 5\}$.   1-3
   a. $\{0\}$ **b.** $\{1\}$ **c.** $\{2\}$ (**d.**) $\{5\}$

5. Translate the following phrase into a variable expression.   1-4
   The difference of seven times n and three.
   a. $7(n - 3)$ **b.** $3 + 7n$ (**c.**) $7n - 3$ **d.** $7(3 - n)$

6. Translate the following sentence into an equation.   1-5
   The product of nine and four less than n is twenty-seven.
   a. $9n - 4 = 27$ (**b.**) $9(n - 4) = 27$
   c. $9(4 - n) = 27$ **d.** $9 + 4 - n = 27$

7. Use the figure and the information beside
   it to write an equation involving x.
   a. $14 + x + x = 28$ **b.** $x + 7 = 28$
   (**c.**) $7x = 28$ **d.** $(7 + x)(7 + x) = 28$

   Rectangle
   Area $= 28$

8. Translate the following problem into an equation.   1-6
   (1) Katie spent $1 more than Mark.   (2) Together they spent $5.
   How much did Mark spend?
   a. $m = m + 1$ **b.** $5 = k + (k + 1)$
   c. $k + 1 = 5$ (**d.**) $(m + 1) + m = 5$

9. Wilt weighs $1\frac{1}{2}$ times as much as Anita. Together they weigh 250 lb. Find   1-7
   Anita's weight. Choices for Anita's weight: 90, 100, 105, 150
   a. 90 lb   (**b.**) 100 lb   **c.** 105 lb   **d.** 150 lb

10. If a surplus of 12 items is represented by 12, determine the opposite of that   1-8
    number and describe the measurement indicated by that opposite.
    a. 12; a gain of 12 items.   **b.** $\frac{1}{12}$; each item is $\frac{1}{12}$ of the total.
    c. $|12|$; there are 12 items.   (**d.**) -12; a shortage of 12 items.

11. Solve $|m| = 4$ over the set of real numbers.   1-9
    a. no solution   **b.** $\{-4\}$
    c. $\{4\}$ (**d.**) $\{-4, 4\}$

12. Which of the following is a true statement?
    a. $-5(0) > |-5| + 0$ **b.** $6 < -(-6)$
    (**c.**) $-\frac{3}{4} > -\frac{5}{4}$ **d.** $6 - |-4| > 9$

Introduction to Algebra   **41**

Chapter Test

Simplify.

1. $5 + (15 \div 5)$ 8

2. $(4 + 12) \cdot 3$ 48   **1-1**

3. $(64 \div 4) + 2$ 18

4. $(12 - 7) \cdot 9$ 45   **1-2**

Evaluate.

5. $7x(y - z)$ if $x = 5$, $y = 8$, and $z = 6$. 70

6. Circumference of a circle: $2\pi r$
   if $r = 49$
   Use $\frac{22}{7}$ as an approximate value for π. 308

Solve if $x \in \{0, 1, 2, 3, 4, 5, 6\}$.

$\{0, 1, 2, 3, 4, 5, 6\}$

7. $56 = 14 + 7x$ {6}

8. $x \cdot x = 0$ {0}

9. $\frac{1}{2}x = \frac{x}{2}$ **1-3**

10. Inga lives 3 miles more than twice as far from school as Brent does. If   **1-4**
    Brent lives b miles from school, then Inga lives __?__ miles from school. $2b + 3$

11. Use the figure and the information below   **1-5**
    it to write an equation involving x.
    $18 = 14 + x$

    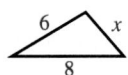

    Perimeter = 18

12. Translate the following problem into an equation.   **1-6**
    (1) Together Jon and Amy spent $29 on a birthday gift.
    (2) Jon spent $5 more than Amy.
    How much did each spend? $a + (a + 5) = 29$

13. Kirsten built a rectangular corral with a fence on three sides. A side of the   **1-7**
    barn served as a short side of the corral. She used 130 m of fencing. The
    length of the corral was 20 m longer than the width. Find the dimensions
    of the corral. Choices for the width: 25, 30, 35 length, 50 m; width, 30 m

**Graph the given numbers on a number line. Draw a separate line for each
exercise. Then list the numbers in increasing order.**

14. $2, 5, -2, -5$ $-5, -2, 2, 5$

15. $0, \frac{1}{4}, -3, 1$ $-3, 0, \frac{1}{4}, 1$ **1-8**

Simplify.

16. $|-2.1| + 3.2$ 5.3

17. $-(-2.75)$ 2.75

18. $-|4 + 1.5|$ -5.5 **1-9**

Complete using one of the symbols >, <, or = to make a true statement.

19. $-(-5)$ __?__ -4 >

20. $-|-10|$ __?__ $|8|$ <

Maintaining Skills

Perform the indicated operations.

Sample 1

12 1
729.35
84.
+ 68.29
881.64

Sample 2

625.3
× 32.1
6253
12506
18759
20072.13

1. 0.0056
    2.3
    18.232
    + 9.41
    29.9476

2. 42.31
    8.79
    + 13.26
    64.36

3. 22.6
    153.3
    + 201.8
    377.7

4. 27
    6.25
    108.1
    + 35.72
    177.07

5. 318
    × 5.2
    1653.6

6. 208.2
    × 10.3
    2144.46

7. 7.51
    × 2.2
    16.522

8. 0.876
    × 0.09
    0.07884

9. 824.2
    × 1.2
    989.04

10. 0.222
    × 11.1
    2.4642

11. 35.83
    + 9.96
    45.79

12. 20.05
    + 8.87
    28.92

Rewrite the fractions using their least common denominator.

Sample 3 $\frac{7}{8}$ and $\frac{2}{3}$

Solution The least common denominator is 24.

$$\frac{7}{8} = \frac{7}{8} \cdot \frac{3}{3} = \frac{21}{24} \qquad \frac{2}{3} = \frac{2}{3} \cdot \frac{8}{8} = \frac{16}{24}$$

13. $\frac{5}{8}$ and $\frac{3}{4}$ $\frac{5}{8}, \frac{6}{8}$
14. $\frac{2}{3}$ and $\frac{3}{5}$ $\frac{10}{15}, \frac{9}{15}$
15. $\frac{2}{7}$ and $\frac{2}{3}$ $\frac{6}{21}, \frac{14}{21}$
16. $\frac{5}{12}$ and $\frac{3}{2}$ $\frac{5}{12}, \frac{18}{12}$

Perform the indicated operations.

Sample 4 $\frac{3}{7} + \frac{2}{3}$

Solution $\frac{3}{7} + \frac{2}{3} = \frac{3}{7} \cdot \frac{3}{3} + \frac{2}{3} \cdot \frac{7}{7} = \frac{9}{21} + \frac{14}{21} = \frac{23}{21}$

Sample 5 $\frac{2}{5} \cdot \frac{7}{8}$

Solution $\frac{2}{5} \cdot \frac{7}{8} = \frac{\overset{1}{\cancel{2}} \cdot 7}{5 \cdot \underset{4}{\cancel{8}}} = \frac{7}{20}$

17. $\frac{3}{5} + \frac{4}{9}$ $\frac{47}{45}$
18. $\frac{2}{7} + \frac{1}{4}$ $\frac{15}{28}$
19. $\frac{3}{8} + \frac{5}{9}$ $\frac{67}{72}$
20. $\frac{7}{10} + \frac{2}{5}$ $\frac{11}{10}$

21. $\frac{5}{13} \cdot \frac{3}{4}$ $\frac{15}{52}$
22. $\frac{5}{9} \cdot \frac{3}{5}$ $\frac{1}{3}$
23. $\frac{10}{11} \cdot \frac{11}{12}$ $\frac{5}{6}$
24. $\frac{5}{6} \cdot \frac{15}{16}$ $\frac{25}{32}$

25. $\frac{2}{3} + \frac{3}{7}$ $\frac{23}{21}$
26. $\frac{9}{10} \cdot \frac{5}{3}$ $\frac{3}{2}$
27. $\frac{7}{8} \cdot \frac{14}{16}$ $\frac{49}{64}$
28. $\frac{9}{13} + \frac{2}{5}$ $\frac{71}{65}$

Introduction to Algebra   **43**

2 Working with Real Numbers

Objectives

2-1 To use number properties to simplify expressions.

2-2 To add real numbers using a number line or properties about opposites.

2-3 To add real numbers using rules for addition.

2-4 To subtract real numbers and to simplify expressions involving differences.

2-5 To use the distributive property to simplify expressions.

2-6 To multiply real numbers.

2-7 To write equations to represent relationships among integers.

2-8 To simplify expressions involving reciprocals.

2-9 To divide real numbers and to simplify expressions involving quotients.

Assignment Guide

See p. T59 for Key to the format of the Assignment Guide

Day	Minimum Course	Average Course	Maximum Course
1	**2-1** 47/1–33 odd, 35 **S** 48/*Mixed Review*	**2-1** 47/1–37 odd **S** 48/*Mixed Review*	**2-1** 47/1–35 odd, 37–40 **S** 48/*Mixed Review*
2	**2-2** 52/1–29 odd, 31–32 **S** 53/*Mixed Review*	**2-2** 52/1–33 odd, 37 **S** 53/*Mixed Review*	**2-2** 52/1–39 odd **S** 53/*Mixed Review*
3	**2-3** 55/1–35 odd **S** 58/*Mixed Review*	**2-3** 55/1–39 odd 56/*P*: 2–12 even **S** 58/*Mixed Review*	**2-3** 55/3–42 mult. of 3 56/*P*: 2–16 even **S** 58/*Mixed Review*
4	**2-3** 56/*P*: 1–10 **2-4** 61/2–46 even	**2-4** 61/2–48 even, 55–58 62/*P*: 2–10 even **S** 63/*Mixed Review*	**2-4** 61/15–60 mult. of 3, 61 62/*P*: 2–12 even **S** 63/*Mixed Review*
5	**2-4** 62/*P*: 1–10 **S** 63/*Mixed Review*	**2-5** 67/3–69 mult. of 3 **S** 69/*Mixed Review* **R** 63/*Self-Test 1*	**2-5** 67/3–75 mult. of 3 **S** 69/*Mixed Review* **R** 63/*Self-Text 1*
6	**2-5** 67/3–54 mult. of 3, 67–68 **S** 69/*Mixed Review* **R** 63/*Self-Test 1*	**2-6** 72/2–34 even, 36–51 mult. of 3 **S** 73/*Mixed Review*	**2-6** 72/3–57 mult. of 3, 59 **S** 73/*Mixed Review*
7	**2-6** 72/1–43 odd **S** 73/*Mixed Review*	**2-7** 77/2–16 even **S** 78/*Mixed Review*	**2-7** 72/2–18 even **S** 78/*Mixed Review*
8	**2-7** 77/1–13 **S** 78/*Mixed Review*	**2-8** 81/1–31 odd **S** 82/*Mixed Review* **R** 78/*Self-Test 2*	**2-8** 81/3–36 mult. of 3 **S** 82/*Mixed Review* **R** 78/*Self-Test 2*
9	**2-8** 81/1–25 odd **S** 82/*Mixed Review* **R** 78/*Self-Test 2*	**2-9** 85/1–33 odd **S** 86/*Mixed Review*	**2-9** 85/1–33 odd, 34–35 **S** 86/*Mixed Review*
10	**2-9** 85/1–27 odd **S** 86/*Mixed Review*	*Prepare for Chapter Test* **R** 86/*Self-Test 3* 89/*Chapter Review* **EP** 641/*Skills;* 665/*Problems*	*Prepare for Chapter Test* **R** 86/*Self-Test 3* 89/*Chapter Review* **EP** 641/*Skills;* 665/*Problems*

Assignment Guide *(continued)*

Day	Minimum Course	Average Course	Maximum Course
11	*Prepare for Chapter Test* **R** 86/*Self-Test 3* 89/*Chapter Review* **EP** 641/*Skills;* 665/*Problems*	*Administer Chapter 2 Test* **R** 91/*Cum. Review:* 1–35 odd **S** 93/*Preparing for College* *Entrance Exams*	*Administer Chapter 2 Test* **R** 91/*Cum. Review:* 1–35 odd **S** 93/*Preparing for College* *Entrance Exams*
12	*Administer Chapter 2 Test* **R** 92/*Maintaining Skills*		

Supplementary Materials Guide

For Use with Lesson	Practice Masters	Tests	Study Guide (Reteaching)	Resource Book		
				Tests	Practice Exercises	Applications (A) Enrichment (E) Technology (T)
2-1			pp. 19–20			p. 179 (A)
2-2	Sheet 5		pp. 21–22			
2-3			pp. 23–24		p. 82	
2-4	Sheet 6	Test 5	pp. 25–26			
2-5			pp. 27–28		p. 83	
2-6	Sheet 7		pp. 29–30			
2-7		Test 6	pp. 31–32		p. 84	
2-8			pp. 33–34			
2-9	Sheet 8	Test 7	pp. 35–36		p. 85	pp. 213–219 (T)
Chapter 2	Sheet 9	Tests 8, 9		pp. 10–13		pp. 191–193 (E)
Cum. Rev. 1–2	Sheet 10					

Overhead Visuals

For Use with Lessons	Visual	Title
2-2	A	Multi-Use Packet 1
2-2	B	Multi-Use Packet 2
2-2, 2-3, 2-4	1	Adding and Subtracting Real Numbers

Software

Software	Computer Activities	Test Generator
	Activity 5	189 test items
For Use with Lessons	2-7	all lessons

Strategies for Teaching

Making Connections to Earlier Math Courses

Comparing previously acquired ideas with new concepts helps students transfer prior learning to new situations. For example, the algebraic representation of the distributive property is related to mental arithmetic techniques (page 65) and to manipulative models of area (page 66) from earlier grades. Other ties to earlier math courses in Chapter 2 occur on pp. 45–46, 50–51, 70–71, and 79–80.

Using Manipulatives

Manipulatives have long been considered to be useful in elementary mathematics courses. Today it is recognized that they can be equally useful in high school mathematics in helping students develop conceptual understanding or in serving as an alternative form of instruction when reteaching is needed. In an Algebra 1 course, manipulatives can help students make the transition from arithmetic to the symbolic representations of algebra. The goal in using manipulatives in Algebra 1 is to have students progress to the point where they can work entirely on the abstract level. Thus, it is important that students understand clearly the relationship between the operations with manipulatives and the abstract operations they model.

2-2 Addition on a Number Line

You can find the sum $3 + (-2)$ using tiles or chips of different colors. In the figure below, a white tile represents $+1$, and a gray tile represents -1.

$$\square \ \square \ \square \ = 3$$
$$\underline{\blacksquare \ \blacksquare \qquad = -2}$$
Sum: $\quad 1 + 0 + 0 \ = 1$

Notice that whenever a white tile and a gray tile are vertically aligned, the pair represents 0. The sum of 3 and -2, therefore, consists of two white-gray pairs with one white tile left over. So the sum is 1.

See the Exploration on p. 686 for an activity in which students use colored tiles or chips to explore addition of integers.

2-4 Subtracting Real Numbers

Unit tiles or chips can also be used to model subtraction. For example, the difference $3 - (-2)$ involves "taking away" two gray tiles from three white ones. To do so, you must first "build up" the three white tiles by adding two white-gray tile pairs (each representing 0). Once the two gray tiles are removed, five white tiles remain. So the difference is 5.

First "build up" 3:

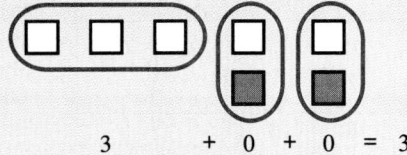

$$3 \qquad + \ 0 \ + \ 0 \ = 3$$

Then "take away" -2:

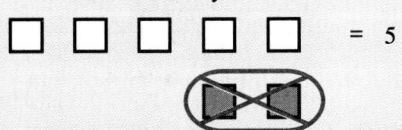

See the Exploration on p. 687 for an activity in which students use colored tiles or chips to explore subtraction of integers.

2-5 The Distributive Property

You can have students explore the distributive property using tiles or manipulatives cut from graph paper. For example, the fact that $3(x + 2) = 3x + 6$ is apparent from the areas of the rectangles shown below.

Have students explore the areas of other pairs of rectangles, both joined and separated.

2-6 Rules for Multiplication

Students can use unit tiles to find a product like $3(-2)$. By taking three groups of two gray tiles each, they should see that $3(-2) = -6$.

2-9 Dividing Real Numbers

Students can use unit tiles to find a quotient like $-6 \div 3$. By separating six gray tiles into three equal groups, they should see that $-6 \div 3 = -2$.

References to Strategies

PE: Pupil's Edition   **TE:** Teacher's Edition   **RB:** Resource Book

Problem Solving Strategies

PE: pp. 53, 69 (Recognizing patterns); pp. 75–78 (Using equations)

Applications

PE: pp. 44, 56–58, 62–63, 74
TE: pp. 44, 49, 59; T83–T84 (Lesson 2-2)
RB: p. 179

Nonroutine Problems

PE: p. 48 (Exs. 37–40, Challenge); p. 53 (Ex. 49, Challenge); p. 58 (Probs. 15, 16); p. 62 (Exs. 61, 62); p. 63 (Ex. 12); p. 69 (Challenge); p. 73 (Exs. 57–60); p. 78 (Exs. 17, 18); p. 86 (Exs. 34, 35)
TE: pp. T83, T84 (Sugg. Extensions)
RB: pp. 191, 192

Communication

PE: p. 64 (Reading Algebra); p. 48 (Ex. 39, convincing argument); p. 53 (Ex. 39c, discussion); p. 62 (Ex. 62, discussion)
TE: pp. T83, 64 (Reading Algebra)

Thinking Skills

PE: pp. 53, 69, 76 (Reasoning and inferencing); pp. 62–63 (Interpreting)
TE: p. 53

Explorations

PE: p. 74 (Product prices); p. 686 (Exploring addition of integers); p. 687 (Exploring subtraction of integers)

Connections

PE: pp. 45–46, 50–51, 70–71, 79–80 (Arithmetic); pp. 44, 57, 73 (Business); p. 44 (Data Analysis); p. 66 (Geometry); pp. 62–63, 87 (History)

Using Technology

PE: pp. 58, 82 (Calculator Key-In); p. 69 (Challenge); p. 74 (Exs.); p. 87 (Computer Key-In)
TE: pp. 58, 69, 74, 82, 87
RB: pp. 179, 213–219
Computer Activities: pp. 10–11

Using Manipulatives/Models

TE: pp. T84–T89 (Lessons 2-2, 2-4, 2-5, 2-6, 2-7, 2-9)
Overhead Visuals: A, B, 1

Cooperative Learning

TE: p. T87 (Lessons 2-6, 2-7)

Teaching Resources

For use in implementing the teaching strategies referenced on the previous page.

Enrichment/Nonroutine Problems
Resource Book, p. 191

Number Arrays (For use with Chapter 2 of text)

In this array of nonnegative integers, notice that the left-hand column consists of the multiples of 5. The multiples of 5 can be thought of as numbers of the form $5n$ where $n \in \{0, 1, 2, 3, \ldots\}$. The numbers in the next column are of the form $5n + 1$; the numbers in the next column are of the form $5n + 2$; the numbers in the next column are of the form $5n + 3$; and the numbers in the last column are of the form $5n + 4$. In what column will the number 54,321 appear? Since 54,321 can be written in the form

$$54,321 = 5(10,864) + 1$$

we can conclude that 54,321 will appear in the second column; that is, the one headed by 1.

In Exercises 1–4, study each listing and determine the answer to this question: In which column will the number 10,000 appear?

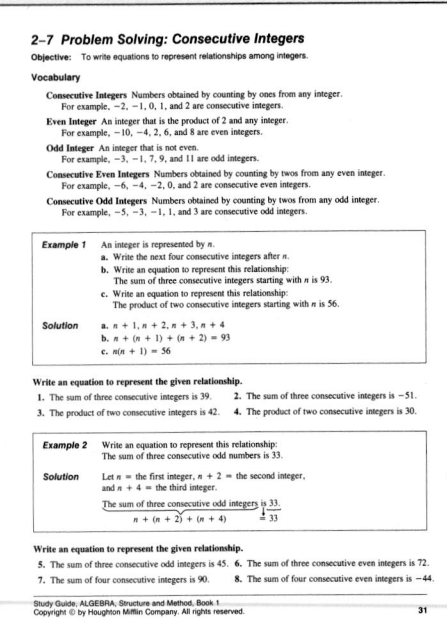

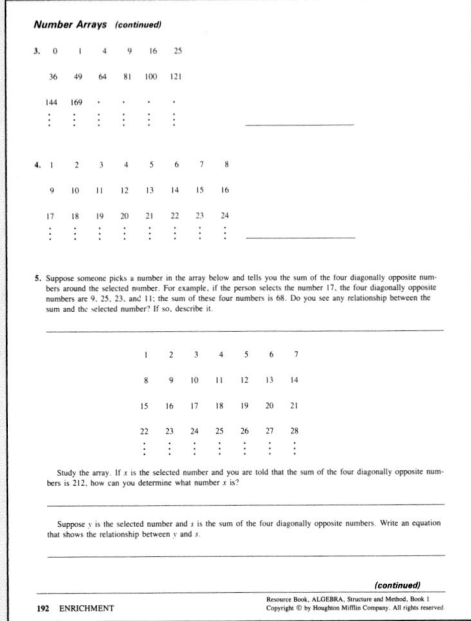

Problem Solving
Study Guide, p. 31

2–7 Problem Solving: Consecutive Integers

Objective: To write equations to represent relationships among integers.

Vocabulary

Consecutive Integers Numbers obtained by counting by ones from any integer.
For example, −2, −1, 0, 1, and 2 are consecutive integers.

Even Integer An integer that is the product of 2 and any integer.
For example, −10, −4, 2, 6, and 8 are even integers.

Odd Integer An integer that is not even.
For example, −3, −1, 7, 9, and 11 are odd integers.

Consecutive Even Integers Numbers obtained by counting by twos from any even integer.
For example, −6, −4, −2, 0, and 2 are consecutive even integers.

Consecutive Odd Integers Numbers obtained by counting by twos from any odd integer.
For example, −5, −3, −1, 1, and 3 are consecutive odd integers.

Example 1 An integer is represented by n.
a. Write the next four consecutive integers after n.
b. Write an equation to represent this relationship:
The sum of three consecutive integers starting with n is 93.
c. Write an equation to represent this relationship:
The product of two consecutive integers starting with n is 56.

Solution
a. $n + 1, n + 2, n + 3, n + 4$
b. $n + (n + 1) + (n + 2) = 93$
c. $n(n + 1) = 56$

Write an equation to represent the given relationship.
1. The sum of three consecutive integers is 39.
2. The sum of three consecutive integers is −51.
3. The product of two consecutive integers is 42.
4. The product of two consecutive integers is 30.

Example 2 Write an equation to represent this relationship:
The sum of three consecutive odd numbers is 33.

Solution Let $n =$ the first integer, $n + 2 =$ the second integer, and $n + 4 =$ the third integer.
$$\underbrace{n + (n + 2) + (n + 4)}_{} \stackrel{\cdot}{=} \underbrace{33}_{}$$

Write an equation to represent the given relationship.
5. The sum of three consecutive odd integers is 45.
6. The sum of three consecutive even integers is 72.
7. The sum of four consecutive integers is 90.
8. The sum of four consecutive even integers is −44.

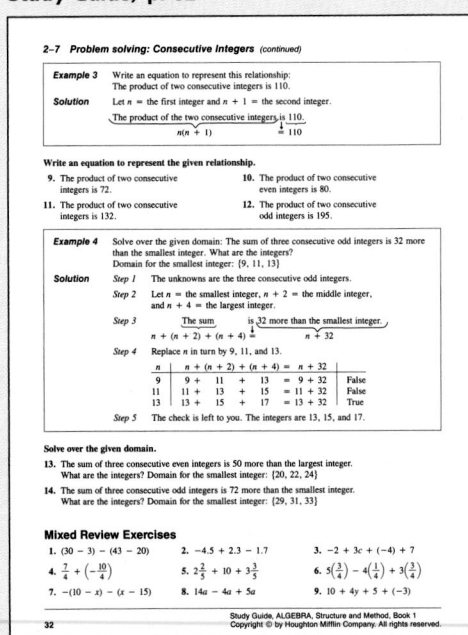

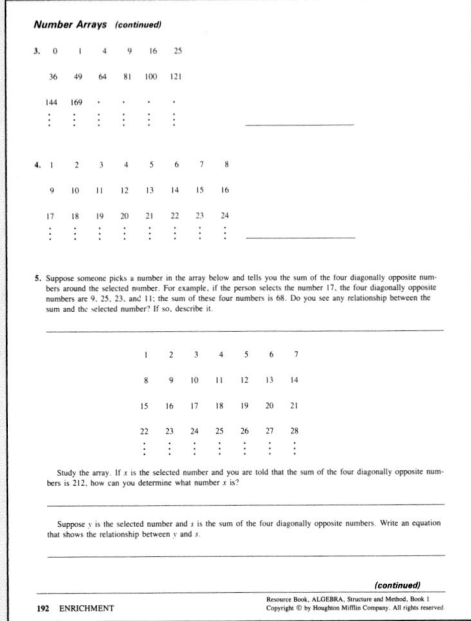

Using Models
Study Guide, p. 21

2-2 Addition On A Number Line

Objective: To add real numbers using a number line or properties about opposites.

Properties	Examples
Identity Property of Addition The sum of a real number and 0 is identical to the number itself. $a + 0 = a$ and $0 + a = a$	$5 + 0 = 5$ and $0 + 5 = 5$
Properties of Opposites Every real number has an opposite. The sum of a real number and its opposite is 0. $a + (-a) = 0$ and $(-a) + a = 0$	$3 + (-3) = 0$ and $(-3) + 3 = 0$
Property of the Opposite of a Sum For all real numbers a and b: $-(a + b) = (-a) + (-b)$	$-(2 + 3) = -5 = (-2) + (-3)$

Example 1 Simplify: **a.** $3 + 4$ **b.** $-3 + (-4)$ **c.** $2 + (-5)$ **d.** $-2 + 5$

Solution

a. $3 + 4 = 7$

b. $-3 + (-4) = -7$

c. $2 + (-5) = -3$

d. $-2 + 5 = 3$

Simplify each expression. If necessary, draw a number line to help you.

1. $4 + 2$ 2. $-4 + (-2)$ 3. $6 + (-9)$
4. $-6 + 9$ 5. $3 + 5$ 6. $-3 + (-5)$
7. $-8 + 4$ 8. $8 + (-4)$ 9. $(-2 + 5) + 4$
10. $(-4 + 7) + 1$ 11. $(-3 + 1) + 2$ 12. $(-6 + 5) + 3$

Application/Using Technology
Resource Book, p. 179

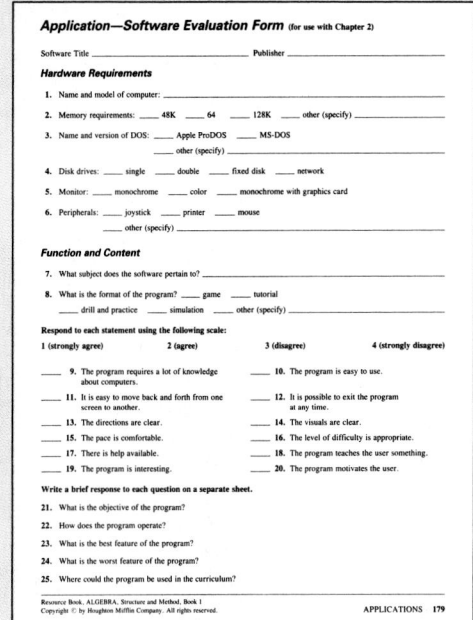

Using Manipulatives/Models
Overhead Visual 1, Sheets 1 and 2

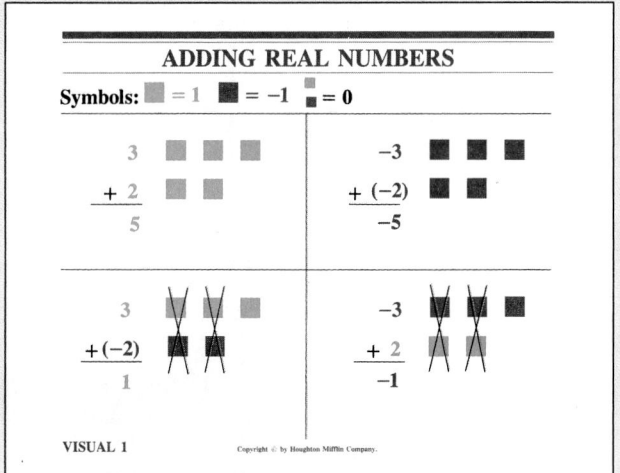

Using Manipulatives/Models
Overhead Visual 1, Sheets 3 and 4

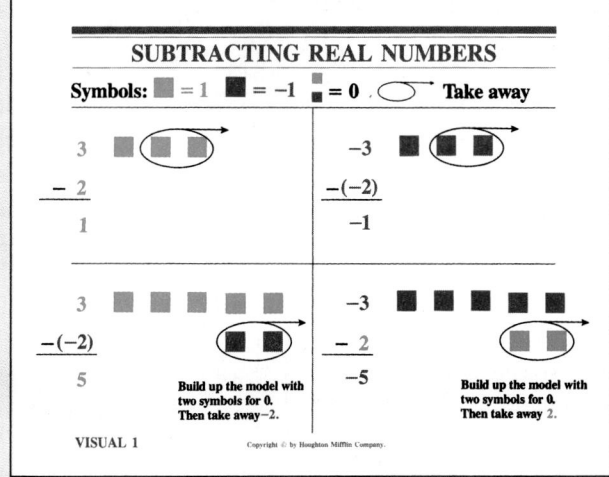

Application

Most large stores have computerized cash registers that do everything from computing change to keeping the inventory. Other businesses use computers to store data and then display it in the form of a graph, as shown in the photo. Computers are revolutionizing the way information is handled.

Research Activities
A few students might want to investigate the use of computers in your school. This could entail making a list of the school's hardware and software and where to find it; or it could involve a detailed discussion of how the software works, how easy it is to use, and where it applies. The report should be made available to all students in the class for reference.

Some colleges take applications by computer, either via a modem or on a disk. Students can investigate which colleges do this, and whether their own school's guidance department has computer links to any of these colleges.

The Mathematical Association of America has a brochure listing the mathematics backgrounds that should be developed in high school to prepare for selected careers. Have students investigate the mathematical demands of careers they are considering, and then share this information with the class, either orally or in writing.

Support Materials
Resource Book   p. 179

2 Working with Real Numbers

Cash registers fill and empty. The activity can be recorded and graphed on a computer. Positive and negative numbers show gains and losses.

44

Addition and Subtraction

2-1 Basic Assumptions

Objective   To use number properties to simplify expressions.

This chapter develops rules for working with positive and negative numbers. The two principal operations are addition and multiplication. Subtraction is related to addition. Later in this chapter you will see that division is related to multiplication.

The rules for working with real numbers are based on several properties that you can accept as facts.

Closure Properties

For all real numbers a and b:

$$a + b \text{ is a unique real number.}$$

$$ab \text{ is a unique real number.}$$

The sum and product of any two real numbers are also real numbers. Moreover, they are *unique*. (This means there is one and only one possible answer when you add or multiply two real numbers.)

Commutative Properties

For all real numbers a and b:

$a + b = b + a$ Example: $2 + 3 = 3 + 2$

$ab = ba$ Example: $4 \cdot 5 = 5 \cdot 4$

The order in which you add or multiply two numbers does not affect the result.

Associative Properties

For all real numbers a, b, and c:

$(a + b) + c = a + (b + c)$ Example: $(5 + 6) + 7 = 5 + (6 + 7)$

$(ab)c = a(bc)$ Example: $(2 \cdot 3)4 = 2(3 \cdot 4)$

When you add or multiply any three real numbers, the grouping (or association) of the numbers does not affect the result.

Working with Real Numbers **45**

Teaching References

Lesson Commentary,
  pp. T83–T89

Assignment Guide,
  pp. T60–T61

Supplementary Materials

  Practice Masters 5–10

  Tests 5–9

  Resource Book
    Practice Exercises,
      pp. 82–85
    Tests, pp. 10–13
    Enrichment Activity,
      pp. 191–193
    Application, p. 179

Study Guide, pp. 19–36

Computer Activity 5

Test Generator

California Standards

Support Workbook
  Explorations for
    Lessons 2-1, 2-3, 2-4

Alternate Test, p. T13

Teaching Suggestions, p. T83

Suggested Extensions, p. T83

Warm-Up Exercises

Complete each sentence with a word that makes the sentence true.

1. Even + Even = _?_   Even
2. Even + Odd = _?_   Odd
3. Odd + Odd = _?_   Even
4. Even × Even = _?_   Even
5. Even × Odd = _?_   Even
6. Odd × Odd = _?_   Odd

Simplify.

7. a. $1 + 4$ 5   **b.** $4 + 1$ 5
8. a. $3 \cdot 2$ 6   **b.** $2 \cdot 3$ 6
9. a. $(1 + 5) + 8$ 14
   b. $1 + (5 + 8)$ 14

Motivating the Lesson

Write 6 + 47 + 92 + 8 + 3 on the chalkboard. Ask students to find the sum as quickly as they can. 156 Ask students in which order they added the numbers together and why. Being able to group numbers in a particular order is the lesson for today.

Chalkboard Examples

Simplify.

1. 21 + 3 + 10
   (21 + 3) + 10
   24 + 10
   34

2. 50 · 9 · 2 · 9
   50 · (9 · 2) · 9
   50 · (2 · 9) · 9
   (50 · 2)(9 · 9)
   100 · 81
   8100

3. 4 + 5y + 3
   (4 + 5y) + 3
   (5y + 4) + 3
   5y + (4 + 3)
   5y + 7

4. (5a)(3b)(4c)
   (5 · 3 · 4)(a · b · c)
   60abc

Check for Understanding

Here is a suggested use of the Oral Exercises to check students' understanding as you teach the lesson.
Oral Exs. 1–3: use after Example 1.
Oral Exs. 4–12: use after Example 2.
Oral Exs. 13–25: use after discussion of the properties of equality.

In the sum $a + b$, a and b are called **terms.** In the product ab, a and b are called **factors.** To find the sum or product of several numbers, you work with two numbers at a time. Examples 1 and 2 show how the commutative and associative properties can sometimes help you to simplify expressions.

Example 1 Simplify $43 + 78 + 7$.

Solution The rule for order of operations tells you to add from left to right: $(43 + 78) + 7$. For mental math it is easiest to add 43 and 7 first. The steps you do almost without thinking about them are shown below. Each step is justified by a property.

$$
\begin{aligned}
(43 + 78) + 7 &= (78 + 43) + 7 && \text{Commutative property of addition} \\
&= 78 + (43 + 7) && \text{Associative property of addition} \\
&= 78 + 50 && \text{Substitution of 50 for } 43 + 7 \\
&= 128 && \text{Substitution of 128 for } 78 + 50
\end{aligned}
$$

Example 2 Simplify: **a.** $7 + 9m + 5$ **b.** $(2x)(3y)(4z)$

Solution   **a.** $7 + 9m + 5 = 9m + (7 + 5)$ **b.** $(2x)(3y)(4z) = (2 \cdot 3 \cdot 4)(xyz)$
$\qquad\qquad\qquad\qquad = 9m + 12$ ***Answer*** $\qquad\qquad\qquad\quad = 24xyz$ ***Answer***

To simplify expressions, you often use the properties listed below.

Properties of Equality

For all real numbers a, b, and c:

Reflexive Property	$a = a$
Symmetric Property	If $a = b$, then $b = a$.
Transitive Property	If $a = b$ and $b = c$, then $a = c$.

Throughout the rest of this book, the domain of each variable is the set of real numbers unless otherwise specified.

Oral Exercises

Simplify each expression. Use the commutative and associative properties to reorder and regroup.

1. $(5 \cdot 83) \cdot 2$ 830
2. $(47 + 39) + 3$ 89
3. $17 + 89 + 3 + 11$ 120
4. $4 + 5x + 2$ 5x + 6
5. $9 + 3y + 4$ 3y + 13
6. $a + 1 + b + 2$ a + b + 3
7. $2(7a)$ 14a
8. $(5n)4$ 20n
9. $(3x)(2y)$ 6xy
10. $(5a)(4b)$ 20ab
11. $(3p)(5q)(2r)$ 30pqr
12. $r(3s)(4t)$ 12rst

46   Chapter 2

Name the property illustrated.

13. $3(14) = (14)3$ Comm. prop. of mult.

14. $(74 + 99) + 1 = 74 + (99 + 1)$ Assoc. prop. of add.

15. $\frac{1}{6} + 9 = 9 + \frac{1}{6}$ Comm. prop. of add.

16. $\frac{1}{5}(15w) = \left(\frac{1}{5} \cdot 15\right)w$ Assoc. prop. of mult.

17. $2.1 + y = y + 2.1$ Comm. prop. of add.

18. $3(8 \cdot 0) = (3 \cdot 8)0$ Assoc. prop. of mult.

19. If $7m = 35$, then $35 = 7m$. Symm. prop. of equality

20. If $3 + p = 12$, then $12 = 3 + p$. Symm. prop. of equality

21. Every real number is equal to itself. Reflex. prop. of equality

22. $(5 + q) + (-3) = (q + 5) + (-3)$ Comm. prop. of add.

23. If $w + 2 = 7$ and $7 = 5 + 2$, then $w + 2 = 5 + 2$. Trans. prop. of equality

24. There is only one real number that is the sum of 0.4 and 2.6. Closure prop. of add.

25. $(r + 37) + 23 + s = r + (37 + 23) + s$ Assoc. prop. of add.

Written Exercises

Simplify.

A

1. $275 + 52 + 25 + 8$ 360

2. $803 + 26 + 47 + 24$ 900

3. $2 \cdot 21 \cdot 5 \cdot 3$ 630

4. $50 \cdot 3 \cdot 3 \cdot 20$ 9000

5. $25 \cdot 74 \cdot 2 \cdot 2$ 7400

6. $8 \cdot 17 \cdot 9 \cdot 25$ 30,600

7. $6\frac{1}{2} + 4\frac{1}{3} + 1\frac{1}{2} + \frac{2}{3}$ 13

8. $56\frac{7}{8} + \frac{3}{5} + \frac{1}{8} + 4\frac{2}{5}$ 62

9. $0.1 + 1.8 + 5.9 + 0.2$ 8

10. $4.75 + 2.95 + 1.05 + 10.25$ 19

11. $3 + 7y + 4$ $7y + 7$

12. $8 + 9z + 4$ $9z + 12$

13. $5 + 2x + 1$ $2x + 6$

14. $5 + 3w + 2$ $3w + 7$

15. $2(5a)$ 10a

16. $3(4n)$ 12n

17. $(7y)(5z)$ 35yz

18. $(6m)(4n)$ 24mn

19. $(8x)(2y)(3z)$ 48xyz

20. $(3p)(4q)(6r)$ 72pqr

Sample $\quad 5x + 3 + 4y + 7 = 5x + 4y + (3 + 7)$
$$= 5x + 4y + 10 \quad \textit{Answer}$$

21. $a + 3 + b + 4$ $a + b + 7$

22. $7 + x + y + 4$ $x + y + 11$

23. $4a + 5 + 3n + 1$ $4a + 3n + 6$

24. $9m + 2 + 7n + 3$ $9m + 7n + 5$

B **25.** $5 + 7x + 3 + 4y + z$ $7x + 4y + z + 8$

26. $8p + 4 + 3q + 87 + 96$ $8p + 3q + 187$

27. $(25b)(25c)(4d)(4e)$ 10,000bcde

28. $(5a)(5b)(5c)(2d)$ 250abcd

Name the property illustrated.

29. $pq = qp$ Comm. prop. of mult.

30. $(25 + 84) + 16 = 25 + (84 + 16)$ Assoc. prop. of add.

31. $x + y = y + x$ Comm. prop. of add.

32. If $3.2 = 8y$, then $8y = 3.2$. Symm. prop. of equality

33. $(3r)s = 3(rs)$ Assoc. prop. of mult.

34. If $x = -3$ and $-3 = z$, then $x = z$. Trans. prop. of equality or subst. prop.

Working with Real Numbers **47**

Name the property that justifies each step.

35. $57 + (25 + 13) = 57 + (13 + 25)$ **a.** __?__ Comm. prop. of add.
$\qquad\qquad\qquad = (57 + 13) + 25$ **b.** __?__ Assoc. prop. of add.
$\qquad\qquad\qquad = 70 + 25$ **c.** __?__ Subst. prop.
$\qquad\qquad\qquad = 95$ **d.** __?__ Subst. prop.

36. $25 \cdot (37 \cdot 8) = 25 \cdot (8 \cdot 37)$ **a.** __?__ Comm. prop. of mult.
$\qquad\qquad\qquad = (25 \cdot 8) \cdot 37$ **b.** __?__ Assoc. prop. of mult.
$\qquad\qquad\qquad = 200 \cdot 37$ **c.** __?__ Subst. prop.
$\qquad\qquad\qquad = (100 \cdot 2) \cdot 37$ **d.** __?__ Subst. prop.
$\qquad\qquad\qquad = 100 \cdot (2 \cdot 37)$ **e.** __?__ Assoc. prop. of mult.
$\qquad\qquad\qquad = 100 \cdot 74$ **f.** __?__ Subst. prop.
$\qquad\qquad\qquad = 7400$ **g.** __?__ Subst. prop.

C 37. a. Find the values of $(7 - 4) - 2$ and $7 - (4 - 2)$. 1; 5
     b. Is subtraction of real numbers associative? no

38. a. Find the values of $(48 \div 8) \div 2$ and $48 \div (8 \div 2)$. 3; 12
     b. Is division of real numbers associative? no

39. Is division of real numbers commutative? Give a convincing argument to justify your answer. No; for example, $10 \div 2 = 5$ but $2 \div 10 = \frac{2}{10} = \frac{1}{5}$.

40. A set of numbers is said to be *closed* under an operation if the result of combining *any* two numbers in the set results in a number that is also in the set. Decide whether or not each set is closed under the operation.
     a. {positive integers}; $\div$ not closed   **b.** {odd integers}; $\times$ closed
     c. {odd integers}; $+$ not closed   **d.** {integers ending in 4 or 6}; $\times$ closed

Mixed Review Exercises

Evaluate if $a = 3$, $x = 5$, $y = 2$, and $z = 6$.

1. $\dfrac{2a - y}{4y - z}$ 2   **2.** $5z(x - y)$ 90   **3.** $\dfrac{3a + x}{4z - (y + 1)}$ $\frac{2}{3}$

Evaluate if $a = -4$, $b = 2$, and $x = -3$.

4. $|a| + |x| - b$ 5   **5.** $2|a| + 7|x|$ 29   **6.** $2|x| - |b| + |a|$ 8
7. $10|x| - 3|b|$ 24   **8.** $2|b| + 3|a|$ 16   **9.** $|-x - 1| - |b - 1|$ 1

Challenge

Change for a dollar consisted of 15 coins (pennies, nickels, and dimes only). At least one of each type of coin was used. How was this done?

5 pennies, 1 nickel, and 9 dimes

2-2 Addition on a Number Line

Objective   To add real numbers using a number line or properties about opposites.

You already know how to add two positive numbers. You can use a number line to help you find the sum of *any* two real numbers. Moves to the left represent negative numbers; moves to the right represent positive numbers.

To find the sum of -3 and -6, first draw a number line. Then, starting at the origin, move your pencil 3 units to the left along your number line. From that position, move your pencil 6 more units to the left. Together, the two moves result in a move of 9 units to the left from the origin. The arrows in the diagram below show the moves.

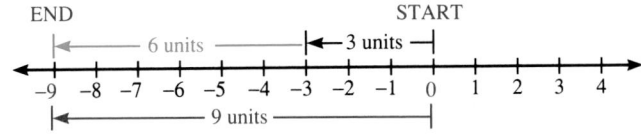

This shows that $-3 + (-6) = -9$.

Note the use of parentheses in "$-3 + (-6)$" to separate the plus sign that means "add" from the minus sign that is part of the numeral for negative six.

To find the sum $-3 + 6$, first move 3 units to the left from the origin. Then, from that position, move 6 units to the right. The two moves result in a move of 3 units to the right of the origin, as shown below.

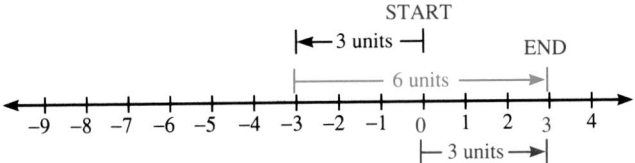

This shows that $-3 + 6 = 3$.

Example 1   Simplify $3 + (-6)$.

Solution

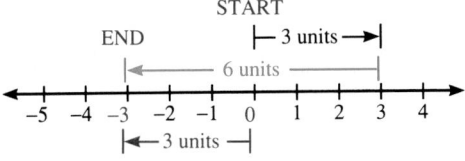

$3 + (-6) = -3$ *Answer*

Working with Real Numbers   **49**

Warm-Up Exercises

A football team has the ball on its 20-yard line. Where is the ball after each of the next two plays?

1. gain 3 yd; 23-yd line
   gain 5 yd; 28-yd line
2. gain 2 yd; 22-yd line
   lose 2 yd; 20-yd line
3. lose 1 yd; 19-yd line
   gain 5 yd; 24-yd line
4. lose 2 yd; 18-yd line
   gain 1 yd; 19-yd line
5. lose 1 yd; 19-yd line
   lose 3 yd; 16-yd line

Motivating the Lesson

In football, yards are lost or gained. The stock market rises or falls. People lose or gain weight. These are examples of positive and negative numbers. Ask students to think of other examples, such as rising and falling temperatures. Point out that adding positive and negative numbers is the topic of today's lesson.

Chalkboard Examples

Simplify.

1. $2 + (-4)$ -2

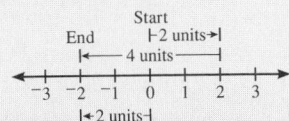

(continued)

Chalkboard Examples
(Continued)

2. $4 + (-4)$ 0

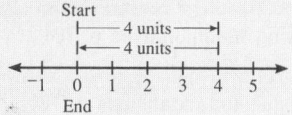

Start
4 units
4 units
-1 0 1 2 3 4 5
End

3. $-2 + (-5)$

$-2 + (-5) = -(2 + 5) = -7$

4. $16 + (-9)$

$16 + (-9) = (7 + 9) + (-9)$
$= 7 + [9 + (-9)]$
$= 7 + 0$
$= 7$

Check for Understanding

Here is a suggested use of the Oral Exercises to check students' understanding as you teach the lesson.
Oral Exs. 1–4: use after Example 1.
Oral Exs. 5–8: use after Example 2.
Oral Exs. 9–20: use after Example 3.

Guided Practice

Simplify each expression. If necessary, draw a number line to help you.

1. $(-4 + 6) - 2$ 0
2. $[3 + (-5)] + 7$ 5
3. $(-3 + 3) + [16 + (-6)]$ 10
4. $2 + x + (-4)$ $x + (-2)$
5. $-9 + (-3t) + (-21)$
$-30 + (-3t)$

Can you visualize $-3 + 0$ on a number line? Think of "adding 0" to mean "moving no units." Then you can see that

$$-3 + 0 = -3 \quad \text{and} \quad 0 + (-3) = -3.$$

These equations illustrate the special property of zero for addition of real numbers: When 0 is added to any real number, the sum is *identical* to that number. We call 0 the **identity element for addition.**

Identity Property of Addition

There is a unique real number 0 such that for every real number a,

$$a + 0 = a \quad \text{and} \quad 0 + a = a.$$

Think of adding a pair of opposites, such as 5 and -5, on a number line as shown below.

Example 2 Simplify: **a.** $5 + (-5)$ **b.** $-5 + 5$

Solution   **a.**   START

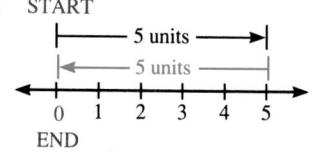

$5 + (-5) = 0$
Answer

b.   START

$-5 + 5 = 0$
Answer

The following property is a formal way of saying that the sum of any number and its opposite is zero.

Property of Opposites

For every real number a, there is a unique real number $-a$ such that

$$a + (-a) = 0 \quad \text{and} \quad (-a) + a = 0.$$

A number and its opposite are called **additive inverses** of each other because their sum is zero, the identity element for addition. Thus, the numeral -5 can be read "negative five," "the opposite of five," or "the additive inverse of five."

From the properties of addition, we can prove the following property of the opposite of a sum. (See Exercise 39.)

50   *Chapter 2*

Property of the Opposite of a Sum

For all real numbers a and b:

$$-(a + b) = (-a) + (-b)$$

The opposite of a sum of real numbers is equal to the sum of the opposites of the numbers.

Summarizing the Lesson

Tell students that they can add real numbers by using a number line as a model for the addition. Ask them to use the number line to explain why addition is commutative.

Example 3 Simplify: **a.** $-8 + (-3)$ **b.** $14 + (-5)$

Solution **a.** $-8 + (-3) = -(8 + 3)$ **b.** $14 + (-5) = (9 + 5) + (-5)$
$$= -11$$
Answer
$$= 9 + [5 + (-5)]$$
$$= 9 + 0$$
$$= 9$$
Answer

Oral Exercises

Give an addition statement illustrated by each diagram.

1.

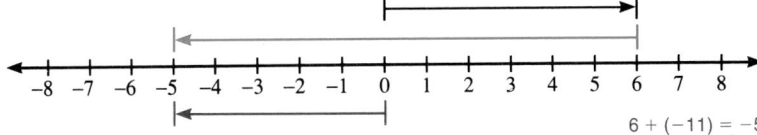

$6 + (-11) = -5$

2.

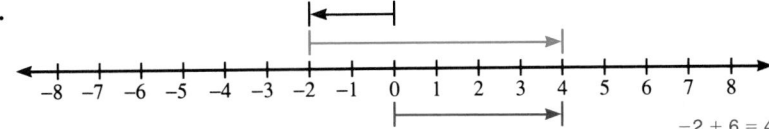

$-2 + 6 = 4$

3.

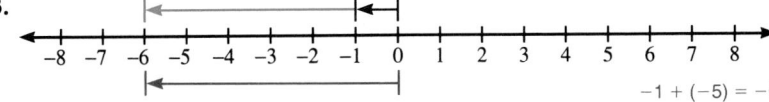

$-1 + (-5) = -6$

4.

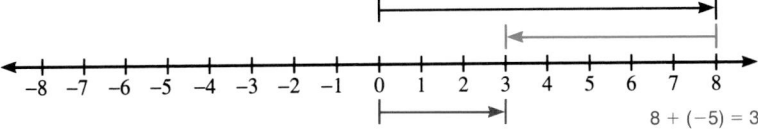

$8 + (-5) = 3$

Working with Real Numbers **51**

Simplify each expression. If necessary, think of moves along a number line.

5. $-2 + 0$ _−2_   **6.** $0 + (-5)$ _−5_   **7.** $-6 + 6$ _0_   **8.** $1 + (-1)$ _0_
9. $-4 + (-8)$ _−12_   **10.** $-7 + (-1)$ _−8_   **11.** $5 + (-1)$ _4_   **12.** $-4 + 9$ _5_
13. $-8 + 7$ _−1_   **14.** $6 + (-4)$ _2_   **15.** $13 + (-18)$ _−5_   **16.** $-1 + (-99)$ _−100_
17. $102 + (-2)$ _100_   **18.** $-100 + 1$ _−99_   **19.** $-10 + 0$ _−10_   **20.** $-45 + 45$ _0_

Written Exercises

Simplify each expression. If necessary, draw a number line to help you.

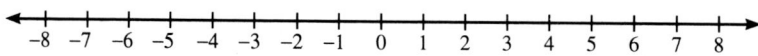

A **1.** $(-4 + 8) + 7$ _11_   **2.** $(-5 + 8) + 2$ _5_
3. $(-9 + 11) + (-2)$ _0_   **4.** $(-3 + 5) + (-2)$ _0_
5. $[3 + (-10)] + 6$ _−1_   **6.** $[5 + (-15)] + 7$ _−3_
7. $[-9 + (-8)] + 9$ _−8_   **8.** $[-5 + (-23)] + 5$ _−23_
9. $22 + [6 + (-11)]$ _17_   **10.** $32 + [8 + (-16)]$ _24_
11. $-26 + [-2 + (-8)]$ _−36_   **12.** $-5 + [-12 + (-18)]$ _−35_
13. $[37 + (-7)] + [1 + (-1)]$ _30_   **14.** $(-3 + 3) + [8 + (-12)]$ _−4_
15. $[0 + (-8)] + [-7 + (-23)]$ _−38_   **16.** $(-4 + 4) + [18 + (-8)]$ _10_
17. $-3 + (-4) + (-6)$ _−13_   **18.** $-5 + (-7) + (-9)$ _−21_
19. $-4 + (-10) + 9 + (-6)$ _−11_   **20.** $-17 + 12 + (-4) + (-13)$ _−22_
21. $-3.2 + (-4.6) + 5.4$ _−2.4_   **22.** $5.9 + (-3.2) + (-7.8)$ _−5.1_
23. $-\dfrac{3}{2} + 5 + \left(-\dfrac{7}{2}\right)$ _0_   **24.** $-\dfrac{9}{5} + (-3) + \left(-\dfrac{6}{5}\right)$ _−6_

Simplify.

Sample $2 + (-3) + n + 7$

Solution Use the commutative and associative properties to reorder and regroup.

$$2 + (-3) + n + 7 = -1 + n + 7$$
$$= n + (-1) + 7$$
$$= n + 6 \quad \textbf{\textit{Answer}}$$

25. $3 + x + (-8)$ _x + (−5)_   **26.** $y + (-2) + 7$ _y + 5_
27. $2n + 5 + (-5)$ _2n_   **28.** $8 + 3n + (-12)$ _3n + (−4)_
29. $13 + 5n + (-21)$ _5n + (−8)_   **30.** $-7 + (-z) + 12$ _−z + 5_

Suggested Assignments

Minimum
  52/1–29 odd, 31–32
S 53/Mixed Review
Average
  52/1–33 odd, 37
S 53/Mixed Review
Maximum
  52/1–39 odd
S 53/Mixed Review

Supplementary Materials

Study Guide   pp. 21–22
Practice Master   5
Overhead Visuals   A, 1

B   **31.** $3a + (-7) + 4b + (-6)$ $3a + 4b + (-13)$ **32.** $-2 + 4n + 9 + (-7)$ $4n$

    33. $7x + (-3) + (-y) + (-7)$ $7x + (-y) + (-10)$ **34.** $-8 + 7c + 11 + (-3)$ $7c$

C   **35.** $b + [a + (-b)]$ a **36.** $-m + (k + m)$ k

    37. $-m + [-h + (m + h)]$ 0 **38.** $[a + (-b)] + [b + (-a)]$ 0

    39. a. Show that $(a + b) + [(-a) + (-b)] = 0$.

                                                        $(a + b) + [(-a) + (-b)] =$

                                                        $[a + (-a)] + [b + (-b)] =$

     b. The opposite of $(a + b)$ is $-(a + b)$. What property tells you $0 + 0 = 0$

        that $(a + b) + [-(a + b)] = 0$? Prop. of opposites.

     c. Explain how the equation in part (a) and the equation in part (b) can

        be used together to prove the property of the opposite of a sum.

        Since the opp. of a number is unique and $-(a + b)$ and $[(-a) + (-b)]$

        both have the sum of zero when added to $(a + b)$, $-(a + b) = (-a) + (-b)$.

Thinking Skills

Exercise 39 guides students through a proof that the opposite of a sum is the sum of its opposites. This logical process is a skill that is often used in mathematics and other areas of study.

Mixed Review Exercises

Simplify.

  1. $7 + 21 \div 7$ 10   **2.** $|-6| + |3|$ 9   **3.** $6 - [-(-2)]$ 4

  4. $\dfrac{4 + (3 \cdot 2)}{2}$ 5   **5.** $\left|\dfrac{1}{3}\right| + \left|-\dfrac{1}{3}\right|$ $\dfrac{2}{3}$ **6.** $\left|-\dfrac{2}{3}\right| - \left|\dfrac{1}{3}\right|$ $\dfrac{1}{3}$

  7. $63 + 25 + 17 + 15$ 120   **8.** $25 \cdot 5 \cdot 20$ 2500   **9.** $(4a)(2b)(3c)$ $24abc$

 10. $5\dfrac{2}{3} + 3\dfrac{1}{4} + 2\dfrac{1}{3} + 6\dfrac{3}{4}$ 18   **11.** $0.7 + 2.4 + 6.3$ 9.4   **12.** $2 \cdot 17 \cdot 5$ 170

Challenge

Recall (page 35) that the triangular numbers are 1, 3, 6, 10, 15, and so on.
1, 4, 9, 16, 25, . . . are called square numbers because they can be represented by dots arranged to form squares.

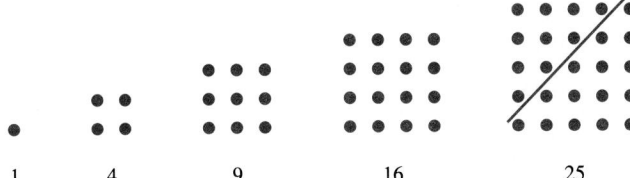

    1   4   9   16   25   and so on

                                                                           2. $4 = 1 + 3$

  1. What are the next two square numbers after 25? 36, 49 $9 = 3 + 6$

                                                                 $16 = 6 + 10$

  2. Verify that each square number from 4 to 100 is the sum of two consecu- $25 = 10 + 15$

      tive triangular numbers. $36 = 15 + 21$

                                                                  $49 = 21 + 28$

  3. Illustrate Exercise 2 by dividing the square array of dots shown above for $64 = 28 + 36$

      25 into two triangular arrays. See diagram above. $81 = 36 + 45$

                                                                      $100 = 45 + 55$

Working with Real Numbers   **53**

Explorations p. 686

Teaching Suggestions p. T84

Suggested Extensions p. T85

Warm-Up Exercises

Simplify.

1. $|11|$ 11
2. $|-7|$ 7
3. $|-7| + |3|$ 10
4. $|-8| - |5|$ 3
5. $-(|3| + |-4|)$ -7
6. $-(|4| - |1|)$ -3

Motivating the Lesson

Write the following examples on the chalkboard:

$(-1) + 5$ 4 $(-2) + 5$ 3
$(-3) + 5$ 2 $(-4) + 5$ 1
$(-5) + 5$ 0 $(-6) + 5$ -1

Have students simplify each using a number line. Ask if they can identify the pattern in these examples. Note that the lesson teaches rules for adding real numbers.

Chalkboard Examples

Simplify.

1. $-11 + (-10) + 10 + 9$
   $-21 + 10 + 9 = -11 + 9 = -2$

Add.

2. -321
   231
   -123 231 -321 543
   312 312 -123 -444
   _____
         543   -444 99

Check for Understanding

Here is a suggested use of the Oral Exercises to check students' understanding as you teach the lesson.
Oral Exs. 1–21: use after Example 2.

2-3 Rules for Addition

Objective   To add real numbers using rules for addition.

Perhaps you have already discovered these rules for adding positive and negative numbers without using a number line.

Rules for Addition	Examples
1. If a and b are both positive, then $$a + b = |a| + |b|.$$	$3 + 7 = 10$
2. If a and b are both negative, then $$a + b = -(|a| + |b|).$$	$-6 + (-2) = -(6 + 2) = -8$
3. If a is positive and b is negative and a has the greater absolute value, then $$a + b = |a| - |b|.$$	$8 + (-5) = 8 - 5 = 3$
4. If a is positive and b is negative and b has the greater absolute value, then $$a + b = -(|b| - |a|).$$	$4 + (-9) = -(9 - 4) = -5$
5. If a and b are opposites, then $$a + b = 0.$$	$2 + (-2) = 0$

A positive and a negative number are said to have *opposite* signs. The rules for adding two nonzero numbers can be restated as follows:

If the numbers have the *same* sign, add their absolute values and prefix their common sign.

If the numbers have *opposite* signs, subtract the lesser absolute value from the greater and prefix the sign of the number having the greater absolute value.

Example 1 shows two methods for adding several numbers.

Example 1   Simplify $7 + (-9) + 15 + (-12)$.

Solution 1   Add the numbers in order from left to right.

$$7 + (-9) + 15 + (-12)$$
$$\underbrace{}\;-2\; + 15 + (-12)$$
$$\underbrace{}\;13\; + (-12)$$
$$\underbrace{}\;1\quad \textit{Answer}$$

Solution 2

1. Add positive numbers.	2. Add negative numbers.	3. Add the sums.
7	−9	22
15	−12	−21
22	−21	1
		Answer

Example 2 Add.
  −291
   379
   185
  −462

Solution

1. Add positive numbers.	2. Add negative numbers.	3. Add the sums.
379	−291	−753
185	−462	564
564	−753	−189
		Answer

Oral Exercises

Add.

1. 7	2. −4	3. −9	4. 13	5. −12	6. −1
7	−3	6	−8	−27	10
14	−7	−3	5	−39	9
7. −16	8. −4	9. −13	10. 35	11. −98	12. 65
7	−19	53	−75	36	−37
−9	−23	40	−40	−62	28

Simplify.

13. −8 + (−13) −21   **14.** −18 + 8 −10   **15.** 14 + (−15) −1

16. 15 + (−9) 6   **17.** 3 + (−12) −9   **18.** −5 + 22 17

19. 4 + (−1) + (−3) 0   **20.** −4 + (−9) + 9 −4   **21.** −3 + (−6) + 9 0

Written Exercises

Add.

A

1. −7	2. −5	3. −34	4. 58	5. 148	6. −173
6	−6	75	−72	−72	412
−1	−11	41	−14	−73	−58
				−31	−93
				−28	88

Working with Real Numbers **55**

Add.

1. 15	**2.** 193
−12	−24
9	−33
6	−61
−22	75
−4	

Simplify.

3. (−9) + (−8) + 10 + 7 0

4. [−7 + 3] + [−4 + (−2)]
−10

5. 10 + (−11) + 12 + (−13) +
14 12

6. 3x + [2 + (−3x)] + (−22)
−20

Summarizing the Lesson
Tell students that they can use the five rules for addition to add quickly two real numbers. Ask a volunteer to name one of the rules of addition and to give an example. Continue until all five rules have been covered.

Suggested Assignments
Minimum
Day 1: 55/1–35 odd
    S 58/Mixed Review
Day 2: 56/P: 1–10
Assign with Lesson 2-4.
Average
    55/1–39 odd
    56/P:2–12 even
    S 58/Mixed Review
Maximum
    55/3–42 mult. of 3
    56/P: 2–16 even
    S 58/Mixed Review

Supplementary Materials

Study Guide   pp. 23–24
Resource Book   p. 82
Overhead Visual   1

Simplify.

7. $-12 + 7 + (-14) + 29$ 10

8. $-16 + (-9) + 8 + 25$ 8

9. $109 + (-56) + (-91) + 26$ -12

10. $-206 + (-75) + 153 + 37$ -91

11. $-[24 + (-5)] + [-(-2 + 6)]$ -23

12. $[-7 + (-1)] + [-(-7 + 1)]$ -2

13. $3.7 + 4.2 + (-2.3) + 0 + 6.4 + 12.8$ 24.8

14. $-7.2 + 11.4 + (-8.1) + (-9.7) + 0.6$ -13

15. $27 + 43 + (-14) + (-57) + 5 + (-36) + (-14)$ -46

16. $46 + (-33) + 18 + 0 + (-93) + (-2) + (-34)$ -98

17. $-\frac{1}{3} + \left(-1\frac{2}{3}\right) + 2$ 0

18. $3 + \left(-\frac{5}{2}\right) + \left(-\frac{7}{2}\right)$ -3

19. $-1\frac{3}{4} + 2\frac{1}{4}$ $\frac{1}{2}$

20. $-3\frac{2}{5} + \left(-1\frac{4}{5}\right)$ $-5\frac{1}{5}$

21. $-\frac{7}{8} + \left(-\frac{11}{8}\right)$ $-\frac{9}{4}$

22. $\frac{16}{3} + \left(-\frac{10}{3}\right)$ 2

Sample $5 + (-7) + (-x) + (-10) = -x + 5 + (-7) + (-10) = -x + (-12)$

23. $-3 + x + (-5) + 4x + (-4)$

24. $2 + (-9) + (-y) + (-11)$ -y + (-18)

25. $-4 + a + 4 + (-a)$ 0

26. $21 + 4b + (-17) + (-12)$ 4b + (-8)

27. $-[8 + (-5)] + (-c) + 3$ -c

28. $-(-9) + 2y + (-9) + 6$ 2y + 6

29. $x + 5 + [(-x) + (-14)]$ -9

30. $4x + [8 + (-5) + (-7)]$ 4x + (-4)

Evaluate each expression if $x = -3$, $y = 6$, and $z = -4$.

B

31. $x + y + (-1)$ 2

32. $-21 + x + z$ -28

-6 **33.** $-15 + (-x) + y$

34. $-z + (-8) + y$ 2

35. $1 + (-y) + z$ -9

-20 **36.** $-y + (-11) + x$

37. $|x + y + z|$ 1

38. $|x + (-y) + z|$ 13

-15 **39.** $-|x + z + (-8)|$

Simplify.

C

40. $-b + [-a + (a + b)]$ 0

41. $-(-x + y) + y$ x

42. $r + s + [-(r + s + t)]$ -t

43. $a + [-(a + b)]$ -b

Problems

a. Write a positive number or a negative number to represent each situation.

b. Compute the sum of the numbers.

c. Answer each question.

Sample   A helicopter flying at an altitude of 2860 ft descended 120 ft and then rose 350 ft. What was its new altitude?

Solution   **a.** 2860, −120, 350   **b.** $2860 + (-120) + 350 = 3090$ **c.** 3090 ft

56   *Chapter 2*

5. a. 698, −250, −1684, −1316, 3700 **b.** 1148 **c.** $1148
6. a. 32, −5, −3, 4, 2, 0 **b.** 30 **c.** $30 per share

A **1.** An elevator started at the eighteenth floor. It then went down seven floors
and up nine floors. At what floor was the elevator then located? **a.** 18, −7, 9
b. 20 **c.** 20th floor

2. A submarine descended to a level 230 m below the surface of the ocean.
Later it ascended 95 m and then dove 120 m. What was the new depth of
the submarine? **a.** −230, 95, −120 **b.** −255 **c.** 255 m below the surface

3. Moira has $784 in her checking account. She deposits $96 and then writes
two checks, one for $18 and the other for $44. What is the new balance in
the account? **a.** 784, 96, −18, −44 **b.** 818 **c.** $818

4. On five plays a football team lost 3 yards, gained 15, gained 8, lost 9, and
lost 4. What was the net yardage on the plays? **a.** −3, 15, 8, −9, −4 **b.** 7 **c.** 7 yards gained

5. In September, the Drama Club treasury
contained $698. The club then pre-
sented a fall play, for which they paid
a royalty of $250. Scenery and cos-
tumes cost $1684, and programs and
other expenses totaled $1316. The sale
of tickets brought in $3700. How much
money was in the treasury after the
play was presented?

6. The stock of the Computer Research
Corporation opened on Monday at $32
per share. It lost $5 that day, dropped
another $3 on Tuesday, but then gained
$4 on Wednesday and $2 on Thursday.
On Friday it was unchanged. What was
its closing price for the week?

7. During a four-day period at the Hotel Gran Via, the numbers of guests
checking in and out were as follows: 32 in and 27 out, 28 in and 31 out,
12 in and 18 out, and 16 in and 25 out. How did the number of guests in
the hotel at the end of the fourth day compare with the number at the start
of the four-day period? **a.** 32, −27, 28, −31, 12, −18, 16, −25 **b.** −13
c. 13 fewer guests on the 4th day

8. During their first year after opening a restaurant, the Habibs had a loss of
$14,250. In their second year of operation, they broke even. During their
third and fourth years, they had gains of $18,180 and $29,470, respectively. What was the restaurant's net gain or loss over the four-year period?
a. −14,250, 0, 18,180, 29,470 **b.** 33,400 **c.** net gain of $33,400

9. A delivery truck traveled 5 blocks west, 3 blocks north, 8 blocks east, and
12 blocks south. After this, where was the truck relative to its starting
point? **a.** −5, 8; 3, −12 **b.** 3; −9 **c.** 3 blocks east and 9 blocks south

10. During an unusual storm, the temperature fell 8° C, rose 5° C, fell 4° C,
and then rose 6° C. If the temperature was 32° C at the outset of the storm,
what was it after the storm was over? **a.** 32, −8, 5, −4, 6 **b.** 31 **c.** 31° C

a. −86, 41, 28, −37 **b.** −54 **c.** 54 m below sea level
B **11.** The lowest point in Death Valley is 86 m below sea level. A helicopter flying at an altitude of 41 m above this point climbed 28 m and then dropped
37 m. At what altitude relative to sea level was it then flying?

12. The rim of a canyon is 156 ft below sea level. If a stranded hiker 71 ft below the rim fired a warning flare that rose 29 ft, to what altitude relative to sea level would the flare rise? **a.** −156, −71, 29 **b.** −198 **c.** 198 ft below sea level

13. Leaving Westwood at 1:00 P.M., Coretta flew to Bay View. The flight took 1.5 hours, but the time zone for Bay View is 2 hours earlier than Westwood's zone. What time was it in Bay View when Coretta landed? **a.** 1, 1.5, −2 **b.** 0.5 **c.** 12:30 P.M.

14. A passenger on a train traveling at 135 km/h walks toward the back of the train at a rate of 7 km/h. What is the passenger's rate of travel with respect to the ground? **a.** 135, −7 **b.** 128 **c.** 128 km/h

Solve.

C **15.** Wes charged $175 for clothing and $287 for camera equipment. He then made two payments of $50 each to his charge account. The next bill showed that he owed a balance of $495.25, including $11.50 in interest charges. How much did Wes owe on the account before making his purchase? $121.75

16. The volume of water in a tank during a five-day period changed as follows: up 375 L, down 240 L, up 93 L, down 164 L, and down 157 L. What was the volume of water in the tank at the beginning of the five-day period if the final volume was 54 L? 147 L

Mixed Review Exercises

Simplify.

1. $5 - 9 \div 3$ 2

2. $3 \cdot 5 \cdot 4 \cdot 20$ 1200

3. $(6 - 4 \div 2) \cdot 3 + 1$ 13

4. $|-7| - 6$ 1

5. $|-1.2| + 1.2$ 2.4

6. $|-15| - |-6|$ 9

7. $\dfrac{7 \cdot 6 + 3 \cdot 7}{(5 + 2)}$ 9

8. $6\frac{1}{7} + 5\frac{2}{3} + 8\frac{6}{7}$ 20$\frac{2}{3}$

9. $3.2 + 1.0 + 4.8$ 9

10. $[15 + (-5)] + 6$ 16

11. $(-8 + 4) + (-6)$ −10

12. $-3 + (-9) + 6 + (-5)$ −11

Calculator Key-In

Most calculators have a change-sign key, $+/-$, that will change a number from positive to negative or from negative to positive. When adding two or more positive and negative numbers, you can add in the usual order, making a number negative by hitting the change-sign key after entering the number.

Exercises

Use your calculator to find the sum.

1. $198 + (-217)$ −19

2. $-612 + 38$ −574

3. $-418 + 27$ −391

4. $-115.8 + 22.4$ −93.4

5. $13.8 + (-21.9)$ −8.1

6. $-319.2 + 45.5$ −273.7

2-4 Subtracting Real Numbers

Objective To subtract real numbers and to simplify expressions involving differences.

The first column below lists a few examples of the subtraction of 2. The second column lists related examples of the addition of -2.

Subtracting 2	Adding -2
$3 - 2 = 1$	$3 + (-2) = 1$
$4 - 2 = 2$	$4 + (-2) = 2$
$5 - 2 = 3$	$5 + (-2) = 3$
$6 - 2 = 4$	$6 + (-2) = 4$

Comparing the entries in the two columns shows that subtracting 2 gives the same result as adding the opposite of 2. This suggests the following:

Definition of Subtraction

For all real numbers a and b, the **difference** $a - b$ is defined by

$$a - b = a + (-b).$$

To subtract b, add the opposite of b.

Example 1 Simplify.
  a. $3 - 12$ **b.** $-7 - 1$ **c.** $-4 - (-10)$ **d.** $y - (y + 6)$

Solution   **a.** $3 - 12 = 3 + (-12) = -9$
  b. $-7 - 1 = -7 + (-1) = -8$
  c. $-4 - (-10) = -4 + 10 = 6$
  d. $y - (y + 6) = y + [-(y + 6)] = y + (-y) + (-6) = -6$

  Note that in part (d), the property of the opposite of a sum is used. The opposite of $(y + 6)$ is $-y + (-6)$.

Using the definition of subtraction, you may replace any difference with a sum. For example,

$$12 - 8 - 7 + 4 \quad \text{means} \quad 12 + (-8) + (-7) + 4.$$

As shown at the right, you may simplify this expression by grouping from left to right. This method is convenient if you are doing the work mentally or with a calculator.

$$
\begin{array}{c}
12 + (-8) + (-7) + 4 \\
\underbrace{}_{4} \ + (-7) + 4 \\
 \underbrace{}_{-3} + 4 \\
 \underbrace{}_{1}
\end{array}
$$

Working with Real Numbers   **59**

Explorations p. 687

Teaching Suggestions p. T85

Using Manipulatives p. T85

Suggested Extensions p. T86

Warm-Up Exercises
Simplify.
1. $16 + (-8)$ 8
2. $(-25) + 12$ -13
3. $(-12) + (-12)$ -24
4. $36 + 24$ 60
5. $(-10) + (-35)$ -45
6. $4 + (-20)$ -16
7. $13 + (-13)$ 0

Motivating the Lesson
Ask students what operation they would use to solve the following problem: What would the temperature be at midnight if this temperature was 27° below the daily high of 24°? subtraction Tell students that today's lesson will focus on subtracting real numbers.

Chalkboard Examples
Simplify.
1. $9 - 12$
   $= 9 + (-12) = -3$
2. $3 - (-4)$
   $= 3 + 4 = 7$
3. $-6 - (-10)$
   $= -6 + 10 = 4$
4. $-y - (-y + 4)$
   $= -y + [-(-y + 4)]$
   $= -y + y + (-4) = -4$
   (continued)

Chalkboard Examples

(continued)

5. 15 decreased by -3
$15 - (-3) = 15 + 3 = 18$

6. The opposite of the difference between y and 7
$-(y - 7) = -[y + (-7)]$
$= (-y) + [-(-7)]$
$= -y + 7$

Simplify.

7. $-(f + 8)$ $-f - 8$

8. $-(-b + 6 - a)$ $b - 6 + a$

9. $m - (-n + 3)$ $m + n - 3$

Check for Understanding

Here is a suggested use of the Oral Exercises to check students' understanding as you teach the lesson.
Oral Exs. 1–12: use after Example 1.
Oral Exs. 13–16: use after Example 3.

Guided Practice

Simplify.

1. $45 - 18$ 27
2. $12 - 35$ -23
3. $32 - (-48)$ 80
4. $-56 - (-6)$ -50
5. $-8.7 - 3.5$ -12.2
6. -23 decreased by -2 -21
7. The difference between -68 and 15, decreased by 30. -113
8. $-(x + 14)$ $-x - 14$
9. $5 - (x + 8)$ $-x - 3$
10. $n - (n - 5)$ 5

For written work, you may want to group positive terms and negative terms:

$$12 - 8 - 7 + 4 = 12 + (-8) + (-7) + 4$$
$$= (12 + 4) + [(-8) + (-7)]$$
$$= 16 + (-15) = 1$$

Certain sums are usually replaced by differences. For example,

$$9 + (-2x) \text{ is usually simplified to } 9 - 2x.$$

Example 2 Simplify: **a.** -30 decreased by -19
   b. The opposite of the difference between a and b

Solution   **a.** First write the expression: $-30 - (-19)$
   Then simplify: $-30 - (-19) = -30 + 19 = -11$ **Answer**

   b. First write the expression: $-(a - b)$. Then simplify:
   $-(a - b) = -[a + (-b)]$ (Definition of subtraction)
   $= (-a) + [-(-b)]$ (Property of the opposite of a sum)
   $= -a + b$ **Answer** (Property of opposites)

The property of the opposite of a sum and the definition of subtraction produce this useful result: *When you find the opposite of a sum or a difference, you change the sign of each term of the sum or difference.*

$$-(a + b) = (-a) + (-b) \qquad -(a - b) = (-a) - (-b)$$
$$= -a - b \qquad\qquad = -a + b$$

Now that you understand the reasoning behind each step, you can simplify some expressions mentally and write only the results, as shown in Example 3.

Example 3 Simplify: **a.** $-(x - 4)$ **b.** $-(-c + 5 - n)$ **c.** $x - (y - 2)$

Solution   **a.** $-x + 4$ **b.** $c - 5 + n$ **c.** $x - y + 2$

Caution: Subtraction is *not* commutative.   Subtraction is *not* associative.
   $8 - 3 = 5$ but $3 - 8 = -5$ $(6 - 4) - 3 = -1$ but $6 - (4 - 3) = 5$

Oral Exercises

Simplify.

1. $2 - 4$ -2 2. $19 - 12$ 7   3. $7 - 5$ 2   4. $7 - 27$ -20
5. $0 - 8$ -8 6. $0 - (-6)$ 6   7. $-16 - 0$ -16 8. $-8 - 2$ -10
9. $3 - (-1)$ 4   10. $7 - (-3)$ 10   11. $-9 - (-13)$ 4   12. $-6 - (-4)$ -2
13. $x - (x + 1)$ -1 14. $n - (n + 4)$ -4 15. $-(a - 3)$ $-a + 3$ 16. $-(w - 5)$ $-w + 5$

Written Exercises

Simplify.

A
1. $25 - 213$ -188
2. $154 - 281$ -127
3. $39 - (-32)$ 71
4. $47 - (-49)$ 96
5. $-19 - (-3)$ -16
6. $-25 - (-9)$ -16
7. $-2.8 - 4.4$ -7.2
8. $-5.1 - 6.7$ -11.8
9. $174 - (-24)$ 198
10. $-106 - (-95)$ -11
11. $1.91 - (-1.03)$ 2.94
12. $2.95 - (-2.55)$ 5.5

13. -21 decreased by 6 -27
14. -6 decreased by -32 26
15. 24 less than -1 -25
16. 15 less than -3 -18
17. $132 - (72 - 61)$ 121
18. $275 - (80 - 65)$ 260
19. $234 - (56 - 87)$ 265
20. $193 - (30 - 75)$ 238
21. $(22 - 33) - (55 - 66)$ 0
22. $(42 - 50) - (73 - 60)$ -21
23. $(3 - 8) - (-15 + 19)$ -9
24. $(42 - 33) - (-7 + 12)$ 4
25. $106 - 492 + 776$ 390
26. $910 - 939 - 201$ -230
27. $12 - (-9) - [5 - (-4)]$ 12
28. $-15 - 6 - [-7 - (-10)]$ -24
29. $4 - 5 + 8 - 17 + 31$ 21
30. $18 - 14 + 15 + 7 - 26$ 0
31. $-6 - 19 + 4 - 8 + 20$ -9
32. $-11 - 43 + 1 - 9 + 30$ -32

33. The difference between 81 and -6, decreased by -29 116
34. -54 decreased by the difference between -37 and 15 -2
35. -46 decreased by the difference between -23 and -61 -84
36. The difference between -59 and 12, decreased by 72 -143

37. $-(x - 7)$ -x + 7
38. $-(4 - y)$ -4 + y or y - 4
39. $x - (x + 5)$ -5
40. $8 - (y + 8)$ -y
41. $5 - (b - 7)$ -b + 12
42. $n - (4 + n)$ -4

Simplify.

B
43. The sum of 8 and y subtracted from z $z - y - 8$
44. The opposite of the sum of -7 and y $7 - y$ or $-y + 7$
45. Five less than the difference between 7 and z -z + 2
46. The opposite of the difference between x and 4 -x + 4
47. $7 + y - (7 - y) - y$ y
48. $s - (-3) - [s + (-3)] - 3$ 3
49. $h + 8 - (-9 + h)$ 17
50. $-(10 - k) - (k - 12)$ 2
51. $(\pi + 2)$ subtracted from $(\pi - 17)$ -19
52. $(7 - 2\pi)$ subtracted from $(11 - 2\pi)$ 4

Evaluate each expression if $a = -4$, $b = 5$, and $c = -1$.

53. $c - |a - b|$ -10
54. $b - c - |a|$ 2
55. $|c - a| - b$ -2
56. $|b - c| - a$ 10
57. $a - |c| - (|a| - b)$ -4
58. $|c| - b - (|a| - c)$ -9
59. $(a - |c|) - |a| - b$ -14
60. $(|c| - b) - |a| - c$ -7

Summarizing the Lesson

Review the two key points of today's lesson by asking:
- What is the definition of subtraction for all real numbers?
- What must be done to find the opposite of a sum or difference?

Use examples as needed to reinforce each point.

Suggested Assignments

Minimum
Day 1: 61/2–46 even
Assign with Lesson 2-3.
Day 2: 62/*P*: 1–10
  S 63/Mixed Review

Average
  61/2–48 even, 55–58
  62/*P*: 2–10 even
  S 63/Mixed Review

Maximum
  61/15–60 mult. of 3, 61
  62/*P*: 2–12 even
  S 63/Mixed Review

Supplementary Materials

Study Guide	pp. 25–26
Practice Master	6
Test Master	5
Overhead Visual	1

In Exercise 61, name the definition or property that justifies each step.

C 61. a. $b + (a - b) = b + [a + (-b)]$ **a.** __?__ Def. of subtraction
$= b + [(-b) + a]$ **b.** __?__ Comm. prop. of add.
$= [b + (-b)] + a$ **c.** __?__ Assoc. prop. of add.
$= 0 + a$ **d.** __?__ Prop. of opposites
$= a$ **e.** __?__ Ident. prop. of add.

b. Use the result of part (a) to complete the following sentence:
$a - b$ is the number to add to b to obtain __?__ . a

62. Suppose you are told that $b - a$ *is the opposite of* $a - b$. Explain how adding $b - a$ to $a - b$ can convince you that this statement is true. Accept reasonable answers.
For example: The sum of a number and its opposite is 0, and a
number has only one opposite. Since $(b - a) + (a - b) =$
$b + (-b) + (-a) + a = 0$, you know that $b - a$ is the opposite of $a - b$.

Problems

**Express the answer to each question as the difference between two real
numbers. Compute the difference. Answer the question and interpret the
sign of the answer.**

Sample   If astronauts traveled from the sunny side of the moon to the dark side,
they would find the temperature 220° C lower than on the sunny side. If
the temperature on the sunny side was 90° C, what was it on the dark side?

Solution $90 - 220 = -130$
The temperature on the dark side of the moon is 130 degrees *below* 0° C.

A **1.** Mars is 141.5 millions of miles from the sun. Earth is 48.6 millions of 92.9 millions
miles closer to the sun than Mars is. How far is Earth from the sun?   of miles

2. The highest recorded weather temperature on Earth is 58.0° C. The difference between that record and the lowest recorded weather temperature is
146.3° C. What is the record low? 88.3° below 0° C

3. The Roman poet Virgil was born in 70 B.C. How old was he on his birthday in 42 B.C.? 28 years old

4. Pythagoras, the Greek mathematician, was born in 582 B.C. and died on
his birthday in 497 B.C. How old was he when he died? 85 years old

5. Krypton boils at 153.4° below 0° C and melts at 157.2° below 0° C. What
is the difference between its boiling and melting points? 3.8° C

6. Including the wind-chill factor, the temperature at Council Bluffs was eight
degrees below zero Celsius at midnight and seventeen below zero at dawn.
What was the change in temperature? fell 9° C

7. Becky Kasai took the subway from a stop 52 blocks east of Central Square
to a stop 39 blocks west of Central Square. How many blocks did she
ride? 91 blocks

8. Glynis drove a golf ball from a point 126 yd north of the ninth hole to a point 53 yd south of the hole. How far did the ball travel? 179 yd

9. Find the difference in altitude between Mt. Rainier, Washington, 4392 m above sea level, and Death Valley, California, 86 m below sea level. 4478 m

10. The difference in altitude between the highest and lowest points in Louisiana is 164.592 m. If Driskill Mountain, the highest point, is 163.068 m above sea level, what is the altitude of New Orleans, the lowest point?
1.524 m below sea level

B 11. In 1972, the Apollo space mission land rover weighed about 475 lb on Earth. Because of low gravity, it weighed 396 lb less on the moon. How much did the land rover weigh on the moon? 79 lb

12. Alonzo has $22; Brad has $29; Caryl has $2; and Diane has $13. Alonzo owes Brad $15 and Caryl $3. Brad owes Caryl $18 and Diane $7. Diane owes Caryl $11 and Alonzo $5. When all debts are paid, how much money will each have?
Alonzo, $9; Brad, $19; Caryl, $34; Diane, $4

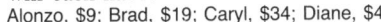

Mixed Review Exercises

Simplify.

1. $|-9| + |7|$ 16

2. $18 \cdot 3 \cdot 5 \cdot 2$ 540

3. $4 + 7x + 3y + 5$ $7x + 3y + 9$

4. $\left|-\frac{2}{5}\right| - \left|\frac{1}{5}\right|$ $\frac{1}{5}$

5. $-\frac{5}{4} + \left(-\frac{7}{4}\right)$ -3

6. $1\frac{1}{3} + \left(-3\frac{2}{3}\right)$ $-2\frac{1}{3}$

7. $[6 + (-12)] + 9$ 3

8. $4.2 - 0.5 + (-3.2)$ 0.5

9. $-6 + [-8 + (-4)]$ -18

10. $-3.2 + 74 + (-2.8)$ 68

11. $-41 + (-28) + 32 + 49$ 12

12. $3 + (-7) + (-12) + (-x)$ $-x - 16$

Self-Test 1

Vocabulary closure properties (p. 45)
commutative properties (p. 45)
associative properties (p. 45)
terms (p. 46)
factors (p. 46)
reflexive property (p. 46)
symmetric property (p. 46)
transitive property (p. 46)

identity element for addition (p. 50)
identity property of addition (p. 50)
property of opposites (p. 50)
additive inverses (p. 50)
property of the opposite of a sum (p. 51)
difference (p. 59)
subtraction (p. 59)

(Self-Test continues on next page.)

Working with Real Numbers **63**

Simplify.

1. $9 \cdot 4 \cdot 7 \cdot 25$ 6300   2. $82 + 31 + x + 18x$ + 131   **Obj. 2-1, p. 45**

3. $3 + (-4)$ −1   4. $(-5 + 6) + 4$ 5   5. $4 + 2x + (-5)$ 2x − 1 **Obj. 2-2, p. 49**

6. $-13 + (-7)$ −20   7. $-201 + (-19) + 20 + 180$ −20   **Obj. 2-3, p. 54**

8. $12 - 26$ −14   9. $9 - (y - 9)$ −y + 18   **Obj. 2-4, p. 59**

Check your answers with those at the back of the book.

Reading Algebra / Independent Study

When you read an algebra textbook, it helps to know the goals of a lesson. The lesson title and the lesson objective (directly below the title) give you a good idea of what you should know when you have finished reading.

Have you noticed that it's useful to skim each lesson first? As you read, look for important words, phrases, and ideas that are in **heavy type,** in *italics,* or in boxes. You need to know the highlighted ideas in order to understand the lesson. The glossary and index can help you find more information about important ideas.

Working through each example in a lesson can help you do some of the Oral and Written Exercises on your own. Doing the exercises will let you know whether you understand the lesson objectives.

The Self-Tests, with answers at the back of the book, will help you review a group of lessons. The Chapter Reviews, Chapter Tests, Cumulative Reviews, Mixed Reviews, and Mixed Problem Solving Reviews will also give you a good idea of your progress. If you do not understand a concept, and re-reading doesn't seem to help, it is a good idea to make a note of the concept so that you can discuss it with your teacher.

Exercises

Skim through Lessons 4-2 and 4-3 (pages 146–154). Then answer the following questions.

1. What should you be able to do when you have finished reading the text of these lessons? Add and subtract polynomials, multiply monomials

2. What new words or phrases are introduced?

3. What is a monomial? a polynomial? Find the definitions of these words in your book.

4. Suppose that you had forgotten the definition of the term *variable.* Where could you look it up? On what page of your textbook is this word first used? Glossary; page 1

5. Lesson 4-2 covers adding and subtracting polynomials. Where could you find information about addition and subtraction in general?
   Index and/or Table of Contents

Reading Algebra

Different purposes demand different types of reading. For previewing or reviewing a lesson, skimming (rapid reading) is used. By contrast, slow reading is used when the student is trying to learn the main ideas and important details of a lesson. For slow reading, it is beneficial for teachers to provide questions in advance that will be discussed upon completion of the reading.

**Additional Answers
Reading Algebra**

2. monomial, constant monomial, constant, polynomial, binomials, trinomials, coefficient, numerical coefficient, similar terms, like terms, simplified, simplified form, degree of a variable in a monomial, degree of a monomial, degree of a polynomial.

3. an expression that is either a numeral, a variable, or the product of a numeral and one or more variables; a sum of monomials

Multiplication

2-5 The Distributive Property

Objective   To use the distributive property to simplify expressions.

The cost of a certain model of cross-country skis is $90. A pair of ski poles costs $12. When Rita bought her family 4 sets of skis and poles, the total cost could have been calculated in two ways:

(1) Total cost:
   4 × (cost of one set of skis and poles)
   4 × (90 + 12) = 4 × 102 = $408

(2) Total cost:
   (4 × cost of skis) + (4 × cost of poles)
   (4 · 90) + (4 · 12) = 360 + 48 = $408

Either way you compute it, the total cost is the same:

$$4(90 + 12) = (4 \cdot 90) + (4 \cdot 12)$$

Note that 4 is *distributed* as a multiplier of each term of the sum 90 + 12. This example illustrates another important property that we use when working with real numbers.

Distributive Property (of multiplication with respect to addition)

For all real numbers a, b, and c:

$$a(b + c) = ab + ac \quad \text{and} \quad (b + c)a = ba + ca.$$

Example 1 shows how the distributive property can make mental math easier.

Example 1 **a.** $5 \cdot 83 = 5(80 + 3)$
$= (5 \cdot 80) + (5 \cdot 3)$
$= 400 + 15$
$= 415$ *Answer*

b. $6(9.5) = 6(9 + 0.5)$
$= (6 \cdot 9) + (6 \cdot 0.5)$
$= 54 + 3$
$= 57$ *Answer*

c. $8\left(2\frac{1}{4}\right) = 8\left(2 + \frac{1}{4}\right)$
$= (8 \cdot 2) + \left(8 \cdot \frac{1}{4}\right)$
$= 16 + 2 = 18$ *Answer*

Working with Real Numbers   **65**

Warm-Up Exercises
Simplify.
1. $4(3 + 1)$ 16
2. $(3)(4) - (8)(4)$ -20
3. $(4)(3) + 4$ 16
4. $(2)(5) - (2)(9)$ -8
5. $3 - (x - 7)$ $-x + 10$
6. $-(x - y + 3)$ $-x + y - 3$

Motivating the Lesson
Ask students to figure the cost of three beverages at $.56 each and three sandwiches at $2.44 each. Discuss the different approaches to finding the solution. Note those methods that illustrate the use of the distributive property, the topic of today's lesson.

Chalkboard Examples
Use the distributive property and mental math to simplify each expression.
1. $6 \cdot 48 = 6(40 + 8)$
$= (6 \cdot 40) + (6 \cdot 8)$
$= 240 + 48$
$= 288$
2. $4(3.25) = 4(3 + 0.25)$
$= (4 \cdot 3) + (4 \cdot 0.25)$
$= 12 + 1$
$= 13$
3. $6\left(4\frac{1}{3}\right) = 6\left(4 + \frac{1}{3}\right)$
$= (6 \cdot 4) + \left(6 \cdot \frac{1}{3}\right)$
$= 24 + 2$
$= 26$
4. $(3x + 4)2$
$= (3x \cdot 2) + (4 \cdot 2)$
$= 6x + 8$

(continued)

Chalkboard Examples

Chalkboard Examples

(continued)

Simplify.

5. $23 \cdot 26 + 77 \cdot 26$
$= (23 + 77)\ 26$
$= (100)26$
$= 2600$

6. Show that $7x + 5x = 12x$
for every real number x.
$7x + 5x = (7 + 5)x$ Dist. prop.
$\quad\quad = 12x$ Subst. prin.

Simplify.

7. $8a - 2a + 10a$
$8a - 2a + 10a = 18a - 2a$
$\quad\quad\quad\quad\quad = 16a$

8. $5n + 7(n - 3)$
$5n + 7(n - 3)$
$= 5n + 7 \cdot n - 7 \cdot 3$
$= 5n + 7n - 21$
$= 12n - 21$

Common Errors

Some students will apply the distributive property to multiplication examples. They write $3(4 \cdot 6)$ as $12 \cdot 18$ and get 216 as their answer. In reteaching, remind them that they can only distribute multiplication with either addition or subtraction.

Check for Understanding

Here is a suggested use of the Oral Exercises to check students' understanding as you teach the lesson.
Oral Exs. 1–8: use after Example 1.
Oral Exs. 9–16: use after Example 2.
Oral Exs. 17–25: use after Example 5.

Example 2 **a.** $5(x + 2) = 5 \cdot x + 5 \cdot 2$ **b.** $(6y + 7)4 = 6y \cdot 4 + 7 \cdot 4$
$\quad\quad\quad\quad\quad\quad\quad = 5x + 10$ *Answer* $= 24y + 28$ *Answer*

Multiplication is distributive with respect to subtraction as well as addition. For example,

$$2(8 - 3) = 2 \cdot 8 - 2 \cdot 3 \quad \text{and} \quad 4(x - 6) = 4 \cdot x - 4 \cdot 6$$
$$\quad\quad\quad = 16 - 6 = 10 \quad\quad\quad\quad\quad\quad = 4x - 24.$$

This principle is stated in general below and will be proved in the next lesson. (See Exercise 60, page 73.)

Distributive Property (of multiplication with respect to subtraction)

For all real numbers a, b, and c:

$$a(b - c) = ab - ac \quad \text{and} \quad (b - c)a = ba - ca.$$

By applying the symmetric property of equality, the distributive properties of multiplication can also be written in the following forms:

$$ab + ac = a(b + c) \quad\quad\quad ba + ca = (b + c)a$$
$$ab - ac = a(b - c) \quad\quad\quad ba - ca = (b - c)a$$

For example, the diagram below illustrates that

$$(3 \cdot 4) + (3 \cdot 2) = 3(4 + 2).$$

Area: $3 \cdot 4$ Area: $3 \cdot 2$ Area: $3(4 + 2)$

Example 3   Simplify $75 \cdot 17 + 25 \cdot 17$.

Solution $75 \cdot 17 + 25 \cdot 17 = (75 + 25)17$
$\quad\quad\quad\quad\quad\quad\quad\quad\quad = (100)17$
$\quad\quad\quad\quad\quad\quad\quad\quad\quad = 1700$ *Answer*

Example 4   Show that $9x + 5x = 14x$ for every real number x.

Solution $9x + 5x = (9 + 5)x$ Distributive property
$\quad\quad\quad\quad = 14x$ Substitution principle

66   *Chapter 2*

The properties of real numbers and equality guarantee that for all values of the variable x, $9x + 5x$ and $14x$ represent the same number. Therefore the two expressions are **equivalent.**

The expression $9x + 5x$ has two terms. The expression $14x$ has one term. Replacing an expression containing variables by an equivalent expression with as few terms as possible is called **simplifying the expression.**

Example 5 Simplify: **a.** $8y - 6y$ **b.** $3n + 7n - 4n$ **c.** $8(n - 1) + 3n$

Solution   **a.** $8y - 6y = (8 - 6)y$ **b.** $3n + 7n - 4n = 10n - 4n$
                $= 2y$ *Answer* $= 6n$ *Answer*

c. $8(n - 1) + 3n = 8 \cdot n - 8 \cdot 1 + 3n$
              $= 8n - 8 + 3n$
              $= 11n - 8$ *Answer*

Oral Exercises

Use the distributive property and mental math to simplify each expression.

1. $2(30 + 5)$ 70 **2.** $7(40 + 1)$ 287 **3.** $4(20 - 1)$ 76 **4.** $5(60 - 2)$ 290

5. $3 \cdot 99$ 297 **6.** $8 \cdot 3\frac{1}{4}$ 26 **7.** $10\left(3\frac{1}{5}\right)$ 32 **8.** $5(7.2)$ 36

For each expression give an equivalent expression without parentheses.

9. $5(a + 2)$ 5a + 10 **10.** $3(x + 4)$ 3x + 12 **11.** $6(n + 3)$ 6n + 18 **12.** $4(a - 1)$ 4a − 4

13. $5(2t - 3)$ 10t − 15 **14.** $9(3n - 2)$ 27n − 18 **15.** $8(b - c)$ 8b − 8c **16.** $7(m + n)$ 7m + 7n

Simplify.

17. $6x + 16x$ 22x **18.** $12y + 8y$ 20y **19.** $2a + 5a$ 7a

20. $3b + b$ 4b **21.** $(-2)x + (-6)x$ −8x **22.** $(-3)y + (-8)y$ −11y

23. $11k - 15k$ −4k **24.** $2c - 4c$ −2c **25.** $3(1 + z) + 7$ 3z + 10

Written Exercises

Simplify.

A **1.** $8(30 + 1)$ 248 **2.** $7(60 + 2)$ 434 **3.** $5(70 - 2)$ 340 **4.** $9(20 - 1)$ 171

  5. $4(50 - 3)$ 188 **6.** $6(80 + 5)$ 510 **7.** $4 \cdot 52$ 208 **8.** $6 \cdot 64$ 384

  9. $4(9.5)$ 38 **10.** $6(9.9)$ 59.4 **11.** $14\left(1\frac{1}{7}\right)$ 16 **12.** $15\left(4\frac{3}{5}\right)$ 69

Working with Real Numbers   **67**

Simplify.
1. $5(30 - 2)$ 140
2. $7 \cdot 28$ 196
3. $12\left(2\frac{5}{6}\right)$ 34
4. $(6.2)(8) + (3.8)(8)$ 80
5. $(-5)r + 10r$ 5r
For each expression write an equivalent expression without parentheses.
6. $6(y + 7)$ 6y + 42
7. $2(6x + 9y)$ 12x + 18y
Simplify.
8. $9k - 7 - 2k$ 7k − 7
9. $4a + 6b - a + 3b$ 3a + 9b

Summarizing the Lesson
Review the definition of the distributive property of multiplication with respect to both addition and subtraction. Have students explain how the distributive property can make mental math easier.

Suggested Assignments
Minimum
    67/3–54 mult. of 3, 67–68
S 69/Mixed Review
R 63/Self-Test 1
Average
    67/3–69 mult. of 3
S 69/Mixed Review
R 63/Self-Test 1
Maximum
    67/3–75 mult. of 3
S 69/Mixed Review
R 63/Self-Test 1

Supplementary Materials
Study Guide   pp. 27–28
Resource Book   p. 83

Simplify.

13. $30 \cdot 18 + 70 \cdot 18$ 1800   **14.** $11 \cdot 43 + 89 \cdot 43$ 4300   **15.** $(13 \cdot 27) - (13 \cdot 27)$ 0

16. $(64 \cdot 81) + (36 \cdot 81)$ 8100 **17.** $(0.75)(32) + (0.25)(32)$ 32   **18.** $(3.6)(25) - (1.6)(25)$ 50

19. $5a + 2a$ 7a   **20.** $7x + 6x$ 13x   **21.** $13y - 4y$ 9y

22. $2n + (-8)n$ (−6)n   **23.** $(-3)p + 7p$ 4p   **24.** $(-8)n - 7n$ (−15)n

For each expression write an equivalent expression without parentheses.

25. $3(x + 2)$ 3x + 6   **26.** $5(a + 7)$ 5a + 35   **27.** $4(n - 2)$ 4n − 8

28. $8(b - 5)$ 8b − 40   **29.** $6(3n + 2)$ 18n + 12   **30.** $7(5n + 3)$ 35n + 21

31. $3(j - k)$ 3j − 3k   **32.** $2(3x - y)$ 6x − 2y   **33.** $(3n + 7)2$ 6n + 14

34. $(4x + 3)3$ 12x + 9   **35.** $(2x + 3y)5$ 10x + 15y   **36.** $(6m + 7n)2$ 12m + 14n

Simplify.

37. $3a + 7 + 5a$ 8a + 7   **38.** $6n + 1 + 3n$ 9n + 1   **39.** $8n - 5 + 4n$ 12n − 5

40. $3p + 8 - 3p$ 8   **41.** $8y - 7y + 4$ y + 4   **42.** $y + 9z - 6z$ y + 3z

> **Sample** $8x + y + 2x + 6y = (8x + 2x) + (y + 6y)$
> $= 10x + 7y$ **Answer**

43. $2a + b + 5a + 3b$ 7a + 4b   **44.** $4c + d + 3c + 2d$ 7c + 3d   **45.** $3s + 5t - t - 2s$ s + 4t

46. $5d - 3e + 4e - d$ 4d + e **47.** $7x + 5y - x - 5y$ 6x   **48.** $6g - 3f + 8f - g$ 5f + 5g

B **49.** $4(x + 3) + 3$ 4x + 15   **50.** $3(n - 1) + 4$ 3n + 1   **51.** $3(a - 7) - 4$ 3a − 25

52. $2(n - 8) + 9$ 2n − 7   **53.** $7 + 2(5 - x)$ −2x + 17   **54.** $8 + 3(4 - y)$ −3y + 20

55. $2 + (x + 3)5$ 5x + 17   **56.** $(y - 5)6 + 15$ 6y − 15   **57.** $5(y + 3) + 7y$ 12y + 15

58. $9(n - 3) + 4n$ 13n − 27   **59.** $3(2x + y + 1)$ 6x + 3y + 3   **60.** $5(7y - 3z + 4)$ 35y − 15z + 20

61. $9(a + b) + 4(3a + 2b)$ 21a + 17b   **62.** $8(k + m) + 15(2k + 5m)$ 38k + 83m

63. $6(r + 5) + 9(r - 2) - 4r$ 11r + 12   **64.** $4(n + 7) + 5(n - 3) - 2n$ 7n + 13

65. $7(c + 2d + 8) + 3(9c - 2)$ 34c + 14d + 50 **66.** $4(5x + 3y + 6) + 14(2y - 1)$ 20x + 40y + 10

In Exercises 67–70, represent each word phrase by a variable expression. Then simplify it.

67. Five times the sum of c and d, increased by twice the sum of $3c$ and d
$5(c + d) + 2(3c + d)$; 11c + 7d

68. Twice the sum of eleven and x, increased by three times the difference between x and seven
$2(11 + x) + 3(x - 7)$; 5x + 1

69. Eight more than the sum of -5 and $15y$, increased by one half of the difference between $12y$ and 8
$8 + (-5 + 15y) + \frac{1}{2}(12y - 8)$; 21y − 1

70. Six more than three times the sum of a and b, increased by five less than b
$6 + 3(a + b) + (b - 5)$; 3a + 4b + 1

Use the 5-step plan to solve each problem over the given domain.

C **71.** If a number is increased by 17 and this sum is multiplied by 4, the result is 77 more than the number. Find the number.
Domain: {2, 3, 4} 3

72. If five is subtracted from twice a number and this difference is tripled, the result is one more than four times the number. Find the number.
Domain: {8, 9, 10} 8

Simplify.

73. $8[5x + 7(3 + 4x)] - 16x - 8$ $248x + 160$

74. $-24 + 3[4y + 2(5y - 8)] - 9y$ $33y - 72$

75. $12(3n + 2p) + 11[n + 3(2n - p - 3)]$ $113n - 9p - 99$

76. $9[7(3a + 2b - 4) + 12(a - 2)] + 3(5a - 8b)$ $312a + 102b - 468$

77. $3[4y - 2(x + 3) + (2 - y)]$ $-6x + 9y - 12$

78. $9[4(2n + r) - 11r] + 3(r - n)$ $69n - 60r$

Mixed Review Exercises

Evaluate if $a = -3$, $b = -2$, $c = 2$, $x = 4$, and $y = 5$.

1. $5x + 2y - c$ 28

2. $(c \cdot c + x) \div 2$ 4

3. $2y - (4x \div c)$ 2

4. $|a| + |b| + (-c)$ 3

5. $c + |-y| + |b|$ 9

6. $3|a| - |b|$ 7

7. $-(-b + x) + y$ -1

8. $b + y + (-2)$ 1

9. $a + x + (-y)$ -4

10. $x - (a - b)$ 5

11. $-a - b + y$ 10

12. $|b + a| - y$ 0

Challenge

1. Copy the diagram.

2. Find each product and write it in the appropriate box. A calculator may be helpful.

   a. $142{,}857 \cdot 1$
   b. $142{,}857 \cdot 2$
   c. $142{,}857 \cdot 3$
   d. $142{,}857 \cdot 4$

3. Predict the following products from the pattern you see in Exercise 2.

   a. $142{,}857 \cdot 5$
   b. $142{,}857 \cdot 6$

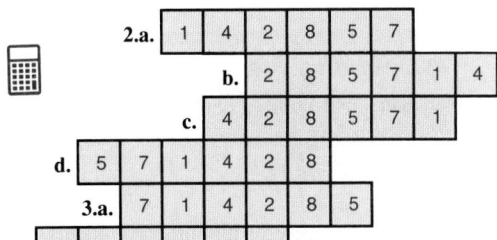

Working with Real Numbers   **69**

Warm-Up Exercises
Multiply.
1. 547 × 1 547
2. 0 × 56,485 0
3. 1 × 737,498 737,498
4. 69 × 35 × 0 × 472 0

Motivating the Lesson
Write the following products
on the chalkboard.
   (7)(3) (7)(2)
   (7)(1) (7)(0)
Ask students to find each
product. Then write these
products:
   (7)(−1) (7)(−2)
Discuss possible answers.
State that the topic of today's lesson is multiplying
real numbers.

2-6 Rules for Multiplication

Objective   To multiply real numbers.

When you multiply any given real number by 1, the product is equal to the given number. For example:

$$4 \cdot 1 = 4 \quad \text{and} \quad 1 \cdot 4 = 4$$

The **identity element for multiplication** is 1.

Identity Property of Multiplication

There is a unique real number 1 such that for every real number a,

$$a \cdot 1 = a \quad \text{and} \quad 1 \cdot a = a.$$

The equations $4 \cdot 0 = 0 \quad \text{and} \quad 0 \cdot 4 = 0$

illustrate the *multiplicative property of zero:*   When one (or at least one) of the factors of a product is zero, the product itself is zero.

Multiplicative Property of Zero

For every real number a:

$$a \cdot 0 = 0 \quad \text{and} \quad 0 \cdot a = 0$$

Would you guess that $4(-1) = -4$? You can verify this product by noticing that

$$4(-1) = (-1) + (-1) + (-1) + (-1) = -4.$$

Multiplying *any* real number by -1 produces the opposite of the number. (See Exercise 59, page 73.)

Multiplicative Property of −1

For every real number a:

$$a(-1) = -a \quad \text{and} \quad (-1)a = -a$$

A special case of this property occurs when the value of a is -1.

$$(-1)(-1) = 1$$

Using the multiplicative property of -1 with the familiar multiplication facts for positive numbers and properties that you have learned, you can compute the product of *any* two real numbers.

70   *Chapter 2*

Example 1 Multiply: **a.** 4(7) **b.** (−4)(7) **c.** 4(−7) **d.** (−4)(−7)

Solution

a. $4(7) = 28$ *Answer*

b. $(−4)(7) = (−1)4(7)$
$= (−1)28$
$= −28$ *Answer*

c. $4(−7) = 4(−1)(7)$
$= 4(7)(−1)$
$= 28(−1)$
$= −28$ *Answer*

d. $(−4)(−7) = (−1)4(−1)7$
$= (−1)(−1)4(7)$
$= 1(28)$
$= 28$ *Answer*

Property of Opposites in Products

For all real numbers a and b:

$$(−a)(b) = −ab \qquad a(−b) = −ab \qquad (−a)(−b) = ab$$

Practice in computing products will suggest to you the following rules for multiplication of positive and negative numbers.

Rules for Multiplication

1. If two numbers have the *same* sign, their product is *positive*.
   If two numbers have *opposite* signs, their product is *negative*.
2. The product of an *even* number of negative numbers is *positive*.
   The product of an *odd* number of negative numbers is *negative*.

Example 2 **a.** $4(−6)(−7)(−5)$ is negative because it has 3 negative factors.
b. $(−2)(−8)(−7)(5)(−6)$ is positive because it has 4 negative factors.
c. $(−9)(3)(0)(−5)$ is zero because it has a zero factor.

Example 3 Simplify: **a.** $(−3x)(−4y)$ **b.** $4p + (−5p)$

Solution

a. $(−3x)(−4y) = (−3)x(−4)y$
$= (−3)(−4)xy$
$= 12xy$ *Answer*

b. $4p + (−5p) = [4 + (−5)]p$
$= (−1)p$
$= −p$ *Answer*

Example 4 Simplify: **a.** $−2(x − 3y)$ **b.** $3p − 4(p − 2)$

Solution

a. $−2(x − 3y) = −2x − (−2)(3y)$
$= −2x − (−6y)$
$= −2x + 6y$
Answer

b. $3p − 4(p − 2) = 3p − (4p − 4 \cdot 2)$
$= 3p − (4p − 8)$
$= 3p − 4p + 8$
$= −p + 8$ *Answer*

Working with Real Numbers   **71**

Multiply.

1. $(-25)(4)$ -100
2. $(16)(-3)$ -48
3. $(-3)(-47)(0)(32)$ 0
4. $(-4)(15p)$ $-60p$
5. $(-7p)(6q)$ $-42pq$
6. $(-1)(3d - e + 8)$
  $-3d + e - 8$
7. $-6(7n - 6)$ $-42n + 36$
8. $-[-4(x - y)]$ $4x - 4y$

Simplify.

9. $6a + 7b - 4a - 3 - 5b$
  $2a + 2b - 3$

Summarizing the Lesson

Have students explain and give an example of:
- the identity property of multiplication
- the multiplicative property of zero
- the multiplicative property of -1
- the rules for multiplication.

Suggested Assignments

Minimum
  72/1–43 odd
S 73/Mixed Review

Average
  72/2–34 even, 36–51
    mult. of 3
S 73/Mixed Review

Maximum
  72/3–57 mult. of 3, 59
S 73/Mixed Review

Oral Exercises

Simplify.

1. $(-3)(-1)$ 3
2. $10(-8)$ -80
3. $(-3)(-9)$ 27
4. $(-8)(-5)$ 40
5. $(-1)(6)(-6)$ 36
6. $2(-6)(-1)$ 12
7. $(-1)(-3)(-5)$ -15
8. $(-2)(-4)(-6)$ -48
9. $7(0)(-12)$ 0
10. $(-11)(-7)(0)$ 0
11. $(-6)(-10g)$ 60g
12. $(-7)(12p)$ $-84p$
13. $(-3p)(-4q)$ 12pq
14. $(4e)(-6f)$ $-24ef$
15. $(-9v)(2w)$ $-18vw$
16. $-2ab - 3ab$ $-5ab$
17. $7c + (-7c)$ 0
18. $-7rs + 2rs$ $-5rs$
19. $-5wz + (-4wz)$ $-9wz$
20. $8u + (-8u)$ 0
21. $-9xy + 8xy$ $-xy$
22. $-3(x - y)$ $-3x + 3y$
23. $-2(a - 5b)$ $-2a + 10b$
24. $-2(c + 5d)$ $-2c - 10d$
25. $-4(3b - 5)$ $-12b + 20$
26. $(x - 7)(-2)$ $-2x + 14$
27. $(-m - n)(-9)$ 9m + 9n
28. $1 - 2(g + h)$ $1 - 2g - 2h$
29. $5 - 2(a - b)$ $5 - 2a + 2b$
30. $-(x - 7) + 4$ $-x + 11$

Written Exercises

Multiply.

A
1. $(-37)(-2)$ 74
2. $23(-5)$ -115
3. $(-4)(10)(-12)$ 480
4. $(-6)(-9)(20)$ 1080
5. $(-3)(-7)(-4)$ -84
6. $(-2)(-8)(-4)$ -64
7. $(-17)(-18)(0)$ 0
8. $54(-47)(0)$ 0
9. $5(-3)(-10)(-2)$ -300
10. $(-4)(25)(-2)(-3)$ -600
11. $(-6)(-1)(-7)(-10)$ 420
12. $(-9)(-5)(-1)(-3)$ 135
13. $(-2a)(-3b)$ 6ab
14. $(-5x)(-3y)$ 15xy
15. $2p(-7q)$ $-14pq$
16. $(-4e)(5t)$ $-20et$
17. $(-7a)(-5c)4$ 140ac
18. $(-x)(-3y)(-z)$ $-3xyz$
19. $-2(x - 3y)$ $-2x + 6y$
20. $-5(c + 2d)$ $-5c - 10d$
21. $-7(3m + 4n)$ $-21m - 28n$
22. $-9(-5y - 8)$ $45y + 72$
23. $(5x - 3)(-7)$ $-35x + 21$
24. $(-4 + 7y)(-2)$ $-14y + 8$
25. $(-1)(a + b - 3)$ $-a - b + 3$
26. $(-1)(2n - y - 5)$ $-2n + y + 5$
27. $(-1)(a - b - c)$ $-a + b + c$
28. $(-1)(-x - y + 7)$ $x + y - 7$
29. $-[(-2)(a + b)]$ $2a + 2b$
30. $-[(-3)(x - y)]$ $3x - 3y$

Simplify.

31. $5x - 7x + 8 + 2x$ 8
32. $3y - 7 - 8y + 5$ $-5y - 2$
33. $14p - 7c - 9c + 11p$ $-16c + 25p$
34. $-y - 3z + 4y - 9z - y$ $2y - 12z$

B
35. $3.4y + 1.6s - (-1.9y) - 3.6s$ $-2s + 5.3y$
36. $-0.8c + 4.1h - (-3.2c) - 0.1h$ $2.4c + 4h$
37. $-8x - 7x - 5x$ $-20x$
38. $-34n + 18n - 4n$ $-20n$
39. $-8(-19) - 7(-19) - 5(-19)$ 380
40. $-34 \cdot 9 + 18 \cdot 9 - 4 \cdot 9$ -180
41. $88(-57) + 13(-57) + (-1)(-57)$ -5700
42. $-63 \cdot 81 + 56 \cdot 81 - 13 \cdot 81$ -1620
43. $-m + \frac{2}{3}m - \frac{1}{2}n + \frac{5}{2}n$ $-\frac{1}{3}m + 2n$
44. $-5a - \left(-\frac{1}{2}b\right) + 3\frac{1}{2}a - \frac{1}{2}b$ $-1\frac{1}{2}a$

45. $7 - 3(r + s)$ $-3r - 3s + 7$

46. $2 + 6(m - n)$ $6m - 6n + 2$

47. $2(x + 5y) + (-3)(7x - y)$ $-19x + 13y$

48. $8(t - u) + 5(2t - 3u)$ $18t - 23u$

49. $-2(2q + w) - 7(w - q)$ $3q - 9w$

50. $-3(7c + d) - 2(10d - c)$ $-19c - 23d$

51. $-4(-e + 3f) - 3[e + (-5f)]$ $e + 3f$

52. $-6[v + (-9w)] + (-5)(3v - w)$ $-21v + 59w$

C **53.** $2[-7(r + 2s) - r] - 3(s + 2r)$ $-22r - 31s$

54. $4[2(-5x + y) - y] - 10(y - 4x)$ $-6y$

55. $-15 + (-3)[2(g - 7) - 2(1 - g)]$
$-12g + 33$

56. $-50 + (-2)[3(1 - f) - 3(-2 + f)]$ $12f - 68$

Write your answer as a variable expression.

57. Sal owned 500 shares of Acme Tube. On Monday morning each share of the stock had gained p points. On Tuesday each share lost one more than twice as many points as it had gained the day before. How much did the total value of Sal's shares of Acme Tube change between the opening of trading on Monday and the closing on Tuesday? $(500p + 500)$ points down

58. A discount store bought 12 dozen radios, each to be sold at $15 above cost. The store sold x of the radios at that price. Each of the remaining radios was sold at $4 below cost. If the store paid $11 for each radio, what was the total income from the sale? (*Hint:* Income = Sales − Cost) $(19x - 576)$ dollars

59. To show that $a(-1)$ is the opposite of a for every real number a, you can show that the sum of $a(-1)$ and a is zero as follows. Name the property that justifies each step.

$a(-1) + a = a(-1) + a(1)$ **a.** __?__ Ident. prop. of mult.

$= a[(-1) + 1]$ **b.** __?__ Dist. prop. (of mult. with respect to add.)

$= a(0)$ **c.** __?__ Prop. of opposites

$= 0$ **d.** __?__ Mult. prop. of 0

Since the unique opposite of a is $-a$, $a(-1) = -a$.

60. Name the property or definition that justifies each step.

$a(b - c) = a[b + (-c)]$ **a.** __?__ Def. of subtraction

$= a(b) + a(-c)$ **b.** __?__ Dist. prop. (of mult. with respect to add.)

$= ab + (-ac)$ **c.** __?__ Prop. of opposites in products

$= ab - ac$ **d.** __?__ Def. of subtraction

Supplementary Materials
Study Guide   pp. 29–30
Practice Master   7

Mixed Review Exercises

Translate each sentence into an equation.

1. Four times a number is 44. $4x = 44$

2. The sum of n and 2 is 32. $n + 2 = 32$

3. Half of a number is twelve. $\frac{1}{2}x = 12$

4. Seven more than twice a number is 11. $2x + 7 = 11$

Simplify.

5. $120 - (14 - 6)$ 112

6. $191 - (9 - 12)$ 194

7. $3 + (-2) + (-y) + 11$ $-y + 12$

8. $4(30 + 2)$ 128

9. $3n + (-7n)$ $-4n$

10. $4(n + 2) + 8$ $4n + 16$

Working with Real Numbers   **73**

Application / *Understanding Product Prices*

You may have noticed the Universal Product Code (UPC) on items in your supermarket. This code is a series of bands of alternating light and dark spaces of varying widths that represent the numbers printed underneath. Many supermarkets have installed electronic check-out counters that contain scanners. These scanners read the UPC on items and send the information to a central computer. The computer "looks up" the price of the item and subtracts the item from the store's inventory of products. The product name and price are then printed on the sales slip. The customer benefits by having a record of the transaction and the store benefits by having up-to-date inventory records.

Manufacturer Code   Product Code

Consumers must make many choices while shopping. Quality, price, and convenience are all important considerations. Sometimes it is difficult to compare the prices of products in different-sized packages. Unit pricing can help you make the comparison. The unit price of an item is its price per unit of measure. Unit prices are often posted on the shelves with the products. The product with the lowest unit price is the best buy provided the quality and the quantity meet your needs.

Example	Find the unit price per liter of lowfat milk: $.95 for 950 mL.
Solution	1 L = 1000 mL, so 950 mL = $\frac{950}{1000}$ L = 0.95 L.
	$.95 ÷ 0.95 L = $1.00 per liter

Exercises

Find the unit price per liter of each item. A calculator may be helpful.

1. Shampoo: $2.40 for 480 mL
$5.00 per liter

2. Chicken noodle soup: $.63 for 315 mL $2.00 per liter

3. Soy sauce: $1.98 for 600 mL
$3.30 per liter

4. Grapefruit juice: $1.44 for 1440 mL $1.00 per liter

Using a Calculator

Students who use a calculator for the exercises should be reminded to estimate to check the reasonableness of their answers. For example, in Exercise 1, 480 mL is about half a liter, so the unit price per liter is about 2 × $2.40.

2-7 Problem Solving: Consecutive Integers

Objective   To write equations to represent relationships among integers.

When you want to be served at a bakery, a deli, or a pizza parlor you often must take a number. The numbers help the clerks keep track of who is next in line.

When you count by ones from any number in the set of integers,

$$\{\ldots, -3, -2, -1, 0, 1, 2, 3, \ldots\},$$

you obtain **consecutive integers.** For example, -2, -1, 0, 1, and 2 are five consecutive integers. Those integers are listed in *natural order,* that is, in order from least to greatest.

Example 1   An integer is represented by n.
  a. Write the next three integers in natural order after n.
  b. Write the integer that immediately precedes n.
  c. Write an equation that states that the sum of four consecutive integers, starting with n, is 66.

Solution   **a.** $n + 1, n + 2, n + 3$
  b. $n - 1$
  c. $n + (n + 1) + (n + 2) + (n + 3) = 66$

Ten is called an *even* integer because $10 = 2 \cdot 5$. An integer that is the product of 2 and any integer is an **even integer.** In natural order, they are

$$\ldots, -6, -4, -2, 0, 2, 4, 6, \ldots$$

An **odd integer** is an integer that is not even. In natural order, the odd integers are

$$\ldots, -5, -3, -1, 1, 3, 5, \ldots$$

If you count by *twos* beginning with any even integer, you obtain **consecutive even integers.** For example:

Three consecutive even integers: 8; 8 + 2, or 10; 10 + 2, or 12

If you count by *twos* beginning with any odd integer, you obtain **consecutive odd integers.** For example:

Three consecutive odd integers: 9; 9 + 2, or 11; 11 + 2, or 13

Working with Real Numbers   **75**

Teaching Suggestions p. T87

Group Activities p. T87

Suggested Extensions p. T88

Warm-Up Exercises

Evaluate each expression if $n = 7$.

1. $n + 1$ 8
2. $n + 2$ 9
3. $2n$ 14
4. $2n + 1$ 15
5. $2n - 1$ 13
6. $n + (n + 1) + (n + 2)$ 24
7. $n + (n + 2) + (n + 4)$ 27

Motivating the Lesson

Ask the class to count by sevens, by nines, by thirteens. Ask if they can write an algebraic expression for counting by sevens. Point out that today's lesson involves writing equations to show relationships among integers.

Chalkboard Examples

An integer is represented by d.

1. Write the next four integers in natural order after d. $d + 1, d + 2, d + 3, d + 4$

2. Write the integer that immediately precedes d. $d - 1$

3. Write an equation that states that the sum of three consecutive integers is 24.
  $d + (d + 1) + (d + 2) = 24$

(continued)

(continued)
Solve over the given domain.

4. The product of two consecutive odd integers is 99. The domain for the smaller integer: {3, 9, 17}.

   Step 1   The unknowns are two consecutive odd integers.

   Step 2   Let n = the smaller integer; $n + 2$ = the larger integer.

   Step 3   The product is 99.
   $n(n + 2) = 99$

   Step 4

n	$n(n + 2) = 99$	
3	$3(3 + 2) = 99$	F
9	$9(9 + 2) = 99$	T
17	$17(17 + 2) = 99$	F

   Step 5   Are 9 and 11 consecutive odd integers whose product is 99?

Check for Understanding

Here is a suggested use of the Oral Exercises to check students' understanding as you teach the lesson.
Oral Exs. 1–8: use after Example 1.
Oral Exs. 9–14: use after Example 2.

Common Errors

Students often represent three consecutive odd integers in natural order as n, $n + 1$, and $n + 3$ because 1 and 3 are odd integers. In reteaching, remind them that two consecutive odd integers differ by 2.

Thus, in natural order, $\qquad$ $n, n + 2, n + 4$

are said to be consecutive even integers if n is even, and consecutive odd integers if n is odd.

Example 2   Solve over the given domain: The sum of three consecutive odd integers is 100 more than the smallest integer. What are the integers?
Domain for the smallest integer: {27, 37, 47}

Solution

Step 1   The unknowns are the 3 consecutive odd integers.

Step 2   Let n = the smallest integer, $n + 2$ = the middle integer, and $n + 4$ = the largest integer.

Step 3 $\underbrace{\text{The sum}}$ is $\underbrace{\text{100 more than the smallest integer.}}$
$n + (n + 2) + (n + 4) =$ $\qquad$ $n + 100$

Step 4

n	$n + (n + 2) + (n + 4) = n + 100$					
27	$27 +$	29	$+$	31	$= 27 + 100$	False
37	$37 +$	39	$+$	41	$= 37 + 100$	False
47	$47 +$	49	$+$	51	$= 47 + 100$	True

Step 5   Are 47, 49, and 51 consecutive odd integers whose sum is 147?
The check is left to you. $\therefore$ the integers are 47, 49, and 51.   **Answer**

Oral Exercises

1. If $w = 3$, what are the values of $w + 1$, $w + 2$, and $w + 3$? 4, 5, 6

2. If $r = 1$, what are the values of $r - 1$, $r - 2$, and $r - 3$? 0, −1, −2

3. The smallest of four consecutive integers is −1. What are the other three integers? 0, 1, 2

4. The greatest of four consecutive integers is 12. What are the other three integers? 9, 10, 11

5. If $x = 15$, represent 14 and 16 in terms of x. 14 = x − 1, 16 = x + 1

6. If $p = 20$, represent 18 and 22 in terms of p. 18 = p − 2, 22 = p + 2

7. If $k = 11$, represent 7, 9, and 13 in terms of k. 7 = k − 4, 9 = k − 2, 13 = k + 2

8. If $e = 12$, represent 8, 10, 14, and 16 in terms of e. 8 = e − 4, 10 = e − 2, 14 = e + 2, 16 = e + 4

9. If m is an odd integer, is $m + 1$ even; odd or is it even? $m + 2$? $m - 1$? odd; even

10. If m and n are even, is $m + n$ odd even; or is it even? $m - n$? mn? even; even

11. If m and n are odd, is $m + n$ odd even; or is it even? $m - n$? mn? even; odd

12. If m is odd and n is even, is $m + n$ odd; odd or is it even? $m - n$? mn? odd; even

13. If n is an integer, is $2n$ odd or even? What are the next two even integers greater than $2n$? What is the next smaller even integer? even; $2n + 2$, $2n + 4$; $2n - 2$

14. If n is an integer, is $2n + 1$ odd or even? What are the next two odd integers greater than $2n + 1$? What is the next smaller odd integer? odd; $2n + 3$, $2n + 5$; $2n - 1$

Written Exercises

Write an equation to represent the given relationship among integers.

Sample   The product of two consecutive integers is 8 more than twice their sum.

Solution   Let x = the first of the integers.
Then $x + 1$ = the second integer.

$$\underbrace{\text{Their product}}_{x(x + 1)} \quad \underset{\downarrow}{\text{is}} \quad \underbrace{\text{8 more than twice their sum.}}_{2[x + (x + 1)] + 8}$$

$\therefore$ the equation is $x(x + 1) = 2[x + (x + 1)] + 8$.   *Answer*

A
1. The sum of two consecutive integers is 43. $x + (x + 1) = 43$
2. The sum of three consecutive integers is 69. $x + (x + 1) + (x + 2) = 69$
3. The sum of four consecutive integers is -106. $x + (x + 1) + (x + 2) + (x + 3) = -106$
4. The sum of four consecutive integers is -42. $x + (x + 1) + (x + 2) + (x + 3) = -42$
5. The sum of three consecutive odd integers is 75. $x + (x + 2) + (x + 4) = 75$
6. The sum of three consecutive odd integers is 147. $x + (x + 2) + (x + 4) = 147$
7. The product of two consecutive even integers is 168. $x(x + 2) = 168$
8. The product of two consecutive odd integers is 195. $x(x + 2) = 195$
9. The sum of four consecutive even integers is -100. $x + (x + 2) + (x + 4) + (x + 6) = -100$
10. The greater of two consecutive even integers is six less than twice the smaller. $x + 2 = 2x - 6$
11. Four cousins were born at two-year intervals. The sum of their ages is 36. $x + (x + 2) + (x + 4) + (x + 6) = 36$
12. The smaller of two consecutive even integers is five more than one half of the greater. $x = \frac{1}{2}(x + 2) + 5$

Solve each problem over the given domain.

B
13. The sum of three consecutive odd integers is 40 more than the smallest. What are the integers? 17, 19, 21
Domain for the smallest: {13, 17, 25}

14. The sum of three consecutive even integers is 30 more than the largest. What are the integers? 14, 16, 18
Domain for the smallest: {14, 18, 20}

15. Find two consecutive integers whose product is 5 less than 5 times their sum. 0, 1; 9, 10
Domain for the smallest: {0, 6, 9}

16. Find two consecutive odd integers whose product is 1 less than 6 times their sum. -1, 1; 11, 13
Domain for the smallest: {-1, 1, 11}

Working with Real Numbers   **77**

Write an equation to represent the given relationship among integers.

1. The sum of two consecutive integers is 93.
$n + (n + 1) = 93.$

2. The sum of three consecutive integers is 192.
$n + (n + 1) + (n + 2) = 192$

3. The product of two consecutive even integers is 120. $n(n + 2) = 120$

4. The largest of three consecutive even integers is three times the smallest.
$n, n + 2, n + 4; n + 4 = 3n$

5. Twice the smaller of two consecutive odd integers is seven more than the larger. $n, n + 2; 2n = (n + 2) + 7$

Summarizing the Lesson

State that today's lesson provided practice in writing equations and in identifying relationships among integers. Have students define and give examples of consecutive integers, consecutive even integers, and consecutive odd integers.

Suggested Assignments

Minimum
77/1–13
S 78/Mixed Review

Average
77/2–16 even
S 78/Mixed Review

Maximum
77/2–18 even
S 78/Mixed Review

Supplementary Materials

Study Guide	pp. 31–32
Test Master	6
Computer Activity	5
Resource Book	p. 84

Write an equation to represent the given relationship among integers. Use this definition:

*The product of any real number and an integer is called a **multiple** of the real number.*

C 17. The lengths in feet of three ropes are consecutive multiples of 3. If each rope were 4 ft shorter, the sum of their lengths would be 42 ft. $(x - 4) + [(x + 3) - 4] + [(x + 6) - 4] = 42$

18. Jim weighs more than Joe but less than Jack. Their weights in kilograms are consecutive multiples of 7. If they each weighed 5 kg less, the sum of their weights would be 195 kg. $(x - 5) + [(x + 7) - 5] + [(x + 14) - 5] = 195$

Mixed Review Exercises

Simplify.

1. $(40 - 7) - (55 - 20)$ −2
2. $-5.3 + 2.1 - 1.7$ −4.9
3. $-4 + 2c + (-1) + 8$ $2c + 3$
4. $\frac{6}{5} + \left(-\frac{9}{5}\right)$ $-\frac{3}{5}$
5. $3\frac{1}{3} + 12 + 2\frac{2}{3}$ 18
6. $6\left(\frac{2}{5}\right) - 5\left(\frac{2}{5}\right) + 3\left(\frac{1}{5}\right)$ 1
7. $-(11 - x) - (x - 13)$ 2
8. $15a - 3a + 7a$ 19a
9. $12 + 5y + 6 + (-2)$ $5y + 16$
10. $(-1)(x + y - z)$ $-x - y + z$
11. $-[-6(a - b)]$ $6a - 6b$
12. $3(-5 + y)$ $3y - 15$

Self-Test 2

Vocabulary distributive property (p. 65)   multiplicative property of −1 (p. 70)
equivalent expressions (p. 67)   property of opposites in products (p. 71)
simplify a variable expression (p. 67)   consecutive integers (p. 75)
identity element for multiplication   natural order (p. 75)
  (p. 70)   even integer (p. 75)
identity property of multiplication   odd integer (p. 75)
  (p. 70)   consecutive even integers (p. 75)
multiplicative property of zero (p. 70)   consecutive odd integers (p. 75)

Simplify.

1. $x + 2y + 3x + 4y$ $4x + 6y$
2. $4(y - 2) + 1$ $4y - 7$ **Obj. 2-5, p. 65**
3. $(-2)a + 4a$ $2a$
4. $2(x + 3) - 2$ $2x + 4$
5. $(-5)(3)(-6)(-2)$ −180
6. $(-4x)(-2y)(7)$ $56xy$ **Obj. 2-6, p. 70**
7. $-3(a + b - c)$ $-3a - 3b + 3c$
8. $18 \cdot 12 + 18 \cdot 10$ 396
9. If $x = 30$, represent 29 and 31 in terms of x. $29 = x - 1, 31 = x + 1$ **Obj. 2-7, p. 75**
10. Write an equation to represent the given relationship among the integers: The greater of two consecutive odd integers is one less than twice the smaller. $x + 2 = 2x - 1$

Check your answers with those at the back of the book.

Quick Quiz

Simplify.

1. $a + 4b - 2a + 7b$
   $-a + 11b$
2. $3(2x - 6) + 1$ $6x - 17$
3. $(-6)t + 3t$ $-3t$
4. $3(t - 4) - 12$ $3t - 24$
5. $(-3)(-4)(-2)(-1)$ 24
6. $(-3w)(5t)(-2)$ $30wt$
7. $-2(x - 2xy + y)$
   $-2x + 4xy - 2y$
8. $16 \cdot 16 + 4 \cdot 16$ 320
9. If $n = 23$, represent 25 and 27 in terms of n.
   $25 = n + 2, 27 = n + 4$
10. Write an equation to represent the given relationship among the integers: The sum of three consecutive integers is 3 times the middle integer.
    $n + (n + 1) + (n + 2) = 3(n + 1)$

Division

2-8 The Reciprocal of a Real Number

Objective   To simplify expressions involving reciprocals.

Two numbers whose product is 1 are called **reciprocals,** or **multiplicative inverses,** of each other. For example:

1. 5 and $\frac{1}{5}$ are reciprocals because $5 \cdot \frac{1}{5} = 1$.

2. $\frac{4}{5}$ and $\frac{5}{4}$ are reciprocals because $\frac{4}{5} \cdot \frac{5}{4} = 1$.

3. -1.25 and -0.8 are reciprocals because $(-1.25)(-0.8) = 1$.

4. 1 is its own reciprocal because $1 \cdot 1 = 1$.

5. -1 is its own reciprocal because $(-1)(-1) = 1$.

6. 0 has no reciprocal because 0 times _any_ number is 0, _not_ 1.

The symbol for the reciprocal, or multiplicative inverse, of a nonzero real number a is $\frac{1}{a}$. Every real number except 0 has a reciprocal.

Property of Reciprocals

For every _nonzero_ real number a, there is a unique real number $\frac{1}{a}$ such that

$$a \cdot \frac{1}{a} = 1 \quad \text{and} \quad \frac{1}{a} \cdot a = 1.$$

Look at the following product:

$$(-a)\left(-\frac{1}{a}\right) = (-1a)\left(-1 \cdot \frac{1}{a}\right) = (-1)(-1)\left(a \cdot \frac{1}{a}\right) = 1 \cdot 1 = 1$$

Therefore, $-a$ and $-\frac{1}{a}$ are reciprocals.

Property of the Reciprocal of the Opposite of a Number

For every _nonzero_ number a,

$$\frac{1}{-a} = -\frac{1}{a}.$$

Read, "The reciprocal of $-a$ is $-\frac{1}{a}$."

Working with Real Numbers   **79**

Warm-Up Exercises

Multiply.

1. $20(-5)$ -100
2. $7a(-3b)$ $-21ab$
3. $76(-85)0$ 0
4. $(-3 + 8y)(-2)$ $6 - 16y$
5. $(-1)(-4x - y + 7)$
   $4x + y - 7$

Motivating the Lesson

Ask the students which number times $\frac{1}{2}$ gives a product of 1. Continue with similar examples. Point out that these pairs of numbers are called _reciprocals,_ the subject of today's lesson.

Chalkboard Examples

Simplify.

1. $\dfrac{1}{-4} \cdot \dfrac{1}{5} = \dfrac{1}{-4 \cdot 5}$

$= \dfrac{1}{-20} = -\dfrac{1}{20}$

2. $9m \cdot \dfrac{1}{9} = \left(9 \cdot \dfrac{1}{9}\right)m$

$= 1m = m$

3. $-64ab\left(-\dfrac{1}{8}\right)$

$= -64\left(-\dfrac{1}{8}\right)(ab) = 8ab$

4. $-\dfrac{1}{6}(-24x + 6y)$

$= -\dfrac{1}{6}(-24x) - \dfrac{1}{6}(6y)$

$= \left(-\dfrac{1}{6}\right)(-24)x - \left(\dfrac{1}{6} \cdot 6\right)y$

$= 4x - y$

Check for Understanding

Here is a suggested use of the Oral Exercises to check students' understanding as you teach the lesson.

Oral Exs. 1–12: use after discussing the properties on page 79.

Oral Exs. 13–25: use after Example 2.

Common Errors

Remind students that 0 is the only number without a reciprocal.

Some students will think that the reciprocal of −4 is a positive number because it is called an inverse. In reteaching, point out that the reciprocal is the multiplicative inverse, not the additive inverse and that it always has the same sign as the number.

Now look at this product:

$$(ab)\left(\dfrac{1}{a} \cdot \dfrac{1}{b}\right) = \left(a \cdot \dfrac{1}{a}\right)\left(b \cdot \dfrac{1}{b}\right) = 1 \cdot 1 = 1$$

Therefore, ab and $\dfrac{1}{a} \cdot \dfrac{1}{b}$ are reciprocals.

Property of the Reciprocal of a Product

For all *nonzero* numbers a and b,

$$\dfrac{1}{ab} = \dfrac{1}{a} \cdot \dfrac{1}{b}.$$

The reciprocal of the product of two nonzero numbers is the product of their reciprocals.

Example 1 Simplify: **a.** $\dfrac{1}{4} \cdot \dfrac{1}{-7}$ **b.** $4y \cdot \dfrac{1}{4}$ **c.** $(-6ab)\left(-\dfrac{1}{3}\right)$

Solution   **a.** $\dfrac{1}{4} \cdot \dfrac{1}{-7} = \dfrac{1}{4(-7)} = \dfrac{1}{-28} = -\dfrac{1}{28}$ *Answer*

b. $4y \cdot \dfrac{1}{4} = \left(4 \cdot \dfrac{1}{4}\right)y = 1y = y$ *Answer*

c. $(-6ab)\left(-\dfrac{1}{3}\right) = (-6)\left(-\dfrac{1}{3}\right)(ab) = 2ab$ *Answer*

Example 2 Simplify $\dfrac{1}{3}(42m - 3v)$.

Solution $\dfrac{1}{3}(42m - 3v) = \dfrac{1}{3}(42m) - \dfrac{1}{3}(3v)$

$= \left(\dfrac{1}{3} \cdot 42\right)m - \left(\dfrac{1}{3} \cdot 3\right)v$

$= 14m - v$ *Answer*

Oral Exercises

State the reciprocal in simplest form.

1. $7 \quad \frac{1}{7}$ **2.** $1 \quad 1$ **3.** $-1 \quad -1$ **4.** $\dfrac{1}{11} \quad 11$

5. $-2 \quad -\frac{1}{2}$ **6.** $\dfrac{3}{4} \quad \frac{4}{3}$ **7.** $0.25 \quad 4$ **8.** $-\dfrac{1}{8} \quad -8$

9. $-\dfrac{13}{5} \quad -\frac{5}{13}$ **10.** $-\dfrac{2}{3} \quad -\frac{3}{2}$ **11.** $\dfrac{1}{w}, \, w \neq 0 \quad w$ **12.** $-\dfrac{1}{s}, \, s \neq 0 \quad -s$

80   *Chapter 2*

Simplify.

13. $\frac{1}{6} \cdot \frac{1}{10}$ $\frac{1}{60}$

14. $\frac{1}{-2} \cdot \frac{1}{-12}$ $\frac{1}{24}$

15. $\frac{1}{6} \cdot \frac{1}{-4}$ $-\frac{1}{24}$

16. $\frac{1}{-x} \cdot \frac{1}{y}$, $x \neq 0$, $y \neq 0$ $-\frac{1}{xy}$

17. $(3a)\frac{1}{3}$ a

18. $\frac{1}{5}(5x)$ x

19. $6w \cdot \frac{1}{6}$ w

20. $\frac{1}{-3}(3ab)$ $-ab$

21. $\frac{1}{2}(10z + 12)$ $5z + 6$

22. $\frac{1}{7}(21g - 14)$ $3g - 2$

23. $-\frac{1}{4}(16m + 32)$ $-4m - 8$

24. $-\frac{1}{6}(54t - 18)$ $-9t + 3$

25. a. $\frac{1}{\frac{2}{3}}$ represents the reciprocal of __?__. $\frac{2}{3}$ **b.** In simplest form $\frac{1}{\frac{2}{3}} = $ __?__. $\frac{3}{2}$

Written Exercises

Simplify each expression.

A **1.** $\frac{1}{5}(-20)$ -4

2. $-\frac{1}{12}(48)$ -4

3. $-1000\left(\frac{1}{100}\right)$ -10

4. $-70\left(\frac{1}{7}\right)$ -10

5. $96\left(-\frac{1}{8}\right)\left(-\frac{1}{12}\right)$ 1

6. $-63\left(-\frac{1}{3}\right)\left(-\frac{1}{21}\right)$ -1

7. $\frac{1}{-3}(36)\left(\frac{1}{4}\right)$ -3

8. $-150\left(\frac{1}{2}\right)\left(-\frac{1}{3}\right)$ 25

9. $4r\left(-\frac{1}{4}\right)$ $-r$

10. $33p\left(-\frac{1}{11}\right)$ $-3p$

11. $\frac{1}{x}(5x)$, $x \neq 0$ 5

12. $7t\left(\frac{1}{t}\right)$, $t \neq 0$ 7

13. $12xy\left(\frac{1}{3}\right)$ $4xy$

14. $15mn\left(\frac{1}{5}\right)$ $3mn$

15. $8ab\left(-\frac{1}{4}\right)$ $-2ab$

16. $9cd\left(\frac{1}{-3}\right)$ $-3cd$

17. $(-4pg)\left(\frac{1}{-2}\right)$ $2pg$

18. $(-36ac)\left(\frac{1}{-9}\right)$ $4ac$

B **19.** $\frac{1}{2}(-16a + 20)$ $-8a + 10$

20. $\frac{1}{3}(18b - 39)$ $6b - 13$

21. $-\frac{1}{5}(-45c + 10d)$ $9c - 2d$

22. $-\frac{1}{8}(56g - 72h)$ $-7g + 9h$

23. $(-42m - 91k)\left(-\frac{1}{7}\right)$ $6m + 13k$

24. $(-39n - 52p)\left(-\frac{1}{13}\right)$ $3n + 4p$

25. $\frac{1}{2}(8u + 10v) - \frac{1}{3}(15u - 3v)$ $-u + 6v$

26. $\frac{1}{5}(-5a + 20b) - \frac{1}{2}(2b - 6a)$ $2a + 3b$

27. $6\left(\frac{1}{3}x - \frac{1}{2}y\right) + 42\left(-\frac{1}{3}y - \frac{1}{7}x\right)$ $-4x - 17y$

28. $-8\left(-\frac{1}{8}p + q\right) + \frac{1}{9}(63p - 9q)$ $8p - 9q$

29. $-\frac{1}{8}(48m - 16) - \frac{1}{4}(84m + 8)$ $-27m$

30. $-5\left(4 - \frac{1}{2}n\right) + \frac{1}{16}(-32n + 8)$ $\frac{1}{2}n - \frac{39}{2}$

C **31.** $-\frac{1}{12}(6r + 4s) + 7\left(\frac{1}{21}s - \frac{1}{14}r\right)$ $-r$

32. $-\frac{1}{20}(5z - 4w) - 6\left(-\frac{1}{30}w - \frac{1}{24}z\right)$ $\frac{2}{5}w$

33. $-3\left[\frac{1}{4}(12n + 1) - \frac{1}{4}\right] + 10n$ n

34. $3s + \left(-\frac{1}{2}\right)\left[6 + 24\left(-\frac{1}{3} + \frac{1}{4}s\right)\right]$ 1

Working with Real Numbers **81**

Guided Practice

Simplify each expression.

1. $\frac{1}{6}(-12)$ -2

2. $112\left(-\frac{1}{4}\right)\left(-\frac{1}{7}\right)$ 4

3. $12at\left(-\frac{1}{3}\right)$ $-4at$

4. $\frac{1}{m}(42mn)$ $42n$

5. $\frac{1}{3}(9x)$ $3x$

6. $\left(-\frac{1}{2}\right)(-4xy)$ $2xy$

Summarizing the Lesson

Today students learned how to simplify expressions involving reciprocals. Ask them to state the following properties and to give an example of each.

• property of reciprocals
• property of the reciprocal of the opposite of a number
• property of the reciprocal of a product.

Suggested Assignments

Minimum
  81/1–25 odd
  S 82/Mixed Review
  R 78/Self-Test 2

Average
  81/1–31 odd
  S 82/Mixed Review
  R 78/Self-Test 2

Maximum
  81/3–36 mult. of 3
  S 82/Mixed Review
  R 78/Self-Test 2

Supplementary Materials

Study Guide   pp. 33–34

Use the five-step plan for solving each problem over the given domain.

35. The sum of a number and its reciprocal is $\frac{13}{6}$. Find the number.

Domain: $\left\{\frac{2}{3}, \frac{3}{4}, \frac{5}{4}, \frac{3}{2}\right\}$ $\frac{2}{3}, \frac{3}{2}$

36. A number is $2\frac{1}{10}$ more than its reciprocal. Find the number.

Domain: $\left\{\frac{2}{5}, \frac{3}{5}, \frac{5}{4}, \frac{5}{2}\right\}$ $\frac{5}{2}$

Mixed Review Exercises

Translate each sentence into an equation.

1. Four more than five times a number is 24. $5x + 4 = 24$

2. Fifteen less than a number is 250. $x - 15 = 250$

3. The sum of two consecutive integers is 67. $x + (x + 1) = 67$

4. The product of two consecutive integers is 42. $x(x + 1) = 42$

Simplify.

5. $(-12)(-5)(-2)$ -120 **6.** $-36(25)(-2)$ 1800 **7.** $(3)(-7)(-2)$ 42

8. $-7(5a - 2d)$ $-35a + 14d$ **9.** $-4(2 + x) - 3(x - 2)$ $-7x - 2$ **10.** $8(x - 1) + 5(2 - x)$
$3x + 2$

Calculator Key-In

Use the reciprocal key on a calculator to find the reciprocal of each number.

1. 0.0625 16 **2.** -32 -0.03125 **3.** 3125 0.00032 **4.** 0.000064 $15,625$

5. For each number in Exercises 1–4, press the reciprocal key twice. Your results illustrate the property: The reciprocal of the reciprocal of a number is __?__. the number

6. a. Copy and complete the table.   **b.** What property does your completed $\frac{1}{ab} = \frac{1}{a} \cdot \frac{1}{b}$ table illustrate?

Answers may vary in the last decimal places.

a	b	$\frac{1}{ab}$	$\frac{1}{a} \cdot \frac{1}{b}$	
4	16	?	?	0.015625; 0.015625
-32	-0.5	?	?	0.0625; 0.0625
0.234	0.654	?	?	6.5344102; 6.5344102
555	222	?	?	0.00000812; 0.00000812

82   *Chapter 2*

2-9 Dividing Real Numbers

Objective   To divide real numbers and to simplify expressions involving quotients.

Dividing by 2 is the same as multiplying by $\frac{1}{2}$: $8 \div 2 = 4$ and $8 \cdot \frac{1}{2} = 4$.

Dividing by 5 is the same as multiplying by $\frac{1}{5}$: $15 \div 5 = 3$ and $15 \cdot \frac{1}{5} = 3$.

The examples above illustrate how division is related to multiplication.

Definition of Division

For every real number a and every *nonzero* real number b, the **quotient** $a \div b$, or $\frac{a}{b}$, is defined by:

$$a \div b = a \cdot \frac{1}{b}.$$

To divide by a nonzero number, multiply by its reciprocal.

You can use the definition of division to express any quotient as a product.

Example 1   **a.** $\dfrac{24}{6} = 24 \div 6 = 24 \cdot \frac{1}{6} = 4$

b. $\dfrac{24}{-6} = 24 \div (-6) = 24\left(-\frac{1}{6}\right) = -4$

c. $\dfrac{-24}{6} = -24 \div 6 = -24 \cdot \frac{1}{6} = -4$

d. $\dfrac{-24}{-6} = -24 \div (-6) = (-24)\left(-\frac{1}{6}\right) = 4$

The four quotients in Example 1 illustrate the following rules.

Rules for Division

If two numbers have the *same* sign, their quotient is *positive*.
If two numbers have *opposite* signs, their quotient is *negative*.

Example 2   **a.** $(-9) \div \left(-\frac{10}{3}\right) = (-9)\left(-\frac{3}{10}\right) = \frac{27}{10}$ *Answer*

b. $\dfrac{-3}{-\frac{1}{3}} = (-3) \div \left(-\frac{1}{3}\right) = (-3)(-3) = 9$ *Answer*

Working with Real Numbers   **83**

Simplify.

5. $-12 \div \left(-\dfrac{5}{6}\right)$

$-12\left(-\dfrac{6}{5}\right) = \dfrac{72}{5}$

6. $\dfrac{-16}{-\dfrac{1}{2}}$ $-16 \div -\dfrac{1}{2} =$

$(-16) \cdot (-2) = 32$

7. $\dfrac{48a}{-8}$ $48a \cdot \left(-\dfrac{1}{8}\right) =$

$(48)\left(-\dfrac{1}{8}\right)a = -6a$

8. $-6 \cdot \dfrac{x}{6}$ $(-6)\left(\dfrac{1}{6}\right)(x) =$

$-1x = -x$

Check for Understanding

Here is a suggested use of the Oral Exercises to check students' understanding as you teach the lesson.
Oral Exs. 1–12: use after Example 1.
Oral Exs. 13–24: use after Example 4.

Guided Practice

Simplify.

1. $-45 \div 9$ -5

2. $-34 \div (-17)$ 2

3. $16 \div \left(-\dfrac{1}{4}\right)$ -64

4. $\dfrac{9}{-\dfrac{1}{7}}$ -63

5. $-30\left(\dfrac{z}{15}\right)$ $-2z$

6. $\dfrac{-416xy}{-4}$ $104xy$

7. Find the average of the given numbers -4, -12, 9, -10, and -3. -4

Example 3 $\dfrac{45x}{-9} = 45x\left(-\dfrac{1}{9}\right) = 45\left(-\dfrac{1}{9}\right)x = -5x$ **Answer**

Example 4 $\dfrac{w}{13} \cdot 13 = w \cdot \dfrac{1}{13} \cdot 13 = w \cdot 1 = w$ **Answer**

Here are some important questions and answers about division of real numbers:

1. Why can you never divide by zero? Dividing by 0 would mean multiplying by the reciprocal of 0. But 0 has no reciprocal (page 79). Therefore, *division by zero has no meaning in the set of real numbers.*

2. Can you divide zero by any number other than zero? Yes, for example,

$$\dfrac{0}{5} = 0 \cdot \dfrac{1}{5} = 0 \quad \text{and} \quad 0 \div (-2) = 0 \cdot \left(-\dfrac{1}{2}\right) = 0.$$

When zero is divided by any nonzero number, the quotient is zero.

3. Is division commutative? No, for example,

$$8 \div 2 = 4 \quad \text{but} \quad 2 \div 8 = 0.25.$$

4. Is division associative? No, for example,

$$(12 \div 3) \div 2 = 4 \div 2 = 2 \quad \text{but} \quad 12 \div (3 \div 2) = 12 \div 1.5 = 8.$$

The following properties of division will be proved in Exercises 34 and 35 on page 86.

For all real numbers a, b, and c such that $c \neq 0$,

$$\dfrac{a+b}{c} = \dfrac{a}{c} + \dfrac{b}{c} \quad \text{and} \quad \dfrac{a-b}{c} = \dfrac{a}{c} - \dfrac{b}{c}.$$

Oral Exercises

Read each quotient as a product. Then simplify.

Sample $8 \div \left(-\dfrac{1}{6}\right)$ **Solution** Eight times negative six; -48

1. $\dfrac{-21}{3}$ -7 **2.** $\dfrac{0}{8}$ 0 **3.** $-25 \div 5$ -5 **4.** $18 \div (-18)$ -1

5. $\dfrac{0}{-9}$ 0 **6.** $\dfrac{-6}{-6}$ 1 **7.** $\dfrac{-2}{2}$ -1 **8.** $\dfrac{49}{-7}$ -7

9. $\dfrac{38}{-2}$ -19 **10.** $\dfrac{-56}{-8}$ 7 **11.** $\dfrac{4}{-64}$ $-\dfrac{1}{16}$ **12.** $\dfrac{-8}{72}$ $-\dfrac{1}{9}$

Simplify.

13. $x \div 1$ x **14.** $x \div (-1)$ $-x$ **15.** $8a \div (-2)$ $-4a$ **16.** $(-18b) \div 3$ $-6b$

17. $(-60a) \div (-5)$ $12a$ **18.** $(-48b) \div (-6)$ $8b$ **19.** $\dfrac{a}{a}$, $a \neq 0$ 1 **20.** $\dfrac{-a}{a}$, $a \neq 0$ -1

21. $6 \cdot \dfrac{n}{6}$ n **22.** $\left(-\dfrac{s}{4}\right)(-4)$ s **23.** $2\left(\dfrac{y}{-2}\right)$ $-y$ **24.** $-3 \cdot \dfrac{n}{3}$ $-n$

Written Exercises

Simplify.

A

1. $-48 \div 6$ -8 **2.** $-64 \div 4$ -16 **3.** $-12 \div (-3)$ 4 **4.** $-24 \div (-8)$ 3

5. $8 \div \left(-\dfrac{1}{2}\right)$ -16 **6.** $12 \div \left(-\dfrac{1}{3}\right)$ -36 **7.** $0 \div \dfrac{3}{4}$ 0 **8.** $-6 \div \left(-\dfrac{1}{4}\right)$ 24

9. $\dfrac{-6}{-\frac{1}{6}}$ 36 **10.** $\dfrac{-8}{-\frac{1}{3}}$ 24 **11.** $\dfrac{-7}{\frac{1}{5}}$ -35 **12.** $\dfrac{9}{-\frac{1}{9}}$ -81

13. $3 \cdot \dfrac{x}{3}$ x **14.** $\dfrac{-w}{4} \cdot 4$ $-w$ **15.** $(-4)\left(\dfrac{-y}{2}\right)$ $2y$ **16.** $(-8)\left(\dfrac{x}{-2}\right)$ $4x$

17. $\dfrac{156a}{12}$ $13a$ **18.** $\dfrac{384b}{-8}$ $-48b$ **19.** $\dfrac{-54x}{6}$ $-9x$ **20.** $\dfrac{-144y}{-24}$ $6y$

In Exercises 21–24, find the average of the given numbers. (The *average* is the sum of the numbers divided by the number of numbers.)

Sample 1   15, -3, -14, -2

Solution $\dfrac{15 + (-3) + (-14) + (-2)}{4} = \dfrac{-4}{4} = -1$ *Answer*

21. $-12, 4, -11, -7$ $-\dfrac{13}{2}$ **22.** $18, -21, -7, 2$ -2

23. $18, -17, -22, 16, 0$ -1 **24.** $18, -17, -22, 16$ $-\dfrac{5}{4}$

Evaluate each expression if $a = -3$, $b = -1$, $c = 2$, and $d = 6$.

Sample 2 $\dfrac{abd}{a + c} = \dfrac{(-3)(-1)(6)}{-3 + 2} = \dfrac{3(6)}{-1} = \dfrac{18}{-1} = -18$ *Answer*

B

25. $\dfrac{b + 5c}{3 - d}$ -3 **26.** $\dfrac{bcd}{(1 - b)a}$ 2 **27.** $\dfrac{abc}{(1 - c)d}$ -1

28. $\dfrac{7a + d}{a + c}$ 15 **29.** $\dfrac{a - 2d}{b + 3c}$ -3 **30.** $\dfrac{4a - d}{abc}$ -3

31. $\dfrac{a - 3b}{bcd}$ 0 **32.** $\dfrac{abc - d}{abc}$ 0 **33.** $\dfrac{(c + a)(c - a)}{b + d}$ -1

Working with Real Numbers   **85**

In Exercises 34 and 35, assume that a, b, and c are any real numbers and $c \neq 0$.

C **34.** Name the property or definition that justifies each step.

$$\frac{a+b}{c} = (a+b) \cdot \frac{1}{c}$$ **a.** __?__ Def. of division

$$= \left(a \cdot \frac{1}{c}\right) + \left(b \cdot \frac{1}{c}\right)$$ **b.** __?__ Dist. prop. (of mult. with respect to add.)

$$= \frac{a}{c} + \frac{b}{c}$$ **c.** __?__ Def. of division

35. Show that $\dfrac{a-b}{c} = \dfrac{a}{c} - \dfrac{b}{c}$. Use the fact that multiplication is distributive with respect to subtraction. (*Hint:* See Exercise 34.)

$$\frac{a-b}{c} = (a-b) \cdot \frac{1}{c} = \left(a \cdot \frac{1}{c}\right) - \left(b \cdot \frac{1}{c}\right) = \frac{a}{c} - \frac{b}{c}$$

Mixed Review Exercises

Solve if $x \in \{0, 1, 2, 3, 4, 5, 6\}$.

1. $x + 3 = 8$ {5}   **2.** $\frac{1}{3}x = 2$ {6}   **3.** $x - 1 = 2$ {3}

4. $3x = 6$ {2}   **5.** $2x + 1 = 5$ {2}   **6.** $x \div 4 = 1$ {4}

Solve over the domain $\{0, 1, 2, 3, 4, 5\}$.

7. $\frac{1}{5}n = 1$ {5}   **8.** $5y - 1 = 14$ {3}   **9.** $x + 2 = 5$ {3}

10. $2x = 4$ {2}   **11.** $x \cdot x \cdot x = 1$ {1}   **12.** $5n = n \cdot 5$ {0, 1, 2, 3, 4, 5}

Self-Test 3

Vocabulary   reciprocals (p. 79)
multiplicative inverse (p. 79)
property of reciprocals (p. 79)
property of the reciprocal of the opposite of a number (p. 79)

property of the reciprocal of a product (p. 80)
division (p. 83)
quotient (p. 83)

State the reciprocal of each expression or number.

1. $3y$, $y \neq 0$ $\frac{1}{3y}$ **2.** $-\frac{1}{2}$ -2 **Obj. 2-8, p. 79**

Simplify.

3. $-30\left(\frac{1}{3}\right)$ -10 **4.** $\frac{1}{6}(24)(-12)$ -48

5. $-81 \div 3$ -27 **6.** $-36 \div (-2)$ 18 **Obj. 2-9, p. 83**

7. $4 \div \frac{1}{2}$ 8 **8.** $\frac{-48x}{12}$ $-4x$

Check your answers with those in the back of the book.

Quick Quiz

State the reciprocal of each expression or number.

1. $3t$, $t \neq 0$ $\frac{1}{3t}$

2. $-\frac{1}{3}$ -3

Simplify.

3. $-15\left(\frac{1}{5}\right)$ -3

4. $\frac{1}{5}(15)(-14)$ -42

5. $-45 \div 9$ -5

6. $-52 \div (-4)$ 13

7. $2 \div \left(\frac{4}{3}\right)$ $\frac{3}{2}$

8. $\frac{63xy}{-3}$ $-21xy$

Computer Key-In

The program below will find the sum of a list of numbers that does not include zero.

```
10 PRINT "TO FIND THE SUM OF SEVERAL"
20 PRINT "NUMBERS (<>0)."
30 PRINT "(TO END, TYPE 0.)"
40 LET S=0
50 PRINT "NUMBER";
60 INPUT N
70 IF N=0 THEN 100
80 LET S=S+N
90 GOTO 50
100 PRINT "SUM=";S
110 END
```

Line 80 is not an equation. It adds each new value of N to S. It means "Take the value of S, add the value of N to it, and then put the new value into S."

Lines 50–90 form a *loop*. Line 90 sends the program back to line 50 for the next value of N to be INPUT. Lines 50–90 will be repeated until line 70 ends the INPUT when 0 is entered. After all of the numbers in the list are INPUT, line 100 prints the final value of S.

Exercises

Use the program above to find the sum of the numbers in each list.

1. 2, −4, 6, −8, 10, −12 –6

2. 1, 4, 9, 16, 25, 36, 49, 64, 81, 100 385

3. 2.25, 3.42, 5.15, 1.98, 4.82 17.62

4. 12.95, 27.59, 21.76, 38.25, 47.34 147.89

Add the three lines below to your program so that it will compute the average of the numbers in the list. The variable C acts as a counter. (You can then type LIST to get a clean copy of the modified program.)

```
45 LET C=0
85 LET C=C+1
105 PRINT "AVERAGE=";S/C
```

5–8. Find the average of the numbers in each list in Exercises 1–4.

5. −1 **6.** 38.5 **7.** 3.524 **8.** 29.578

Historical Note / Why We Call It "Algebra"

The word "algebra" comes from the title of a ninth-century mathematical book by the mathematician and astronomer Muhammed ibn-Musa al-Khwarizmi. The book, *hisab al-jabr w' al muqabalah* ("the science of reduction and comparison"), deals with solving equations. While the entire work may not have been original, it was the first time that algebra was systematically discussed as a separate branch of mathematics.

Al-Khwarizmi's book made its way into Europe and was translated into Latin in the twelfth century as *Ludus algebrae et almucgrabalaeque*. The title was eventually shortened to "algebra."

Working with Real Numbers **87**

Computer Key-In Commentary

Ask students what would happen if Line 40 were omitted. It serves the same function as clearing a calculator before beginning to add. (Line 45 has the same function for the counter.) Ask why the program can't include zero as an addend. Point out that zero was selected to conclude the adding because it doesn't change the sum when included as an addend.

Chapter Summary

1. A number line can be used to find the sum of two real numbers.

2. Opposite and absolute values are used in the rules for adding real numbers (page 54) and multiplying real numbers (page 71).

3. Real-number properties are statements about numbers that are accepted as true and that form the basis for computation in arithmetic and in algebra. The statements in the chart below are true for all real values of each variable except as noted.

4. Useful properties about addition and multiplication:

   Property of the opposite of a sum: $\qquad -(a + b) = (-a) + (-b)$

   Multiplicative property of zero: $\qquad a \cdot 0 = 0 \cdot a = 0$

   Multiplicative property of -1: $\qquad a(-1) = (-1)a = -a$

   Property of opposites in products: $\qquad (-a)(b) = -ab$
   $$a(-b) = -ab$$
   $$(-a)(-b) = ab$$

   Property of the reciprocal of a product: $\quad \dfrac{1}{ab} = \dfrac{1}{a} \cdot \dfrac{1}{b}; \ a \neq 0, \ b \neq 0$

5. Subtraction and division are defined as follows: $\quad a - b = a + (-b)$
   $$a \div b = \frac{a}{b} = a \cdot \frac{1}{b}; \ b \neq 0$$

Properties of Real Numbers

Equality: Reflexive property $\quad a = a$

Symmetric property $\quad$ If $a = b$, then $b = a$.

Transitive property $\quad$ If $a = b$ and $b = c$, then $a = c$.

Substitution principle If $a = b$, then b may be substituted for a in any expression.

	Addition	Multiplication
Properties of closure	$a + b$ is a unique real number.	ab is a unique real number.
Commutative properties	$a + b = b + a$	$ab = ba$
Associative properties	$(a + b) + c = a + (b + c)$	$(ab)c = a(bc)$
Identity properties	$a + 0 = 0 + a = a$	$a \cdot 1 = 1 \cdot a = a$
Property of opposites	$a + (-a) = (-a) + a = 0$	
Property of reciprocals		$a \cdot \dfrac{1}{a} = \dfrac{1}{a} \cdot a = 1, \ a \neq 0$
Distributive property	$a(b + c) = ab + ac$ and $(b + c)a = ba + ca$ $a(b - c) = ab - ac$ and $(b - c)a = ba - ca$	

Chapter Review

Supplementary Materials
Practice Master   9
Resource Book   pp. 191–193

Give the letter of the correct answer.

1. Simplify $125 + 62 + 75 + 38$.   2-1
   a. 310   **b.** 301   **c.** 290   **(d.)** 300

2. Simplify $(16p)(5q)$.
   a. $21pq$ **(b.)** $80pq$ **c.** $21p + q$ **d.** $80(p + q)$

3. Simplify $13 - 5x + (-17)$.   2-2
   a. $-22x$ **(b.)** $-5x - 4$ **c.** -9 **d.** $5x + 30$

4. Simplify $33 + [7 + (-12)]$
   a. 52   **b.** -52 **(c.)** 28   **d.** -28

5. Simplify $[-6 + (-1)] + [-(-6 + 1)]$.   2-3
   a. -12 **(b.)** -2 **c.** 0   **d.** 2

6. Ten passengers got on an empty bus. Then 3 more passengers got on,
   5 got off, and 2 more got on. How many passengers were left inside?
   (a.) 10   **b.** 9   **c.** 8   **d.** 20

7. Simplify $x + 9 - (x - 7)$.   2-4
   a. 2   **(b.)** 16   **c.** $2x + 16$ **d.** $2x + 2$

8. Simplify $(23 \cdot 32) - (13 \cdot 32)$.   2-5
   a. 360   **b.** 330   **(c.)** 320   **d.** 640

9. Simplify $3 + 7(r - 4)$.
   a. $10r - 40$ **b.** $10r - 28$ **(c.)** $7r - 25$ **d.** $7r - 31$

10. Simplify $(-2)(6)(-1)(8)$.   2-6
    (a.) 96   **b.** -48 **c.** 48   **d.** -96

11. Simplify $2(3c - 2d) - 4(c - 3d)$.
    a. $2c - 14d$ **b.** $10c + 10d$ **c.** $10c - 14d$ **(d.)** $2c + 8d$

12. Choose the equation that represents the following: The smaller of two   2-7
    consecutive even integers is eight less than twice the greater.
    a. $x = 8 - 2(x + 2)$ **(b.)** $x = 2(x + 2) - 8$
    c. $x + 2 = 8 - 2(x + 2)$ **d.** $x + 2 = 2(x + 2) - 8$

13. Simplify $(-63st)\left(-\dfrac{1}{9}\right)$.   2-8
    a. $7s + 1$ **b.** $-7st$ **(c.)** $7st$ **d.** $7s - t$

14. Simplify $12\left(\dfrac{1}{4}x + \dfrac{1}{3}\right) - \dfrac{1}{2}(12x - 6)$.
    (a.) $-3x + 7$ **b.** $3x + 7$ **c.** 4   **d.** $-5x + 3$

15. Simplify $\dfrac{72x}{-9}$.   2-9
    a. $-648x$ **b.** $8x$ **c.** -8 **(d.)** $-8x$

16. Evaluate $\dfrac{a + 15b}{c}$ if $a = -6$, $b = 9$, and $c = -3$.
    (a.) -43 **b.** 137   **c.** -13 **d.** -47

Chapter Test

Simplify.

1. $16 + p + q + 5p + q + 21$ 2. $25 \cdot 12 \cdot 4$ 1200   **2-1**

3. $-5 + [-9 + (-9)]$ −23   4. $3n - 6 + (-9)$ $3n - 15$ **2-2**

5. $\left(-1\frac{3}{5}\right) + \frac{2}{5} + 1$ $-\frac{1}{5}$ 6. $-7 + 5 - 4$ −6   **2-3**

7. Samantha left home with $42.51. The subway fare was $1.20. At the station she bought a magazine for $1.95. Lunch cost $4.36. After work she bought a skirt on sale for $26.00. Her subway fare home was also $1.20. At the station Shelly gave Samantha $5 to pay back a loan. How much money did Samantha have at the end of the day? $12.80

Simplify.

8. $(25 - 31) - (-6 + 11)$ −11   9. $x - (-8) - [x + (-8)]$ 16   **2-4**

10. Kara left home $2\frac{2}{3}$ hours before she arrived at the airport. How long had she been gone from home when she had been at the airport for $1\frac{2}{3}$ hours? $4\frac{1}{3}$ h

Simplify.

11. $(23)(0.25) - (7)(0.25)$ 4   12. $(6x + 3)4$ $24x + 12$ **2-5**

13. $5(b - 1) + 8$ $5b + 3$ 14. $7(2c - 4d + 6)$ $14c - 28d + 42$

15. $-16(-3)$ 48   16. $(-11 + 11)19$ 0   **2-6**

17. $(-9)(8)(-1)(-3)$ −216   18. $7x - y + 2x + 3y$ $9x + 2y$

19. Write an equation to represent the following relationship among integers: The sum of three consecutive even integers is 30 more than the smallest integer. $x + (x + 2) + (x + 4) = x + 30$ **2-7**

20. State the reciprocal of -1. −1   21. State the reciprocal of $\frac{5}{7}$. $\frac{7}{5}$ **2-8**

Simplify.

22. $\left(-\frac{1}{17}\right)(85)\left(\frac{1}{5}\right)$ −1   23. $-\frac{1}{7}(-56m + 49n)$ $8m - 7n$

24. $\dfrac{-13}{\frac{1}{6}}$ −78   25. $\dfrac{343w}{-7}$ −49w **2-9**

Cumulative Review *(Chapters 1 and 2)*

Simplify.

1. $(56 \div 7) - (26 \div 13)$ 6

2. $\dfrac{12 + 72}{6 + 8}$ 6

3. $|-12| - |-6|$ 6

4. $-|20| \div |-4|$ -5

5. $38 + [(-3) + 16]$ 51

6. $3[27 \div (12 \div 4)]$ 27

7. $2 + 10 \cdot 15 \div 5$ 32

8. $2\frac{5}{9} + 7\frac{1}{8} + 8\frac{4}{9}$ $18\frac{1}{8}$

9. $-120 - (-17)$ -103

10. $6(2x + 3) - 3(7 - 3x)$ $21x - 3$

11. $3(x + 2y) + 5(2x + y)$ $13x + 11y$

12. $(-9)(-5)(4) - 9(5)$ 135

13. $-18 - 4 - [(-6) + 12]$ -28

14. $\frac{1}{12}(-552xy) \div (-23)$ $2xy$

15. $\frac{6}{7}(4a - 3b) - \frac{3}{7}(8a - 6b)$ 0

Evaluate each expression if $x = -3$, $y = 4$, and $z = 5$.

16. $-z + (-x + 7)$ 5

17. $x - |y| + |z|$ -2

18. $\dfrac{(x + 6)(z - y)}{(x + y)}$ 3

Write the numbers in order from least to greatest.

19. $0, -2, 4, \frac{1}{2}, -\frac{1}{2}, -3$ $-3, -2, -\frac{1}{2}, 0, \frac{1}{2}, 4$

20. $-5, |5|, -\frac{1}{3}, -\frac{2}{3}, |-3|$ $-5, -\frac{2}{3}, -\frac{1}{3}, |-3|, |5|$

21. Graph the numbers $-4, 4, 3, 2, -\frac{1}{2}$, and 0 on a number line.

Solve.

22. $|y| = 7$ {7, -7}

23. $|-x| = 10$ {10, -10}

24. $-|y| = -3$ {3, -3}

25. $c + 12 = 0$ {-12}

26. $b \cdot 1 = 9$ {9}

27. $a + 25 = 25$ {0}

Solve if $x \in \{-5, -3, 0, 3, 5\}$.

28. $4x + 2 = 14$ {3}

29. $\frac{1}{3}x - 2 = -3$ {-3}

30. $6 = 2x - 4$ {5}

Translate each phrase or sentence into a variable expression or an equation.

31. Five more than the product of seven and y $7y + 5$

32. Two less than the sum of x and the opposite of a, decreased by three times y.
$[(x + (-a)) - 2] - 3y$

33. The opposite of x is four less than eight. $-x = 8 - 4$

34. The sum of two consecutive integers is one less than twice the greater integer.
$x + (x + 1) = 2(x + 1) - 1$

Solve.

35. Paul got into an elevator on the fourth floor. Before he got out, the elevator went up seven floors and down eight floors. On what floor did he get out?
the third floor

Maintaining Skills

Perform the indicated operations.

Sample 1
$$\begin{array}{r} \overset{811 \;\; 218}{\cancel{9}1\cancel{7}.\cancel{3}\cancel{8}} \\ -\;\;\; 55.19 \\ \hline 862.19 \end{array}$$

Sample 2
$$2.6\overline{)7.150} \quad 2.75$$
$$\begin{array}{r} 5\;2 \\ \hline 1\;95 \\ 1\;82 \\ \hline 130 \\ 130 \\ \hline 0 \end{array}$$

1. $\begin{array}{r} 49.92 \\ -\;38.6 \\ \hline 11.32 \end{array}$

2. $\begin{array}{r} 575.25 \\ -\;\;\;9.009 \\ \hline 566.241 \end{array}$

3. $\begin{array}{r} 337.14 \\ -\;\;45.32 \\ \hline 291.82 \end{array}$

4. $\begin{array}{r} 700.07 \\ -\;\;\;\;38 \\ \hline 662.07 \end{array}$

5. $\begin{array}{r} 3.4276 \\ -\;0.828 \\ \hline 2.5996 \end{array}$

6. $\begin{array}{r} 16.8 \\ -\;9.25 \\ \hline 7.55 \end{array}$

7. $\begin{array}{r} 5.52 \\ -\;4.763 \\ \hline 0.757 \end{array}$

8. $\begin{array}{r} 877.3 \\ -\;94.3 \\ \hline 783 \end{array}$

9. $0.02\overline{)1.10}$ 55

10. $0.8\overline{)0.036}$ 0.045

11. $5.1\overline{)3376.2}$ 662

12. $1.9\overline{)860.7}$ 453

13. $3.4\overline{)0.0085}$ 0.0025

14. $0.05\overline{)2.367}$ 47.34

15. $0.25\overline{)48}$ 192

16. $0.34\overline{)1156}$ 3400

Express each fraction in simplest form.

Sample 3 $\dfrac{16}{24}$

Solution $\dfrac{16}{24} = \dfrac{2 \cdot 8}{3 \cdot 8} = \dfrac{2}{3}$

17. $\dfrac{14}{49}$ $\frac{2}{7}$

18. $\dfrac{21}{24}$ $\frac{7}{8}$

19. $\dfrac{39}{52}$ $\frac{3}{4}$

20. $\dfrac{27}{54}$ $\frac{1}{2}$

21. $\dfrac{63}{81}$ $\frac{7}{9}$

22. $\dfrac{27}{33}$ $\frac{9}{11}$

Perform the indicated operations. Express the answers in simplest form.

Sample 4 $\dfrac{5}{6} - \dfrac{2}{13}$ Note that the least common denominator is 78.

Solution $\dfrac{5}{6} - \dfrac{2}{13} = \left(\dfrac{5}{6} \cdot \dfrac{13}{13}\right) - \left(\dfrac{2}{13} \cdot \dfrac{6}{6}\right) = \dfrac{65}{78} - \dfrac{12}{78} = \dfrac{65 - 12}{78} = \dfrac{53}{78}$

Sample 5 $\dfrac{7}{18} \div \dfrac{14}{15}$

Solution $\dfrac{7}{18} \div \dfrac{14}{15} = \dfrac{7}{18} \cdot \dfrac{15}{14} = \dfrac{7 \cdot \overset{5}{\cancel{15}}}{\underset{6}{\cancel{18}} \cdot \underset{2}{\cancel{14}}} = \dfrac{5}{12}$

23. $\dfrac{2}{3} - \dfrac{1}{6}$ $\frac{1}{2}$

24. $\dfrac{5}{7} - \dfrac{2}{3}$ $\frac{1}{21}$

25. $\dfrac{3}{4} - \dfrac{15}{21}$ $\frac{1}{28}$

26. $\dfrac{3}{4} - \dfrac{5}{12}$ $\frac{1}{3}$

27. $\dfrac{4}{5} - \dfrac{2}{11}$ $\frac{34}{55}$

28. $\dfrac{3}{7} - \dfrac{11}{28}$ $\frac{1}{28}$

29. $\dfrac{5}{6} \div \dfrac{5}{2}$ $\frac{1}{3}$

30. $\dfrac{12}{21} \div \dfrac{8}{14}$ 1

31. $\dfrac{21}{25} \div \dfrac{9}{20}$ $\frac{28}{15}$

32. $\dfrac{10}{7} \div \dfrac{7}{10}$ $\frac{100}{49}$

33. $\dfrac{24}{25} \div \dfrac{5}{6}$ $\frac{144}{125}$

34. $\dfrac{24}{25} \div \dfrac{6}{5}$ $\frac{4}{5}$

Preparing for College Entrance Exams

Strategy for Success

Familiarize yourself with the test you will be taking well before the test date. This will help you to become comfortable with the types of questions and directions that may appear on the test. Sample tests, with explanations, are available for many standardized tests. The Preparing for College Entrance Exams tests at the end of even-numbered chapters in this book will give you helpful hints and practice in taking such tests.

Decide which is the best of the choices given and write the corresponding letter on your answer sheet.

1. Write an expression that corresponds to the following word sentence. The sum of two consecutive even integers is 20 less than their product. D
   (A) $n(n + 1) = n + (n + 1) - 20$ (B) $n + (n + 1) = n(n + 1) - 20$
   (C) $n(n + 2) = n + (n + 2) - 20$ (D) $n + (n + 2) = n(n + 2) - 20$

2. Michael's weight is 85 lb less than twice the weight of his sister Stacy. Which equation represents the relationship between Michael's weight, m, and Stacy's weight, s? D
   (A) $s = 2m - 85$ (B) $s = 2m + 85$ (C) $m = 2s + 85$ (D) $m = 2s - 85$

3. Simplify the expression $73(19 + 31) - 48(24 + 26)$. A
   (A) 1250   (B) 6050   (C) 1200   (D) 1750

4. On a number line, point A has coordinate -4 and point B has coordinate 8. What is the coordinate of the point one fourth of the way from A to B? C
   (A) 2   (B) -2 (C) -1 (D) 5   (E) 6

5. The operation $*$ is defined for all real numbers a and b by $a * b = ab + a + b$. Which of the following properties does $*$ have? C
   I. Closure   II. Commutativity
   (A) I only   (B) II only   (C) I and II
   (D) None of the above

6. Suppose x is a nonzero real number. Which of the following is (are) always true? A
   I. $\frac{1}{|x|} > 0$ II. $|x| > x$ III. $|x| > -x$
   (A) I only   (B) II only   (C) III only
   (D) II and III only   (E) I and III only

7. a, b, c, and d are positive numbers. Which of the following guarantees that $\frac{a - b}{c - d} < 0$? C
   (A) $a > b$ and $c > d$ (B) $a < b$ and $c < d$ (C) $a > b$ and $c < d$
   (D) $|a - b| > 0$ and $|c - d| > 0$ (E) $|a - b| > 0$ and $|c - d| < 0$

Working with Real Numbers   **93**

3 Solving Equations and Problems

Objectives

3-1 To solve equations using addition or subtraction.

3-2 To solve equations using multiplication or division.

3-3 To solve equations by using more than one transformation.

3-4 To use the five-step plan to solve word problems.

3-5 To solve equations with the variable on both sides.

3-6 To organize the facts of a problem in a chart.

3-7 To solve problems involving cost, income, and value.

3-8 To prove statements in algebra.

Assignment Guide

See p. T59 for Key to the format of the Assignment Guide

Day	Minimum Course		Average Course		Maximum Course	
1	**3-1**	97/1–29 odd 98/*P*: 2, 3, 5, 8	**3-1**	97/1–39 odd 98/*P*: 1–9 odd	**3-1** **S**	97/3–57 mult. of 3 98/*P*: 6–18 mult. of 3 100/*Mixed Review*
2	**3-1** **S**	97/26–42 even 99/*P*: 9, 11, 13 100/*Mixed Review*	**3-1** **S** **3-2**	98/40–48 even 99/*P*: 10, 12, 13 100/*Mixed Review* 104/3–21 mult. of 3	**3-2** **S**	104/3–51 mult. of 3 105/*P*: 8, 10, 12, 15, 17 106/*Mixed Review*
3	**3-2** **S**	104/1–35 odd 105/*P*: 1–13 odd 106/*Mixed Review*	**3-2** **S** **3-3**	104/24–39 mult. of 3 105/*P*: 7–15 odd 106/*Mixed Review* 109/1–11 odd	**3-3** **S**	109/3–60 mult. of 3 110/*Mixed Review*
4	**3-3**	109/1–39 odd	**3-3** **S**	110/15–57 mult. of 3 110/*Mixed Review*	**3-4** **R**	113/*P*: 2–26 even 111/*Self-Test 1*
5	**3-3** **S**	110/32–48 even 110/*Mixed Review*	**3-4** **R**	113/*P*: 1–21 odd 111/*Self-Test 1*	**3-4** **S**	114/*P*: 27–33 115/*Mixed Review*
6	**3-4** **R**	113/*P*: 1–17 odd 111/*Self-Test 1*	**3-4** **S**	114/*P*: 23–26, 27, 29, 31 115/*Mixed Review*	**3-5** **S**	118/3–48 mult. of 3 118/*P*: 3–18 mult. of 3 120/*Mixed Review*
7	**3-4** **S**	113/*P*: 8–22 even 115/*Mixed Review*	**3-5** **S**	118/6–42 mult. of 3 118/*P*: 3–18 mult. of 3 120/*Mixed Review*	**3-6** **R**	122/*P*: 2–8 even, 10–14 120/*Self-Test 2*
8	**3-5**	118/1–29 odd 118/*P*: 1–6	**3-6** **R**	122/*P*: 1–3, 6, 7, 9, 11, 12 120/*Self-Test 2*	**3-6** **S** **3-7**	124/*P*: 15, 17, 19, 20 125/*Mixed Review* 127/*P*: 2–10 even
9	**3-5** **S**	118/16–32 even 119/*P*: 7–9 120/*Mixed Review*	**3-6** **S** **3-7**	124/*P*: 14, 16, 18, 19 125/*Mixed Review* 127/*P*: 2, 4, 6	**3-7** **S**	128/*P*: 11–18 129/*Mixed Review*
10	**3-6** **R**	122/*P*: 1–6 120/*Self-Test 2*	**3-7** **S**	128/*P*: 7–17 odd 129/*Mixed Review*	**3-8** **S**	131/2–8 even, 9–11 133/*Mixed Review*
11	**3-6** **S** **3-7**	124/*P*: 8–11 125/*Mixed Review* 127/*P*: 1–5	**3-8** **S**	131/1–9 odd 133/*Mixed Review*	*Prepare for Chapter Test* **R** 134/*Self-Test 3* 135/*Chapter Review* **EP** 643/*Skills;* 666/*Problems*	

Assignment Guide (continued)

Day	Minimum Course	Average Course	Maximum Course
12	**3-7** 128/P: 6–11 **S** 129/*Mixed Review*	*Prepare for Chapter Test* **R** 134/*Self-Test 3* 135/*Chapter Review* **EP** 643/*Skills;* 666/*Problems*	*Administer Chapter 3 Test* **R** 137/*Cum. Review:* 1–39 odd **S** 139/*Mixed Problem Solving:* 1–17 odd
13	*Prepare for Chapter Test* **R** 134/*Self-Test 3* 135/*Chapter Review:* 1–11 **EP** 643/*Skills;* 666/*Problems*	*Administer Chapter 3 Test* **R** 137/*Cum. Review:* 1–39 odd **S** 139/*Mixed Problem Solving:* 1–17 odd	
14	*Administer Chapter 3 Test* **R** 138/*Maintaining Skills* **S** 139/*Mixed Problem Solving:* 1–7 odd		

Supplementary Materials Guide

For Use with Lesson	Practice Masters	Tests	Study Guide (Reteaching)	Resource Book		
				Tests	Practice Exercises	Mixed Review (MR) Prob. Solving (PS) Applications (A) Enrichment (E) Technology (T) Thinking Skl. (TS)
3-1			pp. 37–38			p. 180 (A)
3-2	Sheet 11		pp. 39–40			
3-3		Test 10	pp. 41–42		p. 86	pp. 213–219 (T)
3-4	Sheet 12		pp. 43–44			p. 222 (TS)
3-5			pp. 45–46		p. 87	
3-6	Sheet 13	Test 11	pp. 47–48			pp. 158–159 (PS)
3-7			pp. 49–50			pp. 160–161 (PS)
3-8	Sheet 14	Test 12	pp. 51–52		p. 88	
Chapter 3	Sheet 15	Tests 13, 14		pp. 14–17		pp. 194–195 (E)
Cum. Rev. 1–3	Sheets 16, 17			pp. 18–19	pp. 89–90	pp. 146–147 (MR)

Software

Software	Computer Activities	Test Generator
	Activities 6–9	168 test items
For Use with Lessons	3-3, 3-7, 3-8	all lessons

Strategies for Teaching

Using Manipulatives and Cooperative Learning

This chapter presents an excellent opportunity to combine the use of manipulatives and cooperative learning groups as teaching strategies. Research shows that sometimes students can understand a concept explained by another student more easily than they can follow the presentation to the class. In addition, cooperative learning groups help students take responsibility for their own learning, improve their use of mathematical language, and become more confident in their own abilities.

Below are some suggestions for combining manipulatives and cooperative learning groups as teaching strategies.

3-1 Transforming Equations: Addition and Subtraction

Divide the class into small groups. Each group should have a balance scale and a collection of unit cubes from a base-ten block set. Give each group two envelopes, one marked "x" containing 4 cubes and one marked "empty." Have each group put the "x" envelope and 5 cubes on one pan of the balance and the "empty" envelope and 9 cubes on the other pan.

Ask the students to write the equation that represents this situation. ($x + 5 = 9$) Then have them remove 5 cubes from each pan and tell what the value of x is. Students can verify their solution by opening the "x" envelope.

See the Exploration on p. 688 for an activity in which students use a balance scale to explore ways to solve equations.

3-2 Transforming Equations: Multiplication and Division

Divide the class into small groups. Each group should have a balance scale and a collection of unit cubes from a base-ten block set. Give each group four envelopes, two marked "x" containing 4 cubes each and two marked "empty." Have each group put the "x" envelopes on one pan of the balance and the "empty" envelopes and 8 cubes on the other pan, as shown below.

Ask the students to write the equation that represents this situation. ($2x = 8$) Then have them separate the 8 cubes into two equal groups. After asking the students to remove one of the groups of cubes as well as an "empty" envelope and an "x" envelope from the balance, have them tell what the value of x is. Students can verify their solution by opening the remaining "x" envelope.

3-3 Using Several Transformations

Have students solve an equation like $3x + 7 = 22$ using a balance scale and a collection of cubes from a base-ten block set.

3-5 Equations with the Variable on Both Sides

Divide the class into small groups. To each group, randomly distribute slips of paper on which are written single steps in the solution of an equation. Have group members then work cooperatively to reassemble the solution.

3-8 Proof in Algebra

Divide the class into small groups. To the members of each group, randomly distribute slips of paper on which are written the (unnumbered) statements and reasons for various proofs in this lesson. Have group members then work cooperatively to reassemble the proofs.

References to Strategies

PE: Pupil's Edition   **TE:** Teacher's Edition   **RB:** Resource Book

Problem Solving Strategies

PE: pp. 98–99 (Recognizing unneeded facts); pp. 121–129 (Using charts or tables); pp. 98–100, 105–106, 112–115 (Using equations); pp. 112–113 (Using five-step plan); pp. 94, 98–99, 112–113 (Using a sketch, diagram, or model)
TE: pp. 99, 115, 124, T93
RB: pp. 158–161

Applications

PE: pp. 94, 98–101, 105–106, 112–115, 119, 122–125, 127–129
TE: p. 94
RB: p. 180

Nonroutine Problems

PE: p. 100 (Probs. 19, 20); p. 115 (Probs. 31–43); p. 119 (Probs. 19, 20); p. 125 (Prob. 20); p. 129 (Probs. 15–18); p. 133 (Exs. 9–11)
RB: pp. 194–195

Communication

TE: p. T91 (Lesson 3-4)

Thinking Skills

PE: pp. 99–100 (Analysis); pp. 105–106 (Interpreting); p. 111 (Synthesis); p. 113 (Recall and transfer); pp. 117, 131–133 (Reasoning and inferencing)
RB: p. 222

Explorations

PE: p. 101 (Car loans); p. 688 (Exploring ways to solve equations)

Connections

PE: pp. 95, 102 (Arithmetic); p. 125 (Astronomy); pp. 111, 117, 120 (Discrete Math); pp. 113–114 (Geometry); pp. 121–125 (Health); p. 115 (History); p. 94 (Physics); p. 100 (Social Science)

Using Technology

PE: pp. 106, 111 (Calculator Key-In); pp. 111, 120, 129 (Exs.)
TE: pp. 106, 111, 120, 129
RB: pp. 213–219
Computer Activities: pp. 12–20

Using Manipulatives/Models

TE: pp. T89–T91 (Lessons 3-1, 3-2, 3-3)

Cooperative Learning

TE: p. T92 (Lesson 3-5); p. T94 (Lesson 3-8)

Teaching Resources

For use in implementing the teaching strategies referenced on the previous page.

Application
Resource Book, p. 180

Application—Number Tricks (for use with Chapter 3)

Many mental mathematics tricks can be explained or demonstrated by using algebraic expressions. The most common of these tricks involves one person, the mind reader, having a second person think of a number, but not stating it out loud. The mind reader then tells the second person to perform a number of specific arithmetic operations on the original number. The second person then states the result of these operations, the mind reader performs one last operation (mentally, of course), and then tells the second person what the original number was.

Write the expressions that demonstrate the following.

1. Think of a number. x
2. Add 17.   _____
3. Double.   _____
4. Subtract 4.   _____
5. Double again.   _____
6. Add 20.   _____
7. Divide by 4.   _____
8. Mind reader subtracts 20.   _____
9. Original number.   _____

Complete the number trick with your own statements and expressions.

1. Think of a number. x
2. Add 18. $x + 18$
3. Multiply by 4. $4x + 72$
4. Subtract 7. $4x + 65$
5. _____   _____
6. _____   _____
7. _____   _____
8. _____ x

Thinking Skills
Resource Book, p. 222

Thinking Skills (For use after Chapter 3)

Applying concepts

1. Suppose you want to open a checking account. Each month Bank A charges a service fee of $4.00 plus $.30 per check written, while Bank B charges a service fee of $6.00 plus $.10 per check written. Complete the columns labeled "Bank A" and "Bank B" in the table to determine the total cost of checking at each bank in one month for the number of checks shown in the first column.

2. In the table at the right, fill in each of the circles using >, =, or < to indicate whether the total cost of checking at Bank A is greater than, equal to, or less than that at Bank B for the number of checks shown.

Number of checks written	Total cost of checking for one month at:		
	Bank A		Bank B
0	_____	◯	_____
2	_____	◯	_____
4	_____	◯	_____
6	_____	◯	_____
8	_____	◯	_____
10	_____	◯	_____
12	_____	◯	_____
14	_____	◯	_____
16	_____	◯	_____
18	_____	◯	_____
20	_____	◯	_____

Interpreting information

3. Whenever the total costs of checking at the two banks are equal, a *break-even point* is reached. From the table, what number of checks written produces a break-even point?

_____

4. Let x = the number of checks written in one month. Based on the information provided in Exercise 1, write a variable expression for the total cost of checking for one month at:
   a. Bank A _____   b. Bank B _____

5. Explain how you can determine the break-even point from the expressions that you wrote in Exercise 4.

6. At which bank would you open a checking account if the average number of checks you planned to write each month was:
   a. less than the break-even point? Explain. _____
   b. greater than the break-even point? Explain. _____

Synthesis

7. For a checking account at Bank C, each month the bank charges a service fee of $4.80 plus $.20 per check written. At which bank (A, B, or C) would you open a checking account if the average number of checks you planned to write each month was:
   a. less than 8? _____   b. between 8 and 12? _____
   c. more than 12? _____

Enrichment/Nonroutine Problems
Resource Book, p. 194

Squares in a Rectangle (For use with Chapter 3 of text)

1. The figure below shows a rectangle that has been divided into nine squares, all of different dimensions. The smallest square has sides 1 unit long, and the sides of two of the other squares have been labeled. Write an equation that will yield the value of x. (*Hint:* First complete the labeling of the sides of the squares. Then, to write the equation to find x, use the fact that opposite sides of a rectangle are equal.)

Equation _____

Solution _____

(continued)

Enrichment/Nonroutine Problems
Resource Book, p. 195

Squares in a Rectangle (continued)

2. This rectangle has been divided into eleven squares. Write an equation that will yield the value of x.

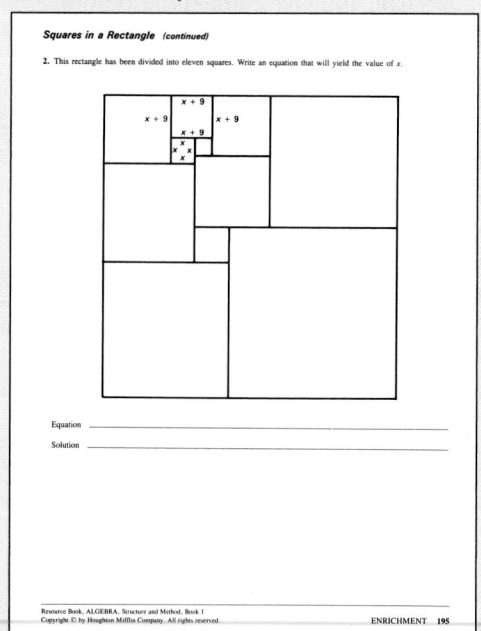

Equation _____

Solution _____

93e

Problem Solving
Resource Book, p. 158

Using Charts in Solving Problems (For use with Lesson 3–6)

By working through the steps in the problems below, you will gain skill in using charts to help solve problems.

Problem 1 The length of a red rectangle is 4 m more than its width. A blue rectangle, which is twice as wide and 2 m longer than the red one, has a perimeter of 42 m. Find the dimensions of both rectangles.

a. What does the problem ask you to find? _____

b. Suppose w represents the width of the red rectangle. Write an expression for the length of the red rectangle. _____

c. The width of the red rectangle is w. The blue rectangle is twice as wide as the red one. Write an expression for the width of the blue rectangle. _____

d. Using the expression for the length of the red rectangle you found in part **b**, write an expression for the length of the blue rectangle. _____

e. Complete this chart using the expressions that you found in parts **b**, **c**, and **d**.

	width	length
red rectangle	w	
blue rectangle		

f. "The blue rectangle has a perimeter of 42" means that
2(length of blue rectangle) + 2(width of blue rectangle) = 42.

Write an equation that states this relationship. _____

g. Solve your equation for w _____. Then find: $w + 4$ _____, $2w$ _____, and $w + 6$ _____.

h. Write your answer to the problem. _____

i. Check your results with the statement of the problem.

Is the length of the red rectangle 4 m more than its width? _____

Is the width of the blue rectangle twice the width of the red one? _____

Is the length of the blue rectangle 2 m more than the length of the red one? _____

(continued)

Problem Solving
Resource Book, p. 159

Using Charts in Solving Problems *(continued)*

Problem 2 Find the total weight of the boxes of cashews in a shipment of 3-lb boxes of cashews and 4-lb boxes of pecans.

(1) There were 20 fewer 4-lb boxes of pecans than 3-lb boxes of cashews.

(2) The total weight of the shipment was 172 lb.

a. Complete: The problem asks you to find the number of pounds of _____ included in the shipment.

b. Let c = the number of 3-lb boxes of cashews. Write an expression for the number of 4-lb boxes of pecans. _____

c. The weight, in pounds, of c 3-lb boxes of cashews is _____.
(Note that this is what you need to find.)

d. Using the expression for the number of 4-lb boxes of pecans you found in part **b**, write an expression for the weight, in pounds, of the boxes of pecans. _____

e. Complete this chart using your answers in parts **b**, **c**, and **d**.

	Weight per box	×	Number of boxes	=	Total weight
Cashews					
Pecans					

f. "The total weight of the shipment was 172 lb" means that
total weight cashews + total weight pecans = 172.

Write an equation that states this relationship. _____

g. Solve your equation for c. _____ Then find the total weight of cashews. _____

h. Write your answer to the problem. _____

i. Check your results with the statement of the problem.

The total weight of cashews is _____. The total weight of pecans is _____.

Do these two weights total 172 lb? _____

Using Technology/Exploration
Computer Activities, p. 18

ACTIVITY 9. Discovering Theorems *(for use with Section 3-8)*

Directions: Write all answers in the spaces provided.

PROBLEM

By choosing several values of a and b, verify that the statement $-(a + b) = (-a) + (-b)$ is true for any numbers.

PROGRAM

```
10  PRINT "WHAT ARE A AND B";
20  INPUT A, B
30  LET L = -(A + B)
40  LET R = (-A) + (-B)
50  PRINT "LEFT IS"; L; "AND RIGHT IS"; R
60  IF L = R THEN 80
70  PRINT "NOT ";
80  PRINT "EQUAL"
90  END
```

PROGRAM CHECK

Type in the program. To test whether you entered it correctly, run the program. Enter 4, 3 after the question. The computer should print

LEFT IS −7 AND RIGHT IS −7
EQUAL

The program should be tested with several values of A and B. If for every value of A and B used the results are equal, there is a strong indication that the original statement is true for all numbers. We suspect that this statement is a theorem, although we have not proved it. To show that the statement is false, it is necessary to find only one set of values for A and B that give results that are not equal.

USING THE PROGRAM

For each of the following, change lines 30 and 40 of the program. Run the new program for the given values of A and B and record the values of L and R. If L and R are equal for all the given A and B pairs, write the theorem that is suggested. Otherwise, write "No theorem."

1. 30 LET L = -(A − B)
    40 LET R = B − A

A	5	1	0	−3
B	3	2	−1	4
L				
R				

_____

(continued)

Using Technology/Exploration
Computer Activities, p. 19

(Activity 9 continued)

For each of the following, change lines 30 and 40 of the program. Run the new program for the given values of A and B and record the values of L and R. If L and R are equal for all the given A and B pairs, write the theorem that is suggested. Otherwise, write "No theorem."

2. 30 LET L = 1 / A + 1 / B
    40 LET R = 1 / (A + B)
    ($A \neq 0$, $B \neq 0$, $A + B \neq 0$)

A	1	3	−2	4
B	1	5	1	−3
L				
R				

3. 30 LET L = -(−A − B)
    40 LET R = A + B

A	3	0	8	−4
B	−3	1	2	−2
L				
R				

4. 30 LET L = A / B + B / A
    40 LET R = (A · A + B · B) / (A · B)
    ($A \neq 0$, $B \neq 0$)

A	2	1	−3	2
B	2	4	−1	−5
L				
R				

5. 30 LET L = ABS(A − B)
    40 LET R = ABS(A) − ABS(B)

A	5	2	−4	1
B	3	2	0	6
L				
R				

6. 30 LET L = 1 / (A / B)
    40 LET R = B / A
    ($A \neq 0$, $B \neq 0$)

A	4	−3	1	−2
B	2	−3	2	4
L				
R				

(continued)

Application

The concept of balance applies to many aspects of the world around us. In Chapter 1 the importance of maintaining a balance between internal and external pressure on the lungs when scuba diving was discussed. Your students have probably heard how pollution upsets the balance of nature. They may also have had the opportunity to observe a tightrope walker at a circus, or to play on a seesaw, and experienced the concept of balance in this way. An equation is a mathematical way to represent a balanced system. When solving equations, this balance must be maintained.

Research Activities
Some students might want to investigate a relationship in nature that illustrates balance. Possible topics include forest and wildlife management, red tide, and acid rain.
  Other students might enjoy designing and building mobiles that can be hung in the classroom.

Motivating the Lesson

Ask, What would happen to the balance in the diagram on page 94 if you added a weight to the left side and added an equal weight to the right side?

3 Solving Equations and Problems

The mobile is in balance, as are the weights in the pans. If a weight is removed from just one side, the balance will be upset. We use the idea of balance to solve equations.

94

Transforming Equations

3-1 Transforming Equations: Addition and Subtraction

Objective   To solve equations using addition or subtraction.

Two soccer teams are tied at half time: 2 to 2. If each team scores 3 goals in the next half, then the score will still be tied:

$$2 + 3 = 2 + 3$$

Two sporting goods stores charge $36 for a soccer ball. If, during a spring sale, each store reduces the price by $5, both stores will still be charging the same price:

$$36 - 5 = 36 - 5$$

The examples above illustrate the following properties of equality.

Addition Property of Equality

If a, b, and c are any real numbers, and $a = b$, then

$$a + c = b + c \quad \text{and} \quad c + a = c + b.$$

If the same number is added to equal numbers, the sums are equal.

Subtraction Property of Equality

If a, b, and c are any real numbers, and $a = b$, then

$$a - c = b - c.$$

If the same number is subtracted from equal numbers, the differences are equal.

Notice that the subtraction property of equality is just a special case of the addition property, since subtracting the number c is the same as adding $-c$. The addition property of equality guarantees that if $a = b$,

$$a + (-c) = b + (-c)$$

or $\qquad a - c = b - c.$

Examples 1 and 2 show how to use the addition and subtraction properties of equality to solve some equations. You add the same number to, or subtract the same number from, each side of the given equation in order to get an equation with the variable alone on one side.

Solving Equations and Problems   **95**

Teaching References
Lesson Commentary,
 pp. T89–T94
Assignment Guide,
 pp. T61–T62
Supplementary Materials
 Practice Masters 11–17
 Tests 10–14
 Resource Book
  Prac. Exs. pp. 86–90
  Tests, pp. 14–19
  En. Act. pp. 194–195
  Mix. Rev. pp. 146–147
  Practice in Problem
   Solving, pp. 158–161
  Application, p. 180
 Study Guide, pp. 37–52
 Computer Activities 6–9
 Test Generator
 California Standards
 Support Workbook
  Exploration for
   Lesson 3-1
Alternate Test, p. T14
Cumulative Review, p. T24

Explorations, p. 688

Teaching Suggestions, p. T89
Using Manipulatives, p. T89
Suggested Extensions, p. T90

Warm-Up Exercises
Simplify.
1. $x + 6 - 6$ x
2. $t - 18 + 18$ t
3. $2 + x - 2$ x
4. $-4 + r + 4$ r
5. $13 - m - 13$ $-m$

Solve.

1. $x - 6 = 12$

$x - 6 + 6 = 12 + 6$

$x = 18$

Check: $x - 6 = 12$

$18 - 6 \overset{?}{=} 12$

$12 = 12$ $\checkmark$

∴ the solution set is $\{18\}$.

2. $y + 7 = -9$

$y + 7 - 7 = -9 - 7$

$y = -16$

Check: $y + 7 = -9$

$-16 + 7 \overset{?}{=} -9$

$-9 = -9$ $\checkmark$

∴ the solution set is $\{-16\}$.

3. $2 = 5 + x$

$2 - 5 = 5 - 5 + x$

$-3 = x$

Check: $2 = 5 + x$

$2 \overset{?}{=} 5 + (-3)$

$2 = 2$ $\checkmark$

∴ the solution set is $\{-3\}$.

Check for Understanding

Here is a suggested use of the Oral Exercises to check students' understanding as you teach the lesson.

Oral Exs. 1–6: use after Example 1.

Oral Exs. 7–21: use after Example 2.

Example 1 Solve $x - 8 = 17$.

Solution

$x - 8 = 17$ {Copy the equation.

$x - 8 + 8 = 17 + 8$ {Add 8 to each side

$x = 25$ {and then simplify.

Because errors may occur in solving equations, you should check that each solution of the final equation satisfies the *original equation*.

Check: $x - 8 = 17 \leftarrow$ original equation

$25 - 8 \overset{?}{=} 17$

$17 = 17$ $\checkmark$ ∴ the solution set is $\{25\}$. **Answer**

The properties of real numbers guarantee in Example 1 that if the original equation, $x - 8 = 17$, is true for some value of x, then the final equation, $x = 25$, is also true for that value of x, and vice versa. Therefore the two equations have the same solution set, $\{25\}$.

Example 2 Solve $-5 = n + 13$.

Solution

$-5 = n + 13$

$-5 - 13 = n + 13 - 13$ {Subtract 13 from each side

$-18 = n$ {and then simplify.

Check: $-5 = n + 13$

$-5 \overset{?}{=} -18 + 13$

$-5 = -5$ $\checkmark$ ∴ the solution set is $\{-18\}$. **Answer**

Equations having the same solution set over a given domain are called **equivalent equations** over that domain. In Example 1, the equations $x - 8 = 17$ and $x = 25$ are equivalent equations. In Example 2, the equations $-5 = n + 13$ and $-18 = n$ are equivalent equations.

It is often possible to change, or *transform*, an equation into a simpler equivalent equation by using substitution or the addition and subtraction properties. The goal is to obtain a simpler equation whose solution or solutions can be easily seen.

Transforming an Equation into an Equivalent Equation

Transformation by Substitution

Substitute an equivalent expression for any expression in a given equation.

Transformation by Addition

Add the same real number to each side of a given equation.

Transformation by Subtraction

Subtract the same real number from each side of a given equation.

Oral Exercises

Describe how to change each equation to produce an equivalent equation with the variable alone on one side. Then state this equivalent equation.

Sample 1 $x - 3 = 5$	**Solution** Add 3 to each side; $x = 8$
Sample 2 $z + 5 = 4$	**Solution** Subtract 5 from each side; $z = -1$

1. $x + 5 = 9$ Subtr. 5; $x = 4$ **2.** $x + 3 = 8$ Subtr. 3; $x = 5$ **3.** $t - 2 = 7$

4. $w - 11 = 4$ Add 11; $w = 15$ **5.** $a + 9 = 1$ Subtr. 9; $a = -8$ **6.** $b + 7 = 6$

7. $6 + n = 0$ Subtr. 6; $n = -6$ **8.** $-4 + y = 0$ Add 4; $y = 4$ **9.** $-5 + m = 5$

10. $-1 + r = -1$ Add 1; $r = 0$ **11.** $-8 + t = -8$ Add 8; $t = 0$ **12.** $-5 = u + 9$

13. $-5 = t - 9$ Add 9; $t = 4$ **14.** $4 = -2 + s$ Add 2; $s = 6$ **15.** $-1 = 5 + k$
Subtr. 5; $k = -6$

16. $z - \frac{1}{4} = \frac{1}{4}$ Add $\frac{1}{4}$; $z = \frac{1}{2}$ **17.** $\frac{4}{5} = \frac{1}{5} + d$ Subtr. $\frac{1}{5}$; $d = \frac{3}{5}$ **18.** $h + 1.7 = -2.1$
Subtr. 1.7, $h = -3.8$

19. $x + 3.2 = 4.5$ Subtr. 3.2; $x = 1.3$ **20.** $-4.2 = z + 2.1$ Subtr. 2.1; $z = -6.3$ **21.** $-1 + x = \frac{1}{3}$ Add 1; $x = 1\frac{1}{3}$

3. Add 2; $t = 9$
6. Subtr. 7; $b = -1$
9. Add 5; $m = 10$
12. Subtr. 9; $u = -14$

Written Exercises

Solve.

A   **1.** $x - 7 = 13$ {20}   **2.** $y - 9 = 17$ {26}   **3.** $z + 8 = 31$ {23}

4. $x + 15 = 27$ {12}   **5.** $-52 + m = 84$ {136}   **6.** $-49 + n = 63$ {112}

7. $t - 25 = -18$ {7}   **8.** $x - 26 = 18$ {44}   **9.** $p + 18 = -32$ {-50}

10. $y + 32 = -45$ {-77}   **11.** $0 = 38 + k$ {-38}   **12.** $0 = z - 14$ {14}

13. $-19 + a = 23$ {42}   **14.** $-32 + b = 82$ {114}   **15.** $c + 9 = 5$ {-4}

16. $x - 8 = 25$ {33}   **17.** $f + 7 = 9 - 2$ {0}   **18.** $g - 6 = 14 - 8$ {12}

19. $z - 57 = -67$ {-10}   **20.** $x - 97 = -105$ {-8}   **21.** $-0.7 + k = -1.7$ {-1}

22. $-1.8 + h = -3.8$ {-2}   **23.** $4.5 = x + 1.6$ {2.9}   **24.** $3.9 = y + 1.2$ {2.7}

Sample 1	$-x + 7 = 2$

Solution $\quad -x + 7 - 7 = 2 - 7$
$\qquad\qquad -x = -5$ { Remember that the opposite of $-x$ is x
$\qquad\qquad\quad x = 5$ { and the opposite of -5 is 5.
$\therefore$ the solution set is {5}. *Answer*

B   **25.** $-x + 6 = 4$ {2}   **26.** $-y + 5 = 17$ {-12}   **27.** $21 - x = 28$ {-7}

28. $9 - y = 16$ {-7}   **29.** $8 = -x + 18$ {10}   **30.** $11 = 32 - y$ {21}

Solving Equations and Problems   **97**

Guided Practice
Solve.
1. $t - 4 = 22$ {26}
2. $-4 = 1 - x$ {5}
3. $d + 26 = -15$ {-41}
4. $9 + r = -3$ {-12}
5. $3.8 = y + 1.2$ {2.6}
6. $y - 4.7 = -6.0$ {-1.3}

Summarizing the Lesson
Have students recall the objective of this lesson and tell how the objective was met. Ask how an equation can be transformed into an equivalent equation by
• addition
• subtraction
• substitution

Suggested Assignments
Minimum
Day 1: 97/1–29 odd
       98/P: 2, 3, 5, 8
Day 2: 97/26–42 even
       99/P: 9, 11, 13
  S 100/Mixed Review
Average
Day 1: 97/1–39 odd
       98/P: 1–9 odd
Day 2: 98/40–48 even
       99/P: 10, 12, 13
  S 100/Mixed Review
Assign with Lesson 3-2.
Maximum
       97/3–57 mult. of 3
       98/P: 6–18 mult. of 3
  S 100/Mixed Review

Supplementary Materials
Study Guide   pp. 37–38

Solve.

31. $-8 - y = 9$ {−17}   **32.** $7 = -12 + e$ {19}   **33.** $13 = -y + 8$ {−5}

34. $(c + 2) + 8 = 4$ {−6}   **35.** $(r + 4) + 2 = 1$ {−5}   **36.** $2 = 10 + (x - 2)$ {−6}

37. $8 = 16 + (y - 1)$ {−7}   **38.** $-2 + (1 + p) = 5$ {6}   **39.** $-3 + (1 + n) = 9$ {11}

40. $(a - 3) + 19 = 125$ {109}   **41.** $(b - 6) + 14 = 100$ {92}   **42.** $4 - (1 + x) = 5$ {−2}

43. $2 - (3 + y) = 6$ {−7}   **44.** $1 = -2 - (4 - w)$ {7}   **45.** $11 = 7 - (1 - q)$ {5}

Sample 2 $|x| + 4 = 13$

Solution $|x| + 4 - 4 = 13 - 4$
$$|x| = 9$$
$$x = 9 \text{ or } x = -9 \qquad \therefore \text{ the solution set is } \{9, -9\} \quad \textbf{\textit{Answer}}$$

C **46.** $|y| - 2 = 8$ {10, −10}   **47.** $|z| + 10 = 28$ {18, −18}   **48.** $-7 + |s| = 0$ {7, −7}

49. $6 + |t| = 14$ {8, −8}   **50.** $|x| + (-2) = 4$ {6, −6}   **51.** $|y| + (-1) = 1$ {2, −2}

52. $0 = -5 + |r|$ {5, −5}   **53.** $2 = 6 + |t|$ no solution   **54.** $-(|a| - 9) = 1$ {8, −8}

55. $-(|x| + 2) = -6$ {4, −4}   **56.** $4 - (2 - |n|) = 2$ {0}   **57.** $7 - (3 - |m|) = 8$ {4, −4}

58. $9 - (|s| + 7) = 4$ no solution   **59.** $-3 + (15 - |a|) = 12$ {0}   **60.** $(|e| - |-8|) + 15 = 7$ {0}

Problems

Write an equation based on the facts of the problem. Then solve the equation and answer the question asked in the problem.

Sample 1   37 less than a number is -19. What is the number?

Solution $n - 37 = -19$
$$n = 18 \qquad \therefore \text{ the number is 18.} \quad \textbf{\textit{Answer}}$$

A **1.** Fifty-one more than a number is -12. What is the number? −63

2. Twenty-two less than a number is -7. What is the number? 15

3. If a number is increased by 28, the result is 7. What is the number? −21

4. If a number is decreased by 8, the result is -21. What is the number? −13

5. If -8 is subtracted from a number, the result is 84. What is the number? 76

6. If -15 is subtracted from a number, the result is -29. What is the number? −44

Sample 2   Wylie hiked into the Grand Canyon from its South Rim, which is 6876 ft above sea level. Walking along the 7.8 mi Bright Angel Trail, he reached the Colorado River in 4 h. At that point he was 2460 ft lower in the Canyon than at his starting point. How far above sea level is the Colorado River at this point?

Solution

Step 1 You are asked to find the river's elevation above sea level at the point where it crosses the Bright Angel Trail. Make a sketch to show the given information.

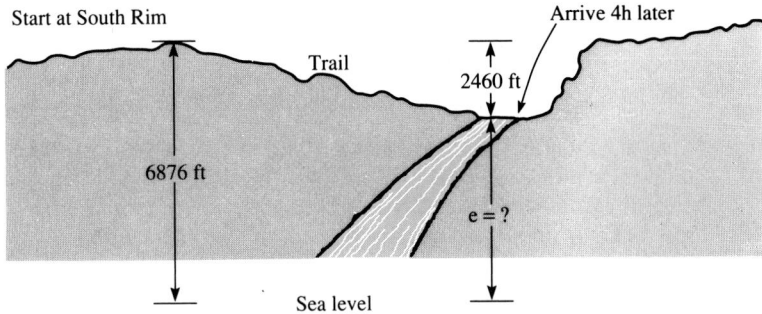

Step 2 Let e = the elevation of the river.

Step 3 $e + 2460 = 6876$

Step 4 $e + 2460 - 2460 = 6876 - 2460$
                    $e = 4416$

Step 5 Check: The check is left to you.

∴ the Colorado River is 4416 ft above sea level at the point where it meets the trail. ***Answer***

Notice that two of the given facts were not used in solving the problem: the length of the trail and the time spent hiking.

7. A lion can run 18 mi/h faster than a giraffe. If a lion can run 50 mi/h, how fast can a giraffe run? 32 mi/h

8. Corita ran the 400-meter dash in 56.8 s. This was 1.3 s less than her previous time. What was her previous time? 58.1 s

9. The desert temperature rose 25° C between 6 A.M. and noon. If the temperature at noon was 18° C, what was the temperature at 6 A.M.? −7° C

10. The temperature at the summit of Mt. Mansfield dropped 17° F between 4 P.M. and 11 P.M. If the temperature at 11 P.M. was −11° F, what was the temperature at 4 P.M.? 6° F

11. Enrico paid $4.75 for a sandwich, a drink, and frozen yogurt. He remembered that the drink and the yogurt were each $1.15 and that the sandwich had too much mustard, but he forgot the price of the sandwich. How much did the sandwich cost? $2.45

12. Ruth Panoyan had 45 sheets of graph paper. She gave five sheets to each of the six students she tutored and put the remaining sheets in her desk. How many did she put in her desk? 15 sheets

Solving Equations and Problems   **99**

Write an equation based on the facts of the problem. Then solve the equation and answer the question asked in the problem.

B **13.** A factory hired 130 new workers during a year in which 27 workers retired and 59 left for other reasons. If there were 498 workers at the end of the year, how many were there at the beginning of the year? 454 workers

14. During one day of trading in the stock market, an investor lost $2500 on one stock, but gained $1700 on another. At the end of trading that day, the investor's holdings in those two stocks were worth $52,400. What were they worth when the market opened that day? $53,200

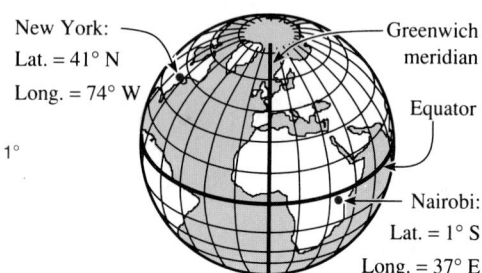

New York:
Lat. = 41° N
Long. = 74° W

Greenwich meridian

Equator

Nairobi:
Lat. = 1° S
Long. = 37° E

15. Longitudes are measured east and west of the Greenwich meridian. How many degrees east of New York City is Nairobi, Kenya? (In the diagram, measurements are given to the nearest degree.) 111°

16. Latitudes are measured north and south of the equator. How many degrees south of New York City is Nairobi? 42°

17. Gino paid $3.23 for two tubes of toothpaste. He paid the regular price of $1.79 for one tube. However, he bought the other one for less because he used a discount coupon. How much was the coupon worth? $.35

18. Kerry bought a picture frame on sale for $4.69. A week later, she returned to buy another frame. However, she had to pay the regular price for the second one. If the two frames cost Kerry $10.64, how much had the store reduced the price for the sale? $1.26

C **19.** At 8:00 P.M. a scavenger hunt started at the town hall. Team 1 drove 5 km east to the golf course, while Team 2 drove 12 km west to the beach. By the time Team 2 had found some seaweed at the beach, Team 1 had already found an orange golf ball and driven 3 km back toward town hall. How far apart were the two teams at this point? 14 km

20. After traveling 387 miles from Los Angeles to San Francisco, Rick noted that his car's odometer read exactly 27972. This number reads the same backwards as forwards. What is the next such number and how far will he have to drive to get it to appear on the odometer? 28082; 110 mi

Mixed Review Exercises

Evaluate if $a = 4$, $b = -6$, $c = -7$, and $d = 5$.

1. $a - |c - b|$ 3

2. $(|b| - a) - (|d| - a)$ 1

3. $2|a| - (-a)$ 12

4. $\dfrac{b - 2c}{b + 2d}$ 2

5. $\dfrac{4d + c + 1}{abc}$ $\frac{1}{12}$

6. $\dfrac{3ab}{c + d}$ 36

Simplify.

7. $(-6)(-7)(10)$ 420

8. $(-9 \cdot 12) + (-9 \cdot 18)$ −270

9. $148a \div (-37)$ −4a

10. $96\left(-\frac{1}{24}\right)\left(-\frac{1}{4}\right)$ 1

11. $-\frac{12b}{5} \cdot (-5)$ 12b

12. $\frac{1}{7}(21a - 7b) - \frac{1}{3}(12b - 6a)$

                                                              $5a - 5b$

Application / *Car Loans*

A car is an expensive purchase. Most people do not have the money to pay for a car with cash. Instead, they pay part of the cash price as a *down payment* and borrow the rest by taking out a loan. The car buyer must pay the lender the amount of money borrowed, which is called the *principal*, plus *interest*.

Example   Miriam bought a $3600 used car. She made a $630 down payment and got a loan for 36 months with payments of $95 per month.
a. Find the total amount paid for the car.
b. Find the amount of interest Miriam had to pay.

Solution   **a.** Total paid = down payment + total of the monthly payments
                   = 630 + 36(95)
                   = 630 + 3420
                   = 4050   ∴ the total paid was $4050.   *Answer*

          b. Interest = total paid − cash price
                 = 4050 − 3600
                 = 450   ∴ Miriam had to pay $450 in interest.   *Answer*

Exercises

a. Find the total amount to be paid on each vehicle.
b. Find the amount of interest the buyer would be paying.

1. Sean bought a $3000 used car by making a $480 down payment and getting a loan for two years with payments of $115 per month. **a.** $3240 **b.** $240

2. The Valley Fruit Stand got a three-year loan at $154 per month to pay for a $5500 used truck. The down payment was $451. **a.** $5995 **b.** $495

3. A $4500 station wagon was advertised in the Daily Gazette. The buyer paid $498 down and made 48 monthly payments of $95 per month. **a.** $5058 **b.** $558

4. Linda bought a used car with a cash price of $10,000. She made a down payment of $620 and paid $220 per month for four years. **a.** $11,180 **b.** $1180

Solving Equations and Problems   **101**

3-2 Transforming Equations: Multiplication and Division

Objective   To solve equations using multiplication or division.

At a hardware store, small construction supplies are often sold by the pound rather than by the number of items.

Suppose a pound of roof nails costs the same as a pound of floor nails. You would expect to pay the same price for *two* pounds of roof nails as for *two* pounds of floor nails, and the same price for *one-half* pound of roof nails as for *one-half* pound of floor nails.

This is an example of the multiplication and division properties of equality.

Multiplication Property of Equality

If a, b, and c are any real numbers, and $a = b$, then

$$ca = cb \qquad \text{and} \qquad ac = bc.$$

If equal numbers are multiplied by the same number, the products are equal.

Division Property of Equality

If a and b are any real numbers, c is any nonzero real number, and $a = b$, then

$$\frac{a}{c} = \frac{b}{c}.$$

If equal numbers are divided by the same *nonzero* number, the quotients are equal.

These properties give you two more ways to transform an equation into an equivalent equation. The others that you have already studied are listed on page 96.

Transforming an Equation into an Equivalent Equation

Transformation by Multiplication:
Multiply each side of a given equation by the same *nonzero* real number.

Transformation by Division:
Divide each side of a given equation by the same *nonzero* real number.

Example 1 Solve $6x = 222$.

Solution

$6x = 222$ $\quad\left\{\right.$ To get x alone on one side, divide each side
$\dfrac{6x}{6} = \dfrac{222}{6}$ $\quad\left.\right\}$ by 6 (or multiply by $\frac{1}{6}$, the reciprocal of 6).

$x = 37$

Check: $6x = 222$

$6(37) \stackrel{?}{=} 222$

$222 = 222$ $\checkmark$ $\therefore$ the solution set is $\{37\}$. **Answer**

Example 2 Solve $8 = -\dfrac{2}{3}t$.

Solution

$8 = -\dfrac{2}{3}t$ $\quad\left\{\right.$ To get t alone on one side, multiply

$-\dfrac{3}{2}(8) = -\dfrac{3}{2}\left(-\dfrac{2}{3}t\right)$ $\quad\left.\right\}$ each side by $-\frac{3}{2}$, the reciprocal of $-\frac{2}{3}$.

$-12 = t$

Check: $8 = -\dfrac{2}{3}t$

$8 \stackrel{?}{=} -\dfrac{2}{3}(-12)$

$8 = 8$ $\checkmark$ $\therefore$ the solution set is $\{-12\}$. **Answer**

Example 3 Solve: **a.** $\dfrac{m}{3} = -5$ **b.** $\dfrac{1}{4}s = 6\dfrac{1}{4}$

Solution

$3\left(\dfrac{m}{3}\right) = 3(-5)$ $\qquad$ $\dfrac{1}{4}s = \dfrac{25}{4}$

$m = -15$ $\qquad$ $4\left(\dfrac{1}{4}s\right) = 4\left(\dfrac{25}{4}\right)$

$\therefore$ the solution set is $\{-15\}$. $\qquad$ $s = 25$

Answer $\qquad$ $\therefore$ the solution set is $\{25\}$.

Answer

You know that zero cannot be a divisor (page 84). Do you know why zero is not allowed as a multiplier in transforming an equation? Look at the following equations.

$$(1) \qquad 5z = 45$$
$$(2) \quad 0 \cdot 5z = 0 \cdot 45$$
$$(3) \quad (0 \cdot 5)z = 0 \cdot 45$$
$$(4) \qquad 0 \cdot z = 0$$

Equation (1) had just one root, namely 9. Equation 4 is satisfied by *any* real number. Since they do not have the same solution set, Equations (1) and (4) are *not* equivalent (see page 96). *In transforming an equation, never multiply by zero.*

Solving Equations and Problems   **103**

---

3. $\dfrac{t}{2} = -5$

$2\left(\dfrac{t}{2}\right) = (2)(-5)$

$t = -10$

Check: $\dfrac{t}{2} = -5$

$\dfrac{-10}{2} \stackrel{?}{=} -5$

$-5 = -5$ $\checkmark$

$\therefore$ the solution set is $\{-10\}$.

4. $\dfrac{2}{3}s = 4\dfrac{1}{3}$

$\left(\dfrac{3}{2}\right)\dfrac{2}{3}s = \left(\dfrac{3}{2}\right)\left(4\dfrac{1}{3}\right)$

$s = \left(\dfrac{3}{2}\right)\left(\dfrac{13}{3}\right)$

$s = \dfrac{13}{2} = 6\dfrac{1}{2}$

Check: $\left(\dfrac{2}{3}\right)s = 4\dfrac{1}{3}$

$\left(\dfrac{2}{3}\right)\left(6\dfrac{1}{2}\right) \stackrel{?}{=} 4\dfrac{1}{3}$

$\left(\dfrac{2}{3}\right)\left(\dfrac{13}{2}\right) \stackrel{?}{=} 4\dfrac{1}{3}$

$4\dfrac{1}{3} = 4\dfrac{1}{3}$ $\checkmark$

$\therefore$ the solution set is $\left\{6\dfrac{1}{2}\right\}$.

Check for Understanding

Here is a suggested use of the Oral Exercises as you teach the lesson.
Oral Exs. 1–4: use after Example 1.
Oral Exs. 5–10: use after Example 2.
Oral Exs. 11–18: use after Example 3.

Guided Practice

Solve.

1. $5x = 75$ $\{15\}$

2. $\dfrac{1}{5}h = 17$ $\{85\}$

3. $\dfrac{1}{2}w = -8$ $\{-16\}$

4. $-\dfrac{2}{7}a = -14$ $\{49\}$

5. $275 = -25x$ $\{-11\}$

6. $39 = -\dfrac{13}{7}x$ $\{-21\}$

Summarizing the Lesson

Have students recall the objective of today's lesson. Ask for examples of equations for which they'd use the multiplication property of equality or the division property of equality to transform the equations and solve them.

Suggested Assignments

Minimum
104/1–35 odd
105/*P*: 1–13 odd
S 106/Mixed Review

Average
Day 1: 104/3–21 mult. of 3
Assign with Lesson 3-1.
Day 2: 104/24–39 mult. of 3
105/*P*: 7–15 odd
S 106/Mixed Review
Assign with Lesson 3-3.

Maximum
104/3–51 mult. of 3
105/*P*: 8, 10, 12, 15, 17
S 106/Mixed Review

Oral Exercises

Describe how you could produce an equivalent equation with the variable alone on one side. Then state the equivalent equation.

1. $8x = 16$ Div. by 8; $x = 2$
2. $5y = 15$ Div. by 5; $y = 3$
3. $3a = -12$ Div. by 3; $a = -4$
4. $-8a = 32$ Div. by −8; $a = -4$
5. $\frac{1}{2}b = 4$ Mult. by 2; $b = 8$
6. $\frac{1}{3}t = 7$ Mult. by 3; $t = 21$
7. $-\frac{1}{10}r = 5$ Mult. by −10; $r = -50$
8. $-\frac{9}{5}m = 9$ Mult. by $-\frac{5}{9}$; $m = -5$
9. $5 = \frac{5}{3}y$ Mult. by $\frac{3}{5}$; $y = 3$
10. $-7 = -\frac{7}{2}x$ Mult. by $-\frac{2}{7}$; $x = 2$
11. $0 = -4k$ Div. by −4; $k = 0$
12. $x \div 8 = -1$ Mult. by 8; $x = -8$
13. $n \div (-5) = 4$ Mult. by −5; $n = -20$
14. $\frac{d}{2} = -6$ Mult. by 2; $d = -12$
15. $-4 = \frac{x}{3}$ Mult. by 3; $x = -12$
16. $-11f = -88$ Div. by −11; $f = 8$
17. $-25p = -75$ Div. by −25; $p = 3$
18. $7 = -\frac{u}{2}$ Mult. by −2; $u = -14$

Written Exercises

Solve.

A
1. $4x = 44$ {11}
2. $5y = 65$ {13}
3. $6y = -18$ {−3}
4. $3t = -27$ {−9}
5. $-8c = 72$ {−9}
6. $-6p = 42$ {−7}
7. $-12a = -36$ {3}
8. $-9z = -63$ {7}
9. $\frac{1}{2}x = 12$ {24}
10. $\frac{1}{3}y = 18$ {54}
11. $\frac{x}{5} = -7$ {−35}
12. $\frac{c}{4} = -9$ {−36}
13. $-\frac{1}{8}b = 8$ {−64}
14. $-\frac{1}{5}t = 17$ {−85}
15. $\frac{2}{3}x = 12$ {18}
16. $\frac{5}{2}y = 10$ {4}
17. $\frac{3}{4}d = -60$ {−80}
18. $\frac{5}{8}c = -20$ {−32}
19. $-\frac{2}{3}t = 22$ {−33}
20. $-\frac{2}{11}p = 14$ {−77}
21. $600 = -25x$ {−24}
22. $-324 = -18c$ {18}
23. $-17d = 0$ {0}
24. $252 = -14y$ {−18}
25. $99 = -\frac{11}{5}x$ {−45}
26. $24 = -\frac{3}{7}t$ {−56}
27. $-6 = \frac{x}{3}$ {−18}
28. $21 = \frac{c}{7}$ {147}

B
29. $\frac{1}{3}y = 2\frac{1}{3}$ {7}
30. $\frac{1}{2}t = 3\frac{1}{2}$ {7}
31. $-1 = 2.5z$ {−0.4}
32. $0 = -4.5y$ {0}
33. $\frac{2}{5}a = 6\frac{2}{5}$ {16}
34. $\frac{3}{2}b = -14\frac{1}{2}$ $\left\{-\frac{29}{3}\right\}$
35. $-\frac{y}{3} = 3\frac{2}{3}$ {−11}
36. $-\frac{x}{2} = 11\frac{1}{2}$ {−23}
37. $-\frac{y}{12} = \frac{1}{4}$ {−3}
38. $-\frac{n}{4} = -\frac{3}{2}$ {6}
39. $0 = -\frac{x}{5}$ {0}
40. $-\frac{5}{3}x = 10$ {−6}

C
41. $2|x| = 18$ {9, −9}
42. $3|y| = 33$ {11, −11}
43. $-7|t| = 42$ no solution
44. $-32 = 8|k|$ no solution
45. $\frac{|x|}{5} = 2$ {10, −10}
46. $\frac{|a|}{8} = 4$ {32, −32}
47. $3 = \frac{|n|}{7}$ {21, −21}
48. $6 = \frac{|m|}{2}$ {12, −12}
49. $\frac{5|c|}{3} = 10$ {6, −6}
50. $\frac{4}{7}|x| = 16$ {28, −28}
51. $7 - \frac{3|a|}{2} = 1$ {4, −4}
52. $10 - \frac{4}{3}|b| = -2$ {9, −9}

Problems

Supplementary Materials
Study Guide   pp. 39–40
Practice Master   11

Write an equation based on the facts of each problem. Then solve the equation and the problem.

A 1. Five times a number is −375. Find the number. −75

2. Negative nine times a number is −108. Find the number. 12

3. One third of a number is −7. Find the number. −21

4. Three quarters of a number is 21. Find the number. 28

5. One hundred twenty seniors are on the honor roll. This represents one third of the senior class. How many seniors are there? 360 seniors

6. Two hundred twenty-five students play a team sport at Lincoln High School. These students represent $\frac{3}{8}$ of the total student population. How many students attend the school? 600 students

7. The perimeter of a square parking lot is 784 m. How long is each side of the lot? 196 m

8. The distance around the United States Pentagon building is one mile. How long is each side? (*Hint:* A regular pentagon has five equal sides.) $\frac{1}{5}$ mi

9. Luis ate three of the eight pizza slices. He paid $2.70 as his share of the cost. How much did the whole pizza cost? $7.20

10. A restaurant charges $2.50 for one eighth of a quiche. At this rate, how much does the restaurant receive for the whole quiche? $20

11. The Eagles won three times as many games as they lost. They won 21 games. How many games did they lose? 7 games

12. Buena Vista High School has five times as many black-and-white monitors as color monitors. The school has 40 black-and-white monitors for computers. How many color monitors does the school have? 8 color monitors

13. How many apples, averaging 0.2 kg each, are included in a 50 kg shipment of apples? 250 apples

14. A 75-watt bulb consumes 0.075 kW · h (kilowatt-hours) of energy when it burns for one hour. How long was the bulb left burning if it consumed 3.3 kW · h of energy? 44 h

B 15. A hard-cover book sells for $16.50. The same title in paperback sells for $4.95. How many hard-cover books must a dealer sell to take in as much money as he/she does for 30 paperback copies? 9 hard-cover books

16. A certain real-estate agent receives $6 for every $100 of a house's selling price. How much was a house sold for if the agent received $10,725? $178,750

Solving Equations and Problems   **105**

17. An employer said that each worker received $24 in fringe benefits for every $100 in wages. At this rate, what wages were earned by a worker whose fringe benefits were valued at $5100? $21,250

18. One kilogram of sea water contains, on average, 35 g of salt. How many grams of sea water contain 4.2 g of salt? 120 g

C **19.** Raul drove $\frac{1}{4}$ mi from Exit 27 to Exit 28 in 18 s. At what rate was he traveling in mi/s? At what rate was he driving in mi/h? (*Hint:* rate · time = distance) $\frac{1}{72}$ mi/s; 50 mi/h

20. A police helicopter clocked a truck over a stretch of highway $\frac{1}{5}$ mi long. The truck traveled the distance in 10 s. At what rate was the truck traveling in mi/s? At what rate was it traveling in mi/h? $\frac{1}{50}$ mi/s; 72 mi/h

Mixed Review Exercises

Evaluate if $a = 2$, $b = -3$, and $c = 4$.

1. $7a - 2b$ 20

2. $(3a - 2b)c$ 48

3. $|b| + |c| - (-c)$ 11

4. $|a| - |b + c|$ 1

5. $\frac{-(5ab)}{2c}$ $\frac{15}{4}$

6. $\frac{2 + a}{c}$ 1

Simplify.

7. $7a + 6 + 9a$ 16a + 6

8. $5n - 9 + 9$ 5n

9. $10p - p + 2$ 9p + 2

10. $-4(m + 2)$ −4m − 8

11. $(x + 7)8$ 8x + 56

12. $3(2y - 5)$ 6y − 15

 Calculator Key-In

Use the division key on a calculator to find a decimal equal to each expression.

Sample 1 $\frac{-36}{8}$ **Solution** $\frac{-36}{8} = -36 \div 8 = -4.5$

1. $\frac{3}{4}$ 0.75

2. $\frac{-5}{8}$ −0.625

3. $\frac{7}{-35}$ −0.2

4. $\frac{-3}{-20}$ 0.15

5. $\frac{1}{40}$ 0.025

6. $\frac{-11}{4}$ −2.75

7. $\frac{12}{-50}$ −0.24

8. $\frac{-7}{-8}$ 0.875

9. $\frac{31}{32}$ 0.96875

10. $\frac{43}{-64}$ −0.671875

11–20. Use the multiplication and reciprocal keys on a calculator to find a decimal equal to each expression in Exercises 1–10. (See Sample 2.) Are your answers the same as before? yes

Sample 2 $\frac{-36}{8}$ **Solution** $\frac{-36}{8} = -36 \cdot \frac{1}{8} = -4.5$

106   *Chapter 3*

3-3 Using Several Transformations

Objective To solve equations by using more than one transformation.

If you start with n, multiply by 5, and subtract 9, you get the expression $5n - 9$. If you start with $5n - 9$, add 9, and divide by 5, you're back to n.

$$n \xrightarrow{\times 5} 5n \xrightarrow{-9} 5n - 9$$

$$5n - 9 \xrightarrow{+9} 5n \xrightarrow{\div 5} n$$

The addition of 9 "undoes" the subtraction of 9. We call addition and subtraction **inverse operations.** The diagram also shows that division by 5 "undoes" multiplication by 5. Multiplication and division are also inverse operations.

For all real numbers a and b,

$$(a + b) - b = a \quad \text{and} \quad (a - b) + b = a.$$

For all real numbers a and all *nonzero* real numbers b,

$$(ab) \div b = a \quad \text{and} \quad (a \div b)b = a.$$

Example 1 Solve $5n - 9 = 71$.

Solution

Use inverse operations:

$$5n - 9 = 71$$
$$5n - 9 + 9 = 71 + 9$$
To undo the subtraction of 9 from $5n$, add 9 to each side.
$$5n = 80$$
$$\frac{5n}{5} = \frac{80}{5}$$
To undo the multiplication of n by 5, divide each side by 5.
$$n = 16$$
$\therefore$ the solution set is $\{16\}$. **Answer**

Example 2 Solve $\frac{1}{2}x + 3 = 9$.

Solution

$$\frac{1}{2}x + 3 = 9$$
To undo the addition of 3 to $\frac{1}{2}x$, subtract 3 from each side.

$$\frac{1}{2}x + 3 - 3 = 9 - 3$$

$$\frac{1}{2}x = 6$$
To undo the multiplication of x by $\frac{1}{2}$, multiply each side by 2, the reciprocal of $\frac{1}{2}$.

$$2\left(\frac{1}{2}x\right) = 2 \cdot 6$$

$$x = 12$$
$\therefore$ the solution set is $\{12\}$. **Answer**

Solving Equations and Problems **107**

Teaching Suggestions, p. T90
Using Manipulatives, p. T91
Suggested Extensions, p. T91

Warm-Up Exercises

Solve.

1. $4w = 48$ $\{12\}$
2. $4 + w = 48$ $\{44\}$
3. $4 - w = 48$ $\{-44\}$
4. $w - 4 = 48$ $\{52\}$
5. $4 = w - 48$ $\{52\}$
6. $4 = w + 48$ $\{-44\}$
7. $\frac{1}{4}w = 48$ $\{192\}$
8. $4 = 48w$ $\left\{\frac{1}{12}\right\}$

Motivating the Lesson

Tell students to choose a number between 1 and 20. Have them multiply it by 2, then add 7. Ask what needs to be done to get back to the original number. Solving equations by using more than one transformation is today's topic.

Chalkboard Examples

Solve.

1. $2x - 7 = 4$
$$2x - 7 + 7 = 4 + 7$$
$$2x = 11$$
$$\frac{2x}{2} = \frac{11}{2}$$
$$x = \frac{11}{2}$$
$\therefore$ the sol. set is $\left\{\frac{11}{2}\right\}$.

2. $\frac{1}{5}x - 9 = 3$
$$\frac{1}{5}x - 9 + 9 = 3 + 9$$
$$\frac{1}{5}x = 12$$
$$5\left(\frac{1}{5}x\right) = 5 \cdot 12$$
$$x = 60$$
$\therefore$ the sol. set is $\{60\}$.

(continued)

3. $\dfrac{k-4}{2} = 13$

$\quad 2\left(\dfrac{k-4}{2}\right) = 2 \cdot 13$

$\quad\quad k - 4 = 26$

$\quad k - 4 + 4 = 26 + 4$

$\quad\quad\quad\quad k = 30$

$\therefore$ the sol. set is $\{30\}$.

4. $40 = 2x + 3x$

$\quad 40 = 5x$

$\quad \dfrac{40}{5} = \dfrac{5x}{5}$

$\quad\; 8 = x$

$\therefore$ the sol. set is $\{8\}$.

5. $8(w + 1) - 3 = 48$

$\quad 8w + 8 - 3 = 48$

$\quad\quad 8w + 5 = 48$

$\quad 8w + 5 - 5 = 48 - 5$

$\quad\quad\quad\quad 8w = 43$

$\quad\quad\quad\; \dfrac{8w}{8} = \dfrac{43}{8}$

$\quad\quad\quad\quad w = \dfrac{43}{8}$

$\therefore$ the sol. set is $\left\{\dfrac{43}{8}\right\}$.

Check for Understanding

Oral Exs. 1–2: use after
Example 1.

Oral Exs. 3–6: use after
Example 2.

Oral Exs. 7–17: use after
Example 4.

Oral Ex. 18: use after
Example 5.

Additional Answers
Oral Exercises

1. Subtr. 3; div. by 5

2. Add 4; div. by 3

3. Add 2; mult. by 4

4. Subtr. 9; mult. by -2

5. Add 6; mult. by 5

6. Add 4; mult. by -3

7. Mult. by $\dfrac{4}{3}$

8. Mult. by $-\dfrac{9}{5}$

9. Add $5x$ and $4x$; div. by 9

Example 3   Solve $\dfrac{w-5}{9} = 2$.

Solution 1 $\dfrac{w-5}{9} = 2$

$\quad\quad 9\left(\dfrac{w-5}{9}\right) = 9 \cdot 2$

$\quad\quad\quad w - 5 = 18$

$\quad w - 5 + 5 = 18 + 5$

$\quad\quad\quad\quad w = 23$

$\therefore$ the solution set is $\{23\}$.   *Answer*

Solution 2 $\dfrac{w-5}{9} = 2$
(condensed) $w - 5 = 18$
$\quad\quad\quad\quad w = 23$

$\therefore$ the solution set is $\{23\}$.
Answer

Examples 4 and 5 show that it is sometimes necessary to use the distributive property and simplify one or both sides of an equation as the first step in solving it.

Example 4   Solve $32 = 7a + 9a$.

Solution 1 $32 = 7a + 9a$.

$\quad\quad 32 = 16a$

$\quad\quad \dfrac{32}{16} = \dfrac{16a}{16}$

$\quad\quad\; 2 = a$

$\therefore$ the solution set is $\{2\}$.   *Answer*

Solution 2 $32 = 7a + 9a$
(condensed) $32 = 16a$
$\quad\quad\quad\; 2 = a$

$\therefore$ the solution set is $\{2\}$.
Answer

Example 5   Solve $4(y + 8) - 7 = 15$.

Solution 1 $4(y + 8) - 7 = 15$ $\quad\quad$ ⎰Use the distributive property

$\quad\quad 4y + 32 - 7 = 15$ $\quad\quad$ ⎱and simplify the left side.

$\quad\quad\quad 4y + 25 = 15$

$\quad 4y + 25 - 25 = 15 - 25$

$\quad\quad\quad\quad\; 4y = -10$

$\quad\quad\quad\quad\; \dfrac{4y}{4} = \dfrac{-10}{4}$

$\quad\quad\quad\quad\quad y = -\dfrac{10}{4} = -\dfrac{5}{2}$ $\quad$ $\therefore$ the solution set is $\left\{-\dfrac{5}{2}\right\}$.   *Answer*

Solution 2 $4(y + 8) - 7 = 15$
(condensed) $4y + 32 - 7 = 15$
$\quad\quad\quad 4y + 25 = 15$
$\quad\quad\quad\quad\; 4y = -10$
$\quad\quad\quad\quad\quad y = -\dfrac{10}{4} = -\dfrac{5}{2}$ $\quad$ $\therefore$ the solution set is $\left\{-\dfrac{5}{2}\right\}$.   *Answer*

At the top of the next page you will find two helpful tips for solving an equation in which the variable is on one side.

108   *Chapter 3*

1. Simplify each side of the equation as needed.
2. If the side containing the variable involves a certain order of operations, apply the inverse operations in the opposite order.

Oral Exercises

Describe how you would solve each equation.

Sample 1 $\frac{1}{5}x + 2 = -1$

Solution First subtract 2 from each side; then multiply each side by 5.

Sample 2 $14 = \frac{2m}{3}$

Solution 1 Multiply each side by 3; then divide each side by 2.

Solution 2 Multiply each side by $\frac{3}{2}$.

1. $5y + 3 = 18$
2. $3y - 4 = 14$
3. $\frac{1}{4}a - 2 = -3$
4. $-\frac{1}{2}b + 9 = 5$
5. $-6 + \frac{y}{5} = 5$
6. $4 = -4 - \frac{x}{3}$
7. $\frac{3n}{4} = -12$
8. $\frac{-5z}{9} = 30$
9. $5x + 4x = 18$
10. $-4n + 7n = -36$
11. $\frac{7}{8}s + 2 = 16$
12. $1 - \frac{4}{5}n = -19$
13. $\frac{y - 2}{3} = 7$
14. $\frac{2}{3}w + 4 = 5$
15. $1 - \frac{2}{9}v = 4$
16. $5 = c + 8c - 4$
17. $10p - p + 2 = -7$
18. $-4(m + 12) = 36$

Written Exercises

Solve.

A
1. $2x - 1 = 11$ {6}
2. $3y - 8 = 16$ {8}
3. $4n + 9 = -3$ {-3}
4. $5c + 7 = -28$ {-7}
5. $-2x + 5 = 19$ {-7}
6. $-8y - 11 = 13$ {-3}
7. $\frac{1}{2}x + 7 = 6$ {-2}
8. $\frac{2}{3}p - 7 = 17$ {36}
9. $\frac{2x}{3} = 8$ {12}
10. $\frac{4y}{5} = 28$ {35}
11. $\frac{x + 5}{3} = 7$ {16}
12. $\frac{z - 5}{4} = 8$ {37}

Solving Equations and Problems **109**

10. Add $-4n$ and $7n$; div. by 3
11. Subtr. 2; mult. by $\frac{8}{7}$
12. Subtr. 1, mult. by $-\frac{5}{4}$
13. Mult. by 3; add 2
14. Subtr. 4; mult. by $\frac{3}{2}$
15. Subtr. 1; mult. by $-\frac{9}{2}$
16. Add c and $8c$; add 4; div. by 9
17. Add $10p$ and $-p$; subtr. 2; div. by 9
18. Div. by -4; subtr. 12

Guided Practice
Solve.
1. $3w - 7 = 8$ {5}
2. $-7x - 9 = -23$ {2}
3. $\frac{1}{3}f - 8 = 10$ {54}
4. $\frac{t - 5}{3} = 11$ {38}
5. $\frac{x + 8}{2} = 14$ {20}
6. $8(6 + r) = 40$ {-1}
7. $4r + 11r - 7 = 8$ {1}

Summarizing the Lesson
Have students recall the objective of today's lesson and the two helpful tips for solving an equation in which the variable is on one side. Have them describe how they would solve the following equations:

$$6(m - 3) = 24$$
$$41 = 4x - 8 + 3x$$

Solve.

13. $\dfrac{1 - x}{2} = 7$ {−13}   **14.** $\dfrac{5 - n}{3} = 4$ {−7}   **15.** $7x - 4x = 54$ {18}

16. $3y - 7y = 28$ {−7}   **17.** $-3n - 5n = 0$ {0}   **18.** $2a - 11a = -27$ {3}

19. $y - 7 + 4y = 13$ {4}   **20.** $2x + 5 - 7x = 15$ {−2}   **21.** $0 = n - 15 - 4n$ {−5}

22. $0 = p + 18 + 5p$ {−3}   **23.** $2(x - 4) = 22$ {15}   **24.** $3(y - 7) = 27$ {16}

25. $35 = 5(n + 2)$ {5}   **26.** $20 = 4(x + 3)$ {2}   **27.** $y + 5 - 4y = -10$ {5}

28. $4w - 3w + 2w = 24$ {8}   **29.** $15 = 8x - 5 + 2x$ {2}   **30.** $32 = 2n - 3n + 5n$ {8}

B **31.** $-\dfrac{1}{2}(x + 4) = 16$ {−36}   **32.** $\dfrac{3}{5}(x + 2) = 12$ {18}

33. $21 = -\dfrac{3}{2}(x - 2)$ {−12}   **34.** $66 = -\dfrac{6}{5}(s + 3)$ {−58}

35. $3(a - 5) + 19 = -2$ {−2}   **36.** $2(b + 8) - 9 = 5$ {−1}

37. $-3 = 4(k + 7) - 15$ {−4}   **38.** $3 = 7(h - 2) + 17$ {0}

39. $4c + 3(c - 2) = -34$ {−4}   **40.** $d + 4(d + 6) = -1$ {−5}

41. $\dfrac{2x - 1}{3} = 5$ {8}   **42.** $\dfrac{4y + 3}{7} = 9$ {15}

43. $0 = \dfrac{8 - 2x}{5}$ {4}   **44.** $7 = \dfrac{4 + 9y}{7}$ {5}

45. $1 - \dfrac{3}{4}(v + 2) = -5$ {6}   **46.** $9 - \dfrac{4}{5}(u - 3) = 1$ {13}

47. $-9 - 3(2q - 1) = -18$ {2}   **48.** $-10 + 4(3p + 10) = 18$ {−1}

49. $-2 = 4(s + 8) - 3s$ {−34}   **50.** $-7 = 3(t - 5) - t$ {4}

51. $(x - 13) - (x - 5) + 2x = 0$ {4}   **52.** $(5 - y) + (6 - y) - (5 - y) = 0$ {6}

53. $b - (1 - 2b) + (b - 3) = -4$ {0}   **54.** $(c + 3) - 2c - (1 - 3c) = 2$ {0}

C **55.** $5m - 3[7 - (1 - 2m)] = 0$ {−18}   **56.** $\dfrac{1}{5}[4(k + 2) - (3 - k)] = 4$ {3}

57. $5(g - 7) + 2[g - 3(g - 5)] = 0$ {5}   **58.** $7n + 2[3(1 - n) - 2(1 + n)] = 14$ {−4}

59. $3|n| - (2|n| - 2) = 9$ {7, −7}   **60.** $(9|x| + 3) - 5|x| - 3 = 12$ {3, −3}

Mixed Review Exercises

Solve.

1. $\dfrac{1}{7}x = -23$ {−161}   **2.** $\dfrac{x}{8} = \dfrac{3}{4}$ {6}   **3.** $\dfrac{1}{5}x = 3\dfrac{1}{5}$ {16}

4. $-3 + x = 1$ {4}   **5.** $2x + 7 = 13$ {3}   **6.** $51 = y + 17$ {34}

7. $-12 + x = -20$ {−8}   **8.** $32 - x = 36$ {−4}   **9.** $-0.25x = 1$ {−4}

10. $2.3 = x + 1$ {1.3}   **11.** $0 = 3x$ {0}   **12.** $18y = 360$ {20}

Computer Exercises

2. An error message results from attempting to divide by zero. There is no solution.

1. Write a BASIC program to solve an equation of the form $Ax + B = C$, where the values of A, B, and C are entered with INPUT statements. Use the program to solve the following equations.

   a. $7x + 8 = 64$ 8

   b. $3x - 2 = -8$ -2

   c. $\frac{2}{5}x + 11 = 7$ -10

   d. $\frac{3}{2}x + 4 = 13$ 6

   e. $\frac{1}{4}x - 9 = 0$ 36

   f. $\frac{3}{10}x + 10.7 = 14$ 11

2. Use the program from Exercise 1 to solve $0x + 9 = 12$. What happens? What is the correct solution? Modify the program from Exercise 1 to print an appropriate response if the value of A is 0.

3. Modify the program from Exercise 1 to solve an equation of the form $A|x| + B = C$. Use this program to solve the following equations.

   a. $|x| + 8 = 10$ {2, -2}

   b. $|x| + 10 = 8$ No sol.

   c. $6|x| + 2 = 5$ {0.5, -0.5}

Self-Test 1

Vocabulary   equivalent equations (p. 96)
transformation by substitution (p. 96)
transformation by addition (p. 96)
transformation by subtraction (p. 96)

transformation by multiplication (p. 102)
transformation by division (p. 102)
inverse operations (p. 107)

Solve.

1. $n - 32 = 6$ {38}

2. $19 + y = 61$ {42}

Obj. 3-1, p. 95

3. $625 = 5y$ {125}

4. $-\frac{1}{2}x = 5\frac{1}{2}$ {-11}

Obj. 3-2, p. 102

5. A rectangle is three times as long as it is wide. If its perimeter is 48 cm, find its dimensions. Draw a diagram first. 6 cm by 18 cm

6. $3x - 4 = 17$ {7}

7. $\frac{1}{2}y + 4 = 16$ {24}

Obj. 3-3, p. 107

Check your answers with those at the back of the book.

Calculator Key-In

You can use a calculator to check whether 16 is a solution of $5n - 9 = 71$. If it is, the calculator will display 71 when you enter $5 \times 16 - 9$.

Exercises

Is the given number a solution of the equation?

1. $6x - 7 = 21$; 3.5 no

2. $22x + 5 = 60$; 2.5 yes

3. $3.9x - 11.2 = 4.6$; 4.2 no

Solving Equations and Problems   **111**

Solving Problems

3-4 Using Equations to Solve Problems

Objective   To use the five-step plan to solve word problems.

The skills that you have gained in solving equations can often help you to solve word problems. Use the five-step plan on page 27 as a guide.

Example 1 Lynne took a taxicab from her office to the airport. She had to pay a flat fee of $2.05 plus $.90 per mile. The total cost was $5.65. How many miles was the taxi trip?

Solution

Step 1 The problem asks for the number of miles traveled in the taxi.

Step 2 Let m = the number of miles.
Then $90m$ = the mileage cost in cents.

Step 3 Flat fee + mileage cost = total cost
$$205 + 90m = 565$$

Step 4 Solve. $90m = 360$
$$m = 4$$

Step 5 *Check:*   4 miles at $.90 per mile: 4($.90) = $3.60

Flat fee + mileage cost: $2.05 + $3.60 = $5.65   √

∴ the taxi trip was 4 mi.   ***Answer***

Example 2 shows that some word problems can be solved more easily if you first draw a diagram.

Example 2 The perimeter of a trapezoid is 90 cm.
The parallel bases are 24 cm and 38 cm long.
The lengths of the other two sides are consecutive odd integers.
What are the lengths of these other two sides?

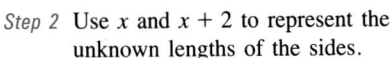
Solution

Step 1 Draw a diagram to help you understand the problem.

Step 2 Use x and $x + 2$ to represent the unknown lengths of the sides.

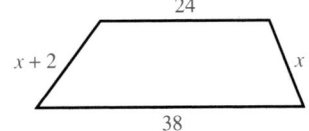

Step 3
$$\text{perimeter} = 90$$
$$38 + x + 24 + (x + 2) = 90$$

Step 4
$$2x + 64 = 90$$
$$2x = 26$$
$$x = 13 \text{ and } x + 2 = 15$$

Step 5 *Check:* Is the sum of the lengths of the sides 90 cm?
$$38 + 13 + 24 + 15 = 90 \quad \checkmark$$
∴ the required lengths are 13 cm and 15 cm.   *Answer*

Problems

Solve each problem using the five-step plan to help you.

A 1. The sum of 38 and twice a number is 124. Find the number. 43

2. Five more than three times a number is 197. Find the number. 64

3. Four less than half of a number is 17. Find the number. 42

4. When one third of a number is decreased by 11, the result is 38. Find the number. 147

5. Four more than two thirds of a number is 22. Find the number. 27

6. Eight less than three quarters of a number is 91. Find the number. 132

7. Find three consecutive integers whose sum is 171. 56, 57, 58

8. Find three consecutive odd integers whose sum is 105. 33, 35, 37

9. Find four consecutive even integers whose sum is 244. 58, 60, 62, 64

10. Find five consecutive integers whose sum is 195. 37, 38, 39, 40, 41

11. Burt's Burger Barn sold 495 hamburgers today. The number sold with cheese was half the number sold without cheese. How many of each kind were sold? with cheese, 165; without cheese, 330

12. A company added a new oil tank that holds 350 barrels of oil more than its old oil tank. Together they hold 3650 barrels of oil. How much does each tank hold? old tank, 1650 barrels; new tank, 2000 barrels

13. Brian has $88 in his savings account. If he saves $3.50 per week, how long will it take him to have $200 in his account? 32 weeks

14. A 1000 L tank now contains 240 L of water. How long will it take to fill the tank using a pump that pumps 25 L per minute? 30.4 min.

Solving Equations and Problems   **113**

Let m = the number of months it will take.
Future stamps = current stamps plus 7 more each month.
$$129 = 45 + 7m$$
$$84 = 7m$$
$$12 = m$$
It will take 12 months for Sarah to have 129 stamps in her collection.
Check: $45 + 7(12) = 45 + 84 = 129$

2. **The length of a rectangle is 3 in. more than the width. Find the length and width if the perimeter of the rectangle is 98 in. Draw a diagram.**

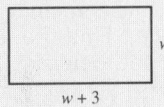

Let w = the width of the rectangle. Then $w + 3$ = the length of the rectangle.
Use the formula $P = 2l + 2w$.
$$98 = 2(w + 3) + 2w$$
$$98 = 2w + 6 + 2w$$
$$98 = 4w + 6$$
$$92 = 4w$$
$$23 = w$$
The length of the rectangle is 26 in. and the width is 23 in.
Check: $2(26) + 2(23) = 52 + 46 = 98$

Guided Practice

Solve each problem using the five-step plan.

1. Six less than five times a number is 74. Find the number. 16

2. Eight less than one half a number is −44. Find the number. −72

(continued)

3. Find four consecutive even integers whose sum is 100. 22, 24, 26, 28

4. Tom has read 143 pages of the 251 pages in a book. If he reads 12 pages a day, how long will it take him to finish the book? 9 days

Solve using the five-step plan. Draw a diagram to help you.

5. The longest side of a triangle is 3 more than twice the shortest side and the remaining side is 2.4 cm. Find the lengths if the perimeter is 12 cm.
2.4 cm, 2.2 cm, 7.4 cm

Summarizing the Lesson

State that the five-step plan was used to solve problems with equations. Ask if students noticed any distinctive feature of the equations they solved in this lesson. If needed, point out that the variable was always on one side of the equation.

Suggested Assignments

Minimum
Day 1: 113/P: 1–17 odd
    R 111/Self-Test 1
Day 2: 113/P: 8–22 even
    S 115/Mixed Review
Average
Day 1: 113/P: 1–21 odd
    R 111/Self-Test 1
Day 2: 114/P: 23–26, 27, 29, 31
    S 115/Mixed Review
Maximum
Day 1: 113/P: 2–26 even
    R 111/Self-Test 1
Day 2: 114/P: 27–33
    S 115/Mixed Review

Solve each problem using the five-step plan. In Exercises 15–26, draw a diagram to help you.

15. The perimeter of a rectangle is 332 cm and the width is 76 cm. Find the rectangle's length. 90 cm

16. The perimeter of a rectangle is 408 cm and the length is 134 cm. Find the rectangle's width. 70 cm

17. In an isosceles triangle, there are two sides, called *legs*, with the same length. The third side is called the *base*. If an isosceles triangle has perimeter 345 cm and base length 85 cm, what is the length of each leg? 130 cm

18. The length of a rectangle is 7 cm more than the width. The perimeter is 78 cm. Find the rectangle's dimensions. 16 cm by 23 cm

19. The width of a rectangle is 15 cm less than the length. The perimeter is 98 cm. Find the rectangle's dimensions. 17 cm by 32 cm

20. The longest side of a triangle is twice as long as the shortest side and the remaining side is 25 cm. If the perimeter is 70 cm, find the lengths of the sides of the triangle. 15 cm, 25 cm, 30 cm

21. A rectangle's length is 8 cm more than three times its width. If the perimeter is 128 cm, find the length and the width. width: 14 cm; length: 50 cm

22. A triangle has sides with lengths in centimeters that are consecutive even integers. Find the lengths if the perimeter is 186 cm. 60 cm, 62 cm, 64 cm

B 23. In any triangle, the sum of the measures of the angles is 180°. In △ABC, ∠A is three times as large as ∠B and also 16° larger than ∠C. Find the measure of each angle. 84°, 28°, 68°

24. In any triangle, the sum of the measures of the angles is 180°. In △ABC, ∠A is twice as large as ∠B. ∠B is 4° larger than ∠C. Find the measure of each angle. 92°, 46°, 42°

25. In △ABC, $\overline{AB}$ is 9 cm shorter than $\overline{AC}$, while $\overline{BC}$ is 3 cm longer than $\overline{AC}$. If the perimeter of the triangle is 48 cm, find the lengths of the three sides. 18 cm, 9 cm, 21 cm

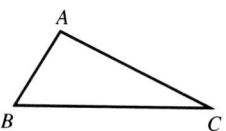

26. In isosceles trapezoid ABCD, the longer base, $\overline{AB}$, is one and one half times as long as the shorter base, $\overline{CD}$. The other two sides, $\overline{AD}$ and $\overline{BC}$, are both 13 cm long.
   a. If the perimeter is 76 cm, find the lengths of $\overline{AB}$ and $\overline{CD}$. AB = 30 cm, CD = 20 cm
   b. If the height of the trapezoid is 12 cm, find its area. 300 cm²
   (*Hint:* Area = ½ × height × sum of base lengths)

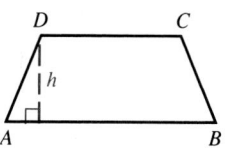

27. Theo has $5 more than Denise and Denise has $11 more than Rudy. Together they have $45. How much money does each have? Theo, $22; Rudy, $6; Denise, $17

28. Chandra has twice as much money as Nora. Nora has $6 less than Lian. Together they have $54. How much money does each have? Lian, $18; Nora, $12; Chandra, $24

A caps 15,800 bottles; B caps 7900 bottles; C caps 16,300 bottles

29. In one day, Machine A caps twice as many bottles as Machine B. Machine C caps 500 more bottles than Machine A. The three machines cap a total of 40,000 bottles in a day. How many bottles does each of the machines cap in one day?

30. The total cost of a sandwich, a glass of milk, and an apple is \$3.50. The milk costs one and a half times as much as the apple. The sandwich costs \$1.40 more than the apple. What is the price of each?
apple, \$.60; milk, \$.90; sandwich, \$2.00

C **31.** With the major options package and destination charge, a sports car cost \$24,416. The base price of the car was ten times the price of the major options package and fifty times the destination charge. What was the base price of the car? \$21,800

32. On the first of three tests, Keiko scored 72 points. On the third test, her score was 1 point more than on the second. Her average on the three tests was 83. What were her scores on the second and third tests? 88 and 89

33. The absolute value of the sum of -7 and twice a number is 23. Find the number. (*Hint:* There are two answers.) 15 or -8

Mixed Review Exercises

Solve.

1. $-5 + y = 1$ {6} **2.** $x - 1.5 = -3$ {−1.5} **3.** $y + 8 = 21$ {13} **4.** $\frac{2}{5}y = 2$ {5}

5. $-21 = \frac{c}{3}$ {−63} **6.** $-\frac{1}{5}x = 20$ {−100} **7.** $41 = y + 11$ {30} **8.** $x - 20 = 37$ {57}

9. $0 = 1.75y$ {0} **10.** $5y + 6 = 16$ {2} **11.** $2x - 5 = 15$ {10} **12.** $2(a - 3) + 6 = -3$ $\left\{-\frac{3}{2}\right\}$

Historical Note / *Variables*

Until the sixteenth century, unknown quantities were represented by words such as "heap," "root," or "thing." Eventually, abbreviations for such words, as well as drawings of squares and cubes, were used to symbolize unknowns.

In the late sixteenth century, a French lawyer, Francois Vietá, who enjoyed studying algebra during his leisure hours, began using vowels for unknowns. An English mathematician, Thomas Harriot, later adopted lowercase letters to stand for variables. In 1637, René Descartes, a French mathematician and philosopher, began using the final letters of the alphabet to represent unknowns.

Problem Solving Strategies

When solving a problem that involves the perimeter or area of a geometric figure, encourage students to *draw and label a diagram* to help them visualize the problem.

Supplementary Materials

Study Guide	pp. 43–44
Practice Master	12

Teaching Suggestions p. T92

Group Activities p. T92

Suggested Extensions p. T92

Warm-Up Exercises

Simplify.

1. $3 + 2x - 2x$ 3
2. $2(4t + 6) - 4t$ $4t + 12$
3. $55 - 2w + 2w$ 55
4. $\frac{2}{5}s + 5 - \frac{2}{5}s$ 5
5. $8 + 5(x - 1) - x$ $4x + 3$
6. $-333u + 22 + 333u$ 22

Motivating the Lesson

Write the following equations on the chalkboard.

$$2x = 6 - x$$
$$2p - 1 = 3p$$
$$8k = k$$

Ask students how these equations differ from those they have previously studied. Solving equations with the variable on both sides is today's topic.

Chalkboard Examples

Solve.

1. $20 + 7x = 9x$
   $20 + 7x - 7x = 9x - 7x$
   $20 = 2x$
   $\frac{20}{2} = \frac{2x}{2}$
   $10 = x$
   $\therefore$ the sol. set is $\{10\}$.

2. $4t = 50 - 6t$
   $4t + 6t = 50 - 6t + 6t$
   $10t = 50$
   $\frac{10t}{10} = \frac{50}{10}$
   $t = 5$
   $\therefore$ the sol. set is $\{5\}$.

3-5 Equations with the Variable on Both Sides

Objective   To solve equations with the variable on both sides.

In the first four lessons of this chapter, the variable appeared on just one side of a given equation. In this lesson, the variable may occur on both sides of the equation. Since variables represent numbers, you may transform an equation by adding a variable expression to each side or by subtracting a variable expression from each side. Then solve the resulting equation as you have in earlier lessons.

Example 1   Solve $6x = 4x + 18$.

Solution 1
$$6x = 4x + 18$$
$$6x - 4x = 4x + 18 - 4x \qquad \text{Subtract } 4x \text{ from each side.}$$
$$2x = 18$$
$$\frac{2x}{2} = \frac{18}{2}$$
$$x = 9$$

Solution 2 $6x = 4x + 18$ *Check:* $6 \cdot 9 \overset{?}{=} 4 \cdot 9 + 18$
(condensed) $2x = 18$ $54 \overset{?}{=} 36 + 18$
$x = 9$ $54 = 54$ $\checkmark$

$\therefore$ the solution set is $\{9\}$.   **Answer**

Example 2   Solve $3y = 15 - 2y$.

Solution $3y = 15 - 2y$ Add $2y$ to both sides.
$5y = 15$
$y = 3$ $\therefore$ the solution set is $\{3\}$.   **Answer**

Example 3   Solve: **a.** $\frac{4}{5}x + 3 = x$ **b.** $\frac{8 + x}{9} = x$

Solution
$$3 = x - \frac{4}{5}x \qquad\qquad 8 + x = 9x$$
$$3 = x\left(1 - \frac{4}{5}\right) \qquad\qquad 8 = 8x$$
$$3 = \frac{1}{5}x \qquad\qquad 1 = x$$
$$15 = x \qquad\qquad \therefore \text{ the solution set}$$
$$\text{is } \{1\}. \quad \textbf{\textit{Answer}}$$
$$\therefore \text{ the solution set}$$
$$\text{is } \{15\}. \quad \textbf{\textit{Answer}}$$

Example 4 Solve $7(a - 2) - 6 = 2a + 8 + a$.

Solution

$$7(a - 2) - 6 = 2a + 8 + a \qquad \left\{ \begin{array}{l} \text{First use the distributive property} \\ \text{and simplify both sides.} \end{array} \right.$$
$$7a - 14 - 6 = 2a + 8 + a$$
$$7a - 20 = 3a + 8$$
$$4a - 20 = 8$$
$$4a = 28$$
$$a = 7 \qquad \therefore \text{ the solution set is } \{7\}. \quad \textbf{\textit{Answer}}$$

It is possible that an equation may have *no* solution, or that it may be satisfied by *every* real number. Examples 5 and 6 illustrate these cases.

Example 5 Solve $3(1 - r) + 5r = 2(r + 1)$.

Solution

$$3 - 3r + 5r = 2r + 2$$
$$3 + 2r = 2r + 2$$
$$3 + 2r - 2r = 2r + 2 - 2r$$
$$3 = 2$$

The given equation is equivalent to the false statement $3 = 2$.
$\therefore$ the equation has no solution. **\textit{Answer}**

We call the set with no members the **empty set,** or the **null set.** It is denoted by the symbol $\emptyset$. The solution set of the equation in Example 5 is $\emptyset$.

Example 6 Solve $\frac{1}{3}(12x - 21) = 4x - 7$.

Solution

$$4x - 7 = 4x - 7$$

The given equation is equivalent to $4x - 7 = 4x - 7$, which is satisfied by every real number. $\therefore$ the solution set is {real numbers}. **\textit{Answer}**

An equation that is true for every value of the variable is called an **identity.** The equation in Example 6 is an identity.

Oral Exercises

Solve. If the equation is an identity or if it has no solution, say so.

1. $4x = 3x + 5$ {5}
2. $4n + 10 = 5n$ {10}
3. $8r + 1 = 9r$ {1}
4. $2p - 1 = 3p$ {−1}
5. $7 + b = b + 7$ identity
6. $2b = 6 + 2b$ no solution
7. $4a = 2a + a$ {0}
8. $8k = k$ {0}
9. $3s = s - 2$ {−1}
10. $3n + 4 = 3n + 5$ no solution
11. $5(x - 2) = 5x - 10$ identity
12. $3(w + 1) = 2w$ {−3}

Solving Equations and Problems **117**

---

3. $\frac{3}{5}x = 4 - \frac{8}{5}x$

$$\frac{3}{5}x + \frac{8}{5}x = 4 - \frac{8}{5}x + \frac{8}{5}x$$
$$\frac{11}{5}x = 4$$
$$\frac{5}{11}\left(\frac{11}{5}x\right) = \frac{5}{11}(4)$$
$$x = \frac{20}{11}$$

$\therefore$ the sol. set is $\left\{\frac{20}{11}\right\}$.

4. $4(r - 9) + 2 = 12r + 14$
$$4r - 36 + 2 = 12r + 14$$
$$4r - 34 = 12r + 14$$
$$-34 = 8r + 14$$
$$-48 = 8r$$
$$-6 = r$$

$\therefore$ the sol. set is $\{-6\}$.

5. $3(x + 2) - x = 2(x + 1)$
$$3x + 6 - x = 2x + 2$$
$$2x + 6 = 2x + 2$$
$$2x - 2x + 6 = 2x - 2x + 2$$
$$6 = 2$$

no solution

6. $2(3y + 5) + 9 =$
$6(y + 3) + 1$
$6y + 19 = 6y + 19$
The resulting equation is an identity. $\therefore$ the sol. set is {real numbers}.

Common Error

Often a student who is solving an equation that is an identity will assume, for example, that getting $4 = 4$ means that the solution is 4. Be sure to point out that this is not the case; show that numerous other values of the variable satisfy the equation.

Check for Understanding

Here is a suggested use of the Oral Exercises to check students' understanding as you teach the lesson.
Oral Exs. 1–4: use after Example 2.
Oral Exs. 5–12: use after Example 6.

Solve each equation.

1. $9x = 2x + 21$ {3}
2. $4t = 60 - 8t$ {5}
3. $2w = 42 + 9w$ {−6}
4. $3(k - 8) = k + 4$ {14}
5. $\dfrac{x + 10}{3} = 2x$ {2}
6. $\dfrac{2x - 7}{2} = 3x$ $\left\{-\dfrac{7}{4}\right\}$

Solve.

7. Find a number whose product with 10 is the same as its sum with 45. 5

8. Find three consecutive integers whose sum is 15 more than twice the middle integer. 14, 15, 16

Summarizing the Lesson

In today's lesson, students solved equations with the variable on both sides. Review the vocabulary of the lesson by asking:
- What is the empty set or null set?
- How is it denoted?
- What is an identity?

Suggested Assignments

Minimum
Day 1: 118/1–29 odd
      118/*P*: 1–6
Day 2: 118/16–32 even
      119/*P*: 7–9
    S 120/Mixed Review
Average
      118/6–42 mult. of 3
      118/*P*: 3–18 mult.
        of 3
    S 120/Mixed Review
Maximum
      118/3–48 mult. of 3
      118/*P*: 3–18 mult.
        of 3
    S 120/Mixed Review

Written Exercises

Solve each equation. If the equation is an identity or if it has no solution, write *identity* or *no solution*.

A

1. $5n = 2n + 6$ {2}
2. $8a = 2a + 30$ {5}
3. $y = 24 - 3y$ {6}
4. $2b = 80 - 8b$ {8}
5. $12n = 34 - 5n$ {2}
6. $3x = 27 - 15x$ $\left\{\dfrac{3}{2}\right\}$
7. $30 = 8 - 2x$ {−11}
8. $51 = 9 - 3x$ {−14}
9. $51a - 56 = 44a$ {8}
10. $39c + 78 = 33c$ {−13}
11. $98 - 4b = -11b$ {−14}
12. $-7a = -12a - 65$ {−13}
13. $4n + 5 = 6n + 7$ {−1}
14. $5p - 9 = 2p + 12$ {7}
15. $3p - 8 = 13 - 4p$ {3}
16. $89 + x = 2 - 2x$ {−29}
17. $71 - 5x = 9x - 13$ {6}
18. $5n + 1 = 5n - 1$ no sol.
19. $2(x - 6) = 3x$ {−12}
20. $4(y - 6) = 7y$ {−8}
21. $8(5 - n) = 2n$ {4}
22. $7(2 - m) = 3m$ $\left\{\dfrac{7}{5}\right\}$
23. $\dfrac{1}{2}x + 5 = x$ {10}
24. $\dfrac{2}{3}x - 7 = x$ {−21}
25. $\dfrac{4 + y}{5} = y$ {1}
26. $\dfrac{x - 2}{3} = x$ {−1}
27. $\dfrac{9 - 2y}{7} = y$ {1}
28. $\dfrac{6 - 4y}{2} = y$ {1}
29. $\dfrac{4n - 28}{3} = 2n$ {−14}
30. $\dfrac{23 - 11c}{7} = 5c$ $\left\{\dfrac{1}{2}\right\}$

B

31. $\dfrac{1}{3}(12 - 6x) = 4 - 2x$ identity
32. $\dfrac{1}{4}(20 - 4a) = 6 - a$ no solution
33. $5(2 + n) = 3(n + 6)$ {4}
34. $3(30 + s) = 4(s + 19)$ {14}
35. $5u + 5(1 - u) = u + 8$ {−3}
36. $2(g - 2) - 4 = 2(g - 3)$ no solution
37. $3(m + 5) - 6 = 3(m + 3)$ identity
38. $3(2 + v) - 4v = v + 16$ {−5}
39. $3(5y + 2) - y = 2(y - 3)$ {−1}
40. $4(3y - 1) + 13 = 5y + 2$ {−1}
41. $6r - 2(2 - r) = 4(2r - 1)$ identity
42. $5x + 2(1 - x) = 2(2x - 1)$ {4}
43. $3 + 4(p + 2) = 2p + 3(p + 4)$ {−1}
44. $4(a + 2) = 14 - 2(3 - 2a)$ identity

C

45. $3x + 2[1 - 3(x + 2)] = 2x$ {−2}
46. $2[5(w + 3) - (w + 1)] = 3(1 + w)$ {−5}
47. $5(2m + 3) - (1 - 2m) = 2[3(3 + 2m) - (3 - m)]$ {1}
48. $3(r + 1) - [2(3 - 2r) - 3(3 - r)] = 2(r + 5) - 4$ {0}

Problems

Solve.

A

1. Find a number that is 96 greater than its opposite. 48
2. Find a number that is 38 less than its opposite. −19
3. Find a number whose product with 9 is the same as its sum with 56. 7
4. Find a number that is 68 greater than three times its opposite. 17

5. Three times a number, decreased by 8, is the same as twice the number, increased by 15. Find the number. 23

6. Four times a number, increased by 25, is 13 less than six times the number. Find the number. 19

7. The greater of two consecutive integers is 15 more than twice the smaller. Find the integers. −14 and −13

8. The greater of two consecutive even integers is 20 more than twice the smaller. Find the integers. −18 and −16

9. Lyle shot three times as many baskets as Cliff, while Kyle shot 12 more baskets than Cliff. If Lyle and Kyle shot the same number of baskets, how many baskets did each of them shoot? Cliff, 6; Kyle and Lyle, 18

10. Dionne has six steel balls of equal mass. If she puts five of them in one pan of a beam balance and one ball and a 100 g mass in the other pan, the pans balance each other. What is the mass of each steel ball? 25 g

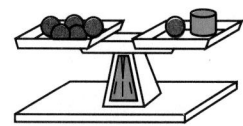

Supplementary Materials

Study Guide   pp. 45–46
Computer Activity   8
Resource Book   p. 87

B 11. The sum of two numbers is 15. Three times one of the numbers is 11 less than five times the other. Find the numbers. 7 and 8

12. The difference of two integers is 9. Five times the smaller is 7 more than three times the larger. Find the numbers. 17 and 26

13. The lengths of the sides of a triangle are consecutive even integers. Find the length of the longest side if it is 22 units shorter than the perimeter. 14 units

14. The length of a rectangle is twice the width. The perimeter is 84 cm more than the width. Make a diagram and find the rectangle's dimensions. 33.6 cm long and 16.8 cm wide

15. Mei's salary starts at $16,000 per year with annual raises of $1500. Janet's starting salary is $19,300 with annual raises of $950. After how many years will the two women be earning the same salary? 6 years

16. A 2000 L tank containing 550 L of water is being filled with water at the rate of 75 L per minute from a full 1600 L tank. How long will it be before the two tanks have the same amount of water? 7 min

17. Eric has twice as much money as Marcia, who has $175 less than Laurel. But Laurel has as much money as Eric and Marcia have together. How much money does each person have? Marcia, $87.50; Eric, $175; Laurel, $262.50

18. A boat weighs 1500 lb more than its motor and 1900 lb more than its trailer. Together the boat and motor weigh five times as much as the trailer. How much does the boat weigh? $2666\frac{2}{3}$ lb

19. Show that it is impossible for three consecutive integers to have a sum that is 200 more than the smallest integer. If $n + (n + 1) + (n + 2) = n + 200$, then $n = 98.5$; not an integer.

20. Is it possible for four consecutive even numbers to have a sum that is ten more than the sum of the smallest two numbers? If so, tell how many solution(s) there are. If there are no solutions, tell why not. yes; one (0, 2, 4, 6)

Solving Equations and Problems   **119**

Simplify.

1. $4 + \left(-\frac{1}{2}\right) + \left(-\frac{3}{2}\right)$ 2

2. $-2\frac{3}{5} + 1\frac{1}{5} - 1\frac{2}{5}$

3. $-212 - (-13)$ -199

4. $17x + (-3)x - 5$ $14x - 5$

5. $-5y + 6 + 20y + 12$ $15y + 18$

6. $7(-3)(-10)(-2)$ -420

Solve.

7. $-3 - x = 9$ $\{-12\}$

8. $5 - (1 + z) = 3$ $\{1\}$

9. $4x = -392$ $\{-98\}$

10. $\frac{1}{2}x = 4\frac{1}{2}$ $\{9\}$

11. $\frac{x}{7} = 6$ $\{42\}$

12. $-12\frac{2}{3} = -\frac{1}{3}x$ $\{38\}$

Using a Computer

In these exercises students will use a computer to solve some equations that have the variable on both sides.

Computer Exercises

For students with some programming experience.

Write a BASIC program to solve an equation of the form $Ax + B = Cx + D$, where the values of A, B, C, and D are entered with INPUT statements. Be sure that the program prints an appropriate message for identities and for equations having no solution. Use the program to solve the following equations.

1. $3x + 4 = 5x + 10$ $\{-3\}$

2. $\frac{1}{2}x + 1 = -2x + 11$ $\{4\}$

3. $4x - 7 = 3 + 4x$ no solution

4. $\frac{1}{2}x + 5 = 5 + \frac{1}{2}x$ identity

5. $3x - 13 = \frac{2}{5}x$ $\{5\}$

6. $3 - x = 4x - 3$ $\{1.2\}$

Self-Test 2

Vocabulary empty set (p. 117) identity (p. 117)
null set (p. 117)

Solve.

1. A $48 sweater costs $6 more than twice as much as the shirt that goes with it. How much does the shirt cost? $21

Obj. 3-4, p. 112

2. $25 - 4n = n$ $\{5\}$

3. $3(x + 1) = 2(x + 5)$ $\{7\}$

Obj. 3-5, p. 116

4. Hilary has three times as much money as Paul. Jeff has $4 less than Hilary and $5 more than Paul. How much money does each have?
Paul, $4.50; Jeff, $9.50; Hilary, $13.50

Check your answers with those at the back of the book.

Quick Quiz

Solve.

1. The length of a rectangle is 5 cm more than 5 times its width. Find the length and the width if the perimeter of the rectangle is 406 cm.
$l = 170$ cm; $w = 33$ cm

2. $36 - 5t = t$ $\{6\}$

3. $8(x + 2) = 5(x - 4)$ $\{-12\}$

4. The green tank contains 23 gallons of water and is being filled at a rate of 4 gallons per minute. The red tank contains 10 gallons of water and is being filled at a rate of 5 gallons per minute. When will the two tanks contain the same amount of water? after 13 min

Extending Your Problem Solving Skills

3-6 Problem Solving: Using Charts

Objective   To organize the facts of a problem in a chart.

Using a chart to organize the facts of a problem can be a helpful problem solving strategy.

Example 1   Organize the given information in a chart:
A roll of carpet 9 ft wide is 20 ft longer than a roll of carpet 12 ft wide.

Solution 1

	Width	Length
First roll	9	l
Second roll	12	$l - 20$

Solution 2

	Width	Length
First roll	9	$l + 20$
Second roll	12	l

Example 2   Solve the problem using the two given facts.
Find the number of Calories in an apple and in a pear.
(1) A pear contains 30 Calories more than an apple.
(2) Ten apples have as many Calories as 7 pears.

Solution

Step 1   The problem asks for the number of Calories in an apple and in a pear.

Step 2   Let $a =$ the number of Calories in an apple.
Then $a + 30 =$ the number of Calories in a pear.

	Calories per fruit $\times$ Number of fruit $=$ Total Calories		
Apple	a	10	$10a$
Pear	$a + 30$	7	$7(a + 30)$

Step 3   Calories in 10 apples = Calories in 7 pears
$$10a = 7(a + 30)$$

Step 4
$$10a = 7a + 210$$
$$3a = 210$$
$$a = 70 \text{ and } a + 30 = 100$$

(Solution continues on the next page.)

Solving Equations and Problems   **121**

Teaching Suggestions, p. T92

Suggested Extensions, p. T93

Warm-Up Exercises
Solve.
1. $4x + 44 = 5x + 55$ $\{-11\}$
2. $4x - 44 = 5x + 55$ $\{-99\}$
3. $4x - 44 = 5x - 55$ $\{11\}$
4. $4x + 44 = 5x - 55$ $\{99\}$

Motivating the Lesson
A chart is helpful in organizing data. Ask students where they have seen charts as a means of presenting data. Ask them to consider the effect on their lives if we didn't have calendars— charts that organize a year's time. Today's lesson involves using charts to organize the facts of a problem.

Chalkboard Examples
Organize the given information in a chart.
1. One board is 4 in. wide and 8 in. longer than a board 2 in. wide.

	Width	Length
1st board	4	$x + 8$
2nd board	2	x

2. Jess bought some boxes of lemonade at seventy cents per box. He bought eight fewer boxes of punch at sixty cents per box.

	No. of boxes	Cents per box	Cost
Lemon.	x	70	$70x$
Punch	$x - 8$	60	$60(x - 8)$

(continued)

121

Chalkboard Examples

(Continued)

Solve the problem using the two given facts. The solution shows Steps 2 through 5.

3. Carrie has 40 more nickels than Joan has dimes. They both have the same amount of money. How many coins does each girl have?

Let x = the number of coins that Joan has. Let $x + 40$ = the number of coins that Carrie has.

	No. of Coins ×	Value per Coin =	Total Value
Carrie	40 + x	5	5(40 + x)
Joan	x	10	10x

$$200 + 5x = 10x$$
$$200 = 5x$$
$$40 = x$$

Check: $10x = 10 \cdot 40 = 400$; $5(40 + x) = 5(40 + 40) = 5(80) = 400$; $400 = 400$

∴ Joan has 40 dimes and Carrie has 80 nickels.

Check for Understanding

Here is a suggested use of the Oral Exercises to check students' understanding as you teach the lesson.
Oral Exs. 1 and 2: use after Example 1.
Oral Ex. 3: use after Example 2.

Guided Practice

Solve the problem using the two given facts. Complete the chart to help you solve the problem.

1. Find how much Kate earned if her earnings were $27 more than the combined earnings of Janet and David.

Step 5 *Check:* (1) 100 Calories is 30 more than 70 Calories. ✓
(2) Ten apples have 10 · 70, or 700 Calories and seven pears have 7 · 100, or 700 Calories. ✓
∴ there are 70 Calories in an apple and 100 Calories in a pear. *Answer*

Oral Exercises

Organize the given information by completing each chart.

1. A swimming pool 25 m long is 13 m narrower than a pool 50 m long.

a.

	Length	Width
1st pool	25	? *w − 13*
2nd pool	50	w

b.

	Length	Width
1st pool	25	w
2nd pool	50	? *w + 13*

2. In game 1, Ellen scored twice as many points as Jody. In game 2 Ellen scored ten fewer points than she did in game 1, while Jody scored 12 more points than she did in game 1.

	Game 1 points	Game 2 points
Ellen	? *2m*	? *2m − 10*
Jody	m	? *m + 12*

3. Use the two given facts to complete the chart. What equation would you write to find the amount of protein in a scrambled egg? $10(x + 1) = 12x$
(1) An egg scrambled with butter and milk has one more gram of protein than an egg fried in butter.
(2) Ten scrambled eggs have as much protein as a dozen fried eggs.

	Protein per egg ×	Number of eggs =	Total protein
Scrambled egg	? *x + 1*	10	? *10(x + 1)*
Fried egg	x	? *12*	? *12x*

Problems

Solve each problem using the two given facts. If a chart is given, first copy and complete the chart to help you solve the problem.

A **1.** Find the number of full 8 hour shifts that Maria worked last month. 14 eight-hour shifts
(1) She worked twice as many 6 hour shifts as 8 hour shifts.
(2) She worked a total of 280 hours. *(Chart on next page)*

122 *Chapter 3*

	Hours per shift × Number of shifts = Total hours worked		
6 h shift	? 6	? 2x	? 12x
8 h shift	? 8	x	? 8x

2. Find the number of round-trip commuter rail tickets sold. 600 round-trip tickets
  (1) Thirty times as many round-trip tickets as 12-ride tickets were sold.
  (2) The total number of tickets sold represented 1440 rides.

	Rides per ticket × Number of tickets sold = Total rides		
12-ride ticket	? 12	n	? 12n
Round-trip ticket	? 2	? 30n	? 60n

3. Find the total weight of the boxes of pecans in a shipment of 3 lb boxes of pecans and 2 lb boxes of walnuts. 306 lb
  (1) There were 24 fewer 2 lb boxes of walnuts than 3 lb boxes of pecans.
  (2) The total weight of the shipment was 462 lb.

	Weight per box × Number of boxes = Total Weight		
Pecans	? 3	? x	? 3x
Walnuts	? 2	? x − 24	?

$2(x - 24)$

4. Find the amount of time Joel spent watching space adventure movies. 9 h
  (1) He saw twice as many $1\frac{1}{2}$ h space movies as he did 2 h mysteries.
  (2) He spent a total of 15 h watching movies.

	Movie length × Number of movies = Total time		
Space movies	? $1\frac{1}{2}$	? 2a	?
Mystery movies	? 2	? a	? 2a

$\left(1\frac{1}{2}\right)2a$

5. Find the number of Calories in an orange and in a peach. Orange, 65 Calories Peach, 35 Calories
  (1) An orange has 30 Calories more than a peach.
  (2) Thirteen peaches have as many Calories as 7 oranges.

6. Find the number of Calories in a stalk of celery and in a carrot.
  (1) A carrot has 13 Calories more than a celery stalk.
  (2) Five carrots and ten celery stalks have only 170 Calories.
  celery, 7 Calories; carrot, 20 Calories

Solve. Use a chart to help you solve the problem.

7. The length of a red rectangle is 15 cm more than its width w. A blue rectangle, which is 5 cm wider and 2 cm shorter than the red one, has perimeter 72 cm. Make a sketch of the rectangles expressing all dimensions in terms of w. Then find the dimensions of each rectangle.
  red rectangle: 9 cm by 24 cm; blue rectangle: 14 cm by 22 cm

Solving Equations and Problems **123**

(1) Janet worked 3 h more than David and 7 h less than Kate.
(2) David earned $7.50/h, Janet $6/h, and Kate $9/h.

	Hours worked ×	Wage per hour =	Total
Janet	$x + 3$	6	$6x + 18$
David	x	7.50	$7.5x$
Kate	$x + 10$	9	$9x + 90$

Kate earned $180.00.

Solve. Use a chart.

2. A stalk of celery contains 7 Calories and a carrot contains 20 Calories. A total of 45 carrots and celery stalks contains a total of 575 Calories. How many carrots are there? 20 carrots

Summarizing the Lesson

A chart can help to organize the information in a problem. In the next lesson students will continue to use charts to solve cost, income, and value problems.

Suggested Assignments

Minimum
Day 1: 122/P: 1–6
   R 120/Self-Test 2
Day 2: 124/P: 8–11
   S 125/Mixed Review
Assign with Lesson 3-7.

Average
Day 1: 122/P: 1–3, 6, 7, 9, 11, 12
   R 120/Self-Test 2
Day 2: 124/P: 14, 16, 18, 19
   S 125/Mixed Review
Assign with Lesson 3-7.

Maximum
Day 1: 122/P: 2–8 even, 10–14
   R 120/Self-Test 2
Day 2: 124/P: 15, 17, 19, 20
   S 125/Mixed Review
Assign with Lesson 3-7.

Solve. Use a chart to help you solve the problem.

8. The length of a rectangle is twice its width w. A second rectangle, which is 8 cm longer and 3 cm narrower than the first rectangle, has perimeter 154 cm. Make a sketch of the rectangles expressing all dimensions in terms of w. Then find the dimensions of each rectangle.
   width: 24 cm, length: 48 cm; width: 21 cm, length, 56 cm

B 9. Brian O'Reilly earns twice as much each week as a tutor than he does pumping gas. His total weekly wages are $150 more than that of his younger sister. She earns one quarter as much as Brian does as a tutor. How much does Brian earn as a tutor? $120

10. Mona Yahuso earns three times as much as an actuary as she does as a writer. Her total income is $40,000 more than that of her brother. He earns half as much as Mona does as an actuary. What is Mona's salary as an actuary? $48,000

11. A roll of carpet 9 ft wide is 30 ft longer than a roll of carpet 15 ft wide. Both rolls have the same area. Make a sketch of the unrolled carpets and find the dimensions of each. 15 ft by 45 ft; 9 ft by 75 ft

12. Leo's garden, which is 6 m wide, has the same area as Jen's garden, which is 8 m wide. Find the lengths of the two rectangular gardens if Leo's garden is 3 m longer than Jen's garden. First make a sketch. Leo, 12 m; Jen, 9 m

13. In March, Rodney sold twice as many cars as Greg. In April, Rodney sold 5 fewer cars than he did in March, while Greg sold 3 more cars than he did in March. If they sold the same number of cars in April, how many cars did each sell in March? Greg, 8; Rodney, 16

14. In one basketball game Maria scored three times as many points as Holly. In the next game, Maria scored 7 fewer points than she did in the first game, while Holly scored 9 more points than she did in the first game. If they scored the same number of points in the second game, how many points did each score in the first game? Holly, 8; Maria, 24

15. Paula mixed 2 cups of sunflower seeds and 3 cups of raisins to make a snack for a hike. She figured that the mixture would provide her with 2900 Calories of food energy. Find the number of Calories per cup of raisins if it is 400 less than the number of Calories per cup of sunflower seeds. 420 Calories

16. The Eiffel Tower is 497 ft taller than the Washington Monument. If each of the monuments were 58 ft shorter, the Eiffel Tower would be twice as tall as the Washington Monument. How tall is each? tower, 1052 ft; monument, 555 ft

17. The upper Angel Falls, the highest waterfall on Earth, are 750 m higher than Niagara Falls. If each of the falls were 7 m lower, the upper Angel Falls would be 16 times as high as Niagara Falls. How high is each waterfall? Angel Falls, 807 m; Niagara Falls, 57 m

18. Nine cartons of juice cost the same as 5 fruit cups. Also, one fruit cup costs 50¢ more than one bowl of soup, while one bowl of soup costs 50¢ more than one carton of juice. What would be the cost of each item: a carton of juice, a fruit cup, and a bowl of soup? fruit cup, $2.25; juice, $1.25; soup, $1.75

19. One serving ($\frac{1}{2}$ cup) of cooked peas contains 45 more Calories than one serving of cooked carrots and 50 more Calories than one serving of cooked green beans. If one serving of carrots and three servings of green beans contain the same number of Calories as one serving of peas, how many Calories are there in one serving of peas? 65 Calories

C 20. The cross-country teams of East High and West High run against each other twice each fall. At the first meet, East's score was two thirds of West's score. At the second meet, East's score increased by seven points and West's score decreased by seven points. In the second meet West's score was three less than East's score. How many points did each team score in each meet? East scored 22 and 29 points; West scored 33 and 26 points.

Mixed Review Exercises

Solve.

1. $25z = 600$ {24}

2. $6 = \frac{2}{5}x$ {15}

3. $12z - 3z = 0$ {0}

4. $195 = 3x$ {65}

5. $7y + 3 = 24$ {3}

6. $-12 + 3y = -36$ {−8}

7. $5x - 2x = 21$ {7}

8. $4(x + 2) = 6x$ {4}

9. $7x - 11 = 2x + 44$ {11}

10. $41 - x = -1 - 7x$ {−7}

11. $-x = 2x - 54$ {18}

12. $5(y + 2) - 3(y - 1) = -27$ {−20}

 Career Note / *Astronomer*

Modern astronomers make few direct observations with telescopes. Instead, they use mathematics and physics to explore the nature of the universe. Their theories are described by mathematical equations that are tested on computers using data from observatories.

Observatories often gather data with radio telescopes and spectroscopes. Radio telescopes are used to detect the invisible x rays and radio waves that are emitted by stars. Spectroscopes, on the other hand, are used to separate a star's visible light into its various wave lengths, to form the star's spectral pattern.

With the aid of a computer, as shown in the photo, an astronomer can analyze a star's spectral pattern to determine whether the star is moving toward or away from the Earth.

Most astronomers work in universities or government space centers as teachers or researchers. They are highly trained in mathematics and physics and most have a Ph.D. in astronomy.

Solving Equations and Problems **125**

Warm-Up Exercises

Multiply each rate in column A by an appropriate number in column B.

A	B
1. 45 mi/h	a. 3 seconds
2. 4 cm/s	b. 23 liters
3. 80 Cal/apple	c. 24 hours
4. 9 g/liter	d. 100 apples

1. c. 1080 mi   **2.** a. 12 cm
3. d. 8000 Cal   **4.** b. 207 g

Motivating the Lesson

A rate is often used to compare two quantities such as 40 miles per hour or $8.00 per ticket. Ask students to think of other familiar rates. Today's lesson shows how certain rates are used in solving problems that involve cost, income, and value.

Chalkboard Examples

Solve. The solution shows Steps 2–5.

An apple sells for 25 cents and a peach sells for 15 cents. A total of 10 pieces of fruit were sold for a total cost of $2.10. How many apples were sold?

Let x = the number of apples sold.
Then $10 - x$ = the number of peaches sold.
Make a chart.

Fruit	No.	$\times$ Price per Fruit =	Cost
Apple	x	25	$25x$
Peach	$10 - x$	15	$15(10 - x)$

3-7 Cost, Income, and Value Problems

Objective   To solve problems involving cost, income, and value.

The word problems in this lesson involve cost, income, and value. Organizing the given facts in a chart will help you to solve such problems. The following formulas will be useful in setting up your charts.

$$\text{Cost} = \text{number of items} \times \text{price per item}$$

$$\text{Income} = \text{hours worked} \times \text{wage per hour}$$

$$\text{Total value} = \text{number of items} \times \text{value per item}$$

Example   Tickets for the senior class play cost $6 for adults and $3 for students. A total of 846 tickets worth $3846 were sold. How many student tickets were sold?

Solution

Step 1 The problem asks for the number of student tickets sold.

Step 2 Let x = the number of student tickets sold.
Then $846 - x$ = the number of adult tickets sold.

Make a chart.

	Number $\times$	Price per ticket =	Cost
Student	x	3	$3x$
Adult	$846 - x$	6	$6(846 - x)$

Step 3 The only fact not recorded in the chart is that the total cost of the tickets was $3846. Write an equation using this fact.

$$\text{Student ticket cost} + \text{adult ticket cost} = 3846$$
$$3x + 6(846 - x) = 3846$$

Step 4
$$3x + 5076 - 6x = 3846$$
$$5076 - 3x = 3846$$
$$-3x = -1230$$
$$x = 410 \leftarrow \text{student tickets}$$
$$846 - x = 436 \leftarrow \text{adult tickets}$$

Step 5 *Check:*   410 student tickets at $3 each cost $1230.
436 adult tickets at $6 each cost $2616.

The total number of tickets is $410 + 436$, or 846.
The total cost of the tickets is $1230 + 2616$, or $3846.   ✓

$\therefore$ 410 student tickets were sold.   **Answer**

126   *Chapter 3*

Oral Exercises

Read each problem and complete the chart. Then give an equation that can be used to solve the problem.

1. Marlee makes $5 an hour working after school and $6 an hour working on Saturdays. Last week she made $64.50 by working a total of 12 hours. How many hours did she work on Saturday? $6s + 5(12 - s) = 64.50$

	Hours worked	× Wage per hour	= Income
Saturdays	s	? 6	? 6s
Weekdays	?	?	?

$$12 - s \qquad 5 \qquad 5(12 - s)$$

2. Ernesto purchased 100 postage stamps worth $9.90. Half of them were 1¢ stamps, and the rest were 14¢ and 22¢ stamps. How many 22¢ stamps did he buy? (*Hint:* In your equation, use 990¢ instead of $9.90.)
$50 + 14(50 - x) + 22x = 990$

	Number	× Price	= Cost
1¢ stamps	? 50	? 1	? 50
14¢ stamps	?	? 14	?
22¢ stamps	x	? 22	?

$$50 - x \qquad\qquad 14(50 - x)$$
$$22x$$

Problems

Solve. Copy and complete the chart first.

A

1. Thirty students bought pennants for the football game. Plain pennants cost $4 each and fancy ones cost $8 each. If the total bill was $168, how many students bought the fancy pennants?
12 students

$$30 - f \qquad 8 \qquad 8f$$
$$4 \qquad 4(30 - f)$$

	Number	× Price	= Cost
Fancy	f	?	?
Plain	?	?	?

2. Adult tickets for the game cost $4 each and student tickets cost $2 each. A total of 920 tickets worth $2446 were sold. How many student tickets were sold? 617 student tickets

$$920 - s \qquad 4 \qquad 4(920 - s)$$

	Number	× Price	= Cost
Adult	?	?	?
Student	s	? 2	? 2s

3. A collection of 40 dimes and nickels is worth $2.90. How many nickels are there? (*Hint:* In your equation, use 290¢ instead of $2.90.) 22 nickels

$$40 - n \qquad 10 \qquad 10(40 - n)$$

	Number	× Value of coin	= Total value
Dimes	?	?	?
Nickels	? n	? 5	? 5n

Solving Equations and Problems **127**

The only fact not recorded on the chart is that 10 pieces of fruit were sold for $2.10. Write an equation using this fact.

$$25(x) + 15(10 - x) = 210$$
$$25x + 150 - 15x = 210$$
$$10x + 150 = 210$$
$$10x = 60$$
$$x = 6$$

6 apples were sold.

Check for Understanding

Here is a suggested use of the Oral Exercises to check students' understanding as you teach the lesson.
Oral Exs. 1 and 2: use after the example.

Guided Practice

Solve. Copy and complete the chart first.

1. Coria and Kip went to the record store during its sale. Together they spent $38.50. If each record cost $3.50 and Kip bought one more than Coria, how many records did each buy?

	No.	× Price	= Cost
Coria	r	3.50	3.5r
Kip	$r + 1$	3.50	$3.5(r + 1)$

Coria bought 5; Kip bought 6

Summarizing the Lesson

Point out that the first step in solving many complicated problems is to organize the data into a chart. Doing so should make it easier to write the equation needed to solve the problem.

Solve. If a chart is given, copy and complete the chart first.

4. A collection of 52 dimes and nickels is worth $4.50. How many nickels are there? 14 nickels

	Number ×	Value of coin (¢) =	Total value (¢)
Dimes	? d	? 10	? 10d
Nickels	?	?	?
	52 − d	5	5(52 − d)

5. Hans paid $1.50 each for programs to the game. He sold all but 20 of them for $3 each and made a profit of $15. How many programs did he buy? (*Hint:* Profit = selling price − purchase price) 50 programs

	Number ×	Price ($) =	Cost ($)
Bought	? b	? 1.5	? 1.5b
Sold	?	?	?
	b − 20	3	3(b − 20)

6. Celia bought 12 apples, ate two of them, and sold the rest at 20¢ more per apple than she paid. Her total profit was $1.00. How much did she sell each apple for? 70¢

	Number ×	Price (¢) =	Cost (¢)
Bought	? 12	? b	? 12b
Sold	?	?	?
	10	b + 20	10(b + 20)

B

7. I have twice as many nickels as quarters. If the coins are worth $4.90, how many quarters are there? 14 quarters

8. I have eight more quarters than dimes. If the coins are worth $6.20, how many dimes are there? 12 dimes

9. The Audio Outlet purchased 60 cassette recorders, gave away three in a contest, and sold the rest at twice their purchase price. If the store's total profit was $1188, how much did the store sell each recorder for? $44

10. The Alan Company bought 80 tickets for a jazz concert. After giving away 20 tickets to customers, the company sold the rest to employees at half of the purchase price. If the company absorbed a $1000 loss on all the tickets, how much did an employee pay for a ticket? $10

11. A plumber makes $4.50 per hour more than his apprentice. During an 8-hour day, their combined earnings total $372. How much does each make per hour? (*Hint:* If you decide to use cents instead of dollars, then use 450 cents per hour and 37200 cents total earnings.) plumber, $25.50; apprentice, $21

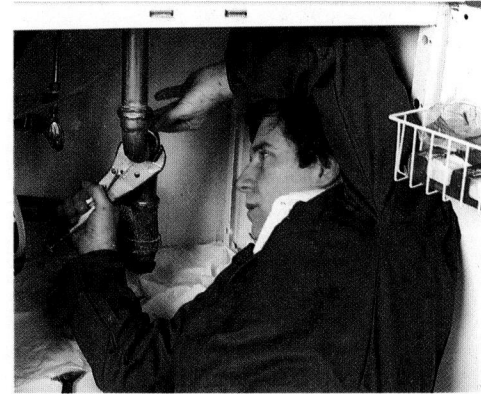

12. Raul works 2 h daily after school, Monday through Friday. On Saturdays he works 8 h at $2 more per hour than on weekdays. If he makes $142 per week, how much does he make per hour on weekdays? $7

128 *Chapter 3*

13. Warren has 40 coins (all nickels, dimes, and quarters) worth $4.05. He has 7 more nickels than dimes. How many quarters does Warren have? 7 quarters

14. Jo has 37 coins (all nickels, dimes, and quarters) worth $5.50. She has 4 more quarters than nickels. How many dimes does Jo have? 9 dimes

15. Rory claims: "I have $20 in quarters, half dollars, and one-dollar bills. I have twice as many quarters as half dollars, and half as many one-dollar bills as half dollars." Give a convincing argument to explain why he must be wrong. Rory would have to have $13\frac{1}{3}$ half dollars, which is impossible.

16. Eleanor claims: "It is possible for 46 pennies and nickels to have a total value of a dollar." Is she right or wrong? Give a convincing argument to justify your answer. Eleanor is wrong; there would have to be $32\frac{1}{2}$ pennies, which is impossible.

C 17. Nadine has seven more nickels than Delano has dimes. If Delano gives Nadine four of his dimes, then Delano will have the same amount of money as Nadine. How much money do they have together? (Assume that Nadine has only nickels and Delano has only dimes.) $3.80

18. Natalie has some nickels, Dirk has some dimes, and Quincy has some quarters. Dirk has five more dimes than Quincy has quarters. If Natalie gives Dirk a nickel, Dirk gives Quincy a dime, and Quincy gives Natalie a quarter, they will all have the same amount of money. How many coins did each have originally?
Natalie, 13 nickels; Dirk, 9 dimes; Quincy, 4 quarters

Mixed Review Exercises

Simplify.

1. $\dfrac{40 \div 5 + 3}{13 - 2}$ 1

2. $36 \div \dfrac{1}{6}$ 216

3. $\dfrac{1}{3}(39y - 6) + 3$ 13y + 1

4. $(-7)(5)(-1)$ 35

5. $4(2x + 7) + 5(-x)$ 3x + 28

6. $7(x + y) + 8(2y + x)$
   15x + 23y

Evaluate if $a = 4$, $b = 5$, and $x = 8$.

7. $\dfrac{5a + b}{x - 3}$ 5

8. $\dfrac{ab}{4x}$ $\dfrac{5}{8}$

9. $3(a + b) - x \div 2$ 23

Computer Exercises

For students with some programming experience.

Jane has a total of 12 coins, some of which are nickels and the rest dimes.

1. Write a BASIC program that uses a FOR . . . NEXT loop to print a chart showing every possible combination of dimes and nickels. The chart should also show the total value of the coins for each combination.

2. Modify the program from Exercise 1 to print the chart for K coins. The value of K should be entered with an input statement.

Using a Computer
In these exercises students will use a computer to chart possible combinations of coins and their total values. Such charts are helpful when applying the trial-and-error (guess-and-check) problem solving strategy.

Warm-Up Exercises

Name the property used in each equation. You may refer to the Glossary of Properties on page 687.

1. $3 + 45 = 45 + 3$
Comm. prop. of add.

2. $(3 \times 2) \times 5 = 3 \times (2 \times 5)$
Assoc. prop. of mult.

3. $4 \times \frac{1}{4} = 1$
Prop. of recip.

4. $246 + 0 = 246$
Iden. prop. of add.

5. $(17) + (-17) = 0$
Prop. of opp.

Motivating the Lesson

Tell students that they can use the properties about the real number system they have learned to prove some further statements about the system. These new statements are known as *theorems* because they can be proved. Proving statements is the topic of today's lesson.

Chalkboard Examples

1. Write the missing reasons. Prove: for all numbers a and b, if $a + b = 0$, then $b = -a$.
Proof:
1. $a + b = 0$ Given
2. $a + (-a) = 0$
   Prop. of opp.
3. $a + b = a + (-a)$
   Trans. prop. of eq.
4. $-a + [a + b] =$
   $-a + [a + (-a)]$
   Add. prop. of eq.
5. $[-a + a] + b =$
   $[-a + a] + (-a)$
   Assoc. prop. of add.

3-8 Proof in Algebra

Objective   To prove statements in algebra.

Some of the properties stated earlier in this book are statements we assume to be true. Others are theorems. A **theorem** is a statement that is shown to be true using a logically developed argument. Logical reasoning that uses given facts, definitions, properties, and other already proved theorems to show that a theorem is true is called a **proof.** Example 1 shows how a theorem is proved in algebra.

Example 1   *Prove:*   For all numbers a and b, $(a + b) - b = a$.

Proof

Statements	Reasons
1. $(a + b) - b = (a + b) + (-b)$	1. Definition of subtraction
2. $(a + b) + (-b) = a + [b + (-b)]$	2. Associative property of addition
3. $b + (-b) = 0$	3. Property of opposites
4. $a + [b + (-b)] = a + 0$	4. Substitution principle
5. $a + 0 = a$	5. Identity property of addition
6. $(a + b) - b = a$	6. Transitive property of equality

Generally, a shortened form of proof is given, in which only the *key reasons* are stated. (The substitution principle and properties of equality are usually not stated.) The proof shown in Example 1 could be shortened to the steps shown below.

Statements	Reasons
1. $(a + b) - b = (a + b) + (-b)$	1. Definition of subtraction
2. $= a + [b + (-b)]$	2. Associative property of addition
3. $= a + 0$	3. Property of opposites
4. $= a$	4. Identity property of addition

Example 2   *Prove:*   For all real numbers a and b such that $a \neq 0$ and $b \neq 0$,
$$\frac{1}{ab} = \frac{1}{a} \cdot \frac{1}{b}. \qquad \text{(Property of the reciprocal of a product)}$$

Proof   Since $\frac{1}{ab}$ is the unique reciprocal of ab, you can prove that $\frac{1}{ab} = \frac{1}{a} \cdot \frac{1}{b}$ by showing that the product of ab and $\frac{1}{a} \cdot \frac{1}{b}$ is 1:

Statements	Reasons
1. $(ab)\left(\frac{1}{a} \cdot \frac{1}{b}\right) = \left(a \cdot \frac{1}{a}\right)\left(b \cdot \frac{1}{b}\right)$	1. Commutative and associative properties of multiplication
2. $= 1 \cdot 1$	2. Property of reciprocals
3. $= 1$	3. Identity property of multiplication

130   *Chapter 3*

Once a theorem has been proved, it can be used as a reason in other proofs. You may refer to the Chapter Summary on page 88 for listings of properties and theorems that you can use as reasons in your proofs in the following exercises.

Oral Exercises

State the missing reasons. Assume that each variable represents any real number.

1. *Prove:* If $a = b$, then $a + c = b + c$.
   (Addition property of equality)

   Proof: 1. $a + c = a + c$ 1. __?__ property of equality Reflexive
            2. $a = b$ 2. Given
            3. $a + c = b + c$ 3. __?__ principle Substitution

2. *Prove:* If $a = b$, then $a - c = b - c$.
   (Subtraction property of equality)

   Proof: 1. $a = b$ 1. __?__ Given
            2. Since c is a real number,   2. Property of opposites
               $-c$ is a real number.
            3. $a + (-c) = b + (-c)$ 3. __?__ property of equality Addition
                                                   (proved in Oral Exercise 1)
            4. $a - c = b - c$ 4. Definition of __?__ subtraction

3. *Prove:* If $a = b$, then $-a = -b$.

   Proof: 1. $a = b$ 1. __?__ Given
            2. $a + (-b) = b + (-b)$ 2. __?__ property of equality Addition
            3. $a + (-b) = 0$ 3. Property of __?__ opposites
            4. $-a + [a + (-b)] = -a + 0$ 4. __?__ property of equality Addition
            5. $(-a + a) + (-b) = -a + 0$ 5. __?__ property of addition Associative
            6. $0 + (-b) = -a + 0$ 6. Property of __?__ opposites
            7. $-b = -a$ 7. __?__ property of addition Identity
            8. $-a = -b$ 8. __?__ property of equality Symmetric

Written Exercises

Write the missing reasons. Assume that each variable represents any real number.

A **1.** *Prove:* If $a = b$, then $ca = cb$.
       (Multiplication property of equality)

   Proof: 1. $ca = ca$ 1. __?__ Reflex. prop. of $=$
            2. $a = b$ 2. Given
            3. $ca = cb$ 3. __?__ Substitution principle

Solving Equations and Problems **131**

6. $0 + b = 0 + (-a)$
   Prop. of opp.
7. $b = -a$
   Iden. prop. of add.

2. Prove:
   $\dfrac{a - b}{c} = \dfrac{a}{c} - \dfrac{b}{c}, c \neq 0.$

   1. $\dfrac{a - b}{c} = (a - b) \cdot \dfrac{1}{c}$
      Def. of div.

   2. $= \left(a \cdot \dfrac{1}{c}\right) - \left(b \cdot \dfrac{1}{c}\right)$
      Dist. prop.

   3. $= \dfrac{a}{c} - \dfrac{b}{c}$ Def. of div.

Check for Understanding

Here is a suggested use of the Oral Exercises to check students' understanding as you teach the lesson.
Oral Exs. 1–3: use after Example 2.

Guided Practice

Write the missing reasons. Assume that each variable represents any real number.
Prove: If $a = b$ and $c = d$, then $ac = bd$.
Proof:
1. $a = b$ Given
2. $ac = bc$ Mult. prop. eq.
3. $c = d$ Given
4. $bc = bd$ Mult. prop. eq.
5. $ac = bd$ Trans prop. eq.

Summarizing the Lesson

Point out that the students have used the properties developed from Chapters 1, 2, and 3 to prove statements about the set of real numbers.

Suggested Assignments

Average
   131/1–9 odd
S 133/Mixed Review
Maximum
   131/2–8 even, 9–11
S 133/Mixed Review

Write the missing reasons in Exercises 2–8. Assume that each variable represents any real number, except as noted.

2. *Prove:*   If $a + c = b + c$, then $a = b$.

    Proof:

1. $\quad a + c = b + c$	1. Given
2. $(a + c) + (-c) = (b + c) + (-c)$	2. __?__ Add. prop. of =
3. $a + [c + (-c)] = b + [c + (-c)]$	3. __?__ Assoc. prop. of add.
4. $\quad a + 0 = b + 0$	4. __?__ Prop. of opposites
5. $\quad\quad a = b$	5. __?__ Identity prop. of add.

3. *Prove:*   If $ac = bc$ and $c \neq 0$, then $a = b$.

    Proof:

1. $\quad ac = bc$	1. Given
2. $(ac) \cdot \dfrac{1}{c} = (bc) \cdot \dfrac{1}{c}$	2. __?__ Mult. prop. of =
3. $a\left(c \cdot \dfrac{1}{c}\right) = b\left(c \cdot \dfrac{1}{c}\right)$	3. __?__ Assoc. prop. of mult.
4. $\quad a \cdot 1 = b \cdot 1$	4. __?__ Prop. of reciprocals
5. $\quad\quad a = b$	5. __?__ Identity prop. of mult.

4. *Prove:*   If $b \neq 0$, then $\dfrac{1}{b}(ba) = a$ and $(ab)\dfrac{1}{b} = a$.

    Proof:

1. $\dfrac{1}{b}(ba) = \left(\dfrac{1}{b} \cdot b\right)a$	1. __?__ Assoc. prop. of mult.
2. $\quad\quad = 1 \cdot a$	2. __?__ Prop. of reciprocals
3. $\quad\quad = a$	3. __?__ Identity prop. of mult.

    From Step 3 prove that $(ab)\dfrac{1}{b} = a$.

4. $\dfrac{1}{b}(ba) = a$	4. (Step 3, above)
5. $(ba)\dfrac{1}{b} = a$	5. __?__ Comm. prop. of mult.
6. $(ab)\dfrac{1}{b} = a$	6. __?__ Comm. prop. of mult.

B   **5.** *Prove:* $-(-b) = b$

    Proof:

1. $\quad\quad b + (-b) = 0$	1. __?__ Prop. of opposites
2. $(-b) + [-(-b)] = 0$	2. __?__ Prop. of opposites
3. $(-b) + [-(-b)] = b + (-b)$	3. __?__ Substitution principle
4. $[-(-b)] + (-b) = b + (-b)$	4. __?__ Comm. prop. of add.
5. $\quad\quad -(-b) = b$	5. Proved in Oral Exercise 2

6. *Prove:* $-(a + b) = (-a) + (-b)$
        (Property of the opposite of a sum)

    Proof: Since $-(a + b)$ is the unique additive inverse of $(a + b)$, we can prove that $-(a + b) = (-a) + (-b)$ by showing that the sum of $(a + b)$ and $[(-a) + (-b)]$ is 0.   *(Proof continues on next page.)*

1. $(a + b) + [(-a) + (-b)] = [(a + b) + (-a)] + (-b)$ 1. $\underset{?}{\text{Assoc. prop. of add.}}$

2. $\qquad\qquad\qquad\qquad = [a + (-a) + b] + (-b)$ 2. $\underset{?}{\text{Assoc., comm. props.}}$

3. $\qquad\qquad\qquad\qquad = [0 + b] + (-b)$ 3. $\underset{?}{\text{Prop. of opposites}}$

4. $\qquad\qquad\qquad\qquad = b + (-b)$ 4. $\underset{?}{\text{Identity prop. of add.}}$

5. $\qquad\qquad\qquad\qquad = 0$ 5. $\underset{?}{\text{Prop. of opposites}}$

7. Prove: $-(a - b) = b - a$

   Proof:

1. $-(a - b) = -[a + (-b)]$ 1. Definition of __?__ subtraction
2. $\qquad\quad = (-a) + [-(-b)]$ 2. Property of the opposite of a sum (proved in Exercise 6)
3. $\qquad\quad = (-a) + b$ 3. Proved in Exercise __?__ 5
4. $\qquad\quad = b + (-a)$ 4. __?__ Comm. prop. of add.
5. $\qquad\quad = b - a$ 5. __?__ Def. of subtr.

8. Prove: $-(-a - b) = a + b$

   Proof:

1. $-(-a - b) = -[-a + (-b)]$ 1. Definition of __?__ subtraction
2. $\qquad\qquad = -(-a) + [-(-b)]$ 2. Property of the opposite of a sum (proved in Exercise 6)
3. $\qquad\qquad = a + b$ 3. Proved in Exercise __?__ 5

Write proofs giving statements and reasons.

C   **9. Prove:** If a and b are any real numbers, c is any nonzero real number, and $a = b$, then $\dfrac{a}{c} = \dfrac{b}{c}$. (*Hint:* Use Exercise 1.)

10. Prove: If a is any nonzero real number, then $\dfrac{a}{a} = 1$.

11. Prove: If a and b are nonzero real numbers, then $\dfrac{1}{\frac{a}{b}} = \dfrac{b}{a}$. (*Hint:* Show that $\dfrac{a}{b} \cdot \dfrac{b}{a} = 1$.)

Mixed Review Exercises

Simplify.

1. $12(12 - 7) \div 6 + 4$ 14   **2.** $-4(-16 + 8)$ 32   **3.** $-7x - 2x + 12x$ 3x

4. $-\dfrac{1}{2}(8 + 2a)$ $-4 - a$ **5.** $\dfrac{1}{2}(2b - 4) + 3$ $b + 1$ **6.** $10 \div \dfrac{1}{2}$ 20

Evaluate if $a = 5$, $b = 4$, $c = 3$, and $x = 6$.

7. $a(b + x)$ 50   **8.** $3|x - a|$ 3   **9.** $b - |x - a|$ 3

10. $\dfrac{b + 2a}{|1 - c|x}$ $\dfrac{7}{6}$ **11.** $\dfrac{5a + x + 4}{b + c}$ 5   **12.** $\dfrac{1}{2}(c - a) + x$ 5

Solving Equations and Problems   **133**

Self-Test 3

Vocabulary   theorem (p. 130)   proof (p. 130)

1. The length of a rectangle is 8 cm more than the width. A second rectangle is 5 cm wider and 6 cm longer than the first rectangle. The second rectangle has a perimeter of 242 cm. Find the dimensions of each rectangle. Make a sketch first. 51 cm by 59 cm; 56 cm by 65 cm   **Obj. 3-6, p. 121**

2. Jeremy had 34 nickels and quarters totaling $4.10. He had two less than twice as many nickels as quarters. How many of each did he have? nickels, 22; quarters, 12   **Obj. 3-7, p. 126**

3. Write the missing reasons.   **Obj. 3-8, p. 130**

   1. $-a + (a + b) = (-a + a) + b$ 1. __?__ Assoc. prop. of add.
   2. $\qquad\qquad = 0 + b$ 2. __?__ Prop. of opposites
   3. $\qquad\qquad = b$ 3. __?__ Identity prop. of add.

Check your answers with those at the back of the book.

Chapter Summary

1. The addition, subtraction, multiplication, and division properties of equality guarantee that:
   a. Adding the same real number to, or subtracting the same real number from, equal numbers gives equal results.
   b. Multiplying or dividing equal numbers by the same nonzero real number gives equal results.

2. Transforming an equation by substitution, by addition or subtraction, or by multiplication or division (not by zero) produces an equivalent equation. These transformations are used in solving equations.

3. Inverse operations are used in solving equations.

4. Equations can be used to solve word problems. Organizing the facts of a word problem in a chart is often helpful.

5. The following formulas are helpful in setting up charts to solve problems about cost, income, and value.

   Cost = number of items × price per item

   Income = hours worked × wage per hour

   Value = number of items × value per item

6. Theorems are proved by logically developing an argument to support them. In such a proof, each step is justified by a definition, property, or previously proven theorem.

Supplementary Materials

Practice Master   15
Resource Book   pp. 194–195

Chapter Review

Write the letter of the correct answer.

1. Solve $20 = 5 + x$.   3-1
   a. 25   **b.** -15 **c.** 15   **d.** -25

2. Solve $y - 17 = 19$.
   a. -36 **b.** 2   **c.** 26   **d.** 36

3. Solve $\frac{1}{9}x = 5$.   3-2

   a. $\frac{5}{9}$ **b.** $5\frac{1}{9}$ **c.** $4\frac{5}{9}$ **d.** 45

4. Solve $4n = -2$.

   a. 6   **b.** 2   **c.** -2 **d.** $-\frac{1}{2}$

5. Solve $\frac{1}{3}x - 3 = -3$.   3-3
   a. 0   **b.** -18 **c.** 18   **d.** 2

6. Solve $b - 3b = 24$.
   a. -8 **b.** -12 **c.** 12   **d.** -6

7. Howard works an 8-hour day at his gas station. He spends twice as much   3-4
   time working on cars as he does waiting on customers. He takes $1\frac{1}{4}$ hours
   to eat lunch and balance his books. How many hours does he spend waiting on customers?

   a. 2 h   **b.** $2\frac{1}{4}$ h   **c.** $1\frac{1}{4}$ h   **d.** $4\frac{1}{2}$ h

8. Solve $2m = 1 - m$.   3-5

   a. $\frac{1}{3}$ **b.** 2   **c.** 1   **d.** 3

9. Solve $3w - 13 = \frac{1}{4}(52 - 12w)$.

   a. $4\frac{1}{3}$ **b.** -1 **c.** no solution   **d.** identity

10. Arthur weighs 34 lb more than Lily. Their combined weight is 180 lb less   3-6
    than four times Lily's weight. How much does Arthur weigh?
    a. 141 lb   **b.** 151 lb   **c.** 107 lb   **d.** 127 lb

11. Nick worked 16 hours last week. He earned $5 per hour at a local restau-   3-7
    rant and $5.50 per hour at a grocery store. If he earned a total of $82, how
    many hours did he work at the grocery store?
    a. 8 h   **b.** 4 h   **c.** 12 h   **d.** 2 h

12. Which of the following properties should be given as the reason for the   3-8
    statement $a(bc) = a(cb)$?
    a. Distributive property   **b.** Associative property of multiplication
    c. Property of opposites   **d.** Commutative property of multiplication

---

Solving Equations and Problems   **135**

Supplementary Materials

Test Masters   13, 14
Resource Book   pp. 14–17

Chapter Test

Solve.

1. $y + 25 = 10$ {−15}   **2.** $73 = h − 13$ {86}   **3-1**
3. $c + 51 = 38$ {−13}   **4.** $x − 38 = 12$ {50}

5. $\dfrac{1}{13}y = 65$ {845}   **6.** $−19v = −114$ {6}   **3-2**

7. $−112 = 16e$ {−7}   **8.** $−\dfrac{x}{21} = 35$ {−735}

9. $12y − 7 = 113$ {10}   **10.** $\dfrac{2}{3}x + 6 = 16$ {15}   **3-3**

11. $\dfrac{3x + 90}{5} = 0$ {−30}   **12.** $−\dfrac{7}{8}(w − 16) = 70$ {−64}

13. In the game of basketball you can score one point for a foul shot, two   **3-4**
points for a regular shot and three points for an outside shot. Manuel
scored 30 points by making eight foul shots and two outside shots. How
many regular shots did he make? Use the five-step plan. 8

**Solve each equation. If the equation is an identity or if it has no solution,
write *identity* or *no solution*.**

14. $7(a − 6) = −3 + 6a$ {39}   **15.** $6(m − 1) = 6(m + 3)$ no solution   **3-5**

Solve. In Exercises 17 and 18, use a chart to help you.

16. Three times a number increased by 44 is the same as the opposite of the
number. Find the number. −11

17. Sean weighs 10 lb more than twice Brad's weight. If Brad gains 10 lb,   **3-6**
together they'll weigh 230 lb. How much does each weigh now? Brad 70 lb; Sean 150 lb

18. When Courtney collected her change she realized that she had five times as   **3-7**
many dimes as quarters. Her dimes and quarters totaled $5.25. How many
quarters did she have? 7

19. Write the missing reasons to justify the multiplicative property of zero.   **3-8**

1.	$0 = 0 + 0$	1. ___?___	Identity prop. of add.
2.	$a \cdot 0 = a(0 + 0)$	2. ___?___	Mult. prop. of =
3.	$a \cdot 0 = a \cdot 0 + a \cdot 0$	3. ___?___	Dist. prop.
4.	But $a \cdot 0 = a \cdot 0 + 0$	4. Identity property of addition	
5.	$\therefore a \cdot 0 + a \cdot 0 = a \cdot 0 + 0$	5. ___?___	Trans. prop. of =
6.	$a \cdot 0 = 0$	6. ___?___	Subtr. prop. of =
7.	$0 \cdot a = 0$	7. ___?___	Comm. prop. of mult.

136   *Chapter 3*

Cumulative Review *(Chapters 1–3)*

Cumulative Review, p. T24

Supplementary Materials
Practice Masters   16, 17
Resource Book, pp. 18–19,
     89–90, 146–147

Simplify.

1. $45 - 2(16 - 6)$ 25   2. $\dfrac{56 \div 7}{16}$ $\frac{1}{2}$ 3. $48 \div (9 + 3)$ 4

4. $|-21| - |-14|$ 7   5. $31 - [35 \div 5]$ 24   6. $48 \div 3 + 7(3)$ 37

7. $-55 - (-42 + 7)$ -20 8. $-22 + 31 + (-44) + 50$ 15   9. $1\frac{1}{3} - 10\frac{1}{4} + 12\frac{2}{3}$ $3\frac{3}{4}$

10. $2.4 + 5.1 - 6.3$ 1.2   11. $9 + x - (5 - x) - 6$ $2x - 2$ 12. $4(x + 3y) - 3(x - 4y)$
                                                                       $x + 24y$

13. $-5(42)\left(-\dfrac{2}{5}\right)\left(-\dfrac{1}{3}\right)$ 14. $-5(-a - b) + 5(a + b)$ 15. $\dfrac{85xy}{5y}$; $y \neq 0$ 17x
          -28 $10a + 10b$

Evaluate if $w = 2$, $x = -3$, $y = \dfrac{1}{2}$, and $z = 3$.

16. $w - |z - x|$ -4 17. $\dfrac{4y - x}{w + z}$ 1   18. $-5(x + w)$ 5   19. $-w + 2x + 4y$ -6

State the coordinate of the given point.

20. The point halfway between F and G. $-\dfrac{1}{2}$
21. The point halfway between B and C. $-4\dfrac{1}{2}$

Solve. If the equation is an identity or has no solution, state that fact.

22. $|x| = 3$ {3, −3}   23. $|y| = -2$ no sol.   24. $x + 7 = 12$ {5}

25. $z + 1 = -3$ {−4}   26. $y + 2 = 9$ {7}   27. $(x - 3) + 17 = 30$ {16}

28. $\dfrac{a}{3} = -14$ {−42}   29. $9 = \dfrac{1}{2}q$ {18}   30. $2x + 6 = -2$ {−4}

31. $\dfrac{1}{2}(2x + 4) = 2x$ {2}   32. $16 = \dfrac{3}{4}k + 1$ {20}   33. $5(z - 3) = 40$ {11}

34. $5y - 2 = 7y + 8$ {−5}   35. $9(2 - b) = b$ $\left\{\dfrac{9}{5}\right\}$ 36. $3(x - 4) = 6(x - 3)$ {2}

Solve.

37. A honeydew melon costs four times as much as a peach. Together they
cost $1.50. How much does each cost?   peach, $.30; melon, $1.20

38. Find three consecutive integers whose sum is 87.   28, 29, 30

39. Thirty-eight employees at High Tech Sales ride to work on the subway.
This represents $\frac{2}{5}$ of the employees. How many employees are there?   95 employees

40. Rory has 30 coins (all nickels and dimes). He has five times as many nickels as dimes. How much money does he have? $1.75

Solving Equations and Problems   **137**

Maintaining Skills

Express each fraction as a mixed number.

| Sample 1 | $\frac{35}{13}$ | Solution | $13\overline{)35}$ $\frac{2}{}$ $\underline{26}$ 9 | $\therefore \frac{35}{13} = 2\frac{9}{13}$ |

1. $\frac{25}{12}$ $\;2\frac{1}{12}$
2. $\frac{45}{6}$ $\;7\frac{1}{2}$
3. $\frac{78}{15}$ $\;5\frac{1}{5}$
4. $\frac{86}{20}$ $\;4\frac{3}{10}$

5. $\frac{91}{12}$ $\;7\frac{7}{12}$
6. $\frac{83}{7}$ $\;11\frac{6}{7}$
7. $\frac{111}{12}$ $\;9\frac{1}{4}$
8. $\frac{115}{13}$ $\;8\frac{11}{13}$

Express each mixed number as a fraction.

| Sample 2 | $5\frac{2}{5}$ | Solution | $5\frac{2}{5} = 5 + \frac{2}{5} = \frac{25}{5} + \frac{2}{5} = \frac{27}{5}$ |

9. $4\frac{1}{6}$ $\;\frac{25}{6}$
10. $8\frac{3}{5}$ $\;\frac{43}{5}$
11. $2\frac{7}{9}$ $\;\frac{25}{9}$
12. $12\frac{3}{4}$ $\;\frac{51}{4}$

13. $3\frac{8}{13}$ $\;\frac{47}{13}$
14. $17\frac{1}{3}$ $\;\frac{52}{3}$
15. $9\frac{11}{12}$ $\;\frac{119}{12}$
16. $10\frac{7}{8}$ $\;\frac{87}{8}$

Perform the indicated operations. Express the answers in simplest form.

Sample 3	$8\frac{2}{3} + 7\frac{5}{6}$	Solution	$8\frac{2}{3} + 7\frac{5}{6} = \frac{26}{3} + \frac{47}{6}$
			$= \frac{52}{6} + \frac{47}{6}$
			$= \frac{99}{6} = \frac{33}{2} = 16\frac{1}{2}$

| Sample 4 | $3\frac{1}{3} \div 7\frac{1}{2}$ | Solution | $3\frac{1}{3} \div 7\frac{1}{2} = \frac{10}{3} \div \frac{15}{2}$ |
| | | | $= \frac{\overset{2}{\cancel{10}}}{3} \cdot \frac{2}{\underset{3}{\cancel{15}}} = \frac{4}{9}$ |

20. 2
24. $2\frac{2}{5}$
28. $1\frac{1}{3}$
32. $27\frac{3}{5}$
36. $41\frac{1}{6}$

17. $8\frac{7}{15} + 9\frac{11}{15}$ $\;18\frac{1}{5}$
18. $5\frac{7}{9} - 6\frac{4}{9}$ $\;-\frac{2}{3}$
19. $7\frac{1}{3} \cdot \left(-\frac{1}{7}\right)$ $\;-1\frac{1}{21}$
20. $4\frac{2}{5} \div 2\frac{1}{5}$

21. $10\frac{1}{5} \div \frac{2}{5}$ $\;25\frac{1}{2}$
22. $20\frac{5}{13} + 8\frac{4}{5}$ $\;29\frac{12}{65}$
23. $6\frac{5}{8} - 3\frac{2}{5}$ $\;3\frac{9}{40}$
24. $6\frac{3}{5} \div 2\frac{3}{4}$

25. $12\frac{9}{10} - 8\frac{3}{5}$ $\;4\frac{3}{10}$
26. $-9\frac{1}{2} + \left(-13\frac{5}{9}\right)$ $\;-23\frac{1}{18}$
27. $11\frac{4}{7} + 10\frac{1}{5}$ $\;21\frac{27}{35}$
28. $8\frac{5}{6} \div 6\frac{5}{8}$

29. $4\frac{10}{11} - 7\frac{1}{2}$ $\;-2\frac{13}{22}$
30. $12\frac{3}{20} \cdot 1\frac{5}{9}$ $\;18\frac{9}{10}$
31. $9\frac{5}{9} - 8\frac{1}{4}$ $\;1\frac{11}{36}$
32. $3\frac{9}{10} \cdot 7\frac{1}{13}$

33. $-5\frac{2}{3} \div 3\frac{1}{2}$ $\;-1\frac{13}{21}$
34. $5\frac{5}{9} \cdot 4\frac{1}{2}$ $\;25$
35. $17\frac{3}{4} + 8\frac{1}{3}$ $\;26\frac{1}{12}$
36. $10\frac{5}{6} \cdot 3\frac{4}{5}$

Mixed Problem Solving

Solve each problem that has a solution. If a problem has no solution, explain why.

A 1. The sum of twice a number and −6 is 9 more than the opposite of the number. Find the number. 5

2. Roger spent $22 on a baseball mitt and softball. If the mitt cost $2 less than 5 times the cost of the softball, find the cost of each. ball, $4; mitt, $18

3. I drove 450 km in 6 h. Find my rate of travel. 75 km/h

4. The Longs' checking account was overdrawn by $35.87. They deposited $580 in the account. Then they wrote checks for $25 and $254.09. Find their new balance. $265.04

5. Alice bought 12 apples and oranges for $2.51. If an apple costs 25¢ and an orange costs 18¢, how many of each did she buy? 7 oranges, 5 apples

6. A rectangle has a perimeter of 48 cm. If the width and the length are consecutive odd integers, find the dimensions of the rectangle. 11 cm by 13 cm

7. The usual July temperature in Windsor, Ontario, 22° C, is 27° above the usual January temperature. Find the usual January temperature. −5° C

8. When 7 is decreased by a number, the result is 10. Find the number. −3

9. Find three consecutive integers such that three times the smallest is equal to the middle number increased by the greatest number. 3, 4, 5

10. What is the difference between the boiling point of mercury, 357° C, and the melting point, −39° C? 396°

11. Ruwa has $125 in $5 bills and $10 bills. If he has four more $5 bills than $10 bills, how many of each does he have? 7 $10 bills, 11 $5 bills

B 12. A store manager bought c calculators for $8 each. All but four were sold for $10 each. The remaining four calculators were not sold. Find the store's profit, in simplified form, in terms of c. $2c - 40$

13. At a city zoo, about $45 of every $100 spent is used for animal care and supplies. One year $216,000 was spent on these uses. Find the total zoo budget that year. $480,000

14. Denise did $\frac{7}{8}$ of the problems on a quiz correctly and five incorrectly. She did all the problems. How many were there? 40

15. On Saturday Kim worked three hours more than Ann did. Together, they worked one hour less than three times the hours Ann worked. How many hours did Kim work? 7 hours

16. A bank contains 44 coins (nickels, dimes, and quarters). There are twice as many dimes as nickels and 8 fewer nickels than quarters. How much money is in the bank? $6.50

17. Sara has twice as much money as Miguel. If she had $6 more, she would have $\frac{4}{3}$ as much money as he has. How much money does each have now? No solution; Miguel can't have a negative amount of money.

Solving Equations and Problems **139**

4 Polynomials

Objectives

4-1 To write and simplify expressions involving exponents.

4-2 To add and subtract polynomials.

4-3 To multiply monomials.

4-4 To find powers of monomials.

4-5 To multiply a polynomial by a monomial.

4-6 To multiply polynomials.

4-7 To transform a formula.

4-8 To solve some word problems involving uniform motion.

4-9 To solve some problems involving area.

4-10 To recognize problems that do not have solutions.

Assignment Guide

See p. T59 for Key to the format of the Assignment Guide

Day	Minimum Course		Average Course		Maximum Course	
1	**4-1** S	143/1–35 odd 144/*Mixed Review*	**4-1** S	143/1–31 odd, 33–45 mult. of 3 144/*Mixed Review*	**4-1** S	143/1–31 odd, 33–48 mult. of 3 144/*Mixed Review*
2	**4-2**	148/2–40 even 150/*P*: 2–8 even	**4-2**	148/3–48 mult. of 3 150/*P*: 2–8 even	**4-2**	148/3–51 mult. of 3 150/*P*: 4–10 even
3	**4-2** S **4-3**	149/42–50 even 150/*P*: 9, 10 150/*Mixed Review* 153/2–18 even	**4-2** S	149/49–54 150/*P*: 9–11 150/*Mixed Review*	**4-2** S	149/53–56 150/*P*: 11–14 150/*Mixed Review*
4	**4-3** S R	153/19–37 odd 154/*Mixed Review* 151/*Self-Test 1*	**4-3** S R	153/3–36 mult. of 3, 38, 41, 42 154/*Mixed Review* 151/*Self-Test 1*	**4-3** S R	153/3–48 mult. of 3 154/*Mixed Review* 151/*Self-Test 1*
5	**4-4** S	156/1–20 157/*Mixed Review*	**4-4** S	156/2–36 even, 39 157/*Mixed Review*	**4-4** S	156/3–51 mult. of 3 157/*Mixed Review*
6	**4-4** **4-5**	157/22–34 even 159/2–18 even	**4-5** S	159/3–36 mult. of 3, 40–42 160/*Mixed Review*	**4-5** S	159/3–42 mult. of 3, 43 160/*Mixed Review*
7	**4-5** S	159/19–37 odd, 40 160/*Mixed Review*	**4-6** S	162/3–42 mult. of 3, 43, 45 164/*Mixed Review*	**4-6** S	162/3–48 mult. of 3, 50 164/*Mixed Review*
8	**4-6**	162/1–31 odd	**4-7** S R	166/2–26 even 166/*Mixed Review* 164/*Self-Test 2*	**4-7** S R	166/4–28 even 166/*Mixed Review* 164/*Self-Test 2*
9	**4-6** S	163/33–43 odd 164/*Mixed Review*	**4-8**	170/*P*: 1–5, 7, 9, 10	**4-8**	170/*P*: 1–11
10	**4-7** S R	166/2–22 even 166/*Mixed Review* 164/*Self-Test 2*	**4-8** S	170/*P*: 11, 13, 15 171/*Mixed Review*	**4-8** S **4-9**	171/*P*: 13–17 odd 171/*Mixed Review* 173/*P*: 2, 4
11	**4-8**	170/*P*: 1–5, 7, 9	**4-9**	173/*P*: 1–6	**4-9** S	173/*P*: 6–9, 10, 12 174/*Mixed Review*

Assignment Guide (continued)

Day	Minimum Course	Average Course	Maximum Course
12	**4-8** 170/*P*: 11, 13 **S** 171/*Mixed Review* **4-9** 173/*P*: 1, 3, 5	**4-9** 174/*P*: 8–11 **S** 174/*Mixed Review*	**4-10** 176/*P*: 2–16 even
13	**4-9** 173/*P*: 7–9 **S** 174/*Mixed Review* **4-10** 176/*P*: 1, 3, 5, 7	**4-10** 176/*P*: 2–14 even	*Prepare for Chapter Test* **R** 177/*Self-Test 3* 178/*Chapter Review* **EP** 645/*Skills;* 668/*Problems*
14	*Prepare for Chapter Test* **R** 177/*Self-Test 3* 178/*Chapter Review* **EP** 645/*Skills;* 668/*Problems*	*Prepare for Chapter Test* **R** 177/*Self-Test 3* 178/*Chapter Review* **EP** 645/*Skills;* 668/*Problems*	*Administer Chapter 4 Test* **R** 181/*Cum. Review:* 1–39 odd **S** 183/*Preparing for College Entrance Exams*
15	*Administer Chapter 4 Test* **R** 182/*Maintaining Skills*	*Administer Chapter 4 Test* **R** 181/*Cum. Review:* 1–39 odd **S** 183/*Preparing for College Entrance Exams*	

Supplementary Materials Guide

For Use with Lesson	Practice Masters	Tests	Study Guide (Reteaching)	Resource Book		
				Tests	Practice Exercises	Prob. Solving (PS) Applications (A) Enrichment (E)
4-1			pp. 53–54			p. 181 (A)
4-2	Sheet 18		pp. 55–56		p. 91	
4-3			pp. 57–58			
4-4	Sheet 19		pp. 59–60		p. 92	
4-5			pp. 61–62			
4-6	Sheet 20	Test 15	pp. 63–64		p. 93	
4-7			pp. 65–66			
4-8	Sheet 21		pp. 67–68		p. 94	pp. 162–165 (PS)
4-9			pp. 69–70			pp. 166–167 (PS)
4-10	Sheet 22	Test 16	pp. 71–72		p. 95	
Chapter 4	Sheet 23	Tests 17, 18		pp. 20–23		p. 196 (E)
Cum. Rev. 1–4		Test 19				

Overhead Visuals

For Use with Lessons	Visual	Title
4-2	2	Geometric Models: Adding and Subtracting Polynomials
4-5, 4-6	3	Geometric Models: Multiplying Polynomials
4-6	6	Geometric Model: $(a + b)^3$

Software

Software	Computer Activities	Test Generator
Software	Activities 10, 11	210 test items
For Use with Lessons	4-1, 4-2	all lessons

Strategies for Teaching

Making Connections to Geometry

Although several connections between algebra and geometry occur throughout the text, Chapters 4 and 5 have particularly strong ties to geometry, both in the use of geometric modeling of algebraic concepts and in problem solving. See the Connections section of the References to Strategies chart on the next page for a listing of pages with ties to Geometry.

Communication and Using Manipulatives

This chapter introduces students to the new terminology of exponents and polynomials and then focuses on applications for the new knowledge. Thus a combined approach of communication and using manipulatives may be an effective teaching strategy. Asking students to verbalize the same exponential expression in different ways and calling attention to the prefixes in words like *monomial, binomial,* and *trinomial* are good ways to develop reading skills while introducing new material. Manipulatives may be used to develop area models for products of monomials and polynomials, as in the Exploration on pp. 689–690.

4-1 Exponents

Stress the use of oral language by having students verbalize in sentences, summarize, repeat, say another way, and read aloud. It is common for a set of symbols to be verbalized in several ways within a lesson. For example, a^2 may be called the square of a, the second power of a, a squared, or a to the second power.

4-2 Adding and Subtracting Polynomials

Write the following monomials on the chalkboard: $-5x^2y^3z$, $2a^7b^9$, and $9pq^2r^3s^4t^5$. Have students state the degree in each variable and the degree of each monomial. If they have difficulty, ask them to think about the factored form of the monomial.

Guide students in understanding the new vocabulary introduced in this lesson by relating the new terms to words they already know. Discuss the words *monorail, bicycle,* and *tripod.* Ask students for the meaning of the prefixes *mono, bi,* and *tri* and for examples of words using each prefix. Relate the meaning of these prefixes to the terms *monomial, binomial,* and *trinomial.*

4-4 Powers of Monomials

You will find it worthwhile to focus on the symbolism used in this lesson. Example 1 and the rules of exponents might be read aloud. Point out that an expression such as $(x^3)^2$ can be read in several different ways—for example, "x cubed to the second power," "x cubed [pause] squared," or "the square of the cube of x." Any word form that makes the meaning clear is acceptable. Ask students to respond to the Oral Exercises with complete sentences—for example, "The square of the fourth power of x is x to the eighth power."

4-5 Multiplying Polynomials by Monomials

Using tiles or manipulatives cut from grid paper (a conveniently sized square to represent one unit, a strip of 10 ones to represent x, and a 10-by-10 square to represent x^2), you can have students confirm that $x^2 + 3x$ is the area of a rectangle with sides of length x and $x + 3$.

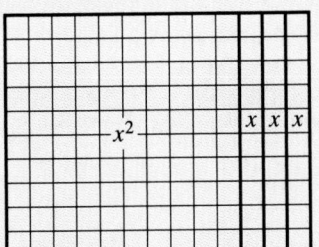

See the Exploration on pp. 689–690 for an activity in which students use tiles to explore monomial and binomial products.

4-6 Multiplying Polynomials

Using tiles or manipulatives cut from grid paper, students can work in pairs to demonstrate that $6x^2 + 19x + 10$ is the area of a rectangle with sides $2x + 5$ and $3x + 2$ as illustrated on page 161.

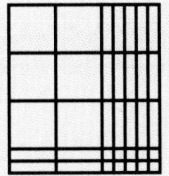

References to Strategies

Problem Solving Strategies

PE: pp. 175–177 (Recognizing no solution); pp. 167–169, 175 (Using charts or tables); pp. 167–169, 172–173 (Using a sketch, diagram, or model)
RB: pp. 162–167

Applications

PE: pp. 140, 145, 165, 167–177
TE: p. 140
RB: p. 181

Nonroutine Problems

PE: p. 154 (Exs. 36–40); p. 157 (Exs. 51–53); p. 160 (Exs. 39–44); pp. 163–164 (Exs. 47–50); p. 171 (Probs. 17–20); p. 174 (Probs. 9–13); pp. 176–177 (Probs. 5, 8, 10–16)

Communication

PE: p. 143 (Exs. 35–36, convincing argument); pp. 176–177 (Exs. 1–16, convincing argument)
TE: pp. T94–T95 (Reading Algebra: 4-1, 4-2, 4-4)

Thinking Skills

PE: pp. 152–157 (Reasoning and inferencing); pp. 154, 160 (Spatial perception)
TE: pp. 154, 156, 161

Explorations

PE: pp. 689–690 (Exploring monomial and binomial products)

Connections

PE: p. 145 (Astronomy); p. 145 (Discrete Math); p. 165 (Engineering); pp. 140–141, 154, 158, 161, 165, 174 (Geometry)
RB: p. 196

Using Technology

PE: p. 145 (Calculator Key-In); pp. 145, 151 (Exs.)
TE: pp. 145, 151, 169
Computer Activities: pp. 21–24

Using Manipulatives/Models

TE: p. T97 (Lessons 4-5, 4-6)
Overhead Visuals: 2, 3, 6

Cooperative Learning

TE: p. T95 (Lesson 4-2); p. T99 (Lesson 4-10)

Teaching Resources

For use in implementing the teaching strategies referenced on the previous page.

Application
Resource Book, p. 181

Application—Floor Plans (for use with Chapter 4)

Part I—Estimating (to be done in class)

1. Draw a floor plan of your bedroom on a sheet of graph paper. In doing so, choose a certain number of squares to represent the width of the doorway.

2. Label the width of the doorway in your drawing with the variable x. Label all other lengths in terms of x.

3. Give a mathematical expression in terms of x in response to each of the following questions based on your floor plan.

   a. How long is the bedroom? _____

   b. How wide is the bedroom? _____

   c. What is the perimeter of the bedroom? _____

   d. What is the area of the floor? _____

Part II—Measuring and Evaluating (to be done at home)

4. Measure and state the actual width of the doorway to your bedroom. _____ in.

5. Evaluate each expression in part (3) using the actual width of the doorway in place of x.

   a. How long is the bedroom? _____ in.

   b. How wide is the bedroom? _____ in.

   c. What is the perimeter of the bedroom? _____ in.

   d. What is the area of the floor? _____ in.^{2}

6. Measure your bedroom. Then answer the following questions based on your actual measurements.

   a. How long is the bedroom? _____ in.

   b. How wide is the bedroom? _____ in.

   c. What is the perimeter of the bedroom? _____ in.

   d. What is the area of the floor? _____ in.^{2}

7. Draw an accurate floor plan on a separate sheet of graph paper. Label each length.

8. Write a paragraph comparing your original floor plan and your revised floor plan, as well as your answers to questions 5 and 6.

Enrichment/Connection
Resource Book, p. 196

Geometric Pictures and Algebraic Facts (For use with Chapter 4 of text)

Each picture illustrates an algebraic fact. Complete each statement.

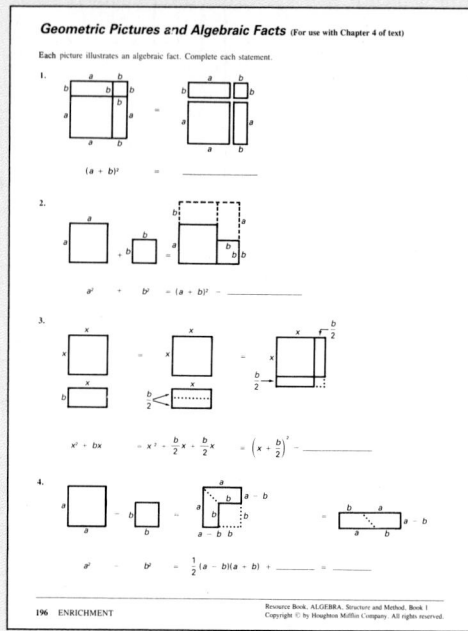

1. $(a + b)^2 = $ _____

2. $a^2 + b^2 = (a + b)^2 - $ _____

3. $x^2 + bx = x^2 + \frac{b}{2}x + \frac{b}{2}x = \left(x + \frac{b}{2}\right)^2 - $ _____

4. $a^2 - b^2 = \frac{1}{2}(a - b)(a + b) + $ _____

Problem Solving
Resource Book, p. 162

Distance-Rate-Time Problems (For use with Lesson 4-8)

By working through the steps in the problems below, you will gain skill in solving problems involving distance, rate, and time.

Problem 1 Two cars left Daisy's Diner at the same time and traveled in opposite directions. One car traveled for 78 min. The other car traveled for 144 min at a rate 5 km/h faster than the first car. If the faster car went twice as far as the slower car, how far did each car travel?

a. Since the rate is given in km/h, express the *times* in hours, using decimals.

Slower car: Time = 78 min = _____ h

Faster car: Time = 144 min = _____ h

b. Let r = the slower car's speed in km/h. Complete the chart.

	Rate	×	Time	=	Distance
Slower car	r				
Faster car					

c. Use the information in the chart to draw a sketch for the problem. Label the sketch.

d. Which given fact is *not* used in the chart? _____

e. Use the chart, the sketch, and the fact in part **d** to write an equation for the problem.

f. Solve the equation, and find a numerical value for each car's speed.

Slower car _____   Faster car _____

g. Notice that finding the cars' speeds does not answer the question in the problem. What does the question ask you to find? _____

h. Write your answer to the question in the problem. _____

i. Check: Did the faster car travel twice as far as the slower car? _____

(continued)

Problem Solving
Resource Book, p. 166

Area Problems
(For use with Lesson 4-9 or with Reading Algebra/Problem Solving Strategies, p. 404)

By working through the steps in the problems below, you will gain skill in solving area problems.

Problem 1 The width of a rectangle is two thirds of the length. If each dimension is decreased by 3 cm, the area is decreased by 66 cm^2. Find the original dimensions.

a. Let x = the length of the first rectangle. Write an expression for the width of the original rectangle. _____

b. Complete the chart.

	Length	×	Width	=	Area
First rectangle	x				
Second rectangle					

c. Write an equation for the problem.

Area of second rectangle = Area of first rectangle − 66 cm^2

_____ = _____ − _____

d. Solve your equation to find the value of x. _____

e. Find the answer to the problem. _____

f. Check your results with the statement of the problem.

Is the width of the original rectangle two thirds of the length? _____

Find the numerical area of each rectangle. What should the difference between these areas be? _____

Is it? _____

(continued)

139e

Using Manipulatives/Models
Overhead Visual 2, Sheets 1 and 2

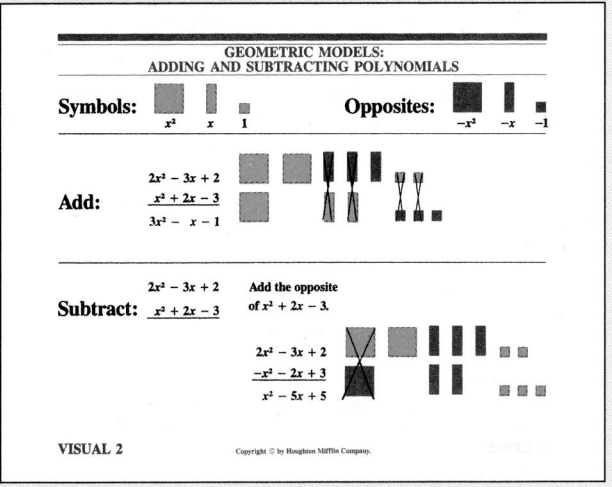

Using Manipulatives/Models
Overhead Visual 3, Sheets 1 and 2

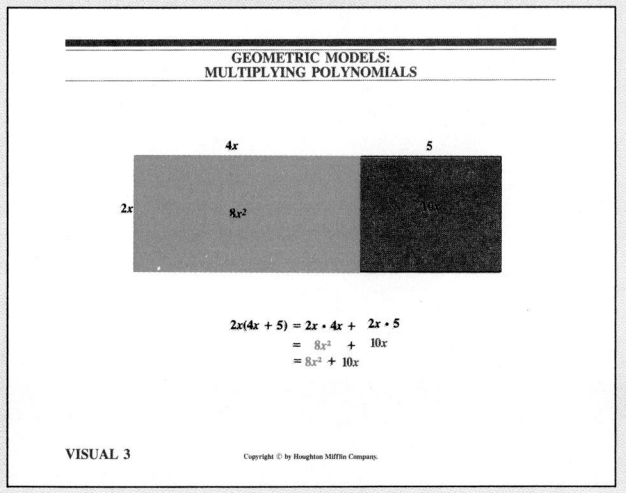

Using Manipulatives/Models
Overhead Visual 3, Sheets 3, 4, and 5

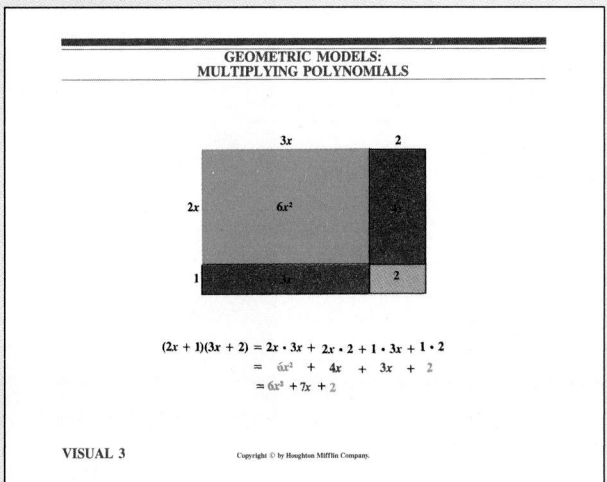

For rectangles, area is the product of length and width. If you're given variable expressions for length and width instead of exact values, you may use exponents to write the product more compactly.

Application

The photo shows some of the tools and materials needed to paint a house. Having the right equipment and supplies is essential when painting or building. A painter must be able to calculate surface area in order to decide how many cans of paint are required. A builder must determine the number of two-by-fours that will be needed in order to estimate construction costs. Painters and builders apply their knowledge of mathematics to come up with these figures.

Research Activities
During class, have students draw floor plans of their bedrooms, from memory, on graph paper. Have them use one to five squares (depending upon the grid size) to represent the width of the doorway. Then tell them to label the width of the doorway x, and to label all other lengths with the appropriate multiples of x. When their diagrams are complete, have students answer the following questions in terms of x: What is the perimeter of the bedroom? How high is the ceiling of the bedroom? What would the total surface area of the walls be?

For homework, have students evaluate the expressions written in class using the actual width of the doorway. Then have them measure their rooms, make a revised drawing, and write about their results.

Support Materials
Resource Book   p. 181

140

Addition and Subtraction

4-1 Exponents

Objective   To write and simplify expressions involving exponents.

The number 25 can be written as $5 \cdot 5$ and is called a *power* of 5. Here is how some powers are defined and written:

First power of 5: $5^1 = 5$ (read "five to the first power")

Second power of 5: $5^2 = 5 \cdot 5$ (read "five to the second power" or "five squared" or "the square of five")

Third power of 5: $5^3 = 5 \cdot 5 \cdot 5$ (read "five to the third power" or "five cubed" or "the cube of five")

Fourth power of 5: $5^4 = 5 \cdot 5 \cdot 5 \cdot 5$ (read "five to the fourth power")

In the expression 5^4 the number 4 is called the **exponent** and the number 5 is called the **base.** We call 5^4 the **exponential form** of $5 \cdot 5 \cdot 5 \cdot 5$. The exponent tells you the number of times the base is used as a factor.

In general, if b is any real number and n is any positive integer, the **nth power of b** is written b^n and is defined as follows:

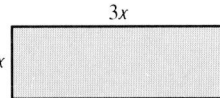

Exponent ——⌐

$$b^n = \underbrace{b \cdot b \cdot b \cdot \ \ldots \ \cdot b}_{n \text{ factors}}$$

Base ——⌐

The expression b^n tells you that b is used as a factor n times.

Example 1   Write each expression in exponential form.

   a. $6 \cdot 6 \cdot 6 \cdot 6$ **b.** $a \cdot a \cdot a \cdot a \cdot a \cdot a$ **c.** $-2 \cdot p \cdot q \cdot 3 \cdot p \cdot q \cdot p$

Solution   **a.** 6^4 **b.** a^6 **c.** $-6p^3q^2$

Example 2   Find the area of the rectangle.

Solution   Area = length × width
   $= 3x \cdot x$
   $= 3x^2$ **Answer**

Polynomials   **141**

Teaching References
Lesson Commentary,
   pp. T94–T99
Assignment Guide,
   pp. T62–T63
Supplementary Materials
   Practice Masters 18–23
   Tests 15–19
   Resource Book
      Practice Exercises,
         pp. 91–95
      Tests, pp. 20–23
      Enrichment Activity,
         p. 196
      Practice in Problem
         Solving/Word Prob-
         lems, pp. 162–167
      Application, p. 181
   Study Guide, pp. 53–72
   Computer Activities 10–11
   Test Generator
   California Standards
   Support Workbook
      Exploration for
      Lessons 4-5 and 4-6
Alternate Test, p. T15

Teaching Suggestions, p. T94
Reading Algebra, pp. T94–T95
Suggested Extensions, p. T95

Warm-Up Exercises
Simplify.
1. $3 \cdot 3$ 9
2. $(-1)(-1)$ 1
3. $2 \cdot 2 \cdot 2$ 8
4. $(-2)(-2)(-2)(-2)(-2)$ -32
5. $4 \cdot 4 \cdot 4$ 64

Motivating the Lesson
A *googol* is the number 1 followed by 100 zeros. By using exponential notation, a topic in today's lesson, we can conveniently express a googol as 10^{100}.

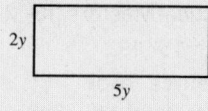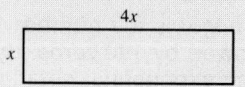
Caution: Be careful when an expression contains both parentheses and exponents.

$(2y)^3$ means $(2y)(2y)(2y)$.   3 is the exponent of the base $2y$.
$2y^3$ means $2 \cdot y \cdot y \cdot y$.   3 is the exponent of the base y.

Example 3 Evaluate x^3 if $x = -5$.   **Solution** Replace x with -5 and simplify.

$$x^3 = (-5)^3 = (-5)(-5)(-5)$$
$$= -125 \quad \textbf{\textit{Answer}}$$

The following steps are used to simplify numerical expressions.

Summary of Order of Operations

1. First simplify expressions within grouping symbols.
2. Then simplify powers.
3. Then simplify products and quotients in order from left to right.
4. Then simplify sums and differences in order from left to right.

Example 4 Simplify: **a.** -3^4 **b.** $(-3)^4$ **c.** $(1 + 5)^2$ **d.** $1 + 5^2$

Solution   **a.** $-3^4 = -(3 \cdot 3 \cdot 3 \cdot 3) = -81$

b. $(-3)^4 = (-3)(-3)(-3)(-3) = 81$

c. $(1 + 5)^2 = 6^2 = 36$

d. $1 + 5^2 = 1 + 5 \cdot 5 = 1 + 25 = 26$

Example 5 Evaluate $(2a + b)^2$ if $a = 3$ and $b = -2$.

Solution
$$(2a + b)^2 = [2 \cdot 3 + (-2)]^2 \quad \text{\{Replace } a \text{ with 3 and } b \text{ with } -2,$$
$$= [6 + (-2)]^2 \quad \text{and simplify.}$$
$$= 4^2$$
$$= 16 \quad \textbf{\textit{Answer}}$$

Example 6 Evaluate $\dfrac{(x - y)^3}{2x + y}$ if $x = 2$ and $y = 5$.

Solution
$$\frac{(x - y)^3}{2x + y} = \frac{(2 - 5)^3}{2 \cdot 2 + 5} \quad \text{\{Replace } x \text{ with 2 and } y \text{ with 5,}$$
$$\text{and then simplify.}$$
$$= \frac{(-3)^3}{4 + 5}$$
$$= \frac{-27}{9}$$
$$= -3 \quad \textbf{\textit{Answer}}$$

142   *Chapter 4*

Oral Exercises

State each expression in exponential form.

1. $x \cdot x \cdot x \cdot x$ x^4
2. $a \cdot a \cdot a \cdot a \cdot a$ a^5
3. $n \cdot y \cdot y \cdot n$ $n^2 y^2$
4. $c \cdot c \cdot y$ $c^2 y$
5. $2 \cdot p \cdot 5 \cdot p$ $10p^2$
6. $a \cdot 3 \cdot a \cdot a \cdot 2 \cdot a$ $6a^4$
7. $(-r)(-r)$ r^2
8. $-r \cdot r$ $-r^2$
9. $(-2) \cdot b \cdot (-4) \cdot b$ $8b^2$
10. $2 \cdot k \cdot k \cdot (-4) \cdot k$ $-8k^3$
11. $a \cdot a \cdot a \cdot 3 \cdot b \cdot b \cdot b$ $3a^3 b^3$
12. $a \cdot a \cdot b \cdot 5 \cdot b \cdot b \cdot a$ $5a^3 b^3$

Simplify.

13. 2^5 32
14. 5^2 25
15. $5 \cdot 2^3$ 40
16. $(5 \cdot 2)^3$ 1000
17. $(-2)^4$ 16
18. -2^4 −16
19. $(2 + 3)^2$ 25
20. $2 + 3^2$ 11

21. An even power of a negative number is a __?__ (positive, negative) number. positive
22. An odd power of a negative number is a __?__ (positive, negative) number. negative

Evaluate if $a = 3$ and $x = 2$.

23. ax^2 12
24. $(ax)^2$ 36
25. $(a + x)^2$ 25
26. $a + x^2$ 7
27. $x^3 - a$ 5
28. $(x - a)^3$ −1
29. $a^3 + x^3$ 35
30. $(a + x)^3$ 125
31. $(x - a)^4$ 1
32. $x^4 - a$ 13
33. $x - a^4$ −79
34. $x^4 - a^4$ −65

35. Study the figures at the right. Explain why the second and third powers of b are called "b squared" and "b cubed."

36. For any positive integer n, $0^n = 0$ and $1^n = 1$. Explain.

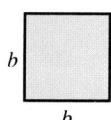 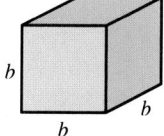

b

Area = __?__ b^2 Volume = __?__ b^3

Written Exercises

Find the area of each rectangle.

A **1.**

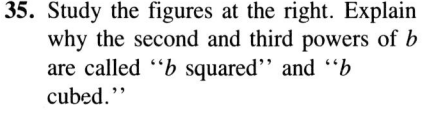

$3y$

2

$6y$

2.

$5x$

$3x$

$15x^2$

3.

$4z$

$2z$

$8z^2$

Write each expression in exponential form.

4. $x \cdot x \cdot x \cdot x \cdot x$ x^5
5. $m \cdot m \cdot m$ m^3
6. $4 \cdot t \cdot t \cdot t$ $4t^3$
7. $c \cdot c \cdot 3 \cdot c$ $3c^3$
8. $-6 \cdot z \cdot z$ $-6z^2$
9. $y \cdot y \cdot (-5)$ $-5y^2$
10. $-3 \cdot x \cdot 2 \cdot x$ $-6x^2$
11. $7 \cdot n \cdot (-2) \cdot n$ $-14n^2$

Polynomials **143**

Write each expression in exponential form.

2. $y \cdot y \cdot y$ y^3
3. $-6 \cdot x \cdot x \cdot 2 \cdot x$ $-12x^3$
4. $3 \cdot a \cdot a \cdot b \cdot (-2) \cdot a \cdot b$ $-6a^3 b^2$

Simplify.

5. -5^2 −25
6. $(-5)^2$ 25
7. $-2 \cdot 4^2$ −32
8. $(-2 \cdot 4)^2$ 64

Additional Answers
Oral Exercises

35. The area of a square with side b is b to the second power. So "b squared" is a natural term for b^2. Similarly, the volume of a cube with side b is b to the third power, so "b cubed" is a natural term for b^3.

36. $0^n = 0 \cdot 0 \cdot 0 \cdot \ldots \cdot 0 = 0$; $1^n = 1 \cdot 1 \cdot 1 \cdot \ldots \cdot 1 = 1$.

Summarizing the Lesson

Tell the students they have learned how to write and simplify expressions with powers. Ask them to identify the base and exponent of a number expressed in exponential form and to summarize the order of operations in evaluating expressions.

Suggested Assignments

Minimum
    143/1–35 odd
S 144/Mixed Review
Average
    143/1–31 odd,
        33–45 mult. of 3
S 144/Mixed Review
Maximum
    143/1–31 odd,
        33–48 mult. of 3
S 144/Mixed Review

Write each expression in exponential form.

12. $a \cdot a \cdot b \cdot b \cdot b$ a^2b^3 **13.** $c \cdot d \cdot c \cdot c$ c^3d **14.** $m \cdot 8 \cdot m \cdot n \cdot n$ $8m^2n^2$ **15.** $u \cdot v \cdot u \cdot u \cdot 9$ $9u^3v$

16. $-3 \cdot x \cdot y \cdot x$ $-3x^2y$ **17.** $r \cdot (-4) \cdot s \cdot s$ $-4rs^2$ **18.** $e \cdot f \cdot e \cdot g \cdot g$ e^2fg^2 **19.** $p \cdot p \cdot q \cdot q \cdot r \cdot s$ p^2q^2rs

Match each phrase with the corresponding algebraic expression.

20. The square of a plus the square of b b   **a.** $(a + b)^3$

21. The square of the sum of a and b d   **b.** $a^2 + b^2$

22. The cube of the quantity a plus b a   **c.** $a^3 + b^3$

23. The sum of the cube of a and the cube of b c   **d.** $(a + b)^2$

Simplify.

24. a. -6^2 -36 **25. a.** $(-2)^2$ 4 **26. a.** $2 \cdot 5^2$ 50 **27. a.** $-4^2 \cdot 3$ -48
b. $(-6)^2$ 36 **b.** -2^2 -4 **b.** $(2 \cdot 5)^2$ 100 **b.** $(-4 \cdot 3)^2$ 144

28. a. $5 - 3^4$ -76 **29. a.** $7 + 3^3$ 34 **30. a.** $2 \cdot 3 - 5^2$ -19 **31. a.** $3 \cdot (4 - 5)^2$ 3
b. $(5 - 3)^4$ 16 **b.** $(7 + 3)^3$ 1000 **b.** $2 \cdot (3 - 5)^2$ 8 **b.** $3 \cdot 4 - 5^2$ -13

Sample $6^3 \div [5^2 - 3^2 - (-2)^2] = 6^3 \div [25 - 9 - 4]$
$$= 216 \div 12$$
$$= 18 \quad Answer$$

B **32.** $(1 \cdot 10^3) + (4 \cdot 10^2) + (9 \cdot 10) + 2$ 1492 **33.** $(1 \cdot 10^3) + (7 \cdot 10^2) + (7 \cdot 10) + 6$ 1776

34. $[2^3 + 3^3] \div [2^3 + (-1)^2]$ $\frac{35}{9}$ **35.** $[5^3 + (-3)^3] \div 7^2$ 2

36. $[3^3 + (-2)^3 + (-1)^3] \div 3^2$ 2 **37.** $(3^4 - 2^4) \div [5^3 \div (4^2 + 3^2)]$ 13

38. $3^2 \div (2^2 - 1) - (5^2 - 3^2) \div (-2)^3$ 5 **39.** $[2^2 \cdot 3^3 - 3 \cdot 2^4] \div [(2 \cdot 3)^2 - 2^4]$ 3

Evaluate if $a = 3$ and $b = -2$.

40. a. $ab - a^2$ -15 **41. a.** $4 + ab^2$ 16 **42. a.** $(2a - b)^3$ 512 **43. a.** $(a + 2b)^3$ -1
b. $a(b - a)^2$ 75 **b.** $(4 + ab)^2$ 4 **b.** $2a - b^3$ 14 **b.** $a^3 + 2b^3$ 11

44. $\dfrac{(2a + b)^2}{2a + b}$ 4 **45.** $\dfrac{a^3 + 2b^3}{a + 2b}$ -11 **46.** $\dfrac{a^4 + b^4}{a + b}$ 97 **47.** $\dfrac{4a}{ab + 4}$ -6

Evaluate each expression for the given value of x.

C **48.** $(x^2 + 4x + 5)(x^2 + x - 2)$, $x = -3$ 8   **49.** $(x^2 - 3x + 1)(x^2 + 2x - 8)$, $x = -4$ 0

Mixed Review Exercises

Solve.

1. $-7x = 56$ {−8}   **2.** $3(n - 4) = 36$ {16}   **3.** $36 = -3x$ {−12}

4. $-n + 8 = 6$ {2}   **5.** $x - 5 = |7 - 12|$ {10}   **6.** $-y + 12 = 8$ {4}

7. $-\dfrac{1}{2}(x + 2) = 3$ {−8}   **8.** $\dfrac{1}{5}x = 10$ {50}   **9.** $3k = -\dfrac{6}{7}$ $\left\{-\dfrac{2}{7}\right\}$

144   *Chapter 4*

Computer Exercises

For students with some programming experience.

1. Write a BASIC program that uses a FOR . . . NEXT loop to print out the value of n^n for $n = 1, 2, 3, 4, 5.$ 1, 4, 27, 256, 3125

2. The symbol 4! is read "four factorial," and its value is $1 \cdot 2 \cdot 3 \cdot 4 = 24.$ Similarly, $6! = 1 \cdot 2 \cdot 3 \cdot 4 \cdot 5 \cdot 6 = 720.$ Write a BASIC program that uses a FOR . . . NEXT loop to print out the value of $n!$ for $n = 1, 2, 3, 4, 5.$ 1, 2, 6, 24, 120

3. Study the data in Exercises 1 and 2. For integers greater than 1, which appears to be larger, $n!$ or n^n? Can you explain why?

 ## Calculator Key-In

Your calculator may have a square key, x^2, or a power key, y^x, to help you simplify powers. Simplify each of the following mentally, then use a calculator to check your answers.

Exercises

1. $(0.1)^2$ 0.01
2. $(0.2)^2$ 0.04
3. $(0.5)^2$ 0.25
4. $(1.1)^2$ 1.21
5. $(0.11)^2$ 0.0121
6. $(0.02)^2$ 0.0004
7. $(0.3)^3$ 0.027
8. $(0.4)^3$ 0.064

Biographical Note / *Hypatia*

Hypatia (A.D. 370–415) is regarded as the first woman mathematician because so little is known about women mathematicians who may have lived before her. She was born in Alexandria, Egypt, when the city was one of the greatest centers of learning in the ancient world. Except for one of her papers that was found in the fifteenth century, our knowledge of Hypatia is based on the letters of her contemporaries and students.

Highly regarded as a mathematician and as an astronomer, Hypatia became a professor of mathematics and philosophy at the University of Alexandria. She lectured on Plato, Aristotle, astronomy, geometry, Diophantine algebra, and the conics of Appollonius. She also invented instruments used in the study of astronomy and apparatus for distilling water, measuring the level of water, and determining the specific gravity of liquids.

After her death in A.D. 415, no significant progress in the mathematics taught by Hypatia was made for centuries.

Polynomials **145**

 Using a Computer

The Computer Exercises include finding the value of n^n and $n!$ for integral values of n.

 Calculator Key-In Commentary

Encourage students with calculators to use them to simplify powers. Experiment with the power key (y^x) to evaluate expressions like 4^7.

This calculator method will be helpful for Oral Exercises 13–20 on page 143 and Written Exercises 24–47 on page 144.

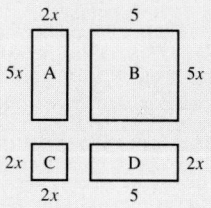
4-2 Adding and Subtracting Polynomials

Objective   To add and subtract polynomials.

Each of the following expressions is a *monomial*: 14, z, $\frac{2}{3}r$, $-6x^2y$.

A **monomial** is an expression that is either a numeral, a variable, or the product of a numeral and one or more variables. A numeral, such as 14, is called a **constant monomial**, or a **constant**.

A sum of monomials is called a **polynomial.** A polynomial such as $x^2 + (-4x) + (-5)$ is usually written as $x^2 - 4x - 5$. Some polynomials have special names:

Binomials (two terms)	$2x - 9$	$2ab + b^2$
Trinomials (three terms)	$x^2 - 4x - 5$	$a^2 + 3ab - 4b^2$

A monomial is considered to be a polynomial of one term.

In the monomial $-3xy^2$, the numeral -3 is called the **coefficient,** or **numerical coefficient.** Two monomials that are exactly alike or are the same except for their numerical coefficients are said to be **similar,** or **like, terms.**

The following monomials are all similar: $-5xy^2$, $16yxy$, xy^2, and $\frac{1}{3}xy^2$. The monomials $-3xy^2$ and $-3x^2y$ are not similar.

A polynomial is **simplified,** or **in simplest form,** when no two of its terms are similar. You may use the distributive property to add similar terms. You may find it helpful at first to copy the polynomial and underline similar terms.

Example 1   Simplify $-6x^3 + 3x^2 + x^2 + 6x^3 - 5$.

Solution $-6x^3 + 3x^2 + x^2 + 6x^3 - 5 = (-6 + 6)x^3 + (3 + 1)x^2 - 5$
$$= 0x^3 + 4x^2 - 5$$
$$= 4x^2 - 5 \quad \textbf{Answer}$$

Example 2   Write the sum of the areas of the rectangles as a polynomial in simplest form.

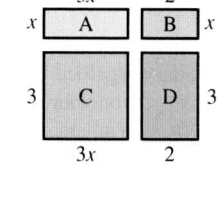

Solution
$$\underset{\text{of A}}{\text{Area}} + \underset{\text{of B}}{\text{Area}} + \underset{\text{of C}}{\text{Area}} + \underset{\text{of D}}{\text{Area}}$$

$$\underset{3x^2}{x \cdot 3x} + \underset{2x}{x \cdot 2} + \underset{9x}{3 \cdot 3x} + \underset{6}{3 \cdot 2}$$

$$3x^2 + 11x + 6 \quad \textbf{Answer}$$

The **degree of a variable in a monomial** is the number of times that the variable occurs as a factor in the monomial. The **degree of a monomial** is the sum of the degrees of its variables. The degree of any nonzero constant monomial, such as 12, is 0.

Example 3 Find the degree of $5x^2yz^4$.

Solution

$$5x^2yz^4$$

The degree of x is 2. ⟶
The degree of y is 1. ⟶
The degree of z is 4. ⟶

∴ the degree of $5x^2yz^4$ is $2 + 1 + 4 = 7$.   **Answer**

The **degree of a polynomial** is the greatest of the degrees of its terms *after it has been simplified*. Since the polynomial $-6x^3 + 3x^2 + x^2 + 6x^3 - 5$ of Example 1 can be simplified to $4x^2 - 5$, its degree is 2, *not* 3.

To find the sum of two polynomials, you add the similar terms.

Example 4 Add $3x^2y + 4xy^2 - 2y^3 + 3$ and $x^2y + 3y^3 - 4$.

Solution 1 First group similar terms and then combine them.

$$(3x^2y + 4xy^2 - 2y^3 + 3) + (x^2y + 3y^3 - 4) =$$
$$(3x^2y + x^2y) + (4xy^2) + (-2y^3 + 3y^3) + (3 - 4) =$$
$$4x^2y + 4xy^2 + y^3 - 1 \quad \textbf{Answer}$$

Solution 2 You can also align similar terms vertically and then add.

$$\begin{array}{l} 3x^2y + 4xy^2 - 2y^3 + 3 \\ \underline{x^2y \qquad\quad + 3y^3 - 4} \\ 4x^2y + 4xy^2 + \ y^3 - 1 \end{array}$$

Subtracting polynomials is like subtracting real numbers. To subtract a real number, you add the opposite of that number. To subtract a polynomial, you add the opposite of *each* term of that polynomial and then simplify.

Example 5 Subtract $-a^2 - 5ab + 4b^2 - 2$ from $3a^2 - 2ab - 2b^2 - 7$.

Solution 1 Add the opposite of $-a^2 - 5ab + 4b^2 - 2$ to $3a^2 - 2ab - 2b^2 - 7$.

$$(3a^2 - 2ab - 2b^2 - 7) - (-a^2 - 5ab + 4b^2 - 2) =$$
$$3a^2 - 2ab - 2b^2 - 7 + a^2 + 5ab - 4b^2 + 2 =$$
$$(3a^2 + a^2) + (-2ab + 5ab) + (-2b^2 + -4b^2) + (-7 + 2) =$$
$$4a^2 + 3ab - 6b^2 - 5 \quad \textbf{Answer}$$

Solution 2 You can also align similar items vertically.

$$\begin{array}{l} 3a^2 - 2ab - 2b^2 - 7 \\ \underline{-a^2 - 5ab + 4b^2 - 2} \end{array} \rightarrow \left\{ \begin{array}{l} \text{Change to the} \\ \text{opposite and add.} \end{array} \right\} \rightarrow \begin{array}{l} 3a^2 - 2ab - 2b^2 - 7 \\ \underline{+a^2 + 5ab - 4b^2 + 2} \\ 4a^2 + 3ab - 6b^2 - 5 \end{array}$$

Polynomials **147**

Guided Practice

Copy the polynomial and underline similar terms. Then simplify the polynomials.

1. $3a^2 - 6a + 2a + 9$
   $3a^2 - 4a + 9$

Add.

2. $6x^2 - 3xy + 2y^2$
   $\underline{3x^2 - 3xy + y^2}$
   $9x^2 - 6xy + 3y^2$

3. $5x + 2y - z + 2$
   $7x + y - 3z + 3$
   $\underline{-2x - 5y + 4z - 1}$
   $10x - 2y + 4$

Subtract.

4. $-2x + 3y - 5z + 2$
   $\underline{4x - 2y - z + 1}$
   $-6x + 5y - 4z + 1$

5. $5x^2 - 2xy + 2y^2$
   $\underline{-4x^2 - 2xy + 3y^2}$
   $9x^2 - y^2$

Simplify.

6. $(3x + 2y - 4) +$
   $(5x - 7y + 9)$
   $8x - 5y + 5$

7. $(6x^2 - 2y + 4) -$
   $(-3x^2 + 4y - 3)$
   $9x^2 - 6y + 7$

Summarizing the Lesson

Ask the students to identify monomials, binomials and trinomials and give their degrees. Tell them they have learned how to add and subtract polynomials by first identifying similar terms.

148

Oral Exercises

Name the similar monomials.

1. $-\underline{2x}$, $\underline{2xy}$, $4y$, $\underline{x}$, $-\underline{xy}$, $-\underline{\underline{y}}$
2. $-\underline{st^2}$, $2s^2t$, $3t^2s$, $-\underline{s^2t}$
3. $3a^4$, $-\underline{4a^3}$, $\underline{a^2}$, $5a^3$, $\underline{3a^2}$
4. $\underline{x^2y^2}$, $\underline{x^2}$, y^2, $-\underline{3x^2y^2}$, $-\underline{\underline{4x^2}}$

In Exercises 5–10, (a) state the degree of each variable in the monomial, and (b) state the degree of the monomial.

5. $-5xy^4z^3$ **a.** x, 1; y, 4; z, 3;   **b.** 8
6. $7ab^3c$ **a.** a, 1; b, 3; c, 1   **b.** 5
7. $-10xyz$ **a.** x, 1; y, 1; z, 1   **b.** 3
8. $-3a^5bc^2$ **a.** a, 5; b, 1; c, 2   **b.** 8
9. $n^2p^2q^2$ **a.** n, 2; p, 2; q, 2   **b.** 6
10. $-2u^4v^6w^2$ **a.** u, 4; v, 6; w, 2   **b.** 12

State the degree of each polynomial. If the polynomial is a binomial or a trinomial, say so.

11. $3x^2 - 7x + 4$ 2; trinomial
12. $-2x^2 - 4x^3 + 6x - 5$ 3
13. $x^3 - x^5$ 5; binomial
14. $p^2q^3 - 3pq^4$ 5; binomial
15. $r^2s - 3rs^3 + 2r^3s^2 + s^4$ 5
16. $2s^2t + 3st^2 - s^2t^2$ 4; trinomial

Add.

17. $2x - 5$
    $\underline{x + 3}$
    $3x - 2$
18. $4m - 3$
    $\underline{3m + 1}$
    $7m - 2$
19. $5n + 6$
    $\underline{-2n + 1}$
    $3n + 7$
20. $4y - 2$
    $\underline{-3y - 9}$
    $y - 11$
21. $3x^2 - 2x + 1$
    $\underline{x^2 - 2x + 3}$
    $4x^2 - 4x + 4$
22. $3y^2 - 5$
    $\underline{2y^2 - 3y + 4}$
    $5y^2 - 3y - 1$
23. $6a - 4b + c$
    $\underline{4a + 4b + c}$
    $10a + 2c$
24. $1 - 2y + 3y^2$
    $\underline{3 - 2y + y^2}$
    $4 - 4y + 4y^2$
25. $3x^3 - 2x^2y + xy^2$
    $\underline{x^3 + x^2y - xy^2}$
    $4x^3 - x^2y$

26–34. In Exercises 17–25, subtract the lower polynomial from the upper one.
26. $x - 8$ 27. $m - 4$ 28. $7n + 5$ 29. $7y + 7$ 30. $2x^2 - 2$ 31. $y^2 + 3y - 9$
32. $2a - 8b$ 33. $-2 + 2y^2$ 34. $2x^3 - 3x^2y + 2xy^2$

Simplify.

35. $(3x - 2y + 5) + (x + 2y - 2)$ $4x + 3$
36. $(2p - q + 1) + (-p - q + 3)$ $p - 2q + 4$
37. $(5r - 2y) - (2r - 3y)$ $3r + y$
38. $(3x + 3y - 5) - (2x - 2y + 5)$ $x + 5y - 10$

Written Exercises

Copy each polynomial and underline similar terms as was done in Example 1, page 146. Then simplify the polynomials.

A

1. $\underline{3x} - \underline{2y} - \underline{x} - \underline{3y}$ $2x - 5y$
2. $\underline{6m} - \underline{6n} - \underline{4m} + \underline{n}$ $2m - 5n$
3. $\underline{3x^2} - \underline{2x} - \underline{2x^2} - \underline{4x}$ $x^2 - 6x - 3$
4. $\underline{n^2} - \underline{4n} - \underline{3n^2} + \underline{7n} + \underline{5n^2}$ $3n^2 + 3n$
5. $\underline{a^2} + \underline{3ab} - \underline{4ab} + \underline{3a^2}$ $4a^2 - ab$
6. $\underline{p^2q} - \underline{q^3} - \underline{3p^2q} + \underline{4q^3}$ $-2p^2q + 3q^3$
7. $\underline{r^2s} - 3rs^2 + 4s^3 - \underline{2r^2s} - 3s^2$
8. $-\underline{3x^2} + \underline{7x^2y} - \underline{x^3} + xy^2 + \underline{4x^3} - \underline{3x^2y}$

148   *Chapter 4*   7. $-r^2s - 3rs^2 - 3s^2 + 4s^3$ 8. $3x^3 - 3x^2 + 4x^2y + xy^2$

Add.

9. $5y - 3$
$\quad \underline{2y + 9}$
$\quad 7y + 6$

10. $4x + 7$
$\quad \underline{x - 2}$
$\quad 5x + 5$

11. $3y + 8$
$\quad \underline{2y - 5}$
$\quad 5y + 3$

12. $7n - 6$
$\quad \underline{n + 4}$
$\quad 8n - 2$

13. $2r - 3x + 5$
$\quad \underline{-r + 3x - 2}$
$\quad r + 3$

14. $-2p + 4q - 7$
$\quad \underline{-4p - 2q + 5}$
$\quad -6p + 2q - 2$

15. $2x^2 - 3x - 4$
$\quad \underline{3x^2 + 4x - 6}$
$\quad 5x^2 + x - 10$

16. $\quad 4 - 3n - 5n^2$
$\quad \underline{-2 + \ n - 3n^2}$
$\quad 2 - 2n - 8n^2$

17. $4x^2 - 3xy - 5y^2$
$\quad \underline{2x^2 + \ xy - 3y^2}$
$\quad 6x^2 - 2xy - 8y^2$

18. $\quad 8p^2 - 5pq + 6q^2$
$\quad \underline{-2p^2 + 5pq - 4q^2}$
$\quad \quad 6p^2 \quad + 2q^2$

19. $3a - 7b - 5c + 2$
$\quad -a + 4b + \ c - 5$
$\quad \underline{2a \quad \quad + 3c + 3}$
$\quad 4a - 3b - c$

20. $\quad 7x - 6y + 4z - 1$
$\quad -3x + 3y - 5z + 3$
$\quad \underline{-2x - \ y + \ z - 4}$
$\quad 2x - 4y - 2$

21–30. In Exercises 9–18, subtract the lower polynomial from the upper one.

21. $3y - 12$ **22.** $3x + 9$ **23.** $y + 13$ **24.** $6n - 10$ **25.** $3r - 6x + 7$
26. $2p + 6q - 12$ **27.** $-x^2 - 7x + 2$ **28.** $6 - 4n - 2n^2$
29. $2x^2 - 4xy - 2y^2$ **30.** $10p^2 - 10pq + 10q^2$

Simplify.

> **Sample 1** $(4x^2 + 2x - 5) + (-x^2 + 3x + 5) = (4x^2 - x^2) + (2x + 3x) + (-5 + 5)$
> $= 3x^2 + 5x$ **Answer**

31. $(2x - 5y + 2) + (5x + 6y - 7)$ $7x + y - 5$

32. $(2p - 7q - 4) + (3q + 2p - 1)$ $4p - 4q - 5$

33. $(2x - 5) - (x - 2)$ $x - 3$

34. $(3m + 5) - (-2m + 3)$ $5m + 2$

35. $(5x - 3t - 7) - (x - 2t - 3)$ $4x - t - 4$

36. $(a - 3b + 5) - (-a + 2b + 3)$

37. $(3n^2 + 5n - 6) + (-n^2 - 3n + 3)$ $2n^2 + 2n - 3$

38. $(y^2 + 6y - 5) + (-y^2 - 3y - 1)$

39. $(3x^2 - 4x - 2) - (-x^2 - 4x + 7)$ $4x^2 - 9$

40. $(y^2 - 3y - 5) - (-y^2 - 7y + 4)$

B **41.** $(u^3 - 3u^2v + 2uv^2) + (3u^2v - 2uv^2 - v^3)$ $u^3 - v^3$ **42.** $(2x^2y - 3xy^2 - y^3) + (2x^2y - xy^2)$

43. $(3a^3 - 2ab^2) - (a^3 - 4ab^2 - b^3)$ $2a^3 + 2ab^2 + b^3$ **44.** $(2p^2q - 3pq^2 + q^3) - (-p^2q + q^3)$

36. $2a - 5b + 2$
38. $3y - 6$
40. $2y^2 + 4y - 9$
42. $4x^2y - 4xy^2 - y^3$
44. $3p^2q - 3pq^2$

Solve.

> **Sample 2** $9x - (3x - 8) = 20$
> $\quad 9x - 3x + 8 = 20$
> $\quad \quad \quad 6x + 8 = 20$
> $\quad \quad \quad \quad \ 6x = 12$
> $\quad \quad \quad \quad \quad x = 2$ $\quad \therefore$ the solution set is $\{2\}$. **Answer**

45. $7x - (3x - 2) = 10$ $\{2\}$

46. $z - (4z - 5) = 8$ $\{-1\}$

47. $(11n - 5) - (3n - 2) = -19$ $\{-2\}$

48. $(2x + 3) - (5x - 7) = 1$ $\{3\}$

49. $(4y - 3) - (4 - y) = 3(y + 3)$ $\{8\}$

50. $3(n - 2) - 2(3 - n) = 4(n - 3)$ $\{0\}$

51. $2 - 3x = 8(5 - x) - (x - 10)$ $\{8\}$

52. $3(4u - 6) = 2(4u - 3) - (u - 8)$ $\{4\}$

C **53.** $(2y^2 - y + 6) - 2(y^2 - 3y + 5) = 11$ $\{3\}$

54. $y(2 - y) = 6 - (y^2 + 3y - 4)$ $\{2\}$

55. $x(3 - x) = x - (x^2 - 2x + 4)$ no sol.

56. $3 - 2x(x - 1) = x(3 - 2x) - (x - 3)$
$\quad \quad \quad$ {all real numbers}

Polynomials **149**

Suggested Assignments

Minimum
Day 1: 148/2–40 even
$\quad \quad$ 150/*P*: 2–8 even
Day 2: 149/42–50 even
$\quad \quad$ 150/*P*: 9, 10
$\quad$ *S* 150/Mixed Review
Assign with Lesson 4-3.

Average
Day 1: 148/3–48 mult. of 3
$\quad \quad$ 150/*P*: 2–8 even
Day 2: 149/49–54
$\quad \quad$ 150/*P*: 9–11
$\quad$ *S* 150/Mixed Review

Maximum
Day 1: 148/3–51 mult. of 3
$\quad \quad$ 150/*P*: 4–10 even
Day 2: 149/53–56
$\quad \quad$ 150/*P*: 11–14
$\quad$ *S* 150/Mixed Review

Supplementary Materials

Study Guide $\quad \quad$ pp. 55–56
Practice Master $\quad \quad$ 18
Computer Activity $\quad \quad$ 11
Resource Book $\quad \quad$ p. 91
Overhead Visual $\quad \quad$ 2

Problems

Write the sum of the areas of the rectangles as a polynomial in simplest form.

A 1.

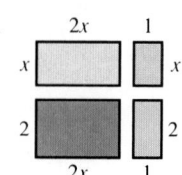

1. $2x^2 + 5x + 2$
2. $5x^2 + 17x + 6$
3. $3x^2 + 4x + 1$
4. $2x^2 + 7x + 6$

2.

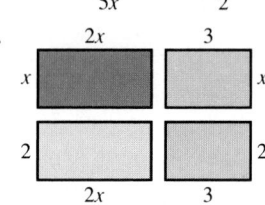

3.

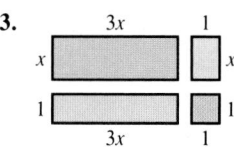

4.

Solve.

5. Find two consecutive integers whose sum is the square of 7. 24, 25

6. Find three consecutive integers whose sum is the square of 6. 11, 12, 13

7. Find four consecutive integers whose sum is twice the cube of 5. 61, 62, 63, 64

8. Find two consecutive odd integers whose sum is the cube of 4. 31, 33

9. The greater of two consecutive integers is 10 less than twice the smaller. Find the integers. 11, 12

10. The greater of two consecutive even integers is 10 less than twice the smaller. Find the integers. 12, 14

B 11. Find three consecutive odd integers such that twice the smallest is 3 more than the greatest integer. 7, 9, 11

12. Find four consecutive integers such that the sum of the two greatest is 17 less than twice the sum of the two smallest. 10, 11, 12, 13

13. Find four consecutive even integers such that the fourth is the sum of the first and second. 4, 6, 8, 10

14. Find four consecutive odd integers such that the sum of the two greatest is four times the smallest. 5, 7, 9, 11

Mixed Review Exercises

Simplify.

1. -5^2 -25 **2.** $(-5)^2$ 25   **3.** $(2^3 + 3^2)$ 17   **4.** $(4 - 6)^2$ 4

Solve.

5. $2(y + 3) - 4 = 3(5 - y)$ $\left\{\frac{13}{5}\right\}$ **6.** $15 = 2(n + 3)$ $\left\{\frac{9}{2}\right\}$ **7.** $5(x + 12) = 15 - 2(2x - 2)$ $\left\{-\frac{41}{9}\right\}$

8. $-\frac{4}{3}(n + 5) = 10$ $\left\{-\frac{25}{2}\right\}$ **9.** $c - 3 = |2 - 9|$ **10.** $\frac{2}{5}(2y + 1) = y - 3$ $\{17\}$

                                                         $\{10\}$

Computer Exercises

For students with some programming experience.

Write a BASIC program to add two polynomials. Using INPUT statements, ask the user to enter the degree of each polynomial. Then ask the user to enter the coefficients of each polynomial in order from least to greatest degree. Store the set of coefficients of each polynomial in an array. Use your program to find the sum of each of the following pairs of polynomials.

1. $3 + 4x + 5x^2$ and $1 + 7x - 2x^2$ $4 + 11x + 3x^2$ **2.** $-5 - 6x^2$ and $2x^2 + x^4$ $-5 - 4x^2 + x^4$

3. $4x + 9x^2$ and $5x^3$ $4x + 9x^2 + 5x^3$ **4.** $7 + 2x + x^3$ and $-3 + 4x + x^2$ $4 + 6x + x^2 + x^3$

Self-Test 1

Vocabulary   power (p. 141)   binomial (p. 146)
                base (p. 141)   trinomial (p. 146)
                exponent (p. 141)   coefficient (p. 146)
                exponential form (p. 141)   similar or like terms (p. 146)
                monomial (p. 146)   polynomial in simplest form (p. 146)
                constant (p. 146)   degree of a monomial (p. 146)
                polynomial (p. 146)   degree of a polynomial (p. 147)

Write in exponential form.

1. $n \cdot m \cdot n \cdot n$ mn^3 **2.** $5 \cdot x \cdot (-3) \cdot x$ $-15x^2$ **3.** $-2 \cdot y \cdot y \cdot 4$ $-8y^2$ **Obj. 4-1, p. 141**

Simplify.

4. $(-2)^4$ 16 **5.** -2^4 -16 **6.** $(3 - 6)^3$ -27

7. $3 - 6^3$ -213 **8.** $2 \cdot (4 - 6)^3$ -16 **9.** $[7^2 + (-1)^4] \div 5^2$ 2

In Exercises 10–12, (a) add the polynomials, and (b) subtract the lower polynomial from the upper one.   **a.** $6x^2 - 12$
                                                   b. $4x^2 + 12x - 4$

10. $7x + 5$ **11.** $5x^2 + 6x - 8$ **12.** $x^2y - 3xy^2 + 7$ **Obj. 4-2, p. 146**

     $\underline{3x - 1}$ **a.** $10x + 4$ $\underline{x^2 - 6x - 4}$ $\underline{-x^2y + 3xy^2 - 4}$ **a.** 3

              b. $4x + 6$ **b.** $2x^2y - 6xy^2 + 11$

13. Find three consecutive even integers such that the greatest is 8 less than twice the smallest. 12, 14, 16

Check your answers with those at the back of the book.

Using a Computer

The Computer Exercises involve writing a BASIC program to add two polynomials.

Quick Quiz

Write in exponential form.

1. $a \cdot b \cdot a \cdot a$ $a^3 b$

2. $6 \cdot y \cdot (-1) \cdot y$ $-6y^2$

3. $-4 \cdot s \cdot s \cdot s$ $-4s^3$

Simplify.

4. $(-6)^2$ 36

5. -6^2 -36

6. $(4 - 7)^3$ -27

7. $4 - 7^3$ -339

8. $3 \cdot (5 - 7)^3$ -24

9. $[6^2 + (-2)^4] \div 2^2$ 13

In Exercises 10–12, (a) add the polynomials, and (b) subtract the lower polynomial from the upper one.

10. $4x + 2$
        $\underline{6x - 5}$
     a. $10x - 3$
     b. $-2x + 7$

11. $6x^2 - 3x - 2$
        $\underline{x^2 - 4x - 5}$
     a. $7x^2 - 7x - 7$
     b. $5x^2 + x + 3$

12. $-5a^2b + ab^2 + 6$
        $\underline{5a^2b - ab^2 - 2}$
     a. 4
     b. $-10a^2b + 2ab^2 + 8$

13. Find three consecutive even integers such that the greatest is 14 less than twice the smallest. 18, 20, 22

Warm-Up Exercises

Simplify.

1. a. $2^3 \cdot 2^5$ 256
   b. 2^8 256

2. a. $3^2 \cdot 3^3$ 243
   b. 3^5 243

3. a. $3^2 \cdot 2^3 \cdot 3 \cdot 2^2$ 864
   b. $3^3 \cdot 2^5$ 864

Motivating the Lesson

The Warm-Up Exercises include skills students will use in today's lesson, except that variables will replace numbers.

Chalkboard Examples

Simplify.

1. $y^4 \cdot y^2$ $y^{4+2} = y^6$

2. $(4n^3)(5n^2)$ $(4 \cdot 5)(n^3 \cdot n^2) =$
     $20n^{3+2} = 20n^5$

3. $(-4x^2y^5)(7xy^4)$
     $(-4)(7)(x^2 \cdot x)(y^5 \cdot y^4) =$
     $-28(x^{2+1})(y^{5+4}) = -28x^3y^9$

4. $\frac{16}{5}x^2y \cdot \frac{15}{4}x^3y^2$
     $\left(\frac{16}{5} \cdot \frac{15}{4}\right)(x^2 \cdot x^3)(y \cdot y^2) =$
     $12x^5y^3$

5. $(2ab^2)(-6a^4b^2) +$
     $(a^2b)(2a^3b^3)$
     $(2)(-6)(a \cdot a^4)(b^2 \cdot b^2) +$
     $2(a^2 \cdot a^3)(b \cdot b^3) =$
     $-12a^5b^4 + 2a^5b^4 =$
     $-10a^5b^4$

Multiplication

4-3 Multiplying Monomials

Objective   To multiply monomials.

Study the following examples. Remember that an exponent indicates the number of times the base is used as a factor.

$$\overbrace{}^{3 \text{ factors}} \quad \overbrace{}^{5 \text{ factors}}$$
$$x^3 \cdot x^5 = \underbrace{(x \cdot x \cdot x) \cdot (x \cdot x \cdot x \cdot x \cdot x)}_{8 \text{ factors}} = x^8$$

$$\overbrace{}^{m \text{ factors}} \quad \overbrace{}^{n \text{ factors}}$$
$$a^m \cdot a^n = \underbrace{(a \cdot a \cdot \ldots \cdot a) \cdot (a \cdot a \cdot \ldots \cdot a)}_{m + n \text{ factors}} = a^{m+n}$$

The following general rule applies when two powers to be multiplied have the *same base*.

Rule of Exponents for Products of Powers

For all positive integers m and n:

$$a^m \cdot a^n = a^{m+n}.$$

To multiply two powers having the same base, you add the exponents.

Example 1   Simplify: **a.** $x^3 \cdot x^5$ **b.** $b^7 \cdot b^4$

Solution   **a.** $x^3 \cdot x^5 = x^{3+5} = x^8$ **b.** $b^7 \cdot b^4 = b^{7+4} = b^{11}$

When you multiply two monomials, you use the rule of exponents along with the commutative and associative properties of multiplication.

Example 2   Simplify $(3n^2)(4n^4)$.

Solution $(3n^2)(4n^4) = (3 \cdot 4)(n^2 \cdot n^4)$ {Commutative and associative properties of multiplication
                $= 12n^6$ {Rule of exponents for products of powers

---

152   *Chapter 4*

Example 3 $(-3a^3b^2)(5ab^4) = (-3 \cdot 5)(a^3 \cdot a)(b^2 \cdot b^4)$
$$= -15a^4b^6 \quad \textbf{Answer}$$

Example 4 $\dfrac{20x^2y}{3} \cdot \dfrac{12x^3y^5}{5} = \left(\dfrac{20}{3} \cdot \dfrac{12}{5}\right)(x^2 \cdot x^3)(y \cdot y^5)$
$$= 16x^5y^6 \quad \textbf{Answer}$$

Example 5 $(3x^4y^6)(-2x^2y) + (8x^3y^2)(x^3y^5) = -6x^6y^7 + 8x^6y^7$
$$= 2x^6y^7 \quad \textbf{Answer}$$

Oral Exercises

Simplify.

1. $x^2 \cdot x^5$ x^7 **2.** $t^4 \cdot t^3$ t^7 **3.** $y^2 \cdot y \cdot y^3$ y^6 **4.** $c \cdot c^6 \cdot c^3$ c^{10}

5. $(2s)(5s)$ $10s^2$ **6.** $(3t)(4t)$ $12t^2$ **7.** $(ab^2)(a^2b)$ a^3b^3 **8.** $(x^2y)(xy^3)$ x^3y^4

9. $(2x^2)(3x^3)$ $6x^5$ **10.** $(4x^4)(5x^5)$ $20x^9$ **11.** $(2ab^3)(a^3b)$ $2a^4b^4$ **12.** $(3mn)(mn^4)$ $3m^2n^5$

13. $(5x^5y)(3x^2y^2)$ $15x^7y^3$ **14.** $(4y^6z)(2yz^4)$ $8y^7z^5$ **15.** $(-3s)(7s^2)$ $-21s^3$ **16.** $(-c^3)(-3c^2)$ $3c^5$

17. $(x^2y^3)(x^3y)$ x^5y^4 **18.** $(r^2s^2)(2rs^3)$ $2r^3s^5$ **19.** $(-t^3)(-t)^3$ t^6 **20.** $(-x^2)(-x)^2$ $-x^4$

Written Exercises

Simplify.

A

1. $n^3 \cdot n^5$ n^8 **2.** $a^2 \cdot a^2$ a^4 **3.** $x^3 \cdot x^4 \cdot x^2$ x^9

4. $n^2 \cdot n^2 \cdot n$ n^5 **5.** $(2x^2)(5x^5)$ $10x^7$ **6.** $(5a^5)(6a^6)$ $30a^{11}$

7. $(m^2n)(mn^4)$ m^3n^5 **8.** $(y^3z)(y^2z^3)$ y^5z^4 **9.** $(2ab)(3ab^5)$ $6a^2b^6$

10. $(5x^2y)(3x^3y^4)$ $15x^5y^5$ **11.** $(4x^5)(-3x^2)$ $-12x^7$ **12.** $(5y^3)(-2y^4)$ $-10y^7$

13. $(-3xy^3)(-2x^3y)$ $6x^4y^4$ **14.** $(3r^2s^3)(-5r^3s)$ $-15r^5s^4$ **15.** $(5a^2b^3c)(2ab^4c^2)$ $10a^3b^7c^3$

16. $(3y^3z)(4y^4z^2)$ $12y^7z^3$ **17.** $(2p^2q)(3pq)(4q)$ $24p^3q^3$ **18.** $(ab^2)(5a^2b^3)(3a^3)$ $15a^6b^5$

19. $(-x^2y^3)(3xy^2)(-2x^3y)$ $6x^6y^6$ **20.** $(-r^2s)(-3rs^3)(-s^2)$ $-3r^3s^6$

21. $\left(\dfrac{2}{3}t^4\right)\left(\dfrac{3}{2}t^2\right)$ t^6 **22.** $\left(\dfrac{2}{7}a^2\right)(21a^5)$ $6a^7$

23. $\dfrac{15a^3b}{2} \cdot \dfrac{8ab^2}{10}$ $6a^4b^3$ **24.** $\dfrac{4h^3k^2}{7} \cdot \dfrac{21hk^5}{2}$ $6h^4k^7$

25. $(3x^3)\left(\dfrac{1}{6}x^2\right)(8x)$ $4x^6$ **26.** $(8c^2)(-d)\left(-\dfrac{1}{4}cd^2\right)$ $2c^3d^3$

27. $(3p^3q)\left(-\dfrac{5}{6}q^3\right)(-p^4)$ $\dfrac{5}{2}p^7q^4$ **28.** $(-a^3b)(-a^2b^2)(-ab^3)$ $-a^6b^6$

29. $(4xy)(2xy^3)(-2y^2)$ $-16x^2y^6$ **30.** $(5b^4)(-3a^2b)(-a^3)$ $15a^5b^5$

Polynomials   **153**

Simplify.

B **31.** $(5x^2)(2x^3) + (3x)(4x^4)$ $22x^5$ **32.** $(2y)(4y^3) + (3y^2)(5y^2)$ $23y^4$

33. $(3a^5)(5a^3) - (6a^2)(a^6)$ $9a^8$ **34.** $(6s^5)(2s^2) - (3s^4)(4s^3)$ 0

Find the perimeter and the area of each shaded region.
(Area of rectangle = length × width.)

35.
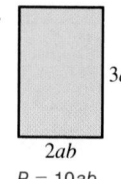
$P = 10ab$
$A = 6a^2b^2$

36.
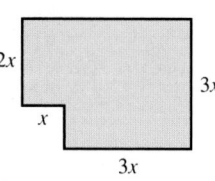
$P = 14x$
$A = 11x^2$

37.
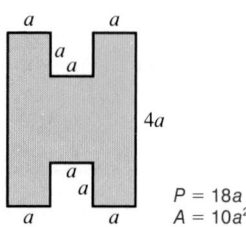
$P = 18a$
$A = 10a^2$

Find the total surface area of each solid.
(The total surface area of a solid is the sum of the areas of all its faces.)

38.
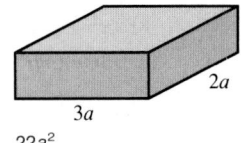
$22a^2$

39.
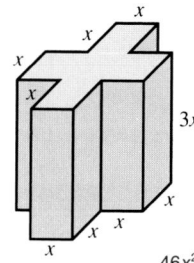
$46x^2$

40.
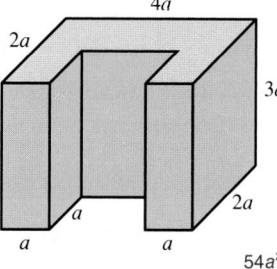
$54a^2$

Simplify.

C **41.** $a^m \cdot a^m$ a^{2m} **42.** $x^{3n} \cdot x^n$ x^{4n} **43.** $3^p \cdot 3^q$ 3^{p+q}

44. $5^x \cdot 5^4$ 5^{x+4} **45.** $4^2 \cdot 4^{x-2}$ 4^x **46.** $(-2)(-2)^{x-2}$ $(-2)^{x-1}$

47. $a^x \cdot a^3$ a^{x+3} **48.** $x^2 \cdot x^n$ x^{2+n} **49.** $2^{x-1} \cdot 2^{x+4}$ 2^{2x+3}

50. $5^{2n} \cdot 5^{n+2} \cdot 5^n$ 5^{4n+2} **51.** $(nx^5)(5x^5)$ $5nx^{10}$ **52.** $(3t^k)(kt^3)$ $3kt^{k+3}$

Mixed Review Exercises

Simplify.

1. $4 + 2^2$ 8 **2.** $(4 + 2)^2$ 36 **3.** $3p^2 + 4q^2 - 2p^2q - q^2$
                                                                                                $3p^2 + 3q^2 - 2p^2q$

4. $3 \cdot 7^2$ 147 **5.** $(3 \cdot 7)^2$ 441 **6.** $3x^2 - 4x + 5 + 6x + 4x^2$
                                                                                                $7x^2 + 2x + 5$

Solve.

7. $4(y + 3) = 3y$ $\{-12\}$ **8.** $15z = 30 + 10z$ $\{6\}$ **9.** $7n - 5 = 2n$ $\{1\}$

10. $\frac{n}{5} + 3 = 6$ $\{15\}$ **11.** $2(x - 4) = 6$ $\{7\}$ **12.** $\frac{y}{2} - 1 = 3$ $\{8\}$

4-4 Powers of Monomials

Objective   To find powers of monomials.

To find a power of a monomial that is already a power, you can use the definition of a power and the rule of exponents for products of powers.

Example 1 $(x^5)^3 = x^5 \cdot x^5 \cdot x^5 = x^{5+5+5} = x^{15}$

Notice that $(x^5)^3 = x^{15}$, or $x^{5 \cdot 3}$. In general:

$$(a^m)^n = \overbrace{a^m \cdot a^m \cdot \ \ldots \ \cdot a^m}^{a^m \text{ is a factor } n \text{ times}} = \overbrace{a^{m+m+\cdots+m}}^{n \text{ terms}} = a^{mn}.$$

Rule of Exponents for a Power of a Power

For all positive integers m and n:

$$(a^m)^n = a^{mn}$$

To find a power of a power, you multiply the exponents.

Example 2 $(u^4)^5 = u^{4 \cdot 5} = u^{20}$ **Example 3** $[(-a)^2]^3 = (a^2)^3 = a^6$

To find a power of a product, you can use the definition of a power and the commutative and associative properties of multiplication.

Example 4 Simplify $(2x)^3$.   **Solution**

$$\begin{aligned}(2x)^3 &= (2x)(2x)(2x) \\ &= (2 \cdot 2 \cdot 2) \cdot (x \cdot x \cdot x) \\ &= 2^3 \cdot x^3 = 8x^3 \quad \textbf{\textit{Answer}}\end{aligned}$$

Both the 2 and the x are cubed when the product $2x$ is cubed. In general:

$$(ab)^m = \overbrace{(ab)(ab)\cdots(ab)}^{ab \text{ is a factor } m \text{ times}} = \overbrace{(a \cdot a \cdot \ \ldots \ \cdot a)}^{m \text{ factors}}\overbrace{(b \cdot b \cdot \ \ldots \ \cdot b)}^{m \text{ factors}} = a^m b^m$$

Rule of Exponents for a Power of a Product

For every positive integer m:

$$(ab)^m = a^m b^m$$

To find a power of a product, you find the power of each factor and then multiply.

Polynomials   **155**

Teaching Suggestions, p. T96
Reading Algebra, p. T96
Suggested Extensions, pp. T96–T97

Warm-Up Exercises

Simplify.
1. $(-2)^3$ -8 2. $(-3)^4$ 81
3. $(-a)^6$ a^6 4. $(-b)^5$ $-b^5$

Find the missing exponent in each of the following.
5. $7^? \cdot 7^5 = 7^8$ 3
6. $n^{10} \cdot n^? = n^{16}$ 6
7. $2^4 \cdot x^3 \cdot 2^? \cdot x = 2^9 x^4$ 5
8. $x^{5 \cdot 2} = x^{5+?} = x^5 \cdot x^?$ 5

Motivating the Lesson

Write on the board:
An easier way to express $2^5 \cdot 2^5$ is $(2^5)^2$.
What would be an easier way to write $4^3 \cdot 4^3 \cdot 4^3 \cdot 4^3 \cdot 4^3 \cdot 4^3$? $(4^3)^6$

Tell students that simplifying expressions that are powers of powers is today's topic.

Chalkboard Examples

Simplify.
1. $(m^3)^4$ m^{12}
2. $(x^2)^5$ x^{10}
3. $[(-b)^4]^5$ $(b^4)^5 = b^{20}$
4. $(2y)^4$
   $(2y)(2y)(2y)(2y) =$
   $(2 \cdot 2 \cdot 2 \cdot 2)(y \cdot y \cdot y \cdot y)$
   $= 16y^4$
5. $(-4mn)^3$
   $(-4)^3 \cdot m^3 \cdot n^3$
   $= -64m^3n^3$

(continued)

Chalkboard Examples

(continued)

6. $(4a^3b^2)^4$

$4^4 \cdot (a^3)^4 \cdot (b^2)^4$

$= 256a^{12}b^8$

Evaluate if $x = 2$.

7. $3x^3$; $(3x)^3$; 3^3x^3

$3 \cdot 2^3 = 3 \cdot 8 = 24$

$(3 \cdot 2)^3 = 6^3 = 216$

$3^3 \cdot 2^3 = 27 \cdot 8 = 216$

Check for Understanding

Here is a suggested use of the Oral Exercises to check students' understanding as you teach the lesson.

Oral Exs. 1–8: use after Example 2.

Oral Exs. 9–12: use after Example 4.

Oral Exs. 13–24: use after Example 7.

Oral Exs. 25–28: use at the end of the lesson.

Common Errors

Some students will write $(3a^2)^3 = 3a^6$. In reteaching, point out that

$(3a^2)^3 = 3a^2 \cdot 3a^2 \cdot 3a^2$

$= 27a^6$.

Thinking Skills

In this lesson and the previous one, students have been asked to look for patterns in examples and to *infer* general rules for working with exponents.

Guided Practice

Evaluate if $a = 2$ and $b = 3$.

1. a^2b^2 36

2. $(ab)^2$ 36

Example 5	Simplify $(-2k)^5$.
Solution	$(-2k)^5 = (-2)^5k^5 = -32k^5$ *Answer*

Example 6	Evaluate if $t = 2$: **a.** $3t^3$ **b.** $(3t)^3$ **c.** 3^3t^3

Solution   **a.** $3t^3 = 3(2)^3$ **b.** $(3t)^3 = (3 \cdot 2)^3$ **c.** $3^3t^3 = 3^3 \cdot 2^3$

$\qquad\qquad\qquad = 3(8) \qquad\qquad\qquad\quad = 6^3 \qquad\qquad\qquad\quad = 27 \cdot 8$

$\qquad\qquad\qquad = 24 \qquad\qquad\qquad\quad = 216 \qquad\qquad\qquad\quad = 216$

In Example 7, both rules of exponents for powers are used.

Example 7	Simplify $(-3x^2y^5)^3$.

Solution $(-3x^2y^5)^3 = (-3)^3(x^2)^3(y^5)^3$

$\qquad\qquad\qquad\qquad\; = -27x^6y^{15}$ *Answer*

Oral Exercises

Simplify.

1. $(a^2)^4$ a^8 **2.** $(x^5)^2$ x^{10} **3.** $(t^6)^3$ t^{18} **4.** $(c^4)^4$ c^{16}

5. **a.** $(t^3)^2$ t^6 **6.** **a.** $(y^5)^3$ y^{15} **7.** **a.** $x^2 \cdot x^4$ x^6 **8.** **a.** $b^4 \cdot b^3$ b^7

     b. $t^3 \cdot t^2$ t^5 **b.** $y^5 \cdot y^3$ y^8 **b.** $(x^2)^4$ x^8 **b.** $(b^4)^3$ b^{12}

9. **a.** $(-z^2)^3$ $-z^6$ **10.** **a.** $(2a^2)^3$ $8a^6$ **11.** **a.** $(3a^4)^2$ $9a^8$ **12.** **a.** $[(-x)^5]^2$ x^{10}

     b. $(-z^3)^2$ z^6 **b.** $(2a^3)^2$ $4a^6$ **b.** $(3a^2)^4$ $81a^8$ **b.** $[(-x)^2]^5$ x^{10}

13. $(2a^3)^5$ $32a^{15}$ **14.** $(-r^3)^4$ r^{12} **15.** $(3t^3)^2$ $9t^6$ **16.** $(2t^2)^4$ $16t^8$

17. $[(-2)^3]^2$ 64 **18.** $[(-1)^7]^3$ -1 **19.** $(-3x^3)^2$ $9x^6$ **20.** $(-2x^2)^3$ $-8x^6$

21. $(a^2b^5)^3$ a^6b^{15} **22.** $(x^3y^3)^2$ x^6y^6 **23.** $(2xy^2)^2$ $4x^2y^4$ **24.** $(-a^2b^3)^3$ $-a^6b^9$

Give the square and the cube of each expression in simplified form.

25. $-2t^2k$ $4t^4k^2$;   **26.** $3rs^4$ $9r^2s^8$;   **27.** $5m^3n$ $25m^6n^2$;   **28.** $-4x^2y^2$ $16x^4y^4$;

        $-8t^6k^3$ $27r^3s^{12}$ $125m^9n^3$ $-64x^6y^6$

Written Exercises

Evaluate if $x = 3$ and $y = 2$.

A   **1.** **a.** $3x^3$ 81 **2.** **a.** $5y^2$ 20 **3.** **a.** xy^2 12 **4.** **a.** xy^3 24

       b. $(3x)^3$ 729 **b.** $(5y)^2$ 100 **b.** x^2y^2 36 **b.** $(xy)^3$ 216

       c. $3^3 \cdot x^3$ 729 **c.** 5^2y^2 100 **c.** $(xy)^2$ 36 **c.** x^3y^3 216

---

156   *Chapter 4*

Simplify.

5. a. $c^5 \cdot c^2$ c^7
   b. $(c^2)^5$ c^{10}
   c. $(c^5)^2$ c^{10}

6. a. $x^4 \cdot x^7$ x^{11}
   b. $(x^4)^7$ x^{28}
   c. $(x^7)^4$ x^{28}

7. a. $(-5a^4)^3$ $-125a^{12}$
   b. $-(5a^4)^3$ $-125a^{12}$
   c. $-5(a^4)^3$ $-5a^{12}$

8. a. $(-2k^5)^6$ $64k^{30}$
   b. $-(2k^5)^6$ $-64k^{30}$
   c. $-2(k^5)^6$ $-2k^{30}$

9. $(7a)^2$ $49a^2$
10. $(-2t)^5$ $-32t^5$
11. $(-4c)^3$ $-64c^3$
12. $(5x)^3$ $125x^3$
13. $(4k^2)^3$ $64k^6$
14. $(6x^3)^2$ $36x^6$
15. $(-3y^3)^3$ $-27y^9$
16. $(-2t^4)^4$ $16t^{16}$
17. $(3a^2b)^3$ $27a^6b^3$
18. $(2x^2y)^5$ $32x^{10}y^5$
19. $(2r^3s^4)^4$ $16r^{12}s^{16}$
20. $(5p^3q^4)^3$ $125p^9q^{12}$

B 21. $(2x)^2(2x)^4$ $64x^6$
22. $(3c)^2(3c)^3$ $243c^5$
23. $(10b)^3(10b)^3$ $1{,}000{,}000b^6$

24. $\left(\frac{1}{2}y\right)^2(2y)^5$ $8y^7$
25. $(3a^2b)^3(2a^3b)$ $54a^9b^4$
26. $(2x^2y^3)^4(-xy^2)^2$ $16x^{10}y^{16}$

27. $\left(\frac{1}{2}p^2q\right)^3(2pq^2)^4$ $2p^{10}q^{11}$
28. $\left(\frac{1}{10}x^3y\right)^3(10y)^4$ $10x^9y^7$
29. $[(2x^2)^2]^2$ $16x^8$

30. $[(-x^3)^2]^3$ x^{18}
31. $(3x^2y)^3(2xy)$ $54x^7y^4$
32. $(5a^2b)^2(5b)^3$ $3125a^4b^5$

Find and simplify (a) the sum and (b) the product of the given monomials.

33. $(3x^3)^2$, $(2x^2)^3$ **a.** $17x^6$ **b.** $72x^{12}$
34. $(a^2)^6$, $(-2a^4)^3$ **a.** $-7a^{12}$ **b.** $-8a^{24}$
35. $a^2(ab^3)^2$, $b^2(a^2b^2)^2$ **a.** $2a^4b^6$ **b.** a^8b^{12}
36. $p(-pq)^4$, $p^3(2pq^2)^2$ **a.** $5p^5q^4$ **b.** $4p^{10}q^8$
37. $a(-ab^2)^3$, $(2a^2b^3)^2$ **a.** $3a^4b^6$ **b.** $-4a^8b^{12}$
38. $(2x)^3(xy)^2$, $(2xy)^2(-x)^3$
   a. $4x^5y^2$ **b.** $-32x^{10}y^4$

Simplify.

C 39. $(x^n)^2$ x^{2n}
40. $(a^x)^3$ a^{3x}
41. $a^x \cdot a^3$ a^{x+3}
42. $x^n \cdot x^2$ x^{n+2}
43. $x^n \cdot x^n$ x^{2n}
44. $a^x \cdot a^x \cdot a^x$ a^{3x}
45. $z^x \cdot z^x \cdot z^x$ z^{3x}
46. $(a^x)^y(a^y)^x$ a^{2xy}
47. $(2r^n)^3(3r^n)^2$ $72r^{5n}$
48. $(2x^n)^3(x^n)^5$ $8x^{8n}$
49. $(3x^n)^2(x^2)^n$ $9x^{4n}$
50. $(t^m)^n \cdot 3(t^n)^m$ $3t^{2mn}$

51. a. Find the volumes of the two cubes shown. $8x^3$; $64x^3$
   b. Which cube has a larger volume? cube on the right
   c. The bigger cube is how many times as large as the smaller cube? 8 times

52. a. Which is larger, $(3^3)^3$ or $3^{(3^3)}$? $3^{(3^3)}$
   b. How many times as large is it? 3^{18} times

53. Show that $16^x \cdot (4^x)^2 = (2^x)^8$.
   $16^x \cdot (4^x)^2 = 16^x \cdot 4^{2x} = (2^4)^x \cdot (2^2)^{2x} = 2^{4x} \cdot 2^{4x} = 2^{8x} = (2^x)^8$

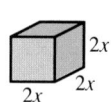
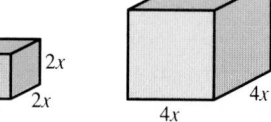

Mixed Review Exercises

Simplify.

1. $(3a^2b)(2ab)(4b)$ $24a^3b^3$
2. $(-x^2y)(2xy)(-4y)$ $8x^3y^3$
3. $(2x^2y^3)^4$ $16x^8y^{12}$
4. $\left(\frac{1}{2}t^3\right)\left(\frac{2}{3}t^2\right)$ $\frac{1}{3}t^5$
5. $6c - 3a - 2c + a$ $4c - 2a$
6. $(3x + 4y + 2) + (2x + y)$ $5x + 5y + 2$
7. $2 \cdot 3^3 + 2 \cdot 3$ 60
8. $-5^2 \cdot 3$ -75
9. $(4^3 + 6^2) \div 5^2$ 4

Simplify.

3. $-(2c^3)^5$ $-32c^{15}$
4. $-2(c^3)^5$ $-2c^{15}$
5. $(6a)^2$ $36a^2$
6. $(-3x)^4$ $81x^4$
7. $(4y^2)^3$ $64y^6$
8. $(-5b^3)^3$ $-125b^9$
9. $(-2x^3y)^3$ $-8x^9y^3$
10. $(3p^3q^4)^2$ $9p^6q^8$

Summarizing the Lesson

Tell the students they have learned how to find powers of powers and powers of products. Ask them to state the rules of exponents (from Lessons 4-3 and 4-4) in their own words and give examples.

Suggested Assignments

Minimum
Day 1: 156/1–20
   S 157/Mixed Review
Day 2: 157/22–34 even
Assign with Lesson 4-5.

Average
   156/2–36 even, 39
   S 157/Mixed Review

Maximum
   156/3–51 mult. of 3
   S 157/Mixed Review

Supplementary Materials

Study Guide   pp. 59–60
Practice Master   19
Resource Book   p. 92

Explorations, pp. 689–690

Teaching Suggestions, p. T97
Using Manipulatives, p. T97
Suggested Extensions, p. T97

Warm-Up Exercises

Simplify.

1. $2(a - 4)$ $2a - 8$

2. $4(2y + 3)$ $8y + 12$

3. $-3(4 - 5x)$ $-12 + 15x$

4. $(6a^2 - 5a + 2) + (7a - 5)$
$6a^2 + 2a - 3$

5. $(2x - 8y) - (x - 3y)$
$x - 5y$

6. $x^3 \cdot x^6$ x^9

7. $-3x^2y^2 \cdot 4xy^3$ $-12x^3y^5$

Motivating the Lesson

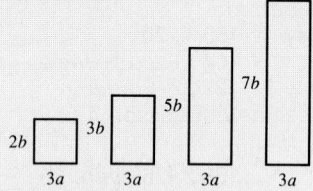

Ask students how they might calculate the total area of the four rectangles. Answers may vary.
$3a(2b + 3b + 5b + 7b)$
Multiplying a polynomial by a monomial is today's topic.

Chalkboard Examples

Simplify.

1. $y(y - 2)$ $y^2 - 2y$

2. $-3b(2b^2 + 4b - 1)$
$-6b^3 - 12b^2 + 3b$

3. $4x^2(5x^2 - 2xy + y^2)$
$20x^4 - 8x^3y + 4x^2y^2$

4. $a[2a - 3(1 - a)]$
$= a(2a - 3 + 3a)$
$= a(5a - 3)$
$= 5a^2 - 3a$

4-5 Multiplying Polynomials by Monomials

Objective   To multiply a polynomial by a monomial.

You can think of the product $x(x + 3)$ as the area of a rectangle as shown in the diagram below.

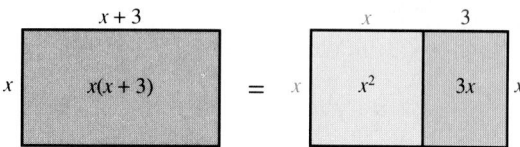

The diagram shows that $x(x + 3) = x^2 + 3x$.

By using the distributive property and the rules of exponents, you can multiply any polynomial by a monomial. You may multiply either horizontally or vertically.

Example 1   Multiply: $x(x + 3)$

Solution 1 $x(x + 3) = x(x) + x(3)$
$= x^2 + 3x$ **Answer**

Solution 2 $x + 3$
x
$x^2 + 3x$ **Answer**

Example 2   Multiply: $-2x(4x^2 - 3x + 5)$

Solution 1 $-2x(4x^2 - 3x + 5) = -2x(4x^2) - 2x(-3x) - 2x(5)$
$= -8x^3 + 6x^2 - 10x$ **Answer**

Solution 2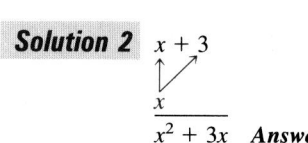
$-8x^3 + 6x^2 - 10x$ **Answer**

Example 3   Multiply: $5xy^2(3x^2 - 4xy + y^2)$

Solution $5xy^2(3x^2 - 4xy + y^2) = 5xy^2(3x^2) - 5xy^2(4xy) + 5xy^2(y^2)$
$= 15x^3y^2 - 20x^2y^3 + 5xy^4$ **Answer**

Example 4 Solve $n(2 - 5n) + 5(n^2 - 2) = 0$.

Solution
$$n(2 - 5n) + 5(n^2 - 2) = 0$$
$$2n - 5n^2 + 5n^2 - 10 = 0$$
$$2n - 10 = 0$$
$$2n = 10$$
$$n = 5 \quad \therefore \text{ the solution set is } \{5\}. \quad \textbf{\textit{Answer}}$$

Oral Exercises

Multiply.

1. $3(x + 2)$ $3x + 6$ 2. $5(t - 2)$ $5t - 10$ 3. $4(3r - 1)$ $12r - 4$

5. $z(3 - z)$ $3z - z^2$ 6. $-x(3 - 2x)$ $-3x + 2x^2$ 7. $-t(-2 - t)$ $2t + t^2$

9. $2x(3x + 2)$ $6x^2 + 4x$ 10. $ab(a + b)$ $a^2b + ab^2$ 11. $a(a^2 - 2a + 3)$ $a^3 - 2a^2 + 3a$

4. $12 - 6y$
8. $ab + 2ac$
4. $6(2 - y)$
8. $a(b + 2c)$
12. $c^2(2 - c - c^2)$ $2c^2 - c^3 - c^4$

Written Exercises

Multiply.

A   1. $4(x - 3)$ $4x - 12$ 2. $-3(y + 3)$ $-3y - 9$ 3. $c(c - 2)$ $c^2 - 2c$ 4. $a(4 - 2a)$ $4a - 2a^2$

5. $3y(y + 5)$ $3y^2 + 15y$ 6. $4x(2x - 3)$ $8x^2 - 12x$ 7. $-2r(7 - 3r)$ $-14r + 6r^2$ 8. $-z(6 - 5z)$ $-6z + 5z^2$

9. $\begin{array}{r} 3y^2 - y - 5 \\ 2y \end{array}$ 10. $\begin{array}{r} 2k^2 - 3k - 7 \\ -3k \end{array}$

9. $6y^3 - 2y^2 - 10y$ 10. $-6k^3 + 9k^2 + 21k$
11. $-2a^3b^2 + 6a^2b^3 - 10ab^4$ 12. $6p^3q^2 - 15p^2q^3 - 9pq^4$

11. $\begin{array}{r} a^2b - 3ab^2 + 5b^3 \\ -2ab \end{array}$ 12. $\begin{array}{r} 2p^3 - 5p^2q - 3pq^2 \\ 3q^2 \end{array}$

13. $3x(x^2 - 2x + 4)$ $3x^3 - 6x^2 + 12x$ 14. $4t(2t^2 - t - 5)$ $8t^3 - 4t^2 - 20t$

15. $pq^2(p^2 - 3pq - 4q^2)$ $p^3q^2 - 3p^2q^3 - 4pq^4$ 16. $2x^2y(2x^2 - 3xy + y^2)$ $4x^4y - 6x^3y^2 + 2x^2y^3$

17. $\frac{1}{3}x^2(6x^2 - 9xy - 3y^2)$ $2x^4 - 3x^3y - x^2y^2$ 18. $\frac{1}{2}s^2t(4t^2 - 10st + 6s^2)$ $2s^2t^3 - 5s^3t^2 + 3s^4t$

Simplify.

Sample
$$4n(n + 5) + n(6 - n) = 4n(n) + 4n(5) + n(6) - n(n)$$
$$= 4n^2 + 20n + 6n - n^2$$
$$= 3n^2 + 26n \quad \textbf{\textit{Answer}}$$

19. $2x(x - 3) + x(5 - x)$ $x^2 - x$ 20. $3x(5 - 2x) + 6x(x - 2)$ $3x$

21. $6r^2(2r - 1) - 3r(4r^2 - 5r)$ $9r^2$ 22. $4y(2y^2 - 3y) - 3y^2(y - 4)$ $5y^3$

23. $-[6y - 3(5y - 4)]$ $9y - 12$ 24. $8n - 2[n - 2(3 - n)]$ $2n + 12$

25. $a[2a - 3(1 - a)] + 5(a - a^2)$ $2a$ 26. $2x[3x - 2(3 + x)] - x^2$ $x^2 - 12x$

Polynomials   **159**

Check for Understanding

Here is a suggested use of the Oral Exercises to check students' understanding as you teach the lesson.
Oral Exs. 1–10: Use after Example 1.
Oral Exs. 11–12: Use after Example 3.

Guided Practice

Multiply.

1. $6(x + 2)$ $6x + 12$

2. $-4(y - 3)$ $-4y + 12$

3. $\begin{array}{r} 2a^2b + ab^2 - ab \\ -ab \\ \hline -2a^3b^2 - a^2b^3 + a^2b^2 \end{array}$

4. $4y(y^2 - 2y + 1)$
$4y^3 - 8y^2 + 4y$

5. $3pq^2(2p^2q - pq + 5q^2)$
$6p^3q^3 - 3p^2q^3 + 15pq^4$

Solve.

6. $2(x - 5) - 6 = 18$ 17

7. $0 = 4(y - 1) - 3(y - 2)$ -2

Summarizing the Lesson

Tell the students they have learned to multiply polynomials by monomials and have solved equations with polynomials.

Suggested Assignments

Minimum
Day 1: 159/2–18 even
Assign with Lesson 4-4.
Day 2: 159/19–37 odd, 40
   S 160/Mixed Review
Average
     159/3–36 mult. of 3, 40–42
   S 160/Mixed Review
Maximum
     159/3–42 mult. of 3, 43
   S 160/Mixed Review

Solve.

27. $2(x - 3) + 5 = 7$ {4}

28. $3(z + 3) - 7 = 8$ {2}

29. $15 = 3(x - 1) + 2(4 - x)$ {10}

30. $0 = 3(1 - 2t) - 5(2 - t)$ {−7}

B **31.** $y(2 - 3y) + 3(y^2 - 4) = 0$ {6}

32. $\frac{1}{2}(12 - 4s^2) - 2s(1 - s) = 8$ {−1}

33. $2(n - 3) + n(2 - n) = 2 - n^2$ {2}

34. $\frac{1}{2}(6c + 4) - 2\left(c + \frac{5}{2}\right) = \frac{2}{3}(9 - 3c)$ {3}

35. $\frac{3}{2}(4x - 6) - x(3 - x) = \frac{1}{3}x(3x + 6)$ {9}

36. $4(y - 7) - 2y(1 - 3y) = 6y^2$ {14}

37. $r^2 - [4 - r(3 - r)] = 2(2r - 3)$ {2}

38. $1 = 2x(x - 2) - [5 - 2x(1 - x)]$ {−3}

39. A rectangular region is divided into two smaller regions with the dimensions shown. $2x^2 + xy$
a. Find the sum of the areas of these two regions.
b. Find the product of the length and width of the original rectangle. $2x^2 + xy$
c. Compare your answers to parts (a) and (b). What property of real numbers does this diagram illustrate? Distributive property

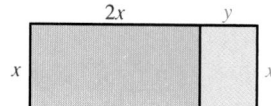

Find the area of each shaded region.

40.

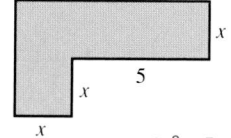

$2x^2 + 5x$

41.

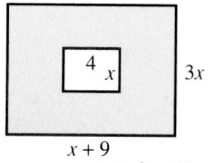

$x + 9$
$3x^2 + 23x$

42.

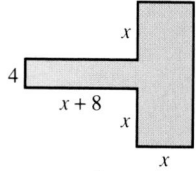

x
$2x^2 + 8x + 32$

Find the total surface area and the volume of each solid shown.

C **43.**

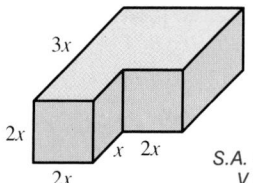

S.A. = $48x^2$
V = $20x^3$

44.

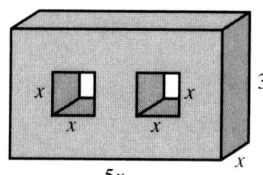

S.A. = $50x^2$
V = $13x^3$

Mixed Review Exercises

Simplify.

1. $(3x^2y)^3$ $27x^6y^3$

2. $(-5r^3y^4)^2$ $25r^6y^8$

3. $(-3n)^3$ $-27n^3$

4. $(2a^3y)^3(3a^2y^2)^2$ $72a^{13}y^7$

5. $(2x^2)(3x^3) + (x^4)(4x)$ $10x^5$

6. $(5n^4)n^2 - n^3(2n^3)$ $3n^6$

7. $(7p - 3q + 5) + (3q + 3p)$ $10p + 5$

8. $(2x + y - 3) - (y + x - 7)$ $x + 4$

9. $(5y^3)^2(3x^2y)^3$ $675x^6y^9$

4-6 Multiplying Polynomials

Objective   To multiply polynomials.

You have learned how to use the distributive property to multiply a polynomial by a monomial:

$$(2x)(3x + 2) = (2x)3x + (2x)2$$

If you replace $(2x)$ in the example by the polynomial $(2x + 5)$, the distributive property can still be used:

$$(2x + 5)(3x + 2) = (2x + 5)3x + (2x + 5)2$$
$$= 6x^2 + 15x + 4x + 10$$
$$= 6x^2 + 19x + 10$$

The product of two polynomials can also be thought of as the area of a rectangle. The diagram also shows that the product of $(2x + 5)$ and $(3x + 2)$ is $6x^2 + 19x + 10$.

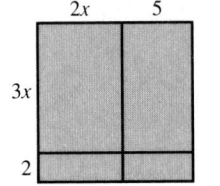

Example 1   Multiply: $(3x - 2)(2x^2 - 5x - 4)$

Solution   You can find the product by arranging your work in vertical form.

Step 1 Multiply by $3x$.	Step 2 Multiply by -2.	Step 3 Add.
$2x^2 - 5x - 4$	$2x^2 - 5x - 4$	$2x^2 - 5x - 4$
$\underline{3x - 2}$	$\underline{3x - 2}$	$\underline{3x - 2}$
$6x^3 - 15x^2 - 12x$	$6x^3 - 15x^2 - 12x$	$6x^3 - 15x^2 - 12x$
	$\underline{\quad - 4x^2 + 10x + 8}$	$\underline{\quad - 4x^2 + 10x + 8}$
		$6x^3 - 19x^2 - 2x + 8$ **Answer**

It often is helpful to rearrange the terms of a polynomial so that the degrees of a particular variable are in either increasing order or decreasing order.

In order of *decreasing* degree of x: $x^4 + 2x^3 - 4x + 2$

In order of *increasing* degree of x: $2 - 4x + 2x^3 + x^4$

In order of *decreasing degree* of x
and *increasing degree* of y: $x^3 - 3x^2y + xy^2 + 2y^3$

Polynomials   **161**

Explorations, pp. 689–690

Teaching Suggestions, p. T97
Using Manipulatives, p. T97
Suggested Extensions, p. T98

Warm-Up Exercises

Example: Multiply 38×46.

$$30 + 8$$
$$\underline{40 + 6}$$
$$1200 + 320$$
$$\underline{180 + 48}$$
$$1200 + 500 + 48 = 1748$$

Multiply as in the example.

1. 42×57

$$40 + 2$$
$$\underline{50 + 7}$$
$$2000 + 100$$
$$\underline{280 + 14}$$
$$2000 + 380 + 14 = 2394$$

2. 34×65

$$30 + 4$$
$$\underline{60 + 5}$$
$$1800 + 240$$
$$\underline{150 + 20}$$
$$1800 + 390 + 20 = 2210$$

Motivating the Lesson

Sometimes a product like 101×99 can be found quickly by multiplying two binomials:

$$100 + 1$$
$$\underline{100 - 1}$$
$$10,000 + 100$$
$$\underline{- 100 - 1}$$
$$10,000 - 1 = 9999$$

This suggests a way to multiply polynomials, the topic of today's lesson.

Thinking Skills

Students recall the use of the distributive property and *apply* it to extend their skills to include the multiplication of two polynomials.

Multiply.

1. $(x + 4)(x - 1)$

$\quad x + 4$
$\quad x - 1$
$\quad \overline{}$
$\quad x^2 + 4x$
$\quad\ \ \underline{-\ x - 4}$
$\quad x^2 + 3x - 4$

2. $(2 - s)(3 + 5s - 4s^2)$

$\quad 3 + 5s - 4s^2$
$\quad 2 - s$
$\quad \overline{}$
$\quad 6 + 10s -\ \ 8s^2$
$\quad\ \ \underline{-\ \ 3s -\ 5s^2 + 4s^3}$
$\quad 6 +\ \ 7s - 13s^2 + 4s^3$

3. $(2y + x)(xy - y^2 + 3x^2)$

$\quad 3x^2 + xy - y^2$
$\quad x + 2y$
$\quad \overline{}$
$\quad 3x^3 +\ \ x^2y -\ \ xy^2$
$\quad\ \ \underline{6x^2y + 2xy^2 - 2y^3}$
$\quad 3x^3 + 7x^2y +\ \ xy^2 - 2y^3$

Here is a suggested use of the Oral Exercises to check students' understanding as you teach the lesson.
Oral Exs. 1–8: use after Example 2.
Oral Exs. 9–14: use at the beginning of the lesson.

Multiply. Use the vertical form.

1. $2x + 4$
$\quad 3x - 1$
$\quad \overline{}$
$\quad 6x^2 + 10x - 4$

2. $3x^2 - 2xy + y^2$
$\quad 2x + y$
$\quad \overline{}$
$\quad 6x^3 - x^2y + y^3$

Multiply. Use the horizontal form.

3. $(a + 2)(a - 3)\ a^2 - a - 6$

To see the advantage of rearranging terms, multiply the polynomials in Example 2 as they are given. Then compare your work with the solution of Example 2.

Example 2 Multiply: $(y + 2x)(x^3 - 2y^3 + 3xy^2 + x^2y)$

Solution

$\begin{array}{l} x^3 - 2y^3 + 3xy^2 + x^2y \\ \underline{y + 2x} \end{array}$ Rearrange in order of decreasing degree of x, $\left.\begin{array}{l} \\ \\ \\ \\ \end{array}\right\}$

$x^3 + x^2y + 3xy^2 - 2y^3$
$\underline{2x + y}$
$2x^4 + 2x^3y + 6x^2y^2 - 4xy^3$
$\underline{\quad x^3y +\ \ x^2y^2 + 3xy^3 - 2y^4}$
$2x^4 + 3x^3y + 7x^2y^2 -\ \ xy^3 - 2y^4$

Oral Exercises

Arrange in order of decreasing degree in the variable printed in color.

1. $5 + 2x^2 - 3x, x$ $\quad 2x^2 - 3x + 5$

2. $3n - 4n^2 + n^3 - 3, n$ $\quad n^3 - 4n^2 + 3n - 3$

3. $a^2b - 2ab^2 + a^3 + 3b^3, a$ $\quad a^3 + a^2b - 2ab^2 + 3b^3$

4. $xy^2 - 3x^2y + 2x^3y - 2y, x$ $\quad 2x^3y - 3x^2y + xy^2 - 2y$

5–8. Repeat Exercises 1–4 after replacing "decreasing" by "increasing."

5. $5 - 3x + 2x^2$ **6.** $-3 + 3n - 4n^2 + n^3$ **7.** $3b^3 - 2ab^2 + a^2b + a^3$ **8.** $-2y + xy^2 - 3x^2y + 2x^3y$

Complete. **9.** $2x + 3; 2x + 3$ **10.** $t - 5; t - 5$ **11.** $a^2 + 2a + 3; a^2 + 2a + 3$ **12.** $y^2 - y + 6; y^2 - y + 6$

9. $(2x + 3)(4x + 1) = (\underline{\ ?\ })4x + (\underline{\ ?\ })1$

10. $(t - 5)(2t - 3) = (\underline{\ ?\ })2t - (\underline{\ ?\ })3$

11. $(a^2 + 2a + 3)(a - 2) = (\underline{\ ?\ })a - (\underline{\ ?\ })2$ **12.** $(y^2 - y + 6)(2y + 3) = (\underline{\ ?\ })2y + (\underline{\ ?\ })3$

13. $(x + 2)(x + 3) = (x + 2)x + (x + 2)3 = (\underline{\ ?\ })x^2 + (\underline{\ ?\ })x + (\underline{\ ?\ })1; 5; 6$

14. $(x - 3)(x + 5) = (x - 3)x + (x - 3)5 = (\underline{\ ?\ })x^2 + (\underline{\ ?\ })x - (\underline{\ ?\ })1; 2; 15$

Written Exercises

Multiply. Use the vertical form.

A **1.** $3x - 5$
$\quad \underline{2x + 1}$
$\quad 6x^2 - 7x - 5$

2. $5t - 1$
$\quad \underline{2t - 3}$
$\quad 10t^2 - 17t + 3$

3. $a^2 - 3a + 4$
$\quad \underline{2a + 3}$
$\quad 2a^3 - 3a^2 - a + 12$

4. $r^2 + 2r - 5$
$\quad \underline{3r - 2}$
$\quad 3r^3 + 4r^2 - 19r + 10$

5. $3x - 2y$
$\quad \underline{2x + 5y}$
$\quad 6x^2 + 11xy - 10y^2$

6. $2a - 5b$
$\quad \underline{a - 3b}$
$\quad 2a^2 - 11ab + 15b^2$

7. $c^2 + 2cd - 3d^2$
$\quad \underline{c - 2d}$
$\quad c^3 - 7cd^2 + 6d^3$

8. $2x^2 - 3xy - y^2$
$\quad \underline{2x + y}$
$\quad 4x^3 - 4x^2y - 5xy^2 - y^3$

Multiply. Use the horizontal form.

9. $(y + 3)(y + 2)\ y^2 + 5y + 6$

10. $(n + 7)(n + 5)\ n^2 + 12n + 35$

11. $(a + 4)(a - 1)\ a^2 + 3a - 4$

12. $(r - 3)(r + 6)\ r^2 + 3r - 18$

13. $(2x - 1)(x - 5)\ 2x^2 - 11x + 5$

14. $(3a - 2)(a - 3)\ 3a^2 - 11a + 6$

15. $(3z - 2)(2z + 3)\ 6z^2 + 5z - 6$

16. $(5k + 2)(2k - 3)\ 10k^2 - 11k - 6$

17. $(4s - 5)(4s + 5)$ $16s^2 - 25$

18. $(3x + 7)(3x - 7)$ $9x^2 - 49$

19. $(a + 2)(a^2 + 3a + 5)$ $a^3 + 5a^2 + 11a + 10$

20. $(x + 3)(x^2 + 2x + 4)$ $x^3 + 5x^2 + 10x + 12$

21. $(m - 1)(m^2 + 2m + 6)$ $m^3 + m^2 + 4m - 6$

22. $(y - 5)(y^2 - 3y - 7)$ $y^3 - 8y^2 + 8y + 35$

23 $(2x - 1)(x^2 - x + 3)$ $2x^3 - 3x^2 + 7x - 3$

24. $(3s + 2)(2s^2 - 2s + 1)$ $6s^3 - 2s^2 - s + 2$

25. $(3z - 2)(3z^2 - z + 4)$ $9z^3 - 9z^2 + 14z - 8$

26. $(2n - 5)(2n^2 - 3n - 2)$
$4n^3 - 16n^2 + 11n + 10$

In each of the following figures, a rectangle has been divided into four smaller rectangles. (a) Find the sum of the areas of the four smaller rectangles. (b) Find the product of the length and width of the original rectangle. (c) Compare your answers to parts (a) and (b).

27.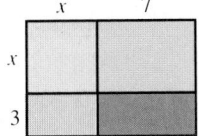
a. $x^2 + 10x + 21$
b. $x^2 + 10x + 21$
c. equal

28.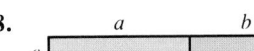
a. $ac + bc + ad + bd$
b. $ac + bc + ad + bd$
c. equal

Multiply using either the horizontal or vertical form. Arrange the terms in each factor in order of decreasing or increasing degree of one of the variables.

29–36. Form of answers may vary as long as correct terms are combined.

B **29.** $(2 + y)(y^2 - 2y + 3)$ $y^3 - y + 6$

30. $(5 + x)(x^2 - 5x + 4)$ $x^3 - 21x + 20$

31. $(2y - 3)(2y - 4 + y^2)$ $2y^3 + y^2 - 14y + 12$

32. $(3y - 4)(y - 2y^2 + 6)$ $-6y^3 + 11y^2 + 14y - 24$

33. $(2 - 3x)(x^2 - 2x + 5)$ $-3x^3 + 8x^2 - 19x + 10$

34. $(1 - 2a)(a^2 - 4 + 3a)$ $-2a^3 - 5a^2 + 11a - 4$

35. $(2r - s)(s^2 + 4r^2 - 4rs)$
$8r^3 - 12r^2s + 6rs^2 - s^3$

36. $(y - 2x)(2x^2 + y^2 - 3xy)$
$-4x^3 + 8x^2y - 5xy^2 + y^3$

Solve.

Sample $(x + 4)(x + 3) = (x + 1)(x + 5)$

Solution
$x^2 + 7x + 12 = x^2 + 6x + 5$
$7x + 12 = 6x + 5$ {Subtract x^2 from both sides.
$x + 12 = 5$ {Subtract $6x$ from both sides.
$x = -7$ {Subtract 12 from both sides.

∴ the solution set is $\{-7\}$. *Answer*

$\{-13\}$

37. $(x + 2)(x - 5) = (x - 1)(x - 3)$ {13}

38. $(x - 3)(x + 7) - (x + 1)(x + 5) = 0$

39. $(2x - 5)(x - 4) + 2x(1 - x) = 0$ $\left\{\frac{20}{11}\right\}$

40. $(3x + 5)(2x - 3) = (x - 1)(6x + 5)$ {5}

41. $(x - 3)(x^2 - 2x + 6) = x(x^2 - 5x + 9)$ {6}

42. $(2n - 3)(n^2 + 3n - 2) = (n - 1)(2n^2 + 5n - 4)$ $\left\{\frac{1}{2}\right\}$

Express as a polynomial. **43.** $x^4 - 6x^3 + 19x^2 - 30x + 25$ **44.** $n^4 + 4n^3 + 2n^2 - 4n + 1$

43. The square of $x^2 - 3x + 5$

44. The square of $n^2 + 2n - 1$

45. The cube of $x + 5$ $x^3 + 15x^2 + 75x + 125$

46. The cube of $a - 3$ $a^3 - 9a^2 + 27a - 27$

47. Given that $(2 - y)^3 = 8 - 12y + 6y^2 - y^3$, find $(2 - y)^4$. $16 - 32y + 24y^2 - 8y^3 + y^4$

48. Subtract the product of $2x - y$ and $x - 2y$ from $x^2 + y^2$. $-x^2 + 5xy - y^2$

Polynomials **163**

---

4. $(5y + 4)(2y - 3)$
$10y^2 - 7y - 12$

5. $(y + 2)(y^2 - 2y + 3)$
$y^3 - y + 6$

6. a. Find the sum of the areas of the four smaller rectangles.

b. Find the product of the length and width of the entire rectangle. Compare the answers.

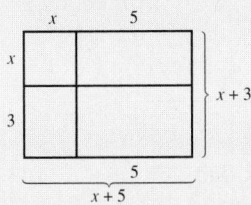

a. $x^2 + 5x + 3x + 15 =$
$x^2 + 8x + 15$
b. $(x + 3)(x + 5) =$
$x^2 + 8x + 15$
Answers are equal.

Summarizing the Lesson

Tell the students that they have learned how to multiply polynomials both in vertical and horizontal form.

Suggested Assignments

Minimum
Day 1: 162/1–31 odd
Day 2: 163/33–43 odd
  S 164/Mixed Review

Average
  162/3–42 mult. of 3,
   43, 45
  S 164/Mixed Review

Maximum
  162/3–48 mult. of 3,
   50
  S 164/Mixed Review

Supplementary Materials

Study Guide   pp. 63–64
Practice Master   20
Test Master   15
Resource Book   p. 93
Overhead Visuals   3, 6

49. When a certain polynomial is divided by $x - 3$, the quotient is $x^2 + x - 2$. Find the polynomial. $x^3 - 2x^2 - 5x + 6$

C 50. a. Multiply:
  (1) $(x + 1)(x^2 - x + 1)$ $x^3 + 1$
  (2) $(x + 1)(x^3 - x^2 + x - 1)$ $x^4 - 1$
  (3) $(x + 1)(x^4 - x^3 + x^2 - x + 1)$ $x^5 + 1$

  b. Using your answers in part (a), predict each product:
  (4) $(x + 1)(x^5 - x^4 + x^3 - x^2 + x - 1)$ $x^6 - 1$
  (5) $(x + 1)(x^6 - x^5 + x^4 - x^3 + x^2 - x + 1)$ $x^7 + 1$

Mixed Review Exercises

Solve.

1. $3(x - 1) = 6$ {3}   **2.** $4(x + 2) - 3 = 21$ {4}   **3.** $6(2a + 2) = 3(a + 10)$ {2}

Evaluate if $w = 3$, $x = -1$, and $y = 4$.

4. $w + |-x| + (-y)$ 0   **5.** $w + x + 3$ 5   **6.** $w - |x - y|$ −2

7. $(w + y)^2$ 49   **8.** $(-x^8)x^2$ −1   **9.** xw^3 −27

Self-Test 2

Simplify.

1. $3x^2x^4$ $3x^6$ **2.** $(-6a^7)(-9a)\left(\frac{1}{3}a\right)$ $18a^9$ **Obj. 4-3, p. 152**

3. $126a\left(-\frac{1}{9}a\right)\left(\frac{1}{7}a^3\right)$ $-2a^5$ **4.** $(ab^2)(a^2b)(a^2b^2)$ a^5b^5

5. $(5xy^2)^3$ $125x^3y^6$ **6.** $(-2x^2y)^3$ $-8x^6y^3$ **Obj. 4-4, p. 155**
7. $-(2x^2y)^3$ $-8x^6y^3$ **8.** $(-3x^3)^2$ $9x^6$

9. $-2n(5 - n)$ $-10n + 2n^2$ **10.** $\frac{1}{7}xy^2(56x^2 - 49xy + y^2)$ **Obj. 4-5, p. 158**
                                                   $8x^3y^2 - 7x^2y^3 + \frac{1}{7}xy^4$

11. Solve $4 - \frac{2}{3}(6a - 15) = -38$. {13}

Multiply.

12. $4x - 5$ **13.** $a^2 + 3a + 2$ **Obj. 4-6, p. 161**
       $\underline{3x + 2}$ $12x^2 - 7x - 10$ $\underline{5a - 4}$ $5a^3 + 11a^2 - 2a - 8$

14. $(6a - 5)(a - 9)$ $6a^2 - 59a + 45$ **15.** $(9 - 7y)(7 - 6y + 8y^2)$ $63 - 103y + 114y^2 - 56y^3$

Check your answers with those at the back of the book.

Simplify.

1. $4x^3 \cdot x^5$ $4x^8$

2. $(-5b^6)(-8b)\left(\frac{1}{10}b\right)$ $4b^8$

3. $84r\left(-\frac{1}{7}r\right)\left(-\frac{1}{4}r^4\right)$ $3r^6$

4. $(xy^2)(x^2y)(x^2y^2)$ x^5y^5

5. $(6a^2b)^3$ $216a^6b^3$

6. $(-2ab^2)^3$ $-8a^3b^6$

7. $-(2ab^2)^3$ $-8a^3b^6$

8. $(-4y^3)^2$ $16y^6$

9. $-3m(6 - m) - 8m$
   $3m^2 - 26m$

10. $\frac{1}{5}rs(25r^2 - 40rs + s^2)$

   $5r^3s - 8r^2s^2 + \frac{1}{5}rs^3$

11. Solve:
   $6 - \frac{3}{4}(12n - 24) = -3$ {3}

Multiply.

12. $5x - 2$
   $\underline{3x + 4}$
   $15x^2 + 14x - 8$

13. $m^2 + 5m + 4$
   $\underline{3m - 2}$
   $3m^3 + 13m^2 + 2m - 8$

14. $(4n - 3)(n - 7)$
   $4n^2 - 31n + 21$

15. $(5 - 3x)(9 - 6x - 8x^2)$
   $45 - 57x - 22x^2 + 24x^3$

164

Problem Solving

4-7 Transforming Formulas

Objective   To transform a formula.

Formulas are used in many applications of mathematics. Example 1 uses a
formula from automotive engineering. It is often helpful to transform such a
formula to express a particular variable in terms of the other variables.

Example 1   A formula for the total piston dis-
placement of an automobile engine is
$P = 0.7854d^2sn$, where d is the diameter of each cylinder, s is the length
of the stroke, and n is the number of
cylinders. Solve this formula for the
variable s in terms of P, d, and n.

Solution $P = 0.7854d^2sn$

To get s alone on one side, divide
both sides by $0.7854d^2n$.

$$\frac{P}{0.7854d^2n} = s \quad \textbf{\textit{Answer}}$$

Note that the formula obtained for s in Example 1 is meaningful only if
$d \neq 0$ and $n \neq 0$. (Of course, neither n nor d will be zero, since the engine
must have cylinders and each cylinder must have a diameter.)

Example 2   Solve the formula for the variable
shown in color: $A = s^2 + 2rs$, r

Solution $A = s^2 + 2rs$ $\left\{ \begin{array}{l} \text{To get } r \text{ alone on one side} \\ \text{first get } 2rs \text{ alone on one side.} \\ \text{Then divide by } 2s. \end{array} \right.$
$A - s^2 = 2rs$
$$\frac{A - s^2}{2s} = r \quad \textbf{\textit{Answer}}$$

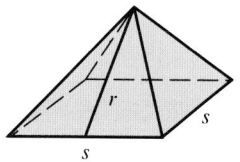

Total Surface Area:
$A = s^2 + 2rs$

The formula obtained in Example 2 is meaningful if $s \neq 0$. (Since s is the
length of a side, $s > 0$.)

Polynomials   **165**

Teaching Suggestions, p. T98

Suggested Extensions, p. T98

Guided Practice

Solve each formula for the given variable. State the restrictions, if any.

1. $V = \pi r^2 h$; h

$h = \dfrac{V}{\pi r^2}$; $r \neq 0$

2. $PV = nrt$; t

$t = \dfrac{PV}{nr}$; $n, r \neq 0$

Summarizing the Lesson

Tell the students they have learned how to solve a formula for one of the variables in the formula. Ask them to write down a formula they know and solve it for one of the variables.

Suggested Assignments

Minimum
166/2–22 even
S 166/Mixed Review
R 164/Self-Test 2

Average
166/2–26 even
S 166/Mixed Review
R 164/Self-Test 2

Maximum
166/4–28 even
S 166/Mixed Review
R 164/Self-Test 2

Additional Answers
Written Exercises

17. $t = \dfrac{v - u}{a}$; $a \neq 0$

18. $y = 3m - x - z$

19. $s = \dfrac{v^2 - u^2}{2a}$; $a \neq 0$

20. $l = \dfrac{2s}{n} - a$; $n \neq 0$

23. $d = \dfrac{Ff + Fg - fg}{F}$; $F \neq 0$

Supplementary Materials
Study Guide   pp. 65–66

Oral Exercises

Solve each equation for the variable shown in color.

1. $b = ax$; x $\quad x = \dfrac{b}{a}$
2. $b = x + a$; x $\quad x = b - a$
3. $c = ax - b$; x $\quad x = \dfrac{c + b}{a}$

4. $s = a + b + c$; c $\quad c = s - a - b$
5. $a = \dfrac{x}{b^2}$; x $\quad x = ab^2$
6. $C = \dfrac{mv^2}{r}$; r $\quad r = \dfrac{mv^2}{C}$

7. $V = Bh$; B $\quad B = \dfrac{V}{h}$
8. $d = rt$; r $\quad r = \dfrac{d}{t}$
9. $E = mc^2$; m $\quad m = \dfrac{E}{c^2}$

10. $F = \dfrac{mv^2}{r}$; r $\quad r = \dfrac{mv^2}{F}$
11. $A = \dfrac{1}{2}bh$; b $\quad b = \dfrac{2A}{h}$
12. $R = \dfrac{kl}{d^2}$; l $\quad l = \dfrac{Rd^2}{k}$

Written Exercises

5. $P = \dfrac{I}{rt}$; $r \neq 0, t \neq 0$
6. $t = \dfrac{A - P}{Pr}$; $P \neq 0, r \neq 0$

7. $h = \dfrac{A - 2a^2}{4a}$; $a \neq 0$
8. $v = \dfrac{s - 16t^2}{t}$; $t \neq 0$

Solve the given formula for the variable shown in color. State the restrictions, if any, for the formula obtained to be meaningful.

$v = \dfrac{m}{d}$; $d \neq 0$

A 1. $C = 2\pi r$; r $\quad r = \dfrac{C}{2\pi}$
2. $F = ma$; a $\quad a = \dfrac{F}{m}$; $m \neq 0$
3. $s = \dfrac{v}{r}$; r $\quad r = \dfrac{v}{s}$; $s \neq 0$
4. $d = \dfrac{m}{v}$; v

5. $I = Prt$; P
6. $A = P + Prt$; t
7. $A = 2a^2 + 4ah$; h
8. $s = vt + 16t^2$; v

9. $A = \dfrac{1}{2}h(a + b)$; h $\quad h = \dfrac{2A}{a + b}$; $a + b \neq 0$
10. $S = \dfrac{n}{2}(a + l)$; n $\quad n = \dfrac{2S}{a + l}$; $a + l \neq 0$
11. $p = 2(l + w)$; w $\quad w = \dfrac{p - 2l}{2}$

12. $A = P(1 + rt)$; r $\quad r = \dfrac{A - P}{Pt}$; $P \neq 0, t \neq 0$
13. $m = \dfrac{x + y}{2}$; y $\quad y = 2m - x$
14. $a = \dfrac{v - u}{t}$; v $\quad v = at + u$

B 15. $S = \dfrac{n}{2}(a + l)$; a $\quad a = \dfrac{2S - nl}{n}$; $n \neq 0$
16. $C = \dfrac{5}{9}(F - 32)$; F $\quad F = \dfrac{9}{5}C + 32$
17. $a = \dfrac{v - u}{t}$; t

18. $m = \dfrac{x + y + z}{3}$; y
19. $v^2 = u^2 + 2as$; s
20. $s = \dfrac{n}{2}(a + l)$; l

21. $S = \dfrac{a}{a - r}$; r $\quad r = \dfrac{Sa - a}{S}$; $S \neq 0$
22. $l = a + (n - 1)d$; n $\quad n = \dfrac{l - a + d}{d}$; $d \neq 0$
23. $F = \dfrac{fg}{f + g - d}$; d

24. $S = \dfrac{a - rl}{1 - r}$; l $\quad l = \dfrac{S - Sr - a}{-r}$; $r \neq 0$
25. $a = \dfrac{180(n - 2)}{n}$; n $\quad n = -\dfrac{360}{a - 180}$; $a \neq 180$
26. $S = \dfrac{r}{1 - r}$; r $\quad r = \dfrac{S}{S + 1}$; $S \neq -1$

C 27. $r = \dfrac{ab}{a + b}$; a $\quad a = \dfrac{br}{b - r}$; $b \neq r$
28. $F = \dfrac{fg}{f + g - d}$; f $\quad f = \dfrac{Fd - Fg}{F - g}$; $F \neq g$
29. $C = K\left(\dfrac{Rr}{R - r}\right)$; R $\quad R = \dfrac{Cr}{C - Kr}$; $C \neq Kr$

Mixed Review Exercises

Simplify.

1. $(y - 5)(y + 3)$ $\quad y^2 - 2y - 15$
2. $(3n - 2)(2n - 4)$ $\quad 6n^2 - 16n + 8$
3. $a[2a - 4(2 + a)]$ $\quad -2a^2 - 8a$
4. $xy(2x + 3y)$ $\quad 2x^2y + 3xy^2$

5. $4x(x^2 - 3x + 2)$ $\quad 4x^3 - 12x^2 + 8x$
6. $(-3x^3)^3$ $\quad -27x^9$
7. $n^2 \cdot n^2 \cdot n^2$ $\quad n^6$
8. $(3a^2)^2 \cdot 4a^3b$ $\quad 36a^7b$

4-8 Rate-Time-Distance Problems

Objective   To solve some word problems involving uniform motion.

An object is in **uniform motion** when it moves without changing its speed, or rate. The examples illustrate three types of problems involving uniform motion. Each is solved by using a chart, a sketch, and the distance formula:

$$\text{Distance} = \text{rate} \times \text{time}$$
$$D = rt$$

Example 1   (Motion in opposite directions) Bicyclists Brent and Jane started at noon from points 60 km apart and rode toward each other, meeting at 1:30 P.M. Brent's speed was 4 km/h greater than Jane's speed. Find their speeds.

Solution

Step 1 The problem asks for Brent's speed and Jane's speed. Draw a sketch.

Step 2 Let r = Jane's speed. Then $r + 4$ = Brent's speed.

Make a chart organizing the given facts and use it to label your sketch. Notice that the time from noon to 1:30 P.M. is 1 h 30 min, or 1.5 h.

	Rate	Time	Distance
Brent	$r + 4$	1.5	$1.5(r + 4)$
Jane	r	1.5	$1.5r$

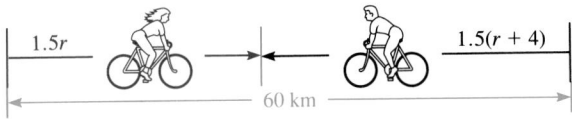

Step 3 The sketch helps you write the equation:
$$1.5(r + 4) + 1.5r = 60$$

Step 4
$$1.5r + 6 + 1.5r = 60$$
$$3r + 6 = 60$$
$$3r = 54$$
$$r = 18 \leftarrow \text{Jane's speed}$$
$$r + 4 = 22 \leftarrow \text{Brent's speed}$$

Step 5 *Check:* In 1.5 h Jane travels $1.5 \cdot 18 = 27$ (km).
Brent travels $1.5 \cdot 22 = 33$ (km). $27 + 33 = 60$ (km) $\checkmark$

∴ Brent's speed was 22 km/h, and Jane's speed was 18 km/h. **Answer**

Polynomials   **167**

Warm-Up Exercises

Complete with an expression involving the given variable.

1. Bill runs at a rate of r mi/h. Will runs twice as fast. Will's rate is __?__ mi/h. $2r$

2. Joshua rides his bike to school in k min. His sister Rachel takes 15 min longer to walk. She spends __?__ min walking to school. $k + 15$

3. Sue and Carol start bicycling toward each other at the same time from homes 9 mi apart. When they meet, Carol has traveled c mi. Sue has traveled __?__ mi. $9 - c$

Motivating the Lesson

Ask the following question:
How would you calculate how long it takes the girls in Warm-Up Exercise 3 to meet?

If needed, point out that it is necessary to know their speeds. State that solving motion problems like this is the topic of today's lesson.

1. What is the distance traveled in 6 h at 60 km/h?
$d = rt = 60 \cdot 6 = 360$ (km)

2. What is the average rate of speed if 275 km are traveled in 5.5 h?
$r = \dfrac{d}{t} = \dfrac{275}{5.5} = 50$ (km/h)

3. How long does it take to travel 288 km at an average rate of 72 km/h?
$t = \dfrac{d}{r} = \dfrac{288}{72} = 4$ (h)

4. Mary Beth and Michael leave school traveling in opposite directions. Michael is walking and Mary Beth is biking, averaging 6 km/h more than Michael. If they are 18 km apart after 1.5 h, what is the rate of each?

Steps 2–4 are given.
M's dist. + MB's dist. = total distance. Let r = Michael's rate.
$1.5r + 1.5(r + 6) = 18$
$1.5r + 1.5r + 9 = 18$
$3r = 9$
Michael: 3 km/h;
Mary Beth: 9 km/h

5. Carla begins biking south at 20 km/h at noon. Dean leaves from the same point 15 min later to catch up with her. If Dean bikes at 24 km/h, how long will it take him to catch up with Carla?

Steps 2–4 are given.
Dean's dist. = Carla's dist.
Let t = Dean's time.
$24t = 20\left(t + \dfrac{1}{4}\right)$
$24t = 20t + 5$
$4t = 5; \ t = 1\dfrac{1}{4}$

$\therefore$ it will take Dean $1\dfrac{1}{4}$ h.

Example 2 (Motion in the same direction) A helicopter leaves Central Airport and flies north at 180 mi/h. Twenty minutes later a plane leaves the airport and follows the helicopter at 330 mi/h. How long does it take the plane to overtake the helicopter?

Solution

Step 1 The problem asks for the plane's flying time before it overtakes the helicopter. Draw a sketch.

Step 2 Let t = plane's flying time.

Make a chart organizing the given facts and use it to label your sketch.

Notice that 20 min must be written as $\frac{1}{3}$ h because the speeds are given in miles per hour.

	Rate ×	Time =	Distance
Helicopter	180	$t + \dfrac{1}{3}$	$180\left(t + \dfrac{1}{3}\right)$
Plane	330	t	$330t$

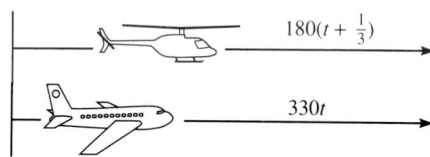

Step 3 When the plane overtakes the helicopter, the distances will be equal.

$$330t = 180\left(t + \dfrac{1}{3}\right)$$

Step 4
$$330t = 180t + 60$$
$$150t = 60$$
$$t = \dfrac{2}{5}$$

Step 5 Check: The helicopter travels at 180 mi/h for $\frac{1}{3}$ h before the plane leaves the airport and $\frac{2}{5}$ h after the plane leaves the airport.

The helicopter covers $\frac{1}{3} \cdot 180 + \frac{2}{5} \cdot 180 = 132$ (mi).

In $\frac{2}{5}$ h the plane travels $\frac{2}{5} \cdot 330 = 132$ (mi). $\checkmark$

$\therefore$ the plane overtakes the helicopter in $\frac{2}{5}$ h, or 24 min. **Answer**

Caution: Some problems, such as the one in Example 2, give the time in *minutes,* and the speed in *hours.* Be sure to write the time in terms of hours when you use the given facts.

168 *Chapter 4*

Example 3 (Round trip) A ski lift carried Maria up a slope at the rate of 6 km/h, and she skied back down parallel to the lift at 34 km/h. The round trip took 30 min. How far did she ski and for how long?

Solution

Step 1 The problem asks for Maria's skiing distance and time. Draw a sketch.

Step 2 Let t = Maria's skiing time. Make a chart.
Notice that 30 min = 0.5 h.

	Rate ×	Time	= Distance
Up	6	$0.5 - t$	$6(0.5 - t)$
Down	34	t	$34t$

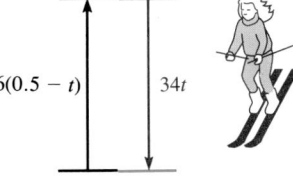

$6(0.5 - t)$ $34t$

Step 3 In round-trip problems, the two distances are equal.
$$34t = 6(0.5 - t)$$

Step 4
$$34t = 3 - 6t$$
$$40t = 3$$
$$t = \frac{3}{40} = 0.075 \text{ and } 34t = 34(0.075) = 2.55 \text{ (km)}$$

Step 5 The check is left to you.
∴ Maria skied for 0.075 h, or 4.5 min, for a distance of 2.55 km. **Answer**

A calculator is helpful for solving problems such as the one above.

Oral Exercises

**Classify each problem as involving (1) motion in opposite directions,
(2) motion in the same direction, or (3) a round trip. Then complete the
table and give an equation.**

motion in opposite directions; $500t + 700(t - 1) = 2100$

1. At noon a private plane left Austin for Los Angeles, 2100 km away, flying at 500 km/h. One hour later a jet left Los Angeles for Austin at 700 km/h. At what time did they pass each other?

	Rate ×	Time	= Distance
Plane	? 500	t	? $500t$
Jet	?	?	?

700     $t - 1$ $700(t - 1)$

2. At 8:00 A.M. the Smiths left a campground, driving at 48 mi/h. At 8:20 A.M. the Garcias left the same campground and followed the same route, driving at 60 mi/h. At what time did they overtake the Smiths?

	Rate ×	Time	= Distance
Smiths	? 48	t	? $48t$
Garcias	?	?	?

60     $t - \frac{1}{3}$ $60\left(t - \frac{1}{3}\right)$

motion in same direction; $48t = 60\left(t - \frac{1}{3}\right)$

Polynomials **169**

6. Mark drove his car to the garage at 48 km/h and then walked back home at 8 km/h. The drive took 10 min less than the walk home. How far did Mark walk and for how long?

Steps 2–4 are given.
dist. out = dist. back. Let t = time walking.
$$48\left(t - \frac{1}{6}\right) = 8t$$
$$48t - 8 = 8t$$
$$40t = 8$$
$$t = \frac{8}{40} = \frac{1}{5}$$
∴ Mark took $\frac{1}{5}$ h, or 12 min, to walk 1.6 km.

Check for Understanding

Here is a suggested use of the Oral Exercises to check students' understanding as you teach the lesson.
Oral Ex. 1: use after Example 1.
Oral Exs. 2, 4: use after Example 2.
Oral Ex. 3: use after Example 3.

 Using a Calculator

Students may find a calculator helpful for checking their answers as well as for solving Problems 1–16 on pp. 170–171.

Problem Solving Strategies

By *using a chart* and the *five-step plan* of Lesson 1-7, facts can be organized to help solve word problems.

169

Guided Practice

Solve.

1. Juan left home on his bicycle at 10:00 A.M., traveling at 21 km/h. At noon, his brother set out after him on his motorcycle, following the same route. If the motorcycle traveled at 63 km/h, what time did Juan's brother overtake him? **1:00 P.M.**

2. Two planes leave Chicago at the same time, one flying east at a speed of 550 mi/h and the other flying west at a speed of 650 mi/h. How long does it take for them to be 2000 miles apart?

$1\frac{2}{3}$ h, or 1 h 40 min

3. A jet flying at a constant speed took 5 hours to fly to San Francisco from St. Louis. On the return trip, a tailwind of 125 mi/h decreased the flying time by 1.25 hours. What was the speed of the plane on the return trip? **500 mi/h**

Common Errors

Problem 7, for example, may be difficult for some students. Because Stacy left one-half hour later than Andrew, some students will represent the time Andrew cycled in hours by x and the time Stacy cycled in hours by $x + \frac{1}{2}$. In reteaching, point out that if Stacy leaves *after* Andrew, then she cycles a *shorter* time than Andrew. Therefore, if Andrew's time in hours is represented by x, then Stacy's time in hours must be represented by $x - \frac{1}{2}$.

---

3. Kwan hiked up a hill at 4 km/h and back down at 6 km/h. His total hiking time was 3 h. How long did the trip up the hill take him? round trip;
$4t = 6(3 - t)$

	Rate	× Time	= Distance
Up	? 4	? t	? 4t
Down	?	?	?
	6	$3 - t$	$6(3 - t)$

4. Jenny had driven for 2 h at a constant speed when road repairs forced her to reduce her speed by 10 mi/h for the remaining 1 h of her 152 mi trip. Find her original speed. motion in same direction; $2r + (r - 10) = 152$

	Rate	× Time	= Distance
At original speed	? r	? 2	? 2r
At slower speed	?	?	?
	$r - 10$	1	$r - 10$

Problems

A **1–4.** Complete the solutions of Oral Exercises 1–4.

Solve. flying east, 650 km/h; flying west, 600 km/h

1. 2:20 P.M. **2.** 9:40 A.M.
3. 1 h 48 min **4.** 54 mi/h

5. Two jets leave Denver at 9:00 A.M., one flying east at a speed 50 km/h greater than the other, which is traveling west. At 11:00 A.M. the planes are 2500 km apart. Find their speeds.

6. At 7:00 A.M. Joe starts jogging at 6 mi/h. At 7:10 A.M. Ken starts off after him. How fast must Ken run in order to overtake him at 7:30 A.M.? 9 mi/h

7. At 9:30 A.M. Andrew left Exeter for Portsmouth, cycling at 12 mi/h. At 10:00 A.M. Stacy left Portsmouth for Exeter, cycling at 16 mi/h. The distance from Exeter to Portsmouth is 20 mi. Find the time when they met. 10:30 A.M.

8. It takes a plane 40 min longer to fly from Boston to Los Angeles at 525 mi/h than it does to return at 600 mi/h. How far apart are the cities? 2800 mi

9. A bus traveled 387 km in 5 h. One hour of the trip was in city traffic. The bus's city speed was just half of its speed on open highway. The rest of the trip was on open highway. Find the bus's city speed. 43 km/h

10. It took Cindy 2 h to bike from Abbott to Benson at a constant speed. The return trip took only 1.5 h because she increased her speed by 6 km/h. How far apart are Abbott and Benson? 36 km

B **11.** Jerry spent 2.5 h biking up Mount Lowe, rested at the top for 30 min, and biked down in 1.5 h. How far did he bike if his rate of ascent was 3 km/h less than his rate of descent? 22.5 km

170 *Chapter 4*

12. Jan can run at 7.5 m/s and Mary at 8.0 m/s. On a race track Jan is given a 25 m head start, and the race ends in a tie. How long is the track? 400 m

13. If Gina leaves now and drives at 66 km/h, she will reach Alton just in time for her appointment. On the other hand, if she has lunch first and leaves in 40 minutes, she will have to drive at 90 km/h to make her appointment. How far away is Alton? 165 km

14. An ultralight plane had been flying for 40 min when a change of wind direction doubled its ground speed. The entire trip of 160 mi took 2 h. How far did the plane travel during the first 40 min? 32 mi

15. A ship must average 22 knots (nautical miles per hour) to make its 10-hour run on schedule. During the first four hours bad weather caused it to reduce speed to 16 knots. What should its average speed be for the rest of the trip to maintain its schedule? 26 knots

16. Jamie ran two laps around a track in 99 s. How long did it take him to run each lap if he ran the first lap at 8.5 m/s and the second at 8.0 m/s? 1st lap, 48 s; 2nd lap, 51 s

In Exercises 17 and 18, cars A and B travel the same road. A's speed is r km/h, and B's speed is s km/h (r < s). When will B overtake A in each situation? Let t = A's time.

C 17. A and B start at the same time, but A starts p km in front of B. when $t = \frac{p}{s-r}$

18. A and B start at the same place, but A starts q hours before B. when $t = \frac{sq}{s-r}$

Suppose that cars A and B described above are d km apart.

19. If A and B start toward each other at the same time, how much later will they meet? when $t = \frac{d}{r+s}$

20. If A and B drive in opposite directions, how far apart will they be after t hours? $(rt + st + d)$ km

Mixed Review Exercises

Solve.

1. $64 = -8x$ {−8}

2. $4(x + 2) = 32$ {6}

3. $(x - 6)(x + 9) = (x + 6)(x - 2)$ {−42}

4. $-5x = -\frac{10}{18}$ $\left\{\frac{1}{9}\right\}$

5. $x - 7 = |2 - 10|$ {15}

6. $(x - 4)(x + 3) = (x - 6)(x + 4)$ {−12}

7. Solve for x: $\frac{bx - 6}{2} = 3$ $x = \frac{12}{b}$

8. Solve for x: $a = 3x + 5$ $x = \frac{a - 5}{3}$

Polynomials **171**

Summarizing the Lesson
Ask the students to describe the three different types of uniform motion problems and give examples of each. Ask them to describe the differences in how the equation is set up.

Suggested Assignments
Minimum
Day 1: 170/P: 1–5, 7, 9
Day 2: 170/P: 11, 13
        S 171/Mixed Review
Assign with Lesson 4-9.

Average
Day 1: 170/P: 1–5, 7, 9, 10
Day 2: 170/P: 11, 13, 15
        S 171/Mixed Review

Maximum
Day 1: 170/P: 1–11
Day 2: 171/P: 13–17 odd
        S 171/Mixed Review
Assign with Lesson 4-9.

Supplementary Materials
Study Guide   pp. 67–68
Practice Master   21
Resource Book   pp. 94,
                  162–165

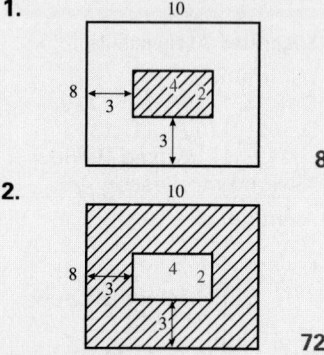
Motivating the Lesson

A 24 in. by 36 in. poster is surrounded by a border 3 in. wide, as in the Warm-Up Exercises. How would you find the area of the border? In today's lesson, you'll need to multiply, and add or subtract polynomials to solve problems like this.

Chalkboard Example

Solve the following problem.

A rectangle is 3 times as long as it is wide. If the length is increased by 6 and the width by 8, the area is increased by 108. Find the original dimensions.

Steps 2–4 are given.
Let w = width.
Then $3w$ = length.
$(3w + 6)(w + 8) = 3w^2 + 108$
$3w^2 + 30w + 48 = 3w^2 + 108$
$30w = 60$
$w = 2$

∴ the width was 2 and the length was 6.

4-9 Area Problems

Objective   To solve some problems involving area.

To solve some problems involving area, you'll need to multiply, and add or subtract, polynomials. Sketches are especially helpful in solving such problems. The units of measure that you'll use most often are square centimeters (cm^2), square meters (m^2), square inches ($in.^2$), and square feet (ft^2).

A photograph 8 in. wide and 10 in. long is surrounded by a border 2 in. wide. To find the area of the border, you subtract the areas of the rectangles.

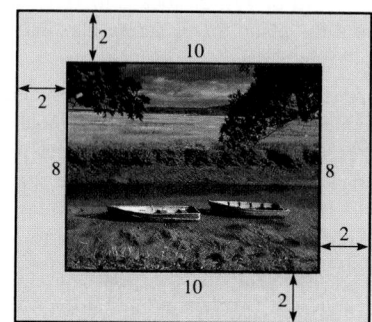

$$\begin{array}{rl} \text{Area of} \\ \text{border} \end{array} = \begin{array}{l} \text{Area of outer} \\ \text{rectangle} \end{array} - \begin{array}{l} \text{Area of inner} \\ \text{rectangle} \end{array}$$
$$= (10 + 4)(8 + 4) - (10)(8)$$
$$= (14)(12) - (10)(8)$$
$$= 168 - 80 = 88$$

Therefore the area of the border is 88 in.^{2}.

Example 1   Hector Herrera made a rectangular fish pond surrounded by a brick walk 2 m wide. He had enough bricks for the area of the walk to be 76 m^2. Find the dimensions of the pond if it is twice as long as it is wide.

Solution

Step 1 The problem asks for the dimensions of the pond. Make a sketch.

Step 2 Let x = the width of the pond. Then $2x$ = the length of the pond. Label your sketch.

Step 3 $\begin{array}{l}\text{Area of}\\\text{walk}\end{array} = \begin{array}{l}\text{Area of}\\\text{pond and walk}\end{array} - \begin{array}{l}\text{Area of}\\\text{pond}\end{array}$

$76 = (2x + 4)(x + 4) - (2x)(x)$

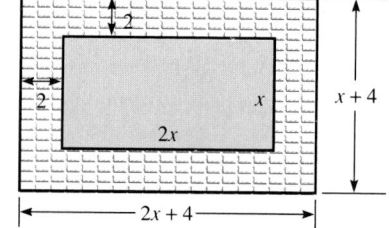

Step 4 $76 = 2x^2 + 12x + 16 - 2x^2$
$76 = 12x + 16$
$60 = 12x$
$5 = x$ and $2x = 10$

Step 5 *Check:* If the dimensions of the pond are 5 m and 10 m, the dimensions of the pond and walk are 9 m and 14 m.

Area of pond and walk = $9 \cdot 14 = 126$ (m^2)
Area of pond = $5 \cdot 10 = 50$ (m^2)
Area of walk = $126 - 50 = 76$ (m^2) ✓

∴ the dimensions of the pond are 10 m and 5 m. **Answer**

172   *Chapter 4*

Oral Exercises

Solve.

1. A rectangle is 5 cm longer than it is wide. If its length and width are both increased by 3 cm, its area is increased by 60 cm². Find the dimensions of the original rectangle. 11 cm by 6 cm

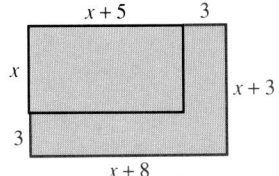

2. A rectangle is 10 m longer than it is wide. If its length and width are both decreased by 2 m, its area is decreased by 48 m². Find its original dimensions. 18 m by 8 m

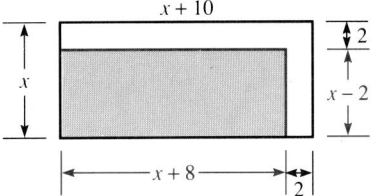

Problems

Solve.

A

1. A rectangle is three times as long as it is wide. If its length and width are both decreased by 2 cm, its area is decreased by 36 cm². Find its original dimensions. Make a sketch as in Oral Exercise 2. 15 cm by 5 cm

2. A rectangle is twice as long as it is wide. If both its dimensions are increased by 4 m, its area is increased by 88 m². Make a sketch as in Oral Exercise 1. Find the dimensions of the original rectangle. 12 m by 6 m

3. A rectangular swimming pool is three times as long as it is wide and is surrounded by a deck 2.5 m wide. Find the dimensions of the pool if the area of the deck is 265 m². 36 m by 12 m

4. A poster is 25 cm taller than it is wide. It is mounted on a piece of cardboard so that there is a 5 cm border on all sides. If the area of the border alone is 1350 cm², what are the dimensions of the poster? 50 cm by 75 cm

5. A brick patio is twice as long as it is wide. It is bordered on all sides by a garden 1.5 m wide. Find the dimensions of the patio if the area of the garden is 54 m². 10 m by 5 m

6. A house has two rooms of equal area. One room is square and the other room is a rectangle 4 ft narrower and 5 ft longer than the square one. Find the area of each room. 400 ft²

B

7. A small city park consists of a rectangular lawn surrounded on all sides by a 330 m² border of flowers 2.5 m wide. Find the area of the lawn if the entire park is 5 m longer than it is wide. 924 m²

Polynomials **173**

Guided Practice

Solve.

1. A rectangle is twice as long as it is wide. If its length is decreased by 4 and its width is decreased by 2, its area is decreased by 24. Find its original dimensions.
   length = 8   width = 4

2. An oil painting is 10 in. longer than it is wide and is bordered on all sides by a 3 in. wide frame. If the area of the frame alone is 402 in.², what are the dimensions of the painting?
   length = 35.5 in.
   width = 25.5 in.

Summarizing the Lesson

Tell students that they have learned how to use polynomials to solve problems involving area.

Suggested Assignments

Minimum
Day 1: 173/*P*: 1, 3, 5
Assign with Lesson 4-8.
Day 2: 173/*P*: 7–9
   S 174/Mixed Review
Assign with Lesson 4-10.

Average
Day 1: 173/*P*: 1–6
Day 2: 174/*P*: 8–11
   S 174/Mixed Review

Maximum
Day 1: 173/*P*: 2, 4
Assign with Lesson 4-8.
Day 2: 173/*P*: 6–9, 10, 12
   S 174/Mixed Review

Problem Solving Strategies

Using a chart or a *diagram* is particularly helpful in solving area problems.

Supplementary Materials

Study Guide   pp. 69–70
Resource Book   pp. 166–167

8. A corner lot that originally was square lost 185 m² of area when one of the adjacent streets was widened by 3 m and the other was widened by 5 m. Find the new dimensions of the lot. (*Hint:* Let x = the length of a side of the original square lot.) 22 m by 20 m

9. The area of a circle of radius r is given by the formula $A = \pi r^2$. Use this fact to find a formula for the shaded area in the figure below. $A = 2\pi rw + \pi w^2$

In Problems 10 and 11, refer to Problem 9.

Use $\frac{22}{7}$ as an approximation for π.

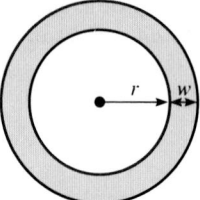

10. Find the radius r if the width w of the shaded region is 2 cm and its area is 176 cm². 13 cm

11. A circular pool is surrounded by a brick walkway 3 m wide. Find the radius of the pool if the area of the walkway is 198 m². 9 m

Exs. 9-11

C 12. A running track 4 m wide goes around a soccer field that is twice as long as it is wide. At each end of the soccer field the track is a semi-circle with inner radius r. Find a formula for the area of the track in terms of π and r.
$A = 8\pi r + 16\pi + 32r$

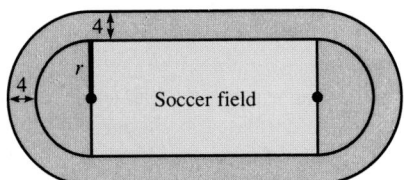

13. **a.** Suppose that you plan to run once around the track described in Problem 12. If you stay 0.5 m from the inner edge of the track, how far will you run? (*Hint:* The circumference of a circle is $2\pi r$. Your answer will be in terms of π and r.) $(2\pi r + 8r + \pi)$ m

   b. Suppose that a friend stays 0.5 m from the outer edge of the track. How much farther does your friend run than you do? 6π m

Mixed Review Exercises

Simplify.

1. $(-5 + 9) + (-8)$ −4
2. $6(c - 2) + (-3)c + 5$ $3c - 7$
3. $(4xy^3)^3$ $64x^3y^9$
4. $y - (-7) - [y + (-7)]$ 14
5. $5^3 \cdot 2^2$ 500
6. $(7 \cdot 4 + 4 \cdot 5) \div (3 \cdot 2)$ 8
7. $-\frac{9}{4} + \frac{5}{4} + 1$ 0
8. $\left(\frac{1}{2}x^4\right)\left(\frac{2}{5}x^3\right)$ $\frac{1}{5}x^7$
9. $-\frac{x}{11}(-143)$ 13x
10. $(-8 + 12) + (-4)$ 0
11. $\left(\frac{1}{3}y^3\right)\left(\frac{3}{5}y\right)$ $\frac{1}{5}y^4$
12. $(3y^2z)^4$ $81y^8z^4$

174   *Chapter 4*

4-10 Problems Without Solutions

Objective   To recognize problems that do not have solutions.

Not all word problems have solutions. Here are some reasons for this:

1. Not enough information is given.
2. The given facts lead to an unrealistic result. (The result satisfies the equation used but not the conditions of the problem situation.)
3. The given facts are contradictory. (They cannot all be true at the same time.)

Example 1   For the first 2 h of her trip Ginny Chang drove at her normal speed, but then road repairs forced her to drive 10 mi/h slower than her normal speed. Still, she made the trip in 3 h. Find her normal speed.

Solution

Step 1   The problem asks for Ginny's normal speed.

Step 2   Let r = Ginny's normal speed. Make a chart showing the given facts.

	Rate	× Time =	Distance
First part of trip	r	2	$2r$
Rest of trip	$r - 10$	1	$r - 10$

All the given facts have been used, but *not enough information has been given* to write an equation.

∴ the problem does not have a solution.

Example 2   A lawn is 8 m longer than it is wide. It is surrounded by a flower bed 5 m wide. Find the dimensions of the lawn if the area of the flower bed is 140 m².

Solution   When you try to solve this problem by letting the dimensions of the lawn be x and $x + 8$, you will obtain the equation $(x + 10)(x + 18) - x(x + 8) = 140$.

This equation is equivalent to $x = -2$. Since the width of the lawn cannot be negative, *the given facts lead to an unrealistic result.*

∴ the problem does not have a solution.

Example 3   Raoul says he has equal numbers of dimes and quarters and three times as many nickels as dimes. The value of his nickels and dimes is 50¢ more than the value of his quarters. How many of each kind of coin does he have?

(Solution on next page)

Polynomials   **175**

Teaching Suggestions, p. T99
Group Activities, p. T99
Suggested Extensions, p. T99

Warm-Up Exercises

1. If 6 cans of soda cost $1.44, what is the cost per can in cents? 24 cents
2. What is the total value in cents of 12 quarters and 9 dimes? 390 cents

Motivating the Lesson

Ask students to name two odd numbers whose product is even. There are none; the product of two odd numbers is always odd. In today's lesson, students will learn to recognize problems that don't have solutions.

Chalkboard Examples

Solve each problem if it has a solution. If a problem has no solution, explain why.

1. For the senior play, twice as many adult tickets as student tickets were sold. If $420 was collected, how many student tickets were sold?
   No sol.; the cost of each type of ticket is needed.
2. Chris has 127 stamps in her stamp collection. She has 4 less than 3 times as many foreign stamps as domestic stamps. How many foreign stamps does she have?

Steps 2–4 are given.
Let x = no. of domestic stamps. Then $3x - 4$ = no. of foreign stamps.
$$x + (3x - 4) = 127$$
$$4x - 4 = 127$$
$$4x = 131$$
$$x = 32.75$$
No sol.; x is not an integer.

(continued)

3. One number is 12 more than three times a second number. Find the numbers if their sum is four times the smaller number.

Steps 2–4 are given.
Let n = second number
$3n + 12$ = first number
$n + 3n + 12 = 4(n)$
$\quad 4n + 12 = 4n$
$\quad\quad\quad 12 = 0$
false statement
No sol.; the given facts are contradictory.

Guided Practice

Solve each problem that has a solution. If it has no solution, explain why.

1. A pool with an area of 296 m² is surrounded by a deck 1.5 m wide. Find the area of the deck.
   No solution. Not enough information.

2. Marcia had three times as many quarters as dimes and five more nickels than dimes. If she had $2.95 in all, how many of each coin did she have?
   3 dimes, 9 quarters, 8 nickels

Summarizing the Lesson

Tell the students that they have learned that not all problems have solutions. Sometimes there are facts missing or the facts lead to contradictory or unrealistic results.

| **Solution** |

Step 1 The problem asks for the numbers of nickels, dimes, and quarters.

Step 2 Let x = the number of dimes and x = the number of quarters. Then $3x$ = the number of nickels.

Step 3 Value of nickels(¢) + Value of dimes(¢) = Value of quarters(¢) + 50
$$15x \quad + \quad 10x \quad = \quad 25x \quad + 50$$

Step 4
$$25x = 25x + 50$$
$$0 = 50$$

The false statement "$0 = 50$" tells you that the *given facts are contradictory*.

∴ the problem does not have a solution.

Problems

4. seven 25¢ stamps, eight 40¢ stamps

Solve each problem that has a solution. If a problem has no solution, explain why.

A 1. A pool is surrounded by a deck 3.5 m wide. Find the area of the pool if the area of the deck is 301 m². No solution; not enough information is given.

2. A child's bank contains $6.30 in dimes and quarters. There are twice as many dimes as quarters. How many of each kind of coin are in the bank?
   28 dimes, 14 quarters

3. In the course of a year, the sum of an investor's gains and losses was $1000. What were his gains that year? His losses? No sol.; not enough info.

4. Kyle spent $4.95 to buy 15 stamps in 25¢ and 40¢ values. How many of each kind of stamp did he buy?

5. Ben weighs 30 lb more than Ann, and their canoe weighs twice as much as Ben. If their canoe weighed 20 lb less, its weight would equal the sum of Ann's and Ben's weights. How much do Ann, Ben, and the canoe each weigh? No sol.; contradictory facts

6. The average of four consecutive even integers is 17. Find the integers. 14, 16, 18, 20

7. A messenger left a construction site and traveled by jeep at 51 km/h. Forty minutes later it was discovered that she had been given the wrong parcel. How fast must a second messenger travel to overtake her in one hour? 85 km/h

8. Jim's sandwich cost the same as the combined cost of his salad and milk. The sandwich cost three times as much as the milk. The salad cost 20¢ more than twice the cost of the milk. How much did Jim's lunch cost?
   No sol.; contradictory facts

9. Find three consecutive odd integers whose sum is 24 more than the greatest of the three integers. 11, 13, 15

---

176 *Chapter 4*

10. Janet has $8.55 in nickels, dimes, and quarters. She has 7 more dimes than nickels and quarters combined. How many of each coin does she have? No sol.; not enough info.

11. At noon a train leaves St. Louis for Chicago. At 1:30 P.M. a train on a parallel track leaves Chicago for St. Louis. If the later train travels 5 mi/h faster than the earlier one, when will they pass each other? No sol.; not enough info.

12. A rectangle is 8 cm longer than it is wide. If the width is increased by 3 cm and the length is decreased by 3 cm, the area is increased by 4 cm². Find the dimensions of the original rectangle. No sol.; contradictory facts

B 13. A bus driven at 49 mi/h for 5 h can cover its route on schedule. During the first 1.5 h, traffic forced the driver to reduce his speed to 42 mi/h. What should the speed of the bus be for the rest of the trip to keep on schedule? 52 mi/h

14. The edges of one cube are 3 cm longer than the edges of another cube. The total surface area of the first cube exceeds the total surface area of the second cube by 234 cm². How long is each edge of the larger cube? 8 cm

15. Jane says she has $8.60 in nickels, dimes, and quarters. She has 6 fewer quarters than nickels and 3 more dimes than twice the number of nickels. How many of each kind of coin does she have? No sol.; unrealistic result

16. At the beginning of the year Alison and Sean together had 24 paperback books. During the year Alison doubled her supply but Sean lost three of his. Together, they had 46 books at the end of the year. How many books did each have at the beginning of the year? No sol.; unrealistic result

Self-Test 3

Vocabulary uniform motion (p. 167)

1. Solve the formula $\frac{PV}{T} = k$ for V. $V = \frac{kT}{P}; P \neq 0$ **Obj. 4-7, p. 165**

Solve each problem. If a problem has no solution, explain why.

2. At 8:00 A.M. two bicyclists are 315 km apart and heading towards each other. At 3:00 P.M. the same day, they both pass Sherwood Park. If the eastbound bicyclist rides at the rate of 20 km/h, find the rate of the westbound bicyclist. 25 km/h **Obj. 4-8, p. 167**

3. A rectangular fish pond is 7 ft longer than it is wide. A wooden walk 1 ft wide is placed around the pond. The area covered by the pond and the walk is 58 ft² greater than the area covered by the pond alone. What are the dimensions of the pond? 17 ft by 10 ft **Obj. 4-9, p. 172**

4. George wants to cash his $280 paycheck for an equal number of $5 bills, $20 bills, and $50 bills. How many of each kind of bill will he get? No. sol.; unrealistic result **Obj. 4-10, p. 175**

Check your answers with those at the back of the book.

Polynomials **177**

Quick Quiz

1. Solve the formula
$$C = \frac{mv^2}{r} \text{ for } m. \quad m = \frac{Cr}{v^2}$$

Solve each problem. If a problem has no solution, explain why.

2. Jack and Janice leave their houses at 10:00 A.M. walking toward each other. They meet at 10:30 A.M. If their houses are 7 km apart, and Jack is walking at 8 km/h, find Janice's rate. 6 km/h

3. A rectangle is 4 cm longer than it is wide. If the length and width are each increased by 3 cm, the new area is 63 cm² greater than the original area. Find the dimensions of the original rectangle. $w = 7$ cm, $l = 11$ cm

4. Robert sold boxes of greeting cards costing $1 and $2. If he sold the same number of $1 boxes as $2 boxes, and collected $52 in all, how many $1 boxes did he sell? no solution; unrealistic result

Chapter Summary

1. The expression b^n is an abbreviation for $\underbrace{b \cdot b \cdot b \cdot \; \ldots \; \cdot b}_{n \text{ factors}}$.
   The base is b and the exponent is n.

2. To simplify expressions that contain powers, follow the steps listed on page 142.

3. To add (or subtract) polynomials, you add (or subtract) their similar terms. Similar terms are monomials that are exactly alike or that differ only in their numerical coefficients.

4. Rules of exponents: $a^m \cdot a^n = a^{m+n}$ $(a^m)^n = a^{mn}$ $(ab)^m = a^m b^m$

5. Polynomials can be multiplied in a vertical or horizontal form by applying the distributive property (page 66). Before multiplying, it is wise to rearrange the terms of each polynomial in order of increasing or decreasing degree in one variable.

6. A formula may be transformed to express a particular variable in terms of the other variables.

7. A chart can be used to solve problems about distances or areas. Formulas to use are:

$$\text{rate} \times \text{time} = \text{distance}$$
$$\text{length} \times \text{width} = \text{area of a rectangle}$$

8. To solve problems involving area, you may find it helpful to make a sketch.

9. Problems may fail to have solutions because of lack of information, contradictory facts, or unrealistic results.

Supplementary Materials

Practice Master   23
Resource Book   p. 196

Chapter Review

Give the letter of the correct answer.

1. Express the cube of the sum of a and b in exponential form.   **4-1**
   a. $a^3 + b^3$ **b.** $(a + b)^3$ **c.** $a^3 b^3$ **d.** $3a^3 b^3$

2. Simplify $9 - 4^3$.
   a. 125 **b.** -125 **c.** -55 **d.** -7

3. Simplify $(xy^2 + 4x^2y - 6) + (5xy^2 - 5x^2y - 7)$.   **4-2**
   a. $6xy - 9x^2y - 1$ **b.** $6xy^2 - x^2y - 13$
   c. $5xy^2 - 13$ **d.** $6xy^2 - x^2y - 1$

4. Solve $x - (15x - 6) = 104$.
   a. $\{-7\}$ **b.** $\left\{-6\frac{1}{8}\right\}$ **c.** $\left\{-6\frac{7}{8}\right\}$ **d.** $\{7\}$

5. Simplify $3x^6\left(-\frac{1}{3}x^6\right)$.   **4-3**
   a. $-9x^6$ **b.** $-x^6$ **c.** $-x^{36}$ **d.** $-x^{12}$

6. Simplify $(3a^4b)(5a^2b^2)(2a^3)$.
 a. $60a^{11}b^3$ **b.** $30a^{10}b^2$ **c.** $150a^{10}b^3$ **d.** $30a^9b^3$

7. Simplify $(-3x^2y^4)^3$.   4-4
 a. $9x^5y^7$ **b.** $-9x^5y^7$ **c.** $27x^6y^{12}$ **d.** $-27x^6y^{12}$

8. Simplify $9n^2\left(\dfrac{1}{3}n\right)^4$.

 a. $3n^8$ **b.** $3n^6$ **c.** $\dfrac{1}{9}n^6$ **d.** $36n^3$

9. Simplify $-6[16a - 8(2a - 2)]$.   4-5
 a. 12 **b.** $-96a$ **c.** 0 **d.** -96

10. Solve $6 - 2(n - 3) = 12$.

 a. $\{0\}$ **b.** $\{6\}$ **c.** $\{-6\}$ **d.** $\left\{-4\dfrac{1}{2}\right\}$

11. Multiply $(4x - 3)(x - 4)$.   4-6
 a. $4x^2 - 19x - 12$ **b.** $4x^2 - 7$ **c.** $4x^2 - 12$ **d.** $4x^2 - 19x + 12$

12. Multiply $(c - 6)(c^2 + 2c + 3)$.
 a. $c^3 + 4c^2 - 15c + 18$ **b.** $c^3 - 12c - 18$
 c. $c^3 - 4c^2 - 9c - 18$ **d.** $c^3 - 17c - 18$

13. Multiply $(a - b)(a^2 + ab + b^2)$.
 a. $a^3 - b^3$ **b.** $a^3 + a^2b + ab^2$
 c. $a - a^2b - ab^2 - b^3$ **d.** $a^3 + 2a^2b + 2ab^2 - b^3$

14. Solve for b in the equation $c + by = a$.   4-7

 a. $b = \dfrac{c + a}{y}$ **b.** $b = \dfrac{a - y}{c}$

 c. $b = \dfrac{a - c}{y}$ **d.** $b = \dfrac{a + y}{c}$

15. Solve for y in the equation $\dfrac{xy + z}{2} = a$.

 a. $y = \dfrac{2a + z}{x}$ **b.** $y = \dfrac{2a - z}{x}$

 c. $y = 2ax - zx$ **d.** $y = 2ax + zx$

16. Laurie left home and ran to the lake at 10 mi/h. She ran back home at   4-8
 8 mi/h. If the entire trip took 27 min, how far did she run in all?
 a. 0.4 mi   **b.** 4 mi   **c.** 4.4 mi   **d.** 2.4 mi

17. A picture is 1 in. longer than it is wide. It is put into a frame $\dfrac{1}{2}$ in. wide.   4-9

 If the area of the frame itself is 8 in.^{2}, how big is the picture?
 a. 3 in. by 4 in.   **b.** 4 in. by 5 in.   **c.** 5 in. by 6 in.   **d.** 7 in. by 8 in.

18. Esteban has 16 coins that total \$3.00. If he has only nickels and quarters,   4-10
 how many quarters does he have?
 a. No solution—not enough facts   **b.** No solution—facts contradict
 c. 5   **d.** 11

Polynomials   **179**

Alternate Test p. T15

Supplementary Materials

Test Masters   17, 18
Resource Book   pp. 20–23

Chapter Test

Write each expression in exponential form.

1. The sum of the cubes of x and y. $x^3 + y^3$ 4-1

2. The quantity ab cubed. $(ab)^3$

3. Simplify $(4^2 - 3 \cdot 1 - 3^2) \div [0 - (-2)^2]$. -1

In Exercises 4–6: a. Add the polynomials.
                      b. Subtract the lower polynomial from the upper one.

4. $9n - 5$ **5.** $6x^2 - 5x - 1$ **6.** $x^2 + 2xy + 3y^2$ 4-2
   $\underline{n + 3}$ **a.** $10n - 2$ $\underline{-6x^2 + 5x + 1}$ $\underline{5x^2 - \ xy - \ y^2}$
            b. $8n - 8$ **a.** 0 **a.** $6x^2 + xy + 2y^2$

Simplify.   **b.** $12x^2 - 10x - 2$ **b.** $-4x^2 + 3xy + 4y^2$

7. $4y^3(-3xy)$ $-12xy^4$ **8.** $(12a^2)\left(\dfrac{2}{3}a^3\right)$ $8a^5$ **9.** $7^2 \cdot 7x^3$ $343x^3$ 4-3

Simplify.

10. 5^4n^4 $625n^4$ **11.** $(2x^3)^5$ $32x^{15}$ **12.** $4n^3\left(\dfrac{1}{2}n\right)^4$ $\dfrac{1}{4}n^7$ 4-4

Multiply.

13. $2x(5 - 4x)$ $10x - 8x^2$ **14.** $-3xy(7x^2 - 8xy + 9y^2)$ 4-5
                                         $-21x^3y + 24x^2y^2 - 27xy^3$

15. Solve $\dfrac{5}{6}(12x - 6) - 4(3x - 1) = 0.$ $\left\{-\dfrac{1}{2}\right\}$

Multiply.

16. $(3x + 2)(2x + 1)$ $6x^2 + 7x + 2$ **17.** $(c + 3)(4c^2 - 6c + 1)$ 4-6
                                    $4c^3 + 6c^2 - 17c + 3$

Solve for the variable shown in color.

18. $F = \dfrac{9}{5}C + 32;\ C$ $C = \dfrac{5}{9}(F - 32)$ **19.** $D = \dfrac{a}{2}(2t - 1);\ a$ $a = \dfrac{2D}{2t - 1};\ t \neq \dfrac{1}{2}$ 4-7

Solve each problem that has a solution. If a problem has no solution, explain why.

20. Lee and Jessie swam towards each other from opposite sides of a lake that   4-8
    is 3.9 km wide. They began swimming at 2:00 P.M. and met at 2:30 P.M.
    Lee's speed was 1 km/h greater than Jessie's speed. Find their speeds.   Lee, 4.4 km/h; Jessie, 3.4 km/h

21. A rectangle is 4 cm longer than it is wide. If the length and width are both   4-9
    decreased by 2 cm, the area is decreased by 24 cm². Find the dimensions
    of the original rectangle. 9 cm by 5 cm

22. Roy says he has more nickels than dimes. If he has $5.20, how many of   4-10
    each coin does he have? No solution; not enough information given.

180   *Chapter 4*

Cumulative Review *(Chapters 1–4)*

Simplify.

1. $(6x - 3) - (4x + 2)$ $2x - 5$ **2.** $\frac{1}{2}(101 - 43)$ 29 **3.** $-2.2 + 3.8 - 5.6 + 4$ 0

4. $15s - (2s - 9)$ $13s + 9$ **5.** $-7 - (-20) \div 2$ 3 **6.** $-\frac{3}{5} + 4\frac{5}{8} - \frac{2}{5} + 7\frac{1}{8}$ $10\frac{3}{4}$

7. $3^3 + 42 \div 3 + 4$ 45 **8.** $(9a - 5) + (4a + 7)$ $13a + 2$ **9.** $-3|6 - 12|$ -18

10. $(5x - 2)(2x + 3)$ $10x^2 + 11x - 6$ **11.** $(4a^3)(5a)^2$ $100a^5$ **12.** $5(3z^2 - 2z + 4)$ $15z^2 - 10z + 20$

13. $-4x^2(3x^2 - 2x - 5)$ $-12x^4 + 8x^3 + 20x^2$ **14.** $(3y^3)(2y^2) - 2(y)(y^4)$ $4y^5$ **15.** $(5 - 4x)(3 + 2x)$ $15 - 2x - 8x^2$

Evaluate each expression if $w = \frac{1}{5}$, $x = -1$, $y = -3$, and $z = 2$.

16. $w(3y + x)$ -2 **17.** $(xz - y)^5$ 1 **18.** $w(z - (-y))$ $-\frac{1}{5}$ **19.** $z(x - 2y)$ 10

Solve. If the equation is an identity or has no solution, state that fact.

20. $|-x| = 9$ $\{9, -9\}$ **21.** $|y - 1| + 4 = 0$ no sol.   **22.** $5 = |x| + 5$ $\{0\}$

23. $c - (-4) = -8$ $\{-12\}$ **24.** $3x - 2 = x + 6$ $\{4\}$ **25.** $42z = -42$ $\{-1\}$

26. $0 = \frac{1}{3}n + 2$ $\{-6\}$ **27.** $-10 = 4m + 2$ $\{-3\}$ **28.** $\frac{1}{4}x = 20$ $\{80\}$

29. $3(2 + x) = -4(x - 5)$ $\{2\}$ **30.** $(11x - 3) - (4 + 2x) = 11$ $\{2\}$

31. $(2n + 9) + (5n - 4) = 6n + 9$ $\{4\}$ **32.** $(4y - 2) + (4 - 2y) = 30$ $\{14\}$

33. $2(c - 1) - 7 = 1$ $\{5\}$ **34.** $(2x - 3)(3x + 1) = (3x - 4)(2x + 2)$ $\{1\}$

Solve each equation for the variable shown in color.

35. $am - bn = c$; m $m = \frac{c + bn}{a}$; $a \neq 0$ **36.** $by - ax = 0$; x $x = \frac{by}{a}$; $a \neq 0$

Solve.

37. One third of the sum of two consecutive odd integers is five less than the smaller integer. Find both integers. 17, 19

38. Randy and Amy left school at the same time and began walking in opposite directions. Randy walked at a rate of 3.6 km/h and Amy walked at a rate of 4.2 km/h. How far apart were they after 10 min? 1.3 km

39. Jessica has 16 dimes and quarters. Whitney has twice as many dimes and $\frac{1}{3}$ as many quarters as Jessica has. If they both have the same amount of money, what coins does each have? Jessica: 10 dimes, 6 quarters Whitney: 20 dimes, 2 quarters

40. A rectangular piece of plywood is trimmed to make a square by cutting a 4-cm strip off the top and a 2-cm strip off one side. If the area of the original piece is 74 cm^2 greater than the area of the square, find the dimensions of the rectangle. 15 cm by 13 cm

Polynomials   **181**

Maintaining Skills

Simplify.

Sample 1 $614 - (821 - 911)$

Solution $614 - (821 - 911) = 614 - (-90) = 614 + 90 = 704$ *Answer*

1. $1921 + (-876)$ 1045
2. $181 + 97 - 64$ 214
3. $(55 - 82) + (91 - 108)$ −44
4. $-78 - 84 - (-92)$ −70
5. $(28 - 86) - (46 - 81)$ −23
6. $284 - (93 - 165)$ 356
7. $35 - (58 + 62)$ −85
8. $-325 + (-726) + 922$ −129
9. $\frac{7}{8} - \left(-\frac{1}{4} + \frac{1}{2}\right)$ $\frac{5}{8}$
10. $\left(\frac{3}{5} - \frac{2}{3}\right) - \frac{5}{9}$ $-\frac{28}{45}$
11. $17.6 - (8.05 - 9.6)$ 19.15
12. $112.72 + (92.04 - 87.6)$ 117.16

Sample 2 $-53(28) + 27(-40)$

Solution $-53(28) + 27(-40) = -1484 + (-1080) = -2564$ *Answer*

Sample 3 $(-814 + 776) \div (-19)$

Solution $(-814 + 776) \div (-19) = -38 \div (-19) = 2$ *Answer*

13. $-12(-16) + 5(-24)$ 72
14. $27(20) - 60(48)$ −2340
15. $-65 - (412 - 385)$ −92
16. $-4(-50) + 8(-25)$ 0
17. $9.25(-2.3)$ −21.275
18. $-6.06(-5.4)$ 32.724
19. $-82.05 \div (-25)$ 3.282
20. $-\frac{24}{35} \div \frac{9}{14}$ $-\frac{16}{15}$
21. $7.24 \div (-0.25)$ −28.96
22. $-\frac{12}{25} \cdot \left(-\frac{35}{42}\right)$ $\frac{2}{5}$
23. $-\frac{18}{35} \cdot \frac{49}{54}$ $-\frac{7}{15}$
24. $-\frac{15}{64} \cdot \left(-\frac{40}{27}\right)$ $\frac{25}{72}$
25. $-2\frac{3}{8} \div \left(-2\frac{1}{8}\right)$ $\frac{19}{17}$

Sample 4 $82 + (-14)^2 \div 7 + 6$

Solution $\begin{aligned} 82 + (-14)^2 \div 7 + 6 &= 82 + 196 \div 7 + 6 \\ &= 82 + 28 + 6 \\ &= 116 \quad \textbf{\textit{Answer}} \end{aligned}$

26. $7 \cdot 8^2 - 6 \cdot 3 - 12 \div 2$ 424
27. $(29 + 7) \div 3^2 + 13 - 2^2$ 13
28. $(0.6)^2 - 1.2^2 \div 8 + 0.27 \div 0.3$ 1.08
29. $-2(0.35 + 0.55)^2 \div 1.8 \div 2$ −0.45
30. $1\frac{4}{5} \div 9 \cdot \frac{1}{2} - \left(\frac{1}{3} + \frac{1}{2}\right)^2$ $-\frac{107}{180}$
31. $-\frac{5}{7}\left[-\left(1\frac{1}{3} - \frac{3}{4}\right)\right] + \frac{1}{3} \div 4$ $\frac{1}{2}$

Preparing for College Entrance Exams

Decide which is the best of the choices given and write the corresponding letter on your answer sheet.

1. *PQRS* is a rectangle. Each of the longer sides is 1 cm shorter than twice a shorter side. The perimeter of the rectangle is 28 cm. Find the length of a longer side. B
   (A) 7 cm   **(B)** 9 cm   **(C)** 5 cm   **(D)** 11 cm

2. Twice the sum of two consecutive integers is 10 less than 5 times the smaller integer. Find the greater integer. C
   (A) 12   **(B)** 14   **(C)** 13   **(D)** -6 **(E)** -8

3. The cost of a cup of soup, a sandwich, and a salad is $4.70. The sandwich costs twice as much as the soup. The salad costs 30¢ more than the soup. What is the cost of the soup? B
   (A) $1.25   **(B)** $1.10   **(C)** $1.15   **(D)** $1.20

4. The Metro Theater has three times as many reserved seats as general admission seats. Reserved seats cost $5 more than general admission seats. Which of the following is (are) sufficient to determine the amount of money collected on a sellout day? D
   I. the number of general admission seats
   II. the cost of a general admission seat   III. the total number of seats
   (A) I only   **(B)** II only   **(C)** III only   **(D)** I and II only

5. Evaluate the expression $(a + b)^2 \div (2a) - b^2$ if $a = 6$ and $b = 4$. A
   (A) $-\dfrac{23}{3}$ **(B)** -13 **(C)** -25 **(D)** $\dfrac{25}{16}$

6. Find $(2n^3)^2$ if $(n + 2)(n + 3) = (4 - n)(12 - n)$. C
   (A) 144   **(B)** 128   **(C)** 256   **(D)** 784

7. Solve for p in the equation $q = 1 + \dfrac{p}{100}$. C
   (A) $p = 100q - 1$ **(B)** $p = \dfrac{q - 1}{100}$ **(C)** $p = 100(q - 1)$ **(D)** $p = 1 + \dfrac{q}{100}$

8. On a 25 km trip to a park, Megan rode her bike for 20 min, then walked the rest of the way. Her walking speed was 18 km/h slower than her biking speed. How long did the trip take? D
   (A) 30 min   **(B)** 40 min   **(C)** 50 min   **(D)** Cannot be determined.

Polynomials   **183**

5 Factoring Polynomials

Objectives

5-1 Factor integers and find the GCF of integers.

5-2 Simplify quotients of monomials and find the GCF of several monomials.

5-3 Divide polynomials by monomials and find monomial factors of polynomials.

5-4 Find the product of two binomials mentally.

5-5 Simplify products of the form $(a + b)(a - b)$ and factor differences of two squares.

5-6 Find squares of binomials and factor perfect square trinomials.

5-7 Factor quadratic trinomials whose quadratic coefficient is 1 and whose constant term is positive.

5-8 Factor quadratic trinomials whose quadratic coefficient is 1 and whose constant term is negative.

5-9 Factor general quadratic trinomials with integral coefficients.

5-10 Factor a polynomial by grouping terms.

5-11 Factor polynomials completely.

5-12 Use factoring in solving polynomial equations.

5-13 Solve problems by writing and factoring quadratic equations.

Assignment Guide

See p. T59 for Key to the format of the Assignment Guide

Day	Minimum Course		Average Course		Maximum Course	
1	5-1	186/1–31 odd, 41–43	5-1	186/3–39 mult. of 3, 41–46	5-1	186/3–48 mult. of 3
	S	187/*Mixed Review*	S	187/*Mixed Review*	5-2	192/3–57 mult. of 3
					S	193/*Mixed Review*
2	5-2	192/2–38 even, 47, 49	5-2	192/1–45 odd	5-3	196/3–54 mult. of 3
						197/*P*: 2–10 even
					S	199/*Mixed Review*
3	5-2	192/39–54 mult. of 3	5-2	192/47–57 odd	5-4	201/3–48 mult. of 3
	S	193/*Mixed Review*	S	193/*Mixed Review*	S	203/*Mixed Review*
	5-3	196/1–17 odd	5-3	196/1–19 odd	R	199/*Self-Test 1*
4	5-3	196/21–49 odd; 197/1, 3, 5	5-3	196/21–51 odd; 197/2, 6, 7	5-5	206/3–66 mult. of 3
	S	199/*Mixed Review*	S	199/*Mixed Review*	S	207/*Mixed Review*
5	5-4	201/2–30 even	5-4	201/3–45 mult. of 3	5-6	210/3–66 mult. of 3
	R	199/*Self-Test 1*	S	203/*Mixed Review*	S	212/*Mixed Review*
			R	199/*Self-Test 1*		
6	5-4	202/32–44 even	5-5	206/3–60 mult. of 3	5-7	215/3–51 mult. of 3, 56
	S	203/*Mixed Review*	S	207/*Mixed Review*	S	216/*Mixed Review*
					R	212/*Self-Test 2*
7	5-5	206/1–43 odd	5-6	210/2–46 even	5-8	218/3–54 mult. of 3, 55
					S	219/*Mixed Review*
8	5-5	207/45–53 odd	5-6	211/48–64 even	5-9	222/3–45 mult. of 3, 46
	S	207/*Mixed Review*	S	212/*Mixed Review*	S	223/*Mixed Review*
	5-6	210/1–19 odd				
9	5-6	210/21–49 odd, 58	5-7	215/3–48 mult. of 3	5-10	225/3–63 mult. of 3
	S	212/*Mixed Review*	S	216/*Mixed Review*	S	226/*Mixed Review*
			R	212/*Self-Test 2*	R	223/*Self-Test 3*
10	5-7	215/2–36 even, 37	5-8	218/3–48 mult. of 3	5-11	228/1–39 odd
	S	216/*Mixed Review*	S	219/*Mixed Review*		
	R	212/*Self-Test 2*				
11	5-8	218/1–33 odd, 36	5-9	222/1–37 odd	5-11	228/41–57 odd
	S	219/*Mixed Review*	S	223/*Mixed Review*	S	229/*Mixed Review*

12	**5-9** 222/1–33 odd **S** 223/*Mixed Review*	**5-10** 225/1–41 odd **R** 223/*Self-Test 3*	**5-12** 232/1–41 odd
13	**5-10** 225/1–15 odd, 21, 23, 25, 39 **R** 223/*Self-Test 3*	**5-10** 226/43–59 odd **S** 226/*Mixed Review*	**5-12** 233/43–55 odd **S** 233/*Mixed Review* **5-13** 235/*P*: 2, 4, 6, 8
14	**5-11** 228/1–6, 11–29 odd **S** 229/*Mixed Review*	**5-11** 228/1–6, 9–51 mult. of 3 **S** 229/*Mixed Review*	**5-13** 236/*P*: 9–31 odd **S** 238/*Mixed Review*
15	**5-12** 232/1–39 odd	**5-12** 232/1–41 odd	**R** 238/*Self-Test 4*; 240/*Ch. Rev.* **EP** 647/*Skills*; 669/*Problems*
16	**5-12** 232/28–44 even **S** 233/*Mixed Review*	**5-12** 232/38–54 even **S** 233/*Mixed Review*	*Administer Chapter 5 Test* **R** 243/*Cum. Review*: 1–41 odd **S** 245/*Mixed Problem Solving*
17	**5-13** 235/*P*: 2–18 even **S** 238/*Mixed Review*	**5-13** 235/*P*: 1–23 odd	
18	**R** 238/*Self-Test 4*; 240/*Ch. Rev.* **EP** 647/*Skills*; 669/*Problems*	**5-13** 236/*P*: 14–30 even **S** 238/*Mixed Review*	
19	*Administer Chapter 5 Test* **R** 244/*Maintaining Skills* **S** 245/*Mix. Pr. Solv.*: 1–5 odd	**R** 238/*Self-Test 4* 240/*Chapter Review* **EP** 647/*Skills*; 669/*Problems*	
20		*Administer Chapter 5 Test* **R** 243/*Cum. Review*: 1–41 odd **S** 245/*Mix. Pr. Solv.*: 1–13 odd	

Supplementary Materials Guide

For Use with Lesson	Practice Masters	Tests	Study Guide (Reteaching)	Resource Book		
				Tests	**Practice**	**Other**
5-1			pp. 73–74			p.182 (Applications)
5-2	Sheet 24		pp. 75–76			
5-3			pp. 77–78		p. 96	
5-4	Sheet 25	Test 20	pp. 79–80			
5-5			pp. 81–82			
5-6	Sheet 26		pp. 83–84	pp. 24–25	p. 97	
5-7			pp. 85–86			
5-8	Sheet 27		pp. 87–88			
5-9		Test 21	pp. 89–90		p. 98	
5-10	Sheet 28		pp. 91–92			
5-11			pp. 93–94		p. 99	
5-12	Sheet 29		pp. 95–96			
5-13	Sheet 30	Test 22	pp. 97–98		p. 100	p. 223 (Thinking Skl.)
Chapter 5	Sheet 31	Tests 23, 24		pp. 26–29		p. 197 (Enrichment)
Cum. Rev. 4–5	Sheet 32					

Overhead Visuals

For Use with Lessons	Visual
5-7, 5-8, 5-9	4
5-7, 5-8, 5-9	5
5-6	6

Software

Computer Activities	Test Generator
Activities 12–14	273 test items
Lessons 5-1, 5-5, 5-8	all lessons

Strategies for Teaching

Using Manipulatives and Cooperative Learning

Students may have used manipulatives in Chapter 4 to model sums and products of monomials and polynomials. The focus of Chapter 5, factoring polynomials, can be illustrated just as easily using manipulatives. One advantage to using manipulatives as area models (aside from making the connection to geometry) is that students can see that factoring is simply a reversal of the multiplication process they learned in Chapter 4. Students may find it helpful to work cooperatively, as they may generate different representations of the manipulative tiles for polynomials with larger coefficients. They might also compare alternative, equally valid plans for factoring certain polynomials.

5-5 Differences of Two Squares

For a change of pace, you may wish to demonstrate $(a + b)(a - b)$ on an overhead projector, as shown in the diagram below, before having the students duplicate the geometric model using manipulatives.

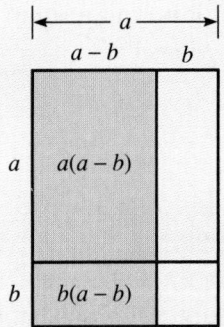

$$
\begin{array}{r}
a - b \\
a + b \\
\hline
a^2 - ab \\
ab - b^2 \\
\hline
a^2 \qquad - b^2
\end{array}
$$

5-6 Squares of Binomials

Using algebra tiles or manipulatives cut from grid paper, students can work in pairs to discover what happens when they square binomials; for example, $(x + 1)^2 = x^2 + 2x + 1$ and $(x + 3)^2 = x^2 + 6x + 9$. Then the geometric model of $(a + b)^2$ on page 208 can be presented as a generalization of their results.

5-7 Factoring Pattern for $x^2 + bx + c$, c positive

If students used manipulatives as suggested on page T97 to make geometric models of the products of polynomials, they can easily reverse the process now. For example, to factor the trinomial $x^2 + 3x + 2$, have them represent it as follows:

Tell them to move the tiles around to try to form a rectangle. Trial and error will yield:

Point out that the length and width of the rectangle are the factors: $x^2 + 3x + 2 = (x + 2)(x + 1)$.

See the Exploration on page 691 for an activity in which students use tiles to factor polynomials.

5-9 Factoring Pattern for $x^2 + bx + c$

Divide the class into groups of three or four students. The goal of each group's activity is to factor $12x^2 + 76x + 24$. Suggest that the members of each group devise a plan for working cooperatively toward the goal. Then have all groups begin at the same time. When the goal has been met by each group, have the class compare the working plans of the fastest and slowest processes.

5-10 Factoring by Grouping

Assign groups of five students to work together as an assembly-line factoring team. Each team member is assigned to carry out one of the first five steps in the Guidelines on page 227. Have the teams work cooperatively on Oral Exercises 7–12 on page 228.

5-13 Using Factoring to Solve Problems

One effective way to handle word problems is to have students work in pairs. Students can often help each other with minor problems and you can concentrate on students with major difficulties.

Another way is to have students work in groups of four using the five-step word problem plan.

1. Assign groups of four students at least four word problems to solve together.
2. One student is responsible for reading the problem carefully and drawing a sketch, chart, or diagram to accompany it. The same student is also responsible for explaining the problem to the group (Steps 1 and 2).
3. The second member is responsible for writing an equation that fits the problem (Step 3).
4. The third member solves the equation (Step 4).
5. The fourth member checks the solutions with the conditions in the problem and determines if the solutions are accurate and reasonable (Step 5).
6. The group members switch roles, go on to the next problem, and repeat the process until every student has had a chance to practice each step.

References to Strategies

PE: Pupil's Edition   **TE:** Teacher's Edition   **RB:** Resource Book

Problem Solving Strategies

PE: pp. 234–235 (Checking solutions); pp. 208, 213–214, 217, 220–221, 239 (Recognizing patterns); pp. 234–238 (Using factoring, using quadratic equations); p. 244 (Using the five-step plan); pp. 238–239 (Using a sketch, diagram, or model)
TE: pp. 217, 221, 234

Applications

PE: pp. 184, 197–199, 229, 235–238
TE: p. 184
RB: p. 182

Nonroutine Problems

PE: p. 188 (Challenge); p. 193 (Exs. 61–62); pp. 198–199 (Probs. 1–11); p. 202 (Exs. 45–49); p. 207 (Exs. 65, 66); pp. 211–212 (Exs. 62–64, 66); p. 223 (Challenge); p. 233 (Ex. 55); pp. 237–238 (Probs. 30–32)
TE: pp. T101, T105 (Sugg. Extensions)

Communication

PE: p. 211 (Exs. 57b, convincing argument); p. 232 (Exs. 7–12, convincing argument)
TE: p. T100 (Reading Algebra, Sugg. Extension); p. 214 (Reading Algebra)

Thinking Skills

TE: pp. 184, 204, 208, 213
RB: p. 223

Explorations

PE: pp. 239, 691

Connections

PE: pp. 185, 195, 203 (Discrete Math); pp. 197–199, 204, 208, 211, 213–214, 221, 236–238 (Geometry); p. 239 (History); pp. 236–237 (Physics)

Using Technology

PE: pp. 187, 203, 205–206, 235–236 (Exs.); pp. 193, 203 (Calculator Key-In); p. 188 (Computer Key-In); p. 223 (Challenge)
TE: pp. 187–188, 193, 203, 205, 235
Computer Activities: pp. 25–30

Using Manipulatives/Models

PE: p. 211 (Exs. 62–64); p. 204 (Exs. 1–3)
TE: pp. T102–T104, 184
Overhead Visuals: 4, 5, 6

Cooperative Learning

TE: p. T81 (Lesson 1-7)

Teaching Resources

For use in implementing the teaching strategies referenced on the previous page.

Application
Resource Book, p. 182

Application—Fibonacci Sequence (for use with Chapter 5)

A sequence is a list of numbers given in a definite order. The sequence 1, 1, 2, 3, 5, ..., where each successive term, other than the first two terms, is the sum of the two terms before it, is called the *Fibonacci sequence* (after the thirteenth-century Italian mathematician Leonardo Fibonacci). This sequence appears naturally in a variety of settings. For example, pine cone ends form clockwise and counterclockwise spirals. Counting these spirals always reveals the Fibonacci sequence.

Suppose the first term of a Fibonacci sequence is x and the second term is y. The third term would be $x + y$ and the fourth term would be $y + (x + y)$, or $x + 2y$.

1. List the fifth through tenth terms of this Fibonacci sequence.

2. Find the sum of the first ten terms.

3. The x- and y- terms of the sum in Exercise 2 have a common factor.

   What is it? _____

4. Factor the sum in Exercise 2. _____

5. Examine the list of terms of the original sequence. One of them is the same as one of the factors in Exercise 4. Write a general rule to find the sum of the first ten terms of a Fibonacci sequence.

A Lucas sequence is defined in the same manner as a Fibonacci sequence except the first term is 1 and the second term is 3.

6. What are the first ten terms of a Lucas sequence whose first two terms are 1 and 3? _____

7. Suppose the first term of a Lucas sequence is x and the second term is $3x$. Is there a rule for finding a sum of terms as there was for the first teñ terms of a Fibonacci sequence? If so, state the rule.

182 APPLICATIONS

Resource Book, ALGEBRA, Structure and Method, Book 1
Copyright © by Houghton Mifflin Company. All rights reserved.

Thinking Skills
Resource Book, p. 223

Thinking Skills (For use after Chapter 5)

Recalling knowledge

1. What is a prime number? _____

Analysis

2. One way to find all prime numbers from 2 to some given number N is to use the *sieve of Eratosthenes*: Start with a list of all integers from 2 to N, as shown at the right. (Here $N = 36$.) Then go through the list and cross off all multiples of 2. Do the same for all multiples of 3 that haven't already been crossed off the list.

	2	3	4	5	6
7	8	9	10	11	12
13	14	15	16	17	18
19	20	21	22	23	24
25	26	27	28	29	30
31	32	33	34	35	36

   a. Why don't you have to cross off any multiples of 4 from the list?

   b. After crossing off any multiples of 5 that haven't already been crossed off, you can stop, because the remaining numbers have to be prime. Why?

3. In the "sieve" of Exercise 2, you "sifted out" all the nonprime numbers from the list. Go back and circle all the prime numbers. Except for 2 and 3, what do you notice about the *location* of the primes in the list?

4. The numbers in the sixth column of the list are all multiples of 6, so they can be written in the general form $6n$ (where $n = 1, 2, 3, ...$). In terms of $6n$, write the general form of the numbers in:

   a. the fifth column _____

   b. the fourth column _____

   c. the third column _____

   d. the second column _____

   e. the first column _____

5. Notice that $6n$ can be factored as $2 \cdot 3 \cdot n$. If any of your answers for Exercise 4 are factorable, write the factored form below. If not, write "not factorable."

   a. _____

   b. _____

   c. _____

   d. _____

   e. _____

Reasoning and drawing inferences

6. How do the results of Exercise 5 support your observation in Exercise 3?

Resource Book, ALGEBRA, Structure and Method, Book 1
Copyright © by Houghton Mifflin Company. All rights reserved.

THINKING SKILLS 223

Enrichment/Nonroutine Problems
Resource Book, p. 197

Factoring (For use with Chapter 5 of text)

Instead of using a calculator to evaluate a numerical expression, it is sometimes easier to rewrite the expression as a simpler one and then evaluate. For example, consider $(876,889)^2 - (123,111)^2$. This expression can be rewritten as

$$(876,889 + 123,111)(876,889 - 123,111) = (1,000,000)(753,778)$$

and the product can be named easily: 753,778,000,000.

Rewrite as a simpler expression.

1. $(1,234,567,890)^2 + (1,234,567,890)(8,765,432,110)$ _____

2. $(1,000,000,011)(999,999,989)$ _____

3. $2(1,234,567,890) - (1,234,567,889)(1,234,567,891)$ _____

4. $(987,654)^2 - (12,346)^2$ _____

5. Find the value of $x^2 - 2xy + y^2$ when $x = 987,654,321$ and $y = 987,654,320$. _____

In Exercises 6–7, you are asked to look at some patterns, generalize, and then show that your generalization is correct.

6. Multiply $(3)(5)$; $(7)(9)$; $(11)(13)$. Use your answers to predict the answer to $(999)(1001)$. Using algebraic expressions, generalize to show that the product of any two consecutive odd numbers is always 1 less than a perfect square.

7. Tell whether each of these sums is divisible by 4: $1 + 2 + 3 + 4$; $28 + 29 + 30 + 31$; $95 + 96 + 97 + 98$. Use your answers to predict whether $999 + 1000 + 1001 + 1002$ is divisible by 4. Using algebraic expressions, generalize to show whether the sum of any four consecutive integers is divisible by 4.

8. Show that $[BC]^2 + [B^2 + C^2][B + C]^2$ is a perfect square.

Resource Book, ALGEBRA, Structure and Method, Book 1
Copyright © by Houghton Mifflin Company. All rights reserved.

ENRICHMENT 197

Problem Solving
Study Guide, p. 97

5–13 Using Factoring to Solve Problems

Objective: To solve problems by writing and factoring quadratic equations.

Example 1 Find two consecutive positive odd integers whose product is 143.

Solution

Step 1	The problem asks for two consecutive positive odd integers.
Step 2	Let $n = $ the first integer. Then $n + 2 = $ the second integer.
Step 3	Use the facts in the problem to write an equation. $n(n + 2) = 143$
Step 4	Solve the equation.

$$n^2 + 2n - 143 = 0$$
$$(n + 13)(n - 11) = 0$$
$$n + 13 = 0 \quad \text{or} \quad n - 11 = 0$$
$$n = -13 \qquad n = 11$$

You are to find positive odd integers, so reject –13. If $n = 11$, then $n + 2 = 13$.

Step 5   Check: $11 \times 13 = 143$.   The integers are 11 and 13.

Example 2 Originally a rectangle was 8 cm by 17 cm. When both dimensions were decreased by the same amount, the area of the rectangle decreased by 66 cm^2. Find the dimensions of the new rectangle.

Solution

Step 1   The problem asks for the dimensions of the new rectangle.

Step 2   Let $x = $ the amount by which each dimension is decreased. Make a sketch. The new dimensions are $17 - x$ and $8 - x$.

Step 3 $\left(\begin{array}{c}\text{Original} \\ \text{area}\end{array}\right) - \left(\begin{array}{c}\text{Decrease} \\ \text{in area}\end{array}\right) = \left(\begin{array}{c}\text{New} \\ \text{area}\end{array}\right)$

$$(17 \cdot 8) - 66 = (17 - x)(8 - x)$$

Step 4
$$136 - 66 = 136 - 25x + x^2$$
$$70 = 136 - 25x + x^2$$
$$0 = 66 - 25x + x^2$$
$$0 = x^2 - 25x + 66$$
$$0 = (x - 3)(x - 22)$$
$$x - 3 = 0 \quad \text{or} \quad x - 22 = 0$$
$$x = 3 \qquad x = 22$$

Step 5   Check in the words of the problem and you'll see that you must reject 22.
The new rectangle is 14 cm long and 5 cm wide.

CAUTION A solution of an equation may not satisfy some of the conditions of the problem. You reject solutions of an equation that do not make sense for the problem.

Study Guide, ALGEBRA, Structure and Method, Book 1
Copyright © by Houghton Mifflin Company. All rights reserved.

97

Using Technology
Computer Activities, p. 25

ACTIVITY 12. *Factors of n* (*for use with Section 5-1*)

Directions: Write all answers in the spaces provided.

PROBLEM

The numbers 1, 2, 3, and 6 are factors of 6 because there is no remainder when each number is divided into 6. Find the factors of any counting number, n, of your choice.

PROGRAM

```
10   PRINT "WHAT IS N";
20   INPUT N
30   PRINT
40   LET C = 0
50   LET T = 0
60   PRINT N; "HAS THESE FACTORS:"
70   FOR I = 1 TO N
80   IF N / I <> INT(N / I) THEN 120
90   LET C = C + 1
100  PRINT I; "      ";
110  LET T = T + I
120  NEXT I
130  PRINT
140  PRINT
150  PRINT "THE NUMBER OF FACTORS IS"; C
160  PRINT "AND THEIR SUM IS"; T
170  END
```

PROGRAM CHECK

Type in the program. To test whether you entered it correctly, run the program. Enter the number 6 after the question. The computer should print

```
6 HAS THESE FACTORS:
1      2      3      6

THE NUMBER OF FACTORS IS 4
AND THEIR SUM IS 12
```

ANALYSIS

This program finds the factors of a number n by actually dividing n by each of the counting numbers between 1 and n inclusive. Each time the division leaves no remainder (remainder equals zero), a factor is found.

USING THE PROGRAM

For each value of n, list all of its factors, the number of its factors, and the sum of its factors.

n	Factors	Number of factors	Sum of factors
1. 24			
2. 13			
3. 27			

(continued)

Using Technology
Computer Activities, p. 26

(Activity 12 continued)

For each value of n, list all of its factors, the number of its factors, and the sum of its factors.

n	Factors	Number of factors	Sum of factors
4. 18			
5. 25			
6. 78			
7. 117			
8. 250			
9. 72			
10. 999			

APPLICATION

1. A number is prime if it has exactly two factors, one and itself. Determine whether each of the following numbers is prime.

   a. 143 _____ b. 157 _____ c. 113 _____ d. 1001 _____ e. 149 _____

2. Find the number of factors for each of the square numbers (1, 4, 9, 16, 25, and so on) from 1 to 100. Which of these square numbers has the most factors?

3. In general, which numbers have exactly three factors?

4. Each of the following numbers is a power of two. Determine the sum of the factors for each number.

   a. 2 _____ b. 4 _____ c. 8 _____ d. 16 _____ e. 32 _____

   f. Guess the sum of the factors of 64. Check your guess using the program. _____

EXTENSION

1. If n is a prime number, what is the sum of its factors? _____
2. The sum of the factors of 496 is 992, which is twice as large as 496. If the sum of the factors of a number (including the number itself) is two times the original number, the number is called a *perfect number*. There are only two perfect numbers less than 30. What are they?

Using Manipulatives/Models
Overhead Visual 4, Sheets 1 and 2

**GEOMETRIC MODELS:
FACTORING $ax^2 + bx + c$**

Factor $2x^2 + 3x + 1$ $= (x + 1)(2x + 1)$

1. Model the polynomial:

2. Try to build a rectangle:

   $x + 1$

   $2x + 1$

   No, try again.

Factor $2x^2 + 2x + 1$ prime polynomial

1. Model the polynomial:

2. Try to build a rectangle:

   No, try again.   No, a rectangle cannot be built.

VISUAL 4

Using Manipulatives/Models
Overhead Visual 6, Sheets 1 and 2

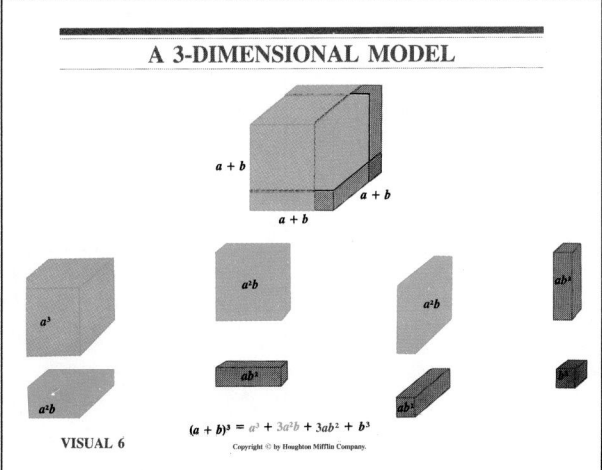

A 3-DIMENSIONAL MODEL

$a + b$

$a + b$

$a + b$

a^3

a^2b

a^2b

ab^2

a^2b

ab^2

ab^2

b^3

$(a + b)^3 = a^3 + 3a^2b + 3ab^2 + b^3$

VISUAL 6

Application

While factoring is a topic studied in algebra, it can be illustrated geometrically, as is done in the diagram. Factoring problems can seem like giant puzzles to students. In solving such puzzles, it is important that students recognize patterns and relationships among the components of the problem in order to determine which parts make up the whole.

Group Activities

The model illustrated in the caption with the photo could be constructed by a student or a group of students, using specific values for *a* and *b*, and presented to the class. A 2-dimensional model of one face of the cube could be done the same way.

An activity where students can explore 3-dimensional puzzles will help foster their spatial perception. Have students bring 3-D puzzles to class. Break the class into groups and give students the opportunity to discuss their puzzles with one another. Ask them to consider such questions as: What approach will you take to solve the puzzle: random trial and error, process of elimination, pattern recognition? Are any of the puzzles solved the same way? Once students have had time to discuss the puzzles, have each group give a presentation of their findings to the class, or, if you prefer, a written summary.

5 Factoring Polynomials

Breaking a polynomial into its factors is like pulling a wooden puzzle apart to reveal its different components. The diagram shows that
$$a^3 + 3a^2b + 3ab^2 + b^3 = (a + b)^3.$$

184

Quotients and Factoring

5-1 Factoring Integers

Objective To factor integers and to find the greatest common factor of several integers.

When you write
$$56 = 8 \cdot 7 \quad \text{or} \quad 56 = 4 \cdot 14,$$
you have *factored* 56. In the first case the factors are 8 and 7. In the second case the factors are 4 and 14. You could also write $56 = \frac{1}{2} \cdot 112$ and call $\frac{1}{2}$ and 112 factors of 56. Usually, however, you are interested only in factors that are integers. To **factor** a number *over* a given set, you write it as a product of numbers in that set, called the **factor set.** In this book *integers will be factored over the set of integers* unless some other set is specified. The factors are then *integral* factors.

You can find the *positive factors* of a given positive integer by dividing it by positive integers in order. Record only the integral factors. Continue until a pair of factors is repeated.

Example 1 Give all the positive factors of 56.

Solution Divide 56 by 1, 2, 3, ...   Stop
$$56 = 1 \cdot 56 = 2 \cdot 28 = 4 \cdot 14 = 7 \cdot 8 \ (= 8 \cdot 7)$$
∴ the positive factors of 56 are 1, 2, 4, 7, 8, 14, 28, and 56.

A **prime number,** or **prime,** is an integer greater than 1 that has no positive integral factor other than itself and 1. The first ten prime numbers are:
$$2, 3, 5, 7, 11, 13, 17, 19, 23, 29$$

To find the **prime factorization** of a positive integer, you express it as a product of primes. Example 2 shows a way to organize your work.

Example 2 Find the prime factorization of 504.

Solution Try the primes in order as divisors. Divide by each prime as many times as possible before going on to the next prime.

$$504 = 2 \cdot 252$$
$$= 2 \cdot 2 \cdot 126$$
$$= 2 \cdot 2 \cdot 2 \cdot 63$$
$$= 2 \cdot 2 \cdot 2 \cdot 3 \cdot 21$$
$$= 2 \cdot 2 \cdot 2 \cdot 3 \cdot 3 \cdot 7$$
$$= 2^3 \cdot 3^2 \cdot 7 \quad \textit{Answer}$$

Factoring Polynomials   **185**

Teaching References

Lesson Commentary,
  pp. T100–T107

Assignment Guide,
  pp. T63–T65

Supplementary Materials
  Practice Masters 24–32
  Tests 20–24
  Resource Book
    Practice Exercises,
      pp. 96–100
    Tests, pp. 24–29
    Enrichment Activity,
      p. 197
    Application, p. 182
  Study Guide, pp. 73–98
  Computer Activities 12–14
  Test Generator
  California Standards
  Support Workbook
    Explorations for
      Lessons 5-4, 5-7
  Alternate Test, p. T16

Teaching Suggestions, p. T100

Reading Algebra, p. T100

Suggested Extensions,
pp. T100–T101

Warm-Up Exercises

Write each expression in exponential form.

1. $2 \cdot 2 \cdot 5 \cdot 5 \cdot 5$ $2^2 \cdot 5^3$

2. $3 \cdot 7 \cdot 7 \cdot 7 \cdot 7$ $3 \cdot 7^4$

3. $2 \cdot 2 \cdot 2 \cdot 2 \cdot 2 \cdot 2$ 2^6

Motivating the Lesson

Ask students, What is the largest prime number you know? Mathematicians are continually trying to find larger prime numbers. The Cray supercomputer found one of the largest known primes: $2^{216091} - 1$, a number with 65,050 digits. Prime numbers and factors are today's topics.

Chalkboard Examples

1. Give all the positive factors of 42. 1, 2, 3, 6, 7, 14, 21, and 42

2. Find the prime factorization of 180. $2^2 \cdot 3^2 \cdot 5$

3. Find the GCF of 36 and 90. 18

Check for Understanding

Here is a suggested use of the Oral Exercises as you teach the lesson.
Oral Exs. 1–6: use after Example 1.
Oral Exs. 7–18: use after Example 2.
Oral Exs. 19–22: use after Example 3.

Guided Practice

List all pairs of factors of each integer.

1. 19 (1)(19) (−1)(−19)

2. 64 (1)(64) (−1)(−64)
   (2)(32) (−2)(−32)
   (8)(8) (−8)(−8)
   (4)(16) (−4)(−16)

Find the prime factorization.

3. 45 $3^2 \cdot 5$

4. 84 $2^2 \cdot 3 \cdot 7$

Summarizing the Lesson

Ask the students to state the definition of a prime number and to give several examples. Tell them they have found the prime factorization of an integer and have found the GCF of groups of integers.

Additional Answers
Written Exercises

2. (1)(22) (−1)(−22)
   (2)(11) (−2)(−11)

4. (1)(18) (−1)(−18)
   (2)(9) (−2)(−9)
   (3)(6) (−3)(−6)

Exponents are generally used for prime factors that occur more than once in a factorization. The prime factorization of an integer is *unique* (there is only one) except for the order of the factors.

A factor of two or more integers is called a **common factor** of the integers. The **greatest common factor (GCF) of two or more integers** is the greatest integer that is a factor of all the given integers.

Example 3 Find the GCF of 882 and 945.

Solution First find the prime factorization of each integer. Then form the product of the *smaller* powers of each common prime factor.

$$882 = 2 \cdot 3^2 \cdot 7^2 \qquad 945 = 3^3 \cdot 5 \cdot 7$$

The common prime factors are 3 and 7.
The smaller powers of 3 and 7 are 3^2 and 7.
∴ the GCF of 882 and 945 is $3^2 \cdot 7$, or 63. **Answer**

Oral Exercises

Give all the positive factors of each number.

1. 12	**2.** 15	**3.** 37	**4.** 1	**5.** 30	**6.** 41
1, 2, 3, 4, 6, 12	1, 3, 5, 15	1, 37	1	1, 2, 3, 5, 6, 10, 15, 30	1, 41

State whether or not the number is prime. Give the prime factorization of the number. 8–15 and 18 are *not* prime.

7. 31 prime **8.** 32 2^5 **9.** 46 $2 \cdot 23$ **10.** 51 $3 \cdot 17$ **11.** 81 3^4 **12.** 39 $3 \cdot 13$

13. 36 $2^2 \cdot 3^2$ **14.** 100 $2^2 \cdot 5^2$ **15.** 45 $3^2 \cdot 5$ **16.** 47 prime **17.** 71 prime **18.** 98 $2 \cdot 7^2$

Find the GCF of each pair of numbers.

19. 15 and 25 5 **20.** 12 and 18 6 **21.** 22 and 35 1 **22.** 23 and 46 23

Written Exercises

Sample List all pairs of factors of each integer. **a.** 20 **b.** −20

Solution **a.** (1)(20) (−1)(−20) **b.** (1)(−20) (−1)(20)
   (2)(10) (−2)(−10)   (2)(−10) (−2)(10)
   (4)(5)   (−4)(−5)   (4)(−5)   (−4)(5)

List all pairs of factors of each integer.

A **1.** 13 **2.** 22 **3.** 24 **4.** 18 **5.** 29
    6. 49 **7.** 40 **8.** 101 **9.** −121 **10.** −52

11. −33   **12.** −48   **13.** 53   **14.** 67   **15.** 26

16. 64   **17.** 68   **18.** 83   **19.** 38   **20.** 74

Find the prime factorization of each number. A calculator may be helpful.

21. 16 2^4 **22.** 34 $2 \cdot 17$ **23.** 69 $3 \cdot 23$ **24.** 65 $5 \cdot 13$

25. 75 $3 \cdot 5^2$ **26.** 88 $2^3 \cdot 11$ **27.** 27 3^3 **28.** 54 $2 \cdot 3^3$

29. 99 $3^2 \cdot 11$ **30.** 120 $2^3 \cdot 3 \cdot 5$ **31.** 104 $2^3 \cdot 13$ **32.** 128 2^7

B   **33.** 125 5^3 **34.** 200 $2^3 \cdot 5^2$ **35.** 450 $2 \cdot 3^2 \cdot 5^2$ **36.** 476 $2^2 \cdot 7 \cdot 17$

37. 1089 $3^2 \cdot 11^2$ **38.** 840 $2^3 \cdot 3 \cdot 5 \cdot 7$ **39.** 782 $2 \cdot 17 \cdot 23$ **40.** 2310 $2 \cdot 3 \cdot 5 \cdot 7 \cdot 11$

Find the GCF of each group of numbers. A calculator may be helpful.

41. 66, 90 6   **42.** 132, 220 44   **43.** 182, 196 14

44. 132, 242 22   **45.** 330, 945 15   **46.** 348, 426 6

C   **47.** 1176, 1617 147   **48.** 1925, 6300 175   **49.** 56, 98, 126 14

50. 105, 126, 210 21   **51.** 141, 198, 364 1   **52.** 90, 126, 252 18

Mixed Review Exercises

Simplify.

1. $\frac{1}{3}(6x + 3) + 2\left(\frac{1}{2}x - 1\right)$ $3x - 1$ **2.** $(5 + 4)^2$ 81   **3.** $3^2 + (2 + 1)^2$ 18

4. $3x - 4 - (2x + 6)$ $x - 10$ **5.** $3ab(2a^2)3a$ $18a^4b$ **6.** $3x^3(4y)2y$ $24x^3y^2$

7. $(3x)^3x$ $27x^4$ **8.** $2n(3n^2 - 4n) + 8n^2$ $6n^3$ **9.** $(-2)^5x^5$ $-32x^5$

10. $x(x^2 + 3) - x^2(x - 2)$ $2x^2 + 3x$ **11.** $(2y + 5)(y + 3)$ $2y^2 + 11y + 15$ **12.** $(x - 4)(3x + 4)$ $3x^2 - 8x - 16$

Computer Exercises

1. Write a BASIC program that uses the INT function to determine whether an integer entered with an INPUT statement is even or odd.

2. Write a BASIC program that uses the INT function to determine whether one integer is a factor of another integer. Each integer should be entered with an INPUT statement.

3. Write a BASIC program that uses the INT function and a FOR . . . NEXT loop to determine whether a number is *composite*. (A composite number is a number, such as 4, 6, 8, 9, and 10, that has two or more prime factors. Use a flag (F) to indicate whether the number is prime (F=0) or composite (F=1). When running your program, enter only integers greater than one.

Factoring Polynomials   **187**

---

6. (1)(49) (−1)(−49)
(7)(7) (−7)(−7)

8. (1)(101) (−1)(−101)

10. (1)(−52) (−1)(52)
(2)(−26) (−2)(26)
(4)(−13) (−4)(13)

12. (1)(−48) (−1)(48)
(2)(−24) (−2)(24)
(3)(−16) (−3)(16)
(4)(−12) (−4)(12)
(6)(−8) (−6)(8)

14. (1)(67) (−1)(−67)

16. (1)(64) (−1)(−64)
(2)(32) (−2)(−32)
(4)(16) (−4)(−16)
(8)(8) (−8)(−8)

18. (1)(83) (−1)(−83)

20. (1)(74) (−1)(−74)
(2)(37) (−2)(−37)

**Computer Key-In
Commentary**

In line 60, the INT (greatest integer) function is used to determine if the quotient is an integer. If Q < >INT (Q), then F does not divide W evenly, and thus is not a factor of W.

In Exercise 4, line 85 *cannot* be IF C > =1 THEN 90 because the program would report 1 as being a prime number.

**Additional Answer
Computer Key-In**

1. One example is given. factors of 30: 1, 30; 2, 15; 3, 10; 5, 6; 6, 5; 10, 3; 15, 2.

Computer Key-In

The BASIC function INT( ) will give the greatest integer less than or equal to whatever number appears inside the parentheses.

$$INT(4)=4 \qquad INT(4.9)=4 \qquad INT(-4.9)=-5$$

This function can be used to find factors of a number.

$$INT(12/3)=12/3, \text{ so } 3 \text{ is a factor of } 12.$$
$$INT(12/5)\neq12/5, \text{ so } 5 \text{ is not a factor of } 12.$$

The following program will PRINT pairs of positive integral factors of a positive integer.

```
10 PRINT "TO FIND POSITIVE INTEGRAL FACTORS"
20 PRINT " OF A POSITIVE INTEGER."
30 INPUT "ENTER A POSITIVE INTEGER > 1: "; W
40 FOR F=1 TO W/2
50 LET Q=W/F
60 IF Q<>INT(Q) THEN 80
70 PRINT F; " AND "; Q; " ARE FACTORS OF "; W
80 NEXT F
90 END
```

No additional factors will be found between W/2 and W.

Exercises

2. If $W/2<N<W$, then $1<W/N<2$ and thus W/N is not an integer.
3. 31 IF W<0 OR W<>INT(W) THEN 30

1. Run the program for the following values of W: 30, 31, 36, 119, 323.

2. Explain why no additional factors of W will be found between $W/2$ and W.

3. Insert a line in the program to test whether the number you INPUT is actually a positive integer. If not, the program should return to line 30.

4. Modify the program to report if the number you INPUT is a prime number. You can do this by adding these four lines to the program:

   35 LET C=0
   75 LET C=C+1   (Type LIST to get a clean copy
   85 IF C>1 THEN 90   of the modified program.)
   86 PRINT W; " IS PRIME."

   5. not prime, prime, prime, not prime, prime

5. RUN the modified program for the following values of W: 1, 2, 11, 51, 53.

6. Challenge: Modify the program you used for Exercise 5 so that it will print out all the prime numbers less than 500.

Challenge

The following problem is from the Egyptian Rhind papyrus:

There are seven houses; in each are seven cats. Each cat kills seven mice. Each mouse would have eaten seven ears of spelt [wheat]. Each ear of spelt will produce seven hekats of grain. How much grain was saved? 7^5, or 16,807 hekats of grain

5-2 Dividing Monomials

Objective   To simplify quotients of monomials and to find the GCF of several monomials.

There are three basic rules used to simplify fractions whose numerators and denominators are monomials. The property of quotients (proved in Exercise 61, page 193) allows you to express a fraction as a product.

Property of Quotients

If a, b, c, and d are real numbers with $b \neq 0$ and $d \neq 0$, then

$$\frac{ac}{bd} = \frac{a}{b} \cdot \frac{c}{d}.$$

Example 1 $\dfrac{15}{21} = \dfrac{3 \cdot 5}{3 \cdot 7} = \dfrac{3}{3} \cdot \dfrac{5}{7} = 1 \cdot \dfrac{5}{7} = \dfrac{5}{7}$

You obtain the following *rule for simplifying fractions* if you let $a = b$ in the property of quotients. (This rule is proved in Exercise 62, page 193.)

If b, c, and d are real numbers with $b \neq 0$ and $d \neq 0$, then

$$\frac{bc}{bd} = \frac{c}{d}.$$

This rule allows you to divide the numerator and the denominator of a fraction by the same nonzero number. In the examples of this lesson, *assume that no denominator equals zero.*

Example 2   Simplify: **a.** $\dfrac{35}{42}$ **b.** $\dfrac{-4xy}{10x}$

Solution   **a.** Divide both numerator and denominator by 7.
The red marks show this.

$$\frac{35}{42} = \frac{5 \cdot \cancel{7}}{6 \cdot \cancel{7}} = \frac{5}{6}$$

b. Divide both numerator and denominator by $2x$.

$$\frac{-4xy}{10x} = \frac{\cancel{2x} \cdot (-2y)}{\cancel{2x} \cdot 5} = \frac{-2y}{5} \text{ or } -\frac{2y}{5}$$

Factoring Polynomials   **189**

Teaching Suggestions, p. T101

Suggested Extensions, p. T101

Warm-Up Exercises

Write the prime factorization of each number.

1. 42 $2 \cdot 3 \cdot 7$

2. 56 $2^3 \cdot 7$

3. What is the GCF of 42 and 56? 14

4. What are the positive factors of 48?
   1, 2, 3, 4, 6, 8, 12, 16, 24, 48

5. What are the positive divisors of 48?
   1, 2, 3, 4, 6, 8, 12, 16, 24, 48

Motivating the Lesson

Ask, Name the greatest common factor of 2^9 and 2^{10}? 2^9 Tell students that finding the GCF of monomials is useful for simplifying quotients of monomials, which is today's topic.

Chalkboard Examples

Simplify.

1. $\dfrac{24}{36}$ $\dfrac{24}{36} = \dfrac{12 \cdot 2}{12 \cdot 3} = \dfrac{12}{12} \cdot \dfrac{2}{3} = 1 \cdot \dfrac{2}{3} = \dfrac{2}{3}$

2. $\dfrac{15}{20}$ $\dfrac{15}{20} = \dfrac{3 \cdot \cancel{5}}{4 \cdot \cancel{5}} = \dfrac{3}{4}$

3. $\dfrac{16xy}{18x}$ $\dfrac{16xy}{18x} = \dfrac{\cancel{2x} \cdot 8y}{\cancel{2x} \cdot 9} = \dfrac{8y}{9}$

4. $\dfrac{x^8}{x^4}$ $\dfrac{x^8}{x^4} = x^{8-4} = x^4$

5. $\dfrac{b^2}{b^6}$ $\dfrac{b^2}{b^6} = \dfrac{1}{b^{6-2}} = \dfrac{1}{b^4}$

6. $\dfrac{p^4}{p^4}$ 1

(continued)

7. Find the GCF of $21x^3y$ and $6x^6y^3$. Since $21 = 3 \cdot 7$ and $6 = 2 \cdot 3$, the GCF of 21 and 6 is 3. The smaller power of x is x^3. The smaller power of y is y.

∴ GCF is $3x^3y$.

Simplify.

8. $\dfrac{-24x^3y^5z}{32xy^2z^4}$

$= \dfrac{-24}{32} \cdot \dfrac{x^3}{x} \cdot \dfrac{y^5}{y^2} \cdot \dfrac{z}{z^4}$

$= \dfrac{-3}{4} \cdot x^2 \cdot y^3 \cdot \dfrac{1}{z^3}$

$= \dfrac{-3x^2y^3}{4z^3}$

Check for Understanding

Here is a suggested use of the Oral Exercises to check students' understanding as you teach the lesson.
Oral Exs. 1–12: use after Example 5.
Oral Exs. 13–36: use after Example 6.

Common Errors

When students divide monomials they often divide the exponents as well. In reteaching, encourage students who make this error to write out the factors of the numerator and denominator and simplify as shown in Example 3.

$\dfrac{a^3}{a^4} = a$ is another error frequently made by students. In reteaching, stress the need for the factor 1 in the numerator, so that $\dfrac{a^3}{a^4} = \dfrac{1}{a}$.

Example 3 Simplify: **a.** $\dfrac{c^7}{c^4}$ **b.** $\dfrac{a^3}{a^8}$ **c.** $\dfrac{b^5}{b^5}$

Solution **a.** $\dfrac{c^7}{c^4} = \dfrac{\cancel{c^4} \cdot c^3}{\cancel{c^4}} = c^3$ **b.** $\dfrac{a^3}{a^8} = \dfrac{\cancel{a^3} \cdot 1}{\cancel{a^3} \cdot a^5} = \dfrac{1}{a^5}$ **c.** $\dfrac{b^5}{b^5} = b^5 \cdot \dfrac{1}{b^5} = 1$

The results of Example 3 show that when you *divide powers* with the same base, you can *subtract* the smaller exponent from the greater if they are different. (Remember: when you *multiply* powers, you *add* the exponents.)

Rule of Exponents for Division

If a is a nonzero real number and m and n are positive integers, then:

If $m > n$:	If $n > m$:	If $m = n$:
$\dfrac{a^m}{a^n} = a^{m-n}.$	$\dfrac{a^m}{a^n} = \dfrac{1}{a^{n-m}}.$	$\dfrac{a^m}{a^n} = 1.$

Example 4 Simplify: **a.** $\dfrac{x^9}{x^5}$ **b.** $\dfrac{x^2}{x^7}$ **c.** $\dfrac{x^3}{x^3}$

Solution **a.** $\dfrac{x^9}{x^5} = x^{9-5} = x^4$ **b.** $\dfrac{x^2}{x^7} = \dfrac{1}{x^{7-2}} = \dfrac{1}{x^5}$ **c.** $\dfrac{x^3}{x^3} = 1$

The **greatest common factor (GCF) of two or more monomials** is the common factor with the *greatest coefficient* and the *greatest degree* in each variable.

Example 5 Find the GCF of $72x^3yz^3$ and $120x^2z^5$.

Solution 1. Find the GCF of the numerical coefficients.
$$72 = 2^3 \cdot 3^2 \quad \text{and} \quad 120 = 2^3 \cdot 3 \cdot 5$$
∴ the GCF of 72 and 120 is $2^3 \cdot 3 = 8 \cdot 3 = 24$.

2. Find the smaller power of each variable that is a factor of *both* monomials.
The smaller power of x is x^2.
y is not a common factor.
The smaller power of z is z^3.

3. Find the product of the GCF of the numerical coefficients and the smaller power of each variable that is a factor of both monomials.
$$24 \cdot x^2 \cdot z^3$$
∴ the GCF of $72x^3yz^3$ and $120x^2z^5$ is $24x^2z^3$. **Answer**

---

190   *Chapter 5*

A quotient of monomials is said to be *simplified* when each base appears only once, when there are no powers of powers, and when the numerator and denominator have no common factors other than 1.

Example 6 Simplify $\dfrac{35x^3yz^6}{56x^5yz}$.

Solution 1 Use the property of quotients and the rule of exponents for division.

$$\frac{35x^3yz^6}{56x^5yz} = \frac{35}{56} \cdot \frac{x^3}{x^5} \cdot \frac{y}{y} \cdot \frac{z^6}{z}$$

$$= \frac{5}{8} \cdot \frac{1}{x^2} \cdot 1 \cdot z^5$$

$$= \frac{5z^5}{8x^2} \quad \textit{Answer}$$

Solution 2 Find the GCF of the numerator and denominator and use the rule for simplifying fractions.

$$\frac{35x^3yz^6}{56x^5yz} = \frac{\cancel{7x^3yz} \cdot 5z^5}{\cancel{7x^3yz} \cdot 8x^2} = \frac{5z^5}{8x^2} \quad \textit{Answer}$$

Oral Exercises

Find the GCF of the given monomials.

1. $3x^2$, $9x^3$ $3x^2$
2. $4c^3$, $8c$ $4c$
3. $15a^4$, $21a^2$ $3a^2$
4. $10b$, $25b^5$ $5b$
5. p^2q^3, p^3q^2 p^2q^2
6. $42ab^2c^3$, $30a^3b^2c$ $6ab^2c$
7. $7xy^3$, $14x^2y^2$ $7xy^2$
8. $4xy^2$, $6x^2y$ $2xy$
9. $6s^2t^2$, $9st^3$ $3st^2$
10. $14a^3b^4$, $21a^2b^5$ $7a^2b^4$
11. $20ax^3$, $30abx$ $10ax$
12. $25p^2qr$, $36pr^3$ pr

Simplify. Assume that no denominator equals 0.

13. $\dfrac{24}{52}$ $\frac{6}{13}$
14. $\dfrac{32}{44}$ $\frac{8}{11}$
15. $\dfrac{10^8}{10^5}$ 1000
16. $\dfrac{10^3}{10^7}$ $\frac{1}{10,000}$
17. $\dfrac{10^6}{10^6}$ 1
18. $\dfrac{6t}{2t}$ 3

19. $\dfrac{8w}{4w}$ 2
20. $\dfrac{9c^3}{3c}$ $3c^2$
21. $\dfrac{3a^2}{6a}$ $\frac{a}{2}$
22. $\dfrac{5w^4}{15w^2}$ $\frac{w^2}{3}$
23. $\dfrac{24b^3}{12b^3}$ 2
24. $\dfrac{12x^5}{-3x^3}$ $-4x^2$

25. $\dfrac{-6p^3}{12p^5}$ $-\frac{1}{2p^2}$
26. $\dfrac{8x^2y}{2xy}$ $4x$
27. $\dfrac{5x^2y^2}{xy}$ $5xy$
28. $\dfrac{r^3s^2}{rs^4}$ $\frac{r^2}{s^2}$
29. $\dfrac{mn^5}{m^3n^2}$ $\frac{n^3}{m^2}$
30. $\dfrac{ab^3}{a^5b}$ $\frac{b^2}{a^4}$

Sample $\dfrac{(4n)^2}{(2n)^3} = \dfrac{16n^2}{8n^3} = \dfrac{\cancel{8n^2} \cdot 2}{\cancel{8n^2} \cdot n} = \dfrac{2}{n}$

31. $\dfrac{(2t)^5}{(2t)^3}$ $4t^2$
32. $\dfrac{(2r)^3}{2r^2}$ $4r$
33. $\dfrac{3s^3}{(3s)^2}$ $\frac{s}{3}$
34. $\dfrac{3x^3y}{(-x)^2y}$ $3x$
35. $\dfrac{-x^4y}{(-x^2)^2}$ $-y$
36. $\dfrac{-(m^3n)}{(-mn)^3}$ $\frac{1}{n^2}$

Guided Practice

Simplify. Assume that no denominator equals 0.

1. $\dfrac{72}{81}$ $\frac{8}{9}$
2. $\dfrac{10^5}{10^7}$ $\frac{1}{100}$
3. $\dfrac{15n}{5n}$ 3
4. $\dfrac{12 \cdot 10^7}{4 \cdot 10^5}$ 300
5. $\dfrac{9y^4}{12y}$ $\frac{3y^3}{4}$
6. $\dfrac{18x^4}{12x^3y}$ $\frac{3x}{2y}$
7. $\dfrac{-7a^2b^3}{28abc}$ $\frac{-ab^2}{4c}$
8. $\dfrac{-12r^2s}{-20rs^2}$ $\frac{3r}{5s}$
9. $\dfrac{(3s)^4}{3s^4}$ 27
10. $\dfrac{(2x^2)^3}{(2x^3)^2}$ 2
11. $\dfrac{(-ab)^7}{ab^7}$ $-a^6$
12. $\dfrac{(-b^3)^4}{(-b^4)^2}$ b^4

Find the missing factor.

13. $18c^9 = (-6c^4)(\underline{\ ?\ })$ $-3c^5$
14. $16x^4y^3 = (8x^2y)(\underline{\ ?\ })$ $(2x^2y^2)$

Summarizing the Lesson

Tell the students they have simplified quotients of monomials and have found the GCF of several monomials. Ask students to give examples of the rule of exponents for division for various positive integers m and n.

Written Exercises

Simplify. Assume that no denominator equals 0.

A
1. $\frac{42}{63}$ $\frac{2}{3}$
2. $\frac{54}{72}$ $\frac{3}{4}$
3. $\frac{10^4}{10^6}$ $\frac{1}{100}$
4. $\frac{10^9}{10^7}$ 100
5. $\frac{12a}{3a}$ 4

6. $\frac{10m}{5m}$ 2
7. $\frac{6 \cdot 10^5}{3 \cdot 10^3}$ 200
8. $\frac{12 \cdot 10^3}{4 \cdot 10^4}$ $\frac{3}{10}$
9. $\frac{4x^5}{8x}$ $\frac{x^4}{2}$
10. $\frac{3n^7}{15n^3}$ $\frac{n^4}{5}$

11. $\frac{12y^3}{4xy}$ $\frac{3y^2}{x}$
12. $\frac{3r^2s}{9rs^2}$ $\frac{r}{3s}$
13. $\frac{-9x^2y^3}{12xy^2}$ $-\frac{3xy}{4}$
14. $\frac{-6pq^2}{-15pq}$ $\frac{2q}{5}$
15. $\frac{-28cd^3}{-21bd^2}$

16. $\frac{42yz^4}{-48xz^3}$ $-\frac{7yz}{8x}$
17. $\frac{xy^2z^3}{x^3y^2z}$ $\frac{z^2}{x^2}$
18. $\frac{r^2s^4t}{r^2st^3}$ $\frac{s^3}{t^2}$
19. $\frac{32a^2bc^3}{20abc}$ $\frac{8ac^2}{5}$
20. $\frac{39x^3y^2z}{52x^2y}$

21. $\frac{(2r)^4}{2r^4}$ 8
22. $\frac{7m^2}{(7m)^2}$ $\frac{1}{7}$
23. $\frac{(3t^2)^3}{(3t^3)^2}$ 3
24. $\frac{(5a^2)^3}{(5a^3)^2}$ 5
25. $\frac{(2ab)^2}{2ab^2}$ $2a$

26. $\frac{(3mn)^2}{3mn^2}$ $3m$
27. $\frac{(-z)^9}{(-z)^6}$ $-z^3$
28. $\frac{(-a)^7}{(-a)^4}$ $-a^3$
29. $\frac{(-xy)^9}{xy^9}$ $-x^8$
30. $\frac{(-t^4)^3}{(-t^2)^5}$ t^2

Find the missing factor.

Sample $48x^3y^2z^4 = (3xy^2z)(\underline{?})$

Solution $\frac{48x^3y^2z^4}{3xy^2z} = 16x^2z^3$

31. $6t^4 = (2t)(\underline{?})$ $3t^3$
32. $12w^6 = (3w^2)(\underline{?})$ $4w^4$
33. $9a^3b^4 = (3a^2b^2)(\underline{?})$ $3ab^2$
34. $18pq^3 = (6pq)(\underline{?})$ $3q^2$
35. $-35x^3y^5 = (7x^2y)(\underline{?})$ $-5xy^4$
36. $-28r^4s^3 = (-7r)(\underline{?})$ $4r^3s^3$
37. $48c^5d^4 = (-3c^3d^2)(\underline{?})$ $-16c^2d^2$
38. $72h^3k = (-8hk)(\underline{?})$ $-9h^2$

B
39. $(3a^3b^2)^3 = (3a^3b^2)^2(\underline{?})$ $3a^3b^2$
40. $(2s^3t)^5 = (2s^3t)^3(\underline{?})$ $4s^6t^2$
41. $(x^2y^3)^3 = (x^4y^5)(\underline{?})$ x^2y^4
42. $(2c^3d^2)^5 = (2c^2d^2)^4(\underline{?})$ $2c^7d^2$
43. $36r^5s^7 = (2r^3s)(6s^4)(\underline{?})$ $3r^2s^2$
44. $48p^5q^4 = (2pq^2)(4pq)(\underline{?})$ $6p^3q$
45. $72x^5y^5 = (2x^2y)^2(3y^3)(\underline{?})$ $6x$
46. $75a^6b^5 = (ab)^3(5a)^2(\underline{?})$ $3ab^2$

Find the GCF of each pair of monomials.

47. $48a^2bc^3$, $72ab^3c^2$ $24abc^2$
48. $36x^2y^2z^2$, $24xy^2z^3$ $12xy^2z^2$
49. $25p^2q^3$, $15p^2q^2$, $35pq^4$ $5pq^2$
50. $56r^4s^3$, $28r^3s^2$, $42r^3s$ $14r^3s$
51. $(x + y)(x - y)$, $2x(x + y)$ $x + y$
52. $4p^2(p - 1)$, $6p(p + 1)^2$ $2p$

Simplify. Assume that no denominator equals 0.

53. $\frac{(a + b)^3}{(a + b)^2}$ $a + b$
54. $\frac{(w + x)^4}{(w + x)^5}$ $\frac{1}{w + x}$
55. $\frac{(x + y)(x - y)}{(x + y)^2}$ $\frac{x - y}{x + y}$
56. $\frac{(r - s)^2}{(r + s)(r - s)}$ $\frac{r - s}{r + s}$

192   *Chapter 5*

Suggested Assignments

Minimum
Day 1: 192/2–38 even, 47, 49
Day 2: 192/39–54 mult. of 3
   S 193/Mixed Review
Assign with Lesson 5-3.

Average
Day 1: 192/1–45 odd
Day 2: 192/47–57 odd
   S 193/Mixed Review
Assign with Lesson 5-3.

Maximum
Lesson 5-2 is covered in the
assignment for Lesson 5-1.

Supplementary Materials

Study Guide   pp. 75–76
Practice Master   24

Simplify. Assume that $x \neq 0$, $y \neq 0$, and n is a positive integer.

C **57.** $\dfrac{136x^{n+1}}{187x^n} \cdot \dfrac{8x}{11}$ **58.** $\dfrac{143(xy)^n}{117xy^n} \cdot \dfrac{11x^{n-1}}{9}$ **59.** $\dfrac{x^{2n+1}y^{n+1}}{(xy^2)^n} \cdot \dfrac{x^{n+1}}{y^{n-1}}$ **60.** $\dfrac{\dfrac{(-xy)^{2n+1}}{x^{2n}y^{n+1}}}{-xy^n}$

Give a reason for each step of the proof. You may use the property of quotients in Exercise 62. Assume that c, d, x, and y are real numbers and that no denominator equals 0.

61. Property of quotients

$\dfrac{ac}{bd} = (ac)\left(\dfrac{1}{bd}\right)$ **a.** ___?___ Def. of division

$= (ac)\left(\dfrac{1}{b} \cdot \dfrac{1}{d}\right)$ **b.** ___?___ Prop. of the reciprocal of a product

$= \left(a \cdot \dfrac{1}{b}\right)\left(c \cdot \dfrac{1}{d}\right)$ **c.** ___?___ ; ___?___ Comm. prop. of mult.; Assoc. prop. of mult.

$= \dfrac{a}{b} \cdot \dfrac{c}{d}$ **d.** ___?___ Def. of division

62. Simplification rule for fractions

$\dfrac{bc}{bd} = \dfrac{b}{b} \cdot \dfrac{c}{d}$ **a.** ___?___

$= \left(b \cdot \dfrac{1}{b}\right) \cdot \dfrac{c}{d}$ **b.** ___?___

$= 1 \cdot \dfrac{c}{d}$ **c.** ___?___

$= \dfrac{c}{d}$ **d.** ___?___

62. a. Prop. of quotients   **b.** Def. of div.   **c.** Prop. of reciprocals   **d.** Identity prop. of mult.

Mixed Review Exercises

Simplify.

1. $\dfrac{1}{5}(-25)$ -5 **2.** $111 \cdot \dfrac{1}{3}$ 37   **3.** $423 \div 9$ 47

4. $6n^4\left(\dfrac{1}{6}n^4\right)$ n^8 **5.** $15 \div \left(-\dfrac{1}{3}\right)$ -45 **6.** $8y \cdot \dfrac{3}{4}y^2$ $6y^3$

Evaluate if $x = 4$, $y = 2$, and $z = -3$

7. $\dfrac{xy}{(1-z)y}$ 1   **8.** $\dfrac{2x}{y-z}$ $\dfrac{8}{5}$ **9.** $7y^3 + 2x$ 64

 Calculator Key-In

When you use a calculator to divide one number by another, any remainder is a decimal. Here's how to write the decimal as a fraction:

1. Subtract the whole number part of the quotient from the entire quotient.
2. Multiply the decimal that remains from the subtraction by the divisor and round to the nearest integer. The result is the remainder.
3. Use the remainder as the numerator and the divisor as the denominator to write the decimal as a fraction.

On some calculators, because of rounding errors, answers may vary.

Find the remainder. Then give the value of the decimal as a fraction.

1. $354 \div 13$ $3; \dfrac{3}{13}$ **2.** $621 \div 7$ $5; \dfrac{5}{7}$ **3.** $753 \div 11$ $5; \dfrac{5}{11}$

4. $1258 \div 15$ $13; \dfrac{13}{15}$ **5.** $3698 \div 36$ $26; \dfrac{13}{18}$ **6.** $5829 \div 45$ $24; \dfrac{8}{15}$

Factoring Polynomials   **193**

Calculator Key-In Commentary

Some calculators have "fraction keys" that avoid converting fractions to decimals and decimals to fractions by operating with fractions directly.

5-3 Monomial Factors of Polynomials

Objective   To divide polynomials by monomials and to find monomial
factors of polynomials.

On page 86 we proved that if a, b, and c are real numbers and $c \neq 0$, then

$$\frac{a+b}{c} = \frac{a}{c} + \frac{b}{c}.$$

This result is also true when a, b, and c are monomials and $c \neq 0$.

Example 1 Divide: $\dfrac{5m + 35}{5}$

Solution $\dfrac{5m + 35}{5} = \dfrac{5m}{5} + \dfrac{35}{5}$

$= m + 7$ *Answer*

To divide a polynomial by a monomial, divide each term of the polynomial by
the monomial and add the results.

In the remaining lessons of this book, assume that no divisor equals 0.

Example 2 Divide: $\dfrac{26uv - 39v}{13v}$

Solution $\dfrac{26uv - 39v}{13v} = \dfrac{26uv}{13v} - \dfrac{39v}{13v}$

$= 2u - 3$ *Answer*

Example 3 Divide: $\dfrac{3x^4 - 9x^3y + 6x^2y^2}{-3x^2}$

Solution $\dfrac{3x^4 - 9x^3y + 6x^2y^2}{-3x^2} = \dfrac{3x^4}{-3x^2} - \dfrac{9x^3y}{-3x^2} + \dfrac{6x^2y^2}{-3x^2}$

$= -x^2 + 3xy - 2y^2$ *Answer*

Example 4 Divide: $\dfrac{x^3y - 4x + 6y}{xy}$

Solution $\dfrac{x^3y - 4x + 6y}{xy} = \dfrac{x^3y}{xy} - \dfrac{4x}{xy} + \dfrac{6y}{xy}$

$= x^2 - \dfrac{4}{y} + \dfrac{6}{x}$ *Answer*

194   *Chapter 5*

We say that one polynomial is **evenly divisible,** or just **divisible,** by another polynomial if the quotient is also a polynomial. Example 3 shows that $3x^4 - 9x^3y + 6x^2y^2$ is divisible by $-3x^2$. Example 4 shows that $x^3y - 4x + 6y$ is *not* divisible by xy because the quotient is not a polynomial.

You *factor* a polynomial by expressing it as a product of other polynomials. Unless otherwise specified, *the factor set for a polynomial having integral coefficients is the set of all polynomials having integral coefficients.*

You can use division to test for factors of a polynomial. Example 3 shows that the divisor, $-3x^2$, is a factor of $3x^4 - 9x^3y + 6x^2y^2$. The quotient is the other factor.

$$3x^4 - 9x^3y + 6x^2y^2 = -3x^2(-x^2 + 3xy - 2y^2)$$

Of course, -3, x, and x^2 (besides $-3x^2$) are all factors of $3x^4 - 9x^3y + 6x^2y^2$, but you should use the *greatest* monomial factor of a polynomial. The **greatest monomial factor of a polynomial** is the GCF of its terms.

Example 5 Factor $5x^2 + 10x$.

Solution 1. The greatest monomial factor of $5x^2 + 10x$ is $5x$.

2. Divide: $\dfrac{5x^2 + 10x}{5x} = \dfrac{5x^2}{5x} + \dfrac{10x}{5x}$
$$= x + 2$$

3. $\therefore 5x^2 + 10x = 5x(x + 2)$ **Answer**

Example 6 Factor $4x^5 - 6x^3 + 14x$.

Solution 1. The greatest monomial factor of $4x^5 - 6x^3 + 14x$ is $2x$.

2. Divide: $\dfrac{4x^5 - 6x^3 + 14x}{2x} = \dfrac{4x^5}{2x} - \dfrac{6x^3}{2x} + \dfrac{14x}{2x}$
$$= 2x^4 - 3x^2 + 7$$

3. $\therefore 4x^5 - 6x^3 + 14x = 2x(2x^4 - 3x^2 + 7)$ **Answer**

Example 7 Factor $8a^2bc^2 - 12ab^2c^2$.

Solution 1. The greatest monomial factor of $8a^2bc^2 - 12ab^2c^2$ is $4abc^2$.

2. Divide: $\dfrac{8a^2bc^2 - 12ab^2c^2}{4abc^2} = \dfrac{8a^2bc^2}{4abc^2} - \dfrac{12ab^2c^2}{4abc^2}$
$$= 2a - 3b$$

3. $\therefore 8a^2bc^2 - 12ab^2c^2 = 4abc^2(2a - 3b)$ **Answer**

With a little practice you will be able to do the division steps mentally. You should check your factorization by multiplying the resulting factors.

Factoring Polynomials   **195**

Check for Understanding

Here is a suggested use of the Oral Exercises to check students' understanding as you teach the lesson.
Oral Exs. 1–9: use after Example 4.
Oral Exs. 10–17: use after Example 7.

Guided Practice

Divide.

1. $\dfrac{9y + 12}{3}$ $3y + 4$

2. $\dfrac{16a + 20b}{4}$ $4a + 5b$

3. $\dfrac{27r^3 - 18r^2 - 36r}{-9r}$
$-3r^2 + 2r + 4$

4. $\dfrac{12p^4q - 8p^3q^2 + 18p^2q^3}{-2p^2q}$
$-6p^2 + 4pq - 9q^2$

Evaluate by factoring first.

5. $9 \cdot 12 + 16 \cdot 12 - 5 \cdot 12$
240

6. $17 \cdot 8 - 40 + 8^2$ 160

Factor.

7. $16a - 18b + 12$
$2(8a - 9b + 6)$

8. $9s^3 + 15s^2$ $3s^2(3s + 5)$

9. $21a^3b - 7a^2b + 14b$
$7b(3a^3 - a^2 + 2)$

Summarizing the Lesson

Tell students they have divided polynomials by monomials and have found monomial factors of polynomials.

Oral Exercises

Divide.

1. $\dfrac{7x + 14}{7}$ $x + 2$

2. $\dfrac{10y - 5}{5}$ $2y - 1$

3. $\dfrac{4u - 6v}{2}$ $2u - 3v$ $2a + 3$

4. $\dfrac{14x - 28y + 21z}{7}$ $2x - 4y + 3z$

5. $\dfrac{36m - 48mn}{6m}$ $6 - 8n$

6. $\dfrac{22ab + 33b}{11b}$

7. $\dfrac{3c^2d - 12cd^2}{3cd}$ $c - 4d$

8. $\dfrac{2a^3b - 6a^2b^2 + 4ab^3}{2ab}$ $a^2 - 3ab + 2b^2$

9. $\dfrac{x^2y^2 + x^2y + xy^2}{xy}$ $xy + x + y$

Find the greatest monomial factor. Then factor the given polynomial.

10. $4y^2 + 8y$

11. $15x^3 - 10x$

12. $ab^2 - a^2b$

13. $6pq + 9qr$

14. $\pi r^2 - 2\pi r$

15. $2x^2y^2 - 12xy$

16. $xy^2z^3 + x^3y^2z$

17. $uv^2r - u^2vs$

10. $4y(y + 2)$
11. $5x(3x^2 - 2)$
12. $ab(b - a)$
14. $\pi r(r - 2)$
15. $2xy(xy - 6)$
16. $xy^2z(z^2 + x^2)$
13. $3q(2p + 3r)$
17. $uv(vr - us)$

Written Exercises

Divide.

A   **1.** $\dfrac{6a + 9}{3}$ $2a + 3$

2. $\dfrac{4x - 6}{2}$ $2x - 3$

3. $\dfrac{24t - 12}{6}$ $4t - 2$

4. $\dfrac{21c + 35}{7}$ $3c + 5$

5. $\dfrac{9m - 18n}{9}$ $m - 2n$

6. $\dfrac{15a + 25b}{5}$ $3a + 5b$

7. $\dfrac{12xy + 27y}{3y}$ $4x + 9$

8. $\dfrac{24mn - 16n}{8n}$ $3m - 2$

9. $\dfrac{10z^2 - 15z - 20}{5}$ $2z^2 - 3z - 4$

10. $\dfrac{3x^2 - 12x - 18}{3}$ $x^2 - 4x - 6$

11. $\dfrac{33y^4 + 11y^3 - 44y^2}{11y}$ $3y^3 + y^2 - 4y$

12. $\dfrac{4u^3 + 10u^2 - 6u}{2u}$ $2u^2 + 5u - 3$

13. $\dfrac{8r^4 - 4r^3 - 6r^2}{-2r^2}$ $-4r^2 + 2r + 3$

14. $\dfrac{9m^5 + 12m^4 - 6m^3}{-m^3}$ $-9m^2 - 12m + 6$

15. $\dfrac{pq^3 - p^3q}{pq}$ $q^2 - p^2$

16. $\dfrac{10a^2b - 15ab^2}{5ab}$ $2a - 3b$

17. $\dfrac{x^2y - xy^2 - xy}{xy}$ $x - y - 1$

18. $\dfrac{6c^3d - 12cd^3 - 15cd}{3cd}$ $2c^2 - 4d^2 - 5$

19. $\dfrac{28r^3s^2 + 42r^2s^3 - 56r^3s^3}{-7r^2s^2}$
$-4r - 6s + 8rs$

20. $\dfrac{30p^4q - 45p^3q^2 + 15p^2q^3}{5p^2q}$
$6p^2 - 9pq + 3q^2$

Evaluate by factoring first.

> **Sample** $11^2 - 7 \cdot 11 = 11 \cdot 11 - 7 \cdot 11 = (11 - 7)11 = 4 \cdot 11 = 44$

21. $65 \cdot 3 + 65 \cdot 7$ 650

22. $43 \cdot 13 - 43 \cdot 3$ 430

23. $7 \cdot 19 - 3 \cdot 19 + 6 \cdot 19$ 190

24. $7 \cdot 13 + 8 \cdot 13 + 5 \cdot 13$ 260

25. $83^2 + 83 \cdot 17$ 8300

27. $13^2 - 5 \cdot 13 + 2 \cdot 13$ 130

29. $7^2 - 28 + 7 \cdot 17$ 140

26. $2 \cdot 9 + 9^2$ 99

28. $12 \cdot 13 - 60 + 12^2$ 240

30. $11^2 - 6 \cdot 11 + 5 \cdot 11$ 110

Factor.

31. $15a - 25b + 20$ $5(3a - 5b + 4)$

33. $6x^2 + 10x$ $2x(3x + 5)$

35. $6p^2q - 9pq$ $3pq(2p - 3)$

37. $7y^3 - 21y^2 - 14y$ $7y(y^2 - 3y - 2)$

32. $18x - 12y + 36$ $6(3x - 2y + 6)$

34. $14c^3 - 21c$ $7c(2c^2 - 3)$

36. $2a^2b^2 + 10ab$ $2ab(ab + 5)$

38. $22y^4 - 33y^3 + 11y^2$ $11y^2(2y^2 - 3y + 1)$

B **39.** $6ab^2 - 8a^2b$ $2ab(3b - 4a)$

41. $-15x^2y^2 - 6xy^2$ $-3xy^2(5x + 2)$

43. $5ax^2 + 10a^2x - 15a^3$ $5a(x^2 + 2ax - 3a^2)$

45. $48a^3b^2 + 72a^2b^3$ $24a^2b^2(2a + 3b)$

47. $96wx^3y^2z^2 - 144w^3xyz^2$
    $48wxy^2z^2(2x^2 - 3w^2)$

40. $4x^2y - 16xy^2$ $4xy(x - 4y)$

42. $-16x^3y - 24x^4y^3$ $-8x^3y(2 + 3xy^2)$

44. $14p^3q^3 - 21p^2q^2 + 35pq$

46. $77r^7s^7 - 84r^8s^4$ $7r^7s^4(11s^3 - 12r)$

48. $84ab^2c^3d^4 + 126a^4b^3c^2$
    $42ab^2c^2(2cd^4 + 3a^3b)$

44. $7pq(2p^2q^2 - 3pq + 5)$

Simplify.

> **Sample** $\dfrac{15x - 25y}{5} - \dfrac{14x - 21y}{7} = (3x - 5y) - (2x - 3y)$
>
> $\qquad\qquad\qquad\qquad\qquad\quad = 3x - 5y - 2x + 3y$
>
> $\qquad\qquad\qquad\qquad\qquad\quad = x - 2y$ **Answer**

49. $\dfrac{4a - 6}{2} + \dfrac{3a + 6}{3}$ $3a - 1$

51. $\dfrac{6p + 9q}{3} - \dfrac{7p + 21q}{7}$ p

53. $\dfrac{x^2y - 3x^2y^2}{xy} + \dfrac{6xy + 9xy^2}{3y}$ $3x$

50. $\dfrac{14x - 21}{7} - \dfrac{10x - 25}{5}$ 2

52. $\dfrac{a^2b + 2ab^2}{ab} - \dfrac{2ab - b^2}{b}$ $-a + 3b$

54. $\dfrac{a^3b^4 - a^4b^3}{a^2b^3} - \dfrac{a^3b^2 - a^2b^3}{a^2b}$ $-a^2 + b^2$

Problems

> **Sample**   Write an expression in factored form for the area A of the shaded region.

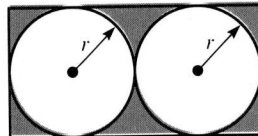

> **Solution**   The length of the rectangle equals the length of four radii ($4r$), and the width equals the length of two radii ($2r$).
>
> $A = $ Area of the rectangle $- (2 \times$ area of a circle$)$
>
> $\quad = (4r \cdot 2r) - 2\pi r^2$
>
> $\quad = 2r^2(4 - \pi)$ **Answer**

Factoring Polynomials   **197**

Suggested Assignments

Minimum

Day 1: 196/1–17 odd
Assign with Lesson 5-2.

Day 2: 196/21–49 odd
   197/*P*: 1, 3, 5
   S 199/Mixed Review

Average

Day 1: 196/1–19 odd
Assign with Lesson 5-2.

Day 2: 196/21–51 odd
   197/*P*: 2, 6, 7
   S 199/Mixed Review

Maximum

   196/3–54 mult. of 3
   197/*P*: 2–10 even
   S 199/Mixed Review

Common Errors

Some students divide only the *first* term of a polynomial by the monomial divisor. In reteaching, remind them that *each* term must be divided by the monomial. Some students may not understand that a division bar may also act as a grouping symbol, as in Exercises 49–54. Emphasize that in those problems, -1 is distributed into the numerator of the second fraction.

Supplementary Materials

Study Guide   pp. 77–78
Resource Book   p. 96

Write an expression in factored form for the area A of each shaded region.

A 1.

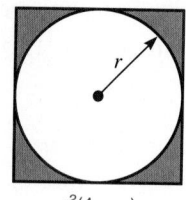

$$r^2(4 - \pi)$$

2.

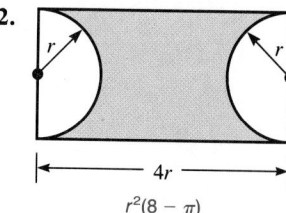

$$4r$$

$$r^2(8 - \pi)$$

3.

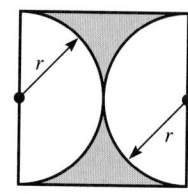

$$2r$$

$$r^2(4 + \pi)$$

4.

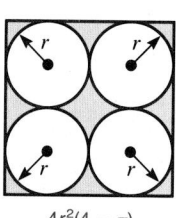

$$r^2(4 - \pi)$$

5.

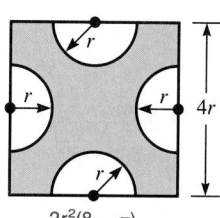

$$4r^2(4 - \pi)$$

6.

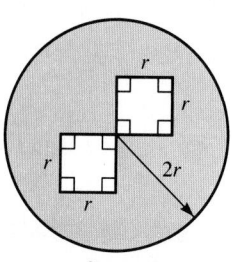

$$4r$$

$$2r^2(8 - \pi)$$

B 7.

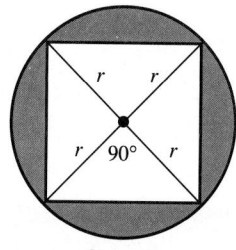

$$2r$$

$$2r^2(2\pi - 1)$$

8.

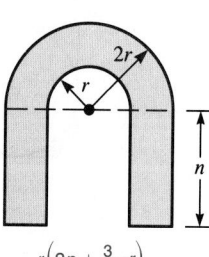

$$90°$$

$$r^2(\pi - 2)$$

9.

$$2r$$

$$n$$

$$r\left(2n + \frac{3}{2}\pi r\right)$$

10.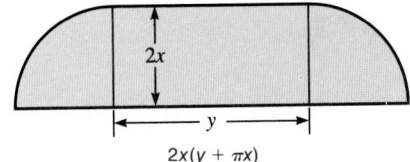

$2x(y + \pi x)$

11.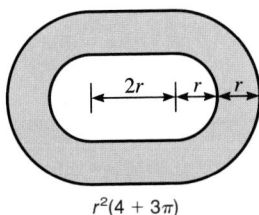

$r^2(4 + 3\pi)$

Mixed Review Exercises

Simplify.

1. $7n^3\left(\dfrac{1}{7}n^3\right)n^6$

2. $9x^2\left(\dfrac{2}{3}x^3\right)$ $6x^5$

3. $4a^2 - 7a^2c + 2a^2 - 3ac^2$ $6a^2 - 7a^2c - 3ac^2$

4. $\dfrac{3x^3y}{6xy^2}$ $\dfrac{x^2}{2y}$

5. $28 \div \left(-\dfrac{1}{4}\right)$ -112

6. $\dfrac{(2a^3)^3}{a^4}$ $8a^5$

7. $(4a)^4$ $256a^4$

8. $5(2^2 - 1) + 3^3 \cdot 2$ 69

9. $(x - 2)(x^2 + 2x + 5)$ $x^3 + x - 10$

Self-Test 1

Vocabulary factor (p. 185)
factor set (p. 185)
prime number (p. 185)
prime factorization (p. 185)
greatest common factor of two or
more integers (p. 186)

greatest common factor of monomials (p. 190)
divisible (p. 195)
greatest monomial factor of a polynomial (p. 195)

1. List all pairs of factors of 45.

$$\begin{array}{ll}(1)(45) & (-1)(-45)\\(3)(15) & (-3)(-15)\\(5)(9) & (-5)(-9)\end{array}$$ **Obj. 5-1, p. 185**

2. Find the prime factorization of 54. $2 \cdot 3^3$

3. Find the greatest common factor of 54 and 45. 9

Simplify.

4. $-\dfrac{21x^2y^5}{7xy^5}$ $-3x$

5. $\dfrac{10m^3n^8}{75m^5n^2}$ $\dfrac{2n^6}{15m^2}$ **Obj. 5-2, p. 189**

Find the missing factor.

6. $27x^4 = 3x^2(\underline{\ ?\ })$ $9x^2$

7. $-35a^2b^5 = (7ab)(\underline{\ ?\ })$ $-5ab^4$

8. Divide: $\dfrac{21t^4 + 15t^3 - 9t^2}{3t^2}$
$7t^2 + 5t - 3$

9. Factor $5m^3 - 20m^2 + 25m$.
$5m(m^2 - 4m + 5)$ **Obj. 5-3, p. 194**

Check your answers with those at the back of the book.

Products and Factors

5-4 Multiplying Binomials Mentally

Objective   To find the product of two binomials mentally.

The following example shows how the distributive property, $(a + b)c = ac + bc$, is used to multiply $(2x + 5)$ by $(3x - 4)$. Notice how the three terms of the product are formed.

Example 1   Write the product $(2x + 5)(3x - 4)$ as a trinomial.

Solution 1   You can do the work horizontally, as shown below, or vertically, as shown at the right.

$$\begin{aligned}(2x + 5)(3x - 4) &= 2x\,(3x - 4) + 5\,(3x - 4) \\ &= 6x^2 - 8x + 15x - 20 \\ &= 6x^2 + 7x - 20\end{aligned}$$

$$\begin{array}{r} 3x - 4 \\ 2x + 5 \\ \hline 6x^2 - 8x \\ 15x - 20 \\ \hline 6x^2 + 7x - 20 \quad \textbf{\textit{Answer}} \end{array}$$

Solution 2   First use the following short method to multiply in your head.

Think of the products of these terms:

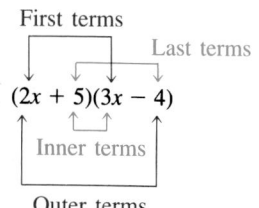

Then write the products:

$$\underbrace{6x^2}_{\substack{\text{First} \\ \text{terms}}} - \underbrace{8x}_{\substack{\text{Outer} \\ \text{terms}}} + \underbrace{15x}_{\substack{\text{Inner} \\ \text{terms}}} - \underbrace{20}_{\substack{\text{Last} \\ \text{terms}}} = 6x^2 + 7x - 20 \quad \textbf{\textit{Answer}}$$

This method is sometimes called the FOIL method.

To write the product $(ax + b)(cx + d)$ as a trinomial:

1. Multiply the first terms of the binomials.

2. Multiply the first term of each binomial by the last term of the other and add these products.

3. Multiply the last terms of the binomials.

Each term of a trinomial like $6x^2 + 7x - 20$ has a standard name. A **quadratic term** is a term of degree two. A **linear term** is a term of degree one. As defined earlier, a *constant term* is one having no variable factor. The trinomial itself is called a **quadratic polynomial** since its term of greatest degree is quadratic.

$$6x^2 + 7x - 20$$

$6x^2$ is the quadratic term. ——
$7x$ is the linear term. ——
-20 is the constant term. ——

Sometimes you may need to evaluate a quadratic polynomial. The Calculator Key-In on page 203 will help you.

Oral Exercises Answers to parts (a), (b), and (c) are given in the side-column.

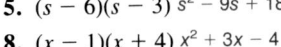

For each product, state (a) the quadratic term, (b) the two terms that form the linear term, (c) the constant term, and (d) the trinomial product.

6. $28 - 11k + k^2$ 9. $r^2 - 2r - 15$
12. $x^2 - 2x - 35$ 15. $2x^2 - 3x - 9$

Sample $(n - 7)(2n + 5)$ **Solution**   **a.** $2n^2$ **b.** $5n$ and $-14n$
c. -35 **d.** $2n^2 - 9n - 35$

$t^2 - 5t + 6$

1. $(x + 1)(x + 3)$ $x^2 + 4x + 3$ 2. $(y + 2)(y + 5)$ $y^2 + 7y + 10$ 3. $(t - 2)(t - 3)$
4. $(u - 4)(u - 1)$ $u^2 - 5u + 4$ 5. $(s - 6)(s - 3)$ $s^2 - 9s + 18$ 6. $(7 - k)(4 - k)$
7. $(y - 3)(y + 5)$ $y^2 + 2y - 15$ 8. $(x - 1)(x + 4)$ $x^2 + 3x - 4$ 9. $(r + 3)(r - 5)$
10. $(s - 3)(s + 3)$ $s^2 - 9$ 11. $(y + 2)(y + 2)$ $y^2 + 4y + 4$ 12. $(x - 7)(x + 5)$
13. $(2y + 3)(y + 1)$ $2y^2 + 5y + 3$ 14. $(n + 1)(2n + 5)$ $2n^2 + 7n + 5$ 15. $(x - 3)(2x + 3)$
16. $(3y - 1)(y + 3)$ $3y^2 + 8y - 3$ 17. $(3r + 1)(r - 2)$ $3r^2 - 5r - 2$ 18. $(1 - 5x)(5 - x)$
18. $5 - 26x + 5x^2$

Written Exercises

3. $y^2 - 7y + 12$
6. $y^2 + 4y - 12$
9. $6 + 5z + z^2$
12. $2r^2 + 11r + 12$

Write each product as a trinomial.

A 1. $(x + 5)(x + 8)$ $x^2 + 13x + 40$ 2. $(x + 7)(x + 6)$ $x^2 + 13x + 42$ 3. $(y - 4)(y - 3)$
4. $(c - 9)(c - 6)$ $c^2 - 15c + 54$ 5. $(z + 4)(z - 7)$ $z^2 - 3z - 28$ 6. $(y + 6)(y - 2)$
7. $(n - 3)(n + 7)$ $n^2 + 4n - 21$ 8. $(u - 10)(u + 9)$ $u^2 - u - 90$ 9. $(3 + z)(2 + z)$
10. $(4 - x)(1 - x)$ $4 - 5x + x^2$ 11. $(2y + 5)(y + 2)$ $2y^2 + 9y + 10$ 12. $(r + 4)(2r + 3)$
13. $(7x - 1)(x + 7)$ $7x^2 + 48x - 7$ 14. $(4k - 1)(k + 4)$ $4k^2 + 15k - 4$ 15. $(2y + 1)(3y + 2)$
16. $(2n + 1)(5n + 2)$ $10n^2 + 9n + 2$ 17. $(2 - 3s)(1 - 2s)$ $2 - 7s + 6s^2$ 18. $(3 - 2r)(2 - 3r)$
19. $(3h - 5)(2h + 1)$ $6h^2 - 7h - 5$ 20. $(3x + 2)(2x - 3)$ $6x^2 - 5x - 6$ 21. $(5n + 4)(4n - 5)$

15. $6y^2 + 7y + 2$
18. $6 - 13r + 6r^2$
21. $20n^2 - 9n - 20$

Sample 1 $(3x - 5y)(4x + y) = 12x^2 + (3xy - 20xy) - 5y^2$
$= 12x^2 - 17xy - 5y^2$ **Answer**

Factoring Polynomials   **201**

Check for Understanding
Here is a suggested use of the Oral Exercises.
Oral Exs. 1–18: use after discussion on p. 201.

Additional Answers
Oral Exercises

1. **a.** x^2 **b.** $3x, x$ **c.** 3
2. **a.** y^2 **b.** $5y, 2y$ **c.** 10
3. **a.** t^2 **b.** $-3t, -2t$ **c.** 6
4. **a.** u^2 **b.** $-u, -4u$ **c.** 4
5. **a.** s^2 **b.** $-3s, -6s$ **c.** 18
6. **a.** k^2 **b.** $-7k, -4k$ **c.** 28
7. **a.** y^2 **b.** $5y, -3y$ **c.** -15
8. **a.** x^2 **b.** $4x, -x$ **c.** -4
9. **a.** r^2 **b.** $-5r, 3r$ **c.** -15
10. **a.** s^2 **b.** $3s, -3s$ **c.** -9
11. **a.** y^2 **b.** $2y, 2y$ **c.** 4
12. **a.** x^2 **b.** $5x, -7x$ **c.** -35
13. **a.** $2y^2$ **b.** $2y, 3y$ **c.** 3
14. **a.** $2n^2$ **b.** $5n, 2n$ **c.** 5
15. **a.** $2x^2$ **b.** $3x, -6x$ **c.** -9
16. **a.** $3y^2$ **b.** $9y, -y$ **c.** -3
17. **a.** $3r^2$ **b.** $-6r, r$ **c.** -2
18. **a.** $5x^2$ **b.** $-x, -25x$ **c.** 5

Suggested Assignments
Minimum
Day 1: 201/2–30 even
  R 199/Self-Test 1
Day 2: 202/32–44 even
  S 203/Mixed Review

Average
  201/3–45 mult. of 3
  S 203/Mixed Review
  R 199/Self-Test 1

Maximum
  201/3–48 mult. of 3
  S 203/Mixed Review
  R 199/Self-Test 1

22. $a^2 + ab - 2b^2$ **23.** $3x^2 - 7xy + 2y^2$

Write each product as a trinomial. See Sample 1 on page 201.

B   **22.** $(a + 2b)(a - b)$

23. $(3x - y)(x - 2y)$

24. $(2r - s)(3r + 2s)$
$6r^2 + rs - 2s^2$

25. $(4h - k)(2h + 3k)$
$8h^2 + 10hk - 3k^2$

26. $(2x + 5y)(2x - 3y)$
$4x^2 + 4xy - 15y^2$

27. $(7a - 2b)(5a - 3b)$
$35a^2 - 31ab + 6b^2$

Sample 2 $(m^2 - 5m)(2m^2 + 4m) = (m^2)(2m^2) + (m^2)(4m) + (-5m)(2m^2) + (-5m)(4m)$
$$= 2m^4 + 4m^3 - 10m^3 - 20m^2$$
$$= 2m^4 - 6m^3 - 20m^2 \quad \textbf{\textit{Answer}}$$

28. $(x^2 - 4x)(3x^2 + 2x)$
$3x^4 - 10x^3 - 8x^2$

29. $(a^2 + 3b)(3a^2 - b)$
$3a^4 + 8a^2b - 3b^2$

30. $(p^2 - q^2)(p^2 + 3q^2)$
$p^4 + 2p^2q^2 - 3q^4$

31. $(p^3 - 4q^3)(p^3 + 3q^3)$
$p^6 - p^3q^3 - 12q^6$

32. $(y^4 - 3y^2)(y^2 + 2)$
$y^6 - y^4 - 6y^2$

33. $(x^4 + x^2y^2)(4x^2 - y^2)$
$4x^6 + 3x^4y^2 - x^2y^4$

Sample 3 $n(n - 3)(2n + 1) = n[2n^2 + (-6n + n) - 3]$
$$= n[2n^2 - 5n - 3]$$
$$= 2n^3 - 5n^2 - 3n \quad \textbf{\textit{Answer}}$$

34. $y(2y - 1)(y + 4)$ $2y^3 + 7y^2 - 4y$

35. $y(4y + 3)(y - 2)$ $4y^3 - 5y^2 - 6y$

36. $y^2(1 - 2y)(2 + 3y)$ $-6y^4 - y^3 + 2y^2$

37. $x^2(4 - x)(2 - 3x)$ $3x^4 - 14x^3 + 8x^2$

Solve.

Sample 4 $(x - 4)(x + 9) = (x + 5)(x - 3)$

Solution $x^2 - 4x + 9x - 36 = x^2 + 5x - 3x - 15$
$$x^2 + 5x - 36 = x^2 + 2x - 15$$
$$5x - 36 = 2x - 15$$
$$3x - 36 = -15$$
$$3x = 21$$
$$x = 7$$

$\therefore$ the solution set is $\{7\}$.   **_Answer_**

38. $(x - 2)(x - 3) = (x - 7)(x + 3)$ $\{27\}$

39. $(y + 4)(y - 3) = (y - 2)(y + 5)$ $\{-1\}$

40. $(2n + 5)(3n - 4) = (n + 2)(6n - 7)$ $\{3\}$

41. $(2x - 1)(8x + 3) = (4x + 5)(4x - 5)$ $\{11\}$

42. $(n + 3)(2n + 3) = (n + 2)^2 + (n - 2)^2$ $\left\{-\frac{1}{9}\right\}$

43. $(2x - 3)(x + 3) = (x - 3)^2 + (x + 3)^2$ $\{9\}$

44. Show that $(ax + b)(cx + d) = acx^2 + (ad + bc)x + bd$.
$(ax + b)(cx + d) = acx^2 + adx + bcx + bd = acx^2 + (ad + bc)x + bd$

In Exercises 45 and 46, find the values of _p_, _q_, and _r_.

C   **45.** $(px + q)(2x + 5) = 6x^2 + 11x + r$
$p = 3, q = -2, r = -10$

46. $(px + 2)(3x + q) = rx^2 + x - 2$
$p = 5, q = -1, r = 15$

Write each product as a trinomial. Assume that _n_ represents a positive integer.

47. $(x^n - y^n)(2x^n + 3y^n)$ $2x^{2n} + x^ny^n - 3y^{2n}$

48. $(2x^n - y^n)(2x^n + y^n)$ $4x^{2n} - y^{2n}$

49. Show that the square of any odd integer is odd. (_Hint:_ If _n_ is an integer, then $2n$ is an even integer and $2n + 1$ is an odd integer.)
$(2n + 1)^2 = 4n^2 + 4n + 1$
$= 2(2n^2 + 2n) + 1$

202   _Chapter 5_

Guided Practice

Write each product as a trinomial.

1. $(y + 3)(y + 4)$
$y^2 + 7y + 12$

2. $(a - 7)(a - 3)$
$a^2 - 10a + 21$

3. $(3x + 1)(x + 2)$
$3x^2 + 7x + 2$

4. $(6k - 3)(2k + 4)$
$12k^2 + 18k - 12$

5. $(5 - 4k)(5 - 4k)$
$25 - 40k + 16k^2$

Summarizing the Lesson

Tell the students they should now be able to multiply binomials mentally. Ask them to write some sample problems and to find the solutions.

Supplementary Materials

Study Guide   pp. 79–80
Practice Master   25
Test Master   20

Mixed Review Exercises

Simplify.

1. $(2x^3y)(-4xy^3)$ $-8x^4y^4$

2. $(5x^2y^5)^3$ $125x^6y^{15}$

3. $(6n + 3)(2n^2 + 3n - 1)$ $12n^3 + 24n^2 + 3n - 3$

4. $\dfrac{10r^2 + 25r - 30}{5}$ $2r^2 + 5r - 6$

5. $\dfrac{(5y)^4}{5y}$ $125y^3$

6. $\dfrac{15 - 9x - 3x^2}{3}$ $5 - 3x - x^2$

Solve.

7. $m = 42 - 2m$ {14}

8. $4x - (2x + 5) = 5$ {5}

9. $4(n + 3) = 3(5 + n)$ {3}

10. $6y + 3 = 63$ {10}

11. $2(x + 1) - 3 = 9$ {5}

12. $3(y - 3) + 7 = 10$ {4}

Computer Exercises

For students with some programming experience.

4. $4x^2 + 28x + 49$ **5.** $9x^2 - 4$ **6.** $36x^2 - 84x + 49$

Write a BASIC program to find the product of $(Ax + B)(Cx + D)$. Enter the values of A, B, C, and D with INPUT statements. Use the program to find the following products. Check the computer's answers by multiplying mentally.

1. $(x + 3)(x + 5)$ $x^2 + 8x + 15$

2. $(x - 4)(2x + 1)$ $2x^2 - 7x - 4$

3. $(4x + 3)(2x - 5)$ $8x^2 - 14x - 15$

4. $(2x + 7)(2x + 7)$

5. $(3x - 2)(3x + 2)$

6. $(6x - 7)(6x - 7)$

7. $(10x + 4)(5x + 2)$ $50x^2 + 40x + 8$

8. $(8x + 9)(9x - 8)$ $72x^2 + 17x - 72$

9. $(12x - 10)(12x + 10)$ $144x^2 - 100$

 Calculator Key-In

You can use a calculator to evaluate a quadratic polynomial for a given value of the variable. One way is to evaluate the polynomial term by term using the calculator's memory to store the partial sums.

Another way is to express the polynomial in a form that suggests a sequence of steps on the calculator. For example, to evaluate $5x^2 - 3x + 6$ you could first rewrite it as follows.

$$5x^2 - 3x + 6 = (5x - 3)x + 6$$

Then to evaluate the polynomial for a particular value, you can just work through the rewritten expression from left to right substituting the appropriate value for x.

Exercises

Evaluate the quadratic polynomial for the given value of the variable.

1. $4x^2 + 5x - 7$; 3 44

2. $6z^2 + 8z - 9$; 4 119

3. $2x^2 + 4x + 5$; -3 11

4. $y^2 - 4y - 3$; 2.5 -6.75

5. $9k^2 - 35k + 50$; 10 600

6. $40y^2 - 25y + 70$; 14 7560

7. $18x^2 - 15x - 10$; -6 728

8. $4y^2 + 4y - 5$; 0.4 -2.76

9. $20z^2 - 15z + 5$; -0.5 17.5

Factoring Polynomials **203**

5-5 Differences of Two Squares

Objective To simplify products of the form $(a + b)(a - b)$ and to factor differences of two squares.

The shaded area below can be thought of as the product $(a + b)(a - b)$. Notice on the right that when you multiply, the product can be simplified to $a^2 - b^2$, the difference of two squares.

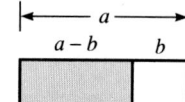

$$\begin{array}{r} a - b \\ a + b \\ \hline a^2 - ab \\ ab - b^2 \\ \hline a^2 \qquad - b^2 \end{array}$$

$$(a + b)(a - b) = a^2 - b^2$$

$$\binom{\text{Sum of two}}{\text{numbers}} \times (\text{Their difference}) = \binom{\text{First}}{\text{number}}^2 - \binom{\text{Second}}{\text{number}}^2$$

Example 1 Write each product as a binomial.
  a. $(x + 3)(x - 3)$ b. $(2n + 5)(2n - 5)$

Solution a. $(x + 3)(x - 3) = x^2 - 3^2$ b. $(2n + 5)(2n - 5) = (2n)^2 - 5^2$
                                   $= x^2 - 9$ $= 4n^2 - 25$
                          Answer   **Answer**

Example 2 Write each product as a binomial.
  a. $(a^2 - 2b)(a^2 + 2b)$ b. $(xy + z^2)(xy - z^2)$

Solution a. $(a^2 - 2b)(a^2 + 2b) = (a^2)^2 - (2b)^2$
                                     $= a^4 - 4b^2$ **Answer**

           b. $(xy + z^2)(xy - z^2) = (xy)^2 - (z^2)^2$
                                   $= x^2y^2 - z^4$ **Answer**

Working in the other direction, if you have the difference of two squares, you can factor the expression:

$$a^2 - b^2 = (a + b)(a - b)$$

Example 3 Factor: **a.** $z^2 - 49$ **b.** $16 - 9x^2$ **c.** $81a^2 - 25x^6$

Solution **a.** $z^2 - 49 = z^2 - 7^2$ **b.** $16 - 9x^2 = (4)^2 - (3x)^2$
$= (z + 7)(z - 7)$ $= (4 + 3x)(4 - 3x)$
Answer **Answer**

c. $81a^2 - 25x^6 = (9a)^2 - (5x^3)^2$
$= (9a + 5x^3)(9a - 5x^3)$ **Answer**

In Examples 3(b) and 3(c) you needed to recognize that both terms of the given binomial were *squares*. A monomial is a *square* if the exponents of all powers in it are even and the numerical coefficient is the square of an integer.

You can use a calculator or the table at the back of the book to see if a given integer is a square. For example, the table shows that 361 is the square of 19.

Example 4 Factor $16r^4 - 625$.

Solution $16r^4 - 625 = (4r^2)^2 - (25)^2$ $\begin{cases} \text{Notice that } 4r^2 - 25 \text{ is also} \\ \text{a difference of two squares.} \end{cases}$
$= (4r^2 + 25)(4r^2 - 25)$
$= (4r^2 + 25)(2r + 5)(2r - 5)$
Answer

Oral Exercises

Square each monomial.

Sample 1 $-7x^2$ **Solution** $(-7x^2)^2 = (-7)^2(x^2)^2 = 49x^4$

1. 8 64 **2.** 5a 25a² **3.** −3t 9t² **4.** 4x² 16x⁴
5. −5y³ 25y⁶ **6.** ab a²b² **7.** 2pq² 4p²q⁴ **8.** m⁸ m¹⁶

Find a monomial whose square is the given monomial.
9–16. Also accept the opposites of the given answers.

Sample 2 **a.** $36m^2$ **b.** $81x^6y^4$ **Solution** **a.** 6m **b.** 9x³y²

9. 9x² 3x **10.** 16c² 4c **11.** 4a⁴ 2a² **12.** 25t⁴ 5t²
13. x²y² xy **14.** 4a²b² 2ab **15.** 49p²q⁴ 7pq² **16.** 9r⁴s⁶ 3r²s³

Factoring Polynomials **205**

5. $64y^4 - 25z^2$
$= (8y^2)^2 - (5z)^2$
$= (8y^2 + 5z)(8y^2 - 5z)$
6. $81m^4 - 16$
$= (9m^2)^2 - (4)^2$
$= (9m^2 + 4)(9m^2 - 4)$
$= (9m^2 + 4)(3m + 2) \cdot$
$(3m - 2)$

  Using a Calculator

A calculator with a square root key ($\sqrt{}$) is helpful in doing Exercises 27–38.

Check for Understanding

Here is a suggested use of the Oral Exercises to check students' understanding as you teach the lesson.
Oral Exs. 1–16: use at the beginning of the lesson.
Oral Exs. 17–22: use after Example 2.
Oral Exs. 23–32: use after Example 4.

Guided Practice

Write each product as a binomial.

1. $(x + 3)(x - 3)$ $x^2 - 9$
2. $(2 + 3b)(2 - 3b)$ $4 - 9b^2$
3. $(6p + 4q)(6p - 4q)$
$36p^2 - 16q^2$
4. $(xy + z^2)(xy - z^2)$
$x^2y^2 - z^4$

Multiply. Use the pattern $(a + b)(a - b) = a^2 - b^2$.

5. $62 \cdot 58$ 3596
6. $99 \cdot 101$ 9999

Factor.

7. $a^2 - 49$ $(a + 7)(a - 7)$
8. $25b^2 - 16$ $(5b + 4)(5b - 4)$
9. $64p^2 - 49q^2$
$(8p + 7q)(8p - 7q)$

205

Common Errors

A common error is to factor $x^2 - 49$ as $(x - 7)(x - 7)$. In reteaching the pattern, encourage students to check their factorization by multiplying the two binomials.

Summarizing the Lesson

Tell the students that they have learned to multiply two binomials that differ only in the sign of the second term. Ask some students to write the pattern on the board and give an example of using the pattern in reverse to factor the difference of two squares.

Suggested Assignments

Minimum
Day 1: 206/1–43 odd
Day 2: 207/45–53 odd
    S 207/Mixed Review
Assign with Lesson 5-6.

Average
    206/3–60 mult. of 3
    S 207/Mixed Review

Maximum
    206/3–66 mult. of 3
    S 207/Mixed Review

Supplementary Materials

Study Guide   pp. 81–82
Computer Activity   13

Express each product as a binomial.

17. $(n + 2)(n - 2)$ $n^2 - 4$ **18.** $(r - 5)(r + 5)$ $r^2 - 25$ **19.** $(2x + 5)(2x - 5)$ $4x^2 - 25$
20. $(4y + 1)(4y - 1)$ $16y^2 - 1$ **21.** $(3s - 2)(3s + 2)$ $9s^2 - 4$ **22.** $(a - 2b)(a + 2b)$ $a^2 - 4b^2$

Tell whether each binomial is the difference of two squares. If it is, factor it.

23. $n^2 - 4$ yes   **24.** $m^2 - 5$ no   **25.** $y^2 - 64$ yes   **26.** $b^2 + 9$ no   **27.** $4x^2 - 1$ yes
28. $x^2 - 9y^2$ yes   **29.** $a^8 + 36$ no   **30.** $a^4 - 9$ yes   **31.** $a^4 - b^2$ yes   **32.** $k^3 - 16$ no
23. $(n + 2)(n - 2)$ **25.** $(y + 8)(y - 8)$ **27.** $(2x + 1)(2x - 1)$ **28.** $(x + 3y)(x - 3y)$
30. $(a^2 + 3)(a^2 - 3)$ **31.** $(a^2 + b)(a^2 - b)$

Written Exercises

Write each product as a binomial.

A   **1.** $(y - 7)(y + 7)$ $y^2 - 49$ **2.** $(m + 8)(m - 8)$ $m^2 - 64$
   3. $(4 + x)(4 - x)$ $16 - x^2$ **4.** $(9 - w)(9 + w)$ $81 - w^2$
   5. $(5y - 2)(5y + 2)$ $25y^2 - 4$ **6.** $(8x - 11)(8x + 11)$ $64x^2 - 121$
   7. $(1 + 3a)(1 - 3a)$ $1 - 9a^2$ **8.** $(7 + 2a)(7 - 2a)$ $49 - 4a^2$
   9. $(3x + 2y)(3x - 2y)$ $9x^2 - 4y^2$ **10.** $(4w + 6z)(4w - 6z)$ $16w^2 - 36z^2$
   11. $(4s + 5t)(4s - 5t)$ $16s^2 - 25t^2$ **12.** $(7p + 5q)(7p - 5q)$ $49p^2 - 25q^2$
   13. $(x^2 - 9y)(x^2 + 9y)$ $x^4 - 81y^2$ **14.** $(2x + n^2)(2x - n^2)$ $4x^2 - n^4$
   15. $(2r^2 + 7s^2)(2r^2 - 7s^2)$ $4r^4 - 49s^4$ **16.** $(3m^2 - 8n^2)(3m^2 + 8n^2)$ $9m^4 - 64n^4$
   17. $(ab - c^2)(ab + c^2)$ $a^2b^2 - c^4$ **18.** $(xy + 3z)(xy - 3z)$ $x^2y^2 - 9z^2$

Multiply. Use the pattern $(a + b)(a - b) = a^2 - b^2$.

Sample 1 $57 \cdot 63$ **Solution** $57 \cdot 63 = (60 - 3)(60 + 3)$
                                                                    $= 3600 - 9$
                                                                    $= 3591$ *Answer*

19. $38 \cdot 42$ 1596   **20.** $53 \cdot 47$ 2491   **21.** $87 \cdot 93$ 8091   **22.** $49 \cdot 51$ 2499
23. $91 \cdot 89$ 8099   **24.** $102 \cdot 98$ 9996   **25.** $74 \cdot 66$ 4884   **26.** $25 \cdot 35$ 875

29. $(2c + 9)(2c - 9)$
32. $(4x + 3)(4x - 3)$
35. $(1 + 3a)(1 - 3a)$

Factor. You may use a calculator or the table of squares.

27. $b^2 - 36$ $(b + 6)(b - 6)$ **28.** $m^2 - 25$ $(m + 5)(m - 5)$ **29.** $4c^2 - 81$
30. $9a^2 - 100$ $(3a + 10)(3a - 10)$ **31.** $25z^2 - 1$ $(5z + 1)$ $(5z - 1)$ **32.** $16x^2 - 9$
33. $169u^2 - 225$ $(13u + 15)(13u - 15)$ **34.** $81n^2 - 121$ $(9n + 11)(9n - 11)$ **35.** $1 - 9a^2$
36. $144 - y^2$ $(12 + y)(12 - y)$ **37.** $49a^2 - 9b^2$ $(7a + 3b)(7a - 3b)$ **38.** $64u^2 - 25v^2$
                                                                    $(8u + 5v)(8u - 5v)$

B   **39.** $16 - c^4$ $(4 + c^2)(2 + c)(2 - c)$ **40.** $625x^4 - 1$ $(25x^2 + 1)(5x + 1)(5x - 1)$ **41.** $u^4 - 81v^4$
   42. $81s^4 - 16t^8$ **43.** $x^8 - y^8$ $(x^4 + y^4)(x^2 + y^2)(x + y)(x - y)$ **44.** $m^{16} - 1$
   $(9s^2 + 4t^4)(3s + 2t^2)(3s - 2t^2)$

206   *Chapter 5*

41. $(u^2 + 9v^2)(u + 3v)(u - 3v)$
44. $(m^8 + 1)(m^4 + 1)(m^2 + 1)(m + 1)(m - 1)$

Factor out the greatest monomial factor. Then factor the remaining binomial.

Sample 2 $3n^5 - 48n^3 = 3n^3(n^2 - 16)$
$$= 3n^3(n + 4)(n - 4) \quad \textit{Answer}$$

45. $5x^3 - 20x$ $5x(x + 2)(x - 2)$

46. $2a^4 - 18a^2$ $2a^2(a + 3)(a - 3)$

47. $36a^2 - 16a^4$ $4a^2(3 + 2a)(3 - 2a)$

48. $50r^8 - 32r^2$ $2r^2(5r^3 + 4)(5r^3 - 4)$

49. $uv^3 - u^3v$ $uv(v + u)(v - u)$

50. $27a^3b - 12ab$ $3ab(3a + 2)(3a - 2)$

51. $2a^5 - 162a$
$2a(a^2 + 9)(a + 3)(a - 3)$

52. $16x^5y^2 - xy^6$
$xy^2(4x^2 + y^2)(2x + y)(2x - y)$

Factor each expression as the difference of two squares. Then simplify the factors.

Sample 3 $u^2 - (u - 5)^2 = [u - (u - 5)][u + (u - 5)]$
$$= 5(2u - 5) \quad \textit{Answer}$$

53. $(x + 4)^2 - x^2$ $8(x + 2)$

54. $t^2 - (t - 1)^2$ $2t - 1$

55. $(s + 2)^2 - (s - 2)^2$ $8s$

56. $9(a + 1)^2 - 4(a - 1)^2$ $(a + 5)(5a + 1)$

Factor, assuming that n is a positive integer.

Sample 4 $x^{2n} - y^6 = (x^n)^2 - (y^3)^2$
$$= (x^n + y^3)(x^n - y^3) \quad \textit{Answer}$$

57. $a^{2n} - b^{2n}$

58. $x^{2n} - 25$

59. $u^{4n} - 4v^{2n}$

60. $45r^{2n} - 5s^{4n}$

61. $x^{4n} - y^{4n}$

62. $a^{4n} - 81b^{4n}$

63. $rt^{4n} - 16r$

64. $x^2 - x^2y^{4n}$

C 65. Show that the square of the sum of two numbers minus the square of their difference is equal to four times their product.

66. Show that the absolute value of the difference of the squares of two consecutive integers is equal to the absolute value of the sum of the integers.

65. $(a + b)^2 - (a - b)^2 = [(a + b) + (a - b)][(a + b) - (a - b)] = (2a)(2b) = 4ab$
66. $|(n + 1)^2 - n^2| = |[(n + 1) + n][(n + 1) - n]| = |(2n + 1) \cdot 1| = |2n + 1| = |n + (n + 1)|$

Mixed Review Exercises

Simplify.

1. $3z(z - 4) + 4z(z + 5)$ $7z^2 + 8z$

2. $(x + 5)(x - 7)$ $x^2 - 2x - 35$

3. $-2(m + 3) - 5m(m - 2)$ $-5m^2 + 8m - 6$

4. $\dfrac{25a^4b}{5a^2}$ $5a^2b$

5. $\dfrac{21a + 3}{3}$ $7a + 1$

6. $\dfrac{24n^3x}{6n^2x}$ $4n$

7. $(a + 1)(2a - 3)$ $2a^2 - a - 3$

8. $5b(b - 2)(3b + 1)$
$15b^3 - 25b^2 - 10b$

9. $(3x)^2\left(\dfrac{1}{3}\right)^2 x$ x^3

10. $\dfrac{12y^3 + 36y^2 - 6y}{6y}$ $2y^2 + 6y - 1$

11. $\dfrac{28x^2 + 42x - 14}{14}$ $2x^2 + 3x - 1$

12. $\dfrac{18x^2y^3z}{x^2y^2z}$ $18y$

Factoring Polynomials **207**

5-6 Squares of Binomials

Objective   To find squares of binomials and to factor perfect square trinomials.

The diagram of the areas below helps you to see what happens when you square the binomial $a + b$.

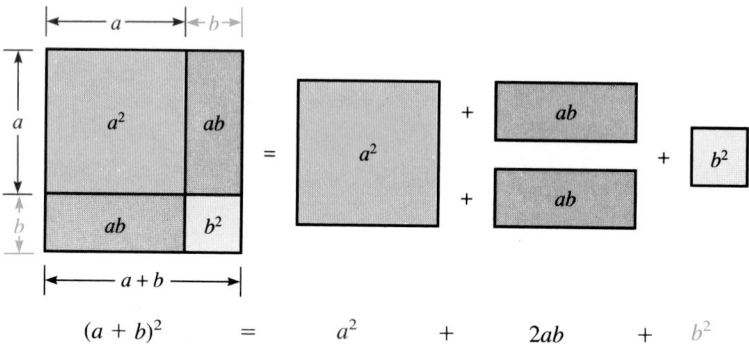

$$(a + b)^2 \quad = \quad a^2 \quad + \quad 2ab \quad + \quad b^2$$

Compare the above result with the algebraic result of multiplying the two binomials.

$$
\begin{array}{r}
a + b \\
a + b \\
\hline
a^2 + ab \\
ab + b^2 \\
\hline
a^2 + 2ab + b^2
\end{array}
$$

1. Square of the first term.
2. Twice the product of the two terms.
3. Square of the last term.

See what happens when you square the binomial difference $a - b$. The middle term in the product has a minus sign. Exercise 64 illustrates this in a diagram.

$$
\begin{array}{r}
a - b \\
a - b \\
\hline
a^2 - ab \\
- ab + b^2 \\
\hline
a^2 - 2ab + b^2
\end{array}
$$

1. Square of the first term.
2. Twice the product of the two terms.
3. Square of the last term.

It will be helpful to memorize these patterns for writing squares of binomials as trinomials.

$$(a + b)^2 = a^2 + 2ab + b^2$$

$$(a - b)^2 = a^2 - 2ab + b^2$$

Example 1 Write each square as a trinomial.
  a. $(x + 3)^2$ **b.** $(7u - 3)^2$ **c.** $(4s - 5t)^2$ **d.** $(3p^2 - 2q^2)^2$

Solution **a.** $(x + 3)^2 = x^2 + 2(x \cdot 3) + 3^2$
                       $= x^2 + 6x + 9$ **Answer**

  b. $(7u - 3)^2 = (7u)^2 - 2(7u \cdot 3) + 3^2$
                    $= (7u)^2 - 2(21u) + 3^2$
                    $= 49u^2 - 42u + 9$ **Answer**

  c. $(4s - 5t)^2 = (4s)^2 - 2(4s \cdot 5t) + (5t)^2$
                    $= (4s)^2 - 2(20st) + (5t)^2$
                    $= 16s^2 - 40st + 25t^2$ **Answer**

  d. $(3p^2 - 2q^2)^2 = (3p^2)^2 - 2(3p^2 \cdot 2q^2) + (2q^2)^2$
                       $= 9p^4 - 2(6p^2q^2) + 4q^4$
                       $= 9p^4 - 12p^2q^2 + 4q^4$ **Answer**

The patterns given at the bottom of page 208 are also useful for factoring:

$$a^2 + 2ab + b^2 = (a + b)^2$$
$$a^2 - 2ab + b^2 = (a - b)^2$$

The expressions on the left sides of these equations are called **perfect square trinomials** because each expression has three terms and is the square of a binomial. To test whether a trinomial is a perfect square, ask three questions as shown in Example 2.

Example 2 Decide whether each trinomial is a perfect square. If it is, factor it.
  a. $4x^2 - 20x + 25$ **b.** $64u^2 + 72uv + 81v^2$

Solution **a.** $4x^2 - 20x + 25$

  1. Is the first term a square?   Yes; $4x^2 = (2x)^2$
  2. Is the last term a square?   Yes; $25 = 5^2$
  3. Is the middle term, neglecting the sign,
     twice the product of $2x$ and 5?   Yes; $20x = 2(2x \cdot 5)$

  $\therefore 4x^2 - 20x + 25$ is a perfect square and equals $(2x - 5)^2$. **Answer**

  b. $64u^2 + 72uv + 81v^2$

  1. Is the first term a square?   Yes; $64u^2 = (8u)^2$
  2. Is the last term a square?   Yes; $81v^2 = (9v)^2$
  3. Is the middle term, neglecting the sign,
     twice the product of $8u$ and $9v$?   No; $72uv \neq 2(8u \cdot 9v)$

  $\therefore 64u^2 + 72uv + 81v^2$ is not a perfect square. **Answer**

Factoring Polynomials   **209**

Decide whether each trinomial is a perfect square. If so, factor it.

5. $9m^2 - 12m + 4$ yes; $(3m - 2)^2$

6. $25y^2 + 5y + 1$ no; since $5y \neq 2(5y \cdot 1)$

Check for Understanding

Here is a suggested use of the Oral Exercises to check students' understanding as you teach the lesson.
Oral Exs. 1–9: use after Example 1.
Oral Exs. 10–18: use after Example 2.
Oral Exs. 19–20: use at the end of the lesson.

Guided Practice

Write each square as a trinomial.

1. $(x - 7)^2$ $x^2 - 14x + 49$

2. $(2p - 5q)^2$
   $4p^2 - 20pq + 25q^2$

3. $(10p^2 - 6q)^2$
   $100p^4 - 120p^2q + 36q^2$

Decide whether each polynomial is a perfect square. If so, factor it. If not, write *not a perfect square.*

4. $x^2 - 6x + 9$ $(x - 3)^2$

5. $9t^2 - 3t + 1$
   not a perfect square

Summarizing the Lesson

Tell the students they have squared binomials and factored perfect square trinomials. Ask them for examples of perfect square trinomials. Then have them factor the trinomials.

Suggested Assignments

Minimum
Day 1: 210/1–19 odd
Assign with Lesson 5-5.
Day 2: 210/21–49 odd, 58
    S 212/Mixed Review

Average
Day 1: 210/2–46 even
Day 2: 211/48–64 even
    S 212/Mixed Review

Maximum
    210/3–66 mult. of 3
    S 212/Mixed Review

Additional Answers
Written Exercises

1. $n^2 + 10n + 25$
2. $z^2 + 16z + 64$
3. $a^2 - 18a + 81$
4. $p^2 - 20p + 100$
5. $16u^2 - 8u + 1$
6. $36c^2 - 12c + 1$
7. $25n^2 - 40n + 16$
8. $9y^2 - 48y + 64$
9. $4r^2 + 36rs + 81s^2$
10. $16u^2 + 56uv + 49v^2$
11. $25p^2 - 60pq + 36q^2$
12. $25a^2 - 80az + 64z^2$
13. $m^2n^2 + 4mn + 4$
14. $p^2q^2 - 8pq + 16$
15. $4a^2b^2 + 4abc^2 + c^4$
16. $36r^2s^2 - 12rs^3 + s^4$
17. $16m^4 + 24m^2n + 9n^2$
18. $169u^2 - 26uv^2 + v^4$
19. $81p^6 + 180p^3 + 100$
20. $121t^4 + 44t^2 + 4$
55. $x^4 - 8x^2 + 16$
    $= (x^2 - 4)^2$
    $= [(x + 2)(x - 2)]^2$
    $= (x + 2)^2(x - 2)^2$
56. $a^4 - 18a^2 + 81$
    $= (a^2 - 9)^2$
    $= [(a + 3)(a - 3)]^2$
    $= (a + 3)^2(a - 3)^2$

You may have to rearrange the terms of a trinomial before you test whether it's a perfect square. For example, if you write $x^2 + 100 - 20x$ as $x^2 - 20x + 100$, you can answer ''yes'' to all three questions.

Oral Exercises

Express each square as a trinomial.

1. $(a + 4)^2$ $a^2 + 8a + 16$
2. $(t - 2)^2$ $t^2 - 4t + 4$
3. $(x - 6)^2$ $x^2 - 12x + 36$
4. $(z + 7)^2$ $z^2 + 14z + 49$
5. $(2y + 1)^2$ $4y^2 + 4y + 1$
6. $(3u - 1)^2$ $9u^2 - 6u + 1$
7. $(5c - 1)^2$ $25c^2 - 10c + 1$
8. $(u^2 - 10)^2$ $u^4 - 20u^2 + 100$
9. $(9 - k^3)^2$ $81 - 18k^3 + k^6$

Decide whether each trinomial is a perfect square.
If it is, factor it.

10. $x^2 + 12x + 36$ $(x + 6)^2$
11. $a^2 + 2a + 1$ $(a + 1)^2$
12. $u^2 - 6u + 9$ $(u - 3)^2$
13. $y^2 - 4y + 16$ no
14. $n^2 + 10n - 25$ no
15. $4c^2 - 12c + 9$ $(2c - 3)^2$
16. $25x^2 + 10xy + y^2$ $(5x + y)^2$
17. $a^2 - 2ab + 4b^2$ no
18. $v^4 - 14v^2 + 49$ $(v^2 - 7)^2$
19. Find the square of 21 by thinking of it as $(20 + 1)^2$. 441
20. Find the square of 29 by thinking of it as $(30 - 1)^2$. 841

Written Exercises

Write each square as a trinomial.

A
1. $(n + 5)^2$
2. $(z + 8)^2$
3. $(a - 9)^2$
4. $(p - 10)^2$
5. $(4u - 1)^2$
6. $(6c - 1)^2$
7. $(5n - 4)^2$
8. $(3y - 8)^2$
9. $(2r + 9s)^2$
10. $(4u + 7v)^2$
11. $(5p - 6q)^2$
12. $(5a - 8z)^2$
13. $(mn + 2)^2$
14. $(pq - 4)^2$
15. $(2ab + c^2)^2$
16. $(-6rs + s^2)^2$
17. $(-4m^2 - 3n)^2$
18. $(-13u + v^2)^2$
19. $(9p^3 + 10)^2$
20. $(-11t^2 - 2)^2$

Decide whether each trinomial is a perfect square.
If it is, factor it. If it is not, write *not a perfect square*.

21. $y^2 + 6y + 9$ $(y + 3)^2$
22. $x^2 - 4x + 4$ $(x - 2)^2$
23. $p^2 - 14p + 49$ $(p - 7)^2$
24. $a^2 + 16a + 64$ $(a + 8)^2$
25. $121 - 22u + u^2$ $(11 - u)^2$
26. $144 + 12y + y^2$
27. $4x^2 + 9 + 12x$ $(2x + 3)^2$
28. $9 + 16c^2 - 24c$ $(4c - 3)^2$
29. $25x^2 - 15xy + 36y^2$
30. $49a^2 + 28ab + 4b^2$ $(7a + 2b)^2$
31. $4s^2 - 36st + 81t^2$ $(2s - 9t)^2$
32. $9u^2 + 30uv + 100v^2$

26., 29., and 32. are not perfect squares.

Factor.

Sample 1 $63n^3 - 84n^2 + 28n = 7n(9n^2 - 12n + 4)$ { First factor out the greatest
                                       $= 7n(3n - 2)^2$ { monomial factor.

33. $8x^2 + 8x + 2$ $2(2x + 1)^2$

35. $9 - 72m + 144m^2$ $9(1 - 4m)^2$

34. $3a^2 - 18a + 27$ $3(a - 3)^2$

36. $125u^2 - 50u + 5$ $5(5u - 1)^2$

B   **37.** $x^5 + 2x^4 + x^3$ $x^3(x + 1)^2$

39. $a^2b + 6ab^2 + 9b^3$ $b(a + 3b)^2$

41. $36p^4 - 48p^3 + 16p^2$ $4p^2(3p - 2)^2$

38. $y^4 - 14y^3 + 49y^2$ $y^2(y - 7)^2$

40. $8u^3 - 24u^2v + 18uv^2$ $2u(2u - 3v)^2$

42. $3x^8 + 48x^5 + 192x^2$ $3x^2(x^3 + 8)^2$

> **Sample 2** $x^2 - y^2 + 6y - 9 = x^2 - (y^2 - 6y + 9)$
> $= x^2 - (y - 3)^2$
> $= [x + (y - 3)][x - (y - 3)]$
> $= (x + y - 3)(x - y + 3)$ **Answer**
>
> { Look for a perfect
>   square trinomial
>   and factor it.

$(u - 1 + v)(u - 1 - v)$
43. $u^2 - 2u + 1 - v^2$

$(p + 2 + q)(p + 2 - q)$
44. $p^2 + 4p + 4 - q^2$

45. $a^2 - b^2 + 6b - 9$
$(a + b - 3)(a - b + 3)$

46. $p^2 - q^2 - 4q - 4$
$(p + q + 2)(p - q - 2)$

Decide whether each polynomial is a perfect square.
If it is, factor it. If it is not, write *not a perfect square*.

47. $x^6 + 10x^3 + 25$ $(x^3 + 5)^2$

49. $p^2q^2 - 12pq + 36$ $(pq - 6)^2$

51. $121 - 33n^2 + 9n^4$ not a perfect square

53. $(x + 1)^2 - 2(x + 1) + 1$ x^2

48. $4 - 4y^2 + y^4$ $(2 - y^2)^2$

50. $a^4 + 2a^2b^4 + b^8$ $(a^2 + b^4)^2$

52. $121c^4 - 264c^2 + 144$ $(11c^2 - 12)^2$

54. $(x + 1)^2 + 2(x + 1) + 1$ $(x + 2)^2$

55. Show that $x^4 - 8x^2 + 16$ can be factored as $(x + 2)^2(x - 2)^2$.

56. Show that $a^4 - 18a^2 + 81$ can be factored as $(a + 3)^2(a - 3)^2$.

57. a. Express $(2x - 3y)^2$ and $(3y - 2x)^2$ as trinomials. $4x^2 - 12xy + 9y^2$; $9y^2 - 12xy + 4x^2$
  b. Explain why $(2x - 3y)^2 = (3y - 2x)^2$ even though $2x - 3y \ne 3y - 2x$.
   $2x - 3y$ and $3y - 2x$ are opposites, and the squares of opposites are equal.

Solve and check.

58. $(x + 2)^2 - (x - 3)^2 = 35$ {4}

60. $(3x + 2)^2 + (4x - 3)^2 = (5x - 1)^2$ {6}

59. $(2x + 5)^2 = (2x + 3)^2$ {−2}

61. $(x + 2)^2 - (x - 2)^2 = (x - 1)^2 - (x - 3)^2$
                {−2}

Copy and cut up the model to show that each diagram illustrates the statement below it.

62.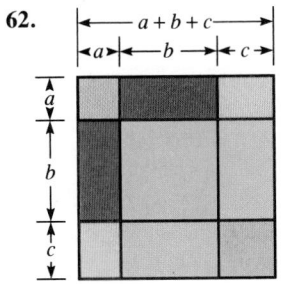

$(a + b + c)^2 =$
$a^2 + b^2 + c^2 + 2ab + 2ac + 2bc$

63.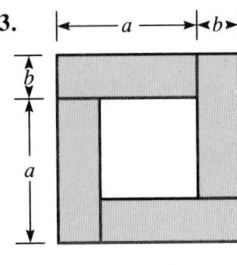

$(a + b)^2 - (a - b)^2 = 4ab$

64.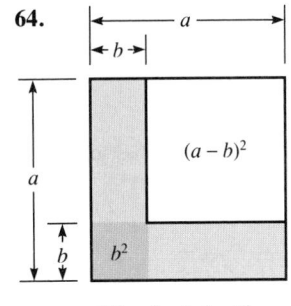

$(a - b)^2 = a^2 - 2ab + b^2$

62.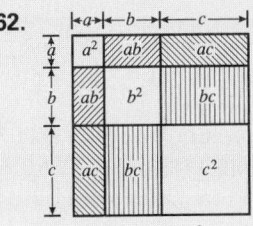

$(a + b + c)^2$

63.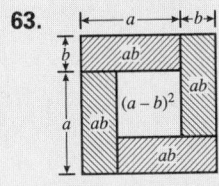

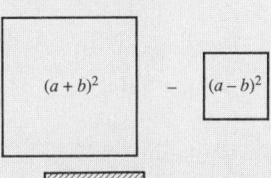

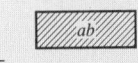

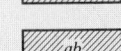

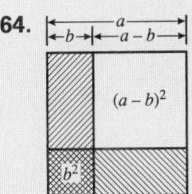

64.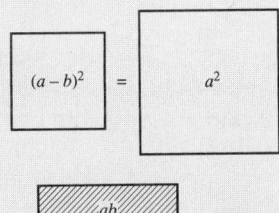

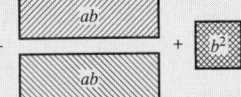

Factoring Polynomials   **211**

C 65. The perimeter of a square garden is 12 m greater than the perimeter of a smaller square garden. The area of the larger garden is 105 m² greater than that of the smaller garden. Find the dimensions of the larger garden. 19 m by 19 m

66. The square of a two-digit number ending in 5 always ends in 25. You find the digits preceding the 25 by multiplying the tens' digit by one more than the tens' digit, as shown. **(a)** Use this rule to find the squares of 25, 55, and 95. **(b)** Let $10n + 5$ represent a two-digit number ending in 5. Show that the square of this number equals $100n(n + 1) + 25$.
(a) 625, 3025, 9025 **(b)** $(10n + 5)^2 = 100n^2 + 100n + 25 = 100n(n + 1) + 25$

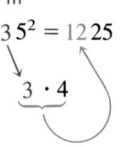

$35^2 = 12\,25$

$3 \cdot 4$

Mixed Review Exercises

Evaluate if $x = 4$ and $y = 2$.

1. $x + y + (-8)$ –2
2. $x - |y| - |3|$ –1
3. $9 + xy^2$ 25
4. $(9 + xy)^2$ 289
5. $(y)^3(-y)^6$ 512
6. $(x^2y^2)^2$ 4096

Simplify.

7. $(4s + 3)(4s - 3)$ $16s^2 - 9$
8. $(x + 9)(x + 3)$ $x^2 + 12x + 27$
9. $(5 - 3)^3$ 8
10. $5 - 3^3$ –22
11. $\dfrac{(a^6)^2}{(a^5)^3}$ $\dfrac{1}{a^3}$
12. $\dfrac{(2xy)^2}{4xy^2}$ x

Self-Test 2

Vocabulary   quadratic term (p. 201)   quadratic polynomial (p. 201)
linear term (p. 201)   perfect square trinomials (p. 209)

Write each product as a polynomial.

1. $(n + 3)(n + 8)$ $n^2 + 11n + 24$
2. $(m - 5)(m - 6)$ $m^2 - 11m + 30$ Obj. 5-4, p. 200
3. $(2y + 7)(3y - 4)$ $6y^2 + 13y - 28$
4. $2x(x - 4)(3x - 2)$ $6x^3 - 28x^2 + 16x$
5. $(x + 9)(x - 9)$ $x^2 - 81$
6. $(9a + 2b)(9a - 2b)$ $81a^2 - 4b^2$ Obj. 5-5, p. 204

Factor.

7. $4n^2 - 81$ $(2n + 9)(2n - 9)$
8. $36x^4 - 16$ $4(3x^2 + 2)(3x^2 - 2)$

Write each square as a trinomial.

9. $(2n + 4)^2$ $4n^2 + 16n + 16$
10. $(3z - 5k)^2$ $9z^2 - 30kz + 25k^2$ Obj. 5-6, p. 208

Factor.

11. $9a^2 + 12a + 4$ $(3a + 2)^2$
12. $16m^2 - 24mn + 9n^2$ $(4m - 3n)^2$

Check your answers with those at the back of the book.

Factoring Patterns

5-7 Factoring Pattern for $x^2 + bx + c$, c positive

Objective   To factor certain quadratic trinomials in which a is 1, b is an integer, and c is a positive integer.

In this lesson, you will study trinomials that can be factored as a product $(x + r)(x + s)$, where r and s are both positive or both negative integers. The diagram shows that the product $(x + r)(x + s)$ and the trinomial $x^2 + (r + s)x + rs$ represent the same total area. Notice that the coefficient of the x-term is the *sum* of r and s, and the constant term is the *product* of r and s.

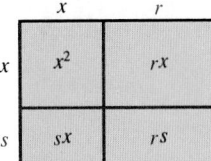

Example 1 $(x + 3)(x + 5) = x^2 + 8x + 15$

sum of 3 and 5 ——┘   └—— product of 3 and 5

Example 2 $(x - 6)(x - 4) = x^2 - 10x + 24$

sum of −6 and −4 ——┘   └—— product of −6 and −4

The examples above suggest the following method for factoring trinomials whose quadratic coefficient is 1 and whose constant term is positive.

1. List the pairs of integral factors whose products equal the constant term.

2. Find the pair of integral factors whose sum equals the coefficient of the linear term.

Examples 1 and 2 suggest that in Step 1 you need to consider only the factors with the *same sign* as the linear term.

Example 3   Factor $y^2 + 14y + 40$.

Solution
1. Since the coefficient of the linear term is positive, list the pairs of positive factors of 40.
2. Find the factors whose sum is 14: 4 and 10.
3. $\therefore y^2 + 14y + 40 = (y + 4)(y + 10)$
   Answer

Factors of 40	Sum of the factors
1 40	41
2 20	22
4 10	14
5 8	13

Factoring Polynomials   **213**

Explorations, p. 691

Teaching Suggestions, p. T103
Using Manipulatives,
   pp. T103–T104
Suggested Extensions, p. T104

Warm-Up Exercises

List each of the following terms and its coefficient for the trinomial $6x^2 - 12x - 4$.

1. quadratic $6x^2$; 6

2. linear $-12x$; -12

3. constant -4

4. Complete.

Positive Factors of 18		Sum of Factors	
1	18		19
2	? 9		? 11
3	? 6		? 9

Negative Factors of 18		Sum of Factors	
-1	-18		-19
-2	? -9		? -11
-3	? -6		? -9

Motivating the Lesson

Tell students that they have learned to multiply two binomials, such as $(x + 2)$ and $(x + 3)$, whose product is $x^2 + 5x + 6$. Ask students, If you are told that the trinomial $x^2 + 4x + 3$ is the product of two binomials, can you find these binomial factors? Factoring trinomials is today's lesson.

Thinking Skills

Students should analyze a quadratic trinomial to see whether it is factorable over the integers. For instance, although $y^2 + 14y + 40$ in Example 3 is factorable, $y^2 + 15y + 40$ is not.

Example 4 Factor $y^2 - 11y + 18$.

Solution 1. Since -11 is negative, think of the negative factors of 18.
2. Select the factors of 18 with sum -11: -2 and -9
3. $\therefore y^2 - 11y + 18 = (y - 2)(y - 9)$ **Answer**

A polynomial that cannot be expressed as a product of polynomials of lower degree is said to be **irreducible.** An irreducible polynomial with integral coefficients whose greatest monomial factor is 1 is a **prime polynomial.**

Example 5 Factor $x^2 - 10x + 14$.

Solution 1. The pairs of negative factors of 14 are: $-1, -14$; $-2, -7$.
2. Neither of these pairs has the sum -10.
3. $\therefore x^2 - 10x + 14$ cannot be factored. It is a prime polynomial. **Answer**

Oral Exercises

The area of each rectangle is represented by the trinomial below it. Use the diagram to factor the trinomial. You may wish to make models from grid paper, using a 10-by-10 square for x^2, a 10-by-1 rectangle for x and a 1-by-1 square for 1.

Sample

	x	?
x	x^2	$?x$
?	$?x$	12

$x^2 + 8x + 12 = (x + ?)(x + ?)$

Solution

	x	6
x	x^2	$6x$
2	$2x$	12

$x^2 + 8x + 12 = (x + 2)(x + 6)$

1.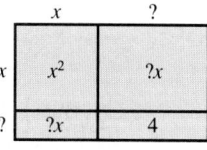

	x	?
x	x^2	$?x$
?	$?x$	4

$x^2 + 5x + 4 =$
$(x + ?)(x + ?)$ 1; 4

2.

	x	?
x	x^2	$?x$
?	$?x$	8

$x^2 + 6x + 8 =$
$(x + ?)(x + ?)$ 2; 4

3.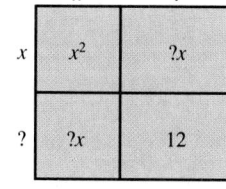

	x	?
x	x^2	$?x$
?	$?x$	12

$x^2 + 7x + 12 =$
$(x + ?)(x + ?)$ 3; 4

214 *Chapter 5*

Find two integers with the given sum and product.

	Example	4.	5.	6.	7.	8.	9.	10.	11.	12.	13.
Sum	$5 = 4 + 1$	5	7	-6	-6	8	10	-9	-11	-10	12
Product	$4 = 4 \cdot 1$	6	6	8	9	15	16	18	24	24	32

4. 2, 3 **5.** 6, 1 **6.** -2, -4 **7.** -3, -3 **8.** 3, 5
9. 8, 2 **10.** -6, -3 **11.** -8, -3 **12.** -6, -4 **13.** 8, 4

For each trinomial tell which two factors of the constant term have a sum equal to the coefficient of the linear term.

Sample $x^2 - 13x + 22$

Solution $(-2)(-11) = 22$ and $-2 + (-11) = -13$
$\therefore$ -2 and -11 are the correct factors.   **Answer**

14. $x^2 + 8x + 7$ 1, 7   **15.** $z^2 - 6z + 5$ -1, -5 **16.** $p^2 - 5p + 6$ -2, -3

17. $y^2 + 7y + 12$ 3, 4   **18.** $c^2 - 15c + 14$ -1, -14 **19.** $u^2 + 11u + 18$ 2, 9

20. $r^2 + 9r + 20$ 4, 5   **21.** $s^2 - 12s + 20$ -2, -10 **22.** $x^2 - 14x + 24$ -2, -12

23. $y^2 + 25y + 24$ 1, 24   **24.** $x^2 + 11x + 28$ 4, 7   **25.** $n^2 - 17n + 30$ -2, -15

Written Exercises

Factor. Check by multiplying the factors. If the polynomial is not factorable, write *prime*.

3. $(r - 4)(r - 2)$
6. $(p - 13)(p - 1)$
9. $(a - 13)(a - 2)$

A **1.** $x^2 + 5x + 4$ $(x + 4)(x + 1)$ **2.** $z^2 + 9z + 8$ $(z + 8)(z + 1)$ **3.** $r^2 - 6r + 8$

4. $c^2 - 10c + 16$ $(c - 8)(c - 2)$ **5.** $y^2 - 9y + 14$ $(y - 7)(y - 2)$ **6.** $p^2 - 14p + 13$

7. $q^2 + 16q + 15$ $(q + 15)(q + 1)$ **8.** $n^2 + 10n + 21$ $(n + 7)(n + 3)$ **9.** $a^2 - 15a + 26$

10. $s^2 - 12s + 40$ prime   **11.** $x^2 + 20x + 36$ $(x + 18)(x + 2)$ **12.** $z^2 + 16z + 39$

13. $u^2 + 12u + 28$ prime   **14.** $x^2 - 22x + 72$ $(x - 4)(x - 18)$ **15.** $42 - 23k + k^2$

16. $64 - 20s + s^2$ $(4 - s)(16 - s)$ **17.** $75 + 20r + r^2$ $(5 + r)(15 + r)$ **18.** $75 + 27u + u^2$

12. $(z + 13)(z + 3)$
15. $(21 - k)(2 - k)$
18. prime

Sample $x^2 - 10xy + 21y^2$

Solution $x^2 - 10xy + 21y^2 = (x - ?)(x - ?)$
$= (x - 3y)(x - 7y)$

Check: $(x - 3y)(x - 7y) = x^2 - 3xy - 7xy + 21y^2$
$= x^2 - 10xy + 21y^2$

21. $(c - 12d)(c - 4d)$
24. $(h - 7k)^2$
27. $(a + 13b)(a + 4b)$

$(p + 17q)(p + 2q)$ $(a + 6b)(a + 4b)$
19. $p^2 + 19pq + 34q^2$ **20.** $a^2 + 10ab + 24b^2$ **21.** $c^2 - 16cd + 48d^2$

22. $x^2 - 15xy + 72y^2$ prime   **23.** $u^2 - 50uv + 49v^2$ **24.** $h^2 - 14hk + 49k^2$

25. $x^2 - 16xy + 45y^2$ prime   **26.** $m^2 + 20mn + 51n^2$ **27.** $a^2 + 17ab + 52b^2$

28. $p^2 + 20pq + 50q^2$ prime   **29.** $r^2 - 15rs + 54s^2$ **30.** $a^2 - 12ab + 27b^2$
                                                                          $(a - 9b)(a - 3b)$
23. $(u - 49v)(u - v)$
26. $(m + 17n)(m + 3n)$ *Factoring Polynomials*   **215**
29. $(r - 9s)(r - 6s)$

31. $(y + 7z)(y + 13z)$ **32.** $(w + 8m)(w + 12m)$

Factor. Check by multiplying the factors.

B **31.** $y^2 + 20yz + 91z^2$ **32.** $w^2 + 20wm + 96m^2$ **33.** $124 - 35y + y^2$
$(4 - y)(31 - y)$

34. $108 - 24y + y^2$ **35.** $112a^2 - 22ab + b^2$ **36.** $117x^2 - 22xy + y^2$
    $(6 - y)(18 - y)$ $(8a - b)(14a - b)$ $(9x - y)(13x - y)$

Find all the integral values of k for which the trinomial can be factored.

Sample $x^2 + kx + 28$

Solution   28 can be factored as a product   (1)(28)   (−1)(−28)
                 of two integers in these ways: (2)(14)   (−2)(−14)
                                                (4)(7)   (−4)(−7)

                 The corresponding values of k are
                 29, 16, 11, −29, −16, and −11.   *Answer*

37. $y^2 + ky + 14$ ±15, ±9   **38.** $x^2 + kx + 10$ ±11, ±7   **39.** $z^2 + kz + 12$ ±13, ±8, ±7

40. $p^2 + kp + 18$ ±19, ±11, ±9 **41.** $n^2 + kn + 9$ ±10, ±6   **42.** $r^2 + kr + 20$ ±21, ±12, ±9

Find all *positive* integral values of k for which the trinomial can be factored.

43. $n^2 + 6n + k$ 5, 8, 9   **44.** $z^2 + 7z + k$ 6, 10, 12

45. $y^2 + 8y + k$ 7, 12, 15, 16   **46.** $x^2 + 9x + k$ 8, 14, 18, 20

Factor completely.

                                           50. $z^2(z + 4)(z - 4)(z + 1)(z - 1)$

C **47.** $(y + 2)^2 - 6(y + 2) + 5$ $(y - 3)(y + 1)$ **48.** $(t + 3)^2 + 8(t + 3) + 15$ $(t + 8)(t + 6)$

    49. $(y + 3)^2 + 6(y + 3) + 9$ $(y + 6)^2$ **50.** $z^6 - 17z^4 + 16z^2$

    51. $x^4 - 5x^2 + 4$ $(x + 2)(x - 2)(x + 1)(x - 1)$ **52.** $r^4 - 29r^2 + 100$ $(r + 5)(r - 5)(r + 2)(r - 2)$

    53. $t^5 - 20t^3 + 64t$ **54.** $(a - 4)^2 + 5(a - 4)(a + 2) + 6(a + 2)^2$
      $t(t + 4)(t - 4)(t + 2)(t - 2)$ $6a(2a + 1)$

    55. Factor $a^{2n} - 30a^n b^{2n} + 209b^{4n}$, where n is a positive integer.

    56. Factor $p^{4n} - 30p^{2n}q^n + 221q^{2n}$, where n is a positive integer.

    55. $(a^n - 11b^{2n})(a^n - 19b^{2n})$ **56.** $(p^{2n} - 13q^n)(p^{2n} - 17q^n)$

Mixed Review Exercises

Solve.

1. $-13 + x = -9$ {4}   **2.** $d + (-5) = -6$ {−1}   **3.** $-15 + b = 8$ {23}

4. $n + 2 = |3 - 6|$ {1}   **5.** $19m = 76$ {4}   **6.** $3p + 18 = -72$ {−30}

7. $-\dfrac{1}{2}x = 12$ {−24}   **8.** $\dfrac{r}{3} - 4 = 5$ {27}   **9.** $-21x = 252$ {−12}

Simplify.

10. $(5y + 7)(5y - 7)$ $25y^2 - 49$ **11.** $(2xy^3)^3$ $8x^3y^9$ **12.** $(2x^2)^6$ $64x^{12}$

216   *Chapter 5*

5-8 Factoring Pattern for $x^2 + bx + c$, c negative

Objective   To factor quadratic trinomials whose quadratic coefficient is 1 and whose constant term is negative.

The factoring that you did in the last lesson had this pattern:

$$x^2 + bx + c = (x + r)(x + s)$$

c positive ⟶   ⟵ r and s are *both positive* or *both negative*.

The factoring that you will do in this lesson has the following pattern:

$$x^2 + bx + c = (x + r)(x + s)$$

c negative ⟶   ⟵ r and s have *opposite* signs.

When you find the product $(x + r)(x + s)$, you obtain

$$x^2 + bx + c = x^2 + (r + s)x + rs$$

Therefore, the method used in this lesson is the same as before. You find two numbers, r and s, whose product is c and whose sum is b. Since c is negative, one of r and s must be negative and the other must be positive.

Example 1   Factor $x^2 - x - 20$.

Solution
1. List the factors of -20 by writing them down or reviewing them mentally.
2. Find the pair of factors with sum -1: 4 and -5.
3. $\therefore x^2 - x - 20 = (x + 4)(x - 5)$ *Answer*

You can check the result by multiplying $(x + 4)$ and $(x - 5)$.

Factors of -20		Sum of the factors
1	-20	-19
-1	20	19
2	-10	-8
-2	10	8
4	-5	-1
-4	5	1

Example 2   Factor $a^2 + 29a - 30$.

Solution
1. The factoring pattern is $(a + ?)(a - ?)$.
2. Find the pair of factors of -30 with sum 29: 30 and -1.
3. $\therefore a^2 + 29a - 30 = (a + 30)(a - 1)$ *Answer*

Example 3   Factor $x^2 - 4kx - 12k^2$.

Solution
1. The factoring pattern is $(x + ?)(x - ?)$.
2. Find the pair of factors of $-12k^2$ with a sum of $-4k$: $2k$ and $-6k$.
3. $\therefore x^2 - 4kx - 12k^2 = (x + 2k)(x - 6k)$ *Answer*

Factoring Polynomials   **217**

Teaching Suggestions, p. T104

Suggested Extensions, p. T104

Warm-Up Exercises

1. Complete.

Factors of -30		Sum	
1	-30	-29	
-1	30	29	
2	? -15	? -13	
-2	? 15	? 13	
? 3	? -10	? -7	
? -3	? 10	? 7	
? 5	? -6	? -1	
? -5	? 6	? 1	

2. Which pair of factors has a sum of 29? -1, 30

Motivating the Lesson

What are *all* the factors of -15? 1, -15 -1, 15   3, -5 -3, 5

Use those factors to write all pairs of binomials whose product has the pattern $x^2 + \_\_x - 15$.
$(x + 1)(x - 15)$,
$(x - 1)(x + 15)$
$(x + 3)(x - 5)$, $(x - 3)(x + 5)$

Give the product of each.
$x^2 - 14x - 15$, $x^2 + 14x - 15$
$x^2 - 2x - 15$, $x^2 + 2x - 15$

Factoring quadratic trinomials like the ones above is the topic today.

Problem Solving Strategies

Students are encouraged to make a chart of all possible pairs of factors of c, the constant term of $x^2 + bx + c$, and the sum of these factors. They can then *eliminate possibilities.*

Factor.

1. $x^2 - x - 30$ $(x + 5)(x - 6)$

2. $w^2 - 2w - 35$
$(w + 5)(w - 7)$

3. $a^2 + 3ab - 18b^2$
$(a + 6b)(a - 3b)$

4. $p^2 - 32p - 33$
$(p + 1)(p - 33)$

5. $t^2 + 10t - 24$
$(t + 12)(t - 2)$

Common Errors

When factoring trinomials of this type, some students think that because c is negative, both factors of c must be negative (especially if b is negative). In reteaching, demonstrate that this is not the case.

Check for Understanding

Here is a suggested use of the Oral Exercises to check students' understanding as you teach the lesson.
Oral Exs. 1–10: use at the beginning of the lesson.
Oral Exs. 11–19: use after Example 2.

Guided Practice

Factor. If the polynomial is not factorable, write *prime*.

1. $y^2 + 4y - 5$
$(y + 5)(y - 1)$

2. $p^2 + p - 12$
$(p + 4)(p - 3)$

3. $x^2 - 14x - 32$
$(x + 2)(x - 16)$

4. $m^2 + 7m - 15$ prime

5. $a^2 - 9a - 8$ prime

Oral Exercises
1. $-1, 3$ 2. $2, -5$ 3. $3, -5$ 4. $-1, 16$ 5. $-3, 6$
6. $2, -9$ 7. $-5, 8$ 8. $5, -5$ 9. $-4, 6$ 10. $2, -12$

Find two integers with the given sum and product.

	Example	1.	2.	3.	4.	5.	6.	7.	8.	9.	10.
Sum	$1 = 3 + (-2)$	2	-3	-2	15	3	-7	1	0	2	-10
Product	$-6 = 3(-2)$	-3	-10	-15	-16	-18	-18	-30	-25	-24	-24

For each trinomial tell which two factors of the constant term have a sum equal to the coefficient of the linear term.

Sample $\quad x^2 - 3x - 28$

Solution $\quad (-7)(4) = -28$ and $-7 + 4 = -3$
$\therefore -7$ and 4 are the correct factors. *Answer*

11. $z^2 + 3z - 4$ $4, -1$ **12.** $z^2 - 4z - 5$ $-5, 1$ **13.** $c^2 - c - 6$ $-3, 2$

14. $p^2 + p - 12$ $4, -3$ **15.** $y^2 - 5y - 14$ $-7, 2$ **16.** $r^2 - 2r - 8$ $-4, 2$

17. $x^2 + 2x - 15$ $5, -3$ **18.** $u^2 - u - 2$ $-2, 1$ **19.** $k^2 + 8k - 9$ $9, -1$

Written Exercises

Factor. Check by multiplying the factors. If the polynomial is not factorable, write *prime*.

3. $(x - 8)(x + 2)$
6. prime
9. $(b - 15)(b + 2)$
12. $(y - 8)(y + 4)$
15. $(y - 24)(y + 3)$

A **1.** $y^2 + 5y - 6$ $(y + 6)(y - 1)$ **2.** $v^2 - 3v - 4$ $(v - 4)(v + 1)$ **3.** $x^2 - 6x - 16$

4. $x^2 + 2x - 8$ $(x + 4)(x - 2)$ **5.** $c^2 - 4c - 12$ $(c - 6)(c + 2)$ **6.** $u^2 - 10u - 9$

7. $n^2 + 2n - 6$ prime **8.** $a^2 - 5a - 24$ $(a - 8)(a + 3)$ **9.** $b^2 - 13b - 30$

10. $p^2 + 7p - 18$ $(p + 9)(p - 2)$ **11.** $y^2 + 12y - 36$ prime **12.** $y^2 - 4y - 32$

13. $x^2 - 25x - 54$ $(x - 27)(x + 2)$ **14.** $t^2 - 16t - 40$ prime **15.** $y^2 - 21y - 72$

16. $z^2 + z - 72$ $(z + 9)(z - 8)$ **17.** $a^2 - ab - 42b^2$ $(a - 7b)(a + 6b)$ **18.** $r^2 - 20rs - 44s^2$

19. $u^2 + 9uv - 70v^2$ **20.** $x^2 - 2xy - 63y^2$ **21.** $h^2 - 25hk - 54k^2$

22. $m^2 + mn - 56n^2$ **23.** $p^2 - 16pq - 36q^2$ **24.** $a^2 - 13ab - 48b^2$

19. $(u + 14v)(u - 5v)$
20. $(x - 9y)(x + 7y)$
22. $(m + 8n)(m - 7n)$
23. $(p - 18q)(p + 2q)$
18. $(r - 22s)(r + 2s)$
21. $(h - 27k)(h + 2k)$
24. $(a + 3b)(a - 16b)$

Sample $\quad 1 - 10x - 24x^2$

Solution $\quad$ Find two factors of $-24x^2$ whose sum is $-10x$: $2x$ and $-12x$.
$\therefore 1 - 10x - 24x^2 = (1 + 2x)(1 - 12x)$ *Answer*

B **25.** $1 - 2n - 48n^2$ $(1 - 8n)(1 + 6n)$ **26.** $1 + 15c - 34c^2$ $(1 + 17c)(1 - 2c)$

27. $x^2 - 10xy - 75y^2$ $(x - 15y)(x + 5y)$ **28.** $a^2 + 5ab - 84b^2$ $(a + 12b)(a - 7b)$

29. $1 + 11pq - 80p^2q^2$ $(1 + 16pq)(1 - 5pq)$

30. $1 - 15mn - 100m^2n^2$ $(1 - 20mn)(1 + 5mn)$

31. $p^2 + 2p - 360$ $(p + 20)(p - 18)$

32. $n^2 + 9n - 400$ $(n + 25)(n - 16)$

33. $-380 + x + x^2$ $(-19 + x)(20 + x)$

34. $-800 - 20a + a^2$ $(-40 + a)(20 + a)$

6. $p^2 + 4pq - 45q^2$
$(p + 9q)(p - 5q)$

7. $m^2 - 34mn - 72n^2$
$(m - 36n)(m + 2n)$

8. $u^2 - 5uv - 10v^2$ prime

9. $r^2 - 7rs - 60$
$(r + 5)(r - 12)$

Find all the integral values of k for which the given polynomial can be factored.

35. $y^2 + ky - 28$
$\pm27, \pm12, \pm3$

36. $c^2 + kc - 20$
$\pm19, \pm8, \pm1$

37. $p^2 + kp - 35$
$\pm34, \pm2$

38. $x^2 + kx - 36$
$\pm35, \pm16, \pm9, \pm5, 0$

Find two negative values of k for which the given polynomial can be factored. (There may be many possible values.) Answers may vary.

39. $r^2 - 2r + k$ $-3, -8$

40. $y^2 + 4y + k$ $-5, -12$

41. $k + 5x + x^2$ $-6, -14$

42. $k - 7r + r^2$ $-8, -18$

43. $k + 4t + t^2$ $-5, -12$

44. $k - 6z + z^2$ $-7, -16$

Factor completely.

C **45.** $x^4 - 3x^2 - 4$ $(x + 2)(x - 2)(x^2 + 1)$

46. $t^4 - 7t^2 - 18$
$(t + 3)(t - 3)(t^2 + 2)$

47. $x^4 - 15x^2y^2 - 16y^4$ $(x + 4y)(x - 4y)(x^2 + y^2)$

48. $(x + 2)^2 - 4(x + 2) - 21$
$(x - 5)(x + 5)$
$(p + q - 5)(p + q + 3)$

49. $(y + 3)^2 + 5(y + 3) - 24$ $y(y + 11)$

50. $(p + q)^2 - 2(p + q) - 15$
$(p + q - 5r)(p + q + 3r)$

51. $(a + b)^2 - (a + b) - 2$ $(a + b - 2)(a + b + 1)$

52. $(p + q)^2 - 2r(p + q) - 15r^2$

53. $(a + b)^2 - c(a + b) - 2c^2$
$(a + b - 2c)(a + b + c)$

54. $(a + b)^4 - (a - b)^4$ $8ab(a^2 + b^2)$

55. Factor $x^{2n} - 4x^ny^{2n} - 221y^{4n}$, where n is a positive integer. $(x^n + 13y^{2n})(x^n - 17y^{2n})$

56. Factor $x^{4n} - 4x^{2n}y^n - 252y^{2n}$, where n is a positive integer. $(x^{2n} + 14y^n)(x^{2n} - 18y^n)$

Summarizing the Lesson

Tell students they have learned how to factor another type of quadratic trinomial, with the coefficient of the quadratic term equal to 1 and the constant term negative. Ask for examples of this type along with the type in Lesson 5-7.

Suggested Assignments

Minimum
218/1–33 odd, 36
S 219/Mixed Review

Average
218/3–48 mult. of 3
S 219/Mixed Review

Maximum
218/3–54 mult. of 3, 55
S 219/Mixed Review

Supplementary Materials

Study Guide   pp. 87–88
Practice Master   27
Computer Activity   14
Overhead Visuals   4, 5

Mixed Review Exercises

Simplify.

1. $(9x^2y)(3xy^2)(2x^2)$ $54x^5y^3$

2. $(3x - 4)(2x + 3)$ $6x^2 + x - 12$

3. $-21x^3 + 14x^2 - 28x$
$-7x(3x^2 - 2x + 4)$

6. $10y^3 + 15y^2 + 25y$

4. $(3x - 4)^2$ $9x^2 - 24x + 16$

5. $(7x^5y^2)^3$ $343x^{15}y^6$

6. $5y(2y^2 + 3y + 5)$

7. $\dfrac{5(xy)^6}{10(xy)^3}$ $\dfrac{x^3y^3}{2}$

8. $\dfrac{-4ab}{-12ab^3}$ $\dfrac{1}{3b^2}$

9. $\dfrac{(-n)^6}{-n^{10}}$ $-\dfrac{1}{n^4}$

10. $(n + 3p)^2$ $n^2 + 6np + 9p^2$

11. $(a - 6)(5a + 2)$ $5a^2 - 28a - 12$

12. $(2y + 7)^2$
$4y^2 + 28y + 49$

Factor.

21. $7ab(ab^2 - 2)$

23. $4(m + 3)(m + 2)$

24. $(c - 13)(c + 2)$

13. $15m - 21n + 9$
$3(5m - 7n + 3)$

14. $121k^2 - 81$ $(11k + 9)(11k - 9)$

15. $a^2 + 18a + 81$
$(a + 9)^2$

16. $a^2 - 13ab + 42b^2$
$(a - 7b)(a - 6b)$

17. $16x^2 + 24x$ $8x(2x + 3)$

18. $64 - n^2$
$(8 + n)(8 - n)$

19. $u^2 - 10u + 25$ $(u - 5)^2$

20. $44 + 15y + y^2$ $(11 + y)(4 + y)$

21. $7a^2b^3 - 14ab$

22. $49w^4 - 16x^2$ $(7w^2 + 4x)(7w^2 - 4x)$

23. $4m^2 + 20m + 24$

24. $c^2 - 11c - 26$

25. $9x^2 - 24xy + 16y^2$ $(3x - 4y)^2$

26. $56 - 15z + z^2$ $(8 - z)(7 - z)$

27. $x^2 - 1$ $(x + 1)(x - 1)$

28. $a^2 + 13a - 68$ $(a + 17)(a - 4)$

29. $25w^6 - 144x^6$
$(5w^3 + 12x^3)(5w^3 - 12x^3)$

30. $25a^2 + 20ab + 4b^2$
$(5a + 2b)^2$

Factoring Polynomials **219**

Motivating the Lesson

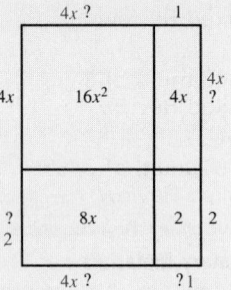

Find the sum of the areas of the four rectangular regions.

$16x^2 + 12x + 2$ Supply the missing dimensions that give the areas shown. Each side of the large rectangle gives a binomial: $4x + 1$ and $4x + 2$. The area of the large rectangle is $(4x + 1)(4x + 2)$. So $16x^2 + 12x + 2 = (4x + 1)(4x + 2)$. These two binomials are the factors of $16x^2 + 12x + 2$. Finding factors is today's topic.

5-9 Factoring Pattern for $ax^2 + bx + c$

Objective   To factor general quadratic trinomials with integral coefficients.

If $ax^2 + bx + c$ $(a > 1)$ can be factored, the factorization will have the pattern

$$(px + r)(qx + s).$$

Example 1 Factor $2x^2 + 7x - 9$.

Solution

Clue 1 Because the trinomial has a negative constant term, one of r and s will be negative and the other will be positive.

Clue 2 You can list the possible factors of the quadratic term, $2x^2$, and the possible factors of the constant term, -9.

Factors of $2x^2$	Factors of -9	
$2x, x$	$1, -9$	$-1, 9$
	$3, -3$	$-3, 3$
	$9, -1$	$-9, 1$

Test the possibilities to see which produces the correct linear term, $7x$. Making a chart will help you do this. Since $(2x + 9)(x - 1)$ gives the correct linear term,

$2x^2 + 7x - 9 = (2x + 9)(x - 1)$.
Answer

Possible factors	Linear term
$(2x + 1)(x - 9)$	$(-18 + 1)x = -17x$
$(2x + 3)(x - 3)$	$(-6 + 3)x = -3x$
$(2x + 9)(x - 1)$	$(-2 + 9)x = 7x$
$(2x - 1)(x + 9)$	$(18 - 1)x = 17x$
$(2x - 3)(x + 3)$	$(6 - 3)x = 3x$
$(2x - 9)(x + 1)$	$(2 - 9)x = -7x$

Example 2 Factor $14x^2 - 17x + 5$.

Solution

Clue 1 Because the trinomial has a positive constant term and a negative linear term, both r and s will be negative.

Clue 2 List the factors of the quadratic term, $14x^2$, and the negative factors of the constant term, 5.

Factors of $14x^2$	Factors of 5
$x, 14x$	$-1, -5$
$2x, 7x$	$-5, -1$

Test the possibilities to see which produces the correct linear term, $-17x$.

Since $(2x - 1)(7x - 5)$ gives the correct linear term,

$14x^2 - 17x + 5 = (2x - 1)(7x - 5)$.
Answer

Possible factors	Linear term
$(x - 1)(14x - 5)$	$(-5 - 14)x = -19x$
$(x - 5)(14x - 1)$	$(-1 - 70)x = -71x$
$(2x - 1)(7x - 5)$	$(-10 - 7)x = -17x$
$(2x - 5)(7x - 1)$	$(-2 - 35)x = -37x$

Remember to check each factorization by multiplying the factors. After some practice you will be able to select the correct factors without writing down all the possibilities.

When the coefficient of the quadratic term is negative, it may be helpful to begin by factoring -1 from each term.

Example 3   Factor $10 + 11x - 6x^2$.

Solution
$$10 + 11x - 6x^2 = -6x^2 + 11x + 10$$
$$= (-1)(6x^2 - 11x - 10)$$
$$= (-1)(2x - 5)(3x + 2)$$
$$= -(2x - 5)(3x + 2) \quad \textbf{\textit{Answer}}$$

{Arrange the terms by decreasing degree.
{Factor -1 from each term.
{Factor the resulting trinomial.

Note: If you factor $10 + 11x - 6x^2$ directly, you will get $(5 - 2x)(2 + 3x)$. Since $(5 - 2x) = -(2x - 5)$, the two answers are equivalent.

Example 4   Factor $5a^2 - ab - 22b^2$.

Solution
$$5a^2 - ab - 22b^2 = (a \quad)(5a \quad)$$
$$= (a + ?)(5a - ?)$$
$$= (a + 2b)(5a - 11b) \quad \textbf{\textit{Answer}}$$

{Write the factors of $5a^2$.
{Test possibilities.

Note: If you write $(a - ?)(5a + ?)$ as the second step, you will not find a combination of factors that produces the desired linear term.

Oral Exercises

The area of the rectangle is represented by the trinomial below. Use the diagram to factor the trinomial.

Sample

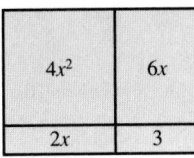

$$4x^2 + 8x + 3$$

Solution

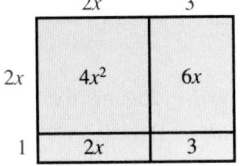

$$4x^2 + 8x + 3 = (2x + 3)(2x + 1)$$

1.

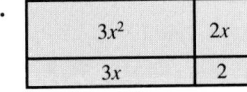

$$3x^2 + 5x + 2$$
$$(3x + 2)(x + 1)$$

2.

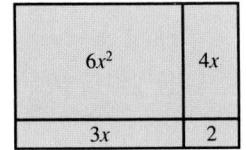

$$6x^2 + 7x + 2 \ (3x + 2)(2x + 1)$$

Factoring Polynomials   **221**

Guided Practice

(continued)

3. $10k^2 - 13k + 4$
$(5k - 4)(2k - 1)$

4. $6m^2 + m - 1$
$(3m - 1)(2m + 1)$

5. $7p^2 + 24p + 12$
prime

6. $20 + 23a - 21a^2$
$(5 - 3a)(4 + 7a)$

7. $3r^2 - 5rs + 2s^2$
$(r - s)(3r - 2s)$

8. $7b^2 - 17ab + 6a^2$
$(7b - 3a)(b - 2a)$

Summarizing the Lesson

Tell the students they have
learned to factor a general
quadratic trinomial, one with
a quadratic coefficient
greater than 1.

Suggested Assignments

Minimum
222/1–33 odd
S 223/Mixed Review

Average
222/1–37 odd
S 223/Mixed Review

Maximum
222/3–45 mult. of 3, 46
S 223/Mixed Review

Supplementary Materials

Study Guide	pp. 89–90
Test Master	21
Resource Book	p. 98
Overhead Visuals	4, 5

For each quadratic trinomial tell whether its factorization will have the form
$$(px + r)(qx + s),$$
$$(px + r)(qx - s),$$
or $(px - r)(qx - s)$,
where p, q, r, and s represent positive integers.

3. $2x^2 + x - 6$ +, −   **4.** $5x^2 - 13x + 6$ −, −   **5.** $4x^2 + 8x + 3$ +, +

6. $4x^2 - 4x - 3$ +, −   **7.** $2x^2 - x - 10$ +, −   **8.** $6x^2 + 5x + 1$ +, +

9. $3x^2 + 4x - 4$ +, −   **10.** $5x^2 - 11x + 2$ −, −   **11.** $8x^2 - 25x + 3$ −, −

12. $9x^2 + 6x - 8$ +, −   **13.** $14x^2 + 13x + 3$ +, +   **14.** $10x^2 - 10x - 9$ +, −

Written Exercises

Factor. Check by multiplying the factors. If the polynomial is not
factorable, write *prime*.

A **1.** $3x^2 + 7x + 2$ $(3x + 1)(x + 2)$ **2.** $2x^2 + 5x + 3$ $(2x + 3)(x + 1)$

3. $3c^2 - 8c + 5$ $(3c - 5)(c - 1)$ **4.** $2x^2 - 15x + 7$ $(2x - 1)(x - 7)$

5. $5y^2 + 4y - 1$ $(5y - 1)(y + 1)$ **6.** $3a^2 + 4a - 4$ $(3a - 2)(a + 2)$

7. $5u^2 - 6u - 2$ prime   **8.** $3r^2 - 2r - 5$ $(3r - 5)(r + 1)$

9. $7x^2 + 8x + 1$ $(7x + 1)(x + 1)$ **10.** $2p^2 + 7p + 3$ $(2p + 1)(p + 3)$

11. $5x^2 - 17x + 6$ $(5x - 2)(x - 3)$ **12.** $7m^2 - 9m + 2$ $(7m - 2)(m - 1)$

13. $3p^2 + 7p - 6$ $(3p - 2)(p + 3)$ **14.** $4c^2 + 4c - 3$ $(2c + 3)(2c - 1)$

15. $4y^2 - y - 3$ $(y - 1)(4y + 3)$ **16.** $6a^2 - 5a - 2$ prime

17. $5 + 7x - 6x^2$ $(5 - 3x)(1 + 2x)$ **18.** $9 + 6k - 8k^2$ $(3 + 4k)(3 - 2k)$

19. $1 - 5b - 8b^2$ prime   **20.** $7 - 12s - 4s^2$ $(7 + 2s)(1 - 2s)$

21. $3m^2 + 11mn + 6n^2$ $(3m + 2n)(m + 3n)$ **22.** $2p^2 - 7pq + 6q^2$ $(2p - 3q)(p - 2q)$

23. $2x^2 + xy - 3y^2$ $(2x + 3y)(x - y)$ **24.** $5a^2 - 2ab - 7b^2$ $(5a - 7b)(a + b)$

B **25.** $9m^2 - 25mn - 6n^2$ $(9m + 2n)(m - 3n)$ **26.** $6h^2 + 17hk + 10k^2$ $(6h + 5k)(h + 2k)$

27. $6r^2 - 11rp + 5p^2$ $(6r - 5p)(r - p)$ **28.** $4x^2 + 16xy - 9y^2$ $(2x + 9y)(2x - y)$

29. $21c^2 + 4c - 12$ $(7c + 6)(3c - 2)$ **30.** $18z^2 + 19z - 12$ $(2z + 3)(9z - 4)$

31. $6 + 7a - 20a^2$ $(2 + 5a)(3 - 4a)$ **32.** $8 + 45r - 18r^2$ $(8 - 3r)(1 + 6r)$

33. $32n^2 - 4n - 15$ $(4n - 3)(8n + 5)$ **34.** $33u^2 - u - 14$ $(3u - 2)(11u + 7)$

35. $21c^2 + 22c - 24$ $(3c - 2)(7c + 12)$ **36.** $35y^2 + 2y - 24$ $(7y + 6)(5y - 4)$

 39. $(2a + 4b - c)(a + 2b + 3c)$ **40.** $(2x - 2y + z)(x - y - 5z)$

C **37.** $2(a + 2)^2 + 5(a + 2) - 3$ $(2a + 3)(a + 5)$ **38.** $2(x - 1)^2 - 9(x - 1) - 5$ $(2x - 1)(x - 6)$

39. $2(a + 2b)^2 + 5(a + 2b)c - 3c^2$ **40.** $2(x - y)^2 - 9(x - y)z - 5z^2$

41. $4x^4 - 17x^2 + 4$ $(2x + 1)(2x - 1)(x + 2)(x - 2)$ **42.** $2x^4 - 15x^2 - 27$ $(2x^2 + 3)(x + 3)(x - 3)$

43. $(y^2 + 3y - 1)^2 - 9$
$(y + 2)(y + 1)(y + 4)(y - 1)$

44. $(a^2 - 4a - 1)^2 - 16$
$(a - 3)(a - 1)(a - 5)(a + 1)$

45. Show that $(15x^2 - 14x + 3)(6x^2 + 19x - 7)(10x^2 + 29x - 21)$ is a *perfect square* by showing that it is the square of a polynomial. $(30x^3 + 77x^2 - 92x + 21)^2$

46. Factor $90a^{8n+1}b^2 - 25a^{4n+1}b^{2n+2} - 240ab^{4n+2}$, where n is a positive integer. $5ab^2(3a^{2n} + 4b^n)(3a^{2n} - 4b^n)(2a^{4n} + 3b^{2n})$

Mixed Review Exercises

Factor.

1. $x^2 - 225$ $(x + 15)(x - 15)$

2. $x^2 - 9x + 20$ $(x - 4)(x - 5)$

3. $r^2 - 5r - 14$

4. $c^2 - 6c + 9$ $(c - 3)^2$

5. $9y^2 - 289x^2$ $(3y + 17x)(3y - 17x)$

6. $4a^4 - 49$

7. $y^2 + 15y + 56$ $(y + 7)(y + 8)$

8. $p^2 + 12p + 36$ $(p + 6)^2$

9. $16y^2 + 24y + 9$

10. $m^2 - m - 72$ $(m - 9)(m + 8)$

11. $n^2 + 15n + 36$ $(n + 12)(n + 3)$

12. $b^2 - 2b - 24$ $(b - 6)(b + 4)$

3. $(r - 7)(r + 2)$
6. $(2a^2 + 7)(2a^2 - 7)$
9. $(4y + 3)^2$

Self-Test 3

Vocabulary   irreducible polynomial (p. 214)   prime polynomial (p. 214)

Factor.

1. $a^2 + 12a + 35$ $(a + 5)(a + 7)$

2. $x^2 - 10x + 16$ $(x - 8)(x - 2)$ **Obj. 5-7, p. 213**

3. $n^2 - 3n - 28$ $(n + 4)(n - 7)$

4. $c^2 + 3cd - 40d^2$ $(c + 8d)(c - 5d)$ **Obj. 5-8, p. 217**

5. $2r^2 - 7r + 6$ $(2r - 3)(r - 2)$

6. $3x^2 + 10xy - 8y^2$ $(3x - 2y)(x + 4y)$ **Obj. 5-9, p. 220**

Challenge

According to the legend, the inventor of the game of chess asked to be rewarded by having one grain of wheat put on the first square of a chessboard, two grains on the second, four grains on the third, eight grains on the fourth, and so on. The total number of grains would be $2^{64} - 1$, which is several thousand times the world's annual wheat yield.

 1. To find how large 2^{64} is approximately, you could enter the number 2 on the calculator and press the squaring button a number of times. How many times must you press this button? 6

2. Factor $2^{64} - 1$ as a difference of squares to show that it is divisible by 3, 5, and 17.

Factoring Polynomials   **223**

Warm-Up Exercises

Find the opposite of each expression.

1. $-4a$ $4a$

2. $-4a + 1$ $4a - 1$

3. $a - b$ $-a + b$, or $b - a$

4. $3x^2 - 2x + 5$
$-3x^2 + 2x - 5$

Name the GCF of the terms in each polynomial. Then factor.

5. $20x - 5$ 5; $5(4x - 1)$

6. $8x + 12x^2$ $4x$;
$4x(2 + 3x)$

Motivating the Lesson

Judy bought a cans of regular soda and b cans of diet soda at a cost of $(n + 1)$ cents per can. How can you calculate her total cost? Write the equation $a(n + 1) + b(n + 1)$ on the chalkboard. Tell students that in today's lesson they will learn how to simplify this expression by using the distributive property.

Common Errors

Students might not realize that $3 - a$ and $-(a - 3)$ are equivalent expressions in Example 2. In reteaching, emphasize the necessity of introducing a factor of -1 in order to get a common group.

General Factoring and Its Application

5-10 Factoring by Grouping

Objective   To factor a polynomial by grouping terms.

A key tool in factoring polynomials is the distributive property:

$$ba + ca = (b + c)a$$

This property is valid not only when a represents a monomial, but also when a represents any polynomial. For example:

If $a = x + 2$, you have $\qquad b(x + 2) + c(x + 2) = (b + c)(x + 2)$

If $a = 3r - s + 7$, you have $\qquad b(3r - s + 7) + c(3r - s + 7) = (b + c)(3r - s + 7)$

Example 1 Factor: **a.** $5(x + y) + w(x + y)$ **b.** $m(m + 4n) - (m + 4n)$

Solution   **a.** $(5 + w)(x + y)$ **b.** $(m - 1)(m + 4n)$

Another helpful tool is recognizing factors that are opposites of each other.

Factor	Opposite				
$x - y$	$-(x - y)$	or	$-x + y$	or	$y - x$
$4 - a^2$	$-(4 - a^2)$	or	$-4 + a^2$	or	$a^2 - 4$
$2n - 3k - 1$	$-(2n - 3k - 1)$	or	$-2n + 3k + 1$	or	$3k - 2n + 1$

Example 2 Factor $5(a - 3) - 2a(3 - a)$.

Solution   Notice that $a - 3$ and $3 - a$ are opposites.

$$5(a - 3) - 2a(3 - a) = 5(a - 3) - 2a[-(a - 3)]$$
$$= 5(a - 3) + 2a(a - 3)$$
$$= (5 + 2a)(a - 3) \quad \textit{Answer}$$

In Example 3 you first group terms with common factors, and then factor.

Example 3 Factor $2ab - 6ac + 3b - 9c$.

Solution 1 $2ab - 6ac + 3b - 9c = (2ab - 6ac) + (3b - 9c)$
$$= 2a(b - 3c) + 3(b - 3c)$$
$$= (2a + 3)(b - 3c) \quad \textit{Answer}$$

---

224   *Chapter 5*

Solution 2 $2ab - 6ac + 3b - 9c = (2ab + 3b) - (6ac + 9c)$
$$= b(2a + 3) - 3c(2a + 3)$$
$$= (b - 3c)(2a + 3) \quad \textbf{\textit{Answer}}$$

Example 4 uses what you know about factoring perfect square trinomials and differences of squares.

Example 4 Factor $4p^2 - 4q^2 + 4qr - r^2$.

Solution $4p^2 - 4q^2 + 4qr - r^2 = 4p^2 - (4q^2 - 4qr + r^2)$ ⟵ A trinomial square
$$= (2p)^2 - (2q - r)^2 \quad ⟵ \text{The difference of two squares.}$$
$$= [2p + (2q - r)][2p - (2q - r)]$$
$$= (2p + 2q - r)(2p - 2q + r) \quad \textbf{\textit{Answer}}$$

In Example 4 you could have tried the grouping $(4p^2 - 4q^2) + (4qr - r^2)$ and factored the groups to obtain $4(p + q)(p - q) + r(4q - r)$. But this doesn't lead anywhere. There are different approaches to factoring a polynomial. You may need to try several before arriving at one that works.

Oral Exercises

Factor.
1. $(a + 3)(a - 2)$ **2.** $(p - 4)(q + 1)$ **3.** $(2r - 5)(r - 3)$
4. $(x - 1)(x + 2y)$ **5.** $(u - v)(u + v)$ **6.** $(h - 2)^2$

1. $a(a - 2) + 3(a - 2)$ **2.** $p(q + 1) - 4(q + 1)$ **3.** $2r(r - 3) - 5(r - 3)$

4. $x(x + 2y) - (x + 2y)$ **5.** $u(u + v) - v(u + v)$ **6.** $h(h - 2) + 2(2 - h)$

7. $x(x - 4) - (4 - x)$ **8.** $m(n - m) - n(m - n)$ **9.** $2r(r - s) + s(s - r)$
     $(x + 1)(x - 4)$ $(m + n)(n - m)$ $(2r - s)(r - s)$

Written Exercises

Factor. Check by multiplying the factors.

11. $(2u + v + 1)(u - 2v)$ **12.** $4b(a - b)$
13. $(x - 1)(2w - 3v + u)$ **14.** $(r + s)(r - s - 2t)$
15. $(s - 2)(s - 2p + 2)$ **16.** $(x + 1)(x - y + 1)$

A   **1.** $3(x + y) + z(x + y)$ $(3 + z)(x + y)$ **2.** $7(r - s) + t(r - s)$ $(7 + t)(r - s)$

     3. $e(f - g) - 4(f - g)$ $(e - 4)(f - g)$ **4.** $w(x - y) - 8(x - y)$ $(w - 8)(x - y)$

     5. $7(r - s) + t(s - r)$ $(7 - t)(r - s)$ **6.** $7(m - n) + p(n - m)$ $(7 - p)(m - n)$

     7. $2a(a + 3) - (3 + a)$ $(2a - 1)(a + 3)$ **8.** $u(v - 2) + 2(2 - v)$ $(u - 2)(v - 2)$

     9. $2x(x - y) + y(y - x)$ $(2x - y)(x - y)$ **10.** $3p(2q - p) - 2q(p - 2q)$ $(3p + 2q)(2q - p)$

   11. $2u(u - 2v) + v(u - 2v) + (u - 2v)$ **12.** $a(a - b) + 4b(a - b) - a(a - b)$

   13. $x(2w - 3v + u) - (2w - 3v + u)$ **14.** $r(r - s - 2t) + s(r - s - 2t)$

   15. $(s^2 - 2ps + 2s) - (2s - 4p + 4)$ **16.** $(x^2 - xy + x) - (y - x - 1)$

   17. $(3t - 3st) + (rs - r)$ $(3t - r)(1 - s)$ **18.** $(9p - 3pq) + (2nq - 6n)$ $(3p - 2n)(3 - q)$

   19. $(12x^2 - 8xy) - 5(3xz - 2yz)$ **20.** $(p^2 - 2pq) - 2(2qr - pr)$ $(p + 2r)(p - 2q)$
          $(4x - 5z)(3x - 2y)$

Factoring Polynomials   **225**

5. $(3q^2 - 4rq + q) -$
$(3q - 4r + 1)$
$(q - 1)(3q - 4r + 1)$

6. $(4y^2 - 3xy) + (9xz - 12yz)$
$(y - 3z)(4y - 3x)$

7. $a^2 + ab - ac - bc$
$(a - c)(a + b)$

8. $p^3 - 3p^2 + 2p - 6$
$(p^2 + 2)(p - 3)$

Factor each expression as a difference of squares.

9. $4b^2 - (b - c)^2$
$(b + c)(3b - c)$

10. $(x + y)^2 - 25z^2$
$(x + y + 5z)(x + y - 5z)$

Summarizing the Lesson

Tell students they have learned how to factor polynomials by grouping terms first.

Suggested Assignments

Minimum
    225/1–15 odd, 21,
    23, 25, 39
    R 223/Self-Test 3

Average
Day 1: 225/1–41 odd
    R 223/Self-Test 3
Day 2: 226/43–59 odd
    S 226/Mixed Review

Maximum
    225/3–63 mult. of 3
    S 226/Mixed Review
    R 223/Self-Test 3

Supplementary Materials

Study Guide   pp. 91–92
Practice Master   28

Factor. Check by multiplying the factors.

21. $3a + ab + 3c + bc$ $(a + c)(3 + b)$

22. $rs + 5r + st + 5t$ $(r + t)(s + 5)$

23. $x^2 - 2x + xy - 2y$ $(x + y)(x - 2)$

24. $u^2 - 2u + uv - 2v$ $(u + v)(u - 2)$

25. $h^2 - hk + hr - kr$ $(h + r)(h - k)$

26. $x^2 - 2xy + 4xz - 8yz$ $(x + 4z)(x - 2y)$

27. $p^3 - 2p^2 + 4p - 8$ $(p^2 + 4)(p - 2)$

28. $3a^3 + a^2 + 6a + 2$ $(a^2 + 2)(3a + 1)$

29. $p^2 - 2pq + pr - 2qr$ $(p + r)(p - 2q)$

30. $u^2 - 3uv - 6uw + 18vw$ $(u - 6w)(u - 3v)$

31. $3hk - 2k - 12h + 8$ $(k - 4)(3h - 2)$

32. $3ab - b - 4 + 12a$ $(b + 4)(3a - 1)$

33. $4z^3 - 6z^2 - 6z + 9$ $(2z^2 - 3)(2z - 3)$

34. $3u^3 - u^2 - 9u + 3$ $(u^2 - 3)(3u - 1)$

35. $(h^2k^2 + 4k^2) + (h^2k + 4k)$ $k(k + 1)(h^2 + 4)$

36. $(a^2b^2 + 2a^2) - (2ab^2 + 4a)$ $a(a - 2)(b^2 + 2)$

37. $x^3 - 3x^2 - x + 3$ $(x + 1)(x - 1)(x - 3)$

38. $n^3 + 2n^2 - 4n - 8$ $(n + 2)^2(n - 2)$

Factor each expression as a difference of squares.

39. $x^2 - (y - z)^2$ $(x + y - z)(x - y + z)$

40. $(a + 2b)^2 - 9c^2$ $(a + 2b + 3c)(a + 2b - 3c)$

41. $(u - 2v)^2 - 4w^2$
$(u - 2v + 2w)(u - 2v - 2w)$

42. $4p^2 - (q - 2r)^2$ $(2p + q - 2r)(2p - q + 2r)$

B **43.** $(a + 2b)^2 - (2b + c)^2$ $(a + 4b + c)(a - c)$

44. $4(x + y)^2 - (2y - z)^2$ $(2x + 4y - z)(2x + z)$

45. $a^2 + 4a + 4 - b^2$ $(a + 2 + b)(a + 2 - b)$

46. $x^2 - 2xy + y^2 - 4$ $(x - y + 2)(x - y - 2)$

47. $u^2 - v^2 + 2v - 1$ $(u + v - 1)(u - v + 1)$

48. $m^2 - n^2 - 2m + 1$ $(m - 1 + n)(m - 1 - n)$

49. $h^2 - 4k^2 - 4h + 4$ $(h - 2 + 2k)(h - 2 - 2k)$

50. $a^2 - b^2 - 2a + 1$ $(a - 1 + b)(a - 1 - b)$

51. $p^2 - q^2 + r^2 - 2pr$ $(p - r + q)(p - r - q)$

52. $4s^2 - 4t^2 + 4s + 1$
$(2s + 1 + 2t)(2s + 1 - 2t)$

Factor.
53. $(x - 2z + 2y)(x - 2z - 2y)$
55. $(a + b + 2)(a + b)$

53. $x^2 - 4y^2 + 4z^2 - 4xz$

54. $m^2 - 9n^2 + 9 - 6m$
$(m - 3 + 3n)(m - 3 - 3n)$

55. $a^2 + b^2 + 2ab + 2a + 2b$

56. $p^2 - q^2 - 2p + 2q$
$(p + q - 2)(p - q)$

57. $x^4 - y^4 - 4x^2 + 4$ $(x^2 - 2 + y^2)(x^2 - 2 - y^2)$

58. $a^4 + b^4 - c^4 + 2a^2b^2$
$(a^2 + b^2 + c^2)(a^2 + b^2 - c^2)$

59. $p^2 + q^2 - r^2 - 2pq + 2r - 1$
$(p - q + r - 1)(p - q - r + 1)$

60. $h^2 - 4k^2 + 4h - 8k$ $(h + 2k + 4)(h - 2k)$

C **61.** Factor $x^4 + 4$ by writing it as $(x^4 + 4x^2 + 4) - 4x^2$, a difference of two squares. $(x^2 + 2x + 2)(x^2 - 2x + 2)$

62. Use the method of Exercise 61 to factor **(a)** $64x^4 + 1$ and **(b)** $x^4 + 4a^4$.

63. Factor $a^{2n+1} + b^{2n+1} + a^{2n}b^{2n} + ab$, where n is a positive integer. $(a + b^{2n})(a^{2n} + b)$

62. a. $(8x^2 + 4x + 1)(8x^2 - 4x + 1)$ **b.** $(x^2 + 2ax + 2a^2)(x^2 - 2ax + 2a^2)$

Mixed Review Exercises

Solve.

1. $-12 + x = -29$ $\{-17\}$

2. $-n + 10 = 2$ $\{8\}$

3. $18 + x = 32$ $\{14\}$

4. $16 = 1 + 3z$ $\{5\}$

5. $10m - 6m = 36$ $\{9\}$

6. $5n - 2n + 8 = 9$ $\left\{\frac{1}{3}\right\}$

7. $14x = 700$ $\{50\}$

8. $-13n = 156$ $\{-12\}$

9. $9b = 108$ $\{12\}$

10. $10n = 2n - 24$ $\{-3\}$

11. $19m = 55 + 14m$ $\{11\}$

12. $10y + 6 = 4(19 - y)$ $\{5\}$

5-11 Using Several Methods of Factoring

Objective To factor polynomials completely.

A polynomial is **factored completely** when it is expressed as the product of a monomial and one or more prime polynomials.

Guidelines for Factoring Completely

1. Factor out the greatest monomial factor first.
2. Look for a difference of squares.
3. Look for a perfect square trinomial.
4. If a trinomial is not a square, look for a pair of binomial factors.
5. If a polynomial has four or more terms, look for a way to group the terms in pairs or in a group of three terms that is a perfect square trinomial.
6. Make sure that each binomial or trinomial factor is prime.
7. Check your work by multiplying the factors.

Example 1 Factor $-4n^4 + 40n^3 - 100n^2$ completely.

Solution $-4n^4 + 40n^3 - 100n^2 = -4n^2(n^2 - 10n + 25)$ ← perfect square trinomial

greatest monomial factor ⬏

$= -4n^2(n - 5)^2$ **Answer**

Example 2 Factor $5a^3b^2 + 3a^4b - 2a^2b^3$ completely.

Solution First rewrite the polynomial in order of decreasing degree in a.

$5a^3b^2 + 3a^4b - 2a^2b^3 = 3a^4b + 5a^3b^2 - 2a^2b^3$

$= a^2b(3a^2 + 5ab - 2b^2)$ ← trinomial

greatest monomial factor ⬏

$= a^2b(3a - b)(a + 2b)$ **Answer**

Example 3 Factor $a^2bc - 4bc + a^2b - 4b$ completely.

Solution $a^2bc - 4bc + a^2b - 4b = b(a^2c - 4c + a^2 - 4)$

$= b[c(a^2 - 4) + (a^2 - 4)]$ {Factor by grouping.

$= b(c + 1)(a^2 - 4)$ ⟵ Difference of squares

$= b(c + 1)(a + 2)(a - 2)$

Answer

Factoring Polynomials **227**

Warm-Up Exercises

Classify each polynomial as one of the following:

a. the difference of two squares
b. a perfect square trinomial
c. a trinomial that is not a perfect square
d. a polynomial with four or more terms
e. none of the above

1. $9y^2 - 24y + 16$ b
2. $a^2 - 9$ a
3. $5x^2 - 3y^2$ e
4. $p^3 - pq^2 - p^2 + q^2$ d
5. $5a^2 + 3a - 2$ c
6. $25x^2 - y^2$ a

Motivating the Lesson

Tell students that they have learned several different types of factoring. Some polynomials require more than one type of factoring. Recognizing when to use several methods of factoring in order to factor a polynomial completely is today's topic.

Chalkboard Examples

Factor completely.

1. $9ay^2 - 4a$
   $= a(9y^2 - 4)$
   $= a(3y + 2)(3y - 2)$
2. $-2x^4 - 12x^3 - 18x^2$
   $= -2x^2(x^2 + 6x + 9)$
   $= -2x^2(x + 3)^2$

(continued)

3. $6n^3 - 21n^2 - 45n$
$= 3n(2n^2 - 7n - 15)$
$= 3n(2n + 3)(n - 5)$

4. $x^3y - xy + 5x^2y - 5y$
$= xy(x^2 - 1) + 5y(x^2 - 1)$
$= (xy + 5y)(x^2 - 1)$
$= y(x + 5)(x + 1)(x - 1)$

Common Errors

Students sometimes forget to factor out the greatest common factor. Point out the importance of this step in Examples 1–3.

Sometimes students factor binomials like Written Exercise 33 incorrectly because they think the sum of the two squares is factorable. In reteaching, remind them that $(a + b)^2 = a^2 + 2ab + b^2$.

Check for Understanding

Here is a suggested use of the Oral Exercises to check students' understanding as you teach the lesson.
Oral Exs. 1–6: use at the beginning of the lesson.
Oral Exs. 7–12: use after Example 2.

Guided Practice

Factor completely.

1. $5a^2 - 20ab + 10b^2$
$5(a^2 - 4ab + 2b^2)$

2. $3x^3 - 12x^2 + 4x$
$x(3x^2 - 12x + 4)$

3. $5a^2 - 20b^2$
$5(a + 2b)(a - 2b)$

4. $4x^2 + 8xy + 4y^2$
$4(x + y)^2$

Oral Exercises

State the greatest monomial factor of each polynomial.

1. $6a^2 - 9ab - 15b^2$ 3
2. $18x - 8x^3$ 2x
3. $15r^3 + 20r^2s - 20rs^2$ 5r
4. $6ab + 9a^2b - 15a^3b$ 3ab
5. $4(z - 4)^2 - 16$ 4
6. $12x^2y - 36xy^2 + 27y^3$ 3y

Factor completely.

7. $10a^2 - 15ab^2$ $5a(2a - 3b^2)$
8. $-4x + 6x^2$ $-2x(2 - 3x)$
9. $t^3 - 9t$ $t(t + 3)(t - 3)$
10. $y^4 + 6y^3 + 9y^2$ $y^2(y + 3)^2$
11. $p^3 - 2p^2q + pq^2$ $p(p - q)^2$
12. $u^3v - uv^3$ $uv(u + v)(u - v)$

Written Exercises

1. $3(2a - 5b)(a + b)$ **2.** $2x(3 + 2x)(3 - 2x)$
3. $5r(3r - 2s)(r + 2s)$ **4.** $3ab(2 + 5a)(1 - a)$
5. $4(z - 2)(z - 6)$ **6.** $3y(2x - 3y)^2$

Factor completely.

A

1–6. The polynomials in Oral Exercises 1–6.

7. $5a^2 + 10ab + 5b^2$ $5(a + b)^2$
8. $6c^2 + 18cd + 12d^2$ $6(c + 2d)(c + d)$
9. $4m^3 - m$ $m(2m + 1)(2m - 1)$
10. $3xy^2 - 27x^3$ $3x(y + 3x)(y - 3x)$
11. $y^4 - 2y^2 - y^3$ $y^2(y - 2)(y + 1)$
12. $-n^4 - 3n^2 - 2n^3$ $-n^2(n^2 + 2n + 3)$
13. $x^2 - xy - x + y$ $(x - 1)(x - y)$
14. $-m^2 + mn + 2m - 2n$ $(2 - m)(m - n)$
15. $-41a + 10 + 21a^2$ $(7a - 2)(3a - 5)$
16. $80 - 120p + 45p^2$ $5(4 - 3p)^2$
17. $a^3 - 2a^2b + 3a^2 - 6ab$ $a(a + 3)(a - 2b)$
18. $8p^3q - 18pq^3$ $2pq(2p + 3q)(2p - 3q)$
19. $6u^2v - 11u^2v^2 - 10u^2v^3$ $u^2v(2 - 5v)(3 + 2v)$
20. $180x^2y - 108xy^2 - 75x^3$ $-3x(5x - 6y)^2$
21. $k(k + 1)(k + 2) - 3k(k + 1)$ $k(k + 1)(k - 1)$
22. $n(n^2 - 1) + n(n - 1)$ $n(n - 1)(n + 2)$
23. $2u^5 - 7u^3 - 4u$ $u(2u^2 + 1)(u + 2)(u - 2)$
24. $81a + 18a^3 + a^5$ $a(a^2 + 9)^2$
25. $r^2 - 6r - 9s^2 + 9$ $(r - 3 + 3s)(r - 3 - 3s)$
26. $x^2 - 4y^2 - 4x + 4$ $(x - 2 + 2y)(x - 2 - 2y)$
27. $u^2 - 4v^2 + 3u - 6v$ $(u + 2v + 3)(u - 2v)$
28. $a^2 - b^2 + ac - bc$ $(a + b + c)(a - b)$
29. $p^2 - 1 - 4q^2 - 4q$ $(p + 2q + 1)(p - 2q - 1)$
30. $x^2 - 2x - 4y^2 - 4y$ $(x - 2y - 2)(x + 2y)$

B

31. $100 + 4x^2 - 16y^2 - 40x$ $4(x - 5 + 2y)(x - 5 - 2y)$
32. $16x^2 + 16y - y^2 - 64$ $(4x + y - 8)(4x - y + 8)$
33. $a^4 - b^4$ $(a^2 + b^2)(a + b)(a - b)$
34. $m^8 - n^8$ $(m^4 + n^4)(m^2 + n^2)(m + n)(m - n)$
35. $2pq + 2pr + q^2 - r^2$ $(2p + q - r)(q + r)$
36. $8a^3 + 4a^2b - 2ab^2 - b^3$ $(2a + b)^2(2a - b)$
37. $(a + b)^2 - (a - c)^2$ $(2a + b - c)(b + c)$
38. $3x^5 + 15x^3 - 108x$ $3x(x + 2)(x - 2)(x^2 + 9)$
39. $x^3 - x^2y - xy^2 + y^3$ $(x + y)(x - y)^2$
40. $4 - 4x^2 - 4y^2 + 8xy$ $4(1 + x - y)(1 - x + y)$
41. $a(a + 2)(a - 3) - 8(a - 3)$ $(a - 3)(a - 2)(a + 4)$
42. $x(x + 1)(x - 4) + 4(x + 1)$ $(x + 1)(x - 2)^2$
43. $16c^{16} - 16$ $16(c^8 + 1)(c^4 + 1)(c^2 + 1)(c + 1)(c - 1)$
44. $(u - v)^3 + v - u$ $(u - v)(u - v + 1)(u - v - 1)$
45. $a(a^2 - 9) - 2(a + 3)^2$ $(a + 3)(a - 6)(a + 1)$
46. $(x - 2)(x^2 - 1) - 6x - 6$ $(x + 1)^2(x - 4)$
47. $9u^2 - 9v^2 - 36w^2 + 36vw$ $9(u + v - 2w)(u - v + 2w)$
48. $x^4 - x^2 + 4x - 4$ $(x^2 - x + 2)(x + 2)(x - 1)$

49. $x^2(x + 2) - x(x + 2) - 12(x + 2)$ $(x + 2)(x + 3)(x - 4)$

50. $(a + b)^3 - 6(a + b)^2 - 7(a + b)$ $(a + b)(a + b + 1)(a + b - 7)$

51. $t^4 - 10t^2 + 9$ $(t + 3)(t - 3)(t + 1)(t - 1)$

52. $16t^4 - 8t^2 + 1$ $(2t + 1)^2(2t - 1)^2$

53. $a^2 + b^2 - c^2 - d^2 - 2ab + 2cd$

54. $(u^2 - v^2)^2 - w^2(u + v)^2$

55. Factor $x^4 + x^2 + 1$ by writing it as $(x^4 + 2x^2 + 1) - x^2$, a difference of squares.

56. Factor $a^4 + a^2b^2 + b^4$. (*Hint:* See Exercise 55.) $(a^2 + ab + b^2)(a^2 - ab + b^2)$

57. Factor $a^3 + b^3$ by writing it as $a^3 + a^2b - a^2b - ab^2 + ab^2 + b^3$ and grouping the terms by pairs. $(a + b)(a^2 - ab + b^2)$

58. Factor $a^3 - b^3$. (*Hint:* See Exercise 57.)
$(a - b)(a^2 + ab + b^2)$

53. $(a - b + c - d)(a - b - c + d)$
54. $(u + v)^2(u - v + w)(u - v - w)$
55. $(x^2 + x + 1)(x^2 - x + 1)$

Mixed Review Exercises

Simplify.

1. $\left(-\frac{1}{4}\right)\left(\frac{1}{5}\right)(40)$ -2

2. $\frac{1}{8}(56)$ 7

3. $-\frac{1}{9}(72)\left(-\frac{1}{8}\right)$ 1

4. $\frac{140b}{7}$ $20b$

5. $52 \div \left(\frac{1}{13}\right)$ 676

6. $625 \div (-5)$ -125

Factor.

7. $x^2 - 12x + 35$ $(x - 7)(x - 5)$

8. $x^2 + 3x - 28$ $(x + 7)(x - 4)$

9. $x^2 - x - 2$ $(x - 2)(x + 1)$

10. $2n^2 + 19n + 9$ $(2n + 1)(n + 9)$

11. $3x^2 + 11x + 10$ $(3x + 5)(x + 2)$

12. $(3x - 12) - 2n(4 - x)$ $(3 + 2n)(x - 4)$

Career Note / *Draftsperson*

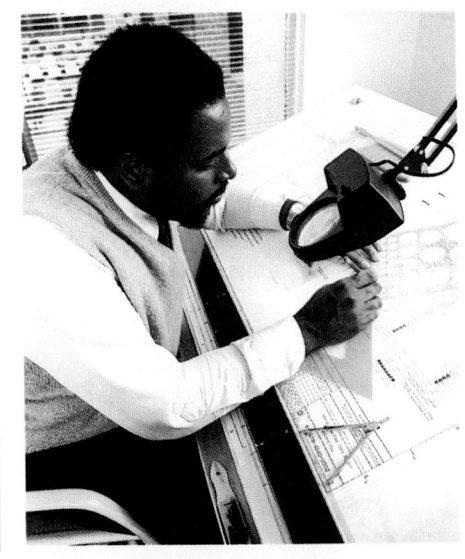

Manufacturers and construction workers rely on detailed plans of buildings and manufactured products as a guide for production. The plans are prepared by a draftsperson using many different tools. For example, he or she may use a compass, a protractor, a triangle, and a calculator. A draftsperson also makes use of math skills, such as working with fractions, making measurements, and making drawings to different scales.

Today draftspersons use computer-aided design (CAD) systems to allow them to see many variations of a design. They often specialize in a particular field of work, such as mechanical, electrical, aeronautical, or architectural drafting. A draftsperson needs coursework in mathematics, mechanical drawing, and drafting.

---

5. $p^4 - p^3 - 6p^2$
$p^2(p - 3)(p + 2)$

6. $s^2r^2 - 4s^4$
$s^2(r + 2s)(r - 2s)$

7. $xy + 3x - 2y - 6$
$(x - 2)(y + 3)$

8. $32b^4 - 48b^3c + 18b^2c^2$
$2b^2(4b - 3c)^2$

9. $y(y + 3)(y + 2) - 4y(y + 2)$
$y(y - 1)(y + 2)$

10. $4p^2 - 1 + 2q - q^2$
$(2p - q + 1)(2p + q - 1)$

Summarizing the Lesson

Ask students to name the various types of polynomials that they have factored in this lesson. Review the guidelines for factoring.

Suggested Assignments

Minimum
     228/1–6, 11–29 odd
   S   229/Mixed Review

Average
     228/1–6, 9–51
       mult. of 3
   S   229/Mixed Review

Maximum
Day 1: 228/1–39 odd
Day 2: 228/41–57 odd
   S   229/Mixed Review

Supplementary Materials

Study Guide   pp. 93–94
Resource Book   p. 99

Factoring Polynomials   **229**

Warm-Up Exercises
Solve.
1. $n - 4 = 0$ {4}
2. $5x - 3 = 0$ $\left\{\frac{3}{5}\right\}$
3. $3u + 4 = 19$ {5}
4. $6(r - 3) = 24$ {7}
5. $5x + 7 = 2x - 5$ {-4}
Complete.
6. $3 \cdot 0 = \underline{\ ?\ }$ 0
7. $\underline{\ ?\ } \cdot 7 = 0$ 0
8. $0 \cdot 0 = \underline{\ ?\ }$ 0
9. $\frac{2}{3} \cdot \underline{\ ?\ } = 0$ 0

Motivating the Lesson
The graph of the equation $y = x^2 + x - 12$ is shown below.

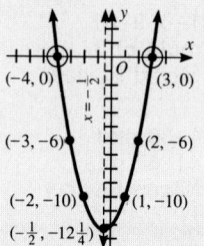

This graph is a curve called a parabola. You will study parabolas later this year. Today you will learn how to find the circled points, which are the solutions to the quadratic equation $x^2 + x - 12 = 0$, or $(x - 3)(x + 4) = 0$.

5-12 Solving Equations by Factoring

Objective To use factoring in solving polynomial equations.

The multiplicative property of zero can be stated as follows:

$$\text{If } a = 0 \text{ or } b = 0, \text{ then } ab = 0. \longleftarrow \text{statement}$$

The statement above is given in "if-then" form. The **converse** of a statement in "if-then" form is obtained by interchanging the "if" and "then" parts of the statement as shown below.

$$\text{If } ab = 0, \text{ then } a = 0 \text{ or } b = 0. \longleftarrow \text{converse}$$

The converse of a true statement is not necessarily true. You can show that the particular converse displayed above *is* true (Exercise 55, page 233).

The words "if and only if" are used to combine a statement and its converse when both are true. The *zero-product property* stated below combines the multiplicative property of zero and its converse.

Zero-Product Property

For all real numbers a and b:

$$ab = 0 \text{ if and only if } a = 0 \text{ or } b = 0.$$

A product of factors is zero if and only if one or more of the factors is zero.

The zero-product property is true for any number of factors. You can use this property to solve certain equations.

Example 1 Solve $(x + 2)(x - 5) = 0$.

Solution One of the factors on the left side must equal zero. Therefore,

$$x + 2 = 0 \quad \text{or} \quad x - 5 = 0$$
$$x = -2 \qquad\qquad x = 5$$

Just by looking at the original equation, you might have seen that when $x = -2$ or $x = 5$ one of the factors will be zero.

Either method gives the solution set {-2, 5}. **Answer**

Example 2 Solve $5n(n - 3)(n - 4) = 0$.

Solution $5n = 0 \quad \text{or} \quad n - 3 = 0 \quad \text{or} \quad n - 4 = 0$
$\qquad\quad n = 0 \qquad\qquad n = 3 \qquad\qquad n = 4$

$\therefore$ the solution set is {0, 3, 4}. **Answer**

---

230 *Chapter 5*

A **polynomial equation** is an equation whose sides are both polynomials. Polynomial equations usually are named by the term of highest degree. If $a \neq 0$:

$$ax + b = 0 \quad \text{is a \textbf{linear equation.}}$$
$$ax^2 + bx + c = 0 \quad \text{is a \textbf{quadratic equation.}}$$
$$ax^3 + bx^2 + cx + d = 0 \quad \text{is a \textbf{cubic equation.}}$$

Many polynomial equations can be solved by factoring and then using the zero-product property. Often the first step is to transform the equation into **standard form** in which one side is zero. The other side should be a simplified polynomial arranged in order of decreasing degree of the variable.

Example 3 Solve the quadratic equation $2x^2 + 5x = 12$.

Solution
1. Transform the equation into standard form. $\quad 2x^2 + 5x - 12 = 0$
2. Factor the left side. $\quad (2x - 3)(x + 4) = 0$
3. Set each factor equal to 0 and solve. $\quad 2x - 3 = 0 \quad$ or $\quad x + 4 = 0$
$$2x = 3 \qquad\qquad x = -4$$
$$x = \frac{3}{2}$$

4. Check the solutions in the original equation.

$$2\left(\frac{3}{2}\right)^2 + 5\left(\frac{3}{2}\right) \overset{?}{=} 12 \qquad\qquad 2(-4)^2 + 5(-4) \overset{?}{=} 12$$

$$2\left(\frac{9}{4}\right) + \frac{15}{2} \overset{?}{=} 12 \qquad\qquad 2(16) - 20 \overset{?}{=} 12$$

$$\frac{9}{2} + \frac{15}{2} = \frac{24}{2} = 12 \ \ \checkmark \qquad\qquad 32 - 20 = 12 \ \ \checkmark$$

$\therefore$ the solution set is $\left\{\frac{3}{2}, -4\right\}$. ***Answer***

Example 4 Solve the cubic equation $18y^3 + 8y + 24y^2 = 0$.

Solution
1. Transform the equation into standard form. $\quad 18y^3 + 24y^2 + 8y = 0$
2. Factor completely. $\quad 2y(9y^2 + 12y + 4) = 0$
$$2y(3y + 2)^2 = 0$$
3. Solve by inspection or by equating each $\quad y = 0$ or $y = -\frac{2}{3}$ or $y = -\frac{2}{3}$
   factor to 0.
4. The check is left to you.

$\therefore$ the solution set is $\left\{0, -\frac{2}{3}\right\}$. ***Answer***

The factorization in Example 4 produced two identical factors. Since the factor $3y + 2$ occurs twice in the factored form of the equation, $-\frac{2}{3}$ is a **double** or **multiple root.** Notice that we list it only once in the solution set.

Factoring Polynomials **231**

Common Errors

Students may try to transform an equation by dividing both sides by a variable expression. See **Caution** at the top of page 232.

Chalkboard Examples

Solve.

1. $(x - 3)(x + 4) = 0$
   $x - 3 = 0$ or $x + 4 = 0$
   $x = 3$ or $x = -4$
   $\therefore$ the solution set is $\{3, -4\}$.

2. $6b(b + 5)(b + 2) = 0$
   $6b = 0$ or $b + 5 = 0$ or $b + 2 = 0$
   $b = 0 \quad b = -5 \quad b = -2$
   $\therefore$ the solution set is $\{0, -5, -2\}$.

3. $5z^2 = 80$
   $5z^2 - 80 = 0$
   $5(z^2 - 16) = 0$
   $5(z + 4)(z - 4) = 0$
   $z + 4 = 0$ or $z - 4 = 0$
   $z = -4 \qquad z = 4$
   $\therefore$ the solution set is $\{4, -4\}$.

4. $6n^2 + 11n = 10$
   $6n^2 + 11n - 10 = 0$
   $(3n - 2)(2n + 5) = 0$
   $3n - 2 = 0$ or $2n + 5 = 0$
   $3n = 2 \qquad\quad 2n = -5$
   $n = \frac{2}{3} \qquad\quad n = \frac{-5}{2}$
   $\therefore$ the solution set is $\left\{\frac{2}{3}, \frac{-5}{2}\right\}$.

5. $18y^3 + 66y^2 - 24y = 0$
   $6y(3y^2 + 11y - 4) = 0$
   $6y(3y - 1)(y + 4) = 0$
   $6y = 0$ or $3y - 1 = 0$ or $y + 4 = 0$
   $y = 0$ or $3y = 1$ or $y = -4$
   $y = \frac{1}{3}$
   $\therefore$ the solution set is $\left\{0, \frac{1}{3}, -4\right\}$.

Here is a suggested use of the Oral Exercises to check students' understanding as you teach the lesson.
Oral Exs. 1–6: use after Example 2.
Oral Exs. 7–12: use after Example 4.
Oral Ex. 13: use at the beginning of the lesson.

Guided Practice

Solve.

1. $(n + 3)(n - 7) = 0$
$\{-3, 7\}$

2. $8y(y - 4) = 0$
$\{0, 4\}$

3. $(2x - 1)(6x + 4) = 0$
$\left\{\frac{1}{2}, \frac{-2}{3}\right\}$

4. $(2n - 4)(3n + 5) = 0$
$\left\{2, \frac{-5}{3}\right\}$

5. $0 = p^2 - 11p + 18$
$\{9, 2\}$

6. $s^2 = 18s - 81$ $\{9\}$

7. $16x^2 = 25$ $\left\{\frac{5}{4}, \frac{-5}{4}\right\}$

8. $8b^2 = 14b + 15$
$\left\{\frac{-3}{4}, \frac{5}{2}\right\}$

9. $0 = 6x^3 - 24x$
$\{0, 2, -2\}$

10. $x^4 - 5x^2 = -4$
$\{2, -2, 1, -1\}$

Summarizing the Lesson

Tell the students they have learned how to solve quadratic equations by getting 0 on one side, factoring, and then using the zero-product property to solve linear equations.

Caution: Never transform an equation by dividing by an expression containing a variable. Notice that in Example 4, the solution 0 would have been lost if both sides of $2y(9y^2 + 12y + 4) = 0$ had been divided by $2y$.

Oral Exercises

Solve.

7–12. Write the equation in standard form and factor the left side. Then set each factor equal to zero and solve.

1. $x(x - 6) = 0$ $\{0, 6\}$ **2.** $2a(a + 1) = 0$ $\{0, -1\}$ **3.** $0 = 3p(2p - 1)$ $\left\{0, \frac{1}{2}\right\}$

4. $(y - 2)(y + 3) = 0$ $\{2, -3\}$ **5.** $0 = (3t - 2)(t - 3)$ $\left\{\frac{2}{3}, 3\right\}$ **6.** $x(2x - 5)(2x + 1) = 0$
$\left\{0, \frac{5}{2}, -\frac{1}{2}\right\}$

Explain how you could solve the given equation. Then solve.

7. $4x^2 - x^3 = 0$ $\{0, 4\}$ **8.** $a^3 = 4a$ $\{0, 2, -2\}$ **9.** $k^2 + 4 = 4k$ $\{2\}$

10. $m^3 - 2m = m^2$ $\{0, -1, 2\}$ **11.** $9x^2 = x^3$ $\{0, 9\}$ **12.** $0 = -n^3 + n$ $\{0, -1, 1\}$

13. Give an example of a true "if-then" statement with a false converse. Answers may vary.
If an animal is a beagle, then it is a dog. (True)
If an animal is a dog, then it is a beagle. (False)

Written Exercises

3. $\{0, -15\}$
6. $\left\{-\frac{7}{2}, \frac{1}{3}\right\}$
12. $\{7, 5\}$ **33.** $\left\{-\frac{7}{3}, \frac{7}{3}\right\}$

Solve.   **7.** $\left\{0, -\frac{1}{2}, -\frac{5}{2}\right\}$ **8.** $\left\{0, \frac{2}{5}, -\frac{5}{2}\right\}$

A   **1.** $(y + 5)(y - 7) = 0$ $\{-5, 7\}$ **2.** $(n + 1)(n + 9) = 0$ $\{-1, -9\}$ **3.** $15n(n + 15) = 0$

4. $2x(x - 20) = 0$ $\{0, 20\}$ **5.** $(2t - 3)(3t - 2) = 0$ $\left\{\frac{3}{2}, \frac{2}{3}\right\}$ **6.** $(2u + 7)(3u - 1) = 0$

7. $3x(2x + 1)(2x + 5) = 0$ **8.** $n(5n - 2)(2n + 5) = 0$ **9.** $y^2 - 3y + 2 = 0$ $\{2, 1\}$

10. $p^2 - p - 6 = 0$ $\{3, -2\}$ **11.** $0 = x^2 + 14x + 48$ $\{-6, -8\}$ **12.** $0 = k^2 - 12k + 35$

13. $m^2 - 36 = 16m$ $\{18, -2\}$ **14.** $r^2 + 9 = 10r$ $\{9, 1\}$ **15.** $s^2 = 4s + 32$ $\{8, -4\}$

16. $x^2 = 20x - 100$ $\{10\}$ **17.** $y^2 = 16y$ $\{0, 16\}$ **18.** $9k^2 = 4k$ $\left\{0, \frac{4}{9}\right\}$

19. $4x^2 - 9 = 0$ $\left\{-\frac{3}{2}, \frac{3}{2}\right\}$ **20.** $25m^2 - 16 = 0$ $\left\{-\frac{4}{5}, \frac{4}{5}\right\}$ **21.** $6n^2 + n = 2$ $\left\{-\frac{2}{3}, \frac{1}{2}\right\}$

22. $3x^2 + x = 2$ $\left\{\frac{2}{3}, -1\right\}$ **23.** $4s - 4s^2 = 1$ $\left\{\frac{1}{2}\right\}$ **24.** $r - 6r^2 = -1$ $\left\{-\frac{1}{3}, \frac{1}{2}\right\}$

25. $7x^2 = 18x - 11$ $\left\{\frac{11}{7}, 1\right\}$ **26.** $2y^2 = 25y + 13$ $\left\{-\frac{1}{2}, 13\right\}$ **27.** $8u^3 - 2u^2 = 0$ $\left\{0, \frac{1}{4}\right\}$

28. $10u^3 - 5u^2 = 0$ $\left\{0, \frac{1}{2}\right\}$ **29.** $0 = 4y^3 - 2y^2$ $\left\{0, \frac{1}{2}\right\}$ **30.** $0 = 10x^3 - 15x^2$ $\left\{0, \frac{3}{2}\right\}$

31. $8y^2 - 9y + 1 = 0$ $\left\{\frac{1}{8}, 1\right\}$ **32.** $6h^2 + 17h + 12 = 0$ $\left\{-\frac{3}{2}, -\frac{4}{3}\right\}$ **33.** $15u^2 - 14u = 49$

34. $25x^2 - 90x = -81$ $\left\{\frac{9}{5}\right\}$ **35.** $4p^2 + 121 = 44p$ $\left\{\frac{11}{2}\right\}$ **36.** $6c^2 - 72 = 11c$ $\left\{-\frac{8}{3}, \frac{9}{2}\right\}$

B   **37.** $4x^3 - 12x^2 + 8x = 0$ $\{0, 2, 1\}$ **38.** $2n^3 - 30n^2 + 100n = 0$ **39.** $9x^3 + 9x = 30x^2$

40. $9x^3 + 25x = 30x^2$ $\left\{0, \frac{5}{3}\right\}$ **41.** $y^4 - 10y^2 + 9 = 0$ **42.** $u^5 - 13u^3 + 36u = 0$
$\{3, -3, 1, -1\}$ $\{0, 3, -3, 2, -2\}$

38. $\{0, 5, 10\}$ **39.** $\left\{0, \frac{1}{3}, 3\right\}$

Sample 1 $(x - 1)(x + 3) = 12$

Solution $x^2 + 2x - 3 - 12 = 0$
$(x - 3)(x + 5) = 0$ ∴ the solution set is $\{3, -5\}$

232   *Chapter 5*

Solve. See Sample 1 on page 232.

43. $(z + 1)(z - 5) = 16$ {7, −3}

44. $(2t - 5)(t - 1) = 2$ $\left\{\frac{1}{2}, 3\right\}$

45. $(x - 2)(x + 3) = 6$ {−4, 3}

46. $(a - 5)(a - 2) = 28$ {9, −2}

47. $x(x - 6) = 4(x - 4)$ {2, 8}

48. $3(m + 2) = m(m - 2)$ {−1, 6}

Find an equation in standard form with integral coefficients that has the given solution set.

Sample 2 $\left\{\frac{2}{3}, -4\right\}$

Solution

$\left(x - \frac{2}{3}\right)(x + 4) = 0$

$3\left(x - \frac{2}{3}\right)(x + 4) = 0$ $\left\{\begin{array}{l}\text{Multiply by 3}\\\text{for integral}\\\text{coefficients.}\end{array}\right.$

$(3x - 2)(x + 4) = 0$

$3x^2 + 10x - 8 = 0$ *Answer*

49. {2, −3}

$x^2 + x - 6 = 0$

50. {−1, 5}

$x^2 - 4x - 5 = 0$

51. $\left\{\frac{5}{2}, -2\right\}$

$2x^2 - x - 10 = 0$

52. $\left\{-\frac{1}{3}, -1\right\}$

$3x^2 + 4x + 1 = 0$

53. $\left\{\frac{1}{3}, \frac{3}{2}\right\}$

$6x^2 - 11x + 3 = 0$

54. $\left\{-\frac{5}{2}, \frac{2}{5}\right\}$

$10x^2 + 21x - 10 = 0$

C **55.** Supply the missing reasons in the proof of: If $ab = 0$, then $a = 0$ or $b = 0$.

Case 1: If $a = 0$, then the theorem is true; there is nothing to prove.

Case 2: Suppose that $a \neq 0$ and show that then $b = 0$.

a.	$ab = 0$	**a.** Given
b.	$\frac{1}{a}$ exists	**b.** __?__ Prop. of reciprocals
c.	$\frac{1}{a}(ab) = \frac{1}{a}(0)$	**c.** __?__ Mult. prop. of equality
d.	$\frac{1}{a}(ab) = 0$	**d.** __?__ Mult. prop. of 0
e.	$\left(\frac{1}{a} \cdot a\right)b = 0$	**e.** __?__ Assoc. prop. of mult.
f.	$1 \cdot b = 0$	**f.** __?__ Prop. of reciprocals
g.	$b = 0$	**g.** __?__ Identity prop. of mult.

Mixed Review Exercises

Evaluate if $x = 2$ and $y = 4$.

1. $(x - y)^4$ 16

2. $x^4 \cdot y^2$ 256

3. $5x^3$ 40

4. $(5x)^3$ 1000

5. $4x + y^2$ 24

6. $4x^2 + y$ 20

7. $4(x + y)^2$ 144

8. $(yx)^2$ 64

9. y^2x^2 64

Simplify.

10. $(3x^3y)(-2xy^5)$ $-6x^4y^6$

11. $(9a)^3$ $729a^3$

12. $-5(x + 2)$ $-5x - 10$

5-13 Using Factoring to Solve Problems

Objective   To solve problems by writing and factoring quadratic equations.

The problems in this lesson all lead to polynomial equations that can be solved by factoring. Sometimes a solution of an equation may not satisfy some of the conditions of the problem. For example, a negative number cannot represent a length or an age. You reject solutions of an equation that do not make sense for the problem.

Example 1   A decorator plans to place a rug in a 9 m by 12 m room so that a uniform strip of flooring around the rug will remain uncovered. How wide will this strip be if the area of the rug is to be half the area of the room?

Solution

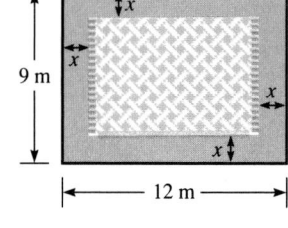

Step 1 The problem asks for the width of the strip.

Step 2 Let x = the width of the strip. Then $12 - 2x$ = the length of the rug and $9 - 2x$ = the width of the rug.

Step 3   Area of the rug = $\frac{1}{2}$(Area of the room)

$(12 - 2x)(9 - 2x) = \frac{1}{2} \cdot 9 \cdot 12$

Step 4 $108 - 42x + 4x^2 = 54$
$\quad 4x^2 - 42x + 54 = 0$
$\quad 2(2x^2 - 21x + 27) = 0$
$\quad 2[(2x - 3)(x - 9)] = 0$
$\quad 2x - 3 = 0 \qquad$ or $\qquad x - 9 = 0$
$\qquad x = \frac{3}{2},$ or 1.5 $\qquad\qquad x = 9$

Step 5 *Check:*   When $x = 1.5$, the area of the rug is $(12 - 2x)(9 - 2x) = 9 \cdot 6 = 54$
$\qquad = \frac{1}{2}$(Area of the room) √

When $x = 9$, the length, $12 - 2x$, and width, $9 - 2x$, are negative. Since a negative length or width is meaningless, reject $x = 9$ as an answer.

∴ the strip around the rug will be 1.5 m wide. ***Answer***

The equation in Step 3 of Example 1 has a root that does not check because this equation does not meet the "hidden" requirements that the rug have positive length ($12 - 2x > 0$) and positive width ($9 - 2x > 0$). Usually it is easier to write only the equation and then check its roots against other conditions stated or implied in the problem.

In the next example both solutions of the equation satisfy the conditions of the problem. You can use the formula

$$h = rt - 4.9t^2$$

to obtain a good approximation of the height h (in meters) of an object t seconds after it is projected upward with an initial speed of r meters per second (m/s).

Example 2   An arrow is shot upward with an initial speed of 34.3 m/s. When will it be at a height of 49 m?

Solution

Step 1   The problem asks for the time when the arrow is 49 m high.

Step 2   Let t = the number of seconds after being shot that the arrow is 49 m high. Let h = the height of arrow = 49 m. Let r = initial speed = 34.3 m/s.

Step 3   Substitute in the formula: $h = rt - 4.9t^2$
$$49 = 34.3t - 4.9t^2$$

Step 4 $4.9t^2 - 34.3t + 49 = 0$
$$4.9(t^2 - 7t + 10) = 0$$
$$4.9(t - 2)(t - 5) = 0$$

Completing the solution and checking the result are left for you. A calculator may be helpful.

∴ the arrow is 49 m high both 2 s and 5 s after being shot.   **Answer**

Problems

Solve.

A   1. If a number is added to its square, the result is 56. Find the number. −8 or 7

    2. If a number is subtracted from its square, the result is 72. Find the number. 9 or −8

    3. A positive number is 30 less than its square. Find the number. 6

    4. A negative number is 42 less than its square. Find the number. −6

    5. Find two consecutive negative integers whose product is 90. −10, −9

    6. Find two consecutive positive odd integers whose product is 143. 11, 13

    7. The sum of the squares of two consecutive positive even integers is 340. Find the integers. 12, 14

    8. The sum of the squares of two consecutive negative even integers is 100. Find the integers. −8, −6

Factoring Polynomials   235

Because negative solutions must frequently be discarded, students sometimes reject negative solutions without checking to see if it is reasonable to do so. In reteaching, encourage careful rereading of the problem as in Step 5 of the five-step plan.

Guided Practice

Solve.

1. If a number is subtracted from its square, the result is 30. Find the number. 6 or −5

2. Find two consecutive positive even integers whose product is 224. 14, 16

3. The sum of the squares of two consecutive negative odd integers is 290. Find the integers. −13, −11

4. The length of a rectangle is 8 cm greater than twice its width. Find the dimensions if the area is 42 cm². 14 cm × 3 cm

5. A rectangle has dimensions 12 in. by 8 in. If a uniform border is added, then the new rectangle has twice the area of the old rectangle. Find the new dimensions. 2 in. border; dimensions are 16 in. × 12 in.

Summarizing the Lesson

Tell the students they have solved problems by writing and factoring quadratic equations.

Solve.

9. The length of a rectangle is 8 cm greater than its width. Find the dimensions of the rectangle if its area is 105 cm². 7 cm by 15 cm

10. The length of a rectangle is 6 cm less than twice its width. Find the dimensions of the rectangle if its area is 108 cm². 9 cm by 12 cm

11. Find the dimensions of a rectangle whose perimeter is 46 m and whose area is 126 m². (*Hint:* Let the width be w. Use the perimeter to find the length in terms of w.) 9 m by 14 m

12. Find the dimensions of a rectangle whose perimeter is 42 m and whose area is 104 m². 8 m by 13 m

13. The sum of two numbers is 25 and the sum of their squares is 313. Find the numbers. (*Hint:* Let one of the numbers be x. Express the other number in terms of x.) 12 and 13

14. The difference of two positive numbers is 5 and the sum of their squares is 233. What are the numbers? 8 and 13

15. Originally the dimensions of a rectangle were 20 cm by 23 cm. When both dimensions were decreased by the same amount, the area of the rectangle decreased by 120 cm². Find the dimensions of the new rectangle. 17 cm by 20 cm

16. Originally a rectangle was twice as long as it was wide. When 4 m were added to its length and 3 m subtracted from its width, the resulting rectangle had an area of 600 m². Find the dimensions of the new rectangle. 40 m by 15 m

In Exercises 17–23, use the formula $h = rt - 4.9t^2$ where h is in meters and the formula $h = rt - 16t^2$ where h is in feet. A calculator may be helpful.

B 17. A ball is thrown upward with an initial speed of 24.5 m/s. When is it 19.6 m high? (Two answers) at 1 s and 4 s

18. A rocket is fired upward with an initial speed of 1960 m/s. After how many minutes does it hit the ground? $6\frac{2}{3}$ min

19. A batter hit a baseball upward with an initial speed of 120 ft/s. How much later did the catcher catch it? 7.5 s

20. Mitch tossed an apple to Kathy, who was on a balcony 40 ft above him, with an initial speed of 56 ft/s. Kathy missed the apple on its way up, but caught it on its way down. How long was the apple in the air? 2.5 s

21. A signal flare is fired upward with initial speed 245 m/s. A stationary balloonist at a height of 1960 m sees the flare pass on the way up. How long after this will the flare pass the balloonist again on the way down? 30 s

236   *Chapter 5*

22. A ball is thrown upward from the top of a 98 m tower with initial speed 39.2 m/s. How much later will it hit the ground? (*Hint:* Consider the top of the tower as level zero. If h is the height of the ball above the top of the tower, then $h = -98$ when the ball hits the ground.) 10 s

23. A rocket is fired upward with an initial velocity of 160 ft/s.
    a. When is the rocket 400 ft high? 5 s after it is fired
    b. How do you know that 400 ft is the greatest height the rocket reaches?
       There is only one time when the rocket is 400 ft high.

Solve.

24. A garden plot 4 m by 12 m has one side along a fence as shown at the right. The area of the garden is to be doubled by digging a border of uniform width on the other three sides. What should the width of the border be? 2 m

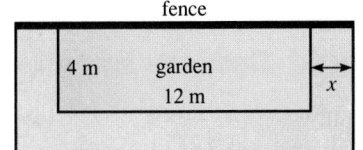

fence

25. Vanessa built a rectangular pen for her dogs. She used an outside wall of the garage for one of the sides of the pen. She had to buy 20 m of fencing in order to build the other sides of the pen. Find the dimensions of the pen if its area is 48 m². 4 m by 12 m or 6 m by 8 m

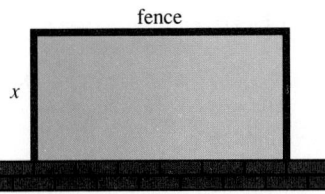

fence

26. A rectangular garden 30 m by 40 m has two paths of equal width crossing through it as shown. Find the width of each path if the total area covered by the paths is 325 m². 5 m

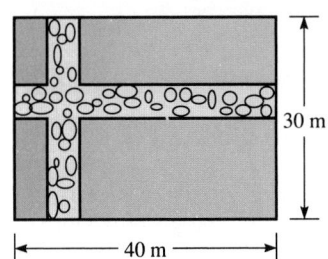

27. A box has a square bottom and top and is 5 cm high. Find its volume if its total surface area is 192 cm². 180 cm³

28. The bottom and top of a box are rectangles twice as long as they are wide. Find the volume of the box if it is 4 ft high and has a total surface area of 220 ft². 200 ft³

29. A 50 m by 120 m park consists of a rectangular lawn surrounded by a path of uniform width. Find the dimensions of the lawn if its area is the same as the area of the path. (*Hint:* Let $x =$ the width of path.) 30 m by 100 m

C 30. The Parkhursts used 160 yd of fencing to enclose a rectangular corral and to divide it into two parts by a fence parallel to one of the shorter sides. Find the dimensions of the corral if its area is 1000 yd². 20 yd by 50 yd

31. Each edge of one cube is 2 cm longer than each edge of another cube. The volumes of the cubes differ by 98 cm³. Find the lengths of the edges of each cube. 3 cm and 5 cm

Factoring Polynomials   237

32. A rectangular sheet of metal is 10 cm longer than it is wide. Squares, 5 cm on a side, are cut from the corners of the sheet, and the flaps are bent up to form an open-topped box having volume 6 L. Find the original dimensions of the sheet of metal. You may wish to make a model. (Recall that $1 \text{ L} = 1000 \text{ cm}^3$.) 40 cm by 50 cm

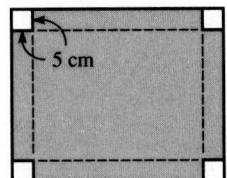

Mixed Review Exercises

Simplify.

1. $(8a^2b)(2ab^2)$ $16a^3b^3$

2. $(5a^2)^3$ $125a^6$

3. $3a(4 - 2b)$ $12a - 6ab$

4. $(6r)\left(\dfrac{1}{3}rs^2\right)$ $2r^2s^2$

5. $\left(\dfrac{1}{8}\right)(16n - 24p)$ $2n - 3p$

6. $(-28x - 14y)\left(-\dfrac{1}{7}\right)$ $4x + 2y$

7. $(3a + 2)(2a^2 + 5 - 7a)$
$6a^3 - 17a^2 + a + 10$

8. $(3b^2y)^2$ $9b^4y^2$

9. $6x(x^2 - 8)$ $6x^3 - 48x$

Factor completely.

10. $-28 + 6m + 10m^2$
$2(5m - 7)(m + 2)$

11. $36a^3 - 9ab^2$
$9a(2a + b)(2a - b)$

12. $21n^2 + 22n - 8$
$(7n - 2)(3n + 4)$

13. $y^4 - y^3 - 12y^2$
$y^2(y - 4)(y + 3)$

14. $15m^2 + 26mn + 8n^2$
$(5m + 2n)(3m + 4n)$

15. $3 + 10x^2 - 17x$
$(5x - 1)(2x - 3)$

Self-Test 4

Vocabulary   factor completely (p. 227)
converse (p. 230)
polynomial equation (p. 231)
linear equation (p. 231)

quadratic equation (p. 231)
cubic equation (p. 231)
standard form of a polynomial equation (p. 231)

Factor completely.

1. $7r - 3rt + 7s - 3st$
$(r + s)(7 - 3t)$

2. $n^2 - 2n + 1 - 100t^4$
$(n - 1 + 10t^2)(n - 1 - 10t^2)$

Obj. 5-10, p. 224

3. $18a^3 - 12a^2 + 2a$
$2a(3a - 1)^2$

4. $21xy - 18x^2 - 6y^2$
$-3(3x - 2y)(2x - y)$

Obj. 5-11, p. 227

Solve.

5. $k^2 - 4k = 32$ $\{8, -4\}$

6. $5m^2 + 20m + 20 = 0$ $\{-2\}$

Obj. 5-12, p. 230

7. $a^3 = 169a$ $\{0, 13, -13\}$

8. $z^3 = z^2 + 30z$ $\{0, 6, -5\}$

9. The length of a rectangle is 9 cm more than its width. The area of the rectangle is 90 cm². Find the dimensions of the rectangle. 6 cm by 15 cm

Obj. 5-13, p. 234

Check your answers with those at the back of the book.

Although Eratosthenes (276–194 B.C.) is best known for determining the diameter and circumference of Earth, one of his greatest contributions to mathematics was his sieve, a method of "sifting out" the primes from the set of positive integers.

To use the sieve of Eratosthenes write out the consecutive integers from 2 through any number, say 100. Then, circle 2 and cross out all numbers in the list that are multiples of 2. Next, circle 3 and cross out every number that is a multiple of 3. Continue in this manner until only the circled numbers remain. These are *prime numbers*.

② ③ 4̸ ⑤ 6̸ ⑦ 8̸ 9̸ 1̸0̸ ⑪ 1̸2̸ ⑬ 1̸4̸ 1̸5̸ 1̸6̸ ⑰ 1̸8̸ ⑲ 2̸0̸
2̸1̸ 2̸2̸ ㉓ 2̸4̸ 2̸5̸ 2̸6̸ 2̸7̸ 2̸8̸ ㉙ 3̸0̸ ㉛ 3̸2̸ 3̸3̸ 3̸4̸ 3̸5̸ 3̸6̸ ㊲ 3̸8̸ 3̸9̸ 4̸0̸
㊶ 4̸2̸ ㊸ 4̸4̸ 4̸5̸ 4̸6̸ ㊼ 4̸8̸ 4̸9̸ 5̸0̸ 5̸1̸ 5̸2̸ ㊽ 5̸4̸ 5̸5̸ 5̸6̸ 5̸7̸ 5̸8̸ ㊾ 6̸0̸
㊅ 6̸2̸ 6̸3̸ 6̸4̸ 6̸5̸ 6̸6̸ ㊇ 6̸8̸ 6̸9̸ 7̸0̸ ㊀ 7̸2̸ ㊂ 7̸4̸ 7̸5̸ 7̸6̸ 7̸7̸ 7̸8̸ ㊈ 8̸0̸
8̸1̸ 8̸2̸ ㊃ 8̸4̸ 8̸5̸ 8̸6̸ 8̸7̸ 8̸8̸ ㊉ 9̸0̸ 9̸1̸ 9̸2̸ 9̸3̸ 9̸4̸ 9̸5̸ 9̸6̸ ㊆ 9̸8̸ 9̸9̸ 1̸0̸0̸

Extra / *Sums and Differences of Cubes*

Both sums and differences of cubes can be factored, as shown by the factoring patterns at the right.

$$x^3 + y^3 = (x + y)(x^2 - xy + y^2)$$
$$x^3 - y^3 = (x - y)(x^2 + xy + y^2)$$

Exercises

1. $(x + y)(x^2 - xy + y^2) = x^3 - x^2y + xy^2 + x^2y - xy^2 + y^3 = x^3 + y^3$
2. $(x - y)(x^2 + xy + y^2) = x^3 + x^2y + xy^2 - x^2y - xy^2 - y^3 = x^3 - y^3$

1. Verify the factoring pattern for the sum of two cubes by multiplying $(x + y)(x^2 - xy + y^2)$.

2. Verify the factoring pattern for the difference of two cubes by multiplying $(x - y)(x^2 + xy + y^2)$.

Factor.

3. $(m + 2)(m^2 - 2m + 4)$
4. $(a - 4)(a^2 + 4a + 16)$
5. $(n + 5)(n^2 - 5n + 25)$
6. $27(1 - 2y)(1 + 2y + 4y^2)$

Sample $m^3 - 27 = m^3 - 3^3 = (m - 3)(m^2 + 3m + 9)$

3. $m^3 + 8$ 4. $a^3 - 64$ 5. $n^3 + 125$ 6. $27 - 216y^3$

7. **a.** Factor $w^6 - 1$ as a difference of cubes to show that
$$w^6 - 1 = (w - 1)(w + 1)(w^4 + w^2 + 1).$$

a. $w^6 - 1 = (w^2)^3 - (1)^3$
$= (w^2 - 1)(w^4 + w^2 + 1)$
$= (w - 1)(w + 1)(w^4 + w^2 + 1)$

b. Factor $w^6 - 1$ as a difference of squares to show that
$$w^6 - 1 = (w - 1)(w + 1)(w^2 + w + 1)(w^2 - w + 1).$$

b. $w^6 - 1 = (w^3)^2 - (1)^2$
$= (w^3 - 1)(w^3 + 1)$
$= (w - 1)(w^2 + w + 1) \times$
$(w + 1)(w^2 - w + 1)$
$= (w - 1)(w + 1) \times$
$(w^2 + w + 1)(w^2 - w + 1)$

c. Show that the factorizations given in parts (a) and (b) are equivalent by writing
$$w^4 + w^2 + 1 = (w^4 + 2w^2 + 1) - w^2$$
and then factoring the difference of squares on the right.

c. $w^4 + w^2 + 1 = (w^4 + 2w^2 + 1) - w^2 = (w^2 + 1)^2 - w^2$
$= (w^2 + 1 - w)(w^2 + 1 + w)$
$= (w^2 - w + 1)(w^2 + w + 1)$

Factoring Polynomials   **239**

Chapter Summary

1. Prime factors of positive integers can be found by using the primes in order as divisors. The *prime factorization* of a positive integer is the expression of the integer as a product of prime factors.

2. The *greatest common factor (GCF) of two or more integers* is the greatest integer that is a factor of all of them. The *greatest common factor of two or more monomials* is the common factor with the greatest coefficient and greatest degree in each variable.

3. The *rule for simplifying fractions* (page 189) and the *rule of exponents for division* (page 190) can be used to simplify quotients of monomials.

4. A method for multiplying binomials mentally is given on page 200.

5. The following factoring patterns are useful in factoring polynomials:

$$a^2 + 2ab + b^2 = (a + b)^2$$
$$a^2 - 2ab + b^2 = (a - b)^2$$
$$a^2 - b^2 = (a + b)(a - b)$$

6. Guidelines for factoring polynomials completely are given on page 227.

7. The *zero-product property* ($ab = 0$ if and only if $a = 0$ or $b = 0$) is useful in solving polynomial equations.

Supplementary Materials

Practice Master   31
Resource Book   p. 197

Chapter Review

Write the letter of the correct answer.

1. List all the pairs of integral factors of -111.   **5-1**
   a. $(-1)(-111)$,   **b.** $(-1)(111)$,   **c.** $(-1)(111)$,   **d.** $(1)(111)$,
   $(-3)(-37)$ $(-3)(37)$ $(1)(-111)$, $(-1)(-111)$,
                                           $(3)(-37)$ $(3)(37)$,
                                           $(-3)(37)$ $(-3)(-37)$

   (c. circled)

2. Find the prime factorization of 72.
   a. $1 \cdot 2^2 \cdot 3^2$ **b.** $2^2 \cdot 3 \cdot 6$ **c.** $2^2 \cdot 3^3$ **d.** $2^3 \cdot 3^2$

   (d. circled)

3. Find the GCF of 14 and 42.
   a. 2   **b.** 7   **c.** 14   **d.** 42

   (c. circled)

4. Simplify $\dfrac{(-5m)^2}{-5m^2}$.   **5-2**
   a. 1   **b.** -1 **c.** 5   **d.** -5

   (d. circled)

5. Find the missing factor: $-105x^3y^6 = (7xy^2)(\underline{\ ?\ })$
   a. $-112x^3y^3$ **b.** $-15y^3y^3$ **c.** $-15x^2y^4$ **d.** $-25x^2y^4$

   (c. circled)

6. Divide: $\dfrac{12c^2 - 30c + 6}{6}$ **5-3**
   a. $2c^2 - 5c$ **b.** $5c^2 - 2c + 16$ **c.** $2c^2 - 5c + 1$ **d.** 2

   (c. circled)

7. Factor $18x^3 - 63x^2 + 9x$.
   a. $9(2x^3 - 7x^2 + x)$
   b. $9x(2x^2 - 7x)$
   c. $9x(2x^2 - 7x + x)$
   d. $9x(2x^2 - 7x + 1)$

8. Express $(k - 1)(k - 1)$ as a polynomial.   5-4
   a. $k^2 + 1$ b. $2k + 1$ **c.** $k^2 - 2k + 1$ d. $k^2 + 2k + 1$

9. Express $(5m + 4n)(m + 4n)$ as a polynomial.
   a. $5m^2 + 8n^2$
   b. $5m^2 + 16n^2$
   c. $5m^2 + 24mn + 8n^2$
   d. $5m^2 + 24mn + 16n^2$

10. Express $(2m - 3n)(2m + 3n)$ as a polynomial.   5-5
    a. $2m^2 - 3n^2$
    b. $4m^2 - 9n^2$
    c. $4m^2 + 12mn - 9n^2$
    d. $4m^2 - 12mn - 9n^2$

11. Factor $49 - x^4$.
    a. $(x^2 + 7)(x^2 - 7)$
    b. $(7 + x^2)(7 - x^2)$
    c. $(x^4 + 7)(x^4 - 7)$
    d. $(7 - x^4)(7 + x^4)$

12. Express $(7r - 3s)^2$ as a polynomial.   5-6
    a. $49r^2 + 9s^2$
    b. $49r^2 - 9s^2$
    c. $49r^2 + 42rs - 9s^2$
    d. $49r^2 - 42rs + 9s^2$

13. Factor $a^2 - 2a + 1$.
    a. not possible   **b.** $(a - 1)^2$ c. $(a + 1)^2$ d. $(a - 2)^2$

14. Factor $a^2 + ab + b^2$.
    a. not possible   b. $(a + b)^2$ c. $(a - b)^2$ d. $(a + b)(a - b)$

15. Factor $y^2 - 7y + 12$.   5-7
    a. not possible   b. $(y - 12)(y - 1)$ **c.** $(y - 3)(y - 4)$

16. Factor $x^2 + 16x + 48$.
    a. $(x + 6)(x + 8)$ b. $(x + 2)(x + 24)$ **c.** $(x + 4)(x + 12)$

17. Factor $n^2 + 12n - 45$.   5-8
    a. $(n - 9)(n + 5)$ **b.** $(n + 15)(n - 3)$ c. $(n - 15)(n + 3)$

18. Factor $x^2 - 14x - 48$.
    a. not possible   b. $(x - 16)(x + 2)$ c. $(x + 4)(x - 12)$

19. Factor $8a^2 - 17a + 2$.   5-9
    a. $(2a - 2)(4a - 1)$ **b.** $(8a - 1)(a - 2)$ c. $(8a - 2)(a - 1)$

20. Factor $3(x - 2) - 4x(2 - x)$.   5-10
    a. $12x(x - 2)$ **b.** $(3 + 4x)(x - 2)$ c. $(4x - 3)(x - 2)$

21. Factor $2x^3y - 50xy$ completely.   5-11
    a. $2y(x^2 - 25x)$ b. $2xy(x - 5)^2$ **c.** $2xy(x + 5)(x - 5)$

22. Factor $m^2 - 9n^2 + 2m - 6n$ completely.
    a. $(m + 2)(m - 3n)$ **b.** $(m + 3n + 2)(m - 3n)$ c. $(m + 3n)(m - 3n)(m - 3n)$

23. Solve $5a(3a - 1)(2a + 4) = 0$.   5-12
    a. $\{0, \frac{1}{3}, -2\}$ b. $\{0, 3, -2\}$ c. $\{0, 3, -\frac{1}{2}\}$ d. $\{0, \frac{1}{3}, -\frac{1}{2}\}$

24. I am thinking of four consecutive integers. The sum of the squares of the   5-13
    second and third is 61. Find the integers.
    a. $\{4, 5, 6, 7\}$
    b. $\{-10, -9, -8, -7\}$
    c. no solution
    d. $\{-4, -5, -6, -7\}$ or $\{4, 5, 6, 7\}$

Chapter Test

List all pairs of integral factors of each integer.

1. -87 $\begin{array}{ll}(1)(-87) & (-1)(87)\\(3)(-29) & (-3)(29)\end{array}$

2. 91 $\begin{array}{ll}(1)(91) & (-1)(-91)\\(7)(13) & (-7)(-13)\end{array}$ **5-1**

Give the prime factorization of each number.

3. 420 $2^2 \cdot 3 \cdot 5 \cdot 7$

4. 168 $2^3 \cdot 3 \cdot 7$

Simplify each fraction.

5. $\dfrac{-70m^5}{-42mn^7}$ $\dfrac{5m^4}{3n^7}$

6. $\dfrac{(-3x)^4}{-39x}$ $-\dfrac{27x^3}{13}$ **5-2**

7. $\dfrac{49ab^2 - 56ab^8}{7ab^2}$ $7 - 8b^6$

8. $\dfrac{-65r^6 + 78r^4 - 52r^2}{-13r^2}$ $5r^4 - 6r^2 + 4$ **5-3**

Evaluate by factoring first.

9. $97 \times 16 - 97 \times 6$ 970

10. $82^2 + 82 \cdot 18$ 8200

Write each product as a polynomial.

11. $(5m - 1)(6m - 5)$ $30m^2 - 31m + 5$

12. $(7x - y)(8x + 9y)$ $56x^2 + 55xy - 9y^2$ **5-4**

13. $(7 - 8x)(7 + 8x)$ $49 - 64x^2$

14. $(c^4 + c^2)(c^4 - c^2)$ $c^8 - c^4$ **5-5**

15. $(x - 9)^2$ $x^2 - 18x + 81$

16. $(4m - 6n)^2$ $16m^2 - 48mn + 36n^2$ **5-6**

Decide whether each trinomial is a perfect square. If it is, factor it. If it is not, write *not a perfect square*.

17. $n^2 + 16k - 64$
not a perfect square

18. $16x^2 - 8x + 1$
$(4x - 1)^2$

19. $a^2 - 9ab + 81b^2$
not a perfect square

Factor completely. If the polynomial is not factorable, write *prime*.

20. $b^2 - 3b + 2$ $(b - 2)(b - 1)$

21. $x^2 - 2x + 4$ prime

22. $a^2 - 6ab + 8b^2$ **5-7**

23. $a^2 - 6a - 40$ $(a - 10)(a + 4)$

24. $z^2 + z - 3$ prime

25. $x^2 + 22xy - 48y^2$ **5-8**

26. $4a^2 - a - 5$ $(4a - 5)(a + 1)$

27. $6y^2 + y - 15$ $(3y + 5)(2y - 3)$

28. $7 - 23r + 6r^2$ **5-9**

29. $5(x - y) + z(y - x)$ $(5 - z)(x - y)$

30. $ax + 2x + a + 2$ $(x + 1)(a + 2)$ **5-10**

31. $x^4 - 1$ $(x^2 + 1)(x + 1)(x - 1)$

32. $x^2y - y^3$ $y(x + y)(x - y)$ **5-11**

33. $9m^3 - 63m^2 + 108m$ $9m(m - 4)(m - 3)$

34. $a^2 + a + ab + b$ $(a + b)(a + 1)$

22. $(a - 4b)(a - 2b)$ **25.** $(x + 24y)(x - 2y)$ **28.** $(7 - 2r)(1 - 3r)$

Solve.

35. $3x^2 - 41x = -60$ $\left\{\dfrac{5}{3}, 12\right\}$ **36.** $5m^2 = 85m$ $\{0, 17\}$

37. $9x^2 = 1$ $\left\{-\dfrac{1}{3}, \dfrac{1}{3}\right\}$ **5-12**

38. The length of a rectangle is 3 cm more than twice the width. The area of the rectangle is 90 cm^2. Find the dimensions of the rectangle. 15 cm by 6 cm   **5-13**

242   *Chapter 5*

Cumulative Review *(Chapters 1–5)*

Simplify. Assume that no denominator equals zero. 9. $3x^2y - x + \frac{8}{9}$

1. $-3.3 + (-27.3 + 10.6)$ −20
2. $-\frac{3}{5}\left(-\frac{9}{17}\right) + \frac{8}{5}\left(-\frac{9}{17}\right) - \frac{9}{17}$
3. $\frac{-168a}{24}$ −7a
   −m + 1
4. $(-4)^2 \div 2 + 2 - 8$ 2
5. $(2z - 3) + (3z - 4)$ 5z − 7
6. $(3m - 4) - (4m - 5)$
7. $(2a^2b)^3(3a^2b)^3$ 216a¹²b⁶
8. $\frac{-45r^3st^2}{25rst}$ $-\frac{9r^2t}{5}$
9. $\frac{27x^3y^2 - 9x^2y + 8xy}{9xy}$
10. $(6rs - 7t)(6rs + 7t)$
    36r²s² − 49t²
11. $(7a + 4)^2$
    49a² + 56a + 16
12. $-t(3t + 5)(2t - 5)$
    −6t³ + 5t² + 25t

Evaluate if $w = -\frac{1}{2}$, $x = 2$, $y = 0$, and $z = -3$.

13. $\frac{(z - 2w) - x}{-y + 1}$ −4
14. $\frac{1}{w}(xy - z)$ −6
15. $(2x + z)^x$ 1
    90 = 2 · 3² · 5; 756 = 2² · 3³ · 7; GCF = 18

16. Find the prime factorizations of 90 and 756 and then find their GCF.

17. $2p^2(3p - pr^2 + 4r^3st)$ 18. $8b(2a + 1)(2a - 1)$ 19. $(2a + 3b)^2$ 20. $(x + 13)(x + 2)$

Factor completely. If the polynomial cannot be factored, write *prime*.

17. $6p^3 - 2p^3r^2 + 8p^2r^3st$
18. $32a^2b - 8b$
19. $4a^2 + 12ab + 9b^2$
20. $x^2 + 15x + 26$
21. $m^2 - 9m + 18$
22. $k^2 - k - 42$
23. $6y^2 + 13y - 5$
24. $x^2 + 4xy + 4y^2 - 16$
25. $a^3 + a^2b - ab^2 - b^3$

21. $(m - 6)(m - 3)$ 22. $(k - 7)(k + 6)$ 23. $(3y - 1)(2y + 5)$ 24. $(x + 2y + 4)(x + 2y - 4)$

25. $(a + b)^2(a - b)$

Solve. If the equation is an identity or has no solution, say so.

26. $9c - 3 = 24$ {3}
27. $|a| - 5 = 3$ {8, −8}
28. $\frac{2}{3}m = 18$ {27}
29. $7(x - 1) = 4x + 5$ {4}
30. $\frac{1}{5}n = -2$ {−10}
31. $10 - x = -2$ {12}
32. $3m - 2 = \frac{1}{2}(8m + 6) - (m + 5)$ identity
33. $2y^2 - 32 = 0$ {−4, 4}
34. $x^2 - 6x + 15 = 6$ {3}
35. $(x + 7)(x + 1) = (x + 2)^2 + 5x$ {3}
36. $8b^2 - 10b = 3$ $\left\{-\frac{1}{4}, \frac{3}{2}\right\}$
37. $x^3 - 9x^2 + 20x = 0$ {0, 5, 4}

38. Marvin has 20 nickels and dimes. He has $\frac{2}{3}$ as many dimes as he does nickels. How many nickels and how many dimes does Marvin have? 12 nickels, 8 dimes

39. The 42 km drive from Oakdale to Ridgemont usually takes 28 min. Because highway construction requires a reduced speed limit, the trip now takes 14 min longer. Find the reduced speed limit in km/h. 60 km/h

40. The sum of the squares of two consecutive integers is 9 greater than 8 times the smaller integer. Find the integers. 4 and 5 or −1 and 0

41. The length of a rectangle is 5 greater than 3 times its width. The area of the rectangle is 22 cm². Find the length and width of the rectangle.
    length, 11 cm; width, 2 cm

Factoring Polynomials   **243**

Maintaining Skills

Review the five-step problem solving plan described on page 27.

Sample The length of a rectangle is 10 cm less than 4 times the width. If the perimeter is 1.3 m, find the dimensions of the rectangle.

Solution

Step 1 Read the problem carefully. It asks for the length and width of the rectangle. Make a sketch.

Step 2 Choose a variable and use it with the given facts to represent the unknowns described in the problem.

Let w = the width.
Then $4w - 10$ = the length.

Step 3 Write an equation based on the given facts:

The perimeter is 1.3 m
$$2w + 2(4w - 10) \overset{?}{=} 130 \qquad (1.3 \text{ m} = 130 \text{ cm})$$

Step 4 Solve the equation and find the unknowns asked for:

$$10w - 20 = 130$$
$$10w = 150$$
$$w = 15; \quad 4w - 10 = 4(15) - 10 = 50$$

Step 5 Check your results with the words of the problem. Give the answer.
∴ the length is 50 cm and the width is 15 cm. **Answer**

Use the five-step plan to solve each problem.

1. The length of a rectangle is 2 cm greater than twice its width. The area of the rectangle is 40 cm². Find the dimensions of the rectangle. 4 cm by 10 cm

2. Three consecutive integers are such that the square of the greatest is 32 less than the sum of the squares of the other two. Find the integers. 7, 8, 9; or −5, −4, −3

3. The bottom of a box is a rectangle with length 5 cm more than the width. The height of the box is 4 cm and its volume is 264 cm³. Find the dimensions of the bottom of the box. 6 cm by 11 cm

4. A painting is 6 cm longer than it is wide. The painting is to be surrounded by a mat that is 2 cm wide and covered by a piece of glass with area 352 cm². Find the dimensions of the painting. 12 cm by 18 cm

5. A ball is thrown upward with an initial speed of 19.6 m/s. When is the ball opposite a roof top that is 14.7 m high? Use the formula $h = rt - 4.9t^2$ where h is the height. (A calculator may be helpful.)
   1 s and 3 s after being thrown

Mixed Problem Solving

Solve each problem that has a solution. If a problem has no solution, explain why.

A

1. Paul earns $4 an hour working at the library and $8 an hour mowing lawns. This week he worked 25 hours and earned $164. How many hours did he work at the library? 9 h

2. The atomic number of nickel, 28, is $3\frac{1}{2}$ times the atomic number of oxygen. Find the atomic number of oxygen. 8

3. Maureen jogged 3 km less than her older sister. If each of them had jogged 4 km less, the total of their distances would have been 15 km. How far did each sister jog? Maureen, 10 km; sister, 13 km

4. The difference between the highest and lowest recorded temperatures in the Yukon is 74.6° C. If the lowest temperature is $-44.4°$ C, find the highest temperature. 30.2° C

5. The sum of two numbers is 5. The sum of their squares is 53. Find the numbers. 7 and -2

6. A can of house paint costs $4 more than a can of wall paint. If 7 cans of house paint cost the same as 9 cans of wall paint, find the cost of each type of paint. wall paint, $14; house paint, $18

7. The width of a rectangle is $\frac{2}{3}$ the length. When each dimension is decreased by 2 cm, the area is decreased by 36 cm². Find the original dimensions of the rectangle. 8 cm by 12 cm

8. I have 30 quarters and dimes worth $5.50. How many dimes do I have? No solution; unrealistic result

9. A submarine traveling 64 m below sea level dived 37 m, dived another 28 m, and then rose 70 m. Find its new depth. 59 m below sea level

10. During July, Ross made deposits of $837.26, wrote checks for $709.74, paid a service charge of $4, and received $3.70 in interest. If his new balance was $528.01, what was his balance at the beginning of the month? $400.79

B

11. A doubles tennis court has the same length as a singles court but is 9 ft wider. The length of a singles court is 3 ft less than three times the width. The area of a doubles court is 2808 ft². Find the area of a singles court. (A calculator will help you to test possible factors.) 2106 ft²

12. At 3:00 P.M. Mark left Pittsburgh and drove toward Cleveland, 208 km away. At 3:30 Carole left Cleveland and headed toward Pittsburgh, driving 2 km/h slower than Mark. If their cars passed each other at 4:30, how fast was each driving? Mark, 84 km/h; Carole, 82 km/h

13. Phil walked to and from school. On his trip home he walked 2 km/h faster and the trip took 5 min less. Find the total distance he walked. No solution; not enough information

14. Find three consecutive even integers such that half their sum is 7 less than the greatest. $-12, -10, -8$

Factoring Polynomials **245**

6 Fractions

Objectives

6-1 To simplify algebraic fractions.

6-2 To multiply algebraic fractions.

6-3 To divide algebraic fractions.

6-4 To express two or more fractions with their least common denominator.

6-5 To add and subtract algebraic fractions.

6-6 To write mixed expressions as fractions in simplest form.

6-7 To divide polynomials.

Assignment Guide

See p. T59 for Key to the format of the Assignment Guide

Day	Minimum Course	Average Course	Maximum Course
1	**6-1** 248/2–30 even	**6-1** 248/2–38 even	**6-1** 248/3–54 mult. of 3 **S** 250/*Mixed Review*
2	**6-1** 249/31–37 odd, 41–45 odd **S** 250/*Mixed Review*	**6-1** 249/39–48 **S** 250/*Mixed Review*	**6-2** 253/3–57 mult. of 3, 59 **S** 254/*Mixed Review*
3	**6-2** 253/1–23 odd, 29, 30, 35–53 odd **S** 254/*Mixed Review*	**6-2** 253/3–54 mult. of 3, 55 **S** 254/*Mixed Review*	**6-3** 256/3–45 mult. of 3 **S** 258/*Mixed Review*
4	**6-3** 256/1–19 odd, 22	**6-3** 256/2–32 even, 33, 36, 39, 42 **S** 258/*Mixed Review*	**6-4** 261/3–45 mult. of 3 **S** 262/*Mixed Review* **R** 258/*Self-Test 1*
5	**6-3** 257/21–41 odd **S** 258/*Mixed Review*	**6-4** 261/2–44 even **S** 262/*Mixed Review* **R** 258/*Self-Test 1*	**6-5** 267/3–30 mult. of 3, 31–34
6	**6-4** 261/1–31 odd, 33, 36, 37, 41 **S** 262/*Mixed Review* **R** 258/*Self-Test 1*	**6-5** 267/2–30 even, 31–33, 35–37	**6-5** 268/36–58 even **S** 268/*Mixed Review* **R** 269/*Self-Test 2*
7	**6-5** 267/1–31 odd, 35, 37, 39	**6-5** 268/34, 38–54 even **S** 268/*Mixed Review*	**6-6** 271/3–45 mult. of 3 **S** 273/*Mixed Review*
8	**6-5** 267/32–46 even **S** 268/*Mixed Review*	**6-6** 271/2–32 even **R** 269/*Self-Test 2*	**6-7** 276/2–30 even, 31, 35
9	**6-6** 271/1–37 odd **R** 269/*Self-Test 2*	**6-6** 272/34, 36, 38, 40 **S** 273/*Mixed Review* **6-7** 276/2–22 even	**6-7** 277/32–34, 36–38 **S** 277/*Mixed Review*
10	**6-6** 272/30–36 even **S** 273/*Mixed Review* **6-7** 276/1–21 odd	**6-7** 276/24–34 even **S** 277/*Mixed Review*	*Prepare for Chapter Test* **R** 277/*Self-Test 3* 280/*Chapter Review* **EP** 649/*Skills*

Assignment Guide (continued)

Day	Minimum Course	Average Course	Maximum Course
11	**6-7** 276/23–33 odd **S** 277/*Mixed Review*	*Prepare for Chapter Test* **R** 277/*Self-Test 3* 280/*Chapter Review* **EP** 649/*Skills*	*Administer Chapter 6 Test* **R** 283/*Cum. Review:* 1–39 odd **S** 285/*Preparing for College* *Entrance Exams*
12	*Prepare for Chapter Test* **R** 277/*Self-Test 3* 280/*Chapter Review* **EP** 649/*Skills*	*Administer Chapter 6 Test* **R** 283/*Cum. Review:* 1–39 odd **S** 285/*Preparing for College* *Entrance Exams*	
13	*Administer Chapter 6 Test* **R** 284/*Maintaining Skills*		

Supplementary Materials Guide

For Use with Lesson	Practice Masters	Tests	Study Guide (Reteaching)	Resource Book Tests	Resource Book Practice Exercises	Resource Book Mixed Review (MR) Applications (A) Enrichment (E)
6-1			pp. 99–100			p. 183 (A)
6-2	Sheet 33		pp. 101–102		p. 101	
6-3		Test 25	pp. 103–104			
6-4	Sheet 34		pp. 105–106		p. 102	
6-5			pp. 107–108			
6-6	Sheet 35		pp. 109–110		p. 103	
6-7	Sheet 36	Test 26	pp. 111–112		p. 104	
Chapter 6	Sheet 37	Tests 27, 28		pp. 30–33		p. 198 (E)
Cum. Rev. 4–6	Sheets 38, 39			pp. 34–35	pp. 105–106	
Cum. Rev. 1–6		Test 29		pp. 36–41	pp. 107–108	pp. 148–150 (MR)

Software

Software	Computer Activities	Test Generator
	Activities 15–18	147 test items
For Use with Lessons	6-5, 6-7	all lessons

Strategies for Teaching

Communication

This chapter requires students to apply what they already know about manipulating fractions to polynomial expressions. A review of terms like *denominator, dividend, divisor, least common denominator, numerator, quotient,* and *reciprocal* may be in order. Some problems students experience in transforming fractions with polynomials, like failing to treat expressions in parentheses as whole units, may occur because they are new to this chapter. Other problems often are the result of sloppy or careless application of familiar rules of fractions. Thus it is important to stress good reading and writing skills to ensure that students' work is organized and steps are not left out. Increased attention to neatness and organization is especially important when students add and subtract fractions with polynomial expressions.

6-1 Simplifying Fractions

It will be helpful to begin this lesson with a review of the rule for simplifying fractions (page 189). Tell students that to simplify a quotient of polynomials they must divide the numerator and the denominator by their greatest common factor.

A common error is for students to cancel single terms of binomial factors. Use the following examples to caution students against this mistake:

$$\frac{2x + 1}{x^2 + 2x + 1} \neq \frac{1}{x^2}$$

$$\frac{(3x + 2) + 1}{(3x + 2)(x + 5)} \neq \frac{1}{x + 5}$$

$$\frac{(x + 5)(x - 2) + (x - 7)(x + 1)}{(x + 5)(x - 7)} \neq (x - 2) - (x + 1)$$

When students cancel common factors have them use a line for each prime factor. Do not permit cancellations like $\dfrac{(x + 2)(2x + 5)}{(2x + 5)(x + 4)} = \dfrac{x + 2}{x + 4}$.

Emphasize the importance of recognizing factors that are opposites of each other. After discussing Example 3, ask students to name the opposite of each expression: $5 + 2t$, $2t - 5$, $5 - 2t$, $-5 - 2t$.

This lesson includes several important instructions in the discussion of the solutions in Examples 1–4, pages 247–248. Have the students read the instructions as you go over the examples and emphasize the importance of reading such helpful tips.

6-2 Multiplying Fractions

With this activity students will practice communicating mathematical ideas orally and in writing.

Have students form groups to discuss an answer to the following question: What should have been done before reaching the solution in the following problem?

$$\frac{21}{12} \cdot \frac{33}{28} = \frac{693}{336} = \frac{3 \times 3 \times 7 \times 11}{2 \times 2 \times 2 \times 2 \times 3 \times 7} = \frac{33}{16}$$

When a group agrees on an answer to the question, it should be written down by the group's recording secretary. The answer must be a clearly written English paragraph including the use of these words: numerator, denominator, common factor, and simplify.

6-3 Dividing Fractions

Have students write a definition for each word and provide an example.

1. reciprocal   2. factor
3. quotient   4. simplify

Have students give the reciprocal.

5. $\dfrac{3}{4}$ $\dfrac{4}{3}$ 6. $-\dfrac{x}{2}$ $-\dfrac{2}{x}$

7. $\dfrac{3x^2}{y^3}$ $\dfrac{y^3}{3x^2}$ 8. $\dfrac{x + y}{x - y}$ $\dfrac{x - y}{x + y}$

6-5 Adding and Subtracting Fractions

It might be helpful for students to organize their work in this lesson in the following way.

1. Factor each denominator but leave space for the multiplication.

$$\frac{x^2}{x^2 - 9} + \frac{1}{x + 3} + \frac{x}{2x + 6} =$$

$$\frac{x^2 \qquad \cdot}{(x + 3)(x - 3) \cdot} +$$

$$\frac{1 \qquad \cdot}{(x + 3) \cdot} + \frac{x \qquad \cdot}{2(x + 3)}$$

2. Write the LCD separately in factored form.
$$\text{LCD} = 2(x + 3)(x - 3)$$

3. Now complete the expression by writing the necessary factor(s) first in the denominators, checking that each denominator is the LCD.

$$\frac{x^2 \qquad \cdot 2}{(x + 3)(x - 3) \cdot 2} +$$

$$\frac{1 \qquad \cdot 2(x - 3)}{(x + 3) \cdot 2(x - 3)} + \frac{x \qquad \cdot (x - 3)}{2(x + 3) \cdot (x - 3)}$$

4. Complete the problem with the students.

6-7 Polynomial Long Division

Have students write their own definition for each word and provide an example.

1. dividend   2. divisor
3. quotient   4. remainder

References to Strategies

Problem Solving Strategies

PE: p. 273 (Recognizing patterns)
TE: p. 273

Applications

PE: pp. 246, 253, 272
TE: p. 246
RB: p. 183

Nonroutine Problems

PE: p. 249 (Exs. 39, 40); p. 254 (Challenge); p. 262 (Ex. 45); p. 263 (Challenge); pp. 267–268 (Exs. 31–34); p. 272 (Exs. 39, 44–46); p. 273 (Challenge); p. 277 (Exs. 31–38)
TE: p. T108 (Sugg. Extension, Lesson 6-2)

Communication

PE: p. 249 (Ex. 39, discussion); p. 254 (Challenge, convincing argument); p. 272 (Ex. 39, convincing argument)
TE: p. T107 (Reading Algebra, Lesson 6-1)

Thinking Skills

PE: pp. 266–268 (Recall and transfer)
TE: p. 266

Explorations

PE: pp. 278–279 (Complex fractions); p. 692 (Exploring GCF and LCM)
RB: p. 198

Connections

PE: pp. 251, 255, 259, 264 (Arithmetic); p. 273 (Discrete Math); pp. 253, 265, 267–268 (Geometry)

Using Technology

PE: pp. 250, 273 (Exs.); p. 258 (Calculator Key-In); p. 263 (Computer Key-In)
TE: pp. 250, 258, 263, 273
Computer Activities: pp. 31–40

Cooperative Learning

TE: p. T108 (Lesson 6-2)

Teaching Resources

For use in implementing the teaching strategies referenced on the previous page.

Application
Resource Book, p. 183

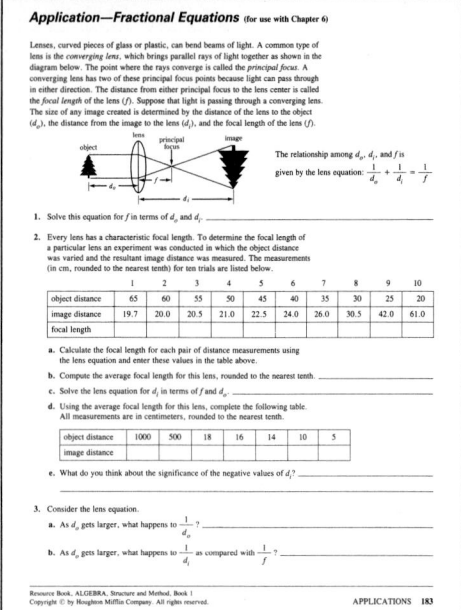

Enrichment/Exploration
Resource Book, p. 198

(Enrichment/Exploration page image — Fractions and Computers)

Reteaching/Practice
Study Guide, p. 105

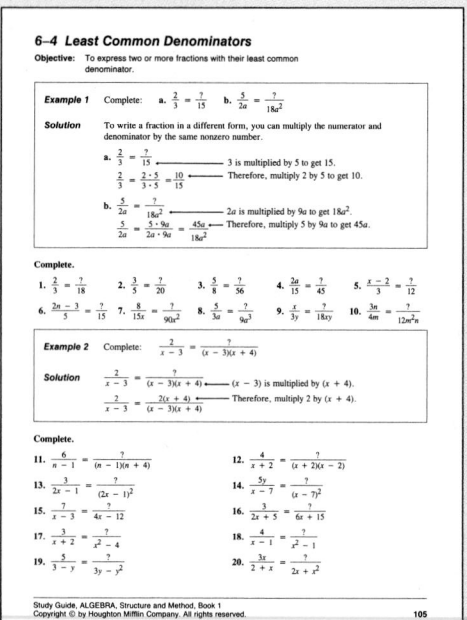

Reteaching/Practice
Study Guide, p. 107

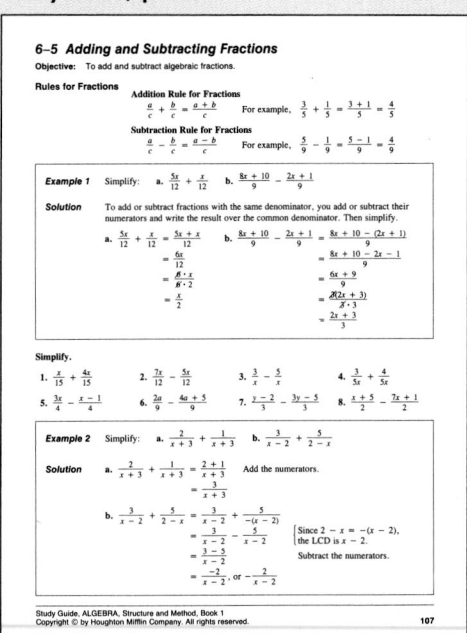

ACTIVITY 16. Exploring Unit Fractions (for use with Section 6-5)

Directions: Write all answers in the spaces provided.

PROBLEM

Can you rewrite any fraction of the form $\frac{1}{n}$ as the sum of two fractions of the form $\frac{1}{a} + \frac{1}{b}$?

PROGRAM

```
10  PRINT "WHAT IS N";
20  INPUT N
30  FOR K = N + 1 TO 2 * N
40  LET L = N * K / (K − N)
50  IF INT(L) <> L THEN 70
60  PRINT "1 /"; N; " = 1 /"; K; " + 1 /"; L
70  NEXT K
80  END
```

PROGRAM CHECK

Type in the program. To test whether you entered it correctly, run the program. Enter the number 4 after the question. The computer should print

$$1 / 4 = 1 / 5 + 1 / 20$$
$$1 / 4 = 1 / 6 + 1 / 12$$
$$1 / 4 = 1 / 8 + 1 / 8$$

These are the different ways that $\frac{1}{4}$ can be written as the sum of two unit fractions (fractions whose numerators are 1).

USING THE PROGRAM

1. For each fraction below record all the ways that it can be written as the sum of two unit fractions.

a. $\frac{1}{5}$ _____

b. $\frac{1}{9}$ _____

c. $\frac{1}{10}$ _____

2. For what values of n between 1 and 16 are there only two ways to write $\frac{1}{n}$ as the sum of two unit fractions?

_____

What is special about these values of n?

_____

(continued)

35

(Activity 16 continued)

3. What is the smallest value of n for which there are 8 ways to write $\frac{1}{n}$ as the sum of two unit fractions?

_____

Find two other values of n, less than 24, that can also be written as the sum of two unit fractions in 8 ways.

_____

ANALYSIS

4. From the data obtained in Problem 1, notice that the first rows of the solutions are

$$1 / 5 = 1 / 6 + 1 / 30$$
$$1 / 9 = 1 / 10 + 1 / 90$$
$$1 / 10 = 1 / 11 + 1 / 110$$

These data suggest that $\frac{1}{n}$ is always equal to $\frac{1}{n + 1} + \frac{1}{n(n + 1)}$. In the space below write an algebraic proof of this statement.

5. From the data obtained in Problem 1, notice that the last rows of the solutions are

$$1 / 5 = 1 / 10 + 1 / 10$$
$$1 / 9 = 1 / 18 + 1 / 18$$
$$1 / 10 = 1 / 20 + 1 / 20$$

What do these data suggest that $\frac{1}{n}$ is equal to? _____

Write an algebraic proof of your answer in the space below.

36

ACTIVITY 17. Partial Fractions (for use with Section 6-5)

Directions: Write all answers in the spaces provided.

PROBLEM

Algebraically, you can add the fractions $\frac{2}{x + 3}$ and $\frac{3}{x + 2}$ to obtain $\frac{5x + 13}{x^2 + 5x + 6}$. This result has the form $\frac{Dx + E}{x^2 + Bx + C}$ and the two original fractions have the form $\frac{M}{x + R}$ and $\frac{N}{x + S}$. Can you reverse this process? That is, can you begin with $\frac{Dx + E}{x^2 + Bx + C}$ and find two fractions of the specified form for which this is the sum?

PROGRAM

```
10  PRINT "WHAT ARE D AND E";
20  INPUT D, E
30  PRINT "WHAT ARE B AND C";
40  INPUT B, C
50  PRINT
60  FOR R = − ABS(C) TO ABS(C)
70  IF R = 0 THEN 110
80  LET S = C/R
90  IF S <> INT(S) THEN 110
100 IF R + S = B THEN 140
110 NEXT R
120 PRINT "X * X +"; B; "X + "; C; "DOES NOT FACTOR"
130 GOTO 210
140 PRINT D; "X + "; E
150 PRINT "— — — — — — — — — — — = "
160 PRINT "X * X +"; B; "X + "; C
170 PRINT
180 PRINT (E − D * R)/(S − R),(E − D * S)/(R − S)
190 PRINT "— — — — — + — "— — — — — —"
200 PRINT "X +"; R, "X +"; S
210 END
```

PROGRAM CHECK

Type in the program. To test whether you entered it correctly, run the program. After the first question, enter 5, 13. After the second question, enter 5, 6. The computer should print

```
      5X + 13
  − − − − − − − − − − − − =
    X * X + 5X + 6

      3                2
  − − − − − −   +   − − − − − −
    X + 2              X + 3
```

(continued)

37

(Activity 17 continued)

USING THE PROGRAM

Run the program to write each fraction of the form $\frac{Dx + E}{x^2 + Bx + C}$ as the sum of two fractions, or state "denominator cannot be factored."

1. $\frac{4x + 10}{x^2 + 6x + 8} =$ _____

2. $\frac{3x + 10}{x^2 + 7x + 12} =$ _____

3. $\frac{x − 5}{x^2 + x + 4} =$ _____

4. $\frac{6x − 22}{x^2 − 8x + 15} =$ _____

5. $\frac{0x + 13}{x^2 − x − 42} =$ _____

6. $\frac{20x + 200}{x^2 + 0x − 100} =$ _____

ANALYSIS

Partial fractions are a useful method for solving certain kinds of more advanced mathematical problems. In order to find two fractions whose sum is

$$\frac{Dx + E}{x^2 + Bx + C},$$

the program does several things. First it factors $x^2 + Bx + C$ into $(x + R)(x + S)$. If it cannot factor the expression, it prints an appropriate message and stops. Next it finds numbers M and N such that

$$\frac{Dx + E}{(x + R)(x + S)} = \frac{M}{x + R} + \frac{N}{x + S}$$

Finally, it prints the resulting fractions that it has found.

APPLICATION

Using algebra, add each of the following pairs of fractions to get a fraction of the form

$$\frac{Dx + E}{x^2 + Bx + C}.$$

Check your work by using the resulting fraction as input into the program.

1. $\frac{1}{x + 2} + \frac{1}{x + 3} =$ _____

2. $\frac{2}{x + 2} + \frac{4}{x + 4} =$ _____

EXTENSION

Suppose you begin with a fraction of the form $\frac{Dx + E}{x^2 + Bx + C}$ that can be simplified. For example, $\frac{x + 2}{x^2 + 5x + 6}$ simplifies to $\frac{1}{x + 3}$. What will your program print for this problem and others like it?

_____

_____

38

245f

Application

Many relationships in photography are fractional in nature. The diagram in the photo shows one such relationship.

The F-stop number on a camera corresponds to the size of the lens opening. The greater the F-stop, the smaller the hole. Shutter speeds dictate the amount of time the film will be exposed. A shutter speed of 125 means the film is exposed for 1/125 of a second.

A photographer must understand how these values affect each other. For example, as available light decreases, the shutter speed can be left constant and the F-stop value decreased, thus providing a larger hole for the light to reach the film. Essentially, with time constant, less light through a larger hole is equivalent to more intense light through a smaller hole.

Research Activities

A few students may wish to do some research to learn more about the diagram and the equation in the photo and give a report. Have them answer questions such as: What kind of lenses are there? How do cameras differ? How do cameras get images "in focus"?

Other students could take pictures with a 35 mm camera to see the effect of different combinations of shutter speeds and F-stops. They should be instructed to keep a record of the setting used for each picture. The results could be displayed on a bulletin board.

Support Materials
Resource Book p. 183

6 Fractions

A fractional equation describes the relationships among these distances: between object and lens (OB), lens and film (OB′), and lens and focal point (OF).

$$\frac{1}{OB} + \frac{1}{OB'} = \frac{1}{OF}$$

246

Algebraic Fractions

6-1 Simplifying Fractions

Objective   To simplify algebraic fractions.

When the numerator and denominator of an algebraic fraction have no common factor other than 1 and -1, the fraction is said to be in *simplest form*. To simplify a fraction, first factor the numerator and the denominator.

Example 1   Simplify $\dfrac{3a + 6}{3a + 3b}$.

Solution $\dfrac{3a + 6}{3a + 3b} = \dfrac{\cancel{3}(a + 2)}{\cancel{3}(a + b)}$ $\begin{cases} \text{Factor the numerator and denominator} \\ \text{and look for common factors.} \end{cases}$

$= \dfrac{a + 2}{a + b}$ $(a \neq -b)$ **Answer**

Remember that you cannot divide by zero. You must *restrict* the variables in a denominator by excluding any values that make the denominator equal to zero. In Example 1, a cannot equal $-b$.

Example 2   Simplify $\dfrac{x^2 - 9}{(2x + 1)(3 + x)}$.

Solution $\dfrac{x^2 - 9}{(2x + 1)(3 + x)} = \dfrac{\cancel{(x + 3)}(x - 3)}{(2x + 1)\cancel{(3 + x)}}$ $\begin{cases} x + 3 \text{ and } 3 + x \\ \text{are equal.} \end{cases}$

$= \dfrac{x - 3}{2x + 1}$ $\left(x \neq -\dfrac{1}{2}, x \neq -3\right)$ **Answer**

Note: To see which values of the variable to exclude, look at the denominator of the *original* fraction. Neither $2x + 1$ nor $3 + x$ can equal zero. Since $2x + 1 \neq 0$ and $3 + x \neq 0$, $x \neq -\frac{1}{2}$ and $x \neq -3$.

Example 3   Simplify $\dfrac{2x^2 + x - 3}{2 - x - x^2}$.

Solution   First factor the numerator and the denominator. If you don't see any common factors, look for opposites.

(Solution continues on next page.)

Teaching References
Lesson Commentary,
   pp. T107–T111
Assignment Guide,
   pp. T64–T66
Supplementary Materials
   Practice Masters 33–39
   Tests 25–29
   Resource Book
      Practice Exercises,
         pp. 101–108
      Tests, pp. 30–41
      Enrichment Activity,
         p. 198
      Mixed Review,
         pp. 148–150
      Application, p. 183
   Study Guide, pp. 99–112
   Computer Activities 15–18
   Test Generator
   California Standards
   Support Workbook
      Exploration for
         Lesson 6-4
   Alternate Test, p. T17
   Cumulative Review, p. T26

Teaching Suggestions, p. T107
Reading Algebra, p. T107
Suggested Extensions, p. T108

Warm-Up Exercises
Factor.
1. $2 - 2y$ $2(1 - y)$
2. $3a + 6b$ $3(a + 2b)$
3. $y^2 - 16$ $(y + 4)(y - 4)$
4. $6x^2 + 7x - 3$
   $(3x - 1)(2x + 3)$

Motivating the Lesson
Discuss ways to simplify the fraction $\dfrac{24}{60}$.

Algebraic fractions are simplified by similar methods, which is the topic of today's lesson.

Chalkboard Examples

Simplify. State the restrictions on the variable.

1. $\dfrac{2t + 6}{5t + 15}$ $\dfrac{2(t + 3)}{5(t + 3)} = \dfrac{2}{5}$; $t \neq -3$

2. $\dfrac{2t + 2}{t^2 - 1}$ $\dfrac{2(t + 1)}{(t + 1)(t - 1)} = \dfrac{2}{t - 1}$; $t \neq 1; t \neq -1$

3. $\dfrac{3x^2 + 5x - 2}{6 + x - x^2}$ $\dfrac{(3x - 1)(x + 2)}{(3 - x)(2 + x)} =$ $\dfrac{3x - 1}{3 - x}$; $x \neq 3; x \neq -2$

4. Solve $4kx + x = 16k^2 + 8k + 1$ for x.
   $x(4k + 1) = (4k + 1)^2$
   $\dfrac{x(4k + 1)}{4k + 1} = \dfrac{(4k + 1)^2}{4k + 1}$
   $x = 4k + 1; k \neq -\dfrac{1}{4}$

Check for Understanding

Here is a suggested use of the Oral Exercises to check students' understanding as you teach the lesson.
Oral Exs. 1–5: use after Example 2.
Oral Exs. 6–16: use after Example 3.

Guided Practice

Simplify. Give any restrictions on the variable.

1. $\dfrac{4p - 4q}{4}$ $p - q$

2. $\dfrac{5p - 5q}{5p + 5q}$ $\dfrac{p - q}{p + q}; p \neq -q$

3. $\dfrac{a^2b^2}{a^2b - b^2a}$ $\dfrac{ab}{a - b}; a \neq b; a \neq 0; b \neq 0$

4. $\dfrac{b^2 - 36}{30 + 7b - 2b^2}$ $-\dfrac{b + 6}{5 + 2b}$; $b \neq 6; b \neq -\dfrac{5}{2}$

5. $\dfrac{2x^2 - 5x - 12}{12x - 3x^2}$ $-\dfrac{2x + 3}{3x}$; $x \neq 0; x \neq 4$

$\dfrac{2x^2 + x - 3}{2 - x - x^2} = \dfrac{(x - 1)(2x + 3)}{(1 - x)(2 + x)}$ $\begin{cases} (x - 1) \text{ and } (1 - x) \text{ are opposites.} \\ (1 - x) = -(x - 1) \end{cases}$

$= \dfrac{\cancel{(x - 1)}(2x + 3)}{-\cancel{(x - 1)}(2 + x)}$

$= \dfrac{2x + 3}{-(2 + x)}$, or $-\dfrac{2x + 3}{x + 2}$ $(x \neq 1, x \neq -2)$ *Answer*

Example 4   Solve $ax - a^2 = bx - b^2$ for x.

Solution
$ax - a^2 = bx - b^2$
$ax - bx = a^2 - b^2$ $\begin{cases} \text{Collect all terms with } x \text{ on one side of the} \\ \text{equation and all other terms on the other side.} \end{cases}$
$(a - b)x = (a + b)(a - b)$ {Factor both sides of the equation.
$x = \dfrac{(a + b)(a - b)}{(a - b)}$ {Divide both sides by the coefficient of x.
$x = a + b$ $(a \neq b)$ *Answer*

Oral Exercises

Simplify. State the restrictions on the variable.   6. $\dfrac{1}{6 - x}$; $x \neq 6, x \neq -6$

1. $\dfrac{3m + 9}{m + 3}$ $3; m \neq -3$

2. $\dfrac{2n + 8}{3n + 12}$ $\dfrac{2}{3}; n \neq -4$

3. $\dfrac{a^2 - 16}{a - 4}$ $a + 4; a \neq 4$

4. $\dfrac{b^2 - 9}{b + 3}$ $b - 3; b \neq -3$

5. $\dfrac{x^2 - 2x + 1}{x - 1}$ $x - 1; x \neq 1$

6. $\dfrac{x + 6}{36 - x^2}$

7. $\dfrac{14 - 2c}{7 - c}$ $2; c \neq 7$

8. $\dfrac{2c - 2d}{2c + 2d}$ $\dfrac{c - d}{c + d}; c \neq -d$

9. $\dfrac{2t - 1}{1 - 2t}$ $-1; t \neq \dfrac{1}{2}$

10. $\dfrac{(2y - 8)^2}{(2y - 8)^3}$ $\dfrac{1}{2y - 8}; y \neq 4$

11. $\dfrac{(x + 5)^2}{5 + x}$ $x + 5; x \neq -5$

12. $\dfrac{(4 - x)(x^2 - 9)}{(x - 4)(x - 3)}$ $-(x + 3); x \neq 4, x \neq 3$

Which of the following fractions *cannot* be simplified?   14 and 16

13. $\dfrac{4x - 6y}{4x + 6y}$ $\dfrac{2x - 3y}{2x + 3y}$

14. $\dfrac{4x - 7y}{7y + 4x}$

15. $\dfrac{4x^2 - y^2}{2x - y}$ $2x + y$

16. $\dfrac{4x^2 + y^2}{2x + y}$

Written Exercises

4. $4; n \neq -4$

8. $\dfrac{6}{y - 5}; y \neq \pm 5$

Simplify. Give any restrictions on the variables.

A   1. $\dfrac{2x + 2y}{4}$ $\dfrac{x + y}{2}$

2. $\dfrac{12m - 15n}{9}$ $\dfrac{4m - 5n}{3}$

3. $\dfrac{5a - 10}{a - 2}$ $5; a \neq 2$

4. $\dfrac{4n + 16}{n + 4}$

5. $\dfrac{3n + 1}{9n + 3}$ $\dfrac{1}{3}; n \neq -\dfrac{1}{3}$

6. $\dfrac{8x - 8y}{8x + 8y}$ $\dfrac{x - y}{x + y}; x \neq -y$

7. $\dfrac{2x - 4}{x^2 - 4}$ $\dfrac{2}{x + 2}; x \neq \pm 2$

8. $\dfrac{6y + 30}{y^2 - 25}$

9. $\dfrac{2xy}{x^2y - y^2x}$

10. $\dfrac{4p^2 - 8p}{4p^3}$

11. $\dfrac{(x + 4)(2x + 1)}{(1 + 2x)(x - 3)}$

12. $\dfrac{(x - 5)(2 + 7x)}{(5 - x)(7x + 2)}$

13. $\dfrac{a^2 + 8a + 16}{16 - a^2}$

14. $\dfrac{25 - b^2}{b^2 + 12b + 35}$

15. $\dfrac{2 - y}{y^2 - 4y + 4}$

16. $\dfrac{(a - 5)^2}{25 - a^2}$

17. $\dfrac{4n^2 + 144}{6n + 36}$

18. $\dfrac{25c + 15d}{50c^2 + 30d^2}$

19. $\dfrac{2n^2 - 5n - 3}{4n^2 - 8n - 5}$

20. $\dfrac{2w^2 + w - 6}{2w + 4}$

21. $\dfrac{3x^2 + 6x}{6x^2 + 7x - 10}$

22. $\dfrac{4b^2 - 5b - 6}{8b^2 + 6b}$

23. $\dfrac{10 - 3a - a^2}{a^2 - 4}$

24. $\dfrac{2y^2 - 9y + 4}{8y - 2y^2}$

25. $\dfrac{x^2 + xy}{x^2 - xy}$

26. $\dfrac{2ab + 2ac + 4a^2}{4b + 4c + 8a}$

27. $\dfrac{r^2 - s^2}{4r^2 + rs - 5s^2}$

28. $\dfrac{3t^2 - 4tv - 7v^2}{t^2 - v^2}$

Solve for x. **35.** $2c + 3d; c \neq -\dfrac{3d}{2}$

B **29.** $cx + dx = c^2 - d^2$ $c - d; c \neq -d$

30. $ax + bx = a^2 + 2ab + b^2$ $x = a + b; a \neq -b$

31. $abx - b = ax - 1$ $\dfrac{1}{a}; a \neq 0, b \neq 1$

32. $3ax + 6 = a^2x + 2a$ $x = -\dfrac{2}{a}; a \neq 0, 3$

33. $5kx - x = 25k^2 - 10k + 1$ $5k - 1; k \neq \dfrac{1}{5}$

34. $4x - 4 = b^2 + 5b - bx$ $x = b + 1; b \neq -4$

35. $2cx + 3dx = 4c^2 + 12cd + 9d^2$

36. $2x + 5k = 6k^2 - 3kx - 6$ $x = 2k - 3; k \neq -\dfrac{2}{3}$

37. $a(x - a) + 6(x + 6) = 0$ $a - 6; a \neq -6$

38. $2n(x - n) = x - 5n + 2$ $x = n - 2; n \neq \dfrac{1}{2}$

39. Miguel wants to evaluate $\dfrac{x^2 - 4y^2}{x - 2y}$ when $x = 3$ and $y = 1$. First he simplifies the fraction to $x + 2y$. Then he substitutes $x = 3$ and $y = 1$, getting 5
for his answer. Miguel also uses the simplified form $x + 2y$ to evaluate the
given fraction when $x = 4$ and $y = 2$, getting 8 for his answer. Tell which
one of these two answers is incorrect and explain why.

40. Donna wants to simplify $\dfrac{x^2 - 4y^2}{x^2 - 2xy}$.

She gives this solution: $\dfrac{x^2 - 4y^2}{x^2 - 2xy} = \dfrac{\cancel{x^2} - 4y^2}{\cancel{x^2} - 2xy} = \dfrac{-4y^2}{-2xy} = \dfrac{2y}{x}$

Choose values of x and y to show that her solution is incorrect. Simplify
the fraction correctly.

Simplify. Give any restrictions on the variables.

41. $\dfrac{25x^2 - 36y^2}{10x^2 + 3xy - 18y^2}$

42. $\dfrac{12x^2 - 5xy - 2y^2}{4y^2 - 4xy - 3x^2}$

43. $\dfrac{6a^3 + 10a^2}{36a^3 - 100a}$

44. $\dfrac{8a^2 + 6ab - 5b^2}{16a^2 - 25b^2}$

Fractions   **249**

Summarizing the Lesson

Tell students that they have
learned to simplify algebraic
fractions and to find restrictions on the variables. Ask
students to name the steps
in simplifying fractions.

Suggested Assignments

Minimum
Day 1: 248/2–30 even
Day 2: 249/31–37 odd,
       41–45 odd
  S 250/Mixed Review
Average
Day 1: 248/2–38 even
Day 2: 249/39–48
  S 250/Mixed Review
Maximum
       248/3–54 mult. of 3
  S 250/Mixed Review

Supplementary Materials

Study Guide   pp. 99–100

Simplify. Give any restrictions on the variables.

45. $\dfrac{x(a + b) - 2(a + b)}{2 - x}$ $-a - b; x \neq 2$

46. $\dfrac{w^4 - 1}{w^4(w + 1) + (w + 1)} \cdot \dfrac{(w^2 + 1)(w - 1)}{w^4 + 1}; w \neq -1$

C **47.** $\dfrac{2x^3 - 13x^2 + 15x}{15x - 7x^2 - 2x^3}$ $\dfrac{5 - x}{5 + x}; x \neq 0, \dfrac{3}{2}, -5$

48. $\dfrac{x^4 - 10x^2 + 9}{3 - 2x - x^2}$ $(3 - x)(x + 1); x \neq -3, 1$

49. $\dfrac{4a^2 - b^2 - 2a + b}{(2a + b)^2 - 1}$ $\dfrac{2a - b}{2a + b + 1}; b \neq 1 - 2a,$ $-(2a + 1)$

50. $\dfrac{x^2 + 2x + 1 - y^2}{(x + 1)^2 + 2y(x + 1) + y^2}$ $\dfrac{x + 1 - y}{x + 1 + y};$ $x \neq -(1 + y)$

For which value(s) of x does each fraction equal zero?

51. $\dfrac{x^2 - 4}{x^2 - 4x + 4}$
$x = -2$

52. $\dfrac{3x^2 + x}{2x - x^3}$
$x = -\dfrac{1}{3}$

53. $\dfrac{x^2 - 2x - 15}{x^2 + 3x - 40}$
$x = -3$

54. $\dfrac{x^4 - x^2}{x^3 + x^2 - 2x}$
$x = -1$

Mixed Review Exercises

Simplify. Assume that no denominator equals zero.

1. $12\left(\dfrac{1}{3}u + \dfrac{1}{4}v\right)$ $4u + 3v$

2. $(-42n^2 + 28p)\left(-\dfrac{1}{4}\right)$ $\dfrac{21n}{2} - 7p$

3. $\dfrac{15a^7b^8}{30a^2b^3}$ $\dfrac{a^5b^5}{2}$

4. $\dfrac{(-3y)^5}{(y^2)^5}$ $\dfrac{-243}{y^5}$

5. $\dfrac{3x^5 + 6x^3 - 12x^2}{x^2}$ $3x^3 + 6x - 12$

6. $(-20)(-7)(-4)(-5)$ 2800

Solve.

7. $-y + 15 = 9$ $\{6\}$

8. $68 = -\dfrac{n}{5}$ $\{-340\}$

9. $5p + 8 = -47$ $\{-11\}$

10. $5(x + 2) + 2 = 27$ $\{3\}$

11. $9y - (7y + 5) = 11$ $\{8\}$

12. $(3n - 6) - (5 - 3n) = 7$ $\{3\}$

Using a Computer

Exercises 1 and 2 use a computer to evaluate fractions and to help generalize a formula from specific examples.

Computer Exercises

For students with some programming experience.

1. a. Write a BASIC program to evaluate each algebraic fraction for $x = 10$, 20, 30, 40, 50.

(1) $\dfrac{x}{x^2 + 1}$

(2) $\dfrac{x^2}{x^2 + 1}$

(3) $\dfrac{x^2}{x + 1}$

b. As the value of x increases, what happens to the value of each of these algebraic fractions? Explain why.

2. a. Write a BASIC program that uses READ . . . DATA statements to evaluate the algebraic fraction $\dfrac{x^5 + 1}{x^4 - x^3 + x^2 - x + 1}$ for $x = 2, 13, 22,$ 50, 99. 3; 14; 23; 51; 100

b. On the basis of your results in part (a), suggest a general formula that evaluates the given fraction for any value of x.

6-2 Multiplying Fractions

Objective   To multiply algebraic fractions.

The property of quotients given in Lesson 5-2 states that

$$\frac{ac}{bd} = \frac{a}{b} \cdot \frac{c}{d}.$$

You can rewrite this result to get the multiplication rule for fractions.

Multiplication Rule for Fractions

$$\frac{a}{b} \cdot \frac{c}{d} = \frac{ac}{bd}$$

Example: $\dfrac{3}{8} \cdot \dfrac{5}{2} = \dfrac{3 \cdot 5}{8 \cdot 2} = \dfrac{15}{16}$

To multiply fractions, you multiply their numerators and multiply their denominators.

Example 1   Multiply: $\dfrac{8}{9} \cdot \dfrac{3}{10}$.

Solution 1 $\dfrac{8}{9} \cdot \dfrac{3}{10} = \dfrac{8 \cdot 3}{9 \cdot 10} = \dfrac{\overset{4}{\cancel{24}}}{\underset{15}{\cancel{90}}} = \dfrac{4}{15}$ $\left\{\begin{array}{l}\text{You can multiply first} \\ \text{and then simplify.}\end{array}\right.$

Solution 2 $\dfrac{\overset{4}{\cancel{8}}}{\underset{3}{\cancel{9}}} \cdot \dfrac{\overset{1}{\cancel{3}}}{\underset{5}{\cancel{10}}} = \dfrac{4}{15}$ $\left\{\begin{array}{l}\text{You can simplify first} \\ \text{and then multiply.}\end{array}\right.$

Example 2   Multiply: **a.** $\dfrac{6x}{y^3} \cdot \dfrac{y^2}{15}$ **b.** $\dfrac{x^2 - x - 12}{x^2 - 5x} \cdot \dfrac{x^2 - 25}{x + 3}$

Solution   **a.** $\dfrac{6x}{y^3} \cdot \dfrac{y^2}{15} = \dfrac{\cancel{3} \cdot 2x}{\cancel{y^2} \cdot y} \cdot \dfrac{\cancel{y^2} \cdot 1}{\cancel{3} \cdot 5} = \dfrac{2x}{5y}$ $(y \neq 0)$

b. $\dfrac{x^2 - x - 12}{x^2 - 5x} \cdot \dfrac{x^2 - 25}{x + 3} = \dfrac{(x - 4)\cancel{(x + 3)}}{x\cancel{(x - 5)}} \cdot \dfrac{(x + 5)\cancel{(x - 5)}}{\cancel{(x + 3)}}$

$\qquad\qquad = \dfrac{(x - 4)(x + 5)}{x}$ $(x \neq 0,\ x \neq 5,\ x \neq -3)$

Answer

Another way to write the answer to Example 2(b) is $\dfrac{x^2 + x - 20}{x}$. The factored form of the answer, as shown in Example 2, is the one we'll show in this book.

Warm-Up Exercises

Simplify.

1. $\dfrac{x^2}{x^3} \cdot \dfrac{1}{x}$; $x \neq 0$

2. $\dfrac{4x^5}{12x^2} \cdot \dfrac{x^3}{3}$; $x \neq 0$

3. $\dfrac{(3c)^3}{(3c)^2}$ $3c$; $c \neq 0$

4. $\dfrac{y^2 - 16}{4 - y}$ $-y - 4$; $y \neq 4$

5. $\dfrac{2x^2 + 7x - 4}{2x - 1}$ $x + 4$; $x \neq \dfrac{1}{2}$

Motivating the Lesson

What are some ways of simplifying $\dfrac{101}{99} \cdot \dfrac{891}{505}$?
Answers will vary.
One way is to first change the numbers to binomials.
$\dfrac{(100 + 1)}{(100 - 1)} \cdot \dfrac{9(100 - 1)}{5(100 + 1)} = \dfrac{9}{5}$
Finding a way to simplify the multiplication of algebraic fractions is today's topic.

Chalkboard Examples

Multiply. Express each product in simplest form.

1. $\dfrac{3}{5} \cdot \dfrac{20}{7} \cdot \dfrac{14}{15}$

$\dfrac{\cancel{3}}{\cancel{5}} \cdot \dfrac{4 \cdot \cancel{5}}{\cancel{7}} \cdot \dfrac{2 \cdot \cancel{7}}{\cancel{3} \cdot 5} = \dfrac{8}{5}$

2. $\dfrac{12y}{z^3} \cdot \dfrac{z}{15}$

$\dfrac{\cancel{3} \cdot 4y}{\cancel{z} \cdot z^2} \cdot \dfrac{\cancel{z}}{\cancel{3} \cdot 5} = \dfrac{4y}{5z^2}$;

$z \neq 0$

(Continued)

251

3. $\dfrac{a-5}{a^3-25a} \cdot (a^2+10a+25)$

$\dfrac{a-5}{a(a^2-25)} \cdot \dfrac{(a+5)(a+5)}{1} =$

$\dfrac{\cancel{(a-5)}}{a\cancel{(a+5)}\cancel{(a-5)}} \cdot \dfrac{\cancel{(a+5)}(a+5)}{1} =$

$\dfrac{a+5}{a};\ a \neq 5;\ a \neq -5;\ a \neq 0$

4. $\left(\dfrac{2}{y}\right)^3 \quad \dfrac{2^3}{y^3} = \dfrac{8}{y^3}$

5. $\left(\dfrac{4y}{z}\right)^3 \cdot \dfrac{3z}{8y} \quad \dfrac{64y^3}{z^3} \cdot \dfrac{3z}{8y} =$

$\dfrac{\cancel{8}y \cdot 8y^2}{\cancel{z} \cdot z^2} \cdot \dfrac{3\cancel{z}}{\cancel{8y}} = \dfrac{24y^2}{z^2}$

Check for Understanding
Here is a suggested use of the Oral Exercises to check students' understanding as you teach the lesson.
Oral Exs. 1–12: use after
    Example 2.
Oral Exs. 13–16: use after
    Example 4.

Guided Practice
Multiply. Express each product in simplest form.

1. $-\dfrac{3}{8} \cdot \dfrac{16}{21} \quad -\dfrac{2}{7}$

2. $\left(-\dfrac{4}{3}\right)^2 \cdot \dfrac{15}{16} \quad \dfrac{5}{3}$

3. $\dfrac{6}{y^6} \cdot \dfrac{y^2}{18} \quad \dfrac{1}{3y^4}$

4. $\dfrac{4u^2v}{9uw} \cdot \dfrac{27w^2}{16v^3} \quad \dfrac{3uw}{4v^2}$

5. $\left(\dfrac{-y}{4}\right)^3 \quad -\dfrac{y^3}{64}$

6. $\left(\dfrac{3n}{7}\right)^2 \quad \dfrac{9n^2}{49}$

7. $-\left(\dfrac{6n}{7m^3}\right)^2 \quad -\dfrac{36n^2}{49m^6}$

8. $\left(-\dfrac{y}{2z}\right)^2 \cdot \left(-\dfrac{6z}{y}\right) \quad -\dfrac{3y}{2z}$

In Example 2(b), the denominators of $\dfrac{x^2-x-12}{x^2-5x} \cdot \dfrac{x^2-25}{x+3}$ equal zero when x is 0, 5, or -3, so the product is restricted to values of x other than 0, 5, and -3.

From now on, assume that the domains of the variables do not include values for which any denominator is zero. Therefore, it will not be necessary to show the excluded values of the variables.

In Chapter 4, you learned the rule of exponents for a power of a product:

For every positive integer m, $(ab)^m = a^m b^m$.

The rule below is similar.

Rule of Exponents for a Power of a Quotient
For every positive integer m,

$$\left(\frac{a}{b}\right)^m = \frac{a^m}{b^m}.$$

Example 3 Simplify $\left(\dfrac{x}{3}\right)^3$.

Solution $\left(\dfrac{x}{3}\right)^3 = \dfrac{x^3}{3^3}$

$= \dfrac{x^3}{27}$ *Answer*

Example 4 Simplify $\left(-\dfrac{c}{2}\right)^2 \cdot \dfrac{4}{3c}$.

Solution $\left(-\dfrac{c}{2}\right)^2 \cdot \dfrac{4}{3c} = \dfrac{c^2}{4} \cdot \dfrac{4}{3c}$

$= \dfrac{\cancel{c} \cdot c}{\cancel{4}} \cdot \dfrac{\cancel{4}}{3\cancel{c}}$

$= \dfrac{c}{3}$ *Answer*

Oral Exercises

Multiply. Express each product in simplest form.

1. $\dfrac{6}{5} \cdot \dfrac{10}{3} \quad 4$

2. $\dfrac{9}{8} \cdot \dfrac{16}{3} \quad 6$

3. $-\dfrac{3}{4} \cdot \dfrac{8}{9} \quad -\dfrac{2}{3}$

4. $\dfrac{a}{b} \cdot \dfrac{b}{a} \quad 1$

5. $\dfrac{2}{x} \cdot \dfrac{x}{14} \quad \dfrac{1}{7}$

6. $\dfrac{n}{6} \cdot \dfrac{16}{n} \quad \dfrac{8}{3}$

7. $\dfrac{5y^2}{3} \cdot \dfrac{6}{y^2} \quad 10$

8. $\dfrac{2a}{3} \cdot \dfrac{a}{4} \quad \dfrac{a^2}{6}$

9. $(3c)^2 \cdot \dfrac{4}{c} \quad 36c$

10. $\dfrac{b}{(2a)^2} \cdot \dfrac{a^2}{b} \quad \dfrac{1}{4}$

11. $\dfrac{(x-1)^2}{8} \cdot \dfrac{4}{x-1} \quad \dfrac{x-1}{2}$

12. $\dfrac{3n-2}{n^2} \cdot \dfrac{n^4}{2-3n} \quad -n^2$

Simplify.

13. $\left(\dfrac{5a}{b}\right)^2 \quad \dfrac{25a^2}{b^2}$

14. $\left(\dfrac{x}{2y}\right)^3 \quad \dfrac{x^3}{8y^3}$

15. $\left(-\dfrac{c^2}{3}\right)^2 \quad \dfrac{c^4}{9}$

16. $\left(-\dfrac{4}{n^2}\right)^3 \quad -\dfrac{64}{n^6}$

252   *Chapter 6*

Written Exercises

Multiply. Express each product in simplest form.

A 1. $\frac{4}{7} \cdot \frac{21}{8}$ $\frac{3}{2}$ 2. $\frac{4}{9} \cdot \frac{3}{16}$ $\frac{1}{12}$ 3. $\frac{15}{4} \cdot \frac{8}{9}$ $\frac{10}{3}$ 4. $-\frac{7}{2} \cdot \frac{10}{28}$ $-\frac{5}{4}$

5. $\frac{3}{5} \cdot \frac{5}{7} \cdot \frac{7}{9}$ $\frac{1}{3}$ 6. $\frac{9}{5} \cdot \frac{2}{3} \cdot \frac{15}{18}$ 1 7. $\left(-\frac{5}{2}\right)^2 \cdot \frac{8}{5}$ 10 8. $(-2)^3 \cdot \frac{35}{16}$ $-\frac{35}{2}$

9. $\frac{6}{x^2} \cdot \frac{x^3}{3}$ $2x$ 10. $\frac{5y}{2} \cdot \frac{4}{15y}$ $\frac{2}{3}$ 11. $\frac{a}{b} \cdot \frac{b}{c} \cdot \frac{c}{d}$ $\frac{a}{d}$ 12. $\frac{4}{x^2} \cdot \frac{7x}{8}$ $\frac{7}{2x}$

13. $\frac{4w}{v} \cdot \frac{v^3}{2w^2}$ $\frac{2v^2}{w}$ 14. $\frac{6a}{11b^4} \cdot \frac{22b}{3a^3}$ $\frac{4}{a^2b^3}$ 15. $\frac{4d^2e}{9ef} \cdot \frac{f^2}{6d}$ $\frac{2df}{27}$ 16. $\frac{2rs^2}{3t} \cdot \frac{9t^2}{4rs}$ $\frac{3st}{2}$

Simplify.

17. $\left(\frac{a}{6}\right)^2$ $\frac{a^2}{36}$ 18. $\left(\frac{c}{5}\right)^3$ $\frac{c^3}{125}$ 19. $\left(\frac{2n}{7}\right)^2$ $\frac{4n^2}{49}$ 20. $\left(\frac{4x}{3}\right)^2$ $\frac{16x^2}{9}$

21. $\left(\frac{2a}{5b^3}\right)^2$ $\frac{4a^2}{25b^6}$ 22. $\left(\frac{4m}{7n^2}\right)^2$ $\frac{16m^2}{49n^4}$ 23. $\left(\frac{-x^2}{10}\right)^4$ $\frac{x^8}{10,000}$ 24. $-\left(\frac{5b^4}{6}\right)^2$ $-\frac{25b^8}{36}$

25. $\left(\frac{a}{b}\right)^2 \cdot \frac{b}{a}$ $\frac{a}{b}$ 26. $\left(\frac{3x}{y}\right)^3 \cdot \frac{y^2}{9}$ $\frac{3x^3}{y}$ 27. $\left(-\frac{x}{4y}\right)^2 \cdot \left(-\frac{4y}{x}\right)$ $-\frac{x}{4y}$ 28. $\left(\frac{3z}{y}\right)^3 \cdot \frac{2yz}{15}$ $\frac{18z^4}{5y^2}$

29. Find the area of a square if each side has length $\frac{2x}{7}$ in. $\frac{4x^2}{49}$ in.^{2}

30. Find the volume of a cube if each edge has length $\frac{4n}{5}$ in. $\frac{64n^3}{125}$ in.^{3}

31. A triangle has base $\frac{3x}{4}$ cm and height $\frac{8}{9x}$ cm. What is its area? $\frac{1}{3}$ cm^2

32. If you travel for $\frac{7t}{60}$ hours at $\frac{80r}{9}$ mi/h, how far have you gone? $\frac{28rt}{27}$ mi.

B 33. Find the total dollar cost of $\frac{4y}{3}$ eggs if they cost d dollars per dozen. $\frac{dy}{9}$ dollars

34. Find the total dollar cost of n dozen pencils if each pencil costs $\frac{2c}{3}$ cents. $\frac{2cn}{25}$ dollars

Simplify.

35. $\frac{c+2}{c^2} \cdot \frac{3c}{c^2-4}$ $\frac{3}{c(c-2)}$ 36. $\frac{x^2-1}{16x} \cdot \frac{4x^2}{5x+5}$ $\frac{x(x-1)}{20}$

37. $\frac{a^2-x^2}{a^2} \cdot \frac{a}{3x-3a}$ $-\frac{a+x}{3a}$ 38. $\frac{3r-rt}{6r^2t} \cdot \frac{3}{9-t^2}$ $\frac{1}{2rt(3+t)}$

39. $(4b^2-3b) \cdot \frac{5b^2}{40b^3-30b^2}$ $\frac{b}{2}$ 40. $\frac{2y}{3y^2+15y} \cdot (3y^3-75y)$ $2y(y-5)$

41. $\frac{10x^4}{6x-12} \cdot \frac{x^2-x-2}{4x}$ $\frac{5x^3(x+1)}{12}$ 42. $\frac{2x^2+5x-3}{x+2} \cdot \frac{9x+18}{1-2x}$ $-9(x+3)$

43. $\frac{n^2-3n+2}{n^2+3n+2} \cdot \frac{8n+8}{4n+8}$ $\frac{2(n-1)(n-2)}{(n+2)^2}$ 44. $\frac{x^2+4x-21}{x^2-6x-16} \cdot \frac{x^2-8x+15}{x^2+9x+14}$ $\frac{(x-3)^2(x-5)}{(x+2)^2(x-8)}$

Fractions   253

9. Find the area of a rectangle if its length is $\frac{x}{8}$ cm and its width is $\frac{4x}{5}$ cm.

$$\frac{x}{8} \cdot \frac{4x}{5} = \frac{x^2}{10}; \ \frac{x^2}{10} \text{ cm}^2$$

Summarizing the Lesson

Tell students that they have learned to multiply fractions and to apply the rule of exponents for a power of a quotient. Ask students to give examples of the multiplication rule for algebraic fractions and the rule of exponents for a power of a quotient.

Suggested Assignments

Minimum
   253/1–23 odd, 29, 30,
     35–53 odd
S 254/Mixed Review
Average
   253/3–54 mult. of 3, 55
S 254/Mixed Review
Maximum
   253/3–57 mult. of 3, 59
S 254/Mixed Review

Common Errors

In multiplying and simplifying fractions, students sometimes forget to write a simplified fractional factor or do not include all factors in their answers. In reteaching, encourage students who make such errors to take the time to write down all steps and to use enough space to show their work.

Supplementary Materials

Study Guide   pp. 101–102
Practice Master   33
Resource Book   p. 101

Simplify.

45. $\dfrac{t^2 - 2t - 8}{4 - t^2} \cdot \dfrac{t^2 - 5t + 6}{t^2 - t - 12}$

46. $\dfrac{a^2 - 7a + 6}{2a^3 - 3a^2} \cdot \dfrac{4a^3 - 9a}{a^2 - 10a + 24}$

47. $\dfrac{3x^2 - 14x - 5}{8x^2 - 12x} \cdot \dfrac{8x^2 - 18}{3x^2 + 4x + 1}$

48. $\dfrac{25 - 16y^2}{6y^3 - 36y^2} \cdot \dfrac{10y + 8y^2}{10 - 3y - 4y^2}$

49. $\dfrac{3d^2 - 9d + 6}{2d^2 - 10d + 12} \cdot \dfrac{6 - 2d}{3 - 3d}$

50. $\dfrac{4c^2 - 8c - 5}{12c^2 + 46c + 40} \cdot \dfrac{20 + 8c}{5 - 2c}$

51. $\left(\dfrac{x - 2}{2}\right)^2 \cdot \left(\dfrac{2}{x - 2}\right)^3$

52. $\left(\dfrac{2n - 1}{3}\right)^4 \cdot \left(\dfrac{9}{2n - 1}\right)^2$

53. $\left(\dfrac{x - y}{x + y}\right)^2 \cdot \dfrac{x^2 + y^2}{x^2 - y^2}$

54. $\dfrac{4a^2 - b^2}{4c^2 - d^2} \cdot \left(\dfrac{2c - d}{2a + b}\right)^2$

C 55. $\dfrac{9x^2 - 1}{6x^2} \cdot \dfrac{12x^2 + 12x}{(1 - 3x)^2} \cdot \dfrac{6 - 18x}{3x^2 + 4x + 1}$

56. $\dfrac{4n^2 - 4}{1 + n^2} \cdot \dfrac{1 - n}{2n} \cdot \dfrac{1 - 2n^2 + n^4}{2 + 2n}$

57. $\dfrac{x^3 + 3x^2 - 4x - 12}{2x^2 - 18} \cdot \dfrac{x^3 - 3x^2 + 3x - 9}{3x^3 - 12x}$

58. $\dfrac{a^2 - (b - c)^2}{2a - 2b + 2c} \cdot \dfrac{6a - 6b + 6c}{b^2 - (a - c)^2}$

59. Find all values of x for which $\dfrac{2x^3 - 2x}{3x^3} \cdot \dfrac{9}{x^2 + 3x + 2}$ is equal to zero.

Mixed Review Exercises

Factor completely.

1. $a^2 + 14a + 45$ $(a + 9)(a + 5)$

2. $x^2 - 7x + 10$ $(x - 5)(x - 2)$

3. $16x^4 - 81$

3. $(2x - 3)(2x + 3)(4x^2 + 9)$

4. $2x^2 + 5x + 1$ prime

5. $625y^2 - 4z^2$

6. $64 + 16c + c^2$

7. $xy + 3y - 4xz - 12z$

8. $9x^2 - 12x + 4$

9. $3x^2 + 14x - 5$

10. $x^4 + 7x^2 - 8x^3$

11. $n^2 + 5n - 14$

12. $y^2 - 5y - 24$

5. $(25y - 2z)(25y + 2z)$ **6.** $(8 + c)^2$ **7.** $(y - 4z)(x + 3)$ **8.** $(3x - 2)^2$
9. $(3x - 1)(x + 5)$ **10.** $x^2(x - 7)(x - 1)$ **11.** $(n - 2)(n + 7)$ **12.** $(y - 8)(y + 3)$

Challenge

What is wrong with this "proof" that $2 = 1$?

$$r = s$$
$$r^2 = rs$$
$$r^2 - s^2 = rs - s^2$$
$$(r + s)(r - s) = s(r - s)$$
$$r + s = s$$
$$s + s = s$$
$$2s = s$$
$$2 = 1$$

The "proof" requires division of both sides by $(r - s)$. But if $r = s$, then $r - s = 0$, and division by zero is undefined.

6-3 Dividing Fractions

Objective   To divide algebraic fractions.

To divide by a real number, you multiply by its reciprocal. You use the same rule to divide algebraic fractions.

Division Rule for Fractions

$$\frac{a}{b} \div \frac{c}{d} = \frac{a}{b} \cdot \frac{d}{c}$$

Example: $\frac{5}{8} \div \frac{2}{9} = \frac{5}{8} \cdot \frac{9}{2} = \frac{45}{16}$

To divide by a fraction, you multiply by its reciprocal.

Example 1   Divide: $\frac{x}{2y} \div \frac{xy}{4}$

Solution $\frac{x}{2y} \div \frac{xy}{4} = \frac{x}{2y} \cdot \frac{4}{xy}$ {Multiply by the reciprocal.

$= \frac{\cancel{x}}{2 \cdot y} \cdot \frac{2 \cdot 2}{\cancel{x} \cdot y}$ {Factor and simplify.

$= \frac{2}{y^2}$ **Answer**

Example 2   Divide: **a.** $\frac{18}{x^2 - 25} \div \frac{24}{x + 5}$ **b.** $\frac{x^2 + 3x - 10}{2x + 6} \div \frac{x^2 - 4}{x^2 - x - 12}$

Solution   **a.** $\frac{18}{x^2 - 25} \div \frac{24}{x + 5} = \frac{18}{x^2 - 25} \cdot \frac{x + 5}{24}$

$= \frac{\cancel{6} \cdot 3}{(x + 5)(x - 5)} \cdot \frac{x + 5}{\cancel{6} \cdot 4}$

$= \frac{3}{4(x - 5)}$ **Answer**

b. $\frac{x^2 + 3x - 10}{2x + 6} \div \frac{x^2 - 4}{x^2 - x - 12} = \frac{x^2 + 3x - 10}{2x + 6} \cdot \frac{x^2 - x - 12}{x^2 - 4}$

$= \frac{(x + 5)(x - 2)}{2(x + 3)} \cdot \frac{(x + 3)(x - 4)}{(x + 2)(x - 2)}$

$= \frac{(x + 5)(x - 4)}{2(x + 2)}$ **Answer**

To simplify an expression that involves more than one operation, follow the order of operations on page 142, as shown in Example 3.

Fractions   **255**

Teaching Suggestions p. T109

Suggested Extensions p. T109

Warm-Up Exercises

Give definitions for each word.

1. reciprocal See Glossary.
2. factor
3. quotient

Give the reciprocal.

4. $\frac{3}{4}$ $\frac{4}{3}$ 5. $-\frac{x}{2}$ $-\frac{2}{x}$

6. $\frac{3x^2}{y^3}$ $\frac{y^3}{3x^2}$ 7. $\frac{x + y}{x - y}$ $\frac{x - y}{x + y}$

Motivating the Lesson

A rectangle has an area of 10, and its width is $\frac{x}{7}$. Find an expression for its length. $A = l \cdot w, \ l = A \div w; \ l = 10 \div \frac{x}{7} = \frac{70}{x}$

Dividing algebraic fractions is today's lesson.

Chalkboard Examples

Divide. Give your answers in simplest form.

1. $\frac{2p}{q} \div \frac{8p}{5q}$

$\frac{2p}{q} \cdot \frac{5q}{8p} = \frac{\cancel{2} \cdot \cancel{p}}{\cancel{q}} \cdot \frac{5 \cdot \cancel{q}}{\cancel{2} \cdot 4 \cdot \cancel{p}} = \frac{5}{4}$

2. $\frac{5t - 10}{t - 5} \div \frac{t - 2}{2}$

$\frac{5t - 10}{t - 5} \cdot \frac{2}{t - 2} = $

$\frac{5(t - 2)}{t - 5} \cdot \frac{2}{t - 2} = \frac{10}{t - 5}$

3. $\frac{y^2 + 3y - 10}{y^2 - 16} \div \frac{2y - 4}{y + 4}$

$\frac{y^2 + 3y - 10}{y^2 - 16} \cdot \frac{y + 4}{2y - 4} = $

$\frac{(y + 5)(y - 2)}{(y + 4)(y - 4)} \cdot \frac{y + 4}{2(y - 2)} = $

$\frac{y + 5}{2(y - 4)}$

(continued)

255

4. $\dfrac{a^2}{b} \cdot \dfrac{2a}{b} \div \left(\dfrac{a}{b}\right)^3$

$\dfrac{a^2}{b} \cdot \dfrac{2a}{b} \cdot \dfrac{b^3}{a^3} =$

$\dfrac{\cancel{a^2}}{\cancel{b}} \cdot \dfrac{2 \cdot \cancel{a}}{\cancel{b}} \cdot \dfrac{\cancel{b} \cdot \cancel{b} \cdot b}{\cancel{a} \cdot \cancel{a^2}} = 2b$

Check for Understanding

Here is a suggested use of the Oral Exercises to check students' understanding as you teach the lesson.
Oral Exs. 1–8: use after Example 1.
Oral Exs. 9–12: use after Example 3.

Guided Practice

Divide. Give your answers in simplest form.

1. $\dfrac{-4}{5} \div \dfrac{-12}{5}$ $\dfrac{1}{3}$

2. $\dfrac{4y}{7} \div \dfrac{y}{14}$ 8

3. $\dfrac{5n}{7} \div \dfrac{10n}{21}$ $\dfrac{3}{2}$

4. $\dfrac{3x^2}{4y^2} \div \dfrac{x}{12xy}$ $\dfrac{9x^2}{y}$

5. $\dfrac{a^2b}{4} \div 2ab^2$ $\dfrac{a}{8b}$

6. $2 \div \left(\dfrac{4y}{5}\right)^2$ $\dfrac{25}{8y^2}$

7. $\dfrac{3+3y}{6} \div \dfrac{1+y}{9}$ $\dfrac{9}{2}$

8. $\dfrac{y^2-16}{4y} \div \dfrac{y-4}{20}$ $\dfrac{5(y+4)}{y}$

9. $\dfrac{1}{a-b} \div \dfrac{1}{b-a}$ -1

10. $\dfrac{y^2-1}{y^2-4} \div \dfrac{y^2+y-2}{y^2-y-2}$ $\dfrac{(y+1)^2}{(y+2)^2}$

Summarizing the Lesson

Tell students that they have learned to divide algebraic fractions in this lesson. Ask students to give the rule for dividing fractions.

Example 3 Simplify $\left(\dfrac{2x}{y}\right)^3 \div \dfrac{x}{y^2} \cdot \dfrac{x}{4}$.

Solution $\left(\dfrac{2x}{y}\right)^3 \div \dfrac{x}{y^2} \cdot \dfrac{x}{4} = \dfrac{8x^3}{y^3} \cdot \dfrac{y^2}{x} \cdot \dfrac{x}{4}$

$= \dfrac{\cancel{4} \cdot 2 \cdot x^3}{y \cdot \cancel{y^2}} \cdot \dfrac{\cancel{y^2}}{\cancel{x}} \cdot \dfrac{\cancel{x}}{\cancel{4}}$

$= \dfrac{2x^3}{y}$ *Answer*

Oral Exercises

Simplify.

1. $\dfrac{5}{7} \div \dfrac{4}{7}$ $\dfrac{5}{4}$

2. $\dfrac{7}{2} \div \dfrac{4}{5}$ $\dfrac{35}{8}$

3. $-\dfrac{1}{4} \div \left(-\dfrac{2}{3}\right)$ $\dfrac{3}{8}$

4. $-\dfrac{4}{7} \div \dfrac{2}{5}$ $-\dfrac{10}{7}$

5. $\dfrac{a}{b} \div \dfrac{c}{d}$ $\dfrac{ad}{bc}$

6. $\dfrac{x}{y} \div \dfrac{y}{x}$ $\dfrac{x^2}{y^2}$

7. $6a \div \dfrac{2}{a}$ $3a^2$

8. $\dfrac{c}{2} \div 2c$ $\dfrac{1}{4}$

9. $\dfrac{y^2}{4} \div \dfrac{y^3}{16}$ $\dfrac{4}{y}$

10. $y \div \dfrac{1}{3y^2}$ $3y^3$

11. $\dfrac{1}{2} \cdot \dfrac{1}{3} \div \dfrac{1}{4}$ $\dfrac{2}{3}$

12. $\dfrac{a}{b} \div \dfrac{c}{d} \cdot \dfrac{e}{f}$ $\dfrac{ade}{bcf}$

Written Exercises

Divide. Give your answers in simplest form.

A 1. $\dfrac{6}{5} \div \dfrac{9}{10}$ $\dfrac{4}{3}$

2. $\dfrac{2}{3} \div \dfrac{5}{9}$ $\dfrac{6}{5}$

3. $\dfrac{a}{6} \div \dfrac{a}{3}$ $\dfrac{1}{2}$

4. $\dfrac{3x}{5} \div \dfrac{x}{15}$ 9

5. $\dfrac{x}{y^2} \div \dfrac{x^2}{y}$ $\dfrac{1}{xy}$

6. $\dfrac{3n^2}{5} \div \dfrac{9n}{20}$ $\dfrac{4n}{3}$

7. $\dfrac{ab}{6} \div \dfrac{b}{a}$ $\dfrac{a^2}{6}$

8. $\dfrac{c}{2d} \div \dfrac{d}{8c}$ $\dfrac{4c^2}{d^2}$

9. $\dfrac{3x^2}{4y} \div \dfrac{xy}{18}$ $\dfrac{27x}{2y^2}$

10. $\dfrac{2n}{3m^2} \div \dfrac{1}{12mn}$ $\dfrac{8n^2}{m}$

11. $\dfrac{xy^2}{3} \div xy$ $\dfrac{y}{3}$

12. $\dfrac{9a^2}{2b} \div 6ab$ $\dfrac{3a}{4b^2}$

13. $1 \div \left(\dfrac{3x}{5}\right)^2$ $\dfrac{25}{9x^2}$

14. $4 \div \left(\dfrac{2}{n}\right)^3$ $\dfrac{n^3}{2}$

15. $\dfrac{2+2b}{6} \div \dfrac{1+b}{9}$ 3

16. $\dfrac{6n-2}{6n} \div \dfrac{3n-1}{27}$ $\dfrac{9}{n}$

17. $\dfrac{x^2-1}{2} \div \dfrac{x+1}{16}$ $8(x-1)$

18. $\dfrac{m^2-9}{2m} \div \dfrac{m-3}{10}$ $\dfrac{5(m+3)}{m}$

19. $\dfrac{1}{x-y} \div \dfrac{1}{y-x}$ -1

20. $\dfrac{1}{8-2a} \div \dfrac{5}{3a-12}$ $-\dfrac{3}{10}$

256   *Chapter 6*

Divide. Give your answers in simplest form.

21. $\dfrac{2x + 2y}{x^2} \div \dfrac{x^2 - y^2}{4x}$ $\dfrac{8}{x(x - y)}$

22. $\dfrac{3}{n^2 - 9} \div \dfrac{3n - 9}{n + 3}$ $\dfrac{1}{(n - 3)^2}$

23. $\dfrac{w^2 - 4}{w^2 - 1} \div \dfrac{w^2 - w - 2}{w^2 + w - 2}$ $\dfrac{(w + 2)^2}{(w + 1)^2}$

24. $\dfrac{x^2 - x - 20}{5x - 25} \div \dfrac{x^2 + 4x - 5}{x^2 - 25}$ $\dfrac{(x + 4)(x - 5)}{5(x - 1)}$

B 25. $\dfrac{4x^2 - 25}{x^2 - 16} \div \dfrac{12x + 30}{2x^2 + 8x}$ $\dfrac{x(2x - 5)}{3(x - 4)}$

26. $\dfrac{2x - y}{2y - x} \div \dfrac{4x^2 - y^2}{4y^2 - x^2}$ $\dfrac{2y + x}{2x + y}$

27. $\dfrac{c^4 - d^4}{5c - 5d} \div \dfrac{c^2 + d^2}{5}$ $c + d$

28. $\dfrac{8 - 2p^4}{3p^4} \div \dfrac{2 + p^2}{6p^2}$ $\dfrac{4(2 - p^2)}{p^2}$

29. $\dfrac{r^2 - t^2}{r^2 + t^2} \div (r + t)$ $\dfrac{r - t}{r^2 + t^2}$

30. $\dfrac{3 - 3n}{n^2 + 2n - 3} \div (2n - 2)$ $-\dfrac{3}{2(n + 3)(n - 1)}$

31. $\dfrac{6 + x - x^2}{x^2 - 13x + 42} \div \dfrac{2x^2 - 5x - 3}{2x^2 - 13x - 7}$ $-\dfrac{(2 + x)}{(x - 6)}$

32. $\dfrac{2x^2 - 11x + 12}{27 - 18x} \div \dfrac{x^3 + 4x^2}{6x^3 - 96x}$ $-\dfrac{2(x - 4)^2}{3x}$

Simplify.

33. a. $\dfrac{3}{8} \cdot \left(\dfrac{2}{3} \div \dfrac{1}{4}\right)$ 1

   b. $\dfrac{3}{8} \cdot \dfrac{2}{3} \div \dfrac{1}{4}$ 1

34. a. $\dfrac{1}{2} \div \dfrac{1}{5} \cdot \dfrac{3}{4}$ $\dfrac{15}{8}$

   b. $\dfrac{1}{2} \div \left(\dfrac{1}{5} \cdot \dfrac{3}{4}\right)$ $\dfrac{10}{3}$

35. a. $\dfrac{r}{5} \div \dfrac{t}{r} \cdot \dfrac{5}{t^2}$ $\dfrac{r^2}{t^3}$

   b. $\dfrac{x}{y^2} \cdot \dfrac{2}{x^2} \div \dfrac{x}{y}$ $\dfrac{2}{x^2 y}$

36. a. $\left(\dfrac{n}{2}\right)^2 \div \dfrac{n}{4} \cdot \dfrac{n}{3}$ $\dfrac{n^2}{3}$

   b. $(2c)^3 \cdot \dfrac{3c}{d} \div \dfrac{6c^3}{d}$ $4c$

37. $\dfrac{c - d}{c + 2d} \cdot \dfrac{2d + c}{d + c} \div \dfrac{d - c}{d + c}$ -1

38. $\dfrac{r^2}{r^2 - s^2} \cdot \dfrac{r - s}{r + s} \div \left(\dfrac{r}{r + s}\right)^2$ 1

39. $\dfrac{2q - 6}{3} \div \left(\dfrac{3 - q}{6}\right)^2$ $\dfrac{-24}{3 - q}$

40. $\left(\dfrac{2p - 7}{9}\right)^3 \div \left(\dfrac{7 - 2p}{3}\right)^4$ $\dfrac{-1}{9(7 - 2p)}$

41. $\dfrac{1}{ab} \div \dfrac{1}{ab^2} \div \dfrac{1}{a^2b}$ a^2b^2

42. $\dfrac{6y}{6y - 14} \div \dfrac{21}{9y - 21} \div \dfrac{y^2}{35}$ $\dfrac{15}{y}$

C 43. $\dfrac{x^2 - 2x}{x^2 - 3x - 4} \cdot \dfrac{x^2 - 25}{x^2 - 4x - 5} \div \dfrac{x^2 + 5x}{5x^2 + 10x + 5}$ $\dfrac{5(x - 2)}{x - 4}$

44. $\dfrac{b^2 + 6b - 7}{6b^2 - 7b - 20} \cdot \dfrac{2b^2 + b - 15}{b^2 + 2b - 3} \div \dfrac{b^2 + 5b - 14}{3b^2 - 2b - 8}$ 1

45. $\dfrac{2d + 2c - cd - c^2}{2 + d} \div \dfrac{d^2 - c^2}{2 + c} \cdot \dfrac{c - d}{c^2 - 4}$ $\dfrac{1}{2 + d}$

46. $\dfrac{x^2 + 2xy + y^2 - 16}{16x^4 - 16y^4} \div \dfrac{x + y - 4}{4x^2 + 4y^2} \cdot \dfrac{x + y}{x + y + 4}$ $\dfrac{1}{4(x - y)}$

Fractions **257**

Suggested Assignments

Minimum
Day 1: 256/1–19 odd, 22
Day 2: 257/21–41 odd
   S 258/Mixed Review
Average
   256/2–32 even, 33,
      36, 39, 42
   S 258/Mixed Review
Maximum
   256/3–45 mult. of 3
   S 258/Mixed Review

Supplementary Materials

Study Guide   pp. 103–104
Test Master   25

258

Mixed Review Exercises

Solve.

1. $4k = 5k - 13$ {13} 2. $4p + 20 = 48$ {7} 3. $(5b - 2) - (3 - 2b) = 9$ {2}

4. $\frac{1}{2}(6x - 2) = 5$ {2} 5. $2n^3 - 8n = 0$ {0, 2, −2} 6. $3x^2 + x = 4$ $\left\{-\frac{4}{3}, 1\right\}$

Give the prime factorization of each number.

7. 256 2^8 8. 156 $2^2 \cdot 3 \cdot 13$ 9. 120 $2^3 \cdot 3 \cdot 5$ 10. 1350 $2 \cdot 3^3 \cdot 5^2$

Self-Test 1

Simplify. Give any restrictions on the variable.

1. $\dfrac{15c - 5c^2}{3c - c^2}$ 5; $c \neq 0,\ c \neq 3$ 2. $\dfrac{4a^2 - 9}{6a^2 + 13a + 6}$ $\dfrac{2a - 3}{3a + 2}$; $a \neq -\dfrac{2}{3},\ a \neq -\dfrac{3}{2}$ **Obj. 6-1, p. 247**

Simplify.

3. $\dfrac{42a}{6c^3} \cdot \dfrac{-4c}{3a^2b}$ $\dfrac{-28}{3abc^2}$ 4. $\left(\dfrac{2x}{3}\right)^3 \cdot \dfrac{27}{48x}$ $\dfrac{x^2}{6}$ **Obj. 6-2, p. 251**

5. $\dfrac{4x^2}{y} \div \dfrac{2xy}{7}$ $\dfrac{14x}{y^2}$ 6. $\dfrac{x^2 - 4}{x^2 - x - 6} \div \dfrac{x - 2}{2x}$ $\dfrac{2x}{x - 3}$ **Obj. 6-3, p. 255**

Check your answers with those at the back of the book.

Calculator Key-In

You can use a calculator to evaluate algebraic fractions for given values of their variables. First evaluate the denominator and store its value in the calculator's memory. (You may want to review the method for evaluating a polynomial given on page 203.) Then evaluate the numerator and divide by what is stored in memory (that is, the value of the denominator).

Evaluate each fraction for the given value of the variable.

1. $\dfrac{5n - 16}{2n}$; $n = 5$ 0.9 2. $\dfrac{7a + 20}{3a}$; $a = 4$ 4

3. $\dfrac{7x^2 + 4x + 12}{x}$; $x = 9$ 68.333333 4. $\dfrac{4m^2 + 11m - 60}{2m + 8}$; $m = -6$ −4.5

5. $\dfrac{a^2 + 8a - 10}{2a}$; $a = 0.5$ −5.75 6. $\dfrac{5y^2 - 22y + 30}{6y - 10}$; $y = -2$ −4.2727273

258 *Chapter 6*

Adding and Subtracting Fractions

Explorations, p. 692

Teaching Suggestions, p. T109

Suggested Extensions, p. T110

6-4 Least Common Denominators

Objective   To express two or more fractions with their least common denominator.

You have learned that you can write a fraction in simpler form by *dividing* its numerator and denominator by the same nonzero number.

$$\frac{bc}{bd} = \frac{c}{d} \quad (b \neq 0)$$

You can rewrite this rule as

$$\frac{c}{d} = \frac{bc}{bd} \quad (b \neq 0)$$

Using this form of the rule, you can write a fraction in a different form by *multiplying* its numerator and denominator by the same nonzero number.

Example 1   Complete: $\frac{3}{7} = \frac{?}{35}$

Solution $\frac{3}{7} = \frac{?}{35}$ ⟵——— 7 is multiplied by 5 to get 35.

$\frac{3}{7} = \frac{3 \cdot 5}{7 \cdot 5} = \frac{15}{35}$ ⟵— Therefore, multiply 3 by 5 to get 15.

Example 2   Complete: $\frac{8}{3a} = \frac{?}{18a^2}$

Solution $\frac{8}{3a} = \frac{?}{18a^2}$ ⟵——— $3a$ is multiplied by $6a$ to get $18a^2$.

$\frac{8}{3a} = \frac{8 \cdot 6a}{3a \cdot 6a} = \frac{48a}{18a^2}$ ⟵— Therefore, multiply 8 by $6a$ to get $48a$.

Example 3   Complete: $\frac{2}{x - 5} = \frac{?}{(x - 5)(x + 1)}$

Solution $\frac{2}{x - 5} = \frac{?}{(x - 5)(x + 1)}$ ⟵——— $x - 5$ is multiplied by $x + 1$.

$\frac{2}{x - 5} = \frac{2(x + 1)}{(x - 5)(x + 1)} = \frac{2(x + 1)}{(x - 5)(x + 1)}$ ⟵— Therefore, multiply 2 by $x + 1$.

Fractions   **259**

Warm-Up Exercises

Complete.

1. $3 \cdot \underline{\ ?\ } = 12$ 4
2. $\underline{\ ?\ } \cdot 6 = 54$ 9
3. $6a^2 = \underline{\ ?\ } \cdot 2a$ $3a$
4. $6a + 2b = 2(\underline{\ ?\ })$ $3a + b$
5. $3x - x^2 = x(\underline{\ ?\ })$ $3 - x$

Motivating the Lesson

Matt wanted to share a pizza among his friends. If Mike wanted $\frac{1}{4}$ of the pizza and Roger wanted $\frac{1}{3}$ of the pizza, in which way can Matt slice the pizza so that each person gets the desired amount? Twelfths.
Solving this problem requires finding the least common denominator. Finding the LCD of algebraic fractions is today's lesson.

Complete.

1. $\dfrac{3}{8} = \dfrac{?}{32}$ 12

2. $\dfrac{7}{4y} = \dfrac{?}{12y^3}$ $21y^2$

3. $\dfrac{t}{t-3} = \dfrac{?}{(t-3)(t+5)}$ $t(t+5)$

Find the LCD for each group of fractions.

4. $\dfrac{3}{5}, \dfrac{5}{8}, \dfrac{5}{12}$ $2^3 \cdot 3 \cdot 5 = 120$

5. $\dfrac{15}{4k-6}, \dfrac{12}{6k-9}$
$4k - 6 = 2(2k - 3)$
$6k - 9 = 3(2k - 3)$
LCD is $6(2k - 3)$.

6. Rewrite $\dfrac{5}{(x+2)(x+3)}$ and
$\dfrac{-3}{x^2+4x+4}$ with their LCD.
$x^2 + 4x + 4 = (x + 2)^2$
The LCD is $(x + 2)^2 \cdot (x + 3)$.
$\dfrac{5}{(x+2)(x+3)} = \dfrac{5(x+2)}{(x+2)^2(x+3)}$
$\dfrac{-3}{x^2+4x+4} = \dfrac{-3}{(x+2)^2} = \dfrac{-3(x+3)}{(x+2)^2(x+3)}$

Check for Understanding

Here is a suggested use of the Oral Exercises to check students' understanding as you teach the lesson.
Oral Exs. 1–8: use after Example 3.
Oral Exs. 9–20: use after Example 6.

You can use the method shown in Examples 1, 2, and 3 to rewrite two or more fractions so that they have equal denominators. When you add and subtract fractions in the next lesson, you'll find that it may simplify your work if you use the *least common denominator* (LCD) of the fractions.

Finding the Least Common Denominator

1. Factor each denominator completely. Write any integral factor as a product of primes.

2. Find the product of the greatest power of each factor occurring in the denominators.

Example 4 Find the LCD of the fractions $\dfrac{3}{4}$, $\dfrac{11}{30}$, and $\dfrac{7}{45}$.

Solution 1. Factor each denominator into prime numbers.

$$4 = 2^2 \qquad 30 = 2 \cdot 3 \cdot 5 \qquad 45 = 3^2 \cdot 5$$

2. Greatest power of 2: 2^2
Greatest power of 3: 3^2
Greatest power of 5: 5

$$2^2 \cdot 3^2 \cdot 5 = 180$$

∴ the LCD is 180. **Answer**

Example 5 Find the LCD of $\dfrac{3}{6x-30}$ and $\dfrac{8}{9x-45}$.

Solution 1. Factor each denominator completely. Factor integers into primes.

$$6x - 30 = 6(x - 5) = 2 \cdot 3(x - 5)$$
$$9x - 45 = 9(x - 5) = 3^2(x - 5)$$

2. Form the product of the greatest power of each factor.
$$2 \cdot 3^2(x - 5), \text{ or } 18(x - 5)$$

∴ the LCD is $18(x - 5)$ **Answer**

Example 6 Rewrite $\dfrac{9}{x^2 - 8x + 16}$ and $\dfrac{5}{x^2 - 7x + 12}$ with their LCD.

Solution $x^2 - 8x + 16 = (x - 4)^2$ $\begin{cases} \text{First find the LCD} \\ \text{of the fractions.} \end{cases}$
$x^2 - 7x + 12 = (x - 3)(x - 4)$
The LCD is $(x - 3)(x - 4)^2$.

(Solution continues on next page.)

Then rewrite each fraction using the LCD.

$$\frac{9}{x^2 - 8x + 16} = \frac{9}{(x-4)^2} = \frac{9(x-3)}{(x-4)^2(x-3)} = \frac{9(x-3)}{(x-3)(x-4)^2}$$

$$\frac{5}{x^2 - 7x + 12} = \frac{5}{(x-3)(x-4)} = \frac{5(x-4)}{(x-3)(x-4)(x-4)} = \frac{5(x-4)}{(x-3)(x-4)^2}$$

Oral Exercises

Complete.

1. $\frac{2}{5} = \frac{?}{10}$ 4

2. $\frac{3}{8} = \frac{?}{40}$ 15

3. $\frac{x}{6} = \frac{?}{30}$ 5x

4. $\frac{a}{3} = \frac{?}{21}$ 7a

5. $\frac{2x}{3} = \frac{?}{9}$ 6x

6. $\frac{a}{b} = \frac{?}{b^2}$ ab

7. $\frac{5}{8n} = \frac{?}{16n^2}$ 10n

8. $\frac{5}{2-x} = \frac{?}{x-2}$ −5

Find the LCD for each group of fractions.

9. $\frac{3}{2}, \frac{7}{10}$ 10

10. $\frac{2}{5}, \frac{1}{9}$ 45

11. $\frac{5}{18}, \frac{5}{12}$ 36

12. $\frac{7}{90}, \frac{11}{60}$ 180

13. $\frac{1}{2}, \frac{1}{3}, \frac{1}{4}$ 12

14. $\frac{2}{5}, \frac{5}{6}, \frac{3}{10}$ 30

15. $\frac{6}{5a}, \frac{11}{20a^2}$ 20a²

16. $\frac{8}{x}, \frac{1}{xy}$ xy

17. $\frac{12}{x^2}, \frac{10}{xy^2}$ x²y²

18. $\frac{2}{3a-b}, \frac{5}{6a-2b}$ 6a − 2b

19. $\frac{3}{x^2+x}, \frac{9}{x+1}, \frac{4}{x}$ x² + x

20. $\frac{4}{y^2-1}, \frac{3}{y+1}, \frac{7}{y-1}$ y² − 1

Written Exercises

Complete.

A

1. $\frac{3}{4} = \frac{?}{28}$ 21

2. $\frac{4}{9} = \frac{?}{27}$ 12

3. $\frac{5x}{3} = \frac{?}{18}$ 30x

4. $\frac{2a}{17} = \frac{?}{51}$ 6a

5. $\frac{x-3}{4} = \frac{?}{12}$ 3(x − 3)

6. $\frac{2n-5}{5} = \frac{?}{25}$ 5(2n − 5)

7. $\frac{6}{15x} = \frac{?}{30x^2}$ 12x

8. $\frac{3}{4a} = \frac{?}{16a^3}$ 12a²

9. $\frac{x}{2y} = \frac{?}{10xy}$ 5x²

10. $\frac{5m}{2n} = \frac{?}{8mn^2}$ 20m²n

11. $\frac{7}{n-3} = \frac{7(n+2)}{(n-3)(n+2)}$?

12. $\frac{4}{x+1} = \frac{?}{(x+1)(x-1)}$ 4(x − 1)

13. $\frac{5}{2n-3} = \frac{?}{(2n-3)^2}$ 5(2n − 3)

14. $\frac{2y}{3y-2} = \frac{2y(3y-2)}{(3y-2)^2}$?

15. $\frac{4}{a-1} = \frac{?}{2a-2}$ 8

16. $\frac{2}{3x-1} = \frac{?}{9x-3}$ 6

17. $\frac{2}{x+1} = \frac{?}{x^2-1}$ 2(x − 1)

18. $\frac{5}{n-3} = \frac{?}{n^2-9}$ 5(n + 3)

19. $\frac{3}{4-y} = \frac{?}{4y-y^2}$ 3y

20. $\frac{2x}{3-x} = \frac{?}{3x-x^2}$ 2x²

Fractions **261**

Complete.

1. $\frac{3}{8} = \frac{?}{40}$ 15

2. $\frac{6x}{5} = \frac{?}{25}$ 30x

3. $\frac{3x-1}{4} = \frac{?}{28}$ 7(3x − 1)

4. $\frac{7n}{3m} = \frac{?}{12m^2n^3}$ 28mn⁴

5. $\frac{3}{y+4} = \frac{?}{(y-2)(y+4)}$
3(y − 2)

6. $\frac{4y}{5y+2} = \frac{?}{(5y+2)^2}$
4y(5y + 2)

Find the LCD for each group of fractions.

7. $\frac{4}{9}, \frac{6}{7}$ 63

8. $\frac{1}{4}, \frac{2}{3}, \frac{3}{5}$ 60

9. $\frac{y+3z}{12}, \frac{2y-z}{18}$ 36

10. $\frac{5}{k+2}, \frac{k-1}{k^2-4}$ (k + 2)(k − 2)

Summarizing the Lesson

Tell students that they have learned to express two or more fractions with their least common denominator. Ask students to tell how they would find the LCD of two fractions.

Suggested Assignments

Minimum
  261/1–31 odd, 33, 36, 37, 41
S 262/Mixed Review
R 258/Self-Test 1
Average
  261/2–44 even
S 262/Mixed Review
R 258/Self-Test 1
Maximum
  261/3–45 mult. of 3
S 262/Mixed Review
R 258/Self-Test 1

Find the LCD for each group of fractions.

21. $\frac{1}{6}, \frac{5}{9}$ 18

22. $\frac{3}{8}, \frac{2}{5}$ 40

23. $\frac{5}{2}, \frac{1}{6}, \frac{3}{5}$ 30

24. $\frac{1}{3}, \frac{2}{9}, \frac{3}{4}$ 36

25. $\frac{a+3b}{8}, \frac{2a-b}{12}$ 24

26. $\frac{n-3}{20}, \frac{n+4}{15}$ 60

27. $\frac{1}{4t}, \frac{7}{16rt^2}$ $16rt^2$

28. $\frac{9}{x^2}, \frac{2}{xy}$ x^2y

29. $\frac{6}{x+1}, \frac{x}{x-2}$ $(x+1)(x-2)$

30. $\frac{b}{b+5}, \frac{2b}{b-5}$ $(b+5)(b-5)$

31. $\frac{7}{m+2}, \frac{m-1}{m^2-4}$ $(m+2)(m-2)$

32. $\frac{3a}{a-1}, \frac{5}{a^2-3a+2}$ $(a-1)(a-2)$

Rewrite each group of fractions with their LCD.

B **33.** $\frac{1}{2xy}, \frac{3}{x^2}, \frac{x}{2x^2y}, \frac{6y}{2x^2y}$

34. $\frac{1}{3mn^2}, \frac{2}{m^2n}, \frac{m}{3m^2n^2}, \frac{6n}{3m^2n^2}$

35. $\frac{11}{6x^2y^2}, \frac{4}{5xy^3}$ $\frac{55y}{30x^2y^3}, \frac{24x}{30x^2y^3}$

36. $\frac{1}{12a^2b}, \frac{5}{18b^2}$

37. $\frac{5}{x-3}, \frac{7}{4x-12}$

38. $\frac{4}{3x-6y}, \frac{1}{5x-10y}$

39. $\frac{6}{x-3}, \frac{4x}{(x-3)^2}$

40. $\frac{9}{(2n+1)^2}, \frac{-2n}{2n+1}$

41. $\frac{3y}{2y-4}, \frac{1}{y^2-4}$

42. $\frac{3}{c^2-6c}, \frac{5}{c^2+6c}$

43. $\frac{x}{x^2-x-6}, \frac{9}{x^2-9}$

44. $\frac{2}{a^2+3a-10}, \frac{4a}{a^2+10a+25}$

C **45.** The product of the first n positive integers, denoted by $n!$, is called
  n **factorial**.
  a. Find $4!$, $5!$, and $6!$. (*Hint:* $3! = 1 \cdot 2 \cdot 3 = 6$) $4! = 24$, $5! = 120$, $6! = 720$
  b. What is the LCD of the fractions $\frac{1}{4!}, \frac{1}{5!}$, and $\frac{1}{6!}$? 720
  c. What is the LCD of the fractions $\frac{1}{n!}$ and $\frac{1}{(n+1)!}$? $(n+1)!$

Mixed Review Exercises

Factor completely.

1. $4n - 8q + 16$ $4(n - 2q + 4)$

2. $3x^2 - 3$ $3(x - 1)(x + 1)$

3. $x^2 - 11x + 18$ $(x-9)(x-2)$

4. $x^2 - 5x - 24$ $(x - 8)(x + 3)$

5. $2x^2 - x - 3$ $(2x - 3)(x + 1)$

6. $x^2 + 16x + 39$ $(x+13)(x+3)$

7. $x^2 + 3x - 28$ $(x + 7)(x - 4)$

8. $x^2 + 22x + 121$ $(x + 11)^2$

9. $n^2 - 9n$ $n(n - 9)$

Write an equation for each sentence.

10. Seven is 4 less than twice the number p. $7 = 2p - 4$

11. The number n decreased by $\frac{1}{2}$ is $5\frac{1}{4}$. $n - \frac{1}{2} = 5\frac{1}{4}$

12. Two thirds of the number k is 16. $\frac{2}{3}k = 16$

The following program will find the LCD for two integral denominators.

```
10 PRINT "TO FIND THE LEAST"
20 PRINT "COMMON DENOMINATOR."
30 INPUT "ENTER TWO DENOMINATORS: "; D1, D2
40 LET M = 1
50 LET Q = (D2*M)/D1
60 IF Q = INT(Q) THEN 90
70 LET M = M + 1
80 GOTO 50
90 PRINT "LCD ("; D1; ", "; D2 ;") = ";
100 PRINT D2 ; " X "; M; " = "; D2*M
110 END
```

Computer Key-In Commentary

In BASIC, a semicolon at the end of a PRINT statement (see line 90) keeps the printing cursor on the same line of type so that a line of printing is not interrupted. This is called "suppressing a line feed."

Exercises

Run this program for each pair of denominators.

1. D1 = 7, D2 = 21 21
2. D1 = 21, D2 = 7 21
3. D1 = 24, D2 = 36 72
4. D1 = 36, D2 = 24 72
5. D1 = 13, D2 = 15 195
6. D1 = 15, D2 = 13 195

7–12. In order to see how the program works, insert

```
55 PRINT D2*M; "/" ; D1; "=" ; (D2*M)/D1
```

and run the program again for the data in Exercises 1–6.

13. How does each RUN where you enter the smaller denominator first (Exercises 1, 3, and 5) compare with each RUN where you enter the smaller denominator last (Exercises 2, 4, and 6)? That is, which RUN requires fewer steps of computation?

14. Explain how to use the program above to find the least common denominator for the three denominators 27, 36, and 30.

Challenge

Two horses approach each other along the same country road, one walking at 5.5 km/h and the other at 4.5 km/h. When the horses are 10 km apart, a horse-fly leaves one horse and flies at 30 km/h to the other. No sooner does the fly reach that horse than it turns around (losing no time on the turn) and returns to the first horse. If the fly continues to fly back and forth between the approaching horses, how far has the fly flown when the horses meet? 30 km

6-5 Adding and Subtracting Fractions

Objective   To add and subtract algebraic fractions.

In Lesson 2-9 you learned that

$$\frac{a+b}{c} = \frac{a}{c} + \frac{b}{c} \quad \text{and} \quad \frac{a-b}{c} = \frac{a}{c} - \frac{b}{c}.$$

You can rewrite these results to get the following rules.

Addition Rule for Fractions

$$\frac{a}{c} + \frac{b}{c} = \frac{a+b}{c}$$

Example: $\dfrac{2}{9} + \dfrac{5}{9} = \dfrac{2+5}{9} = \dfrac{7}{9}$

Subtraction Rule for Fractions

$$\frac{a}{c} - \frac{b}{c} = \frac{a-b}{c}$$

Example: $\dfrac{4}{5} - \dfrac{1}{5} = \dfrac{4-1}{5} = \dfrac{3}{5}$

To add or subtract fractions with the same denominator, you add or subtract
their numerators and write the result over the common denominator.

To simplify an expression involving fractions, you write it as a single fraction in simplest form.

Example 1   Simplify: **a.** $\dfrac{3c}{16} + \dfrac{5c}{16}$ **b.** $\dfrac{5x+4}{10} - \dfrac{3x-8}{10}$

Solution   **a.** $\dfrac{3c}{16} + \dfrac{5c}{16} = \dfrac{3c+5c}{16} = \dfrac{8c}{16}$

$\qquad\qquad\qquad\qquad = \dfrac{\cancel{8} \cdot c}{\cancel{8} \cdot 2}$

$\qquad\qquad\qquad\qquad = \dfrac{c}{2}$ ***Answer***

b. $\dfrac{5x+4}{10} - \dfrac{3x-8}{10} = \dfrac{5x+4-(3x-8)}{10}$

$\qquad\qquad\qquad\qquad = \dfrac{5x+4-3x+8}{10}$

$\qquad\qquad\qquad\qquad = \dfrac{2x+12}{10}$

$\qquad\qquad\qquad\qquad = \dfrac{\cancel{2}(x+6)}{\cancel{2} \cdot 5}$

$\qquad\qquad\qquad\qquad = \dfrac{x+6}{5}$ ***Answer***

Example 2 Simplify: **a.** $\dfrac{3}{x+4} + \dfrac{1}{x+4}$ **b.** $\dfrac{2}{x-3} + \dfrac{7}{3-x}$

Solution

a. $\dfrac{3}{x+4} + \dfrac{1}{x+4} = \dfrac{3+1}{x+4} = \dfrac{4}{x+4}$ *Answer*

b. $\dfrac{2}{x-3} + \dfrac{7}{3-x} = \dfrac{2}{x-3} + \dfrac{7}{-(x-3)}$ $\begin{cases}\text{Since } 3-x = -(x-3), \\ \text{the LCD is } x-3.\end{cases}$

$\qquad = \dfrac{2}{x-3} - \dfrac{7}{x-3}$

$\qquad = \dfrac{2-7}{x-3}$

$\qquad = \dfrac{-5}{x-3}$, or $-\dfrac{5}{x-3}$ *Answer*

Example 3 Simplify $\dfrac{a}{4} - \dfrac{5+12a}{18}$.

Solution Since the denominators are different, rewrite the fractions using their least common denominator, 36.

$\dfrac{a}{4} - \dfrac{5+12a}{18} = \dfrac{a \cdot 9}{4 \cdot 9} - \dfrac{(5+12a) \cdot 2}{18 \cdot 2}$

$\qquad = \dfrac{9a - 2(5+12a)}{36}$

$\qquad = \dfrac{9a - 10 - 24a}{36}$

$\qquad = \dfrac{-15a - 10}{36}$, or $-\dfrac{5(3a+2)}{36}$ *Answer*

Example 4 Find the perimeter of the rectangle shown at the right.

Solution $\begin{array}{l}\text{Perimeter of}\\ \text{a rectangle}\end{array} = (2 \times \text{length}) + (2 \times \text{width})$

$\qquad = 2 \cdot \dfrac{a-1}{4} + 2 \cdot \dfrac{a}{12}$

$\qquad = \dfrac{a-1}{2} + \dfrac{a}{6}$

$\qquad = \dfrac{3(a-1)}{6} + \dfrac{a}{6}$

$\qquad = \dfrac{3a - 3 + a}{6}$

$\qquad = \dfrac{4a-3}{6}$ *Answer*

(rectangle with top side labeled $\dfrac{a-1}{4}$ and right side labeled $\dfrac{a}{12}$)

Fractions **265**

---

3. $\dfrac{m}{3} - \dfrac{6m+3}{12}$

$\dfrac{m \cdot 4}{3 \cdot 4} - \dfrac{6m+3}{12} =$

$\dfrac{4m - (6m+3)}{12} =$

$\dfrac{4m - 6m - 3}{12} = \dfrac{-2m - 3}{12}$

4. Find the perimeter of the rectangle.

(rectangle with left side labeled $\dfrac{n}{3}$ and bottom labeled $\dfrac{n+1}{4}$)

$P = 2l + 2w$

$\quad = 2\left(\dfrac{n+1}{4}\right) + 2\left(\dfrac{n}{3}\right)$

$\quad = \dfrac{n+1}{2} + \dfrac{2n}{3}$

$\quad = \dfrac{3(n+1)}{6} + \dfrac{2 \cdot 2n}{6}$

$\quad = \dfrac{3n + 3 + 4n}{6} = \dfrac{7n+3}{6}$

Simplify.

5. $\dfrac{5}{6y} - \dfrac{7}{12y^3}$

$\dfrac{5 \cdot 2y^2}{6y \cdot 2y^2} - \dfrac{7}{12y^3} =$

$\dfrac{10y^2}{12y^3} - \dfrac{7}{12y^3} = \dfrac{10y^2 - 7}{12y^3}$

6. $\dfrac{n}{n+3} + \dfrac{n+9}{n^2 + 8n + 15}$

$\dfrac{n}{n+3} + \dfrac{n+9}{(n+3)(n+5)} =$

$\dfrac{n(n+5)}{(n+3)(n+5)} +$

$\dfrac{n+9}{(n+3)(n+5)} =$

$\dfrac{n^2 + 5n + n + 9}{(n+3)(n+5)} =$

$\dfrac{n^2 + 6n + 9}{(n+3)(n+5)} =$

$\dfrac{\cancel{(n+3)}(n+3)}{\cancel{(n+3)}(n+5)} = \dfrac{n+3}{n+5}$

Check for Understanding

A suggested use of the Oral Exercises to check students' understanding as you teach the lesson.

Oral Exs. 1–10, 17–18: use after Example 1.

Oral Exs. 11–16, 19–20: use after Example 3.

The addition and subtraction rules for expressions involving fractions are generalized from arithmetic. The ability to *transfer* what has been learned in arithmetic and *apply* it in the study of algebra is important to students' success.

Common Errors

Many students make errors when subtracting algebraic expressions because they think of, for example, $-\frac{2-x}{8}$ as $\frac{-2-x}{8}$. In reteaching, remind them that the fraction bar is a grouping symbol and that

$$-\frac{2-x}{8} = \frac{-(2-x)}{8} = \frac{-2+x}{8}.$$

Guided Practice

Simplify.

1. $\frac{3y}{8} + \frac{y}{8}$ $\frac{y}{2}$

2. $\frac{5}{n} - \frac{8}{n}$ $\frac{-3}{n}$

3. $\frac{4y}{9} - \frac{3y-1}{9}$ $\frac{y+1}{9}$

4. $\frac{x}{x+3} + \frac{4}{x+3}$ $\frac{x+4}{x+3}$

5. $\frac{5}{2y-1} - \frac{2y}{1-2y}$ $\frac{5+2y}{2y-1}$

6. $\frac{12}{mn^2} - \frac{5}{mn}$ $\frac{12-5n}{mn^2}$

7. $\frac{y}{6y-2} + \frac{4}{3y-1}$ $\frac{y+8}{2(3y-1)}$

8. $\frac{3x-1}{4} + \frac{2x+2}{6}$ $\frac{13x+1}{12}$

9. $\frac{2x+4}{5} - \frac{x-1}{4}$ $\frac{3x+21}{20}$

10. $\frac{3r+4}{6} + \frac{4r}{3} - \frac{r-2}{4}$

    $\frac{19r+14}{12}$

Example 5   Simplify $\frac{3}{2x} - \frac{1}{8x^2}$.

Solution $\dfrac{3}{2x} - \dfrac{1}{8x^2} = \dfrac{3 \cdot 4x}{2x \cdot 4x} - \dfrac{1}{8x^2}$

$$= \frac{12x}{8x^2} - \frac{1}{8x^2} = \frac{12x-1}{8x^2} \quad \textbf{Answer}$$

Example 6   Simplify $\frac{a-3}{a^2-2a} - \frac{a-4}{a^2-4}$.

Solution $\dfrac{a-3}{a^2-2a} - \dfrac{a-4}{a^2-4} = \dfrac{a-3}{a(a-2)} - \dfrac{a-4}{(a-2)(a+2)}$

$$= \frac{(a-3)(a+2)}{a(a-2)(a+2)} - \frac{a(a-4)}{a(a-2)(a+2)}$$

$$= \frac{a^2-a-6-(a^2-4a)}{a(a-2)(a+2)}$$

$$= \frac{a^2-a-6-a^2+4a}{a(a-2)(a+2)}$$

$$= \frac{3a-6}{a(a-2)(a+2)}$$

$$= \frac{3\cancel{(a-2)}}{a\cancel{(a-2)}(a+2)}$$

$$= \frac{3}{a(a+2)} \quad \textbf{Answer}$$

Oral Exercises

Simplify.

1. $\frac{4}{5} + \frac{3}{5}$ $\frac{7}{5}$ 2. $\frac{7}{9} - \frac{4}{9}$ $\frac{1}{3}$ 3. $\frac{x}{8} + \frac{3x}{8}$ $\frac{x}{2}$

4. $\frac{7a}{12} - \frac{a}{12}$ $\frac{a}{2}$ 5. $\frac{4}{x} - \frac{1}{x}$ $\frac{3}{x}$ 6. $\frac{7}{2x} + \frac{3}{2x}$ $\frac{5}{x}$

7. $\frac{3}{x+2} + \frac{x}{x+2}$ $\frac{3+x}{x+2}$ 8. $\frac{n}{n+4} - \frac{5}{n+4}$ $\frac{n-5}{n+4}$ 9. $\frac{x}{x+7} + \frac{7}{x+7}$ 1

10. $\frac{2x}{2x-1} - \frac{1}{2x-1}$ 1   11. $\frac{4}{a-b} + \frac{1}{b-a}$ $\frac{3}{a-b}$ 12. $\frac{3}{x-5} - \frac{1}{5-x}$ $\frac{4}{x-5}$

13. $\frac{x}{2} + \frac{x}{8}$ $\frac{5x}{8}$ 14. $\frac{y}{4} - \frac{y}{6}$ $\frac{y}{12}$ 15. $\frac{6}{a} + \frac{3}{2a}$ $\frac{15}{2a}$ 16. $\frac{5}{n} - \frac{4}{n^2}$

17. $\frac{6y}{5} - \frac{y+3}{5}$ $\frac{5y-3}{5}$ 18. $\frac{n^2}{4} - \frac{n^2-4}{4}$ 1   19. $\frac{3c}{2} + \frac{c+1}{4}$ $\frac{7c+1}{4}$ 20. $\frac{x+1}{4} - \frac{x}{6}$ $\frac{x+3}{12}$

16. $\frac{5n-4}{n^2}$

Written Exercises

Simplify.

21. $\dfrac{4 + 5x}{5(x + 1)}$ **22.** $\dfrac{4x - 3}{2(x - 3)}$ **23.** $\dfrac{10x + 5}{12}$ **24.** $\dfrac{37b - 6}{40}$

A

1. $\dfrac{x}{12} + \dfrac{3x}{12}$ $\dfrac{x}{3}$

2. $\dfrac{7x}{15} - \dfrac{4x}{15}$ $\dfrac{x}{5}$

3. $\dfrac{2}{n} - \dfrac{6}{n}$ $\dfrac{-4}{n}$

4. $\dfrac{5}{3x} + \dfrac{9}{3x}$ $\dfrac{14}{3x}$

5. $\dfrac{2x}{3} - \dfrac{x - 1}{3}$ $\dfrac{x + 1}{3}$

6. $\dfrac{3a}{10} - \dfrac{5a + 1}{10}$ $\dfrac{-2a - 1}{10}$

7. $\dfrac{y - 3}{4} - \dfrac{3y - 5}{4}$ $\dfrac{1 - y}{2}$

8. $\dfrac{x + 3}{4} - \dfrac{9x + 11}{4}$ $-2x - 2$

9. $\dfrac{2}{x + 3} + \dfrac{5}{x + 3}$ $\dfrac{7}{x + 3}$

10. $\dfrac{9}{y - 6} - \dfrac{3}{y - 6}$ $\dfrac{6}{y - 6}$

11. $\dfrac{x}{x - 2} + \dfrac{1}{x - 2}$ $\dfrac{x + 1}{x - 2}$

12. $\dfrac{n}{n - 2} - \dfrac{3n - 1}{n - 2}$ $\dfrac{-2n + 1}{n - 2}$

13. $\dfrac{3}{x - 5} + \dfrac{2}{5 - x}$ $\dfrac{1}{x - 5}$

14. $\dfrac{5}{4y - 1} - \dfrac{3}{1 - 4y}$ $\dfrac{8}{4y - 1}$

15. $\dfrac{5c}{c - d} + \dfrac{5d}{d - c}$ 5

16. $\dfrac{6}{3 - 2x} - \dfrac{4x}{2x - 3}$ $\dfrac{6 + 4x}{3 - 2x}$

17. $\dfrac{2}{x} + \dfrac{3}{x^2}$ $\dfrac{2x + 3}{x^2}$

18. $\dfrac{8}{ab} - \dfrac{6}{ab^2}$ $\dfrac{8b - 6}{ab^2}$

19. $\dfrac{1}{2x^2} - \dfrac{5}{4x}$ $\dfrac{2 - 5x}{4x^2}$

20. $\dfrac{4}{3xy} + \dfrac{3}{2x^2}$ $\dfrac{8x + 9y}{6x^2y}$

21. $\dfrac{4}{5(x + 1)} + \dfrac{x}{x + 1}$

22. $\dfrac{2x}{x - 3} - \dfrac{3}{2(x - 3)}$

23. $\dfrac{1 + 2x}{4} + \dfrac{1 + 2x}{6}$

24. $\dfrac{5b + 2}{8} + \dfrac{3b - 4}{10}$

25. $\dfrac{3y - 2}{6} - \dfrac{y - 3}{9}$ $\dfrac{7y}{18}$

26. $\dfrac{a - 6}{15} + \dfrac{4 - a}{10}$ $\dfrac{-a}{30}$

27. $\dfrac{5n - 2}{12} - \dfrac{3(n - 3)}{8}$

28. $\dfrac{3(a - b)}{20} - \dfrac{5(a + b)}{12}$

29. $\dfrac{4x + 3}{3} - \dfrac{7x}{4} + \dfrac{x - 3}{6}$

30. $\dfrac{2m}{5} - \dfrac{m + 4}{4} + \dfrac{2 - m}{10}$

27. $\dfrac{n + 23}{24}$ **28.** $-\dfrac{8a + 17b}{30}$ **29.** $\dfrac{-x + 2}{4}$ **30.** $\dfrac{m - 16}{20}$

Find the perimeter of each figure.

B

31.

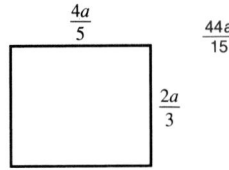

32.

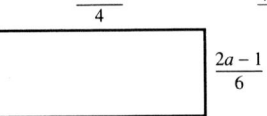

33.

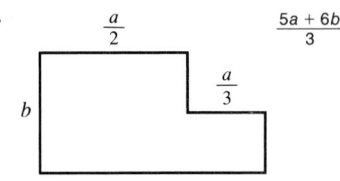

Fractions   **267**

Summarizing the Lesson

Tell students that they have learned to add and subtract algebraic fractions. Ask students to state the rule for adding or subtracting algebraic fractions using the least common denominator.

Suggested Assignments

Minimum
Day 1: 267/1–31 odd, 35, 37, 39
Day 2: 267/32–46 even
   S 268/Mixed Review
Average
Day 1: 267/2–30 even, 31–33, 35–37
Day 2: 268/34, 38–54 even
   S 268/Mixed Review
Maximum
Day 1: 267/3–30 mult. of 3, 31–34
Day 2: 268/36–58 even
   S 268/Mixed Review
   R 269/Self-Test 2

Supplementary Materials

Study Guide   pp. 107–108
Computer Activities
            15, 16, 17

Find the perimeter of the figure.

34.

$\dfrac{3x}{4}$

$\dfrac{x}{6}$

$\dfrac{x}{4}$ $\dfrac{x}{4}$

$\dfrac{3x}{4}$

$\dfrac{14x}{3}$

$\dfrac{x}{6}$

$\dfrac{3x}{4}$

Simplify.

35. $\dfrac{1}{x-1} + \dfrac{1}{x}\ \dfrac{2x-1}{x(x-1)}$

36. $\dfrac{3}{y-6} - \dfrac{1}{y}\ \dfrac{2y+6}{y(y-6)}$

37. $\dfrac{2}{x-3} + \dfrac{4}{x+3}\ \dfrac{6x-6}{(x-3)(x+3)}$

38. $\dfrac{3}{x+4} - \dfrac{4}{x-2}\ \dfrac{-x-22}{(x+4)(x-2)}$

39. $\dfrac{a+1}{a} - \dfrac{a}{a+1}\ \dfrac{2a+1}{a(a+1)}$

40. $\dfrac{x}{x+y} + \dfrac{y}{x-y}\ \dfrac{x^2+y^2}{x^2-y^2}$

41. $\dfrac{x}{x^2-1} + \dfrac{4}{x+1}\ \dfrac{5x-4}{x^2-1}$

42. $\dfrac{2y}{y^2-25} - \dfrac{y}{y-5}$

43. $\dfrac{2m}{2m-1} + \dfrac{1}{1-2m}$

44. $\dfrac{3a}{a-2b} + \dfrac{6b}{2b-a}$

45. $\dfrac{d+2}{d^2-1} - \dfrac{3}{2d+2}$

46. $\dfrac{2n}{n^3-5n^2} + \dfrac{2}{n^2+5n}$

47. $\dfrac{a}{ab-b^2} + \dfrac{b}{ab-a^2}$

48. $\dfrac{x}{x-x^2} - \dfrac{1}{x-x^3}$

49. $\dfrac{n}{n^2+4n} - \dfrac{n}{(n+4)^2}$

50. $\dfrac{1}{a^2+4a+4} + \dfrac{1}{a^2-4}$

51. $\dfrac{x-11}{x^2-9} - \dfrac{x-7}{x^2-3x}$

52. $\dfrac{c-2}{c^2+c-2} - \dfrac{c+2}{c^2-3c+2}$

C 53. $\dfrac{x^2+1}{x^2-1} + \dfrac{1}{x+1} + \dfrac{1}{x-1}\ \dfrac{x+1}{x-1}$

54. $\dfrac{x}{2x-1} + \dfrac{x-1}{2x+1} - \dfrac{2x}{4x^2-1}\ \dfrac{2x-1}{2x+1}$

55. $\dfrac{a+2}{a^2+5a+6} - \dfrac{2+a}{4-a^2} + \dfrac{2-a}{a^2+a-6}\ \dfrac{1}{a-2}$

56. $\dfrac{x-3}{2x+6} - \dfrac{x+3}{3x-9} - \dfrac{5x^2+27}{6x^2-54}$

57. $\dfrac{b+1}{(b-1)^2} + \dfrac{2-2b}{(b-1)^3} + \dfrac{1}{b-1}$

58. $\dfrac{4}{c^2-4cd} - \dfrac{1}{cd-4d^2} - \dfrac{2}{cd}$

56. $-\dfrac{2x^2+15x+9}{3(x+3)(x-3)}$ 57. $\dfrac{2}{b-1}$ 58. $\dfrac{-3}{cd}$

Mixed Review Exercises

Simplify.

1. $-8^2 \cdot 3$ -192

2. $(4 \cdot 6 - 13)^2$ 121

3. $(-4x^2)^3$ $-64x^6$

4. $5y(y-4) + 2y(y+11)$ $7y^2 + 2y$

5. $n^2(n+8) - (2n^2-6)n$ $-n^3 + 8n^2 + 6n$

6. $(5x^2y)(3x^3y^2)(6y^3)$ $90x^5y^6$

7. $\left(\dfrac{12x^2y^2}{5}\right)\left(\dfrac{-10xy^2}{3}\right)$ $-8x^3y^4$

8. $-\dfrac{1}{6}(-42x+12y)$ $7x - 2y$

9. $(3n-5p+2) - (-n+6p+1)$ $4n - 11p + 1$

Self-Test 2

Vocabulary   least common denominator (LCD)
(p. 260)

Find the missing numerators.

1. $\dfrac{3n}{20c} = \dfrac{?}{50c^3}$ $\dfrac{15c^2 n}{2}$

2. $\dfrac{5}{1-a} = \dfrac{?}{a-a^2}$ $5a$

Obj. 6-4, p. 259

Find the LCD for each group of fractions.

3. $\dfrac{3}{4x-8}, \dfrac{-12}{x^2-4x+4}$ $4(x-2)^2$

4. $\dfrac{5}{a}, \dfrac{4}{b}, \dfrac{3}{a-b}$ $ab(a-b)$

Simplify.

5. $\dfrac{32c+3}{6c} - \dfrac{2c+9}{6c}$ $\dfrac{5c-1}{c}$

6. $\dfrac{4}{3ab} + \dfrac{8}{7ab^2}$ $\dfrac{28b+24}{21ab^2}$

Obj. 6-5, p. 264

7. $\dfrac{x}{x-y} + \dfrac{y}{y-x}$ 1

8. $\dfrac{1}{n-1} - \dfrac{n}{5(n-1)}$ $\dfrac{5-n}{5(n-1)}$

Check your answers with those at the back of the book.

Biographical Note / *Srinivasa Ramanujan*

Srinivasa Ramanujan (1887–1920) was a self-taught mathematician. At 16 he was awarded a scholarship to Government College in India for his proficiency in mathematics. However, he became so absorbed in his mathematical studies that he neglected to study English and lost his scholarship. He continued to study mathematics on his own, discovering over 100 theorems.

Friends convinced Ramanujan to write to G. H. Hardy, one of the leading number theorists at Cambridge University in England. Ramanujan sent about 120 of the theorems he had discovered. Convinced of Ramanujan's exceptional ability, Hardy brought him to England, where he was admitted to Trinity College. Hardy was not always sure how to teach a student with such profound mathematical insight but so little formal training; nevertheless Ramanujan progressed rapidly. While in England he did a great deal of work in number theory.

In 1918 Ramanujan was elected a fellow of the Royal Society and of Trinity College.

Fractions   **269**

Warm-Up Exercises

Complete.

1. $5 = \frac{5}{?}$ 1   **2.** $12 = \frac{12}{?}$ 1

3. $6 = \frac{?}{3}$ 18   **4.** $4 = \frac{?}{8}$ 32

5. $3 = \frac{?}{4}$ 12   **6.** $5 = \frac{?}{6}$ 30

Motivating the Lesson

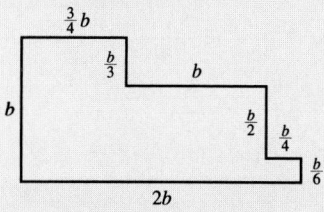

How would you find the perimeter of the figure?
Add the sides. $P = 6b$
Adding mixed expressions is the topic today.

Chalkboard Examples

Write as a fraction in simplest form.

1. $-4\frac{2}{3} = -4 + \frac{-2}{3} =$

$\frac{-4}{1} + \frac{-2}{3} = \frac{-12}{3} + \frac{-2}{3} =$

$\frac{-14}{3}$

2. $3t - \frac{2}{t} = \frac{3t}{1} - \frac{2}{t} =$

$\frac{3t^2}{t} - \frac{2}{t} = \frac{3t^2 - 2}{t}$

3. $\frac{x}{x-1} - 5 =$

$\frac{x}{x-1} - \frac{5}{1} \cdot \frac{(x-1)}{(x-1)} =$

$\frac{x - 5(x-1)}{x-1} =$

$\frac{x - 5x + 5}{x - 1} = \frac{-4x + 5}{x - 1}$

Polynomial Division

6-6 Mixed Expressions

Objective   To write mixed expressions as fractions in simplest form.

A mixed number like $2\frac{3}{4}$ represents the sum of an integer and a fraction. You can write a mixed number as a single fraction in simplest form.

Example 1   Write $2\frac{3}{4}$ as a fraction in simplest form.

Solution $2\frac{3}{4} = 2 + \frac{3}{4}$

$= \frac{2}{1} + \frac{3}{4}$ {Write 2 as $\frac{2}{1}$.

$= \frac{8}{4} + \frac{3}{4}$ {LCD = 4

$= \frac{11}{4}$ **Answer**

The sum or difference of a polynomial and a fraction is called a **mixed expression.**

Example 2   Write each expression as a fraction in simplest form.

a. $c + \frac{5}{c}$ **b.** $5 - \frac{x-3}{x+2}$

Solution   **a.** $c + \frac{5}{c} = \frac{c}{1} + \frac{5}{c}$ {Write c as $\frac{c}{1}$.

$= \frac{c^2}{c} + \frac{5}{c}$ {LCD = c

$= \frac{c^2 + 5}{c}$ **Answer**

b. $5 - \frac{x-3}{x+2} = \frac{5}{1} - \frac{x-3}{x+2}$ {Write 5 as $\frac{5}{1}$.

$= \frac{5(x+2)}{x+2} - \frac{x-3}{x+2}$ {LCD = $x+2$

$= \frac{5x + 10 - x + 3}{x+2}$

$= \frac{4x + 13}{x+2}$ **Answer**

Example 3 Write as a fraction in simplest form: $x + \dfrac{5x + 2}{x - 1} - \dfrac{7}{x - 1}$

Solution $x + \dfrac{5x + 2}{x - 1} - \dfrac{7}{x - 1} = \dfrac{x(x - 1)}{x - 1} + \dfrac{5x + 2}{x - 1} - \dfrac{7}{x - 1}$

$$= \dfrac{x^2 - x + 5x + 2 - 7}{x - 1}$$

$$= \dfrac{x^2 + 4x - 5}{x - 1}$$

$$= \dfrac{(x - 1)(x + 5)}{x - 1}$$

$$= \dfrac{x + 5}{1} = x + 5 \quad \textit{Answer}$$

Oral Exercises

State each expression as a fraction in simplest form. 12. $\dfrac{2b + 1}{b + 1}$

1. $2\frac{1}{8}$ $\frac{17}{8}$

2. $5\frac{2}{3}$ $\frac{17}{3}$

3. $-5\frac{2}{9}$ $-\frac{47}{9}$

4. $-4\frac{4}{7}$ $-\frac{32}{7}$

5. $1 + \dfrac{1}{x}$ $\dfrac{x + 1}{x}$

6. $2 + \dfrac{4}{a}$ $\dfrac{2a + 4}{a}$

7. $n - \dfrac{3}{n}$ $\dfrac{n^2 - 3}{n}$

8. $\dfrac{2}{y} + y$ $\dfrac{2 + y^2}{y}$

9. $2 - \dfrac{a}{b}$ $\dfrac{2b - a}{b}$

10. $3 - \dfrac{1}{x + 1}$ $\dfrac{3x + 2}{x + 1}$

11. $\dfrac{5}{x - 1} - 2$ $\dfrac{7 - 2x}{x - 1}$

12. $\dfrac{b}{b + 1} + 1$

13. $2 + \dfrac{3}{x + 1}$ $\dfrac{2x + 5}{x + 1}$

14. $4 - \dfrac{1}{y + 3}$ $\dfrac{4y + 11}{y + 3}$

15. $\dfrac{3n}{3n + 2} + 2$ $\dfrac{9n + 4}{3n + 2}$

16. $1 - \dfrac{2a}{a + 1}$ $\dfrac{-a + 1}{a + 1}$

Written Exercises
15. $\dfrac{6x^2 + 5x}{x + 1}$ 16. $\dfrac{4y^2 - 19y}{y - 5}$

Write each expression as a fraction in simplest form.

A 1. $4\frac{1}{5}$ $\frac{21}{5}$

2. $2\frac{3}{8}$ $\frac{19}{8}$

3. $8 + \dfrac{1}{x}$ $\dfrac{8x + 1}{x}$

4. $3 + \dfrac{7}{a}$ $\dfrac{3a + 7}{a}$

5. $3a - \dfrac{2}{a}$ $\dfrac{3a^2 - 2}{a}$

6. $5x - \dfrac{3}{x}$ $\dfrac{5x^2 - 3}{x}$

7. $\dfrac{a}{b} - 3$ $\dfrac{a - 3b}{b}$

8. $2 - \dfrac{c}{d}$ $\dfrac{2d - c}{d}$

9. $5 - \dfrac{4}{x + 2}$ $\dfrac{5x + 6}{x + 2}$

10. $8 + \dfrac{y}{y - 1}$ $\dfrac{9y - 8}{y - 1}$

11. $\dfrac{x}{x + 2} + 6$ $\dfrac{7x + 12}{x + 2}$

12. $\dfrac{a + 3}{a} - 3$ $\dfrac{-2a + 3}{a}$

13. $4 + \dfrac{2n + 1}{n + 1}$ $\dfrac{6n + 5}{n + 1}$

14. $2 - \dfrac{k - 3}{k - 4}$ $\dfrac{k - 5}{k - 4}$

15. $6x - \dfrac{x}{x + 1}$

16. $4y + \dfrac{y}{y - 5}$

17. $8n - \dfrac{2}{n + 1}$ $\dfrac{8n^2 + 8n - 2}{n + 1}$

18. $5a + \dfrac{a - 5}{2a + 3}$ $\dfrac{10a^2 + 16a - 5}{2a + 3}$

19. $2a^2 - \dfrac{a - 1}{2a + 5}$ $\dfrac{4a^3 + 10a^2 - a + 1}{2a + 5}$

20. $y^2 - \dfrac{3y + 1}{y + 2}$ $\dfrac{y^3 + 2y^2 - 3y - 1}{y + 2}$

Fractions **271**

Check for Understanding

Oral Exs. 1–4: use after
    Example 1.
Oral Exs. 5–16: use after
    Example 3.

Guided Practice

Write each expression as a
fraction in simplest form.

1. $3\frac{3}{7}$ $\frac{24}{7}$ 2. $6 + \dfrac{1}{y}$ $\dfrac{6y + 1}{y}$

3. $4a - \dfrac{3}{a}$ $\dfrac{4a^2 - 3}{a}$

5. $4 - \dfrac{3y - 1}{y - 1}$ $\dfrac{y - 3}{y - 1}$

6. $\dfrac{2x - 5}{x + 2} - 3x$ $\dfrac{-3x^2 - 4x - 5}{x + 2}$

Summarizing the Lesson

Ask students to tell how
they would find the sum or
the difference of a polynomial and a fraction.

Suggested Assignments

Minimum
Day 1: 271/1–37 odd
   R 269/Self-Test 2
Day 2: 272/30–36 even
   S 273/Mixed Review
Assign with Lesson 6-7.

Average
Day 1: 271/2–32 even
   R 269/Self-Test 2
Day 2: 272/34, 36, 38, 40
   S 273/Mixed Review
Assign with Lesson 6-7.

Maximum
    271/3–45 mult. of 3
   S 273/Mixed Review

271

Write each expression as a fraction in simplest form.

B **21.** $x - \dfrac{8}{x + 1} - \dfrac{6x - 2}{x + 1}$

22. $y - \dfrac{4(y + 1)}{y + 2} - \dfrac{4}{y + 2}$

23. $\dfrac{b - 1}{b} - \dfrac{3}{b - 2} + 1$

24. $\dfrac{x}{x + 1} - \dfrac{x + 1}{x} + 2$

25. $\dfrac{3a}{a + 1} + \dfrac{2}{a - 1} - 1$

26. $2 - \dfrac{x}{x - 3} - \dfrac{1}{x + 3}$

27. $a - 1 - \dfrac{a^2 + a - 5}{a + 2}$

28. $2a + 3b - \dfrac{2a^2 - b^2}{2a - 3b}$

29. $3x - \dfrac{x^2}{2x + 3} - 2$

30. $(x + 4)\left(\dfrac{4}{x} - 1\right)$

31. $\left(a + \dfrac{2}{a}\right)\left(a - \dfrac{2}{a}\right)$

32. $\left(2x + \dfrac{3}{x}\right)\left(x - \dfrac{2}{x}\right)$

33. $\left(\dfrac{a + b}{a} - 1\right)\left(\dfrac{a}{b} + 1\right)\ \dfrac{a + b}{a}$

34. $\left(y - \dfrac{2}{y + 1}\right)\left(1 - \dfrac{1}{y + 2}\right)\ y - 1$

35. $\left(\dfrac{m}{n} - \dfrac{n}{m}\right) \div \left(\dfrac{1}{m} + \dfrac{1}{n}\right)\ m - n$

36. $\left(9 - \dfrac{1}{x^2}\right) \div (3x - 1)\ \dfrac{3x + 1}{x^2}$

37. $\left(1 - \dfrac{2}{a}\right) \div \left(1 - \dfrac{4}{a^2}\right)\ \dfrac{a}{a + 2}$

38. $1 + \dfrac{2x}{2x - 1} - \dfrac{8x^2}{4x^2 - 1}\ \dfrac{1}{2x + 1}$

39. As an algebra exercise, Amy, Don, and Julie were asked to simplify

$$1 - \dfrac{8x}{x^2 - x} - \dfrac{2x}{1 - x}.$$

Amy used a common denominator of $x(x - 1)(1 - x)$. Don used $x(x - 1)$, and Julie used $x - 1$. Explain why any of these three denominators could be used.

40. It took Jan y hours to drive 200 km. If she had increased her speed by 10 km/h and driven for 2 h less, how far could she have gone? (*Hint:* Make a chart. Answer in terms of y.)

41. Ted bought n rolls of film for a total of $40. He then sold all but 2 of them for $1 more per roll than he paid. How much did he receive for the rolls of film that he sold?

40. $\dfrac{10y^2 + 180y - 400}{y}$ km **41.** $\dfrac{n^2 + 38n - 80}{n}$ dollars

Write each expression as a fraction in simplest form.

C **42.** $\left(1 - \dfrac{b^2 + c^2 - a^2}{2bc}\right) \div \left(1 - \dfrac{a^2 + b^2 - c^2}{2ab}\right)\ \dfrac{a(a + b - c)}{c(c - a + b)}$

43. $\left(2 - \dfrac{n}{n + 1} + \dfrac{n}{1 - n}\right) \div \left(\dfrac{1}{n - 1} - \dfrac{1}{n + 1}\right)\ -1$

44. Find the values of A and B if $\dfrac{A}{x + 2} + \dfrac{B}{x - 2} = \dfrac{4}{x^2 - 4}$. $A = -1, B = 1$

45. Find the values of C and D if $\dfrac{C}{x - 2} + \dfrac{D}{x + 1} = \dfrac{6x}{x^2 - x - 2}$. $C = 4, D = 2$

46. Simplify: $\left(1 - \dfrac{1}{2}\right)\left(1 - \dfrac{1}{3}\right)\left(1 - \dfrac{1}{4}\right)\left(1 - \dfrac{1}{5}\right) \ldots \left(1 - \dfrac{1}{n}\right)\ \dfrac{1}{n}$

Mixed Review Exercises

Simplify.

1. $\dfrac{5a + 5b}{5a + 10}$ $\dfrac{a + b}{a + 2}$

2. $\dfrac{a^2 - 9a + 14}{49 - a^2} - \dfrac{a - 2}{7 + a}$

3. $\dfrac{5x^2}{3y^3} \div \dfrac{10xy}{9}$ $\dfrac{3x}{2y^4}$

4. $\dfrac{n^2 - 4}{2} \div \dfrac{n + 2}{8}$ $4(n - 2)$

5. $\dfrac{8}{y^5} \cdot \dfrac{y^7}{4}$ $2y^2$

6. $(-4b^2)^2$ $16b^4$

Find the least common denominator.

7. $\dfrac{1}{2xy}, \dfrac{3}{x^2}$ $2x^2y$

8. $\dfrac{5}{b^2}, \dfrac{2}{ab}$ ab^2

9. $\dfrac{2}{x - 1}, \dfrac{3}{1 + x}, \dfrac{1}{1 - x^2}$
$1 - x^2$, or $x^2 - 1$

Computer Exercises

For students with some programming experience.

In the Computer Exercises on page 145, you wrote a BASIC program to evaluate $n!$ for a value of n entered with an INPUT statement.

1. Write a BASIC program to find the value of each of the following.

$1 + \dfrac{1}{1!} + \dfrac{1}{2!}$ 2.5

$1 + \dfrac{1}{1!} + \dfrac{1}{2!} + \dfrac{1}{3!}$ 2.6666667

$1 + \dfrac{1}{1!} + \dfrac{1}{2!} + \dfrac{1}{3!} + \dfrac{1}{4!}$ 2.7083333

$1 + \dfrac{1}{1!} + \dfrac{1}{2!} + \dfrac{1}{3!} + \dfrac{1}{4!} + \dfrac{1}{5!}$ 2.7166667

$1 + \dfrac{1}{1!} + \dfrac{1}{2!} + \dfrac{1}{3!} + \dfrac{1}{4!} + \dfrac{1}{5!} + \dfrac{1}{6!}$ 2.7180556

$1 + \dfrac{1}{1!} + \dfrac{1}{2!} + \dfrac{1}{3!} + \dfrac{1}{4!} + \dfrac{1}{5!} + \dfrac{1}{6!} + \dfrac{1}{7!}$ 2.718254

2. Based upon your results from Exercise 1, what do you think happens to the

sum $1 + \dfrac{1}{1!} + \dfrac{1}{2!} + \dfrac{1}{3!} + \cdots + \dfrac{1}{n!}$ as n becomes larger? It approaches 2.7182818. (This is the irrational number e.)

Challenge
Answers may vary. For example, 11, 23, and 35 satisfy all three conditions.

Find at least three numbers that satisfy all three conditions:

(1) there is a remainder of 1 when the number is divided by 2;
(2) there is a remainder of 2 when the number is divided by 3;
(3) there is a remainder of 3 when the number is divided by 4.

Fractions **273**

Supplementary Materials
Study Guide   pp. 109–110
Practice Master   35
Resource Book   p. 103

Problem Solving Strategies

Students *look for a general pattern* in summing reciprocals of factorials in the computer exercises.

  Using a Computer

In these exercises a computer is used to find the sum of the reciprocals of consecutive factorials. The exercises also lead students to suggest the value that this sum approaches when more and more terms are added.

Teaching Suggestions, p. T111

Suggested Extensions, p. T111

Warm-Up Exercises

1. Use long division to divide.

$$\begin{array}{r} 16\frac{1}{27} \\ 27\overline{)433} \end{array}$$

Use the example above to identify each term.

2. dividend 433
3. divisor 27
4. quotient 16
5. remainder 1

Rewrite each polynomial in descending degree of *x*.

6. $32x - 15 + 45x^2$
   $45x^2 + 32x - 15$
7. $6 + 4x^5 + x - x^4 + x^2$
   $4x^5 - x^4 + x^2 + x + 6$

Motivating the Lesson

Tell students that they have learned in arithmetic how to divide one number by another number. They will see in today's lesson that they already know how to divide one polynomial by another polynomial because the method is the same. Working with different terms is like working with different place values. As with ordinary long division, sometimes one or more zeros may need to be inserted.

6-7 Polynomial Long Division

Objective To divide polynomials.

Dividing polynomials is very much like dividing real numbers. Compare the polynomial division to the numerical long division shown below.

Long Division	**Polynomial Division**
Step 1 $\begin{array}{r} 4 \\ 23\overline{)949} \\ -92 \\ \hline 29 \end{array}$	*Step 1* $\begin{array}{r} 2x \\ 4x+1\overline{)8x^2+6x+3} \\ 8x^2+2x \\ \hline 4x+3 \end{array}$ ← Subtract.
Step 2 $\begin{array}{r} 41 \\ 23\overline{)949} \\ -92 \\ \hline 29 \\ -23 \\ \hline 6 \end{array}$	*Step 2* $\begin{array}{r} 2x+1 \\ 4x+1\overline{)8x^2+6x+3} \\ 8x^2+2x \\ \hline 4x+3 \\ 4x+1 \\ \hline 2 \end{array}$ ← Subtract.
Check: $949 \stackrel{?}{=} 41 \cdot 23 + 6$ $949 \stackrel{?}{=} 943 + 6$ $949 = 949$ ✓	*Check:* $8x^2 + 6x + 3 \stackrel{?}{=} (2x + 1)(4x + 1) + 2$ $8x^2 + 6x + 3 \stackrel{?}{=} (8x^2 + 6x + 1) + 2$ $8x^2 + 6x + 3 = 8x^2 + 6x + 3$ ✓
$\therefore \frac{949}{23} = 41\frac{6}{23}$	$\therefore \frac{8x^2 + 6x + 3}{4x + 1} = 2x + 1 + \frac{2}{4x + 1}$

In both divisions above, the answer was written in the following form:

$$\frac{\text{Dividend}}{\text{Divisor}} = \text{Quotient} + \frac{\text{Remainder}}{\text{Divisor}}$$

The following formula was used to check both divisions:

$$\text{Dividend} = \text{Quotient} \times \text{Divisor} + \text{Remainder}$$

When you divide polynomials, always arrange the terms in each polynomial in order of decreasing degree of the variable.

Example 1 Divide: $\dfrac{34x - 16 + 15x^2}{5x - 2}$

Solution First rewrite $34x - 16 + 15x^2$ in order of decreasing degree of x as $15x^2 + 34x - 16$.

$$
\begin{array}{r}
3x + 8 \\
5x - 2 \overline{)15x^2 + 34x - 16} \\
\underline{15x^2 - 6x} \\
40x - 16 \\
\underline{40x - 16} \\
0
\end{array}
$$

Check: $15x^2 + 34x - 16 \stackrel{?}{=} (3x + 8)(5x - 2) + 0$

 $15x^2 + 34x - 16 = 15x^2 + 34x - 16$ $\checkmark$

$\therefore \dfrac{15x^2 + 34x - 16}{5x - 2} = 3x + 8$ **Answer**

In Example 1 the remainder is 0. Thus, both $3x + 8$ and $5x - 2$ are *factors* of $15x^2 + 34x - 16$.

Example 2 Divide $\dfrac{2a^3 + 5}{a - 3}$. Write the answer as a mixed expression.

Solution Using zero coefficients, insert missing terms in decreasing degree of a in $2a^3 - 5$. Then divide.

$$
\begin{array}{r}
2a^2 + 6a + 18 \\
a - 3 \overline{)2a^3 + 0a^2 + 0a + 5} \\
\underline{2a^3 - 6a^2} \\
6a^2 + 0a \\
\underline{6a^2 - 18a} \\
18a + 5 \\
\underline{18a - 54} \\
59
\end{array}
$$

$\left\{\begin{array}{l}\text{Division ends when the remainder is} \\ \text{either 0 or of lesser degree than the} \\ \text{divisor.}\end{array}\right.$

Check: $2a^3 + 5 \stackrel{?}{=} (2a^2 + 6a + 18)(a - 3) + 59$

 $2a^3 + 5 \stackrel{?}{=} 2a^3 + 6a^2 + 18a - 6a^2 - 18a - 54 + 59$

 $2a^3 + 5 \stackrel{?}{=} 2a^3 + (6a^2 - 6a^2) + (18a - 18a) - 54 + 59$

 $2a^3 + 5 = 2a^3 + 5$ $\checkmark$

$\therefore \dfrac{2a^3 + 5}{a - 3} = 2a^2 + 6a + 18 + \dfrac{59}{a - 3}$ **Answer**

Chalkboard Examples

Divide.

1. $\dfrac{19x - 21 + 12x^2}{4x - 3}$

$$
\begin{array}{r}
3x + 7 \\
4x - 3 \overline{)12x^2 + 19x - 21} \\
\underline{12x^2 - 9x} \\
28x - 21 \\
\underline{28x - 21} \\
0
\end{array}
$$

2. $\dfrac{y^3 + 4}{y - 1}$

$$
\begin{array}{r}
y^2 + y + 1 + \dfrac{5}{y - 1} \\
y - 1 \overline{)y^3 + 0y^2 + 0y + 4} \\
\underline{y^3 - y^2} \\
y^2 + 0y \\
\underline{y^2 - y} \\
y + 4 \\
\underline{y - 1} \\
5
\end{array}
$$

Check for Understanding

A suggested use of the Oral Exercises to check students' understanding as you teach the lesson.

Oral Exs. 1–3: use after Example 1.

Oral Exs. 4–6: use after reviewing the formulas on p. 274.

Oral Ex. 7: use after Example 1.

Guided Practice

Divide. Write the answer as a polynomial or a mixed expression.

1. $\dfrac{x^2 - 3x - 4}{x - 4}$ $x + 1$

2. $\dfrac{-6 + n^2 + 5n}{n + 6}$ $n - 1$

3. $\dfrac{4x^3 - 2x^2 + 6x - 5}{2x + 1}$

$2x^2 - 2x + 4 - \dfrac{9}{2x + 1}$

(continued)

276

Guided Practice (continued)

4. $\dfrac{y^4 + 1}{y + 1}$

$y^3 - y^2 + y - 1 + \dfrac{2}{y + 1}$

Summarizing the Lesson

Tell students that they have learned to divide polynomials. Ask students to compare polynomial division to long division and to identify the dividend, divisor, quotient and remainder.

Oral Exercises

How would you rewrite the terms of the divisor and the dividend before doing the long division? Do not divide.

1. $\dfrac{x^2 + 3x^3 + 5x - 2}{x + 1}$
$x + 1; 3x^3 + x^2 + 5x - 2$

2. $\dfrac{x^3 + 8}{x + 2}$
$x + 2; x^3 + 0x^2 + 0x + 8$

3. $\dfrac{2 - 2x^3 + x^2}{3 + 2x}$ $2x + 3;$
$-2x^3 + x^2 + 0x + 2$

Use the given information to find the dividend.

4. divisor = 5
quotient = 11
remainder = 2   57

5. divisor = $x + 1$
quotient = $x - 1$
remainder = 3 $x^2 + 2$

6. divisor = $x^2 + 1$
quotient = $2x$
remainder = $7x + 5$

$2x^3 + 9x + 5$

7. When $x^3 - x - 6$ is divided by $x - 2$, the quotient is $x^2 + 2x + 3$ and the remainder is 0. This means that __?__ and __?__ are factors of __?__ .

  $x - 2$ $x^2 + 2x + 3$ $x^3 - x - 6$

Written Exercises

Divide. Write the answer as a polynomial or a mixed expression.

A 1. $\dfrac{x^2 + 5x + 6}{x + 2}$ $x + 3$

2. $\dfrac{x^2 - x - 12}{x - 4}$ $x + 3$

3. $\dfrac{n^2 - 3n - 54}{n - 9}$ $n + 6$

4. $\dfrac{n^2 - 11n - 26}{n + 2}$ $n - 13$

5. $\dfrac{y^2 - 2y + 5}{y + 1}$

6. $\dfrac{a^2 - 3a + 7}{a - 2}$

7. $\dfrac{x^2 - 3x - 9}{x - 3}$

8. $\dfrac{z^2 - 8z - 12}{z + 4}$

9. $\dfrac{4 + n^2 - 2n}{n - 6}$

10. $\dfrac{s + s^2 - 8}{s + 4}$

11. $\dfrac{x^2 + 4}{x + 2}$

12. $\dfrac{y^2 - 9}{y + 9}$

13. $\dfrac{3x^2 + 10x - 9}{3x - 2}$

14. $\dfrac{2a^2 - 5a - 10}{2a + 1}$

15. $\dfrac{8 + 4x^2}{2x + 1}$

16. $\dfrac{9y^2 + 6}{3y - 1}$

17. $\dfrac{n^3 - 2n^2 + n + 2}{n + 2}$

18. $\dfrac{a^3 + 2a^2 + 3a + 4}{a - 1}$

19. $\dfrac{a^3 + 8}{a - 2}$

20. $\dfrac{n^3 - 1}{n - 1}$ $n^2 + n + 1$

21. $\dfrac{12x^3 - 2x^2 + x - 9}{3x + 1}$
$4x^2 - 2x + 1 - \dfrac{10}{3x + 1}$

22. $\dfrac{8n^3 - 6n^2 + 10n + 15}{4n + 1}$
$2n^2 - 2n + 3 + \dfrac{12}{4n + 1}$

B 23. $\dfrac{3x^4 - 4x^3 - x^2 - 16x - 12}{3x + 2}$ $x^3 - 2x^2 + x - 6$

24. $\dfrac{6x^4 - x^3 - 11x^2 + 9x - 2}{2x - 1}$ $3x^3 + x^2 - 5x + 2$

25. $\dfrac{2n^4 - n^3 - 2n + 1}{2n - 1}$ $n^3 - 1$

26. $\dfrac{8y^4 + 10y^3 + 12y + 15}{4y + 5}$ $2y^3 + 3$

27. $\dfrac{z^4 + 16}{z + 2}$ $z^3 - 2z^2 + 4z - 8 + \dfrac{32}{z + 2}$

28. $\dfrac{b^4 + 84}{b - 3}$ $b^3 + 3b^2 + 9b + 27 + \dfrac{165}{b - 3}$

29. $\dfrac{n^4 - n^3 + 3n^2 - 2n + 2}{n^2 + 2}$ $n^2 - n + 1$

30. $\dfrac{x^3 + 3x^2 - 4x - 12}{x^2 + 5x + 6}$ $x - 2$

276   Chapter 6

31. The volume of a rectangular solid is $12n^3 + 8n^2 - 3n - 2$. The length of the solid is $2n + 1$ and the width is $2n - 1$. Find the height. $3n + 2$

32. Divide $a^4 + a^2 - 20$ by $a - 2$.
  a. Use long division. $a^3 + 2a^2 + 5a + 10$
  b. Factor $a^4 + a^2 - 20$ first. Then divide by $a - 2$. $(a + 2)(a^2 + 5)$
  c. Show that your answers to parts (a) and (b) are the same.

33. Factor $2n^3 - 14n + 12$ completely given that $n + 3$ is a factor. $2(n + 3)(n - 1)(n - 2)$

34. Factor $4x^3 - 12x^2 - 37x - 15$ completely given that $2x + 1$ is a factor. $(2x + 1)(2x + 3)(x - 5)$

C 35. Find the value of k if $x - 3$ is a factor of $4x^2 - 15x + k$. 9

36. Find the value of k if $2x - 1$ is a factor of $4x^3 - 6x^2 - 4x + k$. 3

37. Find the value of k if $y + 3$ is a factor of $y^3 + y^2 + ky + 3$. -5

38. When $4x^4 + x^3 - 7x^2 + 3x + k$ is divided by $x - 1$, the remainder is 5. Find the value of k. 4

Mixed Review Exercises

Simplify.

1. $\dfrac{x + 4}{2} + \dfrac{2x - 1}{2}$ $\dfrac{3x + 3}{2}$

2. $\dfrac{a^2}{a + 3} - \dfrac{9}{a + 3}$ $a - 3$

3. $\dfrac{2}{y} + \dfrac{1}{3}$ $\dfrac{6 + y}{3y}$

4. $\dfrac{5c + 1}{6c} + \dfrac{3}{2c}$ $\dfrac{5c + 10}{6c}$

5. $\dfrac{2z + 1}{6} - \dfrac{3z - 5}{9}$ $\dfrac{13}{18}$

6. $\dfrac{x}{x^2 - 25} - \dfrac{1}{2x + 10}$ $\dfrac{1}{2(x - 5)}$

7. $x + \dfrac{2}{x}$ $\dfrac{x^2 + 2}{x}$

8. $4 + \dfrac{n}{n + 1}$ $\dfrac{5n + 4}{n + 1}$

9. $y + 3 + \dfrac{2y - 1}{y - 2}$ $\dfrac{y^2 + 3y - 7}{y - 2}$

Self-Test 3

Vocabulary mixed expression (p. 270)

Write each expression as a fraction in simplest form.

1. $3 - \dfrac{8}{y}$ $\dfrac{3y - 8}{y}$ **2.** $5n + \dfrac{1}{n}$ $\dfrac{5n^2 + 1}{n}$ **3.** $a - \dfrac{a - 1}{a + 1}$ $\dfrac{a^2 + 1}{a + 1}$ **Obj. 6-6, p. 270**

Divide. Write the answer as a polynomial or a mixed expression.

4. $\dfrac{-2 + 3y^2 + y}{y + 1}$ $3y - 2$ **5.** $\dfrac{5b^3 + b^2 + b + 16}{b + 2}$ $5b^2 - 9b + 19 - \dfrac{22}{b + 2}$ **Obj. 6-7, p. 274**

Check your answers with those at the back of the book.

Suggested Assignments

Day 1: 276/1–21 odd
Assign with Lesson 6-6.
Day 2: 276/23–33 odd
  S 277/Mixed Review

Average
Day 1: 276/2–22 even
Assign with Lesson 6-6.
Day 2: 276/24–34 even
  S 277/Mixed Review

Maximum
Day 1: 276/2–30 even, 31, 35
Day 2: 277/32–34, 36–38
  S 277/Mixed Review

Supplementary Materials

Study Guide   pp. 111–112
Practice Masters   36–38
Test Masters   26–29
Computer Activity   18
Resource Book   p. 104

Quick Quiz

Write each expression as a fraction in simplest form.

1. $6 - \dfrac{4}{a}$ $\dfrac{6a - 4}{a}$

2. $3y - \dfrac{2}{y}$ $\dfrac{3y^2 - 2}{y}$

3. $n - \dfrac{n + 1}{n - 1}$ $\dfrac{n^2 - 2n - 1}{n - 1}$

Divide. Write the answer as a polynomial or a mixed expression.

4. $\dfrac{y + 6y^2 - 40}{2y - 5}$ $3y + 8$

5. $\dfrac{2y^3 + 9y^2 - 36}{y + 3}$

$2y^2 + 3y - 9 - \dfrac{9}{y + 3}$

Extra / Complex Fractions

A complex fraction is a fraction whose numerator or denominator contains one or more fractions. To express a complex fraction as a simple fraction, use one of the methods below.

Method 1: Simplify the numerator and denominator. Express the fraction as a quotient using the ÷ sign. Multiply by the reciprocal of the divisor.

Method 2: Find the LCD of all the simple fractions. Multiply the numerator and the denominator of the complex fraction by the LCD.

Example Simplify $\dfrac{\frac{1}{a} + \frac{1}{b}}{\frac{b}{2a} - \frac{a}{2b}}$.

Solution *Method 1:*

$$\frac{\frac{1}{a} + \frac{1}{b}}{\frac{b}{2a} - \frac{a}{2b}} = \frac{\frac{b+a}{ab}}{\frac{b^2 - a^2}{2ab}}$$

$$= \frac{b+a}{ab} \div \frac{b^2 - a^2}{2ab}$$

$$= \frac{\cancel{b+a}}{\cancel{ab}} \cdot \frac{2a\cancel{b}}{(\cancel{b+a})(b-a)}$$

$$= \frac{2}{b-a}$$

Method 2:

The LCD of all the simple fractions is $2ab$.

$$\frac{\frac{1}{a} + \frac{1}{b}}{\frac{b}{2a} - \frac{a}{2b}} = \frac{\left(\frac{1}{a} + \frac{1}{b}\right)2ab}{\left(\frac{b}{2a} - \frac{a}{2b}\right)2ab}$$

$$= \frac{2b + 2a}{b^2 - a^2}$$

$$= \frac{2(\cancel{b+a})}{(\cancel{b+a})(b-a)}$$

$$= \frac{2}{b-a}$$

Exercises

Simplify. Use either Method 1 or Method 2.

A 1. $\dfrac{\frac{m}{8}}{\frac{5m}{8}}$ $\frac{1}{5}$

2. $\dfrac{\frac{3a}{4}}{\frac{15a}{12}}$ $\frac{3}{5}$

3. $\dfrac{\frac{u}{v^2}}{\frac{u}{v}}$ $\frac{1}{v}$

4. $\dfrac{\frac{6e}{3}}{\frac{7e}{}}$ $14e^2$

5. $\dfrac{\frac{1}{4} + \frac{1}{8}}{\frac{1}{4} - \frac{1}{8}}$ 3

6. $\dfrac{\frac{1}{6} + \frac{1}{3}}{\frac{1}{2} + \frac{1}{5}}$ $\frac{5}{7}$

7. $\dfrac{\frac{5}{6} - \frac{5}{7}}{\frac{5}{6} + \frac{5}{7}}$ $\frac{1}{13}$

8. $\dfrac{\frac{3}{x}}{\frac{1}{x} - \frac{1}{3x}}$ $\frac{9}{2}$

9. $\dfrac{\frac{9c^2}{5d^4}}{\frac{3c^2}{10d^3}}$ $\frac{6}{d}$

10. $\dfrac{\frac{n^2 - 25}{n}}{n - 5}$ $\frac{n+5}{n}$

11. $\dfrac{\frac{r}{s} + 2}{1 - \frac{r}{s}}$ $\frac{r + 2s}{s - r}$

12. $\dfrac{\frac{2w}{3} + 2}{\frac{2w}{5(w-3)}}$ $\dfrac{5w}{3} - \dfrac{15}{w}$

Simplify.

B **13.** $\dfrac{z - \dfrac{5z}{z+5}}{z + \dfrac{5z}{z-5}}$ $\dfrac{z-5}{z+5}$

14. $\dfrac{1 - \dfrac{6}{s^2+2}}{\dfrac{4s+2}{s^2+2}+1}$ $\dfrac{s-2}{s+2}$

15. $\dfrac{k + \dfrac{k-3}{k+1}}{k - \dfrac{2}{k+1}}$ $\dfrac{k+3}{k+2}$

16. $\dfrac{\dfrac{1}{c} - \dfrac{1}{3-3c}}{\dfrac{1}{1-c} - \dfrac{3}{c}}$ $-\dfrac{1}{3}$

17. $\dfrac{\dfrac{e}{e-f} - \dfrac{f}{e+f}}{\dfrac{f}{e-f} + \dfrac{e}{e+f}}$ 1

18. $\dfrac{1-2u}{1+\dfrac{1}{2u}} \div \dfrac{1+2u}{1-\dfrac{1}{2u}}$ $\dfrac{(2u-1)^2}{(2u+1)^2}$

19. $\dfrac{\dfrac{2}{z+1}-2}{\dfrac{2-z}{z^2-1}-2}$ $\dfrac{2z(z-1)}{2z^2+z-4}$

20. $\dfrac{\dfrac{m-n}{m+n}+\dfrac{n}{m}}{\dfrac{m}{n}-\dfrac{m-n}{m+n}}$ $\dfrac{n}{m}$

21. If $x = \dfrac{y-1}{y+1}$ and $y = \dfrac{1}{1-z}$, express x in terms of z. $\dfrac{z}{2-z}$

22. If $a = \dfrac{b-c}{1+bc}$ and $b = \dfrac{1}{z-1}$ and $c = \dfrac{1}{z+1}$, find a in terms of z. $\dfrac{2}{z^2}$

23. Sam drives d km at 50 km/h and returns the same distance at 30 km/h. Show that the average speed is 37.5 km/h. (*Hint:* Average speed = total distance divided by total time.)

24. A cyclist travels 12 km on a level road at x km/h and then goes 9 km on a downhill road at $2x$ km/h. Find her average speed in terms of x. (See *Hint* for Exercise 23.) $\dfrac{14x}{11}$ km/h

25. If n items can be purchased for 50 cents, how many items can be purchased for 50 cents after the price per item is decreased by 10 cents? $\dfrac{5n}{5-n}$ items

26. If $a = \dfrac{1-c}{1+c}$ and $c = \dfrac{1+b}{1-b}$, show that $a + b = 0$.

Simplify.

27. $\left(\dfrac{w}{6} - \dfrac{6}{w}\right) \div \left(\dfrac{6}{w} - 4 + \dfrac{w}{2}\right)$

28. $\left(\dfrac{x}{4-x^2} + \dfrac{1}{x-2}\right) \div \left(1 - \dfrac{2}{2+x}\right)$

29. $\left(\dfrac{1}{n-n^2} - \dfrac{1}{n^2+n}\right) \div \left(\dfrac{1}{n^2+1} - \dfrac{1}{n^2-1}\right)$

30. $\left(\dfrac{c^2+d^2}{cd} - 2\right) \div \left(\dfrac{4c^2-4d^2}{2cd}\right)$

31. $\left(\dfrac{9e^2-5}{e-1} - \dfrac{1}{6}\right) \div \left(1 - \dfrac{e-9e^2}{e-1}\right)$

32. $\left(\dfrac{u^2+v^2}{u^2-v^2}\right) \div \left(\dfrac{u-v}{u+v} - \dfrac{u+v}{u-v}\right)$

C **33.** $\dfrac{r}{2}\left(\dfrac{r^2-s^2}{r^2s+rs^2}\right)\left(\dfrac{1}{r-s}\right)\left(\dfrac{1}{r+s}\right) \div \dfrac{1}{r+s}$

34. $\left(\dfrac{4x^2-y^2}{3xy}\right) \div \left(\dfrac{2x^2-y^2}{xy} + 1\right)$

35. $1 - \dfrac{1}{1-\dfrac{1}{c-2}}$

36. $2 + \dfrac{1}{1+\dfrac{2}{a+\dfrac{1}{a}}}$

Fractions **279**

Chapter Summary

1. A fraction can be simplified by factoring its numerator and its denominator and dividing each by their common factors.

2. The *rule of exponents for a power of a quotient* (page 252) is sometimes used when simplifying fractions.

3. The following rules are used with fractions.

Multiplication Rule $\qquad$ Division Rule

$$\frac{a}{b} \cdot \frac{c}{d} = \frac{ac}{bd} \qquad\qquad \frac{a}{b} \div \frac{c}{d} = \frac{a}{b} \cdot \frac{d}{c}$$

Addition Rule $\qquad$ Subtraction Rule

$$\frac{a}{c} + \frac{b}{c} = \frac{a+b}{c} \qquad\qquad \frac{a}{c} - \frac{b}{c} = \frac{a-b}{c}$$

4. When adding or subtracting fractions with different denominators, rewrite the fractions using their *least common denominator (LCD)*. Then apply the appropriate rule. (See page 264.)

5. The sum or difference of a polynomial and a fraction is called a *mixed expression*. A mixed expression can be expressed as a fraction in simplest form.

6. When dividing polynomials, arrange the terms of the *divisor and dividend* in order of decreasing degree of a variable. Wherever the dividend is missing a term, insert one with a zero coefficient.

Supplementary Materials

Practice Master   37
Resource Book   p. 198

Chapter Review

Give the letter of the correct answer.

1. Express $\dfrac{9x^2 - 9}{1 - x^2}$ in simplest form.   **6-1**

   a. 0   **(b.)** -9 **c.** $\dfrac{9(x-1)}{x+1}$ **d.** $\dfrac{9(x+1)(x-1)}{x^2+1}$

2. Express $\dfrac{15xy}{10x^2y - y^2x}$ in simplest form.

   a. $\dfrac{3}{2x-y}$ **(b.)** $\dfrac{15}{10x-y}$ **c.** $\dfrac{5}{3x}$ **d.** $\dfrac{5}{2x-y}$

3. Express $\left(-\dfrac{2}{5}\right)^3 \left(-\dfrac{25}{4}\right)$ in simplest form.   **6-2**

   (a.) $\dfrac{2}{5}$ **b.** $-\dfrac{5}{2}$ **c.** $-\dfrac{2}{5}$ **d.** $\dfrac{5}{2}$

4. Express $\dfrac{2ab}{15} \cdot \dfrac{25}{3ab^2}$ in simplest form.

   a. $10b$ **(b.)** $\dfrac{10}{9b}$ **c.** $\dfrac{10}{9b^2}$ **d.** $\dfrac{10}{3b}$

5. Express $5ab^2 \div \dfrac{10a}{b}$ in simplest form.   **6-3**

   a. $\dfrac{b}{2}$ **(b.)** $\dfrac{b^3}{2}$ **c.** $\dfrac{50a^2}{b}$ **d.** $2b^3$

6. Express $\dfrac{x^2 - 36}{6x + 36} \div (6 - x)$ in simplest form.

   (a.) $-\dfrac{1}{6}$ **b.** 6 **c.** $\dfrac{1}{6}$ **d.** -6

7. Complete: $\dfrac{2}{x - 3} = \dfrac{?}{x^2 - 6x + 9}$ **6-4**

   a. 2 **b.** $2(x + 3)$ **c.** $2(9)$ **(d.)** $2(x - 3)$

8. Find the LCD for $\dfrac{4n}{9n - 6}$ and $\dfrac{2n}{15(3n - 2)^2}$.

   a. $15(3n - 2)$ **b.** $45(3n - 2)^2$ **(c.)** $15(3n - 2)^2$ **d.** $5(3n - 2)$

9. Simplify $\dfrac{3x}{x - 2} + \dfrac{6}{2 - x}$.   **6-5**

   a. $\dfrac{3x + 6}{x - 2}$ **b.** -3 **(c.)** 3 **d.** $\dfrac{3x - 6}{2 - x}$

10. Simplify $\dfrac{n - 9}{36} - \dfrac{n - 35}{108}$.

   a. $\dfrac{n - 2}{27}$ **(b.)** $\dfrac{n + 4}{54}$ **c.** $2n + 8$ **d.** $\dfrac{n - 31}{54}$

11. Write $7 + \dfrac{x + 2}{x - 2}$ as a fraction in simplest form.   **6-6**

   a. $\dfrac{6x}{x - 2}$ **b.** $\dfrac{4(x - 3)}{x - 2}$ **(c.)** $\dfrac{8x - 12}{x - 2}$ **d.** $\dfrac{-6x + 16}{x - 2}$

12. Simplify $y + 3 + \dfrac{1}{y - 3}$.

   (a.) $\dfrac{y^2 - 8}{y - 3}$ **b.** $\dfrac{y + 4}{y - 3}$ **c.** $\dfrac{y^2 - 8}{y^2 - 9}$ **d.** $\dfrac{y^2 - 10}{y - 3}$

13. When $x^3 - 3x^2 + 3x + 4$ is divided by $x - 2$, what is the remainder?   **6-7**

   a. 2 **b.** 4 **(c.)** 6 **d.** 8

14. Divide $\dfrac{27x^3 + 8}{3x - 2}$. Write the answer as a polynomial or a mixed expression.

   a. $9x^2 + 4$ **(b.)** $9x^2 + 6x + 4 + \dfrac{16}{3x - 2}$

   c. $9x^2 + 6x + 4$ **d.** $9x^2 - 6x + 4$

Chapter Test

Simplify. Give the restrictions on the variable.

1. $\dfrac{5x + 35}{x^2 - 49}$ $\dfrac{5}{x-7}$; $x \neq 7,\ x \neq -7$

2. $\dfrac{64 - n^2}{n^2 - 4n - 32}$ $-\dfrac{n+8}{n+4}$; $n \neq 8,\ n \neq -4$ **6-1**

3. $\dfrac{3x^2 - 6x - 24}{3x^2 + 2x - 8}$ $\dfrac{3(x-4)}{3x-4}$; $x \neq \dfrac{4}{3}$; $x \neq -2$

4. $\dfrac{15y^2 - 30y - 45}{5y^2 + 10y - 15}$ $\dfrac{3(y-3)(y+1)}{(y+3)(y-1)}$; $y \neq -3,\ y \neq 1$

Express in simplest form.

5. $\left(-\dfrac{n^3}{7}\right)^2$ $\dfrac{n^6}{49}$

6. $\dfrac{(3b)^2}{5} \cdot \dfrac{b^3}{5}$ $\dfrac{9b^5}{25}$

7. $\left(\dfrac{3a}{b}\right)^2 \cdot \dfrac{7ab}{54}$ $\dfrac{7a^3}{6b}$ **6-2**

8. $\dfrac{9}{11} \div \dfrac{11}{9}$ $\dfrac{81}{121}$

9. $\dfrac{4}{7} \div \dfrac{4}{7}$ 1

10. $\dfrac{5x^2}{4y^2} \div 20xy$ $\dfrac{x}{16y^3}$ **6-3**

11. $18 \div \left(\dfrac{3n}{2}\right)^3$ $\dfrac{16}{3n^3}$

12. $\dfrac{6a + 36}{6a} \div \dfrac{a^2 - 36}{a^2}$ $\dfrac{a}{a-6}$

13. $\dfrac{y}{2x^3} \div \left(\dfrac{y}{2x}\right)^2$ $\dfrac{2}{xy}$

Complete.

14. $\dfrac{7n}{16m} = \dfrac{?}{32m^2n}$ $14mn^2$

15. $\dfrac{3}{x+5} = \dfrac{?}{x^2 - 25}$ $3(x-5)$ **6-4**

Rewrite each group of fractions with their LCD.

16. $\dfrac{3}{8x},\ \dfrac{5}{12y^2},\ \dfrac{5}{6x^2y}$ $\dfrac{9xy^2}{24x^2y^2},\ \dfrac{10x^2}{24x^2y^2},\ \dfrac{20y}{24x^2y^2}$

17. $\dfrac{x-4}{15},\ \dfrac{x+2}{10}$ $\dfrac{2(x-4)}{30},\ \dfrac{3(x+2)}{30}$

Simplify.

18. $\dfrac{x}{x-9} + \dfrac{1}{x-9} - \dfrac{19-x}{x-9}$ 2

19. $\dfrac{x-1}{3} + \dfrac{3-2x}{6}$ $\dfrac{1}{6}$ **6-5**

20. $\dfrac{6n+3}{n-5} - \dfrac{4n+9}{5-n}$ $\dfrac{2(5n+6)}{n-5}$

21. $\dfrac{2}{y^2 - 2y} - \dfrac{3}{y^2 - y - 2}$ $-\dfrac{1}{y(y+1)}$

Write each expression as a fraction in simplest form.

22. $12 - \dfrac{n}{5}$ $\dfrac{60-n}{5}$

23. $2 + \dfrac{6}{y-7}$ $\dfrac{2(y-4)}{y-7}$ **6-6**

24. $4x - \dfrac{x+1}{x-1}$ $\dfrac{4x^2 - 5x - 1}{x-1}$

25. $\dfrac{x}{x+2} + \dfrac{2}{x-2} + 1$ $\dfrac{2x^2}{(x+2)(x-2)}$

Divide. Write the answer as a polynomial or a mixed expression.

26. $\dfrac{45 - 13n + n^2}{n-5}$ $n - 8 + \dfrac{5}{n-5}$

27. $\dfrac{2x^3 - x^2 - 5x - 2}{2x+1}$ $x^2 - x - 2$ **6-7**

Cumulative Review (Chapters 1–6)

Perform the indicated operations. Express the answers in simplest form. Assume that no denominator is zero. 5. $20x^2 + 3x - 9$ 6. $-10y^4 + 35y^3 - 5y$

1. $0.3(-0.5)^2 + 0.7(-0.5)^2$ 0.25

2. $\dfrac{45x^3y^2z^5}{-30(xyz)^2} - \dfrac{3xz^3}{2}$

3. $(4x^3yz^2)^3$ $64x^9y^3z^6$

4. $(8a - 9b) + (5a + 6b)$ $13a - 3b$

5. $(5x - 3)(4x + 3)$

6. $-5y(2y^3 - 7y^2 + 1)$

7. $(-13t + 6s) - (4t + 9s)$
$-17t - 3s$

8. $(-2b + 7c)^2$
$4b^2 - 28bc + 49c^2$

9. $(4t^2s - 9)(4t^2s + 9)$
$16t^4s^2 - 81$

Evaluate if $a = -1$, $b = 1$, $c = -2$, and $d = 3$.

10. $\dfrac{a + b}{c} - cd$ 6

11. $(a - b)^2 \div (c + d)^2$ 4

12. $(a^2 + b^2) \div c^2 + d$ $3\frac{1}{2}$

13. $a^2b(6a + 5ab - 3b)$ **14.** $(7x + 1)^2$ **15.** $2t(2t - 7)^2$ **16.** $n^2(n + 3)(n + 5)$

Factor completely. If the polynomial cannot be factored, write _prime_.

13. $6a^3b + 5a^3b^2 - 3a^2b^2$ **14.** $49x^2 + 14x + 1$ **15.** $8t^3 - 56t^2 + 98t$

16. $n^4 + 8n^3 + 15n^2$ **17.** $m^2 + 12m + 30$ **18.** $t^2 - 13t + 22$

19. $y^3 + 4y^2 - 32y$ **20.** $5c^2 + 8c - 4$ **21.** $4x^2 - 1 + 2x - 1$
17. prime **18.** $(t - 11)(t - 2)$ **19.** $y(y + 8)(y - 4)$ **20.** $(5c - 2)(c + 2)$ **21.** $2(2x - 1)(x + 1)$

Solve. If the equation is an identity or if it has no solution, write _identity_ or _no solution_. **25.** $\{-6\}$ **26.** $\{0, 5\}$ **27.** $\left\{-\frac{3}{4}, \frac{3}{4}\right\}$

22. $6y - 3 = 27$ {5}

23. $\frac{1}{4}a - 3 = 9$ {48}

24. $6 - \frac{3}{4}d = -3$ {12}

25. $(n + 2)^2 = (n + 4)(n - 2)$ **26.** $10m^2 - m^3 = 25m$ **27.** $16c^2 - 9 = 0$

28. $t^2 + 12t + 15 = -5$ {−2, −10} **29.** $x^2 - 6x = 7$ {7, −1} **30.** $6y^3 + 13y^2 - 5y = 0$
$\left\{0, \frac{1}{3}, -\frac{5}{2}\right\}$

Perform the indicated operations. Express the answers in simplest form.

31. $\dfrac{x^2 + 5x + 4}{2x^2 + 3x + 1} \cdot \dfrac{1 + 2x}{x^2 - 16}$

32. $\dfrac{1}{4x - 8} + \dfrac{x}{x^2 - 3x + 2}$

33. $\dfrac{a^2 - b^2}{(cd)^3} \div \dfrac{a + b}{c^2d}$

34. $\dfrac{3}{a^2 + 6a + 9} - \dfrac{a + 1}{a^2 - 9}$

35. $\dfrac{10y^3 + 7y^2 - 52y + 44}{5y - 4}$

36. $x - \dfrac{x + 1}{x - 5}$

37. Jan worked 38 h last week. She worked four times as many 8-hour shifts as 6-hour shifts. How many 8-hour shifts did she work? four 8-hour shifts

38. Jeremy has 24 quarters and half dollars. If he had twice as many half dollars and half as many quarters, he would have $2 more. How much money does he have? $8

39. It took Emily 25 min to ride her bicycle to the repair shop and 1 h 15 min to walk back home. If Emily can ride her bicycle 8 km/h faster than she can walk, how far is the repair shop from her house? 5 km

40. Find two numbers whose difference is 3 and whose squares total 65. 4 and 7, −4 and −7

Fractions **283**

Cumulative Review p. T26

Supplementary Materials
Practice Masters   38, 39
Test Master   29
Resource Book, pp. 34–35,
   36–38, 39–41, 105–106,
   107–108, 148–150

Additional Answers
Cumulative Review

31. $\dfrac{1}{x - 4}$

32. $\dfrac{5x - 1}{4(x - 2)(x - 1)}$

33. $\dfrac{a - b}{cd^2}$

34. $\dfrac{-a^2 - a - 12}{(a + 3)^2(a - 3)}$

35. $2y^2 + 3y - 8 + \dfrac{12}{5y - 4}$

36. $\dfrac{x^2 - 6x - 1}{x - 5}$

Maintaining Skills

Express each fraction as a decimal to the nearest hundredth.

Sample 1 $\frac{11}{13}$ **Solution** $13\overline{)11.000}^{\,0.846}$ $\frac{11}{13} \approx 0.85$

1. $\frac{23}{25}$ 0.92   **2.** $\frac{35}{20}$ 1.75   **3.** $\frac{10}{4}$ 2.50   **4.** $\frac{49}{50}$ 0.98   **5.** $\frac{81}{25}$ 3.24   **6.** $\frac{5}{3}$ 1.67

7. $\frac{51}{30}$ 1.70   **8.** $\frac{7}{8}$ 0.88   **9.** $\frac{14}{6}$ 2.33   **10.** $\frac{41}{24}$ 1.71   **11.** $\frac{15}{22}$ 0.68   **12.** $\frac{21}{17}$ 1.24

Express each percent as a fraction in simplest form.

Sample 2 4.8%   **Solution** $\frac{4.8}{100} = \frac{48}{1000} = \frac{6}{125}$

13. 62% $\frac{31}{50}$ **14.** 12% $\frac{3}{25}$ **15.** 85% $\frac{17}{20}$ **16.** 0.5% $\frac{1}{200}$ **17.** 0.03% $\frac{3}{10,000}$ **18.** 9.2% $\frac{23}{250}$

Express each decimal as a percent.

Sample 3 0.73   **Solution** **(1)** $0.73 = \frac{73}{100} = 73\%$ **(2)** $0.73 = 73\%$

19. 0.91 91%   **20.** 0.07 7%   **21.** 0.8 80%   **22.** 12 1200%   **23.** 0.032 3.2%   **24.** 1.23 123%

Find each number.

Sample 4 24% of 35   **Solution** $0.24 \times 35 = 8.4$

25. 32% of 85 27.2   **26.** 12% of 80 9.6   **27.** 0.2% of 40 0.08
28. 15.6% of 50 7.8   **29.** 130% of 40 52   **30.** 312% of 20 62.4

Find the value of each variable.

Sample 5 35% of $x = 7$ **Solution** $0.35x = 7;\ x = \frac{7}{0.35} = \frac{700}{35} = 20$

Sample 6 $n\%$ of 75 = 33   **Solution** $\frac{n}{100} \cdot 75 = 33;\ \frac{n}{100} = \frac{33}{75};\ n = 44$

31. 30% of $z = 21$ 70   **32.** 15% of $m = 6$ 40   **33.** 5% of $y = 0.6$ 12
34. 24% of $t = 108$ 450   **35.** $p\%$ of 50 = 30 60   **36.** $a\%$ of 45 = 18 40
37. $t\%$ of 105 = 21 20   **38.** 28 = $n\%$ of 112 25   **39.** 51 = $x\%$ of 150 34

Preparing for College Entrance Exams

Strategy for Success

In some problems, especially those involving length, width, area, perimeter, or relative position, it may help to draw a sketch. Use any available space in the test booklet. Be careful to make no assumptions in drawing the figure. Use only the information specifically given in the problem.

Decide which is the best of the choices given and write the corresponding letter on your answer sheet.

1. How many integral values of k are there for which $x^2 + kx + 24$ is factorable? E
   (A) 0   (B) 2   (C) 4   (D) 6   (E) 8

2. Which of the polynomials is prime? B
   (A) $35x^2 + 76x + 33$ (B) $4x^2 - 26x + 13$
   (C) $121y^2 + 176$ (D) $21x^2 + 40x - 21$

3. What solutions does the equation $10x^3 - 7x^2 - 12x = 0$ have? D
   (A) $0, -\dfrac{5}{4}, \dfrac{2}{3}$ (B) $\dfrac{5}{4}, -\dfrac{2}{3}$ (C) $\dfrac{4}{5}, -\dfrac{3}{2}$ (D) $0, -\dfrac{4}{5}, \dfrac{3}{2}$

4. A rectangular garden 9 ft by 12 ft includes a uniform border of woodchips around a rectangular bed of flowers. If the flowers take up half the area of the garden, find the perimeter of the flower bed. B
   (A) 27 ft   (B) 30 ft   (C) 33 ft   (D) 54 ft   (E) 51 ft

5. Express $\dfrac{4t + v}{t + v} - \dfrac{4t^2 - v^2}{t^2 - v^2}$ in simplest form. Assume that no denominator is zero. D
   (A) $\dfrac{2tv}{t^2 - v^2}$ (B) $\dfrac{8tv + 2v^2}{v^2 - t^2}$ (C) $\dfrac{5tv}{t^2 - v^2}$ (D) $\dfrac{3tv}{v^2 - t^2}$

6. Which of the following are factors of $6x^3 + 29x^2 - 7x - 10$? C
   I. $3x - 1$ II. $2x + 2$ III. $x + 5$
   (A) I only   (B) II only   (C) III only   (D) I and III only
   (E) II and III only

7. Express $\dfrac{(3n - 5)^4}{(2n + 1)^2} \div \dfrac{(5 - 3n)^4}{2n^2 + 7n + 3}$ in simplest form. B
   (A) $\dfrac{(3n - 5)^4(n + 3)}{(5 - 3n)^4(2n + 1)}$ (B) $\dfrac{n + 3}{2n + 1}$ (C) $\dfrac{2n + 1}{n + 3}$
   (D) $\dfrac{(3n - 5)^4(2n + 1)}{(5 - 3n)^4(n + 3)}$ (E) $n + 3$

7 Applying Fractions

Objectives

7-1 To solve problems involving ratios.

7-2 To solve problems using proportions.

7-3 To solve equations with fractional coefficients.

7-4 To solve fractional equations.

7-5 To work with percents and decimals.

7-6 To solve problems involving percents.

7-7 To solve mixture problems.

7-8 To solve work problems.

7-9 To use negative exponents.

7-10 To use scientific notation.

Assignment Guide

See p. T59 for Key to the format of the Assignment Guide

Day	Minimum Course		Average Course		Maximum Course	
1	7-1	289/1–25 odd, 31–33 291/P: 2, 4, 6, 8	7-1	289/2–34 even 291/P: 2, 4, 6, 8, 10	7-1 S	289/3–45 mult. of 3 291/P: 3–18 mult. of 3 292/Mixed Review
2	7-1 S 7-2	290/18, 20, 28, 32, 34 291/P: 10, 12 292/Mixed Review 295/1–15 odd	7-1 S 7-2	290/36, 38, 40, 42 291/P: 12, 14, 16 292/Mixed Review 295/3–30 mult. of 3	7-2 S	295/3–48 mult. of 3 296/P: 3, 6, 9, 12, 13 297/Mixed Review
3	7-2 S	295/17–35 odd 296/P: 3, 5, 7, 9 297/Mixed Review	7-2 S	295/33–45 mult. of 3 296/P: 3, 5, 7, 9, 11 297/Mixed Review	7-3 S R	299/3–33 mult. of 3 300/P: 3–15 mult. of 3 301/Mixed Review 297/Self-Test 1
4	7-3 R	299/1–15 odd 300/P: 1, 3, 5 297/Self-Test 1	7-3 R	299/1–4, 6–21 mult. of 3 300/P: 2, 4, 6, 8 297/Self-Test 1	7-4	305/3–36 mult. of 3 306/P: 2, 4, 6
5	7-3 S 7-4	299/14, 16, 18 300/P: 7, 9, 10 301/Mixed Review 305/1–6	7-3 S 7-4	300/25–27 301/P: 10, 12, 14 301/Mixed Review 305/1–6, 8, 10, 12	7-4 S	306/39, 40 307/P: 8, 10, 12, 14 308/Mixed Review
6	7-4 S	305/7–29 odd 306/P: 1–3, 5 308/Mixed Review	7-4 S	306/14–32 even 306/P: 2, 4, 6, 8, 10 308/Mixed Review	7-5 S R	312/3–60 mult. of 3 313/P: 3–15 mult. of 3 314/Mixed Review 308/Self-Test 2
7	7-5 R	312/1–31 odd 313/P: 1–3 308/Self-Test 2	7-5 S R	312/3–48 mult. of 3 313/P: 2, 5, 8, 10, 12 314/Mixed Review 308/Self-Test 2	7-6 S	317/3–21 mult. of 3 318/P: 3–15 mult. of 3 320/Mixed Review
8	7-5 S	312/34–40 even 314/P: 5–7 314/Mixed Review	7-6 S	317/3–21 mult. of 3 318/P: 3, 5, 7, 9, 11 320/Mixed Review	7-7 R	324/P: 1–8, 9, 12, 15, 18, 21 320/Self-Test 3
9	7-6 S	317/1–15 odd 318/P: 1, 3, 5, 7, 9 320/Mixed Review	7-7 R	324/P: 1–8, 10, 12, 14, 16 320/Self-Test 3	7-7 S 7-8	325/P: 22–25 325/Mixed Review 328/P: 1–8

Assignment Guide (continued)

Day	Minimum Course	Average Course	Maximum Course
10	**7-7** 324/*P*: 1–8, 10, 12, 16 **R** 320/*Self-Test 3* **S** 325/*Mixed Review*: 5–10	**7-7** 325/*P*: 18, 20, 22 **S** 325/*Mixed Review* **7-8** 328/*P*: 1–8, 10	**7-8** 329/*P*: 9, 12, 15, 18, 21–23 **S** 330/*Mixed Review*
11	**7-8** 328/*P*: 1–11 odd **S** 330/*Mixed Review*	**7-8** 329/*P*: 11–14, 16, 18, 20 **S** 330/*Mixed Review*	**7-9** 333/3–69 mult. of 3 335/*P*: 3, 5 **S** 335/*Mixed Review* **R** 330/*Self-Test 4*
12	**7-9** 333/1–27 odd, 29–31 335/*P*: 1, 2 **S** 335/*Mixed Review* **R** 330/*Self-Test 4*	**7-9** 333/3–30 mult. of 3, 36–66 mult. of 3; 335/*P*: 1–3 **S** 335/*Mixed Review* **R** 330/*Self-Test 4*	**7-10** 339/3–30 mult. of 3 339/*P*: 1, 2 **S** 340/*Mixed Review*
13	**7-10** 339/3–21 mult. of 3 **R** 341/*Self-Test 5*: 1–3, 10–12	**7-10** 339/3–30 mult. of 3 339/*P*: 1, 2 **S** 340/*Mixed Review*	*Prepare for Chapter Test* **R** 341/*Self-Test 5* 342/*Chapter Review* **EP** 651/*Skills*; 670/*Problems*
14	*Prepare for Chapter Test* **R** 342/*Chapter Review* **EP** 651/*Skills* 670/*Problems*	*Prepare for Chapter Test* **R** 341/*Self-Test 5* 342/*Chapter Review* **EP** 651/*Skills*; 670/*Problems*	*Administer Chapter 7 Test* **R** 345/*Cum. Review*: 1–39 odd **S** 347/*Mixed Problem Solving*: 1–13 odd
15	*Administer Chapter 7 Test* **R** 346/*Maintaining Skills* **S** 347/*Mixed Problem Solving*: 1–7 odd	*Administer Chapter 7 Test* **R** 345/*Cum. Review*: 1–39 odd **S** 347/*Mixed Problem Solving*: 1–13 odd	

Supplementary Materials Guide

For Use with Lesson	Practice Masters	Tests	Study Guide (Reteaching)	Resource Book		
				Tests	Practice Exercises	Prob. Solving (PS) Applications (A) Enrichment (E) Thinking Skl. (TS)
7-1			pp. 113–114			p. 184 (A)
7-2	Sheet 40		pp. 115–116		p. 109	pp. 224–225 (TS)
7-3			pp. 117–118			
7-4	Sheet 41		pp. 119–120		p. 110	
7-5		Test 30	pp. 121–122			
7-6	Sheet 42		pp. 123–124		p. 111	
7-7			pp. 125–126			pp. 168–170 (PS)
7-8	Sheet 43		pp. 127–128		p. 112	pp. 171–172 (PS)
7-9			pp. 129–130		p. 113	
7-10	Sheet 44	Test 31	pp. 131–132	pp. 42–45		
Chapter 7	Sheet 45	Tests 32, 33				p. 199 (E)

Software

Software	Computer Activities	Test Generator
	Activities 19–22	210 test items
For Use with Lessons	7-1, 7-4, 7-5, 7-10	all lessons

Strategies for Teaching

Problem Solving

One of the goals of an algebra course is to familiarize students with standard problem solving techniques and to give students enough practice with these techniques so that they can use them confidently and successfully to solve algebra problems. Chapter 7 allows students to hone their problem solving skills while applying their new knowledge of fractions learned in Chapter 6. Some of the problem solving strategies covered in the chapter include applying standard formulas, recogniz-

ing similar types of problems, using charts, tables, or diagrams, using dimensional analysis, and using estimation. These rather specific strategies are not the only ones that students can use in solving algebra problems. Other more general strategies, such as looking for a pattern or drawing a diagram, provide an approach to solving a problem rather than a specific method of solution.

Making Connections to Real-World Applications

Chapter 7 is rich in problem solving activities with real-world applications, such as the physics connection on p. 340 and the social science connection on p. 333. For a complete list of real-world applications, see the Applications and Connections sections of the References to Strategies chart on the next page.

7-1 Ratios

Emphasize the three ways of expressing ratios stated on page 287. Point out that because ratios can be expressed as fractions, they have the properties of fractions. These properties can be used to simplify ratios, as shown in Example 2 on page 287.

7-2 Proportions

See the Exploration on p. 693 for an activity in which students explore applications of proportions using real data and computer-generated data.

Some students have difficulty solving problems involving proportions because they do not set up the proportion correctly. Point out that there is a choice in the order of the first ratio, but that the second ratio

must correspond to the first. For example, if the first ratio is $\dfrac{\text{number of miles}}{\text{number of gallons}}$, the second ratio must also have the number of miles in the numerator and the number of gallons in the denominator.

7-5 Percents

Some students may have learned how to solve percent problems by using proportions. Point out that the "proportion method" is an acceptable alternative to the solutions presented in Examples 3–5 on p. 310.

7-6 Percent Problems

When discussing percent-of-increase and percent-of-decrease problems, be sure to stress the formula given in the box on page 315. Point out that the change in price is always found by subtracting the original price from the new price, where a positive difference indicates an increase and a negative difference indicates a decrease. Also point out that the change in price is always compared with the *original* price, not the new price, to obtain the percent of increase or decrease.

Encourage students to estimate the answer to a percent problem before actually solving it. In this way the reasonableness of the answer can be judged. In Example 4 on page 316, for instance, students might guess that an equal amount of money ($3000) is invested at 6% and at 11%. If so, the total interest would be 0.06(3000) + 0.11(3000), or $510. Since the actual interest is $460, something more than $3000 must be invested at the lower rate (and something less than $3000 at the higher rate).

7-7 Mixture Problems

The sketch below might be used to explain Example 1 on page 321.

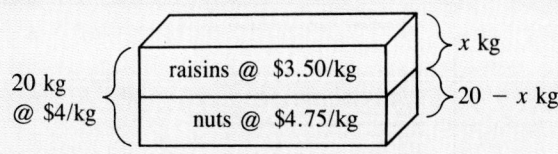

References to Strategies

Problem Solving Strategies

PE: p. 294 (Checking solution); pp. 322, 327 (Recognizing similar types); pp. 307, 321–324, 326–328 (Using charts or tables); p. 302 (Using dimensional analysis); p. 294 (Using estimation)
TE: pp. 294, 302, 321, 323, 328
RB: pp. 168–172

Applications

PE: pp. 286, 288–297, 300–303, 306–308, 313–330, 333, 335–337, 339–341
TE: p. 286
RB: p. 184

Nonroutine Problems

PE: p. 290 (Exs. 43–45); p. 292 (Probs. 17–19, Challenge); p. 296 (Exs. 46–50); p. 297 (Probs. 10–13); p. 301 (Prob. 16); p. 308 (Probs. 13, 14); p. 314 (Prob. 15); p. 325 (Probs. 24, 25); p. 330 (Probs. 22, 23); pp. 334–335 (Exs. 68–71); pp. 339–340 (Probs. 1–3)

Communication

PE: p. 296 (Ex. 46, convincing argument)
TE: pp. T112, T115 (Sugg. Extension); pp. T114–T115 (Reading Algebra)

Thinking Skills

PE: pp. 290, 302–303 (Applying concepts); pp. 305–306 (Analysis); pp. 312–314 (Recall and transfer); p. 347 (Interpreting)
RB: pp. 224–225

Explorations

PE: pp. 302–303 (Units); p. 693 (Exploring Applications of Proportions)
RB: p. 199

Connections

PE: pp. 287, 336–337, 339–340 (Astronomy); pp. 313–319 (Business); pp. 322–325 (Chemistry); pp. 287, 296, 320 (Data Analysis); p. 320 (Discrete Math); p. 341 (Engineering); pp. 291, 300–301 (Geometry); p. 303 (History); pp. 336–340 (Physics); pp. 318, 333, 335 (Social Science)

Using Technology

PE: pp. 309–314, 318–320, 335 (Exs.); p. 341 (Calculator Key-In)
TE: pp. 309, 313, 318, 319, 335, 341
Computer Activities: pp. 41–50

Using Manipulatives/Models

TE: p. T112 (Lesson 7-1); p. T116 (Lesson 7-8); p. T117 (Lesson 7-10)

Cooperative Learning

TE: p. T112 (Lesson 7-2); p. 286

Teaching Resources

For use in implementing the teaching strategies referenced on the previous page.

Application
Resource Book, p. 184

Application—Applying Fractions (for use with Chapter 7)

This is a cooperative activity for a group of two or more students.

You are going to drop a ball from a given altitude and record the height of successive bounces. Drop the ball on a smooth, hard, horizontal surface close to a vertical wall. Stand a meter stick against the wall so that the zero mark is on the floor. Record the height of a bounce by establishing a horizontal sight line across the top of the ball at the top of its path on any given bounce. Use at least four different balls and record the height of the first five bounces for each of them when the ball is initially dropped from a height of one meter (measure from the top of the ball). Record the type of ball and the height of each bounce in the table (values in centimeters).

Type of ball	Bounce Number 1	2	3	4	5	Average Bounce
Example	75	60	45	30	15	45
A						
B						
C						
D						

List the ratio of the first to second, second to third, third to fourth, and fourth to fifth bounce for each ball in the table at the right (simplify each expression).

Type of Ball	1st/2nd	2nd/3rd	3rd/4th	4th/5th
Example	5/4	4/3	3/2	2/1
A				
B				
C				
D				

Ratio of

1. Is there a pattern among the different ratios for any given ball? _____
2. Is there a pattern between the ratio of the first to second bounce for the different balls? _____ Second to third? _____ Third to fourth? _____
   Fourth to fifth? _____
3. Use the height from the first five bounces for any ball to predict the height of the sixth bounce of that ball. Check your prediction. _____
4. If a ball is dropped from a height of two meters, will the heights of the successive bounces be doubled?
5. Do any patterns discovered in the one meter drops still hold for a two meter drop?
6. Are there patterns for the two meter drops that do not exist for the one meter drops?
7. Is there a pair of measurements for any given ball that is twice those of a different pair of measurements for the same ball?
   From one ball to another?

184 APPLICATIONS

Resource Book, ALGEBRA, Structure and Method, Book 1
Copyright © by Houghton Mifflin Company. All rights reserved.

Enrichment/Exploration
Resource Book, p. 199

Experimenting with Fractions (For use with Chapter 7 of text)

The expression at the right may look strange to you. It can, however, be evaluated easily. Since $\frac{1}{1} = 1$, the expression equals $\frac{1}{1+1}$, or $\frac{1}{2}$.

$$\cfrac{1}{1+\cfrac{1}{1}}$$

Evaluate each of the following. Express your answer as a fraction.

1. $1 + \cfrac{1}{1+\cfrac{1}{1}}$

2. $\cfrac{1}{1+\cfrac{1}{1+\cfrac{1}{1}}}$

3. If the expression in Exercise 1 is represented as a, how would you represent the expression in Exercise 2? What is the relationship between the expressions in Exercises 1 and 2?

Evaluate each of the following.

4. $\cfrac{1}{1-\cfrac{1}{1+\cfrac{1}{1+\cfrac{1}{1}}}}$

5. $1 + \cfrac{1}{1-\cfrac{1}{1+\cfrac{1}{1+\cfrac{1}{1}}}}$

Try to express each of the following numbers using expressions similar to the ones in Exercises 2, 4, and 5.

6. $\frac{4}{5}$

7. $\frac{8}{13}$

Resource Book, ALGEBRA, Structure and Method, Book 1
Copyright © by Houghton Mifflin Company. All rights reserved.

ENRICHMENT 199

Thinking Skills
Resource Book, p. 224

Thinking Skills (For use after Chapter 7)

Recalling knowledge

1. Explain what is meant by *ratio.*
2. (To complete this exercise, you may need to use a geometry text or some reference book with geometric formulas.) State the formula for the volume of:
   a. a rectangular prism (that is, a box) _____
   b. a right circular cylinder _____
   c. a right circular cone _____

Applying concepts

3. Since there are 12 in. in 1 ft, the ratio $\frac{1\text{ in.}}{1\text{ ft}} = \frac{1}{12}$.
   Give the value of each of the following ratios.
   a. $\frac{1\text{ in.}^2}{1\text{ ft}^2}$ _____
   b. $\frac{1\text{ in.}^3}{1\text{ ft}^3}$ _____

4. The dimensions of Rectangles A and B and of Boxes C and D are shown at the right. Give the value of each of the following ratios.
   a. $\frac{\text{Area of Rectangle A}}{\text{Area of Rectangle B}}$ _____
   b. $\frac{\text{Volume of Box C}}{\text{Volume of Box D}}$ _____

Reasoning and drawing inferences

5. If two two-dimensional figures, A and B, have the same shape but each dimension of Figure B is k times the corresponding dimension of Figure A, then what is the value of the ratio $\frac{\text{Area of Figure A}}{\text{Area of Figure B}}$?

6. If two three-dimensional figures, A and B, have the same shape but each dimension of Figure B is k times the corresponding dimension of Figure A, then what is the value of the ratio $\frac{\text{Volume of Figure A}}{\text{Volume of Figure B}}$?

(continued)

224 THINKING SKILLS

Resource Book, ALGEBRA, Structure and Method, Book 1
Copyright © by Houghton Mifflin Company. All rights reserved.

Thinking Skills
Resource Book, p. 225

Thinking Skills (Chapter 7) (continued)

Spatial perception

7. When a two-dimensional figure is rotated about a given line, a three-dimensional *solid of rotation* results. For example, when Rectangle A, shown at the right, is rotated about the given line, the resulting solid of rotation is a right circular cylinder with base radius 3 and height 4. Describe the result of rotating each of the following about the given line.
   a. Rectangle B _____
   b. Rectangle C _____

Analysis

In Exercises 8–10, V_A, V_B, and V_C represent the volumes of the solids of rotation described in Exercise 7.

8. What is the value of the ratio $\frac{V_B}{V_A}$? _____

9. Note that $V_C = V_A - V_B$. Use this equation to derive a formula for the ratio $\frac{V_C}{V_A}$ in terms of V_A and V_B. _____

10. Use the results of Exercises 8 and 9 to find the value of the ratio $\frac{V_C}{V_A}$.

Synthesis

Let V_A, V_B, and V_C represent the volumes of the solids of rotation that result when Rectangle A and Right Triangles B and C, shown at the right, are rotated about the given lines.

11. Describe the result of rotating each of the following about the given line.
   a. Right Triangle B _____
   b. Right Triangle C _____

12. Find the value of each of the following ratios.
   a. $\frac{V_B}{V_A}$ _____
   b. $\frac{V_C}{V_A}$ _____

Resource Book, ALGEBRA, Structure and Method, Book 1
Copyright © by Houghton Mifflin Company. All rights reserved.

THINKING SKILLS 225

285e

Problem Solving
Resource Book, p. 168

Mixture Problems (For use with Lesson 7-7)

By working through the steps in the problems below, you will gain skill in solving mixture problems.

Problem 1 A food processing company produces grated cheese made from parmesan and romano cheeses. Parmesan costs $3.50 per kilogram and romano costs $5.00 per kilogram. How many kilograms of each type of cheese should be used to produce 100 kg of the mixture worth $3.95 per kilogram?

a. Complete: The number of kilograms of each type of cheese used must be between _____ kg and _____ kg.

b. What formula do you need to use to solve this problem?

_____

c. Let *p* = the number of kilograms of parmesan cheese used. Write an expression for the number of kilograms of romano cheese used. _____

d. Complete the chart.

	Number of kilograms	×	Price per kilogram	=	Cost
Parmesan	*p*				
Romano					
Mixture					

e. Cost of parmesan used + cost of romano used = _____

f. Write an equation for the problem. _____

g. Solve the equation to find the value of *p*.

h. Answer the question. _____

i. Check by substituting each amount in dollars:

cost of parmesan used + cost of romano used = cost of mixture

$ _____ + $ _____ = $ _____

Problem 2 Suppose you invest $4000 in tax-free bonds that pay $10\frac{1}{4}$% annual interest. At what annual interest rate do you need to invest $1000 in a certificate of deposit to achieve an average rate of interest of 10%?

a. Express $10\frac{1}{4}$% and 10% as decimals. _____

b. What formula do you need to solve the problem? _____

(continued)

Problem Solving
Resource Book, p. 171

Work Problems (For use with Lesson 7-8)

By working through the steps in the problems below, you will gain skill in solving work problems.

Problem 1 A computer can process the Gonzales Electronics Company's payroll in 8 hours. An older back-up computer needs 10 hours to process the payroll. How long would it take the two computers working together to do the job?

a. What is the work rate of the faster computer? _____ job per hour

b. What is the work rate of the slower computer? _____ job per hour

c. Let *h* = the number of hours needed for the computers to do the job together. Complete the chart.

	Work rate	×	Time	=	Work done
Faster computer			*h*		
Slower computer			*h*		

d. To solve the problem, you use the fact that if a job is completed, the fractional parts of the job must have a sum of _____.

e. Write an equation for the problem. _____

f. Solve the equation. _____

g. Answer the question. _____

h. Check by completing the following.

Find the fractional part of the job done by the faster computer. _____

Find the fractional part of the job done by the slower computer. _____

What should the sum of these fractional parts be? _____ Is it? _____

Problem 2 Pipe A can fill an empty swimming pool in 4 hours, and pipe B can fill it in 6 hours. One day pipe A was temporarily out of order, so the pool manager started to fill the pool at 12:00 noon using only pipe B. At 1:30 P.M., when pipe A had been repaired, the two pipes were used to finish the job. At what time was the pool full?

a. What is pipe A's work rate? _____ job per _____

b. What is pipe B's work rate? _____ job per _____

c. Let *x* = the number of hours pipe A was used. Write an expression for the number of hours that pipe B was used. _____

(continued)

Problem Solving/Reteaching
Study Guide, p. 123

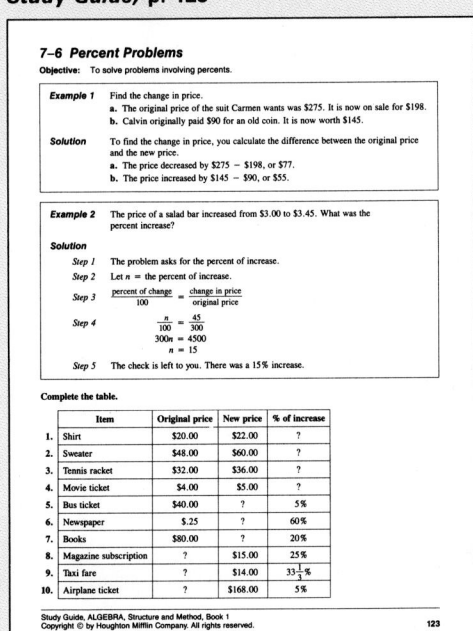

7-6 Percent Problems

Objective: To solve problems involving percents.

Example 1	Find the change in price.
	a. The original price of the suit Carmen wants was $275. It is now on sale for $198.
	b. Calvin originally paid $90 for an old coin. It is now worth $145.
Solution	To find the change in price, you calculate the difference between the original price and the new price.
	a. The price decreased by $275 − $198, or $77.
	b. The price increased by $145 − $90, or $55.

Example 2	The price of a salad bar increased from $3.00 to $3.45. What was the percent increase?
Solution	
Step 1	The problem asks for the percent of increase.
Step 2	Let *n* = the percent of increase.
Step 3	$\frac{\text{percent of change}}{100} = \frac{\text{change in price}}{\text{original price}}$
Step 4	$\frac{n}{100} = \frac{45}{300}$
	$300n = 4500$
	$n = 15$
Step 5	The check is left to you. There was a 15% increase.

Complete the table.

	Item	Original price	New price	% of increase
1.	Shirt	$20.00	$22.00	?
2.	Sweater	$48.00	$60.00	?
3.	Tennis racket	$32.00	$36.00	?
4.	Movie ticket	$4.00	$5.00	?
5.	Bus ticket	$40.00	?	5%
6.	Newspaper	$.25	?	60%
7.	Books	$80.00	?	20%
8.	Magazine subscription	?	$15.00	25%
9.	Taxi fare	?	$14.00	$33\frac{1}{3}$%
10.	Airplane ticket	?	$168.00	5%

Problem Solving/Using Technology
Computer Activities, p. 41

ACTIVITY 19. *Ratio Problems* (*for use with Section 7-1*)

Directions: Write all answers in the spaces provided.

PROBLEM

Two numbers are in the ratio 7:8 and their sum is 360. What are the two numbers?

PROGRAM

```
10  PRINT "WHAT IS THE SUM OF THE NUMBERS";
20  INPUT S
30  PRINT "WHAT IS THE RATIO (ENTER A:B AS A, B)";
40  INPUT A, B
50  PRINT
60  PRINT "THE NUMBERS ARE";
70  PRINT A • S / (A + B); "AND"; B • S / (A + B)
80  END
```

PROGRAM CHECK

Type in the program. To test whether you entered it correctly, run the program. Enter 360 after the first question. After the second question enter 7, 8. The computer should print

THE NUMBERS ARE 168 AND 192

ANALYSIS

If two numbers are in the ratio of *A* to *B*, then for any nonzero number *n*, the ratio of *An* to *Bn* is also *A* to *B*. For example, if the two numbers are in the ratio 7 to 8, then choosing various values of *n* could generate a list such as:

n	First number	Second number	Ratio
2	14	16	7:8
10	70	80	7:8
18	126	144	7:8
24	168	192	7:8
30	210	240	7:8

If it is also known that the sum of the two numbers whose ratio is 7 to 8 is 360, then you would choose 168 and 192.

(continued)

Application

The ratio shown in the caption is called the gear ratio of a multi-speed bicycle. The ratio indicates that with fewer teeth on the rear gear, as in the top diagram, each rotation of the pedals turns the rear tire more times. Such high gears require more power, but yield greater speeds, and are often used on flat surfaces. The bottom diagram shows a configuration for a low gear. A large number of teeth on the rear gear results in fewer rotations of the rear wheel. Low gears demand less power, but produce slower speeds. They are primarily used to climb hills.

Group Activities
Have students examine the gears on a multi-speed bicycle and note the number of teeth on a front gear (to which the pedals are attached) and on a rear gear (to which the rear wheel is attached). You can then have students determine the number of times that the rear wheel spins for every complete turn of the pedals. For example, if a front gear has 45 teeth and a rear gear has 15 teeth, then the rear wheel spins $\frac{45}{15}$, or 3, times for every turn of the pedals.

You can also have students use this information to calculate how many complete turns of the pedals are needed to travel one mile if the diameter of the bicycle's wheels is 27 in.

This ratio tells how many times the wheels spin for each turn of the pedals:

$$\frac{\text{Teeth in front gear}}{\text{Teeth in rear gear}}$$

286

Ratio and Proportion

7-1 Ratios

Objective   To solve problems involving ratios.

The distance from Earth to the moon is about 240,000 mi. The distance from Jupiter to one of its moons, Io, is about 260,000 mi. One way to compare these distances is to write their quotient, or *ratio:*

$$\frac{240{,}000}{260{,}000} = \frac{12}{13}$$

The simplest form of this ratio is $\frac{12}{13}$.

The **ratio** of one number to another is the quotient when the first number is divided by the second number and the second number is not zero. You can write a ratio in three ways:

1. as a quotient using a division sign
2. as a fraction
3. as a ratio using a colon

Example 1   The ratio of 7 to 4 can be written as $7 \div 4$, $\frac{7}{4}$, or $7:4$.

You may find it easier to simplify a ratio if you first rewrite it as a fraction.

Example 2   Write each ratio in simplest form.

    a. $32:48$ **b.** $25x:20x$ **c.** $\dfrac{9x^2y}{6xy^2}$

Solution   **a.** First rewrite the ratio as a fraction. Then simplify.

$$32:48 = \frac{32}{48} = \frac{2}{3}, \text{ or } 2:3$$

b. First rewrite the ratio as a fraction. Then simplify.

$$25x:20x = \frac{25x}{20x} = \frac{5}{4}, \text{ or } 5:4$$

c. $\dfrac{9x^2y}{6xy^2} = \dfrac{3x}{2y}$

Applying Fractions   **287**

Teaching References

Lesson Commentary, pp. T111–T117

Assignment Guide, pp. T65–T67

Supplementary Materials
Practice Masters 40–45
Tests 30–33
Resource Book
Prac. Exs. pp. 109–113
Tests, pp. 42–45
En. Act. p. 199
Practice in Problem Solving, pp. 168–172
Application, p. 184
Study Guide, pp. 113–132
Computer Activities 19–22
Test Generator
California Standards Support Workbook
Exploration for Lesson 7-2
Alternate Test p. T18

Teaching Suggestions p. T111
Using Manipulatives p. T112
Suggested Extensions p. T112

Warm-Up Exercises

Simplify.

1. $\dfrac{24t}{26t}$ $\dfrac{12}{13}$ **2.** $\dfrac{8ab^2}{6a^2b}$ $\dfrac{4b}{3a}$

3. Solve: $4x + 5x + 6x = 180$ $\{12\}$

Motivating the Lesson

A *golden rectangle* is a special rectangle in which the ratio of its length to its width is $\dfrac{1 + \sqrt{5}}{2}$. The ancient Greeks often used this ratio in architecture. This ratio, called the *golden ratio,* frequently appears in nature and in art. Simplifying ratios is today's lesson.

1. Express the ratio of 3 to 8 in three different ways.

$3 \div 8, \frac{3}{8}, 3{:}8$

Write each ratio in simplest form.

2. $45x{:}30x \quad \frac{3}{2}$ 3. $\frac{18ab^2}{14a^2b} \quad \frac{9b}{7a}$

4. 5 days : 18 hours

$= \dfrac{5 \text{ days}}{18 \text{ hours}} =$

$\dfrac{120 \text{ hours}}{18 \text{ hours}} = \dfrac{20}{3}$, or 20:3

5. Write the ratio of the weight of a 20 g marble to a 30 kg bowling ball.

$\dfrac{20 \text{ g}}{30 \text{ kg}} = \dfrac{20 \text{ g}}{30,000 \text{ g}} = \dfrac{1}{1500}$

6. The ratio of boys to girls enrolled in chemistry classes is 5:4. If the total number of students taking chemistry is 981, how many boys and girls are enrolled in chemistry?

Step 2: Let $5x$ = number of boys

Let $4x$ = number of girls

Step 3: $5x + 4x = 981$

Step 4: $\quad 9x = 981$

$\quad x = 109$

∴ Number of boys = $5x$ = $5 \cdot 109 = 545$

Number of girls = $4x$ = $4 \cdot 109 = 436$

7. The heights of three brothers are in the ratio 13:14:15. Their combined heights equal 210 inches. Find the height of each brother.

Let the heights be $13x$, $14x$, and $15x$. Then

$13x + 14x + 15x = 210$

$\qquad 42x = 210$

$\qquad x = 5$

∴ the heights of the brothers are 65 in., 70 in., and 75 in.

You can use ratios to compare two quantities *of the same kind,* such as two heights, two masses, or two time periods, as shown below.

To write the ratio of two quantities of the same kind:

1. First express the measures in the same unit.
2. Then write their ratio.

Example 3 Write each ratio in simplest form. **a.** 3 h : 15 min   **b.** 9 in. : 5 ft

Solution **a.** 3 h : 15 min $= \dfrac{3 \text{ h}}{15 \text{ min}} = \dfrac{180 \text{ min}}{15 \text{ min}} = \dfrac{12}{1}$, or 12:1

b. 9 in. : 5 ft $= \dfrac{9 \text{ in.}}{5 \text{ ft}} = \dfrac{9 \text{ in.}}{60 \text{ in.}} = \dfrac{3}{20}$, or 3:20

Example 4 Write the ratio of the height of a tree 4 m tall to the height of a sapling 50 cm tall in simplest form.

Solution 1 1. Express both heights in *centimeters.*

tree: 4 m = 400 cm

sapling: 50 cm

2. The ratio is the quotient

$\dfrac{400 \text{ cm}}{50 \text{ cm}} = \dfrac{400}{50} = \dfrac{8}{1}$, or 8:1.   **Answer**

Solution 2 1. Express both heights in *meters.*

tree: 4 m

sapling: 50 cm = 0.5 m

2. The ratio is the quotient

$\dfrac{4 \text{ m}}{0.5 \text{ m}} = \dfrac{4}{0.5} = \dfrac{8}{1}$, or 8:1.   **Answer**

When you solve a word problem, you may need to express a ratio in a different form. If two numbers are in the ratio 3:5, you can use $3x$ and $5x$ to represent them, because $\dfrac{3x}{5x} = \dfrac{3}{5}$.

Example 5 Jenna plants alfalfa and wheat on 160 acres on her farm. If the ratio of acres of alfalfa to acres of wheat is 3:5, how many acres of each crop are planted?

Solution

Step 1 The problem asks for the number of acres of alfalfa and the number of acres of wheat.

Step 2 Let $3x$ = the number of acres of alfalfa. Let $5x$ = the number of acres of wheat.

Step 3 $3x + 5x = 160$

Step 4 $\qquad 8x = 160$
$\qquad\quad x = 20$

Number of acres of alfalfa = $3x = 3 \cdot 20 = 60$
Number of acres of wheat = $5x = 5 \cdot 20 = 100$

Step 5 *Check:* Are the numbers of acres of alfalfa to acres of wheat in the ratio 3:5?

$$\frac{60}{100} = \frac{3}{5} \quad \checkmark$$

∴ there are 60 acres of alfalfa and 100 acres of wheat.   ***Answer***

If three numbers are in the ratio 3:7:11, then the ratio of the first to the second is 3:7 and the ratio of the second to the third is 7:11. Therefore, you can use $3x$, $7x$, and $11x$ to represent the numbers.

Example 6   The lengths of the sides of a triangle are in the ratio 3:4:5. The perimeter of the triangle is 24 in. Find the lengths of each side.

Solution   Let the lengths of the sides be $3x$, $4x$, and $5x$.
Then $3x + 4x + 5x = 24$
$\qquad\qquad\quad 12x = 24$
$\qquad\qquad\qquad x = 2$
∴ the lengths of the sides are 6 in., 8 in., and 10 in.   ***Answer***

Oral Exercises

State each ratio in simplest form.

1. 5:15 1:3   **2.** 18:24 3:4   **3.** 49:35 7:5   **4.** 9:48 3:16

5. $4x:6x$ 2:3   **6.** $20t:35t$ 4:7   **7.** $\dfrac{\pi(3r)^2}{\pi r^2}$ $\frac{9}{1}$ **8.** $\dfrac{(2s)^3}{s^3}$ $\frac{8}{1}$

9. 4 h to 20 min 12:1   **10.** 5 m to 25 cm 20:1   **11.** 1 kg to 50 g 20:1

12. Two numbers are in the ratio 10:3. Represent the numbers using a variable. $10x$ and $3x$

Written Exercises

Write each ratio in simplest form.

A   **1.** 14:21 2:3   **2.** 55:33 5:3   **3.** $24x:8x$ 3:1   **4.** $6y:9y$ 2:3

5. $\dfrac{s^2}{(3s)^2}$ $\frac{1}{9}$ **6.** $\dfrac{27m^5}{45m^2}$ $\frac{3m^3}{5}$ **7.** $\dfrac{64a^3b}{16ab^4}$ $\frac{4a^2}{b^3}$ **8.** $\dfrac{72rs^5}{12r^2s^2}$ $\frac{6s^3}{r}$

Applying Fractions   **289**

Check for Understanding
Here is a suggested use of the Oral Exercises to check students' understanding as you teach the lesson.
Oral Exs. 1–8: use after Example 2.
Oral Exs. 9–11: use after Example 3.
Oral Ex. 12: use after Example 5.

Guided Practice
Write each ratio in simplest form.

1. 66:44 3:2

2. $28x:21x$ 4:3

3. $\dfrac{32a^4}{24a^2}$ $\dfrac{4a^2}{3}$

4. $\dfrac{63r^2s^2}{81rs^4}$ $\dfrac{7r}{9s^2}$

5. 45 min:3 h 1:4

6. The ratio of wins to losses for a soccer team that played 42 games and had 24 wins. 4:3

7. Find the ratio of the areas of a pair of rectangles if one rectangle has sides 7 cm and 9 cm and the other rectangle has sides 6 cm and 7 cm. 3:2

8. Find two numbers in the ratio 5:7 whose sum is 48. 20 and 28

9. A certain snack mixture is made by mixing almonds, raisins and peanuts in the ratio 3:8:9. How much of each ingredient is needed to make 540 g of the mixture? 81 g almonds, 216 g raisins, 243 g peanuts

Summarizing the Lesson

Students have learned that the ratio of one number to another is the quotient of the two numbers if the second number is not zero. Ask the students to give several examples of ratios.

Suggested Assignments

Minimum
Day 1: 289/1–25 odd, 31–33
      291/*P*: 2, 4, 6, 8
Day 2: 290/18, 20, 28, 32, 34
      291/*P*: 10, 12
  S 292/Mixed Review
Assign with Lesson 7-2.

Average
Day 1: 289/2–34 even
      291/*P*: 2, 4, 6, 8, 10
Day 2: 290/36, 38, 40, 42
      291/*P*: 12, 14, 16
  S 292/Mixed Review
Assign with Lesson 7-2.

Maximum
      289/3–45 mult. of 3
      291/*P*: 3–18 mult. of 3
  S 292/Mixed Review

Supplementary Materials

Study Guide   pp. 113–114
Computer Activity   19

Common Errors

Students sometimes express ratios such as
4 h:20 min as $\frac{4}{20}$, or $\frac{1}{5}$,
instead of $\frac{240}{20}$, or $\frac{12}{1}$. In reteaching, emphasize that the two quantities in the quotient must be expressed in the same units.

Write each ratio in simplest form.

12. 1:10
16. 1:4000

9. 20 min:2 h 1:6   10. 4 h:45 min 16:3   11. 6 m:120 cm 5:1   12. 18 cm:1.8 m

13. 6 wk:3 days 14:1   14. 9 days:3 wk 3:7   15. 5 km:450 cm 10,000:9   16. 200 cm:8 km

17. 1 lb:7 oz 16:7   18. 13 oz:2 lb 13:32   19. 150 g:3 kg 1:20   20. 2 kg:90 g
                                                                               200:9

21. The ratio of school days to nonschool days in a year with 365 days and 180 days of school. 36:37

22. The student-teacher ratio in a school with 2592 students and 144 teachers. 18:1

23. The ratio of new airplanes to old airplanes in a fleet of 720 planes of which 240 are old. 2:1

24. The ratio of raisins to nuts in a mixture containing 3 c raisins and $1\frac{1}{4}$ c nuts. 12:5

25. **a.** The ratio of seniors taking a math course to seniors enrolled in a school if 105 out of 270 seniors enrolled are taking a math course. 7:18
    b. The ratio of seniors taking a math course to seniors not taking a math course in the school in part (a). 7:11

26. **a.** The ratio of fiction books to nonfiction books in a library containing 1050 fiction books and 1890 nonfiction books. 5:9
    b. The ratio of nonfiction to fiction books in the library in part (a). 9:5

Find the ratio of (a) the perimeters and (b) the areas of each pair of figures.

a. 14:19 **b.** 8:15

27. A rectangle with sides 8 cm and 6 cm and one with sides 10 cm and 9 cm.

28. A rectangle with length 12 cm and perimeter 30 cm and one with length 10 cm and perimeter 30 cm. **a.** 1:1 **b.** 18:25

29. A square with sides 60 cm and one with sides 1 m. **a.** 3:5 **b.** 9:25

30. A square with sides 24 in. and one with sides 2 yd. **a.** 1:3 **b.** 1:9

Find the ratio of *x* to *y* determined by each equation. (*Hint:* In Exercises 37–45, collect *x*-terms on one side and *y*-terms on the other. Then factor.)

Sample $3x = 7y$

Solution $3x = 7y$ Divide both sides by 3.

$x = \frac{7}{3}y$ Divide both sides by *y*.

$\frac{x}{y} = \frac{7}{3}$, or 7:3   ***Answer***

B 31. $8x = 5y$ 5:8   32. $7x = 4y$ 4:7   33. $14x = 12y$ 6:7

34. $10x = 26y$ 13:5   35. $kx = 2y$ 2:*k*   36. $3x = ky$ *k*:3
                                                                              1:1
37. $4(x + y) = 8(x - y)$ 3:1 38. $8(2x - 3y) = 6(x + y)$ 3:1 39. $ax + by = ay + bx$

40. $cx - ay = aby - bcx$ 41. $ax - a^2y = bx - b^2y$ 42. $r^2x = sy + ry + s^2x$
    a:*c* $(a + b)$:1   1:$(r - s)$

C 43. $x^2 + 2y^2 = 2xy + y^2$ 44. $2(x^2 + y^2) = 5xy$ 45. $\frac{x}{y} + 1 = \frac{x + y}{x}$
       1:1   1:2 or 2:1
                                                                  1:1, −1:1, or 1:−1

Problems

Solve.

A 1. Find two numbers in the ratio 4:5 whose sum is 45. 20 and 25

2. Find two numbers in the ratio 3:7 whose sum is 50. 15 and 35

3. Together there are 180 players and coaches in the town soccer league. If the player-coach ratio is 9:1, how many players are there? 162 players

4. In a survey of 700 voters, the ratio of men to women taking part was 17:18. How many women took part in the survey? 360 women

5. The perimeter of a rectangle is 96 cm. Find the dimensions of the rectangle if the ratio of the length to the width is 7:5. 28 cm by 20 cm

6. The perimeter of a rectangle is 68 ft. Find the dimensions of the rectangle if the ratio of the length to the width is 9:8. 18 ft by 16 ft

7. The lengths of the three sides of a triangle are in the ratio 3:5:6. The perimeter of the triangle is 21 cm. Find the length of each side of the triangle. $4\frac{1}{2}$ cm, $7\frac{1}{2}$ cm, and 9 cm

8. The measures of the angles of a triangle are in the ratio 1:2:3. Find the measures. (*Hint:* The sum of the measures of the angles of a triangle is 180°.) 30°, 60°, and 90°

9. Concrete can be made by mixing cement, sand, and gravel in the ratio 3:6:8. How much gravel is needed to make 850 m³ of concrete? 400 m³

10. A new alloy is made by mixing 8 parts of iron, 3 parts of zinc, and 1 part of tungsten. How much of each metal is needed to make 420 m³ of the alloy? 280 m³ of iron, 105 m³ of zinc, and 35 m³ of tungsten

B 11. Ling drives her car 18 mi/h faster than Eddie rides his bike. The ratio of the distances they can travel in 1 h 30 min is 5:2. Find their rates of speed. (*Hint:* Make a rate-time-distance chart.) Eddie, 12 mi/h; Ling, 30 mi/h

12. The ratio of Aldo's cycling speed to José's cycling speed is 6:5. José leaves school at 3 P.M. and Aldo leaves at 3:10 P.M. By 3:30, Aldo is only 2 km behind José. How fast is each cycling? (*Hint:* Make a rate-time-distance chart.) Aldo, 24 km/h; José, 20 km/h

13. A collection of dimes and nickels is worth $5.60. The ratio of the number of dimes to nickels is 3:2. Find the number of each type of coin. (*Hint:* Make a coin value chart.) 42 dimes and 28 nickels

14. In a collection of nickels, dimes, and quarters worth $6.90, the ratio of the number of nickels to dimes is 3:8. The ratio of the number of dimes to quarters is 4:5. Find the number of each type of coin. (*Hint:* Make a coin value chart.) 6 nickels, 16 dimes, 20 quarters

Applying Fractions   **291**

15. The Office Mart purchased a supply of mechanical pencils and ball-point pens. The ratio of pencils to pens was $5:9$. The pencils cost $1 each, the pens cost 25¢ each, and the total bill was $290. How many pencils were purchased? (*Hint:* Make a number-price-cost chart.)

200 pencils

16. The Beach Hut purchased a supply of sunglasses and visors. The ratio of sunglasses to visors was $7:4$. Each pair of sunglasses cost $6.00, each visor cost $4.50, and the total bill was $720. How many pairs of sunglasses were purchased? (*Hint:* Make a number-price-cost chart.) 84 pairs of sunglasses

C 17. The ratio of the sum of two positive integers to their difference is $7:5$. If the sum of the two numbers is at most 25, find all possible values for the pair of numbers. 1 and 6; 2 and 12; 3 and 18

18. There are 2820 cars in Farmington. The ratio of medium-size cars to compacts is $7:5$, and the ratio of compacts to full-size cars is $8:9$. How many full-size cars are there? 900 full-size cars

19. Find two numbers such that their sum, their difference, and their product have the ratio $3:2:5$. 10 and 2

Mixed Review Exercises

Solve.

1. $4x = 24 - 2x$ {4}
2. $4(x - 7) + x = 2$ {6}
3. $5(4 + n) = 2(9 + 2n)$ {−2}
4. $\frac{z + 4}{3} = -12$ {−40}
5. $\frac{16 - 2y}{2} = 3y$ {2}
6. $-\frac{c}{9} = 4$ {−36}
7. $(r + 2)(r - 5) = 0$ {−2, 5}
8. $3x^2 + 12x - 36 = 0$ {−6, 2}
9. $3(x - 2) = 4(x - 3)$ {6}

Simplify.

10. $\frac{3b + 1}{2c} + \frac{b}{c}$ $\frac{5b + 1}{2c}$
11. $3x + \frac{5}{x}$ $\frac{3x^2 + 5}{x}$
12. $\frac{3a}{4} + \frac{4a + 1}{4}$ $\frac{7a + 1}{4}$

Challenge

Fill 2 5-liter containers. Pour both into an 8-liter container. What will not fit equals 2 L of the solution.

To conduct an experiment, a scientist needed exactly 2 L of a solution. After searching the storeroom, she could find only 5-liter containers and 8-liter containers. How could the scientist measure exactly 2 L of the solution?

7-2 Proportions

Objective   To solve problems using proportions.

An equation that states that two ratios are equal is called a **proportion.** Usually you write a proportion in one of two ways:

$$2:3 = 4:6 \quad \text{or} \quad \frac{2}{3} = \frac{4}{6}$$

Both can be read as "2 is to 3 as 4 is to 6."

In the proportion $a:b = c:d$, a and d are called the **extremes,** and b and c are called the **means.** You can use the multiplication property of equality to show that in any proportion the product of the extremes equals the product of the means (see Oral Exercise 9). That is:

$$\text{If } \frac{a}{b} = \frac{c}{d}, \text{ then } ad = bc.$$

You can use this fact to solve proportions.

Example 1   Solve: **a.** $\dfrac{3}{x} = \dfrac{5}{4}$ **b.** $\dfrac{4}{21} = \dfrac{-2}{15a}$ **c.** $\dfrac{3}{n} = 8$

Solution

a. $3 \cdot 4 = x \cdot 5$
$12 = 5x$
$\dfrac{12}{5} = x$

∴ the solution is
$\dfrac{12}{5}$, or 2.4.
Answer

b. $4(15a) = 21(-2)$
$60a = -42$
$a = \dfrac{-42}{60}$
$a = \dfrac{-7}{10}$

∴ the solution is
$\dfrac{-7}{10}$, or -0.7.
Answer

c. $\dfrac{3}{n} = \dfrac{8}{1}$
$3 \cdot 1 = n \cdot 8$
$3 = 8n$
$\dfrac{3}{8} = n$

∴ the solution is
$\dfrac{3}{8}$, or 0.375.
Answer

Example 2   Solve: **a.** $\dfrac{x-4}{3} = \dfrac{2}{15}$ **b.** $\dfrac{2n-3}{5} = \dfrac{n+2}{6}$

Solution

a. $15(x - 4) = 2 \cdot 3$
$15x - 60 = 6$
$15x = 66$
$x = \dfrac{66}{15}$
$x = \dfrac{22}{5}$

∴ the solution is $\dfrac{22}{5}$,
or 4.4. ***Answer***

b. $6(2n - 3) = 5(n + 2)$
$12n - 18 = 5n + 10$
$7n - 18 = 10$
$7n = 28$
$n = 4$

∴ the solution is 4.
Answer

Applying Fractions   **293**

Explorations p. 693

Teaching Suggestions p. T112
Group Activities p. T112
Suggested Extensions p. T112

Warm-Up Exercises

Solve.

1. $5 = 6x$ $\left\{\dfrac{5}{6}\right\}$

2. $6(12a) = -2(18)$ $\left\{-\dfrac{1}{2}\right\}$

3. $5y(20) = -6(-16)$ $\left\{\dfrac{24}{25}\right\}$

4. $3(x + 4) = 18$ $\{2\}$

5. $-2(4 - y) = 3y$ $\{-8\}$

Motivating the Lesson

If a baseball player's batting average is .350, or $\dfrac{350}{1000}$, this means that he would get 350 hits for every 1000 times at bat. How would you calculate how many hits he had out of 400 times at bat? This problem can be solved using a proportion.

Chalkboard Examples

Solve.

1. $\dfrac{x}{3} = \dfrac{5}{12}$
$12 \cdot x = 5 \cdot 3$
$12x = 15$
$x = \dfrac{15}{12} = \dfrac{5}{4}$, or 1.25

2. $\dfrac{3x + 1}{5} = \dfrac{x}{2}$
$2(3x + 1) = 5x$
$6x + 2 = 5x$
$x = -2$

3. $\dfrac{x - 5}{12} = \dfrac{x + 2}{5}$
$5(x - 5) = 12(x + 2)$
$5x - 25 = 12x + 24$
$-7x = 49$
$x = -7$

(continued)

4. An investment of $1200 paid interest of $102. How much interest would $1600 invested at the same rate for the same amount of time pay?

$$\frac{1200}{102} = \frac{1600}{x}$$
$$1200x = 102 \cdot 1600$$
$$x = \frac{102 \cdot 1600}{1200}$$
$$x = 136; \ \$136$$

5. A typist types an essay of 1260 words in 15 min. At that rate, how long would it take to type an essay of 2100 words?

$$\frac{y}{2100} = \frac{15}{1260}$$
$$1260y = 15 \cdot 2100$$
$$y = \frac{15 \cdot 2100}{1260}$$
$$y = 25; \ 25 \text{ min}$$

Problem Solving Strategy

Encourage students to *estimate the answer* to each problem before solving it. They can use the estimate to check the reasonableness of an answer.

Check for Understanding

Here is a suggested use of the Oral Exercises as you teach the lesson.
Oral Exs. 1–9: use after Example 2.

Guided Practice

Solve.

1. $\frac{y}{3} = \frac{5}{8}$ $\left\{\frac{15}{8}\right\}$

2. $\frac{3}{4y} = \frac{5}{7}$ $\left\{\frac{21}{20}\right\}$

3. $\frac{15}{z} = 6$ $\left\{\frac{5}{2}\right\}$

4. $-8 = \frac{9b}{5}$ $\left\{-\frac{40}{9}\right\}$

Example 3 With a 5 lb bag of flour the cooking class can make 120 date-nut muffins. How many muffins can they make with a 2 lb bag of flour?

Solution

Step 1 The problem asks for the number of muffins made with 2 lb of flour.

Step 2 Let x = the number of muffins made with 2 lb of flour.

Step 3 5 lb makes 120 muffins.
2 lb makes x muffins. ← Note that since 2 lb is less than half of 5 lb, you can estimate that the answer is less than 60 muffins.
$$\frac{5}{120} = \frac{2}{x}$$

Step 4 Solve. $5x = 240$
$$x = 48$$

Step 5 Since $48 < 60$, the answer is reasonable. The check is left to you.

∴ 48 muffins can be made with 2 lb of flour. *Answer*

Example 4 About 8 gal of gas filled the tank after Greg drove 224 mi. How many miles can he expect to drive on a full tank of about 13 gal?

Solution

Step 1 The problem asks for the number of miles he can drive on 13 gal.

Step 2 Let x = the number of miles.

Step 3 224 mi on 8 gal
x mi on 13 gal
$$\frac{224}{8} = \frac{x}{13}$$

Step 4 Solve. $224 \cdot 13 = 8x$
$$2912 = 8x$$
$$364 = x$$

Step 5 The check is left to you. ∴ He can drive 364 mi on a full tank. *Answer*

Oral Exercises

For each proportion give the equation that states that the product of the extremes equals the product of the means. Do not solve.

1. $\frac{5}{3} = \frac{2}{x}$
$5x = 3 \cdot 2$

2. $\frac{3}{y} = \frac{7}{8}$
$3 \cdot 8 = y \cdot 7$

3. $\frac{4x}{5} = \frac{9}{2}$
$4x(2) = 5 \cdot 9$

4. $\frac{-1}{n} = \frac{6}{-13}$
$(-1)(-13) = n \cdot 6$

5. $\dfrac{y-3}{4} = \dfrac{5}{2}$

$(y-3)\cdot 2 = 4\cdot 5$

6. $\dfrac{4}{9} = \dfrac{a-2}{3}$

$4\cdot 3 = 9\cdot(a-2)$

7. $\dfrac{3}{5+d} = \dfrac{3}{d}$

$3\cdot d = (5+d)\cdot 3$

8. $\dfrac{x+1}{8} = \dfrac{x-1}{7}$

$(x+1)\cdot 7 = 8\cdot(x-1)$

9. If you multiply both sides of the proportion $\dfrac{a}{b} = \dfrac{c}{d}$ by bd, what equation do you get? $ad = bc$

Written Exercises

Solve.

A   **1.** $\dfrac{x}{5} = \dfrac{3}{4}$ $\left\{\dfrac{15}{4}\right\}$ **2.** $\dfrac{y}{3} = \dfrac{4}{7}$ $\left\{\dfrac{12}{7}\right\}$ **3.** $\dfrac{8}{5} = \dfrac{4}{3x}$ $\left\{\dfrac{5}{6}\right\}$ **4.** $\dfrac{6n}{5} = \dfrac{3}{1}$ $\left\{\dfrac{5}{2}\right\}$

5. $\dfrac{3n}{7} = \dfrac{4}{5}$ $\left\{\dfrac{28}{15}\right\}$ **6.** $\dfrac{8}{5k} = \dfrac{2}{5}$ $\{4\}$ **7.** $\dfrac{7}{6} = \dfrac{2a}{3}$ $\left\{\dfrac{7}{4}\right\}$ **8.** $\dfrac{3}{8} = \dfrac{9}{4k}$ $\{6\}$

9. $\dfrac{18x}{13} = \dfrac{36}{39}$ $\left\{\dfrac{2}{3}\right\}$ **10.** $\dfrac{15x}{64} = \dfrac{45}{32}$ $\{6\}$ **11.** $\dfrac{24}{25} = \dfrac{6y}{7}$ $\left\{\dfrac{28}{25}\right\}$ **12.** $\dfrac{10}{21} = \dfrac{5}{16a}$ $\left\{\dfrac{21}{32}\right\}$

13. $\dfrac{15a}{36} = \dfrac{45}{12}$ $\{9\}$ **14.** $\dfrac{81}{64} = \dfrac{27n}{40}$ $\left\{\dfrac{15}{8}\right\}$ **15.** $\dfrac{12t}{-7} = \dfrac{30}{14}$ $\left\{-\dfrac{5}{4}\right\}$

16. $\dfrac{-15}{25} = \dfrac{4x}{-15}$ $\left\{\dfrac{9}{4}\right\}$ **17.** $\dfrac{4}{x} = 5$ $\left\{\dfrac{4}{5}\right\}$ **18.** $\dfrac{5}{2n} = 3$ $\left\{\dfrac{5}{6}\right\}$

19. $-4 = \dfrac{8b}{5}$ $\left\{-\dfrac{5}{2}\right\}$ **20.** $4 = \dfrac{20}{-9w}$ $\left\{-\dfrac{5}{9}\right\}$ **21.** $\dfrac{x-5}{4} = \dfrac{3}{2}$ $\{11\}$

22. $\dfrac{y-3}{8} = \dfrac{3}{4}$ $\{9\}$ **23.** $2 = \dfrac{6+4n}{7}$ $\{2\}$ **24.** $5 = \dfrac{4-3y}{5}$ $\{-7\}$

25. $\dfrac{5n-3}{4} = \dfrac{5n+3}{6}$ $\{3\}$ **26.** $\dfrac{6x-2}{7} = \dfrac{5x+7}{8}$ $\{5\}$ **27.** $\dfrac{3+2y}{8} = \dfrac{1-y}{5}$ $\left\{-\dfrac{7}{18}\right\}$

28. $\dfrac{2n-9}{7} = \dfrac{3-n}{4}$ $\left\{\dfrac{19}{5}\right\}$ **29.** $\dfrac{4x+5}{5} = \dfrac{2x+7}{7}$ $\{0\}$ **30.** $\dfrac{4x+12}{8} = \dfrac{x+3}{2}$

identity

B   **31.** $\dfrac{4(2x-11)}{13} = -(x+5)$ $\{-1\}$ **32.** $2x-2 = \dfrac{5(x-3)}{11}$ $\left\{\dfrac{7}{17}\right\}$ **33.** $\dfrac{3+2x}{3-2x} = -3$ $\{3\}$

34. $-5 = \dfrac{4-7x}{4+7x}$ $\left\{-\dfrac{6}{7}\right\}$ **35.** $\dfrac{15}{x+7} = \dfrac{45}{x+21}$ $\{0\}$ **36.** $\dfrac{36}{2x-3} = \dfrac{72}{2x+3}$ $\left\{\dfrac{9}{2}\right\}$

Sample   Find the ratio of x to y: $\dfrac{9x-8y}{2} = \dfrac{7x-6y}{3}$

Solution

$$3(9x-8y) = 2(7x-6y)$$

$$27x - 24y = 14x - 12y \quad \left\{ \begin{array}{l} \text{Collect } x\text{-terms on one} \\ \text{side and } y\text{-terms on} \\ \text{the other.} \end{array} \right.$$

$$13x = 12y$$

$$x = \dfrac{12}{13}\,y$$

$$\dfrac{x}{y} = \dfrac{12}{13}$$

Applying Fractions   **295**

---

5. $3 = \dfrac{2+4y}{6}$ $\{4\}$

6. $\dfrac{t-4}{5} = \dfrac{2}{3}$ $\left\{\dfrac{22}{3}\right\}$

7. $\dfrac{4b+6}{6} = \dfrac{4b+8}{8}$ $\{0\}$

8. $\dfrac{6b-5}{3} = \dfrac{12b-10}{6}$ identity

9. Cira earns \$10.20 for 3 hours of work. How much does she earn in 5 hours at the same rate of pay? \$17.00

10. A car travels 88 mi on $\frac{1}{4}$ tank of gas. How much gas does it need to travel 264 mi? $\frac{3}{4}$ tank

11. If 75 shares of a certain stock sell for \$940, how much do 120 shares cost? \$1504

Summarizing the Lesson

Students have learned how to solve proportions and problems using proportions. Ask them to give examples of the rule *the product of the extremes equals the product of the means.*

Suggested Assignments

Minimum
Day 1: 295/1–15 odd
Assign with Lesson 7-1.
Day 2: 295/17–35 odd
       296/*P*: 3, 5, 7, 9
   S 297/Mixed Review

Average
Day 1: 295/3–30 mult. of 3
Assign with Lesson 7-1.
Day 2: 295/33–45 mult. of 3
       296/*P*: 3, 5, 7, 9, 11
   S 297/Mixed Review

Maximum
       295/3–48 mult. of 3
       296/*P*: 3, 6, 9, 12, 13
   S 297/Mixed Review

Common Errors

Students sometimes solve proportions incorrectly because they try to simplify fractions by "canceling" a factor from the numerator on one side of the equals sign and the denominator on the other side. In reteaching, use an example such as $\frac{12a}{16} = \frac{8}{18}$ to point out that this is not correct.

Find the ratio of x to y. See the sample on page 295.

37. $\dfrac{3x + 2y}{5} = \dfrac{4x - 7y}{6}$ $\frac{47}{2}$

38. $\dfrac{9x + 3y}{4} = \dfrac{3x + 9y}{5}$ $\frac{7}{11}$

39. $\dfrac{x + y}{x - y} = \dfrac{3}{2}$ $\frac{5}{1}$

40. $\dfrac{4}{5} = \dfrac{x - y}{x + y}$ $\frac{9}{1}$

41. $\dfrac{d}{c} = \dfrac{x - y}{x + y}$ $\frac{d + c}{c - d}$

42. $\dfrac{x + y}{x - y} = \dfrac{a}{b}$ $\frac{b + a}{a - b}$

43. $\dfrac{cy}{d - c} = \dfrac{dx}{d^2 - c^2}$ $\frac{c(d + c)}{d}$

44. $\dfrac{b - a}{ay} = \dfrac{b^2 - a^2}{bx}$ $\frac{a(b + a)}{b}$

45. Solve $\dfrac{p}{t} = \dfrac{P}{T}$ for P. Then solve for T. $P = \frac{pT}{t}$; $T = \frac{Pt}{p}$

46. If $\dfrac{x}{y} = \dfrac{z}{w}$, which of the following must also be true? Explain. a and c

    (a) $\dfrac{x}{z} = \dfrac{y}{w}$ (b) $\dfrac{x}{w} = \dfrac{y}{z}$ (c) $\dfrac{w}{y} = \dfrac{z}{x}$

If $\frac{x}{y} = \frac{z}{w}$, then $xw = yz$. Likewise, $xw = zy$ in (a) and $wx = yz$ in (b), which are equivalent statements.

When the means of a proportion are equal, each mean is called the *mean proportional* between the two extremes. Find the positive mean proportional between the following extremes.

C **47.** 5 and 125 25

48. 4 and 64 16

49. $\dfrac{3}{2}$ and $\dfrac{2}{27}$ $\frac{1}{3}$

50. $\dfrac{4}{5}$ and $\dfrac{5}{16}$ $\frac{1}{2}$

Problems

Solve. Use estimation to check the reasonableness of your answer.

A **1.** Six oranges cost $.99. How much do ten oranges cost? $1.65

2. Three cans of cat food cost $.87. How much do eight cans cost? $2.32

3. Maria drove 111 mi in 3 h. About how far could she drive in 5 h? 185 mi

4. A truck uses 8 L of gasoline to go 120 km. How much gasoline will it use to go 300 km? 20 L

5. A car that sold for $11,800 has a sales tax of $767. How much does a car cost if its sales tax is $637? $9800

6. A recipe for $2\frac{1}{2}$ dozen whole-wheat muffins requires 600 g of flour. How many muffins can be made with 900 g of flour? $3\frac{3}{4}$ dozen or 45 muffins

7. At a fixed interest rate, an investment of $4000 earns $210. How much do you need to invest at the same rate to earn $336? $6400

8. An ad claims that in a recent poll, three out of four dentists recommended brushing with a certain brand of toothpaste. If there were 92 dentists polled, how many favored this brand? 69 dentists

B **9.** A consumer survey was taken in a town with 18,000 homes. Of the 360 homes surveyed, 48 had computers. On the basis of this survey, estimate the number of homes in the town that have computers. 2400 homes

10. A 25-acre field yields 550 bushels of wheat each year. How many more acres should be planted so that the yearly yield will be 660 bushels? 5 more acres

11. a. A photograph that measures 20 cm by 15 cm is enlarged so that its length becomes 28 cm. What does the width become? 21 cm

    b. Find these ratios: $\dfrac{\text{new length}}{\text{old length}}, \dfrac{\text{new perimeter}}{\text{old perimeter}}, \dfrac{\text{new area}}{\text{old area}}$ $\dfrac{7}{5}, \dfrac{7}{5}, \dfrac{49}{25}$

12. On a map, 1 cm represents 10 km, and Wyoming is a rectangle 44.5 cm by 59.1 cm. Find the area of Wyoming in km². 262,995 km²

C 13. Mahogany weighs 33.94 lb per ft³, whereas pine weighs 23.45 lb per ft³. Which weighs more: a mahogany board that is $5\frac{1}{2}$ in. by 1 in. by 6 ft or a pine board that is $3\frac{1}{2}$ in. by $1\frac{1}{2}$ in. by 8 ft? Mahogany board

Mixed Review Exercises

Find the LCD for each group of fractions.

1. $\dfrac{1}{4x^2y}, \dfrac{5}{xy}$ $4x^2y$

2. $\dfrac{w+4}{4}, \dfrac{2w-6}{12}$ 12

3. $\dfrac{4}{9}, \dfrac{7}{12}$ 36

4. $\dfrac{1}{6}, \dfrac{1}{5}, \dfrac{2}{12}$ 60

5. $\dfrac{3}{x-3}, \dfrac{6}{x+3}$ x^2-9

6. $\dfrac{x}{3y}, \dfrac{x+1}{2}$ $6y$

Simplify.

7. $\dfrac{6}{2(x-1)} + \dfrac{4}{x-1}$ $\dfrac{7}{x-1}$

8. $\dfrac{2r}{3} + \dfrac{r+1}{12}$ $\dfrac{9r+1}{12}$

9. $\dfrac{3a}{10} + \dfrac{4a+1}{8}$ $\dfrac{32a+5}{40}$

10. $|-7.4| - |2.6|$ 4.8

11. $-|3.2 + 1.1|$ -4.3

12. $9 + 3 \cdot 5$ 24

Self-Test 1

Vocabulary   ratio (p. 287)   means (p. 293)
              proportion (p. 293)   extremes (p. 293)

Write each ratio in simplest form.

1. 48 min:1 h   4:5

2. 2 m:5 cm   40:1

                                                  Obj. 7-1, p. 287

3. The ratio of trucks to vans at a rental lot was 9:11. If the lot had a total of 80 trucks and vans, how many trucks were on the lot? 36 trucks

Solve.

4. $\dfrac{17}{25} = \dfrac{m}{150}$ {102}

5. $\dfrac{2}{3n} = 14$ $\left\{\dfrac{1}{21}\right\}$

6. $\dfrac{x-5}{3} = \dfrac{x+2}{4}$ {26}   Obj. 7-2, p. 293

Check your answers with those at the back of the book.

Teaching Suggestions p. T112

Suggested Extensions p. T113

Warm-Up Exercises

Find the LCD.

1. $\frac{x}{5}, \frac{y}{7}$ 35

2. $\frac{y+1}{4}, \frac{y-2}{6}, \frac{y}{5}$ 60

3. $\frac{3a}{2}, \frac{a+1}{7}, 5a$ 14

4. $\frac{1}{2}, \frac{4m}{3}, \frac{3m}{5}$ 30

Motivating the Lesson

Tell students that in the Warm-Up Exercises they found LCDs. Today they'll use this skill to solve equations with fractional coefficients.

Chalkboard Examples

Solve.

1. $\frac{n}{3} + \frac{n}{4} = 7$

$$12\left(\frac{n}{3} + \frac{n}{4}\right) = 12(7)$$

$$12\left(\frac{n}{3}\right) + 12\left(\frac{n}{4}\right) = 84$$

$$4n + 3n = 84$$

$$7n = 84$$

$$n = 12$$

2. $\frac{y-1}{3} - \frac{y+1}{5} = 2$

$$15\left(\frac{y-1}{3} - \frac{y+1}{5}\right) = 15(2)$$

$$15\left(\frac{y-1}{3}\right) - 15\left(\frac{y+1}{5}\right) = 30$$

$$5(y-1) - 3(y+1) = 30$$

$$5y - 5 - 3y - 3 = 30$$

$$2y - 8 = 30$$

$$2y = 38$$

$$y = 19$$

Check for Understanding

Oral Exs. 1–9: use after Example 2.

7-3 Equations with Fractional Coefficients

Objective   To solve equations with fractional coefficients.

You can solve an equation with fractional coefficients by using the least common denominator of all the fractions in the equation. Multiply both sides of the equation by this LCD and then solve the resulting equation.

Example 1   Solve: **a.** $\frac{x}{7} + \frac{x}{3} = 10$ **b.** $\frac{3a}{5} - \frac{a}{2} = \frac{1}{20}$

Solution   **a.** The LCD of the fractions is 21 .

$$21\left(\frac{x}{7} + \frac{x}{3}\right) = 21(10)$$

$$21\left(\frac{x}{7}\right) + 21\left(\frac{x}{3}\right) = 210$$

$$3x + 7x = 210$$

$$10x = 210$$

$$x = 21$$

∴ the solution set is $\{21\}$.
Answer

b. The LCD of the fractions is 20 .

$$20\left(\frac{3a}{5} - \frac{a}{2}\right) = 20\left(\frac{1}{20}\right)$$

$$20\left(\frac{3a}{5}\right) - 20\left(\frac{a}{2}\right) = 1$$

$$4(3a) - 10a = 1$$

$$12a - 10a = 1$$

$$2a = 1$$

$$a = \frac{1}{2}$$

∴ the solution set is $\left\{\frac{1}{2}\right\}$.
Answer

Example 2   Solve: **a.** $\frac{x}{3} - \frac{x+2}{5} = 2$ **b.** $2n + \frac{n}{3} = \frac{n}{4} + 5$

Solution   **a.** The LCD of the fractions is 15 .

$$15\left(\frac{x}{3} - \frac{x+2}{5}\right) = 15(2)$$

$$15\left(\frac{x}{3}\right) - 15\left(\frac{x+2}{5}\right) = 30$$

$$5x - 3(x+2) = 30$$

$$5x - 3x - 6 = 30$$

$$2x = 36$$

$$x = 18$$

∴ the solution set is $\{18\}$.
Answer

b. The LCD of the fractions is 12 .

$$12\left(2n + \frac{n}{3}\right) = 12\left(\frac{n}{4} + 5\right)$$

$$12(2n) + 12\left(\frac{n}{3}\right) = 12\left(\frac{n}{4}\right) + 12(5)$$

$$24n + 4n = 3n + 60$$

$$28n = 3n + 60$$

$$25n = 60$$

$$n = \frac{60}{25} = \frac{12}{5}$$

∴ the solution set is $\left\{\frac{12}{5}\right\}$.
Answer

---

298   *Chapter 7*

Oral Exercises

State the least common denominator of the fractions in each equation. Then state the equation with integral coefficients that results when both sides are multiplied by the LCD.

6. 21; $7x - 3(x + 2) = 42$

1. $\frac{x}{3} + \frac{x}{2} = 1$ 6; $2x + 3x = 6$ 2. $\frac{3y}{8} + \frac{y}{4} = 10$ 8; $3y + 2y = 80$ 3. $\frac{3n}{10} - \frac{n}{5} = \frac{1}{2}$ 10; $3n - 2n = 5$

4. $\frac{2a}{3} - \frac{3a}{2} = -\frac{5}{6}$ 6; $4a - 9a = -5$ 5. $\frac{y}{2} - \frac{y + 5}{3} = 0$ 6; $3y - 2(y + 5) = 0$ 6. $\frac{x}{3} - \frac{x + 2}{7} = 2$

7. $\frac{x + 1}{6} + \frac{x + 5}{4} = 1$ 8. $\frac{y + 3}{2} + \frac{y + 2}{3} = -2$ 9. $\frac{1}{6}(y + 4) - \frac{1}{2}(y - 2) = \frac{5}{12}$

12; $2(x + 1) + 3(x + 5) = 12$ 6; $3(y + 3) + 2(y + 2) = -12$ 12; $2(y + 4) - 6(y - 2) = 5$

Written Exercises

A **1–4.** Solve the equations in Oral Exercises 1–4. 1. $\left\{\frac{6}{5}\right\}$ 2. {16} 3. {5} 4. {1}

Solve.

5. $\frac{w}{3} + \frac{w}{4} = \frac{7}{4}$ {3}

6. $\frac{3c}{10} + \frac{c}{5} = \frac{3}{2}$ {3}

7. $\frac{3a}{5} - \frac{a}{2} = \frac{1}{20}$ $\left\{\frac{1}{2}\right\}$

8. $\frac{7m}{8} - \frac{3m}{5} = \frac{11}{2}$ {20}

9. $\frac{x}{5} - \frac{x + 4}{7} = 0$ {10}

10. $\frac{x}{6} - \frac{x + 3}{5} = 1$ {−48}

11. $\frac{4y + 1}{3} - \frac{2y + 1}{5} = \frac{3}{5}$ $\left\{\frac{1}{2}\right\}$

12. $\frac{x + 2}{15} - \frac{x - 3}{5} = \frac{2}{3}$ $\left\{\frac{1}{2}\right\}$

13. $3u - \frac{u}{5} = 1 + \frac{8u}{10}$ $\left\{\frac{1}{2}\right\}$

14. $x - \frac{3x}{2} = \frac{3x}{4} - \frac{5}{6}$ $\left\{\frac{2}{3}\right\}$

15. $0 = 3m - \frac{3m - 7}{8}$ $\left\{-\frac{1}{3}\right\}$

16. $0 = 2x + \frac{2x - 8}{7}$ $\left\{\frac{1}{2}\right\}$

B 17. $\frac{n + 3}{3} - \frac{n}{4} = \frac{n - 2}{5}$ {12}

18. $\frac{x + 4}{3} - \frac{x}{7} = \frac{x + 7}{5}$ {−7}

Sample $\frac{1}{4}(n + 2) - \frac{1}{6}(n - 2) = \frac{3}{2}$

$12\left[\frac{1}{4}(n + 2) - \frac{1}{6}(n - 2)\right] = 12\left(\frac{3}{2}\right)$ The LCD is 12.

$3(n + 2) - 2(n - 2) = 6(3)$

$3n + 6 - 2n + 4 = 18$

$n + 10 = 18$

$n = 8$

∴ the solution set is {8}. *Answer*

Applying Fractions   **299**

Guided Practice

Solve.

1. $\frac{4x}{8} - \frac{x}{6} = \frac{1}{12}$ $\left\{\frac{1}{4}\right\}$

2. $\frac{a - 2}{4} - \frac{a}{3} = -\frac{2}{5}$ $\left\{-\frac{6}{5}\right\}$

3. $\frac{x + 1}{3} - \frac{x + 2}{4} = \frac{1}{2}$ {8}

4. $2y - \frac{y}{2} = \frac{y}{3} - 7$ {−6}

5. $0 = 4n - \frac{4n + 5}{6}$ $\left\{\frac{1}{4}\right\}$

6. One third of a number is four more than one fifth of the number. Find the number. 30

7. Min saved $\frac{1}{6}$ of her earnings and used $\frac{2}{3}$ for food and clothes. She has $15 left. How much did she earn? $90

Summarizing the Lesson

Students have solved equations and problems with fractional coefficients.

Suggested Assignments

Minimum
Day 1: 299/1–15 odd
    300/*P*: 1, 3, 5
  R 297/Self-Test 1
Day 2: 299/14, 16, 18
    300/*P*: 7, 9, 10
  S 301/Mixed Review
Assign with Lesson 7-4.

Average
Day 1: 299/1–4, 6–21
    mult. of 3
    300/*P*: 2, 4, 6, 8
  R 297/Self-Test 1
Day 2: 300/25–27
    301/*P*: 10, 12, 14
  S 301/Mixed Review
Assign with Lesson 7-4.

Maximum
    299/2–33 mult. of 3
    300/*P*: 3–15 mult. of 3
  S 301/Mixed Review
  R 297/Self-Test 1

Solve. See the sample on page 299.

19. $\frac{1}{2}(x + 4) - \frac{2}{3}(x - 1) = 3$ {−2}

20. $\frac{2}{3}(x - 1) - \frac{1}{5}(2x - 3) = 1$ {4}

21. $0 = \frac{1}{2}(n + 3) - \frac{1}{4}(n + 4)$ {−2}

22. $1 = \frac{1}{3}(x + 6) - \frac{1}{6}(9 - x)$ {1}

23. $\frac{6b - 4}{3} - 2 = \frac{18 - 4b}{3} + b$ {4}

24. $h - \frac{h + 1}{4} = \frac{2h + 3}{5} + 1$ $\left\{\frac{37}{7}\right\}$

25. $\frac{1}{4}\left(y - \frac{1}{3}\right) - \frac{1}{6}(y - 3) = \frac{2}{3}$ {3}

26. $\frac{2}{3}(x - 1) - \frac{1}{5}(x - 2) = \frac{x + 2}{3}$ {7}

C 27. $\frac{1}{2}(2x + 5) - x = \frac{3}{4}\left(\frac{6x + 7}{3}\right)$ $\left\{\frac{1}{2}\right\}$

28. $\frac{2}{5}\left(x + \frac{3}{2}\right) - \frac{5}{6}(2x + 1) = -\frac{44}{15}$ $\left\{\frac{81}{38}\right\}$

29. $\frac{7}{3}(2x + 3) + \frac{3}{4}\left(\frac{x}{5} - \frac{15}{2}\right) = \frac{11}{8}$ {0}

30. $\frac{3}{4}(x - 2) - \frac{2}{3}\left(x - \frac{1}{2}\right) = \frac{x + 1}{2}$ {−4}

Solve for x in terms of the other variable.

31. $\frac{x + 3a}{10} - \frac{x - a}{2} = \frac{x}{5}$ $\left\{\frac{4a}{3}\right\}$

32. $\frac{x + k}{4} - \frac{2x - 3k}{2} = \frac{k + 5x}{6}$ {k}

33. $\frac{m^2 + 10m + 25}{2x} = m^2 + 5m$ $\left\{\frac{m + 5}{2m}\right\}$

34. $\frac{a^2 + 6a + 9}{x} = a^2 + 3a$ $\left\{\frac{a + 3}{a}\right\}$

Problems

Solve.

A 1. One fourth of a number is two more than one fifth of the number. Find the number. 40

2. One eighth of a number is ten less than one third of the number. Find the number. 48

3. Two numbers are in the ratio 5:2. One half of their sum is $10\frac{1}{2}$. Find the numbers. 15 and 6

4. Three numbers are in the ratio 3:5:6. One fourth of their sum is $1\frac{1}{2}$ more than the smallest number. Find the numbers. 9, 15, and 18

5. The width of a poster is $\frac{4}{5}$ of its length. It takes 36 ft of metal framing to frame the poster. Find the dimensions of the poster. 8 ft by 10 ft

6. The length of a rectangular garden is $\frac{3}{2}$ of its width. It takes 50 m of edging to create a border. Find the dimensions of the garden. 15 m by 10 m

7. Scott spent one ninth of his allowance on a newspaper, and two fifths of his allowance on a snack. If he has $2.20 left, how much does he get for an allowance? $4.50

8. Terri spent three eighths of her monthly salary on rent, and one third of her monthly salary on food. If she has $294 left, what is her monthly salary? $1008

9. A rectangle is 9 cm longer than it is wide. The width is one seventh of the perimeter. Find the length and the width. 15 cm and 6 cm

10. The lengths of the sides of a triangle are consecutive integers. Half of the perimeter is 14 more than the length of the longest side. Find the perimeter. 90

B 11. Erica hiked up a mountain trail at 3 km/h and returned at 4 km/h. The entire trip took 5 h 10 min, including the half hour she spent at the top. How long was the trail? 8 km—one way

12. Consuela walked from her home to the fitness center at 6 km/h. She stayed 45 min, and then got a ride back at 48 km/h. If she returned 1.5 h after starting out, find the distance from home to the fitness center. 4 km

13. One eighth of Al's coins are quarters and the rest are nickels. If the total value of the coins is $3.60, how many of each type of coin does he have? 6 quarters and 42 nickels

14. Two thirds of a pile of coins are nickels, one fourth are dimes, and the rest are quarters. If the total value of the coins is $4.75, how many of each type of coin are there? 40 nickels, 15 dimes, 5 quarters

C 15. Hannah bought some apples at the price of 3 apples for 95¢. She sold three fourths of them at 45¢ each, making a profit of 75¢. How many apples did Hannah keep? 9 apples

16. Diophantus was a famous Greek mathematician who lived and worked in Alexandria, Egypt, probably in the third century A.D. After he died, someone described his life in this puzzle:

> He was a boy for $\frac{1}{6}$ of his life.
> After $\frac{1}{12}$ more, he acquired a beard.
> After another $\frac{1}{7}$, he married.
> In the fifth year after his marriage his son was born.
> The son lived half as many years as his father.
> Diophantus died 4 years after his son.

How old was Diophantus when he died? 84 years old

Mixed Review Exercises

Write each ratio in simplest form.

1. 8 days:4 wk 2:7
2. $15x:90x$ 1:6
3. 16:12 4:3
4. $\dfrac{16mn^2}{40mn}$ $\dfrac{2n}{5}$
5. $\dfrac{48x^2y}{36x^3y^2}$ $\dfrac{4}{3xy}$
6. $\dfrac{21a^4}{35ab^2}$ $\dfrac{3a^3}{5b^2}$

Solve.

7. $\dfrac{7}{2n} = \dfrac{3}{6}$ {7}
8. $\dfrac{x+2}{7} = \dfrac{5}{3}$ $\left\{\dfrac{29}{3}\right\}$
9. $\dfrac{2a+3}{5} = \dfrac{a+8}{4}$ $\left\{\dfrac{28}{3}\right\}$
10. $3x - 2 = 14$ $\left\{\dfrac{16}{3}\right\}$
11. $|x| = 5$ {5, −5}
12. $8x + 3 = 9x + 1$ {2}

Applying Fractions **301**

Application / Units of Measurement in Problem Solving

A *rate* is a ratio that compares the amounts of two different kinds of measurements. For example, suppose a greenhouse is selling four begonia plants for $1. Then the rate $\frac{4 \text{ plants}}{\$1}$ tells how many plants you get for a certain amount of money. The rate $\frac{\$1}{4 \text{ plants}}$ tells how much you pay for a certain number of plants. The *unit price* is the price of one unit. In this case the unit price is $\frac{\$.25}{1 \text{ plant}}$, which can be written $.25/plant and read as *$.25 per plant*.

When you solve a problem involving rates, you can think of multiplying and dividing the units just as you do the numbers to determine the appropriate unit for your answer to the problem.

Example 1 Rosario spent $8.28 for two bags of dog biscuits. If there are 36 biscuits per bag, find the unit cost per biscuit.

Solution To find the unit cost per biscuit, you divide the total cost by the total number of biscuits.

Total cost: $8.28

Total number of biscuits: $2 \text{ bags} \times \frac{36 \text{ biscuits}}{1 \text{ bag}} = 72 \text{ biscuits}$

Unit cost: $\frac{\$8.28}{72 \text{ biscuits}} = \frac{\$.115}{1 \text{ biscuit}}$, or 11.5¢/biscuit.   *Answer*

Example 2 What does it cost to carpet a room 10 ft by 12 ft at $12 per square foot?

Solution Area: $10 \text{ ft} \times 12 \text{ ft} = 120 \text{ ft}^2$

Cost: $\frac{\$12}{1 \text{ ft}^2} \times 120 \text{ ft}^2 = \$1440$ *Answer*

Carrying units throughout your computation is also helpful when you want to express a measurement in terms of a larger or smaller unit.

Example 3 An interplanetary probe travels 40,200 km/h. Express this speed in meters per second.

Solution Set up units to "cancel out." Notice that to divide by 60 min/h you multiply by $\frac{1 \text{ h}}{60 \text{ min}}$.

$\frac{40,200 \text{ km}}{1 \text{ h}} \cdot \frac{1000 \text{ m}}{1 \text{ km}} \cdot \frac{1 \text{ h}}{60 \text{ min}} \cdot \frac{1 \text{ min}}{60 \text{ s}} \approx 11,167 \text{ m/s}$ *Answer*

Exercises

Write the appropriate unit.

1. $\dfrac{39¢}{1 \text{ dozen}} \times 2 \text{ dozen} = 78 \underline{\ \ ?\ \ } ¢$

2. $\dfrac{45 \text{ mi}}{1 \text{ h}} \cdot 2 \text{ h} = 90 \underline{\ \ ?\ \ } \text{ mi}$

3. $9 \text{ ft} \times 12 \text{ ft} = 108 \underline{\ \ ?\ \ } \text{ ft}^2$

4. $\dfrac{60 \text{ mi}}{1 \text{ h}} \div \dfrac{60 \text{ min}}{1 \text{ h}} = 1 \underline{\ \ ?\ \ } \text{ mi/min}$

5. $\dfrac{55 \text{ mi}}{1 \text{ h}} \times \dfrac{5280 \text{ ft}}{1 \text{ mi}} \div \dfrac{60 \text{ min}}{1 \text{ h}} = 4840 \underline{\ \ ?\ \ } \text{ ft/min}$

6. The gas tank in an XR-5 car holds up to 15 gal.
   a. If the car averages 36 mi/gal in highway driving, how far can the car be driven on one tank of gas? 540 mi/tank
   b. If the car is driven at an average speed of 48 mi/h, how many hours can the car be driven on one tank of gas? $11\frac{1}{4}$ h/tank

7. The Truongs bought a new refrigerator that uses 102 kW · h (kilowatt-hours) of electricity per month. If electricity cost $0.125 per kW · h, find the operating cost of the refrigerator for one day in June. 42.5¢/day

8. This week the Super-Buy store is selling two 2.5-ounce packages of sliced salami for $1. What is the cost per pound? $3.20/lb

Historical Note / *Broken Numbers*

The word "fraction" comes from the Latin verb *frangere*, meaning "to break." A fraction is thus a "broken number," or a part of a number.

The Babylonians used special symbols to represent commonly used fractions such as $\frac{1}{2}$, $\frac{1}{3}$, and $\frac{2}{3}$. However, fractions having denominators of base sixty, called sexagesimals, were used in astronomical calculations and in mathematical texts. Because the denominators of the fractions were restricted to a certain base, a positional notation was used to represent these fractions. Thus, ◄◄ intended as a fraction meant $\frac{20}{60}$. The many integer divisors of sixty made it easier to simplify fractional computations. Sexagesimal fractions were also used in ancient Greece and then in Europe until the sixteenth century, when they were replaced by decimals.

Like the Babylonians, the Egyptians had special symbols for commonly used fractions. In hieroglyphics the symbol ⬭ was placed over the symbol for a whole number to express its reciprocal. This symbol was replaced by a dot in cursive writing and was later adopted by the English, who wrote $\dot{2}$ for $\frac{1}{2}$.

The Egyptians attempted to avoid computational difficulties by expressing fractions as sums of unit fractions, that is, fractions having a numerator of one. There were numerous rules for forming unit fractions. For example, $\frac{2}{43}$ might have been expressed as

$$\frac{1}{24} + \frac{1}{258} + \frac{1}{1032} \text{ or } \frac{1}{30} + \frac{1}{86} + \frac{1}{645}.$$

Applying Fractions **303**

7-4 Fractional Equations

Objective   To solve fractional equations.

An equation with a variable in the denominator of one or more terms is called a **fractional equation.** To solve a fractional equation you can multiply both sides of the equation by the LCD. You can also solve a fractional equation as you would solve a proportion when the equation consists of one fraction equal to another (see Solution 2 of Example 2).

Example 1   Solve: $\dfrac{3}{x} - \dfrac{1}{4} = \dfrac{1}{12}$

Solution
$$12x\left(\frac{3}{x} - \frac{1}{4}\right) = 12x\left(\frac{1}{12}\right)$$
$$12x\left(\frac{3}{x}\right) - 12x\left(\frac{1}{4}\right) = x$$
$$36 - 3x = x$$
$$36 = 4x$$
$$9 = x$$

Multiply both sides of the equation by the LCD, $12x$. (Notice that x cannot equal 0 because $\dfrac{3}{0}$ has no meaning.)

$Check:$ $\dfrac{3}{9} - \dfrac{1}{4} \stackrel{?}{=} \dfrac{1}{12}$

$\dfrac{1}{3} - \dfrac{1}{4} \stackrel{?}{=} \dfrac{1}{12}$

$\dfrac{4}{12} - \dfrac{3}{12} \stackrel{?}{=} \dfrac{1}{12}$

$\dfrac{1}{12} = \dfrac{1}{12}$ $\checkmark$

$\therefore$ the solution set is $\{9\}$.   **Answer**

Example 2   Solve: $\dfrac{2-x}{3-x} = \dfrac{4}{9}$

Solution 1   Multiply both sides by the LCD, $9(3-x)$. (Notice that x cannot equal 3.)
$$9(3-x)\left(\frac{2-x}{3-x}\right) = 9(3-x)\left(\frac{4}{9}\right)$$
$$9(2-x) = (3-x)(4)$$
$$18 - 9x = 12 - 4x$$
$$6 = 5x$$
$$\frac{6}{5} = x$$

$\therefore$ the solution set is $\left\{\dfrac{6}{5}\right\}$.   **Answer**

Solution 2   Solve as a proportion.
$$\frac{2-x}{3-x} = \frac{4}{9}$$
$$9(2-x) = 4(3-x)$$
$$18 - 9x = 12 - 4x$$
$$6 = 5x$$
$$\frac{6}{5} = x$$

$\therefore$ the solution set is $\left\{\dfrac{6}{5}\right\}$.

Answer

Example 3 Solve: $\dfrac{2}{b^2 - b} - \dfrac{2}{b - 1} = 1.$

Solution

$$b(b-1)\left(\dfrac{2}{b(b-1)} - \dfrac{2}{b-1}\right) = b(b-1)(1)$$

$$b(b-1)\left(\dfrac{2}{b(b-1)}\right) - b(b-1)\left(\dfrac{2}{b-1}\right) = b(b-1)$$

$$2 - 2b = b^2 - b$$

$$0 = b^2 + b - 2$$

$$0 = (b-1)(b+2)$$

$$b = 1 \text{ or } b = -2$$

⎧ Multiply both sides of
⎪ the equation by the LCD,
⎨ $b(b-1)$. (Notice that b
⎪ cannot equal 0 or 1.)
⎩

Check: Since b cannot equal 1 in the original equation, you need to check only -2 in the equation.

$$\dfrac{2}{(-2)^2 - (-2)} - \dfrac{2}{-2 - 1} \stackrel{?}{=} 1$$

$$\dfrac{2}{6} - \dfrac{2}{-3} \stackrel{?}{=} 1$$

$$\dfrac{1}{3} + \dfrac{2}{3} = 1 \ \checkmark$$

$\therefore$ the solution set is $\{-2\}$. **Answer**

Caution: Multiplying both sides of an equation by a variable expression sometimes results in an equation that has an extra root. You must check each root of the transformed equation to see if it satisfies the original equation.

Oral Exercises

1. $4x$; $x + 8 = 3x$ **2.** $2x$; $6 + x = 2x$ **3.** $12y$; $48 - 3y = y$

State the LCD of the fractions in each equation. Then state the equation that results when both sides are multiplied by the LCD.

1. $\dfrac{1}{4} + \dfrac{2}{x} = \dfrac{3}{4}$ **2.** $\dfrac{3}{x} + \dfrac{1}{2} = 1$ **3.** $\dfrac{4}{y} - \dfrac{1}{4} = \dfrac{1}{12}$

4. $\dfrac{9}{2a} - \dfrac{5}{a} = -\dfrac{1}{4}$ **5.** $\dfrac{n}{n-2} = \dfrac{6}{5}$ **6.** $\dfrac{1+b}{1-b} = \dfrac{4}{3}$
$4a$; $18 - 20 = -a$ $5(n-2)$; $5n = 6(n-2)$ $3(1-b)$; $3(1+b) = 4(1-b)$

Written Exercises

A   **1–6.** Solve the equations in Oral Exercises 1–6.

1. $\{4\}$ **2.** $\{6\}$ **3.** $\{12\}$
4. $\{2\}$ **5.** $\{12\}$ **6.** $\left\{\dfrac{1}{7}\right\}$

Solve and check. If the equation has no solution, write *No solution*.

7. $\dfrac{6}{n} - \dfrac{1}{4} = \dfrac{8}{2n}$ $\{8\}$ **8.** $\dfrac{3}{2a} - \dfrac{5}{6} = \dfrac{2}{3a}$ $\{1\}$ **9.** $\dfrac{6-x}{4-x} = \dfrac{3}{5}$ $\{9\}$

10. $\dfrac{5-m}{7-m} = \dfrac{2}{3}$ $\{1\}$ **11.** $1 = \dfrac{x+5}{x-2}$ No solution   **12.** $2 = \dfrac{x-4}{x-2}$ $\{0\}$

Applying Fractions   **305**

---

3. $\dfrac{n+1}{n+2} - \dfrac{10}{n^2 - 4} = 0$ $n \neq \pm 2$
The LCD is $(n+2)(n-2)$ and the solution set is $\{-3, 4\}$.

Check for Understanding

Oral Exs. 1–4: use after Example 1.
Oral Exs. 5–6: use after Example 2.

Guided Practice

Solve and check. If the equation has no solution, write *No solution*.

1. $\dfrac{1}{6} + \dfrac{2}{x} = \dfrac{2}{3}$ $\{4\}$

2. $\dfrac{6}{5y} - \dfrac{2}{2y} = \dfrac{1}{4}$ $\left\{\dfrac{4}{5}\right\}$

3. $\dfrac{z}{z-1} = \dfrac{9}{8}$ $\{9\}$

4. $6 = \dfrac{y-2}{y+3}$ $\{-4\}$

5. $\dfrac{5y-1}{1-5y} = \dfrac{1}{4}$ No solution

6. $\dfrac{1}{8} = \dfrac{3x-1}{3x+1}$ $\left\{\dfrac{3}{7}\right\}$

7. $\dfrac{3+b}{2b} = \dfrac{1}{b}$ $\{-1\}$

Summarizing the Lesson

Students have solved fractional equations by first finding the LCD of all the denominators and then multiplying both sides of the equation by the LCD.

Suggested Assignments

Minimum
Day 1: 305/1–6
Assign with Lesson 7-3.
Day 2: 305/7–29 odd
       306/*P*: 1–3, 5
   S 308/Mixed Review
          (continued)

Suggested Assignments

(continued)

Average
Day 1: 305/1–6, 8, 10, 12
Assign with Lesson 7-3.
Day 2: 306/14–32 even
          306/*P*: 2, 4, 6, 8, 10
     S 308/Mixed Review
Maximum
Day 1: 305/3–36 mult. of 3
          306/*P*: 2, 4, 6
Day 2: 306/39, 40
          307/*P*: 8, 10, 12, 14
     S 308/Mixed Review

Supplementary Materials

Study Guide   pp. 119–120
Practice Master   41
Computer Activity   20
Resource Book   p. 110

Common Errors

Some students forget to multiply constant terms of fractional equations by the LCD. In reteaching, encourage these students to write out their work as shown in the solution to Example 3 on page 305.

Students may also include extraneous roots that are not solutions in their answers. Be sure to emphasize the *Caution* on page 305.

Solve and check. If the equation has no solution, write *No solution*.

13. $\dfrac{3y - 6}{y - 2} = 2$ No sol.

14. $\dfrac{2x - 4}{x - 2} = \dfrac{1}{3}$ No sol.

15. $\dfrac{1}{2} = \dfrac{3 - 2m}{4m - 6}$ No sol.

16. $\dfrac{1}{4} = \dfrac{2w + 1}{2w + 4}$ {0}

17. $\dfrac{3y - 6}{y - 2} = 3$

{All reals except 2}

18. $\dfrac{y - 2}{4y - 8} = \dfrac{1}{4}$

{All reals except 2}

19. $\dfrac{2 + c}{3c} = \dfrac{1}{c}$ {1}

20. $\dfrac{a + 1}{6} = \dfrac{2}{a}$ {−4, 3}

B 21. $\dfrac{3}{2a + 1} = \dfrac{3}{2a - 1}$ No sol.

22. $\dfrac{5}{3 + 4x} = \dfrac{4}{4x + 3}$ No sol.

23. $\dfrac{1}{x} - \dfrac{2x}{x + 1} = 0$ $\left\{-\dfrac{1}{2}, 1\right\}$

24. $\dfrac{1}{z - 3} + \dfrac{3}{9 - 3z} = 0$

{All reals except 3}

25. $\dfrac{1}{y - 3} = \dfrac{6}{y^2 - 9}$ No sol.

26. $\dfrac{4}{a^2 - 4a} = \dfrac{-1}{4 - a}$ No sol.

27. $\dfrac{4}{x + 1} - \dfrac{1}{x} = 1$ {1}

28. $\dfrac{3}{x - 1} + \dfrac{2}{x} = 4$ $\left\{\dfrac{1}{4}, 2\right\}$

29. $1 = \dfrac{3}{y + 2} + \dfrac{1}{y - 2}$ {0, 4}

30. $-2 = \dfrac{1}{1 + x} - \dfrac{3}{1 - x}$ {0, −2}

31. $\dfrac{x}{x + 1} + \dfrac{x + 1}{x} = \dfrac{5}{2}$ {−2, 1}

32. $\dfrac{y + 1}{y - 1} - \dfrac{y - 1}{y + 1} = \dfrac{8}{3}$

33. $\dfrac{n - 2}{n} - \dfrac{n - 3}{n - 6} = \dfrac{1}{n}$ {3}

34. $\dfrac{5}{y - 5} - \dfrac{3}{y + 5} = \dfrac{2}{y}$ $\left\{-\dfrac{5}{4}\right\}$

35. $\dfrac{3}{x - 4} + \dfrac{2}{x^2 - 16} = 0$

36. $\dfrac{2}{c^2 - 2c} + \dfrac{1}{2 - c} = 1$ {−1} **37.** $\dfrac{1}{x - 4} + \dfrac{2}{x^2 - 16} = \dfrac{3}{x + 4}$ {9} **38.** $\dfrac{3a}{a - 1} - \dfrac{4}{a + 1} = \dfrac{4}{a^2 - 1}$

C 39. $\dfrac{3}{2x} - \dfrac{x}{4x^2 - 1} = \dfrac{7}{4x + 2}$ $\left\{1, \dfrac{3}{4}\right\}$

40. $\dfrac{x - 2}{x^2 - x - 6} = \dfrac{1}{x^2 - 4} + \dfrac{3}{2x + 4}$ {1, 4}

32. $\left\{-\dfrac{1}{2}, 2\right\}$ 35. $\left\{-\dfrac{14}{3}\right\}$ 38. $\left\{0, \dfrac{1}{3}\right\}$

Problems

Sample The sum of a number and its reciprocal is $\dfrac{26}{5}$. Find the number.

Solution Let x be the number. Then $\dfrac{1}{x}$ is its reciprocal.

$$x + \dfrac{1}{x} = \dfrac{26}{5}$$

$$5x\left(x + \dfrac{1}{x}\right) = 5x\left(\dfrac{26}{5}\right)$$

$$5x^2 + 5 = 26x$$

$$5x^2 - 26x + 5 = 0$$

$$(5x - 1)(x - 5) = 0$$

$$x = \dfrac{1}{5} \quad \text{or} \quad x = 5$$

∴ the number is $\dfrac{1}{5}$ or 5. *Answer*

Solve.

1. The sum of a number and its reciprocal is $\dfrac{25}{12}$. Find the number. $\dfrac{4}{3}$ or $\dfrac{3}{4}$

2. The sum of a number and its reciprocal is $\dfrac{13}{6}$. Find the number. $\dfrac{2}{3}$ or $\dfrac{3}{2}$

3. The sum of the reciprocals of two consecutive odd integers is $\frac{8}{15}$. Find the integers. 3 and 5

4. The sum of the reciprocals of two consecutive even integers is $\frac{11}{60}$. Find the integers. 10 and 12

5. The numerator of a fraction is 1 more than the denominator. If the numerator and the denominator are both increased by 2, the new fraction will be $\frac{1}{4}$ less than the original fraction. Find the original fraction. $\frac{3}{2}$

6. The numerator of a fraction is 1 less than the denominator. If the numerator and the denominator are both increased by 4, the new fraction will be $\frac{1}{8}$ more than the original fraction. Find the original fraction. $\frac{3}{4}$

B 7. The sum of two numbers is 10 and the sum of their reciprocals is $\frac{5}{12}$. Find the numbers. 4 and 6

8. Two numbers differ by 11. When the larger number is divided by the smaller, the quotient is 2 and the remainder is 4. Find the numbers. 18 and 7

9. Tina hiked 15 km up a mountain trail. Her return trip along the same trail took 30 min less because she was able to increase her speed by 1 km/h. How long did it take her to climb up and down the mountain? 5.5 h

	Rate	× Time =	Distance
Up	x	$\frac{15}{x}$	15
Down	?	?	?
	$x+1$	$\frac{15}{x}-0.5$	15

10. Jacqui commutes 30 mi to her job each day. She finds that if she drives 10 mi/h faster, it takes her 6 min less to get to work. Find her new speed. 60 mi/h

	Rate	× Time =	Distance
Slower	x	$\frac{30}{x}$	30
Faster	?	?	?
	$x+10$	$\frac{30}{x}-\frac{1}{10}$	30

11. The cost of a bus trip was $180. The people who signed up for the trip agreed to split the cost equally. However, six people did not show up, so that those who did go each had to pay $1.50 more. How many people actually went on the trip? 24 people

	Number ×	Price =	Cost
Planned	? x	? $\frac{180}{x}$	? 180
Actual	?	?	?
	$x-6$	$\frac{180}{x}+1.50$	180

12. The $75 cost for a party was to be shared equally by all those attending. Since five more people attended than was expected, the price per person dropped by 50¢. How many people attended the party? 30 people

	Number ×	Price =	Cost
Planned	? x	? $\frac{75}{x}$	? 75
Actual	?	?	?
	$x+5$	$\frac{75}{x}-0.50$	75

Applying Fractions **307**

Solve.

13. Cindy and Dave left the dock to canoe downstream. Fifteen minutes later Tammy left by motorboat with the supplies. Since the motorboat traveled twice as fast as the canoe, it caught up with the canoe 3 km from the dock. What was the speed of the motorboat? 12 km/h

14. An experienced plumber made $600 for working on a certain job. His apprentice, who makes $3 per hour less, also made $600. However, the apprentice worked 10 h more than the plumber. How much does the plumber make per hour? $15 per hour

Mixed Review Exercises

Solve.

1. $\frac{2a}{5} + \frac{3a}{10} = 14$ {20}

2. $\frac{x}{5} - \frac{x}{3} = 4$ {−30}

3. $\frac{1}{3}(y + 3) + \frac{1}{4}(y + 1) = 3$ {3}

4. $\frac{3}{7} = \frac{5a}{14}$ $\left\{\frac{6}{5}\right\}$

5. $\frac{-9}{7t} = \frac{3}{28}$ {−12}

6. $\frac{z}{6} = \frac{12}{5}$ $\left\{\frac{72}{5}\right\}$

Simplify.

7. $(7 - 2)^3$ 125

8. $4x^2(2x^2 - 7 + 3x)$ $8x^4 + 12x^3 - 28x^2$

9. $6 \cdot 2^3$ 48

10. $(4n^2 - n) + (9 + n^2)$ $5n^2 - n + 9$

11. $(5z^3)(2y^2z)$ $10y^2z^4$

12. $(3pq^2)^3$ $27p^3q^6$

Self-Test 2

Vocabulary   fractional equation (p. 304)

Solve.

1. $\frac{5k}{48} - \frac{2k}{9} = \frac{17}{18}$ {−8}

2. $20 = c + \frac{c - 2}{8}$ {18}

Obj. 7-3, p. 298

3. $\frac{3x + 4}{5} = \frac{x - 3}{2}$ {−23}

4. $\frac{m + 6}{10} - \frac{m}{15} = \frac{2}{5}$ {−6}

Solve and check. If the equation has no solution, write *No solution*.

5. $\frac{3a - 1}{a + 1} = 4$ {−5}

6. $\frac{2}{n - 3} - \frac{1}{2n - 6} = 0$ No solution

Obj. 7-4, p. 304

7. The sum of the reciprocals of two consecutive integers is $\frac{5}{6}$. Find the integers. 2 and 3

Check your answers with those at the back of the book.

Quick Quiz

Solve.

1. $\frac{7y}{8} - \frac{3y}{5} = \frac{11}{10}$ {4}

2. $15 = n + \frac{n + 6}{6}$ {12}

3. $\frac{2t - 1}{3} = \frac{4t + 3}{5}$ {−7}

4. $\frac{n - 1}{6} - \frac{n}{7} = \frac{2}{3}$ {35}

Solve and check. If the equation has no solution, write *No solution*.

5. $\frac{4y + 3}{y - 2} = 5$ {13}

6. $\frac{6}{y - 4} + \frac{1}{2y - 8} = 0$ No solution

7. The sum of the reciprocals of two consecutive integers is $\frac{15}{56}$. Find the integers. 7, 8

Percent Problems

7-5 Percents

Objective   To work with percents and decimals.

The word **percent** means "hundredths" or "divided by 100." The symbol %
is used to represent percent.

Example 1 a. $29 \text{ percent} = 29\% = \frac{29}{100} = 0.29$

b. $2.6 \text{ percent} = 2.6\% = \frac{2.6}{100} = \frac{26}{1000} = 0.026$

c. $637 \text{ percent} = 637\% = \frac{637}{100} = 6\frac{37}{100} = 6.37$

d. $0.02 \text{ percent} = 0.02\% = \frac{0.02}{100} = \frac{2}{10,000} = 0.0002$

e. $\frac{1}{4} \text{ percent} = \frac{1}{4}\% = 0.25\% = \frac{0.25}{100} = \frac{25}{10,000} = 0.0025$

f. $33\frac{1}{3} \text{ percent} = 33\frac{1}{3}\% = \frac{100}{3}\% = \frac{100}{3} \div 100 = \frac{1}{3}$

Example 2   Write each number as a percent: a. $\frac{3}{5}$ b. $\frac{1}{3}$ c. 4.7

Solution   a. $\frac{3}{5} = \frac{x}{100}$ b. $\frac{1}{3} = \frac{x}{100}$ c. $4.7 = \frac{x}{100}$

$5x = 300$ $3x = 100$ $\frac{4.7}{1} = \frac{x}{100}$

$x = 60$ $x = 33\frac{1}{3}$ $x = 470$

$\therefore \frac{3}{5} = \frac{60}{100}$ $\therefore \frac{1}{3} = \frac{33\frac{1}{3}}{100}$ $\therefore 4.7 = \frac{470}{100}$

$= 60\%$ $= 33\frac{1}{3}\%$ $= 470\%$

Answer   *Answer*   *Answer*

   Most calculators have a key with the % symbol that will help you solve or
check percent problems. You can also enter a percent as a decimal or use your
calculator and division by 100 to find the decimal form of a percent.
   In percent problems the word "of" means "multiply" and the word "is"
means "equals."

Applying Fractions   **309**

Teaching Suggestions p. T113
Reading Algebra p. T114
Suggested Extensions p. T114

Warm-Up Exercises

Divide by 100. Write the
quotient as a decimal.

1. 75 0.75 **2.** 2 0.02

3. 450 4.5 **4.** 0.8 0.008

5. 9.4 0.094

6. 7.03 0.0703

Motivating the Lesson

One serving of a breakfast
cereal weighs 20 g with 18 g
of carbohydrates and 2 g of
protein. What percent of the
cereal is carbohydrates? protein? 90%; 10% Tell stu-
dents that to solve this
problem and similar prob-
lems they need to know
how to work with percents
and decimals, which is today's lesson.

Using a Calculator

Percent problems are most
easily solved by using a calculator. Encourage students
to use one when possible.

Chalkboard Examples

Express as a fraction in simplest form.

1. 36% $\frac{9}{25}$ **2.** 180% $\frac{9}{5}$

3. $\frac{3}{4}\%$ $\frac{3}{400}$ **4.** $37\frac{1}{2}\%$ $\frac{3}{8}$

Write each number as a
percent.

5. $\frac{7}{8}$ $\frac{7}{8} = \frac{x}{100}$

$8x = 700$

$x = 87.5$

$\therefore \frac{7}{8} = \frac{87.5}{100} = 87.5\%$

(continued)

309

(continued)

6. 6.9

$$\frac{6.9}{1} = \frac{x}{100}$$

$$x = 690$$

$$\therefore 6.9 = \frac{690}{100} = 690\%$$

7. 48% of 125 is what number?

$$0.48 \cdot 125 = 60$$

$$\therefore 48\% \text{ of } 125 \text{ is } 60.$$

8. 9 is 36% of what number?

$$9 = \frac{36}{100} \cdot x$$

$$25 = x$$

$$\therefore 9 \text{ is } 36\% \text{ of } 25.$$

9. What percent of 225 is 99?

$$\frac{x}{100} \cdot 225 = 99$$

$$225x = 9900$$

$$x = 44$$

$$\therefore 44\% \text{ of } 225 \text{ is } 99.$$

Solve.

10. $2.8x = 12.6 + 0.7x$

$$10(2.8x) = 10(12.6 + 0.7x)$$

$$28x = 126 + 7x$$

$$x = 6$$

$$\therefore \text{ the solution set is } \{6\}.$$

11. A dealer pays $5500 for a car and wants to make a profit of 15%. What should be the selling price?

1. Find 15% of $5500:
$0.15 \cdot 5500 = 825$
∴ the profit should be $825.

2. Add the profit to the cost:
$5500 + $825 = $6325
∴ the selling price should be $6325.

Example 3 15% of 180 is what number?

Solution 1 $\dfrac{15}{100} \cdot 180 = x$

$$\frac{2700}{100} = x$$

$$27 = x$$

$$\therefore 15\% \text{ of } 180 \text{ is } 27. \quad \textbf{\textit{Answer}}$$

Solution 2 $0.15 \cdot 180 = x$

$$27 = x$$

$$\therefore 15\% \text{ of } 180 \text{ is } 27. \quad \textbf{\textit{Answer}}$$

Example 4 23 is 25% of what number?

Solution $23 = \dfrac{25}{100} \cdot x$

$$2300 = 25x$$

$$\frac{2300}{25} = x$$

$$92 = x \quad \therefore 23 \text{ is } 25\% \text{ of } 92. \quad \textbf{\textit{Answer}}$$

Example 5 What percent of 64 is 48?

Solution $\dfrac{x}{100} \cdot 64 = 48$

$$\frac{64x}{100} = 48$$

$$64x = 4800$$

$$x = 75 \quad \therefore 75\% \text{ of } 64 \text{ is } 48. \quad \textbf{\textit{Answer}}$$

When you solve an equation with decimal coefficients, you can multiply both sides of the equation by a power of 10 (10, 100, and so on) to get an equivalent equation with integral coefficients.

Example 6 Solve $1.2x = 36 + 0.4x$.

Solution $10(1.2x) = 10(36 + 0.4x)$ {Multiply both sides by 10 when the coefficients are tenths.

$$12x = 360 + 4x$$

$$8x = 360$$

$$x = 45 \quad \therefore \text{ the solution set is } \{45\}. \quad \textbf{\textit{Answer}}$$

Example 7 Solve $94 = 0.15x + 0.08(1000 - x)$.

Solution $100(94) = 100[0.15x + 0.08(1000 - x)]$ {Multiply both sides by 100 when the coefficients are hundredths.

$$9400 = 15x + 8(1000 - x)$$

$$9400 = 15x + 8000 - 8x$$

$$1400 = 7x$$

$$200 = x \quad \therefore \text{ the solution set is } \{200\}. \quad \textbf{\textit{Answer}}$$

310 *Chapter 7*

Example 8 During a sale, a sporting goods store gave a 40% discount on sleeping bags. How much did Ross pay for a sleeping bag with an original price of $75?

Solution 1 1. Find 40% of $75: $0.40 \cdot 75 = 30$

2. Subtract the amount of discount from the original price:

$$\begin{array}{r} 75 \\ -30 \\ \hline 45 \end{array}$$

∴ Ross paid $45 for the sleeping bag. *Answer*

Solution 2 1. If the sleeping bag was discounted 40%, it then cost $100\% - 40\% = 60\%$ of its original price.

2. Find 60% of $75: $0.60 \cdot 75 = 45$

∴ Ross paid $45. *Answer*

Oral Exercises

Express each number as a percent.

1. 0.833 83.3%   **2.** 0.07 7%   **3.** 2.3 230%   **4.** 0.015 1.5%   **5.** 0.003 0.3%

6. $\frac{1}{2}$ 50%   **7.** 9 900%   **8.** 10 1000%   **9.** $\frac{5}{4}$ 125%   **10.** $\frac{9}{50}$ 18%

Express as a fraction in simplest form.

11. 12% $\frac{3}{25}$ **12.** 70% $\frac{7}{10}$ **13.** 6% $\frac{3}{50}$ **14.** $\frac{1}{2}$% $\frac{1}{200}$ **15.** $10\frac{2}{3}$% $\frac{8}{75}$

Express as a fraction and then as a mixed number.

16. 105%   **17.** 250%   **18.** 175%   **19.** 420%   **20.** 375%
$\frac{21}{20}$ or $1\frac{1}{20}$ $\frac{5}{2}$ or $2\frac{1}{2}$ $\frac{7}{4}$ or $1\frac{3}{4}$ $\frac{21}{5}$ or $4\frac{1}{5}$ $\frac{15}{4}$ or $3\frac{3}{4}$

Express as a decimal.

21. 35% 0.35   **22.** 4% 0.04   **23.** 0.5% 0.005   **24.** 125% 1.25   **25.** $9\frac{1}{2}$% 0.095

Applying Fractions   **311**

Check for Understanding

Here is a suggested use of the Oral Exercises to check students' understanding as you teach the lesson.
Oral Exs. 1–10: use after Example 2.
Oral Exs. 11–25: use after Example 1.
Oral Exs. 26–33: use after Example 7.

Guided Practice

Write as a fraction in simplest form.

1. 95% $\frac{19}{20}$ **2.** $67\frac{1}{2}$% $\frac{27}{40}$

3. 48% of 250 is what number? 120

4. 18 is 9% of what number? 200

5. What percent of 60 is 150? 250%

Solve.

6. If the original price of an item is $54 and it is discounted 20%, what is the new price? $43.20

7. Ron makes 15% commission on every pair of shoes he sells. How much commission does he make in one week if he sold $480 worth of shoes? $72

8. Gina's net paycheck includes the following deductions: 15% federal income tax, 7.9% Social Security tax, and 2% medical insurance. If Gina's gross pay (pay before deductions) is $220, what is her net paycheck? $165.22

9. Doris received a rebate of $5.00 on her toaster. This represents 20% of the cost. How much did the toaster cost? $25.00

Summarizing the Lesson

This lesson included conversions among decimals, fractions, and percents and solving problems using percents. Ask students to name a situation where knowledge of percents would be helpful.

Suggested Assignments

Minimum
Day 1: 312/1–31 odd
       313/P: 1–3
     R 308/Self-Test 2
Day 2: 312/34–40 even
       314/P: 5–7
     S 314/Mixed Review

Average
       312/3–48 mult. of 3
       313/P: 2, 5, 8, 10, 12
     S 314/Mixed Review
     R 308/Self-Test 2

Maximum
       312/3–60 mult. of 3
       313/P: 3–15 mult. of 3
     S 314/Mixed Review
     R 308/Self-Test 2

Supplementary Materials

Study Guide   pp. 121–122
Test Master   30
Computer Activity 21

Tell whether you would multiply by 10, 100, or 1000 to eliminate the decimal coefficients in each equation. Then state the equation that would result if you did the multiplication.

26. $0.3x = 1.2 + 2.3x$ 10; 3x = 12 + 23x

27. $0.24x = 3.2(10 - x)$ 100; 24x = 320(10 − x)

28. $1.2x + 0.95 = 0.02(3 - x)$

29. $15.2(1000 - x) = 2.8$ 10; 152(1000 − x) = 28

30. $0.1x - 0.01 = .001$ 1000; 100x − 10 = 1

31. $3.2x = 0.32$ 100; 320x = 32

32. $4.06x = 100$ 100; 406x = 10,000

33. $0.03 + 10x = 3.6$ 100; 3 + 1000x = 360

28. 100; 120x + 95 = 2(3 − x)

Written Exercises

Write as a fraction in simplest form.

A
1. 25% $\frac{1}{4}$
2. 40% $\frac{2}{5}$
3. $37\frac{1}{2}\%$ $\frac{3}{8}$
4. 85% $\frac{17}{20}$

5. 60% $\frac{3}{5}$
6. $66\frac{2}{3}\%$ $\frac{2}{3}$
7. 72% $\frac{18}{25}$
8. 16% $\frac{4}{25}$

9. 4% $\frac{1}{25}$
10. $2\frac{1}{2}\%$ $\frac{1}{40}$
11. 360% $\frac{18}{5}$
12. 150% $\frac{3}{2}$

13. 32% of 300 is what number? 96

14. 6% of 145 is what number? 8.7

15. 1% of 3200 is what number? 32

16. $6\frac{1}{4}\%$ of 500 is what number? 31.25

17. $\frac{1}{2}\%$ of 12 is what number? 0.06

18. 9.2% of 180 is what number? 16.56

19. 8.1% of 250 is what number? 20.25

20. 110% of 30 is what number? 33

21. 8 is 20% of what number? 40

22. 15 is 25% of what number? 60

23. 21 is 6% of what number? 350

24. 99 is 180% of what number? 55

25. 4.2 is 75% of what number? 5.6

26. 32.4 is 45% of what number? 72

27. What percent of 45 is 7.2? 16%

28. What percent of 7.2 is 45? 625%

29. What percent of 150 is 3? 2%

30. What percent of 3 is 150? 5000%

31. What percent of 250 is 50? 20%

32. What percent of 50 is 250? 500%

Complete the tables.

	Original price	% Discount	Price decrease	New price
33.	$12	25%	? $3	? $9
34.	$18	20%	? $3.60	? $14.40
35.	$75	10%	? $7.50	? $67.50
36.	$240	15%	? $36	? $204

	Original price	% Markup	Price increase	New price
B **37.**	$44	25%	? $11	? $55
38.	$85	20%	? $17	? $102
39.	$160	30%	? $48	? $208
40.	$25	6%	? $1.50	? $26.50

Solve.

41. $1.8x = 36$ {20}

42. $0.06x = 120$ {2000}

43. $0.05t = 2.3t - 6.75$ {3}

44. $0.21x = 1.2 - 0.15x$ $\left\{\frac{10}{3}\right\}$

45. $41 = 0.75y + 1.3y$ {20}

46. $0.05a + 0.5a = 4.4$ {8}

47. $2 + 0.08x = 0.2x + 8$ {−50}

48. $0.47x - 20 = 0.09x + 3.25$ $\left\{\frac{2325}{38}\right\}$

49. $90 = x + 0.04(180 - x)$ {86.25}

50. $0.4x + 0.24(x - 5) = 0.08$ {2}

51. $0.02 = 3.685x - 0.075(100 - x)$ {2}

52. $0.05x + 0.065(5000 - x) = 295$ {2,000}

53. $0.06(1000 - x) + 0.05x = 700$ {−64,000}

54. $0.1x - 0.01(10 - x) + 0.01(100 - x) = 19$ {181}

55. $\frac{0.2x - 0.1}{5} = 3(x - 0.5)$ {0.5}

56. $5(x - 0.4) = \frac{0.5x - 0.5}{2}$ $\left\{\frac{7}{19}\right\}$

Complete the table below.

	Amount invested	× Annual interest rate	= Annual simple interest
57.	$400	7.5%	? $30
58.	$60,000	9.5%	? $5700
59.	$1000	? 10.5%	$105
60.	$2500	? 11%	$275
61.	? $850	16%	$136
62.	? $12,000	7.25%	$870

Problems

Solve. You may wish to use a calculator.

A **1.** The Chess Club has a goal of 36 new members. So far, they have 30. What percent of the club's goal have they achieved? $83\frac{1}{3}$%

2. Laura makes a 10.5% commission on each of her sales. How much does she make when she sells a house for $85,000? $8,925

3. A health research fund drive has raised $18,700. That is 22% of the goal. What is the goal? $85,000

Applying Fractions **313**

4. Because an item is slightly damaged, a stock clerk reduces the price by $6. This represents a 15% reduction. What was the original price? $40

5. Carl makes a 2% commission on each of his sales. When he sold a new car, he made $190. How much did the car cost? $9500

6. Last year Molly was given a 3% bonus on her regular yearly salary. The bonus amounted to $720. What is her regular yearly salary? $24,000

7. Where Sondra lives, there is a 3% state sales tax, a $1\frac{1}{2}$% county sales tax, and a 1% municipal sales tax. How much tax will Sondra pay if she buys a $340 bicycle? $18.70

8. Mario invests $4000 in bonds paying $11\frac{1}{2}$% interest and $5000 in bank accounts paying 9.1% interest. Which investment yields more interest in one year? How much more? Bonds yield $5 more each year.

B **9.** A $120 coat goes on sale for $96. By what percent was the coat discounted? 20%

10. A sporting goods dealer estimates that an $85 tennis racket will cost 6% more next year. What will be the new price? $90.10

11. A dealer buys a new car for $8400. How much do you have to pay for the car if the dealer makes a 20% profit and there is a 5% sales tax? $10,584

12. In a nation of 221 million people, the urban population is 2.25 times the rural population. Find the rural and urban populations. rural: 68 million; urban: 153 million

13. A fertilizer is to be diluted with water so that the fertilizer is just 1% of the solution. How much water should be mixed with 5 cm³ of fertilizer? 495 cm³ of water

14. Lucinda bought two record albums and a compact disc for a total of $28.00. The price of each record album was $66\frac{2}{3}$% of the price of the compact disc. How much did Lucinda pay for a record album? $8

C **15.** The price of a share of stock rose 10% on Monday. The price then fell 10% on Tuesday to $59.40 per share. What was the price of a share of stock before trading began on Monday? $60

Mixed Review Exercises

Factor completely. 5. $5pq(pq^2 + 2p - 3q)$

1. $3a^2b + 6a$ $\;3a(ab + 2)$

2. $3y^3 + 6y^2 + 3y$ $\;3y(y + 1)^2$

3. $(m + 2)(m + 3)$
6. $(4a - 3)(a + 1)$

4. $x^2 - 9y^2$ $\;(x - 3y)(x + 3y)$

5. $5p^2q^3 + 10p^2q - 15pq^2$

3. $m^2 + 5m + 6$

6. $4a^2 + a - 3$

7. $a(a + b) + 4(a + b)$
$\;(a + b)(a + 4)$

8. $x^2 + 6x + 9$
$\;(x + 3)^2$

9. $t^2 - 2t - 15$
$\;(t + 3)(t - 5)$

7-6 Percent Problems

Objective   To solve problems involving percents.

Whenever a price is changed, you can find the percent of increase or the percent of decrease by using the following formula:

$$\frac{\text{percent of change}}{100} = \frac{\text{change in price}}{\text{original price}}$$

To find the change in price, you calculate the difference between the original price and the new price.

Example 1   Find the change in price.

a. The original price of the car Jasmine wants was $10,000. It is now on sale for $8,999.

b. Jerry originally paid $600 per month to rent his apartment. It now costs him $650.

Solution   a. The price *decreased* by $10,000 − $8999, or $1001.

b. The price *increased* by $650 − $600, or $50.

Example 2   To attract business, the manager of a musical instruments store decreased the price of an alto saxophone from $500 to $440. What was the percent of decrease?

Solution

Step 1   The problem asks for the percent of decrease.

Step 2   Let x = the percent of decrease.

Step 3 $\dfrac{\text{percent of change}}{100} = \dfrac{\text{change in price}}{\text{original price}}$

Step 4 $\dfrac{x}{100} = \dfrac{60}{500}$

$500x = 6000$

$x = 12$

Step 5   The check is left to you.

∴ there was a 12% decrease.

Teaching Suggestions p. T114

Suggested Extensions p. T114

Warm-Up Exercises

Tell whether the change stated in each sentence is an *increase* or *decrease*.

1. The tax will rise from 8% to 12% after January 1st. Increase

2. The unemployment rate dropped from 6% to 5%. Decrease

3. The price of the 100% wool sweater was reduced 20%. Decrease

4. The cost of living rose $\frac{1}{10}$ of a percent in July. Increase

5. All items were marked down by 30%. Decrease

6. The enrollment at the college went up 10%. Increase

Motivating the Lesson

Use the Warm-Up Exercises to motivate the lesson. Ask students to give more examples of percent of increase or decrease.

Chalkboard Examples

Solve.

1. Alyce originally paid $6500 for a car 3 years ago. The same car costs $7400 today. What is the change in price?
   Find the change in price by subtracting $6500 from $7400.
   $7400 − $6500 = $900.
   ∴ the price increased $900.

(continued)

Solutions show Steps 2 through 4.

2. The Fergusons' real estate taxes went from $1560 to $1638. What was the percent of increase?

Let x = the percent of increase.

$$\frac{\text{percent of change}}{100} =$$

$$\frac{\text{change in price}}{\text{original price}}$$

$$\frac{x}{100} = \frac{78}{1560}$$

$$1560x = 7800$$

$$x = 5$$

∴ There was a 5% increase.

3. The number of registered voters in Franklin increased by 14% over last year. There are now 9633 registered voters. How many were there last year?

Let x = the number of voters last year. Then $9633 - x$ = the change in the number of voters.

$$\frac{\text{percent of change}}{100} =$$

$$\frac{\text{change in number of voters}}{\text{number of voters last year}}$$

$$\frac{14}{100} = \frac{9633 - x}{x}$$

$$14x = 963{,}300 - 100x$$

$$114x = 963{,}300$$

$$x = 8450$$

∴ There were 8450 voters last year.

4. Jerry has $8000 invested in stocks that give him a total annual income of $550. If part of the stocks pay 8% a year and the remainder of the stocks pay 6.5% a year, how much money is invested in the stocks at each rate?

Example 3 Ricardo paid $27 for membership in the Video Club. This was an increase of 8% from last year. What was the price of membership last year?

Solution

Step 1 The problem asks for the original price.

Step 2 Let x = the original price. Then $27 - x$ = the change in price.

Step 3 $\dfrac{\text{percent of change}}{100} = \dfrac{\text{change in price}}{\text{original price}}$

$$\frac{8}{100} = \frac{27 - x}{x}$$

Step 4
$$8x = 2700 - 100x$$
$$108x = 2700$$
$$x = 25$$

Step 5 The check is left to you.

∴ the membership cost $25 last year. *Answer*

Amount invested × Annual interest rate = Annual simple interest

---

Example 4 Sheila invests part of $6000 at 6% interest and the rest at 11% interest. Her total annual income from these investments is $460. How much is invested at 6% and how much at 11%?

Solution

Step 1 The problem asks for the amounts invested at 6% and at 11%.

Step 2 Let x = the amount invested at 6%.
Then $6000 - x$ = the amount invested at 11%.

	Amount invested × Rate =		Interest
At 6%	x	0.06	0.06x
At 11%	$6000 - x$	0.11	0.11(6000 − x)

Step 3 $0.06x + 0.11(6000 - x) = 460$ ⟵ Total interest

Step 4 $100[0.06x + 0.11(6000 - x)] = 100(460)$ Multiply both sides by 100.
$$6x + 11(6000 - x) = 46{,}000$$
$$6x + 66{,}000 - 11x = 46{,}000$$
$$-5x = -20{,}000$$
$$x = 4000$$

Step 5 The check is left to you.

∴ $4000 is invested at 6%; $2000 at 11%. *Answer*

Oral Exercises

Complete each table.

	Item	Original price	New price	Price increase	% of increase
1.	Jeans	$25.00	$30.00	? $5	? 20%
2.	School lunch	$1.60	$2.00	? $0.40	? 25%
3.	Haircut	$10.00	$14.00	? $4	? 40%
4.	Record	$6.00	$7.50	? $1.50	? 25%

	Item	Original price	New price	Price decrease	% of decrease
5.	Sweater	$60.00	$45.00	? $15	? 25%
6.	Fly rod	$20.00	$15.00	? $5	? 25%
7.	Skis	$240.00	$160.00	? $80	? $33\frac{1}{3}$%
8.	Radio	$45.00	$36.00	? $9	? 20%

State the equation you would use to find x.

	Original price	New price	% of change
9.	x	$88	10% price increase
10.	x	$75	25% price increase
11.	x	$21	15% price decrease
12.	x	$48	30% price decrease

9. $\frac{10}{100} = \frac{88 - x}{x}$

10. $\frac{25}{100} = \frac{75 - x}{x}$

11. $\frac{15}{100} = \frac{x - 21}{x}$

12. $\frac{30}{100} = \frac{x - 48}{x}$

Written Exercises

Complete the table.

		Item	Original price	New price	% of increase
A	**1.**	Sneakers	$30.00	$33.00	? 10%
	2.	Record album	$12.00	$15.00	? 25%
	3.	Bike	$250.00	$300.00	? 20%
	4.	Sandwich	$1.80	$2.10	? $16\frac{2}{3}$%
	5.	Paint	$20.00	$22.50	? 12.5%

Applying Fractions **317**

Let x = the amount invested at 8%.
Then $8000 - x$ = the amount invested at 6.5%.

Amount Invested	× Rate =	Interest
x	0.08	$0.08x$
$8000 - x$	0.065	$0.065(8000 - x)$

$0.08x + 0.065(8000 - x) = 550$
$1000[0.08x + 0.065(8000 - x)]$
$\qquad = 1000(550)$
$80x + 65(8000 - x) = 550,000$
$80x + 520,000 - 65x =$
$\qquad\qquad 550,000$
$\qquad 15x = 30,000$
$\qquad\quad x = 2000$
$8000 - x = 6000$

$\therefore$ $2000 is invested at 8%; $6000 is invested at 6.5%.

Check for Understanding

Oral Exs. 1–8: use after Example 2.
Oral Exs. 9–12: use after Example 3.

Guided Practice

1. Complete each table.

Item	Orig. Price	New Price	Percent Increase
Compact Disk	$12	$15	25%
Personal Computer	$790	$884.80	12%
Bicycle	$110	$125.40	14%

Item	Orig. Price	Sale Price	Percent Decrease
Cassette Tape	$9.90	$7.92	20%
Type-writer	$230	$210.45	8.5%
Running Shoes	$70	$59.50	15%

Solve.

2. Hildi bought a sweater for $38.25 after it had been marked down 15%. What was the original price of the sweater? $45

317

Complete the tables.

	Item	Original price	New price	% of increase
6.	Skis	$220.00	$253.00	?15%
7.	Video tape	$6.00	$?$6.30	5%
8.	Phone call	$2.80	$?$3.36	20%
9.	Hammer	$?$6.40	$8.00	25%
10.	Saw	$?$20	$22.00	10%
11.	Backpack	$?$65	$72.80	12%
12.	Stereo	$?$550	$566.50	3%

	Item	Original price	New price	% of decrease
13.	Shirt	$25.00	$20.00	?20%
14.	Pants	$36.00	$27.00	?25%
15.	Notebook	$2.00	$1.65	?17.5%
16.	Hiking boots	$120.00	$108.00	?10%
17.	Soccer ball	$32.00	$25.60 $?	20%
18.	Spaghetti sauce	$2.20	$1.87 $?	15%
19.	Shoes	$?$78	$68.25	12.5%
20.	Shampoo	$?$2.20	$2.09	5%
21.	Skates	$?$70	$59.50	15%

Problems

Solve. You may wish to use a calculator.

A **1.** The population at Dos Pueblos High increased from 1800 students ten years ago to 1926 students last year. What was the percent of increase? 7%

2. The Golds' home was assessed this year at a value of $162,000. Last year it had been assessed at $150,000. What was the percent of increase? 8%

3. A $200 coat is on sale for $166. What is the percent of discount? 17%

4. Elena bought some shares of stock at $28 per share and sold them all at $24.50 per share. What was the percent of her loss? 12.5%

5. While on vacation, Allison noted that a $5.50 breakfast actually cost $5.83 because of the sales tax. What is the sales tax rate? 6%

6. The number of paid subscribers to *The Wildlife Monthly* has declined from 3340 people to 2430 people. What is the percent of decrease? about $27\frac{1}{4}$%

7. Yvonne paid $11,448 for a new automobile. This amount included the 6% sales tax. What was the price of the automobile without the tax? $10,800

8. Emily Ling is a real estate broker who earns a 12% commission on each house she sells. If she earned $21,600 on the sale of a house, what was the selling price of the house? $180,000

9. At the Runners' Shop anniversary sale, running shoes were on sale at a 15% discount. If Alonzo paid $35.70 for a pair of running shoes, what was the original price? $42

10. The number of students at Westwood High School with a driver's license is now 558. This is 24% more than last year. How many students had a driver's license last year? 450 students

B 11. Yolanda invests $6000. Some of the money is invested in stocks paying 6% a year and some in bonds paying 11% year. She receives a total of $580 each year from these investments. How much money is invested in stocks and how much money in bonds? $1600 in stocks, $4400 in bonds

12. Craig invested $4000 in bank certificates and bonds. The certificates pay 5.5% interest and the bonds pay 11% interest. His interest income is $352 this year. How much money was invested in bank certificates? $1600

13. The Creative Arts Fund must raise $2500 next year by investing $30,000 in federal notes paying 9% and in municipal bonds paying 8%. The treasurer wants to invest as much as possible in the bonds, even though they pay less, because the bonds are for projects in the local area. How much should the treasurer invest in bonds? $20,000

14. Bruce invested in stock paying a $10\frac{1}{2}$% dividend. Maya invested $4000 more than Bruce in tax-free bonds paying $7\frac{1}{2}$% annual simple interest. If Maya's income from investment is $75 more than Bruce's, find how much money each invested. Bruce, $7500; Maya, $11,500

15. Jesse invested $2000 more in stocks than in bonds. The bonds paid 7.2% interest and stocks paid 6%. The income from each investment was the same. How much interest did he receive in all? $1440

16. Half of Roberta's money is invested at 12% interest, one third at 11%, and the rest at 9%. Her total annual income from investments is $1340. How much money has Roberta invested? $12,000

Computer Exercises

For students with some programming experience.

1. Suppose that you deposit $100 in a bank account that pays 6% interest per year. At the end of one year, you will have $100 + 100(0.06) = 106. At the end of the second year, you will have $106 + 106(0.06) = 112.36. Write a BASIC program to display in chart form how much money you will have at the end of 1, 2, 3, 4, . . . , 10 years.

Applying Fractions **319**

Using a Computer

A computer is used to calculate the balance in a savings account paying simple interest. It is also used to calculate the percent of increase or decrease on given pairs of data.

**Additional Answers
Computer Exercises**

1.
YEAR	AMOUNT
1	$106
2	$112.36
3	$119.10
4	$126.25
5	$133.82
6	$141.85
7	$150.36
8	$159.38
9	$168.95
10	$179.08

2. Write a BASIC program using an array to store data entered with INPUT statements. The program should calculate and print the percent of increase or decrease between each consecutive pair of data. If the percent of change is the same for each consecutive pair, the data are increasing (or decreasing) exponentially. RUN the program for the following sets of data.

a.

Years after 1989	Population of Muddville
1	207
2	200
3	193
4	186
5	179

−3.38%
−3.5%
−3.63%
−3.76%

Is the population of Muddville decreasing exponentially? no

b.

Hours after start of experiment	Number of bacteria
1	500
2	705
3	994
4	1402
5	1977

41%
40.99%
41.05%
41.01%

Is the number of bacteria increasing exponentially? yes

Mixed Review Exercises

Solve.

1. $\dfrac{3x + 1}{x - 2} = 7$ $\left\{\dfrac{15}{4}\right\}$

2. $\dfrac{a + 3}{4} = \dfrac{1}{a}$ {−4, 1}

3. $\dfrac{5}{n} = \dfrac{13}{6n}$ No solution

4. $1.4x = 28$ {20}

5. $m^2 + 3m + 2 = 0$ {−1, −2}

6. $0.5x + 5.6 = 1.2x$ {8}

Simplify.

7. $(z + 3)9$ $9z + 27$

8. $-4(x - 3y)$ $-4x + 12y$

9. $9a + 7 - 2a + b$ $7a + b + 7$

10. $16t\left(-\dfrac{1}{2}\right)$ $-8t$

11. $(-5b)(-6c)$ $30bc$

12. $\dfrac{1}{7}(-21xz)$ $-3xz$

Self-Test 3

Vocabulary   percent (p. 309)

Express as a fraction in simplest form.

1. 65% $\dfrac{13}{20}$

2. $72\dfrac{1}{2}\%$ $\dfrac{29}{40}$

3. 510% $\dfrac{51}{10}$ **Obj. 7-5, p. 309**

4. Find 16% of 85. 13.6

5. 3.75 is 60% of what number? 6.25

6. What percent of 70 is 245? 350%   7. What percent of 300 is 225? 75%

8. Last year an accountant earned $28,000. This year she received a 6% raise. How much was the raise? $1680

9. A $162 suit is on sale for $108. What is the percent of discount? $33\dfrac{1}{3}\%$ **Obj. 7-6, p. 315**

Check your answers with those at the back of the book.

320   *Chapter 7*

Mixture and Work Problems

Teaching Suggestions p. T114
Reading Algebra p. T115
Suggested Extensions p. T115

7-7 Mixture Problems

Objective   To solve mixture problems.

Supermarkets sometimes sell
a mixture of two or more items.
Similarly, a chemist can make
a solution of a certain strength
by mixing solutions of different
strengths. When you solve a
mixture problem, it is helpful
to make a chart.

Example 1   A health food store sells a mixture of raisins and roasted nuts. Raisins sell for
$3.50/kg and nuts sell for $4.75/kg. How many kilograms of each should be
mixed to make 20 kg of this snack worth $4.00/kg?

Solution

Step 1 The problem asks for the number of kilograms of raisins and the number of
kilograms of nuts.

Step 2 Let x = the number of kilograms of raisins.
Then $20 - x$ = the number of kilograms of nuts.

	Number of kg × Price per kg = Cost		
Raisins	x	3.50	$3.5x$
Nuts	$20 - x$	4.75	$4.75(20 - x)$
Mixture	20	4.00	80

Step 3 Cost of raisins + cost of nuts = total cost of mixture
$$3.5x + 4.75(20 - x) = 80$$

Step 4 $350x + 475(20 - x) = 8000$ Multiply both sides by 100.
$$350x + 9500 - 475x = 8000$$
$$-125x = -1500$$
$$x = 12$$
$$20 - x = 8$$

Step 5 The check is left to you.

$\therefore$ 12 kg of raisins and 8 kg of nuts are needed.   *Answer*

Warm-Up Exercises

Complete.

1. The sum of two numbers
   is 25. If one number is y,
   the other number is
   __?__. $25 - y$

2. If x mL of acid is added
   to 300 mL of water, the
   total volume of the solution is __?__ mL. $300 + x$

3. If the total weight of a
   mixture is 8 kg and part
   of the mixture weighs
   $8 - x$ kg, then the other
   part of the mixture
   weighs __?__ kg. x

4. If, in a collection of 50
   dimes and quarters, there
   are q quarters, then there
   are __?__ dimes. $50 - q$

Motivating the Lesson

Ask students, Do you know
how much water it takes to
dilute 1 L of a 5% acid solution to make it 2%? $1\frac{1}{2}$ L

Chemists, druggists, grocers,
and others frequently use
percents to mix solutions or
ingredients. Calculating the
amounts needed to make
certain mixtures is the topic
today.

Problem Solving Strategies

The examples and problems
in this lesson use the *five-
step plan* for solving word
problems.

Solve. Solutions show
Steps 2 through 4.

1. A grocer makes a natural breakfast cereal by mixing oat cereal costing $2 per kilogram with dried fruits costing $9 per kilogram. How many kilograms of each are needed to make 60 kg of cereal costing $3.75 per kilogram?

Let x = no. of kg of cereal
Then $60 - x$ = no. of kg of dried fruits.

	No. of kg	× Price per kg	= Total cost
Cereal	x	2	$2x$
Fruits	$60 - x$	9	$9(60 - x)$
Mix	60	3.75	225

$2x + 9(60 - x) = 225$
$2x + 540 - 9x = 225$
$-7x = -315$
$x = 45$
$60 - x = 15$
45 kg of cereal; 15 kg of dried fruits

2. How many liters of water must be added to 20 L of a 24% acid solution to make a solution that is 8% acid?

Let x = no. of L of water.

	No. of L	× % Acid	= Amt. Acid
Acid	20	24	4.8
Water	x	0	0
Mix	$20 + x$	8	$0.08(20 + x)$

$0.08(20 + x) = 4.8$
$8(20 + x) = 480$
$160 + 8x = 480$
$8x = 320$
$x = 40$
40 L of water must be added.

Example 2 An auto mechanic has 300 mL of battery acid solution that is 60% acid. He must add water to this solution to dilute it so that it is only 45% acid. How much water should he add?

Solution

Step 1 The problem asks for the number of milliliters of water to be added.

Step 2 Let x = the number of milliliters of water to be added.

	Total amount	× % acid	= Amount of acid
Original solution	300	60%	0.60(300)
Water	x	0%	0
New solution	$300 + x$	45%	$0.45(300 + x)$

Step 3 Original amount of acid + added acid = new amount of acid
$$0.60(300) + 0 = 0.45(300 + x)$$

Step 4
$$60(300) = 45(300 + x)$$
$$18{,}000 = 13{,}500 + 45x$$
$$4500 = 45x$$
$$100 = x$$

Step 5 The check is left to you.
∴ 100 mL of water should be added. **Answer**

Examples 1 and 2 are really very much alike. You can see this in the charts and in Step 3 of each solution. In fact, mixture problems are similar to investment problems, coin problems, and certain distance problems.

Oral Exercises

Read each problem and complete the chart. Use the chart to give an equation to solve the problem. Do not solve.

1. The owner of the Fancy Food Shoppe wants to mix cashews selling at $8.00/kg and pecans selling at $7.00/kg. How many kilograms of each kind of nut should be mixed to get 8 kg worth $7.25/kg? $8x + 7(8 - x) = 58$

	Number of kg	× Price per kg	= Total cost	
Cashews	x	? $8.00	?	$8x$
Pecans	? $8 - x$	? $7.00	?	$7(8 - x)$
Mixture	? 8	? $7.25	?	$58

2. A chemist has 40 mL of a solution that is 50% acid. How much water should he add to make a solution that is 10% acid? $0.50(40) + 0 = 0.10(40 + x)$

	Total amount ×	% acid =	Amount of acid	
Original solution	? 40	? 50%	?	0.50(40)
Water added	x	? 0	?	0
New solution	? 40 + x	? 10%	?	0.10(40 + x)

3. If 800 mL of a juice drink is 15% grape juice, how much grape juice should be added to make a drink that is 20% grape juice?
$0.15(800) + 1.00x = 0.20(800 + x)$

	Total amount ×	% juice =	Amount of juice	
Original drink	? 800	? 15%	?	0.15(800)
Juice added	x	? 100%	?	1.00x
New drink	? 800 + x	? 20%	?	0.20(800 + x)

4. A chemist mixes 12 L of a solution that is 45% acid with 8 L of a solution that is 70% acid. What is the percent of acid of the mixture?
$20x = 0.45(12) + 0.70(8)$

	Total amount ×	% acid =	Amount of acid
1st Solution	? 12	? 45%	? 0.45(12)
2nd Solution	? 8	? 70%	? 0.70(8)
Mixture	? 20	x	? 20x

5. A grocer mixes 5 lb of egg noodles costing 80¢/lb with 2 lb of spinach noodles costing $1.50/lb. What will the cost per pound of the mixture be?
$5(0.80) + 2(1.50) = 7x$

	Number of lb ×	Cost per lb =	Total cost
Egg noodles	? 5	? 0.80	? 5(0.80)
Spinach noodles	? 2	? 1.50	? 2(1.50)
Mixture	? 7	x	? 7x

6. Susan drove for 2 h at 85 km/h and then for 3 h more at 95 km/h. What was her average speed for the entire trip? $2(85) + 3(95) = 5x$

	Rate ×	Time =	Distance
1st part of trip	? 85	? 2	? 2(85)
2nd part of trip	? 95	? 3	? 3(95)
Entire trip	x	? 5	? 5x

Applying Fractions **323**

---

3. How many kilograms of water must be evaporated from 12 kg of a 5% salt solution to produce a solution that is 30% salt?
Let x = no. of kg of water.

	No. kg ×	% salt =	Amt. Salt
Original	12	5	0.6
Water	x	0	0
New	12 − x	30	0.30(12 − x)

$$0.30(12 - x) = 0.6$$
$$30(12 - x) = 60$$
$$360 - 30x = 60$$
$$300 = 30x$$
$$10 = x$$

10 kg of water must be evaporated.

Check for Understanding

Here is a suggested use of the Oral Exercises to check students' understanding as you teach the lesson.
Oral Exs. 1–8: use after Example 2.

Problem Solving Strategies

Problems 1–25 *use a chart* to organize the information in mixture problems.

Guided Practice

Solve.

1. How many liters of pure ethanol must be added to 10L of a 96% gasoline solution to produce a solution that is 80% gasoline? 2 L

2. How many kg of a 45% copper alloy must be added to 62 kg of a 60% copper alloy to form an alloy which is 50% copper? 124 kg

(continued)

Guided Practice

(continued)

3. A grocer wants to mix nuts costing $5 per kilogram with nuts costing $8 per kilogram to make a 10 kg mixture selling for $6 a kilogram. How much of each type should be mixed?

$6\frac{2}{3}$ kg of nuts at $5/kg

$3\frac{1}{3}$ kg of nuts at $8/kg

Summarizing the Lesson

Students have learned to solve liquid and dry mixture problems by using a chart and the five-step plan for solving word problems.

Suggested Assignments

Minimum
324/*P*: 1–8, 10, 12, 16
R 320/Self-Test 3
S 325/Mixed Review: 5–10

Average
Day 1: 324/*P*: 1–8, 10, 12, 14, 16
   R 320/Self-Test 3
Day 2: 325/*P*: 18, 20, 22
   S 325/Mixed Review
Assign with Lesson 7-8.

Maximum
Day 1: 324/*P*: 1–8, 9, 12, 15, 18, 21
   R 320/Self-Test 3
Day 2: 325/*P*: 22–25
   S 325/Mixed Review
Assign with Lesson 7-8.

Supplementary Materials

Study Guide   pp. 125–126
Resource Book   pp. 168–170

---

7. Sam invested $2000 at $5\frac{1}{4}\%$ annual interest and $3000 at $8\frac{1}{2}\%$ annual interest. What percent interest is he earning on his total investment?

	Amount invested × Rate = Interest			
Investment A	? 2000	$5\frac{1}{4}$?%	?	2000(0.0525)
Investment B	? 3000	$8\frac{1}{2}$?%	?	3000(0.085)
Total Investments	? 5000	x	?	5000x

8. Gina has a pile of 50 dimes and nickels worth $4.30. How many coins of each type does she have? $0.10x + 0.05(50 - x) = 4.30$

	Number of coins × Value per coin = Total value			
Dimes	x	? 0.10	?	0.10x
Nickels	? 50 − x	? 0.05	?	0.05(50 − x)
Collection	? 50	——	?	4.30

Problems

A   **1–8.** Solve the problems in Oral Exercises 1–8. **1.** 2 kg cashews, 6 kg pecans **2.** 160 mL water **3.** 50 mL juice **4.** 55% acid **5.** $1.00/lb **6.** 91 km/h **7.** 7.2% **8.** 36 dimes and 14 nickels

Solve.

9. How many liters of water must be added to 50 L of a 30% acid solution in order to produce a 20% acid solution? 25 L

10. How many milliliters of water must be added to 60 mL of a 15% iodine solution in order to dilute it to a 10% iodine solution? 30 mL

11. A spice mixture is 25% thyme. How many grams of thyme must be added to 12 g of the mixture to increase the thyme content to 40%? 3 g

12. A grocer mixes two kinds of nuts. One kind costs $5.00/kg and the other $5.80/kg. How many kilograms of each type are needed to make 40 kg of a blend worth $5.50/kg? 15 kg of $5.00/kg, 25 kg of $5.80/kg

13. Joanne makes a mixture of dried fruits by mixing dried apples costing $6.00/kg with dried apricots costing $8.00/kg. How many kilograms of each are needed to make 20 kg of a mixture worth $7.20/kg? 8 kg dried apples, 12 kg dried apricots

14. A farm stand owner mixes apple juice and cranberry juice. How much should he charge if he mixes 8 L of apple juice selling for 45¢/L with 10 L of cranberry juice selling for $1.08/L? 80¢/L

15. If you drive for 2 h at 80 km/h, how fast must you drive during the next hour in order to have an average speed of 75 km/h? 65 km/h

---

324   *Chapter 7*

16. If Sylvia works overtime, she is paid $1\frac{1}{2}$ times as much per hour as usual. After working her usual 40 h last week, she worked an additional 4 h overtime. If she made $552 last week, find her usual hourly wage. $12/h

B **17.** A chemist wishes to mix some pure acid with some water to produce 16 L of a solution that is 30% acid. How much pure acid and how much water should be mixed? 4.8 L of acid, 11.2 L of water

18. How many liters of water must be evaporated from 10 L of a 40% salt solution to produce a 50% solution? 2 L

19. How many liters of water must be evaporated from 20 L of a 30% salt solution to produce a 50% solution? 8 L

20. A wholesaler has 100 kg of mixed nuts that sell for $4.00/kg. In order to make the price more attractive, she plans to mix in some cheaper nuts worth $3.20/kg. If the wholesaler wants to sell the mixture for $3.40/kg, how many kilograms of the cheaper nuts should be used? 300 kg

21. A securities broker advised a client to invest a total of $21,000 in bonds paying 12% interest and in certificates of deposit paying $5\frac{1}{4}$% interest. The annual income from these investments was $2250. Find out how much was invested at each rate. $17,000 at 12%, $4,000 at $5\frac{1}{4}$%

22. A collection of 50 coins is worth $5.20. There are 12 more nickels than dimes, and the rest of the coins are quarters. How many coins of each type are in the collection? 26 nickels, 14 dimes, 10 quarters

23. **(a)** If you bike for 2 h at 30 km/h and for 2 h at 20 km/h, what is your average speed for the whole trip? **(b)** If you bike for 60 km at 30 km/h and return at 20 km/h, what is your average speed for the whole trip? **(a)** 25 km/h **(b)** 24 km/h

C **24.** The ratio of nickels to dimes to quarters is $3:8:1$. If all the coins were dimes, the amount of money would be the same. Show that there are infinitely many solutions to this problem.

25. A grocer wants to make a mixture of three dried fruits. He decides that the ratio of pounds of banana chips to apricots to dates should be $3:1:1$. Banana chips cost $1.17/lb, apricots cost $3.00/lb, and dates cost $2.30/lb. What is the cost per pound of the mixture? about $1.76

Mixed Review Exercises

Evaluate.

1. 9% of 60 + 0.4% of 230 6.32

2. What percent of 45 is 18? 40%

3. What percent of 160 is 12? 7.5%

4. 16 is $12\frac{1}{2}$% of what number? 128

Evaluate if $a = 2$, $b = 3$, $x = 5$, and $y = 4$.

5. $|-5| + y$ 9   **6.** $\dfrac{7 - 2b}{3 + b}$ $\frac{1}{6}$ **7.** $\frac{1}{7}(9x + y)$ 7   **8.** xy^2 80   **9.** $2a + 5b$ 19   **10.** $(x - b)^2$ 4

Applying Fractions   325

Additional Answers
Problems

24.

	No. × Value =		Total Value
Nickels	3x	5	15x
Dimes	8x	10	80x
Quarters	x	25	25x
All Dimes	12x	10	120x

$15x + 80x + 25x = 120x$
$120x = 120x$.
Since this equation is an identity, there are infinitely many solutions.

1. If it takes Margaret 3 hours to clean her room, what part of the job can she do in 1 hour? $\frac{1}{3}$

2. If Toni can mow $\frac{1}{3}$ of the lawn in $\frac{3}{4}$ of an hour, how long does it take to mow the entire lawn? $2\frac{1}{4}$ h

Solve.

3. $\frac{x}{2} + \frac{x}{3} = 1$ $\left\{\frac{6}{5}\right\}$

4. $\frac{1}{2} + \frac{x+1}{4} = 1$ $\{1\}$

Motivating the Lesson

Paul can wash and wax a car in 4 hours. If Chris can do the same job in 3 hours, how much of the job could they do in one hour working together? $\frac{1}{4} + \frac{1}{3} = \frac{7}{12}$ job

Determining how long it takes for both of them to get the whole job done involves work problems, which is the topic today.

Chalkboard Examples

Solve. Solutions show Steps 2 through 4.

1. Theresa can paint a room in 4 h. Her work rate is the part of the job she can do in 1 h. What is her work rate? $\frac{1}{4}$ job per hour

---

7-8 Work Problems

Objective   To solve work problems.

You can use the following formula to solve work problems.

$$\text{work rate} \times \text{time} = \text{work done}$$
$$rt = w$$

"Work rate" means the fractional part of a job done in a given unit of time.

Example 1   Sheri can rake the lawn in 2 h. Her work rate is the part of the job she can do in 1 h. ∴ her work rate is $\frac{1}{2}$ job per hour.

To finish a job, the sum of the fractional parts of the work done must be 1.

Example 2   Josh can split a cord of wood in 4 days. His father can split a cord in 2 days. How long will it take them to split a cord of wood if they work together?

Solution

Step 1   The problem asks for the number of days the job will take them.

Step 2   Let x = the number of days needed to do the job together.

Josh and his father will each work x days.

Since Josh can do the whole job in 4 days, his work rate is $\frac{1}{4}$ job per day.

His father's work rate is $\frac{1}{2}$ job per day.

	Work rate	× Time =	Work done
Josh	$\frac{1}{4}$	x	$\frac{x}{4}$
Father	$\frac{1}{2}$	x	$\frac{x}{2}$

Step 3   Josh's part of the job + Father's part of the job = Whole job

$$\frac{x}{4} \qquad + \qquad \frac{x}{2} \qquad = \qquad 1$$

Step 4 $4\left(\frac{x}{4} + \frac{x}{2}\right) = 4(1)$ Multiply by the LCD, 4.

$$x + 2x = 4$$
$$3x = 4$$
$$x = \frac{4}{3}, \text{ or } 1\frac{1}{3}$$

Step 5 The check is left to you.

$\therefore$ it would take them $1\frac{1}{3}$ days to do the job together.   ***Answer***

Example 3   Robot A takes 6 min to weld a fender. Robot B takes only $5\frac{1}{2}$ min. If they work together for 2 min, how long will it take Robot B to finish welding the fender by itself?

Solution

Step 1   The problem asks for the amount of time it will take Robot B to finish welding the fender.

Step 2   Let x = the number of minutes needed for Robot B to finish.

Robot B's work rate is $\dfrac{1}{5\frac{1}{2}} = \dfrac{1}{\frac{11}{2}} = \dfrac{2}{11}$.

	Work rate × Time = Work done		
Robot A	$\frac{1}{6}$	2	$\frac{2}{6}$, or $\frac{1}{3}$
Robot B	$\frac{2}{11}$	$2 + x$	$\frac{2}{11}(2 + x)$

Step 3   A's part of job + B's part of job = Whole job

$$\frac{1}{3} \quad + \quad \frac{2}{11}(2 + x) \quad = \quad 1$$

Step 4 $\qquad 33\left[\dfrac{1}{3} + \dfrac{2}{11}(2 + x)\right] = 33(1)$ Multiply by the LCD, 33.

$$11 + 6(2 + x) = 33$$
$$11 + 12 + 6x = 33$$
$$6x = 10$$
$$x = \frac{5}{3}, \text{ or } 1\frac{2}{3}$$

Step 5   The check is left to you.

$\therefore$ it will take $1\frac{2}{3}$ min for Robot B to finish welding.   ***Answer***

The charts used for work problems look similar to the charts used for other problems. The following formulas show the similarities among some types of problems you have studied.

Work done by A + work done by B = *total* work done

Acid in solution A + acid in solution B = *total* acid in mixture

Interest from banks + interest from bonds = *total* interest

Distance by bike + distance by car = *total* distance traveled

Applying Fractions   **327**

---

2. One printing press can finish a job in 8 h. The same job would take a second press 12 h. How long would it take both presses together?

Let x = no. of hours it would take both.

	Work rate	× Time	= Work done
1st	$\frac{1}{8}$	x	$\frac{x}{8}$
2nd	$\frac{1}{12}$	x	$\frac{x}{12}$

$$\frac{x}{8} + \frac{x}{12} = 1$$
$$24\left(\frac{x}{8} + \frac{x}{12}\right) = 24(1)$$
$$24\left(\frac{x}{8}\right) + 24\left(\frac{x}{12}\right) = 24$$
$$3x + 2x = 24$$
$$x = 4\frac{4}{5}$$

It would take $4\frac{4}{5}$ h.

3. An installer can carpet a room in 3 h. An assistant takes $4\frac{1}{2}$ h to do the same job. If the assistant helps for 1 h and then is called away, how long will it take the installer to finish?

Let n = no. of hours it will take to finish.

	Work rate	× Time	= Work done
I	$\frac{1}{3}$	$n + 1$	$\frac{n+1}{3}$
A	$1 \div \frac{9}{2} = \frac{2}{9}$	1	$\frac{2}{9}$

$$\frac{n+1}{3} + \frac{2}{9} = 1$$
$$9\left(\frac{n+1}{3} + \frac{2}{9}\right) = 9 \cdot 1$$
$$9\left(\frac{n+1}{3}\right) + 9\left(\frac{2}{9}\right) = 9$$
$$3n + 3 + 2 = 9$$
$$3n = 4$$
$$n = \frac{4}{3} = 1\frac{1}{3}$$

It would take the installer $1\frac{1}{3}$ h to finish.

Examples 2–3 *use a chart* to organize information and the *five-step plan* to solve work problems.

Check for Understanding

Here is a suggested use of the Oral Exercises to check students' understanding as you teach the lesson.
Oral Exs. 1–4: use after Example 1.
Oral Exs. 5–8: use after Example 3.

Guided Practice

Solve.

1. A pipe can fill a pool in 9 h. What part of the pool can it fill in 1 h? in y h?
$\frac{1}{9}$, $\frac{y}{9}$

2. Jack can paint a room in 7 h, and Karen can paint the same room in 5 h. If they work together, what part of the job can they paint in 2 h? in x h?
$\frac{24}{35}$, $\frac{12x}{35}$

3. It takes Marie $1\frac{1}{2}$ h to deliver newspapers every morning. Hal can deliver the papers alone in 1 h. How fast can they deliver the papers if they work together? $\frac{3}{5}$ h

4. A mail handler needs 3 h to sort an average day's mail, but with an assistant, it takes 2 h. How long would it take the assistant to sort the mail working alone? 6 h

Oral Exercises

State the work rate.

1. Beatrice can wallpaper a room in 8 h. $\frac{1}{8}$ room per hour

2. Marty read a novel in 10 h. $\frac{1}{10}$ novel per hour

3. Annie can wax her car in 45 min. $\frac{4}{3}$ car per hour or $\frac{1}{45}$ car per min

4. A hose can fill a swimming pool in 3 days. $\frac{1}{3}$ pool per day

Complete the charts. Do not solve the problems.

5. Using a new lawn mower, Abby can mow the lawn in 2 h. Her sister Carla uses an older mower and takes 3 h to mow the same lawn. How long will it take them if they work together?

	Work rate × Time = Work done		
Abby	? $\frac{1}{2}$	x	? $\frac{x}{2}$
Carla	? $\frac{1}{3}$	? x	? $\frac{x}{3}$

6. Phil can paint the garage in 12 h, and Rick can do it in 10 h. They work together for 3 h. How long will it take Rick to finish the job alone?

	Work rate × Time = Work done		
Phil	? $\frac{1}{12}$	3	? $\frac{1}{4}$
Rick	? $\frac{1}{10}$	$x + 3$	? $\frac{x+3}{10}$

7. Chuck can shovel the snow off his driveway in 40 min. He shovels for 20 min and then is joined by Joan. If they shovel the remaining snow in 10 min, how long would it have taken Joan to shovel the driveway alone?

	Work rate × Time = Work done		
Chuck	? $\frac{1}{40}$	? 30	? $\frac{3}{4}$
Joan	$\frac{1}{x}$	? 10	? $\frac{10}{x}$

8. Brett usually takes 50 min to groom the horses. After working 10 min, he was joined by Angela and they finished the grooming in 15 min. How long would it have taken Angela working alone?

	Work rate × Time = Work done		
Brett	? $\frac{1}{50}$	? 25	? $\frac{1}{2}$
Angela	$\frac{1}{x}$	? 15	? $\frac{15}{x}$

Problems

A

1. Rita takes 3 h to type a report. What part of the typing can she do in 2 h? in x h? $\frac{2}{3}$; $\frac{x}{3}$

2. Franklin can do a job in 6 h and Mike can do it in 4 h. What part of the job can they do by working together for 2 h? for y h? $\frac{5}{6}$; $\frac{5y}{12}$

3. Jake can wallpaper a room in 10 h and Maura can do it in 8 h. What part of the job can they do by working together for 2.5 h? for h h? $\frac{9}{16}$; $\frac{9h}{40}$

4. One drain pipe can empty a swimming pool in 6 h. Another pipe takes 3 h. If both pipes are used at the same time to drain the pool, what part of the job is completed in 2 h? in x h? whole job; $\frac{x}{2}$

5–8. Solve the problems stated in Oral Exercises 5–8.

5. $1\frac{1}{5}$ h   **6.** $4\frac{1}{2}$ h   **7.** 40 min   **8.** 30 min

Solve.

9. It takes Sally 15 min to pick the apples from the tree in her backyard. Lisa can do it in 25 min. How long will it take them working together? $9\frac{3}{8}$ min

10. It takes Gary 1 h to milk all of the cows, and it takes Dana 1.5 h. How long will it take them to do the job together? 0.6 h or 36 min

11. A roofing contractor estimates that he can shingle a house in 20 h and that his assistant can do it in 30 h. How long will it take them to shingle the house working together? 12 h

12. Stan can load his truck in 24 min. If his brother helps him, it takes them 15 min to load the truck. How long does it take Stan's brother alone? 40 min

4.5 h; 9 h

B **13.** One printing machine works twice as fast as another. When both machines are used, they can print a magazine in 3 h. How many hours would each machine require to do the job alone?

14. Arthur can do a job in 30 min, Bonnie can do it in 40 min, and Claire can do it in 60 min. How long will it take them if they work together? $13\frac{1}{3}$ min

15. It takes my father 3 h to plow our cornfield with his new tractor. Using the old tractor it takes me 5 h. If we both plow for 1 h before I go to school, how long will it take him to finish the plowing? $1\frac{2}{5}$ h

16. Phyllis can rake our lawn in 50 min, and I can do it in 40 min. If she rakes for 5 min before I join her, how long will it take us to finish? 20 min

17. One pump can fill a water tank in 3 h, and another pump takes 5 h. When the tank was empty, both pumps were turned on for 30 min and then the faster pump was turned off. How much longer did the slower pump have to run before the tank was filled? $3\frac{2}{3}$ h

18. Pipe A can fill a swimming pool in 12 h. After it has been used for $4\frac{1}{2}$ h, Pipe B is also used, and the pool is filled in another $4\frac{1}{2}$ h. How long would it take for the Pipe B to fill the pool by itself? 18 h

19. Ramona can do a job in 12 days. After she has worked for 4 days, she is joined by Carlotta and it takes them 2 days working together to finish the job. How long would it have taken Carlotta to do the whole job herself? 4 days

20. The fill pipe for a tank can fill the tank in 4 h, and the drain pipe can drain it in 2 h. If both pipes are accidentally opened, how long will it take to empty a half-filled tank? 2 h

Applying Fractions   **329**

Solve.

1. How many liters of water must be evaporated from 216 L of a 5% salt solution to produce a solution that is 45% salt? 192 L

2. The owner of a spice shop mixes oregano costing $4.00 per ounce with basil costing $2.40 per ounce. How many ounces of each are needed to produce 8 ounces of a mixture costing $3.00 per ounce?
3 oz of oregano, 5 oz of basil

3. Carmen can weed the garden in 24 min. If Kim helps, they can finish in 8 min. How long would it take Kim working alone? 12 min

4. One pipe can fill a tank in 18 h. A second pipe can fill the tank in 14 h. How long would it take both pipes together to fill the tank? $7\frac{7}{8}$ h

21. Nicholas and Marilyn are addressing invitations to the junior class picnic. Nicholas can address one every 30 s and Marilyn can do one every 40 s. How long will it take them to address 140 invitations? 40 min or 2400 s

C 22. Jeff can weed the garden in 4 h. His wife Brenda takes the same amount of time. After they worked together for 1 h, their son Rory helped them finish in $\frac{1}{2}$ h. How long would it have taken Rory by himself? 2 h

23. If three pipes are all opened, they can fill an empty swimming pool in 3 h. The largest pipe alone takes one third the time that the smallest pipe takes and half the time the other pipe takes. How long would it take each pipe to fill the pool by itself? largest pipe, $5\frac{1}{2}$ h;   medium pipe, 11 h;   smallest pipe, $16\frac{1}{2}$ h

Mixed Review Exercises

Complete the table.

	Item	Original price	New price	Percent of increase
1.	Shoes	$ 34.00	$40.12	? 18%
2.	Wallpaper	$130.00	$? $143	10%
3.	Tote Bag	$? $22	$26.40	20%

Solve.

4. $\frac{1}{c+3} + \frac{4}{2c+6} = 3$ {−2}

5. $\frac{8}{n} = \frac{16}{7}$ {3.5}

6. $\frac{x+3}{7} = \frac{x+5}{14}$ {−1}

7. $5a - 1 = 3(a + 7)$ {11}

8. $-0.6 + k = 0.8$ {1.4}

9. $-9p = 0$ {0}

Self-Test 4

Solve.

1. How many liters of water must be evaporated from 50 L of a 10% salt solution to produce a 20% salt solution? 25 L
   Obj. 7-7, p. 321

2. How many kilograms of nuts must be added to 1.8 kg of plain banana bread batter to produce a batter that is 10% nuts? 0.2 kg

3. Fran can write a computer program in 9 days. If Doug helps her, they can write the program in 6 days. How long would it take Doug to write the program by himself? 18 days
   Obj. 7-8, p. 326

4. The main engine on a rocket can use up the fuel in 60 s. The reserve engine can use it up in 80 s. How long can both run at the same time? $34\frac{2}{7}$ s

Check your answers with those at the back of the book.

Problems Involving Exponents

7-9 Negative Exponents

Objective To use negative exponents.

You have learned the meaning of a^n when n is a positive number. For example:

$$2^3 = 8 \qquad 2^2 = 4 \qquad 2^1 = 2$$

In this lesson you'll consider the meaning of expressions like 2^0 and 2^{-1} that have zero and negative integers as exponents.

Definition of a^{-n}

If a is a nonzero real number and n is a positive integer,

$$a^{-n} = \frac{1}{a^n}.$$

Example 1 **a.** $10^{-3} = \frac{1}{10^3} = \frac{1}{1000}$ **b.** $5^{-4} = \frac{1}{5^4} = \frac{1}{625}$ **c.** $16^{-1} = \frac{1}{16^1} = \frac{1}{16}$

The rule of exponents for division (page 190) will help you understand why a^{-n} is defined as $\frac{1}{a^n}$. Recall that for $m > n$, $\frac{a^m}{a^n} = a^{m-n}$. For example,

$$\frac{a^7}{a^3} = a^{7-3} = a^4.$$

You can also apply this rule when $m < n$, that is, when $m - n$ is a negative number. For example,

$$\frac{a^3}{a^7} = a^{3-7} = a^{-4}.$$

Since $\frac{a^3}{a^7}$ and $\frac{a^7}{a^3}$ are reciprocals, a^4 and a^{-4} must also be reciprocals. Thus,

$$a^{-4} = \frac{1}{a^4}.$$

If $m = n$, you can still apply $\frac{a^m}{a^n} = a^{m-n}$. For example, $\frac{a^5}{a^5} = a^{5-5} = a^0$. But

you already know that $\frac{a^5}{a^5} = 1$. This leads to the following definition.

Applying Fractions **331**

Warm-Up Exercises

Simplify.

1. $\frac{x^9}{x^3}$ x^6 **2.** $\frac{x^3}{x^9}$ $\frac{1}{x^6}$

3. $\frac{x^3}{x^3}$ 1

Evaluate.

4. 5^0 1 **5.** $\frac{1}{4^2}$ $\frac{1}{16}$

6. $\left(\frac{1}{3^2}\right)^3$ $\frac{1}{3^6} = \frac{1}{729}$

7. $\frac{2^3}{2^6}$ $\frac{1}{2^3} = \frac{1}{8}$

Motivating the Lesson

In Lesson 5-2 you learned the rule of exponents for division. Today's lesson will expand this rule.

Chalkboard Examples

Evaluate.

1. 11^{-2} $= \frac{1}{11^2} = \frac{1}{121}$

2. $\frac{6}{6^{-2}}$ $= 6^{1-(-2)} = 6^3 = 216$

4. Simplify $(4x^{-2})^3$.

$64x^{(-2)(3)} = 64x^{-6} = \frac{64}{x^6}$

5. In t hours the number of bacteria in a culture will grow to be approximately $n(2.72)^{2t}$ where n is the original number of bacteria. At 1 P.M. the culture has 50 bacteria. About how many bacteria does the culture have at 4 P.M.? at noon?

$50(2.72)^6 \approx 20{,}248$

$50(2.72)^{-2} = \frac{50}{(2.72)^2}$

≈ 7

331

Check for Understanding

Here is a suggested use of the Oral Exercises to check students' understanding as you teach the lesson.

Oral Exs. 1–10: use after Example 1.

Oral Exs. 11–24: use after Example 2.

Oral Ex. 25: use after Example 3.

Common Errors

Some students may still confuse expressions such as $8a^{-2}$ with expression such as $(8a)^{-2}$. In reteaching, point out that $8a^{-2} = \dfrac{8}{a^2}$, whereas $(8a)^{-2} = \dfrac{1}{(8a)^2} = \dfrac{1}{64a^2}$.

Guided Practice

Simplify. Give your answers using positive integers.

1. 4^{-3} $\dfrac{1}{64}$ 2. $5^7 \cdot 5^{-9}$ $\dfrac{1}{25}$

3. $(12^{-1})^{-2}$ 144

4. $\dfrac{4}{4^{-3}}$ 256

5. $\dfrac{8^3 \cdot 8^{-2}}{8^4}$ $\dfrac{1}{512}$

6. $\left(\dfrac{5^0 \cdot 2}{2^{-2}}\right)^{-4}$ $\dfrac{1}{4096}$

7. $(4 \cdot 3)^{-2}$ $\dfrac{1}{144}$

8. $4 \cdot 3^{-2}$ $\dfrac{4}{9}$

9. $(3^{-1} + 3^2)^{-1}$ $\dfrac{3}{28}$

10. $(3^{-1} \cdot 3^2)^{-1}$ $\dfrac{1}{3}$

(continued)

Definition of a^0

If a is a nonzero real number,

$$a^0 = 1.$$

The expression 0^0 has no meaning.

All the rules for positive exponents also hold for zero and negative exponents.

Summary of Rules for Exponents	Examples
Let m and n be any integers. Let a and b be any nonzero integers.	
1. Products of Powers: $b^m b^n = b^{m+n}$	$2^3 \cdot 2^{-5} = 2^{3+(-5)} = 2^{-2} = \dfrac{1}{2^2} = \dfrac{1}{4}$
2. Quotients of Powers: $b^m \div b^n = b^{m-n}$	$6^3 \div 6^7 = 6^{3-7} = 6^{-4} = \dfrac{1}{6^4} = \dfrac{1}{1296}$
3. Power of a Power: $(b^m)^n = b^{mn}$	$(2^3)^{-2} = 2^{-6} = \dfrac{1}{2^6} = \dfrac{1}{64}$
4. Power of a Product: $(ab)^m = a^m b^m$	$(3x)^{-2} = 3^{-2} \cdot x^{-2} = \dfrac{1}{3^2} \cdot \dfrac{1}{x^2} = \dfrac{1}{9x^2}$
5. Power of a Quotient: $\left(\dfrac{a}{b}\right)^m = \dfrac{a^m}{b^m}$	$\left(\dfrac{3}{5}\right)^{-2} = \dfrac{3^{-2}}{5^{-2}} = \dfrac{\frac{1}{3^2}}{\frac{1}{5^2}} = \dfrac{1}{3^2} \cdot \dfrac{5^2}{1} = \dfrac{5^2}{3^2} = \dfrac{25}{9}$

Example 2 Simplify. Give your answers using positive exponents.

    a. $\dfrac{5}{5^{-3}}$ **b.** $(b^{-1})^{-3}$ **c.** $(3x^{-1})^2$

Solution   **a.** $\dfrac{5^1}{5^{-3}} = 5^{1-(-3)}$ Use Rule 2.

                $= 5^4$

                $= 625$

     b. $(b^{-1})^{-3} = b^{(-1)(-3)}$ Use Rule 3.

                $= b^3$

     c. $(3x^{-1})^2 = 9x^{-2}$ Use Rules 4 and 3.

              $= \dfrac{9}{x^2}$ Use the rule for negative exponents.

Positive and negative exponents are often used in problems involving population growth, interest, or energy consumption.

---

332   *Chapter 7*

Oral Exercises

Simplify. In Exercises 17–24, give answers using positive exponents.

1. 10^{-1} $\frac{1}{10}$ 2. 6^{-1} $\frac{1}{6}$ 3. 5^{-1} $\frac{1}{5}$ 4. 1^{-1} 1

5. 10^{-2} $\frac{1}{100}$ 6. 6^{-2} $\frac{1}{36}$ 7. 5^{-2} $\frac{1}{25}$ 8. 1^{-2} 1

9. 2^{-3} $\frac{1}{8}$ 10. 4^{-3} $\frac{1}{64}$ 11. $7^{-4} \cdot 7^3$ $\frac{1}{7}$ 12. $3^6 \cdot 3^{-8}$ $\frac{1}{9}$

13. $(3^{-1})^2$ $\frac{1}{9}$ 14. $(3^{-1})^{-2}$ 9   15. $\dfrac{10}{10^{-2}}$ 1000   16. $\dfrac{10^{-3}}{10^{-5}}$ 100

17. $(5x)^{-2}$ $\frac{1}{25x^2}$ 18. $(3^{-1} \cdot 4^{-1})^{-1}$ 12   19. $\left(\dfrac{1}{2} \cdot \dfrac{1}{4}\right)^{-1}$ 8   20. $\left(\dfrac{3}{2}\right)^{-2}$ $\frac{4}{9}$

21. $a^{-1}b^2$ $\frac{b^2}{a}$ 22. $\dfrac{c^{-2}}{d^{-3}}$ $\frac{d^3}{c^2}$ 23. $(5x^2)^{-1}$ $\frac{1}{5x^2}$ 24. $(2y^{-2})^3$ $\frac{8}{y^6}$

25. The electrical energy consumption in a city has been increasing. In n years the annual electrical consumption will be approximately $C = 1.3(1.07)^n$ billion kilowatt-hours. What value of n should be substituted to find the value of C **(a)** now? **(b)** 10 years from now? **(c)** 10 years ago? **(a)** 0 **(b)** 10 **(c)** −10

Written Exercises

Simplify.

A 1. 5^{-1} $\frac{1}{5}$ 2. 4^{-1} $\frac{1}{4}$ 3. 3^{-2} $\frac{1}{9}$ 4. 2^{-2} $\frac{1}{4}$

5. 9^{-2} $\frac{1}{81}$ 6. 8^{-2} $\frac{1}{64}$ 7. 3^{-3} $\frac{1}{27}$ 8. 2^{-3} $\frac{1}{8}$

9. 2^{-4} $\frac{1}{16}$ 10. 3^{-4} $\frac{1}{81}$ 11. 1^{-6} 1   12. 6^{-1} $\frac{1}{6}$

13. 4^{-2} $\frac{1}{16}$ 14. $3^7 \cdot 3^{-9}$ $\frac{1}{9}$ 15. $(2^{-3})^{-1}$ 8   16. $(4^{-1})^{-3}$ 64

17. $\dfrac{3}{3^{-2}}$ 27   18. $\dfrac{6^{-2}}{6^{-3}}$ 6   19. $\dfrac{7^{-2} \cdot 7}{7^{-1}}$ 1   20. $\dfrac{3^{-5} \cdot 3^3}{3^{-4}}$ 9

21. $\left(\dfrac{3^{-1}}{3}\right)^2$ $\frac{1}{81}$ 22. $\left(\dfrac{8^4}{8^{-4}}\right)^0$ 1   23. $\dfrac{(2^{-3} \cdot 4^2)^{-1}}{2^{-1}}$ 1   24. $\left(\dfrac{3^0 \cdot 2}{2^{-2}}\right)^{-3}$ $\frac{1}{512}$

25. $\left(\dfrac{2}{3}\right)^{-4}$ $\frac{81}{16}$ 26. $\left(\dfrac{5}{4}\right)^{-2}$ $\frac{16}{25}$ 27. $\left(\dfrac{4}{5}\right)^{-3}$ $\frac{125}{64}$ 28. $\left(\dfrac{7}{6}\right)^{-1}$ $\frac{6}{7}$

Applying Fractions   **333**

Summarizing the Lesson

The rules for exponents were extended to include negative exponents, and a^0 was defined.

Suggested Assignments

Minimum
  333/1–27 odd, 29–31
  335/P: 1, 2
S 335/Mixed Review
R 330/Self-Test 4

Average
  333/3–30 mult. of 3,
    36–66 mult. of 3
  335/P: 1–3
S 335/Mixed Review
R 330/Self-Test 4

Maximum
  333/3–69 mult. of 3
  335/P: 3, 5
S 335/Mixed Review
R 330/Self-Test 4

Supplementary Materials
Study Guide   pp. 129–130

Simplify.

$\frac{9}{49}$

29. a. $(2 \cdot 3)^{-3}$ $\frac{1}{216}$ **30. a.** $(4 \cdot 5)^{-2}$ $\frac{1}{400}$ **31. a.** $(2^{-1} + 2^{-2})^{-1}$ $\frac{4}{3}$ **32. a.** $(2 + 3^{-1})^{-2}$

b. $2 \cdot 3^{-3}$ $\frac{2}{27}$ **b.** $4 \cdot 5^{-2}$ $\frac{4}{25}$ **b.** $(2^{-1} \cdot 2^{-2})^{-1}$ 8 **b.** $(2 \cdot 3^{-1})^{-2}$ $\frac{9}{4}$

33. Why is b^{-1} not defined when $b = 0$? 0 has no reciprocal.

34. Suppose that you did not know that $b^0 = 1$. Explain how you could arrive at this fact by using the laws of exponents to simplify $b^2 \cdot b^0 = b^2$.
$b^2 \cdot 1$ also $= b^2$; $\therefore$ $b^0 = 1$ or $b^2 \cdot b^0 = b^{2+0} = b^2$

Simplify. Give your answers using positive exponents.

B **35.** $3x^{-2}$ $\frac{3}{x^2}$ **36.** $2n^{-3}$ $\frac{2}{n^3}$ **37.** $(3x)^{-2}$ $\frac{1}{9x^2}$ **38.** $(5m)^{-2}$ $\frac{1}{25m^2}$

39. $x^{-1}y^2$ $\frac{y^2}{x}$ **40.** $a^{-2}b^{-3}$ $\frac{1}{a^2b^3}$ **41.** $(m^{-3})^4$ $\frac{1}{m^{12}}$ **42.** $(x^{-2})^3$ $\frac{1}{x^6}$

43. $m^{-3} \cdot m^4$ m **44.** $a^5 \cdot a^{-2}$ a^3 **45.** $(3x^{-2})^3$ $\frac{27}{x^6}$ **46.** $(4n^{-1})^2$ $\frac{16}{n^2}$

47. $2x^5 \cdot x^{-5}$ 2 **48.** $3x^{-2} \cdot (3x^2)^{-1}$ $\frac{1}{x^4}$ **49.** $(a^2 \cdot a^{-5})^2$ $\frac{1}{a^6}$ **50.** $(b^5 \cdot b^{-7})^3$ $\frac{1}{b^6}$

51. $\frac{y^3}{y^{-5}}$ y^8 **52.** $\frac{u^{-4}}{u^{10}}$ $\frac{1}{u^{14}}$ **53.** $\frac{c^{-5}}{c^2}$ $\frac{1}{c^7}$ **54.** $\frac{d^{-3}}{d^{-5}}$ d^2

55. $\left(\frac{a^{-6}}{a^{-2}}\right)^{-1}$ a^4 **56.** $\left(\frac{b^{-3}}{b^{-6}}\right)^4$ b^{12} **57.** $\left(\frac{n^{-3}}{n}\right)^{-2}$ n^8 **58.** $\left(\frac{y^5}{y^{-2}}\right)^{-3}$ $\frac{1}{y^{21}}$

Simplify. Use the table of powers of 5.

Sample $\dfrac{3125}{0.008} = \dfrac{5^5}{5^{-3}}$
$= 5^8$
$= 390{,}625$
Answer

$5^1 = 5$	$5^{-1} = 0.2$
$5^2 = 25$	$5^{-2} = 0.04$
$5^3 = 125$	$5^{-3} = 0.008$
$5^4 = 625$	$5^{-4} = 0.0016$
$5^5 = 3125$	$5^{-5} = 0.00032$
$5^6 = 15{,}625$	$5^{-6} = 0.000064$
$5^7 = 78{,}125$	$5^{-7} = 0.0000128$
$5^8 = 390{,}625$	$5^{-8} = 0.00000256$

59. 3125×0.008 25 **60.** $0.0000128 \times 78{,}125$ 1 **61.** $(78{,}125)^{-1}$ 0.0000128

62. $(0.0016)^{-2}$ 390,625 **63.** $\dfrac{0.2}{0.00000256}$ 78,125 **64.** $\dfrac{0.000064}{25}$ 0.00000256

65. $\dfrac{(3125)^2}{15{,}625}$ 625 **66.** $\dfrac{(625)^4}{78{,}125}$ 1,953,125 **67.** $(0.0000128)^3(390{,}625)^2$
0.00032

Exponents can be fractions as well as integers. Exercises 68–71 will help you see how fractional exponents can be defined.

C **68.** If Rule 1 for integral exponents were to hold for fractional exponents, then $9^{\frac{1}{2}} \cdot 9^{\frac{1}{2}} = 9^{\frac{1}{2}+\frac{1}{2}} = 9^1$. Therefore, $9^{\frac{1}{2}}$ ought to be defined as the number ___?___. 3

69. If Rule 1 for integral exponents were to hold for fractional exponents, then $16^{\frac{1}{2}} \cdot 16^{\frac{1}{2}} = 16^1$. Therefore, $16^{\frac{1}{2}}$ ought to be defined as the number ___?___. 4

334 *Chapter 7*

70. If Rule 3 for integral exponents were to hold for fractional exponents, then $(8^{\frac{1}{3}})^3 = 8^{\frac{1}{3} \cdot 3} = 8^1$. Therefore, $8^{\frac{1}{3}}$ ought to be defined as the number ___?___. 2

71. How could you define $(x^2)^{\frac{1}{4}}$ and $(x^3)^{\frac{1}{3}}$? (*Hint:* See Exercises 68–70.) x^1

Problems

Solve. A calculator may be helpful. 1.09⁻⁴ kg or 0.7084252 kg; 1.09⁻⁸ kg or 0.5018663 kg

A **1.** If you have 1 kg of radioactive iodine, it will gradually decay so that d days later you will have 1.09^{-d} kg. Find how many kilograms you will have 4 days later and 8 days later.

2. The value V of a new \$12,000 automobile y years after it is purchased is given by the formula $V = 12{,}000(1.4)^{-y}$. Copy and complete the table at the right. \$12,000; \$8571.43; \$6122.45; \$4373.18; \$2231.21; \$414.86

Years	0	1	2	3	5	10
Value (V)	?	?	?	?	?	?

3. The population of a certain state t years from now will be about $P = 12(1.03)^t$ million. Estimate to the nearest million the population **(a)** now, **(b)** 10 years from now, and **(c)** 10 years ago.
(a) 12 million
(b) 16 million
(c) 9 million

4. The cost of living in a certain city has been increasing so that an item costing one dollar today may cost $(1.08)^t$ dollars in t years. **(a)** How much may today's one-dollar item cost in 3 years? **(b)** How much in 9 years? **(c)** How much did today's one-dollar item cost 9 years ago?
(a) \$1.26
(b) \$2.00
(c) \$0.50

5. A microbiologist has a bacteria culture whose growth rate can be described by $N = n(2.72)^{2t}$, where n is the original number of bacteria and N is the number after t hours. At noon the culture has 100 bacteria. Find, to the nearest whole number, the number on the same day at:
(a) 2 P.M.   **(b)** 10 A.M.   **(c)** 6 P.M.   **(d)** 6 A.M.
　　5474　　　　　　2　　　　16,399,358　　　　0

A calculator is recommended for Problems 1–5 which use formulas with exponents.

Using a Calculator

Mixed Review Exercises

Simplify. Give restrictions on the variables.

1. $\dfrac{30x^2z^2}{18x^3z}$ $\dfrac{5z}{3x}; x \neq 0, z \neq 0$

2. $\dfrac{y^2 + 10y + 25}{y^2 + 7y + 10}$ $\dfrac{y+5}{y+2}; y \neq -5, y \neq -2$

3. $\left(\dfrac{-3p}{q}\right)^2$ $\dfrac{9p^2}{q^2}; q \neq 0$

4. $\dfrac{8}{5mn} - \dfrac{2}{m}$ $\dfrac{2(4-5n)}{5mn}; m \neq 0, n \neq 0$ **5.** $4 - \dfrac{2a}{a-2}$ $\dfrac{2(a-4)}{a-2}, a \neq 2$

6. $\dfrac{x^2 - 9}{x^2 + 5x + 6}$ $\dfrac{x-3}{x+2}; x \neq -3, x \neq -2$

Divide. Write your answer as a polynomial or as a mixed expression.

7. $\dfrac{4x^2 + 2x + 36}{x + 4}$ $4x - 14 + \dfrac{92}{x+4}$

8. $\dfrac{16}{x^2 - 9} \div \dfrac{24}{x^2 + 8x + 15}$ $\dfrac{2(x+5)}{3(x-3)}$

9. $\dfrac{a^3 + 27}{a - 3}$ $a^2 + 3a + 9 + \dfrac{54}{a-3}$

Applying Fractions **335**

Warm-Up Exercises

Express each number as a power of 10. Use negative exponents when appropriate.

1. 100 10^2

2. 10 10^1

3. 1 10^0

4. $\frac{1}{10}$ 10^{-1}

5. $\frac{1}{100}$ 10^{-2}

Motivating the Lesson

If light travels at a speed of about 270,000 km/sec, about how far does it travel in one year?
8,500,000,000,000 km
This distance is called a *light year.* A nearby star, Tau Ceti, is 11.9 light years away. How many kilometers is it? 1×10^{14} km   Dealing with such large numbers is easier with scientific notation, the topic today.

Chalkboard Examples

Write each number in scientific notation.

1. 64,830,000,000,000
   6.483×10^{13}

2. 0.00000000089
   8.9×10^{-10}

Write each number in decimal form.

3. 6.47×10^9 6,470,000,000

4. 7.83×10^{-7} 0.000000783

7-10 Scientific Notation

Objective   To use scientific notation.

Some numbers are so large or so small that they are difficult to read or to write. For example, consider the following measurements:

diameter of the solar system: 118,000,000,000 km

diameter of a silver atom: 0.00000000000025 km

Scientific notation makes it easier to work with such numbers. To write a positive number in **scientific notation,** you express it as the product of a number greater than or equal to 1 but less than 10 and an integral power of 10. Study the following examples.

Number	Number Written in Scientific Notation	Movement of the Decimal Point
118,000,000,000	1.18×10^{11}	11 places
4,709,000,000	4.709×10^9	9 places
0.000152	1.52×10^{-4}	4 places
0.00000000000025	2.5×10^{-13}	13 places

Notice that when a positive number greater than or equal to 10 is written in scientific notation, the power of 10 used is positive. When the number is less than 1, the power of 10 used is negative.

Example 1   Write each number in scientific notation.

   a. 58,120,000,000
   b. 0.00000072

Solution   **a.** Move the decimal point *left* 10 places to get a number between 1 and 10.
$$58,120,000,000 = 5.812 \times 10^{10}$$

   b. Move the decimal point *right* 7 places to get a number between 1 and 10.
$$0.00000072 = 7.2 \times 10^{-7}$$

Example 2 Write each number in decimal form.

 a. 4.95×10^8 **b.** 7.63×10^{-5}

Solution **a.** Move the decimal point 8 places.   **b.** Move the decimal point 5 places.

$4.95 \times 10^8 = 495,000,000$ $7.63 \times 10^{-5} = 0.0000763$

Numbers written in scientific notation can be multiplied and divided easily by using the rules of exponents.

Example 3 Simplify. Write your answers in scientific notation.

 a. $\dfrac{3.2 \times 10^7}{2.0 \times 10^4}$ **b.** $(2.5 \times 10^3)(6.0 \times 10^2)$ **c.** 0.4×10^6

Solution **a.** $\dfrac{3.2 \times 10^7}{2.0 \times 10^4} = \dfrac{3.2}{2.0} \times \dfrac{10^7}{10^4}$ $\begin{cases} \text{Subtract exponents} \\ \text{when you divide.} \end{cases}$

$= 1.6 \times 10^{7-4}$

$= 1.6 \times 10^3$ **Answer**

b. $(2.5 \times 10^3)(6.0 \times 10^2) = (2.5 \times 6.0)(10^3 \times 10^2)$ $\begin{cases} \text{Add exponents} \\ \text{when you multiply.} \end{cases}$

$= (15)(10^{3+2})$

$= (15)(10^5)$

$= 1.5 \times 10^6$ **Answer**

c. $0.4 \times 10^6 = (4 \times 10^{-1})(10^6)$

$= 4 \times 10^5$ **Answer**

Example 4 The distance from the sun to Mercury is approximately 6×10^8 km. The distance from the sun to Pluto is approximately 5.9×10^9 km. Find the ratio of the first distance to the second.

Solution $\dfrac{\text{Distance from sun to Mercury}}{\text{Distance from sun to Pluto}} = \dfrac{6 \times 10^8}{5.9 \times 10^9}$

$= \dfrac{6}{5.9} \times \dfrac{10^8}{10^9}$

$= \dfrac{6}{5.9} \times 10^{8-9}$

$= \dfrac{6}{5.9} \times 10^{-1}$

$= \dfrac{6}{5.9} \times \dfrac{1}{10}$

$= \dfrac{6}{59}$ **Answer**

To see how your calculator handles very large numbers, see the Calculator Key-In on page 341.

Simplify. Express answer in scientific notation.

5. $\dfrac{9.3 \times 10^{12}}{3.0 \times 10^4} = \dfrac{9.3}{3.0} \times \dfrac{10^{12}}{10^4} =$

$3.1 \times 10^{12-4} = 3.1 \times 10^8$

6. $(6.2 \times 10^5)(3.5 \times 10^8)$

$= (6.2 \times 3.5)(10^5 \times 10^8)$

$= 21.7 \times 10^{13}$

$= 2.17 \times 10^{14}$

7. 0.8×10^5

$= (8 \times 10^{-1})(10^5)$

$= 8 \times 10^4$

8. The slightly oval path of the earth around the sun causes it to be as much as 2.5×10^6 km further from the sun than its average distance away, 1.5×10^8 km. Find the ratio of the first number to the second number.

$\dfrac{2.5 \times 10^6}{1.5 \times 10^8} = \dfrac{2.5}{1.5} \times \dfrac{10^6}{10^8} =$

$\dfrac{5}{3} \times \dfrac{1}{10^2} = \dfrac{5}{300} = \dfrac{1}{60}$

Write each number in expanded notation using powers of 10.

9. $48,307 = 40,000 + 8000 + 300 + 0 + 7 =$
$4 \cdot 10^4 + 8 \cdot 10^3 + 3 \cdot 10^2 + 0 \cdot 10^1 + 7 \cdot 10^0$

10. $0.8432 = 0.8 + 0.04 + 0.003 + 0.0002 =$
$8 \cdot 10^{-1} + 4 \cdot 10^{-2} + 3 \cdot 10^{-3} + 2 \cdot 10^{-4}$

11. $64.91 = 60 + 4 + 0.9 + 0.01 = 6 \cdot 10^1 + 4 \cdot 10^0 + 9 \cdot 10^{-1} + 1 \cdot 10^{-2}$

Complete each statement by writing a power of 10.

12. $1 \text{ L} = \underline{\ ?\ } \text{ mL}$ 10^3

13. $1 \text{ g} = \underline{\ ?\ } \text{ kg}$ 10^{-3}

Check for Understanding

Oral Exs. 1–6: use after Example 1.
Oral Exs. 7–12: use after Example 5.
Oral Exs. 13–18: use at the beginning of the lesson.
Oral Exs. 19–24: use after Example 3.

Guided Practice

Rewrite each number in decimal form.

1. The area of the U.S. is 3.6×10^6 mi². 3,600,000

2. The length of time it takes a super-computer to do a calculation, 1×10^{-9} second. 0.000000001

Complete each statement by writing a power of 10.

3. a. 1 m = __?__ mm 10^3
    b. 1 mm = __?__ m 10^{-3}

Write each number in
a) scientific notation and
b) expanded notation.

4. 0.00075 a) 7.5×10^{-4}
    b) $0 \cdot 10^0 + 0 \cdot 10^{-1} + 0 \cdot 10^{-2} + 0 \cdot 10^{-3} + 7 \cdot 10^{-4} + 5 \cdot 10^{-5}$

5. 20,940,000
    a) 2.094×10^7
    b) $2 \cdot 10^7 + 0 \cdot 10^6 + 9 \cdot 10^5 + 4 \cdot 10^4 + 0 \cdot 10^3 + 0 \cdot 10^2 + 0 \cdot 10^1 + 0 \cdot 10^0$

Solve. Write your answer in scientific notation.

6. Jupiter is approximately 778.3 million kilometers away from the sun. If light travels at a rate of about 3.0×10^5 km/s, about how long does it take for light from the sun to reach Jupiter?
2.5943333×10^3 s, or about 2.6×10^3 s

Our decimal number system is based on powers of 10.

Example 5 Write each number in *expanded notation* using powers of 10.

Solution
a. $8572 = 8000 + 500 + 70 + 2$
$= 8 \cdot 10^3 + 5 \cdot 10^2 + 7 \cdot 10^1 + 2 \cdot 10^0$ **Answer**

b. $0.3946 = 0.3 + 0.09 + 0.004 + 0.0006$
$= 3 \cdot 10^{-1} + 9 \cdot 10^{-2} + 4 \cdot 10^{-3} + 6 \cdot 10^{-4}$ **Answer**

c. $25.03 = 20 + 5 + 0.0 + 0.03$
$= 2 \cdot 10^1 + 5 \cdot 10^0 + 0 \cdot 10^{-1} + 3 \cdot 1^{-2}$ **Answer**

The metric system is also based upon powers of 10. To change from one metric unit to another, you simply multiply by a power of 10.

Example 6 Complete each statement by writing a power of 10.
a. 1 km = __?__ m
b. 1 mL = __?__ L

Solution
a. To change from kilometers to meters, multiply by 10^3.
$1 \text{ km} = 10^3 \text{ m}$

b. To change from milliliters to liters, multiply by 10^{-3}.
$1 \text{ mL} = 10^{-3} \text{ L}$

Oral Exercises

7. $3 \cdot 10^4 + 8 \cdot 10^3 + 5 \cdot 10^2$
8. $4 \cdot 10^6 + 0 \cdot 10^5 + 7 \cdot 10^4$
9. $3 \cdot 10^7 + 6 \cdot 10^6 + 0 \cdot 10^5 + 4 \cdot 10^4$

Express each number in scientific notation.

1. 38,500 3.85×10^4

2. 4,070,000 4.07×10^6

3. 36,040,000 3.604×10^7

4. 0.000409 4.09×10^{-4}

5. 0.0000028 2.8×10^{-5}

6. 0.0000000902 9.02×10^{-8}

7–12. Express each number in Exercises 1–6 in expanded notation.

10. $4 \cdot 10^{-4} + 0 \cdot 10^{-5} + 9 \cdot 10^{-6}$
11. $2 \cdot 10^{-5} + 8 \cdot 10^{-6}$
12. $9 \cdot 10^{-8} + 0 \cdot 10^{-9} + 2 \cdot 10^{-10}$

State each number as a single power of 10.

13. $10^5 \cdot 10^{-2} \cdot 10^4$ 10^7

14. $\dfrac{10^9 \cdot 10^8}{10}$ 10^{16}

15. $\dfrac{10^8}{10^6 \cdot 10^6}$ 10^{-4}

16. $\dfrac{10^5}{10^{-2}}$ 10^7

17. $\dfrac{10^{-9}}{10^{-2}}$ 10^{-7}

18. $\dfrac{10^{-1} \cdot 10^{-4}}{10^{-3}}$ 10^{-2}

Simplify. Express your answers in scientific notation.

19. $(2 \times 10^5)(4 \times 10^6)$ 8×10^{11}

20. $\dfrac{6 \times 10^7}{2 \times 10^2}$ 3×10^5

21. $(3 \times 10^8)(6 \times 10^{-4})$ 1.8×10^5

22. $\dfrac{6 \times 10^5}{12 \times 10^{-4}}$ 5×10^8

23. $\dfrac{9 \times 10^{-5}}{3 \times 10^{-3}}$ 3×10^{-2}

24. $\dfrac{(4 \times 10^4)(9 \times 10^{-2})}{2 \times 10^5}$ 1.8×10^{-2}

Written Exercises

Rewrite each number in decimal form.

A 1. The speed of light is 3.0×10^8 m/s. 300,000,000

2. The diameter of the sun is about 1.39×10^9 m. 1,390,000,000

3. The mass of the sun is about 2.0×10^{30} kg. 2,000,000,000,000,000,000,000,000,000,000

4. The frequency of an AM radio wave is 1.4×10^6 hertz (cycles per second). 1,400,000

5. The wavelength of ultraviolet light is 1.36×10^{-6} cm. 0.00000136

6. The wavelength of gamma rays is 3.0×10^{-10} cm. 0.0000000003

7. The diameter of the nucleus of a hydrogen atom is 5.0×10^{-17} cm. 0.00000000000000005

8. The mass of an atom of helium is 6.65×10^{-24} g. 0.00000000000000000000000665

Complete each statement by writing a power of 10.

9. **a.** 1 kg = __?__ g 10^3
   b. 1 g = __?__ kg 10^{-3}

10. **a.** 1 m = __?__ cm 10^2
    b. 1 cm = __?__ m 10^{-2}

11. **a.** 1 kg = __?__ mg 10^6
    b. 1 mg = __?__ kg 10^{-6}

12. **a.** 1 mm = __?__ cm 10^{-1}
    b. 1 cm = __?__ mm 10^1

13. **a.** 1 km = __?__ mm 10^6
    b. 1 mm = __?__ km 10^{-6}

14. **a.** 1 g = __?__ mg 10^3
    b. 1 mg = __?__ g 10^{-3}

15–26. **(a)** See below. **(b)** See Additional Answers.
Write each number in (a) scientific notation and (b) expanded notation.

15. 2500 2.5×10^3
16. .0123 1.23×10^{-2}
17. 0.0000000024 2.4×10^{-9}
18. 26,870,000 2.687×10^7

19. 3,030,000 3.03×10^6
20. 0.0000485 4.85×10^{-5}
21. 0.0000909 9.09×10^{-5}
22. 798,100,000 7.981×10^8

B 23. 98.6% 9.86×10^{-1}
24. 2.3 million 2.3×10^6
25. 12 billion 1.2×10^{10}
26. 200 trillion 2×10^{14}

Simplify. Express your answers in scientific notation.

27. $(3 \times 10^{-8})(1.2 \times 10^4)$ 3.6×10^{-4}

28. $\dfrac{2.5 \times 10^{-5}}{5 \times 10^4}$ 5×10^{-10}

29. $\dfrac{1.08 \times 10^8}{3 \times 10^{-10}}$ 3.6×10^{17}

30. $\dfrac{(5 \times 10^7)(9 \times 10^{-3})}{3 \times 10^{-2}}$ 1.5×10^7

31. $\dfrac{(2 \times 10^5)^2}{(8 \times 10^{-3})(5 \times 10^{12})}$ 1×10^0

32. $\dfrac{(4 \times 10^{-5})^3}{(2 \times 10^{-7})^2}$ 1.6×10^0

Problems

Solve. Write your answers in scientific notation.

A 1. **a.** Find the number of kilometers in a light year. A light year is the distance that light travels in one year. Light travels at the rate of 3.0×10^5 km/s. Assume a year is 365 days. about 9.5×10^{12} km

   b. The Andromeda galaxy is approximately 1.5×10^6 light years from Earth. Find the distance in kilometers. about 1.4×10^{19} km

15. **b.** $2 \cdot 10^3 + 5 \cdot 10^2 + 0 \cdot 10^1$

16. **b.** $0 \cdot 10^{-1} + 1 \cdot 10^{-2} + 2 \cdot 10^{-3} + 3 \cdot 10^{-4}$

17. **b.** $2 \cdot 10^{-9} + 4 \cdot 10^{-10}$

18. **b.** $2 \cdot 10^7 + 6 \cdot 10^6 + 8 \cdot 10^5 + 7 \cdot 10^4$

19. **b.** $3 \cdot 10^6 + 0 \cdot 10^5 + 3 \cdot 10^4$

20. **b.** $4 \cdot 10^{-5} + 8 \cdot 10^{-6} + 5 \cdot 10^{-7}$

21. **b.** $9 \cdot 10^{-5} + 0 \cdot 10^{-6} + 9 \cdot 10^{-7}$

22. **b.** $7 \cdot 10^8 + 9 \cdot 10^7 + 8 \cdot 10^6 + 1 \cdot 10^5$

23. **b.** $9 \cdot 10^{-1} + 8 \cdot 10^{-2} + 6 \cdot 10^{-3}$

24. **b.** $2 \cdot 10^6 + 3 \cdot 10^5$

25. **b.** $1 \cdot 10^{10} + 2 \cdot 10^9$

26. **b.** $2 \cdot 10^{14}$

Summarizing the Lesson

In this lesson, students have expressed decimal numbers in scientific notation and solved problems using scientific notation.

Suggested Assignments

Minimum
   339/3–21 mult. of 3
R 341/Self Test 5: 1–3, 10–12

Average
   339/3–30 mult. of 3
   339/*P*: 1, 2
S 340/Mixed Review

Maximum
   339/3–30 mult. of 3
   339/*P*: 1, 2
S 340/Mixed Review

c. The distance from Earth to the star Alpha Centauri is about 4.07×10^{13} km. Use the result of Problem 1 to find how long it takes light from this star to reach Earth. about 4.3 years

d. How long does it take light from the sun to reach Earth? The sun is 1.5×10^8 km from Earth. about 500 s or $8\frac{1}{3}$ min

2. A sheet of paper is 0.015 cm thick. Suppose that you rip it in half, place the two halves together and rip them in half. Then you place the four pieces you now have in a stack and then rip the stack in half. If it were possible to continue this process of stacking the cut pieces and ripping the stacks apart for 50 times, the stack would have 2^{50} pieces. (*Hint:* $2^{50} \approx 1.13 \times 10^{15}$)

a. How high would the stack reach? 1.695×10^{13} cm

b. Would it be higher than your room? yes

c. Higher than the tallest redwood tree (83 m)? yes

d. Higher than the world's tallest building (443.18 m)? yes

e. Higher than the moon (384,432 m)? yes

f. Higher than the sun (1.5×10^8 km)? yes

3. The diagram shows the repetitive pattern of an electromagnetic wave. The frequency of such a wave is the number of repetitions, or cycles, per second. A typical television wave could have a frequency of 1.3×10^8 cycles per second. The wavelength, L, is the distance from the peak of one wave to the peak of the next. The frequency, F, and wavelength, L, in centimeters, are related by the following formula:

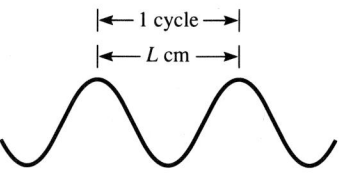

$$F \cdot L = 3.0 \times 10^{10} = \text{speed of light in cm/s}$$

Use this formula to complete the table below.

	a. Television	**b.** Red light	**c.** Violet light	**d.** x rays
Frequency F	1.3×10^8	4.0×10^{14}	?	?
Wavelength L	?	?	1.3×10^{-8}	1×10^{-11}

2.3×10^2	7.5×10^{-5}	2.3×10^{18}	3.0×10^{21}

Mixed Review Exercises

Simplify. Give your answers using positive exponents.

1. $-[y + (-21)] + 2y + 3$ $y + 24$

2. $(x^{-2}y^5)^3$ $\dfrac{y^{15}}{x^6}$

3. $(13 - 25) - (8 - 28)$ 8

4. $55:22$ 5:2

5. $[4 + (-6)] + 7$ 5

6. $3t + [(-6) + (-2) + 9]$ 3t + 1

7. $\left(\dfrac{c^{-3}}{c^3}\right)^2$ $\dfrac{1}{c^{12}}$

8. $-\dfrac{5}{2} + 5 + \left(-\dfrac{1}{2}\right)$ 2

9. $\dfrac{14b^3c^2}{12c^3b}$ $\dfrac{7b^2}{6c}$

Self-Test 5

Vocabulary scientific notation (p. 336) expanded notation (p. 338)

Simplify. Give your answers using positive exponents.

1. $(3^{-2})^{-5}$ 3^{10}

2. $\dfrac{2^{-3}}{2^0}$ $\dfrac{1}{2^3}$ or $\dfrac{1}{8}$

3. $-\dfrac{2^0}{2^{-3}}$ $-(2^3)$ or -8 **Obj. 7-9, p. 331**

4. x^{-5} $\dfrac{1}{x^5}$

5. $4a^{-2}$ $\dfrac{4}{a^2}$

6. $(3a^2)^{-4}$ $\dfrac{1}{81a^8}$

7. $x^3 \cdot x^{-3}$ 1

8. $b^{-7} \cdot b^5$ $\dfrac{1}{b^2}$

9. $(a^3 \cdot a^{-6})^2$ $\dfrac{1}{a^6}$

Express each number in (a) scientific notation and (b) expanded notation.

10. 47 million   **11.** 0.00000006   **12.** 12.34   **Obj. 7-10, p. 336**

10. (a) 4.7×10^7 **(b)** $4 \cdot 10^7 + 7 \cdot 10^6$

Check your answers with those at the back of the book.

11. (a) $6 \cdot 10^{-8}$ **(b)** $6 \cdot 10^{-8}$

12. (a) 1.234×10^1 **(b)** $1 \cdot 10^1 + 2 \cdot 10^0 + 3 \cdot 10^{-1} + 4 \cdot 10^{-2}$

Calculator Key-In

To display very large numbers, most calculators use a form of exponential notation similar to scientific notation. Try this on a calculator:

Press the 9 key until the display is filled with 9's. Next, estimate what the answer would be if you were to multiply this number by 2. Write your estimate. Now multiply by 2 on the calculator. Compare the displayed answer with your estimate. They should be two different forms of the same number.

Enter 9's again. Predict what the calculator will display when you multiply by 20. Try it. Were you right? What will be displayed if you multiply by 400 instead of 20? yes; 4×10^{10}

Career Note / *Electrical Engineer*

Electrical engineers work with physicists, chemists, metallurgists, mathematicians, and statisticians to design the parts that go into electronic products such as computers, stereos, televisions, and telephones. They may work in research, in development, or in quality control.

A bachelor's degree or a master's degree is usually needed since most engineers specialize in highly technical areas. Electrical engineers must always stay informed of new developments in their field of engineering.

Applying Fractions   **341**

Chapter Summary

1. A *ratio* of two numbers is their quotient. The ratio 6 to 8 can be written as 6:8 or more simply as $3 \div 4$, $\frac{3}{4}$, or 3:4. If the ratio of two numbers is 5:7, you can express the numbers as $5x$ and $7x$.

2. A *proportion* is an equation stating that two ratios are equal. In a proportion the product of the extremes is equal to the product of the means. Thus,
$$\text{if } \frac{a}{b} = \frac{c}{d}, \text{ then } ad = bc.$$

3. You can eliminate fractions from *equations with fractional coefficients* and from *fractional equations* by multiplying both sides of the equation by the LCD. Similarly, you can eliminate decimals from equations by multiplying each side by a suitable power of 10.

4. *Percent* means "hundredths" or "divided by 100." Percent problems usually involve finding a percent of a number, finding what percent one number is of another, or finding a number when a percent of the number is known. (See the example on pages 309–311.) When solving word problems, it is often convenient to express the percent as a decimal. For example,
$$7\frac{1}{2}\% = 7.5\% = 0.075.$$

5. The similarities among mixture, coin, investment, work, and distance problems can be seen in the charts and equations used to solve them.

6. Exponents can be positive, negative, or zero. The rules for positive exponents continue to hold for zero and negative exponents.

7. Expressing very large or very small numbers in *scientific notation* makes these numbers easier to use in calculations.

Supplementary Materials

Practice Master   45
Resource Book   p. 199

Chapter Review

1. State the ratio of 5 h:35 min in simplest form.   7-1

   a. $\frac{7}{1}$ **(b.)** $\frac{60}{7}$ **c.** $\frac{7}{60}$ **d.** $\frac{53}{60}$

2. In a ceramics class the ratio of students making projects they intend to keep to students making projects they intend to give as gifts is 3:5. If there are 24 students in the class, how many of the students intend to keep the projects they are making?

   a. 3   **b.** 12   **(c.)** 9   **d.** 15

3. Solve $\frac{x+3}{44} = \frac{42}{24}$.   7-2

   a. $\frac{11}{42}$ **b.** $\frac{77}{3}$ **c.** 77   **(d.)** 74

4. Chanda is drawing a map. If she lets 1.5 cm represent 175 km, how long should she draw a segment that represents 875 km?

   a. 20 cm **b.** 5 cm **(c.)** 7.5 cm **d.** 2.0 cm

5. Solve $\frac{x}{4} - \frac{x+4}{5} = 1$.   7-3

   a. 4 **b.** 16 **(c.)** 36 **d.** 14

6. Solve $\frac{1}{a-1} + \frac{3}{3a-1} = 0$.   7-4

   (a.) $\frac{2}{3}$ **b.** 0 **c.** $\frac{3}{2}$ **d.** no solution

7. Express $16\frac{2}{3}\%$ as a fraction in simplest form.   7-5

   a. $\frac{50}{3}$ **b.** $\frac{5}{3}$ **(c.)** $\frac{1}{6}$ **d.** $\frac{1}{60}$

8. 72% of 72 is what number?

   a. 100 **b.** 1 **c.** $\frac{18}{25}$ **(d.)** 51.84

9. 18 is 6% of what number?

   a. 3 **(b.)** 300 **c.** 1.08 **d.** $\frac{3}{50}$

10. What percent of 36 is 27?

    a. $\frac{4}{3}\%$ **b.** $\frac{3}{4}\%$ **(c.)** 75% **d.** 7.5%

11. A team won 57 games and lost 18. What percent did the team win?

    a. 24% **(b.)** 76% **c.** 3.16% **d.** 31%

12. Monty saves 20% by buying a record on sale for $6.36. What was the original price of the record?   7-6

    (a.) $7.95 **b.** $9.54 **c.** $7.99 **d.** $8.48

13. A chemist has 10 cm³ of a 20% salt solution. How many cubic centimeters of water should she add to produce a 5% salt solution?   7-7

    a. 13 cm³ **b.** 18 cm³ **c.** 22 cm³ **(d.)** 30 cm³

14. Anita can paint the shed in 5 h. If Kris helps her, they can paint the shed in 3 h. How long would it take Kris to paint the shed alone?   7-8

    (a.) $7\frac{1}{2}$ h **b.** $3\frac{3}{5}$ h **c.** $5\frac{1}{3}$ h **d.** 6 h

15. Simplify $(2x^3)^{-2}$.   7-9

    a. $\frac{1}{4x}$ **b.** $\frac{1}{2x^6}$ **c.** $\frac{1}{4x^3}$ **(d.)** $\frac{1}{4x^6}$

16. Express 234 million in scientific notation.   7-10

    a. 234×10^6 **(b.)** 2.34×10^8 **c.** 2.34×10^{-8} **d.** 2.34×10^6

Chapter Test

Express each ratio in simplest form.

1. 21 days:35 wk 3:35

2. 63 cm:0.9 cm 70:1

7-1

Solve.

3. The ratio of time Sean spent writing an essay to the time he spent revising it was 4:1. If he spent a total of $2\frac{1}{2}$ h writing and revising the essay, how long did it take him to write it? 2 h

4. $\frac{104}{x} = \frac{13}{2}$ {16}

5. $\frac{16}{3y} = \frac{12}{5}$ $\left\{\frac{20}{9}\right\}$

7-2

6. $\frac{3x}{10} = \frac{5x}{6}$ {0}

7. $\frac{4a+1}{7} = \frac{3a-4}{3}$ $\left\{\frac{31}{9}\right\}$

8. $2n + \frac{3n}{5} = 5 - \frac{n}{10}$ $\left\{\frac{50}{27}\right\}$

9. $\frac{3y+5}{2} - \frac{3y+2}{5} = \frac{3}{10}$ {−2}

7-3

10. $\frac{1}{b} + \frac{3b}{5b-2} = 0$ $\left\{\frac{1}{3}, -2\right\}$

11. $\frac{2c+3}{2c+6} = \frac{1}{c}$ $\left\{-2, \frac{3}{2}\right\}$

7-4

Express as a fraction in simplest form.

12. 49% $\frac{49}{100}$

13. $73\frac{1}{2}$% $\frac{147}{200}$

14. 540% $\frac{27}{5}$

7-5

15. 22% of 78 is what number? 17.16

16. 48 is 32% of what number? 150

17. What percent of 945 is 315? $33\frac{1}{3}$%

Solve.

18. The number of people at this year's walkathon was 12% higher than last year. If 1344 people walked this year, how many people walked last year? 1200

7-6

19. How many liters of grape juice must be added to 14 L of cranberry juice to make a drink that is 16% grape juice? $2\frac{2}{3}$ L

7-7

20. Working alone, Mandi can complete a project in 7 h. It would take Colin 3 h to complete the same project. If they work together, how long will it take them to complete the project? 2.1 h

7-8

Simplify. Give answers using positive exponents.

21. $3^{-5} \cdot 3^4$ $\frac{1}{3}$

22. $\frac{5^0}{5^{-2}}$ 25

23. $(4m^2)^{-3}$ $\frac{1}{64m^6}$

7-9

24. $12x^{-5}$ $\frac{12}{x^5}$

25. $(a^{-3})^2$ $\frac{1}{a^6}$

26. $n^2 \cdot n^{-6}$ $\frac{1}{n^4}$

27. Express 0.000128 in scientific notation. 1.28×10^{-4}

7-10

Cumulative Review (Chapters 1–7)

4. $-3x^3y^5 + 4x^5y^3 + 14x^2y^2$

Simplify. Give your answers using positive exponents.

8. $15b^2c^2 - 2bc - 24$ 9. $2x^3 - 11x^2y + 11xy^2 - 3y^3$

1. $24 \div 2 + 2^2 - 4^3 \div 2^4$ 12   2. $\left(\dfrac{18}{36}\right)\left(\dfrac{3}{17}\right) + \left(\dfrac{1}{2}\right)\left(\dfrac{3}{17}\right)$ $\dfrac{3}{17}$ 3. $(-2m^3n^4)(8m^5n^3)$ $-16m^8n^7$

$100b^2 + 180b + 81$

4. $x^2y^2(-3xy^3 + 4x^3y + 14)$ 5. $(-4a^2b^3c)^2$ $16a^4b^6c^2$ 6. $(10b + 9)^2$

7. $(5t^2v - 6)^2$ $25t^4v^2 - 60t^2v + 36$ 8. $(3bc - 4)(5bc + 6)$ 9. $(2x - y)(x^2 - 5xy + 3y^2)$

10. $\dfrac{x^2 - 12x + 36}{x - 3} \cdot \dfrac{x^2 - 9}{x^2 - x - 30}$ $\dfrac{(x - 6)(x + 3)}{x + 5}$ 11. $\dfrac{3z - 1}{xyz^3} \div \dfrac{9xz^2 - x}{yz^2}$ $\dfrac{1}{x^2z(3z + 1)}$

12. $\dfrac{t}{t + 5} + \dfrac{t + 4}{t^2 + 2t - 15}$ $\dfrac{t^2 - 2t + 4}{(t + 5)(t - 3)}$ 13. $\dfrac{12b^2 + b - 6}{3b - 2}$ $4b + 3$

14. $\left(\dfrac{y^3}{y - 4}\right)^3$ $\dfrac{y^9}{(y - 4)^3}$ 15. $\left(\dfrac{x^{-7}}{x - 4}\right)^{-2}$ $x^{14}(x - 4)^2$

16. What percent of 400 is 336? 84%   17. 56 is what percent of 600? $9\frac{1}{3}\%$

18. $6st^2(-3s^2 + 4st + 6t)$ 19. $(7z - 2)^2$ 20. $4(5t + 4x)(5t - 4x)$

Factor completely. If the polynomial cannot be factored, write *prime*.

18. $-18s^3t^2 + 24s^2t^3 + 36st^3$ 19. $49z^2 - 28z + 4$ 20. $-64x^2 + 100t^2$

21. $6b^2 + 27b + 27$ $3(2b + 3)(b + 3)$ 22. $18t^2 + 27t + 12$ $3(6t^2 + 9t + 4)$ 23. $12x^2 + 47x - 4$ $(12x - 1)(x + 4)$

Solve. If the equation is an identity or has no solution, state that fact.

24. $-7x + 2 = -33$ {5}   25. $\dfrac{2}{3}t - 8 = 12$ {30}

26. $(n + 4)^2 = (n + 2)^2 + 4(n + 3)$ identity   27. $4y^2 + 28y + 49 = 0$ $\left\{-\frac{7}{2}\right\}$

28. $m^2 + 14 + 9m = 0$ {−7, −2}   29. $y^3 - 12y^2 + 11y = 0$ {0, 1, 11}

30. $0.02(700 - x) + 0.5x = 20$ {12.5}   31. $\dfrac{n - 3}{n + 3} + \dfrac{1}{n - 3} = \dfrac{18}{n^2 - 9}$ {−1, 6}

Express in scientific notation.

32. 67 billion
    6.7×10^{10}
33. 0.0000043
    4.3×10^{-6}
34. $(7.3 \times 10^5)(2.0 \times 10^{-2})$
    1.46×10^4

35. The product of two consecutive odd integers is 22 less than the square of the greater integer. Find the integers. 9 and 11

36. Three numbers are in the ratio 3:4:5 and their sum is 144. Find the numbers. 36, 48, and 60

37. A stereo receiver that normally costs $425 at Berman's would cost an employee $340. What is the percent of the employee's discount? 20%

38. How many liters of water should be added to 20 L of a 30% acid solution to make a solution that is 10% acid? 40 L

39. One pipe can fill a tank in 2 h. A second pipe can fill it in $1\frac{3}{4}$ h. How long will it take to fill the tank with both pipes open? 56 min or $\frac{14}{15}$ h

Maintaining Skills

Simplify.

Sample 1 $-5(a + 3b) - 4(-2a + b) = -5a - 15b + 8a - 4b$
$$= 3a - 19b \quad \textbf{\textit{Answer}}$$

1. $7a^2 + 2 - 5a + 2a^2 + 6$ $9a^2 - 5a + 8$ **2.** $-4c + 2d - 3 - 5d + 3c - 6$ $^{-c - 3d - 9}$

3. $(12 - 2x) + (-8x + 5x)$ $12 - 5x$ **4.** $(3m - 2n) - (-4m + 3n)$ $^{7m - 5n}$

5. $4(x - 3z) - 8(-x + z)$ $12x - 20z$ **6.** $-2(5y^2 - 2y) + 3(-3y + 1)$ $^{-10y^2 - 5y + 3}$

7. $-2(5x + 3) + 4(3x - 2y)$ $2x - 8y - 6$ **8.** $-3(5x - y) + 5x(2y + 2)$ $-5x + 3y + 10xy$

9. $\frac{3}{4}(8a - 2b) - \frac{2}{3}(9a + b)$ $-\frac{13}{6}b$ **10.** $\frac{2}{3}(-12j - k) + \frac{1}{6}(18j + 8k)$ $-5j + \frac{2}{3}k$

Sample 2 $(-4x^2yz)(-5xy^4z^3) = [(-4)(-5)](x^2 \cdot x)(y \cdot y^4)(z \cdot z^3)$
$$= 20x^3y^5z^4 \quad \textbf{\textit{Answer}}$$

11. $(-2a^2b^2)(3ab^2c)$ $-6a^3b^4c$ **12.** $(4st^2)(-s^3t)(-2s^2t^2)$ $8s^6t^5$

13. $(4m^2np)\left(-\frac{1}{4}m^3np^2\right)$ $-m^5n^2p^3$ **14.** $(-5a^2b^3)(2a^3b^2) + (a^4b)(6ab^4)$ $-4a^5b^5$

Sample 3 $(-9a^3b^2)^3 = (-9)^3(a^3)^3(b^2)^3 = -729a^9b^6 \quad \textbf{\textit{Answer}}$

15. $(2x^2y^3)^4$ $16x^8y^{12}$ **16.** $(-11m^4n^3)^2$ $121m^8n^6$

17. $(r^3s^2t)^4(rst)^3$ $r^{15}s^{11}t^7$ **18.** $-9(fg^3)^2(-2f^3g)^2$ $-36f^8g^8$

19. $(2c^2d^2e)^6 + (-2c^4d^4e^2)^3$ $56c^{12}d^{12}e^6$ **20.** $-ab(a^3b^2)^4 + a^3b^4(-a^2b)^5$ $-2a^{13}b^9$

Multiply.

Sample 4 $5x^2y(3x^2 - 4xy + 2y^2) = 15x^4y - 20x^3y^2 + 10x^2y^3 \quad \textbf{\textit{Answer}}$

21. $3ab^2(a^2 - ab + b^2)$ $3a^3b^2 - 3a^2b^3 + 3ab^4$ **22.** $-4m^2n(3mn^2 - 2m + n^3)$ $^{-12m^3n^3 + 8m^3n - 4m^2n^4}$

23. $c^2d^3(d^4 - 2d^2c + c^3)$ $c^2d^7 - 2c^3d^5 + c^5d^3$ **24.** $-xy(5x^3y^2 - 2x^2y + 7y^5)$ $-5x^4y^3 + 2x^3y^2 - 7xy^6$

Sample 5 $(2r - 5s)(-3r + 2s) = 2r(-3r + 2s) - 5s(-3r + 2s)$
$$= -6r^2 + 4rs + 15rs - 10s^2$$

25. $z^2 + 5z - 24$ **26.** $14d^2 + 45d - 14$ $= -6r^2 + 19rs - 10s^2 \quad \textbf{\textit{Answer}}$ **27.** $y^2 + 8y - 20$

28. $10y^2 - 31y + 15$ **29.** $12z^2 - 9z - 3$ **30.** $15c^2 + 29c + 12$

25. $(z - 3)(z + 8)$ **26.** $(2d + 7)(7d - 2)$ **27.** $(y - 2)(y + 10)$

28. $(2y - 5)(5y - 3)$ **29.** $(4z + 1)(3z - 3)$ **30.** $(3c + 4)(5c + 3)$

31. $(9d - 3)(9d + 3)$ $81d^2 - 9$ **32.** $(4y + 5)^2$ $16y^2 + 40y + 25$ **33.** $(x^2 - 6)(x^2 + 6)$ $x^4 - 36$

34. $(3a - 4)(7a + 2)$ $21a^2 - 22a - 8$ **35.** $(y - 3)(3y^2 - 4y + 1)$ $3y^3 - 13y^2 + 13y - 3$ **36.** $(b - 7)(-2b^2 + 5b - 2)$ $-2b^3 + 19b^2 - 37b + 14$

Mixed Problem Solving

Solve each problem that has a solution. If a problem has no solution, explain why.

A **1.** The home team scored 50 points more than half the number scored by the visitors. Their scores totaled 194 points. Which team won? By how many points? home team; by 2 points

2. How many kilograms of salt must be added to 12 kg of an 8% salt solution to make a solution that is 20% salt? 1.8 kg

3. An apple is 85% water. If an apple contains 187 mg of water, find the weight of the apple. 220 mg

4. The ratio of the lengths of two pieces of ribbon is 1:3. If 4 ft were cut from each piece, the sum of the new lengths would be 4 ft. How long would each piece be? No solution; one new ribbon would be −1 ft long.

5. Mia went downtown by bus, traveling at 60 km/h. She walked home at 6 km/h. Her total traveling time was 2.75 h. How far did she travel? 30 km

6. A wholesaler mixed coffee beans worth $6/kg with another kind worth $8.80/kg. The 16 kg mixture was worth $6.70/kg. How many kilograms of each type were used? 12 kg of $6/kg beans; 4 kg of $8.80/kg beans

7. I can weed the garden in 90 min. My friend needs 20 min more. How long will it take us to do the job together? 49.5 min

8. A $24 jigsaw is on sale for $18.60. Find the percent of discount. 22.5%

9. A child's movie ticket costs $3 and an adult's ticket cost $5. If $236 was collected for one show, how many of each type of ticket were sold? No solution; not enough information

B **10.** The sum of two numbers is 40. When the greater number is divided by the smaller, the quotient is 4 and the remainder is 5. Find the numbers. 33 and 7

11. Miriam drove x km at 80 km/h. On her return trip, a detour added 10 km and reduced her speed to 60 km/h. Find her total traveling time in simplified form, in terms of x. $\frac{7x + 40}{240}$ h

12. The sum of the squares of two consecutive odd integers is 2 more than 6 times their sum. Find the numbers. 5 and 7 or −1 and 1

13. I invested $2000 more in stocks paying 11% than in an account paying 6%. If my average interest rate was $9\frac{1}{2}$%, how much did I invest in all? $5,000

14. A photograph is 2 cm longer than it is wide. It is in a frame that is 2 cm wide. Including the frame, the area is 255 cm². Find the dimensions of the photograph. 11 cm by 13 cm

8 Introduction to Functions

Objectives

8-1 To solve equations in two variables over given domains of the variables.

8-2 To graph ordered pairs and linear equations in two variables.

8-3 To find the slope of a line.

8-4 To use the slope-intercept form of a linear equation.

8-5 To find an equation of a line given the slope and one point on the line, or given two points on the line.

8-6 To understand what a function is and to define a function by using tables and graphs.

8-7 To define a function by using equations.

8-8 To graph linear and quadratic functions.

8-9 To use direct variation to solve problems.

8-10 To use inverse variation to solve problems.

Assignment Guide

See p. T59 for Key to the format of the Assignment Guide

Day	Minimum Course		Average Course		Maximum Course	
1	**8-1**	351/1–23 odd, 29, 33, 37	**8-1**	351/1–35 odd, 39–41	**8-1**	351/1–45 odd
	S	352/*Mixed Review*	S	352/*Mixed Review*	S	352/*Mixed Review*
2	**8-2**	357/1–37 odd, 45	**8-2**	357/1–39 odd, 45, 46	**8-2**	357/1–35 odd, 43–48
	S	358/*Mixed Review*	S	358/*Mixed Review*	S	358/*Mixed Review*
3	**8-3**	363/1–33 odd, 37	**8-3**	363/1–39 odd	**8-3**	363/1–35 odd, 38, 40, 42
	S	365/*Mixed Review*	S	365/*Mixed Review*	S	365/*Mixed Review*
	R	358/*Self-Test 1*	R	358/*Self-Test 1*	R	358/*Self-Test 1*
4	**8-4**	368/1–27 odd	**8-4**	368/1–35 odd	**8-4**	368/3–45 mult. of 3
	S	369/*Mixed Review*	S	369/*Mixed Review*	S	369/*Mixed Review*
5	**8-4**	368/28–38 even	**8-4**	369/37–43 odd	**8-5**	372/3–42 mult. of 3
	8-5	372/2–16 even	**8-5**	372/1–15 odd	S	373/*Mixed Review*
6	**8-5**	372/17–35 odd	**8-5**	372/17–39 odd	**8-6**	377/1–9 odd, 10
	S	373/*Mixed Review*	S	373/*Mixed Review*	R	373/*Self-Test 2*
7	**8-6**	377/1–6	**8-6**	377/1–9 odd, 10	**8-7**	380/1–27 odd
	S	377/*Mixed Review*	S	377/*Mixed Review*	S	377/*Mixed Review*
	R	373/*Self-Test 2*	R	373/*Self-Test 2*		
8	**8-7**	380/1–23 odd	**8-7**	380/1–43 odd	**8-7**	381/24–48 even
			S	382/*Mixed Review*	S	382/*Mixed Review*
9	**8-7**	381/24–34 even	**8-8**	386/1–29 odd, 31, 33	**8-8**	386/1–41 odd
		382/*Mixed Review*	S	387/*Mixed Review*	S	387/*Mixed Review*
10	**8-8**	386/1–21 odd	**8-9**	393/1–21 odd	**8-9**	393/3–24 mult. of 3
	S	387/*Mixed Review*	R	388/*Self-Test 3*		395/*P*: 3–15 mult. of 3
					S	396/*Mixed Review*
					R	388/*Self-Test 3*
11	**8-9**	393/1–21 odd	**8-9**	395/*P*: 1–11 odd	**8-10**	399/3–18 mult. of 3
	R	388/*Self-Test 3*	S	396/*Mixed Review*		400/*P*: 3–18 mult. of 3
			8-10	399/1–13 odd	S	402/*Mixed Review*

12	8-9 395/P: 1–9 odd S 396/*Mixed Review* 8-10 399/1–11 odd	8-10 400/15–19 odd; P: 1–13 odd S 402/*Mixed Review*	R 403/*Self-Test 4* 405/*Chapter Review* EP 653/*Skills;* 674/*Problems*
13	8-10 400/15, 17 400/P: 1–9 odd S 402/*Mixed Review*	R 403/*Self-Test 4* 405/*Chapter Review* EP 653/*Skills;* 674/*Problems*	*Administer Chapter 8 Test* R 409/*Cum. Review: 1–33 odd* S 411/*College Entrance Exams*
14	R 403/*Self-Test 4* 405/*Chapter Review* EP 653/*Skills;* 674/*Problems*	*Administer Chapter 8 Test* R 409/*Cum. Review: 1–33 odd* S 411/*College Entrance Exams*	
15	*Administer Chapter 8 Test* R 410/*Maintaining Skills*		

Supplementary Materials Guide

For Use with Lesson	Practice Masters	Tests	Study Guide (Reteaching)	Resource Book		
				Tests	Practice	Other
8-1			pp. 133–134			p. 185 (Application)
8-2	Sheet 46		pp. 135–136		p. 114	p. 206 (Technology)
8-3			pp. 137–138		p. 115	
8-4	Sheet 47		pp. 139–140			pp. 206–207 (Tech.)
8-5		Test 34	pp. 141–142		p. 116	p. 226 (Thinking Skl.)
8-6	Sheet 48		pp. 143–144			
8-7			pp. 145–146		p. 117	
8-8	Sheet 49	Test 35	pp. 147–148		p. 118	pp. 208–209 (Tech.)
8-9			pp. 149–150			
8-10	Sheet 50	Test 36	pp. 151–152		p. 119	p. 210 (Technology)
Chapter 8	Sheet 51	Tests 37, 38		pp. 46–49		pp. 200–201 (Enrich.)
Cum. Rev. 7–8	Sheets 52, 53					
Cum. Rev. 5–8		Test 39				

Overhead Visuals

For Use with Lessons	Visual	Title
8-2, 8-3, 8-4, 8-8, 8-10	A	Multi-Use Packet 1
8-1, 8-2, 8-3, 8-4, 8-8, 8-10	B	Multi-Use Packet 2
8-3, 8-4, 8-5	7	Exploring Slopes and Linear Systems
8-4	8	Graphing $y = mx + b$
8-9, 8-10	9	Variation

Software

	Algebra Plotter Plus	Using Algebra Plotter Plus	Computer Activities	Test Generator
Software	Line Plotter, Parabola Plotter, Parabola Quiz, Conics Plotter, Function Plotter,	Scripted Demo, pp. 18–21 Enrichment, p. 31 Activity Sheets, pp. 43–46	Activities 23–26	210 test items
For Use with Lessons	8-2, 8-3, 8-4, 8-8, 8-9, 8-10	8-2, 8-3, 8-4, 8-8, 8-9, 8-10	8-1, 8-4, 8-6	all lessons

Strategies for Teaching

Using Technology

Recent research in cognitive psychology has emphasized the importance of learning by doing. When students participate actively in exploring and discovering mathematical concepts, they understand and remember the concepts better, and at the same time they develop problem solving skills and confidence in their own mathematical ability.

In the past, technical difficulties (such as the time involved in drawing graphs or performing calculations) have limited the amount of exploration that could be done in the classroom. The availability of user-friendly graphing software and graphing calculators has made exploration a more feasible and more interesting method of instruction.

See the Exploration on p. 694 for an activity in which students use graphing software or a graphing calculator to explore linear equations.

The following activity for graphing software or graphing calculator can be used to introduce the concept of slope in Lesson 8-3 on p. 360. In the script, **T** indicates a teacher comment and **S** the corresponding student response.

T1. (Teacher) Graph the lines $y = 1x$ and $y = 2x$.
S1. (Student) Draws graphs.
T2. Notice that both lines pass through the origin and both rise from left to right. What makes the lines different?
S2. One line is steeper than the other.
T3. What is the equation of the steeper line?
S3. $y = 2x$
T4. Slope is a measure of the steepness of a line. It is defined as the ratio of vertical change to horizontal change as you move from one point to another point on a line. For example, the slope of $y = 1x$ is $\frac{1}{1}$, or 1, because you must move 1 unit up to get back to the line after moving 1 unit to the right from the origin. What, then, is the slope of the line $y = 2x$?
S4. $\frac{2}{1}$, or 2

T5. If you were to graph lines with greater slopes, how would they appear?
S5. The lines would become more vertical.
T6. Look at the y-axis, which is a vertical line. As you move from the origin to another point on the line, say (0, 1), what is the amount of:
a. horizontal change? **b.** vertical change?
S6. **a.** 0   **b.** 1
T7. Since slope is the ratio of vertical change to horizontal change, what can we say about the slope of a vertical line like the y-axis?
S7. The ratio $\frac{1}{0}$ is undefined, so the slope of a vertical line is undefined.
T8. In fact, we say that a vertical line has *no* slope. Now look at the x-axis, a horizontal line. As you move from the origin to another point on the line, say (1, 0), what is the amount of:
a. horizontal change? **b.** vertical change?
S8. **a.** 1   **b.** 0
T9. Since slope is the ratio of vertical change to horizontal change, what can you say about the slope of a horizontal line like the x-axis?
S9. The ratio $\frac{0}{1}$ equals 0, so the slope of a horizontal line is 0.
T10. Although lines with positive slope are indeed slanted, the converse is not true. That is, not all slanted lines have positive slope. Some have negative slope. To investigate negative slope, graph the lines $y = 1x$ and $y = -1x$.
S10. Draws graphs.
T11. To indicate a downward movement, we use a negative sign. So there is a vertical change of -1 unit for each horizontal change of 1 unit on the line $y = -1x$. This means that the slope of the line is $\frac{-1}{1}$, or -1. What would you expect the slope of the line $y = -2x$ to be?
S11. -2
T12. In the fourth quadrant, would you expect the graph of $y = -2x$ to lie above or below the graph of $y = -1x$?
S12. Below

T13. Confirm your expectation by graphing $y = -2x$. (The line will appear dashed.)

S13. Draws graph.

T14. Let's summarize all that we've discussed.

    a. Since slope is a measure of the steepness of a line, a line that is "flat" (that is, horizontal) has what slope?

    b. With regard to slope, how are slanted lines that *rise* from left to right distinguished from slanted lines that *fall*?

    c. Suppose two lines both rise or both fall from left to right. With regard to slope, how are the lines distinguished?

    d. What is the slope of a vertical line?

S14. **a.** 0

    b. Rising lines have positive slopes; falling lines have negative slopes.

    c. The absolute value of the slope of the steeper line is greater.

    d. A vertical line has no slope.

References to Strategies

PE: Pupil's Edition   **TE:** Teacher's Edition   **RB:** Resource Book

Problem Solving Strategies

PE: p. 382 (Recognizing patterns); pp. 395–396 (Alternate methods); p. 404 (Checking solution, Choosing a strategy, Using five-step plan, Using estimation)

TE: p. 395

Applications

PE: pp. 348, 350, 352, 358–359, 365, 369, 378, 395–396, 398, 400–402

TE: p. 348

RB: p. 185

Nonroutine Problems

PE: p. 352 (Exs. 44, 45); pp. 357–358 (Exs. 44–48); p. 365 (Exs. 39–42); p. 369 (Exs. 41–45); p. 373 (Exs. 38–42); p. 377 (Exs. 9, 10); p. 381 (Exs. 47, 48); p. 382 (Challenge); p. 387 (Exs. 31, 32, 41, 42); p. 395 (Exs. 23, 24); p. 396 (Prob. 15); p. 402 (Probs. 15–18)

TE: p. T122 (Sugg. Extension, Lesson 8-9)

Communication

PE: p. 404 (Reading Algebra)

TE: p. T121 (Reading Algebra, Lessons 8-7, 8-8)

Thinking Skills

PE: pp. 350, 393 (Analysis); pp. 364, 369 (Applying concepts); pp. 377, 378, 382 (Reasoning and inferencing); pp. 377, 378 (Synthesis)

TE: pp. 350, 378

RB: p. 226

Explorations

PE: pp. 370, 378, 389–390, 694

RB: pp. 206–210

Algebra Plotter Plus: pp. 18–21, 31, 43–46

Connections

PE: pp. 377–378 (Data Analysis); pp. 382, 388 (Discrete Math); pp. 358, 365, 396, 400 (Geometry); p. 396 (Health); p. 359 (History); pp. 394–395, 398, 400–402 (Physics); p. 348 (Social Science); pp. 374–378 (Statistics)

Using Technology

PE: pp. 352, 354, 357, 368, 382, 384, 386–388, 399, 402 (Exs.); pp. 365, 403 (Calculator Key-In); p. 359 (Computer Key-In)

TE: pp. 352, 354, 359, 365, 367, 368, 382, 385, 388, 399, 402, 403

RB: pp. 206–210

Computer Activities: pp. 51–59

Algebra Plotter Plus: pp. 18–21, 31, 43–46

Using Manipulatives/Models

TE: p. T119 (Lesson 8-3); p. T120 (Lesson 8-6)

Overhead Visuals: A, B, 7, 8, 9

Cooperative Learning

TE: p. T120 (Lesson 8-4)

RB: p. 185

Teaching Resources

For use in implementing the teaching strategies referenced on the previous page.

Application/Cooperative Learning
Resource Book, p. 185

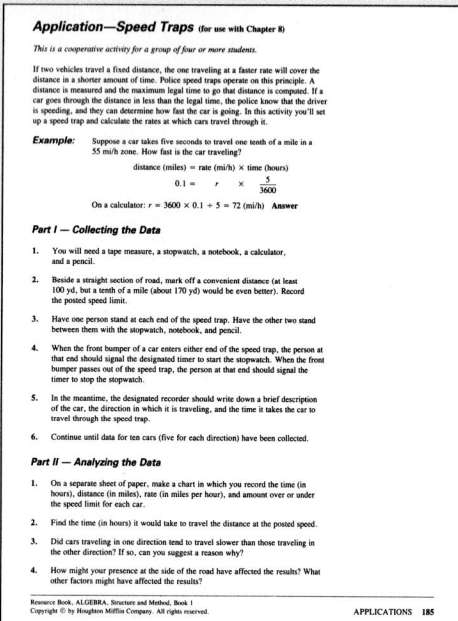

Application—Speed Traps (for use with Chapter 8)

This is a cooperative activity for a group of four or more students.

If two vehicles travel a fixed distance, the one traveling at a faster rate will cover the distance in a shorter amount of time. Police speed traps operate on this principle. A distance is measured and the maximum legal time to go that distance is computed. If a car goes through the distance in less than the legal time, the police know that the driver is speeding, and they can determine how fast the car is going. In this activity you'll set up a speed trap and calculate the rates at which cars travel through it.

Example: Suppose a car takes five seconds to travel one tenth of a mile in a 55 mi/h zone. How fast is the car traveling?

distance (miles) = rate (mi/h) × time (hours)

$$0.1 = r \times \frac{5}{3600}$$

On a calculator: $r = 3600 \times 0.1 \div 5 = 72$ (mi/h) **Answer**

Part I — Collecting the Data

1. You will need a tape measure, a stopwatch, a notebook, a calculator, and a pencil.

2. Beside a straight section of road, mark off a convenient distance (at least 100 yd, but a tenth of a mile (about 170 yd) would be even better). Record the posted speed limit.

3. Have one person stand at each end of the speed trap. Have the other two stand between them with the stopwatch, notebook, and pencil.

4. When the front bumper of a car enters either end of the speed trap, the person at that end should signal the designated timer to start the stopwatch. When the front bumper passes out of the speed trap, the person at that end should signal the timer to stop the stopwatch.

5. In the meantime, the designated recorder should write down a brief description of the car, the direction in which it is traveling, and the time it takes the car to travel through the speed trap.

6. Continue until data for ten cars (five for each direction) have been collected.

Part II — Analyzing the Data

1. On a separate sheet of paper, make a chart in which you record the time (in hours), distance (in miles), rate (in miles per hour), and amount over or under the speed limit for each car.

2. Find the time (in hours) it would take to travel the distance at the posted speed.

3. Did cars traveling in one direction tend to travel slower than those traveling in the other direction? If so, can you suggest a reason why?

4. How might your presence at the side of the road have affected the results? What other factors might have affected the results?

Thinking Skills
Resource Book, p. 226

Thinking Skills (For use after Chapter 8)

Interpreting information

1. Consider the line $x - 2y = 2$.

   a. Find the slope. What does this number tell you about the line? _____

   b. Find the y-intercept. What does this number tell you about the line? _____

Applying concepts

2. Suppose a repairman charges a service-call fee of $40 for coming to your home and an hourly fee of $15 for the work that he does. What is the total charge if the repair takes:

   a. 1 hour? _____ b. 2 hours? _____ c. 3 hours? _____

3. Let t = the repair time, and let c = the total charge. Using your answers to Exercise 2, form ordered pairs (t, c) and plot them on the axes at the right. The three points should all lie on a single line. Draw the line.

4. a. Find an equation in slope-intercept form of the line in Exercise 3. _____

   b. What do you notice about the slope and y-intercept of the line?

5. Suppose a second repairman charges a service-call fee of $30 and an hourly fee of $20. Based on the results of Exercise 4, write an equation relating repair time t and total charge c for the second repairman. _____

6. Using the axes provided for Exercise 3, graph the equation from Exercise 5. (To distinguish the lines, label the original one "Repairman 1" and the new one "Repairman 2.")

Analysis

7. Look at your graph of time versus charge for the two repairmen. For each of the following amounts of time, which repairman would you call if you thought the repair would take that long? How does the graph support your answer?

   a. 1 hour: _____

   b. 2 hours: _____

   c. 3 hours: _____

Enrichment/Connection
Resource Book, p. 200

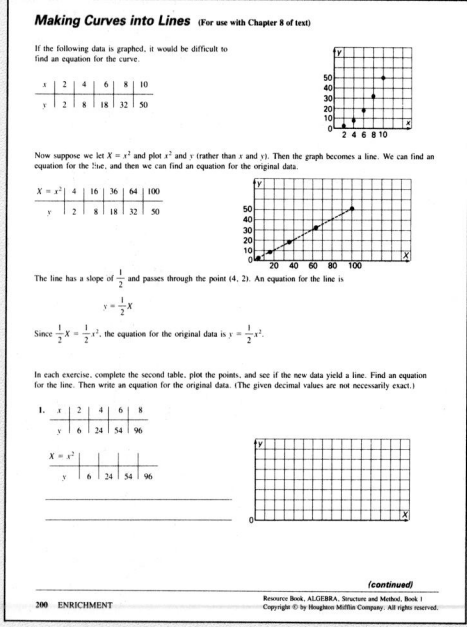

Making Curves into Lines (For use with Chapter 8 of text)

If the following data is graphed, it would be difficult to find an equation for the curve.

x	2	4	6	8	10
y	2	8	18	32	50

Now suppose we let $X = x^2$ and plot x^2 and y (rather than x and y). Then the graph becomes a line. We can find an equation for the line, and then we can find an equation for the original data.

$X = x^2$	4	16	36	64	100
y	2	8	18	32	50

The line has a slope of $\frac{1}{2}$ and passes through the point (4, 2). An equation for the line is

$$y = \frac{1}{2}X$$

Since $\frac{1}{2}X = \frac{1}{2}x^2$, the equation for the original data is $y = \frac{1}{2}x^2$.

In each exercise, complete the second table, plot the points, and see if the new data yield a line. Find an equation for the line. Then write an equation for the original data. (The given decimal values are not necessarily exact.)

1.

x	2	4	6	8
y	6	24	54	96

$X = x^2$				
y	6	24	54	96

(continued)

Using Technology/Exploration
Resource Book, p. 208

Using a Computer or a Graphing Calculator

To complete these activities, you should use a computer with graphics software (such as ALGEBRA PLOTTER PLUS) or a graphing calculator.

Exploring Parabolas (For use with Lesson 8-8)

1. Graph these equations: $y = x^2 + x$, $y = x^2 - 2x$, $y = x^2 + 4x$

   a. The graph of each equation is a U-shaped curve called a *parabola*. Notice that each parabola has a lowest point, called the *vertex*. For each parabola, locate the vertex and complete the table below.

Equation	Vertex
$y = x^2 + x$	$\left(-\frac{1}{2}, -\frac{1}{4}\right)$
$y = x^2 - 2x$	(? , ?) _____
$y = x^2 + 4x$	(? , ?) _____

   b. The equations have the form $y = x^2 + bx$. In terms of the number b, what is the x-coordinate of the vertex? _____

   c. Predict the x-coordinate of the vertex of the parabola $y = x^2 - 3x$: _____ Confirm your prediction by graphing.

2. Graph these equations: $y = x^2 + x$, $y = \frac{1}{2}x^2 + x$, $y = \frac{1}{4}x^2 + x$

   a. Complete the table below.

Equation	Vertex
$y = x^2 + x$	(? , ?)
$y = \frac{1}{2}x^2 + x$	(? , ?)
$y = \frac{1}{4}x^2 + x$	(? , ?)

   b. The equations have the form $y = ax^2 + x$. In terms of the number a, what is the x-coordinate of the vertex? _____

   c. Predict the x-coordinate of the vertex of the parabola $y = 2x^2 + x$: _____ Confirm your prediction by graphing.

3. a. Look at your answers to part (b) of Exercises 1 and 2. Suppose you are given an equation having the form $y = ax^2 + bx$. In terms of the numbers a and b, what would you predict the x-coordinate of the vertex of the parabola to be? _____

(continued)

Using Technology/Exploration
Using Algebra Plotter Plus, p. 43

Graphs of Linear Equations in Standard Form

Use the Line Plotter program of Algebra Plotter Plus. Select EQUATIONS. Then use the right-arrow key to move to the standard form and fill in the blanks for the missing coefficients. Press the <ESC> key and select DRAW.

1. Graph these equations: $x - y = 1$, $2x - y = 1$, $3x - y = 1$
   a. Write the equation whose graph is the steepest.
   b. The y-coordinate of a point where a graph crosses the y-axis is called the y-intercept of the graph. What do you notice about the y-intercepts of the graphs of the given equations?

2. Graph these equations: $x + 2y = 1$, $x - 2y = 1$
   The equations differ only in the sign of the coefficient of y. How do the graphs reflect this difference?

3. Graph these equations: $x + y = 2$, $x + y = -3$, $x + y = 0$
   The equations have the form $x + y = C$. What effect does changing the number C have on the graph of $x + y = C$?

4. Graph these equations: $x + y = 2$, $x - 2y = 4$, $x + 4y = 6$
   a. Complete the table below.

Equation	y-intercept
$x + y = 2$	
$x - 2y = 4$	
$x + 4y = 6$	

   b. The equations have the form $x + By = C$. Describe how the numbers B and C determine the y-intercept of the graph of $x + By = C$.

43

Using Technology/Exploration
Using Algebra Plotter Plus, p. 44

Slope-Intercept Form

Use the Line Plotter program of Algebra Plotter Plus. You must first select EQUATIONS and fill in the blanks for the missing coefficients, then press the <ESC> key and select DRAW.

1. Graph this equation: $y = 2x$
   Choose any point on the graph. If you move 1 unit to the right of this point, describe how you must move vertically to get back to the line.

2. Graph this equation: $y = -3x$
   Choose any point on the graph. If you move 1 unit to the right of this point, describe how you must move vertically to get back to the line.

3. Based on the results of Exercises 1 and 2, describe how the line $y = mx$ looks for:
   a. positive values of m
   b. negative values of m

4. For what value of m would the graph of $y = mx$ be horizontal?

5. Graph these equations: $y = \frac{1}{2}x + 3$, $y = \frac{1}{2}x$, $y = \frac{1}{2}x - 3$
   a. How are the three lines geometrically related?
   b. What can you say about the slopes of the three lines?
   c. What general conclusion do parts (a) and (b) suggest?

6. Graph these equations: $y = -x + 2$, $y = 3x - 4$, $y = 0x + 1$
   a. Locate the point where each line crosses the y-axis. The y-coordinate of this point is called the y-intercept of the line. Complete the table below.

Equation	y-intercept
$y = -x + 2$	
$y = 3x - 4$	
$y = 1$	

   b. The equations have the form $y = mx + b$. What do you notice about the y-intercepts of the graphs of such equations?

7. Try to complete the table below before graphing the given equations.

Equation	Slope	y-intercept
$y = -\frac{3}{2}x$		
$y = 2x + 1$		
$y = -3.5$		

   Now examine the graphs of the given equations to confirm the entries in the table.

44

Using Models/Exploration
Overhead Visual 7, Sheets 1 and 2

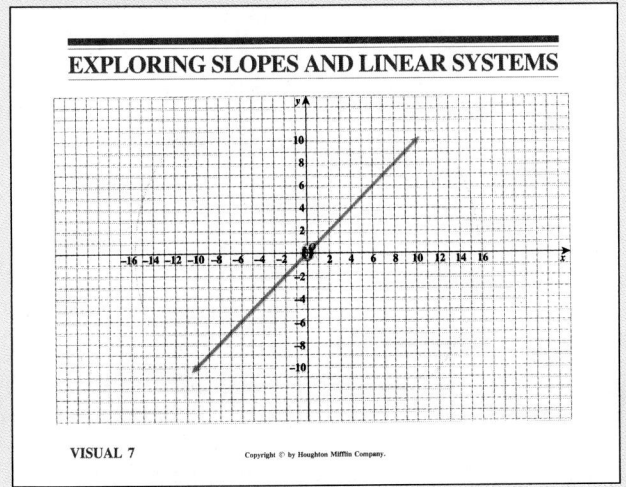

EXPLORING SLOPES AND LINEAR SYSTEMS

VISUAL 7   Copyright © by Houghton Mifflin Company.

Using Models
Overhead Visual 8, Sheets 1 and 2

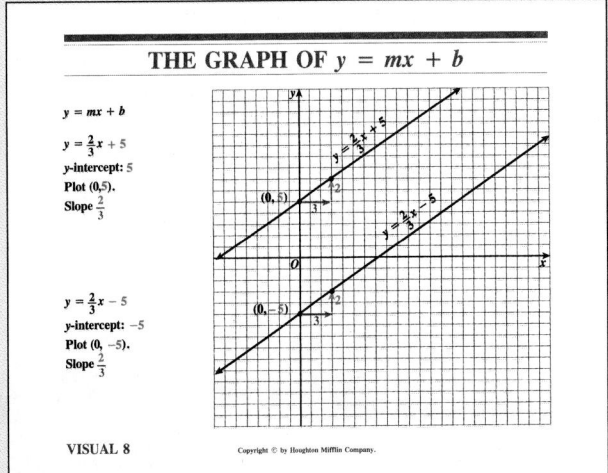

THE GRAPH OF $y = mx + b$

$y = mx + b$

$y = \frac{2}{3}x + 5$
y-intercept: 5
Plot (0, 5).
Slope $\frac{2}{3}$

$y = \frac{2}{3}x - 5$
y-intercept: -5
Plot (0, -5).
Slope $\frac{2}{3}$

VISUAL 8   Copyright © by Houghton Mifflin Company.

347f

Application

Each point on a globe has two numbers associated with it that tells its location with respect to a grid of latitude and longitude lines. Points on a map are also located with the use of a grid and a coordinate system. If you want to find a specific town on a map, you simply find the coordinates of that town in the appropriate table and then trace the grid lines to that location. Points on the graph of an equation in two variables are also located using a grid and a coordinate system.

Group Activities
Your students can apply map-reading skills and math skills by planning a tour of the United States. The formula $d = rt$ will help them to estimate the amount of time it will take to drive from one destination to the next. They should be instructed to estimate expenses, using travel guides to find admission prices and hotel or campsite costs. Their itineraries, time lines, and lists of expenses can be handed in.

You may wish to have some students report to the class on these questions: What are *Great Circle Routes?* How are they used in aviation and in sailing? How do aviation and nautical maps differ from land maps?

As the class begins to learn how to graph equations of lines, it might be useful to have a student investigate graphing calculators and then give the other students a lesson on their use.

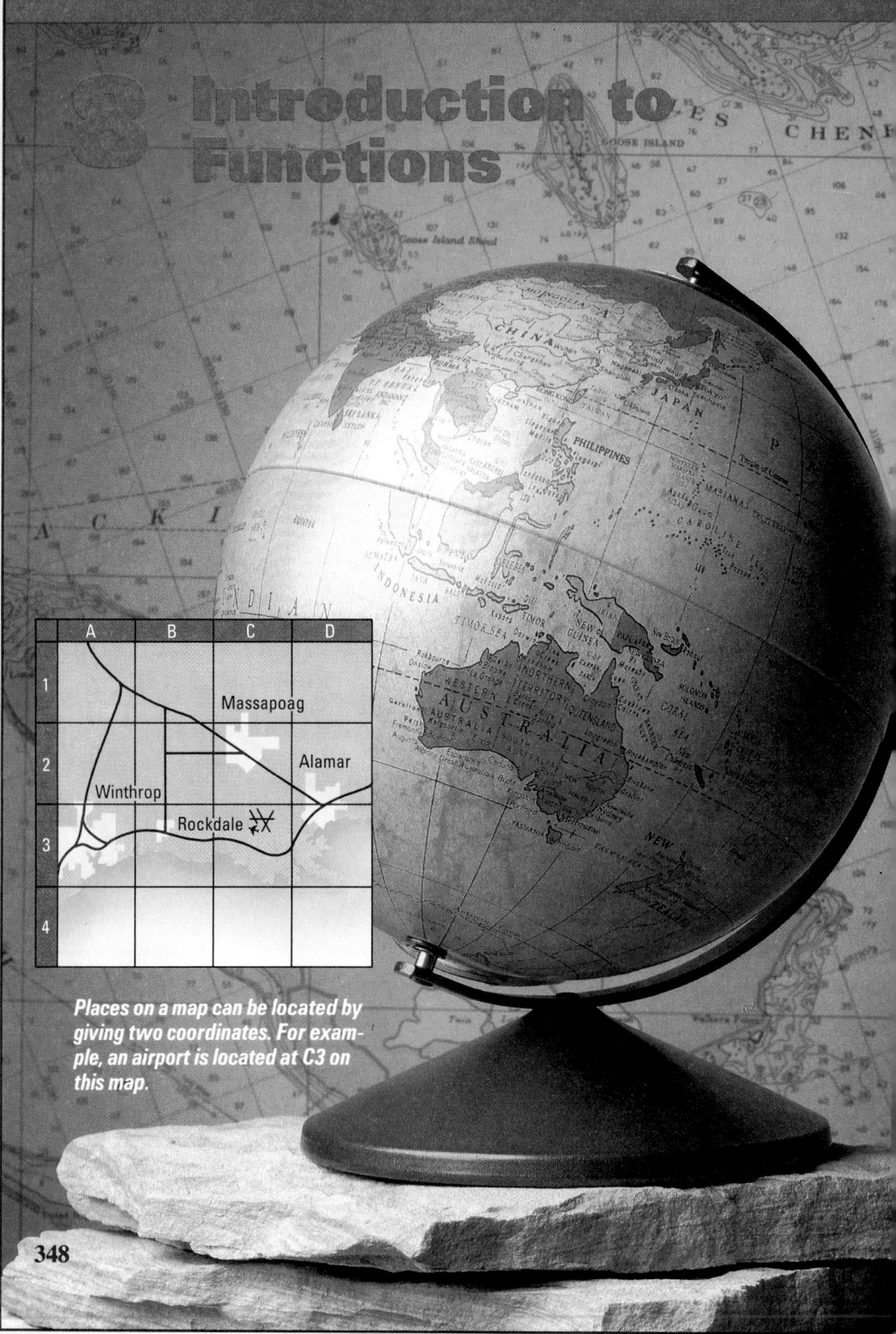

Introduction to Functions

3

Places on a map can be located by giving two coordinates. For example, an airport is located at C3 on this map.

348

Using Two Variables

8-1 Equations in Two Variables

Objective   To solve equations in two variables over given domains of the variables.

In earlier chapters, you worked with equations that contained only one variable. In this chapter, you will work with equations that contain two variables.

One-variable equations	Two-variable equations
$2x - 3 = 7$	$4x + 3y = 10$
$1 - y = 9$	$xy = 6$
$x^2 + 5x + 4 = 0$	$x^2 + y^2 = 4$

The solutions to equations in one variable are numbers. The solutions to equations in two variables are *pairs* of numbers. For example, the pair of numbers $x = 1$ and $y = 2$ is a **solution** of the equation

$$4x + 3y = 10 \text{ because } 4 \cdot 1 + 3 \cdot 2 = 10.$$

The solution $x = 1$ and $y = 2$ can be written as $(1, 2)$, with the x-value written first. A pair of numbers, such as $(1, 2)$, for which the order of the numbers is important, is called an **ordered pair.**

Example 1   State whether each ordered pair of numbers is a solution of $4x + 3y = 10$.

a. $(4, -2)$ **b.** $(-2, 6)$

c. $\left(\frac{3}{2}, \frac{4}{3}\right)$ **d.** $(3, -1)$

Solution   Substitute each ordered pair in the equation $4x + 3y = 10$.

a. $(4, -2)$ is a solution because $4(4) + 3(-2) = 10.$

b. $(-2, 6)$ is a solution because $4(-2) + 3(6) = 10.$

c. $\left(\frac{3}{2}, \frac{4}{3}\right)$ is a solution because $4\left(\frac{3}{2}\right) + 3\left(\frac{4}{3}\right) = 10.$

d. $(3, -1)$ is *not* a solution because $4(3) + 3(-1) \neq 10.$

The equation $4x + 3y = 10$ has many solutions. However, if both x and y are required to be whole numbers, then $(1, 2)$ is the only solution. When you find the set of all solutions of an equation, whether it is a one- or two-variable equation, you have **solved** the equation.

Introduction to Functions   **349**

Teaching References

Lesson Commentary, pp. T117–T122

Assignment Guide, pp. T66–T68

Supplementary Materials
  Practice Masters 46–53
  Tests 34–39
  Resource Book
    Prac. Exs. pp. 114–119
    Tests, pp. 46–49
    En. Act. p. 200
    Application, p. 185
    Using Technology, pp. 206–210
  Study Guide, pp. 133–152
  Computer Activities 23–26
  Test Generator
  California Standards
  Support Workbook
    Explorations for Lessons 8-3, 8-4, 8-8
  Alternate Test p. T19

Teaching Suggestions, p. T117

Suggested Extensions, p. T118

Warm-Up Exercises

Evaluate each expression if $x = 12$.

1. $5x - 2$ 58   **2.** $\frac{2}{3}x + 7$ 15

3. $18 - \frac{5}{4}x$ 3

Motivating the Lesson

Suppose you have 20 cents consisting of only nickels and dimes. What combination of coins do you have?
2 dimes; 4 nickels; or 2 nickels and 1 dime
Can you write an equation that describes this problem?
$5n + 10d = 20$

In this section students will explore the solutions of equations in two variables.

1. Is $(5, -1)$ a solution of the equation $x - y = 4$?
No, because $5 - (-1) = 5 + 1 = 6 \neq 4$.

2. Solve $3x + 4y = 12$ if x and y are whole numbers.

$$y = 3 - \frac{3}{4}x$$

x	$y = 3 - \frac{3}{4}x$	Solution
0	$3 - 0 = 3$	$(0, 3)$
1	$3 - \frac{3}{4} = \frac{9}{4}$	No
2	$3 - \frac{3}{2} = \frac{3}{2}$	No
3	$3 - \frac{9}{4} = \frac{3}{4}$	No
4	$3 - 3 = 0$	$(4, 0)$

∴ the solutions are $(0, 3)$ and $(4, 0)$.

3. The sum of 4 times one whole number and 2 times another whole number is 6. Find the numbers.
Substitute 0, 1, and 2 for x in the equation $4x + 2y = 6$ and check to see if y is a whole number. The sol. are $(0, 3)$ and $(1, 1)$.

Check for Understanding

Here is a suggested use of the Oral Exercises as you teach the lesson.
Oral Exs. 1–8: use after Example 1.
Oral Exs. 9–16: use after Example 2.

Thinking Skills

The *analysis* at the bottom of the charts in Examples 2 and 3 explains why we can stop looking for other whole number solutions.

Example 2 Solve $(x + 1)y = 3$ if x and y are whole numbers.

Solution

1. Solve the equation for y in terms of x.

$$y = \frac{3}{x + 1}$$

2. Replace x with successive whole numbers and find the corresponding values of y. If y is a whole number, you have found a solution pair.

∴ the solutions are $(0, 3)$ and $(2, 1)$. **Answer**

x	$y = \frac{3}{x + 1}$	Solution
0	$\frac{3}{0 + 1} = 3$	$(0, 3)$
1	$\frac{3}{1 + 1} = \frac{3}{2}$	No
2	$\frac{3}{2 + 1} = 1$	$(2, 1)$

Values of x greater than 2 give fractional values of y.

Example 3 Dawn spent \$13 on pens and notebooks. The pens cost \$2 each and the notebooks cost \$3 each. How many of each did she buy?

Solution

Step 1 The problem asks for the number of pens and the number of notebooks Dawn bought.

Step 2 Let p = number of pens, and n = the number of notebooks.

	Number	× Price =	Cost
Pens	p	2	$2p$
Notebooks	n	3	$3n$

Step 3 Since the total cost is \$13, you have: $2p + 3n = 13$.

Step 4 Solve for p: $2p = 13 - 3n$

$$p = \frac{13 - 3n}{2}$$

Both n and p must be whole numbers because Dawn cannot buy a negative or fractional number of pens or notebooks.

Step 5 Check that $(1, 5)$ and $(3, 2)$ are solutions of the problem:

$2(5) + 3(1) = 13$ ✓
$2(2) + 3(3) = 13$ ✓

∴ Dawn bought either 1 notebook and 5 pens or 3 notebooks and 2 pens. **Answer**

n	$p = \frac{13 - 3n}{2}$	Solution
1	$\frac{13 - 3}{2} = 5$	$(1, 5)$
2	$\frac{13 - 6}{2} = \frac{7}{2}$	No
3	$\frac{13 - 9}{2} = 2$	$(3, 2)$
4	$\frac{13 - 12}{2} = \frac{1}{2}$	No

Values of n greater than 4 give negative values of p.

When solving equations in two variables, we will give the numbers in a solution pair in the alphabetical order of the variables. Therefore, in Example 3 the solutions were given as (n, p) instead of (p, n).

Oral Exercises

State whether each ordered pair is a solution of the given equation.

1. $x - y = 5$
(9, 4), (7, 3)
yes   no

2. $x + 2y = 8$
(3, 3), (0, 4)
no   yes

3. $3x + y = 6$
(2, 0), (3, −1)
yes   no

4. $12 - y = 3x$
$(5, -3), \left(\frac{1}{3}, 11\right)$
yes   yes

5. $y = x^2$
(−3, 9), (4, 2)
yes   no

6. $x^2 + y^2 = 10$
(1, 3), (−3, −1)
yes   yes

7. $st = 6$
$(3, -2), \left(\frac{9}{2}, \frac{4}{3}\right)$
no   yes

8. $a^2 - 4b^2 = 0$
(−2, 1), (1, 2)
yes   no

Solve each equation for y in terms of x.

9. $2x + y = 4$
$y = 4 - 2x$

10. $3x - y = 7$
$y = 3x - 7$

11. $x = 4 + 3y$
$y = \frac{x - 4}{3}$

12. $2x + 5y = 9$
$y = \frac{9 - 2x}{5}$

Solve each equation if x and y are whole numbers.

13. $x + y = 3$
(0, 3), (1, 2),
(2, 1), (3, 0)

14. $x + 2y = 7$
(1, 3), (3, 2),
(5, 1), (7, 0)

15. $2xy = 8$
(1, 4), (2, 2),
(4, 1)

16. $x^2 = -y^2$
(0, 0)

Written Exercises

State whether each ordered pair is a solution of the given equation.

A

1. $5x + 2y = 23$
(3, 4), (7, −6)
yes   yes

2. $4m - 5n = 9$
(6, 7), (6, 3)
no   yes

3. $3a - 2b = 13$
(3, −2), (5, −1)
yes   no

4. $3a - 5b = 21$
(7, 0), (−2, −3)
yes   no

5. $2x + 3y = 13$
(5, 1), (11, −3)
yes   yes

6. $5x - 4y = 9$
(7, 6), (−3, −6)
no   yes

7. $3a - 4b = 11$
$\left(\frac{1}{3}, -\frac{5}{2}\right), \left(-\frac{5}{3}, -4\right)$
yes   yes

8. $3m - 2n = 6$
$(0, 3), \left(\frac{5}{3}, -\frac{1}{2}\right)$
no   yes

9. $x^2 - 3y^2 = 15$
(4, −1), (−4, 1)
no   no

10. $2x^2 + 3y^2 = 57$
(−3, 5), (4, −5)
no   no

11. $4st = t$
$\left(-\frac{1}{4}, -3\right), \left(\frac{1}{4}, 0\right)$
no   yes

12. $s^3 = 4s^2t$
$\left(-2, -\frac{1}{2}\right), \left(0, \frac{2}{3}\right)$
yes   yes

Solve each equation if x and y are whole numbers.

13. $2x + y = 6$ **14.** $5x + y = 7$ **15.** $3x + 2y = 8$ **16.** $2x + 5y = 10$

17. $3x + 7y = 7$ **18.** $x + 3y = 9$ **19.** $x + 2y = 9$ **20.** $3x + y = 7$

B

21. $xy = 4$ **22.** $xy = 12$ **23.** $3xy = 9$ **24.** $5xy = 30$

25. $xy + 7 = 23$ **26.** $xy + 6 = 12$ **27.** $2xy + 5 = 15$ **28.** $4xy + 8 = 36$

29. $(x + 2)y = 5$ **30.** $(x + 6)y = 7$ **31.** $y(4 - x) = 4$ **32.** $y(3 - x) = 6$

33. $xy = 4 - x$ **34.** $xy = 6 - x$ **35.** $xy + x = 9$ **36.** $xy + x = 12$

Introduction to Functions   **351**

Supplementary Materials

Study Guide   pp. 133–134
Computer Activity   23
Overhead Visual   B

5 small and 3 large posters, or 9 small and 2 large posters

37. Lisa bought some small posters costing $2 each and some large posters costing $8 each. If she spent $34, how many of each kind of poster did she buy? (There is more than one solution.)

38. Linda and Bill Gomez spent $100 for some spruce trees. Some were blue spruce priced at $20 each, and the rest were green spruce priced at $10 each. How many of each kind of spruce did the Gomezs buy? (There is more than one solution.) 2 blue and 6 green, or 3 blue and 4 green, or 4 blue and 2 green

39. Ed McDonald spent $280 for some baby pigs and some chickens. The pigs cost $40 each and the chickens $3 each. If Ed bought more than one pig, how many pigs and how many chickens did he buy? 4 pigs, 40 chickens

40. The perimeter of the figure at the right is 60. Find x and y if they represent positive integers. $x = 2, y = 3$

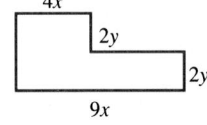

Solve for y.

C **41.** $\dfrac{2x - y}{2} = \dfrac{1 - y}{3}$ $y = 6x - 2$

42. $\dfrac{5y + x}{4} = \dfrac{3x - 2y}{3}$ $y = \dfrac{9x}{23}$

43. $\dfrac{1}{x} + \dfrac{1}{y} = \dfrac{1}{2}$ $y = \dfrac{2x}{x - 2}$

44. Let c and d be positive integers with $c < d$. What is the greatest value for c if $5c + 4d = 79$? 7

45. If a and b are positive two-digit integers, how many solutions are there of the equation $2a + 3b = 100$? 9 solutions: (35, 10), (32, 12), (29, 14), (26, 16), (23, 18), (20, 20), (17, 22), (14, 24), (11, 26)

Mixed Review Exercises

Write each number in scientific notation.

1. 308,000,000 3.08×10^8

2. 0.000437 4.37×10^{-4}

3. 119 million 1.19×10^8

4. 0.0000216 2.16×10^{-5}

5. 49,000 4.9×10^4

6. 56,201,000 5.6201×10^7

Simplify. Give answers in terms of positive exponents.

7. $\dfrac{3n^3}{6n}$ $\dfrac{n^2}{2}$

8. $(5x)^{-3}$ $\dfrac{1}{125x^3}$

9. $\dfrac{48x^4y^3}{16x^3y^2}$ $3xy$

10. $\dfrac{b^{-4}}{b^3}$ $\dfrac{1}{b^7}$

Computer Exercises

For students with some programming experience

Write a BASIC program that determines whether an ordered pair entered with an INPUT statement is a solution to a given equation. Run the program for the following equations with the given ordered pairs.

1. $3x - 2y = 1$; (3, 4), (4, 6) yes; no

2. $4x + y = 10$; $(-3, 2)$, $(5, -10)$ no; yes

3. $xy + y^2 = 6$; (1, 2), (6, 0) yes; no

4. $x^2 + y^2 = 25$; $(-4, -3)$, (0, 5) yes; yes

5. $x^2y + xy^2 = 0$; $(-1, -1)$, $(1, -1)$ no; yes

6. $x^2 + (xy)^2 = 45$; $(3, -2)$, (3, 2) yes; yes

352   *Chapter 8*

8-2 Points, Lines, and Their Graphs

Objective   To graph ordered pairs and linear equations in two variables.

You know how to graph a number as a point on a number line. You can graph, or **plot,** an ordered pair as a point in a "number plane." You can make a "number plane" as follows:

1. Draw a horizontal number line. This number line is called the **horizontal axis.**

2. Draw a second number line intersecting the first at right angles so that both number lines have the same zero point, or **origin** (*O*). The second number line is called the **vertical axis.**

3. Indicate the positive direction on each axis by an arrowhead. The positive direction is to the right on the horizontal axis and upward on the vertical axis.

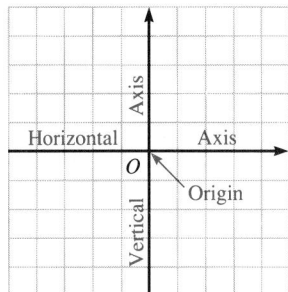

The horizontal axis is often labeled with an *x* and referred to as the **x-axis.** The vertical axis is often labeled with a *y* and referred to as the **y-axis.**

   The diagram at the right shows a point *A* that is the **graph of the ordered pair** (3, 2). Point *A* is located by moving 3 units to the right of the origin and 2 units up. The numbers 3 and 2 are called the **coordinates** of point *A*; 3 is the **x-coordinate,** or **abscissa,** of *A*, and 2 is the **y-coordinate,** or **ordinate,** of *A*. Although there is a difference between the ordered pair of numbers (3, 2) and the point *A*, it is customary to stress their association by referring to the point as *A*(3, 2).

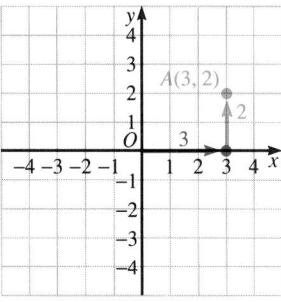

Example 1   Plot each point in a number plane.

   a. *B*(−2, 4)   **b.** *C*(4, −2)   **c.** *D*(−3, −2)

Solution

a.

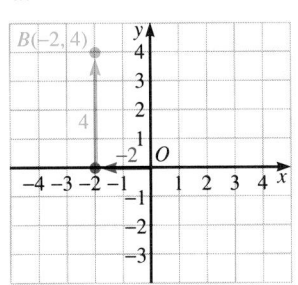

b.

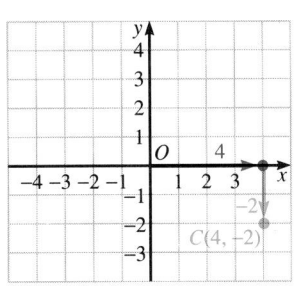

c.

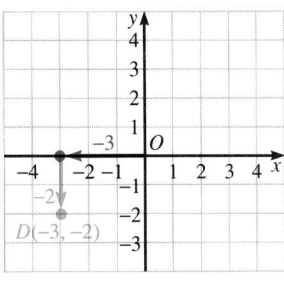

Introduction to Functions   **353**

Teaching Suggestions p. T118

Suggested Extensions p. T118

Warm-Up Exercises

Complete each sentence with the appropriate term.

1. Any value of a variable that makes an open sentence a true statement is called a __?__ of the sentence. solution

2. A pair of numbers for which the order of the numbers is important is called an __?__.
ordered pair

Motivating the Lesson

Tell students that the skills they use to locate a place on a map will be used in today's lesson.

Chalkboard Examples

1. Plot each point in a number plane: (1, 3), (−3, 4), (0, −2), (3, −3), (2, 0), and (−2, −1).

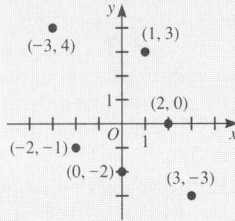

2. Graph *x* + 2*y* = 4 in a coordinate plane.
Let *y* = 0; *x* = 4: Sol. (4, 0)
Let *x* = 0; *y* = 2: Sol. (0, 2)
Another sol. is (−2, 3).

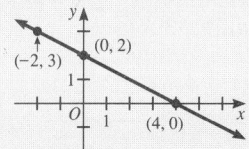

3. a. Graph $x = 4$ in a coordinate plane.

b. Graph $y = -2$ in a coordinate plane.

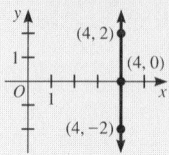

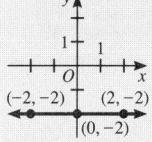

The x- and y-axes are also called **coordinate axes** and the number plane is often called a **coordinate plane.** The coordinate axes separate a coordinate plane into four **quadrants** as shown in the figure at the right. Points *on* the coordinate axes are not considered to be in any quadrant.

The **graph of an equation** in two variables consists of all the points that are the graphs of the solutions of the equation. For example, the equation $x + 2y = 6$ has the ordered pairs $(0, 3)$, $(2, 2)$, $(4, 1)$, $(6, 0)$, and $(-2, 4)$ as some of its solutions. These solutions are graphed at the left below. There are many other solutions, such as $(1, 2\frac{1}{2})$ and $(6.2, -0.1)$. The graphs of all the solutions lie on the straight line shown at the right below. This line is the graph of the equation $x + 2y = 6$.

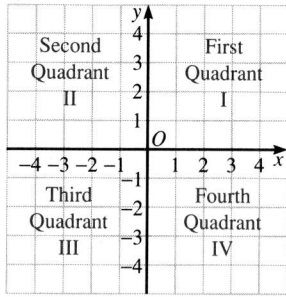

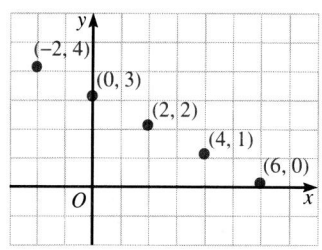

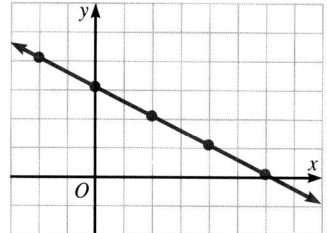

The equation $x + 2y = 6$ is called a **linear equation** because its graph is a line.

If you have a computer or a graphing calculator, you may wish to investigate the graphs of other equations of the form $ax + by = c$ described below.

All linear equations in the variables x and y can be written in the form

$$ax + by = c$$

where a, b, and c are real numbers with a and b not both zero. If a, b, and c are integers, the equation is said to be in **standard form.**

Linear equations in standard form	**Linear equations not in standard form**	**Nonlinear equations**
$2x - 5y = 7$	$\frac{1}{2}x + 4y = 12$	$x^2y + 3y = 4$
$4x + 9y = 0$	$y = 3x - 2$	$xy = 6$
$y = 3$	$x + y - 1 = x - y + 1$	$\frac{1}{x} + 3y = 1$

Since two points determine a line, you need to find only two solutions of a linear equation in order to graph it. However, it is a good idea to find a third solution as a check. The easiest solutions to find are those where the line crosses the x-axis ($y = 0$) and the y-axis ($x = 0$).

354   *Chapter 8*

Example 2 Graph $2x - 3y = 6$ in a coordinate plane.

Solution Let $y = 0$:

$2x - 3(0) = 6$

$2x = 6$

$x = 3$: *Solution* $(3, 0)$

Let $x = 0$:

$2(0) - 3y = 6$

$-3y = 6$

$y = -2$: *Solution* $(0, -2)$

A third solution, such as $(6, 2)$, can be used as a check.

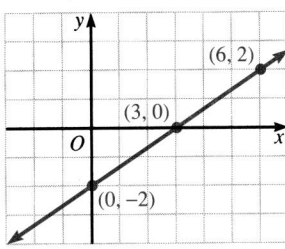

Example 3 **a.** Graph $x = -2$ in a coordinate plane.

b. Graph $y = 3$ in a coordinate plane.

Solution **a.** The equation $x = -2$ places no restriction on y.
All points with x-coordinate -2 are graphs of solutions.
The graph of $x = -2$ is a vertical line.

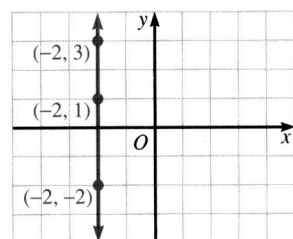

b. The equation $y = 3$ places no restriction on x.
All points with y-coordinate 3 are graphs of solutions.
The graph of $y = 3$ is a horizontal line.

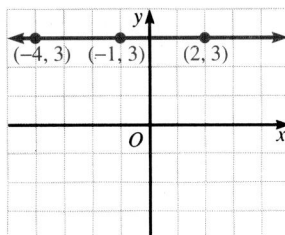

Introduction to Functions   **355**

(continued)

Check for Understanding

Here is a suggested use of the Oral Exercises to check students' understanding as you teach the lesson.

Oral Exs. 1–12: use after Example 1.

Oral Exs. 13–20: use after discussion of coordinate axes, coordinate plane and quadrants.

Oral Exs. 21–26: use after Example 3.

Guided Practice

Plot each of the given points in a coordinate plane.

1. $T(0, -7)$ **2.** $V(-4, 2)$

3. $Z\left(4\frac{1}{2}, -2\right)$

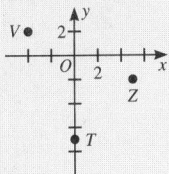

Graph each equation.

4. $x + y = 0$

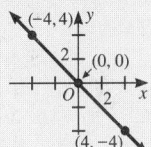

5. $2x + y = 10$

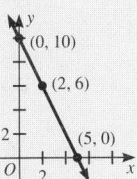

6. $x = -4$

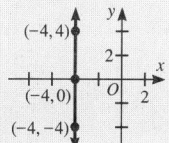

7. $y = 1$

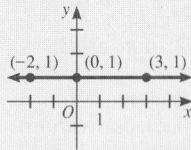

Summarizing the Lesson

Draw a coordinate grid on the chalkboard. Review the key vocabulary of the lesson by having students identify the *x*- and *y*-axes, the origin, the different quadrants, and so on.

Suggested Assignments

357/1–37 odd, 45
S 358/Mixed Review

Average
357/1–39 odd, 45, 46
S 358/Mixed Review

Maximum
357/1–35 odd, 43–48
S 358/Mixed Review

Supplementary Materials

Study Guide   pp. 135–136
Practice Master   46
Resource Book   p. 114
Overhead Visual   A

Additional Answers
Written Exercises

1–12.

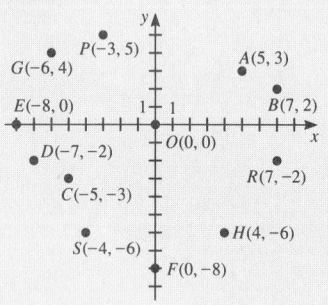

Oral Exercises

Exercises 1–20 refer to the diagram below.

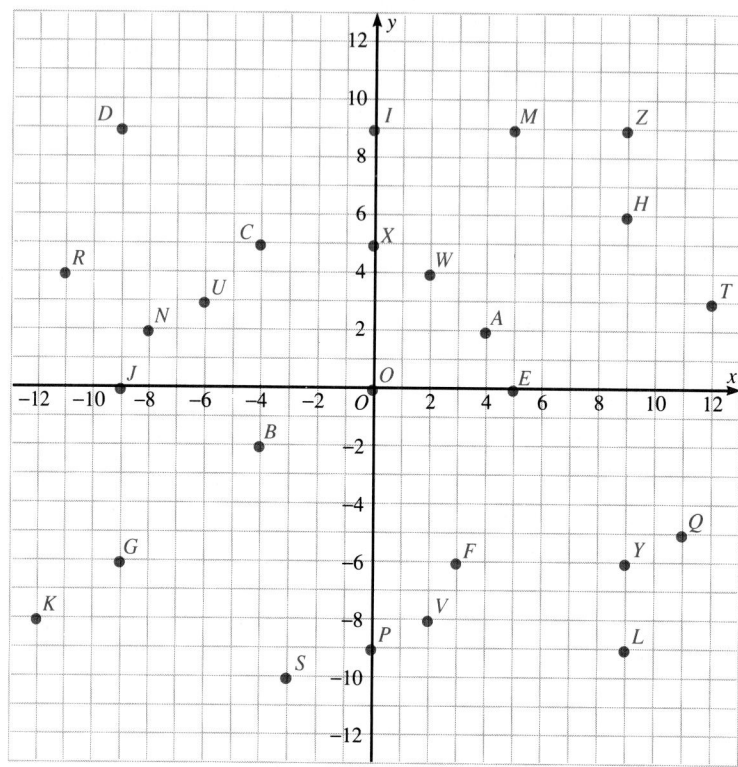

Name the point that is the graph of each ordered pair.

1. $(2, 4)$ W   **2.** $(4, 2)$ A   **3.** $(-6, 3)$ U   **4.** $(3, -6)$ F

5. $(9, 6)$ H   **6.** $(9, -6)$ Y   **7.** $(0, -9)$ P   **8.** $(-9, 0)$ J

9. $(0, 9)$ I   **10.** $(11, -5)$ Q   **11.** $(-11, 4)$ R   **12.** $(-3, -10)$ S

Give the coordinates and the quadrant (if any) of each point.

13. M (5, 9); I   **14.** L (9, −9); IV   **15.** D (−9, 9); II   **16.** B (−4, −2); III

17. E (5, 0)   **18.** V (2, −8); IV   **19.** G (−9, −6); III   **20.** X (0, 5)

Describe the graphs of the following equations.

21. $x = 2$ vert. line through (2, 0)   **22.** $x = -1$ vert. line through (−1, 0)   **23.** $x = 0$ y-axis

24. $y = -3$ horiz. line through (0, −3)   **25.** $y = 4$ horiz. line through (0, 4)   **26.** $y = 0$ x-axis

Give the coordinates of the points where the graph of each equation crosses the x-axis and the y-axis.

27. $2x + y = 10$ (5, 0); (0, 10) **28.** $5x - y = 25$ (5, 0); (0, −25) **29.** $6x + 4y = 24$ (4, 0); (0, 6)

Classify each equation as a linear equation in standard form, a linear equation not in standard form, or a nonlinear equation.

linear not in standard form

linear in standard form
30. $2x + 5y = 2$ **31.** $\dfrac{2}{x} + \dfrac{3}{y} = 3$ nonlinear   **32.** $\dfrac{x}{4} + \dfrac{y}{7} = 1$

33. $x^2 + y^2 = 16$ nonlinear   **34.** $x + y = x - y$ **35.** $xy = 9$ nonlinear
                        linear not in standard form

Written Exercises

Plot each of the given points in a coordinate plane.

 A

1. $A(5, 3)$ **2.** $B(7, 2)$ **3.** $C(-5, -3)$ **4.** $D(-7, -2)$

5. $E(-8, 0)$ **6.** $F(0, -8)$ **7.** $G(-6, 4)$ **8.** $H(4, -6)$

9. $O(0, 0)$ **10.** $P(-3, 5)$ **11.** $R(7, -2)$ **12.** $S(-4, -6)$

Refer to the diagram on page 356. Name the point(s) described.

13. The point on the positive x-axis E

14. The point on the negative y-axis P

15. The points on the vertical line through point Z Z, H, Y, L

16. The points on the horizontal line through point Y G, F, Y

17. The x-coordinate is zero. I, X, O, P

18. The y-coordinate is zero. J, O, E

19. The points on the axes 9 units from the origin J, I, P

20. The points on the axes 5 units from the origin X, E

21. The points having equal x- and y-coordinates Z, O

22. The points having opposite x- and y-coordinates D, L, O

23. The point in Quadrant IV nearest the y-axis V

24. The point in Quadrant III nearest the x-axis B

Graph each equation. You may wish to verify your graphs on a computer or a graphing calculator.

25. $x - y = 10$ **26.** $x + y = 6$ **27.** $y = 2x + 5$ **28.** $y = -2x + 4$

29. $2x + y = 6$ **30.** $x - 3y = 9$ **31.** $4x - 3y = 12$ **32.** $2x + 5y = 10$

33. $x = 4$ **34.** $y = 2$ **35.** $y = -3$ **36.** $x = -6$

B **37.** $\dfrac{x}{2} = \dfrac{y}{3}$ **38.** $\dfrac{x}{4} + y = 0$ **39.** $\dfrac{1}{3}x + \dfrac{1}{6}y = 3$ **40.** $\dfrac{y}{4} - \dfrac{x}{3} = \dfrac{1}{2}$

41. $\dfrac{x}{3} + \dfrac{y}{2} = 6$ **42.** $\dfrac{x}{2} + \dfrac{y}{2} = 12$ **43.** $\dfrac{1}{5}x + \dfrac{1}{4}y = 2$ **44.** $\dfrac{x - y}{2} = \dfrac{x + y}{4}$

Introduction to Functions   **357**

26.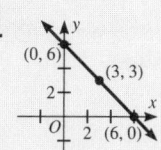

28.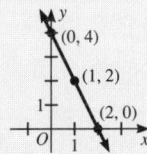

30.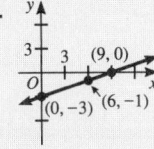

32.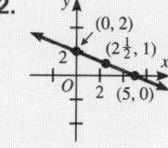

34.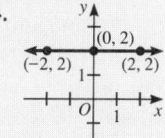

36.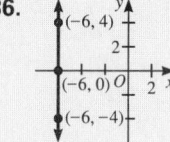

38.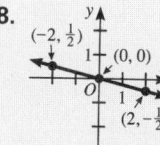

40.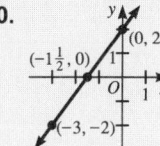

(continued)

42.

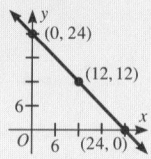

44.

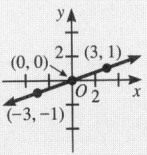

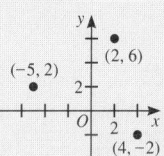
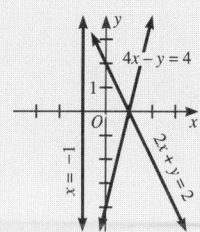
Plot the points *A*, *B*, *C*, and *D*. Then connect *A* to *B*, *B* to *C*, *C* to *D*, and *D* to *A*. Is the resulting figure best described as a square, a rectangle, a parallelogram, or a trapezoid?

                             parallelogram   square

45. $A(-3, -4)$, $B(5, -2)$, $C(6, 4)$, $D(-2, 2)$ **46.** $A(-2, 0)$, $B(0, -4)$, $C(4, -2)$, $D(2, 2)$

47. $A(-4, -1)$, $B(-6, 5)$, $C(3, 8)$, $D(5, 2)$ **48.** $A(-1, 4)$, $B(0, 1)$, $C(4, -1)$, $D(7, 0)$

                   rectangle   trapezoid

Mixed Review Exercises

State whether each ordered pair is a solution of the given equation.

1. $2x + y = 5$ **2.** $3a + 2b = 9$ **3.** $x + 4y = 13$ **4.** $5m + 3n = 9$

   (5, −5), (2, −1)   (3,0), $\left(2, \dfrac{3}{2}\right)$ (3, 2), (−3, 4)   (4, −3), (3, −2)

   yes   no   yes   yes   no   yes   no   yes

Solve.

5. $x^2 + 3x + 2 = 0$ {−1, −2}   **6.** $-z + 13 = 2$ {11}   **7.** $4t^2 - 20t + 24 = 0$ {2, 3}

8. $\dfrac{14 - 3y}{2} = 2$ $\left\{\dfrac{10}{3}\right\}$ **9.** $6x + 12 = 3x - 15$ {−9}   **10.** $12 = \dfrac{4}{5}(n)$ {15}

Self-Test 1

Vocabulary   solution (p. 349)   *x*-coordinate (p. 353)

                        ordered pair (p. 349)   abscissa (p. 353)

                        plot (p. 353)   *y*-coordinate (p. 353)

                        horizontal axis (p. 353)   ordinate (p. 353)

                        origin (p. 353)   coordinate axes (p. 354)

                        vertical axis (p. 353)   coordinate plane (p. 354)

                        x-axis (p. 353)   quadrants (p. 354)

                        y-axis (p. 353)   graph of an equation (p. 354)

                        graph of an ordered pair (p. 353)   linear equation (p. 354)

                        coordinates (p. 353)   standard form (p. 354)

State whether each ordered pair is a solution of the given equation.

1. $2x + 4y = 12$ **2.** $3x + 5y = 30$ **Obj. 8-1, p. 349**

   (2, 2), $\left(7, \dfrac{1}{2}\right)$ (3, 5), (10, 0)

   yes   no   no   yes

Solve each equation if *x* and *y* are whole numbers.

3. $2x + 3y = 12$ (0, 4), (3, 2), (6, 0)   **4.** $5y + 2x = 20$ (0, 4), (5, 2), (10, 0)

(Self-Test continues on next page.)

358   *Chapter 8*

Plot each of the given points in a coordinate plane.

5. $(3, 7)$ **6.** $(-2, 4)$ **7.** $(-5, -2)$ Obj. 8-2, p. 353

Graph the equation.

8. $y = -3$ **9.** $x + y = 8$ **10.** $2x + 3y = 6$

Check your answers with those at the back of the book.

 ## Computer Key-In

The following program will find the intercepts where a linear equation $Px + Qy = R$ crosses the x-axis and the y-axis when P, Q, and R are entered with an INPUT statement. The program will report if the graph does not cross either the x-axis or the y-axis.

```
10 PRINT "INPUT P, Q, R";
20 INPUT P, Q, R
30 PRINT
40 IF P< >0 THEN 70
50 PRINT "THE GRAPH DOES NOT CROSS THE X-AXIS."
60 GOTO 120
70 IF Q< >0 THEN 110
80 PRINT "THE GRAPH DOES NOT CROSS THE Y-AXIS."
90 PRINT "THE GRAPH CROSSES THE X-AXIS AT" ; R/P
100 GOTO 130
110 PRINT "THE GRAPH CROSSES THE X-AXIS AT" ; R/P
120 PRINT "THE GRAPH CROSSES THE Y-AXIS AT" ; R/Q
130 END
```

Exercises

RUN the program for the following linear equations.

1. $2x - 3y = 6$ x-axis at 3, y-axis at −2

2. $8x + y = 12$ x-axis at 1.5, y-axis at 12

3. $7x + 0y = -14$ x-axis at −2, does not cross y-axis

4. $0x - 5y = 2$ does not cross x-axis, y-axis at −0.4

5. $3x + 3y = 8$ x-axis at 2.6666667, y-axis at 2.6666667

6. $6x - 4y = 9$ x-axis at 1.5, y-axis at −2.25

Historical Note / Coordinates

The ancient Egyptians and Romans used the idea of coordinates in land surveying. The Egyptian hieroglyphic for a surveyed district was a grid.

In the seventeenth century two French mathematicians, Pierre de Fermat and René Descartes, used a version of coordinates in their work. In fact, the coordinate plane described on pages 353 and 354 is sometimes called a rectangular Cartesian coordinate plane in honor of Descartes.

Introduction to Functions   **359**

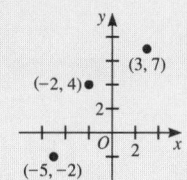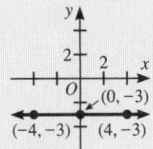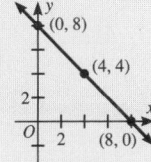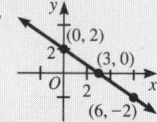

Warm-Up Exercises

Evaluate when $y = 1$ and $x = -1$.

1. $\dfrac{5-y}{2-x}$ $\dfrac{4}{3}$

2. $\dfrac{-6-y}{-3-x}$ $\dfrac{7}{2}$

3. $\dfrac{y-4}{x-2}$ 1

4. $\dfrac{y-(-4)}{x-(-2)}$ 5

5. $\dfrac{1-y}{x-1}$ 0

Motivating the Lesson

Point out that as the steepness of a hill or staircase increases, more energy is required during the climb. A number can denote the steepness of a line; this number is called the slope of the line, the topic of today's lesson.

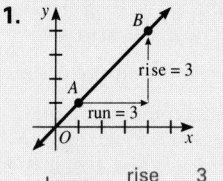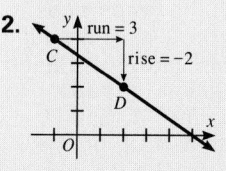
Linear Equations

8-3 Slope of a Line

Objective   To find the slope of a line.

You can describe the steepness, or *slope,* of an airplane's flight path shortly after takeoff by giving the ratio of its vertical *rise* to its horizontal *run,* as shown below.

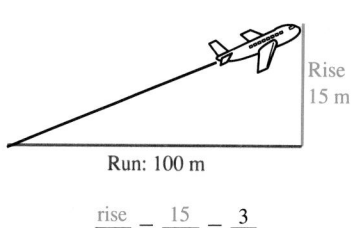

$$\frac{\text{rise}}{\text{run}} = \frac{15}{100} = \frac{3}{20}$$

To describe the slope of a straight line, first choose any two points on the line. Then count the units in the rise and the units in the run from one point to the other. The ratio of the rise to the run is the slope of the line.

Example 1

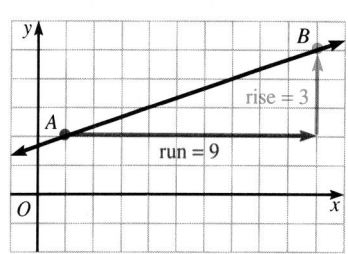

$\text{slope} = \dfrac{\text{rise}}{\text{run}} = \dfrac{3}{9} = \dfrac{1}{3}$

Example 2

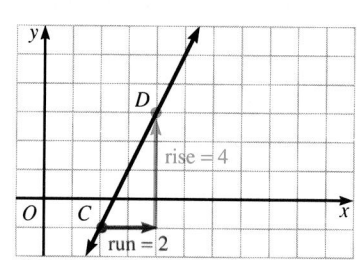

$\text{slope} = \dfrac{\text{rise}}{\text{run}} = \dfrac{4}{2} = 2$

Example 1 and Example 2 show lines that have a *positive* slope. Lines that rise more steeply as you move from left to right have a greater slope. Example 3 and Example 4 on the next page show lines that fall as you move from left to right. The rise of these lines is *negative,* and so is their slope.

360   *Chapter 8*

Example 3

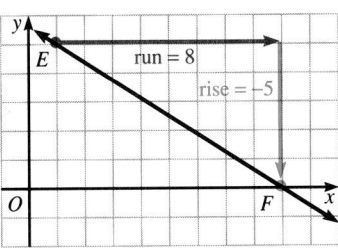

$$\text{slope} = \frac{\text{rise}}{\text{run}} = \frac{-5}{8} = -\frac{5}{8}$$

Example 4

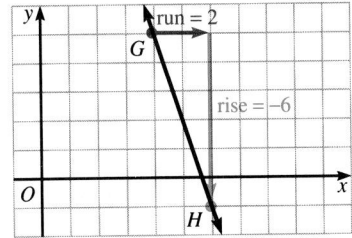

$$\text{slope} = \frac{\text{rise}}{\text{run}} = \frac{-6}{2} = -3$$

In Example 4, notice that each horizontal change of 1 unit produces a negative change of 3 units in the vertical direction. There is a constant change in y per unit change in x.

The slope of a line can be determined by using the coordinates of a pair of points that lie on the line.

$$\mathbf{slope} = \frac{\text{rise}}{\text{run}} = \frac{\text{vertical change}}{\text{horizontal change}} = \frac{\text{difference between } y\text{-coordinates}}{\text{difference between } x\text{-coordinates}}$$

Suppose that

(x_1, y_1), read "x sub 1, y sub 1," and

(x_2, y_2), read "x sub 2, y sub 2,"

are any two different points on a line. We have the following *slope formula*.

$$\mathbf{slope} = \frac{y_2 - y_1}{x_2 - x_1} \quad (x_1 \neq x_2)$$

Example 5 Find the slope of the line through the points $(-2, 3)$ and $(4, 8)$.

Solution 1 $\quad \text{slope} = \dfrac{8 - 3}{4 - (-2)} = \dfrac{5}{6}$

Solution 2 $\quad \text{slope} = \dfrac{3 - 8}{-2 - 4} = \dfrac{-5}{-6} = \dfrac{5}{6}$

Example 5 illustrates the fact that when you find the slope of a line, the order in which you consider the points is not important. However, you *must use the same order* for finding both the difference between the y-coordinates and the difference between the x-coordinates. If you don't, your result will be the opposite of the slope.

Introduction to Functions **361**

---

3. Find the slope of the line through the points $(1, 6)$ and $(3, -2)$.
   slope $= \dfrac{-2 - 6}{3 - 1} = \dfrac{-8}{2} = -4$

4. Find the slope of the line with equation
   $2x - 3y = 18$.
   Find two points on the line, say $(0, -6)$ and $(9, 0)$. The slope is
   $\dfrac{0 - (-6)}{9 - 0} = \dfrac{6}{9} = \dfrac{2}{3}$.

5. Find the slope of the line $x = -5$.
   Two points on the line are $(-5, 0)$ and $(-5, 1)$.
   slope $= \dfrac{1 - 0}{-5 - (-5)} = \dfrac{1}{0}$
   (undefined)
   $\therefore$ the line has no slope.

Check for Understanding

Here is a suggested use of the Oral Exercises to check students' understanding as you teach the lesson.
Oral Exs. 1, 2, 5–8: use after Example 4.
Oral Exs. 3, 4, 9, 10: use after Example 7.

Common Errors

Perhaps because x-coordinates are usually written first and considered first in graphing points, some students may incorrectly think of the slope as $\dfrac{x_2 - x_1}{y_2 - y_1}$. In reteaching, point out that "rise" sounds like "y's" to help these students remember that the vertical change, or numerator of the slope ratio, is the difference of the y-coordinates.

Guided Practice

Find the slope of the line through the given points.

1. $(1, 2)$, $(-3, -4)$ $\frac{3}{2}$

2. $(7, -6)$, $(-5, 2)$ $-\frac{2}{3}$

Find the slope of each line. If the line has no slope, say so.

3. $6x - 2y = 14$ 3

4. $3x + 4y = 7$ $-\frac{3}{4}$

5. $y + 5 = -3$ 0

Through the given point, draw a line with the given slope.

6. $K(1, 1)$; slope -1

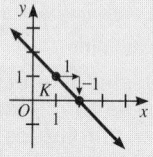

Summarizing the Lesson

Remind students that the steepness of a nonvertical line is measured by a real number. The slope can be found from the graph, two known points, or the equation.

Suggested Assignments

Minimum
  363/1–33 odd, 37
S 365/Mixed Review
R 358/Self-Test 1

Average
  363/1–39 odd
S 365/Mixed Review
R 358/Self-Test 1

Maximum
  363/1–35 odd, 38, 40, 42
S 365/Mixed Review
R 358/Self-Test 1

Example 6 Find the slope of the line with equation $2x + 4y = 12$.

Solution
1. Find any two points on the line.
   If $x = 0$: $4y = 12$, so $y = 3$.
   If $y = 0$: $2x = 12$, so $x = 6$.
   Two points: $(0, 3)$ and $(6, 0)$

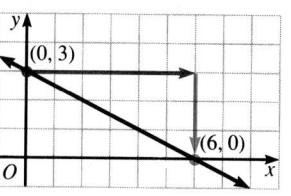

2. slope $= \frac{y_2 - y_1}{x_2 - x_1}$

   $= \frac{0 - 3}{6 - 0} = -\frac{1}{2}$ **Answer**

Note that *any* two points of a line can be used to calculate its slope. For instance, in Example 6 we could have used the points $(2, 2)$ and $(4, 1)$, and the slope would still be $-\frac{1}{2}$.

A basic property of a straight line is that its slope is constant.

Example 7 Find the slope of each line.
  a. $y = 3$ **b.** $x = 4$

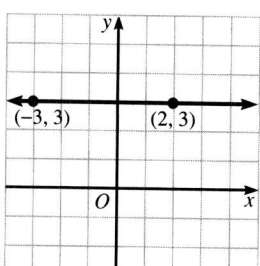

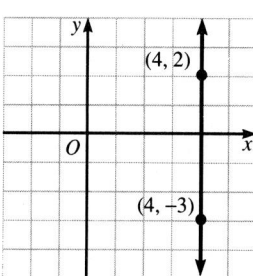

Solution   **a.** slope $= \frac{3 - 3}{-3 - 2} = \frac{0}{-5} = 0$ **b.** slope $= \frac{-3 - 2}{4 - 4} = \frac{-5}{0}$ (undefined)

∴ the slope is 0. **Answer**   ∴ the line has no slope. **Answer**

Example 7 shows the following properties about slopes.

The slope of every horizontal line is 0.
A vertical line has no slope.

Oral Exercises

Use the figure at the right.

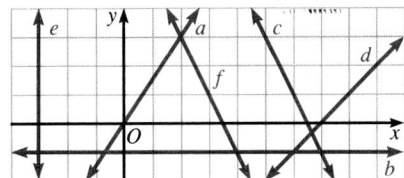

1. Which lines have positive slope? a, d
2. Which lines have negative slope? c, f
3. Which line has zero slope? b
4. Which line has no slope? e

Find the slope of each line.

5. $\frac{3}{4}$
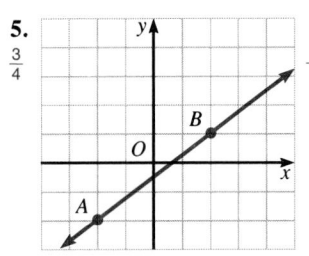

6. $-\frac{6}{5}$
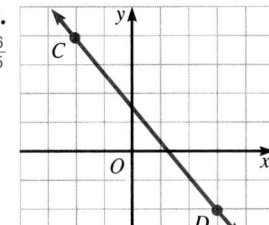

7. $\frac{1}{5}$
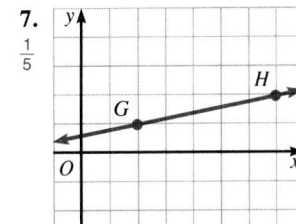

8. $-\frac{5}{2}$
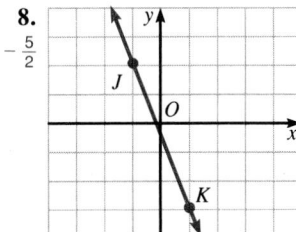

9. 0
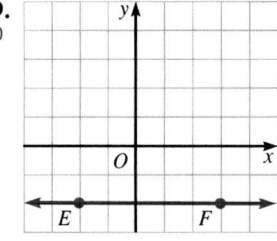

10.
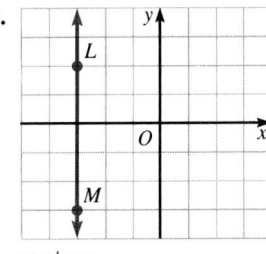
no slope

Written Exercises

Find the slope of the line through the given points.

A

1. $(8, 4), (6, 5) -\frac{1}{2}$ **2.** $(-4, 2), (-6, 5) -\frac{3}{2}$ **3.** $(-6, 3), (-4, 5)$ 1

4. $(0, 7), (2, 3)$ −2   **5.** $(-5, 3), (6, 5) \frac{2}{11}$ **6.** $(-4, 3), (4, 9) \frac{3}{4}$

7. $(-2, -3), (0, -1)$ 1   **8.** $(6, 3), (2, 0) \frac{3}{4}$ **9.** $(4, 8), (1, 3) \frac{5}{3}$

10. $(-8, -7), (-6, -4) \frac{3}{2}$ **11.** $(0, -3), (3, -1) \frac{2}{3}$ **12.** $(-2, 7), (-5, -7) \frac{14}{3}$

Find the slope of each line. If the line has no slope, say so.

13. $y = 2x + 1$ 2   **14.** $y = 3x - 2$ 3   **15.** $y = 8 - 2x$ −2   **16.** $y = 12 - 4x$ −4

17. $3x + 2y = 6 -\frac{3}{2}$ **18.** $2x + 5y = 10 -\frac{2}{5}$ **19.** $3x - 5y = 10 \frac{3}{5}$ **20.** $x - 3y = 9 \frac{1}{3}$

21. $y = 3$ 0   **22.** $y + 4 = 0$ 0   **23.** $x = 2$ no slope   **24.** $3x - 5 = 0$ no slope

Introduction to Functions   **363**

Supplementary Materials
Study Guide   pp. 137–138
Resource Book   p. 115
Overhead Visual   7

25.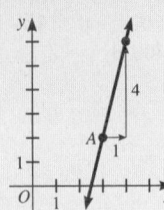

26.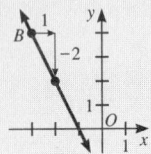

27.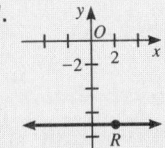

28.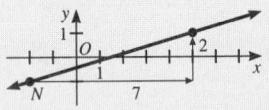

29.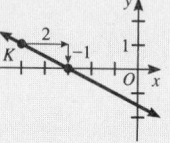

30.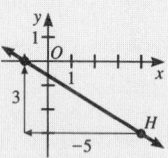

(continued)

Through the given point, draw a line with the given slope.

Sample $P(-2, 1)$; slope -3

Solution   1. Plot point P.

2. Write the slope as $\dfrac{-3}{1}$.

From P, measure 1 unit to the right and 3 units down to locate a second point, T. Draw the line through P and T.

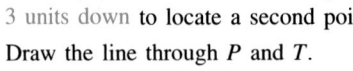

25. $A(3, 2)$; slope 4

26. $B(-3, 4)$; slope -2

27. $R(2, -7)$; slope 0

28. $N(-2, -1)$; slope $\dfrac{2}{7}$

29. $K(-5, 1)$; slope $-\dfrac{1}{2}$

30. $H(4, -3)$; slope $-\dfrac{3}{5}$

Points that lie on the same line are said to be *collinear*. Determine whether the given points are collinear.

Sample   **a.** $(3, 5)$, $(4, 7)$, and $(7, 13)$

b. $(8, 9)$, $(5, 3)$, and $(2, -2)$

Solution   1. Make a table of the coordinates in order of increasing x-coordinates.

2. Find the changes in the x-coordinates and y-coordinates as you move from one point to the next.

3. If the ratio $\dfrac{\text{vertical change}}{\text{horizontal change}}$ is constant, the points are collinear. Otherwise, they are not.

a.

x	y
3	5
4	7
7	13

$1\{\quad\}2$
$3\{\quad\}6$

$$\frac{2}{1} = \frac{6}{3}$$

$\therefore$ the points are collinear.

b.

x	y
2	-2
5	3
8	9

$3\{\quad\}5$
$3\{\quad\}6$

$$\frac{5}{3} \neq \frac{6}{3}$$

$\therefore$ the points are not collinear.

B **31.** $(1, 4)$, $(3, 0)$, $(5, -4)$ collinear

32. $(8, 1)$, $(6, 5)$, $(4, 8)$ not collinear

33. $(-5, 9)$, $(-1, 1)$, $(1, -4)$ not collinear

34. $(-3, 7)$, $(0, 5)$, $(6, 1)$ collinear

35. $(0, -1)$, $(1, -2)$, $(2, -4)$, $(-1, 0)$ not collinear

36. $(1, -1)$, $(-1, 2)$, $(-3, 5)$, $(-5, 8)$ collinear

37. The vertices of a triangle are $A(-4, 6)$, $B(5, 6)$, and $C(-4, -2)$. Find the slope of each side of the triangle. $\overline{AB}$, 0; $\overline{AC}$, no slope; $\overline{BC}$, $\frac{8}{9}$

38. The vertices of a rectangle are $M(-2, -3)$, $N(3, 2)$, $P(10, -5)$, and $Q(5, -10)$. Find the slope of each side of the rectangle. $\overline{NP}$ and $\overline{MQ}$, -1; $\overline{MN}$ and $\overline{PQ}$, 1

39. Determine the slope of the line through the points $(4, 6)$ and $(0, 4)$. Find the value of y if $(8, y)$ lies on this line. $\frac{1}{2}$; 8

40. The slope of a line through the point $(1, 3)$ is 1.5. If the point $(-3, y)$ lies on the line, find the value of y. -3

C 41. The vertices of a square are $A(3, 5)$, $B(11, 3)$, $C(9, -5)$, and $D(1, -3)$. Use the idea of slope to show that the point $M(6, 0)$ lies on the diagonal joining A and C, and on the diagonal joining B and D.

42. The vertices of a right triangle are $P(-4, 2)$, $Q(-4, -6)$, and $R(6, -6)$. Use the idea of slope to show that $S(1, -2)$ lies on one of the sides of the triangle.

41. The slopes of $\overline{AC}$ and $\overline{AM}$ are both $-\frac{5}{3}$; thus M lies on $\overline{AC}$. The slopes of $\overline{DB}$ and $\overline{DM}$ are both $\frac{3}{5}$; thus M lies on $\overline{DB}$.

42. $\overline{PQ}$ has no slope; the slope of $\overline{QR} = 0$ and the slope of $\overline{PR} = -\frac{4}{5}$. Since the slope of $\overline{SP} = -\frac{4}{5}$, S lies on $\overline{PR}$.

Mixed Review Exercises

Solve.

1. $\frac{x + 3}{3} + \frac{x}{2} = 0$ $\left\{-\frac{6}{5}\right\}$

2. $-5 = \frac{9b}{4}$ $\left\{-\frac{20}{9}\right\}$

3. $\frac{3 + z}{2z} = \frac{3}{z}$ {3}

4. $-5(y + 3) = 30$ {-9}

5. $|z| = 1.7$ {-1.7, 1.7}

6. $3m(m - 5) = 0$ {0, 5}

Evaluate if $x = 2$, $y = 1$, $a = -3$, and $b = 4$.

7. $\frac{a + 4b}{2a - b}$ $-\frac{13}{10}$

8. $5(x + 2y)$ 20

9. $\frac{1}{3}(4x + y)$ 3

10. $(xy^2)^2$ 4

11. $(3a - 2b) + 7$ -10

12. $(2y^3)^3$ 8

Calculator Key-In

You can use a calculator to find the slope of a straight line through two given points (x_1, y_1) and (x_2, y_2).

1. First enter $x_2 - x_1$ and store the result in memory.
2. Then enter $y_2 - y_1$ and divide the result by the value stored in memory.

The result of the division in Step 2 is the slope.

Find the slope of the line through the given points.

1. $(2, 0)$, $(3, 7)$ 7

2. $(3, 2.8)$, $(2.22, -5)$ 10

3. $(-0.8, 5.7)$, $(3.2, -2)$ -1.925

4. $(3, 2.5)$, $(6.2, 7)$ 1.40625

5. $(-1, -2)$, $(-5, -6)$ 1

6. $(3, 4.4)$, $(-1.5, 7.1)$ -0.6

Using a Calculator

Remind students who use this calculator method that slopes that are fractions will be given in decimal form. If they try to calculate the slope of a vertical line, their calculators will probably display an error message.

Warm-Up Exercises

Solve each equation for y in terms of x. Find the value for y if $x = 0$.

1. $2y = 4x - 10$
   $y = 2x - 5$; $y = -5$
2. $3x + y = 43$
   $y = -3x + 43$; $y = 43$
3. $4y - 7 = 2x + 9$
   $y = \frac{1}{2}x + 4$; $y = 4$

Motivating the Lesson

When a linear equation is solved for y in terms of x, it is easy to determine the slope of its graph and a special point on its graph. Tell students that this information will enable them to draw the graph quickly without having to make a table of ordered pairs.

Chalkboard Examples

1. Find the slope and y-intercept of $y = -2x + \frac{1}{2}$.

   $m = -2$ and $b = \frac{1}{2}$

   $\therefore$ the slope is -2 and the y-intercept is $\frac{1}{2}$.

2. Use only the slope and y-intercept to graph $y = x - 3$. Slope is 1; y-int. is -3. Plot $(0, -3)$. Move 1 unit to the right and one unit up to locate a second point.

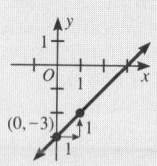

8-4 The Slope-Intercept Form of a Linear Equation

Objective   To use the slope-intercept form of a linear equation.

The points with coordinates $(-2, -4)$, $(-1, -2)$, $(0, 0)$, $(1, 2)$, and $(2, 4)$ are on the graph of the linear equation

$$y = 2x.$$

The graph, shown at the right, is the straight line that has slope $\frac{2}{1}$, or 2, and that passes through the origin.

The graph

$$y = -\frac{1}{3}x,$$

also shown at the right, is a line that has slope $-\frac{1}{3}$ and that passes through the origin.

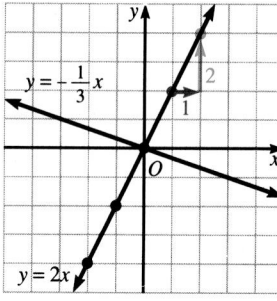

For every real number m, the graph of the equation

$$y = mx$$

is the line that has slope m and passes through the origin.

The graphs of the linear equations $y = 2x$ and $y = 2x + 4$ are shown at the right. The lines have the same slope, but they cross the y-axis at different points. The y-coordinate of a point where a graph crosses the y-axis is called the **y-intercept** of the graph.

To determine the y-intercept of a line, replace x with 0 in the equation of the line:

$y = 2x$	$y = 2x + 4$
$y = 2(0) = 0$	$y = 2(0) + 4 = 4$
y-intercept: 0	y-intercept: 4

If you write $y = 2x$ as $y = 2x + 0$, you can see that the constant term of each equation is the y-intercept of each graph:

$$y = 2x + 0 \qquad\qquad y = 2x + 4$$

For all real numbers m and b, the graph of the equation

$$y = mx + b$$

is the line whose slope is m and whose y-intercept is b.

This is called the **slope-intercept form** of an equation of a line.

366   *Chapter 8*

Example 1 Find the slope and y-intercept of $y = \frac{3}{5}x + 2$.

Solution For $y = \frac{3}{5}x + 2$, we have $m = \frac{3}{5}$ and $b = 2$.

∴ the slope is $\frac{3}{5}$ and the y-intercept is 2. *Answer*

Example 2 Use only the slope and y-intercept to graph $y = -\frac{3}{4}x + 6$.

Solution The slope is $-\frac{3}{4}$. The y-intercept is 6.

Since the y-intercept is 6, plot $(0, 6)$.

Since the slope is $-\frac{3}{4}$, move 4 units to the
right of $(0, 6)$ and 3 units down to locate a
second point.
Draw the line through the two points.

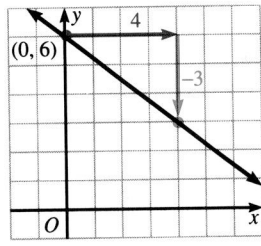

Example 3 Use only the slope and y-intercept to graph $2x - 5y = 10$.

Solution Solve for y to transform the equation into the form $y = mx + b$.

$$2x - 5y = 10$$
$$-5y = -2x + 10$$
$$y = \frac{2}{5}x - 2$$

The slope is $\frac{2}{5}$. The y-intercept is -2.

Since the y-intercept is -2, plot $(0, -2)$.

Since the slope is $\frac{2}{5}$, move 5 units to the
right of $(0, -2)$ and 2 units up to locate a
second point.
Draw the line through the two points.

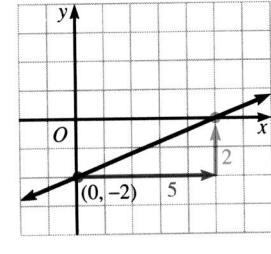

If you have a computer or a graphing calculator, you can use it to investigate the relationships among the graphs of equations that have the same slope,
but different y-intercepts.

Lines in the same plane that do not intersect are **parallel.** The following
relationships exist between parallel lines and their slopes.

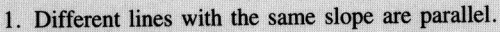

1. Different lines with the same slope are parallel.

2. Parallel lines that are not vertical have the same slope.

Introduction to Functions **367**

---

3. Use only the slope and
   y-intercept to graph $x + 2y = 6$.
   $$x + 2y = 6$$
   $$2y = -x + 6$$
   $$y = -\frac{1}{2}x + 3$$

   The slope is $-\frac{1}{2}$ and the
   y-intercept is 3.

   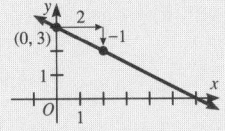

4. Show that the lines
   whose equations are
   $2x - y = 0$ and $2x - y = 4$
   are parallel.
   Write each equation in
   slope-intercept form:
   $y = 2x$ and $y = 2x - 4$.
   Since both lines have the
   same slope and *different*
   y-intercepts, the lines
   are parallel.

Check for Understanding

Here is a suggested use of
the Oral Exercises as you
teach the lesson.
Oral Exs. 1–6: use after
  Example 1.
Oral Exs. 7–12: use after
  Example 3.

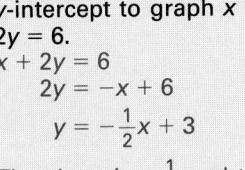

**Using a Computer or a
Graphing Calculator**

You may want to have stu-
dents discover for them-
selves the relationship between lines with the same
slope by using a computer
or a graphing calculator to
graph $y = 2x + b$ for various
values of b such as -3, -2,
$-\frac{1}{2}$, 0, $\frac{1}{2}$, 2, and 3.

Support Materials
  Disk for Algebra
    Menu Item: Line Plotter
Resource Book p. 206

Find the slope and *y*-intercept of each line.

1. $y = -\frac{2}{5}x - 5$ $-\frac{2}{5};\ -5$

2. $y = 4 - x$ $-1;\ 4$

3. $y = 2$ $0;\ 2$

Use only the slope and *y*-intercept to graph each equation.

4. $y = \frac{3}{2}x - 4$

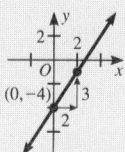

5. $3x + y = 2$

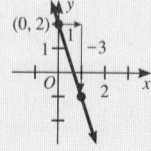

Common Errors

Some students will think that the coefficient of *x* is the slope of the graph of a linear equation when the equation is in standard form. In reteaching, point out that $y = mx + b$ means that the coefficient of *y* must be 1.

Using a Computer or a Graphing Calculator

You might suggest that students use a computer or a graphing calculator to verify graphs in Exs. 13–30.

Example 4 Show that the lines whose equations are $2x + y = 8$ and $2x + y = 6$ are parallel.

Solution 1. Write each equation in slope-intercept form:

$$y = -2x + 8 \qquad\qquad y = -2x + 6$$

2. Find the slope and *y*-intercept of each line.

For $y = -2x + 8$:	For $y = -2x + 6$:
slope = -2	slope = -2
y-intercept = 8	*y*-intercept = 6

Since both lines have the *same* slope and *different* *y*-intercepts, they're parallel.

Oral Exercises

State the slope and *y*-intercept of each line.

1. $y = 3x + 7$ 3; 7 **2.** $y = -2x - 1$ -2; -1 **3.** $y = \frac{1}{2}x + 4$ $\frac{1}{2}$; 4 **4.** $y = \frac{2}{3}x - 5$ $\frac{2}{3}$; -5

5. $y = 5x$ 5; 0 **6.** $y = -3x$ -3; 0 **7.** $y - 6x = 4$ 6; 4 **8.** $y - 2x = 7$ 2; 7

9. $3x + y = 8$ -3; 8 **10.** $4x + y = 10$ -4; 10 **11.** $-2x + y = 7$ 2; 7 **12.** $-3x + y = 8$ 3; 8

Written Exercises

Find the slope and *y*-intercept of each line.

A **1.** $y = 2x + 1$ 2; 1 **2.** $y = 3x - 4$ 3; -4 **3.** $y = \frac{1}{2}x - 3$ $\frac{1}{2}$; -3

4. $y = \frac{2}{3}x + 3$ $\frac{2}{3}$; 3 **5.** $y = -\frac{1}{2}x + 6$ $-\frac{1}{2}$; 6 **6.** $y = -\frac{1}{3}x - 2$ $-\frac{1}{3}$; -2

7. $y = 8 - 2x$ -2; 8 **8.** $y = 9 - 3x$ -3; 9 **9.** $y = x$ 1; 0

10. $y = -x$ -1; 0 **11.** $y = -4$ 0; -4 **12.** $y = 4$ 0; 4

Use only the slope and *y*-intercept to graph each equation. You may wish to verify your graphs on a computer or a graphing calculator.

13. $y = -x + 5$ **14.** $y = 2x - 3$ **15.** $y = \frac{2}{3}x + 4$

16. $y = \frac{4}{5}x - 3$ **17.** $y = -\frac{1}{2}x + 4$ **18.** $y = -\frac{3}{4}x - 5$

19. $x + y = 8$ **20.** $2x + y = 6$ **21.** $3x - y = 6$

22. $2x - y = -4$ **23.** $3x + y = 9$ **24.** $2x + y = -4$

B **25.** $3x - 5y = 10$ **26.** $4x - 3y = 9$ **27.** $x + 5y = 5$

28. $6x + 4y = 8$ **29.** $3x = 2y$ **30.** $4y = 3$

Show that the lines whose equations are given are parallel.

31. $2x - 3y = 7$
$-2x + 3y = 4$

32. $x - 2y = 1$
$-2x + 4y = 9$

33. $x - y = 4$
$y - x = 4$

34. $4x - y = 1$
$-8x + 2y = 2$

35. $\frac{1}{2}x + \frac{1}{2}y = 5$
$2x + 2y = 3$

36. $\frac{1}{3}x - \frac{1}{3}y = 2$
$3x - 3y = 1$

37. Write an equation of the line that has y-intercept 7 and is parallel to the graph of $y = 5x - 3$. $y = 5x + 7$

38. Write an equation of the line that is parallel to the graph of $y - 3x = 4$ and has the same y-intercept as the graph of $4y + x = 36$. $y = 3x + 9$

39. In the equation $2y + px = 5$, for what value of p is the graph of the equation parallel to the graph of $x + y = 5$? the graph of $x - y = 5$? 2; -2

40. In the equation $dy + 3x = 2$, for what value of d is the graph of the equation parallel to the graph of $x - 3y = 0$? the y-axis? -9, 0

In Exercises 41–43, use the points $A(5, 3)$, $B(2, 6)$, and $C(-2, 0)$.

41. Find r if the line joining A to $(r, 2r)$ is parallel to the line joining B and C. -9

42. Find s if the line joining B to $(s + 4, s)$ is parallel to the line joining A and C. 12

43. Find t if the line joining C to $(-3t, 2t + 1)$ is parallel to the line joining A and B. 3

C **44.** A radio beacon is located at $(-1, 0)$ and another at $(2, -1)$. A navigator's equipment tells her that the line joining her position to the first beacon has slope -5 and the line joining her position to the second beacon has slope 3. What is the navigator's approximate location? $\left(\frac{1}{4}, -6\frac{1}{4}\right)$

45. Using the standard form of a linear equation, $ax + by = c$, find a formula for the slope and a formula for the y-intercept in terms of the coefficients, assuming that $b \neq 0$. $m = -\frac{a}{b}$; y-int. $= \frac{c}{b}$

Mixed Review Exercises

Find the slope of the line through each pair of given points.

1. $(-3, 1)$, $(-2, 3)$ 2
2. $(1, 2)$, $(4, 3)$ $\frac{1}{3}$
3. $(-2, 5)$, $(-1, 2)$ -3
4. $(1, 5)$, $(3, 13)$ 4

Factor.

5. $3s^2 + 7s + 4$ $(3s + 4)(s + 1)$

6. $20x^2 + 15x$ $5x(4x + 3)$

7. $3p^2 - 24p + 48$ $3(p - 4)^2$

8. $81y^2 - 16z^2$ $(9y - 4z)(9y + 4z)$

9. $-3x(x + y) + 4(x + y)$ $(x + y)(-3x + 4)$

10. $m^2 - 9mn - 36n^2$ $(m - 12n)(m + 3n)$

Introduction to Functions **369**

Summarizing the Lesson

Have students recall that when a linear equation is written in the slope-intercept form, they can immediately tell the slope of its graph and where the graph crosses the y-axis.

Suggested Assignments

Minimum
Day 1: 368/1–27 odd
    S 369/Mixed Review
Day 2: 368/28–38 even
Assign with Lesson 8-5.

Average
Day 1: 368/1–35 odd
    S 369/Mixed Review
Day 2: 369/37–43 odd
Assign with Lesson 8-5.

Maximum
    368/3–45 mult. of 3
    S 369/Mixed Review

Supplementary Materials

Study Guide   pp. 139–140
Practice Master   47
Computer Activities 24, 25
Overhead Visuals   7, 8

Additional Answers
Written Exercises

14.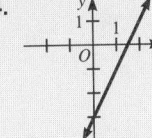

16.

18.

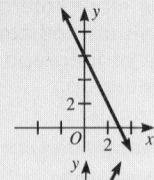
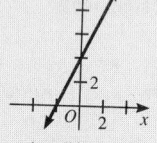
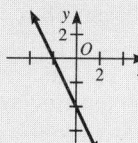
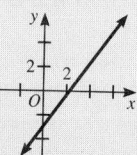
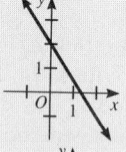
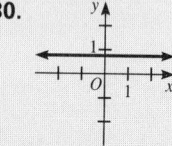
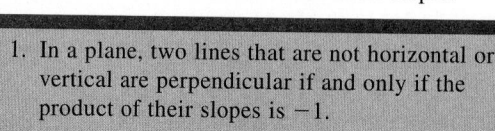

Extra / *Perpendicular Lines*

In a coordinate plane, the x-axis and the y-axis intersect to form right angles. Any two lines that intersect to form right angles are **perpendicular.** The graphs of $y = 2x + 1$ and $y = -\frac{1}{2}x - 2$ shown are perpendicular. This is because the following relationships can be shown to exist between lines and their slopes.

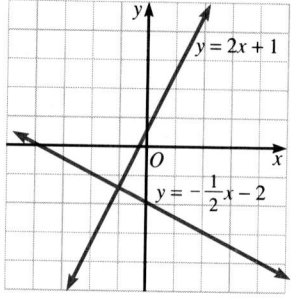

1. In a plane, two lines that are not horizontal or vertical are perpendicular if and only if the product of their slopes is -1.

2. In a plane, vertical lines and horizontal lines are perpendicular.

Example Show that the graphs of $y = \frac{3}{4}x - 1$ and $6y + 8x = 7$ are perpendicular.

Solution
1. Write $6y + 8x = 7$ in slope-intercept form: $y = -\frac{4}{3}x + \frac{7}{6}$
2. The slope of $y = \frac{3}{4}x - 1$ is $\frac{3}{4}$. The slope of $y = -\frac{4}{3}x + \frac{7}{6}$ is $-\frac{4}{3}$.
3. $\frac{3}{4}\left(-\frac{4}{3}\right) = -1$ ∴ the lines are perpendicular. ***Answer***

Exercises

Find the slope of the line perpendicular to the graph of each line.

1. $y = \frac{3}{2}x + 7$ $-\frac{2}{3}$
2. $y = \frac{4}{5}x - 2$ $-\frac{5}{4}$
3. $y = -\frac{3}{8}x + 5$ $\frac{8}{3}$
4. $2x + y = 3$ $\frac{1}{2}$
5. $3x - 5y = 110$ $-\frac{5}{3}$
6. $y = -x$ 1
7. $y = 1$ no slope
8. $x = 3$ 0
9. $x - 3y - 8 = 0$ -3

Tell whether the graphs of each pair of equations are parallel, perpendicular, or neither.

10. $3x + 6y = 8$
$y = 2x - 8$ perpendicular
11. $3x + y = 7$
$y = -3x + 2$ parallel
12. $2x + 5y = 7$
$2x + 5y = 9$ parallel
13. $2x - 8y = 9$
$12x + 3y = 7$ perpendicular
14. $y = x + 5$
$y = 8 - x$ perpendicular
15. $4x + 6y = 9$
$2x + 3y = 5$ parallel

16. Show that the graphs of $y = 4 - 3x$ and $3y - x = 12$ have the same y-intercept and are perpendicular.

17. The graph of $y = \frac{2}{3}x - 12$ intersects the y-axis at $Q(0, -12)$ and is perpendicular to a line joining Q to the point $P(x, 0)$. Find x. -8

8-5 Determining an Equation of a Line

Objective   To find an equation of a line given the slope and one point on the line, or given two points on the line.

You have learned to graph a line when given its equation. Now you will learn to find an equation of a line when given information about its graph.

Example 1   Write an equation of a line that has slope 2 and y-intercept 3.

Solution   Substitute 2 for m and 3 for b in $y = mx + b$.
The equation is $y = 2x + 3$.   **Answer**

Example 2   Write an equation of a line that has slope -4 and x-intercept 3.

Solution   The x-$intercept$ is the x-coordinate of the point where a line crosses the x-axis. In this example, this point is $(3, 0)$.

1. Substitute -4 for m in $y = mx + b$.
$$y = -4x + b$$

2. To find b, substitute 3 for x and 0 for y in $y = -4x + b$.
$$y = -4x + b$$
$$0 = -4(3) + b$$
$$0 = -12 + b$$
$$12 = b$$

$\therefore$ the equation is $y = -4x + 12$.   **Answer**

Example 3   Write an equation of the line passing through the points $(-2, 5)$ and $(4, 8)$.

Solution
1. Find the slope: $\dfrac{y_2 - y_1}{x_2 - x_1} = \dfrac{8 - 5}{4 - (-2)} = \dfrac{3}{6} = \dfrac{1}{2}$

   Substitute $\frac{1}{2}$ for m in $y = mx + b$.
   $$y = \frac{1}{2}x + b$$

2. Choose one of the points, say $(4, 8)$. Substitute 4 for x and 8 for y.
   $$y = \frac{1}{2}x + b$$
   $$8 = \frac{1}{2}(4) + b$$
   $$8 = 2 + b$$
   $$6 = b$$

$\therefore$ the equation is $y = \frac{1}{2}x + 6$.   **Answer**

Introduction to Functions   **371**

Teaching Suggestions p. T120
Suggested Extensions p. T120

Warm-Up Exercises

Given that $y = mx + b$, find the value of b for each set of values for y, m, and x.

1. $y = 10$, $m = 2$, $x = 1$
   $b = 8$
2. $y = 4$, $m = 4$, $x = -2$
   $b = 12$
3. $y = 7$, $m = -3$, $x = 11$
   $b = 40$
4. $y = 5$, $m = -2$, $x = -4$
   $b = -3$

Motivating the Lesson

Point out that in the last lesson the focus was mainly on drawing the graph of a given equation. Determining an equation of a given line is the topic of today's lesson.

Chalkboard Examples

1. Write an equation of a line that has slope 4 and y-intercept -6. $y = 4x - 6$

2. Write an equation of a line that has slope -3 and x-intercept $\frac{1}{3}$.

   $y = -3x + b$; $x = \frac{1}{3}$ when $y = 0$.
   $0 = -3\left(\frac{1}{3}\right) + b$
   $0 = -1 + b$
   $1 = b$
   $\therefore$ the equation is
   $y = -3x + 1$

3. Write an equation of the line passing through the points $(1, 1)$ and $(2, 4)$.
   Slope $= \frac{4 - 1}{2 - 1} = 3$
   $y = 3x + b$
   $1 = 3(1) + b$
   $-2 = b$
   $y = 3x - 2$

Note that in the second step of Example 3 we could have used the point $(-2, 5)$. The resulting equation would have been the same.

Oral Exercises

Give the equation in slope-intercept form of each line described.

1. slope -5, y-intercept 8 $y = -5x + 8$

2. slope $\frac{2}{3}$, y-intercept -7 $y = \frac{2}{3}x - 7$

3. slope 3, passes through (0, 4) $y = 3x + 4$

4. y-intercept 2, x-intercept 2 $y = -x + 2$

5. slope $\frac{1}{2}$, passes through (0, 0) $y = \frac{1}{2}x$

6. passes through (1, 4) and (2, 5) $y = x + 3$

Written Exercises

Write an equation in slope-intercept form of each line described.

A   **1.** slope 2; y-intercept 5 $y = 2x + 5$

2. slope -3; y-intercept 4 $y = -3x + 4$

3. slope $-\frac{1}{2}$; y-intercept 7 $y = -\frac{1}{2}x + 7$

4. slope $\frac{2}{3}$; y-intercept 9 $y = \frac{2}{3}x + 9$

5. slope $\frac{1}{2}$; x-intercept 4 $y = \frac{1}{2}x - 2$

6. slope $-\frac{1}{3}$; x-intercept 3 $y = -\frac{1}{3}x + 1$

7. slope 2; passes through $(-5, 1)$ $y = 2x + 11$

8. slope 3; passes through (4, 1) $y = 3x - 11$

9. slope -2; passes through (3, 5) $y = -2x + 11$

10. slope -1; passes through (8, 5)
$y = -x + 13$

11. slope $\frac{1}{2}$; passes through $(4, -1)$ $y = \frac{1}{2}x - 3$

12. slope $\frac{1}{3}$; passes through (6, 0) $y = \frac{1}{3}x - 2$

13. slope $-\frac{3}{4}$; passes through $(8, -3)$
$y = -\frac{3}{4}x + 3$

14. slope $-\frac{2}{5}$; passes through (5, 7)
$y = -\frac{2}{5}x + 9$

15. slope 0; passes through (1, 3) $y = 3$

16. slope 0; passes through $(-5, 4)$ $y = 4$

Write an equation in slope-intercept form of the line passing through the given points. **22.** $y = -\frac{1}{3}x + \frac{10}{3}$ **25.** $y = 5x - 1$

17. (0, 7), (1, 9) $y = 2x + 7$

18. (0, 3), (2, −1) $y = -2x + 3$

19. (5, 2), (7, 0)
$y = -x + 7$

20. (−3, 4), (3, −4) $y = -\frac{4}{3}x$

21. (8, 1), (1, 8) $y = -x + 9$

22. (−2, 4), (4, 2)

23. (3, −1), (6, 7) $y = \frac{8}{3}x - 9$

24. (−3, −1), (1, −4) $y = -\frac{3}{4}x - \frac{13}{4}$

25. (0, −1), (1, 4)

26. (−1, −2), (0, 3) $y = 5x + 3$

27. (−2, 0), (2, −3) $y = -\frac{3}{4}x - \frac{3}{2}$

28. (3, 0), (−2, 5)
$y = -x + 3$

Write an equation in slope-intercept form for each line described.

B   **29.** y-intercept -2; x-intercept 5 $y = \frac{2}{5}x - 2$

30. y-intercept -5; x-intercept 3
$y = \frac{5}{3}x - 5$

31. x-intercept 6; y-intercept -3 $y = \frac{1}{2}x - 3$

32. x-intercept -4; y-intercept -2
$y = -\frac{1}{2}x - 2$

33. horizontal line through (3, 5) $y = 5$

34. horizontal line through $(-2, -1)$ $y = -1$

372   *Chapter 8*

Write an equation in standard form for each line described.

35. The line that passes through $(-1, 3)$ and is parallel to $3x - y = 4$. $3x - y = -6$

36. The line that is parallel to $x - 2y + 7 = 0$ and contains $(-4, 0)$. $x - 2y = -4$

37. The line that passes through $(-4, -5)$ and has the same y-intercept as $x + 3y + 9 = 0$. $x - 2y = 6$

38. The line that contains $(7, 1)$, $(p, 0)$, and $(0, p)$ for $p \neq 0$. $x + y = 8$

39. **a.** Can the equation of the line through $(2, 5)$ and $(2, 8)$ be written in slope-intercept form? Why or why not? no; there is no slope or y-intercept.
    b. Write the equation of the line in standard form. $x = 2$

40. A horizontal line intersects a vertical line at $(-3, 7)$. Give the equation of each line in standard form. horizontal line, $y = 7$; vertical line, $x = -3$

C 41. A line passes through $(-2, 3)$, $(2, 5)$, and $(6, k)$. Find k. 7

42. A line with x-intercept -4 passes through $(2, 6)$ and $(p, 10)$. Find p. 6

Mixed Review Exercises

Simplify.

1. $\left(\frac{4}{3}t^3\right)(12t^2)$ $16t^5$

2. $\frac{1}{2}(4s^2 - 8st)$ $2s^2 - 4st$

3. $(7pq^2)^2$ $49p^2q^4$

4. $(-3m^2n^4)^3$ $-27m^6n^{12}$

5. $3 \cdot 4 - 3^2$ 3

6. $(3a^3b)(-6ab^2)$ $-18a^4b^3$

7. $2 \cdot (8 - 4)^3$ 128

8. $(8x + 3y) - (3x + y)$ $5x + 2y$

Self-Test 2

Vocabulary   slope (p. 361)
collinear (p. 364)
y-intercept (p. 366)

slope-intercept form of
an equation (p. 366)
parallel (p. 367)
x-intercept (p. 371)

1. Find the slope of the line that passes through $(4, 7)$ and $(1, 3)$. $\frac{4}{3}$ **Obj. 8-3, p. 360**

2. Find the slope of the line whose equation is $y = 4$. 0

3. Find the slope and y-intercept of the line $3x - 7y = 28$. $\frac{3}{7}$; -4 **Obj. 8-4, p. 366**

4. Use only the slope and y-intercept to graph $2x + 3y = -6$.

5. Write an equation in slope-intercept form of the line with slope 3 that passes through the point $(-2, -1)$. $y = 3x + 5$ **Obj. 8-5, p. 371**

6. Write an equation in slope-intercept form of the line through the points $(5, 0)$ and $(0, -5)$. $y = x - 5$

Check your answers with those at the back of the book.

Suggested Assignments

Minimum
Day 1: 372/2–16 even
Assign with Lesson 8-4.
Day 2: 372/17–35 odd
S 373/Mixed Review

Average
Day 1: 372/1–15 odd
Assign with Lesson 8-4.
Day 2: 372/17–39 odd
S 373/Mixed Review

Maximum
372/3–42 mult. of 3
S 373/Mixed Review

Additional Answer
Self-Test 2

4.

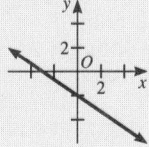

Quick Quiz

1. Find the slope of the line that passes through $(2, 2)$ and $(-4, 10)$. $-\frac{4}{3}$

2. Find the slope of the line whose equation is $y = -5$. 0

3. Find the slope and y-intercept of the line $3x + 9y = 1$. $-\frac{1}{3}$; $\frac{1}{9}$

4. Use only the slope and y-intercept to graph $4x + y = 8$. Line through $(0, 8)$ with slope -4.

5. Write an equation in slope-intercept form of the line with slope 5 that passes through the point $(-1, 2)$. $y = 5x + 7$

6. Write an equation in slope-intercept form of the line through the points $(0, 8)$ and $(2, 12)$. $y = 2x + 8$

Functions

8-6 Functions Defined by Tables and Graphs

Objective   To understand what a function is and to define a function by using tables and graphs.

A **function** is defined by a correspondence among elements in two sets, the **domain** and the **range.** It assigns to each member of the domain *exactly one* member of the range.

You can define a function either by describing the correspondence between elements of the domain and the elements of the range or by describing a set of ordered pairs. In some cases it is possible to list all the ordered pairs, as shown in Example 1.

Example 1   The birthday function matches each person with his or her birthday. Some of these pairings are shown below.

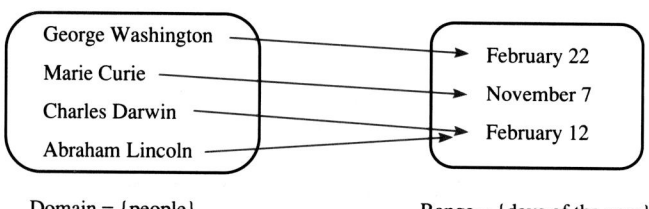

Domain = {people}   Range = {days of the year}

Write each pairing as an ordered pair.

Solution   (George Washington, February 22)
(Marie Curie, November 7)
(Charles Darwin, February 12)
(Abraham Lincoln, February 12)

The table at the right shows the average height in feet associated with each of several types of trees. This association is a function. The table provides a rule by assigning one height to each tree. The domain of the function is the set of first coordinates:

{Douglas fir, Juniper, Oak, Poplar, Yew}

The range of the function is the set of second coordinates:

{10, 12, 25, 30, 40}

Tree	Height (feet)
Douglas fir	40
Juniper	10
Oak	25
Poplar	30
Yew	12

374   *Chapter 8*

It is easier to compare the heights if the facts are displayed in a *bar graph*.

Example 2 Draw a bar graph for the function in the table on page 374.

Solution Choose one axis for the members of the domain, say the horizontal axis. List the members of the range on the left along the vertical axis. For each member of the domain draw a vertical bar to represent the corresponding value in the range of the function. Start the scale of the bars at zero, so that their relative lengths are correct.

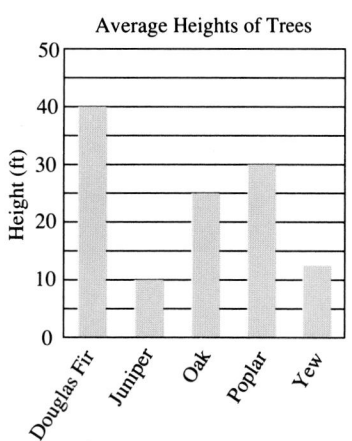

Average Heights of Trees

When a measurement varies over time we say that it is a function of time. For functions of this type it is better to use a *broken-line* graph to display the facts.

Example 3 Draw a broken-line graph for the function in the table below.

Year	1900	1920	1940	1960	1980
United States population (in millions)	76	106	132	179	227

Solution List the members of the domain along the horizontal axis. For each member of the domain plot a point to represent the corresponding value in the range of the function. Then connect the points by line segments.

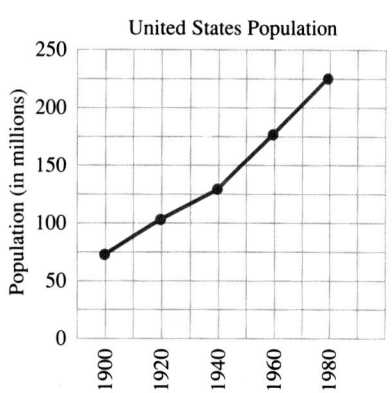

United States Population

Introduction to Functions **375**

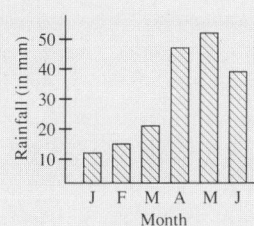
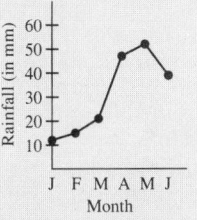
Check for Understanding

Here is a suggested use of the Oral Exercises. Oral Exs. 1–6: use before Example 2.

Summarizing the Lesson

Remind the students that a function can be defined by a chart or a graph. In each case a member of the domain is matched with exactly one member of the range. More than one member of the domain can be matched with the same member of the range.

Suggested Assignments

Minimum
  377/1–6
S 377/Mixed Review
R 373/Self-Test 2
Average
  377/1–9 odd, 10
S 377/Mixed Review
R 373/Self-Test 2
Maximum
  377/1–9 odd, 10
R 373/Self-Test 2

Note that the line segments in the graph of Example 3 do not necessarily show the actual population. However, they do help you to estimate the population and to see the trend over time.

Note that the line segments in the graph of Example 3 do not necessarily show the actual population. However, they do help you to estimate the population and to see the trend over time.

Oral Exercises

State the domain and range of the function shown by each table. Then give each correspondence as a set of ordered pairs.

Additional Answers
Oral Exercises

1. Domain: {Jog, Swim, Tennis, Walk, Bicycling} Range: {120, 210, 270, 330}; {(Jog, 210), (Swim, 270), (Tennis, 210), (Walk, 120), (Bicycling, 330)}

2. Domain: {Human, Horse, Mouse, Tomato, Corn}; Range: {24, 40, 46, 64}; {(Human, 46), (Horse, 64), (Mouse, 40), (Tomato, 24), (Corn, 40)}

3. Domain: {Sit com., Basketball Game, Drama, News, Documen., Hockey game, Movie}; Range: {4.1, 6.2, 6.9, 10.8, 12.0, 14.2, 16.3} {(Sit. com., 10.8), (Basketball game, 6.2), (Drama, 12.0), (News, 16.3), (Docum. 14.2), (Hockey game, 4.1), (Movie, 6.9)}

4. Domain: {Air cond., Dryer, Range, Refrig., TV, Heater, Other} Range: {5, 8, 9, 15, 20, 38}; {(Air cond., 8), (Dryer, 5), (Range, 15), (Refrig. 20), (TV, 9), (Heater, 38), (Other, 5)}

5. Domain: {1940, 1950, 1960, 1970, 1980, 1990} Range: {$.30, $.60, $1.25, $2.00, $3.25, $5.00}; {(1940, $.30), (1950, $.60), (1960, $1.25), (1970, $2.00) (1980, $3.25), (1990, $5.00)}

6. Domain: {1967, 1970, 1973, 1976, 1979, 1982, 1985}; Range: {100, 116.3, 133.1, 170.5, 217.4, 289.1, 317.4};

(continued)

1.

Activity	Calories burned
Jogging	210
Swimming	270
Tennis	210
Walking	120
Bicycling	330

2.

Species	Chromosomes
Human	46
Horse	64
Mouse	40
Tomato	24
Corn	40

3.

Tuesday night television	Nielsen rating
Situation comedy	10.8
Basketball game	6.2
Drama	12.0
News	16.3
Documentary	14.2
Hockey game	4.1
Movie	6.9

4.

Appliance	Percent of total electrical energy used in the house
Air conditioner	8
Clothes dryer	5
Electric range	15
Refrigerator	20
TV	9
Water heater	38
All others	5

5.

Cost of seeing a movie at the Bijou Theater						
Year	1940	1950	1960	1970	1980	1990
Cost	$.30	$.60	$1.25	$2.00	$3.25	$5.00

6.

Consumer Price Index (CPI)							
Year	1967	1970	1973	1976	1979	1982	1985
CPI	100	116.3	133.1	170.5	217.4	289.1	317.4

Written Exercises

A **1–4.** Draw a bar graph for the function shown in each table in Oral Exercises 1–4.

5–6. Draw a broken-line graph for each function shown in Oral Exercises 5 and 6.

B **7.** Use the broken-line graph you drew in Exercise 5 to estimate the cost of seeing a movie in 1955 and in 1975. $.90; $2.50

8. Use the broken-line graph you drew in Exercise 6 to estimate the CPI in 1980 and in 1984. 230; 300

Exercises 9 and 10 require you to find data. Sources that you may use are results of experiments in your science classes, surveys that you conduct in your class or neighborhood, or reference materials in your library. Answers will vary.

9. Find data suitable for presentation as a bar graph, and then draw the graph.

10. Find data suitable for presentation on a broken-line graph, and then draw the graph.

9. Example: Paper carriers and number of customers on route
10. Example: Year and price of a pound of beef.

Mixed Review Exercises

Write an equation in slope-intercept form of each line described.

1. passes through (2, 4) and (4, 6) $y = x + 2$

2. slope 5; passes through (1, 7) $y = 5x + 2$

3. slope $\frac{1}{3}$; y-intercept -4 $y = \frac{1}{3}x - 4$

4. passes through $(-4, 3)$ and $(0, -3)$

$y = -\frac{3}{2}x - 3$

Graph each equation.

5. $y = -3x + 1$ **6.** $x + y = 9$ **7.** $y = \frac{1}{2}x - 5$ **8.** $x = -3$

 Career Note / *Statistician*

Statisticians plan surveys and analyze data. To plan a survey, statisticians decide how many people to contact and what types of questions to ask them. Statisticians then analyze the data and present it in reports. They often use tables and graphs to give a clear picture of the results.

Statisticians need a strong mathematics background. A degree in mathematics or statistics, or in some field using statistics with a minor in statistics, is usually the minimum educational background.

Introduction to Functions **377**

{(1967, 100), (1970, 116.3), (1973, 133.1)
(1976, 170.5)
(1979, 217.4)
(1982, 289.1)
(1985, 317.4)}

**Additional Answers
Written Exercises**

2.

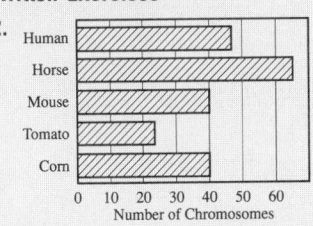

4.

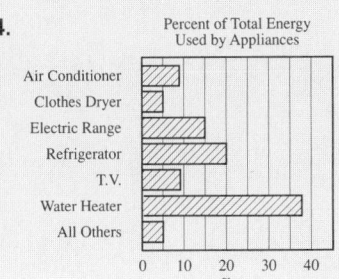

6.

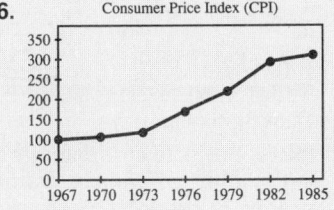

Supplementary Materials

Study Guide	pp. 143–144
Practice Master	48
Computer Activity	26

Application / *Line of Best Fit*

Can your adult height be predicted from that of your father or mother? Will your future income be related to the number of years you attend school? When there is a clear relationship between two measurements, researchers can base predictions on data gathered about many, many people. For each person, there must be a pair of measurements.

For example, to predict a person's height at age 24 from that person's height at age 14, researchers begin by collecting data such as that shown in the chart below for a group of adults. Each pair of heights can be plotted as a point (*x*, *y*) on a graph.

Height at 14	Height at 24
62 in.	73 in.
59 in.	67 in.
58 in.	67 in.
61 in.	70 in.
64 in.	76 in.
60 in.	69 in.

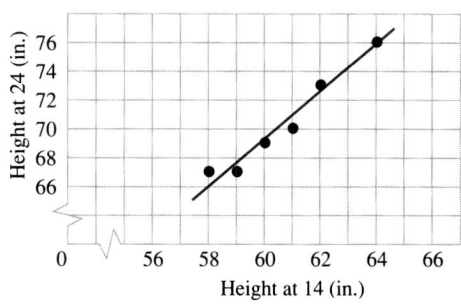

If the data were plotted for many more people, the graph would contain many more points. These points tend to cluster around a line (shown in red) called the line of best fit, since it fits closer to the points than any other line. Mathematicians have derived exact formulas for determining the line of best fit, but you can fit a line quite well "by eye." From graphs based on extensive data gathered over a period of several years, predictions are made.

Projects Answers will vary.

1. **a.** Gather the following data from your classmates: the height of each girl and her mother; the height of each boy and his father.

   b. For each girl, plot (*x*, *y*) on a graph such that the *x*-coordinate is the girl's height and the *y*-coordinate is her mother's height. Make a second graph in the same way using the boy's data.

   c. On each graph, draw the line that seems to fit the points of the graph most closely. (You may wish to use a computer program to draw the line.)

   d. Determine the heights of other students in the same age group as your class. Predict the heights of their mothers or fathers from your graphs. Find out how good your estimates are. (*Note:* Your estimates may be inaccurate, but if you based your graph on more data and estimated heights for a larger group of people, your estimates would be better.)

2. Using Project 1 as a model, design a statistical experiment to study a problem of your own choice.

8-7 Functions Defined by Equations

Objective   To define a function by using equations.

Tickets to the senior class play cost $5. Production expenses are $500. The class's profit, p will depend on n, the number of tickets sold.

$$\text{profit} = \$5 \cdot (\text{number of tickets}) - \$500 \quad \text{or} \quad p = 5n - 500$$

The equation $p = 5n - 500$ describes a correspondence between the number of tickets sold and the profit. This correspondence is a function whose domain is the set of tickets that could possibly be sold.

$$\text{domain } D = \{0, 1, 2, \ldots\}.$$

The range is the set of profits that are possible, including "negative profits," or losses, if too few tickets are sold.

$$\text{range } R = \{-500, -495, -490, \ldots\}.$$

If we call this profit function P, we can use **arrow notation** and write the rule

$$P: n \rightarrow 5n - 500,$$

which is read "the function P that assigns $5n - 500$ to n" or "the function P that pairs n with $5n - 500$." We could also use **functional notation:**

$$P(n) = 5n - 500$$

which is read "P of n equals $5n - 500$" or "the value of P at n is $5n - 500$."

To specify a function completely, you must describe the domain of the function as well as give the rule. The numbers assigned by the rule then form the range of the function.

Example 1   List the range of

$$g: x \rightarrow 4 + 3x - x^2$$

if the domain $D = \{-1, 0, 1, 2\}$.

Solution   In $4 + 3x - x^2$ replace x with each member of D to find the members of the range R.

$\therefore R = \{0, 4, 6\}$ **Answer**

x	$4 + 3x - x^2$
-1	$4 + 3(-1) - (-1)^2 = 0$
0	$4 + 3(0) - 0^2 = 4$
1	$4 + 3(1) - 1^2 = 6$
2	$4 + 3(2) - 2^2 = 6$

Note that the function g in Example 1 assigns the number 6 to both 1 and 2. In listing the range of g, however, you name 6 only once.

Members of the range of a function are called **values of the function.** In Example 1, the values of the function g are 0, 4, and 6. To indicate that the function g assigns to 2 the value 6, you write

$$g(2) = 6,$$

which is read "g of 2 equals 6" or "the value of g at 2 is 6." Note that $g(2)$ is *not* the product of g and 2. It names the number that g assigns to 2.

Introduction to Functions   **379**

Teaching Suggestions p. T121
Reading Algebra p. T121
Suggested Extensions p. T121

Warm-Up Exercises

Evaluate the following expressions if $x = -2$.

1. $2x^2 + 3x + 9$ 11

2. $4 - x^2 + 2x$ -4

3. $x^3 - x$ -6

4. $(3x)^2$ 36

5. $(x + 4)^{-1}$ $\dfrac{1}{2}$

Motivating the Lesson

Point out that defining a function with a table or a graph can be unwieldy for very large sets of data. Defining a function with a rule allows you to find any value of the function by applying the rule. Today's topic is defining a function by using an equation as the rule.

Chalkboard Examples

1. List the range of
$f: t \rightarrow 4t - 3$ if the domain $D = \{0, 1, 2, 3\}$.

t	$4t - 3$
0	$4(0) - 3 = -3$
1	$4(1) - 3 = 1$
2	$4(2) - 3 = 5$
3	$4(3) - 3 = 9$

$\therefore R = \{-3, 1, 5, 9\}$

Given $g: x \rightarrow 4x - x^2$, with the set of real numbers as the domain, find:

2. $g(1)$ $4(1) - 1^2 = 3$

3. $g(-1)$ $4(-1) - (-1)^2 = -5$

4. $g(2)$ $4(2) - 2^2 = 4$

Example 2 Given $f: x \rightarrow x^2 - 2x$ with the set of real numbers as the domain.
Find: **a.** $f(4)$ **b.** $f(-3)$ **c.** $f(2)$

Solution First write the equation: $f(x) = x^2 - 2x$
Then substitute: **a.** $f(4) = 4^2 - 2 \cdot 4 = 16 - 8 = 8$
b. $f(-3) = (-3)^2 - 2(-3) = 9 - (-6) = 15$
c. $f(2) = 2^2 - 2 \cdot 2 = 4 - 4 = 0$

You may use whatever variable you wish to define a function. For example, $G: t \rightarrow t^2 - 2t$ with the set of real numbers as the domain is the same function as f in Example 2.

Oral Exercises

State the range of each function.

1. $F: x \rightarrow x + 5, D = \{0, 1, 2\}$ {5, 6, 7}   2. $H: y \rightarrow y - 3, D = \{-2, 0, 2\}$ {-5, -3, -1}
3. $p(w) = w^2 + 3, D = \{-3, 0, 3\}$ {3, 12}   4. $g(r) = 2r^3, D = \{-2, 0, 2\}$ {-16, 0, 16}
5. $M(x) = 3x^2 - 7, D = \{-2, 0, 2\}$ {-7, 5}   6. $Q(n) = 3n^3 + 2, D = \{-1, 0, 1\}$ {-1, 2, 5}

Given the functions $g: x \rightarrow 3x - 6$ and $h: t \rightarrow t^2$, find the following values.

7. $g(5)$ 9   8. $g(7)$ 15   9. $g(-7)$ -27   10. $g(0)$ -6   11. $g(2)$ 0
12. $h(0)$ 0   13. $h(-3)$ 9   14. $h(5)$ 25   15. $h(8)$ 64   16. $h(-8)$ 64

Complete each statement about the function $P: n \rightarrow 5n - 500$.

17. The value of P at 200 is __?__. 500   18. The value of P at 500 is __?__. 2000
19. The value of P at __?__ is 0. 100   20. The value of P at __?__ is -250. 50

Written Exercises

Find the range of each function.

A   1. $g: x \rightarrow 5x + 1, D = \{-1, 0, 1\}$ {-4, 1, 6}   2. $f: x \rightarrow 3x - 4, D = \{1, 2, 3\}$ {-1, 2, 5}
3. $s(z) = 5 - 4z, D = \{-2, 0, 2\}$ {-3, 5, 13}   4. $h(y) = 1 - 2y, D = \{-3, 0, 1\}$ {-1, 1, 7}
5. $G: a \rightarrow 4a^2 - 1, D = \{-1, 0, 1\}$ {-1, 3}   6. $H: b \rightarrow b^2 + 3, D = \{0, 2, 4\}$ {3, 7, 19}
7. $F(x) = x^2 + 4x - 3, D = P\{1, 2, 4\}$ {2, 9, 29}   8. $M(x) = x^2 + 5x + 2, D = \{-1, -2, -4\}$
9. $P(z) = z^2 - 5z + 6, D = \{2, 3, 4\}$ {0, 2}   10. $N(a) = a^2 - 3a - 2, D = \{-2, -1, 0\}$
11. $q: c \rightarrow c^3 + c^2 + 3c, D = \{0, 1, 3\}$ {0, 5, 45}   12. $K: x \rightarrow x^3 - 5x^2 + 6x, D = \{0, 2, 3\}$
   8. {-4, -2}   **10.** {-2, 2, 8}   **12.** {0}

Find the values for each given function with the set of real numbers as the domain.

13. $f(x) = 5x - 9$ a. $f(3)$ 6   b. $f(-3)$ -24   c. $f(-8)$ -49

14. $p(x) = 8 - 4x$ a. $p(2)$ 0   b. $p(0)$ 8   c. $p(-2)$ 16

15. $R: t \rightarrow t + 1$ a. $R(3)$ 4   b. $R(-2)$ -1   c. $R(-5)$ -4

16. $G: n \rightarrow n - 2$ a. $G(0)$ -2   b. $G(2)$ 0   c. $G(-3)$ -5

17. $h(a) = 3a^2 - 2$ a. $h(4)$ 46   b. $h(-5)$ 73   c. $h(0)$ -2

18. $k(t) = 3t^2 + 9$ a. $k(5)$ 84   b. $k(-2)$ 21   c. $k(-3)$ 36

19. $g(x) = x^2 - 2$ a. $g(5)$ 23   b. $g(-5)$ 23   c. $g(0)$ -2

20. $h(y) = 3y^2 + 2$ a. $h(2)$ 14   b. $h(-2)$ 14   c. $h(-4)$ 50

21. $R: y \rightarrow y^3 + 8$ a. $R(0)$ 8   b. $R(-2)$ 0   c. $R(2)$ 16

22. $N: t \rightarrow t^3 - 27$ a. $N(3)$ 0   b. $N(-3)$ -54   c. $N(0)$ -27

B 23. $f: x \rightarrow x^2 + 3x$ a. $f(7)$ 70   b. $f(-7)$ 28   c. $f(-3)$ 0

24. $g: t \rightarrow 5t^2 - 7t$ a. $g(3)$ 24   b. $g(-3)$ 66   c. $g(0)$ 0

25. $P(y) = y - y^3$ a. $P(3)$ -24   b. $P(1)$ 0   c. $P(-1)$ 0

26. $m(y) = y(1 - 2y)$ a. $m\left(-\dfrac{1}{2}\right)$ -1   b. $m\left(\dfrac{1}{2}\right)$ 0   c. $m(0)$ 0

27. $Z: x \rightarrow |3x - 1|$ a. $Z\left(\dfrac{1}{3}\right)$ 0   b. $Z(0)$ 1   c. $Z\left(\dfrac{2}{3}\right)$ 1

28. $Q: m \rightarrow |3 - 6m|$ a. $Q(-2)$ 15   b. $Q\left(\dfrac{1}{2}\right)$ 0   c. $Q\left(-\dfrac{1}{2}\right)$ 6

For each function, (a) find $f(0)$, (b) solve $f(x) = 0$.

29. $f(x) = 3x - 12$ -12; {4}   30. $f(x) = 4x + 7$ 7; $\left\{-\dfrac{7}{4}\right\}$ 31. $f(x) = 5x - 1$ -1; $\left\{\dfrac{1}{5}\right\}$

32. $f(x) = 2 - 3x$ 2; $\left\{\dfrac{2}{3}\right\}$ 33. $f(x) = -\dfrac{1}{2}x + 7$ 7; {14}   34. $f(x) = 3 - \dfrac{1}{2}x$ 3; {6}

35. $f(x) = x^2 - 2x - 3$ -3; {-1, 3}   36. $f(x) = x^2 - 13x + 40$ 40; {5, 8}   37. $f(x) = x^4 - x^2$

38. $f(x) = \dfrac{x + 1}{x - 2}$ $-\dfrac{1}{2}$; {-1}   39. $f(x) = \dfrac{x^2 - 1}{x^2 + 1}$ -1; {1, -1}   40. $f(x) = \dfrac{x^2 - 3x + 2}{x + 1}$

37. 0; {-1, 0, 1}   40. 2; {1, 2}

Given that $f(x) = 3x + 4$ and $g(x) = -x^2$, find each of the following.

41. $\dfrac{1}{2}g(6)$ -18   42. $2f(5)$ 38   43. $f(1) + g(1)$ 6   44. $f(2) \cdot g(2)$ -40

In Exercises 45–47, let $f(x) = x^2$ and $g(x) = 2x$. Find each of the following. (*Hint:* To find $g[f(2)]$, first find $f(2)$.)

C 45. a. $g(1)$ 2   b. $f(1)$ 1   c. $g[f(1)]$ 2   d. $f[g(1)]$ 4

46. a. $g(-2)$ -4   b. $f(-2)$ 4   c. $g[f(-2)]$ 8   d. $f[g(-2)]$ 16

47. Is there any real number x for which $f[g(x)] = g[f(x)]$? If there is such a number, find it. If there is no such number, explain why not. 0

48. If $f(x) = x + 1$, and $g[f(x)] = x$, what is $g(x)$? $g(x) = x - 1$

Introduction to Functions   **381**

Suggested Assignments

Minimum
Day 1: 380/1–23 odd
Day 2: 381/24–34 even
    382/Mixed Review

Average
    380/1–43 odd
    S 382/Mixed Review

Maximum
Day 1: 380/1–27 odd
    S 377/Mixed Review
Day 2: 381/24–48 even
    S 382/Mixed Review

Supplementary Materials

Study Guide   pp. 145–146
Computer Activity   25
Resource Book   p. 117

Simplify.

1. $\dfrac{4n-1}{3n^3} + \dfrac{3}{n}$ $\dfrac{9n^2+4n-1}{3n^3}$

2. $7\frac{1}{4} + 3\frac{2}{3} + 2\frac{3}{4} + 5\frac{1}{3}$ 19

3. $(-15)\left(\dfrac{y}{5}\right)$ $-3y$

4. $(-3)(3a - 2b + c)$ $-9a + 6b - 3c$

5. $-[9 + (-2)] + (-x) + 8$ $1 - x$

6. $3(4m - 7)$

7. $-120\left(\dfrac{1}{2}\right)\left(\dfrac{1}{5}\right)$ -12

8. $\dfrac{3ef^2}{2e^3} \cdot \dfrac{4de^2}{6ef}$ $\dfrac{df}{e}$

9. $\dfrac{x^2 - y^2}{x^2 + 2xy + y^2}$

6. $12m - 21$ **9.** $\dfrac{x-y}{x+y}$

Computer Exercises

For students with some programming experience

Write a BASIC program to calculate the value of a function for values of x entered with READ . . . DATA statements. (Recall that the BASIC statement that corresponds to $f(x) = x^2$ is DEF FNA(X) = X*X.) Run the program for the functions and values of x given below.

1. $f(x) = 3x - 7$; $x = -2, 0, 1, 10$ $-13, -7, -4, 23$

2. $f(x) = x^2 + 3x + 2$; $x = 0, 1, -1, -2$ $2, 6, 0, 0$

3. $f(x) = \dfrac{1}{x^2 + 1}$; $x = -10, -2, 0, 2, 10$ $0.0099009, 0.2, 1, 0.2, 0.0099009$

4. $f(x) = 4x - x^3$; $x = -3, -2, -1, 0, 1, 2, 3$ $15, 0, -3, 0, 3, 0, -15$

Challenge

1. **a.** Find each sum.

$$\dfrac{1}{1 \cdot 2} + \dfrac{1}{2 \cdot 3} = \underline{\ ?\ }\ \ \dfrac{2}{3}$$

$$\dfrac{1}{1 \cdot 2} + \dfrac{1}{2 \cdot 3} + \dfrac{1}{3 \cdot 4} = \underline{\ ?\ }\ \ \dfrac{3}{4}$$

$$\dfrac{1}{1 \cdot 2} + \dfrac{1}{2 \cdot 3} + \dfrac{1}{3 \cdot 4} + \dfrac{1}{4 \cdot 5} = \underline{\ ?\ }\ \ \dfrac{4}{5}$$

b. If this pattern were continued for 100 fractions, what would the sum be? $\dfrac{100}{101}$

c. If this pattern were continued for n fractions, what would the sum be? $\dfrac{n}{n+1}$

2. **a.** Find each sum.

$$\dfrac{1}{1 \cdot 3} + \dfrac{1}{3 \cdot 5} = \underline{\ ?\ }\ \ \dfrac{2}{5}$$

$$\dfrac{1}{1 \cdot 3} + \dfrac{1}{3 \cdot 5} + \dfrac{1}{5 \cdot 7} = \underline{\ ?\ }\ \ \dfrac{3}{7}$$

$$\dfrac{1}{1 \cdot 3} + \dfrac{1}{3 \cdot 5} + \dfrac{1}{5 \cdot 7} + \dfrac{1}{7 \cdot 9} = \underline{\ ?\ }\ \ \dfrac{4}{9}$$

b. If this pattern were continued for 50 fractions, what would the sum be? $\dfrac{50}{101}$

c. If this pattern were continued for n fractions, what would the sum be? $\dfrac{n}{2n+1}$

382   *Chapter 8*

8-8 Linear and Quadratic Functions

Objective To graph linear and quadratic functions.

The function g defined by
$$g(x) = 2x - 3$$
is called a *linear function*. If its domain is the set of all real numbers, then the straight line that is the graph of
$$y = g(x) = 2x - 3$$
is the **graph** of g. The slope of the graph is 2. The y-intercept is -3.

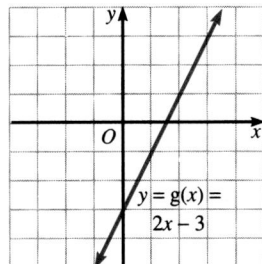

A function f defined by $f(x) = mx + b$ is a **linear function.**

If the domain of f is the set of real numbers, then its graph is the straight line with slope m and y-intercept b.

Now consider the function h defined by
$$h(x) = x^2 - 2x - 2.$$

If the domain of h is the set of all real numbers, then the graph of h is the graph of
$$y = h(x) = x^2 - 2x - 2.$$

Example 1 Graph the function h defined by the equation $y = h(x) = x^2 - 2x - 2$.

Solution Find the coordinates of selected points as shown in the table below. Plot the points and connect them with a smooth curve.

x	$x^2 - 2x - 2 = y$
-2	$(-2)^2 - 2(-2) - 2 =$ 6
-1	$(-1)^2 - 2(-1) - 2 =$ 1
0	$0^2\ \ - 2(0)\ - 2 = -2$
1	$1^2\ \ - 2(1)\ - 2 = -3$
2	$2^2\ \ - 2(2)\ - 2 = -2$
3	$3^2\ \ - 2(3)\ - 2 =$ 1
4	$4^2\ \ - 2(4)\ - 2 =$ 6

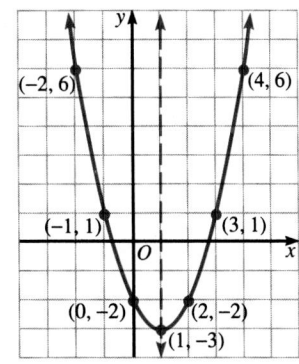

Introduction to Functions **383**

Teaching Suggestions p. T121
Reading Algebra p. T121
Suggested Extensions p. T122

Warm-Up Exercises

Graph the given ordered pairs in a coordinate plane and tell whether they form a straight line.

1. (2, 6), (−1, 6), (3, 5) no
2. (1, 2), (3, 4), (5, 6) yes

Motivating the Lesson

In this section, students will investigate the graphs of quadratic functions. They will see that the quadratic function does not behave the same way as does a linear function.

Chalkboard Examples

1. Graph the function f defined by the equation
$$y = f(x) = x^2 - 6x + 4.$$

x	$x^2 - 6x + 4 = y$
0	$0^2 - 6(0) + 4 = 4$
1	$1^2 - 6(1) + 4 = -1$
2	$2^2 - 6(2) + 4 = -4$
3	$3^2 - 6(3) + 4 = -5$
4	$4^2 - 6(4) + 4 = -4$
5	$5^2 - 6(5) + 4 = -1$
6	$6^2 - 6(6) + 4 = 4$

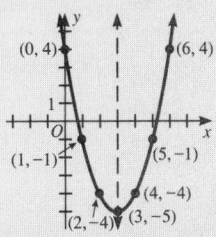

(continued)

2. Graph the function g defined by the equation $y = g(x) = -x^2 + 4x + 1$.

x	$-x^2 + 4x + 1 = y$
-1	$-(-1)^2 + 4(-1) + 1$ $= -4$
0	$-0^2 + 4(0) + 1 = 1$
1	$-1^2 + 4(1) + 1 = 4$
2	$-2^2 + 4(2) + 1 = 5$
3	$-3^2 + 4(3) + 1 = 4$
4	$-4^2 + 4(4) + 1 = 1$
5	$-5^2 + 4(5) + 1 = -4$

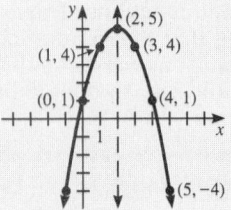

3. Find the vertex of the graph of

$A: x \rightarrow 3x^2 - 12x + 1$. Use the vertex and four other points to graph A. Identify and draw the axis of symmetry.

$$-\frac{b}{2a} = -\frac{-12}{6} = 2$$

The x-coordinate of vertex is 2 and the y-coordinate is -11:

$y = 3(2)^2 - 12(2) + 1 = -11$

vertex: $(2, -11)$
other points: $(0, 1)$, $(1, -8)$, $(3, -8)$, and $(4, 1)$

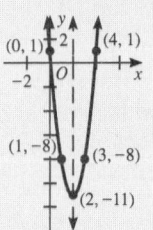

The curve shown in Example 1 is a **parabola.** This parabola opens upward and has a **minimum point,** or lowest point, at $(1, -3)$. The y-coordinate of this point is the **least value** of the function.

The vertical line $x = 1$, containing the minimum point, is called the **axis of symmetry** of the parabola. If you fold the graph along the axis of symmetry, the two halves of the parabola coincide.

Example 2 Graph the function k defined by the equation $y = k(x) = -x^2 + 2x + 2$.

Solution

x	$-x^2 + 2x + 2 = y$
-2	$-(-2)^2 + 2(-2) + 2 = -6$
-1	$-(-1)^2 + 2(-1) + 2 = -1$
0	$-0^2 + 2(0) + 2 = 2$
1	$-1^2 + 2(1) + 2 = 3$
2	$-2^2 + 2(2) + 2 = 2$
3	$-3^2 + 2(3) + 2 = -1$
4	$-4^2 + 2(4) + 2 = -6$

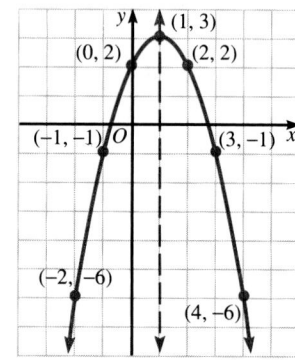

The graph in Example 2 is a parabola that opens downward and has a **maximum point,** or highest point, at $(1, 3)$. The y-coordinate of this point is the **greatest value** of the function. Notice that the maximum point $(1, 3)$ lies on the axis of symmetry.

A function f defined by $f(x) = ax^2 + bx + c$ $(a \neq 0)$ is a **quadratic function.**

If the domain of f is the set of real numbers, then the graph of f is a parabola.
If a is positive, the parabola opens upward.
If a is negative, the parabola opens downward.

The minimum or maximum point of a parabola is called the **vertex.** Notice that in Examples 1 and 2 the points, except the vertex, occur in *pairs that have the same y-coordinate.* The average of the x-coordinates of any such pair of points is the x-coordinate of the vertex.

If you have a computer or a graphing calculator, you can compare the graphs of $y = x^2 - 4x$ and $y = x^2 - 4x + 3$. For quadratic equations, such as $y = x^2 - 4x$ and $y = x^2 - 4x + 3$, that differ only in the constant term, the x-coordinates of the vertices are the same. You can find a formula for the x-coordinate of the vertex of $y = ax^2 + bx + c$, as shown on the next page, by using the two points where the graph of $y = ax^2 + bx$ crosses the x-axis, that is, the points where $y = 0$.

384   *Chapter 8*

$$y = ax^2 + bx$$

Let $y = 0$:
$$0 = ax^2 + bx$$
$$0 = x(ax + b)$$
$$x = 0 \text{ or } ax + b = 0$$
$$\therefore x = 0 \text{ or } x = -\frac{b}{a}$$

The average of these x-coordinates is $-\frac{b}{2a}$.

The x-coordinate of the vertex of the parabola $y = ax^2 + bx + c$ $(a \neq 0)$ is $-\frac{b}{2a}$. The axis of symmetry is the line $x = -\frac{b}{2a}$.

Unless otherwise stated, you may assume that the domain of each linear or quadratic function is the set of real numbers.

Example 3 Find the vertex of the graph of $H: x \rightarrow 2x^2 + 4x - 3$.
Use the vertex and four other points to graph H.
Identify and draw the axis of symmetry.

Solution 1. x-coordinate of vertex $= -\dfrac{b}{2a} = -\dfrac{4}{2 \cdot 2} = -\dfrac{4}{4} = -1$

2. To find the y-coordinate of the vertex, substitute -1 for x.
$$y = 2x^2 + 4x - 3$$
$$y = 2(-1)^2 + 4(-1) - 3$$
$$= 2 - 4 - 3 = -5$$
$\therefore$ the vertex is $(-1, -5)$.

3. For values of x, select two numbers greater than -1 and two numbers less than -1 to obtain paired points with the same y-coordinate.

x	$2x^2 + 4x - 3 = y$
-3	$2(-3)^2 + 4(-3) - 3 = 3$
-2	$2(-2)^2 + 4(-2) - 3 = -3$
-1	$2(-1)^2 + 4(-1) - 3 = -5$
0	$2(0)^2 + 4(0) - 3 = -3$
1	$2(1)^2 + 4(1) - 3 = 3$

Vertex is the row with $x = -1$.

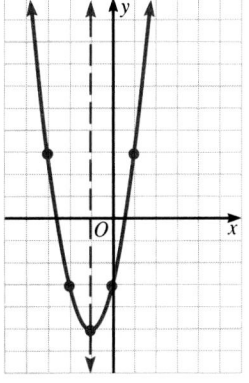

4. Plot the points. Connect them with a smooth curve.

5. The axis of symmetry is the line $x = -1$ (shown as a dashed line on the graph).

Introduction to Functions **385**

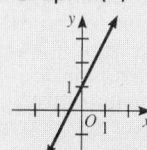
Using a Computer or a Graphing Calculator

A computer or a graphing calculator can be used to compare the graphs of $y = x^2 - 4x$ and $y = x^2 - 4x + 3$. You may wish to have students discover how the graph of $y = x^2 + c$ changes as the value of c changes. Also, students can investigate the changes in the graph of $y = ax^2$ as the value of a changes. For Written Exs. 1–6 and 19–30, they can use a computer or graphing calculator to check their work.

Support Materials
  Disk for Algebra
  Menu Items:
    Line Plotter
    Parabola Plotter
  Resource Book   p. 208

Check for Understanding

Oral Exs. 1–6: use after definition of a linear function.
Oral Exs. 7–18; use after definition of vertex.

Guided Practice

1. Graph $f(x) = 2x + 1$.

2. Find the coordinates of the vertex. Then give the equation of the axis of symmetry and the least or the greatest value of the function.

   a. $g(x) = 4x^2 - 1$
      $(0, -1); x = 0; -1$

   b. $k(x) = -x^2 + 2x + 1$
      $(1, 2); x = 1; 2$

(continued)

(continued)
Find the vertex and the axis of symmetry of the graph of each equation. Use the vertex and at least four other points to graph the equation.

3. $y = -\frac{1}{2}x^2$ (0, 0); $x = 0$

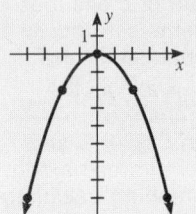

4. $y = x^2 + x - 12$
$\left(-\frac{1}{2}, -12\frac{1}{4}\right)$; $x = -\frac{1}{2}$

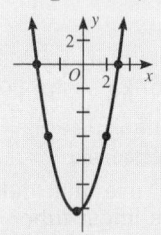

Summarizing the Lesson

The graph of a quadratic function, such as $f(x) = ax^2 + bx + c$ ($a \neq 0$), is a parabola. If a is positive, the vertex is a minimum point (parabola opens up). If a is negative, the vertex is a maximum point (parabola opens down).

Suggested Assignments

Minimum
386/1–21 odd
S 387/Mixed Review

Average
386/1–29 odd, 31, 33
S 387/Mixed Review

Maximum
386/1–41 odd
S 387/Mixed Review

Oral Exercises

State the slope and y-intercept of the graph of each linear function.

1. $f: x \rightarrow -3x + 9$ –3; 9   **2.** $g: x \rightarrow 4x - 8$ 4; –8   **3.** $p(x) = 4 + \frac{3}{2}x$ $\frac{3}{2}$; 4

4. $t(x) = -\frac{2}{3}x - \frac{2}{3}$; 0   **5.** $t(x) = 0$ 0, 0   **6.** $f(x) = 5$ 0; 5

State whether the graph of each quadratic function opens upward or downward.

7. $y = x^2 - 3x + 4$ up   **8.** $y = -2x^2 + x + 1$ down   **9.** $y = 9 - x^2$ down

10. $x^2 - 9 = y$ up   **11.** $3x^2 - 3x = y$ up   **12.** $y = -\frac{1}{3}x^2$ down

State whether the graph of each quadratic function has a minimum or a maximum point.

13. $f: x \rightarrow x^2 - 2x + 1$ min.   **14.** $g: x \rightarrow 3 - 2x - x^2$ max.   **15.** $h: x \rightarrow 3x^2 - x$ min.

16. $P: x \rightarrow 1 - x^2$ max.   **17.** $T: x \rightarrow 8x^2 + x - 6$ min.   **18.** $f: x \rightarrow \frac{2}{5}x^2$ min.

Written Exercises

Draw the graph of each linear function. You may wish to verify your graphs on a computer or a graphing calculator.

A   **1.** $g: x \rightarrow x - 3$ **2.** $f: x \rightarrow -x + 1$ **3.** $q(x) = 2 - \frac{1}{3}x$

     4. $d(x) = -\frac{3}{4}x$ **5.** $r(x) = -7$ **6.** $n(x) = 0$

Find the coordinates of the vertex. Then give the equation of the axis of symmetry and the least value of the function.

7. $f(x) = x^2 - 5$ (0, –5); $x = 0$; –5   **8.** $g(x) = x^2 + 4$ (0, 4); $x = 0$; 4   **9.** $h(x) = x^2 - x - 6$ $\left(\frac{1}{2}, -6\frac{1}{4}\right)$; $x = \frac{1}{2}$; $-6\frac{1}{4}$

10. $t(x) = 4 - 10x + 5x^2$
(1, –1); $x = 1$; –1   **11.** $G(x) = 9x^2 - 4$
(0, –4); $x = 0$; –4   **12.** $F(x) = \frac{1}{4}x^2$
(0, 0); $x = 0$; 0

Find the coordinates of the vertex. Then give the equation of the axis of symmetry and the greatest value of the function.

13. $g(x) = -x^2 - 3x$ **14.** $f(x) = 4x - x^2$ (2, 4); $x = 2$; 4   **15.** $H(x) = -x^2 - 8x - 15$
(–4, 1); $x = -4$; 1

16. $K(x) = 1 - 3x - 6x^2$
$\left(-\frac{1}{4}, 1\frac{3}{8}\right)$; $x = -\frac{1}{4}$; $1\frac{3}{8}$ **17.** $f(x) = x - 2x^2$
$\left(\frac{1}{4}, \frac{1}{8}\right)$; $x = \frac{1}{4}$; $\frac{1}{8}$ **18.** $h(x) = 1 - \frac{1}{3}x^2$
(0, 1); $x = 0$; 1

13. $\left(-1\frac{1}{2}, 2\frac{1}{4}\right)$; $x = -1\frac{1}{2}$; $2\frac{1}{4}$

Find the vertex and the axis of symmetry of the graph of each equation. Use the vertex and at least four other points to graph the equation. You may wish to verify your graphs on a computer or a graphing calculator.

19. $y = 2x^2$ (0, 0); x = 0   **20.** $y = 3 - x^2$ (0, 3); x = 0   **21.** $y = 3x^2$ (0, 0); x = 0

22. $y = -3x^2$ (0, 0); x = 0   **23.** $y = \frac{1}{2}x^2$ (0, 0); x = 0   **24.** $y = -\frac{1}{2}x^2$ (0, 0); x = 0

25. $y = x^2 - 4x$ (2, −4); x = 2   **26.** $y = -x^2 + 2x$ (1, 1); x = 1   **27.** $y = -x^2 - 5x + 6$

28. $y = x^2 - 3x - 10$ **29.** $y = 4 - \frac{1}{3}x^2$ (0, 4); x = 0   **30.** $y = 6 + 6x - \frac{1}{3}x^2$

$\left(1\frac{1}{2}, -12\frac{1}{4}\right)$; x = $1\frac{1}{2}$ **27.** $\left(-2\frac{1}{2}, 12\frac{1}{4}\right)$; x = $-2\frac{1}{2}$ **30.** (9, 33); x = 9

You may wish to use a computer or a graphing calculator to do Ex. 31–32.

B **31. a.** On the same set of axes draw the graphs of $y = x^2$, $y = x^2 + 1$, and $y = x^2 - 2$.

    b. Use your results in part (a) to describe the changes in the graph of $y = x^2 + c$ as the value of c increases; as c decreases. graph rises; graph lowers

32. a. On the same set of axes draw the graphs of $y = \frac{1}{2}x^2$, $y = x^2$, and $y = 2x^2$.

    b. On the same set of axes draw the graphs of $y = -\frac{1}{2}x^2$, $y = -x^2$, and $y = -2x^2$.

    c. Use your results in parts (a) and (b) to describe the change in the graph of $y = ax^2$ as $|a|$ increases. The parabola becomes a narrower curve.

The *zeros* of a function f are the values of x for which $f(x) = 0$. In Exercises 33–40, find (a) $f(0)$; (b) the zeros of f.

33. $f(x) = 2x + 10$ 10; {−5}   **34.** $f(x) = 3x - 9$ −9; {3}

35. $f(x) = 4x - 11$ −11; $\left\{2\frac{3}{4}\right\}$ **36.** $f(x) = 5x + 8$ 8; $\left\{-1\frac{3}{5}\right\}$

37. $f(x) = x^2 - 6x + 8$ 8; {2, 4}   **38.** $f(x) = x^2 - 8x + 15$ 15; {3, 5}

39. $f(x) = x^2 + 8x + 12$ 12; {−6, −2}   **40.** $f(x) = x^2 + 9x + 20$ 20; {−5, −4}

41. Interpret the zeros of the function f in terms of the graph of f. x-intercept

42. Interpret $f(0)$ in terms of the graph of f. y-intercept

Mixed Review Exercises

Find the range of each function.

1. $H: x \rightarrow 3x^2 + 2$, $D = \{0, 1, 2\}$ {2, 5, 14}   **2.** $f(a) = 2a - 4$, $D = \{-2, 0, 2\}$ {−8, −4, 0}

3. $M(b) = b^3 + 7$, $D = \{-1, 1, 3\}$ {6, 8, 34}   **4.** $K: z \rightarrow z^2 - z$, $D = \{1, 2, 3\}$ {0, 2, 6}

Translate each phrase into a variable expression.

5. 7 times the sum of a number and 4 7(x + 4)   **6.** The difference between a number and 3   x − 3

7. The product of a number and 9 9x   **8.** 5 less than one third of a number $\frac{1}{3}x - 5$

Introduction to Functions   **387**

Supplementary Materials

Study Guide   pp. 147–148
Practice Master   49
Test Master   35
Resource Book   p. 118
Overhead Visual   B

Additional Answers
Written Exercises

2.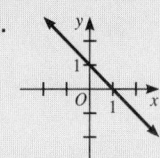

4.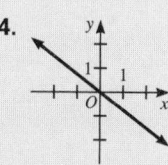

6.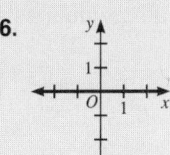

20.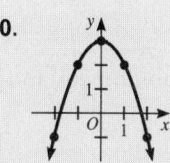

22.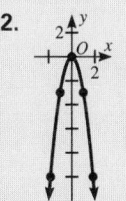

24.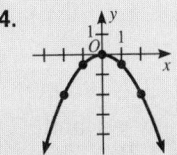

(continued on p. 404)

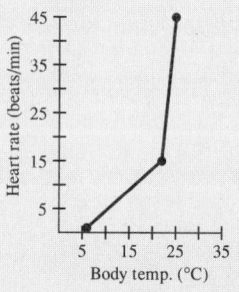
Computer Exercises

For students with some programming experience

Write a BASIC program that determines the vertex of the graph of a quadratic equation $y = Ax^2 + Bx + C$ when A, B, and C are entered with an INPUT statement. The program should also give three points on each side of the vertex that can be used to graph the quadratic equation. Run the program for the following quadratic equations.

1. $y = x^2$
2. $y = -x^2 + 2x + 2$
3. $y = x^2 - 4x + 3$
4. $y = x^2 - 4x$
5. $y = 2x^2 + 4x - 3$
6. $y = -x^2 - 5x + 6$

Self-Test 3

Vocabulary
function (p. 374)
domain of a function (p. 374)
range of a function (p. 374)
bar graph (p. 375)
broken-line graph (p. 375)
arrow notation (p. 379)
functional notation (p. 379)
value of function (p. 379)
graph (p. 383)

linear function (p. 383)
parabola (p. 384)
minimum point (p. 384)
least value (p. 384)
axis of symmetry (p. 384)
maximum point (p. 384)
greatest value (p. 384)
quadratic function (p. 384)
vertex (p. 384)

1. The table below defines a function.　　　　　　　　　　**Obj. 8-6, p. 374**
   a. State the domain and range of the function.
   b. Graph the function by means of a bar graph or a broken-line graph, whichever is more suitable. **a.** $D = \{1985, 1986, 1987, 1988, 1989, 1990\}$
   $R = \{0.75, 0.90, 1.12, 1.43, 1.65, 2.05\}$

Earnings per share of Common Foods Corp.						
Year	1985	1986	1987	1988	1989	1990
Earnings per share ($)	0.75	0.90	1.12	1.43	1.65	2.05

2. Find the range of g if $g: n \rightarrow n^2 + 2n + 3$ and $R = \{2, 3, 6, 11, 18\}$　　**Obj. 8-7, p. 379**
   $D = \{-1, 0, 1, 2, 3\}$.

3. Given $f(x) = 7x - 3$, find:　　**a.** $f(2)$ 11　　**b.** $f(-1)$ −10　　**c.** $f(0)$ −3

4. Find the coordinates of the vertex of $f(x) = x^2 + 8x + 10$. Then　　**Obj. 8-8, p. 383**
   give the least value of the function. $(-4, -6)$; −6

5. Find the coordinates of the vertex and the equation of the axis of symmetry of the graph of $y = 2x^2 - 4x + 1$. Use the vertex and at least four other points to graph the equation. $(1, -1)$; $x = 1$

Check your answers with those at the back of the book.

388 *Chapter 8*

Extra / *Relations*

The diagram at the right shows how each number in the set

$$D = \{0, 1, 2, 3\}$$

is paired with one or more numbers in the set

$$R = \{-1, 1, 2, 3\}.$$

The same pairing is shown in the table next to the diagram and in the list of ordered pairs shown below.

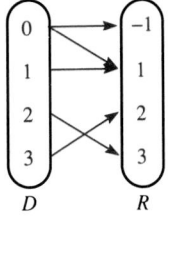

D	R
0	-1
0	1
1	1
2	3
3	2

$$\{(0, -1), (0, 1), (1, 1), (2, 3), (3, 2)\}$$

Notice that this pairing assigns to the number 0 in D two different numbers, -1 and 1, in R. Therefore, the pairing is *not* a function with domain D and range R, since in a function each member of the domain is assigned *exactly one* member of the range. The pairing described above is an example of a *relation*.

A **relation** is any set of ordered pairs.
The set of first coordinates of the ordered pairs is the **domain** of the relation.
The set of second coordinates is the **range.**

The figure at the right shows the graphs of all the ordered pairs that form the relation described above. We call this set the **graph of the relation.**

A function is a special kind of relation.

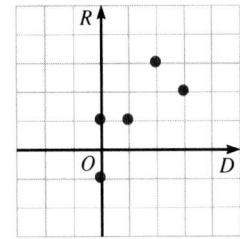

A function is a relation in which different ordered pairs have different first coordinates.

Therefore, in the graph of a function, there is only one point plotted for each value in the domain.

Exercises

1. $D = \{2, 3\}$; $R = \{0, 3, 4, 6\}$
2. $D = \{1, 2, 3, 4\}$; $R = \{-1, 3, 5, 8\}$
3. $D = \{1, 2, 3, 4\}$; $R = \{-3, -1, 0, 6\}$
4. $D = \{0, 5\}$; $R = \{0, 1, 2, 4\}$

State the domain and range of each relation. Is the relation a function?

1. $\{(3, 4), (2, 3), (3, 6), (2, 0)\}$ no

2. $\{(1, -1), (2, 3), (3, 5), (4, 8)\}$ yes

3. $\{(2, -1), (3, 0), (4, 6), (1, -3)\}$ yes

4. $\{(5, 0), (5, 1), (5, 2), (0, 4)\}$ no

5. $\{(-1, 1), (1, 1), (2, 4), (-2, 4)\}$ yes
$D = \{-2, -1, 1, 2\}$; $R = \{1, 4\}$

6. $\{(4, 2), (4, -2), (9, 3), (9, -3)\}$ no
$D = \{4, 9\}$; $R = \{-3, -2, 2, 3\}$

Introduction to Functions   **389**

3. Given $t(n) = 4n - 1$, find:
a. $t(3)$ 11   **b.** $t(-2)$ -9
c. $t(0)$ -1

4. Find the coordinates of the vertex of
$f(x) = x^2 - 2x - 3$. $(1, -4)$
Then give the least value of the function. -4

5. Find the coordinates of the vertex and the equation of the axis of symmetry of the graph of
$y = -x^2 + 6x - 9$. Use the vertex and at least four other points to graph the equation. $(3, 0)$; $x = 3$

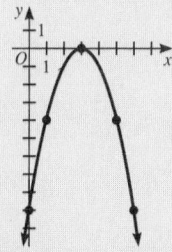

Additional Answers
Self-Test 3

1. b.

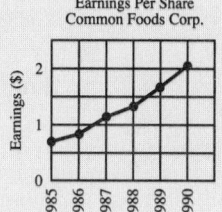

Earnings Per Share
Common Foods Corp.

5.

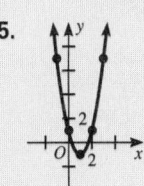

Give the domain and range of the relation graphed in each diagram. Is the relation a function?

7. 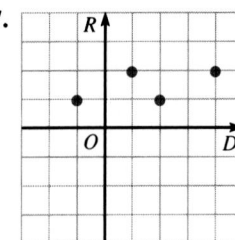 **8.** 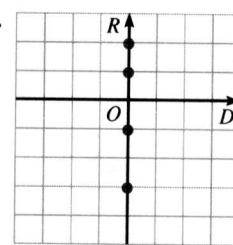 **9.**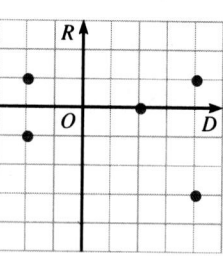

10. 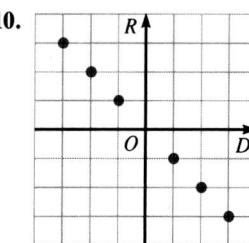 **11.** 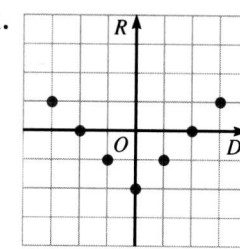 **12.**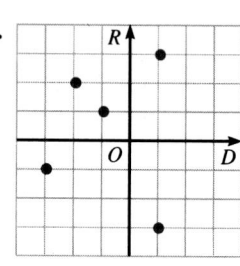

In Exercises 13–18, graph each relation and determine whether it is a function. If it is not a function, explain how that fact shows up on the graph.

13. $\{(-4, 2), (-1, 3), (4, 4), (4, -3)\}$

14. $\{(0, -1), (1, -2), (2, -3), (-1, 2)\}$

15. $\{(-3, 2), (0, 1), (3, -2), (-3, 0)\}$

16. $\{(-1, 1), (0, 0), (1, 1), (2, 4)\}$

17. $\{(0, 0), (1, 2), (2, 9), (-2, -7)\}$

18. $\{(1, 0), (2, 3), (3, -1), (1, 5)\}$

19. Consider the set of all ordered pairs of real numbers (x, y) that satisfy the equation $|y| = |x|$. Is this set of ordered pairs a relation? Is it a function? Justify your answers.

20. The circle shown at the right is the graph of the equation $x^2 + y^2 = 4$. Do the coordinates of the points of the circle form a relation? a function? Why or why not? If the points form a relation or a function, what are the domain and range?

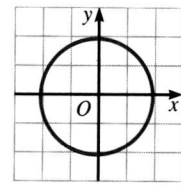

In Exercises 21–24, consider the set of all ordered pairs (x, y) as described. Is the set a relation? Is it a function?

21. (x, y), where x is the name of a telephone subscriber in your town and y is the subscriber's telephone number. yes; no

22. (x, y), where x is the name of each mother in your town and y is the name of her child. yes; no

23. (x, y), where x is each man in London, England, and y is his right thumbprint. yes, yes

24. (x, y), where x is any nonvertical line in the coordinate plane and y is its slope. yes; yes

390   *Chapter 8*

Variation

8-9 Direct Variation

Objective   To use direct variation to solve problems.

The table below shows the mass m of a gold bar whose volume is V cubic centimeters.

Volume in cubic centimeters: V	Mass in grams: m
1	19.3
2	38.6
3	57.9
4	77.2
5	96.5

You can see that $m = 19.3V$. This equation defines a linear function. Note that if the volume of the bar is doubled, the mass is doubled; if the volume is tripled, the mass is tripled, and so on. You can say that the mass *varies directly* as the volume. This function is an example of a *direct variation*.

A **direct variation** is a function defined by an equation of the form
$$y = kx, \text{ where } k \text{ is a nonzero constant.}$$
You can say that y *varies directly as* x.
The constant k is called the **constant of variation.**

When the domain is the set of real numbers, the graph of a direct variation is a straight line with slope k that passes through the origin.

Example 1   Given that m varies directly as n and that $m = 42$ when $n = 2$, find the following.
    a. the constant of variation   **b.** the value of m when $n = 3$

Solution   Let $m = kn$.
    a. Substitute $m = 42$ and $n = 2$: $42 = k \cdot 2$
                                    $21 = k$ *Answer*
    b. Substitute $k = 21$ and $n = 3$: $m = 21 \cdot 3 = 63$ *Answer*

2. The amount a babysitter earns is directly proportional to the number of hours worked. If $7 is earned for 4 hours of work, how much is earned for 10 hours of work? $\frac{7}{4} = \frac{x}{10}$; $x = 17.5$

$17.50 is earned.

Check for Understanding

Here is a suggested use of the Oral Exercises to check students' understanding as you teach the lesson.
Oral Exs. 1–12: use after Example 1.
Oral Exs. 13–24: use after discussion of constant of proportionality.

Guided Practice

Find the constant of variation.

1. y varies directly as x and $y = 18$ when $x = 6$. 3

2. y varies directly as x and $y = \frac{1}{3}$ when $x = \frac{1}{2}$. $\frac{2}{3}$

3. s is directly proportional to p and $s = 60$ when $p = 5$. 12

4. s is directly proportional to p and $s = 256$ when $p = 16$. 16

(x_1, y_1) and (x_2, y_2) are ordered pairs of the same direct variation. Find each missing value.

5. $x_1 = 6$, $y_1 = 5$
   $x_2 = 3$, $y_2 = \underline{\ ?\ }$ $2\frac{1}{2}$

6. $x_1 = 27$, $y_1 = 72$
   $x_2 = 24$, $y_2 = \underline{\ ?\ }$ 64

Suppose (x_1, y_1) and (x_2, y_2) are two ordered pairs of a direct variation defined by $y = kx$ and that neither x_1 nor x_2 is zero. Since (x_1, y_1) and (x_2, y_2) must satisfy $y = kx$, you know that

$$y_1 = kx_1 \text{ and } y_2 = kx_2.$$

From these equations you can write the ratios

$$\frac{y_1}{x_1} = k \text{ and } \frac{y_2}{x_2} = k.$$

Since each ratio equals k, the ratios are equal.

$$\frac{y_1}{x_1} = \frac{y_2}{x_2}, \text{ read ``}y_1 \text{ is to } x_1 \text{ as } y_2 \text{ is to } x_2\text{.''}$$

This equation, which states that two ratios are equal, is a proportion (page 293). For this reason, k is sometimes called the **constant of proportionality,** and y is said to be *directly proportional to x.*

When you use a proportion to solve a problem, you will find it helpful to recall that the product of the extremes equals the product of the means.

Example 2 The amount of interest earned on savings is directly proportional to the amount of money saved. If $104 interest is earned on $1300, how much interest will be earned on $1800 in the same period of time?

Solution 1

Step 1 The problem asks for the interest on $1800 if the interest on $1300 is $104.

Step 2 Let i, in dollars, be the interest on d dollars.

$$i_1 = 104 \qquad i_2 = \underline{\ ?\ }$$
$$d_1 = 1300 \qquad d_2 = 1800$$

Step 3 An equation can be written in the form $\dfrac{i_1}{d_1} = \dfrac{i_2}{d_2}$.

$$\frac{104}{1300} = \frac{i_2}{1800}$$

Step 4
$$104(1800) = 1300i_2$$
$$187{,}200 = 1300i_2$$
$$144 = i_2$$

Step 5 The check is left to you.

$\therefore$ the interest earned on $1800 will be $144. **Answer**

Solution 2 To solve Example 2 by the method shown in Example 1, first write the equation $i = kd$. Then solve for the constant of variation, k, by using the fact that $i = 104$ when $d = 1300$. Use the value of k to find the value of i when $d = 1800$. You may wish to complete the problem this way.

You will find the exercises and problems of this lesson easier if you understand *both* methods.

---

392 *Chapter 8*

Oral Exercises

State whether or not each equation defines a direct variation. For each direct variation, state the constant of variation.

1. $y = 3x$ yes; 3   **2.** $p = 9s$ yes; 9   **3.** $xy = 4$ no   **4.** $d = 3.3t$ yes; 3.3

5. $\frac{1}{2}x = 7$ no   **6.** $\frac{y}{x} = -5$ yes; –5   **7.** $p = \frac{4}{q}$ no   **8.** $C = \pi d$ yes; π

9. $A = \pi r^2$ no   **10.** $\frac{c}{d} = 1$ yes; 1   **11.** $y = 3x^2$ no   **12.** $\frac{x}{y} = \frac{5}{2}$ yes; $\frac{2}{5}$

State whether or not the given ordered pairs are in the same direct variation.

Sample   (6, 8), (9, 12), (18, 24)

Solution $\frac{8}{6} = \frac{4}{3}$, $\frac{12}{9} = \frac{4}{3}$, $\frac{24}{18} = \frac{4}{3}$. Since the ratios are equal, the ordered pairs are in the direct variation $y = \frac{4}{3}x$.

13. (2, 4), (6, 12), (10, 20) yes   **14.** (1, 3), (−6, −18), (5, 15) yes

15. (1, 1), (2, 1), (3, 3) no   **16.** (−1, 2), (2, −4), (4, −8) yes

State whether or not the statement is true. If it is not true, explain why.

17. Every linear function is a direct variation.   No; for example, the linear function $x + 3 = y$ is not a direct variation.

18. All direct variations are linear functions. yes

19. Some linear functions are direct variations. yes

20. No function is both a linear function and a direct variation. No; a direct variation assigns one value of y for every value of x; ∴ it is a linear function.

State whether or not each formula shows a direct variation.

21. $\frac{x_1}{y_1} = \frac{x_2}{y_2}$ yes   **22.** $\frac{x_1}{x_2} = \frac{y_1}{y_2}$ yes   **23.** $\frac{y_1}{x_2} = \frac{y_2}{x_1}$ no   **24.** $\frac{y_2}{x_2} = \frac{y_1}{x_1}$ yes

Written Exercises

In Exercises 1–6, find the constant of variation.

A   **1.** y varies directly as x, and $y = 9$ when $x = 54$. $\frac{1}{6}$

2. y varies directly as x, and $y = 6$ when $x = 72$. $\frac{1}{12}$

3. t varies directly as s, and $t = -16$ when $s = -2$. 8

4. h varies directly as m, and $h = 112$ when $m = -16$. −7

5. W is directly proportional to m, and $W = 150$ when $m = 6$. 25

6. P is directly proportional to t, and $P = 210$ when $t = 14$. 15

Introduction to Functions   **393**

Summarizing the Lesson
Have students recall that, if y varies directly as x, then the function is given by the equation $y = kx$ for some value of k. Many problems involving direct variation can be solved by using the fact that the ratio of the two quantities involved is always constant.

Suggested Assignments
Minimum
Day 1: 393/1–21 odd
   R 388/Self-Test 3
Day 2: 395/P:1–9 odd
   S 396/Mixed Review
Assign with Lesson 8-10.

Average
Day 1: 393/1–21 odd
   R 388/Self-Test 3
Day 2: 395/P: 1–11 odd
   S 396/Mixed Review
Assign with Lesson 8-10.

Maximum
   393/3–24 mult. of 3
   395/P: 3–15 mult. of 3
   S 396/Mixed Review
   R 388/Self-Test 3

Supplementary Materials
Study Guide   pp. 149–150
Overhead Visual   9

7. y varies directly as x, and $y = 450$ when $x = 6$. Find y when $x = 10$. 750

8. d varies directly as z, and $d = 6$ when $z = 48$. Find d when $z = 20$. 2.5

9. h is directly proportional to a, and $h = 425$ when $a = 8.5$. Find h when $a = 12$. 600

10. r is directly proportional to A, and $r = 14$ when $A = 87.5$. Find r when $A = 25$. 4

(x_1, y_1) and (x_2, y_2) are ordered pairs of the same direct variation. Find each missing value.

11. $x_1 = 15$, $y_1 = 9$
$x_2 = 40$, $y_2 = \underline{\ ?\ }$ 24

12. $x_1 = 45$, $y_1 = \underline{\ ?\ }$ 75
$x_2 = 60$, $y_2 = 100$

13. $x_1 = 3.6$, $y_1 = 3$ 1.2
$x_2 = \underline{\ ?\ }$, $y_2 = 1$

14. $x_1 = \underline{\ ?\ }$, $y_1 = 7$ 5.95
$x_2 = 7.65$, $y_2 = 9$

15. $x_1 = \frac{1}{10}$, $y_1 = \frac{1}{6}$
$x_2 = \frac{2}{5}$, $y_2 = \underline{\ ?\ }$ $\frac{2}{3}$

16. $x_1 = \frac{6}{5}$, $y_1 = \underline{\ ?\ }$
$x_2 = \frac{2}{3}$, $y_2 = \frac{1}{9}$ $\frac{1}{5}$

For each direct variation described, write (a) a formula and (b) a proportion.

Sample   The speed, v, of a skydiver in free fall is directly proportional to the number, t, of seconds of fall. After 2 s, the speed is 19.6 m/s.

Solution   **a.** $v = kt$; $v = 19.6$ when $t = 2$.

$19.6 = k(2)$, so $k = \dfrac{19.6}{2} = 9.8$

$\therefore v = 9.8t$

b. Let $v_1 = 19.6$ and $t_1 = 2$.

$\dfrac{19.6}{2} = \dfrac{v_2}{t_2}$

B **17.** The length, L, of the shadow of a tree at any moment varies directly with the height, h, of the tree. At a certain moment, a tree 20 ft tall casts a shadow 14 ft long.

18. The heat, H, required to melt a substance varies directly with its mass, m. Forty-nine calories of heat are needed to melt one gram of copper.

19. The weight, M, of an object on the moon is directly proportional to the weight, E, on Earth. An object weighing 168 lb on Earth weighs 28 lb on the moon.

20. Distance, m, on a map varies directly with the actual distance, d. On a certain map, 1 in. represents 10 mi.

21. At any given temperature, the electrical resistance of a wire is directly proportional to the length. At 20° C, 500 m of No. 18 gauge copper wire has a resistance of 10.295 ohms. $R = 0.02059l$; $\dfrac{10.295}{500} = \dfrac{R_2}{l_2}$

22. Under constant pressure, the volume, V, of a dry gas is directly proportional to its temperature, T, in Kelvin. A sample of oxygen occupies a volume of 5 L at 300 K. $V = \dfrac{1}{60}T$; $\dfrac{5}{300} = \dfrac{V_2}{T_2}$

Let (x_1, y_1) and (x_2, y_2) be ordered pairs of direct variation. Suppose that no coordinate is 0. Show that each given statement is true.

C 23. $\dfrac{y_1}{x_1} = \dfrac{y_2}{x_2}$ 　　　　　　　24. $\dfrac{y_1}{y_2} = \dfrac{x_1}{x_2}$

Problems

Solve.

A 1. An employee's wages are directly proportional to the time worked. If an employee earns \$100 for 5 h, how much will the employee earn for 18 h? $360

2. A certain car uses 15 gal of gasoline in 3 h. If the rate of gasoline consumption is constant, how much gasoline will the car use on a 35-hour trip? 175 gal

3. The amount of money that a magazine pays for an article varies directly as the number of words in the article. If the magazine pays \$720 for a 1200-word article, how much will be paid for an article of 1500 words? $900

4. The distance traveled by a truck at a constant speed varies directly with the length of time it travels. If the truck travels 168 mi in 4 h, how far will it travel in 7 h? 294 mi

5. The number of words typed is directly proportional to the time spent typing. If a typist can type 275 words in 5 min, how long will it take the typist to type a 935-word essay? 17 min

6. When an electric current is 32 A (amperes), the electromotive force is 288 V (volts). Find the force when the current is 65 A if the force varies directly as the current. 585 V

7. The area covered by a painter is directly proportional to the number of hours worked. A painter covered 52 m² in the first 8 h on the job. How large an area will the painter cover in 24 h? 156 m²

8. A restaurant buys 20 lb of ground beef to prepare 110 servings of chili. At this rate, how many servings can be made with 30 lb of ground beef? 165 servings

9. A mass of 25 g stretches a spring 10 cm. If the distance a spring is stretched is directly proportional to the mass, what mass will stretch the spring 22 cm? 55 g

10. The amount of chlorine needed for a pool varies directly as the size of the pool. If 5 units of chlorine is the amount needed for 2500 L of water, how much chlorine is needed for 3750 L of water? 7.5 units

B 11. Thermometer F is marked off into 180 equal units. Thermometer C is marked off into 100 equal units. A reading of 66.6 degrees on thermometer F is equal to a reading of how many degrees on thermometer C? 37 degrees

12. The odometer on the Goldmans' car was not measuring distance correctly. For a 220-mi trip the odometer registered only 216.7 mi. On the return trip, the Goldmans had to detour due to road repairs. If the odometer registered 453.1 mi for the round trip, how many actual miles was the detour? 20 mi

Introduction to Functions　　**395**

23. Since (x_1, y_1) and (x_2, y_2) are ordered pairs of a direct variation and neither is $(0, 0)$, $\dfrac{x_1}{y_1}$ and $\dfrac{x_2}{y_2}$ are equivalent fractions, so $\dfrac{x_1}{y_1} = \dfrac{x_2}{y_2}$; $x_1 y_2 = x_2 y_1$; $y_2 = \dfrac{x_2 y_1}{x_1}$; $\dfrac{y_2}{x_2} = \dfrac{y_1}{x_1}$ or $\dfrac{y_1}{x_1} = \dfrac{y_2}{x_2}$.

24. We know that $\dfrac{x_1}{y_1} = \dfrac{x_2}{y_2}$ (see Ex. 23); $x_1 y_2 = x_2 y_1$; $x_1 = \dfrac{x_2 y_1}{y_2}$; $\dfrac{x_1}{x_2} = \dfrac{y_1}{y_2}$, or $\dfrac{y_1}{y_2} = \dfrac{x_1}{x_2}$

Problem Solving Strategies
Although the problems in this set cover a wide variety of applications, students should *recognize a common problem type:* direct variation. They should also be aware of the two *alternate methods of solution:* the use of the formula $y = kx$ and the use of a proportion. The next lesson will introduce another problem type: inverse variation.

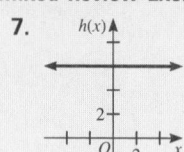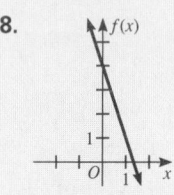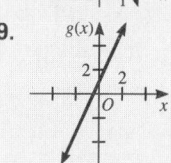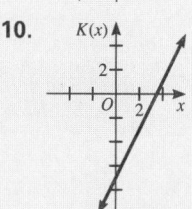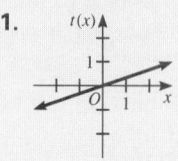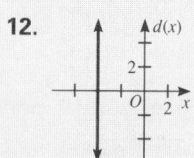
13. On a map, 1 cm represents an actual distance of 75 m. Find the area of a piece of land that is represented on the map by a rectangle measuring 11.5 cm by 18.5 cm. 1,196,718.75 m²

14. In a scale model of a sailboat, an object that is 6 ft tall is represented by a figure 8 in. high. How many feet tall should the mast of the sailboat be in the model if the actual mast of the sailboat is 38 ft tall? $4\frac{2}{9}$ ft

C 15. If the circumference of a circle varies directly as the diameter, and the diameter varies directly as the radius, show that the circumference varies directly as the radius. If $C = k_1 d$ and $d = k_2 r$, then $C = k_1(k_2 r)$ or $C = (k_1 \cdot k_2)r$ and C varies directly as r.

Mixed Review Exercises

Multiply.

1. $(2p + 3)(3p + 1)$ $6p^2 + 11p + 3$

2. $(4x - 2)(x^2 + 3x - 6)$ $4x^3 + 10x^2 - 30x + 12$

3. $-3s(5 - 4s)$ $-15s + 12s^2$

4. $(3c + 2)(3c - 2)$ $9c^2 - 4$

5. $(t + 2)(3t - 5)$ $3t^2 + t - 10$

6. $(7y - 3)(2y + 4)$ $14y^2 + 22y - 12$

Draw the graph of each function.

7. $h(x) = 6$

8. $f: x \rightarrow -3x + 4$

9. $g(x) = \frac{5}{2}x + 1$

10. $K: x \rightarrow 2x - 7$

11. $t(x) = \frac{1}{3}x$

12. $d: x \rightarrow -4$

▨ Biographical Note / *Hsien Wu*

Hsien Wu attended school in China and came to the United States to attend the Massachusetts Institute of Technology. He received his Ph.D. in biochemistry from Harvard University in 1917.

Wu developed methods to analyze small samples of blood. This was a major breakthrough as previous methods required large samples, a procedure that was not advantageous for the patient.

In 1924 Wu was appointed to head the biochemistry department at Peking Union Medical College. He conducted studies in eating habits and health, nutrition, and food composition. His many research papers made Wu the foremost nutritionist in China. He was appointed to a number of international committees and was made director of the Nutrition Institute of China.

8-10 Inverse Variation

Objective   To use inverse variation to solve problems.

The table shows the time, t, that it takes a car to travel a distance of 40 mi at the speed of r mi/h. You can see that

$$rt = 40.$$

Notice that if the speed is increased, the time is decreased, so that the product is always 40. You can say that the time *varies inversely* as the rate. This example illustrates an *inverse variation*.

Rate in mi/h: r	Time in hours: t
20	2
30	$\frac{4}{3}$
40	1
50	$\frac{4}{5}$

An **inverse variation** is a function defined by an equation of the form

$$xy = k, \text{ where } k \text{ is a nonzero constant,}$$

or $y = \dfrac{k}{x}$, where $x \neq 0$.

You say that y *varies inversely as* x or that y *is inversely proportional to* x. The constant k is the **constant of variation.**

The graph of an inverse function is not a straight line, since the equation

$$xy = k$$

is not linear. The term xy is of degree 2.

Example 1   Graph the equation $xy = 1$.

Solution

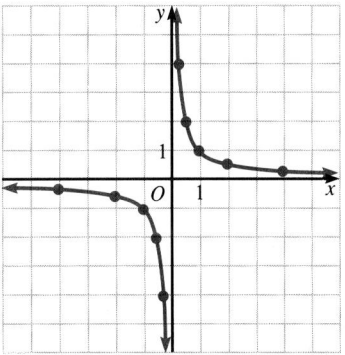

x	y
-4	$-\frac{1}{4}$
-2	$-\frac{1}{2}$
-1	-1
$-\frac{1}{2}$	-2
$-\frac{1}{4}$	-4

x	y
$\frac{1}{4}$	4
$\frac{1}{2}$	2
1	1
2	$\frac{1}{2}$
4	$\frac{1}{4}$

The graph of $xy = 1$ shown in Example 1 is called a *hyperbola*. Since neither x nor y can have the value 0, the graph does not intersect either the x-axis or the y-axis.

Introduction to Functions   **397**

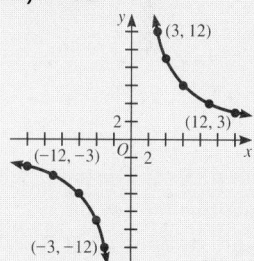

Here is a suggested use of
the Oral Exercises.

Oral Exs. 1–18: use after the
discussion of direct variation and inverse varia-
tion.

Guided Practice

Graph the equation if both
the domain and the range
are the nonzero real num-
bers.

1. $xy = 2$

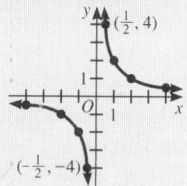

2. Refer to the lever at balance shown on p. 398.
Find m_1 if
$d_1 = \frac{1}{7}$, $m_2 = 21$, $d_2 = \frac{1}{3}$.
49

(x_1, y_1) and (x_2, y_2) are
ordered pairs of the same
inverse variation. Find the
missing value.

3. $x_1 = 20$, $y_1 = 7$,
$x_2 = 4$, $y_2 = \_?\_$ 35

4. $x_1 = 64$, $y_1 = \frac{3}{8}$,
$x_2 = \_?\_$, $y_2 = 6$ 4

Summarizing the Lesson

Remind students that if y
varies inversely as x then
the function is given by the
rule $y = \frac{k}{x}$. Many problems
involving inverse variation
can be solved by using the
fact that the product of the
two quantities in the variation is constant.

For every nonzero value of k, the graph of $xy = k$ is a **hyperbola**.

When k is positive, the branches of the graph are in Quadrants I and III.
When k is negative, the branches of the graph are in Quadrants II and IV.

Let (x_1, y_1) and (x_2, y_2) be two ordered pairs of the same inverse variation.
Since the coordinates must satisfy the equation $xy = k$, you know that

$$x_1 y_1 = k \text{ and } x_2 y_2 = k,$$

or
$$x_1 y_1 = x_2 y_2.$$

You can compare the equations for direct variation and inverse variation.

Direct Variation	**Inverse Variation**
$y = kx$	$xy = k, \quad \text{or} \quad y = \dfrac{k}{x}$
$\dfrac{y_1}{x_1} = \dfrac{y_2}{x_2}$	$x_1 y_1 = x_2 y_2$

The equations above show that *for direct variation the quotients of the
coordinates are constant and for inverse variation the products of the coordinates are constant.*

One example of an inverse variation is the law of the lever. A *lever* is a
bar pivoted at a point called the *fulcrum*. If masses m_1 and m_2 are placed at
distances d_1 and d_2 from the fulcrum, and the bar is balanced, then

$$m_1 d_1 = m_2 d_2.$$

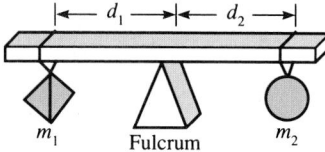

Example 2   If a 24 g mass is 30 cm from the fulcrum of a lever, how far from the fulcrum is a 45 g mass that balances the 24 g mass?

Solution   Let $m_1 = 24$, $d_1 = 30$, and $m_2 = 45$, $d_2 = \_?\_$.
Use $m_1 d_1 = m_2 d_2$.
$$24 \cdot 30 = 45 d_2$$
$$\frac{720}{45} = d_2$$
$$16 = d_2$$
$\therefore$ the distance of the 45 g mass from the fulcrum is 16 cm.   **Answer**

398   *Chapter 8*

Oral Exercises

State whether each equation defines an inverse variation or a direct variation. k is a nonzero constant.

1. $\dfrac{y}{x} = k$ direct

2. $y = \dfrac{k}{x}$ inverse

3. $p = \dfrac{k}{z}$ inverse

4. $xy = 25$ inverse

5. $d = 40t$ direct

6. $m = \dfrac{1}{d}$ inverse

7. $\dfrac{c_1}{d_1} = \dfrac{c_2}{d_2}$ direct

8. $a_1b_1 = a_2b_2$ inverse

9. $\dfrac{1}{4} = rt$ inverse

10. $\dfrac{m}{n} = \dfrac{5}{8}$ direct

11. $\dfrac{x}{y} = \dfrac{1}{k}$ direct

12. $kxy = 5$ inverse

Complete the ordered pairs so they satisfy the given inverse variation.

13. $xy = 12$ and $(x, y) = (2, \underline{\ ?\ })$ 6 $(\underline{\ ?\ }, 4)$ 3 $(-6, \underline{\ ?\ })$ −2

14. $mn = 60$ and $(m, n) = (10, \underline{\ ?\ })$ 6 $(\underline{\ ?\ }, 5)$ 12 $(-2, \underline{\ ?\ })$ −30

15. $144 = pq$ and $(p, q) = (8, \underline{\ ?\ })$ 18 $(-3, \underline{\ ?\ })$ −48 $(\underline{\ ?\ }, 12)$ 12

16. $xy = -1$ and $(x, y) = (-1, \underline{\ ?\ })$ 1 $\left(\dfrac{1}{4}, \underline{\ ?\ }\right)$ −4 $(\underline{\ ?\ }, 2)$ −$\dfrac{1}{2}$

17. If $rs = k$, and r is tripled while k remains the same, how does s change?

18. If $d = rt$, and t is halved while d remains constant, how does r change?

17. s changes to $\dfrac{1}{3}$ its initial value   **18.** r is doubled

Written Exercises

Graph each equation if both the domain and the range are the set of nonzero real numbers. You may wish to verify your graphs on a computer or a graphing calculator.

A   **1.** $xy = 6$ **2.** $xy = 4$ **3.** $xy = -1$ **4.** $xy = -16$

    5. $x = \dfrac{9}{y}$ **6.** $y = \dfrac{2}{x}$ **7.** $\dfrac{x}{2} = \dfrac{-2}{y}$ **8.** $\dfrac{x}{3} = \dfrac{4}{y}$

Exercises 9 and 10 refer to the lever at balance shown on page 398. Find the missing value.

  9. $m_1 = 12$, $m_2 = 9$, $d_1 = 30$, $d_2 = \underline{\ ?\ }$ 40   **10.** $m_1 = \underline{\ ?\ }$, $m_2 = 60$, $d_1 = 5$, $d_2 = 9$ 108

(x_1, y_1) and (x_2, y_2) are ordered pairs of the same inverse variation. Find the missing value.

11. $x_1 = 4$, $y_1 = 54$, $x_2 = 8$, $y_2 = \underline{\ ?\ }$ 27   **12.** $x_1 = 32$, $y_1 = 9$, $x_2 = \underline{\ ?\ }$, $y_2 = 12$ 24

13. $x_1 = \underline{\ ?\ }$, $y_1 = 19.5$, $x_2 = 11.7$, $y_2 = 10.5$ 6.3   **14.** $x_1 = 10$, $y_1 = \underline{\ ?\ }$, $x_2 = 8$, $y_2 = \dfrac{1}{4}$ $\dfrac{1}{5}$

Introduction to Functions   **399**

Using a Computer or a Graphing Calculator

Once students have drawn their own graphs for Written Exercises 1–8, you may wish to have them check their work using a computer or a graphing calculator.

Support Materials
  Disk for Algebra
  Menu Items:
    Function Plotter
  Resource Book   p. 210

Suggested Assignments

Minimum
Day 1: 399/1–11 odd
Assign with Lesson 8-9.
Day 2: 400/15, 17
    400/P: 1–9 odd
    S 402/Mixed Review

Average
Day 1: 399/1–13 odd
Assign with Lesson 8-9.
Day 2: 400/15–19 odd
    400/P: 1–13 odd
    S 402/Mixed Review

Maximum
  399/3–18 mult. of 3
  400/P: 3–18 mult. of 3
S 402/Mixed Review

Additional Answers
Written Exercises

1.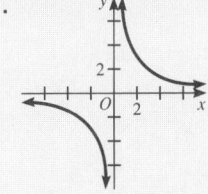

2.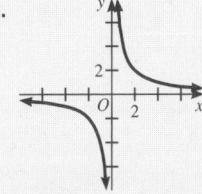

(continued)

Additional Answers
Written Exercises
(continued)

3.

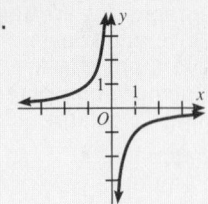

4.

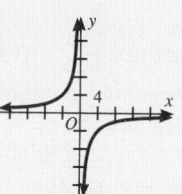

5.

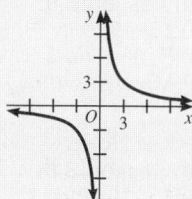

6.

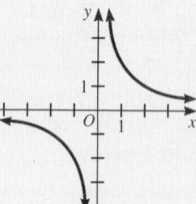

7.

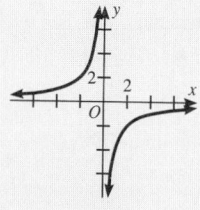

8.

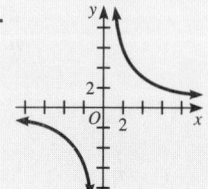

For each inverse variation described, state (a) a formula and (b) a proportion.

Sample   The height, h, of a right circular cylinder of fixed volume varies inversely as the area, A, of the base. A cylinder 6 in. high has a base of 20 in².

Solution   **a.** $Ah = k$; $h = 6$ when $A = 20$.
$20(6) = k$, so $k = 120$

$$\therefore Ah = 120, \quad \text{or} \quad h = \frac{120}{A}$$

b. $A_1h_1 = A_2h_2$
Divide by h_1h_2 to obtain the proportion:

$$\frac{A_1}{h_2} = \frac{A_2}{h_1}$$

Let $A_1 = 20$ and $h_1 = 6$. $\dfrac{20}{h_2} = \dfrac{A_2}{6}$

B   15. Length l and width w of a rectangle of given area vary inversely. When the length is 18, the width is 5.

16. The force, f, needed to move a rock varies inversely as the length, l, of the crowbar used. When the length is 2 m, the force needed is 1.5 N (newtons).

17. The frequency, f, of a periodic wave is inversely proportional to the length, l, of the wave. The frequency is 2.5 Hz (hertz) when the wavelength is 0.60 m.

18. The time, t, required to drive between two cities is inversely proportional to the average speed, r. The trip took 3 h at an average speed of 52 mi/h.

19. At a fixed temperature, the volume, V, of a gas varies inversely as the pressure, P. A volume of 465 cm³ of a gas is at a pressure of 725 mm.

20. The amount of current, I, flowing through a circuit is inversely proportional to the amount of resistance, R, of the circuit. In a circuit with a resistance of 18 ohms, the current is 0.25 amperes.

15. **a.** $lw = 90$
b. $\dfrac{18}{w_2} = \dfrac{l_2}{5}$

16. **a.** $fl = 3$
b. $\dfrac{1.5}{l_2} = \dfrac{f_2}{2}$

17. **a.** $fl = 1.5$
b. $\dfrac{2.5}{l_2} = \dfrac{f_2}{0.60}$

18. **a.** $rt = 156$
b. $\dfrac{52}{t_2} = \dfrac{r_2}{3}$

19. **a.** $PV = 337,125$
b. $\dfrac{725}{V_2} = \dfrac{P_2}{465}$

20. **a.** $IR = 4.5$
b. $\dfrac{0.25}{R_2} = \dfrac{I_2}{18}$

Problems

Solve.

A   1. The number of days needed to remodel a house varies inversely as the number of people working on the job. It takes 18 weeks for 4 people to complete the project. If the job has to be finished in 8 weeks, how many people are needed? 9 people

2. Three friends on a fishing trip pay $100 each to share the rent of a cottage. The cost per person varies inversely as the number of people sharing the rent. How many people would have to share the rent of the cottage to make the cost $60 per person? 5 people

400   *Chapter 8*

3. A rectangle has length 36 cm and width 28 cm. Find the length of another rectangle of equal area whose width is 21 cm. 48 cm

4. The winner of a race ran the distance in 45 s at an average speed of 9.6 m/s. The runner who came in last finished in 48 s. What was the last runner's average speed? 9 m/s

5. A fifteen-centimeter pulley runs at 250 r/min (revolutions per minute). How fast does the five-centimeter pulley it drives revolve, if the number of revolutions per minute varies inversely as the diameter? 750 r/min

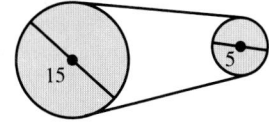

6. A gear with 42 teeth revolves at 1200 r/min and meshes with a gear having 72 teeth. What is the speed of the second gear if the rotational speed of a gear varies inversely with the number of teeth? 700 r/min

7. The number of chairs on a ski lift varies inversely as the distance between them. When they are 10 m apart, the ski lift can accommodate 32 chairs. If 40 evenly spaced chairs are used on the lift, what is the space between them? 8 m

8. The number of plants used to fill a row of given length in a garden varies inversely as the distance between the plants. If 75 plants are used to fill the row when planted 20 cm apart, how many plants are used to fill the row when planted 15 cm apart? 100 plants

9. A string on a violin is 25.8 cm long and produces a tone whose frequency is 440 Hz. What is the length of a string needed to produce a tone of frequency 516 Hz, if the frequency of a vibrating string is inversely proportional to its length? 22 cm

10. The frequency of a vibrating string is inversely proportional to its diameter. A violin string with diameter 0.50 mm produces a tone of frequency 440 Hz. What is the frequency of the tone produced by a similar string whose diameter is 0.55 mm? 400 Hz

In Exercises 11–14, apply the law of the lever.

11. Sara weighs 106 lb and Levon weighs 156 lb. If Levon sits 6 ft from the seesaw support, how far from the support must Sara sit to balance the seesaw? about 8.8 ft

12. One end of a pry bar is under a 350 kg boulder. The fulcrum of the bar is 15 cm from the boulder and 175 cm from the other end of the bar. What mass at that end of the bar will balance the boulder? 30 kg

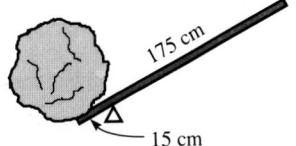

B 13. An 18 kg mass is placed at one end of a steel bar that is 1 m long. A 35 kg mass is placed at the other end. Where should the fulcrum be placed to balance the bar? about 66 cm from the 18 kg mass

14. A lever has a 500 kg steel ball on one end and a 300 kg log on the other end. The lever is balanced. The steel ball is 1 m closer to the fulcrum than the log. How far from the fulcrum is the log? 2.5 m

Introduction to Functions   **401**

Supplementary Materials

Study Guide   pp. 151–152
Practice Masters   50
Test Master   36
Resource Book   p. 119
Overhead Visual   9

The following formula holds for the wave motion of sound:

$$fl = v.$$

f is the frequency (number of cycles per second), l is the wavelength (in meters), and v is the speed of sound (about 335 m/s in air). Use this information in the following problems. 15. $\frac{1}{2}$ the wavelength of the lower note

15. The frequency of a note an octave above a given note is twice that of the given note. How does the wavelength of the higher note compare with that of the lower note? See above.

16. If the wavelength of a note is $\frac{3}{2}$ that of a given note, how do the frequencies compare? See below.

17. An open organ pipe produces a sound wave that has a length that is twice the length of the pipe. Find the length of an open pipe that will produce the note A with the frequency 440. Give the answer to the nearest tenth of a meter. 0.4 m

18. A stopped organ pipe produces a sound wave that has a length that is four times the length of the pipe. What is the frequency of the sound produced by a stopped organ pipe that is 2 m long? about 42 cycles/s

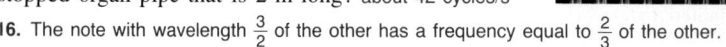

16. The note with wavelength $\frac{3}{2}$ of the other has a frequency equal to $\frac{2}{3}$ of the other.

Mixed Review Exercises

Show that the lines whose equations are given are parallel.

1. $2x + 3y = 3$ 2. $2x + 10y = 3$ 3. $x - y = 5$ 4. $-4x + 6y = 1$
   $2x + 3y = 6$ $x + 5y = 2$ $y - x = 5$ $2x - 3y = 2$

Find the constant of variation.

5. t varies directly as s, and $t = 24$ when $s = -4$. -6
6. y varies directly as x, and $y = 14$ when $x = 70$. $\frac{1}{5}$
7. m is proportional to n, and $m = 63$ when $n = 7$. 9

Computer Exercises

For students with some programming experience

Write a BASIC program to determine whether a set of ordered pairs represents a direct variation, an inverse variation, or neither. At least three ordered pairs should be entered with INPUT statements. Run the program for the data below.

1. $(2, 3)$, $(8, 12)$, $(10, 15)$, $(-24, -36)$ direct   2. $(12, -4)$, $(-16, 3)$, $(-15, 3.2)$ inverse
3. $(0, 0)$, $(3, 4)$, $(9, 8)$, $(-2, -3)$ neither   4. $(2, 1.6)$, $(12, 9.6)$, $(5, 4)$, $(9, 7.2)$ direct

402   *Chapter 8*

Calculator Key-In

You can use a calculator to solve a direct variation or an inverse variation.

For a direct variation, first set up the equation

$$\frac{y_1}{x_1} = \frac{y_2}{x_2}$$

and then use your calculator to multiply and divide to find the missing value.

For an inverse variation, first set up the equation

$$x_1 y_1 = x_2 y_2$$

and then use your calculator to multiply and divide to find the missing value.

Find the missing value.

1. $\dfrac{y_1}{12} = \dfrac{14}{8}$ 21

2. $\dfrac{13}{x_1} = \dfrac{6}{9}$ 19.5

3. $\dfrac{93}{21} = \dfrac{y_2}{35}$ 155

4. $\dfrac{y_1}{4.2} = \dfrac{5.6}{3.2}$ 7.35

5. $\dfrac{1.2}{x_1} = \dfrac{5}{1.5}$ 0.36

6. $\dfrac{2.6}{6.5} = \dfrac{y_2}{4.5}$ 1.8

7. $12(24) = 15y_2$ 19.2

8. $15y_1 = (16)36$ 38.4

9. $4(65) = 50y_2$ 5.2

10. $1.2(0.8) = 1.6y$ 0.6

11. $(10.8)12 = 14.4y_2$ 9

12. $(4.8)(600) = 400y_2$ 7.2

Self-Test 4

Vocabulary   direct variation (p. 391)
constant of variation (p. 391)
constant of proportionality (p. 392)

inverse variation (p. 397)
hyperbola (p. 398)

(x_1, y_1) and (x_2, y_2) **are ordered pairs of the same direct variation. Find each missing value.**

1. $x_1 = 10$, $y_1 = 25$
$x_2 = 2$, $y_2 = \underline{\ ?\ }$ 5

2. $x_1 = 24$, $y_1 = 64$
$x_2 = \underline{\ ?\ }$, $y_2 = 8$ 3

Obj. 8-9, p. 391

3. A worker's earnings are directly proportional to the number of hours worked. If $60 is earned for 4 h of work, how much is earned for 35 h? $525

(x_1, y_1) and (x_2, y_2) **are ordered pairs of the same inverse variation. Find each missing value.**

4. $x_1 = 20$, $y_1 = \underline{\ ?\ }$ 3
$x_2 = 5$, $y_2 = 12$

5. $x_1 = 8$, $y_1 = 16$
$x_2 = 4$, $y_2 = \underline{\ ?\ }$ 32

Obj. 8-10, p. 397

6. Four friends on a ski trip pay $210 each to share the rent of a cabin. The cost per person varies inversely as the number of persons. How many people sharing the rent would make the cost $120 per person? 7 people

Check your answers with those at the back of the book.

Calculator Key-In Commentary

To use a calculator to solve Exercise 1, enter 12 × 14 ÷ 8. For Exercise 2, enter 13 × 9 ÷ 6.

Quick Quiz

(x_1, y_1) and (x_2, y_2) are ordered pairs of the same direct variation. Find each missing value.

1. $x_1 = 5$, $y_1 = 15$
$x_2 = 6$, $y_2 = \underline{\ ?\ }$ 18

2. $x_1 = 25$, $y_1 = 10$
$x_2 = \underline{\ ?\ }$, $y_2 = 12$ 30

3. The distance a spring is stretched is directly proportional to the force applied. If a force of 12 newtons stretches a spring 8 cm, what force will stretch the spring 10 cm? 15 newtons

(x_1, y_1) and (x_2, y_2) are ordered pairs of the same inverse variation. Find each missing value.

4. $x_1 = 5$, $y_1 = 30$
$x_2 = 6$, $y_2 = \underline{\ ?\ }$ 25

5. $x_1 = 6$, $y_1 = 16$
$x_2 = \underline{\ ?\ }$, $y_2 = 12$ 8

6. For a constant temperature, the volume of gas in a cylinder varies inversely with the pressure. If a certain gas is compressed to a volume of 3 m³ it has a pressure of 100 pascals. Find the volume of the gas under a pressure of 300 pascals. 1 m³

26.
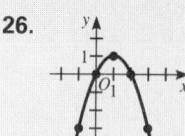

28.
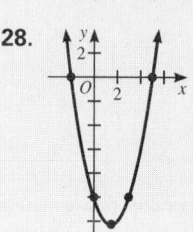

30.
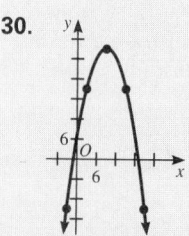

32. a.
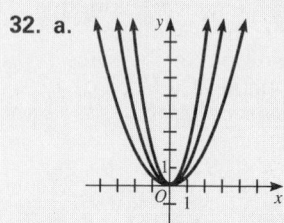

b.
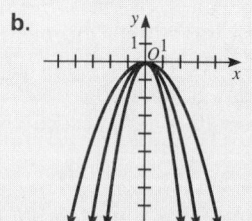

Reading Algebra / *Problem-Solving Strategies*

To be a successful problem solver, you must first master the art of reading word problems. Read each problem slowly and carefully. Here are some questions you can ask yourself as you begin to work a problem.

- Will it help to organize the information in a chart?
- Is there a standard formula to use?
- Will drawing a sketch or making a model help to visualize the problem?
- Is it reasonable to use a trial-and-error (guess-and-check) approach?

If you are having trouble understanding a word problem or figuring out how to begin solving it, there are a number of things you can do. The first is rereading. Perhaps you overlooked something when you first read the problem. Then, attempt to break the problem down. You may be able to use the parts that you understand to make sense of the parts that you do not. Sometimes, substituting simpler data and solving a simpler, related problem may help you see how to solve the given problem.

When you have chosen a strategy and found an answer, check your answer to be sure it makes sense. For example, the length of a room cannot be negative. Estimate before solving and use your estimate to check that your answer is within a reasonable range. Then check your answer in the words of the problem for accuracy. The time you spend on planning and checking will be well worthwhile.

Exercises

1. A coin box contains $26.50 in dimes and quarters. There are 157 coins altogether. How many of each type of coin are in the box? 85 dimes, 72 quarters

2. The length of a rectangle is 4 cm more than twice the width. The perimeter is 56 cm. Find the length and the width. length, 20 cm; width, 8 cm

3. Two planes leave an airport at the same time flying in opposite directions. The first plane is traveling at a speed of 1100 km/h. After 4 h, the planes are 7600 km apart. Find the speed of the second plane. 800 km/h

4. The trip from Winston to Carver takes 8 min longer during rush hour, when the average speed is 75 km/h, than in off-peak hours, when the average speed is 90 km/h. Find the distance between the two towns. 60 km

5. A rectangle is 5 cm longer than it is wide. If the length is doubled and the width is tripled, the area is increased by 420 cm². Find the original dimensions. 7 cm by 12 cm

6. The sum of two numbers is 11 and the sum of their squares is 65. Find the numbers. 4 and 7

7. The edges of one cube are 2 cm longer than the edges of another. The volume of the smaller cube is 152 cm³ less than the volume of the larger cube. Find the lengths of the edges of each cube. smaller, 4 cm; larger, 6 cm

8. A soccer league signed up 440 players. The ratio of returning players to new players was 4:7. How many players were new? 280 players

Chapter Summary

1. The solution set of a linear equation in two variables is the set of all ordered pairs of numbers that make the equation into a true statement.

2. Ordered pairs of real numbers can be graphed as points in a coordinate plane. The graph of a linear equation in two variables is a line.

3. The slope of a line can be found by using any two points on the line. Different lines with the same slope are parallel.

4. An equation of a line can be found from: (a) the slope and the y-intercept; (b) the slope and any point on the line; (c) two points on the line.

5. A function can be defined by a correspondence, a table, an equation, or a set of ordered pairs.

6. The value of a function F at 2 is denoted by $F(2)$. Any value of a function can be found by replacing the variable in the defining equation of the function by the given number.

7. A linear function is defined by a linear equation. Its graph is a line.

8. A quadratic function is defined by an equation of the form $y = ax^2 + bx + c$, $a \neq 0$. Its graph is a parabola that opens upward if a is positive or downward if a is negative.

9. A direct variation is a linear function defined by an equation of the form $y = kx$, $k \neq 0$.

10. An inverse variation is a function defined by an equation of the form $xy = k$, $k \neq 0$, or $y = \dfrac{k}{x}$, $k \neq 0$.

Chapter Review

Give the letter of the correct answer.

1. Which ordered pair is a solution of $3x - 2y = 5$?   **8-1**
   a. $(1, -1)$ **b.** $(2, 1)$ **c.** $(-1, 1)$ **d.** $(-2, 1)$

2. Solve $2x + 3y = 9$ if x and y are whole numbers.
   a. $(0, 3), (1, 3)$ **b.** $(0, 3), (3, 1)$ **c.** $(3, 0), (1, 3)$ **d.** $(3, 0), (3, 1)$

3. In which quadrant is the graph of $(-3, 5)$?   **8-2**
   a. I   **b.** II   **c.** III   **d.** IV

4. Where is the graph of $(-3, 0)$ in the coordinate plane?
   a. in Quadrant II   **b.** in Quadrant III   **c.** on the x-axis   **d.** on the y-axis

Supplementary Materials
Practice Master   51
Resource Book   pp. 200–201

Introduction to Functions   **405**

5. Find the slope of the line that passes through $(4, 4)$ and $(-4, 6)$. 8-3

    a. -4 **b.** 0 **c.** $-\dfrac{1}{4}$ **d.** no slope

6. Find the slope of the line whose equation is $y + 3 = 0$.

    a. 3 **b.** 0 **c.** -3 **d.** no slope

7. Find the slope and y-intercept of the line whose equation is $y = \dfrac{3}{2}x - 2$. 8-4

    a. $m = -2, b = \dfrac{3}{2}$ **b.** $m = 2, b = \dfrac{3}{2}$ **c.** $m = \dfrac{3}{2}, b = 2$ **d.** $m = \dfrac{3}{2}, b = -2$

8. Write an equation in slope-intercept form of the line that is parallel to $y = -\dfrac{1}{3}x$ and that has y-intercept 5.

    a. $y = -\dfrac{1}{3}x + 5$ **b.** $y = 5x - \dfrac{1}{3}$ **c.** $y = -\dfrac{1}{3}x - 5$ **d.** $5y = -\dfrac{1}{3}x$

9. Find the equation of a line with slope $-\dfrac{4}{3}$ that passes through $(12, -3)$. 8-5

    a. $y = -\dfrac{4}{3}x - 19$ **b.** $y = -\dfrac{4}{3}x + 19$ **c.** $y = -\dfrac{4}{3}x + 13$ **d.** $y = -\dfrac{4}{3}x - 13$

10. Write an equation in standard form of the line that passes through the points $(0, -7)$ and $(-7, 0)$.

    a. $-x + y = 7$ **b.** $-x + y = -7$ **c.** $x + y = -7$ **d.** $y = -7$

11. Write the range of the function $\{(-1, 1), (0, 0), (1, 0), (2, 6)\}$. 8-6

    a. $\{0, 1, 2, 3, 4, 5, 6\}$ **b.** $\{-1, 0, 1, 2\}$

    c. $\{(-1, 1), (1, 1)\}$ **d.** $\{0, 1, 6\}$

12. Find $G(0)$ given $G(x) = 4 - 8x$. 8-7

    a. 0 **b.** 2 **c.** 8 **d.** 4

13. Find $F(-1)$ given $F: x \rightarrow 5 - x^2$.

    a. 25 **b.** 7 **c.** 4 **d.** 5

14. Find the vertex and give the least value of $f(x) = x^2 + 8x + 3$. 8-8

    a. $(-4, -13); -13$ **b.** $(4, 13); 13$ **c.** $(-4, 13); 13$ **d.** $(4, -13); -13$

15. Find the vertex and give the greatest value of $f(x) = 2x - x^2$.

    a. $(2, 1); 1$ **b.** $(1, 2); 2$ **c.** $(1, 1); 1$ **d.** $(1, 0); 0$

16. Find the constant of variation if y varies directly as x, and $y = 95$ when $x = 19$. 8-9

    a. 5 **b.** $\dfrac{1}{5}$ **c.** 19 **d.** 95

17. Find the missing value if $(75, 30)$ and $(\underline{\ ?\ }, 18)$ are ordered pairs of the same inverse variation. 8-10

    a. 125 **b.** 75 **c.** 45 **d.** 7.2

Chapter Test

State whether each ordered pair is a solution of the given equation.

1. $3x - 2y = 12$
   $(-2, 3), (4, 0)$
   no   yes

2. $7x + 5y = -3$
   $(-1, -2), (-4, -5)$
   no   no

8-1

Solve each equation if x and y are whole numbers.

3. $2x + 5y = 12$ (1, 2), (6, 0)

4. $2x + 3y = 15$ (0, 5), (3, 3), (6, 1)

Plot each of the given points in a coordinate plane.

5. $(5, 3)$ 6. $(0, 6)$ 7. $(3, -4)$ 8. $(-2, 5)$

8-2

Graph each equation.

9. $y = 3x - 4$

10. $y = \frac{1}{2}x + 2$

Find the slope of the line passing through the two given points.

11. $(-6, 0), (8, -7)$ $-\frac{1}{2}$

12. $(-5, 7), (8, 7)$ 0

8-3

13. $(9, 5), (9, -5)$ no slope

14. $(-2, 4), (3, -1)$ -1

Find the slope of each line whose equation is given.

15. $y = -3x + 2$ -3

16. $x + y = 0$ -1

17. $3x - 5y = 15$ $\frac{3}{5}$

18. $2x + 4y = 1$ $-\frac{1}{2}$

Give the slope and y-intercept of each line. Are any of the lines parallel? If so, which? yes; **20.** and **21.**

19. $y = 3x + 2$ 3; 2

20. $y = -\frac{2}{3}x + 4$ $-\frac{2}{3}$; 4

8-4

21. $y = -\frac{2}{3}x - 3$ $-\frac{2}{3}$; -3

22. $y = \frac{9}{4}x + 6$ $\frac{9}{4}$; 6

Change each equation to slope-intercept form. Then draw the graph using only the slope and y-intercept. See Additional Answers for graphs.

23. $5x - y = 1$ $y = 5x - 1$

24. $-x + 3y + 6 = 0$ $y = \frac{1}{3}x - 2$

25. $2y = 7$ $y = 0 \cdot x + \frac{7}{2}$

26. $x + 2y - 6 = 0$ $y = -\frac{1}{2}x + 3$

Write an equation in slope-intercept form of the line that has the given slope and passes through the given point.

27. slope -3; $(0, -1)$ $y = -3x - 1$

28. slope $\frac{5}{2}$; $(-6, 7)$ $y = \frac{5}{2}x + 22$

8-5

29. slope 0; $\left(2, -\frac{1}{4}\right)$ $y = -\frac{1}{4}$

30. slope $\frac{3}{4}$; $(-3, -4)$ $y = \frac{3}{4}x - \frac{7}{4}$

Introduction to Functions   **407**

Alternate Test p. T19

Supplementary Materials
Test Masters   37, 38
Resource Book   p. 46–49

Additional Answers
Chapter Test

5–8.
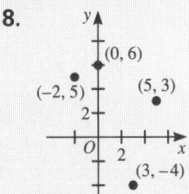

9.
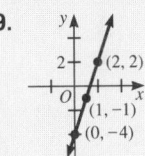

10.
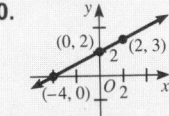

23.
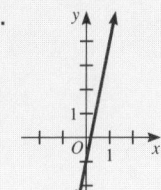

24.
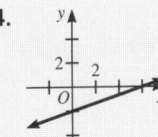

25.
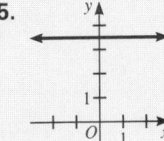

(continued)

26.

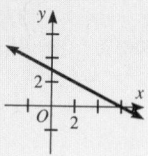

32. b.

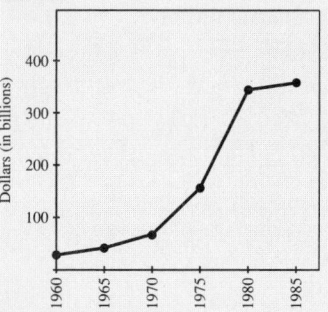

37.

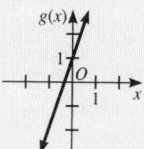

38.

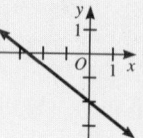

39.

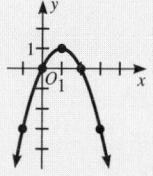

---

31. Write an equation in slope-intercept form of the line passing through the points $(-4, -6)$ and $(4, 10)$. $y = 2x + 2$

32. The table below shows a function.
    a. State the domain and range of the function.
    b. Graph the function by means of a bar graph or a broken-line graph, whichever is more suitable. broken-line graph

8-6

Value of U.S. Exports in Billions of Dollars	
Year	Value
1960	$29
1965	$41
1970	$66
1975	$156
1980	$345
1985	$359

Find the range of each function.

33. $F(t) = 2t - 2$, $D = \{-1, 0, 2\}$ $\{-4, -2, 2\}$

34. $g: x \to x^2 - 1$, $D = \{-1, 0, 1\}$ $\{-1, 0\}$

8-7

35. If $f: x \to \dfrac{2x}{3} - 1$, find: **a.** $f(3)$ 1   **b.** $f(-3)$ -3

36. If $f(x) = \dfrac{2x - 1}{3}$, find: **a.** $f(3)$ $\frac{5}{3}$ **b.** $f(-3)$ $-\frac{7}{3}$

Draw the graph of each function.

37. $g: x \to 3x + 1$

38. $t(x) = -\dfrac{3}{4}x - 2$

8-8

39. Find the coordinates of the vertex and the equation of the axis of symmetry of the graph of the equation $y = 2x - x^2$. Use the vertex and at least four other points to graph the equation. $(1, 1)$; $x = 1$

(x_1, y_1) and (x_2, y_2) are ordered pairs of the same direct variation. Find the missing value.

40. $x_1 = 72$, $y_1 = 3$
    $x_2 = \underset{48}{\underline{\ \ ?\ \ }}$, $y_2 = 2$

41. $x_1 = \underset{5.6}{\underline{\ \ ?\ \ }}$, $y_1 = 70$
    $x_2 = 2$, $y_2 = 25$

8-9

(x_1, y_1) and (x_2, y_2) are ordered pairs of the same inverse variation. Find the missing value.

42. $x_1 = 20$, $y_1 = 5$
    $x_2 = \underset{2}{\underline{\ \ ?\ \ }}$, $y_2 = 50$

43. $x_1 = 10$, $y_1 = 75$
    $x_2 = 30$, $y_2 = \underline{\ \ ?\ \ }$ 25

8-10

Cumulative Review *(Chapters 1–8)*

Supplementary Materials
Test Master   39
Practice Masters   52, 53

Simplify.

1. $(7p - 2r) - (-3p + 4r)$ $10p - 6r$

2. $(8b - 4c)(2b + 3c)$ $16b^2 + 16bc - 12c^2$

3. $3y^3z(10y^2 + 4yz - 7z^3)$ $30y^5z + 12y^4z^2 - 21y^3z^4$

4. $(2x^3y^2z^4)^4 \div (4x^2yz^3)^2$ $x^8y^6z^{10}$

5. $(3m - 5n)^2$ $9m^2 - 30mn + 25n^2$

6. $(3.2 \times 10^{-8})(1.5 \times 10^{12})$ 4.8×10^4

Factor completely.

7. $20x^2 + 13x - 15$ $(4x + 5)(5x - 3)$

8. $4y^2 - 12y + 9$ $(2y - 3)^2$

9. $3z^2 - 21z - 24$ $3(z + 1)(z - 8)$

Express in simplest form. Assume that no denominator is zero.

10. $\dfrac{b^2 + 2b + 1}{b^2 - 2b - 3}$ $\dfrac{b + 1}{b - 3}$

11. $\dfrac{x^2 + 4x + 3}{x + 1} \cdot \dfrac{(x^2 - 1)}{2x^2 + x - 1}$ $\dfrac{(x + 3)(x - 1)}{2x - 1}$

12. $\dfrac{3z^2 + 8z - 3}{3z^2 + 5z - 2} \div \dfrac{z^2 + 6z + 9}{z^3 - 4z}$ $\dfrac{z(z - 2)}{z + 3}$

13. $\dfrac{r}{r - 4} - \dfrac{r}{r + 4} - 5$ $\dfrac{-5r^2 + 8r + 80}{(r - 4)(r + 4)}$

Write an equation in slope-intercept form for each line described.

14. The line with slope -3 that passes through $(2, -2)$. $y = -3x + 4$

15. The line that passes through $(5, 2)$ and $(2, 5)$. $y = -x + 7$

16. The line that contains $(1, 3)$ and is parallel to $2x + y = 4$. $y = -2x + 5$

17. Find the range of the function $f: x \rightarrow x^2 + 2x + 1$ with domain $\{-3, -2, -1, 0, 1, 2, 3\}$. $\{0, 1, 4, 9, 16\}$

Graph each equation.

18. $3x + 5y = 10$

19. $y = x^2 - x + 1$

20. Find the coordinates of the vertex and the equation of the axis of symmetry of the graph of $y = 2x^2 + 3x + 4$. $\left(-\dfrac{3}{4}, \dfrac{23}{8}\right); x = -\dfrac{3}{4}$

Solve each equation. Assume that no denominator is zero.

21. $4(x + 3) = 3(3x - 7)$ $\left\{\dfrac{33}{5}\right\}$

22. $2|x| + 1 = 5$ $\{2, -2\}$

23. $y\%$ of $50 = 27$ $\{54\}$

24. $9a^2 - 12a + 4 = 0$ $\left\{\dfrac{2}{3}\right\}$

25. $49t^2 - 36 = 0$ $\left\{-\dfrac{6}{7}, \dfrac{6}{7}\right\}$

26. $10t^2 + t = 3$ $\left\{-\dfrac{3}{5}, \dfrac{1}{2}\right\}$

27. $\dfrac{1}{x + 1} + 1 = x + 2$ $\{0, -2\}$

28. $\dfrac{a + 2}{a - 1} = \dfrac{a + 1}{a + 4}$ $\left\{-\dfrac{3}{2}\right\}$

29. $\dfrac{2z}{z - 3} - \dfrac{1}{z + 1} = -1$ $\left\{0, \dfrac{1}{3}\right\}$

30. $m\%$ of $60 = 48$ $\{80\}$

31. $2(x + 7) = 5(3x - 5)$ $\{3\}$

32. $\dfrac{1}{3}(m + 2) = m - 4$ $\{7\}$

33. The number of units manufactured varies directly with the number of hours worked. If 10 units are manufactured in 4 h, how many units are manufactured in 14 h? 35 units

34. For a given distance, the speed at which a car travels varies inversely as the time it travels. If it takes 1.5 h to travel a distance at 84 km/h, how long would it take to travel the same distance at 90 km/h? 1.4 h

Additional Answers
Cumulative Review

18.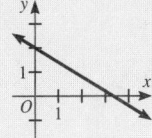

19.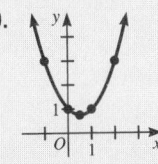

Introduction to Functions   **409**

Maintaining Skills

Factor completely. If the polynomial cannot be factored, write "prime."

Sample 1 $24x^2y - 60xy^4$ **Solution** $24x^2y - 60xy^4 = 12xy(2x - 5y^3)$

$5b^2c^3(5 + 3b^3c)$
1. $25b^2c^3 + 15b^5c^4$ **2.** $12m^3 - 15mn^2 - 8n^2$ prime $3u^4v(3u + 12v - 5v^2)$
                                              3. $9u^5v + 36u^4v^2 - 15u^4v^3$

4. $-vx^3 + 40x^2v^3 - v^6$ **5.** $-24x^7y^5 + 32x^6y^3 - 8x^2y^4$ **6.** $20m^6n^6 - 4m^6n^5 + 24m^5n^7$
$v(-x^3 + 40x^2v^2 - v^5)$ $8x^2y^3(-3x^5y^2 + 4x^4 - y)$ $4m^5n^5(5mn - m + 6n^2)$

Sample 2 $81y^4 - 16$

Solution $81y^4 - 16 = (9y^2 + 4)(9y^2 - 4) = (9y^2 + 4)(3y + 2)(3y - 2)$

Sample 3 $9y^2 + 30y + 25$

Solution $9y^2 + 30y + 25 = (3y)^2 + 2(3y \cdot 5) + 5^2 = (3y + 5)^2$
                                                  12. $(1 + 2y^2)(1 - 2y^2)(1 + 4y^4)$

7. $z^3 - 121z$ $z(z - 11)(z + 11)$ **8.** $27bc^2 - 12b$ $3b(3c - 2)(3c + 2)$ **9.** $-x^6 + 49$ $(7 - x^3)(7 + x^3)$

10. $9x^2 - 12x + 4$ $(3x - 2)^2$ **11.** $25m^4 + 9$ prime   **12.** $1 - 16y^8$

13. $16a^2 - 40a + 25$ **14.** $4n^2 - 16n + 16$ $4(n - 2)^2$ **15.** $25x^2 + 30x + 9$
      $(4a - 5)^2$ $(5x + 3)^2$

Sample 4 $g^2 - 2g - 35$ **Solution** $g^2 - 2g - 35 = (g + 5)(g - 7)$

19. $(7d - c)(c + 2d)$ $(y - 6)(y - 3)$
16. $z^2 + 8z - 16$ prime   **17.** $n^2 + 11n + 18$ $(n + 2)(n + 9)$ **18.** $y^2 - 9y + 18$

19. $-c^2 + 5cd + 14d^2$ **20.** $2d^2 + 18d - 72$ **21.** $x^2 + 10x + 21$

22. $4c^2 - 36c + 32$ **23.** $n^2 - 5np + 6p^2$ **24.** $7f + f^2 - 30$
     $4(c - 1)(c - 8)$ **20.** $2(d + 12)(d - 3)$ **21.** $(x + 3)(x + 7)$
                                   23. $(n - 3p)(n - 2p)$ **24.** $(f + 10)(f - 3)$

Sample 5 $3cd + 21d - 2c - 14$

Solution $3cd + 21d - 2c - 14 = 3d(c + 7) - 2(c + 7) = (3d - 2)(c + 7)$

     $(r - 2s)(y + 3)$ $(2x - y)(y + 3)$ $(s + 2t + 3)(s - 2t - 3)$
25. $ry - 2sy + 3r - 6s$ **26.** $2xy - y^2 + 6x - 3y$ **27.** $s^2 - 4t^2 - 12t - 9$

28. $x^2 - 10x + 25 - y^2$ **29.** $16a^2 - 9b^2 + 30b - 25$ **30.** $m^2t - 5m^2 + 5t - 25$
     $(x - 5 + y)(x - 5 - y)$ $(4a + 3b - 5)(4a - 3b + 5)$ $(m^2 + 5)(t - 5)$

Sample 6 $10p^2 - 19p - 15$

Solution   Test the possibilities for the first terms: $10p$ and p; $5p$ and $2p$
          Test the possibilities for the second terms: -15 and 1; 15 and -1; -5 and 3;
          5 and -3.   **32.** $(5n - 1)(2n + 1)$
          $10p^2 - 19p - 15 = (5p + 3)(2p - 5)$ **33.** $2(3m + 2)(m - 2)$

         $(3b + 5)(b - 1)$ **35.** $z(5z + 2)(5z + 1)$ **36.** $(2 + 3y)(7 - 3y)$
31. $3b^2 + 2b - 5$ **32.** $10n^2 + 3n - 1$ **33.** $6m^2 - 8m - 8$
     $(3a - 1)(2a + 3)$
34. $6a^2 + 7a - 3$ **35.** $25z^3 + 15z^2 + 2z$ **36.** $14 + 15y - 9y^2$

37. $-7y^2 - 20y + 3$ **38.** $22n + 8n^2 - 6$ **39.** $12b^2 - 14b - 10$
     $(3 + y)(1 - 7y)$ $2(4n - 1)(n + 3)$ $2(3b - 5)(2b + 1)$

Preparing for College Entrance Exams

Strategy for Success

Depending upon how a multiple-choice test is scored, it may not be wise to guess. However, if you can eliminate several of the possible answers, guessing may be worthwhile. For example, suppose you do not know the answer to a problem, but your knowledge of algebra tells you the answer must be a positive integer. This may help you improve your chances of guessing correctly.

Decide which is the best of the choices given and write the corresponding letter on your answer sheet.

1. A total of $15,000 was invested in accounts earning 6% annual simple interest and in bonds earning 10% annual simple interest. If twice as much of the $15,000 had been invested in bonds, the earnings would have been $160 higher. How much was invested in bonds? A

   (A) $4000   **(B)** $7000   **(C)** $8000   **(D)** $11,000

2. Identify the point(s) on the line that contains $(-4, 3)$ and has slope $-\frac{1}{4}$. A

   I. $(8, 0)$ II. $(-1, -3)$ III. $(-12, -13)$

   (A) I only   **(B)** II only   **(C)** III only
   (D) I, II, and III   **(E)** None of the above

3. A rectangle has area 24. The graph of the length as a function of the width D

   (A) is a parabola that opens upward.   **(B)** is a parabola that opens downward.
   (C) is a hyperbola.   **(D)** is one branch of a hyperbola.
   (E) cannot be determined from the given information.

4. The inlet pipe on a water tank can fill the tank in 8 hours. When the tank was full, both the inlet pipe and the drain pipe were accidentally opened. Twenty-four hours later, the tank was empty. How many hours would it take to empty a full tank if only the drain were open? A

   (A) 6 hours   **(B)** 9 hours   **(C)** 10 hours   **(D)** 12 hours

5. A runner won a 5 km road race with a time of exactly 15 min. An observer, using a watch that was running fast, clocked the winning time as 15 min 24 s. To the nearest tenth of a minute, how many minutes does the observer's watch gain in a day? B

   (A) 24.0 min   **(B)** 38.4 min   **(C)** 58.4 min   **(D)** 61.0 min   **(E)** 61.6 min

6. Find an equation of the line that intersects the y-axis at the same point as the line containing $(2, 2)$ and $(-4, -1)$ and that is parallel to the line containing $(6, 6)$ and $(-3, 3)$. A

   (A) $x - 3y = -3$ **(B)** $x - 2y = -8$ **(C)** $x + 2y = 8$ **(D)** $2x + y = 4$

9 Systems of Linear Equations

Objectives

9-1 To use graphs to solve systems of linear equations.

9-2 To use the substitution method to solve systems of linear equations.

9-3 To use systems of linear equations in two variables to solve problems.

9-4 To use addition or subtraction to solve systems of linear equations in two variables.

9-5 To use multiplication with the addition-or-subtraction method to solve systems of linear equations.

9-6 To use systems of equations to solve wind and water current problems.

9-7 To use systems of equations to solve digit, age, and fraction problems.

Assignment Guide

See p. T59 for Key to the format of the Assignment Guide

Day	Minimum Course		Average Course		Maximum Course	
1	**9-1** S	415/1–17 odd, 18 416/*Mixed Review*	**9-1** S	415/1–21 odd 416/*Mixed Review*	**9-1** S	415/1–23 odd 416/*Mixed Review*
2	**9-2** S	419/1–17 odd 420/*Mixed Review*	**9-2** S	419/1–19 odd 420/*Mixed Review*	**9-2** S	419/1–39 odd 420/*Mixed Review*
3	**9-2**	419/18–30 even	**9-2**	419/18–40 even	**9-3** S	424/*P*: 1–21 odd 425/*Mixed Review*
4	**9-3** S	424/*P*: 1–9 odd 425/*Mixed Review*	**9-3** S	424/*P*: 1–9 odd 425/*Mixed Review*	**9-4** S	427/1–27 odd 429/*Mixed Review*
5	**9-3**	424/*P*: 11–19	**9-3**	424/*P*: 6–22 even	**9-4**	428/28–31 428/*P*: 1–9 odd
6	**9-4** S	427/1–11 odd, 17, 20 429/*Mixed Review*	**9-4** S	427/1–19 odd 429/*Mixed Review*	**9-5** R	432/3–45 mult. of 3 433/3, 6, 9, 12, 15, 18
7	**9-4**	427/12, 15, 18, 19 428/*P*: 1–4	**9-4**	428/22, 24, 26, 28 428/*P*: 1, 3, 5, 7	**9-5** S	434/*P*: 1–23 odd 436/*Mixed Review*
8	**9-5** R	432/1–21 odd 433/2, 5, 8, 11, 14	**9-5** R	432/3–33 mult. of 3 433/3, 6, 9, 12, 15	**9-5** R	435/*P*: 25–31 odd 437/*Self-Test 1*
9	**9-5** S	434/*P*: 1–15 odd 436/*Mixed Review*	**9-5** S	434/*P*: 1–17 odd 436/*Mixed Review*	**9-6** S	440/*P*: 3–21 mult. of 3, 23 443/*Mixed Review*
10	**9-5** **9-6** R	434/*P*: 12, 14, 16 440/*P*: 1–4, 7 437/*Self-Test 1*	**9-5** **9-6** R	435/*P*: 19, 21, 25 440/*P*: 1–11 odd 437/*Self-Test 1*	**9-7** S	447/*P*: 1–21 odd 449/*Mixed Review*
11	**9-6** S **9-7**	440/*P*: 5, 6, 9, 10, 11 443/*Mixed Review* 447/*P*: 1–7	**9-6** S **9-7**	442/*P*: 12, 15, 18, 21 443/*Mixed Review* 447/*P*: 1–6, 7, 9	**9-7** R	448/*P*: 23–33 odd 450/*Self-Test 2*
12	**9-7** S	447/*P*: 9–13 449/*Mixed Review*	**9-7** S	448/*P*: 14–28 even 449/*Mixed Review*	*Prepare for Chapter Test* R EP	 451/*Chapter Review* 656/*Skills*; 675/*Problems*

Assignment Guide (continued)

Day	Minimum Course	Average Course	Maximum Course
13	*Prepare for Chapter Test* **R** 450/*Self-Test 2* 451/*Chapter Review:* 1–8 **EP** 656/*Skills;* 675/*Problems*	*Prepare for Chapter Test* **R** 450/*Self-Test 2* 451/*Chapter Review* **EP** 656/*Skills;* 675/*Problems*	*Administer Chapter 9 Test* **R** 453/*Cum. Review:* 1–31 odd **S** 455/*Mix. Prob. Solv.:* 1–13 odd
14	*Administer Chapter 9 Test* **R** 454/*Maintaining Skills* **S** 455/*Mixed Problem Solving:* 2–6 even	*Administer Chapter 9 Test* **R** 453/*Cum. Review:* 1–39 odd **S** 455/*Mix. Prob. Solv.:* 1–13 odd	

Supplementary Materials Guide

For Use with Lesson	Practice Masters	Tests	Study Guide (Reteaching)	Resource Book		
				Tests	Practice Exercises	Mixed Review (MR) Prob. Solving (PS) Applications (A) Enrichment (E) Technology (T)
9-1			pp. 153–154			p. 186 (A) pp. 210–211 (T)
9-2	Sheet 54		pp. 155–156		p. 120	
9-3			pp. 157–158			
9-4	Sheet 55		pp. 159–160			
9-5	Sheet 56	Test 40	pp. 161–162		p. 121	
9-6			pp. 163–164		p. 122	pp. 173–175 (PS)
9-7	Sheet 57	Test 41	pp. 165–166		p. 123	pp. 176–177 (PS)
Chapter 9	Sheet 58	Tests 42, 43		pp. 50–53		p. 202 (E)
Cum. Rev. 7–9	Sheets 59, 60			pp. 54–55	pp. 124–125	
Cum. Rev. 1–9						pp. 151–154 (MR)

Overhead Visuals

For Use with Lesson	Visual	Title
9-1	A	Multi-Use Packet 1
9-1	B	Multi-Use Packet 2
9-1	7	Exploring Slopes and Linear Systems

Software

Software	Algebra Plotter Plus	Using Algebra Plotter Plus	Computer Activities	Test Generator
Software	Line Plotter	Scripted Demo, pp. 21–22 Enrichment, pp. 32–33 Activity Sheet, p. 47	Activities 27–29	147 test items
For Use with Lessons	9-1, 9-4	9-1, 9-4	9-1, 9-5, 9-7	all lessons

Strategies for Teaching

Explorations and Problem Solving

To begin this chapter, you may want students to do the Exploration on p. 695. In this activity, students explore the idea of systems of linear equations before learning methods of solution. Using graphing software or a graphing calculator, students see more than one equation on a set of axes. This gives students an informal introduction and a solid foundation for the chapter.

Many of the common difficulties students experience with systems of linear equations can be minimized by emphasizing sound problem solving techniques. Students may have trouble deciding how to represent two quantities with variables and also how to choose the most efficient method (graphing, substitution, addition-or-subtraction) for solving a system. Remind students who are having difficulty translating word problems into equations that they should not get discouraged and that they should break down the information in the problem into more manageable pieces. Review activities for writing equations may be helpful. Emphasize that planning is an integral part of problem solving by telling students to look for key characteristics in systems of equations before they actually try solving them. They might notice, for example, that a system has a variable with a coefficient of 1, suggesting that using the substitution method would be easier and more accurate than graphing the system.

9-2 The Substitution Method

Introduce the substitution method as a technique that gives more accurate solutions than the graphing method. For example, the system

$$x + y = 12$$
$$6x - 7y = -2$$

is easily solved by substitution but difficult to solve by graphing. Point out that the substitution method is usually used only when at least one of the four coefficients of the variables is 1 or -1.

A common error is shown in the following example. Caution students against solving for $-y$ or for $-x$.

$$2x - y = 3 \rightarrow -y = 3 - 2x$$
$$3x + 2y = 8$$
$$3x + 2(3 - 2x) = 8$$

Emphasize the importance of solving for x, not $-x$, or y, not $-y$, before substituting.

9-3 Solving Problems with Two Variables

The two solutions of Example 1 show that some problems can be solved using either one equation and one variable or two equations and two variables. Stress that students should use systems of equations in this lesson to gain practice in writing and solving systems.

For most students, the chief difficulty in solving the problems in this lesson is in identifying two independent relationships on which to base two equations in two variables. The Oral Exercises provide excellent practice in setting up systems of equations.

For practice, have students write equations using n as the variable for the following.

1. 7 more than a number is 55. $n + 7 = 55$
2. 16 is 5 less than a number. $16 = n - 5$
3. 6 less than twice Sarah's age is 20. $2n - 6 = 20$
4. Dave earned \$56.30, which was \$4.50 less than Ned's earnings. $56.30 = n - 4.50$

9-4 The Addition-or-Subtraction Method

Instruct students to write equations in standard form before deciding to add or subtract. (See Written Exercises 19–27.) Remind students to write similar terms in the same column to avoid addition or subtraction errors. Point out that all the systems in Written Exercises 1–18 have been designed so that the coefficients of one variable are the same or are opposites. In the next lesson students will learn to solve systems that cannot be solved simply by adding or subtracting. Remind students that after the value of one variable is known, the value of the second variable should be found by substitution.

9-5 Multiplication with the Addition-or-Subtraction Method

In this lesson, if a student uses the addition-or-subtraction method immediately, the resulting equation will still contain two variables. In order to eliminate a variable, one must find an equivalent system in which the coefficients of this variable are equal or opposites.

It may be helpful to point out that the required coefficients of the variable to be eliminated are equal to a common multiple of its original coefficients, prefer-ably the LCM. In Example 2 the LCM of the coefficients of a is 15.

Be sure to assign some of the Mixed Practice exercises on page 433 to ensure that students are comfortable with the graphing method, the substitution method, and the addition-or-subtraction method.

9-7 Puzzle Problems

Emphasize the value of making a chart when solving digit or age problems. Remind students to check their results against the conditions of the problem. Caution them that the sum of the digits of a number is not the same as the number. The number 345 has 12 as the sum of its digits.

When you discuss fraction problems, you may need to review the procedure for solving proportions.

References to Strategies

PE: Pupil's Edition   **TE:** Teacher's Edition   **RB:** Resource Book

Problem Solving Strategies

PE: pp. 421–422, 438–439, 444–445 (Using charts or tables); pp. 421–424, 428–429, 434–436 (Using two variables)
TE: p. 423
RB: pp. 173–177

Applications

PE: pp. 412, 416, 421–424, 425, 434–436, 438–442, 444–449
TE: p. 412
RB: p. 186

Nonroutine Problems

PE: p. 416 (Exs. 22–24); p. 420 (Exs. 37–41); p. 424 (Probs. 21, 22); p. 425 (Challenge); p. 428 (Exs. 29–31); p. 429 (Probs. 9, 10); p. 432–433 (Exs. 36–46); p. 435–436 (Probs. 27–32); p. 437 (Challenge); p. 442 (Prob. 23); p. 449 (Probs. 31–34)
TE: p. T126 (Sugg. Extensions, Lessons, 9-6, 9-7)

Thinking Skills

PE: p. 437 (Reasoning/inference; recall and transfer)
TE: p. 437

Explorations

PE: p. 695
Algebra Plotter Plus: pp. 21–22, 32–33, 47

Connections

PE: pp. 422–424, 434 (Business); p. 434 (Chemistry); p. 436 (Discrete Math); p. 443 (Engineering); pp. 416, 434, 436 (Geometry); p. 425 (Health); p. 450 (History)

Using Technology

PE: pp. 414–415; pp. 416, 436 (Exs.)
TE: pp. 414, 416, 438
RB: pp. 210–211
Computer Activities: pp. 60–65
Algebra Plotter Plus: pp. 21–22, 32–33, 47

Using Manipulatives/Models

TE: p. T125 (Lesson 9-6)
Overhead Visuals: A, B, 7

Cooperative Learning

TE: p. T123 (Lesson 9-1); p. 412

Teaching Resources

For use in implementing the teaching strategies referenced on the previous page.

Application
Resource Book, p. 186

Application—Musical Lines (for use with Chapter 9)

This is a cooperative activity for a group of students.

Musical notation can be thought of as a graph, in which the x-axis represents the passage of constant units of time (beats) and the y-axis represents the pitch (or tone) of the notes. In the following exercises, you will place notes on the horizontal lines to create a simplified form of musical notation. (In traditional notation, notes can be placed between the horizontal staff lines as well as on them.) Each horizontal grid line represents a possible pitch. The vertical distance between each pair of lines represents a pitch interval called a half-step. After twelve such intervals, you arrive at a note with the same name, but an octave higher (its frequency is twice as great). These 12 pitches form what is called a chromatic scale; C, C#, D, D# E, F, F#, G, G#, A, A#, B. (The sharp pitches, denoted by the # symbol, are the black keys on a piano.)

Part I—Understanding the Graph

1. Refer to the graph above. This graph represents two players each playing a chromatic scale at the same time. Which player's scale is moving up in pitch? _____ Which player's scale is moving down in pitch? _____

2. Because Player 2 moves up one half-step for each beat played, the slope of Player 2's scale is +1. What is the slope of Player 1's scale? _____

3. What pitch letter is the y-intercept of Player 1's scale? _____ What is its numerical value? _____ What pitch letter is the y-intercept of Player 2's scale? _____ What is its numerical value? _____

4. Write an equation in slope-intercept form for each player. Use numbers rather than pitch letters to represent the y-intercepts. Player 1: _____ Player 2: _____

5. Beat number 2 (the third note each player plays) is a G# for Player 1 and a D for Player 2. Name the pitches that are played during beat number 6 (the seventh note each player plays). Player 1: _____ Player 2: _____

6. Connect each statement with its meaning.

Statements	Meanings
A vertical line can be drawn joining two notes.	The same pitch is played at the same time.
A horizontal line can be drawn joining two notes.	Different pitches are played at the same time.
Two musical lines intersect at a note.	The same pitch is played at different times.

Part II—Creating and Playing Musical Lines

7. Make a graph of the musical lines $y = x + 2$ (Player 1), $y = -x + 8$ (Player 2), and $y = x + 4$ (Player 3). Name the intersection points for these three lines. _____ Is there a time when all three players are playing the same pitch? _____

8. If a player jumps up more than one half-step per note, the melody might be called an *arpeggio* instead of a scale, and the slope of the musical line would be greater than 1. Make a graph of the musical lines $y = 3x$, $y = -2x + 10$, and $y = -\frac{1}{2}x + 7$. (*Note:* Player 3 will hit a note only on even-numbered beats.) Under your graph, write the names of the first five pitches played by each player. What is the pitch that all three players play at the same time? _____ What beat does this occur on? _____

Enrichment/Exploration
Resource Book, p. 202

Patterns in Systems of Equations (For use with Chapter 9 of text)

Solve each system of equations.

1. $2x + 2y = 15$
   $x + 2y = 15$ _____

2. $3x - y = 8$
   $-x + 3y = 8$ _____

3. $2x + 3y = 5$
   $3x + 2y = 5$ _____

4. $5x - 2y = 9$
   $-2x + 5y = 9$ _____

5. Find the pattern in Exercises 1–4. Then predict the values that are the solution to the following system of equations.
   $987x + 13y = 100$
   $13x + 987y = 100$ _____

6. Why are the x- and y-values equal in the above examples? _____

7. Solve this system of three equations.
   $x + 2y + 3z = 3$
   $2x + 3y + z = 3$
   $3x + y + 2z = 3$ _____

One way to solve a system of equations such as
   $x + 2y = 5$
   $2x + y = 1$

is to add the equations as they are. You will then have $3x + 3y = 6$. Dividing both sides by 3, you obtain $x + y = 2$. It is now fairly easy to rewrite the first equation $x + 2y = 5$ as $(x + y) + y = 5$, which is the same as $2 + y = 5$. Therefore, $y = 3$. Since $x + 2y = 5$, you obtain $x + 6 = 5$, so $x = -1$.

Use the technique described above to solve each of these systems of equations.

8. $x + 3y = 7$
   $3x + y = 5$ _____

9. $x + y = 4$
   $y + z = -7$
   $x + z = 5$ _____

10. $x + y - z = 4$
    $x - y + z = 1$
    $-x + y + z = 5$ _____

Problem Solving
Resource Book, p. 173

Wind and Water Current Problems (For use with Lesson 9–6)

By working through the steps in the problems below, you will gain skill in solving two-variable uniform motion problems.

Problem 1 A canoeist travels with the current at 17 km/h and travels against the current at 6 km/h. Find the canoe's rate in still water and the rate of the current.

a. Let r = the canoe's rate in km/h (in still water), and let c = the rate of the current in km/h. Write an expression for the rate of the canoe when it is traveling downstream (that is, with the current). _____

b. Write an expression for the rate of the canoe when it is traveling upstream (that is, against the current). _____

c. Use the facts in the problem to write a system of two equations.

_____

d. Solve for r. _____

e. Solve for c. _____

f. Write your answer to the problem. _____

g. Check: Show that the values for r and c yield results that agree with the original statement of the problem.

Canoe's rate with the current = _____ + _____ = _____

Canoe's rate against the current = _____ − _____ = _____

(continued)

Problem Solving
Resource Book, p. 176

Digit Problems (For use with Lesson 9–7)

By working through the steps in the problems below, you will gain skill in solving digit problems.

Problem 1 The sum of the digits of a two-digit number is 11. If the digits are reversed, the new number is 45 less than the original number. What is the original number?

a. Let t = the tens digit of the *original* number.
   Let u = the units digit of the *original* number.
   Write an expression for the value of the original number. _____

b. Complete the chart.

	Tens	Units	Value
Original number			
New number			

c. Use the facts in the first sentence of the problem to write an equation. _____

d. Use the facts in the second sentence of the problem to write another equation. _____

e. Write the equation of part **d** in simplified form. _____

f. Use your equations from parts **c** and **e** to write a system of two equations.

_____

g. Solve the system. $t =$ _____ , $u =$ _____

h. What is the original number? _____
   What is the new number? _____

i. Answer the question in the problem. _____

j. Check your results with the statement of the problem.
   What is the sum of the digits of the original number? _____
   Which number is greater—the original number or the new number? How much greater is it? _____

(continued)

Using Technology/Exploration
Using Algebra Plotter Plus, p. 47

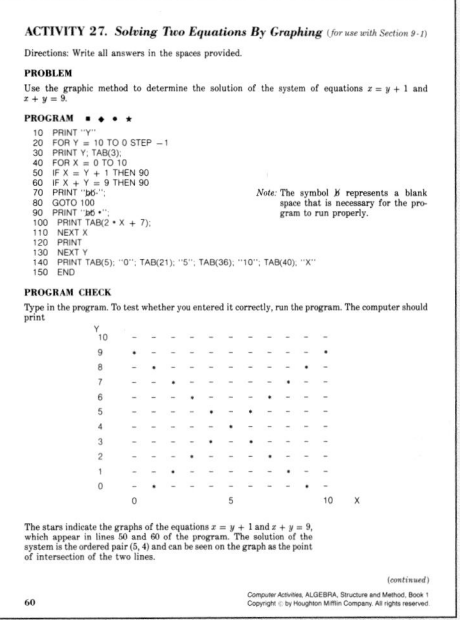

Solving Systems of Linear Equations

[Algebra Plotter Plus] [Book 1: Lesson 9-1]

Use the Line Plotter program of Algebra Plotter Plus. Select EQUATIONS and use the right-arrow key to move to the standard form.

1. Graph this system: $2x + y = 3$
   $x - 3y = 5$

   Write the coordinates of the point of intersection: (_____ , _____)

   This is called a *solution* of the system. Check the solution by substituting the x- and y-coordinates of the point of intersection into each equation of the system. You should get a true statement each time.

2. Graph this system: $2x + 2y = 1$
   $x - 2y = 4$

   a. The coordinates of the point of intersection for the system are *not* integers. Estimate the coordinates from the graph: (_____ , _____)
   b. To obtain a better approximation of the solution, select ZOOM and move the cross hairs near the point of intersection. Press ‹RETURN› or ‹ENTER› and use the arrow keys to change the size of the rectangle that indicates the portion of the graph to be magnified. Then press ‹RETURN› or ‹ENTER› and the computer will automatically draw the magnified graph. Now give a better estimate of the coordinates of the point of intersection: (_____ , _____)

3. Graph this system: $x - y = 1$
   $3x + 4y = 0$

   Find the solution of the system to the nearest tenth: (_____ , _____)
   (*Note:* If you used ZOOM in the previous exercise, you may first need to return the scale to the standard values. Select SCALE and use arrow keys to move to the "Standard Scale" option, then highlight "Yes.")

4. Graph this system: $-2x + y = 13$
   $5x + 4y = -30$

   Find the solution of the system to the nearest tenth: (_____ , _____)
   (*Note:* If the point of intersection is off the screen, you will need to rescale to see where the lines intersect. Select SCALE and redefine the minimum and maximum x-values before using DRAW.)

5. Graph this system: $6x - 4y = 3$
   $9x - 6y = 8$

   a. What do you notice about the lines? _____
      What can you say about the solution of the system? _____
   b. By replacing the constant 8 in the second equation with some other constant, you can make the graph of the system be two coinciding lines. What should the constant be? _____ What can you say about the solution of the system when the lines coincide? _____

Using Technology
Computer Activities, p. 60

ACTIVITY 27. *Solving Two Equations By Graphing* (*for use with Section 9-1*)

Directions: Write all answers in the spaces provided.

PROBLEM

Use the graphic method to determine the solution of the system of equations $x = y + 1$ and $x + y = 9$.

PROGRAM ■ ♦ ● ★

```
 10  PRINT "Y"
 20  FOR Y = 10 TO 0 STEP -1
 30  PRINT Y; TAB(3);
 40  FOR X = 0 TO 10
 50  IF X = Y + 1 THEN 90
 60  IF X + Y = 9 THEN 90
 70  PRINT "b6";
 80  GOTO 100
 90  PRINT "b6 •";
100  PRINT TAB(2 * X + 7);
110  NEXT X
120  PRINT
130  NEXT Y
140  PRINT TAB(5); "0"; TAB(21); "5"; TAB(36); "10"; TAB(40); "X"
150  END
```

Note: The symbol ᛒ represents a blank space that is necessary for the program to run properly.

PROGRAM CHECK

Type in the program. To test whether you entered it correctly, run the program. The computer should print

```
Y
10  -   -   -   -   -   -   *
 9  •   -   -   -   -   -   •
 8  -   •   -   -   -   *   -
 7  -   -   •   -   -   *   -
 6  -   -   -   •   -   *   -
 5  -   -   -   •   -   *   -
 4  -   -   -   -   *   -   -
 3  -   -   -   *   -   •   -
 2  -   -   •   -   -   -   •
 1  -   •   -   -   -   -   •
 0  •   -   -   -   -   •   -

    0           5         10   X
```

The stars indicate the graphs of the equations $x = y + 1$ and $x + y = 9$, which appear in lines 50 and 60 of the program. The solution of the system is the ordered pair $(5, 4)$ and can be seen on the graph as the point of intersection of the two lines.

(*continued*)

Using Models/Exploration
Overhead Visual 7, Sheets 1, 3, and 4

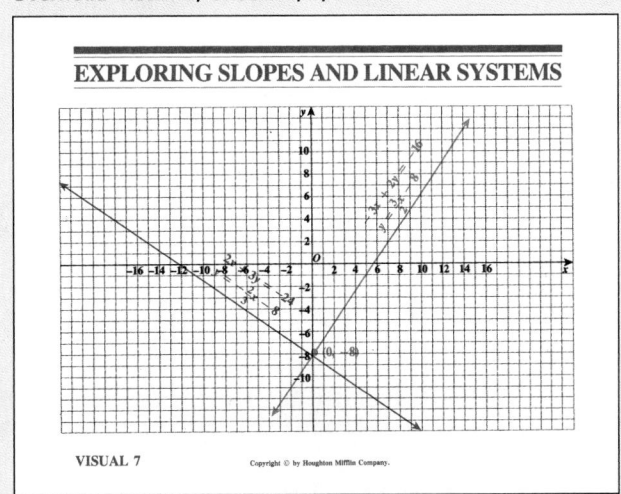

EXPLORING SLOPES AND LINEAR SYSTEMS

VISUAL 7

Application

Two forms of standardized notation are used to record the moves in a chess game. In both forms, the rows and columns are given names, and the squares where they intersect are identified by a pair of these names.

In *descriptive (English) notation,* a column is labeled according to the pieces that initially occupy it. For example, *Q* is the label for the column where the queens begin. The rows are numbered relative to the two players. Thus, row 3 for Black will be row 5 for White.

In *algebraic notation,* both the rows and the columns are labeled relative to the side where the white pieces begin. The rows are labeled with the numbers 1 through 8, and the columns are labeled with the letters *a* through *h.* Computer-chess software uses such notation.

Group Activities

Chess players use the problem solving strategies of trial and error and alternate solutions. You may have some students play a game of chess outside of class, and record their moves using the algebraic notation described above. Later, have a group of students try to reconstruct the game based on the written record. In addition, ask them to evaluate moves in which pieces were taken, and to suggest other moves that would have saved those pieces.

Many newspapers have a chess column. You may have a few students collect some of these columns and explain them to the class.

9 Systems of Linear Equations

Wherever the legal paths of chess pieces cross, conflict can occur and a piece may be taken. This chapter will show you how to find the intersection of two such paths or lines.

412

Solving Systems of Linear Equations

9-1 The Graphing Method

Objective   To use graphs to represent the solution of a system of linear equations as a point in the plane.

Two or more equations in the same variables form a **system of equations.** The examples below give systems that consist of two equations in the variables x and y. A **solution** of a system of two equations in two variables is a pair of values x and y that satisfies each equation in the system. Since this solution satisfies each equation, the point corresponding to the ordered pair (x, y) must lie on the graph of both equations.

Example 1   Solve the system by graphing: $2x - y = 8$
$$x + y = 1$$

Solution   Graph $2x - y = 8$ and $x + y = 1$ in the same coordinate plane. The only point on *both* lines is the *intersection point* $(3, -2)$ The only solution of *both* equations is $(3, -2)$ You can check that $(3, -2)$ is a solution of the system by substituting $x = 3$ and $y = -2$ in *both* equations.

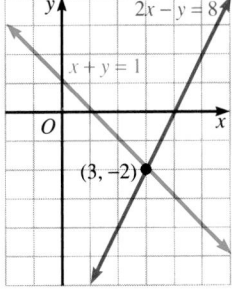

$$2x - y = 8 \qquad x + y = 1$$
$$2(3) - (-2) = 8 \;\checkmark \qquad 3 + (-2) = 1 \;\checkmark$$

∴ the system has the solution $(3, -2)$.   **Answer**

Example 2   Solve the system by graphing: $x - 2y = -6$
$$x - 2y = 2$$

Solution   When you graph the equations in the same coordinate plane, you see that the lines have the same slope but different y-intercepts. The graphs are *parallel lines*. Since the lines do not intersect, there is no point that represents a solution of both equations.

∴ the system has no solution.   **Answer**

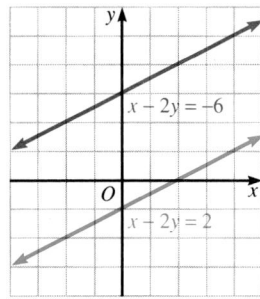

Systems of Linear Equations   **413**

Teaching References

Lesson Commentary,
   pp. T123–T126

Assignment Guide,
   pp. T67–T69

Supplementary Materials

   Practice Masters 54–60

   Tests 40–43

   Resource Book
      Prac. Exs. pp. 120–125
      Tests, pp. 50–55
      En. Act. p. 202
      Mix. Rev. pp. 151–154
      Practice in Problem
         Solving, pp. 173–177
      Application, p. 186
      Using Technology,
         pp. 210–211

   Study Guide pp. 153–166

   Computer Activities 27–29

   Test Generator

   California Standards

   Support Workbook
      Exploration for
      Lesson 9-1

Alternate Test p. T20

Cumulative Review p. T28

Explorations p. 695

Teaching Suggestions p. T123

Group Activities p. T123

Suggested Extensions p. T123

Warm-Up Exercises

Give the slope and y-intercept.

1. $y = 2x + 1$ slope is 2; y-intercept is 1.

2. $y = 3 - x$ slope is -1; y-intercept is 3.

3. $2x + y = 6$ slope is -2; y-intercept is 6.

4. $x + 2y = 8$ slope is $-\frac{1}{2}$; y-intercept is 4.

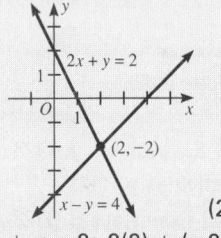
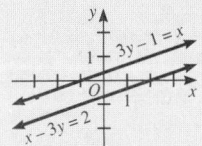
414

Example 3 Solve the system by graphing: $2x + 3y = 6$
                                              $4x + 6y = 12$

Solution When you graph the equations in the same coordinate plane, you see that the graphs *coincide*. The equations are equivalent. Every point on the line represents a solution of both equations.

∴ the system has infinitely many solutions. **Answer**

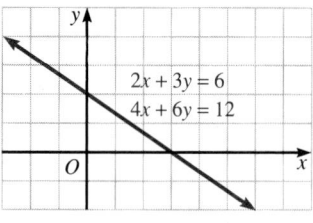

All the examples show how to solve a system of linear equations by the *graphing method*. If you have a computer or a graphing calculator, you can easily solve or estimate the solution to a system of equations by this method.

The Graphing Method

To solve a system of linear equations in two variables, draw the graph of each linear equation in the same coordinate plane.

1. If the lines intersect, there is only one solution, namely, the intersection point.
2. If the lines are parallel, there is no solution.
3. If the lines coincide, there are infinitely many solutions.

Oral Exercises

State whether the given ordered pair is a solution of the system.

1. (5, 3) no

   $2x - y = 7$
   $x + y = 2$

2. (−1, 4) no

   $4x + 3y = 8$
   $3x + y = 0$

3. (2, −2) yes

   $9x = 10 - 4y$
   $y = 3x - 8$

State the solution of each system.

4.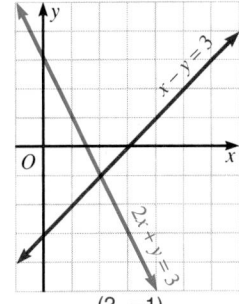

$(2, -1)$

5.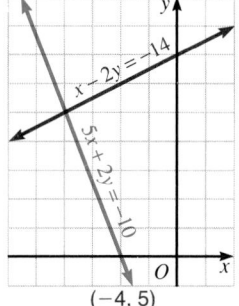

$(-4, 5)$

6.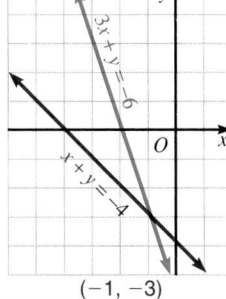

$(-1, -3)$

7. Suppose the graphs of a pair of linear equations appear to intersect at the point $(-1, 4)$. How can you check whether $(-1, 4)$ really is a solution of the system? See if $(-1, 4)$ satisfies both equations.

8. If a system of linear equations has no solution, what do you know about the graphs of the equations? The lines are parallel.

9. Suppose $(1, 5)$ and $(3, 7)$ are known to be solutions of a system of two linear equations. Are there any other solutions? Yes, infinitely many.

Written Exercises

Solve each system by the graphing method.

A

1. $y = x$
$y = 6 - x$ $(3, 3)$

2. $y = -x$
$y = x + 9$ $\left(-\frac{9}{2}, \frac{9}{2}\right)$

3. $y = -x + 2$
$y = 2x + 5$ $(-1, 3)$

4. $y = 3x + 1$
$y = 3x - 8$
no solution

5. $x - y = 6$
$2x + y = 0$ $(2, -4)$

6. $4x + y = -3$
$5x - y = -6$ $(-1, 1)$

7. $3x - 9y = 0$
$-x + 3y = -3$
no solution

8. $-2x + y = -1$
$x + y = 5$
$(2, 3)$

9. $y = \frac{1}{2}x + 1$
$4x - 8y = -8$
infinitely many

10. $2y - x = 2$
$x - 2y = 8$
no solution

11. $y - 2x = -5$
$y - x = -3$
$(2, -1)$

12. $6x + 4y = 2$
$3x + 2y = 1$
infinitely many

Solve each system by the graphing method. Estimate the coordinates of the intersection point to the nearest half unit. You may wish to check your graphs using a computer or a graphing calculator.

B

13. $x + y = 3$
$x - y = 4$
$\left(3\frac{1}{2}, -\frac{1}{2}\right)$

14. $x + y = -2$
$2x - y = 10$
$\left(2\frac{1}{2}, -4\frac{1}{2}\right)$

15. $3x + 5y = 15$
$x - y = 4$
$\left(4\frac{1}{2}, \frac{1}{2}\right)$

16. $2y - 3x = 9$
$4y + 3x = 12$
$\left(-\frac{1}{2}, 3\frac{1}{2}\right)$

The graphing method of solving a system of equations is particularly useful when the equations are not linear. Estimate the solutions of each nonlinear system below by studying the graphs. Check whether your estimate satisfies both equations.

17. $y = x^2$ and $y = 8 - x^2$

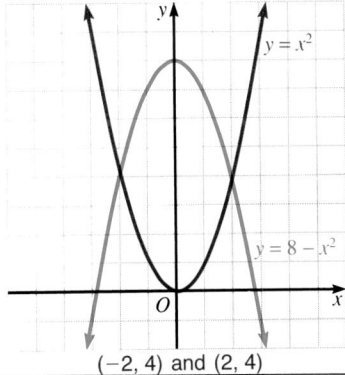

$(-2, 4)$ and $(2, 4)$

18. $y = x^2 - 2x$ and $y = -x^2 + 6x - 6$

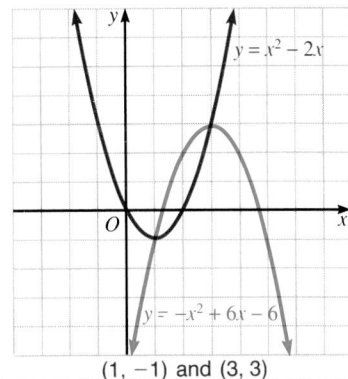

$(1, -1)$ and $(3, 3)$

Systems of Linear Equations **415**

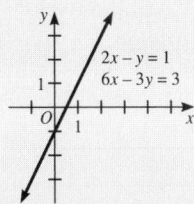

19. Where on the graph of $5x - 2y = 15$ is the x-coordinate equal to the y-coordinate? $(5, 5)$

20. Where on the graph of $3x - y = 12$ are the x- and y-coordinates opposites of each other? $(3, -3)$

21. Where on the graph of $4x + y + 12 = 0$ is the y-coordinate twice the x-coordinate? $(-2, -4)$

22. The triangular region shown is enclosed by the x-axis and by the graphs of $x + 2y = 8$ and $y = \frac{3}{2}x$. Find the area of this region. (*Hint:* Area of a triangle $= \frac{1}{2} \times$ base $\times$ height.) 12 sq. units

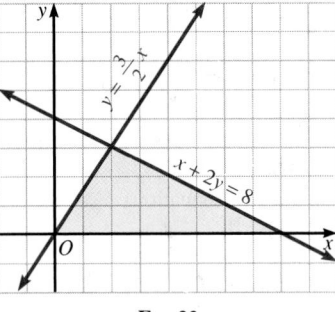

Ex. 22

C **23.** Find the area of the triangular region enclosed by the y-axis and the graphs of $6x + 5y = 30$ and $2x - y = 2$. 10 sq. units

24. Find the area of the region whose vertices are the points of intersection of the graphs of $2x + y = 5$, $y = x - 4$, and $y = 5$. 27 sq. units

Mixed Review Exercises

Simplify. Give answers using positive exponents.

1. $\dfrac{15s^3t}{3s^2t^3} \cdot \dfrac{5s}{t^2}$

2. $(a^{-3}b^2)^4 \cdot \dfrac{b^8}{a^{12}}$

3. $\dfrac{14m^6n}{35m^4n^3} \cdot \dfrac{2m^2}{5n^2}$

4. $(x^2y)^{-2} \dfrac{1}{x^4y^2}$

5. $p^5p^{-2}p^3$

6. $\dfrac{x^4y^3}{x^{-3}y} \cdot x^7y^2$

Using a Computer

These exercises ask students to write a BASIC program that will determine if a system of linear equations has a solution over a given domain. The program must allow students to input the coefficients, and must report the outcomes.

Computer Exercises

For students with some programming experience

Write a BASIC program to print out a table of ordered pairs for each of two linear equations $Ax + By = C$ and $Dx + Ey = F$, where A, B, C, D, E, and F are entered with INPUT statements. If the two equations have an ordered pair in common, the program should report that the ordered pair is a solution of the system of equations. Run the program for the following pairs of equations with the given values of x.

1. $2x - 7y = 9$
 $x + y = 0$
    $x \in \{0, 1, 2, 3, 4, 5\}$ $(1, -1)$ is a solution.

2. $x + 3y = 1$
 $\frac{1}{2}x - 4y = -5$
    $x \in \{-3, -2, -1, 0, 1\}$ $(-2, 1)$ is a solution.

3. $4x - 3y = 0$
 $2x + y = 2$
    $x \in \{0, 1, 2, 3, 4\}$ No pairs in common.

4. $3x - 4y = -6$
 $3x - 2y = 0$
    $x \in \{-2, -1, 0, 1, 2\}$ $(2, 3)$ is a solution.

416   *Chapter 9*

9-2 The Substitution Method

Objective   To use the substitution method to solve the systems of linear equations.

There are several ways to solve a system of equations. In the *substitution method* we use either equation to solve for one variable in terms of the other. The substitution method then calls for obtaining a third equation involving only one variable. The examples below show this method.

Example 1 Solve: $x + y = 15$
$4x + 3y = 38$

Solution   Solve the first equation for y.

$$x + y = 15$$
$$y = 15 - x$$

Substitute this expression for y in the other equation, and solve for x.

$$4x + 3y = 38$$
$$4x + 3(15 - x) = 38$$
$$4x + 45 - 3x = 38$$
$$x + 45 = 38$$
$$x = -7$$

Substitute the value of x in the equation in Step 1, and solve for y.

$$y = 15 - x$$
$$y = 15 - (-7)$$
$$y = 22$$

Check $x = -7$ and $y = 22$ in *both* equations.

$x + y = 15$	$4x + 3y = 38$
$-7 + 22 \stackrel{?}{=} 15$	$4(-7) + 3(22) \stackrel{?}{=} 38$
$15 = 15$ ✓	$38 = 38$ ✓

∴ the solution is $(-7, 22)$.   **Answer**

Example 2 Solve: $2x - 3y = 4$
$x + 4y = -9$

Solution   Solve the second equation for x since x has a coefficient of 1.

$$x + 4y = -9$$
$$x = -9 - 4y$$

Substitute this expression for x in the other equation, and solve for y.

$$2x - 3y = 4$$
$$2(-9 - 4y) - 3y = 4$$
$$-18 - 8y - 3y = 4$$
$$-11y = 22$$
$$y = -2$$

Substitute the value of y in the equation in Step 1, and solve for x.

$$x = -9 - 4y$$
$$x = -9 - 4(-2)$$
$$x = -1$$

The check in *both* equations is left to you.

∴ the solution is $(-1, -2)$.   **Answer**

Systems of Linear Equations   **417**

Teaching Suggestions p. T123

Suggested Extensions p. T123

Warm-Up Exercises

For each equation find the value of y when $x = -2$.
1. $y = -7x + 2$ $y = 16$
2. $3x + y = 1$ $y = 7$
3. $x + 4y = 10$ $y = 3$
4. $x = 2y - 7$ $y = 2\frac{1}{2}$
5. $(x + 1)(y - 4) = 3$ $y = 1$

Motivating the Lesson

The graphing method for solving systems of linear equations is not always useful when the coordinates of the intersection point are difficult to read. Other methods exist for solving systems of linear equations. One of these methods, the substitution method, is the topic of today's lesson.

Chalkboard Examples

Solve by the substitution method.

1. $2x + y = 9$ $y = -2x + 9$
$x + 4y = 1$
$x + 4(-2x + 9) = 1$
$x - 8x + 36 = 1$
$-7x = -35$
$x = 5$
$y = -2x + 9$
$= -2(5) + 9$
$= -1$
The solution is $(5, -1)$.

2. $x - 2y = y$ $x = 3y$
$2x - 5y = 4$
$2(3y) - 5y = 4$
$6y - 5y = 4$
$y = 4$
$x = 3y = 3(4) = 12$
The solution is $(12, 4)$.

(continued)

417

Chalkboard Examples

(continued)

3. $y = 4x - 5$
$8x - 2y = 20$
$8x - 2(4x - 5) = 20$
$8x - 8x + 10 = 20$
$10 = 20$
false; no solution

4. $2x - y = 1 \quad y = 2x - 1$
$3y + 3 = 6x$
$3(2x - 1) + 3 = 6x$
$6x - 3 + 3 = 6x$
$6x = 6x$
true for all values of x;
infinitely many solutions

Check for Understanding

Here is a suggested use of the Oral Exercises to check students' understanding as you teach the lesson.
Oral Exs. 1–6: use after Example 2.
Oral Exs. 7–12: use after Example 4.

Guided Practice

Solve by the substitution method.

1. $m = 4n$
$3m + 2n = 28 \quad (8, 2)$

2. $y - 2x = -17$
$x + y = 16 \quad (11, 5)$

3. $3w - 2z = 5$
$w + z = 15 \quad (7, 8)$

4. $2a + 5b = 16$
$\frac{a}{2} + \frac{b}{4} = 1 \quad \left(\frac{1}{2}, 3\right)$

Summarizing the Lesson

Tell students that they have learned to solve systems of linear equations using the substitution method. Ask them to describe the substitution method in their own words and to explain why it is useful. Point out that this information appears on p. 418.

The substitution method is most convenient to use when the coefficient of one of the variables is 1 or -1 as in Examples 1 and 2.

The Substitution Method

To solve a system of linear equations in two variables:

1. Solve one equation for one of the variables.
2. Substitute this expression in the other equation and solve for the other variable.
3. Substitute this value in the equation in Step 1 and solve.
4. Check the values in both equations.

Example 3 Solve by the substitution method: $2x - 8y = 6$
$x - 4y = 8$

Solution $x - 4y = 8$
$x = 8 + 4y$

$2x - 8y = 6$
$2(8 + 4y) - 8y = 6$
$16 + 8y - 8y = 6$
$16 = 6 \leftarrow$ False

The false statement indicates that there is *no* ordered pair (x, y) that satisfies both equations. (If you graph the equations, you'll see that the lines are parallel.)

$\therefore$ the system has no solution.   ***Answer***

Example 4 Solve by the substitution method: $\dfrac{y}{2} = 2 - x$
$6x + 3y = 12$

Solution $\dfrac{y}{2} = 2 - x$ $\begin{cases} \text{Multiply both sides by 2} \\ \text{to solve for } y. \end{cases}$
$y = 4 - 2x$

$6x + 3y = 12$
$6x + 3(4 - 2x) = 12$
$6x + 12 - 6x = 12$
$12 = 12 \leftarrow$ True

Every ordered pair (x, y) that satisfies one of the equations also satisfies the other. (If you graph the equations, you'll see that the lines coincide.)

$\therefore$ the system has infinitely many solutions.   ***Answer***

418   *Chapter 9*

Oral Exercises

For each system, solve one of the equations for one of the variables.

1. $x - 2y = 0$
$x + y = 6$

2. $3x + 2y = 10$
$x + y = 10$

3. $5a + 3b = 1$
$3a - b = 4$

4. $8m - n = 12$
$2m - 3n = 18$

5. $2s + 5t = 14$
$\frac{s}{2} = \frac{t}{4}$

6. $3p - 10 = 4q$
$\frac{p}{6} + \frac{q}{3} = 0$

Solve by the substitution method.

7. $x = 6$
$y = x - 5$ (6, 1)

8. $b = a - 2$
$b = 1$ (3, 1)

9. $m = -2$
$2n = m$ (−2, −1)

10. $y = 3x$
$x + y = 8$ (2, 6)

11. $d = 4c$
$c + d = 20$ (4, 16)

12. $y = x - 2$
$x + y = 12$ (7, 5)

Written Exercises

Solve by the substitution method.

A **1.** $y = 6x$
$x + y = 28$ (4, 24)

2. $y = 2x$
$5x - y = 30$ (10, 20)

3. $a = 3b$
$a - b = 12$ (18, 6)

4. $m = 4n$
$3m - 2n = 20$ (8, 2)

5. $s = t + 2$
$2t + s = 17$ (7, 5)

6. $c = 3d - 4$
$c + d = 16$ (11, 5)

7. $3x + 1 = y$
$2x + 3y = 25$ (2, 7)

8. $3a = 2b - 6$
$a = b - 1$ (−4, −3)

9. $4f - 3h = 0$
$f + 4h = 19$ (3, 4)

10. $3n + 5m = 7$
$m - 4n = 6$ (2, −1)

11. $2a - b = 17$
$3a + 4b = -13$ (5, −7)

12. $3y - x = -9$
$2y + 5x = 11$ (3, −2)

13. $2r + 3s = 0$
$r + 5 = 6s$ $\left(-1, \frac{2}{3}\right)$

14. $3x + 2y = 11$
$x - 2 = -4y$ $\left(4, -\frac{1}{2}\right)$

15. $2a - b = 1$
$a = \frac{3}{5}b$ (3, 5)

16. $3x + 2y = 550$
$x = \frac{4}{5}y$ (100, 125)

17. $c - d = 8$
$\frac{c}{5} = d + 4$ (5, −3)

18. $\frac{y}{2} - x = 1$
$x + y + 7 = 0$ (−3, −4)

19. $2u + v = 9$
$\frac{u}{2} - \frac{1}{2} = -v$ $\left(\frac{17}{3}, -\frac{7}{3}\right)$

20. $\frac{m}{3} + \frac{n}{3} = 2$
$2m + 3n = 10$ (8, −2)

21. $\frac{y}{2} + \frac{x}{2} = 7$
$3y + 2x = 48$ (−6, 20)

22. $3b - 2a = 4$
$\frac{b}{2} - \frac{2a}{3} = 1$ $\left(-1, \frac{2}{3}\right)$

23. $\frac{r}{2} + \frac{s}{3} = 1$
$\frac{r}{4} + \frac{2s}{3} = -1$ (4, −3)

24. $\frac{c}{2} - \frac{d}{5} = -4$
$\frac{2c}{3} - \frac{3d}{5} = -7$ (−6, 5)

Systems of Linear Equations   **419**

Common Errors

Some students will forget to find the value of the second variable after finding the value of the first. In reaching, stress that the solution to a system of equations is a set of ordered pairs.

419

Supplementary Materials

Study Guide   pp. 155–156
Practice Master   54
Resource Book   p. 120

Solve by the substitution method.

B **25.** $x + y = 1000$
$0.05x + 0.06y = 57$ (300, 700)

26. $a + b = 5000$
$0.08a = 0.06b - 20$ (2000, 3000)

27. $\dfrac{x + y}{2} = 10$
$2x = 3y$ (12, 8)

28. $\dfrac{3d + e}{4} = \dfrac{d + 1}{2}$
$\dfrac{d - e}{4} = 1$ (3, −1)

29. $\dfrac{3p - q}{4} = p + 1$
$\dfrac{5p + q}{2} = p$ (2, −6)

30. $2x - \dfrac{y + 2}{2} = 22$
$3x + \dfrac{y + 2}{3} = 7$ (5, −26)

Determine whether each of the following systems has no solution or infinitely many solutions. If there are infinitely many solutions, give three of them.

33. infinitely many; (7, 1), (14, 2), (0, 0)

31. $5y - 2x = 3$
$6x = 15y - 1$
no solution

32. $3y - 6x = 24$
$8 + 2x = y$

33. $2x = 14y$
$\dfrac{x - y}{3} = \dfrac{x + y}{4}$

32. infinitely many; (0, 8), (1, 10), (2, 12)

Solve each system by (a) the graphing method; (b) the substitution method.

34. $y = 3x - 7$
$6x - 2y = 12$
no solution

35. $y = \dfrac{2}{3}x - 5$
$4x - 6y = 30$
infinitely many

36. $4x + y = 20$
$\dfrac{1}{2}y = -2x + 10$
infinitely many

37. The graphs of the equations $ax + 4y = 6$ and $x + by = -8$ intersect at $(-2, 3)$. Find a and b. $a = 3, b = -2$

38. The graphs of $ax + by = 13$ and $ax - by = -3$ intersect at $(1, 4)$. Find a and b.
$a = 5, b = 2$

Use the substitution method to solve each system.

C **39.** $x + y + z = 180$
$y = 3x$ $x = 20$
$z = 5x$ $y = 60$
            $z = 100$

40. $a + b + c = 62$
$a = 2c - 5$ $a = 19$
$b = 3c - 5$ $b = 31$
                $c = 12$

41. $x + y + 2z = 1$ $x = \dfrac{3}{2}$
$x - y = 1$
$x - z = 2$ $y = \dfrac{1}{2}$

$z = -\dfrac{1}{2}$

Mixed Review Exercises

Solve each system by the graphing method.

1. $3x + 2y = 5$
$y = x - 5$ (3, −2)

2. $x + y = 9$
$2y - x = 6$ (4, 5)

3. $y = 4x$
$x - y = 3$ (−1, −4)

4. $y = \dfrac{1}{2}x$
$x + 2y = 8$ (4, 2)

5. $3x + 4y = 0$
$3x - y = 15$ (4, −3)

6. $5x + y = -12$
$4x - y = 3$ (−1, −7)

Write an equation in slope-intercept form for each line described.

7. slope − 4, passes through (2, −7)
$y = -4x + 1$

8. slope $\dfrac{2}{3}$, passes through (6, 6)
$y = \dfrac{2}{3}x + 2$

9. slope $-\dfrac{1}{2}$, y-intercept −6 $y = -\dfrac{1}{2}x - 6$

10. passes through (3, 8) and (0, −1)
$y = 3x - 1$

11. passes through (2, −4) and (5, −7)
$y = -x - 2$

12. slope 0, y-intercept 2 $y = 2$

420   *Chapter 9*

9-3 Solving Problems with Two Variables

Objective   To use systems of linear equations in two variables to solve problems.

You have learned to solve problems using equations in one variable. Now you can solve problems with equations in two variables. Example 1 compares these two methods.

Example 1   John has 15 coins, all dimes and quarters, worth $2.55. How many dimes and how many quarters does John have?

Solution 1 (Using one variable)

Step 1 The problem asks for the number of dimes and the number of quarters.

Step 2 Let x = the number of dimes. Then $15 - x$ = the number of quarters. Make a chart.

	Number $\times$	Value per coin =	Total Value
Dimes	x	10	$10x$
Quarters	$15 - x$	25	$25(15 - x)$

Step 3 The only fact not recorded in this chart is the total value of the coins, $2.55 (or 255 cents). Use this fact to write an equation.
$$10x + 25(15 - x) = 255$$

Step 4 $10x + 375 - 25x = 255$
$$-15x = -120$$
$$x = 8$$
$$15 - x = 7$$

Step 5 The check is left to you.

∴ John has 8 dimes and 7 quarters. *Answer*

Solution 2 (Using two variables)

Step 1 The problem asks for the number of dimes and the number of quarters.

Step 2 Let d = the number of dimes and q = the number of quarters. Make a chart.

	Number $\times$	Value per coin =	Total Value
Dimes	d	10	$10d$
Quarters	q	25	$25q$

(Solution continues on the next page.)

Systems of Linear Equations   **421**

Teaching Suggestions p. T124
Suggested Extensions p. T124

Warm-Up Exercises

Using n as the variable, write an equation.

1. 7 more than a number is 55. $n + 7 = 55$

2. 16 is 5 less than a number. $16 = n - 5$

3. 6 less than twice Sarah's age is 20. $2n - 6 = 20$

4. 47 is 11 more than three times Neil's age. $47 = 11 + 3n$

5. Dave earned $56.30. This was $4.50 less than Ned's earnings. What did Ned earn? $56.30 = n - 4.50$

Motivating the Lesson

Cary has 15 coins, all dimes and nickels, worth $1.40. How many nickels does she have? This type of problem can be solved by using an equation with one variable. Today's lesson shows that a system of equations with two variables can also be used.

Chalkboard Examples

Solve, using two equations in two variables.

1. The sum of two numbers is 5. The larger number exceeds twice the smaller number by 14. Find the numbers.
   Let n = larger number and k = smaller number
   $n + k = 5$
   $n - 2k = 14$; $n = 2k + 14$
   $2k + 14 + k = 5$
   $3k = -9$
   $k = -3$
   $n = 2(-3) + 14 = 8$
   The numbers are 8 and −3.
   (continued)

421

2. A pet shop sold 23 puppies and kittens one week. They sold 9 more puppies than kittens. How many of each did they sell?

Let p = number of puppies and k = number of kittens

$p + k = 23$
$p = k + 9$

$k + 9 + k = 23$
$\quad\quad 2k = 14$
$\quad\quad\ \ k = 7$
$\quad\quad\ \ p = 7 + 9 = 16$

The shop sold 16 puppies and 7 kittens.

3. A bank teller has 112 $5-bills and $10-bills for a total of $720. How many of each does the teller have?

Let f = no. of $5-bills and t = no. of $10-bills

$f + t = 112;\ t = 112 - f$
$5f + 10t = 720$

$5f + 10(112 - f) = 720$
$5f + 1120 - 10f = 720$
$\quad\quad\quad 400 = 5f$
$\quad\quad\quad\quad f = 80$
$\quad\quad\quad\ \ t = 112 - 80$
$\quad\quad\quad\quad\ \ = 32$

The teller has 80 $5-bills and 32 $10-bills.

Check for Understanding

Here is a suggested use of the Oral Exercises to check students' understanding as you teach the lesson.
Oral Exs. 3–12: use after Example 3.

Step 3 The two facts not recorded in the chart are the total number of coins, 15, and the total value, $2.55. Use these facts to write a system of equations.

$$d + q = 15$$
$$10d + 25q = 255$$

Step 4 $\quad\quad\quad\quad\quad q = 15 - d \quad$ {Find q in terms of d.

$10d + 25(15 - d) = 255 \quad\quad$ {Substitute.
$10d + 375 - 25d = 255$
$\quad\quad\quad\quad -15d = -120$
$\quad\quad\quad\quad\quad\ d = 8$

$\quad\quad\quad q = 15 - d$
$\quad\quad\quad q = 15 - 8$
$\quad\quad\quad q = 7$

Step 5 The check is left to you.
$\therefore$ John has 8 dimes and 7 quarters. **Answer**

Example 2 Ann and Betty together have $60. Ann has $9 more than twice Betty's amount. How much money does each have?

Solution Let a = the amount of Ann's money and b = the amount of Betty's money.

Ann and Betty together have $60. $\quad\quad \rightarrow a + b = 60$
Ann has $9 more than twice Betty's amount. $\rightarrow a = 2b + 9$

The system of the two equations above can be used to solve the problem. The rest of the solution is left to you (see Oral Exercise 1).

Example 3 Joan Wu has $8000 invested in stocks and bonds. The stocks pay 4% interest, and the bonds pay 7% interest. If her annual income from the stocks and bonds is $500, how much is invested in bonds?

Solution Let s = the amount invested in stocks and b = the amount invested in bonds. Make a chart.

	Principal	× Rate	= Interest
Stocks	s	0.04	$0.04s$
Bonds	b	0.07	$0.07b$
Total	8000		500

The total amount invested is $8000. $\quad\quad \rightarrow s + b = 8000$
The total amount of interest earned is $500 $\rightarrow 0.04s + 0.07b = 500$

The rest of the solution is left to you (see Oral Exercise 2).

---

422 *Chapter 9*

You can use either one variable or two variables to solve problems like those in the examples. The advantage of using two variables is that it is sometimes easier to write the equations that will solve the problem.

Oral Exercises

1. Complete the solution to Example 2. Ann, $43; Betty, $17
2. Complete the solution to Example 3. bonds, $6000; stocks, $2000

Give a system of equations that can be used to solve each problem.

In Exercises 3–6 use n, d, and q for the number of nickels, the number of dimes, and the number of quarters, respectively.

3. Sam has 30 nickels and dimes worth $2.40. How many nickels does he have?
$$n + d = 30$$
$$5n + 10d = 240$$

4. Kelley has 24 dimes and quarters worth $3.60. How many quarters does she have?
$$d + q = 24$$
$$10d + 25q = 360$$

5. Bruce has $5.50 in dimes and quarters. He has 8 more quarters than dimes. How many quarters does he have?
$$d + 8 = q$$
$$10d + 25q = 550$$

6. Luis and Julia have the same number of coins. Luis has only dimes and Julia has only quarters. If Julia has $1.80 more than Luis does, how many coins does each have?
$$d = q$$
$$10d + 180 = 25q$$

In Exercises 7–12, use whatever variables seem appropriate.

7. Dick and Connie purchased a radio for $128. Dick paid $36 more than Connie. How much did each pay?
$$d + c = 128$$
$$c + 36 = d$$

8. Annette and June bowled together and had a combined score of 425. June's score was 25 less than Annette's score. Find their scores.
$$a + j = 425$$
$$a - 25 = j$$

9. Steve has $3 more than twice as much as Tracy. Together they have $57. How much does each have?
$$s + t = 57$$
$$2t + 3 = s$$

10. The length of a rectangle is 5 cm less than three times its width. If the perimeter is 70 cm, find the dimensions.

11. A radio station broadcasts programs and commercials 20 hours everyday. The ratio of the time spent on commercials to the programming time is 1:4. How much time each day does the station spend broadcasting commercials?

12. A person invests $5000 in treasury notes and bonds. The notes pay 8% annual interest and the bonds pay 10% annual interest. If the annual income is $480, how much is invested in treasury notes?
$$n + b = 5000$$
$$0.08n + 0.1b = 480$$

10. $l = 3w - 5$ 11. $c + p = 20$
$2l + 2w = 70$ $\dfrac{c}{p} = \dfrac{1}{4}$

Systems of Linear Equations   **423**

Suggested Assignments

Minimum
Day 1: 424/*P*: 1–9 odd
    S 425/Mixed Review
Day 2: 424/*P*: 11–19

Average
Day 1: 424/*P*: 1–9 odd
    S 425/Mixed Review
Day 2: 424/*P*: 6–22 even

Maximum
    424/*P*: 1–21 odd
    S 425/Mixed Review

Supplementary Materials

Study Guide   pp. 157–158

Problems

1. 12 nickels 2. 8 quarters 3. 18 quarters 4. 12 coins each
5. Dick, $82; Connie, $46 6. Annette, 225; June, 200
7. Tracy, $18; Steve, $39
8. 10 cm × 25 cm
9. 4 h 10. $1000

A **1–10.** Solve the problems given in Oral Exercises 3–12.

Solve, using two equations in two variables.

B **11.** The sum of two numbers is 100. Five times the smaller is 8 more than the larger. Find the numbers. 18 and 82

12. One number is 12 more than half another number. The two numbers total 60. Find the numbers. 28 and 32

13. Lisa and Beverly had just $5 to spend for an after-school snack. They could have bought 2 hamburgers and 1 carton of milk with no change back or 1 hamburger and 2 cartons of milk with 40 cents change back. How much does a carton of milk cost? $1.40

14. If you buy six pens and one mechanical pencil, you'll get only $1 change from your $10 bill. But if you buy four pens and two mechanical pencils, you'll get $2 change. How much does each pen and each pencil cost? pen, $1.25 pencil, $1.50

15. Marty Lister invested $9000 in stocks and bonds. The stocks paid 5% and the bonds 8%, giving an annual income of $525. How much did he invest in bonds? $2500

16. Melinda Bowen receives an annual income of $234.50 from investing one amount of money at 6% and another amount at 5%. If the investments were interchanged, her income would increase by $5.10. Find the amounts she invested. $1900 at 6%; $2410 at 5%

17. A car and a bike set out at noon from the same point headed in the same direction. At 1:00 P.M., the car is 60 km ahead of the bike. Find how fast each travels, given that the car travels four times as fast as the bike. bike, 20 km/h; car, 80 km/h

18. A grocer mixes together some cashews costing $8 per kilogram with some Brazil nuts costing $10 per kilogram. The grocer sold 12 kg of the mixture for $8.50 per kilogram. How many kilograms of cashews were in the mixture the grocer sold? 9 kg

19. One number is 16 more than another. If the smaller number is subtracted from two thirds of the larger number, the result is one fourth of the sum of the two numbers. Find the numbers. 8 and 24

20. If Bill rides his bike 3 mi to Fred's house and then walks with Fred the remaining 1 mi to school, it will take him 30 min. But if he rides the entire distance, it will take him only 20 min. Find his biking speed and walking speed. biking, 12 mi/h; walking, 4 mi/h

Solve each problem by using a system of three equations in three variables.

C **21.** I have 30 coins, all nickels, dimes, and quarters, worth $4.60. There are two more dimes than quarters. How many of each kind of coin do I have? 4 nickels, 14 dimes, 12 quarters

22. Carl, Diane, and Ed together have $46. Carl has half as much as Diane, and Ed has $2 less than Diane. How much does each have? Carl, $9.60; Diane, $19.20; Ed, $17.20

Mixed Review Exercises

Solve.

1. $\frac{1}{2}s + 8 = 3$ $\{-10\}$

2. $\frac{1}{4}y = 2\frac{1}{4}$ $\{9\}$

3. $\frac{x+2}{3} = 11$ $\{31\}$

4. $4(a + 3) = 12 - 2(a - 18)$ $\{6\}$

5. $-12 + n = 5$ $\{17\}$

6. $3x + 14 = x + 4$ $\{-5\}$

Solve by the substitution method.

7. $y = \frac{1}{2}x - \frac{5}{2}$
$2x + 10 = 4y$ no solution

8. $b - 2a = -1$
$3b + a = 18$ (3, 5)

9. $y = 3x - 2$ no solution
$\frac{y-1}{3} = x$

10. $y = x - 3$
$x + y = 5$ (4, 1)

11. $3c - 4d = 6$
$2c + d = -7$ (−2, −3)

12. $q = 3p$
$2p + q = 15$ (3, 9)

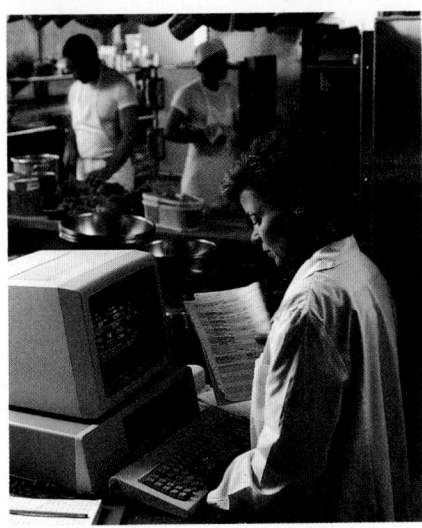

Challenge

The numbers 21 and 22 can be written using five 4's and mathematical symbols as shown below.

$$21 = 4 \cdot 4 + 4 + 4 \div 4 \qquad 22 = 44 \div \sqrt{4} \div (4 \div 4)$$

Which of the numbers 23 through 29 can you write using five 4's and mathematical symbols?

Additional Answers
Challenge

All; Answers may vary

$23 = 44 \div \sqrt{4} + 4 \div 4$

$24 = \sqrt{4} \cdot 4 \cdot 4 - 4 - 4$

$25 = (\sqrt{4} + \sqrt{4} + 4 \div 4)^{\sqrt{4}}$

$26 = 44 \div \sqrt{4} + \sqrt{4} + \sqrt{4}$

$27 = 44 \div 4 + 4 \cdot 4$

$28 = 4 \cdot 4 + 4 \cdot 4 - 4$

$29 = (4 + 4 \div 4)^{\sqrt{4}} + 4$

9-4 The Addition-or-Subtraction Method

Objective To use addition or subtraction to solve systems of linear equations in two variables.

When solving a system of two equations, you can sometimes add or subtract the equations to obtain a new equation with just one variable. This method is called the *addition-or-subtraction method*.

Example 1 (The Addition Method)   Solve: $5x - y = 12$
$3x + y = 4$

Solution

1. Add similar terms of the two equations.

$5x - y = 12$
$3x + y = 4$
$\overline{}$
$8x = 16$

$\left\{\begin{array}{l}\text{The } y\text{-terms are}\\\text{eliminated.}\end{array}\right.$

2. Solve the resulting equation.

$x = 2$

3. Substitute 2 for x in either of the original equations to find y.

$3x + y = 4$
$3(2) + y = 4$
$y = -2$

4. Check $x = 2$ and $y = -2$ in *both* original equations.

$3x + y = 4$
$3(2) + (-2) \stackrel{?}{=} 4$
$4 = 4$ ✓

$5x - y = 12$
$5(2) - (-2) \stackrel{?}{=} 12$
$12 = 12$ ✓

∴ the solution is (2, −2).   **Answer**

Example 2 (The Subtraction Method)   Solve: $6c + 7d = -15$
$6c - 2d = 12$

Solution

1. Subtract similar terms of the two equations.

$6c + 7d = -15$
$6c - 2d = 12$
$\overline{}$
$9d = -27$

$\left\{\begin{array}{l}\text{The } c\text{-terms are}\\\text{eliminated.}\end{array}\right.$

2. Solve the resulting equation.

$d = -3$

3. Substitute -3 for d in either of the original equations to find c.

$6c + 7d = -15$
$6c + 7(-3) = -15$
$6c = 6$
$c = 1$

4. The check in both original equations is left to you.

∴ the solution is (1, −3). **Answer**

426   Chapter 9

Notice that in Example 2 the coefficients of c are the *same*, and in Example 1 the coefficients of y are *opposites*. Whenever two equations have the same or opposite coefficients for one of their terms, the addition-or-subtraction method can be used.

The Addition-or-Subtraction Method

To solve a system of linear equations in two variables:

1. Add or subtract the equations to eliminate one variable.
2. Solve the resulting equation for the other variable.
3. Substitute in either original equation to find the value of the first variable.
4. Check in both original equations.

Oral Exercises

Use the addition method to solve for x.

1. $3x + 2y = 7$
$5x - 2y = 1$ $x = 1$

2. $x - 5y = 1$
$2x + 5y = 17$ $x = 6$

3. $4y + 3x = 9$
$-4y - x = 7$ $x = 8$

Use the subtraction method to solve for s.

4. $3t + 5s = 10$
$3t + s = 2$ $s = 2$

5. $4s - 5t = 7$
$2s - 5t = 3$ $s = 2$

6. $3s + 4t = 18$
$-2s + 4t = 8$ $s = 2$

Use the addition-or-subtraction method to solve for one of the variables.

7. $3a + 2b = 11$
$2a - 2b = 4$ $a = 3$

8. $3p + 2q = 19$
$3p - 5q = 5$ $q = 2$

9. $-4s + 7t = 10$
$4s - 2t = 5$ $t = 3$

Written Exercises

Solve by the addition-or-subtraction method.

A
1. $x + y = 7$
$x - y = 3$ (5, 2)

2. $a + b = 5$
$a - b = 7$ (6, −1)

3. $3n - 2t = 16$
$5n + 2t = 8$ $\left(3, -\frac{7}{2}\right)$

4. $3c + 5d = 17$
$3c + 8d = 5$ $\left(\frac{37}{3}, -4\right)$

5. $12n + 3m = 18$
$5n + 3m = 4$ (−2, 2)

6. $3a - 5b = 31$
$7a - 5b = 59$ (7, −2)

7. $6p - 7q = 28$
$-6p + 3q = -12$ (0, −4)

8. $4a - 7b = 13$
$2a - 7b = 3$ (5, 1)

9. $2c + 3d = 0$
$5c - 3d = 21$ (3, −2)

10. $-3x + 5y = 45$
$3x + 13y = 9$ (−10, 3)

11. $12p - 18q = 14$
$-15p - 18q = -4$ $\left(\frac{2}{3}, -\frac{1}{3}\right)$

12. $9y + 5z = 1$
$-9y - 10z = 2$ $\left(\frac{4}{9}, -\frac{3}{5}\right)$

Systems of Linear Equations **427**

Check for Understanding
Oral Exs. 1–3: use after Example 1.
Oral Exs. 4–9: use after Example 2.

Guided Practice
Solve by the addition-or-subtraction method.

1. $x + y = 17$
$x - y = 1$ (9, 8)

2. $a - 3b = -1$
$2a + 3b = 16$ (5, 2)

3. $-3n + 9m = 6$
$3n + 4m = 7$ (1, 1)

4. $8q + 12r = 20$
$5q + 12r = -1$ (7, −3)

5. $9x - 10y = 2$
$9x + 2y = -22$ (−2, −2)

6. $a - 2b = 0$
$a + 2b = 12$ (6, 3)

7. $2.58d - 0.03e = 15$
$1.72d + 0.03e = 19.4$
(8, 188)

Summarizing the Lesson
Tell students that they have learned the addition-or-subtraction method for solving systems of linear equations in two variables. Ask them to explain what special feature of the given system is necessary for this method to work. Remind students that the method is outlined on p. 427.

Suggested Assignments
Minimum
Day 1: 427/1–11 odd, 17, 20
    S 429/Mixed Review
Day 2: 427/12, 15, 18, 19
    428/*P*: 1–4
        (continued)

Suggested Assignments

(continued)
Average
Day 1: 427/1–19 odd
    S 429/Mixed Review
Day 2: 428/22, 24, 26, 28
    428/*P*: 1, 3, 5, 7
Maximum
Day 1: 427/1–27 odd
    S 429/Mixed Review
Day 2: 428/28–31
    428/*P*: 1–9 odd

Supplementary Materials

Study Guide   pp. 159–160
Practice Master   55

Solve by the addition-or-subtraction method.

13. $21x - 16y = -1$
$33x + 16y = 19$ $\left(\frac{1}{3}, \frac{1}{2}\right)$

14. $-28g + 15h = -18$
$-28g - 40h = -29$ $\left(\frac{3}{4}, \frac{1}{5}\right)$

(150, 200)
15. $0.02x + 0.03y = 9$
$0.02x + 0.05y = 13$

16. $0.07a - 0.03b = 12$
$0.01a + 0.03b = 12$
    (300, 300)

17. $\frac{1}{2}x + \frac{1}{3}y = 4$
$\frac{5}{2}x - \frac{1}{3}y = 8$
  (4, 6)

18. $\frac{3}{4}x - \frac{1}{6}y = -12$
$\frac{5}{4}x - \frac{1}{6}y = -22$
  (−20, −18)

Solve by either the substitution method or the addition-or-subtraction method.

B **19.** $a = 6b + 3$
$a + 2b = 5$ $\left(\frac{9}{2}, \frac{1}{4}\right)$

20. $x - 5y = 2$
$2x + y = 4$ (2, 0)

21. $4(x - 2y) = 8$
$x + 6y = 2$ (2, 0)

22. $4(a - 2b) = 8$
$2(a + 4b) = -8$ (0, −1)

23. $n = 2 - 6m$
$\frac{1}{2}n - m = 1$ (0, 2)

24. $\frac{1}{3}a - \frac{2}{3}b = 1$ $\left(-\frac{11}{3}, -\frac{10}{3}\right)$
$a + b + 7 = 0$

25. $y = \frac{2}{3}x$
$x + 6y = 30$ (6, 4)

26. $\frac{5a}{6} - \frac{b}{3} = 6$
$a + 2b = 0$ (6, −3)

27. $3n + 1 = \frac{p}{4}$
$n = \frac{p + 1}{15}$ $\left(\frac{5}{3}, 24\right)$

28. a. Use the graph shown at the right to
estimate the solution of the system
$$7x + 5y = 25$$
$$2x - 5y = 15 \quad \left(4\frac{1}{2}, -1\right) \text{ or}$$
to the nearest half unit. $\left(4\frac{1}{2}, -1\frac{1}{2}\right)$

b. Use algebra to find the exact solution
of this system. $\left(4\frac{4}{9}, -1\frac{2}{9}\right)$

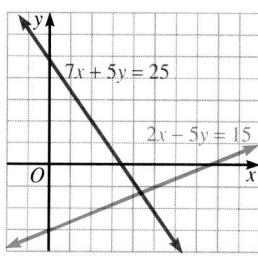

29. The graphs of $ax + by = 18$ and $ax - by = 6$
intersect at (3, −2). Find a and b. $a = 4, b = -3$

C **30.** The graphs of $5x - 3y = 35$, $7x - 3y = 43$, and $4x - ay = 61$ all intersect
in the same point. Find a. 9

They both reduce to the same equation: $y = \frac{1}{4}x$.

31. Show that the graphs of $\dfrac{x - 2y}{x + 2y} = \dfrac{1}{3}$ and $\dfrac{x - y}{x + y} = \dfrac{3}{5}$ coincide.

Problems

**Solve using two equations in two variables. Use either the substitution
method or the addition-or-subtraction method.**

A **1.** The sum of two numbers is 21 and their difference is 5. What are the numbers? 13 and 8

2. The sum of two numbers is 64. Twice the smaller number is 10 less than
the larger number. Find the numbers. 18 and 46

3. There are 812 students in a school. There are 36 more girls than boys.
How many girls are there? 424 girls

428   *Chapter 9*

4. Three pizzas and four sandwiches cost $34. Three pizzas and seven sandwiches cost $41.50. How much does a pizza cost? $8.00

B **5.** There are 26 times as many students in Lincoln High School as teachers. When all the teachers and students are seated in the 900-seat school auditorium, only 9 seats are unoccupied. How many students are at Lincoln High? 858 students

6. At an amusement park you get 5 points for each bull's eye you hit, but you lose 10 points for every miss. After 30 tries, Yolanda lost 90 points. How many bull's eyes did she have? 14

7. Since my uncle's farmyard appeared to be overrun with chickens and dogs, I asked him how many of each he had. Being a puzzler as well as a farmer, my uncle replied that his dogs and chickens had a total of 148 legs and 60 heads. How many dogs and how many chickens does my uncle have?

8. A shipment of 18 cars, some weighing 3000 lb apiece and the others 5000 lb each, has a total weight of 30 tons. Find the number of each kind of car. **7.** 14 dogs, 46 chickens
8. 15 at 3000 lb, 3 at 5000 lb

C **9.** If Tom gives Maria 30 cents, they will have equal amounts of money. But if Maria then gives Tom 50 cents, he will have twice as much money as she does. How much money does each have now? Maria, $1.20; Tom $1.80

10. In a running and swimming race, the athletes must run 2 mi and swim 1 mi. It took Peggy 42 min to do this, but if she were able to run the total 3 mi, it would have taken only 18 min. At what rate did she swim the mile? 2 mi/h

Mixed Review Exercises

Simplify.

1340

1. $7x^3 + 5x^2 - 3x + 6x^2$
$7x^3 + 11x^2 - 3x$

2. $3 \cdot 4^2$ 48

3. $(1 \cdot 10^3) + (3 \cdot 10^2) + (4 \cdot 10)$

4. $-2[3n - 2(n - 1)] -2n - 4$

5. $(6x^4y^3)\left(\frac{3}{2}xy^2\right)$ $9x^5y^5$

6. $(3a^3)^2$ $9a^6$

7. $(-2p^2q)^3$ $-8p^6q^3$

8. $3x[4x + 3(2 - x)]$
$3x^2 + 18x$

9. $(6ab)(-3a^2b)(2a^3b^2)$ $-36a^6b^4$

10. $\left(-\frac{1}{15}\right)(105)\left(\frac{1}{7}\right)$ -1

11. $\dfrac{-8}{\frac{1}{3}}$ -24

12. $\frac{1}{6}(-54m + 36n)$ $-9m + 6n$

9-5 Multiplication with the Addition-or-Subtraction Method

Objective To use multiplication with the addition-or-subtraction method to solve systems of linear equations.

The two equations in a system don't always have the same or opposite coefficients for one of their terms. Before you can use the addition-or-subtraction method to solve the system you need a step that gives an equivalent system that has the same or opposite coefficients for one of the terms.

Example 1 Solve: $4x - 5y = 23$
$3x + 10y = 31$

Solution
1. Multiply both sides of the first equation by 2 so that the y-terms are opposites.

$2(4x - 5y) = 2(23) \rightarrow 8x - 10y = 46$
$3x + 10y = 31 \quad \rightarrow \underline{ 3x + 10y = 31}$

2. Add similar terms.

$11x = 77$

3. Solve the resulting equation.

$x = 7$

4. Substitute 7 for x in either original equation to find the value of y.

$4x - 5y = 23$
$4(7) - 5y = 23$
$-5y = -5$
$y = 1$

5. The check in both original equations is left to you.

∴ the solution is $(7, 1)$. **Answer**

Example 2 Solve: $3a + 4b = 2$
$5a + 9b = 1$

Solution
1. Transform *both* equations by multiplication so that a-terms are the same.

$5(3a + 4b) = 5(2) \rightarrow 15a + 20b = 10$
$3(5a + 9b) = 3(1) \rightarrow \underline{15a + 27b = 3}$

2. Subtract similar terms.

$-7b = 7$

3. Solve the resulting equation.

$b = -1$

4. Substitute -1 for b in either original equation to find the value of a.

$3a + 4b = 2$
$3a + 4(-1) = 2$
$3a = 6$
$a = 2$

5. The check is left to you.

∴ the solution is $(2, -1)$. **Answer**

Example 3 Solve: $\dfrac{5x}{3} + y = 7$

$$x + \dfrac{y}{4} = \dfrac{7}{2}$$

Solution When a system has fractions, it is usually convenient to eliminate the fractions first.

1. Multiply each equation by the LCD of its denominators.

$$3\left(\dfrac{5x}{3} + y\right) = 3(7) \ \rightarrow 5x + 3y = 21$$

$$4\left(x + \dfrac{y}{4}\right) = 4\left(\dfrac{7}{2}\right) \rightarrow 4x + \ y = 14$$

2. Multiply the second equation by 3 so that the y-terms are the same.

$$\begin{array}{l} 5x + 3y = 21 \quad \rightarrow \quad 5x + 3y = 21 \\ 3(4x + y) = 3(14) \rightarrow \underline{12x + 3y = 42} \end{array}$$

$$\qquad\qquad\qquad\qquad -7x \quad\ \ = -21$$

3. Subtract similar terms.

4. Solve the resulting equation.

$$x = 3$$

5. Substitute 3 for x in either original equation to find the value of y.

$$\dfrac{5x}{3} + y = 7$$

$$\dfrac{5(3)}{3} + y = 7$$

$$5 + y = 7$$

$$y = 2$$

6. The check is left to you.

$\therefore$ the solution is (3, 2). **Answer**

Oral Exercises

Explain how to use multiplication with the addition-or-subtraction method to solve each system by answering these questions:

a. Which variable will you eliminate?
b. Which equation(s) will you transform by multiplication?
c. By what number(s) will you multiply?
d. Will you then add or subtract similar terms?

Answers may vary.

1. $2x + \ y = 8$ **a.** y **c.** 2
    $3x - 2y = 5$ **b.** 1st   **d.** +

2. $3a + 5b = 3$ **a.** a **c.** 3
    $a + 2b = 13$ **b.** 2nd   **d.** −

3. $3x - 2t = 4$ **a.** t **c.** 2
    $2x + \ t = 5$ **b.** 2nd   **d.** +

4. $4x - 3y = 7$ **a.** y **c.** 3
    $5x - \ y = 6$ **b.** 2nd   **d.** −

5. $4p - \ q = 6$ **a.** q **c.** 3
    $2p - 3q = 8$ **b.** 1st   **d.** −

6. $4x - 3y = 8$ **a.** y **c.** 3
    $2x + \ y = 14$ **b.** 2nd   **d.** +

7. $5p - 2q = 1$ **a.** q **c.** 5; 2
    $4p + 5q = 47$ **b.** both   **d.** +

8. $2c - 3d = -1$ **a.** d **c.** 4; 3
    $3c - 4d = -3$ **b.** both   **d.** −

9. $3r - 2s = 15$ **a.** s **c.** 3; 2
    $7r - 3s = 15$ **b.** both   **d.** −

2. $\quad 4s - \ 5t = 3$
$\quad\ \ 3s + \ 2t = -15$

$\quad\ \ 8s - 10t = 6$
$\quad \underline{15s + 10t = -75}$
$\qquad\ 23s = -69$
$\qquad\quad\ s = -3$

$\quad -9 + 2t = -15$
$\qquad\ \ 2t = -6$
$\qquad\quad t = -3$
$\therefore$ the solution is $(-3, -3)$.

3. $\quad \dfrac{3x}{2} + y = 6$
$\quad\ \ x + \ y = 5$

$\quad 3x + 2y = 12$
$\quad\ \ x + \ y = 5$

$\quad 3x + 2y = 12$
$\quad \underline{3x + 3y = 15}$
$\qquad\ -y = -3$
$\qquad\quad y = 3$

$\quad x + 3 = 5$
$\qquad x = 2$
$\therefore$ the solution is (2, 3).

Check for Understanding

Here is a suggested use of the Oral Exercises as you teach the lesson.
Oral Exs. 1–6: use after Example 1.
Oral Exs. 7–9: use after Example 2.

Guided Practice

Solve each system by using multiplication with the addition-or-subtraction method.

1. $\quad 4x - 2y = 10$
$\quad\ \ 3x - \ y = 12$ (7, 9)

2. $\quad 5a + 3b = 43$
$\quad -a + 7b = -1$ (8, 1)

3. $\quad m + 2n = 6$
$\quad -2m + 4n = 28$ (−4, 5)

4. $\quad 2s + 3t = 35$
$\quad\ \ 5s - 4t = 7$ (7, 7)

5. $\quad 4w - 4z = -8$
$\quad -3w + 5z = 0$ (−5, −3)

431

Written Exercises

Solve each system by using multiplication with the addition-or-subtraction method.
1. $(3, 2)$ **2.** $(-59, 36)$ **3.** $(1, 2)$ **4.** $(1, -1)$ **5.** $(1, -2)$ **6.** $(5, 4)$
7. $(3, 7)$ **8.** $(-5, -3)$ **9.** $(-3, -12)$

18. $\left(5, \frac{1}{3}\right)$

21. $\left(4, -\frac{1}{2}\right)$

A **1–9.** Solve the systems given in Oral Exercises 1–9.

10. $3c - 8d = 7$
$c + 2d = -7$ $(-3, -2)$

11. $3a + b = 4$
$a - 2b = 6$ $(2, -2)$

12. $x + y = 7$ $(5, 2)$
$3x - 2y = 11$

13. $4x + 5t = 22$
$5x - t = 13$ $(2, 3)$

14. $2n + 5a = 14$
$6n + 7a = 10$ $(4, -3)$

15. $3p + 4q = 4$ $(4, -2)$
$5p + 2q = 16$

16. $3t - 8z = 34$
$7t + 4z = -34$ $(-2, -5)$

17. $2c - 7d = 41$
$6c + 5d = -7$ $(3, -5)$

18. $4r + 9s = 23$
$-7r + 3s = -34$

19. $4b + 13c = -24$
$12b - 5c = 16$ $\left(\frac{1}{2}, -2\right)$

20. $18a - 5b = 17$
$6a + 10b = -6$ $\left(\frac{2}{3}, -1\right)$

21. $3p + 8q = 8$
$5p - 2q = 21$

22. $4x + 15t = 10$
$3x + 10t = 5$ $(2, -5)$

23. $6n + 8c - 4 = 0$
$9n + 10c - 7 = 0$ $\left(-\frac{1}{2}, \frac{4}{3}\right)$

24. $6z - 5t + 10 = 0$
$4z - 7t + 25 = 0$

$\left(5, \frac{5}{2}\right)$

B **25.** Show that the equations $6n + 4c = 5$ and $9n + 6c = 8$ have no common solution.

26. Show that the equations $8a - 10b = \frac{1}{3}$ and $20a - 25b = \frac{5}{6}$ have many solutions.

Solve each system by using multiplication with the addition-or-subtraction method.

27. $0.4x + 1.5y = -5.7$
$-0.2x + 0.8y = -1.8$
$(-3, -3)$

28. $0.9x - 2.1y = 12.3$
$4.6x - 6.3y = 40.7$
$(2, -5)$

29. $0.3x + 0.5y = 31$
$0.2x - 0.1y = -1$
$(20, 50)$

30. $0.05x + 0.06y = 215$
$x + y = 400$
$(-19{,}100, 19{,}500)$

31. $\dfrac{a}{4} + \dfrac{b}{3} = 2$
$\dfrac{a}{2} - b = -1$ $(4, 3)$

32. $\dfrac{x}{2} - y = 9$
$x + \dfrac{y}{2} = 8$ $(10, -4)$

33. $\dfrac{a}{6} + \dfrac{b}{4} = \dfrac{3}{2}$
$\dfrac{2a}{3} = \dfrac{b}{2}$ $(3, 4)$

34. $\dfrac{p}{8} + \dfrac{q}{6} = 1$
$\dfrac{p}{q} = -\dfrac{2}{3}$ $(-8, 12)$

35. $\dfrac{x}{2} + \dfrac{y}{3} = -4$
$\dfrac{x}{5} + \dfrac{y}{5} = -2$
$(-4, -6)$

C **36.** Determine whether the graphs of $3x - 4y = 3$, $6x + 6y = 13$, and $9x + 2y = 16$ intersect in a single point. yes; $\left(\frac{5}{3}, \frac{1}{2}\right)$

37. The point $(8, -3)$ is the intersection of the graphs of $ax + by = 25$ and $3ax - 5by = 3$. Find a and b. $a = 2, b = -3$

Solve for x and y by the method you prefer. $\left(\text{Hint: Let } \dfrac{1}{x} = a \text{ and } \dfrac{1}{y} = b.\right)$

38. $\dfrac{1}{x} + \dfrac{1}{y} = 1$
$\dfrac{3}{x} - \dfrac{2}{y} = 8$ $\left(\frac{1}{2}, -1\right)$

39. $\dfrac{1}{x} + \dfrac{1}{y} = 5$
$\dfrac{3}{x} - \dfrac{5}{y} = -9$ $\left(\frac{1}{2}, \frac{1}{3}\right)$

40. $\dfrac{8}{x} + \dfrac{15}{y} = 33$ $\left(\frac{2}{3}, \frac{5}{7}\right)$
$\dfrac{4}{x} - \dfrac{35}{y} = -43$

Solve for x and y in terms of a and b.

41. $ax + y = 5$
$3ax - 2y = 0 \left(\dfrac{2}{a}, 3\right)$

42. $ax + by = 1$
$3ax - 2by = 4 \left(\dfrac{6}{5a}, -\dfrac{1}{5b}\right)$

43. $ax - by = 1 \left(\dfrac{a+b}{a^2+b^2}, \dfrac{a-b}{a^2+b^2}\right)$
$bx + ay = 1$

Solve for x, y, and z. (*Hint:* Eliminate one variable from the first two equations and then eliminate the same variable from the second two equations. This will give two new equations in two variables. Your answer will be an ordered triple of the form (x, y, z).)

44. $x + y + z = 7$
$2x - y + z = 4$
$3x + 2y + z = 11$ $(1, 2, 4)$

45. $x + y + z = 4$
$2x - y + z = 0$
$x - y + 2z = -3$ $(2, 3, -1)$

46. $6x + 4y - z = -7$
$-5x + 6y + 2z = 14$
$3x - 2y - 3z = -13 \left(-1, \dfrac{1}{2}, 3\right)$

Mixed Practice

Solve by the graphing method.

A **1.** $y - x = 4$
$y = 3x + 2$ $(1, 5)$

2. $x + y = 1$
$5x + y = -7$ $(-2, 3)$

3. $4x + 2y = 6$
$x - y = 3$ $(2, -1)$

Solve by the substitution method.

4. $a = 3b$
$a - 5b = 16$ $(-24, -8)$

5. $8c - d = -3$
$4c + 5d = 15$ $(0, 3)$

6. $9p = 2q - 6$
$3p - q = 12$ $(-10, -42)$

Solve by the addition-or-subtraction method.

7. $2a + 3b = -1$
$a - 3b = 4$ $(1, -1)$

8. $5x - 9y = -3$
$4x - 3y = 6$ $(3, 2)$

9. $2p + 3q + 1 = 0$
$3p + 5q + 2 = 0$ $(1, -1)$

Solve by whatever method you prefer.

B **10.** $y = x + 2$
$2x + y = 11$ $(3, 5)$

11. $x + y = 9$
$x - 3y = -3$ $(6, 3)$

12. $3x - 2y = 1$
$4y = 7 + 3x$ $(3, 4)$

13. $3x + 5y = 14$
$2x - y = -1 \left(\dfrac{9}{13}, \dfrac{31}{13}\right)$

14. $2a - 4b = 6$
$7 + a = -3b$ $(-1, -2)$

15. $r - s = 4$
$r - 6 = 2(s - 6)$ $(14, 10)$

16. $a - 2b = 10$
$a + b = 2(b + 6)$ $(14, 2)$

17. $t + u = 11$
$(10t + u) - (10u + t) = 27$ $(7, 4)$

18. $u - t = 5$
$10t + u = 3(t + u)$ $(2, 7)$

19. $4x + 3y = 1$
$6x - 2y = 21 \left(\dfrac{5}{2}, -3\right)$

20. $3a + 4b = -25$
$2a - 3b = 6$ $(-3, -4)$

21. $5n - 2m = 1$
$4n + 5m = 47$ $(7, 3)$

22. $0.04x - 0.06y = 40$
$x + y = 6000$ $(4000, 2000)$

23. $2.4 = 0.3x + 0.4y$
$5x = 2 + 6y$ $(4, 3)$

24. $3a + 2b = 4$
$\dfrac{1}{3}(2a + b) = 1$ $(2, -1)$

25. $\dfrac{1}{3}(3a - 2b) = -3$

$3(a - b) = -9$ $(-3, 0)$

26. $\dfrac{5c}{4} + d = \dfrac{11}{2}$

$c + \dfrac{d}{3} = 3$ $(2, 3)$

27. $2x - \dfrac{5}{2}y = 13$

$\left(\dfrac{40}{9}, -\dfrac{74}{45}\right)$ $\dfrac{x}{3} + \dfrac{y}{3} = \dfrac{14}{15}$

Systems of Linear Equations **433**

Additional Answers
Written Exercises

25. Solving the system by using multiplication with the addition-or-subtraction method gives a false statement. Thus, there is no ordered pair that is a solution.

26. Solving the system by using multiplication with the addition-or-subtraction method gives a true statement. Thus, every ordered pair satisfying either equation is a solution. The system has infinitely many solutions.

Supplementary Materials
Study Guide   pp. 161–162
Practice Master   56
Test Master   40
Computer Activity   28
Resource Book   p. 121

Problems

Solve by whatever method you prefer, using one or two variables.

A 1. The sum of two numbers is 25 and their difference is 7. Find the numbers. 16 and 9

2. One number is 4 less than eleven times another. The sum of the two numbers is 92. Find the numbers. 84 and 8

3. Cory has $24 more than twice as much as Stan. Together they have $150. How much money does each have? Stan, $42; Cory, $108

4. Marcia has $84 less than three times as much as Sue. Together they have $132. How much money does Marcia have? $78

5. The length of a rectangle is 5 more than twice the width. The perimeter is 130. What is the area? 900 sq. units

6. A rectangle is five times as long as it is wide. If it were 24 cm shorter and 24 cm wider, it would be a square. What are its dimensions? 12 cm by 60 cm

7. Phil has 50 nickels and dimes worth $4.15. How many dimes does he have? 33

8. Sally has $21.40 in dimes and quarters, for a total of 100 coins. How many of each kind of coin does Sally have? 76 quarters, 24 dimes

9. The bill for five glasses of apple juice and four salads is $9.50, but the bill for four glasses of apple juice and five salads is $10.30. What would be the bill for a glass of juice and a salad? $2.20

10. Three pens and two notebooks cost $8.25. Two pens and three notebooks cost $8.00. How much would two pens and two notebooks cost? $6.50

11. A movie theater charges $5 for an adult's ticket and $2 for a child's ticket. One Saturday the theater sold 785 tickets for $3280. How many child's tickets were sold for the movie that Saturday? 215 child's tickets

12. Six grapefruit cost as much as a dozen oranges. The cost of a dozen grapefruit and two dozen oranges is $12. How much does one grapefruit cost? 50¢

13. A chemist has 1000 g of a solution that is 40% acid. How many grams of water must be added to reduce the acidity to 25%? 600 g

14. A chemist has 800 g of a dye solution that is 20% of its original strength. How much dye must be added to increase the strength to 50%? 480 g

15. Edna Britten's income from two stocks each year totals $280. Stock A pays dividends at the rate of 5% and stock B at the rate of 6%. If she has invested a total of $5000, how much is invested in each stock? A, $2000; B, $3000

16. Beatrice Roberts receives $375 per year from a $6000 investment in stocks and bonds. The bonds pay 10% interest and the stocks pay 5% in dividends. How much is invested in stocks? $4500

B 17. Ted's bill for 6 cans of grape juice and 4 cans of orange juice was $13.20. When he got home, he found that he should have bought 4 cans of grape juice and 6 cans of orange juice. Although he mixed up the order, Ted did save 60 cents. How much does each can cost? grape, $1.20; orange, $1.50

18. Joe Tyson is the place kicker for his college foot-ball team. Last season he kicked 38 times and never missed. Each field goal scored 3 points and each point after touchdown scored 1 point for a total of 70 points. How many field goals did Joe kick last season? 16 field goals

19. A store received $823 from the sale of 5 tape decks and 7 radios. The receipts from the tape decks exceeded the receipts from the radios by $137. What is the cost of a radio? $49

20. Rebecca has 45 coins, all nickels and dimes. The total value of the coins is $3.60. How many of each type of coin does Rebecca have? 18 nickels, 27 dimes

21. Before last weekend's hiking trip, Juanita mixed 3 kg of peanuts and raisins as an energy snack. The peanuts cost $4.25 per kilogram and the raisins cost $3.50 per kilogram. The whole mix cost $12. How many kilograms of peanuts did Juanita have? 2 kg

22. A grocer prepares a mixture of 30 lb of dried fruit to sell for $4.10 per pound. For the mixture he uses two types of dried fruit, one selling at $4.30 per pound, the other at $3.90 per pound. How much of each type should he use for the mixture? 15 lb of each type

23. A car traveled at a steady speed for 120 km. Due to a mechanical prob-lem, it returned at half that speed. If the total time for the round trip was 4 h 30 min, find the two speeds. 80 km/h, 40 km/h

24. Larry can paint the walls of his apartment in 8 h. After he has worked for 3 h, Patrick joins him, and together they finish the job in 2 h. How long would it take Patrick to do the entire painting job without Larry? $5\frac{1}{3}$ h

25. Todd has 48 words to spell for a puzzle. As an incentive, his mother offers to pay him 10 cents for each word he spells correctly, if Todd will pay her 6 cents for each word he spells incorrectly. If Todd makes $1.92, how many words does he spell correctly? 30 words

26. Elsa works at the China Emporium on Saturdays packing dishes for ship-ment. She receives 12 cents for each piece she packs successfully and is fined 18 cents for each piece she breaks. If she handles 188 pieces and is paid $20.16, how many pieces does she break? 8 pieces

27. Does the equation $2x + 6y = 35$ have any whole-number solutions? Why or why not? If x and y are both whole numbers, $2x + 6y$ is even. But 35 is odd. Hence, $2x + 6y \neq 35$ if x and y are whole numbers.

28. Find the area enclosed between the x-axis and the graphs of $x + y = 20$ and $3x - 2y = 0$. 120 sq. units

C 29. On a simple pan balance, 3 apples and 1 banana exactly balance 10 plums. Also, 1 apple and 6 plums balance 1 banana. How many plums will bal-ance one banana? 7 plums

Systems of Linear Equations **435**

30. Roger, Sue, and Tim have $155 among them. Roger has $5 more than Sue and Tim together. If Sue gives Tim $5, he will have twice as much as she does. How much does each have? Sue, $30; Tim, $45; Roger, $80

31. If the length of a rectangle is increased by 12 and the width is decreased by 8, the area is unchanged. The area is also unchanged if the original length is increased by 5 and the original width is decreased by 4. Find the original dimensions of the rectangle. 28 by 30

32. If Alexandra increases her usual driving speed by 15 km/h, it will take her 2 h less to make a trip to her grandparents' house. If she decreases her usual speed by 15 km/h, it will take her 3 h more than usual to make the trip. How long is the trip? 900 km

Mixed Review Exercises

Factor completely.

1. $6 - 36t + 54t^2$ $6(1 - 3t)^2$ **2.** $12m^2n - 24mn^3$ $12mn(m - 2n^2)$ **3.** $25c^2 - 36d^2$ $(5c - 6d)(5c + 6d)$

4. $x^2 + 7x + 12$ $(x + 3)(x + 4)$ **5.** $2y^2 + 11y + 15$ $(2y + 5)(y + 3)$ **6.** $p^2 - 3p - 10$ $(p + 2)(p - 5)$

Find the constant of variation.

7. y varies directly as x, and $y = 68$ when $x = 17$. 4

8. t varies directly as s, and $t = -24$ when $s = 72$. $-\frac{1}{3}$

9. p is directly proportional to n, and $p = 36$ when $n = 54$. $\frac{2}{3}$

10. h is directly proportional to b, and $h = 35$ when $b = 5$. 7

Using a Computer
The exercises in this section ask students to use multiplication with the addition-or-subtraction method to verify the given solutions to a system of linear equations. Students are asked to write a BASIC program to solve a system of equations and to run the program for four given systems of linear equations.

Computer Exercises

For students with some programming experience

1. Use multiplication with the addition-or-subtraction method to verify that the solution of the system

$$\begin{matrix} Ax + By = C \\ Dx + Ey = F \end{matrix} \quad \text{is} \quad \left(\frac{CE - BF}{AE - BD}, \frac{AF - CD}{AE - BD} \right).$$

2. Using the result in Exercise 1, write a BASIC program to solve a system of linear equations in two variables. Provide for the case $AE - BD = 0$.

3. Run the program for each of the following.

a. $3x + 4y = -25$
  $2x - 3y = 6$ $(-3, -4)$

b. $5x + 4y = 22$
  $3x + y = 9$ $(2, 3)$

c. $2x + 4y = 11$
  $3x + 6y = 17$ no solution

d. $2x + y = 8$
  $3x - 2y = 5$ $(3, 2)$

Self-Test 1

Vocabulary   system of equations (p. 413)   system of simultaneous equations
   solution of a system (p. 413)   (p. 413)
   intersection point (p. 413)

Solve by the graphing method.

1. $y - 3x = -1$
   $y = x + 3$ (2, 5)

2. $x - 3y = -10$
   $2x + y = 1$ (−1, 3)

Obj. 9-1, p. 413

Solve by the substitution method.

3. $m - 4n = -5$
   $m = 2n - 4$ $\left(-3, \frac{1}{2}\right)$

4. $a - 2b = 1$
   $3a - b = -4$ $\left(-\frac{9}{5}, -\frac{7}{5}\right)$

Obj. 9-2, p. 417

5. Solve by using two equations in two variables: The talent show ticket committee sold a total of 805 tickets in advance. The student tickets cost $3 each and the adult tickets cost $4 each. If the total receipts were $1740, how many of each type of ticket were sold? no solution

Obj. 9-3, p. 421

Solve by the addition-or-subtraction method.

6. $a - 3b = 0$
   $a + 3b = 0$ (0, 0)

7. $3c + 5d = 20$
   $-2c + 5d = 20$ (0, 4)

Obj. 9-4, p. 426

Solve by using multiplication with the addition-or-subtraction method.

8. $s + 2t = -7$
   $3s - 8t = 7$ (−3, −2)

9. $2x + 3y = 12$
   $3x + 2y = 13$ (3, 2)

Obj. 9-5, p. 430

Check your answers with those at the back of the book.

Challenge

The diagrams show some equalities of mass among spheres, cubes, cylinders, and cones. What is the least number of objects that will balance the final scale?
1 sphere and 1 cube

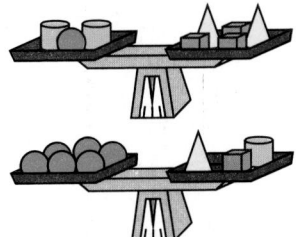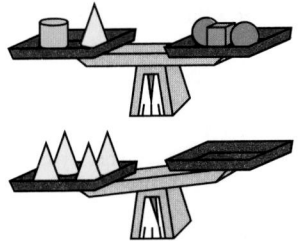

Systems of Linear Equations   **437**

Teaching Suggestions p. T125

Using Manipulatives p. T125

Suggested Extensions p. T126

Applications

9-6 Wind and Water Current Problems

Objective   To use systems of equations to solve wind and water current problems.

Suppose that you can paddle a canoe at the rate, or speed, of 3 mi/h in still water. If you paddle downstream on a river with a current of 1 mi/h, your speed is increased to $3 + 1$, or 4 mi/h. If you paddle upstream against the current, your speed is reduced to $3 - 1$, or 2 mi/h. Since the current increases your speed downstream by as much as it decreases your speed upstream, you might think that the current has no effect on the total travel time. However, the calculations below show that the current actually increases the total time for the round trip and decreases the average speed for the round trip.

Suppose that you travel 12 mi downstream and 12 mi back upstream. The time for each trip can be found by using the relationship

$$\text{Time} = \text{Distance} \div \text{Rate},$$

which is another form for the basic relationship

$$\text{Distance} = \text{Rate} \times \text{Time}.$$

	No current			1 mi/h current		
	Rate	× Time	= Distance	Rate	× Time	= Distance
Downstream	3	4	12	$3 + 1 = 4$	$12 \div 4 = 3$	12
Upstream	3	4	12	$3 - 1 = 2$	$12 \div 2 = 6$	12

Total distance = $12 + 12 = 24$ (miles)   Total distance = $12 + 12 = 24$ (miles)
Total time = $4 + 4 = 8$ (hours)   Total time = $3 + 6 = 9$ (hours)
Average speed = $\dfrac{\text{Total distance}}{\text{Total time}} = \dfrac{24 \text{ mi}}{8 \text{ h}} = 3$ mi/h   Average speed = $\dfrac{24 \text{ mi}}{9 \text{ h}} = 2\frac{2}{3}$ mi/h

The principles illustrated above apply to wind currents as well as water currents. Thus, if

   r = the rate of a plane when there is no wind

and

   w = the rate of the wind,

then

   $r + w$ = the rate of the plane flying with the wind

and

   $r - w$ = the rate of the plane flying against the wind.

---

438   *Chapter 9*

Example A jet can travel the 6800 km distance between New York and Paris in 6 h 48 min with the wind. The return trip against the same wind takes 8 h. Find the rate of the jet in still air and the rate of the wind.

Solution

Step 1 The problem asks for the rate of the jet in still air and the rate of the wind.

Step 2 Let r = the rate in km/h of the jet in still air and let w = the rate in km/h of the wind. The time 6 h 48 min is $6\frac{48}{60}$ h, or 6.8 h.

	Rate	× Time	= Distance
With the wind	$r + w$	6.8	6800
Against the wind	$r - w$	8	6800

Step 3 Use the information in the chart to write two equations:

$$6.8(r + w) = 6800, \quad \text{or} \quad r + w = 1000$$
$$8(r - w) = 6800, \quad \text{or} \quad r - w = 850$$

Step 4
$$
\begin{array}{r}
r + w = 1000 \\
r - w = 850 \\
\hline
2r = 1850 \\
r = 925
\end{array}
$$

$$925 + w = 1000$$
$$w = 75$$

Step 5 The check is left to you.

∴ the rate of the jet is 925 km/h and the rate of the wind is 75 km/h.

Answer

Oral Exercises

Complete the table. All rates are in km/h.

	Rate of plane in still air	Rate of wind	Rate of plane with wind	Rate of plane against wind
1.	700	50	? 750	? 650
2.	825	100	? 925	? 725
3.	900	w	900 + w ?	900 − w ?
4.	p	w	? $p + w$	? $p - w$

Chalkboard Examples

Solve:

A plane can fly 3750 km in 3 h with the wind. The plane takes 5 h to travel the same distance flying against that wind. Find the rate of the plane in still air and the speed of the wind.

Let r = rate of plane in still air in km/h

w = rate of wind in km/h

with wind	$(r + w)3 = 3750$ $r + w = 1250$
against wind	$(r - w)5 = 3750$ $r - w = 750$

$$
\begin{array}{r}
r + w = 1250 \\
r - w = 750 \\
\hline
2r = 2000 \\
r = 1000
\end{array}
$$

$$1000 + w = 1250$$
$$w = 250$$

∴ the rate of the plane in still air is 1000 km/h and the speed of the wind is 250 km/h.

Check for Understanding

Here is a suggested use of the Oral Exercises to check students' understanding as you teach the lesson.

Oral Exs. 1–8: use after discussion on p. 438.

Oral Exs. 9–16: use after the Example.

Guided Practice

Let r = rate of plane in still air and w = rate of wind. Write an equation that expresses each fact.

1. The rate of a plane flying against the wind is 900 km/h. $r - w = 900$

(continued)

Guided Practice

(continued)

2. The plane takes 3 h to fly 3000 km with the wind.

$\frac{3000}{r + w} = 3$

Suppose you can row at a rate of 6 km/h in still water. You are going to travel 8 km up a river and then return. The rate of the current is 2 km/h. Complete each blank.

3. Time upstream = __?__
2 h

4. Time downstream = __?__
1 h

5. Average speed = __?__
$5\frac{1}{3}$ km/h

Solve.

6. Jim can row a boat 30 km downstream in 3 h, but it takes him 5 h to return. What is Jim's rate in still water? What is the rate of the current? 8 km/h; 2 km/h

7. An airplane flies 3000 mi in 4 h, but takes 5 h to make the return trip. What is the plane's speed in still air? 675 mi/h What is the speed of the wind? 75 mi/h

---

Additional Answers
Oral Exercises

9. The rate of the rowboat traveling with the current is 12 km/h.

10. The rate of the rowboat traveling against the current is 8 km/h.

11. The rate of the swimmer traveling with the current is 3 km/h.

12. The rate of the swimmer traveling against the current is 1 km/h.

The following rates are given in km/h.

$$r = \text{rate of a rowboat in still water}$$
$$s = \text{rate of a swimmer in still water}$$
$$c = \text{rate of the current of Silver River}$$

Explain what rate each expression represents.

5. $r + c$boat
with current

6. $r - c$boat
against current

7. $s + c$swimmer
with current

8. $s - c$swimmer
against current

Each equation below states some fact about a rowboat or swimmer. What is this fact?

9. $r + c = 12$ **10.** $r - c = 8$ **11.** $s + c = 3$ **12.** $s - c = 1$

Match each equation with its corresponding statement on the right.

(*Hint:* $\frac{\text{Distance}}{\text{Rate}} = \text{Time}$)

13. $\frac{30}{r + c} = 2$c

a. A rowboat traveled 20 km upstream and 30 km downstream in 2 h.

14. $\frac{30}{r - c} = 2$b

b. A rowboat traveled 30 km upstream in 2 h.

15. $\frac{30}{r + c} = \frac{20}{r - c}$d

c. A rowboat traveled 30 km downstream in 2 h.

16. $\frac{30}{r + c} + \frac{20}{r - c} = 2$a

d. A rowboat traveled 30 km downstream and 20 km upstream in the same amount of time.

Problems

Let r = rate in km/h of the rowboat in still water and c = rate in km/h of the current. Write an equation that expresses each fact.

A   **1.** The rate of the rowboat going downstream is 15 km/h. $r + c = 15$

2. The rate of the rowboat going upstream is 10 km/h. $r - c = 10$

3. The rowboat takes 3 hours to go 24 km upstream. $\frac{24}{r - c} = 3$

4. The rowboat takes 2 hours to go 20 km upstream. $\frac{20}{r - c} = 2$

Solve.

5. Jim's motorboat travels downstream at the rate of 15 km/h. Going upstream it travels at 7 km/h. Write an equation that expresses each fact. What is the rate of the current? $r + c = 15$ and $r - c = 7$; 4 km/h

6. Camille can swim against the current at 1.5 m/s and with the current at 3.5 m/s. Write an equation that expresses each fact. How fast can she swim in still water? $s - c = 1.5$ and $s + c = 3.5$; 2.5 m/s

Complete each table.

7. A motorboat travels at 10 km/h in still water. The boat makes a trip 30 km downstream and 30 km back.

	No current			5 km/h current		
	Rate × Time = Distance			Rate × Time = Distance		
Downstream	? 10	? 3	30	? 15	? 2	30
Upstream	? 10	? 3	30	? 5	? 6	30

Total distance = <u>?</u> 60 km Total distance = <u>?</u> 60 km
Total time = <u>?</u> 6 h Total time = <u>?</u> 8 h
Average speed = <u>?</u> 10 km/h Average speed = <u>?</u> 7.5 km/h

8. In a canoe race Norma travels 300 m upstream and then returns. Norma can paddle at a rate of 5 m/s in still water, and the rate of the current is 1 m/s.

	Rate × Time = Distance		
Upstream	? 4	? 75	? 300
Downstream	? 6	? 50	? 300

Total distance = <u>?</u> 600 m
Total time = <u>?</u> 125 s
Average speed = <u>?</u> 4.8 m/s

9. Flying with no wind, a plane makes a 600 km trip in 3 h. On the return trip, the plane flies with a 50 km/h wind.

	Rate × Time = Distance		
No wind	? 200	? 3	? 600
With wind	? 250	? 2.4	? 600

Total distance = <u>?</u> 1200 km
Total time = <u>?</u> 5.4 h
Average speed = <u>?</u> $222.\overline{2}$ km/h

10. Flying with no wind, a plane makes an 840 mi trip in 6 h. On the return trip, the plane flies with a 70 mi/h wind.

	Rate × Time = Distance		
No wind	? 140	? 6	? 840
With wind	? 210	? 4	? 840

Total distance = <u>?</u> 1680 mi
Total time = <u>?</u> 10 h
Average speed = <u>?</u> 168 mi/h

Solve.

11. A plane travels 8400 km against the wind in 7 h. With the wind, the plane makes the return trip in 6 h. Find the speed of the plane in still air and the speed of the wind. in still air 1300 km/h; wind 100 km/h

Systems of Linear Equations   **441**

12. In a canoe race, a team paddles downstream 480 m in 60 s. The same team makes the trip upstream in 80 s. Find the team's rate in still water and the rate of the current. in still water, 7 m/s; current, 1 m/s

13. A sailboat travels 12 mi downstream in only 2 h. The return trip upstream takes 3 h. Find the speed of the sailboat in still water and the rate of the current. in still water, 5 mi/h; current, 1 mi/h

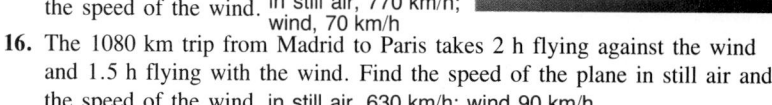

14. It takes an airplane 1 h 30 min to fly 600 km against the wind. The return trip with the wind takes only 1 h. Find the total flying time for the round trip if there was no wind. 2.4 h

15. The 4200 km trip from New York to San Francisco takes 6 h flying against the wind but only 5 h returning. Find the speed of the plane in still air and the speed of the wind. in still air, 770 km/h; wind, 70 km/h

16. The 1080 km trip from Madrid to Paris takes 2 h flying against the wind and 1.5 h flying with the wind. Find the speed of the plane in still air and the speed of the wind. in still air, 630 km/h; wind 90 km/h

B 17. Len is planning a three-hour trip down the Allenem River and back to his starting point. He knows that he can paddle in still water at 3 mi/h and that the rate of the current is 2 mi/h. How much time can he spend going downstream? How far downstream can he travel? 0.5 h; 2.5 mi

18. A motorboat has a four-hour supply of gasoline. How far from the marina can it travel if the rate going out against the current is 20 mi/h and the rate coming back with the current is 30 mi/h? 48 mi

19. A motorboat goes 36 km downstream in the same amount of time that it takes to go 24 km upstream. If the current is flowing at 3 km/h, what is the rate of the boat in still water? 15 km/h

20. The rate of the current in the Susanna River is 4 km/h. If a canoeist can paddle 5 km downstream in the same amount of time that she can paddle 1 km upstream, how fast can she paddle in still water? 6 km/h

21. The steamboat River Queen travels at the rate of 30 km/h in still water. If it can travel 45 km upstream in the same amount of time that it takes to go 63 km downstream, what is the rate of the current? 5 km/h

22. An airplane whose speed in still air is 760 km/h can travel 2000 km with the wind in the same amount of time that it takes to fly 1800 km against the wind. What is the speed of the wind? 40 km/h

C 23. A plane has a speed of p km/h in still air. It makes a round trip, flying with and against a wind of w km/h. Show that its average speed is $\dfrac{p^2 - w^2}{p}$ km/h.

Mixed Review Exercises

Solve each system using multiplication with the addition-or-subtraction method.

1. $3x + 2y = 11$
$x - y = 7$ $(5, -2)$

2. $5a + 4b = 3$
$2a + 3b = 3$ $\left(-\dfrac{3}{7}, \dfrac{9}{7}\right)$

3. $7p + 2q = 10$
$p + 3q = -4$ $(2, -2)$

Simplify.

4. $\dfrac{9b^2 + b - 2}{12b + 4}$ $\dfrac{9b^2 + b - 2}{4(3b + 1)}$

5. $\dfrac{4}{x - 2} + \dfrac{5}{2 - x}$ $\dfrac{1}{2 - x}$

6. $(-2t^2)^2 \cdot \dfrac{4s}{t}$ $16st^3$

7. $\dfrac{4r^2 - t^2}{r^2 - t^2} \div \dfrac{2r - t}{5}$ $\dfrac{5(2r + t)}{(r + t)(r - t)}$

8. $\dfrac{3p + 2}{8} - \dfrac{2p + 1}{6}$ $\dfrac{p + 2}{24}$

9. $2a - 1 - \dfrac{a - 2}{a + 3}$ $\dfrac{2a^2 + 4a - 1}{a + 3}$

 Biographical Note / *Emily Warren Roebling*

Emily Warren Roebling (1843–1903) helped supervise the completion of the Brooklyn Bridge. She was married to Washington Roebling, an engineer whose father, John Roebling, was commissioned to build the bridge. Emily and Washington Roebling went to Europe, where Washington studied the experimental method of using watertight chambers of compressed air to sink underwater foundations. Soon after their return to the United States, John Roebling died and Washington Roebling became the chief engineer. He was disabled with caisson disease (the bends) ten years before the bridge was completed.

To continue the project, Emily Roebling studied calculus and cable construction. She learned to read bridge specifications, to determine the stress various materials could tolerate, and to calculate catenary curves. As acting chief engineer, she negotiated with representatives of construction supply firms, inspected the work, and delivered instructions to the assistant engineers.

Nine months before the completion of the bridge, the board of trustees tried to dismiss Washington Roebling as chief engineer. As a result of the presentation Emily Roebling made before the American Society of Civil Engineers, Washington Roebling retained his position.

The Brooklyn Bridge is a tribute to Emily Roebling's intense involvement in its construction. A plaque in her honor was placed on the bridge in 1950 by the Brooklyn Engineers Club.

Warm-Up Exercises

Evaluate $100h + 10t + u$ for the following values of the variables.

1. $h = 7, t = 3, u = 4$ 734
2. $h = 9, t = 0, u = 6$ 906
3. $h = 5, t = 1, u = 0$ 510
4. $h = 0, t = 6, u = 2$ 62
5. $h = 4, t = 0, u = 0$ 400

Motivating the Lesson

Robert is five years older than Toni. Three years ago he was twice as old as she was. How old are they now? Since the numbers are simple, it is easy to find that Robert is 13 and Toni is 8. In today's lesson, systems of linear equations are used to solve age problems like this one, as well as digit and fraction problems.

9-7 Puzzle Problems

Objective   To use systems of equations to solve digit, age, and fraction problems.

Digit problems are based on our decimal system of numeration. Note the value of 537, 604, and a number with digits h, t, and u shown below.

Hundreds digit	Tens digit	Units digit	Value
5	3	7	$5 \cdot 100 + 3 \cdot 10 + 7 \cdot 1$
6	0	4	$6 \cdot 100 + 0 \cdot 10 + 4 \cdot 1$
h	t	u	$h \cdot 100 + t \cdot 10 + u \cdot 1$

Example 1   (Digit Problem)

The sum of the digits in a two-digit number is 12. The new number obtained when the digits are reversed is 36 more than the original number. Find the original number.

Solution

Step 1   The problem asks for the original number.

Step 2   Let t = the tens digit of the original number.
Let u = the units digit of the original number.

	Tens	Units	Value
Original number	t	u	$10t + u$
Number with digits reversed	u	t	$10u + t$

Step 3   Use the facts of the problem to write two equations.

$$t + u = 12 \quad \{\text{Sum of the digits of the original number is 12.}$$
$$(10u + t) - (10t + u) = 36 \quad \{\text{Difference between new number and original}$$
$$10u + t - 10t - u = 36 \quad \{\text{number is 36.}$$
$$9u - 9t = 36$$
$$9(u - t) = 36$$
$$u - t = 4$$

Step 4 $u + t = 12$
$\underline{u - t = 4}$
$2u = 16$
$u = 8$ 　　　$u - t = 4$ 　　$\{\text{Substitute 8 for } u \text{ in}$
　　　　　　　　$8 - t = 4$ 　　$\{\text{the second equation.}$
　　　　　　　　$t = 4$

Step 5   The check is left to you.

$\therefore$ the original number is 48.   ***Answer***

The technique of using more than one variable and organizing the given facts in a chart is also useful when solving age and fraction problems.

Example 2 (Age problem)

Mimi is four years older than Ronald. Five years ago she was twice as old as he was. Find their ages now.

Solution

Step 1 The problem asks for Mimi's age and Ronald's age now.

Step 2 Let m = Mimi's age now, and let r = Ronald's age now. Make a chart.

Age	Now	5 years ago
Mimi	m	$m - 5$
Ronald	r	$r - 5$

Step 3 Use the facts of the problem to write two equations.

$m = 4 + r$ {now
$m - 5 = 2(r - 5)$ {five years ago

Step 4 Simplify the equations and solve.

$m = 4 + r \rightarrow m - r = 4$
$m - 5 = 2(r - 5) \rightarrow \underline{m - 2r = -5}$
$r = 9$

$m - r = 4$
$m - 9 = 4$
$m = 13$

Step 5 The check is left to you.

$\therefore$ Mimi is 13 years old and Ronald is 9.   **Answer**

Example 3 (Fraction problem)

The numerator of a fraction is 3 less than the denominator. If the numerator and denominator are each increased by 1, the value of the resulting fraction is $\frac{3}{4}$. Find the original fraction.

Solution

Step 1 The problem asks for the original fraction.

Step 2 Let n = the numerator of the original fraction and d = the denominator of the original fraction. Then $\frac{n}{d}$ = the original fraction.

(Solution continues on next page.)

Systems of Linear Equations   **445**

Chalkboard Examples

Solve.

1. The sum of the digits in a two-digit number is 15. If the digits are reversed, the new number obtained is 9 more than the original. Find the original number.

Let t = tens digit of original number;
u = units digit of original number

	Tens	Units	Values
Old	t	u	$10t + u$
New	u	t	$10u + t$

$t + u = 15$
$10t + u + 9 = 10u + t$
$9t - 9u = -9 \rightarrow t - u = -1$
$t - u = -1$
$\underline{t + u = 15}$
$2t = 14$
$t = 7$

$7 + u = 15$
$u = 8$

$\therefore$ the number is 78.

2. Nine years ago, Frank was half as old as Marilyn. Now his age is two thirds her age. Find their ages now.

Let f = Frank's age now;
m = Marilyn's age now

Age	Now	9 years ago
Frank	f	$f - 9$
Marilyn	m	$m - 9$

$f = \frac{2}{3}m$

$f - 9 = \frac{1}{2}(m - 9)$

$\frac{2}{3}m - 9 = \frac{1}{2}m - \frac{9}{2}$

$4m - 54 = 3m - 27$
$m = 27$

$f = \frac{2}{3} \cdot 27 = 18$

$\therefore$ Frank is 18 and Marilyn is 27.

3. The denominator of a fraction is 2 more than the numerator. If 3 is added to both the numerator and denominator, the new fraction is equal to $\frac{5}{6}$. Find the original fraction.

Let n = numerator of original fraction and d = denominator of original fraction.

$$d = n + 2$$

$$\frac{n+3}{d+3} = \frac{5}{6}$$

$6(n + 3) = 5(d + 3)$

$6n + 18 = 5d + 15$

$6n + 18 = 5(n + 2) + 15$

$6n + 18 = 5n + 10 + 15$

$n = 7$

$d = 7 + 2$

$= 9$

∴ The original fraction is $\frac{7}{9}$.

Check for Understanding

Oral Exs. 1–8: use after Example 1.
Oral Exs. 9–18: use after Example 2.
Oral Exs. 19–22: use after Example 3.

Guided Practice

Solve each of the following problems about two-digit numbers.

1. The sum of the digits of a two-digit number is 10. If the digits are reversed, the number is increased by 72. What is the original number? **19**

2. A number is ten times the sum of its digits. The tens digit is two greater than the units digit. Find the number. **20**

Step 3 Use the facts of the problem to write two equations.

$$n = d - 3$$

$$\frac{n+1}{d+1} = \frac{3}{4}, \quad \text{or} \quad 4(n + 1) = 3(d + 1)$$

Step 4 Simplify the equations and solve.

$$
\begin{array}{ccccc}
n = d - 3 & \rightarrow & n - d = -3 & \rightarrow & 4n - 4d = -12 \\
4(n + 1) = 3(d + 1) & \rightarrow & \underline{4n - 3d = -1} & \rightarrow & \underline{4n - 3d = -1} \\
& & & & -d = -11 \\
& & & & d = 11 \\
& & & & \\
& & & & n = d - 3 \\
& & & & n = 11 - 3 \\
& & & & n = 8
\end{array}
$$

Step 5 The check is left to you.

∴ the original fraction is $\frac{8}{11}$. ***Answer***

Oral Exercises

A two-digit number has tens digit t and units digit u. Express the following in terms of t and u.

1. The value of the two-digit number. $10t + u$

2. The value of the two-digit number obtained by reversing the digits. $10u + t$

3. The tens digit exceeds the units digit by 5. $t = u + 5$

4. The units digit exceeds the tens digit by 8. $u = t + 8$

5. The tens digit is one half the units digit. $t = \frac{1}{2}u$

A three-digit number has hundreds digit h, tens digit t, and units digit u. Express the following as equations.

6. The sum of the digits is 20. $h + t + u = 20$

7. The tens digit is three times the sum of the other two digits. $t = 3(h + u)$

8. The number obtained by reversing the order of the digits exceeds the original number by 99. $100u + 10t + h = 100h + 10t + u + 99$

Let b = Bob's age now and c = Claire's age now. Express the following in terms of b and c.

9. Bob's age in 4 years $b + 4$

10. Claire's age in 4 years $c + 4$

11. Bob's age 2 years ago $b - 2$

12. Claire's age 2 years ago $c - 2$

13. The sum of their ages in 4 years $b + c + 8$

14. The sum of their ages 2 years ago $b + c - 4$

15. Bob is half as old as Claire. $b = \frac{1}{2}c$

16. Claire is twice as old as Bob. $c = 2b$

17. Four years ago, Bob was one-third as old as Claire was. $b - 4 = \frac{1}{3}(c - 4)$

18. Next year, the sum of Bob's age and Claire's age will be 26. $(b + 1) + (c + 1) = 26$

A fraction is represented by $\frac{n}{d}$. Express in terms of n and d the new fraction obtained by doing each of the following.

19. Increase both the numerator and the denominator by 4. $\frac{n + 4}{d + 4}$

20. Decrease both the numerator and the denominator by 7. $\frac{n - 7}{d - 7}$

21. Interchange the numerator and the denominator. $\frac{d}{n}$

22. Increase the numerator by 5 and decrease the denominator by 3. $\frac{n + 5}{d - 3}$

Problems

Write an equation expressing each fact.

A **1.** The sum of the digits of a two-digit number is 15. $t + u = 15$

2. The sum of the digits of a three-digit number is 10. $h + t + u = 10$

3. A two-digit number is four times the sum of its digits. $4(t + u) = 10t + u$

4. A three-digit number is sixteen times the sum of its digits. $100h + 10t + u = 16(h + t + u)$

5. When the digits of a two-digit number are reversed, the new number is 18 more than the original number. $(10t + u) + 18 = 10u + t$

6. When the digits of a three-digit number are reversed, the new number is 198 less than the original number. $(100h + 10t + u) - 198 = 100u + 10t + h$

Solve each of the following problems about two-digit numbers.

7. A two-digit number is four times the sum of its digits. The tens digit is 3 less than the units digit. What is the number? 36

8. The sum of the digits of a two-digit number is one third of the number. The units digit is 5 more than the tens digit. What is the number? 27

9. When the digits of a two-digit number are reversed, the new number is 36 more than the original number. The units digit is twice the tens digit. What is the original number? 48

10. When the digits of a two-digit number are reversed, the new number is 54 less than the original number. If the sum of its digits is 8, what is the original number? 71

Solve by using a system of two equations in two variables.

11. Nicole is 5 years older than Pierre. Last year she was twice as old as he was. How old is each now? Nicole, 11 years old; Pierre, 6 years old

12. Cecilia is 24 years younger than Joe. Six years ago she was half as old as he was. How old is each now? Joe, 54 years old; Cecilia, 30 years old

13. Steve is three times as old as Theresa. In four years he will be twice as old as she will be. How old is each now? Steve, 12 years old; Theresa, 4 years old

Systems of Linear Equations **447**

Solve by using a system of two equations in two variables.

3. Carole is twice Lorraine's age. In six years, the sum of their ages will be 30. How old are they now? Carole, 12; Lorraine, 6

4. Seven years ago, my father's age was five times mine. Right now, his age is the sum of our two ages 7 years ago. How old am I? 14

5. If 5 is subtracted from the numerator of a fraction, the value of the resulting fraction is $\frac{1}{4}$. If 6 is added to the denominator of the original fraction, the value of the new fraction is $\frac{1}{2}$. What is the original fraction? $\frac{7}{8}$

Summarizing the Lesson
Tell students that they have learned to use systems of equations to solve digit, age, and fraction puzzles. Ask them to tell the steps they would take to solve puzzle problems.

Suggested Assignments
Minimum
Day 1: 447/P: 1–7
Assign with Lesson 9-6.
Day 2: 447/P: 9–13
    S 449/Mixed Review

Average
Day 1: 447/P: 1–6, 7, 9
Assign with Lesson 9-6.
Day 2: 448/P: 14–28 even
    S 449/Mixed Review

Maximum
Day 1: 447/P: 1–21 odd
    S 449/Mixed Review
Day 2: 448/P: 23–33 odd
    R 450/Self-Test 2

14. Four years ago, Marion was $\frac{2}{3}$ as old as Les was. Now she is $\frac{3}{4}$ as old as he is. How old is each now? Les, 16 years old; Marion, 12 years old

15. The denominator of a fraction is 8 more than the numerator. If 3 is added to both the numerator and the denominator, the value of the resulting fraction is $\frac{1}{2}$. What is the original fraction? $\frac{5}{13}$

16. The denominator of a fraction is 9 more than the numerator. If the numerator is decreased by 3 and the denominator is increased by 3, the value of the resulting fraction is $\frac{1}{4}$. What is the original fraction? $\frac{8}{17}$

17. If 1 is subtracted from the numerator of a fraction, the value of the resulting fraction is $\frac{1}{2}$. However, if 7 is added to the denominator of the original fraction, the value of the resulting fraction is $\frac{1}{3}$. Find the original fraction. $\frac{5}{8}$

18. If the numerator of a fraction is increased by 4, the value of the resulting fraction is $\frac{3}{4}$. If the denominator of the original fraction is increased by 2, the value of the resulting fraction is $\frac{1}{2}$. Find the original fraction. $\frac{11}{20}$

21. Golden Gate Bridge, 1937; Brooklyn Bridge, 1883

B **19.** Next year, Lyle will be twice as old as Sean will be. Four years ago, he was three times as old as Sean was. How old is each now? Lyle, 19 years old; Sean, 9 years old

20. Mary is three years older than her twin brothers. Next year, the sum of the ages of the three will be exactly 102. How old are they now? Mary, 35 years old; twins, 32 years old

21. The Golden Gate Bridge was completed 54 years after the Brooklyn Bridge was. In 1983, the Golden Gate Bridge was $\frac{23}{50}$ as old as the Brooklyn Bridge. When was each bridge completed? See above.

22. In 1985, the Lincoln Memorial was $1\frac{1}{2}$ times as old as the Jefferson Memorial. If the Lincoln Memorial was built 21 years before the Jefferson Memorial, give the year when each was built.
Jefferson Memorial, 1943; Lincoln Memorial, 1922

Solve each of the following problems about three-digit numbers.

23. A number between 300 and 400 is forty times the sum of its digits. The tens digit is 6 more than the units digit. Find the number. 360

24. A three-digit number, which is divisible by 10, has a hundreds digit that is one less than its tens digit. The number also is 52 times the sum of its digits. Find the number. 780

25. The sum of the three digits is 12. The tens digit exceeds the hundreds digit by the same amount that the units digit exceeds the tens digit. If the digits are reversed, the new number exceeds the original number by 198. Find the original number. 345

26. The sum of the three digits is 9. The tens digit is 1 more than the hundreds digit. When the digits are reversed, the new number is 99 less than the original number. Find the original number. 342

Solve by using a system of two equations in two variables.

27. A father, being asked his age and that of his son, said, "If you add 4 to my age and divide the sum by 4, you will have my son's age. But 6 years ago I was $7\frac{1}{2}$ times as old as my son." Find their ages. son, 10 years old; father, 36 years old

28. The two digits in the numerator of a fraction whose value is $\frac{4}{7}$ are reversed in its denominator. The reciprocal of the fraction is the value obtained when 16 is added to the original numerator and 5 is subtracted from the original denominator. Find the original fraction. $\frac{12}{21}$

29. The numerator equals the sum of the two digits in the denominator. The value of the fraction is $\frac{1}{4}$. When both numerator and denominator are increased by 3, the resulting fraction has the value $\frac{1}{3}$. Find the original fraction. $\frac{6}{24}$

30. The two digits in the numerator of a fraction are reversed in its denominator. If 1 is subtracted from both the numerator and the denominator, the value of the resulting fraction is $\frac{1}{2}$. The fraction whose numerator is the difference and whose denominator is the sum of the units and tens digits equals $\frac{2}{5}$. Find the original fraction. $\frac{37}{73}$

C 31. Laura is 3 times as old as Maria was when Laura was as old as Maria is now. In 2 years, Laura will be twice as old as Maria was 2 years ago. Find their present ages. Laura, 18 years old; Maria, 12 years old

32. Find a two-decimal-place number between 0 and 1 such that the sum of its digits is 9 and such that if the digits are reversed the number is increased by 0.27. 0.36

33. Cindy's age equals the sum of Paul's age and Sue's age. Two years ago, Cindy was 4 times as old as Sue was, and two years from now, Cindy will be 1.4 times as old as Paul will be. How old is each now? Cindy, 26 years old; Paul, 18 years old; (*Hint:* Use a system of three equations in three variables.) Sue, 8 years old

34. A man is three times as old as his son was at the time when the father was twice as old as his son will be two years from now. Find the present age of each person if the sum of their ages is 55 years.
son, 16 years old; father, 39 years old

Mixed Review Exercises

Simplify.

1. $(27 - 12) - (4 - 7)$ 18
2. $4 + 6 \div 3$ 6
3. $|10| + 3 - |2|$ 11
4. $7 - (18 \div 6)$ 4
5. $[40 + (-4)] + [1 + (-3)]$ 34
6. $4 \cdot (15 - 3)$ 48

Solve.

7. $\frac{x + 4}{3} - \frac{x}{4} = \frac{2}{3}$ $\{-8\}$
8. $\frac{3n + 5}{2} = \frac{n - 1}{5}$ $\left\{-\frac{27}{13}\right\}$
9. $\frac{4 + c}{2 + c} = \frac{1}{2}$ $\{-6\}$
10. $|x| = 7.7$ $\{-7.7, 7.7\}$
11. $3.3 = 70t - 0.2$ $\{0.05\}$
12. $-\frac{1}{6}p = 14$ $\{-84\}$

Solve by using a system of two equations in two variables.

1. A runner goes 12 km/h with the wind and 8 km/h against the wind. What is the speed of the wind? 2 km/h

2. When the digits of a two-digit number are reversed, the new number is 54 more than the original number. Find the number if the units digit is 4 times the tens digit. 28

3. Jack's age next year will be twice Jill's age. Last year the sum of their ages was 32. How old is each now? Jill is 11; Jack is 23.

4. The denominator of a fraction is 4 more than the numerator. When 7 is added to both denominator and numerator, the new fraction equals $\frac{5}{7}$. Find the original fraction. $\frac{3}{7}$

Self-Test 2

Solve by using a system of two equations in two variables.

1. A jet travels at a rate of 798 mi/h with the wind. Going against the same wind, the jet travels at a rate of 762 mi/h. What is the rate of the jet in still air? What is the rate of the wind? 780 mi/h; 18 mi/h

   Obj. 9-6, p. 438

2. The sum of the digits in a two-digit number is 15. If the digits are reversed, the number is decreased by 27. What is the number? 96

   Obj. 9-7, p. 444

3. Five years ago, Jerry was $\frac{2}{3}$ as old as Jeff. Ten years from now, he will be $\frac{5}{6}$ as old as Jeff will be. How old is each now? Jerry, 15 years old; Jeff, 20 years old

4. The numerator of a fraction is 3 less than the denominator. If 5 is added to each, the value of the resulting fraction is $\frac{3}{4}$. Find the original fraction. $\frac{4}{7}$

Check your answers with those at the back of the book.

Historical Note / *The Equality Symbol*

The Englishman Robert Recorde is credited with the invention of the equals sign. He wrote a mathematics book called *Whetstone of Witte*, which was published in 1557. In that book he used the symbol ══ "to avoid the tedious repetition of the words 'is equal to.'" He said that he chose a pair of line segments of the same length because "no two things could be more equal." Eventually, the segments shortened until the symbol became =.

Another English mathematician, Thomas Harriot, who served as Sir Walter Raleigh's tutor in mathematics, later helped popularize the equality symbol by persuading other mathematicians of the day to adopt this notation. It was Harriot who invented two of the most useful mathematical symbols, the symbols $>$ and $<$.

Chapter Summary

1. The solution of systems of linear equations in two variables can be estimated by using the graphing method. Solutions can be computed algebraically by using the following methods:

   substitution method
   addition-or-subtraction method
   multiplication with the addition-or-subtraction method

2. Systems of linear equations in two variables may be used to solve word problems involving wind, water current, age, fractions, and digits, as well as other types.

450 *Chapter 9*

Chapter Review

Supplementary Materials
Practice Master   58
Resource Book   p. 202

Give the letter of the correct answer.

1. The solution of the system $\begin{array}{l} 2x + \ y = 13 \\ 5x - 2y = 19 \end{array}$ is $(5, 3)$.   9-1

   How are the graphs of the two equations related?

   a. The graphs are parallel.
   b. The graphs coincide.
   c. The graphs intersect at $(5, 3)$.
   d. The graphs intersect at $(5, 0)$ and $(0, 3)$.

2. Solve by the substitution method: $\begin{array}{l} 2x + \ y = 6 \\ 3x - 2y = 2 \end{array}$ 9-2

   a. $(2, 2)$ **b.** $(-2, -2)$ **c.** $(3, 0)$ **d.** $(0, -2)$

3. Solve by using two equations in two variables: One positive integer is 17   9-3
   more than a second positive integer. If the sum of the first integer and
   twice the second integer is 152, find each integer.

   a. 54, 37   **b.** 45, 28   **c.** 55, 28   **d.** 62, 45

4. Solve by the addition-or-subtraction method: $\begin{array}{l} a + 3b = 9 \\ 2a + 3b = 15 \end{array}$ 9-4

   a. $(-6, 5)$ **b.** $(1, 6)$ **c.** $\left(8, \frac{1}{3}\right)$ **d.** $(6, 1)$

5. Solve by using multiplication with the addition-or-subtraction method: 9-5

   $$3s - 5t = 27$$
   $$s + 4t = -8$$

   a. $(14, 3)$ **b.** $(4, 3)$ **c.** $(3, 14)$ **d.** $(4, -3)$

6. A boat travels downstream at 37 mi/h. The same boat travels upstream at   9-6
   17 mi/h. Find the rate of the current.

   a. 20 mi/h   **b.** 10 mi/h   **c.** 27 mi/h   **d.** 54 mi/h

7. The sum of the digits of a two-digit number is 8. If the digits are reversed,   9-7
   the number is increased by 54. Find the original number.

   a. 71   **b.** 17   **c.** 26   **d.** 62

8. Two years ago, Rick's age was 1 year less than twice Barbara's age. Four
   years from now, Rick will be 8 years more than half Barbara's age. How
   old is Rick?

   a. 1   **b.** 3   **c.** 7   **d.** 9

9. The denominator of a fraction is 7 more than the numerator. If 5 is added
   to each, the value of the resulting fraction is $\frac{1}{2}$. Find the original fraction.

   a. $\frac{7}{14}$ **b.** $\frac{9}{2}$ **c.** $\frac{5}{12}$ **d.** $\frac{2}{9}$

Systems of Linear Equations   **451**

Chapter Test

Solve by the graphing method.   **9-1**

1. $x - 2y = 9$
    $3x - y = 7$ $(1, -4)$

2. $y = 2x - 1$
    $2x - 4y = 10$ $(-1, -3)$

Solve by the substitution method.   **9-2**

3. $8m + n = 3$
    $5m + 2n = -27$ $(3, -21)$

4. $3a - 4b = 17$ $\left(\frac{19}{5}, -\frac{7}{5}\right)$
    $a + 2b = 1$

5. Show that the following system has infinitely many solutions:

    $y = 3x - 4$ The equations are equivalent; ∴ there are infinitely many solutions.
    $6x - 2y = 8 \rightarrow -2y = -6x + 8 \rightarrow y = 3x - 4$

6. Show that the following system has no solution:

                  $-4x + y = -3 \rightarrow -8x + 2y = -6$
    $y = 4x - 3$
    $2y - 8x = -8$ $-8x + 2y = -8 \rightarrow -8x + 2y = -8$
                              $0 = 2$; ∴ there is no solution

7. Solve using two equations in two variables: Jason bought a total of 7 post-cards for $1.80. If the small postcards cost 20¢ each and the large ones cost 30¢ each, how many postcards of each size did he buy?   **9-3**
                       3 small postcards; 4 large postcards

Solve by the addition-or-subtraction method.   **9-4**

8. $4x - 5y = 0$
   $8x + 5y = -60$ $(-5, -4)$

9. $10p + 4q = 2$
   $10p - 8q = 26$ $(1, -2)$

Solve by using multiplication with the addition-or-subtraction method.   **9-5**

10. $-8r + s = -17$
    $5r - 3s = -6$ $(3, 7)$

11. $2x + 5y = 16$
    $5x - 3y = -22$ $(-2, 4)$

Solve by using a system of two equations in two variables.

12. Gretchen paddles a canoe upstream at 3 mi/h. Traveling downstream, she travels at 8 mi/h. What is Gretchen's paddling rate in still water and what is the rate of the current? paddling rate, 5.5 mi/h; current rate, 2.5 mi/h   **9-6**

13. Six years ago, Joe Foster was two years more than five times as old as his daughter. Six years from now, he will be 11 years more than twice as old as she will be. How old is Joe? 43 years old   **9-7**

14. The numerator of a fraction is 4 less than the denominator. If 17 is added to each, the value of the fraction is $\frac{5}{6}$. Find the original fraction. $\frac{3}{7}$

Cumulative Review (Chapters 1–9)

4. $10c^3 + 14c^2 - 7c - 3$ **6.** $49x^3 - 21bx^2 + 21bx - 9b^2$ **8.** $\dfrac{b^2 - 5b - 1 - 4b^3}{(1 + 2b)(1 - 2b)}$

Perform the indicated operations. Express the answers in simplest form. Assume that no denominator is zero. **1.** $7p^2q + 4p - 21q^3$

1. $(28p^4q^3 + 16p^3q^2 - 84p^2q^5) \div (2pq)^2$

2. $(-2x^3yz^2)^4(x^2y^2)^3$ $16x^{18}y^{10}z^8$

3. $4j^4(jk^3 - 6j^2k + 7k^4)$ $4j^5k^3 - 24j^6k + 28j^4k^4$ **4.** $(5c - 3)(2c^2 + 4c + 1)$

5. $(21z - 3)(2z + 4)$ $42z^2 + 78z - 12$

6. $(7x^2 + 3b)(7x - 3b)$

7. $\dfrac{15t^2 - 11t - 12}{3t - 4}$ $5t + 3$

8. $\dfrac{3}{2b - 1} + \dfrac{b^2 + 2}{1 - 4b^2} + b$

9. $\dfrac{x^2 - 7x + 10}{x^2 - 4} \div \dfrac{x + 3}{x^2 - x - 6}$ $\dfrac{(x - 5)(x - 3)}{(x + 3)}$

10. $(10y^2 + 27y - 15) \div (2y + 7)$ $5y - 4 + \dfrac{13}{2y + 7}$

11. $(1.7 \times 10^5)(0.4 \times 10^6)$ 6.8×10^{10}

12. $\left(\dfrac{m^{-4}}{m^{-5}}\right)^{-3}$ $\dfrac{1}{m^3}$

Factor completely. If the polynomial cannot be factored, write "prime."

13. $49x^2 + 98xy + 81y^2$ prime **14.** $64x^4 - 81y^4$ **15.** $30x^2 + 15x + 1$ prime

16. $28y^2 + 37y + 12$ $(4y + 3)(7y + 4)$ **17.** $8y^2 - 26y + 5$ prime **14.** $(8x^2 - 9y^2)(8x^2 + 9y^2)$ **18.** $16y^2 - 25x^2 + 10x - 1$ $(4y - 5x + 1)(4y + 5x - 1)$

Solve. Assume that no denominator is zero. If the equation is an identity or has no solution, say so.

19. $16 - \dfrac{1}{2}|m| = 5$ $\{22, -22\}$ **20.** $\dfrac{1}{5}(x - 6) = 34 - 3x$ $\{11\}$ **21.** $196x^2 - 16 = 0$ $\left\{-\dfrac{2}{7}, \dfrac{2}{7}\right\}$

22. $18t^2 + 53t - 3 = 0$ $\left\{-3, \dfrac{1}{18}\right\}$ **23.** $\dfrac{2x + 1}{x - 3} + \dfrac{x + 3}{2x + 1} = \dfrac{2x}{3 - x}$ $\left\{-\dfrac{4}{3}, \dfrac{2}{3}\right\}$

Write an equation in standard form for each line described.

24. slope $\dfrac{1}{4}$, passes through (12, 2) $x - 4y = 4$

25. passes through (1, 0) and (2, −3) $3x + y = 3$

Solve algebraically.

26. $4x + 3y = 12$
$3y - 8x = -12$ $\left(2, \dfrac{4}{3}\right)$

27. $5x = y + 3$
$3x + 2y = 20$ (2, 7)

28. $2x + 5y = 9$
$3x - 2y = 4$ (2, 1)

29. The sum of the digits of a two-digit number is 6. When the digits are reversed, the resulting number is 6 greater than 3 times the original number. Find the original number. 15

30. It took a cyclist 6 h to travel 48 mi going against the wind. The next day on the return trip, it took the cyclist 3 h, traveling with the wind. What was the speed of the cyclist? 12 mi/h

31. How many kilograms of nuts worth $5/kg should be mixed with 6 kg of nuts worth $9/kg to produce a mix worth $6.50/kg? 10 kg

Systems of Linear Equations **453**

Supplementary Materials

Practice Masters 59, 60
Resource Book,
pp. 54–55, 124–125,
151–154

Maintaining Skills

Simplify. Assume that no denominator is zero.

Sample 1 $\dfrac{5x + 15}{2x} \cdot \dfrac{4x^3}{x^2 + 6x + 9} = \dfrac{5(x + 3)}{2x} \cdot \dfrac{4x^3}{(x + 3)^2} = \dfrac{20x^3(x + 3)}{2x(x + 3)^2} = \dfrac{10x^2}{x + 3}$

1. $\dfrac{ab}{4a - 4b} \cdot \dfrac{a^2 - ab}{ab}$ $\dfrac{a}{4}$

2. $\dfrac{2x - 14}{-5x} \cdot \dfrac{5x^3}{3x - 21}$ $-\dfrac{2x^2}{3}$

3. $\dfrac{8f + 24g}{2f - 4g} \cdot \dfrac{4f - 8g}{2f + 6g}$ 8

4. $\dfrac{m + 2}{2m - 6} \cdot \dfrac{m^2 - 5m + 6}{2m + 4}$ $\dfrac{m - 2}{4}$

5. $\dfrac{3z - 6}{5z} \cdot \dfrac{z^2 - z - 6}{z^2 - 4}$ $\dfrac{3(z - 3)}{5z}$

6. $\dfrac{x^2 - 4}{x^2 - 9} \cdot \dfrac{2x^2 + 6x}{x - 2}$

7. $\dfrac{3n^2 + 2n - 1}{5n^2 - 9n - 2} \cdot \dfrac{10n^2 - 13n - 3}{2n^2 - n - 3}$ $\dfrac{3n - 1}{n - 2}$

8. $\dfrac{y^2 + 12y + 36}{36 - y^2} \cdot \dfrac{y^2 - 5y - 6}{2y^2 - 2y - 84}$

6. $\dfrac{2x(x + 2)}{x - 3}$ **8.** $\dfrac{y + 1}{2(7 - y)}$

Sample 2 $\dfrac{2m^2 + 5m + 2}{m^2 + 4m + 3} \div \dfrac{m + 2}{2m^2 + 7m + 3}$

Solution $\dfrac{(2m + 1)(m + 2)}{(m + 3)(m + 1)} \cdot \dfrac{(2m + 1)(m + 3)}{m + 2} = \dfrac{(2m + 1)^2}{m + 1}$

9. $\dfrac{10a - 10b}{ab} \div \dfrac{2a - 2b}{a^2 b^2}$ $5ab$

10. $\dfrac{16m^2 - n^2}{6m + 3n} \div \dfrac{4mn - n^2}{2mn + n^2}$ $\dfrac{4m + n}{3}$

11. $\dfrac{2b^2 + 17b + 21}{b + 1} \div (b + 7)$ $\dfrac{2b + 3}{b + 1}$

12. $\dfrac{x^2 + x}{-x^2 - 2x - 1} \div \dfrac{x^2 - 3x}{2x^2 - 2}$ $\dfrac{2(x - 1)}{3 - x}$

13. $\dfrac{c^2 - c - 6}{c^2 + 2c - 15} \div \dfrac{c^2 - 4c - 5}{c^2 - 25}$ $\dfrac{c + 2}{c + 1}$

14. $\dfrac{6y^2 - y - 2}{12y^2 + 5y - 2} \div \dfrac{8y^2 - 6y + 1}{4y^2 - 1}$

15. $\dfrac{r^2 - r - 20}{r^2 - 6r + 5} \cdot \dfrac{r^2 - 36}{r^2 - 9} \div \dfrac{r^2 + 7r + 12}{r^2 + 5r - 6}$ $\dfrac{(r - 6)(r + 6)^2}{(r - 3)(r + 3)^2}$

$\dfrac{(3y - 2)(2y + 1)^2}{(3y + 2)(4y - 1)^2}$

Sample 3 $\dfrac{b}{b - 2} - \dfrac{2}{b^2 - 4} + 1$ **18.** $\dfrac{1}{b^2}$ **21.** $\dfrac{v^2 - v + 8}{(v + 1)(v - 1)}$ **24.** $\dfrac{2(x^2 + 2x + 3)}{(x - 1)(x + 2)}$

Solution $\dfrac{b(b + 2) - 2 + (b + 2)(b - 2)}{(b + 2)(b - 2)} = \dfrac{b^2 + 2b - 2 + b^2 - 4}{(b + 2)(b - 2)} = \dfrac{2(b^2 + b - 3)}{(b + 2)(b - 2)}$

16. $\dfrac{2t - 3}{r^2 t} + \dfrac{r - t}{r^2 t}$ $\dfrac{t - 3 + r}{r^2 t}$

17. $\dfrac{x + 2y}{x - y} + \dfrac{x + y}{x - y}$ $\dfrac{2x + 3y}{x - y}$

18. $\dfrac{3b + 2}{b^3} - \dfrac{2b + 2}{b^3}$

19. $\dfrac{w - 2}{w - 3} - \dfrac{w^2 + w}{w - 3}$ $\dfrac{2 + w^2}{3 - w}$

20. $z + \dfrac{z - 1}{z + 1} + 1$ $\dfrac{z(z + 3)}{z + 1}$

21. $\dfrac{8}{v^2 - 1} + \dfrac{v}{v + 1}$

22. $\dfrac{s}{s - t} - \dfrac{s}{s + t}$ $\dfrac{2st}{s^2 - t^2}$

23. $\dfrac{3b}{2b - 1} - b$ $\dfrac{2b(2 - b)}{2b - 1}$

24. $\dfrac{x + 3}{x - 1} + \dfrac{x}{x + 2}$

25. $\dfrac{d - 3}{2d + 1} + \dfrac{1}{d + 1}$ $\dfrac{d^2 - 2}{(2d + 1)(d + 1)}$

26. $\dfrac{v + 4}{v + 2} - \dfrac{v + 2}{v + 4}$ $\dfrac{4(v + 3)}{(v + 2)(v + 4)}$

27. $\dfrac{t}{t^2 - 4} - \dfrac{5t}{4 - t^2}$

28. $\dfrac{2b}{b + 2} + \dfrac{b + 1}{b} - 1$

$\dfrac{2b^2 + b + 2}{b(b + 2)}$

29. $\dfrac{x + 4}{x - 4} - \dfrac{x - 4}{x + 3} + 2$

$\dfrac{2x^2 + 13x - 28}{(x - 4)(x + 3)}$

30. $\dfrac{3a + b}{a^2 - b^2} - \dfrac{1}{a + b}$

27. $\dfrac{6t}{t^2 - 4}$ **30.** $\dfrac{2}{a - b}$

454   *Chapter 9*

Mixed Problem Solving

Solve each problem that has a solution. If a problem has no solution, explain why.

A 1. As the altitude increases from sea level to 6000 m, the air pressure decreases from 101.3 kilopascals to 47.2 kilopascals. Find the approximate percent decrease in air pressure. 53.4%

2. The ratio of boys to girls in a sophomore class of 460 students is 11:12. How many girls are there? 240 girls

3. The sum of the squares of two consecutive even integers is 34. Find the integers. No solution; contradictory facts

4. Eight ears of corn and a cantaloupe cost $2.37. Six ears of corn and 3 cantaloupes cost $3.51. What does a cantaloupe cost? 77¢

5. An airplane travels 1800 km in 6 h flying with the wind. It travels only two thirds as far in the same time against the wind. Find the speed of the wind. 50 km/h

6. At 9:00 A.M. two boys began hiking at 6 km/h. At 10:30 A.M. their mother started after them in her car at 60 km/h, bringing a friend to join them. At what time did she catch up with them? 10:40 A.M.

7. The amount of tax is directly proportional to the cost of an item. If the tax on a $12,300 car is $738, find the tax on a $9450 car. $567

8. The tens digit of a two-digit number is 1 more than 3 times the units digit. Subtracting 45 from the number reverses it. Find the original number. 72

B 9. Ramon can do the weekly billing in 2 h. Luann needs 3 h. If Ramon works for 30 min and is then joined by Luann, how long will it take them to finish? 54 min

10. The rectangular base of a radio receiver is twice as long as it is wide. A design engineer finds that in order to fit the receiver into the space available on an airplane, she must decrease the length by 7 in. and increase the width by 2 in. If this change decreases the area of the base by 32 in.^{2}, what were the original dimensions of the receiver? 6 in. by 12 in.

11. How many kilograms of water must be evaporated from 8 kg of a 25% salt solution to produce a 40% salt solution? 3 kg

12. The value of a fraction is $\frac{3}{4}$. When 7 is added to its numerator, the resulting fraction is equal to the reciprocal of the original fraction. Find the original fraction. $\frac{9}{12}$

13. The Kwons invested $6000, part at $7\frac{1}{4}$% and part at 10%, and earned $567 in interest. How much did they invest at each rate? $1200 at $7\frac{1}{4}$%, $4800 at 10%

14. I have dimes and quarters worth $1.15. How many of each could I have? (*Hint:* There is more than one solution.) 1 quarter and 9 dimes, or 3 quarters and 4 dimes

10 Inequalities

Objectives

10-1 To review the concept of order and to graph inequalities in one variable.

10-2 To transform inequalities in order to solve them.

10-3 To solve problems that involve inequalities.

10-4 To find the solution sets of combined inequalities.

10-5 To solve equations and inequalities involving absolute value.

10-6 To extend your skill in solving open sentences that involve absolute value.

10-7 To graph linear inequalities in two variables.

10-8 To graph the solution set of a system of two linear inequalities in two variables.

Assignment Guide

See p. T59 for Key to the format of the Assignment Guide

Day	Minimum Course		Average Course		Maximum Course	
1	**10-1** **S**	459/1–35 odd 461/*Mixed Review*	**10-1** **S**	459/1–37 odd 461/*Mixed Review*	**10-1** **S**	459/1–29 odd, 36–40 461/*Mixed Review*
2	**10-2** **S**	466/1–10, 12, 15, 22, 23, 41 467/*Mixed Review*	**10-2** **S**	466/1–10, 12–45 mult. of 3 467/*Mixed Review*	**10-2** **S**	466/1–10, 12–48 mult. of 3, 51, 56, 61, 63 467/*Mixed Review*
3	**10-2** **10-3** **S**	467/26, 35, 43 471/1–11 odd 475/*Mixed Review*	**10-3** **S**	471/1–15 odd 473/*P*: 2, 5, 10, 13, 15 475/*Mixed Review*	**10-3** **S**	471/3–18 mult. of 3 473/*P*: 3–21 mult. of 3 475/*Mixed Review*
4	**10-3** **10-4** **R**	472/6, 8, 10; 473/*P*: 1–3 480/1–15 odd 475/*Self-Test 1*	**10-4** **S** **R**	480/1–15 odd, 23–26 481/*Mixed Review* 475/*Self-Test 1*	**10-4** **S** **R**	480/3–39 mult. of 3 481/*Mixed Review* 475/*Self-Test 1*
5	**10-4** **S** **10-5**	480/12–22 even 481/*Mixed Review* 484/1–6	**10-5** **S**	484/3–36 mult. of 3 485/*Mixed Review*	**10-5** **S**	484/3–36 mult. of 3 485/*Mixed Review*
6	**10-5** **S** **10-6**	485/13–21 odd 485/*Mixed Review* 488/1–5	**10-6** **S**	488/1–21 odd 488/*Mixed Review*	**10-6** **S**	488/1–25 odd 488/*Mixed Review*
7	**10-6** **S** **10-7**	488/9–12 488/*Mixed Review* 492/1–11 odd	**10-7** **S** **R**	492/3–33 mult. of 3 494/*Mixed Review* 489/*Self-Test 2*	**10-7** **S** **R**	492/3–39 mult. of 3 494/*Mixed Review* 489/*Self-Test 2*
8	**10-7** **S** **10-8**	492/10, 12–14, 25–28 494/*Mixed Review* 496/1–11 odd	**10-8** **S**	496/1–17 odd 498/*Mixed Review*	**10-8** **S**	496/3–24 mult. of 3 498/*Mixed Review*
9	*Prepare for Chapter Test* **R** **EP**	 489/*Self-Test 2* 501/*Chapter Review* 657/*Skills;* 677/*Problems*	**10-8** **R**	496/16, 18–22 498/*Self-Test 3*	*Prepare for Chapter Test* **R** **EP**	 498/*Self-Test 3* 501/*Chapter Review* 657/*Skills;* 677/*Problems*

Assignment Guide (continued)

Day	Minimum Course	Average Course	Maximum Course
10	*Administer Chapter 10 Test* **R** 504/*Maintaining Skills*	*Prepare for Chapter Test* **R** 501/*Chapter Review* **EP** 657/*Skills;* 677/*Problems*	*Administer Chapter 10 Test* **R** 503/*Cum. Review:* 1–39 odd **S** 505/*Prep. for Coll. Ent.* *Exams*
11		*Administer Chapter 10 Test* **R** 503/*Cum. Review:* 1–39 odd **S** 505/*Prep. for Coll. Ent.* *Exams*	

Supplementary Materials Guide

For Use with Lesson	Practice Masters	Tests	Study Guide (Reteaching)	Resource Book		
				Tests	Practice Exercises	Applications (A) Enrichment (E) Technology (T)
10-1			pp. 167–168			p. 187 (A)
10-2	Sheet 61		pp. 169–170		p. 126	
10-3		Test 44	pp. 171–172		p. 127	
10-4	Sheet 62		pp. 173–174		p. 128	
10-5			pp. 175–176			
10-6	Sheet 63		pp. 177–178		p. 129	
10-7		Test 45	pp. 179–180			p. 212 (T)
10-8	Sheet 64		pp. 181–182		p. 130	
Chapter 10	Sheet 65	Tests 46, 47		pp. 56–59		p. 203 (E)

Overhead Visuals

For Use with Lessons	Visual	Title
10-1 through 10-8	A	Multi-Use Packet 1
10-1 through 10-8	B	Multi-Use Packet 2
10-5	10	Absolute Value in Sentences
10-7, 10-8	11	Graphing Linear Inequalities and Systems

Software

Software	Algebra Plotter Plus	Using Algebra Plotter Plus	Computer Activities	Test Generator
Software	Absolute Value Plotter, Inequality Plotter	Scripted Demo, pp. 22–24 Enrichment, pp. 33–34 Activity Sheets, pp. 48–49	Activities 30–32	168 test items
For Use with Lessons	10-7, 10-8	10-7, 10-8	10-4, 10-5, 10-8	all lessons

Strategies for Teaching

Communication

Translating word phrases into mathematical expressions requires extra care when inequalities are involved, since different symbols may yield different solution sets. Thus it might be helpful to remind students to pay close attention to reading and writing algebra skills when translating expressions. Students may also have trouble understanding the subtleties in logic governing rules for multiplying (or dividing) inequalities by negative numbers, distinguishing between conjunctions and disjunctions, and applying absolute value signs. Tell students that careful reading of all definitions and properties often explains the rationale behind rules.

10-1 Order of Real Numbers

Begin with a review of the inequality signs and their meanings, and of how to graph a real number on a number line. Review the meaning of solution of an open sentence in general, and show that possible solutions of an inequality can be tested by substituting values for the variable in the inequality.

Emphasize the difference between the symbols $<$ and $\leq$, and between $>$ and $\geq$. Also, remind students that a statement such as $x \geq 5$ is equivalent to the statement $5 \leq x$.

The significance of the words "and" and "or" is developed more thoroughly in Lesson 10-4, but begin to stress the idea of true and false statements.

$$\left.\begin{array}{l} -5 < -2 \text{ and } -2 < 0 \text{ true} \\ -1 < -2 \text{ and } -2 < 0 \text{ false} \end{array}\right\}$$ An "and" statement is true only if both parts are true.

$$\left.\begin{array}{ll} 5 > 2 \text{ or } 5 < 9 & \text{true} \\ 7 > 4 \text{ or } 7 = 4 & \text{true} \\ -2 > 0 \text{ or } -2 < -4 & \text{false} \end{array}\right\}$$ An "or" statement is true if either part is true.

Define the "greatest integer" symbol [ ] as follows: $[x]$ is the greatest integer that is less than or equal to x. For example, $[5] = 5$, $[-3] = -3$, $[2.3] = 2$, and $[-9.6] = -10$.

As an extension, have students solve each inequality over the domain {the positive real numbers}.

1. $[x] > 3$ **2.** $[x] \leq 5$ **3.** $2 < [x] < 6$

1. {the real numbers greater than or equal to 4}
2. {the positive real numbers less than 6}
3. {the real numbers less than 6 and greater than or equal to 3}

10-3 Solving Problems Involving Inequalities

This section builds on previous work. The emphasis should be on writing the inequalities. Once this has been done, solutions should not pose a major difficulty; students simply use the methods developed in Lesson 10-2. The Written Exercises allow students to concentrate on the crucial skill of translating problems into mathematical terms, without concerning themselves with the mechanics of solving the inequalities.

The list at the bottom of page 469, while not exhaustive, should help students develop a feel for which inequality sign is implied by a given expression.

The five-step plan for solving word problems encourages students to read and reread problems and to break them down into comprehensible portions. Encourage students to read word problems with pencil in hand, to jot notes as they read, and to refine their notes when rereading.

10-4 Solving Combined Inequalities

The mathematical meanings of the words "or" and "and" are matters of definition. The word "or," in particular, has more than one meaning in ordinary English and, hence, must be clearly defined in a mathematical context. The meaning used is usually expressed "either or both" in ordinary English. Encourage students to work through the Extra on pages

476–477 if they haven't already done so. It can be helpful to explain solutions of conjunctions and disjunctions in terms of intersections and unions.

Many students will benefit from a graphic breakdown of combined inequalities. Advise students to graph the two component inequalities individually, then look for the overlapping portion (intersection).

10-6 Absolute Value of Products in Open Sentences

Use many numerical examples along with those that follow Example 1 to remind students that the absolute value of a product is the product of the absolute values. Generalize the results with a concise statement:

$$|ab| = |a| \, |b|.$$

Point out that this statement says that if a number is factored from an absolute value quantity, it must be positive. For example, $|3x| = 3|x|$ and $|-3x| = 3|x|$.

10-7 Graphing Linear Inequalities

Review how to graph a line using slope-intercept form. The steps in the box on page 491 and in Example 1 involve expressing a line in slope-intercept form. Graphing this line produces the boundary of the half-plane that is the graph of the inequality under consideration. Relate the symbols $\leq$, $\geq$, $<$, and $>$ to the inclusion or exclusion of the boundary line in the graph and remind students to use care in drawing either a solid or a dashed boundary line.

References to Strategies

PE: Pupil's Edition   **TE:** Teacher's Edition   **RB:** Resource Book

Problem Solving Strategies

PE: pp. 469–474 (Using five-step plan); pp. 468–474 (Using inequalities)
TE: pp. 463, 470, 483
RB: pp. 220–221

Applications

PE: pp. 456, 461, 470–474, 477, 489, 499–500
TE: p. 456
RB: p. 187

Nonroutine Problems

PE: p. 460 (Exs. 39–42); p. 467 (Exs. 51–66);
p. 474 (Probs. 21–23); p. 475 (Challenge);
p. 481 (Exs. 39, 40); p. 488 (Exs. 19–25);
p. 493 (Exs. 34–39); pp. 497–498 (Exs. 19–28)
RB: p. 203

Communication

PE: p. 468 (Reading Algebra); p. 475 (Challenge, convincing argument)
TE: p. T128 (Reading Algebra, Sugg. Extension)

Thinking Skills

TE: pp. 459, 470, 487

Explorations

PE: pp. 476, 494, 499–500, 696
RB: p. 212
Algebra Plotter Plus: pp. 22–24, 33–34, 48, 49

Connections

PE: pp. 476, 499–500 (Discrete Math); pp. 470–471, 473–474 (Geometry); pp. 461, 489 (Health); p. 477 (History); p. 456 (Physics)

Using Technology

PE: pp. 460, 481, 494 (Exs.); p. 498 (Calculator Key-In)
TE: pp. 460, 481, 494, 498, 500
RB: p. 212
Computer Activities: pp. 66–72
Algebra Plotter Plus: pp. 22–24, 33–34, 48, 49

Using Manipulatives/Models

TE: p. T127 (Lesson 10-2); p. T128 (Lesson 10-4)
Overhead Visuals: A, B, 10, 11

Cooperative Learning

TE: p. T129 (Lesson 10-6)

Teaching Resources

For use in implementing the teaching strategies referenced on the previous page.

Application
Resource Book, p. 187

Application—Postal Rates (for use with Chapter 10)

The United States Postal Service uses inequalities as a means of setting postage rates. For a given mail class, letters and packages are classified by weight ranges and postal rates are set for each range. The general formula for postage rates for first class mail is: $.25 for the first ounce plus $.20 for each additional ounce or fraction thereof. Thus, the price of a letter weighing 6 oz is the same as that of a letter weighing 5.1 oz.

1. If letter weights were restricted to integer values (in ounces), then the relationship between cost and weight would be linear. State the linear equation for this circumstance. (Let c = cost, and let w = weight.)

2. The Postal Service provides tables for calculating postage rates for mail of various weights. The tables are based on the rule above. Below is a sample table for first class mail. Complete the table.

For pieces not exceeding	Rate	For pieces not exceeding	Rate
1 oz	$.25	7 oz	___
2 oz	$.45	8 oz	___
3 oz	$.65	9 oz	___
4 oz	___	10 oz	___
5 oz	___	11 oz	___
6 oz	___	12 oz	___

3. What is the postage rate for a first class letter weighing 3.4 oz? ___

4. The information in the table above could be presented using inequalities. State an inequality for the information given in line 3 of the table:
   If ___, then c = $.65.

5. Suppose you had a postage bill of $3.00 for mailing four first class letters.
   a. List three possibilities for the individual weights of the four letters.

   b. What is the maximum weight of the four letters? ___

6. Investigate postal rates for types of mail other than first class.

Enrichment/Nonroutine Problems
Resource Book, p. 203

Reciprocals of Integers (For use with Chapter 10 of text)

1. Find three different positive integers A, B, and C such that $\frac{1}{A} + \frac{1}{B} = \frac{1}{C}$. Then compare your answer with those of your classmates to see if you can recognize some patterns.

2. Add these two expressions and simplify the answer.
$$\frac{1}{x(x+y)} + \frac{1}{y(x+y)}$$

3. How can the given expressions and the result in Exercise 2 help you to find other values of A, B, and C that satisfy the equation $\frac{1}{A} + \frac{1}{B} = \frac{1}{C}$ (Exercise 1)?

4. Find four different positive integers A, B, C, and D such that $\frac{1}{A} + \frac{1}{B} + \frac{1}{C} = \frac{1}{D}$.

Using Technology/Exploration
Resource Book, p. 212

Using a Computer or a Graphing Calculator

To complete these activities, you should use a computer with graphics software (such as ALGEBRA PLOTTER PLUS) or a graphing calculator.

Equations Involving Absolute Value (For use with Chapter 10, p. 494)

1. Graph these equations: $y = |x|$, $y = |x| + 1$, $y = |x| - 2$
   a. Each V-shaped graph has a lowest point, called the *vertex*. Locate the vertex of each graph and complete the table below.

Equation	Vertex	
$y = |x|$	(0, 0)	
$y = |x| + 1$	(? , ?)	___
$y = |x| - 2$	(? , ?)	___

   b. The equations have the form $y = |x| + c$. Using the number c, give the coordinates of the vertex of the graph of $y = |x| + c$ ___

2. Graph these equations: $y = |x|$, $y = |x - 1|$, $y = |x + 2|$
   a. Complete the table below.

Equation	Vertex	
$y = |x|$	(0, 0)	
$y = |x - 1|$	(? , ?)	___
$y = |x + 2|$	(? , ?)	___

   b. The equations have the form $y = |x + b|$. Using the number b, give the coordinates of the vertex of the graph of $y = |x + b|$: ___

3. Based on the results of Exercises 1 and 2, try to complete the table below before graphing the given equations.

Equation	Vertex	
$y = |x - 3| - 1$	(? , ?)	___
$y = |x - 2| + 2$	(? , ?)	___
$y = |x + 1| - 4$	(? , ?)	___

Now examine the graphs of the given equations to confirm the entries in the table.

4. Find an equation involving absolute value for which the graph of the equation has its vertex at:
   a. $(-2, 4)$ ___   b. $(1, -3)$ ___
   Confirm your equations by graphing.

Using Technology/Exploration
Using Algebra Plotter Plus, p. 49

Linear Programming | Algebra Plotter Plus | | Book 1: Lesson 10-8 Application |

Use the Inequality Plotter program of Algebra Plotter Plus.

1. Suppose the feasible region for a linear programming problem is given by:
$x \geq 0$
$y \geq 0$
$x + y \leq 9$
$x + 2y \leq 16$
$4x + y \leq 24$

Since the first two inequalities imply that the feasible region lies entirely in the first quadrant, you need not plot them. Instead, you should set the SCALE to display the intervals $0 \leq x \leq 12$ and $0 \leq y \leq 10$. Then select INEQUALITIES and use the arrow keys to fill in the blanks for the other three inequalities. The region that contains the densest shading is the feasible region. List the five vertices of the feasible region:

(___ , ___), (___ , ___), (___ , ___), (___ , ___), (___ , ___)

2. For the feasible region of Exercise 1, suppose you are given the objective function $P = 3x + 2y$. To determine the minimum or maximum value of P in the feasible region, you need only check the values of P at the vertices.

For example, one of the vertices in your list for Exercise 1 should have been the origin, as shown in the table below. Complete the table for the other vertices from your list.

	x	y	$3x + 2y = P$
	0	0	$3(0) + 2(0) = 0$
a.			
b.			
c.			
d.			

   e. The minimum value of P is ___, which is found when $x =$ ___ and $y =$ ___.
   f. The maximum value of P is ___, which is found when $x =$ ___ and $y =$ ___.

3. Use the feasible region of Exercise 1 to find the minimum and maximum values of the objective function $P = 4x + 5y$.
   a. The minimum value of P is ___, which is found when $x =$ ___ and $y =$ ___.
   b. The maximum value of P is ___, which is found when $x =$ ___ and $y =$ ___.

Using Models
Overhead Visual 11, Sheets 1 and 4

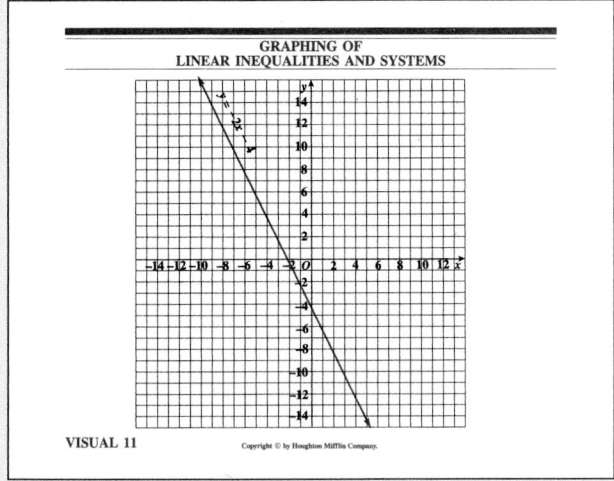

Using Models
Overhead Visual 11, Sheets 1 and 5

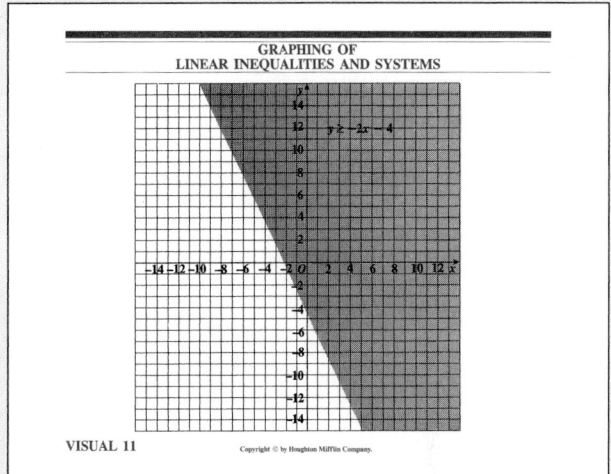

Using Models
Overhead Visual 11, Sheets 1 and 3

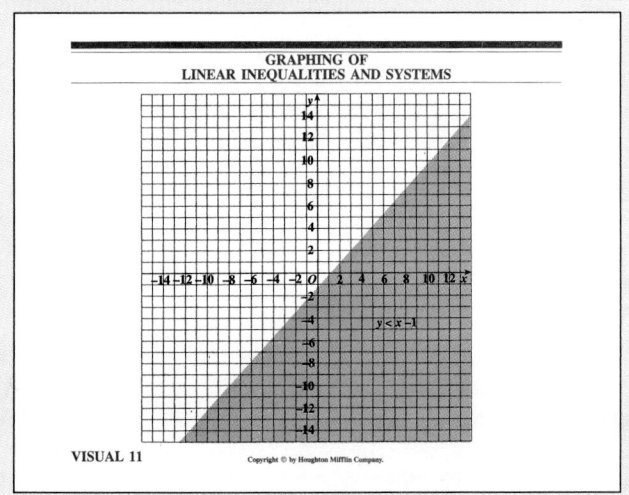

Using Models
Overhead Visual 11, Sheets 1, 3, and 5

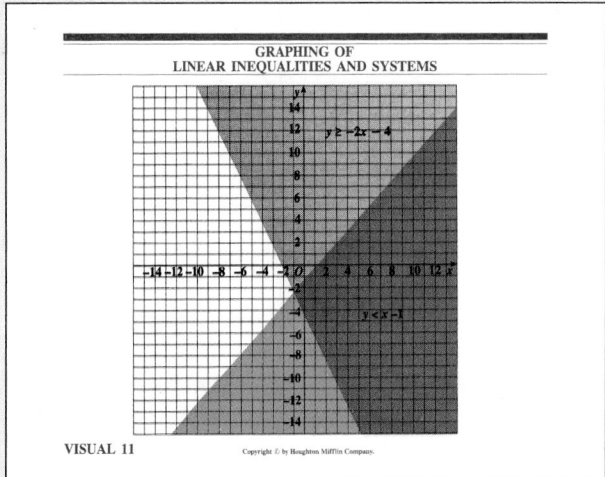

Application

The effects of temperature on water are shown. The three states of water occur within specific temperature ranges. These ranges can be expressed using inequalities, one each for steam, water, and ice.

Many compounds change from solids to liquids, and from liquids to gases when their temperatures exceed certain limits. Inequalities are used to denote the temperature range for each state of a compound.

Research Activities

Temperature affects plastics in many different ways. A student who would like to do an extensive project may wish to investigate the melting point of various plastics. The student should be able to explain, in general terms, why some plastic bags can be placed in an oven without melting, while others melt upon touching a hot object.

As a fact finding project, students may explore other situations where inequalities can be used to express ranges of numbers. Possibilities include weight classes for wrestling and boxing, load limits on bridges, height limits under bridges, and speed limits (maximum and minimum). Results can be shared with the class.

Above the boiling point ($t > 212°F$) *water is steam. Below the freezing point* ($t < 32°F$) *it's ice. In between* ($32°F < t < 212°F$), *it's liquid.*

456

Inequalities in One Variable

10-1 Order of Real Numbers

Objective To review the concept of order and to graph inequalities in one variable.

A number line shows order relationships among real numbers.

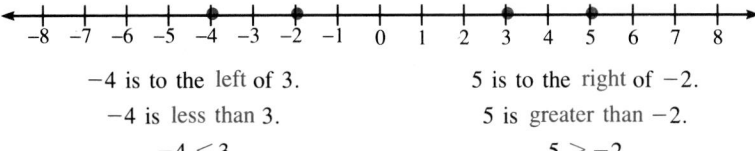

-4 is to the left of 3.   5 is to the right of -2.

-4 is less than 3.   5 is greater than -2.

$\qquad -4 < 3 \qquad\qquad\qquad\qquad 5 > -2$

The value of a variable may be unknown, but you may know that it's greater than or equal to another number. For example,

$\qquad x \geq 5$ is read "x is greater than or equal to 5."

$\qquad x \geq 5$ is another way of writing "$x > 5$ or $x = 5$."

Example 1 Translate the statement into symbols.

    a. -3 is greater than -5. **b.** x is less than or equal to 8.

Solution   **a.** $-3 > -5$ **b.** $x \leq 8$

To show that x is *between* -4 and 2, you write

$$-4 < x < 2,$$

which is read

    "-4 is less than x and x is less than 2,"

or

    "x is greater than -4 and less than 2."

The same comparisons are stated in the sentence $2 > x > -4$.

When all the numbers are known, you can determine whether the statements are true or false.

Example 2 Classify each statement as true or false.

    a. $-4 < 1 < 2$ **b.** $-4 < 8 < 2$

    c. $7 \geq 6$ **d.** $6 \geq 6$ *(Solution is on next page.)*

Inequalities **457**

Teaching References

Lesson Commentary, pp. T126–T130

Assignment Guide, pp. T68–T70

Supplementary Materials
Practice Masters 61–65

Tests 44–47

Resource Book
Practice Exercises, pp. 126–130
Tests, pp. 56–59
Enrichment Activity, p. 203
Application, p. 187
Using Technology, p. 212

Study Guide, pp. 167–182

Computer Activities 30–32

Test Generator

California Standards Support Workbook
Exploration for Lesson 10-2

Alternate Test, p. T21

Teaching Suggestions p. T126

Suggested Extensions p. T127

Warm-Up Exercises

Graph each set of numbers on a single number line.

1. $-3, 2, -5, 0, -0.5$

2. $1.5, 0.8, -0.2, 0.2, -1.5$

3. $-25, -40, 15, -5, 25$

(continued)

Warm-Up Exercises

(continued)
Find the value of the expression if $x = -2$ and $y = 5$.

4. $x^2 - 3x + 4$ 14

5. $4y - (y - 7)$ 22

6. $(x + y)(x - y)$ -21

Motivating the Lesson

The water temperature in an aquarium must be more than 50° F and less than 80° F for goldfish to survive. Will they survive if the temperature is 65° F? Yes, since 65 is a solution of the inequality $50 < x < 80$. Inequalities like these are today's topic.

Chalkboard Examples

1. Translate into symbols: y is greater than or equal to -5. $y \geq -5$

2. Classify each statement as true or false.
 a. $-1 < 3 < 2$ False since $3 < 2$ is false.
 b. $|-2| + |-5| \geq |-2 - 5|$ True since $7 = 7$.
 c. $|-1| \leq |-9|$ $1 < 9$ is true.

3. Solve $2n + 2 > 5$ if $n \in \{0, 1, 2, 3, 4\}$.
 Replace n with each of its values in turn:
 $2(0) + 2 > 5$ False
 $2(1) + 2 > 5$ False
 $2(2) + 2 > 5$ True
 $2(3) + 2 > 5$ True
 $2(4) + 2 > 5$ True
 ∴ solution set is $\{2, 3, 4\}$.

4. Graph $-2 < m \leq 3$ over the domain {the real numbers}.

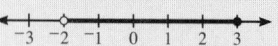

Solution   **a.** $-4 < 1 < 2$ is true since *both* $-4 < 1$ *and* $1 < 2$ are true.

 b. $-4 < 8 < 2$ is false since $-4 < 8$ is true but $8 < 2$ is false.

 c. For $7 \geq 6$ to be true, *either* $7 > 6$ *or* $7 = 6$ must be true. $7 \geq 6$ is true since $7 > 6$ is true.

 d. $6 \geq 6$ is true since $6 = 6$ is true.

The statements given in Examples 1 and 2 are *inequalities*. An **inequality** is formed by placing an inequality symbol ($>$, $<$, $\geq$, $\leq$) between numerical or variable expressions, called the **sides** of the inequality.

As with equations, an inequality containing a variable is called an *open sentence* (page 10). You solve an inequality by finding the values from the *domain* of the variable for which the inequality is a true statement. Such values are called **solutions of the inequality.** All the solutions make up the **solution set of the inequality.**

Example 3 Solve $y + 5 \leq 7$ if $y \in \{-1, 0, 1, 2, 3, 4\}$.

Solution Replace y with each of its values in turn:

$$y + 5 \leq 7$$

$-1 + 5 \leq 7$ True	$2 + 5 \leq 7$ True
$0 + 5 \leq 7$ True	$3 + 5 \leq 7$ False
$1 + 5 \leq 7$ True	$4 + 5 \leq 7$ False

∴ the solution set is $\{-1, 0, 1, 2\}$. **Answer**

When you graph the numbers in the solution set of an inequality on a number line, you are drawing the **graph of the inequality.** The graph of the inequality $y + 5 \leq 7$ in Example 3 is shown below.

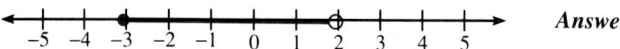

Example 4 Graph $-3 \leq x < 2$ over the domain {the real numbers}.

Solution For the inequality to be a true statement, x must represent any number between -3 and 2, including -3 but not 2.

Answer

---

458   *Chapter 10*

Notice that the graph in Example 4 includes all the points on the number line from the graph of −3 up to, but not including, the graph of 2. The open circle shows that 2 is not a solution.

Oral Exercises

Classify each statement as true or false.

1. $6 \geq 3$ T
2. $17 \leq 23$ T
3. $-10 \leq -15$ F
4. $-1 > -2$ T

5. $4 > -4 > -1$ F
6. $-5 < 5 < 9$ T
7. $3 > 0 > -5$ T
8. $-1.5 < 0.5 < 2.5$ T

9. $|-4| \geq 0$ T
10. $|-2| > |-8|$ F
11. $2^4 < 4^2$ F
12. $\frac{1}{2} \leq \left(\frac{1}{2}\right)^2$ F

Match each graph with its description.

13.
d

14.
b

15.
g

16.
c

17.
f

18.
a

19.
h

20.
e

a. The real numbers greater than or equal to 0.
b. $\{-2, 0, 2\}$
c. The real numbers between -1 and 3.
d. $\{-3, -1, 0, 2\}$
e. The real numbers less than 0.
f. The real numbers greater than -1 and less than or equal to 2.
g. The real numbers greater than or equal to -1.
h. The real numbers less than or equal to -2.

Written Exercises

Translate each statement into symbols.

A
1. 4 is greater than -7. $4 > -7$
2. -5 is less than -3. $-5 < -3$
3. -12 is less than or equal to -9. $-12 \leq -9$
4. 6 is greater than or equal to 2. $6 \geq 2$
5. 3 is greater than 2 and less than 3.5. $2 < 3 < 3.5$
6. 0 is greater than $-\frac{1}{2}$ and less than 1. $-\frac{1}{2} < 0 < 1$

Inequalities   **459**

Check for Understanding

Here is a suggested use of the Oral Exercises as you teach the lesson.
Oral Exs. 1–12: use after Example 2.
Oral Exs. 13–20: use after Example 4.

Common Errors

Students are often unclear about when to use open and closed dots. Review these symbols.

Thinking Skills

Students are asked to *translate* from verbal expressions to mathematical symbols including inequality signs.

Guided Practice

Translate each statement into symbols.
1. 3 is greater than or equal to -4. $3 \geq -4$
2. -7 is between -15 and -1. $-15 < -7 < -1$
3. The number n is greater than 0 and less than 5. $0 < n < 5$
Classify as true or false.
4. $|-15| \leq |-14|$ False
5. $-3 > -5 > -6$ True
Solve each inequality if $x \in \{-2, -1, 0, 1, 2, 3\}$.
6. $2x < 1$ $\{-2, -1, 0\}$
7. $7 - x \leq 7$ $\{0, 1, 2, 3\}$

Summarizing the Lesson

Tell students that they now know how to graph simple inequalities. Ask them to explain how to find the solution of a given inequality over a given domain.

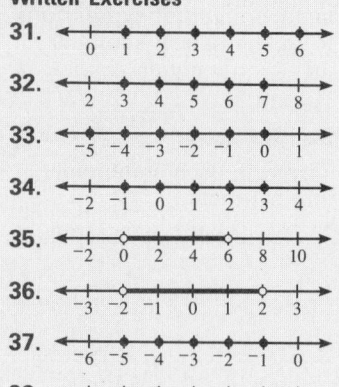
Translate each statement into symbols.

7. -8 is between 0 and -10. $-10 < -8 < 0$

8. 5 is between -9 and 9. $-9 < 5 < 9$

9. 4.6 is greater than 4 and 4 is greater than 0. $0 < 4 < 4.6$

10. -1.5 is less than -1 and -1 is less than 2. $-1.5 < -1 < 2$

11. The number n is greater than 10. $n > 10$

12. The number n is less than 20. $n < 20$

13. The absolute value of -2 is greater than 1. $|-2| > 1$

14. The absolute value of n is less than or equal to n. $|n| \le n$

Classify each statement as true or false.

15. $|-3| > -3$ T   **16.** $0 \le |-2|$ T   **17.** $|-25| < |-10|$ F   **18.** $|-0.5| \le -0.5$ F

19. $\left|-\frac{1}{2}\right| \ge 0$ T   **20.** $-6 < 1 < 7$ T   **21.** $6 > 0 > 2$ F   **22.** $-5 < -4 < 4$ T

23. $\{-4, -3, -2, -1, 0, 1\}$ **24.** $\{2, 3, 4\}$ **25.** $\{-3, -2, -1, 0, 1, 2, 3, 4\}$ **26.** $\{-4, -3, -2, -1, 0\}$
Solve each inequality if $x \in \{-4, -3, -2, -1, 0, 1, 2, 3, 4\}$.

23. $4x < 8$ **24.** $3x \ge 6$ **25.** $-3x \le 9$ **26.** $x + 2 < 3$

27. $-5 - x \le 1$ **28.** $1 - x \ge 0$ **29.** $x^2 \ge 10$ **30.** $x^2 \le 4$
27. $\{-4, -3, -2, -1, 0, 1, 2, 3, 4\}$ **28.** $\{-4, -3, -2, -1, 0, 1\}$ **29.** $\{-4, 4\}$ **30.** $\{-2, -1, 0, 1, 2\}$

Graph each inequality over the given domain.

B   **31.** $1 \le x \le 6$; {the positive integers}   **32.** $2 < h < 8$; {the positive integers}

33. $-5 \le x < 1$; {the integers}   **34.** $3 \ge t \ge -1$; {the integers}

35. $6 > u > 0$; {the real numbers}   **36.** $-2 < m < 2$; {the real numbers}

37. $-5 \le h < 1$; {the negative integers}   **38.** $4 \ge n > -5$; {the negative integers}

For each statement in Exercises 39–42: Answers may vary.

a. Find a pair of values of x and y for which the statement is true.

b. Find a pair of values of x and y for which the statement is false.   a. (0, 1)
b. (−1, 1)

C   **39.** If $x \ge y$, then $|x| \le |y|$. a. (−2, −3) b. (3, 2)   **40.** If $x \le 0$ and $y > 0$, then $xy \ge 0$.

41. If $x > y$, then $xy > y^2$.
a. (2, 1) b. (2, −1)   **42.** $|x + y| > x + y$
a. (2, −3) b. (2, 3)

Computer Exercises

For students with some programming experience

Write a BASIC program to find the solution set of an inequality for a specified domain of the variable. Run the program to find the solution set of each of the following inequalities for the given domain.

1. $2x - 5 < 7$; $x \in \{0, 1, 2, \ldots, 10\}$ $\{0, 1, 2, 3, 4, 5\}$

2. $x^2 - x < 6$; $x \in \{-4, -3, -2, \ldots, 1, 2, 3, 4\}$ $\{-1, 0, 1, 2\}$

3. $|4 - 5x| > 13$; $x \in \{0, 1, 2, 3, 4, 5\}$ $\{4, 5\}$

4. $x^2 + 3x + 4 < 10$; $x \in \{-3, -2, -1, 0, 1, 2, 3\}$ $\{-3, -2, -1, 0, 1\}$

5. $x^2 - 4x + 1 > 6$; $x \in \{0, 1, 2, 3, \ldots, 8, 9, 10\}$ $\{6, 7, 8, 9, 10\}$

Mixed Review Exercises

Solve.

1. $x - 5 = 13$ {18}

2. $14 = 2(c + 1)$ {6}

3. $5 - 2a = 17$ {−6}

4. $\dfrac{s}{5} = -10$ {−50}

5. $\dfrac{21}{y} = \dfrac{7}{9}$ {27}

6. $\dfrac{3x + 1}{5} = \dfrac{x + 12}{4}$ {8}

7. $5(2 + n) = 4(n - 6)$ {−34}

8. $(x + 4)(x + 7) = (x + 5)^2$ {−3}

9. $\dfrac{b}{5} + 8 = b$ {10}

10. $\dfrac{x}{4} = \dfrac{x - 3}{5}$ {−12}

11. $\dfrac{3p}{10} + \dfrac{p}{5} = \dfrac{1}{2}$ {1}

12. $\dfrac{1}{3}(x + 9) = 3$ {0}

Biographical Note / Daniel Hale Williams

Daniel Hale Williams (1856–1931) was a pioneer in heart surgery. After serving as a surgeon's apprentice for almost two years, Williams attended Chicago Medical College, and received his diploma in 1883. Dr. Williams opened a medical practice in Chicago's South Side, where he often performed surgery in his office or in patients' homes. Realizing a need for a hospital that would admit and give quality care to all, as well as provide training for doctors and nurses, Williams helped found Provident Hospital, the first interracial hospital in the United States. Williams's colleagues, impressed by his extraordinary techniques and skill, often observed him as he performed surgery.

Dr. Williams's most famous case occurred on July 9, 1893. A young man who had been stabbed in the chest was admitted to the hospital. Risking both his career and his reputation, Williams opened the patient's chest cavity, something no doctor had done before. He cleansed the wound, rejoined an artery, and stitched the membrane surrounding the heart. The operation saved the patient's life and won Williams the praise of the medical world.

The following year Williams was appointed chief surgeon of Freedmen's Hospital in Washington, D.C. Williams completely reorganized and modernized the hospital, adding departments in bacteriology and pathology, and instituting training programs for nurses and interns. In addition to the many honors he received, Williams was elected vice president of the National Medical Association, which he had actively helped to organize.

Inequalities **461**

10-2 Solving Inequalities

Objective   To transform inequalities in order to solve them.

Only the first of the following statements is true:

$$-7 < 4 \qquad -7 = 4 \qquad -7 > 4$$
$$\text{True} \qquad\quad \text{False} \qquad\quad \text{False}$$

When you compare real numbers, you take the *property of comparison* for granted.

Property of Comparison

For all real numbers a and b, one and only one of the following statements is true:

$$a < b, \qquad a = b, \qquad \text{or} \qquad a > b.$$

Suppose you know two facts about the graphs of three numbers a, b, and c.

1. The graph of a is to the left of the graph of b: $a < b$
2. The graph of b is to the left of the graph of c: $b < c$

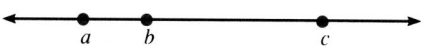

From the graphs above, you can see that the graph of a is to the left of the graph of c: $a < c$.

The facts above illustrate the following property:

Transitive Property of Order

For all real numbers a, b, and c:

1. If $a < b$ and $b < c$, then $a < c$;
2. If $c > b$ and $b > a$, then $c > a$.

What happens when the same number is added to or subtracted from each side of an inequality?

$$\begin{array}{ccc} 3 & < & 6 \\ 3 + 4 & \underline{\ ?\ } & 6 + 4 \\ 7 & < & 10 \end{array} \qquad\qquad \begin{array}{ccc} 3 & < & 6 \\ 3 - 4 & \underline{\ ?\ } & 6 - 4 \\ -1 & < & 2 \end{array}$$

These numerical examples suggest the property of order stated on the next page. (Remember that subtracting a number is the same as adding the opposite of that number.)

462   *Chapter 10*

Addition Property of Order

For all real numbers, a, b, and c:

1. If $a < b$, then $a + c < b + c$;
2. If $a > b$, then $a + c > b + c$.

What happens when each side of the inequality $-4 < 3$ is multiplied by a nonzero real number?

Multiply by 2:
Is $2(-4) < 2(3)$?
Yes, $-8 < 6$.

Multiply by -2:
Is $-2(-4) < -2(3)$?
No, $8 > -6$.

These examples suggest that multiplying each side of an inequality by a *negative* number *reverses the direction,* or order, of the inequality.

Multiplication Property of Order

For all real numbers, a, b, and c such that

$c > 0$ (c is positive):

1. If $a < b$, then $ac < bc$;
2. If $a > b$, then $ac > bc$.

$c < 0$ (c is negative):

1. If $a < b$, then $ac > bc$;
2. If $a > b$, then $ac < bc$.

Multiplying both sides of an inequality by zero does not produce an inequality; the result is the identity $0 = 0$.

The properties that have been stated guarantee that the following transformations of a given inequality always produce an **equivalent inequality,** that is, one with the same solution set.

Transformations That Produce an Equivalent Inequality

1. Substituting for either side of the inequality an expression equivalent to that side.

2. Adding to (or subtracting from) each side of the inequality the same real number.

3. Multiplying (or dividing) each side of the inequality by the same positive number.

4. Multiplying (or dividing) each side of the inequality by the same negative number *and reversing the direction of the inequality*.

To solve an inequality, you usually try to transform it into a simple equivalent inequality whose solution set can be easily seen.

Inequalities   **463**

Solve each inequality and graph its solution set.

2. $2 - 3u \geq 8$
$-3u \geq 6$
$u \leq -2$
{the real numbers less than or equal to -2}

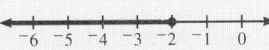

3. $2t - 4 + 5(5 + t) \geq 0$
$2t - 4 + 25 + 5t \geq 0$
$7t + 21 \geq 0$
$7t \geq -21$
$t \geq -3$
{the real numbers greater than or equal to -3}

4. $2(3 - 2x) > 10 - 4x$
$6 - 4x > 10 - 4x$
$6 > 10$
no solution

5. $4y - (1 + y) < 2y + (1 + y)$
$3y - 1 < 3y + 1$
$-1 < 1$
{all real numbers}

Check for Understanding

Here is a suggested use of the Oral Exercises to check students' understanding as you teach the lesson.
Oral Exs. 1–12: use after Example 1.
Oral Exs. 13–18: use after Example 3.

Problem Solving Strategies

A strategy commonly used in algebra involves *transforming a problem into a simpler equivalent problem* in order to solve it. The goal of using transformations with inequalities is to arrive at an equivalent sentence whose solution is easily seen.

Guided Practice

Solve each inequality.

1. $x - 7 \leq 16$ {the real numbers less than or equal to 23}

2. $\frac{p}{-13} < -3$ {the real numbers greater than 39}

3. $a + 4 < a + 1$ no solution

Solve each inequality. Graph the solution set, if there is one.

4. $7j \geq 16j - 18$ {the real numbers less than or equal to 2}

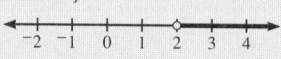

5. $6(2 - x) < 3(x - 2)$ {the real numbers greater than 2}

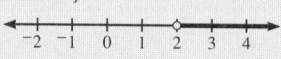

6. $\frac{3}{8}y + 1 \geq \frac{9}{8}$ {the real numbers greater than or equal to $\frac{1}{3}$}

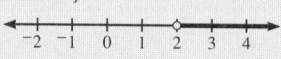

Example 1   Tell how to transform the first inequality into the second one.

  a. $m - 9 < 2$ **b.** $-8k \geq 16$
         $m < 11$ $k \leq -2$

Solution   **a.** Add 9 to each side.   **b.** Divide each side by -8 and reverse the direction of the inequality.

You may assume that the domain of all variables is the set of real numbers unless otherwise stated.

Example 2   Solve $6x - 3 < 7 + 4x$ and graph its solution set.

Solution

$$6x - 3 < 7 + 4x$$
$$6x - 3 + 3 < 7 + 4x + 3 \qquad \text{Add 3 to each side.}$$
$$6x < 10 + 4x$$
$$6x - 4x < 10 + 4x - 4x \qquad \text{Subtract } 4x \text{ from each side.}$$
$$2x < 10$$
$$\frac{2x}{2} < \frac{10}{2} \qquad \text{Divide each side by 2.}$$
$$x < 5$$

∴ the solution set is {the real numbers less than 5}.

The graph is: 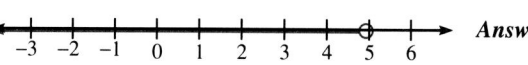 *Answer*

To solve an inequality, you take the same steps used to solve equations:

1. Simplify each side of the inequality as needed.
2. Use the inverse operations to undo any additions or subtractions.
3. Use the inverse operations to undo any multiplications or divisions.

Example 3   Solve $2(w - 8) + 9 \geq 3(4 - w) - 4$ and graph its solution set.

Solution

$$2(w - 8) + 9 \geq 3(4 - w) - 4$$
$$2w - 16 + 9 \geq 12 - 3w - 4$$
$$2w - 7 \geq 8 - 3w$$
$$5w \geq 15$$
$$w \geq 3$$

∴ the solution set is {the real numbers greater than or equal to 3}.

464   *Chapter 10*

The graph is:

Answer

Some inequalities have no solution, and some inequalities are true for all real numbers.

Example 4 Solve $4x > 4(x + 2)$ and graph its solution set.

Solution

$4x > 4(x + 2)$

$4x > 4x + 8$

$0 > 8$

Since $0 > 8$ is false, the original inequality has no solution. There is no graph. *Answer*

Example 5 Solve $y + 5 < 7y - 6(y - 1)$ and graph its solution set.

Solution

$y + 5 < 7y - 6(y - 1)$

$y + 5 < 7y - 6y + 6$

$y + 5 < y + 6$

$5 < 6$

Since $5 < 6$ is true, the original inequality is true for every real number.

∴ the solution set is {the real numbers}, and the graph is the entire number line.

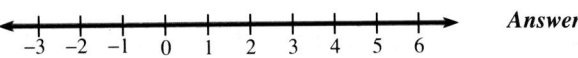
Answer

Oral Exercises

Tell how to transform the first inequality to obtain the second one.

1. $t + 3 < 7$
$\quad t < 4$

2. $r - 5 > 7$
$\quad r > 12$

3. $-1 < x - 2$
$\quad 1 < x$

4. $y + 6 < 0$
$\quad y < -6$

5. $4p < 20$
$\quad p < 5$

6. $3m < -18$
$\quad m < -6$

7. $-6a < 18$
$\quad a > -3$

8. $\frac{x}{2} > 4$
$\quad x > 8$

9. $2 > \frac{v}{7}$
$\quad 14 > v$

10. $\frac{r}{-3} \leq -5$
$\quad r \geq 15$

11. $3y \leq \frac{1}{2}$
$\quad y \leq \frac{1}{6}$

12. $-\frac{t}{2} \geq 0$
$\quad t \leq 0$

Inequalities **465**

Summarizing the Lesson

Tell students that the objective was to learn how to use transformations to solve inequalities. Ask them to explain how the transformations for inequalities are similar to and different from those for equations.

Additional Answers
Oral Exercises

1. Subtr. 3 from both sides.
2. Add 5 to both sides.
3. Add 2 to both sides.
4. Subtr. 6 from both sides.
5. Div. both sides by 4.
6. Div. both sides by 3.
7. Div. both sides by -6 and reverse the direction of the inequality.
8. Mult. both sides by 2.
9. Mult. both sides by 7.
10. Mult. both sides by -3 and reverse the direction of the inequality.
11. Div. both sides by 3.
12. Mult. both sides by -2 and reverse the direction of the inequality.
13. Add 5 to both sides; $y < 13$
14. Subtr. 1 from both sides; $5 < x$
15. Div. both sides by 10; $p > 10$
16. Div. both sides by -2 and reverse the direction of the inequality; $4 < c$
17. Mult. both sides by 2; $w \geq 24$
18. Mult. both sides by -3 and reverse the direction of the inequality; $-6 \geq r$

Explain how to transform each inequality in order to solve it. Then state the transformed inequality.

13. $y - 5 < 8$ **14.** $6 < x + 1$ **15.** $10p > 100$

16. $-8 > -2c$ **17.** $\frac{w}{2} \geq 12$ **18.** $2 \leq -\frac{r}{3}$

Written Exercises

Solve each inequality in Exercises 1–10 and write the letter of its graph.

A

1. $y - 2 \geq 7$ d

2. $10 < z + 8$ a

3. $6p < 24$ j

4. $18 \leq 6v$ h

5. $-28 > -7m$ b

6. $\frac{d}{2} > -10$ g

7. $2 - g > 0$ e

8. $3 \leq \frac{x}{-2}$ i

9. $b - 1 < b - 2$ f

10. $t + 2 > t + 1$ c

a.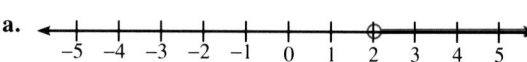

b.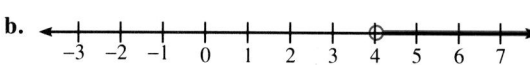

c.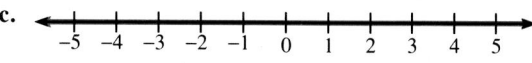

d.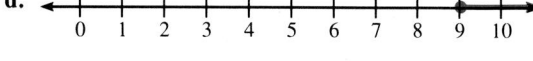

e.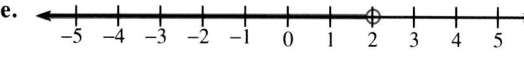

f.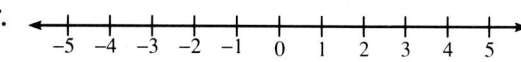

g.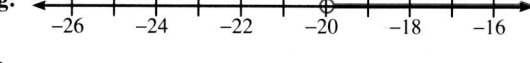

h.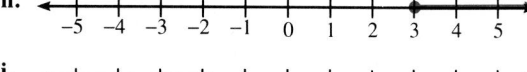

i.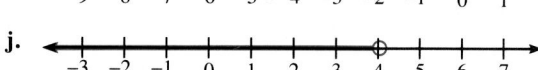

j.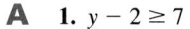

Solve each inequality. Graph the solution set, if there is one.

11. $n - 4 > 11$ **12.** $a + 3 < 11$ **13.** $-\frac{y}{2} > 4$

14. $4q < 12$ **15.** $36 < \frac{x}{-9}$ **16.** $-6 > \frac{s}{3}$

17. $-6m \geq 6$ **18.** $-5w \leq 15$ **19.** $\frac{x}{2} - 4 > -6$

20. $2v + 1 > 7$ **21.** $-\frac{d}{3} \geq 0$ **22.** $7 \geq 2k - 7$

23. $\frac{3}{2}t - 7 < 2$

24. $-4 \geq 4 - \frac{u}{2}$

25. $-1 < 9 + \frac{2}{3}g$

26. $5 + \frac{x}{3} \leq 6$

27. $12 - \frac{3}{2}c > 0$

28. $0 > 6 - \frac{2}{3}d$

29. $5y < 4y + 6$

30. $3f - 4 < 2f + 5$

31. $4r - 5 < 5r + 7$

32. $8 - 2b > 4 - b$

33. $2(x - 4) \leq 6$

34. $8 < 2(4 - m)$

35. $-5(x + 3) < -5x + 1$

36. $7a < 3 + 7(a - 1)$

37. $5(1 - t) > 4(3 - t)$

38. $4(2 - v) \geq -(v - 5)$

39. $\frac{5}{6}r + 1 \geq \frac{4}{3}$

40. $\frac{3}{4} < 6 - \frac{1}{2}a$

B 41. $5(x - 1) > \frac{5}{4}x$

42. $\frac{1}{2}y \geq 2(y - 3)$

43. $n - \frac{5}{2} > \frac{3}{4}(n - 6)$

44. $3w - \frac{1}{2}(2w + 8) > 0$

45. $5(5 - k) - 7(7 + k) < 0$

46. $5(v - 1) > 3(v + 4) - 5$

47. $4\left(r - \frac{1}{2}\right) - 3 \leq 5(r - 1) + 4$

48. $4(t + 1) - 2(t - 1) \leq 3 - t$

49. $5 - a + 6(a - 2) \geq 5(a + 1)$

50. $5(2b + 1) - 3(b + 1) < 7b + 5$

Given that a and b are real numbers such that $a > b$, describe the real numbers c, if any, for which each statement is true.

All real numbers   No real numbers   All pos. real numbers   All neg. real numbers

C 51. $a + c > b + c$ **52.** $a - c < b - c$ **53.** $ac > bc$ **54.** $ac < bc$

55. $ac = bc$ **56.** $\frac{a}{c} > \frac{b}{c}$ **57.** $\frac{a}{c} < \frac{b}{c}$ **58.** $ac^2 < bc^2$

0   All pos. real numbers   All neg. real numbers   No real numbers

Given that a and b are real numbers such that $a > b > 0$, classify each of the following statements as true or false. If you classify a statement as false, give an example of values for which it is false.

59. $a > 0$ T   **60.** $a^2 > a$ F; $a = \frac{1}{2}$ **61.** $\frac{a}{b} > 0$ T   **62.** $a + b > b$ T

63. $a^2 > b$ F;   **64.** $a - b > 0$ T   **65.** $\frac{a}{b} > \frac{b}{a}$ T   **66.** $a^2 > b^2$ T
    $a = \frac{1}{2}, b = \frac{1}{3}$

Mixed Review Exercises

Classify each statement as true or false.

1. $-(-2) < |-3|$ T

2. $|-3| \geq |3|$ T

3. $|-13| < |-12|$ F

4. $5(4 + 3 \cdot 2) = 70$ F

5. $2x + 10 = 2(x + 5)$ T

6. $(x + 3)(x + 7) = x^2 + 10x$ F

Solve.

7. $3f - 4 = 2f + 5$ {9}

8. $0 = 2x + 5$ $\left\{-\frac{5}{2}\right\}$

9. $a(a + 5) = (a - 9)(a - 7)$ {3}

10. $4y - 2(y + 1) = -6$ {−2}

11. $p - 2(6 - p) = -p$ {3}

12. $3b + 2(b + 1) = b + 6$ {1}

23. {the real numbers less than 6}

24. {the real numbers greater than or equal to 16}

25. {the real numbers greater than −15}

26. {the real numbers less than or equal to 3}

27. {the real numbers less than 8}

28. {the real numbers greater than 9}

29. {the real numbers less than 6}

30. {the real numbers less than 9}

31. {the real numbers greater than −12}

32. {the real numbers less than 4}

33. {the real numbers less than or equal to 7}

34. {the real numbers less than 0}

35. {all real numbers}

36. no solution

37. {the real numbers less than −7}

38. {the real numbers less than or equal to 1}

39. {the real numbers greater than or equal to $\frac{2}{5}$}

40. {the real numbers less than $\frac{21}{2}$}

41. {the real numbers greater than $\frac{4}{3}$}

42. {the real numbers less than or equal to 4}

43. {the real numbers greater than −8}

44. {the real numbers greater than 2}

45. {the real numbers greater than −2}

46. {the real numbers greater than 6}

(continued)

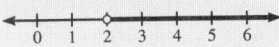
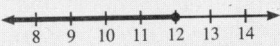

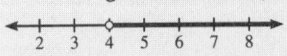
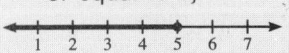
Reading Algebra / *Inequalities*

When working with inequalities, it is important to read both the symbols and the words slowly and carefully. Unlike equations, which involve only one sign, $=$, inequalities can contain any of the four inequality symbols, $<$, $>$, $\leq$, or $\geq$. Whichever symbol is used determines what your answer will be. For example, the equation $2x + 6 = 14$ is equivalent to $x = 4$, and the solution set is simply {4}. However, the inequalities

$$2x + 6 < 14, \qquad 2x + 6 > 14, \qquad 2x + 6 \leq 14, \qquad \text{and } 2x + 6 \geq 14$$

all have different solution sets.

$2x + 6 < 14$ is equivalent to $x < 4$. The solution set is {the real numbers less than 4}.

$2x + 6 > 14$ is equivalent to $x > 4$. The solution set is {the real numbers greater than 4}.

$2x + 6 \leq 14$ is equivalent to $x \leq 4$. The solution set is {the real numbers less than or equal to 4}.

$2x + 6 \geq 14$ is equivalent to $x \geq 4$. The solution set is {the real numbers greater than or equal to 4}.

Word problems involving inequalities also require very careful reading. An important step in solving this type of problem is determining which inequality symbol to use. Is the problem asking for a number that is less than, greater than, less than or equal to, or greater than or equal to a particular number or expression? Before you write your inequality you should be certain that you will use the correct symbol.

Exercises

For each of the following:

a. Determine whether the inequality symbol means less than, greater than, less than or equal to, or greater than or equal to.

b. Determine whether the graph has a closed circle or an open circle and whether the graph goes to the right or the left of that circle.

c. Solve and graph the solution.

1. $x - 3 > 12$

2. $3y + 1 > 7$

3. $5 \geq 2y - 3$

4. $12 + y \leq 24$

5. $-9 < 21 + 2m$

6. $-6 \leq 6 - k$

7. $18 - 3y > 0$

8. $1 + 3r \geq 5 - r$

9. $2x - 3 < 4x + 5$

10. $21 - 15x < -8x - 7$

11. $4(t - 2) > 5(t - 3)$

12. $6(z - 5) \leq 15 + 5(7 - 2z)$

10-3 Solving Problems Involving Inequalities

Objective   To solve problems that involve inequalities.

Example 1   Molly set her car's trip odometer at zero at the start of her trip home. When the odometer showed that she had driven 16 mi, a highway sign showed her that she was still more than 25 mi from her home. What is the minimum total distance, to the nearest mile, that she will have traveled when she arrives home?

Solution

Step 1   The problem asks for the minimum total distance Molly will have traveled.

Step 2   Choose a variable to represent the total distance.
Let d = the total distance in miles.
Then $d - 16$ = the distance from the sign to home.

Step 3   Use the variable to write an inequality based on the given information.
The distance from the sign to home is more than 25 mi.

$$d - 16 \qquad > \qquad 25$$

Step 4   Solve the open sentence: $d - 16 > 25$
$$d > 41$$

The smallest integer that is greater than 41 is 42.
Thus the minimum distance traveled is 42 mi.

Step 5   *Check:*   Is the distance from the sign to home more than 25 mi?
$$42 - 16 \overset{?}{>} 25$$
$$26 > 25 \quad \checkmark$$

Is the distance the least possible?
Suppose the distance is the next smaller integer, 41.
$$41 - 16 \overset{?}{>} 25$$
$$25 > 25 \quad \text{False}$$

∴ the minimum total distance Molly will have traveled is 42 mi.   *Answer*

To translate phrases such as "is at least" and "is no less than" or "is at most" and "is no more than" into mathematical terms, you use the symbols $\geq$ or $\leq$. For example:

The age of the tree is at least 70 years:	$a \geq 70$
The rent is no less than $400 per month:	$r \geq 400$
The price of the paperback book is at most $5.95:	$p \leq 5.95$
Her time in the 10 km race was no more than 40 min:	$t \leq 40$

Inequalities   **469**

Teaching Suggestions p. T127
Reading Algebra p. T128
Suggested Extensions p. T128

Warm-Up Exercises

Express each quantity in terms of k.

1. the value in cents of k quarters $25k$

2. the time needed to travel 100 km at k km/h $\dfrac{100}{k}$

3. the area of a rectangle measuring 23 m by k m $23k$

4. the cost of a k-minute telephone call, if the first minute costs $0.40 and each additional minute is $0.30 $0.40 + 0.30(k - 1)$

5. the perimeter of a rectangle that measures 2.5 ft by k ft $5 + 2k$

Motivating the Lesson

Part of being human is solving problems. Problems, mathematical and otherwise, don't come nicely packaged and organized for us. We have to be able to take problems in their "raw" form and convert them into a mathematically manageable form, as is done in today's lesson.

Chalkboard Examples

1. Before going shopping, Mel had $28. After cashing a check, he had more than $75. What is the amount of the check Mel cashed?
Let c = amount of check.
$28 + c > 75$, so $c > 47$.
∴ Mel cashed a check for more than $47.

(continued)

2. Postage is $.25 for the first ounce and $.20 for each additional ounce. How heavy a package, to the nearest ounce, can Marcella send if she wants to spend no more than $2.25?
   Let w = weight in oz of package.
   $0.25 + 0.20(w - 1) \le 2.25$
   $0.25 + 0.20w - 0.20 \le 2.25$
   $0.05 + 0.20w \le 2.25$
   $0.20w \le 2.20$
   $w \le 11$
   ∴ Marcella can send a package weighing 11 oz or less.

3. The width of a poster is 8 cm less than the length. The perimeter is more than 184 cm. If the measurements are both integers, find the minimum dimensions of the poster.
   Let L = length in cm.
   $2L + 2(L - 8) > 184$
   $2L + 2L - 16 > 184$
   $4L - 16 > 184$
   $4L > 200$
   $L > 50$
   ∴ the minimum dimensions are 51 cm by 43 cm.

Thinking Skills

In these problems, a mathematical solution is not enough. Students need to *evaluate* solutions to see whether they meet all the criteria of the problem.

Problem Solving Strategies

The *five-step plan for solving problems* is used in Section 10-3. It provides a framework for analyzing problems and formulating a solution. Emphasize the checking process.

Example 2 Mike wants to rent a car for his vacation. The rental costs $125 a week plus $.15 a mile. How far to the nearest mile can Mike travel if he wants to spend at most $200?

Solution

Step 1 The problem asks for the number of miles Mike can travel.

Step 2 Let m = the number of miles Mike can travel.

Step 3 Cost of car rental is at most $200.

$$125 + 0.15m \quad \le \quad 200$$

Step 4 $125 + 0.15m \le 200$
$0.15m \le 75$
$m \le 500$

∴ Mike can travel 500 mi or less and still spend no more than $200.

Step 5 *Check:* Is the number of miles the most possible?
Suppose Mike traveled 501 mi.
$$125 + 0.15(501) \overset{?}{\le} 200$$
$$200.15 \le 200 \quad \text{False}$$

∴ Mike can travel at most 500 mi. **Answer**

Example 3 The width of a rectangular computer screen is 20 cm less than twice the length. The perimeter is at least 53 cm. Find the minimum dimensions, in centimeters, of the screen if each dimension is an integer.

Solution

Step 1 The problems asks for the minimum length and width in centimeters.

You are told that:
a. the length and width are integers;
b. the width is 20 cm less than twice the length;
c. the perimeter is at least 53 cm.

Step 2 Let l = the length in centimeters.
Then $2l - 20$ = the width in centimeters.

Step 3 The perimeter is at least 53 cm.

$$2l + 2(2l - 20) \quad \ge \quad 53$$

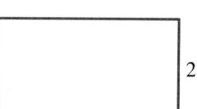

$2l - 20$

l

Step 4 $2l + 2(2l - 20) \geq 53$

$2l + 4l - 40 \geq 53$

$6l - 40 \geq 53$

$6l \geq 93$

$l \geq 15.5$

∴ the minimum integral length is 16 cm.
The minimum width is $2(16) - 20$, or 12 cm.

Step 5 Check: Is the perimeter at least 56 cm?

$2(16) + 2(12) \overset{?}{\geq} 56$

$56 \geq 56$ ✓

Are the dimensions the least possible?
Suppose the length is the next smaller integer, 15.
Then the width would be $2(15) - 20$, or 10 cm.
Is the perimeter at least 56 cm?

$2(15) + 2(10) \overset{?}{\geq} 56$

$50 \geq 56$ False

∴ the dimensions are 16 cm and 12 cm. **Answer**

Written Exercises

For each of the following:
a. Choose a variable to represent the number indicated in color.
b. Use the variable to write an inequality based on the given information.
   (Do not solve.)

A 1. Ilene, who is not yet 21 years old, is two years older than Ida.
   (Ida's age) **a.** i **b.** $i + 2 < 21$

2. After addressing 75 envelopes, a political volunteer has fewer than 26 envelopes left to address. **a.** e **b.** $e - 75 < 26$
   (the total number of envelopes the volunteer needs to address)

3. A sales executive traveled a certain number of kilometers by airplane and then one tenth as far by automobile. Her total trip was more than 3000 km.
   a. x **b.** $x + 0.1x > 3000$

4. Clark and John cut the grass of a neighbor's lawn. Clark started the job and then John finished the job, working $\frac{1}{2}$ hour longer than Clark. The job took at least 2 hours. **a.** c **b.** $c + \left(c + \frac{1}{2}\right) \geq 2$
   (the number of hours Clark worked)

5. Beth's balance in her checking account is $75. She must deposit enough money in her account to be able to pay the telephone bill, which is $110.
   (the amount of deposit) **a.** d **b.** $75 + d \geq 110$

Inequalities **471**

Guided Practice

Choose a variable to represent the number indicated in parentheses, and use it to write an inequality based on the given information. (Do not solve.)

1. Maria, who is older than her 12-year-old brother, is 4 years younger than Sue. (Sue's age)
   $s - 4 > 12$

2. The sum of four consecutive integers is at most 100. (smallest integer)
   $n + (n + 1) + (n + 2) + (n + 3) \leq 100$

3. Fred has one third as many $10 bills as $20 bills. He has at least $300. (number of $20 bills)
   $20t + 10 \cdot \frac{1}{3}t \geq 300$

Solve.

4. After serving 45 lb of poultry, a caterer had more than 10 lb left. How many pounds of poultry did the caterer have originally? more than 55 lb

5. Sonya is a waitress. She earns $200 a week plus a 15% tip on the cost of each meal she serves. What must be the total cost of the meals she serves in order for her to earn at least $425 each week? $1500 or more

6. The length of a rectangle is 6 cm shorter than its width. The perimeter is at least 60 cm. What are the smallest possible dimensions for the rectangle? 12 cm by 18 cm

For each of the following:

a. Choose a variable to represent the number indicated in color.

b. Use the variable to write an inequality based on the given information. (Do not solve.)

6. The length of a rectangle is 4 cm longer than the width. The perimeter is no more than 28 cm. **a.** w **b.** $2w + 2(w + 4) \leq 28$

7. In a marathon Peter ran 15 more kilometers than half the number Juan ran. Peter ran at most 36 km. **a.** j **b.** $\frac{j}{2} + 15 \leq 36$

8. The cost for Rhoda to operate her car for one month was at least \$190. The cost for gas and repairs was one half the amount of the monthly payment on the car loan. **a.** p **b.** $p + \frac{p}{2} \geq 190$

9. The sum of three consecutive odd integers is no less than 51. (the middle integer) **a.** m **b.** $(m - 2) + m + (m + 2) \geq 51$

10. The product of two consecutive odd integers is at most 255. (the greater integer) **10. a.** g **b.** $g(g - 2) \leq 255$

                    11. a. t **b.** $86t + 78t \geq 650$

B 11. Two trucks start from the same point at the same time, but travel in opposite directions. One truck travels at 86 km/h, the other at 78 km/h. After some hours of traveling, the trucks are at least 650 km apart.

12. If a motorist drove 10 mi/h faster, then he would travel farther in 3 h than he does in 4 h at his present speed. **a.** s **b.** $3(s + 10) > 4s$

13. A coin bank containing only nickels, dimes, and quarters has twice as many nickels as dimes and one third as many quarters as nickels. The total value of the coins does not exceed \$2.80. (the number of dimes) **a.** d **b.** $10d + 5(2d) + 25\left(\frac{2d}{3}\right) \leq 280$

14. At a school cafeteria, a student paid \$1.25 for a whole-wheat muffin and a glass of milk. The milk cost less than two thirds of the cost of the muffin. **a.** m **b.** $125 - m < \frac{2}{3}m$

15. A dowel 25 cm long is cut into two pieces. One piece is at least 1 cm longer than twice the length of the shorter piece. **a.** s **b.** $25 - s \geq 2s + 1$

16. The greater of two consecutive even integers is at most 50 less than five times the smaller. **a.** s **b.** $s + 2 \leq 5s - 50$

17. The sum of two consecutive even integers is no more than 100 less than one eighth of the smaller integer. **a.** s **b.** $s + (s + 2) \leq \frac{s}{8} - 100$

18. The sum of three consecutive odd integers is more than 60 decreased by twice the smallest of the three integers. (the greatest integer) **a.** g **b.** $(g - 4) + (g - 2) + g > 60 - 2(g - 4)$

In Exercises 19–20, express in symbols the property that is stated in words.

C 19. The absolute value of the sum of two real numbers is no greater than the sum of the absolute values of the numbers. $|a + b| \leq |a| + |b|$

20. The sum of the squares of two integers is no less than twice the product of the integers. $m^2 + n^2 \geq 2mn$

Problems

Solve. **8.** Shelley, at least 21 cassettes; Terry, at most 29 cassettes

A **1.** After selling a dozen copies of the *Daily Bulletin,* a newsdealer had fewer less than 87 copies than 75 copies left. How many copies did the newsdealer have originally?

2. A house and lot together cost more than $89,000. The house costs $1000 more than seven times the cost of the lot. How much does the lot cost? more than $11,000

3. Martha wants to rent a car for a week and to pay no more than $130. How far can she drive if the car rental costs $94 a week plus $.12 a mile? 300 mi or less

4. Jordan's salary is $1250 a month plus a 5% commission on all his sales. What must the amount of his sales be to earn at least $1500 each month? $5000 or more

5. The sum of two consecutive integers is less than 55. Find the pair of integers with the greatest sum. 26 and 27

6. The sum of two consecutive even integers is at most 400. Find the pair of integers with the greatest sum. 198 and 200

7. Two trucks start from the same point at the same time and go in opposite directions. One truck travels at 88 km/h and the other travels at 72 km/h. How long must they travel to be at least 672 km apart? at least 4.2 h

8. Between them, Terry and Shelley have 50 cassettes. If Shelley has more than two thirds as many cassettes as Terry, at least how many cassettes does Shelley have? At most how many does Terry have?

9. A bag contains 100 marbles, some red, the rest blue. If there are no more than $1\frac{1}{2}$ times as many red marbles as blue ones in the bag, at most how many red marbles are in the bag? At least how many blue ones are in the bag? 60 red marbles; 40 blue marbles

10. Ken has 22 coins, some of which are dimes and the rest are quarters. Altogether, the coins are worth more than $3.40. At least how many of the coins are quarters? At most how many are dimes? at least 9 quarters; at most 13 dimes

11. The length of a rectangle is 4 cm longer than the width, and the perimeter is at least 48 cm. What are the smallest possible dimensions for the rectangle? 10 cm by 14 cm

12. A pair of consecutive integers has the property that 7 times the smaller is less than 6 times the greater. What are the greatest such integers? 5 and 6

B **13.** At 1 P.M. two trains, traveling toward each other, leave from towns that are 312 km apart. One train averages at most 82 km/h, and the other at most 74 km/h. What is the earliest possible time for them to meet? 3 P.M.

Inequalities   **473**

14. If Maura were able to increase her average cycling speed by 3.5 km/h, she would be able to cover in 2 h a distance at least as great as that which now takes 3 h. What is her best average speed at present? 7 km/h

15. There are three exams in a marking period. A student received grades of 75 and 81 on the first two exams. What grade must the student earn on the last exam to get an average of no less than 80 for the marking period? 84

16. Betty earns a salary of $14,000 per year plus an 8% commission on all her sales. How much must her sales be if her annual income is to be no less than $15,600? at least $20,000

17. A mechanic earns $20 an hour, but 25% of his earnings are deducted for taxes and various types of insurance. What is the least number of hours the mechanic must work in order to have no less than $450 in after-tax income? 30 h

18. At least how many grams of copper must be alloyed with 387 g of pure silver to produce an alloy that is no more than 90% pure silver? 43 g

19. Randy walked at the rate of 5.2 km/h in a straight path from his campsite to a ranch. He returned immediately on horseback at the rate of 7.8 km/h. Upon his return, he found that he had been gone no more than 3.5 h. At most how far is it from his campsite to the ranch? 10.92 km

20. The length of a rectangle exceeds the width by 10 cm. If each dimension were increased by 3 cm, the area would be no less than 111 cm^2 more. What are the least possible dimensions of the rectangle? 12 cm by 22 cm

C 21. During the first week of their vacation trip, the Gomez family spent $200 more than three fifths of their vacation money and had more than $400 less than half of it left. If they started their trip with a whole number of dollars, what was the greatest amount of vacation money they could have had? $1999

22. Three consecutive integers have the property that the difference of the squares of the middle integer and the least integer exceeds the largest integer by more than 3. Find the three smallest consecutive integers having this property. 5, 6, and 7

23. Verna decided to sell her collection of paperback books. To Fred, she sold 2 books, and one fifth of what was left. Later to Joan she sold 6 books, and one fifth of what then remained. If she sold more books to Fred than to Joan, what was the least possible number of books in her original collection? 97 books

474 *Chapter 10*

Mixed Review Exercises

Solve.

1. $|s| = 7$ $\{-7, 7\}$

2. $|2 - 5| = k$ $\{3\}$

3. $|y| - 2 = 10$ $\{-12, 12\}$

4. $3|b| = 12$ $\{-4, 4\}$

5. $x = |-2 - (-6)|$ $\{4\}$

6. $p = -|7 - 10|$ $\{-3\}$

Factor completely.

7. $x^2 + 15x + 36$ $(x + 3)(x + 12)$

8. $x^3 - 5x^2 - 24x$ $x(x + 3)(x - 8)$

9. $49x^2 - 25$ $(7x - 5)(7x + 5)$

10. $2y^2 + y - 3$ $(2y + 3)(y - 1)$

11. $x^2 + 6xy + 9y^2$ $(x + 3y)^2$

12. $16x^3 - 4x$ $4x(2x - 1)(2x + 1)$

Self-Test 1

Vocabulary   inequality (p. 458)   sides of an inequality (p. 458)   solutions of an inequality (p. 458)   solution set of an inequality (p. 458)   graph of an inequality (p. 458)   equivalent inequalities (p. 463)

1. Translate "-3 is between -7 and -2" into symbols. $-7 < -3 < -2$ **Obj. 10-1, p. 457**

2. Solve $4x + 7 \le 15$ if the domain of x is $\{-3, -2, -1, 0, 1, 2, 3\}$. $\{-3, -2, -1, 0, 1, 2\}$

Solve and graph.

3. $r - 4 < -3$ **4.** $5 - 3t \le 20$ **Obj. 10-2, p. 462**

Solve.

5. A purse contains 26 coins, some of which are dimes and the rest nickels. Altogether, the coins are worth more than $2.10. At least how many dimes are in the purse? at least 17 dimes   **Obj. 10-3, p. 469**

Check your answers with those at the back of the book.

Challenge

What is wrong with the following "proof" that $0 > 3$?

$$a > 3$$
$$3a > 3(3)$$
$$3a - a^2 > 9 - a^2$$
$$a(3 - a) > (3 - a)(3 + a) \leftarrow \text{If you divide by } 3 - a, \text{ which is negative}$$
$$a > 3 + a \qquad \text{(because } a > 3\text{), then the inequality must}$$
$$\therefore 0 > 3 \qquad \text{be reversed so that } Step\ 5 \text{ is } a < 3 + a.$$

Inequalities   **475**

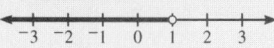
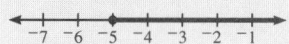
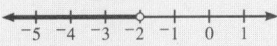
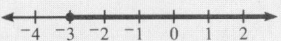

The diagrams below, called *Venn diagrams,* show how shading can be used to represent the relationships among the sets:

$$A = \{1, 2, 3, 4, 5\}$$
$$B = \{2, 4, 6\}$$
$$C = \{7, 8\}$$

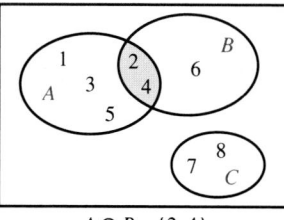

$$A \cap B = \{2, 4\}$$

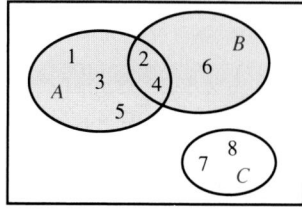

$$A \cup B = \{1, 2, 3, 4, 5, 6\}$$

To find the *intersection* of A and B, we shade the region consisting of those members and only those members *common to both* set A and set B. From the diagram at the left above, you can see that the intersection of $\{1, 2, 3, 4, 5\}$ and $\{2, 4, 6\}$ is $\{2, 4\}$. This is written

$$\{1, 2, 3, 4, 5\} \cap \{2, 4, 6\} = \{2, 4\}.$$

Notice in the diagrams that the regions A and C do not overlap. Two sets, such as A and C, that have no members in common are called *disjoint sets.* Their intersection is the empty set: $A \cap C = \emptyset$.

In the diagram at the right above, we shade the region consisting of the members that belong to *at least one* of the sets A and B, in order to find the *union* of A and B. This diagram shows that the union of $\{1, 2, 3, 4, 5\}$ and $\{2, 4, 6\}$ is $\{1, 2, 3, 4, 5, 6\}$. This is written

$$\{1, 2, 3, 4, 5\} \cup \{2, 4, 6\} = \{1, 2, 3, 4, 5, 6\}.$$

Exercises

Refer to the diagram and list the members of each of the following sets.

{0, 1, 2, 5, 6, 7, 8, 9}

1. $D \cap E$ {6, 9}

2. $D \cup E$

3. $E \cup F$ {0, 3, 4, 5, 6, 7, 8, 9}

4. $E \cap F$ {6, 7, 8}

5. $(D \cap E) \cap F$ {6}

6. $D \cup (E \cap F)$ {1, 2, 5, 6, 7, 8, 9}

7. $D \cap (E \cup F)$ {5, 6, 9}

8. $(D \cup E) \cup F$ {0, 1, 2, 3, 4, 5, 6, 7, 8, 9}

9. $(D \cap F) \cup (E \cap F)$ {5, 6, 7, 8}

10. Express $\{6, 7, 8, 9\}$ in terms of D, E, and F.
$(D \cap E) \cup (E \cap F)$

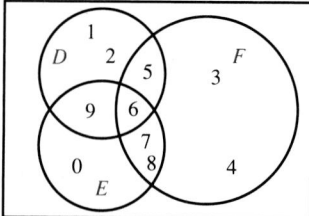

11. $\cup = \{-4, -3, -2, -1, 0\}$; $\cap = \{-3, -2\}$ 12. $\cup = \{-1, 0, 1, 2, 3\}$; $\cap = \{0, 1\}$

Specify the union and the intersection of the given sets. If the sets are disjoint, say so. 13. $\cup = \{3, 4, 5, 6, 7, 8\}$; $\cap = \emptyset$ (disjoint)   14. $\cup = \{5, 6, 7, 8, 9\}$; $\cap = \{6, 8\}$

11. $\{-2, -3, -4\}$, $\{-3, -2, -1, 0\}$

13. $\{3, 5, 7\}$, $\{4, 6, 8\}$

15. $\{3, 4, 6, 8, 12\}$, $\{2, 4, 6, 8, 10\}$
$\cup = \{2, 3, 4, 6, 8, 10, 12\}$; $\cap = \{4, 6, 8\}$

12. $\{-1, 0, 1\}$, $\{0, 1, 2, 3\}$

14. $\{6, 8\}$, $\{5, 6, 7, 8, 9\}$

16. $\{-5, -4, -3\}$, $\{-2, -1, 0\}$
$\cup = \{-5, -4, -3, -2, -1, 0\}$; $\cap = \emptyset$ (disjoint)

In Exercises 17–24, refer to the number lines shown and describe each set.

$P = \{$the real numbers greater than $-1\}$
$Q = \{$the real numbers between -3 and $3\}$
$R = \{$the real numbers less than $2\}$

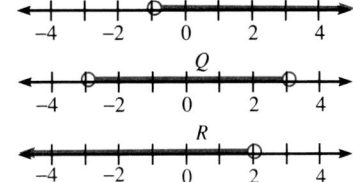

17. $P \cap R$ 18. $P \cap Q$ 19. $P \cup Q$

20. $P \cup R$ 21. $Q \cap R$ 22. $Q \cup R$

23. $P \cap (Q \cap R)$ 24. $P \cup (Q \cap R)$

For each of Exercises 25 and 26, make two enlarged copies of the diagram shown at the right. Shade the regions representing the sets named.

25. $X \cap (Y \cup Z)$; $(X \cap Y) \cup (X \cap Z)$

26. $X \cup (Y \cap Z)$; $(X \cup Y) \cap (X \cup Z)$

27. State a "distributive axiom" that appears to be true on the basis of Exercise 25.

28. State a "distributive axiom" that appears to be true on the basis of Exercise 26.

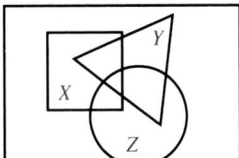

29. Copy the diagram at the right and write in the remaining members of these sets:

$$J = \{1, 3, 5, 7, 9\}$$
$$K = \{-3, -1, 1, 3, 4\}$$
$$L = \{1, 2, 3, 4, 5, 6, 7\}$$
$$M = \{3, 4, 5, 6, 7\}$$

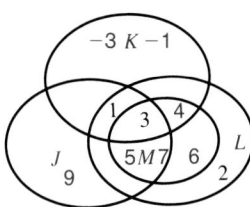

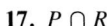 **Historical Note / *The Seqt of a Pyramid***

To check the uniform slope of the faces of a pyramid, the ancient Egyptians determined the pyramid's seqt. "Seqt" was the ratio of rise to run. (Modern architects use the same ratio to describe slope.) The units of measurement were fingers, hands, and cubits. There were four fingers in a hand and seven hands in a cubit.

Problems 56 and 57 of the Rhind mathematical papyrus, a collection of practical problems copied from an earlier document by the scribe Ahmes about 1550 B.C., deal with the seqt of a pyramid. Problem 56 asks for the seqt of a pyramid 250 cubits high having a square base of 360 cubits on a side. Problem 57 asks for the height of a pyramid having a square base 140 cubits on a side and a seqt of 5 hands and 1 finger per cubit.

Inequalities   477

Additional Answers
Extra

17. {the real numbers between -1 and 2}

18. {the real numbers between -1 and 3}

19. {the real numbers greater than -3}

20. {the real numbers}

21. {the real numbers between -3 and 2}

22. {the real numbers less than 3}

23. {the real numbers between -1 and 2}

24. {the real numbers greater than -3}

25–26. The two diagrams for each exercise are identical.

25.

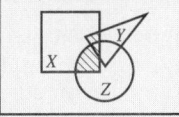

26.

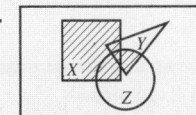

27. $X \cap (Y \cup Z) = (X \cap Y) \cup (X \cap Z)$

28. $X \cup (Y \cap Z) = (X \cup Y) \cap (X \cup Z)$

29.

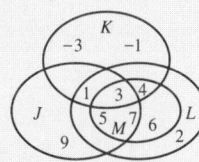

Teaching Suggestions p. T128
Using Manipulatives p. T128
Suggested Extensions p. T128

Warm-Up Exercises

As a review of Lessons 10-2 and 10-3, have students write a paragraph outlining the transformations used in solving the inequality $5 - 3x > -4$.

Answers will vary.

$5 - 3x > -4$

$\quad -3x > -9$ Add -5

$\qquad x < 3$ Divide by -3 and reverse the direction of the inequality.

Motivating the Lesson

In ordinary language we use words such as "and," "or," and "but" to form compound sentences. In algebra, open sentences can be combined. In this lesson students will learn the special mathematical meanings of "and" and "or."

Chalkboard Examples

Draw the graph of each open sentence.

1. conjunction: $x > -3$ and $x \le -3$ No real number can be both greater than -3 and less than or equal to -3. Empty set, no graph.

2. disjunction: $x > -3$ or $x \le -3$ Every real number is either greater than -3 or less than or equal to -3. {all real numbers}

10-4 Solving Combined Inequalities

Objective   To find the solution sets of combined inequalities.

Each of the four sentences below involves one or two inequalities.

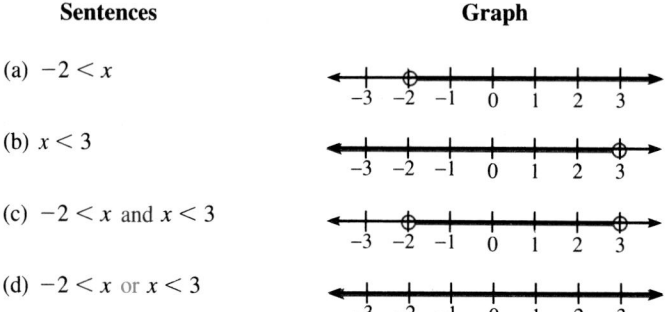

| Sentences | Graph |

(a) $-2 < x$

(b) $x < 3$

(c) $-2 < x$ and $x < 3$

(d) $-2 < x$ or $x < 3$

The sentence in (c) is formed by joining the sentences in (a) and (b) by the word *and*. Such a sentence is called a **conjunction**. To **solve a conjunction** of two open sentences in a given variable, you find the values of the variable for which *both* sentences are true. Note that the conjunction $-2 < x$ and $x < 3$ can be written as

$$-2 < x < 3.$$

The graph of the conjunction consists of the points common to *both* the graph of $-2 < x$ and the graph of $x < 3$. (Notice where the graphs in (a) and (b) overlap.)

In (d) above, the inequalities in (a) and (b) have been joined by the word *or*. Such a sentence is called a **disjunction**. To **solve a disjunction** of two open sentences, you find the values of the variable for which *at least one* of the sentences is true (that is, one or the other or both are true). The graph consists of all points that are in the graph of (a), the graph of (b), or both.

Remember (page 457) that the disjunction

$$y > 2 \text{ or } y = 2$$

is usually written "$y \ge 2$." Similarly, "$y \le 2$" means

$$y < 2 \text{ or } y = 2.$$

Example 1   Draw the graph of each open sentence.

   a. conjunction: $t < 5$ and $t \ge 5$ **b.** disjunction: $t < 5$ or $t \ge 5$

Solution   **a.** No real number can be less than 5 and also greater than or equal to 5.

∴ the solution set is the empty set, and it has no graph.   *Answer*

b. Every real number is either less than 5 or greater than or equal to 5.

∴ the solution set is {the real numbers}, and its graph contains every point.

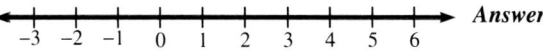   *Answer*

To solve conjunctions and disjunctions of inequalities, you use the transformations listed on page 463.

Example 2   Solve the conjunction $-3 \leq x - 2 < 4$ and graph its solution set.

Solution   To solve the inequality $-3 \leq x - 2 < 4$, you solve the conjunction:

$$-3 \leq x - 2 \qquad \text{and} \qquad x - 2 < 4$$
$$-3 + 2 \leq x - 2 + 2 \qquad \Big| \qquad x - 2 + 2 < 4 + 2$$
$$-1 \leq x \qquad \text{and} \qquad x < 6$$

$$-1 \leq x < 6$$

∴ the solution set is $\{-1,$ and all the real numbers between -1 and $6\}$.

The graph is:

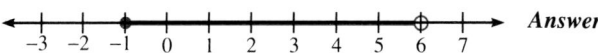   *Answer*

Below is a more compact way of solving the conjunction in Example 2:

$$-3 \leq x - 2 < 4$$
$$-3 + 2 \leq x - 2 + 2 < 4 + 2$$
$$-1 \leq x < 6$$

Example 3   Solve the disjunction $2w - 1 < 3$ or $3w \geq w + 10$ and graph its solution set.

Solution
$$2w - 1 < 3 \qquad \text{or} \qquad 3w \geq w + 10$$
$$2w - 1 + 1 < 3 + 1 \qquad \Big| \qquad 3w - w \geq w + 10 - w$$
$$2w < 4 \qquad \qquad 2w \geq 10$$
$$w < 2 \qquad \text{or} \qquad w \geq 5$$

∴ the solution set is $\{5,$ and the real numbers greater than 5 or less than 2$\}$.

The graph is:

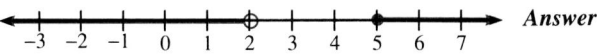   *Answer*

Inequalities   **479**

Solve each open sentence and graph its solution set.

3. $-2 < m + 1 \leq 4$
  $-2 < m + 1$ and $m + 1 \leq 4$
  $-3 < m$ and $m \leq 3$
  {3, and the real numbers between -3 and 3}

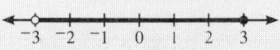

4. $1 + 5y < -4$ or $4y > y + 9$
  $5y < -5$ or $3y > 9$
  $y < -1$ or $y > 3$
  {the real numbers less than -1 or greater than 3}

Check for Understanding

Here is a suggested use of the Oral Exercises to check students' understanding as you teach the lesson.

Oral Exs. 1–12: use after the discussion of sentences (a)-(d) and the discussion of conjunction and disjunction on page 478.

Common Errors

Students sometimes feel compelled to give a solution for any open sentence. In reteaching, remind them that there are open sentences with no solution at all, as well as those that are true for all values of the variable.

Guided Practice

Draw the graph of each open sentence.

1. $s \leq 4$ or $s > 7$

2. $-4 \leq m \leq 4$

(continued)

480

Guided Practice (continued)

Solve each open sentence. Graph the solution set.

3. $-5 < m + 3 \le 1$ {−2, and the real numbers between −8 and −2}

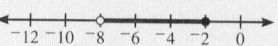

4. $-31 \le 5x + 1 \le 41$ $\left\{-6\frac{2}{5}, 8,\text{ and the real numbers between } -6\frac{2}{5}\text{ and } 8\right\}$

5. $2x + 3 \le -2$ or $2x + 3 \ge 5$ $\{-\frac{5}{2}, 1,\text{ and the real numbers greater than 1 or less than } -\frac{5}{2}\}$

6. $5x - 3 < 7$ or $5x - 3 > 12$ {the real numbers greater than 3 or less than 2}

Summarizing the Lesson

Ask students to compare conjunctions and disjunctions. Have them explain how various combinations of inequalities are graphed.

Suggested Assignments

Minimum
Day 1: 480/1–15 odd
  R 475/Self-Test 1
Assign with Lesson 10-3.
Day 2: 480/12–22 even
  S 481/Mixed Review
Assign with Lesson 10-5.

Average
  480/1–15 odd, 23–26
  S 481/Mixed Review
  R 475/Self-Test 1

Maximum
  480/3–39 mult. of 3
  S 481/Mixed Review
  R 475/Self-Test 1

Supplementary Materials

Study Guide   pp. 173–174
Practice Master   62
Computer Activity   30
Resource Book   p. 128

Oral Exercises

Match each graph with one of the open sentences in a–g.

1. ——— f
2. ——— g
3. ——— a
4. ——— c
5. ——— d
6. ——— b
7. ——— e

a. $t > 2$
b. $-2 < t < 2$
c. $-2 \le t \le 2$
d. $t \le 2$
e. $t \le -2$ or $t > 2$
f. $t < 2$
g. $t \ge 2$ or $t < -2$

Match each open sentence with an equivalent inequality in a–e.

8. $x = 3$ or $x < 3$ c
9. $x < 3$ and $x > -1$ d
10. $x \le 3$ and $x > -1$ b
11. $x = 3$ or $x > 3$ e
12. $x \le 3$ and $x \ge -1$ a

a. $-1 \le x \le 3$
b. $-1 < x \le 3$
c. $x \le 3$
d. $-1 < x < 3$
e. $x \ge 3$

Written Exercises

Draw the graph of each open sentence.

A
1. $-3 < t \le 2$
2. $r > 3$ or $r \le -2$
3. $1 \le n \le 5$
4. $s < -2$ or $s \ge 0$

Solve each open sentence. Graph the solution set, if there is one.

5. $-2 < a + 1 < 3$
6. $-2 < y - 2 \le 1$
7. $-4 < -3 + d \le 2$
8. $-6 \le 3 + r < 4$
9. $-2 \le 2a + 4 < 8$
10. $-2 < 2b - 1 \le 5$
11. $-5 \le 3m + 1 < 4$
12. $-8 < 3n + 7 \le 1$
13. $y - 2 < -5$ or $y - 2 > 5$
14. $h + 5 \le -2$ or $h + 5 \ge 2$
15. $2x + 1 \le -3$ or $2x + 1 \ge 3$
16. $1 + 2y < -9$ or $1 + 2y > 9$

17. $3n - 1 \leq -5$ or $5 \leq 3n - 1$

18. $2d - 5 < -7$ or $7 < 2d - 5$

B 19. $-6 \leq -x \leq 2$

20. $-8 \leq -2x \leq 6$

21. $-4 \leq 2 - t < 3$

22. $-2 < 3 - y \leq 1$

23. $-5 < 1 - 2x \leq 7$

24. $-7 < -1 - 3x \leq 8$

25. $-2m < 4$ and $12 + 2m < 0$

26. $-6r > 18$ or $12 + 3r \geq 0$

27. $-8 \leq -1 - s < -3$

28. $-9 < -10 - p \leq -4$

29. $5 - v > 7$ or $v - 5 > 7$

30. $t - 5 \geq 2$ or $5 - t \geq 2$

31. $5 - 2p \geq 11$ or $5 - 2p < -1$

32. $7 - 3q \geq 10$ and $3q - 7 \geq 2$

33. $2d - 5 \geq -8$ and $-2d - 5 < d - 3$

34. $9 - y \leq 3 - 2y$ and $-1 - 2y \geq -5$

C 35. $6 - c < 2c + 3 \leq 8 + c$

36. $5 - d \leq 3 - 2d$ or $d + 2 > 3d - 2$

37. $2(1 - w) \geq 6$ or $4w - 5 \leq 3w - 1$

38. $1 - 4m \leq 3 - 5m \leq m - 3$

39. Find an example of real values of a, b, c, and d for which the following statement is **(a)** true and **(b)** false. Answers may vary; examples are given.

If $a > b$ and $c > d$, then $ac > bd$. **a.** $2 > 1$ and $3 > 2$, and $2 \cdot 3 > 1 \cdot 2$; True

40. Find a value of k so that the solution set of

b. $1 > -2$ and $2 > -3$, and $1 \cdot 2 > (-2)(-3)$; False

$$k - 5 \leq x - 6 \leq 3$$

will be the same as the solution set of

$$3x - 7 \leq 2(1 + x) \text{ and } 5x - 7 \geq 23. \quad k = 5$$

Computer Exercises

For students with some programming experience

The sum of two positive integers must be no more than 10, but their product must be at least 9. Write a BASIC program to list all the ordered pairs (x, y) that satisfy these requirements.

Mixed Review Exercises

Choose a variable and use the variable to write an inequality.

$t \leq 78$

1. The net is at least 10 yd away. $n \geq 10$

2. The temperature cannot exceed 78°F.

3. The weight is at most 150 lb. $w \leq 150$

4. The trip takes at least 3 h. $t \geq 3$

5. The cost is not less than \$17. $c \geq 17$

6. The gap is smaller than 2 cm. $g < 2$

7. Her score was at most 340 points. $s \leq 340$

8. Jane owns at least 5 pairs of shoes. $s \geq 5$

Evaluate each expression if $k = -4$, $m = 7$, and $x = 4$.

9. $|k - m|$ 11

10. $|m - k|$ 11

11. $|m - x|$ 3

12. $|x - m|$ 3

13. $|k - x|$ 8

14. $|x - k|$ 8

Inequalities **481**

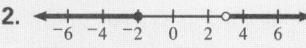 **Using a Computer**

The problem posed involves a conjunction. Students will probably search through values of x and y, using loops, to find those combinations that satisfy both conditions in the conjunction.

Warm-Up Exercises

Supply the missing number(s) that make each statement true. If there are none, so state.

1. $|-8| = \underline{\ ?\ }$ 8

2. $|\underline{\ ?\ }| = 6$ 6 or -6

3. $|\underline{\ ?\ }| < 2$ any real number between 2 and -2

4. $|\underline{\ ?\ }| < 0$ none

Motivating the Lesson

Sometimes you may see mileage signs along the highway. Suppose one sign says "Richmond 72 miles" and a later sign says "Richmond 37 miles." How far apart are the two signs? Finding the answer to this question involves finding the distance between two points, which is the basis of today's lesson.

Chalkboard Examples

Solve.

1. $|r + 4| = 1$ r is a number whose distance from -4 is 1; $r + 4 = -1$ or $r + 4 = 1$; $\{-5, -3\}$

Solve each inequality and graph its solution set.

2. $|w + 2| < 3$ The distance between w and -2 must be less than 3; $-3 < w + 2 < 3$; {the real numbers between -5 and 1}

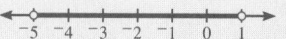

3. $|x - 3| > 1$ The distance between x and 3 must be greater than 1; $x - 3 < -1$ or $x - 3 > 1$; {the real numbers less than 2 or greater than 4}

10-5 Absolute Value in Open Sentences

Objective   To solve equations and inequalities involving absolute value.

You learned in Lesson 1-9 (page 37) that $|a|$ is the distance between the graph of a number a and the origin on a number line.

$|x| = 3$ means x is 3 units from 0:	$x = -3$ or $x = 3$.
$|x| < 3$ means x is less than 3 units from 0:	$-3 < x < 3$.
$|x| > 3$ means x is more than 3 units from 0:	$x < -3$ or $x > 3$.

On a number line, the distance between the graphs of two numbers a and b is the absolute value of the difference of a and b. Notice that $|a - b| = |b - a|$.

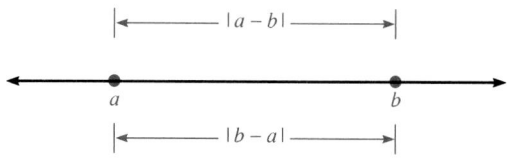

The following examples show how to solve equations and inequalities by two methods: (1) by graphing and (2) by writing the open sentence as a conjunction or a disjunction.

Example 1   Solve $|y - 2| = 4$.

Solution 1   To satisfy the equation $|y - 2| = 4$, y must be a number whose distance from 2 is 4. Thus, to arrive at y, start at 2 and move 4 units in either direction on the number line.

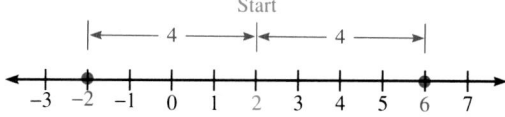

You arrive at 6 and -2 as the values of y.

$\therefore$ the solution set is $\{-2, 6\}$.   **Answer**

Solution 2   Note that $|y - 2| = 4$ is equivalent to the disjunction

$$y - 2 = -4 \quad \text{or} \quad y - 2 = 4$$
$$y = -2 \quad \text{or} \quad y = 6$$

$\therefore$ the solution set is $\{-2, 6\}$.   **Answer**

Example 2 Solve $|x + 1| \leq 3$ and graph its solution set.

Solution 1 Because $x + 1 = x - (-1)$, $|x + 1| \leq 3$ is equivalent to
$$|x - (-1)| \leq 3.$$
Therefore, the distance between x and -1 must be no more than 3.

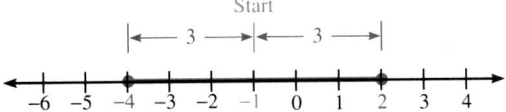

So, starting at -1, the numbers up to and including 2 will satisfy the given inequality, along with the numbers down to and including -4. Thus, the given inequality is equivalent to
$$-4 \leq x \leq 2.$$
∴ the solution set is $\{-4, 2$, and the real numbers between -4 and $2\}$. The graph is shown above.   ***Answer***

Solution 2 $|x + 1| \leq 3$ is equivalent to the conjunction:
$$-3 \leq x + 1 \leq 3$$
$$-3 - 1 \leq x + 1 - 1 \leq 3 - 1$$
$$-4 \leq x \leq 2$$
∴ the solution set and graph are as in Solution 1.   ***Answer***

Example 3 Solve $|t - 3| > 2$ and graph its solution set.

Solution 1 The distance between t and 3 must be greater than 2, as shown in the graph below.

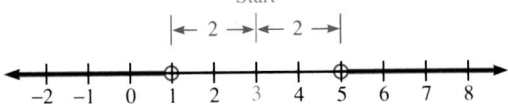

Therefore, the given inequality is equivalent to the disjunction
$$t < 1 \quad \text{or} \quad t > 5.$$
∴ the solution set is {the real numbers less than 1 or greater than 5}. The graph is shown above.   ***Answer***

Solution 2 $|t - 3| > 2$ is equivalent to the disjunction:
$$t - 3 < -2 \quad \text{or} \quad t - 3 > 2$$
$$t < 1 \qquad \text{or} \qquad t > 5$$
∴ the solution set and graph are as in Solution 1.   ***Answer***

Inequalities   **483**

Guided Practice

(continued)

4.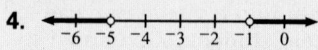

$|x + 3| > 2$

Solve each open sentence and graph its solution set.

5. $|t - 6| = 3$ $\{3, 9\}$

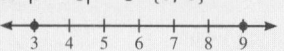

6. $|m| < 9$ {the real numbers between -9 and 9}

7. $|x - 1| \geq 3.5$ $\{-2.5, 4.5,$ and the real numbers greater than 4.5 or less than $-2.5\}$

Additional Answers
Oral Exercises

1. **a.** The distance between x and 0 is 4.
   b. $x = 4$ or $x = -4$

2. **a.** The distance between y and 0 is 3.
   b. $y = 3$ or $y = -3$

3. **a.** The distance between r and 0 is greater than 5.
   b. $r > 5$ or $r < -5$

4. **a.** The distance between p and 0 is less than 6.
   b. $-6 < p < 6$

5. **a.** The distance between n and 1 is less than or equal to 3.
   b. $-3 \leq n - 1 \leq 3$

6. **a.** The distance between n and 2 is greater than 3.
   b. $n - 2 > 3$ or $n - 2 < -3$

7. **a.** The distance between v and -5 is greater than 2.
   b. $v + 5 > 2$ or $v + 5 < -2$

8. **a.** The distance between v and -5 is less than 2.
   b. $-2 < v + 5 < 2$

Oral Exercises

In Exercises 1–12:

a. Translate the equation or inequality into a word sentence about the distance between numbers.

b. State a conjunction or disjunction equivalent to the given sentence.

Sample $|r + 2| > 7$

Solution   **a.** The distance between r and -2 is greater than 7.
   b. $r + 2 > 7$ or $r + 2 < -7$

1. $|x| = 4$ 2. $|y| = 3$ 3. $|r| > 5$

4. $|p| < 6$ 5. $|n - 1| \leq 3$ 6. $|n - 2| > 3$

7. $|v + 5| > 2$ 8. $|v + 5| < 2$ 9. $4 \leq |1 - s|$

10. $3 > |2 - q|$ 11. $1 > |2 + m|$ 12. $8 \leq |3 + w|$

In Exercises 13–18, match each open sentence with its graph.

13. $|x| \leq 3$ f

14. $|x| \geq 3$ a

15. $|x - 3| = 2$ e

16. $|x + 1| > 1$ d

17. $|x - 1| = 2$ b

18. $|3 - x| < 2$ c

a. A number line from -5 to 5.

b. A number line from -5 to 5.

c. A number line from -5 to 5.

d. A number line from -5 to 5.

e. A number line from -5 to 5.

f. A number line from -5 to 5.

Written Exercises

In Exercises 1–6:

a. Translate the equation or inequality into a word sentence about the distance between numbers.

b. State a conjunction or disjunction equivalent to the given sentence.

A   1. $|x - 5| = 1$ 2. $|y + 2| = 2$ 3. $|r + 3| > 5$

     4. $|p - 7| < 4$ 5. $|n - 4| \leq 1$ 6. $|n + 6| \geq 3$

Write an equation or an inequality involving absolute value to describe each graph. Use x as the variable.

Sample

Solution
The center point of the graph is 1. Since 1 is 2 units from 3 and 2 units from -1, and x represents a number *between* -1 and 3, the distance between x and 1 must be less than 2.

$\therefore |x - 1| < 2$ *Answer*

7. $|x| < 2$ **8.** $|x| \geq 2$
9. $|x + 1| = 2$ **10.** $|x - 2| = 1$
11. $|x - 1| \geq 3$ **12.** $|x + 3| < 3$

7.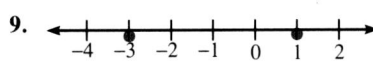

8.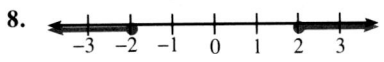

9.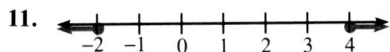

10.

11.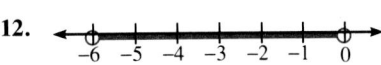

12.

Solve each open sentence and graph its solution set.

13. $|m - 6| = 8$ **14.** $|k + 7| = 3$ **15.** $|3 + x| = 5$
16. $|7 - y| = 4$ **17.** $|r| < 2.5$ **18.** $|s| \geq 1.5$
19. $|y + 5| > 8$ **20.** $|t + 4| < 10$ **21.** $|6 - p| \leq 2$
22. $|4 - v| \geq 5$ **23.** $|-2 - a| \geq 4$ **24.** $|-1 - b| \leq 6$

B **25.** $3|s| - 2 \geq 7$ **26.** $4|p| - 1 < 15$ **27.** $|2 - z| + 3 > 8$
28. $|2 - q| - 3 < 1$ **29.** $4 - 3|r| \geq -7$ **30.** $4 - 3|y| < 1$
31. $6 - |2 - p| \leq 4$ **32.** $8 - |1 - x| > 7$ **33.** $2(3|a| - 1) \leq 10$

C **34.** $|x - 2| = \frac{x}{3}$ **35.** $|y + 1| = \frac{y}{2}$ **36.** $|y - 4| = y - 4$
37. $|t - 4| > t - 4$ **38.** $|n + 5| < n + 5$ **39.** $|n + 5| \geq n + 5$

Mixed Review Exercises

Solve each inequality and graph its solution set.

1. $x - 5 < 4$ **2.** $\frac{x}{2} + 5 < 1$ **3.** $10 < 5(2 + m)$

4. $-1 < x + 5 < 2$ **5.** $h + 1 \leq 10$ or $h - 5 > 7$ **6.** $3 \leq -x \leq 10$

Simplify. Assume that no denominator is zero.

7. $\frac{20x}{3y^2} \div 5xy \quad \frac{4}{3y^3}$ **8.** $\left(\frac{2a}{b}\right)^3 \cdot \left(\frac{4b^2}{3a}\right) \quad \frac{32a^2}{3b}$ **9.** $\frac{x + 4}{3} - \frac{2x}{9} \quad \frac{x + 12}{9}$ **10.** $3x + \frac{x}{7} \quad \frac{22x}{7}$

Inequalities   **485**

10-6 Absolute Values of Products in Open Sentences

Objective   To extend your skill in solving open sentences that involve absolute value.

Example 1   Solve $|2p - 3| = 7$.

Solution $|2p - 3| = 7$ is equivalent to the disjunction:

$$2p - 3 = -7 \qquad \text{or} \qquad 2p - 3 = 7$$
$$2p - 3 + 3 = -7 + 3 \qquad\qquad 2p - 3 + 3 = 7 + 3$$
$$2p = -4 \qquad\qquad 2p = 10$$
$$\frac{2p}{2} = \frac{-4}{2} \qquad\qquad \frac{2p}{2} = \frac{10}{2}$$
$$p = -2 \qquad \text{or} \qquad p = 5$$

$\therefore$ the solution set is $\{-2, 5\}$.   **Answer**

You can use a number line to solve the open sentence in Example 1. First consider the following statements about the absolute value of a product of two numbers.

$$|-7 \cdot 4| = |-28| = 28 = 7 \cdot 4 = |-7| \cdot |4|$$
$$|(-5) \cdot (-3)| = |15| = 15 = 5 \cdot 3 = |-5| \cdot |-3|$$

The statements above suggest that the absolute value of a product of numbers equals the products of their absolute values: $|ab| = |a| \cdot |b|$. Using this property, you see that:

$$|2p - 3| = 7$$
$$\left|2\left(p - \frac{3}{2}\right)\right| = 7$$
$$|2| \cdot \left|p - \frac{3}{2}\right| = 7$$
$$2\left|p - \frac{3}{2}\right| = 7$$
$$\left|p - \frac{3}{2}\right| = \frac{7}{2}$$

Therefore, the distance between p and $\frac{3}{2}$ is $\frac{7}{2}$.

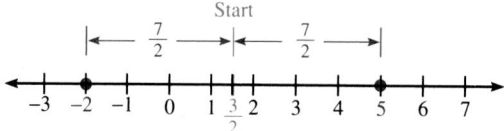

Starting at $\frac{3}{2}$ the numbers -2 and 5 are exactly $\frac{7}{2}$ units away in either direction. Therefore, the solution set is $\{-2, 5\}$.

Example 2 Solve $|10 - 2k| \geq 6$ and graph its solution set.

Solution 1

$$|10 - 2k| \geq 6$$
$$|(-2)(k - 5)| \geq 6$$
$$|-2| \cdot |k - 5| \geq 6$$
$$2|k - 5| \geq 6$$
$$\therefore \quad |k - 5| \geq 3$$

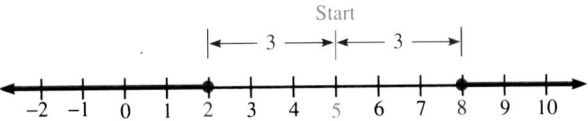

The distance between k and 5 must be 3 or more, as shown above. Thus the given inequality is equivalent to the disjunction

$$k \leq 2 \quad \text{or} \quad k \geq 8.$$

$\therefore$ the solution set is $\{2, 8,$ and the real numbers less than 2 or greater than $8\}$. The graph is shown above.

Answer

Solution 2 $|10 - 2k| \geq 6$ is equivalent to the disjunction

$10 - 2k \leq -6$	or	$10 - 2k \geq 6$
$-2k \leq -16$		$-2k \geq -4$
$k \geq 8$	or	$k \leq 2$

$\therefore$ the solution set and graph are as given in Solution 1. *Answer*

Oral Exercises

Express each given absolute value as the product of a number and the absolute value of a difference.

Sample $|16 - 8y|$

Solution $|16 - 8y| = |(-8)(y - 2)| = 8|y - 2|$

1. $|3x - 27|$ $3|x - 9|$ **2.** $|5m - 20|$ $5|m - 4|$ **3.** $|22 - 11p|$ $11|p - 2|$ **4.** $|12 - 4c|$ $4|c - 3|$

5. $|2k + 10|$ $2|k - (-5)|$ **6.** $|7n + 42|$ $7|n - (-6)|$ **7.** $|5r - 4|$ $5\left|r - \frac{4}{5}\right|$ **8.** $|2b - 9|$ $2\left|b - \frac{9}{2}\right|$

Inequalities **487**

---

2. $|3k - 2| \leq 7$
$$-7 \leq 3k - 2 \leq 7$$
$$-5 \leq 3k \leq 9; \quad -\frac{5}{3} \leq k \leq 3;$$
$\left\{-\frac{5}{3}, 3,$ and the real numbers between $-\frac{5}{3}$ and $3\right\}$

Check for Understanding

Here is a suggested use of the Oral Exercises as you teach the lesson.
Oral Exs. 1–8: use after Example 1.

Thinking Skills

By a simple change of form, students can broaden the range of applicability of a skill learned earlier. Expressions in absolute values can be *transformed* from the $ax + b$ form to the $x + c$ form for which techniques were developed in Section 10-5.

Guided Practice

Solve each open sentence and graph its solution set.

1. $|5x| = 20$ $\{4, -4\}$

2. $|4y - 12| > 16$ $\{$the real numbers greater than 7 or less than $-1\}$

3. $|3x + 5| < 1$ $\left\{$the real numbers between -2 and $-\frac{4}{3}\right\}$

(continued)

Guided Practice
(continued)

4. $\left|\dfrac{t}{2} - 1\right| < 3$ {the real numbers between -4 and 8}

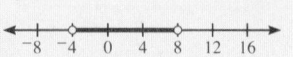

$$\begin{array}{ccccccccc} \leftarrow & + & \circ & + & + & + & \circ & + & + & \rightarrow \\ & -8 & -4 & 0 & 4 & 8 & 12 & 16 \end{array}$$

Summarizing the Lesson

Tell students they have learned to solve a new type of absolute value open sentence by extending the last lesson. Ask students to give an expression that is equivalent to $6 - 2k$ and has a coefficient of 1 for the k term.

Suggested Assignments

Minimum
Day 1: 488/1–5
Assign with Lesson 10-5.
Day 2: 488/9–12
S 488/Mixed Review
Assign with Lesson 10-7.

Average
    488/1–21 odd
    S 488/Mixed Review

Maximum
    488/1–25 odd
    S 488/Mixed Review

Supplementary Materials

Study Guide   pp. 177–178
Practice Master   63
Resource Book   p. 129
Overhead Visual   A

Additional Answers
Written Exercises

2. $\{-7, 7\}$

4. $\{-6, 6$ and the real numbers between -6 and $6\}$

6. $\{-\frac{5}{3}, 3\}$

8. $\{-\frac{6}{5}, 2$ and the real numbers less than $-\frac{6}{5}$ or greater than $2\}$

(continued)

Written Exercises

Solve each open sentence and graph its solution set.

A
1. $|3x| = 12$
2. $|5y| = 35$
3. $\left|\dfrac{y}{4}\right| \geq 1$

4. $\left|\dfrac{t}{3}\right| \leq 2$
5. $|2a - 1| = 9$
6. $|3b - 2| = 7$

7. $|4d - 11| \leq 3$
8. $|5h - 2| \geq 8$
9. $|3 + 4n| \leq 15$

10. $|1 + 8c| > 23$
11. $\left|\dfrac{y}{5} - 2\right| \geq 4$
12. $\left|\dfrac{x}{2} - 3\right| \leq 2$

B
13. $|1 - (3 - 2x)| < 18$
14. $|6 - (2y - 3)| \leq 9$
15. $4 + 3|5n + 1| = 13$
16. $2|3k - 7| + 11 = 19$
17. $5 - 4|2 - 3t| > 21$
18. $21 - 4|2 - 5w| > 13$

Classify each of the following sentences as true for all real values of the variable or false for some real value. If you classify a sentence as false, give at least one value of the variable for which it is false.

C
19. $|a^2| = a^2$ True
20. $|-a^2| = a^2$ True

21. $\left|\dfrac{a}{3}\right| = \dfrac{a}{3}$ False; $a = -1$
22. $|a - 3| < |a + 3|$ False; $a = -10$

23. $|a + 1| \leq |a| + 1$ True
24. $|a| - 1 \leq |a - 1|$ True

25. During January in Colton the absolute value of the temperature in degrees Celsius never exceeded $10°$. In degrees Fahrenheit, what were the greatest and least possible temperatures in Colton that month?

(*Hint:* $C = \dfrac{5}{9}(F - 32)$, where C and F are the temperatures in degrees Celsius and Fahrenheit, respectively.)
greatest, $50°$F; least, $14°$F

Mixed Review Exercises

Give the slope and *y*-intercept of each line.

1. $y = 4x + 2$ $m = 4$; *y*-int. $= 2$
2. $4y = 20x - 8$ $m = 5$; *y*-int. $= -2$
3. $2x + 3y + 9 = 0$ $m = -\dfrac{2}{3}$; *y*-int. $= -3$

4. $y = 9$ $m = 0$; *y*-int. $= 9$
5. $3x - y - 11 = 0$ $m = 3$; *y*-int. $= -11$
6. $x = -2y + 8$ **6.** $m = -\dfrac{1}{2}$; *y*-int. $= 4$

Graph each equation.

7. $y = -2x + 1$

8. $y = 3x - 2$

9. $x = -6$

10. $y = 5$

11. $y = \frac{3}{2}x + 5$

12. $y = -\frac{1}{3}x - 4$

Self-Test 2

Vocabulary   conjunction (p. 478)   disjunction (p. 478)

solve a conjunction (p. 478)   solve a disjunction (p. 478)

Solve each open sentence and graph its solution set.

1. $3x - 1 > 8$ or $2 - x > 0$

2. $-2 \leq y + 4 < 5$ Obj. 10-4, p. 478

3. $3m + 1 \leq -5$ or $3m - 1 \geq 5$

4. $-5 \leq 3x + 1 < 4$

5. $|p - 2| = 3$

6. $|3 - n| \geq 7$ Obj. 10-5, p. 482

7. $|1 - x| = 6$

8. $|x + 4| < 2$

9. $|4s - 13| \leq 7$

10. $|2p - 4| = 10$ Obj. 10-6, p. 486

11. $|4m - 7| = 1$

12. $|1 - 6a| < 13$

Check your answers with those at the back of the book.

Career Note / *Pharmacist*

The primary responsibility of a pharmacist is to prepare and dispense medicine prescribed by doctors. Pharmacists are experts in the use, composition, and effect of drugs. Occasionally, it is necessary for pharmacists to "compound" or mix ingredients for a prescription. However, the vast majority of medicines are now prepared by manufacturers rather than by pharmacists.

Many pharmacies offer more than medical and health supplies. An individual owning or managing such a pharmacy orders and sells merchandise, supervises personnel, and handles the finances of the business.

At least five years of study beyond high school are required to receive a degree from a college of pharmacy. During the first few years of study, mathematics and basic science courses are emphasized.

Inequalities   **489**

Quick Quiz

Solve each open sentence and graph its solution set.

1. $5x - 1 \leq -6$ or $3 - x \leq 1$
{-1, 2, and the real numbers less than -1 or greater than 2}

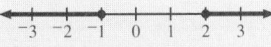

2. $-3 < 2x - 1 < 5$
{the real numbers between -1 and 3}

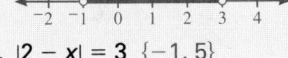

3. $|2 - x| = 3$ {-1, 5}

4. $|x - 2| < 5$
{the real numbers between -3 and 7}

5. $|3x + 2| = 7$ $\left\{-3, \frac{5}{3}\right\}$

6. $|2x + 1| \geq 1$
{-1, 0, and the real numbers less than -1 or greater than 0}

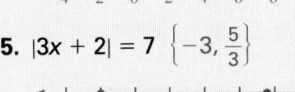

489

Warm-Up Exercises

Give the slope and
y-intercept of the line.

1. $y = 2x + 3$ 2; 3

2. $x - y = 5$ 1; −5

3. $2x - 4y = 8$ $\frac{1}{2}$; −2

4. $x = 3y + 6$ $\frac{1}{3}$; −2

5. $y = -3$ 0; −3

Motivating the Lesson

An international border divides land into three parts: the border itself, one nation, and the other nation. Similarly, a line separates a plane into three parts. These parts, a line and two half-planes, make up the graphs of inequalities, which is the subject of today's lesson.

Chalkboard Examples

Graph each inequality.

1. $3x + y \le 3$ $y \le -3x + 3$

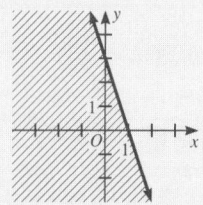

2. $y < 1$

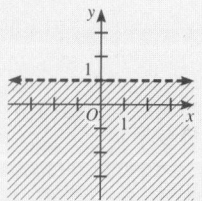

(continued)

490

10-7 Graphing Linear Inequalities

Objective   To graph linear inequalities in two variables.

The graph of the linear equation

$$y = x + 3$$

separates the coordinate plane into three sets of points:

> the points *on* the line,
> the points *above* the line,
> the points *below* the line.

The regions above and below the line are called **open half-planes,** and the line is the **boundary** of each half-plane.

If you start at any point on the line, say $P(2, 5)$, and move upward from P, the y-coordinate increases. If you move downward from P, the y-coordinate decreases.

Thus, the upper open half-plane is the graph of the inequality

$$y > x + 3,$$

and the lower open half-plane is the graph of the inequality

$$y < x + 3.$$

The graphs of

$$y > x + 3, \qquad y = x + 3, \qquad \text{and} \qquad y < x + 3$$

completely cover the coordinate plane. The upper half-plane and the boundary line together form the graph of

$$y \ge x + 3.$$

The lower half-plane and the boundary line together form the graph of

$$y \le x + 3.$$

The graph of an open half-plane and its boundary is called a **closed half-plane.**

The graphs of inequalities are shown by shading. If the boundary line is part of a graph, it is drawn as a solid line. If the boundary line is *not* part of the graph, it is drawn as a dashed line. This is shown by the diagrams at the top of the next page.

490   *Chapter 10*

(a) $y > x + 3$ (b) $y \geq x + 3$ (c) $y < x + 3$ (d) $y \leq x + 3$

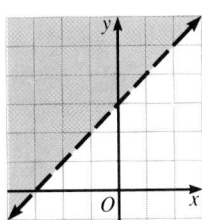 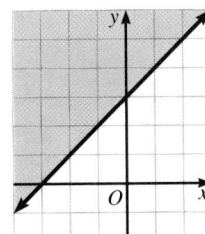 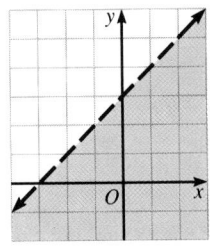 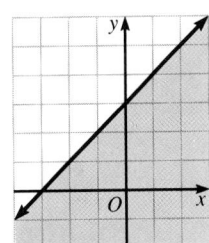

In general, you follow these steps.

To graph a linear inequality in the variables x and y, when the coefficient of y is not zero:

1. Transform the given inequality into an equivalent inequality that has y alone as one side.

2. Graph the equation of the boundary. Use a solid line if the symbol $\geq$ or $\leq$ is used; use a dashed line if $>$ or $<$ is used.

3. Shade the appropriate region.

Example 1 Graph $3x - 2y \geq -4$.

Solution   1. Transform the inequality:

$$3x - 2y \geq -4$$
$$-2y \geq -4 - 3x$$
$$y \leq 2 + \frac{3}{2}x$$

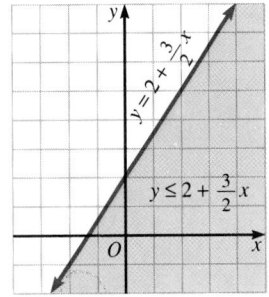

2. Draw the boundary line $y = 2 + \frac{3}{2}x$ as a *solid* line, since the symbol $\leq$ includes the equals sign.

3. Shade the region *below* the line since the symbol $\leq$ includes the less than sign.

Check: Choose a point of the graph not on the boundary, say $(0, 0)$. See whether its coordinates satisfy the given inequality:

$$3x - 2y \geq -4$$
$$3(0) - 2(0) \overset{?}{\geq} -4$$
$$0 \geq -4 \quad \checkmark$$

Thus, $(0, 0)$ is in the solution set, and the correct region has been shaded.

Inequalities   **491**

---

3. $x \geq -2$

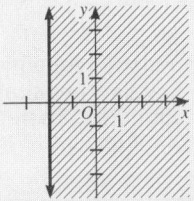

Guided Practice

Graph each inequality.

1. $y > -2$

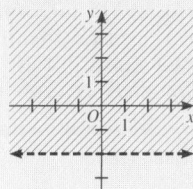

2. $y \leq 2x - 1$

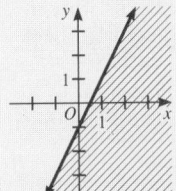

(continued)

Guided Practice

(continued)
Transform each inequality into an equivalent inequality with y as one side. Then graph the inequality.

3. $y - 2x \le -2$ $y \le 2x - 2$

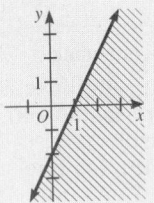

4. $x + 2y > 6$ $y > -\frac{1}{2}x + 3$

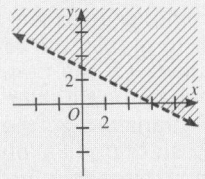

Summarizing the Lesson

Ask students to reread the objective on p. 490. Then have them outline the three basic steps in graphing a linear inequality in two variables. Point out that these steps are set apart in the textbook for easy reference.

Suggested Assignments

Minimum
Day 1: 492/1–11 odd
Assign with Lesson 10-6.
Day 2: 492/10–14, 25–28
   S 494/Mixed Review
Assign with Lesson 10-8.

Average
      492/3–33 mult. of 3
   S 494/Mixed Review
   R 489/Self-Test 2

Maximum
      492/3–39 mult. of 3
   S 494/Mixed Review
   R 489/Self-Test 2

Example 2   Graph $y > 2$

Solution   Graph $y = 2$ as a dashed horizontal line. Any point above that horizontal line has a y-coordinate that satisfies $y > 2$. Therefore, the graph of $y > 2$ is the open half-plane above the graph of $y = 2$.

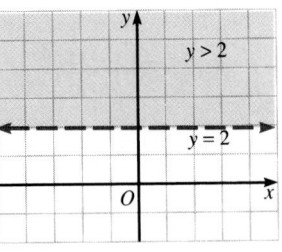

Example 3   Graph $x < -3$.

Solution   Graph $x = -3$ as a dashed vertical line. Any point to the left of that vertical line has an x-coordinate that satisfies $x < -3$. Therefore, the graph of $x < -3$ is the open half-plane to the left of the graph of $x = -3$.

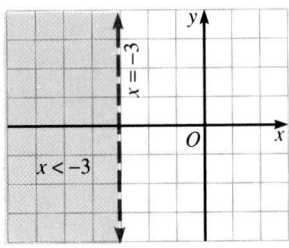

Oral Exercises

State whether the given points belong to the graph of the given inequality.

1. $x \ge 2$; (2, 3), (−2, 3), (0, 0) yes, no, no

no, yes; no
2. $y < -3$; (2, −3), (4, −4), (0, 0)

3. $y < x + 4$; (4, 2), (−1, 4), (0, 0) yes, no, yes

yes, yes, no
4. $y \le 2x - 1$; (2, 0), (1, 1), (0, 0)

5. $2x + y < 0$; (−1, −1), (1, 1), (0, 0)
yes, no, no

6. $x - 3y \ge -2$; (1, −1), (−1, 1), (0, 0)
yes, no, yes

Transform each inequality into an equivalent inequality having y alone as one side. Then state the equation of the boundary of the graph.

7. $x + y < 5$ $y = -x + 5$

8. $-x + y > 1$ $y = x + 1$

9. $4x + y \ge 7$ $y = -4x + 7$

10. $2x + y \le -2$ $y = -2x - 2$

11. $2x + 3y > 0$ $y = -\frac{2}{3}x$

12. $15x + 5y < 0$ $y = -3x$

13. $5y < x$ $y = \frac{1}{5}x$

14. $2x > -3y$ $y = -\frac{2}{3}x$

15. $x - y \ge 1$ $y = x - 1$

16. $12x - 6y \le 0$ $y = 2x$

17. $x - 6y > 24$
$y = \frac{x}{6} - 4$

18. $6 > x - y$ $y = x - 6$

Written Exercises

Graph each inequality.

A
1. $y \ge 4$

2. $y > 4$

3. $x < 1$

4. $x \le 1$

5. $x > 0$

6. $y < 0$

7. $y \ge -1$

8. $x \le -4$

9. $y < x + 5$

10. $y > -x + 1$

11. $y \le 3 - x$

12. $y \ge 1 - 3x$

21. $y \le -\frac{3}{2}x - 2$

Transform each inequality into an equivalent inequality with y as one side.
Then graph the inequality. See Additional Answers for graphs.

$y \ge \frac{1}{3}x + 2$

13. $x + y < 1$ $y < -x + 1$ **14.** $x - y \ge 3$ $y \le x - 3$ **15.** $x - 3y \le -6$

16. $2x + y > -4$ $y > -2x - 4$ **17.** $4x - y > 6$ $y < 4x - 6$ **18.** $y - 2x \le -3$
$y \le 2x - 3$

19. $3x - 2y \ge 8$ $y \le \frac{3}{2}x - 4$ **20.** $3y - 2x < 0$ $y < \frac{2}{3}x$ **21.** $7x + 4y \le x - 8$

22. $3y - 1 > 2x - 7$ **23.** $4(x - y) \ge 3x + 2$ **24.** $5y - 8 < 2(x + 2y)$
$y > \frac{2}{3}x - 2$ $y \le \frac{1}{4}x - \frac{1}{2}$ $y < 2x + 8$

In each of Exercises 25–33, write an inequality whose graph is shown.

B **25.**

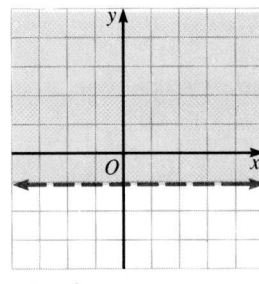

$y > -1$

26.

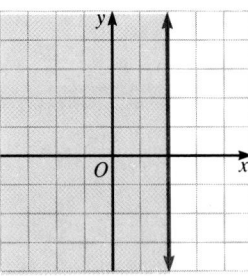

$x \le 2$

27.

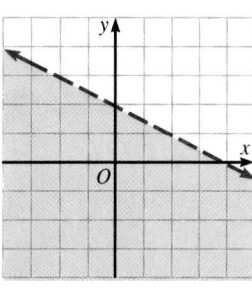

$y < -\frac{1}{2}x + 2$

28.

$y < -\frac{3}{2}x$

29.

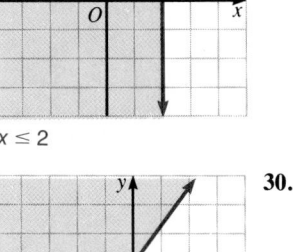

$y \ge \frac{4}{3}x + 4$

30.

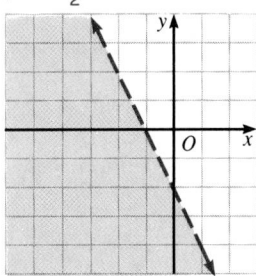

$y < -2x - 2$

31.

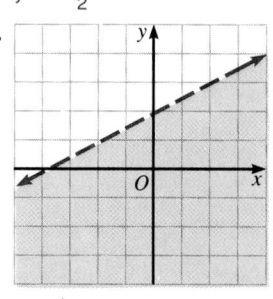

$y < \frac{1}{2}x + 2$

32.

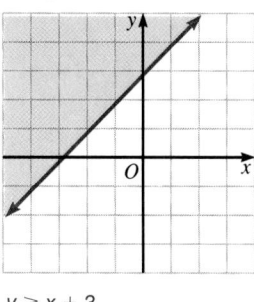

$y \ge x + 3$

33.

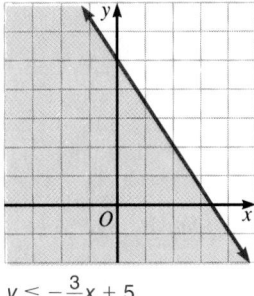

$y \le -\frac{3}{2}x + 5$

Graph each of the following in a coordinate plane.

C **34.** $y = |x|$ **35.** $y = -|x|$ **36.** $y > |x|$

37. $y \le |x|$ **38.** $|y| > 2$ **39.** $|y| < 2$

Inequalities **493**

Supplementary Materials

Study Guide   pp. 179–180
Test Master   45
Overhead Visual   11

Additional Answers
Written Exercises

2.

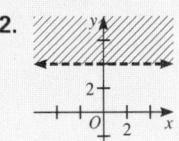

4.

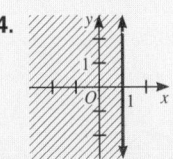

6.

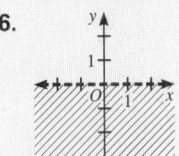

8.

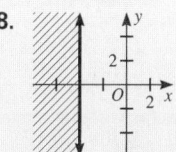

10.

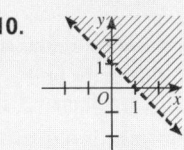

12.

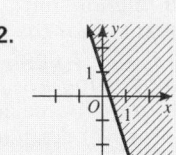

14.

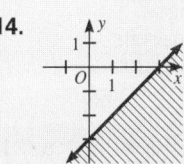

(continued)

493

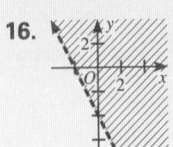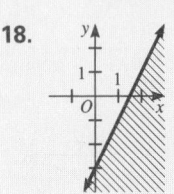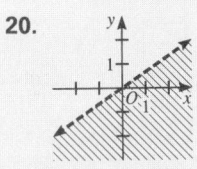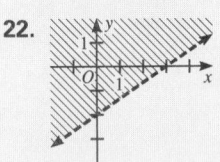

Mixed Review Exercises

Solve each system by whatever method you prefer.

1. $y = 3x$
   $x - y = 4(-2, -6)$

2. $m + n = 9$
   $m - n = 5(7, 2)$

3. $10p + 4q = 2$
   $10p - 12q = 34(1, -2)$

Solve each open sentence and graph its solution set.

4. $|4p| = 20$

5. $|3p + 3| = 15$

6. $|3x| < 21$

7. $|2y + 5| \geq 6$

8. $-6 \leq x + 1 < 5$

9. $2x + 5 > 7$ or $2 - x \geq 2$

Extra / The Graph of $y = |ax + b| + c$

The graph of $y = |x|$ is the V-shape shown in black in the drawings below. You can verify this by making a table of values and plotting the corresponding points. Study the different graphs shown in color below. Compare each graph with the graph of $y = |x|$.

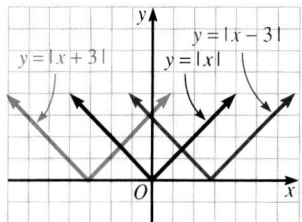
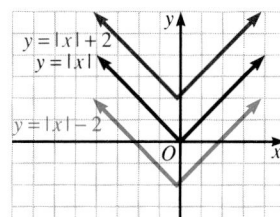
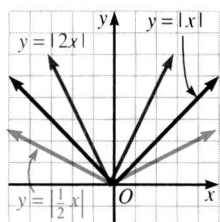

You can see that if you move the graph of $y = |x|$ *to the left* or *to the right* b units, you get the graph of $y = |x + b|$ or of $y = |x - b|$. If you move the graph of $y = |x|$ *up* or *down* c units, you get the graph of $y = |x| + c$ or of $y = |x| - c$. Also, you can see that the graph of $y = |ax|$ is narrower or wider than the graph of $y = |x|$, depending on the factor a.

If you have a computer or a graphing calculator, you may wish to explore what effect the changes in the values of a, b, and c have on the graph of $y = |ax + b| + c$.

Exercises

Graph each set of equations in the same coordinate plane. You may wish to check your graphs using a computer or a graphing calculator.

1. a. $y = |x - 3| + 2$
   b. $y = |2x - 3| + 2$
   c. $y = |-2x - 3| + 2$

2. a. $y = |2x + 1|$
   b. $y = -|2x + 1|$
   c. $y = \left|\frac{1}{2}x + 1\right| - 3$

494   *Chapter 10*

494

10-8 Systems of Linear Inequalities

Objective To graph the solution set of a system of two linear inequalities in two variables.

You can use graphs to find the solution set of a system of linear inequalities.

Example Graph the solution set of the system: $y - x - 3 \le 0$
$2x + 3y > -6$

Solution

1. Transform each inequality into an equivalent one with y as one side.

$$y - x - 3 \le 0 \rightarrow y \le x + 3$$

$$2x + 3y > -6 \rightarrow y > -\frac{2}{3}x - 2$$

2. Draw the graph of $y = x + 3$, the boundary for the first inequality. Use a solid line and shade the region below this line to show the graph of $y \le x + 3$ (red shading)

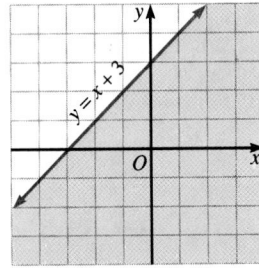

3. In the same coordinate system, draw the graph of $y = -\frac{2}{3}x - 2$, the boundary for the second inequality. Use a dashed line, and shade the region above this line to show the graph of $y > -\frac{2}{3}x - 2$ (blue shading)

4. The doubly shaded region (the intersection of red and blue shadings) is the graph of the solution set of the given system.

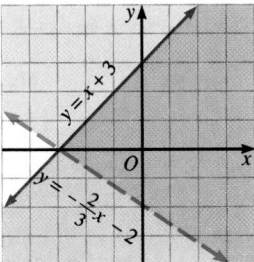

Teaching Suggestions p. T130

Suggested Extensions p. T130

Warm-Up Exercises

Solve each system.

1. $x = -5$
$y = x + 3$ $(-5, -2)$

2. $y + x = 6$
$y - 2x = -6$ $(4, 2)$

3. $5x + 2y = 7$
$x - 2y = -1$ $(1, 1)$

4. $3x - 5y = 13$
$x + 2y = 8$ $(6, 1)$

5. $6x - 5y = 5$
$5x + 2y = -2$ $(0, -1)$

Motivating the Lesson

In Section 10-7 students learned to graph the solution of an inequality. When two or more inequalities are graphed together it is called graphing a system of inequalities, the topic of today's lesson.

Chalkboard Examples

Graph the solution set of the system.

1. $y > 1$
$x < 3$

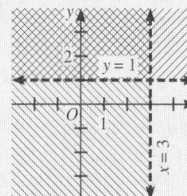

2. $x - y > 2$
$x + 2y \ge 1$

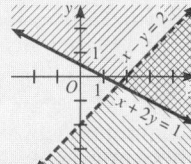

Check for Understanding

Here is a suggested use of the Oral Exercises as you teach the lesson.
Oral Exs. 1–23: use after Example .

Guided Practice

Graph each pair of inequalities and indicate the solution set of the system with crosshatching or shading.

1. $y \le -3$
   $x > 2$

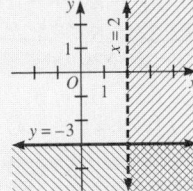

2. $y \ge 1 - 2x$
   $y \le 2 + x$

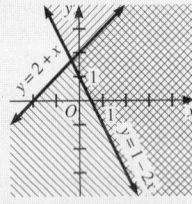

Summarizing the Lesson

Tell students they have learned to graph the solution of a system of inequalities. Ask them to explain the steps used in solving such a system. Mention that solving a system of linear inequalities is the basis of linear programming, an application of mathematics that is discussed on pages 499–500.

Supplementary Materials

Study Guide   pp. 181–182
Practice Masters   64
Computer Activity   32
Resource Book   p. 130
Overhead Visual   11

Oral Exercises

Give a system of two linear inequalities whose solution set is shown by the shaded region in each graph.

1.
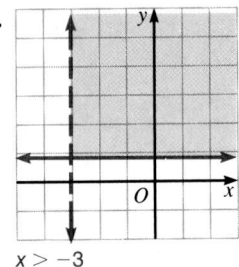
$x > -3$
$y \ge 1$

2.
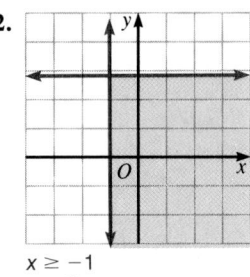
$x \ge -1$
$y \le 3$

3.
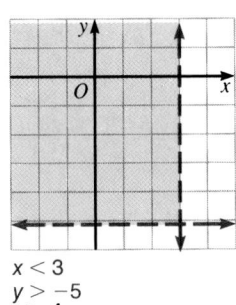
$x < 3$
$y > -5$

State whether or not each ordered pair is a solution of the system: $y \ge 4$ and $x < 5$.

4. (0, 0) no   **5.** (5, 4) no   **6.** (4, 4) yes   **7.** (−2, 4) yes   **8.** (−2, −4) no
9. (4, 5) yes   **10.** (5, 9) no   **11.** (4, 3) no   **12.** (0, 8) yes   **13.** (0, 4) yes

State whether each point belongs to the graph of the solution set of the system: $y \le 2$ and $x - y \le 5$.

14. (0, −5) yes   **15.** (8, 2) no   **16.** (−8, 2) yes   **17.** (−8, 3) no   **18.** (0, 2) yes
19. (0, 0) yes   **20.** (7, 2) yes   **21.** (0, −6) no   **22.** (−4, −5) yes   **23.** (−9, 2) yes

---

Written Exercises

Graph each pair of inequalities and indicate the solution set of the system with crosshatching or shading.

A **1.** $y < 0$ **2.** $y \le 5$ **3.** $y > 3$ **4.** $y < -4$
        $x \le 0$ $x \ge 1$ $x < -2$ $x > 4$

   5. $x < y$ **6.** $y > 3x$ **7.** $x \le 3$ **8.** $x > -2$
        $y > 2$ $x < 1$ $y > 5 - x$ $y \le 2x + 7$

   9. $y \le x + 1$ **10.** $y < 4x + 4$ **11.** $y > 2x - 3$ **12.** $y < 5x + 3$
        $y \ge 2 - x$ $y > -4x + 4$ $y < 2x + 6$ $y > 5 - 5x$

B **13.** $x - y \ge 4$ **14.** $x + y \ge 5$ **15.** $3x - y > -1$
        $x + y \le 6$ $x - 2y > 8$ $x - y > -4$
   16. $x - y < 7$ **17.** $3x - 4y < -12$ **18.** $2x - 5y > 0$
        $x - 3y > 15$ $3x + 4y > 0$ $x - 4y \le -8$

496   *Chapter 10*

Write a system of linear inequalities whose solution set is shown by the shaded region in each graph.

19.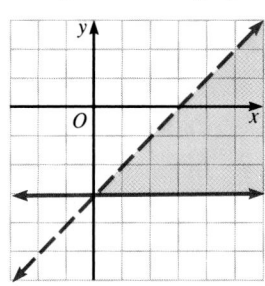

$y \geq -3$
$y < x - 3$

20.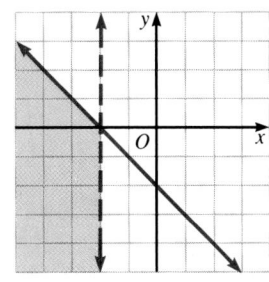

$x < -2$
$y \leq -x - 2$

21.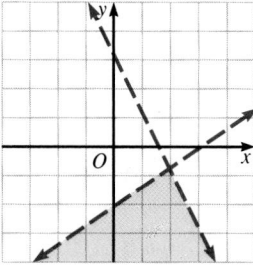

$y < \frac{2}{3}x - 2$
$y < -2x + 3$

22.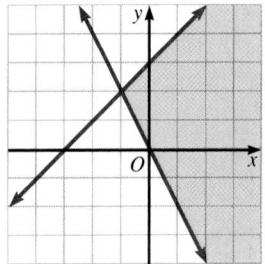

$y \leq x + 3$
$y \geq -2x$

Sample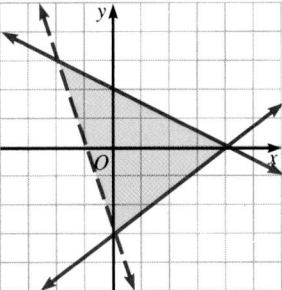

Solution $y \geq \frac{3}{4}x - 3$

$y > -3x - 3$

$y \leq -\frac{1}{2}x + 2$

23. $x \leq 3$
$y \leq \frac{1}{2}x + 2$
$y \geq -\frac{1}{4}x - 1$

24. $x > -2$
$x < 4$
$y \leq \frac{1}{3}x + \frac{8}{3}$
$y \geq -\frac{1}{3}x - \frac{8}{3}$

C **23.**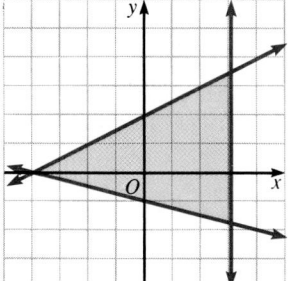

24.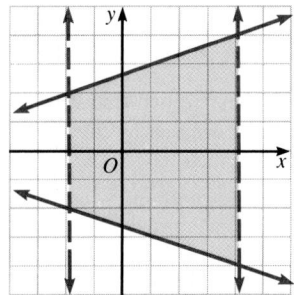

Inequalities **497**

Suggested Assignments

Minimum
        496/1–11 odd
Assign with Lesson 10-7.

Average
Day 1: 496/1–17 odd
        S 498/Mixed Review
Day 2: 496/16, 18–22
        R 498/Self-Test 3

Maximum
        496/3–24 mult. of 3
        S 498/Mixed Review

**Additional Answers
Written Exercises**

2.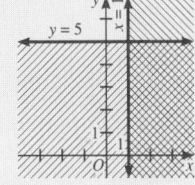

4.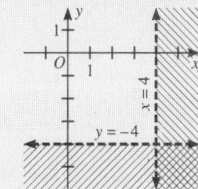

6.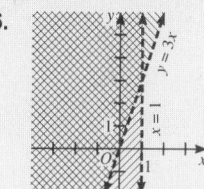

8.

10.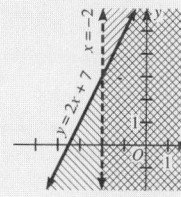

(continued on p. 499) **497**

Quick Quiz

Graph each inequality in a coordinate plane.

1. $y < 2$

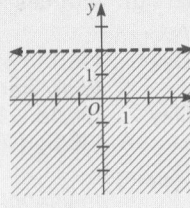

2. $2x - y \geq 4$

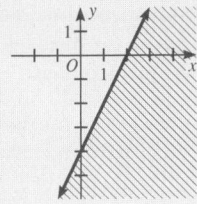

3. Graph the solution set of the system:
$x + y < 2$
$x - 2y \leq 4$

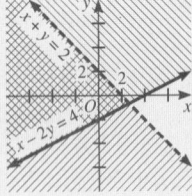

Graph each system of inequalities. Determine exactly the *corner points* of the graph of the solution set of the system, that is, the points where boundary lines intersect. See Additional Answers for graphs.

$(-3, 3), (-3, -1),$
$(3, 1), (3, -1)$

25. $y \leq x$
$y \geq -x$
$x \leq 4$
$(0, 0), (4, 4), (4, -4)$

26. $y \geq 2x$
$3y < x$
$y \geq -3$
$(0, 0), \left(-\dfrac{3}{2}, -3\right), (-9, -3)$

27. $2x - y \geq 4$
$x \leq -1$
$|y| \leq 2$ No sol.

28. $x + 3y \leq 6$
$y \geq -1$
$|x| \leq 3$

Mixed Review Exercises

2. $\dfrac{12a}{36}, \dfrac{8}{36}, \dfrac{3(a+1)}{36}$

Rewrite each group of fractions with their LCD.

3. $\dfrac{k(k+5)}{(k+5)^2}, \dfrac{3k}{(k+5)^2}$

1. $\dfrac{1}{6}, \dfrac{4}{15}, \dfrac{3}{5}$ $\dfrac{5}{30}, \dfrac{8}{30}, \dfrac{18}{30}$

2. $\dfrac{a}{3}, \dfrac{2}{9}, \dfrac{a+1}{12}$

3. $\dfrac{k}{k+5}, \dfrac{3k}{k^2 + 10k + 25}$

4. $\dfrac{2y+3}{y-6}, \dfrac{4}{y}, \dfrac{y}{5}$

5. $\dfrac{8}{x+2}, \dfrac{x}{x-2}$

6. $\dfrac{1}{x^2 - 16}, \dfrac{5}{4-x}, \dfrac{x}{4+x}$

Evaluate each expression if $a = \dfrac{3}{5}$, $b = \dfrac{1}{2}$, and $c = \dfrac{5}{12}$.

7. $a + b \div c$ $\dfrac{9}{5}$

8. $b(c - a) - \dfrac{11}{120}$

9. $a - (b + c) - \dfrac{19}{60}$

10. $\dfrac{1}{2}(a + b + c)$ $\dfrac{91}{120}$

11. $c + \dfrac{1}{2}(b - c)$ $\dfrac{11}{24}$

12. $b - \dfrac{1}{2}(a - b)$ $\dfrac{9}{20}$

Self-Test 3

Vocabulary   open half-plane (p. 490)   closed half-plane (p. 490)
boundary (p. 490)

Graph each inequality in a coordinate plane.

1. $x > -2$ **2.** $x + 3y \leq 9$ Obj. 10-7, p. 490

3. Graph the solution set of the system: $x - y > 5$ Obj. 10-8, p. 495
$3x + y \geq -1$

Check your answers with those at the back of the book.

Calculator Key-In

You can compare two fractions with the aid of a calculator. First change each fraction to a decimal by dividing the numerator by the denominator. Then compare the decimals.

True or false?

1. $\dfrac{5}{8} > \dfrac{9}{20} > \dfrac{6}{13}$ False

2. $\dfrac{17}{23} < \dfrac{18}{24} < \dfrac{19}{25}$ True

3. $\dfrac{90}{101} > \dfrac{91}{102} > \dfrac{92}{103}$ False

---

Using a Calculator

Some students have been told that they can't compute with fractions on a calculator. Converting fractions to decimals provides a way around this. Since some of these fractions become repeating, nonterminating decimals, it might be helpful to discuss rounding and comparing decimals.

Application / Linear Programming

Business decisions aim at making some quantities, such as profit, as large as possible, and other quantities, such as cost, as small as possible. A decision to maximize or minimize a quantity is usually subject to conditions *(constraints)*. If the quantity can be represented by a linear equation, and the constraints can be represented by a system of linear inequalities, the decision problem can be solved by using a branch of mathematics called *linear programming*.

Example A machine shop makes two parts, I and II, each requiring the use of three machines, A, B, and C. Each Part I requires 4 min on Machine A, 4 min on Machine B, and 5 min on Machine C. Each Part II requires 5 min on Machine A, 1 min on Machine B, and 6 min on Machine C. The shop makes a profit of $8 on each Part I and $5 on each Part II. However, the number of units of Part II produced must not be less than half the number of Part I. Also, each day, the shop has only 120 min of Machine A, 72 min of Machine B, and 180 min of Machine C available for the production of Parts I and II. What should the daily production be to maximize the shop's profit?

Solution Let x = the number of units of Part I.
Let y = the number of units of Part II.
Let P = the total profit on Parts I and II.

The data in the problem are summarized in the following chart.

Part	Number	Minutes on Machine A	B	C	Profit per Unit
I	x	4	4	5	$8
II	y	5	1	6	$5
Available Time		120	72	180	

The information in the chart can be expressed by these inequalities:

$4x + 5y \le 120$ (Total time on Machine A must not exceed 120 min.)
$4x + y \le 72$ (Total time on Machine B must not exceed 72 min.)
$5x + 6y \le 180$ (Total time on Machine C must not exceed 180 min.)

$y \ge \dfrac{1}{2}x$ (Number of units of Part II must not be less than half the number of Part I.)

$\left.\begin{matrix} x \ge 0 \\ y \ge 0 \end{matrix}\right\}$ (A negative number of parts cannot be produced.)

You want to find values of x and y that are subject to these inequalities (constraints) and that maximize the total profit, P, where $P = 8x + 5y$.

(Solution continues on the next page.)

Inequalities **499**

Additional Answers
Application

1. a.
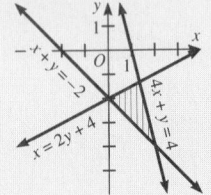

3. a. $6c + 12s \leq 2400$;
   $12c + 16s \leq 3600$;
   $c \geq 0$; $s \geq 0$
  b.
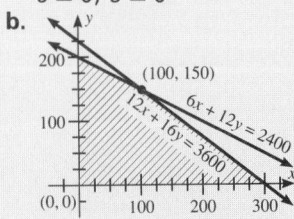

  c. The farmer can plant 200 acres of soybeans and no corn or 150 acres of soybeans and 100 acres of corn.

500

Step 1 Graph the solution set of this system of inequalities. The solution set, which is shaded, is called the *feasible region*.

Step 2 Find the points of the feasible region where the boundary lines intersect. These points, called *corner points*, are (0, 0), (16, 8), (15, 12), and (0, 24).

A remarkable fact, proved in more advanced mathematics courses, is that if a maximum or minimum value of a *linear expression ax + by* exists, it must occur at a corner point of the feasible region. You use this fact in the next step.

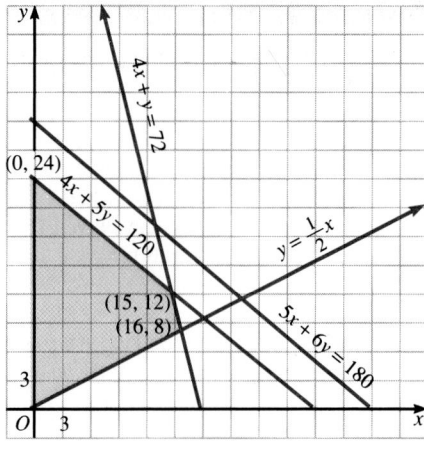

Step 3 Evaluate $P = 8x + 5y$ at each corner point.

(0, 0): $P = 8(0) + 5(0) = 0$ (15, 12): $P = 8(15) + 5(12) = 180$
(16, 8): $P = 8(16) + 5(8) = 168$ (0, 24): $P = 8(0) + 5(24) = 120$

The maximum value of P, $180, occurs at (15, 12). The shop should produce 15 units of Part I and 12 units of Part II each day. **Answer**

Exercises

1. **a.** Draw the graph of the solution set of the system: $x \geq 2y + 4$
                                                                    $x + y \geq -2$
                                                                    $4x + y \leq 4$
   b. Find the corner points of the solution set. $(0, -2)$, $(2, -4)$, $\left(\frac{4}{3}, -\frac{4}{3}\right)$
   c. Find the maximum and minimum values of $4x + 7y$ subject to the inequalities in part (a). maximum, -4; minimum, -20

2. Find x and y to maximize $R = x + 3y$ subject to the constraints $x \geq 2$, $y \geq 1$, $x + 2y \leq 8$, and $x + y \leq 6$. (2, 3)

3. **a.** A farmer plants two crops, corn and soybeans. The expenses are $6 for each acre of corn and $12 for each acre of soybeans. Each acre of corn requires 12 bushels of storage, and each acre of soybeans requires 16 bushels of storage. The farmer has at most 3600 bushels of storage available and $2400 to spend on expenses. Choose variables for the number of acres of corn and soybeans planted. Write four inequalities that express the conditions of the problem.
   b. Graph the solution set of the system of inequalities described in part (a). State the coordinates of the corner points for this feasible region.
   c. Suppose that the farmer earns a profit of $24 for each acre of corn and $48 for each acre of soybeans. Find two ways the farmer can satisfy the conditions while maximizing the profits. (Notice that a linear programming problem can have more than one solution.)

500 *Chapter 10*

Chapter Summary

1. The symbols $>$, $<$, $\geq$, and $\leq$ are used to express inequalities. $-2 < 4 < 9$ (or $9 > 4 > -2$) means that 4 is between -2 and 9.

2. Open inequalities can be solved by transformations to obtain simpler equivalent inequalities whose solution sets can be seen at a glance. The graph of the solution set of an inequality in one variable can be shown on a number line.

3. Sentences joined by "and" are conjunctions. A conjunction of two statements is true if and only if both statements are true. Sentences joined by "or" are disjunctions. A disjunction of two statements is true if at least one of the statements is true.

4. The distance between the graphs of two numbers a and b on a number line is the absolute value of the difference between a and b. This concept can be used to solve open sentences involving the absolute value of a variable. These open sentences also may be written as equivalent conjunctions or disjunctions.

5. The solution set of a linear inequality in two variables is an open or closed half-plane.

6. The graph of the solution set of a system of inequalities consists of the points common to the graphs of all the inequalities in the system.

Chapter Review

Give the letter of the correct answer.

1. Which statement is true? 10-1
   a. $-3 < -5 < -7$ b. $6 > -4 > 2$
   c. $-9 < -4 < 0$ d. $-5 > 2 > 1$

2. Find the solution set of $1 - x \leq 0$ if $x \in \{-4, -2, 0, 2, 4\}$.
   a. $\{-4, -2, 0, 2, 4\}$ b. $\{-4, -2\}$ c. $\{2, 4\}$ d. $\{0\}$

3. Find an inequality equivalent to $-4x < 12$. 10-2
   a. $x > -48$ b. $x < -16$ c. $x > -3$ d. $x < -3$

4. Find an inequality equivalent to $3(3 + y) < 5(5 + y)$.
   a. $y < -8$ b. $y > -8$ c. $y < 8$ d. $y > 8$

5. Write as an inequality: "The sum of two consecutive odd integers is at most 35." 10-3
   a. $n + (n + 1) > 35$ b. $n + (n + 1) < 35$
   c. $n + (n + 2) \geq 35$ d. $n + (n + 2) \leq 35$

Inequalities   **501**

Additional Answers
Written Exercises
(continued from p. 481)

24. $\{-3$ and the real numbers between -3 and $2\}$

26. $\{$the real numbers$\}$

28. $\{-6$ and the real numbers between -6 and $-1\}$

30. $\{3, 7,$ and the real numbers greater than 7 or less than $3\}$

32. no solution

34. $\{$the real numbers less than or equal to $-6\}$

36. $\{$the real numbers less than $2\}$

38. $\{1, 2,$ and the real numbers between 1 and $2\}$

Supplementary Materials
Practice Master   65
Resource Book   p. 203

Additional Answers
Chapter Test

3. {the real numbers less than or equal to 4}

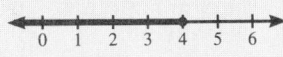

5. {−1 and the real numbers between −1 and 2}

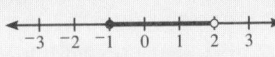

6. {−8, −2, and the real numbers less than −8 or greater than −2}

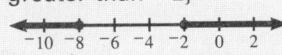

7. {−1, 5}

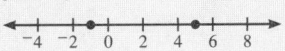

8. {the real numbers between −13 and 11}

9. {−1, 7}

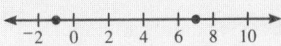

10. {−3, 4, and the real numbers between −3 and 4}

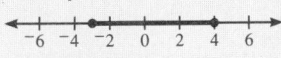

11.

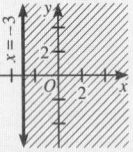

12.

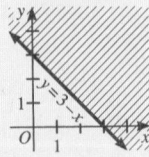

(continued)

502

---

6. Which is the graph of the disjunction $x < -2$ or $x > 4$? **10-4**

   (a.) ··· **b.** ··· **c.** ···

7. Which is the graph of the conjunction $-6 \leq x$ and $x < 4$?

   a. ··· **(b.)** ···

   c. ··· **d.** ···

8. Which open sentence states that the distance from r to 3 is greater than 4? **10-5**
   a. $r - 3 > 4$ **b.** $r - 3 \geq 4$ **(c.)** $|r - 3| > 4$ **d.** $|r - 3| \geq 4$

9. Which inequality is equivalent to $|8n - 4| < 12$? **10-6**
   a. $|2n - 1| < 12$ **(b.)** $|2n - 1| < 3$
   c. $|4n - 2| < 12$ **d.** $|2n - 1| > -3$

10. What is the equation of the boundary of the graph of $x - 2y > 4$? **10-7**
    a. $y = 2x - 4$ **(b.)** $y = \frac{1}{2}x - 2$ **c.** $y \leq \frac{1}{2}x - 2$ **d.** $y \geq 2x - 4$

11. Which point belongs to the graph of the solution set of the system: **10-8**
    $x < 2$
    $y \leq 2x + 3$
    a. $(0, 5)$ **(b.)** $(0, -5)$ **c.** $(-5, 0)$ **d.** $(-3, 5)$

Chapter Test

1. Classify the statement as true or false: $4 > -\frac{1}{2} > -2$. True **10-1**

2. Find the solution set of $y + 1 < 3$ if $y \in \{-2, -1, 0, 1, 2\}$. {−2, −1, 0, 1}

3. Solve the inequality $5 \geq 2x - 3$ and graph the solution set on a number line. **10-2**

4. Of all pairs of consecutive odd integers whose sum is greater than 75, find the pair whose sum is the least. 37, 39 **10-3**

Solve each open sentence and graph its solution set.

5. $-1 \leq 2c + 1 < 5$ 6. $k + 5 \leq -3$ or $k + 5 \geq 3$ **10-4**

7. $|2 - y| = 3$ 8. $|y + 1| < 12$ **10-5**

9. $|6 - 2x| = 8$ 10. $|2m - 1| \leq 7$ **10-6**

Graph each inequality in a coordinate plane.

11. $x \geq -3$ 12. $y \geq 3 - x$ **10-7**

13. Graph the solution set of the system: $y < 2x + 2$ **10-8**
    $y > 2 - 2x$

Cumulative Review *(Chapters 1–10)*

5. $3c^3 - 10c^2d + 16cd^2 - 16d^3$

Simplify. Assume that no denominator is zero.

1. $(-7b + 2) + (8b - 5)$ $b - 3$

2. $-3x^2(4x^3 - 2x^2 - 11x)$ $-12x^5 + 6x^4 + 33x^3$

3. $(3x^3y^4)^5 \div (9xy^8)$ $27x^{14}y^{12}$

4. $(3x + 5y)(7x - 4y)$ $21x^2 + 23xy - 20y^2$

5. $(3c^2 - 4cd + 8d^2)(c - 2d)$

6. $(5t - 7v)^2$ $25t^2 - 70tv + 49v^2$

7. $\dfrac{3x^2 - 8x - 3}{9x^2 + 9x + 2} \dfrac{x - 3}{3x + 2}$

8. $(12m^3n^2 - 11r^3)(12m^3n^2 + 11r^3)$ $144m^6n^4 - 121r^6$

9. $\dfrac{4.8 \times 10^{25}}{2.0 \times 10^{11}}$ 2.4×10^{14}

10. $\dfrac{z^2 + 8z + 16}{z^2 + 7z + 12} \cdot \dfrac{z^2 - 9}{z^2 + z - 12}$ 1

11. $\dfrac{y^3 + 4y^2 + 3y}{y^2 + 7y + 10} \div \dfrac{y^2 + 3y}{y^3 + 2y^2}$ $\dfrac{y^2(y + 1)}{y + 5}$

12. $2 + \dfrac{4}{b - 1} - \dfrac{3b}{b^2 - 1}$ $\dfrac{2b^2 + b + 2}{b^2 - 1}$

Factor completely.

13. $30z^2 + 240z + 96$ $6(5z^2 + 40z + 16)$

14. $81r^4 - 1$ $(3r - 1)(3r + 1)(9r^2 + 1)$

15. $16z^2 - y^2 - 10y - 25$ $(4z - y - 5)(4z + y + 5)$

Write an equation in standard form for each line described.

16. The line that contains $(-1, 10)$ and $(4, -5)$. $3x + y = 7$

17. The line that has slope $\dfrac{1}{2}$ and contains $(5, 6)$. $x - 2y = -7$

Graph each inequality.

18. $|x - 3| \le 7$

19. $4y + 5 < -7$ or $2y - 1 > 3$

20. Graph the solution set of the system: $\begin{aligned} x + y &< 2 \\ 2x - y &\le 0 \end{aligned}$

Solve each equation, inequality, or system. Assume that no denominator is zero.

26. $\{1, 2\}$ 29. $\{-5, 0, 2\}$

21. $|z| - 3 = 4$ $\{7, -7\}$

22. $5q - 8 = 22$ $\{6\}$

23. $|z + 1| = 10$ $\{-11, 9\}$

24. $b^2 - 8 = 1$ $\{3, -3\}$

25. $5(d - 3) = 3(2d - 5)$ $\{0\}$

26. $(x - 2)(x - 1) = 0$

27. $x^2 + 11x + 10 = 0$ $\{-10, -1\}$

28. $2b^2 + 9b - 5 = 0$ $\left\{-5, \dfrac{1}{2}\right\}$

29. $z^3 + 3z^2 - 10z = 0$

30. $\dfrac{18}{x} = \dfrac{3 + 3x}{x}$ $\{5\}$

31. $\dfrac{b + 1}{b + 2} - \dfrac{b + 2}{b + 1} = \dfrac{1}{b + 2}$ $\left\{-\dfrac{4}{3}\right\}$

32. $\dfrac{1}{a^2 - a} = \dfrac{3}{a} - 1$ $\{2\}$

33. $y = 5x - 1$
$2x + 3y = 14$ $(1, 4)$

34. $3r + 2s = -4$
$4r - 2s = -10$ $(-2, 1)$

35. $6m + 5n = 4$
$4m + 3n = 2$ $(-1, 2)$

36. $1 + 3t \le 10$

37. $2 - b > 7$

38. $2|3x - 1| + 1 < 5$

39. Marcy can do a job alone in 5 h. If Mark helps her, they can do the job together in 3 h. How long would Mark take working alone? $7\dfrac{1}{2}$ h

40. The units' digit of a two-digit number is 1 less than the tens' digit. Nine times the tens' digit is less than the number with the digits reversed. Find the least such number. 65

Inequalities   **503**

13.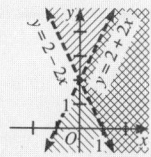

Additional Answers
Cumulative Review

18.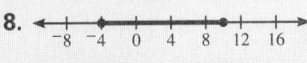

19.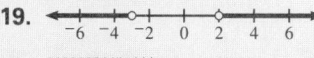

20.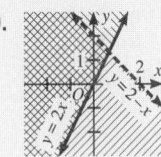

36. {the real numbers less than or equal to 3}

37. {the real numbers less than -5}

38. {the real numbers between $-\dfrac{1}{3}$ and 1}

503

504

504

Additional Answers
Written Exercises

(continued from p. 484)

2. a. The distance between y and -2 is equal to 2.
   b. $y + 2 = 2$ or $y + 2 = -2$

4. a. The distance between p and 7 is less than 4.
   b. $-4 < p - 7 < 4$

6. a. The distance between n and -6 is greater than or equal to 3.
   b. $n + 6 \geq 3$ or $n + 6 \leq -3$

14. $\{-10, -4\}$

16. $\{3, 11\}$

18. $\{-1.5, 1.5,$ and the real numbers greater than 1.5 or less than $-1.5\}$

20. {the real numbers between -14 and 6}

22. $\{-1, 9,$ and the real numbers greater than 9 or less than $-1\}$

24. $\{-7, 5,$ and the real numbers between -7 and 5}

26. {the real numbers between -4 and 4}

28. {the real numbers between -2 and 6}

30. {the real numbers greater than 1 or less than -1}

32. {the real numbers between 0 and 2}

34. $\{\frac{3}{2}, 3\}$

36. {the real numbers greater than or equal to 4}

38. no solution

Maintaining Skills

Solve. If the equation is an identity or has no solution, say so. Assume that no denominator is zero.

Sample 1 $12t^2 - 3 = 5t$

Solution
$$12t^2 - 5t - 3 = 0$$
$$(4t - 3)(3t + 1) = 0$$

$4t - 3 = 0$ or $3t + 1 = 0$

$4t = 3$ $3t = -1$

$t = \dfrac{3}{4}$ or $t = -\dfrac{1}{3}$

The check is left to you. ∴ the solution set is $\left\{\dfrac{3}{4}, -\dfrac{1}{3}\right\}$.

1. $t^2 - 6t - 40 = 0 \{-4, 10\}$ **2.** $x^2 = 15x - 56 \{7, 8\}$ **3.** $y^2 + 12y + 36 = 0 \{-6\}$

4. $n^2 + 400 = 40n \{20\}$ **5.** $5z^2 + 4z = 1 \left\{-1, \dfrac{1}{5}\right\}$ **6.** $10m^2 + 29m + 10 = 0$ $\left\{-\dfrac{5}{2}, -\dfrac{2}{5}\right\}$

7. $8 + 14z = 15z^2$ $\left\{-\dfrac{2}{5}, \dfrac{4}{3}\right\}$ **8.** $21b^2 + 25b + 6 = 0$ $\left\{-\dfrac{1}{3}, -\dfrac{6}{7}\right\}$ **9.** $9d^2 + 7d = 16$ $\left\{-\dfrac{16}{9}, 1\right\}$

Sample 2 $\dfrac{z + 3}{z + 1} + \dfrac{z}{z - 2} = \dfrac{2}{z - 2}$

Solution Note that $z \neq -1$ and $z \neq 2$.

$$(z + 1)(z - 2)\left[\dfrac{z + 3}{z + 1} + \dfrac{z}{z - 2}\right] = (z + 1)(z - 2)\left(\dfrac{2}{z - 2}\right)$$
$$(z - 2)(z + 3) + z(z + 1) = 2(z + 1)$$
$$z^2 + z - 6 + z^2 + z = 2z + 2$$
$$2z^2 = 8$$
$$z^2 = 4$$
$$z = 2 \text{ or } z = -2$$

The check is left to you. ∴ the solution set is $\{-2\}$.

10. $\dfrac{1}{x} + \dfrac{3}{x} = 4 \{1\}$ **11.** $\dfrac{2}{3} + \dfrac{2}{t} = \dfrac{10}{3t} \{2\}$ **12.** $\dfrac{5}{y} - \dfrac{4}{y} = \dfrac{1}{y}$ {the real numbers except 0}

13. $\dfrac{a + 5}{a} + \dfrac{2}{a^2} = 1 \left\{-\dfrac{2}{5}\right\}$ **14.** $y - \dfrac{y}{y + 1} = \dfrac{1}{y + 1} \{1\}$ **15.** $\dfrac{3}{4b - 6} - \dfrac{1}{2b - 3} = 0$ No sol.

16. $\dfrac{3x}{x + 1} - \dfrac{1}{x} = \dfrac{x + 1}{x} \left\{-\dfrac{1}{2}, 2\right\}$ **17.** $\dfrac{b - 2}{b + 2} + \dfrac{b}{b - 2} = 2 \{6\}$ **18.** $\dfrac{1}{t} - \dfrac{1}{t + 1} = \dfrac{t + 2}{t^2 + t}$ No sol.

19. $\dfrac{x^2 + 12}{x^2 - 4} - \dfrac{1}{x - 2} = \dfrac{3}{x - 2}$ No solution   **20.** $\dfrac{5}{d - 1} - \dfrac{10}{d^2 - 1} = 3 \left\{\dfrac{2}{3}\right\}$ **21.** $\dfrac{b^2 + 1}{b^2 - 1} = \dfrac{b}{b - 1} + \dfrac{2}{b + 1}$ No solution

Preparing for College Entrance Exams

Strategy for Success

Remember that you are asked to determine the *best* answer. More than one answer may be "right" to some degree. Do not choose the first answer that seems reasonable. Be sure to check all possible choices before determining which is the best answer.

Decide which is the best of the choices given and write the corresponding letter on your answer sheet.

1. Which method(s) could be used to solve: $3x - y = 6$ D
$$x + y = 6$$

   I. Graphing   II. Multiplication with Addition-or-Subtraction   III. Substitution
   (A) I only   **(B)** II only   **(C)** III only
   (D) I, II, and III   **(E)** I and III only

2. The length of a rectangle is 3 cm less than twice its width. A second rectangle is such that each of its dimensions is the reciprocal of the corresponding dimension of the first rectangle. The perimeter of the second rectangle is $\frac{1}{5}$ the perimeter of the first. Find the perimeter of the first rectangle. B
   (A) 6 cm   **(B)** 9 cm   **(C)** 12 cm   **(D)** 18 cm

3. How many sets of three consecutive positive even integers are there such that three times the sum of the first two integers is less than five times the third integer? D
   (A) none   **(B)** two   **(C)** four   **(D)** six   **(E)** eight

4. Two notebooks and three packages of pencils cost $7. It would cost $3 more to buy three notebooks and four packages of pencils. How much would it cost to buy one notebook and one package of pencils? C
   (A) $1   **(B)** $2   **(C)** $3   **(D)** $4

5. The sum of a positive integer and the square of the next consecutive integer is 131. Find the sum of the two integers. C
   (A) 19   **(B)** 20   **(C)** 21   **(D)** 22   **(E)** 23

6. Identify the inequality whose graph is shown at the right. B
   (A) $x + 3y \le 6$ **(B)** $x + 3y \ge 6$
   (C) $3x - y \le 3$ **(D)** $3x - y \ge 3$

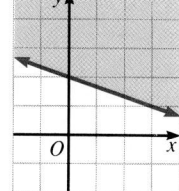

Inequalities   **505**

**Additional Answers
Written Exercises**

(continued from p. 494)

24.

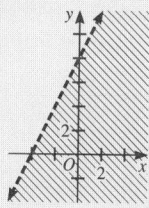

34.

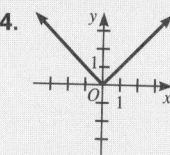

36.

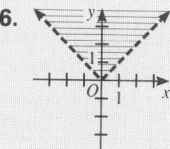

38.

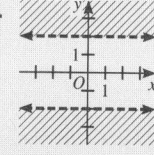

**Additional Answers
Extra**

(continued from p. 494)

1.

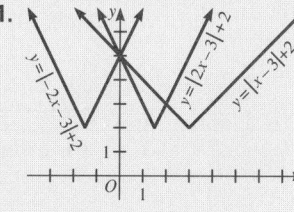

2.

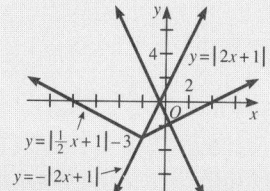

11 Rational and Irrational Numbers

Objectives

11-1 To learn and apply some properties of rational numbers.

11-2 To express rational numbers as decimals or fractions.

11-3 To find the square roots of numbers that have rational square roots.

11-4 To simplify radicals and to find decimal approximations of irrational square roots.

11-5 To find square roots of variable expressions and to use them to solve equations and problems.

11-6 To use the Pythagorean theorem and its converse to solve geometric problems.

11-7 To simplify products and quotients of radicals.

11-8 To simplify sums and differences of radicals.

11-9 To multiply binomials containing square-root radicals and to rationalize binomial denominators that contain square-root radicals.

11-10 To solve simple radical equations.

Assignment Guide

See p. T59 for Key to the format of the Assignment Guide

Day	Minimum Course	Average Course	Maximum Course
1	**11-1** 510/1–31 odd S 511/*Mixed Review*	**11-1** 510/1–35 odd S 511/*Mixed Review*	**11-1** 510/2–38 even S 511/*Mixed Review*
2	**11-2** 515/1–37 odd S 516/*Mixed Review*	**11-2** 515/1–39 odd S 516/*Mixed Review*	**11-2** 515/2–42 even S 516/*Mixed Review*
3	**11-3** 519/1–35 odd S 520/*Mixed Review*	**11-3** 519/3–45 mult. of 3 S 520/*Mixed Review*	**11-3** 519/3–48 mult. of 3 S 520/*Mixed Review*
4	**11-4** 522/1–35 odd S 523/*Mixed Review* R 520/*Self-Test 1*	**11-4** 522/3–45 mult. of 3 S 523/*Mixed Review* R 520/*Self-Test 1*	**11-4** 522/3–48 mult. of 3 S 523/*Mixed Review* R 520/*Self-Test 1*
5	**11-5** 526/1–37 odd 527/*P*: 1, 3, 5 S 528/*Mixed Review*	**11-5** 526/3–48 mult. of 3 527/*P*: 2, 5, 8 S 528/*Mixed Review*	**11-5** 526/3–51 mult. of 3 527/*P*: 3, 6, 9, 12 S 528/*Mixed Review*
6	**11-6** 532/1–21 odd 533/*P*: 1, 3 S 534/*Mixed Review*	**11-6** 532/3–27 mult. of 3 533/*P*: 2, 5, 8 S 534/*Mixed Review*	**11-6** 532/3–30 mult. of 3 533/*P*: 3, 6, 9, 12 S 534/*Mixed Review*
7	**11-7** 538/1–25 odd R 534/*Self-Test 2*	**11-7** 538/3–51 mult. of 3 S 539/*Mixed Review* R 534/*Self-Test 2*	**11-7** 538/3–57 mult. of 3 S 539/*Mixed Review* R 534/*Self-Test 2*
8	**11-7** 538/14–36 even S 539/*Mixed Review*	**11-8** 541/3–33 mult. of 3 S 542/*Mixed Review*	**11-8** 541/3–36 mult. of 3 S 542/*Mixed Review*
9	**11-8** 541/1–14 S 533/*P*: 5	**11-9** 545/3–42 mult. of 3 S 546/*Mixed Review*	**11-9** 545/3–45 mult. of 3 S 546/*Mixed Review*
10	**11-8** 541/15–27 S 542/*Mixed Review*	**11-10** 548/2–42 even S 550/*Mixed Review*	**11-10** 548/3–48 mult. of 3 549/*P*: 3, 6, 9, 10 S 550/*Mixed Review*

Assignment Guide (continued)

Day	Minimum Course	Average Course	Maximum Course
11	**11-9** 545/1–27 odd, 31 **S** 546/*Mixed Review*	**11-10** 549/P: 1–6, 8, 10 **R** 550/*Self-Test 3*	**R** 550/*Self-Test 3* 555/*Chapter Review* **EP** 659/*Skills;* 677/*Problems*
12	**11-10** 548/1–25 odd; 549/P: 1–3 **S** 550/*Mixed Review*	**R** 555/*Chapter Review* **EP** 659/*Skills;* 677/*Problems*	*Administer Chapter 11 Test* **R** 557/*Cum. Review:* 1–41 odd **S** 559/*Mix. Pr. Sol.:* 1–13 odd
13	**R** 550/*Self-Test 3* 555/*Chapter Review* **EP** 659/*Skills;* 677/*Problems*	*Administer Chapter 11 Test* **R** 557/*Cum. Review:* 1–41 odd **S** 559/*Mix. Pr. Sol.:* 1–13 odd	
14	*Administer Chapter 11 Test* **R** 558/*Maintaining Skills* **S** 559/*Mix. Pr. Sol.:* 2, 4, 6		

Supplementary Materials Guide

For Use with Lesson	Practice Masters	Tests	Study Guide (Reteaching)	Resource Book		
				Tests	Practice Exercises	Applications (A) Enrichment (E) Thinking Skl. (TS)
11-1			pp. 183–184			p. 188 (A)
11-2	Sheet 66		pp. 185–186		p. 131	
11-3		Test 48	pp. 187–188			
11-4	Sheet 67		pp. 189–190		p. 132	
11-5			pp. 191–192			
11-6	Sheet 68	Test 49	pp. 193–194		p. 133	p. 227 (TS)
11-7			pp. 195–196			
11-8	Sheet 69		pp. 197–198		p. 134	
11-9			pp. 199–200			
11-10	Sheet 70	Test 50	pp. 201–202		p. 135	
Chapter 11	Sheet 71	Tests 51, 52		pp. 60–63		p. 204 (E)
Cum. Rev. 10–11	Sheet 72					

Overhead Visuals

For Use with Lesson	Visual	Title
11-4	B	Multi-Use Packet 2
11-6	12	The Pythagorean Theorem

Software

Software	Algebra Plotter Plus	Using Algebra Plotter Plus	Computer Activities	Test Generator
	Function Plotter	Enrichment, pp. 34–35	Activities 33–35	210 test items
For Use with Lessons	11-4, 11-10	11-4, 11-10	11-2, 11-8, 11-10	all lessons

Strategies for Teaching

Using Manipulatives and Using Technology

The key mathematical ideas explored in Chapter 11 include expressing rational numbers as decimals and fractions, finding square roots, applying the Pythagorean theorem, and simplifying radical equations. Manipulatives can serve as useful models for illustrating perfect squares and the Pythagorean theorem. See the Exploration on pp. 698–699 for an activity in which students make models and use manipulatives to explore irrational numbers by creating segments having irrational length.

The chapter is also particularly suited for using calculators and computers as learning tools. See the Exploration on p. 697 for an activity in which students use calculators to explore terminating and repeating decimals. Calculators have obvious timesaving benefits for activities like finding and checking decimal approximations for fractions and square roots. Beyond this, computers can be used as extended learning tools to illustrate alternative methods for finding irrational square roots and solving simple radical equations.

11-3 Rational Square Roots

Students can "see" numbers that are perfect squares and their square roots if you demonstrate the following activity with unit squares and an overhead projector. Then have students use manipulatives to "see" other perfect squares.

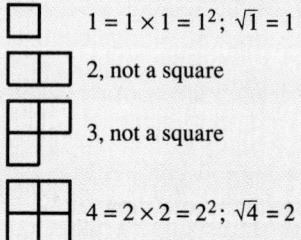

$1 = 1 \times 1 = 1^2; \sqrt{1} = 1$

2, not a square

3, not a square

$4 = 2 \times 2 = 2^2; \sqrt{4} = 2$

11-4 Irrational Square Roots

You can have students approximate the square root of a positive number a by graphing the parabola $y = x^2 - a$. For example, have the students graph $y = x^2 - 2$ on a computer or graphing calculator. By zooming in on the point where the parabola crosses the positive x-axis, the students can obtain approximations of the point's x-coordinate, which is $\sqrt{2}$. Likewise, the students can approximate $\sqrt{3}$ by zooming in on the point where the parabola $y = x^2 - 3$ crosses the positive x-axis. You might ask students to explain why this method works. (On the x-axis, $y = 0$, so the equation becomes $0 = x^2 - a$. The roots of this equation are $\pm \sqrt{a}$.)

11-6 The Pythagorean Theorem

In addition to discussing the proof given on page 529, you can have students investigate the Pythagorean theorem independently. Give each student a piece of graph paper and these directions: Draw a right triangle with legs 3 units and 4 units long. Then draw squares using each side of the right triangle as a side of the square.

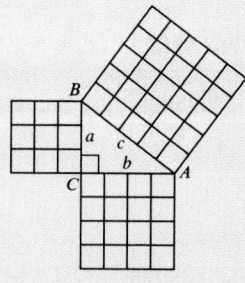

Have students count the unit squares to verify that $c^2 = a^2 + b^2$. (Have them devise their own methods for counting the unit squares in the square on the hypotenuse.)

11-10 Simple Radical Equations

One method for solving an equation of the form $f(x) = g(x)$ involves graphing the equations $y = f(x)$ and $y = g(x)$ on the same set of axes and then determining the x-coordinate of each point where the two curves intersect. For example, have the students solve the radical equation $\sqrt{x + 2} = 4 - x$ by graphing $y = \sqrt{x + 2}$ and $y = 4 - x$. (Note that the expression $\sqrt{x + 2}$ is typically entered as $\sqrt{\ }(X + 2)$ on a graphing calculator and as SQR(X + 2) on a computer.) Ask the students for the x-coordinate of the point of intersection of the two curves. [2] Then have them substitute this value into the equation $\sqrt{x + 2} = 4 - x$ to confirm that it is a solution. (To provide more of a challenge, ask the students to solve $\sqrt{x + 2} = 5 - x$ by graphing. In this case the x-coordinate of the point of intersection is irrational $\left(\dfrac{11 - \sqrt{29}}{2}\right)$, so the students must zoom in to get a reasonable approximation. [2.8])

An alternate approach to solving an equation of the form $f(x) = g(x)$ involves rewriting the equation as $f(x) - g(x) = 0$. When $y = f(x) - g(x)$ is graphed, any x-intercepts will be solutions of the equation. For example, the students can solve $\sqrt{x + 2} = 4 - x$ by graphing $y = \sqrt{x + 2} + x - 4$ and determining the x-coordinates of the points where the graph crosses the x-axis.

References to Strategies

PE: Pupil's Edition   **TE:** Teacher's Edition   **RB:** Resource Book

Problem Solving Strategies

PE: p. 533 (Using a sketch, diagram, or model); pp. 527, 529–533 (Using square roots)

Applications

PE: pp. 506, 527, 533, 549–550
TE: p. 506
RB: p. 188

Nonroutine Problems

PE: pp. 510–511 (Exs. 33–38); p. 516 (Exs. 41–43); p. 520 (Challenge); p. 527 (Probs. 10–12); p. 533 (Probs. 9–12); p. 534 (Challenge); p. 536 (Challenge); p. 546 (Exs. 41–44); p. 549 (Exs. 47–50); p. 550 (Probs. 9–11)
TE: p. T135 (Sugg. Extension, Lesson 11-7)

Communication

PE: pp. 524, 543 (Extra, convincing argument); p. 529 (convincing argument)
TE: p. T132 (Lesson 11-2)

Thinking Skills

RB: p. 227

Explorations

PE: pp. 524, 535–536, 543, 551–553, 697, 698–699
RB: p. 204
Algebra Plotter Plus: pp. 34–35

Connections

PE: pp. 507–508, 521–522 (Discrete Math); pp. 527, 532–533, 549 (Geometry); pp. 523–524 (History); pp. 549–550 (Physics)

Using Technology

PE: pp. 515, 517, 519, 521–523, 527, 532–534 (Exs.); pp. 528, 554 (Calculator Key-In)
TE: pp. 515, 517, 519, 521, 523, 527–528, 532–534, 554
Computer Activities: pp. 73–79
Algebra Plotter Plus: pp. 34–35

Using Manipulatives/Models

TE: p. T133 (Lesson 11-3); p. T134 (Lesson 11-6)
Overhead Visuals: B, 12

Cooperative Learning

TE: p. T136 (Lesson 11-8)

Teaching Resources

For use in implementing the teaching strategies referenced on the previous page.

Application
Resource Book, p. 188

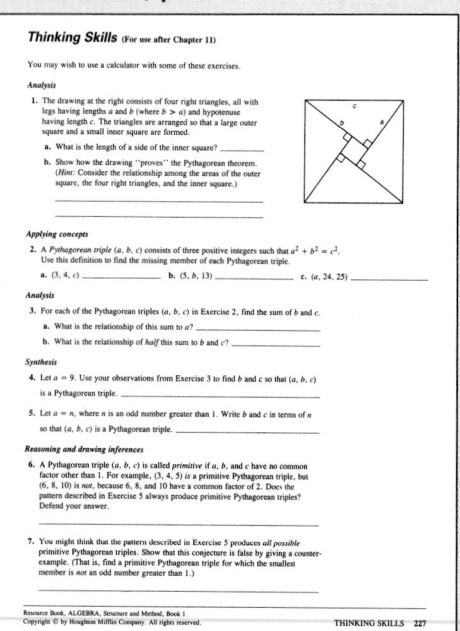

Application—The Number π (for use with Chapter 11)

No matter how large or small a circle is, the ratio of the circumference of the circle to its diameter always remains the same. This special ratio, or number, is called π (pi). If you can find a value for π, then you can use this value to find the circumference, the diameter, and the area of any circle.

Part I—Collecting the Data

1. Take a coin of any size. Draw a straight line on a piece of paper. Roll the coin along the line until the coin has gone through one revolution, marking the beginning and the end of the revolution.

   Measure the line segment to find the circumference of the coin. $C =$ _____

   Measure the diameter of the coin. $d =$ _____

   Divide the circumference by the diameter. $\dfrac{C}{d} =$ _____

2. Measure the circumference of the top of a wastebasket using a tape measure. $C =$ _____

   Measure the diameter of the wastebasket. $d =$ _____

   Divide the circumference by the diameter. $\dfrac{C}{d} =$ _____

3. Continue computing the value of the ratio $\dfrac{C}{d}$ for several circular objects such as different coins, cups, plates, or wheels.

Item	Circumference	Diameter	$\dfrac{C}{d}$

Part II—Analyzing the Data

4. The exact value of π can never be computed because π is an irrational number. Decimal approximations for π have been computed to thousands of decimal places. Some calculators give 3.1415927 as an approximation for π which is correct to six decimal places. Compare the values you found in Part I with this value of π.

5. In the past, mathematicians had to find clever ways to find an approximation for π. Some of these approximations are given below. The more terms or factors you use, the better your approximation will be. Use a calculator (one with a square root key and a memory) to find the value of each approximation using the number of terms or factors shown. Which approximation is the most accurate? _____

   a. $\pi \approx 2 + \left(\sqrt{0.5} \cdot \sqrt{0.5 + 0.5\sqrt{0.5}} \cdot \sqrt{0.5 + 0.5\sqrt{0.5 + 0.5\sqrt{0.5}}} \right)$ (Vieta, 16th century)

   b. $\pi \approx 4 \cdot \left(1 - \dfrac{1}{3} + \dfrac{1}{5} - \dfrac{1}{7} + \dfrac{1}{9} - \dfrac{1}{11} + \dfrac{1}{13} - \dfrac{1}{15} \right)$ (Leibniz, 17th century)

   c. $\pi \approx 2\sqrt{3} \cdot \left(1 - \dfrac{1}{3 \cdot 3} + \dfrac{1}{3^2 \cdot 5} - \dfrac{1}{3^3 \cdot 7} + \dfrac{1}{3^4 \cdot 9} - \dfrac{1}{3^5 \cdot 11} \right)$ (Sharpe, 16th century)

Enrichment/Exploration
Resource Book, p. 204

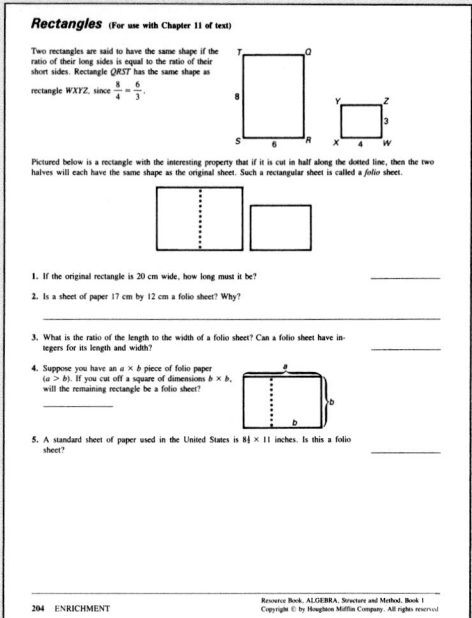

Rectangles (For use with Chapter 11 of text)

Two rectangles are said to have the same shape if the ratio of their long sides is equal to the ratio of their short sides. Rectangle $QRST$ has the same shape as rectangle $WXYZ$, since $\dfrac{8}{4} = \dfrac{6}{3}$.

Pictured below is a rectangle with the interesting property that if it is cut in half along the dotted line, then the two halves will each have the same shape as the original sheet. Such a rectangular sheet is called a *folio* sheet.

1. If the original rectangle is 20 cm wide, how long must it be? _____

2. Is a sheet of paper 17 cm by 12 cm a folio sheet? Why? _____

3. What is the ratio of the length to the width of a folio sheet? Can a folio sheet have integers for its length and width? _____

4. Suppose you have an $a \times b$ piece of folio paper $(a > b)$. If you cut off a square of dimensions $b \times b$, will the remaining rectangle be a folio sheet? _____

5. A standard sheet of paper used in the United States is $8\frac{1}{2} \times 11$ inches. Is this a folio sheet? _____

Thinking Skills
Resource Book, p. 227

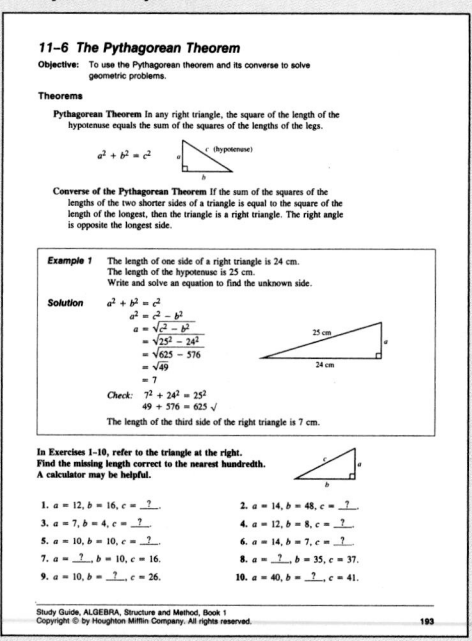

Thinking Skills (For use after Chapter 11)

You may wish to use a calculator with some of these exercises.

Analysis

1. The drawing at the right consists of four right triangles, all with legs having lengths a and b (where $b > a$) and hypotenuse having length c. The triangles are arranged so that a large outer square and a small inner square are formed.

   a. What is the length of a side of the inner square? _____

   b. Show how the drawing "proves" the Pythagorean theorem. (*Hint:* Consider the relationship among the areas of the outer square, the four right triangles, and the inner square.) _____

Applying concepts

2. A *Pythagorean triple* (a, b, c) consists of three positive integers such that $a^2 + b^2 = c^2$. Use this definition to find the missing member of each Pythagorean triple.

   a. $(3, 4, c)$ _____   b. $(5, b, 13)$ _____   c. $(a, 24, 25)$ _____

Analysis

3. For each of the Pythagorean triples (a, b, c) in Exercise 2, find the sum of b and c.

   a. What is the relationship of this sum to a? _____

   b. What is the relationship of *half* this sum to b and c? _____

Synthesis

4. Let $a = 9$. Use your observations from Exercise 3 to find b and c so that (a, b, c) is a Pythagorean triple. _____

5. Let $a = n$, where n is an odd number greater than 1. Write b and c in terms of n so that (a, b, c) is a Pythagorean triple. _____

Reasoning and drawing inferences

6. A Pythagorean triple (a, b, c) is called *primitive* if a, b, and c have no common factor other than 1. For example, $(3, 4, 5)$ *is* a primitive Pythagorean triple, but $(6, 8, 10)$ is *not*, because 6, 8, and 10 have a common factor of 2. Does the pattern described in Exercise 5 always produce primitive Pythagorean triples? Defend your answer. _____

7. You might think that the pattern described in Exercise 5 produces *all possible* primitive Pythagorean triples. Show that this conjecture is false by giving a counterexample. (That is, find a primitive Pythagorean triple for which the smallest member is *not* an odd number greater than 1.) _____

Connection (Geometry)
Study Guide, p. 193

11–6 The Pythagorean Theorem

Objective: To use the Pythagorean theorem and its converse to solve geometric problems.

Theorems

Pythagorean Theorem In any right triangle, the square of the length of the hypotenuse equals the sum of the squares of the lengths of the legs.

$$a^2 + b^2 = c^2$$

c (hypotenuse)

Converse of the Pythagorean Theorem If the sum of the squares of the lengths of the two shorter sides of a triangle is equal to the square of the length of the longest, then the triangle is a right triangle. The right angle is opposite the longest side.

Example 1	The length of one side of a right triangle is 24 cm. The length of the hypotenuse is 25 cm. Write and solve an equation to find the unknown side.
Solution	$a^2 + b^2 = c^2$ $a^2 = c^2 - b^2$ $a = \sqrt{c^2 - b^2}$ $= \sqrt{25^2 - 24^2}$ $= \sqrt{625 - 576}$ $= \sqrt{49}$ $= 7$ **Check:** $7^2 + 24^2 = 25^2$ $49 + 576 = 625$ ✓ The length of the third side of the right triangle is 7 cm.

In Exercises 1–10, refer to the triangle at the right. Find the missing length correct to the nearest hundredth. A calculator may be helpful.

1. $a = 12$, $b = 16$, $c = \underline{\ ?\ }$
2. $a = 14$, $b = 48$, $c = \underline{\ ?\ }$
3. $a = 7$, $b = 4$, $c = \underline{\ ?\ }$
4. $a = 12$, $b = 8$, $c = \underline{\ ?\ }$
5. $a = 10$, $b = 10$, $c = \underline{\ ?\ }$
6. $a = 14$, $b = 7$, $c = \underline{\ ?\ }$
7. $a = \underline{\ ?\ }$, $b = 10$, $c = 16$.
8. $a = \underline{\ ?\ }$, $b = 35$, $c = 37$.
9. $a = 10$, $b = \underline{\ ?\ }$, $c = 26$.
10. $a = 40$, $b = \underline{\ ?\ }$, $c = 41$.

ACTIVITY 33. Fractions for Repeating Decimals (for use with Section 11-2)

Directions: Write all answers in the spaces provided.

PROBLEM

Every repeating decimal can be expressed as a fraction. In the repeating decimal $2.\overline{45}$, for example, we will call 2 the integer part and 45 the block of repeating digits. Express $2.\overline{45}$ as a fraction.

PROGRAM

```
10   PRINT "WHAT IS THE INTEGER PART OF THE NUMBER";
20   INPUT A
30   PRINT "WHAT IS THE BLOCK OF REPEATING DIGITS";
40   INPUT B
50   PRINT "HOW MANY DIGITS IN THE REPEATING BLOCK";
60   INPUT S
70   LET P = INT(10 ↑ S + .5)
80   LET D = P − 1
90   LET N = D * A + B
100  PRINT
110  PRINT A; "."; B; B; ". . ."
120  PRINT "="; N; "/"; D
130  END
```

PROGRAM CHECK

Type in the program. To test whether you entered it correctly, run the program. Enter 2 after the first question, 45 after the second question, and 2 after the third question. The computer should print

```
        2. 45 45 45 . . .
        = 243 / 99
```

IMPROVING THE PROGRAM

You may have noticed in the check that the program does not reduce fractions. Add the following lines to the program, so that all answers will be expressed in simplest form.

```
130  LET E = N
140  LET F = D
150  IF E = 0 THEN 200
160  LET R = F − E * INT(F / E)
170  LET F = E
180  LET E = R
190  GOTO 150
200  LET N = N / F
210  LET D = D / F
220  IF N = D * A + B THEN 270
230  PRINT "="; N; "/"; D
240  IF D = 1 THEN 260
250  GOTO 270
260  PRINT "="; N
270  END
```

(continued)

73

(Activity 33 continued)

As a check for the revised program, enter the numbers 2, 45, and 2 in response to the questions. This time the computer should print

```
        2. 45 45 45 . . .
        = 243 / 99
        = 27 / 11
```

USING THE PROGRAM

Run the program to find the fraction for each of these repeating decimals.

1. $0.\overline{1}$ _____   2. $2.\overline{12}$ _____

3. $0.\overline{123}$ _____   4. $2.\overline{142857}$ _____

5. $3.\overline{30}$ _____   6. $5.\overline{3210}$ _____

7. $7.\overline{7}$ _____   8. $1.\overline{9}$ _____

9. $2.\overline{9}$ _____   10. $3.\overline{9}$ _____

ANALYSIS

11. Examine the results of Problems 8–10. How would you write 6.999... in simplest form? _____

12. Examine your answer to Problem 4. How would you write $21.\overline{428571}$ as a fraction? _____

EXTENSION

Although the program is not designed to convert $1.2\overline{37}$ to a fraction, you can do so as follows:
1. Multiply $1.2\overline{37}$ by 100 to get $123.\overline{7}$.
2. Run the program for $123.\overline{7}$ to get a fraction.
3. Divide the fraction obtained by the computer by 100 to get the correct answer.

Using this process, find the fraction for each of these repeating decimals.

13. $1.2\overline{37}$ _____

14. $0.4\overline{9}$ _____

15. $0.24\overline{9}$ _____

16. Without using the computer, guess the fraction in simplest form for $0.1\overline{9}$. _____

17. Examine your answers to Problems 14, 15, and 16. Can you find a more common decimal for each of the given repeating decimals? _____

74

Using Models/Exploration
Overhead Visual 12, Sheets 1, 2, 3, and 4

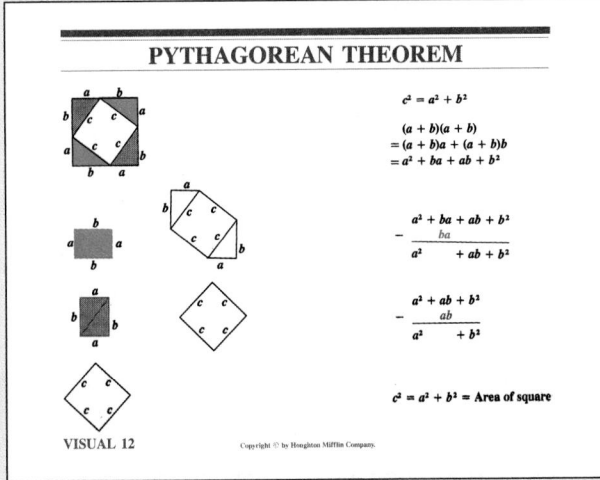

PYTHAGOREAN THEOREM

$$c^2 = a^2 + b^2$$

$$(a + b)(a + b)$$
$$= (a + b)a + (a + b)b$$
$$= a^2 + ba + ab + b^2$$

$$\begin{array}{r} a^2 + ba + ab + b^2 \\ -\quad\quad ba \quad\quad\quad \\ \hline a^2 \quad\quad + ab + b^2 \end{array}$$

$$\begin{array}{r} a^2 + ab + b^2 \\ -\quad ab \quad\quad \\ \hline a^2 \quad\quad + b^2 \end{array}$$

$$c^2 = a^2 + b^2 = \text{Area of square}$$

VISUAL 12

505f

Application

Theodolites, such as that shown in the photo, are the instruments that people generally associate with surveying. They are used to measure angles. This is done by focusing the telescope on an object and reading the angle on a circular scale. Other instruments used in surveying include steel tapes, compasses, and levels. They are used to measure distance, direction, and elevation.

It is not efficient to measure every dimension of a plot of land using surveying tools. A surveyor takes only a few measurements, and then calculates the other dimensions using geometry and trigonometry.

Group Activities
Students may enjoy seeing how surveying equipment is used. You can invite a surveyor to give a demonstration to your class using the school's baseball field as an example. You can ask students to answer these questions: Are the bases 90 ft apart? Are the angles between bases 90°? Can the bases be 90 ft apart and not form a square? If one of the angles is a right angle, and all of the lengths between bases are 90 ft, must the paths between bases form a square? Have students make drawings to support their conclusions.

A few students may wish to write reports about the use of surveying tools in engineering or map making. Alternately, a student may wish to explore the difference between plane surveys and geodetic surveys, and discuss his or her findings with the class.

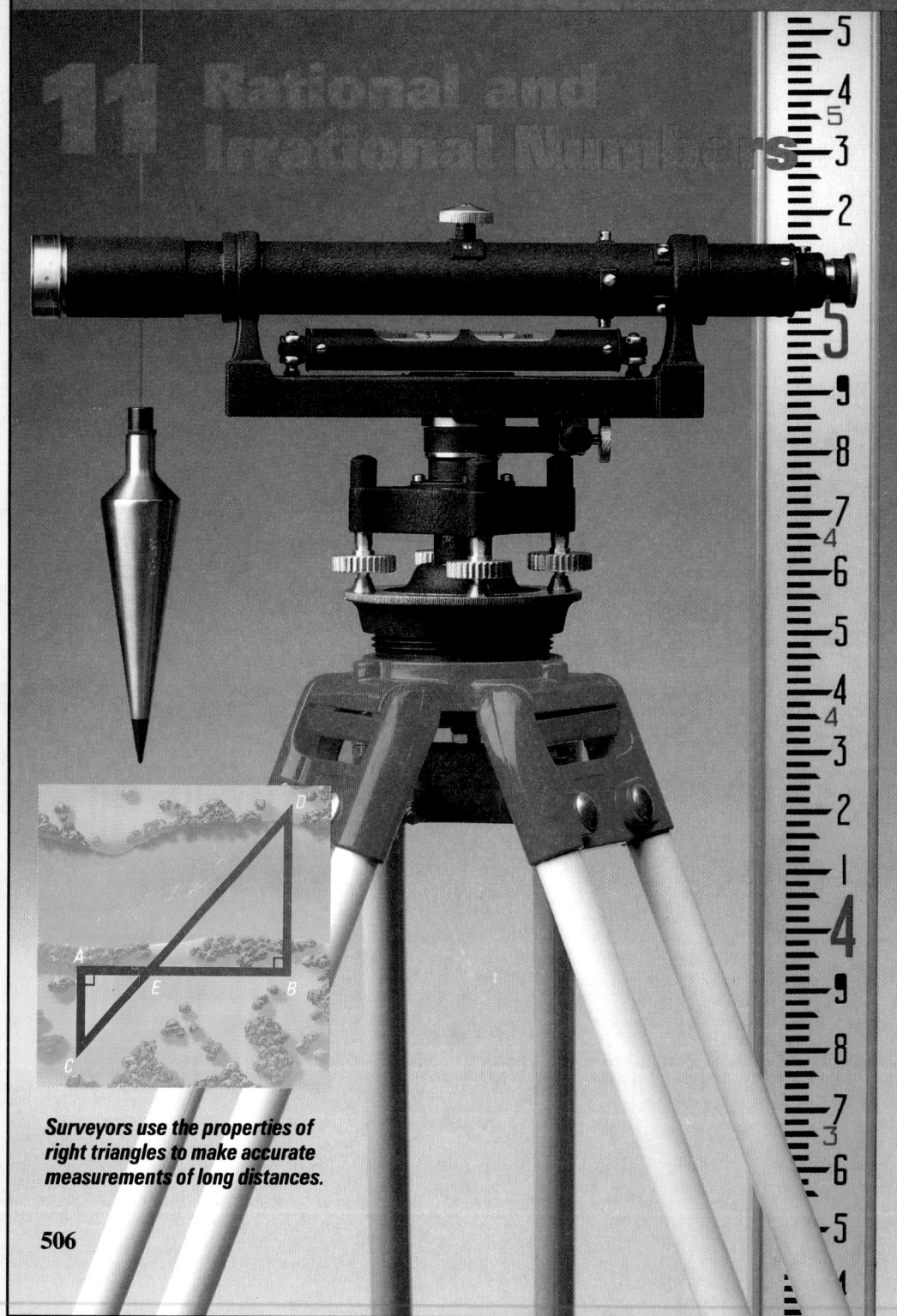

Surveyors use the properties of right triangles to make accurate measurements of long distances.

506

Rational Numbers

11-1 Properties of Rational Numbers

Objective   To learn and apply some properties of rational numbers.

In Chapter 1, you learned that the positive numbers, the negative numbers, and zero are called real numbers.

A real number that can be expressed as the quotient of two integers is called a **rational number.**

Each number below is a rational number.

$$0 = \frac{0}{1} \qquad 7 = \frac{7}{1} \qquad 5\frac{2}{3} = \frac{17}{3} \qquad 0.43 = \frac{43}{100} \qquad -\frac{4}{9} = \frac{-4}{9}$$

A rational number can be written as a quotient of integers in an unlimited number of ways.

Example 1   Write as a quotient of integers: **a.** 3   **b.** $-1\frac{4}{5}$ **c.** 48%   **d.** 0.6

Solution   **a.** $3 = \frac{6}{2} = \frac{12}{4} = \frac{-15}{-5} = \ldots$ **b.** $-1\frac{4}{5} = \frac{-9}{5} = \frac{18}{-10} = \ldots$

   c. $48\% = \frac{48}{100} = \frac{24}{50} = \ldots$ **d.** $0.6 = \frac{6}{10} = \frac{12}{20} = \ldots$

   To determine which of two rational numbers is greater, you can write them with the same positive denominator and compare their numerators.

Example 2   Which rational number is greater, $\frac{8}{3}$ or $\frac{17}{7}$?

Solution   The LCD is 21.

   $\frac{8}{3} = \frac{56}{21}$ and $\frac{17}{7} = \frac{51}{21}$.

   Compare $\frac{56}{21}$ and $\frac{51}{21}$.

   Since $56 > 51$, $\frac{56}{21} > \frac{51}{21}$.

   $\therefore \frac{8}{3} > \frac{17}{7}$ **Answer**

Rational and Irrational Numbers   **507**

Teaching References
Lesson Commentary,
   pp. T131–T137
Assignment Guide,
   pp. T69–T71
Supplementary Materials
   Practice Masters 66–72
   Tests 48–52
   Resource Book
      Practice Exercises,
         pp. 131–135
      Tests, pp. 60–63
      Enrichment Activity,
         p. 204
      Application, p. 188
   Study Guide, pp. 183–202
   Computer Activities 33–35
   Test Generator
   California Standards
   Support Workbook
      Explorations for
         Lessons 11-2, 11-6
   Alternate Test, p. T22

Teaching Suggestions, p. T131

Suggested Extensions, p. T131

Warm-Up Exercises

Replace the __?__ with <, =, or > to make a true statement.

1. -8 __?__ 4   <

2. -3 __?__ -7 >

3. $4(-3)$ __?__ $-7 - 5$ =

Write each number as a fraction in simplest form.

4. $2\frac{3}{5}$ $\frac{13}{5}$

5. 0.25 $\frac{1}{4}$

6. 27% $\frac{27}{100}$

Motivating the Lesson

Stock A increased by $1\frac{3}{4}$ points. Stock B increased by $1\frac{5}{8}$ points. Which stock showed the greater increase? (Stock A) Tell students that to find this answer, it is helpful to understand some properties of rational numbers, which is the topic of today's lesson.

Chalkboard Examples

1. Write as a quotient of integers.

   a. $2\frac{3}{7}$ **b.** 0.54

   a. $2\frac{3}{7} = \frac{17}{7} = \frac{34}{14} = \cdots$

   b. $0.54 = \frac{54}{100} = \frac{-27}{-50} = \cdots$

2. Which rational number is greater, $-\frac{11}{4}$ or $-\frac{25}{9}$?

   The LCD is 36.

   $-\frac{11}{4} = \frac{-99}{36}$ and

   $-\frac{25}{9} = \frac{-100}{36}$

   Since $-99 > -100$,

   $\frac{-99}{36} > \frac{-100}{36}$.

   $\therefore -\frac{11}{4} > -\frac{25}{9}$

3. Replace the __?__ with $<$, $=$, or $>$ to make a true statement.

   $-3\frac{4}{13}$ __?__ $-\frac{36}{11}$

   Write $-3\frac{4}{13}$ as $-\frac{43}{13}$.

   $-\frac{43}{13} = \frac{-43}{13}$ and

   $-\frac{36}{11} = \frac{-36}{11}$.

   $\frac{-43}{13}$ __?__ $\frac{-36}{11}$

   $(-43)(11)$ __?__ $(13)(-36)$

   $-473 < -468$

   $\therefore -3\frac{4}{13} < -\frac{36}{11}$

For all integers a and b and all positive integers c and d:

1. $\dfrac{a}{c} > \dfrac{b}{d}$ if and only if $ad > bc$.

2. $\dfrac{a}{c} < \dfrac{b}{d}$ if and only if $ad < bc$.

(See Exercise 36 on page 511 for a proof of the second statement.)

Thus, $\dfrac{4}{7} > \dfrac{3}{8}$ because $(4)(8) > (3)(7)$;

$\dfrac{7}{9} < \dfrac{4}{5}$ because $(7)(5) < (4)(9)$.

Example 3 Replace the __?__ with $<$, $=$, or $>$ to make a true statement.

   a. $-\dfrac{5}{8}$ __?__ $-\dfrac{7}{13}$.

   b. $6\dfrac{4}{7}$ __?__ $\dfrac{53}{9}$.

Solution **a.** $-\dfrac{5}{8} = \dfrac{-5}{8}$ and $-\dfrac{7}{13} = \dfrac{-7}{13}$.

   $\dfrac{-5}{8}$ __?__ $\dfrac{-7}{13}$

   $(-5)(13)$ __?__ $(-7)(8)$

   $-65 < -56$

   $\therefore -\dfrac{5}{8} < -\dfrac{7}{13}$

   Answer

   b. Write $6\dfrac{4}{7}$ as $\dfrac{46}{7}$.

   $\dfrac{46}{7}$ __?__ $\dfrac{53}{9}$

   $(46)(9)$ __?__ $(53)(7)$

   $414 > 371$

   $\therefore 6\dfrac{4}{7} > \dfrac{53}{9}$

   Answer

Rational numbers differ from integers in several ways. For example, given any integer, there is a next greater integer: -8 follows -9, 1 follows 0, 24 follows 23, and so on. However, there is no "next greater" rational number after a given rational number. This property of rational numbers is called the *density property*.

The Density Property for Rational Numbers

Between every pair of different rational numbers there is another rational number.

The density property implies that it is possible to find an unlimited or endless number of rational numbers between two given rational numbers. For example, if a and b are rational numbers and $a < b$, then the number halfway from a to b is $a + \dfrac{1}{2}(b - a)$; the number one third of the way from a to b is $a + \dfrac{1}{3}(b - a)$; and so on.

508 *Chapter 11*

Example 4 Find a rational number between $\frac{3}{4}$ and $\frac{5}{6}$.

Solution Choose, for example, the number halfway between $\frac{3}{4}$ and $\frac{5}{6}$. This number can be expressed as:

$$\frac{3}{4} + \frac{1}{2}\left(\frac{5}{6} - \frac{3}{4}\right) = \frac{3}{4} + \frac{1}{2}\left(\frac{10}{12} - \frac{9}{12}\right)$$

$$= \frac{3}{4} + \frac{1}{2}\left(\frac{1}{12}\right)$$

$$= \frac{3}{4} + \frac{1}{24}$$

$$= \frac{18}{24} + \frac{1}{24}$$

$$= \frac{19}{24}$$

Check: Is $\frac{3}{4} < \frac{19}{24}$?   Is $\frac{19}{24} < \frac{5}{6}$?

Is $(3)(24) < (19)(4)$?   Is $(19)(6) < (5)(24)$?

$72 < 76$ ✓ $114 < 120$ ✓

∴ $\frac{19}{24}$ is a rational number between $\frac{3}{4}$ and $\frac{5}{6}$.   **Answer**

The number halfway between two numbers is also their average since

$$a + \frac{1}{2}(b - a) = \frac{2a}{2} + \frac{b - a}{2} = \frac{a + b}{2}.$$

Oral Exercises

Express each number as a quotient of two integers.

Sample   5.34   **Solution** $\frac{534}{100}$

1. 4.6 $\frac{46}{10}$ **2.** -3.5 $-\frac{35}{10}$ **3.** $-2\frac{3}{4}$ $-\frac{11}{4}$ **4.** 61% $\frac{61}{100}$

5. -7 $-\frac{7}{1}$ **6.** 32 $\frac{32}{1}$ **7.** $0\frac{0}{a}, a \neq 0$ **8.** $\frac{3}{11} + \left(-\frac{7}{11}\right)$ $-\frac{4}{11}$

Which rational number in each pair is the greater?

9. $\frac{7}{13}, \frac{9}{13}$ $\frac{9}{13}$ **10.** $-\frac{4}{7}, -\frac{5}{7}$ $-\frac{4}{7}$ **11.** $-5, \frac{1}{2}$ $\frac{1}{2}$

12. $\frac{1}{4}, \frac{1}{5}$ $\frac{1}{4}$ **13.** $\frac{5}{8}, \frac{3}{4}$ $\frac{3}{4}$ **14.** $-\frac{9}{2}, -\frac{13}{3}$ $-\frac{13}{3}$

15. How many integers are between -4 and -2? How many rational numbers?

16. How many integers are between 100 and 101? How many rational numbers?

17. Is -7 a real number? an integer? a rational number?   **17.** yes; yes; yes

15. one (-3); an infinite number
16. none; an infinite number

Rational and Irrational Numbers   **509**

---

4. Find a rational number between $-\frac{5}{8}$ and $-\frac{1}{3}$.

The number halfway between $-\frac{5}{8}$ and $-\frac{1}{3}$ can be expressed as:

$$-\frac{5}{8} + \frac{1}{2}\left[-\frac{1}{3} - \left(-\frac{5}{8}\right)\right]$$

$$= -\frac{5}{8} + \frac{1}{2}\left(-\frac{1}{3} + \frac{5}{8}\right)$$

$$= -\frac{5}{8} + \frac{1}{2}\left(-\frac{8}{24} + \frac{15}{24}\right)$$

$$= -\frac{5}{8} + \frac{1}{2}\left(\frac{7}{24}\right)$$

$$= -\frac{5}{8} + \frac{7}{48}$$

$$= -\frac{30}{48} + \frac{7}{48}$$

$$= -\frac{23}{48}$$

Check: Is $-\frac{5}{8} < -\frac{23}{48}$?

Is $-5(48) < (-23)(8)$?
$-240 < -184$ ✓

Is $-\frac{23}{48} < -\frac{1}{3}$?

Is $(-23)(3) < (-1)(48)$?
$-69 < -48$ ✓

∴ $-\frac{23}{48}$ is a rational number

between $-\frac{5}{8}$ and $-\frac{1}{3}$.

Replace the __?__ with $<$, $=$, or $>$ to make a true statement.

1. $\frac{1}{7}$ __?__ $\frac{4}{35}$ $>$

2. $-\frac{5}{12}$ __?__ $-\frac{40}{9}$ $>$

3. $\frac{158}{15}$ __?__ $10\frac{3}{8}$ $>$

Arrange each group of numbers in order from least to greatest.

4. $\frac{2}{3}, \frac{1}{2}, \frac{3}{4}, \frac{1}{2}, \frac{2}{3}, \frac{3}{4}$

5. $-6.2, -6\frac{1}{3}, -\frac{77}{12}$

$-\frac{77}{12}, -6\frac{1}{3}, -6.2$

Find the number halfway between the given numbers.

6. $\frac{5}{8}$ and $\frac{1}{4}$ $\frac{7}{16}$

7. $-3\frac{1}{6}$ and $1\frac{2}{9}$ $-\frac{35}{36}$

Tell the students they have learned to compare rational numbers using two methods. One method is to write the numbers using the LCD and then compare the numerators. The other method is to compare the product of the extremes with that of the means. Ask students to define the density property for rational numbers.

Minimum
510/1–31 odd
S 511/Mixed Review

Average
510/1–35 odd
S 511/Mixed Review

Maximum
510/2–38 even
S 511/Mixed Review

Written Exercises

Replace the __?__ with $<$, $=$, or $>$ to make a true statement.

A 1. $\frac{1}{9}$ __?__ $\frac{4}{27}$ $<$ 2. $\frac{11}{15}$ __?__ $\frac{2}{3}$ $>$ 3. $-\frac{3}{4}$ __?__ $-\frac{9}{13}$ $<$ 4. $-\frac{7}{8}$ __?__ $-\frac{5}{6}$ $<$

5. $\frac{3}{4}$ __?__ $\frac{24}{32}$ $=$ 6. $\frac{12}{19}$ __?__ $\frac{17}{24}$ $<$ 7. $-18\frac{2}{5}$ __?__ $-\frac{131}{7}$ $>$ 8. $-\frac{214}{14}$ __?__ $-15\frac{2}{3}$ $>$

Arrange each group of numbers in order from least to greatest. $-5, 5.6, \frac{107}{18}$

9. $\frac{4}{7}, \frac{3}{8}, \frac{5}{9}, \frac{3}{8}, \frac{5}{9}, \frac{4}{7}$ 10. $\frac{3}{5}, \frac{5}{7}, \frac{2}{9}, \frac{2}{9}, \frac{3}{5}, \frac{5}{7}$ 11. $5.6, \frac{107}{18}, -5$

12. $-3.8, -\frac{35}{8}, -3$ 13. $\frac{7}{24}, \frac{4}{15}, \frac{5}{16}, \frac{1}{2}$ 14. $-\frac{3}{7}, -\frac{5}{6}, -\frac{3}{5}, -\frac{7}{9}$

$-\frac{35}{8}, -3.8, -3$ $\frac{4}{15}, \frac{7}{24}, \frac{5}{16}, \frac{1}{2}$ $-\frac{5}{6}, -\frac{7}{9}, -\frac{3}{5}, -\frac{3}{7}$

Find the number halfway between the given numbers.

15. $\frac{5}{9}$ and $\frac{4}{7}$ $\frac{71}{126}$ 16. $\frac{7}{11}$ and $\frac{3}{4}$ $\frac{61}{88}$ 17. $-\frac{4}{25}$ and $-\frac{9}{50}$ $-\frac{17}{100}$

18. $-\frac{5}{39}$ and $-\frac{6}{117}$ $-\frac{7}{78}$ 19. $2\frac{3}{4}$ and $-3\frac{3}{4}$ $-\frac{1}{2}$ 20. $-5\frac{1}{5}$ and $8\frac{2}{3}$ $1\frac{11}{15}$

If $x \in \{0, 1, 2, 3\}$, state whether each fraction increases or decreases in value as x takes on its values in increasing order.

Sample $\frac{x}{4}$ becomes $\frac{0}{4}, \frac{1}{4}, \frac{2}{4}, \frac{3}{4}$. $\therefore$ the fraction increases.

B 21. $\frac{x}{3}$ 22. $\frac{x}{5}$ 23. $\frac{7}{x+1}$ 24. $\frac{x+1}{6}$ 25. $\frac{9-2x}{5}$ 26. $\frac{14}{12-3x}$

increases   increases   decreases   increases   decreases   increases

27. Find the number one-third of the way from $\frac{1}{6}$ to $\frac{4}{5}$. $\frac{17}{45}$

28. Find the number one-fourth of the way from $\frac{5}{8}$ to $1\frac{1}{4}$. $\frac{25}{32}$

29. Find the number one-fifth of the way from $-\frac{2}{3}$ to $\frac{3}{5}$. $-\frac{31}{75}$

30. Find the number three-fourths of the way from $\frac{1}{2}$ to $\frac{8}{9}$. $\frac{19}{24}$

31. Find a rational number between $\frac{1}{3}$ and $\frac{3}{4}$. example: $\frac{13}{24}$

32. Find a rational number between $-\frac{1}{6}$ and $-\frac{1}{4}$. example: $-\frac{1}{5}$

33. Write an expression in simplest form for the number halfway between $\frac{3a}{7}$ and $-\frac{a}{12}$. $\frac{29a}{168}$

34. Write an expression in simplest form for the number two-thirds of the way from $-\frac{7b}{5}$ to $-\frac{2b}{3}$. $-\frac{41b}{45}$

35. a. Brian and Lou agreed to share equally the profits from their lawn mowing business. At the end of one week, Brian had earned $27.50 and Lou had earned $35.50. Brian said, "You owe me half the difference, which is $4.00." Was he right? yes

   b. In general, suppose Brian received a dollars and Lou received b dollars, where $b > a$. Show that if Lou gives Brian $\frac{1}{2}(b - a)$ dollars, then each will have exactly the same amount of money.

C 36. Supply the missing reasons in the proof of the following theorem:

For all integers a and b and all positive integers c and d, $\frac{a}{c} < \frac{b}{d}$ if and only if $ad < bc$.

Proof: If $\frac{a}{c} < \frac{b}{d}$, then $ad < bc$.

1. $\frac{a}{c} < \frac{b}{d}$ 1. Given

2. $\frac{ad}{cd} < \frac{bc}{cd}$ $\left(\text{since } \frac{d}{d} = \frac{c}{c} = 1\right)$ 2. _?_ Mult. rule for fractions

3. $ad < bc$ 3. _?_ Mult. prop. of order

$\therefore$ if $\frac{a}{c} < \frac{b}{d}$, then $ad < bc$.

Proof: If $ad < bc$, $\frac{a}{c} < \frac{b}{d}$.

1. $ad < bc$ 1. Given

2. $\frac{ad}{cd} < \frac{bc}{cd}$ (since $cd > 0$)   2. _?_ Mult. prop. of order

3. $\frac{a}{c} < \frac{b}{d}$ 3. _?_ Rule for simplifying fractions

$\therefore$ if $ad < bc$, then $\frac{a}{c} < \frac{b}{d}$.

$\therefore \frac{a}{c} < \frac{b}{d}$ if and only if $ad < bc$.

State conditions for w and z that make the following true.

37. $\frac{x}{w} > \frac{x}{z}$; $x > 0$
$w < z$ and $wz > 0$; or $z < 0 < w$

38. $\frac{x}{w - z} < \frac{x}{z - w}$; $x > 0$
$z > w$

Mixed Review Exercises

Solve each inequality and graph its solution.

1. $3y + 4 \leq 10$ **2.** $|0.5 + x| < 10$ **3.** $10 + 6|2 - k| \geq 22$

4. $|3 + z| \geq 5$ **5.** $4 \leq 2x + 4 < 6$ **6.** $6 \leq 2 - 4m$

Write as a fraction in simplest form.

7. 35% $\frac{7}{20}$ **8.** 0.6 $\frac{3}{5}$ **9.** 4.4 $\frac{22}{5}$ **10.** $3 \cdot 10^{-4}$ $\frac{3}{10,000}$ **11.** $62\frac{1}{2}\%$ $\frac{5}{8}$ **12.** $\frac{1}{4}\%$ $\frac{1}{400}$

Rational and Irrational Numbers   **511**

Teaching Suggestions p. 131
Reading Algebra p. 132
Suggested Extensions p. 132

Motivating the Lesson

The population of Turkey is about 0.0625 times the population of India. Ask students if they know what fraction expresses this same relationship? $\frac{1}{16}$

Expressing rational numbers as fractions or decimals is the topic of today's lesson.

Warm-Up Exercises

Divide. If necessary, round to the nearest thousandth.

1. $125)\overline{50}$ 0.4

2. $12)\overline{7}$ 0.583

3. $9)\overline{20}$ 2.222

4. $5)\overline{0.62}$ 0.124

Chalkboard Examples

Express each rational number as a decimal.

1. $\frac{7}{8}$ 0.875

2. $2\frac{2}{3}$ 2.66 . . .

Express each decimal as a fraction in simplest form.

3. 0.48 $\frac{48}{100} = \frac{12}{25}$

4. $0.\overline{342}$

$1000N = 342.\overline{342}$

$\underline{\quad N = \quad\ 0.\overline{342}}$

$999N = 342$

$N = \frac{342}{999} = \frac{38}{111}$

$\therefore 0.\overline{342} = \frac{38}{111}$

11-2 Decimal Forms of Rational Numbers

Objective   To express rational numbers as decimals or fractions.

Any common fraction can be written as a decimal by dividing the numerator by the denominator. If the remainder is zero, the decimal is called a **terminating, ending,** or **finite decimal.**

Example   Express $\frac{3}{8}$ as a decimal.

Solution

$$
\begin{array}{r}
0.375 \\
8)\overline{3.000} \\
\underline{2\ 4} \\
60 \\
\underline{56} \\
40 \\
\underline{40} \\
0
\end{array}
$$

The division at the left shows that $\frac{3}{8}$ can be expressed as the terminating decimal 0.375. **Answer**

If you don't reach a remainder of zero when dividing the numerator by the denominator, continue to divide until the remainders begin to repeat.

Example 2   Express each rational number as a decimal: **a.** $\frac{5}{6}$ **b.** $\frac{7}{11}$ **c.** $3\frac{2}{7}$

Solution

a. $\frac{5}{6} \rightarrow$
$$
\begin{array}{r}
0.833 \\
6)\overline{5.000} \\
\underline{4\ 8} \\
20 \\
\underline{18} \\
20 \\
\underline{18} \\
2
\end{array}
$$
$\therefore \frac{5}{6} = 0.833 \ldots$

b. $\frac{7}{11} \rightarrow$
$$
\begin{array}{r}
0.6363 \\
11)\overline{7.0000} \\
\underline{6\ 6} \\
40 \\
\underline{33} \\
70 \\
\underline{66} \\
40 \\
\underline{33} \\
7
\end{array}
$$
$\therefore \frac{7}{11} = 0.6363 \ldots$

c. $3\frac{2}{7} = \frac{23}{7} \rightarrow$
$$
\begin{array}{r}
3.2857142 \\
7)\overline{23.0000000} \\
\underline{21} \\
2\ 0 \\
\underline{1\ 4} \\
60 \\
\underline{56} \\
40 \\
\underline{35} \\
50 \\
\underline{49} \\
10 \\
\underline{7} \\
30 \\
\underline{28} \\
20 \\
\underline{14} \\
6
\end{array}
$$
$\therefore 3\frac{2}{7} = 3.285714285714 \ldots$

The decimal quotients shown in Example 2 are **nonterminating, unending,** or **infinite.** The dots indicate that the decimals continue without end. We write:

$$\frac{5}{6} = 0.833\ldots \qquad \frac{7}{11} = 0.6363\ldots \qquad 3\frac{2}{7} = 3.285714285714\ldots$$

They are also called **repeating** or **periodic** because the same digit or block of digits repeats unendingly. A bar is used to indicate the block of digits that repeat, as shown below.

$$\frac{5}{6} = 0.8\overline{3} \qquad \frac{7}{11} = 0.\overline{63} \qquad 3\frac{2}{7} = 3.\overline{285714}$$

When you divide a positive integer n by a positive integer d, the remainder r at each step must be zero or a positive integer less than d. For example, if the divisor is 6, the remainders will be 0, 1, 2, 3, 4, or 5, and the division will terminate or begin repeating within 5 steps after only zeros remain to be brought down. In general:

> For every integer n and every positive integer d, the decimal form of the rational number $\frac{n}{d}$ either terminates or eventually repeats in a block of fewer than d digits.

To express a terminating decimal as a common fraction, express the decimal as a common fraction with a power of ten as the denominator. This fraction is then usually expressed in simplest form.

Example 3 Express each terminating decimal as a fraction in simplest form.

　　　　　a. 0.38　　　　　　　**b.** 0.425

Solution **a.** $0.38 = \frac{38}{100} = \frac{19}{50}$　　**b.** $0.425 = \frac{425}{1000} = \frac{17}{40}$

The following examples show how to express a repeating decimal as a common fraction.

Example 4 Express $0.5\overline{42}$ as a fraction in simplest form.

Solution Let N = the number $0.5\overline{42}$.
Let n = the number of digits in the block of repeating digits.

Multiply N by 10^n.
Since $0.5\overline{42}$ has 2 digits in the repeating block, $n = 2$.
Therefore, multiply both sides of the equation $N = 0.5\overline{42}$ by 10^2, or 100.

$$100N = 100(0.5\overline{42})$$

(Solution continues on the next page.)

Rational and Irrational Numbers　　**513**

Express each rational number as a terminating or repeating decimal.

1. $\frac{3}{4}$ 0.75

2. $-\frac{5}{9}$ $-0.\overline{5}$

Express each rational number as a fraction in simplest form.

5. -0.8 $-\frac{4}{5}$

6. 2.15 $\frac{43}{20}$

7. $0.\overline{7}$ $\frac{7}{9}$

8. $-0.\overline{123}$ $-\frac{41}{333}$

Summarizing the Lesson

Tell students that today they have learned to express rational numbers as fractions and decimals. In particular, they have learned how to convert repeating decimals to common fractions.

Since $0.5\overline{42} = 0.54242\ldots$, $0.5\overline{42}$ can also be written as $0.54\overline{42}$

Then

$$100(0.5\overline{42}) = 100(0.54\overline{42})$$
$$= 54.2\overline{42}$$

Subtract N from $100N$.

$$100N = 54.2\overline{42}$$
$$\underline{N =\ \ 0.5\overline{42}}$$
$$99N = 53.7$$

Solve for N.

$$N = \frac{53.7}{99} = \frac{537}{990} = \frac{179}{330}$$

$\therefore 0.5\overline{42} = \frac{179}{330}$ ***Answer***

Example 5 Express $-0.\overline{375}$ as a fraction in simplest form.

Solution First, express $0.\overline{375}$ as a common fraction.

Let $N =$ the number.

$$1000N = 375.\overline{375}$$
$$\underline{N =\ \ \ \ 0.\overline{375}}$$
$$999N = 375$$

Since there are 3 digits in the repeating block, multiply N by 10^3, or 1000. Then subtract.

$$N = \frac{375}{999} = \frac{125}{333}$$

Since $0.\overline{375} = \frac{125}{333}$, $-0.\overline{375} = -\frac{125}{333}$. ***Answer***

All terminating decimals and all repeating decimals represent rational numbers that can be written in the form $\frac{n}{d}$, where n is an integer and d is a positive integer.

It is often convenient to use an approximation of a lengthy decimal. For example, you may approximate $\frac{7}{13}$ as 0.53846, 0.538, or 0.54.

To round a decimal:
1. If the first digit dropped is greater than or equal to 5, add 1 to the last digit retained.
2. If the first digit dropped is less than 5, don't change the last digit retained.

Example 6 shows decimals being rounded to various decimal places. The symbol $\approx$ means "is approximately equal to."

514 *Chapter 11*

Example 6 **a.** $0.41\overline{6} \approx 0.417$ (to the nearest thousandth)
                        ≈ 0.42 (to the nearest hundredth)

         b. $0.4\overline{16} \approx 0.416$ (to the nearest thousandth)
                        ≈ 0.42 (to the nearest hundredth)

         c. $0.5\overline{3} \approx 0.54$ (to the nearest hundredth)
                       ≈ 0.5 (to the nearest tenth)

         d. $3.4\overline{81} \approx 3.5$ (to the nearest tenth)
                       ≈ 3 (to the nearest unit)

         e. $0.\overline{681} \approx 0.7$ (to the nearest tenth)
                       ≈ 1 (to the nearest unit)

Oral Exercises

Round each number to the nearest tenth.

1. 5.358 5.4   **2.** -0.729 -0.7 **3.** $4.\overline{6}$ 4.7   **4.** $3.48\overline{2}$ 3.5   **5.** $-0.2\overline{7}$ -0.3

6–10. Round the numbers in Exercises 1–5 to the nearest hundredth.

6. 5.36   **7.** -0.73 **8.** 4.67   **9.** 3.48   **10.** -0.28

Tell whether the decimal form terminates or repeats.

11. $\dfrac{1}{2}$ **12.** $-\dfrac{5}{6}$ **13.** $\dfrac{7}{4}$ **14.** $\dfrac{59}{2000}$ **15.** $\dfrac{18}{7}$ **16.** $-\dfrac{8}{13}$

    terminates   repeats   terminates   terminates   repeats   repeats

Written Exercises

Express each rational number as a terminating or repeating decimal.

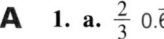

1. a. $\dfrac{2}{3}$ $0.\overline{6}$ **2. a.** $\dfrac{9}{2}$ 4.5   **3. a.** $-\dfrac{4}{9}$ $-0.\overline{4}$ **4. a.** $-\dfrac{3}{5}$ -0.6

    b. $\dfrac{2}{30}$ $0.0\overline{6}$ **b.** $\dfrac{9}{200}$ 0.045   **b.** $-\dfrac{4}{9000}$ $-0.000\overline{4}$ **b.** $-\dfrac{3}{50}$ -0.06

5. $\dfrac{11}{8}$ 1.375   **6.** $\dfrac{11}{12}$ $0.91\overline{6}$ **7.** $\dfrac{15}{11}$ $1.\overline{36}$ **8.** $\dfrac{4}{7}$ $0.\overline{571428}$

9. $-\dfrac{7}{18}$ $-0.3\overline{8}$ **10.** $-\dfrac{15}{32}$ -0.46875 **11.** $3\dfrac{9}{20}$ 3.45   **12.** $2\dfrac{5}{11}$ $2.\overline{45}$

13. $\dfrac{3}{11}$ $0.\overline{27}$ **14.** $-6\dfrac{3}{4}$ -6.75 **15.** $-\dfrac{18}{37}$ $-0.\overline{486}$ **16.** $\dfrac{22}{37}$ $0.\overline{594}$

Express each rational number as a fraction in simplest form.

17. 0.2 $\dfrac{1}{5}$ **18.** 0.66 $\dfrac{33}{50}$ **19.** 0.325 $\dfrac{13}{40}$ **20.** 3.8 $\dfrac{19}{5}$

21. $0.\overline{4}$ $\dfrac{4}{9}$ **22.** $1.\overline{15}$ $\dfrac{38}{33}$ **23.** $-0.28\overline{3}$ $-\dfrac{17}{60}$ **24.** 2.39 $\dfrac{12}{5}$

25. $0.\overline{07}$ $\dfrac{7}{99}$ **26.** $-1.\overline{36}$ $-\dfrac{15}{11}$ **27.** $-2.\overline{3}$ $-\dfrac{7}{3}$ **28.** $0.\overline{857142}$ $\dfrac{6}{7}$

Rational and Irrational Numbers   **515**

Suggested Assignments

Minimum
    515/1–37 odd
S 516/Mixed Review

Average
    515/1–39 odd
S 516/Mixed Review

Maximum
    515/2–42 even
S 516/Mixed Review

Supplementary Materials

Study Guide   pp. 185–186
Practice Master   66
Computer Activity   33
Resource Book   p. 131

Using a Calculator

Students may wish to check their answers to Written Exercises 1–28 by using a calculator.

Find the number halfway between the given numbers.

Sample $\frac{3}{4}$ and 0.756   **Solution** $\frac{3}{4} = \frac{75}{100} = 0.75$

$$0.75 + \frac{1}{2}(0.756 - 0.75) = 0.75 + \frac{1}{2}(0.006)$$
$$= 0.75 + 0.003$$
$$= 0.753 \quad \textbf{\textit{Answer}}$$

B **29.** $\frac{1}{4}$ and 0.259 0.2545   **30.** $\frac{5}{8}$ and 0.634 0.6295   **31.** 0.44 and $0.\overline{4}$ $0.44\overline{2}$

32. 0.77 and $0.\overline{7}$ $0.773\overline{8}$ **33.** 0.83 and $\frac{5}{6}$ $0.831\overline{6}$ **34.** 0.121 and $\frac{1}{8}$ 0.123

Express both numbers as fractions. Then find their product.

35. $\frac{3}{5}$ and 0.75 $\frac{3}{5}, \frac{3}{4}; \frac{9}{20}$ **36.** 0.875 and $\frac{5}{7}$ $\frac{7}{8}, \frac{5}{7}; \frac{5}{8}$ **37.** $0.\overline{6}$ and $\frac{7}{12}$ $\frac{2}{3}, \frac{7}{12}; \frac{7}{18}$

38. $\frac{9}{20}$ and $0.\overline{5}$ $\frac{9}{20}, \frac{5}{9}; \frac{1}{4}$ **39.** $0.\overline{407}$ and $0.2\overline{7}$ $\frac{11}{27}, \frac{5}{18}; \frac{55}{486}$ **40.** $0.3\overline{5}$ and $1.3\overline{36}$ $\frac{16}{45}, \frac{147}{110}; \frac{392}{825}$

C **41. a.** Express $\frac{1}{9}, \frac{5}{9}$, and $\frac{8}{9}$ as repeating decimals. $0.\overline{1}$; $0.\overline{5}$; $0.\overline{8}$

   b. Express $\frac{1}{27}, \frac{5}{27}$, and $\frac{8}{27}$ as repeating decimals. $0.\overline{037}$; $0.\overline{185}$; $0.\overline{296}$

   c. What is the relationship between the numbers in (a) and (b)?

42. a. Express $\frac{1}{7}$ and $\frac{6}{7}$ as repeating decimals. $0.\overline{142857}$; $0.\overline{857142}$

   b. What is the relationship between the blocks of digits that repeat in (a)?

   c. Express $\frac{3}{7}, \frac{4}{7}$, and $\frac{5}{7}$ as decimals. $0.\overline{428571}$; $0.\overline{571428}$; $0.\overline{714285}$

43. Since $\frac{1}{99} = 0.\overline{01}$, $\frac{n}{99} = n(0.\overline{01})$ for $1 \le n < 100$.
$0.\overline{08}$; $0.\overline{32}$; $0.\overline{87}$

   a. Confirm the fact above by expressing $\frac{8}{99}, \frac{32}{99}$, and $\frac{87}{99}$ as decimals.

   b. Express 1 as $\frac{99}{99}$ to show that $0.\overline{9} = 1$. $1 = \frac{99}{99} = 99\left(\frac{1}{99}\right) = 99(0.\overline{01}) = .\overline{99} = 0.\overline{9}$

   c. Use the method of Example 4 to show that $0.\overline{9} = 1$.

Mixed Review Exercises

Find the prime factorization of each number.

1. 200 $2^3 \cdot 5^2$ **2.** 98 $2 \cdot 7^2$ **3.** 1089 $3^2 \cdot 11^2$ **4.** 2250 $2 \cdot 3^2 \cdot 5^3$ **5.** 392 $2^3 \cdot 7^2$ **6.** 576 $2^6 \cdot 3^2$

Solve.

7. $(y + 3)(y - 4) = 0$ {−3, 4}   **8.** $(a + 5)^2 = 9$ {−2, −8}   **9.** $y^2 = -36$ No sol.

10. $k^3 - 16k = 0$ {0, −4, 4}   **11.** $|x + 2| = 10$ {−12, 8}   **12.** $k + 4 < 16$ {the real numbers less than 12}

11-3 Rational Square Roots

Objective   To find the square roots of numbers that have rational square roots.

On page 107, you learned that subtraction "undoes" addition, and that division by a nonzero number "undoes" multiplication. Similarly, squaring a number can be undone by finding a square root.

If $a^2 = b$, then a is a **square root** of b.

Because $7^2 = 49$ and $(-7)^2 = 49$, both 7 and -7 are square roots of 49.

The symbol $\sqrt{}$ is used to write the **principal,** or positive, square root of a positive number.

$\qquad \sqrt{49} = 7$ is read "The *positive* square root of 49 equals 7."

A negative square root is associated with the symbol $-\sqrt{}$.

$\qquad -\sqrt{49} = -7$ is read "The *negative* square root of 49 equals -7."

It is often convenient to use *plus-or-minus* notation:

$\qquad \pm\sqrt{49}$ means the positive *or* negative square root of 49.

In the expression $\sqrt{49}$, the number written beneath the radical sign, such as 49, is called the **radicand.** On scientific calculators you press the key labeled $\sqrt{}$ to find the square root of a number.

For all positive real numbers a:

Every positive real number a has two square roots: $\sqrt{a}$ and $-\sqrt{a}$.
The symbol $\sqrt{a}$ denotes the principal square root of a.
Zero has only one square root, namely zero itself; that is, $\sqrt{0} = 0$.

It follows from the definition of square root that $(\sqrt{a})^2 = a$.

Because the square of every real number is either positive or zero, *negative numbers do not have square roots in the set of real numbers.* If you try to take the square root of a negative number on a calculator, the display will indicate an error.

Notice that $\sqrt{4 \cdot 25} = \sqrt{100} = 10$ and $\sqrt{4} \cdot \sqrt{25} = 2 \cdot 5 = 10$. Therefore $\sqrt{4 \cdot 25} = \sqrt{4} \cdot \sqrt{25}$.

Product Property of Square Roots

For any nonnegative real numbers a and b:

$$\sqrt{ab} = \sqrt{a} \cdot \sqrt{b}$$

Rational and Irrational Numbers   **517**

Teaching Suggestions p. T132
Using Manipulatives p. T133
Suggested Extensions p. T133

Warm-Up Exercises

Is the statement true or false?

1. $8^2 = 16$ false
2. The square of 13 is 169. true
3. $(5 \cdot 3)^2 = 5^2 \cdot 3^2$ true
4. $(24)^2 = (2^3 \cdot 3)^2$ true
5. $\left(\dfrac{3}{5}\right)^2 = \dfrac{9}{5}$ false
6. $2^2 + 9^2 = 11^2$ false

Motivating the Lesson

Pose to the class the following question: What positive number squared equals 81? 9
Is there another number whose square is 81? yes; -9
Each of these numbers is called a square root of 81. Finding the square root of a number is the topic today.

   Using a Calculator

Encourage students with calculators to explore the procedure for the correct use of the square-root key.

Chalkboard Examples

Find the following:
1. $\sqrt{900}\ \ = \sqrt{9 \cdot 100}$
$\qquad\quad\ = \sqrt{9} \cdot \sqrt{100}$
$\qquad\quad\ = 3 \cdot 10 = 30$
2. $\sqrt{1296}\ = \sqrt{2^2 \cdot 3^2 \cdot 6^2}$
$\qquad\qquad = \sqrt{2^2} \cdot \sqrt{3^2} \cdot \sqrt{6^2}$
$\qquad\qquad = 2 \cdot 3 \cdot 6 = 36$

(continued)

Check for Understanding

Here is a suggested use of the Oral Exercises to check students' understanding as you teach the lesson.
Oral Exs. 1–10: use after Example 2.
Oral Exs. 11–24: use after Example 3.

Common Errors

In simplifying expressions such as those given in Oral Exercises 16–20 and Written Exercises 45–48, students may incorrectly assume that $\sqrt{a^2 - b^2} = \sqrt{a^2} - \sqrt{b^2}$. In reteaching, show that $\sqrt{5^2 - 3^2} \neq \sqrt{5^2} - \sqrt{3^2}$. Some students may think that $\sqrt{0.09} = 0.03$. Remind them that $(0.03)(0.03) = 0.0009$, not 0.09.

Guided Practice

Find the indicated square root.

1. $\sqrt{25}$ 5

2. $-\sqrt{900}$ -30

3. $\pm\sqrt{676}$ ± 26

4. $\sqrt{\dfrac{64}{625}}$ $\dfrac{8}{25}$

5. $-\sqrt{\dfrac{729}{3364}}$ $-\dfrac{27}{58}$

Example 1 Find $\sqrt{225}$.   **Solution** $\sqrt{225} = \sqrt{9 \cdot 25}$
$= \sqrt{9} \cdot \sqrt{25}$
$= 3 \cdot 5$
$= 15$ *Answer*

If you cannot see any squares that divide the radicand, begin by factoring the radicand (page 185).

Example 2 Find $\sqrt{2304}$.   **Solution** $\sqrt{2304} = \sqrt{2^2 \cdot 3^2 \cdot 8^2}$
$= \sqrt{2^2} \cdot \sqrt{3^2} \cdot \sqrt{8^2}$
$= 2 \cdot 3 \cdot 8$
$= 48$ *Answer*

Notice that $\sqrt{\dfrac{100}{25}} = \sqrt{4} = 2$ and $\dfrac{\sqrt{100}}{\sqrt{25}} = \dfrac{10}{5} = 2$. Therefore $\sqrt{\dfrac{100}{25}} = \dfrac{\sqrt{100}}{\sqrt{25}}$.
This result suggests another property of square roots.

Quotient Property of Square Roots

For any nonnegative real number a and any positive real number b:

$$\sqrt{\dfrac{a}{b}} = \dfrac{\sqrt{a}}{\sqrt{b}}$$

Example 3 Find the indicated square root: **a.** $\sqrt{\dfrac{36}{121}}$ **b.** $\pm\sqrt{\dfrac{144}{3025}}$

Solution   **a.** $\sqrt{\dfrac{36}{121}} = \dfrac{\sqrt{36}}{\sqrt{121}} = \dfrac{6}{11}$

     b. $\pm\sqrt{\dfrac{144}{3025}} = \pm\dfrac{\sqrt{144}}{\sqrt{3025}} = \pm\dfrac{12}{\sqrt{5^2 \cdot 11^2}} = \pm\dfrac{12}{55}$

Oral Exercises

Find the indicated square roots.

1. $\sqrt{16}$ 4   **2.** $-\sqrt{81}$ -9 **3.** $\sqrt{25}$ 5   **4.** $-\sqrt{144}$ -12 **5.** $\pm\sqrt{169}$ ± 13 43

6. $\sqrt{15^2}$ 15   **7.** $\sqrt{84^2}$ 84   **8.** $-\sqrt{52^2}$ -52 **9.** $(\sqrt{6})^2$ 6   **10.** $(\sqrt{43})^2$ 11

11. $-\sqrt{\dfrac{1}{25}}$ $-\dfrac{1}{5}$ **12.** $\sqrt{\dfrac{1}{64}}$ $\dfrac{1}{8}$ **13.** $-\sqrt{\dfrac{100}{49}}$ $-\dfrac{10}{7}$ **14.** $\sqrt{\dfrac{81}{16}}$ $\dfrac{9}{4}$ **15.** $-\sqrt{\dfrac{121}{36}}$ $\dfrac{6}{}$

16. $\sqrt{5^2 - 4^2}$ 3   **17.** $\sqrt{5^2} - \sqrt{4^2}$ 1   **18.** $\sqrt{13^2 - 5^2}$ 12   **19.** $\sqrt{13^2} - \sqrt{5^2}$ 8   **20.** $\sqrt{10^2 - 6^2}$ 8

Sample $\sqrt{\left(\dfrac{3}{7}\right)^2} = \sqrt{\dfrac{3^2}{7^2}} = \dfrac{\sqrt{3^2}}{\sqrt{7^2}} = \dfrac{3}{7}$

21. $\sqrt{\left(\dfrac{2}{5}\right)^2}$ $\dfrac{2}{5}$
22. $\sqrt{\left(\dfrac{12}{29}\right)^2}$ $\dfrac{12}{29}$
23. $\left(\sqrt{\dfrac{7}{11}}\right)^2$ $\dfrac{7}{11}$
24. $\left(\sqrt{\dfrac{5}{23}}\right)^2$ $\dfrac{5}{23}$

Written Exercises

Find the indicated square root.

A
1. $\sqrt{36}$ 6
2. $\sqrt{64}$ 8
3. $\sqrt{100}$ 10
4. $\sqrt{121}$ 11

5. $-\sqrt{400}$ −20
6. $-\sqrt{196}$ −14
7. $\sqrt{625}$ 25
8. $\sqrt{576}$ 24

9. $\pm\sqrt{2500}$ ± 50
10. $\pm\sqrt{1225}$ ± 35
11. $-\sqrt{\dfrac{81}{1600}}$ $-\dfrac{9}{40}$
12. $-\sqrt{\dfrac{225}{49}}$ $-\dfrac{15}{7}$

13. $\pm\sqrt{\dfrac{121}{25}}$ $\pm\dfrac{11}{5}$
14. $\pm\sqrt{\dfrac{1}{256}}$ $\pm\dfrac{1}{16}$
15. $\sqrt{\dfrac{144}{441}}$ $\dfrac{4}{7}$
16. $\sqrt{\dfrac{529}{576}}$ $\dfrac{23}{24}$

17. $-\sqrt{\dfrac{484}{100}}$ $-\dfrac{11}{5}$
18. $-\sqrt{\dfrac{324}{729}}$ $-\dfrac{2}{3}$
19. $\sqrt{\dfrac{361}{2304}}$ $\dfrac{19}{48}$
20. $\sqrt{\dfrac{1156}{289}}$ 2

Sample 1 $\sqrt{\dfrac{18}{32}} = \sqrt{\dfrac{2 \cdot 9}{2 \cdot 16}} = \sqrt{\dfrac{9}{16}} = \dfrac{3}{4}$

B
21. $-\sqrt{\dfrac{28}{63}}$ $-\dfrac{2}{3}$
22. $-\sqrt{\dfrac{12}{75}}$ $-\dfrac{2}{5}$
23. $\sqrt{\dfrac{99}{44}}$ $\dfrac{3}{2}$
24. $\sqrt{\dfrac{20}{45}}$ $\dfrac{2}{3}$

25. $\pm\sqrt{\dfrac{175}{28}}$ $\pm\dfrac{5}{2}$
26. $\pm\sqrt{\dfrac{92}{207}}$ $\pm\dfrac{2}{3}$
27. $\sqrt{\dfrac{7}{175}}$ $\dfrac{1}{5}$
28. $\sqrt{\dfrac{5}{180}}$ $\dfrac{1}{6}$

29. $\pm\sqrt{\dfrac{33}{132}}$ $\pm\dfrac{1}{2}$
30. $\pm\sqrt{\dfrac{180}{845}}$ $\pm\dfrac{6}{13}$
31. $-\sqrt{\dfrac{3200}{648}}$ $-\dfrac{20}{9}$
32. $-\sqrt{\dfrac{1682}{20,000}}$ $-\dfrac{29}{100}$

Suggested Assignments
Minimum
519/1–35 odd
S 520/Mixed Review
Average
519/3–45 mult. of 3
S 520/Mixed Review
Maximum
519/3–48 mult. of 3
S 520/Mixed Review

Supplementary Materials
Study Guide   pp. 187–188
Test Master   48

Find the indicated square root. Express as a decimal. You may wish to use a calculator to check your answers.

Sample 2 $\sqrt{0.64} = \sqrt{\dfrac{64}{100}} = \dfrac{\sqrt{64}}{\sqrt{100}} = \dfrac{8}{10} = 0.8$

36. −0.8
40. ± 3.5

33. $\sqrt{0.04}$ 0.2
34. $\sqrt{0.09}$ 0.3
35. $-\sqrt{0.81}$ −0.9
36. $-\sqrt{0.64}$

37. $\sqrt{1.21}$ 1.1
38. $\sqrt{2.25}$ 1.5
39. $\pm\sqrt{7.84}$ ± 2.8
40. $\pm\sqrt{12.25}$

41. $\sqrt{0.0196}$ 0.14
42. $\sqrt{0.0289}$ 0.17
43. $\sqrt{0.0009}$ 0.03
44. $\sqrt{0.000049}$ 0.007

Evaluate the expression $\sqrt{x^2 - y^2} - (\sqrt{x})^2$ for the given values of x and y.

45. $x = 5$, $y = 3$ −1
46. $x = 17$, $y = 15$ −9

47. $x = 20$, $y = 16$ −8
48. $x = 37$, $y = 12$ −2

Rational and Irrational Numbers   **519**

Mixed Review Exercises

Express as a fraction in simplest form.

1. 0.125 $\frac{1}{8}$ 2. -6.4 $-\frac{32}{5}$ 3. $0.\overline{3}$ $\frac{1}{3}$ 4. $2.\overline{16}$ $\frac{214}{99}$ 5. $\frac{1}{2}\left(\frac{4}{5} - \frac{2}{3}\right)$ $\frac{1}{15}$ 6. $\frac{2}{3}\left(\frac{x}{4} - \frac{2x}{7}\right)$ $-\frac{x}{42}$

Factor completely.

7. $4b^2 - 12b - 72$ $4(b+3)(b-6)$

8. $16t^2 - 8t - 9v^2 + 1$ $(4t - 1 + 3v)(4t - 1 - 3v)$

9. $64k^3 - k$ $k(8k+1)(8k-1)$

10. $9w^2 - 24wy + 16y^2$ $(3w - 4y)^2$

11. $2x^2 - 9xy - 5y^2$ $(2x + y)(x - 5y)$

12. $3 - 2ab - 5a^2b^2$ $(3 - 5ab)(1 + ab)$

Challenge

Solve the systems if a, b, and c are positive integers:
$$4a - 11b + 12c = 22$$
$$a + 5b - 4c = 17 \quad (7, 6, 5)$$

Self-Test 1

Vocabulary   rational number (p. 507)   principal square root (p. 517)
               terminating decimal (p. 512)   radical sign (p. 517)
               repeating decimal (p. 513)   radical (p. 517)
               square root (p. 517)   radicand (p. 517)

Find the number halfway between the given numbers.

1. $\frac{5}{8}$ and $\frac{4}{9}$ $\frac{77}{144}$ 2. $\frac{5}{4}$ and $\frac{4}{3}$ $\frac{31}{24}$ 3. $4\frac{1}{6}$ and $5\frac{1}{8}$ $4\frac{31}{48}$ **Obj. 11-1, p. 507**

Replace the ___?___ with <, =, or > to make a true statement.

4. $\frac{11}{3}$ ___?___ $\frac{7}{5}$ $>$ 5. $-\frac{13}{7}$ ___?___ $-\frac{9}{5}$ $<$ 6. $\frac{32}{20}$ ___?___ $\frac{37}{22}$ $<$

Express each rational number as a decimal.

7. $\frac{12}{25}$ 0.48 8. $\frac{13}{4}$ 3.25 9. $\frac{7}{30}$ $0.2\overline{3}$ 10. $\frac{24}{35}$ $0.6\overline{857142}$ **Obj. 11-2, p. 512**

11. Express $0.2\overline{02}$ as a fraction in simplest form. $\frac{20}{99}$

Find the indicated square root.

12. $\sqrt{1089}$ 33 13. $\sqrt{\dfrac{64}{2025}}$ $\frac{8}{45}$ 14. $\sqrt{2.56}$ 1.6 **Obj. 11-3, p. 517**

Check your answers with those at the back of the book.

---

520   *Chapter 11*

Quick Quiz

Find the number halfway between the given numbers.

1. $\frac{7}{10}$ and $\frac{2}{3}$ $\frac{41}{60}$

2. $\frac{6}{5}$ and $\frac{3}{2}$ $\frac{27}{20} = 1\frac{7}{20}$

3. $2\frac{1}{6}$ and $3\frac{1}{9}$ $2\frac{23}{36}$

Replace the ___?___ with <, =, or > to make a true statement.

4. $\frac{13}{4}$ ___?___ $\frac{10}{3}$ $<$

5. $-\frac{17}{8}$ ___?___ $-\frac{15}{7}$ $>$

6. $\frac{31}{18}$ ___?___ $\frac{35}{21}$ $>$

Express each rational number as a decimal.

7. $\frac{3}{8}$ 0.375 8. $\frac{14}{5}$ 2.8

9. $\frac{11}{15}$ $0.7\overline{3}$ 10. $\frac{25}{28}$ 0.89285714

11. Express $0.3\overline{13}$ as a fraction in simplest form. $\frac{31}{99}$

Find the indicated square root.

12. $\sqrt{1521}$ 39

13. $\sqrt{\dfrac{81}{1225}}$ $\frac{9}{35}$

14. $\sqrt{3.24}$ 1.8

Irrational Numbers

Teaching Suggestions p. T133

Suggested Extensions p. T133

11-4 Irrational Square Roots

Objective   To simplify radicals and to find decimal approximations of irrational square roots.

You can use the product property of square roots to simplify radicals when the radicand has a factor that is the square of an integer other than 1.

Example 1   Simplify: **a.** $\sqrt{324}$ **b.** $\sqrt{75}$ **c.** $2\sqrt{112}$ **d.** $\sqrt{891}$

Solution   **a.** $\sqrt{324} = \sqrt{9 \cdot 36} = \sqrt{9} \cdot \sqrt{36} = 3 \cdot 6 = 18$

   b. $\sqrt{75} = \sqrt{25 \cdot 3} = \sqrt{25} \cdot \sqrt{3} = 5\sqrt{3}$

   c. $2\sqrt{112} = 2\sqrt{16 \cdot 7} = 2 \cdot 4\sqrt{7} = 8\sqrt{7}$

   d. $\sqrt{891} = \sqrt{81 \cdot 11} = 9\sqrt{11}$

Since integers such as 3, 7, and 11 are not squares of integers, numbers such as $\sqrt{3}$, $\sqrt{7}$, and $\sqrt{11}$ are not in the set of rational numbers. These numbers are in another major subset of the real numbers called the set of *irrational numbers*. Their exact values cannot be expressed as either terminating or repeating decimals. However, you can use a calculator or the table of square roots at the back of the book to find the decimal approximation of an irrational square root. For example, $\sqrt{3} \approx 1.732$, $\sqrt{7} \approx 2.646$, and $\sqrt{11} \approx 3.317$.

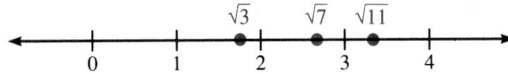

Irrational numbers are real numbers that cannot be expressed in the form $\frac{a}{b}$, where a and b are integers.

Irrational square roots are not the only irrational numbers. For example, π is an irrational number, as is $0.13579111315. \ldots$

The set of real numbers is made up of the rational numbers and the irrational numbers. The real numbers have all the properties that you have studied so far in this course. In addition, the set of real numbers has the *property of completeness*.

Rational and Irrational Numbers   **521**

Warm-Up Exercises
From the set $\left\{-8, -3.7, 0.\overline{5},\right.$ $\sqrt{\frac{49}{81}}, \left.\sqrt{144}\right\}$, identify the following type of numbers.
1. Integers $-8, \sqrt{144}$
2. Rational   the entire set
3. Real   entire set

Motivating the Lesson
Ask students how they might simplify $\sqrt{8}$. $2\sqrt{2}$
Point out that some square roots do not simplify to a rational number. These are called irrational numbers, which is the topic of today's lesson.

   Using a Calculator
Emphasize to the students that when a calculator is used to find an irrational square root, the answer displayed is a decimal approximation of the irrational square root. Since different calculators round differently, students should know that this approximate value may vary from calculator to calculator.

Chalkboard Examples
Simplify.
1. $\sqrt{216}$ $= \sqrt{36 \cdot 6}$
$= \sqrt{36} \cdot \sqrt{6}$
$= 6\sqrt{6}$
2. $3\sqrt{125}$ $= 3\sqrt{25 \cdot 5}$
$= 3 \cdot 5\sqrt{5} = 15\sqrt{5}$
3. $\sqrt{1920}$ $= \sqrt{64 \cdot 30}$
$= 8\sqrt{30}$
(continued)

4. Approximate $\sqrt{637}$ to the nearest tenth.

$\sqrt{637} = \sqrt{7^2 \cdot 13} = 7\sqrt{13}$
From the table: $\sqrt{13} \approx 3.606$
$7\sqrt{13} \approx 7(3.606) = 25.242$
$\therefore \sqrt{637} \approx 25.2$

Check for Understanding

Oral Exs. 1–10: use after discussion on page 521.
Oral Exs. 11–15: use after Example 1.
Oral Exs. 16–20: use after Example 2.

Common Errors

When simplifying square roots, students may not do so completely. For example, they may write $\sqrt{32} = 2\sqrt{8}$. In reteaching, remind them to check for a perfect square as a factor of the radicand. Thus, $2\sqrt{8} = 2\sqrt{4} \cdot \sqrt{2} = 4\sqrt{2}$. Reteaching, suggest to students that when factoring the original radicand, they should look for the largest perfect square factor. This will assure complete simplification. Thus, $\sqrt{32} = \sqrt{16 \cdot 2} = 4\sqrt{2}$.

Guided Practice

Simplify.
1. $\sqrt{18}$ $3\sqrt{2}$
2. $3\sqrt{12}$ $6\sqrt{3}$
3. $\sqrt{196}$ 14
4. $\sqrt{960}$ $8\sqrt{15}$
5. $8\sqrt{2592}$ $288\sqrt{2}$

Property of Completeness

Every decimal number represents a real number, and every real number can be represented as a decimal.

The product and quotient properties of square roots can be used with a table of square roots to approximate irrational square roots if you don't have a calculator.

Example 2 Approximate each square root to the nearest hundredth.
  a. $\sqrt{684}$ **b.** $\sqrt{0.8}$

Solution   **a.** $\sqrt{684} = \sqrt{2^2 \cdot 3^2 \cdot 19}$ **b.** $\sqrt{0.8} = \dfrac{\sqrt{80}}{\sqrt{100}}$
$= \sqrt{2^2 \cdot 3^2} \cdot \sqrt{19}$
$= 6\sqrt{19}$ $\approx \dfrac{8.944}{10} = 0.8944$

From the table: $\sqrt{19} \approx 4.359$ $\therefore \sqrt{0.8} \approx 0.89$ ***Answer***
$6\sqrt{19} \approx 6(4.359) = 26.154$
$\therefore \sqrt{684} \approx 26.15$ ***Answer***

Oral Exercises

State whether each number represents a rational or an irrational number.

1. $\sqrt{17}$ irr.   **2.** $\sqrt{49}$ rat.   **3.** $\sqrt{11}$ irr.   **4.** $\sqrt{1.21}$ rat.   **5.** $5 + \sqrt{2}$ irr.
6. $(\sqrt{2})^4$ rat.   **7.** $\sqrt{3} - \sqrt{3}$ rat.   **8.** 7π irr.   **9.** $2.\overline{91}$ rat.   **10.** $1.23456789\ldots$ irr.

Simplify.

11. $\sqrt{50}$ $5\sqrt{2}$ **12.** $\sqrt{150}$ $5\sqrt{6}$ **13.** $\sqrt{98}$ $7\sqrt{2}$ **14.** $\sqrt{128}$ $8\sqrt{2}$ **15.** $\sqrt{220}$ $2\sqrt{55}$

Approximate each square root to the nearest tenth. Use your calculator or the table at the back of the book.

16. $\sqrt{500}$ 22.4   **17.** $\sqrt{1200}$ 34.6   **18.** $\sqrt{2800}$ 52.9   **19.** $\sqrt{4300}$ 65.6   **20.** $\sqrt{6300}$ 79.4

Written Exercises

Simplify.

A **1.** $\sqrt{63}$ $3\sqrt{7}$ **2.** $\sqrt{28}$ $2\sqrt{7}$ **3.** $\sqrt{98}$ $7\sqrt{2}$ **4.** $\sqrt{50}$ $5\sqrt{2}$ **5.** $\sqrt{75}$ $5\sqrt{3}$
  6. $\sqrt{24}$ $2\sqrt{6}$ **7.** $\sqrt{256}$ 16   **8.** $\sqrt{120}$ $2\sqrt{30}$ **9.** $2\sqrt{48}$ $8\sqrt{3}$ **10.** $6\sqrt{108}$ $36\sqrt{3}$
  11. $5\sqrt{72}$ $30\sqrt{2}$ **12.** $9\sqrt{90}$ $27\sqrt{10}$ **13.** $\sqrt{529}$ 23   **14.** $\sqrt{324}$ 18   **15.** $6\sqrt{45}$ $18\sqrt{5}$

16. $14\sqrt{75}$ $70\sqrt{3}$ **17.** $\sqrt{361}$ 19 **18.** $\sqrt{864}$ $12\sqrt{6}$ **19.** $10\sqrt{125}$ $50\sqrt{5}$ **20.** $3\sqrt{160}$ $12\sqrt{10}$
21. $\sqrt{192}$ $8\sqrt{3}$ **22.** $\sqrt{432}$ $12\sqrt{3}$ **23.** $5\sqrt{600}$ $50\sqrt{6}$ **24.** $4\sqrt{363}$ $44\sqrt{3}$ **25.** $6\sqrt{245}$ $42\sqrt{5}$
26. $5\sqrt{567}$ $45\sqrt{7}$ **27.** $\sqrt{5625}$ 75 **28.** $\sqrt{9200}$ **29.** $7\sqrt{1200}$ **30.** $5\sqrt{2050}$ $25\sqrt{82}$
$20\sqrt{23}$ $\qquad\qquad$ $140\sqrt{3}$

In Exercises 31–50, use your calculator or the table at the back of the book.

Approximate each square root to the nearest tenth.

B **31.** $\sqrt{800}$ 28.3 **32.** $\sqrt{500}$ 22.4 **33.** $-\sqrt{700}$ -26.5 **34.** $-\sqrt{600}$ -24.5
35. $-\sqrt{5900}$ -76.8 **36.** $-\sqrt{4800}$ -69.3 **37.** $\pm\sqrt{7800}$ ± 88.3 **38.** $\pm\sqrt{5600}$ ± 74.8

Approximate each square root to the nearest hundredth.

39. $\sqrt{68}$ 8.25 **40.** $\sqrt{42}$ 6.48 **41.** $-\sqrt{0.5}$ -0.71 **42.** $-\sqrt{0.3}$ -0.55
43. $\pm\sqrt{0.87}$ ± 0.93 **44.** $\pm\sqrt{0.73}$ ± 0.85 **45.** $-\sqrt{0.07}$ -0.26 **46.** $-\sqrt{0.08}$ -0.28

Approximate each square root to the nearest whole number.

47. $\sqrt{150,000}$ 387 **48.** $\sqrt{240,000}$ 490 **49.** $\sqrt{420,000}$ 648 **50.** $\sqrt{580,000}$ 762

Mixed Review Exercises

Find the indicated square roots.

1. $\sqrt{400}$ 20 **2.** $-\sqrt{169}$ -13 **3.** $\sqrt{\dfrac{25}{81}}$ $\dfrac{5}{9}$

4. $-\sqrt{\dfrac{49}{225}}$ $-\dfrac{7}{15}$ **5.** $\sqrt{176^2}$ 176 **6.** $\sqrt{\left(\dfrac{3}{8}\right)^2}$ $\dfrac{3}{8}$

Simplify.

7. $(17x)^2$ $289x^2$ **8.** $(3y^4z^9)^2$ $9y^8z^{18}$ **9.** $(2x + 3y)^2$ $4x^2 + 12xy + 9y^2$
10. $[15(a + 2)]^2$ $225a^2 + 900a + 900$ **11.** $(11a^4b^{11}c)^2$ $121a^8b^{22}c^2$ **12.** $(6z^3 + 5y^4)(6z^3 - 5y^4)$ $36z^6 - 25y^8$

Historical Note / π

The number π occurs naturally as the ratio of the circumference of a circle to its diameter. It is not possible to get an exact value for π since it is an irrational number.

   The first known approximation (other than just using 3) was given in the Rhind mathematical papyrus as $(\frac{4}{3})^4$, or $3.1604\ldots$. This was used until 240 B.C. when Archimedes calculated π to be between $\frac{223}{71}$ and $\frac{22}{7}$, or 3.14, to two decimal places. Four hundred years later this approximation was improved slightly to $\frac{377}{120}$, or 3.1416. In China, Tsu Ch'ung-chih gave a value for π of $\frac{355}{113}$, or $3.1415929\ldots$, which is correct to six decimal places. Indian mathematicians used $\frac{62,832}{20,000}$, although this was later refined to $\frac{754}{240}$.

Rational and Irrational Numbers **523**

Summarizing the Lesson

Today's lesson extended the definition of real numbers (see p. 32) to include irrational numbers. Ask students to define real and irrational numbers in their own words and to give examples of each type of number.

Suggested Assignments

Minimum
   522/1–35 odd
S 523/Mixed Review
R 520/Self-Test 1

Average
   522/3–45 mult. of 3
S 523/Mixed Review
R 520/Self-Test 1

Maximum
   522/3–48 mult. of 3
S 523/Mixed Review
R 520/Self-Test 1

 Using a Calculator

Students can use the $\sqrt{}$ key on a calculator to approximate square roots for Oral Exercises 16–20 and to check their answers to Written Exercises 1–30. For example, to check that $6\sqrt{45} = 18\sqrt{5}$, students can see that
$6\sqrt{45} \approx 40.249224$ and
$18\sqrt{5} \approx 40.249224$.

Supplementary Materials

Study Guide   pp. 189–190
Practice Master   67
Resource Book   p. 132

Following the Middle Ages, European mathematicians once again tried to get better approximations for π. In 1706, the calculation had reached 100 decimal places. William Jones became the first person to use the symbol π to represent the number. By 1737, π was in general use.

In 1767 π was shown to be an irrational number. This did not stop people from calculating more decimal places. In 1948 the last calculation by hand was done to 808 places. Since 1949 computers have been used to approximate π. The first attempt in 1949 produced 2037 decimal places (after 70 hours of computer time). By 1967 the value had been calculated to over 500,000 places.

Additional Answers
Extra

Assume that 3 has a rational square root. Then $\sqrt{3}$ $= \dfrac{p}{q}$, where p and q are positive integers that have no common prime factor. If $\sqrt{3} = \dfrac{p}{q}$, then $3 = \dfrac{p^2}{q^2}$, and p^2 and q^2 have no common prime factor. Then $3q^2 = p^2$. Thus p^2 and p are divisible by 3. Therefore let $p = 3m$. Then $3q^2 = (3m)^2 = 9m^2$, and $q^2 = 3m^2$. Thus, both q^2 and q are divisible by 3. This contradicts the assumption that p and q have no common prime factor. $\therefore$ 3 does not have a rational square root.

Extra / Irrationality of $\sqrt{2}$

The following proof shows that 2 does not have a rational square root. You begin by assuming that 2 has a rational square root and then show that this assumption leads to a contradiction. Hence, the original assumption that 2 has a rational square root must be false.

1. Assume that 2 has a rational square root.

2. Then, $\sqrt{2} = \dfrac{a}{b}$, where a and b are positive integers that have no common prime factor; that is, $\dfrac{a}{b}$ is in simplest form.

3. If $\sqrt{2} = \dfrac{a}{b}$, then $2 = \dfrac{a^2}{b^2}$. Since a^2 has the same prime factors as a, and b^2 has the same prime factors as b, a^2 and b^2 have no common prime factors. Thus, $\dfrac{a^2}{b^2}$ is in simplest form.

4. Multiplying both sides of the equation $\dfrac{a^2}{b^2} = 2$ by b^2, you have $a^2 = 2b^2$.

    Thus, a must be even because its square is even. (Recall that the square of an even integer is even and that the square of an odd integer is odd.)

5. Since a is even, you can write $a = 2n$ for some integer n. Then, substituting $2n$ for a in $a^2 = 2b^2$, you have $(2n)^2 = 2b^2$, $4n^2 = 2b^2$, or $2n^2 = b^2$.

6. Since $2n^2 = b^2$, b must be even because its square is even. Therefore, you may write $b = 2m$ for some integer m.

7. Therefore, both a and b have 2 as a factor. This contradicts the fact that a and b have no common prime factor.

8. Hence the assumption that 2 has a rational root is false since it leads to a contradiction.

Exercise

Prove that $\sqrt{3}$ is irrational.

524   *Chapter 11*

11-5 Square Roots of Variable Expressions

Objective   To find square roots of variable expressions and to use them to solve equations and problems.

Is it always true that $\sqrt{x^2} = x$? Recall that the symbol $\sqrt{}$ names the principal, or positive, square root of a positive number. Thus, when $x = -9$, you have

$$\sqrt{(-9)^2} = \sqrt{81} = 9.$$

Therefore, it is not always true that $\sqrt{x^2} = x$. If x is positive, $\sqrt{x^2} = x$, but if x is negative, then $\sqrt{x^2} = -x$. In either case, it *is* true that

$$\sqrt{x^2} = |x|.$$

When you are finding square roots of variable expressions, you must be careful to use absolute value signs when needed to ensure that your answer is positive.

Example 1   Simplify:

     a. $\sqrt{196y^2}$ **b.** $\sqrt{36x^8}$ **c.** $\sqrt{m^2 - 6m + 9}$ **d.** $\sqrt{18a^3}$

Solution   **a.** $\sqrt{196y^2} = \sqrt{196} \cdot \sqrt{y^2} = 14|y|$

     b. $\sqrt{36x^8} = \sqrt{36} \cdot \sqrt{(x^4)^2} = 6x^4$ (x^4 is always nonnegative.)

     c. $\sqrt{m^2 - 6m + 9} = \sqrt{(m - 3)^2} = |m - 3|$

     d. $\sqrt{18a^3} = \sqrt{9 \cdot 2 \cdot a^2 \cdot a} = \sqrt{9} \cdot \sqrt{a^2} \cdot \sqrt{2a} = 3a\sqrt{2a}$

Example 2   Solve $9x^2 = 64$.

Solution 1
$$9x^2 = 64$$
$$9x^2 - 64 = 0$$
$$(3x + 8)(3x - 8) = 0$$
$$3x = -8 \text{ or } 3x = 8$$
$$x = -\frac{8}{3} \text{ or } x = \frac{8}{3}$$

Solution 2
$$9x^2 = 64$$
$$x^2 = \frac{64}{9}$$
$$x = \pm\sqrt{\frac{64}{9}}$$
$$x = \pm\frac{8}{3}$$

Check: $9\left(\frac{8}{3}\right)^2 \overset{?}{=} 64$ and $9\left(-\frac{8}{3}\right)^2 \overset{?}{=} 64$

                $64 = 64$ ✓   and $64 = 64$ ✓

$\therefore$ the solution set is $\left\{\frac{8}{3}, -\frac{8}{3}\right\}$.   **Answer**

The second solution of Example 2 is based upon the following property.

Rational and Irrational Numbers   **525**

Teaching Suggestions p. T134

Suggested Extensions p. T134

Warm-Up Exercises

Complete.

1. $m^4 = (\underline{\ ?\ })^2$ m^2
2. $r^3 = (\underline{\ ?\ })r$ r^2
3. $s^6 = (\underline{\ ?\ })^2$ s^3
4. $t^{40} = (\underline{\ ?\ })^2$ t^{20}

Factor.

5. $c^2 - 14c + 49$ $(c - 7)^2$
6. $c^2 - 49$ $(c + 7)(c - 7)$
7. $4a^2 + 20a + 25$ $(2a + 5)^2$

Motivating the Lesson

The Warm-Up Exercises today reviewed factoring involving variables. Tell students that they will use this skill to find the square roots of variable expressions, which is the topic of today's lesson.

Chalkboard Examples

Simplify.

1. $\sqrt{400z^6}$
    $\sqrt{400} \cdot \sqrt{z^6} = 20|z^3|$
2. $\sqrt{162y^{12}}$
    $\sqrt{81} \cdot \sqrt{2} \cdot \sqrt{y^{12}} = 9y^6\sqrt{2}$
3. $\sqrt{100 + 20n + n^2}$
    $\sqrt{(10 + n)^2} = |10 + n|$
4. Solve $45r^2 - 500 = 0$.
    $45r^2 = 500$
    $r^2 = \frac{500}{45} = \frac{100}{9}$
    $r = \pm\sqrt{\frac{100}{9}} = \pm\frac{10}{3}$
    $\therefore$ the solution set is
    $\left\{\frac{10}{3}, -\frac{10}{3}\right\}$.

Property of Square Roots of Equal Numbers

For any real numbers r and s:

$$r^2 = s^2 \text{ if and only if } r = s \text{ or } r = -s.$$

Oral Exercises

Simplify.
1. $\sqrt{25x^2}$ $5|x|$
2. $\sqrt{144y^2}$ $12|y|$
3. $\sqrt{81a^4}$ $9a^2$
4. $\sqrt{64x^2y^2}$ $8|xy|$
5. $\sqrt{0.09c^2}$ $0.3|c|$
6. $\sqrt{\dfrac{x^2}{49}}$ $\dfrac{|x|}{7}$
7. $\sqrt{\dfrac{16}{a^4}}$ $\dfrac{4}{a^2}$
8. $\sqrt{\dfrac{x^4y^4}{64}}$ $\dfrac{x^2y^2}{8}$
9. $\sqrt{\dfrac{r^6s^6}{36}}$ $\dfrac{|r^3s^3|}{6}$
10. $\sqrt{\dfrac{m^{16}}{100n^8}}$ $\dfrac{m^8}{10n^4}$

Written Exercises

Simplify. 13. $\pm 3|x|y\sqrt{6y}$ 14. $\pm 2|r^3|s^2\sqrt{14}$ 16. $-20|a^3|b^2$

A
1. $\sqrt{121a^2}$ $11|a|$
2. $\sqrt{100z^2}$ $10|z|$
3. $\sqrt{28x^2}$ $2|x|\sqrt{7}$
4. $\sqrt{32b^4}$ $4b^2\sqrt{2}$
5. $-\sqrt{9c^4}$ $-3c^2$
6. $-\sqrt{64x^2}$ $-8|x|$
7. $-\sqrt{25d^6}$ $-5|d^3|$
8. $-\sqrt{16d^8}$ $-4d^4$
9. $\sqrt{80a^2b^2}$ $4|ab|\sqrt{5}$
10. $\sqrt{49a^2b^2}$ $7|ab|$
11. $\sqrt{75r^3}$ $5r\sqrt{3r}$
12. $\sqrt{80n^6}$ $4|n^3|\sqrt{5}$
13. $\pm\sqrt{54x^2y^3}$
14. $\pm\sqrt{56r^6s^4}$
15. $-\sqrt{144x^2z^2}$ $-12|xz|$
16. $-\sqrt{400a^6b^4}$
17. $\pm\sqrt{\dfrac{100f^{10}}{121}}$ $\pm\dfrac{10|f^5|}{11}$
18. $\pm\sqrt{\dfrac{256}{400s^{12}}}$ $\pm\dfrac{4}{5s^6}$
19. $\sqrt{\dfrac{x^4y^6}{4r^2}}$ $\dfrac{x^2|y^3|}{2|r|}$
20. $\sqrt{\dfrac{45m^3n^2}{5mn^4}}$ $\dfrac{3|m|}{|n|}$
21. $\sqrt{\dfrac{64g^{18}}{8100h^{20}}}$ $\dfrac{4|g^9|}{45h^{10}}$
22. $\sqrt{\dfrac{324r^{50}}{49}}$ $\dfrac{18|r^{25}|}{7}$
23. $-\sqrt{3.24x^4}$ $-1.8x^2$
24. $\sqrt{1.96k^6}$ $1.4|k^3|$
25. $\sqrt{y^2 - 8y + 16}$ $|y - 4|$
26. $\sqrt{m^2 - 12m + 36}$ $|m - 6|$

Solve. 31. $\{10, -10\}$ 32. $\{9, -9\}$ 30. $\{7, -7\}$ 34. $\{3, -3\}$
27. $x^2 = 25$ $\{5, -5\}$
28. $n^2 = 64$ $\{8, -8\}$
29. $x^2 - 4 = 0$ $\{2, -2\}$
30. $d^2 - 49 = 0$
31. $0 = a^2 - 100$
32. $0 = m^2 - 81$
33. $2m^2 - 50 = 0$ $\{5, -5\}$
34. $50b^2 - 450 = 0$
35. $81y^2 - 16 = 0$ $\left\{\dfrac{4}{9}, -\dfrac{4}{9}\right\}$
36. $9c^2 - 64 = 0$ $\left\{\dfrac{8}{3}, -\dfrac{8}{3}\right\}$
37. $0 = 81z^2 - 49$ $\left\{\dfrac{7}{9}, -\dfrac{7}{9}\right\}$
38. $0 = 80p^2 - 125$ $\left\{\dfrac{5}{4}, -\dfrac{5}{4}\right\}$

Find both roots of each equation to the nearest tenth.
  39. $\{24.9, -24.9\}$ 40. $\{12.4, -12.4\}$ 42. $\{0.5, -0.5\}$

B
39. $x^2 = 618$
40. $a^2 = 154$
41. $0.38 = r^2$ $\{0.6, -0.6\}$
42. $0.29 = k^2$
43. $c^2 - 212 = 0$
44. $w^2 - 204 = 0$
45. $y^2 - 10.25 = 0$
46. $n^2 - 13.08 = 0$
47. $9z^2 = 513$ $\{7.5, -7.5\}$
48. $7z^2 = 133$ $\{4.4, -4.4\}$
49. $0 = 4b^2 - 0.48$ $\{0.3, -0.3\}$
50. $0 = 6n^2 - 0.42$ $\{0.3, -0.3\}$

C
51. $0.13m^2 = 9.36$ $\{8.5, -8.5\}$
52. $9k^2 = 168$ $\{4.3, -4.3\}$
53. $(x + 1)^2 + (x - 1)^2 = 176$ $\{9.3, -9.3\}$
54. $(a + 3)^2 + (a - 3)^2 = 256$ $\{10.9, -10.9\}$

Problems

Solve. Find each answer to the nearest tenth. Use 3.14 for π. A calculator may be helpful.

Using a Calculator

A calculator may be helpful when solving exercises in the Problems section.

Supplementary Materials

Study Guide   pp. 191–192

A 1. Find the length of a side of a square whose area is 300 cm². 17.3 cm

2. Find the length of a side of a square whose area is the same as that of a rectangle 24 cm by 30 cm. 26.8 cm

3. The length of the base of a triangle is 3 times the length of its altitude. Find the length of the base if the area of the triangle is 54 m². 18 m

4. Find the length of a side of a square if its area is the same as the area of a triangle with an altitude of 18 cm and a base of 11 cm. 9.9 cm

5. The search for a missing boat covered a circular region with an area of 164 km². What was the radius of the search region? 7.2 km

6. If the area of the figure at the right below is 600 mm², find s. 6.1 mm

B 7. The formula $s = 4.9t^2$ gives the approximate distance traveled in t seconds by an object falling from rest. How long does it take a rock falling from rest to travel 1587.6 m? 18 s

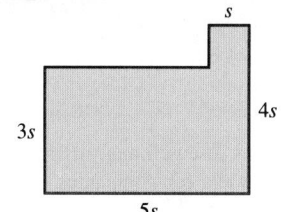

Ex. 6

8. A circle inside a square just touches its sides. If the area of the circle is 341.9 cm², what is the length of a side of the square? 20.9 cm

9. An old water pipe is to be replaced by a new one so that twice as much water can flow through the pipe. What is the ratio of the radius of the new pipe to that of the old pipe? $\frac{\sqrt{2}}{1} \approx \frac{1.4}{1}$

Let a, b, and c be the lengths of the sides of a triangle. Let $s = \frac{1}{2}(a + b + c)$. Then the area, A, of the triangle is $A = \sqrt{s(s - a)(s - b)(s - c)}$. Find the area, to the nearest tenth, of a triangle with sides of the given lengths.

C 10. 8 cm, 10 cm, and 14 cm 39.2 cm²

11. 14 m, 19 m, and 25 m 131.9 m²

12. 6 cm, 6 cm, and 6 cm 15.6 cm²

Rational and Irrational Numbers   **527**

Mixed Review Exercises

Simplify.

1. $\pm\sqrt{250}$ $\pm 5\sqrt{10}$

2. $-6\sqrt{76}$ $-12\sqrt{19}$

3. $5\sqrt{396}$ $30\sqrt{11}$

4. $2^{-2} - 3^{-2}$ $\dfrac{5}{36}$

5. $6^2 \cdot 3^{-3}$ $\dfrac{4}{3}$

6. $(4x^3)^2(-2x^5)^{-3}$ $-\dfrac{2}{x^9}$

Evaluate if $x = 9$, $y = 4$, and $n = 1$.

7. $x^2 + y^2$ 97

8. $x^2 y^2$ 1296

9. $x^2 - n^2$ 80

10. $\sqrt{\dfrac{n}{x}}$ $\dfrac{1}{3}$

11. $\sqrt{\dfrac{x}{y}}$ $\dfrac{3}{2}$

12. $(\sqrt{y})^4$ 16

 ## Calculator Key-In

Use a calculator and the formula $A = \sqrt{s(s-a)(s-b)(s-c)}$ where $s = \frac{1}{2}(a + b + c)$ to find the approximate area of each triangle whose sides are given. Give your answers to the nearest hundredth.

1. 7 cm, 11 cm, and 14 cm 37.95 cm^2

2. 13 mm, 18 mm, and 27 mm 101.03 mm^2

3. 12 m, 12 m, and 16 m 71.55 m^2

4. 48 mm, 64 mm, and 84 mm 1527.22 mm^2

5. 2.8 m, 3.9 m, and 5.7 m 4.92 m^2

6. 15.8 cm, 16.9 cm, and 23.4 cm 133.47 cm^2

7. 9.2 cm, 11.8 cm, and 17.1 cm 51.51 cm^2

8. 37.1 m, 46.4 m, and 69.7 m 794.04 m^2

 ## Career Note / Operations Research Analyst

Operations research analysts find more efficient ways for companies to control inventory, schedule personnel, predict future needs, and allocate resources. An operations research analyst may be asked to find the ideal number of parts for a manufacturing company to have on hand. When working on such problems mathematicians often use a method called linear programming (see the Extra on pages 499–500).

Operations research analysts approach a problem by breaking it down and learning everything they can about each part of the problem. They then use computers and statistics to examine possible solutions. When their analysis is complete, they make recommendations to the decision-making managers of the company.

11-6 The Pythagorean Theorem

Objective To use the Pythagorean theorem and its converse to solve geometric problems.

The Pythagorean theorem can be used to find the lengths of sides of right triangles. The hypotenuse of a right triangle is the side opposite the right angle. It is the longest side. The other two sides of a right triangle are called the legs of the triangle.

The Pythagorean Theorem

In any right triangle, the square of the length of the hypotenuse equals the sum of the squares of the lengths of the legs. For the triangle shown,

$$a^2 + b^2 = c^2.$$

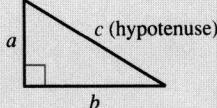

The diagrams below suggest a proof of the Pythagorean theorem. Each diagram shows a square, $(a + b)$ units on a side, divided into other figures. The diagrams suggest different expressions for the area of the square. Equating these expressions leads to the equation $a^2 + b^2 = c^2$.

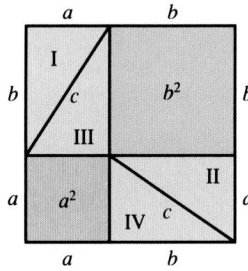

$$(a + b)^2 = a^2 + b^2 + 4\left(\tfrac{1}{2}ab\right) \qquad (a + b)^2 = c^2 + 4\left(\tfrac{1}{2}ab\right)$$

$$a^2 + b^2 + 4\left(\tfrac{1}{2}ab\right) = c^2 + 4\left(\tfrac{1}{2}ab\right)$$

$$\therefore a^2 + b^2 = c^2$$

Example 1 The length of one side of a right triangle is 28 cm. The length of the hypotenuse is 53 cm. Write and solve an equation for the length of the unknown side.

Solution
$$a^2 + b^2 = c^2 \qquad a = \sqrt{c^2 - b^2}$$
$$a^2 = c^2 - b^2 \qquad = \sqrt{53^2 - 28^2}$$
$$= \sqrt{2809 - 784} = \sqrt{2025} = 45 \; \textit{(Check on next page.)}$$

Rational and Irrational Numbers **529**

Explorations pp. 698–699

Teaching Suggestions p. T134
Using Manipulatives p. T134
Suggested Extensions p. T135

Warm-Up Exercises

Evaluate each expression for the given values. Round answers to the nearest hundredth.

1. $\sqrt{a^2 + b^2}$; $a = 3$, $b = 4$ 5
2. $\sqrt{c^2 - a^2}$; $a = 6$, $c = 10$ 8
3. $\sqrt{a^2 + b^2}$; $a = 4$, $b = 7$
   8.06
4. $\sqrt{c^2 - b^2}$; $b = 3$, $c = 9$
   8.49

Motivating the Lesson

Suppose Sean is painting the upper trim on his house at a height of 12 ft. If he must place his ladder 5 ft from the base of the house to avoid the shrubs, what is the minimum length of the ladder he must use? (13 ft) Tell students that to answer this question, they can use the Pythagorean theorem, the topic of today's lesson.

Chalkboard Examples

1. One leg of a right triangle measures 36 cm. The hypotenuse is 39 cm long. Write and solve an equation for the length of the unknown side.
$$a^2 + b^2 = c^2$$
$$b^2 = c^2 - a^2$$
$$b = \sqrt{c^2 - a^2}$$
$$= \sqrt{39^2 - 36^2}$$
$$= \sqrt{1521 - 1296}$$
$$= \sqrt{225} = 15$$
Check:
$$36^2 + 15^2 \stackrel{?}{=} 39^2$$
$$1521 = 1521 \; \checkmark$$

(continued)

2. State whether or not the three given numbers could represent the lengths of the sides of a right triangle.

a. 16, 30, 34

$$a^2 + b^2 = c^2$$
$$16^2 + 30^2 \stackrel{?}{=} 34^2$$
$$256 + 900 \stackrel{?}{=} 1156$$
$$1156 = 1156 \checkmark$$

∴ 16, 30, and 34 could form a right triangle.

b. 11, 11, 16

$$a^2 + b^2 = c^2$$
$$11^2 + 11^2 \stackrel{?}{=} 16^2$$
$$121 + 121 \stackrel{?}{=} 256$$
$$242 \neq 256$$

∴ 11, 11, and 16 could not form a right triangle.

3. To the nearest hundredth, what is the length of a diagonal of a rectangle whose width is 12 cm and whose length is 42 cm?

$$a^2 + b^2 = c^2$$
$$\sqrt{a^2 + b^2} = c$$
$$\sqrt{12^2 + 42^2} = c$$
$$\sqrt{1908} = c$$
$$\sqrt{6^2 \cdot 53} = c$$
$$6\sqrt{53} = c$$
$$6(7.280) \approx c$$
$$43.68 \approx c$$

Check:
$$12^2 + 42^2 \stackrel{?}{\approx} (43.68)^2$$
$$1908 \approx 1907.94$$

Check for Understanding

Here is a suggested use of the Oral Exercises as you teach the lesson.

Oral Exs. 1–3: use before Example 1.

Oral Exs. 4–5: use after Example 1.

Check: $28^2 + 45^2 \stackrel{?}{=} 53^2$ ∴ the length of the third side of
$2809 = 2809$ $\checkmark$ the right triangle is 45 cm. **Answer**

To draw a line segment with a length of $\sqrt{2}$ units, draw a right triangle whose legs are each 1 unit long, as shown in the following diagram.

Then:

$$a^2 + b^2 = c^2$$
$$1^2 + 1^2 = c^2$$
$$1 + 1 = c^2$$
$$2 = c^2$$
$$\pm\sqrt{2} = c$$

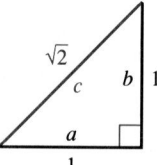

∴ the length of the hypotenuse is $\sqrt{2}$ units.

The following diagrams show that a segment $\sqrt{2}$ units long can be used to construct a segment $\sqrt{3}$ units long, that a segment $\sqrt{3}$ units long can be used to construct a segment $\sqrt{4}$ units long, and so on.

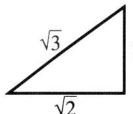 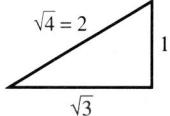 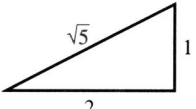 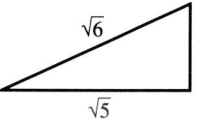

A series of such triangles can be used to locate irrational square roots such as $\sqrt{2}$, $\sqrt{3}$, and $\sqrt{5}$ on the number line. The arcs are drawn to transfer the length of the hypotenuse of each triangle to the x-axis. Note that $-\sqrt{2}$ is located $\sqrt{2}$ units to the left of O.

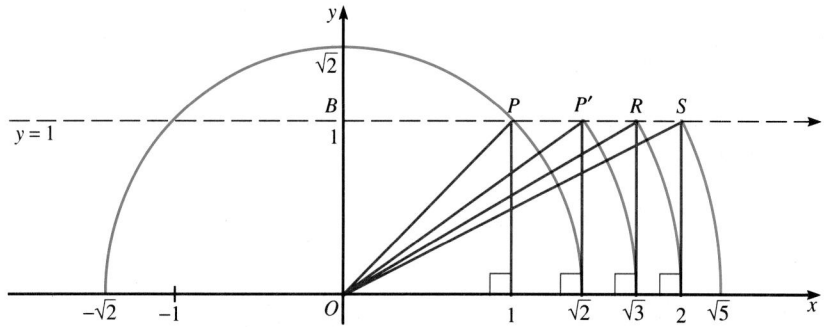

The converse of the Pythagorean theorem is also true. It can be used to see if a given triangle is a right triangle.

Converse of the Pythagorean Theorem

If the sum of the squares of the lengths of the two shorter sides of a triangle is equal to the square of the length of the longest, then the triangle is a right triangle. The right angle is opposite the longest side.

530   *Chapter 11*

Example 2 State whether or not the three given numbers could represent the lengths of the sides of a right triangle.

    a. 8, 15, 17   **b.** 16, 24, 30

Solution   **a.** $a^2 + b^2 = c^2$ **b.** $a^2 + b^2 = c^2$

$$8^2 + 15^2 \overset{?}{=} 17^2 \qquad\qquad 16^2 + 24^2 \overset{?}{=} 30^2$$
$$64 + 225 \overset{?}{=} 289 \qquad\qquad 256 + 576 \overset{?}{=} 900$$
$$289 = 289 \ \checkmark \qquad\qquad\qquad 832 \neq 900$$

∴ 8, 15, and 17 could form   ∴ 16, 24, and 30 could not form
a right triangle. **Answer**   a right triangle. **Answer**

Example 3 To the nearest hundredth, what is the length of a diagonal of a rectangle whose width is 18 cm and whose length is 30 cm?

Solution
$$a^2 + b^2 = c^2$$
$$\sqrt{a^2 + b^2} = c$$
$$\sqrt{18^2 + 30^2} = c$$
$$\sqrt{1224} = c$$
$$\sqrt{2^2 \cdot 3^2 \cdot 34} = c$$
$$6\sqrt{34} = c$$
$$6(5.831) \approx c$$
$$34.99 \approx c$$

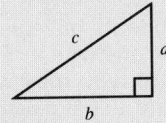

18 cm

30 cm

Check: $18^2 + 30^2 \overset{?}{\approx} (34.99)^2$
              $1224 \approx 1224.3 \ \checkmark$

∴ the length of a diagonal of the rectangle is 34.99 cm. **Answer**

Oral Exercises

Evaluate.

1. $\sqrt{6^2 + 8^2}$ 10   **2.** $\sqrt{5^2 - 3^2}$ 4   **3.** $\sqrt{13^2 - 5^2}$ 12

State and solve an equation for the length of the unknown side.

4.

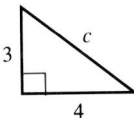

3

4

c

$$a^2 \ + \ b^2 \ = c^2$$
$$(\underline{\ ?\ 3})^2 + (\underline{\ ?\ 4})^2 = c^2$$
$$25\underline{\ ?\ } = c^2$$
$$5\underline{\ ?\ } = c$$

5.

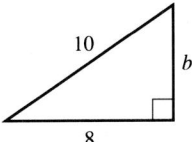

10

8

b

$$a^2 \ + \ b^2 \ = c^2$$
$$8\,(\underline{\ ?\ })^2 + \ b^2 \ = (\underline{\ ?\ })^2 \ 10$$
$$b^2 = \underline{\ ?\ } \ 36$$
$$b = \underline{\ ?\ } \ 6$$

Rational and Irrational Numbers   **531**

Guided Practice

In Exercises 1–3, refer to the triangle below. Find the missing length correct to the nearest hundredth.

c

a

b

1. $a = 6$, $b = 8$, $c = \underline{\ ?\ }$ 10

2. $a = \underline{\ ?\ }$, $b = 9$, $c = 11$
  6.32

3. $a = 15$, $b = \underline{\ ?\ }$, $c = 22$
  16.09

State whether or not the three given numbers could represent the lengths of the sides of a right triangle.

4. 4, 8, 10 no

5. 15, 36, 39 yes

Make a sketch. Approximate the square root to the nearest hundredth.

6. Find the length of a diagonal of a rectangle whose dimensions are 80 cm by 150 cm. 170 cm

Summarizing the Lesson

Tell students that the Pythagorean theorem applies to many areas of mathematics, including analytic geometry, trigonometry, and vectors. Have students write the Pythagorean theorem on their papers and explain it in words.

Suggested Assignments

Minimum
    532/1–21 odd
    533/*P*: 1, 3
S 534/Mixed Review

Average
    532/3–27 mult. of 3
    533/*P*: 2, 5, 8
S 534/Mixed Review

Maximum
    532/3–30 mult. of 3
    533/*P*: 3, 6, 9, 12
S 534/Mixed Review

Using a Calculator

Once students have simplified their answers in Exercises 1–10, you may want to have them use a calculator to find the decimal approximations to the nearest hundredth.

Supplementary Materials

Study Guide   pp. 193–194
Practice Master   68
Test Master   49
Resource Book   p. 133
Overhead Visual   12

Using a Computer

Students with programming experience can write a BASIC program for the Computer Exercises that will use the converse of the Pythagorean theorem to determine whether three numbers could represent the lengths of the sides of a right triangle.

532

Written Exercises

In Exercises 1–10, refer to the triangle at the right. Find the missing length correct to the nearest hundredth. A calculator may be helpful.

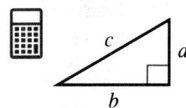

A 1. $a = 10$, $b = 24$, $c = $ _?_ 26

2. $a = 5$, $b = 12$, $c = $ _?_ 13

3. $a = 8$, $b = 5$, $c = $ _?_ 9.43

4. $a = 13$, $b = 9$, $c = $ _?_ 15.81

5. $a = 8$, $b = 8$, $c = $ _?_ 11.31

6. $a = 16$, $b = 8$, $c = $ _?_ 17.89

7. $a = $ _?_ , $b = 21$, $c = 29$ 20

8. $a = $ _?_ , $b = 11$, $c = 17$ 12.96

9. $a = 6$, $b = $ _?_ , $c = 40$ 39.55

10. $a = 5$, $b = $ _?_ , $c = 8$ 6.24

State whether or not the three given numbers could represent the lengths of the sides of a right triangle.

11. 20, 21, 29 yes

12. 3, 9, 11 no

13. 12, 16, 20 yes

14. 16, 32, 36 no

15. 15, 20, 25 yes

16. 17, 34, 39 no

B 17. $2a$, $3a$, $4a$ no

18. $3a$, $4a$, $5a$ yes

19. $8a$, $15a$, $17a$ yes

20. $6a$, $7a$, $8a$ no

In Exercises 21–26, refer to the diagram for Exercises 1–10. Find the missing length correct to the nearest hundredth.

21. $a = b = 12$, $c = $ _?_ 16.97

22. $a = 15$, $b = \frac{1}{5}a$, $c = $ _?_ 15.30

23. $a = 18$, $b = \frac{1}{3}a$, $c = $ _?_ 18.97

24. $a = \frac{1}{2}b$, $b = 14$, $c = $ _?_ 15.65

25. $a = \frac{4}{5}b$, $b = 20$, $c = $ _?_ 25.61

26. $a = \frac{5}{7}b$, $b = 28$, $c = $ _?_ 34.41

In Exercises 27–30, refer to the diagram for Exercises 1–10. Find a and b correct to the nearest hundredth.

C 27. $a = b$, $c = 60$ $a = b = 42.43$

28. $a = 3b$, $c = 20$ $a = 18.96$; $b = 6.32$

29. $a = \frac{1}{3}b$, $c = 30$ $a = 9.49$; $b = 28.46$

30. $a = \frac{2}{3}b$, $c = 52$ $a = 28.85$; $b = 43.27$

Computer Exercises

Write a BASIC program that will report whether three positive numbers entered with INPUT statements could represent the lengths of the sides of a right triangle. RUN the program for the following series of numbers.

1. 14, 48, 50 yes

2. 0.8, 1.5, 1.7 yes

3. 27, 36, 45 yes

Problems

Make a sketch for each problem. Approximate each square root to the nearest hundredth. A calculator may be helpful.

A 1. Find the length of each diagonal of a rectangle whose dimensions are 33 cm by 56 cm. 65 cm

2. A guywire 20 m long is attached to the top of a telephone pole. The guywire is just able to reach a point on the ground 12 m from the base of the telephone pole. Find the height of the telephone pole. 16 m

3. A baseball diamond is a square 90 ft on a side. What is the length from first base to third base? 127.28 ft

4. The dimensions of a rectangular doorway are 200 cm by 90 cm. Can a table top with a diameter of 210 cm be carried through the doorway? yes

5. The base of an isosceles triangle is 18 cm long. The equal sides are each 24 cm long. Find the altitude. 22.25 cm

B 6. A right triangle has sides whose lengths in feet are consecutive even integers. Determine the length of each side. 6 ft, 8 ft, 10 ft

7. The longer leg of a right triangle is 6 cm longer than 6 times the shorter leg and also 1 cm shorter than the hypotenuse. Find the perimeter of the triangle. 182 cm

8. Find the area of a triangle with three sides of length 4 cm. (*Hint:* Find the height first.) 6.93 cm^2

C 9. What is the length of each diagonal of a cube that is 45 cm on each side? 77.94 cm

10. Show that a triangle with sides of lengths $x^2 + y^2$, $2xy$, and $x^2 - y^2$ is a right triangle. Assume that $x > y$.

11. What is the length of each diagonal of a rectangular box with length 55 cm, width 48 cm, and height 70 cm? Would a meter stick fit in the box? 101.14 cm; yes

12. Gary is standing on a dock 2.0 m above the water. He is pulling in a boat that is attached to the end of a 5.2 m rope. If he pulls in 2.3 m of rope, how far did he move the boat? 2.7 m

Rational and Irrational Numbers **533**

Mixed Review Exercises

Simplify.

1. $\sqrt{16x^{16}y^2}\ 4x^8|y|$

2. $\sqrt{c^2 - 10c + 25}\ |c - 5|$

3. $\sqrt{50a^5(b+4)^2}$
$5a^2|b+4|\sqrt{2a}$

Write as a fraction in simplest form.

4. $(3 \cdot 10^{-4})^2\ \dfrac{9}{100,000,000}$

5. $(2x^{-3}y^{-5})^2\ \dfrac{4}{x^6y^{10}}$

6. $\dfrac{7}{8} \div \dfrac{8}{7}\ \dfrac{49}{64}$

7. $\dfrac{a-1}{6} + \dfrac{3-2a}{9}\ \dfrac{3-a}{18}$

8. $5y + \dfrac{3-y}{y-3}\ 5y - 1$

9. $\dfrac{3r^2}{8x} \div 24rx\ \dfrac{r}{64x^2}$

10. $\left(-\dfrac{k^2}{6}\right)^3 - \dfrac{k^6}{216}$

11. $\dfrac{2r^3 - 10r^2 - 28r}{2r - 14}\ r^2 + 2r$

12. $\dfrac{2s^2 + 9s - 5}{5 + s}\ 2s - 1$

Self-Test 2

Vocabulary   irrational numbers (p. 521)   Pythagorean theorem (p. 529)

Approximate each square root to the nearest tenth. Use a calculator or the table at the back of the book as necessary.

1. $\sqrt{0.81}\ 0.9$

2. $\sqrt{1700}\ 41.2$

3. $-\sqrt{0.88}\ -0.9$

Obj. 11-4, p. 521

Simplify.

4. $\sqrt{144m^2n^2}\ 12|mn|$

5. $-\sqrt{81x^8y^6}\ -9x^4|y^3|$

6. $\sqrt{0.25a^4}\ 0.5a^2$

Obj. 11-5, p. 525

Solve.

7. $w^2 = 64\ \{-8, 8\}$

8. $n^2 - 49 = 0\ \{-7, 7\}$

9. $36y^2 - 25 = 0\ \left\{-\dfrac{5}{6}, \dfrac{5}{6}\right\}$

10. Find c correct to the nearest hundredth if $a = 14$ and $b = 17$. 22.02

Obj. 11-6, p. 529

11. Is a triangle with sides 9, 12, and 14 units long a right triangle? no

Check your answers with those at the back of the book.

Challenge

The following "Problem of the Hundred Fowl" dates to sixth-century China:
If a rooster is worth 5 yuan, a hen is worth 3 yuan, and 3 chicks are worth 1 yuan, how many of each, 100 in all, would be worth 100 yuan? Assume that at least 5 roosters are required. 8 roosters, 11 hens, and 81 chicks, *or* 12 roosters, 4 hens, and 84 chicks

534   *Chapter 11*

Using a Calculator

You may want to have students use a calculator to approximate square roots in Self-Test 2.

Quick Quiz

Approximate each square root to the nearest tenth. Use a calculator or the table at the back of the book as necessary.

1. $\sqrt{0.16}\ 0.4$

2. $\sqrt{2100}\ 45.8$

3. $-\sqrt{0.55}\ -0.7$

Simplify.

4. $\sqrt{25a^2b^2}\ 5|ab|$

5. $-\sqrt{121x^4y^{10}}\ -11x^2|y^5|$

6. $\sqrt{0.49b^8}\ 0.7b^4$

Solve.

7. $y^2 = 400\ \{-20, 20\}$

8. $m^2 - 100 = 0\ \{-10, 10\}$

9. $4c^2 - 25 = 0\ \left\{-\dfrac{5}{2}, \dfrac{5}{2}\right\}$

10. Find the hypotenuse of a right triangle whose legs are 5 cm and 8 cm. State your answer correct to the nearest hundredth. 9.43 cm

11. Is a triangle with sides 6, 9, and 14 units long a right triangle? no

Extra / The Distance Formula

The distance between two points on the *x*-axis or on a line parallel to that axis is the absolute value of the difference between their *x*-coordinates. Using the notation $A'B'$ to denote the distance from A' to B', you can write the following:

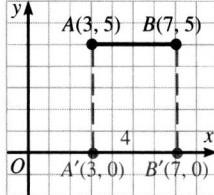

$$A'B' = |3 - 7| = |7 - 3| = 4$$

$$AB = |3 - 7| = |7 - 3| = 4$$

The distance between two points on the *y*-axis or on a line parallel to that axis is the absolute value of the difference between their *y*-coordinates.

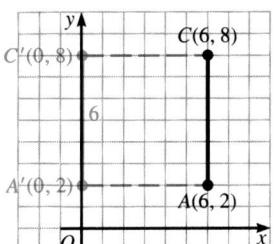

$$A'C' = |2 - 8| = |8 - 2| = 6$$

$$AC = |2 - 8| = |8 - 2| = 6$$

To find the distance between two points not on an axis or a line parallel to an axis, use the Pythagorean theorem:

$$AC = \sqrt{(AB)^2 + (BC)^2}$$
$$= \sqrt{(9 - 3)^2 + (6 - 4)^2}$$
$$= \sqrt{6^2 + 2^2}$$
$$= \sqrt{36 + 4}$$
$$= \sqrt{40}$$
$$= 2\sqrt{10}$$

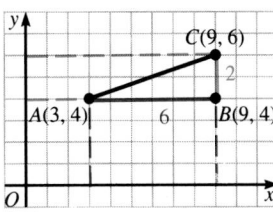

This method for finding the distance between any two points can be generalized in the distance formula.

The Distance Formula

For any points $P_1(x_1, y_1)$ and $P_2(x_2, y_2)$.

$$P_1P_2 = \sqrt{(x_2 - x_1)^2 + (y_2 - y_1)^2}$$

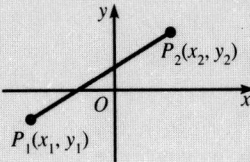

Rational and Irrational Numbers   **535**

Example Find the distance between points $P(-5, 4)$ and $Q(3, -2)$.

Solution 1 $PQ = \sqrt{(3 - (-5))^2 + (-2 - 4)^2}$
$= \sqrt{8^2 + (-6)^2}$
$= \sqrt{64 + 36}$
$= \sqrt{100}$
$= 10$ **Answer**

Solution 2 $QP = \sqrt{(-5 - 3)^2 + (4 - (-2))^2}$
$= \sqrt{(-8)^2 + (6)^2}$
$= \sqrt{64 + 36}$
$= \sqrt{100}$
$= 10$ **Answer**

Exercises

Use the distance formula to find the distance between the given points to the nearest tenth.

1. $(-6, 0)$, $(4, 0)$ 10

2. $(0, -9)$, $(0, 7)$ 16

3. $(3, 4)$, $(9, 7)$ 6.7

4. $(10, 3)$, $(-4, 9)$ 15.2

5. $(-5, -3)$, $(-9, -6)$ 5

6. $(7, -2)$, $(4, -6)$ 5

7. $(-4, 6)$, $(5, 2)$ 9.8

8. $(-4, 7)$, $(-9, -5)$ 13

9. $(4, -4)$, $(9, -8)$ 6.4

10. $(3, -7)$, $(12, -8)$ 9.1

11. $(-2, 1)$, $(-8, -5)$ 8.5

12. $(10, -11)$, $(-9, 3)$ 23.6

13. Use the distance formula to show that the point $M(-2, -3)$ is equidistant from points $A(3, 9)$ and $B(-7, -15)$.

14. Show that the points $R(-4, -1)$, $S(3, 6)$, and $T(2, 7)$ are the vertices of a right triangle.

Challenge

1. On the same set of axes, graph the following line segments to draw a picture.

$x = 0$, $2 \le y \le 7$

$x = 6$, $0 \le y \le 5$

$x = 18$, $4 \le y \le 9$

$x + 3y = 6$, $0 \le x \le 6$

$x + 3y = 21$, $0 \le x \le 6$

$x - y = -7$, $0 \le x \le 3$

$x - 3y = 6$, $6 \le x \le 18$

$x - 3y = -9$, $6 \le x \le 18$

$x - 3y = -27$, $3 \le x \le 15$

$5x + 3y = 45$, $3 \le x \le 6$

$5x + 3y = 117$, $15 \le x \le 18$

2. Draw a picture on graph paper using line segments. Write a set of equations and inequalities to describe your picture as in Exercise 1.

536 *Chapter 11*

Radical Expressions

11-7 Multiplying, Dividing, and Simplifying Radicals

Objective   To simplify products and quotients of radicals.

You can use the product and quotient properties of square roots together with the commutative, associative, and distributive properties to multiply, divide, and simplify square-root radicals.

Example 1 Simplify $3\sqrt{2} \cdot 4\sqrt{18}$.

Solution $3\sqrt{2} \cdot 4\sqrt{18} = (3 \cdot 4)(\sqrt{2} \cdot \sqrt{18})$
$= 12\sqrt{36}$
$= 12 \cdot 6$
$= 72$ *Answer*

Example 2 Simplify $\sqrt{\dfrac{3}{7}} \cdot \sqrt{\dfrac{14}{27}}$.

Solution $\sqrt{\dfrac{3}{7}} \cdot \sqrt{\dfrac{14}{27}} = \sqrt{\dfrac{3}{7} \cdot \dfrac{14}{27}} = \sqrt{\dfrac{3 \cdot 14}{7 \cdot 27}} = \sqrt{\dfrac{2}{9}} = \dfrac{\sqrt{2}}{\sqrt{9}} = \dfrac{\sqrt{2}}{3}$

You can eliminate the radical from the denominator by multiplying a radical expression by an appropriate value of 1. For example:

$$\dfrac{\sqrt{5}}{\sqrt{7}} = \dfrac{\sqrt{5} \cdot \sqrt{7}}{\sqrt{7} \cdot \sqrt{7}} = \dfrac{\sqrt{5 \cdot 7}}{(\sqrt{7})^2} = \dfrac{\sqrt{35}}{7} \leftarrow \text{no radical in denominator}$$

The process of expressing $\dfrac{\sqrt{5}}{\sqrt{7}}$ as $\dfrac{\sqrt{35}}{7}$ is called **rationalizing the denominator.** As you can see, it is easier to name the decimal value of $\dfrac{\sqrt{35}}{7}$ than of $\dfrac{\sqrt{5}}{\sqrt{7}}$. Of course with a calculator it may not matter. In general:

An expression having a square-root radical is in **simplest form** when:
1. no integral radicand has a perfect-square factor other than 1,
2. no fractions are under a radical sign, and
3. no radicals are in a denominator.

Rational and Irrational Numbers   **537**

Teaching Suggestions p. T135

Suggested Extensions p. T135

Warm-Up Exercises
Name the illustrated property or properties.
1. $\sqrt{4 \cdot 7} = \sqrt{4} \cdot \sqrt{7}$ product property of square roots
2. $\sqrt{\dfrac{5}{9}} = \dfrac{\sqrt{5}}{\sqrt{9}}$ quotient property of square roots
3. $(3\sqrt{5})\sqrt{6} = 3(\sqrt{5} \cdot \sqrt{6})$ associative
4. $(\sqrt{7} \cdot 4)(\sqrt{3}) = (4\sqrt{7})(\sqrt{3})$ commutative
5. $5\sqrt{2} \cdot 3\sqrt{8} = (5 \cdot 3)\sqrt{2} \cdot \sqrt{8}$ associative and commutative

Motivating the Lesson
Multiplication and division of radicals are today's topics. Students will need these skills when solving simple radical equations.

Chalkboard Examples
Simplify.
1. $5\sqrt{3} \cdot 8\sqrt{21}$
$(5 \cdot 8)(\sqrt{3} \cdot \sqrt{21}) =$
$40\sqrt{63} = 40\sqrt{9 \cdot 7} =$
$40 \cdot 3\sqrt{7} = 120\sqrt{7}$

2. $\sqrt{\dfrac{10}{3}} \cdot \sqrt{\dfrac{27}{32}} = \sqrt{\dfrac{10}{3} \cdot \dfrac{27}{32}} =$
$\sqrt{\dfrac{10 \cdot 27}{3 \cdot 32}} = \sqrt{\dfrac{45}{16}} = \dfrac{\sqrt{45}}{\sqrt{16}} =$
$\dfrac{\sqrt{9 \cdot 5}}{\sqrt{16}} = \dfrac{3\sqrt{5}}{4}$

3. $\dfrac{\sqrt{75}}{2\sqrt{18}} = \dfrac{5\sqrt{3}}{2 \cdot 3\sqrt{2}} = \dfrac{5\sqrt{3}}{6\sqrt{2}} \cdot$
$\dfrac{\sqrt{2}}{\sqrt{2}} = \dfrac{5\sqrt{6}}{6(\sqrt{2})^2} = \dfrac{5\sqrt{6}}{12}$

(continued)

4. $\sqrt{2\frac{2}{3}} \cdot \sqrt{1\frac{1}{4}}$

$\sqrt{\frac{8}{3}} \cdot \sqrt{\frac{5}{4}} =$

$\sqrt{\frac{8}{3} \cdot \frac{5}{4}} = \sqrt{\frac{10}{3}} =$

$\frac{\sqrt{10}}{\sqrt{3}} \cdot \frac{\sqrt{3}}{\sqrt{3}} = \frac{\sqrt{10 \cdot 3}}{(\sqrt{3})^2} =$

$\frac{\sqrt{30}}{3}$

Multiply. Assume that all variables represent positive real numbers.

5. $4\sqrt{a^2b^2}(3\sqrt{b})$

$4(3)\sqrt{a^2b^2 \cdot b} = 12ab\sqrt{b}$

6. $\sqrt{x}(\sqrt{x} - 3)$

$(\sqrt{x})^2 - 3\sqrt{x} = x - 3\sqrt{x}$

Check for Understanding

Here is a suggested use of the Oral Exercises to check students' understanding as you teach the lesson.
Oral Exs. 1–8: use after Example 2.
Oral Exs. 9–10: use after Example 3.

Guided Practice

Simplify. Assume that all variables represent positive real numbers.

1. $7\sqrt{2} \cdot 5\sqrt{2}$ 70

2. $\sqrt{7} \cdot \sqrt{42}$ $7\sqrt{6}$

3. $4\sqrt{507}$ $52\sqrt{3}$

4. $\sqrt{3\frac{1}{3}} \cdot \sqrt{4\frac{4}{5}}$ 4

5. $\sqrt{\frac{6}{5}} \cdot \sqrt{\frac{50}{9}}$ $\frac{2\sqrt{15}}{3}$

6. $\frac{3\sqrt{20}}{\sqrt{15}}$ $2\sqrt{3}$

7. $\sqrt{8}(7 - \sqrt{14})$
    $14\sqrt{2} - 4\sqrt{7}$

8. $(3\sqrt{8})(-\sqrt{6})(4\sqrt{15})$
    $-144\sqrt{5}$

Example 3 Simplify: **a.** $\dfrac{3}{\sqrt{5}}$ **b.** $\sqrt{\dfrac{7}{8}}$ **c.** $\dfrac{9\sqrt{3}}{\sqrt{24}}$ **d.** $\sqrt{3\frac{3}{7}} \cdot \sqrt{2\frac{1}{3}}$

Solution **a.** $\dfrac{3}{\sqrt{5}} = \dfrac{3}{\sqrt{5}} \cdot \dfrac{\sqrt{5}}{\sqrt{5}} = \dfrac{3\sqrt{5}}{(\sqrt{5})^2} = \dfrac{3\sqrt{5}}{5}$

b. $\sqrt{\dfrac{7}{8}} = \dfrac{\sqrt{7}}{\sqrt{8}} = \dfrac{\sqrt{7}}{2\sqrt{2}} = \dfrac{\sqrt{7}}{2\sqrt{2}} \cdot \dfrac{\sqrt{2}}{\sqrt{2}} = \dfrac{\sqrt{7 \cdot 2}}{2(\sqrt{2})^2} = \dfrac{\sqrt{14}}{4}$

c. $\dfrac{9\sqrt{3}}{\sqrt{24}} = \dfrac{9\sqrt{3}}{2\sqrt{6}} = \dfrac{9\sqrt{3}}{2\sqrt{6}} \cdot \dfrac{\sqrt{6}}{\sqrt{6}} = \dfrac{9\sqrt{18}}{2(\sqrt{6})^2} = \dfrac{9\sqrt{9 \cdot 2}}{2 \cdot 6} = \dfrac{9 \cdot 3\sqrt{2}}{2 \cdot 6} = \dfrac{9\sqrt{2}}{4}$

d. $\sqrt{3\frac{3}{7}} \cdot \sqrt{2\frac{1}{3}} = \sqrt{\dfrac{24}{7}} \cdot \sqrt{\dfrac{7}{3}} = \sqrt{\dfrac{24 \cdot 7}{7 \cdot 3}} = \sqrt{8} = 2\sqrt{2}$

Example 4 Multiply. Assume that all variables represent positive real numbers.
   a. $3\sqrt{ab^2}(-2\sqrt{a})$ **b.** $\sqrt{r}(5 - \sqrt{r})$

Solution **a.** $3\sqrt{ab^2}(-2\sqrt{a}) = 3(-2)\sqrt{ab^2 \cdot a} = -6\sqrt{a^2b^2} = -6ab$

   b. $\sqrt{r}(5 - \sqrt{r}) = 5\sqrt{r} - (\sqrt{r})^2 = 5\sqrt{r} - r$

Oral Exercises

Simplify.

1. $\sqrt{2} \cdot \sqrt{5}$ $\sqrt{10}$ **2.** $\dfrac{\sqrt{32}}{\sqrt{2}}$ 4   **3.** $\dfrac{\sqrt{45}}{\sqrt{5}}$ 3   **4.** $4\sqrt{2} \cdot \sqrt{3}$ $4\sqrt{6}$ **5.** $\sqrt{3} \cdot \sqrt{6}$ $3\sqrt{2}$

6. $\sqrt{3} \cdot \sqrt{12}$ 6   **7.** $\dfrac{\sqrt{18}}{\sqrt{3}}$ $\sqrt{6}$ **8.** $\dfrac{\sqrt{48}}{\sqrt{2}}$ $2\sqrt{6}$ **9.** $\dfrac{\sqrt{5}}{\sqrt{15}}$ $\dfrac{\sqrt{3}}{3}$ **10.** $\sqrt{\dfrac{2}{7}}$ $\dfrac{\sqrt{14}}{7}$

Written Exercises

Simplify. Assume that all variables represent positive real numbers.

A **1.** $5\sqrt{3} \cdot 2\sqrt{3}$ 30   **2.** $4\sqrt{7} \cdot 2\sqrt{7}$ 56   **3.** $\sqrt{3} \cdot \sqrt{3} \cdot \sqrt{4}$ 6   **4.** $\sqrt{5} \cdot \sqrt{5} \cdot \sqrt[15]{9}$

5. $2\sqrt{5} \cdot \sqrt{7}$ $2\sqrt{35}$ **6.** $6\sqrt{2} \cdot \sqrt{5}$ $6\sqrt{10}$ **7.** $\sqrt{3} \cdot \sqrt{27}$ 9   **8.** $\sqrt{5} \cdot \sqrt{20}$ 10

9. $\sqrt{11} \cdot \sqrt{44}$ 22   **10.** $\sqrt{7} \cdot \sqrt{35}$ $7\sqrt{5}$ **11.** $6\sqrt{72}$ $36\sqrt{2}$ **12.** $9\sqrt{242}$ $99\sqrt{2}$

13. $\sqrt{\dfrac{3}{8}} \cdot \sqrt{\dfrac{8}{3}}$ 1   **14.** $\sqrt{\dfrac{4}{9}} \cdot \sqrt{\dfrac{18}{4}}$ $\sqrt{2}$ **15.** $\sqrt{\dfrac{8}{11}} \cdot \sqrt{\dfrac{22}{32}}$ $\dfrac{\sqrt{2}}{2}$ **16.** $\sqrt{\dfrac{7}{3}} \cdot \sqrt{\dfrac{3}{28}}$ $\dfrac{1}{2}$

17. $\sqrt{\dfrac{3}{4}} \cdot \sqrt{\dfrac{8}{9}}$ $\dfrac{\sqrt{6}}{3}$ **18.** $\sqrt{\dfrac{4}{5}} \cdot \sqrt{\dfrac{10}{36}}$ $\dfrac{\sqrt{2}}{3}$ **19.** $\sqrt{3\frac{3}{5}} \cdot \sqrt{2\frac{1}{2}}$ 3   **20.** $\sqrt{2\frac{2}{5}} \cdot \sqrt{1\frac{2}{3}}$ 2

21. $\sqrt{\dfrac{10}{13}} \cdot \sqrt{\dfrac{1}{2}}$ $\dfrac{\sqrt{65}}{13}$ **22.** $\sqrt{\dfrac{15}{11}} \cdot \sqrt{\dfrac{1}{3}}$ $\dfrac{\sqrt{55}}{11}$ **23.** $\dfrac{6\sqrt{7}}{\sqrt{35}}$ $\dfrac{6\sqrt{5}}{5}$ **24.** $\dfrac{5\sqrt{48}}{\sqrt{39}}$ $\dfrac{20\sqrt{13}}{13}$

25. $3\sqrt{\dfrac{48}{9}}$ $4\sqrt{3}$ **26.** $7\sqrt{\dfrac{40}{49}}$ $2\sqrt{10}$ **27.** $\dfrac{14\sqrt{320}}{2\sqrt{5}}$ 56 **28.** $\dfrac{15\sqrt{6}}{\sqrt{90}}$ $\sqrt{15}$

29. $\sqrt{5}(\sqrt{5} - 2)$ $5 - 2\sqrt{5}$ **30.** $\sqrt{7}(6 - \sqrt{2})$ $6\sqrt{7} - \sqrt{14}$

31. $(3\sqrt{2})(-2\sqrt{8})(3\sqrt{27})$ $-216\sqrt{3}$ **32.** $(3\sqrt{5})(-\sqrt{10})(\sqrt{27})$ $-45\sqrt{6}$

B **33.** $(4\sqrt{a^2b})(3\sqrt{b})$ $12ab$ **34.** $(5\sqrt{mn^2})(-2\sqrt{m})$ $-10mn$

     35. $(-x\sqrt{x^2y})(y\sqrt{xy^2})$ $-x^2y^2\sqrt{xy}$ **36.** $(-r\sqrt{r^2s})(-s\sqrt{r^2s})$ r^3s^2

     37. $\sqrt{m}(\sqrt{m^3} + 6)$ $m^2 + 6\sqrt{m}$ **38.** $\sqrt{x}(\sqrt{x^5} + 7)$ $x^3 + 7\sqrt{x}$

     39. $(\sqrt{5x})(\sqrt{2x})(3\sqrt{10x^2})$ $30x^2$ **40.** $(\sqrt{3a})(\sqrt{2a})(2\sqrt{6a^2})$ $12a^2$

     41. $\sqrt{32} \cdot \sqrt{2x} \cdot \sqrt{3x}$ $8x\sqrt{3}$ **42.** $\sqrt{27} \cdot \sqrt{3n} \cdot \sqrt{5n}$ $9n\sqrt{5}$

     43. $(2\sqrt{5x})^2$ $20x$ **44.** $2n(\sqrt{7n})^2$ $14n^2$

     45. $3x\sqrt{\dfrac{x}{y}} \cdot \sqrt{\dfrac{9x}{y}}$ $\dfrac{9x^2}{y}$ **46.** $3q\sqrt{\dfrac{3q}{2r}} \cdot \sqrt{\dfrac{q}{r}}$ $\dfrac{3q^2\sqrt{6}}{2r}$

49. $24m^2 - 120m^3\sqrt{m}$ **50.** $24x^2\sqrt{3} - 30x^3\sqrt{2x}$

C **47.** $\sqrt{3a}(\sqrt{12a} - 2\sqrt{8a^2})$ $6a - 4a\sqrt{6a}$ **48.** $\sqrt{6x}(\sqrt{3x} - 4\sqrt{8x^2})$ $3x\sqrt{2} - 16x\sqrt{3x}$

     49. $3\sqrt{8m^3}(2\sqrt{2m} - 5\sqrt{8m^4})$ **50.** $2\sqrt{6x^3}(3\sqrt{8x} - 5\sqrt{3x^4})$

     51. $(2\sqrt{3y^3})^3$ $24y^4\sqrt{3y}$ **52.** $(5\sqrt{2x^3})^3$ $250x^4\sqrt{2x}$

     53. $(\sqrt{10xy})^3(x\sqrt{5x^3y} - y\sqrt{10xy^3})$ **54.** $(\sqrt{18ab})^3(a\sqrt{3a^2b} + b\sqrt{5ab^2})$

             $50x^4y^2\sqrt{2} - 100x^2y^4$ $54a^3b^2\sqrt{6a} + 54a^2b^3\sqrt{10b}$

Rationalize the numerator.

> **Sample** $\dfrac{\sqrt{5}}{\sqrt{7}} = \dfrac{\sqrt{5} \cdot \sqrt{5}}{\sqrt{7} \cdot \sqrt{5}} = \dfrac{(\sqrt{5})^2}{\sqrt{7 \cdot 5}} = \dfrac{5}{\sqrt{35}}$ ← no radical in numerator

55. $\dfrac{\sqrt{11}}{\sqrt{3}}$ $\dfrac{11}{\sqrt{33}}$ **56.** $\dfrac{\sqrt{2}}{\sqrt{5}}$ $\dfrac{2}{\sqrt{10}}$ **57.** $\dfrac{\sqrt{6}}{\sqrt{13}}$ $\dfrac{6}{\sqrt{78}}$ **58.** $\dfrac{\sqrt{7}}{\sqrt{15}}$ $\dfrac{7}{\sqrt{105}}$ **59.** $\dfrac{\sqrt{19}}{\sqrt{8}}$ $\dfrac{19}{2\sqrt{38}}$

Mixed Review Exercises

Solve.

1. $x^2 = 169$ {13, −13}   **2.** $2s^2 - 200 = 0$ {10, −10}   **3.** $25z^2 - 1 = 15$ $\left\{\dfrac{4}{5}, -\dfrac{4}{5}\right\}$

4. $\dfrac{1}{c} + \dfrac{1}{3} = \dfrac{1}{2}$ {6}   **5.** $\dfrac{5}{9} = \dfrac{25}{y}$ {45}   **6.** $\dfrac{8b - 5}{5b - 4} = \dfrac{13}{8}$ {12}

Simplify.

7. $19x + 2(3x - 4) + 5$ $25x - 3$ **8.** $12a + 7 - (8a - 17)$ $4a + 24$ **9.** $4(2b - 6) - 5(b - 4)$ $3b - 4$

10. $(-5c^2d)(-4cd^4)$ $20c^3d^5$ **11.** $-4m + 3 + 11m - 4$ $7m - 1$ **12.** $x(x + 2) + (x - 4)(2x + 1)$ $3x^2 - 5x - 4$

Rational and Irrational Numbers   **539**

11-8 Adding and Subtracting Radicals

Objective   To simplify sums and differences of radicals.

You can use the distributive property to simplify the sum of $4\sqrt{7}$ and $5\sqrt{7}$ because each term has $\sqrt{7}$ as a common factor.

Example 1 Simplify $4\sqrt{7} + 5\sqrt{7}$.

Solution $4\sqrt{7} + 5\sqrt{7} = (4 + 5)\sqrt{7} = 9\sqrt{7}$

On the other hand, terms that have unlike radicands *cannot* be combined.

Example 2 Simplify $3\sqrt{6} - 2\sqrt{13} + 5\sqrt{6}$.

Solution $3\sqrt{6} - 2\sqrt{13} + 5\sqrt{6} = (3 + 5)\sqrt{6} - 2\sqrt{13} = 8\sqrt{6} - 2\sqrt{13}$

By expressing each radical in simplest form, you can sometimes combine terms in sums and differences of radicals.

Example 3 Simplify $7\sqrt{3} - 4\sqrt{6} + 2\sqrt{48} - 6\sqrt{54}$.

Solution $7\sqrt{3} - 4\sqrt{6} + 2\sqrt{48} - 6\sqrt{54} = 7\sqrt{3} - 4\sqrt{6} + 2\sqrt{16 \cdot 3} - 6\sqrt{9 \cdot 6}$
$$= 7\sqrt{3} - 4\sqrt{6} + 2(4\sqrt{3}) - 6(3 \cdot \sqrt{6})$$
$$= 7\sqrt{3} - 4\sqrt{6} + 8\sqrt{3} - 18\sqrt{6}$$
$$= 15\sqrt{3} - 22\sqrt{6} \quad \textbf{Answer}$$

To simplify sums or differences of square-root radicals:
1. Express each radical in simplest form.
2. Use the distributive property to add or subtract radicals with like radicands.

Oral Exercises

State the terms in each expression that can be expressed with the same radicand. Simplify the expression if possible. 6. not possible 9. $4\sqrt{17}$

1. $3\sqrt{5} + 2\sqrt{5}$ $\ 5\sqrt{5}$ 2. $8\sqrt{3} - 5\sqrt{3}$ $\ 3\sqrt{3}$ 3. $4\sqrt{11} - 8\sqrt{11}$ $\ -4\sqrt{11}$

4. $6\sqrt{7} + 9\sqrt{7} + 2\sqrt{7}$ $\ 17\sqrt{7}$ 5. $8\sqrt{14} - 5\sqrt{14} + \sqrt{3}$ 6. $3\sqrt{17} - 3\sqrt{13} + 5\sqrt{11}$

7. $12\sqrt{3} - 7\sqrt{3}$ $\ 5\sqrt{3}$ 8. $8\sqrt{15} - 5\sqrt{15} + 7\sqrt{15}$ 9. $6\sqrt{17} - 5\sqrt{17} + 3\sqrt{17}$

10. $\sqrt{27} - \sqrt{3}$ $\ 2\sqrt{3}$ 11. $\sqrt{48} + \sqrt{3}$ $\ 5\sqrt{3}$ 12. $\sqrt{24} + \sqrt{6}$ $\ 3\sqrt{6}$

5. $3\sqrt{14} + \sqrt{3}$ 8. $10\sqrt{15}$

Written Exercises

Simplify.

3. $-20\sqrt{17}$
6. $-7\sqrt{6}$
9. $10\sqrt{7} - 6\sqrt{5}$

A

1. $8\sqrt{3} - 6\sqrt{3}$ $2\sqrt{3}$

2. $9\sqrt{5} + 4\sqrt{5}$ $13\sqrt{5}$

3. $-13\sqrt{17} - 7\sqrt{17}$

4. $5\sqrt{80} - 12\sqrt{5}$ $8\sqrt{5}$

5. $5\sqrt{3} + 2\sqrt{75}$ $15\sqrt{3}$

6. $-2\sqrt{24} - 3\sqrt{6}$

7. $3\sqrt{32} - 4\sqrt{63}$ $12\sqrt{2} - 12\sqrt{7}$

8. $3\sqrt{45} + 7\sqrt{36}$ $9\sqrt{5} + 42$

9. $5\sqrt{28} - 2\sqrt{45}$

10. $-4\sqrt{75} + 3\sqrt{147}$ $\sqrt{3}$

11. $-11\sqrt{8} - 7\sqrt{12}$ $-22\sqrt{2} - 14\sqrt{3}$

12. $\sqrt{150} - 5\sqrt{96}$ $-15\sqrt{6}$

13. $9\sqrt{13} - 6\sqrt{11} + \sqrt{13}$ $10\sqrt{13} - 6\sqrt{11}$

14. $-4\sqrt{2} + 6\sqrt{72} - 8\sqrt{32}$ 0

15. $5\sqrt{28} + 2\sqrt{7} - \sqrt{14}$ $12\sqrt{7} - \sqrt{14}$

16. $-3\sqrt{72} + 6\sqrt{52} - 7\sqrt{128}$

17. $-\sqrt{338} - \sqrt{200} + \sqrt{162}$ $-14\sqrt{2}$

18. $4\sqrt{112} + 5\sqrt{56} - 9\sqrt{126}$

16. $-74\sqrt{2} + 12\sqrt{13}$
18. $16\sqrt{7} - 17\sqrt{14}$

Sample

$$\sqrt{15} - \sqrt{\frac{3}{5}} = \sqrt{15} - \frac{\sqrt{3}}{\sqrt{5}}$$

$$= \sqrt{15} - \frac{\sqrt{3}}{\sqrt{5}} \cdot \frac{\sqrt{5}}{\sqrt{5}}$$

$$= \sqrt{15} - \frac{\sqrt{15}}{5}$$

$$= \frac{5\sqrt{15} - \sqrt{15}}{5}$$

$$= \frac{4\sqrt{15}}{5} \quad \textit{Answer}$$

B

19. $\sqrt{55} - 7\sqrt{\frac{5}{11}}$ $\frac{4\sqrt{55}}{11}$

20. $\sqrt{3} - \sqrt{\frac{1}{3}}$ $\frac{2\sqrt{3}}{3}$

21. $3\sqrt{18} + \sqrt{\frac{2}{25}}$ $\frac{46\sqrt{2}}{5}$

22. $2\sqrt{75} + \sqrt{\frac{3}{16}}$ $\frac{41\sqrt{3}}{4}$

23. $\sqrt{\frac{5}{11}} - \sqrt{\frac{11}{5}}$ $-\frac{6\sqrt{55}}{55}$

24. $\sqrt{\frac{2}{7}} - \sqrt{\frac{7}{2}}$ $-\frac{5\sqrt{14}}{14}$

25. $4\sqrt{\frac{5}{6}} - \sqrt{\frac{3}{10}}$ $\frac{17\sqrt{30}}{30}$

26. $5\sqrt{\frac{16}{3}} - \sqrt{\frac{9}{2}}$ $\frac{40\sqrt{3} - 9\sqrt{2}}{6}$

27. $3\sqrt{3} - 2\sqrt{12} + 4\sqrt{\frac{1}{3}}$ $\frac{\sqrt{3}}{3}$

28. $8\sqrt{10} - 3\sqrt{40} + 5\sqrt{\frac{1}{10}}$ $\frac{5\sqrt{10}}{2}$

29. $2\sqrt{\frac{7}{2}} + 4\sqrt{\frac{7}{8}} - \frac{1}{2}\sqrt{98}$ $\frac{4\sqrt{14} - 7\sqrt{2}}{2}$

30. $3\sqrt{\frac{5}{12}} + \sqrt{\frac{12}{5}} - \frac{1}{3}\sqrt{60}$ $\frac{7\sqrt{15}}{30}$

31. $5\sqrt{3}(\sqrt{6} + 2\sqrt{8})$ $15\sqrt{2} + 20\sqrt{6}$

32. $5\sqrt{2}(4\sqrt{8} - 2\sqrt{12})$ $80 - 20\sqrt{6}$

Simplify. Assume that all variables represent positive real numbers.

C

33. $2\sqrt{49x^3} - 3\sqrt{16x^5}$ $14x\sqrt{x} - 12x^2\sqrt{x}$

34. $4\sqrt{72s^4} - 2s\sqrt{200s^2}$ $4s^2\sqrt{2}$

35. $\sqrt{\frac{x^2}{16} + \frac{x^2}{25}}$ $\frac{x\sqrt{41}}{20}$

36. $\sqrt{\frac{x^2}{49} - \frac{x^2}{121}}$ $\frac{6x\sqrt{2}}{77}$

37. $\sqrt{\frac{x^2}{a^2} + \frac{x^2}{b^2}}$ $\frac{x\sqrt{a^2 + b^2}}{ab}$

38. $\sqrt{\frac{x}{a}} - \sqrt{\frac{a}{x}}$ $\frac{\sqrt{ax}(x - a)}{ax}$

Rational and Irrational Numbers   **541**

Mixed Review Exercises

Write each equation in slope-intercept form.

1. $2y = 6x + 10$ $y = 3x + 5$　**2.** $5y - x + 10 = 0$ $y = \frac{1}{5}x - 2$　**3.** $3x - y = 3$ $y = 3x - 3$

4. $5x + 5y = 4$ $y = -x + \frac{4}{5}$　**5.** $x = 2y + 6$ $y = \frac{1}{2}x - 3$　**6.** $2x - 7y = 0$ $y = \frac{2}{7}x$

7. $x = -y + 11$ $y = -x + 11$　**8.** $7 - x + 11y = 0$ $y = \frac{1}{11}x - \frac{7}{11}$　**9.** $12x - 4 = -2y$
$y = -6x + 2$

For each parabola whose equation is given, find the coordinates of the vertex and the equation of the axis of symmetry.

10. $y = -4x^2$ $(0, 0); x = 0$　**11.** $y = x^2 - 6x + 9$ $(3, 0); x = 3$　**12.** $y = 5 - 2x^2$ $(0, 5); x = 0$

Solve. Assume that no denominator is zero.

13. $\frac{4x}{5} = \frac{10x}{.9}$ $\{0\}$

14. $\frac{4}{b + 6} = \frac{-1}{2b + 3}$ $\{-2\}$

15. $11 - \frac{10}{x} = x$ $\{1, 10\}$

16. $\frac{3}{t} = \frac{-7}{2t^2 - 1}$ $\left\{\frac{1}{3}, -\frac{3}{2}\right\}$

17. $\frac{1}{y} + \frac{2 - y}{y + 3} = \frac{1}{y + 3}$ $\{3, -1\}$

18. $\frac{p + 2}{4p - 1} = \frac{p}{4p + 3}$ $\left\{-\frac{1}{2}\right\}$

▨ Biographical Note / *Juan de la Cierva*

Juan de la Cierva was born in Murcia, Spain, in 1895. He attended school there and later graduated from the Special Technical College in Madrid.

Juan de la Cierva was interested in aircraft design. At age 17, de la Cierva and two friends assembled a biplane using the wreckage from a French aircraft. This airplane became the first Spanish-built plane to fly. De la Cierva later designed and built a monoplane and the world's second trimotor, a plane powered by three engines.

After the crash of the trimotor, de la Cierva designed a new type of aircraft, the autogiro. This aircraft resembled a cross between a helicopter and an airplane. The large rotor at the top of the plane was not powered, but moved when air passed over the blades. De la Cierva hoped that this design would eliminate crashes caused by engines stalling at low speeds. In 1923, one of his autogiros flew successfully.

In 1928 de la Cierva was able to fly an autogiro across the English Channel. The concept of the autogiro reached its high point in 1933 with a model that could take off in a space of six yards and was capable of a speed of 100 mi/h.

Extra / Proving Divisibility Tests

You may have learned the following divisibility tests in an earlier course.

Divisibility by	Test
2	Number must end in 0, 2, 4, 6, or 8
3	Sum of digits must be divisible by 3
4	Last two digits must be divisible by 4 (81,736 is divisible by 4 because 36 is.)
5	Number must end in 0 or 5
6	Number must pass tests for both 2 and 3
8	Last 3 digits must be divisible by 8 (145,320 is divisible by 8 because 320 is.)
9	Sum of digits must be divisible by 9

These tests rely on our decimal system of numeration. They can be proved by writing expressions for the values of the numbers involved.

Example Prove the divisibility test for 9 for a three-digit number.

Solution A three-digit number with digits h, t, and u has a value of

$$100h + 10t + u = (99h + 9t) + (h + t + u).$$

Since $99h + 9t$ is divisible by 9, the entire right-hand side of the equation is divisible by 9 if and only if the sum of the digits, $h + t + u$, is divisible by 9.

Exercises

1. Prove the test for divisibility by 3 for a three-digit number.

2. The number 87,154,316 can be written as $(871,543) \cdot 100 + 16$. Explain why you need look only at the last two digits to see if the original number is divisible by 4.

3. Prove the test for divisibility by 4 for a six-digit number.

4. Prove the test for divisibility by 8 for a six-digit number. (*Hint:* See Exercise 3.)

5. Prove that a six-digit number is divisible by 11 if and only if the sum of the first, third, and fifth digits minus the sum of the second, fourth, and sixth digits is divisible by 11.

6. Devise a test to check whether eleven-digit numbers are divisible by 11.

Rational and Irrational Numbers **543**

2. $871,453 \cdot 100$ is divisible by 4 because 100 is divisible by 4. Thus, the number is divisible by 4 because 16 is divisible by 4.

3. Let a, b, c, h, t, u be the digits of a 6-digit number whose value is $a \cdot 10^5 + b \cdot 10^4 + c \cdot 10^3 + h \cdot 10^2 + t \cdot 10 + u = 100(a \cdot 10^3 + b \cdot 10^2 + c \cdot 10 + h) + 10t + u$. Since 4 divides 100, 4 divides the number if and only if 4 divides $10t + u$.

4. Let a, b, c, h, t, u be the digits of a 6-digit number whose value is $a \cdot 10^5 + b \cdot 10^4 + c \cdot 10^3 + h \cdot 10^2 + t \cdot 10 + u = 1000(a \cdot 10^2 + b \cdot 10 + c) + 100h + 10t + u$. Since 8 divides 1000, 8 divides the number if and only if 8 divides $(100h + 10t + u)$.

5. Let the 6-digit number be represented by $a \cdot 10^5 + b \cdot 10^4 + c \cdot 10^3 + h \cdot 10^2 + t \cdot 10 + u$. This can be rewritten as $11 \cdot 10^4 \cdot a + 11(b - a)10^3 + 11(c - b + a)10^2 + 11(h - c + b - a)10 + 11(t - h + c - b + a) + (u - t + h - c + b - a)$. The first 5 terms are divisible by 11. Thus, the number is divisible by 11 if and only if $u - t + h - c + b - a$ is divisible by 11.

6. The number is divisible by 11 if and only if the sum of the odd-place digits minus the sum of the even-place digits is divisible by 11.

11-9 Multiplication of Binomials Containing Radicals

Objective   To multiply binomials containing square-root radicals and to rationalize binomial denominators that contain square-root radicals.

In Chapter 5, you learned some special methods of multiplying binomials. We can use these methods when multiplying binomials containing square-root radicals.

Example 1   Simplify $(6 + \sqrt{11})(6 - \sqrt{11})$.

Solution   The pattern is $(a + b)(a - b) = a^2 - b^2$.
$$(6 + \sqrt{11})(6 - \sqrt{11}) = 6^2 - (\sqrt{11})^2$$
$$= 36 - 11$$
$$= 25 \quad \textit{Answer}$$

Example 2   Simplify $(3 + \sqrt{5})^2$.

Solution   The pattern is $(a + b)^2 = a^2 + 2ab + b^2$.
$$(3 + \sqrt{5})^2 = 3^2 + 2[(3)(\sqrt{5})] + (\sqrt{5})^2$$
$$= 9 + 6\sqrt{5} + 5$$
$$= 14 + 6\sqrt{5} \quad \textit{Answer}$$

Example 3   Simplify $(2\sqrt{3} - 5\sqrt{7})^2$.

Solution   The pattern is $(a - b)^2 = a^2 - 2ab + b^2$.
$$(2\sqrt{3} - 5\sqrt{7})^2 = (2\sqrt{3})^2 - 2[(2\sqrt{3})(5\sqrt{7})] + (5\sqrt{7})^2$$
$$= (2\sqrt{3})^2 - 2[(2)(5)(\sqrt{3})(\sqrt{7})] + (5\sqrt{7})^2$$
$$= 4(3) - 20\sqrt{21} + 25(7)$$
$$= 12 - 20\sqrt{21} + 175$$
$$= 187 - 20\sqrt{21} \quad \textit{Answer}$$

If b and d are both nonnegative, then the binomials
$$a\sqrt{b} + c\sqrt{d} \quad \text{and} \quad a\sqrt{b} - c\sqrt{d}$$
are called **conjugates** of one another. Conjugates differ only in the sign of one term. If a, b, c, and d are all integers, then the product
$$(a\sqrt{b} + c\sqrt{d})(a\sqrt{b} - c\sqrt{d})$$
will be an integer (see Example 1). Conjugates can be used to rationalize binomial denominators that contain radicals.

544   *Chapter 11*

Example 4

Rationalize the denominator of $\dfrac{3}{5 - 2\sqrt{7}}$.

Solution

$$\dfrac{3}{5 - 2\sqrt{7}} = \dfrac{3}{5 - 2\sqrt{7}} \cdot \dfrac{5 + 2\sqrt{7}}{5 + 2\sqrt{7}}$$

$$= \dfrac{3(5 + 2\sqrt{7})}{25 - (2\sqrt{7})^2}$$

$$= \dfrac{15 + 6\sqrt{7}}{25 - 28}$$

$$= \dfrac{15 + 6\sqrt{7}}{-3}$$

$$= \dfrac{15}{-3} + \dfrac{6\sqrt{7}}{-3}$$

$$= -5 - 2\sqrt{7} \quad \textbf{\textit{Answer}}$$

Oral Exercises

Complete. Express in simplest form.

1. $(\sqrt{5} + 3)(\sqrt{5} - 3) = 5 - \underline{\ 9\ }_? = \underline{\ -4\ }_?$

2. $(8 - \sqrt{6})(8 + \sqrt{6}) = 64 - \underline{\ 6\ }_? = \underline{\ 58\ }_?$

3. $(\sqrt{2} + 3)^2 = 2 + \underline{\ ?\ }_{6\sqrt{2}} + 9 = 11 + \underline{\ ?\ }_{6\sqrt{2}}$

4. $(6 - \sqrt{11})^2 = 36 - \underline{\ ?\ }_{12\sqrt{11}} + \underline{\ 11\ }_? = \underline{\ ?\ }_{47 - 12\sqrt{11}}$

State the conjugate of each binomial.

5. $8 + 4\sqrt{5}$
$\quad 8 - 4\sqrt{5}$

6. $-7 - 3\sqrt{11}$
$\quad -7 + 3\sqrt{11}$

7. $-4 + 6\sqrt{7}$
$\quad -4 - 6\sqrt{7}$

8. $5 - 8\sqrt{13}$
$\quad 5 + 8\sqrt{13}$

Written Exercises

Simplify.

A

1. $(2 + \sqrt{3})(2 - \sqrt{3})$ 1

2. $(4 + \sqrt{11})(4 - \sqrt{11})$ 5

3. $(\sqrt{15} + 6)(\sqrt{15} - 6)$ -21

4. $(\sqrt{19} - 9)(\sqrt{19} + 9)$ -62

5. $(\sqrt{3} - \sqrt{2})(\sqrt{3} + \sqrt{2})$ 1

6. $(\sqrt{15} - \sqrt{3})(\sqrt{15} + \sqrt{3})$ 12

7. $(2 + \sqrt{7})^2$ $11 + 4\sqrt{7}$

8. $(8 - \sqrt{6})^2$ $70 - 16\sqrt{6}$

9. $(2\sqrt{2} - 3)^2$ $17 - 12\sqrt{2}$

10. $(4\sqrt{10} + 3)^2$ $169 + 24\sqrt{10}$

11. $(\sqrt{13} - 2\sqrt{5})^2$ $33 - 4\sqrt{65}$

12. $(3\sqrt{7} - \sqrt{3})^2$ $66 - 6\sqrt{21}$

13. $(2\sqrt{7} + \sqrt{3})(2\sqrt{7} - \sqrt{3})$ 25

14. $(3\sqrt{5} - \sqrt{2})(3\sqrt{5} + \sqrt{2})$ 43

15. $(6\sqrt{5} - \sqrt{7})(6\sqrt{5} + \sqrt{7})$ 173

16. $(8\sqrt{11} + 2\sqrt{6})(8\sqrt{11} - 2\sqrt{6})$ 680

17. $(4\sqrt{3} - 5)(2\sqrt{3} + 3)$ $9 + 2\sqrt{3}$

18. $(6\sqrt{2} + 4)(3\sqrt{2} - 5)$ $16 - 18\sqrt{2}$

B

19. $(2\sqrt{5} - 6\sqrt{7})(3\sqrt{5} + \sqrt{7})$ $-12 - 16\sqrt{35}$

20. $(7\sqrt{13} + 2\sqrt{6})(2\sqrt{13} + 3\sqrt{6})$ $218 + 25\sqrt{78}$

21. $(4\sqrt{11} - 2\sqrt{2})(6\sqrt{11} + 8\sqrt{2})$ $232 + 20\sqrt{22}$

22. $(8\sqrt{6} - 2\sqrt{3})(2\sqrt{6} - 3\sqrt{3})$ $114 - 84\sqrt{2}$

Rational and Irrational Numbers **545**

---

4. Rationalize the denominator of $\dfrac{6}{3 - 2\sqrt{3}}$.

$$\dfrac{6}{3 - 2\sqrt{3}} \cdot \dfrac{3 + 2\sqrt{3}}{3 + 2\sqrt{3}} =$$

$$\dfrac{6(3 + 2\sqrt{3})}{9 - (2\sqrt{3})^2} = \dfrac{18 + 12\sqrt{3}}{9 - 12} =$$

$$\dfrac{18 + 12\sqrt{3}}{-3} = \dfrac{18}{-3} + \dfrac{12\sqrt{3}}{-3} =$$

$$-6 - 4\sqrt{3}$$

Check for Understanding

Oral Exs. 1–2: use after Example 1.
Oral Exs. 3–4: use after Example 3.
Oral Exs. 5–8: use after Example 4.

Guided Practice

Simplify.

1. $(5 + \sqrt{7})(5 - \sqrt{7})$ 18

2. $(4 + \sqrt{6})^2$ $22 + 8\sqrt{6}$

3. $(3\sqrt{3} - \sqrt{10})^2$ $37 - 6\sqrt{30}$

4. $(5\sqrt{3} - 2\sqrt{6})(5\sqrt{3} + 2\sqrt{6})$ 51

5. $(7\sqrt{5} + 11)(2\sqrt{5} - 6)$ $4 - 20\sqrt{5}$

Summarizing the Lesson

Tell students they have learned to multiply binomials with radicals. They have also learned how to rationalize binomial denominators that contain radicals by using conjugates.

Suggested Assignments

Minimum
545/1–27 odd, 31
S 546/Mixed Review

Average
545/3–42 mult. of 3
S 546/Mixed Review

Maximum
545/3–45 mult. of 3
S 546/Mixed Review

Rationalize the denominator of each fraction.

23. $\dfrac{1}{1 + \sqrt{5}}$ $\dfrac{-1 + \sqrt{5}}{4}$

24. $\dfrac{1}{2 + \sqrt{3}}$ $2 - \sqrt{3}$

25. $\dfrac{3}{\sqrt{5} - 2}$ $3\sqrt{5} + 6$

26. $\dfrac{1}{\sqrt{7} - 3}$ $\dfrac{-3 - \sqrt{7}}{2}$

27. $\dfrac{1 + \sqrt{7}}{2 - \sqrt{7}}$ $-3 - \sqrt{7}$

28. $\dfrac{4 + \sqrt{5}}{3 - \sqrt{5}}$ $\dfrac{17 + 7\sqrt{5}}{4}$

29. $\dfrac{\sqrt{3} - 4}{\sqrt{7} + 2}$

30. $\dfrac{\sqrt{5} - 2}{\sqrt{3} + 1}$

31. $\dfrac{7}{2\sqrt{5} + 1}$

32. $\dfrac{5}{3\sqrt{7} - 5}$

33. $\dfrac{4 + 2\sqrt{2}}{2\sqrt{5} - 3}$

34. $\dfrac{6 - 2\sqrt{3}}{3\sqrt{2} + 3}$

If $f(x) = x^2 - 5x - 7$, find the value of each function.

Sample $f(\sqrt{7}) = (\sqrt{7})^2 - 5(\sqrt{7}) - 7$
$= 7 - 5\sqrt{7} - 7$
$= -5\sqrt{7}$ *Answer*

35. $f(\sqrt{6})$ $-1 - 5\sqrt{6}$

36. $f(\sqrt{10})$ $3 - 5\sqrt{10}$

37. $f(\sqrt{2} + 1)$ $-9 - 3\sqrt{2}$

38. $f(\sqrt{3} + 2)$ $-10 - \sqrt{3}$

39. $f(-2 + \sqrt{11})$ $18 - 9\sqrt{11}$

40. $f(\sqrt{7} - 2)$ $14 - 9\sqrt{7}$

41. Show that $(4 + \sqrt{7})$ and $(4 - \sqrt{7})$ are roots of the equation $x^2 - 8x + 9 = 0$.

42. Show that $(5 + \sqrt{3})$ and $(5 - \sqrt{3})$ are roots of the equation $y^2 - 10y + 22 = 0$.

43. Show that $\left(\dfrac{2}{3} + \dfrac{\sqrt{7}}{3}\right)$ and $\left(\dfrac{2}{3} - \dfrac{\sqrt{7}}{3}\right)$ are roots of the equation $3x^2 - 4x - 1 = 0$.

C   44. Write an expression in simplest form for the area of a triangle whose base is $\dfrac{4\sqrt{5} - 2}{5}$ units and whose height is $\dfrac{\sqrt{5} + 6}{2}$ units. $\dfrac{4 + 11\sqrt{5}}{10}$ square units

Simplify each expression, assuming that the value of each variable is nonnegative.

45. $(x + \sqrt{y})(x - \sqrt{y})$
$x^2 - y$

46. $(x - 3\sqrt{2})^2$
$x^2 - 6x\sqrt{2} + 18$

47. $(3a\sqrt{b} - c)(5a\sqrt{b} + 3c)$
$15a^2b + 4ac\sqrt{b} - 3c^2$

Mixed Review Exercises

Simplify. Assume the radicands are nonnegative real numbers.

1. $\sqrt{18x^8}$ $3x^4\sqrt{2}$

2. $4\sqrt{15x} \cdot 3\sqrt{5}$ $60\sqrt{3x}$

3. $6\sqrt{8} - 4\sqrt{2}$ $8\sqrt{2}$

4. $4\sqrt{63} + 5\sqrt{28}$ $22\sqrt{7}$

5. $\sqrt{\dfrac{3}{5}} \cdot \sqrt{\dfrac{5}{9}}$ $\dfrac{\sqrt{3}}{3}$

6. $\sqrt{1\dfrac{5}{6}} \cdot \sqrt{4\dfrac{1}{6}}$ $\dfrac{5\sqrt{11}}{6}$

7. $(3 - 5k^2)^2$
$9 - 30k^2 + 25k^4$

8. $(2p + 7z)^2$
$4p^2 + 28pz + 49z^2$

9. $(6ab + x)(6ab - x)$
$36a^2b^2 - x^2$

Solve.

10. $7p - 3 = 6(p + 2)$ $\{15\}$

11. $x^2 - 14x + 45 = 0$
$\{5, 9\}$

12. $36g^2 = 16$ $\left\{\dfrac{2}{3}, -\dfrac{2}{3}\right\}$

546   *Chapter 11*

11-10 Simple Radical Equations

Objective To solve simple radical equations.

Skydivers must plan carefully before free-falling from an airplane. The formula they use to determine the velocity of their free falling is $v = \sqrt{2gd}$, where v is the velocity in m/s, $g = 9.8$ m/s^2, and d is the distance in meters.

An equation like $v = \sqrt{2gd}$ that has a variable in the radicand is called a **radical equation.** Simple radical equations are solved by isolating the radical on one side of the equals sign and then squaring both sides of the equation.

Example 1 Solve $140 = \sqrt{2(9.8)d}$.

Solution

$$140 = \sqrt{2(9.8)d}$$
$$140 = \sqrt{19.6d}$$
$$(140)^2 = (\sqrt{19.6d})^2$$
$$19{,}600 = 19.6d$$
$$1000 = d$$

Check: $140 \overset{?}{=} \sqrt{2(9.8)(1000)}$
$140 \overset{?}{=} \sqrt{19{,}600}$
$140 = 140$ ✓

∴ the solution set is $\{1000\}$. ***Answer***

Example 2 Solve $\sqrt{5x + 1} + 2 = 6$.

Solution

$$\sqrt{5x + 1} + 2 = 6$$
$$\sqrt{5x + 1} = 4$$
$$5x + 1 = 16$$
$$5x = 15$$
$$x = 3$$

Check: $\sqrt{5(3) + 1} + 2 \overset{?}{=} 6$
$\sqrt{15 + 1} + 2 \overset{?}{=} 6$
$\sqrt{16} + 2 \overset{?}{=} 6$
$4 + 2 \overset{?}{=} 6$
$6 = 6$ ✓

∴ the solution set is $\{3\}$. ***Answer***

When you square both sides of an equation, the new equation may not be equivalent to the original equation. Therefore, you must *check every possible root in the original equation* to see whether it is indeed a root. By the multiplication property of equality, any root of the original equation is also a root of the squared equation. Thus, you are sure to find all the roots of the original equation among the roots of the squared equation.

Rational and Irrational Numbers **547**

Teaching Suggestions p. T136

Suggested Extensions p. T137

Warm-Up Exercises

Square each expression.

1. $\sqrt{m}$ m **2.** $2\sqrt{5a}$ $20a$

3. $\sqrt{3c^2}$ $3c^2$

4. $\sqrt{2r - 5}$ $2r - 5$

5. $\sqrt{\dfrac{5z + 8}{3}}$ $\dfrac{5z + 8}{3}$

Motivating the Lesson

In physics, there are laws describing the motion of a pendulum. One of the formulas is $t = 2\pi\sqrt{\dfrac{L}{980}}$ where t is the time of vibration and L is the length of the string in centimeters. Tell the students they'll learn to solve equations involving radicals today.

Chalkboard Examples

Solve.

1. $\sqrt{\dfrac{3x}{2}} = 120$

$$\left(\sqrt{\dfrac{3x}{2}}\right)^2 = (120)^2$$
$$\dfrac{3x}{2} = 14{,}400$$
$$3x = 28{,}800$$
$$x = 9600$$

Check: $\sqrt{\dfrac{3 \cdot 9600}{2}} \overset{?}{=} 120$
$\sqrt{14{,}400} \overset{?}{=} 120$
$120 = 120$

∴ the solution set is $\{9600\}$.

2. $\sqrt{6y - 2} - 3 = 7$
$$\sqrt{6y - 2} = 10$$
$$(\sqrt{6y - 2})^2 = 10^2$$
$$6y - 2 = 100$$
$$6y = 102$$
$$y = 17$$

(continued)

Check: $\sqrt{6 \cdot 17 - 2} - 3 \overset{?}{=} 7$

$\sqrt{100} - 3 \overset{?}{=} 7$

$7 = 7$

∴ the solution set is {17}.

3. $\sqrt{5x^2 + 16} - 3x = 0$

$\sqrt{5x^2 + 16} = 3x$

$5x^2 + 16 = 9x^2$

$16 = 4x^2$

$4 = x^2$

$x = 2$ or $x = -2$

Check:

$\sqrt{5(2)^2 + 16} - 3(2) \overset{?}{=} 0$

$\sqrt{20 + 16} - 6 \overset{?}{=} 0$

$\sqrt{36} - 6 \overset{?}{=} 0$

$6 - 6 = 0$

$\sqrt{5(-2)^2 + 16} - 3(-2) \overset{?}{=} 0$

$\sqrt{20 + 16} + 6 \overset{?}{=} 0$

$\sqrt{36} + 6 \overset{?}{=} 0$

$6 + 6 \neq 0$

∴ the solution set is {2}.

Check for Understanding

Oral Exs. 1–9: use after
Example 1.

Oral Exs. 10–15: use after
Example 2.

Guided Practice

Solve.

1. $\sqrt{z} = 16$ {256}

2. $\sqrt{2m} = 4$ {8}

3. $\sqrt{x} + 6 = 14$ {64}

4. $\sqrt{\dfrac{x}{3}} = 7$ {147}

5. $\sqrt{z + 2} = 3$ {7}

6. $\sqrt{5x} - 6 = 4$ {20}

7. $\sqrt{4m - 3} + 6 = 10$ $\left\{\dfrac{19}{4}\right\}$

8. $\sqrt{3x} = 2\sqrt{15}$ {20}

Example 3 Solve $\sqrt{11x^2 - 63} - 2x = 0$.

Solution $\sqrt{11x^2 - 63} - 2x = 0$

$\sqrt{11x^2 - 63} = 2x$ $\begin{cases}\text{Set apart the radical on} \\ \text{one side of the equation.}\end{cases}$

$11x^2 - 63 = 4x^2$ {Square both sides.

$7x^2 = 63$

$x^2 = 9$

$x = 3$ or $x = -3$

Check: $\sqrt{11(3)^2 - 63} - 2(3) \overset{?}{=} 0$

$\sqrt{99 - 63} - 6 \overset{?}{=} 0$

$\sqrt{36} - 6 \overset{?}{=} 0$

$6 - 6 = 0$ ✓

$\sqrt{11(-3)^2 - 63} - 2(-3) \overset{?}{=} 0$

$\sqrt{99 - 63} + 6 \overset{?}{=} 0$

$\sqrt{36} + 6 \overset{?}{=} 0$

$6 + 6 \neq 0$

-3 is not a solution.

∴ the solution set is {3}. *Answer*

Oral Exercises

Solve.

1. $\sqrt{x} = 7$ {49}   **2.** $\sqrt{y} = 8$ {64}   **3.** $\sqrt{d} = 10$ {100}

4. $\sqrt{y} = 5$ {25}   **5.** $\sqrt{4a} = 10$ {25}   **6.** $\sqrt{4m} = 8$ {16}

7. $\sqrt{m} = -1$ No solution   **8.** $\sqrt{k} = 0$ {0}   **9.** $\sqrt{z^2} = 6$ {6, −6}

State the first step in the solution of each equation.

10. $\sqrt{3x} = 9$ $3x = 81$ **11.** $\sqrt{5a + 9} = 12$ $5a + 9 = 144$ **12.** $\sqrt{5z - 1} = 7$ $5z - 1 = 49$

13. $\sqrt{x - 5} + 1 = 8$ $\sqrt{x - 5} = 7$ **14.** $2\sqrt{5b} = 6$ $\sqrt{5b} = 3$ **15.** $\sqrt{9x} - 5 = 13$ $\sqrt{9x} = 18$

Written Exercises

Solve.

A   **1.** $\sqrt{x} = 3$ {9}   **2.** $\sqrt{y} = 14$ {196}   **3.** $4 = \sqrt{2x}$ {8}

4. $9 = \sqrt{3a}$ {27}   **5.** $\sqrt{8x} = \dfrac{2}{5}$ $\left\{\dfrac{1}{50}\right\}$ **6.** $\sqrt{4n} = \dfrac{1}{3}$ $\left\{\dfrac{1}{36}\right\}$

7. $1 = \sqrt{m} - 3$ {16}   **8.** $7 = \sqrt{z} - 2$ {81}   **9.** $\dfrac{2}{3} + \sqrt{b} = 1$ $\left\{\dfrac{1}{9}\right\}$

10. $\sqrt{y} - \dfrac{1}{2} = 2$ $\left\{\dfrac{25}{4}\right\}$ **11.** $3 = \sqrt{\dfrac{x}{2}}$ {18}   **12.** $8 = \sqrt{\dfrac{s}{5}}$ {320}

13. $\sqrt{x + 1} = 3$ {8}   **14.** $\sqrt{m + 5} = 1$ {−4}   **15.** $20 = 5\sqrt{2x}$ {8}

16. $5 = 2\sqrt{3x}$ $\left\{\dfrac{25}{12}\right\}$ **17.** $\sqrt{4x} + 2 = 6$ {4}   **18.** $\sqrt{3x} + 4 = 7$ {3}

---

19. $4 = \sqrt{8a} + 3 \left\{\frac{1}{8}\right\}$ **20.** $3 = \sqrt{4x + 1}$ {2}   **21.** $\sqrt{5y - 2} + 3 = 9 \left\{\frac{38}{5}\right\}$

22. $\sqrt{5m - 5} + 6 = 7 \left\{\frac{6}{5}\right\}$ **23.** $\sqrt{x} = 3\sqrt{7}$ {63}   **24.** $\sqrt{r} = 5\sqrt{2}$ {50}

B   **25.** $8 = \sqrt{\frac{5a}{4}} - 2$ {80}   **26.** $14 = \sqrt{\frac{7x}{3}} + 2 \left\{\frac{432}{7}\right\}$ **27.** $\sqrt{\frac{2x + 9}{5}} = 3$ {18}

28. $\sqrt{\frac{2n - 4}{8}} = 2$ {18}   **29.** $4 = \sqrt{\frac{7k - 10}{9}}$ {22}   **30.** $3 = \sqrt{\frac{4x - 5}{7}}$ {17}

31. $15\sqrt{2} = 5\sqrt{t}$ {18}   **32.** $5\sqrt{10} = 6\sqrt{m} \left\{\frac{125}{18}\right\}$ **33.** $\sqrt{2a^2 - 5} = 11$

34. $\sqrt{2m^2 - 10} = 4$ **35.** $10 = 2\sqrt{3c^2 - 2}$ **36.** $36 = 4\sqrt{4m^2 + 5}$

37. $\sqrt{5b^2 - 36} = 2b$ {6}   **38.** $\sqrt{19x^2 - 51} = 4x$ {$\sqrt{17}$}   **39.** $\sqrt{x^2 + 1} = 1 - x$ {0}

40. $\sqrt{x^2 + 9} = 3 - x$ {0}   **41.** $\sqrt{3a^2 - 32} = a$ {4}   **42.** $\sqrt{13b^2 + 33} = 4b$ {$\sqrt{11}$}

33. {$3\sqrt{7}, -3\sqrt{7}$}   **34.** {$\sqrt{13}, -\sqrt{13}$}   **35.** {3, −3}   **36.** {$\sqrt{19}, -\sqrt{19}$}

C   **43.** $\sqrt{x^2 + 6x} = 4$ {−8, 2}   **44.** $\sqrt{a^2 + 3a} = 2$ {1, −4}

45. $\sqrt{15x^2 - 12x} = 9x$ {0}   **46.** $\sqrt{20y^2 - 13y} = 5y$ {0}

47. $\sqrt{x} + 6 = \sqrt{16x}$ {4}   **48.** $3\sqrt{a} + 7 = \sqrt{16a}$ {49}

Solve each system of equations.

49. $3\sqrt{a} + 5\sqrt{b} = 31$
$5\sqrt{a} - 5\sqrt{b} = -15$ (4, 25)

50. $5\sqrt{x} - 2\sqrt{y} = 4\sqrt{2}$
$2\sqrt{x} + 3\sqrt{y} = 13\sqrt{2}$ (8, 18)

Problems

Solve.

A   **1.** The square root of three times a number is 15. Find the number. 75

2. Twice the square root of a number is 22. Find the number. 121

3. One eighth of the square root of a number is 3. Find the number. 576

4. The square root of one eighth of a number is 3. Find the number. 72

5. When 4 times a number is increased by 5, the square root of the result is 11. Find the number. 29

6. When 23 is subtracted from the square root of three times a number, the result is 16. Find the number. 507

B   **7.** The radius (r) of a cylinder is related to its volume (V) and its height (h) by the formula $r = \sqrt{\frac{V}{\pi h}}$. Find the volume of a cylinder whose radius is 15 cm and whose height is 36 cm. Express your answer in terms of π. 8100π cm^3

8. The time it takes a free-falling object to fall can be found by using the formula $t = \sqrt{\frac{2s}{g}}$, where t is in seconds, $g = 9.8$ m/s^2, and s is the distance in meters. Find the distance an object falls in 15 s. 1102.5 m

Rational and Irrational Numbers   **549**

9. The current I that flows through an electrical appliance is determined by $I = \sqrt{\dfrac{P}{R}}$, where P is the power required and R is the resistance of the appliance. The current is measured in amperes (A), the power in watts (W), and the resistance in ohms (Ω). An electric hair dryer has a resistance of 60 Ω and draws 4.5 A of current. How much power does it use? 1215 W

26 and 24

C 10. The geometric mean of two positive numbers is the positive square root of their product. Find two consecutive positive even integers whose geometric mean is $4\sqrt{39}$.

11. The period of a pendulum (T) is the amount of time (in seconds) it takes the pendulum to make a complete swing back and forth. The period is determined by the formula $T = 2\pi\sqrt{\dfrac{l}{9.8}}$ where l is the length of the pendulum in meters. Find the length of a pendulum with a period of 8 seconds. Give your answer to the nearest tenth. (Use 3.14 for π.) 15.9 m

Mixed Review Exercises

Express in simplest form.

1. $(5 + \sqrt{6})(5 - \sqrt{6})$ 19
2. $(2 + \sqrt{5})^2$ $9 + 4\sqrt{5}$
3. $\dfrac{2}{3 + \sqrt{11}}$ $-3 + \sqrt{11}$
4. $\dfrac{2 + \sqrt{5}}{1 - \sqrt{5}}$ $\dfrac{-7 - 3\sqrt{5}}{4}$
5. $3\sqrt{5}(\sqrt{15} - 2\sqrt{5})$ $15\sqrt{3} - 30$
6. $(2\sqrt{3} + 1)(\sqrt{3} - 4)$ $2 - 7\sqrt{3}$

Factor completely.

7. $7a^2 - 14a + 7$ $7(a - 1)^2$
8. $t^3 - 4t^2 - 45t$ $t(t - 9)(t + 5)$
9. $6x(x + 2) + 4(x + 2)$ $2(3x + 2)(x + 2)$
10. $y^3 + y^2 - 6y - 6$ $(y^2 - 6)(y + 1)$
11. $4g^5 - 100g$ $4g(g^2 + 5)(g^2 - 5)$
12. $36x^2 + 24xy + 4y^2$ $4(3x + y)^2$

Self-Test 3

Vocabulary   simplest form of a radical (p. 537)   conjugate (p. 544)
rationalizing the denominator (p. 537)   radical equation (p. 547)

Simplify.

1. $2\sqrt{3} \cdot 5\sqrt{3}$ 30
2. $\sqrt{\dfrac{5}{4}} \cdot \sqrt{\dfrac{12}{15}}$ 1   Obj. 11-7, p. 537
3. $6\sqrt{7} + \sqrt{13} - 4\sqrt{13} + \sqrt{7}$ $7\sqrt{7} - 3\sqrt{13}$
4. $5\sqrt{48} - 8\sqrt{27}$ $-4\sqrt{3}$ Obj. 11-8, p. 540
5. $(3 - \sqrt{6})^2$ $15 - 6\sqrt{6}$
6. $(\sqrt{2} + \sqrt{3})(\sqrt{2} - \sqrt{3})$ -1 Obj. 11-9, p. 544

550

Rationalize the denominator.

7. $\dfrac{2}{\sqrt{7} - 3}$ $-3 - \sqrt{7}$

8. $\dfrac{\sqrt{5}}{\sqrt{5} + 4}$ $\dfrac{-5 + 4\sqrt{5}}{11}$

Solve.

9. $4 + \sqrt{m} = 9$ $\{25\}$

10. $\sqrt{5x - 2} + 3 = 6$ $\left\{\dfrac{11}{5}\right\}$

Obj. 11-10, p. 547

Check your answers with those at the back of the book.

Extra / *Fractional Exponents*

In Chapter 4, you learned the rule of exponents for products of powers:

For all positive integers m and n, $a^m \cdot a^n = a^{m+n}$.

Thus, you can simplify $2^4 \cdot 2^5$ as follows:

$$2^4 \cdot 2^5 = 2^{4+5} = 2^9.$$

If the rule of exponents for products of powers were to hold for all positive numbers, and not just for positive integers, what would be the value of n in the equation $2^n \cdot 2^n = 2$? Of course, $n = \frac{1}{2}$, as the following shows.

Since

$$2^n \cdot 2^n = 2^{n+n} = 2^{2n}$$

you have

$$2^{2n} = 2^1.$$

The bases are equal (and not -1, 0, or 1). Therefore, the exponents must be equal. Thus, $2n = 1$, or $n = \frac{1}{2}$, and you have $2^{1/2} \cdot 2^{1/2} = 2$.

Because $\sqrt{2} \cdot \sqrt{2} = 2$ and $(-\sqrt{2})(-\sqrt{2}) = 2$, it makes sense to define $2^{1/2}$ as either the positive or negative square root of 2. Selecting the positive, or principal, square root, we define

$$2^{1/2} = \sqrt{2}.$$

Radicals are not restricted to square roots. The symbol $\sqrt[n]{a}$ is used to indicate the principal nth root of a, where n is a positive integer. Thus, you can have third (or cube) roots, fourth roots, fifth roots, and so on. As you have seen, the *root index, n,* is omitted when $n = 2$.

Just as the inverse of squaring a number is finding the square root of that number, the inverse of cubing a number is finding the cube root. For example, since $2^3 = 8$, $\sqrt[3]{8}$, read "the cube root of 8," is 2. Likewise, since $(-2)^3 = -8$, $\sqrt[3]{-8} = -2$.

While $\sqrt[3]{-8}$ is a real number, $\sqrt{-8}$ is not. In general, you can find *odd* roots of negative numbers but not even roots.

If n is an odd positive integer, $\sqrt[n]{a^n} = a$.

If n is an even positive integer, $\sqrt[n]{a^n} = |a|$.

Rational and Irrational Numbers   **551**

Example 1 Solve $4^n \cdot 4^n \cdot 4^n = 4$

Solution
$$4^n \cdot 4^n \cdot 4^n = 4$$
$$4^{3n} = 4^1 \qquad \text{Since the bases are equal, the exponents are equal.}$$
$$3n = 1$$
$$n = \frac{1}{3}$$

Is it always possible to find the nth root of a? Think of a^n. Since a^n is always positive when n is an even integer, $\sqrt[n]{a}$, and hence $a^{1/n}$, its exponential form, do not name a real number if n is even and $a < 0$. For example, since $2^4 = (-2)^4 = 16$, $\sqrt[4]{-16}$, or $(-16)^{1/4}$, does not name a real number. Thus, we have the following definition.

For all integers $n > 1$,
$$a^{1/n} = \sqrt[n]{a}.$$
When $a < 0$ and n is even, neither $a^{1/n}$ nor $\sqrt[n]{a}$ names a real number.

Example 2 Write each of the following radicals in exponential form.

a. $\sqrt{5}$ b. $\sqrt[3]{7}$ c. $\sqrt[5]{2}$ d. $\sqrt[7]{-12}$

Solution   a. $\sqrt{5} = \sqrt[2]{5^1} = 5^{1/2}$ b. $\sqrt[3]{7} = \sqrt[3]{7^1} = 7^{1/3}$

c. $\sqrt[5]{2} = \sqrt[5]{2^1} = 2^{1/5}$ d. $\sqrt[7]{-12} = \sqrt[7]{(-12)^1} = (-12)^{1/7}$

Example 3 Simplify: a. $49^{1/2}$ b. $64^{1/3}$ c. $(-32)^{1/5}$ d. $(-81)^{1/4}$

Solution   a. $49^{1/2} = \sqrt{49} = 7$

b. $64^{1/3} = \sqrt[3]{64} = \sqrt[3]{4^3} = 4$

c. $(-32)^{1/5} = \sqrt[5]{-32} = \sqrt[5]{(-2)^5} = -2$

d. $(-81)^{1/4} = \sqrt[4]{-81}$, which does not name a real number.

You know that $\sqrt[3]{7} = 7^{1/3}$. How would you write $(\sqrt[3]{7})^2$ in exponential form? If the rule of exponents for a power of a power is to be true for all positive exponents, then
$$(\sqrt[3]{7})^2 = (7^{1/3})^2 = 7^{(1/3)2} = 7^{2/3}.$$

If $\sqrt[n]{a}$ is a real number and m and n are positive integers, then $(\sqrt[n]{a})^m = a^{m/n}$.

Example 4 Write each of the following radicals in exponential form.

  a. $(\sqrt[3]{5})^2$ **b.** $(\sqrt{6})^5$ **c.** $(\sqrt[5]{2})^3$ **d.** $(\sqrt[5]{10})^4$

Solution **a.** $(\sqrt[3]{5})^2 = (5^{1/3})^2 = 5^{2/3}$ **b.** $(\sqrt{6})^5 = (6^{1/2})^5 = 6^{5/2}$

  c. $(\sqrt[5]{2})^3 = (2^{1/5})^3 = 2^{3/5}$ **d.** $(\sqrt[5]{10})^4 = (10^{1/5})^4 = 10^{4/5}$

Example 5 Simplify.

  a. $4^{3/2}$ **b.** $32^{4/5}$ **c.** $(-27)^{2/3}$ **d.** $(-16)^{5/2}$

Solution **a.** $4^{3/2} = (4^{1/2})^3 = (\sqrt{4})^3 = 2^3 = 8$

  b. $32^{4/5} = (32^{1/5})^4 = (\sqrt[5]{32})^4 = (\sqrt[5]{2^5})^4 = 2^4 = 16$

  c. $(-27)^{2/3} = [(-27)^{1/3}]^2 = (\sqrt[3]{-27})^2 = (\sqrt[3]{(-3)^3})^2 = (-3)^2 = 9$

  d. $(-16)^{5/2} = [(-16)^{1/2}]^5 = (\sqrt{-16})^5$, which does not name a real number.

Exercises

Write each of the following radicals in exponential form.

A **1.** $\sqrt{6}$ $6^{1/2}$ **2.** $\sqrt{10}$ $10^{1/2}$ **3.** $\sqrt[3]{11}$ $11^{1/3}$ **4.** $\sqrt[7]{5}$ $5^{1/7}$

  5. $\sqrt[4]{2}$ $2^{1/4}$ **6.** $\sqrt[5]{3}$ $3^{1/5}$ **7.** $\sqrt[3]{-15}$ $(-15)^{1/3}$ **8.** $\sqrt[4]{14}$ $14^{1/4}$

  9. $\sqrt[6]{10}$ $10^{1/6}$ **10.** $\sqrt[5]{-12}$ $(-12)^{1/5}$ **11.** $(\sqrt[3]{4})^2$ $4^{2/3}$ **12.** $(\sqrt[6]{8})^5$ $8^{5/6}$

  13. $(\sqrt{2})^3$ $2^{3/2}$ **14.** $(\sqrt{7})^5$ $7^{5/2}$ **15.** $(\sqrt[4]{3})^5$ $3^{5/4}$ **16.** $(\sqrt[7]{5})^3$ $5^{3/7}$

Simplify. If the expression does not name a real number, say so.

B **17.** $64^{1/2}$ 8   **18.** $8^{1/3}$ 2   **19.** $27^{1/3}$ 3

  20. $100^{1/2}$ 10   **21.** $(-64)^{1/3}$ -4 **22.** $(-625)^{1/4}$

  23. $(-1296)^{1/4}$ **24.** $(-343)^{1/3}$ -7 **25.** $32^{3/5}$ 8

  26. $16^{3/4}$ 8   **27.** $9^{5/2}$ 243   **28.** $81^{3/4}$ 27

  29. $(-9)^{3/2}$ **30.** $(-1000)^{2/3}$ 100   **31.** $36^{3/2}$ 216

  32. $25^{3/2}$ 125   **33.** $125^{4/3}$ 625   **34.** $243^{4/5}$ 81

22, 23, 29. Not a real number

Solve.

C **35.** $5^n \cdot 5^n = 5$ $\left\{\frac{1}{2}\right\}$ **36.** $3^n \cdot 3^n \cdot 3^n \cdot 3^n = 3$ $\left\{\frac{1}{4}\right\}$ **37.** $2^n \cdot 2^n \cdot 2^n = 2^{\left\{\frac{1}{3}\right\}}$ $\left\{\frac{3}{2}\right\}$

  38. $6^{(1/2)n} \cdot 6^{(1/2)n} = 36$ $\{2\}$ **39.** $4^{(1/3)n} \cdot 4^{(1/3)n} = 16$ $\{3\}$ **40.** $7^{(7/5)n} \cdot 7^{(3/5)n} = 343$

Rational and Irrational Numbers   **553**

Calculator Key-In

Many calculators have a square-root key. It is possible to use this key to find the fourth root, eighth root, sixteenth root, and so on, of a number. You do this by working with powers of 2. If you have a scientific calculator you may be able to use a special key to find $\sqrt[n]{a}$ for other values of *n* that are not powers of two.

Find the indicated roots of each number.

Sample   Eighth root of 32

Solution   Express 8 as a power of 2: $8 = 2^3$

This tells you that you need to press the $\sqrt{}$ key three times.

1.5422108   *Answer*

1. Fourth root of 48 2.632148
2. Fourth root of 196 3.7416574
3. Eighth root of 150 1.8707313
4. Eighth root of 38 1.5756979
5. Sixteenth root of 164 1.3753959
6. Thirty-second root of 200 1.1800684

Chapter Summary

1. A rational number can be expressed as a fraction in simplest form, $\frac{a}{b}$, where *a* and *b* are integers and $b > 0$. Rational numbers in fractional form can be expressed as either terminating or repeating decimals by dividing.

2. Irrational numbers are represented by nonterminating, nonrepeating decimals which may be rounded to a convenient number of places for use in computation. These numbers cannot be represented in fractional form.

3. Square roots may be rational or irrational. Irrational square roots may be approximated using a calculator or a table of square roots.

4. Some quadratic equations can be solved using the property of square roots of equal numbers (page 526).

5. Many problems involving right triangles can be solved using the Pythagorean theorem:
$$a^2 + b^2 = c^2.$$

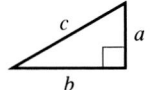

6. Radical expressions can be added, subtracted, multiplied, and divided. The product and quotient properties of square roots (pages 517–518) are useful in simplifying expressions involving radicals. Divisions can often be simplified by rationalizing the denominator.

Chapter Review

Supplementary Materials
Practice Master   71
Resource Book   p. 204

Give the letter of the correct answer.

1. Find the rational number halfway between $\frac{1}{2}$ and $\frac{5}{8}$.   11-1

   a. $\frac{7}{16}$ **(b.)** $\frac{9}{16}$ **c.** $\frac{4}{7}$ **d.** $\frac{3}{8}$

2. Compare $\frac{3}{4}$ and $\frac{11}{15}$.

   (a.) $\frac{3}{4} > \frac{11}{15}$ **b.** $\frac{11}{15} > \frac{3}{4}$ **c.** $\frac{3}{4} = \frac{11}{15}$

3. Express $\frac{5}{11}$ as a decimal.   11-2

   a. 0.45 **b.** $0.\overline{454}$ **(c.)** $0.\overline{45}$ **d.** $0.0\overline{45}$

4. Express $0.\overline{57}$ as a fraction in simplest form.

   a. $\frac{57}{100}$ **b.** $\frac{57}{99}$ **c.** $\frac{575}{1000}$ **(d.)** $\frac{19}{33}$

5. Find $\sqrt{1764}$.   11-3

   a. 420 **(b.)** 42 **c.** 4.2 **d.** 0.42

6. Find $\sqrt{\frac{576}{400}}$.

   a. $\frac{12}{5}$ **b.** $\frac{3}{4}$ **(c.)** $\frac{6}{5}$ **d.** $\frac{8}{5}$

7. Approximate $\sqrt{2700}$ to the nearest hundredth. Use a calculator or the table   11-4
   of square roots at the back of the book.

   a. 5.196 **(b.)** 51.96 **c.** 519.6 **d.** 51.9

8. Simplify $\sqrt{96}$.

   a. $6\sqrt{4}$ **b.** $16\sqrt{6}$ **(c.)** $4\sqrt{6}$ **d.** $8\sqrt{6}$

9. Simplify $\sqrt{2.25a^4b^2c^6}$.   11-5

   (a.) $1.5a^2|bc^3|$ **b.** $1.5\sqrt{a^4b^2c^6}$ **c.** $1.5a^2bc^3$

10. Solve $5n^2 - 405 = 0$.

    a. $\{9\}$ **(b.)** $\{9, -9\}$ **c.** $\{3, -3\}$ **d.** $\{81, -81\}$

11. The shorter sides of a right triangle are 16 cm and 30 cm long. Find the   11-6
    length of the hypotenuse.

    a. 14 cm   **b.** 46 cm   **(c.)** 34 cm   **d.** 1156 cm

12. Can a right triangle have sides 15 m, 36 m, and 20 m long?

    a. yes   **(b.)** no

13. Simplify $\sqrt{15} \cdot \sqrt{12}$.   11-7

    (a.) $6\sqrt{5}$ **b.** $9\sqrt{20}$ **c.** $12\sqrt{5}$ **d.** $5\sqrt{6}$

14. Simplify $\sqrt{16} + 3\sqrt{8} - 2\sqrt{2}$.   11-8

    a. $4 + 3\sqrt{8} - 2\sqrt{2}$ **b.** $4 + 5\sqrt{2}$ **(c.)** $4 + 4\sqrt{2}$ **d.** $8\sqrt{2}$

Rational and Irrational Numbers   **555**

15. Multiply $(4 + \sqrt{7})(4 - \sqrt{7})$.   **11-9**

    a. 16   **b.** 23   **c.** $16 - 2\sqrt{7}$ **(d.)** 9

16. Rationalize the denominator of $\dfrac{\sqrt{3}}{\sqrt{3} - 2}$.

    a. $\dfrac{\sqrt{3}}{5}$ **(b.)** $-3 - 2\sqrt{3}$ **c.** $\dfrac{3 + 2\sqrt{3}}{5}$ **d.** $3 + 2\sqrt{3}$

17. Solve $\sqrt{5x + 1} - 6 = 8$.   **11-10**

    (a.) 39   **b.** 3   **c.** 51   **d.** $\dfrac{13}{5}$

Chapter Test

1. Find the rational number halfway between $\dfrac{5}{16}$ and $\dfrac{7}{8}$. $\dfrac{19}{32}$ **11-1**

2. Arrange $\dfrac{4}{21}$, $\dfrac{2}{15}$, and $\dfrac{5}{27}$ in order from least to greatest. $\dfrac{2}{15}, \dfrac{5}{27}, \dfrac{4}{21}$

3. Express $\dfrac{7}{12}$ as a decimal. $0.58\overline{3}$ **11-2**

4. Express $0.1\overline{6}$ as a fraction in simplest form. $\dfrac{1}{6}$

5. Find $\sqrt{\dfrac{225}{900}}$. $\dfrac{1}{2}$ **6.** Find $\sqrt{0.0049}$. 0.07 **11-3**

7. Approximate $\sqrt{3400}$ to the nearest tenth. Use a calculator or the table of   **11-4**
square roots at the back of the book. 58.3

8. Simplify $\sqrt{150}$. $5\sqrt{6}$ **9.** Simplify $4\sqrt{216}$. $24\sqrt{6}$

10. Simplify $\sqrt{121a^4b^{10}}$. $11a^2|b^5|$ **11.** Solve $3a^2 - 108 = 0$. $\{6, -6\}$ **11-5**

12. In a right triangle, the hypotenuse is 19 m long, and one of the shorter   **11-6**
sides is 8 m long. Find the length of the other side to the nearest
hundredth. 17.23 m

13. Is a triangle with sides 14 units, 40 units, and 50 units long a right
triangle? no

Simplify.

14. $\sqrt{\dfrac{4}{5}} \cdot \sqrt{\dfrac{35}{4}}$ $\sqrt{7}$ **15.** $\dfrac{6\sqrt{18}}{18\sqrt{6}}$ $\dfrac{\sqrt{3}}{3}$ **11-7**

16. $4\sqrt{2} + \sqrt{72}$ $10\sqrt{2}$ **17.** $3\sqrt{24} - 4\sqrt{54}$ $-6\sqrt{6}$ **11-8**

18. $(\sqrt{5} + 3)^2$ $14 + 6\sqrt{5}$ **19.** $(\sqrt{7} - \sqrt{2})(\sqrt{7} + \sqrt{2})$ 5 **11-9**

20. Rationalize the denominator of $\dfrac{3}{5 - 2\sqrt{3}}$. $\dfrac{15 + 6\sqrt{3}}{13}$

21. Solve $\sqrt{3x + 2} = 4$. $\left\{\dfrac{14}{3}\right\}$ **11-10**

556   *Chapter 11*

Cumulative Review *(Chapters 1–11)*

Simplify. Assume that no denominator is zero.

1. $-21 - 2 \cdot 6 \div 3$ **2.** $(2ab^2)^2(3a^2 + 5ab + b^2)$ **3.** $(4a^3b + 9c^2)^2$

4. $(-3p + 2q)(12p - q)$ **5.** $(3.2 \times 10^{-4})^2$ **6.** $(6x^2 - 13x - 28) \div (2x - 7)$

7. $\dfrac{96 - 40x + 4x^2}{x^2 - 8x + 16} \cdot \dfrac{x^2 + 5x - 6}{2x^2 - 72}$ **8.** $\dfrac{3x^2 - 14x + 15}{x^2 + 10x + 25} \div \dfrac{3x^2 + 10x - 25}{x^2 - 25}$

9. $\dfrac{t - 3}{t + 2} + \dfrac{1}{t} - 5$ **10.** $\sqrt{720}$ **11.** $\sqrt{112} - \sqrt{63}$ **12.** $2\sqrt{3}(5\sqrt{6} + 4\sqrt{2})$

13. $\dfrac{5\sqrt{75}}{\sqrt{90}} \dfrac{5\sqrt{30}}{6}$ **14.** $\dfrac{5}{\sqrt{6} + 1} \sqrt{6} - 1$ **15.** $\sqrt{\dfrac{2}{3}} + \sqrt{\dfrac{5}{6}} \dfrac{2\sqrt{6} + \sqrt{30}}{6}$

Factor completely.

16. $16y^4 - 8y^2 + 1$
$(2y + 1)^2(2y - 1)^2$

17. $4c^2 - 4cd + d^2 - 9$
$(2c - d - 3)(2c - d + 3)$

18. $12c^2 - 17c - 5$
$(4c + 1)(3c - 5)$

Graph the solution set. (In Exercise 19, use a number line.)

19. $|2 - x| \le 4$ **20.** $2x - 3y = 3$ **21.** $2x + y < 6$

22. Write an equation in standard form of the line that contains $(0, 2)$ and $(-1, 8)$.
$6x + y = 2$

23. Find the least value of the function $f: x \to x^2 - 4x + 4$. 0

24. Express $0.\overline{5}$ and $0.\overline{15}$ as fractions. Then find their sum. $0.\overline{5} = \frac{5}{9}$, $0.\overline{15} = \frac{5}{33}$; $\frac{70}{99}$, or $0.\overline{70}$

25. Graph the solution set of the system: $x + y < 4$
$y - 2x \ge 0$

Solve each equation, inequality, or system. Assume that no denominator is zero. If there is no solution, say so.

26. $2y - 3 = |-15|$ {9}   **27.** $y\%$ of $75 = 12$ {16}   **28.** $\dfrac{1}{3}y - 2 = \dfrac{1}{2}$ $\left\{\dfrac{15}{2}\right\}$

29. $4d^2 - 12d + 9 = 0$ $\left\{\dfrac{3}{2}\right\}$ **30.** $2n^2 + 5n - 3 = 0$ $\left\{\dfrac{1}{2}, -3\right\}$ **31.** $\dfrac{1}{x} + \dfrac{3 - x}{x + 6} = \dfrac{x - 1}{2x + 12}$

32. $x - 2y = 8$
$3x + 2y = 9$ $\left(\dfrac{17}{4}, -\dfrac{15}{8}\right)$

33. $2x - 5y = -1$
$3x - 10y = -1$ $\left(-1, -\dfrac{1}{5}\right)$

34. $2x + 11y = 3$ $\{4, -1\}$
$5x + 28y = 7$ $(7, -1)$

35. $5 \le 2x - 1 \le 9$ **36.** $4|y - 2| > 12$ **37.** $7 - 3b < 9$

38. $2\sqrt{t} = 3\sqrt{2}$ $\left\{\dfrac{9}{2}\right\}$ **39.** $\sqrt{2p - 1} = p$ {1}   **40.** $\sqrt{z^2 + 7} = z - 1$
No solution

41. The hypotenuse of a right triangle is 9 cm long and another side is 5 cm long. Find the length of the third side to the nearest hundredth. Use a calculator or the table of square roots at the back of the book. 7.48 cm

42. Two groups entering a museum each paid $70. One group included ten adults and four children. The other included five adults and sixteen children. Find the admission price for children and for adults. adults, $6; children, $2.50

Rational and Irrational Numbers   **557**

 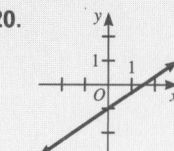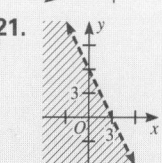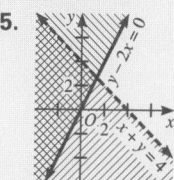

Maintaining Skills

Solve each system. Use either method shown below.

Sample 1 $x - 2y = 1$
$3x - 5y = 6$

Solution   (Substitution Method) Solve one equation for one of the variables (in this case, x), and substitute in the other equation.

$$\begin{array}{ll} x - 2y = 1 & \rightarrow \quad x = 2y + 1 \\ 3x - 5y = 6 & \qquad 3(2y + 1) - 5y = 6 \\ & \qquad\quad 6y + 3 - 5y = 6 \\ & \qquad\qquad\quad y + 3 = 6 \\ & \qquad\qquad\qquad\quad y = 3 \end{array}$$

$$x = 2(3) + 1 = 7$$

The check is left to you. $\therefore$ the solution is $(7, 3)$.

Sample 2 $7x - 2y = 4$
$3x + \ y = 11$

Solution   (Multiplication with the Addition-or-Subtraction Method)

$$\begin{array}{lll} 7x - 2y = 4 & 7x - 2y = 4 & 7(2) - 2y = 4 \\ 3x + \ y = 11 \underline{\quad \times 2} \rightarrow & \underline{6x + 2y = 22} & 14 - 2y = 4 \\ & 13x \qquad = 26 & -2y = -10 \\ & \qquad\quad x = 2 & y = 5 \end{array}$$

The check is left to you. $\therefore$ the solution is $(2, 5)$.

1. $x + y = 1$
$2x + y = 0 (-1, 2)$

2. $x + y = 3$
$2x - y = 6 (3, 0)$

3. $2x + \ y = 15$
$x + 2y = 15 (5, 5)$

4. $3x + 4y = -2$
$4x + 3y = -12 (-6, 4)$

5. $2x + 3y = 2$
$8x + 9y = 7 \left(\frac{1}{2}, \frac{1}{3}\right)$

6. $9x + 4y = 5$
$y = 4x \qquad \left(\frac{1}{5}, \frac{4}{5}\right)$

7. $4x + 5 = y$
$2x + y = 1 \left(-\frac{2}{3}, \frac{7}{3}\right)$

8. $y - x = 20$
$2x + 3y = 10 (-10, 10)$

9. $3x - 4y = 9$
$x + 2y = 13 (7, 3)$

10. $5x - 6y = 2$
$4y - 5x = 12 (-8, -7)$

11. $x + 10y = 2$
$\frac{1}{3}x + \ y = 3 (12, -1)$

12. $\frac{4}{5}x - \frac{1}{2}y = 18$
$\frac{1}{2}x - \frac{3}{4}y = 20 (10, -20)$

13. $y = 7x$
$5x - 8y = 0 (0, 0)$

14. $x - 2y = 5$
$-2x + 3y = -5 (-5, -5)$

15. $2x + \ 3y = 11$
$3x + 14y = 7 (7, -1)$

16. $5x + 6y = 4$
$3x + 6y = 3 \left(\frac{1}{2}, \frac{1}{4}\right)$

17. $4x + 3y = 8$
$5x + 4y = 13 (-7, 12)$

18. $5x - 6y = 1$
$2x - 3y = 7 (-13, -11)$

19. $6x - 5y = 0$
$5x - 3y = 7 (5, 6)$

20. $2x - 7y = 9$
$x + 8y = 16 (8, 1)$

21. $3x - 5y = 7$
$-2x + 7y = 10 (9, 4)$

Mixed Problem Solving

Solve each problem that has a solution. If a problem has no solution, explain why.

in still water, 11 km/h; current, 1 km/h

A **1.** A boat travels 4 km in 20 min with the current. The return trip takes 24 min. Find the speed of the current and the speed of the boat in still water.

2. Half the square root of twice a number is 5. Find the number. 50

3. The base of a triangle of a given area varies inversely as the height. A triangle has a base of 18 cm and a height of 10 cm. Find the height of a triangle of equal area and with base 15 cm. 12 cm

4. Two trains leave a station at noon traveling in opposite directions. The speeds of the trains are 80 km/h and 100 km/h. At what time will the trains be 225 km apart? 1:15 P.M.

Saturn, 10 km/s; Mars, 24 km/s

5. The average orbital speed of Saturn is 14 km/s slower than the speed of Mars. The speed of Saturn is also $\frac{5}{12}$ the speed of Mars. Find each speed.

6. A fraction's value is $\frac{3}{5}$. If its numerator and denominator are both increased by 3, the resulting fraction equals $\frac{5}{8}$. Find the original fraction. $\frac{27}{45}$

7. The Robinsons bought a computer at 25% off the usual price. The total cost, including a 4% tax on the sale price, was $1170. Find the usual price excluding taxes. $1500

8. How many liters of water should be added to 24 L of an 18% acid solution to form a 15% solution? 4.8 L

B **9.** Sandy can complete her paper route in 45 min. When her sister Kris helps her, it takes them 18 min to complete the route. How long would it take Kris alone to complete the route? 30 min

10. Isabel invested $8000, part in an account paying 6% interest and part in bonds paying 8%. If she had reversed the amounts invested, she would have received $100 less. How much did she invest in each? $1500 at 6%; $6500 at 8%

11. The numbers of nickels and quarters in a bank are in the ratio 23:25. If the coins are worth $7, how many of each type are there? No solution; unrealistic result

12. The length of a rectangle is 1 cm shorter than a diagonal. The length is 2 cm longer than twice the width. Find the perimeter of the rectangle. 34 cm

13. Find the price per kilogram when 8 kg of almonds worth x dollars per kilogram are mixed with 4 kg of raisins worth $x + 2$ dollars per kilogram. Give your simplified answer in terms of x. $\frac{3x + 2}{3}$ dollars per kg

Rational and Irrational Numbers **559**

12 Quadratic Functions

Objectives

12-1 To solve quadratic equations involving perfect squares.

12-2 To solve quadratic equations by completing the square.

12-3 To learn the quadratic formula and use it to solve equations.

12-4 To use the discriminant to find the number of roots of the equation $ax^2 + bx + c = 0$ and the number of x-intercepts of the graph of the related equation $y = ax^2 + bx + c$.

12-5 To choose the best method for solving a quadratic equation.

12-6 To use quadratic equations to solve problems.

12-7 To use quadratic direct variation and inverse variation as a square in problem solving.

12-8 To solve problems involving joint variation and combined variation.

Assignment Guide

See p. T59 for Key to the format of the Assignment Guide

Day	Minimum Course		Average Course		Maximum Course	
1	**12-1**	563/1–31 odd	**12-1**	563/1–39 odd	**12-1**	563/3–48 mult. of 3, 49
	S	563/*Mixed Review*	**S**	563/*Mixed Review*	**S**	563/*Mixed Review*
2	**12-2**	566/1–10	**12-2**	566/1–27 odd	**12-2**	566/2–30 even
	S	563/33	**S**	566/*Mixed Review*	**S**	566/*Mixed Review*
3	**12-2**	566/11–18	**12-3**	569/1–31 odd	**12-3**	569/1–31 odd
	S	566/*Mixed Review*	**S**	570/*Mixed Review*	**S**	570/*Mixed Review*
4	**12-3**	569/1–12	**12-4**	574/1–17 odd	**12-4**	574/1–19 odd
	S	570/*Mixed Review*	**S**	575/*Mixed Review*	**S**	575/*Mixed Review*
5	**12-3**	569/13–18	**12-5**	577/1–27 odd	**12-5**	577/1–31 odd
	R	575/*Self-Test 1*, 1–5	**S**	578/*Mixed Review*	**S**	578/*Mixed Review*
		595/*Ch. Review:* 1–3, 5–6	**R**	575/*Self-Test 1*	**R**	575/*Self-Test 1*
6	*Administer Chapter 12 Test* *(through Lesson 12-3)*		**12-6**	580/*P:* 1–13 odd	**12-6**	580/*P:* 1–15 odd
			S	581/*Mixed Review*	**S**	581/*Mixed Review*
7			**12-7**	586/*P:* 1–5, 7, 9	**12-7**	586/*P:* 1–11 odd
			S	587/*Mixed Review*	**S**	587/*Mixed Review*
			R	582/*Self-Test 2*	**R**	582/*Self-Test 2*
8			**12-8**	590/1–6; *P:* 1–11 odd	**12-8**	590/1–9 odd
			S	592/*Mixed Review*		590/*P:* 1–13 odd
					S	592/*Mixed Review*
9			*Prepare for Chapter Test*		*Prepare for Chapter Test*	
			R	594/*Self-Test 3*	**R**	594/*Self-Test 3*
				595/*Chapter Review*		595/*Chapter Review*
			EP	662/*Skills;* 679/*Problems*	**EP**	662/*Skills;* 679/*Problems*
10			*Administer Chapter 12 Test*		*Administer Chapter 12 Test*	
					R	597–598/*Cumulative Review:* 3–84, mult. of 3
					S	599/*Prep. for Coll. Ent. Exams*

Supplementary Materials Guide

For Use with Lesson	Practice Masters	Tests	Study Guide (Reteaching)	Resource Book		
				Tests	Practice Exercises	Mixed Review (MR) Applications (A) Enrichment (E)
12-1			pp. 203–204			p. 189 (A)
12-2	Sheet 73		pp. 205–206		p. 136	
12-3		Test 53	pp. 207–208		p. 137	
12-4	Sheet 74		pp. 209–210		p. 138	
12-5			pp. 211–212			
12-6			pp. 213–214		p. 139	
12-7			pp. 215–216			
12-8	Sheet 75	Test 54	pp. 217–218		p. 140	
Chapter 12	Sheet 76	Tests 55, 56		pp. 64–67		p. 205 (E)
Cum. Rev. 10–12	Sheets 77, 78			pp. 68–69	pp. 141–142	
Cum. Rev. 9–12		Test 57				
Cum. Rev. 7–12		Test 58		pp. 70–72	pp. 143–145	
Cum. Rev. 1–12	Sheets 79, 80			pp. 73–78		pp. 155–157 (MR)

Overhead Visuals

For Use with Lessons	Visual	Title
12-4	A	Multi-Use Packet 1
12-4	B	Multi-Use Packet 2
12-2, 12-5	13	Geometric Models: Completing the Square

Software

Software	Algebra Plotter Plus	Using Algebra Plotter Plus	Computer Activities	Test Generator
	Parabola Plotter	Scripted Demo, pp. 24–25 Enrichment, p. 35	Activities 36, 37	168 test items
For Use with Lessons	12-1, 12-4	12-1, 12-4	12-4, 12-6	all lessons

Strategies for Teaching

Communication and Problem Solving

Chapter 12 introduces completing the square and the quadratic formula as alternatives for solving quadratic equations. Students then add these new approaches to previously learned methods and formulate an integrated plan for solving word problems with quadratics. Students learn to choose a method for solving quadratics based on key characteristics of the equation. As in Chapter 9, planning is emphasized as an integral part of the problem solving process. It may be helpful to use reading activities as a review of general properties of quadratics to help students integrate new material into a problem solving approach.

12-2 Completing the Square

For the following perfect square trinomial

$$4a^2 + 20a + 25$$

have students identify the quadratic term, the constant term, and the coefficient of the linear term. Then have them factor the trinomial. $4a^2$; 25; 20; $(2a + 5)^2$

12-3 The Quadratic Formula

The derivation of the quadratic formula on page 567 may be difficult for some students to understand. Nevertheless, it is worthwhile to discuss the derivation step by step. Emphasize that the formula is obtained by completing the square of the general quadratic equation $ax^2 + bx + c = 0$. While students should not be expected to derive the formula, they should memorize it. Encourage students to write the formula every time they use it to help avoid errors.

Students often make errors substituting for a, b, and c. Stress the importance of expressing an equation in the form $ax^2 + bx + c = 0$ before applying the quadratic formula. Students may want to write and refer to a "skeleton form" of the formula:

$$x = \frac{-(\ ) \pm \sqrt{(\ )^2 - 4(\ )(\ )}}{2(\ )}$$

If a student asks about equations for which $b^2 - 4ac < 0$, point out that such an equation has no *real* roots.

12-4 Graphs of Quadratic Equations: The Discriminant

See the Exploration on p. 700 for an activity in which students use graphing software or a graphing calculator to explore the graphs of quadratic equations by focusing on the discriminant.

12-5 Methods of Solution

Be sure students realize that more than one method may be suitable for solving a particular quadratic equation. Encourage students to use the guidelines on page 576 to select a method that will simplify the computations.

Stress that any quadratic equation can be solved by applying the quadratic formula. Students should memorize the quadratic formula.

It may be helpful to assign and/or discuss as many of the A-level and B-level Written Exercises as possible. These exercises provide the full range of forms of quadratic equations, reinforcing the four methods of solution.

The discriminant can be used to determine if a quadratic equation in the form $ax^2 + bx + c = 0$ can be factored or not. If a, b, and c are integers and $b^2 - 4ac$ is greater than zero and a perfect square, the given quadratic equation can be solved by factoring and the solutions will be rational numbers.

Have students determine if the following can be solved by factoring. **1.** yes **2.** yes **3.** no **4.** yes

1. $x^2 + 5x - 14 = 0$ **2.** $12x^2 - 5x - 2 = 0$

3. $4x^2 - 3x - 3 = 0$ **4.** $14x^2 - 25x + 6 = 0$

12-6 Solving Problems Involving Quadratic Equations

As you discuss the example on page 579, point out that Step 4 yields a solution in simplest radical form: $x = -2 \pm \sqrt{29}$. Stress that practical problems require solutions that make sense under the given conditions. In this particular case:

1. An answer in radical form is not useful.
2. Only the positive root makes sense.
3. Answers must be rounded to usable approximations.
4. The check using approximate values cannot be exact.

Emphasize the importance of always going back to the words of the problem as a final test.

12-7 Direct and Inverse Variation Involving Squares

Have students define each of the following terms in their own words and give two examples of each. They may use the Glossary to check their definitions.

1. Direct variation   see glossary; $y = 3x$
2. Inverse variation   see glossary; $xy = 8$
3. Constant of proportionality
   see glossary; in $y = 3x$, $k = 3$

References to Strategies

PE: Pupil's Edition   **TE:** Teacher's Edition   **RB:** Resource Book

Problem Solving Strategies

PE: pp. 579, 584 (Checking solution); pp. 579–581 (Using quadratic equations)
TE: p. 580

Applications

PE: pp. 560, 580–581, 583, 586–593
TE: p. 560
RB: p. 189

Nonroutine Problems

PE: p. 563 (Ex. 49); p. 566 (Exs. 28–30); p. 569 (Exs. 29–31); p. 574 (Exs. 19, 20); p. 578 (Exs. 28–31); p. 581 (Prob. 15); p. 587 (Probs. 11, 12); p. 590 (Exs. 7–10); p. 592 (Probs. 11–14)
RB: p. 205

Communication

PE: p. 577 (Ex. 13, convincing argument)
TE: pp. T139, 586 (Reading Algebra)

Thinking Skills

TE: pp. 572, 577, 587

Explorations

PE: pp. 570, 581–582, 583, 593, 700
Algebra Plotter Plus: pp. 24–25, 35

Connections

PE: p. 591 (Astronomy); pp. 570, 575 (Discrete Math); pp. 580, 586–591 (Geometry); pp. 560, 578, 583, 586–587, 591–593 (Physics)

Using Technology

PE: pp. 565–566, 569–570, 575, 579, 586–587, 590–592 (Exs.)
TE: pp. 565, 569, 570, 575, 579, 587, 590
Computer Activities: pp. 80–83
Algebra Plotter Plus: pp. 24–25, 35

Using Manipulatives/Models

TE: p. T140 (Lesson 12-7)
Overhead Visuals: A, B, 13

Cooperative Learning

TE: p. T138 (Lesson 12-3)

Teaching Resources

For use in implementing the teaching strategies referenced on the previous page.

Application
Resource Book, p. 189

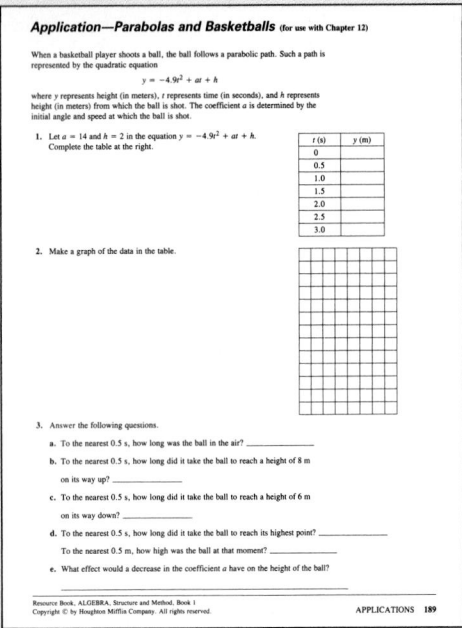

Application—Parabolas and Basketballs (for use with Chapter 12)

When a basketball player shoots a ball, the ball follows a parabolic path. Such a path is represented by the quadratic equation

$$y = -4.9t^2 + at + h$$

where y represents height (in meters), t represents time (in seconds), and h represents height (in meters) from which the ball is shot. The coefficient a is determined by the initial angle and speed at which the ball is shot.

1. Let $a = 14$ and $h = 2$ in the equation $y = -4.9t^2 + at + h$. Complete the table at the right.

t (s)	y (m)
0	
0.5	
1.0	
1.5	
2.0	
2.5	
3.0	

2. Make a graph of the data in the table.

3. Answer the following questions.

   a. To the nearest 0.5 s, how long was the ball in the air? _____

   b. To the nearest 0.5 s, how long did it take the ball to reach a height of 8 m on its way up? _____

   c. To the nearest 0.5 s, how long did it take the ball to reach a height of 6 m on its way down? _____

   d. To the nearest 0.5 s, how long did it take the ball to reach its highest point? _____

   To the nearest 0.5 m, how high was the ball at that moment? _____

   e. What effect would a decrease in the coefficient a have on the height of the ball?

Enrichment/Nonroutine Problems
Resource Book, p. 205

Exponents and Polynomials (For use with Chapter 12 of text)

1. Here are 3^8 dots arranged in a square. How many dots are there on each side of the square? Try to find the answer without actually counting the dots.

2. Suppose a square array of dots contains M^{2N} dots. How many dots are there along each side of the square? _____

In Exercises 3–5, multiply to find each product. Then look for a pattern that you can use to answer the question in Exercise 6.

3. $(x - 1)(x^2 + x + 1)$ _____

4. $(x - 1)(x^3 + x^2 + x + 1)$ _____

5. $(x - 1)(x^4 + x^3 + x^2 + x + 1)$ _____

6. What do you think the product of $x - 1$ and $x^{100} + x^{99} + x^{98} + \cdots + x + 1$ will be? _____

In Exercises 7–10, multiply to find each product. Then look for a pattern that you can use to answer the question in Exercise 11.

7. $(x + 1)(x^2 - x + 1)$ _____

8. $(x + 1)(x^3 - x^2 + x - 1)$ _____

9. $(x + 1)(x^4 - x^3 + x^2 - x + 1)$ _____

10. $(x + 1)(x^5 - x^4 + x^3 - x^2 + x - 1)$ _____

11. What do you think the product of $x + 1$ and $x^{100} - x^{99} + x^{98} - \cdots - x + 1$ will be? _____

Thinking Skills
Study Guide, p. 211

12–5 Methods of Solution

Objective: To choose the best method for solving a quadratic equation.

Methods for Solving a Quadratic Equation	When to Use the Method
1. Using the quadratic formula	1. If an equation is in the form $ax^2 + bx + c = 0$, especially if you use a calculator.
2. Factoring	2. If an equation is in the form $ax^2 + bx = 0$, or if the factors are easily seen.
3. Using the property of square roots of equal numbers	3. If an equation is in the form $ax^2 + c = 0$.
4. Completing the square	4. If an equation is in the form $x^2 + bx + c = 0$ and b is an even number.

Example Solve each quadratic equation using the most appropriate method.

    a. $6x^2 - 54 = 0$ b. $2x^2 - 7x + 5 = 0$

    c. $2t^2 - 28t = 0$ d. $n^2 + 6n - 16 = 0$

Solution
a. $6x^2 - 54 = 0$ The equation has the form $ax^2 + c = 0$.
$6x^2 = 54$ Therefore, use the property of square roots of equal numbers.
$x^2 = 9$
$x = \pm 3$
The solution set is $\{-3, 3\}$.

b. $2x^2 - 7x + 5 = 0$ The equation has the form $ax^2 + bx + c = 0$.

$x = \dfrac{-(-7) \pm \sqrt{(-7)^2 - 4(2)(5)}}{2(2)}$ Therefore, use the quadratic formula.

$= \dfrac{7 \pm \sqrt{49 - 40}}{4}$

$= \dfrac{7 \pm \sqrt{9}}{4}$

$= \dfrac{7 \pm 3}{4}$

$x = \dfrac{7 + 3}{4} = \dfrac{10}{4}$ or $x = \dfrac{7 - 3}{4} = \dfrac{4}{4}$

The solution set is $\left\{\dfrac{5}{2}, 1\right\}$.

c. $2t^2 - 28t = 0$ The equation has the form $ax^2 + bx = 0$.
$2t(t - 14) = 0$ Therefore, factor.
$2t = 0$ or $t - 14 = 0$
$t = 0$ or $t = 14$
The solution set is $\{0, 14\}$.

Problem Solving
Study Guide, p. 213

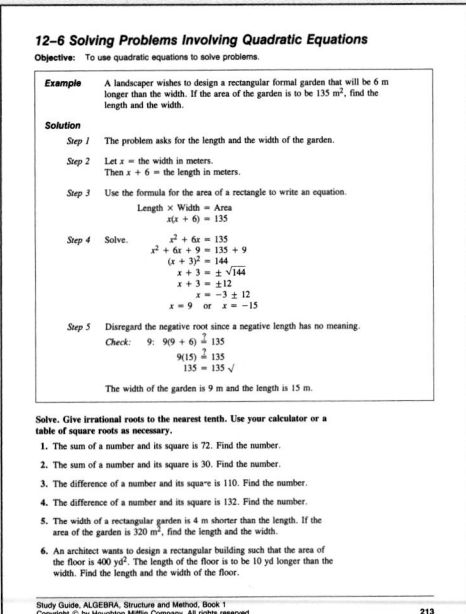

12–6 Solving Problems Involving Quadratic Equations

Objective: To use quadratic equations to solve problems.

Example A landscaper wishes to design a rectangular formal garden that will be 6 m longer than the width. If the area of the garden is to be 135 m², find the length and the width.

Solution

Step 1   The problem asks for the length and the width of the garden.

Step 2   Let $x =$ the width in meters.
Then $x + 6 =$ the length in meters.

Step 3   Use the formula for the area of a rectangle to write an equation.

Length × Width = Area
$x(x + 6) = 135$

Step 4   Solve. $x^2 + 6x = 135$
$x^2 + 6x + 9 = 135 + 9$
$(x + 3)^2 = 144$
$x + 3 = \pm \sqrt{144}$
$x + 3 = \pm 12$
$x = -3 \pm 12$
$x = 9$ or $x = -15$

Step 5   Disregard the negative root since a negative length has no meaning.

Check: $9: 9(9 + 6) \overset{?}{=} 135$
$9(15) \overset{?}{=} 135$
$135 = 135 \;\checkmark$

The width of the garden is 9 m and the length is 15 m.

Solve. Give irrational roots to the nearest tenth. Use your calculator or a table of square roots as necessary.

1. The sum of a number and its square is 72. Find the number.

2. The sum of a number and its square is 30. Find the number.

3. The difference of a number and its square is 110. Find the number.

4. The difference of a number and its square is 132. Find the number.

5. The width of a rectangular garden is 4 m shorter than the length. If the area of the garden is 320 m², find the length and the width.

6. An architect wants to design a rectangular building such that the area of the floor is 400 yd². The length of the floor is to be 10 yd longer than the width. Find the length and the width of the floor.

Using Technology
Computer Activities, p. 80

ACTIVITY 36. *The Quadratic Formula* (*for use with Section 12-4*)

Directions: Write all answers in the spaces provided.

PROBLEM

Use the quadratic formula to solve any quadratic equation $Ax^2 + Bx + C = 0$ that has real roots.

PROGRAM

```
10 PRINT "WHAT ARE A, B, C";
20 INPUT A, B, C
30 LET D = B • B − 4 • A • C
40 IF D >= 0 THEN 70
50 PRINT "NO REAL ROOTS"
60 GOTO 90
70 PRINT "THE ROOTS ARE:"
80 PRINT (−B + SQR(D))/(2 • A), "AND", (−B − SQR(D))/(2 • A)
90 END
```

PROGRAM CHECK

Type in the program. To test whether you entered it correctly, run the program. Input 1, 4, 3 after the question. The computer should print

THE ROOTS ARE:
−1   AND   −3

USING THE PROGRAM

Run the program to solve each of these equations.

Solutions

1. $x^2 − 5x + 6 = 0$ _____
2. $x^2 − 8x − 7 = 0$ _____
3. $x^2 + 6x + 9 = 0$ _____
4. $x^2 + 8x − 7 = 0$ _____
5. $x^2 − 16 = 0$ _____
6. $2x^2 − 8x + 3 = 0$ _____
7. $x^2 + 5x + 6 = 0$ _____
8. $x^2 − 7x = 0$ _____
9. $x^2 + x + 1 = 0$ _____
10. $3x^2 − 20 = 0$ _____

(continued)

Using Technology
Computer Activities, p. 81

(*Activity 36 continued*)

Run the program to solve each of these equations.

Solutions

11. $2x^2 − 11x = 0$ _____
12. $2x^2 + 3x + 4 = 0$ _____
13. $3x^2 + 3x + 3 = 0$ _____
14. $x^2 − 8x + 16 = 0$ _____

ANALYSIS

Examine your solutions carefully. Generalize your results to answer the following questions.

1. If r and s are the roots of $Ax^2 + Bx + C = 0$, what are the roots of $Ax^2 − Bx + C = 0$?

2. If $x = 0$ is a solution of $Ax^2 + Bx + C = 0$, what can you conclude about A, B, or C?

3. If r and s are roots of $Ax^2 + Bx + C = 0$ ($C < 0$, $B = 0$), how are r and s related?

4. If $A = B = C$, what do you conclude about the solution of $Ax^2 + Bx + C = 0$?

5. If $Ax^2 + Bx + C = 0$ has a double root, what is the polynomial $Ax^2 + Bx + C$ called?

Using Models
Overhead Visual 13, Sheets 1 and 2

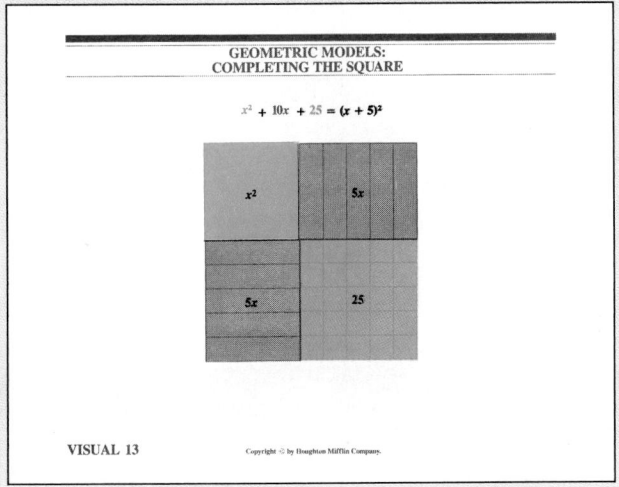

GEOMETRIC MODELS:
COMPLETING THE SQUARE

$x^2 + 10x + 25 = (x + 5)^2$

VISUAL 13

Using Models
Overhead Visual 13, Sheets 3 and 4

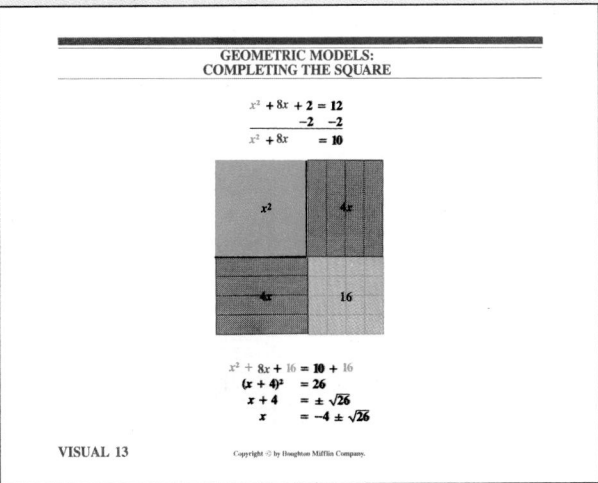

GEOMETRIC MODELS:
COMPLETING THE SQUARE

$$x^2 + 8x + 2 = 12$$
$$\underline{ -2 \quad -2}$$
$$x^2 + 8x = 10$$

$$x^2 + 8x + 16 = 10 + 16$$
$$(x + 4)^2 = 26$$
$$x + 4 = \pm\sqrt{26}$$
$$x = -4 \pm \sqrt{26}$$

VISUAL 13

Application

The basketball in the photo would follow a linear path and maintain a constant speed if not for gravity. This force accelerates objects toward the ground. That is why a projectile's path is parabolic. The initial speed of an object is reduced by gravity until the object stops rising and begins its downward swing.

The formula shown in the caption gives a fairly accurate picture of a projectile's path. It is an elaborate version of the familiar formula $d = rt$ that reflects the influence of gravity. There are other factors that affect the path of a projectile, such as wind, but gravity has the greatest impact.

Group Activities
Students can explore values of quadratic functions before learning to deal with them algebraically. Have them make a table of values for the equation in the caption. They should be told that h is in meters and t is in seconds. They may let a equal 14 and use half-second intervals from 0 to 3. They may disregard the height of the ballplayer and round answers to the nearest tenth.

Once they have made their tables, the students should graph the results and answer these questions: In how many seconds will the ball reach its highest point? How high will it be at that moment? When will the ball be 5.8 m high?

Support Materials
Resource Book   p. 189

12 Quadratic Functions

The path of a ball thrown upward is a parabola. The height of the ball at a time t is given by the quadratic equation $h = -4.9t^2 + at$, where the coefficient a depends on the initial angle and speed of the ball.

560

Quadratic Equations

12-1 Quadratic Equations with Perfect Squares

Objective   To solve quadratic equations involving perfect squares.

In Chapter 5 you learned how to solve certain quadratic equations by factoring. In Chapter 11 you learned how to solve quadratic equations of the form $x^2 = k$. This lesson extends what you learned in Chapter 11 to any quadratic equation involving a *perfect square*. Later in this chapter you'll learn more general methods that can be used to solve any quadratic equation and to determine its number of roots.

The property of square roots of equal numbers (page 526) leads you to the following information about the roots of $x^2 = k$.

If $k > 0$, then $x^2 = k$ has two real-number roots: $x = \pm\sqrt{k}$.

If $k = 0$, then $x^2 = k$ has one real-number root: $x = 0$.

If $k < 0$, then $x^2 = k$ has no real-number roots.

Examples 1 and 2 show you how to use this information about roots to solve some quadratic equations.

Example 1 Solve: **a.** $m^2 = 49$ **b.** $5r^2 = 45$

Solution **a.** $m^2 = 49$ **b.** $5r^2 = 45$
$\qquad\qquad m = \pm\sqrt{49}$ $\qquad r^2 = 9$
$\qquad\qquad m = \pm 7$ $\qquad r = \pm\sqrt{9} = \pm 3$
$\qquad$ ∴ the solution set is $\{7, -7\}$.   ∴ the solution set is $\{3, -3\}$.

Example 2 Solve $(x + 6)^2 = 64$.

Solution $(x + 6)^2 = 64$
$\qquad\qquad x + 6 = \pm 8$
$\qquad\qquad x = -6 \pm 8$
$\qquad\quad x = 2 \ $ or $\ x = -14$
$\qquad$ Check: $(2 + 6)^2 \stackrel{?}{=} 64 \qquad\qquad (-14 + 6)^2 \stackrel{?}{=} 64$
$\qquad\qquad\qquad\quad (8)^2 \stackrel{?}{=} 64 \qquad\qquad\qquad (-8)^2 \stackrel{?}{=} 64$
$\qquad\qquad\qquad\qquad 64 = 64 \ \checkmark \qquad\qquad\quad 64 = 64 \ \checkmark$
$\qquad$ ∴ the solution set is $\{2, -14\}$. *Answer*

Quadratic Functions   **561**

Teaching References
Lesson Commentary, pp. T137–T140
Assignment Guide, pp. T70–T71
Supplementary Materials
  Practice Masters 73–80
  Tests 53–58
  Resource Book
    Prac. Exs. pp. 136–145
    Tests, pp. 64–78
    En. Act. p. 205
    Mix. Rev. pp. 155–157
    Application, p. 189
  Study Guide, pp. 203–218
  Computer Activities 36–37
  Test Generator
  California Standards
  Support Workbook
    Appendix: *If and only if* and Exploration for Lesson 12-4
Alternate Test, p. T23
Cumulative Review, p. T30

Teaching Suggestions p. T137

Suggested Extensions p. T137

Warm-Up Exercises

Check to see whether the given set is the solution for the equation.

1. $4x^2 = 9$ $\left\{\frac{3}{2}, \frac{-3}{2}\right\}$ yes

2. $25a^2 = 50$ $\{\sqrt{2}, -\sqrt{2}\}$ yes

3. $(c - 3)^2 = 16$ $\{7, -7\}$ no

4. $(3t + 2)^2 = -25$ $\left\{1, \frac{-7}{3}\right\}$ no

Motivating the Lesson

Tell students that today they will use their knowledge of perfect squares, radicals, and factoring to solve equations like those in the Warm-Up Exercises.

Solve.

1. $9r^2 = 121$ $r^2 = \dfrac{121}{9}$

$$r = \pm\sqrt{\dfrac{121}{9}}$$

$$r = \pm\dfrac{11}{3}$$

∴ the sol. set is
$\left\{\dfrac{11}{3}, -\dfrac{11}{3}\right\}$.

2. $(x - 3)^2 = 100$
$x - 3 = \pm 10$
$x = 3 \pm 10$
Check:
$(13 - 3)^2 = 10^2 = 100$ ✓
$(-7 - 3)^2 = (-10)^2 = 100$ ✓
∴ the sol. set is {13, −7}.

3. $7(x + 8)^2 = -28$
$(x + 8)^2 = -4$
∴ there is no real-no. sol.

4. $m^2 - 10m + 25 = 16$
$(m - 5)^2 = 16$
$m - 5 = \pm 4$
$m = 5 \pm 4$
∴ the sol. set is {9, 1}.

5. $6(x + 9)^2 - 4 = 32$
$6(x + 9)^2 = 36$
$(x + 9)^2 = 6$
$x + 9 = \pm\sqrt{6}$
$x = -9 \pm \sqrt{6}$;
$\{-9 + \sqrt{6}, -9 - \sqrt{6}\}$

Check for Understanding

Oral Exs. 1–6: use after
    Example 3.
Oral Exs. 7–9: use after
    Example 1.

Guided Practice

Solve. Express irrational solutions in simplest radical
form. If the equation has no
solution, write "no solu-
tion."

1. $x^2 = 81$ {±9}

2. $m^2 = \dfrac{49}{169}$ $\left\{\pm\dfrac{7}{13}\right\}$

3. $15x^2 = 120$ $\{\pm 2\sqrt{2}\}$

An expression such as $(x + 1)^2$, x^2, or $(5x - 3)^2$ is called a **perfect square.** Whenever an equation can be expressed in the form

$$\text{perfect square} = k \qquad (k \geq 0),$$

you can solve the equation by the method shown in Examples 1 and 2. (You may find it helpful to review Lesson 5-6 about squares of binomials.)

Example 3 Solve: **a.** $5(x - 4)^2 = 40$ **b.** $y^2 + 6y + 9 = 49$

Solution **a.** $5(x - 4)^2 = 40$ **b.** $y^2 + 6y + 9 = 49$
$(x - 4)^2 = 8$ $(y + 3)^2 = 49$
$x - 4 = \pm\sqrt{8}$ $y + 3 = \pm 7$
$x = 4 \pm \sqrt{8}$ $y = -3 \pm 7$
$x = 4 \pm 2\sqrt{2}$ $y = 4$ or $y = -10$
The check is left to you.   The check is left to you.
∴ the solution set is   ∴ the solution set is {4, −10}.
$\{4 + 2\sqrt{2}, 4 - 2\sqrt{2}\}$. **Answer**   **Answer**

The perfect squares occurring in Example 3 are $(x - 4)^2$ and $(y + 3)^2$. Note that Example 3(b) could also have been solved by factoring.

An equation that has a negative number as one side and a perfect square as the other side has no real-number solutions. This is so because *the square of any real number is always a nonnegative real number*.

Example 4 Solve $2(3x - 5)^2 + 15 = 7$.

Solution $2(3x - 5)^2 + 15 = 7$
$2(3x - 5)^2 = -8$
$(3x - 5)^2 = -4$

∴ there is no real-number solution. **Answer**

Oral Exercises

Express each trinomial as the square of a binomial.

Sample $y^2 + 8y + 16 = (y + 4)^2$

1. $x^2 + 6x + 9$ $(x + 3)^2$ **2.** $x^2 - 4x + 4$ $(x - 2)^2$ **3.** $x^2 + 10x + 25$ $(x + 5)^2$

4. $x^2 + 16x + 64$ $(x + 8)^2$ **5.** $x^2 - 14x + 49$ $(x - 7)^2$ **6.** $x^2 - 20x + 100$ $(x - 10)^2$

Solve.

7. $5r^2 = 180$ {6, −6} **8.** $y^2 = \dfrac{1}{121}$ $\left\{\dfrac{1}{11}, -\dfrac{1}{11}\right\}$ **9.** $4x^2 = 32$ $\{2\sqrt{2}, -2\sqrt{2}\}$

Written Exercises

Solve. Express irrational solutions in simplest radical form. If the equation has no solution, write "no solution."

A **1.** $x^2 = 64$ $\{\pm 8\}$ **2.** $(y - 7)^2 = 0$ $\{7\}$ **3.** $t^2 = \dfrac{100}{169}$ $\left\{\pm \dfrac{10}{13}\right\}$

4. $a^2 = -9$ no sol.   **5.** $3x^2 = 108$ $\{\pm 6\}$ **6.** $6t^2 = 156$ $\{\pm \sqrt{26}\}$

7. $14t^2 = 126$ $\{\pm 3\}$ **8.** $x^2 - 48 = 0$ $\{\pm 4\sqrt{3}\}$ **9.** $x^2 + 32 = 0$ no sol.

10. $m^2 - 54 = 0$ $\{\pm 3\sqrt{6}\}$ **11.** $6x^2 - 18 = 0$ $\{\pm \sqrt{3}\}$ **12.** $7m^2 - 42 = 0$ $\{\pm \sqrt{6}\}$

13. $4y^2 + 7 = 19$ $\{\pm \sqrt{3}\}$ **14.** $4r^2 - 7 = 29$ $\{\pm 3\}$ **15.** $3z^2 - 18 = 3$ $\{\pm \sqrt{7}\}$

16. $(x + 6)^2 = 16$ $\{-10, -2\}$ **17.** $(y - 6)^2 = 13$ $\{6 \pm \sqrt{13}\}$ **18.** $(y + 2)^2 = 12$ $\{-2 \pm 2\sqrt{3}\}$

19. $(s - 7)^2 = 28$ $\{7 \pm 2\sqrt{7}\}$ **20.** $(z - 3)^2 = 32$ $\{3 \pm 4\sqrt{2}\}$ **21.** $2(x - 5)^2 = 18$ $\{2, 8\}$

22. $5(m - 8)^2 = 25$ $\{8 \pm \sqrt{5}\}$ **23.** $8(x + 3)^2 = 56$ $\{-3 \pm \sqrt{7}\}$ **24.** $6(z + 5)^2 = 42$ $\{-5 \pm \sqrt{7}\}$

B **25.** $x^2 + 6x + 9 = 16$ $\{1, -7\}$ **26.** $x^2 - 14x + 49 = 64$ $\{15, -1\}$ **27.** $r^2 - 22r + 121 = 4$ $\{9, 13\}$

28. $y^2 - 18y + 81 = 144$ $\{21, -3\}$ **29.** $\dfrac{1}{5}x^2 - \dfrac{5}{49} = 0$ $\left\{\pm \dfrac{5}{7}\right\}$ **30.** $\dfrac{1}{4}t^2 - \dfrac{9}{64} = 0$ $\left\{\pm \dfrac{3}{4}\right\}$

31. $\dfrac{1}{5}r^2 - 2 = \dfrac{5}{6}$ $\left\{\pm \dfrac{\sqrt{510}}{6}\right\}$ **32.** $\dfrac{1}{6}x^2 - 4 = \dfrac{5}{6}$ $\{\pm \sqrt{29}\}$ **33.** $t^2 + 18t + 81 = 225$ $\{6, -24\}$

34. $0.49x^2 + 2 = 3.96$ $\{\pm 2\}$ **35.** $1.44z^2 - 1.36 = -0.64$ $\left\{\pm \dfrac{\sqrt{2}}{2}\right\}$ **36.** $5(t + 2)^2 = \dfrac{3}{5}$ $\left\{\dfrac{-10 \pm \sqrt{3}}{5}\right\}$

37. $4(x - 2)^2 = \dfrac{1}{49}$ $\left\{\dfrac{27}{14}, \dfrac{29}{14}\right\}$ **38.** $\left(y - \dfrac{3}{7}\right)^2 = -\dfrac{8}{9}$ no sol.   **39.** $\left(z - \dfrac{3}{5}\right)^2 = \dfrac{7}{16}$ $\left\{\dfrac{12 \pm 5\sqrt{7}}{20}\right\}$

Solve each equation by factoring.

40. $7y^3 - 28y = 0$ $\{0, \pm 2\}$ **41.** $7a^3 - 175a = 0$ $\{0, \pm 5\}$ **42.** $\dfrac{1}{4}t^3 - 16t = 0$ $\{0, \pm 8\}$

43. $4b^3 - \dfrac{1}{4}b = 0$ $\left\{0, \pm \dfrac{1}{4}\right\}$ **44.** $8x^3 = 392x$ $\{0, \pm 7\}$ **45.** $8x^3 = 512x$ $\{0, \pm 8\}$

Solve.

C **46.** $3(5x - 2)^2 = 27$ $\left\{1, -\dfrac{1}{5}\right\}$ **47.** $5(6x - 1)^2 = 5$ $\left\{0, \dfrac{1}{3}\right\}$ **48.** $2(7x - 2)^2 + 5 = 11$ $\left\{\dfrac{2 \pm \sqrt{3}}{7}\right\}$

49. How many different real-number solutions does $a(x + b)^2 = c$ have if:

    a. $a > 0$ and $c > 0$? 2   **b.** $a < 0$ and $c < 0$? 2

    c. $a < 0$ and $c > 0$? none   **d.** $a > 0$ and $c = 0$? 1

Mixed Review Exercises

1. $x^2 - 22x + 121$ **2.** $4x^2 + 20x + 25$

Express each square as a trinomial.

1. $(x - 11)^2$ **2.** $(2x + 5)^2$ **3.** $(6x - 7)^2$ $36x^2 - 84x + 49$ **4.** $(-3c + 4)^2$ $9c^2 - 24c + 16$

5. $\left(x + \dfrac{1}{2}\right)^2$ $x^2 + x + \dfrac{1}{4}$ **6.** $\left(x + \dfrac{1}{3}\right)^2$ $x^2 + \dfrac{2}{3}x + \dfrac{1}{9}$ **7.** $\left(\dfrac{1}{2}x + \dfrac{2}{3}\right)^2$ **8.** $\left(\dfrac{1}{3}x + \dfrac{3}{4}\right)^2$

7. $\dfrac{1}{4}x^2 + \dfrac{2}{3}x + \dfrac{4}{9}$ **8.** $\dfrac{1}{9}x^2 + \dfrac{1}{2}x + \dfrac{9}{16}$ *Quadratic Functions*   **563**

4. $x^2 + 16 = 0$ no sol.

5. $9m^2 + 1 = 28$ $\{\pm \sqrt{3}\}$

6. $(y - 2)^2 = 48$ $\{2 \pm 4\sqrt{3}\}$

7. $7(3x - 1)^2 = 252$ $\left\{\dfrac{7}{3}, \dfrac{-5}{3}\right\}$

Common Errors

Once students have the equation in the form

    perfect square = k,

they often will name only one square root of k. Thus, they do not find the entire solution set. For example, for $(x + 3)^2 = 49$, they may write $x + 3 = 7$, followed by $x = -3 + 7 = 4$. In reteaching, show them that -10 is also a solution and point out their error.

Summarizing the Lesson

Tell students they have learned to solve quadratic equations involving perfect squares. For the equation in the form $x^2 = k$, ask them how many real-number roots exist when: (a) $k > 0$, (b) $k = 0$, and (c) $k < 0$. 2, 1, 0
Point out that such information is summarized on page 561 for easy review.

Suggested Assignments

Minimum
  563/1–31 odd
S 563/Mixed Review

Average
  563/1–39 odd
S 563/Mixed Review

Maximum
  563/3–48 mult. of 3, 49
S 563/Mixed Review

Supplementary Materials

Study Guide   pp. 203–204

Warm-Up Exercises

Write the following perfect square trinomial on the board:

$$4a^2 + 20a + 25.$$

Have each student identify the quadratic term, the constant term, and the coefficient of the linear term. Then have them factor the trinomial.
$4a^2$; 25; 20; $(2a + 5)^2$

Motivating the Lesson

Tell students that quadratic equations used to model natural phenomena do not always involve perfect squares, as did the equations in the previous lesson. Students will learn to solve more general quadratic equations today.

Chalkboard Examples

Complete the square. Then write the trinomial as the square of a binomial.

1. $x^2 - 20x +$?

$\left(\frac{20}{2}\right)^2 = 100$; $(x - 10)^2$

2. $x^2 + 11x +$?

$\left(\frac{11}{2}\right)^2 = \frac{121}{4}$; $\left(x + \frac{11}{2}\right)^2$

Solve by completing the square. Give irrational roots in simplest radical form.

3. $y^2 - 24y + 23 = 0$

$y^2 - 24y = -23$

$y^2 - 24y + 12^2 = -23 + 144$

$(y - 12)^2 = 121$

$y - 12 = \pm 11$

$y = 12 \pm 11$

∴ the sol. set is {23, 1}.

12-2 Completing the Square

Objective   To solve quadratic equations by completing the square.

In Lesson 12-1 you learned that it is always possible to solve a quadratic equation that has the form

$$\text{perfect square} = k \quad (k \geq 0).$$

If a quadratic equation does not have this form, it may be possible to transform it into one that does by a method called **completing the square.**

   Study the perfect squares below. The main idea behind completing the square is shown.

$$(x + 4)^2 = x^2 \underbrace{+ 8x}_{} + 16 \qquad\qquad (x - 5)^2 = x^2 \underbrace{- 10x}_{} + 25$$
$$\left(\frac{8}{2}\right)^2 = 16 \qquad\qquad\qquad \left(-\frac{10}{2}\right)^2 = 25$$

$$(x + a)^2 = x^2 \underbrace{+ 2ax}_{} + a^2$$
$$\left(\frac{2a}{2}\right)^2 = a^2$$

In each case, notice that the coefficient of x^2 is 1 and that the constant term is *the square of half the coefficient of x.*

Method of Completing the Square

For $x^2 + bx +$ _?_ :

1. Find half the coefficient of x: $\frac{b}{2}$

2. Square the result of Step 1: $\left(\frac{b}{2}\right)^2$

3. Add the result of Step 2 to $x^2 + bx$: $x^2 + bx + \left(\frac{b}{2}\right)^2$

4. You have completed the square: $x^2 + bx + \left(\frac{b}{2}\right)^2 = \left(x + \frac{b}{2}\right)^2$

Example 1   Complete the square.

   a. $x^2 + 14x +$ _?_   **b.** $x^2 - 9x +$ _?_

Solution   **a.** $x^2 \underbrace{+ 14x}_{} + 49 = (x + 7)^2$ **b.** $x^2 \underbrace{- 9x}_{} + \frac{81}{4} = \left(x - \frac{9}{2}\right)^2$

$\left(\frac{14}{2}\right)^2 = 49$ $\left(-\frac{9}{2}\right)^2 = \frac{81}{4}$

564   *Chapter 12*

Example 2 Solve $x^2 - 3x - 18 = 0$ by completing the square.

Solution

$$x^2 - 3x - 18 = 0$$
$$x^2 - 3x = 18$$

$$x^2 - 3x + \left(-\frac{3}{2}\right)^2 = 18 + \left(-\frac{3}{2}\right)^2 \qquad \begin{cases} \text{Half the coefficient of } x \\ \text{is } -\frac{3}{2}. \text{ Square it and add} \\ \text{the result to } both \text{ sides.} \end{cases}$$

$$x^2 - 3x + \frac{9}{4} = 18 + \frac{9}{4}$$

perfect square $\longrightarrow \left(x - \frac{3}{2}\right)^2 = \frac{81}{4} \longleftarrow$ constant

$$x - \frac{3}{2} = \pm\frac{9}{2}$$

$$x = \frac{3}{2} \pm \frac{9}{2} = \frac{3 \pm 9}{2}$$

$$x = 6 \quad \text{or} \quad x = -3$$

The check is left to you.

∴ the solution set is $\{6, -3\}$.   **Answer**

Example 3 Solve $5x^2 + 8x + 1 = 0$ by completing the square.
Give irrational roots in simplest form.

Solution

$$5x^2 + 8x + 1 = 0$$
$$5x^2 + 8x = -1 \qquad \begin{cases} \text{Divide both sides by 5 so that} \\ \text{the coefficient of } x^2 \text{ will be 1.} \end{cases}$$
$$x^2 + \frac{8}{5}x = -\frac{1}{5}$$

$$x^2 + \frac{8}{5}x + \left(\frac{4}{5}\right)^2 = -\frac{1}{5} + \left(\frac{4}{5}\right)^2$$

$$x^2 + \frac{8}{5}x + \frac{16}{25} = -\frac{1}{5} + \frac{16}{25}$$

$$\left(x + \frac{4}{5}\right)^2 = \frac{11}{25}$$

$$x + \frac{4}{5} = \pm\sqrt{\frac{11}{25}}$$

$$x = -\frac{4}{5} \pm \frac{\sqrt{11}}{5} = \frac{-4 \pm \sqrt{11}}{5}$$

$$x = \frac{-4 + \sqrt{11}}{5} \quad \text{or} \quad x = \frac{-4 - \sqrt{11}}{5}$$

The check is left to you.

∴ the solution set is $\left\{\dfrac{-4 + \sqrt{11}}{5}, \dfrac{-4 - \sqrt{11}}{5}\right\}$.   **Answer**

You can use a calculator or the table of square roots on page 682 to find decimal approximations of the irrational roots in Example 3.

$$\frac{-4 + \sqrt{11}}{5} \approx \frac{-4 + 3.32}{5} = \frac{-0.68}{5} = -0.136 \approx -0.1$$

$$\frac{-4 - \sqrt{11}}{5} \approx \frac{-4 - 3.32}{5} = \frac{-7.32}{5} = -1.464 \approx -1.5$$

Quadratic Functions   **565**

---

4. $3x^2 + 4x - 1 = 0$

$$3x^2 + 4x = 1$$

$$x^2 + \frac{4}{3}x = \frac{1}{3}$$

$$x^2 + \frac{4}{3}x + \left(\frac{2}{3}\right)^2 = \frac{1}{3} + \left(\frac{2}{3}\right)^2$$

$$x^2 + \frac{4}{3}x + \frac{4}{9} = \frac{1}{3} + \frac{4}{9}$$

$$\left(x + \frac{2}{3}\right)^2 = \frac{7}{9}$$

$$x + \frac{2}{3} = \pm\sqrt{\frac{7}{9}}$$

$$x = -\frac{2}{3} \pm \frac{\sqrt{7}}{3}$$

$$\left\{\frac{-2 + \sqrt{7}}{3}, \frac{-2 - \sqrt{7}}{3}\right\}$$

Check for Understanding

Oral Exs. 1–6: use after
Example 1.

Common Errors

In completing the square, some students may not take half the coefficient of the middle term, especially if it is an odd number or a fraction. In reteaching, encourage such students to write their work off to the side.

Using a Calculator

Students can use a calculator to find approximations of square roots, both here and in Written Exercises 1–12.

Guided Practice

Solve by completing the square. Give irrational roots in simplest radical form, and then approximate them to the nearest tenth.

1. $x^2 - 6x = -8$ $\{2, 4\}$

2. $x^2 + 10x - 3 = 0$
$\{-5 + 2\sqrt{7},$
$-5 - 2\sqrt{7}\}; \{0.3, -10.3\}$

3. $x^2 - 5x = 23$ $\left\{\dfrac{5 + 3\sqrt{13}}{2},\right.$

$\left.\dfrac{5 - 3\sqrt{13}}{2}\right\}; \{7.9, -2.9\}$

(continued)

565

Guided Practice (continued)

4. $4a^2 + 8a = 27$

$\left\{-1 + \dfrac{\sqrt{31}}{2}, -1 - \dfrac{\sqrt{31}}{2}\right\};$
$\{1.8, -3.8\}$

Solve by (a) completing the square and (b) factoring.

5. $6n^2 - 10n + 4 = 0$ $\left\{1, \dfrac{2}{3}\right\}$

Summarizing the Lesson

Tell students that they have learned how to complete the square. Have them outline the steps for this method orally while you write the steps on the board.

Suggested Assignments

Minimum
Day 1: 566/1–10
  S 563/33
Day 2: 566/11–18
  S 566/Mixed Review

Average
  566/1–27 odd
  S 566/Mixed Review

Maximum
  566/2–30 even
  S 566/Mixed Review

Supplementary Materials

Study Guide   pp. 205–206
Practice Master   73
Resource Book   p. 136
Overhead Visual   13

Additional Answers
Written Exercises

2. $\{\sqrt{26} - 4, -\sqrt{26} - 4\};$
$\{1.1, -9.1\}$

4. $\{-25, 7\}$ **6.** $\{-15, 21\}$

8. $\{3\sqrt{2} - 4, -3\sqrt{2} - 4\};$
$\{0.2, -8.2\}$

10. $\left\{\dfrac{\sqrt{13} - 1}{2}, \dfrac{-\sqrt{13} - 1}{2}\right\};$
$\{1.3, -2.3\}$

12. $\left\{\dfrac{\sqrt{73} + 7}{2}, \dfrac{-\sqrt{73} + 7}{2}\right\};$
$\{7.8, -0.8\}$

Oral Exercises

Complete the square.

1. $z^2 + 18z + \underline{\ ?\ } = (z + \underline{\ ?\ })^2$ 81; 9

2. $k^2 - 12k + \underline{\ ?\ } = (k - \underline{\ ?\ })^2$ 36; 6

3. $m^2 + 5m + \underline{\ ?\ } = (m + \underline{\ ?\ })^2$ $\dfrac{25}{4}; \dfrac{5}{2}$

4. $r^2 - 11r + \underline{\ ?\ } = (r - \underline{\ ?\ })^2$ $\dfrac{121}{4}; \dfrac{11}{2}$

5. $t^2 + 1.6t + \underline{\ ?\ } = (t + \underline{\ ?\ })^2$ 0.64; 0.8

6. $q^2 - \dfrac{2}{3}q + \underline{\ ?\ } = (q - \underline{\ ?\ })^2$ $\dfrac{1}{9}; \dfrac{1}{3}$

Written Exercises

Solve by completing the square. Give irrational roots in simplest radical form and then approximate them to the nearest tenth. You may wish to use a calculator.

A **1.** $x^2 - 4x = 17$ **2.** $y^2 + 8y = 10$ **3.** $w^2 + 6w = -3$

4. $c^2 + 18c - 175 = 0$ **5.** $v^2 - 20v + 19 = 0$ **6.** $z^2 - 6z - 307 = 8$

7. $y^2 + 18y + 32 = 226$ **8.** $2b^2 + 16b = 4$ **9.** $5x^2 - 20x = 10$

10. $w^2 + w = 3$ **11.** $x^2 - 5x = 2$ **12.** $c^2 - 7c - 2 = 4$

Solve the equations by (a) completing the square and (b) factoring.

13. $x^2 - 12x + 35 = 0$ $\{5, 7\}$ **14.** $y^2 + 15y + 56 = 0$ $\{-8, -7\}$ **15.** $z^2 - 2z - 35 = 0$ $\{-5, 7\}$

16. $3c^2 - 7c = 6$ $\left\{3, -\dfrac{2}{3}\right\}$ **17.** $2y^2 = 9y - 9$ $\left\{3, \dfrac{3}{2}\right\}$ **18.** $4n^2 + 12n + 5 = 0$
$\left\{-\dfrac{5}{2}, -\dfrac{1}{2}\right\}$

Solve. Write irrational roots in simplest radical form.

B **19.** $\dfrac{x^2}{4} - x = 3$ $\{6, -2\}$ **20.** $\dfrac{2y^2}{3} - y - 3 = 0$ $\left\{3, -\dfrac{3}{2}\right\}$ **21.** $m^2 - 3 = \dfrac{11m}{2}$ $\left\{6, -\dfrac{1}{2}\right\}$

22. $a^2 + \dfrac{a}{3} = 3$ $\left\{\dfrac{-1 \pm \sqrt{109}}{6}\right\}$ **23.** $\dfrac{3m^2}{4} - 3 = \dfrac{m}{2}$ $\left\{\dfrac{1 \pm \sqrt{37}}{3}\right\}$ **24.** $\dfrac{y^2}{2} - \dfrac{y}{4} = 3$ $\left\{\dfrac{1 \pm \sqrt{97}}{4}\right\}$

25. $x + 1 = \dfrac{2 + x}{4x}$ $\left\{\dfrac{-3 \pm \sqrt{41}}{8}\right\}$ **26.** $y - 2 = \dfrac{3y - 2}{2y}$ $\left\{\dfrac{7 \pm \sqrt{33}}{4}\right\}$ **27.** $9t = \dfrac{6t - 1}{t + 2}$ $\left\{\dfrac{-2 \pm \sqrt{3}}{3}\right\}$

28. $\left\{\dfrac{-b \pm \sqrt{b^2 - 4}}{2}\right\}$

Solve for x in terms of a, b, and c. $\left\{\dfrac{b \pm \sqrt{b^2 - 4c}}{2}\right\}$ $\left\{\dfrac{-b \pm \sqrt{b^2 - 4ac}}{2a}\right\}$

C **28.** $x^2 + bx + 1 = 0$ **29.** $x^2 - bx + c = 0$ **30.** $ax^2 + bx + c = 0$

Mixed Review Exercises

Simplify.

1. $\sqrt{188}$ $2\sqrt{47}$ **2.** $\sqrt{2400}$ $20\sqrt{6}$ **3.** $\sqrt{10x^4y^9}$ $x^2y^4\sqrt{10y}$ **4.** $\sqrt{120a^6b^7c^5}$ $2|a^3b^3|c^2\sqrt{30bc}$

5. $\dfrac{z}{4 - z} + \dfrac{6}{z + 4}$ **6.** $1 + \dfrac{b^2}{2b + 1}$ **7.** $3(2x - 1) + (3x + 5)(5x + 3)$
$15x^2 + 40x + 12$

5. $\dfrac{z^2 - 2z + 24}{16 - z^2}$ **6.** $\dfrac{b^2 + 2b + 1}{2b + 1}$

12-3 The Quadratic Formula

Objective   To learn the quadratic formula and use it to solve equations.

In Lesson 5-12, you learned that the standard form of a quadratic equation is given by

$$ax^2 + bx + c = 0,$$

where $a \neq 0$. Solving this equation by completing the square gives a formula for finding all real-number solutions of any quadratic equation.

$$ax^2 + bx + c = 0$$

$$ax^2 + bx = -c$$

$$x^2 + \frac{b}{a}x = -\frac{c}{a}$$

$$x^2 + \frac{b}{a}x + \left(\frac{b}{2a}\right)^2 = -\frac{c}{a} + \left(\frac{b}{2a}\right)^2 \qquad \text{Complete the square.}$$

$$\left(x + \frac{b}{2a}\right)^2 = -\frac{c}{a} + \frac{b^2}{4a^2}$$

$$\left(x + \frac{b}{2a}\right)^2 = \frac{b^2 - 4ac}{4a^2}$$

$$x + \frac{b}{2a} = \pm\sqrt{\frac{b^2 - 4ac}{4a^2}} \qquad \text{If } b^2 - 4ac \geq 0.$$

$$x = -\frac{b}{2a} \pm \sqrt{\frac{b^2 - 4ac}{4a^2}}$$

$$x = -\frac{b}{2a} \pm \frac{\sqrt{b^2 - 4ac}}{2a}$$

$$x = \frac{-b \pm \sqrt{b^2 - 4ac}}{2a}$$

The last equation in the solution above is called the **quadratic formula.** It gives the roots of the quadratic equation $ax^2 + bx + c = 0$ in terms of the coefficients a, b, and c. In this solution, notice the assumptions that $a \neq 0$ and that $b^2 - 4ac \geq 0$.

The Quadratic Formula

If $ax^2 + bx + c = 0$, $a \neq 0$, and $b^2 - 4ac \geq 0$,

then $\qquad\qquad x = \dfrac{-b \pm \sqrt{b^2 - 4ac}}{2a}.$

Quadratic Functions   **567**

Teaching Suggestions p. T138
Group Activities p. T138
Suggested Extensions p. T138

Warm-Up Exercises

Evaluate each expression if $x = 3$, $y = -2$, and $z = -7$.

1. $x^2 - 5y$ 19
2. $6 \pm \sqrt{2 + yz}$ 2 or 10
3. $\pm\sqrt{-2y - 4x}$ undefined
4. $10 \pm \dfrac{\sqrt{4 - xz}}{5}$ 9 or 11
5. $\dfrac{10 \pm \sqrt{4 - xz}}{5}$ 1 or 3

Motivating the Lesson

Write the following equations on the chalkboard.

$$x^2 + 8x + 6 = 0$$
$$7x^2 + 5x - 6 = 0$$

Ask students to compare the degree of difficulty involved in solving these equations by completing the square. Today's lesson will derive the quadratic formula, which will work for any quadratic equation and is especially useful for types like the second example above.

Chalkboard Examples

Solve by using the quadratic formula. Give irrational roots in simplest radical form and then approximate them to the nearest tenth.

1. $3x^2 + x - 4 = 0$

$$x = \frac{-(1) \pm \sqrt{(1)^2 - 4(3)(-4)}}{2(3)}$$

$$= \frac{-1 \pm \sqrt{1 + 48}}{6}$$

$$= \frac{-1 \pm \sqrt{49}}{6} = \frac{-1 \pm 7}{6}$$

$$x = \frac{-1 + 7}{6} = 1 \text{ or}$$

$$x = \frac{-1 - 7}{6} = \frac{-4}{3}$$

$$\left\{1, \frac{-4}{3}\right\}$$

(continued)

567

2. $3y^2 = 6y - 1$

$3y^2 - 6y + 1 = 0$

$y = \dfrac{-(-6) \pm \sqrt{(-6)^2 - 4(3)(1)}}{2(3)}$

$= \dfrac{6 \pm \sqrt{24}}{6} = \dfrac{6 \pm 2\sqrt{6}}{6}$

$= \dfrac{2(3 \pm \sqrt{6})}{6} = \dfrac{3 \pm \sqrt{6}}{3}$

Since $\sqrt{6} \approx 2.45$,

$y \approx \dfrac{3 + 2.45}{3} \approx 1.8$ or

$y \approx \dfrac{3 - 2.45}{3} \approx 0.2$

$\left\{\dfrac{3 \pm \sqrt{6}}{3}\right\}$, or $\{1.8, 0.2\}$

Check for Understanding

Oral Exs. 1–12: use after
  Example 2.

Common Errors

Students may confuse the values of a, b, and c if the quadratic equation is not given in the standard form $ax^2 + bx + c = 0$. (Emphasize the paragraph following Example 1.) Students may also be confused about the values of b and c if the quadratic equation lacks either a linear or a constant term. In reteaching, point out that $b = 0$ if there is no linear term and that $c = 0$ if there is no constant term.

Guided Practice

Use the quadratic formula to solve each equation. Give irrational roots in simplest radical form.

1. $r^2 - r - 12 = 0$ $\{4, -3\}$

2. $t^2 + 3t + 1 = 0$ $\left\{\dfrac{-3 \pm \sqrt{5}}{2}\right\}$

Example 1 Use the quadratic formula to solve $9x^2 + 12x - 1 = 0$. Give irrational roots in simplest radical form and then approximate them to the nearest tenth.

Solution $9x^2 + 12x - 1 = 0$

$x = \dfrac{-b \pm \sqrt{b^2 - 4ac}}{2a}$, where $a = 9$, $b = 12$, and $c = -1$

$x = \dfrac{-(12) \pm \sqrt{(12)^2 - 4(9)(-1)}}{2(9)} = \dfrac{-12 \pm \sqrt{144 + 36}}{18}$

$= \dfrac{-12 \pm \sqrt{180}}{18} = \dfrac{-12 \pm \sqrt{36 \cdot 5}}{18} = \dfrac{-12 \pm 6\sqrt{5}}{18}$

$= \dfrac{6(-2 \pm \sqrt{5})}{18} = \dfrac{-2 \pm \sqrt{5}}{3}$

Since $\sqrt{5} \approx 2.24$, $x \approx \dfrac{-2 + 2.24}{3} = \dfrac{0.24}{3} \approx 0.1$

or $x \approx \dfrac{-2 - 2.24}{3} = \dfrac{-4.24}{3} \approx -1.4$

The check is left to you.

$\therefore$ the solution set is $\left\{\dfrac{-2 + \sqrt{5}}{3}, \dfrac{-2 - \sqrt{5}}{3}\right\}$, or $\{0.1, -1.4\}$. **Answer**

Remember to write a quadratic equation in the form
$$ax^2 + bx + c = 0$$
before using the quadratic formula. For example, to solve
$$4x^2 = 9x - 1,$$
first rewrite the equation as
$$4x^2 - 9x + 1 = 0$$
so that you can easily identify the values of a, b, and c.

Example 2 Use the quadratic formula to solve $x^2 = x - 8$.

Solution $x^2 = x - 8$

$x^2 - x + 8 = 0$ $\begin{cases} \text{Rewrite the equation} \\ \text{in standard form.} \end{cases}$

$x = \dfrac{-b \pm \sqrt{b^2 - 4ac}}{2a}$, where $a = 1$, $b = -1$, and $c = 8$.

$x = \dfrac{-(-1) \pm \sqrt{(-1)^2 - 4(1)(8)}}{2(1)} = \dfrac{1 \pm \sqrt{1 - 32}}{2} = \dfrac{1 \pm \sqrt{-31}}{2}$

Since $\sqrt{b^2 - 4ac} = \sqrt{-31}$, and $\sqrt{-31}$ does not represent a real number, the equation has *no real-number solution*. **Answer**

Oral Exercises

Read each equation in standard form. Then tell what the values of a, b, and c are for each equation.

1. $3x^2 + 5x - 2 = 0$ 3, 5, −2
2. $3a^2 - 9a + 5 = 0$ 3, −9, 5
3. $2p^2 + 7p - 3 = 0$ 2, 7, −3
4. $5d^2 + 9d = 2$ 5, 9, −2
5. $x^2 - 7x = 4$ 1, −7, −4
6. $y^2 = 6y - 7$ 1, −6, 7
7. $8m^2 = m + 5$ 8, −1, −5
8. $6 - q^2 = 4q$ 1, 4, −6
9. $5x^2 = 7x$ 5, −7, 0
10. $z = 10z^2$ 10, −1, 0
11. $8x^2 = 3$ 8, 0, −3
12. $12t^2 = 0$ 12, 0, 0

Written Exercises

Use the quadratic formula to solve each equation. Give irrational roots in simplest radical form and then approximate them to the nearest tenth. You may wish to use a calculator.

A
1. $x^2 - 3x - 10 = 0$
2. $2s^2 - 3s - 2 = 0$
3. $5z^2 - 11z + 2 = 0$
4. $2y^2 - 6y - 8 = 0$
5. $z^2 - 5z - 6 = 0$
6. $m^2 + 8m + 7 = 0$
7. $x^2 - 6x - 11 = 0$
8. $k^2 - 3k - 1 = 0$
9. $r^2 + 8r + 5 = 0$
10. $n^2 - 6n - 1 = 0$
11. $7x^2 + 2x - 2 = 0$
12. $-2z^2 + 8z + 5 = 0$
13. $-4x^2 + 2x + 3 = 0$
14. $j^2 - 6j = 13$
15. $4y^2 - 12y = -7$
16. $4v^2 = 10v - 5$
17. $3x^2 + 8x = 2$
18. $2r = 5 - 4r^2$

Solve.

B
19. $a^2 + 0.7a - 0.1 = 0$
20. $3x^2 - 1.8x + 0.03 = 0$
21. $4r^2 = 0.6r + 0.5$
22. $t^2 + \frac{3}{2}t + \frac{2}{3} = 0$
23. $2c^2 + \frac{1}{2}c + \frac{2}{3} = 0$
24. $x + \frac{1}{x} = \frac{3}{x} + 3$
25. $\frac{3}{2}x^2 + \frac{1}{3}x + \frac{2}{3} = 0$ no real-number solution
26. $\frac{1}{3} - \frac{2}{2y+1} = \frac{3}{y}$ $\left\{ \frac{23 \pm \sqrt{601}}{4} \right\}$; {11.9, −0.4}
27. $\frac{3x}{x+2} - \frac{x+1}{x-1} = 0$ $\left\{ \frac{3 \pm \sqrt{13}}{2} \right\}$; {3.3, −0.3}
28. $\frac{w+3}{w-1} - \frac{7}{w+5} = 3$ $\left\{ \frac{-11 \pm \sqrt{417}}{4} \right\}$; {2.4, −7.9}

The roots of a quadratic equation $ax^2 + bx + c = 0$ are

$$\frac{-b + \sqrt{b^2 - 4ac}}{2a} \quad \text{and} \quad \frac{-b - \sqrt{b^2 - 4ac}}{2a}.$$

C
29. Find the sum of the roots of $ax^2 + bx + c = 0$. $-\frac{b}{a}$
30. Find the product of the roots of $ax^2 + bx + c = 0$. $\frac{c}{a}$
31. Write a quadratic equation whose roots are $2 \pm \sqrt{5}$. (*Hint:* Find the sum and the product of the roots. Then use the results of Exercises 29 and 30 to find values for a, b, and c.)   Answers may vary. Example: $x^2 - 4x - 1 = 0$

---

3. $1 - s^2 = s$ $\left\{ \frac{-1 \pm \sqrt{5}}{2} \right\}$
4. $5m^2 + 8m$ $\left\{ \frac{-4 \pm \sqrt{11}}{5} \right\}$
5. $5x^2 = 6x + 5$ $\left\{ \frac{3 \pm \sqrt{34}}{5} \right\}$

 Using a Calculator

Students can approximate the irrational roots in their answers to the Written Exs. using a calculator.

Summarizing the Lesson

Tell students they have learned to use the quadratic formula to solve quadratic equations. Ask them to state the formula.

Suggested Assignments

Minimum
Day 1: 569/1–12
    S 570/Mixed Review
Day 2: 569/13–18
    R 575/Self-Test 1: 1–5
    595/ Ch. Rev. 1–6

Average
  569/1–31 odd
S 570/Mixed Review

Maximum
  569/1–31 odd
S 570/Mixed Review

Exercise Notes

See the side column on p. 571 for more about Exs. 29–31.

Additional Answers
Written Exercises

2. $\left\{ -\frac{1}{2}, 2 \right\}$ 4. $\{-1, 4\}$
6. $\{-7, -1\}$
8. $\left\{ \frac{3 \pm \sqrt{13}}{2} \right\}$; {3.3, −0.3}
10. $\{3 \pm \sqrt{10}\}$; {6.2, −0.2}
12. $\left\{ \frac{4 \pm \sqrt{26}}{2} \right\}$; {4.5, −0.5}

(continued)

Mixed Review Exercises

Solve each open sentence and graph its solution set.

1. $|x - 4| \le 7$

2. $2|y + 7| = 10 \{-12, -2\}$

3. $|3p + 5| < 7$

4. $0 < 2z + 1 \le 9$

5. $\sqrt{x} = 9 \{81\}$

6. $\sqrt{6n + 1} = 5 \{4\}$

7. $3\sqrt{3p} = 18 \{12\}$

8. $|9 + 2k| = 15 \{-12, 3\}$

9. $4|4 - m| = 20 \{-1, 9\}$

Solve by completing the squares.

10. $y^2 - 10y + 16 = 0 \{2, 8\}$

11. $2p^2 + 12p = 0 \{0, -6\}$

12. $c^2 - c = 6 \{-2, 3\}$

Computer Exercises

For students with some programming experience

1. Write a program that will solve quadratic equations by using the quadratic formula. Provide an output if $b^2 - 4ac$ is negative.

Answers may vary. Irrational answers are given to the nearest hundredth.
Use your program to solve the following equations.

2. $2x^2 + 7x + 3 = 0 \{-0.5, -3\}$

3. $4x^2 - 7x + 3 = 0 \{1, 0.75\}$

4. $3x^2 - 8x + 2 = 0 \{2.39, 0.28\}$

5. $x^2 - 4x + 2 = 0 \{3.41, 0.59\}$

6. $x^2 - 6x + 9 = 0 \{3\}$

7. $x^2 - 2x + 3 = 0$ no real-number solution

Extra / Imaginary Numbers

You know that there are no real-number solutions to the equation $x^2 = -16$. If you take another course in algebra, you'll learn that equations like this have solutions that are *imaginary numbers*. The imaginary number i is defined to be the square root of -1. All imaginary numbers involve i. Some examples are $3i$, $-\dfrac{5i}{2}$, and $2i\sqrt{3}$.

$$i = \sqrt{-1}, \quad \text{and} \quad i^2 = -1$$

The definition of i allows us to solve $x^2 = -16$ over the set of imaginary numbers.

Example Solve $x^2 = -16$.

Solution $x = \pm\sqrt{-16} = \pm\sqrt{16} \cdot \sqrt{-1} = \pm 4\sqrt{-1} = \pm 4i$

570 *Chapter 12*

In general:

$$\text{If } r > 0, \text{ then } \sqrt{-r} = i\sqrt{r}.$$

We write $i\sqrt{r}$ rather than $\sqrt{r}\,i$ to avoid confusion with $\sqrt{ri}$.

An interesting pattern occurs when you find i^n for increasing powers of n:

$i^1 = \sqrt{-1} = i$	i	$i^5 = i^2 \cdot i^3 = (-1)(-i) = i$	i
$i^2 = -1$	-1	$i^6 = i^3 \cdot i^3 = (-i)(-i) = i^2 = -1$	-1
$i^3 = i \cdot i^2 = i(-1) = -i$	$-i$	$i^7 = i^3 \cdot i^4 = (-i)(1) = -i$	$-i$
$i^4 = i^2 \cdot i^2 = (-1)(-1) = 1$	1	$i^8 = i^4 \cdot i^4 = 1(1) = 1$	1

Likewise, it can be shown that $i^9 = i$, $i^{10} = -1$, $i^{11} = -i$, $i^{12} = 1$, and so on.

Exercises

Simplify each expression to i, -1, $-i$, or 1.

1. i^{14} -1
2. i^{23} $-i$
3. i^{17} i
4. i^{36} 1
5. i^{19} $-i$
6. i^{27} $-i$

Simplify.

Sample a. $-\sqrt{-12}$ b. $\sqrt{96} \cdot \sqrt{-54}$ c. $\sqrt{\dfrac{-16}{25}}$

Solution a. $-\sqrt{-12} = -\sqrt{-1 \cdot 2^2 \cdot 3} = -2i\sqrt{3}$

b. $\sqrt{96} \cdot \sqrt{-54} = \sqrt{4^2 \cdot 6} \cdot \sqrt{-1 \cdot 3^2 \cdot 6}$
$= 4\sqrt{6} \cdot 3i\sqrt{6} = 12i \cdot 6 = 72i$

c. $\sqrt{\dfrac{-16}{25}} = \dfrac{\sqrt{-16}}{\sqrt{25}} = \dfrac{\sqrt{-1 \cdot 4^2}}{\sqrt{5^2}} = \dfrac{4i}{5}$

7. $\sqrt{-49}$ $7i$
8. $-\sqrt{-500}$ $-10i\sqrt{5}$
9. $\sqrt{96}$ $4\sqrt{6}$
10. $-\sqrt{-144}$ $-12i$
11. $\sqrt{12} \cdot \sqrt{-75}$ $30i$
12. $\sqrt{-3} \cdot \sqrt{48}$ $12i$
13. $\sqrt{18} \cdot \sqrt{-108}$ $18i\sqrt{6}$
14. $(\sqrt{-4} \cdot \sqrt{9})^2$ -36
15. $\sqrt{\dfrac{16}{-81}}$ $\dfrac{4i}{9}$
16. $-\sqrt{\dfrac{-25}{64}}$ $-\dfrac{5i}{8}$
17. $-\sqrt{\dfrac{-49}{121}}$ $-\dfrac{7i}{11}$
18. $\dfrac{\sqrt{-150}}{-\sqrt{54}}$ $-\dfrac{5i}{3}$

Solve.

19. $x^2 = -100$ $\{\pm 10i\}$
20. $x^2 + 63 = 0$ $\{\pm 3i\sqrt{7}\}$
21. $x^2 = -98$ $\{\pm 7i\sqrt{2}\}$
22. $x^2 + 272 = 0$ $\{\pm 4i\sqrt{17}\}$

Quadratic Functions **571**

Exercise Notes

Exs. 29–31 focus on the relationship between the sum and product of the roots of a quadratic equation and the coefficients of that equation. The results of these exercises can be generalized as follows: The general quadratic equation $ax^2 + bx + c = 0$ ($a \neq 0$) can be rewritten as $x^2 - \left(-\dfrac{b}{a}\right)x + \dfrac{c}{a} = 0$. From Exs. 29 and 30, the sum of the roots is $-\dfrac{b}{a}$ and the product of the roots is $\dfrac{c}{a}$. Thus, the general equation can be stated as: $x^2 - (\text{sum of roots})x + (\text{product of roots}) = 0$.

Ex 31.

Another way to solve this exercise is to use the Zero-Product Property and the relationship between a quadratic equation and its roots. [See pp. 230, 233 (Exs. 49–54), and 546 (Exs. 41–43).] A quadratic equation with roots $2 \pm \sqrt{5}$ is: $(x - (2 + \sqrt{5}))(x - (2 - \sqrt{5})) = 0$. Multiplying the left side of this equation and simplifying yields $x^2 - 4x - 1 = 0$.

12-4 Graphs of Quadratic Equations: The Discriminant

Objective   To use the discriminant to find the number of roots of the equation $ax^2 + bx + c = 0$ and the number of x-intercepts of the graph of the related equation $y = ax^2 + bx + c$.

You learned in Lesson 8-8 that the graph of the function defined by the quadratic equation

$$y = x^2 - 2x - 3$$

is the parabola shown at the right. The x-coordinate of a point where the curve intersects the x-axis is called an **x-intercept** of the curve. This parabola has two x-intercepts, −1 and 3, because $y = 0$ for both of these values of x. You can also see that the equation

$$x^2 - 2x - 3 = 0, \quad \text{or} \quad (x + 1)(x - 3) = 0,$$

has −1 and 3 as roots.

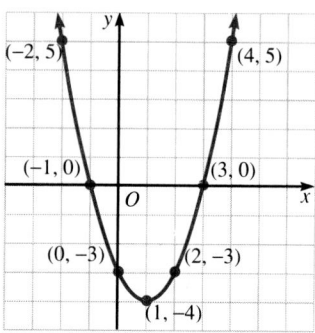

The roots of any quadratic equation of the form

$$ax^2 + bx + c = 0$$

are the x-intercepts of the graph of the related equation

$$y = ax^2 + bx + c.$$

The algebraic fact that a quadratic equation can have two, one, or no real-number roots corresponds to the geometric fact that a parabola can have two, one, or no x-intercepts, as illustrated in the following examples.

Example 1

Equation: $x^2 + 4x + 1 = 0$ *Related equation:* $y = x^2 + 4x + 1$

Solution: *Graph:*

$$x = \frac{-(4) \pm \sqrt{(4)^2 - 4(1)(1)}}{2(1)}$$

$$= \frac{-4 \pm \sqrt{12}}{2} = \frac{-4 \pm 2\sqrt{3}}{2}$$

$$= -2 \pm \sqrt{3}$$

∴ the solution set is $\{-2 + \sqrt{3}, -2 - \sqrt{3}\}$.

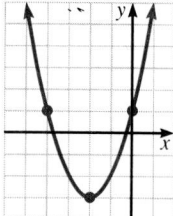

Number of roots: two real-number roots   *Number of x-intercepts:* two

Example 2

Equation: $x^2 + 2x + 1 = 0$

Solution:

$$x = \frac{-(2) \pm \sqrt{(2)^2 - 4(1)(1)}}{2(1)}$$

$$= \frac{-2 \pm \sqrt{0}}{2}$$

$$= -1$$

∴ the solution set is $\{-1\}$.

Number of roots: one real-number root

Related equation: $y = x^2 + 2x + 1$

Graph:

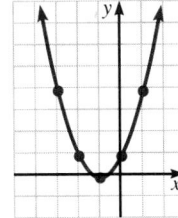

Number of x-intercepts: one

Example 3

Equation: $x^2 - 4x + 7 = 0$

Solution:

$$x = \frac{-(-4) \pm \sqrt{(-4)^2 - 4(1)(7)}}{2(1)}$$

$$= \frac{4 \pm \sqrt{-12}}{2}$$

There is no real-number root since $\sqrt{-12}$ does not represent a real number.

Number of roots: no real-number roots

Related equation: $y = x^2 - 4x + 7$

Graph:

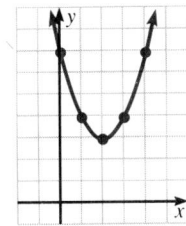

Number of x-intercepts: none

In Examples 1, 2, and 3, the value of $b^2 - 4ac$ in the quadratic formula is shown in color. This value is the key to the number of real roots, as shown in the following chart.

	Value of $b^2 - 4ac$	Number of different real roots of $ax^2 + bx + c = 0$	Number of x-intercepts of the graph of $y = ax^2 + bx + c$
Case 1	positive	2	2
Case 2	zero	1 (a double root)	1
Case 3	negative	0	0

Note that when $b^2 - 4ac$ is negative, there is no real-number root of the equation $ax^2 + bx + c = 0$ because square roots of negative numbers do not exist in the set of real numbers.

Because the value of $b^2 - 4ac$ discriminates, or points out differences, among the three cases shown in the box, it is called the **discriminant** of the quadratic equation.

Quadratic Functions   **573**

2. Graph the related equation.

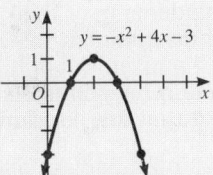

3. Find the number of real-number roots (or x-intercepts). There are 2 real-number roots (or 2 x-intercepts).

Find the value of the discriminant. Then tell how many real-number roots the equation has.

4. $4x^2 + 4x + 1 = 0$

$b^2 - 4ac = (4)^2 - 4(4)(1)$
$= 16 - 16$
$= 0$

∴ there is one (double) real-number root.

5. $2x^2 - 3x + 5 = 0$

$b^2 - 4ac = (-3)^2 - 4(2)(5)$
$= 9 - 40$
$= -31$

∴ there are no real-number roots.

Using the discriminant, determine (a) how many x-intercepts the parabola has, and (b) whether its vertex lies above, below, or on the x-axis.

6. $y = x^2 + 2x - 1$

a. $b^2 - 4ac$
$= (2)^2 - 4(1)(-1) = 8$
∴ there are two x-intercepts.

b. Since the coefficient of x^2 is positive, the graph opens up to intersect the x-axis.
∴ the vertex lies below the x-axis.

Check for Understanding

Oral Exs. 1–8: use after discussing the chart on page 573.

Oral Exercises

The value of the discriminant of an equation is given. Tell how many different real-number roots the equation has.

1. 31 two　　　**2.** -8 none　　　**3.** 0 one　　　**4.** 1 two　　　**5.** 49 two

State the value of the discriminant.

6. $x^2 - 5x + 7 = 0$ -3　　　**7.** $-2x^2 + 3x + 2 = 0$ 25　　　**8.** $6x^2 - 7x - 4 = 0$ 145

Written Exercises

6. -20; none　**9.** 21; two

Write the value of the discriminant of each equation. Then use it to decide how many different real-number roots the equation has. (Do not solve.)

A　**1.** $x^2 - 5x + 4 = 0$ 9; two　　**2.** $r^2 - 3r + 9 = 0$ -27; none　　**3.** $n^2 - 16n + 64 = 0$ 0; one

4. $2z^2 + 5z - 3 = 0$ 49; two　　**5.** $9y^2 - 12y + 4 = 0$ 0; one　　**6.** $3t^2 - 4t + 3 = 0$

7. $4m^2 + 20m + 25 = 0$ 0; one　　**8.** $3a^2 - 2a - 6 = 0$ 76; two　　**9.** $-5b^2 + b + 1 = 0$

10. $-4q^2 + 3q - 2 = 0$　　**11.** $2c^2 - 1.4c + 0.1 = 0$　　**12.** $\frac{1}{2}d^2 - 2d + 2 = 0$
-23; none　　　　　　　　　1.16; two　　　　　　　　　　0; one

Without drawing the graph of the given equation, determine (a) how many x-intercepts the parabola has and (b) whether its vertex lies above, below, or on the x-axis.

Sample　　$y = 5x - x^2 + 6$

Solution　　**a.** The x-intercepts of the graph are the roots of the equation
$$5x - x^2 + 6 = 0, \quad \text{or} \quad -x^2 + 5x + 6 = 0.$$
Its discriminant is $(5)^2 - 4(-1)(6)$, or 49.
The equation has two real-number roots.
The parabola has two x-intercepts.

b. Since the coefficient of x^2 is negative, the parabola opens downward (see page 384). Its vertex must be above the x-axis (otherwise the parabola would not intersect the x-axis in two points).

B　**13.** $y = x^2 - 5x + 5$ two; below　　**14.** $y = -x^2 + 3x + 6$ two; above　　**15.** $y = x^2 + 16 - 8x$ one; on

16. $y = 2x^2 + 4x + 3$ none; above　　**17.** $y = 7x + 2 - 3x^2$ two; above　　**18.** $y = 4x^2 + 2x - 1$ two; below

C　**19.** Find k so that the equation $9x^2 + 12x + k = 0$ has one real-number (double) root. 4

20. Find k so that the equation $4x^2 + 12kx + 9 = 0$ has one real-number (double) root. $-1, 1$

574　　*Chapter 12*

Mixed Review Exercises

Simplify. Assume no denominator equals zero.

1. $\dfrac{\sqrt{3}-3}{\sqrt{6}} \cdot \dfrac{\sqrt{2}-\sqrt{6}}{2}$

2. $\sqrt{\dfrac{12c^3}{5}} \cdot \sqrt{\dfrac{3c^5}{20}}$ $\dfrac{3c^4}{5}$

3. $6\sqrt{8}-15\sqrt{2}+\sqrt{18}$ 0

4. $\dfrac{2x+14}{x^3+8x^2+7x} \cdot \dfrac{2}{x^2+x}$

5. $\dfrac{b}{b+1}+\dfrac{5}{4b+4}$ $\dfrac{4b+5}{4(b+1)}$

6. $(6.2 \cdot 10^4)(8.1 \cdot 10^3)$ 5.022×10^8

Find the vertex and the axis of symmetry of the graph of each equation.

7. $y=4x^2$ $(0, 0)$; $x = 0$

8. $y=x^2+10x+25$ $(-5, 0)$; $x = -5$

9. $y=2x^2+3$ $(0, 3)$; $x = 0$

10. $y=-x^2+9x-3$ $\left(4\frac{1}{2}, 17\frac{1}{4}\right)$; $x = 4\frac{1}{2}$

11. $y=6-5x+\frac{1}{3}x^2$ $\left(7\frac{1}{2}, -12\frac{3}{4}\right)$; $x = 7\frac{1}{2}$

12. $y=-2x^2+3x$ $\left(\frac{3}{4}, 1\frac{1}{8}\right)$; $x = \frac{3}{4}$

Computer Exercises
For students with some programming experience

Write a BASIC program that computes the value of the discriminant of a quadratic equation $AX^2 + BX + C = 0$, where the values of A, B, and C are entered with INPUT statements. The program should then report the number of real roots of the equation. Run the program for the following equations.

1. $2x^2-3x-1=0$ 2

2. $4x^2+28x+49=0$ 1 double root

3. $x^2-x+1=0$ 0

Self-Test 1

Vocabulary   perfect square (p. 562)
completing the square (p. 564)
quadratic formula (p. 567)

x-intercept (p. 572)
discriminant (p. 573)

Solve.

1. $6x^2=54$ $\{-3, 3\}$

2. $(x-3)^2=7$ $\{3 \pm \sqrt{7}\}$

Obj. 12-1, p. 561

Solve by completing the square.

3. $a^2-12a+35=0$ $\{5, 7\}$

4. $x^2-6x-16=0$ $\{-2, 8\}$

Obj. 12-2, p. 564

Solve by using the quadratic formula.

5. $2x^2-3x-2=0$ $\left\{2, -\frac{1}{2}\right\}$

6. $t^2-3t-6=0$ $\left\{\dfrac{3 \pm \sqrt{33}}{2}\right\}$

Obj. 12-3, p. 567

Give the number of real roots.

7. $2y^2-2y+8=0$ none

8. $c^2-c+3=0$ none

Obj. 12-4, p. 572

Check your answers with those at the back of the book.

Quadratic Functions   **575**

Supplementary Materials
Study Guide   pp. 209–210
Practice Master   74
Computer Activity   36
Resource Book   p. 138

Using a Computer

You may wish to have students with BASIC programming experience write a computer program using the discriminant. The program should take the coefficients of a quadratic equation as input values and output the number of real-number roots.

Quick Quiz

Solve.

1. $5c^2=180$ $\{-6, 6\}$

2. $(y-3)^2=12$
$\{3+2\sqrt{3}, 3-2\sqrt{3}\}$

Solve by completing the square.

3. $a^2-14a+13=0$ $\{13, 1\}$

4. $x^2+4x-12=0$ $\{2, -6\}$

Solve by using the quadratic formula.

5. $2m^2+5m-1=0$
$\left\{\dfrac{-5+\sqrt{33}}{4}, \dfrac{-5-\sqrt{33}}{4}\right\}$

6. $x^2-4x-2=0$
$\{2+\sqrt{6}, 2-\sqrt{6}\}$

Give the number of real roots.

7. $3n^2-4n+1=0$ two

8. $y^2-2y+4=0$ none

Using Quadratic Equations

12-5 Methods of Solution

Objective   To choose the best method for solving a quadratic equation.

You have learned four methods for solving quadratic equations. Although the quadratic formula can be used to solve any quadratic equation in the form $ax^2 + bx + c = 0$, one of the other methods may be easier. Here are some guidelines to help you decide which method to use.

Methods for Solving a Quadratic Equation

Method	When to Use the Method
1. Using the quadratic formula	1. If an equation is in the form $ax^2 + bx + c = 0$, especially if you use a calculator.
2. Factoring	2. If an equation is in the form $ax^2 + bx = 0$, or if the factors are easily seen.
3. Using the property of square roots of equal numbers	3. If an equation is in the form $ax^2 + c = 0$.
4. Completing the square	4. If an equation is in the form $x^2 + bx + c = 0$ and b is an even number.

Example   Solve each quadratic equation using the most appropriate method.

a. $12x^2 - 108 = 0$ **b.** $4x^2 - 12x + 7 = 0$
c. $4t^2 - 56t = 0$ **d.** $n^2 + 8n - 2 = 0$

Solution   **a.** $12x^2 - 108 = 0$
$$12x^2 = 108$$
$$x^2 = 9$$
$$x = \pm 3$$
∴ the solution set is $\{3, -3\}$.   **Answer**

$\left\{\begin{array}{l}\text{Use the property of square} \\ \text{roots of equal numbers,} \\ \text{since the equation has} \\ \text{the form } ax^2 + c = 0.\end{array}\right.$

b. $4x^2 - 12x + 7 = 0$
$$x = \frac{-(-12) \pm \sqrt{(-12)^2 - 4(4)(7)}}{2(4)}$$
$$= \frac{12 \pm \sqrt{32}}{8} = \frac{12 \pm 4\sqrt{2}}{8} = \frac{3 \pm \sqrt{2}}{2}$$
∴ the solution set is $\left\{\frac{3 + \sqrt{2}}{2}, \frac{3 - \sqrt{2}}{2}\right\}$.   **Answer**

$\left\{\begin{array}{l}\text{Use the quadratic formula,} \\ \text{since the equation has the} \\ \text{form } ax^2 + bx + c = 0.\end{array}\right.$

c. $4t^2 - 56t = 0$ Form: $ax^2 + bx = 0$

$4t(t - 14) = 0$ Factor.

$4t = 0$ or $t - 14 = 0$

$t = 0$ or $t = 14$

$\therefore$ the solution set is $\{0, 14\}$.   **Answer**

d. $n^2 + 8n - 2 = 0$ Form: $x^2 + bx + c = 0$

$n^2 + 8n = 2$ Complete the square.

$n^2 + 8n + 16 = 2 + 16$

$(n + 4)^2 = 18$

$n + 4 = \pm\sqrt{18}$

$n = -4 \pm 3\sqrt{2}$

$\therefore$ the solution set is $\{-4 + 3\sqrt{2}, -4 - 3\sqrt{2}\}$.   **Answer**

Oral Exercises

s = the property of square roots of equal numbers   f = factoring
q = the quadratic formula   c = completing the square

State which method you would use to solve each quadratic equation. Answers may vary.

1. $x^2 + 5x - 6 = 0$ f
2. $x^2 - 2x = 1$ c
3. $11x^2 = 44$ s

4. $8x^2 + 11x = 0$ f
5. $x^2 + 7x + 2 = 0$ q
6. $3x^2 - 5x = 4$ q

7. $x^2 + 6x = 5$ c
8. $2x^2 + 7x + 3 = 0$ f
9. $5x^2 - 20x = 0$ f

10. $(x - 2)^2 = 7$ s
11. $x^2 - 8x + 1 = 3$ c
12. $4x^2 - 2x - 3 = 0$ q

13. Explain why the quadratic formula can be used to solve all quadratic equations. Any quadratic equation can be expressed in the form $ax^2 + bx + c = 0$.   .

Written Exercises

A   **1–12.** Solve the quadratic equations given in Oral Exercises 1–12. Write the answers in simplest radical form.

Solve each quadratic equation by using the most appropriate method. Write irrational answers in simplest radical form.

13. $5x^2 + 19x = 4$ $\left\{\frac{1}{5}, -4\right\}$ **14.** $x^2 - 8x = 11$ $\{4 \pm 3\sqrt{3}\}$ **15.** $3x^2 = 2x + 7$ $\left\{\frac{1 \pm \sqrt{22}}{3}\right\}$

16. $\frac{2x^2}{3} + \frac{3x}{4} = 1$ $\left\{\frac{-9 \pm \sqrt{465}}{16}\right\}$ **17.** $\frac{(y + 3)^2}{4} = 5$ $\{-3 \pm 2\sqrt{5}\}$ **18.** $0.75x^2 - 0.3x + 0.03 = 0$ $\left\{\frac{1}{5}\right\}$

19. $1.4x^2 - 0.7x = 0.2$ $\left\{\frac{7 \pm \sqrt{161}}{28}\right\}$ **20.** $\frac{1}{3x} = \frac{2x - 3}{2}$ $\left\{\frac{9 \pm \sqrt{129}}{12}\right\}$ **21.** $\frac{4x - 3}{2x - 3} = \frac{5x - 3}{x + 1}$ $\left\{\frac{2}{3}, 3\right\}$

B   **22.** $5x(x - 3) + 4(x + 4) = 31 - 7x^2$ $\left\{-\frac{3}{4}, \frac{5}{3}\right\}$ **23.** $2x(x - 3) + 7(x^2 - 1) = 2$ $\left\{\frac{1 \pm \sqrt{10}}{3}\right\}$

24. $(x + 3)^2 + 6(x + 3) = 16$ $\{-1, -11\}$ **25.** $9(x - 4)^2 + 4(x - 4) = 0$ $\left\{\frac{32}{9}, 4\right\}$

26. $(3x + 2)(x - 1) - 13 = 2x(2 - x)$ $\left\{\frac{1 \pm \sqrt{13}}{2}\right\}$ **27.** $(3x - 5)^2 = (8x + 3)^2$ $\left\{-\frac{8}{5}, \frac{2}{11}\right\}$

Quadratic Functions   **577**

---

4. $r^2 + 9r + 8 = 0$ Method 2
$(r + 8)(r + 1) = 0$
$r = -8$ or $r = -1$; $\{-8, -1\}$

Check for Understanding

Oral Exs. 1–13: use after discussion of methods.

Thinking Skills

Students should be able to *analyze* a quadratic equation and then decide which method to use for solving.

Guided Practice

Solve each quadratic equation by using the most appropriate method. Write irrational answers in simplest radical form.

1. $10x^2 = 90$ $\{\pm 3\}$

2. $x^2 + 7x - 8 = 0$ $\{-8, 1\}$

3. $7x^2 + 3x - 1 = 0$
$\left\{\frac{-3 \pm \sqrt{37}}{14}\right\}$

4. $x^2 + 16x = 0$ $\{0, -16\}$

5. $\frac{2x^2}{9} + \frac{x}{6} = \frac{1}{2}$ $\left\{\frac{-3 \pm 3\sqrt{17}}{8}\right\}$

Summarizing the Lesson

Ask students to list the four methods for solving quadratic equations and to explain when to use each.

Suggested Assignments

Average
   577/1–27 odd
S 578/Mixed Review
R 575/Self-Test 1

Maximum
   577/1–31 odd
S 578/Mixed Review
R 575/Self-Test 1

Additional Answers
Written Exercises

1. $\{-6, 1\}$

2. $\{1 \pm \sqrt{2}\}$

(continued)

Solve. Be sure that you have found all real roots of each equation. Write irrational answers in simplest form. (*Hint:* Substitute y for x^2.)

C 28. $9x^4 - 14x^2 + 5 = 0 \left\{\pm\dfrac{\sqrt{5}}{3}, \pm 1\right\}$ 29. $4x^4 + 21x^2 - 18 = 0 \left\{\pm\dfrac{\sqrt{3}}{2}\right\}$

30. $3x^4 - 7x^2 = 0 \left\{0, \pm\dfrac{\sqrt{21}}{3}\right\}$ 31. $9x^4 - 64 = 0 \left\{\pm\dfrac{2\sqrt{6}}{3}\right\}$

Mixed Review Exercises

Evaluate if $x = 1$, $y = 8$, and $z = -9$. Write irrational expressions in simplest radical form.

1. $\pm\sqrt{y^2 - 4xz} \;\pm 10$ 2. $-\sqrt{y^2 + 4zx} \;-2\sqrt{7}$ 3. $\sqrt{z^2 - 4xy} \;7$

4. $\sqrt{z^2 + 4xy} \;\sqrt{113}$ 5. $\pm\sqrt{x^2 - 4yz} \;\pm 17$ 6. $\sqrt{x^2 + 4yz}$ no real-number sol.

Solve. Write irrational roots in simplest radical form. 7. $\left\{-\dfrac{3}{2}, \dfrac{5}{2}\right\}$ 8. $\left\{-7, \dfrac{11}{2}\right\}$

7. $4x^2 - 4x - 15 = 0$ 8. $2d^2 + 3d - 77 = 0$ 9. $2(x + 4)(x + 7) = (2x + 1)(x - 9) - 3$ $\left\{-\dfrac{68}{39}\right\}$

10. $c^2 - 4c - 2 = 0$ 11. $3p^2 - 4p + 1 = 0$ 12. $12y^2 + 24y = 5$

$\{2 \pm \sqrt{6}\}$ $\left\{\dfrac{1}{3}, 1\right\}$ $\left\{\dfrac{-6 \pm \sqrt{51}}{6}\right\}$

Biographical Note / *Albert Einstein*

Albert Einstein was born in Ulm, Germany in 1879. He attended school in Munich and went to college in Switzerland. As he excelled only in mathematics and science, Einstein was unable to secure a teaching position after his graduation in 1901 and ended up working as a minor official in the Swiss patent office. The job, however, left him time to work on his scientific studies.

In 1905 Einstein published three important papers that were to have a far-reaching effect on science. One paper helped to establish the quantum, or particle, theory of light, and for this research Einstein was awarded the 1921 Nobel Prize in physics. A second paper contained equations that described molecular motion and that could be used to determine the size of molecules.

However, it was Einstein's paper on the special theory of relativity that made him famous. This theory replaced Isaac Newton's theories of the universe when dealing with objects whose speeds

approached that of light.

Einstein became a professor at the University of Zurich. He eventually took a position with the Institute of Advanced Studies in Princeton, New Jersey. At the time of his death in 1955, Einstein, like Newton, left science greatly different from the way it was before his work.

12-6 Solving Problems Involving Quadratic Equations

Objective   To use quadratic equations to solve problems.

Example   The parks commission wants a new rectangular sign with an area of 25 m² for the visitor center. The length of the sign is to be 4 m longer than the width. To the nearest tenth of a meter, what will be the length and the width of the sign?

Solution

Step 1 The problem asks for the length and width of the sign.

Step 2 Let x = the width in meters.
Then $x + 4$ = the length in meters.

Step 3 Use the formula for the area of a rectangle to write an equation.
$$x(x + 4) = 25$$

Step 4 Solve $x(x + 4) = 25$.
$$x^2 + 4x = 25$$
$$x^2 + 4x + 4 = 25 + 4 \qquad \text{Complete the square.}$$
$$(x + 2)^2 = 29$$
$$x + 2 = \pm\sqrt{29}$$
$$x = -2 \pm \sqrt{29}$$

 Use your calculator or the table of square roots on page 682 to approximate the roots to the nearest tenth:
$$-2 + \sqrt{29} \approx -2 + 5.39 = 3.39 \approx 3.4$$
$$-2 - \sqrt{29} \approx -2 - 5.39 = -7.39 \approx -7.4$$

Step 5 Discard the negative root since a negative length has no meaning.

Check 3.4:
$$3.4(3.4 + 4) \stackrel{?}{=} 25$$
$$3.4(7.4) \stackrel{?}{=} 25$$
$$25.16 \approx 25 \quad \checkmark$$

The numbers are approximately equal, so the approximate solution is correct.

∴ the width of the sign is 3.4 m and the length is 7.4 m.   *Answer*

Teaching Suggestions p. T139
Reading Algebra p. T139
Suggested Extensions p. T140

Warm-Up Exercises

Arrange in order the five steps used to solve word problems.

a. Reread problem and write equations.

b. Check results with the problem. Give answer.

c. Choose a variable and use it with given facts to describe the unknown in the problem.

d. Read the problem, deciding what is given and what is asked. Draw a sketch if possible.

e. Solve the equation and find the unknowns.

Order of steps is d, c, a, e, b.

Motivating the Lesson

Tell students that sometimes word problems involve solving quadratic equations. Today's lesson and related Problems provide practice with a variety of these.

  Using a Calculator

A calculator is helpful for estimating irrational square roots. Problems 1–15 on pp. 580–581 are appropriate for using a calculator.

Chalkboard Examples

An altitude of a triangle measures 2 cm less than twice the length of the base. If the triangle has an area of 6 cm², find the length of the base and the altitude. (Steps 2–4 are given)
Let x = the base in cm. Then $2x - 2$ = the altitude in cm.
(continued)

$A = \frac{1}{2}bh$

$6 = \frac{1}{2}x(2x - 2)$

$6 = x^2 - x$

$0 = x^2 - x - 6$

$0 = (x - 3)(x + 2)$

$x = 3$ or -2

-2 cannot be a solution.

∴ the base is 3 cm and the altitude is 4 cm.

Problem Solving Strategy

Students must *consider the reasonableness* of their answers in order to eliminate, when necessary, unrealistic solutions.

Guided Practice

Solve. Give irrational roots to the nearest tenth.

1. The length of a rectangular table is 5 in. more than twice its width. Its area is 1950 in.². Find its dimensions.
   length 65 in., width 30 in.

2. The sum of a number and its square is 156. Find the number.
   12 or −13

3. The altitude of a triangle is 9 cm less than the base. The area is 143 cm². What are the altitude and the base? 13 cm, 22 cm

4. If the side of a square is increased by 3 m, its area is 121 m². Find the length of a side of the original square. 8 m

Problems

Solve. Give irrational roots to the nearest tenth. Use your calculator or the table of square roots on page 682 as necessary.

A

1. The width of a rectangular park is 5 m shorter than its length. If the area of the park is 300 m², find the length and the width. 20 m, 15 m

2. The length of a rectangle is 3 times the width. The area of the rectangle is 75 cm². Find the length and the width. 15 cm, 5 cm

3. The sum of a number and its square is 56. Find the number. 7 or −8

4. The difference of a number and its square is 182. Find the number. 14 or −13

5. The length of the base of a triangle is 4 times its altitude. If the area of the triangle is 162 cm², find the altitude.

   (*Hint:* Area of a triangle = $\frac{1}{2}$ × base × height.) 9 cm

6. The altitude of a triangle is 5 m less than its base. The area of the triangle is 42 m². Find the base. 12 m

7. If the sides of a square are increased by 3 cm, its area becomes 100 cm². Find the length of the sides of the original square. 7 cm

8. Holly has a rectangular garden that measures 12 m by 14 m. She wants to increase the area to 255 m² by increasing the width and length by the same amount. What will be the dimensions of the new garden? length 17 m, width 15 m

9. Cindy and Olaf leave the same point at the same time. Cindy is bicycling west at a rate of 2 mi/h faster than Olaf, who is traveling south. After one hour, they are 10 mi apart. How fast is each person traveling? (*Hint:* Use the Pythagorean theorem.) Olaf, 6 mi/h; Cindy, 8 mi/h

B

10. Working alone, Colleen can paint a house in 2 h less than James. Working together, they can paint the house in 10 h. How long would it take James to paint the house by himself? 21.0 h

11. Together Maria and Johannes can pick a bushel of apples in 16 min. Maria takes 4 min more to pick a bushel than Johannes does. Find the time it takes each person to pick a bushel of apples alone. Maria, 34.1 min; Johannes, 30.1 min

12. The Computer Club went on a field trip to a computer museum. The trip cost $240 to be paid for equally by each club member. The day before the trip, 4 students decided not to go. This increased the cost by $2 per student. How many students went to the computer museum? 20

13. The Math Club bought a $72 calculator for club use. If there had been 2 more students in the club, each would have had to contribute 50 cents less. How many students were in the club? 16

14. Judith can ride her bike 2 mi/h faster than Kelly. Judith takes 48 min less to travel 50 mi than Kelly does. What is each person's speed in miles per hour? Judith, 12.2 mi/h; Kelly, 10.2 mi/h

C **15.** Pipe A can fill a tank in 4 h. Pipe B can fill the tank in 9 h less than the time it takes pipe C, a drain pipe, to empty the tank. When all 3 pipes are open, it takes 2 h to fill the tank. How much time is required for pipe C to empty the tank if pipes A and B are closed? 12 h

Mixed Review Exercises

Solve.

1. $\dfrac{\sqrt{n}}{3} = \dfrac{\sqrt{5}}{1}$ {45}

2. $\dfrac{\sqrt{x-3}}{6} = \dfrac{3}{2}$ {84}

3. $\dfrac{\sqrt{5t}}{8} = \dfrac{1}{4}$ $\left\{\dfrac{4}{5}\right\}$

4. $\dfrac{13}{7} = \dfrac{20}{m}$ $\left\{10\dfrac{10}{13}\right\}$

5. $m^2 = 14m - 45$ {5, 9}

6. $y - \dfrac{7}{y+2} - \dfrac{3y-1}{y+2} = 5$ {8}

In Exercises 7–9, (x_1, y_1) and (x_2, y_2) are ordered pairs of the same direct variation. Find the missing value.

7. $x_1 = 1,\ y_1 = 3$
   $x_2 = 4,\ y_2 = \underline{\ ?\ }$ 12

8. $x_1 = 10,\ y_1 = \underline{\ ?\ }$ 25
   $x_2 = 2,\ y_2 = 5$

9. $x_1 = 24,\ y_1 = 64$
   $x_2 = \dfrac{\underline{\ ?\ }}{3},\ y_2 = 8$

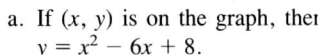

Extra / *Quadratic Inequalities*

The graph of the quadratic function $y = x^2 - 6x + 8$ can be used to illustrate the solutions of the following:

   (1) $x^2 - 6x + 8 = 0$
   (2) $x^2 - 6x + 8 > 0$
   (3) $x^2 - 6x + 8 < 0$

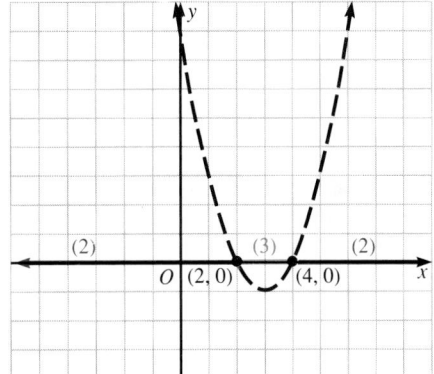

The solution set of quadratic equation **(1)** is {**2, 4**}. These two values of x are called the *zeros* of the quadratic function.

   To solve quadratic inequality (2), you reason as follows:

a. If (x, y) is on the graph, then $y = x^2 - 6x + 8$.

b. If (x, y) is above the x-axis, then $y > 0$.

c. Therefore, if (x, y) is on the graph *and* above the x-axis, then $y = x^2 - 6x + 8 > 0$.

d. Therefore, the solution set for **(2)** is {$x < 2$ or $x > 4$} because these values of x give points that are on the graph above the x-axis.

Similar reasoning shows that the solution set for (3) is {$2 < x < 4$} because these values of x give points on the graph below the x-axis.

Quadratic Functions **581**

Summarizing the Lesson

Tell students that in today's lesson, their skills for solving quadratic equations were applied to word problems.

Suggested Assignments

Average
   580/*P*: 1–13 odd
   S 581/Mixed Review

Maximum
   580/*P*: 1–15 odd
   S 581/Mixed Review

Supplementary Materials

Study Guide   pp. 213–214
Practice Master   75
Computer Activity   37
Resource Book   p. 139

1.

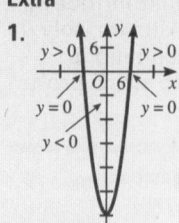

2.

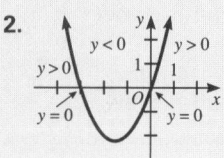

3.

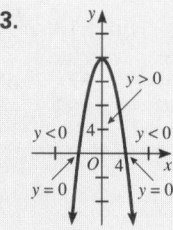

4.

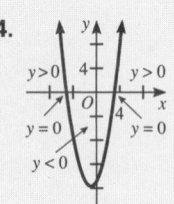

5.

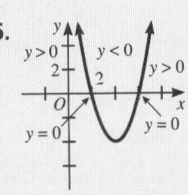

6.

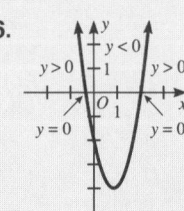

Example　Solve for x.

(1) $x^2 + 2x + 1 = 0$

(2) $x^2 + 2x + 1 > 0$

(3) $x^2 + 2x + 1 < 0$

Solution　Use the graph of $y = x^2 + 2x + 1$.

(1) Factor the quadratic equation
$x^2 + 2x + 1 = 0$.
Since $(x + 1)(x + 1) = 0$,
$x = -1$.

(2) Since the graph lies above the
x-axis for all x except -1,
$x^2 + 2x + 1 > 0$ for all $x \neq -1$.

(3) There are no values of x for which
$x^2 + 2x + 1 < 0$, since the graph
does not go below the x-axis.

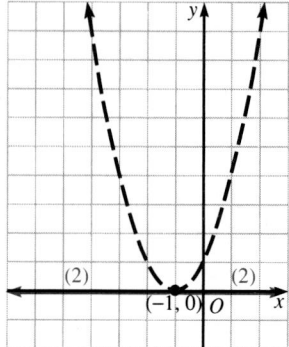

Exercises

Graph each quadratic equation. Solve for x when (1) $y = 0$, (2) $y > 0$, and (3) $y < 0$.

1. $y = x^2 - 36$ 　　　**2.** $y = 3x + x^2$ 　　　**3.** $y = 16 - x^2$

4. $y = x^2 + 2x - 15$ 　**5.** $y = x^2 - 8x + 12$ 　**6.** $y = 3x^2 - 5x - 2$

Find the values of x for which each expression represents a real number.

7. $\sqrt{x^2 - 3x}$
$x \leq 0$ or $x \geq 3$

8. $\sqrt{x^2 + 4x + 3}$
$x \leq -3$ or $x \geq -1$

9. $\sqrt{x^2 - 10x + 21}$
$x \leq 3$ or $x \geq 7$

Self-Test 2

Solve the following quadratic equations using the most convenient method.

1. $3(x + 2)^2 = 12 \{-4, 0\}$ 　　**2.** $2x^2 + 6x + 3 = 0$ $\left\{\dfrac{-3 \pm \sqrt{3}}{2}\right\}$ 　　Obj. 12-5, p. 576

3. $x^2 - 10x = 20 \{5 \pm 3\sqrt{5}\}$ 　　**4.** $3x^2 + 9x = 0 \{-3, 0\}$

Solve.

5. The length of a rectangle is twice the width. The area of the
rectangle is 200 cm². Find the length and the width. 20 cm, 10 cm 　　Obj. 12-6, p. 579

6. The perimeter of a rectangular wading pool is 172 m and its
area is 1800 m². Find the length and width of the pool. 50 m, 36 m

Check your answers with those at the back of the book.

Application / Boyle's Gas Law

Air and other gases have characteristics of temperature, pressure, and volume much the same as do liquids, such as water. Air temperature is measured in degrees, volume in cubic centimeters or liters, and pressure in millimeters.

Robert Boyle, a seventeenth-century English scientist, investigated many properties of air and gases. He conducted experiments to see how the pressure of a gas in an enclosed space is related to its volume. His discovery is used today in the modern internal combustion engine and in a simple pump for inflating basketballs or tires.

Boyle observed that pressure on a confined gas reduces its volume. In fact, he found that with a constant temperature, the volume of a gas varies inversely with the pressure exerted on it. This statement, known as Boyle's Law, can be written in these two ways.

$$pV = k, \text{ where } k \text{ is a constant,}$$
$$V \text{ is the volume, and}$$
$$p \text{ is the pressure}$$

or

$$pV = p'V', \text{ where } p' \text{ and } V' \text{ are the new}$$
$$\text{pressure and the new volume,}$$
$$\text{respectively.}$$

Example A gas has a volume of 600 mL at a pressure of 760 mm. What is the volume of the gas at a pressure of 800 mm?

Solution
$$pV = p'V'$$
$$760 \times 600 = 800V'$$
$$\frac{760 \times 600}{800} = V'$$
$$570 = V'$$
$$\therefore \text{ the volume is 570 mL.}$$

Exercises

1. A certain gas has a volume of 420 cm³ at a pressure of 720 mm. What will its volume be if the pressure is increased to 840 mm? 360 cm³

2. A gas kept at 760 mm of pressure occupies 2 L. What pressure must be exerted for the volume to decrease to 1.9 L? 800 mm

3. A certain gas has a volume of 500 cm³ at a pressure of 750 mm. If the pressure is decreased to 625 mm, what is the resulting volume? 600 cm³

4. A gas occupies 2 m³ of space at 760 mm of pressure. It is compressed to 1 m³ of space. What is the new pressure? 1520 mm

5. An underinflated balloon contains 9 m³ of helium when the pressure is 760 mm. What is the volume of the balloon when it reaches an altitude where the pressure is 304 mm? 22.5 m³

Quadratic Functions **583**

Define each of the following terms and give two examples of each. You may use the Glossary to help you.

1. **Direct variation**
   A function defined by an equation of the form $y = kx$, where k is a nonzero constant. Possible examples: $y = 3x$; $y = -\frac{1}{2}x$

2. **Inverse variation**
   A function defined by an equation of the form $xy = k$, where k is a nonzero constant. Possible examples: $xy = 8$; $xy = -12$

3. **Constant of proportionality**
   The constant k in the equations for variation $y = kx$ and $xy = k$; also called constant of variation. Possible examples: in $y = 3x$, $k = 3$; in $xy = -12$, $k = -12$.

Motivating the Lesson

Point out that the area of a square can be found by multiplying $\frac{1}{2}$ times the square of the length of the diagonal: $A = \frac{1}{2}d^2$. As d increases (or decreases), so does the value of A. Today's lesson will explore this kind of relationship.

Variation

12-7 Direct and Inverse Variation Involving Squares

Objective To use quadratic direct variation and inverse variation as a square in problem solving.

In Lessons 8-9 and 8-10 you learned about direct and inverse variation. In the world around us, there are many examples in which a quantity varies either directly or inversely *as the square* of another quantity. For example, the surface area of a sphere varies directly as the square of the radius: $S = 4\pi r^2$. This is an example of a *quadratic direct variation*.

A **quadratic direct variation** is a function defined by an equation of the form

$$y = kx^2, \text{ where } k \text{ is a nonzero constant.}$$

You say that y *varies directly as* x^2 or that y *is directly proportional to* x^2.

If (x_1, y_1) and (x_2, y_2) are ordered pairs of the same quadratic variation, and neither x_1 nor x_2 is zero, then

$$\frac{y_1}{x_1^2} = \frac{y_2}{x_2^2}.$$

Example 1 Given that a varies directly as the square of d, and $a = 45$ when $d = 3$, find the value of d when $a = 60$.

Solution 1 Use $a = kd^2$.
$$45 = k(3)^2$$
$$45 = 9k$$
$$5 = k$$
$$\therefore \quad a = 5d^2$$
For $a = 60$:
$$60 = 5d^2$$
$$12 = d^2$$
$$\pm\sqrt{12} = d$$
$$\pm 2\sqrt{3} = d \quad \textbf{Answer}$$

Solution 2 Use $\dfrac{a_1}{d_1^2} = \dfrac{a_2}{d_2^2}$.
$$\frac{45}{3^2} = \frac{60}{d_2^2}$$
$$\frac{45}{9} = \frac{60}{d_2^2}$$
$$45d_2^2 = 540$$
$$d_2^2 = 12$$
$$d_2 = \pm\sqrt{12}$$
$$d_2 = \pm 2\sqrt{3} \quad \textbf{Answer}$$

Remember to examine your solution to see if each one makes sense. For example, if d represents a length, you can discard the negative solution since a negative length has no meaning.

584   *Chapter 12*

The intensity of sound *varies inversely as the square* of the distance of a listener from the source of sound. Therefore, if you halve the distance between yourself and a trumpeter, the intensity of the sound that reaches your ears will be quadrupled.

An **inverse variation as the square** is a function defined by an equation of the form

$$x^2y = k, \text{ where } k \text{ is a nonzero constant,}$$

or

$$y = \frac{k}{x^2}, \text{ where } x \neq 0.$$

You say that y *varies inversely as* x^2 or y *is inversely proportional to* x^2.

If (x_1, y_1) and (x_2, y_2) are ordered pairs of the function defined by $x^2y = k$, then

$$x_1^2y_1 = x_2^2y_2.$$

Example 2 Given that h varies inversely as the square of r, and that $h = 2$ when $r = 3$, find the value of r when $h = \frac{3}{10}$.

Solution 1 Use $h = \frac{k}{r^2}$.

$$2 = \frac{k}{3^2}$$
$$18 = k$$
$$\therefore \quad h = \frac{18}{r^2}$$

For $h = \frac{3}{10}$:

$$\frac{3}{10} = \frac{18}{r^2}$$
$$3r^2 = 180$$
$$r^2 = 60$$
$$r = \pm\sqrt{60}$$
$$= \pm2\sqrt{15} \quad \textbf{Answer}$$

Solution 2 Use $r_1^2h_1 = r_2^2h_2$.

$$3^2(2) = r_2^2\left(\frac{3}{10}\right)$$
$$18 = \frac{3r_2^2}{10}$$
$$3r_2^2 = 180$$
$$r_2^2 = 60$$
$$r_2 = \pm\sqrt{60}$$
$$= \pm2\sqrt{15} \quad \textbf{Answer}$$

Remember that in a particular situation you must examine each root to see if it makes sense.

Solve.

1. If y varies directly as x^2 and $x = 6$ when $y = 24$, find y when $x = 9$.

Solution 1

$$y = kx^2$$
$$24 = k(6)^2$$
$$24 = 36k$$
$$\frac{2}{3} = k$$
$$\therefore y = \frac{2}{3}x^2$$

For $x = 9$:
$$y = \frac{2}{3}(9)^2$$
$$= 54$$

Solution 2

$$\frac{y_1}{x_1^2} = \frac{y_2}{x_2^2}$$
$$\frac{24}{6^2} = \frac{y_2}{9^2}$$
$$\frac{24}{36} = \frac{y_2}{81}$$
$$y_2 = \frac{81(24)}{36}$$
$$= 54$$

2. If m varies inversely as the square of t, and $m = 45$ when $t = 1.2$, find the value of t when $m = 20$.

Solution 1

$$m = \frac{k}{t^2}$$
$$45 = \frac{k}{(1.2)^2}$$
$$64.8 = k$$
$$\therefore m = \frac{64.8}{t^2}$$

For $m = 20$:
$$20 = \frac{64.8}{t^2}$$
$$20t^2 = 64.8$$
$$t^2 = 3.24$$
$$t = \pm\sqrt{3.24}$$
$$= \pm1.8$$

Solution 2

$$m_1t_1^2 = m_2t_2^2$$
$$45(1.2)^2 = 20t_2^2$$
$$64.8 = 20t_2^2$$
$$t_2^2 = 3.24$$
$$t_2 = \pm\sqrt{3.24}$$
$$= \pm1.8$$

Guided Practice

Solve.

1. The distance an object falls in a vacuum is directly proportional to the square of the time it has been falling. After 4 s, a ball has fallen 576 ft. How long will it take to fall 1296 ft? 6 s

2. The area of a circle varies directly as the square of its radius. If a circle has a 5 ft radius and an approximate area of 78.5 ft^2, what is the approximate area of a circle with radius of 8 ft? 200.96 ft^2

3. The time needed to fill a tank varies inversely as the square of the radius of the hose. If a hose of radius 4 cm takes 2.5 min to fill the tank, how long will it take to fill the same tank with a hose of 5 cm radius? 1.6 min

Oral Exercises

Translate each statement into a formula. Use k as the constant of variation where needed.

1. The kinetic energy, e, of a moving body varies directly as the square of its velocity, v. $e = kv^2$

2. The force, F, between two point charges of static electricity is inversely proportional to the square of the distance, d, between them. $Fd^2 = k$, or $F = \dfrac{k}{d^2}$

3. The weight, w, of an object is inversely proportional to the square of its distance, d, from the center of Earth. $wd^2 = k$, or $w = \dfrac{k}{d^2}$

4. The area, A, of the surface of a steel ball is directly proportional to the square of the diameter, d, of the ball. $A = kd^2$

5. The time, t, required to fill a pool varies inversely as the square of the radius, r, of the hose. $tr^2 = k$, or $t = \dfrac{k}{r^2}$

6. The quantity, Q, of heat energy in an electrical circuit is directly proportional to the square of the current, I. $Q = kI^2$

Problems

Solve. Give irrational roots to the nearest tenth. You may wish to use a calculator.

A 1. The amount of material needed to cover a ball is directly proportional to the square of its diameter. A ball with a diameter of 12 cm needs 452 cm^2 of material to cover it. If 1017 cm^2 of material is to be used, what is the diameter of the ball? 18 cm

2. The price of a diamond varies directly as the square of its mass in carats. If a 1.5 carat diamond costs \$2700, find the mass in carats of a diamond that costs \$4800. 2 carats

3. The distance it takes an automobile to stop varies directly as the square of its speed. If the stopping distance for a car traveling at 80 km/h is 175 m, what is the stopping distance for a car traveling at 64 km/h? 112 m

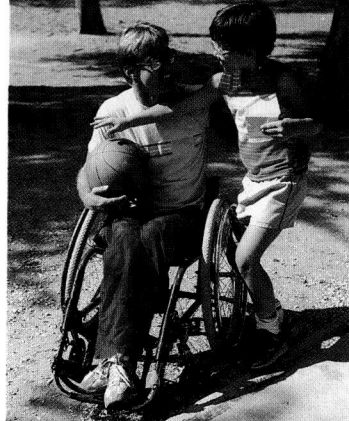

4. The height that a person is above the water is directly proportional to the square of the distance the person can see across the ocean. If the captain of a ship is 4 m above the water, he can see about 30 km across the ocean. How far can the captain see if he is 10 m above the water? 47.4 km

5. The height of a cylinder of a given volume is inversely proportional to the square of the radius. A cylinder of radius 6 cm has a height of 24 cm. What is the radius of a cylinder of equal volume whose height is 96 cm? 3 cm

586   *Chapter 12*

586

6. The brightness of the light on an object varies inversely as the square of the distance from the object to the light source. At a distance of 1.2 m from a light source, the brightness on a book page was measured at 25 lm/m² (lumens per square meter). If the page were moved 0.4 m closer to the light source, what would the brightness measure? 56.25 lm/m²

7. The length of a pendulum varies directly as the square of the time in seconds that it takes to swing from one side to the other. If it takes a 100 cm pendulum 1 s to swing from one side to the other, how many seconds does it take a 150 cm pendulum to swing? 1.2 s

8. The exposure time needed for a photograph is inversely proportional to the square of the radius of the camera lens. If the lens radius is 1 cm, the exposure time needed is 0.01 s. Find the radius of the lens for an exposure time of 0.0025 s. 2 cm

B 9. The height of a circular cylinder of given volume varies inversely as the square of the radius of the base. How many times greater is the radius of a cylinder 3 m high than the radius of a cylinder 6 m high with the same volume? 1.4 times as great

10. The strength of a radio signal is inversely proportional to the square of the distance from the source of the signal. An observer is 200 m away from a source. She then moves to a position closer to the source. The strength of the signal at the second position is 16 times as strong as at the first position. How far is she from the source of the signal? 50 m

C 11. The volume of a sphere varies directly as the cube of the radius. If the ratio of the radii of two spheres is 4:3, what is the ratio of the volumes of the spheres? 64:27

12. The heat emitted from a star is directly proportional to the fourth power of the surface temperature of the star. If the ratio of the amount of heat emitted from two stars is 16:81, what is the ratio of their surface temperatures? 2:3

Mixed Review Exercises

Solve for the indicated variable. State any restrictions.

1. $3x^2 - 2y = 1$; y $\frac{3x^2 - 1}{2}$

2. $A = \frac{h(b + c)}{2}$; h $\frac{2A}{b + c}$; $b \neq -c$

3. $A = \frac{h(b + c)}{2}$; b $\frac{2A - hc}{h}$; $h \neq 0$

4. $1 - x = ax$; x $\frac{1}{a + 1}$; $a \neq -1$

5. $t = \frac{V - k^2}{g}$; V $k^2 + tg$; $g \neq 0$

6. $Er^2 = k$; r $\pm\frac{\sqrt{kE}}{E}$; $E \neq 0$, $kE \geq 0$

Write an equation, in standard form, of the line passing through the given points.

7. (4, 1), (0, −7) $2x - y = 7$

8. (3, 2), (−6, −4) $2x - 3y = 0$

9. (4, 3), (−4, 7) $x + 2y = 10$

10. (−1, −1), (7, 23) $3x - y = -2$

11. (0, −4), (−12, −6) $x - 6y = 24$

12. (0, −10), (13, −5) $5x - 13y = 130$

Quadratic Functions   **587**

Summarizing the Lesson

Tell students they have learned to use quadratic direct variation and inverse variation involving squares in solving problems. Point out that an equation that represents each type of variation is boxed in their textbooks for easy review. Have them find and read the information.

 Using a Calculator

Some students who succeed in setting up their work correctly for the problems on pages 586–587 may then make errors in arithmetic. The use of calculators can help you focus on those students who need help analyzing the problem.

Thinking Skills

In solving the problems in this lesson, students will need to *evaluate* their solutions to see whether a negative solution makes sense in the problem situation.

Suggested Assignments

Average
  586/*P*: 1–5, 7, 9
S 587/Mixed Review
R 582/Self-Test 2

Maximum
  586/*P*: 1–11 odd
S 587/Mixed Review
R 582/Self-Test 2

Supplementary Materials

Study Guide   pp. 215–216

12-8 Joint and Combined Variation

Objective   To solve problems involving joint variation and combined variation.

If Danalee earns \$750 next summer and puts her earnings into a savings account, the amount of simple interest, I, she will receive depends on her bank's interest rate, r, and on the length of time, t, that she leaves the money in the account. That is:

$$I = 750rt$$

The interest is directly proportional to the product of the rate and the time. This is an example of a *joint variation*.

If a variable varies directly as the product of two or more other variables, the resulting relationship is called a **joint variation.** You can express the relationship in the forms

$$z = kxy, \text{ where } k \text{ is a nonzero constant,}$$

and $\dfrac{z_1}{x_1 y_1} = \dfrac{z_2}{x_2 y_2}.$

You say that z *varies jointly as x and y.*

Example 1   The volume of a right circular cone varies jointly as the height, h, and the square of the radius, r. If $V_1 = 320\pi$, $h_1 = 15$, $r_1 = 8$, $h_2 = 12$, and $r_2 = 16$, find V_2.

Solution

$$\frac{V_1}{h_1 r_1^2} = \frac{V_2}{h_2 r_2^2}$$

$$\frac{320\pi}{15(8)^2} = \frac{V_2}{12(16)^2}$$

$$15(64)V_2 = 12(256)(320\pi)$$

$$V_2 = 1024\pi \quad \textbf{\textit{Answer}}$$

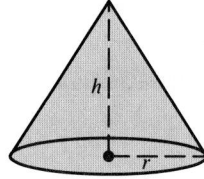

If a variable varies *directly* as one variable and *inversely* as another, the resulting relationship is called a **combined variation.** You can express the relationship in the forms

$$zy = kx \left(\text{or } z = \frac{kx}{y} \right), \text{ where } k \text{ is a nonzero constant,}$$

and $\dfrac{z_1 y_1}{x_1} = \dfrac{z_2 y_2}{x_2}.$

588   *Chapter 12*

Example 2 The power, P, of an electric current varies directly as the square of the voltage, V, and inversely as the resistance, R. If 6 volts applied across a resistance of 3 ohms produces 12 watts of power, how much voltage applied across a resistance of 6 ohms will produce 13.5 watts of power?

Solution Let $P_1 = 12$, $V_1 = 6$, $R_1 = 3$, $P_2 = 13.5$, and $R_2 = 6$. $V_2 = \underline{}$

$$\frac{P_1 R_1}{V_1^2} = \frac{P_2 R_2}{V_2^2}$$

$$\frac{12(3)}{6^2} = \frac{(13.5)(6)}{V_2^2}$$

$$12(3)V_2^2 = 36(13.5)(6)$$

$$V_2^2 = 81$$

$$V_2 = \pm\sqrt{81} = \pm 9$$

Discard the negative root since a negative voltage has no meaning.

∴ the amount of voltage is 9 volts.   **Answer**

Oral Exercises

Translate each statement into a formula. Use k as the constant of variation where needed.

1. T varies jointly as s and p. $T = ksp$

2. V varies directly as d and inversely as t. $Vt = kd$

3. a varies directly as the square of b and inversely as c. $ac = kb^2$

4. Q varies directly as m and inversely as the square of t. $Qt^2 = km$

5. y varies directly as the square of x and inversely as the square of z. $yz^2 = kx^2$

6. V varies jointly with l, w, and h. $V = klwh$

7. The total force, F, of a liquid varies jointly as the area of the surface, A, the depth of liquid, h, and the density, d. $F = kAhd$

8. The volume, V, of a cylinder varies jointly as its height, h, and the square of its radius, r. $V = khr^2$

9. The heat, H, produced by an electric lamp varies jointly as the resistance, R, and the square of the current, C. $H = kRC^2$

10. The pressure, P, of a gas varies directly as its temperature, T, and inversely as its volume, V. $PV = kT$

11. The centrifugal force, F, of an object moving in a circular path is directly proportional to the square of its velocity, v, and inversely proportional to the diameter, d, of its path. $Fd = kv^2$

12. The acceleration, a, of a moving object is directly proportional to the distance, d, it travels and inversely proportional to the square of the time, t, it travels. $at^2 = kd$

Quadratic Functions   **589**

Guided Practice

Solve.

1. x varies directly as y and inversely as z. If $x = 50$ when $y = 75$ and $z = 9$, find x when $y = 2$ and $z = 72$. $\frac{1}{6}$

2. m varies jointly as n and the square of p. If $m = 40$ when $n = 20$ and $p = 2$, find m when $n = 30$ and $p = 3$. 135

3. P varies directly as the square of s and inversely as q. If $P = 50$ when $s = 5$ and $q = 3$, find P when $s = 4$ and $q = 4$. 24

4. The number of persons needed to do a job varies directly as the amount of work to be done and inversely as the time in which the job must be done. If 4 people can wash 5 cars in 1 h, how many people will be needed to wash 200 cars in 8 h? 20 people

Summarizing the Lesson

Tell students they have solved problems involving joint variation and combined variation. Have them express these relationships as equations. Point out that such information is boxed in their texts for easy review.

 Using a Calculator

The problems in this lesson are appropriate for solving and checking on a calculator.

Translate each statement into a formula. Use k as the constant of variation where needed.

13. The kinetic energy, e, of a moving object varies jointly as the mass, m, of the object and the square of the velocity, v. $e = kmv^2$

14. The wind resistance, R, of an object varies jointly as the area, A, of its surface facing the wind and the square of the speed, s, of the wind. $R = kAs^2$

Written Exercises

Solve. Give irrational roots to the nearest tenth. You may wish to use a calculator.

A 1. c varies directly as a and inversely as b. If $c = 15$ when $a = 18$ and $b = 40$, find c when $a = 36$ and $b = 25$. 48

2. d varies jointly as r and t. If $d = 45$ when $r = 15$ and $t = 14$, find d when $r = 21$ and $t = 8$. 36

3. m varies jointly as v and the square of u. If $m = 9$ when $v = 15$ and $u = 6$, find u when $m = 60$ and $v = 25$. 12, -12

4. c varies inversely as the square of h and directly as n. If $c = 1$ when $h = 11$ and $n = 50$, find h when $c = 3.63$ and $n = 6$. 2, -2

5. The square of y varies inversely as x and directly as z. If $y = 3$ when $x = 12$ and $z = 21$, find y when $x = 8$ and $z = 28$. 4.2, -4.2

6. a varies directly as r and inversely as the square of v. If $a = 15$ when $r = 27$ and $v = 8$, find v when $r = 4.5$ and $a = 10$. 4, -4

B 7. x varies jointly as u and v. How does x change when both u and v are doubled? when u is doubled and v is halved? quadrupled; remains the same

8. m varies directly as the square of r and inversely as s. How does m change when both r and s are doubled? when both r and s are tripled? doubled; tripled

9. In the formula $h^2 = \frac{3r^2}{\pi d}$, how does h change when r is doubled and d is halved? h is 2.8 times as large.

10. In the formula $t^2 = \frac{Fs}{r}$, how does t change when F remains constant, s is tripled, and r is halved? t is 2.4 times as large.

Problems

Solve. Give irrational roots to the nearest tenth. You may wish to use a calculator.

A 1. The volume of a pyramid varies jointly as the height and the area of the base. A pyramid 20 cm high has base area of 63 cm^2 and a volume of 420 cm^3. What is the volume if the height is 8 cm and the area of the base is 39 cm^2? 104 cm^3

2. The lateral surface area of a cylindrical jar varies jointly as the diameter and the height of the jar. For a diameter of 10.4 cm and a height of 18 cm, the lateral surface area is 588 cm^2. What is the height if the lateral surface area is 294 cm^2 and the diameter is 7.8 cm? 12 cm

In Exercises 3 and 4, apply the statement: The number of persons needed to do a job varies directly as the amount of work to be done and inversely as the time in which the job must be done.

3. If 5 students in a typing pool can type 280 pages in 2 days, how many students will be needed to type 2100 pages in 3 days? 25 students

4. If 3 people can mow 300 m^2 of grass in 0.5 h, how long will it take 7 people to mow 7000 m^2? 5 h

5. The cost of running an appliance varies jointly as the number of watts used, the hours of operation, and the cost per kilowatt-hour. A 6000 watt convection oven operates for 10 min for 15¢ at a cost of 7.5¢ per kilowatt-hour. What is the cost of cooking two meals if each meal takes 70 min to cook? $2.10

6. The volume of a cone varies jointly as its height and the square of its radius. A certain cone has a volume of 702π cm^3, a height of 15 cm, and a radius of 12 cm. Find the radius of another cone that has a height of 27 cm and a volume of 576π cm^3. 8.1 cm

7. The distance a car travels from rest varies jointly as its acceleration and the square of the time of motion. A car travels 250 m from rest in 5 s at an acceleration of 20 m/s^2. How many seconds will it take the car to travel 1800 m at acceleration of 25 m/s^2? 12 s

8. The resistance of a wire to the transmission of electricity varies directly as the length of the wire and inversely as the square of the radius of a cross section of the wire. An 800 m wire has a radius of 0.48 cm and a resistance of 0.3125 ohms. If another wire made from the same metal has a length of 500 m and a resistance of 0.5 ohms, what is its radius? 0.3 cm

B 9. Using the mass of the sun as the unit of mass, and measuring distance in astronomical units (AU) and time in years, the total mass of a double star is directly proportional to the cube of the maximum distance between the stars and inversely proportional to the square of the period (the time it takes each star to revolve about the other). The double star Sirius has a period of 50.0 years, a maximum distance of 41.0 AU, and a total mass of 3.45. What is the total mass of Capella if its period is 0.285 years and the maximum distance is 1.51 AU? 5.30

10. For a two-year period, the growth factor of an investment varies directly as the square root of the final value and inversely as the square root of the original investment. A $2000 investment with a growth factor of 1.5 yields $4500 in 2 years. Find the growth factor of a $1600 investment that yields $4900 in 2 years. 1.75

Suggested Assignments
Average
  590/1–6
  590/*P*: 1–11 odd
S 592/Mixed Review
Maximum
  590/1–9 odd
  590/*P*: 1–13 odd
S 592/Mixed Review

Supplementary Materials
Study Guide   pp. 217–218
Practice Master   75
Test Master   54
Resource Book   p. 140

Quadratic Functions   591

11. The heat lost through a windowpane varies jointly as the difference of the inside and outside temperatures and the window area, and inversely as the thickness of the pane. In one hour, 49.5 joules of heat are lost through a pane 40 cm by 28 cm that is 0.8 cm thick, when the temperature difference is 44° C. How many joules are lost in one hour through a pane 0.5 cm thick having an area that is 0.25 times the area of the other pane, when the temperature difference is 40° C? 18 joules

12. The wind pressure on a plane varies jointly as the surface area and the square of the speed of the wind. With a wind speed of 12 mi/h, the pressure on a 4 ft by 1.5 ft rectangle is 20 lb. What is the speed of the wind when the pressure on a 2 ft by 2 ft square is 30 lb? 18 mi/h

C 13. The heat generated by a stove element varies jointly as the resistance and the square of the current. What is the effect on the heat generated in the following cases?

    a. The current is unchanged but the resistance is doubled. doubled

    b. The resistance is unchanged but the current is doubled. quadrupled

    c. The current is tripled and the resistance is doubled. 18 times as large

14. The power in an electric circuit varies directly as the square of the voltage and inversely as the resistance. What is the effect on the power in the following cases?

    a. The resistance is constant and the voltage is halved. one fourth as large

    b. The voltage is constant and the resistance is halved. doubled

    c. The voltage is tripled and the resistance is quadrupled. 2.25 times as large

Mixed Review Exercises

Solve each system.

1. $3x - 2y = 1$
   $x - y = 0$ (1, 1)

2. $x + y = 10$
   $x - 2y = 16$ (12, −2)

3. $2x - 5y = 3$
   $-x + 5y = 6$ (9, 3)

4. $5x + 3y = 5$
   $4x + 3y = 10$ (−5, 10)

5. $x - y = 0$
   $x + y = 4$ (2, 2)

6. $x + y = 3$
   $2x + 3y = -2$ (11, −8)

Multiply.

7. $(2x + 1)(4x + 2)$ $8x^2 + 8x + 2$

8. $(8s + 4)(5 + 6s)$ $48s^2 + 64s + 20$

9. $(7t - 2y)(7t + 2y)$ $49t^2 - 4y^2$

10. $(3p - 4k)^2$ $9p^2 - 24pk + 16k^2$

11. $(r - 2)^2$ $r^2 - 4r + 4$

12. $(xy - 2)(3xy + 4)$ $3x^2y^2 - 2xy - 8$

Application / *Illumination*

Suppose you had to use a flashlight to help you see an object at a very close range. You would need to hold the light close to the object to make it clearer and brighter. To see a larger area, you would put more distance between the light and the object.

Scientists have measured how illumination is related to distance and brightness. The brightness, or intensity (I), of a light source is measured in units called candelas (cd). A 100-watt bulb gives about 130 cd. Illumination is the amount of light energy per second that falls on a unit area. Illumination is measured in luxes (lx).

Illumination is directly proportional to the intensity of the source. If the intensity is doubled, the illumination is doubled. Illumination on a surface is also dependent on its distance from the source. The farther the light source is from the surface, the lower the illumination.

Specifically, illumination (E) on a surface perpendicular to a light source varies inversely as the square of the distance (r) from the light source:

$$E = \frac{I}{r^2}$$

Thus, if the distance from the light source is doubled, the illumination is one fourth of what it was originally. If the distance is tripled, the illumination is one ninth. This equation is called the *law of illumination*.

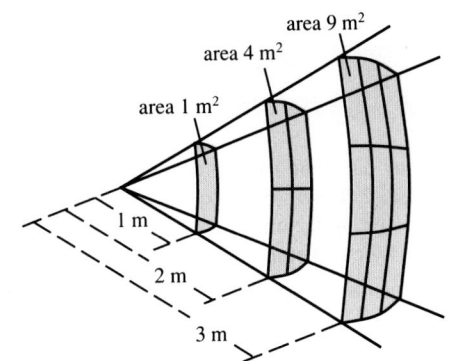

Example

What illumination is provided on the surface of a table 3 m directly below a 99 cd lamp?

Solution

Use the formula to solve for E: $E = \dfrac{99}{3^2} = \dfrac{99}{9} = 11$

∴ the illumination is 11 lx.

Exercises

1. What illumination is provided on a surface 4 m from a 160 cd lamp? 10 lx

2. If a light is giving 315 cd from 3 m above a desk top, what illumination is provided? 35 lx

3. If a lamp gives 216 cd, how far must it be placed from a table surface to provide 24 lx of illumination? 3 m

4. What illumination does a 120 cd lamp provide at a distance of 2 m? 30 lx

5. What illumination is provided on the surface of a desk 2.5 m directly below a 125 cd lamp? 20 lx

Quadratic Functions   **593**

Quick Quiz

1. If y varies inversely as the square of x, and $y = 40$ when $x = 5$, find the value of y when $x = 2$. 250

2. a varies directly as the square of b and inversely as c. If $a = 12$ when $b = 6$ and $c = 9$, find a when $b = 4$ and $c = 6$. 8

Self-Test 3

Vocabulary   quadratic direct variation (p. 584)   joint variation (p. 588)
inverse variation as the square   combined variation (p. 588)
(p. 585)

1. The distance that the signal from a radio station travels varies directly as the square of the number of kilowatts (kW) it produces. A 40 kW station can broadcast a distance of 64 km. How far could the station broadcast if it produced 70 kW? 196 km

    Obj. 12-7, p. 584

2. The mass of a circular coin varies jointly as the thickness and the square of the radius of the coin. A silver coin 2 cm in radius and 0.2 cm thick has a mass of 26.4 g. What is the mass of a silver coin 4 cm in radius and 0.3 cm thick? 158.4 g

    Obj. 12-8, p. 588

Check your answers with those at the back of the book.

Chapter Summary

1. Any quadratic equation can be solved using the quadratic formula (see item 2 below). Some quadratic equations, however, may be more easily solved by factoring, applying the property of square roots of equal numbers, or by completing the square.

2. When $ax^2 + bx + c = 0$ and $a \neq 0$, the quadratic formula is expressed as:

$$x = \frac{-b \pm \sqrt{b^2 - 4ac}}{2a}$$

3. The graph of a quadratic equation of the form $y = ax^2 + bx + c$ is a parabola. The x-intercepts of the parabola correspond to the roots of the related quadratic equation $ax^2 + bx + c = 0$.

4. The discriminant, $b^2 - 4ac$, is used to determine the number of roots of a quadratic equation.

    If $b^2 - 4ac > 0$, there are two real-number roots.
    If $b^2 - 4ac = 0$, there is one (double) real-number root.
    If $b^2 - 4ac < 0$, there are no real-number roots.

5. Several kinds of variation have been described (k is a nonzero constant):

    a. A quadratic direct variation is a quadratic function defined by an equation of the form $y = kx^2$.

    b. An inverse variation as the square is a function defined by an equation of the form $x^2 y = k$ $\left(\text{or } y = \dfrac{k}{x^2} \right)$.

    c. A joint variation is defined by an equation of the form $z = kxy$.

    d. A combined variation is defined by an equation of the form $zy = kx$ or $z = \dfrac{kx}{y}$.

594   *Chapter 12*

Chapter Review

Supplementary Materials
Practice Master 76
Resource Book p. 205

Write the letter of the correct answer.

Solve.

1. $2x^2 - 128 = 0$ 12-1

    a. $\{64\}$ **b.** $\{64, -64\}$ **c.** $\{8\}$ **d.** $\{8, -8\}$

2. $(a - 25)^2 = 9$

    a. $\{22, 28\}$ **b.** $\{2, -8\}$ **c.** $\{2, -2\}$ **d.** $\{2, 8\}$

Solve by completing the square.

3. $x^2 - 4x - 77 = 0$ 12-2

    a. $\{11, 7\}$ **b.** $\{-11, -7\}$ **c.** $\{11, -7\}$ **d.** $\{-11, 7\}$

4. $c^2 - 10c - 20 = 0$

    a. $\{-5 + 3\sqrt{5}, -5 - 3\sqrt{5}\}$ **b.** $\{3\sqrt{5} + 5, 3\sqrt{5} - 5\}$

    c. $\{5 + 3\sqrt{5}, 5 - 3\sqrt{5}\}$ **d.** $\{-3\sqrt{5} + 5, -3\sqrt{5} - 5\}$

Solve by using the quadratic formula.

5. $5z^2 + 11z + 2 = 0$ 12-3

    a. $\left\{-2, -\frac{1}{5}\right\}$ **b.** $\left\{2, \frac{1}{5}\right\}$ **c.** $\left\{2, -\frac{1}{5}\right\}$ **d.** $\left\{-2, \frac{1}{5}\right\}$

6. $10y^2 - y - 3 = 0$

    a. $\left\{-\frac{3}{5}, -\frac{1}{2}\right\}$ **b.** $\left\{\frac{3}{5}, \frac{1}{2}\right\}$ **c.** $\left\{-\frac{3}{5}, \frac{1}{2}\right\}$ **d.** $\left\{\frac{3}{5}, -\frac{1}{2}\right\}$

7. Give the discriminant of $2x^2 - 3x - 2 = 0$. 12-4

    a. -25 **b.** 25 **c.** -5 **d.** 5

8. How many real roots does $x^2 + 2x + 5 = 0$ have?

    a. 0 **b.** 1 **c.** 2 **d.** 3

9. Give the best method for solving $2y^2 + 8y = 0$. 12-5

    a. Factoring **b.** Property of square roots of equal numbers

    c. Completing the square **d.** Quadratic formula

Solve.

10. The dimensions of a sheet of paper can be represented by consecutive odd integers. If the area of the paper is 143 cm^2, find the dimensions. 12-6

    a. $l = 9 \text{ cm}$ **b.** $l = 11 \text{ cm}$ **c.** $l = 15 \text{ cm}$ **d.** $l = 13 \text{ cm}$
    $w = 7 \text{ cm}$ $w = 9 \text{ cm}$ $w = 13 \text{ cm}$ $w = 11 \text{ cm}$

11. If y varies inversely as x^2, and x is halved, then y is __?__.

    a. doubled   **(b.)** quadrupled   **c.** divided by 4   **d.** halved

12-7

12. If r varies directly as the cube of t and inversely as the square of s, and $r = \frac{1}{2}$ when $s = 6$ and $t = 2$, find r when $s = 12$ and $t = 4$.

12-8

    a. $\frac{1}{4}$ **b.** 0   **c.** $\frac{1}{2}$ **(d.)** 1

Alternate Test p. T23

Supplementary Materials

Test Masters   55, 56
Resource Book   pp. 64–67

Chapter Test

Solve.

1. $36x^2 = 49 \left\{ \pm \frac{7}{6} \right\}$

2. $3(a - 5)^2 = 21 \ \{5 \pm \sqrt{7}\}$

12-1

Solve by completing the square.

3. $c^2 + 2c - 15 = 0 \ \{3, -5\}$

4. $b^2 - 4b - 10 = 0 \ \{2 \pm \sqrt{14}\}$

12-2

Solve by using the quadratic formula.

5. $3z^2 - 6z - 9 = 0 \ \{3, -1\}$

6. $y^2 + 6y - 23 = 0 \ \{-3 \pm 4\sqrt{2}\}$

12-3

Give the number of real roots.

7. $2x^2 + 3x + 2 = 0$ none

8. $x^2 + 4x - 4 = 0$ two

12-4

Solve by using the most appropriate method.

9. $7x^2 - 3x = 0 \left\{ 0, \frac{3}{7} \right\}$

10. $3x^2 - 10x - 4 = 0 \left\{ \frac{5 \pm \sqrt{37}}{3} \right\}$

12-5

Solve. Approximate irrational roots to the nearest tenth.

11. A garden is currently 4 m wide and 7 m long. If the area of the garden is to be doubled by increasing the width and the length by the same number of meters, find the new dimensions of the garden. length 9.1 m, width 6.1 m

12-6

12. The area of a square is directly proportional to the square of its diagonal. If the area of a square having a diagonal 16 cm long is 128 cm^2, what is the area of a square having a diagonal 24 cm long? 288 cm^2

12-7

13. If v varies jointly as b and h, and $v = 50$ when $b = 25$ and $h = 6$, find h when $b = 36$ and $v = 108$. 9

12-8

Cumulative Review (Chapters 1–12)

Evaluate if $a = -1$, $b = 1$, $c = 0$, $d = 3$, and $e = -\frac{5}{2}$.

1. $a(b - e)$ $-\frac{7}{2}$

2. $(b \div d + e)^a$ $-\frac{6}{13}$

3. $c \div e$ 0

4. $(ad)^2 - (ad)^3$ 36

5. $(de + ab)^c$ 1

6. $d \div e^a$ $-\frac{15}{2}$

Simplify. Assume that no denominator is zero. Each variable represents a positive real number.

7. $5 \cdot 58 - 7 \cdot 58 - (-58)$ -58

8. $6^2 \div 3^2 + 4 \div 3$ $\frac{16}{3}$

9. $(6 - 13)(6 + 13)$ -133

10. $3x - (0.4x + 1.2y)$ $2.6x - 1.2y$

11. $15(3x - 4) + 5 - 9c$ $45x - 55 - 9c$

12. $\left(-\frac{1}{8}x^5y^3z\right)(-24x^2y)$ $3x^7y^4z$

13. $-\frac{3}{5}a^3b(-20ab^2 - 15b^3)$ $12a^4b^3 + 9a^3b^4$

14. $(5x^3y^2)^2(3x^4y^3)^2$ $225x^{14}y^{10}$

15. $\frac{-72wx^4y^5z}{-96x^3y^7z}$ $\frac{3wx}{4y^2}$

16. $\frac{(3r^3s^4)^3}{(-9r^5s^6)^2}$ $\frac{1}{3r}$

17. $(4u^2 - 2u + 1)(2u + 1)$ $8u^3 + 1$

18. $a - 2(3a - 2)$ $-5a + 4$

19. $(9z - 3)(5z + 4)$ $45z^2 + 21z - 12$

20. $(3a^3 - 2)^2$ $9a^6 - 12a^3 + 4$

21. $(8r^3t - 3v)(8r^3t + 3v)$ $64r^6t^2 - 9v^2$

22. $(3.4 \times 10^{12})(0.2 \times 10^{-3})$ 6.8×10^8

23. $\frac{12c^2 - 26cd + 12d^2}{12c^2 - 44cd + 24d^2}$ $\frac{2c - 3d}{2c - 6d}$

24. $(18x^2 - x - 4) \div (9x + 4)$ $2x - 1$

25. $(27x^3 + 64) \div (3x + 4)$ $9x^2 - 12x + 16$

26. $\frac{b^2 + b - 12}{b + 2} \cdot \frac{b^2 - 4}{b^2 - 5b - 6}$ $\frac{(b + 4)(b - 3)(b - 2)}{(b - 6)(b + 1)}$

27. $\frac{3z^2 - 8z - 16}{z^2 + 6z + 9} \div \frac{z^2 - 3z - 4}{z + 3}$ $\frac{3z + 4}{(z + 1)(z + 3)}$

28. $\frac{85k^8 + 51k^4 - 17k^2}{-17k^4}$ $\frac{-5k^6 - 3k^2 + 1}{k^2}$

29. $\frac{4a - 4}{3} - \frac{5 - 2a}{3}$ $2a - 3$

30. $\frac{n + 1}{2n - 3} - \frac{4}{n + 1} + 3$ $\frac{7n^2 - 9n + 4}{(2n - 3)(n + 1)}$

31. $\frac{3}{m + 3} - \frac{1}{2m - 6}$ $\frac{5m - 21}{2(m + 3)(m - 3)}$

32. $-\sqrt{2.25x^6z^3}$ $-1.5|x^3|z\sqrt{z}$

33. $3\sqrt{5}(\sqrt{180} - \sqrt{81})$ $90 - 27\sqrt{5}$

34. $(3\sqrt{2} + 1)^2$ $19 + 6\sqrt{2}$

35. $\sqrt{\frac{18a^7}{7}} \cdot \sqrt{\frac{112}{2a^5}}$ $12a$

36. $\sqrt{108} - \sqrt{24} + \sqrt{6}$ $6\sqrt{3} - \sqrt{6}$

37. $3\sqrt{80} + \frac{2\sqrt{35}}{\sqrt{7}}$ $14\sqrt{5}$

38. $\frac{3\sqrt{5} - 4}{\sqrt{2} - 3}$ $\frac{3\sqrt{10} - 4\sqrt{2} + 9\sqrt{5} - 12}{-7}$

39. $(2\sqrt{5} + 4\sqrt{2})(6\sqrt{5} + 4\sqrt{2})$ $92 + 32\sqrt{10}$

Factor completely. If the polynomial cannot be factored, write "prime."

40. $49r^2 + 56rs + 16s^2$

41. $4t^5 + 9t^3$

42. $30x^2 + 91x - 30$

43. $-16z^4 - 48z^3 - 64z^2$

44. $125a^4 - 45a^2$

45. $12a^2 - 5a - 12$

46. $2a^3 - a^2b - 8a + 4b$

47. $c^2 - 8c + 16$

48. $-10p^2 + 27p + 28$

Quadratic Functions **597**

Cumulative Review p. T30

Supplementary Materials

| Test Masters | 57, 58 |
| Practice Masters | 77–80 |

Resource Book,
pp. 141–142, 143–145,
155–157, 68–69, 70–72,
73–75, 76–78

Additional Answers
Cumulative Review

40. $(7r + 4s)^2$

41. $t^3(4t^2 + 9)$

42. $(3x + 10)(10x - 3)$

43. $-16z^2(z^2 + 3z + 4)$

44. $5a^2(5a - 3)(5a + 3)$

45. prime

46. $(2a - b)(a - 2)(a + 2)$

47. $(c - 4)^2$

48. $-(2p - 7)(5p + 4)$

63. $\{-2, 8$, and the real numbers less than -2 or greater than $8\}$

64. $\{$the real numbers between $\frac{1}{3}$ and $6\}$

65. $\{-\frac{3}{2}, 2$, and the real numbers between $-\frac{3}{2}$ and $2\}$

66. $\{$the real numbers greater than $\frac{1}{3}\}$

73.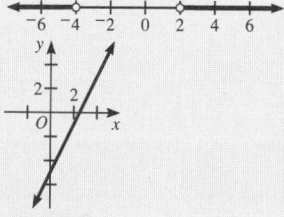

74.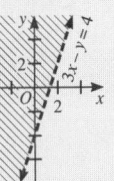

75.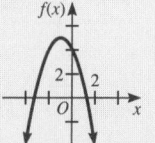

77.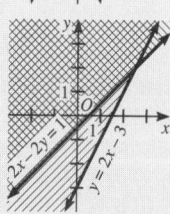

79.

Solve each equation, inequality, or system. Assume that no denominator is zero. If there is no solution, write "no solution."

49. $\frac{1}{5}x - 2 = \frac{2}{3} \left\{\frac{40}{3}\right\}$

50. $15 - 3(y + 1) = 14 - 5y \{1\}$

51. $7w + 4 = |-39| \{5\}$

52. $16 = 4.8x - 2.48 \{3.85\}$

53. 35% of $t = 105 \{300\}$

54. $3|x| + 5 = 9 \left\{\pm\frac{4}{3}\right\}$

55. $z^2 - 9z + 18 = 0 \{3, 6\}$

56. $9t^2 - 24t + 16 = 0 \left\{\frac{4}{3}\right\}$

57. $12b^2 + 5b = 2$ $\left\{-\frac{2}{3}, \frac{1}{4}\right\}$

58. $(3a - 2)(4a + 1) = 5$ $\left\{-\frac{7}{12}, 1\right\}$

59. $\begin{aligned} 3x + 4y &= 2 \\ -5x + 4y &= -2 \end{aligned}$ $\left(\frac{1}{2}, \frac{1}{8}\right)$

60. $\begin{aligned} 2x + y &= 7 \\ x - 2y &= 11 \end{aligned}$ $(5, -3)$

61. $\frac{x-2}{8} - \frac{2x+1}{12} = \frac{1}{3} \{-16\}$

62. $\frac{3x+2}{x-1} = \frac{3x+4}{x+1} \left\{-\frac{3}{2}\right\}$

63. $|t - 3| \geq 5$

64. $-4 < 3t - 5 < 13$

65. $0 \leq 4 - 2t \leq 7$

66. $\frac{1}{3} - \frac{7}{2}t < -\frac{5}{6}$

67. $-2\sqrt{t - 1} = 6$ no sol.

68. $\sqrt{x^2 + 1} = x - 1$ no sol.

69. $\sqrt{3r + 1} = 2r - 6$ $\{5\}$

70. $\frac{1}{2}m^2 + 2m + 2 = 0 \{-2\}$

71. $3t^2 - 5t + 1 = 0 \left\{\frac{5 \pm \sqrt{13}}{6}\right\}$

72. $3t^2 + 2t - 7 = 0$ $\left\{\frac{-1 \pm \sqrt{22}}{3}\right\}$

Graph the solution set. (In Exercise 73, use a number line.)

73. $|x + 1| > 3$

74. $2x - y = 5$

75. $3x - y < 4$

76. Write an equation in standard form of the line containing $(-1, 1)$ and $(6, -1)$. $2x + 7y = 5$

77. Graph the function $f(x) = 4 - 2x - x^2$.

78. Write $0.4\overline{25}$ as a fraction in simplest form. $\frac{421}{990}$

79. Graph the solution set of the system:

$$y \geq 2x - 3$$
$$2x - 2y \leq 1$$

80. Find the length, to the nearest hundredth of a meter, of the diagonal of a rectangle that is 10 m by 9 m. (Use a calculator or the table of square roots on page 682.) 13.45 m

81. A plumber and an assistant finished a job in 4 h. The job would have taken the plumber 6 h working alone. How long would the job have taken the assistant working alone? 12 h

82. a varies directly as b and inversely as the square of c, and $a = 10$ when $b = 8$ and $c = 2$. Find a when $b = 20$ and $c = 5$. 4

83. During a canoe trip, Roberto paddled twice as many hours as Edward, and Jim paddled for one hour. If the three of them paddled less than a total of ten hours, what is the number of hours that Roberto could have paddled? less than 6 h

84. During a 3000 mi flight, a plane encountered a strong tail wind that increased its speed by 100 mi/h. This increase in speed shortened the flying time by one hour. Find the speed of the plane relative to the ground. 500 mi/h

Preparing for College Entrance Exams

Strategy for Success

Take your time and be sure to read each question and all the possible answers carefully. Although it is important to work quickly, you must be sure not to work so quickly that you lose accuracy. Remember that no partial credit is given.

Decide which is the best of the choices given and write the corresponding letter on your answer sheet.

1. Which number is $\frac{3}{5}$ of the way from $-\frac{4}{7}$ to $1\frac{1}{8}$? D

    (A) $\frac{31}{56}$ **(B)** $\frac{95}{56}$ **(C)** $\frac{93}{280}$ **(D)** $\frac{25}{56}$ **(E)** $\frac{57}{56}$

2. The length of a rectangle is four times the width. The area is 184.96 m². Find the width of the rectangle to the nearest tenth of a meter. C
    (A) 6.4 m **(B)** 6.6 m **(C)** 6.8 m **(D)** 7.2 m **(E)** 7.4 m

3. Two sides of a right triangle are 8 cm and 15 cm long. Find the length of the hypotenuse to the nearest tenth of a centimeter. B
    (A) 12.9 cm **(B)** 17.0 cm **(C)** 13.0 cm
    (D) No such triangle is possible.
    (E) Cannot be determined from the given information.

4. Evaluate $\frac{x(x+1)}{x+2}$ if $x = \sqrt{3}$. A

    (A) $3 - \sqrt{3}$ **(B)** $\sqrt{3} - 3$ **(C)** $-3 - \sqrt{3}$ **(D)** $\frac{1 + \sqrt{3}}{2}$

5. The sum of a positive integer and the square of the next consecutive integer is 131. Find the sum of the two integers. C
    (A) 19 **(B)** 20 **(C)** 21 **(D)** 22 **(E)** 23

6. The graph of an equation of the form $y = ax^2 + bx + c$ is shown at the right. Identify the true statement(s). D
    I. $0 < a < 1$
    II. $b^2 > 4c$
    III. $c > 0$
    (A) I only **(B)** II only **(C)** III only
    (D) I and II only **(E)** I, II, and III

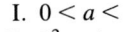

7. The equation $ax^2 + 3x + c = 0$ has two distinct roots. Which of the following is (are) possible? E
    I. $a = 1, c = 2$ II. $a = -1, c = -2$ III. $a = -1, c = 2$
    (A) I only **(B)** II only **(C)** III only
    (D) I and II only **(E)** I, II, and III

Teaching References

Lesson Commentary,
  pp. T141–T144

Assignment Guide,
  p. T71

Supplementary Materials
  Study Guide, pp. 219–240
  Computer Activities 38
  Disk for Algebra

Teaching Suggestions p. T141

Looking Ahead

Probability

Sample Spaces and Events

Objective   To specify the sample space and events for a random experiment.

So far you have been solving mathematical problems that deal with definite situations. You'll now consider the branch of mathematics called *probability*, which deals with the possibility, or likelihood, that an event will happen. For example, a food company can use the data from a survey to determine the probability that a new cereal will be successful in the marketplace.

Suppose you toss a coin many times in exactly the same way. On each toss it will land with either a head or a tail up. However, you can't predict with certainty which it will be. An activity repeated under essentially the same conditions is called a **random experiment** when the outcome can't be predicted.

Although you don't know before a toss whether the result will be a head or a tail, you do know that only these two outcomes are possible. The set of all possible outcomes of a random experiment is called the **sample space** of the experiment. For the coin-tossing experiment, if the outcomes are denoted by H and T, then the sample space is $\{H, T\}$.

Any possible subset of the sample space of an experiment is called an **event.** When an event involves a single member of the sample space, it is called a **simple event.** In the coin-tossing experiment, there are two simple events: $\{H\}$ and $\{T\}$.

Example 1   For the experiment of spinning the pointer of the green spinner at the right, give:

a. the sample space for the experiment.

b. the event that an even number results.

c. the event that a number greater than 6 results.

Solution **a.** {1, 2, 3, 4, 5, 6, 7, 8}

b. {2, 4, 6, 8}

c. {7, 8}

Suppose you now have two spinners, one blue and one red. A simple event in this experiment can be represented by the ordered pair (*b, r*), where *b* is the number from the blue spinner and *r* is the number from the red spinner. The ordered pair (4, 2) represents the simple event, "blue spinner shows 4 and red spinner shows 2."

Example 2 For the two-spinner experiment, give:

a. the sample space for the experiment.

b. the event that the sum of the numbers on the two spinners equals 4.

c. the event that the sum of the numbers on the two spinners is less than 4.

Solution **a.** {(1, 1), (1, 2), (1, 3), (2, 1), (2, 2), (2, 3), (3, 1), (3, 2), (3, 3), (4, 1), (4, 2), (4, 3)}

b. {(1, 3), (2, 2), (3, 1)}

c. {(1, 1), (1, 2), (2, 1)}

Oral Exercises

A penny and a nickel are tossed. The sample space is {(*H, H*), (*H, T*), (*T, H*), (*T, T*)}. State each event.

1. Two tails up {(*T, T*)}

2. One head up and one tail up
{(*H, T*), (*T, H*)}

3. Exactly one tail up {(*H, T*), (*T, H*)}

4. At least one head up
{(*H, H*), (*H, T*), (*T, H*)}

Each letter of the word FLOWER is written on a separate card. The cards are shuffled. Then one card is drawn at random.

5. What is the sample space for this experiment? {F, L, O, W, E, R}

6. What is the event that the letter on the card is a vowel? {O, E}

7. What is the event that the letter on the card is neither L nor W? {F, O, E, R}

Each of the numbers from 1 to 8 is written on a separate card. The cards are shuffled. Then one card is drawn at random.

8. What is the sample space for this experiment? {1, 2, 3, 4, 5, 6, 7, 8}

9. What is the event that the number on the card is even? {2, 4, 6, 8}

10. What is the event that the number on the card is not less than 5? {5, 6, 7, 8}

Probability   **601**

---

2. For her birthday, Sara may choose to go to a movie (*M*) or a skating rink (*S*). She may also choose to go with either Dan (*D*), Barbara (*B*), or Vincent (*V*). Specify:

a. the sample space of the activity and person.
{(*M, D*), (*M, B*), (*M, V*), (*S, D*), (*S, B*), (*S, V*)}

b. the event she goes with Barbara.
{(*M, B*), (*S, B*)}

c. the event she goes with a boy. {(*M, D*), (*M, V*), (*S, D*), (*S, V*)}

Check for Understanding

Oral Exs. 1–10: use after Example 2.

Guided Practice

1. Each of the numbers 2, 5, 8, 10, and 15 is written on a separate card. The cards are shuffled and then one is drawn at random. Give:

a. the sample space. {2, 5, 8, 10, 15}

b. the event the number is even. {2, 8, 10}

c. the event the number is a multiple of 5. {5, 10, 15}

d. the event the number is divisible by 10. {10}

2. One bag contains a penny, a nickel, and a dime. A second bag contains a nickel, a dime, and a quarter. One coin is drawn from each bag. Give:

a. the sample space.
{(*P, N*), (*P, D*), (*P, Q*), (*N, N*), (*N, D*), (*N, Q*), (*D, N*), (*D, D*), (*D, Q*)}

b. the event that 15¢ is drawn. {(*N, D*), (*D, N*)}

(continued)

Guided Practice

(continued)

c. the event that less than 15¢ is drawn.
{(P, N), (P, D), (N, N)}

d. the event a quarter is drawn.
{(P, Q), (N, Q), (D, Q)}

Summarizing the Lesson

Tell students that today they have learned to specify a sample space and events for a random experiment.

Suggested Assignments

Maximum
602/1–7

Additional Answers
Written Exercises

1. {A, B, C, D, E, F, G, H, I, J, K}

2. {(Y, Y), (Y, G), (Y, B),
(R, Y), (R, G), (R, B)}

3. {(2, 1), (2, 4), (2, 9), (4, 1),
(4, 4), (4, 9), (8, 1), (8, 4),
(8, 9), (15, 1), (15, 4),
(15, 9)}

4. {(3, 1), (3, 5), (3, 10),
(3, 15), (3, 20), (6, 1), (6, 5),
(6, 10), (6, 15), (6, 20),
(9, 1), (9, 5), (9, 10), (9, 15),
(9, 20)}

5. {(O, O, O), (O, O, F),
(O, F, O), (O, F, F),
(F, O, O), (F, F, O),
(F, O, F), (F, F, F)}

6. {(1, 1), (1, 2), (1, 3), (2, 1),
(2, 2), (2, 3), (3, 1), (3, 2),
(3, 3), (4, 1), (4, 2), (4, 3)}

7. {p, n, d, (p, n), (p, d),
(n, d), (p, n, d)}

Supplementary Materials

Study Guide   pp. 219–220

Written Exercises

For the experiments described in Exercises 1–7, first give the sample space and then give each event. For sample spaces, see side-column.

A 1. Each of the letters A, B, C, D, E, F, G, H, I, J, and K is written on a card. The cards are shuffled, and then one card is drawn at random.

   a. The letter is a vowel.   **b.** The letter is not a vowel.   **c.** The letter is C, F, or H.
   {A, E, I}   {B, C, D, F, G, H, J, K}   {C, F, H}

2. A bowl contains a yellow marble and a red marble. A second bowl contains a yellow, a green, and a blue marble. One marble is taken at random from each bowl.
{(Y, Y), (Y, G), (R, Y), (R, G)}

   a. One marble is green.   **b.** At least one marble is yellow.   **c.** Neither marble is blue.
   {(Y, G), (R, G)}   {(Y, Y), (Y, G), (Y, B), (R, Y)}

3. A hat contains cards numbered 2, 4, 8, and 15. A second hat contains cards numbered 1, 4, and 9. One card is drawn at random from each hat.

   a. Both numbers are the same. {(4, 4)}

   b. Both numbers are odd. {(15, 1), (15, 9)}   {(4, 9), (8, 9), (15, 1),

   c. The sum of the numbers is greater than 12. (15, 4), (15, 9)}

   d. The sum of the numbers is less than 6. {(2, 1), (4, 1)}

4. A spinner is divided into three equal sections numbered 3, 6, and 9. A second spinner is divided into five equal sections numbered 1, 5, 10, 15, and 20. Each pointer is spun.

   a. Both numbers are odd. {(3, 1), (3, 5), (3, 15), (9, 1), (9, 5), (9, 15)}

   b. Exactly one number is odd. {(3, 10), (3, 20), (6, 1), (6, 5), (6, 15), (9, 10), (9, 20)}

   c. The sum of the numbers is between 12 and 21. {(3, 10), (3, 15), (6, 10), (9, 5), (9, 10)}

   d. The product of the numbers is greater than 60. {(6, 15), (6, 20), (9, 10), (9, 15), (9, 20)}

B 5. There are three on-off switches on a light panel. Each switch controls O = on and F = off one light.   **c.** {(O, O, F), (O, F, O), (O, F, F), (F, O, O), (F, O, F), (F, F, O), (F, F, F)}

   a. All three lights are on.   **b.** At least two lights are off.   **c.** At least one light is off.
   {(O, O, O)}   {(O, F, F), (F, O, F), (F, F, O), (F, F, F)}

6. Refer to the two-spinner experiment of Example 2. As before, the ordered pair (b, r) represents a simple event.

   a. $b + r > 4$ {(2, 3), (3, 2), (3, 3), (4, 1), (4, 2), (4, 3)}   **b.** $b < r$ {(1, 2), (1, 3), (2, 3)}

   c. $b + r$ is a multiple of 3   **d.** $b \cdot r > b + r$
   {(1, 2), (2, 1), (3, 3), (4, 2)}   {(2, 3), (3, 2), (3, 3), (4, 2), (4, 3)}

C 7. A coin collection consists of a penny, a nickel, and a dime. Either 1, 2, or 3 coins are randomly selected.

   a. The total amount is even. {d, (p, n), (p, n, d)}

   b. The total amount is odd. {p, n, (p, d), (n, d)}

   c. The total amount is greater than 2¢ and less than 16¢. {n, d, (p, n), (p, d), (n, d)}

   d. The total amount is less than 6¢ or greater than 15¢. {p, n, (p, n, d)}

---

602   *Looking Ahead*

Probability

Objective   To find the probability that an event will happen.

Suppose you toss a coin repeatedly. The sample space is $\{H, T\}$. Assuming that the coin is fair, the two simple events $\{H\}$ and $\{T\}$ are *equally likely* to happen. That is, for a large number of tosses, you would expect the number of heads, or the number of tails, to be about one half the number of tosses.

The **probability** of an event is the ratio of the number of outcomes favoring the event to the total number of possible outcomes. We write the ratio as a fraction. In the case of a tossed coin, if the probability of $\{H\}$ is written as $P(H)$ and the probability of $\{T\}$ as $P(T)$, then

$$P(H) = P(T) = \frac{1}{2}.$$

The probability of an impossible event is 0. For example, the probability that the result of the toss of a coin is both heads and tails is 0.

$$P(H \text{ and } T) = 0$$

The probability of an event that is certain is 1. For example, the probability that the result of the toss of a coin is either heads or tails is 1.

$$P(H \text{ or } T) = 1$$

Thus, for any probability P,

$$0 \leq P \leq 1.$$

The jar shown at the right contains 5 differently colored marbles. The sample space is $\{B, G, Y, R, W\}$. If you randomly pick a marble, the five simple events are equally likely to occur. Thus,

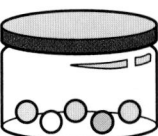

$$P(B) = P(G) = P(Y) = P(R) = P(W) = \frac{1}{5}.$$

In general, if $\{a_1, a_2, a_3, \ldots, a_n\}$ is a sample space with n equally likely simple events, then

$$P(a_1) = P(a_2) = P(a_3) = \cdots = P(a_n) = \frac{1}{n}.$$

The sum of the probabilities assigned to all simple events in a sample space of a random experiment is 1. For example, in the experiment of randomly picking a marble,

$$P(B) + P(G) + P(Y) + P(R) + P(W) = \frac{1}{5} + \frac{1}{5} + \frac{1}{5} + \frac{1}{5} + \frac{1}{5} = 1.$$

Thus, for the general sample space $\{a_1, a_2, a_3, \ldots, a_n\}$,

$$P(a_1) + P(a_2) + P(a_3) + \cdots + P(a_n) = 1.$$

Probability   **603**

Teaching Suggestions p. T141
Using Manipulatives p. T141
Group Activities p. T141

Warm-Up Exercises

There are 3 roses, 6 daisies, and 9 carnations in a bouquet. Write the fraction that represents each quantity.

1. the part of the bouquet made up of daisies
   $\frac{6}{18}$, or $\frac{1}{3}$

2. the part of the bouquet made up of roses
   $\frac{3}{18}$, or $\frac{1}{6}$

3. the part of the bouquet made up of orchids
   $\frac{0}{18}$, or 0

Motivating the Lesson

Ask the students whether they think it's likely that the sun will set today, that it will rain, that the sky will fall. Today they will study the likelihood of some events.

Chalkboard Examples

Given a spinner with 8 equal sections numbered 1, 2, 3, 4, 5, 6, 7, and 8, find the probability of each event.

1. *Event A:* The spinner stops on an odd number.
   Event A = $\{1, 3, 5, 7\}$
   $P(A) = \frac{4}{8} = \frac{1}{2}$

2. *Event B:* The spinner stops on a multiple of 2 or 3.
   Event B = $\{2, 3, 4, 6, 8\}$
   $P(B) = \frac{5}{8}$

3. *Event C:* The spinner stops on a number that is not divisible by 4.
   Event C = $\{1, 2, 3, 5, 6, 7\}$
   $P(C) = \frac{6}{8} = \frac{3}{4}$

Common Errors

Some students may think that the probability of an event is the number of simple events rather than the ratio of this number to the number of events in the entire sample space. In reteaching, emphasize that probability is expressed as a ratio greater than or equal to zero and less than or equal to 1.

Guided Practice

Two spinners both have four equal sections numbered 1, 2, 3, and 4.

1. Give the sample space.
   {(1, 1), (1, 2), (1, 3), (1, 4), (2, 1), (2, 2), (2, 3), (2, 4), (3, 1), (3, 2), (3, 3), (3, 4), (4, 1), (4, 2), (4, 3), (4, 4)}

2. Given that $P(x)$ means the probability of getting x as the sum, find the following probabilities.
   a. $P(6)$ $\frac{3}{16}$ b. $P(2)$ $\frac{1}{16}$
   c. $P(3 \text{ or } 4)$ $\frac{5}{16}$
   d. $P(\text{even number})$ $\frac{1}{2}$
   e. $P(\text{not } 7)$ $\frac{7}{8}$

Thinking Skills

In the study of probability, students learn to *draw inferences* about the likelihood of an event's happening by considering all possible outcomes.

Example A glass bowl contains 3 red marbles, 2 blue marbles, and 1 green marble. A marble is drawn at random from the bowl. Find the probability of each event.

  a. *Event A:* The marble drawn is blue.

  b. *Event B:* The marble drawn is either blue or green.

  c. *Event C:* The marble drawn is not green.

Solution The sample space is {red 1, red 2, red 3, blue 1, blue 2, green}.

  a. Since there are 2 blue marbles, *Event A* has 2 equally likely outcomes. So $P(A) = \frac{2}{6} = \frac{1}{3}$.

  b. Since there are 2 blue marbles and 1 green marble, *Event B* has 3 equally likely outcomes. So $P(B) = \frac{3}{6} = \frac{1}{2}$.

  c. If the marble is not green, then it must be either red or blue. Since there are 3 red marbles and 2 blue marbles, *Event C* has 5 equally likely outcomes. So $P(C) = \frac{5}{6}$.

Oral Exercises

A letter is selected randomly from the word PARABOLA. Name the probability of each event.

1. The letter is a vowel. $\frac{1}{2}$

2. The letter is a consonant. $\frac{1}{2}$

3. The letter is an A. $\frac{3}{8}$

4. The letter is a B. $\frac{1}{8}$

A cube whose sides are numbered 1, 2, 3, 4, 5, and 6 is tossed. Name the probability of each event.

5. The number is odd. $\frac{1}{2}$

6. The number is prime. $\frac{1}{2}$

7. The number is less than 7. 1

8. The number is greater than 0. 1

9. The number is not an integer. 0

10. The number is 3 or 5. $\frac{1}{3}$

11. Explain why the probability of an event cannot be greater than 1. By definition of probability, an event with n possible outcomes has a maximum probability of $\frac{n}{n}$, or 1.

Written Exercises

Solve.

A 1. A box contains 4 opals, 5 garnets, and 6 pearls. A jewel is selected at random from the box. Find the probability of the event that the jewel is:

  a. an opal $\frac{4}{15}$
  b. either an opal or a pearl $\frac{2}{3}$
  c. a garnet $\frac{1}{3}$
  d. not a garnet $\frac{2}{3}$

604 *Looking Ahead*

2. One card is drawn at random from a deck of 13 hearts, 13 diamonds, 13 clubs, and 13 spades. Find the probability of the event that the card is:

   a. a 5 $\frac{1}{13}$

   b. a red 7 $\frac{1}{26}$

   c. a club $\frac{1}{4}$

   d. the king of hearts $\frac{1}{52}$

   e. a 3 or 7 $\frac{2}{13}$

   f. an 8, 9, or 10 $\frac{3}{13}$

3. There are 24 students in your algebra class. The students are to explain a problem at the board. Each student determines his or her turn by taking a number at random from a jar. The jar contains the numbers 1–24. Find the probability of the event that:

   a. you are the first person to explain a problem. $\frac{1}{24}$

   b. you are one of the first 9 people to explain a problem. $\frac{3}{8}$

   c. your number is between 8 and 16 (not including 8 or 16). $\frac{7}{24}$

   d. your number is divisible by 5. $\frac{1}{6}$

4. The results of rolling two numbered cubes are shown in the table at the right. Copy and complete the table. Then use it to find the probability of each event listed below. $P(5)$ means "the probability of getting a sum of 5."

	1	2	3	4	5	6
6	(6, 1)	(6, 2)	(6,3) ?	(6,4) ?	(6,5) ?	(6,6) ?
5	(5, 1)	(5, 2)	(5,3) ?	(5,4) ?	(5,5) ?	(5,6) ?
4	(4, 1)	(4, 2)	(4,3) ?	(4,4) ?	(4,5) ?	(4,6) ?
3	(3, 1)	(3, 2)	(3,3) ?	(3,4) ?	(3,5) ?	(3,6) ?
2	(2, 1)	(2, 2)	(2, 3)	(2, 4)	(2,5) ?	(2,6) ?
1	(1, 1)	(1, 2)	(1, 3)	(1, 4)	(1, 5)	(1,6) ?

   a. $P(5)$ $\frac{1}{9}$

   b. $P(\text{not }5)$ $\frac{8}{9}$

   c. $P(4 \text{ or } 7)$ $\frac{1}{4}$

   d. $P(12)$ $\frac{1}{36}$

   e. $P(13)$ 0

   f. $P(2 \text{ or } 8)$ $\frac{1}{6}$

   g. $P(\text{not }6)$ $\frac{31}{36}$

   h. $P(\text{even number})$ $\frac{1}{2}$

   i. $P(\text{odd number})$ $\frac{1}{2}$

B 5. A penny, a nickel, and a dime are tossed. Find the probability of the event that the coins give:

   a. 3 heads $\frac{1}{8}$

   b. exactly two tails $\frac{3}{8}$

   c. at least 2 heads $\frac{1}{2}$

   d. one or two heads $\frac{3}{4}$

6. A spinner is divided into three equal sections numbered 1, 2, and 3. A second spinner is divided into four equal sections numbered 2, 4, 6, and 7. Each pointer is spun. Find the probability of each event.

   a. $P(1, 4)$ $\frac{1}{12}$

   b. $P(2, \text{not }2)$ $\frac{1}{4}$

   c. $P(3, 6)$ $\frac{1}{12}$

   d. $P(\text{even number, even number})$ $\frac{1}{4}$

   e. $P(\text{sum is }7)$ $\frac{1}{6}$

   f. $P(\text{sum is less than }8)$ $\frac{7}{12}$

C 7. A bag contains 1 red marble, 2 green marbles, and 3 white marbles. Two marbles are randomly selected. Find the probability of the event that the marbles are:

   a. 1 red and 1 green $\frac{2}{15}$

   b. 1 green and 1 white $\frac{2}{5}$

   c. neither red nor green $\frac{1}{5}$

   d. neither red nor white $\frac{1}{15}$

   e. two of the same color $\frac{4}{15}$

   f. 1 red and a green or a white $\frac{1}{3}$

Probability **605**

Summarizing the Lesson

Tell students that they have learned how to find the probability of some events. Have them write the probability of an event that is certain, and of an event that is impossible.

Suggested Assignments

Maximum
  604/1–7

Supplementary Materials

Study Guide   pp. 221–222

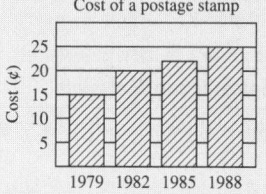
Statistics

Frequency Distributions

Objective   To recognize and analyze frequency distributions.

Thirty-one students received the following scores on a test.

77 67 91 63 81 89 100 73 67 85 89 89 95 83 79 89
66 83 88 97 74 77   88 89 95 79 83 95 83 98 94

A collection of data is more meaningful when you have organized the data. The table at the right arranges the scores in decreasing order and also tells how many students received each score. The information given in this table is called a **frequency distribution.**

Another way to describe a frequency distribution is to draw a graph called a **histogram,** as shown below. In a histogram, data are grouped into convenient intervals. The intervals in this histogram of test scores are 60–65, 65–70, and so on. A test score of 75 is considered to be in the interval 70–75, while a score of 80 is in the interval 75–80. A "boundary" score in a histogram like the one below is usually included in the interval to its left.

Score	Number of Students
100	1
98	1
97	1
95	3
94	1
91	1
89	5
88	2
85	1
83	4
81	1
79	2
77	2
74	1
73	1
67	2
66	1
63	1

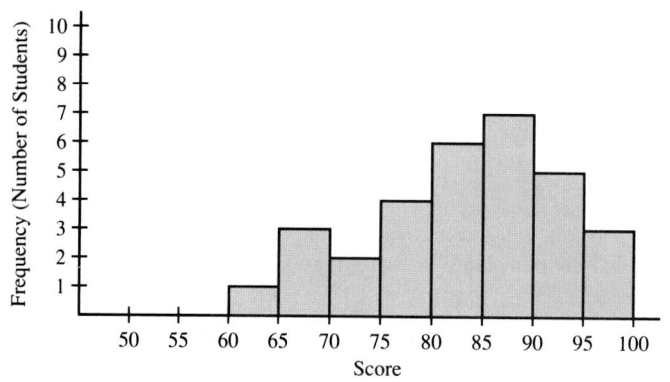

Frequency distributions are often analyzed using numbers called *statistics*. The *mean, median,* and *mode* are statistics used in analyzing a distribution. The **mean** of a collection of data is the sum of the data divided by the number of items of data. The sum of the test scores given for the 31 students is 2606. Then the mean (*M*) of the test scores is

$$M = \frac{\text{sum of data}}{\text{number of items}} = \frac{2606}{31} = 84.06 \approx 84.$$

606   *Looking Ahead*

The **median** of a frequency distribution is the middle number when the data are arranged in order. If the number of data is even, the average of the two numbers closest to the middle is the median. Arranging the test scores in increasing order gives:

63 66 67 67 73 74 77 77 79 79 81 83 83 83 83 85
88 88 89 89 89 89 89 91 94 95 95 95 97 98 100

The median is 85, which is the sixteenth score.

The **mode** is the most frequently occurring number in a frequency distribution. A set of data may have one or more modes or none at all. From the frequency table, the mode of the test scores is 89. The mode is most useful in analyzing nonnumerical data, such as color or taste preferences.

Another important statistic is the *range,* which is used to indicate the spread of the data in a distribution. The **range** of a frequency distribution is the difference between the highest and the lowest values. For example, the range of the data in the table is $100 - 63$, or 37.

Example Two numbered cubes are rolled 10 times. The product of the numbers after each roll are, in increasing order, 2, 6, 8, 12, 18, 20, 24, 24, 30, and 36. Find the mean, the median, the mode, and the range of the data.

Solution $M = \dfrac{2 + 6 + 8 + 12 + 18 + 20 + 24 + 24 + 30 + 36}{10} = \dfrac{180}{10} = 18$

Since there is an even number of data, the median is the average of the two middle scores.

$$\text{median} = \frac{18 + 20}{2} = \frac{38}{2} = 19$$

Since 24 is the score that occurs most frequently, it is the mode.

The range is the difference between 36 and 2, or 34.

Computers and calculators, especially graphing calculators, are very useful when doing a statistical analysis of data.

Oral Exercises

1. The histogram at the right shows the frequency distribution for the number of points scored in a game by a high school basketball team for a season of 18 games.

   State the number of games in which the team scored:

   a. between 50 and 60 points 3

   b. between 90 and 100 points 1

   c. between 60 and 80 points 11

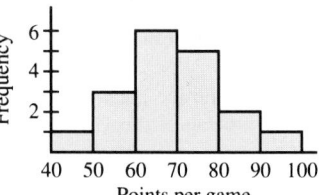

Statistics **607**

---

c. The most any of these numbers occurs is twice. Both 13 and 17 occur twice, so they are the modes.

d. range $= 17 - 13 = 4$

Check for Understanding

Oral Exs. 1–4: use after the Example.

 Using a Computer or a Graphing Calculator

Histograms can be drawn using a computer or a graphing calculator. You may wish to have students use one of these tools to draw the histogram in Written Exercise 10.

The program "Statistical Spreadsheet" on the Disk for Algebra can be used to compute the mean and median for a given distribution. A calculator can also be used for this purpose.

Support Materials
   Disk for Algebra
      Menu Item: Statistics
         Spreadsheet

Guided Practice

Find (a) the mean, (b) the median, (c) the mode, and (d) the range.

1. Seven members of a basketball team scored 6, 11, 3, 19, 8, 14, and 9 points during a game.
   (a) 10 (b) 9
   (c) none (d) 16

2. The heights (in meters to the nearest hundredth) of a group of ninth graders are 1.65, 1.72, 1.61, 1.75, 1.58, 1.63, 1.61, 1.73, 1.65, and 1.61.
   (a) 1.65 (b) 1.64
   (c) 1.61 (d) 0.17

(continued)

3. Draw a histogram for the
data in Exercise 1 using
the intervals 0–5, 5–10,
and so on.

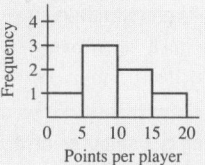

Points per player

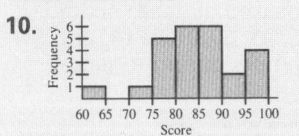
2. In four days Michelle earned \$5, \$3, \$9, and \$3. For her earnings, find:
 a. the mean \$5   **b.** the mode \$3   **c.** the median \$4   **d.** the range \$6

3. In five successive baseball games, the Apex Cougars scored 3, 2, 0, 6, and
4 runs. For this distribution, find:
 a. the mean 3   **b.** the mode none   **c.** the median 3   **d.** the range 6

4. If the range for a given set of data is 0, explain why the mean, median,
and mode are all equal. Since the highest value and the lowest value of the data
are equal, each value in the distribution is the same.

Written Exercises

For the data in Exercises 1–6, find (a) the mean, (b) the median, (c) the mode,
and (d) the range. Wherever appropriate, give answers to the nearest tenth.

A **1.** 53, 32, 49, 24, 62 44; 49; none; 38   **2.** 8, 15, 41, 31, 15 22; 15; 15; 33

3. 32, 29, 40, 17, 32, 22 28.7; 30.5; 32; 23   **4.** 11, 9, 19, 9, 19, 9, 13 12.7; 11; 9; 10

5. 61, 53, 52, 56, 61, 53, 56 56; 56; 53 and
                         56 and 61; 9   **6.** 72, 78, 63, 49, 81, 50, 66 65.6; 66;
                                                                      none; 32

7. In six debate matches David scored 81, 92, 85, 81, 84, and 92. Find the
mean, the median, the mode, and the range of his scores. 85.8; 84.5; 81 and 92; 11

8. Find the mean and range for the average monthly temperatures given in
degrees Celsius: $-1.5°$, $-2°$, $5°$, $16.5°$, $20°$, $24.5°$, $28°$, $33.5°$, $29.5°$,
$18.5°$, $6°$, $2.5°$. 15.0°; 35.5°

9. For ten consecutive days, Lara ran 8, 10, 7, 9, 10, 11, 12, 11, 12, and 12
laps around the track. To the nearest tenth of a lap, find the mean, the
median, the mode, and the range. 10.2; 10.5; 12; 5

10. In a class of 25 students, the test scores were 78, 90, 95, 76, 65, 80, 90,
96, 100, 98, 84, 88, 81, 76, 100, 94, 90, 83, 73, 85, 90, 81, 79, 81, and
88. First make a frequency table. Then group the data into the intervals
60–65, 65–70, and so on. Draw a histogram for the data.

B **11.** Vin needs an average of 90% in 6 classes in order to participate in a Scholastic Fair this summer. He knows his percentages in 5 classes: 85, 98, 87,
85, and 89. What percentage must he have in the sixth class? 96%

12. If each score on an algebra test is increased by 10 points, how does this
affect the: increases   increases by 10   increases by 10   stays the same
 a. mean? by 10   **b.** mode?   **c.** median?   **d.** range?

13. If each number in a set of data is multiplied by three, how does this affect the:
 a. mean?   **b.** mode?   **c.** median?   **d.** range?

14. The mean of 8 numbers is 17. What is the sum of the numbers? 136

   13a–d. Each statistic is multiplied by 3.

C **15.** Find the mean of 12 numbers if the mean of the first three is 32 and the
mean of the last nine numbers is 40. 38

16. Felicia has a score of 89 for each of her first eight geometry tests. Her
score on the ninth test is 96. What does her score for the tenth test have to
be for a final mean score of 90? 92

Extra / *Measures of Variation*

Objective   To calculate measures of variation for a given distribution.

You learned previously (pages 606–607) that the mean, median, and mode are important numbers for analyzing a set of data. Statisticians are also interested in how the data are dispersed, or spread, throughout the distribution. The statistics used to measure this dispersion are called measures of variation.

The range (page 607) is a *weak* measure of variation because it uses only two values of the distribution. For example, compare the range values for the following two groups of data.

    Group A: 11, 12, 14, 14, 14, 14, 19   Range = 19 − 11 = 8
    Group B: 11, 12, 14, 16, 17, 17, 18   Range = 18 − 11 = 7

Groups A and B have almost the same range, but the data in Group A are more clustered together than in Group B. Although the range is easy to calculate, it can be a misleading measure of variation.

Strong measures of variation use the distance of each value of the distribution from the mean, M. The **variance,** denoted by σ^2 (σ is the Greek letter sigma), is the mean of the squares of the distance of each data item (x_i) from the mean. For a distribution of n data items,

$$\sigma^2 = \frac{(x_1 - M)^2 + (x_2 - M)^2 + \cdots + (x_n - M)^2}{n}.$$

The **standard deviation,** denoted by σ, is the principal square root of the variance.

Example 1   Calculate, to the nearest tenth, the variance and standard deviation for the data 6, 7, 9, 10, and 13.

Solution   First find the mean: $M = \dfrac{6 + 7 + 9 + 10 + 13}{5} = 9$

Make a table to find the square of the distance of each data item from the mean ($M = 9$).

x_i	$x_i - M$	$(x_i - M)^2$
6	−3	9
7	−2	4
9	0	0
10	1	1
13	4	16

Since $n = 5$, the variance is:

$$\sigma^2 = \frac{9 + 4 + 0 + 1 + 16}{5} = 6$$

Answer

Then the standard deviation is:

$$\sigma = \sqrt{\sigma^2} = \sqrt{6} \approx 2.4 \quad \textbf{\textit{Answer}}$$

A useful statistic for identifying the relative position of an individual value within a distribution is the distance that a data item is from the mean *in terms of the standard deviation*. This distance is called the *standard score*, or *z-score*. For a distribution with mean M and standard deviation σ, a data item x_i has a standard score given by

$$z = \frac{x_i - M}{\sigma}.$$

Example 2 Find to the nearest tenth the standard score for each data item in the distribution in Example 1.

Solution In Example 1, $M = 9$ and $\sigma = 2.4$. The standard scores are computed at the right. Notice the data item 13 has 1.7 as its standard score. This means that 13 is 1.7 standard deviations from the mean 9.

x_i	$\frac{x_i - M}{\sigma}$ = standard score
6	$\frac{6-9}{2.4} \approx -1.3$
7	$\frac{7-9}{2.4} \approx -0.8$
9	$\frac{9-9}{2.4} = 0$
10	$\frac{10-9}{2.4} \approx 0.4$
13	$\frac{13-9}{2.4} \approx 1.7$

Exercises

1. Explain why the standard deviation for 7, 7, 7, 7, 7, and 7 is 0.

2. Groups A and B on page 609 have almost the same range. Explain why Group B must have a higher variance than Group A. Verify this by finding the variance for each group.

3. Golf scores for a 9-hole course for six players were 38, 41, 48, 45, 38, and 36.

   a. Find the mean golf score. 41
   b. Find the standard deviation to the nearest tenth. 4.2
   c. Find the standard score to the nearest tenth for each score. See margin

x_i	stand. score
36	−1.2
38	−0.7
41	0
45	1.0
48	1.7

4. A set of test scores had a mean of 26 and a standard deviation of 5. Find the standard score for each of the following scores from the distribution.

   a. 31 1   b. 22 −0.8   c. 17 −1.8   d. 29 0.6   e. 26 0   f. 40 2.8

5. Two factories compared the number of items their workers could produce in an hour:

   Factory I: $M = 235$, $\sigma = 14$
   Factory II: $M = 235$, $\sigma = 6$

In which factory were the production rates of the workers more nearly alike? How do you know? Factory II; the standard deviation is less, thus there must have been less of a difference between each data item and the mean.

6. On a chapter test, you received a standard score of 3.4. If the mean score was 76 and the standard deviation was 5, what was your actual score? 93

610 *Looking Ahead*

Presenting Statistical Data

Objective   To construct stem-and-leaf plots and box-and-whisker plots.

Statisticians organize data they have collected in order to present it in a useful form. You have learned that bar graphs, broken-line graphs (page 375), and histograms (page 606) can be used to summarize data.

Another way to organize data is by a **stem-and-leaf plot.** In this type of display the raw data values themselves are incorporated into a frequency distribution. This method is illustrated for the following set of thirty scores.

83	71	92	79	74	80	63	86	84	74
100	81	94	98	79	62	50	82	56	67
75	86	83	96	57	100	87	67	98	44

First the *stems* (in black), derived by dropping the unit's digit from each score, are written in order to the left of a vertical line. For each score the *leaf*, or unit's digit (in red), is then recorded to the right of the corresponding stem. For the score of 84, for example, the leaf 4 is recorded to the right of the stem 8. The leaves are separated by commas, using equal space for each leaf. Then the plot can be rotated to become a histogram, displaying the shape of the frequency distribution. Unlike a standard histogram, the stem-and-leaf plot still retains every individual score in coded form.

Stem	Leaf
4	4
5	0, 6, 7
6	3, 2, 7, 7
7	1, 9, 4, 4, 9, 5
8	3, 0, 6, 4, 1, 2, 6, 3, 7
9	2, 4, 8, 6, 8
10	0, 0

Researchers often wish to compare pairs of data, such as these semester mathematics (M) and history (H) averages collected from twenty students.

M	83	90	64	49	73	81	71	60	79	62	85	72	78	66	93	81	74	85	66	76
H	76	85	75	67	88	90	88	78	90	57	93	71	96	71	91	54	81	78	81	82

Scatter graphs or *diagrams* often are used to show researchers whether a relationship exists between two measurements. Researchers can then base predictions on the patterns they observe in these relationships. The diagram shown in the Application on page 378 is a scatter graph. Each pair of points in the table above can be plotted on a scatter graph to investigate the relationship between the mathematics and history averages.

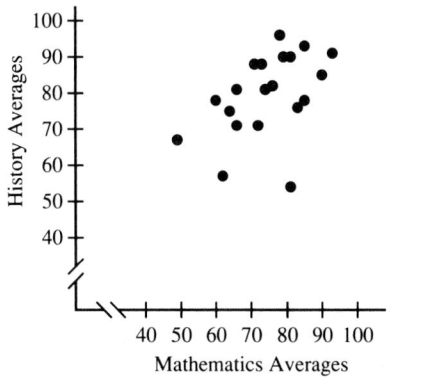

Statistics   **611**

Teaching Suggestions p. T142
Group Activities p. T142

Warm-Up Exercises

1. Graph the values -3, 0, -1.5, 5, and 3.5 on a number line.

2. Find the median and the range of the data in Exercise 1. 0 ; 8

Motivating the Lesson

Ask the students to name and describe some kinds of graphs newspapers use to show data (for example, pictographs, bar graphs, and circle graphs). In today's lesson they'll construct two new kinds of graphs for presenting statistical data.

Chalkboard Examples

The ages of 9 cousins are 20, 27, 12, 31, 10, 14, 23, 27, and 22. Use these data to construct:

1. a stem-and-leaf plot
   Arrange the data in order.
   10 12 14 20 22 23 27 27 31

Stem	Leaf
1	0, 2, 4
2	0, 2, 3, 7, 7
3	1

2. a box-and-whisker plot
   lowest age: 10
   median age: 22
   highest age: 31
   first quartile age: 14
   third quartile age: 27

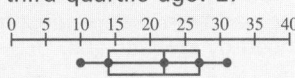

Check for Understanding

Here is a suggested use of
the Oral Exercises to check
students' understanding as
you teach the lesson.
Oral Ex. 1: use after the
discussion of stem-
and-leaf plots on
p. 611.
Oral Ex. 2: use after the
discussion on p. 612.

Guided Practice

The stem-and-leaf plot
below shows ages in
months of 11 ninth graders.

18 | 4 3 1
17 | 5 2 3 4
16 | 8 6 7 8

1. List the ages in order.
166, 167, 168, 168, 172,
173, 174, 175, 181, 183,
184

2. Find the:
  a. lowest age 166
  b. highest age 184
  c. range 18
  d. median range 173
  e. first quartile age 168
  f. third quartile age 178

3. Make a box-and-whisker
plot for the data.

Summarizing the Lesson

Tell students that they have
learned several ways to represent data. Ask students to
tell when stem-and-leaf
plots, scatter graphs, and
box-and-whisker graphs are
used by statisticians.

The averages can also be compared by using **box-and-whisker plots.** To
construct a box-and-whisker plot, the following values must be identified for
each set of data: highest score, lowest score, median score, and first and third
quartile scores.

Recall that the median of a set of scores is the middle score when the data
are arranged in order. The first quartile score is the median of the bottom half
of the data, and the third quartile score is the median of the upper half of the
data. In the example on the previous page, the mathematics averages, in order,
are:

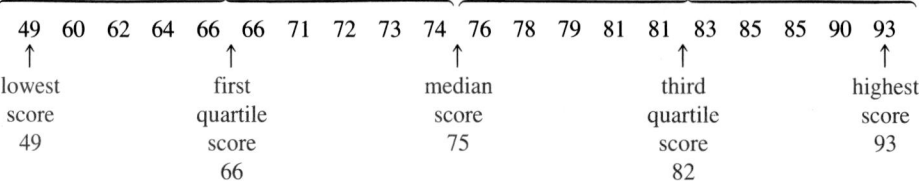

Identify these five special values with dots below a number line.

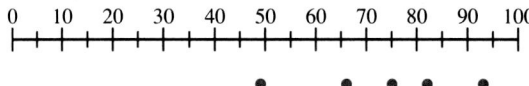

Next, make a box with the two quartile scores on the outer sides. Draw a line
inside the box, through the median dot. Finally, draw "whiskers" from the
sides of the box to the dots of the lowest and highest scores.

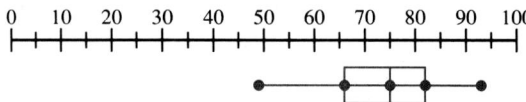

Verify the given box-and-whisker plot for the set of history averages (median:
81; lowest score: 54; highest score: 96; first quartile: 73; third quartile: 89).

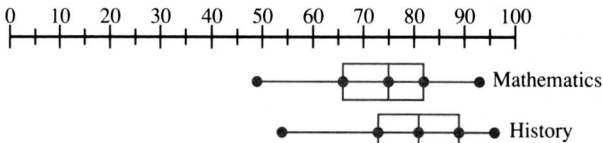

Notice that the box encloses the middle half of the data while the whiskers
show the range. By studying the box-and-whisker plot for each set of data, you
can easily compare the ranges and the locations of the middle halves of the distributions.

612 *Looking Ahead*

Oral Exercises

1. Use the distribution of scores given by the stem-and-leaf plot at the left below to list the original scores in order.

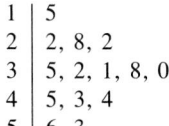

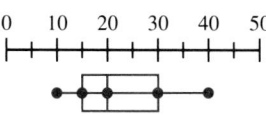

15, 22, 22, 28, 30, 31, 32, 35, 38, 43, 44, 45, 53, 56

2. Use the box-and-whisker plot at the right above to state the value of the:
   a. first quartile 15   b. median 20   c. third quartile 30   d. range 30

Written Exercises

1a. 51, 53, 54, 62, 63, 65, 68, 70, 71, 73, 76, 77, 79, 84, 84, 88, 90, 95

A

1. Use the distribution of scores given by the stem-and-leaf plot shown at the right.
   a. List the original scores of the distribution in order.
   b. What are the median, the mode, and the range of the scores?
      72, 84, 44

   5 | 3, 1, 4
   6 | 8, 2, 3, 5
   7 | 7, 3, 6, 9, 0, 1
   8 | 4, 8, 4
   9 | 5, 0

2. Twenty students reported the amount of money they earned last week in part-time jobs. They earned (in dollars) 102, 115, 87, 91, 80, 73, 114, 145, 137, 135, 127, 120, 86, 100, 134, 129, 133, 88, 75, and 109. Construct a stem-and-leaf plot for their earnings.

   7 | 3, 5
   8 | 7, 0, 6, 8
   9 | 1
   10 | 2, 0, 9
   11 | 5, 4
   12 | 7, 0, 9
   13 | 7, 5, 4, 3
   14 | 5

3. Eleven students were asked to rate a presentation given by a speaker on a scale from 1 to 10, with 10 as the highest score. The results were 7, 9, 8, 5, 8, 10, 9, 7, 8, 6, and 4. Find the:
   a. median 8   b. first quartile score 6   c. third quartile score 9
   d. highest score 10   e. lowest score 4   f. range 6

4. Make a box-and-whisker plot for the data in Exercise 3.

Use the following data for Exercises 5–7: Fifteen cars were road tested on both city streets and highways. The resulting fuel economy data were recorded.

City (mi/gal)	22	21	28	19	28	30	21	20	19	28	22	24	21	24	28
Highway (mi/gal)	24	27	32	23	29	38	24	25	24	30	23	26	26	26	31

B

5. For the city driving test, find the median, first quartile score, third quartile score, highest score, and lowest score. 22; 21; 28; 30; 19

6. For the highway driving test, find the median, first quartile score, third quartile score, highest score, and lowest score. 26; 24; 30; 38; 23

7. Using the same number-line scale, construct box-and-whisker plots to compare the mi/gal figures for city and highway driving.

Suggested Assignments
Maximum
   613/1–7
   615/1–3

Supplementary Materials
Study Guide   pp. 225–226
Overhead Visual   14

**Additional Answers
Written Exercises**

4.

7.

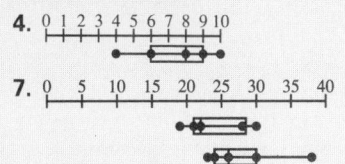

Thinking Skills

In this Application students are asked to *draw inferences* from survey results and graphs and to use *reasoning* to determine whether results are reported in a misleading way.

Application / *Misuse of Statistics*

In today's world statistics plays an increasingly important role in decision making. Decisions are usually based on conclusions drawn from a study of a particular fact about a large population. If people do not use statistics correctly, either by accident or on purpose, faulty conclusions can be drawn.

Data are often collected by a survey. Since it is not practical to survey an entire group, statisticians must select a small part of the population, a sample, that is representative of the total population. Misleading statistics can be produced if the data collection for a given population is faulty. There are two important things to consider when a sample is used: the way in which the sample is selected and the size of the sample.

Example 1 Study each advertisement. Do you agree with the conclusion of the ad?

a.
Users of BRUSH Toothpaste have 30% fewer cavities.

Data obtained in interviews with 50 people in Thompsonville.

b.
ROCK MUSIC IS THE WINNER!
43% of all listeners prefer rock music to jazz.

936 students at CENTER HIGH SCHOOL were surveyed.

Solution

a. In this advertisement, only 50 people were surveyed. This is a very small number of people on which to base the conclusion that BRUSH toothpaste reduces cavities for everyone.

b. The sample of 936 people used in this advertisement is large, but the way in which this sample was selected is not correct. This sample is probably not representative of the entire population because it does not indicate which music students in other high schools or adults prefer. Surveys must be conducted so that they represent the entire population.

Graphs are often used to summarize data in a form that is easy to read. Choices must be made about how to draw a particular graph. Sometimes graphs of the same data can be made to tell different stories.

Example 2 Study and compare the two different broken-line graphs of the same data shown on the next page. Do you think profits are growing during the years 1982 to 1988?

614 *Looking Ahead*

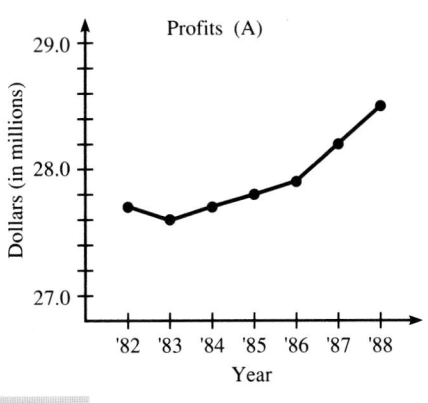

Solution Each of these graphs shows the same data, yet they tell very different stories. Graph A makes it seem that the profits are definitely growing. Graph B makes it seem that the profits are not changing much. The different stories come from using two different scales on the vertical axes. (Notice that the range of the values for the vertical axis of Graph A is 2 whereas the range of the values for the vertical axis of Graph B is 6.) While nothing in either graph is untrue, the graph you might use to describe the data would depend on which story you wanted to tell.

Exercises

Analyze each advertisement. Do you think that the use of statistics is misleading? Give a reason for your answer.

1.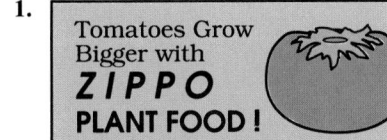

2.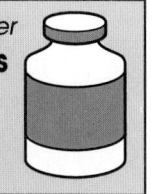

3. The table shows the salaries of a company's employees.

   a. Find the median salary for these ten employees.

   b. Find the mean salary for these ten employees.

   c. Do you think the mean or the median is the better description of what most people earn at this company? Give a reason for your answer.

   d. If you want to tell the story that all ten employees earn similar salaries, what scale would you use on the vertical axis of your graph? Draw the broken-line graph.

   e. If you want to tell the story that there is a large difference between some of the salaries, what scale would you use on the vertical axis of your graph? Draw the broken-line graph.

Yearly Salaries	
$21,500	$22,000
$21,750	$22,000
$21,750	$22,350
$21,800	$47,500
$22,000	$53,000

Statistics **615**

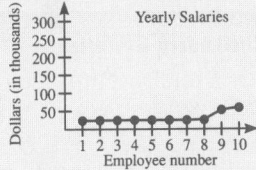
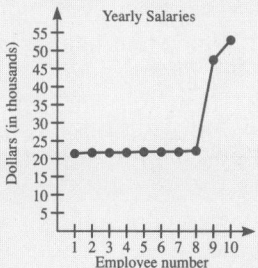

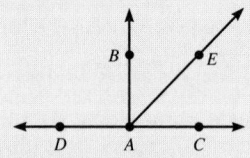
Geometry

Points, Lines, and Angles

Objective To represent points, lines, and angles and to measure angles.

You have shown relationships among numbers by representing them as points on a number line. Likewise, you have shown relationships among ordered pairs of numbers by representing them as points in a coordinate plane. The study of *points, lines,* and *planes* is the subject of the branch of mathematics called *geometry*.

Geometric points and *lines* are abstract ideas, not actual objects. A point has no size; a line has no thickness. To illustrate these abstract ideas, however, you draw figures that do have size and thickness. To represent the idea of a geometric point, you draw a dot. To represent the idea of a geometric line, you draw a straight line.

A line consists of infinitely many points. Any two points determine a line. A line determined by points A and B is denoted by $\overleftrightarrow{AB}$ or $\overleftrightarrow{BA}$. The arrowheads indicate that the line extends in both directions without end.

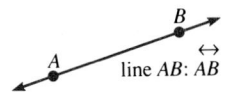

line AB: $\overleftrightarrow{AB}$

The part of $\overleftrightarrow{AB}$ that consists of points A and B and all points of $\overleftrightarrow{AB}$ between A and B is called a **line segment,** or a **segment.** The segment is denoted by $\overline{AB}$ or $\overline{BA}$. The length of $\overline{AB}$ is denoted by AB.

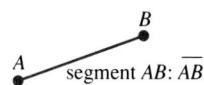

segment AB: $\overline{AB}$

The part of $\overleftrightarrow{AB}$ that starts at point A and extends without ending through point B is a **ray,** denoted by $\overrightarrow{AB}$. A is called the **endpoint** of $\overrightarrow{AB}$.

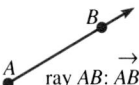

ray AB: $\overrightarrow{AB}$

An **angle** is a figure formed by two different rays that have the same endpoint. The rays are called the **sides** of the angle and the common endpoint is called the **vertex** of the angle. The angle shown at the right is formed by $\overrightarrow{AB}$ and $\overrightarrow{AC}$. It is denoted by $\angle A$, $\angle BAC$, or $\angle CAB$. When three letters are used to name an angle, the middle letter is always the vertex.

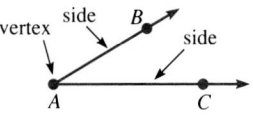

616 *Looking Ahead*

To find the **degree measure** of an angle, you use a protractor. Using the outer scale, you can see that the degree measure of ∠POQ is 60. You will see this fact written as m∠POQ = 60, m∠POQ = 60°, or ∠POQ = 60°. For simplicity, we will use ∠POQ = 60°. Also, ∠POR = 90° and ∠POS = 150°.

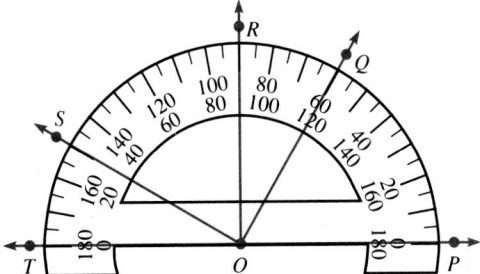

Angles are classified according to their measures.

> An **acute angle** has measure between 0° and 90°.
> A **right angle** has measure 90°.
> An **obtuse angle** has measure between 90° and 180°.
> A **straight angle** has measure 180°.

The degree measure of ∠QOR in the diagram above is found by subtracting 60 from 90: ∠QOR = 30°. Do you see that ∠ROS = 60° and ∠QOS is a right angle? To state that ∠POQ and ∠ROS have equal measures, write ∠POQ = ∠ROS.

Oral Exercises

Exercises 1–8 refer to the diagram below.

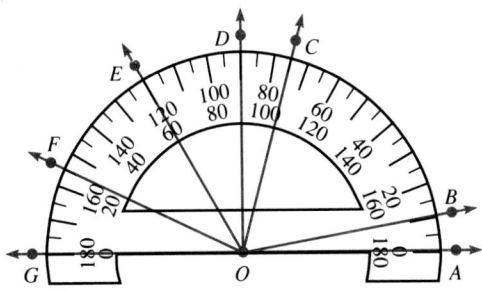

State the measure of the angle.

1. ∠AOC 75° **2.** ∠EOF 35° **3.** ∠BOE 110° **4.** ∠BOF 145°

Name an angle whose measure is given.

5. 15° ∠COD **6.** 65° ∠BOC or ∠DOF **7.** 90° ∠AOD or ∠DOG **8.** 80° ∠COF or ∠BOD

Geometry   **617**

---

3. Name four rays.
$\overrightarrow{AB}, \overrightarrow{AD}, \overrightarrow{DC}, \overrightarrow{AE}$

4. a. Name two angles that appear to be acute.
∠EAB, ∠CAE

  b. Name one angle that appears to be obtuse.
∠DAE

Check for Understanding

Here is a suggested use of the Oral Exercises to check students' understanding as you teach the lesson.
Oral Exs. 1–8: use after the discussion on p. 617.

Guided Practice

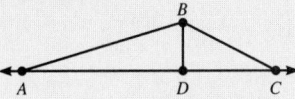

Refer to the diagram above.

1. Name six different line segments. $\overline{AD}, \overline{AC}, \overline{AB}, \overline{BC}, \overline{BD}, \overline{DC}$

2. Name four angles that appear to be acute.
∠BAC, ∠BCA, ∠ABD, ∠DBC

3. Name one angle that appears to be obtuse.
∠ABC

4. Name one angle that appears to be straight.
∠ADC

Summarizing the Lesson

Tell students that they have learned the physical representations of points and lines and that definitions were given for line segment, ray, and angle. The use of a protractor was explained and special angles were classified by measure.

Written Exercises

In Exercises 1–4, name five different line segments in each diagram.

A **1.**

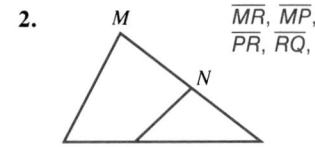

$\overline{WX}$, $\overline{WY}$, $\overline{WZ}$, $\overline{XY}$, $\overline{XZ}$, $\overline{YZ}$

2.

$\overline{MR}$, $\overline{MP}$, $\overline{MN}$, $\overline{NP}$,
$\overline{PR}$, $\overline{RQ}$, $\overline{QP}$, $\overline{NQ}$

3.

$\overline{AE}$, $\overline{BC}$, $\overline{EB}$, $\overline{ED}$, $\overline{DB}$,
$\overline{AC}$, $\overline{AD}$, $\overline{DC}$

4.

$\overline{HF}$, $\overline{HK}$, $\overline{FK}$, $\overline{FG}$, $\overline{KG}$

Measure the given angle and classify it as acute, obtuse, right, or straight.

5. ∠*DOE* acute

6. ∠*AOC* obtuse

7. ∠*EOG* right

8. ∠*BOH* acute

9. ∠*EOH* obtuse

10. ∠*AOE* straight

11. ∠*DOF* acute

12. ∠*FOH* right

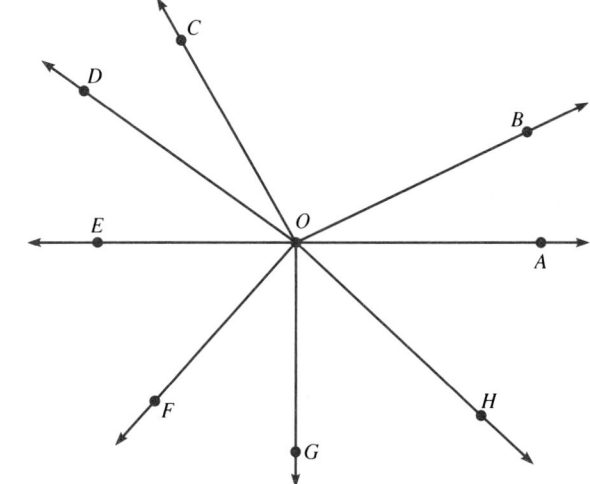

Graph the solution set of each sentence. Identify the graph as a point, a line, a line segment, or a ray.

B **13.** $x \leq 2$ ray

14. $-5 \leq x \leq -1$ line segment

15. $x = -4$ point

16. $-7 \leq x + 2 \leq 11$ line segment

17. $3x - 4 = 1$ point

18. $x + 5 = x - 2 + 7$ line

C **19.** $x - 3 \geq 1$ and $x + 2 \leq 10$ line segment

20. $1 + x \geq 5$ or $x - 3 \leq 9$ line

21. $2x \geq 8$ or $-3x \geq -9$ two rays

22. $3x + 7 \geq 1$ and $4x - 3 \geq 17$ ray

---

618   *Looking Ahead*

 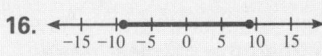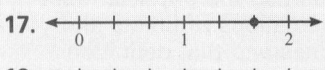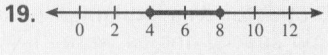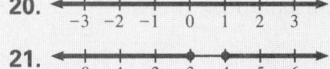

Pairs of Angles

Objective   To learn the names and properties of special pairs of angles.

The diagram at the right shows two lines intersecting at
O and forming $\angle AOB$, $\angle AOC$, $\angle COD$, and $\angle DOB$.
Two angles such as $\angle AOB$ and $\angle COD$ whose sides are
rays in the same lines but in opposite directions are
called **vertical angles**. Another pair of vertical
angles is $\angle AOC$ and $\angle DOB$. Vertical angles have equal
measures. You can use a protractor to see that $\angle AOB$
has the same measure as $\angle COD$ and $\angle AOC$ has the
same measure as $\angle DOB$.

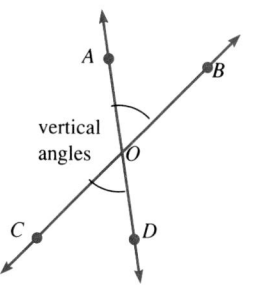

   Two angles are **complementary angles** if the sum
of their measures is 90°. Each angle is called a **complement** of the other. The
diagram at the left below shows a pair of complementary angles.

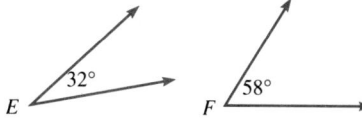

$\angle E$ and $\angle F$ are complementary.
$\angle E$ is a complement of $\angle F$.
$\angle F$ is a complement of $\angle E$.

$\angle G$ and $\angle H$ are supplementary.
$\angle G$ is a supplement of $\angle H$.
$\angle H$ is a supplement of $\angle G$.

   Two angles are **supplementary angles** if the sum of their measures is
180°. Each angle is called a **supplement** of the other. The diagram at the right
above shows a pair of supplementary angles.

Example   The measure of a supplement of an angle is 10° more than five times the
measure of its complement. Find the measure of the angle.

Solution   Let n = the measure of the angle in degrees.
Then $90 - n$ = the measure of its complement,
and $180 - n$ = the measure of its supplement.

$$180 - n = 5(90 - n) + 10$$
$$180 - n = 450 - 5n + 10$$
$$4n = 280$$
$$n = 70$$

The measure of the complement is $(90 - 70)°$, or 20°.
The measure of the supplement is $(180 - 70)°$, or 110°.
Check: $110 \overset{?}{=} 5(20) + 10$
   $110 = 110$ $\checkmark$

∴ the measure of the angle is 70°.   ***Answer***

Teaching Suggestions, p. T143

Warm-Up Exercises

Complete.

Two different __?__ that have
the same endpoint form an
angle. The common end-
point is called the __?__ of
the angle. An acute angle
has measure between __?__ °
and __?__ °, and an obtuse
angle has measure between
__?__ ° and __?__ °.   rays, vertex,
0, 90, 90, 180

Motivating the Lesson

To introduce today's lesson,
have students draw two intersecting lines on a piece of
paper. Have them measure
the angles formed and write
down their measurements.
Ask students what they notice about the measure-
ments. Students may see
that some of the measures
are equal and that some of
the measures add up to 180.

Chalkboard Examples

The sum of the measures of
a complement and a supplement of an angle is 134°.
Find the measure of the
angle.

Let n = measure of angle in
degrees.
$90 - n$ = measure of its
comp.
$180 - n$ = measure of its
supp.

$90 - n + 180 - n = 134$
$270 - 2n = 134$
$-2n = -136$
$n = 68$

measure of comp. = 22°
measure of supp. = 112°
Check: 22 + 112 = 134
∴ the measure of the angle
is 68°.

Oral Exercises

State the measure of a complement of an angle with the given measure.

1. 20° 70°   **2.** 87° 3°   **3.** 45° 45°   **4.** 33° 57°   **5.** $x°$ $(90 - x)°$ **6.** $7x°$ $(90 - 7x)°$

State the measure of a supplement of an angle with the given measure.

7. 40° 140°   **8.** 90° 90°   **9.** 153° 27°   **10.** 12° 168°   **11.** $y°$ $(180 - y)°$ **12.** $21t°$ $(180 - 21t)°$

Classify each statement as true or false.

13. The measures of two complementary angles are never equal. false

14. If the measures of the supplements of two angles are equal, then the measures of the angles are equal. true

15. The complement of an acute angle is obtuse. false

16. The supplement of an acute angle is an obtuse angle. true

17. A supplement of a right angle is a right angle. true

18. If two supplementary angles are vertical, then the angles are both right angles. true

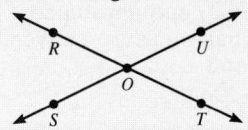
Written Exercises

In Exercises 1–4, use the diagram at the right. Assume that the measures of ∠EAB and ∠ABF are equal.

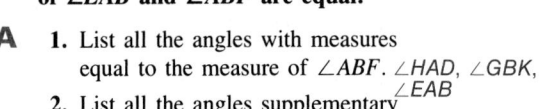
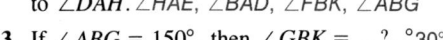

A

1. List all the angles with measures equal to the measure of ∠ABF. ∠HAD, ∠GBK, ∠EAB

2. List all the angles supplementary to ∠DAH. ∠HAE, ∠BAD, ∠FBK, ∠ABG

3. If ∠ABG = 150°, then ∠GBK = __?__ ° 30°

4. If ∠EAH = 135°, then ∠ABG = __?__ ° 135°

5. The smaller of two complementary angles measures 50° less than the larger. Find the measures of the two angles. 70° and 20°

6. The larger of two supplementary angles measures 8 times the smaller. Find the measures of the two angles. 20°, 160°

7. Find the measure of an angle that is 74° more than the measure of its supplement. 127°

8. Find the measure of an angle that is $\frac{1}{4}$ of the measure of its complement. 18°

B

9. The sum of the measures of a complement and a supplement of an angle is 144°. Find the measure of the angle. 63°

10. The measure of a supplement of an angle exceeds 10 times the measure of its complement by 9°. Find the measure of the angle. 81°

Triangles

Objective   To learn some properties of triangles.

A **triangle** is the figure formed by three segments joining three points not on the same line. Each segment is a **side** of the triangle. Each of the three points is a **vertex** (vertices) of the triangle.

"Triangle *ABC*" can be written △*ABC*.

Sides of △*ABC*: $\overline{AB}$, $\overline{BC}$, $\overline{CA}$
Vertices of △*ABC*: *A*, *B*, *C*
Angles of △*ABC*: ∠*A*, ∠*B*, ∠*C*

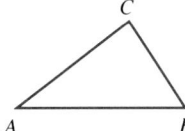

In any triangle, the sum of the measures of the angles is 180°. To check this statement for a particular triangle, measure each angle with a protractor and then find the sum of the measures. You can also show this by tearing off the corners of a paper triangle and fitting them together so that they form a straight angle, as shown below.

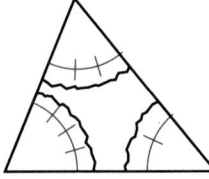
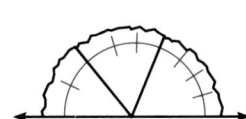

Here are some special triangles:

Right triangle
The small square in the right triangle indicates the right angle: ∠*C* = 90°

$(AC)^2 + (BC)^2 = (AB)^2$

(Recall the Pythagorean theorem and its converse on pages 529 and 530.)

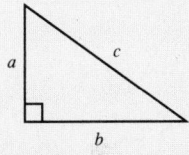

Isosceles triangle
$MN = NP$; ∠*M* = ∠*P*
Base: $\overline{MP}$
Base angles: ∠*M* and ∠*P*

Equilateral triangle
$RS = ST = TR$
∠*R* = ∠*S* = ∠*T* = 60°

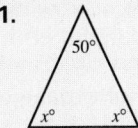

Geometry   **621**

Teaching Suggestions p. T143
Using Manipulatives p. T143

Warm-Up Exercises

1. Complete:
   The __?__ theorem states that the sum of the squares of the lengths of the __?__ of a right triangle is equal to the __?__ of the length of the __?__.
   Pythagorean, legs, square, hypotenuse

2. Refer to the diagram. Find the missing side.

   a. $a = 3$, $b = $__?__, $c = 5$ 4
   b. $a = $__?__, $b = 12$, $c = 13$ 5
   c. $a = \sqrt{2}$, $b = \sqrt{2}$, $c = $__?__   2

Motivating the Lesson

Tell students that the properties of triangles studied in this lesson are some of the properties that will be encountered in a geometry course.

Chalkboard Examples

Identify each triangle as right, isosceles, or equilateral. Then find the value of *x*.

1.

   isosceles
   $x + x + 50 = 180$
   $2x + 50 = 180$
   $2x = 130$
   $x = 65$

   (continued)

621

2.

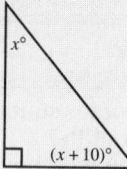

right
$x + (x + 10) + 90 = 180$
$\qquad 2x + 100 = 180$
$\qquad\qquad 2x = 80$
$\qquad\qquad\quad x = 40$

3.

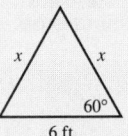

equilateral
$x = 6$ ft

Check for Understanding

Oral Exs. 1–8: use after the discussion of special triangles on p. 621.

Guided Practice

The measures of two angles of a triangle are given. Find the measure of the third angle.

1. 68°, 37° 75°

2. $x°$, $2x°$ $(180 - 3x)°$

3. Determine if △DEF is a right triangle if $DE = 26$, $EF = 10$, and $DF = 24$.
yes

4. If △GHI is isosceles, with $\angle I = \angle H$, $IH = 10$ cm and $GH = 8$ cm, find GI. 8 cm

5. If △ABC is a right triangle with $\angle A = 90°$, $AC = 9$, $BC = 15$, find AB. 12

Oral Exercises

Identify △ABC as right, isosceles, or equilateral.

1. $\angle A = 90°$ right

2. $AB = BC = CA$ equilateral

3. $AB = 12$, $AC = 12$, $BC = 9$ isosceles

4. $AB = 3$, $BC = 4$, $CA = 5$ right

5. $\angle B = 38°$, $\angle C = 38°$ isosceles

6. $\angle C = 16°$, $\angle A = 74°$ right

7. $\angle A = 60°$, $\angle B = 60°$ equilateral

8. $\angle A = 40°$, $\angle B = 100°$ isosceles

Written Exercises

The measures of two angles of a triangle are given. Find the measure of the third angle.

A **1.** 28°, 59° 93° **2.** 122°, 41° 17° **3.** 38°, 52° 90°

4. 15°, 27° 138° **5.** 90°, 24° 66° **6.** 138°, 21° 21°

In Exercises 7–12, use the converse of the Pythagorean theorem to determine whether or not the triangle is a right triangle.

7. △ABC: $AB = 9$, $BC = 8$, $AC = 13$ no **8.** △DEF: $EF = 8$, $FD = 10$, $DE = 6$ yes

9. △GHI: $GH = HI = 12$, $GI = 16$ no **10.** △JKL: $JK = 15$, $KL = 17$, $JL = 8$ yes

11. △MNO: $MN = 24$, $MO = 10$, $NO = 26$ **12.** △PQR: $PQ = 10$, $QR = 12$, $PR = 8$ no
yes

13. If △STU is a right triangle with $\angle T = 90°$, $TU = 12$, and $ST = 9$, find SU. 15

14. If △XYZ is a right triangle with $\angle Z = 90°$, $XZ = 12$, and $YZ = 5$, find XY. 13

15. If △ABC is a right triangle with $\angle A = 90°$, $AB = 24$, and $BC = 30$, find AC. 18

16. If △DEF is isosceles, $DE = DF$, and $\angle D = 50°$, find $\angle E$. 65°

17. If △GHI is isosceles, $GH = GI$, and $\angle H = 20°$, find $\angle G$. 140°

18. If △MNO is a right isosceles triangle and $\angle M = 90°$, find the measures of $\angle N$ and $\angle O$. 45° and 45°

In Exercises 19–26, $\angle C = 90°$ in △ABC. Given the lengths of the other two sides, find the length of the third side in simplest radical form.

B **19.** $AC = 4$, $BC = 12$ $4\sqrt{10} = AB$ **20.** $AC = 3$, $BC = 6$ $AB = 3\sqrt{5}$

21. $AC = 6$, $AB = 10$ $BC = 8$ **22.** $BC = 9$, $AB = 41$ $AC = 40$

23. $BC = 16$, $AB = 24$ $AC = 8\sqrt{5}$ **24.** $AC = 11$, $AB = 25$ $BC = 6\sqrt{14}$

C **25.** $AC = BC = x$ $AB = x\sqrt{2}$ **26.** $AC = y$, $AB = 2y$ $BC = y\sqrt{3}$

---

622 *Looking Ahead*

Problems

Solve.

A 1. In a right triangle, the measure of one acute angle is four times the measure of the other. Find the measures of the two acute angles. 18° and 72°

2. Find the measure of each angle of an isosceles triangle if the measure of the third angle is 10 times the measure of each base angle. 15°, 15°, 150°

3. In a triangle, the measure of the second angle is 7 times the measure of the first angle, and the measure of the third angle is 10 times the measure of the first angle. Find the measure of each angle. 10°, 70°, 100°

4. The measures of the angles of a triangle are in the ratio 4:5:6. Find the measure of each angle. 48°, 60°, 72°

5. The measure of the second angle of a triangle is three times the measure of the first angle, and the measure of the third angle is twice the measure of the second angle. Find the measure of each angle. 18°, 54°, 108°

6. The measure of the second angle of a triangle is 4 times the measure of the first angle, and the measure of the third angle is 63° less than the measure of the second angle. Find the measure of each angle. 27°, 108°, 45°

7. The measures of two angles of a triangle are equal. The measure of the third angle is $\frac{1}{2}$ of the sum of the measures of the first two angles. Find the measure of each angle. 60°, 60°, 60°

8. The measure of the second angle of a triangle is twice the measure of the first angle, and the measure of the third angle is 5° more than 4 times the measure of the first angle. Find the measure of each angle. 25°, 50°, 105°

B 9. The measure of the second angle of a triangle is 5° more than four times that of the first, and the measure of the third angle is 27° less than three times that of the second. Find the measure of each angle. 11°, 49°, 120°

10. In a triangle, the measure of the third angle is 3° more than twice the measure of the second angle. The measure of the first angle is 24° more than twice the measure of the third angle. Find the measure of each angle. 114°, 21°, 45°

11. The measure of the first angle of a triangle is 2° less than twice the measure of the second angle. The measure of the third angle is 35° more than half the measure of the first angle. Find the measure of each angle. 72°, 37°, 71°

C 12. In a triangle, the measure of the second angle is six times the measure of the first angle. The measure of the third angle is 18° less than the sum of the measures of the second angle and the square of the first angle. Find the measure of each angle. 9°, 54°, 117°

13. The measure of the second angle of a triangle is 22° more than the measure of the complement of the first angle, and the measure of the third angle is 49° less than the measure of the supplement of the first angle. Find the measure of each angle. 63°, 49°, 68°

Geometry **623**

Motivating the Lesson

A building casts a 5 m shadow at the same time a 9 m pole casts a 2 m shadow. Tell students that the height of the building can be found by solving a proportion. The geometric principle behind this solution is the topic of today's lesson.

Chalkboard Examples

1.

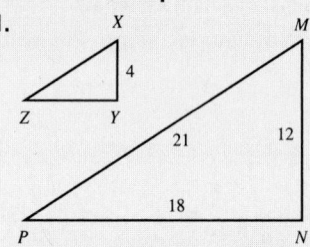

In the diagram $\triangle MNP \sim \triangle XYZ$. Find YZ and ZX.

$\frac{YZ}{18} = \frac{4}{12}$, $YZ = 6$

$\frac{ZX}{21} = \frac{4}{12}$, $ZX = 7$

2.

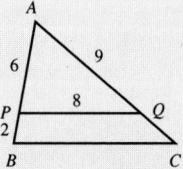

In the diagram $\triangle APQ \sim \triangle ABC$. Find QC and BC.

(continued)

Similar Triangles

Objective   To solve problems involving similar triangles.

An object viewed under a magnifying lens appears larger than it is, but its shape is not changed. Two figures that have the same shape are called *similar*.

Two triangles are **similar triangles** when the measures of two angles of one triangle equal the measures of two angles of the other triangle. (Since the sum of the measures of the angles of a triangle is 180°, you can see that the remaining angles also have equal measures.) The triangles shown below are similar.

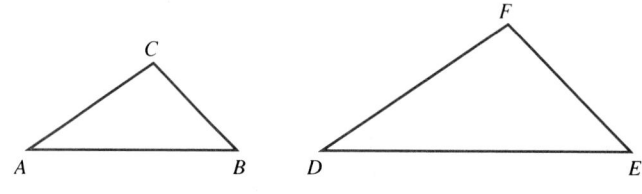

$$\angle A = \angle D = 35°, \quad \angle B = \angle E = 45°, \quad \angle C = \angle F = 100°$$

You show that the triangles ABC and DEF are similar by writing

$$\triangle ABC \sim \triangle DEF.$$

Notice that the vertices of angles with equal measures are written in corresponding positions in the names of the triangles. Angles with equal measures in similar triangles are called **corresponding angles.** The sides opposite corresponding angles are called **corresponding sides.** $\overline{AB}$ corresponds to $\overline{DE}$, and so on. *It is a geometric fact that the lengths of corresponding sides of similar triangles are proportional.* For the triangles shown above,

$$\frac{AB}{DE} = \frac{BC}{EF} = \frac{CA}{FD}.$$

Example 1   In the diagram $\triangle ABC \sim \triangle DEF$. Find AC and BC.

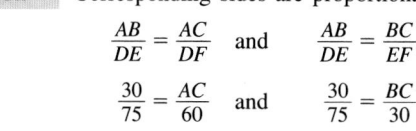

Solution   Corresponding sides are proportional:

$$\frac{AB}{DE} = \frac{AC}{DF} \quad \text{and} \quad \frac{AB}{DE} = \frac{BC}{EF}$$

$$\frac{30}{75} = \frac{AC}{60} \quad \text{and} \quad \frac{30}{75} = \frac{BC}{30}$$

$$75(AC) = 1800 \quad \text{and} \quad 75(BC) = 900$$

$$AC = 24 \quad \text{and} \quad BC = 12 \quad \textbf{\textit{Answer}}$$

624   *Looking Ahead*

Example 2 In the diagram, $\triangle ABC \sim \triangle AEF$. Find EF and AF.

Solution Corresponding sides are proportional:

$$\frac{BC}{EF} = \frac{AB}{AE} \quad \text{and} \quad \frac{AC}{AF} = \frac{AB}{AE}$$

$$\frac{6}{EF} = \frac{12}{20} \quad \text{and} \quad \frac{9}{AF} = \frac{12}{20}$$

$$12(EF) = 120 \quad \text{and} \quad 12(AF) = 180$$

$$EF = 10 \quad \text{and} \quad AF = 15 \quad \textbf{\textit{Answer}}$$

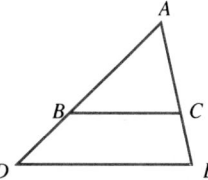

$\frac{AP}{AB} = \frac{AQ}{AC}, \frac{6}{8} = \frac{9}{AC},$

$AC = 12, QC = 3$

$\frac{AP}{PQ} = \frac{AB}{BC}, \frac{6}{8} = \frac{8}{BC},$

$BC = \frac{32}{3},$ or $10\frac{2}{3}$

Check for Understanding

Oral Exs. 1–3: use after
  Example 2.

Oral Exercises

2. $\overline{AB}$ and $\overline{AD}$, $\overline{AC}$ and $\overline{AE}$, $\overline{BC}$ and $\overline{DE}$

In the diagram for Exercises 1–3, $\triangle ABC \sim \triangle ADE$.

$\angle ABC$ and $\angle ADE$, $\angle ACB$ and $\angle AED$, $\angle A$ and $\angle A$

1. Name the corresponding angles.

2. Name the corresponding sides.

3. Name three equal ratios.
$$\frac{AB}{AD} = \frac{AC}{AE} = \frac{BC}{DE}$$

Guided Practice

In $\triangle ABC$, $\angle A = 80°$ and
$\angle B = 70°$. In $\triangle DEF$, $\angle F = 80°$, and $\angle D = 70°$.

1. Write the corresponding
  angles. $\angle A$ and $\angle F$; $\angle B$
  and $\angle D$; $\angle C$ and $\angle E$

2. Complete: $\triangle ABC \sim \triangle \underset{FDE}{\underline{?}}$

3. Write 3 equal ratios.
  $\frac{AB}{FD} = \frac{BC}{DE} = \frac{AC}{FE}$

$\triangle XYZ \sim \triangle MNR$. $XY = 15$,
$YZ = 21$, $XZ = 24$, $MN = 10$

4. Find NR. 14

5. Find MR. 16

Written Exercises

A 1. In $\triangle RST$, $\angle R = 50°$ and $\angle S = 70°$. In $\triangle XYZ$, $\angle Y = 50°$ and $\angle Z = 70°$.
  a. Write the corresponding angles. $\angle S$ and $\angle Z$; $\angle R$ and $\angle Y$; $\angle T$ and $\angle X$
  b. Write the corresponding sides. $\overline{RS}$ and $\overline{YZ}$; $\overline{ST}$ and $\overline{ZX}$; $\overline{RT}$ and $\overline{YX}$
  c. Complete: $\triangle RST \sim \triangle \underline{\ ?\ }$ YZX

2. In $\triangle JKL$ and $\triangle MNP$, $\angle K = \angle M = 35°$, and $\angle L = \angle N = 88°$. Write three equal ratios.
$\frac{JK}{PM} = \frac{KL}{MN} = \frac{JL}{PN}$

Classify each statement as true or false.

3. All right triangles are similar. false

4. All isosceles triangles are similar. false

5. All equilateral triangles are similar. true

6. All isosceles right triangles are similar. true

7. If $\triangle ABC \sim \triangle BCA$, then $\triangle ABC$ is equilateral. true

In Exercises 8–11, $\triangle ABC \sim \triangle DEF$. Find the lengths of the sides not given.

8. $AB = 3$, $BC = 5$, $AC = 6$, $DE = 9$ $EF = 15$; $DF = 18$

9. $DE = 15$, $EF = 21$, $DF = 12$, $AC = 8$ $AB = 10$; $BC = 14$

10. $AB = 24$, $BC = 16$, $AC = 32$, $EF = 12$ $DE = 18$; $DF = 24$

11. $AB = BC = 10$, $AC = 15$, $DE = 14$ $EF = 14$; $DF = 21$

Summarizing the Lesson

Tell students that they have
learned to use properties of
similar triangles to find unknown lengths. Ask students
to state a geometric fact
regarding the lengths of corresponding sides of similar
triangles.

Suggested Assignments

Maximum
  625/1–15 odd
  626/P: 3, 6, 9

Geometry **625**

In Exercises 12–15, $\triangle ABC \sim \triangle DEF$. Find the lengths of the sides not given.

B 12. $AB = 4$, $BC = 6$, $DE = 6$, $DF = 12$ $EF = 9$; $AC = 8$

13. $AB = 16$, $AC = 20$, $DF = 15$, $EF = 18$ $DE = 12$; $BC = 24$

14. $BC = 21$, $AC = 28$, $DE = 25$, $DF = 20$ $AB = 35$; $EF = 15$

15. $AC = 32$, $BC = 18$, $DE = 39$, $DF = 48$ $AB = 26$; $EF = 27$

C 16. In $\triangle RST$ at the right, $\angle RTS = 90°$ and $\angle TUR = 90°$.
Complete the following statement:

$\triangle RTS \sim \triangle\ \underline{\ ?\ } \sim \triangle\ \underline{\ ?\ }$
$TUSRUT$

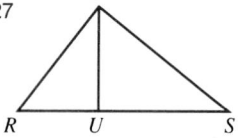

Problems

Solve.

A 1. The sides of a triangle have lengths of 6 cm, 10 cm, and 12 cm. If the longest side of a similar triangle is 18 cm, find its shortest side. 9 cm

2. Leigh is 5 ft tall and casts a shadow 2 ft long at the same time a tree casts a shadow 26 ft long. How tall is the tree? 65 ft

3. A sign 4 m high casts a shadow 3 m long at the same time a building casts a shadow 27 m long. How tall is the building? 36 m

4. An isosceles triangle has two sides of length 28 cm and a base of 35 cm. The base of a similar triangle is 15 cm. Find the perimeter of the smaller triangle. 39 cm

5. To find the length of a swamp, two similar triangles were roped off. The measurements are shown on the diagram. How long is the swamp? 225 m

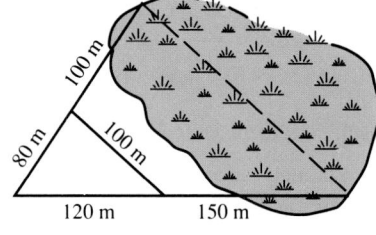

B 6. $\overline{AC}$ and $\overline{DE}$ intersect at point B and $\triangle ABE \sim \triangle CBD$. If $AB = x$, $BC = 4x$, $BD = 20$, and $DC = 32$, find EB. 5

7. Chen walks 5 m up a ramp and is 2 m above the ground. If he were to walk 10 m farther, how far above the ground would he be? 6 m

8. From a point on the ground 7 m from the base of a tree 8 m tall, it is possible to see the top of a building 400 m tall just over the top of the tree. How far is the point from the base of the building? 350 m

C 9. A boy whose eye level at A is 1.5 m above the ground wants to find the height ED of a tree. He places a mirror flat on the ground 15 m from the tree. If he stands at a point B, which is 2 m from the mirror at C, he can see the reflection of the top of the tree. Find the height of the tree. 11.25 m

Trigonometry

Trigonometric Ratios

Objective   To find the sine, cosine, and tangent of an acute angle.

In the branch of mathematics called *trigonometry* you study the measurement of triangles. Any acute angle, such as $\angle A$ in the diagram, can be made an angle of a right triangle ABC. The legs opposite and adjacent to this angle are labeled. Ratios of the lengths of the sides of $\triangle ABC$ are called **trigonometric ratios** of $\angle A$. These ratios have special names and symbols.

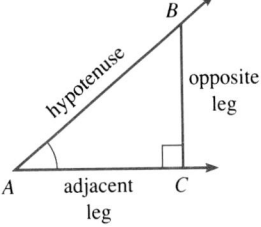

$$\textbf{sine} \text{ of } \angle A \;=\; \frac{\text{length of leg opposite } \angle A}{\text{length of hypotenuse}} = \frac{BC}{AB}$$
(symbol: $\sin A$)

$$\textbf{cosine} \text{ of } \angle A \;=\; \frac{\text{length of leg adjacent to } \angle A}{\text{length of hypotenuse}} = \frac{AC}{AB}$$
(symbol: $\cos A$)

$$\textbf{tangent} \text{ of } \angle A \;=\; \frac{\text{length of leg opposite } \angle A}{\text{length of leg adjacent to } \angle A} = \frac{BC}{AC}$$
(symbol: $\tan A$)

Example 1   Find the sine, cosine, and tangent of $\angle A$ and of $\angle B$.

Solution $\sin A = \dfrac{8}{17}$ $\sin B = \dfrac{15}{17}$

$\cos A = \dfrac{15}{17}$ $\cos B = \dfrac{8}{17}$

$\tan A = \dfrac{8}{15}$ $\tan B = \dfrac{15}{8}$

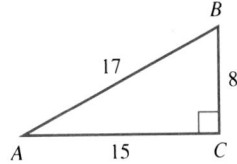

Example 2   Find the sine, cosine, and tangent of $\angle Q$.

Solution $a^2 + 6^2 = 14^2$ $\begin{cases} \text{Use the Pythagorean} \\ \text{theorem to find } RQ. \end{cases}$
$a^2 + 36 = 196$
$a^2 = 160$
$a = 4\sqrt{10}$

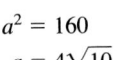

$\sin Q = \dfrac{6}{14} = \dfrac{3}{7}$ $\cos Q = \dfrac{4\sqrt{10}}{14} = \dfrac{2\sqrt{10}}{7}$ $\tan Q = \dfrac{6}{4\sqrt{10}} = \dfrac{3\sqrt{10}}{20}$

Trigonometry   **627**

Teaching Suggestions p. T144

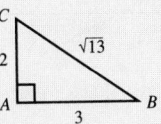
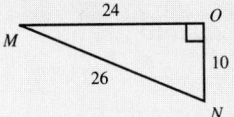

2. Find the sine, cosine, and tangent of $\angle A$.

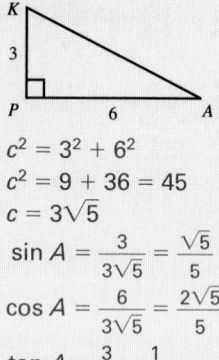

$c^2 = 3^2 + 6^2$

$c^2 = 9 + 36 = 45$

$c = 3\sqrt{5}$

$\sin A = \dfrac{3}{3\sqrt{5}} = \dfrac{\sqrt{5}}{5}$

$\cos A = \dfrac{6}{3\sqrt{5}} = \dfrac{2\sqrt{5}}{5}$

$\tan A = \dfrac{3}{6} = \dfrac{1}{2}$

Check for Understanding

Oral Exs. 1–13: use after Example 1.

Guided Practice

For the right triangle shown, find $\sin A$, $\cos A$, $\tan A$, $\sin B$, $\cos B$, $\tan B$. Write irrational answers in simplest radical form.

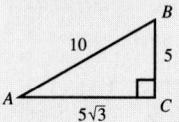

$\sin A = \dfrac{1}{2}$ $\cos A = \dfrac{\sqrt{3}}{2}$

$\tan A = \dfrac{\sqrt{3}}{3}$ $\sin B = \dfrac{\sqrt{3}}{2}$

$\cos B = \dfrac{1}{2}$ $\tan B = \dfrac{\sqrt{3}}{1}$

Summarizing the Lesson

Tell students that they have learned how to find the sine, cosine, and tangent of an acute angle. Ask them to define these terms.

The values of the trigonometric ratios of an angle depend only on the measure of the angle and not on the particular right triangle that contains the angle. For example, in the two right triangles below, $\angle A$ and $\angle D$ have equal measures. It can be shown that the trigonometric ratios of $\angle A$ and $\angle D$ are also equal.

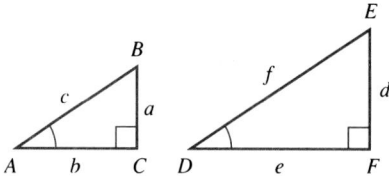

Since $\angle A = \angle D = 30°$ and $\angle C = \angle F = 90°$, the triangles are similar and their corresponding sides are proportional:

$$\frac{a}{d} = \frac{c}{f}$$

Multiplying both ratios by $\dfrac{d}{c}$, you obtain the equivalent proportion

$$\frac{a}{c} = \frac{d}{f}, \text{ or } \sin A = \sin D.$$

You can show similarly that $\cos A = \cos D$ and $\tan A = \tan D$.

Because the values of $\sin A$, $\cos A$, and $\tan A$ depend only on the measure of $\angle A$ and not on the triangle containing $\angle A$, you can think of these trigonometric ratios as the values of three functions each having the set of acute angles as its domain. These functions are called **trigonometric functions.**

Oral Exercises

State the value of each trigonometric ratio for the triangle shown.

$\dfrac{5}{13}$ **1.** $\sin A \ \dfrac{12}{13}$

2. $\cos A$

3. $\tan A \ \dfrac{12}{5}$

$\dfrac{5}{13}$ **4.** $\sin B$

5. $\cos B \ \dfrac{12}{13}$

$\dfrac{5}{12}$ **6.** $\tan B$

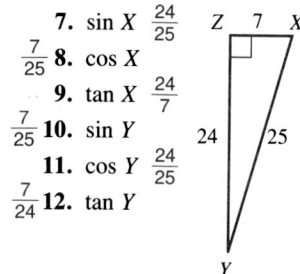

7. $\sin X \ \dfrac{24}{25}$

$\dfrac{7}{25}$ **8.** $\cos X$

9. $\tan X \ \dfrac{24}{7}$

$\dfrac{7}{25}$ **10.** $\sin Y$

11. $\cos Y \ \dfrac{24}{25}$

$\dfrac{7}{24}$ **12.** $\tan Y$

13. Explain why the sine and the cosine of an acute angle are always less than 1.

Because the side opposite and the side adjacent are always less than the hypotenuse. Thus $\dfrac{\text{opp}}{\text{hyp}}$ and $\dfrac{\text{adj}}{\text{hyp}}$ must be less than 1.

628 *Looking Ahead*

Written Exercises

For each right triangle shown, find sin A, cos A, tan A, sin B, cos B, and tan B. Write irrational answers in simplest radical form.

A 1.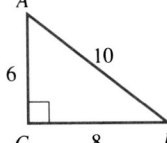

2.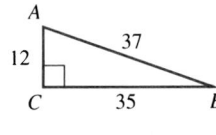

3.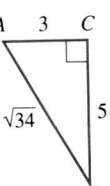

4.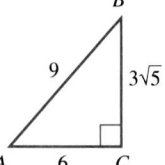

5.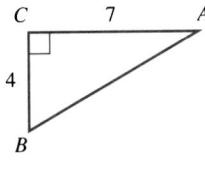

6.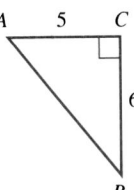

7.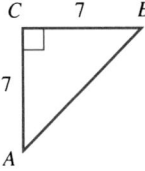

8.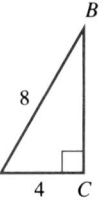

9.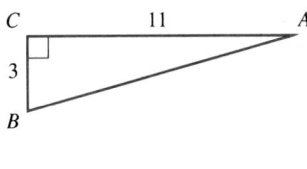

In Exercises 10–13, $\triangle ABC$ is a right triangle with $\angle C$ as the right angle. Show that the following statements are true.

B 10. $\sin A = \cos B$ $\quad \sin A = \dfrac{a}{c}$; $\cos B = \dfrac{a}{c}$

11. $\cos A = \sin B$ $\quad \cos A = \dfrac{b}{c}$; $\sin B = \dfrac{b}{c}$

12. $(\sin A)^2 + (\cos A)^2 = 1$

13. $\tan A = \dfrac{\sin A}{\cos A}$

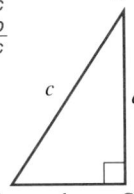

C 14. If $\sin R = \dfrac{3}{5}$, find cos R. $\quad \dfrac{4}{5}$

15. If $\sin Z = \dfrac{3}{8}$, find the sine of the complement of $\angle Z$. $\quad \dfrac{\sqrt{55}}{8}$

16. If $\tan X = \dfrac{11}{60}$, find sin X and cos X. $\quad \dfrac{11}{61}$ and $\dfrac{60}{61}$

Trigonometry   629

Additional Answers
Written Exercises

2. $\sin A = \dfrac{35}{37}$, $\cos A = \dfrac{12}{37}$

$\tan A = \dfrac{35}{12}$, $\sin B = \dfrac{12}{37}$

$\cos B = \dfrac{35}{37}$, $\tan B = \dfrac{12}{35}$

4. $\sin A = \dfrac{\sqrt{5}}{3}$, $\cos A = \dfrac{2}{3}$

$\tan A = \dfrac{\sqrt{5}}{2}$, $\sin B = \dfrac{2}{3}$

$\cos B = \dfrac{\sqrt{5}}{3}$, $\tan B = \dfrac{2\sqrt{5}}{5}$

6. $\sin A = \dfrac{6\sqrt{61}}{61}$,

$\cos A = \dfrac{5\sqrt{61}}{61}$

$\tan A = \dfrac{6}{5}$, $\sin B = \dfrac{5\sqrt{61}}{61}$

$\cos B = \dfrac{6\sqrt{61}}{61}$, $\tan B = \dfrac{5}{6}$

8. $\sin A = \dfrac{\sqrt{3}}{2}$, $\cos A = \dfrac{1}{2}$

$\tan A = \sqrt{3}$, $\sin B = \dfrac{1}{2}$

$\cos B = \dfrac{\sqrt{3}}{2}$, $\tan B = \dfrac{\sqrt{3}}{3}$

12. $(\sin A)^2 + (\cos A)^2 =$
$\left(\dfrac{a}{c}\right)^2 + \left(\dfrac{b}{c}\right)^2 = \dfrac{a^2}{c^2} + \dfrac{b^2}{c^2} =$
$\dfrac{a^2 + b^2}{c^2} = \dfrac{c^2}{c^2} = 1$

13. $\dfrac{\sin A}{\cos A} = \dfrac{\frac{a}{c}}{\frac{b}{c}} = \dfrac{a}{c} \cdot \dfrac{c}{b} = \dfrac{a}{b}$
$= \tan A$

Supplementary Materials
Study Guide   pp. 235–236

Values of Trigonometric Ratios

Objective To find values of trigonometric ratios for given angles, and measures of angles for given trigonometric ratios.

Values of the trigonometric ratios are needed to solve practical problems involving right triangles. A few values can be easily computed using the properties of special triangles and the Pythagorean theorem. For an isosceles right triangle:

$$\sin 45° = \frac{1}{\sqrt{2}} = \frac{\sqrt{2}}{2} \approx 0.707$$

$$\cos 45° = \frac{1}{\sqrt{2}} = \frac{\sqrt{2}}{2} \approx 0.707$$

$$\tan 45° = \frac{1}{1} = 1$$

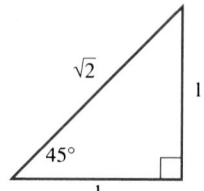

It is not possible to give *exact* values of the trigonometric ratios for most angles. You can use a scientific calculator or the table on page 683 to find approximate values of sin A, cos A, and tan A for any angle A with a whole-number measure from 1° to 89°.

Example 1 Find the values of sin 58°, cos 58°, and tan 58°.

Solution 1 Using a Table
Locate 58° in the left-hand column of the portion of the table shown at the right, then read across the row to find:

sin 58° ≈ 0.8480
cos 58° ≈ 0.5299
tan 58° ≈ 1.6003 *Answer*

Angle	Sine	Cosine	Tangent
1°	.0175	.9998	.0175
56°	.8290	.5592	1.4826
57°	.8387	.5446	1.5399
58°	.8480	.5299	1.6003
59°	.8572	.5150	1.6643
60°	.8660	.5000	1.7321

For convenience, you may write = instead of ≈ in statements such as these.

Solution 2 Using a Calculator

To find the value for sin 58°, you enter 58 and then press the sin key to get 0.8480481.

∴ to the nearest ten-thousandth, sin 58° = 0.8480. Likewise, you enter 58 and then press the cos key or the tan key to get:

cos 58° ≈ 0.5299193, or cos 58° = 0.5299
tan 58° ≈ 1.6003345, or tan 58° = 1.6003 *Answer*

630 *Looking Ahead*

A trigonometric table or a calculator can also be used to approximate the measure of an angle if one of its trigonometric ratios is given.

Example 2 Find the measure of ∠A to the nearest degree.

  a. cos A = 0.5150   **b.** sin A = 0.8368

Solution 1 Using a Table

  a. Locate the value 0.5150 in the cosine column, if possible. Since it is there, read across the row to the left-hand column to find that the angle has a measure of 59°. *Answer*

  b. Since 0.8368 is not listed in the sine column, locate the entries between which 0.8368 lies:

  sin 56° = 0.8290 and sin 57° = 0.8387, so the measure of ∠A must be between 56° and 57°.

  Since 0.8368 is closer to 0.8387 than it is to 0.8290, ∠A = 57°, to the nearest degree. *Answer*

Solution 2 Using a Calculator

  Most calculators have the inverse keys ($\sin^{-1}$, $\cos^{-1}$, $\tan^{-1}$, or inv sin, inv cos, inv tan) that give the measure of an acute angle.

  a. Enter 0.5150, then press the $\cos^{-1}$ key to get 59.002545°.

  ∴ to the nearest degree, ∠A = 59°. *Answer*

  b. Enter 0.8368, then press the $\sin^{-1}$ key to get 56.803734°.

  ∴ to the nearest degree, ∠A = 57°. *Answer*

Oral Exercises

For Exercises 1–12, use a calculator or the portion of the table of trigonometric ratios shown on the previous page.

State the value of each trigonometric ratio.

1. sin 59° 0.8572   **2.** cos 56° 0.5592   **3.** tan 1° 0.0175

4. tan 60° 1.7321   **5.** sin 57° 0.8387   **6.** cos 59° 0.5150

Find the measure of angle A to the nearest degree.

7. sin A = 0.8290 56°   **8.** cos A = 0.9998 1°   **9.** tan A = 1.5399 57°

10. cos A = 0.5100 59°   **11.** tan A = 1.6832 59°   **12.** sin A = 0.8475 58°

13. Explain why sin 10° = cos 80° by referring to the diagram and the definitions on page 627.
Suppose in the diagram on page 627 ∠A = 10° and
∠B = 80°. Then sin ∠A = $\frac{BC}{AB}$ and the cos ∠B = $\frac{BC}{AB}$. Thus sin ∠A = cos ∠B. *Trigonometry*   **631**

2. Use a calculator or the table on page 683 to find the measure of ∠A to the nearest degree.
  a. cos A = 0.8290 34°
  b. tan A = 5.3812 79°
  c. cos A = 0.9 26°

Common Errors

When a value is not listed in the table, students may have difficulty in determining the closer value. It may be easier for students if they write the values in a list, as shown below. For sin A = 0.8368:

                                        difference

sin 56° ≈ 0.8290 ⎱
                            ⎰ 0.0078
sin A = 0.8368   ⎱
                            ⎰ 0.0019
sin 57° ≈ 0.8387

∴ the measure of ∠A is closer to 57°.

Check for Understanding

Oral Exs. 1–6: use after Example 1.
Oral Exs. 7–13: use after Example 2.

Guided Practice

1. Use a calculator or the table on page 683 to find sin A, cos A, and tan A for the given measure of angle A.
  a. 53° 0.7986, 0.6018, 1.3270
  b. 76° 0.9703, 0.2419, 4.011

2. Use a calculator or the table on page 683 to find the measure of angle A to the nearest degree.
  a. sin A = 0.4813 29°
  b. cos A = 0.4813 61°
  c. tan A = 0.4813 26°

Written Exercises

Use a calculator or the table on page 683 to find sin A, cos A, and tan A for the given measure of angle A.

A
1. 20°   2. 40°   3. 15°
4. 39°   5. 68°   6. 83°
7. 24°   8. 59°   9. 4°
10. 71°   11. 45°   12. 35°

Use a calculator or the table on page 683 to find the measure of angle A to the nearest degree.

13. sin A = 0.9781 78°   14. cos A = 0.6561 49°
15. tan A = 0.1584 9°   16. tan A = 0.9431 43°
17. sin A = 0.8431 57°   18. cos A = 0.4128 66°
19. cos A = 0.9243 22°   20. tan A = 8.2198 83°
21. sin A = 0.5801 35°   22. sin A = 0.2340 14°
23. tan A = 0.8724 41°   24. cos A = 0.9913 8°
25. tan A = 0.3712 20°   26. sin A = 0.9299 68°
27. cos A = 0.8300 34°   28. tan A = 3.2276 73°

Complete with >, <, or = to make a true statement.

B
29. If $\angle A > \angle B$, then sin A __?__ sin B. >
30. If $\angle A > \angle B$, then cos A __?__ cos B. <
31. If $\angle A$ is a complement of $\angle B$, then sin A __?__ cos B. =

C
32. If $\angle A$ = 23°, show that sin $(2A)$ = $2 \cdot$ sin $A \cdot$ cos A.
33. If $\angle B$ = 36°, show that cos $(2B)$ = $(\cos B)^2 - (\sin B)^2$.

///////////////////////////////////////

Challenge

Is the reasoning logical in each case?

1. The sum of the measures of the angles of a triangle is 180°. The sum of the measures of $\angle A$, $\angle R$, and $\angle Z$ is 180°. Therefore, $\angle A$, $\angle R$, and $\angle Z$ are the angles of a triangle. no

2. A square is a rectangle with four sides of equal length. A rectangle has four right angles. Therefore, a square has four right angles. yes

3. A parallelogram is a figure in geometry. Geometry is a branch of mathematics. Therefore, a parallelogram is a figure in mathematics. yes

632   *Looking Ahead*

Problem Solving Using Trigonometry

Objective   To use trigonometric ratios to solve problems.

Trigonometric ratios can be used to solve practical problems involving right triangles. You can find values for these ratios by using the table on page 683 or a scientific calculator.

Example 1   A radio transmission tower is 83 m high. A support wire is attached to the tower 25 m from the top. If the support wire and the ground form an angle of 42°, what is the length of the support wire?

Solution   Draw a triangle and label the different values. First, find how high on the tower the support wire is attached:

$$83 - 25 = 58$$

Since $\triangle ABC$ is a right triangle,

$$\sin 42° = \frac{58}{x}, \text{ or } x = \frac{58}{\sin 42°}.$$

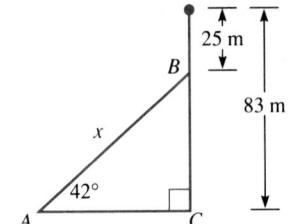

From the table on page 683 or a calculator, $\sin 42° = 0.6691$.

Then $x = \frac{58}{0.6691} \approx 86.7.$

∴ to the nearest tenth of a meter, the support wire is 86.7 m long.

In surveying and navigation problems involving right triangles, the terms *angle of elevation* and *angle of depression* are used. In the diagram below, $\angle CBA$ is an angle of elevation, since the point A is elevated with respect to an observer at B. $\angle DAB$ is an angle of depression, since the point B is depressed with respect to an observer at A.

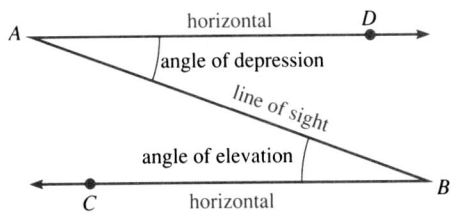

Teaching Suggestions, p. T144

Warm-Up Exercises

1. Find the measure of $\angle A$ to the nearest degree if $\sin A = \frac{28}{45}$.   38°

2. Solve for x to the nearest whole number if $0.4831 = \frac{61}{x}$.   126

3. Solve for y to the nearest whole number if $2.8914 = \frac{y}{250}$.   723

Motivating the Lesson

A navigator discovers that his plane has flown 10° off course for five hundred miles. He needs to find how far away he is from the correct path. Tell students that using trigonometric ratios to solve problems such as the one above is today's topic.

Chalkboard Examples

Solve each problem.

1. How long to the nearest foot is the ladder that is leaning against the building?

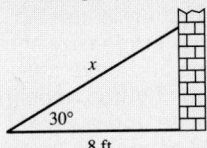

$$\cos 30° = \frac{8}{x}$$
$$x \cdot \cos 30° = 8$$
$$x = \frac{8}{\cos 30°}$$
$$x = \frac{8}{0.8660}$$
$$x \approx 9.2$$

∴ to the nearest foot, the ladder is 9 ft long.

(continued)

2. The length of a ramp is 25 m. The angle of depression of the ramp is 13°. What is the ramp's height to the nearest meter?

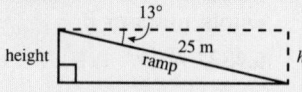

$$\sin 13° = \frac{h}{25}$$
$$h = 25 (\sin 13°)$$
$$h = 25(0.2250)$$
$$h = 5.6$$
∴ to the nearest meter, the ramp is 6 m high.

Check for Understanding

Oral Exs. 1–6: use after Example 2.

Problem Solving Strategies

Students *draw diagrams* and use the definitions of the trigonometric ratios to solve problems in this lesson.

Common Errors

Students may have difficulty determining which trigonometric function to use. In reteaching, emphasize the definitions and have students draw figures, labeling the opposite and adjacent legs after naming the hypotenuse.

Example 2 At a point 166 m from the base of the World Trade Center in New York City, the angle of elevation to the top is 68°. To the nearest meter, what is the height of the World Trade Center?

Solution Draw a triangle and label the different values. You want to find x, the height of the World Trade Center. Since △ABC is a right triangle,

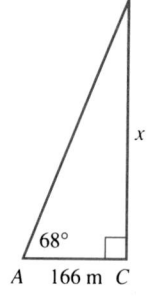

$$\tan 68° = \frac{x}{166}, \text{ or}$$
$$x = 166(\tan 68°).$$

From the table on page 683 or a calculator, tan 68° = 2.4751.

Then x = 166(2.4751)
= 410.8666.

∴ to the nearest meter, the World Trade Center is 411 m high. **Answer**

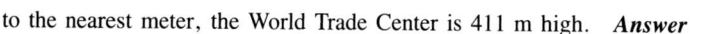

Oral Exercises

State whether you would use the sine, the cosine, or the tangent ratio to find x for each figure.

1.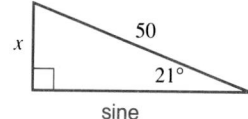

   sine

2.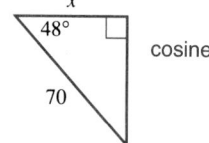

   cosine

3.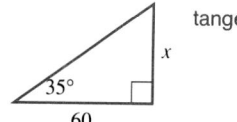

   tangent

4.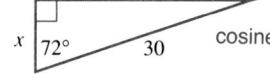

   cosine

5.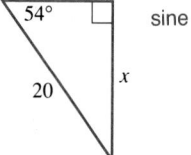

   sine

6.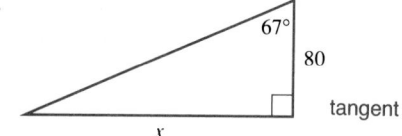

   tangent

634 *Looking Ahead*

Written Exercises

Use the table on page 683 or a calculator as needed.

A **1–6.** In Oral Exercises 1–6, find the value of x to the nearest whole number.
1. 18 **2.** 47 **3.** 42 **4.** 9 **5.** 16 **6.** 188

In a right △ABC, ∠C = 90°. Find the lengths of the other sides of the triangle to the nearest whole number.

7. ∠A = 39°, AB = 53 AC = 41; BC = 33   **8.** ∠B = 21°, AB = 12 AC = 4; BC = 11

9. ∠B = 80°, AC = 48 AB = 49; BC = 8   **10.** ∠A = 65°, BC = 28 AC = 13; AB = 31

In a right △DEF, ∠E = 90°. Find the measures of ∠D and ∠F to the nearest degree.

Sample   DE = 16, DF = 25

Solution

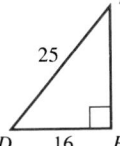

$$\cos \angle D = \frac{DE}{DF}$$

$$\cos \angle D = \frac{16}{25}$$

$$\cos \angle D = 0.6400$$

$$\angle D = 50°$$

Since the sum of the measures of the angles of a triangle is 180°,
∠F = 180° − (90° + 50°).
∠F = 40°

B **11.** DE = 48, EF = 36 ∠D = 37°; ∠F = 53°   **12.** DF = 30, EF = 25 ∠F = 34°; ∠D = 56°

13. EF = 42, DF = 54 ∠F = 39°; ∠D = 51°   **14.** DE = 63, EF = 81 ∠D = 52°; ∠F = 38°

15. In the right △XYZ, ∠Y = 90°, ∠X = 41°, and XZ = 95. Find XY and ZY to the nearest whole number. XY = 72; ZY = 62

16. In the right △RST, ∠S = 90°, RT = 120, ∠T = 30°. Find RS and TS to the nearest whole number. RS = 60; TS = 104

Problems

Solve each problem, drawing a sketch for each. Express distances to the nearest unit and angle measures to the nearest degree. Use the table on page 683 or a calculator as needed.

A **1.** How far is the ladder from the foot of the building? 16 m

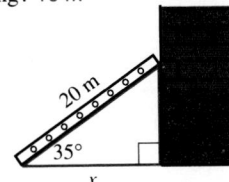

2. How long is the cable that supports the pole? 1478 cm

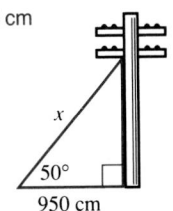

Trigonometry   **635**

3. How high is the cliff? 226 m

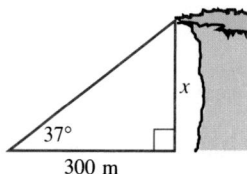

4. How far is the boy from the monument? 70 m

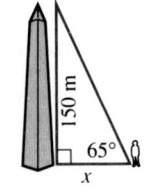

5. How far below sea level will a porpoise be if it swims 250 m at a 12° angle of depression? 52 m

6. The length of a water ski jump is 720 cm and the angle of elevation is 35°. Find the height of the ski jump. 413 cm

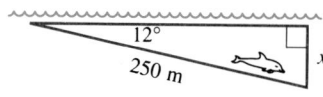

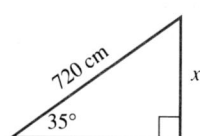

7. A bird rises 20 m vertically over a horizontal distance of 80 m. What is the angle of elevation? 14°

8. If a plane flies 1° off course for 6000 km, how far away will the plane be from the correct path? 105 km

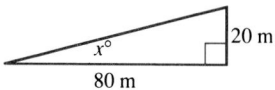

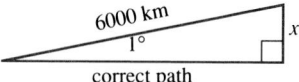

B **9.** An escalator is 15 m in length with a 37° incline. How high is the escalator? 9 m

10. From the top of a 20 m lighthouse, the angle of depression of the nearest point on the beach is 8°. Find the distance from the bottom of the lighthouse to the beach. 142 m

11. A hot air balloon with an altitude of 120 m is directly over a bridge that is 313 m from the balloon's landing point. The navigator finds the angle of depression to the landing point. What will be the angle of depression she finds? 21°

12. A submarine travels through the water at a steady rate of 360 m/min on a diving path that forms a 4° angle of depression with the surface of the water. After 5 min, how far below the surface is the submarine? 126 m

C **13.** From the top of a 65 m lighthouse, an airplane was observed directly over a whale in the water. The angle of elevation of the airplane was 16° and the angle of depression of the whale was 46°. How far was the whale from the base of the lighthouse? How high was the plane flying? 63 m; 83 m

14. A car is traveling on a level road toward a mountain 2 km high. The angle of elevation from the car to the top of the mountain changes from 6° to 15°. How far has the car traveled? 12 km

Summary

1. Probability is the branch of mathematics that is concerned with the possibility that an event will happen. For any event with probability P, $0 \leq P \leq 1$.

2. Data can be summarized and analyzed using statistics. This can be done by using histograms, frequency distributions, stem-and-leaf plots, and box-and-whisker plots.

3. Geometry is the branch of mathematics that is concerned with the properties of sets of points such as lines, rays, angles, and triangles.

4. Two angles whose sides are rays in the same lines but in opposite directions are called vertical angles. Two angles are complementary if the sum of their measures is 90°. Two angles are supplementary if the sum of their measures is 180°.

5. The sum of the measures of the angles of a triangle is 180°. Some special triangles are right triangles, isosceles triangles, and equilateral triangles.

6. Similar triangles have the same shape but not necessarily the same size. Their corresponding angles have the same measure and corresponding sides are proportional.

7. Trigonometry is the branch of mathematics that includes the measurement of triangles.

   Three trigonometric ratios are $\sin A = \dfrac{a}{c}$, $\cos A = \dfrac{b}{c}$, and $\tan A = \dfrac{a}{b}$. Approximate values for these ratios are given in the table on page 683. Trigonometric ratios can be used to solve problems involving right triangles.

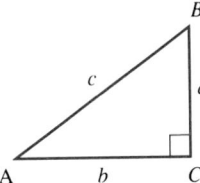

Review

Give the letter of the correct answer.

1. A cube with letters A, B, C, D, E, and F is rolled. Specify the event that the letter turned up is a vowel.

   a. $\{A, B, C, D, E, F\}$ **b.** $\{A, E, I, O, U\}$
   c. $\{A, E\}$ **d.** $\{B, C, D, F\}$

2. A spinner is divided into five equal sections, numbered 1, 2, 3, 4, and 5. The pointer is spun. Find the probability that the number on which the pointer stops is odd.

   a. 0   **b.** 1   **c.** $\dfrac{1}{5}$ **d.** $\dfrac{3}{5}$

---

3. Find the mean for the data 42, 44, 46, 53, 55:

   a. 48   **b.** 46   **c.** 42   **d.** 55

4. Find the range for the data 33, 43, 57, 61, 76:

   a. 54   **b.** 57   **c.** 43   **d.** 76

5. The histogram at the right shows the frequency distribution for the height in centimeters of all the students in the Drama Club. How many of these students are between 150 and 170 cm?

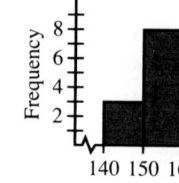

   a. 11   **b.** 7

   c. 12   **d.** 6

6. Find the first quartile score for the data:

$$2, 4, 4, 5, 7, 8, 8$$

   a. 5.4   **b.** $\frac{10}{3}$ **c.** $\frac{15}{2}$ **d.** 4

7. Which angle is a right angle?

   a. $\angle A = 99°$ **b.** $\angle B = 60°$ **c.** $\angle C = 90°$ **d.** $\angle D = 45°$

8. Find the measure of the supplement of an angle with measure 63°.

   a. 17°   **b.** 127°   **c.** 117°   **d.** 27°

9. Find the complement of an angle with measure $x°$.

   a. $(90 - x)°$ **b.** $(90 + x)°$ **c.** $(180 - x)°$ **d.** $(180 + x)°$

10. What is the sum of the measures of the angles of a right triangle?

   a. 45°   **b.** 90°   **c.** 180°   **d.** 360°

11. If $\triangle ABC \sim \triangle DEF$, $\frac{AB}{DE} = \frac{12}{5}$, and $CA = 8$, find FD.

   a. $\frac{3}{5}$ **b.** $\frac{3}{10}$ **c.** 1   **d.** $\frac{10}{3}$

12. Use the diagram to find $\cos A$.

   a. $\frac{3}{4}$ **b.** $\frac{4}{5}$

   c. $\frac{3}{5}$ **d.** $\frac{4}{3}$

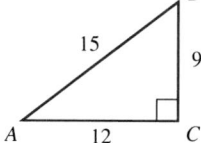

13. Use the table on page 683 to find sin 54°.

   a. 1.3764   **b.** 0.5878   **c.** 0.8090   **d.** 0.1584

14. The angle of elevation to the top of a tree from a point on the ground 800 cm from the base of the tree is 47°. Find the height of the tree to the nearest centimeter.

   a. 600 cm   **b.** 858 cm   **c.** 585 cm   **d.** 546 cm

Extra Practice: Skills

Chapter 1

Simplify each expression. (1-1, 1-2)

1. $5 + (4 \times 8)$ 37
2. $(3 + 7) \times 2$ 20
3. $(30 \times 3) + (5 \times 2)$ 100
4. $(40 \div 4) - (9 - 5)$ 6
5. $(30 + 3) \times (4 + 2)$ 198
6. $(40 - 4) \div (9 - 5)$ 9
7. $9 + 7 - 2 \times 8 \div 4$ 12
8. $32 \div 8 + 3 \times 7 - 6$ 19
9. $4 \times 6 - 16 \div 2 + 7$ 23

Evaluate each expression if $e = 2$, $f = 3$, $g = 4$, $u = 0$, $v = 5$, and $w = 1$. (1-1, 1-2)

10. $ev - f$ 7
11. $5g + 4w$ 24
12. $(uv) + (fg)$ 12
13. $w(v - f) + g$ 6
14. $(3g) \cdot (e + u)$ 24
15. $(v - u)w + g$ 9
16. $(e + f)(g + v)$ 45
17. $e(u + v - w)$ 8
18. $(4e - 2f)(v + w)$ 12
19. $\frac{e + g}{v - f}$ 3
20. $\frac{gv - 5e}{5 - 3u}$ 2
21. $f(we + v) + \frac{g}{e}$ 23

Solve each equation if $x \in \{0, 1, 2, 3, 4, 5, 6\}$. (1-3)

22. $7 + x = 12$ {5}
23. $x - 4 = 2$ {6}
24. $8 - x = 3$ {5}
25. $x - x = 0$ {0, 1, 2, 3, 4, 5, 6}
26. $6x = 18$ {3}
27. $0 = 5x$ {0}
28. $8x = 32$ {4}
29. $x \cdot x = 36$ {6}
30. $x \cdot x = 1$ {1}
31. $\frac{1}{2}x = 2$ {4}
32. $\frac{1}{3}x = 2$ {6}
33. $x \cdot x = 5x$ {0, 5}
34. $3x + 9 = 26$ ∅
35. $15 = 9x - 3$ {2}
36. $4x = x \cdot 4$ {0, 1, 2, 3, 4, 5, 6}
37. $x(9 - x) = 0$ {0}

Translate each phrase into a variable expression. (1-4)

38. Three more than twice the number m $2m + 3$
39. Four less than half the number z $\frac{1}{2}z - 4$
40. Two more than eight times the number k $8k + 2$
41. The difference of five times a number w and one $5w - 1$
42. Three times the sum of a number h and six $3(h + 6)$

Complete each statement with a variable expression. (1-4)

43. In x weeks there are __?__ days. $7x$
44. In y yards there are __?__ feet. $3y$
45. A house is x years old. Four years ago it was __?__ years old. $x - 4$
46. Tony weighs w lb. Ray is 7 lb heavier than Tony. Ray weighs __?__ lb. $w + 7$
47. My car is 5 years older than my sister's car. If my car is n years old, then her car is __?__ years old. $n - 5$

In Exercises 48–50, (1-5)

a. **Choose a variable to represent the number described by the words in parentheses.**

b. **Write an equation that represents the given information.**

48. A package of a dozen pencils costs $1.39. (Cost of one pencil in cents) **a.** c **b.** $12c = 1.39$

49. The perimeter of a square is 52 m. (Length of a side in meters) **a.** s **b.** $4s = 52$

50. All but 5 of the 34 invited guests came to the party. (Number of guests at the party) **a.** g **b.** $g + 5 = 34$

Translate each problem into an equation. Drawing a sketch may help you. (1-6)

51. Henry is 4 years older than Celia. If the product of their ages is 140, find each person's age. Let x = Celia's age; $x(x + 4) = 140$

52. The length of a rectangle is 5 cm more than its width. If the area of the rectangle is 176 cm², find the dimensions of the rectangle.
Let x = width of rectangle; $x(x + 5) = 176$

Solve using the five-step plan. Write out each step. A choice of possible numbers for one unknown is given. (1-7)

53. The number of tickets Cynthia sold is 12 less than half the number Holly sold. Together they sold 114 tickets. How many tickets did each sell? Choices for the number Holly sold: 68, 72, 84 Cynthia, 30; Holly, 84

54. Jim weighs 40 lb more than Stephanie. Stephanie weighs three fourths as much as Jim. How much does each weigh? Choices for Stephanie's weight: 100 lb, 118 lb, 120 lb Jim, 160 lb; Stephanie, 120 lb

Write a number to represent each situation. Then write the opposite of that situation and write a number to represent it. (1-8)
400; 400 ft below sea level; −400   −50; a deposit of $50; 50

55. 400 ft above sea level   **56.** A bank withdrawal of $50

57. Ten losses −10; ten wins; 10   **58.** Seven floors up 7; seven floors down, −7

Graph the given numbers on a number line. (1-8)

59. $5, -2, \frac{1}{2}, 3, -4$ **60.** $-3, 0, 1, -2.5, 2$

Simplify. (1-9)

61. $-(7 - 4)$ −3   **62.** $[-(-8)] + 10$ 18   **63.** $3 + [-(-6)]$ 9   **64.** $2 + |-9|$ 11

65. $|-3| + |0|$ 3   **66.** $|6| - |6|$ 0   **67.** $|-3.2| + |-0.8|$ 4   **68.** $|-4.7| + |4.7|$ 9.4

Replace each __?__ with one of the symbols < or > to make a true statement. (1-9)

69. $9 - 8$ __?__ -1 >   **70.** 7 __?__ $6 + 5$ <   **71.** $|0|$ __?__ 1 <

72. -4.3 __?__ -4.4 >   **73.** $-(7 + 3)$ __?__ $|-14|$ <   **74.** $-\dfrac{3}{7}$ __?__ $-\dfrac{2}{7}$ <

Chapter 2

Simplify. (2-1)

1. $237 + 75 + 13 + 25$ 350
2. $456 + 29 + 44 + 21$ 550
3. $0.2 + 16.4 + 2.8 + 0.6$ 20
4. $3.75 + 4.85 + 1.25 + 3.15$ 13
5. $6\frac{3}{8} + 1\frac{2}{7} + 4\frac{5}{8} + 3\frac{5}{7}$ 16
6. $25\frac{3}{4} + \frac{4}{5} + \frac{1}{4} + 2\frac{1}{5}$ 29
7. $8 + 3m + 4$ $3m + 12$
8. $15 + 5f + 7$ $5f + 22$
9. $9 + 6w + 3$ $6w + 12$
10. $5(7u)$ $35u$
11. $(8n)(11)$ $88n$
12. $(4b)9$ $36b$
13. $(3p)(4q)(5r)$ $60pqr$
14. $(2x)(5k)(7l)$ $70klx$
15. $(10w)(3h)(2m)$ $60hmw$

Simplify. If necessary, draw a number line to help you. (2-2)

16. $(-4 + 8) + 9$ 13
17. $(-7 + 10) + (-3)$ 0
18. $[16 + (-21)] + 4$ -1
19. $[-5 + (-13)] + 6$ -12
20. $[0 + (-7)] + [-8 + (-22)]$ -37
21. $[27 + (-7)] + [1 + (-1)]$ 20
22. $-3 + (-4) + (-9)$ -16
23. $(-5) + (-8) + (-6)$ -19
24. $-7.2 + (-3.5) + 10.7$ 0
25. $5.4 + (-3.1) + (-7.9)$ -5.6

Add. (2-3)

26. $9 + 8 + (-3) + 4$ 18
27. $-6 + (-7) + 10 + 2$ -1
28. $112 + (-32) + (-40) + (-25)$ 15
29. $-265 + (-88) + 105 + 95$ -153
30. $-[24 + (-8)] + [-(-4 + 6)]$ -18
31. $[-9 + (-2)] + [-(-9 + 2)]$ -4

Evaluate each expression if $x = 2$, $y = -5$, and $z = 3$. (2-3)

32. $-8 + x + (-y)$ -1
33. $-z + y + (-4)$ -12
34. $1 + (-x) + z$ 2
35. $|x + y + z|$ 0
36. $x + (-z) + (-12)$ -13
37. $-|z + (-y) + x|$ -10

Simplify. (2-4, 2-5)

38. $48 - 218$ -170
39. $53 - (-47)$ 100
40. $-18 - (-5)$ -13
41. $-27 - 56$ -83
42. $133 - (62 - 59)$ 130
43. $186 - (40 - 69)$ 215
44. $(33 - 44) - (66 - 77)$ 0
45. $(54 - 32) - (-8 + 13)$ 17
46. $[14 - (-8) - [6 - (-3)]$ 13
47. $-18 - 7 - [-6 - (-11)]$ -30
48. $6 + x - (6 - x) - x$ x
49. $y - (-4) - [y + (-4)] - 4$ 4
50. $30\left(\frac{1}{6} + \frac{1}{3}\right)$ 15
51. $\frac{1}{5}(24) + \frac{1}{5}(16)$ 8
52. $\frac{1}{4}(16 + 12)$ 7
53. $(0.25)(34) + (0.75)(34)$ 34
54. $(37 \times 22) - (7 \times 22)$ 660
55. $(16 \times 58) - (6 \times 58)$ 580
56. $14m + 7m$ $21m$
57. $15q + (-8)q$ $7q$
58. $53n - 110n$ $-57n$
59. $79a - 37a$ $42a$
60. $3u + 7u + 8$ $10u + 8$
61. $7(c + 3) + 6$ $7c + 27$

Simplify. (2-5, 2-6)

62. $26 + 4(h + 3)$ $4h + 38$ **63.** $8(j - 4) + 17$ $8j - 15$ **64.** $23 + 6(t - 2)$ $6t + 11$

65. $5x + 9 + 3x + 11$ $8x + 20$ **66.** $(-5)m + 3 + 13m + 17$ $8m + 20$

67. $14u - 8 - 12u + 13$ $2u + 5$ **68.** $4h + 8k + (-2)h + 12k$ $2h + 20k$

69. $9f + 3g - 7f + 7g$ $2f + 10g$ **70.** $10x + 14y - 6x - 3y$ $4x + 11y$

71. $(-27)(-5)$ 135 **72.** $38(-2)$ -76 **73.** $(-4)45$ -180

74. $(-8)(-6)(30)$ 1440 **75.** $(-5)(-9)(-3)$ -135 **76.** $(-13)(-14)(0)$ 0

77. $5(-4)(-12)(-2)$ -480 **78.** $-3(-2 - 9)$ 33 **79.** $(-17 + 6)(-1)$ 11

80. $(-6 \times 13) + (-6 \times 15)$ -168 **81.** $[27 \times (-5)] - (27 \times 5)$ -270

82. $-16 \times (-1) - [-16 \times (-11)]$ -160 **83.** $7(-m + 6p)$ $-7m + 42p$

84. $-5(2u - h)$ $-10u + 5h$ **85.** $-4(6n - 9v)$ $-24n + 36v$ $5l + 5$

86. $-x + 7 + 6x - 5$ $5x + 2$ **87.** $4 - t - 8 - 7t$ $-8t - 4$ **88.** $-l + 9 + 6l - 4$

89. $3(x + 4y) + (-4)(8x - y)$ $-29x + 16y$ **90.** $-4(2u + v) + 5(u - v)$ $-3u - 9v$

91. $-2(3c + d) - 3(5d - c)$ $-3c - 17d$ **92.** $7(e - f) - 3(2e - 3f)$ $e + 2f$

Write an equation to represent the given relationship among integers. (2-7)

93. The sum of three consecutive integers is 75. $x + (x + 1) + (x + 2) = 75$

94. The sum of three consecutive odd integers is 87. $x + (x + 2) + (x + 4) = 87$

95. The sum of three consecutive even integers is 138. $x + (x + 2) + (x + 4) = 138$

96. The product of two consecutive integers is 156. $x(x + 1) = 156$

97. The greater of two consecutive odd integers is eight more than three times the lesser. $x + 2 = 3x + 8$

98. The smaller of two consecutive even integers is one less than half of the greater. $x = \frac{1}{2}(x + 2) - 1$

Simplify each expression. (2-8, 2-9)

99. $-\frac{1}{11}(55)$ -5 **100.** $-5000\left(\frac{1}{50}\right)$ -100 **101.** $-\frac{1}{9}(-63)$ 7

102. $112\left(-\frac{1}{7}\right)\left(-\frac{1}{2}\right)$ 8 **103.** $-\frac{1}{5}(80)$ $\frac{1}{4}$ -4 **104.** $6uv\left(-\frac{1}{6}\right)$ $-uv$

105. $44xy\left(\frac{1}{4}\right)$ $11xy$ **106.** $\frac{1}{m}(3mn)$, $m \neq 0$ $3n$ **107.** $(8fg)\left(\frac{1}{f}\right)$, $f \neq 0$ $8g$

108. $\frac{1}{5}(-35a + 15)$ $-7a + 3$ **109.** $(27h - 18)\frac{1}{3}$ $9h - 6$ $8e - 10f$

110. $-\frac{1}{4}(-32e + 40f)$

111. $(42x - 63y)\left(-\frac{1}{7}\right)$ $-6x + 9y$ **112.** $\frac{1}{12}(-480 - 144m)$ $-40 - 12m$ **113.** $(-50p - 100q)\left(-\frac{1}{10}\right)$ $5p + 10q$

114. $-392 \div 56$ -7 **115.** $216 \div (-27)$ -8 **116.** $55 \div \left(-\frac{1}{5}\right)$ -275 **117.** $0 \div (-29)$ 0

118. $\frac{-36}{-\frac{1}{6}}$ 216 **119.** $\frac{8}{-\frac{1}{5}}$ -40 **120.** $\frac{-12}{\frac{1}{4}}$ -48 **121.** $\frac{0}{-\frac{1}{3}}$ 0

122. $\dfrac{168m}{-12}$ $-14m$ **123.** $\dfrac{252a}{-8} - \dfrac{63}{2}a$ **124.** $\dfrac{-756x}{7x}$, $x \neq 0$ -108 **125.** $\dfrac{-253u}{-23u}$, $u \neq 0$ 11

126. $-\dfrac{c}{17}(-17)$ c **127.** $-9 \cdot \dfrac{x}{9}$ $-x$ **128.** $\dfrac{8w}{7} \cdot 7$ $8w$ **129.** $-\dfrac{5h}{3}(-3)$ $5h$

Chapter 3

Solve. Check your answers.   (3-1, 3-2, 3-3)

1. $a - 13 = 17$ {30}   **2.** $c + 8 = 22$ {14}   **3.** $s - 20 = -12$ {8}

4. $y + 14 = -33$ {−47}   **5.** $15 + h = 0$ {−15}   **6.** $0 = k - 13$ {13}

7. $f - 4 = |16|$ {20}   **8.** $g + 7 = |-2|$ {−5}   **9.** $-x + 6 = 9$ {−3}

10. $23 - y = 47$ {−24}   **11.** $-5 - m = 7$ {−12}   **12.** $13 = -q + 8$ {−5}

13. $(e + 4) + 3 = 9$ {2}   **14.** $6 = 10 + (n + 3)$ {−7}   **15.** $-5 + (1 + z) = 8$ {12}

16. $13u = 338$ {26}   **17.** $-396 = 22a$ {−18}   **18.** $-12x = -444$ {37}   **19.** $126 = -9w$ {−14}

20. $\dfrac{1}{7}t = 13$ {91}   **21.** $\dfrac{1}{8}h = -8$ {−64}   **22.** $11 = -\dfrac{1}{4}v$ {−44}   **23.** $-10 = -\dfrac{1}{5}m$ {50}

24. $-42 = \dfrac{n}{7}$ {−294}   **25.** $-\dfrac{c}{4} = 32$ {−128}   **26.** $-\dfrac{m}{27} = 0$ {0}   **27.** $-\dfrac{m}{3} = -40$ {120}

28. $4x = -\dfrac{2}{7}$ $\left\{-\dfrac{1}{14}\right\}$ **29.** $-\dfrac{3}{2} = -9z$ $\left\{\dfrac{1}{6}\right\}$ **30.** $\dfrac{1}{4}v = 2\dfrac{3}{4}$ {11}   **31.** $3\dfrac{1}{2} = \dfrac{1}{2}u$ {7}

32. $5k + 8 = 43$ {7}   **33.** $7h - 6 = 36$ {6}   **34.** $-3 + 3m = -45$ {−14}

35. $2n + 8n = 80$ {8}   **36.** $9v - 5v = 44$ {11}   **37.** $3c - 8c = 65$ {−13}

38. $\dfrac{n}{5} + 9 = -11$ {−100}   **39.** $-\dfrac{x}{3} - 2 = 7$ {−27}   **40.** $\dfrac{5}{6}u + 15 = 0$ {−18}

41. $x - 5 - 6x = -25$ {4}   **42.** $0 = y - 14 - 3y$ {−7}   **43.** $e + 3e + 4e = 48$ {6}

44. $5(k + 3) = -10$ {−5}   **45.** $-\dfrac{4}{3}(n - 6) = 12$ {−3}   **46.** $2(v + 7) - 9 = 19$ {7}

Solve each problem using the five-step plan to help you.   (3-4)

47. The sum of 37 and three times a number is 67. Find the number. 10

48. Four times a number, decreased by 24, is −20. Find the number. 1

49. The perimeter of a rectangle is 108. If the length is 33, find the width. 21

50. A large bucket holds 3 L more than twice as much as a small bucket. It took 2 small buckets and 5 large buckets to fill a 63 L tank. How much does a large bucket hold? 11 L

51. The lengths, in meters, of the sides of a triangle are consecutive even integers. The perimeter is 18 m. How long are the sides? 4 m, 6 m, 8 m

52. Bruce's savings account contains $122 more than his younger brother's account. Together, they have $354. Find the amount in each account.
Bruce, $238; brother, $116

Extra Practice   **643**

Solve each equation. If the equation is an identity or if it has no solution, write (3-5)
identity or *no solution.* **62.** identity **63.** $\left\{\dfrac{11}{8}\right\}$ **64.** $\left\{-\dfrac{5}{3}\right\}$

53. $10w = 8w + 14$ {7} **54.** $x = 45 - 4x$ {9} **55.** $48 - 6k = -12k$ {−8}

56. $9m + 3 = 6m + 21$ {6} **57.** $27 + u = 3 - 3u$ {−6} **58.** $4n + 1 = -1 + 4n$ no sol.

59. $2(v - 8) = 6v$ {−4} **60.** $3x = 5(x - 6)$ {15} **61.** $7y - 3 = 6(y + 2)$ {15}

62. $\dfrac{1}{3}(18 - 9c) = 6 - 3c$ **63.** $m - 5 = \dfrac{1}{2}(12 - 14m)$ **64.** $\dfrac{4}{5}(25x - 15) = 50x + 38$

65. $5(3 + h) = 4(h + 2)$ {−7} **66.** $(6x - 3)2 = (4x + 7)3$ **67.** $7(n - 3) = 5(n - 3)$ {3}
no solution

Solve. Use a chart to help you solve the problem. (3-6, 3-7)

68. Jay's salary is $\dfrac{2}{3}$ of his wife's salary. In January, when they both get $2000 raises, their combined income will be $49,000. What are their current salaries? Jay, $18,000; wife, $27,000

69. Erin's three test scores were consecutive odd integers. If her next test score is 18 points more than the highest score of the three tests, her total number of points will be 328. Find Erin's test scores. 75, 77, 79, 97

70. Julius weighs twice as much as each of his twin brothers. If each of the twins gains 5 lb and Julius gains twice that amount, the sum of the three brothers' weights will be 240 lb. How much does each weigh now?
Julius, 110 lb; twins, 55 lb each

71. The width of a rectangle is 6 cm less than the length. A second rectangle, with a perimeter of 54 cm, is 3 cm wider and 2 cm shorter than the first. What are the dimensions of each rectangle? 16 cm by 10 cm; 14 cm by 13 cm

72. Martha has some nickels and dimes worth $6.25. She has three times as many nickels as dimes. How many nickels does she have? 75 nickels

73. Elliot paid $1.50 a dozen for some flowers. He sold all but 5 dozen of them for $2 a dozen, making a profit of $18. How many dozen flowers did he buy? 56 dozen

10 cans dog food; 12 cans cat food
74. Rachel spent $16.18 for some cans of dog food costing 79 cents each and some cans of cat food costing 69 cents each. She bought two more cans of cat food than of dog food. How many cans of each did she buy?

75. Victor earns $3 an hour working after school and $4 an hour working on Saturdays. Last week he earned $43, working a total of 13 h. How many hours did he work on Saturday? 4 h

State a reason for each step in Exercises 76–78. (3-8)

76. $6 + (15 + 4) = 6 + (4 + 15)$ __?__ Comm. prop. of add.
$\qquad = (6 + 4) + 15$ __?__ Assoc. prop. of add.
$\qquad = 10 + 15 = 25$ __?__ Substitution principle

77. $20 + (-4) = (16 + 4) + (-4)$ __?__ Substitution principle
$\qquad = 16 + [4 + (-4)]$ __?__ Assoc. prop. of add.
$\qquad = 16 + 0$ __?__ Prop. of opposites
$\qquad = 16$ __?__ Ident. prop. of add.

644 *Extra Practice*

78. $-7 + 19 = 19 + (-7)$ __?__ Comm. prop. of add.
$\qquad\qquad = 12 + 7 + (-7)$ __?__ Substitution principle
$\qquad\qquad = 12 + 0$ __?__ Prop. of opposites
$\qquad\qquad = 12$ __?__ Identity prop. of add.

Chapter 4

Simplify.   **(4-1)**

1. 7^3 343   **2.** $(-5)^4$ 625   **3.** $-3 \cdot 2^4$ -48 **4.** $(-2 \cdot 5)^3$ -1000

5. $7 + 5^2$ 32   **6.** $(8 - 4)^3$ 64   **7.** $6 - 2^5$ -26 **8.** $(4 + 7)^2$ 121

9. $5^3 \div (3^2 + 4^2)$ 5   **10.** $(8^2 - 6^2) \div 7$ 4   **11.** $4(9^2 - 4^3)$ 68

Evaluate if $a = -3$ and $b = 2$.   **(4-1)**

12. $3a + b^2$ -5 **13.** $(3a + b)^2$ 49   **14.** $4a - b^3$ -20 **15.** $(4a - b)^3$ -2744

16. $7 + ab^2$ -5 **17.** $(7 + ab)^2$ 1   **18.** $-\dfrac{3a}{b^2}$ $\dfrac{9}{4}$ **19.** $\left(-\dfrac{3a}{b}\right)^2$ $\dfrac{81}{4}$

Add.   **(4-2)**

20. $4x - 3$ **21.** $\quad 3b + 4$ **22.** $5m + 8$ **23.** $-2t - 7$
$\underline{7x + 8}$ $11x + 5$ $\underline{-2b - 6}$ $b - 2$ $\underline{4m + 3}$ $9m + 11$ $\underline{\;6t - 3\;}$ $4t - 10$

24. $\quad 5k - 6l + 4$ **25.** $6x^2 - 2xy + 3y^2$
$\underline{-5k + 8l + 2}$ $2l + 6$ $\underline{4x^2 - \;xy - \;y^2}$ $10x^2 - 3xy + 2y^2$

26. $\quad 2m^2 - 3mn - 5n$ **27.** $\quad 5a^2 - 6ab$
$\underline{-8m^2 \qquad\;\; - \;n}$ $-6m^2 - 3mn - 6n$ $\underline{-2a^2 + 9ab - b^2}$ $3a^2 + 3ab - b^2$

28–35. In Exercises 20–27, subtract the lower polynomial from the upper one.

Simplify. **41.** $60j^5k^3l^5$ **44.** $-\dfrac{28u^4v^4}{3}$ **(4-3, 4-4)**

36. $e^6 \cdot e^3 \cdot e$ e^{10} **37.** $(4f^3)(2f^4)$ $8f^7$ **38.** $(-3c^2d)(-4cd^2)$ $12c^3d^3$

39. $(-2gh^2)(5g^3h)$ $-10g^4h^3$ **40.** $(3mn)(6m^2n)(2n^2)$ $36m^3n^4$ **41.** $(-5j^4k^2)(4jl^3)(-3kl^2)$

42. $\left(\dfrac{8}{3}x^5y\right)\left(\dfrac{9}{2}xy^6\right)$ $12x^6y^7$ **43.** $(-6a^3)\left(\dfrac{1}{6}a^3\right)$ $-a^6$ **44.** $(3u^2v)(-7v^3)\left(\dfrac{4}{9}u^2\right)$

45. $3^w \cdot 3^{5-w} \cdot 3$ 729   **46.** $4^2 \cdot 4^{a+1} \cdot 4^a$ 4^{2a+3} **47.** $2^5 \cdot 2^{b+3} \cdot 2^{3-b}$ 2048

48. $(3p^5)(5p^2) + (7p^3)(2p^4)$ $29p^7$ **49.** $(8d^3)(2d^7) - (3d^6)(4d^4)$ $4d^{10}$

50. $(w^5)^2$ w^{10} **51.** $(x^2)^5$ x^{10} **52.** $y^2 \cdot y^5$ y^7 **53.** $z^n \cdot z^n$ z^{2n}

54. $(a^n)^3$ a^{3n} **55.** $(b^3)^n$ b^{3n} **56.** $c^3 \cdot c^n$ c^{n+3} **57.** $d^n \cdot d^n \cdot d^n$ d^{3n}

58. $(5f)^2$ $25f^2$ **59.** $(gh)^4$ g^4h^4 **60.** $(6m^3)^2$ $36m^6$ **61.** $(4mn^5)^3$ $64m^3n^{15}$

62. $(2u^3v)^5$ $32u^{15}v^5$ **63.** $(3a^5b^4)^2$ $9a^{10}b^8$ **64.** $(-7x^4)^2$ $49x^8$ **65.** $-(8x^5)^3$ $-512x^{15}$

66. $(3k)^2(3k)^4$ $729k^6$ **67.** $(-2x^3)^3 \cdot (5x^2)^2$ $-200x^{13}$ **68.** $-(4t^2)^2(3t)^3$ $-432t^7$ **69.** $(5x^2y)^3 \cdot 3xy^2$ $375x^7y^5$

Extra Practice   **645**

Additional Answers

28. $-3x - 11$

29. $5b + 10$

30. $m + 5$

31. $-8t - 4$

32. $10k - 14l + 2$

33. $2x^2 - xy + 4y^2$

34. $10m^2 - 3mn - 4n$

35. $7a^2 - 15ab + b^2$

41. $60j^5k^3l^5$

44. $-\dfrac{28u^4v^4}{3}$

Multiply. $\hspace{6cm}$ (4-5, 4-6)

70. $\overset{7x + 21}{7(x + 3)}$ $\quad$ 71. $\overset{5y - 20}{5(y - 4)}$ $\quad$ 72. $\overset{-3n + 6}{-3(n - 2)}$ $\quad$ 73. $\overset{-8 - 32m}{-8(1 + 4m)}$

74. $3n(n + 5)$ $\quad$ 75. $-4t(3 - 2t)$ $\quad$ 76. $6k(2k - 7)$ $\quad$ 77. $-5h(8h + 3)$
$\quad$ $3n^2 + 15n$ $\qquad$ $-12t + 8t^2$ $\qquad$ $12k^2 - 42k$ $\qquad$ $-40h^2 - 15h$

78. $9a(a^2 - 3a - 4)\, 9a^3 - 27a^2 - 36a$ $\qquad$ 79. $-5b^2(3b^2 - 2b + 6)$
$\hspace{9cm} -15b^4 + 10b^3 - 30b^2$

80. $\frac{1}{3}c(6c^2 - 3cd + 9d^2)$ $\qquad\qquad$ 81. $\frac{1}{2}uv^2(10u^2 - 4uv + 8v^2)$
$\quad$ $2c^3 - c^2d + 3cd^2$ $\hspace{5cm}$ $5u^3v^2 - 2u^2v^3 + 4uv^4$

82. $(m + 4)(m + 2)$ $\qquad$ 83. $(n - 3)(n + 5)$ $\qquad$ 84. $(a - 6)(a - 7)$

85. $(5x - 2)(x + 7)$ $\qquad$ 86. $(4y - 2)(3y - 1)$ $\qquad$ 87. $(6m + 4)(5m + 3)$

88. $(u + 3)(u^2 + 2u + 5)$ $\qquad$ 89. $(v - 1)(3v^2 + 4v + 7)$ $\qquad$ 90. $(3c - 5)(2c^2 - c + 8)$
$\quad$ $u^3 + 5u^2 + 11u + 15$ $\hspace{2.5cm}$ $3v^3 + v^2 + 3v - 7$ $\hspace{2cm}$ $6c^3 - 13c^2 + 29c - 40$

91. $\overset{7x - 4y}{\underset{3x - 2y}{}}$ $\qquad$ 92. $\overset{5a - 8b}{\underset{4a + b}{}}$ $\qquad$ 93. $\overset{e^2 + ef + f^2}{\underset{e + f}{}}$ $\qquad$ 94. $\overset{3m^2 - 4mn + n^2}{\underset{5m + n}{}}$

$21x^2 - 26xy + 8y^2$ $\quad$ $20a^2 - 27ab - 8b^2$ $\quad$ $e^3 + 2e^2f + 2ef^2 + f^3$ $\quad$ $15m^3 - 17m^2n + mn^2 + n^3$

Solve the given formula for the variable shown in color. State the restrictions, $\hspace{1cm}$ (4-7)
if any, for the formula obtained to be meaningful.

95. $A = \frac{1}{2}ap;\ a$ $\qquad$ 96. $V = \frac{1}{3}Bh;\ h$ $\qquad$ 97. $A = \frac{1}{2}h(b_1 + b_2);\ b_1$

98. $y = mx + b;\ b$ $\qquad$ 99. $A = \pi r^2;\ r$ $\qquad$ 100. $S = (n - 2)180;\ n$

101. $F = \frac{9}{5}C + 32;\ C$ $\qquad$ 102. $P = \frac{A}{1 + rt};\ A$ $\qquad$ 103. $r = \frac{I}{Pt};\ t$

Solve. Use a chart to help you solve the problem. $\hspace{4cm}$ (4-8)

104. Two buses leave a depot at the same time, one traveling north and the other south. The speed of the northbound bus is 15 mi/h greater than the speed of the southbound bus. After 3 h on the road, the buses are 255 mi apart. What are their speeds? 35 mi/h, 50 mi/h

105. Exactly 10 min after Alex left his grandparents' house, his cousin Alison set out from there to overtake him. Alex drives at 36 mi/h. Alison drives at 40 mi/h. How long did it take Alison to overtake Alex? 90 min

106. A plane flew from the Sky City airport to the Plainsville airport at 800 km/h and then returned to Sky City at 900 km/h. The return trip took 30 min less than the flight to Plainsville. How far apart are the airports and how long did the trip to Plainsville take? 3600 km; 4.5 h

107. A poster is three times as long as it is wide. It is framed by a mat such $\hspace{1cm}$ (4-9) that there is a 4 in. border around the poster. Find the dimensions of the poster if the area of the mat is 488 in². 13.25 in. by 39.75 in.

108. A square piece of remnant material is on sale. A rectangular piece of the same material, whose length is 1 yd longer than a side of the square and whose width is $\frac{5}{9}$ yd shorter than a side of the square, is also on sale. If the square and the rectangle have the same area and you purchase both remnants, how much material will you get? $3\frac{1}{8}$ yd²

Additional Answers

82. $m^2 + 6m + 8$

83. $n^2 + 2n - 15$

84. $a^2 - 13a + 42$

85. $5x^2 + 33x - 14$

86. $12y^2 - 10y + 2$

87. $30m^2 + 38m + 12$

95. $a = \frac{2A}{p};\ p \neq 0$

96. $h = \frac{3V}{B};\ B \neq 0$

97. $b_1 = \frac{2A - b_2h}{h};\ h \neq 0$

98. $b = y - mx$

99. $r = \sqrt{\frac{A}{\pi}},\ A \geq 0$

100. $n = \frac{S + 360}{180}$

101. $C = \frac{5}{9}(F - 32)$

102. $A = P + Prt$

103. $t = \frac{I}{Pr};\ Pr \neq 0$

646 $\quad$ *Extra Practice*

Chapter 5

List all pairs of factors of each integer. (5-1)

1. 42　　　　　**2.** 80　　　　　**3.** 91　　　　　**4.** 72　　　　　**5.** 52

6–10. Find the prime factorization of each integer in Exercises 1–5.

6. $2 \cdot 3 \cdot 7$　**7.** $2^4 \cdot 5$　**8.** $7 \cdot 13$　**9.** $2^3 \cdot 3^2$　**10.** $2^2 \cdot 13$

Give the GCF of each group of numbers. (5-1)

11. 126, 168 42　　**12.** 144, 84 12　　**13.** 65, 52 13　　**14.** 90, 330 30

Simplify. Assume that no denominator equals 0. (5-2)

15. $\dfrac{12x^5}{4x}$　$3x^4$　**16.** $\dfrac{25m^4n}{-15mn^6}$　$-\dfrac{5m^3}{3n^5}$　**17.** $\dfrac{-7ab}{21ab^5}$　$-\dfrac{1}{3b^4}$　**18.** $\dfrac{-8(uv)^7}{-10(uv)^5}$　$\dfrac{4u^2v^2}{5}$

19. $\dfrac{(w^4)^2}{(w^5)^4}$　$\dfrac{1}{w^{12}}$　**20.** $\dfrac{(5k)^2}{5k^2}$　5　**21.** $\dfrac{(-3y)^3}{(y^3)^2}$　$-\dfrac{27}{y^3}$　**22.** $\dfrac{(2c^5)(4c^3)}{(8c^2)^3}$　$\dfrac{c^2}{64}$

Divide. (5-3)

23. $\dfrac{12e + 8}{4}$　$3e + 2$　　　　**24.** $\dfrac{6x - 9y + 12}{3}$　$2x - 3y + 4$　　　**25.** $\dfrac{2x^3 + 6x^2 + x}{x}$ $2x^2 + 6x + 1$

26. $\dfrac{18ab - 24a^2}{-6a}$　$-3b + 4a$　　**27.** $\dfrac{15m - 25m^2 - 5m^3}{5m}$　$3 - 5m - m^2$　　**28.** $\dfrac{28h^5k^3 - 35hk^2}{7hk^2}$ $4h^4k - 5$

Factor each polynomial as the product of its greatest monomial factor and another polynomial. (5-3)

29. $15w^2 - 10w + 5$ $5(3w^2 - 2w + 1)$　　**30.** $9x^2 + 18x$ $9x(x + 2)$　　**31.** $7u^3 + 14u^2$ $7u^2(u + 2)$

32. $12a^3 - 6a^2 + 18a$ $6a(2a^2 - a + 3)$　　**33.** $15c^2 + 3cd$ $3c(5c + d)$　　**34.** $8m^2n - 24mn^2$ $8mn(m - 3n)$

Write each product as a trinomial. (5-4)

35. $(x + 5)(x + 3)$ $x^2 + 8x + 15$　**36.** $(b - 2)(b - 4)$ $b^2 - 6b + 8$　**37.** $(n - 3)(n + 7)$

38. $(e - 8)(e + 6)$ $e^2 - 2e - 48$　**39.** $(3 + m)(2 + m)$ $6 + 5m + m^2$　**40.** $(3f + 2)(f + 5)$

41. $(4y - 3)(2y - 1)$ $8y^2 - 10y + 3$　**42.** $(8z + 7)(z - 2)$ $8z^2 - 9z - 14$　**43.** $(5n - 3)(4n - 2)$

44. $a(6a - 4)(5a - 3)$ $30a^3 - 38a^2 + 12a$　**45.** $h(3h + 7)(4h + 9)$ $12h^3 + 55h^2 + 63h$　**46.** $2x(9x - 1)(2x + 3)$ $36x^3 + 50x^2 - 6x$

Write each product as a binomial. (5-5)

47. $(k - 5)(k + 5)$ $k^2 - 25$　**48.** $(3 - y)(3 + y)$ $9 - y^2$　**49.** $(4d - 8)(4d + 8)$ $16d^2 - 64$

50. $(w^2 - 6)(w^2 + 6)$ $w^4 - 36$　**51.** $(5m^2 + n)(5m^2 - n)$ $25m^4 - n^2$　**52.** $(ab + c^2)(ab - c^2)$ $a^2b^2 - c^4$

Factor. You may use a calculator or the table of squares. (5-5)

53. $16e^2 - 9$　　**54.** $36u^2 - 25$　　**55.** $81 - f^2$　　　**56.** $144a^2 - 64b^2$

57. $49 - 100y^2$ $(7 - 10y)(7 + 10y)$　**58.** $v^4 - w^4$ $(v - w)(v + w)(v^2 + w^2)$　**59.** $s^6 - 4$ $(s^3 - 2)(s^3 + 2)$　**60.** $16x^8 - 625$

60. $(2x^2 - 5)(2x^2 + 5)(4x^4 + 25)$　　　*Extra Practice*　　**647**

Express each square as a trinomial. (5-6)

61. $(g + 7)^2$ $g^2 + 14g + 49$

62. $(k - 3)^2$ $k^2 - 6k + 9$

63. $(2x + 6)^2$ $4x^2 + 24x + 36$

64. $(5y - 3)^2$ $25y^2 - 30y + 9$

65. $(2m + 3n)^2$ $4m^2 + 12mn + 9n^2$

66. $(7a - 5b)^2$ $49a^2 - 70ab + 25b^2$

67. $(ef - 8)^2$ $e^2f^2 - 16ef + 64$

68. $(-4 + 9f)^2$ $81f^2 - 72f + 16$

Factor. (5-6)

69. $x^2 - 6x + 9$ $(x - 3)^2$

70. $e^2 + 18e + 81$ $(e + 9)^2$

71. $4 - 28h + 49h^2$ $(2 - 7h)^2$

72. $64x^2 + 80xy + 25y^2$ $(8x + 5y)^2$

73. $4m^2 - 36mn + 81n^2$ $(2m - 9n)^2$

74. $16w^2 + 24wz + 9z^2$ $(4w + 3z)^2$

Factor. Check by multiplying the factors. If the polynomial is not factorable, write *prime*. (5-7, 5-8, 5-9)

75. $k^2 + 8k + 7$

76. $v^2 - 9v + 20$

77. $a^2 - 2a + 1$

78. $35 + 12u + u^2$

79. $n^2 - 16n + 48$

80. $w^2 + 18w + 80$

81. $x^2 + 13xy + 42y^2$

82. $m^2 - 10mn + 21n^2$

83. $e^2 - 15ef + 44f^2$

84. $c^2 + 3c - 18$

85. $x^2 - 2x - 35$

86. $k^2 + 8k - 32$

87. $h^2 - 7h - 18$

88. $b^2 + 7b - 30$

89. $y^2 - 4y - 45$

90. $a^2 - 2ab - 3b^2$

91. $u^2 + 3uv - 4v^2$

92. $m^2 - mn - 20n^2$

93. $2x^2 + 11x + 12$

94. $10e^2 - 12e + 3$

95. $10d^2 + d - 3$

96. $-10 - 26y - 12y^2$

97. $-7 - 39z - 18z^2$

98. $-10 + 24z - 8z^2$

99. $15x^2 + 13xy + 2y^2$

100. $8a^2 - 22ab + 12b^2$

101. $14m^2 - mn - 3n^2$

Factor. Check by multiplying.

102. $8(m - 3) - 5m(3 - m)$ $(m - 3)(5m + 8)$

103. $6a(a + 2) + 4(a + 2)$

104. $u(u - 2v) - (2v - u)$ $(u - 2v)(u + 1)$

105. $b(b - 2)(b + 1) - 3 - 3b$

106. $a^2 + 2a + ab + 2b$ $(a + 2)(a + b)$

107. $7cw + 3c - 7w^2 - 3w$

108. $n^3 + n^2 - 6n - 6$ $(n + 1)(n^2 - 6)$

109. $64 - 64m^2 + m^4 - m^6$

103. $2(a + 2)(3a + 2)$ (5-10)

105. $(b - 3)(b + 1)^2$

107. $(7w + 3)(c - w)$

109. $(1 + m)(1 - m)(64 + m^4)$

Factor completely. Check by multiplying. (5-11)

110. $42x^3 + 68x^2 + 16x$

111. $60y^3 - 18y^2 - 6y$

112. $12x^5 - 20x^4 + 3x^3$

113. $16a^4 - 144a^2$

114. $4n^5 - 100n$

115. $28w^7 - 102w^5$

116. $36m^2 + 24mn + 4n^2$

117. $24cd - 12c^2 - 12d^2$

118. $-7x^3 + 14x^2y - 7xy^2$

119. $\{-13, -8\}$ **120.** $\{16, 27\}$ **121.** $\left\{2, \dfrac{5}{3}\right\}$

Solve and check.   **122.** $\left\{\dfrac{5}{6}, -\dfrac{5}{6}\right\}$ **123.** $\left\{0, -\dfrac{3}{4}\right\}$ **124.** $\left\{0, -\dfrac{7}{2}, \dfrac{4}{3}\right\}$ (5-12)

119. $(a + 13)(a + 8) = 0$

120. $(f - 16)(f - 27) = 0$

121. $(2x - 4)(3x - 5) = 0$

122. $(6h - 5)(6h + 5) = 0$

123. $7w(4w + 3) = 0$

124. $m(2m + 7)(3m - 4) = 0$

125. $a^2 + 7a + 6 = 0$ $\{-1, -6\}$

126. $q^2 - 21q = -20$ $\{1, 20\}$

127. $d^2 = 14d - 45$ $\{5, 9\}$

128. $y^2 - 7y - 18 = 0$ $\{-2, 9\}$

129. $c^2 - 36 = -5c$ $\{4, -9\}$

130. $h^2 = -3h + 54$ $\{6, -9\}$

131. $6 - 23z - 4z^2 = 0$ $\left\{\dfrac{1}{4}, -6\right\}$

132. $3m^2 + 1 = 4m$ $\left\{1, \dfrac{1}{3}\right\}$

133. $2n^2 = 10 + n$ $\left\{-2, \dfrac{5}{2}\right\}$

134. $e^2 - 49 = 0$ $\{7, -7\}$

135. $36g^2 = 16$ $\left\{\dfrac{2}{3}, -\dfrac{2}{3}\right\}$

136. $w^3 - 9w = 0$ $\{0, 3, -3\}$

137. The sum of a number and its square is 56. Find the number. 7 or -8 (5-13)

138. Find two consecutive negative odd integers whose product is 143. -13 and -11

139. The length of a rectangle is 5 cm less than twice the width. If the area of the rectangle is 88 cm^2, find the dimensions of the rectangle. 8 cm by 11 cm

140. Find two numbers that total 12 and whose squares total 74. 5 and 7

Chapter 6

Simplify. Give the restrictions on the variable. (6-1)

1. $\dfrac{5m - 15}{m - 3}$ 5, $m \neq 3$ **2.** $\dfrac{2a + 1}{6a + 3}$ $\dfrac{1}{3}$, $a \neq -\dfrac{1}{2}$ **3.** $\dfrac{7c - 7d}{7c + 7d}$ $\dfrac{c - d}{c + d}$; $c \neq -d$ **4.** $\dfrac{6k - k^2}{36 - k^2}$ $\dfrac{k}{6 + k}$; $k \neq 6$, $k \neq -6$

5. $\dfrac{3uv}{u^2v - v^2u}$ $\dfrac{3}{u - v}$; $u \neq 0$, $v \neq 0$, $u \neq v$ **6.** $\dfrac{8w^3}{8w^2 - 12w}$ $\dfrac{2w^2}{2w - 3}$; $w \neq 0$, $w \neq \dfrac{3}{2}$ **7.** $\dfrac{x^2 - 64}{x^2 - x - 56}$ $\dfrac{x + 8}{x + 7}$; $x \neq -7$, $x \neq 8$ **8.** $\dfrac{(e - 7)^2}{49 - e^2}$ $\dfrac{7 - e}{7 + e}$; $e \neq -7$, $e \neq 7$

9. $\dfrac{15m + 6n}{25m^2 - 4n^2}$ $\dfrac{3}{5m - 2n}$; $m \neq -\dfrac{2}{5}n$, $m \neq \dfrac{2}{5}n$ **10.** $\dfrac{a^2 + ab}{a^2 - ab}$ $\dfrac{a + b}{a - b}$; $a \neq 0$, $a \neq b$

11. $\dfrac{(k - 3)(7k - 2)}{(2 - 7k)(k - 3)}$ -1; $k \neq 3$, $k \neq \dfrac{2}{7}$ **12.** $\dfrac{3x^2 + 17xy + 20y^2}{3x^2 - xy - 10y^2}$ $\dfrac{x + 4y}{x - 2y}$; $x \neq -\dfrac{5}{3}y$, $x \neq 2y$

13. $\dfrac{14 - 9t + t^2}{t^2 - 4}$ $\dfrac{t - 7}{t + 2}$; $t \neq 2$, $t \neq -2$ **14.** $\dfrac{u^2 - v^2}{u^2 + 2uv + v^2}$ $\dfrac{u - v}{u + v}$; $u \neq -v$

15. $\dfrac{(5w - x)^5}{(x - 5w)^7}$ $-\dfrac{1}{(5w - x)^2}$; $w \neq \dfrac{x}{5}$ **16.** $\dfrac{(4s - 6)^2(3s - 2)}{(2 - 3s)(6 - 4s)}$ $4s - 6$; $s \neq \dfrac{2}{3}$, $s \neq \dfrac{3}{2}$

Multiply. Express each product in simplest form. (6-2)

17. $\dfrac{5}{8} \cdot \dfrac{32}{15}$ $\dfrac{4}{3}$ **18.** $\dfrac{4}{3} \cdot \dfrac{3}{5} \cdot \dfrac{5}{7}$ $\dfrac{4}{7}$ **19.** $\left(\dfrac{-2}{5}\right)^2 \cdot \dfrac{15}{16}$ $\dfrac{3}{20}$ **20.** $\left(-\dfrac{3}{2}\right)^3 \cdot \dfrac{24}{9}$ -9

21. $\dfrac{e}{f} \cdot \dfrac{f}{g} \cdot \dfrac{g}{h}$ $\dfrac{e}{h}$ **22.** $\dfrac{5}{w} \cdot \dfrac{w^2}{10}$ $\dfrac{w}{2}$ **23.** $\dfrac{8m}{3} \cdot \dfrac{9}{12m}$ 2 **24.** $\dfrac{a^2}{3b} \cdot \dfrac{b^2}{4a}$ $\dfrac{ab}{12}$

25. $\dfrac{14v}{12v^2} \cdot \dfrac{4uw^2}{7v^2}$ $\dfrac{2uw^2}{3v^3}$ **26.** $\dfrac{a + 5}{a} \cdot \dfrac{a^2}{a^2 - 25}$ $\dfrac{a}{a - 5}$

27. $\dfrac{4x - xy}{8x^2y} \cdot \dfrac{2}{16 - y^2}$ $\dfrac{1}{4xy(4 + y)}$ **28.** $\dfrac{m + n}{m - n} \cdot \dfrac{m^2 - n^2}{3m + 3n}$ $\dfrac{m + n}{3}$

Simplify. Use the rules of exponents for a power of a product and a power of a quotient. (6-2)

29. $(5k^3)^2$ $25k^6$ **30.** $\left(\dfrac{x}{7}\right)^2$ $\dfrac{x^2}{49}$ **31.** $\left(\dfrac{3x}{4}\right)^2$ $\dfrac{9x^2}{16}$ **32.** $\left(\dfrac{2m}{3n^2}\right)^3$ $\dfrac{8m^3}{27n^6}$

33. $\left(-\dfrac{x^2}{5}\right)^3$ $-\dfrac{x^6}{125}$ **34.** $\left(\dfrac{e}{f}\right)^3 \cdot \dfrac{e}{f}$ $\dfrac{e^4}{f^4}$ **35.** $\left(\dfrac{4c}{d}\right)^3 \cdot \dfrac{c^2}{8}$ $\dfrac{8c^5}{d^3}$ **36.** $\left(\dfrac{7a}{b}\right)^2 \cdot \dfrac{3ab}{14}$ $\dfrac{21a^3}{2b}$

Divide. Express the answers in simplest form. (6-3)

37. $\frac{4}{9} \div \frac{16}{3}$ $\frac{1}{12}$

38. $\frac{a^2}{4} \div \frac{a}{12}$ $3a$

39. $\frac{m}{3n} \div \frac{mn}{6}$ $\frac{2}{n^2}$

40. $\frac{8x^2}{5y} \div 4xy$ $\frac{2x}{5y^2}$

41. $\frac{e+f}{5} \div \frac{3e+3f}{15}$ 1

42. $\frac{u^2-v^2}{u^2+v^2} \div (u+v)$ $\frac{u-v}{u^2+v^2}$

43. $\frac{5}{n^2-25} \div \frac{5n-15}{n+5}$ $\frac{1}{(n-3)(n-5)}$

44. $\frac{4n-12}{4} \div \frac{5n-15}{8}$ $\frac{8}{5}$

45. $\frac{x^4-y^4}{2x^2+8x} \div \frac{x^2+y^2}{x^2-16}$ $\frac{(x-y)(x+y)(x-4)}{2x}$

46. $\frac{4a^2-25}{6a^2} \div \frac{12a-30}{3a^4}$ $\frac{a^2(2a+5)}{12}$

47. $\frac{m^2+n^2}{8s-10t} \div \frac{7m+7n}{4t-6s}$ $\frac{(2t-3s)(m^2+n^2)}{7(4s-5t)(m+n)}$

Simplify. (6-3)

48. $\frac{1}{3} \div \frac{2}{6} \cdot \frac{5}{7}$ $\frac{5}{7}$

49. $\frac{x}{7} \div \frac{y^2}{x} \cdot \frac{7}{y}$ $\frac{x^2}{y^3}$

50. $\frac{e^2}{3} \cdot \frac{f^2}{e} \div \frac{e}{f}$ $\frac{f^3}{3}$

51. $\left(\frac{c}{3}\right)^2 \div \frac{c}{9} \cdot \frac{c}{3}$ $\frac{c^2}{3}$

52. $\left(\frac{w}{4}\right)^2 \div \left(\frac{w}{8} \cdot \frac{w}{2}\right)$ 1

53. $\frac{a-b}{a+3b} \cdot \frac{3b+a}{b+a} \div \frac{b-a}{b+a}$ -1

Complete. (6-4)

54. $\frac{5x}{11} = \frac{?}{33}$ $15x$

55. $\frac{h-4}{7} = \frac{?}{14}$ $2h-8$

56. $\frac{3k-5}{2} = \frac{?}{8}$ $12k-20$

57. $\frac{6m-n}{7} = \frac{?}{35}$ $30m-5n$

58. $\frac{c}{d} = \frac{?}{c^3d}$ c^4

59. $\frac{4s}{5t} = \frac{?}{15st^2}$ $12s^2t$

60. $\frac{8}{7d+2} = \frac{?}{(7d+2)^2}$ $56d+16$

61. $\frac{5}{e-1} = \frac{?}{e^2-1}$ $5e+5$

62. $\frac{3}{h-2} = \frac{?}{2-h}$ -3

63. $\frac{5}{z-3} = \frac{?}{z^2-3z}$ $5z$

64. $\frac{w}{w+4} = \frac{?}{w^2+4w}$ w^2

65. $\frac{3}{a^2b} = \frac{?}{a^3b^2}$ $3ab$

Write each group of fractions with their LCD. (6-4)

66. $\frac{2}{3}, \frac{4}{5}, \frac{3}{7}$ $\frac{70}{105}, \frac{84}{105}, \frac{45}{105}$

67. $\frac{x-2}{16}, \frac{x+3}{12}$ $\frac{3x-6}{48}, \frac{4x+12}{48}$

68. $\frac{3m-n}{10}, \frac{3m+n}{15}$

69. $\frac{1}{3cd}, \frac{4}{cd^2}$ $\frac{d}{3cd^2}, \frac{12}{3cd^2}$

70. $\frac{7}{e+f}, \frac{5}{e}, \frac{6}{f}$ $\frac{7ef}{ef(e+f)}, \frac{5ef+5f^2}{ef(e+f)}, \frac{6e^2+6ef}{ef(e+f)}$

71. $\frac{2w}{3x-9}, \frac{1}{x^2-9}$

Simplify. (6-5)

72. $\frac{3}{a} + \frac{5}{a} - \frac{4}{a}$ $\frac{4}{a}$

73. $\frac{7}{2x} + \frac{6}{2x} - \frac{5}{2x}$ $\frac{4}{x}$

74. $\frac{u}{7} - \frac{3u+5}{7}$

75. $\frac{k+3}{5} - \frac{2k+7}{5}$ $\frac{-k-4}{5}$

76. $\frac{c}{c-3} + \frac{1}{c-3} - \frac{8-c}{c-3}$ $\frac{2c-7}{c-3}$

77. $\frac{4}{g-3} - \frac{3}{3-g}$

78. $\frac{3m}{m-n} + \frac{3n}{n-m}$ 3

79. $\frac{5}{y^2} + \frac{3}{y}$ $\frac{5+3y}{y^2}$

80. $\frac{4}{5x} - \frac{1}{15x^2}$

81. $\frac{1}{5wx} - \frac{3}{10w}$ $\frac{2-3x}{10wx}$

82. $\frac{3k-2}{2k^3} + \frac{6}{k^2}$ $\frac{15k-2}{2k^3}$

83. $\frac{2}{3(x+2)} + \frac{x}{x+2}$

84. $\dfrac{5a-4}{6}+\dfrac{a-2}{9}$ $\dfrac{17a-16}{18}$ **85.** $\dfrac{2h+4}{8}-\dfrac{h}{4}+\dfrac{3h-2}{10}$ $\dfrac{3(h+1)}{10}$ **86.** $\dfrac{4(m-n)}{16}-\dfrac{3(m+n)}{12}-\dfrac{n}{2}$

87. $\dfrac{3}{x+2}-\dfrac{1}{x+3}$ $\dfrac{2x+7}{(x+2)(x+3)}$ **88.** $\dfrac{3z}{z^2-16}+\dfrac{z}{z-4}$ $\dfrac{z(z+7)}{(z+4)(z-4)}$ **89.** $\dfrac{u}{u-4}+\dfrac{3}{4-u}$ $\dfrac{u-3}{u-4}$

Write each expression as a fraction in simplest form. (6-6)

90. $7\dfrac{1}{3}$ $\dfrac{22}{3}$ **91.** $5+\dfrac{1}{n}$ $\dfrac{5n+1}{n}$ **92.** $4m-\dfrac{3}{m}$ $\dfrac{4m^2-3}{m}$ **93.** $\dfrac{x}{y}+3$ $\dfrac{x+3y}{y}$

94. $6-\dfrac{5}{k+3}$ $\dfrac{6k+13}{k+3}$ **95.** $\dfrac{n}{n-2}+7$ $\dfrac{8n-14}{n-2}$ **96.** $\dfrac{x+3}{x}-2$ $\dfrac{3-x}{x}$ **97.** $8h-\dfrac{h}{h+3}$

98. $3y+\dfrac{y}{2y+7}$ **99.** $5-\dfrac{e+3}{e^2-1}$ **100.** $a+\dfrac{5a+3}{a+3}$ **101.** $2w-\dfrac{w+3}{w-3}$

102. $n-\dfrac{7}{n+2}-\dfrac{3n-1}{n+2}$ **103.** $\dfrac{v}{u+v}+\dfrac{u}{v-u}+1$ **104.** $\dfrac{x}{x-4}+\dfrac{x}{x+4}-3$

Divide. Write the answer as a polynomial or mixed expression. (6-7)

105. $\dfrac{x^2+7x+10}{x+2}$ **106.** $\dfrac{y^2-2y-35}{y-7}$ **107.** $\dfrac{a^2-5a-3}{a+2}$ **108.** $\dfrac{n^2-16}{n+4}$

109. $\dfrac{7+k^2-4k}{k-5}$ **110.** $\dfrac{8y^2+6}{2y-1}$ **111.** $\dfrac{b^3-1}{b+1}$ **112.** $\dfrac{x^3+5}{x+3}$

113. $\dfrac{w^3+w^2+2w-4}{w-1}$ w^2+2w+4 **114.** $\dfrac{u^3+2u^2-16}{u-2}$ u^2+4u+8 **115.** $\dfrac{2n^2-13n+20}{2n-5}$ $n-4$

116. $\dfrac{2-9h+7h^2}{7h-2}$ $h-1$ **117.** $\dfrac{v^3+v^2+v+1}{v-2}$ $v^2+3v+7+\dfrac{15}{v-2}$ **118.** $\dfrac{5n^2+6n^3+9}{3+2n}$ $3n^2-2n+3$

Chapter 7

Write each ratio in simplest form. (7-1)

1. 40 s : 2 min 1:3 **2.** 4 m : 250 cm 8:5 **3.** 3 kg : 45 g 200:3
4. $6y : 15y$ 2:5 **5.** $36d^2 : 10d$ 18d:5 **6.** $(4a)^2 : 6a$ 8a:3

7. The ratio of old cars to new cars if there are 180 cars and 55 are new. 25:11

8. The ratio of wins to losses for a baseball team that played 84 games and won 48 of them. 4:3

Solve each proportion. (7-2)

9. $\dfrac{3}{5}=\dfrac{x}{15}$ $\{9\}$ **10.** $\dfrac{5}{7}=\dfrac{25}{a}$ $\{35\}$ **11.** $\dfrac{24}{7}=\dfrac{4}{c}$ $\left\{\dfrac{7}{6}\right\}$

12. $\dfrac{3x}{2}=\dfrac{2}{5}$ $\left\{\dfrac{4}{15}\right\}$ **13.** $\dfrac{15a}{64}=\dfrac{45}{32}$ $\{6\}$ **14.** $\dfrac{17d}{25}=\dfrac{51}{125}$ $\left\{\dfrac{3}{5}\right\}$

15. $\dfrac{x-4}{x}=\dfrac{7}{9}$ $\{18\}$ **16.** $\dfrac{3w}{10w+2}=\dfrac{2}{7}$ $\{4\}$ **17.** $\dfrac{8a-5}{5a-4}=\dfrac{13}{8}$ $\{12\}$

Additional Answers

97. $\dfrac{h(8h+23)}{h+3}$

98. $\dfrac{2y(3y+11)}{2y+7}$

99. $\dfrac{5e^2-e-8}{(e+1)(e-1)}$

100. $\dfrac{a^2+8a+3}{a+3}$

101. $\dfrac{2w^2-7w-3}{w-3}$

102. $n-3$

103. $\dfrac{2v^2}{(v+u)(v-u)}$

104. $\dfrac{-x^2+48}{(x+4)(x-4)}$

105. $x+5$

106. $y+5$

107. $a-7+\dfrac{11}{a+2}$

108. $n-4$

109. $k+1+\dfrac{12}{k-5}$

110. $4y+2+\dfrac{8}{2y-1}$

111. $b^2-b+1-\dfrac{2}{b+1}$

112. $x^2-3x+9-\dfrac{22}{x+3}$

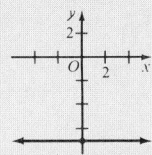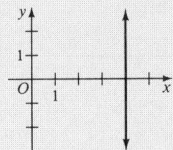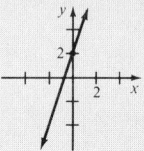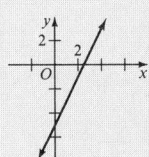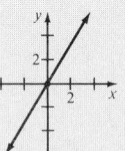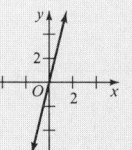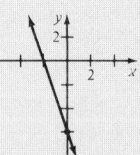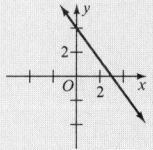
Solve and check. If the equation has no solution, write *No Solution*. (7-3, 7-4)

18. $\frac{a}{3} - \frac{a}{9} = 2$ {9}

19. $\frac{2x}{3} - \frac{x}{2} = 12$ {72}

20. $\frac{6}{7}x - \frac{1}{2}x = 5$ {14}

21. $\frac{2}{3}x - \frac{5}{9}x = -1$ {−9}

22. $\frac{y+2}{2} = \frac{2y}{3}$ {6}

23. $\frac{x+1}{5} - \frac{3}{2} = \frac{3x-6}{10}$ {−7}

24. $\frac{12}{z} = \frac{4+4z}{z}$ {2}

25. $\frac{1}{x} + \frac{1}{3} = \frac{1}{2}$ {6}

26. $\frac{4}{5y} + \frac{y-2}{y} = -\frac{1}{5}$ {1}

27. $\frac{c}{c+3} = \frac{2}{5}$ {2}

28. $\frac{3m+5}{6} - \frac{10}{m} = \frac{m}{2}$ {12}

29. $\frac{h}{2h+4} - \frac{1}{h+2} = 1$ {−6}

Evaluate. (7-5)

30. 80% of 700 560

31. 45% of 450 202.5

32. 3.25% of 48 1.56

33. 18 is 60% of what number? 30

34. 63 is 150% of what number? 42

35. What percent of 180 is 45? 25%

36. What percent of 36 is 54? 150%

Solve. (7-5, 7-6, 7-7, 7-8)

37. $1.2x = 48$ {40}

38. $0.6z = 180$ {300}

39. $0.08y = 64$ {800}

40. $0.4a - 0.7 = 2.9$ {9}

41. $0.3b + 0.03b = 99$ {300}

42. $0.05c = 6.6 - 0.06c$ {60}

43. How many kilograms of zinc are contained in 30 kg of an alloy containing 28% zinc? 8.4 kg

44. Ed Jefferson bought a new suit that cost $140. If he also paid $6.30 in sales tax, find the sales tax rate. 4.5%

45. A camera that originally cost $150 is on sale at 15% off the original price. Find the sale price. $127.50

46. How many kilograms of water must be added to 12 kg of a 30% salt solution to produce a 20% solution? 6 kg

47. How many kilograms of water must be evaporated from 40 kg of a 10% salt solution to produce a 25% solution? 24 kg

48. A coin-sorting machine can sort a certain number of coins in 15 min. A second machine can sort the same number of coins in 30 min. How long would it take both machines working together to do the job? 10 min

49. An air conditioner takes 20 min to cool a room. If a second air conditioner is used together with the first, it takes only 12 min to cool the room. How long would it take the second air conditioner alone to cool the room? 30 min

Evaluate. (7-9)

50. 6^{-2} $\frac{1}{36}$

51. 5^{-3} $\frac{1}{125}$

52. 7^{-2} $\frac{1}{49}$

53. 9^{-3} $\frac{1}{729}$

54. $2^{-4} \cdot 2^{-3}$ $\frac{1}{128}$

55. $(6^{-2})^{-1}$ 36

56. $\frac{3^{-4}}{3^{-3}}$ $\frac{1}{3}$

57. $\frac{8^{-2}}{8^{-4}}$ 64

652 *Extra Practice*

Simplify. Give answers in terms of positive exponents. $\dfrac{1}{a^2b^3}$ (7-9)

58. $5y^{-2}$ $\dfrac{5}{y^2}$　　**59.** $(9y)^{-3}$ $\dfrac{1}{729y^3}$　　**60.** x^2y^{-5} $\dfrac{x^2}{y^5}$　　**61.** $a^{-2}b^{-3}$

62. $uv^{-2}w^{-1}$ $\dfrac{u}{v^2w}$　　**63.** $d^{-4}e^2f^{-2}$ $\dfrac{e^2}{d^4f^2}$　　**64.** $(a^{-2}b^3)^2$ $\dfrac{b^6}{a^4}$　　**65.** $(x^{-4}y^{-5}z^3)^{-3}$

$$\dfrac{x^{12}y^{15}}{z^9}$$ (7-10)

Write each of the following numbers in scientific notation.

6.43×10^{11}

66. 64,800,000　6.48×10^7　　**67.** 147,000,000　1.47×10^8　　**68.** 643 billion

69. 0.0000098　9.8×10^{-6}　　**70.** 0.000000006　6×10^{-9}　　**71.** 0.00000000001

$$1 \times 10^{-11}$$

Chapter 8

State whether each ordered pair of numbers is a solution of the given equation. (8-1)

no; no

1. $x - 2y = 6$　　**2.** $x + 3y = 9$　　**3.** $2x - y = 5$
(3, 0), (0, −3) no; yes　　(3, 2), (−3, 4) yes; yes　　(4, −1), (1, −7)

4. $2x + 3y = 7$　　**5.** $4x + 2y = 6$　　**6.** $-3x + 4y = -7$
(1, 2), (5, −1) no; yes　　$\left(\dfrac{3}{2}, 0\right)$, (1, 1) yes; yes　　(1, −1), $\left(2, \dfrac{1}{4}\right)$ yes; no

Solve each equation if x and y are whole numbers. (8-1)

(0, 4), (3, 0)

7. $x + 2y = 8$ (0, 4), (2, 3),　　**8.** $3x + y = 5$ (0, 5), (1, 2)　　**9.** $4x + 3y = 12$
(4, 2), (6, 1),
10. $xy = 5$ (8, 0)　　**11.** $x + 4y = 10$　　**12.** $2xy + 12 = 14$
(1, 5), (5, 1)　　(2, 2), (6, 1), (10, 0)　　(1, 1)

Graph each equation. (8-2)

13. $y = -7$　　**14.** $x = 4$　　**15.** $y = 3x + 2$

16. $y = 2x - 5$　　**17.** $5x = 3y$　　**18.** $8x - 2y = 0$

19. $3x + y = -6$　　**20.** $4x + 3y = 12$　　**21.** $2x + 3y = 7$

Find the slope of the line through the given points. (8-3)

22. (1, 2), (4, 6) $\dfrac{4}{3}$　　**23.** (−7, 1), (−1, 2) $\dfrac{1}{6}$　　**24.** (−1, 6), (0, 0) −6

25. (−4, −3), (2, −3) 0　　**26.** (2, 1), (8, −2) $-\dfrac{1}{2}$　　**27.** (−7, −7), (6, −4) $\dfrac{3}{13}$

Find the slope of each line. If the line has no slope, say so.

28. $y = 7x - 3$ 7　　**29.** $x = 5$ no slope　　**30.** $3x - 2y = 8$ $\dfrac{3}{2}$

31. $y - 9 = 0$ 0　　**32.** $5x + 4y = 16$ $-\dfrac{5}{4}$　　**33.** $y = 1 - x$ −1

Determine whether the given points are collinear. (8-3)

34. (2, 1), (0, −3), (4, 5), (−2, −7) yes　　**35.** (0, 4), (9, −2), (−3, 6), (6, 0) yes

36. (−3, −2), (2, −4), (6, −5), (−5, 2) no　　**37.** (−5, 3), (0, 3), (5, 3), (−2, 3) yes

Extra Practice　**653**

(continued)

21.
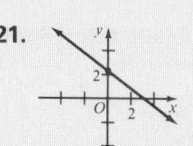

Additional Answers, p. 654

38.
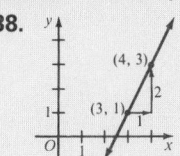

39.
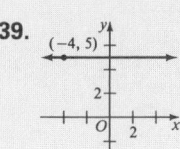

40.
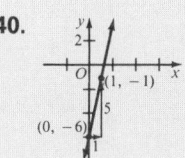

41.
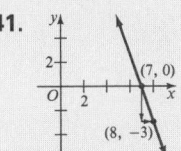

42.
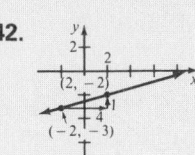

43.
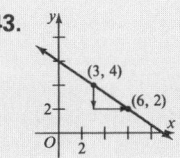

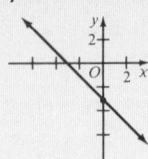
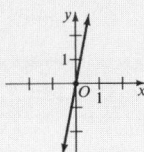
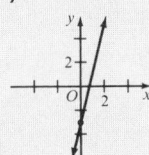
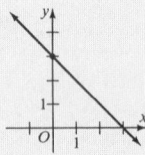
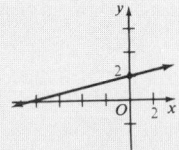
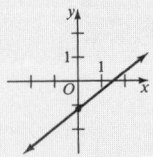
Through the given point, draw a line with the given slope. (8-3)

38. $P(3, 1)$; slope 2   **39.** $P(-4, 5)$; slope 0   **40.** $P(0, -6)$; slope 5

41. $P(7, 0)$; slope -3 **42.** $P(-2, -3)$; slope $\frac{1}{4}$ **43.** $P(3, 4)$; slope $-\frac{2}{3}$

Change each equation to the slope-intercept form. Use only the slope and (8-4)
y-intercept to draw the graph of each equation.

44. $x + y = -3$ **45.** $7x = 2y$ **46.** $4x - y = 3$

47. $2x + 2y = 6$ **48.** $-x + 5y = 10$ **49.** $3x - 4y - 5 = 0$

Use the slope-intercept form to show that the lines whose equations are (8-4)
given are parallel.

50. $x - y = 2$ **51.** $3x - 2y = 6$ **52.** $-x - 5y = 1$
      $y - x = -3$ $-2y = 12 - 3x$ $2x + 10y = 2$

Write an equation in slope-intercept form of the line that has the given (8-5)
slope and y-intercept.

$y = \frac{1}{3}x + 6$

53. $m = 3$, $b = \frac{1}{2}$ $y = 3x + \frac{1}{2}$ **54.** $m = -4$, $b = \frac{3}{5}$ $y = -4x + \frac{3}{5}$ **55.** $m = \frac{1}{3}$, $b = 6$

56. $m = 0$, $b = -3.5$ **57.** $m = -\frac{3}{7}$, $b = \frac{3}{8}$ **58.** $m = -1.5$, $b = 2.7$
     $y = -3.5$ $y = -\frac{3}{7}x + \frac{3}{8}$ $y = -1.5x + 2.7$

Write an equation in slope-intercept form of the line that has the given (8-5)
slope and passes through the given point.

     $y = 3x + 4$ $y = -2x + 2$ $y = \frac{3}{4}x - 2$

59. $m = 3$; $(-3, -5)$ **60.** $m = -2$; $(3, -4)$ **61.** $m = \frac{3}{4}$; $(0, -2)$

62. $m = 0$; $\left(\frac{1}{2}, 3\right)$ **63.** $m = -\frac{1}{5}$; $(-5, 0)$ **64.** $m = \frac{7}{3}$; $(3, 7)$
     $y = 3$ $y = -\frac{1}{5}x - 1$ $y = \frac{7}{3}x$

Write an equation in slope-intercept form of the line passing through the points. (8-5)

65. $(2, 1)$, $(6, 4)$ $y = \frac{3}{4}x - \frac{1}{2}$ **66.** $(2, -1)$, $(1, -7)$ $y = 6x - 13$ **67.** $(0, 0)$, $(6, -1)$

68. $(-3, 2)$, $(-3, -4)$ $x = -3$ **69.** $(-2, 8)$, $(1, 2)$ $y = -2x + 4$ **70.** $(6, -4)$, $(-7, -7)$

State the domain and range of the function shown by each table.   **67.** $y = -\frac{1}{6}x$ (8-6)

70. $y = \frac{3}{13}x - \frac{70}{13}$

71.
Longest Suspension Bridges	
Mackinac Straits	3800 ft
Humber Estuary	4626 ft
Golden Gate	4200 ft
Ataturk	3524 ft
Verrazano Narrows	4260 ft

72.
Airports in U.S.	
1930	1782
1940	2331
1950	6403
1960	6881
1970	11,261

73. Make a bar graph for the function shown in Exercise 71.

74. Make a broken-line graph for the function shown in Exercise 72.

Given $f: x \rightarrow 5 - 3x$, find the following values of f. (8-7)

75. $f(4)$ -7 **76.** $f\left(-\dfrac{1}{3}\right)$ 6 **77.** $f(0)$ 5 **78.** $f(-5)$ 20

Given $G(n) = n^3 + 2n$, find the following values of G. (8-7)

79. $G(0)$ 0 **80.** $G(-2)$ -12 **81.** $G\left(\dfrac{1}{2}\right)$ $\dfrac{9}{8}$ **82.** $G(3)$ 33

Find all the values of each function. (8-7)

83. $h(x) = 5 - 2x - x^2$, $D = \{1, 2, 3\}$
$\{2, -3, -10\}$

84. $M(u) = \dfrac{6}{4u + 2}$, $D = \{-1, 0, 1\}$
$\{-3, 3, 1\}$

Find the range of each function. $\{-10, 10, 2\}$ (8-7)

85. $r: z \rightarrow -3 - 4z$, $D = \{-2, -1, 0\}$ $\{5, 1, -3\}$

86. $N: s \rightarrow \dfrac{10}{s - 3}$, $D = \{2, 4, 8\}$

87. $G: w \rightarrow (w - 1)(w + 1)$, $D = \{-2, 0, 2\}$
$\{3, -1\}$

88. $k: v \rightarrow v^2 - 4v + 2$, $D = \{3, 4, 5\}$
$\{-1, 2, 7\}$

Find the vertex and the axis of symmetry of the graph of each equation. (8-8)
Use the vertex and at least four other points to graph the equation.

89. $y = 4x^2$ $(0, 0)$; $x = 0$ **90.** $y = -2x^2$ $(0, 0)$; $x = 0$ **91.** $y = \dfrac{1}{5}x^2$ $(0, 0)$; $x = 0$

92. $y = -x^2 + 3x$
$\left(\dfrac{3}{2}, \dfrac{9}{4}\right)$; $x = \dfrac{3}{2}$

93. $y = x^2 - 2x + 5$
$(1, 4)$; $x = 1$

94. $y = 4 - \dfrac{1}{2}x^2$
$(0, 4)$; $x = 0$

Find the vertex. Then give the least value of the function. (8-8)

95. $f: x \rightarrow x^2 + 7x$
$\left(-\dfrac{7}{2}, -\dfrac{49}{4}\right)$; $-\dfrac{49}{4}$

96. $g: x \rightarrow x^2 - 3x - 4$
$\left(\dfrac{3}{2}, -\dfrac{25}{4}\right)$; $-\dfrac{25}{4}$

97. $h: x \rightarrow \dfrac{1}{2}x^2$
$(0, 0)$; 0

Find the vertex. Then give the greatest value of the function. (8-8)

98. $f(x) = x - 3x^2$ $\left(\dfrac{1}{6}, \dfrac{1}{12}\right)$; $\dfrac{1}{12}$ **99.** $g(x) = 2 - \dfrac{1}{3}x^2$ $(0, 2)$; 2 **100.** $h(x) = -x^2 - x - 1$
$\left(-\dfrac{1}{2}, -\dfrac{3}{4}\right)$; $-\dfrac{3}{4}$

In Exercises 101 and 102, find the constant of variation. (8-9)

101. y varies directly as x, and $y = 12$ when $x = 60$. $\dfrac{1}{5}$

102. q is directly proportional to p, and $q = 144$ when $p = 24$. 6

103. If n varies directly as m, and $n = 300$ when $m = 5$, find n when $m = 15$. 900

104. If b is directly proportional to a, and $b = 28.7$ when $a = 4.1$, find b when $a = 13$. 91

(x_1, y_1) and (x_2, y_2) are ordered pairs of the same direct variation. (8-9)
Find each missing value.

105. $x_1 = 35$, $y_1 = 7$
$x_2 = 105$, $y_2 = \underline{\ ?\ }$ 21

106. $x_1 = 5.2$, $y_1 = 5$
$x_2 = \underline{\ ?\ }$, $y_2 = 1$ 1.04

107. $x_1 = \dfrac{3}{8}$, $y_1 = \underline{\ ?\ }$ $\dfrac{3}{32}$
$x_2 = \dfrac{2}{5}$, $y_2 = \dfrac{1}{10}$

Extra Practice **655**

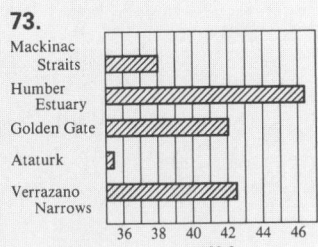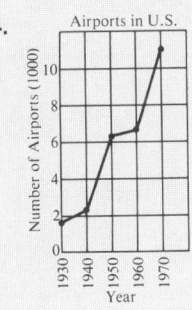

89.

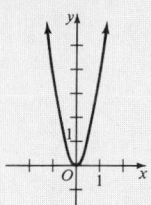

90.

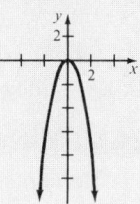

91.

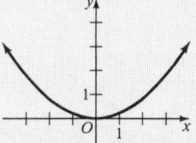

92.

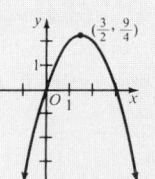

93.

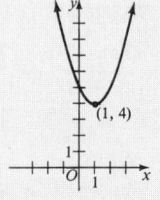

94.

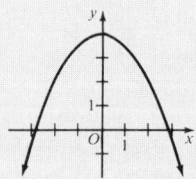

For each variation described, state (a) a formula and (b) a proportion.   (8-9, 8-10)

108. The circumference, C, of a circle is directly proportional to the diameter, d, of the circle.   **a.** $C = kd$ **b.** $\frac{C_1}{d_1} = \frac{C_2}{d_2}$

109. The elongation, e, of a coil spring varies directly as the mass, m, suspended from it. **a.** $e = km$ **b.** $\frac{e_1}{m_1} = \frac{e_2}{m_2}$

110. The length, l, of the shadow of a vertical object at a given time and location varies directly with the height, h, of the object. **a.** $l = kh$ **b.** $\frac{l_1}{h_1} = \frac{l_2}{h_2}$

111. The monthly rent, r, for each roommate in an apartment is inversely proportional to the number, n, of roommates. **a.** $rn = k$ **b.** $r_1n_1 = r_2n_2$

112. The height, h, of a triangle of constant area varies inversely as the base length, b. **a.** $hb = k$ **b.** $h_1b_1 = h_2b_2$

113. The number of tickets remaining to be sold, n, varies inversely as the number of tickets sold, s. **a.** $ns = k$ **b.** $n_1s_1 = n_2s_2$

Graph each equation if the domain and the range are both the set of non-zero real numbers.   (8-10)

114. $xy = 4$ **115.** $3xy = 1$ **116.** $x = \frac{10}{y}$ **117.** $\frac{x}{2} = \frac{4}{y}$

(x_1, y_1) and (x_2, y_2) are ordered pairs of the same inverse variation. Find each missing value.   (8-10)

118. $x_1 = 5$, $y_1 = 8$ **119.** $x_1 = 0.6$, $y_1 = 1.2$ **120.** $x_1 = \frac{1}{4}$, $y_1 = \underset{10}{?}^{\frac{1}{3}}$
$x_2 = 4$, $y_2 = \underset{10}{\underline{?}}$ $x_2 = \underset{1.8}{\underline{?}}$, $y_2 = 0.4$ $x_2 = \frac{1}{6}$, $y_2 = \frac{1}{2}$

Chapter 9

Solve each system by the graphic method.   (9-1)

1. $x + y = 6$
$x - y = 2$ (4, 2)

2. $x + y = 9$
$y = 2x$ (3, 6)

3. $x + y = 0$
$x + 2y = 2$ (−2, 2)

4. $y = 3 - x$
$x + y = 5$ No solution

5. $y = \frac{2}{3}x + 1$
$y = -\frac{2}{3}x + 5$ (3, 3)

6. $y = \frac{1}{2}x + 1$
$x + 2 = 2y$
Infinite number of solutions

Solve by the substitution method.   (9-2)

7. $3x + y = 5$
$y = 2x$ (1, 2)

8. $m - 3n = -4$
$2m + 6n = 5$ $\left(-\frac{3}{4}, \frac{13}{12}\right)$

9. $2a + b = 4$
$b = 1 - a$ (3, −2)

10. $4c - 3d = 9$
$2c - d = 5$ (3, 1)

11. $x + 3y = 2$
$2x + 3y = 7$ (5, −1)

12. $3x - 2y = 5$
$x + 2y = 15$ (5, 5)

Solve by using a system of two equations in two variables.   (9-3)

13. On a jury there are 3 fewer men than twice the number of women. If there
    were 2 more women on the jury, the numbers of men and women would
    be equal. How many men are on the jury? 7 men

14. Janet and Lynn live 8 mi apart in opposite directions from their office. If
    Lynn lives 1 mi less than twice as far from the office as Janet does, how
    far does each live from the office? Janet, 3 mi; Lynn, 5 mi

Solve by the addition-or-subtraction method.   (9-4)

15. $r - s = -3$
    $r + s = 9$ (3, 6)

16. $c + 2n = -20$
    $c - 2n = 30$ $\left(5, -\dfrac{25}{2}\right)$

17. $x - 3y = 2$
    $x + 4y = 16$ (8, 2)

18. $6r + 5y = -8$
    $2r - 5y = -16$ (−3, 2)

19. $12m + 3n = 51$
    $7m - 3n = 44$ (5, −3)

20. $8g + 7h = 26$
    $8g - 10h = 60$
    (5, −2)

Solve by using multiplication with the addition-or-subtraction method.   (9-5)

21. $v + w = 3$
    $3v - 5w = 17$ (4, −1)

22. $4a - 3b = -1$
    $a - b = -1$ (2, 3)

23. $3x - y = 3$
    $x + 3y = 11$ (2, 3)

24. $3x + 4y = -25$
    $2x - 3y = 6$ (−3, −4)

25. $2w - 3z = -1$
    $3w + 4z = 24$ (4, 3)

26. $5a - 2b = 0$
    $2a - 3b = -11$
    (2, 5)

Solve by using a system of two equations in two variables.   (9-6, 9-7)

27. A plane can fly 1120 km in 80 min with the wind. Flying against the same
    wind, the plane travels the same distance in 84 min. Find the speed of the
    wind and the speed of the plane in still air. 20 km/h; 820 km/h

28. The sum of the digits of a two-digit number is 7. With the digits reversed
    the number is 5 times the tens digit of the original number. Find the origi-
    nal number. 52

29. In five years Jenny will be two thirds as old as her aunt. Three years ago
    she was half as old as her aunt is now. How old are Jenny and her aunt
    now? Jenny, 17 years old; aunt, 28 years old

30. The numerator of a fraction is 1 less than the denominator. If 1 is sub-
    tracted from the numerator, and the denominator is unchanged, the resulting
    fraction has a value of $\dfrac{3}{4}$. Find the original fraction. $\dfrac{7}{8}$

Chapter 10

Classify each statement as true or false.   (10-1)

1. $-8 > 7 > 6$ False

2. $-5 < -4 < 5$ True

3. $-1.5 < -1 < -0.05$ True

4. $-\dfrac{1}{2} < 0 < 1$ True

5. $7 > 0 > 2$ False

6. $-10 < -15 < -20$ False

7. $|-0.6| < 0.4$ False

8. $\left|-\dfrac{1}{3}\right| \geq 0$ True

9. $|5 - 3| \leq |3 - 5|$ True

Extra Practice   **657**

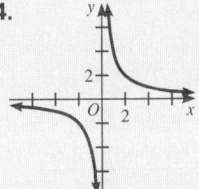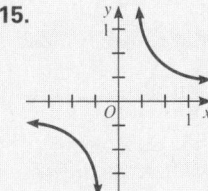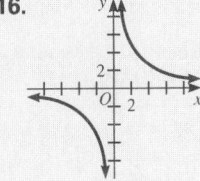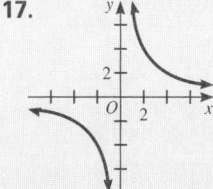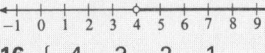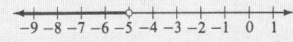

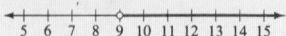
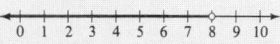
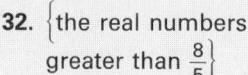
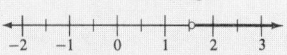
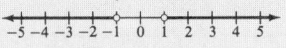
Solve each inequality if $x \in \{-4, -3, -2, -1, 0, 1, 2, 3, 4\}$. (10-1)

10. $5x \le 15$
$\{-4, -3, -2, -1, 0, 1, 2, 3\}$

11. $-7x > 14$
$\{-4, -3\}$

12. $-4 - x \ge 0$
$\{-4\}$

13. $x^2 < 10$
$\{-3, -2, -1, 0, 1, 2, 3\}$

Graph each inequality over the given domain. (10-1)

14. $4 < x$; {the positive numbers}

15. $-6 \le k < 2$; {the negative integers}

16. $3 > t \ge -4$; {the integers}

17. $-2 < n < 2$; {the real numbers}

Solve each inequality and graph its solution set. (10-2)

18. $e - 8 > 12$

19. $13 > n + 9$

20. $4q < -20$

21. $-\frac{x}{7} < 14$

22. $\frac{m}{3} - 5 > -2$

23. $-3 > 7 + \frac{4}{5}k$

24. $5v + 3 > 18$

25. $48 - 6y < 0$

26. $7n < 6n + 8$

27. $8f - 5 > 4f + 11$

28. $-6(v - 3) \le 42$

29. $5(m + 2) > 4(m - 1)$

30. $\frac{4}{9}h + 3 \le \frac{1}{3}$

31. $2(w - 1) < \frac{3}{2}w$

32. $2x - \frac{1}{4}(3x + 8) > 0$

In Exercises 33–37: (10-3)

a. Choose a variable to represent the number indicated in color.

b. Use the variable to write an inequality based on the given information. (Do not solve.)

33. Marquita sold 9 fewer magazine subscriptions than twice the number Juanita sold. Marquita sold at most 43 subscriptions. **a.** x **b.** $2x - 9 \le 43$

34. Rick, who is not yet 16 years old, is 3 years older than Sam. (Sam's age) **a.** s **b.** $s + 3 < 16$

35. Andrea lives 10 mi less than half as far as Roger lives from the beach. Andrea lives at least 25 mi from the beach. **a.** y **b.** $\frac{1}{2}y - 10 \ge 25$

36. The number of San Marcos High School students who ride the bus is one third the number who walk or ride their bikes. The total number of students is at least 1800. **a.** n **b.** $n + \frac{1}{3}n \ge 1800$

37. Six years ago, Buford was less than half as old as he is now. (His present age) **a.** b **b.** $b - 6 < \frac{1}{2}b$

Solve each open sentence and graph its solution set. (10-4)

38. $-3 < n + 5 < 7$

39. $-6 < -6 + w \le 2$

40. $-4 \le 3a - 1 < 5$

41. $-1 \le 8m + 7 \le 23$

42. $u - 2 < -5$ or $u - 2 \ge 4$

43. $k + 6 \le -3$ or $k + 6 > 2$

44. $4n + 3 < -1$ or $4n + 3 > 7$

45. $2x - 2 \le -8$ or $8 < 2x - 2$

46. $-5e < 15$ and $6 + 3e < 0$

47. $h - 4 \ge 2$ or $4 - h \ge 2$

Solve each open sentence and graph its solution set. (10-5, 10-6)

48. $|v - 6| = 3$ **49.** $|8 - k| = 5$ **50.** $|m| > 2\frac{1}{2}$

51. $|x| \leq 1.5$ **52.** $|y + 5| > 2$ **53.** $|3 + z| \leq 4$

54. $|7 - f| < 6$ **55.** $|-4 - g| > 7$ **56.** $|-a - 2| \geq 1$

57. $4|s| + 2 \leq 8$ **58.** $5 - 3|z| < 14$ **59.** $9 - |3 - b| > 2$

60. $|8k| = 16$ **61.** $\left|\frac{a}{2}\right| \geq 3$ **62.** $\left|\frac{c}{4}\right| \leq 1$

63. $|5x - 3| = 17$ **64.** $|7 + 6n| < 19$ **65.** $|2w - 3| > 5$

66. $\left|\frac{u}{3} + 4\right| = 1$ **67.** $\left|\frac{v}{2} - 1\right| \leq 3$ **68.** $\left|\frac{a}{4} + 2\right| \geq 1$

69. $|5 - (3 - 2x)| < 6$ **70.** $7 + 3|2m + 1| = 13$ **71.** $10 - 6|2 - k| \geq 22$

Graph each inequality. (10-7)

72. $x < 3$ **73.** $x \geq -4$ **74.** $y > 0$ **75.** $y \leq -2$

76. $y > x - 1$ **77.** $y \leq -x + 2$ **78.** $y < 3 + 4x$ **79.** $y \geq -5x - 1$

Transform each inequality into an equivalent inequality with y as one side. (10-7)
Then graph the inequality. See Additional Answers for graphs.

80. $x - y \geq 5$ $y \leq x - 5$ **81.** $4x + y \leq -2$ $y \leq -4x - 2$ **82.** $x - 3y > 6$ $y < \frac{1}{3}x - 2$

83. $6x - y < 2$ $y > 6x - 2$ **84.** $y - 5x \geq 3$ $y \geq 5x + 3$ **85.** $4y - 5x < 0$ $y < \frac{5}{4}x$

86. $7x + 6y \geq x - 3$ $y \geq -x - \frac{1}{2}$ **87.** $3y - 2 > 6x - 4$ $y > 2x - \frac{2}{3}$ **88.** $8y - 7 \leq 3(x + 2y)$ $y \leq \frac{3}{2}x + \frac{7}{2}$

Graph each pair of inequalities and indicate the solution set of the system (10-8)
with crosshatching or shading.

89. $y \leq 0$ **90.** $y \geq -3$ **91.** $y > 4x$ **92.** $x \geq -1$
$\quad\ x > 0$ $\quad\ x \leq 2$ $\quad\ x < 3$ $\quad\ y < 2x - 5$

93. $y < x + 3$ **94.** $y \leq 5x - 4$ **95.** $x + y > 2$ **96.** $3x - 4y \leq 0$
$\quad\ y > 3 - x$ $\quad\ y \geq 2x + 1$ $\quad\ x - y < 6$ $\quad\ x - 2y \geq -6$

Chapter 11

Replace the _?_ with $<$, $=$, or $>$ to make a true statement. (11-1)

1. $\frac{17}{23} \underset{<}{\_?\_} \frac{15}{19}$ **2.** $-\frac{87}{29} \underset{=}{\_?\_} -\frac{39}{13}$ **3.** $\frac{197}{6} \underset{<}{\_?\_} 33\frac{2}{7}$

Arrange each group of numbers in order from least to greatest. (11-1)

4. $-\frac{39}{8}, -4.7, -\frac{41}{9}$ **5.** $\frac{5}{7}, \frac{2}{3}, \frac{11}{15}, \frac{12}{17}$ **6.** $-\frac{4}{9}, -\frac{5}{8}, -\frac{6}{11}, -\frac{5}{7}$

---

4. $-\frac{39}{8}, -4.7, -\frac{41}{9}$ **5.** $\frac{2}{3}, \frac{12}{17}, \frac{5}{7}, \frac{11}{15}$ **6.** $-\frac{5}{7}, -\frac{5}{8}, -\frac{6}{11}, -\frac{4}{9}$ *Extra Practice* **659**

---

48. $\{3, 9\}$

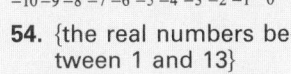

50. $\left\{\text{the real numbers greater than } 2\frac{1}{2} \text{ or less than } -2\frac{1}{2}\right\}$

52. the real numbers less than -7 or greater than $-3\}$

54. {the real numbers between 1 and 13}

56. $\{-3, -1,$ and the real numbers greater than -1 or less than $-3\}$

58. {all real numbers}

60. $\{-2, 2\}$

62. $\{-4, 4,$ and the real numbers between -4 and $4\}$

64. $\left\{\text{the real numbers between } -\frac{13}{3} \text{ and } 2\right\}$

66. $\{-15, -9\}$

68. $\{-12, -4,$ and the real numbers less than -12 or greater than $-4\}$

70. $\left\{-\frac{3}{2}, \frac{1}{2}\right\}$

71. No solution

(continued)

72.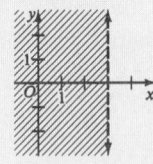

74.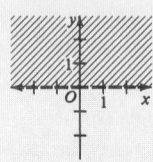

76.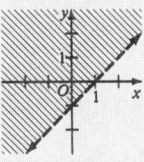

78.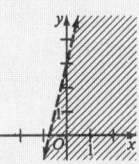

80. $y \le x - 5$

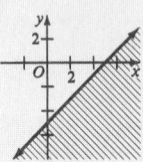

82. $y < \frac{1}{3}x - 2$

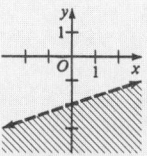

84. $y \ge 5x + 3$

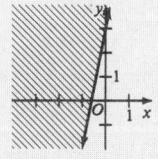

(continued)

Find the number halfway between the given numbers. (11-1)

7. $\frac{27}{41}, \frac{31}{37}$ $\frac{1135}{1517}$

8. $-\frac{17}{140}, -\frac{11}{32}$ $-\frac{521}{2240}$

9. $-5\frac{2}{7}, 9\frac{1}{4}$ $\frac{111}{56}$

If $x \in \{0, 1, 2, 3\}$ state whether each fraction increases or decreases in value as x takes on its values in increasing order. (11-1)

10. $\frac{5}{x + 1}$ decreases

11. $\frac{x - 3}{7}$ increases

12. $\frac{8}{x + 2}$ decreases

13. $\frac{6 - x}{4}$ decreases

14. $\frac{10}{5 + 2x}$ decreases

Express each rational number as a terminating or repeating decimal. (11-2)

15. $\frac{4}{9}$ $0.\overline{4}$

16. $-\frac{29}{24}$ $-1.208\overline{3}$

17. $3\frac{11}{20}$ 3.55

18. $-7\frac{5}{11}$ $-7.\overline{45}$

19. $\frac{41}{55}$ $0.7\overline{45}$

Express each rational number as a fraction in simplest form. (11-2)

20. 0.77 $\frac{77}{100}$

21. $0.\overline{6}$ $\frac{2}{3}$

22. $-0.31\overline{8}$ $-\frac{287}{900}$

23. $2.\overline{37}$ $\frac{235}{99}$

24. $0.\overline{4135}$ $\frac{4135}{9999}$

Find the number halfway between the given numbers. (11-2)

25. $\frac{5}{8}$ and 0.63 0.6275

26. 0.66 and $0.\overline{6}$ 0.663

27. $\frac{7}{11}$ and $0.6\overline{28}$ $0.6\overline{32}$

Express both numbers as fractions. Then find their product. (11-2)

28. $\frac{2}{5}$ and 0.85 $\frac{2}{5}, \frac{17}{20}; \frac{17}{50}$

29. $0.\overline{4}$ and $\frac{2}{3}$ $\frac{4}{9}, \frac{2}{3}; \frac{8}{27}$

30. -2.2 and $0.\overline{3}$ $-\frac{11}{5}, \frac{1}{3}; -\frac{11}{15}$

Find the indicated square roots. (11-3)

31. $\sqrt{441}$ 21

32. $\sqrt{784}$ 28

33. $\sqrt{2704}$ 52

34. $\sqrt{5184}$ 72

35. $\sqrt{10816}$ 104

36. $\sqrt{0.04}$ 0.2

37. $\sqrt{0.64}$ 0.8

38. $\sqrt{1.96}$ 1.4

39. $\sqrt{0.0144}$ 0.12

40. $\sqrt{0.0036}$ 0.06

41. $\sqrt{\frac{81}{225}}$ $\frac{3}{5}$

42. $\sqrt{\frac{1}{289}}$ $\frac{1}{17}$

43. $\sqrt{\frac{324}{1936}}$ $\frac{9}{22}$

44. $\sqrt{\frac{32}{50}}$ $\frac{4}{5}$

45. $\sqrt{\frac{320}{405}}$ $\frac{8}{9}$

Simplify. (11-4)

46. $\sqrt{63}$ $3\sqrt{7}$

47. $\sqrt{176}$ $4\sqrt{11}$

48. $2\sqrt{52}$ $4\sqrt{13}$

49. $4\sqrt{99}$ $12\sqrt{11}$

50. $5\sqrt{175}$ $25\sqrt{7}$

51. $10\sqrt{162}$ $90\sqrt{2}$

52. $\sqrt{192}$ $8\sqrt{3}$

53. $\sqrt{672}$ $4\sqrt{42}$

54. $\sqrt{224}$ $4\sqrt{14}$

55. $\sqrt{2646}$ $21\sqrt{6}$

Approximate to the nearest tenth by using a calculator or the square root table at the back of the book. (11-4)

56. $\sqrt{720}$ 26.8

57. $-\sqrt{800}$ -28.3

58. $\sqrt{440}$ 21.0

59. $\sqrt{8400}$ 91.7

60. $-\sqrt{5400}$ -73.5

Simplify. (11-5)

61. $\sqrt{169m^2}$ $13|m|$

62. $\sqrt{48a^2}$ $4|a|\sqrt{3}$

63. $\sqrt{125x^4}$ $5x^2\sqrt{5}$

64. $\sqrt{54e^3}$ $3|e|\sqrt{6e}$

65. $-\sqrt{36t^6}$ $-6|t^3|$

66. $\sqrt{98u^2v^2}$ $7|uv|\sqrt{2}$

67. $-2\sqrt{72x^3y^2}$ $-12|xy|\sqrt{2x}$

68. $\sqrt{324r^4s^6}$ $18r^2|s^3|$

69. $-\sqrt{4.84w^4}$ $-2.2w^2$

70. $\sqrt{5.76c^6}$ $2.4|c^3|$

71. $\sqrt{\dfrac{a^4 b^6}{12 c^2}}$ **72.** $\sqrt{\dfrac{48 u^5 v^2}{4 u v^4}}$ **73.** $\sqrt{\dfrac{144 k^8}{256}}$ $\dfrac{3k^4}{4}$ **74.** $\sqrt{\dfrac{3600}{81 m^{36}}}$ $\dfrac{20}{3 m^{18}}$; $m \neq 0$ **75.** $\sqrt[4]{\dfrac{225 x^{40}}{16}}$ $\dfrac{15 x^{20}}{4}$

76. $\sqrt{x^2 + 8x + 16}$ $|x + 4|$ **77.** $\sqrt{a^2 - 4a + 4}$ $|a - 2|$ **78.** $\sqrt{81 + 18k + k^2}$ $|9 + k|$

Solve. **71.** $\dfrac{a^2|b^3|\sqrt{3}}{6|c|}$; $c \neq 0$ **72.** $\dfrac{2u^2\sqrt{3}}{|v|}$; $u \neq 0,\ v \neq 0$ **(11-5)**

79. $g^2 = 49$ $\{-7, 7\}$ **80.** $h^2 - 64 = 0$ $\{-8, 8\}$ **81.** $25m^2 = 16$ $\left\{-\dfrac{4}{5}, \dfrac{4}{5}\right\}$

82. $9x^2 - 4 = 0$ $\left\{-\dfrac{2}{3}, \dfrac{2}{3}\right\}$ **83.** $6y^2 - 54 = 0$ $\{-3, 3\}$ **84.** $32t^2 - 27 = 0$
$\left\{-\dfrac{3\sqrt{6}}{8}, \dfrac{3\sqrt{6}}{8}\right\}$
(11-5)

Find both roots of each equation to the nearest tenth.

85. $a^2 = 132$ $\{-11.5, 11.5\}$ **86.** $b^2 - 208 = 0$ $\{-14.4, 14.4\}$ **87.** $11c^2 = 473$ $\{-6.6, 6.6\}$

In Exercises 88–95, refer to the right tri-angle shown at the right. Find the missing length correct to the nearest hundredth.

(11-6)

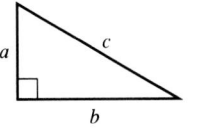

88. $a = 3,\ b = 4,\ c = $ _?_ 5.00 **89.** $a = 5,\ b = 8,\ c = $ _?_ 9.43

90. $a = $ _?_ , $b = 9,\ c = 13$ 9.38 **91.** $a = $ _?_ , $b = 10,\ c = 15$ 11.18

92. $a = 8,\ b = $ _?_ , $c = 16$ 13.86 **93.** $a = 20,\ b = $ _?_ , $c = 30$ 22.36

94. $a = 12,\ b = \dfrac{3}{4}a,\ c = $ _?_ 15.00 **95.** $a = \dfrac{2}{3}b,\ b = 15,\ c = $ _?_ 18.03

State whether or not the three numbers given could represent the lengths of the sides of a right triangle. **(11-6)**

96. 21, 28, 35 yes **97.** 9, 9, 12 no **98.** 45, 60, 75 yes

99. 31, 41, 51 no **100.** $6a, 8a, 10a, a > 0$ yes **101.** $5a, 7a, 9a, a > 0$ no

Simplify. **(11-7)**

102. $\sqrt{3} \cdot 4\sqrt{3}$ 12 **103.** $2\sqrt{5} \cdot 3\sqrt{5}$ 30 **104.** $\sqrt{7} \cdot \sqrt{6} \cdot \sqrt{2}$ $2\sqrt{21}$

105. $\sqrt{7} \cdot \sqrt{7} \cdot \sqrt{4}$ 14 **106.** $5\sqrt{2} \cdot \sqrt{3}$ $5\sqrt{6}$ **107.** $8\sqrt{162}$ $72\sqrt{2}$

108. $\sqrt{\dfrac{5}{9}} \cdot \sqrt{\dfrac{9}{5}}$ 1 **109.** $\sqrt{\dfrac{7}{5}} \cdot \sqrt{\dfrac{45}{14}}$ $\dfrac{3\sqrt{2}}{2}$ **110.** $\sqrt{5\dfrac{5}{6}} \cdot \sqrt{2\dfrac{4}{7}}$ $\sqrt{15}$

111. $\dfrac{1}{4}\sqrt{\dfrac{16}{3}} \cdot \dfrac{1}{2}\sqrt{\dfrac{3}{2}}$ $\dfrac{\sqrt{2}}{4}$ **112.** $\dfrac{12\sqrt{20}}{4\sqrt{3}}$ $2\sqrt{15}$ **113.** $\dfrac{11\sqrt{6}}{\sqrt{98}}$ $\dfrac{11\sqrt{3}}{7}$

Simplify. Assume all variables represent positive real numbers. **(11-7)**

114. $(3\sqrt{y})(-5\sqrt{x^2 y})$ $-15xy$ **115.** $\sqrt{n}(\sqrt{n^3} + 3)$ $n^2 + 3\sqrt{n}$ **116.** $(7\sqrt{3})(-4\sqrt{6})(5\sqrt{22})$ $-840\sqrt{11}$

Simplify. **(11-8)**

117. $9\sqrt{3} - 5\sqrt{3}$ $4\sqrt{3}$ **118.** $7\sqrt{2} + 6\sqrt{2}$ $13\sqrt{2}$ **119.** $3\sqrt{54} - 2\sqrt{6}$ $7\sqrt{6}$

120. $4\sqrt{28} + 6\sqrt{112}$ $32\sqrt{7}$ **121.** $-10\sqrt{18} - 5\sqrt{32}$ $-50\sqrt{2}$ **122.** $\sqrt{242} - 3\sqrt{363}$
$11\sqrt{2} - 33\sqrt{3}$

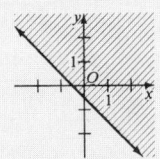
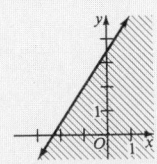
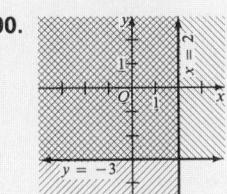
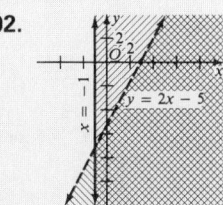
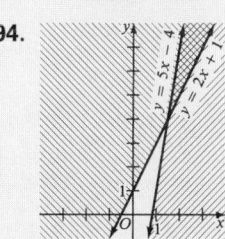
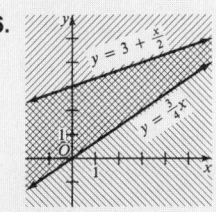

Simplify.

$\dfrac{20\sqrt{7}}{7} + \dfrac{3\sqrt{2}}{4}$ (11-8)

123. $\sqrt{8} - \sqrt{\dfrac{5}{6}}$ $2\sqrt{2} - \dfrac{\sqrt{30}}{6}$ **124.** $\sqrt{\dfrac{2}{3}} - \sqrt{\dfrac{3}{2}} - \dfrac{\sqrt{6}}{6}$ **125.** $5\sqrt{\dfrac{16}{7}} + \sqrt{\dfrac{9}{8}}$

126. $3\sqrt{63} + 2\sqrt{28} - \sqrt{35}$ $13\sqrt{7} - \sqrt{35}$ **127.** $\sqrt{120} - \sqrt{270} + \sqrt{300}$ $10\sqrt{3} - \sqrt{30}$

128. $2\sqrt{\dfrac{5}{3}} + 4\sqrt{\dfrac{3}{8}} - \dfrac{1}{2}\sqrt{68}$ $\dfrac{2\sqrt{15}}{3} + \sqrt{6} - \sqrt{17}$ **129.** $3\sqrt{5}(\sqrt{75} - 2\sqrt{12})$ $3\sqrt{15}$

Simplify.   (11-9)

130. $(5 - \sqrt{3})(5 + \sqrt{3})$ 22   **131.** $(\sqrt{7} + 6)(\sqrt{7} - 6)$ -29

132. $(\sqrt{6} - \sqrt{5})(\sqrt{6} + \sqrt{5})$ 1   **133.** $(4 + \sqrt{2})^2$ $18 + 8\sqrt{2}$

134. $(5 - \sqrt{5})^2$ $30 - 10\sqrt{5}$ **135.** $(3\sqrt{2} - 4)^2$ $34 - 24\sqrt{2}$

136. $(\sqrt{11} + 3\sqrt{7})^2$ $74 + 6\sqrt{77}$ **137.** $2\sqrt{6}(5\sqrt{2} - 4\sqrt{3})$ $20\sqrt{3} - 24\sqrt{2}$

138. $(4\sqrt{5} - 6)(2\sqrt{7} + 7)$ **139.** $(3\sqrt{14} + 2\sqrt{7})(5\sqrt{14} + 3\sqrt{7})$

$8\sqrt{35} - 12\sqrt{7} + 28\sqrt{5} - 42$ $252 + 133\sqrt{2}$

Rationalize the denominator of each fraction.   (11-9)

140. $\dfrac{5}{3 + \sqrt{7}}$ $\dfrac{15 - 5\sqrt{7}}{2}$ **141.** $\dfrac{2 + \sqrt{3}}{1 - \sqrt{5}}$ $\dfrac{2 + \sqrt{3} + 2\sqrt{5} + \sqrt{15}}{4}$

Solve.   (11-10)

142. $\sqrt{m} = 7$ $\{49\}$ **143.** $\sqrt{6x} = \dfrac{3}{2}$ $\left\{\dfrac{3}{8}\right\}$ **144.** $\sqrt{a} - 5 = 4$ $\{81\}$

145. $\dfrac{1}{5} + \sqrt{y} = 1$ $\left\{\dfrac{16}{25}\right\}$ **146.** $\sqrt{\dfrac{x}{3}} = 6$ $\{108\}$ **147.** $\sqrt{n-2} = 9$ $\{83\}$

148. $4\sqrt{5t} = 8$ $\left\{\dfrac{4}{5}\right\}$ **149.** $\sqrt{3z} + 2 = 5$ $\{3\}$ **150.** $\sqrt{4k-5} + 1 = 8$ $\left\{\dfrac{27}{2}\right\}$

151. $\sqrt{\dfrac{5u}{2}} - 3 = -2$ $\left\{\dfrac{2}{5}\right\}$ **152.** $\sqrt{\dfrac{4c-3}{7}} = 3$ $\left\{\dfrac{33}{2}\right\}$ **153.** $8\sqrt{n} = 24\sqrt{5}$ $\{45\}$

Chapter 12

10. $\{5 + \sqrt{6}, 5 - \sqrt{6}\}$ **11.** $\{-4 + 3\sqrt{3}, -4 - 3\sqrt{3}\}$
12. $\{1 + \sqrt{15}, 1 - \sqrt{15}\}$ **13.** $\{-7 + \sqrt{21}, -7 - \sqrt{21}\}$
14. $\left\{\dfrac{7}{2}, -\dfrac{13}{2}\right\}$ **15.** $\left\{\dfrac{1 + 2\sqrt{6}}{3}, \dfrac{1 - 2\sqrt{6}}{3}\right\}$

Solve. Express irrational solutions in simplest radical form. If the equation   (12-1)
has no solution, write "no solution."

1. $m^2 = \dfrac{25}{49}$ $\left\{-\dfrac{5}{7}, \dfrac{5}{7}\right\}$ **2.** $5a^2 = 60$ $\{-2\sqrt{3}, 2\sqrt{3}\}$ **3.** $w^2 + 52 = 0$ No sol.

4. $x^2 - 108 = 0$ $\{-6\sqrt{3}, 6\sqrt{3}\}$ **5.** $7u^2 - 112 = 0$ $\{-4, 4\}$ **6.** $4c^2 + 7 = 23$ $\{-2, 2\}$

7. $3t^2 - 12 = -3$ $\{-\sqrt{3}, \sqrt{3}\}$ **8.** $2n^2 + 9 = 4$ No sol.   **9.** $(v + 5)^2 = 16$ $\{-9, -1\}$

10. $(z - 5)^2 = 6$ **11.** $3(k + 4)^2 = 81$ **12.** $4(f - 1)^2 = 60$

13. $2(h + 7)^2 = 42$ **14.** $(2x + 3)^2 = 100$ **15.** $7(3y - 1)^2 = 168$

16. $e^2 + 6e + 9 = 64$ $\{-11, 5\}$ **17.** $a^2 - 12a + 36 = 49$ $\{-1, 13\}$ **18.** $m^2 + 18m + 81 = 36$
                                                                $\{-15, -3\}$

Solve by completing the square. Give irrational roots in simplest form and   (12-2)
then approximate them to the nearest tenth.

19. $x^2 + 16x = -15$ $\{-15, -1\}$ **20.** $y^2 - 8y + 7 = 0$ $\{1, 7\}$ **21.** $n^2 - 12n - 202 = 8$

22. $4a^2 + 10a = 12$ **23.** $b^2 - 3b = 5$ **24.** $3c^2 + 6c - 1233 = 0$

Solve the equations by (a) completing the square and (b) factoring.   (12-2)

25. $e^2 - 10e + 21 = 0$ $\{3, 7\}$ **26.** $4f^2 - 18f = 10$ $\left\{5, -\frac{1}{2}\right\}$ **27.** $6h^2 + 9h - 42 = 0$

$\left\{2, -\frac{7}{2}\right\}$ (12-2)

Solve. Write irrational roots in simplest radical form.

28. $\frac{m^2}{3} - 2m = 7$ **29.** $n^2 + \frac{n}{2} = 5$ $\left\{2, -\frac{5}{2}\right\}$ **30.** $\frac{x^2}{2} - \frac{x}{4} = 2$

$\{3 + \sqrt{30}, 3 - \sqrt{30}\}$ $\left\{\frac{1 + \sqrt{65}}{4}, \frac{1 - \sqrt{65}}{4}\right\}$

Use the quadratic formula to solve each equation. Give irrational roots in   (12-3)
simplest radical form and then approximate them to the nearest tenth.

31. $z^2 + 7z + 3 = 0$ **32.** $w^2 + 8w - 4 = 0$ **33.** $2u^2 - 10u - 6 = 0$

34. $5y^2 = -9y - 1$ **35.** $3k^2 + 2 = 5k$ **36.** $6m = 3 - 2m^2$

37. $x^2 + 0.3x - 0.2 = 0$ **38.** $n^2 + \frac{2}{3}n - \frac{1}{2} = 0$ **39.** $\frac{1}{2}y^2 - \frac{7}{2}y = 1$

Write the value of the discriminant of each equation. Then use it to decide   (12-4)
how many different real-number roots the equation has. (Do not solve the equations.)
                                    −131; none   0; one
40. $x^2 - 6x + 2 = 0$ 28; two   **41.** $5n^2 + 3n + 7 = 0$ **42.** $-2t^2 + 4t - 2 = 0$

43. $3k^2 - 1.2k + 1.1 = 0$ **44.** $3s^2 + 6s + 3 = 0$ 0; one   **45.** $\frac{1}{3}b^2 - b - 3 = 0$
     −11.76; none   5; two

Without drawing the graph of the given equation, determine (a) how many   (12-4)
x-intercepts the parabola has, and (b) whether its vertex lies above, below, or
on the *x*-axis.

46. $y = 3x^2 + 2x - 5$ **47.** $y = -6 + 3x - 2x^2$ **48.** $y = x^2 - 4x + 16$
   a. two b. below   a. zero b. below   a. zero b. above

Solve each equation by the most appropriate method. Write irrational   (12-5)
answers in simplest radical form.

49. $x^2 + 7x + 12 = 0$ $\{-3, -4\}$ **50.** $13x^2 = 52$ $\{-2, 2\}$

51. $5x^2 - 9x = 0$ $\left\{0, \frac{9}{5}\right\}$ **52.** $3x^2 - 11x = 2$ $\left\{\frac{11 + \sqrt{145}}{6}, \frac{11 - \sqrt{145}}{6}\right\}$

53. $x^2 + 8x + 3 = 0$ $\{-4 + \sqrt{13}, -4 - \sqrt{13}\}$ **54.** $(x - 3)^2 = 6$ $\{3 + \sqrt{6}, 3 - \sqrt{6}\}$

55. $6x^2 + 4x = 1$ $\left\{\frac{-2 + \sqrt{10}}{6}, \frac{-2 - \sqrt{10}}{6}\right\}$ **56.** $\frac{(x + 4)^2}{3} = 8$ $\{-4 + 2\sqrt{6}, -4 - 2\sqrt{6}\}$

57. $\frac{3}{4}x^2 - \frac{2}{3}x = 1$ $\left\{\frac{4 + 2\sqrt{31}}{9}, \frac{4 - 2\sqrt{31}}{9}\right\}$ **58.** $\frac{1}{2x} = \frac{3x - 2}{3}$ $\left\{\frac{2 + \sqrt{22}}{6}, \frac{2 - \sqrt{22}}{6}\right\}$

59. $1.2x^2 - 0.4x = 0.2$ $\left\{\frac{1 + \sqrt{7}}{6}, \frac{1 - \sqrt{7}}{6}\right\}$ **60.** $\frac{2x - 1}{4x + 3} = \frac{x + 1}{3x - 2}$ $\left\{\frac{7 + \sqrt{51}}{2}, \frac{7 - \sqrt{51}}{2}\right\}$

61. $4x(x - 2) + 3(x + 8) = 27 + 5x^2$ **62.** $(x + 6)^2 + 2(x - 1) = 13$
                                            $\{-7 + 2\sqrt{7}, -7 - 2\sqrt{7}\}$

61. $\left\{\frac{-5 + \sqrt{13}}{2}, \frac{-5 - \sqrt{13}}{2}\right\}$

Extra Practice   **663**

**Solve. Give irrational roots to the nearest tenth. Use your calculator or the
Table of Square Roots at the back of the book as necessary.**

(12-6)

63. The length of a rectangle is 6 times the width. The area of the rectangle is
    84 cm². Find the length and width. length, 22.2 cm; width, 3.7 cm

64. The difference of a number and its square is 56. Find the number. 8 or −7

65. The altitude of a triangle is 2 m less than the base. The area of the triangle
    is 84 m². Find the base. 14 m

66. Theresa is crocheting an afghan that is already 30 in. wide by 40 in. long.
    If she continues to crochet by increasing the width and the length by the
    same number of inches until the afghan's area is doubled, what will be the
    new dimensions? 44.2 in. by 54.2 in.

**Translate each statement into a formula. Use *k* as the constant of variation
where needed.**

(12-7, 12-8)

67. The height, h, of a right circular cylinder of a given volume is inversely
    proportional to the square of the radius, r. $hr^2 = k$

68. Wind pressure, p, on a flat surface varies directly as the square of the wind
    velocity, v. $\frac{p}{v^2} = k$

69. The lateral area, L, of a cylinder varies jointly as the radius, r, of the
    base, and the height, h. $L = krh$

70. The volume, V, of a cone varies jointly as the height, h, and the square of
    the radius, r, of the base. $V = khr^2$

71. The rate of speed, r, of a moving body varies inversely as the time trav-
    eled, t, and directly as the distance traveled, d. $\frac{rt}{d} = k$

72. Centrifugal force, F, varies inversely as the radius, r, of the circular path,
    and directly as the square of the velocity, v, of a moving body. $\frac{Fr}{v^2} = k$

Extra Practice: Problem Solving

Chapter 1

Use the five-step plan to solve each problem.   (1-7)

1. A train is traveling at an average speed of 90 km/h. How far will it travel in 2.5 h? 225 km

2. If a number is decreased by 27, the result is 36. Find the number. 63

3. A football team finished its 12-game season with no ties. The team won twice as many games as it lost. How many games did the team win? 8 games

4. A store sold 102 record albums during a two-day sale. Twice as many albums were sold the second day as the first. How many albums were sold the first day? 34 albums

5. If three times a number is increased by 11, the result is 68. Find the number. 19

6. A bank contains 57 nickels, dimes, and quarters. There are 8 more dimes than quarters and 5 more nickels than dimes. How much money is in the bank? $6.25

Chapter 2

Solve.   (2-3)

1. A football team gained 23 yd on one play. However, the ball was brought back to the line of scrimmage and then the team was given a 15 yd penalty. How far was the ball from where it would have been had no penalty been assessed? 38 yd

2. An elevator left the twenty-sixth floor of a building and went up eight floors, then down twelve, and back up four. On what floor was the elevator then? 26th floor

3. At the beginning of the month the Cranes had $250 in their vacation fund. They were able to add $10 per week for four weeks. Then they had to take out $85 for emergency household repairs. How much was in the fund at the end of the month? $205

4. A neighborhood association collected $85 in dues, earned $280 at a garage sale, and got $124 in donations. The association needs $500 to build a playground. How much more must it collect? $11

5. An 8:00 A.M. flight from Boston to Minneapolis took three hours. The time in Minneapolis is one hour earlier than Boston. What time was it in Minneapolis when the flight arrived? 10:00 A.M.

6. A train is traveling at the rate of 100 km/h. A conductor is walking toward the back of the train at 5 km/h. What is the conductor's speed relative to the ground? 95 km/h

Solve. (2-4)

1. Neon freezes at $-248.61°$ C and boils at $-246.09°$ C. Find the difference between the boiling point and the freezing point. 2.52° C

2. The highest point in California is Mount Whitney at 4418 m above sea level. The lowest point is Death Valley at 86 m below sea level. Find the difference in altitude. 4504 m

3. A candidate goes door to door along Main Street from a point 16 blocks west of campaign headquarters to a point 12 blocks east of headquarters. How many blocks has she gone? 28 blocks

4. Find the difference in degrees of longitude between Chicago at about 88° W and Rome at about 12° E. 100°

5. Mount Everest at 8848 m above sea level is 9245 m higher than the Dead Sea. Find the altitude of the Dead Sea. 397 m below sea level

6. One winter day the temperature in Marshview reached a record high of 18.3° C. That was 22.7° C higher than the average temperature for that day. Find the average temperature. $-4.4°$ C

Chapter 3

Solve. (3-1)

1. A number increased by 13 is -5. Find the number. -18

2. A glass of milk costs 70¢. If a glass of milk and a sandwich cost $2.50, how much does the sandwich cost? $1.80

3. Fifteen less than a number is 43. Find the number. 58

4. A plane flew 145 km/h faster when it was flying with the wind than it would have flown in still air. If its speed with the wind was 970 km/h, find the speed of the plane in still air. 825 km/h

5. The Booster Club had $425 in its treasury. The members earned $642 selling refreshments. They donated $320 to the football team for bus rentals. How much money did they have left? $747

6. Seventy-six tickets were sold in advance for a museum field trip. Thirteen tickets were sold the day of the trip. Seven people had to return their tickets and did not go. How many people went altogether? 82 people

Solve. (3-2)

1. The opposite of seven times a number is 238. Find the number. -34

2. One fourth of a number is 73. Find the number. 292

3. A 2.5 kg bag of apples costs $1.40. Find the cost per kilogram of the apples. 56¢

4. Frank works the same number of hours each week at a part-time job. In the last 8 weeks he worked 68 h. How many hours does Frank work each week? 8.5 h

5. A rectangle is 24 cm long and has a perimeter of 72 cm. Find the width. 12 cm

6. A restaurant cuts its large pizza into 8 slices and sells each slice for 90¢. If the pizzas were cut into 6 slices, how much would the restaurant have to charge for each slice to make the same amount? $1.20

Solve. (3-4)

1. If you subtract 34 from the product of 15 and a number, you get 146. Find the number. 12

2. The perimeter of a rectangle is 152 cm. The width is 35 cm. Find the length. 41 cm

3. Charlene paid $131.44, including tax, for a desk. The tax was 31 cents less than $\frac{1}{16}$ the cost of the desk. Find the cost of the desk. $124

4. Twin Cinema I seats 150 more people than Twin Cinema II. If the cinemas seat 1250 people altogether, find the number of seats in Twin Cinema II. 550 seats

5. A bank contains 36 nickels, dimes, and quarters. There are 4 more dimes than quarters and twice as many nickels as quarters. How many of each coin are in the bank? 8 quarters, 12 dimes, 16 nickels

6. The longest side of a triangle is 8 cm longer than the shortest side and 5 cm longer than the third side. If the perimeter of the triangle is 56 cm, find the lengths of the three sides. 23 cm, 15 cm, 18 cm

Solve. (3-5)

1. The larger of two consecutive integers is 10 more than twice the smaller. Find the integers. −9 and −8

2. Find a number whose product with 6 is the same as its sum with 45. 9

3. Five times a number, increased by 3, is the same as three times the number, increased by 27. Find the number. 12

4. The sum of two numbers is 20. Twice one number is 4 more than four times the other. Find the numbers. 14 and 6

5. The lengths of the sides of a triangle are consecutive odd integers. If the perimeter is 1 less than four times the shortest side, find the length of each side. 7, 9, 11

6. A sandwich costs 20¢ more than a salad plate. Six sandwiches cost as much as seven salad plates. Find the cost of each. sandwich, $1.40; salad plate, $1.20

Solve. (3-6)

1. Kevin works 3 times as many hours in a week as Karen does. If each were to work 6 h more per week, Kevin would be working twice as many hours as Karen does. How many hours does each work now? Kevin, 18 h; Karen, 6 h

2. Aaron, Betsy, and Charita work part-time at the public library. Betsy works 4 h more each week than Aaron, and together they work half as many hours as Charita. How long does each person work if their total time is 45 h? Aaron, 5.5 h; Betsy, 9.5 h; Charita, 30 h

3. Zach's last quiz score was 30 points less than twice his first score. What was his first quiz score if the sum of his two scores is 150? 60

4. The length of a rectangle is 18 cm more than the width. A second rectangle is 6 cm shorter and 3 cm wider than the first and has a perimeter of 126 cm. Find the dimensions of each rectangle. 24 cm by 42 cm; 27 cm by 36 cm

5. Becky has as many dimes as Ryan and Amy have together. Ryan has 2 more dimes than Amy, and Amy has one third as many dimes as Becky has. How many dimes does each have? Becky, 6; Ryan, 4; Amy, 2 dimes

6. A cup of skim milk has 10 more than half the calories of a cup of whole milk. A cup of whole milk has 40 more calories than a glass of apple juice. If the total number of calories in one cup of each is 370, find the number of calories in each. whole milk, 160 calories; skim milk, 90 calories; apple juice, 120 calories

Solve. (3-7)

1. A collection of quarters and dimes is worth $6.75. The number of dimes is 4 less than three times the number of quarters. How many of each are there? 13 quarters, 35 dimes

2. A total of 720 people attended the school basketball game. Adult tickets cost $2.50 each and student tickets cost $1.50 each. If $1220 worth of tickets were sold, how many students and how many adults attended? 580 students, 140 adults

3. A worker earns $9 per hour for a regular workday and $13.50 per hour for additional hours. If the worker was paid $114.75 for an 11-hour workday, what is the length of a regular workday? 7.5 h

4. Carrots cost 75¢ per kilogram and potatoes cost 70¢ per kilogram. A shopper bought 9 kg of the vegetables for $6.60. How many kilograms of each did the shopper buy? 6 kg of carrots, 3 kg of potatoes

5. A collection of 102 nickels, dimes, and quarters is worth $13.60. There are 14 more nickels than dimes. How many quarters are there? 36 quarters

Chapter 4

Solve. (4-8)

1. Two trains leave a station at the same time, heading in opposite directions. One train is traveling at 80 km/h, the other at 90 km/h. How long will it take for the trains to be 425 km apart? 2.5 h

2. Grace leaves home at 8:00 A.M. Ten minutes later, Will notices Grace's lunch and begins bicycling after her. If Grace walks at 5 km/h and Will cycles at 15 km/h, how long will it take him to catch up with her? 5 min

3. A jet took one hour longer flying to Lincoln from Adams at 800 km/h than to return at 1200 km/h. Find the distance from Lincoln to Adams. 2400 km

4. Gene spent 10 min riding his bicycle to a friend's house. He left his bike there and, with his friend, walked for 15 min to the gym. Gene rides his bicycle 10 km/h faster than he walks. If the entire trip covered a distance of 2.75 km, how far is it from his friend's house to the gym? 0.65 km

5. At noon, Sheila left a boat landing and paddled her canoe 20 km downstream and 20 km back. If she traveled 10 km/h downstream and 4 km/h upstream, what time did she arrive back at the landing? 7:00 P.M.

Solve. (4-9)

1. A rectangle is 4 m longer than it is wide. If the length and width are both increased by 5 m, the area is increased by 115 m^2. Find the original dimensions. 7 m by 11 m

2. A rectangle is 3 cm longer and 2 cm narrower than a square with the same area. Find the dimensions of each figure. 4 cm by 9 cm; 6 cm by 6 cm

3. A rectangular swimming pool is 4 m longer than it is wide. It is surrounded by a cement walk 1 m wide. The area of the walk is 32 m^2. Find the dimensions of the pool. 5 m by 9 m

4. When the length of a square is increased by 6 and the width is decreased by 4, the area remains unchanged. Find the dimensions of the square. 12 by 12

5. A print is 10 cm longer than it is wide. It is mounted in a frame 1.5 cm wide. The area of the frame is 399 cm^2. Find the dimensions of the print.
60 cm by 70 cm

Solve. (4-10)

1. Find two consecutive integers whose sum is 104. No solution

2. A plane averaged 1000 km/h on the first half of a round trip, but heavy winds slowed its speed on the return trip to 600 km/h. If the entire trip took 6 h, find the total distance. 4500 km

3. Jill earned 12 more points on her quiz than Jack. If they both get 8 bonus points, Jill will have three times as many points as Jack does. How many points does each have? No solution

4. The side of a square is 2 cm longer than the side of a second square. The area of the first square exceeds that of the second by 220 cm^2. Find the side of each square. 56 cm and 54 cm

5. Find three consecutive integers whose sum is four times the greatest integer.
−5, −4, −3

Chapter 5

Solve. (5-13)

1. The sum of a number and its square is 132. Find the number. 11 or −12

2. The sum of the squares of two consecutive positive odd integers is 202. Find the numbers. 9, 11

3. A rectangle is 8 cm longer than it is wide. The area is 240 cm². Find the dimensions. 12 cm by 20 cm

4. The sum of two numbers is 12 and the sum of their squares is 74. Find the numbers. 5 and 7

5. A rectangular flower garden is planted in a rectangular yard that is 16 m by 12 m. The garden occupies $\frac{1}{6}$ of the area of the yard and leaves a uniform strip of grass around the edges. Find the dimensions of the garden. 4 m by 8 m

6. The edge of one cube is 4 cm longer than the edge of a second cube. The volumes of the cubes differ by 316 cm³. Find the length of the edge of each cube. 3 cm; 7 cm

Chapter 7

Solve. (7-1)

1. Two numbers are in the ratio 2:3 and their sum is 125. Find the numbers. 50, 75

2. The measures of the angles of a triangle are in the ratio 2:3:5. Recall that the sum of the measures of the angles of a triangle is 180°. Find the measure of each angle. 36°, 54°, 90°

3. Three numbers are in the ratio 2:3:5 and their sum is 200. Find the numbers. 40, 60, 100

4. The ratio of teachers to assistants to children at a day care center is 2:1:9. Of the 96 people at the center, how many are children? 72 children

5. A collection of quarters, dimes, and nickels is worth $22.80. If the ratio of quarters to dimes to nickels is 5:3:7, how many coins are there? 180 coins

6. Two trains leave a station at the same time heading in opposite directions. After 2 h, the trains are 376 km apart. If the ratio of their speeds is 22:25, find the speed of each train. 88 km/h, 100 km/h

Solve. (7-2)

1. A 1.5-lb steak costs $5.80. Find the cost of a 2-lb steak. $7.73

2. A poll showed that 400 voters out of 625 favor Question 1 in the town election. If there are 7500 voters altogether, how many can be expected to vote in favor of the question? 4800

3. Group-rate admissions to a museum cost $140.70 for a group of 42. How much would it cost for a group of 50? $167.50

4. The tax on a restaurant meal that costs $24 is $1.44. Find the tax on a meal that costs $35. $2.10

5. The Sommers' scale is inaccurate. If it registers 120 lb for Karen, who actually weighs 116 lb, how much will it register for Neil, who actually weighs 174 lb? 180 lb

6. On a wall map, 1 cm represents 25 km. Colorado is represented by a rectangle 25.8 cm long and 18.4 cm wide. Find the approximate area of Colorado in square kilometers. 296,700 km^2

Solve. (7-3)

1. Juan spent $2 more on books than Sylvia did. If they each spent $4 less, Sylvia would have spent exactly $\frac{5}{6}$ of what Juan spent. How much did each spend? Juan, $16; Sylvia, $14

2. Three fifths of a number added to one fourth of the number is 51. Find the number. 60

3. Bart's age is one third of his mother's age. Seven years ago, his age was one fifth of hers. How old are both now? Bart, 14 years old; mother, 42 years old

4. A rectangle is 11 cm narrower than it is long. The length is two sevenths of the perimeter. Find the length and the width. length, 44 cm; width, 33 cm

5. Two thirds of the coins in a collection of quarters and dimes are quarters. The collection is worth $12. How many dimes are there? 20 dimes

6. A bus, traveling at 90 km/h, takes 15.2 h longer to get from Ardmore to Zepher than a plane flying at 850 km/h. How far is it from Ardmore to Zepher? 1530 km

Solve. (7-4)

1. The sum of a number and its reciprocal is $\frac{25}{12}$. Find the number. $\frac{3}{4}$ or $\frac{4}{3}$

2. The sum of a number and its reciprocal is $\frac{29}{10}$. Find the number. $\frac{5}{2}$ or $\frac{2}{5}$

3. The denominator of a fraction is 2 more than the numerator. If the numerator and denominator are increased by 2, the new fraction is $\frac{4}{15}$ greater than the original fraction. Find the original fraction. $\frac{1}{3}$

4. The denominator of a fraction is 2 more than the numerator. The sum of the fraction and its reciprocal is $\frac{34}{15}$. Find the fraction. $\frac{3}{5}$

5. If the speed limit is decreased by 10 km/h on a 100 km stretch of a highway, the trip will take a half hour longer than usual. What is the usual speed limit? 50 km/h

6. Sue can ride her bike 14 km/h faster than she can walk. It takes 17.5 min longer to walk 2.5 km than to ride. Find Sue's walking speed. 6 km/h

Solve. (7-5)

1. If there is a 6% tax on clothing, find the tax on a suit that costs $175. $10.50

2. A real estate agent makes a 7% commission on all sales. How much does the agent make on a sale of $182,500? $12,775

3. A discount store sold a sweater for $32. If the discount was 20%, find the original price. $40

4. If the Gannons' $84 monthly gas bill goes up 8%, what will be their new monthly payment? $90.72

Extra Practice   **671**

5. An $840 personal computer is discounted 25%. What is the final cost? $630

6. How much greater is the income on $3600 invested at 12% than on $4200 invested at 8%? $96

Solve. (7-6)

1. Last season, when a football team was doing poorly, weekly attendance averaged 42,000. This season weekly attendance averages 56,700. What is the percent of increase? 35%

2. A single monthly issue of *Sports Spotlight* costs $2.25 at the newsstand. A yearly subscription of 12 issues costs $21.60. Find the percent of discount from the newsstand price. 20%

3. Enrollment in the summer recreation program this year increased by 16% to 1711 people. How many people enrolled last year? 1475

4. The Katchners invested $7500 at 8% and $3500 at 5%. Find the total annual income from the two investments. $775

5. The Ozakas invested a sum of money at 10%. They could have earned the same interest by investing $1600 less at 12%. How much did they invest? $9600

6. The Sanjurjos invested three fourths of their money at 12% and the rest at 8%. If their annual income from the investment is $1320, how much have they invested? $12,000

Chemistry

Solve. (7-7)

1. How many liters of water must be added to 20 L of a 75% acid solution to produce a solution that is 15% acid? 80 L

2. How many liters of acid should be added to 4 L of a 10% acid solution to make a solution that is 80% acid? 14 L

3. A chemist mixes 16 L of a 40% acid solution and 24 L of a 16% acid solution. What is the percent of acid of the mixture? 25.6%

4. How many kilograms of water must be evaporated from 84 kg of a 5% salt solution to produce a solution that is 35% salt? 72 kg

Grocery

Solve. (7-7)

1. Students working at a refreshment stand mixed cranberry juice at 50¢ per liter and apple juice at 35¢ per liter to make 120 L of a fruit drink worth 40¢ per liter. How many liters of each did they use?
   40 L of cranberry juice; 80 L of apple juice

premium blend, 14.4 kg; regular blend, 21.6 kg

2. A grocer mixes a premium blend worth $17 per kilogram with a blend worth $7 per kilogram to make 36 kg of a blend worth $11 per kilogram. How many kilograms of each type are included?

3. A butcher mixes 12 lb of ground pork at $1.25 per pound with 24 lb of ground beef at $2 per pound to sell as meat loaf mix. What should be the cost per pound of the mixture? $1.75

4. How many kilograms of cranberries at $2.10 per kilogram should a grocer mix with 10 kg of pineapple chunks at $1.20 per kilogram to make a relish worth $1.35 per kilogram? 2 kg

Investment and Wages

Solve. (7-7)

1. A worker earns $1\frac{1}{2}$ times the regular wage for overtime. In one week the worker's total income was $625 for 35 h of regular work plus 10 h of overtime. What is the regular hourly wage? $12.50

2. The Esperanzas invested part of their $8000 at 12% and part at 8%. If their annual investment income is $825, how much is invested at each rate? $4625 at 12%; $3375 at 8%

3. The Lees invested two thirds of their money at 12.5%, one fourth at 8%, and the rest at 6%. If their annual investment income is $1625, how much did they invest altogether? $15,000

4. An investor has $10,000 invested in two stocks. If one stock pays 15% and the other 16%, and the total annual income is $1520, how much is invested in each? $2000 at 16%; $8000 at 15%

Solve. (7-8)

1. Joe can do a job in 6 h and Charlie can do the same job in 5 h. What part of the job can they finish by working together for 2 h? $\frac{11}{15}$

2. Charlotte can finish her paper route in 2 h. When Ralph helps, they finish in 45 min. How long would it take Ralph working alone? 1 h 12 min

3. A crew of 2 could put siding on a house in 30 h. Another crew of 3 could do the same job in 24 h. How long would it take all 5 people working together? 13 h 20 min

4. Flora can finish her chores in 4 h. One week, after Flora worked alone for 1 h, she was joined by her younger sister Fiona and they finished the job in 2 h. How long would it have taken Fiona working alone? 8 h

5. One pipe can fill a tank in 50 min and a second pipe can fill it in 90 min. When the tank was empty, the first pipe was opened for 20 min, then shut. How long will it take the second pipe to finish the job? 54 min

6. One machine can produce an order of Wonder Widgets in 45 min. A second machine takes 60 min, and a third takes 90 min. How long would it take all three working together? 20 min

Solve.
a. 10,000 **b.** 9709 **c.** 10,300   (7-9)

1. The population of a certain area in t years is expected to be $10(1.03)^t$ thousand people. Find the population (a) now, (b) last year, and (c) next year.

2. A certain isotope has a half-life of 100 years. Starting with 100 g of the isotope, in t years there will be $100(0.5)^{t/100}$ g left. (a) How much will be **a.** 0.09766 g left in 1000 years? (b) How much was there 1000 years ago? **b.** 102,400 g

3. A certain bacteria culture quadruples every 2 days. The number present t days from now will be $1,000,000(4)^{t/2}$. How many bacteria were there 2 weeks ago? about 61 bacteria

4. A $10,000 investment earning 8%, compounded annually, will be worth $10,000(1.08)^t$ in t years. What was the amount 4 years ago? $7350.29

5. The growth rate of a certain city is such that its population t years from now is given by the formula $12,000(1.06)^t$. What was the population 10 years ago? about 6701 people

6. In one country the cost of living has been increasing so that an item costing one dollar now will cost $(1.05)^t$ dollars t years from now. How much did today's one-dollar item cost 5 years ago? 78¢

Solve.   (7-10)

1. The speed of light is about 3.00×10^5 km/s. The average distance from Earth to the moon is about 3.84×10^5 km. How long does it take light reflected from Earth to reach the moon? 1.28 s

2. At its farthest, the moon is about 4.07×10^5 km from Earth. At its closest, it is about 3.56×10^5 km from Earth. Find the difference between the two distances. 5.1×10^4 km

3. The average distance from the sun to Pluto is about 6.10×10^9 km. About how long does it take light from the sun to reach Pluto? (See Exercise 1 above.) 2.03×10^4 s

4. **a.** A parsec is about 3.3×10^3 light years. The star Deneb is about 5.0×10^2 parsecs from the sun. How many light years is that? 1.65×10^6
   b. A light year is about 9.5×10^{12} km. Find the distance from Deneb to the sun in kilometers. 1.5675×10^{19} km

5. The approximate wavelength of visible light is 6.0×10^3 Angstrom units. An Angstrom unit is equal to 1.0×10^{-8} cm. Find the wavelength of visible light in centimeters. 6.0×10^{-5} cm

Chapter 8

Solve.   (8-9)

1. A beam bends 1.6 cm with a mass of 32 kg on it. If the amount of bending is directly proportional to the mass, find the amount of bending caused by a mass of 62 kg. 3.1 cm

674 *Extra Practice*

2. A baker uses 18 cups of flour to make 48 sandwich rolls. How many cups of flour are needed to make 104 sandwich rolls? 39 cups

3. A grocer uses 22 kg of premium nuts in making 54 kg of a mixture. How much of the premium nuts is needed for 81 kg of the mixture? 33 kg

4. On a scale drawing, a child 4 ft tall is represented by a figure 6 in. tall. How tall a figure should be used to represent an 11 ft elephant? 16.5 in

5. On a map, 1 cm represents 60 km. Find the actual area of a region represented on the map by a rectangle 7.5 cm by 8.4 cm. 226,800 km^2

6. A factory is to be built in the shape of a rectangular solid. The actual building will be 62 m long, 30 m wide, and 12 m high. A scale model is built with a scale of 1 cm to 5 m. Find the volume of the model. 178.56 cm^3

Solve. (8-10)

1. The time required to drive a given distance is inversely proportional to the speed. If it takes 7.5 h to cover a distance at 84 km/h, how long will it take at 90 km/h? 7 h

2. A gear with 36 teeth revolves at 800 r/min and meshes with a gear with 24 teeth. Find the speed of the second gear if the speed varies inversely as the number of teeth. 1200 r/min

3. How much would you have to invest at 8% to earn as much interest as $1250 invested at 12%? $1875

4. A room is to be partitioned into a row of carrels. If each carrel is 1.8 m wide, there will be room for 16 carrels. How many carrels will fit if each is 1.92 m wide? 15

5. A mass of 18 g and a mass of 22 g are on the ends of a meter stick. Where should a fulcrum be placed to balance the meter stick? 0.55 m from the mass of 18 g or 0.45 m from the mass of 22 g

6. A lever has a mass of 400 g on one end and a mass of 250 g on the other. The lever is balanced when the mass of 400 g is 0.75 m closer to the fulcrum than the other mass. How far from the fulcrum is the mass of 250 g? 2 m

Chapter 9

Solve. (9-3)

1. A collection of 77 quarters and dimes is worth $12.50. How many quarters are there? 32 quarters

2. The sum of two numbers is 32. One number is 4 more than the other. Find the numbers. 14, 18

3. The length of a rectangle is 3 less than twice the width. The perimeter is 54. Find the dimensions. width, 10; length, 17

4. The sum of two numbers is 66. If the smaller number is subtracted from two thirds of the larger number, the result is one third the positive difference of the original numbers. Find the numbers. 22, 44

5. If 1 is subtracted from the numerator of a fraction, the resulting fraction is $\frac{1}{3}$. If 2 is subtracted from the denominator, the resulting fraction is $\frac{1}{2}$. Find the original fraction. $\frac{5}{12}$

6. If 2 is added to the numerator of a fraction, the resulting fraction is $\frac{2}{3}$. If 1 is subtracted from the denominator, the resulting fraction is $\frac{1}{2}$. Find the original fraction. $\frac{4}{9}$

Solve. (9-4)

1. The sum of two numbers is 36 and their difference is 6. Find the numbers. 21, 15

2. The sum of two numbers is 73. When the smaller number is subtracted from twice the greater number, the result is 50. Find the numbers. 41, 32

3. There are 158 members in the soccer program. There are 16 more boys than girls. How many boys are there? 87 boys

4. If Cathy walks for 2 h and rides her bicycle for 1 h, she can travel 36 km. If she walks for 2 h and rides her bicycle for 2 h, she can travel 56 km. How fast can she walk? How fast can she ride her bicycle? walk, 8 km/h; bike, 20 km/h

5. Craig has 38 quarters and dimes. If he had twice as many quarters, he would have $11. How many of each coin does he have? 18 quarters, 20 dimes

6. Olivia has $30 more than Carl. If they each had $7 less, the sum of their funds would equal the amount that Olivia has now. How much money does each have now? Olivia, $44; Carl, $14

Solve. (9-5)

1. The sum of two numbers is 51 and their difference is 13. Find the numbers. 19, 32

2. A collection of 27 nickels and dimes is worth $1.95. How many of each coin are there? 15 nickels, 12 dimes

3. The side of a square house is 24 ft long, and the house is located on a lot which is 50 ft longer than it is wide. The perimeter of the lot is 20 ft more than 5 times the perimeter of the house. Find the length of the lot. 150 ft

4. Museum passes cost $5 for adults and $2 for children. One day the museum sold 1820 passes for $6100. How many of each type were sold? 820 adult passes, 1000 children's passes

5. In a math contest, each team is asked 50 questions. The teams earn 15 points for each correct answer and lose 8 for each incorrect answer. One team finished with a score of 566. How many questions did this team answer correctly? 42 questions

6. A grocer mixes two types of nuts, Brand A and Brand B. If the mix includes 4 kg of Brand A and 6 kg of Brand B, the mix will cost $6.20 per kilogram. If it includes 2 kg of Brand A and 8 kg of Brand B, it will cost $5.60 per kilogram. Find the cost per kilogram of each brand. Brand A, $8/kg; Brand B, $5/kg

Solve. (9-6)

1. A boat can travel 16 km/h against the current. The same boat can travel 30 km/h with the current. Find the rate of the boat in still water and the rate of the current. boat, 23 km/h; current, 7 km/h

2. A jet flies with the wind at 1100 km/h and against the same wind at 750 km/h. Find the rate of the wind and the speed of the jet in still air.

3. A swimmer can swim 4 km with the current in 24 min. The same distance would take 40 min against the current. Find the rate of the current and the speed of the swimmer. current, 2 km/h; swimmer, 8 km/h

4. A plane flies the first half of a 5600 km flight into the wind in 3.5 h. The return trip, with the same wind, takes 2.5 h. Find the speed of the wind and the speed of the plane in still air. wind, 160 km/h; plane, 960 km/h

5. A plane has a speed of 840 km/h in still air. It can travel 3120 km with the wind in the same time it would take to travel 1920 km against the wind. Find the speed of the wind. 200 km/h

6. A rowboat can travel a distance of 66 km in 3 h with the current. The rowboat can travel 33 km in 3 h against the current. Find the rate of the current and the rate of the rowboat in still water.
current, 5.5 km/h; rowboat, 16.5 km/h

Chapter 10

Solve. (10-3)

1. The sum of two consecutive integers is less than 83. Find the pair of such integers with the greatest sum. 40, 41

2. A collection of quarters and dimes is worth more than $20. There are twice as many quarters as dimes. At least how many dimes are there? 34 dimes

3. Four members of a bowling team had scores of 240, 180, 220, and 200. Find the lowest score a fifth person must get to maintain an average for the group of at least 220. 260

4. The sum of three consecutive even integers is less than 80. Find the greatest such integers. 24, 26, 28

5. When road repairs begin, the current speed limit will be cut by 40 km/h. It will then take at least 3.6 h to cover the same distance that can be covered in 2 h now. What is the speed limit now? 90 km/h

6. The length of a rectangle is 1 cm greater than twice the width. If each dimension were increased by 5 cm, the area would be at least 150 cm^2 greater. Find the least possible dimensions. 8 cm by 17 cm

Chapter 11

Solve. (11-5)

1. A square has an area of 184 cm^2. Find the length of a side to the nearest tenth of a centimeter. 13.6 cm

2. A square has the same area as a rectangle that is 25 m by 18 m. Find the length of a side of the square to the nearest tenth of a meter. 21.2 m

3. A square has the same area as a triangle that has a base of 8 cm and a height of 5 cm. Find the length of a side of the square to the nearest tenth of a centimeter. 4.5 cm

4. A circle inside a square just touches its sides. The area of the circle is 226.08 m². Find the length of a side of the square to the nearest tenth of a meter. Use 3.14 as an approximation for π. 17.0 m

5. A circular wading pool covers an area of 34.54 m². Find the radius of the pool to the nearest tenth of a meter. Use 3.14 as an approximation for π. 3.3 m

6. A circular flower bed is surrounded by a crushed-stone walk that is 1 m wide. If the area of the whole region is 21.98 m², find the radius of the flower bed to the nearest tenth of a meter. Use 3.14 as an approximation for π. 1.6 m

Solve. Approximate each square root to the nearest hundredth. (11-6)

1. A small park in the shape of a rectangle has dimensions 50 m by 20 m. A road through the park follows the diagonal of the rectangle. Find the length of the road. 53.85 m

2. A rope from the top of a mast of a sailboat is attached to a point 2 m from the mast. If the rope is 6 m long, how tall is the mast? 5.66 m

3. The length of one leg of a right triangle is one centimeter less than twice the length of the second leg. The hypotenuse is one centimeter more than twice the length of the second leg. Find the length of each leg. 8 cm, 15 cm

4. The bottom of a 7 m ramp is 5 m from the base of a loading platform. Find the height of the platform. 4.90 m

5. The length of the longer leg of a right triangle is 3 cm more than the length of the shorter leg. The length of the hypotenuse is 3 cm more than the length of the longer leg. Find the length of each leg. 9 cm, 12 cm

Solve. (11-10)

1. One fourth the square root of a number is 7. Find the number. 784

2. When 8 is subtracted from 3 times a number, the square root of the result is 10. Find the number. 36

3. Four times the square root of a number is 28. Find the number. 49

4. When 5 is subtracted from the square root of twice a number, the result is 9. Find the number. 98

5. The geometric mean of two positive numbers is the positive square root of their product. Find two consecutive even integers whose geometric mean is $8\sqrt{15}$. 30, 32

6. Find two consecutive positive odd integers whose geometric mean is $15\sqrt{3}$. 25, 27

Chapter 12

Solve. (12-6)

1. The sum of a number and its square is 30. Find the number. 5 or −6

2. The foundation of a house is 13 m by 7 m. If the builder increases each dimension by the same amount, the area of the foundation will increase to 135 m². Find the new dimensions. 15 m by 9 m

3. The perimeter of a rectangular yard is 138 m and the area is 540 m². Find the dimensions of the yard. 9 m by 60 m

4. The sum of the squares of two consecutive even integers is 340. Find the integers. 12 and 14, or −14 and −12

5. One work crew can finish a job in 18 h less than a second crew. Working together, they can finish the job in 40 h. How long would each crew take working alone? 72 h and 90 h

6. One number is 2 more than 3 times another. The sum of their squares is 212. Find the numbers. 4 and 14, or −5.2 and −13.6

Solve. (12-7)

1. The stopping distance of a car varies directly as the square of its speed. If the stopping distance is 112 m at 64 km/h, find the stopping distance at 56 km/h. 85.75 m

2. The price of a diamond varies directly as the square of its mass. If a 1.4 carat diamond costs $1764, find the cost of a similar stone with a mass of 1.7 carats. $2601

3. The height of a cone of given volume is inversely proportional to the square of the radius of the base. If a cone that is 4 units high has a base with radius 3 units, find the height of a cone of equal volume with a base of radius 6 units. 1 unit

4. The time needed to fill a tank varies inversely as the square of the radius of the hose. If a hose of radius 3.5 cm takes 8 min to fill a tank, how long will it take using a hose of radius 2 cm? 24.5 min

5. The force between two magnets varies inversely as the square of the distance between them. Two magnets are initially 4 cm apart. They are moved 8 cm farther apart. What is the effect on the force? It is $\frac{1}{9}$ as large as it was.

6. The distance an object falls varies directly as the square of the time it falls. If an object falls 175.5 m in 6 s, how long would it take to fall 487.5 m? 10 s

Solve. (12-8)

1. The cost of operating an appliance varies jointly as the number of watts, hours of operation, and the cost per kilowatt-hour. It costs 45¢ to operate a 3000-watt air conditioner for 2 h at a cost of 7.5¢ per kilowatt-hour. Find the cost of operating a 1200-watt dishwasher for 40 min. 6¢

2. The number of persons needed to do a job varies directly as the amount of work to be done and inversely as the time in which the job is to be done. If 8 factory workers can produce 520 items in 4 days, how many workers will be needed to produce 585 items in 3 days? 12 workers

3. If 2 painters can cover 320 ft^2 in 3 h, how long will it take 3 painters to cover 840 ft^2? (See Exercise 2 above.) $5\frac{1}{4}$ h

4. The mass of a metal disc varies directly as the thickness and the square of the radius. A disc 2 cm thick with radius 5 cm has a mass of 840 g. Find the mass of a disc of the same metal that has radius 3 cm and is 0.5 cm thick. 75.6 g

Table 1 / Squares of Integers from 1 to 100

Number	Square	Number	Square	Number	Square	Number	Square
1	1	26	676	51	2601	76	5776
2	4	27	729	52	2704	77	5929
3	9	28	784	53	2809	78	6084
4	16	29	841	54	2916	79	6241
5	25	30	900	55	3025	80	6400
6	36	31	961	56	3136	81	6561
7	49	32	1024	57	3249	82	6724
8	64	33	1089	58	3364	83	6889
9	81	34	1156	59	3481	84	7056
10	100	35	1225	60	3600	85	7225
11	121	36	1296	61	3721	86	7396
12	144	37	1369	62	3844	87	7569
13	169	38	1444	63	3969	88	7744
14	196	39	1521	64	4096	89	7921
15	225	40	1600	65	4225	90	8100
16	256	41	1681	66	4356	91	8281
17	289	42	1764	67	4489	92	8464
18	324	43	1849	68	4624	93	8649
19	361	44	1936	69	4761	94	8836
20	400	45	2025	70	4900	95	9025
21	441	46	2116	71	5041	96	9216
22	484	47	2209	72	5184	97	9409
23	529	48	2304	73	5329	98	9604
24	576	49	2401	74	5476	99	9801
25	625	50	2500	75	5625	100	10,000

Table 2 / Square Roots of Integers from 1 to 100

Exact square roots are shown in red. For the others, rational approximations are given correct to three decimal places.

Number	Positive Square Root	Number	Positive Square Root	Number	Positive Square Root	Number	Positive Square Root
N	$\sqrt{N}$	N	$\sqrt{N}$	N	$\sqrt{N}$	N	$\sqrt{N}$
1	1	26	5.099	51	7.141	76	8.718
2	1.414	27	5.196	52	7.211	77	8.775
3	1.732	28	5.292	53	7.280	78	8.832
4	2	29	5.385	54	7.348	79	8.888
5	2.236	30	5.477	55	7.416	80	8.944
6	2.449	31	5.568	56	7.483	81	9
7	2.646	32	5.657	57	7.550	82	9.055
8	2.828	33	5.745	58	7.616	83	9.110
9	3	34	5.831	59	7.681	84	9.165
10	3.162	35	5.916	60	7.746	85	9.220
11	3.317	36	6	61	7.810	86	9.274
12	3.464	37	6.083	62	7.874	87	9.327
13	3.606	38	6.164	63	7.937	88	9.381
14	3.742	39	6.245	64	8	89	9.434
15	3.873	40	6.325	65	8.062	90	9.487
16	4	41	6.403	66	8.124	91	9.539
17	4.123	42	6.481	67	8.185	92	9.592
18	4.243	43	6.557	68	8.246	93	9.644
19	4.359	44	6.633	69	8.307	94	9.695
20	4.472	45	6.708	70	8.367	95	9.747
21	4.583	46	6.782	71	8.426	96	9.798
22	4.690	47	6.856	72	8.485	97	9.849
23	4.796	48	6.928	73	8.544	98	9.899
24	4.899	49	7	74	8.602	99	9.950
25	5	50	7.071	75	8.660	100	10

Table 3 / *Trigonometric Ratios*

Angle	Sine	Cosine	Tangent	Angle	Sine	Cosine	Tangent
1°	.0175	.9998	.0175	46°	.7193	.6947	1.0355
2°	.0349	.9994	.0349	47°	.7314	.6820	1.0724
3°	.0523	.9986	.0524	48°	.7431	.6691	1.1106
4°	.0698	.9976	.0699	49°	.7547	.6561	1.1504
5°	.0872	.9962	.0875	50°	.7660	.6428	1.1918
6°	.1045	.9945	.1051	51°	.7771	.6293	1.2349
7°	.1219	.9925	.1228	52°	.7880	.6157	1.2799
8°	.1392	.9903	.1405	53°	.7986	.6018	1.3270
9°	.1564	.9877	.1584	54°	.8090	.5878	1.3764
10°	.1736	.9848	.1763	55°	.8192	.5736	1.4281
11°	.1908	.9816	.1944	56°	.8290	.5592	1.4826
12°	.2079	.9781	.2126	57°	.8387	.5446	1.5399
13°	.2250	.9744	.2309	58°	.8480	.5299	1.6003
14°	.2419	.9703	.2493	59°	.8572	.5150	1.6643
15°	.2588	.9659	.2679	60°	.8660	.5000	1.7321
16°	.2756	.9613	.2867	61°	.8746	.4848	1.8040
17°	.2924	.9563	.3057	62°	.8829	.4695	1.8807
18°	.3090	.9511	.3249	63°	.8910	.4540	1.9626
19°	.3256	.9455	.3443	64°	.8988	.4384	2.0503
20°	.3420	.9397	.3640	65°	.9063	.4226	2.1445
21°	.3584	.9336	.3839	66°	.9135	.4067	2.2460
22°	.3746	.9272	.4040	67°	.9205	.3907	2.3559
23°	.3907	.9205	.4245	68°	.9272	.3746	2.4751
24°	.4067	.9135	.4452	69°	.9336	.3584	2.6051
25°	.4226	.9063	.4663	70°	.9397	.3420	2.7475
26°	.4384	.8988	.4877	71°	.9455	.3256	2.9042
27°	.4540	.8910	.5095	72°	.9511	.3090	3.0777
28°	.4695	.8829	.5317	73°	.9563	.2924	3.2709
29°	.4848	.8746	.5543	74°	.9613	.2756	3.4874
30°	.5000	.8660	.5774	75°	.9659	.2588	3.7321
31°	.5150	.8572	.6009	76°	.9703	.2419	4.0108
32°	.5299	.8480	.6249	77°	.9744	.2250	4.3315
33°	.5446	.8387	.6494	78°	.9781	.2079	4.7046
34°	.5592	.8290	.6745	79°	.9816	.1908	5.1446
35°	.5736	.8192	.7002	80°	.9848	.1736	5.6713
36°	.5878	.8090	.7265	81°	.9877	.1564	6.3138
37°	.6018	.7986	.7536	82°	.9903	.1392	7.1154
38°	.6157	.7880	.7813	83°	.9925	.1219	8.1443
39°	.6293	.7771	.8098	84°	.9945	.1045	9.5144
40°	.6428	.7660	.8391	85°	.9962	.0872	11.4301
41°	.6561	.7547	.8693	86°	.9976	.0698	14.3007
42°	.6691	.7431	.9004	87°	.9986	.0523	19.0811
43°	.6820	.7314	.9325	88°	.9994	.0349	28.6363
44°	.6947	.7193	.9657	89°	.9998	.0175	57.2900
45°	.7071	.7071	1.0000				

Introducing Explorations

The following sixteen pages provide you with activities for exploring various concepts of algebra. The activities give you a chance to discover for yourself some of the ideas presented in this textbook. They carefully lead you to interesting conclusions and applications; they will make some of the abstract concepts of algebra easier to understand.

Some of the questions in these activities are open-ended. They ask you to describe, explain, analyze, design, summarize, write, predict, check, generalize, and recognize patterns. Often there is more than one correct way to answer a question. You can work on these activities by yourself or in small groups. You will need to use the materials listed below.

With these explorations we hope you enjoy exploring algebra!

Use With Lessons	Titles	Materials	Pages
1-8	Exploring Density of Real Numbers	calculator	685
2-3	Exploring Addition of Integers	integer chips (2 colors)	686
2-4	Exploring Subtraction of Integers	integer chips (2 colors)	687
3-1	Exploring Ways to Solve Equations	balance, washers, envelopes	688
4-5, 4-6	Exploring Monomial and Binomial Products	algebra tiles	689–690
5-7	Exploring Polynomial Factors	algebra tiles	691
6-4	Exploring GCF and LCM	none needed	692
7-2	Exploring Applications of Proportions	phone book, computer	693
8-4	Exploring Linear Equations	computer or graphing calculator	694
9-1	Exploring Systems of Linear Equations	computer or graphing calculator	695
10-2	Exploring Properties of Equality and Order	none needed	696
11-2	Exploring Decimals	calculator	697
11-6	Exploring Irrational Numbers	ruler, protractor, geoboard and rubber bands or dot paper	698–699
12-4	Exploring Quadratic Equations	computer or graphing calculator	700

Explorations

Exploring Density of Real Numbers

Use with Lesson 1-8

In this activity, you will use a calculator in finding a number between two given numbers.

Explore by Multiplying

1. **a.** Choose a positive integer less than 10 and use your calculator to multiply it by $\frac{1}{2}$. Graph the number you chose and the product on a number line.
   b. Multiply the product by $\frac{1}{2}$, and graph it on the same number line.
   c. Continue the process three more times.
   d. Describe what would happen if you continued this process. Will you reach zero? If so, when? If not, why not?   No. The product approaches, but never reaches, zero.

2. Repeat Exercise **1**, but choose a negative integer greater than ⁻10.

3. What can you conclude from these explorations?   This process of multiplying by $\frac{1}{2}$ produces numbers that approach zero from *either* side of zero on the number line.

Explore by Finding Averages

4. **a.** Choose two integers between 5 and 15, and find their average. Graph the numbers you chose and their average on a number line.
   b. Find the average of the larger number and the average you found in part **a.** Graph the result.
   c. Find the average of the larger number and the average you found in part **b.** Graph the result.
   d. Describe what you observe.   The average approaches, but never reaches, the larger number.

5. **a.** Choose two numbers between 5 and 15, different from those you chose in Exercise **4a.** Find their average. Graph the numbers and their average.
   b. Repeat steps **4b–4c,** but this time use the smaller number and the resulting average each time. Describe what you observe.   The average approaches, but never reaches, the smaller number.

Use What You Have Observed

6. **a.** How can you find a number between 0 and any other number x?   Multiply x by $\frac{1}{2}$.
   b. How can you find a number between any two given numbers?   Find their average.

7. A set of numbers is said to be **dense** if, for any two numbers in the set, we can find another number that is between those two numbers and is also a member of that set. Are these sets of numbers dense? Explain your answer.
   a. All proper fractions   Yes
   b. All integers   No

Explorations   **685**

Purpose
To have students explore the property of density of real numbers.

Materials
calculator

Background
Encourage students to find averages beyond the number of times specified to get an increased sense of how this process can generate infinitely many numbers between any two numbers.

For Discussion
Have students classify all sets of numbers with which they are familiar (whole numbers, integers, rationals, etc.) as dense or not dense.

Additional Answers

1. Sample answer: 8, 4, 2, 1, 0.5, 0.25
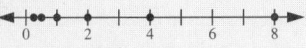

2. Sample answer: −6, −3, −1.5, −0.75, −0.375, −0.1875

4. Sample answer: 7 and 12; averages: 9.5, 10.75, 11.375

5. Sample answer: 7 and 13; averages: 10, 8.5, 7.75
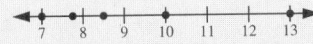

7. **a.** By averaging you can always find a fraction between two fractions.
   b. No integer exists between consecutive integers.

Purpose

To have students use a physical model to explore addition of integers.

Materials

at least 10 each of two different colors of plastic chips, tiles, or construction paper cutouts

Background

This activity leads to discovery of some of the rules for addition on p. 54. It also serves as a prerequisite activity for the next exploration, which uses the same model for subtraction.

Cooperative Learning

Students can work in small groups. As one student performs part of the activity, another can draw the steps, while a third records the numerical results. They can then change roles.

Further Exploration

Students can use chips to explore that addition is commutative and associative.

Additional Answers

1. a.
$1 + (-1) = 0$

b.

$-2 + 2 = 0$

d.

$3 + (-3) = 0$

(continued on p. 687)

686

Exploring Addition of Integers

Use before Lesson 2-3

In this activity, you will use two different colors of plastic chips to help you develop rules for adding different combinations of positive and negative numbers. Each chip will have an absolute value of 1. Choose one color for positive integers and one color for negative integers. Here, one blue chip represents +1 and one red chip represents −1.

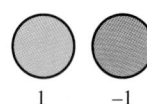
1   −1

Explore the Property of Opposites

1. a. Use the chips to represent $1 + (-1)$.
   b. Use the chips to represent $(-2) + 2$.
   c. What integer is represented by the sum of the chips in each part above? 0
   d. Use three pairs of chips to represent zero.
   e. Describe a general way to show that the sum of an integer and its opposite is zero, using the chips. Use an equal number of red chips and blue chips.

Explore the Identity Property of Addition

2. a. What sum is represented by the chips shown at the right? $2 + 0$
   b. What integer is represented by the sum of the chips in part **a**? 2
   c. Use both red and blue chips to represent the number −2.

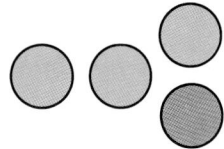

Explore Addition

3. a. Use chips to represent the sums $2 + 1$ and $-2 + (-1)$.
   b. Think about the signs of the addends and also the signs of their sums. What do you notice? The signs of the addends and their sums are the same.
   c. Can you think of an example in which adding two numbers having the same sign yields a sum with the opposite sign? No

4. In both cases in Exercise **3**, the signs of the addends were the same. What happens when the signs of the addends are different?
   a. Use chips to represent $1 + (-2)$ and $2 + (-1)$, and find the sums.
   b. What is the sign of the sum in each case? The first is negative, the second positive.
   c. How do the absolute values and signs of the addends affect the sign of the sum?
   The sign of the number with greater absolute value determines the sign of the sum.

Use What You Have Observed

5. Use your observations to find each sum. Then check by using colored chips.
   a. $3 + 5$ 8   **b.** $-3 + (-5)$ −8 **c.** $-3 + 5$ 2   **d.** $3 + (-5)$ −2

Exploring Subtraction of Integers

Use before Lesson 2-4

On the previous page, you used colored chips to model addition of integers.
This activity builds on what you have learned to explore subtraction.

Explore Subtraction

1. Use the chips to find the difference $4 - 3$.

   a. Start with 4 blue chips.
   b. Take away 3 blue chips.
   c. Count the remaining chips. How many are left? 1
   d. Write a number sentence that expresses your result. $4 - 3 = 1$

2. Use the chips to find the difference $-4 - (-3)$. Follow steps similar to those
   in Exercise **1.** Start with 4 red chips; take away 3 red chips; 1 red chip remains;
   $$-4 - (-3) = -1$$

3. Use the chips to find the difference $4 - (-3)$.
   a. In terms of chips, how can you represent $4 - (-3)$? by removing 3 red
   chips from 4 blue chips
   b. Start with 4 blue chips.
   c. There are no red chips to remove. Add zero by using a combination of
      3 blue chips and 3 red chips.
   d. Take away 3 red chips. Name the chips that remain. There are 7 blue chips left.
   e. Write a number sentence that expresses the result. $4 - (-3) = 7$

4. Use the chips to find the difference $-4 - 3$.
   a. What chips will you start with? 4 red chips
   b. What chips must you take away? 3 blue chips
   c. What combination of red and blue chips will you add in order to take
      away the chips you need to? 3 pairs of red and blue chips
   d. Take away the necessary chips. Name the chips that remain. There are 7 red chips left.
   e. Write a number sentence that expresses the result. $-4 - 3 = -7$

Use What You Have Observed

5. Use chips to compute and compare $-5 - (-3)$ with $-3 - (-5)$. $-5 - (-3) = -2$ (2 red chips); $-3 - (-5) = 2$ (2 blue chips)

6. Use chips to find each sum and difference.
   a. $4 - 3$ and $4 + (-3)$ 1, 1   b. $4 - (-2)$ and $4 + 2$ 6, 6
   c. $4 - 5$ and $4 + (-5)$ −1, −1   d. $-5 - 3$ and $-5 + (-3)$ −8, −8

7. Analyze your answers in Exercise **6,** and look for a pattern. Is the following
   statement true or false? "Subtracting one number, b, from another, a, gives
   the same result as adding the opposite of b to a." true

Explorations **687**

Purpose
To have students use a
physical model to explore
subtraction of integers.

Materials
at least 10 each of two different colors of plastic chips

Background
This activity builds on the
previous one. In Exercise **5,**
some students may not recognize that only 2 more red
chips (with 2 blue chips)
need be introduced for the
second subtraction. If students introduce 5 red chips
(with 5 blue chips), guide
them to see that after removing 5 red chips, any pair
of 1 red and 1 blue chip
may also be removed be-
cause its sum is zero.
  Exercise **5** can be used to
discuss that subtraction is
not commutative.

Additional Answers
5.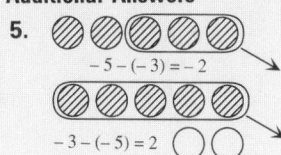

Additional Answers, p. 686

2. c.

3. a.

4. a.

687

Purpose

To use physical models to solve equations by using subtraction or addition.

Materials

double pan balance, metal washers, envelopes

Background

Ahead of time, prepare one envelope marked **X**, containing 7 washers, and one marked **Y**, containing 11 washers, for each student or group of students. Alternatively, small identical boxes or bags and pennies can be used.

Point out that it is necessary to use the empty envelope to balance the envelope containing the unknown quantity of washers.

Encourage students to write equations for each step in Exercises **4** and **5**.

Additional Answers

1. a. The pans balance;
   $6 = 6$
b. The pans balance; 8;
   $6 + 2 = 6 + 2$, or $8 = 8$
c. The pans balance; 5;
   $8 - 3 = 8 - 3$, or
   $5 = 5$
d. The pans do not balance; $5 - 1 \neq 5 - 2$, or
   $4 \neq 3$, or $4 > 3$
e. If the same number of washers is added to or subtracted from each pan, the pans stay in balance.

2. b. 3; the envelope marked **X** now balances the empty envelope and the washers on the other pan.

(continued on p. 689)

688

Exploring Ways to Solve Equations

Use before Lesson 3-1

In this activity, you will use a double pan balance to explore properties of equality and to solve equations. Each pan of the balance represents one side of the equation.

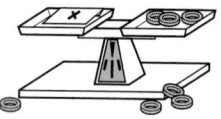

Explore Properties of Equality

1. a. Start with the empty pans in balance. Place 6 metal washers on each pan. What do you notice? Write an equation represented by the balance.
   b. Add 2 more washers to each pan. What happens? How many washers are on each side? Write an equation represented by the balance.
   c. Remove 3 washers from each pan. What happens? How many washers are on each side? Write an equation represented by the balance.
   d. Remove 1 washer from the left pan and 2 washers from the right pan. What happens? Write an inequality represented by the balance.
   e. What conclusion can you draw from these results?

Explore by Subtracting

2. For this activity your teacher will give you an envelope marked X, which contains some washers, and an empty envelope.
   a. Start with the empty pans in balance. Place envelope X, together with 3 washers, on one pan. Place the empty envelope, together with 10 washers, on the other pan. What happens? Write an equation.   The pans balance; $x + 3 = 10$
   b. Remove 1 washer from each pan until only envelope X is left on one pan. How many washers did you remove from each side of the balance? Describe the results.
   c. How many washers are on the side with the empty envelope? How many washers must be in envelope X? Write an equation.   7; 7; $x = 7$

Explore by Adding

3. For this activity your teacher will give you an envelope marked Y, which contains some washers, and an empty envelope.
   a. Start with the empty pans in balance. Without looking inside, remove 4 washers from envelope Y, and place it on one pan. Place 7 washers and the empty envelope on the other pan. What happens? Write an equation.
   b. Replace the 4 washers you removed from envelope Y. Add an equal number of washers to the other side. Write an equation. $y = 11$

Use What You Have Observed

4. Explain how you can solve each equation.
   a. $x + 6 = 10$ **b.** $y - 6 = 7$ **c.** $x + 75 = 203$ **d.** $y - 173 = 511$

Exploring Monomial and Binomial Products

Use before Lessons 4-5 and 4-6

In this activity, you will use square and rectangular tiles like those shown below to represent products of monomials and binomials.

x-by-x tile:

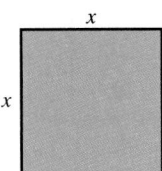

Area = x^2

1-by-x tile:

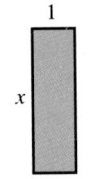

Area = x

1-by-1 tile:

Area = 1

Explore the Product of a Monomial and a Binomial

1. Build a rectangle by placing one 1-by-x tile next to one x-by-x tile as shown.
   a. What *monomial* represents the length of one side of the rectangle? x
      What *binomial* represents the length of one side of the rectangle? x + 1
   b. Express the area of the rectangle as the product of a monomial and a binomial. x(x + 1)
   c. What is the area of the x-by-x tile? x^2
      What is the area of the 1-by-x tile? x
   d. How is the area of the rectangle related to the areas of the tiles? The area of the rectangle is the sum of the areas of the tiles.
   e. Write an expression that shows the relationship described in part **d.** x(x + 1) = x^2 + x

2. Use tiles as described below to find the product 2x(x + 2).
   a. Place two x-by-x tiles and two 1-by-x tiles together as shown.
   b. Complete the rectangle by including two more 1-by-x tiles.
   c. What are the lengths of the sides of the rectangle? 2x, x + 2
   d. Use the expressions from part **c** to express the area of the rectangle. 2x(x + 2)
   e. Find the sum of the areas of the tiles that form the rectangle. $2x^2$ + 4x
   f. What is the product 2x(x + 2)? $2x^2$ + 4x

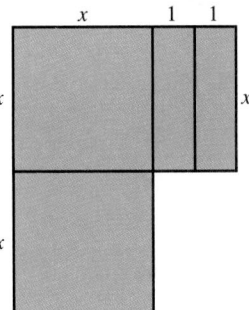

(Continued on next page.)

Explorations   **689**

Purpose
To use a physical model to introduce finding the product of a monomial and a binomial and the product of two binomials. Use before or with Lessons 4-5 and 4-6.

Materials
square tiles of two dimensions—x by x and 1 by 1—and rectangular tiles of dimension 1 by x

Background
If tiles are not available, provide students with templates and have them cut tiles from construction or graph paper ahead of time. (See p. T97.) Lead students to understand that this activity provides a connection between geometric and algebraic concepts. Exercises **1, 2, 4a–b,** and **5** can be used with Lesson 4-5, whereas Exercises **3, 4c–d,** and **6** can be used with Lesson 4-6.

Cooperative Learning
Students can work in groups of 2, 3, or 4, taking turns and/or discussing which tiles to choose for building the rectangles.

Additional Answers, p. 688
3. a. The pans balance;
      y − 4 = 7
4. a. Subtract 6 from each side of the equation.
   b. Add 6.
   c. Subtract 75.
   d. Add 173.

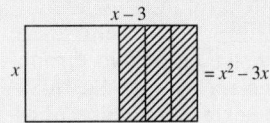 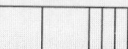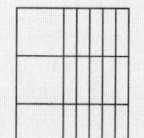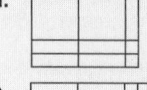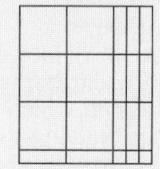

Exploring Monomial and Binomial Products

Use before Lessons 4-5 and 4-6 (continued)

Explore the Product of Two Binomials

3. Use tiles as described below to find the product of $x + 1$ and $x + 3$.

a. Place one x-by-x tile and four 1-by-x tiles as shown.

b. What tiles must you include to complete the rectangle?   three 1-by-1 tiles

c. What are the lengths of the sides of the rectangle? $x + 1$, $x + 3$

d. What is the sum of the areas of the tiles? $x^2 + 4x + 3$

e. What is the product $(x + 1)(x + 3)$? $x^2 + 4x + 3$

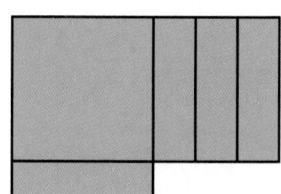

Use What You Have Observed

4. Write the product represented by each tile model. Then find the product.

a.
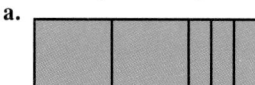
$x(2x + 3) = 2x^2 + 3x$

b.
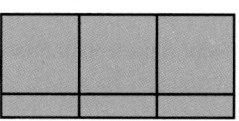
$3x(x + 1) = 3x^2 + 3x$

c.
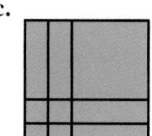
$(x + 2)(x + 2) = x^2 + 4x + 4$

d.
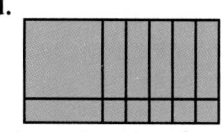
$(x + 1)(x + 5) = x^2 + 6x + 5$

5. Find each product by using tiles. Refer to Exercises **1** and **2** as a guide.

a. $x(2x + 3)$
$2x^2 + 3x$

b. $3x(2x + 1)$
$6x^2 + 3x$

c. $(x + 5)3x$
$3x^2 + 15x$

6. Find each product by using tiles. Refer to Exercise **3** as a guide.

a. $(x + 2)(2x + 1)$
$2x^2 + 5x + 2$

b. $(2x + 3)(3x + 1)$
$6x^2 + 11x + 3$

c. $(x + 3)^2$
$x^2 + 6x + 9$

Exploring Polynomial Factors

Use before Lesson 5-7

In this activity, you will use the square and rectangular tiles from the previous exploration to find the factors of polynomials.

Explore Monomial Factors

1. Represent $x^2 + 3x$ with one x-by-x tile and three 1-by-x tiles as shown.

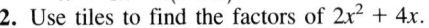

  a. Arrange the tiles to form a rectangle. What is the area of this rectangle in terms of the areas of the tiles? $x^2 + 3x$

  b. What is the length of the rectangle? $x + 3$
  What is the width of the rectangle? x

  c. Express the area of the rectangle as the product of its length and width. $x(x + 3)$

  d. Write an expression that shows the factors of $x^2 + 3x$.
  $x^2 + 3x = x(x + 3)$

2. Use tiles to find the factors of $2x^2 + 4x$.   two x-by-x tiles and

  a. What tiles can you use to represent the given expression?   four 1-by-x tiles

  b. Arrange the tiles to form a rectangle that has a width of x. What is the length of the rectangle? $2x + 4$

  c. Write an expression that shows these factors of the given expression. $2x^2 + 4x = x(2x + 4)$

  d. Rearrange the tiles to form a different rectangle. What are the lengths of the sides of this rectangle? $2x, x + 2$

  e. Write an expression that shows another way to factor the given expression.
  $2x^2 + 4x = 2x(x + 2)$

Explore Binomial Factors

3. Use tiles to factor $x^2 + 7x + 12$.

  a. What tiles will you start with?   One x-by-x tile, seven 1-by-x tiles, and twelve 1-by-1 tiles

  b. Arrange the tiles to form a rectangle.

  c. What are the lengths of the sides of the rectangle? $x + 4, x + 3$

  d. What are the factors of $x^2 + 7x + 12$? $(x + 4)(x + 3)$

Use What You Have Observed

4. Write the polynomial and its factors represented by the tiles.

  a. 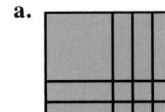   **b.** 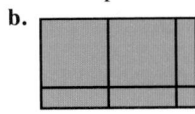   **c.**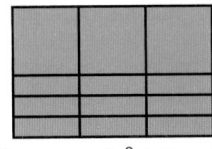

$x^2 + 5x + 6 = (x + 3)(x + 2)$ $2x^2 + 3x + 1 = (2x + 1)(x + 1)$ $3x^2 + 9x = 3x(x + 3)$

5. Use tiles to find the factors of each polynomial.

  a. $2x^2 + x$ $x(2x + 1)$ **b.** $x^2 + 2x + 1$ $(x + 1)^2$ **c.** $3x^2 + 7x + 2$ $(3x + 1)(x + 2)$

Purpose

To use a physical model to introduce the monomial and binomial factors of certain polynomials. Use as an activity before Lesson 5-7.

Materials

square tiles of two dimensions—x by x and 1 by 1—and rectangular tiles of dimension 1 by x

Background

In Exercise **2**, point out that the solution in part **e** is said to be *factored completely*. The solution in part **c** is not factored completely since one of the factors, $2x + 4$, is factorable further. Ask students whether or not it makes sense that a polynomial can have several different factors. Have students think about a number and its factors (for example, $12 = 3 \cdot 4$, and $12 = 2 \cdot 6$).

Cooperative Learning

Students can work in groups of 3 or 4, taking turns and/or discussing which tiles to choose for building the rectangles.

Additional Answers

3. b.

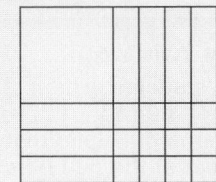

Exploring GCF and LCM

Use before Lesson 6-4

In this activity, you will explore the connection between the factored forms of the greatest common factor (GCF) and the least common multiple (LCM) of two numbers. You will need to use the following definitions:

To find the GCF and LCM of two numbers, first find the prime factorization of each number.
The **GCF** is the product of the *smaller* powers of each *common* prime factor.
The **LCM** is the product of the *larger* powers of each prime factor.

Explore Using Whole Numbers

1. **a.** Find the factored form of the GCF of 18 and 24 as described above. $2 \cdot 3$
   b. What prime factors of 18 and 24 are *not* included in the GCF? $2^3, 3^2$
   c. Find the factored form of the LCM of 18 and 24 as described above. $2^3 \cdot 3^2$
   d. What prime factors of 18 and 24 are *not* included in the LCM? 2, 3
   e. What do you observe about your answers to parts **a–d**? The factors not included in the GCF form the LCM, and those not included in the LCM form the GCF.
2. **a.** Find the factored form of the product of 18 and 24. $2^4 \cdot 3^3$
   b. How is the product related to the GCF and LCM? The product of the two numbers is equal to the product of the GCF and the LCM.

Explore Using Algebraic Expressions

3. **a.** Using the following two expressions $N = ab^2c^3$ and $P = a^2bc^2d$, find the GCF of N and P. abc^2
   b. What factors of N and P are not included in the GCF? $a^2b^2c^3d$
   c. Find the factored form of the LCM of N and P. $a^2b^2c^3d$
   d. What factors of N and P are not included in the LCM? abc^2
   e. What do you observe about your answers to parts **a–d**? The factors not included in the GCF form the LCM and those not included in the LCM form the GCF.
4. **a.** Find the factored form of the product of N and P. $a^3b^3c^5d$
   b. How is the product related to the GCF and LCM? The product of the two expressions is equal to the product of the GCF and the LCM.

Use What You Have Observed

5. Find the GCF of 48 and 60. Then use the GCF and the product of 48 and 60 to find the LCM of these two numbers. 12; 240

6. For fractions, the least common denominator (LCD) is the LCM of the denominators of the fractions. Use the method of Exercise **5** to find the LCD for each pair of fractions.

   a. $\frac{1}{4}, \frac{1}{6}$ 12   **b.** $\frac{7}{12}, \frac{5}{18}$ 36   **c.** $\frac{3}{25}, \frac{4}{15}$ 75

Purpose

To have students discover the relationship between the product of any two numbers and the GCF and LCM of those numbers. Students also develop a way to find the LCD by first finding the GCF.

Background

Students have already considered finding GCFs by using prime factorization. (See pages 186 and 190.) The concept of LCM will be used in the upcoming lesson when finding LCDs.

It might be useful to review the concepts of powers (p. 141) and of multiples (p. 78), which should be familiar to students from earlier courses. The *least common multiple* is the smallest number that contains the two given numbers as factors. Thus 12 is the LCM of 3 and 4.

Students should be encouraged to think about why the process used in the exploration works with two numbers but not with three. (See Further Exploration.)

For Exercise **6**, point out that the method provides a nice shortcut for finding an LCD if you can easily determine the GCF by inspection.

Further Exploration

Have students examine sets of three numbers to see if the same principle (that the product of the numbers is equal to the product of the GCF and the LCM) holds true. What must be true of the three numbers for this principle to hold true? The numbers must have no common factors.

Exploring Applications of Proportions

Use with Lesson 7-2

In this activity, you will use real data or randomly generated data along with proportions to make estimates in real-life situations.

Explore Using Real Data

1. Use a local phone book for the data in this exercise.   Results will vary.
   a. Use the number of listings in one column to write and solve a proportion to estimate the number of listings in the entire book.
   b. Count the listings on one page that use only initials for first names.
   c. Find a ratio that represents the following: $\dfrac{\text{number of listings with initials}}{\text{number of listings}}$
   d. Use a proportion to estimate the number of listings in the entire phone book that use initials.

Explore Using Randomly-Generated Data

2. Since it is impractical to identify every member of a given wildlife population, population samples are frequently used to make estimates of entire populations. Follow the example below.
   a. Use a computer to generate 200 random numbers from 1 to 1000.
   b. Generate a second set of 200 random numbers from 1 to 1000.
   c. Assume the first set of numbers represents the initial portion of a wildlife population that was captured, tagged, and released. Assume the second set of numbers represents a second captured portion. Based on the two sets of numbers, how many animals were captured both times?   Answers will vary (but should be approx. 40).
   d. Parts **a–c** are a model of a capture-recapture method used to estimate wildlife populations. This method uses the following proportion:

   $$\frac{\text{number of animals initially tagged and released}}{\text{total population of animals}} = \frac{\text{number of tagged animals in second sample}}{\text{total number of animals in second sample}}$$

   Use this proportion to find how many animals you should have expected to capture both times in part **c**. $\dfrac{200}{1000} = \dfrac{x}{200}$; $x = 40$ animals

Use What You Have Observed

3. To estimate how many fish are in Lake Rainbow, fish-and-wildlife rangers captured, tagged, and released 100 fish. Later, they captured a second sample of 100 fish and found that 8 of them had been previously tagged. What is the fish population of Lake Rainbow? $\dfrac{100}{p} = \dfrac{8}{100}$; $p = 1250$ fish

4. Design a method for determining how many students in your school participate in a certain extracurricular activity.

Explorations   **693**

Exploring Linear Equations

Use before Lesson 8-4

In this activity, you will use a graphing calculator or a computer with graphing software to graph linear equations. You will be able to watch the lines change as you change values of different parts of the equation.

For $y = mx + b$, choose a value for m and choose a value for b.

Explore Changes in the Value of m

1. **a.** Use the software to graph the equation you selected above.
   b. Increase the value of m by 1, and graph this equation.
   c. Increase the value of m by 1 several more times. Graph each equation.
   d. How are the graphs alike? How are they different? How are the equations alike? How are they different?

2. **a.** Use the software to graph the original equation you selected above.
   b. Decrease the value of m by 1 several times. Graph each equation.
   c. How are the graphs alike? How are they different? How are the equations alike? How are they different?

3. Write a statement that summarizes your results in Exercises **1** and **2**. For an equation of the form $y = mx + b$, the value of m determines the slant, or slope, of the line.

Explore Changes in the Value of b

4. **a.** Use the software to graph the original equation you selected above.
   b. Increase the value of b by 1 several times. Graph each equation.
   c. How are the graphs alike? different? How are the equations alike? different?

5. **a.** Use the software to graph the original equation you selected above.
   b. Decrease the value of b by 1 several times. Graph each equation.
   c. How are the graphs alike? different? How are the equations alike? different?

6. Write a statement that summarizes your results in Exercises **4** and **5**. For an equation of the form $y = mx + b$, b determines the point $(0, b)$ on the y-axis that the line goes through.

Use What You Have Observed

7. How are the graphs of $y = 2x + 5$ and $y = 3x + 5$ related? First make a prediction; then graph the lines to check. They both pass through the point $(0, 5)$, but the second line would be steeper.

8. How are the graphs of $y = 2x + 5$ and $y = 2x + 1$ related? First make a prediction; then graph the lines to check. They are parallel (have the same slope); the first line intersects the y-axis at $(0, 5)$; the second one intersects the y-axis at $(0, 1)$.

Exploring Systems of Linear Equations

Use before Lesson 9-1

In this activity, you will use a graphing calculator or a computer with graphing software to graph more than one linear equation on the same pair of axes. You will be able to see how the graphs are related to each other as you form new equations by changing values of different parts of the equations.

For $ax + by = c$, choose a value for a, for b, and for c. For example, you might let $a = 1$, $b = -2$, and $c = \frac{1}{2}$.

Explore Changes in the Value of c

1. **a.** Use the software to graph the equation you selected above.
   b. Choose a different value for c, and graph this equation on the same set of axes. How are the two graphs related?   The lines are parallel.
   c. Repeat step **b** four more times. Summarize the results of changing the value of c.   The lines are parallel to the original line.

Explore Multiplying by a Constant

2. **a.** Use the software to graph the original equation you selected above.
   b. Choose any number and multiply each term of the original equation by this number; then graph this equation on the same set of axes. How are the two graphs related?   The lines are the same; the graphs coincide.
   c. Repeat step **b** four more times. Summarize the results of multiplying each term of the original equation by a different constant each time.
   The lines coincide with the original line.

Explore Changes in the Value of a or b

3. **a.** Use the software to graph the original equation you selected above.
   b. Choose a different value for a only or for b only, and graph this equation on the same set of axes. How are the graphs related?   The lines intersect in one point.
   c. Is the point of intersection a solution of the original equation? Is it a solution of the new equation?   yes; yes
   d. Repeat step **b** four more times. Summarize the results of changing the value of a or b.   The lines all intersect the original line in one point.

Use What You Have Observed

4. Explain how the graphs of $2x - 3y = -\frac{1}{2}$ and $2x - 3y = 0$ are related.
   They are parallel. Only the value of c is different in each.
5. Explain how the graphs of $-3x + y = -2$ and $6x - 2y = 4$ are related.
   The graphs coincide. The first equation multiplied by -2 yields the second equation.
6. Explain how the graphs of $3x + 2y = 5$ and $3x + 4y = 5$ are related.
   They intersect in one point. The value of b, but not a, is different.

Purpose
To have students discover how the graphs of linear equations may be related.

Materials
graphing calculator or computer with graphing software

Background
Software that displays multiple graphs is best for this activity. Alternatively, printouts or transparencies of individual graphs can be used.
  For software that requires equations to be in the form $y = f(x)$, have students select their values, then solve for y in terms of x.

Discussion Questions

1. If two linear equations are graphed on the same pair of axes, how may the resulting two lines be related? They may be parallel, may coincide, or may intersect

2. For each of the possibilities described above, how many ordered pairs (x, y) are solutions for both lines? parallel: none; coincident: infinitely many; intersecting: one

Additional Answers, p. 694

4. **c.** The lines are parallel (have the same slope); each line goes through a different point $(0, b)$ on the y-axis; the equations are alike except for the value of b.

5. **c.** same as **4c**

Exploring Properties of Equality and Order

Use before Lesson 10-2

In Lesson 2-1, you used three important properties of the equals relationship.

For all real numbers a, b, and c:

Reflexive Property	$a = a$
Symmetric Property	If $a = b$, then $b = a$.
Transitive Property	If $a = b$ and $b = c$, then $a = c$.

Do you think these properties hold true for other relationships? Let's see.

Explore Relationships in Real Situations

1. Think of the relationship "is next door to." Let a, b, and c represent houses. Write how each property would be stated.
   a. reflexive property a is next door to a.
   b. symmetric property   If a is next door to b, then b is next door to a.
   c. transitive property   If a is next door to b and b is next door to c, then a is next door to c.

2. Which of the properties in Exercise 1 hold true in real life? Use the diagram to help you decide.   symmetric

3. Determine which of the properties, if any, hold true for each relationship. Let a, b, and c represent people. Use diagrams to help you decide.
   a. is shorter than   transitive
   b. is the sibling (brother or sister) of   symmetric, transitive
   c. is the classmate of   symmetric
   d. is older than   transitive

Explore Relationships in Mathematics

4. Think of the relationship "is a factor of." Let a, b, and c represent numbers. Write how each property would be stated.   **a.** a is a factor of a.   **b.** If a is a factor of b, then b is a factor of a.
   a. reflexive property   **b.** symmetric property   **c.** transitive property
   c. If a is a factor of b and b is a factor of c, then a is a factor of c.

5. Which of the properties in Exercise 4 hold true?   reflexive and transitive

6. Determine which properties, if any, hold true for each relationship.
   a. is a multiple of   reflexive, transitive
   b. is *not* equal to   symmetric
   c. is less than   transitive
   d. is greater than   transitive

Use What You Have Observed

7. Suppose you want to list 4 people (all of different ages) in increasing order of age. They will not tell you their ages but they will answer "yes" or "no" when asked if each is older than another. What is the fewest possible number of questions needed to list them properly?   5

8. Which property was helpful in solving Exercise 7?   transitive

Exploring Decimals

Use with Lesson 11-2

In this activity you will use a calculator to explore which fractions can be expressed as terminating decimals and which can be expressed as repeating decimals.

Explore Decimal Forms of Unit Fractions

1. a. Use a calculator to find the decimal form of $\frac{1}{2}$ by dividing 1 by 2. 0.5

   b. Find the decimal form of the next ten unit fractions: $0.\overline{3}$, 0.25, 0.2, $0.1\overline{6}$, $0.\overline{142857}$, $\frac{1}{3}, \frac{1}{4}, \frac{1}{5}, \frac{1}{6}, \cdots, \frac{1}{12}$. Make a table of your results. 0.125, $0.\overline{1}$, 0.1, $0.\overline{09}$, $0.08\overline{3}$

   c. Which fractions have decimal forms that terminate? $\frac{1}{2}, \frac{1}{4}, \frac{1}{5}, \frac{1}{8}, \frac{1}{10}$

   d. Which fractions have decimal forms that repeat? $\frac{1}{3}, \frac{1}{6}, \frac{1}{7}, \frac{1}{9}, \frac{1}{11}, \frac{1}{12}$

   e. Find the prime factors of the denominator for each fraction in parts **c** and **d**. Compare the two sets of results.

   f. What seems to be true of the fractions with denominators having prime factors of only 2 and/or 5? Their decimal forms are terminating.

   g. What seems to be true of the fractions with denominators having prime factors other than 2 or 5? Their decimal forms are repeating.

2. Predict whether the decimal form of each fraction will terminate or repeat. Then check with a calculator.

   a. $\frac{1}{13}$ repeats   **b.** $\frac{1}{20}$ terminates **c.** $\frac{1}{27}$ repeats   **d.** $\frac{1}{200}$ terminates

Explore the Fraction Forms of Decimals

3. b. 5, $2^2 \cdot 5^2$, $2^3 \cdot 5$, $2^4 \cdot 5^4$

3. a. Write each of the following decimals in fraction form:
   0.4, 0.29, 0.325, 0.4791 $\frac{4}{10} = \frac{2}{5}, \frac{29}{100}, \frac{325}{1,000} = \frac{13}{40}, \frac{4,791}{10,000}$

   b. Write the prime factorization of each denominator from part **a.**

   c. What do you observe about the factored forms of all the denominators? Does this agree or disagree with your results in Exercise **1**?
   Their only prime factors are 2 and 5; agree

Use What You Have Observed

4. What generalization can you make about the denominators of fractions in simplest form that represent terminating decimals? They are the product of prime factors of 2 and/or 5.

5. What generalization can you make about the denominators of fractions in simplest form that represent repeating decimals? They are the product of prime factors that include at least one prime other than 2 or 5.

Explorations   **697**

Purpose

To lead students to the following generalizations for any fraction in simplest form:

1. If the prime factors of the denominator include only 2 and/or 5, the equivalent decimal is terminating.

2. If the denominator contains some prime factor other than 2 or 5, the equivalent decimal is repeating.

Use with Lesson 11-2.

Materials

calculator

Background

The generalizations above apply only to fractions in simplest form. In $\frac{36}{60}$, which equals 0.6, the denominator has a prime factor other than 2 or 5, but when simplified, as $\frac{3}{5}$, it does not.

Note that students' calculators may round repeating decimals. For example, $\frac{1}{7} = 0.\overline{142857}$ may be displayed as 0.14256. Also, $\frac{1}{11} = 0.\overline{09}$ may be displayed as 0.0909091. Instruct students to do long division if they are unsure whether a decimal repeats or not.

Additional Answers

1. e. c: 2, 2^2, 5, 2^3, $5 \cdot 2$
   d: 3, $3 \cdot 2$, 7, 3^2, 11, $2^2 \cdot 3$
   The denominators for **c** have only 2 and/or 5 as prime factors. The denominators for **d** have other primes besides 2 and 5.

Purpose

To have students explore the relationship between sides of a right triangle and to have them discover two methods of drawing segments with irrational lengths.

Materials

ruler, protractor, geoboard and rubber bands or dot paper

Background

Students will need to use the Pythagorean theorem to find the hypotenuse of each new triangle. Have them leave their answers in radical form rather than using a decimal approximation. This will enable students to see the patterns.

In Exercise **4,** students should generate the Wheel of Theodorus as shown below.

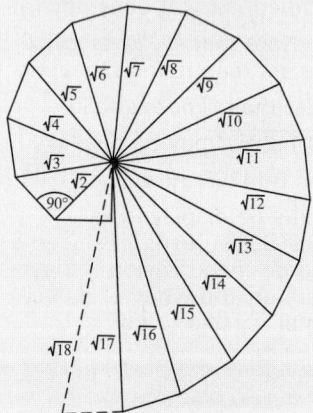

Theodorus of Cyrene (circa 465–399 B.C.) was the mathematics tutor of Plato. He demonstrated that $\sqrt{3}$, $\sqrt{5}$, $\sqrt{6}$, $\sqrt{7}$, $\sqrt{8}$, $\sqrt{10}$, $\sqrt{11}$, $\sqrt{12}$, $\sqrt{13}$, $\sqrt{14}$, $\sqrt{15}$, and $\sqrt{17}$ are irrational. A mystery that mathematical historians have pondered is

Exploring Irrational Numbers

Use after Lesson 11-6

In this activity you will explore relationships between sides of a right triangle and then explore two methods of creating segments having irrational lengths.

Explore the Sides of a Right Triangle

1. **a.** Find the length of the hypotenuse of a right triangle with both legs having a length of 1. $\sqrt{2}$
   b. Using your answer to part **a** as the length of one leg and 1 as the length of the other leg, find the length of the hypotenuse of this new triangle. $\sqrt{3}$
   c. Using your answer to part **b** as the length of one leg and 1 as the length of the other leg, find the length of the hypotenuse of this new triangle. $\sqrt{4} = 2$
   d. Continue this process, finding the length of the hypotenuse of the next five new triangles formed by the procedure above. $\sqrt{5}$, $\sqrt{6}$, $\sqrt{7}$, $\sqrt{8} = 2\sqrt{2}$, $\sqrt{9} = 3$
   e. What pattern do you notice? The new hypotenuse is the square root of the number that is one more than the radicand of the longer leg.

2. **a.** Find the length of the hypotenuse of a right triangle with both legs having a length of 2. $2\sqrt{2}$
   b. Using your answer to part **a** as the length of one leg and 2 as the length of the other leg, find the length of the hypotenuse of this new triangle. $2\sqrt{3}$
   c. Using your answer to part **b** as the length of one leg and 2 as the length of the other leg, find the length of the hypotenuse of this new triangle. $2\sqrt{4} = 4$
   d. Continue this process, finding the length of the hypotenuse of the next five new triangles formed. $2\sqrt{5}$, $2\sqrt{6}$, $2\sqrt{7}$, $2\sqrt{8} = 4\sqrt{2}$, $2\sqrt{9} = 6$
   e. What pattern do you notice? The new hypotenuse is 2 times the square root of the number that is one more than the radicand of the longer leg.

Generalize What You Have Observed

3. If the lengths of the legs of a right triangle are x and $x\sqrt{y}$, what will be the length of the hypotenuse? $x\sqrt{y + 1}$

Explore Using Diagrams

4. **a.** Use a ruler and a protractor to draw a right triangle with legs of length 1 in. each, as shown at the right.
   b. At point A, draw a 1-in. segment that is perpendicular to $\overline{AB}$ and connect the end of this segment to point B to form a new right triangle. Label the new vertex C.

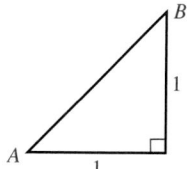

(Continued on next page.)

Exploring Irrational Numbers

Use after Lesson 11-6 (continued)

4. c. What are the lengths of the sides of triangle *ABC*?   1, $\sqrt{2}$, $\sqrt{3}$

  d. At point *C*, draw a 1-in. segment that is perpendicular to $\overline{CB}$ and connect the end of this segment to point *B* to form a new right triangle. Label the new vertex *D*.

  e. What are the lengths of the sides of triangle *CBD*?   1, $\sqrt{3}$, $\sqrt{4} = 2$

  f. Continue drawing new right triangles until your diagram will overlap your first triangle. The diagram you have generated is called the *Wheel of Theodorus*.

  g. What lengths of irrational measure have you constructed? $\sqrt{2}$, $\sqrt{3}$, $\sqrt{5}$, $\sqrt{6}$, $\sqrt{7}$, $\sqrt{8}$, $\sqrt{10}$, $\sqrt{11}$, $\sqrt{12}$, $\sqrt{13}$, $\sqrt{14}$, $\sqrt{15}$, $\sqrt{17}$

Explore Using a Geoboard or Dot Paper

5. a. The right triangle built on the geoboard at the right has legs of length 2 and 3. What is the length of the hypotenuse? $\sqrt{13}$

  b. Use a geoboard or dot paper to build a triangle with legs of length 1 and 2. What is the length of the hypotenuse? Is it irrational? $\sqrt{5}$; yes

  c. Build another triangle with a hypotenuse of irrational length. Give the lengths of the legs and hypotenuse.   Possible answer: 3, 5, $\sqrt{34}$

  d. Build a square with sides of length 2. Then build the diagonal and find its length. $2\sqrt{2}$

  e. Build a rectangle with width of 2 and length of 5. Then build the diagonal and find its length. $\sqrt{29}$

Use What You Have Observed

6. Describe two ways to construct a segment with length $\sqrt{17}$.

7. Can you construct a segment with length $\sqrt{21}$ using a Wheel of Theodorus?   Yes using a geoboard?   No

8. How can you construct a segment with length $5\sqrt{7}$ in.?

---

why Theodorus started with $\sqrt{3}$ and stopped at $\sqrt{17}$. The most prevalent belief is that he started with $\sqrt{3}$ because the irrationality of $\sqrt{2}$ had already been demonstrated by others, notably Pythagoras, and he ended with $\sqrt{17}$ because that is where the construction named after him began to overlap. However, the latter is merely conjecture and the Wheel of Theodorus is not part of the various proofs of irrationality given by Theodorus.

For Discussion

1. Can the Wheel of Theodorus be used to construct a segment for any length $\sqrt{n}$, where *n* is a positive integer? Yes

2. Which irrational lengths can you construct on a geoboard? Any irrational that can be expressed in the form $\sqrt{x^2 + y^2}$ where *x* and *y* are integers

---

Additional Answers

6. Use the Wheel of Theodorus or build a right triangle with legs 1 and 4 on a geoboard.

7. Yes, continue the Wheel of Theodorus until you construct a triangle with hypotenuse of length $\sqrt{21}$; no, since $\sqrt{21}$ cannot be expressed as $\sqrt{x^2 + y^2}$ where *x* and *y* are integers.

8. Begin a new Wheel of Theodorus using a right triangle with legs that measure 5 in. each. Using perpendicular segments of 5 in., draw five more triangles of the wheel. The last hypotenuse yields $5\sqrt{7}$ in.

Purpose

To have students explore the relationship between the discriminant of a quadratic equation and the number of times the graph of the related function crosses the *x*-axis and to estimate roots of equations to the nearest tenth. Use as an activity to be completed in conjunction with Lesson 12-4.

Materials

Computer with graphing software or graphing calculator

Background

Provide instructions for the class on how to use the software or calculator. Encourage students to try three sets of values for each of Exercises **1–3**. For the first set, let *a*, *b*, and *c* have integral values. For the second, let *a*, *b*, and *c* have rational values. For the third, let *a*, *b*, and *c* be any real numbers, including irrational numbers. Students should discover that results regarding the number of roots do not change.

Cooperative Learning

This activity can be done by pairs or small groups of students.

Further Exploration

Have students explore the nature of the roots when $b^2 - 4ac > 0$ and is a perfect square. The values for *a*, *b*, and *c* should be integral. The roots are two rational numbers.

Exploring Quadratic Equations

Use with Lesson 12-4

In this activity, you will use a computer with graphing software or a graphing calculator to graph quadratic equations. You will then change the scale of the graph, if necessary, to find the number of real roots and to estimate these roots.

Explore $ax^2 + bx + c = 0$, where $b^2 - 4ac = 0$

1. a. Choose values for *a*, *b*, and *c* such that $b^2 - 4ac = 0$. For example, let $a = 2$, $b = 4$, and $c = 2$. Graph the resulting equation $y = ax^2 + bx + c$.
   b. In how many points does the graph intersect the *x*-axis?   One
   c. Enlarge the scale on the *x*-axis, if necessary, until you can estimate the root(s) to the nearest tenth.
   d. Repeat steps **a–c** for a different set of values.

Explore $ax^2 + bx + c = 0$, where $b^2 - 4ac > 0$

2. a. Choose values for *a*, *b*, and *c*, such that $b^2 - 4ac > 0$, and graph the resulting equation $y = ax^2 + bx + c$.
   b. In how many points does the graph intersect the *x*-axis?   Two
   c. Enlarge the scale on the *x*-axis, if necessary, until you can estimate these root(s) to the nearest tenth.
   d. Repeat steps **a–c** for a different set of values.

Explore $ax^2 + bx + c = 0$, where $b^2 - 4ac < 0$

3. a. Choose values for *a*, *b*, and *c*, such that $b^2 - 4ac < 0$, and graph the resulting equation $y = ax^2 + bx + c$.
   b. In how many points does the graph intersect the *x*-axis?   None
   c. What can you conclude about the real roots for this equation?   There are none.
   d. Repeat steps **a–c** for a different set of values.

Use What You Have Observed

4. How many real roots does $3x^2 - 8x + 9 = 0$ have? How do you know?
   none, because $b^2 - 4ac < 0$
5. How many real roots does $x^2 - \sqrt{12}x + 3 = 0$ have? How do you know?
   Graph the related equation and estimate the root(s) to the nearest tenth.
   one, because $b^2 - 4ac = 0$; $x \approx 1.7$
6. How many real roots does $3x^2 - 6x + 1 = 0$ have? How do you know?
   Graph the related equation and estimate the root(s) to the nearest tenth.
   two, because $b^2 - 4ac > 0$; $x \approx 1.8$, $x \approx 0.2$
7. Make up quadratic equations that have no roots, one root, and two roots. Graph your equations to verify the number of roots.   Answers may vary.

Portfolio Projects

To make a portfolio, an artist selects a variety of original work to represent the range of his or her skills. Each of the following projects will give you a chance to create a finished product that you will be proud to add to your algebra portfolio.

The projects will help you develop your ability to present and communicate your ideas. They will also help you develop your problem-solving and reasoning abilities as you make connections between what you know and what is new. Your individual insight and creativity will help shape the mathematics you discover.

Let these projects be springboards for further exploration. Feel free to expand them to include new questions or areas of interest that arise. Most of all, have fun!

Hailstone Sequences (Chapter 1)

A *sequence* is an ordered list of numbers. The rules given below generate some interesting sequences, called *hailstone sequences*. Begin with any positive integer n.

Step 1 If the integer is even, then the next number is $\frac{1}{2}n$.

If the integer is odd, then the next number is $3n + 1$.

Step 2 For each number you obtain, repeat step (1) to find the next number.

Here is an example:

Start with $n = 10$.

10 is even, so the next number is $\frac{1}{2}(10) = 5$.

5 is odd, so the next number is $3 \cdot 5 + 1 = 16$.

1. Continue listing numbers of the sequence above until a pattern becomes clear.

2. The diagram at the right represents the sequence in Exercise 1. Draw a similar diagram of the sequence that begins with **(a)** $n = 6$ and **(b)** $n = 18$.

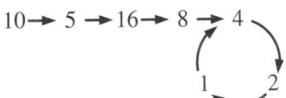

3. Draw diagrams of at least five more hailstone sequences.

4. Investigate the following questions: Does every hailstone sequence end in a loop? If so, do they all end in the same loop? What is the longest stretch of numbers before a hailstone sequence enters a loop? What is the highest value reached by a hailstone sequence?

5. Investigate the consequences of changing the rules for generating a hailstone sequence. Again, begin with any positive integer n. Then:

Divide the integer by 3.

If the remainder is 0, then the next number is $\frac{1}{3}n$.

If the remainder is 1, then the next number is $4n - 1$.

If the remainder is 2, then the next number is $4n + 1$.

Portfolio Projects

In the side columns you will find a combination of hints, comments, answers, and ideas for extensions.

Chapter 1

The name "hailstone" is a whimsical reference to the way the terms of these sequences seem, like hailstones in the sky, to rise and fall chaotically, but eventually land on the ground (reach 1).

1. 8, 4, 2, 1, 4, 2, 1, ... The sequence 4, 2, 1 repeats.

2. **a.** $6 \to 3 \to 10 \to 5 \to$
$16 \to 8 \to 4 \to 2 \to 1 \to$
$4 \to 2 \to 1$

   b. $18 \to 9 \to 28 \to 14 \to$
$7 \to 22 \to 11 \to 34 \to$
$17 \to 52 \to 26 \to 13 \to$
$40 \to 20 \to 10 \to 16 \to$
$8 \to 4 \to 2 \to 1 \to$
$4 \to 2 \to 1$

3. Diagrams will vary.

4. Students should conjecture that every hailstone sequence eventually reaches the loop 4, 2, 1. (No proof of this conjecture has been found, but it has been verified for all integers up to at least 1 trillion.)

   Conjectures about the longest stretch of numbers before looping and about the highest value reached will vary. Have students try starting with $n = 27$. This sequence has 109 terms before entering the loop; the highest term is 9232.

5. Every hailstone sequence using the given rules seems eventually to reach the loop 3, 1. (This sequence has been verified for integers up to at least 100,000.)

Diagramming Operations (Chapter 2)

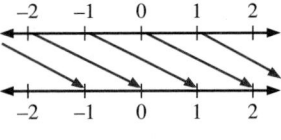

The diagram at the right represents the arithmetic operation "add 2." Notice, for example, that an arrow joins -1 on the upper number line to $-1 + 2$, or 1, on the lower number line. Similarly, an arrow joins each number n on the upper number line to $n + 2$ on the lower number line.

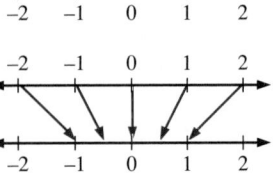

1. Describe the operation represented by the diagram at the right in words and with an algebraic expression.

2. Draw a diagram to represent each operation, and write an algebraic expression to describe the operation.
   a. Subtract 1   **b.** Multiply by 3   **c.** Take the reciprocal

The diagram at the left below represents two operations applied one after the other. The upper and middle number lines represent the first operation, and the middle and lower number lines represent the second operation. The combined operations are represented by the diagram at the right below, in which the middle number line has been eliminated and each pair of arrows has been replaced by one arrow.

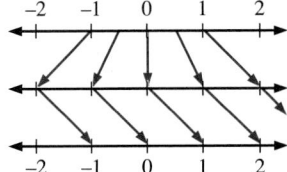

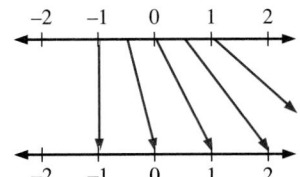

3. **a.** Describe in words the two operations represented by the diagram at the left above. Write an algebraic expression to describe the combined operations represented by the diagram at the right above.

   b. What two operations would you use to *reverse the directions* of the arrows, that is, to move from the lower to the middle and upper number lines? Write an algebraic expression to describe the combined operations represented by the diagram at the right with the arrows reversed.

ISBNs and Check Digits (Chapter 3)

Every book published after 1968 has a 10-digit ISBN, or *International Standard Book Number*. The diagram at the right shows how to interpret the first 9 digits of an ISBN. The last digit of an ISBN is a *check digit*, which allows a person or a computer to tell if a mistake was made in one of the other nine digits.

The book is published in an English-speaking country.

The publisher is Houghton Mifflin Company.

0 - 395 - 67608 - 8

The title is *Algebra, Structure and Method, Book 1.*

The check digit is chosen so that when the digits of the ISBN are inserted in order into the blanks of the expression shown below, the result of the calculation is divisible by 11.

$1 \cdot \underline{} + 2 \cdot \underline{} + 3 \cdot \underline{} + 4 \cdot \underline{} + 5 \cdot \underline{} + 6 \cdot \underline{} + 7 \cdot \underline{} + 8 \cdot \underline{} + 9 \cdot \underline{} + 10 \cdot \underline{}$

For example, the "check calculation" for the ISBN 0-395-67608-8 is:

$1 \cdot 0 + 2 \cdot 3 + 3 \cdot 9 + 4 \cdot 5 + 5 \cdot 6 + 6 \cdot 7 + 7 \cdot 6 + 8 \cdot 0 + 9 \cdot 8 + 10 \cdot 8 = 319 = 11 \cdot 29$

1. Find the ISBNs of two books (they usually appear on the copyright page). Do the check calculation for each book. Verify that the result is divisible by 11.

2. Find the correct check digit n for (a) 0-231-10245-n and (b) 0-101-10200-n.

3. A typist enters ISBNs into a computer, which checks them to see if they are valid. Show by example that the typist could type two wrong digits without the computer detecting the errors. Is it possible for the typist to enter only a single wrong digit without the error being detected? Explain.

4. Why do you think that 11 was chosen as the number that must divide evenly into the result of the check calculation? Would some other number, such as 7 or 8 or 12, work just as well? Explain.

5. Devise your own code that uses a check digit and give the check calculation formula for your code.

Bumper-to-Bumper (Chapter 4)

Traffic volume and *traffic density* are two measures of the number of cars on a highway at any given time. The average speed maintained by cars on a highway depends in part on both the traffic volume and the traffic density.

Traffic volume is the number of cars per hour (cars/h) that pass a given point.
Traffic density is the average number of cars per mile (cars/mi).

1. Suppose that there are 2 cars in every mile of highway, and that they are traveling at an average speed of 50 mi/h. What is the traffic volume? Draw a picture and explain your method.

2. Find the traffic volume for a highway on which cars are traveling at an average speed of 40 mi/h with a density of 15 cars/mi.

3. For a given stretch of highway, let s = the average speed in mi/h of cars on the highway, let v = the traffic volume in cars/h, and let d = the traffic density in cars/mi. Write a formula relating these three variables.

4. For any fixed average speed, what happens to the traffic volume as traffic density increases? Will this always happen? Explain.

5. Two lanes of bumper-to-bumper traffic merge into one lane. The cars are moving at an average speed of 10 mi/h before the merge. If the traffic volume is the same before and after the merge, then what is the average speed of the cars immediately after the merge? Explain your reasoning.

In Exs. 3 and 4, expect students' explanations to be much less sophisticated than those given here.

3. For example, if a typist enters 0-331-10246-3 instead of 0-231-10245-3, the check calculation is 154 = 11 · 14. This error would not be detected. To see why one wrong digit is always detectable, let S be the check calculation for a correctly entered ISBN. Then S is divisible by 11. Suppose the ISBN's nth digit d is incorrectly entered as D. Now the check calculation is $S + n(D - d)$. Since D and d are both integers from 0–9, $|D - d|$ is also an integer from 0–9. Also, n is an integer from 1–10. Since S is divisible by 11, $S + n(D - d)$ is divisible by 11 only if $n(D - d)$ is divisible by 11. But this is not possible since both n and $|D - d|$ are less than 11, which is prime.

4. See the discussion in Ex. 3 above. Note that the product $n(D - d)$ is potentially divisible by any positive integer less than 11. Thus, 11 is the smallest positive integer that allows a single wrong digit to be detected every time.

Chapter 4

1. 100 cars/h
2. 600 cars/h
3. $v = sd$
4. Traffic volume increases until cars are so close together that drivers must reduce their speed to avoid collisions. Then traffic volume decreases.
5. 20 mi/h; $v = s_1 d_1 = s_2 d_2$; since $d_2 = (1/2)d_1$, $s_2 = 2s_1 = 2 \cdot 10 = 20$ mi/h.

Note: This project may be too long for some students. Have them choose the exercises they find most interesting. Students will find it helpful to use a calculator.

1. 79 and 157 are prime. Methods will vary. For example: Divide the given number by each prime in order. If a prime is a factor, then the given number is not prime. Test primes until a prime factor is found or until the square of the prime being tested is greater than the given number. In the latter case, the given number is prime.

2. When $x = 0, 1, 2,$ and 3, $x^2 + x + 17 = 17, 19, 23,$ and 29, respectively; all primes. Examples: When $x = 16, 16^2 + 16 + 17 = 289 = 17 \cdot 17$; when $x = 17,$ $17^2 + 17 + 17 = 17 \cdot 19.$

3. $2^{11} - 1 = 2047 = 23 \cdot 89$

4. Goldbach's Conjecture states that every even number greater than 2 can be written as the sum of two primes. $6 = 3 + 3,$ $8 = 3 + 5, 10 = 3 + 7,$ $12 = 5 + 7, 14 = 3 + 11,$ $16 = 5 + 11, 18 = 7 + 11,$ $20 = 7 + 13, 22 = 5 + 17,$ and $24 = 7 + 17.$

5. Answers will vary.

Chapter 6

1. a. $\dfrac{11}{4}$ b. $\dfrac{11}{49}$

2. a. $1 + \dfrac{1}{2 + \dfrac{1}{2 + \dfrac{1}{2}}}$

   b. $\dfrac{1}{3 + \dfrac{1}{5}}$

Pursuing Primes *(Chapter 5)*

For centuries, people have tried to find formulas that generate prime numbers. Formulas have been found that work in some cases, but never in *all*. In Exercises 2 and 3, you will investigate two of these formulas. First, though, you should establish an efficient method of testing a number for primeness, which is the purpose of Exercise 1. Exercise 4 involves a little research. Exercise 5 is a game you can play that relies on knowing prime numbers and factors of numbers.

1. Which of the following numbers are prime: 79, 157, 253, and 679? Describe an efficient method of testing whether a number is prime.

2. A polynomial formula that has been tried as a prime-number generator is $x^2 + x + 17$. Show that the formula gives a prime number for $x = 0, 1, 2,$ and 3. Find a positive integer for which the formula does not produce a prime.

3. In the seventeenth century, the French abbot Marin Mersenne looked for primes that can be written in the form $2^p - 1$, where p is a prime number. (In 1975, the postmark pictured at the right commemorated the discovery of the *Mersenne prime* $2^{11213} - 1$.) Find a prime number p less than 20 for which $2^p - 1$ is *not* prime.

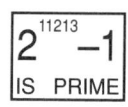

4. In a book on mathematics, find Goldbach's Conjecture and then demonstrate that it is true for at least the first 10 even numbers greater than 4.

5. In this solitaire game, your goal is to get the highest score you can by taking numbers according to the rules given below. Play the game several times and then describe your strategy for choosing the numbers you take.

   Begin with a list of the first 20 positive integers. Take a number that has at least one of the remaining numbers as a factor. Then eliminate from the list all factors of the number you took. Continue to take numbers in this way for as long as you can. Your score is the sum of all the numbers you take.

Continued Fractions *(Chapter 6)*

The expression shown at the right could be described as the sum of an integer and a fraction that has within it two other fractions. The numerators of all the fractions are 1. Such an expression is called a *continued fraction*. To evaluate the continued fraction, start at the bottom and work your way up:

$$1 + \cfrac{1}{2 + \cfrac{1}{1 + \cfrac{1}{4}}}$$

$$1 + \cfrac{1}{2 + \cfrac{1}{1 + \frac{1}{4}}} = 1 + \cfrac{1}{2 + \cfrac{1}{\frac{5}{4}}} = 1 + \cfrac{1}{2 + \frac{4}{5}} = 1 + \cfrac{1}{\frac{14}{5}} = 1 + \frac{5}{14} = \frac{19}{14}$$

To write a fraction in continued-fraction form, follow the steps illustrated by the example at the top of the next page.

$$\underbrace{\frac{37}{10}}_{\substack{\text{Split off} \\ \text{the integer} \\ \text{part of } \frac{37}{10}.}} = 3 + \underbrace{\frac{7}{10}}_{\substack{\text{Write } \frac{7}{10} \\ \text{as } 1 \div \frac{10}{7}.}} = 3 + \cfrac{1}{\underbrace{\frac{10}{7}}_{\substack{\text{Split off} \\ \text{the integer} \\ \text{part of } \frac{10}{7}.}}} = 3 + \cfrac{1}{1 + \underbrace{\frac{3}{7}}_{\substack{\text{Write } \frac{3}{7} \\ \text{as } 1 \div \frac{7}{3}.}}} = 3 + \cfrac{1}{1 + \cfrac{1}{\underbrace{\frac{7}{3}}_{\substack{\text{Split off} \\ \text{the integer} \\ \text{part of } \frac{7}{3}.}}}} = 3 + \cfrac{1}{1 + \cfrac{1}{2 + \cfrac{1}{3}}} \left.\begin{array}{l} \\ \\ \\ \\ \end{array}\right\} \begin{array}{l} \text{Stop when} \\ \text{all the} \\ \text{numerators} \\ \text{are 1.} \end{array}$$

1. Evaluate each continued fraction: **a.** $2 + \cfrac{1}{1 + \cfrac{1}{3}}$ **b.** $\cfrac{1}{4 + \cfrac{1}{2 + \cfrac{1}{5}}}$

2. Write each fraction in continued-fraction form: **a.** $\frac{17}{12}$ **b.** $\frac{5}{16}$

3. By trying several examples, discover and describe how to find the continued-fraction form of any fraction of the type $\frac{n}{n+1}$, where n is a positive integer.

4. By trying several examples, discover and describe the relationship between the continued-fraction forms of a fraction and its reciprocal.

A Transportation Problem (Chapter 7)

A certain construction company often moves lumber to construction sites by helicopter. The lumber can be loaded inside the helicopter or it can be carried below the helicopter, attached by a cable. Packing the lumber inside the helicopter takes more time than simply attaching the lumber with a cable, but the helicopter can fly faster if it carries the lumber inside rather than underneath. Here are the facts:

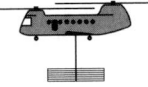

Loading the lumber into the helicopter takes 30 minutes and unloading it takes 20 minutes. Carrying the lumber inside, the helicopter travels 144 mi/h.

Attaching the lumber by cable takes 15 minutes, and detaching it takes only 10 minutes. Carrying its load underneath, the helicopter travels 120 mi/h.

It costs $300 per hour to fly the helicopter and $40 per hour to load and unload the lumber (whether loading it inside or attaching it by cable).

The company management asks you to answer two questions:

1. For what distances is each method of transporting lumber most economical?

2. Sometimes the company has a rush job that requires them to transport the lumber as quickly as possible, regardless of cost. For what distances does it make sense for them to take the time to load the lumber inside the helicopter?

Prepare a written report for the company management giving your solutions.

---

3. The continued-fraction form of $\frac{n}{n+1}$ is $\cfrac{1}{1 + \cfrac{1}{n}}$. For example, $\frac{5}{6} = \cfrac{1}{1 + \cfrac{1}{5}}$.

4. If F is the continued-fraction form of any fraction, then $\frac{1}{F}$ is the continued-fraction form of the reciprocal of the fraction. For example,

$$\frac{11}{4} = 2 + \cfrac{1}{1 + \cfrac{1}{3}} \text{ (Ex. 1(a))}$$

and $\frac{4}{11} = \cfrac{1}{2 + \cfrac{1}{1 + \cfrac{1}{3}}}$

Chapter 7

1. At a distance of 40 mi, the total costs are equal: $116.67. Under 40 mi, the total cost is less if the lumber is carried below the helicopter. Over 40 mi, the total cost is less if the lumber is carried inside the helicopter.

2. At 300 mi, the time required is the same for both methods: 2 h 55 min. Under 300 mi, the total time required is less if the lumber is carried below the helicopter. Over 300 mi, the total time required is less if the lumber is carried inside the helicopter.

Chapter 8

1. Divide the height of the riser by the depth of the tread.

2. Answers will vary. Possible range of slopes: 0.6 to 0.8.

3. Measurements will vary. Slopes are likely to range from about 0.5 to about 0.9, and to average about 0.7.

4. Answers will vary.

Extension: Ask students to make scatter diagrams of ordered pairs (riser height, tread depth) for private buildings and for public buildings. Students can compare scatter plots and present their conclusions in a report.

Chapter 9

1. a. $y = 2x + 240$

  b. The intersection point is (20, 280).

  c. It means that if Zack and Zoe watch 20 movies, they will spend the same amount of money ($280) whether they buy the VCR or continue to go to the cinema. If they plan to watch more than 20 movies, they will save money by buying the VCR. If they plan to watch less than 20 movies, it would not be economical to buy the VCR.

2. Answers will vary. For example, buying a washing machine and dryer and then paying for the hot water vs. taking laundry to a laundromat.

Slopes of Staircases *(Chapter 8)*

Materials: *Ruler or tape measure*

The horizontal parts of a staircase are called *treads* and the vertical parts are called *risers*.

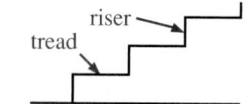

1. How would you use the height of the risers and the depth of the treads to measure the slope of a staircase?

2. Many communities have building-code requirements that place restrictions on the slope of a staircase. Why do you think this is so? (How will the slope of a staircase affect your sense of comfort and safety when you use the stairs?) By drawing pictures, estimate a good range of slopes for staircases.

3. Measure the riser height and tread depth of staircases in a number of buildings, both public (such as your school) and private (such as your home). Include different types of stairs, such as front stairs, back stairs, attic stairs, and basement stairs. Find the average slope, and the smallest and largest slopes of the staircases you measure. For each staircase, rate or otherwise describe the sense of comfort and safety you feel walking up and down the stairs.

4. Find a set of recommended specifications for the design of stairs. (You could find this in a reference book or you could call a local building inspector to find out what the building-code requirements are in your community.) How closely do the staircases you measured conform to these recommendations?

Breaking Even *(Chapter 9)*

Zack and Zoe spend $14 every time they go to the local cinema. They're thinking about buying a VCR for $240 and renting tapes for $2 each. The graph shows the couple's total expenses if they continue to go to the cinema (red dots) and if they buy a VCR and rent tapes (blue dots). Each set of colored dots is linear.

1. a. The red dots lie on the line with equation $y = 14x$. What is an equation for the set of blue dots?

  b. Graph the two equations in part (a) and find the intersection point of the two lines. You may want to use a graphing calculator or a computer with graphing software.

  c. The point you found in part (b) is called a *break-even* point. Explain what this means for Zack and Zoe.

2. Find other situations in which making some investment, such as buying a VCR, lowers a regularly-occurring expense, such as the cost of watching a movie. Use graphs, equations, and words to analyze the situations, especially with regard to break-even points and what they mean.

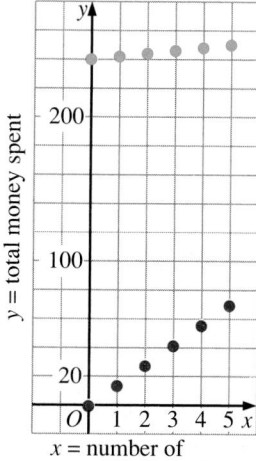

706   *Portfolio Projects*

The Classified Ads *(Chapter 10)*

Suppose you have been hired to lay out the classified ads for a newspaper. Classified ads may appear only in the bottom 20 cm of any given page, and each page of the newspaper is divided into 6 columns. Ads are one column wide, and no ad can begin at the bottom of one column and then end at the top of another column. You want to do the job efficiently, keeping wasted space to a minimum, but you don't want to spend too much time "tinkering" with the placement of the ads. Instead, you need a general procedure that you can use day after day to position the ads using as few columns as possible.

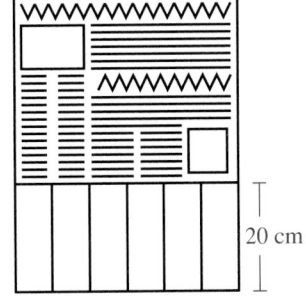

For today's paper, the ads are of the following lengths:

5 cm, 8 cm, 4 cm, 6 cm, 4 cm, 2.5 cm, 3.5 cm, 5 cm, 7 cm, 7.5 cm, 6 cm, 6.5 cm, 3.5 cm, 2 cm, 6 cm, 4 cm, 7 cm, 5 cm, 5 cm, 5.5 cm, 4.5 cm, 6 cm, 5 cm

Using the lengths given above as an example, devise a systematic approach to the problem of positioning the ads. Can you fit all of today's ads in the 20 cm at the bottom of one page or must you use part of a second page? Describe your procedure in detail so that someone else could use it and get the same results. Make up another set of lengths of ads and use your procedure to position the ads.

A Swimming Race *(Chapter 11)*

Six swimmers are about to begin a 50 m race, which will cover one length of the pool. Each swimmer stands in the middle of his or her lane, which is 2.75 m wide. The race will begin when the starter, standing at the side of the pool 3 m from the starting end, fires the starting pistol. The moment they hear the starting signal, the swimmers will dive into the pool and the timers (one for each lane) will start their stop-watches. As each swimmer finishes the race, the timer for that swimmer's lane will stop his or her watch.

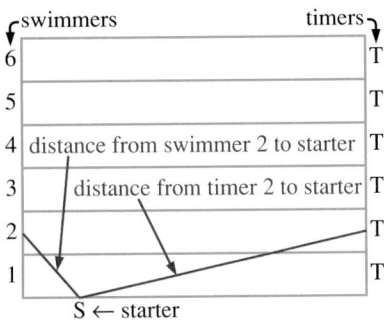

Because the swimmers and timers are different distances from the starter, each one will hear the sound of the gun at a slightly different time. As a result, there may be a discrepancy between a given swimmer's actual and recorded times.

Suppose that the swimmer in lane 2 wins the race with a recorded time of 30.87 s. The swimmer in lane 6 comes in second with a recorded time of 30.88 s. Assuming that under the conditions of this race the speed of sound is 343 m/s, show that the swimmer in lane 6 may actually have won. Write up your solution in detail.

Note: Students should use a spreadsheet or a calculator that allows them to do iterations without re-entering the operations at each step. Decimals should not be rounded off.

Students will find that the results of the iteration process can vary: the sequence of values may approach a limit (a solution of the equation); or the sequence of values may approach infinity, cycle periodically, or behave unpredictably. Thus, students may need to try more than one initial guess, and they may need to try more than one way of rewriting a given equation.

1. The values settle down to $x \approx -4$.
2. The values eventually settle down to $x \approx 1$.
3. $x^2 + 3x - 4 = 0$; $(x + 4)(x - 1) = 0$; $x = -4$ or $x = 1$
4. a. $x = 1$ or $x = 3$
   b. $x \approx -0.8090$ or $x \approx -0.3090$ (Students may have difficulty finding the second solution. Suggest that they write the equation in the form $x = \dfrac{\sqrt{1 - 2x}}{2}$, and then ask them what initial guess values would keep the expression under the radical positive for all iterations.)
5. The sequence of values never approaches a limit. It either approaches infinity, cycles periodically, or behaves unpredictably.

Solving Equations by Iteration *(Chapter 12)*

Have you ever tried to solve a quadratic equation by getting the x^2 term alone on one side of the equation and then dividing both sides by x? For example:

$$x^2 + 3x - 4 = 0$$
$$x^2 = -3x + 4$$

Although x is "alone," you still don't know a value of x that makes the equation true. $\left.\rule{0pt}{18pt}\right\} \longrightarrow x = -3 + \dfrac{4}{x}$

With the equation $x^2 + 3x - 4 = 0$ written in the form $x = -3 + \dfrac{4}{x}$, you can, however, use a method called *solving by iteration* to the find a solution. The steps of the process are illustrated below.

(1) Start by *guessing* a solution.

Guess $x = 2$.

(2) Substitute the guess into the expression on the right side of the equation.

$-3 + \dfrac{4}{x} = -3 + \dfrac{4}{2} = -1$

(3) Use the result as a new guess for a solution.

Guess $x = -1$.

(4) Repeat step 2 with the new guess.

$-3 + \dfrac{4}{x} = -3 + \dfrac{4}{-1} = -7$

(5) Use the result as a new guess for a solution.

Guess $x = -7$.

(6) With each guess, repeat steps 2 and 3 until the value of the new guess is the same as the value of the old guess.

$new\ guess = -3 + \dfrac{4}{old\ guess}$

1. Continue the process shown above from $x = -7$, until the values of the guesses settle down to one number. By substituting this number for x, show that the number is a solution of the equation $x = -3 + \dfrac{4}{x}$, and also of the equation $x^2 + 3x - 4 = 0$.

2. Show that another way to get x "alone" in the equation $x^2 + 3x - 4 = 0$ is to write the equation in the form $x = \dfrac{4 - x^2}{3}$. Then try solving by iteration. What is the result?

3. Use the quadratic formula or solve by factoring to confirm that the values of x you found in Exercises 1 and 2 are the solutions of the equation $x^2 + 3x - 4 = 0$.

4. Solve by iteration. Find as many solutions as you can. Use the quadratic formula or solving by factoring to confirm your solutions.
   a. $x^2 - 4x + 3 = 0$ b. $4x^2 + 2x - 1 = 0$

5. Write a quadratic equation that has no real solutions and then try to solve it by iteration. Describe what happens.

Appendix

Preparing for College Entrance Exams

If you plan to attend college, you will most likely be required to take college entrance examinations. Some of these exams attempt to measure the extent to which your verbal and mathematical reasoning skills have been developed. Others test your knowledge of specific subject areas. Usually the best preparation for college entrance examinations is to follow a strong academic program in high school, to study, and to read as extensively as possible. The following test-taking strategies may prove useful:

- Familiarize yourself with the type of test you will be taking well in advance of the test date. Sample tests, with accompanying explanatory material, are available for many standardized tests. By working through this sample material, you become comfortable with the types of questions and directions that will appear on the test and you develop a feeling for the pace at which you must work in order to complete the test.

- Find out how the test is scored so that you know whether it is advantageous to guess.

- Skim sections of the test before starting to answer the questions, to get an overview of the questions. You may wish to answer the easiest questions first. In any case, do not waste time on questions you do not understand; go on to those that you do.

- Mark your answer sheet carefully, checking the numbering on the answer sheet about every five questions to avoid errors caused by misplaced answer markings.

- Write in the test booklet if it is helpful; for example, cross out incorrect alternatives and do mathematical calculations.

- Work carefully, but do not take time to double-check your answers unless you finish before the deadline and have extra time.

- Arrive at the test center early and come well prepared with any necessary supplies such as sharpened pencils and a watch.

College entrance examinations that test general reasoning abilities, such as the Scholastic Aptitude Test, usually include questions dealing with basic algebraic concepts and skills. The College Board Achievement Tests in mathematics (Level I and Level II) include many questions on algebra. The following first-year algebra topics often appear on these exams. For each of the topics listed on pages 710 – 711, a page reference to the place in your textbook where this topic is discussed has been provided. As you prepare for college entrance exams, you may wish to review the topics on these pages.

Types of Numbers (pages 31–32, 75, 185)

Positive integers	$\{1, 2, 3, 4, \ldots\}$
Negative integers	$\{-1, -2, -3, -4, \ldots\}$
Integers	$\{\ldots, -4, -3, -2, -1, 0, 1, 2, 3, 4, \ldots\}$
Odd numbers	$\{1, 3, 5, 7, 9, \ldots\}$
Even numbers	$\{0, 2, 4, 6, 8, \ldots\}$
Consecutive integers	$\{n, n + 1, n + 2, \ldots\}$ (n = an integer)
Consecutive even integers	$\{n, n + 2, n + 4, \ldots\}$ (n = even integer)
Consecutive odd integers	$\{n, n + 2, n + 4, \ldots\}$ (n = odd integer)
Prime numbers	$\{2, 3, 5, 7, 11, 13, \ldots\}$

Properties (See the Glossary of Properties on pages 721–722.)

Rules for Operations on Positive and Negative Numbers
(pages 54, 71)

Rules for Addition

1. If a and b are both positive, then
$$a + b = |a| + |b|.$$

2. If a and b are both negative, then
$$a + b = -(|a| + |b|).$$

3. If a is positive and b is negative and a has the greater absolute value, then
$$a + b = |a| - |b|.$$

4. If a is positive and b is negative and b has the greater absolute value, then
$$a + b = -(|b| - |a|).$$

5. If a and b are opposites, then
$$a + b = 0.$$

Rules for Multiplication

1. If two numbers have the *same* sign, their product is *positive*.
If two numbers have *opposite* signs, their product is *negative*.

2. The product of an *even* number of negative numbers is *positive*.
The product of an *odd* number of negative numbers is *negative*.

Factoring (pages 185–186, 194–195, 204–227)

Integers	$a^2 + 2ab + b^2$
$a^2 - b^2$	$a^2 - 2ab + b^2$
$ax^2 + bx$	$ax^2 + bx + c$

Algebraic Fractions (pages 247–279)

Simplification	Multiplication
Addition	Division

Graphing (pages 31–32, 353–355, 366–368, 383–385, 457–458, 478–479, 490–492, 495, 572–573)

Points on a number line
Inequalities on a number line
Points and lines in a number plane
Inequalities in a number plane
Quadratic functions

Percents (pages 309–311, 315–316)

Converting decimals and
  fractions to percents
Percents greater than 100
Percents less than 1
Percent problems

Solving Equations (pages 95–96, 102–103, 230–232, 561–562, 567–568, 573)

Transformation by substitution (p. 96)
Transformation by addition (p. 96)
Transformation by subtraction (p. 96)
Transformation by multiplication (p. 102)
Transformation by division (p. 102)

Factoring (pp. 230–232)
$x^2 = k$ (p. 561)
Quadratic formula (p. 567)
Discriminant (p. 573)

Simultaneous Equations (pages 413–414, 417–418, 426–427, 430–431)

The graphic method
The substitution method
The addition-or-subtraction method
Multiplication with the addition-or-subtraction method

Variation (pages 391–392, 397–398, 584–585, 588–589)

Direct variation
Inverse variation
Direct variation involving powers
Inverse variation involving powers
Joint variation
Combined variation

Word Problems (pages 23–24, 26, 27–28, 75–76, 112–113, 121–122, 126, 165, 167–169, 172, 175–176, 234–235, 287–289, 293–294, 302, 315–316, 321–322, 326–327, 350, 421–423, 438–439, 444–446, 469–471, 579, 588–589)

Age	Percent
Area	Proportion
Consecutive integers	Ratio
Cost and value	Uniform motion
Digit	Wind and water current
Fraction	Without solutions
Investment	Work
Mixture	

Types of Questions

The types of questions you can expect may include five-choice *Multiple–Choice* questions, four-choice *Quantitative Comparison* questions, or *Grid–in* questions. Here is an example of a **Multiple–Choice** question:

If $4x + 4x + 4x = 72$, what is the value of $x + 3$?
(A) 6
(B) 7
(C) 8
(D) 9   *the correct answer*
(E) 10

Quantitative Comparison questions give you two quantities and ask you to compare them. Here is an example of a Quantitative Comparison question:

Column A	Column B
7^2	$4^2 + 3^2$

You must choose whether the quantity in Column A is greater, the quantity in column B is greater, the two quantities are equal, or if you cannot determine which is greater from the information given. For this example, the quantity in Column A is greater.

Grid–in questions emphasize active problem solving and critical thinking by asking you to grid the answer directly on the answer sheet rather than recognize it from among the choices. Using the same example as the Multiple–Choice question, the answer is still 9, but you would have to grid 9 on the answer sheet rather than choose (D).

Calculator Use

Some college entrance exams allow students to use calculators. If calculator use is permitted, bring a familiar calculator with you to the test center, but don't plan to use it for every problem. First decide how to solve the problem, and then decide if a calculator will help with the computation. For example, suppose you are given the numbers 1, 4, 82, 93, 45, 232, and 19. If you are asked to find the median, the middle value listed, using a calculator will not help. You should list the numbers in order and choose 45. If you are asked to find the mean, the average of the numbers, using a calculator may help. You should add $1 + 4 + 82 + 93 + 45 + 232 + 19$ and then divide by 7 to get 68. In general, calculators help solve problems involving data, number patterns, or guess-and-check problem solving strategies.

A-2 Point-Slope Form

Objective   To derive linear equations using the point-slope formula.

Use after Chapter 8

A shipping company charges $10 to ship a package weighing 3 lb or less. For every pound over 3 lb, it charges an additional $.50 per pound. The graph of this pricing scheme consists of pieces of two lines. The lines can be described algebraically.

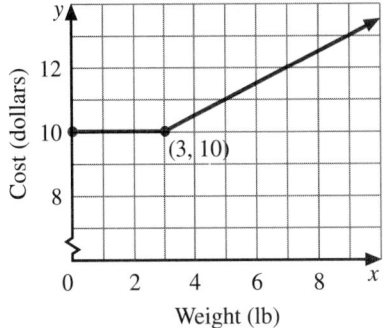

For weights ≤ 3 lb: $y = 10$
For weights > 3 lb: $y = 10 + 0.50(x - 3)$
$ $ number of pounds over 3

The second equation features the coordinates of a point on the line, (3, 10), as well as the slope of the line, 0.50.
When you know the coordinates of a point on a line, (x_0, y_0), and the slope of the line, m, you can use the *point-slope* formula to write an equation of the line:

Point-slope formula	Example
$y - y_0 = m(x - x_0)$	$y - 10 = 0.50(x - 3)$

Example 1   Write an equation in point-slope form of the line through the point (7, 8) with slope 4.

Solution
$$y - y_0 = m(x - x_0)$$
$$y - 8 = 4(x - 7)$$

Equations of Perpendicular Lines

When two lines are perpendicular, their slopes have a product of –1. In other words, if the slope of one line is m, then the slope of a line perpendicular to it is $-\dfrac{1}{m}$. You can use this fact to write an equation.

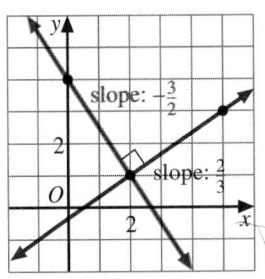

Example 2 Line A has equation $y = 3x - 7$ and passes through the point $(-2, 6)$. Line B passes through the same point and is perpendicular to Line A. Write an equation of Line B in slope-intercept form .

Solution First write an equation in point-slope form. Then rewrite it in slope-intercept form.

$$y - y_0 = m(x - x_0)$$
$$y - 6 = -\frac{1}{3}(x - (-2)) \qquad \left\{\begin{array}{l}\text{The slope of Line } A \text{ is } 3, \\ \text{so the slope of Line } B \text{ is } -\frac{1}{3}.\end{array}\right.$$
$$y - 6 = -\frac{1}{3}(x + 2)$$
$$y = 6 - \frac{1}{3}x - \frac{2}{3}$$
$$y = -\frac{1}{3}x + \frac{16}{3}$$

Written Exercises

For answers to this appendix, see the Additional Answers following the Selected Answers.

For Exercises 1–8, a point and the slope of a line are given. Write an equation in point-slope form.

1. $(1, 2)$; 3 **2.** $(5, 9)$; 2 **3.** $(3, 4)$; $-\frac{1}{2}$ **4.** $(-2, 4)$; 5

5. $(-3, -8)$; 5 **6.** $(1, -7)$; $-\frac{2}{3}$ **7.** $(0, 3)$; $\frac{4}{7}$ **8.** $(0, b)$; m

9. An equation of a line is $y - 2 = \frac{3}{4}(x - 5)$. Write an equation in slope-intercept form. Then write an equation in standard form.

For Exercises 10 and 11, write an equation in slope-intercept form for the line described.

10. a. The line through $(2, 5)$ that is parallel to the line $y = \frac{4}{3}x + 1$

 b. The line through $(2, 5)$ that is perpendicular to the line $y = \frac{4}{3}x + 1$

11. a. The line through $(-7, 6)$ that is parallel to the line $4x + 2y = 9$

 b. The line through $(-7, 6)$ that is perpendicular to the line $4x + 2y = 9$

12. Read the first three paragraphs on page 378. Notice that the red line passes approximately through the point $(62, 73)$.

 a. Estimate the slope of the line and write an equation for the line in point-slope form.

 b. A boy is 70 in. tall at age 14. Use your equation from part (a) to predict his height at age 24.

A-3 Inductive and Deductive Reasoning

Objective   To identify and use inductive and deductive reasoning.

Use after Chapter 12

Suppose you observe the following pattern:

$$1 = 1$$
$$1 + 3 = 4 \qquad \text{The sum of the first 2 odd integers is } 2^2.$$
$$1 + 3 + 5 = 9 \qquad \text{The sum of the first 3 odd integers is } 3^2.$$
$$1 + 3 + 5 + 7 = 16 \qquad \text{The sum of the first 4 odd integers is } 4^2.$$

Based on the pattern, you could use inductive reasoning to make the following generalization:

The sum of the first n positive odd integers is n^2.

Inductive reasoning involves making a general statement based on a number of observations.

You can test the statement above for many different values of n. Observing that the statement is true for many values of n is not the same as *proving* that it is true for all values of n, however. You can use *deductive reasoning* to *prove* that the statement is true for all values of n. **Deductive reasoning** uses known facts, definitions, and accepted properties in a logical order to reach a conclusion or to show that a statement is true.

Example   Prove that the sum of the first n positive odd integers is n^2.

Solution   Let $S =$ the sum of the first n odd integers. First write an equation.

$$S = 1 + 3 + 5 + \ldots + (2n - 3) + (2n - 1) \qquad \left\{ \begin{array}{l} \text{The } n\text{th even integer is } 2n, \text{ so the} \\ n\text{th odd integer is } 1 \text{ less than } 2n. \end{array} \right.$$

$$\begin{array}{rcccccccc} S = & 1 & + & 3 & + \ldots + & (2n-3) & + & (2n-1) \\ + \quad S = & (2n-1) & + & (2n-3) & + \ldots + & 3 & + & 1 \\ \hline 2S = & 2n & + & 2n & + \ldots + & 2n & + & 2n \end{array}$$

$\left\{ \begin{array}{l} \text{Now write } S \text{ as a "forward sum"} \\ \text{and a "backward sum." Add the} \\ \text{two equations, term by term.} \end{array} \right.$

$$2S = n(2n) \qquad \text{The term } 2n \text{ occurs } n \text{ times.}$$
$$2S = 2n^2$$
$$S = n^2$$

Using Counterexamples

You may wonder why it is important to prove a statement like the one in the Example. After all, the statement appears to be true for all values of n. To see why a deductive proof is important, consider the following statement:

For every positive integer n, $n^2 + n + 41$ is a prime number.

If you test the statement for different values of n, it appears to be true.

When $n = 1$, $1^2 + 1 + 41 = 43$ prime
When $n = 2$, $2^2 + 2 + 41 = 47$ prime
When $n = 3$, $3^2 + 3 + 41 = 53$ prime

Testing many numbers may lead you to believe that the statement above is true, but you would be wrong! For example:

When $n = 41$, $41^2 + 41 + 41 = 1763$ not prime because $1763 = 43 \cdot 41$

In fact, $n^2 + n + 41$ is prime when $n = 1, 2, 3, \ldots, 39$, but it is not prime when $n = 40$ or 41. These values of n are called *counterexamples*.

Proving that a statement is false requires just one counterexample. Proving that a statement is true requires a deductive proof.

Written Exercises

For answers to this appendix, see the Additional Answers following the Selected Answers.

For Exercises 1–3, tell whether each argument uses *inductive* or *deductive* reasoning.

1. Tim is Veronica's cousin. Since David is Veronica's twin brother, Tim is also David's cousin.

2. The school librarian notices that many students are requesting books about different countries in Africa. The librarian concludes that one of the social studies classes must be studying about Africa.

3. Julie notices that each term in the sequence 1, 3, 9, 27, … is found by multiplying the previous term by 3. She concludes that the next two terms are 81 and 243.

4. Study the equations and algebraic reasoning shown below the two colored figures on page 529. Is the final equation $a^2 + b^2 = c^2$ reached by using *inductive* or *deductive* reasoning?

5. Give an example of inductive reasoning. Then give an example of deductive reasoning. How are the two types of reasoning different?

6. Look for a pattern in the statements below:

$$2 = 1 \cdot 2$$
$$2 + 4 = 2 \cdot 3$$
$$2 + 4 + 6 = 3 \cdot 4$$

   a. Write the next two statements in the pattern.

   b. Use inductive reasoning to write a general statement.

   c. Use deductive reasoning to prove your statement. *Hint:* Start by letting S = the sum of the first n positive even integers. Then write two equations and add them vertically, term by term:

$$S = \quad 2 \quad + \quad 4 \quad + \ldots + (2n - 2) + (2n)$$
$$+ \quad S = (2n) + (2n - 2) + \ldots + \quad 4 \quad + \quad 2$$

7. Consider the equation $(x + 3)(x + 4) = x^2 + 7x + 12$.

   a. How are the numbers 7 and 12 related to the numbers 3 and 4?

   b. Does this relationship work when you multiply $(x + 5)(x + 8)$?

   c. Use inductive reasoning to multiply $(x + a)(x + b)$.

   d. Use deductive reasoning and the FOIL method to show that your generalization in part (c) is true for all values of a and b.

Provide a counterexample for each statement to show that it is false.

8. $(n + 2)^3 = n^3 + 2^3$

9. $|a + b| = |a| + |b|$

10. $x^2 > x$ for all values of x.

11. If $a > 0$, then $a^3 > a$.

Tell whether each statement is *True* or *False*. If it is false, give a counterexample.

12. For every positive integer n, $n^2 + n + 11$ is a prime number.

13. Perfect square numbers always end in 1, 4, 5, 6, or 9.

14. The result of multiplying the sum of the first n positive even integers by 4 and then adding 1 is always a perfect square.

15. Use deductive reasoning to prove that the statement in Exercise 14 is always true. (*Hint:* Look back at Exercise 6(c).)

A-4 Hypothesis and Conclusion

Objective   To identify the hypothesis and the conclusion of a statement.

Use after Appendix A-3

Logical arguments are based on statements that can be expressed in this form:

"If statement p is true, then statement q is true."

Statement p is called the *hypothesis*. Statement q is called the *conclusion*.

Hypothesis	Conclusion
(1) If a and b are even integers,	then $a + b$ is an even integer.
(2) If $x \neq 0$,	then $x^2 > 0$.

Example 1   Peggy says that $n^2 > n^3$ for all negative numbers n. Write Peggy's statement as an if-then statement. Identify the hypothesis and the conclusion.

Solution   If n is a negative number, then $n^2 > n^3$.
Hypothesis: n is a negative number. Conclusion: $n^2 > n^3$

Whenever you try to prove that an "If p, then q" statement is true, you use the hypothesis as the starting point, assuming it is true. Then you can use deductive reasoning to prove that the conclusion is true.

Example 2   Prove that this statement is true: If $2(x + 3) = -8$, then $x = -7$.

Solution   Use properties of real numbers to prove the statement.

$$2(x + 3) = -8$$
$$2x + 6 = -8 \quad \text{Distributive property}$$
$$2x = -14 \quad \text{Addition property of equality}$$
$$x = -7 \quad \text{Multiplication property of equality}$$

The Converse of a Statement

A statement that contains a hypothesis and a conclusion has a *converse*. In the **converse** of a statement, the hypothesis and the conclusion are reversed. Even though a statement may be true, its converse is not necessarily true.

Statement	Converse
(1) If a and b are even integers, then $a + b$ is an even integer	If $a + b$ is an even integer, then a and b are even integers.
(2) If $x \neq 0$, then $x^2 > 0$.	If $x^2 > 0$, then $x \neq 0$.

Example 3	Tell whether the converse of each statement at the bottom of page 718 is true or false. Justify your reasoning.
Solution	(1) Let $a = 3$ and $b = 5$. Then $a + b = 3 + 5 = 8$, an even integer. But 3 and 5 are not even, so the converse of statement (1) is false.
	(2) If $x^2 > 0$, then $x \neq 0$ because $0^2 = 0$. The converse of statement (2) is true.

Written Exercises

For answers to this appendix, see the Additional Answers following the Selected Answers.

For Exercises 1–4, write the hypothesis and the conclusion of each statement. Tell whether the statement is *true* or *false*. Justify your reasoning.

1. If the current month is September, then there are 30 days in the month.

2. If a and b are negative, then ab is positive.

3. Joe lives in New England if he lives in Vermont.

4. $|a + b| = |a| + |b|$ if a and b are both positive.

5. Give the converse of each statement in Exercises 1–4. Tell whether the converse is *true* or *false*. Justify your reasoning.

6. After trying many different pairs of numbers, Jim stated that the sum of any two odd integers is always even.

   a. Identify the hypothesis and the conclusion of Jim's statement. Then write an if-then statement.

   b. Write the converse of your statement from part (a). Tell whether the converse is *true* or *false*. Justify your reasoning.

7. Write the converse of the statement in Example 1. Then try different values of n to see whether the converse is *true* or *false*. Explain your reasoning.

8. Consider the inequality $|x| - 1 \geq 0$. For what values of x is the inequality true? For what values is it not true? Based on your observations, write an if-then statement about the inequality $|x| - 1 \geq 0$. Identify the hypothesis and the conclusion of your statement.

Tell whether each statement is *sometimes true*, *always true*, or *never true*. Explain your reasoning.

9. For real numbers a and b, $|a \cdot b| = |a| \cdot |b|$.

10. If a and b are nonzero real numbers and $a > b$, then $\dfrac{1}{a} > \dfrac{1}{b}$.

11. If a and b are real numbers and $a > b$, then $ax > bx$.

12. If $2x^2 - 12x + 18 = 0$, then $x = 3$.

13. If m and n are prime numbers, then mn is also prime.

14. If m and n are prime numbers, then $m + n$ is also prime.

A-5 Indirect Reasoning

Objective To use indirect reasoning in a logical argument.

Use after Appendix A-4

Sharon King returns home to find that a large slice of freshly baked rhubarb pie has been eaten. The only people with access to the house are her husband, son, and daughter. Since her husband is out of town and her daughter hates rhubarb, she concludes that her son must have eaten the pie.

Sharon does not reason directly that her son ate the pie. Instead, she uses *indirect reasoning*. In other words, she shows that all other alternatives are impossible. **Indirect reasoning** is used in mathematics as well.

Example Use indirect reasoning to prove the following statement:
If n^2 is odd, then n is odd.

Solution Start by identifying the hypothesis and the conclusion of the statement. Then try to show that the alternative conclusion leads to a contradiction in the statement.

Hypothesis and known fact: n^2 is odd.
Desired conclusion: n is odd.
Alternative Conclusion: n is even.

Assume temporarily that the alternative conclusion is true. If n is even, then n can be described as the product of 2 and some integer k. Then n^2 is as follows:

$$n^2 = (2k)^2 = 4k^2 = 2(2k^2)$$

Notice that n^2 has a factor of 2. This implies that n^2 is even, which contradicts the known fact that n^2 is odd. The desired conclusion must be accepted, and the original statement is true.

Written Exercises

For answers to this appendix, see the Additional Answers following the Selected Answers.

Use indirect reasoning to prove each statement.

1. If n^3 is negative, then n is negative.

2. If n^2 is even, then n is even.

3. If $x > 3$, then $|x| - 3 > 0$.

4. If an equation in the form $ax^2 + bx + c = 0$ has no real-number solutions, then the graph of the related equation $y = ax^2 + bx + c = 0$ has no x-intercepts.

5. If n^2 is a multiple of 3, then n is a multiple of 3. (*Hint:* The desired conclusion is that n is 3 times some integer k. There are two alternative conclusions you must consider: $n = 3k + 1$ or $n = 3k + 2$.)

Glossary of Properties

addition property of equality (p. 95): If a, b, and c are any real numbers, and $a = b$, then $a + c = b + c$ and $c + a = c + b$.

addition property of order (p. 463): For all real numbers a, b, and c:
1. If $a < b$, then $a + c < b + c$;
2. If $a > b$, then $a + c > b + c$.

associative properties (p. 45): For all real numbers a, b, and c:
$$(a + b) + c = a + (b + c)$$
$$(ab)c = a(bc)$$

closure properties (p. 45): For all real numbers a and b:

$a + b$ is a unique real number.
ab is a unique real number.

commutative properties (p. 45): For all real numbers a and b:
$$a + b = b + a$$
$$ab = ba$$

density property for rational numbers (p. 508): Between every pair of different rational numbers there is another rational number.

distributive property (of multiplication with respect to addition) (p. 65): For all real numbers a, b, and c,
$$a(b + c) = ab + ac \text{ and}$$
$$(b + c)a = ba + ca.$$

distributive property (of multiplication with respect to subtraction) (p. 66): For all real numbers a, b, and c,
$$a(b - c) = ab - ac \text{ and}$$
$$(b - c)a = ba - ca.$$

division property of equality (p. 102): If a and b are any real numbers, c is any nonzero real number, and $a = b$, then
$$\frac{a}{c} = \frac{b}{c}.$$

identity property of addition (p. 50): There is a unique real number 0 such that for every real number a, $a + 0 = a$ and $0 + a = a$.

identity property of multiplication (p. 70): There is a unique real number 1 such that for every real number a, $a \cdot 1 = a$ and $1 \cdot a = a$.

multiplication property of equality (p. 102): If a, b, and c are any real numbers, and $a = b$, then $ca = cb$ and $ac = bc$.

multiplication property of order (p. 463): For all real numbers a, b, and c such that $c > 0$:
1. If $a < b$, then $ac < bc$;
2. If $a > b$, then $ac > bc$.

For all real numbers a, b, and c such that $c < 0$:
1. If $a < b$, then $ac > bc$;
2. If $a > b$, then $ac < bc$.

multiplicative property of −1 (p. 70): For every real number a, $a(-1) = -a$ and $(-1)a = -a$.

multiplicative property of zero (p. 70): For every real number a, $a \cdot 0 = 0$ and $0 \cdot a = 0$.

product property of square roots (p. 517): For any nonnegative real numbers a and b, $\sqrt{ab} = \sqrt{a} \cdot \sqrt{b}$.

property of comparison (p. 462): For all real numbers a and b, one and only one of the following statements is true: $a < b$, $a = b$, $a > b$.

property of completeness (p. 522): Every decimal represents a real number, and every real number can be represented by a decimal.

property of the opposite of a sum (p. 51): For all real numbers a and b: $-(a + b) = (-a) + (-b)$.

property of opposites (p. 50): For every real number a, there is a unique real number $-a$ such that $a + (-a) = 0$ and $(-a) + a = 0$.

property of opposites in products (p. 71): For all real numbers a and b, $(-a)(b) = -ab$, $a(-b) = -ab$, and $(-a)(-b) = ab$.

property of quotients (p. 189): If a, b, c, and d are real numbers with $b \neq 0$ and $d \neq 0$, then $\dfrac{ac}{bd} = \dfrac{a}{b} \cdot \dfrac{c}{d}$.

property of the reciprocal of the opposite of a number (p. 79): For every non-zero number a, $\dfrac{1}{-a} = -\dfrac{1}{a}$.

property of the reciprocal of a product (p. 80): For all nonzero numbers a and b, $\dfrac{1}{ab} = \dfrac{1}{a} \cdot \dfrac{1}{b}$.

property of reciprocals (p. 79): For every nonzero real number a, there is a unique real number $\dfrac{1}{a}$ such that $a \cdot \dfrac{1}{a} = 1$ and $\dfrac{1}{a} \cdot a = 1$.

property of square roots of equal numbers (p. 526): For any real numbers r and s: $r^2 = s^2$ if and only if $r = s$ or $r = -s$.

quotient property of square roots (p. 518): For any nonnegative real number a and any positive real number b, $\sqrt{\dfrac{a}{b}} = \dfrac{\sqrt{a}}{\sqrt{b}}$.

reflexive property of equality (p. 46): If a is a real number, then $a = a$.

substitution principle (p. 2): An expression may be replaced by another expression that has the same value.

subtraction property of equality (p. 95): If a, b, and c are any real numbers, and $a = b$, then $a - c = b - c$.

symmetric property of equality (p. 46): If a and b are real numbers, and $a = b$, then $b = a$.

transitive property of equality (p. 46): For all real numbers, a, b, and c, if $a = b$ and $b = c$, then $a = c$.

transitive property of order (p. 462): For all real numbers a, b, and c,
1. If $a < b$ and $b < c$, then $a < c$;
2. If $c > b$ and $b > a$, then $c > a$.

zero-product property (p. 230): For all real numbers a and b, $ab = 0$ if and only if $a = 0$ or $b = 0$.

Glossary of Terms

abscissa (p. 353): The first coordinate in an ordered pair of numbers associated with a point in a coordinate plane. Also called *x-coordinate*.

absolute value (pp. 37, 482): The positive number of any pair of opposite nonzero real numbers is the absolute value of each number. The absolute value of 0 is 0. The absolute value of a number a is denoted by $|a|$.

acute angle (p. 617): An angle with measure between 0° and 90°.

addition-or-subtraction method (pp. 426–427): A method of solving a system of two equations; one variable is eliminated by adding or subtracting the equations.

additive inverses (p. 50): A number and its opposite.

angle (p. 616): A figure formed by two different rays that have the same endpoint.

area: The area of a region is the number of square units it contains.

arrow notation (p. 379): A notation used in defining a function; for example, $P: n \rightarrow 5n - 500$.

average (p. 85): The average of a set of numbers is the sum of the numbers divided by the number of numbers.

axes (p. 354): *See* coordinate axes.

axis of symmetry of a parabola (p. 384): The line containing the maximum or minimum point of the parabola.

base of a power (p. 141): The number that is used as a factor a given number of times; in 2^5, 2 is the base.

BASIC (p. 111): A programming language.

binomial (p. 146): A polynomial of only two terms.

boundary (p. 490): A line that separates the coordinate plane into three sets of points: the points *on* the line; the points *above* the line; the points *below* the line.

box-and-whisker plot (p. 612): A display of data useful for comparing two distributions.

closed half-plane (p. 490): The graph of an open half-plane and its boundary.

coefficient (p. 146): In the monomial $15a^2b^2$, 15 is the coefficient, or *numerical coefficient*.

collinear points (p. 364): Points that lie on the same line.

combined variation (p. 588): If a variable varies directly as one variable and inversely as another, the resulting relationship is a combined variation (expressed by $zy = kx$, k a nonzero constant).

common factor (p. 186): A factor of two or more integers is called a common factor of the integers.

complementary angles (p. 619): Two angles are complementary if the sum of their measures is 90°. Each angle is a *complement* of the other.

completing the square (p. 564): A method of transforming a quadratic equation so that it is in the form "perfect square = k" ($k \geq 0$).

complex fraction (p. 278): A fraction whose numerator or denominator contains one or more fractions.

conjugates (p. 544): If b and d are both nonnegative, then the binomials $a\sqrt{b} + c\sqrt{d}$ and $a\sqrt{b} - c\sqrt{d}$ are conjugates of one another.

conjunction (p. 478): A sentence formed by joining two open sentences by the word *and*.

consecutive even integers (p. 75): Integers obtained by counting by twos, beginning with any even integer.

consecutive integers (p. 75): Numbers obtained by counting by ones from any number in the set of integers.

consecutive odd integers (p. 75): Integers obtained by counting by twos, beginning with any odd integer.

constant (monomial) (pp. 146, 201): A monomial consisting of a numeral only; a term with no variable factor.

constant of variation (pp. 391, 397): The nonzero constant k in a direct variation defined by $y = kx$ or in an inverse variation defined by $xy = k$. Also called *constant of proportionality*.

converse (p. 230): The converse of a statement in "if-then" form is obtained by interchanging the "if" and "then" parts of the statement.

coordinate axes (p. 354): The x- and y-axes in the coordinate plane.

coordinate plane (p. 354): A plane in which an ordered pair can be located by reference to two intersecting number lines.

coordinate of a point (p. 31): The number paired with that point on a number line.

coordinates of a point (p. 353): The abscissa and ordinate of the point, written as an ordered pair of numbers.

cosine (p. 627): The cosine of an acute angle A in a right triangle $=$
$$\frac{\text{length of leg adjacent to } \angle A}{\text{length of hypotenuse}}.$$

cubic equation (p. 231): A polynomial equation with a term of degree 3 as its term of highest degree.

degree (p. 617): A unit of angle measurement.

degree of a monomial (p. 146): The sum of the degrees of the variables in the monomial.

degree of a polynomial (p. 147): The greatest of the degrees of its terms after it has been simplified.

degree of a variable in a monomial (p. 146): The number of times that the variable occurs as a factor in the monomial.

difference (p. 59): *See* subtraction.

direct variation (p. 391): A function defined by an equation of the form $y = kx$, where k is a nonzero constant. We say that y is directly proportional to x. (*See also* quadratic direct variation.)

discriminant (p. 573): For a quadratic equation in the form $ax^2 + bx + c = 0$, the value of $b^2 - 4ac$ is called the discriminant.

disjoint sets (p. 476): Two sets that have no members in common.

disjunction (p. 478): A sentence formed by joining two open sentences by the word *or*.

distance formula (p. 535): For any points $P_1(x_1, y_1)$ and $P_2(x_2, y_2)$,
$$P_1P_2 = \sqrt{(x_2 - x_1)^2 + (y_2 - y_1)^2}.$$

divisible (p. 195): One polynomial is (evenly) divisible by another polynomial if the quotient is also a polynomial.

division (p. 83): For every real number a and every nonzero real number b, the quotient $a \div b$, or $\frac{a}{b}$, is defined by $a \div b = a \cdot \frac{1}{b}$.

domain of a function (p. 374): *See under* function.

domain of a variable (p. 10): The given set of numbers that the variable may represent.

double root (p. 231): *See* multiple root.

empty set (p. 117): The set with no members; the null set.

endpoint (p. 616): The starting point of a ray.

equation (p. 10): A statement formed by placing an equals sign between two numerical or variable expressions.

equilateral triangle (p. 621): A triangle with all sides of equal length.

equivalent equations (p. 96): Equations that have the same solution set over a given domain.

equivalent expressions (p. 67): Expressions that represent the same number for all values of the variable that they contain.

equivalent inequality (p. 463): An inequality that has the same solution set as a given inequality.

equivalent system (p. 430): A system of equations having the same solution set as another system.

evaluating a variable expression (p. 2): Replacing each variable in the expression by a given value and simplifying the result.

even integer (p. 75): An integer that is the product of 2 and any integer.

event (p. 600): Any possible subset of the sample space resulting from an experiment.

expanded notation (p. 338): A way of writing numbers that uses powers of 10 to express place values.

exponent (p. 141): In a power, the number that indicates how many times the base is used as a factor; in 6^5, 5 is the exponent.

exponential form of a power (p. 141): The expression n^4 is the exponential form of $n \cdot n \cdot n \cdot n$.

extremes (p. 293): In the proportion $a:b = c:d$, a and d are the extremes.

factor (p. 46): When two or more numbers are multiplied, each of the numbers is a factor of the product.

factor set (p. 185): The name given to the set over which a number is factored.

factored completely (p. 227): A polynomial is factored completely when it is expressed as the product of a monomial and one or more prime polynomials.

factoring (p. 185): Factoring a number over a given set is writing the number as a product of numbers in that set.

factors (p. 46): Numbers that are multiplied together to produce a product.

finite decimal (p. 512): *See* terminating decimal.

formula (p. 15): An equation that states a rule about a relationship.

fraction (pp. 83, 247): An expression in the form $\frac{a}{b}$, $b \neq 0$.

fractional equation (p. 304): An equation with a variable in the denominator of one or more terms.

frequency distribution (p. 606): A summary of data that displays the items according to frequency of occurrence.

function (p. 374): A correspondence between two sets, the *domain* and the *range*, that assigns to each member of the domain *exactly one* member of the range.

functional notation (p. 379): A notation used in defining a function; for example, $P(n) = 5n - 500$.

graph of an equation in two variables (p. 354): All the points that are the graphs of the solutions of the equation.

graph of a function (p. 383): The graph of the equation that defines the function.

graph of an inequality (p. 458): The graph representing all the numbers in the solution set of the sentence.

graph of a number (p. 31): The point on a number line that is paired with the number.

graph of an ordered pair (p. 353): The point in a coordinate plane associated with an ordered pair of real numbers.

graph of a relation (p. 389): The graphs of all the ordered pairs that form the relation.

graphing method (p. 414): A method of solving a system of equations in two variables.

greatest common factor (GCF) of integers (p. 186): The greatest integer that is a factor of two or more given integers.

greatest common factor (GCF) of two or more monomials (p. 190): The common factor with the greatest coefficient and the greatest degree in each variable.

greatest monomial factor of a polynomial (p. 195): The GCF of the terms of the polynomial.

greatest value of a function (p. 384): The y-coordinate of the highest point of the graph of the function.

grouping symbol (p. 6): A device used to enclose an expression that should be simplified before other operations are performed. Examples: parentheses, brackets, fraction bar.

half-plane (p. 490): *See* closed half-plane *and* open half-plane.

histogram (p. 606): A graph that describes a frequency distribution.

horizontal axis (p. 353): The horizontal number line in a coordinate plane. Also called the *x-axis*.

hyperbola (pp. 397–398): The graph of $xy = k$ for any nonzero value of k.

hypotenuse (p. 529): In a right triangle, the side opposite the right angle.

identity (p. 117): An equation that is true for every value of the variable(s).

identity element for addition (p. 50): Zero (0).

identity element for multiplication (p. 70): One (1).

imaginary numbers (p. 570): Numbers that involve the imaginary unit i, defined as $\sqrt{-1}$.

inequality (p. 458): A statement formed by placing an inequality symbol between numerical or variable expressions.

inequality symbols (pp. 32, 457): Symbols used to show the order of two real numbers. The symbol $\neq$ means "is not equal to."

infinite decimal (p. 513): *See* nonterminating decimal.

integers (p. 31): The set consisting of the positive integers, the negative integers, and zero.

intersection of sets (p. 476): For any two sets A and B, the set consisting of those members and only those members common to A and B.

inverse operations (p. 107): Operations that "undo" each other – for example, multiplication and division.

inverse variation (p. 397): A function defined by an equation of the form $xy = k$, where k is a nonzero constant.

inverse variation as the square (p. 585): A function defined by an equation of the form $x^2y = k$, where k is a nonzero constant.

irrational numbers (p. 521): Real numbers that cannot be expressed in the form $\frac{a}{b}$, where a and b are integers.

irreducible polynomial (p. 214): A polynomial that cannot be expressed as a product of polynomials of lower degree.

isosceles triangle (p. 621): A triangle having two sides of equal length. The third side is called the *base*. The angles opposite the equal sides are the *base angles*.

joint variation (p. 588): If a variable varies directly as the product of two or more other variables, the resulting relationship is a joint variation (expressed by $z = kxy$, k a nonzero constant).

least common denominator (LCD) (p. 260): The least positive common multiple of the denominators of two or more given fractions.

least value of a function (p. 384): The y-coordinate of the lowest point of the graph of the function.

legs of a right triangle (p. 529): The sides that form the right angle.

like terms (p. 146): *See* similar terms.

line segment (p. 616): The part of a line that consists of two points and all points between them. Also called *segment*.

linear equation (pp. 231, 354): A polynomial equation of degree one.

linear equation in two variables (p. 354): Any equation equivalent to one of the form $ax + by = c$, where a, b, and c are real numbers with a and b not both zero. Its graph is a line.

linear function (p. 383): A function defined by $f(x) = mx + b$.

linear programming (p. 499): A branch of mathematics concerned with problems that involve maximizing or minimizing a quantity.

linear term (p. 201): A term of degree one.

maximum point of a parabola (p. 384): The highest point; the point whose y-coordinate is the greatest value of the corresponding function.

mean (p. 606): The sum of the data in a collection divided by the number of items.

mean proportional (p. 296): When the means of a proportion are equal, each mean is called the mean proportional between the two extremes.

means (p. 293): In the proportion $a:b = c:d$, b and c are the means.

median (p. 607): In a frequency distribution, the middle number or the average of the two middle numbers when the data are arranged in order.

minimum point of a parabola (p. 384): The lowest point; the point whose y-coordinate is the least value of the corresponding function.

mixed expression (p. 270): The sum or difference of a polynomial and a fraction.

mixed number (p. 270): The sum of an integer and a fraction.

mode (p. 607): The most frequently occurring number in a frequency distribution.

monomial (p. 146): An expression that is either a numeral, a variable, or the product of a numeral and one or more variables.

multiple (p. 78): The product of any real number and an integer is a multiple of the real number.

multiple root (p. 231): A solution of an equation that occurs more than once.

multiplicative inverses (p. 79): *See* reciprocals.

natural order of integers (p. 75): Order from least to greatest.

negative integers (p. 31): The numbers -1, -2, -3, -4, and so on.

negative number (p. 31): A number paired with a point on the negative side of a number line.

negative side (p. 31): On a horizontal number line, the side to the left of the origin.

nonterminating decimal (p. 513): When a common fraction is written as a decimal by dividing the numerator by the denominator, the result is a nonterminating decimal if a digit or block of digits repeats endlessly as the remainder. Also called *unending, infinite, repeating,* or *periodic decimal.*

null set (p. 117): The set with no members; the empty set.

numeral (p. 1): An expression that names a particular number; a numerical expression.

numerical coefficient (p. 146): *See* coefficient.

numerical expression (p. 1): An expression that names a particular number; a numeral.

obtuse angle (p. 617): An angle with measure between 90° and 180°.

odd integer (p. 75): An integer that is not even.

open half-plane (p. 490): Either of the two regions into which a boundary line separates the coordinate plane.

open sentence (p. 10): A sentence containing one or more variables.

opposite of a number (p. 36): Each of the numbers in a pair such as 6 and −6 or −2.5 and 2.5. Also called *additive inverse*.

ordered pair (p. 349): A pair of numbers for which the order of the numbers is important; $(2, -3)$ is an ordered pair.

ordinate (p. 353): The second coordinate in an ordered pair of numbers associated with a point in a coordinate plane. Also called *y-coordinate*.

origin (pp. 31, 353): The zero point on a number line. The intersection of the axes on a coordinate plane.

parabola (p. 384): The graph of $f(x) = ax^2 + bx + c$, where the domain is the set of real numbers and $a \neq 0$.

parallel lines (p. 367): Lines in the same plane that do not intersect; nonvertical lines that have the same slope.

percent (p. 309): Another way of saying *hundredths,* or *divided by 100*. Usually denoted by the symbol %.

perfect square (p. 562): An expression such as x^2, $(x + 1)^2$, or $(5x - 3)^2$.

perfect square trinomial (p. 209): An expression with three terms that is the square of a binomial.

perimeter: The perimeter of a plane figure is the distance around it.

periodic decimal (p. 513): *See* nonterminating decimal.

perpendicular lines (p. 370): Any two lines that intersect to form right angles.

plot a point (p. 353): Locate the graph of an ordered pair of real numbers in a coordinate plane.

polynomial (p. 146): A sum of monomials.

polynomial equation (p. 231): An equation whose sides are both polynomials.

positive integers (p. 31): The numbers 1, 2, 3, 4, and so on.

positive number (p. 31): A number paired with a point on the positive side of a number line.

positive side (p. 31): On a horizontal number line, the side to the right of the origin.

power of a number (p. 141): The product when a number is multiplied by itself a given number of times; $4 \times 4 \times 4$, or 4^3, is the third power of 4.

prime factorization (p. 185): Expressing a positive integer as a product of primes.

prime number (prime) (p. 185): An integer greater than 1 that has no positive integral factor other than itself and 1.

prime polynomial (p. 214): An irreducible polynomial with integral coefficients whose greatest monomial factor is 1.

principal square root (p. 517): The positive square root of a positive number; denoted by the symbol $\sqrt{}$.

probability (p. 600): The branch of mathematics that deals with the possibility that an event will happen.

probability of an event (p. 603): The ratio of the number of outcomes favoring the event to the total number of outcomes.

proof (p. 130): Logical reasoning that uses given facts, definitions, properties, and previously proved theorems to show that a theorem is true.

proportion (p. 293): An equation that states that two ratios are equal.

Pythagorean theorem (p. 529): In any right triangle, the square of the length of the hypotenuse equals the sum of the squares of the lengths of the legs. (The converse is also true.)

quadrant (p. 354): One of the four regions into which the coordinate axes separate the plane.

quadratic direct variation (p. 584): A function defined by an equation of the form $y = kx^2$, where k is a nonzero constant.

quadratic equation (p. 231): A polynomial equation whose term of highest degree is quadratic.

quadratic formula (p. 567): The solutions of a quadratic equation in the form $ax^2 + bx + c = 0$, $a \neq 0$ and $b^2 - 4ac \geq 0$, are given by the formula

$$x = \frac{-b \pm \sqrt{b^2 - 4ac}}{2a}.$$

quadratic function (p. 384): A function defined by $f(x) = ax^2 + bx + c$ ($a \neq 0$).

quadratic polynomial (p. 201): A trinomial whose term of greatest degree is quadratic.

quadratic term (p. 201): A term of degree two.

quotient (p. 83): *See* division.

radical (p. 517): An expression in the form $\sqrt{a}$.

radical equation (p. 547): An equation containing a radical with a variable in the radicand.

radical sign (p. 517): The symbol $\sqrt{}$.

radicand (p. 517): The symbol written beneath a radical sign.

random experiment (p. 600): An activity whose outcome can't be predicted when the activity is repeated under essentially the same conditions.

range of a frequency distribution (p. 607): The difference between the highest and the lowest values.

range of a function (p. 374): *See under* function.

rate (p. 302): A ratio that compares the amounts of two different kinds of measurements, for example, meters per second.

ratio (p. 287): The ratio of one number to another is the quotient when the first number is divided by the second number (not zero).

rational expression (p. 507): An expression for a rational number.

rational number (p. 507): A real number that can be expressed as the quotient of two integers.

rationalizing the denominator (p. 537): The process of eliminating a radical from the denominator of a fraction.

ray (p. 616): The part of a line that consists of a point A and all points of the line on one side of A.

real number (p. 32): Any number that is either positive, negative, or zero.

reciprocals (p. 79): Two numbers whose product is 1; also called *multiplicative inverses*.

relation (p. 389): Any set of ordered pairs. The set of first coordinates of the ordered pairs is the *domain* of the relation; the set of second coordinates is the *range*.

repeating decimal (p. 513): *See* nonterminating decimal.

right angle (p. 617): An angle with measure 90°.

right triangle (p. 621): A triangle having one right angle.

root of a sentence: *See* solution of a sentence.

sample space (p. 600): The set of all possible outcomes of a random experiment.

satisfy an open sentence (p. 10): Any solution of the sentence satisfies the sentence.

scientific notation (p. 336): A positive number in scientific notation is expressed as the product of a number greater than or equal to 1 but less than 10, and an integral power of 10.

sides of an angle (p. 616): The two rays that form the angle.

sides of an equation (p. 10): The two expressions joined by the equals sign.

sides of an inequality (p. 458): The expressions joined by an inequality symbol.

sides of a triangle (p. 621): The three segments that form the triangle.

similar terms (p. 146): Two monomials that are exactly alike or are the same except for their numerical coefficients. Also called *like terms*.

similar triangles (p. 624): Two triangles are similar if the measures of two angles of one triangle equal the measures of two angles of the other. Angles with equal measures are called *corresponding angles*. Sides opposite corresponding angles are called *corresponding sides*.

simple event (p. 600): An event that involves a single member of a sample space.

simplest form of an algebraic fraction (p. 247): A form of the fraction in which the numerator and denominator have no common factor other than 1 and -1.

simplest form of an expression having a square-root radical (p. 537): The form of the expression in which no integral radicand has a square factor other than 1; no fractions are under a radical sign; no radicals are in a denominator.

simplest form of a polynomial (p. 146): A polynomial is in simplest form when no two of its terms are similar.

simplifying an expression (p. 67): Replacing an expression containing variables by an equivalent expression with as few terms as possible.

simplifying a numerical expression (p. 2): Replacing the expression by the simplest name for its value.

simultaneous equations (p. 413): *See under* system of (simultaneous) equations.

sine (p. 627): The sine of an acute angle A in a right triangle =
$$\frac{\text{length of leg opposite } \angle A}{\text{length of hypotenuse}}.$$

slope of a line (p. 361): If (x_1, y_1) and (x_2, y_2) are two different points on a line, the slope of the line is given by $\frac{y_2 - y_1}{x_2 - x_1}$. A horizontal line has slope 0; a vertical line has no slope.

slope-intercept form of an equation (p. 366): The equation of a line in the form $y = mx + b$, where m is the slope and b is the y-intercept.

solution of an equation in two variables (p. 349): An ordered pair of numbers that make the sentence true.

solution of a sentence (pp. 10, 458): Any value of a variable that turns an open sentence into a true statement.

solution of a system of two equations in two variables (p. 413): An ordered pair that satisfies both equations at the same time.

solution set of an open sentence (pp. 10, 458): The set of all solutions of the sentence.

solve a conjunction (p. 478): To find the values of the variable for which both open sentences in the conjunction are true.

solve a disjunction (p. 478): To find the values of the variable for which at least one of the open sentences in the disjunction is true.

solve an equation (p. 349): To find the set of all solutions of the equation.

solve an open sentence (p. 10): To find the solution set of the sentence.

solve a system of two equations in x and y (p. 413): To find all ordered pairs (x, y) that make both equations true.

square root (p. 517): If $a^2 = b$, then a is a square root of b.

standard deviation (p. 609): In a frequency distribution, the principal square root of the variance.

standard form of a linear equation (p. 354): $ax + by = c$, where a, b, and c are integers and a and b are not both zero.

standard form of a polynomial equation (p. 231): A form of the equation in which one side is zero and the other is a simplified polynomial arranged in order of decreasing degree of the variable.

stem-and-leaf plot (p. 611): A way of displaying a frequency distribution.

straight angle (p. 617): An angle with measure 180°.

substitution method (p. 418): A method of solving a system of linear equations in two variables.

subtraction (p. 59): For all real numbers a and b, the difference $a - b$ is defined by $a - b = a + (-b)$.

supplementary angles (p. 619): Two angles are supplementary if the sum of their measures is 180°. Each angle is a *supplement* of the other.

system of (simultaneous) equations (p. 413): Two or more equations in the same variables.

tangent (p. 627): The tangent of an acute angle A in a right triangle $=$
$$\frac{\text{length of leg opposite } \angle A}{\text{length of leg adjacent to } \angle A}.$$

terminating decimal (p. 512): When a common fraction is written as a decimal by dividing the numerator by the denominator, the result is a terminating decimal if the remainder is zero. Also called *ending decimal* or *finite decimal*.

terms (p. 46): In the sum $a + b$, a and b are called terms.

theorem (p. 130): A statement that is shown to be true by use of a logically developed argument.

transformations (pp. 96, 102, 463): Operations on an equation or an inequality that produce a simpler equivalent statement.

triangle (p. 621): A figure formed by three segments joining three points not on the same line. Each segment is a *side,* and each point is a *vertex,* of the triangle.

trigonometric functions (p. 628): The functions sine, cosine, and tangent, each having the set of acute angles as domain.

trigonometric ratios (p. 627): Ratios of the lengths of the sides of a right triangle.

trinomial (p. 146): A polynomial of only three terms.

uniform motion (p. 167): Motion without change in speed, or rate.

union of sets (p. 476): For any two sets A and B, the set whose members belong to at least one of the sets A and B.

unit price (p. 302): The price of one unit of a given item.

value of a numerical expression (p. 1): The number named by the expression.

values of a function (p. 379): Members of the range of the function.

values of a variable (p. 1): The numbers that can be represented by the variable.

variable (p. 1): A symbol used to represent one or more numbers.

variable expression (p. 1): An expression that contains a variable.

variance (p. 609): In a frequency distribution, the mean of the squares of the distance of each score from the mean.

vertex of an angle (p. 616): The common endpoint of the rays forming the angle.

vertex of a parabola (p. 384): The maximum or minimum point of the graph.

vertical angles (p. 619): Two angles whose sides are rays in the same line, but in opposite directions.

vertical axis (p. 353): The vertical number line in a coordinate plane.

vertices of a triangle (p. 621): *See under* triangle.

whole numbers (p. 31): The set consisting of zero and all the positive integers.

work rate (p. 326): The fractional part of a job done in a given unit of time.

x-axis (p. 353): The horizontal axis in the coordinate plane.

x-coordinate (p. 353): *See* abscissa.

x-intercept (pp. 371, 572): The x-coordinate of a point where a graph intersects the x-axis.

y-axis (p. 353): *See* vertical axis.

y-coordinate (p. 353): *See* ordinate.

y-intercept (p. 366): The y-coordinate of a point where a graph crosses the y-axis.

zeros of a quadratic function (p. 581): The members of the solution set of the related quadratic equation.

Index

Abscissa, 353
Absolute value, 37
  in open sentences, 482–488
Acute angle, 617
Addition
  of fractions, 264–268
  of integers, 686
  identity element for, 50
  on a number line, 49–53
  of polynomials, 146–150
  properties of, 50, 51
  of radicals, 540–541
  of real numbers, 54–58
  rules for, 54, 264
  of similar terms, 146
  transforming equations by,
    95–96
Addition-or-subtraction method,
  426–433
Addition property
  of equality, 95
  of order, 463
Additive inverse(s), 50
Algebra (historical note), 87
Angle(s), 616–617, 619–620
  complementary, 619
  corresponding, 624
  degree measure of, 617
  of depression, 633
  of elevation, 633
  supplementary, 619
  of a triangle, 621, 624
  vertical, 619
Applications
  architecture, 8, 229, 477
  astronomy, 30, 125, 145
  bicycle gears, 286
  Boyle's gas law, 583
  business, 44
  car loans, 101
  energy, 5, 333, 550, 589, 591,
    592
  engineering, 165, 341, 443
  games, 184, 412, 560
  health, 121–122, 396, 425, 461,
    489
  illumination, 593
  line of best fit, 378
  linear programming, 499–500
  map coordinates, 100, 348, 359
  misuse of statistics, 614–615

  photography, 172, 246, 297, 587
  physics, xviii, 94, 398, 456
  surveying, 359, 506, 633
  understanding product prices, 74
  units of measurement in problem
    solving, 302
  See also Problems.
Approximation
  of irrational square root, 521,
    522, 565
  of repeating decimal, 514–515
Area formulas and problems, 4,
  8, 9, 15, 21, 143, 150, 154,
  160, 163, 165, 172–174,
  197–199, 290, 416
Arrow notation, 379
Associative properties, 45
Average, 85, 509. *See also* Mean.
Axes, coordinate, 353
Axioms. *See* Properties.
Axis
  horizontal, 353
  of symmetry, 384, 385
  vertical, 353

Bar graph, 375, 606
Base of an isosceles triangle, 621
Base of a power, 141
BASIC. *See* Computer Exercises
  and Computer Key-In.
between, **meaning of,** 457
Binomials, 146
  containing square-root radicals,
    544–545
  factoring products of, 205–207,
    691
  multiplying mentally, 200–202
  product of, 200–202, 689–690
  squares of, 208–212
Biographical Note
  de la Cierva, Juan, 542
  Einstein, Albert, 578
  Hypatia, 145
  Mitchell, Maria, 30
  Ramanujan, Srinivasa, 269
  Roebling, Emily Warren, 443
  Williams, Daniel Hale, 461
  Wu, Hsien, 396
Boundary of a half-plane, 490
Box-and-whisker plot, 612

Broken-line graph, 375–376

Calculator Key-In, 13, 58, 82,
  106, 111, 145, 193, 203, 258,
  341, 365, 403, 498, 528, 554
Calculators
  graphing, 354, 357, 367, 368,
    384, 386, 387, 399, 414, 415,
    494, 607, 694, 695, 700
  suggestions for when to use, 7,
    169, 205, 235, 309, 337, 517,
    521, 565, 630, 631, 633
  use in exercises, 69, 74, 187,
    206, 223, 236, 313, 318, 335,
    519, 522, 523, 527, 532, 533,
    534, 566, 569, 580, 586, 631,
    632, 635, 685, 697
Cancellation rule for fractions,
  189
Career Note
  astronomer, 125
  bilingual math teacher, 40
  draftsperson, 229
  electrical engineer, 341
  nutritionist, 425
  operations research analyst, 528
  pharmacist, 489
  statistician, 377
Challenge problems, 9, 35, 48,
  53, 69, 188, 223, 254, 263,
  273, 292, 382, 425, 437, 475,
  520, 534, 536, 632
Chapter Review. *See* Reviews.
Chapter Summary. *See*
  Summaries.
Chapter Test. *See* Tests.
Charts used in problem solving,
  121–125, 126–129, 167–169,
  175, 307, 321–324, 326–328,
  421–422, 438–439, 444–445
Closed half-plane, 490
Closure
  properties of, 45
  under an operation, 48
Coefficient(s), 146
  decimal, 310
College Entrance Exams,
  Preparing for, 93, 183, 285,
  411, 505, 599, 709–711
Commutative properties, 45

solving, by the quadratic
formula, 567–569, 576
standard form of, 231, 567
Quadratic formula, 567
Quadratic function(s), 383–385,
561–596
graphs of, 383–385, 581–582
Quadratic inequalities, 581–582
Quadratic polynomial, 201
Quadratic term, 201
Quadratic trinomials. *See under*
Factoring.
Quartile, 612
Quotient(s), 14
of monomials, 191
of polynomials, 274
power of a, 252
of powers, 190
property of, 189
**Quotient property of square
roots,** 518

Radical, 517
Radical equation(s), 547–550
Radical expression(s), 537–551
addition and subtraction of,
540–541
multiplication of binomials
containing, 544–545
products and quotients of,
537–539
rationalizing the denominator of
a, 537, 545
simplest form of, 537
simplifying, 537–539
Radical sign, 517
Radicand, 517
Random experiment, 600–601
Range
of frequency distribution, 607,
609
of function, 374
of relation, 389
Rate, 302
of motion, 438
Ratio(s), 287–292
three numbers in, 289
trigonometric, 627–636
Rational expression, 247, 507
See also Fractions.
Rational number(s), 507
comparing, 507–508
decimal forms of, 512–516
properties of, 507–511
Rationalizing the denominator,
537, 545
Ray, 616

Reading Algebra
independent study, 64
inequalities, 468
problem solving, 26
problem-solving strategies, 404
reading your algebra book, xiv–
xv
symbols, xvi–xvii
Real number(s), 32
addition of, 54–58
division of, 83–86
exploring density of, 685
multiplication of, 70–73
and the number line, 32,
457–458
reciprocal of, 79–80
subtraction of, 59–63
Reciprocal(s), 79
of opposite of a number, 79
of a product, 80
property of, 79
Reflexive property of equality, 46
Relation(s), 389–390
graphs of, 389
Repeating decimal, 513–514, 697
Reviews
chapter, 41, 89, 135, 178–179,
240–241, 280–281, 342–343,
405–406, 451, 501–502,
555–556, 595–596, 637–638
cumulative, 91, 137, 181, 243,
283, 345, 409, 453, 503, 557,
597–598
mixed problem solving, 139,
245, 347, 455, 559
mixed review exercises, *at end
of each lesson*
See also Extra Practice,
Maintaining Skills, *and* Tests.
Right angle, 617
Right triangle(s), 529–530, 621
exploring, 698–699
Pythagorean theorem and
converse, 529, 530
trigonometric ratios associated
with angles in, 627–628
Root(s)
double, 231
multiple, 231
of open sentences, 10
of quadratic equations, 231, 561,
572, 573, 700
Rounding decimals, 514–551

Sample space, 600
Scatter graphs, 378, 611

Science. *See* Applications,
Formulas, *and* Problems.
Scientific notation, 336–340
Segment, 616
Self-Tests. *See* Tests.
Set(s), 10
disjoint, 476
empty, 117
factor, 185, 195
intersection of, 476
of irrational numbers, 521
members of, 10
null, 117
of rational numbers, 507–508
of real numbers, 31–32,
521–522
solution, 10
union of, 476
Sides
of an angle, 616
corresponding, 624
of an equation, 10
of an inequality, 458
of a triangle, 621, 624
Similar terms, 146
Similar triangles, 624–626, 628
Simple interest, 4, 313, 316, 392
Simplest form
of expression having a square-
root radical, 537
of fractions, 189, 247
of polynomials, 146
Simplifying
expressions, 2, 6–7, 46, 79–82,
142
fractions, 189–191, 247–250
polynomials, 146
radical expressions, 537–539
sums and differences of radicals,
540–541
Simultaneous equations, 413
See also Systems of linear
equations.
Sine, 627, 628, 630
Slope of a line, 360–365
**Slope-intercept form of a linear
equation,** 366–369
Solution, 10, 349, 458
of a system of equations,
413–414
See also Root(s).
Solution set(s)
of an inequality, 458
of a sentence, 10
Solving equations, 10–11
exploring ways of, 688
by factoring, 230–233

Acknowledgments

Book designed by Ligature, Inc.

Technical Art by Precision Graphics

Illustrations by Gary Torrisi

Cover design by Ligature, Inc.

Cover and chapter opener photos by John Payne Photo, Ltd.;
   Luis Casteneda/Image Bank/Chicago (background photo)

Photos

xiv	Peter Chapman	229	Jeff Zaruba/After Image
xv	Peter Chapman	234	E.A. McGee/FPG
5	Ray Pfortner/Peter Arnold, Inc.	236	MacDonald Photography/Picture Cube
15	Joe Outland/FPG	267	Alese and Mort Pechter/Stock Market
15	Tad Goodale	268	Michael Radigan/Stock Market
25	Arthur Grace/Stock Boston	272	Rui Coutinho/Nawrocki
29	Warren Morgan/Focus on Sports	291	Sal Maimone/Shostal Associates
32	Tad Goodale	292	Bob Daemmrich/Uniphoto
40	Kevin Galvin/Bruce Coleman	294	Charles Ronear/Nawrocki
57	Lou Jones	303	George Meinzinger/After Image
63	NASA	311	Peter Chapman
65	Hanson Carroll/Peter Arnold, Inc.	314	Renaud W. Granel/Index Stock
74	Cody/FPG	315	Ken Sexton/Nawrocki
75	Elliot Smith	321	Index Stock
101	James Ballard	326	Runk/Schoenberg/Grant Heilman
102	Gabe Palmer/Stock Market	329	Frank Rossotto/Stock Market
105	Frank Fisher/After Image	341	Brownie Harris/Stock Market
112	D.P. Hershkowitz/Bruce Coleman	360	Reed Chestner/Nawrocki
115	Edward L. Miller/Light Images	369	Gus Schonefeld/Berg and Associates
125	National Optical Astronomy Observatory	377	Caroline Brown/Fran Heyl Associates
128	Stuart Cohen/Stock Market	391	Tom Tracy/FPG
165	Cy Furlan/Berg and Associates	394	Cynthia Matthews/Stock Market
170	Robert C. Dawson/After Image	402	Alan Goldsmith/Stock Market
171	Vince Streano/Click/Chicago	422	Ken O'Donoghue
172	Alan C. Ross/Photo Researchers, Inc.	425	Gabe Palmer/Stock Market
176	Gabe Palmer/Stock Market	428	Julie Habel/Westlight
198	R.L. Goddard/Berg and Associates	435	Howard Zyrb/FPG
223	Ed Lettau/Photo Researchers, Inc.	442	Wendell Metzen/Bruce Coleman
		448	Henley and Savage/Stock Market

Photos *(continued)*

473 Coco McCoy/Rainbow
474 Michael Hayman/After Image
488 Sylvia Schlender/Nawrocki
489 Bob Daemmrich/Image Works
527 H. Armstrong Roberts
528 Camerique/H. Armstrong Roberts
533 Index Stock
547 Keith Kent/Peter Arnold, Inc.
550 Mark Antman/Image Works
579 Steve Raye/Taurus Photos
585 Tibor Bognar/Stock Market
586 Bob Daemmrich
592 Michael Amberger/Stock Market
600 Caroline Brown/Fran Heyl Associates
663 Mark and Chris Beattie/After Image

Answers to Selected Exercises

Chapter 1 Variables and Equations

Written Exercises, pages 3–4 **1.** 8 **3.** 60
5. 6 **7.** 29 **9.** 340 **11.** 2 **13.** 10 **15.** 6
17. 15 **19.** 13 **21.** 10 **23.** 56 **25.** 1
27. 5 **29.** 0 **31.** 58 **33.** 300 **35.** 60
37. 98.6 **39.** 1250 **41.** 3 **43.** any number
45. $\frac{1}{2}$ **47.** 0, 2 **49.** 1, 3

Mixed Review Exercises, page 5 **1.** 0.36
2. 29.32 **3.** 4 **4.** 3.4 **5.** 219 **6.** 1.62
7. 151.914 **8.** 16 **9.** $\frac{29}{30}$ **10.** $\frac{5}{8}$ **11.** $\frac{4}{3}$
12. $\frac{1}{8}$ **13.** $\frac{4}{15}$ **14.** $\frac{7}{20}$ **15.** $\frac{26}{21}$ **16.** $\frac{8}{3}$

Application, page 5 **1.** 2.016 kW · h

Written Exercises, pages 8–9 **1. a.** 20
b. 44 **3. a.** 5 **b.** 1 **5.** 3 **7.** 2 **9. a.** 13
b. 20 **11. a.** 6 **b.** 42 **13. a.** 17 **b.** 27
15. a. 72 **b.** 108 **17.** 0 **19.** 40 **21.** 4
23. $\frac{11}{2}$ **25.** 78 **27.** 8 **29.** 54 **31.** 384
33. 16.28 **35.** $12 \neq 6$ **37.** $30 = 30$
39. $5 \cdot (8 - 6) \div 2$ **41.** $5 \cdot (8 - 6 \div 2)$
43. $5 \cdot (2 + 8 - 4) \div 2$
45. $[(5 \cdot 2) + 8 - 4] \div 2$

Mixed Review Exercises, page 9 **1.** 3 **2.** 436
3. 144 **4.** 12 **5.** 4 **6.** 55 **7.** 23 **8.** 10
9. 5 **10.** 5 **11.** 60 **12.** 32

Challenge, page 9 **a.** 110 **b.** 5050

Written Exercises, pages 11–12 **1.** {4} **3.** {5}
5. {5} **7.** {4} **9.** {2} **11.** {0} **13.** {3}
15. {4} **17.** {1} **19.** {0, 1, 2, 3, 4, 5} **21.** 4
23. 8 **25.** 2 **27.** {4} **29.** {2} **31.** {8}
33. {7} **35.** {0, 2} **37.** {0, 6} **39. a.** More
than one **b.** None **c.** One; {4}
41. a. One; {2} **b.** More than one **c.** None
For Exs. 43–45, answers may vary. Examples
are given. **43.** $1 \cdot x = 3$, $x + 1 = 4$
45. $x - x = 0$, $4x \div 2 = x + x$

Mixed Review Exercises, page 12 **1.** 132
2. 10 **3.** 3 **4.** $\frac{7}{8}$ **5.** 6 **6.** 2 **7.** 22 **8.** 12
9. 88 **10.** 55 **11.** 2.4 **12.** 6

Calculator Key-In, page 13 **1.** 0 **3.** 0.1
5. 333,333 **7. a.** 100 **b.** 0 **c.** 37

Self-Test 1, page 13 **1.** 22 **2.** 84 **3.** 23
4. 6 **5.** {5} **6.** {3}

Written Exercises, pages 16–18 **1.** $8 + n$
3. $n - 11$ **5.** $\frac{1}{2}n$ **7.** $\frac{17}{d}$ **9.** $11x$ **11.** $7 + 2y$
13. $\frac{1}{2}n - 8$ **15.** $5 + \frac{n}{8}$ **17.** i **19.** g **21.** h
23. b **25.** c **27.** $f + 3$ **29.** $m - 10$
31. $17 - x$ **33. a.** $s - 3$ **b.** $d + 3$
35. a. $g - 12$ **b.** $b + 12$ **37.** $(3r)$ mi
39. $(5p)$ cents **41.** $5l$ **43.** $(3p + 2n)$ cents
45. 180 min; $60h$ min **47.** 3 years; $\frac{m}{12}$ years
49. $10c$; $10(c - 5)$ **51.** $n - 5$
53. $(p + 29) + 2p + (p + 42)$

Mixed Review Exercises, page 18 **1.** 13
2. 64 **3.** 12 **4.** 27 **5.** 26 **6.** 16 **7.** {4}
8. {4} **9.** {1} **10.** {0} **11.** {3} **12.** {2}
13. {4} **14.** {3}

Written Exercises, pages 20–22 **1.** a **3.** a
5. b **7.** b **9.** e **11.** b **13.** d **15.** h
17. $24 = x + 17$ **19.** $12 = 7 + x$
21. $40 = 8x$ **23.** s; $4s = 116$
25. c; $c + 7 = 50$ **27.** d; $d + 12 = 120$
29. p; $\frac{1}{8}p = 0.95$ **31.** t; $462 = 132t$
33. l; $\frac{1}{100}l = 8.5$ **35.** r; $24 - r = 3 + 2r$

Mixed Review Exercises, page 22 **1.** {4}
2. {6} **3.** {5} **4.** {6} **5.** {3} **6.** {2} **7.** {5}
8. {0, 1, 2, 3, 4, 5, 6} **9.** $n - 5$ **10.** $5 + n$
11. $\frac{5}{n}$ **12.** $2(5 + n)$

Problems, pages 24–26 **1.** $s + (s + 5) = 73$
3. $w + (4 + w) = 12$ **5.** $w + (3 + w) = 25$
7. $t + 8 = 2t$ **9.** $c + (5 + c) = 33$
11. $b + (2 + b) = 34$ **13.** $x + (x + 1) = 9$
15. $2(2w) + 2w = 60$
17. $30 = 7 + x + (x + 1)$
19. $x + (x + 1) + [(x + 1) + 2] = 12$
21. $x + (x + 1) + [2 + (1 + x)] = 10$

Answers to Selected Exercises **1**

Mixed Review Exercises, page 26   1. {1}
2. {2}   **3.** {4}   **4.** {4}   **5.** {5}   **6.** {5}   **7.** {2}
8. {4}   **9.** $\frac{1}{3}x$ **10.** $4x - 2$ **11.** $5 + 2x$
12. $\frac{1}{4}x - 4$

Reading Algebra, page 26   1. Twice as much milk as apple juice and three times as much milk as fruit punch was served; a total of 660 cartons was served.   **3.** No; the amount of apple juice served was $\frac{1}{2}x$, not $2x$, and the amount of punch served was $\frac{1}{3}x$, not $3x$.

Problems, pages 28–29   1. water color, 8; oil painting, 24   **3.** smaller, 64; larger, 121   **5.** car, 159 km; bus, 477 km   **7.** 44 Republicans; 56 Democrats   **9.** Ramon, $90; Elena, $135   **11.** school, 18 m   **13.** width, 11 m; length, 23 m   **15.** width, 12 ft; length, 27 ft   **17.** Luis, 115 lb; Carla, 110 lb; Rita, 108 lb

Mixed Review Exercises, page 29   1. 10   **2.** 4   **3.** 24   **4.** 153   **5.** $6x = 36$ **6.** $6 = x - 2$ **7.** $2 + 2x = 10$ **8.** $\frac{1}{3}x = 6$

Self-Test 2, page 30   1. $8(n + 4)$
2. $2x = 2 + x$ **3.** $x + (2 + 2x) = 11$
4. length, 11 ft; width, 5 ft

Written Exercises, pages 33–35   1. ⁻5, 5; five steps up   **3.** 190, ⁻190; 190 m below sea level   **5.** 18, ⁻18; a loss of $18   **7.** ⁻15, 15; 15 km east   **9.** 85, ⁻85; payments of $85   **11.** ⁻1, 1; one foot above ground   **13.** ⁻50, 50; a profit of $50   **15.** $6 > ⁻9$ **17.** $⁻8 > ⁻10$ **19.** $6 < 6.5$ **21.** $⁻13 < 0$ **23.** S, F   **25.** N, R   **27.** Q, A, U   **29.** M, T, P   **31.** $⁻1 < 3, 3 > ⁻1$ **33.** $0 < 2, 2 > 0$ **35.** $⁻6 < ⁻2, ⁻2 > ⁻6$ **37.** $0 < 5, 5 > 0$ **39.** <   **41.** <   **43.** >   **45.** >   **47.** ⁻2, ⁻1, 1, 2

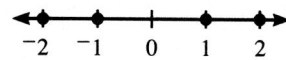

49. ⁻1, ⁻0.5, 0, 1.5

51. $⁻3, -1\frac{2}{3}, -\frac{1}{3}, 0$

53. $-1\frac{1}{4}, -\frac{1}{4}, \frac{3}{4}, 2\frac{1}{4}$

55. Cora, Freida, Stu, Janelle   **57.** 3

Mixed Review Exercises, page 35   1. 24   **2.** 24   **3.** 6   **4.** 3   **5.** 15   **6.** 14   **7.** $30 - x = 12$ **8.** $x + 4 = 2$ **9.** $6x = 2$ **10.** $\frac{1}{4}x = 1$

Challenge, page 35   1. 21, 28, 36, 45, 55

Written Exercises, pages 38–39   1. -12 **3.** 0   **5.** 19   **7.** 8   **9.** 11   **11.** 14   **13.** $\frac{3}{2}$ **15.** 4   **17.** 1   **19.** 0   **21.** >   **23.** <   **25.** =   **27.** $|-5| > 2$ **29.** $-(-2) > -(-1)$ **31.** {0}   **33.** $\left\{\frac{1}{2}, -\frac{1}{2}\right\}$ **35.** No sol. because the absolute value of a number cannot be negative.   **37.** {1, −1}   **39.** 3.5   **41.** 2.3   **43.** 6.3   **45.** (a) is false. 0 is a real number and $|0| = 0$, which is not a positive number.

Mixed Review Exercises, page 39   1. 1   **2.** 7   **3.** 2   **4.** 8   **5.** 1   **6.** 13   **7.** $-3, 3$ **8.** $-50, 50$ **9.** $1000, -1000$ **10.** $0.5, -0.5$

Self-Test 3, page 39
1.

2. -7 **3.** 14   **4.** -3 **5.** $\frac{2}{3}$

Chapter Review, page 41   1. d   **3.** b   **5.** c   **7.** c   **9.** b   **11.** d

Maintaining Skills, page 43   1. 29.9476   **3.** 377.7   **5.** 1653.6   **7.** 16.522   **9.** 989.04   **11.** 45.79   **13.** $\frac{5}{8}, \frac{6}{8}$ **15.** $\frac{6}{21}, \frac{14}{21}$ **17.** $\frac{47}{45}$ **19.** $\frac{67}{72}$ **21.** $\frac{15}{52}$ **23.** $\frac{5}{6}$ **25.** $\frac{23}{21}$ **27.** $\frac{49}{64}$

Chapter 2 Working with Real Numbers

Written Exercises, pages 47–48   1. 360   **3.** 630   **5.** 7400   **7.** 13   **9.** 8   **11.** $7y + 7$ **13.** $2x + 6$ **15.** $10a$ **17.** $35yz$ **19.** $48xyz$ **21.** $a + b + 7$ **23.** $4a + 3n + 6$ **25.** $7x + 4y + z + 8$ **27.** $10,000bcde$

29. Comm. prop. of mult.   **31.** Comm. prop. of add.   **33.** Assoc. prop. of mult.
35. a. Comm. prop. of add.   **b.** Assoc. prop. of add.   **c.** Subst. prop.   **d.** Subst. prop.
37. a. 1; 5   **b.** no   **39.** No; for example, $10 \div 2 = 5$ but $2 \div 10 = \frac{1}{5}$.

Mixed Review Exercises, page 48   **1.** 2   **2.** 90   **3.** $\frac{2}{3}$ **4.** 5   **5.** 29   **6.** 8   **7.** 24   **8.** 16   **9.** 1

Challenge, page 48   5 pennies, 1 nickel, and 9 dimes

Written Exercises, pages 52–53   **1.** 11   **3.** 0   **5.** -1 **7.** -8 **9.** 17   **11.** -36 **13.** 30   **15.** -38 **17.** -13 **19.** -11 **21.** -2.4 **23.** 0   **25.** $x + (-5)$ **27.** $2n$ **29.** $5n + (-8)$ **31.** $3a + 4b + (-13)$ **33.** $7x + (-y) + (-10)$ **35.** a **37.** 0
39. a. $(a + b) + [(-a) + (-b)] = [a + (-a)] + [b + (-b)] = 0 + 0 = 0$ **b.** Prop. of opposites   **c.** Since the opp. of a number is unique and $-(a + b)$ and $[(-a) + (-b)]$ both have the sum of zero when added to $(a + b)$, $-(a + b) = (-a) + (-b)$.

Mixed Review Exercises, page 53   **1.** 10   **2.** 9   **3.** 4   **4.** 5   **5.** $\frac{2}{3}$ **6.** $\frac{1}{3}$ **7.** 120   **8.** 2500   **9.** $24abc$ **10.** 18   **11.** 9.4   **12.** 170

Challenge, page 53
1. 36, 49   **3.** $25 = 10 + 15$

Written Exercises, pages 55–56   **1.** -1 **3.** 41   **5.** -28 **7.** 10   **9.** -12 **11.** -23 **13.** 24.8   **15.** -46 **17.** 0   **19.** $\frac{1}{2}$ **21.** $-\frac{9}{4}$ **23.** $x + (-4)$ **25.** 0   **27.** $-c$ **29.** -9 **31.** 2   **33.** -6 **35.** -9 **37.** 1   **39.** -15 **41.** x **43.** $-b$

Problems, pages 56–58   **1.** 20th floor   **3.** $818   **5.** $1148   **7.** 13 fewer guests on the 4th day   **9.** 3 blocks east and 9 blocks south   **11.** 54 m below sea level   **13.** 12:30 P.M.   **15.** $121.75

Mixed Review Exercises, page 58   **1.** 2   **2.** 1200   **3.** 13   **4.** 1   **5.** 2.4   **6.** 9   **7.** 9   **8.** $20\frac{2}{3}$ **9.** 9   **10.** 16   **11.** -10 **12.** -11

Calculator Key-In, page 58   **1.** -19 **3.** -391 **5.** -8.1

Written Exercises, pages 61–62   **1.** -188 **3.** 71   **5.** -16 **7.** -7.2 **9.** 198   **11.** 2.94   **13.** -27 **15.** -25 **17.** 121   **19.** 265   **21.** 0   **23.** -9 **25.** 390   **27.** 12   **29.** 21   **31.** -9 **33.** 116   **35.** -84 **37.** $-x + 7$ **39.** -5 **41.** $-b + 12$ **43.** $z - y - 8$ **45.** $-z + 2$ **47.** y **49.** 17   **51.** -19 **53.** -10 **55.** -2 **57.** -4 **59.** -14 **61. a.** Def. of subtraction; Comm. prop. of add.; Assoc. prop. of add.; Prop. of opposites; Ident. prop. of add.   **b.** a

Problems, pages 62–63   **1.** 92.9 millions of miles   **3.** 28 years old   **5.** 3.8°C   **7.** 91 blocks   **9.** 4478 m   **11.** 79 lb

Mixed Review Exercises, page 63   **1.** 16   **2.** 540   **3.** $7x + 3y + 9$ **4.** $\frac{1}{5}$ **5.** -3 **6.** $-2\frac{1}{3}$ **7.** 3   **8.** 0.5   **9.** -18 **10.** 68   **11.** 12   **12.** $-x - 16$

Self-Test 1, pages 63–64   **1.** 6300   **2.** $x + 131$ **3.** -1 **4.** 5   **5.** $2x - 1$ **6.** -20 **7.** -20 **8.** -14 **9.** $-y + 18$

Reading Algebra, page 64   **1.** Add and subtract polynomials, multiply monomials   **3.** A monomial is an expression that is either a numeral, a variable, or the product of a numeral and one or more variables. A polynomial is a sum of monomials.   **5.** Index and/or Table of Contents

Written Exercises, pages 67–69   **1.** 248   **3.** 340   **5.** 188   **7.** 208   **9.** 38   **11.** 16   **13.** 1800   **15.** 0   **17.** 32   **19.** $7a$ **21.** $9y$ **23.** $4p$ **25.** $3x + 6$ **27.** $4n - 8$ **29.** $18n + 12$ **31.** $3j - 3k$ **33.** $6n + 14$ **35.** $10x + 15y$ **37.** $8a + 7$ **39.** $12n - 5$ **41.** $y + 4$ **43.** $7a + 4b$ **45.** $s + 4t$ **47.** $6x$ **49.** $4x + 15$ **51.** $3a - 25$ **53.** $-2x + 17$ **55.** $5x + 17$ **57.** $12y + 15$ **59.** $6x + 3y + 3$ **61.** $21a + 17b$ **63.** $11r + 12$ **65.** $34c + 14d + 50$ **67.** $5(c + d) + 2(3c + d)$; $11c + 7d$ **69.** $8 + (-5 + 15y) + \frac{1}{2}(12y - 8)$; $21y - 1$ **71.** 3   **73.** $248x + 160$ **75.** $113n - 9p - 99$ **77.** $-6x + 9y - 12$

Mixed Review Exercises, page 69   **1.** 28   **2.** 4
3. 2   **4.** 3   **5.** 9   **6.** 7   **7.** −1   **8.** 1   **9.** −4
10. 5   **11.** 10   **12.** 0

Challenge, page 69   **3. a.** 714,285
b. 857,142

Written Exercises, pages 72–73   **1.** 74
3. 480   **5.** −84   **7.** 0   **9.** −300   **11.** 420
13. $6ab$ **15.** $-14pq$ **17.** $140ac$
19. $-2x + 6y$ **21.** $-21m - 28n$
23. $-35x + 21$ **25.** $-a - b + 3$
27. $-a + b + c$ **29.** $2a + 2b$ **31.** 8
33. $-16c + 25p$ **35.** $-2s + 5.3y$ **37.** $-20x$
39. 380   **41.** −5700   **43.** $-\frac{1}{3}m + 2n$
45. $-3r - 3s + 7$ **47.** $-19x + 13y$
49. $3q - 9w$ **51.** $e + 3f$ **53.** $-22r - 31s$
55. $-12g + 33$ **57.** $(500p + 500)$ points down
59. a. Ident. prop. of mult.   **b.** Dist. prop. (of
mult. with respect to add.)   **c.** Prop. of opposites   **d.** Mult. prop. of 0

Mixed Review Exercises, page 73   **1.** $4x = 44$
2. $n + 2 = 32$ **3.** $\frac{1}{2}x = 12$ **4.** $2x + 7 = 11$
5. 112   **6.** 194   **7.** $-y + 12$ **8.** 128   **9.** $-4n$
10. $4n + 16$

Application, page 74   **1.** \$5.00 per liter
3. \$3.30 per liter

Written Exercises, pages 77–78
1. $x + (x + 1) = 43$
3. $x + (x + 1) + (x + 2) + (x + 3) = -106$
5. $x + (x + 2) + (x + 4) = 75$
7. $x(x + 2) = 168$
9. $x + (x + 2) + (x + 4) + (x + 6) = -100$
11. $x + (x + 2) + (x + 4) + (x + 6) = 36$
13. 17, 19, 21   **15.** 0, 1; 9, 10
17. $(x - 4) + [(x + 3) - 4] + [(x + 6) - 4] = 42$

Mixed Review Exercises, page 78   **1.** −2
2. −4.9   **3.** $2c + 3$ **4.** $-\frac{3}{5}$ **5.** 18   **6.** 1
7. 2   **8.** $19a$ **9.** $5y + 16$ **10.** $-x - y + z$
11. $6a - 6b$ **12.** $3y - 15$

Self-Test 2, page 78   **1.** $4x + 6y$ **2.** $4y - 7$
3. $2a$ **4.** $2x + 4$ **5.** −180   **6.** $56xy$
7. $-3a - 3b + 3c$ **8.** 396   **9.** $29 = x - 1$,
$31 = x + 1$ **10.** $x + 2 = 2x - 1$

Written Exercises, pages 81–82   **1.** −4
3. −10   **5.** 1   **7.** −3   **9.** $-r$ **11.** 5   **13.** $4xy$

15. $-2ab$ **17.** $2pg$ **19.** $-8a + 10$
21. $9c - 2d$ **23.** $6m + 13k$ **25.** $-u + 6v$
27. $-4x - 17y$ **29.** $-27m$ **31.** $-r$ **33.** n
35. $\frac{2}{3}, \frac{3}{2}$

Mixed Review Exercises, page 82
1. $5x + 4 = 24$ **2.** $x - 15 = 250$
3. $x + (x + 1) = 67$ **4.** $x(x + 1) = 42$
5. −120   **6.** 1800   **7.** 42   **8.** $-35a + 14d$
9. $-7x - 2$ **10.** $3x + 2$

Calculator Key-In, page 82   **1.** 16
3. 0.00032   **5.** the number

Written Exercises, pages 85–86   **1.** −8   **3.** 4
5. −16   **7.** 0   **9.** 36   **11.** −35   **13.** x
15. $2y$ **17.** $13a$ **19.** $-9x$ **21.** $-\frac{13}{2}$
23. −1   **25.** −3   **27.** −1   **29.** −3   **31.** 0
33. −1   **35.** $\frac{a - b}{c} = (a - b) \cdot \frac{1}{c} =$
$\left(a \cdot \frac{1}{c}\right) - \left(b \cdot \frac{1}{c}\right) = \frac{a}{c} - \frac{b}{c}$

Mixed Review Exercises, page 86   **1.** {5}
2. {6}   **3.** {3}   **4.** {2}   **5.** {2}   **6.** {4}   **7.** {5}
8. {3}   **9.** {3}   **10.** {2}   **11.** {1}
12. {0, 1, 2, 3, 4, 5}

Self-Test 3, page 86   **1.** $\frac{1}{3y}$ **2.** −2   **3.** −10
4. −48   **5.** −27   **6.** 18   **7.** 8   **8.** $-4x$

Computer Key-In, page 87   **1.** −6   **3.** 17.62
5. −1   **7.** 3.524

Chapter Review, page 89   **1.** d   **3.** b   **5.** b
7. b   **9.** c   **11.** d   **13.** c   **15.** d

Cumulative Review, page 91   **1.** 6   **3.** 6
5. 51   **7.** 32   **9.** −103   **11.** $13x + 11y$
13. −28   **15.** 0   **17.** −2
19. $-3, -2, -\frac{1}{2}, 0, \frac{1}{2}, 4$
21.

23. {10, −10}   **25.** {−12}   **27.** {0}   **29.** {−3}
31. $7y + 5$ **33.** $-x = 8 - 4$ **35.** the third
floor

Maintaining Skills, page 92   **1.** 11.32
3. 291.82   **5.** 2.5996   **7.** 0.757   **9.** 55
11. 662   **13.** 0.0025   **15.** 192   **17.** $\frac{2}{7}$ **19.** $\frac{3}{4}$

21. $\frac{7}{9}$ **23.** $\frac{1}{2}$ **25.** $\frac{1}{28}$ **27.** $\frac{34}{55}$ **29.** $\frac{1}{3}$

31. $\frac{28}{15}$ **33.** $\frac{144}{125}$

Preparing for College Entrance Exams,
page 93 **1.** D **3.** A **5.** C **7.** C

Chapter 3 Transforming Equations

Written Exercises, pages 97–98 **1.** {20}
3. {23} **5.** {136} **7.** {7} **9.** {−50}
11. {−38} **13.** {42} **15.** {−4} **17.** {0}
19. {−10} **21.** {−1} **23.** {2.9} **25.** {2}
27. {−7} **29.** {10} **31.** {−17} **33.** {−5}
35. {−5} **37.** {−7} **39.** {11} **41.** {92}
43. {−7} **45.** {5} **47.** {18, −18}
49. {8, −8} **51.** {2, −2} **53.** no solution
55. {4, −4} **57.** {4, −4} **59.** {0}

Problems, pages 98–100 **1.** −63 **3.** −21
5. 76 **7.** 32 mi/h **9.** −7°C **11.** $2.45
13. 454 employees **15.** 111° **17.** $.35
19. 14 km

Mixed Review Exercises, pages 100–101 **1.** 3
2. 1 **3.** 12 **4.** 2 **5.** $\frac{1}{12}$ **6.** 36 **7.** 420
8. −270 **9.** −4a **10.** 1 **11.** 12b
12. 5a − 5b

Application, page 101 **1. a.** $3240 **b.** $240
3. a. $5058 **b.** $558

Written Exercises, page 104 **1.** {11} **3.** {−3}
5. {−9} **7.** {3} **9.** {24} **11.** {−35}
13. {−64} **15.** {18} **17.** {−80} **19.** {−33}
21. {−24} **23.** {0} **25.** {−45} **27.** {−18}
29. {7} **31.** {−0.4} **33.** {16} **35.** {−11}
37. {−3} **39.** {0} **41.** {9, −9}
43. no solution **45.** {10, −10} **47.** {21, −21}
49. {6, −6} **51.** {4, −4}

Problems, pages 105–106 **1.** −75 **3.** −21
5. 360 seniors **7.** 196 m **9.** $7.20
11. 7 games **13.** 250 apples **15.** 9 hard-cover
books **17.** $21,250 **19.** $\frac{1}{72}$ mi/s; 50 mi/h

Mixed Review Exercises, page 106 **1.** 20
2. 48 **3.** 11 **4.** 1 **5.** $\frac{15}{4}$ **6.** 1 **7.** 16a + 6
8. 5n **9.** 9p + 2 **10.** −4m − 8 **11.** 8x + 56
12. 6y − 15

Calculator Key-In, page 106 **1.** 0.75 **3.** −0.2
5. 0.025 **7.** −0.24 **9.** 0.96875 **11–20.** yes

Written Exercises, pages 109–110 **1.** {6}
3. {−3} **5.** {−7} **7.** {−2} **9.** {12} **11.** {16}
13. {−13} **15.** {18} **17.** {0} **19.** {4}
21. {−5} **23.** {15} **25.** {5} **27.** {5} **29.** {2}
31. {−36} **33.** {−12} **35.** {−2} **37.** {−4}
39. {−4} **41.** {8} **43.** {4} **45.** {6} **47.** {2}
49. {−34} **51.** {4} **53.** {0} **55.** {−18}
57. {5} **59.** {7, −7}

Mixed Review Exercises, page 110 **1.** {−161}
2. {6} **3.** {16} **4.** {4} **5.** {3} **6.** {34}
7. {−8} **8.** {−4} **9.** {−4} **10.** {1.3}
11. {0} **12.** {20}

Computer Exercises, page 111 **1. a.** 8
b. −2 **c.** −10 **d.** 6 **e.** 36 **f.** 11
3. a. {2, −2} **b.** no solution **c.** {0.5, −0.5}

Self-Test 1, page 111 **1.** {38} **2.** {42}
3. {125} **4.** {−11} **5.** 6 cm by 18 cm **6.** {7}
7. {24}

Calculator Key-In, page 111 **1.** no **3.** no

Problems, pages 113–115 **1.** 43 **3.** 42
5. 27 **7.** 56, 57, 58 **9.** 58, 60, 62, 64
11. with cheese, 165; without cheese, 330
13. 32 weeks **15.** 90 cm **17.** 130 cm
19. 17 cm by 32 cm **21.** width, 14 cm; length,
50 cm **23.** $m\angle A = 84$, $m\angle B = 28$, $m\angle C = 68$
25. AB = 9; AC = 18; BC = 21 **27.** Theo,
$22; Rudy, $6; Denise, $17 **29.** Mach. A,
15,800 bottles; Mach. B, 7900 bottles; Mach. C,
16,300 bottles **31.** $21,800 **33.** 15 or −8

Mixed Review Exercises, page 115 **1.** {6}
2. {−1.5} **3.** {13} **4.** {5} **5.** {−63}
6. {−100} **7.** {30} **8.** {57} **9.** {0} **10.** {2}
11. {10} **12.** $\left\{-\frac{3}{2}\right\}$

Written Exercises, page 118 **1.** {2} **3.** {6}
5. {2} **7.** {−11} **9.** {8} **11.** {−14}
13. {−1} **15.** {3} **17.** {6} **19.** {−12}
21. {4} **23.** {10} **25.** {1} **27.** {1}
29. {−14} **31.** identity **33.** {4} **35.** {−3}
37. identity **39.** {−1} **41.** identity **43.** {−1}
45. {−2} **47.** {1}

Problems, pages 118–119 **1.** 48 **3.** 7 **5.** 23
7. −14, −13 **9.** Cliff, 6; Kyle and Lyle, 18
11. 7, 8 **13.** 14 units **15.** 6 years

17. Marcia, $87.50; Eric, $175; Laurel, $262.50
19. If $n + (n + 1) + (n + 2) = n + 200$, then $n = 98.5$, which is not an integer. ∴ it is impossible.

Mixed Review Exercises, page 120 **1.** 2
2. $-1\frac{2}{5}$ **3.** -199 **4.** $14x - 5$ **5.** $15y + 18$
6. -420 **7.** $\{-12\}$ **8.** $\{1\}$ **9.** $\{-98\}$
10. $\{9\}$ **11.** $\{42\}$ **12.** $\{38\}$

Computer Exercises, page 120 **1.** $\{-3\}$
3. no solution **5.** $\{5\}$

Self-Test 2, page 120 **1.** $21 **2.** $\{5\}$ **3.** $\{7\}$
4. Paul, $4.50; Jeff, $9.50; Hilary, $13.50

Problems, pages 122–125 **1.** 14 shifts
3. 306 lb **5.** orange, 65 Calories; peach, 35 Calories **7.** red, 9 cm by 24 cm; blue, 14 cm by 22 cm **9.** $120 **11.** 15 ft by 45 ft; 9 ft by 75 ft **13.** Greg, 8; Rodney, 16
15. 420 Calories **17.** Angel Falls, 807 m; Niagara Falls, 57 m **19.** 65 Calories

Mixed Review Exercises, page 125 **1.** $\{24\}$
2. $\{15\}$ **3.** $\{0\}$ **4.** $\{65\}$ **5.** $\{3\}$ **6.** $\{-8\}$
7. $\{7\}$ **8.** $\{4\}$ **9.** $\{11\}$ **10.** $\{-7\}$ **11.** $\{18\}$
12. $\{-20\}$

Problems, pages 127–129 **1.** 12 students
3. 22 nickels **5.** 50 programs **7.** 14 quarters
9. $44 **11.** plumber, $25.50; apprentice, $21
13. 7 quarters **15.** Solution involves a fractional number of coins. **17.** $3.80

Mixed Review Exercises, page 129 **1.** 1
2. 216 **3.** $13y + 1$ **4.** 35 **5.** $3x + 28$
6. $15x + 23y$ **7.** 5 **8.** $\frac{5}{8}$ **9.** 23

Written Exercises, pages 131–133
1. (1) Reflex. prop. of =; (3) Substitution principle **3.** (2) Mult. prop. of =; (3) Assoc. prop. of mult.; (4) Prop. of reciprocals; (5) Identity prop. of mult. **5.** (1) Prop. of opposites; (2) Prop. of opposites; (3) Substitution principle or Trans. prop. of equality; (4) Comm. prop. of add. **7.** (1) Subtraction; (3) 5; (4) Comm. prop. of add.; (5) Def. of subtr.
9. (1) $a = b$ (Given)

   (2) $a \cdot \dfrac{1}{c} = b \cdot \dfrac{1}{c}$ (Mult. prop. of =)

   (3) $\dfrac{a}{c} = \dfrac{b}{c}$ (Def. of div.)

11. (1) $\dfrac{a}{b} \cdot \dfrac{b}{a} = \left(a \cdot \dfrac{1}{b}\right)\left(b \cdot \dfrac{1}{a}\right)$ (Def. of division)

   (2) $\dfrac{a}{b} \cdot \dfrac{b}{a} = \left(a \cdot \dfrac{1}{a}\right)\left(b \cdot \dfrac{1}{b}\right)$ (Commutative and associative props. of mult.)

   (3) $\dfrac{a}{b} \cdot \dfrac{b}{a} = 1 \cdot 1$ (Prop. of reciprocals)

   (4) $\dfrac{a}{b} \cdot \dfrac{b}{a} = 1$ (Identity prop. of mult.)

   (5) $\dfrac{a}{b} \cdot \left(\dfrac{1}{\frac{a}{b}}\right) = 1$ (Prop. of reciprocals)

   (6) $\dfrac{a}{b} \cdot \dfrac{1}{\frac{a}{b}} = \dfrac{a}{b} \cdot \left(\dfrac{b}{a}\right)$ (Substitution)

   (7) $\dfrac{1}{\frac{a}{b}} = \dfrac{b}{a}$ (Div. prop. of =)

Mixed Review Exercises, page 133 **1.** 14
2. 32 **3.** $3x$ **4.** $-4 - a$ **5.** $b + 1$ **6.** 20
7. 50 **8.** 3 **9.** 3 **10.** $\frac{7}{6}$ **11.** 5 **12.** 5

Self-Test 3, page 134 **1.** 51 cm by 59 cm; 56 cm by 65 cm **2.** nickels, 22; quarters, 12
3. (1) Assoc. prop. of add.; (2) Prop. of opposites; (3) Identity prop. of add.

Chapter Review, page 135 **1.** c **3.** d **5.** a
7. b **9.** a **11.** b

Cumulative Review, page 137 **1.** 25 **3.** 4
5. 24 **7.** -20 **9.** $3\frac{3}{4}$ **11.** $2x - 2$ **13.** -28
15. $17x$ **17.** 1 **19.** -6 **21.** $-4\frac{1}{2}$
23. no solution **25.** $\{-4\}$ **27.** $\{16\}$ **29.** $\{18\}$
31. $\{2\}$ **33.** $\{11\}$ **35.** $\left\{\frac{9}{5}\right\}$ **37.** peach, $.30; melon, $1.20 **39.** 95 employees

Maintaining Skills, page 138 **1.** $2\frac{1}{12}$ **3.** $5\frac{1}{5}$
5. $7\frac{7}{12}$ **7.** $9\frac{1}{4}$ **9.** $\frac{25}{6}$ **11.** $\frac{25}{9}$ **13.** $\frac{47}{13}$
15. $\frac{119}{12}$ **17.** $18\frac{1}{5}$ **19.** $-1\frac{1}{21}$ **21.** $25\frac{1}{2}$
23. $3\frac{9}{40}$ **25.** $4\frac{3}{10}$ **27.** $21\frac{27}{35}$ **29.** $-2\frac{13}{22}$
31. $1\frac{11}{36}$ **33.** $-1\frac{13}{21}$ **35.** $26\frac{1}{12}$

Mixed Problem Solving Review, page 139
1. 5 **3.** 75 km/h **5.** 7 oranges, 5 apples
7. $-5°C$ **9.** 3, 4, 5 **11.** 7 $10 bills, 11 $5 bills **13.** $480,000 **15.** 7 h **17.** no solution

Chapter 4 Addition and Subtraction

Written Exercises, pages 143–144   **1.** $6y$
3. $8z^2$ **5.** m^3 **7.** $3c^3$ **9.** $-5y^2$ **11.** $-14n^2$
13. c^3d **15.** $9u^3v$ **17.** $-4rs^2$ **19.** p^2q^2rs
21. d **23.** c **25. a.** 4   **b.** -4 **27. a.** -48
b. 144   **29. a.** 34   **b.** 1000   **31. a.** 3
b. -13 **33.** 1776   **35.** 2   **37.** 13   **39.** 3
41. a. 16   **b.** 4   **43. a.** -1 **b.** 11   **45.** -11
47. -6 **49.** 0

Mixed Review Exercises, page 144   **1.** $\{-8\}$
2. $\{16\}$ **3.** $\{-12\}$ **4.** $\{2\}$ **5.** $\{10\}$ **6.** $\{4\}$
7. $\{-8\}$ **8.** $\{50\}$ **9.** $\left\{-\dfrac{2}{7}\right\}$

Calculator Key-In, page 145   **1.** 0.01
3. 0.25   **5.** 0.0121   **7.** 0.027

Written Exercises, pages 148–149
1. $\underline{3x} - \underline{\underline{2y}} - \underline{x} - \underline{\underline{3y}};\ 2x - 5y$
3. $\underline{3x^2} - \underline{\underline{2x}} - \underline{2x^2} - \underline{\underline{4x}} - 3;\ x^2 - 6x - 3$
5. $\underline{a^2} + \underline{\underline{3ab}} - \underline{4ab} + \underline{\underline{3a^2}};\ 4a^2 - ab$
7. $\underline{r^2s} - 3rs^2 + \underline{\underline{4s^3}} - \underline{2r^2s} - 3s^2;$
$-r^2s - 3rs^2 - 3s^2 + 4s^3$ **9.** $7y + 6$
11. $5y + 3$ **13.** $r + 3$ **15.** $5x^2 + x - 10$
17. $6x^2 - 2xy - 8y^2$ **19.** $4a - 3b - c$
21. $3y - 12$ **23.** $y + 13$ **25.** $3r - 6x + 7$
27. $-x^2 - 7x + 2$ **29.** $2x^2 - 4xy - 2y^2$
31. $7x + y - 5$ **33.** $x - 3$ **35.** $4x - t - 4$
37. $2n^2 + 2n - 3$ **39.** $4x^2 - 9$ **41.** $u^3 - v^3$
43. $2a^3 + 2ab^2 + b^3$ **45.** $\{2\}$ **47.** $\{-2\}$
49. $\{8\}$ **51.** $\{8\}$ **53.** $\{3\}$ **55.** no sol.

Problems, page 150   **1.** $2x^2 + 5x + 2$
3. $3x^2 + 4x + 1$ **5.** 24, 25   **7.** 61, 62, 63, 64
9. 11, 12   **11.** 7, 9, 11   **13.** 4, 6, 8, 10

Mixed Review Exercises, pages 150–151
1. -25 **2.** 25   **3.** 17   **4.** 4   **5.** $\left\{\dfrac{13}{5}\right\}$ **6.** $\left\{\dfrac{9}{2}\right\}$
7. $\left\{-\dfrac{41}{9}\right\}$ **8.** $\left\{-\dfrac{25}{2}\right\}$ **9.** $\{10\}$ **10.** $\{17\}$

Self-Test 1, page 151   **1.** mn^3 **2.** $-15x^2$
3. $-8y^2$ **4.** 16   **5.** -16 **6.** -27 **7.** -213
8. -16 **9.** 2   **10. a.** $10x + 4$ **b.** $4x + 6$
11. a. $6x^2 - 12$ **b.** $4x^2 + 12x - 4$ **12. a.** 3
b. $2x^2y - 6xy^2 + 11$ **13.** 12, 14, 16

Written Exercises, pages 153–154   **1.** n^8
3. x^9 **5.** $10x^7$ **7.** m^3n^5 **9.** $6a^2b^6$ **11.** $-12x^7$
13. $6x^4y^4$ **15.** $10a^3b^7c^3$ **17.** $24p^3q^3$

19. $6x^6y^6$ **21.** t^6 **23.** $6a^4b^3$ **25.** $4x^6$
27. $\dfrac{5}{2}p^7q^4$ **29.** $-16x^2y^6$ **31.** $22x^5$ **33.** $9a^8$
35. $P = 10ab;\ A = 6a^2b^2$ **37.** $P = 18a;$
$A = 10a^2$ **39.** $46x^2$ **41.** a^{2m} **43.** 3^{p+q}
45. 4^x **47.** a^{x+3} **49.** 2^{2x+3} **51.** $5nx^{10}$

Mixed Review Exercises, page 154   **1.** 8
2. 36   **3.** $3p^2 + 3q^2 - 2p^2q$ **4.** 147   **5.** 441
6. $7x^2 + 2x + 5$ **7.** $\{-12\}$ **8.** $\{6\}$ **9.** $\{1\}$
10. $\{15\}$ **11.** $\{7\}$ **12.** $\{8\}$

Written Exercises, pages 156–157   **1. a.** 81
b. 729   **c.** 729   **3. a.** 12   **b.** 36   **c.** 36
5. a. c^7 **b.** c^{10} **c.** c^{10} **7. a.** $-125a^{12}$
b. $-125a^{12}$ **c.** $-5a^{12}$ **9.** $49a^2$ **11.** $-64c^3$
13. $64k^6$ **15.** $-27y^9$ **17.** $27a^6b^3$ **19.** $16r^{12}s^{16}$
21. $64x^6$ **23.** $1{,}000{,}000b^6$ **25.** $54a^9b^4$
27. $2p^{10}q^{11}$ **29.** $16x^8$ **31.** $54x^7y^4$ **33. a.** $17x^6$
b. $72x^{12}$ **35. a.** $2a^4b^6$ **b.** a^8b^{12} **37. a.** $3a^4b^6$
b. $-4a^8b^{12}$ **39.** x^{2n} **41.** a^{x+3} **43.** x^{2n}
45. z^{3x} **47.** $72r^{5n}$ **49.** $9x^{4n}$ **51. a.** $8x^3;\ 64x^3$
b. right   **c.** 8 times
53. $16^x \cdot (4^x)^2 = 16^x \cdot 4^{2x} = (2^4)^x \cdot (2^2)^{2x} =$
$2^{4x} \cdot 2^{4x} = 2^{8x} = (2^x)^8$

Mixed Review Exercises, page 157   **1.** $24a^3b^3$
2. $8x^3y^3$ **3.** $16x^8y^{12}$ **4.** $\dfrac{1}{3}t^5$ **5.** $4c - 2a$
6. $5x + 5y + 2$ **7.** 60   **8.** -75 **9.** 4

Written Exercises, pages 159–160   **1.** $4x - 12$
3. $c^2 - 2c$ **5.** $3y^2 + 15y$ **7.** $-14r + 6r^2$
9. $6y^3 - 2y^2 - 10y$
11. $-2a^3b^2 + 6a^2b^3 - 10ab^4$
13. $3x^3 - 6x^2 + 12x$ **15.** $p^3q^2 - 3p^2q^3 - 4pq^4$
17. $2x^4 - 3x^3y - x^2y^2$ **19.** $x^2 - x$ **21.** $9r^2$
23. $9y - 12$ **25.** $2a$ **27.** $\{4\}$ **29.** $\{10\}$
31. $\{6\}$ **33.** $\{2\}$ **35.** $\{9\}$ **37.** $\{2\}$
39. a. $2x^2 + xy$ **b.** $2x^2 + xy$ **c.** Distributive
prop.   **41.** $3x^2 + 23x$ **43.** S.A. $= 48x^2;$
$V = 20x^3$

Mixed Review Exercises, page 160   **1.** $27x^6y^3$
2. $25r^6y^8$ **3.** $-27n^3$ **4.** $72a^{13}y^7$ **5.** $10x^5$
6. $3n^6$ **7.** $10p + 5$ **8.** $x + 4$ **9.** $675x^6y^9$

Written Exercises, pages 162–164
1. $6x^2 - 7x - 5$ **3.** $2a^3 - 3a^2 - a + 12$
5. $6x^2 + 11xy - 10y^2$ **7.** $c^3 - 7cd^2 + 6d^3$
9. $y^2 + 5y + 6$ **11.** $a^2 + 3a - 4$
13. $2x^2 - 11x + 5$ **15.** $6z^2 + 5z - 6$
17. $16s^2 - 25$ **19.** $a^3 + 5a^2 + 11a + 10$
21. $m^3 + m^2 + 4m - 6$
23. $2x^3 - 3x^2 + 7x - 3$

25. $9z^3 - 9z^2 + 14z - 8$ **27. a.** $x^2 + 10x + 21$
b. $x^2 + 10x + 21$ **c.** equal **29.** $y^3 - y + 6$
31. $2y^3 + y^2 - 14y + 12$
33. $-3x^3 + 8x^2 - 19x + 10$
35. $8r^3 - 12r^2s + 6rs^2 - s^3$
37. $\{13\}$ **39.** $\left\{\dfrac{20}{11}\right\}$ **41.** $\{6\}$
43. $x^4 - 6x^3 + 19x^2 - 30x + 25$
45. $x^3 + 15x^2 + 75x + 125$
47. $16 - 32y + 24y^2 - 8y^3 + y^4$
49. $x^3 - 2x^2 - 5x + 6$

Mixed Review Exercises, page 164 **1.** $\{3\}$
2. $\{4\}$ **3.** $\{2\}$ **4.** 0 **5.** 5 **6.** -2 **7.** 49
8. -1 **9.** -27

Self-Test 2, page 164 **1.** $3x^6$ **2.** $18a^9$
3. $-2a^5$ **4.** a^5b^5 **5.** $125x^3y^6$ **6.** $-8x^6y^3$
7. $-8x^6y^3$ **8.** $9x^6$ **9.** $-10n + 2n^2$
10. $8x^3y^2 - 7x^2y^3 + \dfrac{1}{7}xy^4$ **11.** $\{13\}$
12. $12x^2 - 7x - 10$ **13.** $5a^3 + 11a^2 - 2a - 8$
14. $6a^2 - 59a + 45$
15. $63 - 103y + 114y^2 - 56y^3$

Written Exercises, page 166 **1.** $r = \dfrac{c}{2\pi}$
3. $r = \dfrac{v}{s}$; $s \neq 0$ **5.** $P = \dfrac{I}{rt}$; $r \neq 0$, $t \neq 0$
7. $h = \dfrac{A - 2a^2}{4a}$; $a \neq 0$ **9.** $h = \dfrac{2A}{a + b}$;
$a + b \neq 0$ **11.** $w = \dfrac{P - 2l}{2}$ **13.** $y = 2m - x$
15. $a = \dfrac{2S - nl}{n}$; $n \neq 0$ **17.** $t = \dfrac{v - u}{a}$; $a \neq 0$
19. $s = \dfrac{v^2 - u^2}{2a}$; $a \neq 0$ **21.** $r = \dfrac{Sa - a}{S}$; $S \neq 0$
23. $d = \dfrac{Ff + Fg - fg}{F}$; $F \neq 0$ **25.** $n = \dfrac{360}{180 - a}$;
$a \neq 180$ **27.** $a = \dfrac{br}{b - r}$; $b \neq r$
29. $R = \dfrac{Cr}{C - Kr}$; $C \neq Kr$

Mixed Review Exercises, page 166
1. $y^2 - 2y - 15$ **2.** $6n^2 - 16n + 8$
3. $-2a^2 - 8a$ **4.** $2x^2y + 3xy^2$
5. $4x^3 - 12x^2 + 8x$ **6.** $-27x^9$ **7.** n^6 **8.** $36a^7b$

Problems, pages 170–171 **1.** 2:20 P.M.
3. 1 h 48 min **5.** east, 650 km/h; west,
600 km/h **7.** 10:30 A.M. **9.** 43 km/h
11. 22.5 km **13.** 165 km **15.** 26 knots
17. when $t = \dfrac{P}{s - r}$ **19.** when $t = \dfrac{d}{r + s}$

Mixed Review Exercises, page 171 **1.** $\{-8\}$
2. $\{6\}$ **3.** $\{-42\}$ **4.** $\left\{\dfrac{1}{9}\right\}$ **5.** $\{15\}$ **6.** $\{-12\}$
7. $x = \dfrac{12}{b}$ **8.** $x = \dfrac{a - 5}{3}$

Problems, pages 173–174 **1.** 15 cm by 5 cm
3. 36 m by 12 m **5.** 10 m by 5 m **7.** 924 m²
9. $A = 2\pi rw + \pi w^2$ **11.** 9 m
13. a. $(2\pi r + 8r + \pi)$ m **b.** 6π m

Mixed Review Exercises, page 174 **1.** -4
2. $3c - 7$ **3.** $64x^3y^9$ **4.** 14 **5.** 500 **6.** 8
7. 0 **8.** $\dfrac{1}{5}x^7$ **9.** $13x$ **10.** 0 **11.** $\dfrac{1}{5}y^4$
12. $81y^8z^4$

Problems, pages 176–177 **1.** No sol.;
insufficient info. **3.** No sol.; insufficient info.
5. No sol.; contradiction **7.** 85 km/h
9. 11, 13, 15 **11.** No. sol.; insufficient info.
13. 52 mi/h **15.** No sol.; unrealistic result

Self-Test 3, page 177 **1.** $V = \dfrac{kT}{P}$; $P \neq 0$
2. 25 km/h **3.** 17 ft by 10 ft **4.** No sol.;
unrealistic result

Chapter Review, pages 178–179 **1.** b **2.** c
3. b **4.** a **5.** d **6.** d **7.** d **8.** c **9.** d
10. a **11.** d **12.** c **13.** a **14.** c **15.** b
16. b **17.** a **18.** d

Cumulative Review, page 181 **1.** $2x - 5$
3. 0 **5.** 3 **7.** 45 **9.** -18 **11.** $100a^5$
13. $-12x^4 + 8x^3 + 20x^2$ **15.** $15 - 2x - 8x^2$
17. 1 **19.** 10 **21.** no sol. **23.** $\{-12\}$
25. $\{-1\}$ **27.** $\{-3\}$ **29.** $\{2\}$ **31.** $\{4\}$ **33.** $\{5\}$
35. $m = \dfrac{c + bn}{a}$; $a \neq 0$ **37.** 17, 19
39. Jessica: 10 dimes, 6 quarters; Whitney:
20 dimes, 2 quarters

Maintaining Skills, page 182 **1.** 1045
3. -44 **5.** -23 **7.** -85 **9.** $\dfrac{5}{8}$ **11.** 19.15
13. 72 **15.** -92 **17.** -21.275 **19.** 3.282
21. -28.96 **23.** $-\dfrac{7}{15}$ **25.** $\dfrac{19}{17}$ **27.** 13
29. -0.45 **31.** $\dfrac{1}{2}$

Preparing for College Entrance Exams,
page 183 **1.** B **3.** B **5.** A **7.** C

Written Exercises, pages 186–187 **1.** $(1)(13)$, $(-1)(-13)$ **3.** $(1)(24)$, $(2)(12)$, $(3)(8)$, $(4)(6)$, $(-1)(-24)$, $(-2)(-12)$, $(-3)(-8)$, $(-4)(-6)$ **5.** $(1)(29)$, $(-1)(-29)$ **7.** $(1)(40)$, $(2)(20)$, $(4)(10)$, $(5)(8)$, $(-1)(-40)$, $(-2)(-20)$, $(-4)(-10)$, $(-5)(-8)$ **9.** $(1)(-121)$, $(-1)(121)$, $(11)(-11)$ **11.** $(1)(-33)$, $(-1)(33)$, $(3)(-11)$, $(-3)(11)$ **13.** $(1)(53)$, $(-1)(-53)$ **15.** $(1)(26)$, $(2)(13)$, $(-1)(-26)$, $(-2)(-13)$ **17.** $(1)(68)$, $(2)(34)$, $(4)(17)$, $(-1)(-68)$, $(-2)(-34)$, $(-4)(-17)$ **19.** $(1)(38)$, $(2)(19)$, $(-1)(-38)$, $(-2)(-19)$ **21.** 2^4 **23.** $3 \cdot 23$ **25.** $3 \cdot 5^2$ **27.** 3^3 **29.** $3^2 \cdot 11$ **31.** $2^3 \cdot 13$ **33.** 5^3 **35.** $2 \cdot 3^2 \cdot 5^2$ **37.** $3^2 \cdot 11^2$ **39.** $2 \cdot 17 \cdot 23$ **41.** 6 **43.** 14 **45.** 15 **47.** 147 **49.** 14 **51.** 1

Mixed Review Exercises, page 187 **1.** $3x - 1$ **2.** 81 **3.** 18 **4.** $x - 10$ **5.** $18a^4b$ **6.** $24x^3y^2$ **7.** $27x^4$ **8.** $6n^3$ **9.** $-32x^5$ **10.** $2x^2 + 3x$ **11.** $2y^2 + 11y + 15$ **12.** $3x^2 - 8x - 16$

Challenge, page 188 7^5 hekats of grain

Written Exercises, pages 192–193 **1.** $\frac{2}{3}$ **3.** $\frac{1}{100}$ **5.** 4 **7.** 200 **9.** $\frac{x^4}{2}$ **11.** $\frac{3y^2}{x}$ **13.** $-\frac{3xy}{4}$ **15.** $\frac{4cd}{3b}$ **17.** $\frac{z^2}{x^2}$ **19.** $\frac{8ac^2}{5}$ **21.** 8 **23.** 3 **25.** $2a$ **27.** $-z^3$ **29.** $-x^8$ **31.** $3t^3$ **33.** $3ab^2$ **35.** $-5xy^4$ **37.** $-16c^2d^2$ **39.** $3a^3b^2$ **41.** x^2y^4 **43.** $3r^2s^2$ **45.** $6x$ **47.** $24abc^2$ **49.** $5pq^2$ **51.** $x + y$ **53.** $a + b$ **55.** $\frac{x - y}{x + y}$ **57.** $\frac{8x}{11}$ **59.** $\frac{x^{n+1}}{y^{n-1}}$ **61. a.** Def. of division **b.** Prop. of the reciprocal of a product **c.** Comm. prop. of mult.; Assoc. prop. of mult. **d.** Def. of division

Mixed Review Exercises, page 193 **1.** -5 **2.** 37 **3.** 47 **4.** n^8 **5.** -45 **6.** $6y^3$ **7.** 1 **8.** $\frac{8}{5}$ **9.** 64

Calculator Key-In, page 193 **1.** $3; \frac{3}{13}$ **3.** $5; \frac{5}{11}$ **5.** $26; \frac{13}{18}$

Written Exercises, pages 196–197 **1.** $2a + 3$ **3.** $4t - 2$ **5.** $m - 2n$ **7.** $4x + 9$

9. $2z^2 - 3z - 4$ **11.** $3y^3 + y^2 - 4y$ **13.** $-4r^2 + 2r + 3$ **15.** $q^2 - p^2$ **17.** $x - y - 1$ **19.** $-4r - 6s + 8rs$ **21.** 650 **23.** 190 **25.** 8300 **27.** 130 **29.** 140 **31.** $5(3a - 5b + 4)$ **33.** $2x(3x + 5)$ **35.** $3pq(2p - 3)$ **37.** $7y(y^2 - 3y - 2)$ **39.** $2ab(3b - 4a)$ **41.** $-3xy^2(5x + 2)$ **43.** $5a(x^2 + 2ax - 3a^2)$ **45.** $24a^2b^2(2a + 3b)$ **47.** $48wxy^2z^2(2x^2 - 3w^2)$ **49.** $3a - 1$ **51.** p **53.** $3x$

Problems, pages 197–199 **1.** $r^2(4 - \pi)$ **3.** $r^2(4 + \pi)$ **5.** $4r^2(4 - \pi)$ **7.** $2r^2(2\pi - 1)$ **9.** $r\left(2n + \frac{3}{2}\pi r\right)$ **11.** $r^2(4 + 3\pi)$

Mixed Review Exercises, page 199 **1.** n^6 **2.** $6x^5$ **3.** $6a^2 - 7a^2c - 3ac^2$ **4.** $\frac{x^2}{2y}$ **5.** -112 **6.** $8a^5$ **7.** $256a^4$ **8.** 69 **9.** $x^3 + x - 10$

Self-Test 1, page 199 **1.** $(1)(45)$, $(-1)(-45)$, $(3)(15)$, $(-3)(-15)$, $(5)(9)$, $(-5)(-9)$ **2.** $2 \cdot 3^3$ **3.** 9 **4.** $-3x$ **5.** $\frac{2n^6}{15m^2}$ **6.** $9x^2$ **7.** $-5ab^4$ **8.** $7t^2 + 5t - 3$ **9.** $5m(m^2 - 4m + 5)$

Written Exercises, pages 201–202 **1.** $x^2 + 13x + 40$ **3.** $y^2 - 7y + 12$ **5.** $z^2 - 3z - 28$ **7.** $n^2 + 4n - 21$ **9.** $6 + 5z + z^2$ **11.** $2y^2 + 9y + 10$ **13.** $7x^2 + 48x - 7$ **15.** $6y^2 + 7y + 2$ **17.** $2 - 7s + 6s^2$ **19.** $6h^2 - 7h - 5$ **21.** $20n^2 - 9n - 20$ **23.** $3x^2 - 7xy + 2y^2$ **25.** $8h^2 + 10hk - 3k^2$ **27.** $35a^2 - 31ab + 6b^2$ **29.** $3a^4 + 8a^2b - 3b^2$ **31.** $p^6 - p^3q^3 - 12q^6$ **33.** $4x^6 + 3x^4y^2 - x^2y^4$ **35.** $4y^3 - 5y^2 - 6y$ **37.** $3x^4 - 14x^3 + 8x^2$ **39.** $\{-1\}$ **41.** $\{11\}$ **43.** $\{9\}$ **45.** $p = 3$, $q = -2$, $r = -10$ **47.** $2x^{2n} + x^ny^n - 3y^{2n}$ **49.** $(2n + 1)^2 = 4n^2 + 4n + 1 = 2(2n^2 + 2n) + 1$

Mixed Review Exercises, page 203 **1.** $-8x^4y^4$ **2.** $125x^6y^{15}$ **3.** $12n^3 + 24n^2 + 3n - 3$ **4.** $2r^2 + 5r - 6$ **5.** $125y^3$ **6.** $5 - 3x - x^2$ **7.** $\{14\}$ **8.** $\{5\}$ **9.** $\{3\}$ **10.** $\{10\}$ **11.** $\{5\}$ **12.** $\{4\}$

Computer Exercises, page 203 **1.** $x^2 + 8x + 15$ **3.** $8x^2 - 14x - 15$ **5.** $9x^2 - 4$ **7.** $50x^2 + 40x + 8$ **9.** $144x^2 - 100$

Calculator Key-In, page 203 **1.** 44 **3.** 11 **5.** 600 **7.** 728 **9.** 17.5

Written Exercises, pages 206–207   **1.** $y^2 - 49$
3. $16 - x^2$ **5.** $25y^2 - 4$ **7.** $1 - 9a^2$
9. $9x^2 - 4y^2$ **11.** $16s^2 - 25t^2$ **13.** $x^4 - 81y^2$
15. $4r^4 - 49s^4$ **17.** $a^2b^2 - c^4$ **19.** 1596
21. 8091   **23.** 8099   **25.** 4884
27. $(b + 6)(b - 6)$ **29.** $(2c + 9)(2c - 9)$
31. $(5z + 1)(5z - 1)$ **33.** $(13u + 15)(13u - 15)$
35. $(1 + 3a)(1 - 3a)$ **37.** $(7a + 3b)(7a - 3b)$
39. $(4 + c^2)(2 + c)(2 - c)$
41. $(u^2 + 9v^2)(u + 3v)(u - 3v)$
43. $(x^4 + y^4)(x^2 + y^2)(x + y)(x - y)$
45. $5x(x + 2)(x - 2)$ **47.** $4a^2(3 + 2a)(3 - 2a)$
49. $uv(v + u)(v - u)$
51. $2a(a^2 + 9)(a + 3)(a - 3)$ **53.** $8(x + 2)$
55. $8s$ **57.** $(a^n + b^n)(a^n - b^n)$
59. $(u^{2n} + 2v^n)(u^{2n} - 2v^n)$
61. $(x^{2n} + y^{2n})(x^n + y^n)(x^n - y^n)$
63. $r(t^{2n} + 4)(t^n + 2)(t^n - 2)$
65. $(a + b)^2 - (a - b)^2 =$
$[(a + b) + (a - b)][(a + b) - (a - b)] =$
$(2a)(2b) = 4ab$

Mixed Review Exercises, page 207
1. $7z^2 + 8z$ **2.** $x^2 - 2x - 35$
3. $-5m^2 + 8m - 6$ **4.** $5a^2b$ **5.** $7a + 1$
6. $4n$ **7.** $2a^2 - a - 3$ **8.** $15b^3 - 25b^2 - 10b$
9. x^3 **10.** $2y^2 + 6y - 1$ **11.** $2x^2 + 3x - 1$
12. $18y$

Written Exercises, pages 210–212
1. $n^2 + 10n + 25$ **3.** $a^2 - 18a + 81$
5. $16u^2 - 8u + 1$ **7.** $25n^2 - 40n + 16$
9. $4r^2 + 36rs + 81s^2$ **11.** $25p^2 - 60pq + 36q^2$
13. $m^2n^2 + 4mn + 4$ **15.** $4a^2b^2 + 4abc^2 + c^4$
17. $16m^4 + 24m^2n + 9n^2$
19. $81p^6 + 180p^3 + 100$ **21.** $(y + 3)^2$
23. $(p - 7)^2$ **25.** $(11 - u)^2$ **27.** $(2x + 3)^2$
29. not a perfect square trinomial
31. $(2s - 9t)^2$ **33.** $2(2x + 1)^2$
35. $9(1 - 4m)^2$ **37.** $x^3(x + 1)^2$
39. $b(a + 3b)^2$ **41.** $4p^2(3p - 2)^2$
43. $(u - 1 + v)(u - 1 - v)$
45. $(a + b - 3)(a - b + 3)$ **47.** $(x^3 + 5)^2$
49. $(pq - 6)^2$ **51.** not a perfect square
trinomial   **53.** x^2 **55.** $x^4 - 8x^2 + 16 =$
$(x^2 - 4)^2 = [(x + 2)(x - 2)]^2 =$
$(x + 2)^2(x - 2)^2$ **57.** $4x^2 - 12xy + 9y^2$;
$9y^2 - 12xy + 4x^2$ **59.** $\{-2\}$ **61.** $\{-2\}$
65. 19 m $\times$ 19 m

Mixed Review Exercises, page 212   **1.** -2
2. -1 **3.** 25   **4.** 289   **5.** 512   **6.** 4096

7. $16s^2 - 9$ **8.** $x^2 + 12x + 27$ **9.** 8
10. -22 **11.** $\dfrac{1}{a^3}$ **12.** x

Self-Test 2, page 212   **1.** $n^2 + 11n + 24$
2. $m^2 - 11m + 30$ **3.** $6y^2 + 13y - 28$
4. $6x^3 - 28x^2 + 16x$ **5.** $x^2 - 81$
6. $81a^2 - 4b^2$ **7.** $(2n + 9)(2n - 9)$
8. $4(3x^2 + 2)(3x^2 - 2)$ **9.** $4n^2 + 16n + 16$
10. $9z^2 - 30kz + 25k^2$ **11.** $(3a + 2)^2$
12. $(4m - 3n)^2$

Written Exercises, pages 215–216
1. $(x + 4)(x + 1)$ **3.** $(r - 4)(r - 2)$
5. $(y - 7)(y - 2)$ **7.** $(q + 15)(q + 1)$
9. $(a - 13)(a - 2)$ **11.** $(x + 18)(x + 2)$
13. prime   **15.** $(21 - k)(2 - k)$
17. $(5 + r)(15 + r)$ **19.** $(p + 17q)(p + 2q)$
21. $(c - 12d)(c - 4d)$ **23.** $(u - 49v)(u - v)$
25. prime   **27.** $(a + 13b)(a + 4b)$
29. $(r - 9s)(r - 6s)$ **31.** $(y + 7z)(y + 13z)$
33. $(4 - y)(31 - y)$ **35.** $(8a - b)(14a - b)$
37. $\pm15, \pm9$ **39.** $\pm13, \pm8, \pm7$
41. $\pm10, \pm6$ **43.** 5, 8, 9   **45.** 7, 12, 15, 16
47. $(y - 3)(y + 1)$ **49.** $(y + 6)^2$
51. $(x + 2)(x - 2)(x + 1)(x - 1)$
53. $t(t + 4)(t - 4)(t + 2)(t - 2)$
55. $(a^n - 11b^{2n})(a^n - 19b^{2n})$

Mixed Review Exercises, page 216   **1.** $\{4\}$
2. $\{-1\}$ **3.** $\{23\}$ **4.** $\{1\}$ **5.** $\{4\}$ **6.** $\{-30\}$
7. $\{-24\}$ **8.** $\{27\}$ **9.** $\{-12\}$ **10.** $25y^2 - 49$
11. $8x^3y^9$ **12.** $64x^{12}$

Written Exercises, pages 218–219
1. $(y + 6)(y - 1)$ **3.** $(x - 8)(x + 2)$
5. $(c - 6)(c + 2)$ **7.** prime
9. $(b - 15)(b + 2)$ **11.** prime
13. $(x - 27)(x + 2)$ **15.** $(y - 24)(y + 3)$
17. $(a - 7b)(a + 6b)$ **19.** $(u + 14v)(u - 5v)$
21. $(h - 27k)(h + 2k)$ **23.** $(p - 18q)(p + 2q)$
25. $(1 - 8n)(1 + 6n)$ **27.** $(x - 15y)(x + 5y)$
29. $(1 + 16pq)(1 - 5pq)$ **31.** $(p + 20)(p - 18)$
33. $(-19 + x)(20 + x)$ **35.** $\pm27, \pm12, \pm3$
37. $\pm34, \pm2$ **39.** $-3, -8$ **41.** $-6, -14$
43. $-5, -12$ **45.** $(x + 2)(x - 2)(x^2 + 1)$
47. $(x + 4y)(x - 4y)(x^2 + y^2)$ **49.** $y(y + 11)$
51. $(a + b - 2)(a + b + 1)$
53. $(a + b - 2c)(a + b + c)$
55. $(x^n + 13y^{2n})(x^n - 17y^{2n})$

Mixed Review Exercises, page 219   **1.** $54x^5y^3$
2. $6x^2 + x - 12$ **3.** $-21x^3 + 14x^2 - 28x$
4. $9x^2 - 24x + 16$ **5.** $343x^{15}y^6$

6. $10y^3 + 15y^2 + 25y$ **7.** $\dfrac{x^3y^3}{2}$ **8.** $\dfrac{1}{3b^2}$

9. $-\dfrac{1}{n^4}$ **10.** $n^2 + 6np + 9p^2$

11. $5a^2 - 28a - 12$ **12.** $4y^2 + 28y + 49$

13. $3(5m - 7n + 3)$ **14.** $(11k + 9)(11k - 9)$

15. $(a + 9)^2$ **16.** $(a - 7b)(a - 6b)$

17. $8x(2x + 3)$ **18.** $(8 + n)(8 - n)$

19. $(u - 5)^2$ **20.** $(11 + y)(4 + y)$

21. $7ab(ab^2 - 2)$ **22.** $(7w^2 + 4x)(7w^2 - 4x)$

23. $4(m + 2)(m + 3)$ **24.** $(c - 13)(c + 2)$

25. $(3x - 4y)^2$ **26.** $(7 - z)(8 - z)$

27. $(x + 1)(x - 1)$ **28.** $(a + 17)(a - 4)$

29. $(5w^3 + 12x^3)(5w^3 - 12x^3)$ **30.** $(5a + 2b)^2$

Written Exercises, pages 222–223
1. $(3x + 1)(x + 2)$ **3.** $(3c - 5)(c - 1)$
5. $(5y - 1)(y + 1)$ **7.** prime
9. $(7x + 1)(x + 1)$ **11.** $(5x - 2)(x - 3)$
13. $(3p - 2)(p + 3)$ **15.** $(y - 1)(4y + 3)$
17. $(5 - 3x)(1 + 2x)$ **19.** prime
21. $(3m + 2n)(m + 3n)$ **23.** $(2x + 3y)(x - y)$
25. $(9m + 2n)(m - 3n)$ **27.** $(6r - 5p)(r - p)$
29. $(7c + 6)(3c - 2)$ **31.** $(2 + 5a)(3 - 4a)$
33. $(4n - 3)(8n + 5)$ **35.** $(3c - 2)(7c + 12)$
37. $(2a + 3)(a + 5)$
39. $(2a + 4b - c)(a + 2b + 3c)$
41. $(2x + 1)(2x - 1)(x + 2)(x - 2)$
43. $(y + 2)(y + 1)(y + 4)(y - 1)$
45. $(30x^3 + 77x^2 - 92x + 21)^2$

Mixed Review Exercises, page 223
1. $(x + 15)(x - 15)$ **2.** $(x - 4)(x - 5)$
3. $(r - 7)(r + 2)$ **4.** $(c - 3)^2$
5. $(3y + 17x)(3y - 17x)$ **6.** $(2a^2 + 7)(2a^2 - 7)$
7. $(y + 7)(y + 8)$ **8.** $(p + 6)^2$ **9.** $(4y + 3)^2$
10. $(m - 9)(m + 8)$ **11.** $(n + 12)(n + 3)$
12. $(b - 6)(b + 4)$

Self-Test 3, page 223 **1.** $(a + 5)(a + 7)$
2. $(x - 8)(x - 2)$ **3.** $(n + 4)(n - 7)$
4. $(c + 8d)(c - 5d)$ **5.** $(2r - 3)(r - 2)$
6. $(3x - 2y)(x + 4y)$

Challenge, page 223 **1.** 6
2. $(2^{32} + 1)(2^{16} + 1)(2^8 + 1)(2^4 + 1)(2^2 + 1) \cdot$
$(2 + 1)(2 - 1); \; 2^4 + 1 = 17, \; 2^2 + 1 = 5,$
$2 + 1 = 3$

Written Exercises, pages 225–226
1. $(3 + z)(x + y)$ **3.** $(e - 4)(f - g)$
5. $(7 - t)(r - s)$ **7.** $(2a - 1)(a + 3)$
9. $(2x - y)(x - y)$ **11.** $(2u + v + 1)(u - 2v)$

13. $(x - 1)(2w - 3v + u)$
15. $(s - 2)(s - 2p + 2)$ **17.** $(3t - r)(1 - s)$
19. $(4x - 5z)(3x - 2y)$ **21.** $(a + c)(3 + b)$
23. $(x + y)(x - 2)$ **25.** $(h + r)(h - k)$
27. $(p^2 + 4)(p - 2)$ **29.** $(p + r)(p - 2q)$
31. $(k - 4)(3h - 2)$ **33.** $(2z^2 - 3)(2z - 3)$
35. $k(k + 1)(h^2 + 4)$
37. $(x + 1)(x - 1)(x - 3)$
39. $(x + y - z)(x - y + z)$
41. $(u - 2v + 2w)(u - 2v - 2w)$
43. $(a + 4b + c)(a - c)$
45. $(a + 2 + b)(a + 2 - b)$
47. $(u + v - 1)(u - v + 1)$
49. $(h - 2 + 2k)(h - 2 - 2k)$
51. $(p - r + q)(p - r - q)$
53. $(x - 2z + 2y)(x - 2z - 2y)$
55. $(a + b + 2)(a + b)$
57. $(x^2 - 2 + y^2)(x^2 - 2 - y^2)$
59. $(p - q + r - 1)(p - q - r + 1)$
61. $(x^2 + 2x + 2)(x^2 - 2x + 2)$
63. $(a + b^{2n})(a^{2n} + b)$

Mixed Review Exercises, page 226 **1.** $\{-17\}$

2. $\{8\}$ **3.** $\{14\}$ **4.** $\{5\}$ **5.** $\{9\}$ **6.** $\left\{\dfrac{1}{3}\right\}$

7. $\{50\}$ **8.** $\{-12\}$ **9.** $\{12\}$ **10.** $\{-3\}$
11. $\{11\}$ **12.** $\{5\}$

Written Exercises, pages 228–229
1. $3(2a - 5b)(a + b)$ **3.** $5r(3r - 2s)(r + 2s)$
5. $4(z - 2)(z - 6)$ **7.** $5(a + b)^2$
9. $m(2m + 1)(2m - 1)$ **11.** $y^2(y - 2)(y + 1)$
13. $(x - 1)(x - y)$ **15.** $(7a - 2)(3a - 5)$
17. $a(a + 3)(a - 2b)$ **19.** $u^2v(2 - 5v)(3 + 2v)$
21. $k(k + 1)(k - 1)$
23. $u(2u^2 + 1)(u + 2)(u - 2)$
25. $(r - 3 + 3s)(r - 3 - 3s)$
27. $(u + 2v + 3)(u - 2v)$
29. $(p + 2q + 1)(p - 2q - 1)$
31. $4(x - 5 + 2y)(x - 5 - 2y)$
33. $(a^2 + b^2)(a + b)(a - b)$
35. $(2p + q - r)(q + r)$
37. $(2a + b - c)(b + c)$
39. $(x + y)(x - y)^2$
41. $(a - 3)(a - 2)(a + 4)$
43. $16(c^8 + 1)(c^4 + 1)(c^2 + 1)(c + 1)(c - 1)$
45. $(a + 3)(a - 6)(a + 1)$
47. $9(u + v - 2w)(u - v + 2w)$
49. $(x + 2)(x + 3)(x - 4)$
51. $(t + 3)(t - 3)(t + 1)(t - 1)$
53. $(a - b + c - d)(a - b - c + d)$
55. $(x^2 + x + 1)(x^2 - x + 1)$
57. $(a + b)(a^2 - ab + b^2)$

Answers to Selected Exercises **11**

Mixed Review Exercises, page 229 **1.** -2
2. 7 **3.** 1 **4.** $20b$ **5.** 676 **6.** -125
7. $(x - 7)(x - 5)$ **8.** $(x + 7)(x - 4)$
9. $(x - 2)(x + 1)$ **10.** $(2n + 1)(n + 9)$
11. $(3x + 5)(x + 2)$ **12.** $(3 + 2n)(x - 4)$

Written Exercises, pages 232–233 **1.** $\{-5, 7\}$
3. $\{0, -15\}$ **5.** $\left\{\frac{3}{2}, \frac{2}{3}\right\}$ **7.** $\left\{0, -\frac{1}{2}, -\frac{5}{2}\right\}$
9. $\{2, 1\}$ **11.** $\{-6, -8\}$ **13.** $\{18, -2\}$
15. $\{8, -4\}$ **17.** $\{0, 16\}$ **19.** $\left\{-\frac{3}{2}, \frac{3}{2}\right\}$
21. $\left\{-\frac{2}{3}, \frac{1}{2}\right\}$ **23.** $\left\{\frac{1}{2}\right\}$ **25.** $\left\{\frac{11}{7}, 1\right\}$
27. $\left\{0, \frac{1}{4}\right\}$ **29.** $\left\{0, \frac{1}{2}\right\}$ **31.** $\left\{\frac{1}{8}, 1\right\}$
33. $\left\{-\frac{7}{5}, \frac{7}{3}\right\}$ **35.** $\left\{\frac{11}{2}\right\}$ **37.** $\{0, 1, 2\}$
39. $\left\{0, \frac{1}{3}, 3\right\}$ **41.** $\{\pm 3, \pm 1\}$ **43.** $\{7, -3\}$
45. $\{-4, 3\}$ **47.** $\{2, 8\}$ **49.** $x^2 + x - 6 = 0$
51. $2x^2 - x - 10 = 0$ **53.** $6x^2 - 11x + 3 = 0$
55. a. Given **b.** Prop. of reciprocals **c.** Mult.
prop. of equality **d.** Mult. prop. of 0
e. Assoc. prop. of mult. **f.** Prop. of reciprocals
g. Identity prop. of mult.

Mixed Review Exercises, page 233 **1.** 16
2. 256 **3.** 40 **4.** 1000 **5.** 24 **6.** 20
7. 144 **8.** 64 **9.** 64 **10.** $-6x^4y^6$ **11.** $729a^3$
12. $-5x - 10$

Problems, pages 235–238 **1.** -8 or 7 **3.** 6
5. $-10, -9$ **7.** 12, 14 **9.** 7 cm × 15 cm
11. 9 m × 14 m **13.** 12, 13
15. 17 cm × 20 cm **17.** at 1 s and 4 s
19. 7.5 s **21.** 30 s **23. a.** 5 s **b.** There is
only one time. **25.** 4 m × 12 m or 6 m × 8 m
27. 180 cm³ **29.** 30 m × 100 m
31. 3 cm, 5 cm

Mixed Review Exercises, page 238 **1.** $16a^3b^3$
2. $125a^6$ **3.** $12a - 6ab$ **4.** $2r^2s^2$ **5.** $2n - 3p$
6. $4x + 2y$ **7.** $6a^3 - 17a^2 + a + 10$ **8.** $9b^4y^2$
9. $6x^3 - 48x$ **10.** $2(5m - 7)(m + 2)$
11. $9a(2a + b)(2a - b)$ **12.** $(7n - 2)(3n + 4)$
13. $y^2(y - 4)(y + 3)$ **14.** $(5m + 2n)(3m + 4n)$
15. $(5x - 1)(2x - 3)$

Self-Test 4, page 238 **1.** $(r + s)(7 - 3t)$
2. $(n - 1 + 10t^2)(n - 1 - 10t^2)$
3. $2a(3a - 1)^2$ **4.** $-3(3x - 2y)(2x - y)$
5. $\{8, -4\}$ **6.** $\{-2\}$ **7.** $\{0, 13, -13\}$
8. $\{0, 6, -5\}$ **9.** 6 cm × 15 cm

Extra, page 239 **1.** $(x + y)(x^2 - xy + y^2) =$
$x^3 - x^2y + xy^2 + x^2y - xy^2 + y^3 = x^3 + y^3$
3. $(m + 2)(m^2 - 2m + 4)$
5. $(n + 5)(n^2 - 5n + 25)$ **7. a.** $w^6 - 1 =$
$(w^2)^3 - (1)^3 = (w^2 - 1)(w^4 + w^2 + 1) =$
$(w - 1)(w + 1)(w^4 + w^2 + 1)$ **b.** $w^6 - 1 =$
$(w^3)^2 - (1)^2 = (w^3 - 1)(w^3 + 1) =$
$(w - 1)(w^2 + w + 1)(w + 1)(w^2 - w + 1) =$
$(w - 1)(w + 1)(w^2 + w + 1)(w^2 - w + 1)$
c. $w^4 + w^2 + 1 = (w^4 + 2w^2 + 1) - w^2 =$
$(w^2 + 1)^2 - w^2 = (w^2 + 1 + w)(w^2 + 1 - w) =$
$(w^2 + w + 1)(w^2 - w + 1)$

Chapter Review, pages 240–241 **1.** c **3.** c
5. c **7.** d **9.** d **11.** b **13.** b **15.** c **17.** b
19. b **21.** c **23.** a

Cumulative Review (Chapters 1–5), page 243
1. -20 **3.** $-7a$ **5.** $5z - 7$ **7.** $216a^{12}b^6$
9. $3x^2y - x + \frac{8}{9}$ **11.** $49a^2 + 56a + 16$
13. -4 **15.** 1 **17.** $2p^2(3p - pr^2 + 4r^3st)$
19. $(2a + 3b)^2$ **21.** $(m - 6)(m - 3)$
23. $(3y - 1)(2y + 5)$ **25.** $(a + b)^2(a - b)$
27. $\{8, -8\}$ **29.** $\{4\}$ **31.** $\{12\}$ **33.** $\{4, -4\}$
35. $\{3\}$ **37.** $\{0, 4, 5\}$ **39.** 60 km/h
41. 2 cm × 11 cm

Maintaining Skills, page 244
1. 4 cm × 10 cm **3.** 6 cm × 11 cm
5. 1 s, 3 s

Mixed Problem Solving, page 245 **1.** 9 h
3. Maureen, 10 km; sister, 13 km **5.** 7, -2
7. 8 cm × 12 cm **9.** 59 m below sea level
11. 2106 ft² **13.** No sol.; insufficient info.

Chapter 6 Fractions

Written Exercises, pages 248–250 **1.** $\frac{x + y}{2}$
3. 5; $a \neq 2$ **5.** $\frac{1}{3}$; $n \neq -\frac{1}{3}$ **7.** $\frac{2}{x + 2}$; $x \neq 2$,
$x \neq -2$ **9.** $\frac{2}{x - y}$; $x \neq 0$, $x \neq y$, $y \neq 0$
11. $\frac{x + 4}{x - 3}$; $x \neq 3$, $x \neq -\frac{1}{2}$ **13.** $\frac{a + 4}{4 - a}$; $a \neq 4$,
$a \neq -4$ **15.** $-\frac{1}{y - 2}$; $y \neq 2$ **17.** $\frac{2(n^2 + 36)}{3(n + 6)}$;
$n \neq -6$ **19.** $\frac{n - 3}{2n - 5}$; $n \neq -\frac{1}{2}$, $n \neq \frac{5}{2}$
21. $\frac{3x}{6x - 5}$; $x \neq -2$, $x \neq \frac{5}{6}$ **23.** $-\frac{5 + a}{a + 2}$;
$a \neq 2$, $a \neq -2$ **25.** $\frac{x + y}{x - y}$; $x \neq 0$, $x \neq y$

27. $\dfrac{r+s}{4r+5s}$; $r \neq s$, $r \neq -\dfrac{5s}{4}$ **29.** $c-d$;

$c \neq -d$ **31.** $\dfrac{1}{a}$; $a \neq 0$, $b \neq 1$ **33.** $5k-1$;

$k \neq \dfrac{1}{5}$ **35.** $2c+3d$; $c \neq -\dfrac{3d}{2}$ **37.** $a-6$;

$a \neq -6$ **39.** 2nd case; variable restriction $x \neq 2y$; in case 2, $x = 2y$, so results are invalid.

41. $\dfrac{5x+6y}{2x+3y}$; $x \neq \dfrac{6y}{5}$, $x \neq -\dfrac{3y}{2}$ **43.** $\dfrac{a}{2(3a-5)}$;

$a \neq 0$, $a \neq \dfrac{5}{3}$, $a \neq -\dfrac{5}{3}$ **45.** $-a-b$; $x \neq 2$

47. $\dfrac{5-x}{5+x}$; $x \neq 0$, $x \neq \dfrac{3}{2}$, $x \neq -5$

49. $\dfrac{2a-b}{2a+b+1}$; $b \neq 1-2a$, $b \neq -(2a+1)$

51. $x = -2$ **53.** $x = -3$

Mixed Review Exercises, page 250

1. $4u + 3v$ **2.** $\dfrac{21n}{2} - 7p$ **3.** $\dfrac{a^5 b^5}{2}$ **4.** $\dfrac{-243}{y^5}$

5. $3x^3 + 6x - 12$ **6.** 2800 **7.** $\{6\}$ **8.** $\{-340\}$

9. $\{-11\}$ **10.** $\{3\}$ **11.** $\{8\}$ **12.** $\{3\}$

Written Exercises, pages 253–254 **1.** $\dfrac{3}{2}$

3. $\dfrac{10}{3}$ **5.** $\dfrac{1}{3}$ **7.** 10 **9.** $2x$ **11.** $\dfrac{a}{d}$ **13.** $\dfrac{2v^2}{w}$

15. $\dfrac{2df}{27}$ **17.** $\dfrac{a^2}{36}$ **19.** $\dfrac{4n^2}{49}$ **21.** $\dfrac{4a^2}{25b^6}$

23. $\dfrac{x^8}{10{,}000}$ **25.** $\dfrac{a}{b}$ **27.** $-\dfrac{x}{4y}$ **29.** $\dfrac{4x^2}{49}$ in.^{2}

31. $\dfrac{1}{3}$ cm^2 **33.** $\dfrac{dy}{9}$ dollars **35.** $\dfrac{3}{c(c-2)}$

37. $-\dfrac{a+x}{3a}$ **39.** $\dfrac{b}{2}$ **41.** $\dfrac{5x^3(x+1)}{12}$

43. $\dfrac{2(n-1)(n-2)}{(n+2)^2}$ **45.** $\dfrac{3-t}{t+3}$

47. $\dfrac{(x-5)(2x+3)}{2x(x+1)}$ **49.** 1 **51.** $\dfrac{2}{x-2}$

53. $\dfrac{(x-y)(x^2+y^2)}{(x+y)^3}$ **55.** $-\dfrac{12}{x}$ **57.** $\dfrac{x^2+3}{6x}$

59. $x = 1$

Mixed Review Exercises, page 254
1. $(a+9)(a+5)$ **2.** $(x-5)(x-2)$
3. $(2x-3)(2x+3)(4x^2+9)$ **4.** prime
5. $(25y-2z)(25y+2z)$ **6.** $(8+c)^2$
7. $(y-4z)(x+3)$ **8.** $(3x-2)^2$
9. $(3x-1)(x+5)$ **10.** $x^2(x-7)(x-1)$
11. $(n-2)(n+7)$ **12.** $(y-8)(y+3)$

Challenge, page 254 The proof requires division of both sides by $(r-s)$. But it is given that $r = s$, so $r - s = 0$, and division by 0 is undefined.

Written Exercises, pages 256–257 **1.** $\dfrac{4}{3}$

3. $\dfrac{1}{2}$ **5.** $\dfrac{1}{xy}$ **7.** $\dfrac{a^2}{6}$ **9.** $\dfrac{27x}{2y^2}$ **11.** $\dfrac{y}{3}$ **13.** $\dfrac{25}{9x^2}$

15. 3 **17.** $8(x-1)$ **19.** -1 **21.** $\dfrac{8}{x(x-y)}$

23. $\dfrac{(w+2)^2}{(w+1)^2}$ **25.** $\dfrac{x(2x-5)}{3(x-4)}$ **27.** $c+d$

29. $\dfrac{r-t}{r^2+t^2}$ **31.** $-\dfrac{2+x}{x-6}$ **33. a.** 1 **b.** 1

35. a. $\dfrac{r^2}{t^3}$ **b.** $\dfrac{2}{x^2 y}$ **37.** -1 **39.** $-\dfrac{24}{3-q}$

41. $a^2 b^2$ **43.** $\dfrac{5(x-2)}{x-4}$ **45.** $\dfrac{1}{2+d}$

Mixed Review Exercises, page 258 **1.** $\{13\}$
2. $\{7\}$ **3.** $\{2\}$ **4.** $\{2\}$ **5.** $\{0, 2, -2\}$
6. $\left\{1, -\dfrac{4}{3}\right\}$ **7.** 2^8 **8.** $2^2 \cdot 3 \cdot 13$ **9.** $2^3 \cdot 3 \cdot 5$
10. $2 \cdot 3^3 \cdot 5^2$

Self-Test 1, page 258 **1.** 5; $c \neq 0$, $c \neq 3$

2. $\dfrac{2a-3}{3a+2}$; $a \neq -\dfrac{2}{3}$, $a \neq -\dfrac{3}{2}$ **3.** $\dfrac{-28}{3abc^2}$

4. $\dfrac{x^2}{6}$ **5.** $\dfrac{14x}{y^2}$ **6.** $\dfrac{2x}{x-3}$

Calculator Key-In, page 258 **1.** 0.9
3. $68.\overline{33}$ **5.** -5.75

Written Exercises, pages 261–262 **1.** 21
3. $30x$ **5.** $3(x-3)$ **7.** $12x$ **9.** $5x^2$
11. $7(n+2)$ **13.** $5(2n-3)$ **15.** 8
17. $2(x-1)$ **19.** $3y$ **21.** 18 **23.** 30 **25.** 24
27. $16rt^2$ **29.** $(x+1)(x-2)$
31. $(m+2)(m-2)$ **33.** $\dfrac{x}{2x^2 y}$, $\dfrac{6y}{2x^2 y}$

35. $\dfrac{55y}{30x^2 y^3}$, $\dfrac{24x}{30x^2 y^3}$ **37.** $\dfrac{20}{4(x-3)}$, $\dfrac{7}{4(x-3)}$

39. $\dfrac{6(x-3)}{(x-3)^2}$, $\dfrac{4x}{(x-3)^2}$

41. $\dfrac{3y(y+2)}{2(y-2)(y+2)}$, $\dfrac{2}{2(y-2)(y+2)}$

43. $\dfrac{x(x+3)}{(x+2)(x-3)(x+3)}$, $\dfrac{9(x+2)}{(x+2)(x-3)(x+3)}$
45. a. $24, 120, 720$ **b.** 720 **c.** $(n+1)!$

Mixed Review Exercises, page 262
1. $4(n-2q+4)$ **2.** $3(x-1)(x+1)$
3. $(x-9)(x-2)$ **4.** $(x-8)(x+3)$
5. $(2x-3)(x+1)$ **6.** $(x+13)(x+3)$
7. $(x+7)(x-4)$ **8.** $(x+11)^2$ **9.** $n(n-9)$

10. $7 = 2p - 4$ **11.** $n - \dfrac{1}{2} = 5\dfrac{1}{4}$

12. $\dfrac{2}{3}k = 16$

Computer Key-In, page 263 **1.** 21 **3.** 72 **5.** 195 **7.** 21 **9.** 72 **11.** 195 **13.** smaller denominator first

Challenge, page 263 30 km

Written Exercises, pages 267–268 **1.** $\frac{x}{3}$

3. $\frac{-4}{n}$ **5.** $\frac{x+1}{3}$ **7.** $\frac{1-y}{2}$ **9.** $\frac{7}{x+3}$

11. $\frac{x+1}{x-2}$ **13.** $\frac{1}{x-5}$ **15.** 5 **17.** $\frac{2x+3}{x^2}$

19. $\frac{2-5x}{4x^2}$ **21.** $\frac{4+5x}{5(x+1)}$ **23.** $\frac{10x+5}{12}$

25. $\frac{7y}{18}$ **27.** $\frac{n+23}{24}$ **29.** $\frac{-x+2}{4}$ **31.** $\frac{44a}{15}$

33. $\frac{5a+6b}{3}$ **35.** $\frac{2x-1}{x(x-1)}$ **37.** $\frac{6x-6}{(x-3)(x+3)}$

39. $\frac{2a+1}{a(a+1)}$ **41.** $\frac{5x-4}{x^2-1}$ **43.** 1

45. $\frac{7-d}{2(d^2-1)}$ **47.** $\frac{a+b}{ab}$ **49.** $\frac{4}{(n+4)^2}$

51. $-\frac{7}{x(x+3)}$ **53.** $\frac{x+1}{x-1}$ **55.** $\frac{1}{a-2}$

57. $\frac{2}{b-1}$

Mixed Review Exercises, page 268 **1.** -192 **2.** 121 **3.** $-64x^6$ **4.** $7y^2+2y$ **5.** $-n^3+8n^2+6n$ **6.** $90x^5y^6$ **7.** $-8x^3y^4$ **8.** $7x-2y$ **9.** $4n-11p+1$

Self-Test 2, page 269 **1.** $\frac{15c^2n}{2}$ **2.** $5a$

3. $4(x-2)^2$ **4.** $ab(a-b)$ **5.** $\frac{5c-1}{c}$

6. $\frac{28b+24}{21ab^2}$ **7.** 1 **8.** $\frac{5-n}{5(n-1)}$

Written Exercises, pages 271–272 **1.** $\frac{21}{5}$

3. $\frac{8x+1}{x}$ **5.** $\frac{3a^2-2}{a}$ **7.** $\frac{a-3b}{b}$ **9.** $\frac{5x+6}{x+2}$

11. $\frac{7x+12}{x+2}$ **13.** $\frac{6n+5}{n+1}$ **15.** $\frac{6x^2+5x}{x+1}$

17. $\frac{8n^2+8n-2}{n+1}$ **19.** $\frac{4a^3+10a^2-a+1}{2a+5}$

21. $x-6$ **23.** $\frac{2b^2-8b+2}{b(b-2)}$ **25.** $\frac{2a^2-a+3}{a^2-1}$

27. $\frac{3}{a+2}$ **29.** $\frac{5x^2+5x-6}{2x+3}$ **31.** $\frac{a^4-4}{a^2}$

33. $\frac{a+b}{a}$ **35.** $m-n$ **37.** $\frac{a}{a+2}$ **39.** $\frac{8x}{x^2-x}$

can be reduced to $\frac{8}{x-1}$. Thus, $x-1$ is the

LCD. Any multiple is a common denominator, so $x(x-1)(1-x)$ and $x(x-1)$ will also work. **41.** $\$\left(\frac{n^2+38n-80}{n}\right)$ **43.** -1 **45.** $C=4$, $D=2$

Mixed Review Exercises, page 273 **1.** $\frac{a+b}{a+2}$

2. $-\frac{a-2}{7+a}$ **3.** $\frac{3x}{2y^4}$ **4.** $4(n-2)$ **5.** $2y^2$ **6.** $16b^4$ **7.** $2x^2y$ **8.** ab^2 **9.** $1-x^2$

Challenge, page 273 Answers may vary; for example, 11, 23, and 35.

Written Exercises, pages 276–277 **1.** $x+3$

3. $n+6$ **5.** $y-3+\frac{8}{y+1}$ **7.** $x-\frac{9}{x-3}$

9. $n+4+\frac{28}{n-6}$ **11.** $x-2+\frac{8}{x+2}$

13. $x+4-\frac{1}{3x-2}$ **15.** $2x-1+\frac{9}{2x+1}$

17. $n^2-4n+9-\frac{16}{n+2}$

19. $a^2+2a+4+\frac{16}{a-2}$

21. $4x^2-2x+1-\frac{10}{3x+1}$

23. x^3-2x^2+x-6 **25.** n^3-1

27. $z^3-2z^2+4z-8+\frac{32}{z+2}$ **29.** n^2-n+1

31. $3n+2$ **33.** $2(n+3)(n-1)(n-2)$ **35.** 9 **37.** -5

Mixed Review Exercises, page 277 **1.** $\frac{3x+3}{2}$

2. $a-3$ **3.** $\frac{6+y}{3y}$ **4.** $\frac{5c+10}{6c}$ **5.** $\frac{13}{18}$

6. $\frac{1}{2(x-5)}$ **7.** $\frac{x^2+2}{x}$ **8.** $\frac{5n+4}{n+1}$

9. $\frac{y^2+3y-7}{y-2}$

Self-Test 3, page 277 **1.** $\frac{3y-8}{y}$ **2.** $\frac{5n^2+1}{n}$

3. $\frac{a^2+1}{a+1}$ **4.** $3y-2$

5. $5b^2-9b+19-\frac{22}{b+2}$

Extra, pages 278–279 **1.** $\frac{1}{5}$ **3.** $\frac{1}{v}$ **5.** 3

7. $\frac{1}{13}$ **9.** $\frac{6}{d}$ **11.** $\frac{r+2s}{s-r}$ **13.** $\frac{z-5}{z+5}$

15. $\frac{k+3}{k+2}$ **17.** 1 **19.** $\frac{2z(z-1)}{2z^2+z-4}$ **21.** $\frac{z}{2-z}$

23. $s_{avg} = \dfrac{d_{total}}{t_{total}}$; $t_{total} = t_1 + t_2$, $t_1 = \dfrac{d}{50}$, $t_2 = \dfrac{d}{30}$

$t_{total} = \dfrac{4d}{75}$; $d_{total} = 2d$; $s_{avg} = \dfrac{2d}{\left(\dfrac{4d}{75}\right)} = 37.5$

25. $\dfrac{5n}{5-n}$ items **27.** $\dfrac{w+6}{3(w-2)}$ **29.** $n^2 + 1$

31. $\dfrac{54e^2 - e - 29}{6(3e+1)(3e-1)}$ **33.** $\dfrac{1}{2s}$ **35.** $\dfrac{1}{3-c}$

Chapter Review, pages 280–281 **1.** b **2.** b
3. a **4.** b **5.** b **6.** a **7.** d **8.** c **9.** c
10. b **11.** c **12.** a **13.** c **14.** b

Cumulative Review, page 283 **1.** 0.25
3. $64x^9y^3z^6$ **5.** $20x^2 + 3x - 9$ **7.** $-17t - 3s$
9. $16t^4s^2 - 81$ **11.** 4
13. $a^2b(6a + 5ab - 3b)$ **15.** $2t(2t - 7)^2$
17. prime **19.** $y(y + 8)(y - 4)$
21. $2(2x - 1)(x + 1)$ **23.** $\{48\}$ **25.** $\{-6\}$
27. $\left\{-\dfrac{3}{4}, \dfrac{3}{4}\right\}$ **29.** $\{7, -1\}$ **31.** $\dfrac{1}{x-4}$
33. $\dfrac{a-b}{cd^2}$ **35.** $2y^2 + 3y - 8 + \dfrac{12}{5y-4}$
37. four 8-hour shifts **39.** 5 km

Maintaining Skills, page 284 **1.** 0.92
3. 2.50 **5.** 3.24 **7.** 1.70 **9.** 2.33 **11.** 0.68
13. $\dfrac{31}{50}$ **15.** $\dfrac{17}{20}$ **17.** $\dfrac{3}{10,000}$ **19.** 91%
21. 80% **23.** 3.2% **25.** 27.2 **27.** 0.08
29. 52 **31.** 70 **33.** 12 **35.** 60 **37.** 20
39. 34

***Preparing for College Entrance Exams,
page 285*** **1.** E **3.** D **5.** D **7.** B

Chapter 7 Applying Fractions

Written Exercises, pages 289–290 **1.** 2:3
3. 3:1 **5.** $\dfrac{1}{9}$ **7.** $\dfrac{4a^2}{b^3}$ **9.** 1:6 **11.** 5:1
13. 14:1 **15.** 10,000:9 **17.** 16:7 **19.** 1:20
21. 36:37 **23.** 2:1 **25. a.** 7:18 **b.** 7:11
27. a. 14:19 **b.** 8:15 **29. a.** 3:5 **b.** 9:25
31. 5:8 **33.** 6:7 **35.** 2:k **37.** 3:1 **39.** 1:1
41. $(a + b):1$ **43.** 1:1 **45.** 1:1, $-1:1$, or
1:-1

Problems, pages 291–292 **1.** 20 and 25
3. 162 players **5.** 28 cm by 20 cm **7.** $4\dfrac{1}{2}$ cm,

$7\dfrac{1}{2}$ cm, and 9 cm **9.** 400 m³ **11.** Eddie,

12 mi/h; Ling, 30 mi/h **13.** 42 dimes and 28
nickels **15.** 200 pencils **17.** 1 and 6; 2 and
12; 3 and 18 **19.** 10 and 2

Mixed Review Exercises, page 292 **1.** $\{4\}$
2. $\{6\}$ **3.** $\{-2\}$ **4.** $\{-40\}$ **5.** $\{2\}$ **6.** $\{-36\}$
7. $\{-2, 5\}$ **8.** $\{-6, 2\}$ **9.** $\{6\}$ **10.** $\dfrac{5b+1}{2c}$
11. $\dfrac{3x^2 + 5}{x}$ **12.** $\dfrac{7a+1}{4}$

Challenge, page 292 Fill 2 5-liter containers
and pour both into an 8-liter container. What
will not fit equals 2 L of the solution.

Written Exercises, pages 295–296 **1.** $\left\{\dfrac{15}{4}\right\}$
3. $\left\{\dfrac{5}{6}\right\}$ **5.** $\left\{\dfrac{28}{15}\right\}$ **7.** $\left\{\dfrac{7}{4}\right\}$ **9.** $\left\{\dfrac{2}{3}\right\}$ **11.** $\left\{\dfrac{28}{25}\right\}$
13. $\{9\}$ **15.** $\left\{-\dfrac{5}{4}\right\}$ **17.** $\left\{\dfrac{4}{5}\right\}$ **19.** $\left\{-\dfrac{5}{2}\right\}$
21. $\{11\}$ **23.** $\{2\}$ **25.** $\{3\}$ **27.** $\left\{-\dfrac{7}{18}\right\}$
29. $\{0\}$ **31.** $\{-1\}$ **33.** $\{3\}$ **35.** $\{0\}$ **37.** $\dfrac{47}{2}$
39. $\dfrac{5}{1}$ **41.** $\dfrac{d+c}{c-d}$ **43.** $\dfrac{c(d+c)}{d}$ **45.** $P = \dfrac{pT}{t}$;
$T = \dfrac{Pt}{p}$ **47.** 25 **49.** $\dfrac{1}{3}$

Problems, pages 296–297 **1.** $1.65
3. 185 mi **5.** $9800 **7.** $6400 **9.** 2400
homes **11. a.** 21 cm **b.** $\dfrac{7}{5}, \dfrac{7}{5}, \dfrac{49}{25}$
13. mahogany board

Mixed Review Exercises, page 297 **1.** $4x^2y$
2. 12 **3.** 36 **4.** 60 **5.** $x^2 - 9$ **6.** $6y$
7. $\dfrac{7}{x-1}$ **8.** $\dfrac{9r+1}{12}$ **9.** $\dfrac{32a+5}{40}$ **10.** 4.8
11. -4.3 **12.** 24

Self-Test 1, page 297 **1.** 4:5 **2.** 40:1 **3.** 36
trucks **4.** $\{102\}$ **5.** $\left\{\dfrac{1}{21}\right\}$ **6.** $\{26\}$

Written Exercises, pages 299–300 **1.** $\left\{\dfrac{6}{5}\right\}$
3. $\{5\}$ **5.** $\{3\}$ **7.** $\left\{\dfrac{1}{2}\right\}$ **9.** $\{10\}$ **11.** $\left\{\dfrac{1}{2}\right\}$
13. $\left\{\dfrac{1}{2}\right\}$ **15.** $\left\{-\dfrac{1}{3}\right\}$ **17.** $\{12\}$ **19.** $\{-2\}$
21. $\{-2\}$ **23.** $\{4\}$ **25.** $\{3\}$ **27.** $\left\{\dfrac{1}{2}\right\}$ **29.** $\{0\}$
31. $\left\{\dfrac{4a}{3}\right\}$ **33.** $\left\{\dfrac{m+5}{2m}\right\}$

Problems, pages 300–301 **1.** 40 **3.** 15 and 6
5. 8 ft by 10 ft **7.** $4.50 **9.** 15 cm by 6 cm
11. 8 km (one way) **13.** 6 quarters and 42
nickels **15.** 9 apples

Mixed Review Exercises, page 301 **1.** 2:7
2. 1:6 **3.** 4:3 **4.** $\frac{2n}{5}$ **5.** $\frac{4}{3xy}$ **6.** $\frac{3a^3}{5b^2}$
7. {7} **8.** $\left\{\frac{29}{3}\right\}$ **9.** $\left\{\frac{28}{3}\right\}$ **10.** $\left\{\frac{16}{3}\right\}$
11. {5, −5} **12.** {2}

Application, page 303 **1.** ¢ **3.** ft^2 **5.** ft/min
7. 42.5¢/day

Written Exercises, pages 305–306 **1.** {4}
3. {12} **5.** {12} **7.** {8} **9.** {9} **11.** No sol.
13. No sol. **15.** No sol. **17.** {All real numbers except 2} **19.** {1} **21.** No sol.
23. $\left\{-\frac{1}{2}, 1\right\}$ **25.** No sol. **27.** {1} **29.** {0, 4}
31. {−2, 1} **33.** {3} **35.** $\left\{-\frac{14}{3}\right\}$ **37.** {9}
39. $\left\{1, \frac{3}{4}\right\}$

Problems, pages 306–308 **1.** $\frac{4}{3}$ or $\frac{3}{4}$ **3.** 3
and 5 **5.** $\frac{3}{2}$ **7.** 4 and 6 **9.** 5.5 h **11.** 24
people **13.** 12 km/h

Mixed Review Exercises, page 308 **1.** {20}
2. {−30} **3.** {3} **4.** $\left\{\frac{6}{5}\right\}$ **5.** {−12} **6.** $\left\{\frac{72}{5}\right\}$
7. 125 **8.** $8x^4 + 12x^3 - 28x^2$ **9.** 48
10. $5n^2 - n + 9$ **11.** $10y^2z^4$ **12.** $27p^3q^6$

Self-Test 2, page 308 **1.** {−8} **2.** {18}
3. {−23} **4.** {−6} **5.** {−5} **6.** No sol.
7. 2 and 3

Written Exercises, pages 312–313 **1.** $\frac{1}{4}$ **3.** $\frac{3}{8}$
5. $\frac{3}{5}$ **7.** $\frac{18}{25}$ **9.** $\frac{1}{25}$ **11.** $\frac{18}{5}$ **13.** 96 **15.** 32
17. 0.06 **19.** 20.25 **21.** 40 **23.** 350
25. 5.6 **27.** 16% **29.** 2% **31.** 20% **33.** $3;
$9 **35.** $7.50; $67.50 **37.** $11; $55 **39.** $48;
$208 **41.** {20} **43.** {3} **45.** {20} **47.** {−50}
49. {86.25} **51.** {2} **53.** {−64,000} **55.** {0.5}
57. $30 **59.** 10.5% **61.** $850

Problems, pages 313–314 **1.** $83\frac{1}{3}$%
3. $85,000 **5.** $9500 **7.** $18.70 **9.** 20%
11. $10,584 **13.** 495 cm^3 of water **15.** $60

Mixed Review Exercises, page 314
1. $3a(ab + 2)$ **2.** $3y(y + 1)^2$
3. $(m + 2)(m + 3)$ **4.** $(x - 3y)(x + 3y)$
5. $5pq(pq^2 + 2p - 3q)$ **6.** $(4a - 3)(a + 1)$
7. $(a + b)(a + 4)$ **8.** $(x + 3)^2$ **9.** $(t + 3)(t - 5)$

Written Exercises, pages 317–318 **1.** 10%
3. 20% **5.** 12.5% **7.** $6.30 **9.** $6.40
11. $65 **13.** 20% **15.** 17.5% **17.** $25.60
19. $78 **21.** $70

Problems, pages 318–319 **1.** 7% **3.** 17%
5. 6% **7.** $10,800 **9.** $42 **11.** $1600 in
stocks, $4400 in bonds **13.** $20,000
15. $1440

Computer Exercises, pages 319–320
1.

Years	$
1	106
2	112.36
3	119.10
4	126.25
5	133.82
6	141.85
7	150.36
8	159.38
9	168.95
10	179.08

Mixed Review Exercises, page 320 **1.** $\left\{\frac{15}{4}\right\}$
2. {−4, 1} **3.** No sol. **4.** {20} **5.** {−1, −2}
6. {8} **7.** $9z + 27$ **8.** $-4x + 12y$
9. $7a + b + 7$ **10.** $-8t$ **11.** $30bc$ **12.** $-3xz$

Self-Test 3, page 320 **1.** $\frac{13}{20}$ **2.** $\frac{29}{40}$ **3.** $\frac{51}{10}$
4. 13.6 **5.** 6.25 **6.** 350% **7.** 75% **8.** $1680
9. $33\frac{1}{3}$%

Problems, pages 324–325 **1.** 2 kg cashews,
6 kg pecans **3.** 50 mL juice **5.** $1.00/lb
7. 7.2% **9.** 25 L **11.** 3 g **13.** 8 kg apples,
12 kg apricots **15.** 65 km/h **17.** 4.8 L acid,
11.2 L water **19.** 8 L **21.** $17,000 at 12%,
$4000 at $5\frac{1}{4}$% **23.** (a) 25 km/h (b) 24 km/h
25. about $1.76

Mixed Review Exercises, page 325 **1.** 6.32
2. 40% **3.** 7.5% **4.** 128 **5.** 9 **6.** $\frac{1}{6}$ **7.** 7
8. 80 **9.** 19 **10.** 4

Problems, pages 328–330   **1.** $\frac{2}{3}$; $\frac{x}{3}$ **3.** $\frac{9}{16}$;

$\frac{9h}{40}$ **5.** $1\frac{1}{5}$ h   **7.** 40 min   **9.** $9\frac{3}{8}$ min   **11.** 12 h

13. 4.5 h; 9 h   **15.** $1\frac{2}{5}$ h   **17.** $3\frac{2}{3}$ h

19. 4 days   **21.** 40 min or 2400 s   **23.** largest,

$5\frac{1}{2}$ h; medium, 11 h; smallest, $16\frac{1}{2}$ h

Mixed Review Exercises, page 330   **1.** 18%
2. \$143   **3.** \$22   **4.** $\{-2\}$ **5.** $\{3.5\}$ **6.** $\{-1\}$
7. $\{11\}$ **8.** $\{1.4\}$ **9.** $\{0\}$

Self-Test 4, page 330   **1.** 25 L   **2.** 0.2 kg
3. 18 days   **4.** $34\frac{2}{7}$ s

Written Exercises, pages 333–335   **1.** $\frac{1}{5}$ **3.** $\frac{1}{9}$

5. $\frac{1}{81}$ **7.** $\frac{1}{27}$ **9.** $\frac{1}{16}$ **11.** 1   **13.** $\frac{1}{16}$ **15.** 8

17. 27   **19.** 1   **21.** $\frac{1}{81}$ **23.** 1   **25.** $\frac{81}{16}$

27. $\frac{125}{64}$ **29. a.** $\frac{1}{216}$ **b.** $\frac{2}{27}$ **31. a.** $\frac{4}{3}$ **b.** 8

33. 0 has no reciprocal.   **35.** $\frac{3}{x^2}$ **37.** $\frac{1}{9x^2}$

39. $\frac{y^2}{x}$ **41.** $\frac{1}{m^{12}}$ **43.** m **45.** $\frac{27}{x^6}$ **47.** 2

49. $\frac{1}{a^6}$ **51.** y^8 **53.** $\frac{1}{c^7}$ **55.** a^4 **57.** n^8

59. 25   **61.** 0.0000128   **63.** 78,125   **65.** 625
67. 0.00032   **69.** 4   **71.** x^1

Problems, page 335   **1.** 0.7084252 kg;
0.5018663 kg   **3. (a)** 12 million   **(b)** 16 million   **(c)** 9 million   **5. (a)** 5474   **(b)** 2
(c) 16,399,358   **(d)** 0

Mixed Review Exercises, page 335   **1.** $\frac{5z}{3x}$;

$x \neq 0$, $z \neq 0$ **2.** $\frac{y+5}{y+2}$; $y \neq -5$, $y \neq -2$

3. $\frac{9p^2}{q^2}$; $q \neq 0$ **4.** $\frac{2(4-5n)}{5mn}$; $m \neq 0$, $n \neq 0$

5. $\frac{2(a-4)}{a-2}$; $a \neq 2$ **6.** $\frac{x-3}{x+2}$; $x \neq -3$, $x \neq -2$

7. $4x - 14 + \frac{92}{x+4}$ **8.** $\frac{2(x+5)}{3(x-3)}$

9. $a^2 + 3a + 9 + \frac{54}{a-3}$

Written Exercises, page 339   **1.** 300,000,000
3. 2,000,000,000,000,000,000,000,000,000,000
5. 0.00000136   **7.** 0.00000000000000005

9. a. 10^3 **b.** 10^{-3} **11. a.** 10^6 **b.** 10^{-6}
13. a. 10^6 **b.** 10^{-6} **15. a.** 2.5×10^3
b. $2 \cdot 10^3 + 5 \cdot 10^2$ **17. a.** 2.4×10^{-9}
b. $2 \cdot 10^{-9} + 4 \cdot 10^{-10}$ **19. a.** 3.03×10^6
b. $3 \cdot 10^6 + 0 \cdot 10^5 + 3 \cdot 10^4$
21. a. 9.09×10^{-5} **b.** $9 \cdot 10^{-5} + 0 \cdot 10^{-6} +$
$9 \cdot 10^{-7}$ **23. a.** 9.86×10^{-1}
b. $9 \cdot 10^{-1} + 8 \cdot 10^{-2} + 6 \cdot 10^{-3}$
25. a. 1.2×10^{10} **b.** $1 \cdot 10^{10} + 2 \cdot 10^9$
27. 3.6×10^{-4} **29.** 3.6×10^{17} **31.** 1×10^0

Problems, pages 339–340   **1. a.** about
9.5×10^{12} km   **b.** about 1.4×10^{19} km

c. about 4.3 years   **d.** about 500 s or $8\frac{1}{3}$ min

3. a. 2.3×10^2 **b.** 7.5×10^{-5} **c.** 2.3×10^{18}
d. 3.0×10^{21}

Mixed Review Exercises, page 340   **1.** $y + 24$

2. $\frac{y^{15}}{x^6}$ **3.** 8   **4.** 5:2   **5.** 5   **6.** $3t + 1$ **7.** $\frac{1}{c^{12}}$

8. 2   **9.** $\frac{7b^2}{6c}$

Self-Test 5, page 341   **1.** 3^{10} **2.** $\frac{1}{2^3}$ or $\frac{1}{8}$

3. $-(2^3)$ or -8 **4.** $\frac{1}{x^5}$ **5.** $\frac{4}{a^2}$ **6.** $\frac{1}{81a^8}$ **7.** 1

8. $\frac{1}{b^2}$ **9.** $\frac{1}{a^6}$ **10. a.** 4.7×10^7

b. $4 \cdot 10^7 + 7 \cdot 10^6$ **11. a.** 6×10^{-8}
b. $6 \cdot 10^{-8}$ **12. a.** 1.234×10^1
b. $1 \cdot 10^1 + 2 \cdot 10^0 + 3 \cdot 10^{-1} + 4 \cdot 10^{-2}$

Chapter Review, pages 342–343   **1.** b   **3.** d
5. c   **7.** c   **9.** b   **11.** b   **13.** d   **15.** d

Cumulative Review, page 345   **1.** 12
3. $-16m^8n^7$ **5.** $16a^4b^6c^2$
7. $25t^4v^2 - 60t^2v + 36$
9. $2x^3 - 11x^2y + 11xy^2 - 3y^3$ **11.** $\frac{1}{x^2z(3z+1)}$

13. $4b + 3$ **15.** $x^{14}(x-4)^2$ **17.** $9\frac{1}{3}\%$

19. $(7z - 2)^2$ **21.** $3(2b + 3)(b + 3)$

23. $(12x - 1)(x + 4)$ **25.** $\{30\}$ **27.** $\left\{-\frac{7}{2}\right\}$

29. $\{0, 1, 11\}$ **31.** $\{-1, 6\}$ **33.** 4.3×10^{-6}

35. 9 and 11   **37.** 20%   **39.** 56 min or $\frac{14}{15}$ h

Maintaining Skills, page 346   **1.** $9a^2 - 5a + 8$
3. $12 - 5x$ **5.** $12x - 20z$ **7.** $2x - 8y - 6$

9. $-\frac{13}{6}b$ **11.** $-6a^3b^4c$ **13.** $-m^5n^2p^3$

15. $16x^8y^{12}$ **17.** $r^{15}s^{11}t^7$ **19.** $56c^{12}d^{12}e^6$

21. $3a^3b^2 - 3a^2b^3 + 3ab^4$
23. $c^2d^7 - 2c^3d^5 + c^5d^3$ **25.** $z^2 + 5z - 24$
27. $y^2 + 8y - 20$ **29.** $12z^2 - 9z - 3$
31. $81d^2 - 9$ **33.** $x^4 - 36$
35. $3y^3 - 13y^2 + 13y - 3$

Mixed Problem Solving, page 347 **1.** home;
2 points **3.** 220 mg **5.** 30 km **7.** 49.5 min
9. No sol.; insufficient info. **11.** $\dfrac{7x + 40}{240}$ h
13. $5,000

Chapter 8 Introduction to Functions

Written Exercises, pages 351–352 **1.** yes; yes
3. yes; no **5.** yes; yes **7.** yes; yes **9.** no; no
11. no; yes **13.** (0, 6), (1, 4), (2, 2), and
(3, 0) **15.** (0, 4) and (2, 1) **17.** (0, 1)
19. (1, 4), (3, 3), (5, 2), (7, 1), and (9, 0)
21. (1, 4), (2, 2), and (4, 1) **23.** (1, 3) and
(3, 1) **25.** (1, 16), (2, 8), (4, 4), (8, 2), and
(16, 1) **27.** (1, 5) and (5, 1) **29.** (3, 1)
31. (0, 1), (2, 2), and (3, 4) **33.** (1, 3), (2, 1),
and (4, 0) **35.** (9, 0), (3, 2), and (1, 8) **37.** 5
small and 3 large or 9 small and 2 large **39.** 4
pigs and 40 chickens **41.** $y = 6x - 2$

43. $y = \dfrac{2x}{x - 2}$ **45.** 9

Mixed Review Exercises, page 352
1. 3.08×10^8 **2.** 4.37×10^{-4} **3.** 1.19×10^8
4. 2.16×10^{-5} **5.** 4.9×10^4 **6.** 5.6201×10^7
7. $\dfrac{n^2}{2}$ **8.** $\dfrac{1}{125x^3}$ **9.** $3xy$ **10.** $\dfrac{1}{b^7}$

Computer Exercises, page 352 **1.** yes; no
2. no; yes **3.** yes; no **4.** yes; yes **5.** no; yes
6. yes; yes

Written Exercises, pages 357–358
1–11.
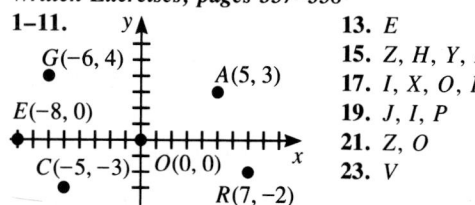
13. E
15. Z, H, Y, L
17. I, X, O, P
19. J, I, P
21. Z, O
23. V

25.
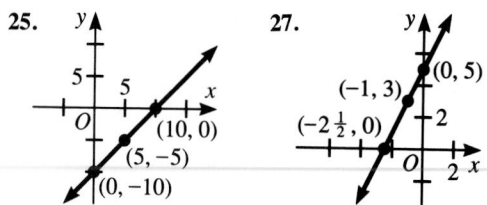
27.

29.
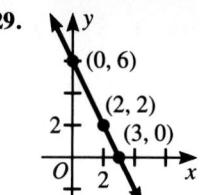
31.
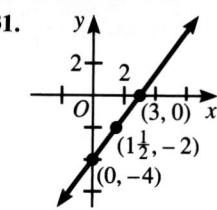

33.
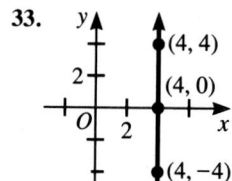
35.
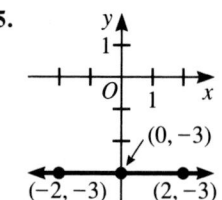

37.
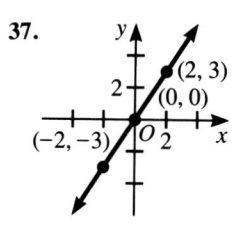
39.
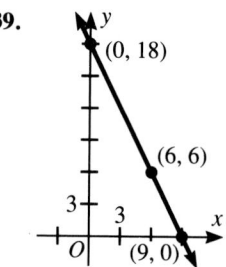

41.
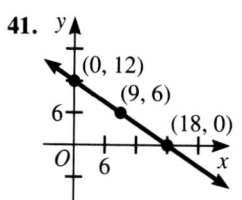
43.
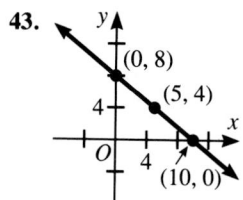

45. parallelogram **47.** rectangle
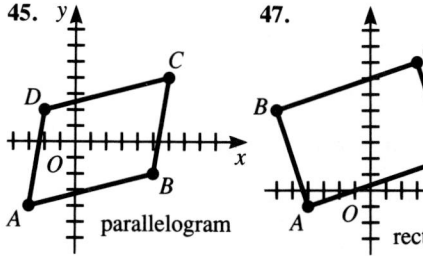

Mixed Review Exercises, page 358 **1.** yes; no
2. yes; yes **3.** no; yes **4.** no; yes
5. $\{-1, -2\}$ **6.** $\{11\}$ **7.** $\{2, 3\}$ **8.** $\left\{\dfrac{10}{3}\right\}$
9. $\{-9\}$ **10.** $\{15\}$

Self-Test 1, page 358 **1.** yes; no **2.** no; yes
3. (0, 4), (3, 2), (6, 0) **4.** (0, 4), (5, 2),
(10, 0)

5–7.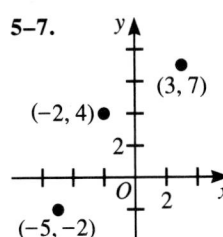

8.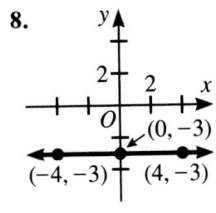

9.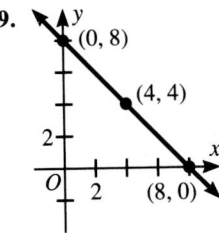

10.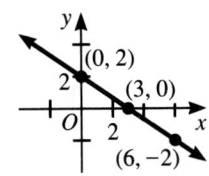

Mixed Review Exercises, page 365 **1.** $\left\{-\frac{6}{5}\right\}$

2. $\left\{-\frac{20}{9}\right\}$ **3.** $\{3\}$ **4.** $\{-9\}$ **5.** $\{1.7, -1.7\}$

6. $\{0, 5\}$ **7.** $-\frac{13}{10}$ **8.** 20 **9.** 3 **10.** 4

11. -10 **12.** 8

Calculator Key-In, page 365 **1.** 7 **3.** -1.925
5. 1

Written Exercises, pages 368–369 **1.** 2; 1

3. $\frac{1}{2}$; -3 **5.** $-\frac{1}{2}$; 6 **7.** -2; 8 **9.** 1; 0

11. 0; -4 **13.**
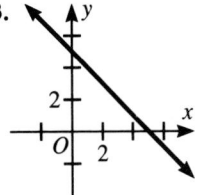

Computer Key-In, page 359 **1.** x-axis at 3, y-axis at -2 **3.** x-axis at -2, does not cross the y-axis **5.** x-axis at 2.6666667, y-axis at 2.6666667

Written Exercises, pages 363–365 **1.** $-\frac{1}{2}$

3. 1 **5.** $\frac{2}{11}$ **7.** 1 **9.** $\frac{5}{3}$ **11.** $\frac{2}{3}$ **13.** 2

15. -2 **17.** $-\frac{3}{2}$ **19.** $\frac{3}{5}$ **21.** 0 **23.** no slope

15.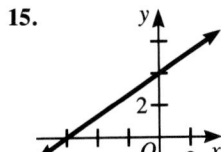

17.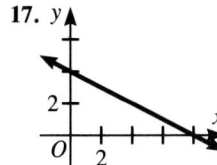

25.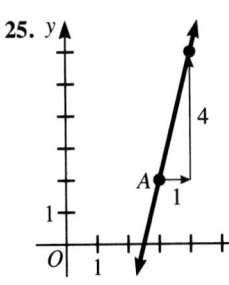

27.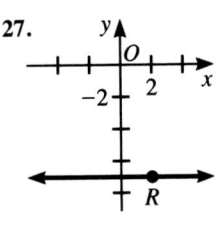

19.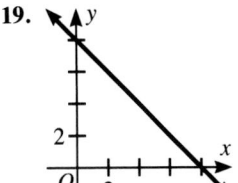

21.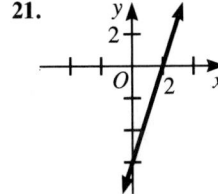

23.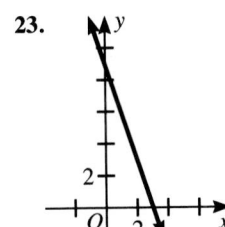

25.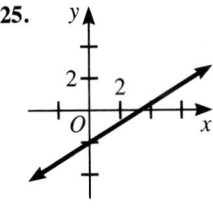

29.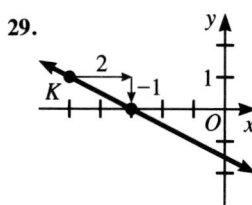

31. collinear **33.** not collinear **35.** not collinear **37.** $\overline{AB}$, 0; $\overline{AC}$, no slope; $\overline{BC}$, $\frac{8}{9}$ **39.** $\frac{1}{2}$; 8

41. The slopes of $\overline{AC}$ and $\overline{AM}$ are both $-\frac{5}{3}$; thus M lies on $\overline{AC}$. The slopes of $\overline{DB}$ and $\overline{DM}$ are both $\frac{3}{5}$; thus M lies on $\overline{DB}$.

27.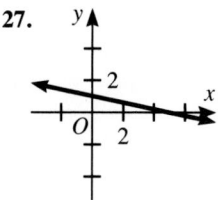

29.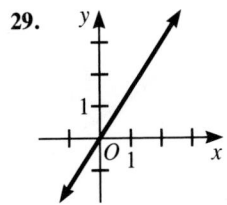

31. both lines have slope of $\frac{2}{3}$ and different y-intercepts **33.** both lines have slope of 1 and different y-intercepts **35.** both lines have slope of -1 and different y-intercepts **37.** $y = 5x + 7$

39. 2; -2 **41.** -9 **43.** 3 **45.** $m = -\frac{a}{b}$ and

$b = \frac{c}{b}$

Mixed Review Exercises, page 369 **1.** 2 **2.** $\frac{1}{3}$
3. -3 **4.** 4 **5.** $(3s + 4)(s + 1)$ **6.** $5x(4x + 3)$
7. $3(p - 4)^2$ **8.** $(9y - 4z)(9y + 4z)$
9. $(x + y)(-3x + 4)$ **10.** $(m - 12n)(m + 3n)$

Extra, page 370 **1.** $-\frac{2}{3}$ **3.** $\frac{8}{3}$ **5.** $-\frac{5}{3}$
7. no slope **9.** -3 **11.** parallel
13. perpendicular **15.** parallel **17.** -8

Written Exercises, pages 372–373
1. $y = 2x + 5$ **3.** $y = -\frac{1}{2}x + 7$

5. $y = \frac{1}{2}x - 2$ **7.** $y = 2x + 11$

9. $y = -2x + 11$ **11.** $y = \frac{1}{2}x - 3$

13. $y = -\frac{3}{4}x + 3$ **15.** $y = 3$ **17.** $y = 2x + 7$
19. $y = -x + 7$ **21.** $y = -x + 9$
23. $y = \frac{8}{3}x - 9$ **25.** $y = 5x - 1$

27. $y = -\frac{3}{4}x - \frac{3}{2}$ **29.** $y = \frac{2}{5}x - 2$

31. $y = \frac{1}{2}x - 3$ **33.** $y = 5$ **35.** $3x - y = -6$

37. $x - 2y = 6$ **39. a.** No; there is no slope or y-intercept. **b.** $x = 2$ **41.** 7

Mixed Review Exercises, page 373 **1.** $16t^5$
2. $2s^2 - 4st$ **3.** $49p^2q^4$ **4.** $-27m^6n^{12}$ **5.** 3
6. $-18a^4b^3$ **7.** 128 **8.** $5x + 2y$

Self-Test 2, page 373 **1.** $\frac{4}{3}$ **2.** 0 **3.** $\frac{3}{7}$; -4

4.

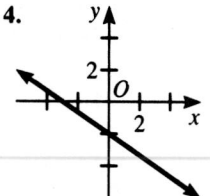

5. $y = 3x + 5$
6. $y = x - 5$

Written Exercises, page 377
1.

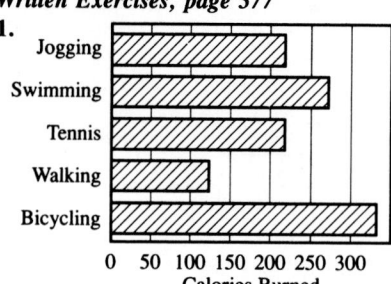

3.

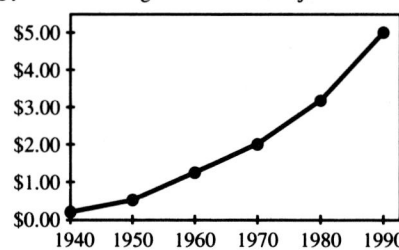

5. Cost of seeing a movie at the Bijou Theater

7. $\$.90$; $\$2.50$ **9.** Answers will vary.

Mixed Review Exercises, page 377
1. $y = x + 2$ **2.** $y = 5x + 2$ **3.** $y = \frac{1}{3}x - 4$

4. $y = -\frac{3}{2}x - 3$

5.

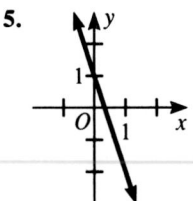

6.

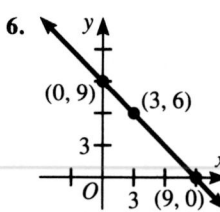

7.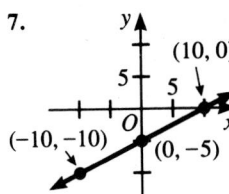

8.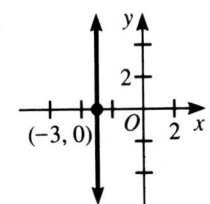

9. $\left(\frac{1}{2}, -6\frac{1}{4}\right)$; $x = \frac{1}{2}$; $-6\frac{1}{4}$ **11.** $(0, -4)$;

$x = 0$; -4 **13.** $\left(-1\frac{1}{2}, 2\frac{1}{4}\right)$; $x = -1\frac{1}{2}$; $2\frac{1}{4}$

15. $(-4, 1)$; $x = -4$; 1 **17.** $\left(\frac{1}{4}, \frac{1}{8}\right)$; $x = \frac{1}{4}$; $\frac{1}{8}$

19. $(0, 0)$; $x = 0$;

21. $(0, 0)$; $x = 0$;

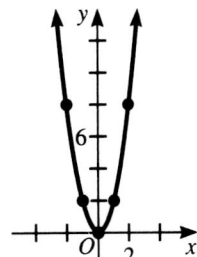
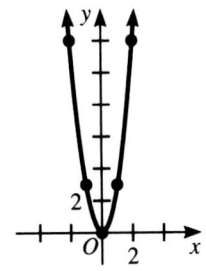

Written Exercises, pages 380–381
1. $\{-4, 1, 6\}$ **3.** $\{-3, 5, 13\}$ **5.** $\{-1, 3\}$
7. $\{2, 9, 29\}$ **9.** $\{0, 2\}$ **11.** $\{0, 5, 45\}$
13. a. 6 **b.** -24 **c.** -49 **15. a.** 4 **b.** -1
c. -4 **17. a.** 46 **b.** 73 **c.** -2 **19. a.** 23
b. 23 **c.** -2 **21. a.** 8 **b.** 0 **c.** 16
23. a. 70 **b.** 28 **c.** 0 **25. a.** -24 **b.** 0
c. 0 **27. a.** 0 **b.** 1 **c.** 1 **29.** -12; $\{4\}$
31. -1; $\left\{\frac{1}{5}\right\}$ **33.** 7; $\{14\}$ **35.** -3; $\{-1, 3\}$
37. 0; $\{-1, 0, 1\}$ **39.** -1; $\{1, -1\}$ **41.** -18
43. 6 **45. a.** 2 **b.** 1 **c.** 2 **d.** 4 **47.** 0

23. $(0, 0)$; $x = 0$;

25. $(2, -4)$; $x = 2$;

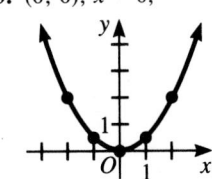
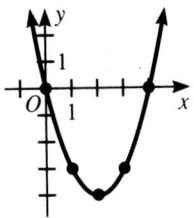

Mixed Review Exercises, page 382
1. $\dfrac{9n^2 + 4n - 1}{3n^3}$ **2.** 19 **3.** $-3y$
4. $-9a + 6b - 3c$ **5.** $1 - x$ **6.** $12m - 21$
7. -12 **8.** $\dfrac{df}{e}$ **9.** $\dfrac{x - y}{x + y}$

Computer Exercises, page 382 **1.** $-13, -7,$
$-4, 23$ **3.** $0.0099, 0.2, 1, 0.2, 0.0099$

Challenge, page 382 **1. a.** $\dfrac{2}{3}; \dfrac{3}{4}; \dfrac{4}{5}$ **b.** $\dfrac{100}{101}$

c. $\dfrac{n}{n + 1}$

Written Exercises, pages 386–387

1.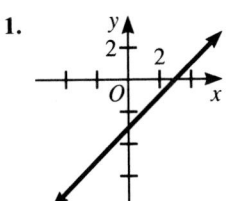

3.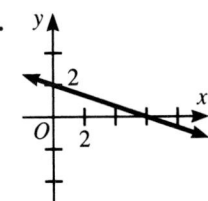

5.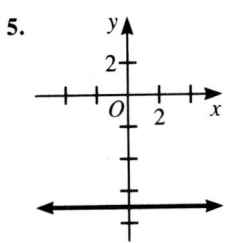

7. $(0, -5)$; $x = 0$; -5

27. $\left(-2\frac{1}{2}, 12\frac{1}{4}\right)$;

$x = -2\frac{1}{2}$;

29. $(0, 4)$; $x = 0$;

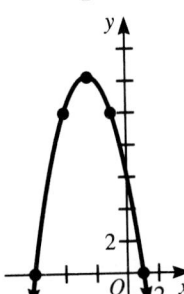
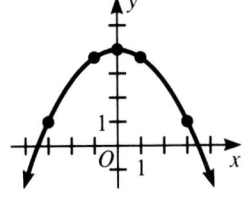

31. a.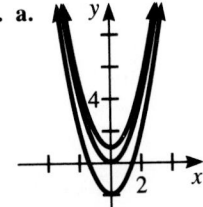

b. graph rises;
graph lowers

33. 10; $\{-5\}$
35. -11; $\left\{2\frac{3}{4}\right\}$
37. 8; $\{2, 4\}$
39. 12; $\{-6, -2\}$
41. x-intercepts

Mixed Review Exercises, page 387
1. {2, 5, 14} **2.** {−8, −4, 0} **3.** {6, 8, 34}
4. {0, 2, 6} **5.** 7(x + 4) **6.** x − 3 **7.** 9x
8. $\frac{1}{3}x - 5$

Computer Exercises, page 388 **1.** (0, 0);
(−3, 9), (−2, 4), (−1, 1); (1, 1)(2, 4)(3, 9)
3. (2, −1); (−1, 8), (0, 3), (1, 0);
(3, 0)(4, 3)(5, 8) **5.** (−1, −5); (−4, 13),
(−3, 3), (−2, −3); (0, −3), (1, 3), (2, 13)

Self-Test 3, page 388
1. a. D = {1985, 1986, 1987, 1988, 1989, 1990};
R = {0.75, 0.90, 1.12, 1.43, 1.65, 2.05}

b.
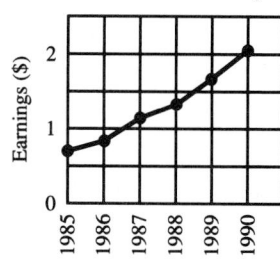
Earnings Per Share
Common Foods Corp.

2. R = {2, 3, 6, 11, 18}
3. a. 11 **b.** −10 **c.** −3
4. (−4, −6); −6
5. (1, −1); x = 1; see
graph at right.

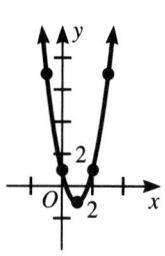

Ex. 5

Extra, pages 389–390 **1.** D = {2, 3};
R = {0, 3, 4, 6}; no **3.** D = {1, 2, 3, 4};
R = {−3, −1, 0, 6}; yes
5. D = {−2, −1, 1, 2}; R = {1, 4}; yes
7. D = {−1, 1, 2, 4}; R = {1, 2}; yes
9. D = {−2, 2, 4}; R = {−3, −1, 0, 1}; no
11. D = {−3, −2, −1, 0, 1, 2, 3};
R = {−2, −1, 0, 1}; yes
13. Not a function;   **15.** Not a function;
(4, 4) and (4, −3)   (−3, 0) and (−3, 2)
have the same   have the same
first coordinate.   first coordinate.

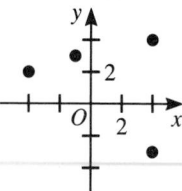   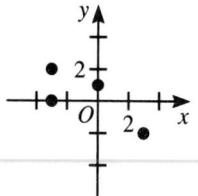

17. Yes, it is a function.
See graph at right.
19. Yes; no; it is
not a function be-
cause all nonzero
x's are paired with
2 y's. **21.** yes; no
23. yes; yes

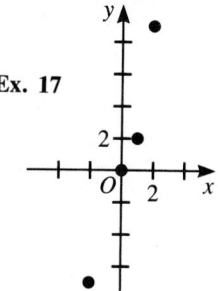
Ex. 17

Written Exercises, pages 393–395 **1.** $\frac{1}{6}$ **3.** 8
5. 25 **7.** 750 **9.** 600 **11.** 24 **13.** 1.2
15. $\frac{2}{3}$ **17. a.** $L = \frac{7}{10}h$ **b.** $\frac{14}{20} = \frac{L_2}{h_2}$
19. a. $M = \frac{1}{6}E$ **b.** $\frac{28}{168} = \frac{M_2}{E_2}$
21. a. $R = 0.02059\,l$ **b.** $\frac{10.295}{500} = \frac{R_2}{l_2}$
23. Since (x_1, y_1) and (x_2, y_2) are ordered pairs
of a direct variation and neither is (0, 0), $\frac{x_1}{y_1}$ and
$\frac{x_2}{y_2}$ are equivalent fractions, so $\frac{x_1}{y_1} = \frac{x_2}{y_2}$;
$x_1y_2 = x_2y_1$; $y_2 = \frac{x_2y_1}{x_1}$; $\frac{y_2}{x_2} = \frac{y_1}{x_1}$, or $\frac{y_1}{x_1} = \frac{y_2}{x_2}$.

Problems, pages 395–396 **1.** $360 **3.** $900
5. 17 min **7.** 156 m² **9.** 55 g **11.** 37 degrees
13. 1,196,718.75 m² **15.** If $C = k_1d$ and
$d = k_2r$, then $C = k_1(k_2r)$ or $C = (k_1 \cdot k_2)r$ and C
varies directly with r.

Mixed Review Exercises, page 396
1. $6p^2 + 11p + 3$ **2.** $4x^3 + 10x^2 - 30x + 12$
3. $-15s + 12s^2$ **4.** $9c^2 - 4$ **5.** $3t^2 + t - 10$
6. $14y^2 + 22y - 12$ **7.**

8.
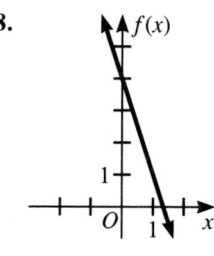

9.
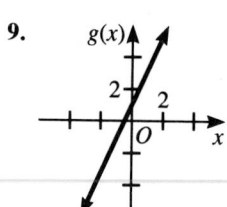

10.
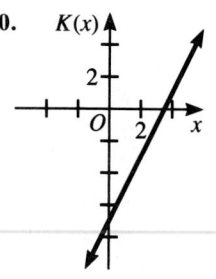

22   *Answers to Selected Exercises*

11.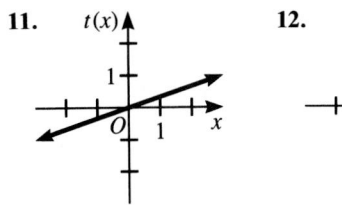
$t(x)$

12.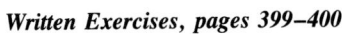
$d(x)$

Written Exercises, pages 399–400

1.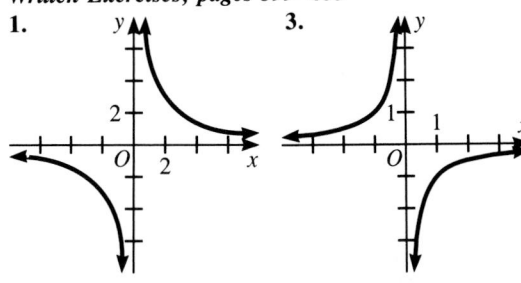

3.

5.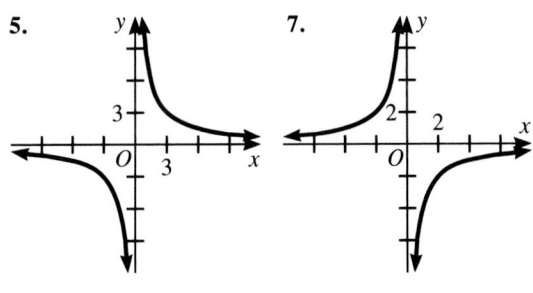

7.

9. 40   **11.** 27   **13.** 6.3   **15. a.** $lw = 90$

b. $\dfrac{5}{l_2} = \dfrac{w_2}{18}$ **17. a.** $fl = 1.5$ **b.** $\dfrac{0.6}{f_2} = \dfrac{l_2}{2.5}$

19. a. $PV = 337{,}125$ **b.** $\dfrac{725}{V_2} = \dfrac{P_2}{465}$

Problems, pages 400–401   **1.** 9 people
3. 48 cm   **5.** 750 r/min   **7.** 8 m   **9.** 22 cm
11. about 8.8 ft   **13.** about 66 cm from the

18 kg mass   **15.** $\dfrac{1}{2}$ the wavelength of the lower

note   **17.** 0.4 m

Mixed Review Exercises, page 402   **1.** Both

lines have a slope of $-\dfrac{2}{3}$ and different y-inter-

cepts.   **2.** Both lines have a slope of $-\dfrac{1}{5}$ and

different y-intercepts.   **3.** Both lines have a
slope of 1 and different y-intercepts.   **4.** Both

lines have a slope of $\dfrac{2}{3}$ and different y-inter-

cepts.   **5.** -6 **6.** $\dfrac{1}{5}$ **7.** 9

Computer Exercises, page 402   **1.** direct
3. neither

Calculator Key-In, page 403   **1.** 21   **3.** 155
5. 0.36   **7.** 19.2   **9.** 5.2   **11.** 9

Self-Test 4, page 403   **1.** 5   **2.** 3   **3.** $525
4. 3   **5.** 32   **6.** 7 people

Reading Algebra, page 404   **1.** 85 dimes, 72
quarters   **3.** 800 km/h   **5.** 7 cm by 12 cm
7. 4 cm; 6 cm

Chapter Review, pages 405–406   **1.** a   **3.** b
5. c   **7.** d   **9.** c   **11.** d   **13.** c   **15.** c   **17.** a

Cumulative Review, page 409   **1.** $10p - 6r$
3. $30y^5z + 12y^4z^2 - 21y^3z^4$
5. $9m^2 - 30mn + 25n^2$ **7.** $(4x + 5)(5x - 3)$

9. $3(z + 1)(z - 8)$ **11.** $\dfrac{(x + 3)(x - 1)}{2x - 1}$

13. $\dfrac{-5r^2 + 8r + 80}{(r - 4)(r + 4)}$ **15.** $y = -x + 7$

17. $\{0, 1, 4, 9, 16\}$

19.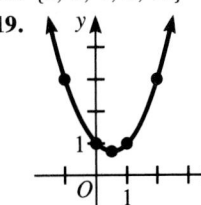

21. $\left\{\dfrac{33}{5}\right\}$ **23.** $\{54\}$ **25.** $\left\{-\dfrac{6}{7}, \dfrac{6}{7}\right\}$

27. $\{0, -2\}$ **29.** $\left\{0, \dfrac{1}{3}\right\}$ **31.** $\{3\}$ **33.** 35 units

Maintaining Skills, page 410
1. $5b^2c^3(5 + 3b^3c)$ **3.** $3u^4v(3u + 12v - 5v^2)$
5. $8x^2y^3(-3x^5y^2 + 4x^4 - y)$
7. $z(z + 11)(z - 11)$ **9.** $(7 - x^3)(7 + x^3)$
11. prime   **13.** $(4a - 5)^2$ **15.** $(5x + 3)^2$
17. $(n + 2)(n + 9)$ **19.** $(7d - c)(2d + c)$
21. $(x + 3)(x + 7)$ **23.** $(n - 3p)(n - 2p)$
25. $(r - 2s)(y + 3)$
27. $(s + 2t + 3)(s - 2t - 3)$
29. $(4a + 3b - 5)(4a - 3b + 5)$
31. $(3b + 5)(b - 1)$ **33.** $2(3m + 2)(m - 2)$
35. $z(5z + 2)(5z + 1)$ **37.** $(3 + y)(1 - 7y)$
39. $2(3b - 5)(2b + 1)$

Preparing for College Entrance Exams,
page 411   **1.** A   **3.** D   **5.** B

Chapter 9 Solving Systems of Linear Equations

Written Exercises, pages 415–416

1.
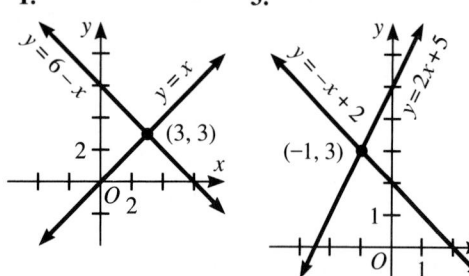

3.

5.
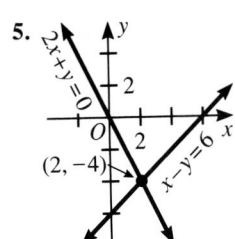

7.
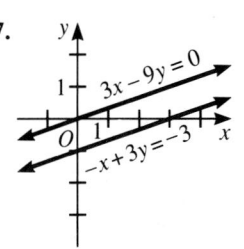

9.
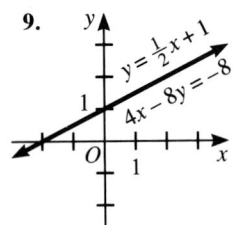

11.
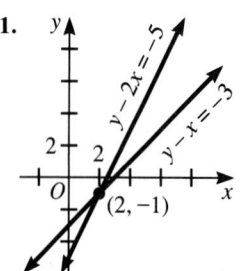

13.
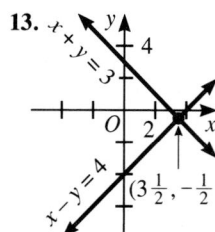

15.
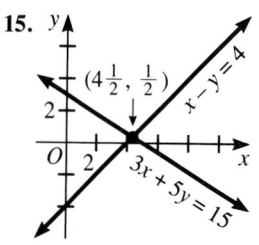

17. $(-2, 4)$ and $(2, 4)$ **19.** $(5, 5)$
21. $(-2, -4)$ **23.** 10 sq. units

Mixed Review Exercises, page 416 **1.** $\frac{5s}{t^2}$

2. $\frac{b^8}{a^{12}}$ **3.** $\frac{2m^2}{5n^2}$ **4.** $\frac{1}{x^4y^2}$ **5.** p^3 **6.** x^7y^2

Computer Exercises, page 416 **1.** $(1, -1)$
3. No pairs in common.

Written Exercises, pages 419–420 **1.** $(4, 24)$
3. $(18, 6)$ **5.** $(7, 5)$ **7.** $(2, 7)$ **9.** $(3, 4)$
11. $(5, -7)$ **13.** $\left(-1, \frac{2}{3}\right)$ **15.** $(3, 5)$
17. $(5, -3)$ **19.** $\left(\frac{17}{3}, -\frac{7}{3}\right)$ **21.** $(-6, 20)$
23. $(4, -3)$ **25.** $(300, 700)$ **27.** $(12, 8)$
29. $(2, -6)$ **31.** no sol. **33.** infinitely many;
$(7, 1), (14, 2), (0, 0)$

35. infinitely many
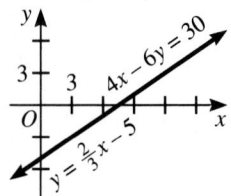

37. $a = 3, b = -2$ **39.** $x = 20, y = 60,$
$z = 100$ **41.** $x = \frac{3}{2}, y = \frac{1}{2}, z = -\frac{1}{2}$

Mixed Review Exercises, page 420

1.
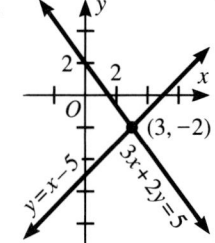

2.
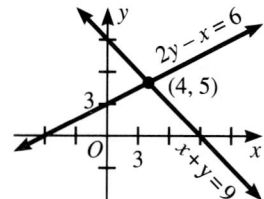

3.
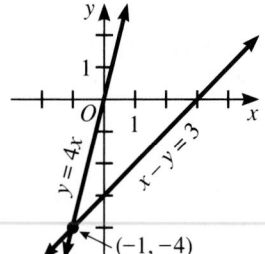

4.

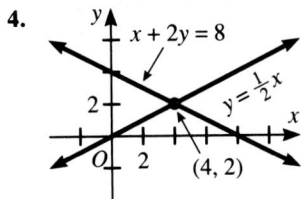

$x + 2y = 8$
$y = \frac{1}{2}x$
$(4, 2)$

5.

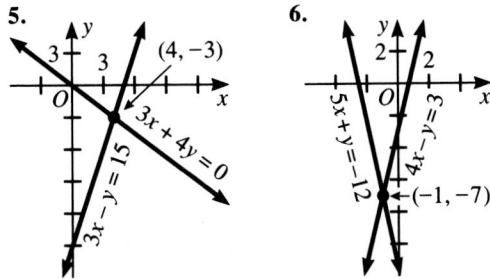

$(4, -3)$
$3x + 4y = 0$
$3x - y = 15$

6.

$5x + y = -12$
$4x - y = 3$
$(-1, -7)$

7. $y = -4x + 1$ **8.** $y = \frac{2}{3}x + 2$

9. $y = -\frac{1}{2}x - 6$ **10.** $y = 3x - 1$

11. $y = -x - 2$ **12.** $y = 2$

Problems, page 424 **1.** 12 nickels **3.** 18 quarters **5.** Dick, $82; Connie, $46 **7.** Tracy, $18; Steve, $39 **9.** 4 hours **11.** 18 and 82 **13.** $1.40 **15.** $2500 **17.** bike, 20 km/h; car, 80 km/h **19.** 8 and 24 **21.** 4 nickels, 14 dimes, 12 quarters

Mixed Review Exercises, page 425 **1.** $\{-10\}$ **2.** $\{9\}$ **3.** $\{31\}$ **4.** $\{6\}$ **5.** $\{17\}$ **6.** $\{-5\}$ **7.** no sol. **8.** (3, 5) **9.** no sol. **10.** (4, 1) **11.** $(-2, -3)$ **12.** (3, 9)

Challenge, page 425 All; Answers may vary;
$23 = 44 \div \sqrt{4} + 4 \div 4$,
$24 = \sqrt{4} \cdot 4 \cdot 4 - 4 - 4$,
$25 = (\sqrt{4} + \sqrt{4} + 4 \div 4)^{\sqrt{4}}$,
$26 = 44 \div \sqrt{4} + \sqrt{4} + \sqrt{4}$,
$27 = 44 \div 4 + 4 \cdot 4$, $28 = 4 \cdot 4 + 4 \cdot 4 - 4$,
$29 = (4 + 4 \div 4)^{\sqrt{4}} + 4$

Written Exercises, pages 427–428 **1.** (5, 2)
3. $\left(3, -\frac{7}{2}\right)$ **5.** $(-2, 2)$ **7.** $(0, -4)$
9. $(3, -2)$ **11.** $\left(\frac{2}{3}, -\frac{1}{3}\right)$ **13.** $\left(\frac{1}{3}, \frac{1}{2}\right)$
15. (150, 200) **17.** (4, 6) **19.** $\left(\frac{9}{2}, \frac{1}{4}\right)$
21. (2, 0) **23.** (0, 2) **25.** (6, 4) **27.** $\left(\frac{5}{3}, 24\right)$

29. $a = 4$, $b = -3$ **31.** They both reduce to the same equation: $y = \frac{1}{4}x$

Problems, pages 428–429 **1.** 13 and 8 **3.** 424 girls **5.** 858 students **7.** 14 dogs, 46 chickens **9.** Maria, $1.20; Tom, $1.80

Mixed Review Exercises, page 429
1. $7x^3 + 11x^2 - 3x$ **2.** 48 **3.** 1340
4. $-2n - 4$ **5.** $9x^5y^5$ **6.** $9a^6$ **7.** $-8p^6q^3$
8. $3x^2 + 18x$ **9.** $-36a^6b^4$ **10.** -1 **11.** -24
12. $-9m + 6n$

Written Exercises, pages 432–433 **1.** (3, 2)
3. (1, 2) **5.** $(1, -2)$ **7.** (3, 7) **9.** $(-3, -12)$
11. $(2, -2)$ **13.** (2, 3) **15.** $(4, -2)$
17. $(3, -5)$ **19.** $\left(\frac{1}{2}, -2\right)$ **21.** $\left(4, -\frac{1}{2}\right)$
23. $\left(-\frac{1}{2}, \frac{4}{3}\right)$ **25.** Solving the system by using multiplication with the addition-or-subtraction method gives a false statement. Thus, there is no ordered pair that is a solution of both equations.
27. $(-3, -3)$ **29.** (20, 50) **31.** (4, 3)
33. (3, 4) **35.** $(-4, -6)$ **37.** $a = 2$, $b = -3$
39. $\left(\frac{1}{2}, \frac{1}{3}\right)$ **41.** $\left(\frac{2}{a}, 3\right)$
43. $\left(\frac{a + b}{a^2 + b^2}, \frac{a - b}{a^2 + b^2}\right)$ **45.** $(2, 3, -1)$

Mixed Practice, page 433
1.

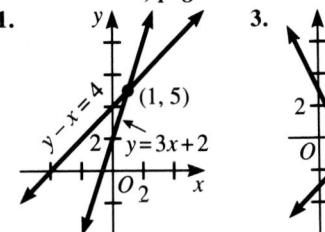

$y - x = 4$
$(1, 5)$
$y = 3x + 2$

3.

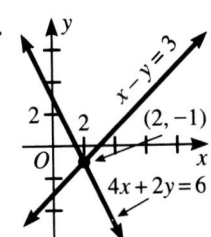

$x - y = 3$
$(2, -1)$
$4x + 2y = 6$

5. (0, 3) **7.** $(1, -1)$ **9.** $(1, -1)$ **11.** (6, 3)
13. $\left(\frac{9}{13}, \frac{31}{13}\right)$ **15.** (14, 10) **17.** (7, 4)
19. $\left(\frac{5}{2}, -3\right)$ **21.** (7, 3) **23.** (4, 3)
25. $(-3, 0)$ **27.** $\left(\frac{40}{9}, -\frac{74}{45}\right)$

Problems, pages 434–436 **1.** 16 and 9
3. Stan, $42; Cory, $108 **5.** 900 sq. units
7. 33 **9.** $2.20 **11.** 215 tickets **13.** 600 g
15. A, $2000; B, $3000 **17.** grape, $1.20; orange, $1.50 **19.** $49 **21.** 2 kg **23.** 80 km/h, 40 km/h **25.** 30 **27.** If x and y are both whole

numbers, then $2x + 6y$ is even. Since 35 is odd, x and y cannot both be whole numbers. **29.** 7 plums **31.** 28 by 30

Mixed Review Exercises, page 436
1. $6(1 - 3t)^2$ **2.** $12mn(m - 2n^2)$
3. $(5c + 6d)(5c - 6d)$ **4.** $(x + 3)(x + 4)$
5. $(2y + 5)(y + 3)$ **6.** $(p + 2)(p - 5)$ **7.** 4
8. $-\frac{1}{3}$ **9.** $\frac{2}{3}$ **10.** 7

Computer Exercises, page 436 **3. a.** $(-3, -4)$
b. $(2, 3)$ **c.** no sol. **d.** $(3, 2)$

Self-Test 1, page 437 **1.** $(2, 5)$ **2.** $(-1, 3)$
3. $\left(-3, \frac{1}{2}\right)$ **4.** $\left(-\frac{9}{5}, -\frac{7}{5}\right)$ **5.** no sol.
6. $(0, 0)$ **7.** $(0, 4)$ **8.** $(-3, -2)$ **9.** $(3, 2)$

Problems, pages 440–442 **1.** $r + c = 15$
3. $\frac{24}{r - c} = 3$ **5.** 4 km/h

7. No current

	Rate	× Time	= Distance
Downstream	10	3	30
Upstream	10	3	30

Total distance = 60 km
Total time = 6 h
Average speed = 10 km/h

5 km/h current

Rate	× Time	= Distance
15	2	30
5	6	30

Total distance = 60 km
Total time = 8 h
Average speed = 7.5 km/h

9.

	Rate	× Time	= Distance
No wind	200	3	600
With wind	250	2.4	600

Total distance = 1200 km
Total time = 5.4 h
Average speed = 222.2 km/h

11. 1300 km/h; 100 km/h **13.** 5 mi/h; 1 mi/h
15. 770 km/h; 70 km/h **17.** 0.5 h; 2.5 mi
19. 15 km/h **21.** 5 km/h **23.** total distance is

$2d$; total time is $\dfrac{d}{p + w} + \dfrac{d}{p - w} = \dfrac{2pd}{p^2 - w^2}$;

Average speed is $\dfrac{2d}{\dfrac{2pd}{p^2 - w^2}} = \dfrac{p^2 - w^2}{p}$

Mixed Review Exercises, page 443 **1.** $(5, -2)$
2. $\left(-\frac{3}{7}, \frac{9}{7}\right)$ **3.** $(2, -2)$ **4.** $\dfrac{9b^2 + b - 2}{4(3b + 1)}$
5. $\dfrac{1}{2 - x}$ **6.** $16st^3$ **7.** $\dfrac{5(2r + t)}{(r + t)(r - t)}$ **8.** $\dfrac{p + 2}{24}$
9. $\dfrac{2a^2 + 4a - 1}{a + 3}$

Problems, pages 447–449 **1.** $t + u = 15$
3. $4(t + u) = 10t + u$
5. $10t + u + 18 = 10u + t$ **7.** 36 **9.** 48
11. Nicole, 11 years old; Pierre, 6 years old
13. Steve, 12 years old; Theresa, 4 years old
15. $\frac{5}{13}$ **17.** $\frac{5}{8}$ **19.** Lyle, 19 years old; Sean, 9
years old **21.** Golden Gate, 1937; Brooklyn,
1883 **23.** 360 **25.** 345 **27.** son, 10 years old;
father, 36 years old **29.** $\frac{6}{24}$ **31.** Laura, 18
years old; Maria, 12 years old **33.** Cindy, 26
years old; Paul, 18 years old; Sue, 8 years old

Mixed Review Exercises, page 449 **1.** 18
2. 6 **3.** 11 **4.** 4 **5.** 34 **6.** 48 **7.** $\{-8\}$
8. $\left\{-\frac{27}{13}\right\}$ **9.** $\{-6\}$ **10.** $\{-7.7, 7.7\}$
11. $\{0.05\}$ **12.** $\{-84\}$

Self-Test 2, page 450 **1.** 780 mi/h; 18 mi/h
2. 96 **3.** Jerry, 15 years old; Jeff, 20 years old
4. $\frac{4}{7}$

Chapter Review, page 451 **1.** c **3.** d **5.** d
7. b **9.** d

Cumulative Review, page 453
1. $7p^2q + 4p - 21q^3$ **3.** $4j^5k^3 - 24j^6k + 28j^4k^4$
5. $42z^2 + 78z - 12$ **7.** $5t + 3$
9. $\dfrac{(x - 5)(x - 3)}{(x + 3)}$ **11.** 6.8×10^{10} **13.** prime
15. prime **17.** prime **19.** $\{22, -22\}$
21. $\left\{-\frac{2}{7}, \frac{2}{7}\right\}$ **23.** $\left\{-\frac{4}{3}, \frac{2}{3}\right\}$ **25.** $3x + y = 3$
27. $(2, 7)$ **29.** 15 **31.** 10 kg

Maintaining Skills, page 454 **1.** $\frac{a}{4}$ **3.** 8
5. $\dfrac{3(z - 3)}{5z}$ **7.** $\dfrac{3n - 1}{n - 2}$ **9.** $5ab$ **11.** $\dfrac{2b + 3}{b + 1}$

13. $\dfrac{c+2}{c+1}$ **15.** $\dfrac{(r-6)(r+6)^2}{(r-3)(r+3)^2}$ **17.** $\dfrac{2x+3y}{x-y}$

19. $\dfrac{2+w^2}{3-w}$ **21.** $\dfrac{v^2-v+8}{(v+1)(v-1)}$ **23.** $\dfrac{2b(2-b)}{2b-1}$

25. $\dfrac{d^2-2}{(2d+1)(d+1)}$ **27.** $\dfrac{6t}{t^2-4}$

29. $\dfrac{2x^2+13x-28}{(x-4)(x+3)}$

Mixed Problem Solving, page 455 **1.** 53.4%
3. No sol.; contradictory facts **5.** 50 km/h
7. $567 **9.** 54 min **11.** 3 kg **13.** $1200 at
$7\frac{1}{4}$%, $4800 at 10%

Chapter 10 Inequalities

Written Exercises, pages 459–460 **1.** $4 > -7$
3. $-12 \le -9$ **5.** $2 < 3 < 3.5$
7. $-10 < -8 < 0$ **9.** $0 < 4 < 4.6$ **11.** $n > 10$
13. $|-2| > 1$ **15.** T **17.** F **19.** T **21.** F
23. $\{-4, -3, -2, -1, 0, 1\}$
25. $\{-3, -2, -1, 0, 1, 2, 3, 4\}$
27. $\{-4, -3, -2, -1, 0, 1, 2, 3, 4\}$
29. $\{-4, 4\}$
31.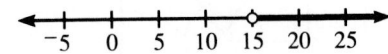
33.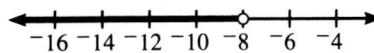
35.
37.

39–41. Answers may vary. **39. a.** $(-2, -3)$
b. $(3, 2)$ **41. a.** $(2, 1)$ **b.** $(2, -1)$

Computer Exercises, page 460
1. $\{0, 1, 2, 3, 4, 5\}$ **3.** $\{4, 5\}$
5. $\{6, 7, 8, 9, 10\}$

Mixed Review Exercises, page 461 **1.** $\{18\}$
2. $\{6\}$ **3.** $\{-6\}$ **4.** $\{-50\}$ **5.** $\{27\}$ **6.** $\{8\}$
7. $\{-34\}$ **8.** $\{-3\}$ **9.** $\{10\}$ **10.** $\{-12\}$
11. $\{1\}$ **12.** $\{0\}$

Written Exercises, pages 466–467 **1.** d **3.** j
5. b **7.** e **9.** f
11. {the real numbers greater than 15}
13. {the real numbers less than -8}

15. {the real numbers less than -324}
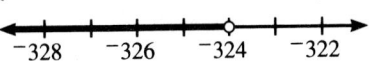
17. {the real numbers less than or equal to -1}
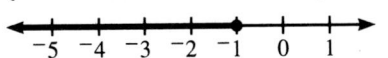
19. {the real numbers greater than -4}
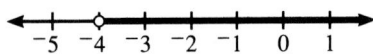
21. {the real numbers less than or equal to 0}
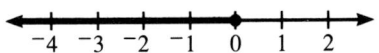
23. {the real numbers less than 6}
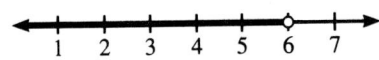
25. {the real numbers greater than -15}
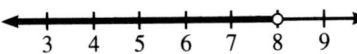
27. {the real numbers less than 8}
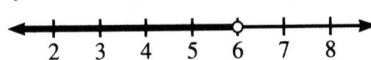
29. {the real numbers less than 6}
31. {the real numbers greater than -12}
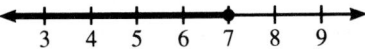
33. {the real numbers less than or equal to 7}
35. {the real numbers}
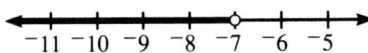
37. {the real numbers less than -7}

39. $\left\{\text{the real numbers greater than or equal to } \frac{2}{5}\right\}$
41. $\left\{\text{the real numbers greater than } \frac{4}{3}\right\}$
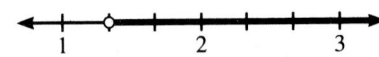
43. {the real numbers greater than -8}
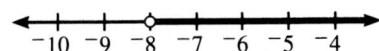

45. {the real numbers greater than -2}

$$\begin{array}{c} \leftarrow\!\!\!+\!\!\!-\!\!\!\circ\!\!\!-\!\!\!+\!\!\!-\!\!\!+\!\!\!-\!\!\!+\!\!\!-\!\!\!+\!\!\!-\!\!\!+\!\!\!\rightarrow \\ -3\ -2\ -1\ \ 0\ \ 1\ \ 2\ \ 3 \end{array}$$

47. {the real numbers greater than or equal to -4}

$$\begin{array}{c} \leftarrow\!\!\!+\!\!\!-\!\!\!\bullet\!\!\!-\!\!\!+\!\!\!-\!\!\!+\!\!\!-\!\!\!+\!\!\!-\!\!\!+\!\!\!-\!\!\!+\!\!\!\rightarrow \\ -5\ -4\ -3\ -2\ -1\ \ 0\ \ 1 \end{array}$$

49. no solution **51.** all real numbers **53.** all pos. real numbers **55.** 0 **57.** all neg. real numbers **59.** T **61.** T **63.** F; $a = \frac{1}{2}$, $b = \frac{1}{3}$ **65.** T

Mixed Review Exercises, page 467 **1.** T **2.** T **3.** F **4.** F **5.** T **6.** F **7.** {9} **8.** $\left\{-\frac{5}{2}\right\}$ **9.** {3} **10.** {-2} **11.** {3} **12.** {1}

Reading Algebra, page 468
1. a. greater than **b.** open; right **c.** {the real numbers greater than 15}

$$\begin{array}{c} \leftarrow\!\!\!+\!\!\!-\!\!\!+\!\!\!-\!\!\!\circ\!\!\!-\!\!\!+\!\!\!-\!\!\!+\!\!\!-\!\!\!+\!\!\!-\!\!\!+\!\!\!\rightarrow \\ 14\ \ 15\ \ 16\ \ 17\ \ 18\ \ 19\ \ 20 \end{array}$$

3. a. greater than or equal to **b.** closed; left **c.** {the real numbers less than or equal to 4}

$$\begin{array}{c} \leftarrow\!\!\!+\!\!\!-\!\!\!+\!\!\!-\!\!\!+\!\!\!-\!\!\!+\!\!\!-\!\!\!+\!\!\!-\!\!\!\bullet\!\!\!-\!\!\!+\!\!\!\rightarrow \\ -1\ \ 0\ \ 1\ \ 2\ \ 3\ \ 4\ \ 5 \end{array}$$

5. a. less than **b.** open; right **c.** {the real numbers greater than -15}

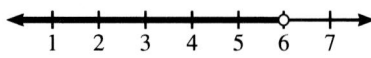

7. a. greater than **b.** open; left **c.** {the real numbers less than 6}

$$\begin{array}{c} \leftarrow\!\!\!+\!\!\!-\!\!\!+\!\!\!-\!\!\!+\!\!\!-\!\!\!+\!\!\!-\!\!\!+\!\!\!-\!\!\!\circ\!\!\!-\!\!\!+\!\!\!\rightarrow \\ 1\ \ 2\ \ 3\ \ 4\ \ 5\ \ 6\ \ 7 \end{array}$$

9. a. less than **b.** open; right **c.** {the real numbers greater than -4}

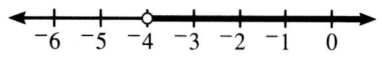

11. a. greater than **b.** open; left **c.** {the real numbers less than 7}

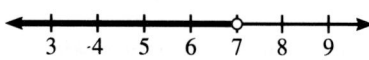

Written Exercises, pages 471–472 **1. a.** i **b.** $i + 2 < 21$ **3. a.** x **b.** $x + 0.1x > 3000$ **5. a.** d **b.** $75 + d \geq 110$ **7. a.** j **b.** $\frac{j}{2} + 15 \leq 36$ **9. a.** m **b.** $(m - 2) + m + (m + 2) \geq 51$ **11. a.** t **b.** $86t + 78t \geq 650$ **13. a.** d **b.** $10d + 5(2d) + 25\left(\frac{2d}{3}\right) \leq 280$ **15. a.** s

b. $25 - s \geq 2s + 1$ **17. a.** s **b.** $s + (s + 2) \leq \frac{s}{8} - 100$ **19.** $|a + b| \leq |a| + |b|$

Problems, pages 473–474 **1.** less than 87 copies **3.** 300 mi or less **5.** 26 and 27 **7.** at least 4.2 h **9.** 60 red marbles; 40 blue marbles **11.** 10 cm by 14 cm **13.** 3 P.M. **15.** 84 **17.** 30 h **19.** 10.92 km **21.** $1999 **23.** 97 books

Mixed Review Exercises, page 475 **1.** {-7, 7} **2.** {3} **3.** {-12, 12} **4.** {-4, 4} **5.** {4} **6.** {-3} **7.** $(x + 3)(x + 12)$ **8.** $x(x + 3)(x - 8)$ **9.** $(7x - 5)(7x + 5)$ **10.** $(2y + 3)(y - 1)$ **11.** $(x + 3y)^2$ **12.** $4x(2x - 1)(2x + 1)$

Self-Test 1, page 475 **1.** $-7 < -3 < -2$ **2.** {$-3, -2, -1, 0, 1, 2$} **3.** {the real numbers less than 1}

$$\begin{array}{c} \leftarrow\!\!\!+\!\!\!-\!\!\!+\!\!\!-\!\!\!+\!\!\!-\!\!\!+\!\!\!-\!\!\!\circ\!\!\!-\!\!\!+\!\!\!-\!\!\!+\!\!\!\rightarrow \\ -3\ -2\ -1\ \ 0\ \ 1\ \ 2\ \ 3 \end{array}$$

4. {the real numbers greater than or equal to -5}

$$\begin{array}{c} \leftarrow\!\!\!+\!\!\!-\!\!\!+\!\!\!-\!\!\!\bullet\!\!\!-\!\!\!+\!\!\!-\!\!\!+\!\!\!-\!\!\!+\!\!\!-\!\!\!+\!\!\!\rightarrow \\ -7\ -6\ -5\ -4\ -3\ -2\ -1 \end{array}$$

5. at least 17 dimes

Challenge, page 475 Step 4: If you divide by $3 - a$, which is negative (because $a > 3$), the inequality must be reversed so that Step 5 is $a < 3 + a$.

Extra, pages 476–477 **1.** {6, 9} **3.** {0, 3, 4, 5, 6, 7, 8, 9} **5.** {6} **7.** {5, 6, 9} **9.** {5, 6, 7, 8} **11.** {$-4, -3, -2, -1, 0$}; {$-3, -2$} **13.** {3, 4, 5, 6, 7, 8}; disjoint sets **15.** {2, 3, 4, 6, 8, 10, 12}; {4, 6, 8} **17.** {the real numbers between -1 and 2} **19.** {the real numbers greater than -3} **21.** {the real numbers between -3 and 2} **23.** {the real numbers between -1 and 2}

25.

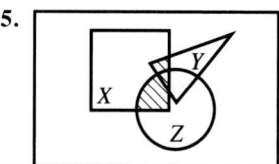

27. $X \cap (Y \cup Z) = (X \cap Y) \cup (X \cap Z)$

29.

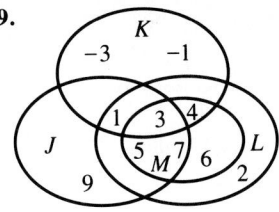

Written Exercises, pages 480–481

1.
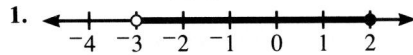

3.
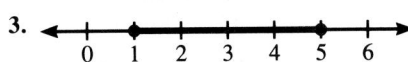

5. {the real numbers between −3 and 2}
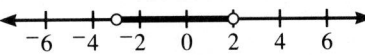

7. {5 and the real numbers between −1 and 5}
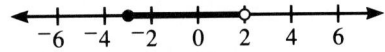

9. {−3 and the real numbers between −3 and 2}

11. {−2 and the real numbers between −2 and 1}

13. {the real numbers less than −3 or greater than 7}

15. {−2, 1, and the real numbers less than −2 or greater than 1}

17. $\left\{-\dfrac{4}{3}, 2, \text{ and the real numbers less than } -\dfrac{4}{3} \text{ or greater than } 2\right\}$

19. {−2, 6, and the real numbers between −2 and 6}

21. {6 and the real numbers between −1 and 6}

23. {−3 and the real numbers between −3 and 3}
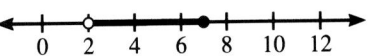

25. no solution

27. {7 and the real numbers between 2 and 7}
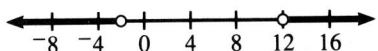

29. {the real numbers less than −2 or greater than 12}

31. {−3 and the real numbers less than −3 or greater than 3}

33. $\left\{\text{the real numbers greater than } -\dfrac{2}{3}\right\}$

35. {5 and the real numbers between 1 and 5}

37. {the real numbers less than or equal to 4}

39. a. $a = 2, b = 1, c = 4, d = 3$ **b.** $a = 1, b = -2, c = 2, d = -3$

Computer Exercises, page 481 (1, 9), (2, 5), (2, 6), (2, 7), (2, 8), (3, 3), (3, 4), (3, 5), (3, 6), (3, 7), (4, 3), (4, 4), (4, 5), (4, 6), (5, 2), (5, 3), (5, 4), (5, 5), (6, 2), (6, 3), (6, 4), (7, 2), (7, 3), (8, 2), and (9, 1).

Mixed Review Exercises, page 481 **1.** $n \ge 10$ **2.** $t \le 78$ **3.** $w \le 150$ **4.** $t \ge 3$ **5.** $c \ge 17$ **6.** $g < 2$ **7.** $s \le 340$ **8.** $s \ge 5$ **9.** 11 **10.** 11 **11.** 3 **12.** 3 **13.** 8 **14.** 8

Written Exercises, pages 484–485 **1. a.** The distance between x and 5 is 1. **b.** $x - 5 = 1$ or $x - 5 = -1$ **3. a.** The distance between r and −3 is greater than 5. **b.** $r + 3 > 5$ or $r + 3 < -5$ **5. a.** The distance between n and 4 is less than or equal to 1. **b.** $-1 \le n - 4 \le 1$ **7.** $|x| < 2$ **9.** $|x + 1| = 2$ **11.** $|x - 1| \ge 3$ **13.** {14, −2}
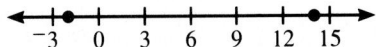

15. $\{-8, 2\}$

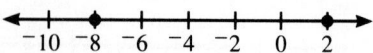

17. {the real numbers between -2.5 and 2.5}

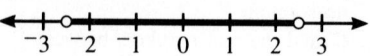

19. {the real numbers less than -13 or greater than 3}

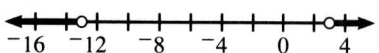

21. {4, 8, and the real numbers between 4 and 8}

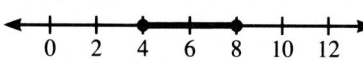

23. $\{-6, 2,$ and the real numbers less than -6 or greater than 2}

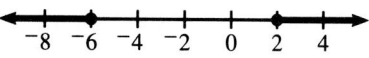

25. $\{-3, 3,$ and the real numbers less than -3 or greater than 3}

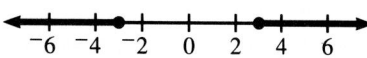

27. {the real numbers less than -3 or greater than 7}

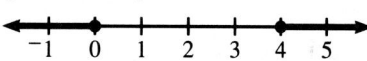

29. $\left\{-\dfrac{11}{3}, \dfrac{11}{3},$ and the real numbers between $-\dfrac{11}{3}$ and $\dfrac{11}{3}\right\}$

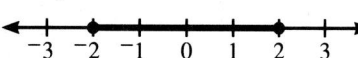

31. {0, 4, and the real numbers less than 0 or greater than 4}

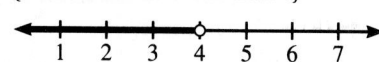

33. $\{-2, 2,$ and the real numbers between -2 and 2}

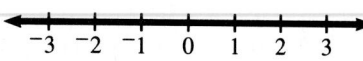

35. no solution

37. {the real numbers less than 4}

39. {the real numbers}

1. {the real numbers less than 9}

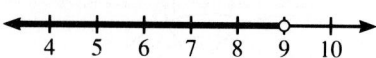

2. {the real numbers less than -8}

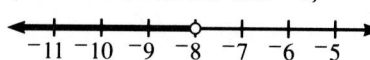

3. {the real numbers greater than 0}

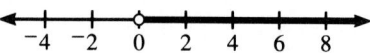

4. {the real numbers between -6 and -3}

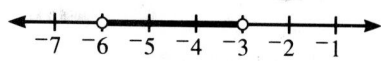

5. {9, and the real numbers less than 9 or greater than 12}

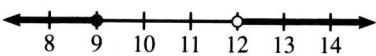

6. $\{-10, -3,$ and the real numbers between -10 and -3}

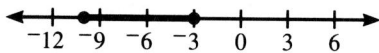

7. $\dfrac{4}{3y^3}$ **8.** $\dfrac{32a^2}{3b}$ **9.** $\dfrac{x+12}{9}$ **10.** $\dfrac{22x}{7}$

1. $\{-4, 4\}$

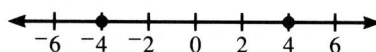

3. $\{-4, 4,$ and the real numbers less than -4 or greater than 4}

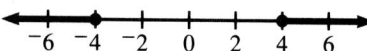

5. $\{-4, 5\}$

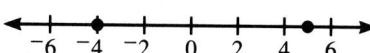

7. $\left\{2, \dfrac{7}{2},$ and the real numbers between 2 and $\dfrac{7}{2}\right\}$

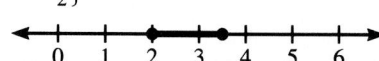

9. $\left\{-\dfrac{9}{2}, 3,$ and the real numbers between $-\dfrac{9}{2}$ and $3\right\}$

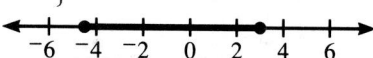

11. $\{-10, 30,$ and the real numbers less than -10 or greater than 30}

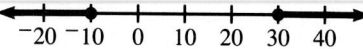

13. {the real numbers between −8 and 10}

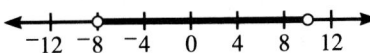

15. $\left\{-\dfrac{4}{5}, \dfrac{2}{5}\right\}$

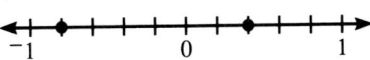

17. no solution   **19.** T   **21.** F; $a = -1$ **23.** T
25. 50°F; 14°F

Mixed Review Exercises, page 488   **1.** 4; 2

2. 5; −2   **3.** $-\dfrac{2}{3}$; −3   **4.** 0; 9   **5.** 3; −11
6. $-\dfrac{1}{2}$; 4

7.
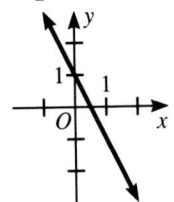

8.
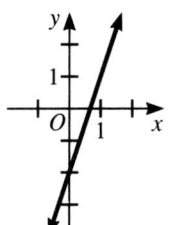

9.
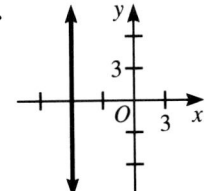

10.
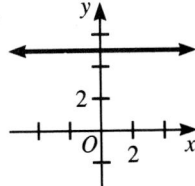

11.
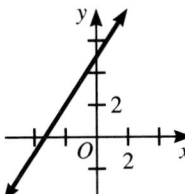

12.
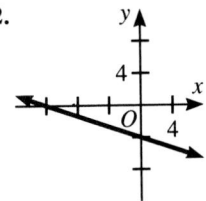

Self-Test 2, page 489
1. {the real numbers less than 2 or greater than 3}

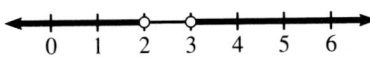

2. {−6 and the real numbers between −6 and 1}

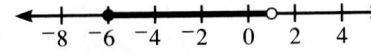

3. {−2, 2, and the real numbers less than −2 or greater than 2}

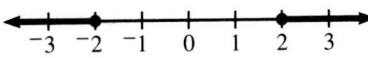

4. {−2 and the real numbers between −2 and 1}

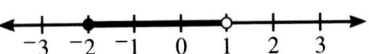

5. {−1, 5}

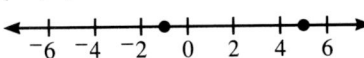

6. {−4, 10, and the real numbers less than −4 or greater than 10}

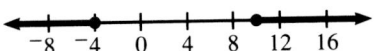

7. {−5, 7}

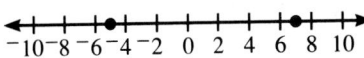

8. {the real numbers between −6 and −2}

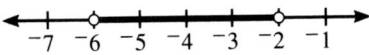

9. $\left\{\dfrac{3}{2}, 5, \text{ and the real numbers between } \dfrac{3}{2} \text{ and } 5\right\}$

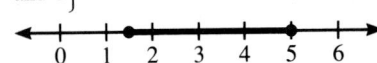

10. {−3, 7}

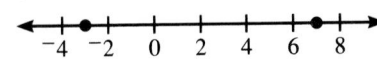

11. $\left\{\dfrac{3}{2}, 2\right\}$

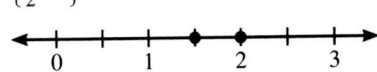

12. $\left\{\text{the real numbers between } -2 \text{ and } \dfrac{7}{3}\right\}$

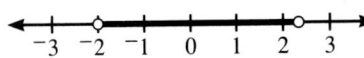

Written Exercises, pages 492–493

1.   **3.**
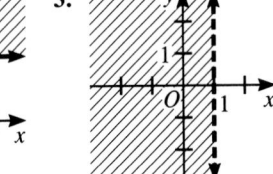

5.   **7.**
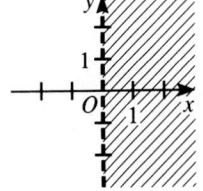
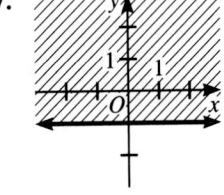

9. 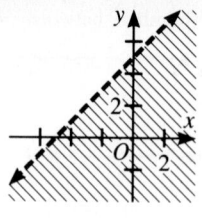 **11.**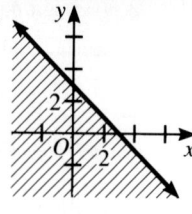

39.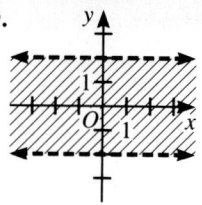

13. $y < -x + 1$ **15.** $y \geq \frac{1}{3}x + 2$

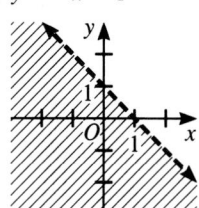 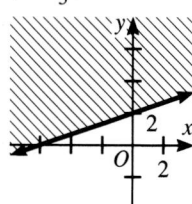

Mixed Review Exercises, page 494
1. $(-2, -6)$ **2.** $(7, 2)$ **3.** $(1, -2)$

4. $\{5, -5\}$

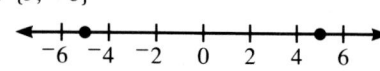

5. $\{-6, 4\}$

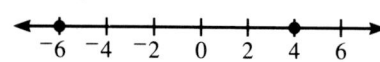

17. $y < 4x - 6$ **19.** $y \leq \frac{3}{2}x - 4$

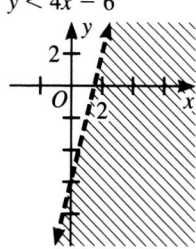 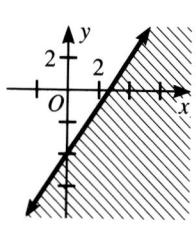

6. {the real numbers between -7 and 7}

7. $\left\{-\frac{11}{2}, \frac{1}{2},\right.$ and the real numbers less than $-\frac{11}{2}$ or greater than $\left.\frac{1}{2}\right\}$

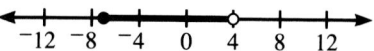

21. $y \leq -\frac{3}{2}x - 2$ **23.** $y \leq \frac{1}{4}x - \frac{1}{2}$

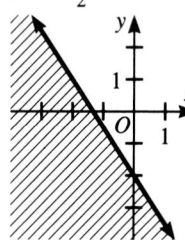 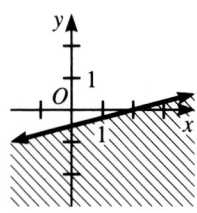

8. {-7 and the real numbers between -7 and 4}

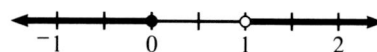

9. {0 and the real numbers less than 0 or greater than 1}

25. $y > -1$ **27.** $y < -\frac{1}{2}x + 2$

29. $y \geq \frac{4}{3}x + 4$ **31.** $y < \frac{1}{2}x + 2$

33. $y \leq -\frac{3}{2}x + 5$

Extra, page 494
1.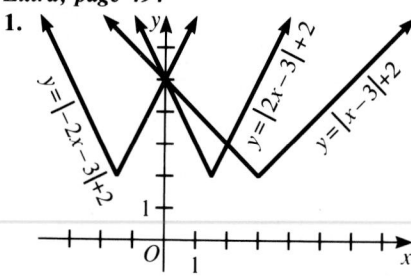

35.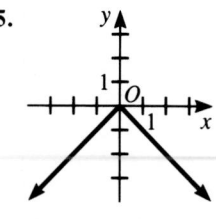

1.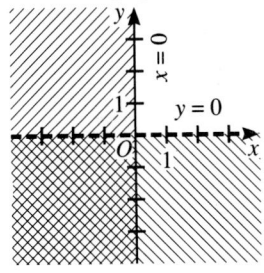

3.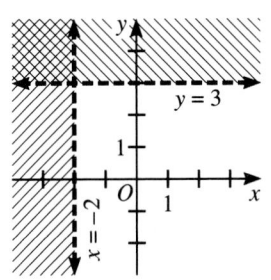

5.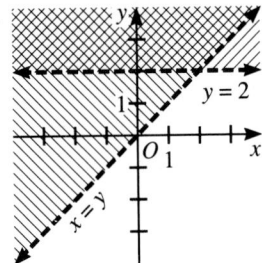

7.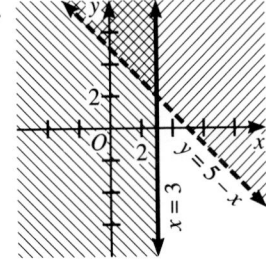

9.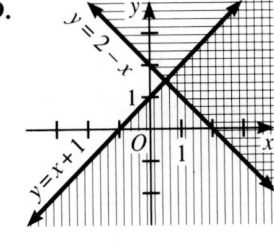

11.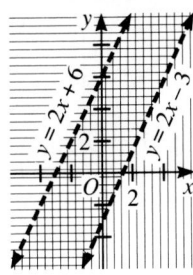

13.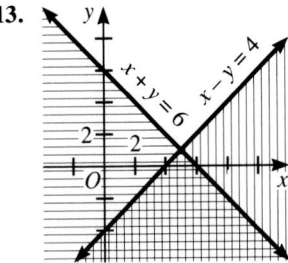

15.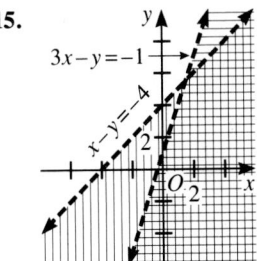

17.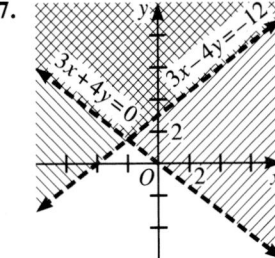

19. $y \geq -3$
$y < x - 3$

21. $y < \frac{2}{3}x - 2$
$y < -2x + 3$

23. $x \leq 3$
$y \leq \frac{1}{2}x + 2$
$y \geq -\frac{1}{4}x - 1$

25. $(0, 0)$,
$(4, 4)$,
$(4, -4)$

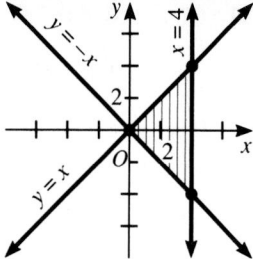

27. no solution

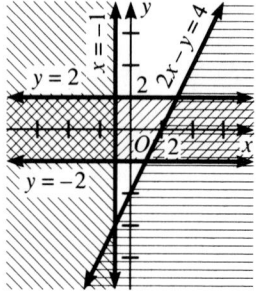

Mixed Review Exercises, page 498   **1.** $\dfrac{5}{30}$, $\dfrac{8}{30}$,

$\dfrac{18}{30}$ **2.** $\dfrac{12a}{36}$, $\dfrac{8}{36}$, $\dfrac{3(a+1)}{36}$ **3.** $\dfrac{k(k+5)}{(k+5)^2}$,

$\dfrac{3k}{(k+5)^2}$ **4.** $\dfrac{5y(2y+3)}{5y(y-6)}$, $\dfrac{20(y-6)}{5y(y-6)}$, $\dfrac{y^2(y-6)}{5y(y-6)}$

5. $\dfrac{8(x-2)}{(x+2)(x-2)}$, $\dfrac{x(x+2)}{(x+2)(x-2)}$ **6.** $-\dfrac{1}{16-x^2}$,

$\dfrac{5(4+x)}{16-x^2}$, $\dfrac{x(4-x)}{16-x^2}$ **7.** $\dfrac{9}{5}$ **8.** $-\dfrac{11}{120}$ **9.** $-\dfrac{19}{60}$

10. $\dfrac{91}{120}$ **11.** $\dfrac{11}{24}$ **12.** $\dfrac{9}{20}$

Self-Test 3, page 498
1.

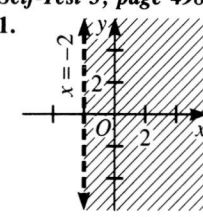

2.

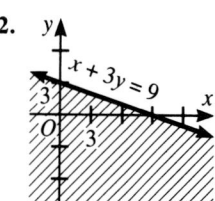

3.

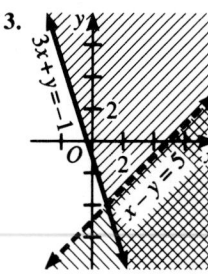

Calculator Key-In, page 498   **1.** F **3.** F

Application, page 500
1. a.

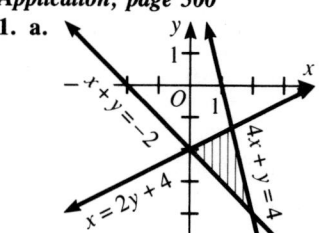

b. $\left(\dfrac{4}{3}, -\dfrac{4}{3}\right)$, $(2, -4)$, $(0, -2)$

c. maximum: -4; minimum: -20

3. a. $6c + 12s \le 2400$; $12c + 16s \le 3600$;
$c \ge 0$; $s \ge 0$

b.

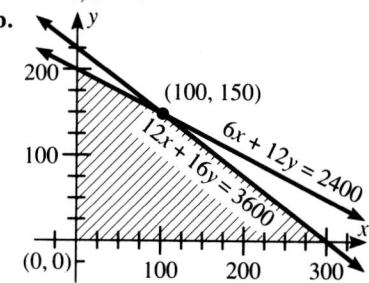

c. 100 acres of corn, 150 acres of soybeans;
0 acres of corn, 200 acres of soybeans

Chapter Review, pages 501–502   **1.** c **3.** c
5. d **7.** b **9.** b **11.** b

Cumulative Review, page 503   **1.** $b - 3$
3. $27x^{14}y^{12}$ **5.** $3c^3 - 10c^2d + 16cd^2 - 16d^3$

7. $\dfrac{x-3}{3x+2}$ **9.** 2.4×10^{14} **11.** $\dfrac{y^2(y+1)}{y+5}$

13. $6(5z^2 + 40z + 16)$
15. $(4z - y - 5)(4z + y + 5)$ **17.** $x - 2y = -7$

19.

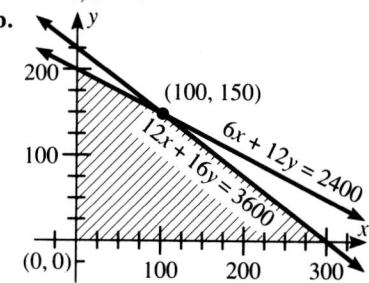

21. $\{7, -7\}$ **23.** $\{-11, 9\}$ **25.** $\{0\}$
27. $\{-10, -1\}$ **29.** $\{-5, 0, 2\}$ **31.** $\left\{-\dfrac{4}{3}\right\}$
33. $(1, 4)$ **35.** $(-1, 2)$ **37.** {the real numbers
less than -5} **39.** $7\dfrac{1}{2}$ h

Maintaining Skills, page 504   **1.** $\{-4, 10\}$
3. $\{-6\}$ **5.** $\left\{-1, \dfrac{1}{5}\right\}$ **7.** $\left\{-\dfrac{2}{5}, \dfrac{4}{3}\right\}$

9. $\left\{-\frac{16}{9}, 1\right\}$ 11. $\{2\}$ 13. $\left\{-\frac{2}{5}\right\}$ 15. no sol.
17. $\{6\}$ 19. no sol. 21. no sol.

Preparing for College Entrance Exams, page 505 **1.** D **3.** D **5.** C

Chapter 11 Rational and Irrational Numbers

Written Exercises, pages 510–511 **1.** < **3.** <
5. = **7.** > **9.** $\frac{3}{8}, \frac{5}{9}, \frac{4}{7}$ **11.** $-5, 5.6, \frac{107}{18}$
13. $\frac{4}{15}, \frac{7}{24}, \frac{5}{16}, \frac{1}{2}$ **15.** $\frac{71}{126}$ **17.** $-\frac{17}{100}$
19. $-\frac{1}{2}$ **21.** increases **23.** decreases
25. decreases **27.** $\frac{17}{45}$ **29.** $-\frac{31}{75}$
31. example: $\frac{13}{24}$ **33.** $\frac{29a}{168}$ **35. a.** yes
37. $w < z$ and $wz > 0$; or $z < 0 < w$

Mixed Review Exercises, page 511
1. {2 and the real numbers less than 2}

2. {the real numbers between -10.5 and 9.5}
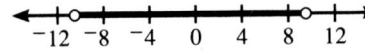
3. {0, 4, and the real numbers less than 0 or greater than 4}
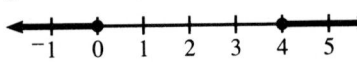
4. {-8, 2, and the real numbers less than -8 or greater than 2}
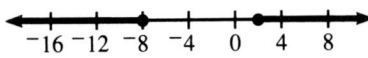
5. {0 and the real numbers between 0 and 1}
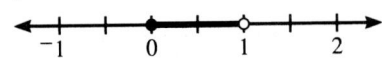
6. {-1 and the real numbers less than -1}

7. $\frac{7}{20}$ **8.** $\frac{3}{5}$ **9.** $\frac{22}{5}$ **10.** $\frac{3}{10,000}$ **11.** $\frac{5}{8}$
12. $\frac{1}{400}$

Written Exercises, pages 515–516 **1. a.** $0.\overline{6}$
b. $0.0\overline{6}$ **3. a.** $-0.\overline{4}$ **b.** $-0.000\overline{4}$ **5.** 1.375
7. $1.3\overline{6}$ **9.** $-0.3\overline{8}$ **11.** 3.45 **13.** $0.\overline{27}$

15. $-0.4\overline{86}$ **17.** $\frac{1}{5}$ **19.** $\frac{13}{40}$ **21.** $\frac{4}{9}$ **23.** $-\frac{17}{60}$
25. $\frac{7}{99}$ **27.** $-\frac{7}{3}$ **29.** 0.2545 **31.** $0.44\overline{2}$
33. $0.831\overline{6}$ **35.** $\frac{3}{5}, \frac{3}{4}; \frac{9}{20}$ **37.** $\frac{2}{3}, \frac{7}{12}; \frac{7}{18}$
39. $\frac{11}{27}, \frac{5}{18}; \frac{55}{486}$ **41. a.** $0.\overline{1}$; $0.\overline{5}$; $0.\overline{8}$
b. $0.\overline{037}$; $0.\overline{185}$; $0.\overline{296}$ **c.** Each decimal in (b) is one third the corresponding decimal in (a).
43. a. $0.\overline{08}$; $0.\overline{32}$; $0.\overline{87}$ **b.** $1 = \frac{99}{99} = 99(0.\overline{01}) = .\overline{99} = 0.\overline{9}$ **c.** $10N = 9.\overline{9}$, $10N - N = 9.\overline{9} - 0.\overline{9}$, $9N = 9$, $N = 1$

Mixed Review Exercises, page 516 **1.** $2^3 \cdot 5^2$
2. $2 \cdot 7^2$ **3.** $3^2 \cdot 11^2$ **4.** $2 \cdot 3^2 \cdot 5^3$ **5.** $2^3 \cdot 7^2$
6. $2^6 \cdot 3^2$ **7.** $\{-3, 4\}$ **8.** $\{-2, -8\}$ **9.** no sol.
10. $\{0, -4, 4\}$ **11.** $\{-12, 8\}$ **12.** {the real numbers less than 12}

Written Exercises, page 519 **1.** 6 **3.** 10
5. -20 **7.** 25 **9.** ± 50 **11.** $-\frac{9}{40}$ **13.** $\pm \frac{11}{5}$
15. $\frac{4}{7}$ **17.** $-\frac{11}{5}$ **19.** $\frac{19}{48}$ **21.** $-\frac{2}{3}$ **23.** $\frac{3}{2}$
25. $\pm \frac{5}{2}$ **27.** $\frac{1}{5}$ **29.** $\pm \frac{1}{2}$ **31.** $-\frac{20}{9}$ **33.** 0.2
35. -0.9 **37.** 1.1 **39.** ± 2.8 **41.** 0.14
43. 0.03 **45.** -1 **47.** -8

Mixed Review Exercises, page 520 **1.** $\frac{1}{8}$
2. $-\frac{32}{5}$ **3.** $\frac{1}{3}$ **4.** $\frac{214}{99}$ **5.** $\frac{1}{15}$ **6.** $-\frac{x}{42}$
7. $4(b + 3)(b - 6)$
8. $(4t - 1 + 3v)(4t - 1 - 3v)$
9. $k(8k + 1)(8k - 1)$ **10.** $(3w - 4y)^2$
11. $(2x + y)(x - 5y)$ **12.** $(3 - 5ab)(1 + ab)$

Challenge, page 520 (7, 6, 5)

Self-Test 1, page 520 **1.** $\frac{77}{144}$ **2.** $\frac{31}{24}$ **3.** $4\frac{31}{48}$
4. > **5.** < **6.** < **7.** 0.48 **8.** 3.25 **9.** $0.2\overline{3}$
10. $0.6857142\overline{}$ **11.** $\frac{20}{99}$ **12.** 33 **13.** $\frac{8}{45}$
14. 1.6

Written Exercises, pages 522–523 **1.** $3\sqrt{7}$
3. $7\sqrt{2}$ **5.** $5\sqrt{3}$ **7.** 16 **9.** $8\sqrt{3}$ **11.** $30\sqrt{2}$
13. 23 **15.** $18\sqrt{5}$ **17.** 19 **19.** $50\sqrt{5}$
21. $8\sqrt{3}$ **23.** $50\sqrt{6}$ **25.** $42\sqrt{5}$ **27.** 75
29. $140\sqrt{3}$ **31.** 28.3 **33.** -26.5 **35.** -76.8
37. ± 88.3 **39.** 8.25 **41.** -0.71 **43.** ± 0.93
45. -0.26 **47.** 387 **49.** 648

Mixed Review Exercises, page 523 **1.** 20
2. -13 **3.** $\frac{5}{9}$ **4.** $-\frac{7}{15}$ **5.** 176 **6.** $\frac{3}{8}$
7. $289x^2$ **8.** $9y^8z^{18}$ **9.** $4x^2 + 12xy + 9y^2$
10. $225a^2 + 900a + 900$ **11.** $121a^8b^{22}c^2$
12. $36z^6 - 25y^8$

Written Exercises, page 526 **1.** $11|a|$
3. $2|x|\sqrt{7}$ **5.** $-3c^2$ **7.** $-5|d^3|$ **9.** $4|ab|\sqrt{5}$
11. $5r\sqrt{3r}$ **13.** $\pm 3|x|y\sqrt{6y}$ **15.** $-12|xz|$
17. $\pm\frac{10|f^5|}{11}$ **19.** $\frac{x^2|y^3|}{2|r|}$ **21.** $\frac{4|g^9|}{45h^{10}}$ **23.** $-1.8x^2$
25. $|y-4|$ **27.** $\{5, -5\}$ **29.** $\{2, -2\}$
31. $\{10, -10\}$ **33.** $\{5, -5\}$ **35.** $\left\{\frac{4}{9}, -\frac{4}{9}\right\}$
37. $\left\{\frac{7}{9}, -\frac{7}{9}\right\}$ **39.** $\{24.9, -24.9\}$
41. $\{0.6, -0.6\}$ **43.** $\{14.6, -14.6\}$
45. $\{3.2, -3.2\}$ **47.** $\{7.5, -7.5\}$
49. $\{0.3, -0.3\}$ **51.** $\{8.5, -8.5\}$
53. $\{9.3, -9.3\}$

Problems, page 527 **1.** 17.3 cm **3.** 18 m
5. 7.2 km **7.** 18 s **9.** $\frac{\sqrt{2}}{1} \approx \frac{1.4}{1}$
11. 131.9 m^2

Mixed Review Exercises, page 528 **1.** $\pm 5\sqrt{10}$
2. $-12\sqrt{19}$ **3.** $30\sqrt{11}$ **4.** $\frac{5}{36}$ **5.** $\frac{4}{3}$
6. $-\frac{2}{x^9}$ **7.** 97 **8.** 1296 **9.** 80 **10.** $\frac{1}{3}$
11. $\frac{3}{2}$ **12.** 16

Calculator Key-In, page 528 **1.** 37.95 cm^2
3. 71.55 m^2 **5.** 4.92 m^2 **7.** 51.51 cm^2

Written Exercises, page 532 **1.** 26 **3.** 9.43
5. 11.31 **7.** 20 **9.** 39.55 **11.** yes **13.** yes
15. yes **17.** no **19.** yes **21.** 16.97
23. 18.97 **25.** 25.61 **27.** $a = b = 42.43$
29. $a = 9.49; b = 28.46$

Computer Exercises, page 532 **1.** yes **3.** yes

Problems, page 533 **1.** 65 cm **3.** 127.28 ft
5. 22.25 cm **7.** 182 cm **9.** 77.94 cm
11. 101.14 cm; yes

Mixed Review Exercises, page 534 **1.** $4x^8|y|$
2. $|c - 5|$ **3.** $5a^2|b + 4|\sqrt{2a}$ **4.** $\frac{9}{100,000,000}$
5. $\frac{4}{x^6y^{10}}$ **6.** $\frac{49}{64}$ **7.** $\frac{3-a}{18}$ **8.** $5y - 1$ **9.** $\frac{r}{64x^2}$
10. $-\frac{k^6}{216}$ **11.** $r^2 + 2r$ **12.** $2s - 1$

Self-Test 2, page 534 **1.** 0.9 **2.** 41.2
3. -0.9 **4.** $12|mn|$ **5.** $-9x^4|y^3|$ **6.** $0.5a^2$
7. $\{-8, 8\}$ **8.** $\{-7, 7\}$ **9.** $\left\{-\frac{5}{6}, \frac{5}{6}\right\}$
10. 22.02 **11.** no

Challenge, page 534 8 roosters, 11 hens, and
81 chicks; or 12 roosters, 4 hens, and 84 chicks

Extra, page 536 **1.** 10 **3.** 6.7 **5.** 5 **7.** 9.8
9. 6.4 **11.** 8.5 **13.** $MA = MB = 13$, therefore
M is equidistant from A and B.

Challenge, page 536
1.

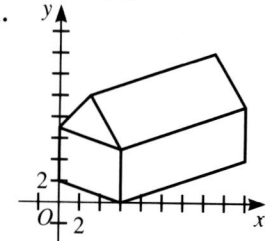

Written Exercises, pages 538–539 **1.** 30 **3.** 6
5. $2\sqrt{35}$ **7.** 9 **9.** 22 **11.** $36\sqrt{2}$ **13.** 1
15. $\frac{\sqrt{2}}{2}$ **17.** $\frac{\sqrt{6}}{3}$ **19.** 3 **21.** $\frac{\sqrt{65}}{13}$ **23.** $\frac{6\sqrt{5}}{5}$
25. $4\sqrt{3}$ **27.** 56 **29.** $5 - 2\sqrt{5}$
31. $-216\sqrt{3}$ **33.** $12ab$ **35.** $-x^2y^2\sqrt{xy}$
37. $m^2 + 6\sqrt{m}$ **39.** $30x^2$ **41.** $8x\sqrt{3}$ **43.** $20x$
45. $\frac{9x^2}{y}$ **47.** $6a - 4a\sqrt{6a}$
49. $24m^2 - 120m^3\sqrt{m}$ **51.** $24y^4\sqrt{3y}$
53. $50x^4y^2\sqrt{2} - 100x^2y^4$ **55.** $\frac{11}{\sqrt{33}}$ **57.** $\frac{6}{\sqrt{78}}$
59. $\frac{19}{2\sqrt{38}}$

Mixed Review Exercises, page 539
1. $\{13, -13\}$ **2.** $\{10, -10\}$ **3.** $\left\{\frac{4}{5}, -\frac{4}{5}\right\}$
4. $\{6\}$ **5.** $\{45\}$ **6.** $\{12\}$ **7.** $25x - 3$
8. $4a + 24$ **9.** $3b - 4$ **10.** $20c^3d^5$
11. $7m - 1$ **12.** $3x^2 - 5x - 4$

Written Exercises, page 541 **1.** $2\sqrt{3}$
3. $-20\sqrt{17}$ **5.** $15\sqrt{3}$ **7.** $12\sqrt{2} - 12\sqrt{7}$
9. $10\sqrt{7} - 6\sqrt{5}$ **11.** $-22\sqrt{2} - 14\sqrt{3}$
13. $10\sqrt{13} - 6\sqrt{11}$ **15.** $12\sqrt{7} - \sqrt{14}$
17. $-14\sqrt{2}$ **19.** $\frac{4\sqrt{55}}{11}$ **21.** $\frac{46\sqrt{2}}{5}$
23. $-\frac{6\sqrt{55}}{55}$ **25.** $\frac{17\sqrt{30}}{30}$ **27.** $\frac{\sqrt{3}}{3}$
29. $\frac{4\sqrt{14} - 7\sqrt{2}}{2}$ **31.** $15\sqrt{2} + 20\sqrt{6}$

33. $14x\sqrt{x} - 12x^2\sqrt{x}$ **35.** $\dfrac{x\sqrt{41}}{20}$

37. $\dfrac{x\sqrt{a^2 + b^2}}{ab}$

Mixed Review Exercises, page 542

1. $y = 3x + 5$ **2.** $y = \dfrac{1}{5}x - 2$ **3.** $y = 3x - 3$

4. $y = -x + \dfrac{4}{5}$ **5.** $y = \dfrac{1}{2}x - 3$ **6.** $y = \dfrac{2}{7}x$

7. $y = -x + 11$ **8.** $y = \dfrac{1}{11}x - \dfrac{7}{11}$

9. $y = -6x + 2$ **10.** $(0, 0)$; $x = 0$ **11.** $(3, 0)$;
$x = 3$ **12.** $(0, 5)$; $x = 0$ **13.** $\{0\}$ **14.** $\{-2\}$

15. $\{1, 10\}$ **16.** $\left\{\dfrac{1}{3}, -\dfrac{3}{2}\right\}$ **17.** $\{3, -1\}$

18. $\left\{-\dfrac{1}{2}\right\}$

Written Exercises, pages 545–546 **1.** 1
3. -21 **5.** 1 **7.** $11 + 4\sqrt{7}$ **9.** $17 - 12\sqrt{2}$
11. $33 - 4\sqrt{65}$ **13.** 25 **15.** 173
17. $9 + 2\sqrt{3}$ **19.** $-12 - 16\sqrt{35}$
21. $232 + 20\sqrt{22}$ **23.** $\dfrac{-1 + \sqrt{5}}{4}$
25. $3\sqrt{5} + 6$ **27.** $-3 - \sqrt{7}$
29. $\dfrac{\sqrt{21} - 2\sqrt{3} - 4\sqrt{7} + 8}{3}$ **31.** $\dfrac{14\sqrt{5} - 7}{19}$
33. $\dfrac{8\sqrt{5} + 12 + 4\sqrt{10} + 6\sqrt{2}}{11}$ **35.** $-1 - 5\sqrt{6}$
37. $-9 - 3\sqrt{2}$ **39.** $18 - 9\sqrt{11}$
41. Show that $(4 + \sqrt{7})^2 - 8(4 + \sqrt{7}) + 9 = 0$
and $(4 - \sqrt{7})^2 - 8(4 - \sqrt{7}) + 9 = 0$. **43.** Show
that $3\left(\dfrac{2}{3} + \dfrac{\sqrt{7}}{3}\right)^2 - 4\left(\dfrac{2}{3} + \dfrac{\sqrt{7}}{3}\right) - 1 = 0$ and
$3\left(\dfrac{2}{3} - \dfrac{\sqrt{7}}{3}\right)^2 - 4\left(\dfrac{2}{3} - \dfrac{\sqrt{7}}{3}\right) - 1 = 0$.
45. $x^2 - y$ **47.** $15a^2b + 4ac\sqrt{b} - 3c^2$

Mixed Review Exercises, page 546 **1.** $3x^4\sqrt{2}$
2. $60\sqrt{3x}$ **3.** $8\sqrt{2}$ **4.** $22\sqrt{7}$ **5.** $\dfrac{\sqrt{3}}{3}$
6. $\dfrac{5\sqrt{11}}{6}$ **7.** $9 - 30k^2 + 25k^4$
8. $4p^2 + 28pz + 49z^2$ **9.** $36a^2b^2 - x^2$ **10.** $\{15\}$
11. $\{5, 9\}$ **12.** $\left\{\dfrac{2}{3}, -\dfrac{2}{3}\right\}$

Written Exercises, pages 548–549 **1.** $\{9\}$
3. $\{8\}$ **5.** $\left\{\dfrac{1}{50}\right\}$ **7.** $\{16\}$ **9.** $\left\{\dfrac{1}{9}\right\}$ **11.** $\{18\}$
13. $\{8\}$ **15.** $\{8\}$ **17.** $\{4\}$ **19.** $\left\{\dfrac{1}{8}\right\}$ **21.** $\left\{\dfrac{38}{5}\right\}$
23. $\{63\}$ **25.** $\{80\}$ **27.** $\{18\}$ **29.** $\{22\}$
31. $\{18\}$ **33.** $\{3\sqrt{7}, -3\sqrt{7}\}$ **35.** $\{3, -3\}$

37. $\{6\}$ **39.** $\{0\}$ **41.** $\{4\}$ **43.** $\{-8, 2\}$ **45.** $\{0\}$
47. $\{4\}$ **49.** $(4, 25)$

Problems, pages 549–550 **1.** 75 **3.** 576
5. 29 **7.** 8100π cm^3 **9.** 1215 W **11.** 15.9 m

Mixed Review Exercises, page 550 **1.** 19
2. $9 + 4\sqrt{5}$ **3.** $-3 + \sqrt{11}$ **4.** $\dfrac{-7 - 3\sqrt{5}}{4}$
5. $15\sqrt{3} - 30$ **6.** $2 - 7\sqrt{3}$ **7.** $7(a - 1)^2$
8. $t(t - 9)(t + 5)$ **9.** $2(3x + 2)(x + 2)$
10. $(y^2 - 6)(y + 1)$ **11.** $4g(g^2 + 5)(g^2 - 5)$
12. $4(3x + y)^2$

Self-Test 3, pages 550–551 **1.** 30 **2.** 1
3. $7\sqrt{7} - 3\sqrt{13}$ **4.** $-4\sqrt{3}$ **5.** $15 - 6\sqrt{6}$
6. -1 **7.** $-3 - \sqrt{7}$ **8.** $\dfrac{-5 + 4\sqrt{5}}{11}$ **9.** $\{25\}$
10. $\left\{\dfrac{11}{5}\right\}$

Extra, page 553 **1.** $6^{1/2}$ **3.** $11^{1/3}$ **5.** $2^{1/4}$
7. $(-15)^{1/3}$ **9.** $10^{1/6}$ **11.** $4^{2/3}$ **13.** $2^{3/2}$
15. $3^{5/4}$ **17.** 8 **19.** 3 **21.** -4 **23.** not a real
number **25.** 8 **27.** 243 **29.** not a real number
31. 216 **33.** 625 **35.** $\left\{\dfrac{1}{2}\right\}$ **37.** $\left\{\dfrac{1}{3}\right\}$ **39.** $\{3\}$

Calculator Key-In, page 554 **1.** 2.632148
3. 1.8707313 **5.** 1.3753959

Chapter Review, pages 555–556 **1.** b **3.** c
5. b **7.** b **9.** a **11.** c **13.** a **15.** d **17.** a

Cumulative Review, page 557 **1.** -25
3. $16a^6b^2 + 72a^3bc^2 + 81c^4$ **5.** 1.024×10^{-7}
7. $\dfrac{2(x - 1)}{x - 4}$ **9.** $-\dfrac{2(2t^2 + 6t - 1)}{t(t + 2)}$ **11.** $\sqrt{7}$
13. $\dfrac{5\sqrt{30}}{6}$ **15.** $\dfrac{2\sqrt{6} + \sqrt{30}}{6}$
17. $(2c - d - 3)(2c - d + 3)$
19.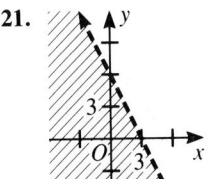

21. **23.** 0
25.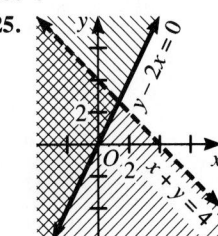

27. $\{16\}$ **29.** $\left\{\dfrac{3}{2}\right\}$
31. $\{4, -1\}$

33. $\left(-1, -\frac{1}{5}\right)$ **35.** $\{3, 5,$ and the real numbers between 3 and 5$\}$ **37.** $\left\{\text{the real numbers greater than } -\frac{2}{3}\right\}$ **39.** $\{1\}$ **41.** 7.48 cm

Maintaining Skills, page 558 **1.** $(-1, 2)$
3. $(5, 5)$ **5.** $\left(\frac{1}{2}, \frac{1}{3}\right)$ **7.** $\left(-\frac{2}{3}, \frac{7}{3}\right)$ **9.** $(7, 3)$
11. $(12, -1)$ **13.** $(0, 0)$ **15.** $(7, -1)$
17. $(-7, 12)$ **19.** $(5, 6)$ **21.** $(9, 4)$

Mixed Problem Solving Review, page 559
1. 1 km/h; 11 km/h **3.** 12 cm **5.** Saturn, 10 km/s; Mars, 24 km/s **7.** \$1500 **9.** 30 min
11. no sol.; unrealistic result **13.** $\frac{3x + 2}{3}$ dollars per kg

Chapter 12 Quadratic Functions

Written Exercises, page 563 **1.** $\{\pm 8\}$
3. $\left\{\pm\frac{10}{13}\right\}$ **5.** $\{\pm 6\}$ **7.** $\{\pm 3\}$ **9.** no sol.
11. $\{\pm\sqrt{3}\}$ **13.** $\{\pm\sqrt{3}\}$ **15.** $\{\pm\sqrt{7}\}$
17. $\{6 \pm \sqrt{13}\}$ **19.** $\{7 \pm 2\sqrt{7}\}$ **21.** $\{2, 8\}$
23. $\{-3 \pm \sqrt{7}\}$ **25.** $\{1, -7\}$ **27.** $\{9, 13\}$
29. $\left\{\pm\frac{5}{7}\right\}$ **31.** $\left\{\pm\frac{\sqrt{510}}{6}\right\}$ **33.** $\{6, -24\}$
35. $\left\{\pm\frac{\sqrt{2}}{2}\right\}$ **37.** $\left\{\frac{27}{14}, \frac{29}{14}\right\}$ **39.** $\left\{\frac{12 \pm 5\sqrt{7}}{20}\right\}$
41. $\{0, \pm 5\}$ **43.** $\left\{0, \pm\frac{1}{4}\right\}$ **45.** $\{0, \pm 8\}$
47. $\left\{0, \frac{1}{3}\right\}$ **49. a.** 2 **b.** 2 **c.** none **d.** 1

Mixed Review Exercises, page 563
1. $x^2 - 22x + 121$ **2.** $4x^2 + 20x + 25$
3. $36x^2 - 84x + 49$ **4.** $9c^2 - 24c + 16$
5. $x^2 + x + \frac{1}{4}$ **6.** $x^2 + \frac{2}{3}x + \frac{1}{9}$
7. $\frac{1}{4}x^2 + \frac{2}{3}x + \frac{4}{9}$ **8.** $\frac{1}{9}x^2 + \frac{1}{2}x + \frac{9}{16}$

Written Exercises, page 566
1. $\{\sqrt{21} + 2, -\sqrt{21} + 2\}$; $\{6.6, -2.6\}$
3. $\{\sqrt{6} - 3, -\sqrt{6} - 3\}$; $\{-0.6, -5.4\}$
5. $\{1, 19\}$ **7.** $\{5\sqrt{11} - 9, -5\sqrt{11} - 9\}$;
$\{7.6, -25.6\}$ **9.** $\{\sqrt{6} + 2, -\sqrt{6} + 2\}$;
$\{4.4, -0.4\}$ **11.** $\left\{\frac{\sqrt{33} + 5}{2}, \frac{-\sqrt{33} + 5}{2}\right\}$;
$\{5.4, -0.4\}$ **13.** $\{5, 7\}$ **15.** $\{-5, 7\}$
17. $\left\{\frac{3}{2}, 3\right\}$ **19.** $\{-2, 6\}$ **21.** $\left\{-\frac{1}{2}, 6\right\}$

23. $\left\{\frac{1 \pm \sqrt{37}}{3}\right\}$ **25.** $\left\{\frac{-3 \pm \sqrt{41}}{8}\right\}$
27. $\left\{\frac{-2 \pm \sqrt{3}}{3}\right\}$ **29.** $\left\{\frac{b \pm \sqrt{b^2 - 4c}}{2}\right\}$

Mixed Review Exercises, page 566 **1.** $2\sqrt{47}$
2. $20\sqrt{6}$ **3.** $x^2y^4\sqrt{10y}$ **4.** $2|a^3b^3|c^2\sqrt{30bc}$
5. $\frac{z^2 - 2z + 24}{16 - z^2}$ **6.** $\frac{b^2 + 2b + 1}{2b + 1}$
7. $15x^2 + 40x + 12$

Written Exercises, page 569 **1.** $\{5, -2\}$
3. $\left\{2, \frac{1}{5}\right\}$ **5.** $\{-1, 6\}$ **7.** $\{3 \pm 2\sqrt{5}\}$;
$\{7.5, -1.5\}$ **9.** $\{-4 \pm \sqrt{11}\}$; $\{-0.7, -7.3\}$
11. $\left\{\frac{-1 \pm \sqrt{15}}{7}\right\}$; $\{0.4, -0.7\}$ **13.** $\left\{\frac{1 \pm \sqrt{13}}{4}\right\}$;
$\{1.2, -0.7\}$ **15.** $\left\{\frac{3 \pm \sqrt{2}}{2}\right\}$; $\{0.8, 2.2\}$
17. $\left\{\frac{-4 \pm \sqrt{22}}{3}\right\}$; $\{0.2, -2.9\}$
19. $\left\{\frac{-0.7 \pm \sqrt{0.89}}{2}\right\}$; $\{0.1, -0.8\}$
21. $\left\{\frac{0.3 \pm \sqrt{2.09}}{4}\right\}$; $\{0.4, -0.3\}$ **23.** no real-number sol. **25.** no real-number sol.
27. $\left\{\frac{3 \pm \sqrt{13}}{2}\right\}$; $\{-0.3, 3.3\}$ **29.** $-\frac{b}{a}$
31. $x^2 - 4x - 1 = 0$

Mixed Review Exercises, page 570
1. $\{-3, 11,$ and the real numbers between -3 and $11\}$

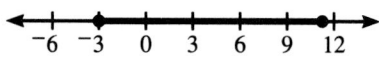

2. $\{-12, -2\}$

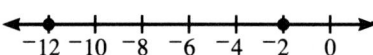

3. $\left\{\text{the real numbers between } -4 \text{ and } \frac{2}{3}\right\}$

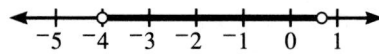

4. $\left\{4 \text{ and the real numbers between } -\frac{1}{2} \text{ and } 4\right\}$

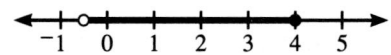

5. $\{81\}$

6. $\{4\}$

7. {12}
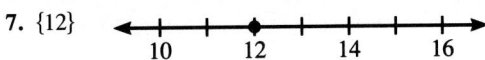

8. {−12, 3}

9. {−1, 9}

10. {2, 8} **11.** {0, −6} **12.** {−2, 3}

Computer Exercises, page 570 **3.** {1, 0.75}
5. {3.41, 0.59} **7.** no real-number solution

Extra, page 571 **1.** −1 **3.** i **5.** −i **7.** 7i
9. $4\sqrt{6}$ **11.** 30i **13.** 18$i\sqrt{6}$ **15.** $\frac{4i}{9}$

17. $-\frac{7i}{11}$ **19.** {±10i} **21.** {±7$i\sqrt{2}$}

Written Exercises, page 574 **1.** 9; two **3.** 0;
one **5.** 0; one **7.** 0; one **9.** 21; two
11. 1.16; two **13.** two; below **15.** one; on
17. two; above **19.** 4

Mixed Review Exercises, page 575
1. $\frac{\sqrt{2} - \sqrt{6}}{2}$ **2.** $\frac{3c^4}{5}$ **3.** 0 **4.** $\frac{2}{x^2 + x}$

5. $\frac{4b + 5}{4(b + 1)}$ **6.** 5.022×10^8 **7.** (0, 0); $x = 0$
8. (−5, 0); $x = -5$ **9.** (0, 3); $x = 0$
10. $\left(4\frac{1}{2}, 17\frac{1}{4}\right)$; $x = 4\frac{1}{2}$ **11.** $\left(7\frac{1}{2}; -12\frac{3}{4}\right)$;
$x = 7\frac{1}{2}$ **12.** $\left(\frac{3}{4}, 1\frac{1}{8}\right)$; $x = \frac{3}{4}$

Computer Exercises, page 575 **1.** 2 **3.** 0

Self-Test 1, page 575 **1.** {−3, 3}
2. {3 ± $\sqrt{7}$} **3.** {5, 7} **4.** {−2, 8}
5. $\left\{2, -\frac{1}{2}\right\}$ **6.** $\left\{\frac{3 \pm \sqrt{33}}{2}\right\}$ **7.** none **8.** none

Written Exercises, pages 577–578 **1.** {−6, 1}
3. {±2} **5.** $\left\{\frac{-7 \pm \sqrt{41}}{2}\right\}$ **7.** −3 ± $\sqrt{14}$

9. {0, 4} **11.** {4 ± $3\sqrt{2}$} **13.** $\left\{\frac{1}{5}, -4\right\}$

15. $\left\{\frac{1 \pm \sqrt{22}}{3}\right\}$ **17.** {−3 ± $2\sqrt{5}$}

19. $\left\{\frac{7 \pm \sqrt{161}}{28}\right\}$ **21.** $\left\{\frac{2}{3}, 3\right\}$ **23.** $\left\{\frac{1 \pm \sqrt{10}}{3}\right\}$

25. $\left\{\frac{32}{9}, 4\right\}$ **27.** $\left\{-\frac{8}{5}, \frac{2}{11}\right\}$ **29.** $\left\{\pm\frac{\sqrt{3}}{2}\right\}$

31. $\left\{\pm\frac{2\sqrt{6}}{3}\right\}$

Mixed Review Exercises, page 578 **1.** ±10
2. $-2\sqrt{7}$ **3.** 7 **4.** $\sqrt{113}$ **5.** ±17 **6.** no
real-number sol. **7.** $\left\{-\frac{3}{2}, \frac{5}{2}\right\}$ **8.** $\left\{-7, \frac{11}{2}\right\}$

9. $\left\{-\frac{68}{39}\right\}$ **10.** {2 ± $\sqrt{6}$} **11.** $\left\{\frac{1}{3}, 1\right\}$
12. $\left\{\frac{-6 \pm \sqrt{51}}{6}\right\}$

Problems, pages 580–581 **1.** 20 m, 15 m
3. 7 or −8 **5.** 9 cm **7.** 7 cm **9.** Olaf,
6 mi/h; Cindy, 8 mi/h **11.** Maria, 34.1 min;
Johannes, 30.1 min **13.** 16 **15.** 12 h

Mixed Review Exercises, page 581 **1.** {45}
2. {84} **3.** $\left\{\frac{4}{5}\right\}$ **4.** $\left\{10\frac{10}{13}\right\}$ **5.** {5, 9} **6.** {8}
7. 12 **8.** 25 **9.** 3

Extra, page 582
1.
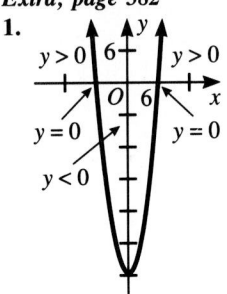

3.
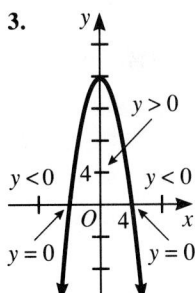

5.
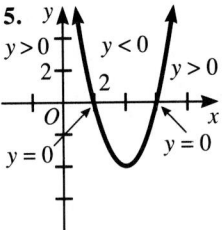

7. $x \le 0$ or $x \ge 3$
9. $x \le 3$ or $x \ge 7$

Self-Test 2, page 582 **1.** {−4, 0}
2. $\left\{\frac{-3 \pm \sqrt{3}}{2}\right\}$ **3.** {5 ± $3\sqrt{5}$} **4.** {−3, 0}
5. 20 cm, 10 cm **6.** 50 m, 36 m

Application, page 583 **1.** 360 cm³
3. 600 cm³ **5.** 22.5 m³

Problems, page 586–587 **1.** 18 cm **3.** 112 m
5. 3 cm **7.** 1.2 s **9.** 1.4 **11.** 64:27

Mixed Review Exercises, page 587 **1.** $\frac{3x^2 - 1}{2}$

2. $\frac{2A}{b + c}$; $b \ne -c$ **3.** $\frac{2A - hc}{h}$; $h \ne 0$

4. $\dfrac{1}{a+1}$; $a \neq -1$ **5.** $k^2 + tg$; $g \neq 0$

6. $\pm\dfrac{\sqrt{kE}}{E}$; $kE \geq 0$, $E \neq 0$ **7.** $2x - y = 7$

8. $2x - 3y = 0$ **9.** $x + 2y = 10$

10. $3x - y = -2$ **11.** $x - 6y = 24$

12. $5x - 13y = 130$

Written Exercises, page 590   **1.** 48   **3.** ± 12
5. ± 4.2 **7.** quadrupled; no change   **9.** h is 2.8
times as large

Problems, pages 590–592   **1.** 104 cm³   **3.** 25
5. \$2.10   **7.** 12 s   **9.** 5.30   **11.** 18 joules
13. a. doubled   **b.** quadrupled   **c.** 18 times as
large

Mixed Review Exercises, page 592   **1.** (1, 1)
2. (12, −2)   **3.** (9, 3)   **4.** (−5, 10)   **5.** (2, 2)
6. (11, −8)   **7.** $8x^2 + 8x + 2$
8. $48s^2 + 64s + 20$ **9.** $49t^2 - 4y^2$
10. $9p^2 - 24pk + 16k^2$ **11.** $r^2 - 4r + 4$
12. $3x^2y^2 - 2xy - 8$

Application, page 593   **1.** 10 lx   **3.** 3 m
5. 20 lx

Self-Test 3, page 594   **1.** 196 km   **2.** 158.4 g

Chapter Review, pages 595–596   **1.** d   **3.** c
5. a   **7.** b   **9.** a   **11.** b

Cumulative Review, pages 597–598   **1.** $-\dfrac{7}{2}$

3. 0   **5.** 1   **7.** −58   **9.** −133
11. $45x - 55 - 9c$ **13.** $12a^4b^3 + 9a^3b^4$
15. $\dfrac{3wx}{4y^2}$ **17.** $8u^3 + 1$ **19.** $45z^2 + 21z - 12$

21. $64r^6t^2 - 9v^2$ **23.** $\dfrac{2c - 3d}{2c - 6d}$

25. $9x^2 - 12x + 16$ **27.** $\dfrac{3z + 4}{(z + 1)(z + 3)}$

29. $2a - 3$ **31.** $\dfrac{5m - 21}{2(m + 3)(m - 3)}$

33. $90 - 27\sqrt{5}$ **35.** $12a$ **37.** $14\sqrt{5}$
39. $92 + 32\sqrt{10}$ **41.** $t^3(4t^2 + 9)$
43. $-16z^2(z^2 + 3z + 4)$ **45.** prime
47. $(c - 4)^2$ **49.** $\left\{\dfrac{40}{3}\right\}$ **51.** {5}   **53.** {300}

55. {3, 6}   **57.** $\left\{-\dfrac{2}{3}, \dfrac{1}{4}\right\}$ **59.** $\left(\dfrac{1}{2}, \dfrac{1}{8}\right)$

61. {−16}   **63.** {−2, 8, and the real numbers
less than −2 or greater than 8}   **65.** $\left\{-\dfrac{3}{2}, 2,\right.$

and the real numbers between $-\dfrac{3}{2}$ and $\left.2\right\}$

67. no sol.   **69.** {5}   **71.** $\left\{\dfrac{5 \pm \sqrt{13}}{6}\right\}$

73.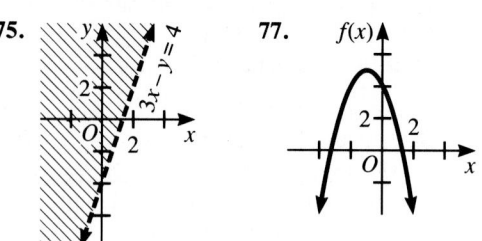

75. **77.**

79. **81.** 12 h
83. less than 6 h
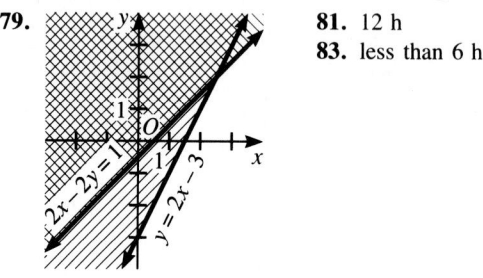

Preparing for College Entrance Exams,
page 599   **1.** D   **3.** B   **5.** C   **7.** E

Looking Ahead

Written Exercises, page 602   **1.** {A, B, C, D,
E, F, G, H, I, J, K};   **a.** {A, E, I}
b. {B, C, D, F, G, H, J, K}   **c.** {C, F, H}
3. {(2, 1), (2, 4), (2, 9), (4, 1), (4, 4), (4, 9),
(8, 1), (8, 4), (8, 9), (15, 1), (15, 4), (15, 9)};
a. {(4, 4)}   **b.** {(15, 1), (15, 9)}   **c.** {(4, 9),
(8, 9), (15, 1), (15, 4), (15, 9)}   **d.** {(2, 1),
(4, 1)}   **5.** {(O, O, O), (O, O, F), (O, F, F),
(O, F, O), (F, O, O), (F, O, F), (F, F, O),
(F, F, F)};   **a.** {(O, O, O)}   **b.** {(O, F, F),
(F, F, O), (F, O, F), (F, F, F)}   **c.** {(O, O, F),
(O, F, F), (O, F, O), (F, O, O), (F, O, F),
(F, F, O), (F, F, F)}   **7.** {p, n, d, (p, n), (p, d),
(n, d), (p, n, d)};   **a.** {d, (p, n), (p, n, d)}
b. {p, n, (p, d), (n, d)}   **c.** {n, d, (p, n), (p, d),
(n, d)}   **d.** {p, n, (p, n, d)}

Written Exercises, pages 604–605   **1. a.** $\dfrac{4}{15}$

b. $\dfrac{2}{3}$ **c.** $\dfrac{1}{3}$ **d.** $\dfrac{2}{3}$ **3. a.** $\dfrac{1}{24}$ **b.** $\dfrac{3}{8}$ **c.** $\dfrac{7}{24}$

d. $\dfrac{1}{6}$ **5. a.** $\dfrac{1}{8}$ **b.** $\dfrac{3}{8}$ **c.** $\dfrac{1}{2}$ **d.** $\dfrac{3}{4}$ **7. a.** $\dfrac{2}{15}$

b. $\dfrac{2}{5}$ **c.** $\dfrac{1}{5}$ **d.** $\dfrac{1}{15}$ **e.** $\dfrac{4}{15}$ **f.** $\dfrac{1}{3}$

Written Exercises, page 608 **1.** 44; 49; none; 38 **3.** 28.7; 30.5; 32; 23 **5.** 56; 56; 53 and 56 and 61; 9 **7.** 85.8; 84.5; 81 and 92; 11 **9.** 10.2; 10.5; 12; 5 **11.** 96% **13. a–d.** Each statistic is multiplied by 3. **15.** 38

Extra, page 610 **1.** The mean is 7 and the difference between each data point and the mean is 0. Therefore the variance and standard deviation are both 0. **3. a.** 41 **b.** 4.2

c.

x_i	standard score
36	-1.2
38	-0.7
41	0
45	1.0
48	1.7

5. Factory II; the standard deviation is lower, so there must have been less of a difference between each worker's productivity and the mean productivity.

Written Exercises, page 613 **1. a.** 51, 53, 54, 62, 63, 65, 68, 70, 71, 73, 76, 77, 79, 84, 84, 88, 90, 95 **b.** 72; 84; 44 **3. a.** 8 **b.** 6 **c.** 9 **d.** 10 **e.** 4 **f.** 6 **5.** 22; 21; 28; 30; 19 **7.**

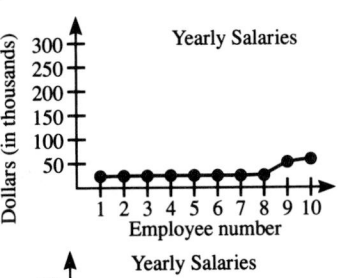

Application, page 615 **1.** no **3. a.** $22,000 **b.** $27,565 **c.** median; only two people earn more than $23,000

d. For the scale on the vertical axis, for example, make each unit $50 (in thousands).

e. For the scale on the vertical axis, for example, make each unit $5 (in thousands).

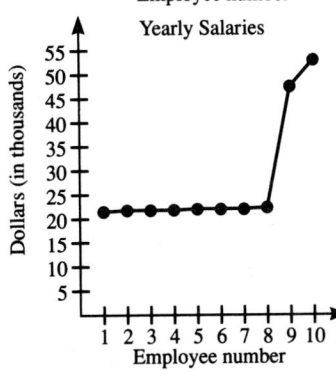

Written Exercises, page 618 **1.** Any 5 of: $\overline{WX}$, $\overline{WY}$, $\overline{WZ}$, $\overline{XY}$, $\overline{XZ}$, $\overline{YZ}$ **3.** Any 5 of: $\overline{AE}$, $\overline{BC}$, $\overline{EB}$, $\overline{ED}$, $\overline{DB}$, $\overline{AC}$, $\overline{AD}$, $\overline{DC}$ **5.** acute **7.** right **9.** obtuse **11.** acute

13. ray

15. point

17. point

19. line segment

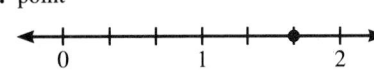

21. two rays

Written Exercises, page 620 **1.** $\angle HAD$, $\angle GBK$, $\angle EAB$ **3.** 30° **5.** 70° and 20° **7.** 127° **9.** 63°

Written Exercises, page 622 **1.** 93° **3.** 90° **5.** 66° **7.** no **9.** no **11.** yes **13.** 15 **15.** 18 **17.** 140° **19.** $4\sqrt{10}$ **21.** 8 **23.** $8\sqrt{5}$ **25.** $x\sqrt{2}$

Problems, page 623 **1.** 18° and 72° **3.** 10°, 70°, 100° **5.** 18°, 54°, 108° **7.** 60°, 60°, 60° **9.** 11°, 49°, 120° **11.** 72°, 37°, 71° **13.** 63°, 49°, 68°

Written Exercises, pages 625–626 **1. a.** $\angle S$, $\angle Z$; $\angle R$, $\angle Y$; $\angle T$, $\angle X$ **b.** $\overline{RS}$, $\overline{YZ}$; $\overline{ST}$, $\overline{ZX}$; $\overline{RT}$, $\overline{YX}$ **c.** YZX **3.** F **5.** T **7.** T **9.** $AB = 10$, $BC = 14$ **11.** $EF = 14$, $DF = 21$ **13.** $DE = 12$, $BC = 24$ **15.** $AB = 26$, $EF = 27$

Problems, page 626 **1.** 9 cm **3.** 36 m **5.** 225 m **7.** 6 m **9.** 11.25 m

Written Exercises, page 629 **1.** $\sin A = \frac{4}{5}$, $\cos A = \frac{3}{5}$, $\tan A = \frac{4}{3}$, $\sin B = \frac{3}{5}$, $\cos B = \frac{4}{5}$, $\tan B = \frac{3}{4}$ **3.** $\sin A = \frac{5\sqrt{34}}{34}$, $\cos A = \frac{3\sqrt{34}}{34}$, $\tan A = \frac{5}{3}$, $\sin B = \frac{3\sqrt{34}}{34}$, $\cos B = \frac{5\sqrt{34}}{34}$,

$\tan B = \frac{3}{5}$ **5.** $\sin A = \frac{4\sqrt{65}}{65}$, $\cos A = \frac{7\sqrt{65}}{65}$,

$\tan A = \frac{4}{7}$, $\sin B = \frac{7\sqrt{65}}{65}$, $\cos B = \frac{4\sqrt{65}}{65}$,

$\tan B = \frac{7}{4}$ **7.** $\sin A = \frac{\sqrt{2}}{2}$, $\cos A = \frac{\sqrt{2}}{2}$,

$\tan A = 1$, $\sin B = \frac{\sqrt{2}}{2}$, $\cos B = \frac{\sqrt{2}}{2}$,

$\tan B = 1$ **9.** $\sin A = \frac{3\sqrt{130}}{130}$,

$\cos A = \frac{11\sqrt{130}}{130}$, $\tan A = \frac{3}{11}$, $\sin B = \frac{11\sqrt{130}}{130}$,

$\cos B = \frac{3\sqrt{130}}{130}$, $\tan B = \frac{11}{3}$ **11.** $\cos A = \frac{b}{c}$;

$\sin B = \frac{b}{c}$ **13.** $\tan A = \frac{a}{b}$; $\dfrac{\sin A}{\cos A} = \dfrac{\frac{a}{c}}{\frac{b}{c}} = \dfrac{a}{b}$

15. $\frac{\sqrt{55}}{8}$

Written Exercises, page 632 **1.** 0.3420,
0.9397, 0.3640 **3.** 0.2588, 0.9659, 0.2679
5. 0.9272, 0.3746, 2.4751 **7.** 0.4067, 0.9135,
0.4452 **9.** 0.0698, 0.9976, 0.0699
11. 0.7071, 0.7071, 1.0000 **13.** 78° **15.** 9°
17. 57° **19.** 22° **21.** 35° **23.** 41° **25.** 20°
27. 34° **29.** > **31.** =

Challenge, page 632 **1.** no **3.** yes

Written Exercises, page 635 **1.** 18 **3.** 42
5. 16 **7.** $AC = 41$, $BC = 33$ **9.** $AB = 49$,
$BC = 8$ **11.** $\angle D = 37°$, $\angle F = 53°$
13. $\angle F = 39°$, $\angle D = 51°$ **15.** $XY = 72$,
$ZY = 62$

Problems, pages 635–636 **1.** 16 m **3.** 226 m
5. 52 m **7.** 14° **9.** 9 m **11.** 21° **13.** 63 m;
83 m

Review, pages 637–638 **1.** c **3.** a **5.** c
7. c **9.** a **11.** d **13.** c

EXTRA PRACTICE: Skills

Chapter 1, pages 639–640 **1.** 37 **3.** 100
5. 198 **7.** 12 **9.** 23 **11.** 24 **13.** 6 **15.** 9
17. 8 **19.** 3 **21.** 23 **23.** {6}
25. {0, 1, 2, 3, 4, 5, 6} **27.** {0} **29.** {6}
31. {4} **33.** {0, 5} **35.** {2} **37.** {0}
39. $\frac{1}{2}z - 4$ **41.** $5w - 1$ **43.** $7x$
45. $x - 4$ **47.** $n - 5$ **49. a.** s **b.** $4s = 52$
51. Let x = Henry's age; $x(x - 4) = 140$

53. Cynthia, 30; Holly, 84 **55.** 400; 400 ft
below sea level; -400 **57.** -10; ten wins; 10
59.

$$\begin{array}{cccccccccccc} \hline -5 & -4 & -3 & -2 & -1 & 0 & 1 & 2 & 3 & 4 & 5 \end{array}$$

61. -3 **63.** 9 **65.** 3 **67.** 4 **69.** > **71.** <
73. <

Chapter 2, pages 641–643 **1.** 350 **3.** 20
5. 16 **7.** $3m + 12$ **9.** $6w + 12$ **11.** $88n$
13. $60pqr$ **15.** $60hmw$ **17.** 0 **19.** -12
21. 20 **23.** -19 **25.** -5.6 **27.** -1
29. -153 **31.** -4 **33.** -12 **35.** 0 **37.** -10
39. 100 **41.** -83 **43.** 215 **45.** 17 **47.** -30
49. 4 **51.** 8 **53.** 34 **55.** 580 **57.** $7q$
59. $42a$ **61.** $7c + 27$ **63.** $8j - 15$
65. $8x + 20$ **67.** $2u + 5$ **69.** $2f + 10g$
71. 135 **73.** -180 **75.** -135 **77.** -480
79. 11 **81.** -270 **83.** $-7m + 42p$
85. $-24n + 36v$ **87.** $-8t - 4$
89. $-29x + 16y$ **91.** $-3c - 17d$
93. $x + (x + 1) + (x + 2) = 75$
95. $x + (x + 2) + (x + 4) = 138$
97. $x + 2 = 3x + 8$ **99.** -5 **101.** 7 **103.** -4
105. $11xy$ **107.** $8g$ **109.** $9h - 6$
111. $-6x + 9y$ **113.** $5p + 10q$ **115.** -8
117. 0 **119.** -40 **121.** 0 **123.** $-\frac{63}{2}a$
125. 11 **127.** $-x$ **129.** $5h$

Chapter 3, pages 643–645 **1.** {30} **3.** {8}
5. {-15} **7.** {20} **9.** {-3} **11.** {-12}
13. {2} **15.** {12} **17.** {-18} **19.** {-14}
21. {-64} **23.** {50} **25.** {-128} **27.** {120}
29. $\left\{\frac{1}{6}\right\}$ **31.** {7} **33.** {6} **35.** {8} **37.** {-13}
39. {-27} **41.** {4} **43.** {6} **45.** {-3} **47.** 10
49. 21 **51.** 4 m, 6 m, 8 m **53.** {7} **55.** {-8}
57. {-6} **59.** {-4} **61.** {15} **63.** $\left\{\frac{11}{8}\right\}$
65. {-7} **67.** {3} **69.** 75, 77, 79, 97
71. 16 cm by 10 cm; 14 cm by 13 cm
73. 56 dozen **75.** 4 h **77.** Substitution principle, Assoc. prop. of add., Prop. of opposites,
Ident. prop. of add.

Chapter 4, pages 645–646 **1.** 343 **3.** -48
5. 32 **7.** -26 **9.** 5 **11.** 68 **13.** 49
15. -2744 **17.** 1 **19.** $\frac{81}{4}$ **21.** $b - 2$
23. $4t - 10$ **25.** $10x^2 - 3xy + 2y^2$
27. $3a^2 + 3ab - b^2$ **29.** $5b + 10$ **31.** $-8t - 4$
33. $2x^2 - xy + 4y^2$ **35.** $7a^2 - 15ab + b^2$
37. $8f^7$ **39.** $-10g^4h^3$ **41.** $60j^5k^3l^5$ **43.** $-a^6$

45. 729 **47.** 2048 **49.** $4d^{10}$ **51.** x^{10} **53.** z^{2n}
55. b^{3n} **57.** d^{3n} **59.** g^4h^4 **61.** $64\,m^3n^{15}$
63. $9a^{10}b^8$ **65.** $-512x^{15}$ **67.** $-200x^{13}$
69. $375x^7y^5$ **71.** $5y - 20$ **73.** $-8 - 32m$
75. $-12t + 8t^2$ **77.** $-40h^2 - 15h$
79. $-15b^4 + 10b^3 - 30b^2$
81. $5u^3v^2 - 2u^2v^3 + 4uv^4$ **83.** $n^2 + 2n - 15$
85. $5x^2 + 33x - 14$ **87.** $30m^2 + 38m + 12$
89. $3v^3 + v^2 + 3v - 7$ **91.** $21x^2 - 26xy + 8y^2$
93. $e^3 + 2e^2f + 2ef^2 + f^3$ **95.** $a = \dfrac{2A}{p}; p \neq 0$
97. $b_1 = \dfrac{2A - b_2h}{h}; h \neq 0$ **99.** $r = \sqrt{\dfrac{A}{\pi}}; A \geq 0$
101. $C = \dfrac{5}{9}(F - 32)$ **103.** $t = \dfrac{I}{Pr}; P \neq 0,$
$r \neq 0$ **105.** 90 min **107.** 13.25 in. by
39.75 in.

Chapter 5, pages 647–649 **1.** 1, 42; 2, 21; 3,
14; 6, 7; −1, −42; −2, −21; −3, −14; −6,
−7 **3.** 1, 91; 7, 13; −1, −91; −7, −13
5. 1, 52; 2, 26; 4, 13; −1, −52; −2, −26; −4,
−13 **7.** $2^4 \cdot 5$ **9.** $2^3 \cdot 3^2$ **11.** 42 **13.** 13
15. $3x^4$ **17.** $-\dfrac{1}{3b^4}$ **19.** $\dfrac{1}{w^{12}}$ **21.** $-\dfrac{27}{y^3}$
23. $3e + 2$ **25.** $2x^2 + 6x + 1$
27. $3 - 5m - m^2$ **29.** $5(3w^2 - 2w + 1)$
31. $7u^2(u + 2)$ **33.** $3c(5c + d)$
35. $x^2 + 8x + 15$ **37.** $n^2 + 4n - 21$
39. $6 + 5m + m^2$ **41.** $8y^2 - 10y + 3$
43. $20n^2 - 22n + 6$ **45.** $12h^3 + 55h^2 + 63h$
47. $k^2 - 25$ **49.** $16d^2 - 64$ **51.** $25m^4 - n^2$
53. $(4e - 3)(4e + 3)$ **55.** $(9 - f)(9 + f)$
57. $(7 - 10y)(7 + 10y)$ **59.** $(s^3 - 2)(s^3 + 2)$
61. $g^2 + 14g + 49$ **63.** $4x^2 + 24x + 36$
65. $4m^2 + 12mn + 9n^2$ **67.** $e^2f^2 - 16ef + 64$
69. $(x - 3)^2$ **71.** $(2 - 7h)^2$ **73.** $(2m - 9n)^2$
75. $(k + 1)(k + 7)$ **77.** $(a - 1)^2$
79. $(n - 4)(n - 12)$ **81.** $(x + 6y)(x + 7y)$
83. $(e - 4f)(e - 11f)$ **85.** $(x - 7)(x + 5)$
87. $(h - 9)(h + 2)$ **89.** $(y - 9)(y + 5)$
91. $(u + 4v)(u - v)$ **93.** $(2x + 3)(x + 4)$
95. $(5d + 3)(2d - 1)$ **97.** prime
99. $(5x + y)(3x + 2y)$ **101.** $(7m + 3n)(2m - n)$
103. $2(a + 2)(3a + 2)$ **105.** $(b - 3)(b + 1)^2$
107. $(7w + 3)(c - w)$
109. $(1 + m)(1 - m)(64 + m^4)$
111. $6y(5y + 1)(2y - 1)$
113. $16a^2(a - 3)(a + 3)$ **115.** $2w^5(14w^2 - 51)$
117. $-12(c - d)^2$ **119.** $\{-13, -8\}$
121. $\left\{2, \dfrac{5}{3}\right\}$ **123.** $\left\{0, -\dfrac{3}{4}\right\}$ **125.** $\{-1, -6\}$

127. $\{5, 9\}$ **129.** $\{4, -9\}$ **131.** $\left\{\dfrac{1}{4}, -6\right\}$
133. $\left\{-2, \dfrac{5}{2}\right\}$ **135.** $\left\{\dfrac{2}{3}, -\dfrac{2}{3}\right\}$ **137.** 7 or −8
139. 8 cm by 11 cm

Chapter 6, pages 649–651 **1.** 5, $m \neq 3$
3. $\dfrac{c - d}{c + d}$; $c \neq -d$ **5.** $\dfrac{3}{u - v}$; $u \neq 0$, $v \neq 0$,
$u \neq v$ **7.** $\dfrac{x + 8}{x + 7}$; $x \neq 8$, $x \neq -7$ **9.** $\dfrac{3}{5m - 2n}$;
$m \neq -\dfrac{2}{5}n$, $m \neq \dfrac{2}{5}n$ **11.** −1; $k \neq 3$, $k \neq \dfrac{2}{7}$
13. $\dfrac{t - 7}{t + 2}$; $t \neq 2$, $t \neq -2$ **15.** $-\dfrac{1}{(x - 5w)^2}$;
$w \neq \dfrac{x}{5}$ **17.** $\dfrac{4}{3}$ **19.** $\dfrac{3}{20}$ **21.** $\dfrac{e}{h}$ **23.** 2
25. $\dfrac{2uw^2}{3v^3}$ **27.** $\dfrac{1}{4xy(4 + y)}$ **29.** $25k^6$ **31.** $\dfrac{9x^2}{16}$
33. $-\dfrac{x^6}{125}$ **35.** $\dfrac{8c^5}{d^3}$ **37.** $\dfrac{1}{12}$ **39.** $\dfrac{2}{n^2}$ **41.** 1
43. $\dfrac{1}{(n - 3)(n - 5)}$ **45.** $\dfrac{(x - y)(x + y)(x - 4)}{2x}$
47. $\dfrac{(2t - 3s)(m^2 + n^2)}{7(4s - 5t)(m + n)}$ **49.** $\dfrac{x^2}{y^3}$ **51.** $\dfrac{c^2}{3}$ **53.** −1
55. $2h - 8$ **57.** $30m - 5n$ **59.** $12s^2t$
61. $5e + 5$ **63.** $5z$ **65.** $3ab$ **67.** $\dfrac{3x - 6}{48}$,
$\dfrac{4x + 12}{48}$ **69.** $\dfrac{d}{3cd^2}$, $\dfrac{12}{3cd^2}$ **71.** $\dfrac{2wx + 6w}{3(x^2 - 9)}$,
$\dfrac{3}{3(x^2 - 9)}$ **73.** $\dfrac{4}{x}$ **75.** $\dfrac{-k - 4}{5}$ **77.** $\dfrac{7}{g - 3}$
79. $\dfrac{5 + 3y}{y^2}$ **81.** $\dfrac{2 - 3x}{10wx}$ **83.** $\dfrac{2 + 3x}{3(x + 2)}$
85. $\dfrac{3(h + 1)}{10}$ **87.** $\dfrac{2x + 7}{(x + 2)(x + 3)}$ **89.** $\dfrac{u - 3}{u - 4}$
91. $\dfrac{5n + 1}{n}$ **93.** $\dfrac{x + 3y}{y}$ **95.** $\dfrac{8n - 14}{n - 2}$
97. $\dfrac{h(8h + 23)}{h + 3}$ **99.** $\dfrac{5e^2 - e - 8}{(e + 1)(e - 1)}$
101. $\dfrac{2w^2 - 7w - 3}{w - 3}$ **103.** $\dfrac{2v^2}{(v + u)(v - u)}$
105. $x + 5$ **107.** $a - 7 + \dfrac{11}{a + 2}$
109. $k + 1 + \dfrac{12}{k - 5}$ **111.** $b^2 - b + 1 - \dfrac{2}{b + 1}$
113. $w^2 + 2w + 4$ **115.** $n - 4$
117. $v^2 + 3v + 7 + \dfrac{15}{v - 2}$

Chapter 7, pages 651–653 **1.** 1:3 **3.** 200:3
5. 18d:5 **7.** 25:11 **9.** $\{9\}$ **11.** $\left\{\dfrac{7}{6}\right\}$ **13.** $\{6\}$
15. $\{18\}$ **17.** $\{12\}$ **19.** $\{72\}$ **21.** $\{-9\}$
23. $\{-7\}$ **25.** $\{6\}$ **27.** $\{2\}$ **29.** $\{-6\}$
31. 202.5 **33.** 30 **35.** 25% **37.** $\{40\}$

39. {800} **41.** {300} **43.** 8.4 kg **45.** $127.50
47. 24 kg **49.** 30 min **51.** $\frac{1}{125}$ **53.** $\frac{1}{729}$
55. 36 **57.** 64 **59.** $\frac{1}{729y^3}$ **61.** $\frac{1}{a^2b^3}$ **63.** $\frac{e^2}{d^4f^2}$
65. $\frac{x^{12}y^{15}}{z^9}$ **67.** 1.47×10^8 **69.** 9.8×10^{-6}
71. 1×10^{-11}

Chapter 8, pages 653–656 **1.** no; yes **3.** no;
no **5.** yes; yes **7.** (0, 4), (2, 3), (4, 2), (6, 1),
(8, 0) **9.** (0, 4), (3, 0) **11.** (2, 2), (6, 1),
(10, 0)

13. 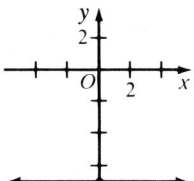 **15.**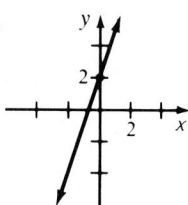

17. 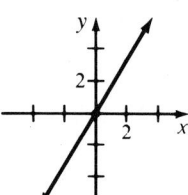 **19.**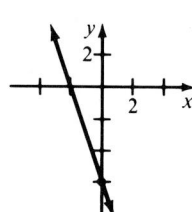

21. 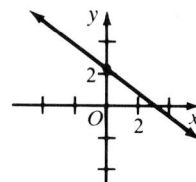 **23.** $\frac{1}{6}$ **25.** 0
27. $\frac{3}{13}$ **29.** no slope
31. 0 **33.** -1
35. yes **37.** yes

39. 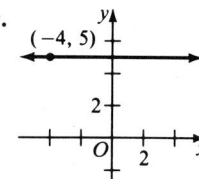 **41.**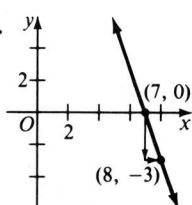

43. 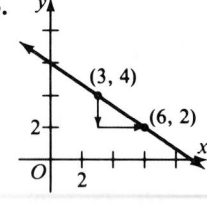 **45.** $y = \frac{7}{2}x$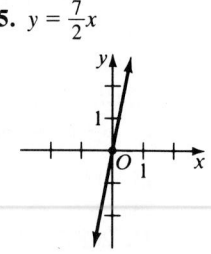

47. $y = -x + 3$ 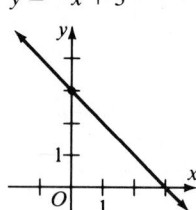 **49.** $y = \frac{3}{4}x - \frac{5}{4}$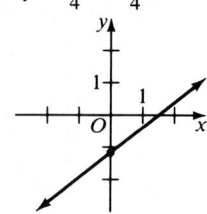

51. $y = \frac{3}{2}x - 3$, $y = \frac{3}{2}x - 6$; Both slopes are
$\frac{3}{2}$, so the lines are parallel. **53.** $y = 3x + \frac{1}{2}$
55. $y = \frac{1}{3}x + 6$ **57.** $y = -\frac{3}{7}x + \frac{3}{8}$
59. $y = 3x + 4$ **61.** $y = \frac{3}{4}x - 2$
63. $y = -\frac{1}{5}x - 1$ **65.** $y = \frac{3}{4}x - \frac{1}{2}$
67. $y = -\frac{1}{6}x$ **69.** $y = -2x + 4$
71. D = {Mackinac Straits, Humber Estuary,
Golden Gate, Ataturk, Verrazano Narrows},
R = {3800 ft, 4626 ft, 4200 ft, 3524 ft, 4260 ft}

73.

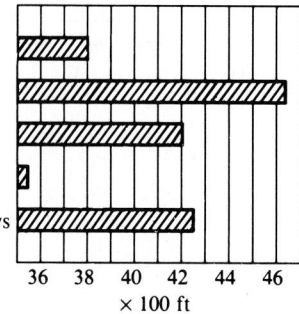

75. -7 **77.** 5 **79.** 0 **81.** $\frac{9}{8}$
83. {2, -3, -10} **85.** {5, 1, -3} **87.** {3, -1}
89. (0, 0); $x = 0$ 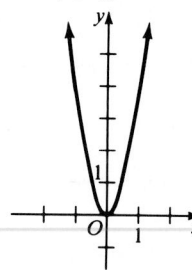 **91.** (0, 0); $x = 0$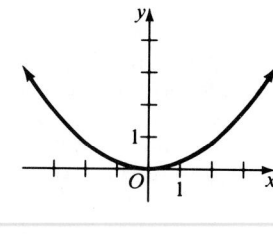

93. $(1, 4)$; $x = 1$

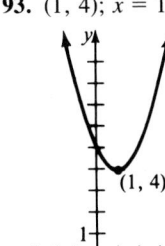

95. $\left(-\dfrac{7}{2}, -\dfrac{49}{4}\right)$; $-\dfrac{49}{4}$

97. $(0, 0)$; 0

99. $(0, 2)$; 2   **101.** $\dfrac{1}{5}$

103. 900   **105.** 21

107. $\dfrac{3}{32}$

109. a. $e = km$ **b.** $\dfrac{e_1}{m_1} = \dfrac{e_2}{m_2}$

111. a. $rn = k$ **b.** $\dfrac{r_1}{n_2} = \dfrac{r_2}{n_1}$

113. a. $ns = k$ **b.** $\dfrac{n_1}{s_2} = \dfrac{n_2}{s_1}$

115.

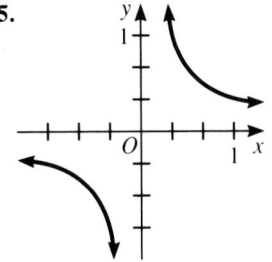

117.

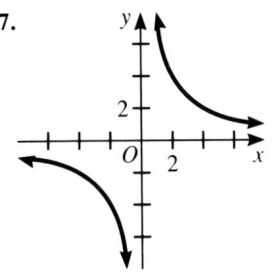

119. 1.8

Chapter 9, pages 656–657   1. $(4, 2)$
3. $(-2, 2)$ **5.** $(3, 3)$ **7.** $(1, 2)$ **9.** $(3, -2)$
11. $(5, -1)$ **13.** 7 men   **15.** $(3, 6)$ **17.** $(8, 2)$
19. $(5, -3)$ **21.** $(4, -1)$ **23.** $(2, 3)$
25. $(4, 3)$ **27.** 20 km/h; 820 km/h   **29.** Jenny,
17 years old; aunt, 28 years old

Chapter 10, pages 657–659   1. False   **3.** True
5. False   **7.** False   **9.** True   **11.** $\{-4, -3\}$
13. $\{-3, -2, -1, 0, 1, 2, 3\}$

15.

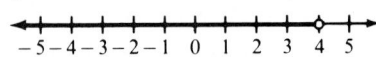

17.

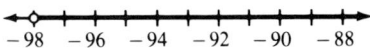

19. {the real numbers less than 4}

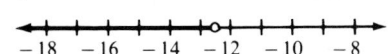

21. {the real numbers greater than -98}

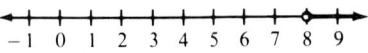

23. $\left\{\text{the real numbers less than } -\dfrac{25}{2}\right\}$

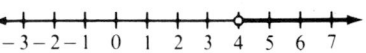

25. {the real numbers greater than 8}

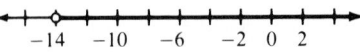

27. {the real numbers greater than 4}

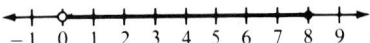

29. {the real numbers greater than -14}

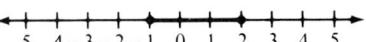

31. {the real numbers less than 4}

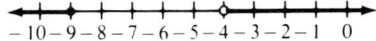

33. a. x **b.** $2x - 9 \le 43$ **35. a.** y
b. $\dfrac{1}{2}y - 10 \ge 25$ **37. a.** b **b.** $b - 6 < \dfrac{1}{2}b$

39. {8, and the real numbers between 0 and 8}

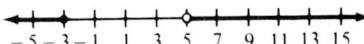

41. $\{-1, 2,$ and the real numbers between -1
and 2$\}$

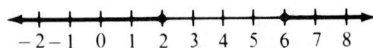

43. $\{-9,$ and the real numbers less than -9 or
greater than $-4\}$

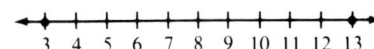

45. $\{-3,$ and the real numbers less than -3 or
greater than 5}

47. {6, 2, and the real numbers greater than 6 or
less than 2}

49. $\{3, 13\}$

51. {−1.5, 1.5, and the real numbers between −1.5 and 1.5}

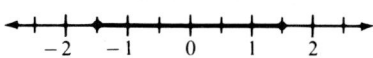

53. {−7, 1, and the real numbers between −7 and 1}

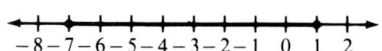

55. {the real numbers less than −11 or greater than 3}

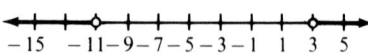

57. $\left\{-\dfrac{3}{2}, \dfrac{3}{2}, \text{ and the real numbers between } -\dfrac{3}{2}\right.$ and $\left.\dfrac{3}{2}\right\}$

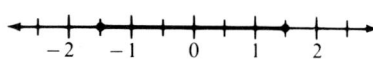

59. {the real numbers between −4 and 10}

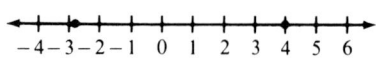

61. {−6, 6, and the real numbers less than −6 or greater than 6}

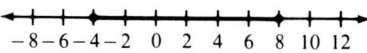

63. $\left\{4, -\dfrac{14}{5}\right\}$

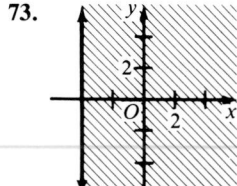

65. {the real numbers less than −1 or greater than 4}

67. {−4, 8, and the real numbers between −4 and 8}

69. {the real numbers between −4 and 2}

71. No solution

73.

75.

77.

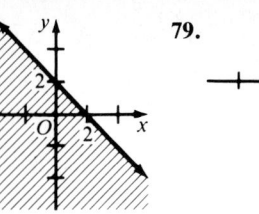

79.

81. $y \le -4x - 2$

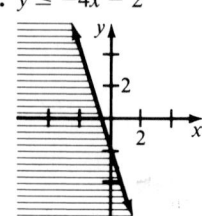

83. $y > 6x - 2$

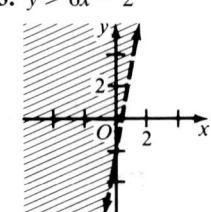

85. $y < \dfrac{5}{4}x$

87. $y > 2x - \dfrac{2}{3}$

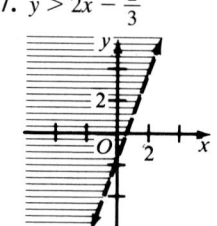

89.

91.

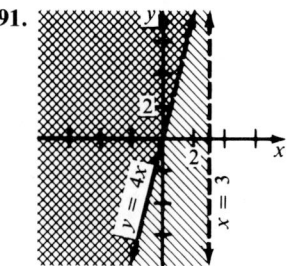

93.

95.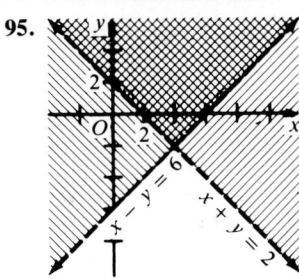

Chapter 11, pages 659–662   1. $<$ **3.** $<$
5. $\frac{2}{3}, \frac{12}{17}, \frac{5}{7}, \frac{11}{15}$ **7.** $\frac{1135}{1517}$ **9.** $\frac{111}{56}$
11. increases **13.** decreases **15.** $0.\overline{4}$ **17.** 3.55
19. $0.7\overline{45}$ **21.** $\frac{2}{3}$ **23.** $\frac{235}{99}$ **25.** 0.6275
27. $0.6\overline{32}$ **29.** $\frac{4}{9}, \frac{2}{3}; \frac{8}{27}$ **31.** 21 **33.** 52
35. 104 **37.** 0.8 **39.** 0.12 **41.** $\frac{3}{5}$ **43.** $\frac{9}{22}$
45. $\frac{8}{9}$ **47.** $4\sqrt{11}$ **49.** $12\sqrt{11}$ **51.** $90\sqrt{2}$
53. $4\sqrt{42}$ **55.** $21\sqrt{6}$ **57.** -28.3 **59.** 91.7
61. $13|m|$ **63.** $5x^2\sqrt{5}$ **65.** $-6|t^3|$
67. $-12|xy|\sqrt{2x}$ **69.** $-2.2w^2$ **71.** $\frac{a^2|b^3|\sqrt{3}}{6|c|}$
73. $\frac{3k^4}{4}$ **75.** $\frac{15x^{20}}{4}$ **77.** $|a-2|$ **79.** $\{-7, 7\}$
81. $\left\{-\frac{4}{5}, \frac{4}{5}\right\}$ **83.** $\{-3, 3\}$ **85.** $\{-11.5, 11.5\}$
87. $\{-6.6, 6.6\}$ **89.** 9.43 **91.** 11.18
93. 22.36 **95.** 18.03 **97.** no **99.** no
101. no **103.** 30 **105.** 14 **107.** $72\sqrt{2}$
109. $\frac{3\sqrt{2}}{2}$ **111.** $\frac{\sqrt{2}}{4}$ **113.** $\frac{11\sqrt{3}}{7}$
115. $n^2 + 3\sqrt{n}$ **117.** $4\sqrt{3}$ **119.** $7\sqrt{6}$
121. $-50\sqrt{2}$ **123.** $2\sqrt{2} - \frac{\sqrt{30}}{6}$
125. $\frac{20\sqrt{7}}{7} + \frac{3\sqrt{2}}{4}$ **127.** $10\sqrt{3} - \sqrt{30}$
129. $3\sqrt{15}$ **131.** -29 **133.** $18 + 8\sqrt{2}$
135. $34 - 24\sqrt{2}$ **137.** $20\sqrt{3} - 24\sqrt{2}$
139. $252 + 133\sqrt{2}$
141. $-\frac{2 + \sqrt{3} + 2\sqrt{5} + \sqrt{15}}{4}$ **143.** $\left\{\frac{3}{8}\right\}$
145. $\left\{\frac{16}{25}\right\}$ **147.** $\{83\}$ **149.** $\{3\}$ **151.** $\left\{\frac{2}{5}\right\}$
153. $\{45\}$

Chapter 12, pages 662–664   1. $\left\{-\frac{5}{7}, \frac{5}{7}\right\}$
3. no solution **5.** $\{-4, 4\}$ **7.** $\{-\sqrt{3}, \sqrt{3}\}$
9. $\{-9, -1\}$ **11.** $\{-4 + 3\sqrt{3}, -4 - 3\sqrt{3}\}$
13. $\{-7 + \sqrt{21}, -7 - \sqrt{21}\}$

15. $\left\{\frac{1 + 2\sqrt{6}}{3}, \frac{1 - 2\sqrt{6}}{3}\right\}$ **17.** $\{-1, 13\}$
19. $\{-15, -1\}$ **21.** $\{6 + \sqrt{246}, 6 - \sqrt{246}\}$;
$\{21.7, -9.7\}$ **23.** $\left\{\frac{3 + \sqrt{29}}{2}, \frac{3 - \sqrt{29}}{2}\right\}$;
$\{4.2, -1.2\}$ **25.** $\{3, 7\}$ **27.** $\left\{2, -\frac{7}{2}\right\}$
29. $\left\{2, -\frac{5}{2}\right\}$ **31.** $\left\{\frac{-7 + \sqrt{37}}{2}, \frac{-7 - \sqrt{37}}{2}\right\}$;
$\{-0.5, -6.5\}$ **33.** $\left\{\frac{5 + \sqrt{37}}{2}, \frac{5 - \sqrt{37}}{2}\right\}$;
$\{5.5, -0.5\}$ **35.** $\left\{1, \frac{2}{3}\right\}$
37. $\left\{\frac{-3 + \sqrt{89}}{20}, \frac{-3 - \sqrt{89}}{20}\right\}$; $\{0.3, -0.6\}$
39. $\left\{\frac{7 + \sqrt{57}}{2}, \frac{7 - \sqrt{57}}{2}\right\}$; $\{7.3, -0.3\}$
41. -131; none **43.** -11.76; none **45.** 5; two
47. a. zero **b.** below **49.** $\{-3, -4\}$
51. $\left\{0, \frac{9}{5}\right\}$ **53.** $\{-4 + \sqrt{13}, -4 - \sqrt{13}\}$
55. $\left\{\frac{-2 + \sqrt{10}}{6}, \frac{-2 - \sqrt{10}}{6}\right\}$
57. $\left\{\frac{4 + 2\sqrt{31}}{9}, \frac{4 - 2\sqrt{31}}{9}\right\}$
59. $\left\{\frac{1 + \sqrt{7}}{6}, \frac{1 - \sqrt{7}}{6}\right\}$
61. $\left\{\frac{-5 + \sqrt{13}}{2}, \frac{-5 - \sqrt{13}}{2}\right\}$ **63.** length,
22.2 cm; width, 3.7 cm **65.** 14 m **67.** $hr^2 = k$
69. $L = krh$ **71.** $\frac{rt}{d} = k$

EXTRA PRACTICE: Problem-Solving

Chapter 1, page 665   (1-7) 1. 225 km
3. 8 games **5.** 19

Chapter 2, page 665   (2-3) 1. 38 yd **3.** $205
5. 10:00 A.M. **(2-4) 1.** $2.52°$ C **3.** 28 blocks
5. 397 m below sea level

Chapter 3, page 666   (3-1) 1. -18 **3.** 58
5. $747 **(3-2) 1.** -34 **3.** 56¢ **5.** 12 cm
(3-4) 1. 12 **3.** $124 **5.** 8 quarters, 12 dimes,
16 nickels **(3-5) 1.** -9 and -8 **3.** 12 **5.** 7,
9, 11 **(3-6) 1.** Kevin, 18 h; Karen, 6 h **3.** 60
5. Becky, 6; Ryan, 4; Amy, 2 dimes
(3-7) 1. 13 quarters, 35 dimes **3.** 7.5 h **5.** 36
quarters

Chapter 4, page 668   (4-8) 1. 2.5 h
3. 2400 km **5.** 7:00 P.M. **(4-9) 1.** 7 m by
11 m **3.** 5 m by 9 m **5.** 60 cm by 70 cm
(4-10) 1. no solution **3.** no solution **5.** -5,
-4, -3

Chapter 5, page 669 *(5-13)* **1.** 11 or –12
3. 12 cm by 20 cm **5.** 4 m by 8 m

Chapter 7, page 670 *(7-1)* **1.** 50, 75 **3.** 40,
60, 100 **5.** 180 coins *(7-2)* **1.** $7.73
3. $167.50 **5.** 180 lb *(7-3)* **1.** Juan, $16;
Sylvia, $14 **3.** Bart, 14; mother, 42 years old
5. 20 dimes *(7-4)* **1.** $\frac{3}{4}$ or $\frac{4}{3}$ **3.** $\frac{1}{3}$
5. 50 km/h *(7-5)* **1.** $10.50 **3.** $40 **5.** $630
(7-6) **1.** 35% **3.** 1475 **5.** $9600
(7-7) **Chemistry 1.** 80 L **3.** 25.6%
Grocery 1. 40 L of cranberry juice; 80 L of
apple juice **3.** $1.75 **Investment and**
Wages 1. $12.50 **3.** $15,000 *(7-8)* **1.** $\frac{11}{15}$
3. 13 h 20 min **5.** 54 min
(7-9) **1. a.** 10,000 **b.** 9709 **c.** 10,300
3. about 61 bacteria **5.** about 6701 people
(7-10) **1.** 1.28 s **3.** 2.03×10^4 s
5. 6.0×10^{-5} cm

Chapter 8, page 674 *(8-9)* **1.** 3.1 cm
3. 33 kg **5.** 226,800 km² *(8-10)* **1.** 7 h
3. $1875 **5.** 0.55 m from the mass of 18 g or
0.45 m from the mass of 22 g

Chapter 9, page 675 *(9-3)* **1.** 32 quarters
3. width, 10; length, 17 **5.** $\frac{5}{12}$ *(9-4)* **1.** 21,
15 **3.** 87 boys **5.** 18 quarters, 20 dimes
(9-5) **1.** 19, 32 **3.** 150 ft **5.** 42 questions
(9-6) **1.** boat, 23 km/h; current, 7 km/h
3. current, 2 km/h; swimmer, 8 km/h
5. 200 km/h

Chapter 10, page 677 *(10-3)* **1.** 40, 41
3. 260 **5.** 90 km/h

Chapter 11, page 677 *(11-5)* **1.** 13.6 cm
3. 4.5 cm **5.** 3.3 m *(11-6)* **1.** 53.85 m
3. 8 cm, 15 cm **5.** 9 cm, 12 cm
(11-10) **1.** 784 **3.** 49 **5.** 30, 32

Chapter 12, page 679 *(12-6)* **1.** 5 or –6
3. 9 m by 60 m **5.** 72 h and 90 h
(12-7) **1.** 85.75 m **3.** 1 unit **5.** It is $\frac{1}{9}$ as
large as it was. *(12-8)* **1.** 6¢ **3.** $5\frac{1}{4}$ h

Explorations

Page 685 *(1-8)* **1. d.** No. The product
approaches, but never reaches, zero. **3.** This
process of multiplying by $\frac{1}{2}$ produces numbers
that approach zero from *either* side of zero on
the number line. **5. b.** The average
approaches, but never reaches, the smaller
number. **7. a.** yes **b.** no

Page 686 *(2-3)* **1. c.** 0 **e.** Use an equal
number of red chips and blue chips. **3. b.** The
signs of the addends and their sums are the
same. **c.** no **5. a.** 8 **b.** –8 **c.** 2 **d.** –2

Page 687 *(2-4)* **1. c.** 1 **d.** $4 - 3 = 1$
3. a. by removing 3 red chips from 4 blue
chips **d.** 7 blue chips **e.** $4 - (-3) = 7$
5. $-5 - (-3) = -2$ (2 red chips); $-3 - (-5) = 2$
(2 blue chips) **7.** true

Page 688 *(3-1)* **1. a.** The pans balance; $6 = 6$
b. The pans balance; 8; $6 + 2 = 6 + 2$, or
$8 = 8$ **c.** The pans balance; 5; $8 - 3 = 8 - 3$,
or $5 = 5$ **d.** The pans do not balance;
$5 - 1 \neq 5 - 2$, or $4 \neq 3$, or $4 > 3$ **e.** If the
same number of washers is added to or
subtracted from each pan, the pans stay in
balance. **3. a.** The pans balance; $y - 4 = 7$
b. $y = 11$

Pages 689–690 *(4-5, 4-6)* **1. a.** x; $x + 1$
b. $x(x + 1)$ **c.** x^2; x **d.** The area of the
rectangle is the sum of the areas of the tiles.
e. $x(x + 1) = x^2 + x$ **3. b.** three 1-by-1 tiles
c. $x + 1$, $x + 3$ **d.** $x^2 + 4x + 3$
e. $x^2 + 4x + 3$ **5. a.** $2x^2 + 3x$ **b.** $6x^2 + 3x$
c. $3x^2 + 15x$

Page 691 *(5-7)* **1. a.** $x^2 + 3x$ **b.** $x + 3$; x
c. $x(x + 3)$ **d.** $x^2 + 3x = x(x + 3)$ **3. a.** One
x-by-x tile, seven 1-by-x tiles, and twelve 1-by-1
tiles **c.** $x + 4$, $x + 3$ **d.** $(x + 4)(x + 3)$
5. a. $x(2x + 1)$ **b.** $(x + 1)^2$
c. $(3x + 1)(x + 2)$

Page 692 *(6-4)* **1. a.** $2 \cdot 3$ **b.** 2^3, 3^2
c. $2^3 \cdot 3^2$ **d.** 2, 3 **e.** The factors not
included in the GCF form the LCM, and those
not included in the LCM form the GCF.
3. a. abc^2 **b.** $a^2b^2c^3d$ **c.** $a^2b^2c^3d$ **d.** abc^2
e. The factors not included in the GCF form
the LCM, and those not included in the LCM
form the GCF. **5.** 12; 240

Page 693 *(7-2)* **3.** 1250 fish

Page 694 *(8-4)* **1. d.** The lines all go through

the same point, (0, *b*); the slant, or slope, of the line is different; the equations are alike except for the value of *m*. **3.** For an equation of the form *y* = *mx* + *b*, the value of *m* determines the slant, or slope, of the line. **5. c.** The lines are parallel (have the same slope); each line goes through a different point (0, *b*) on the *y*-axis; the equations are alike except for the value of *b*. **7.** They both pass through the point (0, 5), but the second line is steeper.

Page 695 (9-1) **1. b.** The lines are parallel. **c.** The lines are parallel to the original line. **3. b.** The lines intersect in one point. **c.** yes; yes **d.** The lines all intersect the original line in one point. **5.** The graphs coincide. The first equation multiplied by −2 yields the second equation.

Page 696 (10-2) **1. a.** *a* is next door to *a*. **b.** If *a* is next door to *b*, then *b* is next door to *a*. **c.** If *a* is next door to *b* and *b* is next door to *c*, then *a* is next door to *c*. **3. a.** transitive **b.** symmetric, transitive **c.** symmetric **d.** transitive **5.** reflexive and transitive **7.** 5

Page 697 (11-2) **1. a.** 0.5 **b.** $0.\overline{3}$, $0.\overline{25}$, 0.2, $0.1\overline{6}$, $0.\overline{142857}$, 0.125, $0.\overline{1}$, 0.1, 0.09, $0.08\overline{3}$ **c.** $\frac{1}{2}, \frac{1}{4}, \frac{1}{5}, \frac{1}{8}, \frac{1}{10}$ **d.** $\frac{1}{3}, \frac{1}{6}, \frac{1}{7}, \frac{1}{9}, \frac{1}{11}, \frac{1}{12}$ **e.** The denominators for (c) have only 2 and/or 5 as prime factors. The denominators for (d) have other primes besides 2 and 5. **f.** Their decimal forms are terminating. **g.** Their decimal forms are repeating. **3. a.** $\frac{4}{10} = \frac{2}{5}$, $\frac{29}{100}$, $\frac{325}{1000} = \frac{13}{40}$, $\frac{4791}{10,000}$ **b.** 5, $2^2 \cdot 5^2$, $2^3 \cdot 5$, $2^4 \cdot 5^4$ **c.** Their only prime factors are 2 and 5; agree. **5.** They are the product of prime factors that include at least one prime other than 2 or 5.

Pages 698–699 (11-6) **1. a.** $\sqrt{2}$ **b.** $\sqrt{3}$ **c.** $\sqrt{4} = 2$ **d.** $\sqrt{5}, \sqrt{6}, \sqrt{7}, \sqrt{8} = 2\sqrt{2}$, $\sqrt{9} = 3$ **e.** The new hypotenuse is the square root of the number that is one more than the radicand of the longer leg. **3.** $x\sqrt{y + 1}$ **5. a.** $\sqrt{13}$ **b.** $\sqrt{5}$; yes **c.** Possible answer: 3, 5, $\sqrt{34}$ **d.** $2\sqrt{2}$ **e.** $\sqrt{29}$ **7.** yes; no

Page 700 (12-4) **1. b.** one **3. b.** none **c.** There are none. **5.** one, because $b^2 - 4ac = 0$; $x \approx 1.7$

Appendices

A–2, page 714 **1.** $y - 2 = 3(x - 1)$ **3.** $y - 4 = -\frac{1}{2}(x - 3)$ **5.** $y + 8 = 5(x + 3)$ **7.** $y - 2 = \frac{4}{7}(x - 0)$ **9.** $y = \frac{3}{4}x - \frac{7}{4}$; $3x - 4y = 7$ **11. a.** $y = -2x + 8$ **b.** $y = \frac{1}{2}x + \frac{19}{2}$

A–3, pages 716–717 **1.** deductive **3.** inductive **5.** Inductive: A chemistry experiment produces the same result 20 times. You conclude that it will always produce the same result. Deductive: a direct two-column proof in geometry. Inductive reasoning makes a general statement based on a mumber of observations. Deductive reasoning uses known facts, definitions, and properties in a logical order to reach a conclusion. **7. a.** 3 + 4 = 7; 3 • 4 = 12 **b.** yes **c.** $(x + a)(x + b) = x^2 + (a + b)x + ab$ **d.** $(x + a)(x + b) = x^2 + xa + ab = x^2 + (a + b)x + ab$ **9.** $a = 2, b = -2$ **11.** $a = 0.5$ **13.** false; $10^2 = 100$ **15.** The sum of the first *n* positive even integers is $n(n + 1)$. $4n(n + 1) + 1 = 4n^2 + 4n + 1 = (2n + 1)^2$. Since $(2n + 1)^2$ is a perfect square, the statement is true.

A–4, page 719 **1.** hypothesis: The current month is September. conclusion: There are 30 days in the month. True; There are 30 days in September. **3.** hypothesis: Joe lives in Vermont. conclusion: Joe lives in New England. True; Vermont is a New England state. **5.** (1) If there are 30 days in the month, then the current month is September. False; April, June, and November all have 30 days. (2) If *ab* is positive, then *a* and *b* are negative. False; *a* and *b* could both be positive. (3) If Joe lives in New England, then he lives in Vermont. False; Joe could live in Maine, New Hampshire, Rhode Island, Connecticut, or Massachusetts. (4) If $|a + b| = |a| + |b|$, then *a* and *b* are both positive. False; *a* and *b* could both be 0. **9.** always true; true when *a* and *b* are both positive or both negative, or when one is zero, or when one is positive and one negative.

A–5, page 720   **1.** hypothesis and known fact: n^3 is negative. desired conclusion: n is negative. alternative conclusion: n is positive or 0. Assume temporarily that the alternative conclusion is true. If n is positive, then n^3 is positive since the cube of a positive number is positive. If $n = 0$, then $n^3 = 0$ since the cube of 0 is 0. This contradicts the known fact that n^3 is negative. The desired conclusion must be accepted and the original statement is true.   **3.** hypothesis and known fact: $x > 3$. desired conclusion: $|x| - 3 > 0$. alternative conclusion: $|x| - 3 \leq 0$. Assume temporarily that the alternative conclusion is true. If $|x| - 3 \leq 0$, then $|x| \leq 3$ contradicts the known fact that x is greater than 3. The desired conclusion must be accepted and the original statement is true.   **5.** hypothesis and known fact: n^2 is a multiple of 3. desired conclusion: n is a multiple of 3. alternative conclusion: n is not a multiple of 3. Assume temporarily that the alternative conclusion is true. Then either $n = 3k + 1$ or $n = 3k + 2$, where k is any integer. If $n = 3k + 1$, then $n^2 = (3k + 1)^2 = 9k^2 + 6k + 1$, or $3(3k^2 + 2k) + 1$. Since $3(3k^2 + 2k)$ is a multiple of 3, $3(3k^2 + 2k) + 1$, or n^2, is not a multiple of 3. If $n = 3k + 2$, then $n^2 = 9k^2 + 12k + 4$, or $3(3k^2 + 4k + 1) + 1$. Since $3(3k^2 + 4k + 1)$ is a multiple of 3, $3(3k^2 + 4k + 1) + 1$, or n^2, is not a multiple of 3. Both cases contradict the known fact that n^2 is a multiple of 3. The desired conclusion must be accepted and the original statement is true.

Additional Answers

Appendices

A–2, page 714 **1.** $y - 2 = 3(x - 1)$ **2.** $y - 9 = 2(x - 5)$ **3.** $y - 4 = -\frac{1}{2}(x - 3)$ **4.** $y - 4 = 5(x + 2)$ **5.** $y + 8 = 5(x + 3)$ **6.** $y + 7 = -\frac{2}{3}(x - 1)$ **7.** $y - 2 = \frac{4}{7}(x - 0)$ **8.** $y - b = m(x - 0)$ **9.** $y = \frac{3}{4}x - \frac{7}{4}; 3x - 4y = 7$

10. a. $y = \frac{4}{3}x + \frac{7}{3}$ **b.** $y = -\frac{3}{4}x + \frac{13}{2}$

11. a. $y = -2x + 8$ **b.** $y = \frac{1}{2}x + \frac{19}{2}$

12. a. Estimates will vary: about $\frac{5}{6}$; $y - 73 = \frac{5}{6}(x - 62)$ **b.** about 80 in.

A–3, pages 716–717 **1.** deductive **2.** inductive **3.** inductive **4.** deductive **5.** Inductive: A chemistry experiment produces the same result 20 times. You conclude that it will always produce the same result. Deductive: a direct two-column proof in geometry. Inductive reasoning makes a general statement based on a mumber of observations. Deductive reasoning uses known facts, definitions, and properties in a logical order to reach a conclusion. **6. a.** $2 + 4 + 6 + 8 = 4 \cdot 5$; $2 + 4 + 6 + 8 + 10 = 5 \cdot 6$ **b.** The sum of the first n positive even integers is $n(n + 1)$. **c.** Let $S = $ sum of first n positive even integers.

$$S = \quad 2 \quad + \quad 4 + \ldots + (2n-2) + \quad (2n)$$
$$\underline{S = \quad (2n) \quad + (2n-2) + \ldots + \quad 4 + \quad 2}$$
$$2S = (2n+2) + (2n+2) + \ldots + (2n+2) + (2n+2)$$

$2S = n(2n + 2) = 2n(n + 1)$. Therefore $S = n(n + 1)$.

7. a. $3 + 4 = 7; 3 \cdot 4 = 12$ **b.** yes **c.** $(x + a)(x + b) = x^2 + (a + b)x + ab$ **d.** $(x + a)(x + b) = x^2 + xa + ab = x^2 + (a + b)x + ab$ **8.** $n = 1$ **9.** $a = 2, b = -2$ **10.** $x = 0.5$ **11.** $a = 0.5$ **12.** false; $n = 11$ **13.** false; $10^2 = 100$ **14.** true **15.** The sum of the first n positive even integers is $n(n + 1)$. $4n(n + 1) + 1 = 4n^2 + 4n + 1 = (2n + 1)^2$. $(2n + 1)^2$ is a perfect square. Therefore the statement is true.

A–4, page 719 **1.** hypothesis: The current month is September. conclusion: There are 30 days in the month. True; There are 30 days in September. **2.** hypothesis: a and b are negative. conclusion: ab is positive. True; The product of two negative numbers is always positive. **3.** hypothesis: Joe lives in Vermont. conclusion: Joe lives in New England. true; Vermont is a New England state. **4.** hypothesis: a and b are both positive. conclusion: $|a + b| = |a| + |b|$ True; since a and b are both positive, $|a + b| = a + b$ and $|a| + |b| = a + b$ **5.** (1) If there are 30 days in the month, then the current month is September. False; April, June, and November all have 30 days. (2) If ab is positive, then a and b are negative. False; a and b could both be positive. (3) If Joe lives in New England, then he lives in Vermont. False; Joe could live in Maine, New Hampshire, Rhode Island, Connecticut, or Massachusetts. (4) If $|a + b| = |a| + |b|$, then a and b are both positive. False; a and b could both be 0. **6. a.** hypothesis: you add two odd integers. conclusion: the sum is even. If you add two odd integers, the sum is even. **b.** If the sum is even, then you are adding two odd integers. False; The sum of two even integers is always even also. **7.** If $n^2 > n^3$, then n is a negative number. False; If $0 < n < 1$, then $n^2 > n^3$, but the numbers between 0 and 1 are positive. **8.** True for $x \geq 1$ or $x \leq -1$; not true for $-1 < x < 1$. If $|x| - 1 \geq 0$, then $x \geq 1$ or $x \leq -1$. hypothesis: $|x| - 1 \geq 0$; conclusion: $x \geq 1$ or $x \leq -1$ **9.** always true; true when a and b are both positive or both negative, or when one is zero, or when one is positive and one negative. **10.** sometimes true; true when a is positive and b is negative, false when both are positive or both are negative **11.** sometimes true; true when x is positivve, false when x is negative or 0 **12.** always true; $0 = 2x^2 - 12x + 18 = 2(x - 3)^2$ means $x = 3$. **13.** never true; 1 is not prime, and for any numbers other than 1, pq has factors p and q. **14.** sometimes true; $2 + 5$ is prime, $2 + 7$ is not prime.

A–5, page 720 **1.** hypothesis and known fact: n^3 is negative. desired conclusion: n is negative. alternative conclusion: n is positive or 0. Assume temporarily that the alternative conclusion is true. If n is positive, then n^3 is positive since the cube of a positive number is positive. If $n = 0$, then $n^3 = 0$ since the cube of 0 is 0. This contradicts the known fact that n^3 is negative. The desired conclusion must be accepted and the original statement is true. **2.** hypothesis and known fact: n^2 is even. desired conclusion: n is even. alternative conclusion: n is odd. Assume temporarily that the alternative conclusion is true. If n is odd, then $n = 2k + 1$, where k is any integer. Then $n^2 = (2k + 1)^2 = 4k^2 + 4k + 1 = 2(2k^2 + 2k) + 1$. Since $2(2k^2 + 2k)$ has a factor of 2, it must be even which implies that $2(2k^2 + 2k) + 1$ must be odd. Thus, n^2 must be odd which contradicts the known fact that n^2 is even. The desired conclusion must be accepted and the original statement is true. **3.** hypothesis and known fact: $x > 3$. desired conclusion: $|x| - 3 > 0$. alternative conclusion: $|x| - 3 \leq 0$. Assume temporarily that the alternative conclusion is true. If $|x| - 3 \leq 0$, then $|x| \leq 3$ which contradicts the known fact that x is greater than 3. The desired conclusion must be accepted and the original statement is true. **4.** hypothesis and known fact: $ax^2 + bx + c = 0$ has no real-number solutions. desired conclusion: the graph of $y = ax^2 + bx + c$ has no x-intercepts. alternative conclusion: the graph of $y = ax^2 + bx + c$ has at least one x-intercept. Assume temporarily that the alternative conclusion is true. If the graph has at least one x-intercept, then the discriminant, $b^2 - 4ac \geq 0$ and the equation $ax^2 + bx + c = 0$ has at least one solution. This contradicts the known fact that $ax^2 + bx + c = 0$ has no real-number solutions. The desired conclusion must be accepted and the original statement is true.
5. hypothesis and known fact: n^2 is a multiple of 3. desired conclusion: n is a multiple of 3. alternative conclusion: n is not a multiple of 3. Assume tem-porarily that the alternative conclusion is true. Then either $n = 3k + 1$ or $n = 3k + 2$, where k is any integer. If $n = 3k + 1$, then $n^2 = (3k + 1)^2 = 9k^2 + 6k + 1$, or $3(3k^2 + 2k) + 1$. Since $3(3k^2 + 2k)$ is a multiple of 3, $3(3k^2 + 2k) + 1$, or n^2, is not a multiple of 3. If $n = 3k + 2$, then $n^2 = 9k^2 + 12k + 4$, or $3(3k^2 + 4k + 1) + 1$. Since $3(3k^2 + 4k + 1)$ is a multiple of 3, $3(3k^2 + 4k + 1) + 1$, or n^2, is not a multiple of 3. Both cases con-tradict the known fact that n^2 is a multiple of 3. The desired conclusion must be accepted and the origi-nal statement is true.